D MAP PAGES

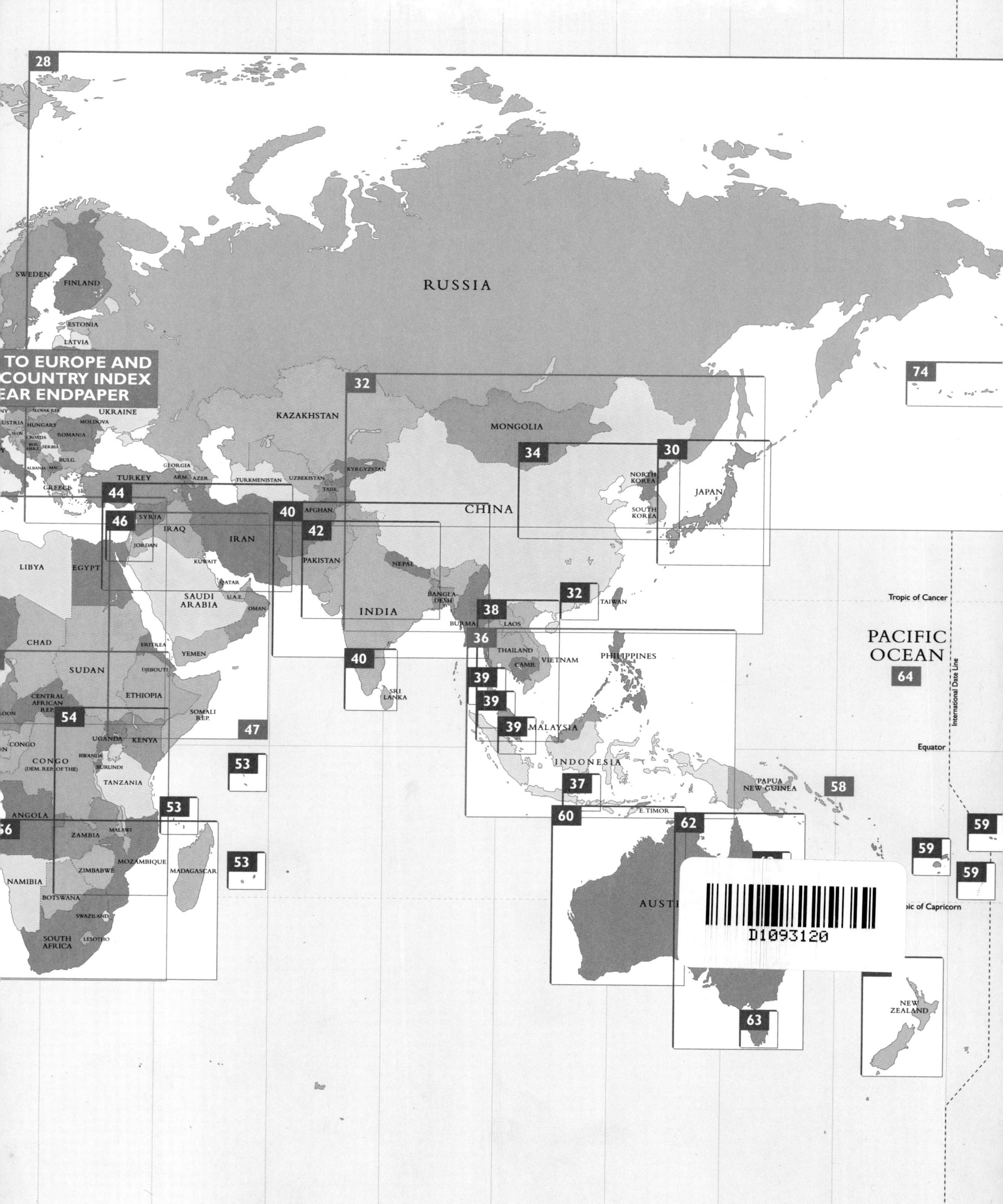

28

TO EUROPE AND
COUNTRY INDEX
EAR ENDPAPER

SWEDEN
FINLAND
ESTONIA
LATVIA

RUSSIA

NY
SLOVAK REP.
USTRIA
HUNGARY   MOLDOVA
SLOV.
CROATIA SERBIA
BOS.
HER.C.
ROMANIA
ALBANIA MAC.
BULG.
GREECE
TURKEY
GEORGIA
ARM. AZER.
UKRAINE

KAZAKHSTAN

MONGOLIA

32

34   30

NORTH
KOREA

SOUTH
KOREA

JAPAN

74

44

46   SYRIA
IRAQ
JORDAN

40   AFGHAN.
42
TURKMENISTAN   UZBEKISTAN
TAJIK.
KYRGYZSTAN

CHINA

LIBYA   EGYPT

SAUDI
ARABIA

KUWAIT
QATAR
U.A.E.
OMAN

PAKISTAN

NEPAL

BANGLA-
DESH

INDIA

IRAN

TAIWAN

Tropic of Cancer

CHAD

SUDAN

CENTRAL
AFRICAN
REP.

ERITREA
YEMEN

DJIBOUTI

ETHIOPIA

SOMALI
REP.

40

SRI
LANKA

BURMA

38   LAOS

36   THAILAND

39   CAMB.   VIETNAM

39

39   MALAYSIA

PHILIPPINES

PACIFIC
OCEAN

64

54

UGANDA   KENYA

47

53

53

INDONESIA

37

PAPUA
NEW GUINEA

58

CONGO   RWANDA
(DEM. REP. OF THE)   BURUNDI
TANZANIA

60   E. TIMOR

62

ANGOLA

ZAMBIA   MALAWI

ZIMBABWE

MOZAMBIQUE

MADAGASCAR

53

59

59

NAMIBIA

BOTSWANA

SWAZILAND

AUSTR

D1093120

59

Tropic of Capricorn

SOUTH
AFRICA   LESOTHO

63

NEW
ZEALAND

International Date Line

Equator

THE ROYAL
GEOGRAPHICAL
SOCIETY

WORLD ATLAS

Philip's are grateful to the following for acting as specialist geography consultants on 'The World in Focus' front section:

Professor D. Brunsden, Kings College, University of London, UK
Dr C. Clarke, Oxford University, UK
Dr I. S. Evans, Durham University, UK
Professor P. Haggett, University of Bristol, UK
Professor K. McLachlan, University of London, UK
Professor M. Monmonier, Syracuse University, New York, USA
Professor M-L. Hsu, University of Minnesota, Minnesota, USA
Professor M. J. Tooley, University of St Andrews, UK
Dr T. Unwin, Royal Holloway, University of London, UK

THE WORLD IN FOCUS
Cartography by Philip's

Picture Acknowledgements
Robin Scagell/Galaxy page 3

Illustrations: Stefan Chabluk

WORLD CITIES
Cartography by Philip's

Page 10, Dublin: The town plan of Dublin is based on Ordnance Survey Ireland by permission of the Government Permit Number 8408. © Ordnance Survey Ireland and Government of Ireland.

Page 11, Edinburgh, and page 15, London: This product includes mapping data licensed from Ordnance Survey® with the permission of the Controller of Her Majesty's Stationery Office. © Crown copyright 2008. All rights reserved. Licence number 100011710.

Vector data courtesy of Gräfe and Unser Verlag GmbH, München, Germany (city-centre maps of Bangkok, Beijing, Cape Town, Jerusalem, Mexico City, Moscow, Singapore, Sydney, Tokyo and Washington D.C.)
The following city maps utilize base data supplied courtesy of MapQuest.com, Inc. (© MapQuest) (Las Vegas, New Orleans, Orlando)

All satellite images in this section courtesy of NPA Group, Edenbridge, Kent (www.satmaps.com)

Published in Great Britain in 2008
by Philip's,
a division of Octopus Publishing Group Limited,
www.octopusbooks.co.uk
2–4 Heron Quays, London E14 4JP
An Hachette Livre UK Company
www.hachettelivre.co.uk

Copyright © 2008 Philip's

Cartography by Philip's

ISBN 978–0–540–09259–8

A CIP catalogue record for this book is available from the British Library.

Printed in Hong Kong

Details of other Philip's titles and services can be found on our website at:
www.philips-maps.co.uk

Royal Geographical Society
with IBG

Advancing geography and geographical learning

PHILIP'S World Atlases are published in association with THE ROYAL GEOGRAPHICAL SOCIETY (with THE INSTITUTE OF BRITISH GEOGRAPHERS).

The Society was founded in 1830 and given a Royal Charter in 1859 for 'the advancement of geographical science'. It holds historical collections of national and international importance, many of which relate to the Society's association with and support for scientific exploration and research from the 19th century onwards. It was pivotal in establishing geography as a teaching and research discipline in British universities close to the turn of the century, and has played a key role in geographical and environmental education ever since.

Today the Society is a leading world centre for geographical learning – supporting education, teaching, research and expeditions, and promoting public understanding of the subject. The Society welcomes those interested in geography as members. For further information, please visit the website at: **www.rgs.org**

THE ROYAL
GEOGRAPHICAL
SOCIETY

WORLD ATLAS

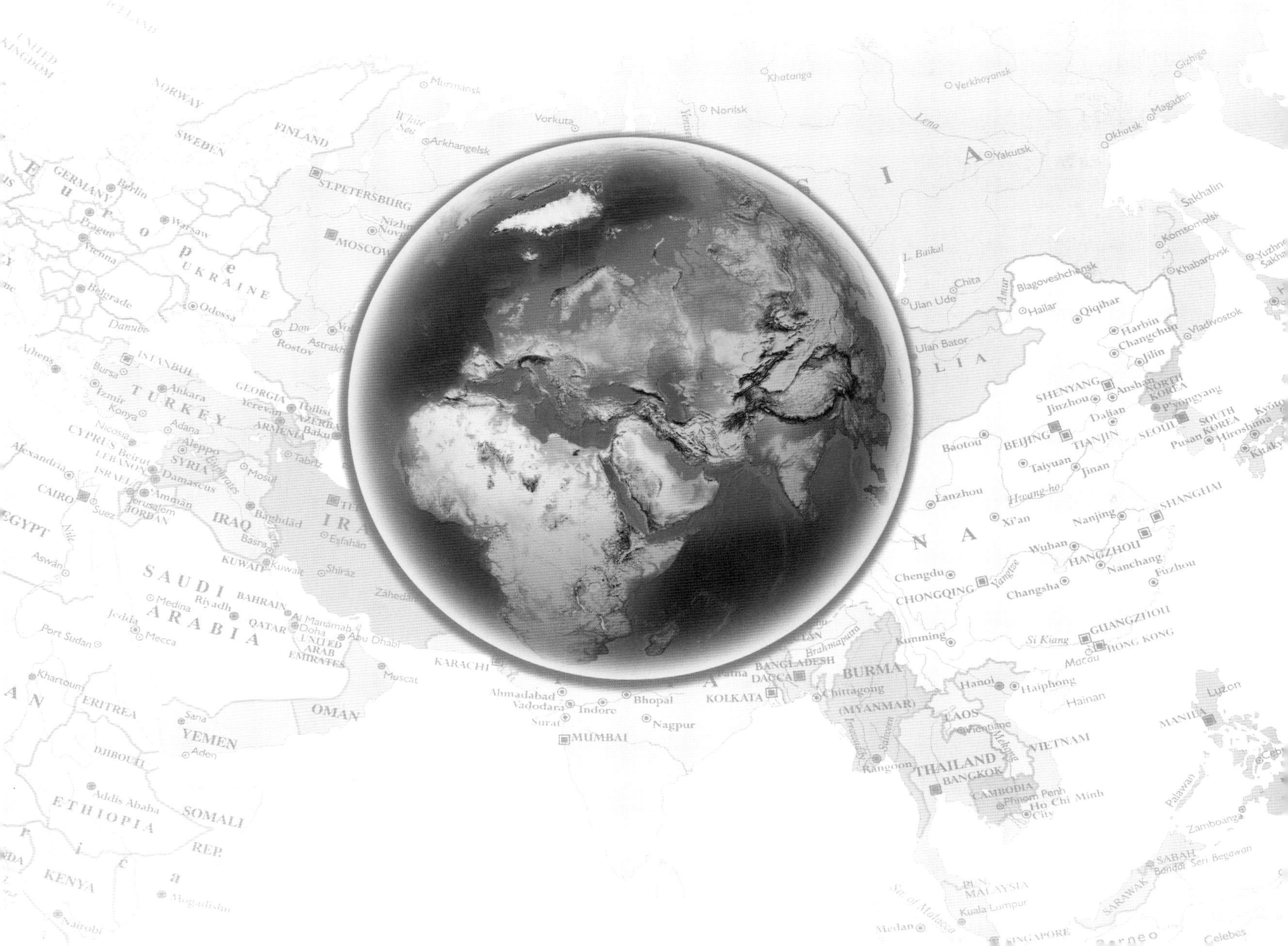

Contents

World Statistics

Countries vi
Physical Dimensions vii
User Guide viii

The World in Focus

Planet Earth 2–3
Restless Earth 4–5
Landforms 6–7
Oceans 8–9
Climate 10–11
Water and Vegetation 12–13
Environment 14–15
Population 16–17
The Human Family 18–19
Wealth 20–21
Quality of Life 22–23
Energy 24–25
Production 26–27
Trade 28–29
Travel and Tourism 30–31

World Cities

Amsterdam 2
Athens 2
Atlanta 3
Baghdad 3
Bangkok 3
Barcelona 4
Beijing 4
Berlin 5
Boston 6
Brussels 6
Budapest 7
Buenos Aires 7
Cairo 7
Cape Town 8
Copenhagen 8
Chicago 9
Delhi 10
Dublin 10
Edinburgh 11
Guangzhou 11
Helsinki 11
Hong Kong 12
Istanbul 12
Jakarta 12
Jerusalem 13
Johannesburg 13
Karachi 13
Kolkata 14
Lagos 14
Las Vegas 14
Lima 14
London 15
Lisbon 16
Los Angeles 16
Madrid 17
Manila 17
Melbourne 18
Mexico City 18
Miami 18
Milan 19
Moscow 19
Montréal 20
Mumbai 20
Munich 21
New Orleans 21
New York 22
Orlando 23
Osaka 23
Oslo 23
Paris 24
Prague 25
Rio de Janeiro 25
Rome 26
San Francisco 26
St Petersburg 27
Santiago 27
São Paulo 27
Seoul 27
Shanghai 28
Singapore 28
Stockholm 29
Sydney 29
Tokyo 30
Tehran 31
Toronto 31
Vienna 32
Warsaw 32
Washington 33
Wellington 33
Index to City Maps 34–39
World Cities Satellite Images 40–48

World Maps

Map Symbols 1

The World: Political
1:95 000 000 2–3

Arctic Ocean
1:35 000 000 4

Antarctica
1:35 000 000 5

Europe

Europe: Physical
1:20 000 000 6

Europe: Political
1:20 000 000 7

Scandinavia 1:6 000 000
Iceland 1:6 000 000
Færoe Islands 1:6 000 000
8–9

Ireland 1:2 000 000
10

Scotland 1:2 000 000
11

England and Wales
1:2 000 000
12–13

British Isles 1:5 000 000
14

Netherlands, Belgium and
Luxembourg 1:2 500 000
15

Central Europe 1:5 000 000
16–17

Eastern Europe and Turkey
1:10 000 000
18–19

France 1:5 000 000
20

Spain and Portugal
1:5 000 000
21

Italy and the Balkan States
1:5 000 000
22–23

The Balearics, the Canaries and
Madeira 1:1 000 000 / 1:2 000 000
24

Malta, Crete, Corfu, Rhodes
and Cyprus
1:1 000 000 / 1:1 300 000
25

Asia

Asia: Physical 1:47 000 000 26

Asia: Political 1:47 000 000 27

Russia and Central Asia
1:20 000 000
28–29

Japan 1:5 000 000
30–31

China and the Far East
1:15 000 000
Hong Kong and Macau 1:1 000 000
32–33

Northern China and Korea
1:6 000 000
34–35

Indonesia and the Philippines
1:12 500 000
Java and Madura 1:7 500 000
Bali 1:2 000 000
36–37

Mainland South-east Asia
1:6 000 000
Ko Phuket 1:1 000 000
Ko Samui 1:1 000 000
Pinang 1:1 000 000
Singapore 1:1 000 000
38–39

South Asia 1:10 000 000
40–41

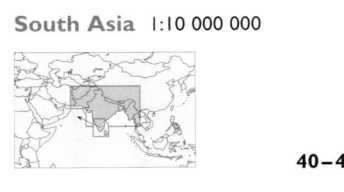

Northern India, Pakistan and Nepal
1:6 000 000
Jammu and Kashmir 1:6 000 000

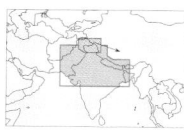

42–43

The Middle East
1:7 000 000

44–45

The Near East 1:2 500 000

46

Arabia and the Horn of Africa 1:15 000 000

47

Africa

Africa: Physical
1:42 000 000   **48**

Africa: Political
1:42 000 000   **49**

Northern Africa
1:15 000 000
Azores 1:15 000 000
Cape Verde Islands 1:10 000 000

50–51

Central and Southern Africa
1:15 000 000
Seychelles 1:2 500 000
Réunion 1:2 500 000
Mauritius 1:2 500 000
Comoros 1:8 000 000

52–53

East Africa 1:8 000 000

54–55

Southern Africa
1:8 000 000
Madagascar 1:8 000 000

56–57

Australia and Oceania

Australia and Oceania: Physical and Political
1:50 000 000   **58**

New Zealand 1:6 000 000
Samoan Islands 1:6 000 000
Fiji 1:6 000 000
Tonga 1:6 000 000
Tahiti and Moorea 1:1 000 000

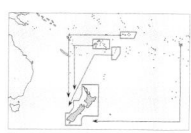

59

Western Australia
1:8 000 000

60–61

Eastern Australia
1:8 000 000
Torres Strait 1:8 000 000
Whitsunday Islands 1:2 500 000
Tasmania 1:8 000 000

62–63

Pacific Ocean
1:54 000 000   **64–65**

North America

North America: Physical
1:35 000 000   **66**

North America: Political
1:35 000 000   **67**

Canada 1:15 000 000

68–69

Western Canada 1:7 000 000

70–71

Eastern Canada 1:7 000 000

72–73

United States 1:15 000 000
Hawai'i 1:15 000 000
Alaska 1:15 000 000

74–75

United States – West
1:6 700 000

76–77

Central and Southern California and Western Washington
1:2 500 000

78–79

United States – Midwest and North-east
1:6 700 000

80–81

North-eastern United States
1:2 500 000

82–83

United States – South
1:6 700 000

84–85

Mexico 1:8 000 000

86–87

Central America and the West Indies 1:8 000 000
Jamaica 1:3 000 000
Guadeloupe 1:2 000 000
Martinique 1:2 000 000
Puerto Rico 1:3 000 000
Virgin Islands 1:2 000 000
St Lucia 1:2 000 000
Barbados 1:2 000 000

88–89

South America

South America: Physical
1:35 000 000   **90**

South America: Political
1:35 000 000   **91**

South America – North
1:16 000 000
Trinidad and Tobago 1:2 500 000

92–93

Central South America
1:8 000 000

94–95

South America – South
1:16 000 000

96

Index to World Maps
97–176

World Statistics: Countries

This alphabetical list includes the principal countries and territories of the world. If a territory is not completely independent, the country it is associated with is named. The area figures give the total area of land, inland water and ice. The population figures are 2007 estimates where available. The annual income is the Gross Domestic Product per capita in US dollars. The figures are the latest available, usually 2007 estimates.

Country/Territory	Area km² Thousands	Area miles² Thousands	Population Thousands	Capital	Annual Income US $
Afghanistan	652	252	31,890	Kabul	800
Albania	28.7	11.1	3,601	Tirana	5,500
Algeria	2,382	920	33,333	Algiers	8,100
American Samoa (US)	0.20	0.08	58	Pago Pago	5,800
Andorra	0.47	0.18	72	Andorra La Vella	38,800
Angola	1,247	481	12,264	Luanda	6,500
Anguilla (UK)	0.10	0.04	14	The Valley	8,800
Antigua & Barbuda	0.44	0.17	69	St John's	10,900
Argentina	2,780	1,074	40,302	Buenos Aires	13,000
Armenia	29.8	11.5	2,972	Yerevan	5,700
Aruba (Netherlands)	0.19	0.07	100	Oranjestad	21,800
Australia	7,741	2,989	20,434	Canberra	37,500
Austria	83.9	32.4	8,200	Vienna	39,000
Azerbaijan	86.6	33.4	8,120	Baku	9,000
Azores (Portugal)	2.2	0.86	236	Ponta Delgada	15,000
Bahamas	13.9	5.4	306	Nassau	22,700
Bahrain	0.69	0.27	709	Manama	34,700
Bangladesh	144	55.6	150,448	Dhaka	1,400
Barbados	0.43	0.17	281	Bridgetown	19,700
Belarus	208	80.2	9,725	Minsk	10,200
Belgium	30.5	11.8	10,392	Brussels	36,500
Belize	23.0	8.9	294	Belmopan	7,800
Benin	113	43.5	9,078	Porto-Novo	1,500
Bermuda (UK)	0.05	0.02	66	Hamilton	69,900
Bhutan	47.0	18.1	2,328	Thimphu	1,400
Bolivia	1,099	424	9,119	La Paz/Sucre	4,400
Bosnia-Herzegovina	51.2	19.8	4,552	Sarajevo	6,600
Botswana	582	225	1,816	Gaborone	14,700
Brazil	8,514	3,287	190,011	Brasília	9,700
Brunei	5.8	2.2	375	Bandar Seri Begawan	25,600
Bulgaria	111	42.8	7,323	Sofia	11,800
Burkina Faso	274	106	14,326	Ouagadougou	1,200
Burma (=Myanmar)	677	261	47,374	Rangoon/Naypyidaw	1,900
Burundi	27.8	10.7	8,391	Bujumbura	800
Cambodia	181	69.9	13,996	Phnom Penh	1,800
Cameroon	475	184	18,060	Yaoundé	2,300
Canada	9,971	3,850	33,390	Ottawa	38,200
Canary Is. (Spain)	7.2	2.8	1,682	Las Palmas/Santa Cruz	19,900
Cape Verde Is.	4.0	1.6	424	Praia	7,000
Cayman Is. (UK)	0.26	0.10	47	George Town	43,800
Central African Republic	623	241	4,369	Bangui	700
Chad	1,284	496	9,886	Ndjaména	1,600
Chile	757	292	16,285	Santiago	14,400
China	9,597	3,705	1,321,852	Beijing	5,300
Colombia	1,139	440	44,380	Bogotá	7,200
Comoros	2.2	0.86	711	Moroni	600
Congo	342	132	3,801	Brazzaville	3,700
Congo (Dem. Rep. of the)	2,345	905	65,752	Kinshasa	300
Cook Is. (NZ)	0.24	0.09	22	Avarua	9,100
Costa Rica	51.1	19.7	4,134	San José	13,500
Croatia	56.5	21.8	4,493	Zagreb	15,500
Cuba	111	42.8	11,394	Havana	4,500
Cyprus	9.3	3.6	788	Nicosia	24,600
Czech Republic	78.9	30.5	10,229	Prague	24,400
Denmark	43.1	16.6	5,468	Copenhagen	37,400
Djibouti	23.2	9.0	496	Djibouti	1,000
Dominica	0.75	0.29	72	Roseau	3,800
Dominican Republic	48.5	18.7	9,366	Santo Domingo	9,200
East Timor	14.9	5.7	1,085	Dili	800
Ecuador	284	109	13,756	Quito	7,100
Egypt	1,001	387	80,335	Cairo	5,400
El Salvador	21.0	8.1	6,948	San Salvador	5,200
Equatorial Guinea	28.1	10.8	551	Malabo	4,100
Eritrea	118	45.4	4,907	Asmara	1,000
Estonia	45.1	17.4	1,316	Tallinn	21,800
Ethiopia	1,104	426	76,512	Addis Ababa	700
Faroe Is. (Denmark)	1.4	0.54	48	Tórshavn	31,000
Fiji	18.3	7.1	919	Suva	4,100
Finland	338	131	5,238	Helsinki	35,500
France	552	213	60,876	Paris	33,800
French Guiana (France)	90.0	34.7	200	Cayenne	8,300
French Polynesia (France)	4.0	1.5	279	Papeete	17,500
Gabon	268	103	1,455	Libreville	13,800
Gambia, The	11.3	4.4	1,688	Banjul	800
Gaza Strip (OPT)*	0.36	0.14	1,482	–	1,100
Georgia	69.7	26.9	4,646	Tbilisi	4,200
Germany	357	138	82,401	Berlin	34,400
Ghana	239	92.1	22,931	Accra	1,400
Gibraltar (UK)	0.006	0.002	28	Gibraltar Town	38,200
Greece	132	50.9	10,706	Athens	30,500
Greenland (Denmark)	2,176	840	56	Nuuk	20,000
Grenada	0.34	0.13	90	St George's	3,900
Guadeloupe (France)	1.7	0.66	453	Basse-Terre	7,900
Guam (US)	0.55	0.21	173	Agana	15,000
Guatemala	109	42.0	12,728	Guatemala City	5,400
Guinea	246	94.9	9,948	Conakry	1,000
Guinea-Bissau	36.1	13.9	1,473	Bissau	600
Guyana	215	83.0	769	Georgetown	5,300
Haiti	27.8	10.7	8,706	Port-au-Prince	1,900
Honduras	112	43.3	7,484	Tegucigalpa	3,300
Hungary	93.0	35.9	9,956	Budapest	19,500
Iceland	103	39.8	302	Reykjavik	39,400
India	3,287	1,269	1,129,866	New Delhi	2,700
Indonesia	1,905	735	234,694	Jakarta	3,400
Iran	1,648	636	65,398	Tehran	12,300
Iraq	438	169	27,500	Baghdad	3,600
Ireland	70.3	27.1	4,109	Dublin	45,600
Israel	20.6	8.0	6,427	Jerusalem	28,800
Italy	301	116	58,148	Rome	31,000
Ivory Coast (=Côte d'Ivoire)	322	125	18,013	Yamoussoukro	1,800
Jamaica	11.0	4.2	2,780	Kingston	4,800
Japan	378	146	127,433	Tokyo	33,800
Jordan	89.3	34.5	6,053	Amman	4,700
Kazakhstan	2,725	1,052	15,285	Astana	11,100
Kenya	580	224	36,914	Nairobi	1,600
Kiribati	0.73	0.28	108	Tarawa	1,800
Korea, North	121	46.5	23,302	Pyŏngyang	1,900
Korea, South	99.3	38.3	49,045	Seoul	24,600
Kosovo	10.9	4.2	2,127	Pristina	1,800
Kuwait	17.8	6.9	2,506	Kuwait City	55,300
Kyrgyzstan	200	77.2	5,284	Bishkek	2,000
Laos	237	91.4	6,522	Vientiane	1,900
Latvia	64.6	24.9	2,260	Riga	17,700
Lebanon	10.4	4.0	3,926	Beirut	10,400
Lesotho	30.4	11.7	2,125	Maseru	1,500
Liberia	111	43.0	3,196	Monrovia	500
Libya	1,760	679	6,037	Tripoli	13,100
Liechtenstein	0.16	0.06	34	Vaduz	25,000
Lithuania	65.2	25.2	3,575	Vilnius	16,700
Luxembourg	2.6	1.0	480	Luxembourg	80,800
Macedonia (FYROM)	25.7	9.9	2,056	Skopje	8,400
Madagascar	587	227	19,449	Antananarivo	1,000
Madeira (Portugal)	0.78	0.30	241	Funchal	22,700
Malawi	118	45.7	13,603	Lilongwe	800
Malaysia	330	127	24,821	Kuala Lumpur/Putrajaya	14,400
Maldives	0.30	0.12	369	Malé	3,900
Mali	1,240	479	11,995	Bamako	1,200
Malta	0.32	0.12	402	Valletta	23,700
Marshall Is.	0.18	0.07	62	Majuro	2,900
Martinique (France)	1.1	0.43	436	Fort-de-France	14,400
Mauritania	1,026	396	3,270	Nouakchott	1,800
Mauritius	2.0	0.79	1,251	Port Louis	11,900
Mayotte (France)	0.37	0.14	209	Mamoudzou	4,900
Mexico	1,958	756	108,701	Mexico City	12,500
Micronesia, Fed. States of	0.70	0.27	108	Palikir	2,300
Moldova	33.9	13.1	4,320	Chişinău	2,200
Monaco	0.001	0.0004	33	Monaco	30,000
Mongolia	1,567	605	2,952	Ulan Bator	2,900
Montenegro	14.0	5.4	685	Podgorica	3,800
Morocco	447	172	33,757	Rabat	3,800
Mozambique	802	309	20,906	Maputo	900
Namibia	824	318	2,055	Windhoek	5,200
Nauru	0.02	0.008	14	Yaren District	5,000
Nepal	147	56.8	28,902	Katmandu	1,100
Netherlands	41.5	16.0	16,571	Amsterdam/The Hague	38,600
Netherlands Antilles (Neths)	0.80	0.31	224	Willemstad	16,000
New Caledonia (France)	18.6	7.2	222	Nouméa	15,000
New Zealand	271	104	4,116	Wellington	27,300
Nicaragua	130	50.2	5,675	Managua	3,200
Niger	1,267	489	12,895	Niamey	700
Nigeria	924	357	135,031	Abuja	2,200
Northern Mariana Is. (US)	0.46	0.18	85	Saipan	12,500
Norway	324	125	4,628	Oslo	55,600
Oman	310	119	3,205	Muscat	19,100
Pakistan	796	307	164,742	Islamabad	2,600
Palau	0.46	0.18	21	Melekeok	7,600
Panama	75.5	29.2	3,242	Panamá	9,000
Papua New Guinea	463	179	5,796	Port Moresby	2,900
Paraguay	407	157	6,669	Asunción	4,000
Peru	1,285	496	28,675	Lima	7,600
Philippines	300	116	91,077	Manila	3,300
Poland	323	125	38,518	Warsaw	16,200
Portugal	88.8	34.3	10,643	Lisbon	21,800
Puerto Rico (US)	8.9	3.4	3,944	San Juan	19,600
Qatar	11.0	4.2	907	Doha	29,400
Réunion (France)	2.5	0.97	788	St-Denis	6,200
Romania	238	92.0	22,276	Bucharest	11,100
Russia	17,075	6,593	141,378	Moscow	14,600
Rwanda	26.3	10.2	9,908	Kigali	1,000
St Kitts & Nevis	0.26	0.10	39	Basseterre	8,200
St Lucia	0.54	0.21	171	Castries	4,800
St Vincent & Grenadines	0.39	0.15	118	Kingstown	3,600
Samoa	2.8	1.1	214	Apia	2,100
San Marino	0.06	0.02	30	San Marino	34,100
São Tomé & Príncipe	0.96	0.37	200	São Tomé	1,200
Saudi Arabia	2,150	830	27,601	Riyadh	20,700
Senegal	197	76.0	12,522	Dakar	1,700
Serbia	77.5	29.9	8,024	Belgrade	7,700
Seychelles	0.46	0.18	82	Victoria	18,400
Sierra Leone	71.7	27.7	6,145	Freetown	800
Singapore	0.68	0.26	4,553	Singapore City	48,900
Slovak Republic	49.0	18.9	5,448	Bratislava	19,800
Slovenia	20.3	7.8	2,009	Ljubljana	27,300
Solomon Is.	28.9	11.2	567	Honiara	600
Somalia	638	246	9,119	Mogadishu	600
South Africa	1,221	471	43,998	Cape Town/Pretoria	10,600
Spain	498	192	40,448	Madrid	33,700
Sri Lanka	65.6	25.3	20,926	Colombo	4,100
Sudan	2,506	967	39,379	Khartoum	2,500
Suriname	163	63.0	471	Paramaribo	7,800
Swaziland	17.4	6.7	1,133	Mbabane	4,800
Sweden	450	174	9,031	Stockholm	36,900
Switzerland	41.3	15.9	7,555	Bern	39,800
Syria	185	71.5	19,315	Damascus	4,500
Taiwan	36.0	13.9	22,859	Taipei	29,800
Tajikistan	143	55.3	7,077	Dushanbe	1,600
Tanzania	945	365	39,384	Dodoma	1,100
Thailand	513	198	65,068	Bangkok	8,000
Togo	56.8	21.9	5,702	Lomé	900
Tonga	0.65	0.25	117	Nuku'alofa	2,200
Trinidad & Tobago	5.1	2.0	1,057	Port of Spain	21,700
Tunisia	164	63.2	10,276	Tunis	7,500
Turkey	775	299	71,159	Ankara	9,400
Turkmenistan	488	188	5,097	Ashkhabad	9,200
Turks & Caicos Is. (UK)	0.43	0.17	22	Cockburn Town	11,500
Tuvalu	0.03	0.01	12	Fongafale	1,600
Uganda	241	93.1	30,263	Kampala	1,100
Ukraine	604	233	46,300	Kiev	6,900
United Arab Emirates	83.6	32.3	4,444	Abu Dhabi	55,200
United Kingdom	242	93.4	60,776	London	35,300
United States of America	9,629	3,718	301,140	Washington, DC	46,000
Uruguay	175	67.6	3,461	Montevideo	10,700
Uzbekistan	447	173	27,780	Tashkent	2,200
Vanuatu	12.2	4.7	212	Port-Vila	2,900
Venezuela	912	352	26,024	Caracas	12,800
Vietnam	332	128	85,262	Hanoi	2,600
Virgin Is. (UK)	0.15	0.06	24	Road Town	38,500
Virgin Is. (US)	0.35	0.13	108	Charlotte Amalie	14,500
Wallis & Futuna Is. (France)	0.20	0.08	16	Mata-Utu	3,800
West Bank (OPT)*	5.9	2.3	2,536	–	1,100
Western Sahara	266	103	383	El Aaiún	N/A
Yemen	528	204	22,231	Sana'	2,400
Zambia	753	291	11,477	Lusaka	1,400
Zimbabwe	391	151	12,311	Harare	500

*OPT = Occupied Palestinian Territory   N/A = Not available

World Statistics: Physical Dimensions

Each topic list is divided into continents and within a continent the items are listed in order of size. The bottom part of many of the lists is selective in order to give examples from as many different countries as possible. The order of the continents is the same as in the atlas, beginning with Europe and ending with South America. The figures are rounded as appropriate.

World, Continents, Oceans

	km²	miles²	%
The World	509,450,000	196,672,000	–
Land	149,450,000	57,688,000	29.3
Water	360,000,000	138,984,000	70.7
Asia	44,500,000	17,177,000	29.8
Africa	30,302,000	11,697,000	20.3
North America	24,241,000	9,357,000	16.2
South America	17,793,000	6,868,000	11.9
Antarctica	14,100,000	5,443,000	9.4
Europe	9,957,000	3,843,000	6.7
Australia & Oceania	8,557,000	3,303,000	5.7
Pacific Ocean	155,557,000	60,061,000	46.4
Atlantic Ocean	76,762,000	29,638,000	22.9
Indian Ocean	68,556,000	26,470,000	20.4
Southern Ocean	20,327,000	7,848,000	6.1
Arctic Ocean	14,056,000	5,427,000	4.2

Ocean Depths

Atlantic Ocean	m	ft
Puerto Rico (Milwaukee) Deep	8,605	28,232
Cayman Trench	7,680	25,197
Gulf of Mexico	5,203	17,070
Mediterranean Sea	5,121	16,801
Black Sea	2,211	7,254
North Sea	660	2,165

Indian Ocean	m	ft
Java Trench	7,450	24,442
Red Sea	2,635	8,454

Pacific Ocean	m	ft
Mariana Trench	11,022	36,161
Tonga Trench	10,882	35,702
Japan Trench	10,554	34,626
Kuril Trench	10,542	34,587

Arctic Ocean	m	ft
Molloy Deep	5,608	18,399

Southern Ocean	m	ft
South Sandwich Trench	7,235	23,737

Mountains

Europe		m	ft
Elbrus	*Russia*	5,642	18,510
Dykh-Tau	*Russia*	5,205	17,076
Shkhara	*Russia/Georgia*	5,201	17,064
Koshtan-Tau	*Russia*	5,152	16,903
Kazbek	*Russia/Georgia*	5,047	16,558
Pushkin	*Russia/Georgia*	5,033	16,512
Katyn-Tau	*Russia/Georgia*	4,979	16,335
Shota Rustaveli	*Russia/Georgia*	4,860	15,945
Mont Blanc	*France/Italy*	4,808	15,774
Monte Rosa	*Italy/Switzerland*	4,634	15,203
Dom	*Switzerland*	4,545	14,911
Liskamm	*Switzerland*	4,527	14,852
Weisshorn	*Switzerland*	4,505	14,780
Taschorn	*Switzerland*	4,490	14,730
Matterhorn/Cervino	*Italy/Switzerland*	4,478	14,691
Grossglockner	*Austria*	3,797	12,457
Mulhacén	*Spain*	3,478	11,411
Zugspitze	*Germany*	2,962	9,718
Olympus	*Greece*	2,917	9,570
Galdhøpiggen	*Norway*	2,469	8,100
Ben Nevis	*UK*	1,342	4,403

Asia		m	ft
Everest	*China/Nepal*	8,850	29,035
K2 (Godwin Austen)	*China/Kashmir*	8,611	28,251
Kanchenjunga	*India/Nepal*	8,598	28,208
Lhotse	*China/Nepal*	8,516	27,939
Makalu	*China/Nepal*	8,481	27,824
Cho Oyu	*China/Nepal*	8,201	26,906
Dhaulagiri	*Nepal*	8,167	26,795
Manaslu	*Nepal*	8,156	26,758
Nanga Parbat	*Kashmir*	8,126	26,660
Annapurna	*Nepal*	8,078	26,502
Gasherbrum	*China/Kashmir*	8,068	26,469
Broad Peak	*China/Kashmir*	8,051	26,414
Xixabangma	*China*	8,012	26,286
Kangbachen	*Nepal*	7,858	25,781
Trivor	*Pakistan*	7,720	25,328
Pik Imeni Ismail Samani	*Tajikistan*	7,495	24,590
Demavend	*Iran*	5,604	18,386
Ararat	*Turkey*	5,165	16,945
Gunong Kinabalu	*Malaysia (Borneo)*	4,101	13,455
Fuji-San	*Japan*	3,776	12,388

Africa		m	ft
Kilimanjaro	*Tanzania*	5,895	19,340
Mt Kenya	*Kenya*	5,199	17,057
Ruwenzori (Margherita)	*Ug./Congo (D.R.)*	5,109	16,762
Meru	*Tanzania*	4,565	14,977
Ras Dashen	*Ethiopia*	4,533	14,872
Karisimbi	*Rwanda/Congo (D.R.)*	4,507	14,787
Mt Elgon	*Kenya/Uganda*	4,321	14,176
Batu	*Ethiopia*	4,307	14,130
Toubkal	*Morocco*	4,165	13,665
Mt Cameroun	*Cameroon*	4,070	13,353

Oceania		m	ft
Puncak Jaya	*Indonesia*	5,029	16,499
Puncak Trikora	*Indonesia*	4,730	15,518
Puncak Mandala	*Indonesia*	4,702	15,427
Mt Wilhelm	*Papua New Guinea*	4,508	14,790
Mauna Kea	*USA (Hawai'i)*	4,205	13,796
Mauna Loa	*USA (Hawai'i)*	4,169	13,681
Aoraki Mt Cook	*New Zealand*	3,753	12,313
Mt Kosciuszko	*Australia*	2,228	7,310

North America		m	ft
Mt McKinley (Denali)	*USA (Alaska)*	6,194	20,321
Mt Logan	*Canada*	5,959	19,551
Pico de Orizaba	*Mexico*	5,610	18,405
Mt St Elias	*USA/Canada*	5,489	18,008
Popocatépetl	*Mexico*	5,452	17,887
Mt Foraker	*USA (Alaska)*	5,304	17,401
Iztaccihuatl	*Mexico*	5,286	17,343
Mt Lucania	*Canada*	5,226	17,146
Mt Steele	*Canada*	5,073	16,644
Mt Bona	*USA (Alaska)*	5,005	16,420
Mt Whitney	*USA*	4,418	14,495
Tajumulco	*Guatemala*	4,220	13,845
Chirripó Grande	*Costa Rica*	3,837	12,589
Pico Duarte	*Dominican Rep.*	3,175	10,417

South America		m	ft
Aconcagua	*Argentina*	6,962	22,841
Bonete	*Argentina*	6,872	22,546
Ojos del Salado	*Argentina/Chile*	6,863	22,516
Pissis	*Argentina*	6,779	22,241
Mercedario	*Argentina/Chile*	6,770	22,211
Huascarán	*Peru*	6,768	22,204
Llullaillaco	*Argentina/Chile*	6,723	22,057
Nevado de Cachi	*Argentina*	6,720	22,047
Yerupaja	*Peru*	6,632	21,758
Sajama	*Bolivia*	6,520	21,391
Chimborazo	*Ecuador*	6,267	20,561
Pico Cristóbal Colón	*Colombia*	5,800	19,029
Pico Bolivar	*Venezuela*	5,007	16,427

Antarctica		m	ft
Vinson Massif		4,897	16,066
Mt Kirkpatrick		4,528	14,855

Rivers

Europe		km	miles
Volga	*Caspian Sea*	3,700	2,300
Danube	*Black Sea*	2,850	1,770
Ural	*Caspian Sea*	2,535	1,575
Dnepr (Dnipro)	*Black Sea*	2,285	1,420
Kama	*Volga*	2,030	1,260
Don	*Black Sea*	1,990	1,240
Petchora	*Arctic Ocean*	1,790	1,110
Oka	*Volga*	1,480	920
Dnister (Dniester)	*Black Sea*	1,400	870
Vyatka	*Kama*	1,370	850
Rhine	*North Sea*	1,320	820
N. Dvina	*Arctic Ocean*	1,290	800
Elbe	*North Sea*	1,145	710

Asia		km	miles
Yangtze	*Pacific Ocean*	6,380	3,960
Yenisey–Angara	*Arctic Ocean*	5,550	3,445
Huang He	*Pacific Ocean*	5,464	3,395
Ob–Irtysh	*Arctic Ocean*	5,410	3,360
Mekong	*Pacific Ocean*	4,500	2,795
Amur	*Pacific Ocean*	4,442	2,760
Lena	*Arctic Ocean*	4,402	2,735
Irtysh	*Ob*	4,250	2,640
Yenisey	*Arctic Ocean*	4,090	2,540
Ob	*Arctic Ocean*	3,680	2,285
Indus	*Indian Ocean*	3,100	1,925
Brahmaputra	*Indian Ocean*	2,900	1,800
Syrdarya	*Aral Sea*	2,860	1,775
Salween	*Indian Ocean*	2,800	1,740
Euphrates	*Indian Ocean*	2,700	1,675
Amudarya	*Aral Sea*	2,540	1,575

Africa		km	miles
Nile	*Mediterranean*	6,695	4,160
Congo	*Atlantic Ocean*	4,670	2,900
Niger	*Atlantic Ocean*	4,180	2,595
Zambezi	*Indian Ocean*	3,540	2,200
Oubangi/Uele	*Congo (D.R.)*	2,250	1,400
Kasai	*Congo (D.R.)*	1,950	1,210
Shaballe	*Indian Ocean*	1,930	1,200
Orange	*Atlantic Ocean*	1,860	1,155
Cubango	*Okavango Delta*	1,800	1,120
Limpopo	*Indian Ocean*	1,770	1,100
Senegal	*Atlantic Ocean*	1,640	1,020

Australia		km	miles
Murray–Darling	*Southern Ocean*	3,750	2,330
Darling	*Murray*	3,070	1,905
Murray	*Southern Ocean*	2,575	1,600
Murrumbidgee	*Murray*	1,690	1,050

North America		km	miles
Mississippi–Missouri	*Gulf of Mexico*	5,971	3,710
Mackenzie	*Arctic Ocean*	4,240	2,630
Missouri	*Mississippi*	4,088	2,540
Mississippi	*Gulf of Mexico*	3,782	2,350
Yukon	*Pacific Ocean*	3,185	1,980
Rio Grande	*Gulf of Mexico*	3,030	1,880
Arkansas	*Mississippi*	2,340	1,450
Colorado	*Pacific Ocean*	2,330	1,445
Red	*Mississippi*	2,040	1,270
Columbia	*Pacific Ocean*	1,950	1,210
Saskatchewan	*Lake Winnipeg*	1,940	1,205

South America		km	miles
Amazon	*Atlantic Ocean*	6,450	4,010
Paraná–Plate	*Atlantic Ocean*	4,500	2,800
Purus	*Amazon*	3,350	2,080
Madeira	*Amazon*	3,200	1,990
São Francisco	*Atlantic Ocean*	2,900	1,800
Paraná	*Plate*	2,800	1,740
Tocantins	*Atlantic Ocean*	2,750	1,710
Orinoco	*Atlantic Ocean*	2,740	1,700
Paraguay	*Paraná*	2,550	1,580
Pilcomayo	*Paraná*	2,500	1,550
Araguaia	*Tocantins*	2,250	1,400

Lakes

Europe		km²	miles²
Lake Ladoga	*Russia*	17,700	6,800
Lake Onega	*Russia*	9,700	3,700
Saimaa system	*Finland*	8,000	3,100
Vänern	*Sweden*	5,500	2,100

Asia		km²	miles²
Caspian Sea	*Asia*	371,000	143,000
Lake Baikal	*Russia*	30,500	11,780
Tonlé Sap	*Cambodia*	20,000	7,700
Lake Balqash	*Kazakhstan*	18,500	7,100
Aral Sea	*Kazakhstan/Uzbekistan*	17,160	6,625

Africa		km²	miles²
Lake Victoria	*East Africa*	68,000	26,300
Lake Tanganyika	*Central Africa*	33,000	13,000
Lake Malawi/Nyasa	*East Africa*	29,600	11,430
Lake Chad	*Central Africa*	25,000	9,700
Lake Bangweulu	*Zambia*	9,840	3,800
Lake Turkana	*Ethiopia/Kenya*	8,500	3,290

Australia		km²	miles²
Lake Eyre	*Australia*	8,900	3,400
Lake Torrens	*Australia*	5,800	2,200
Lake Gairdner	*Australia*	4,800	1,900

North America		km²	miles²
Lake Superior	*Canada/USA*	82,350	31,800
Lake Huron	*Canada/USA*	59,600	23,010
Lake Michigan	*USA*	58,000	22,400
Great Bear Lake	*Canada*	31,800	12,280
Great Slave Lake	*Canada*	28,500	11,000
Lake Erie	*Canada/USA*	25,700	9,900
Lake Winnipeg	*Canada*	24,400	9,400
Lake Ontario	*Canada/USA*	19,500	7,500
Lake Nicaragua	*Nicaragua*	8,200	3,200

South America		km²	miles²
Lake Titicaca	*Bolivia/Peru*	8,300	3,200
Lake Poopo	*Bolivia*	2,800	1,100

Islands

Europe		km²	miles²
Great Britain	*UK*	229,880	88,700
Iceland	*Atlantic Ocean*	103,000	39,800
Ireland	*Ireland/UK*	84,400	32,600
Novaya Zemlya (N.)	*Russia*	48,200	18,600
Sicily	*Italy*	25,500	9,800
Corsica	*France*	8,700	3,400

Asia		km²	miles²
Borneo	*South-east Asia*	744,360	287,400
Sumatra	*Indonesia*	473,600	182,860
Honshu	*Japan*	230,500	88,980
Sulawesi (Celebes)	*Indonesia*	189,000	73,000
Java	*Indonesia*	126,700	48,900
Luzon	*Philippines*	104,700	40,400
Hokkaido	*Japan*	78,400	30,300

Africa		km²	miles²
Madagascar	*Indian Ocean*	587,040	226,660
Socotra	*Indian Ocean*	3,600	1,400
Réunion	*Indian Ocean*	2,500	965

Oceania		km²	miles²
New Guinea	*Indonesia/Papua NG*	821,030	317,000
New Zealand (S.)	*Pacific Ocean*	150,500	58,100
New Zealand (N.)	*Pacific Ocean*	114,700	44,300
Tasmania	*Australia*	67,800	26,200
Hawai'i	*Pacific Ocean*	10,450	4,000

North America		km²	miles²
Greenland	*Atlantic Ocean*	2,175,600	839,800
Baffin Is.	*Canada*	508,000	196,100
Victoria Is.	*Canada*	212,200	81,900
Ellesmere Is.	*Canada*	212,000	81,800
Cuba	*Caribbean Sea*	110,860	42,800
Hispaniola	*Dominican Rep./Haiti*	76,200	29,400
Jamaica	*Caribbean Sea*	11,400	4,400
Puerto Rico	*Atlantic Ocean*	8,900	3,400

South America		km²	miles²
Tierra del Fuego	*Argentina/Chile*	47,000	18,100
Falkland Is. (E.)	*Atlantic Ocean*	6,800	2,600

User Guide

The reference maps which form the main body of this atlas have been prepared in accordance with the highest standards of international cartography to provide an accurate and detailed representation of the Earth. The scales and projections used have been carefully chosen to give balanced coverage of the world, while emphasizing the most densely populated and economically significant regions. A hallmark of Philip's mapping is the use of hill shading and relief colouring to create a graphic impression of landforms: this makes the maps exceptionally easy to read. However, knowledge of the key features employed in the construction and presentation of the maps will enable the reader to derive the fullest benefit from the atlas.

Map sequence

The atlas covers the Earth continent by continent: first Europe; then its land neighbour Asia (mapped north before south, in a clockwise sequence), then Africa, Australia and Oceania, North America and South America. This is the classic arrangement adopted by most cartographers since the 16th century. For each continent, there are maps at a variety of scales. First, physical relief and political maps of the whole continent; then a series of larger-scale maps of the regions within the continent, each followed, where required, by still larger-scale maps of the most important or densely populated areas. The governing principle is that by turning the pages of the atlas, the reader moves steadily from north to south through each continent, with each map overlapping its neighbours.

Map presentation

With very few exceptions (for example, for the Arctic and Antarctica), the maps are drawn with north at the top, regardless of whether they are presented upright or sideways on the page. In the borders will be found the map title; a locator diagram showing the area covered; continuation arrows showing the page numbers for maps of adjacent areas; the scale; the projection used; the degrees of latitude and longitude; and the letters and figures used in the index for locating place names and geographical features. Physical relief maps also have a height reference panel identifying the colours used for each layer of contouring.

Map symbols

Each map contains a vast amount of detail which can only be conveyed clearly and accurately by the use of symbols. Points and circles of varying sizes locate and identify the relative importance of towns and cities; different styles of type are employed for administrative, geographical and regional place names. A variety of pictorial symbols denote features such as glaciers and marshes, as well as man-made structures including roads, railways, airports and canals.

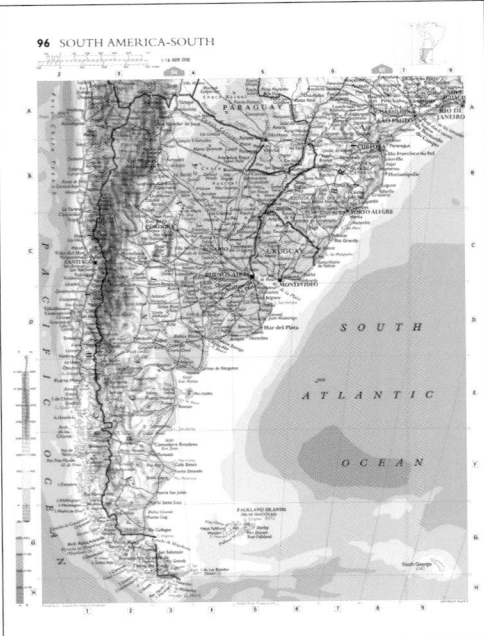

International borders are shown by red lines. Where neighbouring countries are in dispute, for example in the Middle East, the maps show the *de facto* boundary between nations, regardless of the legal or historical situation. The symbols are explained on the first page of the World Maps section of the atlas.

Map scales

The scale of each map is given in the numerical form known as the 'representative fraction'. The first figure is always one, signifying one unit of distance on the map; the second figure, usually in millions, is the number by which the map unit must be multiplied to give the equivalent distance on the Earth's surface. Calculations can easily be made in centimetres and kilometres, by dividing the Earth units figure by 100 000 (i.e. deleting the last five 0s). Thus 1:1 000 000 means 1 cm = 10 km. The calculation for inches and miles is more laborious, but 1 000 000 divided by 63 360 (the number of inches in a mile) shows that the ratio 1:1 000 000 means approximately 1 inch = 16 miles. The table below provides distance equivalents for scales down to 1:50 000 000.

LARGE SCALE		
1:1 000 000	1 cm = 10 km	1 inch = 16 miles
1:2 500 000	1 cm = 25 km	1 inch = 39.5 miles
1:5 000 000	1 cm = 50 km	1 inch = 79 miles
1:6 000 000	1 cm = 60 km	1 inch = 95 miles
1:8 000 000	1 cm = 80 km	1 inch = 126 miles
1:10 000 000	1 cm = 100 km	1 inch = 158 miles
1:15 000 000	1 cm = 150 km	1 inch = 237 miles
1:20 000 000	1 cm = 200 km	1 inch = 316 miles
1:50 000 000	1 cm = 500 km	1 inch = 790 miles
SMALL SCALE		

Measuring distances

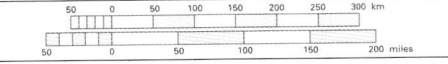

Although each map is accompanied by a scale bar, distances cannot always be measured with confidence because of the distortions involved in portraying the curved surface of the Earth on a flat page. As a general rule, the larger the map scale (i.e. the lower the number of Earth units in the representative fraction), the more accurate and reliable will be the distance measured. On small-scale maps such as those of the world and of entire continents, measurement may only be accurate along the 'standard parallels', or central axes, and should not be attempted without considering the map projection.

Latitude and longitude

Accurate positioning of individual points on the Earth's surface is made possible by reference to the geometrical system of latitude and longitude. Latitude *parallels* are drawn west–east around the Earth and numbered by degrees north and south of the Equator, which is designated 0° of latitude. Longitude *meridians* are drawn north–south and numbered by degrees east and west of the *prime meridian*, 0° of longitude, which passes through Greenwich in England. By referring to these co-ordinates and their subdivisions of minutes ($^{1}/_{60}$th of a degree) and seconds ($^{1}/_{60}$th of a minute), any place on Earth can be located to within a few hundred metres. Latitude and longitude are indicated by blue lines on the maps; they are straight or curved according to the projection employed. Reference to these lines is the easiest way of determining the relative positions of places on different maps, and for plotting compass directions.

Name forms

For ease of reference, both English and local name forms appear in the atlas. Oceans, seas and countries are shown in English throughout the atlas; country names may be abbreviated to their commonly accepted form (for example, Germany, not The Federal Republic of Germany). Conventional English forms are also used for place names on the smaller-scale maps of the continents. However, local name forms are used on all large-scale and regional maps, with the English form given in brackets only for important cities – the large-scale map of Russia and Central Asia thus shows Moskva (Moscow). For countries which do not use a Roman script, place names have been transcribed according to the systems adopted by the British and US Geographic Names Authorities. For China, the Pin Yin system has been used, with some more widely known forms appearing in brackets, as with Beijing (Peking). Both English and local names appear in the index, the English form being cross-referenced to the local form.

THE WORLD IN FOCUS

PLANET EARTH	2	WATER & VEGETATION	12	QUALITY OF LIFE	22
RESTLESS EARTH	4	ENVIRONMENT	14	ENERGY	24
LANDFORMS	6	POPULATION	16	PRODUCTION	26
OCEANS	8	THE HUMAN FAMILY	18	TRADE	28
CLIMATE	10	WEALTH	20	TRAVEL & TOURISM	30

Planet Earth

Sun Mercury Mars Saturn Neptune

Venus Earth Jupiter Uranus

The Solar System

A minute part of one of the billions of galaxies (collections of stars) that populate the Universe, the Solar System lies about 26,000 light-years from the centre of our own galaxy, the 'Milky Way'. Thought to be about 5 billion years old, it consists of a central Sun with eight planets and their moons revolving around it, attracted by its gravitational pull. The planets orbit the Sun in the same direction – anti-clockwise when viewed from above the Sun's north pole – and almost in the same plane. Their orbital distances, however, vary enormously.

The Sun's diameter is 109 times that of the Earth, and the temperature at its core – caused by continuous thermonuclear fusions of hydrogen into helium – is estimated to be 15 million degrees Celsius. It is the Solar System's only source of light and heat.

Profile of the Planets

	Mean distance from Sun (million km)	Mass (Earth = 1)	Period of orbit (Earth days/years)	Period of rotation (Earth days)	Equatorial diameter (km)	Number of known satellites*
Mercury	57.9	0.06	87.97 days	58.65	4,879	0
Venus	108.2	0.82	224.7 days	243.02	12,104	0
Earth	149.6	1.00	365.3 days	1.00	12,756	1
Mars	227.9	0.11	687.0 days	1.029	6,792	2
Jupiter	778	317.8	11.86 years	0.411	142,984	63
Saturn	1,427	95.2	29.45 years	0.428	120,536	60
Uranus	2,871	14.5	84.02 years	0.720	51,118	27
Neptune	4,498	17.2	164.8 years	0.673	49,528	13

Number of known satellites at mid-2008

All planetary orbits are elliptical in form, but only Mercury follows a path that deviates noticeably from a circular one. In 2006, Pluto was demoted from its former status as a planet and is now regarded as a member of the Kuiper Belt of icy bodies at the fringes of the Solar System.

The Seasons

Seasons occur because the Earth's axis is tilted at an angle of approximately 23½°. When the northern hemisphere is tilted to a maximum extent towards the Sun, on 21 June, the Sun is overhead at the Tropic of Cancer (latitude 23½° North). This is midsummer, or the summer solstice, in the northern hemisphere.

On 22 or 23 September, the Sun is overhead at the equator, and day and night are of equal length throughout the world. This is the autumnal equinox in the northern hemisphere. On 21 or 22 December, the Sun is overhead at the Tropic of Capricorn (23½° South), the winter solstice in the northern hemisphere. The overhead Sun then tracks north until, on 21 March, it is overhead at the equator. This is the spring (vernal) equinox in the northern hemisphere.

In the southern hemisphere, the seasons are the reverse of those in the north.

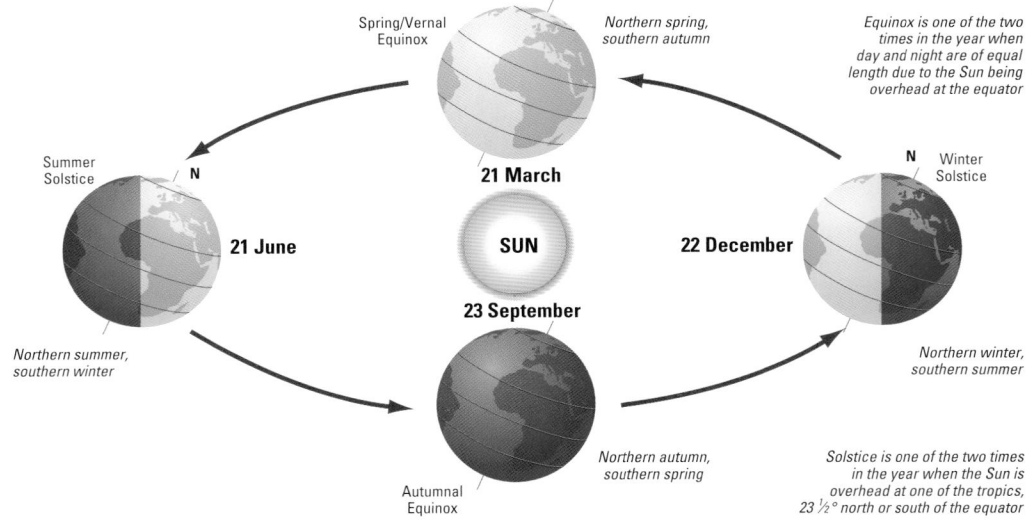

Spring/Vernal Equinox

Northern spring, southern autumn

Equinox is one of the two times in the year when day and night are of equal length due to the Sun being overhead at the equator

Summer Solstice

N

21 March

N Winter Solstice

21 June **SUN** **22 December**

23 September

Northern summer, southern winter

Northern winter, southern summer

Autumnal Equinox

Northern autumn, southern spring

Solstice is one of the two times in the year when the Sun is overhead at one of the tropics, 23½° north or south of the equator

Day and Night

The Sun appears to rise in the east, reach its highest point at noon, and then set in the west, to be followed by night. In reality, it is not the Sun that is moving but the Earth rotating from west to east. The moment when the Sun's upper limb first appears above the horizon is termed sunrise; the moment when the Sun's upper limb disappears below the horizon is sunset.

At the summer solstice in the northern hemisphere (21 June), the Arctic has total daylight and the Antarctic total darkness. The opposite occurs at the winter solstice (21 or 22 December). At the equator, the length of day and night are almost equal all year.

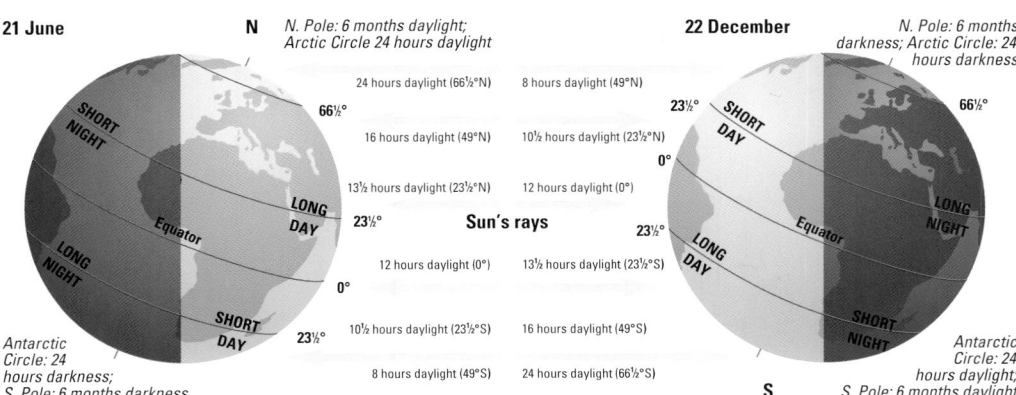

21 June N N. Pole: 6 months daylight; Arctic Circle 24 hours daylight

24 hours daylight (66½°N)

8 hours daylight (49°N)

66½°

16 hours daylight (49°N)

10½ hours daylight (23½°N)

SHORT NIGHT

LONG DAY

13½ hours daylight (23½°N)

12 hours daylight (0°)

23½° **Sun's rays**

Equator

LONG NIGHT

12 hours daylight (0°)

13½ hours daylight (23½°S)

0°

10½ hours daylight (23½°S)

16 hours daylight (49°S)

SHORT DAY 23½°

Antarctic Circle: 24 hours darkness; S. Pole: 6 months darkness

8 hours daylight (49°S)

24 hours daylight (66½°S)

22 December N. Pole: 6 months darkness; Arctic Circle: 24 hours darkness

23½° 66½°

0°

23½°

SHORT DAY

LONG NIGHT

Equator

LONG DAY

SHORT NIGHT

Antarctic Circle: 24 hours daylight; S. Pole: 6 months daylight

S

Time

Year: The time taken by the Earth to revolve around the Sun, or 365.24 days.

Leap Year: A calendar year of 366 days, 29 February being the additional day. It offsets the difference between the calendar and the solar year.

Month: The 12 calendar months of the year are approximately equal in length to a lunar month.

Week: An artificial period of 7 days, not based on astronomical time.

Day: The time taken by the Earth to complete one rotation on its axis.

Hour: 24 hours make one day. The day is divided into hours a.m. (ante meridiem or before noon) and p.m. (post meridiem or after noon), although most timetables now use the 24-hour system, from midnight to midnight.

Sunrise

Sunset

The Moon

The Moon rotates more slowly than the Earth, taking just over 27 days to make one complete rotation on its axis. Since this corresponds to the Moon's orbital period around the Earth, the Moon always presents the same hemisphere towards us, and we never see the far side. The interval between one New Moon and the next is 29½ days – this is called a lunation, or lunar month. The Moon shines only by reflected sunlight, and emits no light of its own. During each lunation the Moon displays a complete cycle of phases, caused by the changing angle of illumination from the Sun.

Phases of the Moon

Mean distance from Earth: 384,401 km; Mean diameter: 3,475 km;
Mass: approximately 1/80 that of Earth; Surface gravity: one-sixth of Earth's;
Daily range of temperature at lunar equator: 280°C; Average orbital speed: 3,681 km/h

| New Moon | Waxing Crescent | First Quarter | Gibbous | Full Moon | Gibbous | Last Quarter | Waning Crescent | New Moon |

Eclipses

When the Moon passes between the Sun and the Earth, the Sun becomes partially eclipsed (1). A partial eclipse becomes a total eclipse if the Moon proceeds to cover the Sun completely (2) and the dark central part of the lunar shadow touches the Earth. The broad geographical zone covered by the Moon's outer shadow (P), has only a very small central area (often less than 100 km wide) that experiences totality. Totality can never last for more than 7½ minutes at maximum, but is usually much briefer than this. Lunar eclipses take place when the Moon moves through the shadow of the Earth, and can be partial or total. Any single location on Earth can experience a maximum of four solar and three lunar eclipses in any single year, while a total solar eclipse occurs an average of once every 360 years for any given location.

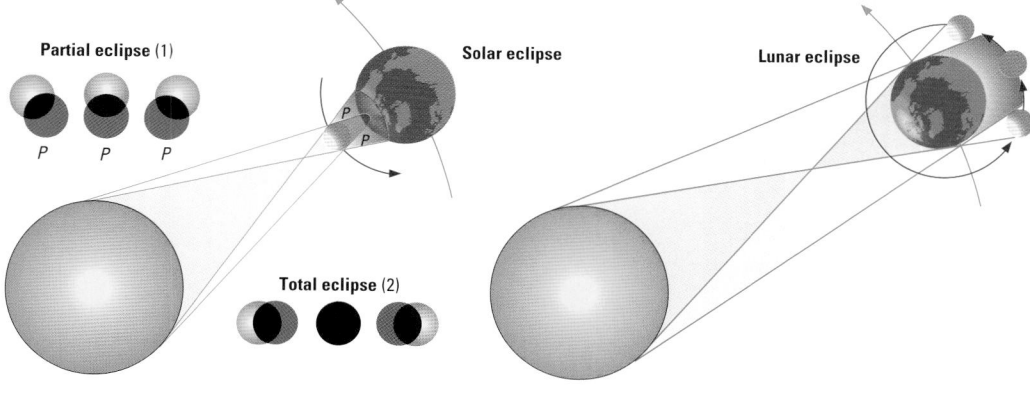

Partial eclipse (1)

Solar eclipse

Lunar eclipse

Total eclipse (2)

Tides

The daily rise and fall of the ocean's tides are the result of the gravitational pull of the Moon and that of the Sun, though the effect of the latter is not as strong as that of the Moon. This effect is greatest on the hemisphere facing the Moon and causes a tidal 'bulge'.

Spring tides occur when the Sun, Earth and Moon are aligned; high tides are at their highest, and low tides fall to their lowest. When the Moon and Sun are furthest out of line (near the Moon's First and Last Quarters), neap tides occur, producing the smallest range between high and low tides.

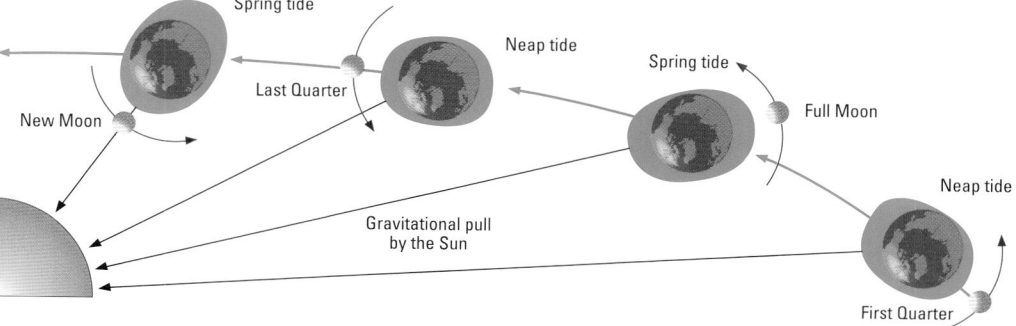

Spring tide

Neap tide

Spring tide

Last Quarter

New Moon

Full Moon

Neap tide

Gravitational pull by the Sun

First Quarter

Restless Earth

The Earth's Structure

Upper mantle (c. 370 km)

Crust (average 5–50 km)

Transitional zone (600 km)

Outer core (2,100 km)

Lower mantle (1,700 km)

Inner core (1,350 km)

Continental Drift

About 200 million years ago the original Pangaea landmass began to split into two continental groups, which further separated over time to produce the present-day configuration.

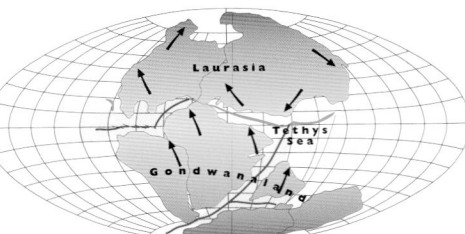

180 million years ago

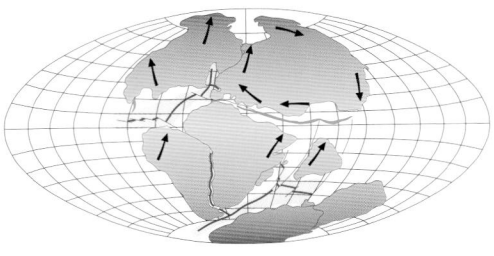

135 million years ago

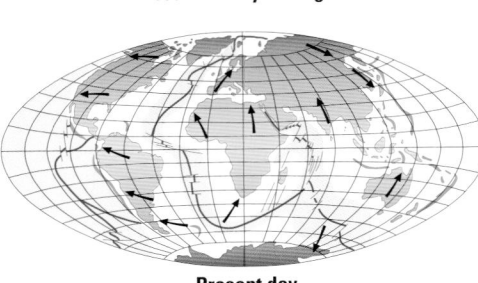

Present day

Trench
Rift
New ocean floor
Zones of slippage

Notable Earthquakes Since 1900

Year	Location	Richter Scale	Deaths
1906	San Francisco, USA	8.3	3,000
1906	Valparaiso, Chile	8.6	22,000
1908	Messina, Italy	7.5	83,000
1915	Avezzano, Italy	7.5	30,000
1920	Gansu (Kansu), China	8.6	180,000
1923	Yokohama, Japan	8.3	143,000
1927	Nan Shan, China	8.3	200,000
1932	Gansu (Kansu), China	7.6	70,000
1933	Sanriku, Japan	8.9	2,990
1934	Bihar, India/Nepal	8.4	10,700
1935	Quetta, India (now Pakistan)	7.5	60,000
1939	Chillan, Chile	8.3	28,000
1939	Erzincan, Turkey	7.9	30,000
1960	S. W. Chile	9.5	2,200
1960	Agadir, Morocco	5.8	12,000
1962	Khorasan, Iran	7.1	12,230
1964	Anchorage, USA	9.2	125
1968	N. E. Iran	7.4	12,000
1970	N. Peru	7.8	70,000
1972	Managua, Nicaragua	6.2	5,000
1974	N. Pakistan	6.3	5,200
1976	Guatemala	7.5	22,500
1976	Tangshan, China	8.2	255,000
1978	Tabas, Iran	7.7	25,000
1980	El Asnam, Algeria	7.3	20,000
1980	S. Italy	7.2	4,800
1985	Mexico City, Mexico	8.1	4,200
1988	N.W. Armenia	6.8	55,000
1990	N. Iran	7.7	36,000
1993	Maharashtra, India	6.4	30,000
1994	Los Angeles, USA	6.6	51
1995	Kobe, Japan	7.2	5,000
1995	Sakhalin Is., Russia	7.5	2,000
1997	N. E. Iran	7.1	2,400
1998	Takhar, Afghanistan	6.1	4,200
1998	Rostaq, Afghanistan	7.0	5,000
1999	Izmit, Turkey	7.4	15,000
1999	Taipei, Taiwan	7.6	1,700
2001	Gujarat, India	7.7	14,000
2002	Baghlan, Afghanistan	6.1	1,000
2003	Boumerdes, Algeria	6.8	2,200
2003	Bam, Iran	6.6	30,000
2004	Sumatra, Indonesia	9.0	250,000
2005	N. Pakistan	7.6	74,000
2006	Java, Indonesia	6.4	6,200
2007	S. Peru	8.0	600
2008	Sichuan, China	7.9	70,000

Earthquakes

Earthquake magnitude is usually rated according to either the Richter or the Modified Mercalli scale, both devised by seismologists in the 1930s. The Richter scale measures absolute earthquake power with mathematical precision: each step upwards represents a tenfold increase in shockwave amplitude. Theoretically, there is no upper limit, but most of the largest earthquakes measured have been rated at between 8.8 and 8.9. The 12–point Mercalli scale, based on observed effects, is often more meaningful, ranging from I (earthquakes noticed only by seismographs) to XII (total destruction); intermediate points include V (people awakened at night; unstable objects overturned), VII (collapse of ordinary buildings; chimneys and monuments fall), and IX (conspicuous cracks in ground; serious damage to reservoirs).

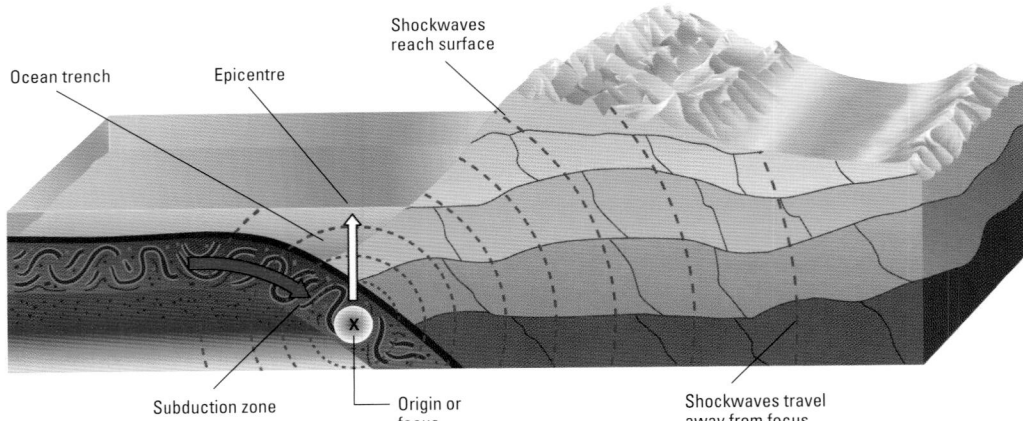

Shockwaves reach surface

Ocean trench

Epicentre

Subduction zone

Origin or focus

Shockwaves travel away from focus

Structure and Earthquakes

Mobile land areas
Submarine zones of mobile land areas
Stable land platforms
Submarine extensions of stable land platforms
Mid-oceanic volcanic ridges
Oceanic platforms

1976 ○ Principal earthquakes and dates (since 1900)

Earthquakes are a series of rapid vibrations originating from the slipping or faulting of parts of the Earth's crust when stresses within build up to breaking point. They usually happen at depths varying from 8 km to 30 km. Severe earthquakes cause extensive damage when they take place in populated areas, destroying structures and severing communications. Most initial loss of life occurs due to secondary causes such as falling masonry, fires and flooding.

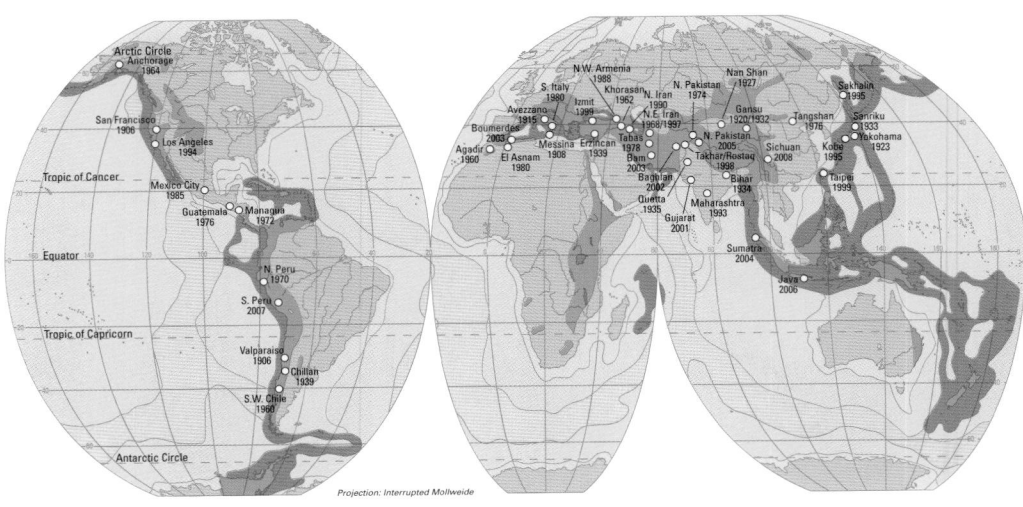

Projection: Interrupted Mollweide

Plate Tectonics

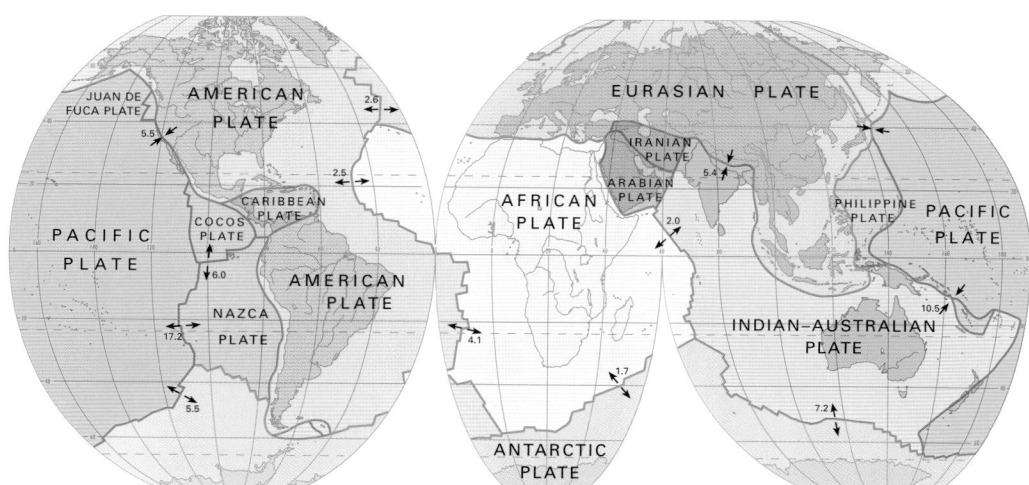

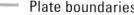 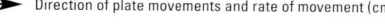
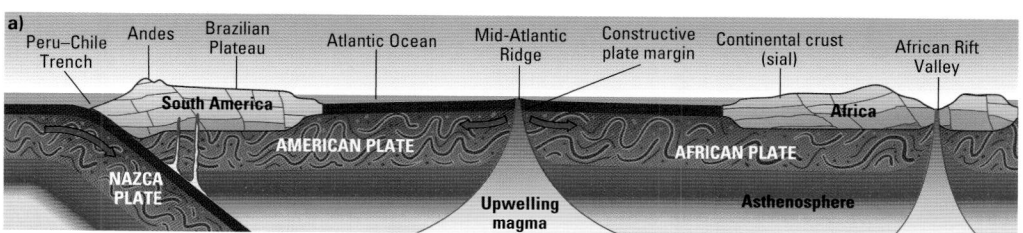

a)

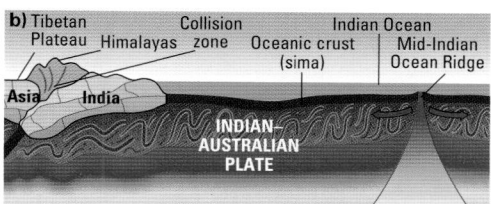

b)

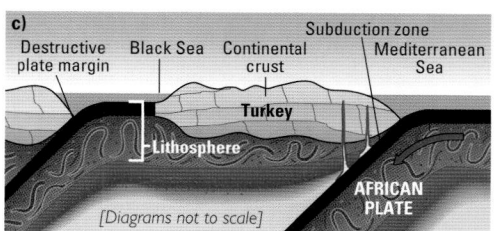

c)

[Diagrams not to scale]

The drifting of the continents is a feature that is unique to Planet Earth. The complementary, almost jigsaw-puzzle fit of the coastlines on each side of the Atlantic Ocean inspired Alfred Wegener's theory of continental drift in 1915. The theory suggested that the ancient super-continent, which Wegener named Pangaea, incorporated all of the Earth's landmasses and gradually split up to form today's continents.

The original debate about continental drift was a prelude to a more radical idea: plate tectonics. The basic theory is that the Earth's crust is made up of a series of rigid plates which float on a soft layer of the mantle and are moved about by continental convection currents within the Earth's interior. These plates diverge and converge along margins marked by seismic activity. Plates diverge from mid-ocean ridges where molten lava pushes upwards and forces the plates apart at rates of up to 40 mm [1.6 in] a year.

The three diagrams, left, give some examples of plate boundaries from around the world. Diagram (a) shows sea-floor spreading at the Mid-Atlantic Ridge as the American and African plates slowly diverge. The same thing is happening in (b) where sea-floor spreading at the Mid-Indian Ocean Ridge is forcing the Indian–Australian plate to collide into the Eurasian plate. In (c) oceanic crust (sima) is being subducted beneath lighter continental crust (sial).

Volcanoes

Volcanoes occur when hot liquefied rock beneath the Earth's crust is pushed up by pressure to the surface as molten lava. Some volcanoes erupt in an explosive way, throwing out rocks and ash, whilst others are effusive and lava flows out of the vent. There are volcanoes which are both, such as Mount Fuji. An accumulation of lava and cinders creates cones of variable size and shape. As a result of many eruptions over centuries, Mount Etna in Sicily has a circumference of more than 120 km [75 miles].

Climatologists believe that volcanic ash, if ejected high into the atmosphere, can influence temperature and weather for several years afterwards. The 1991 eruption of Mount Pinatubo in the Philippines ejected more than 20 million tonnes of dust and ash 32 km [20 miles] into the atmosphere and is believed to have accelerated ozone depletion over a large part of the globe.

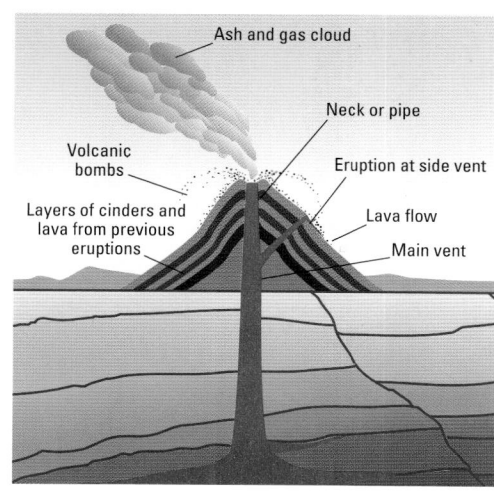

Distribution of Volcanoes

Volcanoes today may be the subject of considerable scientific study but they remain both dramatic and unpredictable: in 1991 Mount Pinatubo, 100 km [62 miles] north of the Philippines capital Manila, suddenly burst into life after lying dormant for more than six centuries. Most of the world's active volcanoes occur in a belt around the Pacific Ocean, on the edge of the Pacific plate, called the 'ring of fire'. Indonesia has the greatest concentration with 90 volcanoes, 12 of which are active. The most famous, Krakatoa, erupted in 1883 with such force that the resulting tidal wave killed 36,000 people and tremors were felt as far away as Australia.

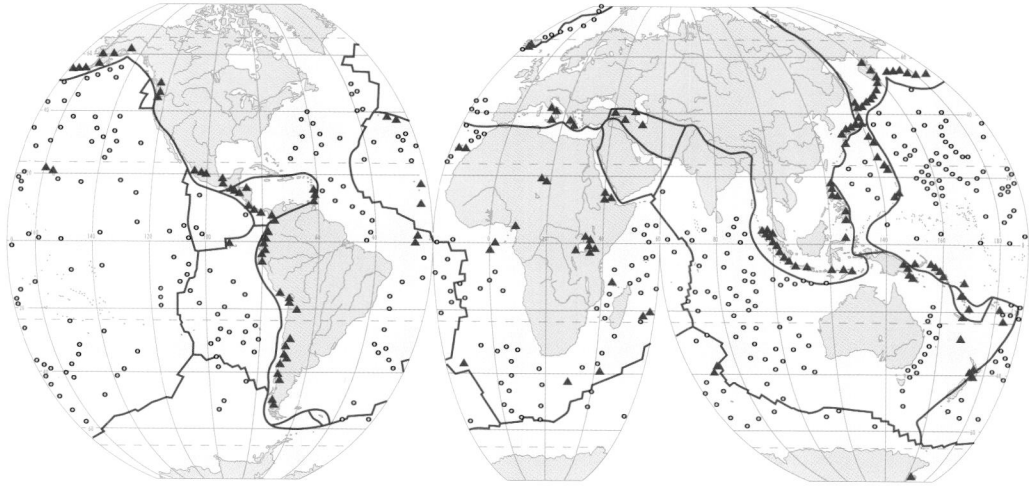

○ Submarine volcanoes

▲ Land volcanoes active since 1700

—— Boundaries of tectonic plates

Landforms

The Rock Cycle

James Hutton first proposed the rock cycle in the late 1700s after he observed the slow but steady effects of erosion.

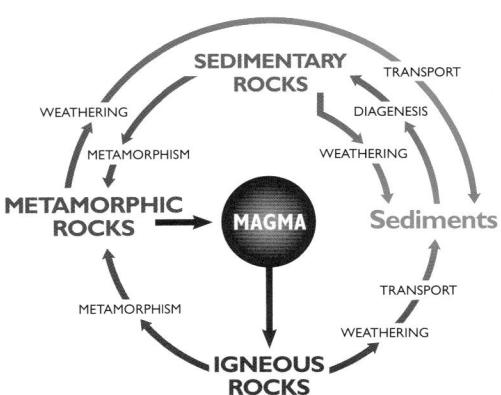

Above and below the surface of the oceans, the features of the Earth's crust are constantly changing. The phenomenal forces generated by convection currents in the molten core of our planet carry the vast segments or 'plates' of the crust across the globe in an endless cycle of creation and destruction. A continent may travel little more than 25 mm [1 in] per year, yet in the vast span of geological time this process throws up giant mountain ranges and creates new land.

Destruction of the landscape, however, begins as soon as it is formed. Wind, water, ice and sea, the main agents of erosion, mount a constant assault that even the most resistant rocks cannot withstand. Mountain peaks may dwindle by as little as a few millimetres each year, but if they are not uplifted by further movements of the crust they will eventually be reduced to rubble and transported away.

Water is the most powerful agent of erosion – it has been estimated that 100 billion tonnes of sediment are washed into the oceans every year. Three

Asian rivers account for 20% of this total; the Huang He, in China, and the Brahmaputra and Ganges in Bangladesh.

Rivers and glaciers, like the sea itself, generate much of their effect through abrasion – pounding the land with the debris they carry with them. But as well as destroying they also create new landforms, many of them spectacular: vast deltas like those of the Mississippi and the Nile, or the deep fjords cut by glaciers in British Columbia, Norway and New Zealand.

Geologists once considered that landscapes evolved from 'young', newly uplifted mountainous areas, through a 'mature' hilly stage, to an 'old age' stage when the land was reduced to an almost flat plain, or peneplain. This theory, called the 'cycle of erosion', fell into disuse when it became evident that so many factors, including the effects of plate tectonics and climatic change, constantly interrupt the cycle, which takes no account of the highly complex interactions that shape the surface of our planet.

Mountain Building

Mountains are formed when pressures on the Earth's crust caused by continental drift become so intense that the surface buckles or cracks. This happens where oceanic crust is subducted by continental crust or, more dramatically, where two tectonic plates collide: the Rockies, Andes, Alps, Urals and Himalayas resulted from such impacts. These are all known as fold mountains because they were formed by the compression of the rocks, forcing the surface to bend and fold like a crumpled rug. The Himalayas are formed from the folded former sediments of the Tethys Sea which was trapped in the collision zone between the Indian and Eurasian plates.

The other main mountain-building process occurs when the crust fractures to create faults, allowing rock to be forced upwards in large blocks; or when the pressure of magma within the crust forces the surface to bulge into a dome, or erupts to form a volcano. Large mountain ranges may reveal a combination of these features; the Alps, for example, have been compressed so violently that the folds are fragmented by numerous faults and intrusions of molten igneous rock.

Over millions of years, even the greatest mountain ranges can be reduced by the agents of erosion (most notably rivers) to a low rugged landscape known as a peneplain.

Types of faults: Faults occur where the crust is being stretched or compressed so violently that the rock strata break in a horizontal or vertical movement. They are classified by the direction in which the blocks of rock have moved. A normal fault results when a vertical movement causes the surface to break apart; compression causes a reverse fault. Horizontal movement causes shearing, known as a strike-slip fault. When the rock breaks in two places, the central block may be pushed up in a horst fault, or sink (creating a rift valley) in a graben fault.

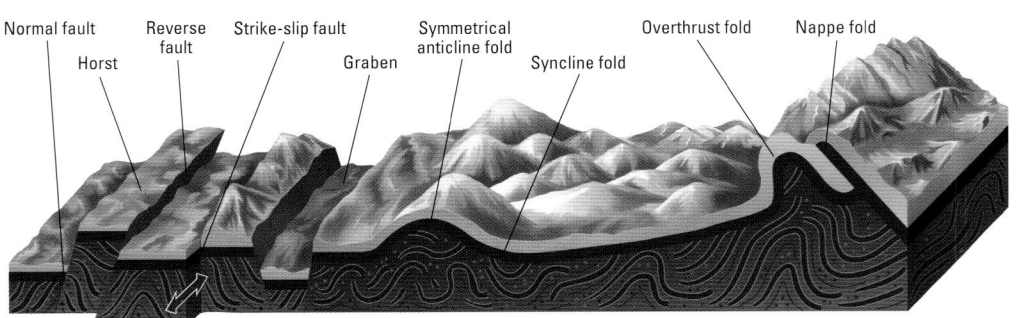

Types of fold: Folds occur when rock strata are squeezed and compressed. They are common, therefore, at destructive plate margins and where plates have collided, forcing the rocks to buckle into mountain ranges. Geographers give different names to the degrees of fold that result from continuing pressure on the rock. A simple fold may be symmetric, with even slopes on either side, but as the pressure builds up, one slope becomes steeper and the fold becomes asymmetric. Later, the ridge or 'anticline' at the top of the fold may slide over the lower ground or 'syncline' to form a recumbent fold. Eventually, the rock strata may break under the pressure to form an overthrust and finally a nappe fold.

Continental Glaciation

Ice sheets were at their greatest extent about 200,000 years ago. The maximum advance of the last Ice Age was about 18,000 years ago, when ice covered virtually all of Canada and reached as far south as the Bristol Channel in Britain.

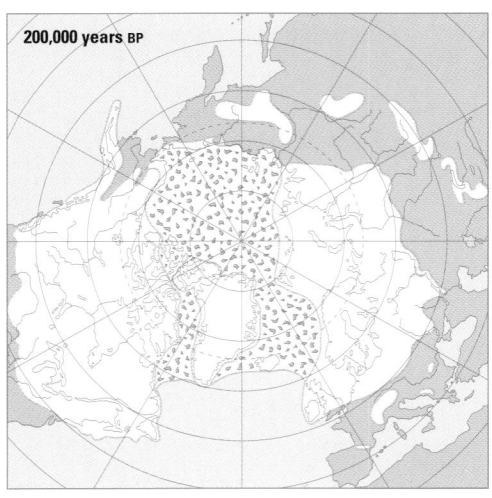

200,000 years BP

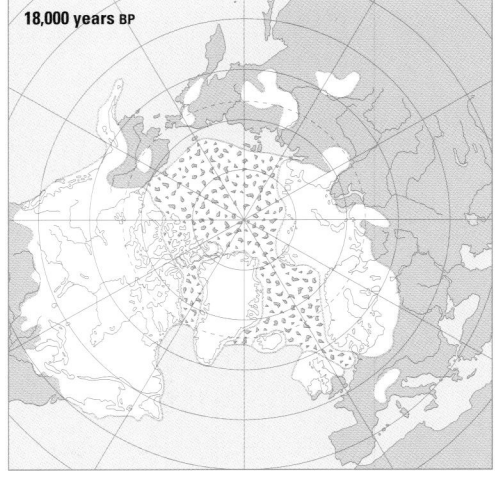

18,000 years BP

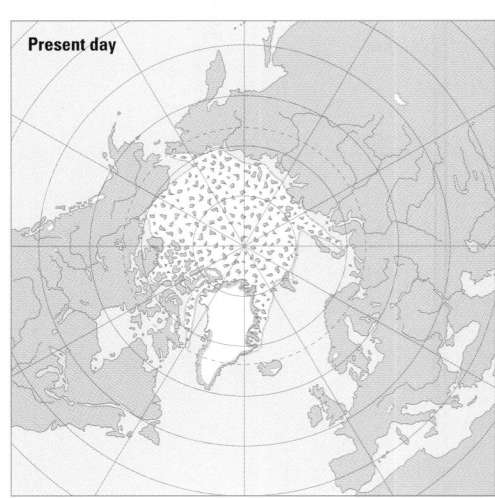

Present day

Natural Landforms

A stylized diagram to show a selection of landforms found in the mid-latitudes.

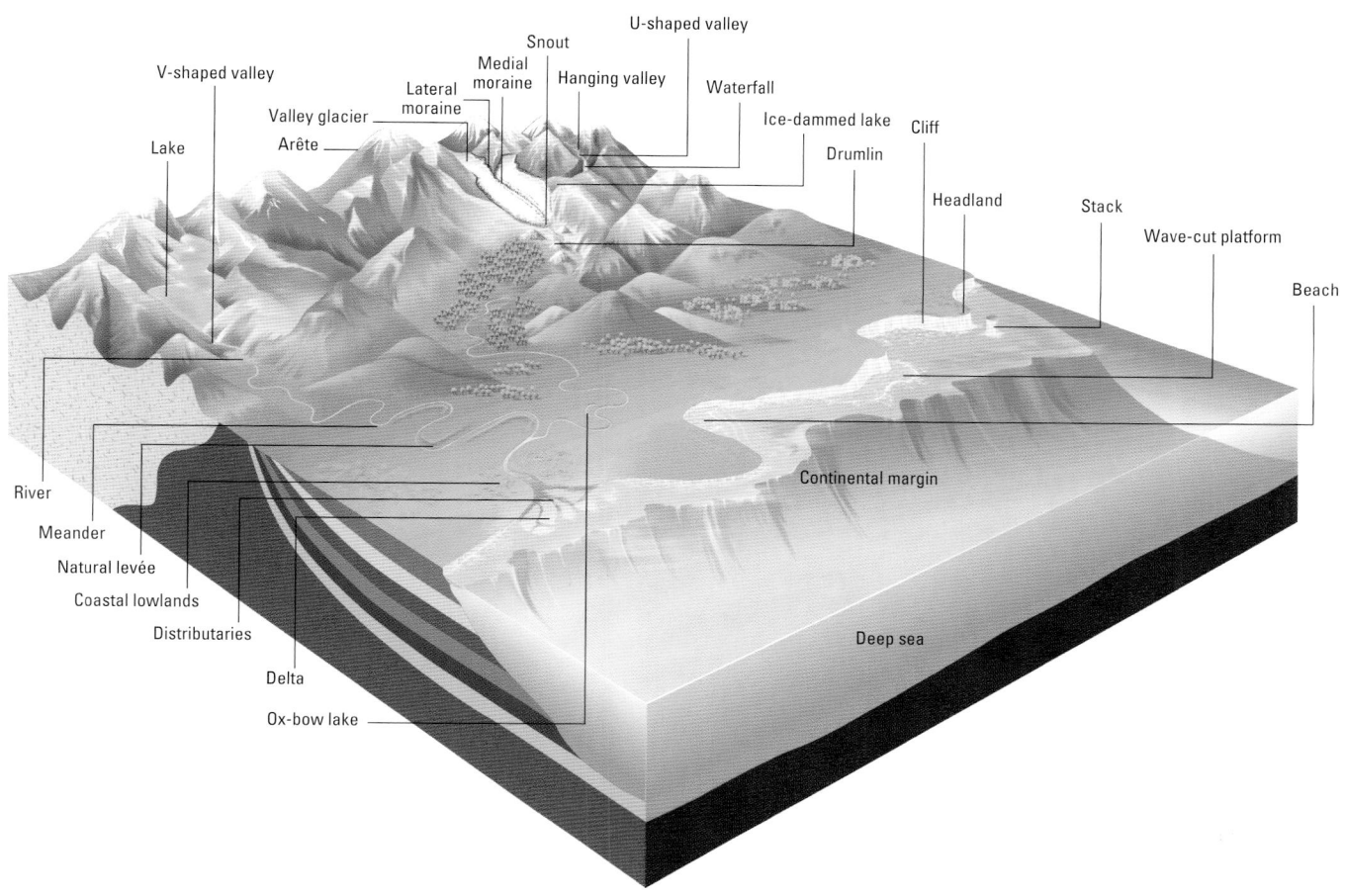

Desert Landscapes

The popular image that deserts are all huge expanses of sand is wrong. Despite harsh conditions, deserts contain some of the most varied and interesting landscapes in the world. They are also one of the most extensive environments – the hot and cold deserts together cover almost 40% of the Earth's surface.

The three types of hot desert are known by their Arabic names: sand desert, called *erg*, covers only about one-fifth of the world's desert; the rest is divided between *hammada* (areas of bare rock) and *reg* (broad plains covered by loose gravel or pebbles).

In areas of *erg*, such as the Namib Desert, the shape of the dunes reflects the character of local winds. Where winds are constant in direction, crescent-shaped *barchan* dunes form. In areas of bare rock, wind-blown sand is a major agent of erosion. The erosion is mainly confined to within 2 m [6.5 ft] of the surface, producing characteristic mushroom-shaped rocks.

Erg

Hammada

Reg

Surface Processes

Catastrophic changes to natural landforms are periodically caused by such phenomena as avalanches, landslides and volcanic eruptions, but most of the processes that shape the Earth's surface operate extremely slowly in human terms. One estimate, based on a study in the United States, suggested that 1 m [3 ft] of land was removed from the entire surface of the country, on average, every 29,500 years. However, the time-scale varies from 1,300 years to 154,200 years depending on the terrain and climate.

In hot, dry climates, mechanical weathering, a result of rapid temperature changes, causes the outer layers of rock to peel away, while in cold mountainous regions, boulders are prised apart when water freezes in cracks in rocks. Chemical weathering, at its greatest in warm, humid regions, is responsible for hollowing out limestone caves and decomposing granites.

The erosion of soil and rock is greatest on sloping land and the steeper the slope, the greater the tendency for mass wasting – the movement of soil and rock downhill under the influence of gravity. The mechanisms of mass wasting (ranging from very slow to very rapid) vary with the type of material, but the presence of water as a lubricant is usually an important factor.

Running water is the world's leading agent of erosion and transportation. The energy of a river depends on several factors, including its velocity and volume, and its erosive power is at its peak when it is in full flood. Sea waves also exert tremendous erosive power during storms when they hurl pebbles against the shore, undercutting cliffs and hollowing out caves.

Glacier ice forms in mountain hollows and spills out to form valley glaciers, which transport rocks shattered by frost action. As glaciers move, rocks embedded into the ice erode steep-sided, U-shaped valleys. Evidence of glaciation in mountain regions includes cirques, knife-edged ridges, or arêtes, and pyramidal peaks.

Oceans

The Great Oceans

Relative sizes of the world's oceans

Pacific
Atlantic
Indian
Southern
Arctic

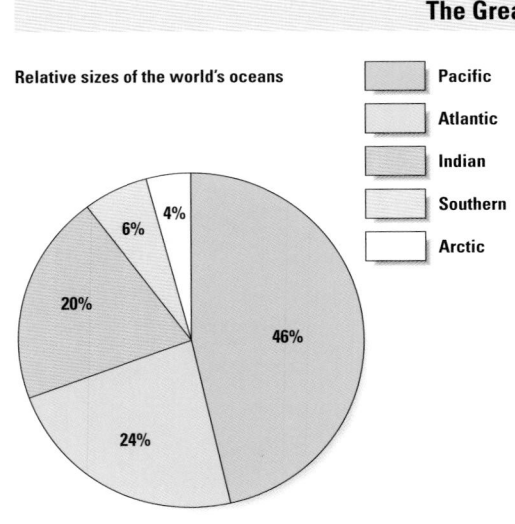

46%
4%
6%
20%
24%

From ancient times to about the 15th century, the legendary 'Seven Seas' comprised the Red Sea, Mediterranean Sea, Persian Gulf, Black Sea, Adriatic Sea, Caspian Sea and Indian Sea.

The Earth is a watery planet: more than 70% of its surface – over 360,000,000 sq km [140,000,000 sq miles] – is covered by the oceans and seas. The mighty Pacific alone accounts for nearly 36% of the total, and more than 46% of the sea area. Gravity holds in around 1,400 million cu. km [320 million cu. miles] of water, of which over 97% is saline.

The vast underwater world starts in the shallows of the seaside and plunges to depths of more than 11,000 m [36,000 ft]. The continental shelf, part of the landmass, drops gently to around 200 m [650 ft]; here the seabed falls away suddenly at an angle of 3° to 6° – the continental slope. The third stage, called the continental rise, is more gradual with gradients varying from 1 in 100 to 1 in 700. At an average depth of 5,000 m [16,500 ft] there begins the aptly-named abyssal plain – massive submarine depths where sunlight fails to penetrate and few creatures can survive.

From these plains rise volcanoes which, taken from base to top, rival and even surpass the tallest continental mountains in height. Mauna Kea, on Hawai'i, reaches a total of 10,203 m [33,400 ft], some 1,355 m [4,500 ft] more than Mount Everest, though scarcely 40% is visible above sea level.

In addition, there are underwater mountain chains up to 1,000 km [600 miles] across, whose peaks sometimes appear above sea level as islands, such as Iceland and Tristan da Cunha.

The Ocean Depths

Average and maximum depths of the world's great oceans, in metres

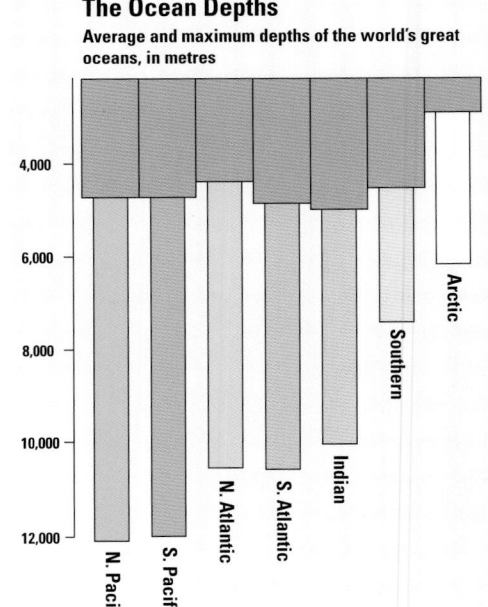

Ocean Currents

January ocean currents

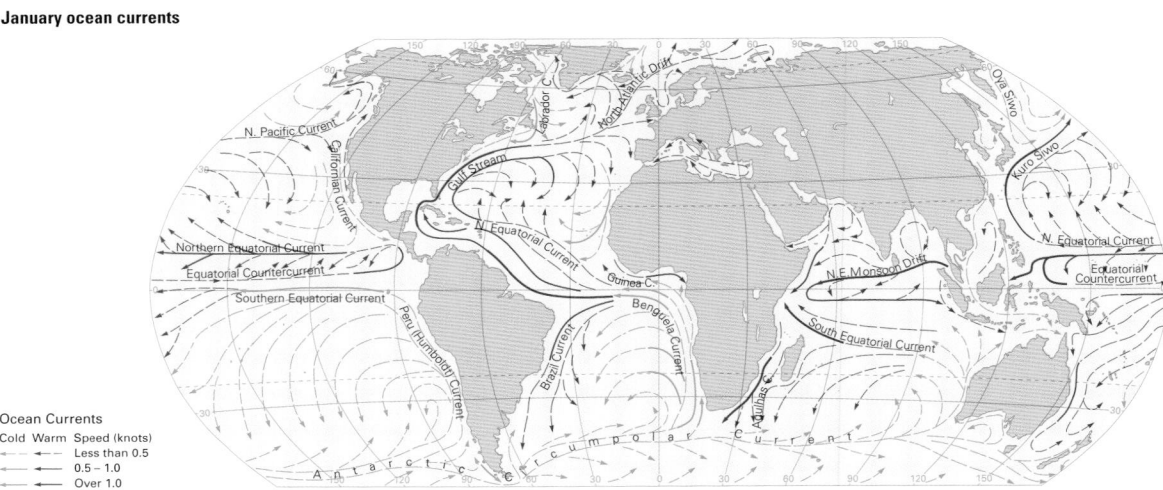

Ocean Currents
Cold Warm Speed (knots)
Less than 0.5
0.5 – 1.0
Over 1.0

July ocean currents

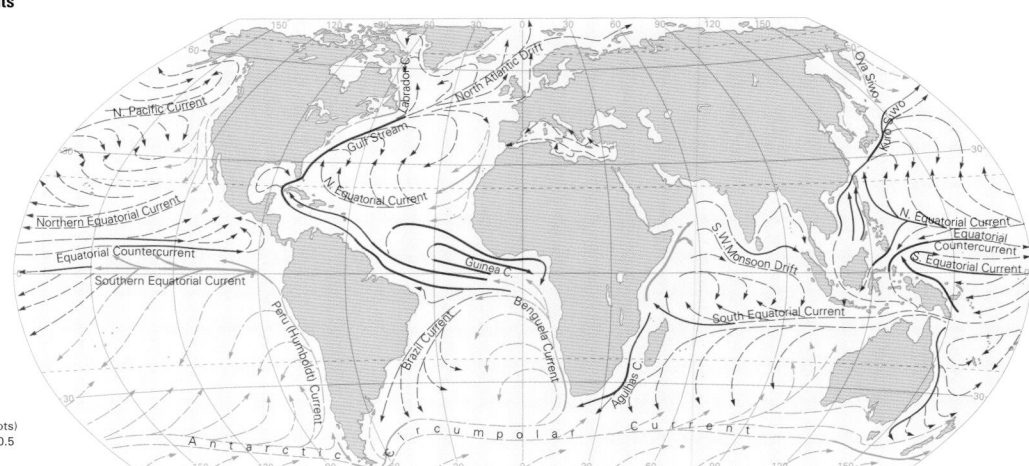

Ocean Currents
Cold Warm Speed (knots)
Less than 0.5
0.5 – 1.0
Over 1.0

Moving immense quantities of energy as well as billions of tonnes of water every hour, the ocean currents are a vital part of the great heat engine that drives the Earth's climate. They themselves are produced by a twofold mechanism. At the surface, winds push huge masses of water before them; in the deep ocean, below an abrupt temperature gradient that separates the churning surface waters from the still depths, density variations cause slow vertical movements.

The pattern of circulation of the great surface currents is determined by the displacement known as the Coriolis effect. As the Earth turns beneath a moving object – whether it is a tennis ball or a vast mass of water – it appears to be deflected to one side. The deflection is most obvious near the Equator, where the Earth's surface is spinning eastwards at 1,700 km/h [1,050 mph]; currents moving polewards are curved clockwise in the northern hemisphere and anti-clockwise in the southern.

The result is a system of spinning circles known as gyres. The Coriolis effect piles up water on the left of each gyre, creating a narrow, fast-moving stream that is matched by a slower, broader returning current on the right. North and south of the Equator, the fastest currents are located in the west and in the east respectively. In each case, warm water moves from the Equator and cold water returns to it. Cold currents often bring an upwelling of nutrients with them, supporting the world's most economically important fisheries.

Depending on the prevailing winds, some currents on or near the Equator may reverse their direction in the course of the year – a seasonal variation on which Asian monsoon rains depend, and whose occasional failure can bring disaster to millions.

World Fishing Areas

Main commercial fishing areas (numbered FAO regions)

Catch by top marine fishing areas, million tonnes (2005)

1.	Pacific, NW	[61]	21.6	22.7%
2.	Pacific, SE	[87]	15.5	16.3%
3.	Pacific, WC	[71]	11.0	11.6%
4.	Atlantic, NE	[27]	10.0	10.5%
5.	Indian, E	[57]	5.6	5.9%
6.	Indian, W	[51]	4.1	4.3%
7.	Atlantic, EC	[34]	3.4	3.6%
8.	Pacific, NE	[67]	3.1	3.3%
9.	Atlantic, NW	[21]	2.4	2.5%
10.	Atlantic, WC	[31]	2.1	2.2%

Principal fishing areas

Leading fishing nations

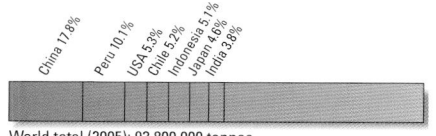

China 17.8% Peru 10.1% USA 5.3% Chile 5.2% Indonesia 5.1% Japan 4.6% India 3.8%

World total (2005): 93,800,000 tonnes
(Marine catch 89.8% Inland catch 10.2%)

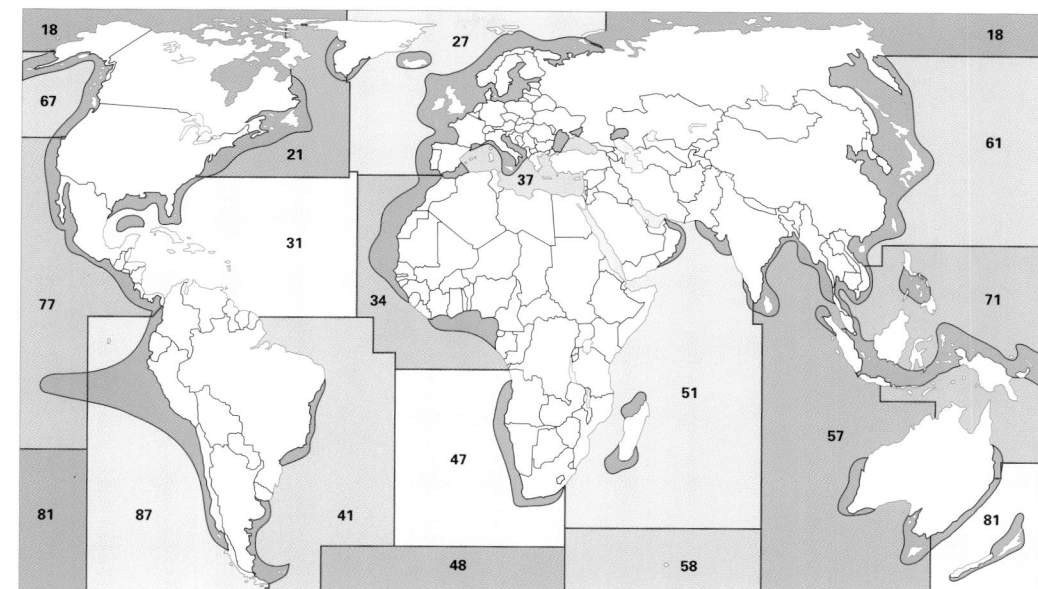

Marine Pollution

Sources of marine oil pollution

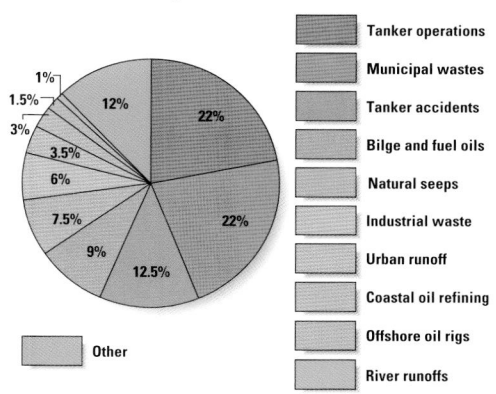

Tanker operations
Municipal wastes
Tanker accidents
Bilge and fuel oils
Natural seeps
Industrial waste
Urban runoff
Coastal oil refining
Offshore oil rigs
River runoffs

Other

Oil Spills

Major oil spills from tankers and combined carriers

Year	Vessel	Location	Spill (barrels) *	Cause
1979	Atlantic Empress	West Indies	1,890,000	collision
1983	Castillo De Bellver	South Africa	1,760,000	fire
1978	Amoco Cadiz	France	1,628,000	grounding
1991	Haven	Italy	1,029,000	explosion
1988	Odyssey	Canada	1,000,000	fire
1967	Torrey Canyon	UK	909,000	grounding
1972	Sea Star	Gulf of Oman	902,250	collision
1977	Hawaiian Patriot	Hawaiian Is.	742,500	fire
1979	Independenta	Turkey	696,350	collision
1993	Braer	UK	625,000	grounding
1996	Sea Empress	UK	515,000	grounding
2002	Prestige	Spain	463,250	storm

Other sources of major oil spills

Year	Source	Location	Spill (barrels)	Cause
1983	Nowruz oilfield	Persian Gulf	4,250,000[†]	war
1979	Ixtoc 1 oilwell	Gulf of Mexico	4,200,000[†]	blow-out
1991	Kuwait	Persian Gulf	2,500,000[†]	war

* 1 barrel = 0.136 tonnes/159 lit./35 Imperial gal./42 US gal. [†] estimated

River Pollution

Sources of river pollution, USA

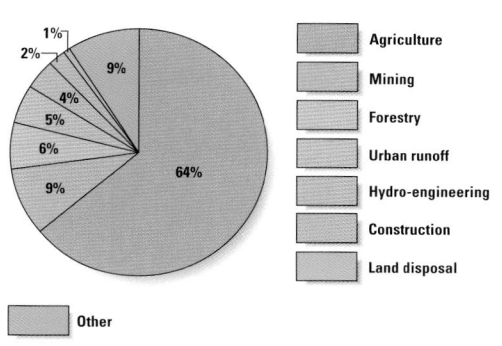

Agriculture
Mining
Forestry
Urban runoff
Hydro-engineering
Construction
Land disposal

Other

Water Pollution

Severely polluted sea areas and lakes

Polluted sea areas and lakes

Areas of frequent oil pollution by shipping

◣ Major oil tanker spills

▲ Major oil rig blow-outs

▼ Offshore dumpsites for industrial and municipal waste

── Severely polluted rivers and estuaries

The most notorious tanker spillage of the 1980s occurred when the *Exxon Valdez* ran aground in Prince William Sound, Alaska, in 1989, spilling 267,000 barrels of crude oil close to shore in a sensitive ecological area. This rates as the world's 28th worst spill in terms of volume.

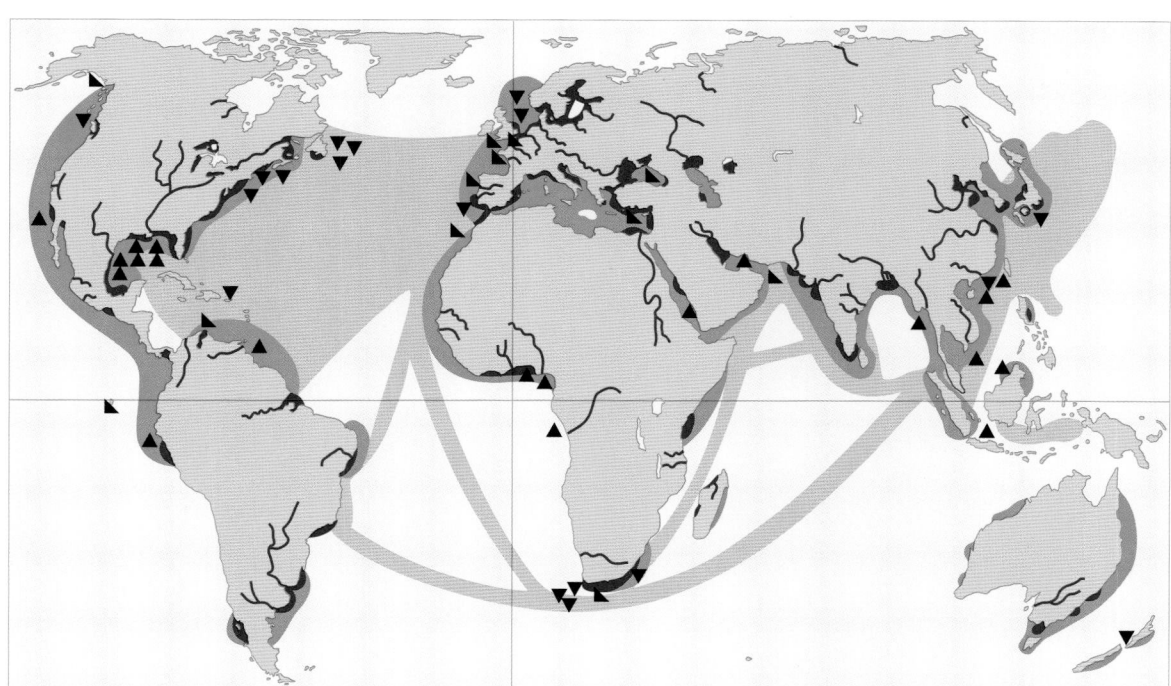

Climate

Climatic Regions

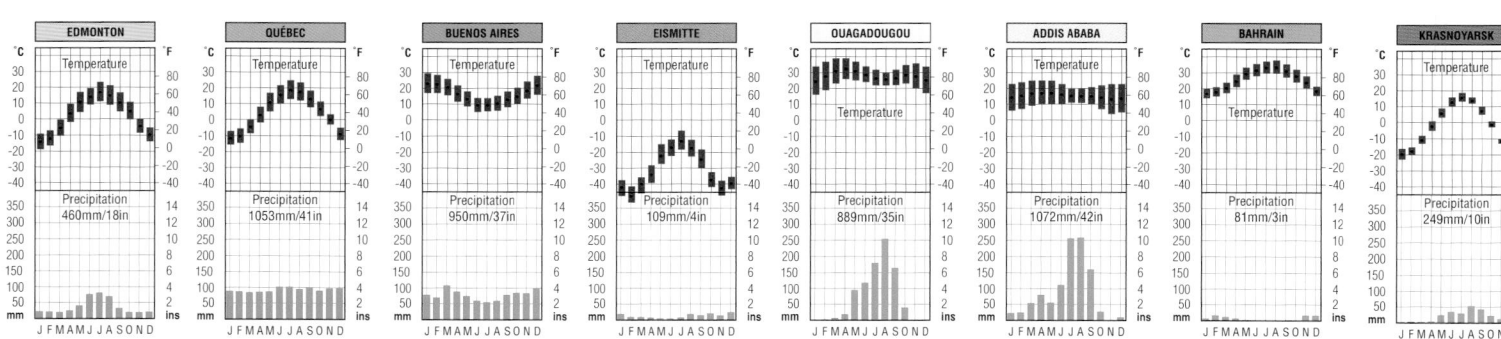

Colour of climate region on map		
Tropical climate (hot with rain all year)	Steppe climate (warm and dry)	Subarctic climate (very cold winter)
Desert climate (hot and very dry)	Mild climate (warm and wet)	Polar climate (very cold and dry)
Savanna climate (hot with dry season)	Continental climate (wet with cold winter)	Mountainous climate (altitude affects climate)

Climate Records

Temperature

Highest recorded shade temperature: Al Aziziyah, Libya, 57.7°C [135.9°F], 13 September 1922.

Highest mean annual temperature: Dallol, Ethiopia, 34.4°C [94°F], 1960–66.

Longest heatwave: Marble Bar, W. Australia, 162 days over 38°C [100°F], 23 October 1923 to 7 April 1924.

Lowest recorded temperature (outside poles): Verkhoyansk, Siberia, –68°C [–93.6°F], 7 February 1982.

Lowest mean annual temperature: Polus Nedostupnosti, Pole of Cold, Antarctica, –57.8°C [–72°F].

Precipitation

Driest place: Quillagua, Chile, mean annual rainfall 0.5 mm [0.02 in], 1964–2001.

Wettest place (12 months): Cherrapunji, Meghalaya, N. E. India, 26,461 mm [1,042 in], August 1860 to July 1861. Cherrapunji also holds the record for the most rainfall in one month: 2,930 mm [115 in], July 1861.

Wettest place (average): Mt Wai-ale-ale, Hawai'i, USA, mean annual rainfall 11,680 mm [459.8 in].

Wettest place (24 hours): Fac Fac, Réunion, Indian Ocean, 1,825 mm [71.9 in], 15–16 March 1952.

Heaviest hailstones: Gopalganj, Bangladesh, up to 1.02 kg [2.25 lb], 14 April 1986 (killed 92 people).

Heaviest snowfall (continuous): Bessans, Savoie, France, 1,730 mm [68 in] in 19 hours, 5–6 April 1969.

Heaviest snowfall (season/year): Mt Baker, Washington, USA, 28,956 mm [1,140 in], June 1998 to June 1999.

Pressure and winds

Highest barometric pressure: Agata, Siberia (at 262 m [862 ft] altitude), 1,083.8 mb, 31 December 1968.

Lowest barometric pressure: Typhoon Tip, Guam, Pacific Ocean, 870 mb, 12 October 1979.

Highest recorded wind speed: Bridge Creek, Oklahoma, USA, 512 km/h [318 mph], 3 May 1999. Measured by Doppler radar monitoring a tornado.

Windiest place: Port Martin, Antarctica, where winds of more than 64 km/h [40 mph] occur for not less than 100 days a year.

Climate

Climate is weather in the long term: the seasonal pattern of hot and cold, wet and dry, averaged over time (usually 30 years). At the simplest level, it is caused by the uneven heating of the Earth. Surplus heat at the Equator passes towards the poles, levelling out the energy differential. Its passage is marked by a ceaseless churning of the atmosphere and the oceans, further agitated by the Earth's diurnal spin and the motion it imparts to moving air and water. The heat's means of transport – by winds and ocean currents, by the continual evaporation and recondensation of water molecules – is the weather itself. There are four basic types of climate, each of which can be further subdivided: tropical, desert (dry), temperate and polar.

Composition of Dry Air

Nitrogen	78.09%	Sulphur dioxide	trace
Oxygen	20.95%	Nitrogen oxide	trace
Argon	0.93%	Methane	trace
Water vapour	0.2–4.0%	Dust	trace
Carbon dioxide	0.03%	Helium	trace
Ozone	0.00006%	Neon	trace

El Niño

In a normal year, south-easterly trade winds drive surface waters westwards off the coast of South America, drawing cold, nutrient-rich water up from below. In an El Niño year (which occurs every 2–7 years), warm water from the west Pacific suppresses upwelling in the east, depriving the region of nutrients. The water is warmed by as much as 7°C [12°F], disturbing the tropical atmospheric circulation. During an intense El Niño, the south-east trade winds change direction and become equatorial westerlies, resulting in climatic extremes in many regions of the world, such as drought in parts of Australia and India, and heavy rainfall in south-eastern USA. An intense El Niño occurred in 1997–8, with resultant freak weather conditions across the entire Pacific region.

Normal year

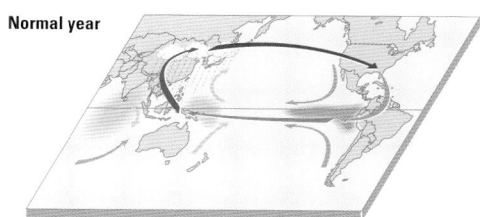

El Niño event

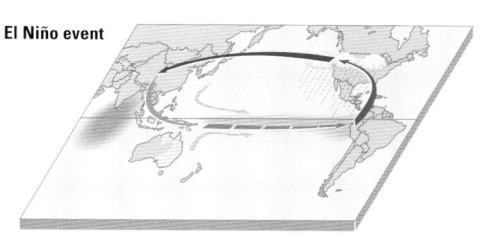

Beaufort Wind Scale

Named after the 19th-century British naval officer who devised it, the Beaufort Scale assesses wind speed according to its effects. It was originally designed as an aid for sailors, but has since been adapted for use on the land.

Scale	Wind speed km/h	mph	Effect
0	0–1	0–1	**Calm** Smoke rises vertically
1	1–5	1–3	**Light air** Wind direction shown only by smoke drift
2	6–11	4–7	**Light breeze** Wind felt on face; leaves rustle; vanes moved by wind
3	12–19	8–12	**Gentle breeze** Leaves and small twigs in constant motion; wind extends small flag
4	20–28	13–18	**Moderate** Raises dust and loose paper; small branches move
5	29–38	19–24	**Fresh** Small trees in leaf sway; wavelets on inland waters
6	39–49	25–31	**Strong** Large branches move; difficult to use umbrellas
7	50–61	32–38	**Near gale** Whole trees in motion; difficult to walk against wind
8	62–74	39–46	**Gale** Twigs break from trees; walking very difficult
9	75–88	47–54	**Strong gale** Slight structural damage
10	89–102	55–63	**Storm** Trees uprooted; serious structural damage
11	103–117	64–72	**Violent storm** Widespread damage
12	118+	73+	**Hurricane**

Conversions

°C = (°F − 32) × 5/9; °F = (°C × 9/5) + 32; 0°C = 32°F
1 in = 25.4 mm; 1 mm = 0.0394 in; 100 mm = 3.94 in

Temperature

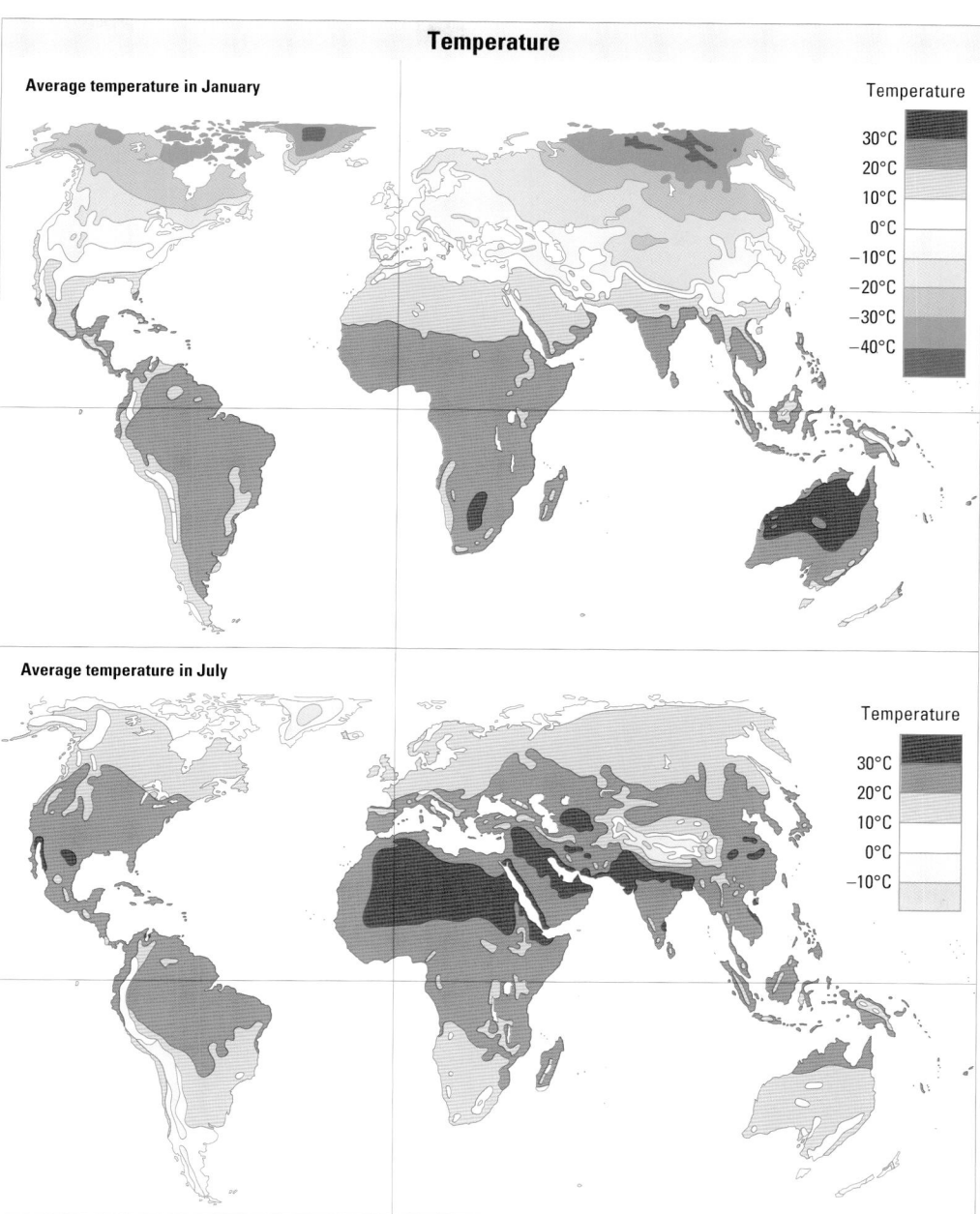

Average temperature in January

Temperature

30°C
20°C
10°C
0°C
−10°C
−20°C
−30°C
−40°C

Average temperature in July

Temperature

30°C
20°C
10°C
0°C
−10°C

Precipitation

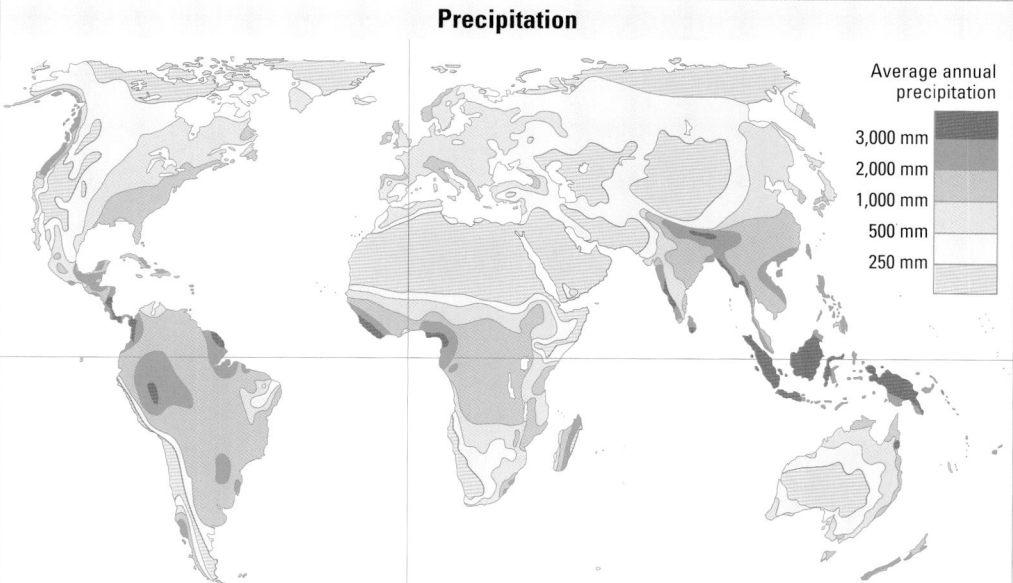

Average annual precipitation

3,000 mm
2,000 mm
1,000 mm
500 mm
250 mm

Water and Vegetation

The Hydrological Cycle

The world's water balance is regulated by the constant recycling of water between the oceans, atmosphere and land. The movement of water between these three reservoirs is known as the hydrological cycle. The oceans play a vital role in the hydrological cycle: 74% of the total precipitation falls over the oceans and 84% of the total evaporation comes from the oceans.

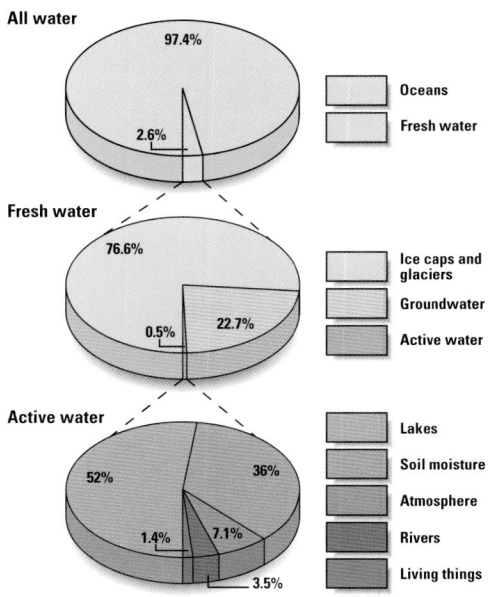

Water Distribution

The distribution of planetary water, by percentage. Oceans and ice caps together account for more than 99% of the total; the breakdown of the remainder is estimated.

All water

97.4% — Oceans
2.6% — Fresh water

Fresh water

76.6% — Ice caps and glaciers
22.7% — Groundwater
0.5% — Active water

Active water

52% — Lakes
36% — Soil moisture
7.1% — Atmosphere
3.5% — Rivers
1.4% — Living things

Water Utilization

Domestic | Industrial | Agriculture

The percentage breakdown of water usage by sector, selected countries (2007)

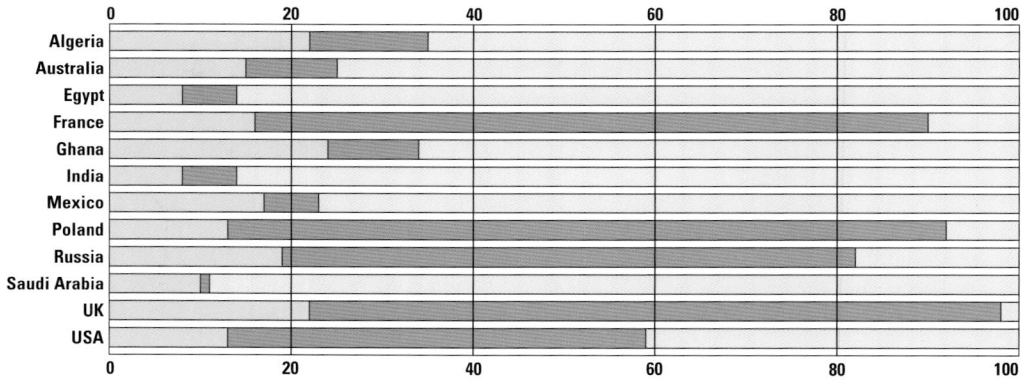

Algeria
Australia
Egypt
France
Ghana
India
Mexico
Poland
Russia
Saudi Arabia
UK
USA

Water Usage

Almost all the world's water is 3,000 million years old, and all of it cycles endlessly through the hydrosphere, though at different rates. Water vapour circulates over days, even hours, deep ocean water circulates over millennia, and ice-cap water remains solid for millions of years.

Fresh water is essential to all terrestrial life. Humans cannot survive more than a few days without it, and even the hardiest desert plants and animals could not exist without some water. Agriculture requires huge quantities of fresh water: without large-scale irrigation most of the world's people would starve. In the USA, agriculture uses 41% and industry 46% of all water withdrawals.

According to the latest figures, the average North American uses 1.3 million litres per year. This is more than six times the average African, who uses just 186,000 litres of water each year. Europeans and Australians use 694,000 litres per year.

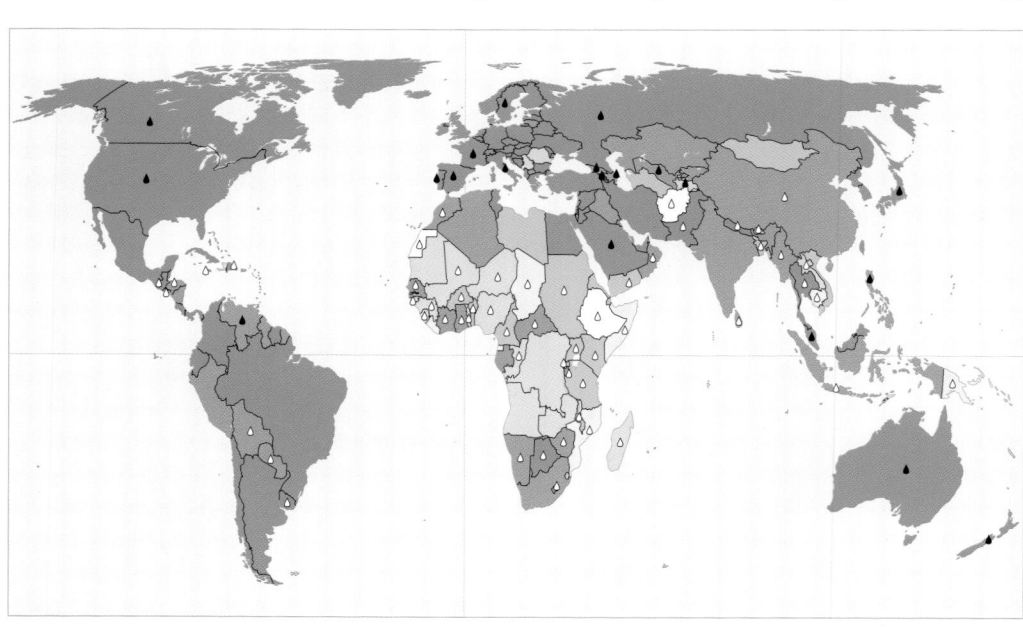

Water Supply

Percentage of total population with access to safe drinking water (2005)

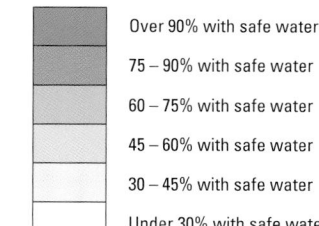

Over 90% with safe water

75 – 90% with safe water

60 – 75% with safe water

45 – 60% with safe water

30 – 45% with safe water

Under 30% with safe water

○ Under 80 litres per person per day domestic water consumption

● Over 320 litres per person per day domestic water consumption

NB: 80 litres of water a day is considered necessary for a reasonable quality of life.

Least well-provided countries

Afghanistan	13%	Papua New Guinea	39%
Ethiopia	22%	Cambodia	41%
Western Sahara	26%	Somalia	42%

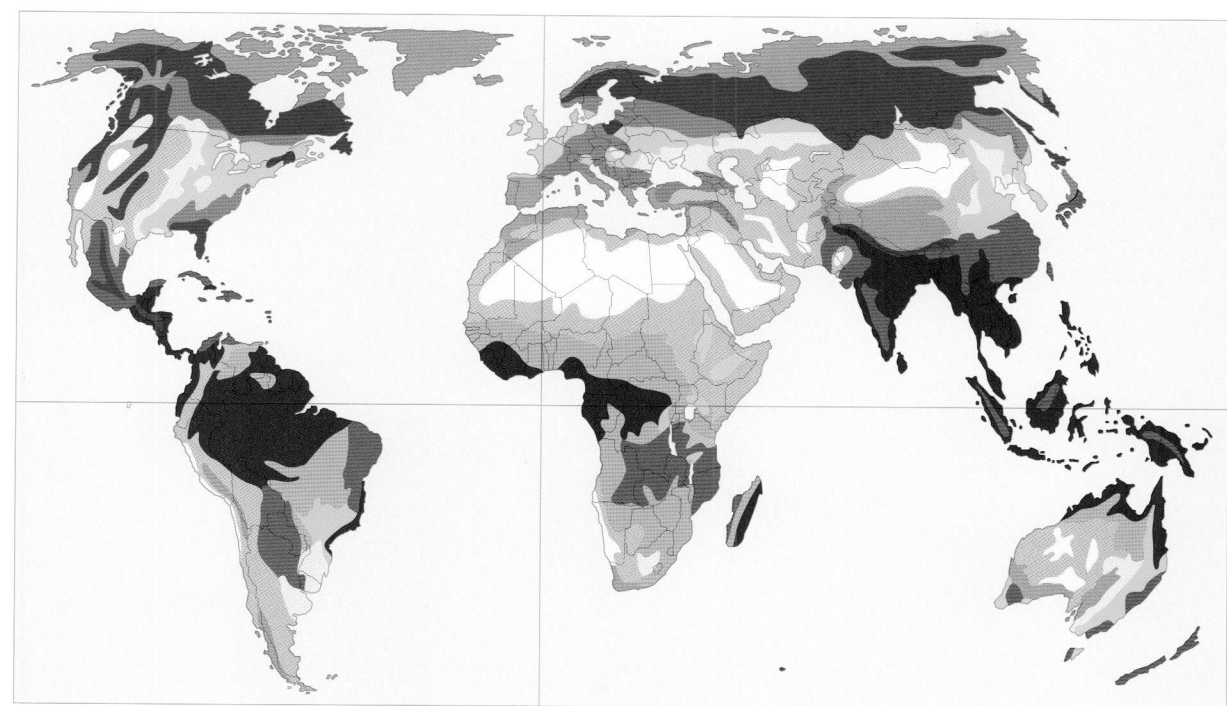

Natural Vegetation

Regional variation in vegetation

- Tundra and mountain vegetation
- Needleleaf evergreen forest
- Mixed needleleaf evergreen & broadleaf deciduous trees
- Broadleaf deciduous woodland
- Mid-latitude grassland
- Evergreen broadleaf and deciduous trees & shrubs
- Semi-desert scrub
- Desert
- Tropical grassland (savanna)
- Tropical broadleaf rainforest and monsoon forest
- Subtropical broadleaf and needleleaf forest

The map shows the natural 'climax vegetation' of regions, as dictated by climate and topography. In most cases, however, agricultural activity has drastically altered the vegetation pattern. Western Europe, for example, lost most of its broadleaf forest many centuries ago, while irrigation has turned some natural semi-desert into productive land.

Land Use by Continent (2005)

- Forest
- Permanent pasture
- Permanent crops
- Arable
- Other

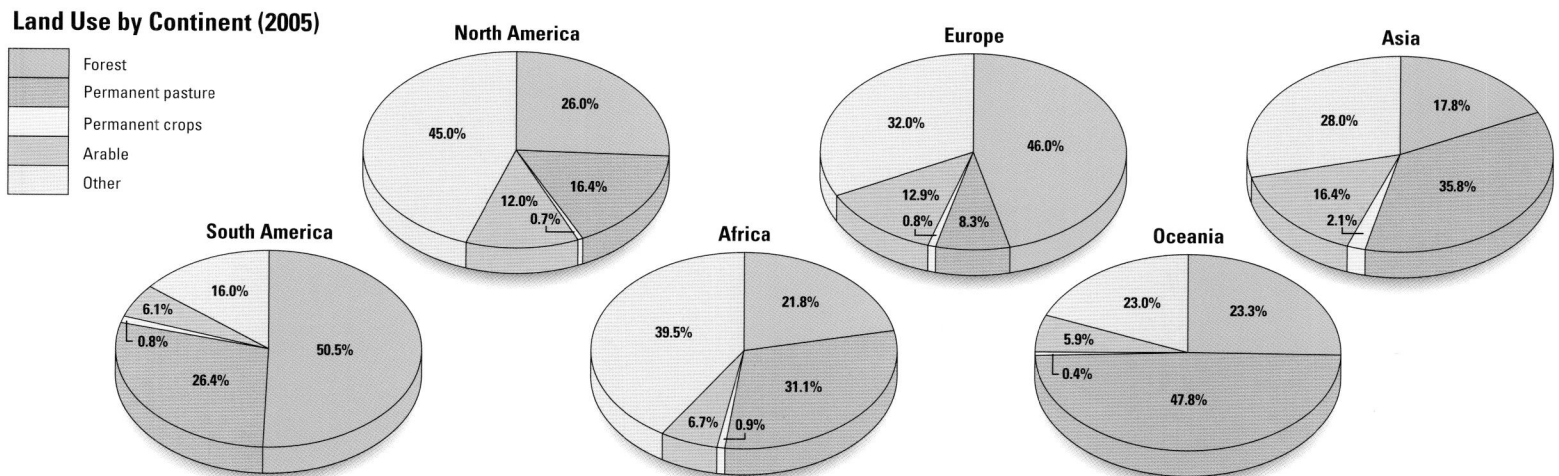

North America
26.0% / 45.0% / 16.4% / 12.0% / 0.7%

Europe
32.0% / 46.0% / 12.9% / 0.8% / 8.3%

Asia
17.8% / 28.0% / 35.8% / 16.4% / 2.1%

South America
16.0% / 6.1% / 0.8% / 50.5% / 26.4%

Africa
21.8% / 39.5% / 31.1% / 6.7% / 0.9%

Oceania
23.0% / 23.3% / 5.9% / 0.4% / 47.8%

Forestry: Production

	Forest and woodland (million hectares)	Annual production (2006, million cubic metres)	
		Fuelwood	Industrial roundwood*
World	*3,869.5*	*1,948.7*	*1762.6*
Europe	1,039.3	152.6	516.7
S. America	885.6	274.6	157.0
Africa	649.9	588.4	66.4
N. & C. America	549.3	131.4	741.9
Asia	547.8	788.9	231.0
Oceania	197.6	12.8	49.6

Paper and Board

Top producers (2006)**		Top exporters (2006)**	
USA	.84,317	Canada	.14,260
China	.57,983	Germany	.13,058
Japan	.29,473	Finland	.12,906
Germany	.22,655	Sweden	.10,849
Canada	.18,176	USA	.9,644

* roundwood is timber as it is felled
** in thousand tonnes

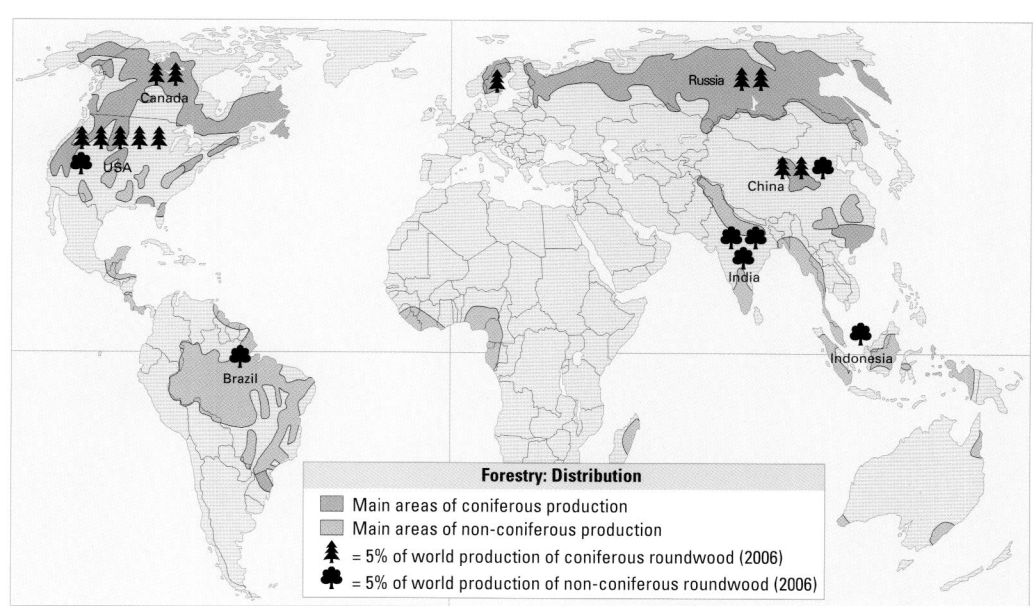

Forestry: Distribution

- Main areas of coniferous production
- Main areas of non-coniferous production
- 🌲 = 5% of world production of coniferous roundwood (2006)
- ♣ = 5% of world production of non-coniferous roundwood (2006)

Environment

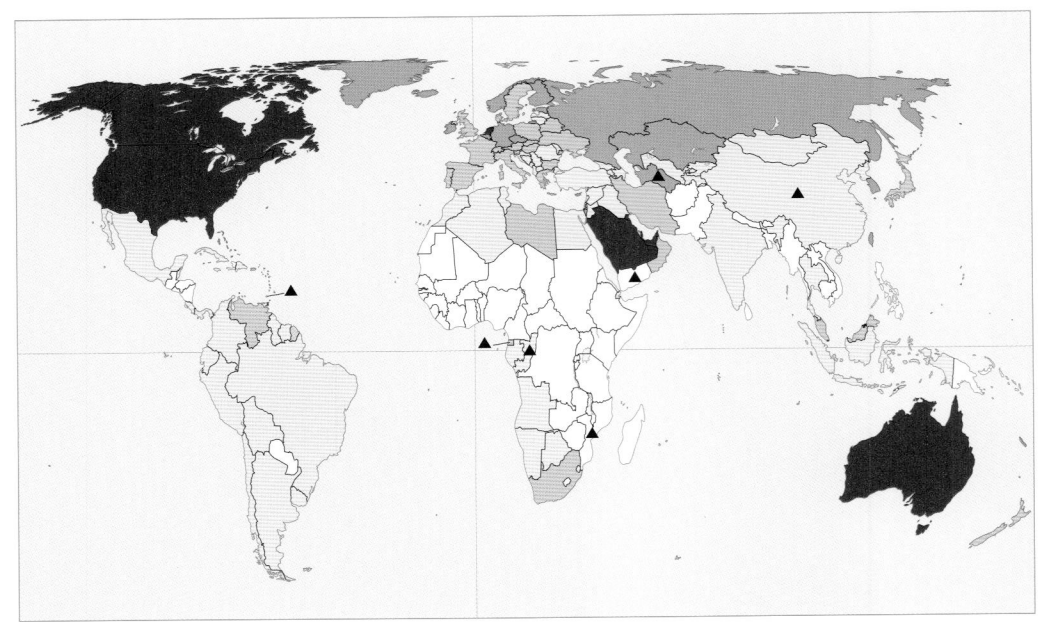

Global Warming

Carbon dioxide emissions in tonnes per capita (2005)

- Over 15
- 10 – 15
- 5 – 10
- 1 – 5
- Under 1
- ▲ Over 75% increase 2000-2005

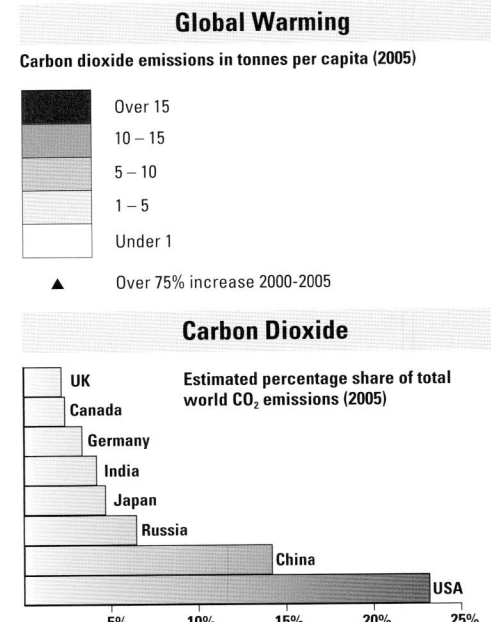

Carbon Dioxide

Estimated percentage share of total world CO₂ emissions (2005)

UK
Canada
Germany
India
Japan
Russia
China
USA

5%   10%   15%   20%   25%

Predicted Change in Precipitation

The difference between actual annual average precipitation, 1960-1990, and the predicted annual average precipitation, 2070-2100.
It should be noted that these predicted annual mean changes mask quite significant seasonal detail.

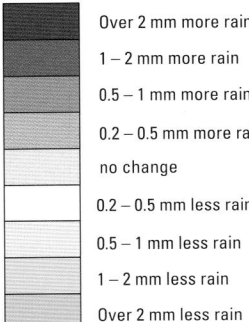

- Over 2 mm more rain
- 1 – 2 mm more rain
- 0.5 – 1 mm more rain
- 0.2 – 0.5 mm more rain
- no change
- 0.2 – 0.5 mm less rain
- 0.5 – 1 mm less rain
- 1 – 2 mm less rain
- Over 2 mm less rain

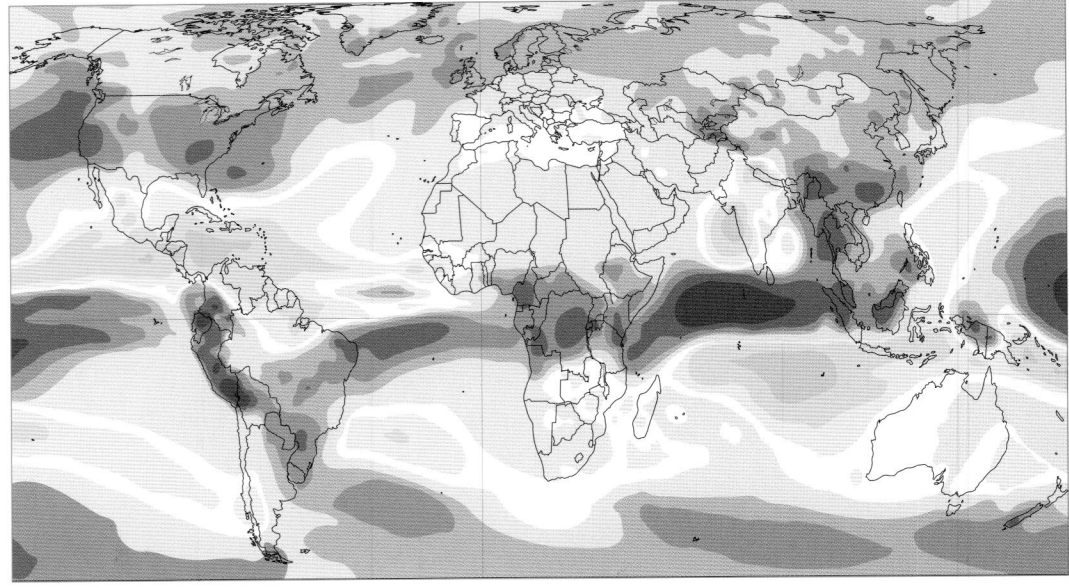

Predicted Change in Temperature

The difference between actual annual average surface air temperature, 1960-1990, and the predicted annual average surface air temperature, 2070-2100.
This map shows the predicted increase, assuming a 'medium growth' of global economy and assuming that no measures to combat the emission of greenhouse gases are taken.

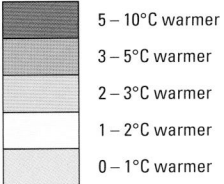

- 5 – 10°C warmer
- 3 – 5°C warmer
- 2 – 3°C warmer
- 1 – 2°C warmer
- 0 – 1°C warmer

Source: The Hadley Centre of Climate Prediction and Research, The Met. Office

Projected Change in Global Warming

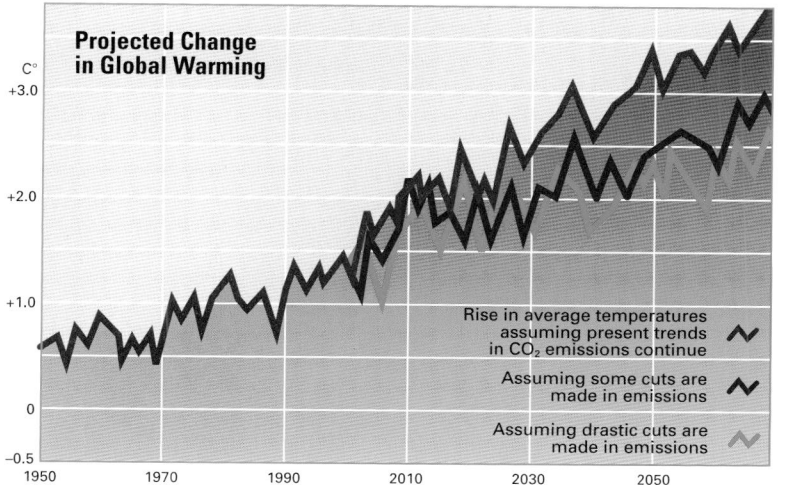

C°
+3.0
+2.0
+1.0
0
−0.5

1950 1970 1990 2010 2030 2050

Rise in average temperatures assuming present trends in CO₂ emissions continue

Assuming some cuts are made in emissions

Assuming drastic cuts are made in emissions

Possible Effect of Sea Level Rise in Florida

Sea levels have risen worldwide by about 2 cm since 1900. If CO₂ emissions continue at the same rate, the sea level is expected to rise by 7.4 m by 2200. The map shows the dramatic effects that such a rise could have on the southern part of Florida in the USA.

Submerged land area if sea level rises 4.5 m

Submerged land area if sea level rises 7.4 m

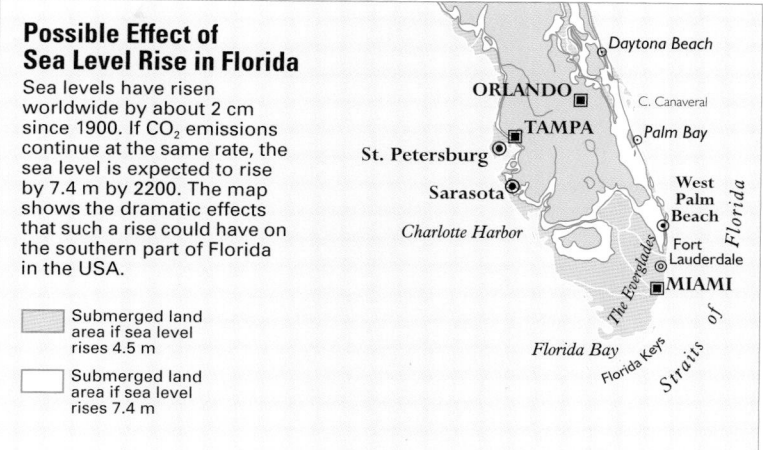

Daytona Beach
ORLANDO
C. Canaveral
TAMPA
Palm Bay
St. Petersburg
Sarasota
West Palm Beach
Charlotte Harbor
Fort Lauderdale
The Everglades
MIAMI
Florida Bay
Florida Keys
Straits of Florida

The Greenhouse Effect

Carbon dioxide is increased by burning fossil fuels and cutting forests

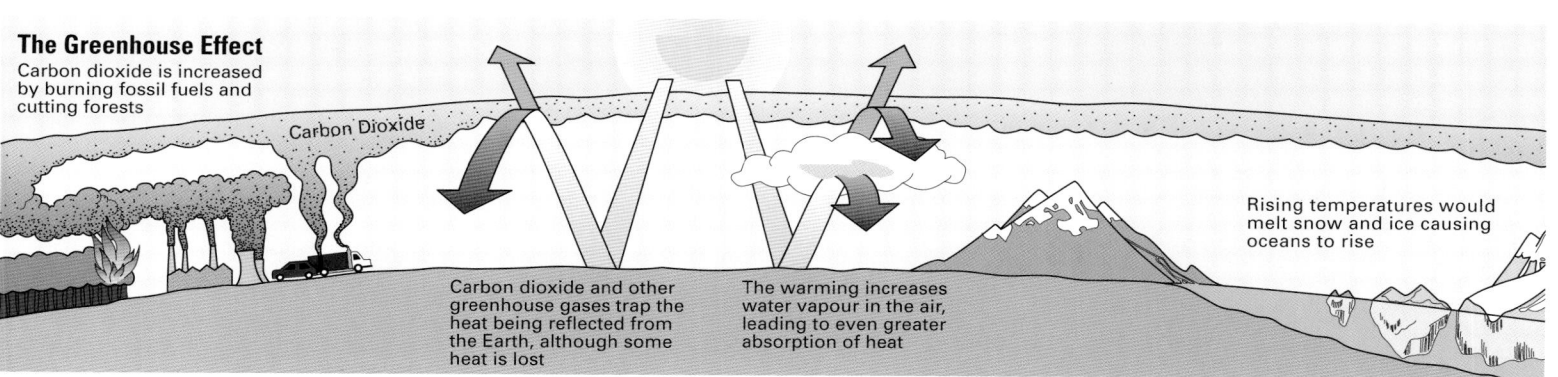

Carbon Dioxide

Carbon dioxide and other greenhouse gases trap the heat being reflected from the Earth, although some heat is lost

The warming increases water vapour in the air, leading to even greater absorption of heat

Rising temperatures would melt snow and ice causing oceans to rise

Desertification

Existing deserts

Areas with a high risk of desertification

Areas with a moderate risk of desertification

Former areas of rainforest

Existing rainforest

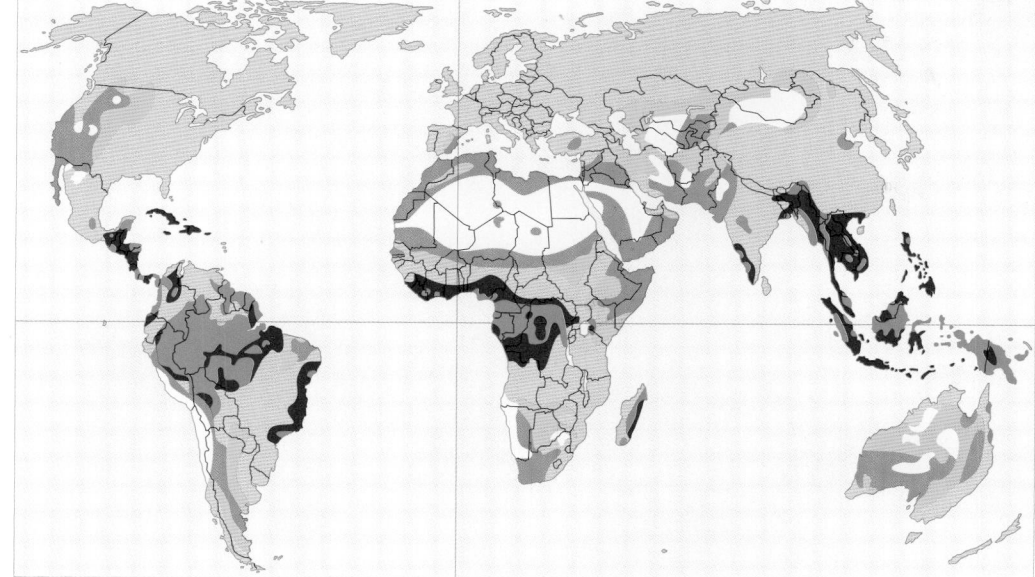

Forest Clearance

Thousands of hectares of forest cleared annually, tropical countries surveyed 1980–85, 1990–95 and 2000–05. Loss as a percentage of remaining stocks is shown in figures on each column. Gain is indicated as a minus figure.

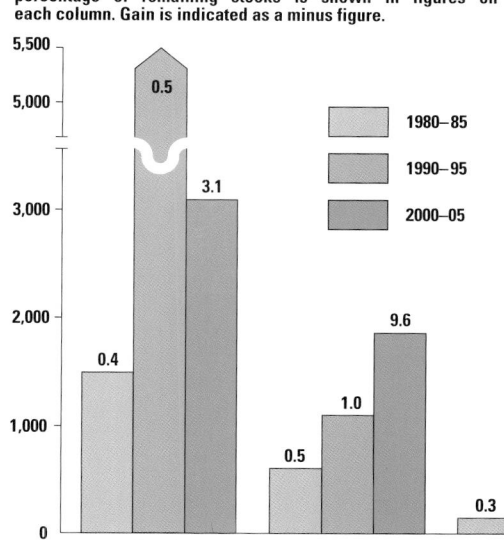

5,500
5,000
3,000
2,000
1,000
0

1980–85
1990–95
2000–05

Brazil 0.4 0.5 3.1
Indonesia 0.5 1.0 9.6
India 0.3 0.0 0.7
Burma 0.3 1.4 4.7
Thailand 2.4 2.6 2.0
Vietnam 0.7 1.4 −12.2
Philippines 1.0 3.5 4.2
Costa Rica 4.0 3.0 −0.6

Deforestation

The Earth's remaining forests are under attack from three directions: expanding agriculture, logging, and growing consumption of fuelwood, often in combination. Sometimes deforestation is the direct result of government policy, as in the efforts made to resettle the urban poor in some parts of Brazil; just as often, it comes about despite state attempts at conservation. Loggers, licensed or unlicensed, blaze a trail into virgin forest, often destroying twice as many trees as they harvest. Landless farmers follow, burning away most of what remains to plant their crops, completing the destruction. Some countries such as Vietnam and Costa Rica have successfully implemented reafforestation programmes.

Population

Demographic Profiles

Developed nations such as the UK have populations evenly spread across the age groups and, usually, a growing proportion of elderly people. The great majority of the people in developing nations, however, are in the younger age groups, about to enter their most fertile years. In time, these population profiles should resemble the world profile (even Nigeria has made recent progress by reducing its birth rate), but the transition will come about only after a few more generations of rapid population growth.

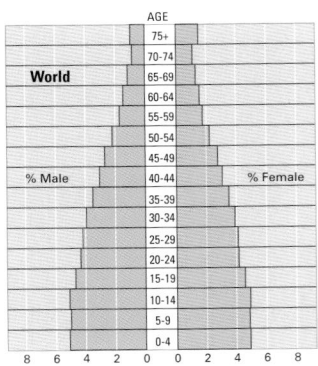

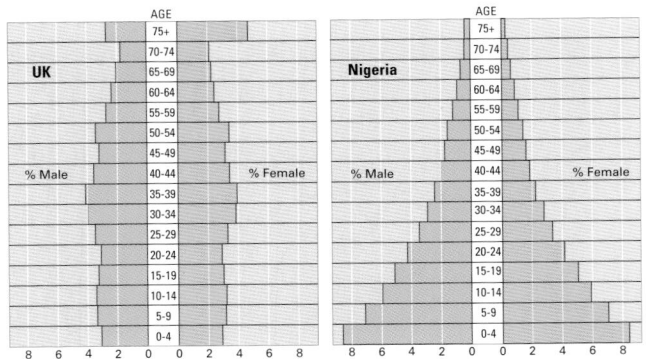

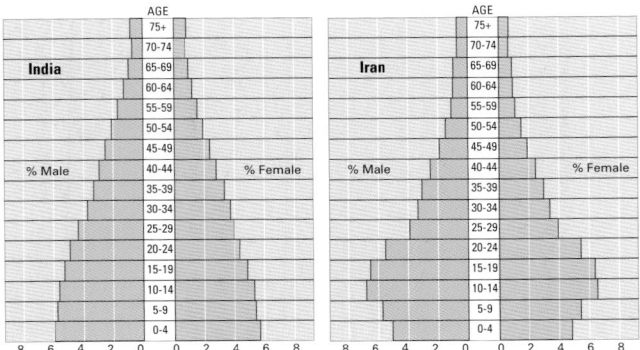

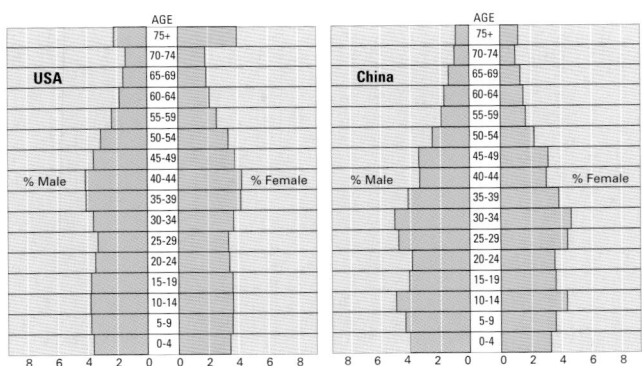

Most Populous Nations, in millions (2007 estimates)

1.	China	1,322	9. Nigeria	135	17. Turkey	71
2.	India	1,130	10. Japan	127	18. Congo (Dem. Rep.)	66
3.	USA	301	11. Mexico	109	19. Iran	65
4.	Indonesia	235	12. Philippines	91	20. Thailand	65
5.	Brazil	190	13. Vietnam	85	21. France	61
6.	Pakistan	165	14. Germany	82	22. UK	61
7.	Bangladesh	150	15. Egypt	80	23. Italy	58
8.	Russia	141	16. Ethiopia	77	24. South Korea	49

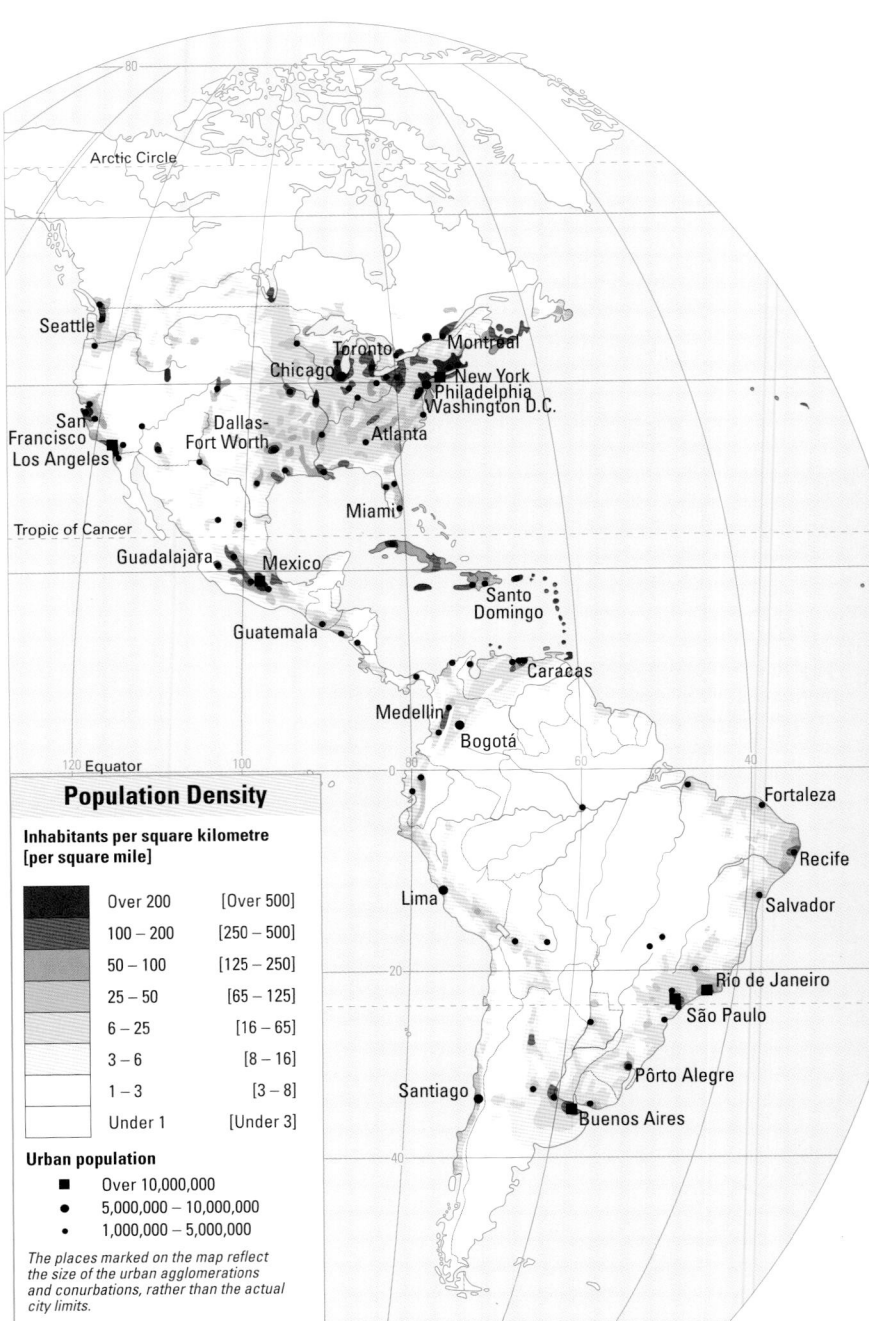

Population Density

Inhabitants per square kilometre [per square mile]

Over 200	[Over 500]
100 – 200	[250 – 500]
50 – 100	[125 – 250]
25 – 50	[65 – 125]
6 – 25	[16 – 65]
3 – 6	[8 – 16]
1 – 3	[3 – 8]
Under 1	[Under 3]

Urban population

- ■ Over 10,000,000
- ● 5,000,000 – 10,000,000
- • 1,000,000 – 5,000,000

The places marked on the map reflect the size of the urban agglomerations and conurbations, rather than the actual city limits.

Continental Comparisons

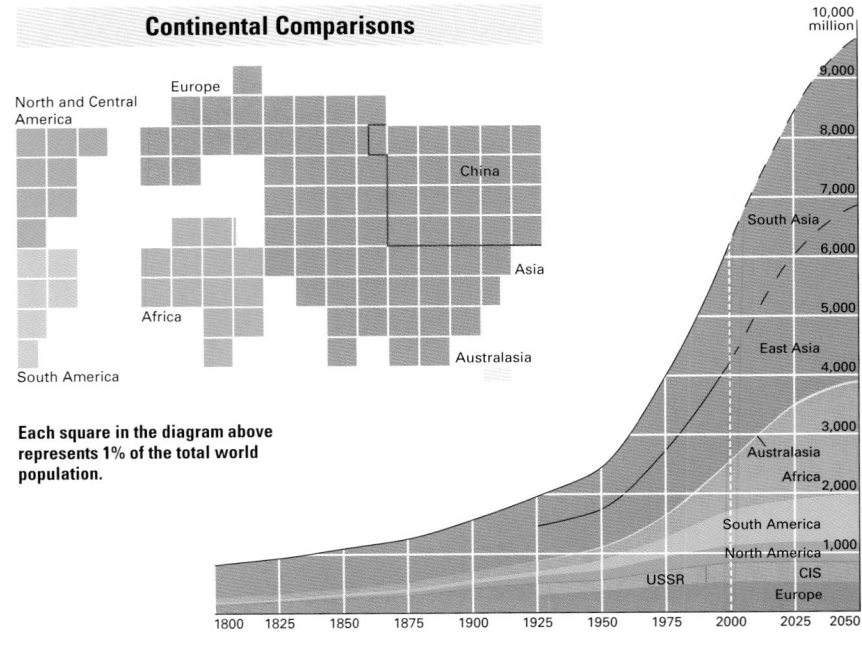

Each square in the diagram above represents 1% of the total world population.

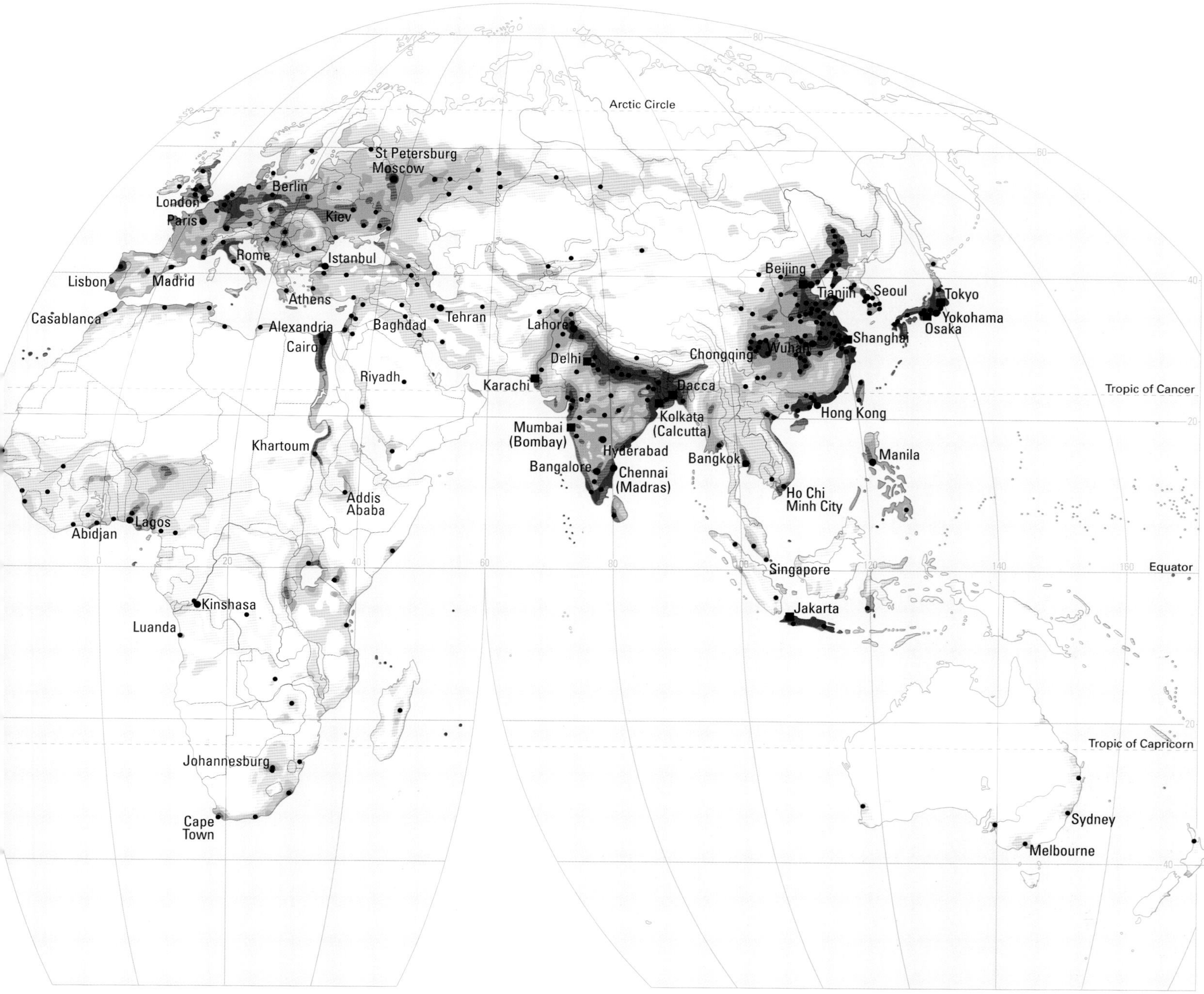

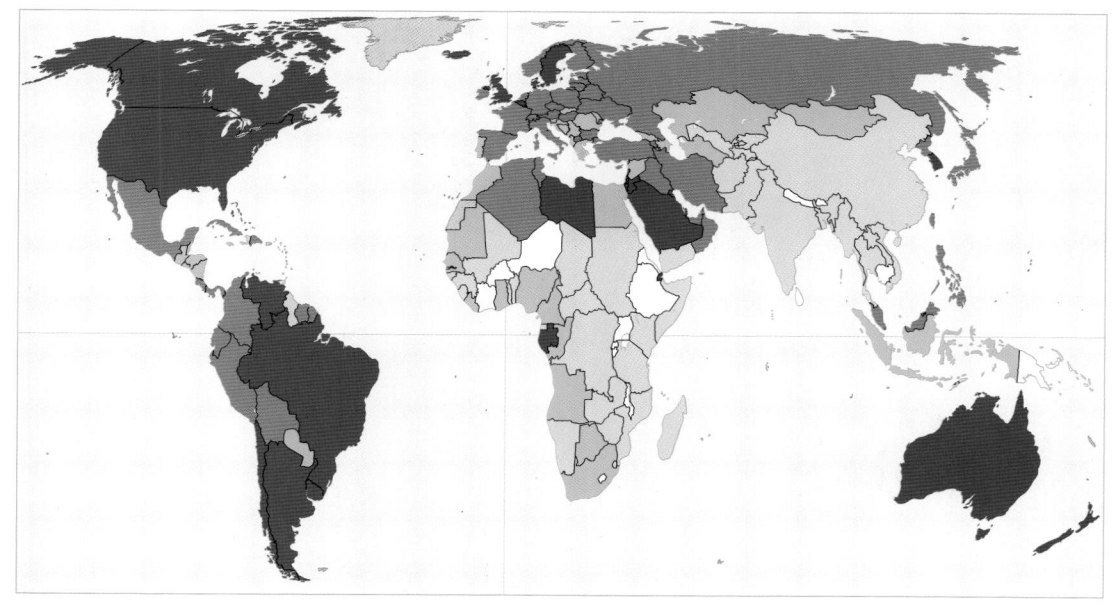

Arctic Circle

St Petersburg
Moscow

Berlin

London
Paris

Kiev

Rome

Lisbon
Madrid

Istanbul

Casablanca

Athens

Alexandria

Baghdad

Tehran

Beijing

Tianjin
Seoul
Tokyo
Yokohama
Osaka

Cairo

Riyadh

Lahore

Delhi

Chongqing
Wuhan
Shanghai

Tropic of Cancer

Karachi

Dacca

Khartoum

Mumbai
(Bombay)

Kolkata
(Calcutta)

Hong Kong

Hyderabad
Bangalore
Chennai
(Madras)

Bangkok

Manila

Addis
Ababa

Ho Chi
Minh City

Lagos
Abidjan

Equator

Singapore

Kinshasa

Jakarta

Luanda

Tropic of Capricorn

Johannesburg

Sydney

Cape
Town

Melbourne

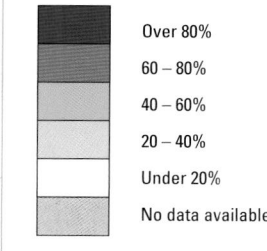

Urban Population

Percentage of total population living in towns and cities (2005)

	Over 80%
	60 – 80%
	40 – 60%
	20 – 40%
	Under 20%
	No data available

Most urbanized		**Least urbanized**	
Singapore	........100%	Burundi	..........10%
Kuwait	...........97%	Bhutan	...........11%
Belgium	..........97%	Trinidad & Tobago	..12%
Bahrain	...........96%	Uganda	...........13%
Qatar	.............95%	Papua New Guinea	.13%

The Human Family

Predominant Languages

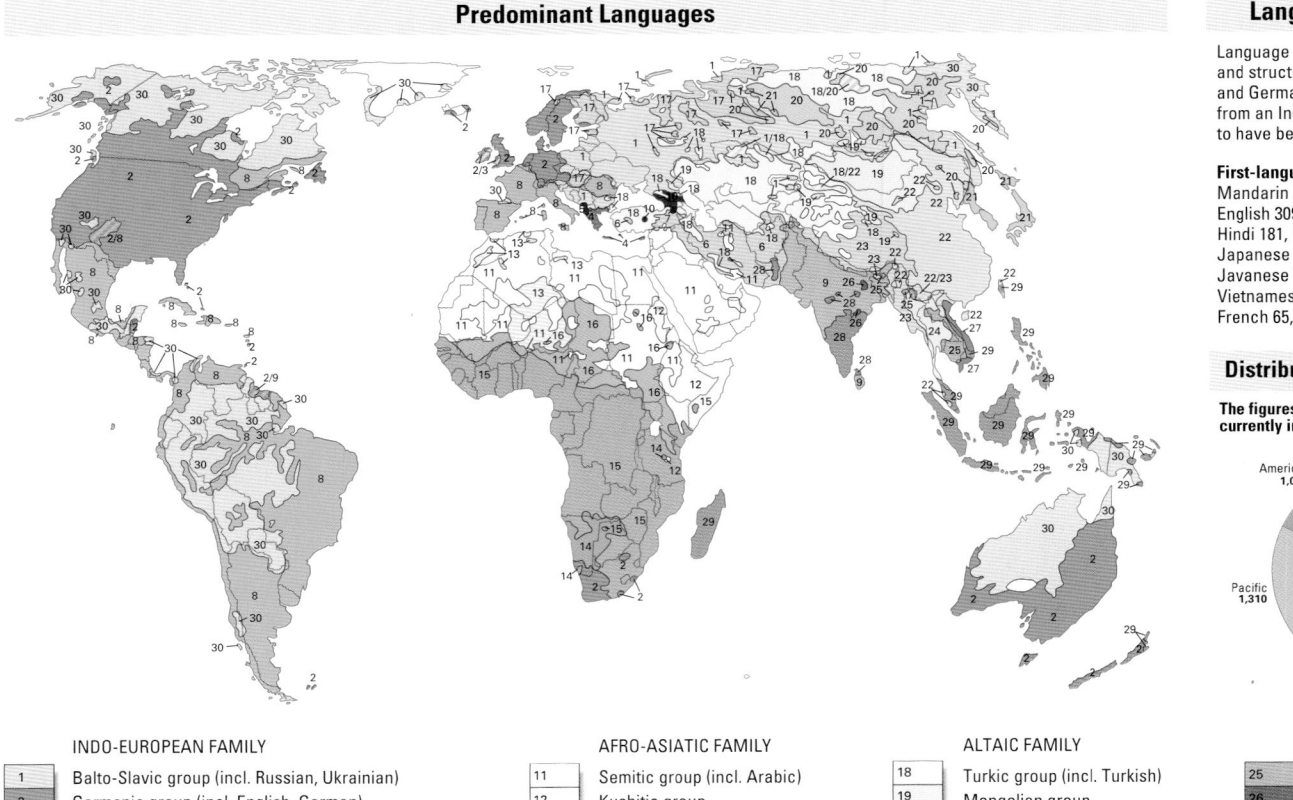

Languages of the World

Language can be classified by ancestry and structure. For example, the Romance and Germanic groups are both derived from an Indo-European language believed to have been spoken 5,000 years ago.

First-language speakers in millions (2005)
Mandarin Chinese 873, Spanish 322, English 309, Portuguese 230, Arabic 206, Hindi 181, Bengali 171, Russian 145, Japanese 122, German 95, Wu Chinese 77, Javanese 75, Telugu 70, Marathi 68, Vietnamese 67, Korean 67, Tamil 65, French 65, Italian 62, Punjabi 60.

Distribution of Living Languages

The figures refer to the number of languages currently in use in the regions shown

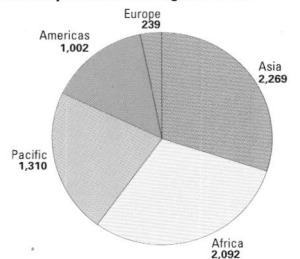

Europe 239
Americas 1,002
Asia 2,269
Pacific 1,310
Africa 2,092

Language Families (map legend)

INDO-EUROPEAN FAMILY
1. Balto-Slavic group (incl. Russian, Ukrainian)
2. Germanic group (incl. English, German)
3. Celtic group
4. Greek
5. Albanian
6. Iranian group
7. Armenian
8. Romance group (incl. Spanish, Portuguese, French, Italian)
9. Indo-Aryan group (incl. Hindi, Bengali, Urdu, Punjabi, Marathi)
10. CAUCASIAN FAMILY

AFRO-ASIATIC FAMILY
11. Semitic group (incl. Arabic)
12. Kushitic group
13. Berber group

14. KHOISAN FAMILY

15. NIGER-CONGO FAMILY

16. NILO-SAHARAN FAMILY

17. URALIC FAMILY

ALTAIC FAMILY
18. Turkic group (incl. Turkish)
19. Mongolian group
20. Tungus-Manchu group
21. Japanese and Korean

SINO-TIBETAN FAMILY
22. Sinitic (Chinese) languages (incl. Mandarin, Wu, Yue)
23. Tibetic-Burmic languages

24. TAI FAMILY

AUSTRO-ASIATIC FAMILY
25. Mon-Khmer group
26. Munda group
27. Vietnamese

28. DRAVIDIAN FAMILY (incl. Telugu, Tamil)

29. AUSTRONESIAN FAMILY (incl. Malay-Indonesian, Javanese)

30. OTHER LANGUAGES

Predominant Religions

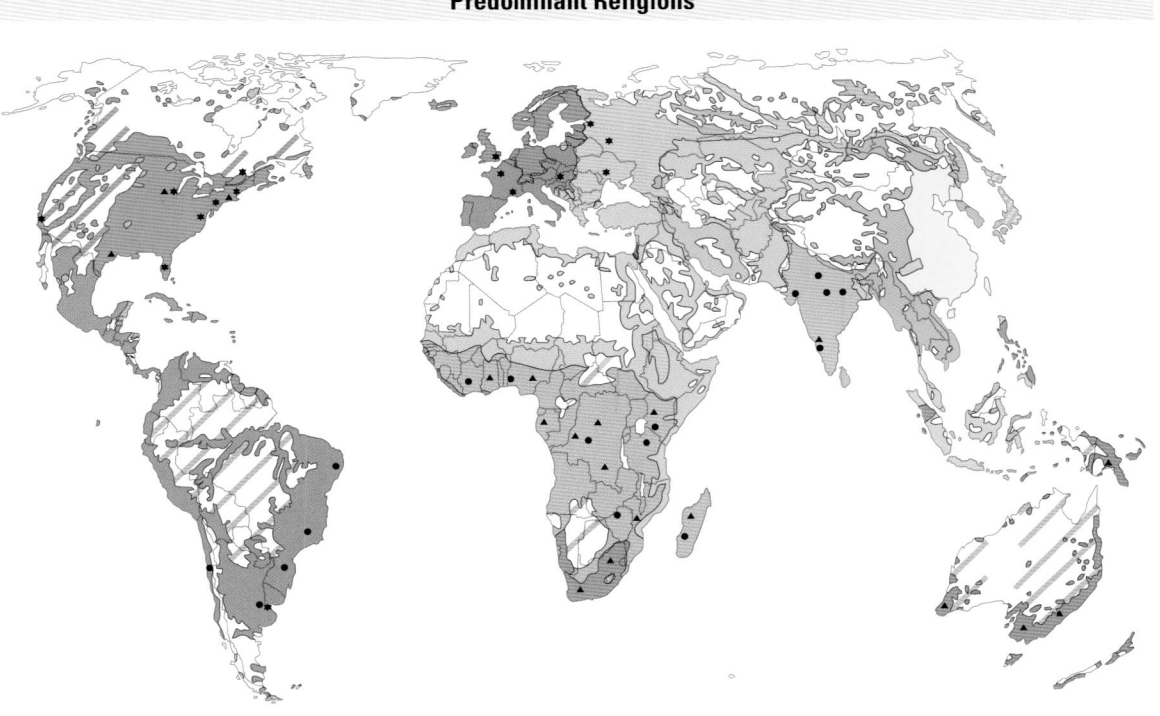

Religious Adherents

Religious adherents in millions (2006)

Christianity	2,100	Hindu	900
Roman Catholic	*1,050*	Chinese folk	394
Protestant	*396*	Buddhism	376
Orthodox	*240*	Ethnic religions	300
Anglican	*73*	New religions	103
Others	*341*	Sikhism	23
Islam	1,070	Spiritism	15
Sunni	*940*	Judaism	14
Shi'ite	*120*	Baha'i	7
Others	*10*	Confucianism	6
Non-religious/		Jainism	4
Agnostic/Atheist	1,100	Shintoism	4

Religions (map legend)

- Roman Catholicism
- Orthodox and other Eastern Churches
- Protestantism
- Sunni Islam
- Shi'ite Islam
- Buddhism
- Hinduism
- Confucianism
- Judaism
- Shintoism
- Tribal Religions

United Nations

Created in 1945 to promote peace and co-operation and based in New York, the United Nations is the world's largest international organization, with 192 members and an annual budget of US $2.1 billion (2007). Each member of the General Assembly has one vote, while the five permanent members of the 15-nation Security Council – China, France, Russia, UK and USA – hold a veto. The Secretariat is the UN's principal administrative arm. The 54 members of the Economic and Social Council are responsible for economic, social, cultural, educational, health and related matters. The UN has 16 specialized agencies – based in Canada, France, Switzerland and Italy, as well as the USA – which help members in fields such as education (UNESCO), agriculture (FAO), medicine (WHO) and finance (IFC). By the end of 1994, all the original 11 trust territories of the Trusteeship Council had become independent.

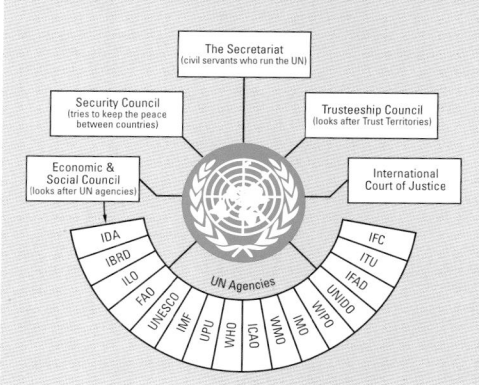

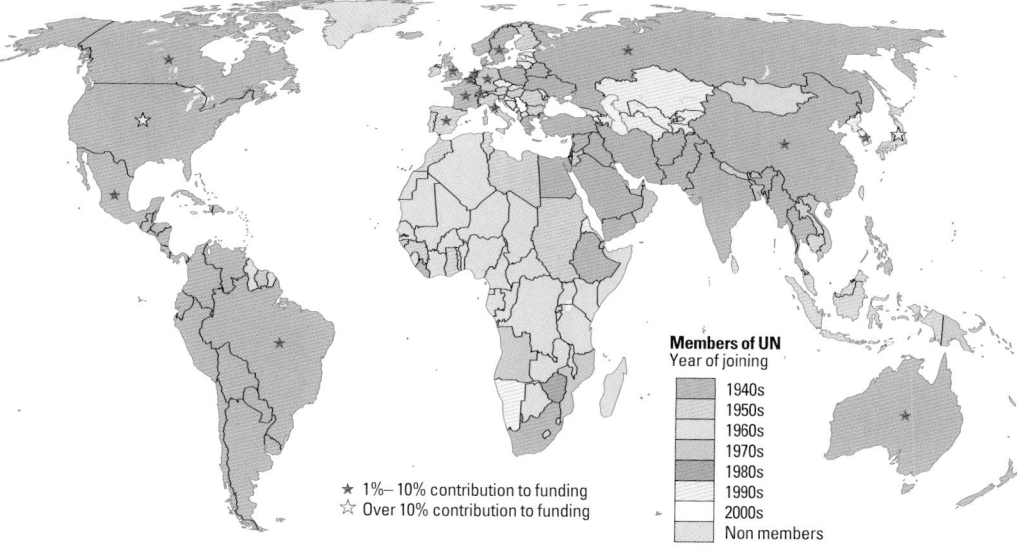

Members of UN
Year of joining

- 1940s
- 1950s
- 1960s
- 1970s
- 1980s
- 1990s
- 2000s
- Non members

★ 1%–10% contribution to funding
☆ Over 10% contribution to funding

MEMBERSHIP OF THE UN In 1945 there were 51 members; by the end of 2006 membership had increased to 192 following the admission of East Timor, Switzerland and Montenegro. There are 2 independent states which are not members of the UN – Taiwan and the Vatican City. All the successor states of the former USSR had joined by the end of 1992. The official languages of the UN are Chinese, English, French, Russian, Spanish and Arabic.

FUNDING The UN regular budget for 2007 was US$ 2.1 billion. Contributions are assessed by the members' ability to pay, with the maximum 24% of the total (USA's share), the minimum 0.01%. The European Union pays over 37% of the budget.

PEACEKEEPING The UN has been involved in 65 peacekeeping operations worldwide since 1948.

International Organizations

ACP African-Caribbean-Pacific (formed in 1963). Members have economic ties with the EU.

APEC Asia-Pacific Economic Co-operation (formed in 1989). It aims to enhance economic growth and prosperity for the region and to strengthen the Asia-Pacific community. APEC is the only intergovernmental grouping in the world operating on the basis of non-binding commitments, open dialogue, and equal respect for the views of all participants. There are 21 member economies.

ARAB LEAGUE (formed in 1945). The League's aim is to promote economic, social, political and military co-operation. There are 22 member nations.

ASEAN Association of South-east Asian Nations (formed in 1967). Cambodia joined in 1999.

AU The African Union replaced the Organization of African Unity (formed in 1963) in 2002. Its 53 members represent over 94% of Africa's population. Arabic, French, Portuguese and English are recognized as working languages.

COLOMBO PLAN (formed in 1951). Its 25 members aim to promote economic and social development in Asia and the Pacific.

COMMONWEALTH The Commonwealth of Nations evolved from the British Empire. Pakistan was suspended in 1999, and Zimbabwe left the Commonwealth in 2002. In response to its continued suspension, Pakistan was reinstated in 2004, but Fiji Islands was suspended in December 2006 following a military coup. It now comprises 16 Queen's realms, 31 republics and 6 indigenous monarchies, giving a total of 53 member states.

EU European Union (evolved from the European Community in 1993). Cyprus, the Czech Republic, Estonia, Hungary, Latvia, Lithuania, Malta, Poland, the Slovak Republic and Slovenia joined the EU in May 2004; Bulgaria and Romania joined in January 2007. The other members are Austria, Belgium, Denmark, Finland, France, Germany, Greece, Ireland, Italy, Luxembourg, Netherlands, Portugal, Spain, Sweden and the UK – together these 27 countries aim to integrate economies, co-ordinate social developments and bring about political union.

LAIA Latin American Integration Association (1980). Its aim is to promote freer regional trade.

NATO North Atlantic Treaty Organization (formed in 1949). It continues after 1991 despite the winding up of the Warsaw Pact. Bulgaria, Estonia, Latvia, Lithuania, Romania, the Slovak Republic and Slovenia became members in 2004.

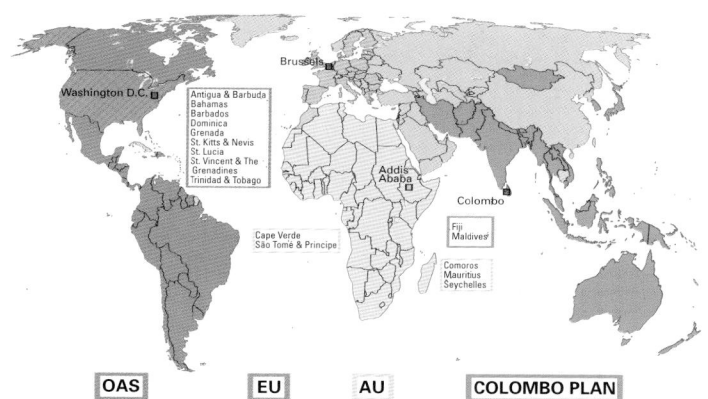

OAS | **EU** | **AU** | **COLOMBO PLAN**

OAS Organization of American States (formed in 1948). It aims to promote social and economic co-operation between developed countries of North America and developing nations of Latin America.

OECD Organization for Economic Co-operation and Development (formed in 1961). It comprises 30 major free-market economies. Poland, Hungary and South Korea joined in 1996, and the Slovak Republic in 2000. 'G8' is its 'inner group' of leading industrial nations, comprising Canada, France, Germany, Italy, Japan, Russia, UK and USA.

OPEC Organization of Petroleum Exporting Countries (formed in 1960). It controls about three-quarters of the world's oil supply. Gabon left the organization in 1996.

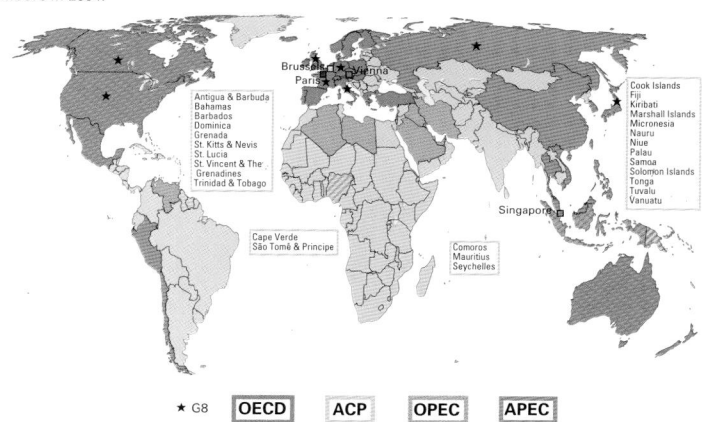

★ G8   **OECD**   **ACP**   **OPEC**   **APEC**

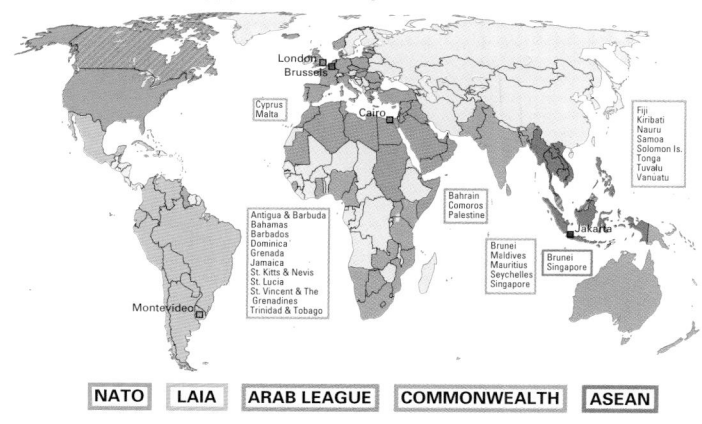

NATO   **LAIA**   **ARAB LEAGUE**   **COMMONWEALTH**   **ASEAN**

Wealth

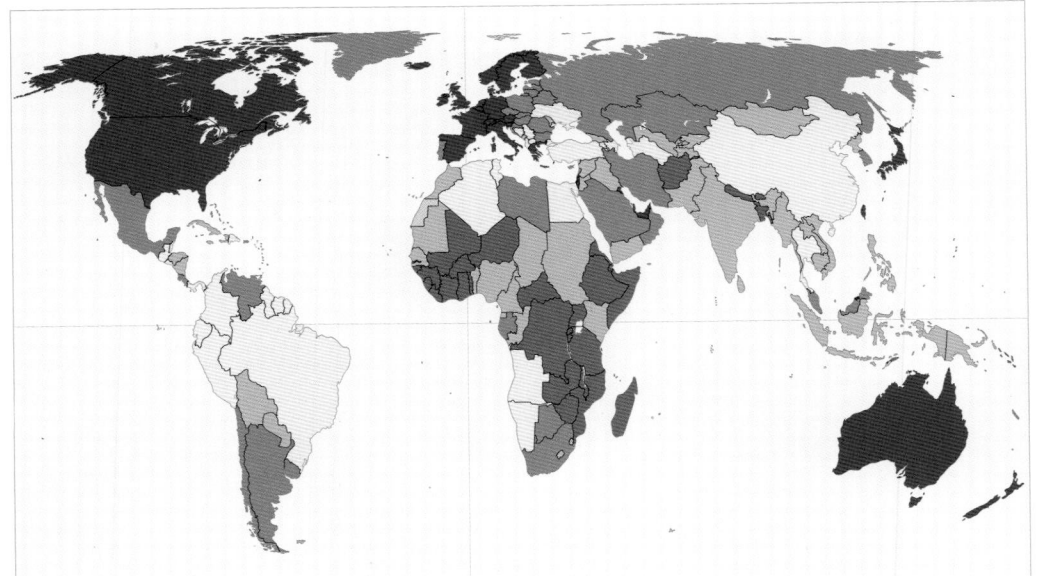

Levels of Income

Gross Domestic Product per capita: the annual value of goods and services divided by the population, using purchasing power parity (PPP) (2007)

 Over 250% of world average

 100% – 250% of world average

[World average per person US$10,000]

50% – 100% of world average

15% – 50% of world average

Under 15% of world average

No data available

Wealth Creation

The Gross Domestic Product (GDP) of the world's largest economies, US$ million (2007)

1.	USA	13,860,000	23.	Argentina	524,000
2.	China	7,043,000	24.	Thailand	520,000
3.	Japan	4,346,000	25.	South Africa	468,000
4.	India	2,965,000	26.	Pakistan	446,000
5.	Germany	2,833,000	27.	Egypt	432,000
6.	UK	2,147,000	28.	Belgium	379,000
7.	Russia	2,076,000	29.	Malaysia	358,000
8.	France	2,067,000	30.	Venezuela	335,000
9.	Brazil	1,838,000	31.	Sweden	333,000
10.	Italy	1,800,000	32.	Greece	326,000
11.	Spain	1,362,000	33.	Ukraine	321,000
12.	Mexico	1,353,000	34.	Colombia	320,000
13.	Canada	1,274,000	35.	Austria	320,000
14.	South Korea	1,206,000	36.	Switzerland	301,000
15.	Iran	853,000	37.	Philippines	299,000
16.	Indonesia	846,000	38.	Nigeria	295,000
17.	Australia	767,000	39.	Hong Kong	293,000
18.	Taiwan	690,000	40.	Algeria	269,000
19.	Turkey	668,000	41.	Norway	257,000
20.	Netherlands	639,000	42.	Czech Republic	249,000
21.	Poland	624,000	43.	Romania	247,000
22.	Saudi Arabia	572,000	44.	Chile	234,000

The Wealth Gap

The world's richest and poorest countries, by Gross Domestic Product per capita in US $ (2007)

Richest countries			Poorest countries		
1.	Luxembourg	80,800	1.	Congo (Dem. Rep.)	300
2.	Norway	55,600	2.	Liberia	500
3.	Kuwait	55,300	3.	Zimbabwe	500
4.	UAE	55,200	4.	Comoros	600
5.	Singapore	48,900	5.	Guinea-Bissau	600
6.	USA	46,000	6.	Solomon Islands	600
7.	Ireland	45,600	7.	Somalia	600
8.	Hong Kong (China)	42,000	8.	Central African Rep.	700
9.	Switzerland	39,800	9.	Ethiopia	700
10.	Iceland	39,400	10.	Niger	700
11.	Austria	39,000	11.	Afghanistan	800
12.	Andorra	38,800	12.	Burundi	800
13.	Netherlands	38,600	13.	East Timor	800
14.	Canada	38,200	14.	Gambia	800
15.	Australia	37,500	15.	Malawi	800
16.	Denmark	37,400	16.	Sierra Leone	800
17.	Sweden	36,900	17.	Mozambique	900
18.	Belgium	36,500	18.	Togo	900
19.	Finland	35,500	19.	Djibouti	1,000
20.	UK	35,000	20.	Eritrea	1,000
21.	Bahrain	34,700	21.	Guinea	1,000

Continental Shares

Shares of population and of wealth (GNI) by continent

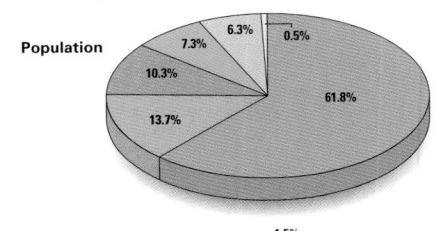

Population

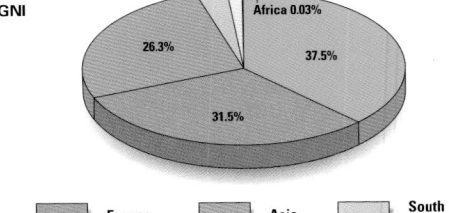

GNI

Europe
Australia
Asia
Africa
South America
North America

Inflation

Average annual rate of inflation (2007)

Over 20%

10% – 20%

5% – 10%

2.5% – 5%

Under 2.5%

No data available

Highest inflation		Lowest inflation	
Zimbabwe	26,470%	Nauru	–3.6%
Burma (Myanmar)	40%	Vanuatu	–1.6%
Venezuela	21%	San Marino	–1.5%
Guinea	20%	Dominica	–0.1%
Tajikistan	20%	Japan	0%

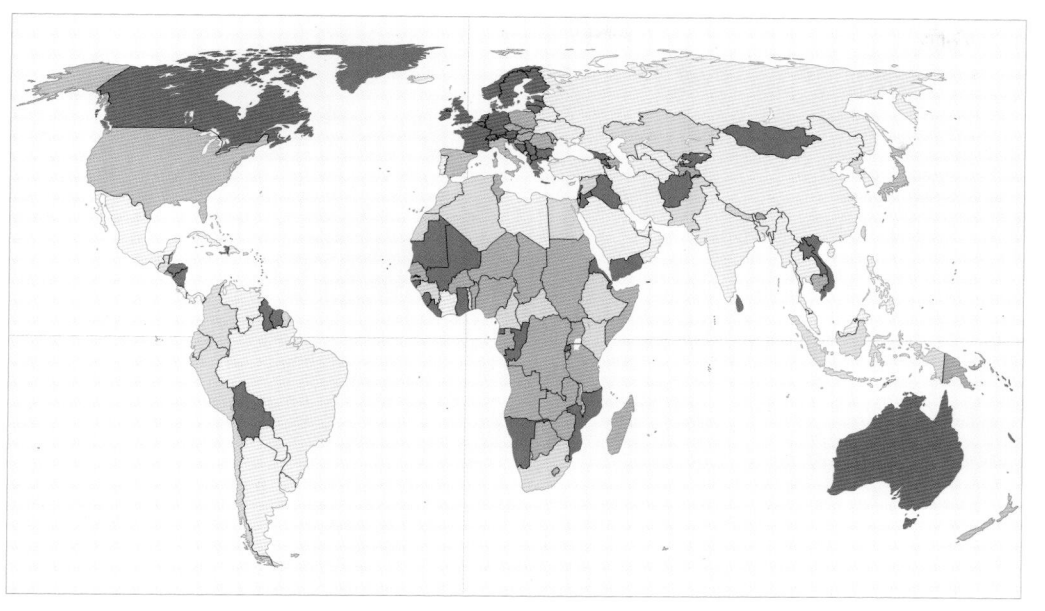

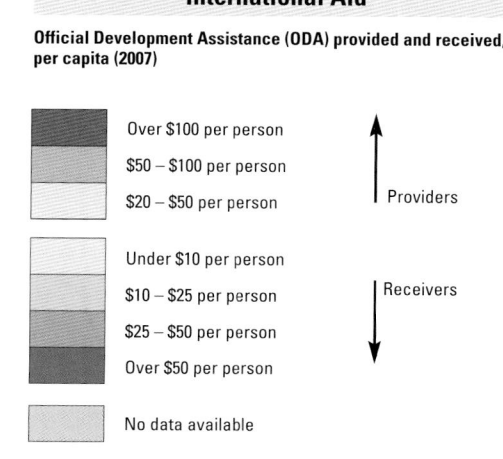

International Aid

Official Development Assistance (ODA) provided and received, per capita (2007)

- Over $100 per person
- $50 – $100 per person
- $20 – $50 per person

Providers

- Under $10 per person
- $10 – $25 per person
- $25 – $50 per person
- Over $50 per person

Receivers

- No data available

Debt and Aid

International debtors and the aid they receive

Although aid grants make a vital contribution to many of the world's poorer countries, they are usually dwarfed by the burden of debt that the developing economies are expected to repay. It is estimated that the total debt burden of developing countries is US$523 billion.

- Debt, US $ per capita (2007)
- Aid, US $ per capita (2007)

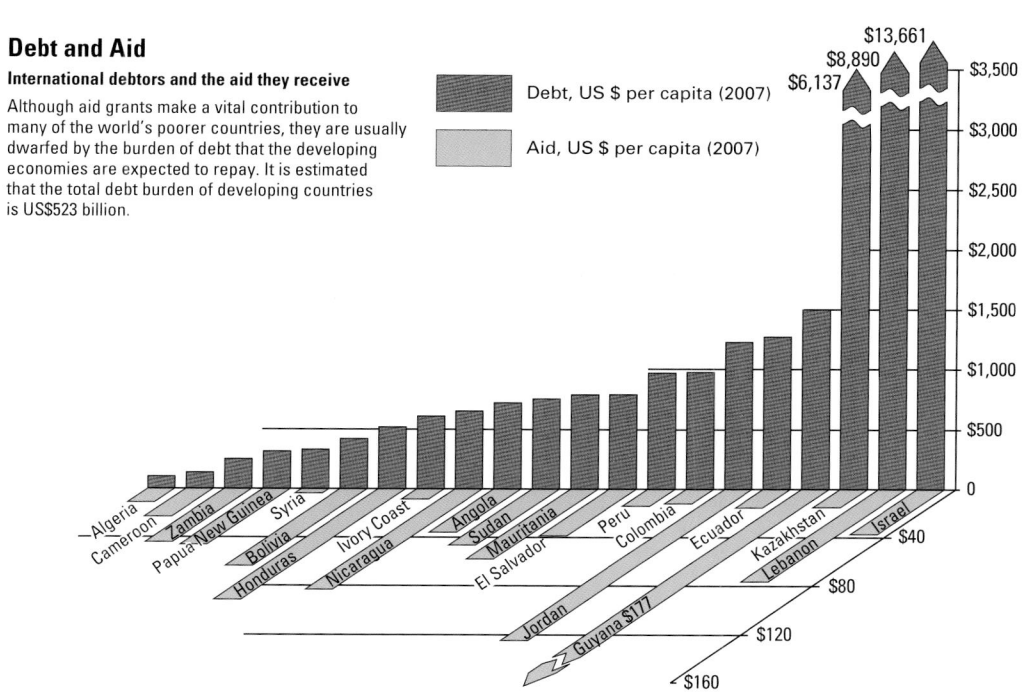

Distribution of Spending

Percentage share of household spending, selected countries

- Food
- Clothing
- Energy & Housing
- Medicine & Education
- Transport
- Other

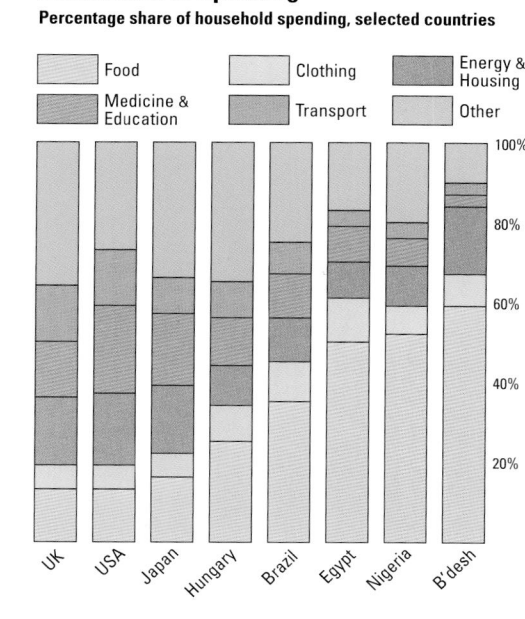

UK, USA, Japan, Hungary, Brazil, Egypt, Nigeria, B'desh

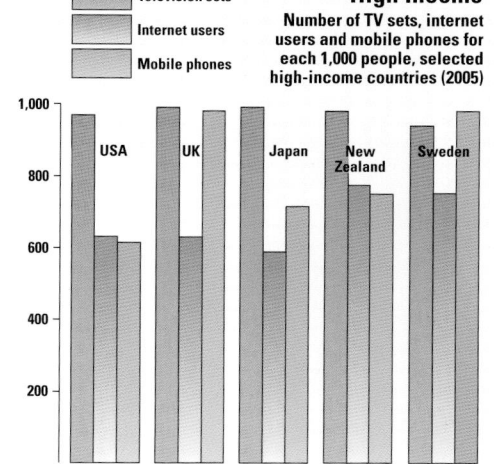

High Income

Number of TV sets, internet users and mobile phones for each 1,000 people, selected high-income countries (2005)

- Television sets
- Internet users
- Mobile phones

USA, UK, Japan, New Zealand, Sweden

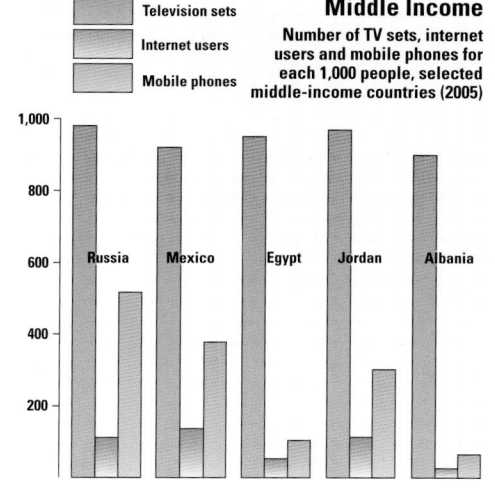

Middle Income

Number of TV sets, internet users and mobile phones for each 1,000 people, selected middle-income countries (2005)

- Television sets
- Internet users
- Mobile phones

Russia, Mexico, Egypt, Jordan, Albania

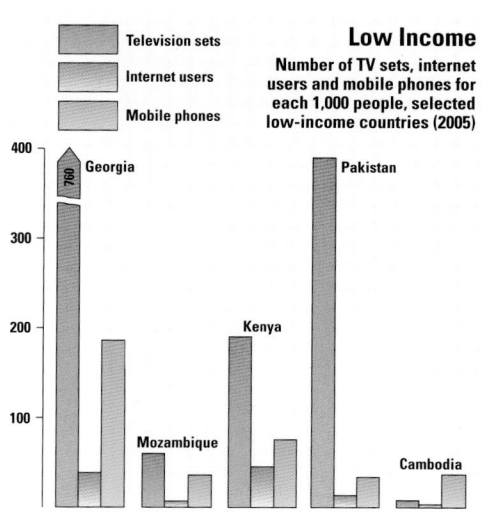

Low Income

Number of TV sets, internet users and mobile phones for each 1,000 people, selected low-income countries (2005)

- Television sets
- Internet users
- Mobile phones

Georgia, Mozambique, Kenya, Pakistan, Cambodia

Quality of Life

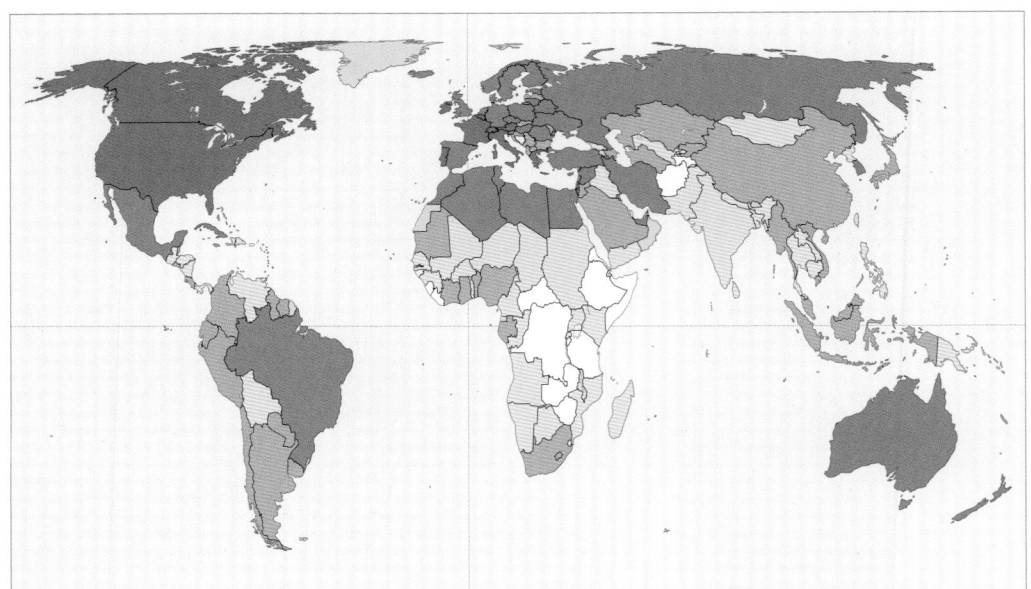

Daily Food Consumption

Average daily food intake in calories per person (2003)

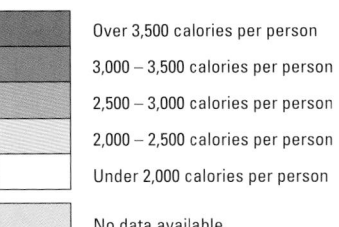

- Over 3,500 calories per person
- 3,000 – 3,500 calories per person
- 2,500 – 3,000 calories per person
- 2,000 – 2,500 calories per person
- Under 2,000 calories per person
- No data available

Hospital Capacity

Hospital beds available for each 1,000 people (2007)

Highest capacity		Lowest capacity	
Japan	14.1	Angola	0.1
Belarus	11.1	Cambodia	0.1
Russia	9.7	Malawi	0.1
Ukraine	8.7	Senegal	0.1
South Korea	8.6	Ethiopia	0.2
Czech Republic	8.4	Nepal	0.2
Germany	8.3	Bangladesh	0.3
Azerbaijan	8.1	Guinea	0.3
Lithuania	8.0	Madagascar	0.3
Hungary	7.9	Mali	0.3
Kazakhstan	7.8	Afghanistan	0.4
Austria	7.6	Chad	0.4
Latvia	7.6	Sierra Leone	0.4
Malta	7.6	Benin	0.5
Iceland	7.5	Nigeria	0.5

Although the ratio of people to hospital beds gives a good approximation of a country's health provision, it is not an absolute indicator. Raw numbers may mask inefficiency and other weaknesses: the high availability of beds in Belarus, for example, has not prevented infant mortality rates over three times as high as in the United Kingdom and the United States.

Life Expectancy

Years of life expectancy at birth, selected countries (2007)

The chart shows combined data for both sexes. On average, women live longer than men worldwide, even in developing countries with high maternal mortality rates. Overall, life expectancy is steadily rising, though the difference between rich and poor nations remains dramatic.

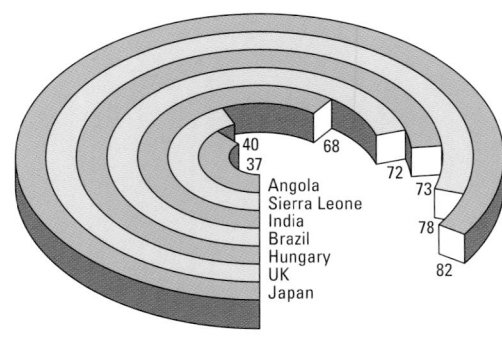

Angola 37
Sierra Leone 40
India 68
Brazil 72
Hungary 73
UK 78
Japan 82

Causes of Death

Causes of death for selected countries by percentage

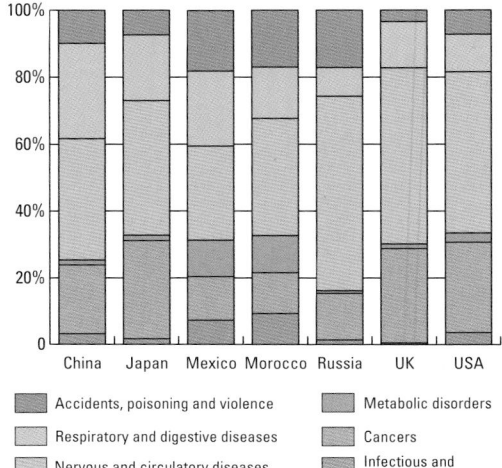

China   Japan   Mexico   Morocco   Russia   UK   USA

- Accidents, poisoning and violence
- Respiratory and digestive diseases
- Nervous and circulatory diseases
- Metabolic disorders
- Cancers
- Infectious and parasitic diseases

Infant Mortality

Number of babies who died under the age of one, per 1,000 live births (2007)

- Over 100 deaths per 1,000 births
- 50 – 100 deaths per 1,000 births
- 25 – 50 deaths per 1,000 births
- 10 – 25 deaths per 1,000 births
- Under 10 deaths per 1,000 births
- No data available

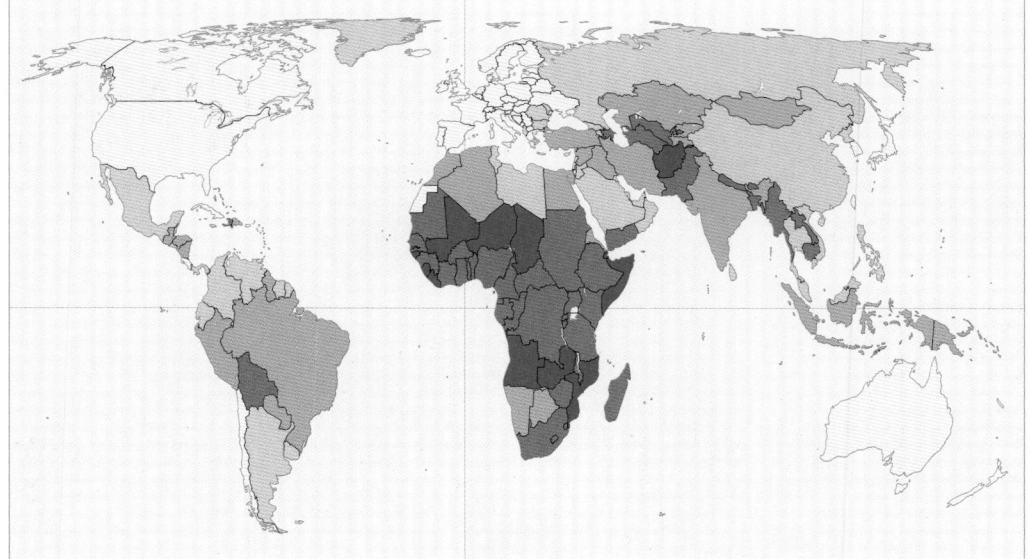

Highest infant mortality		Lowest infant mortality	
Angola	184 deaths	Singapore	2 deaths
Sierra Leone	158 deaths	Sweden	3 deaths
Afghanistan	157 deaths	Hong Kong (China)	3 deaths
Liberia	150 deaths	Japan	3 deaths
Niger	117 deaths	Iceland	3 deaths

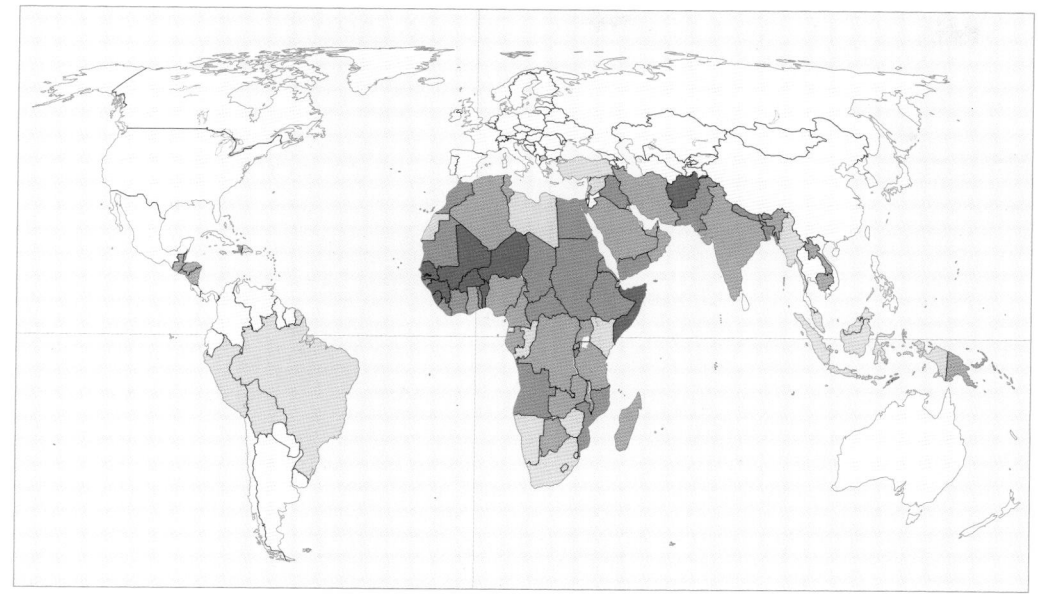

Illiteracy

Percentage of the total adult population unable to read or write (2005)

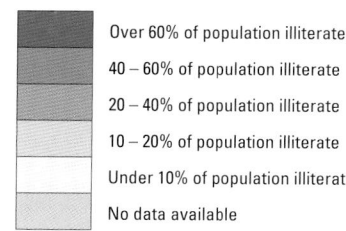

- Over 60% of population illiterate
- 40 – 60% of population illiterate
- 20 – 40% of population illiterate
- 10 – 20% of population illiterate
- Under 10% of population illiterate
- No data available

Countries with the highest and lowest illiteracy rates

Highest		Lowest	
Burkina Faso	87	Australia	0
Niger	83	Denmark	0
Mali	81	Finland	0
Sierra Leone	69	Liechtenstein	0
Guinea	64	Luxembourg	0

Fertility and Education

Fertility rates compared with female education, selected countries (2000–05)

Percentage of females aged 12–17 in secondary education

Fertility rate: average number of children borne per woman

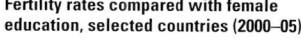 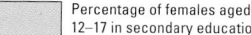 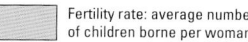

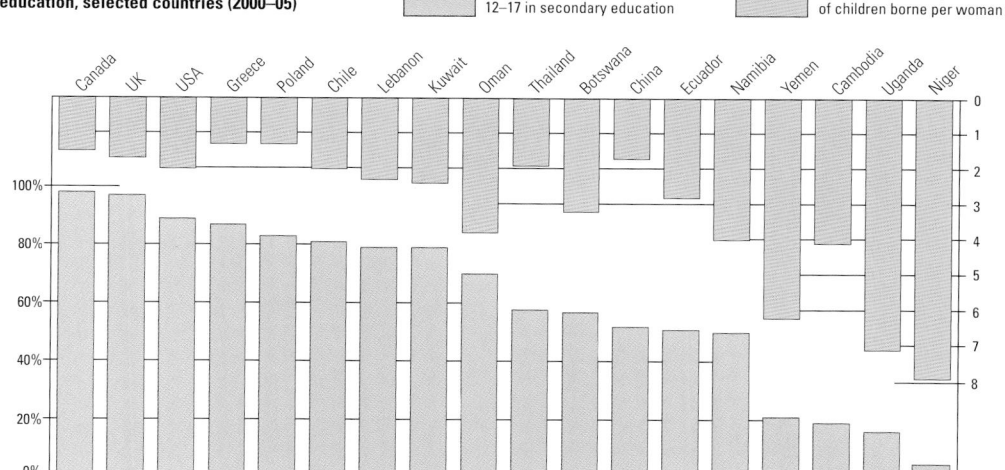

Living Standards

At first sight, most international contrasts in living standards are swamped by differences in wealth. The rich not only have more money, they have more of everything, including years of life. Those with only a little money are obliged to spend most of it on food and clothing, the basic maintenance costs of their existence; air travel and tourism are unlikely to feature on their expenditure lists. However, poverty and wealth are both relative: slum dwellers living on social security payments in an affluent industrial country have far more resources at their disposal than an average African peasant, but feel their own poverty nonetheless. A middle-class Indian lawyer cannot command a fraction of the earnings of a counterpart living in New York, London or Rome; nevertheless, he rightly sees himself as prosperous.

The rich not only live longer, on average, than the poor, they also die from different causes. Infectious and parasitic diseases, all but eliminated in the developed world, remain a scourge in the developing nations. On the other hand, more than two-thirds of the populations of OECD nations eventually succumb to cancer or circulatory disease.

Human Development Index

The Human Development Index (HDI), calculated by the UN Development Programme, gives a value to countries using indicators of life expectancy, education and standards of living (2005). Higher values show more developed countries.

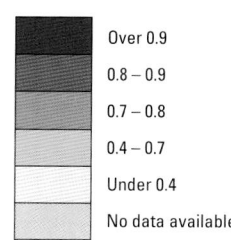

- Over 0.9
- 0.8 – 0.9
- 0.7 – 0.8
- 0.4 – 0.7
- Under 0.4
- No data available

Highest values		Lowest values	
Iceland	0.968	Sierra Leone	0.336
Norway	0.968	Burkina Faso	0.370
Australia	0.962	Guinea-Bissau	0.374
Ireland	0.959	Niger	0.374
Sweden	0.95	Mali	0.380

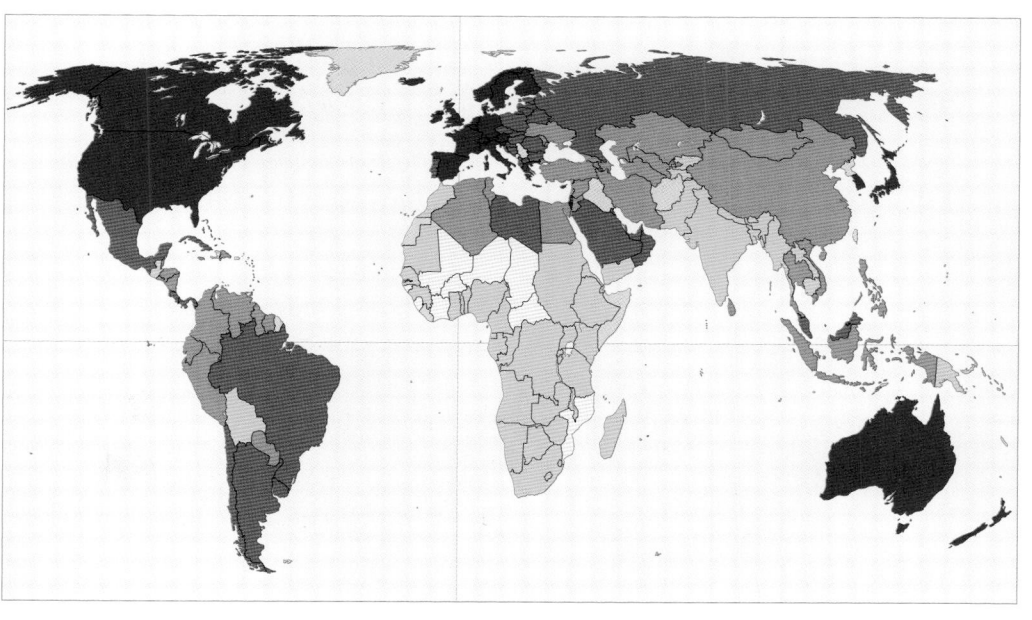

Energy

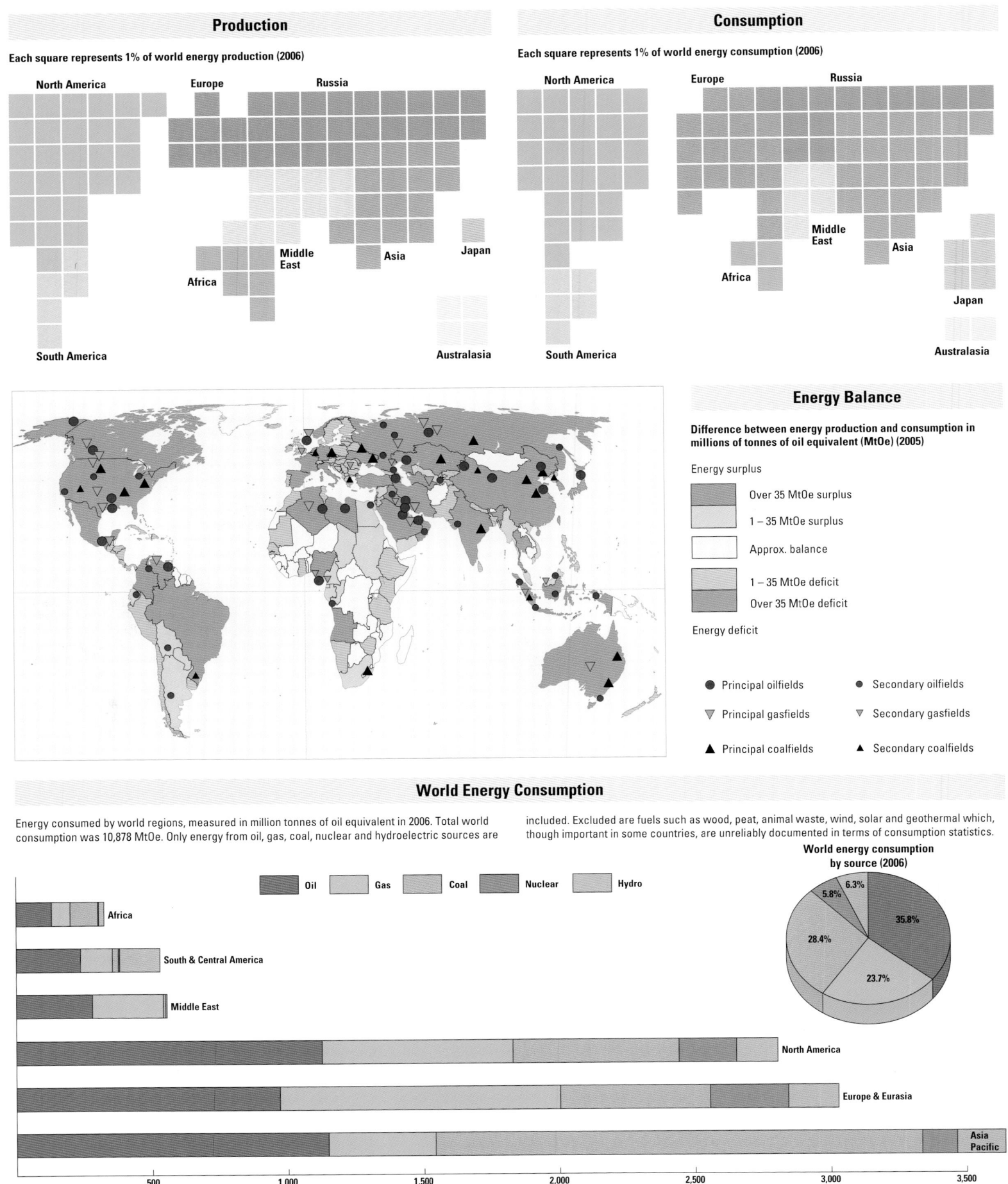

Production

Each square represents 1% of world energy production (2006)

North America Europe Russia

Africa Middle East Asia Japan

South America Australasia

Consumption

Each square represents 1% of world energy consumption (2006)

North America Europe Russia

Middle East Asia

Africa

South America Japan Australasia

Energy Balance

Difference between energy production and consumption in millions of tonnes of oil equivalent (MtOe) (2005)

Energy surplus

Over 35 MtOe surplus

1 – 35 MtOe surplus

Approx. balance

1 – 35 MtOe deficit

Over 35 MtOe deficit

Energy deficit

● Principal oilfields ● Secondary oilfields

▽ Principal gasfields ▽ Secondary gasfields

▲ Principal coalfields ▲ Secondary coalfields

World Energy Consumption

Energy consumed by world regions, measured in million tonnes of oil equivalent in 2006. Total world consumption was 10,878 MtOe. Only energy from oil, gas, coal, nuclear and hydroelectric sources are included. Excluded are fuels such as wood, peat, animal waste, wind, solar and geothermal which, though important in some countries, are unreliably documented in terms of consumption statistics.

Oil Gas Coal Nuclear Hydro

Africa

South & Central America

Middle East

North America

Europe & Eurasia

Asia Pacific

500 1,000 1,500 2,000 2,500 3,000 3,500

million tonnes of oil equivalent

World energy consumption by source (2006)

6.3%

5.8%

35.8%

28.4%

23.7%

Source: BP Statistical Review of World Energy 2007

24

Energy

Energy is used to keep us warm or cool, fuel our industries and our transport systems, and even feed us; high-intensity agriculture, with its use of fertilizers, pesticides and machinery, is heavily energy-dependent. Although we live in a high-energy society, there are vast discrepancies between rich and poor; for example, a North American consumes 13 times as much energy as a Chinese person. But even developing nations have more power at their disposal than was imaginable a century ago.

The distribution of energy supplies, most importantly fossil fuels (coal, oil and natural gas), is very uneven. In addition, the diagrams and map opposite show that the largest producers of energy are not necessarily the largest consumers. The movement of energy supplies around the world is therefore an important component of international trade. In 2006, total world movements in oil amounted to 2,590 million tonnes.

As the finite reserves of fossil fuels are depleted, renewable energy sources, such as solar, hydro-thermal, wind, tidal and biomass, will become increasingly important around the world.

Nuclear Power

Major producers by percentage of world total and by percentage of domestic electricity generation (2006)

Country	% of world total production	Country	% of nuclear as proportion of domestic electricity
1. USA	29.6%	1. France	78.7%
2. France	16.1%	2. Lithuania	64.2%
3. Japan	10.9%	3. Slovak Rep.	57.3%
4. Germany	6.0%	4. Belgium	54.7%
5. Russia	5.4%	5. Ukraine	48.4%
6. South Korea	5.3%	6. Switzerland	47.1%
7. Canada	3.4%	7. Bulgaria	43.4%
8. Ukraine	3.2%	8. Sweden	41.5%
9. UK	2.6%	9. Armenia	40.5%
10. Sweden	2.4%	10. South Korea	38.6%

Although the 1980s were a bad time for the nuclear power industry (fears of long-term environmental damage were heavily reinforced by the 1986 disaster at Chernobyl), the industry picked up in the early 1990s. Sixteen countries currently rely on nuclear power to supply over 25% of their electricity requirements. There are over 400 operating nuclear power stations worldwide, with over 100 more planned or under construction.

Hydroelectricity

Major producers by percentage of world total and by percentage of domestic electricity generation (2004)

Country	% of world total production	Country	% of hydroelectric as proportion of domestic electricity
1. Canada	12.2%	1. Bhutan	100%
2. China	11.9%	= Paraguay	100%
3. Brazil	11.6%	= Lesotho	100%
4. USA	9.8%	4. Mozambique	99.8%
5. Russia	6.0%	5. Congo	99.7%
6. Norway	3.9%	= Congo (Dem. Rep.)	99.7%
7. Japan	3.4%	= Uganda	99.7%
8. India	3.0%	8. Nepal	99.6%
9. Sweden	2.3%	9. Zambia	99.5%
10. France	2.2%	10. Norway	98.8%

Countries heavily reliant on hydroelectricity are usually small and non-industrial: a high proportion of hydroelectric power more often reflects a modest energy budget than vast hydroelectric resources. The USA, for instance, produces only 6.7% of its power requirements from hydroelectricity; yet that 6.7% amounts to more than seven times the hydropower generated by most of Africa.

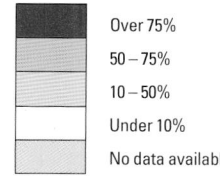

Fuel Exports

Fuels as a percentage of total value of exports (2005)

- Over 75%
- 50 – 75%
- 10 – 50%
- Under 10%
- No data available

In the 1970s, oil exports became a political issue when OPEC sought to increase the influence of developing countries in world affairs by raising oil prices and restricting production. But its power was short-lived, following a fall in demand for oil in the 1980s, due to an increase in energy efficiency and development of alternative resources. However, with the heavy energy demands of the Asian economies early in the 21st century, both oil and gas prices have risen sharply.

Conversion Rates

1 barrel = 0.136 tonnes or 159 litres or 35 Imperial gallons or 42 US gallons

1 tonne = 7.33 barrels or 1,185 litres or 256 Imperial gallons or 261 US gallons

1 tonne oil = 1.5 tonnes hard coal or 3.0 tonnes lignite or 12,000 kWh

1 Imperial gallon = 1.201 US gallons or 4.546 litres or 277.4 cubic inches

Measurements

For historical reasons, oil is traded in 'barrels'. The weight and volume equivalents (shown right) are all based on average-density 'Arabian light' crude oil.

The energy equivalents given for a tonne of oil are also somewhat imprecise: oil and coal of different qualities will have varying energy contents, a fact usually reflected in their price on world markets.

World Coal Reserves

World coal reserves (including lignite) by region and country, billion tonnes (2006)

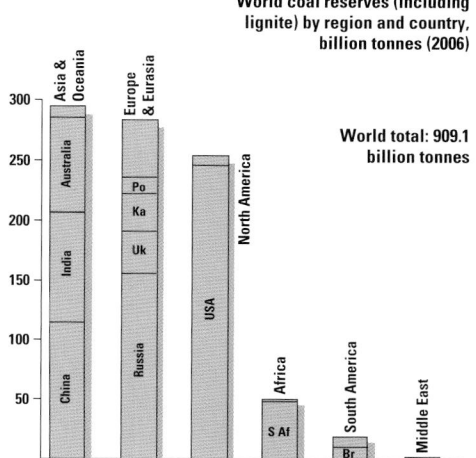

World total: 909.1 billion tonnes

World Gas Reserves

World natural gas reserves by region and country, billion tonnes of oil equivalent (2006)

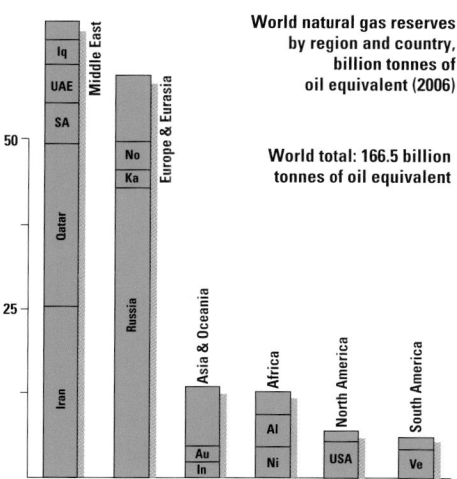

World total: 166.5 billion tonnes of oil equivalent

World Oil Reserves

World oil reserves by region and country, billion tonnes (2006)

World total: 163.6 billion tonnes

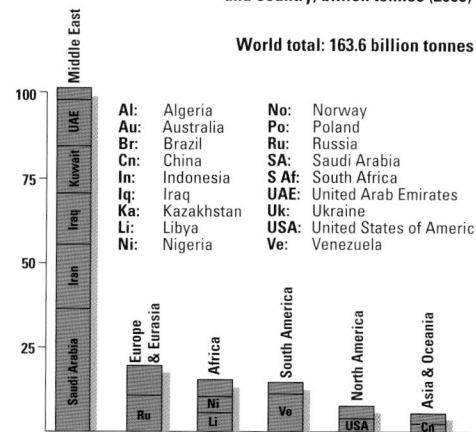

Al:	Algeria	**No:**	Norway
Au:	Australia	**Po:**	Poland
Br:	Brazil	**Ru:**	Russia
Cn:	China	**SA:**	Saudi Arabia
In:	Indonesia	**S Af:**	South Africa
Iq:	Iraq	**UAE:**	United Arab Emirates
Ka:	Kazakhstan	**Uk:**	Ukraine
Li:	Libya	**USA:**	United States of America
Ni:	Nigeria	**Ve:**	Venezuela

Production

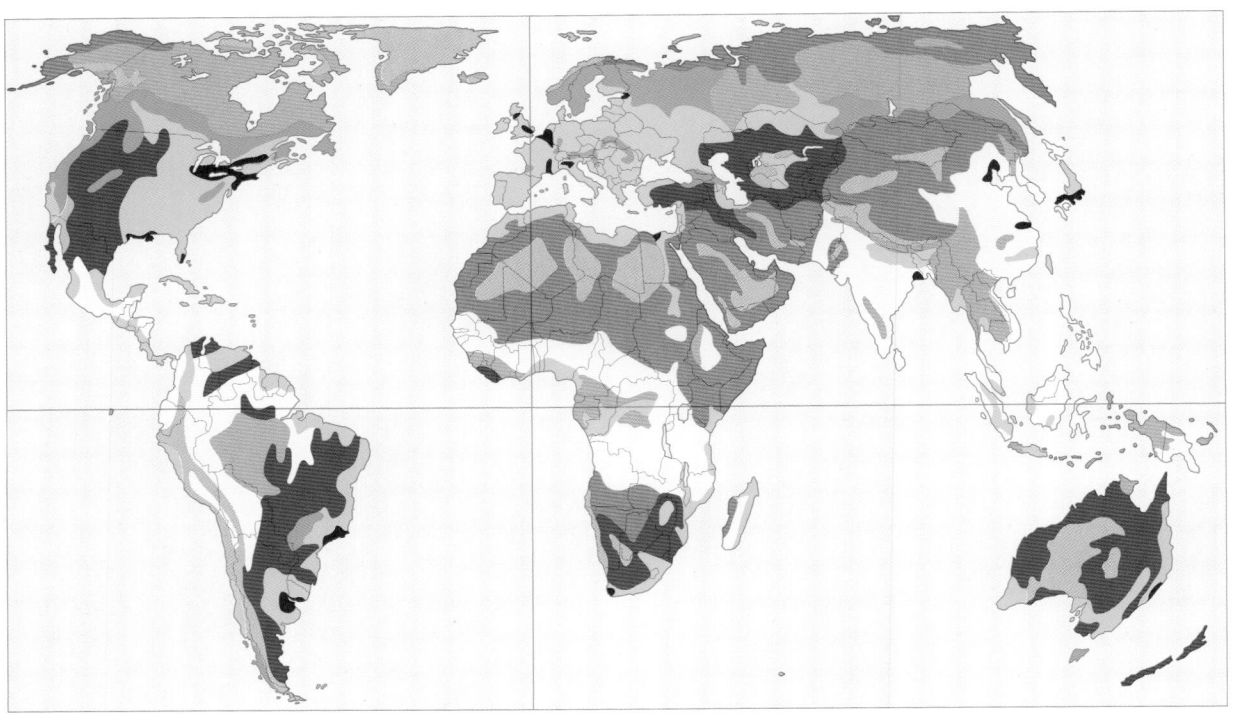

Agriculture

Predominant type of farming or land use

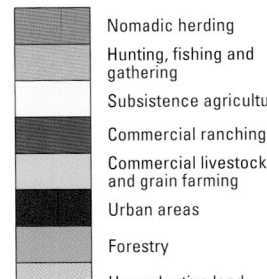

- Nomadic herding
- Hunting, fishing and gathering
- Subsistence agriculture
- Commercial ranching
- Commercial livestock and grain farming
- Urban areas
- Forestry
- Unproductive land

The development of agriculture has transformed human existence more than any other. The whole business of farming is constantly developing: due mainly to the new varieties of rice and wheat, world grain production has more than doubled since 1965. New machinery and modern agricultural techniques enable relatively few farmers to produce enough food for the world's 6 billion or so people.

Staple Crops

Wheat

China 17.2% India 11.4% USA 9.5% Russia 7.4% France 5.8% Canada 4.5% Germany 3.7%

World total (2006): 605,946,000 tonnes

Maize

USA 38.5% China 20.9% Brazil 6.1%

World total (2006): 695,228,000 tonnes

Oats

Russia 21.1% Canada 15.6% Australia 8.1% USA 5.9% China 5.0% Poland 4.5% Spain 4.0%

World total (2006): 23,101,000 tonnes

Millet

India 31.8% Nigeria 24.2% Niger 10.1% China 5.7%

World total (2006): 31,781,000 tonnes

Rice

China 29.0% India 21.5% Indonesia 8.6% Bangladesh 6.9% Vietnam 5.6% Thailand 4.6% Burma 4.0%

World total (2006): 634,606,000 tonnes

Potatoes

China 22.3% Russia 12.2% India 7.6% USA 6.3% Ukraine 6.2%

World total (2006): 315,100,000 tonnes

Soya

USA 39.6% Brazil 23.6% Argentina 18.3% China 7.0%

World total (2006): 221,501,000 tonnes

Cassava

Nigeria 20.2% Brazil 11.8% Thailand 10.0% Indonesia 8.8% Congo (D.R.) 6.6% Mozambique 5.1%

World total (2006): 226,337,000 tonnes

Sugars

Sugar cane

Brazil 32.7% India 20.2% China 7.2% Mexico 3.6% Thailand 3.4% Pakistan 3.2%

World total (2006): 1,392,365,000 tonnes

Sugar beet

Russia 12.0% France 11.7% USA 11.3% Ukraine 8.7% Germany 8.1% Turkey 5.6% Poland 4.3% Italy 4.2%

World total (2006): 256,407,000 tonnes

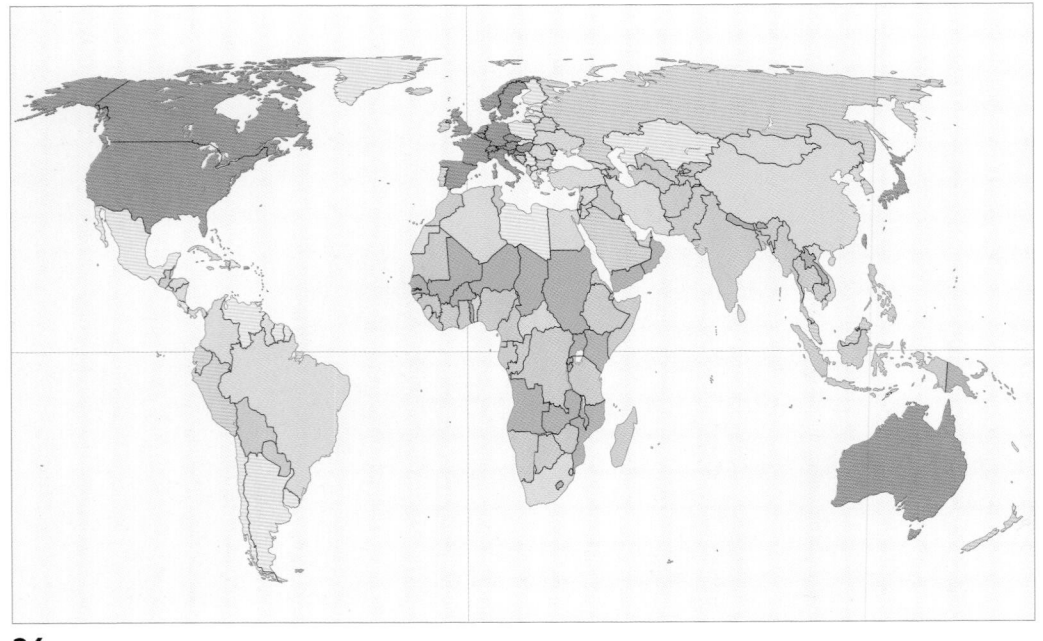

Employment

The number of workers employed in manufacturing for every 100 workers engaged in agriculture (2006)

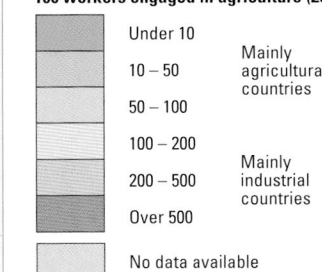

Under 10	Mainly agricultural countries
10 – 50	
50 – 100	
100 – 200	Mainly industrial countries
200 – 500	
Over 500	
No data available	

Countries with the highest and lowest number of workers employed in manufacturing per 100 workers engaged in agriculture (2006)

Highest		Lowest	
Bahrain	7,900	Burundi	2.5
San Marino	4,200	Yemen	5.0
Micronesia	3,822	Oman	5.0
USA	3,271	Rwanda	5.6
Liechtenstein	2,350	Malawi	5.6

Mineral Production

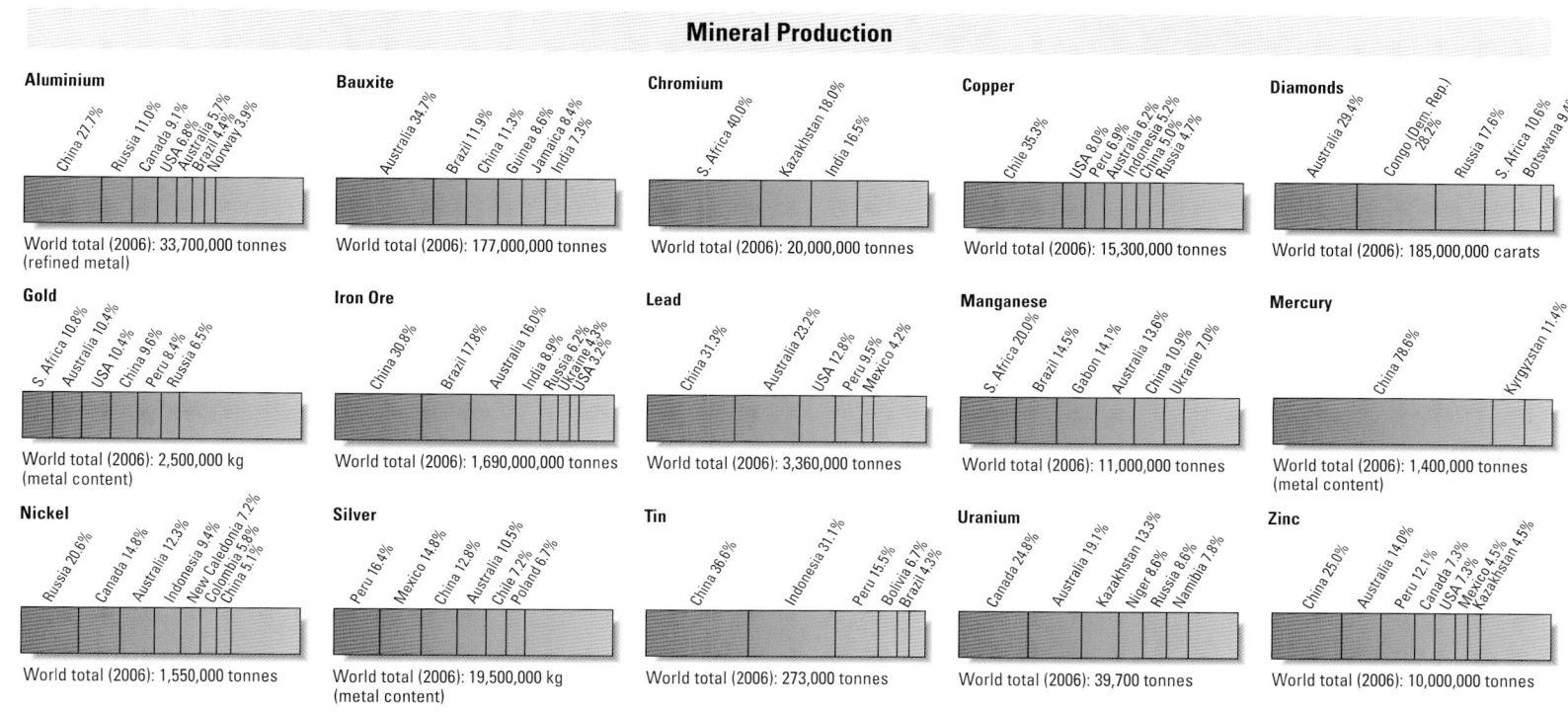

Aluminium
China 27.7% · Russia 11.0% · Canada 9.1% · USA 6.8% · Australia 5.7% · Brazil 4.4% · Norway 3.9%
World total (2006): 33,700,000 tonnes (refined metal)

Bauxite
Australia 34.7% · Brazil 11.9% · China 11.3% · Guinea 8.6% · Jamaica 8.4% · India 7.3%
World total (2006): 177,000,000 tonnes

Chromium
S. Africa 40.0% · Kazakhstan 18.0% · India 16.5%
World total (2006): 20,000,000 tonnes

Copper
Chile 35.3% · USA 8.0% · Peru 6.9% · Australia 6.2% · Indonesia 5.2% · Russia 4.7% · China 3.0%
World total (2006): 15,300,000 tonnes

Diamonds
Australia 29.4% · Congo (Dem. Rep.) 28.2% · Russia 17.6% · S. Africa 10.6% · Botswana 9.4%
World total (2006): 185,000,000 carats

Gold
S. Africa 10.8% · Australia 10.4% · USA 10.4% · China 9.6% · Peru 8.4% · Russia 6.5%
World total (2006): 2,500,000 kg (metal content)

Iron Ore
China 30.8% · Brazil 17.8% · Australia 16.0% · India 8.9% · Russia 6.2% · Ukraine 4.3% · USA 3.2%
World total (2006): 1,690,000,000 tonnes

Lead
China 31.3% · Australia 23.2% · USA 12.8% · Peru 9.5% · Mexico 4.2%
World total (2006): 3,360,000 tonnes

Manganese
S. Africa 20.0% · Brazil 14.5% · Gabon 14.1% · Australia 13.6% · China 10.9% · Ukraine 7.0%
World total (2006): 11,000,000 tonnes

Mercury
China 78.6% · Kyrgyzstan 11.4%
World total (2006): 1,400,000 tonnes (metal content)

Nickel
Russia 20.6% · Canada 14.8% · Australia 12.3% · Indonesia 9.4% · New Caledonia 7.2% · Colombia 5.8% · China 5.1%
World total (2006): 1,550,000 tonnes

Silver
Peru 16.4% · Mexico 14.8% · China 12.8% · Australia 10.5% · Chile 7.2% · Poland 6.7%
World total (2006): 19,500,000 kg (metal content)

Tin
China 38.6% · Indonesia 31.1% · Peru 15.5% · Bolivia 6.7% · Brazil 4.3%
World total (2006): 273,000 tonnes

Uranium
Canada 24.8% · Australia 19.1% · Kazakhstan 13.3% · Niger 8.6% · Russia 8.6% · Namibia 7.8%
World total (2006): 39,700 tonnes

Zinc
China 25.0% · Australia 14.0% · Peru 12.1% · Canada 7.3% · USA 7.3% · Mexico 4.5% · Kazakhstan 4.5%
World total (2006): 10,000,000 tonnes

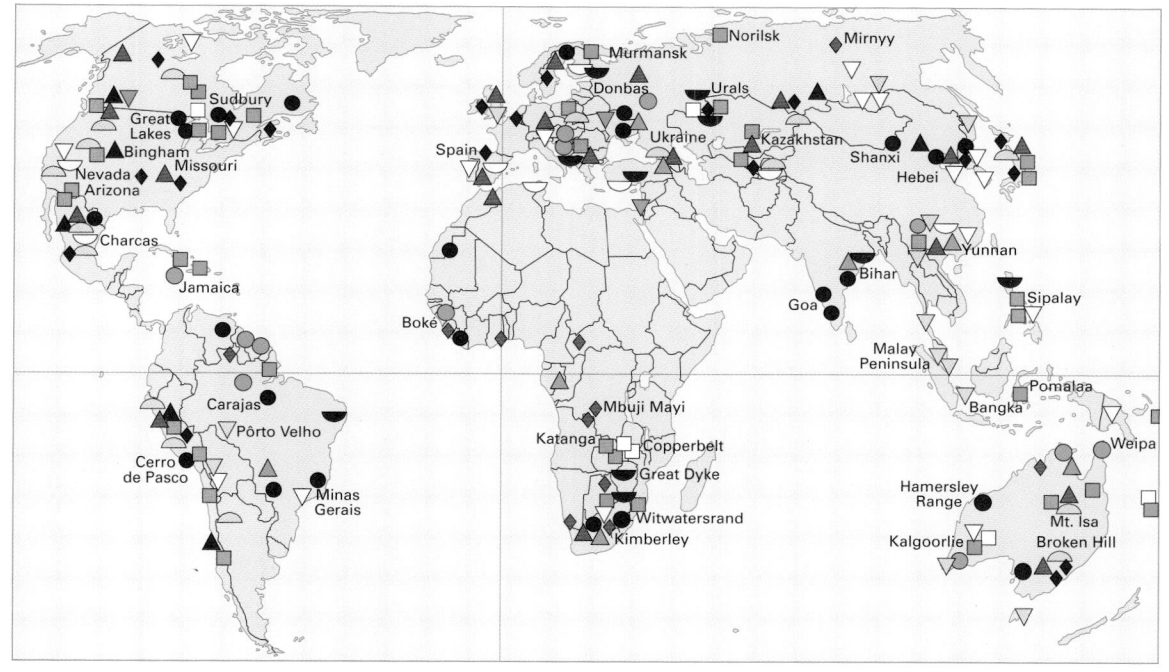

Mineral Distribution

The map shows the richest sources of the most important minerals (major mineral locations are named)

- Bauxite
- Chromium
- Cobalt
- Copper
- Diamonds
- Gold
- Iron ore
- Lead
- Manganese
- Mercury
- Molybdenum
- Nickel
- Potash
- Silver
- Tin
- Tungsten
- Zinc

The map does not show undersea deposits, most of which are considered inaccessible.

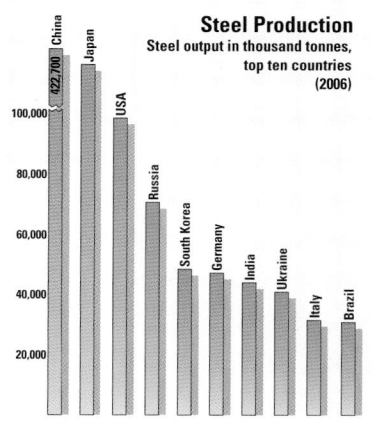

Steel Production
Steel output in thousand tonnes, top ten countries (2006)

422,700 China · Japan · USA · Russia · South Korea · Germany · India · Ukraine · Italy · Brazil

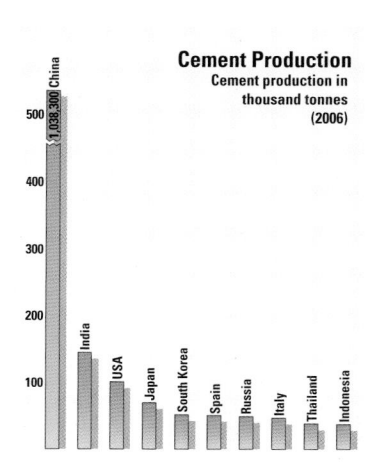

Cement Production
Cement production in thousand tonnes (2006)

1,038,300 China · India · USA · Japan · South Korea · Spain · Russia · Italy · Thailand · Indonesia

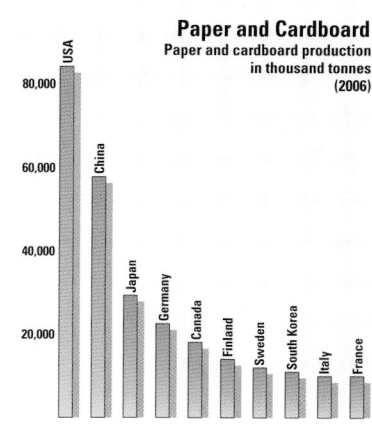

Paper and Cardboard
Paper and cardboard production in thousand tonnes (2006)

USA · China · Japan · Germany · Canada · Finland · Sweden · South Korea · Italy · France

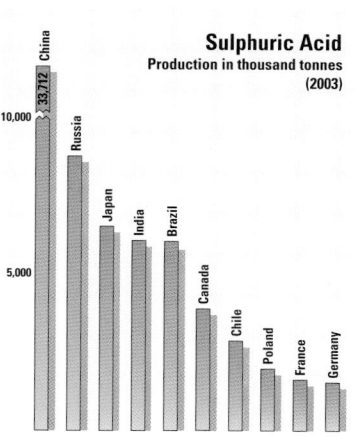

Sulphuric Acid
Production in thousand tonnes (2003)

33,712 China · Russia · Japan · India · Brazil · Canada · Chile · Poland · France · Germany

Trade

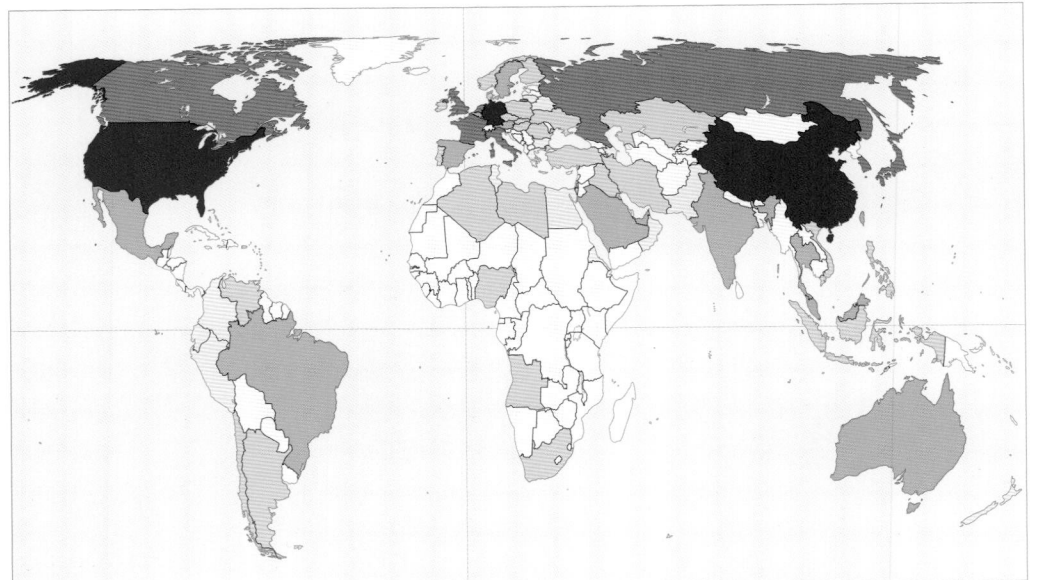

Share of World Trade

Percentage share of total world exports by value (2007)

- Over 5% of world trade
- 2.5 – 5% of world trade
- 1 – 2.5% of world trade
- 0.25 – 1% of world trade
- 0.1 – 0.25% of world trade
- Under 0.1% of world trade

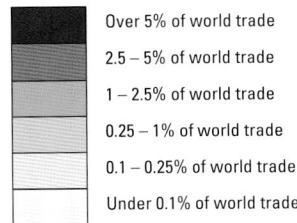

Largest share of world trade		Smallest share of world trade	
Germany	9.8%	East Timor	0.0%
China	8.8%	Eritrea	0.0%
USA	8.2%	Burundi	0.0%
Japan	4.8%	Rwanda	0.0%
France	4.0%	Guinea-Bissau	0.0%

The Main Trading Nations

The imports and exports of the top ten trading nations as a percentage of world trade (2006). Each country's trade in manufactured goods is shown in dark blue

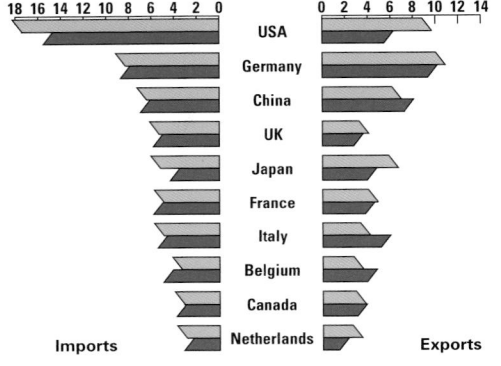

Imports — Exports

Major exports

Leading manufactured items and their exporters (2007)

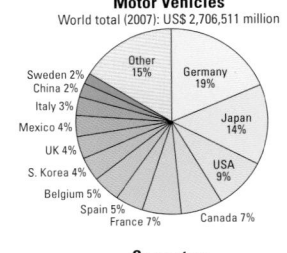

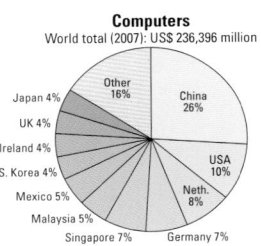

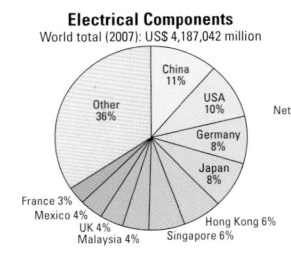

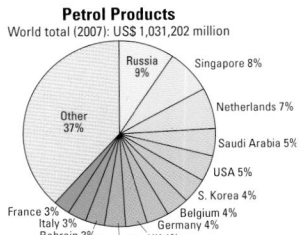

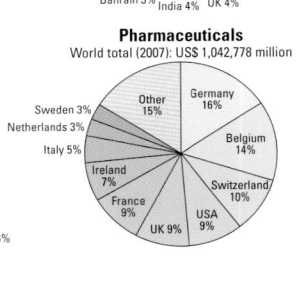

Balance of Trade

Value of exports in proportion to the value of imports (2007)

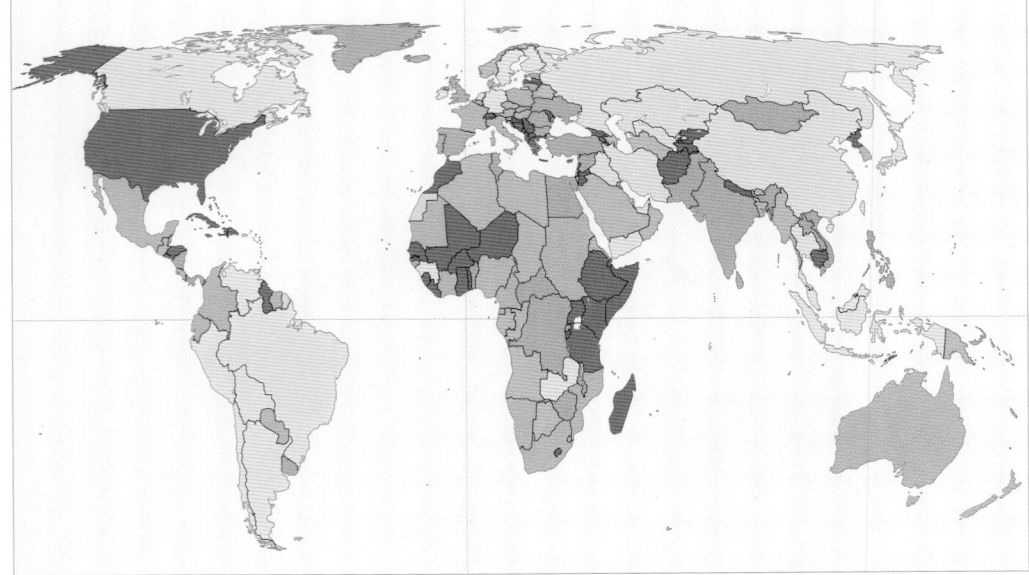

- More than 40%   Imports exceed exports by:
- 10 – 40%
- 10% either side
- 10 – 40%
- More than 40%   Exports exceed imports by:
- No data available

The total world trade balance should amount to zero, since exports must equal imports on a global scale. In practice, at least $100 billion in exports go unrecorded, leaving the world with an apparent deficit and many countries in a better position than public accounting reveals. However, a favourable trade balance is not necessarily a sign of prosperity: many poorer countries must maintain a high surplus in order to service debts, and do so by restricting imports below the levels needed to sustain successful economies.

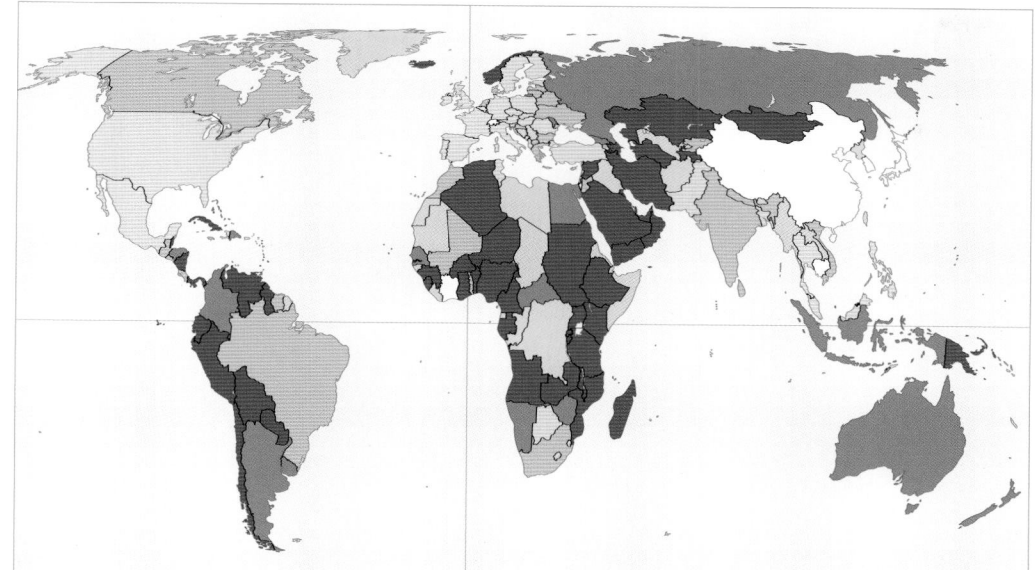

Primary exports as a percentage of total export value (2005)

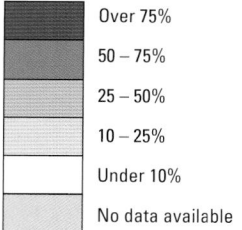

Over 75%

50 – 75%

25 – 50%

10 – 25%

Under 10%

No data available

Primary exports are raw materials or partly processed products that form the basis for manufacturing. They are the necessary requirements of industries and include agricultural products, minerals, fuels and timber, as well as many semi-manufactured goods such as cotton, which has been spun but not woven, wood pulp or flour. Many developed countries have few natural resources and rely on imports for the majority of their primary products. The countries of South-east Asia export hardwoods to the rest of the world, while many South American countries are heavily dependent on coffee exports.

Merchant Fleets

Merchant fleets in thousand gross registered tonnage (2006). Although a large number of vessels are registered in Liberia and Panama, they are not part of the national fleet

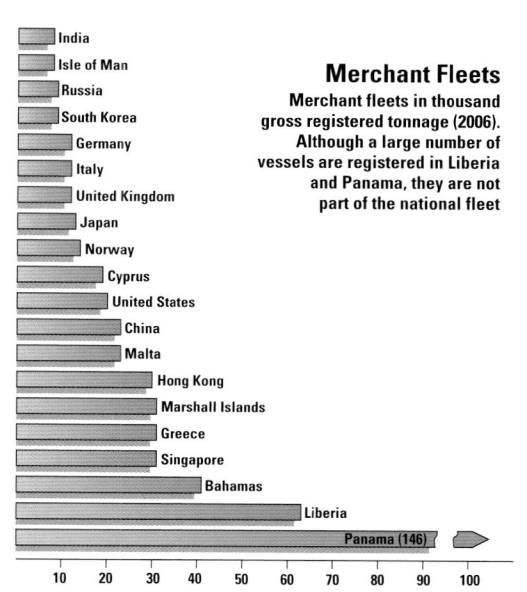

India
Isle of Man
Russia
South Korea
Germany
Italy
United Kingdom
Japan
Norway
Cyprus
United States
China
Malta
Hong Kong
Marshall Islands
Greece
Singapore
Bahamas
Liberia
Panama (146)

10 20 30 40 50 60 70 80 90 100

Top Ten Ports

Total container traffic, in million TEU (2006) ('TEU' stands for Twenty-foot Equivalent Unit, the equivalent of a standard container)

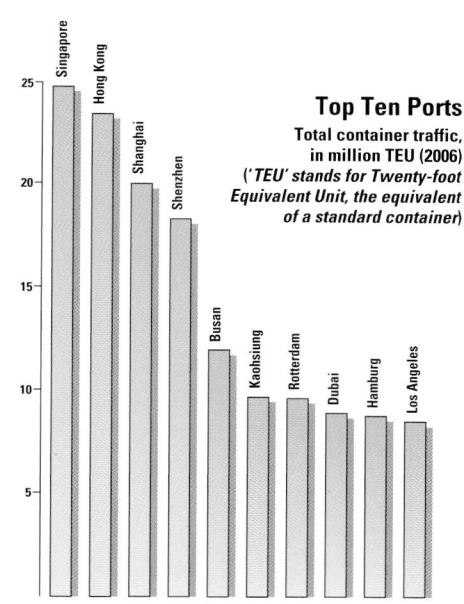

Types of Vessels

World fleet by type of vessel (2006)

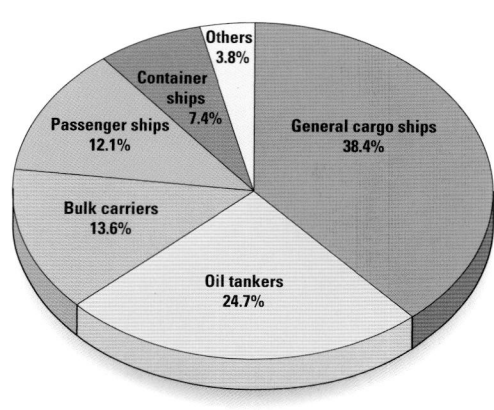

Others 3.8%
Container ships 7.4%
Passenger ships 12.1%
General cargo ships 38.4%
Bulk carriers 13.6%
Oil tankers 24.7%

Exports Per Capita

Value of exports in US $, divided by total population (2006)

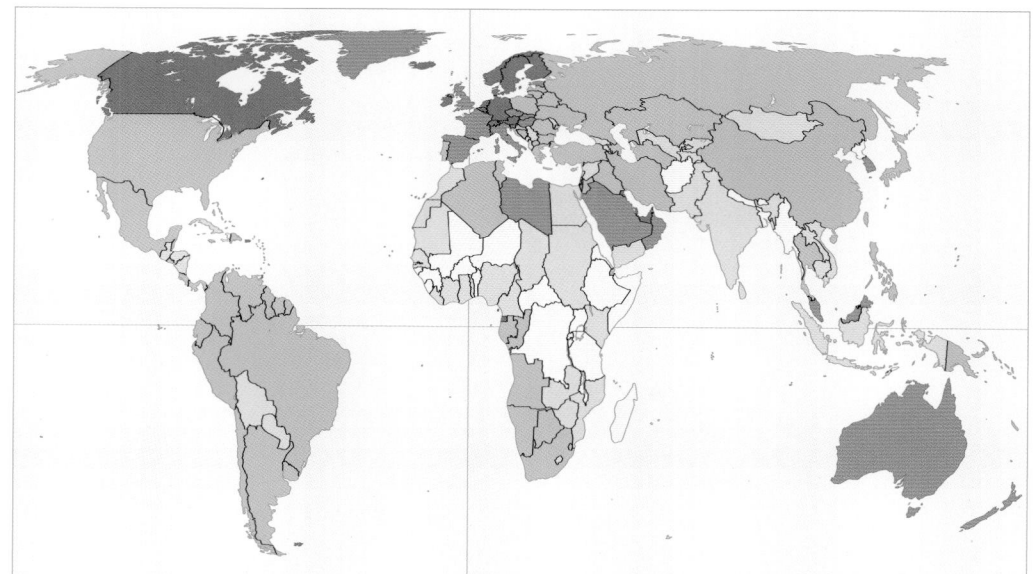

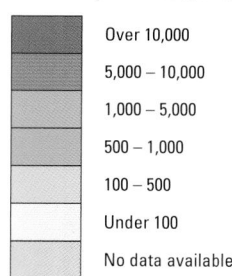

Over 10,000

5,000 – 10,000

1,000 – 5,000

500 – 1,000

100 – 500

Under 100

No data available

Highest per capita

Hong Kong	$88,121
Liechtenstein	$72,675
Singapore	$63,132
United Arab Emirates	$52,676
Luxembourg	$41,209

Travel and Tourism

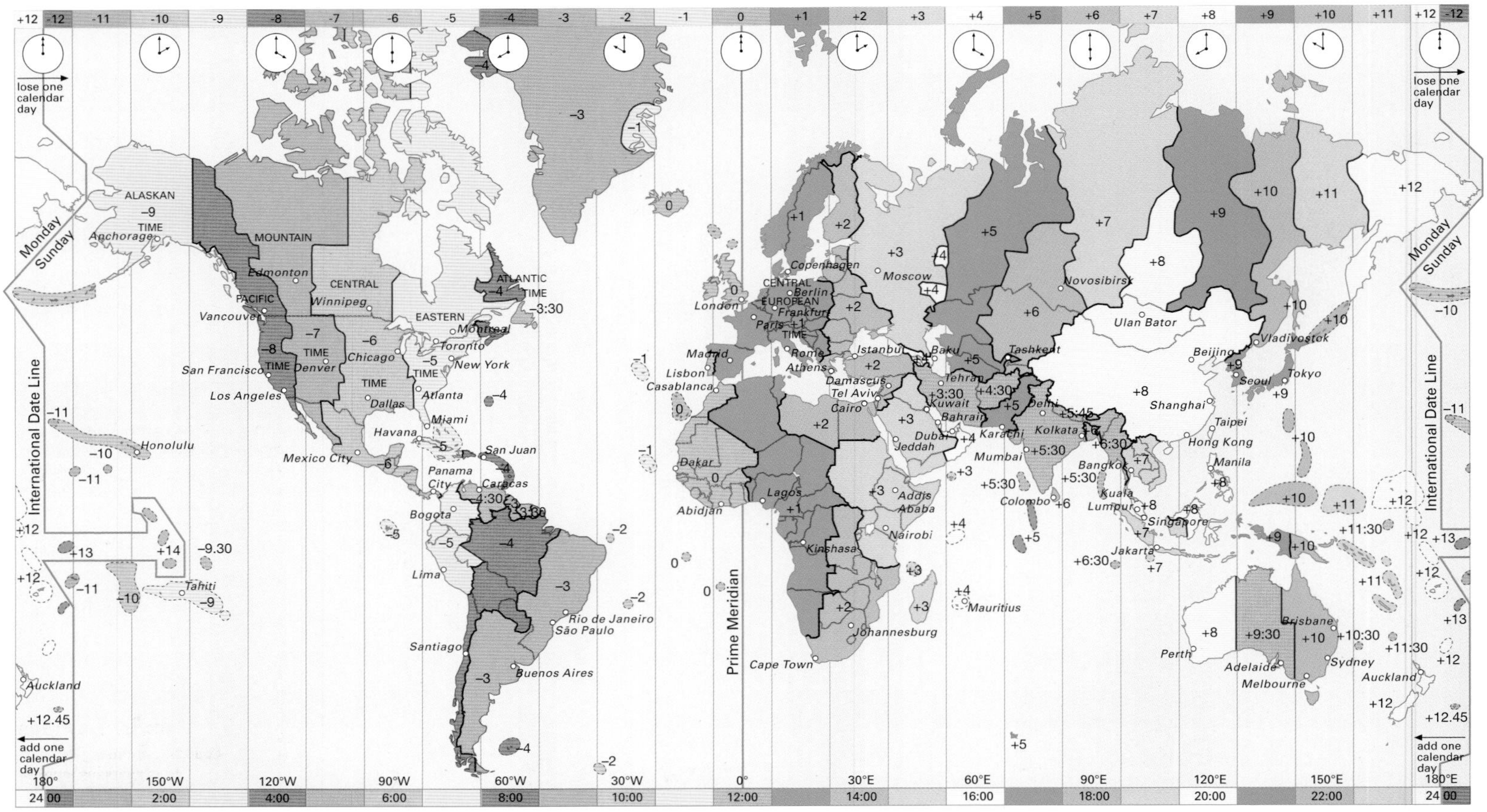

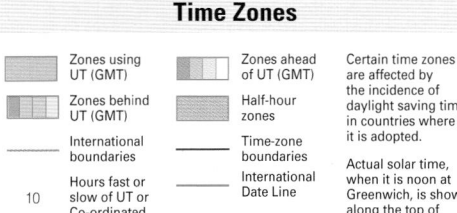

Projection: Mercator

Time Zones

Zones using UT (GMT)	Zones ahead of UT (GMT)	Certain time zones are affected by the incidence of daylight saving time in countries where it is adopted.
Zones behind UT (GMT)	Half-hour zones	
International boundaries	Time-zone boundaries	Actual solar time, when it is noon at Greenwich, is shown along the top of the map.
10 Hours fast or slow of UT or Co-ordinated Universal Time	International Date Line	

The world is divided into 24 time zones, each centred on meridians at 15° intervals, which is the longitudinal distance the sun travels every hour. The meridian running through Greenwich, London, passes through the middle of the first zone.

Rail and Road: The Leading Nations

Total rail network ('000 km)	Passenger km per head per year	Total road network ('000 km)	Vehicle km per head per year	Number of vehicles per km of roads
1. USA 233.8	Japan 1,891	USA 6,378.3	USA...................12,505	Hong Kong 287
2. Russia 85.5	Switzerland 1,751	India 3,319.6	Luxembourg 7,989	Qatar....................284
3. Canada 73.2	Belarus 1,334	China 1,765.2	Kuwait 7,251	UAE......................232
4. India 63.1	France 1,203	Brazil 1,724.9	France 7,142	Germany 195
5. China 60.5	Ukraine...............1,100	Canada...............1,408.8	Sweden 6,991	Lebanon 191
6. Germany...............36.1	Russia 1,080	Japan 1,171.4	Germany 6,806	Macau 172
7. Argentina...............34.2	Austria...............1,008	France 893.1	Denmark 6,764	Singapore 167
8. France...............29.3	Denmark 999	Australia 811.6	Austria...................6,518	South Korea 160
9. Mexico...............26.5	Netherlands 855	Spain 664.9	Netherlands 5,984	Kuwait 156
10. South Africa...............22.7	Germany 842	Russia 537.3	UK 5,738	Taiwan 150
11. Brazil...............22.1	Italy 811	Italy...............479.7	Canada 5,493	Israel 111
12. Ukraine 22.1	Belgium...............795	UK 371.9	Italy...................4,852	Malta 110

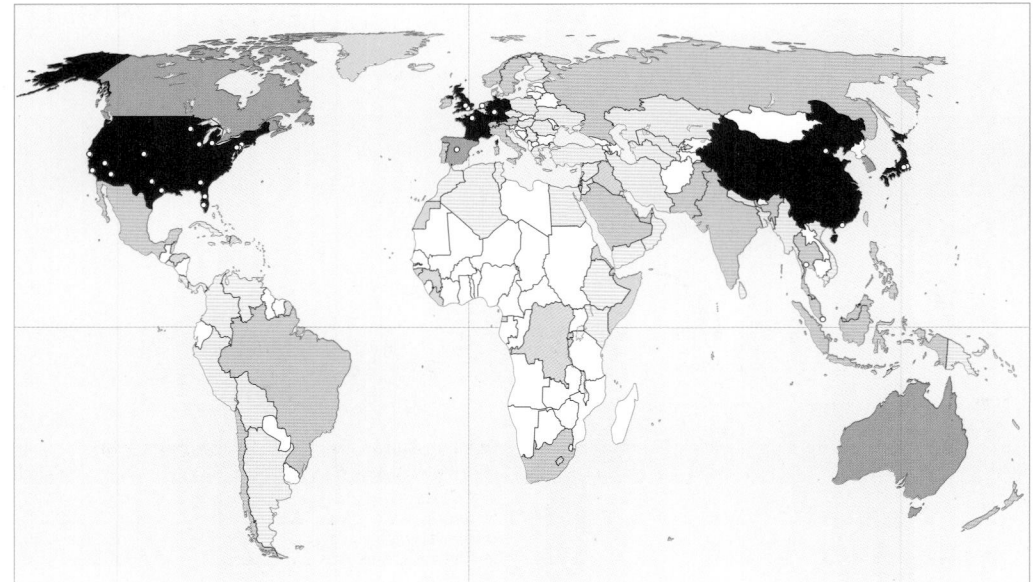

Air Travel

Passenger kilometres flown on scheduled flights (the number of passengers in thousands – international and domestic – multiplied by the distance flown from the airport of origin)

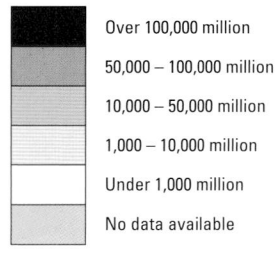

	Over 100,000 million
	50,000 – 100,000 million
	10,000 – 50,000 million
	1,000 – 10,000 million
	Under 1,000 million
	No data available
○	Major airports (handling over 30 million passengers)

World's busiest airports (total passengers)		World's busiest airports (international passengers)	
1. Atlanta	(Hartsfield)	1. London	(Heathrow)
2. Chicago	(O'Hare)	2. Paris	(Charles de Gaulle)
3. London	(Heathrow)	3. Amsterdam	(Schipol)
4. Tokyo	(Haneda)	4. Frankfurt	(International)
5. Los Angeles	(International)	5. Hong Kong	(International)

CARTOGRAPHY BY PHILIP'S. COPYRIGHT PHILIP'S

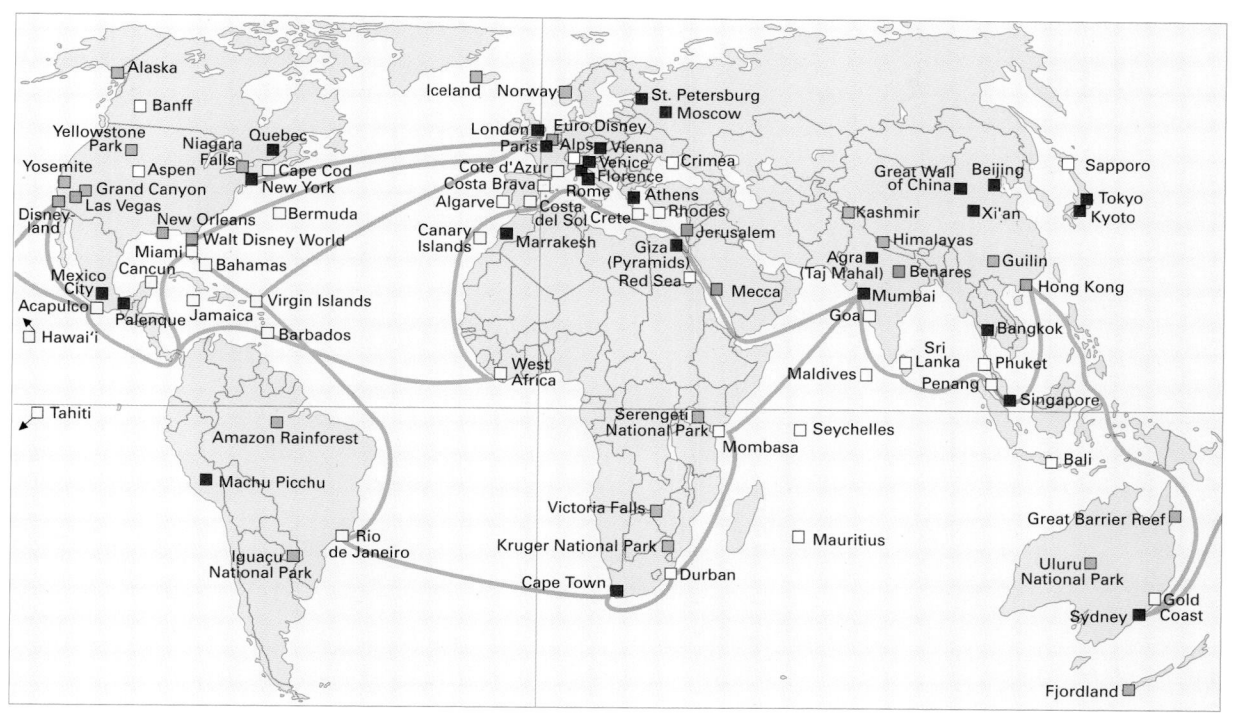

Destinations

- ■ Cultural and historical centres
- □ Coastal resorts
- □ Ski resorts
- ▨ Centres of entertainment
- ▨ Places of pilgrimage
- ▨ Places of great natural beauty
- ── Popular holiday cruise routes

Visitors to the USA

Overseas arrivals to the USA, in thousands (2006)

1.	Canada	15,995
2.	Mexico	13,400
3.	UK	4,176
4.	Japan	3,673
5.	Germany	1,386
6.	France	790
7.	South Korea	758
8.	Australia	603
9.	Italy	533
10.	Brazil	525

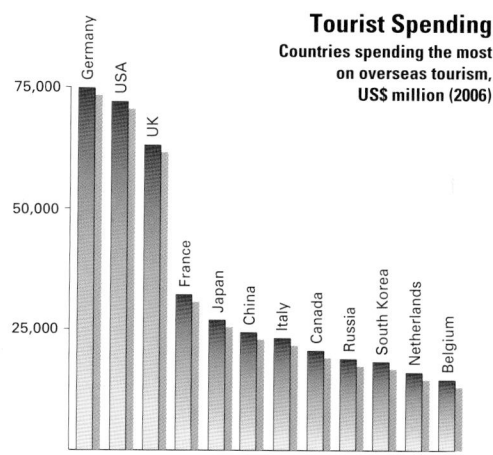

Tourist Spending

Countries spending the most on overseas tourism, US$ million (2006)

Importance of Tourism

		Arrivals from abroad (2006)	% of world total (2006)
1.	France	76,001,000	9.0%
2.	Spain	55,577,000	6.6%
3.	USA	46,085,000	5.4%
4.	China	41,761,000	4.9%
5.	Italy	36,513,000	4.3%
6.	UK	29,970,000	3.5%
7.	Germany	21,500,000	2.5%
8.	Mexico	20,617,000	2.4%
9.	Turkey	20,273,000	2.4%
10.	Austria	19,952,000	2.4%
11.	Russia	19,940,000	2.4%
12.	Canada	19,152,000	2.3%

The 846 million international arrivals in 2006 represented an additional 43 million over 2005's level – making a new record year for the industry. Growth was common to all regions, but particularly strong in Asia and the Pacific, and in the Middle East.

Tourist Earnings

Countries receiving the most from overseas tourism, US$ million (2006)

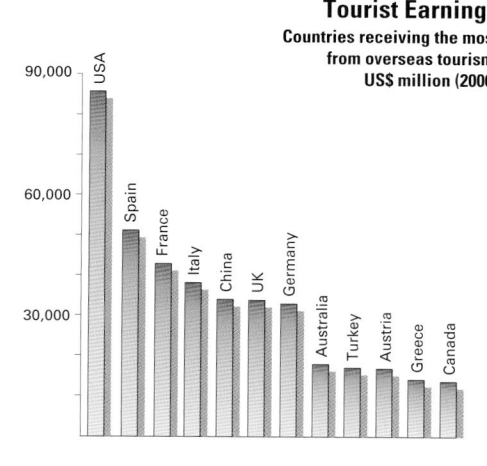

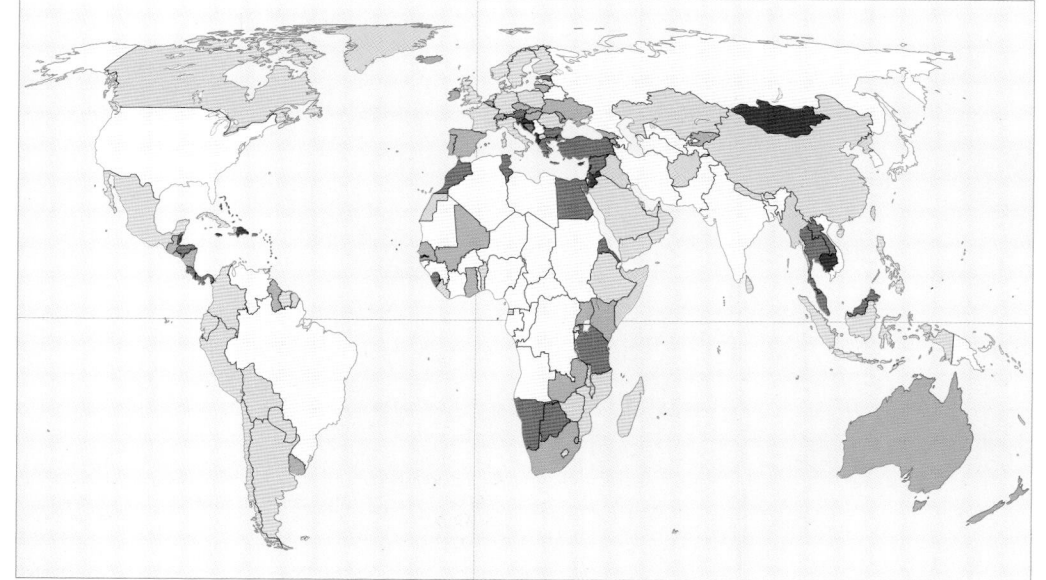

Tourism

Tourism receipts as a percentage of Gross National Income (2005)

- ▨ Over 10%
- ▨ 5 – 10%
- ▨ 2.5 – 5%
- ▨ 1 – 2.5%
- □ Under 1%
- ▨ No data available

Countries most dependent on tourism (highest tourism receipts as a percentage of GNI, 2005)

1.	Palau	63.0%
2.	St Lucia	44.8%
3.	Bahamas	40.2%
4.	Antigua & Barbuda	36.9%
5.	Maldives	36.5%

– MT EVEREST, CHINA/NEPAL –

Part of the Himalaya range, Mt Everest – the highest mountain in the world at 8,850 m (29,035 ft) – lies just north of centre in this image. The two arms of the Rongbuk glacier flow away from the triangular shaded north wall, with the Kangshung glacier due east. The international boundary between China and Nepal bisects the peak, which was first climbed on 28 May 1953.

WORLD CITIES

AMSTERDAM	2	HONG KONG	12	MUMBAI	20	TEHRAN	31
ATHENS	2	ISTANBUL	12	MUNICH	21	TORONTO	31
ATLANTA	3	JAKARTA	12	NEW ORLEANS	21	VIENNA	32
BAGHDAD	3	JERUSALEM	13	NEW YORK	22	WARSAW	32
BANGKOK	3	JOHANNESBURG	13	ORLANDO	23	WASHINGTON	33
BARCELONA	4	KARACHI	13	OSAKA	23	WELLINGTON	33
BEIJING	4	KOLKATA	14	OSLO	23		
BERLIN	5	LAGOS	14	PARIS	24	INDEX	34–39
BOSTON	6	LAS VEGAS	14	PRAGUE	25		
BRUSSELS	6	LIMA	14	RIO DE JANEIRO	25		
BUDAPEST	7	LONDON	15	ROME	26	WORLD CITIES	
BUENOS AIRES	7	LOS ANGELES	16	SAN FRANCISCO	26	SATELLITE IMAGES	
CAIRO	7	LISBON	16	ST PETERSBURG	27	CAPE TOWN	40
CAPE TOWN	8	MADRID	17	SANTIAGO	27	KARACHI	41
COPENHAGEN	8	MANILA	17	SÃO PAULO	27	LONDON	42
CHICAGO	9	MELBOURNE	18	SEOUL	27	MELBOURNE	43
DELHI	10	MEXICO CITY	18	SHANGHAI	28	NEW ORLEANS	44
DUBLIN	10	MIAMI	18	SINGAPORE	28	NEW YORK	45
EDINBURGH	11	MILAN	19	STOCKHOLM	29	SAN FRANCISCO	46
GUANGZHOU	11	MOSCOW	19	SYDNEY	29	SANTIAGO	47
HELSINKI	11	MONTRÉAL	20	TOKYO	30	TOKYO	48

CITY MAPS

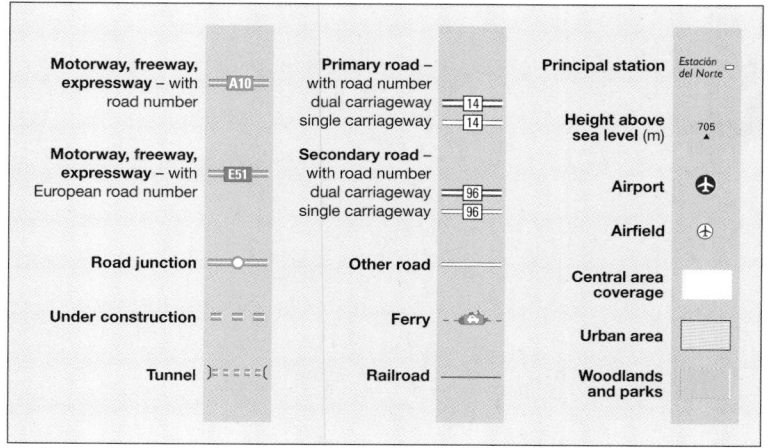

CENTRAL AREA MAPS

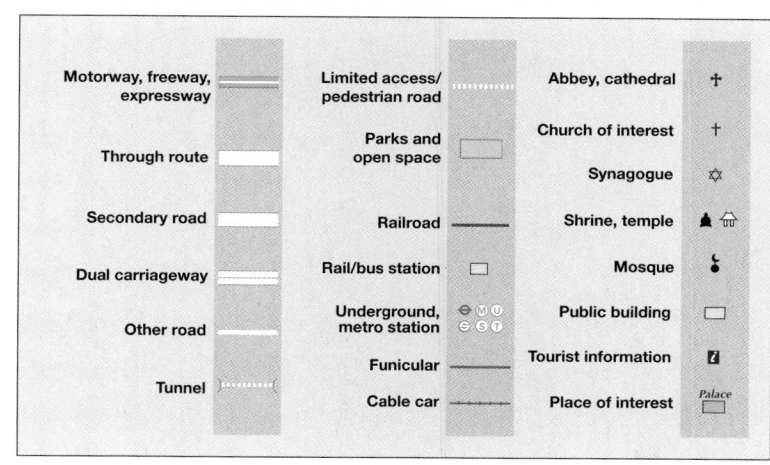

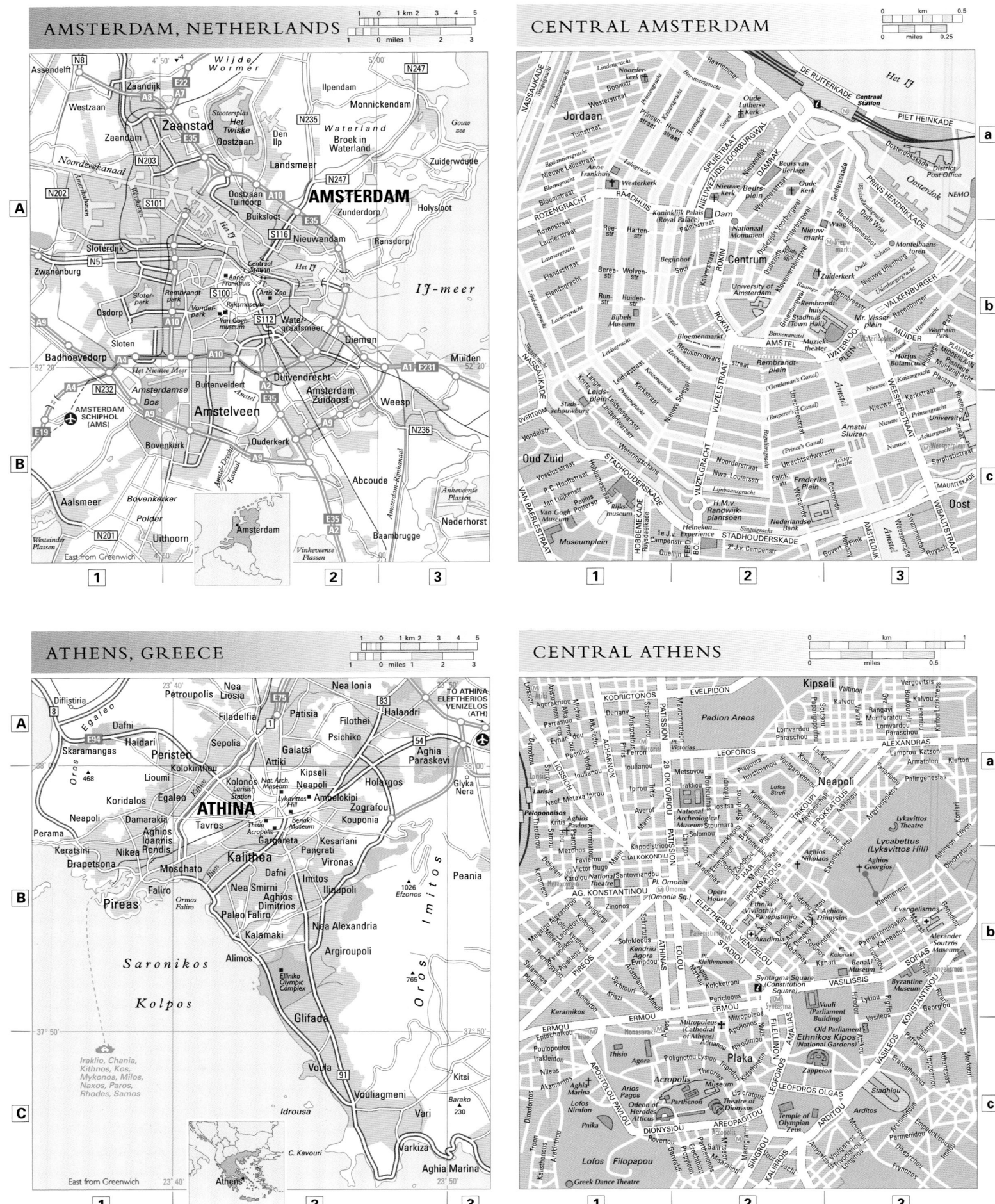

AMSTERDAM, NETHERLANDS

CENTRAL AMSTERDAM

ATHENS, GREECE

CENTRAL ATHENS

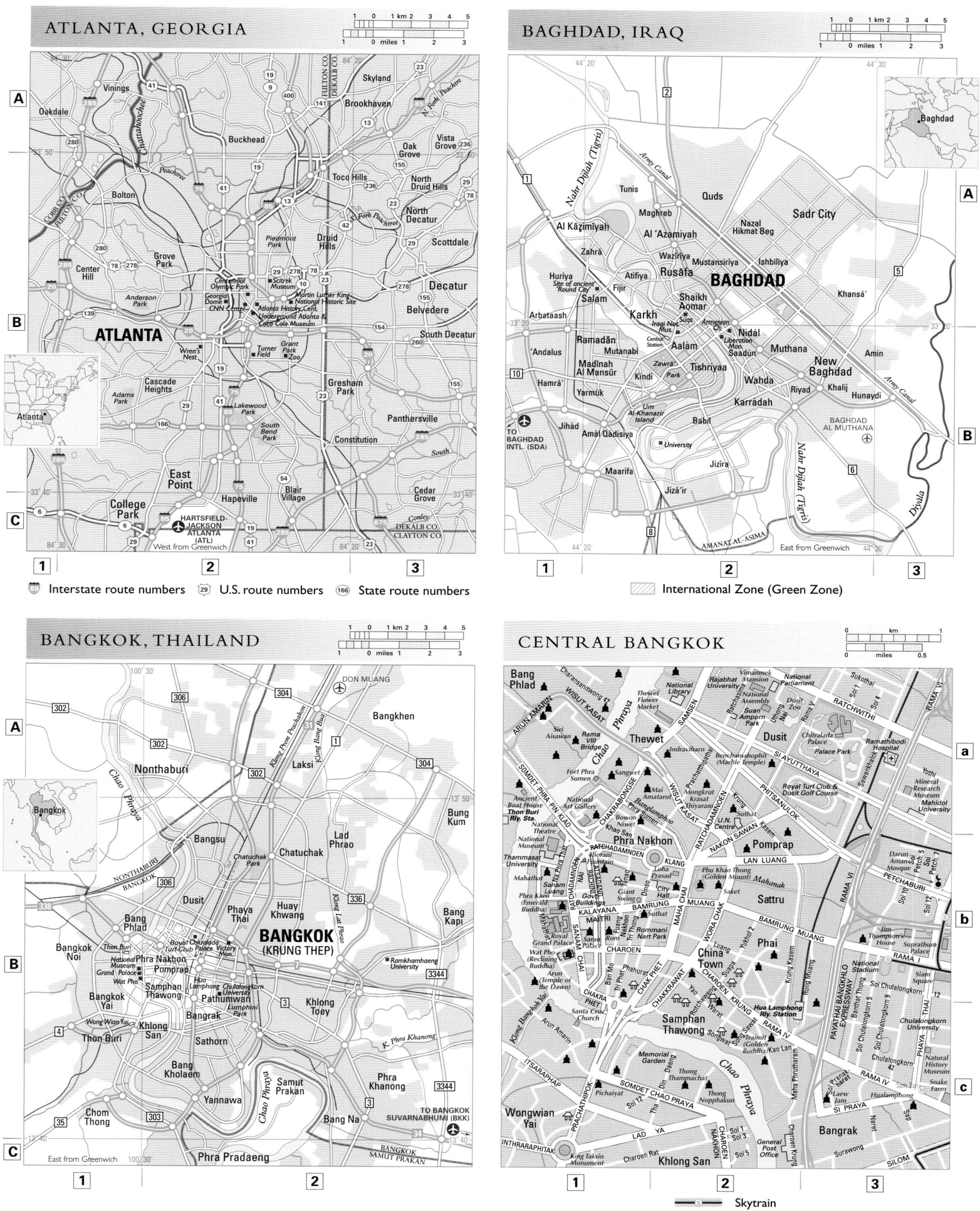

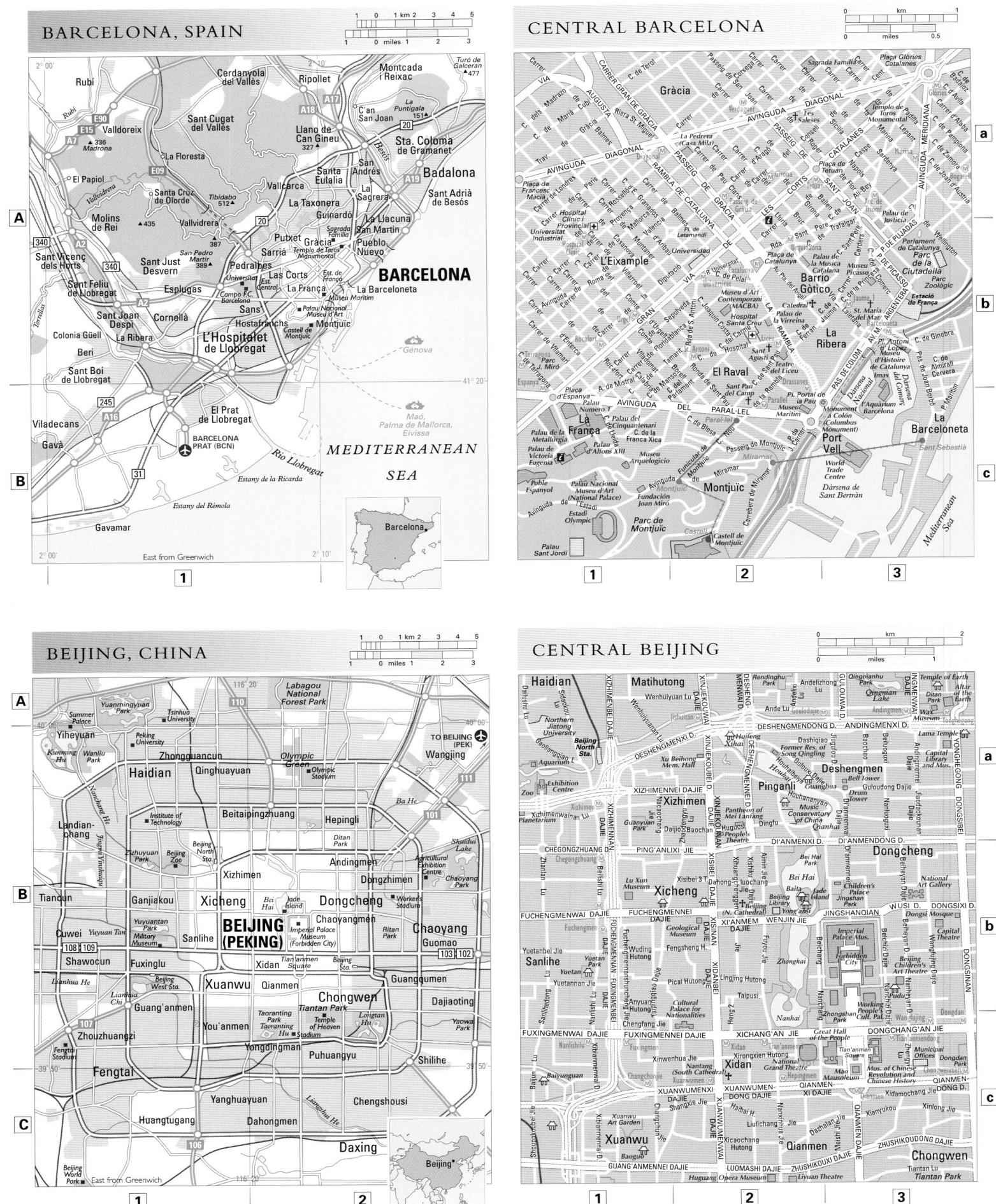

BERLIN, GERMANY

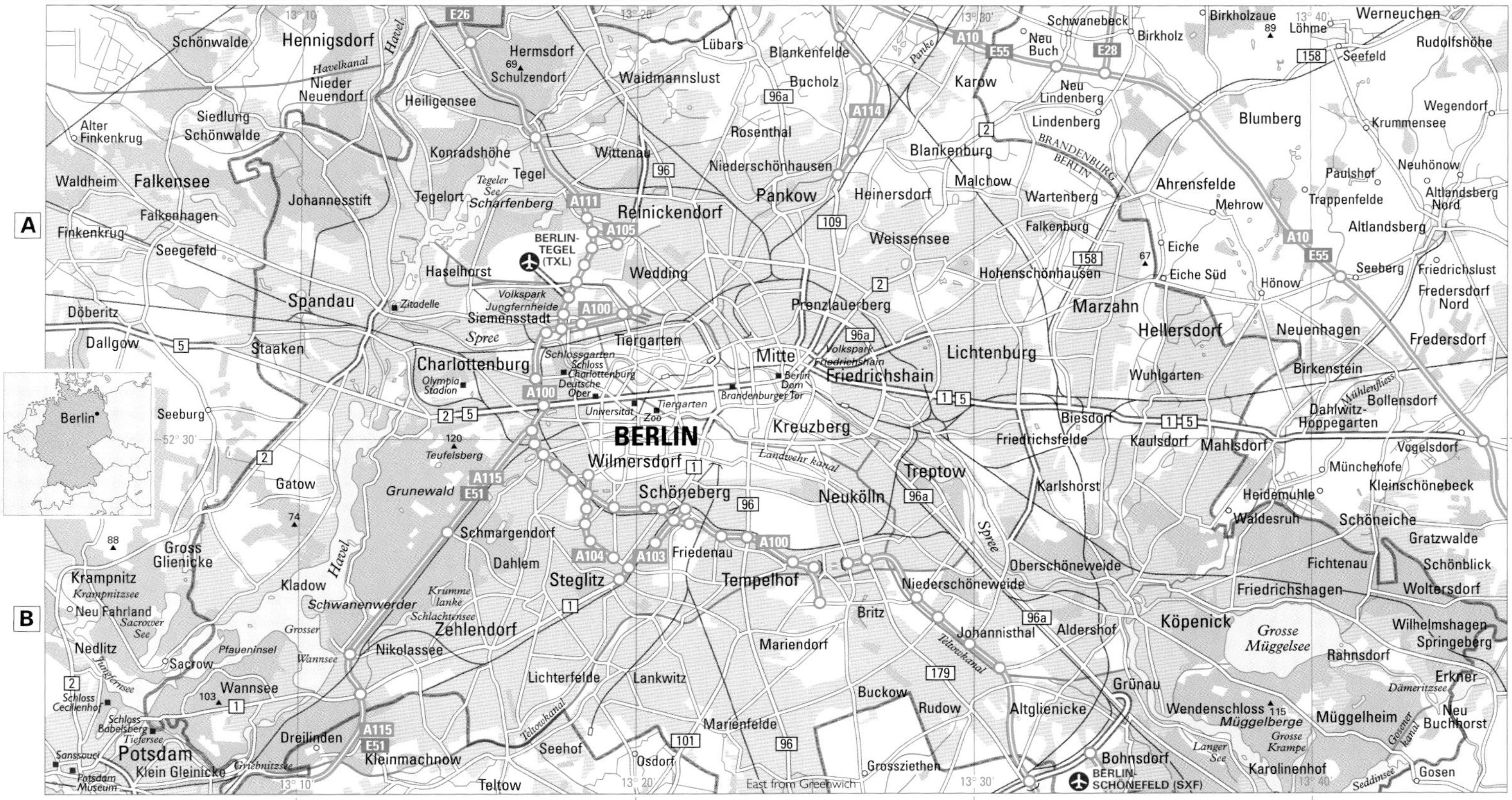

1 0 1 km 2 3 4 5
1 0 miles 1 2 3

Schönwalde · Hennigsdorf · Hermsdorf · Lübars · Blankenfelde · Schwanebeck · Birkholzaue · Werneuchen
Alter Finkenkrug · Nieder Neuendorf · Schulzendorf · Waidmannslust · Bucholz · Karow · Neu Buch · Birkholz · Löhme · Seefeld · Rudolfshöhe
Waldheim · Falkensee · Johannesstift · Heiligensee · Rosenthal · Niederschönhausen · Neu Lindenberg · Blumberg · Krummensee · Wegendorf
Falkenhagen · Tegelort · Tegel · Konradshöhe · Wittenau · Pankow · Heinersdorf · Lindenberg · Ahrensfelde · Mehrow · Trappenfelde · Altlandsberg Nord
Finkenkrug · Siedlung Schönwalde · Scharfenberg · BERLIN-TEGEL (TXL) · Reinickendorf · Weissensee · Falkenberg · Eiche · Eiche Süd · Hönow · Seeberg · Altlandsberg
Seegeld · Spandau · Haselhorst · Wedding · Prenzlauerberg · Hohenschönhausen · Marzahn · Neuenhagen · Friedrichslust
Döberitz · Siemensstadt · Tiergarten · Mitte · Lichtenburg · Wuhlgarten · Birkenstein · Fredersdorf Nord
Dallgow · Staaken · Charlottenburg · Friedrichshain · Biesdorf · Kaulsdorf · Mahlsdorf · Fredersdorf
Gatow · Olympia Stadion · Universität · Zoo · Brandenburger Tor · Kreuzberg · Friedrichsfelde · Dahlwitz-Hoppegarten · Vogelsdorf
Teufelsberg · BERLIN · Wilmersdorf · Schöneberg · Treptow · Karlshorst · Münchehofe · Kleinschönebeck
Grunewald · Schmargendorf · Neukölln · Oberschöneweide · Heidemühle · Schöneiche · Gratzwalde
Seeburg · Schwanenwerder · Dahlem · Friedenau · Tempelhof · Niederschöneweide · Waldesruh · Schönblick
Gross Glienicke · Kladow · Steglitz · Britz · Johannisthal · Aldershof · Köpenick · Friedrichshagen · Woltersdorf
Krampnitz · Nikolassee · Zehlendorf · Mariendorf · Grosse Müggelsee · Rahnsdorf · Wilhelmshagen Springeberg
Nedlitz · Neu Fahrland · Wannsee · Lichterfelde · Lankwitz · Grünau · Müggelberge · Erkner
Sacrow · Marienfelde · Buckow · Rudow · Altglienicke · Wendenschloss · Müggelheim · Neu Buchhorst
Potsdam · Dreilinden · Kleinmachnow · Seehof · Marienfelde · Grossziethen · Bohnsdorf · Karolinenhof · Gosen
Potsdam Museum · Klein Gleinicke · Teltow · East from Greenwich · BERLIN-SCHÖNEFELD (SXF)

CENTRAL BERLIN

0 km 1
0 miles 0.5

Tiergarten · Charlottenburg · Mitte · Kreuzberg · Wilmersdorf · Schöneberg
Scheunenviertel · Hauptbahnhof Lehrter bahnhof · Alexanderplatz
Zoologischer Garten · Brandenburger Tor · Unter den Linden · Museuminsel
Kaiser Wilhelm Gedächtniskirche · Potsdamer Platz · Checkpoint Charlie

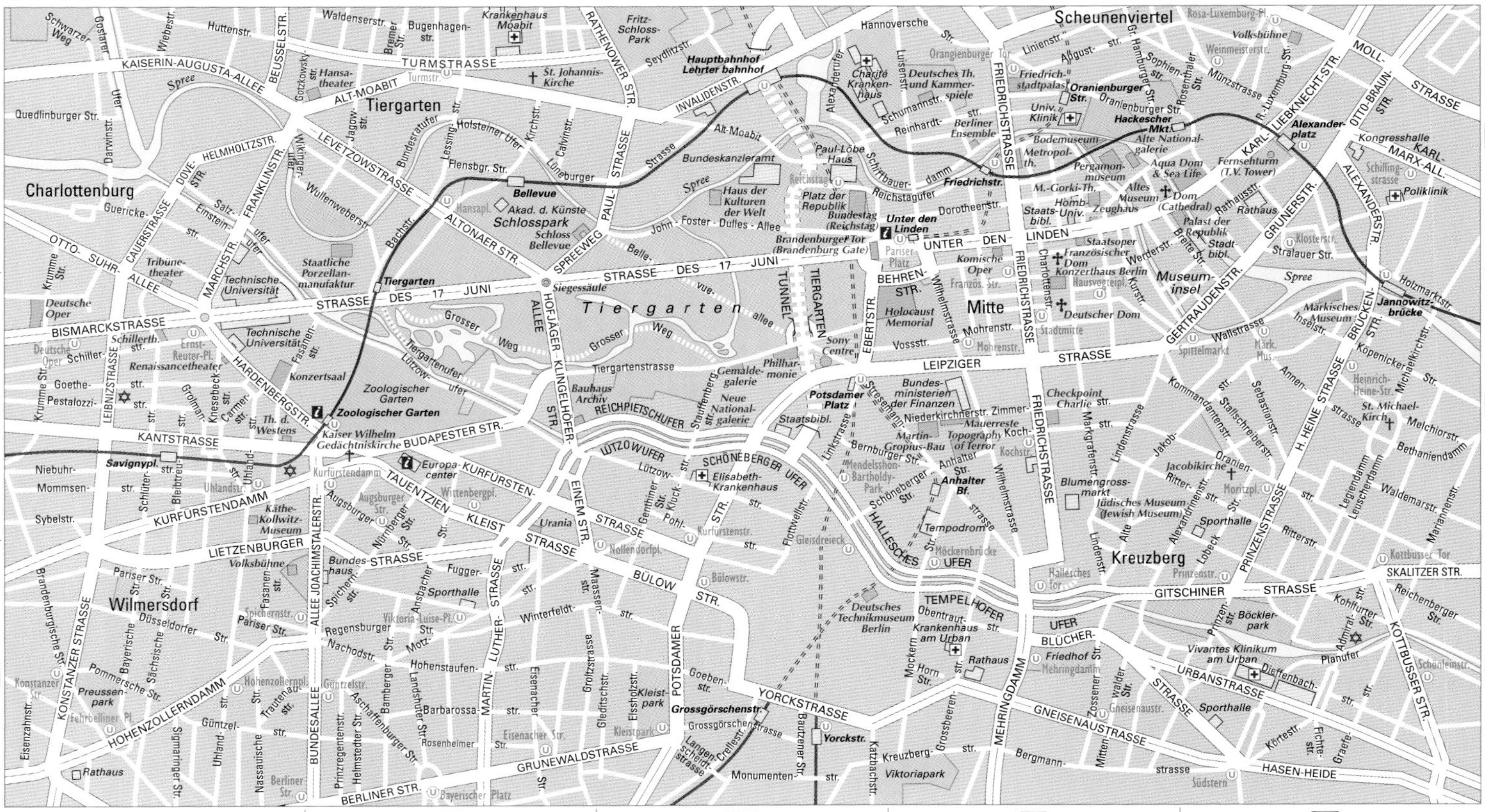

COPYRIGHT PHILIP'S

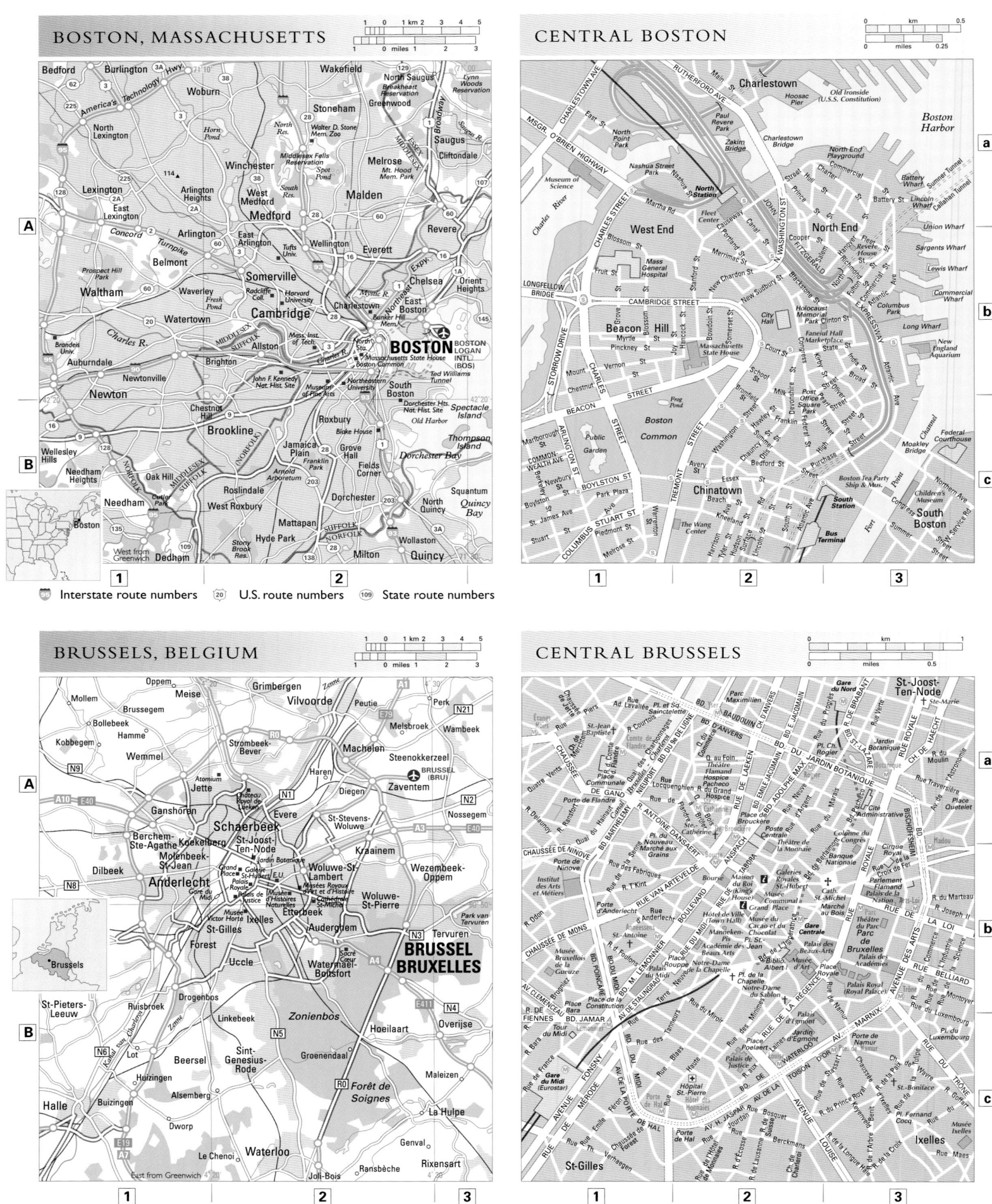

BOSTON, MASSACHUSETTS

CENTRAL BOSTON

BRUSSELS, BELGIUM

CENTRAL BRUSSELS

Interstate route numbers   U.S. route numbers   State route numbers

COPYRIGHT PHILIP'S

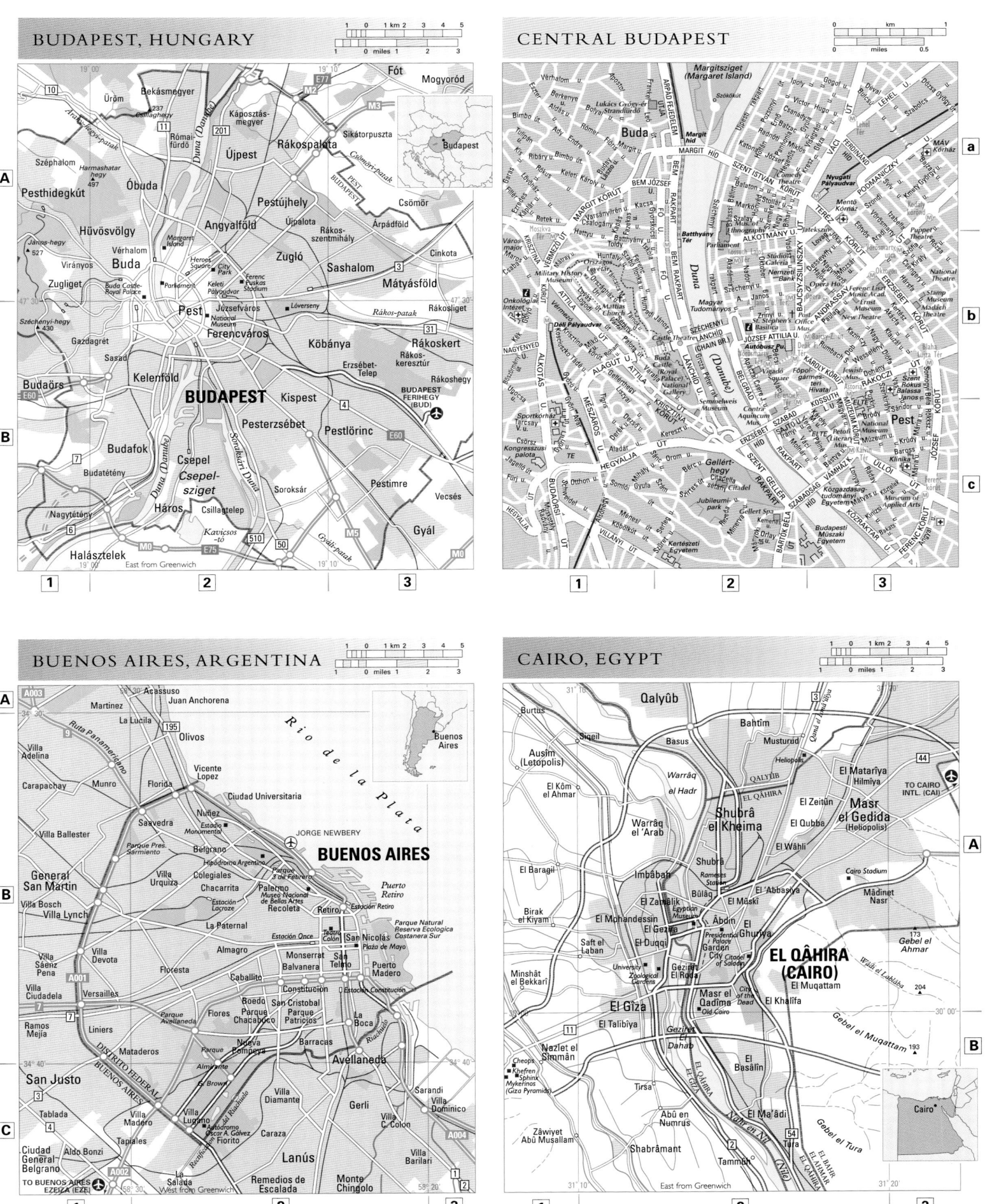

BUDAPEST, HUNGARY

CENTRAL BUDAPEST

BUENOS AIRES, ARGENTINA

CAIRO, EGYPT

COPYRIGHT PHILIP'S

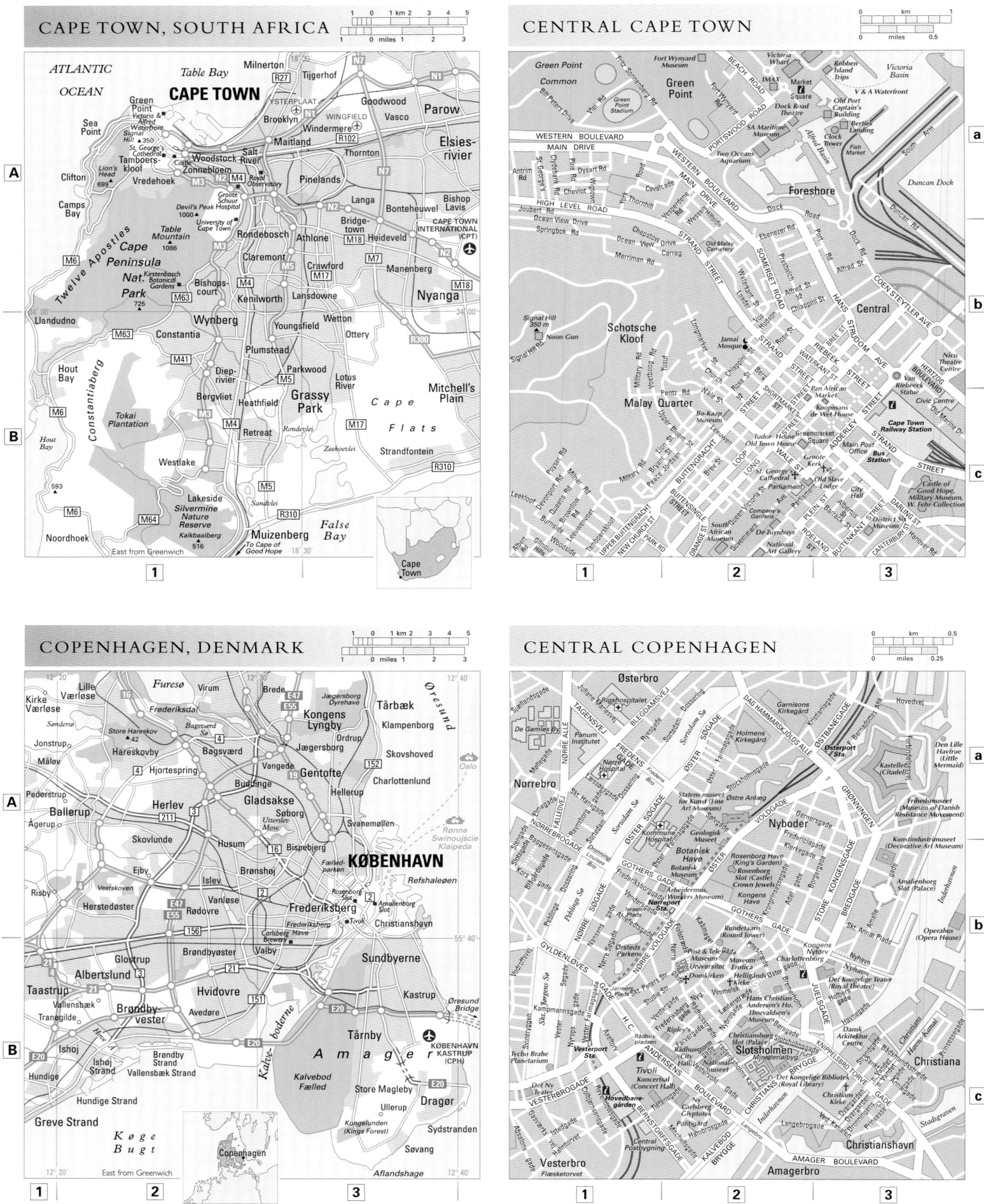

CHICAGO, ILLINOIS

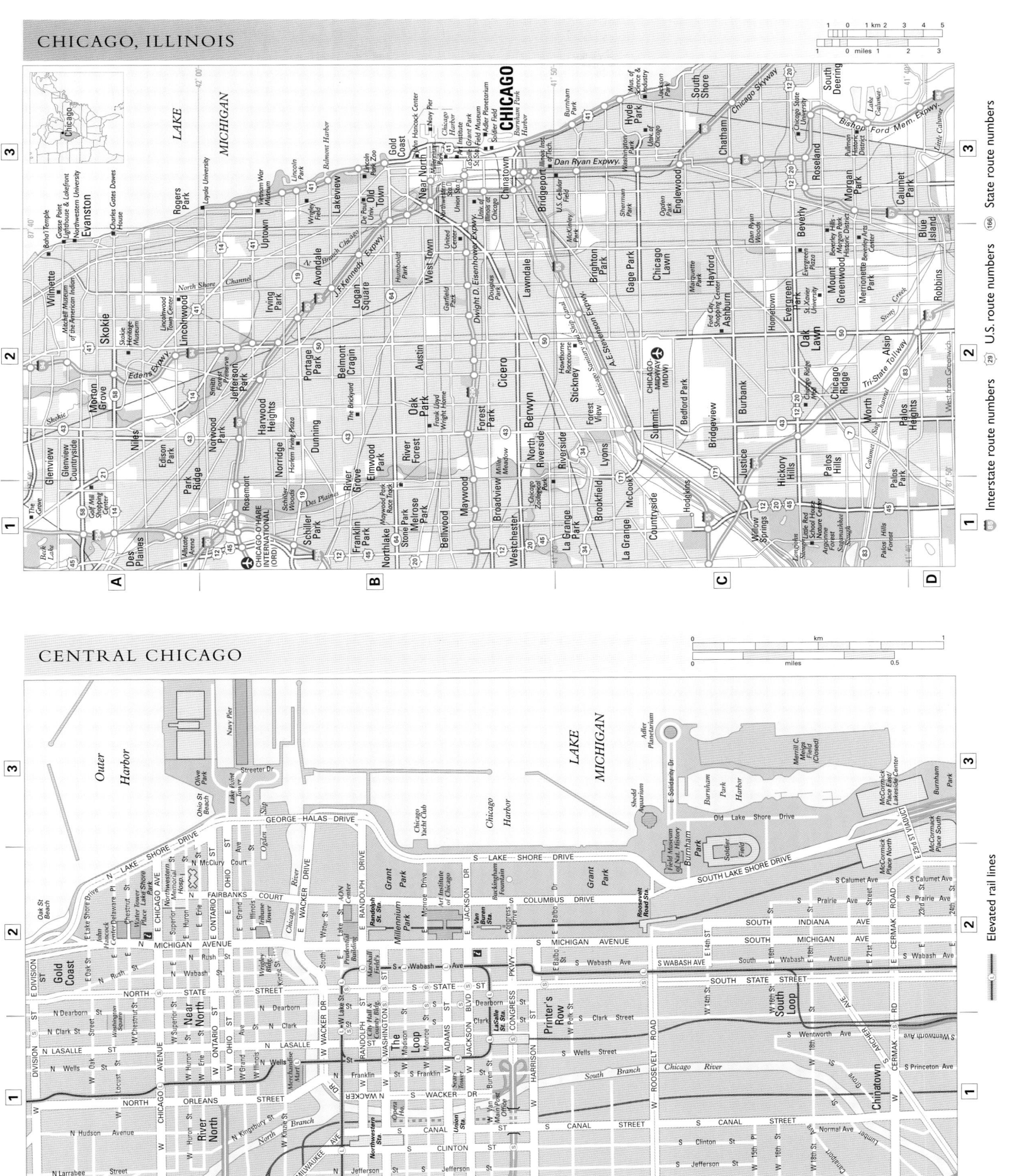

LAKE MICHIGAN

Inset map (top left): Chicago

Grosse Point Lighthouse & Lakefront
Baha'i Temple
Charles Gates Dawes House
Northwestern University
Evanston
Wilmette
Mitchell Museum of the American Indian

The Grove
Glenview
Glenview Countryside
Golf Mill Shopping Center
Morton Grove
Niles
Skokie
Skokie Heritage Museum
Lincolnwood Town Center
Lincolnwood
Lincolnwood
Rogers Park
Loyola University

Back Lake
Des Plaines
Allstate Arena
Rosemont
CHICAGO-O'HARE INTERNATIONAL (ORD)
Park Ridge
Edison Park
Norridge
Harwood Heights
Norwood Park
Dunning
Schiller Park
Des Plaines
Schiller Woods
Franklin Park
River Grove
Maywood Park Race Track
Stone Park
Melrose Park
Northlake
Bellwood
Maywood
Broadview
Westchester
Bellwood

North Shore Channel
Edens Expwy
Smith Forest Preserve
Jefferson Park
Portage Park
Irving Park
Avondale
Uptown
Lakeview
Wrigley Field
Vietnam War Museum
Belmont Harbor
Lincoln Park Zoo
Lincoln Park
Gold Coast
Near North

Logan Square
Humboldt Park
Belmont Cragin
Oak Park
Frank Lloyd Wright Home
Forest Park
River Forest
North Riverside
Riverside
Miller Meadow
Broadview
La Grange Park
La Grange
Brookfield
Chicago Zoological Park
Brookfield
McCook

J.F.Kennedy Expwy
West Town
Garfield Park
Douglas Park
Dwight D. Eisenhower Expwy
Austin
Cicero
Berwyn
Stickney
Forest View
Summit
Countryside
Willow Springs

United Center
Northwestern Sta.
Union Sta.
Univ. of Ill. at Chic.
Chinatown
Bridgeport
U.S. Cellular Field
McKinley Park
Brighton Park
Gage Park
Chicago Lawn
Marquette Park
A.E.Stevenson Expwy
CHICAGO MIDWAY (MDW)
Bedford Park
Burbank
Chicago Ridge

CHICAGO
Navy Pier
Lincoln Park Zoo
Chicago Art Institute
Field Museum
Soldier Field
Adler Planetarium
Burnham Harbor
Grant Park
Burnham Park

Mus. of Science & Industry
Jackson Park
Univ. of Chicago
Hyde Park
South Shore
Chicago Skyway
Chatham
Englewood
Washington Park
Dan Ryan Expwy
Roseland
Morgan Park
Beverly
Evergreen Park
Mount Greenwood
Oak Lawn
Hometown
Ashburn
Hickory Hills
Palos Hills
Palos Heights
Palos Park
Palos Hills Forest

South Deering
Lake Calumet
Calumet Park
Blue Island
Robbins
Alsip
Tri-State Tollway

Bishop Ford Mem. Expwy
Pullman Historic District
Calumet
West from Greenwich

Legend (right margin):
Interstate route numbers
State route numbers
U.S. route numbers

CENTRAL CHICAGO

Outer Harbor
Navy Pier
Olive Park
Lake Point Tower
Ohio St Beach
Streeter Dr
LAKE MICHIGAN
Chicago Harbor
Chicago Yacht Club
Adler Planetarium
E. Solidarity Dr
Shedd Aquarium
Field Museum of Nat. History
Soldier Field
Burnham Park Harbor
Meigs Field (Closed)
Old Lake Shore Drive
McCormick Place East/Lakeside Center
McCormick Place North
McCormick Place South
Burnham Park

Oak St Beach
Gold Coast
N Lake Shore Drive
E Lake Shore Dr
Water Tower Place
N Michigan Avenue
John Hancock Center
Near North
Northwestern Memorial Hosp.
McClurg Court
Fairbanks Court
Olympia Centre
Chicago Tribune Building
Wrigley Bldg.
Marshall Field's
AON Center
Prudential Building
Millennium Park
Grant Park
Art Institute of Chicago
Buckingham Fountain

River North
Merchandise Mart
Northwestern Sta.
Union Sta.
The Loop
LaSalle St. Sta.
Sears Tower
Printer's Row
Van Buren St. Sta.
Roosevelt Road Sta.
South Loop
Chinatown

GEORGE HALAS DRIVE
N LAKE SHORE DRIVE
E CHICAGO AVE
MICHIGAN AVENUE
E WACKER DRIVE
E RANDOLPH
LAKE SHORE DRIVE
SOUTH LAKE SHORE DRIVE
COLUMBUS DRIVE
SOUTH STATE STREET
SOUTH MICHIGAN AVENUE
SOUTH INDIANA AVE
CERMAK ROAD
ROOSEVELT ROAD
CONGRESS PKWY
S WACKER DR
W WACKER DR
CANAL STREET
MILWAUKEE AVE
ARCHER AVE
Wentworth Ave

Elevated rail lines

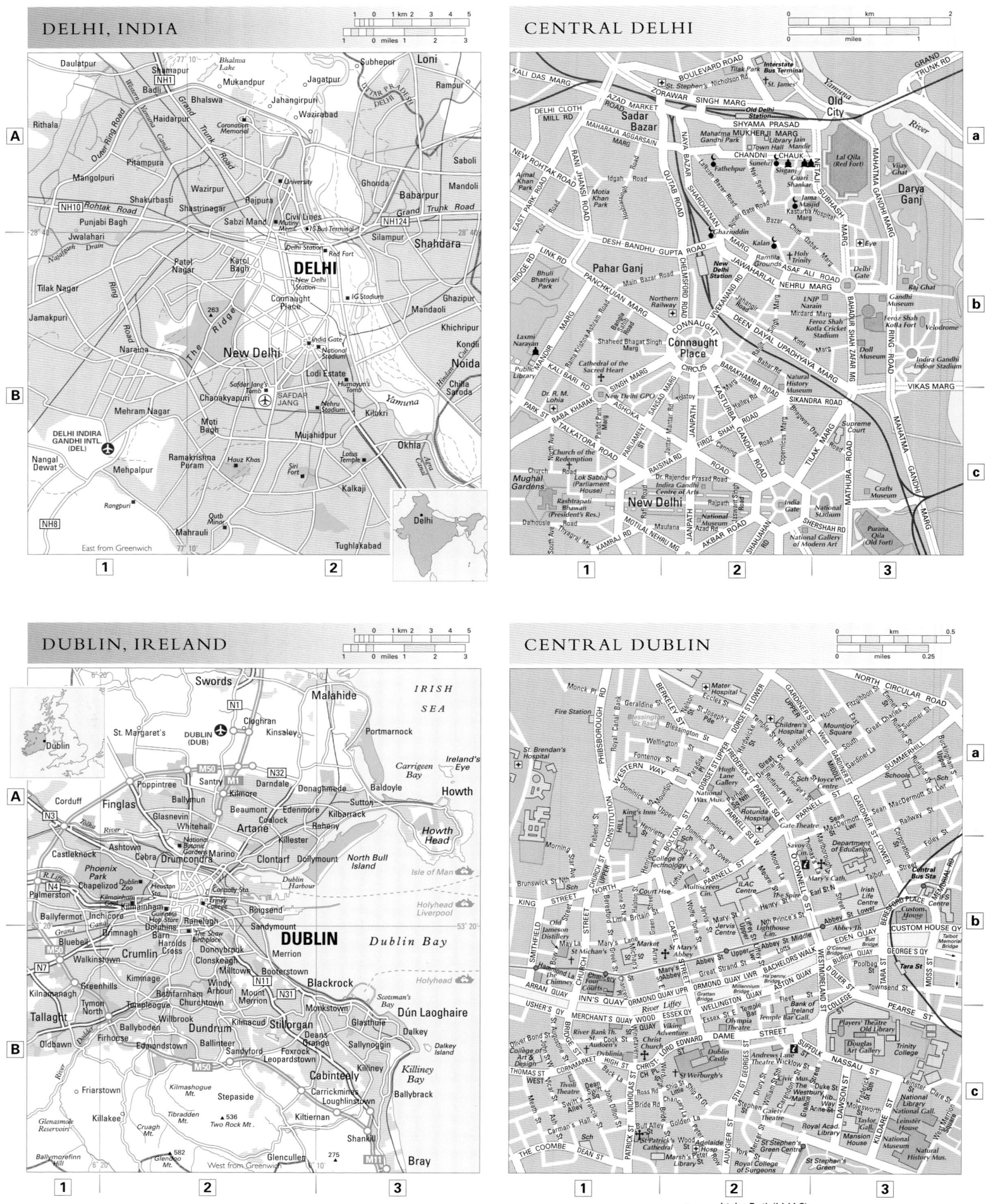

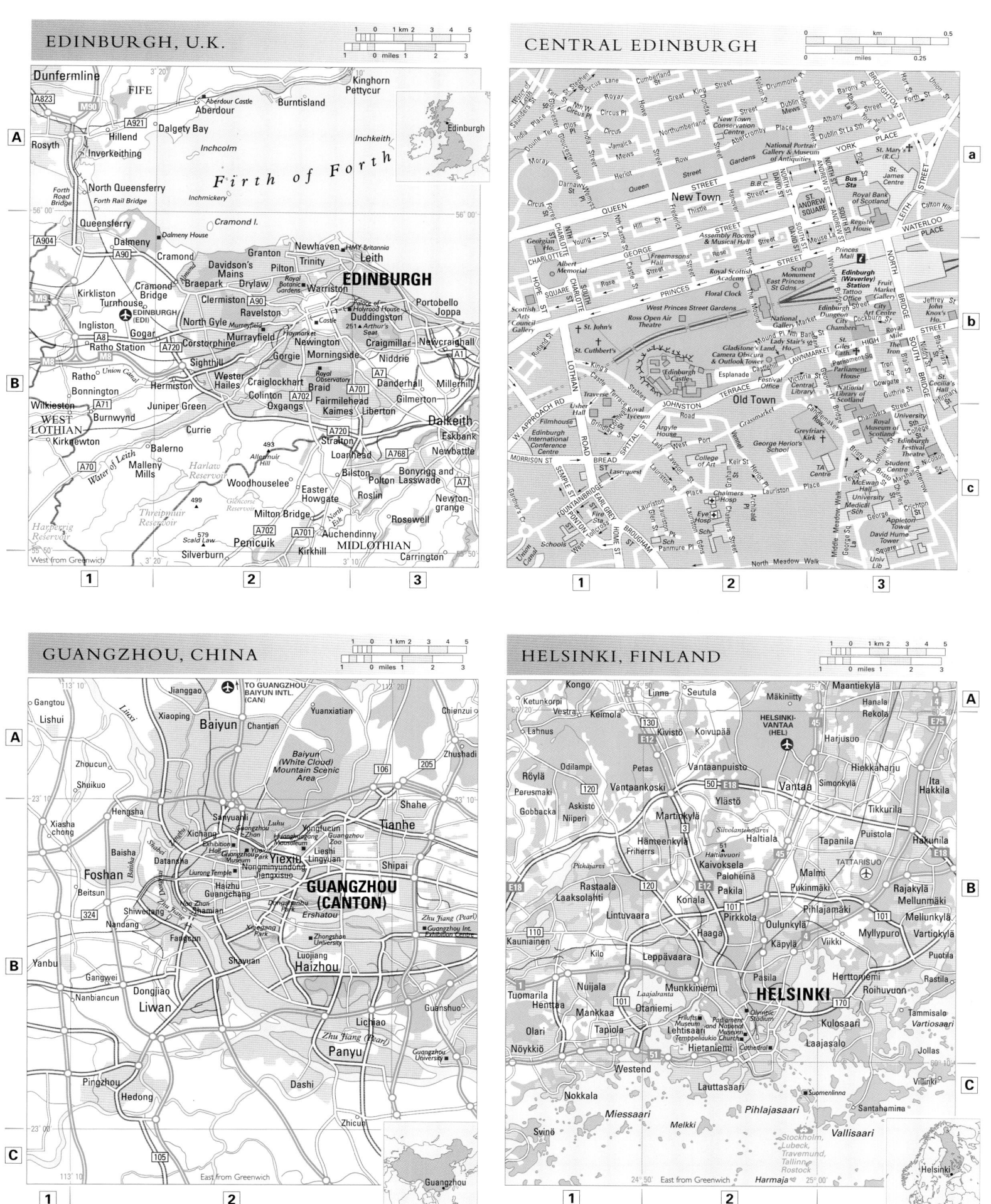

EDINBURGH, U.K.

CENTRAL EDINBURGH

GUANGZHOU, CHINA

HELSINKI, FINLAND

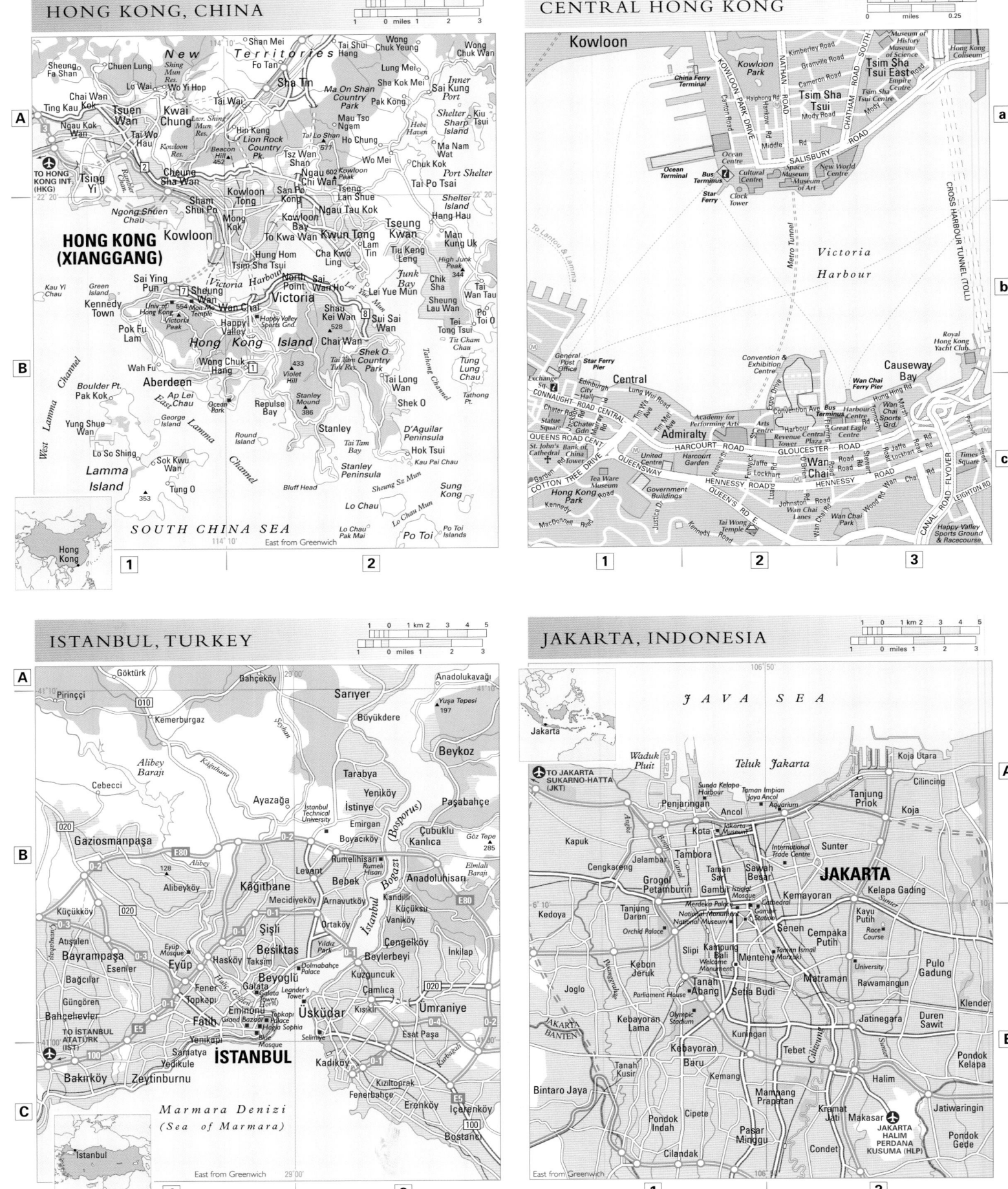

HONG KONG, CHINA

CENTRAL HONG KONG

ISTANBUL, TURKEY

JAKARTA, INDONESIA

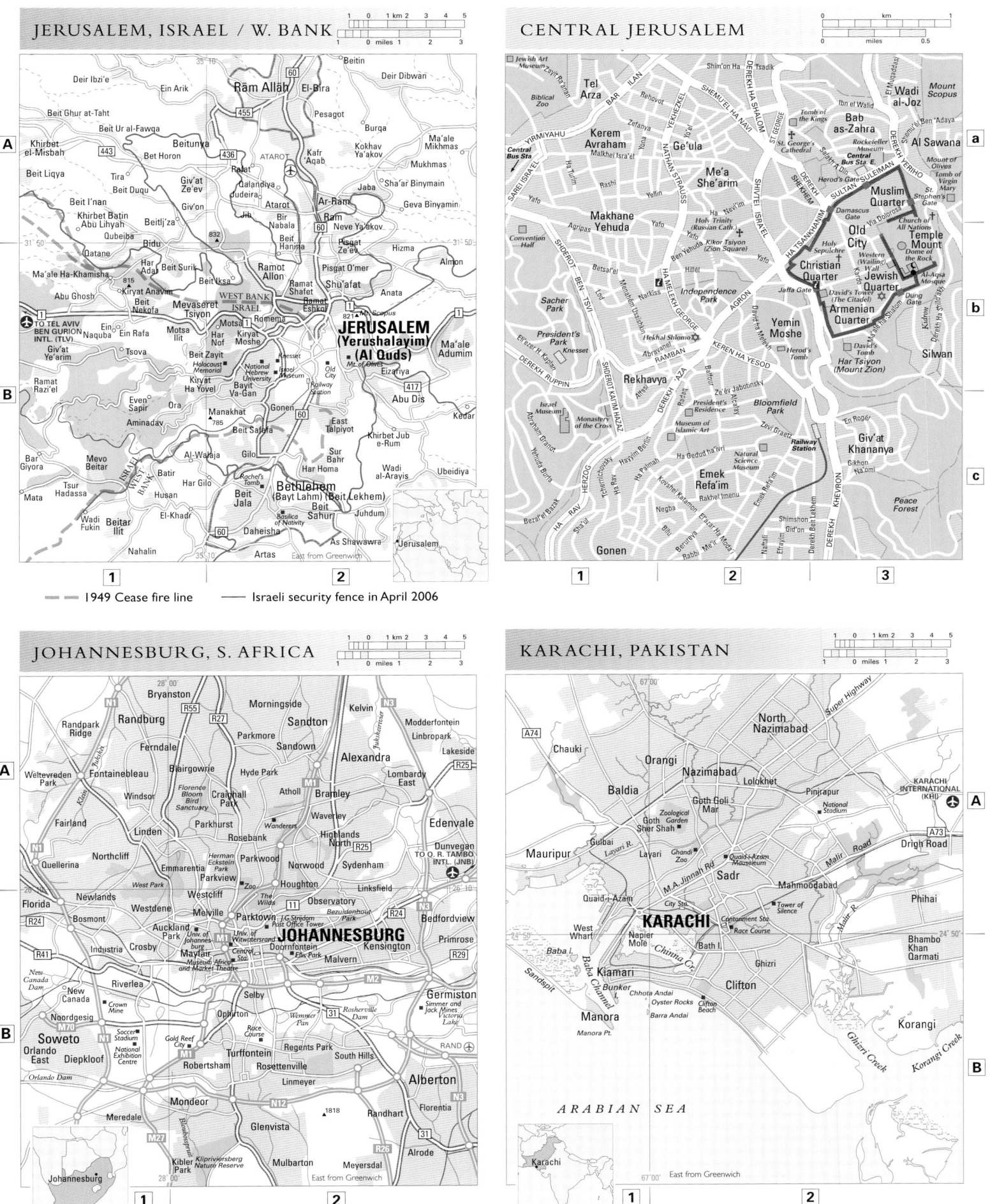

JERUSALEM, ISRAEL / W. BANK

Deir Ibzi'e
Ein Arik
Beitin
Deir Dibwan
Ram Allah
El-Bira
Beit Ghur at-Taht
455
Pesagot
Burqa
Ma'ale
Mikhmas
Beit Ur al-Fawqa
60
Kokhav
Ya'akov
Kafr
'Aqab
Mukhmas
Khirbet
el-Misbah
443
Beitunya
Bet Horon
436
ATAROT
Qalandiya
Judeira
Jaba
Sha'ar Binymin
Geva Binyamin
Beit Liqya
Tira
Giv'at
Ze'ev
Atarot
Giv'on
Jib
Ar-Ram
Bir
Nabala
60
Ram
Neve Ya'akov
Khirbet Batin
Abu Lihyah
Beitlj'za
Qubeiba
832
Beit
Hanina
Hizma
Almon
Qatane
Bidu
31° 50'
Pisgat
Ze'ev
Pisgat O'mer
Har Adar
Beit Surik
Ramot
Allon
Ramat
Shafet
Shu'afat
Anata
Ma'ale Ha-Khamisha
815
Beit Iksa
821 Mt Scopus
Kiryat Anavim
WEST BANK
Abu Ghosh
Mevaseret
Tsiyon
ISRAEL
Ramat
Eshkol
Ma'ale
Adumim
Beit
Nekofa
Motsa
1
JERUSALEM
(Yerushalayim)
(Al Quds)
TO TEL AVIV
BEN GURION
INTL. (TLV)
Ein
Naquba
Ein Rafa
Motsa
Ilit
Kiryat
Moshe
Har
Nof
Giv'at
Ye'arim
Tsova
Beit Zayit
National
Hebrew
Holocaust
Memorial
Bayit
Va-Gan
Israel
Museum
Old
City
Eizariya
Ramat
Razi'el
Even
Sapir
Ora
Kiryat
Ha Yovel
Railway
Station
417
Aminadav
785
Manakhat
Gonen
Abu Dis
Beit Safafa
East
Talpiyot
Khirbet Jub
e-Rum
Bar
Giyora
Mevo
Beitar
Batir
Al-Walaja
Gilo
Sur
Bahr
Kedar
Tsur
Hadassa
Mata
Har Gilo
Husan
Har Homa
Wadi
al-Arayis
Ubeidiya
Wadi
Fukin
Beitar
Ilit
Rachel's
Tomb
Bethlehem
(Bayt Lahm) (Beit Lekhem)
Nahalin
El-Khadr
60
Beit
Jala
Beit
Sahur
Basilica
of Nativity
Juhdam
Daheisha
35° 10'
As Shawawra
Artas
East from Greenwich
Jerusalem

- - - 1949 Cease fire line
— Israeli security fence in April 2006

CENTRAL JERUSALEM

Jewish Art
Museum
Zayit Ra'anan
Shim'on Ha Tsadik
Sheikh el Walid
Wadi
al-Joz
Mount
Scopus
Tel
Arza
Biblical
Zoo
Zefanya
Tomb of
the Kings
Ben 'Adaya
Al Sawana
Kerem
Avraham
Malkhei Isra'el
Bab
as-Zahra
Rockefeller
Museum
Ge'ula
St. George's
Cathedral
Mount of
Olives
Central
Bus Sta
Yellin
Me'a
She'arim
Herod's Gate
Central
Bus Sta. E.
Tomb of
Virgin
Mary
St.
Stephen's
Gate
Makhane
Yehuda
Holy Trinity
(Russian Cath.)
Muslim
Quarter
Church of
All Nations
Convention
Hall
Yafo
Ben Yehuda
Kikar Tsiyon
(Zion Square)
Holy
Sepulchre
Old
City
Temple
Mount
Dome of
the Rock
Hillel
Christian
Quarter
Western
(Wailing)
Wall
Jewish
Quarter
Al-Aqsa
Mosque
Sacher
Park
Independence
Park
Jaffa Gate
David's Tower
(The Citadel)
Armenian
Quarter
Dung
Gate
President's
Park
Hekhal Shlomo
Yemin
Moshe
Silwan
Knesset
David's
Tomb
Har Tsiyon
(Mount Zion)
Rekhavya
Israel
Museum
President's
Residence
Bloomfield
Park
En Rogel
Monastery
of the Cross
Museum of
Islamic Art
Giv'at
Khananya
Emek
Refa'im
Natural
Science
Museum
Railway
Station
Gikhon
Na'omi
Peace
Forest
Gonen
Shimshon
Gid'on
East from Greenwich

JOHANNESBURG, S. AFRICA

N1
Bryanston
Randpark
Ridge
Randburg
R55
R27
Morningside
Kelvin
N3
Modderfontein
Sandton
Weltevreden
Park
Ferndale
Parkmore
Sandown
Linbropark
Fontainebleau
Blairgowrie
Hyde Park
Lakeside
R25
Windsor
Florence
Bloom
Bird
Sanctuary
Craighall
Park
Atholl
Bramley
Alexandra
Lombardy
East
Fairland
Linden
Parkhurst
Waverley
Edenvale
Quellerina
Northcliff
Rosebank
Parkwood
Highlands
North
R25
Dunvegan
TO O. R. TAMBO
INTL. (JNB)
N1
Herman
Eckstein
Park
Norwood
Sydenham
Emmarentia
Parkview
West Park
Zoo
Houghton
Linksfield
Florida
Newlands
Westcliff
The Wilds
Observatory
R24
Bedfordview
R24
Bosmont
Westdene
Melville
11
J.G Strijdom
Post Office Tower
Bezuidenhout
Park
N3
R41
Auckland
Park
Univ. of
Johannesburg
Univ. of
Witwatersrand
JOHANNESBURG
Primrose
New
Canada
Dam
Industria
Crosby
Mayfair
Central
Sta.
Museum Africa
and Market Theatre
Doornfontein
Ellis Park
Malvern
Kensington
R29
New
Canada
Riverlea
Crown
Mine
Selby
Ophirton
Rosherville
Dam
Simmer and
Jack Mines
Victoria
Lake
Germiston
Noordgesig
Soweto
Orlando
East
Diepkloof
Soccer
Stadium
Gold Reef
City
Wemmer
Pan
Race
Course
M2
RAND
Orlando Dam
National
Exhibition
Centre
M1
Turffontein
Regents Park
South Hills
Alberton
N3
Robertsham
Rosettenville
Linmeyer
Mondeor
N12
Randhart
Florentia
Meredale
1818
31
Alrode
Kibler
Park
Glenvista
Mulbarton
Meyersdal
R26
M27
Klipriviersberg Nature Reserve
East from Greenwich
Johannesburg

KARACHI, PAKISTAN

67° 00'
Super Highway
A74
Chauki
North
Nazimabad
Orangi
Nazimabad
Lolokhet
KARACHI
INTERNATIONAL
(KHI)
Baldia
Goth Goli
Mar
Pinjrapur
National
Stadium
A73
Mauripur
Gulbai
Zoological
Garden
Goth
Sher Shah
Lavari
Ghandi
Zoo
Layari R.
Quaid-i-Azam
Mausoleum
Drigh Road
Sadr
Mahmoodabad
M.A. Jinnah Rd
Quaid-i-Azam
City Stn.
Tower of
Silence
Phihai
West
Wharf
KARACHI
Cantonment Stn.
Race Course
Bhambo
Khan
Qarmati
Napier
Mole
Chinna Cr.
Bath I.
Ghizri
Baba I.
Kiamari
Manora
Clifton
Korangi
Manora Pt.
Chhota Andai
Oyster Rocks
Clifton
Beach
Sandspit
Bunker
Barra Andai
Ghizri Creek
Korangi Creek
ARABIAN SEA
67° 00'
East from Greenwich
Karachi

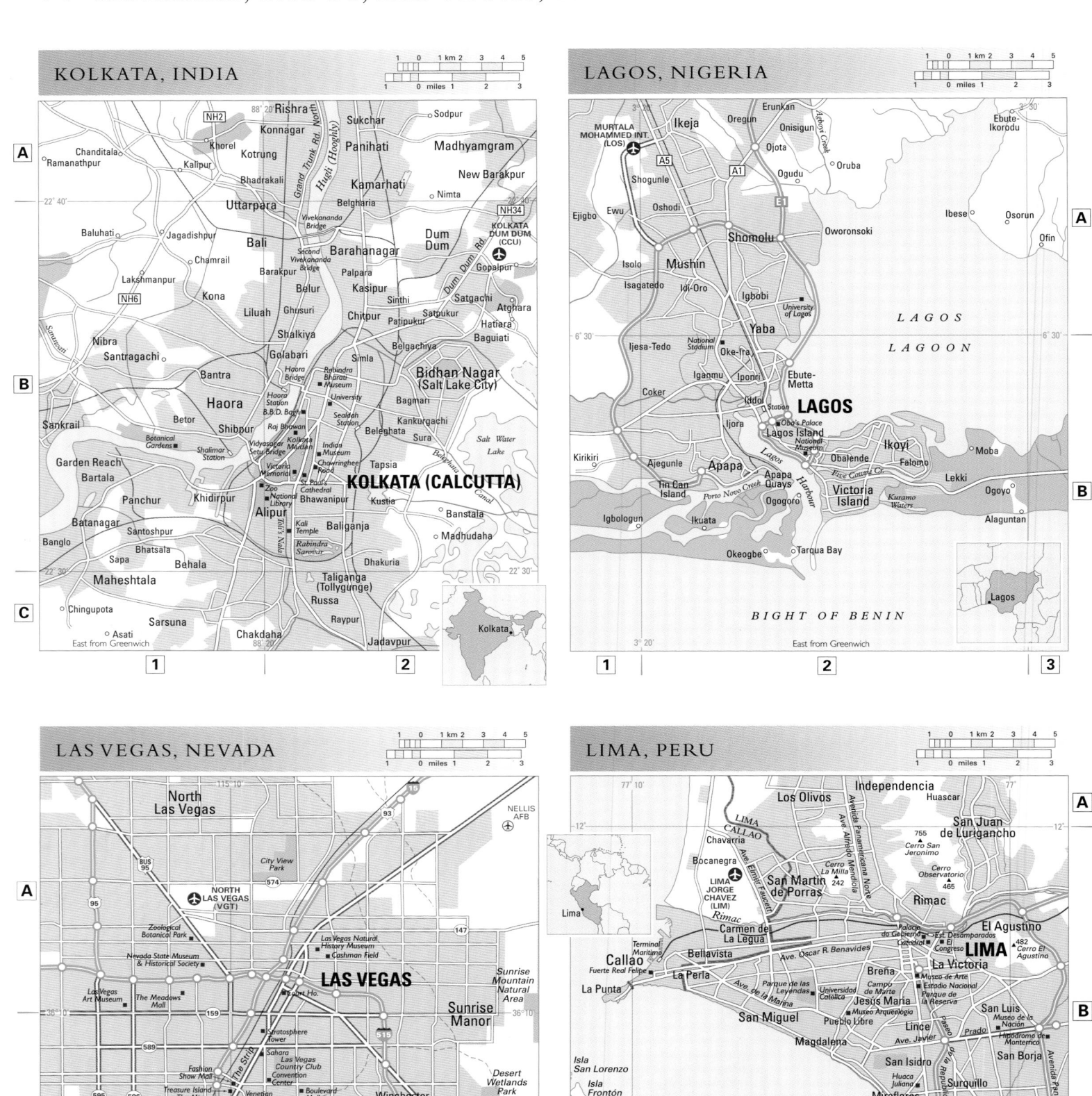

KOLKATA, INDIA

LAGOS, NIGERIA

LAS VEGAS, NEVADA

LIMA, PERU

🛣 Interstate route numbers   🛣 U.S. route numbers   🛣 State route numbers

COPYRIGHT PHILIP'S

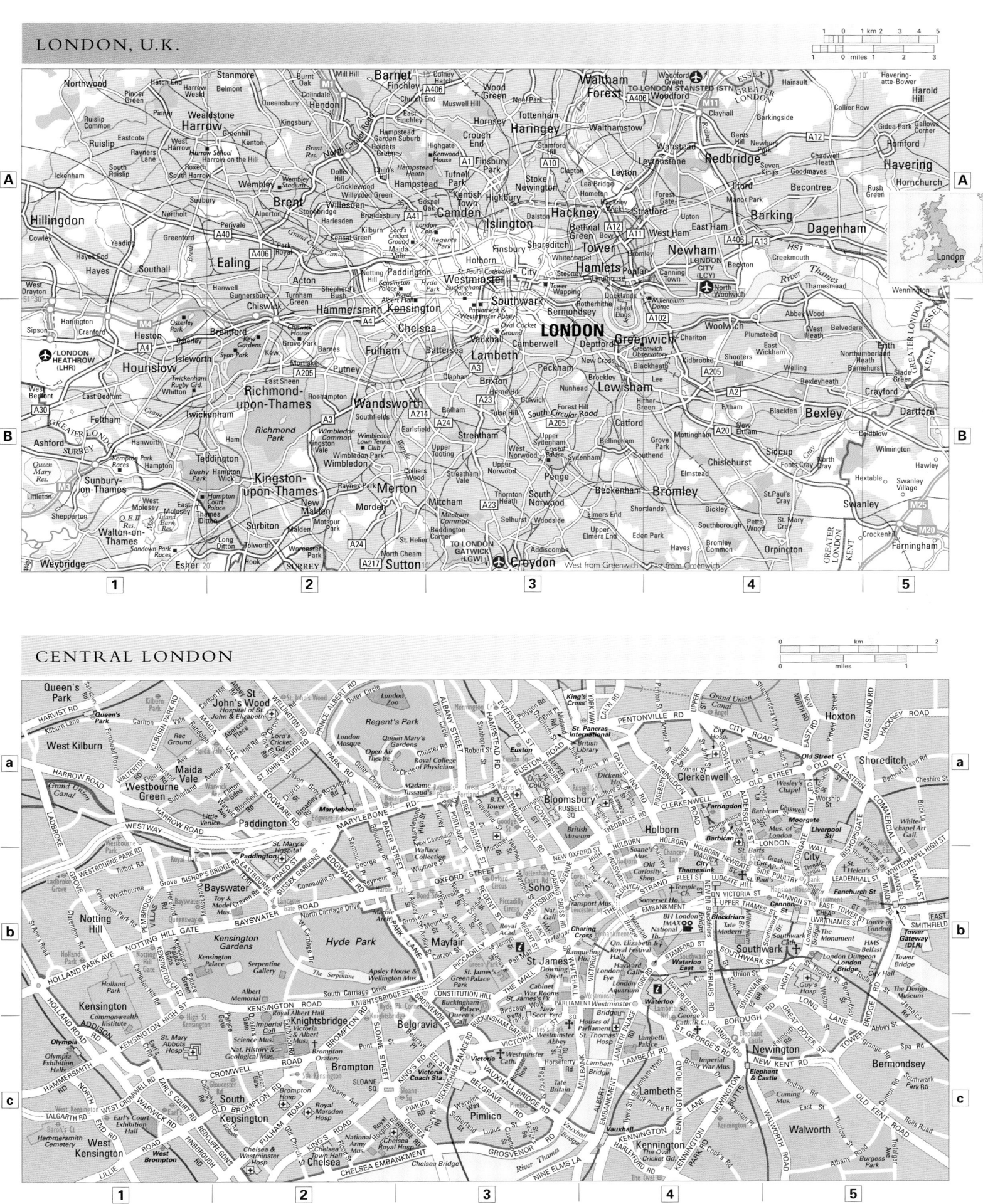

LONDON, U.K.

CENTRAL LONDON

Congestion Charging Zone

COPYRIGHT PHILIP'S

LISBON, PORTUGAL

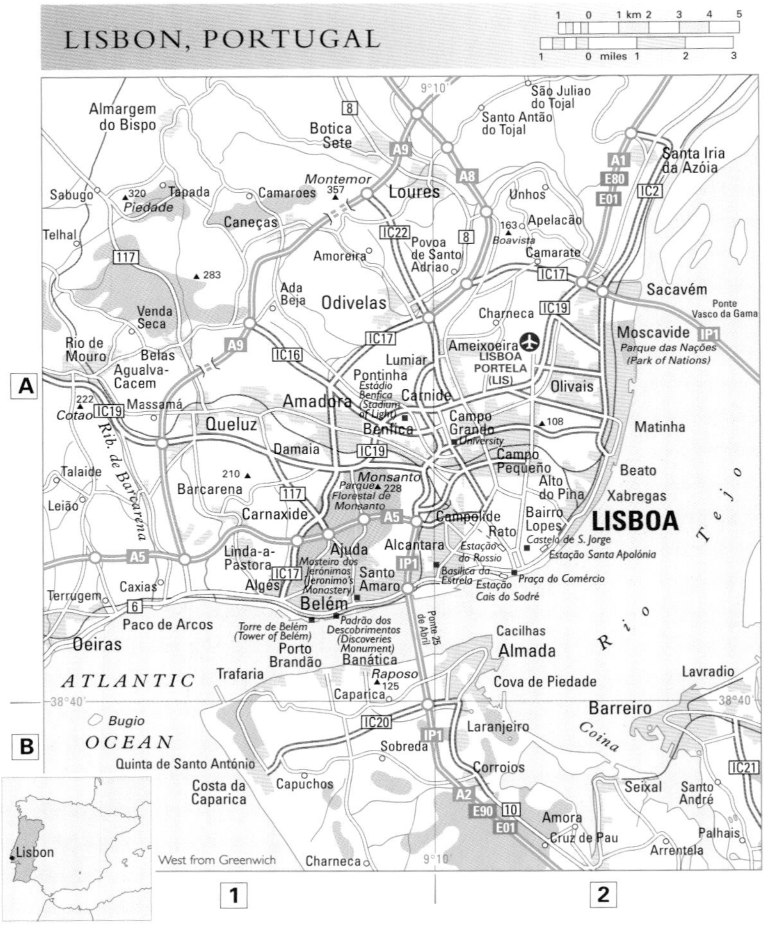

km
miles

Almargem do Bispo
Botica Sete
Santo Antão do Tojal
São Julião do Tojal
Santa Iria da Azóia
Sabugo
Tapada
Piedade
Montemor
Camarões
Loures
Unhos
Apelacão
Telhal
Caneças
Póvoa de Santo Adrião
Boavista do
Camarate
Venda Seca
Amoreira
Odivelas
Charneca
Sacavém
Ponte Vasco da Gama
Rio de Mouro
Belas
Aguálva-Cacem
Lumiar
Pontinha
Catride
Moscavide
Parque das Nações (Park of Nations)
LISBOA PORTELA (LIS)
Cotao
Massamá
Amadora
Benfica
Estádio (Stadium) of Light
Campo Grande
University
Olivais
A
Queluz
Damaia
Campo Pequeno
Matinha
Talaide
Barcarena
Monsanto
Parque Florestal de Monsanto
Alto do Pina
Beato
Carnaxide
Xabregas
Bairro Lopes
LISBOA
Leião
Linda-a-Pastora
Ajuda
Mosteiro dos Jerónimos (Jerónimos Monastery)
Santo Amaro
Alcântara
Estação do Rossio
Basílica da Estrela
Estação Santa Apolónia
Caxias
Algés
Belém
Padrão dos Descobrimentos (Discoveries Monument)
Estação Cais do Sodré
Praça do Comércio
Terrugem
Torre de Belém (Tower of Belém)
Porto Brandão
Banática
Raposo
Cacilhas
Almada
Lavradio
ATLANTIC
Oeiras
Paço de Arcos
Trafaria
Cova de Piedade
Bugio
OCEAN
Capuchos
Quinta de Santo António
Costa da Caparica
Capucha
Sobreda
Laranjeiro
Barreiro
B
Corroios
Seixal
Santo André
Amora
Cruz de Pau
Palhais
Arrentela
Charneca
West from Greenwich

Lisbon

1 | **2**

CENTRAL LISBON

km
miles

Palacio de Justiça
Instituto Superior Técnico
Penitenciária
Praça Duque Saldanha
Rua Marquês da Fronteira
Parque
Estefânia
Eduardo VII
Pavilhão dos Desportos
Penha França
Amoreiros
Anjos
Hospital M. Bombarda
Rato
Hospital de Santa Marta
Bairro Lopes
Academia das Ciências
Jardim Botânico
Graça
Palácio de Assembleia Nacional
Instituto de Medicina Legal
Bairro Alto
Restauradores
Theatro Nac. de Dona Maria II
Estação do Rossio
Igreja de Graça
Estação Santa Apolónia
Museu do Arqueologia
Praça Rossio
Castelo de São Jorge (St. George's Castle)
Sé Catedral
Museu de Arte Decorativas
Alfama
Military Museum
Elevador de Santa Justa
Baixa
Praça do Comércio
AV. VINTE E QUATRO DE JULHO
Estação Cais do Sodré
Estação Fluvial
Rio Tejo (Tagus)

a | b | c

1 | **2** | **3**

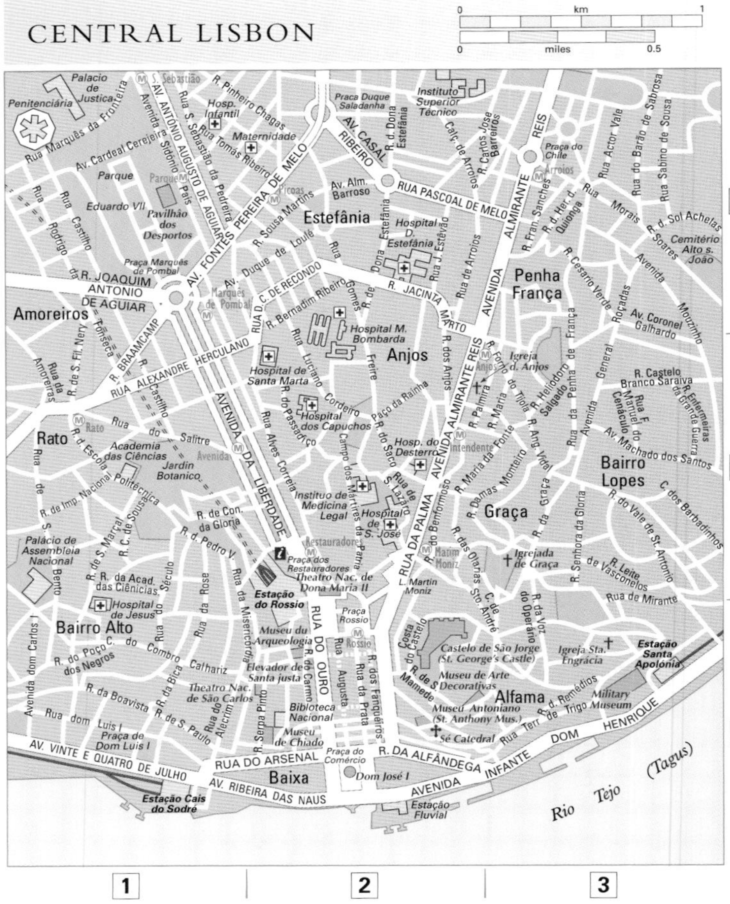

LOS ANGELES, CALIFORNIA

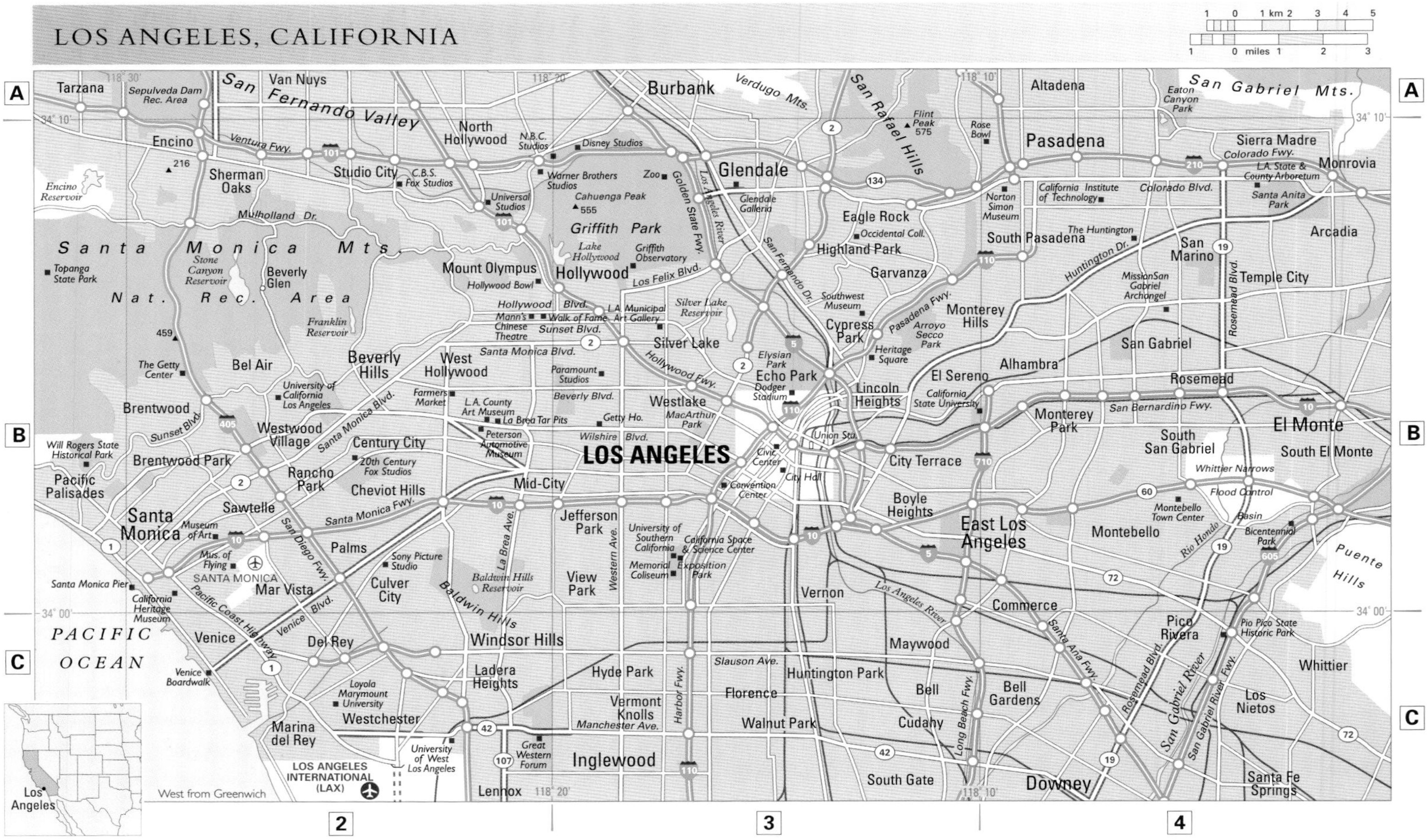

km
miles

Tarzana
Van Nuys
San Fernando Valley
Burbank
Verdugo Mts.
San Rafael Hills
Altadena
Eaton Canyon Park
San Gabriel Mts.
A
Encino
Ventura Fwy.
North Hollywood
N.B.C. Studios
Disney Studios
Flint Peak 576
Rose Bowl
Pasadena
Sierra Madre
Monrovia
Encino Reservoir
Sherman Oaks
Studio City
C.B.S. Fox Studios
Warner Brothers Studios
Cahuenga Peak 555
Zoo
Glendale
Glendale Galleria
Norton Simon Museum
California Institute of Technology
Colorado Blvd.
L.A. State & County Arboretum
Santa Anita Park
Arcadia
Topanga State Park
Stone Canyon Reservoir
Beverly Glen
Mulholland Dr.
Griffith Park
Lake Hollywood
Griffith Observatory
Eagle Rock
Occidental Coll.
Highland Park
South Pasadena
The Huntington
San Marino
Temple City
Santa Monica Mts.
Nat. Rec. Area
Mount Olympus
Hollywood Bowl
Hollywood
Los Feliz Blvd.
Garvanza
Huntington Dr.
Mission San Gabriel Archangel
Franklin Reservoir
Hollywood Blvd.
L.A. Municipal Art Gallery
Silver Lake Reservoir
Southwest Museum
Rosemead Blvd.
The Getty Center
Mann's Chinese Theatre
Walk of Fame
Sunset Blvd.
Silver Lake
Cypress Park
Pasadena Fwy.
Arroyo Seco Park
Alhambra
San Gabriel
Bel Air
Beverly Hills
West Hollywood
Santa Monica Blvd.
Hollywood Fwy.
Elysian Park
Heritage Square
El Sereno
Rosemead
Brentwood
University of California Los Angeles
Paramount Studios
Beverly Blvd.
Getty Ho.
Westlake
Echo Park
Dodger Stadium
Lincoln Heights
California State University
Monterey Park
San Bernardino Fwy.
El Monte
B
Will Rogers State Historical Park
Westwood Village
Century City
Farmers Market
L.A. County Art Museum
La Brea Tar Pits
Wilshire Blvd.
MacArthur Park
LOS ANGELES
Union Sta.
Civic Center
City Hall
City Terrace
Boyle Heights
South San Gabriel
South El Monte
Pacific Palisades
Brentwood Park
Westwood
Sunset Blvd.
Rancho Park
20th Century Fox Studios
Peterson Automotive Museum
Cheviot Hills
Mid-City
Jefferson Park
University of Southern California
Convention Center
East Los Angeles
Montebello
Montebello Town Center
Whittier Narrows Flood Control Basin
Bicentennial Park
Puente Hills
Santa Monica
Museum of Art
Mus. of Flying
SANTA MONICA
Palms
Sony Picture Studio
California Space & Science Center
Memorial Coliseum
Exposition Park
Vernon
Commerce
Pico Rivera
Pio Pico State Historic Park
Santa Monica Pier
California Heritage Museum
Pacific Coast Highway
Mar Vista
Culver City
Baldwin Hills Reservoir
View Park
Los Angeles River
Maywood
PACIFIC
OCEAN
Venice
Del Rey
Windsor Hills
Baldwin Hills
Hyde Park
Slauson Ave.
Huntington Park
Bell
Bell Gardens
Los Nietos
Whittier
C
Venice Boardwalk
Loyola Marymount University
Ladera Heights
Vermont Knolls
Manchester Ave.
Florence
Cudahy
Santa Fe Springs
Marina del Rey
Westchester
University of West Los Angeles
Great Western Forum
Walnut Park
LOS ANGELES INTERNATIONAL (LAX)
Inglewood
Lennox
South Gate
Downey
West from Greenwich

Los Angeles

2 | **3** | **4**

Interstate route numbers   State route numbers

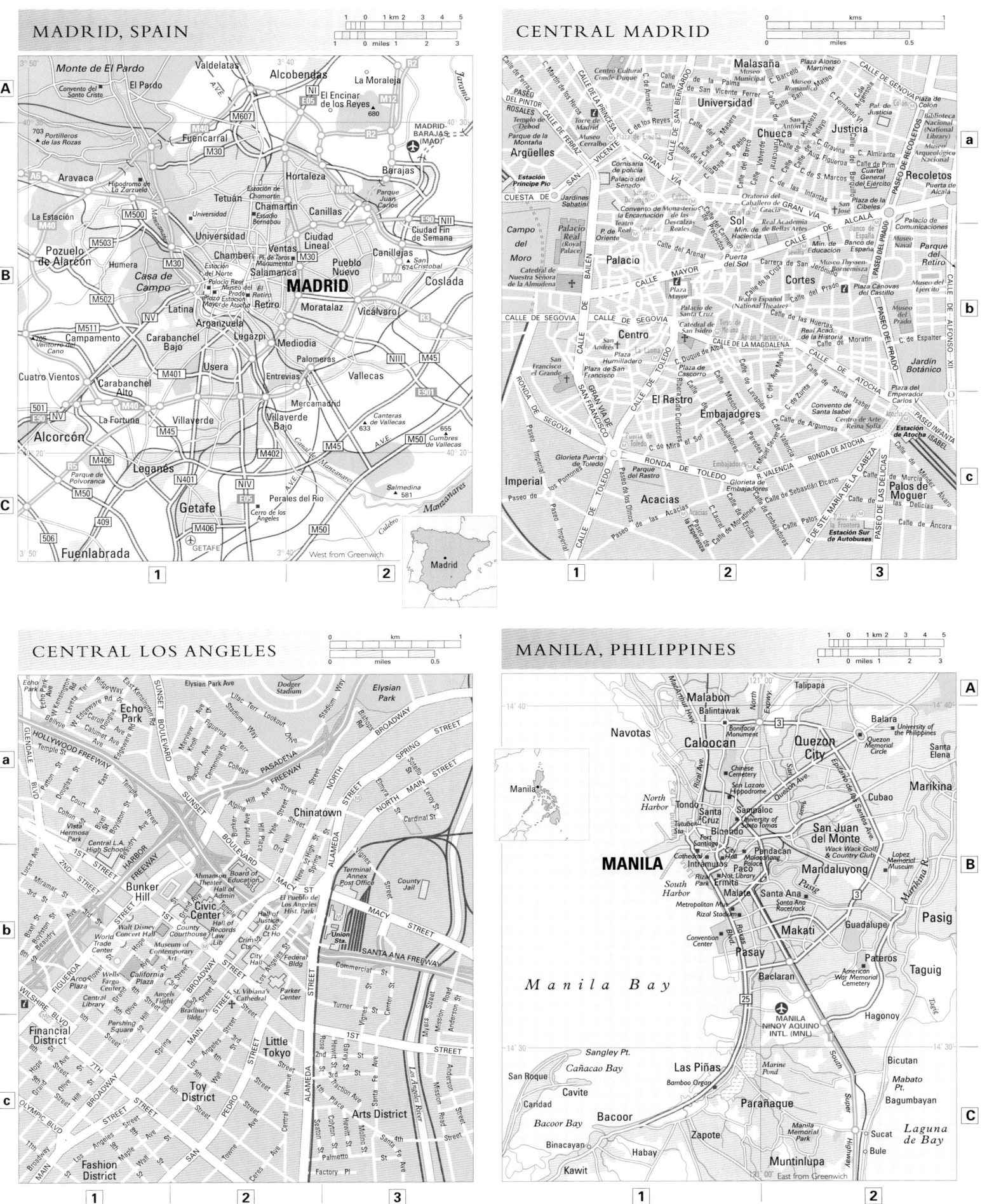

MADRID, SPAIN

1 km 2 3 4 5
miles 1 2 3

Monte de El Pardo
Valdelatas
Alcobendas
La Moraleja
Convento del Santo Cristo
El Pardo
El Encinar de los Reyes
MADRID-BARAJAS (MAD)
Portilleros de las Rozas
Fuencarral
Barajas
Aravaca
Hipodromo de la Zarzuela
Hortaleza
Parque Juan Carlos
La Estación
Tetuán
Chamartin
Canillas
Ciudad Fin de Semana
Universidad
Estadio Bernabeu
Ciudad Lineal
San Cristobal
Pozuelo de Alarcón
Humera
Chamberí
Ventas
Pueblo Nuevo
Casa de Campo
Salamanca
MADRID
Coslada
Latina
El Retiro
Moratalaz
Vicálvaro
Campamento
Arganzuela
Legazpi
Mediodia
Palomeras
Vallecas
Cuatro Vientos
Carabanchel Alto
Usera
Entrevias
Mercamadrid
Canteras de Vallecas
Cumbres de Vallecas
Alcorcón
La Fortuna
Villaverde
Villaverde Bajo
Salmedina
Leganés
Parque de Polvoranca
Perales del Rio
Getafe
Cerro de los Angeles
Fuenlabrada
West from Greenwich

Madrid

CENTRAL MADRID

kms
miles 0.5

Malasaña
Plaza Alonso Martínez
Centro Cultural Conde Duque
Universidad
Justicia
Recoletos
Argüelles
Chueca
Biblioteca Nacional (National Library)
Museo Arqueológico Nacional
Estación Principe Pio
Puerta de Alcalá
Campo del Moro
Palacio Real (Royal Palace)
Sol
Parque del Retiro
Palacio
Catedral de Nuestra Señora de la Almudena
Cortes
Plaza Mayor
Centro
Catedral de San Isidro
El Rastro
Embajadores
Jardín Botánico
Imperial
Acacias
Palos de Moguer
Estación de Atocha

CENTRAL LOS ANGELES

km
miles 0.5

Echo Park
Elysian Park Ave
Dodger Stadium
Elysian Park
Echo Park
HOLLYWOOD FREEWAY
Chinatown
Central L.A. High Schools
Bunker Hill
Civic Center
Little Tokyo
Financial District
Union Sta.
Toy District
Arts District
Fashion District

MANILA, PHILIPPINES

1 km 2 3 4 5
miles 1 2 3

Talipapa
Malabon
Balintawak
Balara
Navotas
Caloocan
Bonifacio Monument
Quezon City
University of the Philippines
Santa Elena
Cubao
Marikina
North Harbor
Tondo
Sampaloc
San Juan del Monte
Santa Cruz
MANILA
Intramuros
Ermita
Santa Ana
Mandaluyong
Makati
Pasig
Malate
Pateros
Taguig
Pasay
Guadalupe
Baclaran
Manila Bay
MANILA NINOY AQUINO INTL. (MNL)
Hagonoy
Sangley Pt.
Las Piñas
Bicutan
Cañacao Bay
Marine Pond
Parañaque
Bagumbayan
Bacoor Bay
Bacoor
Muntinlupa
Kawit
East from Greenwich

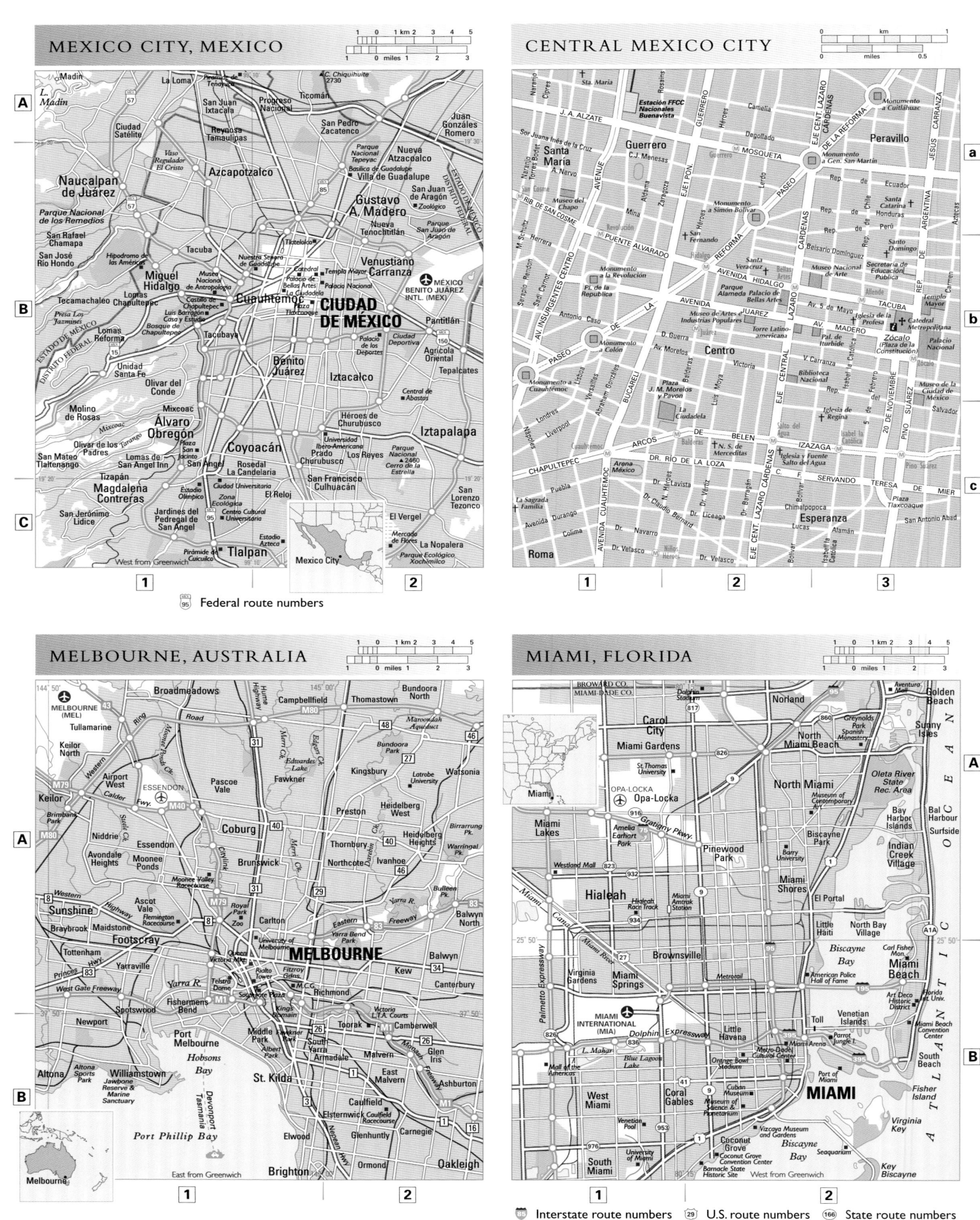

MEXICO CITY, MEXICO

Federal route numbers

CENTRAL MEXICO CITY

MELBOURNE, AUSTRALIA

MIAMI, FLORIDA

Interstate route numbers   U.S. route numbers   State route numbers

COPYRIGHT PHILIP'S

MILAN, ITALY

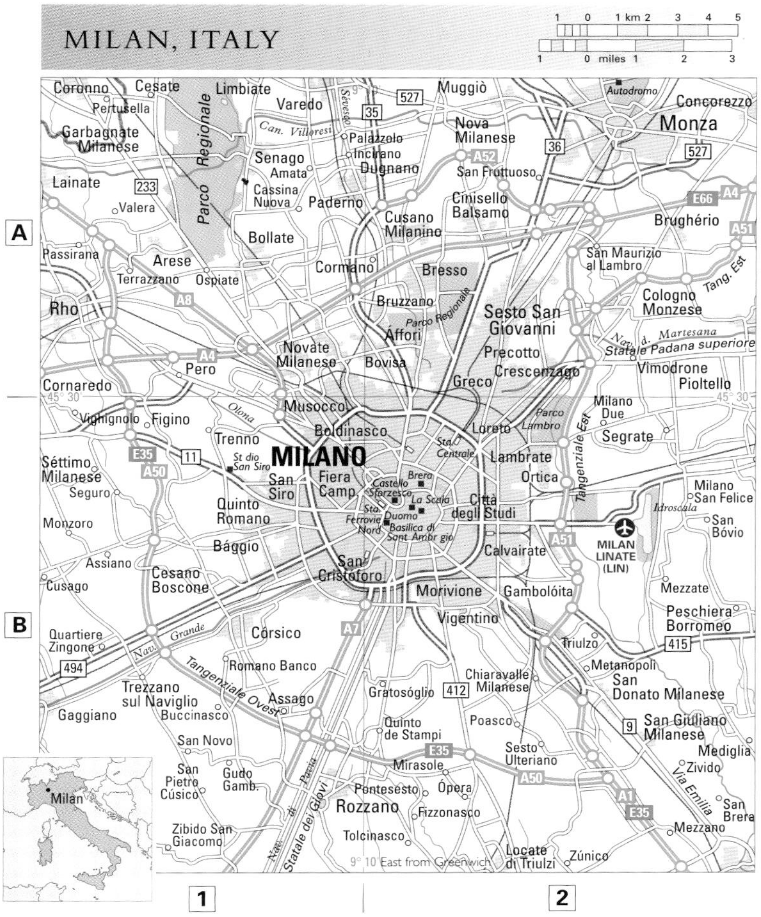

1 0 1 km 2 3 4 5
1 0 miles 1 2 3

Corúnno · Ceśate · Limbiate · Varedo · Muggiò · Autodromo · Concorezzo
Pertusella · Garbagnate Milanese · Parcó Regionale · Palazzolo · Inchino · Dugnano · Nova Milanese · Monza
Lainate · Senago · Amata · Cassina Nuova · Paderno · San Fruttuoso · Brughério
233 · Valera · Bollate · Cormano · Cusano Milanino · Bresso · San Maurizio al Lambro · Cologno Monzese
A · Passirana · Arese · Terrazzano · Ospiate · Bruzzano · Áffori · Precotto · Crescenzago · Vimodrone · Pioltello
Rho · Cornaredo · Pero · Novate Milanese · Bovisa · Greco · Milano Due
Séttimo Milanese · Vighignolo · Figino · Trenno · Musocco · Boldinasco · MILANO · Loreto · Lambrate · Ortica · Milano San Felice
Seguro · Monzoro · Quinto Romano · San Siro · Fiera Camp. · Brera · Sta. Centrale · Città degli Studi · San Bóvio
Assiano · Bággio · Castello · Duomo · La Scala · Calvairate · MILAN LINATE (LIN)
B · Cusago · Cesano Boscone · San Cristoforo · Morivione · Vigentino · Gamboloíta · Peschiera Borromeo
Quartiere Zingone · Córsico · Triulzo · Metanopoli · San Donato Milanese
Gaggiano · Trezzano sul Naviglio · Buccinasco · Romano Banco · Assago · Gratosóglio · Chiaravalle Milanese · Poasco · San Giuliano Milanese
San Novo · Quinto de Stampi · Mirasole · Sesto Ulteriano · Zivido · Mediglia
San Pietro Cúsico · Gudo Gamb. · Ópera · Fizzonasco · San Brera
Zibido San Giacomo · Rozzano · Pontesésto · Locate di Triulzi · Zúnico · Mezzano

Milán

9° 10 East from Greenwich

1   2

CENTRAL MOSCOW

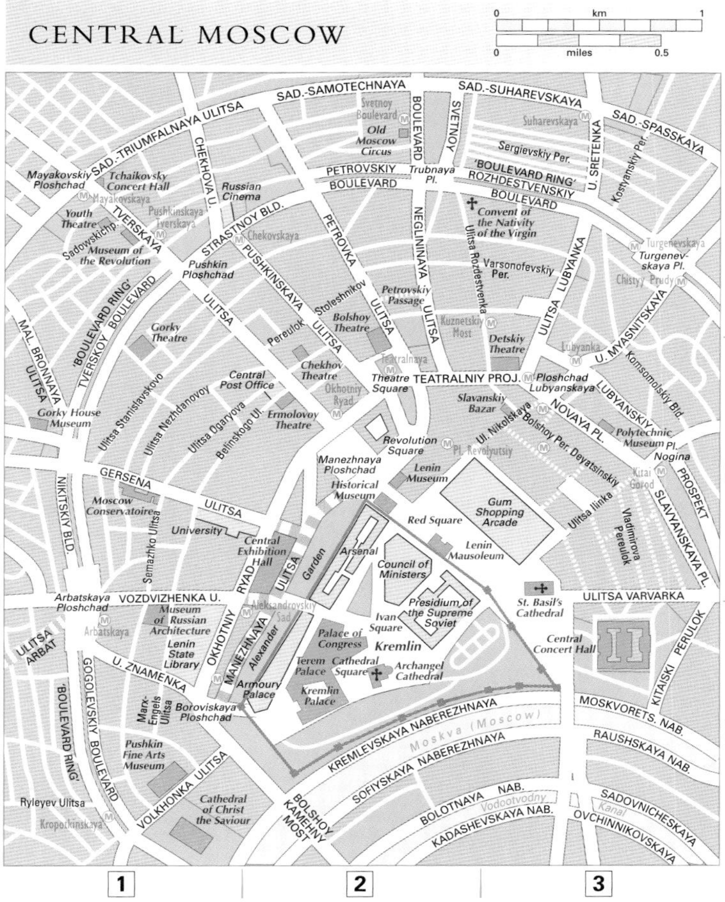

0 km 1
0 miles 0.5

SAD.-SAMOTECHNAYA · SAD.-SUHAREVSKAYA · SAD.-SPASSKAYA
Mayakovsky Ploshchad · Tchaikovsky Concert Hall · Old Moscow Circus · Svetnoy Boulevard · SVETNOY · BOULEVARD · Sergievsky Per. · U. SRETENKA
Youth Theatre · SAD.-TRIUMFALNAYA ULITSA · CHEKHOVA U. · Russian Cinema · PETROVSKIY · BOULEVARD 'ROZHDESTVENSKIY BOULEVARD · Trubnaya Pl. · 'BOULEVARD RING'
a · Museum of the Revolution · TVERSKAYA · STRASTNOY BOULEVARD · PETROVKA · NEGLINNAYA · Ploshchad · Convent of the Nativity of the Virgin · ULITSA LUBYANKA · Turgenevskaya Pl.
Pushkin Ploshchad · PUSHKINSKAYA · ULITSA · Bolshoi Theatre · Petrovsky Passage · Kuznetski Most · Detskiy Theatre · U. MYASNITSKAYA
MAI. BRONNAYA ULITSA · Chekhov Theatre · Central Post Office · Theatre · TEATRALNIY PROJ. · Teatralny Square · Ploshchad Lubyanskaya · NOVAYA PL.
b · Gorky House Museum · GERSENA · ULITSA · Ermolovoy Theatre · Revolution Square · Manezhnaya Ploshchad · Red Square · Polytechnic Museum
NIKITSKIY BLD. · Moscow Conservatoire · University · Central Exhibition Hall · Garden · Arsenal · Lenin Museum · Lenin Mausoleum · Gum Shopping Arcade · SLAVYANSKAYA PL.
Arbatskaya Ploshchad · VOZDVIZHENKA U. · Museum of Russian Architecture · OKHOTNIY RYAD · Alexander Garden · Ivan Square · Council of Ministers · Presidium of the Supreme Soviet · St. Basil's Cathedral · ULITSA VARVARKA
ULITSA ARBAT · U. ZNAMENKA · Lenin State Library · MANEZHNAYA · Palace of Congress · Kremlin · Terem Palace · Cathedral Square · Archangel Cathedral · Central Concert Hall
Armoury Palace · Kremlin Palace · MOSKVORETS. NAB.
'BOULEVARD RING' · GOGOLEVSKY BOULEVARD · Marx Engels Ulitsa · Borovitskaya Ploshchad · KREMLEVSKAYA NABEREZHNAYA · Moskva (Moscow) · RAUSHSKAYA NAB.
c · Pushkin Fine Arts Museum · SOFIYSKAYA NABEREZHNAYA · SADOVNICHESKAYA
Ryleyev Ulitsa · VOLKHONKA ULITSA · Cathedral of Christ the Saviour · BOLSHOY KAMENNY MOST · BOLOTNAYA NAB. · OVCHINNIKOVSKAYA
Kropotkinskaya · KADASHEVSKAYA NAB. · Vodootvodny

1   2   3

MOSCOW, RUSSIA

1 0 1 km 2 3 4 5
1 0 miles 1 2 3

A · Putilkovo · Bratsevo · TO MOSCOW SHEREMETYEVO INTL. (SVO) · Degunino · Vladykino · Babushkin · MOSKVA OBLAST · GOROD MOSKVA · Medvezhiy Ozyora · Medvezhiy Ozyora
Novonikolyskoye · Mitino · Khimki-Khovrino · Losiny Ostrov National Park · Almazova
Chernyovo · Penyagino · Tushino · M10 · Nikolskiy · Petrovsko-Razumovskoye · M8 · Pekhra-Pokrovskoye
Krasnogorsk · Golyevo · Pavshino · Timiryazev Park · Ostankino · Abramtsevo · Vostochnyy · Balashikha
Myakinino · M9 · Strogino · Pokrovsko-Sresnevo · Leningradskiy Prospekt · Petrovsky Park · Bogorodskoye · Galyanovo · Gorenki · Novaya
Arkhangelskoye · Troitse-Lykovo · Frunze · Sokolniki Park · Izmaylovo · Pekhra-Yakovievskaya · M7
Zakharkovo · Rublovo · Khorosovo · Dzerzhinskiy · Izmaylovskiy Park · Vishnyaki
B · Razdory · Krylatskoye · Tatarovo · Mnevniki · MOSKVA (Moscow) · Sverdlov · Leningrad Station · Yaroslov Station · Kazan Station · Bauman · Kursk Station · Novogireyevo · Nikolyskoye · Saltykovka
Barvikha · Cherepkovo · MOSKVA · Krasno-Presnenskaya · Bolshoy Theatre · Red Square, St. Basil's Cath. · Lenin Museum · Reutov · Kutsino
Romashkovo · Kuntsevo · Fili-Mazilovo · Kremlin · Tretiakov Art Gallery · Perovo · Kuskovo · Serebryanka · Zheleznodorozhnyy
Poduskino · Davydkovo · Kiev Station · Novodevichy Convent · Pavelet Station · Plyushchevo · Veshnyaki · Fenino
Nemchinovka · Novoivanovskoye · Aminyevo · Lomonosov Moscow State University · Gorky Park · Moskvoretsky · Zhdanov · Vykhino · Kosino · Kozhukhovo · Temnikovo
Lochino · Ochakovo · Ramenki · Moscow Circus · Oktyabrskiy · Tekstilyshchik · Kuzyminki · Mikhelysona · Marusino
Mamonovo · Bakovka · Zarechie · Leninskiy Prospekt · Leninskiye Gory · Nagatino · Lyublino · Lyubertsy · Nekrasovka
Odintsovo · M1 · Meshcherskiy · Nikulino · Cheryomushki · Dyakovo · Maryino · Kotelniki · Tomilino · Kraskovo · Korenevo
C · Choboty · Solntsevo · Troparevo · Zyuzino · Volkhonka-Zil · Kuryanovo · Zhulebino · Kapotnya · Chkalova · Malakhovka
Peredelkino · Orlovo · Belyayevo Bogorodskoye · Bittsevsky Forest Park · Brateyevo · M5
Vnukovo · Rasskazovka · Rumyantsevo · M3 · Chertanovo · Lenino · M4 · M6 · TO DOMODEDOVO INTL. (DME) · Borisovo · Tokarevo · Dzerzhinskiy
East from Greenwich

Moscow

1   2   3   4   5   6

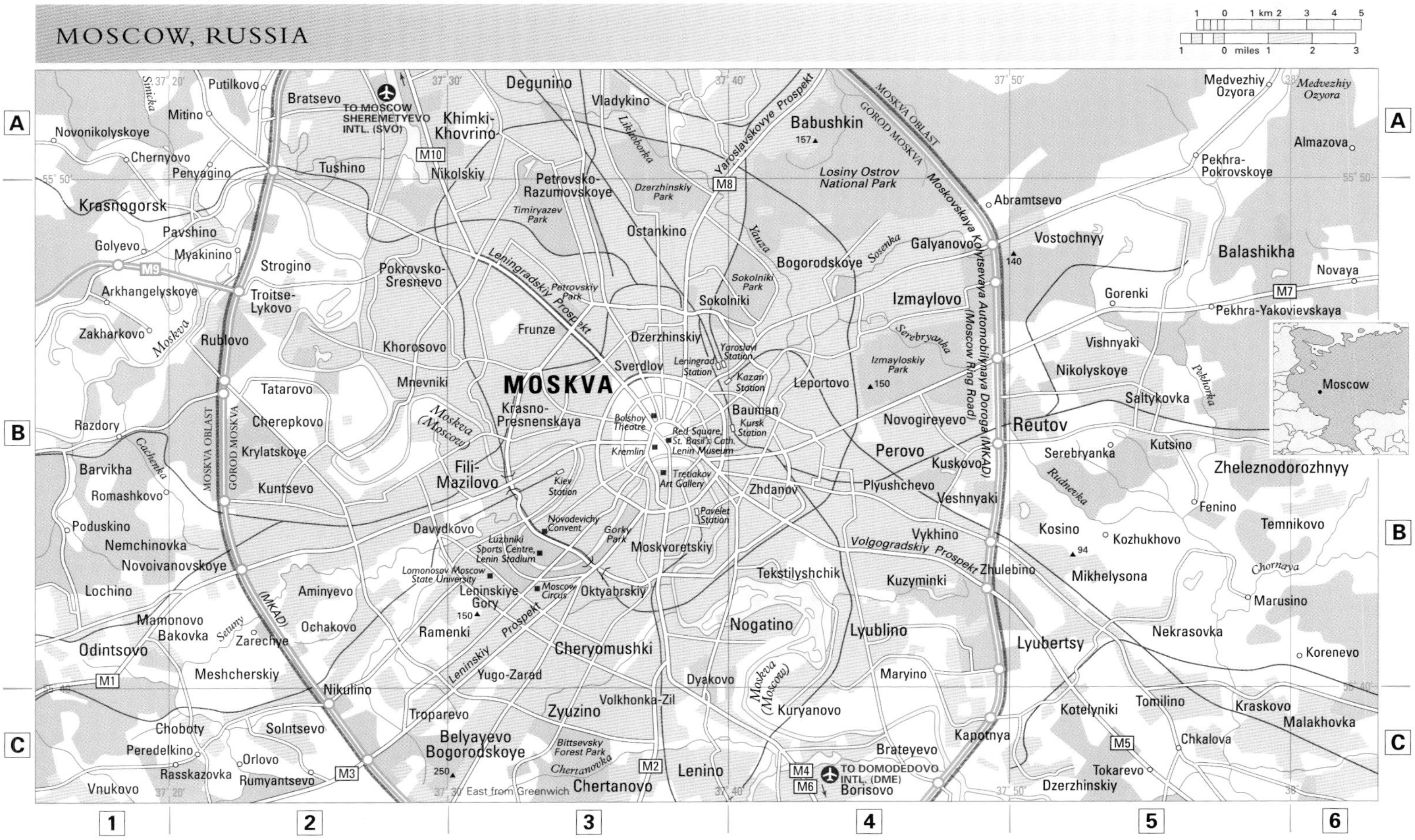

COPYRIGHT PHILIP'S

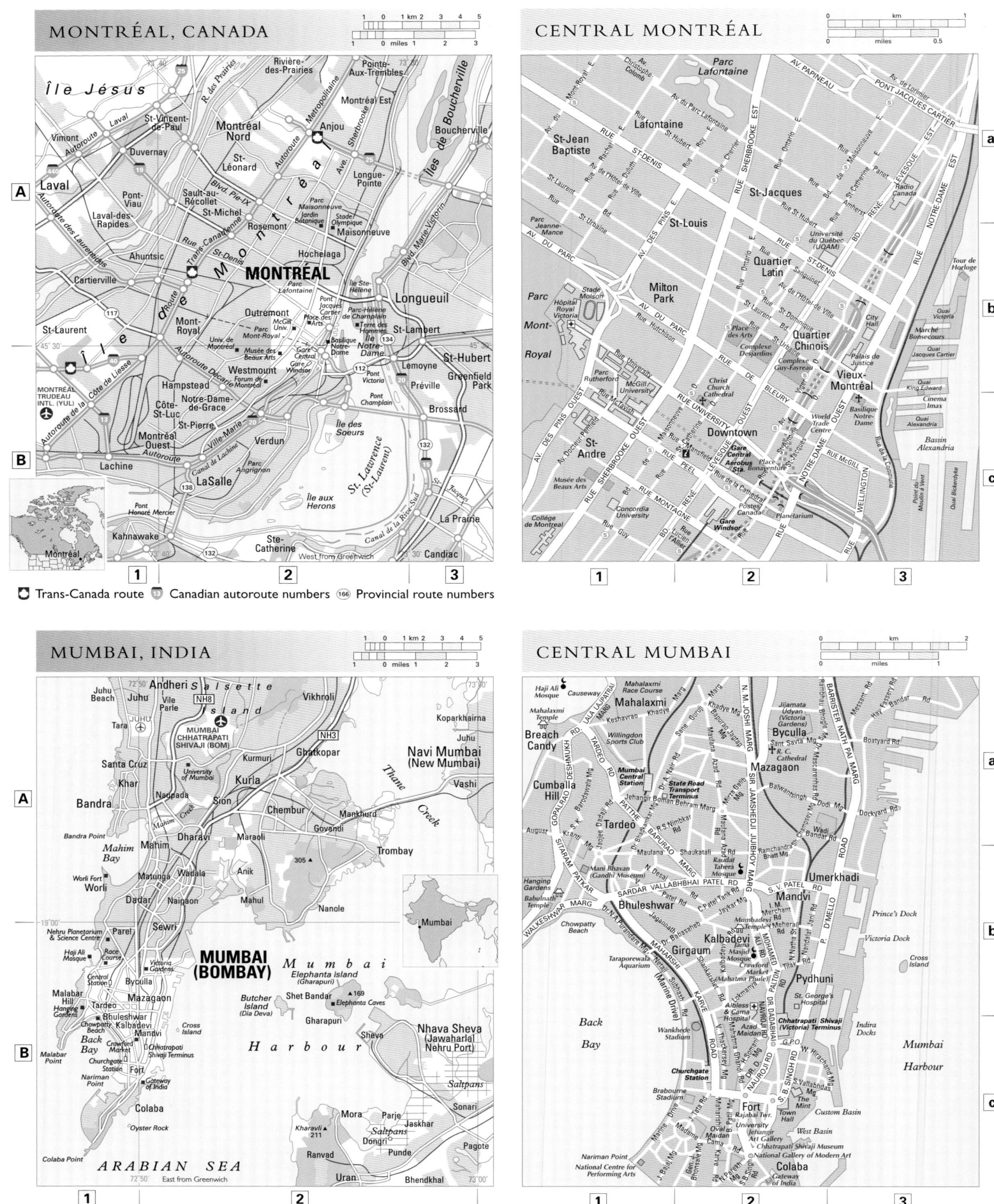

MONTRÉAL, CANADA

CENTRAL MONTRÉAL

MUMBAI, INDIA

CENTRAL MUMBAI

Trans-Canada route Canadian autoroute numbers Provincial route numbers

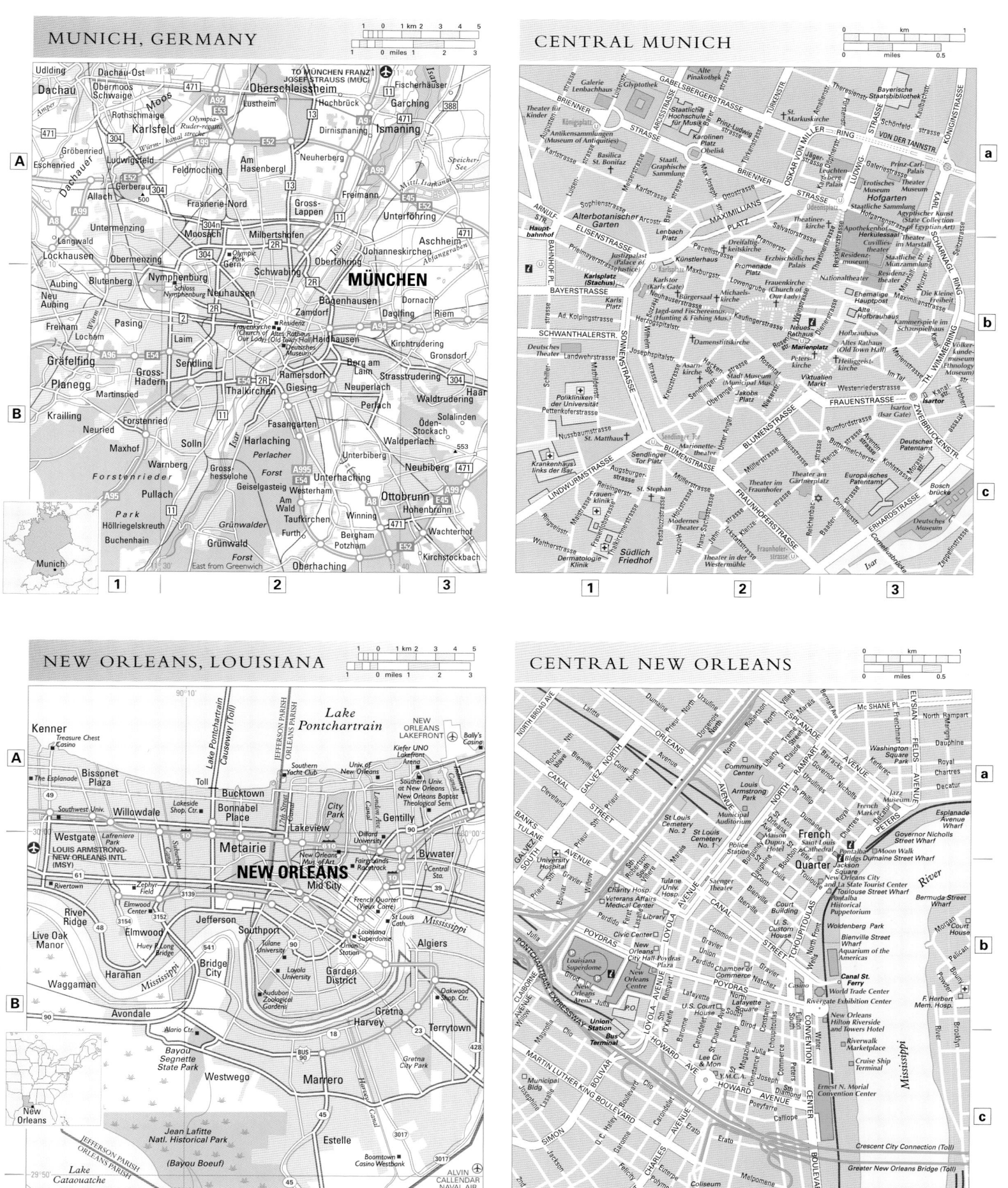

NEW YORK, NEW YORK

1 0 1 km 2 3 4 5
1 0 miles 1 2 3

Interstate route numbers
U.S. route numbers
State route numbers

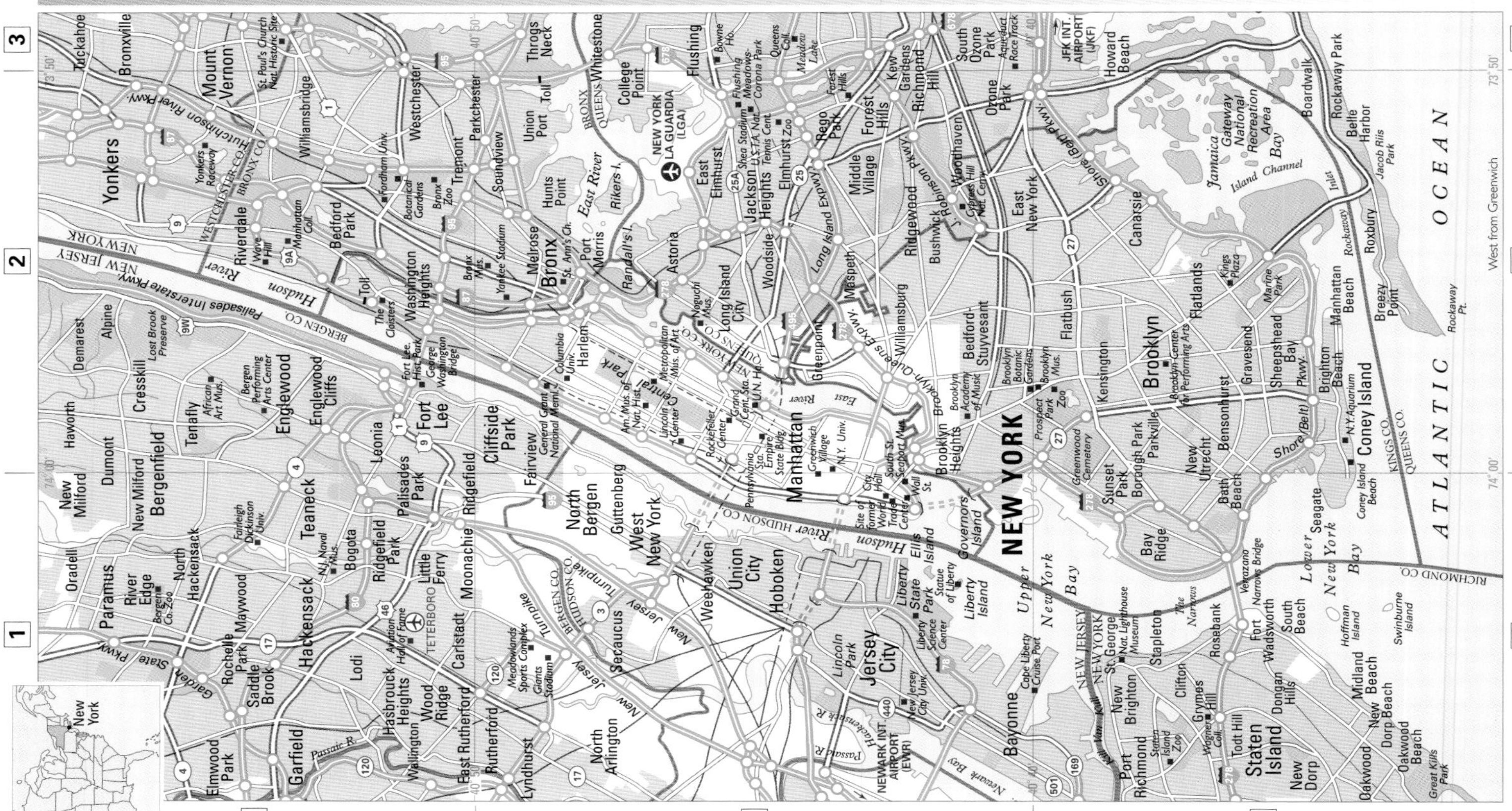

ATLANTIC OCEAN

West from Greenwich

Yonkers · Mount Vernon · Bronxville · Tuckahoe · Westchester · Williamsbridge · Throgs Neck · Whitestone · Flushing · Bowne · Queens · South Ozone Park · JFK INT AIRPORT (JFK) · Howard Beach · Rockaway Park · Belle Harbor

Riverdale · Bedford Park · Washington Heights · Tremont · Soundview · College Point · Union Port Toll · BRONX · Port Morris · Astoria · Long Island City · Woodside · Elmhurst · Jackson Heights · Rego Park · Forest Hills · Middle Village · Ridgewood · Bushwick · East New York · Canarsie · Jamaica Bay · Rockaway Pt.

Englewood · Englewood Cliffs · Fort Lee · Cliffside Park · Fairview · Manhattan · Harlem · Central Park · Rockefeller Center · Lincoln Tunnel · Greenwich Village · Brooklyn Heights · Brooklyn · Flatbush · Gravesend · Sheepshead Bay · Brighton Beach · Coney Island

Paramus · Hackensack · Teaneck · Ridgefield Park · North Bergen · West New York · Union City · Hoboken · Jersey City · Liberty Island · Ellis Island · Governors Island · NEW YORK · Upper New York Bay · Verrazano Bridge · Bay Ridge · Sunset Park · Borough Park · Bensonhurst · Bath Beach

Garfield · Lodi · Hasbrouck Heights · Wood Ridge · East Rutherford · Rutherford · Lyndhurst · North Arlington · Secaucus · Bayonne · New Brighton · Port Richmond · Staten Island · New Dorp · Oakwood

NEWARK INT AIRPORT (EWR) · KINGS CO · QUEENS CO · RICHMOND CO · BERGEN CO · HUDSON CO · NEW JERSEY · NEW YORK

CENTRAL NEW YORK

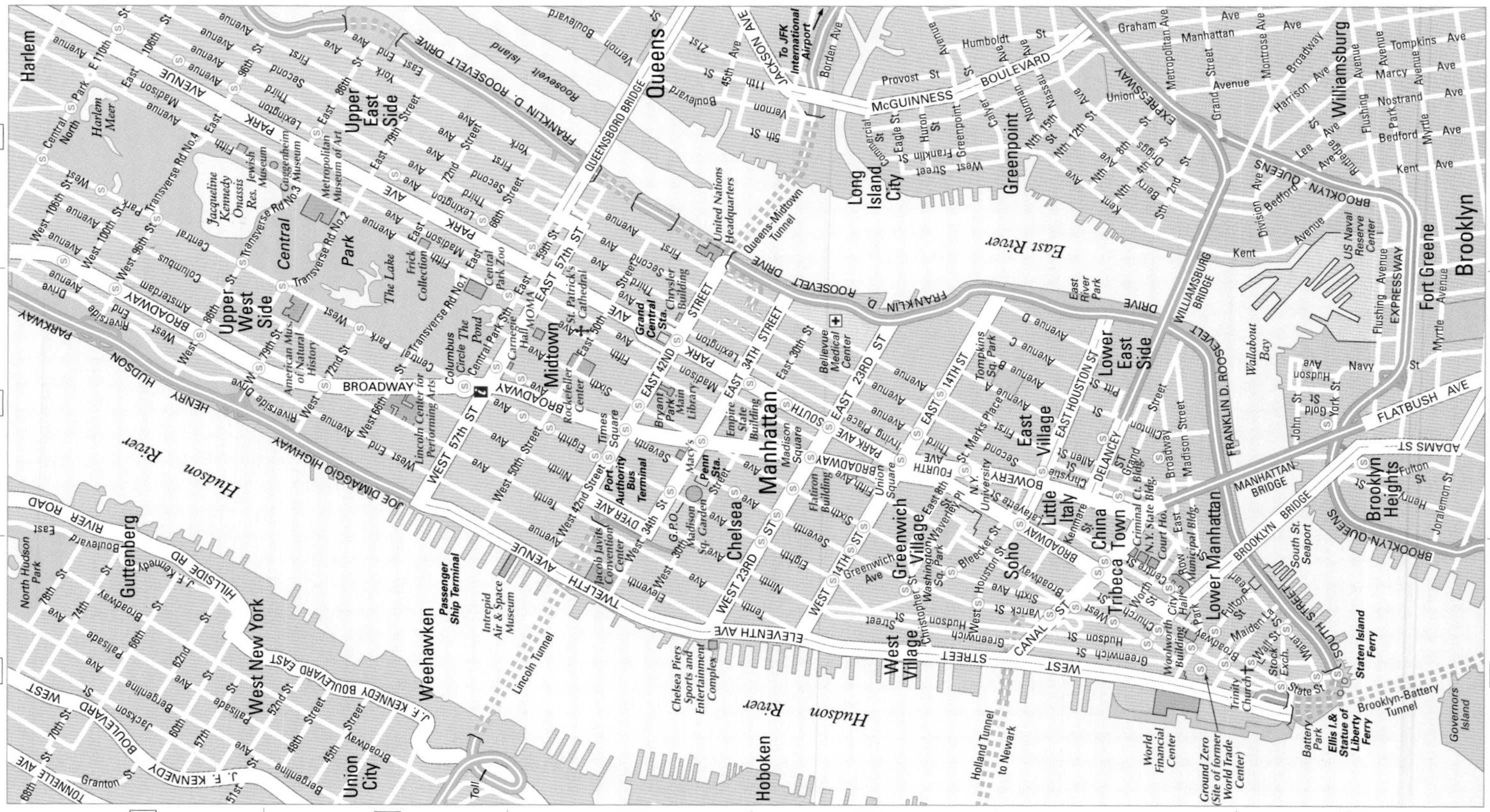

0 km 2
0 miles 1

Harlem · Upper East Side · Upper West Side · Central Park · Midtown · Manhattan · Chelsea · Greenwich Village · East Village · Lower East Side · Little Italy · China Town · Soho · Tribeca · Lower Manhattan

Queens · Long Island City · Greenpoint · Williamsburg · Fort Greene · Brooklyn · Brooklyn Heights

Hudson River · East River · Hudson River

Guttenberg · West New York · Union City · Weehawken · Hoboken

American Museum of Natural History · Metropolitan Museum of Art · Jacqueline Kennedy Onassis Res. · Central Park Zoo · MoMA · St Patrick's Cathedral · Grand Central Sta. · Chrysler Building · United Nations Headquarters · Rockefeller Center · Lincoln Center for Performing Arts · Columbus Circle · Times Square · Port Authority Bus Terminal · Penn Sta. · G.P.O. · Madison Square · Empire State Building · Flatiron Building · Bellevue Medical Center · Union Square · Washington Square · Bowery · World Financial Center · Ground Zero Site of former World Trade Center · Battery Park · Ellis I. & Statue of Liberty · Staten Island Ferry · Brooklyn-Battery Tunnel · Governors Island

FRANKLIN D. ROOSEVELT DRIVE · JOE DiMAGGIO HIGHWAY · HENRY HUDSON PARKWAY · QUEENSBORO BRIDGE · WILLIAMSBURG BRIDGE · MANHATTAN BRIDGE · BROOKLYN BRIDGE · BROOKLYN-QUEENS EXPRESSWAY · FLATBUSH AVE · McGUINNESS BOULEVARD · JACKSON AVE · To JFK International Airport

COPYRIGHT PHILIP'S

PARIS, FRANCE

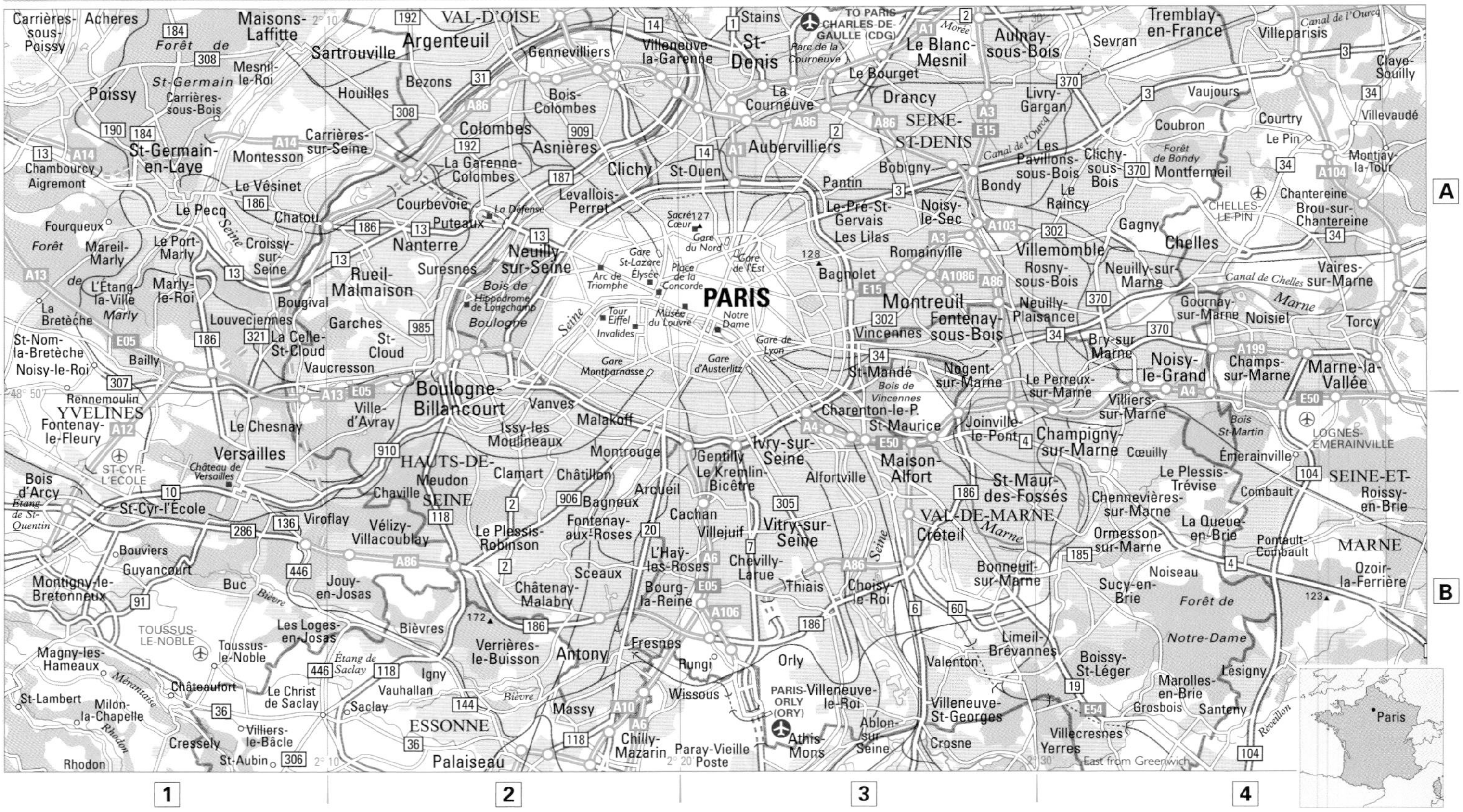

VAL-D'OISE

Carrières-sous-Poissy · Achères · Maisons-Laffitte · Argenteuil · Gennevilliers · Villeneuve-la-Garenne · Stains · St-Denis · TO PARIS CHARLES-DE-GAULLE (CDG) · Le Blanc-Mesnil · Aulnay-sous-Bois · Sevran · Tremblay-en-France · Villeparisis

Sartrouville · Bezons · Bois-Colombes · La Courneuve · Le Bourget · Livry-Gargan · Vaujours · Courtry · Le Pin · Villevaudé

Poissy · Houilles · Colombes · Asnières · Clichy · St-Ouen · Aubervilliers · Bobigny · Drancy · Les Pavillons-sous-Bois · Clichy-sous-Bois · Montfermeil · Chantereine · Brou-sur-Chantereine · Montjay-la-Tour

St-Germain-en-Laye · Carrières-sur-Seine · La Garenne-Colombes · Levallois-Perret · Pantin · Le Pré-St-Gervais · Les Lilas · Romainville · Villemomble · Rosny-sous-Bois · Neuilly-sur-Marne · Gagny · Chelles · CHELLES-LE-PIN · Vaires-sur-Marne

Le Pecq · Chatou · Courbevoie · Puteaux · La Défense · Neuilly-sur-Seine · Gare St-Lazare · Gare du Nord · Gare de l'Est · Bagnolet · Montreuil · Fontenay-sous-Bois · Noisy-le-Grand · Champs-sur-Marne · Marne-la-Vallée · LOGNES EMERAINVILLE

Nanterre · Rueil-Malmaison · Suresnes · Arc de Triomphe · Notre Dame · **PARIS** · Tour Eiffel · Musée du Louvre · Place de la Concorde · Sacré Cœur · Vincennes · St-Mandé · Le Perreux-sur-Marne · Villiers-sur-Marne · Bry-sur-Marne · Noisiel · Torcy

Bougival · Garches · St-Cloud · Boulogne · Gare Montparnasse · Gare de Lyon · Gare d'Austerlitz · Charenton-le-P. · St-Maurice · Joinville-le-Pont · Champigny-sur-Marne · Le Plessis-Trévise · Émerainville

Boulogne-Billancourt · Vanves · Malakoff · Issy-les-Moulineaux · Ivry-sur-Seine · Maison-Alfort · St-Maur-des-Fossés · Chennevières-sur-Marne · La Queue-en-Brie · Combault

YVELINES · HAUTS-DE-SEINE · Meudon · Clamart · Montrouge · Gentilly · Le Kremlin-Bicêtre · Alfortville · VAL-DE-MARNE · Ormesson-sur-Marne · SEINE-ET-ROISSY-EN-BRIE

Versailles · Châtillon · Bagneux · Cachan · Vitry-sur-Seine · Créteil · Bonneuil-sur-Marne · Noiseau · MARNE · Ozoir-la-Ferrière

Le Chesnay · Viroflay · Vélizy-Villacoublay · Le Plessis-Robinson · Fontenay-aux-Roses · L'Haÿ-les-Roses · Chevilly-Larue · Villejuif · Choisy-le-Roi · Sucy-en-Brie · Forêt de Notre-Dame

Sceaux · Châtenay-Malabry · Bourg-la-Reine · Thiais · Boissy-St-Léger

St-Cyr-l'École · Bouviers · Guyancourt · Buc · Bièvres · Verrières-le-Buisson · Antony · Fresnes · Orly · Valenton · Limeil-Brévannes · Marolles-en-Brie · Lesigny

ESSONNE · Igny · Massy · Rungis · Wissous · PARIS ORLY (ORY) · Villeneuve-le-Roi · Villeneuve-St-Georges · Crosne · Yerres · Villecresnes · Santeny

Palaiseau · Chilly-Mazarin · Paray-Vieille-Poste · Athis-Mons · Ablon-sur-Seine

CENTRAL PARIS

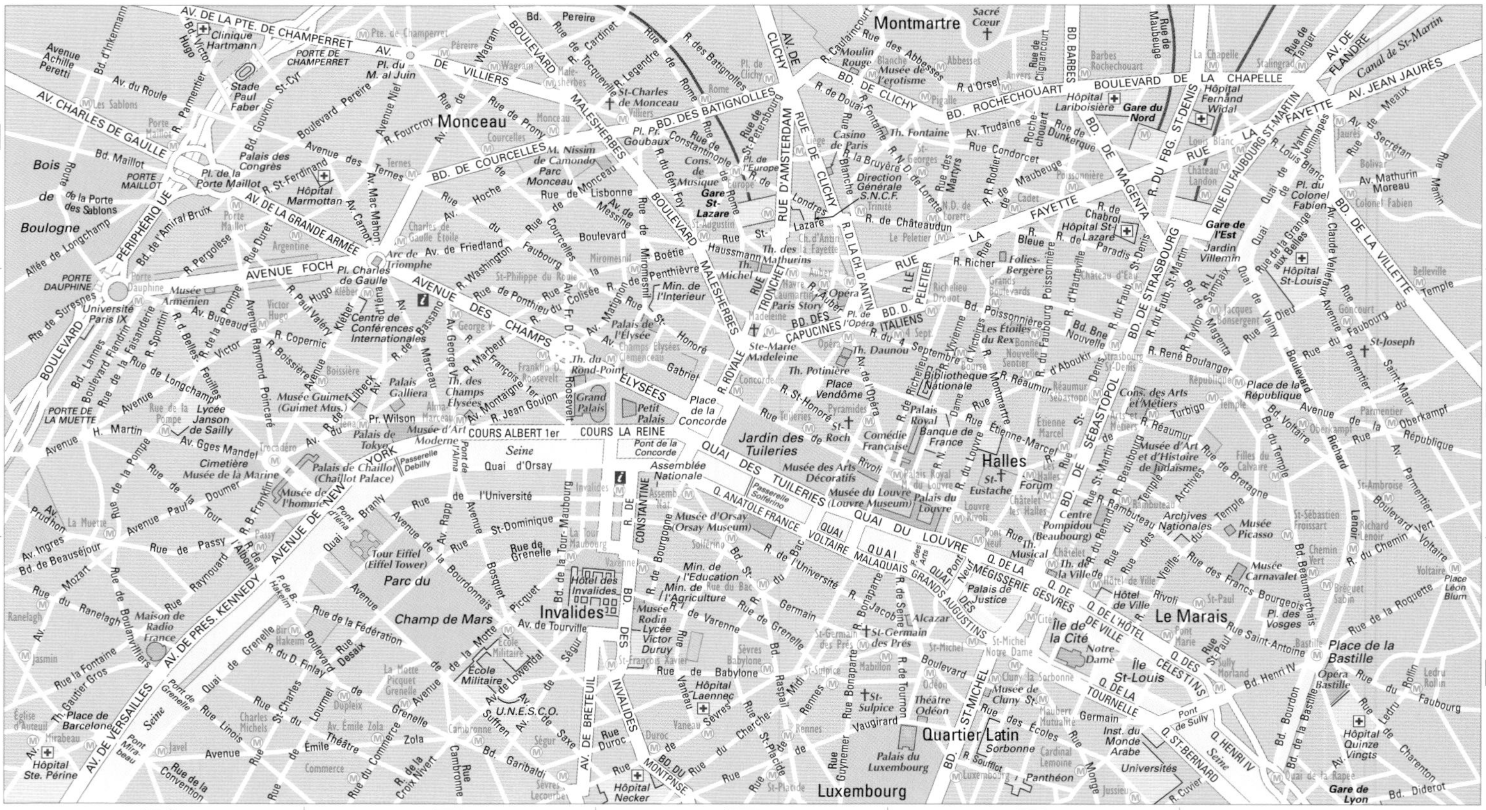

Montmartre · Sacré Cœur · Moulin Rouge · Gare du Nord · Gare de l'Est

Monceau · Parc Monceau · Gare St-Lazare · Opéra · Bibliothèque Nationale · Musée d'Art et d'Histoire du Judaïsme

Bois de Boulogne · PORTE MAILLOT · Arc de Triomphe · Pl. Charles de Gaulle · AVENUE DES CHAMPS ELYSÉES · Place de la Concorde · Jardin des Tuileries · Musée du Louvre · Halles · Centre Pompidou Beaubourg · Archives Nationales · Musée Picasso

PORTE DAUPHINE · AVENUE FOCH · Palais de Chaillot · Musée de l'Homme · Tour Eiffel · Champ de Mars · Invalides · Assemblée Nationale · Musée d'Orsay · Hôtel de Ville · Île de la Cité · Notre Dame · Île St-Louis · Le Marais · Place de la Bastille

Maison de Radio France · U.N.E.S.C.O. · École Militaire · St-Germain-des-Prés · Quartier Latin · Sorbonne · Panthéon · Luxembourg · Palais du Luxembourg · Gare de Lyon

PRAGUE, CZECH REPUBLIC

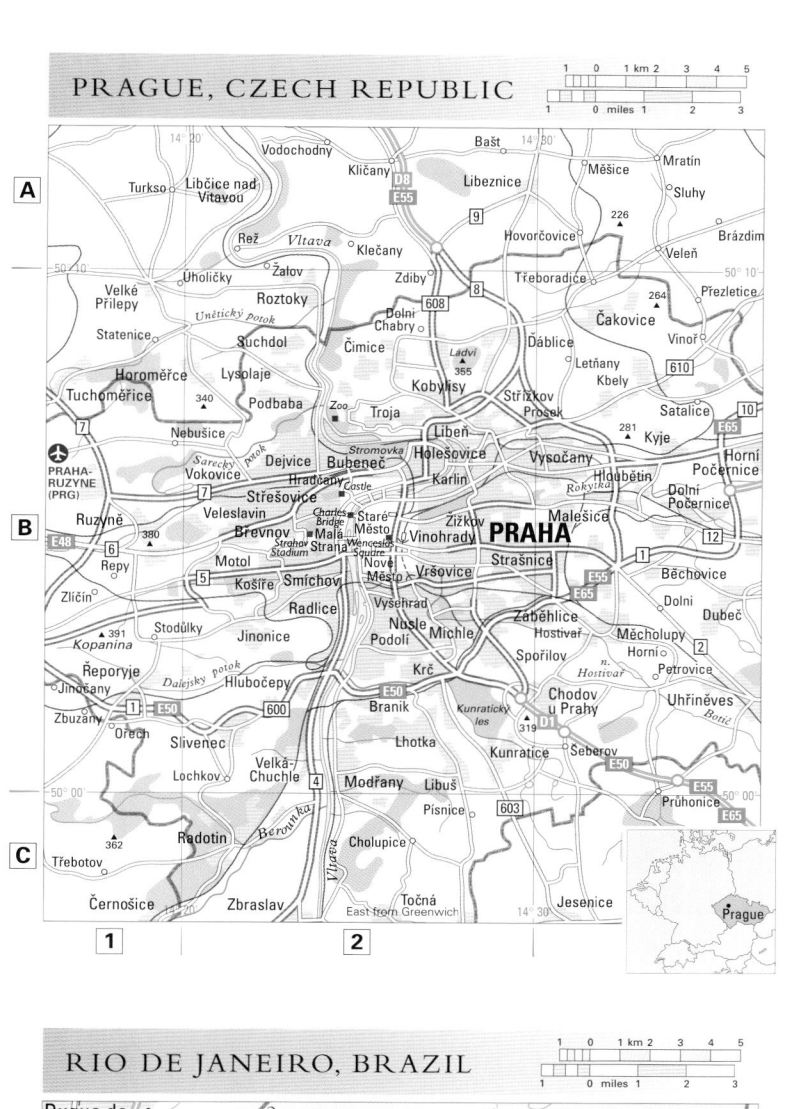

CENTRAL PRAGUE

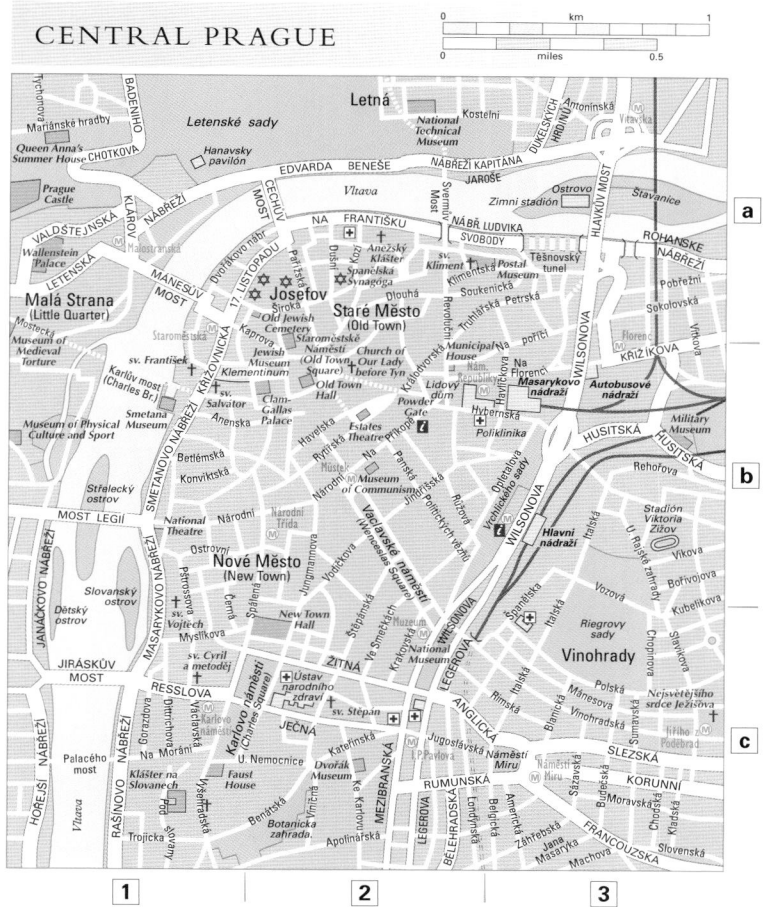

RIO DE JANEIRO, BRAZIL

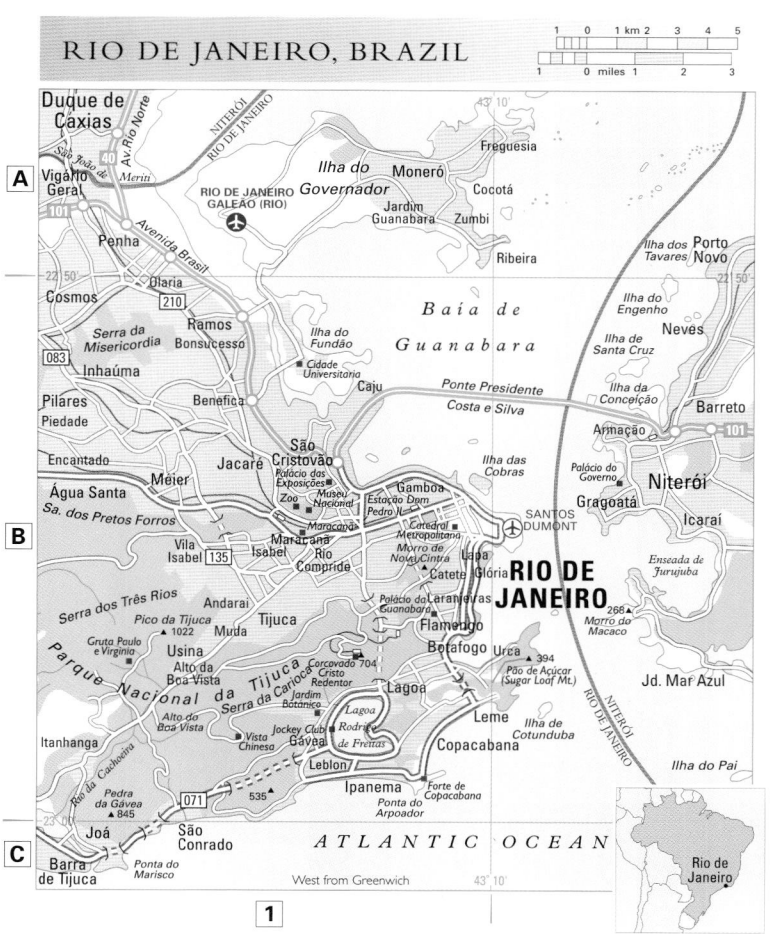

CENTRAL RIO DE JANEIRO

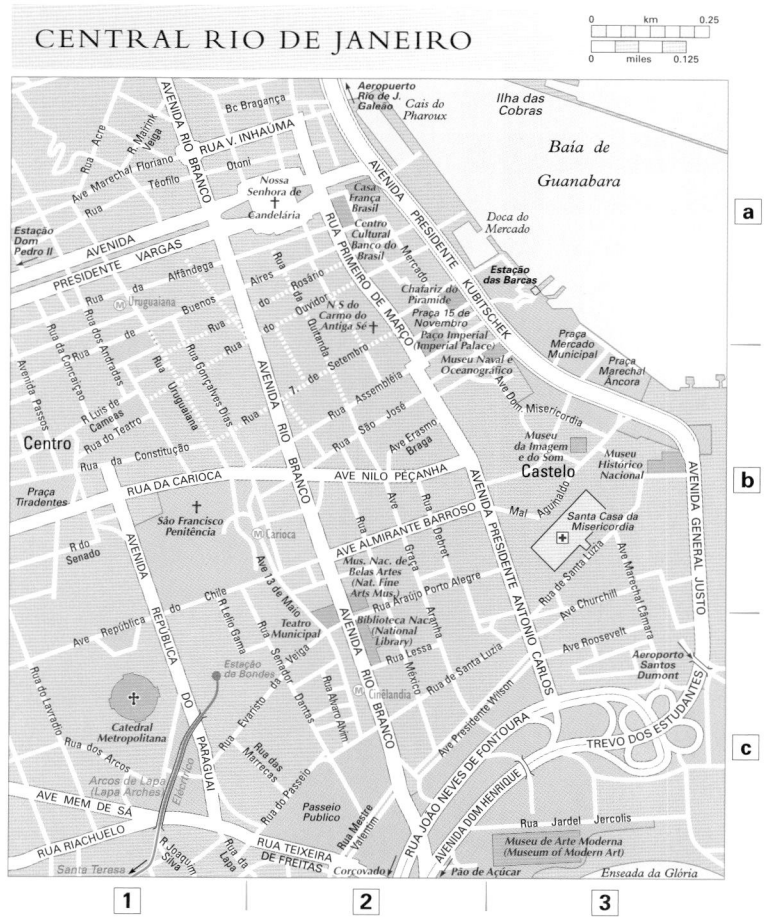

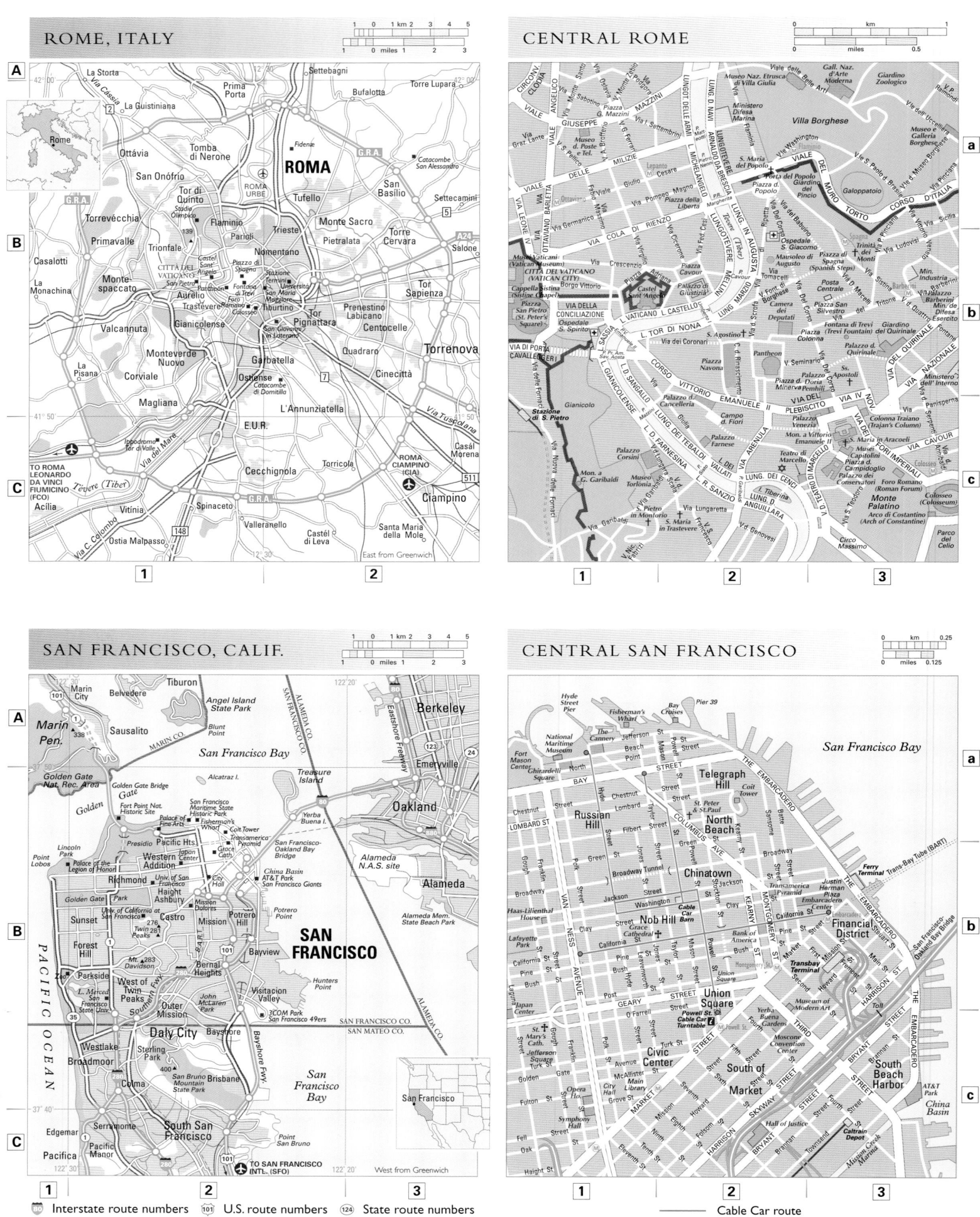

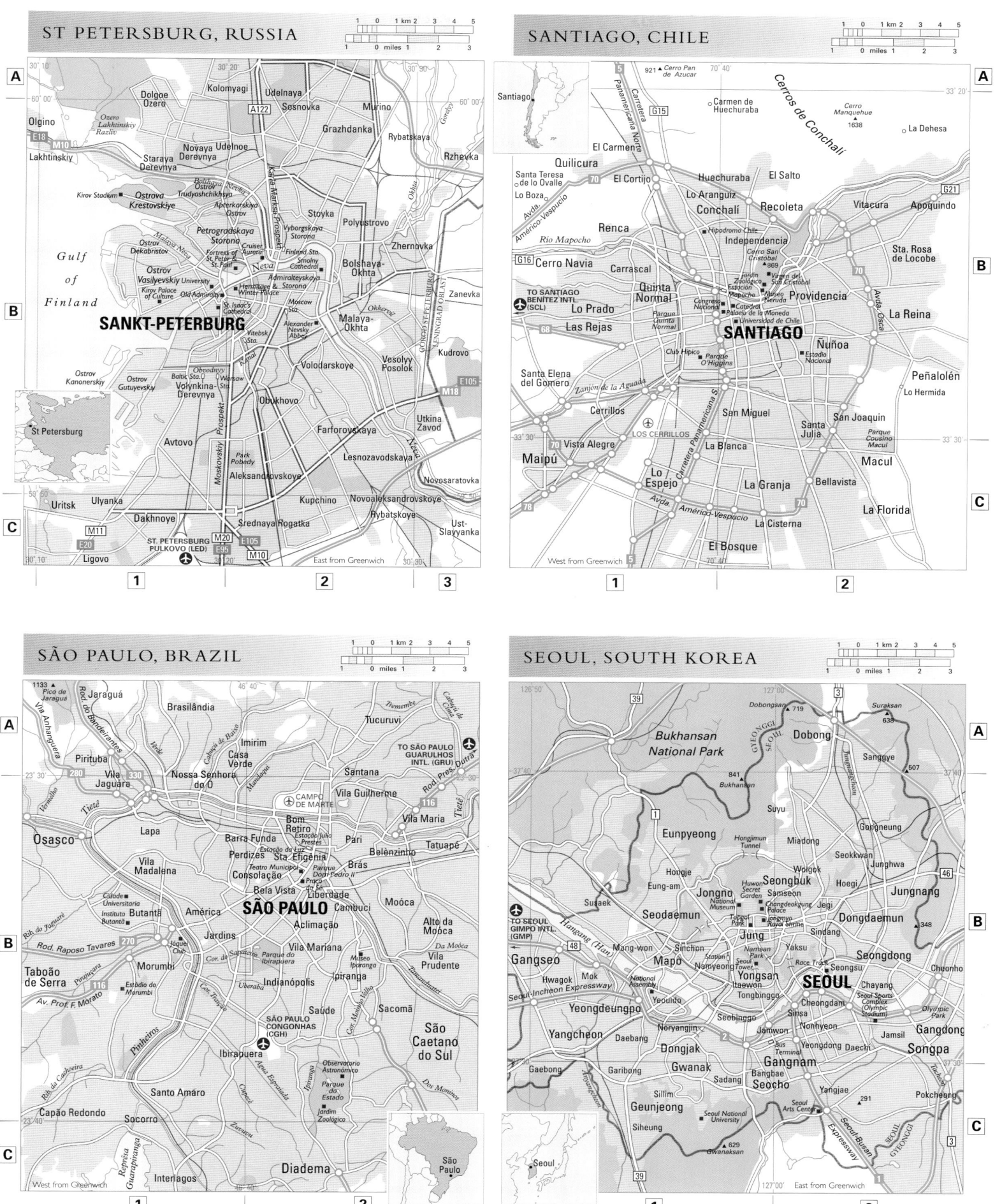

ST PETERSBURG, RUSSIA

SANTIAGO, CHILE

SÃO PAULO, BRAZIL

SEOUL, SOUTH KOREA

COPYRIGHT PHILIP'S

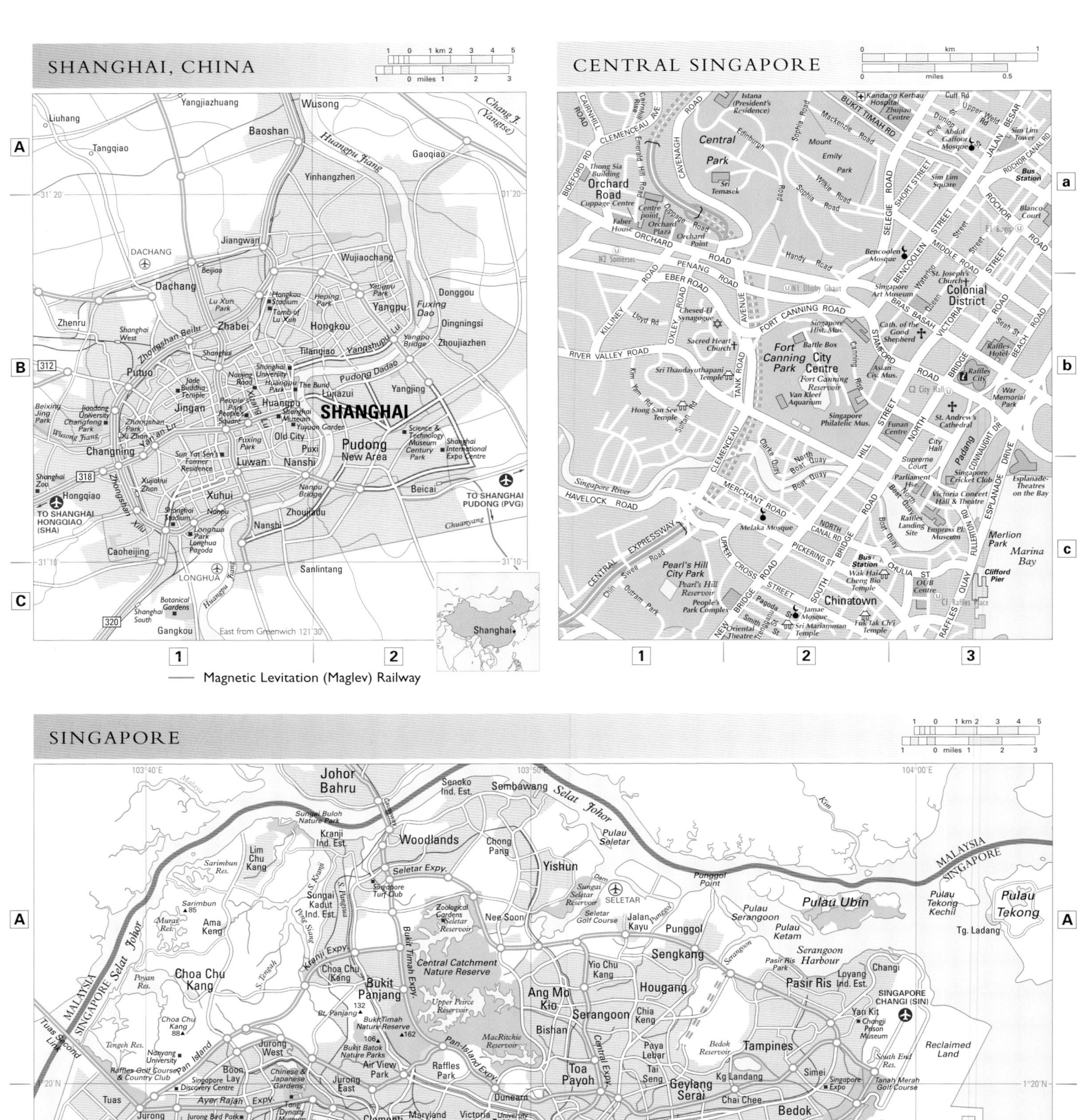

SHANGHAI, CHINA

— Magnetic Levitation (Maglev) Railway

CENTRAL SINGAPORE

SINGAPORE

STOCKHOLM, SWEDEN

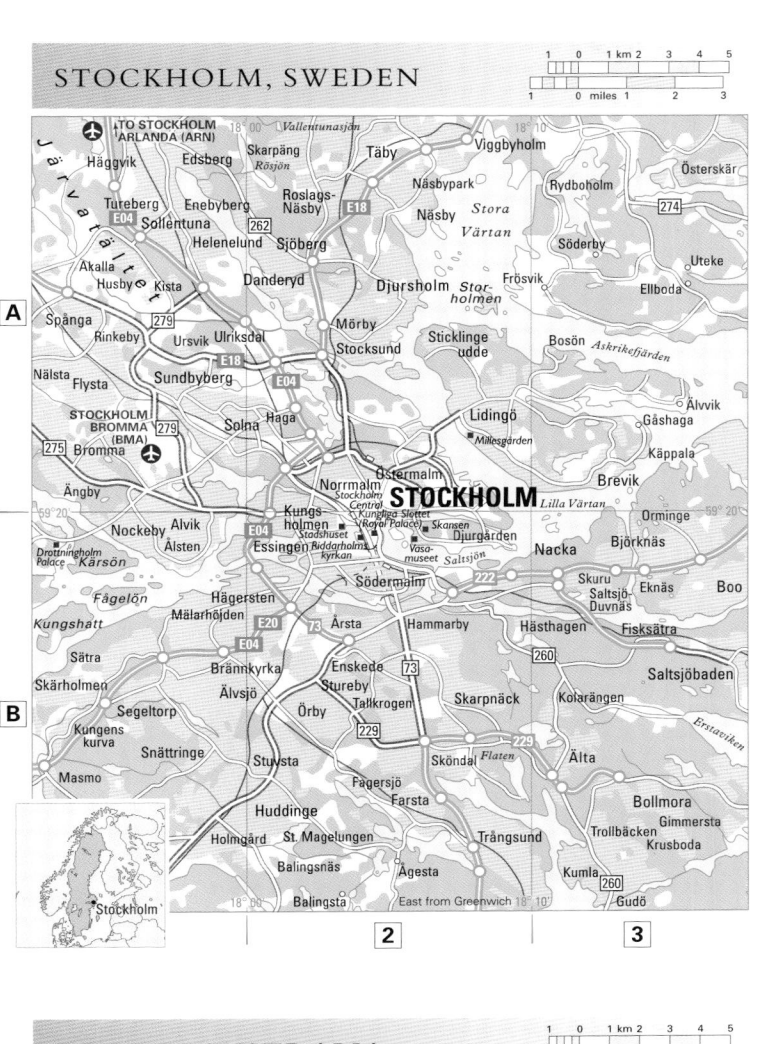

CENTRAL STOCKHOLM

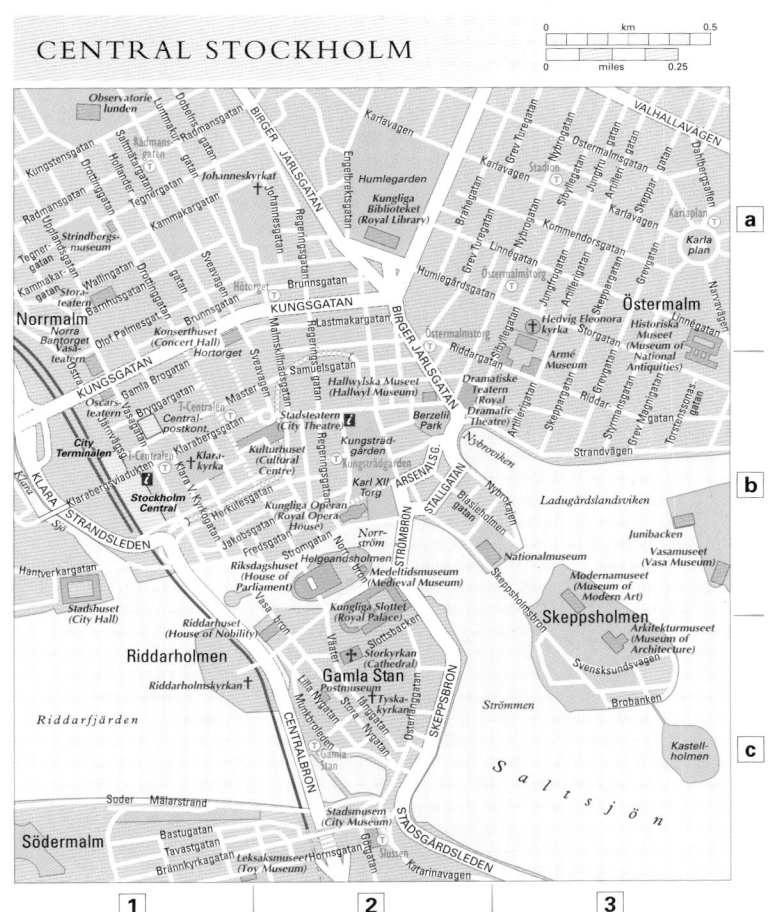

SYDNEY, AUSTRALIA

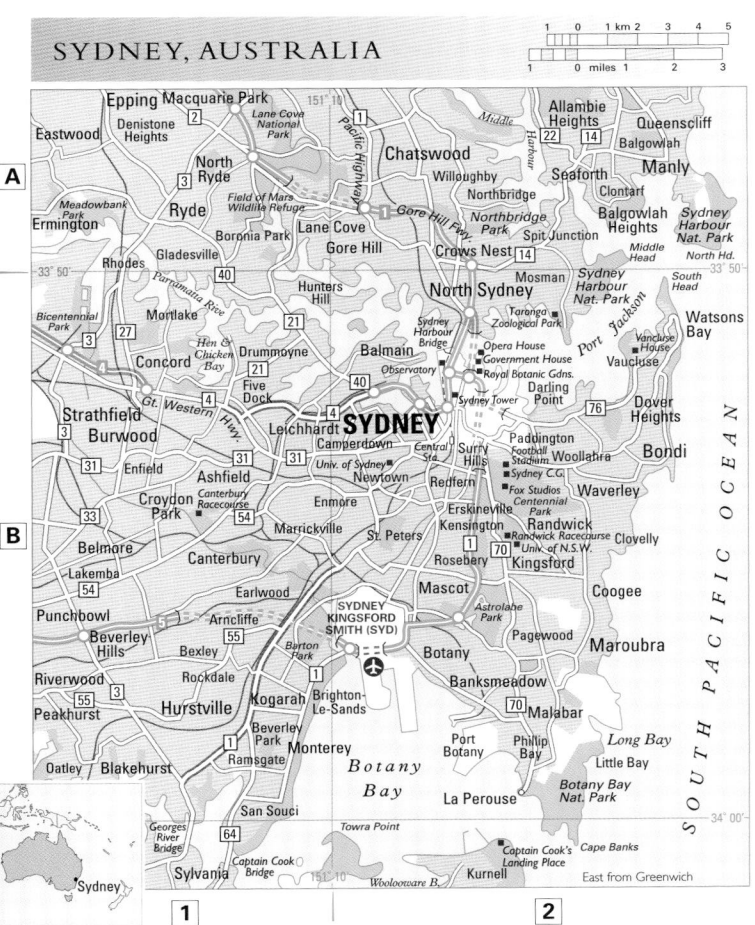

CENTRAL SYDNEY

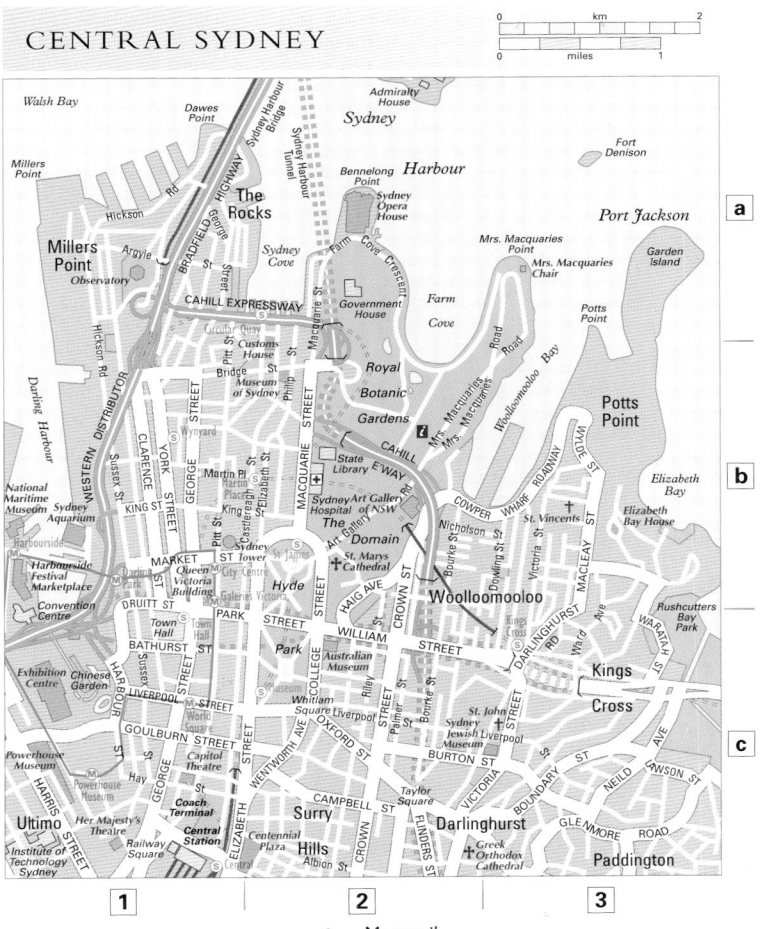

—Ⓜ— Monorail

TOKYO, JAPAN

1 0 1 km 2 3 4 5
1 0 miles 1 2 3

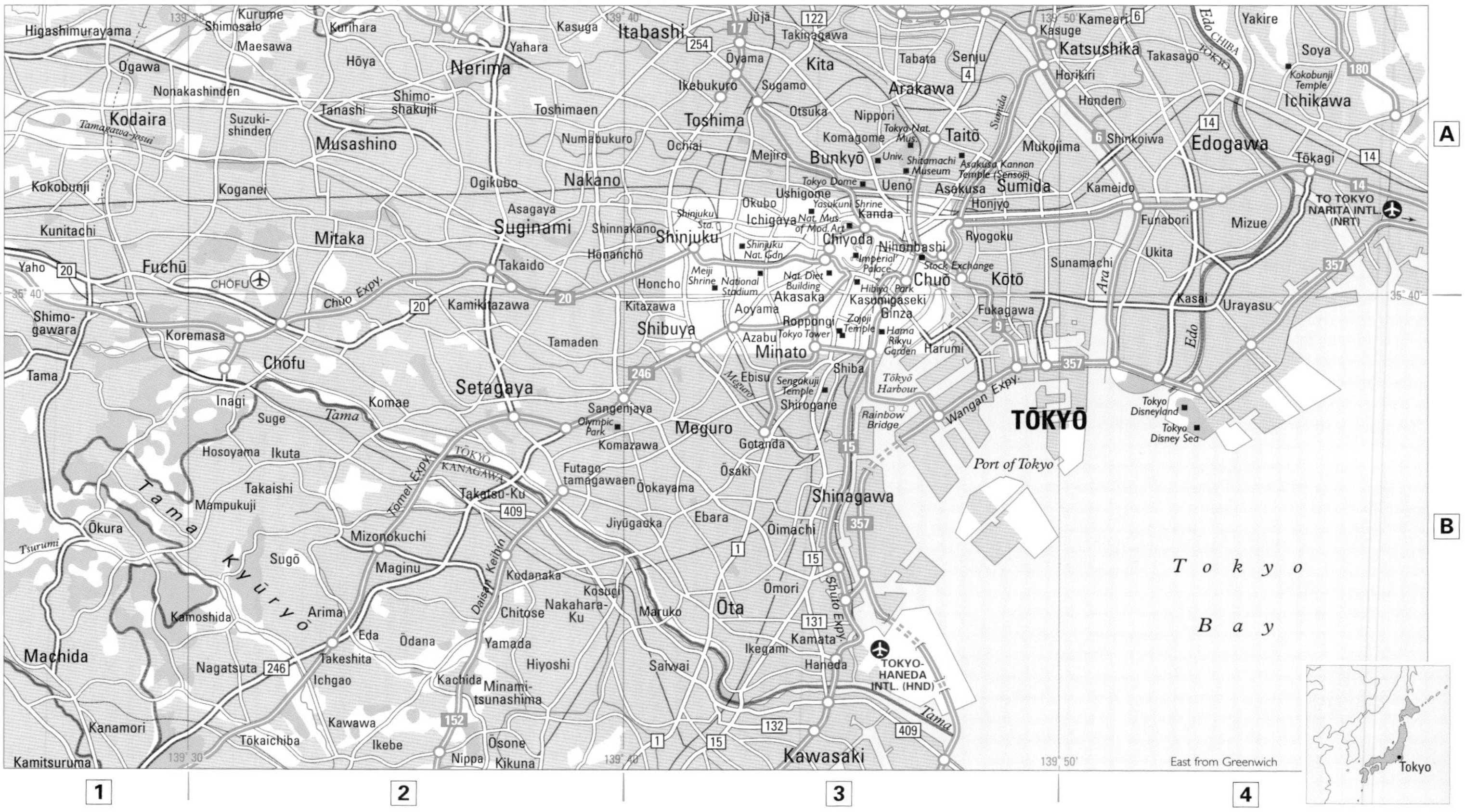

CENTRAL TOKYO

0 km 1
0 miles 0.5

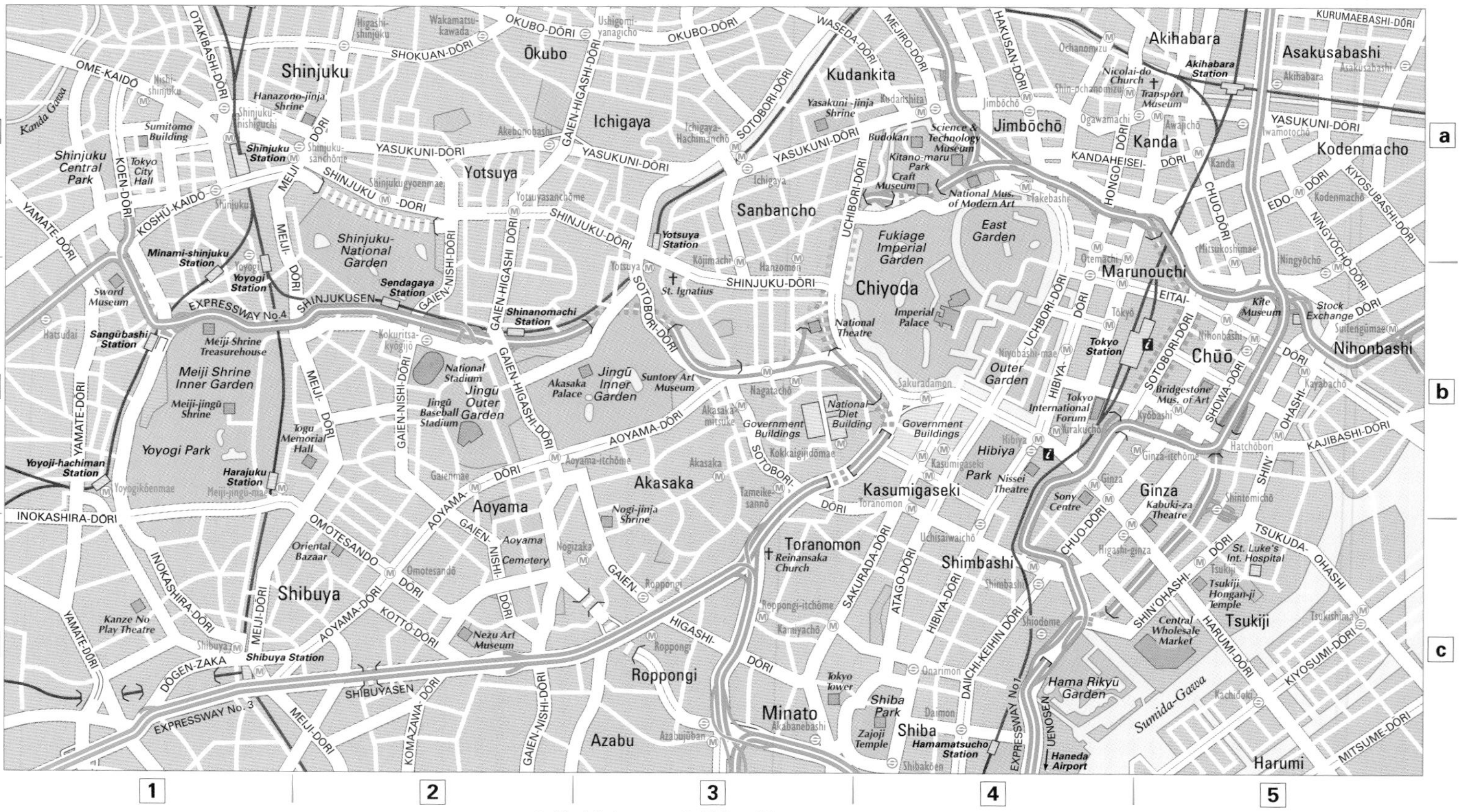

Toei Subway Tokyo Metro

TEHRAN, IRAN

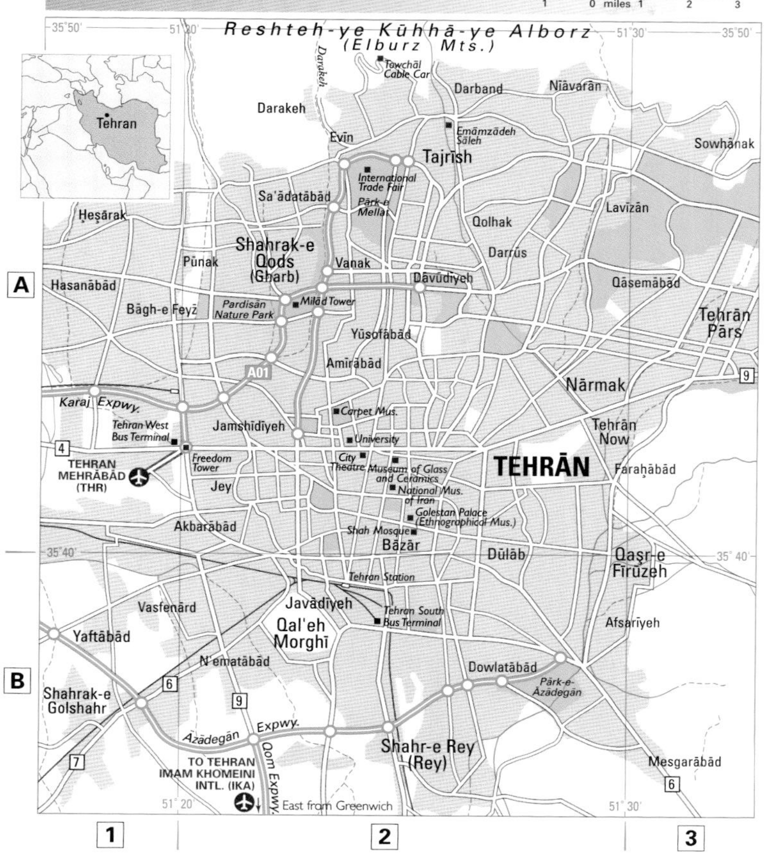

1 0 1 km 2 3 4 5
0 miles 1 2 3

35°50′ 51°20′ 51°30′ 35°50′

Reshteh-ye Kūhhā-ye Alborz
(Elburz Mts.)

Towchāl Cable Car

Darband
Darakeh
Darbard
Niāvarān
Evīn
Emāmzādeh Sāleh
Sowhānak
Tajrīsh
Sa'ādatābād
International Trade Fair
Park-e Mellat
Qolhak
Lavīzān
Heşārak
Shahrak-e Qods (Gharb)
Vanak
Dāvūdīyeh
Qāsemābād
A Hasanābād
Pardisan Nature Park
Mīlād Tower
Darrūs
Tehrān Pārs
Bāgh-e Feyż
Pūnak
Yūsofābād
Amīrābād
Karaj Expwy
A01
Nārmak
Tehran West Bus Terminal
Jamshīdīyeh
Carpet Mus.
Tehrān Now
4
TEHRAN MEHRĀBĀD (THR)
Freedom Tower
University
City Theatre
Museum of Glass and Ceramics
TEHRĀN
9
Jey
Akbarābād
National Mus. of Iran
Golestan Palace (Ethnographical Mus.)
Farahābād
35°40′
Shah Mosque
Bāzār
Dūlāb
Qasr-e Fīrūzeh
35°40′
Tehran Station
Vasfenārd
Javādīyeh
Qal'eh Morghī
Tehran South Bus Terminal
Afsarīyeh
Yaftābād
N'ematābād
Dowlatābād
Park-e Āzādegān
B Shahrak-e Golshahr
6
9
Āzādegān Expwy
Qom Expwy
Shahr-e Rey (Rey)
Mesgarābād
7
51°20′
TO TEHRAN IMAM KHOMEINI INTL. (IKA)
East from Greenwich
51°30′
6

1 **2** **3**

CENTRAL TORONTO

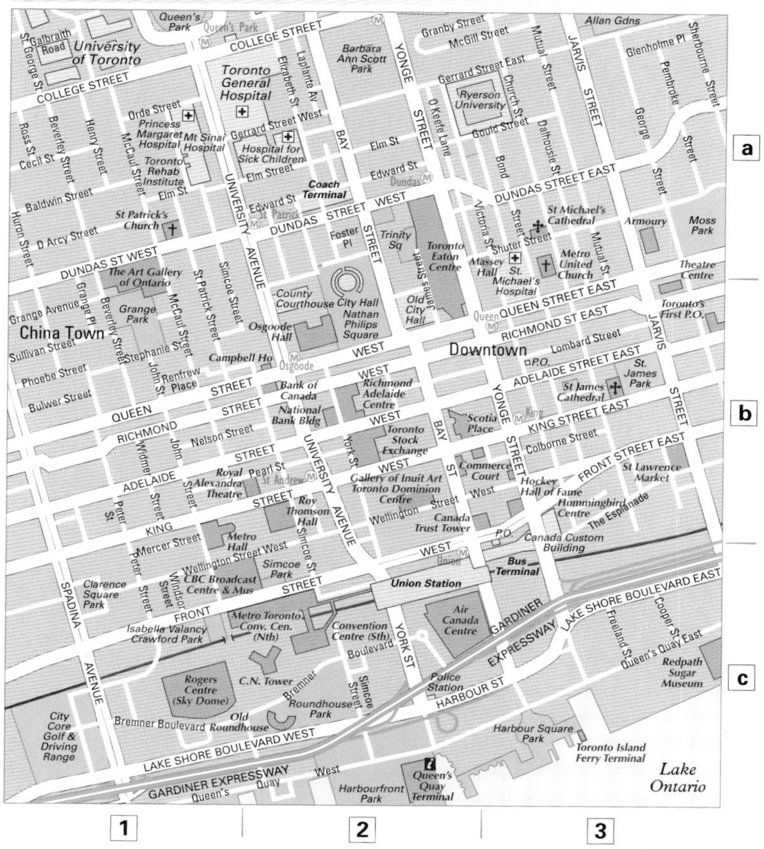

0 km 0.5
0 miles 0.25

Queen's Park
Galbraith Road
University of Toronto
COLLEGE STREET
Barbara Ann Scott Park
Granby Street
McGill Street
Allan Gdns
Glenholme St
Sherbourne Street
Pembroke
a
COLLEGE STREET
St George St
Orde Street
Gerrard Street East
YONGE
Ross St
Beverley Street
Henry Street
Princess Margaret Hospital
Mt Sinai Hospital
Gerrard Street West
Elm St
D Keefe Lane
D St
Bond
George
Baldwin Street
McCaul Street
Toronto Rehab Institute
Hospital for Sick Children
Elm Street
Edward St
Coach Terminal
St Michael's Cathedral
Armoury
Moss Park
Cecil St
Huron Street
D Arcy Street
St Patrick's Church
The Art Gallery of Ontario
DUNDAS ST WEST
Foster Pl
Trinity Sq
DUNDAS STREET EAST
Massey Hall
Metro United Church
St Michael's Hospital
Theatre Centre
A
Grange Avenue
Grange Park
Beverley Street
St Patrick Street
Simcoe Street
County Courthouse
City Hall
Nathan Phillips Square
Old City Hall
QUEEN STREET EAST
Toronto's First P.O.
China Town
Sullivan Street
Stephanie St
Osgoode
Campbell Ho
Downtown
Lombard Street
St James Park
Phoebe Street
Renfrew Place
QUEEN
Bank of Canada
Richmond Adelaide Centre
St James Cathedral
b
Bulwer Street
STREET
National Bank Bldg
WEST
ADELAIDE STREET EAST
Colborne Street
RICHMOND
Nelson Street
Toronto Stock Exchange
Scotia Place
KING STREET EAST
Widmer
John
Peter
ADELAIDE
Royal Alexandra Theatre
St Andrew St
Pearl St
Gallery of Inuit Art
Commerce Court
Hockey Hall of Fame
FRONT STREET EAST
St Lawrence Market
KING
Toronto Dominion Centre
Canada Trust Tower
Hummingbird Centre
The Esplanade
Mercer St
Wellington
P.O.
Canada Custom Building
WEST
Roy Thomson Hall
Simcoe Park
WEST
Bus Terminal
SPADINA
Clarence Square Park
CBC Broadcast Centre & Mus
FRONT
Union Station
Air Canada Centre
LAKE SHORE BOULEVARD EAST
c
Isabella Valancy Crawford Park
Metro Toronto Conv. Cen. (Nth)
Convention Centre (Sth)
YORK ST
Police Station
GARDINER
Cooper St East
Queen's Quay East
Redpath Sugar Museum
AVENUE
Rogers Centre (Sky Dome)
C.N. Tower
Roundhouse Park
Boulevard
HARBOUR ST
EXPRESSWAY
City Core Golf & Driving Range
Bremner Boulevard
Old Roundhouse
Roundhouse Park
Simcoe St
Harbour Square Park
LAKE SHORE BOULEVARD WEST
Toronto Island Ferry Terminal
Lake Ontario
GARDINER EXPRESSWAY
Queen's
Quay
West
Harbourfront Park
Queen's Quay Terminal

1 **2** **3**

TORONTO, CANADA

1 0 1 km 2 3 4 5
1 0 miles 1 2 3

79°40′ 79°30′ 79°20′

Boyd Conservation Area
7 407
East Don
Markham
Metro Toronto Zoo
401
Fairport
Vaughan
Thornhill
The Promenade
Concord
Brown
Little Rouge
West Rouge
Rouge Hill
27
Humber
Pine Grove
7
Edgeley
Newtonbrook
48
Agincourt
Malvern
401
Highland Creek
2A
Port Union
Woodbridge
407
Fisherville
G. Ross Lord Park
Willowdale
11
East Don Parkland
404
Fairview Mall
Scarborough Town Centre
Morningside Park
West Hill
Humber Summit
Black Creek Pioneer Village
York University
Northmount
Lansing
401
Bendale
Woburn
Beaumonte Heights
Black Creek
North York
York Mills
East Don
Wexford
Creek Hague Park
Eastpoint Park
A
Clairville Reservoir
407
400
Armour Heights
Don Mills
Scarborough
Cliffside
Humberwood Park
427
Woodbine Centre
Kipling Heights
Downsview
Yorkdale Shopping Centre
Lawrence Heights
11A
York Univ
Don
Wilket Creek Park
Sunnybrook Health Science Centre
Ontario Science Centre
Thorncliffe
Danforth
Bluffers Park
Malton
Woodbine Race Track
Rexdale
Humberlea
401
Weston
Forest Hill
11
Leaside
Dentonia Park
409
York
Cedarvale Park
Casa Loma
East York
5
Scarborough Bluffs
TORONTO LESTER B. PEARSON INTL. (YYZ)
Humber Valley Village
Mount Dennis
Royal Ontario Museum
Riverdale Park
Don Valley Pkwy
Birch Cliff
9
Ashbridge's Bay Park
43°40′
University of Toronto
Parliament Buildings
9
Kew Gardens
Etobicoke
27
Swansea
High Park
Old City Hall
Old Fort York
C.N. Tower & Rogers Centre
Union Sta.
Gardiner Expy
43°40′
410
Hanlon
Islington
Kingsway
Humber
Parkdale
Exhibition Place
TORONTO CITY CENTRE (ISLAND)
TORONTO
Tommy Thompson Park
B
401
Markland Wood
427
Humber Bay
5
Summerville
Way
Humber Bay Park
Ontario Place
Island Park
Toronto Harbour
B
10
Burnhamthorpe
Elizabeth
Toronto Islands
LAKE ONTARIO
403
Square One
Dixie Mall
New Toronto
2
Humber College
Samuel Smith Park
Gibraltar Point
Cooksville
Mississauga
Long Branch
79°30′
79°20′
West from Greenwich
79°10′
Toronto

1 **2** **3** **4**

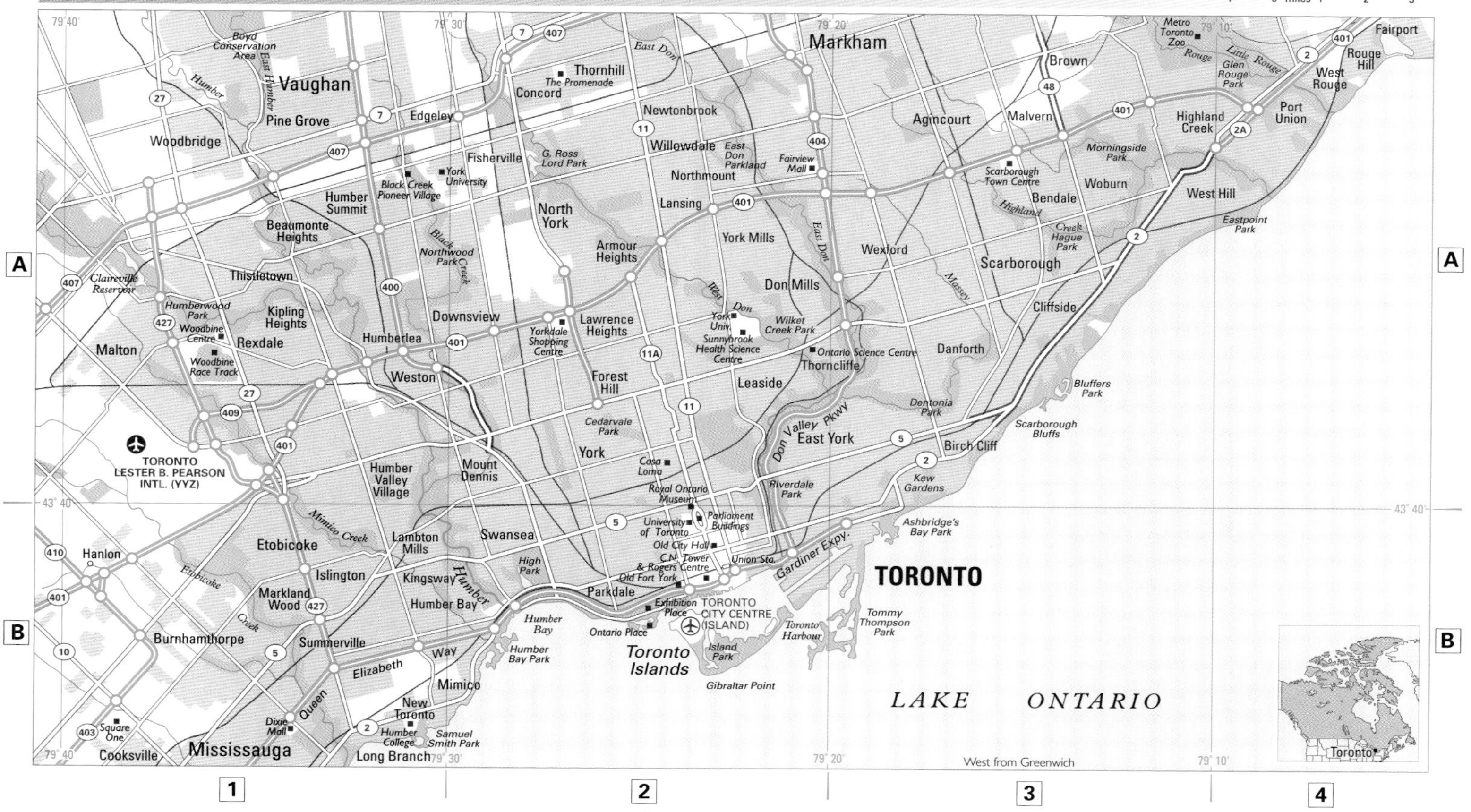

427 Provincial route numbers

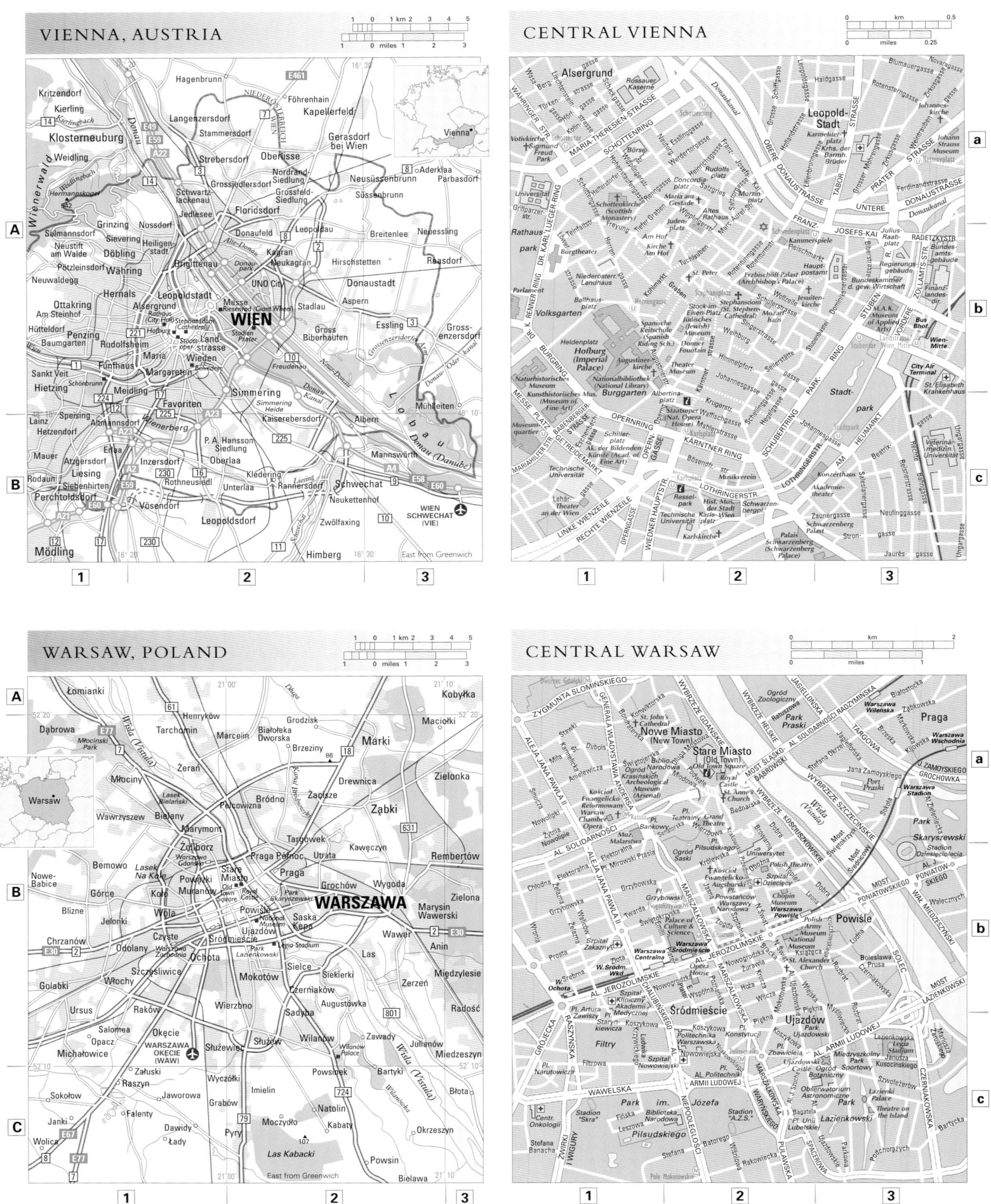

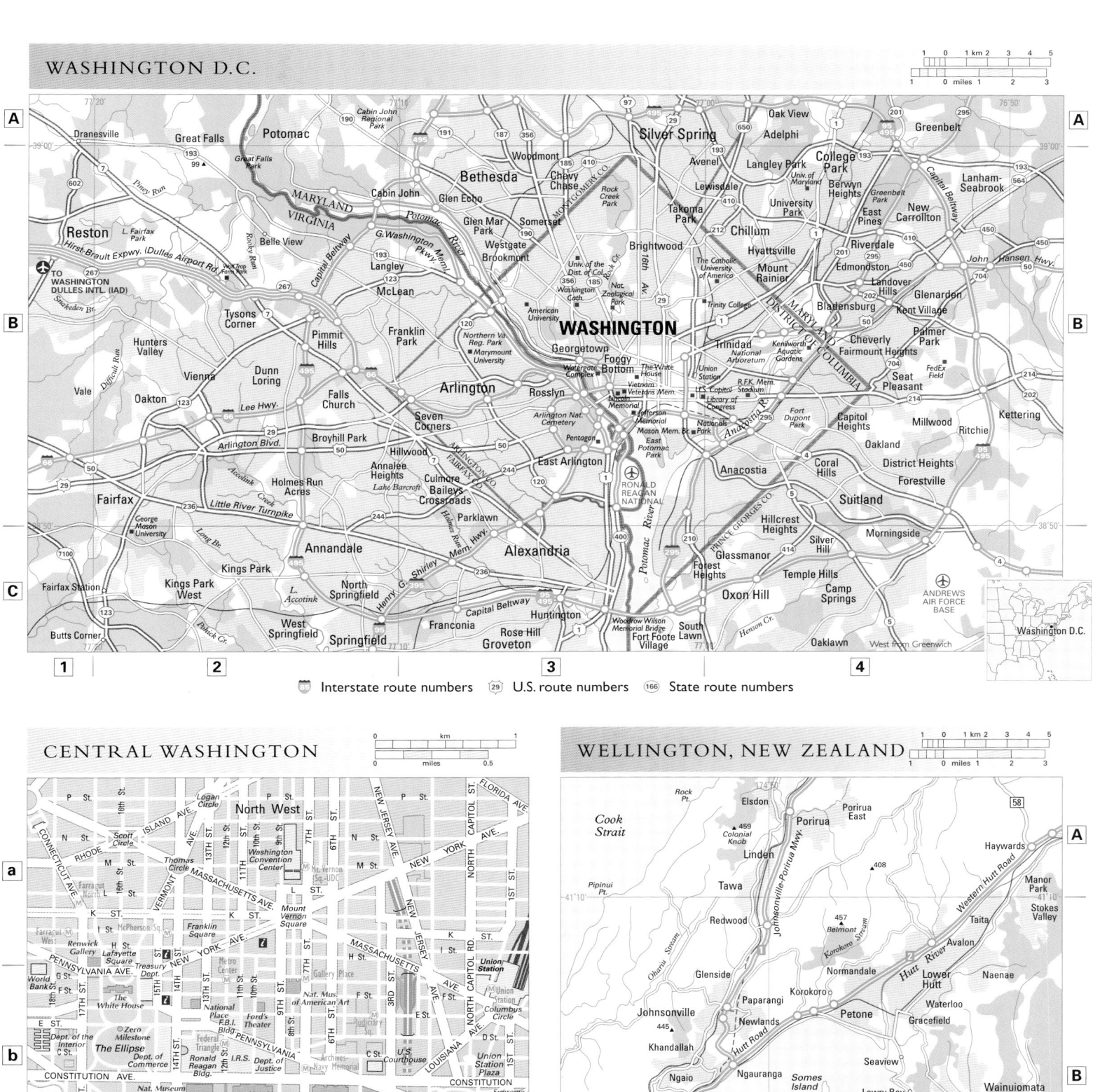

WASHINGTON D.C.

Interstate route numbers · U.S. route numbers · State route numbers

CENTRAL WASHINGTON

WELLINGTON, NEW ZEALAND

COPYRIGHT PHILIP'S

INDEX TO CITY MAPS

The index contains the names of all the principal places and features shown on the City Maps. Each name is followed by an additional entry in italics giving the name of the City Map within which it is located.

The number in bold type which follows each name refers to the number of the City Map page where that feature or place will be found.

The letter and figure which are immediately after the page number give the grid square on the map within which the feature or place is situated.

The letter represents the latitude and the figure the longitude. The full geographic reference is provided in the border of the City Maps.

The location given is the centre of the city, suburb or feature and is not necessarily the name. Rivers, canals and roads are indexed to their name. Rivers carry the symbol → after their name.

An explanation of the alphabetical order rules and a list of the abbreviations used are to be found at the beginning of the World Map Index.

A

Aalām Baghdad 3 B2
Aalsmeer Amsterdam 2 B1
Abbey Wood London 15 B4
Abcoude Amsterdam 2 B2
Ābdîn Cairo 7 A2
Abeno Osaka 23 B2
Aberdeen Hong Kong 12 B1
Aberdour Edinburgh 11 A2
Aberdour Castle Edinburgh 11 A2
Abfanggraben → Munich 21 A3
Ablon-sur-Seine Paris 24 B3
Abramtsevo Moscow 19 B3
Abu Dis Jerusalem 13 B2
Abû en Numrus Cairo 7 B2
Abu Ghosh Jerusalem 13 B1
Acassuso Buenos Aires 7 A2
Accotink, L. Washington 33 C2
Accotink Cr. → Washington 33 B2
Achères Paris 24 A1
Acilia Rome 26 C1
Aclimação São Paulo 27 B2
Acropolis Athens 2 B2
Acton London 15 A2
Açúcar, Pão de Rio de Janeiro 25 B2
Ada Beja Lisbon 16 A1
Adams Park Atlanta 3 B2
Addiscombe London 15 B3
Adelphi Washington 33 A4
Aderklaa Vienna 32 A3
Adler Planetarium Chicago 9 B3
Admiralteyskaya Storona St. Petersburg 27 B2
Àffori Milan 19 A2
Aflandshage Copenhagen 8 B3
Afsarīyeh Tehran 31 B2
Agboyi Cr. → Lagos 14 A2
Ågerup Copenhagen 8 A1
Ågesta Stockholm 29 B2
Aghia Marina Athens 2 C3
Aghia Paraskevi Athens 2 A2
Aghios Dimitrios Athens 2 B2
Aghios Ioannis Rendis Athens 2 B1
Agincourt Toronto 31 A3
Agra Canal Delhi 10 B2
Agricola Oriental Mexico City 18 B2
Água Espraiada → São Paulo 27 B2
Agualva-Cacem Lisbon 16 A1
Ahrensfelde Berlin 5 A4
Ahuntsic Montreal 20 A1
Ai → Osaka 23 A2
Aigremont Paris 24 A1
Air View Park Singapore 28 A2
Airport West Melbourne 18 A1
Ajegunle Lagos 14 B2
Aji Osaka 23 A1
Ajuda Lisbon 16 A1
Akalla Stockholm 29 A1
Akasaka Tokyo 30 A3
Akbarābād Tehran 31 A2
Akershus Slott Oslo 23 A3
Al 'Āzamīyah Baghdad 3 A2
Al Quds = Jerusalem Jerusalem 13 B2
Al-Walaja Jerusalem 13 B1
Alaguntan Lagos 14 B2
Alameda San Francisco 26 B3
Alameda Memorial State Beach Park San Francisco 26 B3
Albern Vienna 32 B2
Albert Park Melbourne 18 B1
Alberton Johannesburg 13 B2
Albertslund Copenhagen 8 B2
Alcantara Lisbon 16 A1
Alcatraz I. San Francisco 26 B2
Alcobendas Madrid 17 A2
Alcorcón Madrid 17 B1
Aldershof Berlin 5 B4
Aldo Bonzi Buenos Aires 7 C1
Aleksandrovskoye St. Petersburg 27 B2
Alexander Nevsky Abbey St. Petersburg 27 B2
Alexandra Johannesburg 13 A2
Alexandra Singapore 28 B2
Alexandria Washington 33 C3
Alfortville Paris 24 B3
Algés Lisbon 16 A1
Algiers New Orleans 21 B2
Alhambra Los Angeles 16 B4
Alibey → Istanbul 12 B1
Alibey Barajı Istanbul 12 B1
Alibeyköy Istanbul 12 B1
Alimos Athens 2 B2
Alipur Kolkata 14 B1
Allach Munich 21 A1
Allambie Heights Sydney 29 A2
Allermuir Hill Edinburgh 11 B2
Allstate Arena Chicago 9 A1
Allston Boston 6 A2
Almada Lisbon 16 A2
Almagro Buenos Aires 7 B2
Almargem do Bispo Lisbon 16 A1
Almirante G. Brown, Parque Buenos Aires 7 C2
Almon Jerusalem 13 B2
Almond → Edinburgh 11 B2
Alna Oslo 23 A4
Alnsjøen Oslo 23 A4
Alperton London 15 A2
Alpine New York 22 A2
Alrode Johannesburg 13 B2
Alsemberg Brussels 6 B2
Alsergrund Vienna 32 A2
Alsip Chicago 9 C2
Ålsten Stockholm 29 B1
Älta Stockholm 29 B3
Altadena Los Angeles 16 A4
Alte-Donau → Vienna 32 A2
Alter Finkenkrug Berlin 5 A1
Altes Rathaus Munich 21 B2
Altglienicke Berlin 5 B4
Altlandsberg Berlin 5 A5
Altlandsberg Nord Berlin 5 A5
Altmannsdorf Vienna 32 B1
Alto da Boa Vista Rio de Janeiro 25 B1
Alto da Moóca São Paulo 27 B2
Alto do Pina Lisbon 16 A2
Altona Melbourne 18 B1
Alvik Stockholm 29 B1
Alvin Callendar Naval Air Station New Orleans 21 B2
Älvsjö Stockholm 29 B2
Älvvik Stockholm 29 A3
Am Hasenbergl Munich 21 A2
Am Steinhof Vienna 32 A1
Am Wald Munich 21 B2
Ama Keng Singapore 28 A2
Amadora Lisbon 16 A1
Amagasaki Osaka 23 A1
Amager Copenhagen 8 B3
Amāl Qādisiya Baghdad 3 B2
Amalienborg Slot Copenhagen 8 A3
Amata Milan 19 A1
Ambelokipi Athens 2 B2
Ameixoeira Lisbon 16 A2
América São Paulo 27 B1
American Police Hall of Fame Miami 18 B2
American Univ. Washington 33 B3
Amin Baghdad 3 B2
Aminadav Jerusalem 13 B1
Amīrābād Tehran 31 A2
Amora Lisbon 16 B2
Amoreira Lisbon 16 A1
Amper → Munich 21 A1
Amstel-Drecht-Kanaal Amsterdam 2 B2
Amstelveen Amsterdam 2 B2
Amsterdam Amsterdam 2 A2
Amsterdam ✕ (AMS) Amsterdam 2 B1
Amsterdam-Rijnkanaal Amsterdam 2 B3
Amsterdam Zuidoost Amsterdam 2 B2
Amsterdamse Bos Amsterdam 2 B1
Anacosta → Washington 33 B4
Anacostia Washington 33 B4
Anadoluhisarı Istanbul 12 B2
Anadolukavağı Istanbul 12 A2
Anata Jerusalem 13 B2
Ancol Jakarta 12 A1
'Andalus Baghdad 3 B1
Andaraí Rio de Janeiro 25 B1
Anderlecht Brussels 6 A1
Anderson Park Atlanta 3 B2
Andingmen Beijing 4 B2
Ang Mo Kio Singapore 28 A3
Ängby Stockholm 29 A1
Angel I. San Francisco 26 A2
Angel Island State Park ⌂ San Francisco 26 A2
Angke, Kali → Jakarta 12 A1
Angyalföld Budapest 7 A2
Anik Mumbai 20 A2
Anin Warsaw 32 B2
Anjou Montreal 20 A2
Annalee Heights Washington 33 B2
Annandale Washington 33 C2
Anne Frankhuis Amsterdam 2 A2
Antony Paris 24 B2
Aoyama Tokyo 30 B3
Ap Lei Chau Hong Kong 12 B1
Apapa Lagos 14 B2
Apapa Quays Lagos 14 B2
Apelação Lisbon 16 A2
Apopka, L. Orlando 23 A1
Apoquindo Santiago 27 B2
Apterkarskiy Ostrov St. Petersburg 27 B2
Ar Kazimiyah Baghdad 3 B1
Ar Ram Jerusalem 13 A2
Ara → Tokyo 30 A4
Arakawa Tokyo 30 A3
Arany-hegyi-patak → Budapest 7 A2
Aravaca Madrid 17 B1
Arbataash Baghdad 3 A1
Arc de Triomphe Paris 24 A2
Arcadia Los Angeles 16 B4
Arcueil Paris 24 B2
Arese Milan 19 A1
Arganzuela Madrid 17 B1
Argenteuil Paris 24 A2
Argiroupoli Athens 2 B2
Argonne Forest Chicago 9 C1
Arima Tokyo 30 B2
Arlanda, Stockholm ✕ (ARN) Stockholm 29 A1
Arlington Boston 6 A1
Arlington Washington 33 B3
Arlington Heights Boston 6 A1
Arlington Nat. Cemetery Washington 33 B3
Armação Rio de Janeiro 25 B2
Armadale Melbourne 18 B2
Armour Heights Toronto 31 A2
Arncliffe Sydney 29 B1
Arnold Arboretum Boston 6 B2
Árpádföld Budapest 7 A3
Arrentela Lisbon 16 B2
Arroyo Seco Park Los Angeles 16 B3
Årsta Stockholm 29 B2
Artane Dublin 10 A2
Artas Jerusalem 13 B2
Arthur's Seat Edinburgh 11 B3
Arts, Place des Montreal 20 A2
As Shawawra Jerusalem 13 B2
Asagaya Tokyo 30 A2
Asahi Osaka 23 A2
Asakusa Tokyo 30 A3
Asati Kolkata 14 C1
Aschheim Munich 21 A3
Ascot Vale Melbourne 18 A1
Ashbridge's Bay Park Toronto 31 B3
Ashburn Chicago 9 C2
Ashburton Melbourne 18 B2
Ashfield Sydney 29 B1
Ashford London 15 B1
Ashtown Dublin 10 A2
Askisto Helsinki 11 B1
Askrikefjärden Stockholm 29 A3
Asnières Paris 24 A2
Aspern Vienna 32 A2
Assago Milan 19 B1
Assendelft Amsterdam 2 A1
Assiano Milan 19 B1
Astoria New York 22 B2
Astrolabe Park Sydney 29 B2
Atarot Jerusalem 13 A2
Atarot ✕ (JRS) Jerusalem 13 A2
Atghara Kolkata 14 B2
Athens = Athina Athens 2 B2
Athina Athens 2 B2
Athina ✕ (ATH) Athens 2 A3
Athinai = Athina Athens 2 B2
Athis-Mons Paris 24 B3
Athlone Cape Town 8 A2
Atholl Johannesburg 13 A2
Atīfiya Baghdad 3 A2
Atişalen Istanbul 12 B1
Atlanta Atlanta 3 B2
Atlanta Hartsfield Int. ✕ (ATL) Atlanta 3 C2
Atlanta Zoo Atlanta 3 B2
Atomium Brussels 6 A2
Attiki Athens 2 A2
Atzgersdorf Vienna 32 B1
Aubervilliers Paris 24 A3
Aubing Munich 21 B1
Auburndale Boston 6 A1
Auchendinny Edinburgh 11 B2
Auckland Park Johannesburg 13 B2
Auderghem Brussels 6 B2
Augustówka Warsaw 32 B2
Aulnay-sous-Bois Paris 24 A3
Aurelio Rome 26 B1
Ausîm Cairo 7 A1
Austerlitz, Gare d' Paris 24 A3
Austin Chicago 9 B2
Avalon Wellington 33 B2
Avedøre Copenhagen 8 B2
Avellaneda Buenos Aires 7 C2
Avenel Washington 33 B4
Avondale Chicago 9 B2
Avondale New Orleans 21 B1
Avondale Heights Melbourne 18 A1
Avtovo St. Petersburg 27 B1
Ayazağa Istanbul 12 B1
Ayer Chawan, Pulau Singapore 28 B2
Ayer Merbau, Pulau Singapore 28 B2
Azabu Tokyo 30 B3
Azcapotzalco Mexico City 18 B1
Azteca, Estadia Mexico City 18 C2
Azucar, Cerro Pan de Santiago 27 A1

B

Baambrugge Amsterdam 2 B2
Baba Channel Karachi 13 B1
Baba I. Karachi 13 B1
Babarpur Delhi 10 A2
Babushkin Moscow 19 A3
Back B. Mumbai 20 B1
Baclaran Manila 17 B2
Bacoor Manila 17 C1
Bacoor B. Manila 17 C1
Badalona Barcelona 4 A2
Badhoevedorp Amsterdam 2 A1
Badli Delhi 10 A1
Bærum Oslo 23 A2
Bağcılar Istanbul 12 B1
Bàggio Milan 19 B1
Bāgh-e-Feyz Tehran 31 A1
Baghdād Baghdad 3 A2
Baghdād al Muthana ✕ (BGW) Baghdad 3 B2
Baghdad Int. ✕ (SDA) Baghdad 3 B1
Bagmari Kolkata 14 B2
Bagneux Paris 24 B2
Bagnolet Paris 24 A3
Bagsværd Copenhagen 8 A2
Bagsværd Sø Copenhagen 8 A2
Baguiati Kolkata 14 B2
Bagumbayan Manila 17 C2
Baha'i Temple Chicago 9 A2
Bahçeköy Istanbul 12 A1
Bahçelievler Istanbul 12 B1
Bahtîm Cairo 7 A2
Baile Átha Cliath = Dublin Dublin 10 A2
Baileys Crossroads Washington 33 B3
Bailly Paris 24 A1
Bairro Lopes Lisbon 16 A2
Baisha Guangzhou 11 B2
Baiyun Guangzhou 11 A2
Baiyun Hill Guangzhou 11 B2
Baiyun Mountain Scenic Area Guangzhou 11 A2
Bakırköy Istanbul 12 C1
Bal Harbor Miami 18 A2
Balara Manila 17 B2
Baldia Karachi 13 A1
Baldoyle Dublin 10 A3
Baldwin, L. Orlando 23 A3
Baldwin Hills Los Angeles 16 B2
Baldwin Hills Res. Los Angeles 16 B2
Balgowlah Sydney 29 A2
Balgowlah Heights Sydney 29 A2
Balham London 15 B3
Bali Kolkata 14 B1
Baliganja Kolkata 14 B2
Balingsnäs Stockholm 29 B2
Balingsta Stockholm 29 B2
Balintawak Manila 17 B1
Ballerup Copenhagen 8 A2
Ballinteer Dublin 10 B2
Ballyboden Dublin 10 B2
Ballybrack Dublin 10 B3
Ballyfermot Dublin 10 A1
Ballymorefinn Hill Dublin 10 B1
Ballymun Dublin 10 A2
Balmain Sydney 29 B2
Baluhati Kolkata 14 B1
Balvanera Buenos Aires 7 B2
Balwyn Melbourne 18 A2
Balwyn North Melbourne 18 A2
Banática Lisbon 16 A1
Bandra Mumbai 20 A1
Bandra Pt. Mumbai 20 A1
Bang Kapi Bangkok 3 B2
Bang Na Bangkok 3 B2
Bangbae Seoul 27 C1
Bangkhen Bangkok 3 A2
Bangkok Bangkok 3 B2
Bangkok Don Muang Int. ✕ (BKK) Bangkok 3 A2
Bangkok Noi Bangkok 3 B1
Bangkok Yai Bangkok 3 B1
Banglo Kolkata 14 B1
Bangrak Bangkok 3 B2
Bangsu Bangkok 3 B2
Banks, C. Sydney 29 C2
Banksmeadow Sydney 29 B2
Banstala Kolkata 14 B2
Bantra Kolkata 14 B1
Baoshan Shanghai 28 A1
Bar Giyora Jerusalem 13 B1
Barahanagar Kolkata 14 B2
Barajas Madrid 17 B2
Barajas, Madrid ✕ (MAD) Madrid 17 B2
Barakpur Kolkata 14 A2
Barcarena Lisbon 16 A1
Barcarena, Rib. de → Lisbon 16 A1
Barcelona Barcelona 4 A2
Barcelona-Prat ✕ (BCN) Barcelona 4 B1
Barcroft, L. Washington 33 B3
Barking London 15 A4
Barkingside London 15 A4
Barnes London 15 B2
Barnet London 15 A2
Barra Andai Karachi 13 B2
Barra Funda São Paulo 27 B2
Barracas Buenos Aires 7 B2
Barrackpur = Barakpur Kolkata 14 A2
Barranco Lima 14 B2
Barreiro Lisbon 16 B2
Barreto Rio de Janeiro 25 B2
Bartala Kolkata 14 B1
Barton Park Sydney 29 B1
Bartyki Warsaw 32 C2
Basus Cairo 7 A2
Batanagar Kolkata 14 B1
Bath Beach New York 22 C1
Bath I. Karachi 13 B2
Batir Jerusalem 13 B1
Batok, Bukit Singapore 28 A2
Battersea London 15 B3
Bauman Moscow 19 B3
Baumgarten Vienna 32 A1
Bay, L. Orlando 23 A2
Bay Harbor Islands Miami 18 A2
Bay Hill Orlando 23 B1
Bay Ridge New York 22 C1
Bayit Va-Gan Jerusalem 13 B2
Bayonne New York 22 B1
Bayou Boeuf New Orleans 21 B1
Bayou Segnette State Park ⌂ New Orleans 21 B2
Bayrampaşa Istanbul 12 B1
Bayshore San Francisco 26 B2
Bayt Lahm Jerusalem 13 B2
Bayview San Francisco 26 B2
Bāzār Tehran 31 A2
Beacon Hill Hong Kong 12 A2
Beato Lisbon 16 A2
Beaumont Dublin 10 A2
Beaumonte Heights Toronto 31 A1
Bebek Istanbul 12 B2
Bĕchovice Prague 25 B3
Beck L. Chicago 9 A1
Beckenham London 15 B3
Beckton London 15 A4
Becontree London 15 A4
Beddington Corner London 15 B3
Bedford Boston 6 A1
Bedford Park Chicago 9 C2
Bedford Park New York 22 A2
Bedford Stuyvesant New York 22 B2
Bedford View Johannesburg 13 B2
Bedok Singapore 28 B3
Bedok, Res. Singapore 28 A3
Beersel Brussels 6 B1
Behala Kolkata 14 B1
Bei Hai Beijing 4 B2
Beicai Shanghai 28 B2
Beijing Beijing 4 B1
Beit Duqu Jerusalem 13 A1
Beit Ghur at-Taht Jerusalem 13 A1
Beit Ghur el-Fawqa Jerusalem 13 A1
Beit Hanina Jerusalem 13 B2
Beit Ij'za Jerusalem 13 A1
Beit Iksa Jerusalem 13 B2
Beit I'nan Jerusalem 13 A1
Beit Jala Jerusalem 13 B2
Beit Lekhem = Bayt Lahm Jerusalem 13 B2
Beit Liqya Jerusalem 13 A1
Beit Nekofa Jerusalem 13 B1
Beit Sahur Jerusalem 13 B2
Beit Sofafa Jerusalem 13 B2
Beit Surik Jerusalem 13 B1
Beit Ur al-Fawqa Jerusalem 13 A1
Beit Zayit Jerusalem 13 B1
Beitaipingzhuan Beijing 4 B1
Beitar Illit Jerusalem 13 B1
Beitin Jerusalem 13 A2
Beitsun Guangzhou 11 B2
Beitunya Jerusalem 13 A2
Beixing Jing Park Shanghai 28 B1
Békásmegyer Budapest 7 A2
Bekkelaget Oslo 23 A3
Bekkestua Oslo 23 A2
Bel Air Los Angeles 16 B2
Bela Vista São Paulo 27 B2
Bélanger Montreal 20 A1
Belas Lisbon 16 A1
Beleghata Kolkata 14 B2
Belém Lisbon 16 A1
Belém, Torre de Lisbon 16 A1
Belênzinho São Paulo 27 B2
Belgachiya Kolkata 14 B2
Belgharia Kolkata 14 B2
Belgrano Buenos Aires 7 B2
Bell Los Angeles 16 C3
Bell Gardens Los Angeles 16 C4
Bellavista Lima 14 B2
Bellavista Santiago 27 C2
Belle Harbor New York 22 C2
Belle Isle Orlando 23 B2
Belle View Washington 33 B2
Bellingham London 15 B3
Bellwood Chicago 9 B1
Belmont Boston 6 A1
Belmont London 15 A2
Belmont, Mt. Wellington 33 B2
Belmont Cragin Chicago 9 B2
Belmont Harbor Chicago 9 B3
Belmore Sydney 29 B1
Belur Kolkata 14 B2
Belvedere Atlanta 3 B3
Belvedere London 15 B4
Belvedere San Francisco 26 A2
Belyayevo Bogorodskoye Moscow 19 C2
Bemowo Warsaw 32 B1
Benaki Museum Athens 2 B2
Bendale Toronto 31 A3
Benefica Rio de Janeiro 25 B1
Benfica Lisbon 16 A1
Benitez Int. ✕ (SCL) Santiago 27 B1
Benito Juárez, Int. ✕ (MEX) Mexico City 18 B2
Bensonhurst New York 22 C2
Berchem-Ste-Agathe Brussels 6 A1
Berg am Laim Munich 21 B2
Bergenfield New York 22 A2
Bergham Munich 21 B2
Bergvliet Cape Town 8 B1
Beri Barcelona 4 A1
Berkeley San Francisco 26 A3
Berlin Berlin 5 A3
Berlin Dom Berlin 5 A3
Berlin Tegel ✕ (TXL) Berlin 5 A2
Bermondsey London 15 B3
Bernabeu, Estadio Madrid 17 B1
Bernal Heights San Francisco 26 B2
Berwyn Chicago 9 B2
Berwyn Heights Washington 33 B4
Besiktas Istanbul 12 B2
Besós → Barcelona 4 A2
Bessie, L. Orlando 23 B1
Bet Horon Jerusalem 13 A1
Bethesda Washington 33 B3
Bethlehem = Bayt Lahm Jerusalem 13 B2
Bethnal Green London 15 A3
Betor Kolkata 14 B1
Beulah Orlando 23 B1
Beulah, L. Orlando 23 A1
Beverley Hills Sydney 29 B1
Beverley Park Sydney 29 B1
Beverly Chicago 9 C3
Beverly Arts Center Chicago 9 C2
Beverly Glen Los Angeles 16 B2
Beverly Hills Los Angeles 16 B2
Beverly Hills -Morgan Park Historic District Chicago 9 C2
Bexley Sydney 29 B1
Bexley □ London 15 B4
Bexleyheath London 15 B4
Beykoz Istanbul 12 B2
Beylerbeyi Istanbul 12 B2
Beyoğlu Istanbul 12 B1
Bezons Paris 24 A2
Bezuidenhout Park Johannesburg 13 B2
Bhadrakali Kolkata 14 A2
Bhalswa Delhi 10 A2
Bhambo Khan Qarmati Karachi 13 B2
Bhatsala Kolkata 14 B1
Bhawanipur Kolkata 14 B2
Bhendkhal Mumbai 20 B2
Bhuleshwar Mumbai 20 B1
Białołeka Dworska Warsaw 32 B2
Bicentennial Park Los Angeles 16 B4
Bicentennial Park Sydney 29 B1
Bickley London 15 B4
Bicutan Manila 17 C2
Bidhan Nagar Kolkata 14 B2
Bidu Jerusalem 13 B1
Bielany Warsaw 32 B1
Bielawa Warsaw 32 C2
Biesdorf Berlin 5 A4
Bièvre → Paris 24 B1
Bièvres Paris 24 B2
Big Sand Lake Orlando 23 B2
Bilston Edinburgh 11 B2
Binacayan Manila 17 C1
Binondo Manila 17 B1
Bintaro Jaya Jakarta 12 B1
Bir Nabala Jerusalem 13 A2
Birak el Kiyam Cairo 7 A1
Birch Cliff Toronto 31 A3
Birkenstein Berlin 5 A5
Birkholz Berlin 5 A4
Birkholzaue Berlin 5 A4
Birrarung Park Melbourne 18 A2
Biscayne Park Miami 18 A2
Bishop Lavis Cape Town 8 A2
Bishopscourt Cape Town 8 A1
Bispebjerg Copenhagen 8 A3
Bissonet Plaza New Orleans 21 A1
Bittsevsky Forest Park Moscow 19 C2
Björknas Stockholm 29 B3
Black Cr. → Toronto 31 A2
Black Creek Pioneer Village Toronto 31 A1
Blackfen London 15 B4
Blackheath London 15 B4
Blackrock Dublin 10 B2
Bladensburg Washington 33 B4
Blair Village Atlanta 3 C2
Blairgowrie Johannesburg 13 A2
Blake House Boston 6 B2
Blakehurst Sydney 29 B1
Blakstad Oslo 23 B1
Blanche, L. Orlando 23 B1
Blankenburg Berlin 5 A3
Blankenfelde Berlin 5 A3
Blizne Warsaw 32 B1
Blota Warsaw 32 C3
Blue Island Chicago 9 D2
Blue Mosque = Sultanahme Camil Istanbul 12 B1
Bluebell Dublin 10 B1
Bluff Hd. Hong Kong 12 B2
Bluffers Park Toronto 31 A3
Blumberg Berlin 5 A4
Blunt Pt. San Francisco 26 A2
Blutenberg Munich 21 B1
Blylaget Oslo 23 B3
Boa Vista, Alto do Rio de Janeiro 25 B1
Boardwalk New York 22 C3
Boavista Lisbon 16 A2
Bobigny Paris 24 A3
Bocanegra Lima 14 B2
Boedo Buenos Aires 7 B2
Bogenhausen Munich 21 B2
Bogorodskoye Moscow 19 B3
Bogota New York 22 A1
Bogstadvatnet Oslo 23 A2
Bohnsdorf Berlin 5 B4
Bois-Colombes Paris 24 A2
Bois-d'Arcy Paris 24 B1
Boissy-St-Léger Paris 24 B4
Boldinasco Milan 19 B1
Bøler Oslo 23 A4
Bollate Milan 19 A1
Bollebeek Brussels 6 A1
Bollensdorf Berlin 5 A5
Bollmora Stockholm 29 B3
Bolshaya Okhta St. Petersburg 27 B2
Bolton Atlanta 3 B2
Bom Retiro São Paulo 27 B2
Bombay = Mumbai Mumbai 20 B2
Bondi Sydney 29 B2
Bondy Paris 24 A3
Bondy, Forêt de Paris 24 A4
Bonifacio Monument Manila 17 B1
Bonnabel Place New Orleans 21 A2
Bonneuil-sur-Marne Paris 24 B4
Bonnington Edinburgh 11 B1
Bonnyrigg and Lasswade Edinburgh 11 B3
Bonsucesso Rio de Janeiro 25 B1
Bonteheuwel Cape Town 8 A2
Boo Stockholm 29 A3
Booterstown Dublin 10 B2
Borisovo Moscow 19 C3
Borle Mumbai 20 A2
Boronia Park Sydney 29 A1
Bosmont Johannesburg 13 B1
Bosön Stockholm 29 A3
Bosporus = İstanbul Boğazı Istanbul 12 B2
Bostancı Istanbul 12 C2
Boston Boston 6 A2
Boston Common Boston 6 A2
Boston Logan Int. ✕ (BOS) Boston 6 A2
Botafogo Rio de Janeiro 25 B1
Botany Sydney 29 B2
Botany B. Sydney 29 B2
Botany Bay △ Sydney 29 B2
Botič → Prague 25 B3
Botica Sete Lisbon 16 A1
Boucherville Montreal 20 A3
Boucherville, Îs. de Montreal 20 A3
Bougival Paris 24 A1
Boulder Pt. Hong Kong 12 B1
Boulogne, Bois de Paris 24 A2
Boulogne-Billancourt Paris 24 A2
Bourg-la-Reine Paris 24 B2
Bouviers Paris 24 B1
Bovenkerk Amsterdam 2 B2
Bovenkerker Polder Amsterdam 2 B2
Bovisa Milan 19 A2
Bow London 15 A3
Boyacıköy Istanbul 12 B2
Boyd Conservation Area Toronto 31 A1
Boyle Heights Los Angeles 16 B3
Braepark Edinburgh 11 B2
Braid Edinburgh 11 B2
Bramley Johannesburg 13 A2
Brandeis Univ. Boston 6 A1
Brandenburger Tor Berlin 5 A3
Brani, Pulau Singapore 28 B3
Branik Prague 25 B2
Brännkyrka Stockholm 29 B2
Brás São Paulo 27 B2
Brasilândia São Paulo 27 A1
Brateyevo Moscow 19 C3
Braybrook Melbourne 18 A1
Brązdim Prague 25 A3
Breakheart Reservation Boston 6 A2
Brede Copenhagen 8 A3
Breezy Point New York 22 C2
Breitenlee Vienna 32 A3
Breña Lima 14 B2
Brent □ London 15 A2
Brent Res. London 15 A2
Brentford London 15 B2
Brentwood Los Angeles 16 B2
Brentwood Park Los Angeles 16 B2
Brera Milan 19 B2
Bresso Milan 19 A2
Brevik Stockholm 29 A3
Břevnov Prague 25 B2
Brickyard, The Chicago 9 B2
Bridge City New Orleans 21 B2
Bridgeport Chicago 9 B3
Bridgetown Cape Town 8 A2
Bridgeview Chicago 9 C2
Brighton Boston 6 A2
Brighton Melbourne 18 B1
Brighton Beach New York 22 C2
Brighton-Le-Sands Sydney 29 B1
Brighton Park Chicago 9 C2
Brightwood Washington 33 B3
Brigittenau Vienna 32 A2
Brimbank Park Melbourne 18 A1
Brisbane San Francisco 26 B2
Britz Berlin 5 B3
Brixton London 15 B3
Broadmeadows Melbourne 18 A1
Broadmoor San Francisco 26 B2
Broadview Chicago 9 B1
Brockley London 15 B3
Bródno Warsaw 32 B2
Bródnowski, Kanal Warsaw 32 B2
Broek Amsterdam 2 A2
Bromley □ London 15 B4
Bromley Common London 15 B4
Bromma Stockholm 29 A1
Bromma ✕ (BMA) Stockholm 29 A1
Brøndby Strand Copenhagen 8 B2
Brøndbyøster Copenhagen 8 B2
Brøndbyvester Copenhagen 8 B2
Brondesbury London 15 A2
Brønnøya Oslo 23 A2
Brønshøj Copenhagen 8 A2
Bronxville New York 22 A3
Brookfield Chicago 9 C1
Brookhaven Atlanta 3 A2
Brookline Boston 6 B2
Brooklyn Cape Town 8 A1
Brooklyn New York 22 C2
Brooklyn Wellington 33 B1
Brooklyn Heights New York 22 B2
Brookmont Washington 33 B3
Brossard Montreal 20 B3
Brou-sur-Chantereine Paris 24 A4
Brown Toronto 31 A3
Brownhill Park Washington 33 B2
Brugherio Milan 19 A2
Brunswick Melbourne 18 A1
Brussegem Brussels 6 A1
Brussel Brussels 6 A2
Brussel ✕ (BRU) Brussels 6 A2
Brussels = Brussel Brussels 6 A2
Bruxelles = Brussel Brussels 6 A2
Bruzzano Milan 19 A2
Bry-sur-Marne Paris 24 A4
Bryan, L. Orlando 23 B2
Bryanston Johannesburg 13 A1
Bryn Oslo 23 A1
Brzeziny Warsaw 32 B2
Bubeneč Prague 25 B2
Buc Paris 24 B1
Buchenhain Munich 21 B1
Buchholz Berlin 5 A3
Buckhead Atlanta 3 A2
Buckingham Palace London 15 A3
Buckow Berlin 5 B3
Bucktown New Orleans 21 A2
Buda Budapest 7 A2
Buda Castle = Budaváripalota Budapest 7 A2
Budafok Budapest 7 B2
Budaörs Budapest 7 B1
Budapest Budapest 7 B2
Budapest ✕ (BUD) Budapest 7 B3
Budatétény Budapest 7 B2
Budaváripalota Budapest 7 A2
Buddinge Copenhagen 8 A3
Buena Vista San Francisco 26 B2
Buenos Aires Buenos Aires 7 B2
Buenos Aires Ezeiza ✕ (EZE) Buenos Aires 7 C1
Bufalotta Rome 26 B2
Bugio Lisbon 16 B1
Buiksloot Amsterdam 2 A2
Buitenveldert Amsterdam 2 B2
Buizingen Brussels 6 B1
Bukhansan Seoul 27 B1
Bukit Panjang Nature Reserve Singapore 28 A2
Bukit Timah Nature Reserve Singapore 28 A2
Bukum, Pulau Singapore 28 B2
Bûlâq Cairo 7 A2
Bule Manila 17 C2
Bulim Singapore 28 A2
Bullen Park Melbourne 18 A2
Bund, The Shanghai 28 B1
Bundoora North Melbourne 18 A2
Bundoora Park Melbourne 18 A2
Bunker Hill Memorial Boston 6 A2
Bunker I. Karachi 13 B1
Bunkyō Tokyo 30 A3
Bunnefjorden Oslo 23 A3
Buona Vista Park Singapore 28 B2
Burbank Chicago 9 C2
Burbank Los Angeles 16 A3
Burden, L. Orlando 23 B1
Burlington Boston 6 A1
Burnham Park Chicago 9 C3
Burnham Park Harbor Chicago 9 B3
Burnhamthorpe Toronto 31 B1
Burnt Oak London 15 A2
Burntisland Edinburgh 11 A2
Burnwynd Edinburgh 11 B1
Burqa Jerusalem 13 A2
Burtus Cairo 7 A1
Burudvatn Oslo 23 A2
Burwood Sydney 29 B1
Bushwick New York 22 B2
Bushy Park London 15 B1
Butantã São Paulo 27 B1
Butcher I. Mumbai 20 B2
Butler, L. Orlando 23 B1
Butts Corner Washington 33 C2
Büyükdere Istanbul 12 B2
Byculla Mumbai 20 B2
Bygdøy Oslo 23 A3
Bywater New Orleans 21 B2

C

C.B.S. Fox Studios Los Angeles 16 B2
C.N.N. Center Atlanta 3 B2
C.N. Tower Toronto 31 B2
Caballito Buenos Aires 7 B2
Cabin John Washington 33 B2
Cabin John Regional Park ⌂ Washington 33 A2
Cabinteely Dublin 10 B3
Cabra Dublin 10 A2
Cabuçú de Baixo → São Paulo 27 A1
Cabuçú de Cima → São Paulo 27 A2
Cachan Paris 24 B2
Cachoeira, Rib. da → São Paulo 27 B1
Cacilhas Lisbon 16 A2
Cahuenga Park Los Angeles 16 B3
Cain, L. Orlando 23 B2
Cairo = El Qâhira Cairo 7 A2
Cairo Int. ✕ (CAI) Cairo 7 A3
Caju Rio de Janeiro 25 B1
Čakovice Prague 25 B3
Calcutta = Kolkata Kolkata 14 B2
California Inst. of Tech. Los Angeles 16 B4
California Los Angeles, Univ. of Los Angeles 16 B2
California State Univ. Los Angeles 16 B3
Callao Lima 14 B1
Caloocan Manila 17 B1
Calumet L. Chicago 9 C3
Calumet Park Chicago 9 C3
Calumet Sag Channel → Chicago 9 C2
Calvairate Milan 19 B2
Camarate Lisbon 16 A2
Camaroes Lisbon 16 A1
Camberwell London 15 B3
Camberwell Melbourne 18 B2
Cambridge Boston 6 A2

Cambuci São Paulo 27 B2
Camden □ London 15 A3
Cameron, Mt. Wellington 33 B2
Çamlica Istanbul 12 B2
Camp Springs Washington 33 C4
Campamento Madrid 17 B1
Campbellfield Melbourne 18 A1
Camperdown Sydney 29 B2
Campo, Casa de Madrid 17 B1
Campo F.C. Barcelona Barcelona 4 A1
Campo Grande Lisbon 16 A2
Campo Pequeño Lisbon 16 A2
Campolide Lisbon 16 A2
Camps Bay Cape Town 8 A1
C'an San Joan Barcelona 4 A2
Cañacao B. Manila 17 C1
Canarsie New York 22 C2
Candiac Montreal 20 B3
Caneças Lisbon 16 A1
Canillas Madrid 17 B2
Canillejas Madrid 17 B2
Canning Town London 15 A4
Canteras de Vallecas Madrid 17 B2
Canterbury Melbourne 18 A2
Canterbury Sydney 29 B1
Canton = Guangzhou Guangzhou 11 B2
Caoheijing Shanghai 28 B1
Capão Redondo São Paulo 27 B1
Caparica Lisbon 16 A2
Caparica, Costa da Lisbon 16 B1
Cape Flats Cape Town 8 B2
Cape Town Cape Town 8 A1
Cape Town Int. ✕ (CPT) Cape Town 8 A2
Capitol Heights Washington 33 B4
Captain Cook Bridge Sydney 29 C1
Captain Cook Landing Place Park Sydney 29 C2
Capuchos Lisbon 16 B1
Carabanchel Alto Madrid 17 B1
Carabanchel Bajo Madrid 17 B1
Carapachay Buenos Aires 7 B1
Caraza Buenos Aires 7 C2
Caridad Manila 17 C1
Carioca, Sa. da Rio de Janeiro 25 B1
Carlstadt New York 22 A1
Carlton Melbourne 18 A1
Carmen de Huechuraba Santiago 27 B1
Carmen de la Legua Lima 14 B2
Carnaxide Lisbon 16 A1
Carnegie Melbourne 18 B2
Carnide Lisbon 16 A1
Carol City Miami 18 A1
Carrascal Santiago 27 B1
Carrickmines Dublin 10 B3
Carrières-sous-Bois Paris 24 A1
Carrières-sous-Poissy Paris 24 A1
Carrières-sur-Seine Paris 24 A2
Carrigeen B. Dublin 10 A3
Cartierville Montreal 20 A1
Casa Loma Toronto 31 A2
Casa Verde São Paulo 27 A1
Casal Morena Rome 26 C2
Casalotti Rome 26 B1
Cascade Heights Atlanta 3 B2
Castèl di Leva Rome 26 C2
Castèl Sant'Angelo Rome 26 B1
Castleknock Dublin 10 A1
Castleton Corners New York 22 C1
Cataouatche, L. New Orleans 21 B1
Catete Rio de Janeiro 25 B1
Catford London 15 B3
Catherine, L. Orlando 23 B2
Caulfield Melbourne 18 B2
Cavite Manila 17 C1
Caxias Lisbon 16 A1
Cebecci Istanbul 12 B1
Cecchignola Rome 26 C2
Cecilienhof, Schloss Berlin 5 B1
Cedar Grove Atlanta 3 C3
Cedarvale Park Toronto 31 A2
Cempaka Putih Jakarta 12 B2
Çengelköy Istanbul 12 B2
Cengkareng Jakarta 12 A1
Centennial Olympic Park Atlanta 3 B2
Centennial Park Sydney 29 B2
Center Hill Atlanta 3 B2
Centocelle Rome 26 B2
Central, Gare Montreal 20 B2
Central Park New York 22 B2
Century City Los Angeles 16 B2
Cerdanyola del Vallès Barcelona 4 A1
Cerillos Santiago 27 B1
Cerro de la Estrella △ Mexico City 18 B2
Cerro de los Angeles Madrid 17 C1
Cerro Navia Santiago 27 B1
Cesano Boscone Milan 19 B1
Cesate Milan 19 A1
Cha Kwo Ling Hong Kong 12 B2
Chacarita Buenos Aires 7 B2
Chadwell Heath London 15 A4
Chai Chee Singapore 28 B3
Chai Wan Hong Kong 12 B2
Chai Wan Kok Hong Kong 12 A1
Chakdaha Kolkata 14 C1
Chamartín Madrid 17 B1
Chamberi Madrid 17 B1
Chambourcy Paris 24 A1
Champigny-sur-Marne Paris 24 B4
Champlain, Pont Montreal 20 B2
Champs-sur-Marne Paris 24 A4
Chamrail Kolkata 14 B1
Chanakyapuri Delhi 10 B2
Chanditala Kolkata 14 A1
Changfeng Park Shanghai 28 B1
Changhai = Shanghai Shanghai 28 B2
Changi Singapore 28 A3
Changi, Singapore ✕ (SIN) Singapore 28 A3
Changning Shanghai 28 B1
Chantereine Paris 24 A4
Chantian Guangzhou 11 A2
Chaoyang Beijing 4 B2
Chaoyangmen Beijing 4 B2
Chapelizod Dublin 10 A1
Chapultepec, Bosque de Mexico City 18 B1
Chapultepec, Castillo de Mexico City 18 B1
Charenton-le-Pont Paris 24 B3
Charleroi, Kanal de → Brussels 6 B1
Charles Bridge = Karlův most Prague 25 B2
Charles Gates Dawes House Chicago 9 A2
Charlestown Boston 6 A2
Charlottenburg Berlin 5 A2
Charlottenburg, Schloss Berlin 5 A2
Charlottenlund Copenhagen 8 A3
Charlton London 15 B4
Charneca Lisbon 16 A2
Charneca Lisbon 16 B1
Chase, L. Orlando 23 B1
Châteaufort Paris 24 B1
Châtenay-Malabry Paris 24 B2
Chatham Chicago 9 C3
Châtillon Paris 24 B2
Chatou Paris 24 A1
Chatpur Kolkata 14 B2
Chatswood Sydney 29 A2
Chatuchak Bangkok 3 B2
Chatuchak Park Bangkok 3 B2
Chauki Karachi 13 A1
Chavarria Lima 14 B2
Chaville Paris 24 B2
Chayang Seoul 27 B2
Chelles Paris 24 A4
Chelles, Canal de Paris 24 A4
Chells-le-Pin ✕ Paris 24 A4
Chelsea Boston 6 A2
Chelsea London 15 B2
Chembur Mumbai 20 A2
Chengshousi Beijing 4 C2
Chennevières-sur-Marne Paris 24 B4
Cheongdam Seoul 27 B2
Cheonho Seoul 27 B2
Cheops Cairo 7 B1
Chertanovka → Moscow 19 C2
Chertanovo Moscow 19 C2
Cheryomushki Moscow 19 B2
Chestnut Hill Boston 6 B1
Cheung Sha Wan Hong Kong 12 A1
Cheverly Washington 33 B4
Chevilly-Larue Paris 24 B3
Cheviot Hills Los Angeles 16 B2
Chevy Chase Washington 33 B3
Chhatrapati Shivaji, Mumbai ✕ (BOM) Mumbai 20 A2
Chia Keng Singapore 28 A3
Chiaravalle Milanese Milan 19 B2
Chicago Chicago 9 B3
Chicago, Univ. of Chicago 9 C3
Chicago Harbor Chicago 9 B3
Chicago Lawn Chicago 9 C2
Chicago-Midway ✕ (MDW) Chicago 9 C2
Chicago O'Hare Int. ✕ (ORD) Chicago 9 B1
Chicago Ridge Chicago 9 C2
Chicago River, North Branch → Chicago 9 B2
Chicago Sanitary and Ship Canal Chicago 9 C2
Chicago State Univ. Chicago 9 C3
Chicago Zoo Chicago 9 B1
Chienzui Guangzhou 11 A3
Chik Sha Hong Kong 12 B2
Child's Hill London 15 A2
Chile, Univ. de Santiago 27 B2
Chilla Saroda Delhi 10 B2
Chillum Washington 33 B4
Chilly-Mazarin Paris 24 B2
Chingupota Kolkata 14 C1
Chinna Cr. → Karachi 13 B2
Chiquihuite, Cerro Mexico City 18 A2
Chislehurst London 15 B4
Chiswick London 15 B2
Chiswick House London 15 B2
Chitose Tokyo 30 B2
Chitralada Palace Bangkok 3 B2
Chiyoda Tokyo 30 A3
Choa Chu Kang Singapore 28 A2
Chodov u Prahy Prague 25 B3
Chōfu Tokyo 30 B2
Choisy-le-Roi Paris 24 B3
Cholupice Prague 25 C2
Chom Thong Bangkok 3 B1
Chong Pang Singapore 28 A2
Chongwen Beijing 4 B2
Chorrillos Lima 14 C2
Chowpatty Beach Mumbai 20 B1
Christianshavn Copenhagen 8 A3
Chrzanów Warsaw 32 B1
Chuen Lung Hong Kong 12 A1
Chuk Kok Hong Kong 12 A2
Chulalongkorn Univ. Bangkok 3 B2
Chuō Tokyo 30 A3
Church End London 15 A2
Church of our Lady = Frauenkirche Munich 21 B2
Churchtown Dublin 10 B2
Ciampino Rome 26 C2
Ciampino ✕ (CIA) Rome 26 C2
Cicero Chicago 9 B2
Cilandak Jakarta 12 B1
Cilincing Jakarta 12 A2
Ciliwung → Jakarta 12 B2
Čimice Prague 25 B2
Cinecittà Rome 26 B2
Cinisello Bálsamo Milan 19 A2
Cinkota Budapest 7 A3
Cipete Jakarta 12 B1
Citta degli Studi Milan 19 B2
Città del Vaticano = Vatican City ■ Rome 26 B1
City, The London 15 A3
City Hall = Rådhus Oslo 23 A3
City Hall = Stadshuset Stockholm 29 B2
City of the Dead Cairo 7 A2
City Park New Orleans 21 A2
City Terrace Los Angeles 16 B3
Ciudad de México Mexico City 18 B2
Ciudad Deportiva Mexico City 18 B2
Ciudad Fin de Semana Madrid 17 B2
Ciudad General Belgrano Buenos Aires 7 C1
Ciudad Lineál Madrid 17 B2
Ciudad Satélite Mexico City 18 A1
Ciudad Universitaria Buenos Aires 7 B2
Ciudad Universitaria Mexico City 18 C1
Claireville Res. Toronto 31 A1
Clamart Paris 24 B2
Clapham London 15 B3
Clapton London 15 A3
Claremont Cape Town 8 A1
Clayhall London 15 A4
Clear, L. Orlando 23 A2
Clermiston Edinburgh 11 B2
Clichy Paris 24 A2
Clichy-sous-Bois Paris 24 A4
Cliffside Toronto 31 A3
Cliffside Park New York 22 B2
Clifton Cape Town 8 A1
Clifton Karachi 13 B2
Clifton New York 22 C1
Clifton Beach Karachi 13 B2
Cliftondale Boston 6 A2
Cloghran Dublin 10 A2
Clonskeagh Dublin 10 B2
Clontarf Dublin 10 A2
Clontarf Sydney 29 A2
Clovelly Sydney 29 B2
Cobras, I. das Rio de Janeiro 25 B2
Coburg Melbourne 18 A1
Cocotá Rio de Janeiro 25 A1
Cœuilly Paris 24 B4
Coina Lisbon 16 B2
Coker Lagos 14 B2
Colaba Mumbai 20 B1
Colaba Pt. Mumbai 20 B1
Colegiales Buenos Aires 7 B2
Colindale London 15 A2
Colinton Edinburgh 11 B2
College Park Atlanta 3 C2
College Park Washington 33 B4
College Point New York 22 B2
Collégien Paris 24 A4
Collier Row London 15 A4
Colliers Wood London 15 B2
Colma San Francisco 26 B2
Colney Hatch London 15 A3
Cologno Monzese Milan 19 A2
Colombes Paris 24 A2
Colonia Güell Barcelona 4 A1
Colonial Knob Wellington 33 A1
Colosseo Rome 26 B1
Colosseum = Colosseo Rome 26 B1
Combault Paris 24 B4
Comércio, Praça do Lisbon 16 A2
Commerce Los Angeles 16 B4
Conceição, I. da Rio de Janeiro 25 B2
Conchali Santiago 27 B2
Concord Sydney 29 B1
Concord Toronto 31 A2
Concorde, Place de la Paris 24 A2
Concorezzo Milan 19 A2
Condet Jakarta 12 A2
Coney Island New York 22 C2
Congonhas São Paulo ✕ (CGH) São Paulo 27 B2
Conley → Atlanta 3 C3
Connaught Place Delhi 10 B2
Consolação São Paulo 27 B2
Constantia Cape Town 8 B1
Constitución Buenos Aires 7 B2
Constitution Atlanta 3 B2
Convention Center Los Angeles 16 B3
Conway Orlando 23 B2
Conway, L. Orlando 23 B2
Coogee Sydney 29 B2
Cooksville Toronto 31 B1
Coolock Dublin 10 A2
Copacabana Rio de Janeiro 25 B1
Copenhagen = København Copenhagen 8 A2
Coral Gables Miami 18 B2
Coral Hills Washington 33 B4
Corcovado, Cristo Redentor Rio de Janeiro 25 B1
Corduff Dublin 10 A1
Cormano Milan 19 A2
Cornaredo Milan 19 A1
Córsico Milan 19 B1
Corstorphine Edinburgh 11 B2
Corviale Rome 26 B1
Coslada Madrid 17 B2
Cossigny Paris 24 B4
Cotao Lisbon 16 A1
Côte-St-Luc Montreal 20 B2
Cotunduba, I. de Rio de Janeiro 25 B2
Coubron Paris 24 A4
Countryside Chicago 9 C1
County Art Museum Los Angeles 16 B2
Courbevoie Paris 24 A2
Courtry Paris 24 A4
Cowley London 15 A1
Coyoacán Mexico City 18 B2
Craighall Park Johannesburg 13 A2
Craiglockhart Edinburgh 11 B2
Craigmillar Edinburgh 11 B3
Cramond Edinburgh 11 B2
Cramond Bridge Edinburgh 11 B1
Cramond I. Edinburgh 11 B2
Cranford London 15 B1
Crawford Cape Town 8 A2
Crayford London 15 B5
Creekmouth London 15 A4
Crescent, L. Orlando 23 A1
Crescenzago Milan 19 A2
Cressely Paris 24 B1
Cresskill New York 22 A2
Créteil Paris 24 B3
Cricklewood London 15 A2
Cristo Redentor, Corcovado Rio de Janeiro 25 B1
Crockenhill London 15 B4
Croissy-Beaubourg Paris 24 B4
Croissy-sur-Seine Paris 24 A1
Crosby Johannesburg 13 B1
Crosne Paris 24 B3
Cross I. Mumbai 20 B2
Crouch End London 15 A3
Crown Mine Johannesburg 13 B1
Crows Nest Sydney 29 A2
Croydon London 15 B3
Croydon Park Sydney 29 B1
Cruagh Mt. Dublin 10 B2
Crumlin Dublin 10 B2
Cruz de Pau Lisbon 16 B2
Crystal Palace London 15 B3
Csepel Budapest 7 B2
Csepelsziget Budapest 7 B2
Csillaghegy Budapest 7 A2
Csillagtelep Budapest 7 B2
Csömör Budapest 7 A3
Csömöri-patak → Budapest 7 A3
Cuatro Vientos Madrid 17 B1
Cuauhtémoc Mexico City 18 B2
Cuban Museum Miami 18 B2
Cubao Manila 17 B2
Çubuklu Istanbul 12 B2
Cudahy Los Angeles 16 C3
Cuicuilco, Pirámide de Mexico City 18 C1
Culmore Washington 33 B3
Culver City Los Angeles 16 B2
Cupecé → São Paulo 27 B1
Currie Edinburgh 11 B2
Cusago Milan 19 B1
Cusano Milanino Milan 19 A2
Cutler Park Boston 6 B1
Çuvuşabaşi → Istanbul 12 B1
Cuwei Beijing 4 B1
Cypress Hills New York 22 B2
Cypress Park Los Angeles 16 B3
Czernriaków Warsaw 32 B2
Czyste Warsaw 32 B1

D

Da Moóca → São Paulo 27 B2
Ďáblice Prague 25 B2
Dąbrowa Warsaw 32 B1
Dachang Shanghai 28 B1
Dachang ✕ Shanghai 28 B1
Dachau Munich 21 A1
Dachau-Ost Munich 21 A1
Dachauer Moos Munich 21 A1
Dadar Mumbai 20 A1
Daebang Seoul 27 B1
Daechi Seoul 27 B2
Dafni Athens 2 B2
Dagenham London 15 A4
Daglfing Munich 21 B2
Dahab, Geziret el Cairo 7 B2
Daheisha Jerusalem 13 B2
Dahlem Berlin 5 B2
Dahlwitz-Hoppegarten Berlin 5 A5
Dahongmen Beijing 4 C2
Dajiaoting Beijing 4 B2
Dakhnoye St. Petersburg 27 C1
Dalejsky potok → Prague 25 B2
Dalgety Bay Edinburgh 11 A1
Dalkeith Edinburgh 11 B3
Dalkey Dublin 10 B3
Dalkey I. Dublin 10 B3
Dallgow Berlin 5 A1
Dalmeny Edinburgh 11 B1
Dalston London 15 A3
Daly City San Francisco 26 B2
Damaia Lisbon 16 A1
Damarakia Athens 2 B1
Dämeritzsee Berlin 5 B5
Dan Ryan Woods Chicago 9 C2
Danderhall Edinburgh 11 B3
Danderyd Stockholm 29 A2
Danforth Toronto 31 A3
Darakeh Tehran 31 A2
Darband Tehran 31 A2
Darling Point Sydney 29 B2
Darndale Dublin 10 A2
Darrūs Tehran 31 A2
Dartford London 15 B5
Dashi Guangzhou 11 B2
Datansha Guangzhou 11 B2
Datun Beijing 4 B2
Daulatpur Delhi 10 A1
Davidson, Mt. San Francisco 26 B2
Davidson's Mains Edinburgh 11 B2
Dāvūdiyeh Tehran 31 A2
Davydkovo Moscow 19 B1
Dawidy Warsaw 32 C1
Daxing Beijing 4 C2
Days Bay Wellington 33 B2
Decatur Atlanta 3 B3
Dedham Boston 6 B1
Degunino Moscow 19 A2
Deir Dibwan Jerusalem 13 A2
Deir Ibzi'e Jerusalem 13 A1
Dejvice Prague 25 B2
Dekabristov, Ostrov St. Petersburg 27 B1
Del Rey Los Angeles 16 C2
Delhi Delhi 10 B2
Delhi Indira Gandhi Int. ✕ (DEL) Delhi 10 B1
Demarest New York 22 A2
Den Ilp Amsterdam 2 A2
Denistone Heights Sydney 29 A1
Dentonia Park Toronto 31 A3
DePaul Univ. Chicago 9 B3
Deptford London 15 B3
Des Plaines Chicago 9 A1
Desert Wetlands Park Las Vegas 14 B2
Deutsche Oper Berlin 5 A2
Deutsches Museum Munich 21 B2
Devil's Peak Cape Town 8 A1
Dhakuria Kolkata 14 B2
Dharavi Mumbai 20 A2
Diadema São Paulo 27 C2
Diegem Brussels 6 A2
Diemen Amsterdam 2 A2
Diepkloof Johannesburg 13 B1
Dieprivier Cape Town 8 B1
Difficult Run → Washington 33 B2
Dilbeek Brussels 6 A1
Dilli = Delhi Delhi 10 B2
Dirnismaning Munich 21 A2
Disney-M.G.M. Studios Orlando 23 B1
Disney Studios Los Angeles 16 B3
District Heights Washington 33 B4
Djakarta = Jakarta Jakarta 12 A2
Djursholm Stockholm 29 A2
Döberitz Berlin 5 A1
Döbling Vienna 32 A2
Dobong Seoul 27 B2
Dobongsan Seoul 27 A2
Docklands London 15 A3
Doctor Phillips Orlando 23 B2
Dodder → Dublin 10 B1
Dodger Stadium Los Angeles 16 B3
Dogs, Isle of London 15 B3
Dolgoe Ozero St. Petersburg 27 A1
Dollis Hill London 15 A2
Dollymount Dublin 10 A2
Dolni Prague 25 B3
Dolni Chabry Prague 25 B2
Dolni Počernice Prague 25 B3
Dolphins Barn Dublin 10 B2
Dom Pedro II, Parque São Paulo 27 B2
Don Mills Toronto 31 A2
Don Muang Int. ✕ (BKK) Bangkok 3 A2
Donaghmede Dublin 10 A3
Donau-Oder Kanal Vienna 32 A3
Donaufeld Vienna 32 A2
Donaupark Vienna 32 A2
Donaustadt Vienna 32 A2
Dongan Hills New York 22 C1
Dongcheng Beijing 4 B2
Dongdaemung Seoul 27 B2
Donggou Shanghai 28 B2
Dongjak Seoul 27 B1
Dongjiao Guangzhou 11 B2
Dongri Mumbai 20 B2
Dongshanhu Park Guangzhou 11 B2
Dongzhimen Beijing 4 B2
Donnybrook Dublin 10 B2
Doornfontein Johannesburg 13 B2
Dorchester Boston 6 B2
Dorchester B. Boston 6 B2
Dorchester Heights Nat. Historical Site ⌂ Boston 6 B2
Dornach Munich 21 B3
Dorval Int., Montréal ✕ (YUL) Montreal 20 B1
Dos Moninos → São Paulo 27 C2
Douglas Park Chicago 9 B2
Dover Heights Sydney 29 B2
Dowlatābād Tehran 31 B2
Down, L. Orlando 23 A1
Downey Los Angeles 16 C4
Downsview Toronto 31 A1
Dragør Copenhagen 8 B3
Drancy Paris 24 A3
Dranesville Washington 33 A1
Drapetsona Athens 2 B1
Dreilinden Berlin 5 B2
Drewnica Warsaw 32 B2
Drigh Road Karachi 13 A2
Drimnagh Dublin 10 B2
Drogenbos Brussels 6 B1
Druid Hills Atlanta 3 B2
Drumcondra Dublin 10 A2
Drummoyne Sydney 29 B1
Drylaw Edinburgh 11 B2
Dubeč Prague 25 B3
Dublin Dublin 10 A2
Dublin ✕ (DUB) Dublin 10 A2
Dublin B. Dublin 10 B3
Dublin Harbour Dublin 10 A2
Duddingston Edinburgh 11 B3
Dugnano Milan 19 A2
Duivendrecht Amsterdam 2 B2
Dūlāb Tehran 31 B2
Dulles Int. ✕ (IAD) Washington 33 B1
Dulwich London 15 B3
Dum Dum Kolkata 14 B2
Dum Dum Int. ✕ (CCU) Kolkata 14 B2
Dumont New York 22 A2
Dún Laoghaire Dublin 10 B3
Dundrum Dublin 10 B2
Dunearn Singapore 28 B2
Dúnleary = Dún Laoghaire Dublin 10 B3
Dunn Loring Washington 33 B2
Dunning Chicago 9 B2
Dunvegan Johannesburg 13 A2
Duomo Milan 19 B2
Duque de Caxias Rio de Janeiro 25 A1
Duren Sawit Jakarta 12 A2
Dusit Bangkok 3 B2
Dworp Brussels 6 B1
Dyakovo Moscow 19 B2
Dyker Beach Park New York 22 C1
Dzerzhinskiy Moscow 19 B2
Dzerzhinskiy Park Moscow 19 B2

E

E.U.R. = Esposizione Universale di Roma Rome 26 C1
Eagle Rock Los Angeles 16 B3
Ealing □ London 15 A2
Earlsfield London 15 B2
Earlwood Sydney 29 B1
East Arlington Boston 6 A2
East Arlington Washington 33 B3
East Bedfont London 15 B1
East Boston Boston 6 A2
East Don → Toronto 31 A2
East Don Parkland Toronto 31 A2
East Elmhurst New York 22 B2
East Finchley London 15 A2
East Flatbush New York 22 C2
East Ham London 15 A4
East Humber → Toronto 31 A1
East Lamma Channel Hong Kong 12 B1
East Las Vegas = Whitney Las Vegas 14 B2
East Lexington Boston 6 A1
East Los Angeles Los Angeles 16 B3
East Molesey London 15 B1
East New York New York 22 B2
East Pines Washington 33 B4
East Point Atlanta 3 B2
East Potomac Park Washington 33 B3
East River → New York 22 B2
East Rutherford New York 22 A1
East Sheen London 15 B2
East Talpiyot Jerusalem 13 B2
East Wickham London 15 B4
East York Toronto 31 A2
Eastbourne Wellington 33 B2
Eastcote London 15 A1
Easter Howgate Edinburgh 11 B2
Eastpoint Park Toronto 31 A4
Eastwood Sydney 29 A1
Eaton Canyon Park Los Angeles 16 A4
Ebara Tokyo 30 B3
Ebisu Tokyo 30 B3
Ebute-Ikorodu Lagos 14 A2
Ebute-Metta Lagos 14 B2
Eda Tokyo 30 B2
Edendale Johannesburg 13 A2
Edenmore Dublin 10 A2
Edgars Cr. → Melbourne 18 A1
Edgeley Toronto 31 A1
Edgemar San Francisco 26 C2
Edgewater New York 22 B2
Edgewood Orlando 23 B2
Edinburgh Edinburgh 11 B2
Edinburgh ✕ (EDI) Edinburgh 11 B1
Edinburgh Castle Edinburgh 11 B2
Edison Park Chicago 9 A2
Edmondston Washington 33 B4
Edmondstown Dublin 10 B2
Edo → Tokyo 30 B4
Edogawa Tokyo 30 A4
Edsberg Stockholm 29 A1
Edwards L. Melbourne 18 A1
Efzonos Athens 2 B2
Egaleo Athens 2 B2
Egaleo, Oros Athens 2 B1
Eiche Berlin 5 A4
Eiche Süd Berlin 5 A4
Eiffel, Tour Paris 24 A2
Ein Arik Jerusalem 13 A1
Ein Naquba Jerusalem 13 B1
Ein Rafa Jerusalem 13 B1
Eizariya Jerusalem 13 B2
Ejby Copenhagen 8 A2
Ejigbo Lagos 14 A1
Ekeberg Oslo 23 A3
Eknäs Stockholm 29 B3
El 'Abbasiya Cairo 7 A2
El Agustino Lima 14 B2
El Agustino, Cerro Lima 14 B3
El Baragil Cairo 7 A1
El Basâtîn Cairo 7 B2
El Bira Jerusalem 13 A2
El Bosque Santiago 27 C2
El Carmen Santiago 27 B1
El Cortijo Santiago 27 B1
El Cristo, Vaso Regulador Mexico City 18 B1
El Duqqi Cairo 7 A2
El Encinar de los Reyes Madrid 17 A2
El Gezira Cairo 7 A2
El Ghuriya Cairo 7 A2
El Giza Cairo 7 A2
El Khadr Jerusalem 13 B1
El Khalîfa Cairo 7 A2
El Kôm el Ahmar Cairo 7 A2
El Ma'âdi Cairo 7 B2
El Matariya Cairo 7 A2
El Mohandessin Cairo 7 A2
El Monte Los Angeles 16 B4
El Muqattam Cairo 7 A2
El Mûskî Cairo 7 A2
El Pardo Madrid 17 A1
El Portal Miami 18 A2
El Prat de Llobregat Barcelona 4 B1
El Qâhira Cairo 7 A2
El Qubba Cairo 7 A2
El Reloj Mexico City 18 C2
El Retiro Madrid 17 B1
El Salto Santiago 27 B2
El Sereno Los Angeles 16 B3
El Talibîya Cairo 7 B2
El Vergel Mexico City 18 C2
El Wâhli Cairo 7 A2
El Zamâlik Cairo 7 A2
El Zeitûn Cairo 7 A2
Eleftherios Venizelos ✕ (ATH) Athens 2 A3
Elephanta Caves Mumbai 20 B2
Elephanta I. Mumbai 20 B2
Ellboda Stockholm 29 A3
Ellenor, L. Orlando 23 B2
Elliniko Olympic Complex Athens 2 B2
Ellis I. New York 22 B1
Elmers End London 15 B3
Elmhurst New York 22 B2
Elmstead London 15 B4
Elmwood New Orleans 21 B1
Elmwood Park Chicago 9 B2
Elmwood Park New York 22 A1
Elsdon Wellington 33 A1
Elsiesrivier Cape Town 8 A2
Elsternwick Melbourne 18 B2
Eltham London 15 B4
Elwood Melbourne 18 B1
Élysée Paris 24 A2
Elysian Park Los Angeles 16 B3
Emāmzādeh Sāleh Tehran 31 A2
Émerainville Paris 24 B4
Emeryville San Francisco 26 A3
Eminönü Istanbul 12 B1
Emirgan Istanbul 12 B2
Emmarentia Johannesburg 13 A2
Empire State Building New York 22 B2
Encantado Rio de Janeiro 25 B1
Encino Los Angeles 16 B2
Encino Res. Los Angeles 16 B1
Enebyberg Stockholm 29 A1
Enfield Sydney 29 B1
Engenho, I. do Rio de Janeiro 25 B2
Englewood Chicago 9 C3
Englewood New York 22 A2
Englewood Cliffs New York 22 A2
Enmore Sydney 29 B2
Enskede Stockholm 29 B2
Enterprise Las Vegas 14 B1
Entrevias Madrid 17 B1
Epcot Orlando 23 B1
Epping Sydney 29 A1
Erenköy Istanbul 12 C2
Erith London 15 B5
Erlaa Vienna 32 B1
Ermington Sydney 29 A1
Ermita Manila 17 B1
Ershatou Guangzhou 11 B2
Erskineville Sydney 29 B2
Erunkan Lagos 14 A2
Erzsébet-Telep Budapest 7 B3
Eschenried Munich 21 A1
Esenler Istanbul 12 B1
Esher London 15 B1
Eskbank Edinburgh 11 B3
Esplugas Barcelona 4 A1
Esposizione Universale di Roma Rome 26 C1
Essendon Melbourne 18 A1
Essendon ✕ (MEB) Melbourne 18 A1
Essingen Stockholm 29 B1
Essling Vienna 32 A3
Est, Gare de l' Paris 24 A3
Estado, Parque do São Paulo 27 B2
Estelle New Orleans 21 B2
Estrela, Basilica da Lisbon 16 A2
Etobicoke Toronto 31 B1
Etobicoke Cr. → Toronto 31 B1
Etterbeek Brussels 6 B2
Eung-am Seoul 27 B1
Eunpyeong Seoul 27 B1
Evanston Chicago 9 A2
Even Sapir Jerusalem 13 B1
Evere Brussels 6 A2
Everett Boston 6 A2
Evergreen Park Chicago 9 C2
Evīn Tehran 31 A2
Ewu Lagos 14 A1
Exhibition Place Toronto 31 B2
Exposições, Palácio das Rio de Janeiro 25 B1
Eyüp Istanbul 12 B1
Ezeiza ✕ (EZE) Buenos Aires 7 C1

F

Fabour, Mt. Singapore 28 B2
Fælledparken Copenhagen 8 A3
Fågelön Stockholm 29 B1
Fagersjö Stockholm 29 B2
Fairfax Washington 33 B2
Fairfax Station Washington 33 C2
Fairland Johannesburg 13 A1
Fairmilehead Edinburgh 11 B2
Fairmount Heights Washington 33 B4
Fairport Toronto 31 A4
Fairview New York 22 B2
Fairview, L. Orlando 23 A2
Falenty Warsaw 32 C1
Faliro Athens 2 B1
Faliro, Ormos Athens 2 B2
Falkenburg Berlin 5 A4
Falkenhagen Berlin 5 A1
Falkensee Berlin 5 A1
Falls Church Washington 33 B2
Falomo Lagos 14 B2
False Bay Cape Town 8 B2
Fangcun Guangzhou 11 B2
Faraḥābād Tehran 31 A2
Farforovskaya St. Petersburg 27 B2
Farningham London 15 B5
Farsta Stockholm 29 B2
Fasanerie-Nord Munich 21 A2
Fasangarten Munich 21 B2
Fatih Istanbul 12 B1
Favoriten Vienna 32 B2
Fawkner Melbourne 18 A1
Fawkner Park Melbourne 18 B1
FedEx Stadium Washington 33 B4
Feijó Lisbon 16 B2
Feldkirchen Munich 21 B3
Feldmoching Munich 21 A2
Feltham London 15 B1
Fener Istanbul 12 B1
Fenerbahçe Istanbul 12 C2
Fengtai Beijing 4 C1
Fengtai Stadium Beijing 4 B1
Ferencváros Budapest 7 B2
Ferihegy, Budapest ✕ (BUD) Budapest 7 B3
Ferndale Johannesburg 13 A2
Fichtenau Berlin 5 B5
Field Museum of Natural History Chicago 9 B3
Fields Corner Boston 6 B2
Fiera Camp Milan 19 B1
Figino Milan 19 B1
Fijir Baghdad 3 A2
Filadelfia Athens 2 A2
Fili-Mazilovo Moscow 19 B1
Filothei Athens 2 A2
Finchley London 15 A2
Fine Arts, Museum of Boston 6 A2
Finglas Dublin 10 A2
Finsbury London 15 A3
Finsbury Park London 15 A3
Fiorito Buenos Aires 7 C2
Firhouse Dublin 10 B2
Fischerhäuser Munich 21 A3
Fisher Island Miami 18 B2
Fishermans Bend Melbourne 18 A1
Fisherville Toronto 31 A2
Fisksätra Stockholm 29 B3
Fitzroy Gardens Melbourne 18 A1
Five Cowrie Cr. → Lagos 14 B2
Five Dock Sydney 29 B1
Fjellstrand Oslo 23 B2
Flamengo Rio de Janeiro 25 B1
Flamingo Orlando 23 B2
Flaminio Rome 26 B1
Flaskebekk Oslo 23 B2
Flatbush New York 22 C2
Flaten Stockholm 29 B2
Flatlands New York 22 C2
Flemington Racecourse Melbourne 18 A1
Flint Pk. Los Angeles 16 B3
Florence Los Angeles 16 C3
Florence Bloom Bird Sanctuary ⌂ Johannesburg 13 A2
Florentia Johannesburg 13 B2
Flores Buenos Aires 7 B2
Flores, Mercado de Mexico City 18 C2
Floresta Buenos Aires 7 B2
Florida Buenos Aires 7 B2
Florida Johannesburg 13 B1
Floridsdorf Vienna 32 A2
Flushing New York 22 B3
Flushing Meadows Corona Park New York 22 B2
Flysta Stockholm 29 A1
Fo Tan Hong Kong 12 A2
Foggy Bottom Washington 33 B3
Föhrenhain Vienna 32 A2
Fontainebleau Johannesburg 13 A1
Fontenay-aux-Roses Paris 24 B2
Fontenay-le-Fleury Paris 24 B1
Fontenay-sous-Bois Paris 24 A3
Foots Cray London 15 B4
Footscray Melbourne 18 A1
Forbidden City = Imperial Palace Museum Beijing 4 B2
Forest Brussels 6 B1
Forest Gate London 15 A4
Forest Heights Washington 33 C3
Forest Hill London 15 B3
Forest Hill Toronto 31 A2
Forest Hills New York 22 B2
Forest Park Chicago 9 B2
Forest Park New York 22 B2
Forest View Chicago 9 C2
Forestville Washington 33 B4
Fornebu Oslo 23 A2
Foro Romano Rome 26 B1
Forstenried Munich 21 B1
Forstenrieder Park Munich 21 B1
Fort Mumbai 20 B1
Fort Dupont Park Washington 33 B4
Fort Foote Village Washington 33 C3
Fort Lee New York 22 A2
Forth, Firth of Edinburgh 11 A3
Forth Rail Bridge Edinburgh 11 A1
Forth Road Bridge Edinburgh 11 A1
Foshan Guangzhou 11 B2
Fót Budapest 7 A3
Fourqueux Paris 24 A1
Fox Studios Sydney 29 B2
Foxrock Dublin 10 B2
Franconia Washington 33 C3
Frank Lloyd Wright Home Chicago 9 B2
Frankel Singapore 28 B3
Franklin Park Boston 6 B2
Franklin Park Chicago 9 B1
Franklin Park Washington 33 B3
Franklin Res. Los Angeles 16 B2
Franz Josef Strauss ✕ (MUC) Munich 21 A2
Frauenkirche Munich 21 B2
Frederiksberg Copenhagen 8 A3
Frederiksdal Copenhagen 8 A2
Fredersdorf Berlin 5 A5
Freguesia Rio de Janeiro 25 A1
Freidrichshain, Volkspark Berlin 5 A3
Freiham Munich 21 B1
Freimann Munich 21 A2
French Quarter New Orleans 21 B2
Fresh Pond Boston 6 A2
Fresnes Paris 24 B3
Freudenau Vienna 32 A2
Friarstown Dublin 10 B1
Friedenau Berlin 5 B3
Friedrichsfelde Berlin 5 B4
Friedrichshagen Berlin 5 B4
Friedrichshain Berlin 5 A3
Friedrichslust Berlin 5 A5
Friherrs Helsinki 11 B1
Frilufts Museum Helsinki 11 B2
Frontón, I. Lima 14 B1
Frunze Moscow 19 B2
Fuchū Tokyo 30 A1
Fuencarral Madrid 17 B1
Fuenlabrada Madrid 17 C1
Fukagawa Tokyo 30 B3
Fukushima Osaka 23 A1
Fulham London 15 B2
Funabori Tokyo 30 A4
Fundão, I. do Rio de Janeiro 25 B1
Fünfhaus Vienna 32 A2
Fureso Copenhagen 8 A2
Fürth Munich 21 B2
Futago-tamagawaen Tokyo 30 B2
Fuxing Dao Shanghai 28 B1
Fuxing Park Shanghai 28 B1
Fuxinglu Beijing 4 B1

G

G. Ross Lord Park Toronto 31 A2
Gaebong Seoul 27 C1
Gage Park Chicago 9 C2
Gagny Paris 24 A4
Galata Istanbul 12 B1
Galata Tower Istanbul 12 B1
Galatsi Athens 2 A2
Galeão, Int. de ✕ (GIG) Rio de Janeiro 25 A1
Galyanovo Moscow 19 B3
Gambir Jakarta 12 A1
Gamboa Rio de Janeiro 25 B1
Gambolóita Milan 19 B2
Gamlebyen Oslo 23 A3
Gangdong Seoul 27 B2
Gangnam Seoul 27 B1
Gangseo Seoul 27 B1
Gangtou Guangzhou 11 A1
Gangwei Guangzhou 11 B2
Ganjiakou Beijing 4 B1
Ganshoren Brussels 6 A1
Gants Hill London 15 A4
Gaoqiao Shanghai 28 A2
Garbagnate Milanese Milan 19 A1
Garbatella Rome 26 B2
Garches Paris 24 A2
Garching Munich 21 A3
Garden City Cairo 7 A2
Garden Reach Kolkata 14 B1
Garder Oslo 23 B2
Garfield New York 22 A1
Garfield Park Chicago 9 B2
Gargareta Athens 2 B2
Garibong Seoul 27 C1
Garvanza Los Angeles 16 B3
Gåshaga Stockholm 29 A3
Gateway ⌂ New York 22 C2
Gateway of India Mumbai 20 B2
Gatow Berlin 5 B1
Gavà Barcelona 4 B1
Gavamar Barcelona 4 B1
Gávea Rio de Janeiro 25 B1
Gávea, Pedra da Rio de Janeiro 25 B1
Gazdagrét Budapest 7 B1
Gaziosmanpaşa Istanbul 12 B1
Gebel el Ahmar Cairo 7 A3
Gebel el Muqattam Cairo 7 A2
Gebel el Tura Cairo 7 B2
Geiselgasteig Munich 21 B2
General San Martin Buenos Aires 7 B1
Gennevilliers Paris 24 A2
Gentilly New Orleans 21 A2
Gentilly Paris 24 B3
Gentofte Copenhagen 8 A3
Genval Brussels 6 B2
George I. Hong Kong 12 B1
Georges River Bridge Sydney 29 C1
Georgetown Washington 33 B3
Georgia Dome Atlanta 3 B2
Gerasdorf bei Wien Vienna 32 A2
Gerberau Munich 21 A1
Gerli Buenos Aires 7 C2
Germiston Johannesburg 13 B2
Gern Munich 21 B2
Getafe Madrid 17 C1
Getty Center, The Los Angeles 16 B2
Geunjeong Seoul 27 C1
Geva Binyamin Jerusalem 13 A2
Geylang Serai Singapore 28 B3
Gharapuri Mumbai 20 B2
Gharb = Shahrak-e Qods Tehran 31 A2
Ghatkopar Mumbai 20 A2
Ghazipur Delhi 10 B2
Ghizri Karachi 13 B2
Ghizri Cr. → Karachi 13 B2
Ghonda Delhi 10 A2
Ghusuri Kolkata 14 B2
Gianicolense Rome 26 B1
Giant Wheel = Riesenrad Vienna 32 A2
Gibraltar Pt. Toronto 31 B2
Gidea Park London 15 A5
Giesing Munich 21 B2
Gilmerton Edinburgh 11 B3
Gilo Jerusalem 13 B2
Gimmersta Stockholm 29 B3
Ginza Tokyo 30 B3
Giv'at Ram Jerusalem 13 B2
Giv'at Ye'arim Jerusalem 13 B1
Giv'at Ze'ev Jerusalem 13 A2
Giv'on Jerusalem 13 A1
Giza = El Giza Cairo 7 A2
Giza Pyramids Cairo 7 B1
Gjersjøen Oslo 23 B3
Gladesville Sydney 29 B1
Gladsakse Copenhagen 8 A2
Glasnevin Dublin 10 A2
Glassmanor Washington 33 C4
Glasthule Dublin 10 B3
Glen Iris Melbourne 18 B2
Glen Mar Park Washington 33 B3
Glen Rouge Park Toronto 31 A4
Glenarden Washington 33 B4
Glenasmole Reservoirs Dublin 10 B1
Glencorse Res. Edinburgh 11 B2
Glencullen Dublin 10 B2
Glendale Los Angeles 16 B3
Glendoo Mt. Dublin 10 B2
Glenhuntly Melbourne 18 B2
Glenside Wellington 33 B1
Glenview Chicago 9 A2
Glenview Countryside Chicago 9 A2
Glenvista Johannesburg 13 B2
Glifada Athens 2 B2
Glostrup Copenhagen 8 B2
Gogar Edinburgh 11 B2
Göktürk Istanbul 12 A1
Golabari Kolkata 14 B2
Golabki Warsaw 32 B1
Gold Coast Chicago 9 B3
Golden Gate San Francisco 26 B2
Golden Gate ⌂ San Francisco 26 A2
Golden Gate Bridge San Francisco 26 B2
Golden Gate Park San Francisco 26 B2
Golden Horn = Haliç Istanbul 12 B1
Golders Green London 15 A2
Golestan Palace Tehran 31 A2
Gollans Stream → Wellington 33 B2
Gonen Jerusalem 13 B2
Gongneung Seoul 27 B2
Goodmayes London 15 A4
Goodwood Cape Town 8 A2
Gopalpur Kolkata 14 B2
Górce Warsaw 32 B1
Gore Hill Sydney 29 A2
Gorelyy → St. Petersburg 27 A3
Gorgie Edinburgh 11 B2
Gorky Park Moscow 19 B2
Gosen Berlin 5 B5
Gosener kanal Berlin 5 B5
Gospel Oak London 15 A3
Gotanda Tokyo 30 B3
Goth Goli Mar Karachi 13 A2
Goth Sher Shah Karachi 13 A1

Gotha *Orlando* 23 A1
Gournay-sur-Marne *Paris* 24 A4
Governador, I. do
  Rio de Janeiro 25 A1
Governors I. *New York* 22 B1
Grabów *Warsaw* 32 B1
Grace, Mt. *Wellington* 33 B2
Gracefield *Wellington* 33 B2
Gràcia *Barcelona* 4 A2
Gräfelfing *Munich* 21 B1
Gragoatá *Rio de Janeiro* 25 B2
Grand Bazaar = Kapali
  Carsi *Istanbul* 12 B1
Grand Central Station
  New York 22 B2
Grand Palace *Bangkok* 3 B2
Grande Place *Brussels* 6 A2
Grankulla = Kauniainen
  Helsinki 11 B1
Grant Park *Chicago* 9 B3
Granton *Edinburgh* 11 B2
Grassy Park *Cape Town* 8 B2
Gratosóglio *Milan* 19 B2
Gratzwalde *Berlin* 5 B5
Gravesend *New York* 22 C2
Grazhdanka *St. Petersburg* 27 B2
Great Falls *Washington* 33 B2
Great Falls Park *Washington* 33 B2
Great Western Forum
  Los Angeles 16 C2
Greco *Milan* 19 A2
Green I. *Hong Kong* 12 B1
Green Point *Cape Town* 8 A1
Greenbelt *Washington* 33 A4
Greenbelt Park *Washington* 33 A4
Greenfield Park *Montreal* 20 B3
Greenford *London* 15 A1
Greenhill *London* 15 A2
Greenhills *Dublin* 10 B1
Greenwich □ *London* 15 B3
Greenwich Observatory
  London 15 B3
Greenwich Village
  New York 22 B2
Greenwood *Boston* 6 A3
Grefsen *Oslo* 23 A3
Gresham Park *Atlanta* 3 B2
Gretna *New Orleans* 21 B2
Gretna City Park
  New Orleans 21 B2
Greve Strand *Copenhagen* 8 B1
Griebnitzsee *Berlin* 5 B1
Griffith Park *Los Angeles* 16 B3
Grimbergen *Brussels* 6 A2
Grinzing *Vienna* 32 A2
Gröbenried *Munich* 21 A1
Grochów *Warsaw* 32 B2
Grodzisk *Warsaw* 32 B1
Groenendaal *Brussels* 6 B2
Grogol Petamburin *Jakarta* 12 A1
Gronsdorf *Munich* 21 B3
Grorud *Oslo* 23 A4
Gross-Glienicke *Berlin* 5 B1
Gross-Hadern *Munich* 21 B1
Gross-Lappen *Munich* 21 A2
Grosse Krampe *Berlin* 5 B5
Grosse Müggelsee *Berlin* 5 B4
Grosse Point Lighthouse
  Chicago 9 A2
Grossenzersdorf *Vienna* 32 A3
Grossenzersdorfer Arm →
  Vienna 32 A3
Grosser Biberhaufen *Vienna* 32 A2
Grosser Wannsee *Berlin* 5 B2
Grosfeld-Siedlung *Vienna* 32 A2
Grosshesselohe *Munich* 21 B2
Grossjedlersdorf *Vienna* 32 A2
Grossziethen *Berlin* 5 B3
Ground Zero *New York* 22 B1
Grove, The *Chicago* 9 A1
Grove Hall *Boston* 6 B2
Grove Park *Atlanta* 3 B2
Grove Park *London* 15 B4
Grove Park *London* 15 B2
Groveton *Washington* 33 C3
Grünau *Berlin* 5 B4
Grunewald *Berlin* 5 B2
Grünwald *Munich* 21 B2
Grünwalder Forst *Munich* 21 B2
Grymes Hill *New York* 22 C1
Guadalupe *Manila* 17 B2
Guadalupe, Basílica de
  Mexico City 18 B2
Guanabara, B. de
  Rio de Janeiro 25 B1
Guanabara, Jardim
  Rio de Janeiro 25 B1
Guanabara, Palácio da
  Rio de Janeiro 25 B1
Guang'anmen *Beijing* 4 B1
Guangqumen *Beijing* 4 B2
Guangzhou *Guangzhou* 11 B2
Guanshuo *Guangzhou* 11 B3
Gudö *Stockholm* 29 B3
Güell, Parque de *Barcelona* 4 A2
Guinardó *Barcelona* 4 A2
Gulbai *Karachi* 13 A1
Güngören *Istanbul* 12 B1
Gunnersbury *London* 15 B2
Guomao *Beijing* 4 B2
Gustavo A. Madero
  Mexico City 18 B2
Guttenberg *New York* 22 B1
Gutuyevskiy, Ostrov
  St. Petersburg 27 B2
Guyancourt *Paris* 24 B1
Gwanak *Seoul* 27 C1
Gwanaksan *Seoul* 27 C1
Gyál *Budapest* 7 B3
Gyáli-patak → *Budapest* 7 B2

H

Haaga *Helsinki* 11 B2
Haar *Munich* 21 B3
Habay *Manila* 17 C1
Hackbridge *London* 15 B3
Hackensack *New York* 22 A1
Hackensack → *New York* 22 B1
Hackney □ *London* 15 A3
Hackney Wick *London* 15 A3
Hadr, Warrâq el *Cairo* 7 A2
Haga *Stockholm* 29 A2
Hägersbrunn *Vienna* 32 A2
Häggvik *Stockholm* 29 A1
Hagonoy *Manila* 17 B2
Hague Park *Toronto* 31 A3
Haidari *Athens* 2 A1
Haidarpur *Delhi* 10 A1
Haidhausen *Munich* 21 B2
Haidian *Beijing* 4 B1
Haight-Ashbury
  San Francisco 26 B2
Hainault *London* 15 A4
Haizhou *Guangzhou* 11 B2
Haizhu Guangchang
  Guangzhou 11 B2
Hakunila *Helsinki* 11 B3
Halandri *Athens* 2 A2

Halásztelek *Budapest* 7 B1
Halic *Istanbul* 12 B1
Halim Perdana Kusuma
  Int. ✈ (HLP) *Jakarta* 12 B2
Halle *Brussels* 6 B1
Haltiala *Helsinki* 11 B2
Haltiavuori *Helsinki* 11 B2
Ham *London* 15 B2
Hämeenkylä *Helsinki* 11 B1
Hammarby *Stockholm* 29 B2
Hamme *Brussels* 6 A1
Hammersmith *London* 15 A2
Hampstead *London* 15 A2
Hampstead *Montreal* 20 B2
Hampstead Garden
  Suburb *London* 15 A2
Hampstead Heath *London* 15 A2
Hampton *London* 15 B1
Hampton Court Palace
  London 15 B1
Hampton Wick *London* 15 B2
Hamrä' *Baghdad* 3 B1
Hanala *Helsinki* 11 A3
Haneda *Tokyo* 30 B3
Haneda, Tōkyō ✈ (HND)
  Tokyo 30 B3
Hang Hau *Hong Kong* 12 B2
Hanging Gardens *Mumbai* 20 B1
Hanlon *Toronto* 31 B1
Hanwell *London* 15 A1
Hanworth *London* 15 B1
Haora *Kolkata* 14 B1
Hapeville *Atlanta* 3 C2
Happy Valley *Hong Kong* 12 B2
Har Adar *Jerusalem* 13 B1
Har Gilo *Jerusalem* 13 B2
Har Homa *Jerusalem* 13 B2
Har Nof *Jerusalem* 13 B2
Harahan *New Orleans* 21 B1
Haren *Brussels* 6 A2
Hareskovby *Copenhagen* 8 A2
Haringey □ *London* 15 A3
Harjusuo *Helsinki* 11 B3
Harlaching *Munich* 21 B2
Harlaw Res. *Edinburgh* 11 B2
Harlem *New York* 22 B2
Harlesden *London* 15 A2
Harlington *London* 15 B1
Harmaja *Helsinki* 11 C2
Harmashatar hegy *Budapest* 7 A2
Harolds Cross *Dublin* 10 B2
Háros *Budapest* 7 B2
Harperrig Res. *Edinburgh* 11 B1
Harrow □ *London* 15 A1
Harrow on the Hill *London* 15 A1
Harrow School *London* 15 A1
Harrow Weald *London* 15 A1
Hartsdale *Amsterdam* 2 A3
Hartsfield-Atlanta Int. ✈
  (ATL) *Atlanta* 3 C2
Harumi *Tokyo* 30 B3
Harvard Univ. *Boston* 6 A3
Harvey *New Orleans* 21 B2
Harwood Heights *Chicago* 9 B2
Hasbrouck Heights
  New York 22 A1
Haselhorst *Berlin* 5 A2
Hasköy *Istanbul* 12 B1
Hasle *Oslo* 23 B2
Haslum *Oslo* 23 B2
Hästhagen *Stockholm* 29 B2
Hataitai *Wellington* 33 B1
Hatch End *London* 15 A1
Hatiara *Kolkata* 14 B2
Hauketo *Oslo* 23 B3
Hauz Khas *Delhi* 10 B2
Havel → *Berlin* 5 A1
Havelkanaal *Berlin* 5 A2
Havering □ *London* 15 A5
Havering-atte-Bower
  London 15 A5
Haworth *New York* 22 A2
Hawthorne Racecourse
  Chicago 9 C2
Hayes *London* 15 B4
Hayes *London* 15 A1
Hayes East *London* 15 A1
Hayford *Chicago* 9 C2
Haywards *Wellington* 33 B2
Heathfield *Cape Town* 8 B1
Heathrow, London ✈
  (LHR) *London* 15 B1
Hebe Haven *Hong Kong* 12 A2
Hedong *Guangzhou* 11 B2
Heidelberg Heights
  Melbourne 18 A2
Heidelberg West *Melbourne* 18 A2
Heidemühle *Berlin* 5 B5
Heideveld *Cape Town* 8 A2
Heiligensee *Berlin* 5 A2
Heiligenstadt *Vienna* 32 A2
Heinersdorf *Berlin* 5 A3
Hélène de Champlain,
  Parc → *Montreal* 20 A2
Helenelund *Stockholm* 29 A1
Heliopolis = Masr el
  Gedida *Cairo* 7 A2
Hellersdorf *Berlin* 5 A4
Hellerup *Copenhagen* 8 A3
Helsingfors = Helsinki
  Helsinki 11 B2
Helsinki *Helsinki* 11 B2
Helsinki-Vantaa ✈ (HEL)
  Helsinki 11 B2
Hen and Chicken B. *Sydney* 29 B1
Henderson *Las Vegas* 14 B2
Hendon *London* 15 A2
Hengsha *Guangzhou* 11 B3
Hennigsdorf *Berlin* 5 A2
Henrykôw *Warsaw* 32 B1
Henson Cr. → *Washington* 33 C4
Henttaa *Helsinki* 11 B1
Heping Park *Shanghai* 28 B2
Hepingli *Beijing* 4 B2
Herlev *Copenhagen* 8 A2
Herman Eckstein Park
  Johannesburg 13 A2
Hermannskogel *Vienna* 32 A1
Hermiston *Edinburgh* 11 B2
Hermitage and Winter
  Palace *St. Petersburg* 27 B1
Hermsdorf *Berlin* 5 A3
Hernals *Vienna* 32 A2
Herne Hill *London* 15 B3
Héroes de Churubusco
  Mexico City 18 C2
Heroes, Í. aux *Montreal* 20 B2
Herstedøster *Copenhagen* 8 A2
Herttoniemi *Helsinki* 11 B3
Heşarak *Tehran* 31 A1
Heston *London* 15 B1
Hetzendorf *Vienna* 32 B1
Hextable *London* 15 B5
Hialeah *Miami* 18 A1
Hiawassa, I. *Orlando* 23 A2
Hickory Hills *Chicago* 9 C2
Hiekkaharju *Helsinki* 11 B3
Hietaniemi *Helsinki* 11 B2
Hietzing *Vienna* 32 A1
Higashi *Osaka* 23 A2
Higashimurayama *Tokyo* 30 A1

Higashinari *Osaka* 23 A2
Higashisumiyoshi *Osaka* 23 B2
Higashiyodogawa *Osaka* 23 A1
High Park *Toronto* 31 B2
Highbury *London* 15 A3
Highgate *London* 15 A3
Highland Cr. → *Toronto* 31 A3
Highland Creek *Toronto* 31 A3
Highland Park *Los Angeles* 16 B3
Highlands North
  Johannesburg 13 A2
Hillcrest Heights
  Washington 33 C4
Hillend *Edinburgh* 11 A1
Hillingdon □ *London* 15 A1
Hillwood *Washington* 33 B3
Hilmîya *Cairo* 7 A2
Hin Keng *Hong Kong* 12 A2
Hirota *Osaka* 23 A1
Hirschstetten *Vienna* 32 A2
History Center *Atlanta* 3 B2
Hither Green *London* 15 B3
Hiyoshi *Tokyo* 30 B2
Hizma *Jerusalem* 13 B2
Hjortekær *Copenhagen* 8 A3
Hjortespring *Copenhagen* 8 A2
Hlubočepy *Prague* 25 B2
Ho Chung *Hong Kong* 12 A2
Hoboken *New York* 22 B1
Hobsons B. *Melbourne* 18 B1
Hochbrück *Munich* 21 A2
Hochelaga *Montreal* 20 A2
Hodgkins *Chicago* 9 C1
Hoegi *Seoul* 27 B2
Hoeilaart *Brussels* 6 B2
Hofburg *Vienna* 32 A2
Hoffman I. *New York* 22 C1
Hohenbrunn *Munich* 21 B3
Hohenschönhausen *Berlin* 5 A4
Holargos *Athens* 2 A2
Holborn *London* 15 A3
Holden, L. *Orlando* 23 B2
Holešovice *Prague* 25 B2
Holland Village *Singapore* 28 B2
Höllriegelskreuth *Munich* 21 B1
Hollywood *Los Angeles* 16 B3
Hollywood Bowl *Los Angeles* 16 B2
Holmenkollen *Oslo* 23 A3
Holmes Run Acres
  Washington 33 B3
Holmgård *Stockholm* 29 B1
Holmlia *Oslo* 23 B4
Holocaust Memorial
  Jerusalem 13 B2
Holyrood House, Palace of
  Edinburgh 11 B3
Holysloot *Amsterdam* 2 A3
Homerton *London* 15 A3
Hometown *Chicago* 9 C2
Hönanchō *Tokyo* 30 A3
Honcho *Tokyo* 30 A3
Honden *Tokyo* 30 A4
Hondo, Rio → *Los Angeles* 16 B4
Hong Kong *Hong Kong* 12 B1
Hong Kong I. *Hong Kong* 12 B2
Hong Kong, Univ. of
  Hong Kong 12 B1
Hongje *Seoul* 27 B1
Hongjimun Tunnel *Seoul* 27 B1
Hongkou *Shanghai* 28 B1
Hongqiao *Shanghai* 28 B1
Honjyo *Tokyo* 30 A4
Honoré Mercier, Pont
  Montreal 20 B1
Hönow *Berlin* 5 A4
Hook *London* 15 B1
Horikiri *Tokyo* 30 A4
Horn Pond *Boston* 6 A1
Hornchurch *London* 15 A5
Horni *Prague* 25 B3
Horní Počernice *Prague* 25 B3
Hornsey *London* 15 A3
Horoměřice *Prague* 25 A1
Hortaleza *Madrid* 17 B2
Hosoyama *Tokyo* 30 B2
Hostafranchs *Barcelona* 4 A1
Hostivař *Prague* 25 B3
Houbětin *Prague* 25 B3
Houghton *Johannesburg* 13 B2
Houilles *Paris* 24 A2
Hounslow □ *London* 15 B1
Hout Bay *Cape Town* 8 B1
Hovedøya *Oslo* 23 B3
Høvik *Oslo* 23 A2
Hovorčovice *Prague* 25 A3
Howard Beach *New York* 22 C2
Howrah = Haora *Kolkata* 14 B1
Howth *Dublin* 10 A3
Howth Hd. *Dublin* 10 A3
Hōya *Tokyo* 30 A2
Hradčany *Prague* 25 B2
Huanghuagang
  Mausoleum *Guangzhou* 11 B2
Huangpu *Shanghai* 28 B1
Huangpu Jiang → *Shanghai* 28 B1
Huangpu Park *Shanghai* 28 B1
Huangtugang *Beijing* 4 C1
Huascar *Lima* 14 A2
Huay Khwang *Bangkok* 3 B2
Huddinge *Stockholm* 29 B2
Huechuraba *Santiago* 27 B2
Huertas de San Beltran
  Barcelona 4 A1
Huizingen *Brussels* 6 B1
Humayun's Tomb *Delhi* 10 B2
Humber → *Toronto* 31 A1
Humber B. *Toronto* 31 B2
Humber Bay *Toronto* 31 B2
Humber Bay Park *Toronto* 31 B2
Humber College *Toronto* 31 B1
Humber Summit *Toronto* 31 A1
Humber Valley Village
  Toronto 31 A1
Humberlea *Toronto* 31 A1
Humberwood Park *Toronto* 31 A1
Humboldt Park *Chicago* 9 B2
Humera *Madrid* 17 B1
Hunaydî *Baghdad* 3 B1
Hundige *Copenhagen* 8 B2
Hundige Strand *Copenhagen* 8 B2
Hunters Hill *Sydney* 29 B1
Hunters Pt. *San Francisco* 26 B2
Hunters Valley *Washington* 33 B2
Huntington *Washington* 33 C3
Huntington Park
  Los Angeles 16 C3
Huriya *Baghdad* 3 A1
Hursville *Sydney* 29 B1
Husan *Jerusalem* 13 B1
Husby *Stockholm* 29 A1
Husum *Copenhagen* 8 A2
Hutt → *Wellington* 33 B2
Huvudsta *Stockholm* 29 A1
Huwon Secret Garden *Seoul* 27 B1
Hvalstad *Oslo* 23 A1
Hvalstrand *Oslo* 23 A2
Hvidovre *Copenhagen* 8 B2
Hwagok *Seoul* 27 B1

Hyattsville *Washington* 33 B4
Hyde Park *Boston* 6 B2
Hyde Park *Chicago* 9 C3
Hyde Park *Johannesburg* 13 A2
Hyde Park *London* 15 A2
Hyde Park *Los Angeles* 16 C3
Hyde Park *Sydney* 29 B2

I

Ibese *Lagos* 14 A2
Ibirapuera *São Paulo* 27 B1
Ibirapuera, Parque do
  São Paulo 27 B1
Icarai *Rio de Janeiro* 25 B2
İçerenköy *Istanbul* 12 C2
Ichgao *Tokyo* 30 B2
Ichigaya *Tokyo* 30 A3
Ichikawa *Tokyo* 30 A4
Ickenham *London* 15 A1
Iddo *Lagos* 14 B2
Idi-Oro *Lagos* 14 A2
Iganmu *Lagos* 14 B2
Igbobi *Lagos* 14 A2
Igbologun *Lagos* 14 B1
Igny *Paris* 24 B2
Ikebe *Tokyo* 30 B2
Ikebukuro *Tokyo* 30 A3
Ikegami *Tokyo* 30 B3
Ikeja *Lagos* 14 A2
Ikeuchi *Osaka* 23 B2
Ikoyi *Lagos* 14 B2
Ikuata *Lagos* 14 B2
ikuno *Osaka* 23 B2
Ikuta *Tokyo* 30 B2
Ila *Oslo* 23 A2
Ilford *London* 15 A4
Ilioupoli *Athens* 2 B2
Illinois at Chicago, Univ.
  of *Chicago* 9 B3
Illinois Institute of
  Technology *Chicago* 9 B3
Ilpendam *Amsterdam* 2 A2
Ilsos → *Athens* 2 B2
Imbâbah *Cairo* 7 A2
Imielin *Warsaw* 32 B2
Imirim *São Paulo* 27 A1
Imitos *Athens* 2 B2
Imitos, Oros *Athens* 2 B2
Inagi *Tokyo* 30 B2
Inchcolm *Edinburgh* 11 A2
Inchicore *Dublin* 10 A1
Inchkeith *Edinburgh* 11 A3
Inchmickery *Edinburgh* 11 A2
Incirano *Milan* 19 A1
Independencia *Lima* 14 A2
Independencia *Santiago* 27 B2
India Gate *Delhi* 10 B2
Indian Creek Village *Miami* 18 A2
Indianópolis *São Paulo* 27 B1
Indira Gandhi Int. ✈
  (DEL) *Delhi* 10 B1
Industria *Johannesburg* 13 B1
Industrial Canal →
  New Orleans 21 B2
Ingierstrand *Oslo* 23 B3
Inglewood *Los Angeles* 16 C3
Ingliston *Edinburgh* 11 B1
Inhaúma *Rio de Janeiro* 25 B1
Inner Port Shelter
  Hong Kong 12 A2
Interlagos *São Paulo* 27 C1
Intramuros *Manila* 17 B1
Inválides *Paris* 24 A3
Inverkeithing *Edinburgh* 11 A1
Inzersdorf *Vienna* 32 B2
Ipanema *Rio de Janeiro* 25 B1
Ipiranga *São Paulo* 27 B1
Ipiranga → *São Paulo* 27 B2
Iponri *Lagos* 14 B2
Ireland's Eye *Dublin* 10 A3
Irving Park *Chicago* 9 B2
Isabel *Rio de Janeiro* 25 B1
Isagatedo *Lagos* 14 A1
Isar → *Munich* 21 A3
Ishbīlīya *Baghdad* 3 A2
Ishøj Strand *Copenhagen* 8 B2
Island Bay *Wellington* 33 B1
Island Park *Toronto* 31 B2
Islev *Copenhagen* 8 A2
Isleworth *London* 15 B2
Islington *London* 15 A3
Islington □ *London* 15 A3
Ismaning *Munich* 21 A3
Ismayloskiy Park *Moscow* 19 B3
Isolo *Lagos* 14 A2
Issy-les-Moulineaux *Paris* 24 A2
Istanbul *Istanbul* 12 B1
Istanbul Boğazı *Istanbul* 12 B2
Istinye *Istanbul* 12 B1
İtä Hakkila *Helsinki* 11 B3
Itaewon *Seoul* 27 B1
Itami *Osaka* 23 A1
Itanhanga *Rio de Janeiro* 25 B1
Ivanhoe *Melbourne* 18 A2
Ivry-sur-Seine *Paris* 24 A3
Ixelles *Brussels* 6 B2
Izmaylovo *Moscow* 19 B3
Iztacalco *Mexico City* 18 B2
Iztapalapa *Mexico City* 18 B2

J

Jaba *Jerusalem* 13 A2
Jacaré *Rio de Janeiro* 25 B1
Jackson Heights *New York* 22 B2
Jackson Park *Chicago* 9 C3
Jacques-Cartier *Montreal* 20 A3
Jacques-Cartier, Pont
  Montreal 20 A2
Jadavpur *Kolkata* 14 C2
Jade Buddha Temple
  Shanghai 28 B1
Jægersborg *Copenhagen* 8 A3
Jægersborg Dyrehave
  Copenhagen 8 A3
Jagadishpur *Kolkata* 14 B1
Jagatpur *Delhi* 10 A2
Jaguaré, Rib. do →
  São Paulo 27 B1
Jahangirpur *Delhi* 10 A2
Jakarta *Jakarta* 12 A1
Jakarta, Teluk *Jakarta* 12 A1
Jalan Kayu *Singapore* 28 A3
Jamaica B. *New York* 22 C2
Jamaica Plain *Boston* 6 B2
Jamakpuri *Delhi* 10 B1
Jamshidiyeh *Tehran* 31 A2
Jamsil *Seoul* 27 B2
Jamwon *Seoul* 27 B2

Janki *Warsaw* 32 C1
Jaraguá *São Paulo* 27 A1
Jaraguá, Pico de *São Paulo* 27 A1
Jardim Paulista *São Paulo* 27 B1
Järvatälstet *Stockholm* 29 A1
Jaskhar *Mumbai* 20 B2
Jatinegara *Jakarta* 12 B2
Jāvādīyeh *Tehran* 31 B2
Jebel Ali *Jerusalem* 13 A2
Jefferson *New Orleans* 21 B2
Jefferson Memorial
  Washington 33 B3
Jefferson Park *Chicago* 9 B2
Jefferson Park *Los Angeles* 16 B3
Jegi *Seoul* 27 B2
Jelambar *Jakarta* 12 A1
Jelonki *Warsaw* 32 B1
Jerónimos, Mosteiro dos
  Lisbon 16 A1
Jersey City *New York* 22 B1
Jerusalem *Jerusalem* 13 B2
Jessamine, L. *Orlando* 23 B2
Jésus, Î. *Montreal* 20 A2
Jesús María *Lima* 14 B2
Jette *Brussels* 6 A1
Jey *Tehran* 31 B2
Jianggao *Guangzhou* 11 A2
Jiangwan *Shanghai* 28 B1
Jib *Jerusalem* 13 A2
Jikebe *Tokyo* 30 B2
Jihād *Baghdad* 3 B1
Jingan *Shanghai* 28 B1
Jinočany *Prague* 25 B1
Jinonice *Prague* 25 B2
Jiulong = Kowloon
  Hong Kong 12 B1
Jiyūgaoka *Tokyo* 30 B3
Jizā'ir *Baghdad* 3 B2
Jizīra *Baghdad* 3 A2
Joglo *Jakarta* 12 B1
Johannesburg *Johannesburg* 13 B2
Johannesburg, Univ. of
  Johannesburg 13 B2
Johanneskirchen *Munich* 21 A2
Johannesstift *Berlin* 5 A2
Johannisthal *Berlin* 5 B4
John F. Kennedy Nat.
  Historic Site △ *Boston* 6 A2
John McLaren Park
  San Francisco 26 B2
Johnsonville *Wellington* 33 B1
Joinville-le-Pont *Paris* 24 B3
Joli-Bois *Brussels* 6 B2
Jollas *Helsinki* 11 B3
Jongmyo Royal Shrine
  Seoul 27 B1
Jongno *Seoul* 27 B1
Jonstrup *Copenhagen* 8 A2
Joppa *Edinburgh* 11 B3
Jorge Chavez, Int. ✈ (LIM)
  Lima 14 B2
Jorge Newbery ✈ (AEP)
  Buenos Aires 7 A2
Jósefa Piłsudskiego Park
  Warsaw 32 B2
Jōtō *Osaka* 23 A2
Jouy-en-Josas *Paris* 24 B2
Juan Anchorena
  Buenos Aires 7 A2
Juan González Romero
  Mexico City 18 A2
Juárez Int. ✈ (MEX)
  Mexico City 18 B2
Judeira *Jerusalem* 13 A2
Juhdum *Jerusalem* 13 B2
Juhu *Mumbai* 20 A2
Jūjā *Tokyo* 30 A3
Jukskeirivier →
  Johannesburg 13 A2
Julianów *Warsaw* 32 B1
Jung *Seoul* 27 B1
Jungfernheide, Volkspark
  Berlin 5 A2
Jungfernsee *Berlin* 5 B1
Junghwa *Seoul* 27 B2
Jungnang *Seoul* 27 B2
Jungnangcheon → *Seoul* 27 B2
Juniper Green *Edinburgh* 11 B2
Junk B. *Hong Kong* 12 B2
Jurong *Singapore* 28 B2
Jurong, Selat *Singapore* 28 B2
Jurong Industrial Estate
  Singapore 28 B2
Jurujuba, Enseada de
  Rio de Janeiro 25 B2
Justice *Chicago* 9 C2
Jwalahari *Delhi* 10 B1

K

Kaapstad = Cape Town
  Cape Town 8 A1
Kabaty *Warsaw* 32 C2
Kadıköy *Istanbul* 12 C2
Kadoma *Osaka* 23 A2
Kafr 'Aqab *Jerusalem* 13 A2
Kāğithane *Istanbul* 12 B1
Kāğithane → *Istanbul* 12 B1
Kagran *Vienna* 32 A2
Kahnawake *Montreal* 20 B1
Kaimes *Edinburgh* 11 B2
Kaisereberstorf *Vienna* 32 B2
Kaivoksela *Helsinki* 11 B2
Kalamaki *Athens* 2 B2
Kalbadevi *Mumbai* 20 B1
Kalipur *Kolkata* 14 A1
Kalithea *Athens* 2 B2
Kalkaji *Delhi* 10 B2
Kalookan = Caloocan
  Manila 17 B1
Kalvebod Fælled *Copenhagen* 8 B3
Kalveboderne *Copenhagen* 8 B3
Kamarhati *Kolkata* 14 A2
Kamata *Tokyo* 30 B3
Kameari *Tokyo* 30 A4
Kameido *Tokyo* 30 A4
Kami-Itabashi *Tokyo* 30 A3
Kamikitazawa *Tokyo* 30 B2
Kamitsuruma *Tokyo* 30 B1
Kamoshida *Tokyo* 30 B2
Kampong Landang
  Singapore 28 B2
Kampong Tanjong
  Penjuru *Singapore* 28 B2
Kampung Bali *Jakarta* 12 A1
Kanamori *Tokyo* 30 B1
Kanda *Tokyo* 30 A3
Kandilli *Istanbul* 12 B2
Kankurgachi *Kolkata* 14 B2
Kanlıca *Istanbul* 12 B2
Kannonskiy, Ostrov
  St. Petersburg 27 B1
Kansai Int. ✈ (KIX) *Osaka* 23 B2
Kanzaki → *Osaka* 23 A1
Kapali Carsi *Istanbul* 12 B1
Kapellerfeld *Vienna* 32 A2
Káposztásmegyer *Budapest* 7 A2

Kapotnya *Moscow* 19 C3
Käppala *Stockholm* 29 A2
Kapuk *Jakarta* 12 A1
Käpylä *Helsinki* 11 B2
Karachi *Karachi* 13 A2
Karachi Int. ✈ (KHI)
  Karachi 13 A2
Karkh *Baghdad* 3 B2
Karlin *Prague* 25 B2
Karlsfeld *Munich* 21 A1
Karlshorst *Berlin* 5 A4
Karlův most *Prague* 25 B2
Karol Bagh *Delhi* 10 B2
Karolinenhof *Berlin* 5 B4
Karori *Wellington* 33 B1
Karow *Berlin* 5 A3
Karrädah *Baghdad* 3 B2
Kärson *Stockholm* 29 B1
Kasai *Tokyo* 30 B4
Kasipur *Kolkata* 14 B2
Kastrup *Copenhagen* 8 B3
Kastrup, København ✈
  (CPH) *Copenhagen* 8 B3
Kasuga *Tokyo* 30 A3
Kasuge *Tokyo* 30 A3
Kasumigaseki *Tokyo* 30 B3
Katong *Singapore* 28 B3
Katsushika *Tokyo* 30 A4
Kau Pai Chau *Hong Kong* 12 B2
Kau Yi Chau *Hong Kong* 12 B1
Kauloon *Tokyo* 30 A3
Kauniainen *Helsinki* 11 B1
Kawasaki *Tokyo* 30 B3
Kawawa *Tokyo* 30 B2
Kawęczyn *Warsaw* 32 B2
Kayu Putih *Jakarta* 12 A2
Kbely *Prague* 25 B3
Kebayoran Baru *Jakarta* 12 B1
Kebayoran Lama *Jakarta* 12 B1
Kebon Jeruk *Jakarta* 12 B1
Kedar *Jerusalem* 13 B2
Kedoya *Jakarta* 12 B1
Keilor *Melbourne* 18 A1
Keilor East *Melbourne* 18 A1
Keilor North *Melbourne* 18 A1
Keimola *Helsinki* 11 A1
Kelapa Gading *Jakarta* 12 A2
Kelenföld *Budapest* 7 B2
Kelvin *Johannesburg* 13 A2
Kemang *Jakarta* 12 B1
Kemayoran *Jakarta* 12 B2
Kemerburgaz *Istanbul* 12 B1
Kempton Park Races
  London 15 B1
Kenilworth *Cape Town* 8 B1
Kennedy Town *Hong Kong* 12 B1
Kenner *New Orleans* 21 A1
Kensal Green *London* 15 A2
Kensington *Johannesburg* 13 B2
Kensington *London* 15 A2
Kensington *New York* 22 C2
Kensington *Sydney* 29 B2
Kensington Palace *London* 15 A2
Kent Village *Washington* 33 B4
Kentish Town *London* 15 A3
Kenton *London* 15 A2
Kenwood House *London* 15 A3
Kepa *Warsaw* 32 B2
Kesariani *Athens* 2 B2
Kettering *Washington* 33 B4
Kew *London* 15 B2
Kew *Melbourne* 18 A2
Kew Gardens *London* 15 B2
Kew Gardens *Toronto* 31 A3
Key Biscayne *Miami* 18 B2
Khalīj *Baghdad* 3 B2
Khandallah *Wellington* 33 B1
Khansā' *Baghdad* 3 A2
Kharavli *Mumbai* 20 B2
Khefren *Cairo* 7 B1
Khichripur *Delhi* 10 B2
Khidirpur *Kolkata* 14 B1
Khimki-Khovrino *Moscow* 19 A2
Khirbet Batin Abu Lihyah
  Jerusalem 13 A2
Khirbet el-Misbah *Jerusalem* 13 B1
Khirbet Jub e-Rum
  Jerusalem 13 B2
Khlong San *Bangkok* 3 B2
Khlong Toey *Bangkok* 3 B2
Khorel *Kolkata* 14 B2
Khorosovo *Moscow* 19 B1
Kiamari *Karachi* 13 B1
Kierling *Vienna* 32 A1
Kierlingbach → *Vienna* 32 A1
Kifisos → *Athens* 2 A1
Kikuna *Tokyo* 30 B2
Kilbarrack *Dublin* 10 A3
Kilbirnie *Wellington* 33 B1
Kilburn *London* 15 A2
Killeen *Dublin* 10 B2
Killester *Dublin* 10 A3
Killiney *Dublin* 10 B3
Killiney B. *Dublin* 10 B3
Kilmacud *Dublin* 10 B2
Kilmainham Gaol *Dublin* 10 A2
Kilmashogue Mt. *Dublin* 10 B2
Kilmore *Dublin* 10 A3
Kilnamanagh *Dublin* 10 B1
Kilo *Helsinki* 11 B2
Kiltiern *Dublin* 10 B2
Kilmage *Dublin* 10 B2
Kindi *Baghdad* 3 B1
Kinghorn *Edinburgh* 11 A2
Kings Domain *Melbourne* 18 A1
Kings Forest =
  Kongelunden *Copenhagen* 8 B3
Kings Park *Washington* 33 C2
Kings Park West
  Washington 33 C2
Kingsbury *London* 15 A2
Kingsbury *Melbourne* 18 A2
Kingsford *Sydney* 29 B2
Kingsford Smith,
  Sydney ✈ (SYD) *Sydney* 29 B2
Kingston-upon-Thames □
  London 15 B2
Kingston Vale *London* 15 B2
Kingsway *Toronto* 31 B1
Kinsaley *Dublin* 10 A3
Kipling Heights *Toronto* 31 A1
Kipseli *Athens* 2 A2
Kirchstockbach *Munich* 21 B3
Kirchtrudering *Munich* 21 B3
Kirikiri *Lagos* 14 B2
Kirke Værløse *Copenhagen* 8 A1
Kirkhill *Edinburgh* 11 B3
Kirkliston *Edinburgh* 11 B1
Kirktewton *Edinburgh* 11 B1
Kirov Palace of Culture
  St. Petersburg 27 B1
Kiryat Anavim *Jerusalem* 13 B1
Kiryat Ha Yovel *Jerusalem* 13 B2
Kısıklı *Istanbul* 12 C2
Kispest *Budapest* 7 B2
Kista *Stockholm* 29 A1
Kita *Tokyo* 30 A3
Kitazawa *Tokyo* 30 B3

Kiu Tsiu *Hong Kong* 12 A2
La Garenne-Colombes *Paris* 24 A2
La Giustiniana *Rome* 26 B1
La Grange *Chicago* 9 C1
La Grange Park *Chicago* 9 C1
La Granja *Santiago* 27 C2
La Guardia, New York ✈
  (LGA) *New York* 22 B2
La Hulpe *Brussels* 6 B2
La Llacuna *Barcelona* 4 A1
La Loma *Mexico City* 18 A1
La Lucila *Buenos Aires* 7 A2
La Maladrerie *Paris* 24 A1
La Milla, Cerro *Lima* 14 A2
La Monachina *Rome* 26 B1
La Moraleja *Madrid* 17 A2
La Nopalera *Mexico City* 18 C2
La Paternal *Buenos Aires* 7 B2
La Perla *Lima* 14 B2
La Perouse *Sydney* 29 C2
La Pisana *Rome* 26 B1
La Prairie *Montreal* 20 B3
La Punta *Lima* 14 B1
La Puntigala *Barcelona* 4 A2
La Queue-en-Brie *Paris* 24 B4
La Reina *Santiago* 27 B2
La Ribera *Barcelona* 4 A1
La Sagrera *Barcelona* 4 A2
La Salada *Buenos Aires* 7 C2
La Scala *Milan* 19 B2
La Storta *Rome* 26 B1
La Taxonera *Barcelona* 4 A2
La Victoria *Lima* 14 B2
Laajalahti *Helsinki* 11 B1
Laajasalo *Helsinki* 11 B3
Laaksolahti *Helsinki* 11 B1
Labagoola National Forest
  Park *Beijing* 4 A2
Lablâba, W. el → *Cairo* 7 A2
Lachine *Montreal* 20 B2
Lachine, Canal de *Montreal* 20 B2
Lad Phrao *Bangkok* 3 B2
Ladera Heights *Los Angeles* 16 C2
Ládví *Prague* 25 B2
Lady *Warsaw* 32 C1
Lafontaine, Parc *Montreal* 20 A2
Lagoa *Rio de Janeiro* 25 B1
Lagos *Lagos* 14 B2
Lagos Harbour *Lagos* 14 B2
Lagos-Ikeja ✈ (LOS) *Lagos* 14 A2
Lagos Island *Lagos* 14 B2
Lagos Lagoon *Lagos* 14 B2
Laguna de B. *Manila* 17 C2
Laim *Munich* 21 B2
Lainate *Milan* 19 A1
Lainz *Vienna* 32 B1
Lake Buena Vista *Orlando* 23 B1
Lake Cain Hills *Orlando* 23 B1
Lake Fairfax Park
  Washington 33 B2
Lakemba *Sydney* 29 B1
Lakeside *Cape Town* 8 B1
Lakeside *Johannesburg* 13 A2
Lakeview *London* 15 A2
Lakeview *New Orleans* 21 A2
Lakewood Park *Atlanta* 3 B2
Lakhtinskiy, St. Petersburg 27 B1
Lakhtinskiy Razliv, Oz.
  St. Petersburg 27 B1
Lakshmanpur *Kolkata* 14 B1
Laksi *Bangkok* 3 A2
Lal Qila *Delhi* 10 B2
Lam Tin *Hong Kong* 12 B2
Lambert *Oslo* 23 A3
Lambeth □ *London* 15 B3
Lambrate *Milan* 19 B2
Lambro, Parco *Milan* 19 B2
Lambton Mills *Toronto* 31 B1
Lamma I. *Hong Kong* 12 B1
Landianchang *Beijing* 4 B1
Landover Hills *Washington* 33 B4
Landsmeer *Amsterdam* 2 A2
Landstrasse *Vienna* 32 A2
Landwehr kanal *Berlin* 5 B3
Lane Cove *Sydney* 29 A1
Lane Cove Nat. Park △
  Sydney 29 A1
Langa *Cape Town* 8 A2
Langenzersdorf *Vienna* 32 A2
Langer See *Berlin* 5 B4
Langley *Washington* 33 B2
Langley Park *Washington* 33 B4
Langwald *Munich* 21 A1
Lanham *Washington* 33 B4
Lankwitz *Berlin* 5 B3
L'Annunziatella *Rome* 26 C2
Lansdowne *Cape Town* 8 A2
Lansing *Toronto* 31 A2
Lanus *Buenos Aires* 7 C2
Lapa *Rio de Janeiro* 25 B1
Laranjeiras *Rio de Janeiro* 25 B1
Largo *Washington* 33 B4
Las Corts *Barcelona* 4 A1
Las Kabacki *Warsaw* 32 C2
Las Pinas *Manila* 17 C1
Las Rejas *Santiago* 27 B1
Las Vegas *Las Vegas* 14 A2
Las Vegas McCarran
  Int. ✈ (LAS) *Las Vegas* 14 B2
LaSalle *Montreal* 20 B2
LaSalle Street Station
  Chicago 9 C2
Lasek Bielański *Warsaw* 32 B1
Lasek Na Kole *Warsaw* 32 B1
Latina *Madrid* 17 B1
Lauttasaari *Helsinki* 11 C2
Laval-des-Rapides *Montreal* 20 A1
Lavižan *Tehran* 31 A2
Lavradio *Lisbon* 16 A2
Lawndale *Chicago* 9 B2
Lawne L. *Orlando* 23 A2
Lawrence Heights *Toronto* 31 A2
Layari *Karachi* 13 A2
Layari → *Karachi* 13 A2
Łazienkowski Park *Warsaw* 32 B2
Le Blanc-Mesnil *Paris* 24 A3
Le Bourget *Paris* 24 A3
Le Bridge *Leon* 15 A3
Leaside *Toronto* 31 A2
Lebbon *Rio de Janeiro* 25 B1
Lee *London* 15 B3
Leganés *Madrid* 17 C1
Legazpi *Madrid* 17 B1
Lehtisaari *Helsinki* 11 B2
Lei Yue Mun *Hong Kong* 12 B2
Leião *Lisbon* 16 A1
Leichhardt *Sydney* 29 B1
Leith *Edinburgh* 11 B3

Lekki Lagos 14 B2
Leme Rio de Janeiro 25 B1
Lemoyne Montreal 20 B3
Lenin Moscow 19 B2
Lenino Moscow 19 C2
Leninskiye Gory Moscow 19 B2
Lennox Los Angeles 16 C2
Leonia New York 22 A2
Leopardstown Dublin 10 B2
Leopoldau Vienna 32 A2
Leopoldsdorf Vienna 32 B2
Leopoldstadt Vienna 32 A2
Leportovo Moscow 19 B3
Leppävaara Helsinki 11 B1
Les Lilas Paris 24 A3
Les Loges-en-Josas Paris 24 B1
Les Pavillons-sous-Bois Paris 24 A4
Lésigny Paris 24 B4
Lesnozavodskaya St. Petersburg 27 B2
Lester B. Pearson Int., Toronto ✈ (YYZ) Toronto 31 A1
L'Étang-la-Ville Paris 24 A1
Letňany Prague 25 B3
Letopolis = Ausîm Cairo 7 A1
Levallois-Perret Paris 24 A2
Levent Istanbul 12 B2
Lewisdale Washington 33 B4
Lewisham □ London 15 B3
Lexington Boston 6 A1
Leyton London 15 A3
Leytonstone London 15 A4
L'Haÿ-les-Roses Paris 24 B3
L'Hospitalet de Llobregat Barcelona 4 A1
Lhotka Prague 25 B2
Liangshui He → Beijing 4 C2
Lianhua Chi Beijing 4 B1
Lianhua He → Beijing 4 B1
Libčice nad Vitavou Prague 25 A2
Libeň Prague 25 B2
Liberdade São Paulo 27 B2
Liberton Edinburgh 11 B3
Liberty I. New York 22 B1
Liberty Osaka Museum Osaka 23 B1
Liberty State Park ⌓ New York 22 B1
Libeznice Prague 25 A2
Libuš Prague 25 B2
Lichiao Guangzhou 11 B2
Lichtenburg Berlin 5 A4
Lichterfelde Berlin 5 B2
Lidingö Stockholm 29 A2
Lieshi Lingyuan Guangzhou 11 B2
Liesing Vienna 32 B1
Liesing → Vienna 32 B2
Ligovo St. Petersburg 27 C1
Lijordet Oslo 23 A2
Likhoborka → Moscow 19 A2
Lilla Värtan Stockholm 29 A3
Lille Værløse Copenhagen 8 A2
Liluah Kolkata 14 B1
Lim Chu Kang Singapore 28 A2
Lima Lima 14 B2
Lima Jorge Chavez, Int. ✈ (LIM) Lima 14 B2
Limbiate Milan 19 A1
Limehouse London 15 A3
Limeil-Brévannes Paris 24 B3
Linate, Milano ✈ (LIN) Milan 19 B2
Linbropark Johannesburg 13 A2
Lincoln Center for Performing Arts New York 22 B2
Lincoln Heights Los Angeles 16 B3
Lincoln Memorial Washington 33 B3
Lincoln Park Chicago 9 B3
Lincoln Park New York 22 B1
Lincoln Park San Francisco 26 B1
Lincoln Park Zoo Chicago 9 B3
Lincolnwood Chicago 9 A2
Linda-a-Pastora Lisbon 16 A1
Linden Johannesburg 13 A2
Linden Wellington 33 A1
Lindenberg Berlin 5 A4
Lindøya Oslo 23 A3
Liniers Buenos Aires 7 B1
Linkebeek Brussels 6 B2
Linksfield Johannesburg 13 A2
Linmeyer Johannesburg 13 B2
Linna Helsinki 11 A2
Lintuvaara Helsinki 11 B1
Lion Rock Country Park ⌓ Hong Kong 12 A2
Lion's Head Cape Town 8 A1
Lioumi Athens 2 B2
Lisboa Lisbon 16 A2
Lisboa ✈ (LIS) Lisbon 16 A2
Lisbon = Lisboa Lisbon 16 A2
Lishui Guangzhou 11 A1
Little B. Sydney 29 B2
Little Calumet → Chicago 9 D3
Little Ferry New York 22 A1
Little Lake Conway Orlando 23 B2
Little Red School House Nature Center Chicago 9 C1
Little Rouge → Toronto 31 A4
Liuhang Shanghai 28 A1
Liurong Temple Guangzhou 11 B2
Live Oak Manor New Orleans 21 B1
Livry-Gargan Paris 24 A4
Liwan Guangzhou 11 B2
Ljan Oslo 23 A3
Llano de can Gineu Barcelona 4 A2
Lo Aranguiz Santiago 27 B2
Lo Boza Santiago 27 B1
Lo Chau Hong Kong 12 B2
Lo Chau Pak Mai Hong Kong 12 B2
Lo Espejo Santiago 27 C1
Lo Hermida Santiago 27 B2
Lo Prado Santiago 27 B1
Lo So Shing Hong Kong 12 B1
Lo Wai Hong Kong 12 A1
Loanhead Edinburgh 11 B3
Lobau Vienna 32 A3
Lobos, Pt. San Francisco 26 B1
Locham Munich 21 B1
Lochkov Prague 25 B2
Lockhausen Munich 21 A1
Lodi New York 22 A1
Lodi Estate Delhi 10 B2
Logan Int., Boston ✈ (BOS) Boston 6 A2
Logan Square Chicago 9 B2
Lognes-Émerainville ✈ (XLG) Paris 24 B4
Löhme Berlin 5 A5
Lolokhet Karachi 13 A2
Lomas Chapultepec Mexico City 18 B1
Lomas de San Angel Inn Mexico City 18 B1
Lombardy East Johannesburg 13 A2
Lomianki Warsaw 32 A1
Lomus Reforma Mexico City 18 B1
London London 15 B3
London Avenue Canal New Orleans 21 A2
London City ✈ (LCY) London 15 A4
London Heathrow ✈ (LHR) London 15 B1
London Zoo London 15 A3
Long B. Sydney 29 B2
Long Branch Toronto 31 B1
Long Brook → Washington 33 C2
Long Ditton London 15 B2
Long Island City New York 22 B2
Longchamp, Hippodrome de Paris 24 A2
Longhua Pagoda Shanghai 28 B1
Longhua Park Shanghai 28 B1
Longjohn Slough Chicago 9 C1
Longtan Hu → Beijing 4 B2
Longue-Pointe Montreal 20 A2
Longueuil Montreal 20 A3
Loni Delhi 10 A2
Loop, The Chicago 9 B3
Lord's Cricket Ground London 15 A2
Loreto Milan 19 B2
Los Angeles Los Angeles 16 B3
Los Angeles Int. ✈ (LAX) Los Angeles 16 C2
Los Cerrillos ✈ (ULC) Santiago 27 B1
Los Nietos Los Angeles 16 C4
Los Olivos Lima 14 A2
Los Remedios △ Mexico City 18 B1
Los Reyes Mexico City 18 B2
Losiny Ostrov △ Moscow 19 A3
Lot Brussels 6 B1
Lotus River Cape Town 8 B2
Lotus Temple Delhi 10 B2
Loughlinstown Dublin 10 B3
Louis Armstrong New Orleans Int. ✈ (MSY) New Orleans 21 A1
Louise, L. Orlando 23 B1
Louisiana Superdome New Orleans 21 B2
Loures Lisbon 16 A1
Louveciennes Paris 24 A1
Louvre, Musée du Paris 24 A3
Lower B. New York 22 C1
Lower Hutt Wellington 33 B2
Lower New York B. = Lower B. New York 22 C1
Lower Shing Mun Res. Hong Kong 12 A1
Lowry Bay Wellington 33 B2
Loyola Univ. Chicago 9 B3
Lu Xun, Tomb of Shanghai 28 B1
Lu Xun Park Shanghai 28 B1
Lübars Berlin 5 A3
Lucy, L. Orlando 23 A2
Ludwigsfeld Munich 21 A1
Luhu Guangzhou 11 B2
Lumiar Lisbon 16 A2
Lundtofte Copenhagen 8 A3
Lung Mei Hong Kong 12 A2
Luojiang Guangzhou 11 B2
Lustheim Munich 21 A2
Luwan Shanghai 28 B1
Luzhniki Sports Centre Moscow 19 B2
Lyndhurst New York 22 B1
Lynn Woods Res. Boston 6 A2
Lyon, Gare de Paris 24 A3
Lyons Chicago 9 C2
Lysaker Oslo 23 A2
Lysakerselva → Oslo 23 A2
Lysolaje Prague 25 B2
Lyublino Moscow 19 B3

M

Ma Nam Wat Hong Kong 12 A2
Ma On Shan Country Park ⌓ Hong Kong 12 A2
Ma'ale Adumim Jerusalem 13 B2
Ma'ale Ha Khamisha Jerusalem 13 B1
Ma'ale Mikhmas Jerusalem 13 A2
Maantiekylä Helsinki 11 A3
Maarifa Baghdad 3 B2
Mabato Pt. Manila 17 C2
Mabel, L. Orlando 23 B1
Macaco, Morro do Rio de Janeiro 25 B2
McCarran Int., Las Vegas ✈ (LAS) Las Vegas 14 B2
McCook Chicago 9 C2
McGill Univ. Montreal 20 A2
Machelen Brussels 6 A2
Machida Tokyo 30 B1
Maciołki Warsaw 32 B2
McKerrow, Mt. Wellington 33 B2
McKinley Park Chicago 9 C2
McLean Washington 33 B2
Macopocho → Santiago 27 B1
MacRitchie Res. Singapore 28 A2
Macul Santiago 27 C2
Madhudaha Kolkata 14 B2
Madhyamgram Kolkata 14 A2
Madin Mexico City 18 A1
Madin, L. Mexico City 18 A1
Madīnat Al Mansūr Baghdad 3 B2
Mâdinet Nasr Cairo 7 A2
Madrid Madrid 17 B1
Madrid Barajas ✈ (MAD) Madrid 17 B2
Madrona Barcelona 4 A1
Maesawa Tokyo 30 A2
Magdalena Lima 14 B2
Magdalena Contreras Mexico City 18 C1
Maghreb Baghdad 3 A2
Maginu Tokyo 30 B2
Magliana Rome 26 B1
Magny-les-Hameaux Paris 24 B1
Maheshtala Kolkata 14 C1
Mahim Mumbai 20 A2
Mahim B. Mumbai 20 A1
Mahlsdorf Berlin 5 A4
Mahmoodabad Karachi 13 A2
Mahrauli Delhi 10 B2
Mahul Mumbai 20 A2
Maida Vale London 15 A2
Maidstone Melbourne 18 A1
Maipú Santiago 27 C1
Maisonneuve, Parc Montreal 20 A2
Maisons-Alfort Paris 24 B3
Maisons-Laffitte Paris 24 A1
Maissoneuve Montreal 20 A2
Maitland Cape Town 8 A1
Makasar Jakarta 12 A2
Makati Manila 17 B2
Mäkiniitty Helsinki 11 A2
Malá Strana Prague 25 B2
Malabar Sydney 29 B2
Malabar Hill Mumbai 20 B1
Malabar Pt. Mumbai 20 B1
Malabon Manila 17 B1
Malacañang Palace Manila 17 B1
Malahide Dublin 10 A3
Malakoff Paris 24 B2
Mälarhöjaen Stockholm 29 B1
Malate Manila 17 B1
Malaya Neva St. Petersburg 27 B1
Malaya Okhta St. Petersburg 27 B2
Malchow Berlin 5 A3
Malden Boston 6 A2
Malden London 15 B2
Maleizen Brussels 6 B3
Malešice Prague 25 B3
Malir → Karachi 13 B2
Malleny Mills Edinburgh 11 B2
Malmi Helsinki 11 B2
Malmøya Oslo 23 A3
Måløv Copenhagen 8 A1
Malton Toronto 31 A1
Malvern Johannesburg 13 B2
Malvern Melbourne 18 B2
Malvern Toronto 31 A3
Mampang Prapatan Jakarta 12 B1
Mampukuji Tokyo 30 B2
Man Budrukh Mumbai 20 A2
Man Khurd Mumbai 20 A2
Manakhat Jerusalem 13 B2
Mandaluyong Manila 17 B2
Mandaoli Delhi 10 B2
Mandaqui → São Paulo 27 A2
Mandoli Delhi 10 A2
Mandvi Mumbai 20 B2
Manenberg Cape Town 8 A2
Mang Kung Uk Hong Kong 12 B2
Mang-won Seoul 27 B1
Mangolpuri Delhi 10 A1
Manguinhos ✈ Rio de Janeiro 25 B1
Manhattan New York 22 B2
Manhattan Beach New York 22 C2
Manila Manila 17 B1
Manila Ninoy Aquino Int. ✈ (MNL) Manila 17 B2
Mankkaa Helsinki 11 B1
Manly Sydney 29 A2
Mann, L. Orlando 23 A2
Mann's Chinese Theatre Los Angeles 16 B2
Mannswörth Vienna 32 B3
Manor Park London 15 A4
Manor Park Wellington 33 A2
Manora Karachi 13 B1
Manora Pt. Karachi 13 B1
Manquehue, Cerro Santiago 27 B2
Manzanares, Canal de Madrid 17 C2
Mapo Seoul 27 B1
Mar Vista Los Angeles 16 B2
Maracanã Rio de Janeiro 25 B1
Maraoli Mumbai 20 A2
Marcelin Warsaw 32 B1
Mareil-Marly Paris 24 A1
Margareten Vienna 32 A2
Maria Vienna 32 A2
Maridalen Oslo 23 A3
Maridalsvatnet Oslo 23 A3
Mariendorf Berlin 5 B3
Marienfelde Berlin 5 B3
Marikina Manila 17 B2
Marikina → Manila 17 B2
Marin City San Francisco 26 A1
Marin Pen. San Francisco 26 A1
Marina del Rey Los Angeles 16 C2
Marino Dublin 10 A2
Marisco, Ponta do Rio de Janeiro 25 C1
Markham Toronto 31 A2
Marki Warsaw 32 B2
Markland Wood Toronto 31 B1
Marly, Forêt de Paris 24 A1
Marly-le-Roi Paris 24 A1
Marne-la-Vallée Paris 24 A4
Marolles-en-Brie Paris 24 B4
Maroubra Sydney 29 B2
Marquette Park Chicago 9 C2
Marrero New Orleans 21 B2
Marrickville Sydney 29 B1
Marsfield Sydney 29 A1
Marsha, L. Orlando 23 B2
Marte, Campo de São Paulo 27 B2
Martesana, Naviglio della Milan 19 A2
Martin Luther King Nat. Historic Site ⌓ Atlanta 3 B2
Martinez Buenos Aires 7 A1
Martinkylä Helsinki 11 B2
Martinsried Munich 21 B1
Maruko Tokyo 30 B3
Maryino Moscow 19 B3
Maryland Singapore 28 B2
Marymont Warsaw 32 B1
Marysin Wawerski Warsaw 32 B2
Marzahn Berlin 5 A4
Mascot Sydney 29 B2
Masmo Stockholm 29 B1
Maspeth New York 22 B2
Masr el Gedida Cairo 7 A2
Masr el Qadîma Cairo 7 A2
Massachusetts Inst. of Tech. Boston 6 A2
Massamá Lisbon 16 A1
Massey → Toronto 31 A3
Massy Paris 24 B2
Mata Jerusalem 13 B1
Matinha Lisbon 16 A2
Matraman Jakarta 12 B2
Matsubara Osaka 23 B2
Mattapan Boston 6 B2
Mátyásföld Budapest 7 A3
Mau Tso Ngam Hong Kong 12 A2
Mauer Vienna 32 B1
Mauripur Karachi 13 A1
Maxhof Munich 21 B1
Mayfair Johannesburg 13 B2
Maywood Chicago 9 B1
Maywood Los Angeles 16 C3
Maywood New York 22 A1
Maywood Park Race Track Chicago 9 B1
Mazagaon Mumbai 20 B2
Meadowbank Park Sydney 29 A1
Měcholupy Prague 25 B3
Měčice Prague 25 A3
Mecidiyeköy Istanbul 12 B2
Medford Boston 6 A2
Mediodia Madrid 17 B2
Meguro Tokyo 30 B3
Meguro → Tokyo 30 B3
Mehpalpur Delhi 10 B1
Mehrābād ✈ (THR) Tehran 31 A1
Mehram Nagar Delhi 10 B1
Mehrow Berlin 5 A4
Meidling Vienna 32 A2
Méier Rio de Janeiro 25 B1
Meiji Shrine Tokyo 30 A3
Meise Brussels 6 A1
Mejiro Tokyo 30 A3
Melbourne Melbourne 18 A1
Melbourne ✈ (MEL) Melbourne 18 A1
Melkki Helsinki 11 C2
Mellunkylä Helsinki 11 B3
Mellunmäki Helsinki 11 B3
Melrose Boston 6 A2
Melrose New York 22 B2
Melrose Park Chicago 9 B1
Melsbroek Brussels 6 A2
Melville Johannesburg 13 B2
Menteng Jakarta 12 B1
Mérantaise → Paris 24 B1
Mercamadrid Madrid 17 B2
Merced, L. San Francisco 26 B2
Meredale Johannesburg 13 B1
Merlimau, Pulau Singapore 28 B2
Merri Cr. → Melbourne 18 A1
Merrion Dublin 10 B2
Merrionette Park Chicago 9 C2
Merton □ London 15 B2
Mesgarābād Tehran 31 B3
Messe Vienna 32 A2
Metairie New Orleans 21 A2
Metanópoli Milan 19 B2
Metro-Dade Cultural Centre Miami 18 B2
Metro Toronto Zoo Toronto 31 A3
Metropolitan Museum of Art New York 22 B2
Meudon Paris 24 B2
Mevaseret Tsiyon Jerusalem 13 B1
Mevo Beitar Jerusalem 13 B1
México Mexico City 18 B2
México, Ciudad de Mexico City 18 B2
Mexico City Int. ✈ (MEX) Mexico City 18 B2
Meyersdal Johannesburg 13 B2
Mezzate Milan 19 B2
Miadong Seoul 27 B2
Miami Miami 18 B2
Miami Beach Miami 18 B2
Miami Canal Miami 18 A1
Miami Int. ✈ (MIA) Miami 18 B1
Miami Shores Miami 18 A2
Miami Springs Miami 18 B1
Miasto Warsaw 32 B2
Michałowice Warsaw 32 B1
Michle Prague 25 B2
Mid-City Los Angeles 16 B2
Mid-City New Orleans 21 B2
Middle Harbour Sydney 29 A2
Middle Hd. Sydney 29 A2
Middle Park Melbourne 18 B1
Middle Village New York 22 B2
Middlesex Fells Reservation Boston 6 A2
Midland Beach New York 22 C1
Midwood New York 22 C2
Miedzeszyn Warsaw 32 B3
Międzylesie Warsaw 32 B3
Miessaari Helsinki 11 C1
Miguel Hidalgo Mexico City 18 B1
Milan = Milano Milan 19 B1
Milanese, Parco Regionale ⌓ Milan 19 A1
Milano Milan 19 B1
Milano Due Milan 19 B2
Milano Linate ✈ (LIN) Milan 19 B2
Milano San Felice Milan 19 B2
Milbertshofen Munich 21 A2
Mill Hill London 15 A2
Millennium Dome London 15 A4
Miller Meadow Chicago 9 B2
Millerhill Edinburgh 11 B3
Milltown Dublin 10 B2
Millwood Washington 33 B4
Milnerton Cape Town 8 A1
Milon-la-Chapelle Paris 24 B1
Milton Boston 6 B2
Milton Bridge Edinburgh 11 B2
Mimico Toronto 31 B2
Mimico Creek → Toronto 31 B1
Minami Osaka 23 A2
Minamitsunashima Tokyo 30 B2
Minato Osaka 23 B1
Minato Tokyo 30 B3
Minshât el Bekkarî Cairo 7 A1
Miraflores Lima 14 B2
Miramar Wellington 33 B1
Misericordia, Sa. da Rio de Janeiro 25 B1
Mission San Francisco 26 B2
Mississauga Toronto 31 B1
Mitaka Tokyo 30 A2
Mitcham London 15 B2
Mitcham Common London 15 B3
Mitchell Museum of the American Indian Chicago 9 A2
Mitchell's Plain Cape Town 8 B2
Mitte Berlin 5 A3
Mittel Isarkanal → Munich 21 A3
Mixcoac Mexico City 18 B1
Miyakojima Osaka 23 A2
Mizonokuchi Tokyo 30 B2
Mizue Tokyo 30 A4
Młocinski Park Warsaw 32 B1
Młociny Warsaw 32 B1
Mnevniki Moscow 19 B1
Moba Lagos 14 B2
Moczydło Warsaw 32 C2
Modderfontein Johannesburg 13 A2
Modřany Prague 25 B2
Mogyoród Budapest 7 A3
Moinho Velho, Cor. → São Paulo 27 B2
Mok Seoul 27 B1
Mokotów Warsaw 32 B2
Molenbeek-St-Jean Brussels 6 A1
Molino de Rosas Mexico City 18 B1
Mollem Brussels 6 A1
Mollins de Rey Barcelona 4 A1
Mondeor Johannesburg 13 B2
Moneda, Palacio de la Santiago 27 B2
Monerò Rio de Janeiro 25 A1
Mong Kok Hong Kong 12 B2
Monkstown Dublin 10 B3
Monnickendam Amsterdam 2 A3
Monrovia Los Angeles 16 B4
Monsanto Lisbon 16 A1
Monsanto, Parque Florestal de Lisbon 16 A1
Mont-Royal Montreal 20 A2
Mont-Royal, Parc Montreal 20 A2
Montana de Montjuich Barcelona 4 A1
Montcada i Reixac Barcelona 4 A2
Monte Chingolo Buenos Aires 7 C2
Montebello Los Angeles 16 B4
Montemor Lisbon 16 A1
Monterey Hills Los Angeles 16 B3
Monterey Park Los Angeles 16 B4
Montespaccato Rome 26 B1
Montesson Paris 24 A1
Monteverde Nuovo Rome 26 B1
Montfermeil Paris 24 A4
Montigny-le-Bretonneux Paris 24 B1
Montjay-la-Tour Paris 24 A4
Montjuïc Barcelona 4 A2
Montparnasse, Gare Paris 24 A2
Montréal Montreal 20 A2
Montréal, Î. de Montreal 20 A2
Montréal, Univ. de Montreal 20 B2
Montréal Est Montreal 20 A2
Montréal-Nord Montreal 20 A2
Montréal-Ouest Montreal 20 B1
Montréal Trudeau Int. ✈ (YUL) Montreal 20 B1
Montreuil Paris 24 A3
Montrouge Paris 24 B2
Montserrat Buenos Aires 7 B2
Monza Milan 19 A2
Monzoro Milan 19 B1
Moóca São Paulo 27 B2
Moonachie New York 22 B1
Moonee Ponds Melbourne 18 A1
Moonee Valley Racecourse Melbourne 18 A1
Moosach Munich 21 A2
Mora Mumbai 20 B2
Moratalaz Madrid 17 B2
Mörby Stockholm 29 A2
Morden London 15 B2
Morée → Paris 24 A3
Morgan Park Chicago 9 C3
Moriguchi Osaka 23 A2
Morivione Milan 19 B2
Morningside Edinburgh 11 B2
Morningside Johannesburg 13 A2
Morningside Washington 33 C4
Morningside Park Orlando 23 B2
Morningside Park Toronto 31 A3
Morro Solar, Cerro Lima 14 C2
Mortlake London 15 B2
Mortlake Sydney 29 B1
Morton Grove Chicago 9 A2
Morumbi São Paulo 27 B1
Moscavide Lisbon 16 A2
Moschato Athens 2 B2
Moscow = Moskva Moscow 19 B2
Moskva Moscow 19 B2
Moskvoretskiy Moscow 19 B2
Mosman Sydney 29 B2
Moti Bagh Delhi 10 B2
Motol Prague 25 B2
Motsa Jerusalem 13 B2
Motsa Illit Jerusalem 13 B1
Motspur Park London 15 B2
Mottingham London 15 B4
Mount Dennis Toronto 31 A2
Mount Greenwood Chicago 9 C2
Mount Hood Memorial Park ⌓ Boston 6 A2
Mount Merrion Dublin 10 B2
Mount Olympus Los Angeles 16 B2
Mount Rainier Washington 33 B4
Mount Vernon New York 22 A3
Müggelberge Berlin 5 B4
Müggelheim Berlin 5 B5
Muggiò Milan 19 A2
Mühleiten Vienna 32 A3
Mühlenfliess → Berlin 5 A5
Muiden Amsterdam 2 A3
Muizenberg Cape Town 8 B1
Mujahidpur Delhi 10 B2
Mukandpur Delhi 10 A2
Mukhmas Jerusalem 13 A2
Muko → Osaka 23 A1
Mukojima Tokyo 30 A3
Mulbarton Johannesburg 13 B2
Mullach Íde = Malahide Dublin 10 A3
Mumbai Mumbai 20 B2
Mumbai Chhatrapati Shivaji Int. ✈ (BOM) Mumbai 20 A2
Mumbai Harbour Mumbai 20 B2
Munch-museum Oslo 23 A3
Münchehofe Berlin 5 B5
München Munich 21 B2
München Franz Josef Strauss Int. ✈ (MUC) Munich 21 A2
Munich = München Munich 21 B2
Munkkiniemi Helsinki 11 B2
Munro Buenos Aires 7 B1
Muntinlupa Manila 17 C2
Murai Res. Singapore 28 A2
Muranów Warsaw 32 B1
Murino St. Petersburg 27 B2
Murrayfield Edinburgh 11 B2
Murtala Mohammed International ✈ (LOS) Lagos 14 A1
Musashino Tokyo 30 A2
Museu Nacional Rio de Janeiro 25 B1
Mushin Lagos 14 A2
Musocco Milan 19 B1
Mustansiriya Baghdad 3 A2
Musturud Cairo 7 A2
Muswell Hill London 15 A3
Mutanabi Baghdad 3 B2
Muthana Baghdad 3 B2
Mykerinos Cairo 7 B1
Myllypuro Helsinki 11 B3
Mystic → Boston 6 A2

N

Nacka Stockholm 29 B3
Naenae Wellington 33 B2
Nærsnes Oslo 23 B1
Nagatsuta Tokyo 30 B2
Nagytétény Budapest 7 B1
Nahalin Jerusalem 13 B1
Najafgarh Drain → Delhi 10 B1
Nakahara Tokyo 30 B2
Nakano Tokyo 30 A2
Namsan Park Seoul 27 B1
Namyeong Seoul 27 B1
Nanbiancun Guangzhou 11 B1
Nanchang He → Beijing 4 B1
Nandang Guangzhou 11 B2
Nangal Dewat Delhi 10 B1
Naniwa Osaka 23 B1
Nanole Mumbai 20 A2
Nanpu Bridge Shanghai 28 B2
Nanshi Shanghai 28 B1
Nanterre Paris 24 A2
Napier Mole Karachi 13 B1
Naraina Delhi 10 B1
Nariman Point Mumbai 20 B1
Nariman Pt. Mumbai 20 B1
Nārmak Tehran 31 A2
Naruo Osaka 23 A1
Näsby Stockholm 29 A2
Näsbypark Stockholm 29 A2
National Arboretum Washington 33 B3
National Zoological Park Washington 33 B3
Nationals Park Washington 33 B3
Nativity, Basilica of Jerusalem 13 B2
Natolin Warsaw 32 C2
Naucalpan de Juárez Mexico City 18 B1
Naupada Mumbai 20 A2
Navi Mumbai Mumbai 20 A2
Naviglio di Pavia Milan 19 B1
Naviglio Grande Milan 19 B1
Navotas Manila 17 B1
Navy Pier Chicago 9 B3
Nazal Hikmat Beg Baghdad 3 A2
Nazimabad Karachi 13 A2
Nazlet el Simmân Cairo 7 B1
Nea Alexandria Athens 2 B2
Nea Ionia Athens 2 A2
Nea Liosia Athens 2 A2
Nea Smirni Athens 2 B2
Neapoli Athens 2 B2
Near North Chicago 9 B3
Nebušice Prague 25 B1
Nederhorst Amsterdam 2 B3
Nedlitz Berlin 5 B1
Nee Soon Singapore 28 A2
Needham Boston 6 B1
Needham Heights Boston 6 B1
Nellis Air Force Base ✈ (LSV) Las Vegas 14 A2
N'emātābād Tehran 31 B2
Nerima Tokyo 30 A3
Nesodden Oslo 23 B3
Nesoddtangen Oslo 23 A3
Nesøya Oslo 23 A2
Neu Aubing Munich 21 B1
Neu Buch Berlin 5 A4
Neu Buchhorst Berlin 5 B5
Neu Fahrland Berlin 5 B1
Neu Lindenberg Berlin 5 A4
Neubiberg Munich 21 B3
Neuenhagen Berlin 5 A4
Neuessling Vienna 32 A3
Neuhausen Munich 21 B2
Neuherberg Munich 21 A2
Neuhönow Berlin 5 A5
Neuilly-Plaisance Paris 24 A4
Neuilly-sur-Marne Paris 24 A4
Neuilly-sur-Seine Paris 24 A2
Neukagran Vienna 32 A2
Neukettenhof Vienna 32 B2
Neukölln Berlin 5 B3
Neuperlach Munich 21 B2
Neuried Munich 21 B1
Neustift am Walde Vienna 32 A1
Neusüssenbrunn Vienna 32 A2
Neuwaldegg Vienna 32 A1
Neve Ya'akov Jerusalem 13 A2
Neves Rio de Janeiro 25 B2
New Baghdād Baghdad 3 B2
New Barakpur Kolkata 14 A2
New Brighton New York 22 C1
New Canada Johannesburg 13 B1
New Canada Dam Johannesburg 13 B1
New Carrollton Washington 33 B4
New Cross London 15 B3
New Delhi Delhi 10 B2
New Dorp New York 22 C1
New Dorp Beach New York 22 C1
New Malden London 15 B2
New Milford New York 22 A1
New Mumbai = Navi Mumbai Mumbai 20 A2
New Orleans New Orleans 21 B2
New Orleans Int. ✈ (MSY) New Orleans 21 A1
New Territories Hong Kong 12 A1
New Toronto Toronto 31 B1
New Utrecht New York 22 C2
New York New York 22 B3
New York La Guardia ✈ (LGA) New York 22 B2
Newark B. New York 22 B1
Newbattle Edinburgh 11 B3
Newbury Park London 15 A4
Newcraighall Edinburgh 11 B3
Newham □ London 15 A4
Newhaven Edinburgh 11 B2
Newington Edinburgh 11 B2
Newlands Johannesburg 13 B1
Newlands Wellington 33 B1
Newport Melbourne 18 B1
Newton Boston 6 B1
Newtonbrook Toronto 31 A2
Newtongrange Edinburgh 11 B3
Newtonville Boston 6 A1
Newtown Sydney 29 B2
Ngaio Wellington 33 B1
Ngau Chi Wan Hong Kong 12 A2
Ngau Tau Kok Hong Kong 12 B2
Ngauranga Wellington 33 B1
Ngong Shuen Chau Hong Kong 12 B1
Ngua Kok Wan Hong Kong 12 A1
Nhava Sheva Mumbai 20 B2
Niāvarān Tehran 31 A2
Nibra Kolkata 14 B1
Nidāl Baghdad 3 B2
Niddrie Edinburgh 11 B3
Niddrie Melbourne 18 A1
Nieder Neuendorf Berlin 5 A2
Niederschöneweide Berlin 5 B3
Niederschönhausen Berlin 5 A3
Niemeyer Rio de Janeiro 25 B1
Nieuwendam Amsterdam 2 A2
Nihonbashi Tokyo 30 A3
Niipperi Helsinki 11 B1
Nikea Athens 2 B1
Nikolassee Berlin 5 B2
Nikolskiy Moscow 19 B1
Niles Chicago 9 A2
Nimta Kolkata 14 A2
Ninoy Aquino Int. ✈ (MNL) Manila 17 B2
Nippa Tokyo 30 B2
Nippori Tokyo 30 A3
Nishi Osaka 23 A1
Nishinari Osaka 23 B1
Nishinomiya Osaka 23 A1
Nishiyodogawa Osaka 23 A1
Niterói Rio de Janeiro 25 B2
Nockeby Stockholm 29 B1
Noel Park London 15 A3
Nogatino Moscow 19 B3
Nogent-sur-Marne Paris 24 A3
Noida Delhi 10 B2
Noiseau Paris 24 B4
Noisiel Paris 24 A4
Noisy-le-Grand Paris 24 A4
Noisy-le-Roi Paris 24 A1
Noisy-le-Sec Paris 24 A3
Nokkala Helsinki 11 C1
Nomentano Rome 26 B2
Nonakashinden Tokyo 30 A2
Nongminyundong Jiangxisuo Guangzhou 11 B2
Nonhyeon Seoul 27 B2
Nonthaburi Bangkok 3 A1
Noordgesig Johannesburg 13 B1
Noordzeekanaal Amsterdam 2 A1
Nord, Gare du Paris 24 A3
Nordmarka Oslo 23 A3
Nordrand-Siedlung Vienna 32 A2
Nordstrand Oslo 23 A3
Normandale Wellington 33 B2
Norridge Chicago 9 B2
Norrmalm Stockholm 29 A2
North Arlington New York 22 B1
North Bay Village Miami 18 A2
North Bergen New York 22 B1
North Bull I. Dublin 10 A3
North Cheam London 15 B2
North Cray London 15 B4
North Decatur Atlanta 3 B3
North Druid Hills Atlanta 3 B3
North Esk → Edinburgh 11 B2
North Gyle Edinburgh 11 B2
North Hackensack New York 22 A1
North Harbor Manila 17 B1
North Hd. Sydney 29 A2
North Hollywood Los Angeles 16 B2
North Las Vegas Las Vegas 14 A1
North Las Vegas ✈ (VGT) Las Vegas 14 A1
North Lexington Boston 6 A1
North Miami Miami 18 A2
North Miami Beach Miami 18 A2
North Nazimabad Karachi 13 A2
North Pt. Hong Kong 12 B2
North Queensferry Edinburgh 11 A1
North Quincy Boston 6 B2
North Res. Boston 6 A2
North Riverside Chicago 9 B2
North Saugus Boston 6 A2
North Shore Channel → Chicago 9 B2
North Springfield Washington 33 C2
North Station Boston 6 A2
North Sydney Sydney 29 B2
North Woolwich London 15 A4
North York Toronto 31 A2
Northbridge Sydney 29 A2
Northbridge Park Sydney 29 A2
Northcliff Johannesburg 13 A1
Northcote Melbourne 18 A2
Northeastern Univ. Boston 6 A2
Northern Virginia Regional Park ⌓ Washington 33 B3
Northlake Chicago 9 B1
Northmount Toronto 31 A2
Northolt London 15 A1
Northumberland Heath London 15 B5
Northwestern Station Chicago 9 B3
Northwestern Univ. Chicago 9 A2
Northwood London 15 A1
Northwood Park Toronto 31 A1
Norwood Johannesburg 13 A2
Norwood Park Chicago 9 B2
Noryangjin Seoul 27 B1
Nossa Senhora do Ó São Paulo 27 B1
Nossegem Brussels 6 A3
Notre-Dame Paris 24 A3
Notre-Dame, Basilique Montreal 20 B2
Notre-Dame, Bois Paris 24 B4
Notre-Dame-de-Grace Montreal 20 B2
Notting Hill London 15 A2
Nova Milanese Milan 19 A2
Novate Milanese Milan 19 A1
Novaya Derevnya St. Petersburg 27 A1
Nové Město Prague 25 B2
Novoaleksandrovskoye St. Petersburg 27 B2
Novodevichy Convent Moscow 19 B2
Novogireyevo Moscow 19 B3
Novosaratovka St. Petersburg 27 B3
Nowe-Babice Warsaw 32 B1
Nöykkiö Helsinki 11 B1
Nueva Atzacoalco Mexico City 18 B2
Nueva Pompeya Buenos Aires 7 C2
Nueva Tenochtitlán Mexico City 18 B2
Nuijala Helsinki 11 B1
Nukui Tokyo 30 A2
Numabukuro Tokyo 30 A2
Nuñez Buenos Aires 7 B2
Nunhead London 15 B3
Ñuñoa Santiago 27 B2
Nusle Prague 25 B2
Nussdorf Vienna 32 A2
Nyanga Cape Town 8 A2
Nymphenburg Munich 21 B2
Nymphenburg, Schloss Munich 21 B2

O

O.R. Tambo Int. ✈ (JNB) Johannesburg 13 A2
Oak Grove Atlanta 3 A3
Oak Hill Boston 6 B1
Oak Lawn Chicago 9 C2
Oak Park Chicago 9 B2
Oak View Washington 33 A4
Oakdale Atlanta 3 A2
Oakland San Francisco 26 B3
Oakland Washington 33 B4
Oaklawn Washington 33 C4
Oakleigh Melbourne 18 B2
Oakton Washington 33 B1
Oakwood Beach New York 22 C1
Oatley Sydney 29 B1
Obalende Lagos 14 B2
Oba's Palace Lagos 14 B2
Oberföhring Munich 21 B2
Oberhaching Munich 21 B2
Oberlaa Vienna 32 B2
Oberlisse Vienna 32 A2
Obermenzing Munich 21 A1
Obermoos Schwaige Munich 21 A1
Oberschleissheim Munich 21 A2
Oberschöneweide Berlin 5 B4
Observatory Johannesburg 13 B2
Óbuda Budapest 7 A2
Obukhovo St. Petersburg 27 B2
Obvodnyy Kanal St. Petersburg 27 B1
Ocean Park Hong Kong 12 B2
Ochota Warsaw 32 B1
Ocoee Orlando 23 A1
Ōdana Tokyo 30 B2
Öden-Stockach Munich 21 B3
Odilampi Helsinki 11 B1
Odivelas Lisbon 16 A1
Odolany Warsaw 32 B1
Oeiras Lisbon 16 A1
Ofin Lagos 14 A3
Ogawa Tokyo 30 A1
Ogden Park Chicago 9 C2
Ogikubo Tokyo 30 A2
Ogogoro Lagos 14 B2
Ogoyo Lagos 14 B2
Ogudu Lagos 14 A2
O'Hare Int., Chicago ✈ (ORD) Chicago 9 B1
Ohariu Stream → Wellington 33 B1
O'Higgins, Parque Santiago 27 B2
Ōimachi Tokyo 30 B3
Ojota Lagos 14 A2
Oke-Ira Lagos 14 B2
Okęcie Warsaw 32 B1
Okęcie, Warszawa ✈ (WAW) Warsaw 32 B1
Okeogbe Lagos 14 B2
Okhla Delhi 10 B2
Okhta → St. Petersburg 27 B2
Okkervil → St. Petersburg 27 B2
Okrzeszyn Warsaw 32 C2
Oksval Oslo 23 A3
Oktyabrskiy Moscow 19 B2
Okubo Tokyo 30 A3
Ōkura Tokyo 30 B1
Olari Helsinki 11 B1
Olaria Rio de Janeiro 25 B1
Old Admiralty St. Petersburg 27 B1
Old City Jerusalem 13 B2
Old City Shanghai 28 B1
Old Fort York Toronto 31 B2
Old Harbor Boston 6 B2
Old Town = Stare Miasto Warsaw 32 B2
Old Town Chicago 9 B3
Old Town Hall = Altes Rathaus Munich 21 B2
Oldbawn Dublin 10 B1
Olgino St. Petersburg 27 A1
Olimpico, Estadio Mexico City 18 C1
Olivais Lisbon 16 A2
Olivar de los Padres Mexico City 18 B1
Olivar del Conde Mexico City 18 B1
Olives, Mt. of Jerusalem 13 B2
Olivia, L. Orlando 23 A1
Olivos Buenos Aires 7 B2
Olona → Milan 19 B1
Olympia, L. Orlando 23 A1
Olympic Green Beijing 4 B2
Olympic Stadium = Turner Field Atlanta 3 B2
Olympic Stadium Beijing 4 B2
Olympic Stadium Helsinki 11 B2
Olympique, Stade Montreal 20 A2
Ōmori Tokyo 30 B3
Onisigun Lagos 14 A2
Ontario Science Centre Toronto 31 A2
Ōokayama Tokyo 30 B3
Oostzaan Tuindorp Amsterdam 2 A2
Opa-Locka Miami 18 A1
Opa-Locka ✈ (OPF) Miami 18 A1
Opacz Warsaw 32 B1
Ophirton Johannesburg 13 B2
Oppegård Oslo 23 B3
Oppem Brussels 6 A1
Oppsal Oslo 23 A4
Ora Jerusalem 13 B1
Oradell New York 22 A1
Oradell Res. New York 22 A1
Orange Bowl Stadium Miami 18 B2
Orangi Karachi 13 A2
Ordrup Copenhagen 8 A3
Orech Prague 25 B1
Oregun Lagos 14 A2
Orient Heights Boston 6 A3
Orlando Orlando 23 A2
Orlando Dam Johannesburg 13 B1
Orlando East Johannesburg 13 B1
Orlando Executive ✈ (ORL) Orlando 23 A2
Orlando Int. ✈ (MCO) Orlando 23 B3
Orlovista Orlando 23 A2
Orly Paris 24 B3
Orly, Paris ✈ (ORY) Paris 24 B3
Ormesson-sur-Marne Paris 24 B4
Ormond Melbourne 18 B2
Ormøya Oslo 23 A3
Orpington London 15 B4
Ortaköy Istanbul 12 B2
Ortica Milan 19 B2
Oruba Lagos 14 A2
Ōsaka Osaka 23 B2
Ōsaka Castle Osaka 23 A2
Ōsaka Harbour Osaka 23 B1
Ōsaka Itami Int. ✈ (ITM) Osaka 23 A1
Ōsaka Kansai Int. ✈ (KIX) Osaka 23 B2
Ōsaki Tokyo 30 B3
Osasco São Paulo 27 B1
Osdorf Berlin 5 B3
Osdorp Amsterdam 2 A1
Oshodi Lagos 14 A2
Oslo Oslo 23 A3
Oslo ✈ (OSL) Oslo 23 A4
Ōsone Tokyo 30 B2
Osorun Lagos 14 A2
Ospiate Milan 19 A1
Ostankino Moscow 19 B2
Osterley London 15 B1
Osterley Park London 15 B1
Östermalm Stockholm 29 A2
Österskär Stockholm 29 A3
Östia Malpasso Rome 26 C1
Ostiense Rome 26 B1
Østmarkkapellet Oslo 23 A4
Østøya Oslo 23 B2
Østre Aker Oslo 23 A3
Ōta Tokyo 30 B3
Otaniemi Helsinki 11 B1
Otari Open Air Museum Wellington 33 B1
Otsuka Tokyo 30 A3
Ottakring Vienna 32 A1
Ottávia Rome 26 B1
Ottery Cape Town 8 B2
Ottobrunn Munich 21 B3
Ouderkerk Amsterdam 2 B2
Oulunkylä Helsinki 11 B2
Ourcq, Canal de l' Paris 24 A3
Outer Mission San Francisco 26 B2
Outremont Montreal 20 A2
Overijse Brussels 6 B3
Owhiro Bay Wellington 33 C1
Oworonsoki Lagos 14 A2
Oxgangs Edinburgh 11 B2
Oxon Hill Washington 33 C4
Oyodo Osaka 23 A1
Oyster Rock Mumbai 20 B1
Oyster Rocks Karachi 13 B2
Ozoir-la-Ferrière Paris 24 B4
Ozone Park New York 22 B2

P

Pacific Heights San Francisco 26 B2
Pacific Manor San Francisco 26 C2
Pacific Palisades Los Angeles 16 B1
Pacifica San Francisco 26 C2
Paco Manila 17 B1

Paco de Arcos Lisbon 16 A1
Paddington London 15 A2
Paddington Sydney 29 B2
Paderno Milan 19 A1
Pagewood Sydney 29 B2
Pagote Mumbai 20 B2
Pai, I. do Rio de Janeiro 25 B2
Pak Kok Hong Kong 12 B1
Pak Kong Hong Kong 12 A2
Pakila Helsinki 11 B2
Palacio Real Madrid 17 B1
Palaiseau Paris 24 B2
Palazzolo Milan 19 A1
Paleo Faliro Athens 2 B2
Palermo Buenos Aires 7 B2
Palhais Lisbon 16 B2
Palisades Park New York 22 A1
Palmer Park Washington 33 B4
Palmerston Dublin 10 A1
Palms Los Angeles 16 B2
Paloheinä Helsinki 11 B2
Palomeras Madrid 17 B2
Palos Heights Chicago 9 D2
Palos Hills Chicago 9 C2
Palos Hills Forest Chicago 9 C1
Palos Park Chicago 9 C1
Palpara Kolkata 14 B2
Panchur Kolkata 14 B1
Pandacan Manila 17 B2
Pandan, Selat Singapore 28 B2
Pandan Res. Singapore 28 B2
Pangrati Athens 2 B2
Pangsua, Sungei → Singapore 28 A2
Panihati Kolkata 14 A2
Panjang, Bukit Singapore 28 A2
Panke → Berlin 5 A3
Pankow Berlin 5 A3
Pantheon Rome 26 B1
Panthersville Atlanta 3 B3
Pantin Paris 24 A3
Pantitlán Mexico City 18 B2
Panyu Guangzhou 11 B2
Paparangi Wellington 33 B1
Papiol Barcelona 4 A1
Paradise Las Vegas 14 B2
Paramount Studios Los Angeles 16 B3
Paramus New York 22 A1
Paranaque Manila 17 B1
Paray-Vieille-Poste Paris 24 B3
Pardisān Nature Park Tehran 31 A2
Parel Mumbai 20 B1
Pari São Paulo 27 B2
Parioli Rome 26 B1
Paris Paris 24 A3
Paris Orly ✕ (ORY) Paris 24 B3
Parje Mumbai 20 B2
Pārk-e Āzādegān Tehran 31 B2
Pārk-e Mellat Tehran 31 A2
Park Ridge Chicago 9 A1
Park Royal London 15 A2
Parkchester New York 22 B2
Parkdale Toronto 31 B2
Parkhurst Johannesburg 13 A2
Parklawn Washington 33 B3
Parkmore Johannesburg 13 A2
Parkside San Francisco 26 B2
Parktown Johannesburg 13 B2
Parkview Johannesburg 13 A2
Parkville New York 22 C2
Parkwood Cape Town 8 B1
Parkwood Johannesburg 13 A2
Parow Cape Town 8 A2
Parque Chacabuco Buenos Aires 7 B2
Parque Patricios Buenos Aires 7 B2
Parramatta → Sydney 29 A1
Paşabahçe Istanbul 12 B2
Pasadena Los Angeles 16 B4
Pasay Manila 17 B1
Pascoe Vale Melbourne 18 A1
Pasig Manila 17 B2
Pasig → Manila 17 B2
Pasila Helsinki 11 B2
Pasing Munich 21 B1
Pasir Panjang Singapore 28 B2
Pasir Ris Singapore 28 A3
Passaic New York 22 A1
Passaic → New York 22 B1
Passirana Milan 19 A1
Patel Nagar Delhi 10 B1
Pateros Manila 17 B2
Pathumwan Bangkok 3 B2
Patipukur Kolkata 14 B2
Patisia Athens 2 A2
Paulo E. Virginia, Gruta Rio de Janeiro 25 B1
Paulshof Berlin 5 A5
Paya Lebar Singapore 28 A3
Peakhurst Sydney 29 B1
Peania Athens 2 B3
Pearson Int. Toronto ✕ (YYZ) Toronto 31 A1
Peckham London 15 B3
Pederstrup Copenhagen 8 A2
Pedralbes Barcelona 4 A1
Pedregal de San Angel, Jardines del Mexico City 18 C1
Peip'ing = Beijing Beijing 4 B1
Peking = Beijing Beijing 4 B1
Pelcowizna Warsaw 32 B2
Peñalolén Santiago 27 B2
Pencarrow Hd. Wellington 33 C2
Peng Siang → Singapore 28 A2
Penge London 15 B3
Penha Rio de Janeiro 25 A1
Penicuik Edinburgh 11 B2
Penjaringan Jakarta 12 A1
Pentagon Washington 33 B3
Penzing Vienna 32 A1
People's Park Shanghai 28 B1
People's Square Shanghai 28 B1
Perales del Rio Madrid 17 C2
Perchtoldsdorf Vienna 32 B1
Perdizes São Paulo 27 B2
Peristeri Athens 2 A2
Perivale London 15 A2
Perk Brussels 6 A2
Perlach Munich 21 B2
Perlacher Forst Munich 21 B2
Pero Milan 19 A1
Peropok, Bukit Singapore 28 B2
Perovo Moscow 19 B3
Pertusella Milan 19 A1
Pesagot Jerusalem 13 A2
Pesanggrahag, Kali → Jakarta 12 B1
Peschiera Borromeo Milan 19 B2
Pesek, Pulau Singapore 28 B2
Pest Budapest 7 B2
Pesterzsébet Budapest 7 B2
Pesthidegkút Budapest 7 A1
Pestimre Budapest 7 B3
Pestlőrinc Budapest 7 B3
Pestújhely Budapest 7 A2
Petas Helsinki 11 B2
Petone Wellington 33 B2
Petrogradskaya Storona St. Petersburg 27 B2
Petroupoli Athens 2 A2
Petrovice Prague 25 B3
Petrovskiy Park Moscow 19 B2
Petrovsko-Razumovskoye Moscow 19 B2
Pettycur Edinburgh 11 A2
Peutie Brussels 6 A2
Pfaueninsel Berlin 5 B1
Phaya Thai Bangkok 3 B2
Phihai Karachi 13 A2
Phillip B. Sydney 29 B2
Phoenix Park Dublin 10 A2
Phra Khanong Bangkok 3 B2
Phra Nakhon Bangkok 3 B2
Phra Pradaeng Bangkok 3 C2
Phranakhon Bangkok 3 B1
Pico Rivera Los Angeles 16 C4
Piedade Lisbon 16 A1
Piedade Rio de Janeiro 25 B1
Piedade, Cova da Lisbon 16 A2
Piedmont Park Atlanta 3 B2
Pierre Elliott Trudeau ✕ (YUL) Montreal 20 B1
Pietralata Rome 26 B2
Pihlajamäki Helsinki 11 B2
Pihlajasaari Helsinki 11 C2
Pilares Rio de Janeiro 25 B1
Pilton Edinburgh 11 B2
Pimmit Hills Washington 33 B2
Pine Castle Orlando 23 B2
Pine Grove Toronto 31 A1
Pine Hills Orlando 23 A2
Pinewood Park Miami 18 A2
Piney Run → Washington 33 B2
Pingzhou Guangzhou 11 B2
Pinheiros → São Paulo 27 B1
Pinjrapur Karachi 13 A2
Pinner London 15 A1
Pinner Green London 15 A1
Pioltello Milan 19 A2
Pipinui Pt. Wellington 33 A1
Piræus = Pireas Athens 2 B1
Piraiévs = Pireas Athens 2 B1
Pirajuçara → São Paulo 27 B1
Pireas Athens 2 B1
Pirinççi Istanbul 12 B1
Pirituba São Paulo 27 A1
Pirkkola Helsinki 11 B2
Pisgat O'mer Jerusalem 13 B2
Pisgat Ze'ev Jerusalem 13 B2
Pisnice Prague 25 C2
Pitampura Delhi 10 A1
Pitkäjärvi Helsinki 11 B1
Planegg Munich 21 B1
Plaza Mayor Madrid 17 B1
Pleasure Island Orlando 23 B1
Plumstead Cape Town 8 B1
Plumstead London 15 B4
Plyushchevo Moscow 19 B3
Po Toi Hong Kong 12 B2
Po Toi O Hong Kong 12 B2
Poasco Milan 19 B2
Podbaba Prague 25 B2
Podoli Prague 25 B2
Pohick Creek → Washington 33 C2
Pointe-Aux-Trembles Montreal 20 A2
Poissy Paris 24 A1
Pok Fu Lam Hong Kong 12 B1
Pokcheong Seoul 27 C2
Polton Edinburgh 11 B3
Polvoranca, Parque de Madrid 17 C1
Polyustrovo St. Petersburg 27 B2
Pomprap Bangkok 3 B2
Pondok Gede Jakarta 12 A2
Pondok Indah Jakarta 12 B1
Pont-Viau Montreal 20 A1
Pontault-Combault Paris 24 B4
Pontinha Lisbon 16 A1
Poplar London 15 A3
Poppintree Dublin 10 A2
Porirua Wellington 33 A2
Porirua East Wellington 33 A2
Port Botany Sydney 29 B2
Port Mearnóg = Portmarnock Dublin 10 A3
Port Melbourne Melbourne 18 B1
Port Nicholson Wellington 33 B2
Port Richmond New York 22 C1
Port Shelter Hong Kong 12 A2
Port Union Toronto 31 A4
Portage Park Chicago 9 B2
Portela, Lisboa ✕ (LIS) Lisbon 16 A2
Porter, L. Orlando 23 A3
Portmarnock Dublin 10 A3
Porto Brandão Lisbon 16 A1
Pôrto Novo Rio de Janeiro 25 A2
Porto Novo Cr. → Lagos 14 B2
Portobello Edinburgh 11 B3
Portrero San Francisco 26 B3
Potomac Washington 33 A2
Potrero Pt. San Francisco 26 B2
Potsdam Berlin 5 B1
Potzham Munich 21 B2
Pötzleinsdorf Vienna 32 A1
Póvoa de Santo Adriao Lisbon 16 A2
Powązki Warsaw 32 B1
Powiśle Warsaw 32 B2
Powsin Warsaw 32 C2
Powsinek Warsaw 32 C2
Poyan Res. Singapore 28 A2
Pozuelo de Alarcón Madrid 17 B1
Prado, Museo del Madrid 17 B1
Prado Churubusco Mexico City 18 B2
Praga Warsaw 32 B2
Prague = Praha Prague 25 B2
Praha Prague 25 B2
Praha ✕ (PRG) Prague 25 B1
Praires, R. des → Montreal 20 A2
Prater Vienna 32 A2
Precotto Milan 19 A2
Prenestino Labicano Rome 26 B2
Prenzlauerberg Berlin 5 A3
Preston Melbourne 18 A1
Pretos Forros, Sa. dos Rio de Janeiro 25 B1
Préville Montreal 20 B3
Přezletice Prague 25 B3
Prima Porta Rome 26 B1
Primavalle Rome 26 B1
Primrose Johannesburg 13 B2
Progreso Nacional Mexico City 18 A2
Prosek Prague 25 B3
Prospect Hill Park Boston 6 A1
Providencia Santiago 27 B2
Průhonice Prague 25 C3
Psichiko Athens 2 A2
Pudong New Area Shanghai 28 B2
Pueblo Libre Lima 14 B2
Pueblo Nuevo Barcelona 4 A2
Pueblo Nuevo Madrid 17 B2
Puerto Madero Buenos Aires 7 B2
Puhuangyu Beijing 4 B2
Puistola Helsinki 11 B3
Pukinmäki Helsinki 11 B2
Pulkovo Int. ✕ (LED) St. Petersburg 27 C1
Pullach Munich 21 B1
Pullman Historic District Chicago 9 C3
Pulo Gadung Jakarta 12 B2
Pūnak Tehran 31 A2
Punchbowl Sydney 29 B1
Punde Mumbai 20 B2
Punggol Singapore 28 A3
Punggol, Sungei → Singapore 28 A3
Punggol Pt. Singapore 28 A3
Punjabi Bagh Delhi 10 A1
Puotila Helsinki 11 B3
Puteaux Paris 24 A2
Putney London 15 B2
Putuo Shanghai 28 B1
Putxet Barcelona 4 A1
Puxi Shanghai 28 B1
Pyramids Cairo 7 B1
Pyry Warsaw 32 C1

Q

Qalandiya Jerusalem 13 A2
Qal'eh Morghī Tehran 31 B2
Qanā el Ismā'ilîya Cairo 7 A2
Qāsemābād Tehran 31 A3
Qasr-e Fīrūzeh Tehran 31 B3
Qatane Jerusalem 13 B1
Qianmen Beijing 4 B2
Qinghuayuan Beijing 4 B1
Qingningsi Shanghai 28 B2
Qolhak Tehran 31 A2
Quadraro Rome 26 B2
Quaid-i-Azam Karachi 13 A1
Quartiere Zingone Milan 19 B1
Qubeiba Jerusalem 13 A1
Quds Baghdad 3 A2
Queen Mary Res. London 15 B1
Queen Victoria Market Melbourne 18 A1
Queensbury London 15 A2
Queenscliffe Sydney 29 A2
Queensferry Edinburgh 11 B1
Queenstown Singapore 28 B2
Quellerina Johannesburg 13 A1
Queluz Lisbon 16 A1
Quezon City Manila 17 B2
Quilicura Santiago 27 B1
Quincy Boston 6 B2
Quincy B. Boston 6 B3
Quinta Normal Santiago 27 B1
Quinto de Stampi Milan 19 B2
Quinto Romano Milan 19 B1
Quirinale Rome 26 B1

R

R.F.K. Memorial Stadium Washington 33 B4
Raasdorf Vienna 32 A3
Radcliffe College Boston 6 A2
Rådhus Oslo 23 A3
Radlice Prague 25 B2
Radość Warsaw 32 B3
Radotin Prague 25 C2
Rafat Jerusalem 13 A2
Raffles Park Singapore 28 B2
Raheny Dublin 10 A3
Rahnsdorf Berlin 5 B5
Rajakylä Helsinki 11 B3
Rajpura Delhi 10 A2
Rákos-patak → Budapest 7 B3
Rákoshegy Budapest 7 B3
Rákoskeresztúr Budapest 7 B3
Rákoskert Budapest 7 B3
Rákosliget Budapest 7 B3
Rákospalota Budapest 7 A2
Rákosszentmihály Budapest 7 A2
Raków Warsaw 32 B1
Ram Jerusalem 13 A2
Rām Allāh Jerusalem 13 A2
Ramadān Baghdad 3 B2
Ramakrishna Puram Delhi 10 B1
Rāmallāh = Rām Allāh Jerusalem 13 A2
Ramanathpur Kolkata 14 A1
Ramat Allon Jerusalem 13 B2
Ramat Eshkol Jerusalem 13 B2
Ramat Razi'el Jerusalem 13 B1
Ramat Shafet Jerusalem 13 B2
Rambler Channel Hong Kong 12 A1
Ramenki Moscow 19 B1
Ramersdorf Munich 21 B2
Rameses Station Cairo 7 A2
Ramos Rio de Janeiro 25 B1
Ramos Mejía Buenos Aires 7 B1
Ramot Jerusalem 13 B2
Rampur Delhi 10 A2
Ramsgate Sydney 29 B1
Rancho Park Los Angeles 16 B2
Rand ✕ (QRA) Johannesburg 13 B2
Randalls I. New York 22 B2
Randburg Johannesburg 13 A1
Randhart Johannesburg 13 B2
Randpark Ridge Johannesburg 13 A1
Randwick Sydney 29 B2
Ranelagh Dublin 10 A2
Rangpuri Delhi 10 B1
Rannersdorf Vienna 32 B2
Ransbèche Brussels 6 B2
Ransdorp Amsterdam 2 A2
Ranvad Mumbai 20 B2
Raposo Lisbon 16 A1
Rastaala Helsinki 11 B1
Rastila Helsinki 11 B3
Raszyn Warsaw 32 C1
Rathfarnham Dublin 10 B2
Ratho Edinburgh 11 B1
Ratho Station Edinburgh 11 B1
Rato Lisbon 16 A2
Ravelston Edinburgh 11 B2
Rawamangun Jakarta 12 B2
Rayners Lane London 15 A1
Raynes Park London 15 B2
Raypur Kolkata 14 C2
Real Felipe, Fuerte Lima 14 B2
Reams, L. Orlando 23 B1
Reclining Buddha = Wat Pho Bangkok 3 B1
Recoleta Buenos Aires 7 B2
Recoleta Santiago 27 B2
Red Fort = Lal Qila Delhi 10 B2
Red Square Moscow 19 B2
Redbridge ☐ London 15 A4
Redfern Sydney 29 B2
Redwood Wellington 33 B1
Refshaleøen Copenhagen 8 A3
Regents Park Johannesburg 13 B2
Regent's Park London 15 A3
Rego Park New York 22 B2
Reinickendorf Berlin 5 A3
Rekola Helsinki 11 B3
Rembertów Warsaw 32 B2
Rembrandtpark Amsterdam 2 A2
Remedios de Escalada Buenos Aires 7 C2
Rémola, Estany del Barcelona 4 B1
Renca Santiago 27 B1
Rennemoulin Paris 24 A1
Řeporyje Prague 25 B1
Repulse Bay Hong Kong 12 B2
Repy Prague 25 B1
Residenz Munich 21 B2
Reston Washington 33 B2
Retiro Buenos Aires 7 B2
Retiro Madrid 17 B1
Retiro, Puerto Buenos Aires 7 B2
Retreat Cape Town 8 B1
Reutov Moscow 19 B4
Réveillon → Paris 24 B4
Revere Boston 6 A2
Rexdale Toronto 31 A1
Reynosa Tamaulipas Mexico City 18 A1
Rho Milan 19 A1
Rhodes Sydney 29 A1
Rhodon Paris 24 B1
Rhodon → Paris 24 B1
Rialto Towers Melbourne 18 A1
Ribeira Rio de Janeiro 25 A1
Ricarda, Estany de la Barcelona 4 B1
Richmond Melbourne 18 A2
Richmond San Francisco 26 B2
Richmond Hill New York 22 B2
Richmond Park London 15 B2
Richmond-upon-Thames ☐ London 15 B2
Ridge, The Delhi 10 B2
Ridgefield New York 22 B1
Ridgefield Park New York 22 A1
Ridgewood New York 22 B2
Riem Munich 21 B3
Riesenrad Vienna 32 A2
Rijksmuseum Amsterdam 2 A2
Rikers I. New York 22 B2
Rimac Lima 14 B2
Ringsend Dublin 10 A2
Rinkeby Stockholm 29 A1
Rio Comprido Rio de Janeiro 25 B1
Rio de Janeiro Rio de Janeiro 25 B1
Rio de Janeiro Galeão ✕ (GIG) Rio de Janeiro 25 A1
Rio de Mouro Lisbon 16 A1
Ripollet Barcelona 4 A1
Ris Oslo 23 A3
Risby Copenhagen 8 A1
Rishra Kolkata 14 A2
Ritchie Washington 33 B4
Rithala Delhi 10 A1
Rive Sud, Canal de la Montreal 20 B2
River Edge New York 22 A1
River Forest Chicago 9 B2
River Grove Chicago 9 B1
River Ridge New Orleans 21 B1
Riverdale New York 22 A2
Riverdale Washington 33 B4
Riverdale Park Toronto 31 A2
Riverlea Johannesburg 13 B1
Riverside Chicago 9 C2
Riverwood Sydney 29 B1
Rivière-des-Praires Montreal 20 A2
Rixensart Brussels 6 B3
Riyad Baghdad 3 B2
Rizal Park Manila 17 B1
Rizal Stadium Manila 17 B1
Røa Oslo 23 A2
Robbins Chicago 9 D2
Robertsham Johannesburg 13 B2
Rochelle Park New York 22 A1
Rock Cr. → Washington 33 B3
Rock Creek Park Washington 33 B3
Rock Pt. Wellington 33 A1
Rockaway Beach New York 22 C3
Rockaway Pt. New York 22 C2
Rockdale Sydney 29 B1
Rockefeller Center New York 22 B2
Rocky Run → Washington 33 B2
Roda, Gezîret el Cairo 7 A2
Roda I. = Roda, Gezîret el Cairo 7 A2
Rodaon Vienna 32 B1
Rødovre Copenhagen 8 A2
Rodrigo de Freitas, L. Rio de Janeiro 25 B1
Roehampton London 15 B2
Rogers Park Chicago 9 A3
Roihuvuori Helsinki 11 B3
Roissy-en-Brie Paris 24 B4
Rokytka → Prague 25 B3
Roma Rome 26 B1
Roma Urbe ✕ Rome 26 B2
Római-Fürdő Budapest 7 A2
Romainville Paris 24 A3
Roman Forum = Foro Romano Rome 26 B1
Romano Banco Milan 19 B1
Rome = Roma Rome 26 B1
Romema Jerusalem 13 B2
Romford London 15 A5
Ronald Reagan Nat. Washington ✕ (DCA) Washington 33 B3
Rondebosch Cape Town 8 A1
Roppongi Tokyo 30 B3
Rose, L. Orlando 23 A1
Rose Bowl Los Angeles 16 B4
Rose Hill Washington 33 C3
Rosebank Johannesburg 13 A2
Rosebank New York 22 C1
Rosebery Sydney 29 B2
Rosedal La Candelaria Mexico City 18 B2
Roseland Chicago 9 C3
Rosemead Los Angeles 16 B4
Rosemont Chicago 9 B1
Rosemont Montreal 20 A2
Rosenborg Slot Copenhagen 8 A3
Rosenthal Berlin 5 A3
Rosettenville Johannesburg 13 B2
Rosewell Edinburgh 11 B3
Rosherville Dam Johannesburg 13 B2
Rösjön Stockholm 29 A2
Roslags-Näsby Stockholm 29 A2
Roslin Edinburgh 11 B3
Roslindale Boston 6 B2
Rosny-sous-Bois Paris 24 A4
Rosslyn Washington 33 B3
Rosyth Edinburgh 11 A1
Rotherhithe London 15 B3
Rothneusiedl Vienna 32 B2
Rothschmaige Munich 21 A1
Rouge Hill Toronto 31 A4
Round I. Hong Kong 12 B2
Roxbury Boston 6 B2
Roxeth London 15 A1
Royal Botanic Gardens Edinburgh 11 B2
Royal Observatory Edinburgh 11 B2
Royal Palace = Kungliga Slottet Stockholm 29 B2
Royal Palace = Palacio Real Madrid 17 B1
Royal Park Melbourne 18 A1
Röylä Helsinki 11 B1
Rozas, Portilleros de las Madrid 17 B1
Roztoky Prague 25 B2
Rozzano Milan 19 B1
Rubí → Barcelona 4 A1
Rudolfsheim Vienna 32 A2
Rudolfshöhe Berlin 5 A5
Rudow Berlin 5 B3
Rueil-Malmaison Paris 24 A2
Ruisbroek Brussels 6 B1
Ruislip London 15 A1
Rumelihisarı Istanbul 12 B2
Rungis Paris 24 B3
Rusāfa Baghdad 3 A2
Rush Green London 15 A5
Russa Kolkata 14 C2
Rutherford New York 22 B1
Ruzyně Prague 25 B1
Ruzyne, Praha ✕ (PRG) Prague 25 B1
Rybatskaya St. Petersburg 27 B2
Rydboholm Stockholm 29 A3
Ryde Sydney 29 A1
Ryogoku Tokyo 30 A3
Rzhevka St. Petersburg 27 B3

S

Sa'ādatābād Tehran 31 A2
Saadūn Baghdad 3 B2
Saavedra Buenos Aires 7 B2
Saboli Delhi 10 A2
Sabugo Lisbon 16 A1
Sabzi Mand Delhi 10 A2
Sacavém Lisbon 16 A2
Saclay Paris 24 B2
Saclay, Étang de Paris 24 B1
Sacomã São Paulo 27 B2
Sacré Cœur Paris 24 A3
Sacrow Berlin 5 B1
Sacrower See Berlin 5 B1
Sadang Seoul 27 C1
Saddle → New York 22 A1
Saddle Brook New York 22 A1
Sadr Karachi 13 A2
Sadr City Baghdad 3 A2
Sadyba Warsaw 32 B2
Safdar Jang's Tomb Delhi 10 B2
Saft el Laban Cairo 7 A2
Saganashkee Slough Chicago 9 C1
Sagene Oslo 23 A3
Sagrada Familia, Templo de Barcelona 4 A2
Sahar, Mumbai ✕ (BOM) Mumbai 20 A2
Sai Kung Hong Kong 12 A2
Sai Wan Ho Hong Kong 12 B2
Sai Ying Pun Hong Kong 12 B1
St-Aubin Paris 24 B1
St-Cloud Paris 24 A2
St-Cyr-l'École Paris 24 B1
St-Cyr-l'École ✕ Paris 24 B1
St-Denis Paris 24 A3
St-Germain, Forêt de Paris 24 A1
St-Germain-en-Laye Paris 24 A1
St-Gilles Brussels 6 B2
St. Helier London 15 B2
St-Hubert Montreal 20 B3
St. Hubert, Galeries Royales Brussels 6 A2
St. Isaac's Cathedral St. Petersburg 27 B1
St-Jacques → Montreal 20 B3
St-Joost-Ten-Node Brussels 6 A2
St. Kilda Melbourne 18 B1
St-Lambert Montreal 20 A3
St-Lambert Paris 24 B1
St-Laurent Montreal 20 A1
St-Léonard Montreal 20 A2
St. Magelungen Stockholm 29 B2
St-Mandé Paris 24 A3
St. Margaret's Dublin 10 A2
St-Martin, Bois Paris 24 B4
St. Mary Cray London 15 B4
St-Maur-des-Fossés Paris 24 B3
St-Maurice Paris 24 B3
St-Michel Montreal 20 A2
St. Nikolaus-Kirken Prague 25 B2
St-Ouen Paris 24 A3
St. Paul's Cray London 15 B4
St. Peters Sydney 29 B2
St. Peter's Square = San Pietro, Piazza Rome 26 B1
St. Petersburg = Sankt-Peterburg St. Petersburg 27 B1
St. Petersburg Pulkovo Int. ✕ (LED) St. Petersburg 27 C1
St-Pierre Montreal 20 B2
St-Pieters Leew Brussels 6 B1
St-Quentin, Étang de Paris 24 B1
St. Stephens Cathedral = Stephansdom Vienna 32 A2
St-Stevens-Woluwe Brussels 6 A2
St-Vincent-de-Paul Montreal 20 A2
St. Xavier Univ. Chicago 9 C2
Ste-Catherine Montreal 20 B2
Ste-Hélène, Î. Montreal 20 A2
Saiwai Tokyo 30 B3
Sakai Osaka 23 B1
Sakai Harbour Osaka 23 B1
Sakra, Pulau Singapore 28 B2
Salam Baghdad 3 A2
Salamanca Madrid 17 B1
Sallynoggin Dublin 10 B3
Salmannsdorf Vienna 32 A1
Salomea Warsaw 32 B1
Salsette I. Mumbai 20 A2
Salt Lake City = Bidhan Nagar Kolkata 14 B2
Salt River Cape Town 8 A1
Salt Water L. Kolkata 14 B2
Saltsjö-Duvnäs Stockholm 29 B3
Samatya Istanbul 12 C1
Sampaio Rio de Janeiro 25 B1
Samphan Thawong Bangkok 3 B2
Samseon Seoul 27 B2
Samuel Smith Park Toronto 31 B1
Samut Prakan Bangkok 3 B2
San Andrés Barcelona 4 A2
San Angel Mexico City 18 B1
San Basilio Rome 26 B2
San Borja Lima 14 B3
San Bóvio Milan 19 B2
San Bruno, Pt. San Francisco 26 C2
San Bruno Mountain State Park ⌂ San Francisco 26 B2
San Cristóbal Buenos Aires 7 B2
San Cristóbal Madrid 17 B2
San Cristóbal, Cerro Santiago 27 B2
San Cristóbal, Virgen del Santiago 27 B2
San Cristoforo Milan 19 B1
San Donato Milanese Milan 19 B2
San Francisco San Francisco 26 B2
San Francisco B. San Francisco 26 B3
San Francisco Culhuacán Mexico City 18 C2
San Fruttuoso Milan 19 A2
San Gabriel Los Angeles 16 B4
San Gabriel → Los Angeles 16 C4
San Giuliano Milanese Milan 19 B2
San Isidro Lima 14 B2
San Jerónimo Lídice Mexico City 18 C1
San Joaquin Santiago 27 B2
San José Rio Hondo Mexico City 18 B1
San Juan → Manila 17 B2
San Juan de Aragón Mexico City 18 B2
San Juan de Aragón, Parque Mexico City 18 B2
San Juan de Lurigancho Lima 14 A2
San Juan del Monte Manila 17 B2
San Juan Ixtacala Mexico City 18 A1
San Just Desvern Barcelona 4 A1
San Justo Buenos Aires 7 C1
San Lorenzo Tezonco Mexico City 18 C2
San Luis Lima 14 B2
San Marino Los Angeles 16 B4
San Martín Barcelona 4 A2
San Martin de Porras Lima 14 B2
San Mateo Tlaltenango Mexico City 18 B1
San Miguel Lima 14 B2
San Miguel Santiago 27 B2
San Nicolás Buenos Aires 7 B2
San Onófrio Rome 26 B1
San Pedro Mártir Barcelona 4 A1
San Pedro Zacatenco Mexico City 18 A2
San Pietro, Piazza Rome 26 B1
San Po Kong Hong Kong 12 A2
San Rafael Chamapa Mexico City 18 B1
San Rafael Hills Los Angeles 16 A3
San Roque Manila 17 B2
San Siro Milan 19 B1
San Souci Sydney 29 B1
San Telmo Buenos Aires 7 B2
San Vicenç dels Horts Barcelona 4 A1
Sandown Johannesburg 13 A2
Sandown Park Races London 15 B1
Sandton Johannesburg 13 A2
Sandvika Oslo 23 A2
Sandyford Dublin 10 B2
Sandymount Dublin 10 A2
Sangenjaya Tokyo 30 B2
Sanggye Seoul 27 B2
Sangley Pt. Manila 17 C1
Sankrail Kolkata 14 B1
Sankt-Peterburg St. Petersburg 27 B1
Sankt Veit Vienna 32 A1
Sanlihe Beijing 4 B1
Sanlintang Shanghai 28 C1
Sans Barcelona 4 A1
Sanssouci Berlin 5 B1
Sant Ambrogio, Basilica di Milan 19 B2
Sant Boi de Llobregat Barcelona 4 A1
Sant Cugat Barcelona 4 A1
Sant Feliu de Llobregat Barcelona 4 A1
Sant Joan Despí Barcelona 4 A1
Santa Ana Manila 17 B2
Santa Anita Park Los Angeles 16 B4
Santa Coloma de Gramenet Barcelona 4 A2
Santa Cruz Manila 17 B1
Santa Cruz Mumbai 20 A1
Santa Cruz, I. de Rio de Janeiro 25 B2
Santa Cruz de Olorde Barcelona 4 A1
Santa Efigênia São Paulo 27 B2
Santa Elena Manila 17 B2
Santa Elena del Gomero Santiago 27 B1
Santa Eulalia Barcelona 4 A2
Santa Fe Springs Los Angeles 16 C4
Santa Iria da Azóia Lisbon 16 A2
Santa Julia Santiago 27 C2
Santa Monica Los Angeles 16 B2
Santa Monica Mts. Los Angeles 16 B2
Santa Rosa de Locobe Santiago 27 B2
Santa Teresa de la Ovalle Santiago 27 B1
Santahamina Helsinki 11 C3
Santana São Paulo 27 A2
Santeny Paris 24 B4
Santiago Santiago 27 B2
Santiago Benítez ✕ (SCL) Santiago 27 B1
Santiago de Surco Lima 14 B2
Santo Amaro Lisbon 16 A1
Santo Amaro São Paulo 27 B1
Santo André Lisbon 16 B2
Santo Antão do Tojal Lisbon 16 A2
Santo Antônio, Qta. de Lisbon 16 B2
Santo Tomas, Univ. of Manila 17 B1
Santos Dumont ✕ (SDU) Rio de Janeiro 25 B2
Santoshpur Kolkata 14 B1
Santragachi Kolkata 14 B1
Santry Dublin 10 A2
Sanyuanli Guangzhou 11 B2
São Caetano do Sul São Paulo 27 B2
São Conrado Rio de Janeiro 25 B1
São Cristóvão Rio de Janeiro 25 B1
São Jorge, Castelo de Lisbon 16 A2
São Julião do Tojal Lisbon 16 A2
São Paulo São Paulo 27 B2
São Paulo Congonhas ✕ (CGH) São Paulo 27 B2
Sapa Kolkata 14 B1
Sapateiro, Cor. do → São Paulo 27 B1
Sarandi Buenos Aires 7 C2
Saraswati → Kolkata 14 A1
Sarecky potok → Prague 25 B2
Sarimbun Singapore 28 A2
Sarimbun Res. Singapore 28 A2
Sarıyer Istanbul 12 B2
Sarriá Barcelona 4 A1
Sarsuna Kolkata 14 C1
Sartrouville Paris 24 A2
Sasad Budapest 7 B2
Sashalom Budapest 7 A3
Saska Warsaw 32 B2
Satalice Prague 25 B3
Satgachi Kolkata 14 B2
Satpukur Kolkata 14 B2
Sätra Stockholm 29 B1
Saúde São Paulo 27 B2
Saugus Boston 6 A2
Saugus → Boston 6 A2
Sault-au-Récollet Montreal 20 A2
Sausalito San Francisco 26 A2
Sawah Besar Jakarta 12 A1
Sawtelle Los Angeles 16 B2
Scald Law Edinburgh 11 B2
Scarborough Toronto 31 A3
Scarborough Bluffs Toronto 31 A3
Sceaux Paris 24 B2
Schaerbeek Brussels 6 A2
Scharfenberg Berlin 5 A2
Schiller Park Chicago 9 B1
Schiller Woods Chicago 9 B1
Schiphol, Amsterdam ✕ (AMS) Amsterdam 2 B1
Schlachtensee Berlin 5 B2
Schlossgarten Berlin 5 A2
Schmargendorf Berlin 5 B2
Schönblick Berlin 5 B5
Schönbrunn Vienna 32 A1
Schöneberg Berlin 5 B3
Schönefeld Berlin 5 B4
Schöneiche Berlin 5 B5
Schönwalde Berlin 5 A1
Schulzendorf Berlin 5 A2
Schwabing Munich 21 B2
Schwanebeck Berlin 5 A4
Schwanenwerder Berlin 5 B2
Schwarzlackenau Vienna 32 A2
Schwechat Vienna 32 B2
Schwechat, Wien ✕ (VIE) Vienna 32 B3
Science and Industry, Museum of Chicago 9 C3
Scitrek Museum Atlanta 3 B2
Scopus, Mt. Jerusalem 13 B2
Scottdale Atlanta 3 B3
Scutari = Üsküdar Istanbul 12 B2
Sea Point Cape Town 8 A1
Seabrook Washington 33 B5
Seacliff San Francisco 26 B2
Seaforth Sydney 29 A2
Seagate New York 22 C1
Seat Pleasant Washington 33 B4
Seaview Wellington 33 B2
SeaWorld Orlando 23 B2
Šeberov Prague 25 B3
Secaucus New York 22 B1
Seddinsee Berlin 5 B5
Seeberg Berlin 5 A5
Seeburg Berlin 5 A1
Seefeld Berlin 5 A5
Seegefeld Berlin 5 A1
Seehof Berlin 5 B2
Segeltorp Stockholm 29 B1
Segrate Milan 19 A2
Seguro Milan 19 B1
Seixal Lisbon 16 B2
Selby Johannesburg 13 B2
Seletar, Pulau Singapore 28 A3
Seletar Hills Singapore 28 A3
Seletar Res. Singapore 28 A2
Selhurst London 15 B3
Sembawang Singapore 28 A2
Senago Milan 19 A1
Sendling Munich 21 B2
Senju Tokyo 30 A3
Senriyama Osaka 23 A2
Sentosa Singapore 28 B2
Seobinggo Seoul 27 B1
Seocho Seoul 27 C1
Seodaemun Seoul 27 B1
Seokkwan Seoul 27 B2
Seongbuk Seoul 27 B2
Seongdong Seoul 27 B2
Seongsu Seoul 27 B2
Seoul Seoul 27 B2
Seoul Nat. Univ. Seoul 27 C1
Seoul Tower Seoul 27 B1
Sepolia Athens 2 A2
Sepulveda Dam Rec. Area ⌂ Los Angeles 16 A2
Serangoon Singapore 28 A3
Serangoon, Pulau Singapore 28 A3
Serangoon, Sungei → Singapore 28 A3
Serangoon Harbour Singapore 28 A3
Seraya, Pulau Singapore 28 B2
Serebryanka → Moscow 19 B3
Serramonte San Francisco 26 C2
Sesto San Giovanni Milan 19 A2
Sesto Ulteriano Milan 19 B2
Setagaya Tokyo 30 B2
Setia Budi Jakarta 12 B1
Settebagni Rome 26 A2
Settecamini Rome 26 B2
Séttimo Milanese Milan 19 B1
Settsu Osaka 23 A2
Seutula Helsinki 11 A2
Seven Corners Washington 33 B3
Seven Kings London 15 A4
Seventeenth Street Canal New Orleans 21 A2
Sévesco → Milan 19 A1
Sevran Paris 24 A4
Sewri Mumbai 20 B2
Sforzesso, Castello Milan 19 B2
Sha Kok Mei Hong Kong 12 A2
Sha Tin Hong Kong 12 A2
Sha'ar Binyamin Jerusalem 13 A2
Shabrâmant Cairo 7 B2
Shah Mosque Tehran 31 A2
Shahdara Delhi 10 A2
Shahe Guangzhou 11 B2
Shahr-e Rey Tehran 31 B2
Shahrak-e Golshahr Tehran 31 B1
Shahrak-e Qods Tehran 31 A2
Shaikh Aomar Baghdad 3 A2
Shakurbasti Delhi 10 A1
Shalkiya Kolkata 14 B2
Sham Shui Po Hong Kong 12 B1
Shamapur Delhi 10 A1
Shamian Guangzhou 11 B2
Shan Mei Hong Kong 12 A2
Shanghai Shanghai 28 B2
Shanghai Hongqiao ✕ (SHA) Shanghai 28 B1
Shanghai Pudong ✕ (PVG) Shanghai 28 B2
Shankill Dublin 10 B3
Sharp I. Hong Kong 12 A2
Shastrinagar Delhi 10 A2
Shau Kei Wan Hong Kong 12 B2
Shawocun Beijing 4 B1
Shayuan Guangzhou 11 B2
Sheen, L. Orlando 23 B1
Sheepshead Bay New York 22 C2
Shek O Hong Kong 12 B2
Shelter I. Hong Kong 12 B2
Shepherds Bush London 15 A2
Shepperton London 15 B1
Sheremetyevo ✕ (SVO) Moscow 19 A2
Sherman Oaks Los Angeles 16 B2
Sherman Park Chicago 9 C2
Sherwood, L. Orlando 23 A2
Shet Bandar Mumbai 20 B2
Sheung Fa Shan Hong Kong 12 A1
Sheung Lau Wan Hong Kong 12 B2
Sheung Wan Hong Kong 12 B1
Sheva Mumbai 20 B2
Sheva Nhava Mumbai 20 B2
Shiba Tokyo 30 B3
Shibpur Kolkata 14 B1
Shibuya Tokyo 30 B3
Shilihe Beijing 4 B2
Shimogawara Tokyo 30 B1
Shimosalo Tokyo 30 A2
Shimoshakujii Tokyo 30 A2
Shinagawa Tokyo 30 B3
Shing Mun Res. Hong Kong 12 A1
Shinjuku Tokyo 30 A3
Shinjuku Nat. Garden Tokyo 30 A3
Shinkoiwa Tokyo 30 A4
Shinnakano Tokyo 30 A3
Shipai Guangzhou 11 B3
Shirinashi → Osaka 23 B1
Shirogane Tokyo 30 B3
Shitennoji Temple Osaka 23 B2
Shiweitang Guangzhou 11 B2
Shogunle Lagos 14 A2
Shomolu Lagos 14 A2
Shooters Hill London 15 B4
Shoreditch London 15 A3
Shortlands London 15 B4
Shu'afat Jerusalem 13 B2
Shubrâ Cairo 7 A2
Shubrâ el Kheima Cairo 7 A2
Shuikou Guangzhou 11 A2
Sidcup London 15 B4
Siebenhirten Vienna 32 B1
Siedlung Berlin 5 A1
Siekierki Warsaw 32 B2
Sielce Warsaw 32 B2
Siemensstadt Berlin 5 A2
Sierra Madre Los Angeles 16 B4
Sievering Vienna 32 A2
Sighthill Edinburgh 11 B2
Signal Hill Cape Town 8 A1
Siheung Seoul 27 C1
Sikátorpuszta Budapest 7 A3
Silampur Delhi 10 B2
Sillim Seoul 27 C1
Silver, L. Orlando 23 A2
Silver Hill Washington 33 C4
Silver Lake Los Angeles 16 B3
Silver Spring Washington 33 A3
Silvermine Nature Reserve Cape Town 8 B1
Silvolantekojärvi Helsinki 11 B2
Simei Singapore 28 A3
Simla Kolkata 14 B2
Simmering Vienna 32 A2
Simmeringer Heide Vienna 32 A2
Simonkylä Helsinki 11 B3
Sinchon Seoul 27 B1
Sindang Seoul 27 B2
Singapore ■ Singapore 28 B3
Singapore, Univ. of Singapore 28 B2
Singapore Changi ✕ (SIN) Singapore 28 A3
Sinki, Selat Singapore 28 B2
Sinsa Seoul 27 B2
Sint-Genesius-Rode Brussels 6 B2
Sion Mumbai 20 A2
Sipson London 15 B1
Siqeil Cairo 7 A1
Şişli Istanbul 12 B1
Skansen Stockholm 29 B2
Skärholmen Stockholm 29 B1
Skarpäng Stockholm 29 A2
Skarpnäck Stockholm 29 B2
Skaryszewski, Park Warsaw 32 B2
Skokie Chicago 9 A2
Skokie → Chicago 9 A2
Skokie Heritage Museum Chicago 9 A2
Skoklefall Oslo 23 A3
Sköndal Stockholm 29 B2
Skovlunde Copenhagen 8 A2
Skovshoved Copenhagen 8 A3
Skuru Stockholm 29 B3
Sky Lake Orlando 23 B2
Skyland Atlanta 3 A3
Slade Green London 15 B5
Slependen Oslo 23 A1
Slipi Jakarta 12 B1
Slivenec Prague 25 B2
Sloten Amsterdam 2 A1
Sloterdijk Amsterdam 2 A1
Sloterpark Amsterdam 2 A1
Sluhy Prague 25 A3
Służew Warsaw 32 B2
Służewiec Warsaw 32 B2
Smíchov Prague 25 B2
Smith Forest Preserve Chicago 9 B2
Smolny St. Petersburg 27 B2
Smolny Cathedral St. Petersburg 27 B2
Snake Creek Canal Miami 18 A2
Snakeden Branch → Washington 33 B1
Snarøya Oslo 23 A2
Snättringe Stockholm 29 B1
Søborg Copenhagen 8 A2
Sobreda Lisbon 16 B1
Söderby Stockholm 29 A3
Södermalm Stockholm 29 B2
Sodpur Kolkata 14 A2
Soeurs, Î. des Montreal 20 B2
Sognsvatn Oslo 23 A3
Soignes, Forêt de Brussels 6 B2
Sok Kwu Wan Hong Kong 12 B1
Sokolniki Moscow 19 B3
Sokolniki Park Moscow 19 B3
Sokołów Warsaw 32 C1
Solalinden Munich 21 B3
Sollentuna Stockholm 29 A1
Solln Munich 21 B2
Solna Stockholm 29 A1
Somerset Washington 33 B3
Somerville Boston 6 A2
Somes I. Wellington 33 B2
Sonari Mumbai 20 B2
Søndersø Copenhagen 8 A2
Songpa Seoul 27 B2
Sony Picture Studio Los Angeles 16 B2
Sord = Swords Dublin 10 A2
Soroksár Budapest 7 B2
Soroksari Duna → Budapest 7 B2
Sosenka → Moscow 19 B3
Sosnovka St. Petersburg 27 B2
Söul = Seoul Seoul 27 B2

Soundview New York 22 B2
South Beach New York 22 C1
South Bend Park Atlanta 3 B2
South Boston Boston 6 A2
South Decatur Atlanta 3 B3
South Deering Chicago 9 C3
South El Monte Los Angeles 16 B4
South Gate Los Angeles 16 B3
South Harbor Manila 17 B1
South Harrow London 15 A1
South Hd. Sydney 29 B2
South Hills Johannesburg 13 A2
South Lawn Washington 33 C3
South Miami Miami 18 B1
South Norwood London 15 B3
South of Market San Francisco 26 B2
South Ozone Park New York 22 B3
South Pasadena Los Angeles 16 B4
South Res. Boston 6 A2
South Ruislip London 15 A1
South San Francisco San Francisco 26 B2
South San Gabriel Los Angeles 16 B4
South Shore Chicago 9 C3
Southall London 15 B1
Southborough London 15 B4
Southend London 15 B3
Southern California, Univ. of Los Angeles 16 B3
Southfields London 15 B2
Southport New Orleans 21 B2
Southwest □ London 15 B2
Southwest Museum Los Angeles 16 B3
Søvang Copenhagen 8 B3
Soweto Johannesburg 13 B1
Sowhānak Tehran 31 A1
Soya Tokyo 30 A3
Spandau Berlin 5 A1
Spånga Stockholm 29 A1
Spanish Monastery Miami 18 A2
Spectacle I. Boston 6 A2
Speicher-See Munich 21 A3
Speising Vienna 32 B1
Sphinx Cairo 7 B1
Spinaceto Rome 26 C1
Spit Junction Sydney 29 A2
Spořilov Prague 25 B3
Spot Pond Boston 6 A2
Spotswood Melbourne 18 A1
Spring Valley Las Vegas 14 B1
Springeberg Berlin 5 B5
Springfield Washington 33 C2
Squantum Boston 6 B2
Srednaya Rogatka St. Petersburg 27 B2
Śródmieście Warsaw 32 B2
Staaken Berlin 5 A1
Stabekk Oslo 23 A2
Stadlau Vienna 32 A2
Stadshuset Stockholm 29 B2
Stains Paris 24 A3
Stamford Hill London 15 A3
Stammersdorf Vienna 32 A2
Stanley Hong Kong 12 A1
Stanley Pen. Hong Kong 12 B2
Stanmore London 15 A2
Stapleton New York 22 C1
Staraya Derevnya St. Petersburg 27 A2
Staré Město Prague 25 B2
Stare Miasto Warsaw 32 B2
Starke, L. Orlando 23 A1
Staten Island Zoo New York 22 C1
Staten Islands Ferry Terminal New York 22 C1
Statenice Prague 25 B1
Stedelijk Museum Amsterdam 2 A2
Steele Creek Melbourne 18 A1
Steenokkerzeel Brussels 6 A2
Steer, L. Orlando 23 A1
Steglitz Berlin 5 B2
Stepaside Dublin 10 B2
Stephansdom Vienna 32 A2
Stepney London 15 A3
Sterling Park San Francisco 26 B2
Sticklinge udde Stockholm 29 A1
Stickney Chicago 9 C2
Stillorgan Dublin 10 B2
Stockholm Stockholm 29 B2
Stockholm Arlanda ✈ (ARN) Stockholm 29 A1
Stocksund Stockholm 29 A2
Stodůlky Prague 25 B1
Stoke Newington London 15 A3
Stokes Valley Wellington 33 B2
Stone Canyon Res. Los Angeles 16 B2
Stone Park Chicago 9 B1
Stonebridge London 15 A2
Stoneham Boston 6 A1
Stony Brook Res. Boston 6 B2
Stony Creek → Chicago 9 C2
Stora Värtan Stockholm 29 A2
Store Hareskov Copenhagen 8 A2
Store Magleby Copenhagen 8 B3
Storholmen Stockholm 29 A2
Stoyka St. Petersburg 27 B2
Straiton Edinburgh 11 B3
Strandfontein Cape Town 8 B2
Strašnice Prague 25 B2
Strasslach Munich 21 B3
Strasstraudering Munich 21 B3
Stratford London 5 B2
Strathfield Sydney 29 B1
Streatham London 15 B3
Streatham Vale London 15 B3
Strebersdorf Vienna 32 A2
Strip, The Las Vegas 14 B2
Střížkov Prague 25 B2
Strombeek-Bever Brussels 6 A2
Stromovka Prague 25 B2
Studio City Los Angeles 16 B2
Stureby Stockholm 29 B2
Stuvsta Stockholm 29 B2
Subhepur Delhi 10 A2
Suburban Canal New Orleans 21 B1
Sucat Manila 17 C2
Suchdol Prague 25 B2
Sucy-en-Brie Paris 24 B4
Sue, L. Orlando 23 A2
Sugamo Tokyo 30 A3
Sugar Loaf Mt. = Açúcar, Pão de Rio de Janeiro 25 B2
Suge Tokyo 30 B2
Suginami Tokyo 30 A2
Sugō Tokyo 30 B2
Sui Sai Wan Hong Kong 12 B1
Suita Osaka 23 A2
Suitland Washington 33 B4
Sukchar Kolkata 14 A2
Sultanahme Camil Istanbul 12 B1
Sumida Tokyo 30 A3
Sumida → Tokyo 30 A3
Sumiyoshi Osaka 23 B1

Sumiyoshi Shrine Osaka 23 B1
Summerville Toronto 31 B1
Summit Chicago 9 C2
Sunamachi Tokyo 30 A4
Sunbury-on-Thames London 15 B1
Sundbyberg Stockholm 29 A1
Sundbyerne Copenhagen 8 B3
Sung Kong Hong Kong 12 B2
Sungei Kadut Industrial Estate Singapore 28 A2
Sungei Selatar Res. Singapore 28 A2
Sunrise Manor Las Vegas 14 A2
Sunrise Mountain Natural Area Las Vegas 14 B2
Sunset Park Las Vegas 14 B2
Sunset Park New York 22 C2
Sunter Jakarta 12 A2
Sunter, Kali → Jakarta 12 B2
Suomenlinna Helsinki 11 C2
Sur Bahr Jerusalem 13 B2
Sura Kolkata 14 B2
Suraksan Seoul 27 A2
Surbiton London 15 B2
Suresnes Paris 24 A2
Surfside Miami 18 A2
Surquillo Lima 14 B2
Surrey Hills Sydney 29 B2
Susaek Seoul 27 B1
Süssenbrunn Vienna 32 A2
Sutton Dublin 10 A3
Sutton London 15 B2
Suyu Seoul 27 B2
Suzukishinden Tokyo 30 A2
Svanemollen Copenhagen 8 A3
Sveaborg = Suomenlinna Helsinki 11 C2
Sverdlov Moscow 19 B2
Svestad Oslo 23 B2
Sviňo Helsinki 11 C1
Swanley London 15 B3
Swansea Toronto 31 B1
Swinburne I. New York 22 C1
Swords Dublin 10 A2
Sydenham Johannesburg 13 A2
Sydney Sydney 29 B2
Sydney, Univ. of Sydney 29 B2
Sydney Harbour △ Sydney 29 B2
Sydney Harbour Bridge Sydney 29 B2
Sydney Kingsford Smith ✈ (SYD) Sydney 29 B2
Sydstranden Copenhagen 8 B3
Sylvania Sydney 29 C1
Syon Park London 15 B2
Szczęśliwice Warsaw 32 B1
Széchnenyi-hegy Budapest 7 B1
Széphalom Budapest 7 A1

T
Taastrup Copenhagen 8 B1
Tabata Tokyo 30 A3
Tablada Buenos Aires 7 C1
Table B. Cape Town 8 A1
Table Mountain △ Cape Town 8 A1
Table Mt. Cape Town 8 A1
Taboão da Serra São Paulo 27 B1
Täby Stockholm 29 A2
Tacuba Mexico City 18 B1
Tacubaya Mexico City 18 B1
Tafelbaai = Table B. Cape Town 8 A1
Taft Orlando 23 B2
Tagig → Manila 17 B2
Taguig Manila 17 B2
Tai Lo Shan Hong Kong 12 A2
Tai Po Tsai Hong Kong 12 A2
Tai Seng Singapore 28 A3
Tai Shui Hang Hong Kong 12 A2
Tai Tam B. Hong Kong 12 B2
Tai Tam Tuk Res. Hong Kong 12 B2
Tai Wai Hong Kong 12 A2
Tai Wan Tau Hong Kong 12 B2
Tai Wo Hau Hong Kong 12 A1
Tainaka Osaka 23 B2
Taishō Osaka 23 B1
Taita Wellington 33 B2
Tajrish Tehran 31 A2
Takaido Tokyo 30 A2
Takaishi Tokyo 30 B2
Takarazuka Osaka 23 A1
Takasago Tokyo 30 A4
Takatsu Tokyo 30 B2
Takeshita Tokyo 30 B2
Takinegawa Tokyo 30 A3
Takoma Park Washington 33 B3
Taksim Istanbul 12 B1
Talaide Lisbon 16 A1
Taliganga Kolkata 14 B2
Talipapa Manila 17 A2
Tallaght Dublin 10 B1
Tallkrogen Stockholm 29 B2
Tama → Tokyo 30 B2
Tama Tokyo 30 B2
Tama Kyūryō Tokyo 30 B2
Tamaden Tokyo 30 B2
Tamagawa-josui → Tokyo 30 A1
Taman Sari Jakarta 12 A1
Tamanduatei → São Paulo 27 B2
Tambora Jakarta 12 A1
Tammisalo Helsinki 11 B3
Tammūh Cairo 7 B2
Tampines Singapore 28 A3
Tanah Abang Jakarta 12 B1
Tanah Kusir Jakarta 12 B1
Tangelo Park Orlando 23 B2
Tanjung Duren Jakarta 12 A1
Tanjung Priok Jakarta 12 A2
Tanum Oslo 23 A1
Tapada Lisbon 16 A1
Tapanila Helsinki 11 B3
Tapiales Buenos Aires 7 C1
Tapiola Helsinki 11 B1
Tapsia Kolkata 14 B2
Tara Mumbai 20 A2
Tarabya Istanbul 12 B2
Tárbæk Copenhagen 8 A3
Tarchomin Warsaw 32 B1
Tardeo Mumbai 20 B1
Targówek Warsaw 32 B2
Tárnby Copenhagen 8 B3
Tarqua Bay Lagos 14 B2
Tathong Channel Hong Kong 12 B2
Tathong Pt. Hong Kong 12 B2
Tatuapé São Paulo 27 B2
Taufkirchen Munich 21 B2
Tavares, I. dos Rio de Janeiro 25 B2
Tavros Athens 2 B2
Tawa Wellington 33 B2
Te Papa Museum Wellington 33
Teaneck New York 22 A1
Tebet Jakarta 12 B2

Tecamachalco Mexico City 18 B1
Ted Williams Tunnel Boston 6 A2
Teddington London 15 B1
Tegel Berlin 5 A2
Tegel, Berlin ✈ (TXL) Berlin 5 A1
Tegeler See Berlin 5 A2
Tegelort Berlin 5 A2
Tehrān = Tehrān Tehran 31 A2
Tehrān Tehran 31 A2
Tehrān Mehrābād ✈ (THR) Tehran 31 A1
Tehrān Pārs Tehran 31 A3
Tei Tong Tsui Hong Kong 12 B2
Tejo, Rio → Lisbon 16 A2
Tekstilyshchik Moscow 19 B3
Telhal Lisbon 16 A1
Telok Blangah Singapore 28 B2
Teltow Berlin 5 B2
Teltow kanal Berlin 5 B3
Tempelhof Berlin 5 B2
Temple City Los Angeles 16 B4
Temple Hills Los Angeles 16 B4
Temple of Heaven Beijing 4 B2
Templeogue Dublin 10 B1
Temppeliaukio Church Helsinki 11 B2
Tenafly New York 22 A2
Tenayuca, Piramide de Mexico City 18 A1
Tengah → Singapore 28 A2
Tennoji Osaka 23 B2
Tepalcates Mexico City 18 B2
Tepeyac △ Mexico City 18 B2
Terrazzano Milan 19 A1
Terre des Hommes Montreal 20 A2
Terrugem Lisbon 16 A1
Terrytown New Orleans 21 B2
Tervuren Brussels 6 B3
Tervuren, Park van Brussels 6 B3
Tetuán Madrid 17 B1
Teufelsberg Berlin 5 B2
Thalkirchen Munich 21 B2
Thames Ditton London 15 B1
Thamesmead London 15 A4
Thana Cr. → Mumbai 20 A2
Thiais Paris 24 B3
Thisio Athens 2 B2
Thistletown Toronto 31 A1
Thomastown Melbourne 18 A2
Thompson I. Boston 6 B3
Thon Buri Bangkok 3 B1
Thornbury Melbourne 18 A2
Thorncliffe Toronto 31 A2
Thornhill Toronto 31 A2
Thornton Cape Town 8 A2
Thornton Heath London 15 B3
Threipmuir Res. Edinburgh 11 B2
Throgs Neck New York 22 B3
Tiancun Beijing 4 B1
Tianhe Guangzhou 11 B3
Tibet, L. Orlando 23 A1
Tibidabo Barcelona 4 A1
Tibradden Mt. Dublin 10 B2
Tiburon San Francisco 26 A2
Tiburtino Rome 26 B2
Ticomán Mexico City 18 A2
Tiefersee Berlin 5 B5
Tiergarten Berlin 5 A3
Tijgerhof Cape Town 8 A1
Tijuca Rio de Janeiro 25 B1
Tijuca, Pico da Rio de Janeiro 25 B1
Tijuca △ Rio de Janeiro 25 B1
Tikkurila Helsinki 11 B3
Tilak Nagar Delhi 10 B1
Tilanqiao Shanghai 28 B1
Timah, Bukit Singapore 28 A2
Timiryazev Park Moscow 19 B2
Tin Can I. Lagos 14 B2
Ting Kau Hong Kong 12 A1
Tira Jerusalem 13 A1
Tirsa Cairo 7 B2
Tishrīyaa Baghdad 3 B2
Tiu Keng Leng Hong Kong 12 B2
Tizapán Mexico City 18 C1
Tlalnepantla → Mexico City 18 A1
Tlalpan Mexico City 18 C2
To Kwai Wan Hong Kong 12 B2
Toa Payoh Singapore 28 A3
Točná Prague 25 B2
Toco Hills Atlanta 3 B2
Todt Hill New York 22 C1
Tōkagi Tokyo 30 A4
Tokai Plantation Cape Town 8 B1
Tōkaichiba Tokyo 30 B1
Tōkyō Tokyo 30 A3
Tōkyō B. = Tōkyō-Wan Tokyo 30 B4
Tōkyō Disneyland Tokyo 30 B4
Tōkyō Haneda ✈ (HND) Tokyo 30 B3
Tōkyō Harbour Tokyo 30 B3
Tōkyō-Wan Tokyo 30 B4
Tolka → Dublin 10 A1
Tollygunge = Taliganga Kolkata 14 B2
Tolworth London 15 B2
Tomba di Nerone Rome 26 B1
Tommy Thompson Park Toronto 31 B3
Tondo Manila 17 B1
Tongbinggo Seoul 27 B1
Tongqiao Shanghai 28 B1
Toorak Melbourne 18 B2
Topanga State Park △ Los Angeles 16 B2
Topkapı Istanbul 12 B1
Topkapı Palaca Istanbul 12 B1
Tor di Quinto Rome 26 B1
Tor Pignattara Rome 26 B2
Tor Sapienza Rome 26 B2
Torcy Paris 24 A4
Toronto Toronto 31 B2
Toronto, Univ. of Toronto 31 B2
Toronto City Centre ✈ (YTZ) Toronto 31 B2
Toronto Harbour Toronto 31 B2
Toronto I. Toronto 31 B2
Toronto Lester B. Pearson Int. ✈ (YYZ) Toronto 31 A1
Torre Lupara Rome 26 B2
Torre Nova Rome 26 B2
Torrejón → Madrid 17 B2
Torrelles → Barcelona 4 A1
Torrevécchia Rome 26 B1
Toshima Tokyo 30 A3
Toshimaen Tokyo 30 A3
Tottenham London 15 A3
Tottenham Melbourne 18 A1
Toussus-le-Noble Paris 24 B1
Toussus-le-Noble ✈ (TNF) Paris 24 B1
Towchal Cable Car Tehran 31 A2
Tower Hamlets □ London 15 A3
Tower of London London 15 A3
Towra Pt. Sydney 29 C1
Toyonaka Osaka 23 A1
Trafaria Lisbon 16 A1
Traição, Cor. → São Paulo 27 B2
Traneglide Copenhagen 8 A3
Trångsund Stockholm 29 B2

Trappenfelde Berlin 5 A5
Trastévere Rome 26 B1
Treasure I. San Francisco 26 B2
Třeboradice Prague 25 B2
Třebotov Prague 25 C1
Tremblay-en-France Paris 24 A4
Tremembe → São Paulo 27 A2
Tremont New York 22 B2
Tremono Milan 19 B1
Treptow Berlin 5 B3
Três Rios, Sa. dos Rio de Janeiro 25 B1
Trevi, Fontana di Rome 26 B1
Trezzano sul Navíglio Milan 19 B1
Trinidad Washington 33 B4
Trinity College Dublin 10 A2
Trinity Edinburgh 11 B2
Trionfale Rome 26 B1
Triulzo Milan 19 B2
Troja Prague 25 B2
Trollbäcken Stockholm 29 B3
Trombay Mumbai 20 A2
Tropareovo Moscow 19 B2
Trudeau, Montréal ✈ (YUL) Montreal 20 B1
Trudyashchikhsya, Ostrov St. Petersburg 27 B1
Tryvasshøgda Oslo 23 A3
Tseng Lan Shue Hong Kong 12 A2
Tseung Kwan Hong Kong 12 A2
Tsim Sha Tsui Hong Kong 12 B1
Tsing Yi Hong Kong 12 A1
Tsova Jerusalem 13 B1
Tsuen Wan Hong Kong 12 A1
Tsur Hadassa Jerusalem 13 B1
Tsurumi → Tokyo 30 B3
Tsz Wan Shan Hong Kong 12 A2
Tuas Singapore 28 B1
Tuchoměřice Prague 25 B1
Tuckahoe New York 22 A2
Tucuruví São Paulo 27 A2
Tufello Rome 26 B2
Tufnell Park London 15 A3
Tufts Univ. Boston 6 A2
Tughlakabad Delhi 10 B2
Tullamarine Melbourne 18 A1
Tulse Hill London 15 B3
Tung Lung Chau Hong Kong 12 B2
Tung O Hong Kong 12 B1
Tunis Baghdad 3 B2
Tuomarila Helsinki 11 B1
Tureberg Stockholm 29 A1
Turffontein Johannesburg 13 B2
Turkey L. Orlando 23 A1
Turkey Lake Park Orlando 23 A1
Turner Field Atlanta 3 B2
Turnham Green London 15 B2
Turnhouse Edinburgh 11 B1
Tuscolana, Via Rome 26 B2
Twelve Apostles Cape Town 8 A1
Twentieth Century Fox Studios Los Angeles 16 B2
Twickenham London 15 B2
Twickenham Rugby Ground London 15 B2
Twin Peaks San Francisco 26 B2
Two Rock Mt. Dublin 10 B2
Tymon North Dublin 10 B1
Tysons Corner Washington 33 B3

U
U.S. Capitol Washington 33 B4
U.S. Cellular Field Chicago 9 C3
Ubeidiya Jerusalem 13 B2
Uberaba → São Paulo 27 B2
Ubin, Pulau Singapore 28 A3
Uccle Brussels 6 B2
Udelnaya St. Petersburg 27 A2
Udelnoe St. Petersburg 27 B2
Uddling Munich 21 A1
Ueno Tokyo 30 A3
Úholičky Prague 25 B1
Uhříněves Prague 25 B3
Uithoorn Amsterdam 2 B1
Ujazdów Warsaw 32 B2
Újpalota Budapest 7 A2
Újpest Budapest 7 A2
Ukita Tokyo 30 A4
Ulerup Copenhagen 8 B3
Ulleval Oslo 23 A3
Ulriksdal Stockholm 29 A1
Ulyanka St. Petersburg 27 B1
Um Al-Khanazir Island Baghdad 3 B2
Umeda Osaka 23 A1
Ümraniye Istanbul 12 B2
Underground Atlanta Atlanta 3 B2
Underhill, L. Orlando 23 B3
Unětický potok → Prague 25 B2
Unhos Lisbon 16 A2
Unidad Santa Fe Mexico City 18 B1
Union City New York 22 B1
Union Port New York 22 B2
Union Station Toronto 31 B2
United Center Chicago 9 B2
United Nations Headquarters New York 22 B2
Universal Studios Los Angeles 16 B2
Universal Studios Orlando 23 B2
Universidad Madrid 17 B1
University Park Washington 33 B4
Unterbiberg Munich 21 B2
Unterföhring Munich 21 A3
Unterhaching Munich 21 B2
Unterlaa Vienna 32 B2
Untermenzing Munich 21 A1
Upper B. New York 22 C1
Upper Elmers End London 15 B3
Upper New York B. = Upper B. New York 22 C1
Upper Norwood London 15 B3
Upper Peirce Res. Singapore 28 A2
Upper Sydenham London 15 B3
Upper Tooting London 15 B3
Upton London 15 A4
Uptown Chicago 9 B2
Uran Mumbai 20 B2
Urayasu Tokyo 30 B4
Urbe ✕ Rome 26 B2
Urca Rio de Janeiro 25 B2
Uritsk St. Petersburg 27 C1
Üröm Budapest 7 A2
Ursus Warsaw 32 B1
Ursvik Stockholm 29 A1
Usera Madrid 17 B1
Ushigome Tokyo 30 A3
Usina Rio de Janeiro 25 B2
Üsküdar Istanbul 12 B2
Ust-Slavyanka St. Petersburg 27 C3
Uteke Stockholm 29 A1
Utrata Warsaw 32 B1
Uttarpara Kolkata 14 B1
Utterslev Mose Copenhagen 8 A2

V
Vaclavské náměstí Prague 25 B2
Vadaul Mumbai 20 A2
Vaires-sur-Marne Paris 24 A4
Valby Copenhagen 8 B2
Valcannuta Rome 26 B1
Valdelatas Madrid 17 A1
Vale Washington 33 B2
Vallcarca Barcelona 4 A1
Valldoreix Barcelona 4 A1
Vallecas Madrid 17 B2
Vallecas, Cumbres de Madrid 17 B2
Vallentunasjön Stockholm 29 A2
Valleranello Rome 26 C1
Vallisaari Helsinki 11 C3
Vallvidrera Barcelona 4 A1
Vallvidrera → Barcelona 4 A1
Van Gogh Museum Amsterdam 2 A2
Vanak Tehran 31 A2
Vanda = Vantaa Helsinki 11 B2
Vangede Copenhagen 8 A3
Vaniköy Istanbul 12 B2
Vanløse Copenhagen 8 A2
Vantaa Helsinki 11 B2
Vantaankoski Helsinki 11 B2
Vantaanpuisto Helsinki 11 B2
Vanves Paris 24 B2
Varedo Milan 19 A1
Varkiza Athens 2 C2
Vartiokylä Helsinki 11 B3
Vartiosaari Helsinki 11 B3
Vasamuseet Stockholm 29 B2
Vasco Cape Town 8 A2
Vasfanārd Tehran 31 B2
Vashi Mumbai 20 A2
Vasilyevsky, Ostrov St. Petersburg 27 B1
Vatican City ■ Rome 26 B1
Vaucluse Sydney 29 B2
Vaucluse House Sydney 29 B2
Vaucresson Paris 24 A1
Vaughan Toronto 31 A1
Vauhallan Paris 24 B2
Vaujours Paris 24 A4
Vauxhall London 15 B3
Vecsés Budapest 7 B3
Veleň Prague 25 B2
Veleslavin Prague 25 B2
Vélizy-Villacoublay Paris 24 B2
Velka-Chuchle Prague 25 B2
Velké Přílepy Prague 25 B1
Venda Seca Lisbon 16 A1
Venetian Islands Miami 18 B2
Venice Los Angeles 16 B2
Ventas Madrid 17 B1
Ventorro del Cano Madrid 17 B1
Venustiano Carranza Mexico City 18 B2
Verde → São Paulo 27 A1
Verdi Athens 2 A2
Verdugo Mts. Los Angeles 16 A2
Verdun Montreal 20 B2
Vérhalom Budapest 7 A2
Vermelho → São Paulo 27 B1
Vermont Knolls Los Angeles 16 C3
Vermont Los Angeles 16 B3
Verrières-le-Buisson Paris 24 B2
Versailles Buenos Aires 7 B1
Versailles Paris 24 B1
Veshnyaki Moscow 19 B3
Vesolyy Posolok St. Petersburg 27 B2
Vestra Helsinki 11 B1
Vestskoven Copenhagen 8 A2
Vicálvaro Madrid 17 B2
Vicente Lopez Buenos Aires 7 B2
Victoria Wellington 33 B1
Victoria, Mt. Wellington 33 B1
Victoria, Pont Montreal 20 B2
Victoria and Alfred Waterfront Cape Town 8 A1
Victoria Gardens Mumbai 20 B2
Victoria Harbour Hong Kong 12 B1
Victoria L. Johannesburg 13 B2
Victoria Lawn Tennis Courts Melbourne 18 B2
Victoria Park Hong Kong 12 B1
Victoria Peak Hong Kong 12 B1
Vienna = Wien Vienna 32 A2
Vienna Washington 33 B2
Vietnam Veterans Memorial Washington 33 B3
Vietnam War Memorial Chicago 9 B2
Vieux Carré = French Quarter New Orleans 21 B2
View Park Los Angeles 16 B2
Vigário Geral Rio de Janeiro 25 A1
Vigentino Milan 19 B2
Viggbyholm Stockholm 29 A2
Vighignolo Milan 19 B1
Viikki Helsinki 11 B3
Vikhroli Mumbai 20 A2
Vila Guilherme São Paulo 27 B2
Vila Isabel Rio de Janeiro 25 B1
Vila Jaguára São Paulo 27 B1
Vila Madalena São Paulo 27 B1
Vila Maria São Paulo 27 B2
Vila Mariana São Paulo 27 B2
Vila Prudente São Paulo 27 B2
Viladecans Barcelona 4 B1
Vile Parle Mumbai 20 A2
Villa Adelina Buenos Aires 7 B1
Villa Ballester Buenos Aires 7 B1
Villa Barilari Buenos Aires 7 C2
Villa Bosch Buenos Aires 7 B1
Villa C. Colon Buenos Aires 7 C2
Villa Ciudadela Buenos Aires 7 B1
Villa de Guadalupe Mexico City 18 B2
Villa Devoto Buenos Aires 7 B1
Villa Diamante Buenos Aires 7 C2
Villa Dominico Buenos Aires 7 C3
Villa Lugano Buenos Aires 7 C1
Villa Lynch Buenos Aires 7 B1
Villa Madero Buenos Aires 7 C1
Villa Sáenz Pena Buenos Aires 7 B1
Vila Urquiza Buenos Aires 7 B1
Villaverde Madrid 17 B1
Villaverde Bajo Madrid 17 B1
Ville-d'Avray Paris 24 B2
Villecresnes Paris 24 B3
Villejuif Paris 24 B3
Villemomble Paris 24 A4
Villeneuve-la-Garenne Paris 24 A2
Villeneuve-le-Roi Paris 24 B3
Villeneuve-St-Georges Paris 24 B3
Villeparisis Paris 24 A4
Villevaudé Paris 24 A4
Villiers-le-Bâcle Paris 24 B1

Villiers-sur-Marne Paris 24 A4
Villinki Helsinki 11 C3
Villoresi, Canale Milan 19 A1
Vilvoorde Brussels 6 A2
Vimodrone Milan 19 B2
Vimont Montreal 20 A1
Vincennes Paris 24 B3
Vincennes, Bois de Paris 24 B3
Vineland Orlando 23 B1
Vinings Atlanta 3 A1
Vinohrady Prague 25 B2
Vinoř Prague 25 B3
Violet Hill Hong Kong 12 B2
Virányos Budapest 7 A1
Virginia, L. Orlando 23 B2
Virginia Gardens Miami 18 B1
Virginia Key Miami 18 B2
Viroflay Paris 24 B2
Vironas Athens 2 B2
Virum Copenhagen 8 A2
Visitacion Valley San Francisco 26 B2
Vista Alegre Lima 14 B3
Vista Alegre Santiago 27 C1
Vista Grove Atlanta 3 A3
Vitacura Santiago 27 B1
Vitínia Rome 26 C1
Vitry-sur-Seine Paris 24 B3
Vizcaya Museum and Gardens Miami 18 B2
Vladykino Moscow 19 A2
Vokovice Prague 25 B2
Volgelsdorf Berlin 5 B5
Volkhonka-Zil Moscow 19 C2
Vollen Oslo 23 B1
Volodarskoye St. Petersburg 27 B2
Volynkina-Derevnya St. Petersburg 27 B1
Voula Athens 2 C2
Vouliagmeni Athens 2 C2
Vredehoek Cape Town 8 A1
Vršovice Prague 25 B2
Vyborgskaya Storona St. Petersburg 27 B2
Vykhino Moscow 19 B3
Vyšehrad Prague 25 B2

W
Wachterhof Munich 21 B3
Wadala Mumbai 20 A2
Wadestown Wellington 33 B1
Wadi al-Arayis Jerusalem 13 B2
Wadi Fukin Jerusalem 13 B1
Waduk Pluit Jakarta 12 A1
Waggaman New Orleans 21 B1
Wah Fu Hong Kong 12 B1
Wahda Baghdad 3 B2
Währing Vienna 32 A2
Waidmannslust Berlin 5 A3
Wainuiomata Wellington 33 B2
Wainuiomata → Wellington 33 B2
Wakefield Boston 6 A2
Waldesruh Berlin 5 B4
Walderlach Munich 21 B2
Waldtrudering Munich 21 B3
Walkinstown Dublin 10 B1
Wall Street New York 22 B1
Walt Disney World Orlando 23 B1
Walter D. Stone Memorial Zoo Boston 6 A2
Waltham Boston 6 A1
Waltham Forest □ London 15 A3
Walthamstone London 15 A3
Walton-on-Thames London 15 B1
Wambeek Brussels 6 A3
Wan Chai Hong Kong 12 B1
Wandle → London 15 B3
Wandsworth □ London 15 B2
Wangjing Beijing 4 B2
Wannsee Berlin 5 B1
Wansdorf Berlin 5 A1
Wanstead London 15 A4
Wapping London 15 A3
Ward I. Wellington 33 B2
Ward L. New York 22 A2
Warnberg Munich 21 B2
Warner Brothers Studios Los Angeles 16 B2
Warrâq el `Arab Cairo 7 A2
Warringal Park Melbourne 18 A2
Warriston Edinburgh 11 B2
Warsaw = Warszawa Warsaw 32 B2
Warszawa Warsaw 32 B2
Warszawa ✕ (WAW) Warsaw 32 B1
Wartenberg Berlin 5 A4
Washington Washington 33 B3
Washington Dulles Int. ✕ (IAD) Washington 33 B1
Washington Heights New York 22 A2
Washington Park Chicago 9 C3
Washington Ronald Reagan Nat. ✕ (DCA) Washington 33 B3
Wat Pho Bangkok 3 B1
Water of Leith → Edinburgh 11 B1
Watergraafsmeer Amsterdam 2 A2
Waterland Amsterdam 2 A2
Waterloo Brussels 6 B2
Waterloo Wellington 33 B2
Watermael-Boitsfort Brussels 6 B2
Watertown Boston 6 A1
Watsonia Melbourne 18 A2
Waverley Boston 6 A1
Waverley Johannesburg 13 A2
Waverley Sydney 29 B2
Wawer Warsaw 32 B2
Wawrzyszew Warsaw 32 B1
Wazirabad Delhi 10 A2
Wazirīya Baghdad 3 B2
Wazirpur Delhi 10 A2
Wealdstone London 15 A1
Wedding Berlin 5 A3
Weehawken New York 22 B1
Weesp Amsterdam 2 B3
Weidling Vienna 32 A1
Weidlingbach Vienna 32 A1
Weissensee Berlin 5 A3
Wellesley Hills Boston 6 B1
Welling London 15 B4
Wellington Wellington 33 B1
Wellington Int. ✕ (WLE) Wellington 33 B1
Welwyn Boston 6 A2
Wembley London 15 A2
Wemmel Brussels 6 A1
Wemmer Pan Johannesburg 13 B2
Wenceslas Square = Vaclavské náměstí Prague 25 B2
Wendenschloss Berlin 5 B4
Wennington London 15 A5
Werneuchen Berlin 5 A5

Worli Mumbai 20 A1
Worth Chicago 9 C2
Wren's Nest Atlanta 3 B2
Wrigley Field Chicago 9 B3
Wuhlgarten Berlin 5 A4
Wujiaochang Shanghai 28 B2
Würm → Munich 21 B1
Wusong Shanghai 28 A1
Wyczółki Warsaw 32 C1
Wygoda Warsaw 32 B2
Wynberg Cape Town 8 B1

 X
Xabregas Lisbon 16 A2
Xianggang = Hong Kong Hong Kong 12 B1
Xiaogang Park Guangzhou 11 B2
Xiaoping Guangzhou 11 B1
Xiasha chong Guangzhou 11 B1
Xichang Guangzhou 11 B2
Xicheng Beijing 4 B1
Xidan Beijing 4 B1
Xizhimen Beijing 4 B1
Xochimilco, Parque Ecológico Mexico City 18 C2
Xuanwu Beijing 4 B1
Xuhui Shanghai 28 B1

 Y
Yaba Lagos 14 A2
Yaftābād Tehran 31 B1
Yahara Tokyo 30 A2
Yaho Tokyo 30 A1
Yakire Tokyo 30 A4
Yaksa Seoul 27 B2
Yamada Osaka 23 A2
Yamada Tokyo 30 B2
Yamato → Osaka 23 B1
Yan Kit Singapore 28 B3
Yanbu Guangzhou 11 B1
Yangcheon Seoul 27 B1
Yanghuayuan Beijing 4 C1
Yangjiae Seoul 27 C2
Yangjiazhuang Shanghai 28 B1
Yangjing Shanghai 28 B1
Yangpu Park Shanghai 28 B2
Yannawa Bangkok 3 B2
Yarmūk Baghdad 3 B2
Yarra Bend Park Melbourne 18 A2
Yarraville Melbourne 18 A1
Yauza → Moscow 19 B4
Yeading London 15 A1
Yedikule Istanbul 12 C1
Yenikapı Istanbul 12 B1
Yeniköy Istanbul 12 B2
Yeongdeungpo Seoul 27 B1
Yeongdong Seoul 27 B2
Yeouido Seoul 27 B1
Yerba Buena I. San Francisco 26 B2
Yerres Paris 24 B4
Yerushalayim = Jerusalem Jerusalem 13 B2
Yiexiu Guangzhou 11 B2
Yiheyuan Beijing 4 B1
Yıldız Park Istanbul 12 B2
Yinhangzhen Shanghai 28 A2
Yishun Singapore 28 A3
Ylästö Helsinki 11 B2
Yodo → Osaka 23 A2
Yongdingman Beijing 4 B2
Yongfucun Guangzhou 11 B2
Yongsan Seoul 27 B2
Yonkers New York 22 A2
York Toronto 31 A2
York Mills Toronto 31 A2
York Univ. Toronto 31 A1
You'anmen Beijing 4 B1
Youngsfield Cape Town 8 B1
Yuanmingyuan Park Beijing 4 A1
Yuanxiatian Guangzhou 11 B2
Yuexiu Park Guangzhou 11 B2
Yugo-Zarad Moscow 19 B2
Yuhalixqui, Volcan Mexico City 18 C2
Yung Shue Wan Hong Kong 12 B1
Yūsofābād Tehran 31 A2

 Z
Zaandam Amsterdam 2 A1
Zaandijk Amsterdam 2 A1
Zaanstad Amsterdam 2 A1
Zábřehlice Prague 25 B2
Zabki Warsaw 32 B2
Zahrā Baghdad 3 A1
Żalov Prague 25 A2
Zahuski Warsaw 32 B2
Zamdorf Munich 21 A2
Zanevka St. Petersburg 27 B2
Zapote Manila 17 C1
Zaventem Brussels 6 A2
Zawady Warsaw 32 B2
Zâwiyet Abû Musallam Cairo 7 B1
Zawrā' Park Baghdad 3 B2
Zbraslav Prague 25 C2
Zbuzany Prague 25 B1
Zdiby Prague 25 B2
Zeekoevlei Cape Town 8 B2
Zehlendorf Berlin 5 B2
Zenne → Brussels 6 A2
Zephyr Field New Orleans 21 B1
Żerań Warsaw 32 B2
Zerzeń Warsaw 32 B2
Zeytinburnu Istanbul 12 C1
Zhabei Shanghai 28 B1
Zhabovo Moscow 19 B3
Zhenru Shanghai 28 B1
Zhernovka St. Petersburg 27 B2
Zhicun Guangzhou 11 B2
Zhongguancun Beijing 4 B1
Zhongshan Park Shanghai 28 B1
Zhoucun Guangzhou 11 B2
Zhoujiadu Shanghai 28 B2
Zhoujiazhen Shanghai 28 A2
Zhulebino Moscow 19 B4
Zielona Warsaw 32 B2
Zielonka Warsaw 32 B2
Zizhuyuan Park Beijing 4 B1
Žižkov Prague 25 B2
Zličin Prague 25 B1
Zografou Athens 2 B2
Żoliborz Warsaw 32 B2
Zonnebloem Cape Town 8 A1
Zugliget Budapest 7 B1
Zuiderwoude Amsterdam 2 A2
Zumbi → São Paulo 27 C1
Zunderdorp Amsterdam 2 A1
Zuvuvu → São Paulo 27 C1
Zwanenburg Amsterdam 2 B1
Zwölfaxing Vienna 32 B2

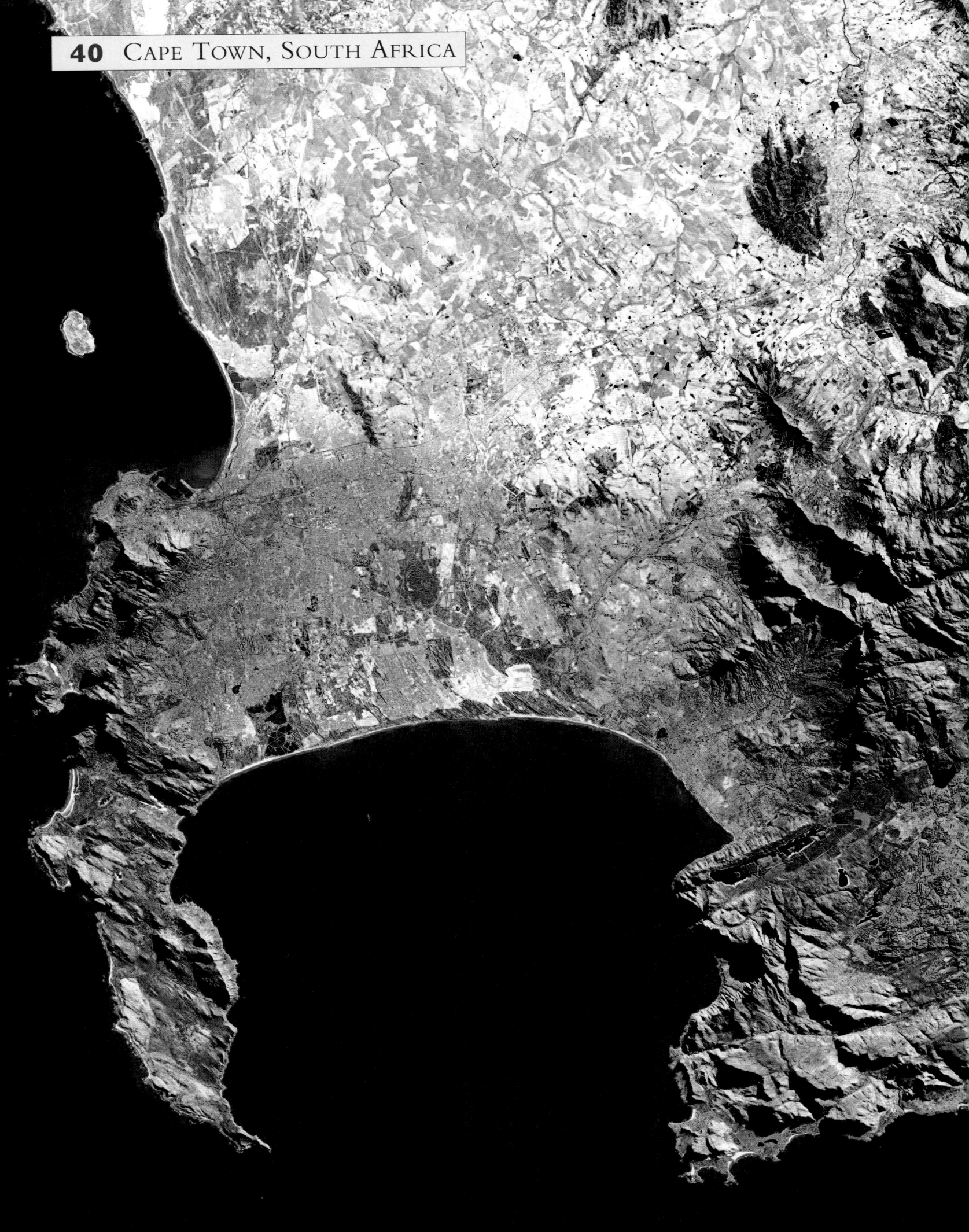

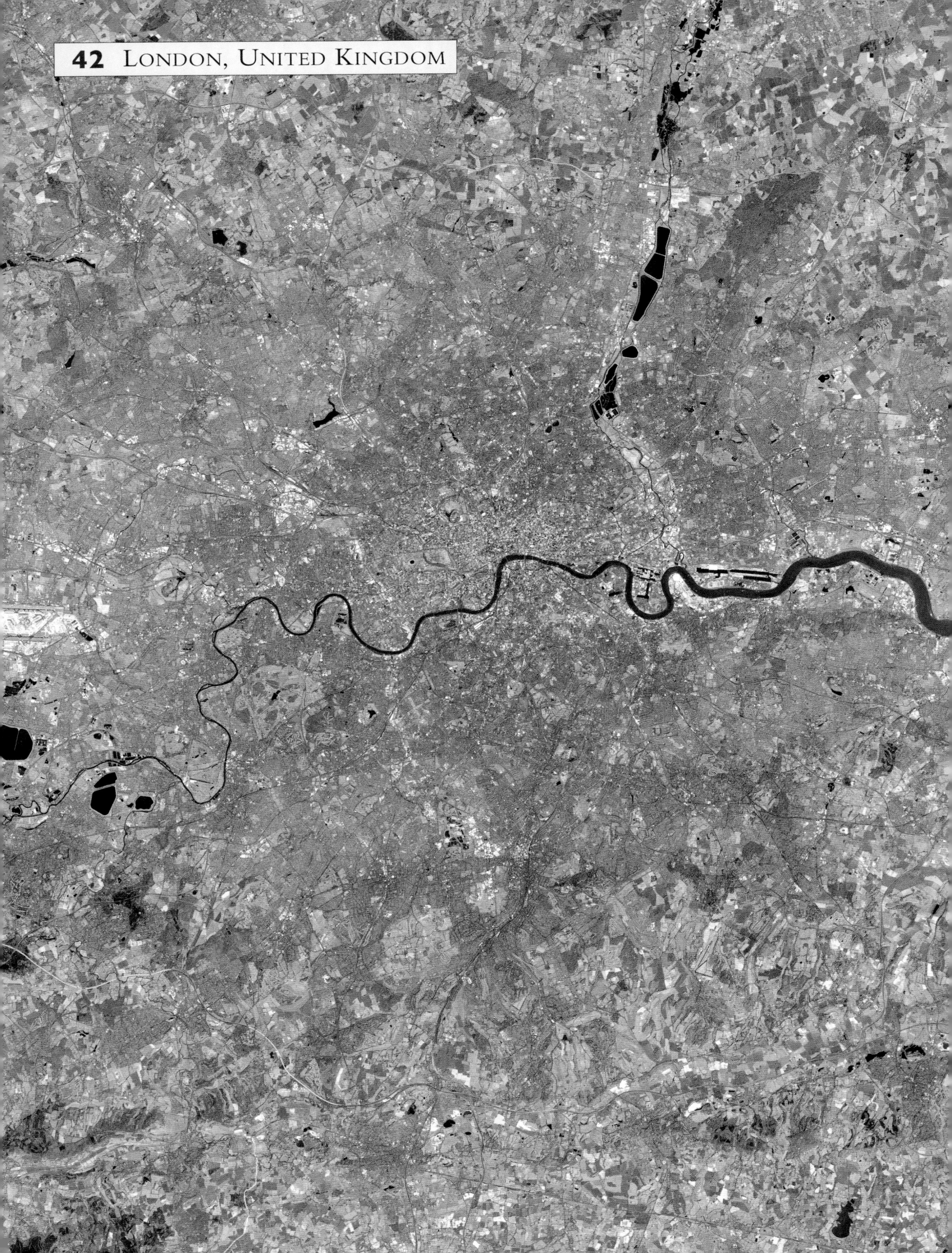

WORLD
MAPS

SETTLEMENTS

■ **PARIS** ◉ **Rotterdam** ◉ **Livorno** ◉ Brugge ◉ Exeter ○ *Torremolinos* ○ *Oberammergau* ○ *Thira*

Settlement symbols and type styles vary according to the scale of each map and indicate the importance
of towns on the map rather than specific population figures

• *Vaduz* Capital cities have red infills

∴ Ruins or archaeological sites

⬠ Urban agglomerations

⌣ Wells in desert

ADMINISTRATION

——— International boundaries

– – – –. International boundaries
(undefined or disputed)

··········· Internal boundaries

National parks

PERU Country names

KENT Administrative
area names

International boundaries show the *de facto* situation where there are rival claims to territory

COMMUNICATIONS

═══ Motorways, freeways
and expressways

——— Principal roads

——— Other roads

+---+ Road tunnels

——— Principal railways

–––– Railways
under construction

——— Other railways

+---+ Railway tunnels

LHR ✈ Principal airports

⊕ Other airports

·········· Principal canals

⤄ Passes

PHYSICAL FEATURES

〜 Perennial streams

– – – Intermittent streams

⬭ Perennial lakes

⠂⠂⠂ Sand deserts

⬬ Intermittent lakes

⚏ Swamps and marshes

❄ Permanent ice
and glaciers

▲ 8850 Elevations in metres

▼ 8500 Sea depths in metres

1134 Height of lake surface
above sea level in metres

ELEVATION AND DEPTH TINTS

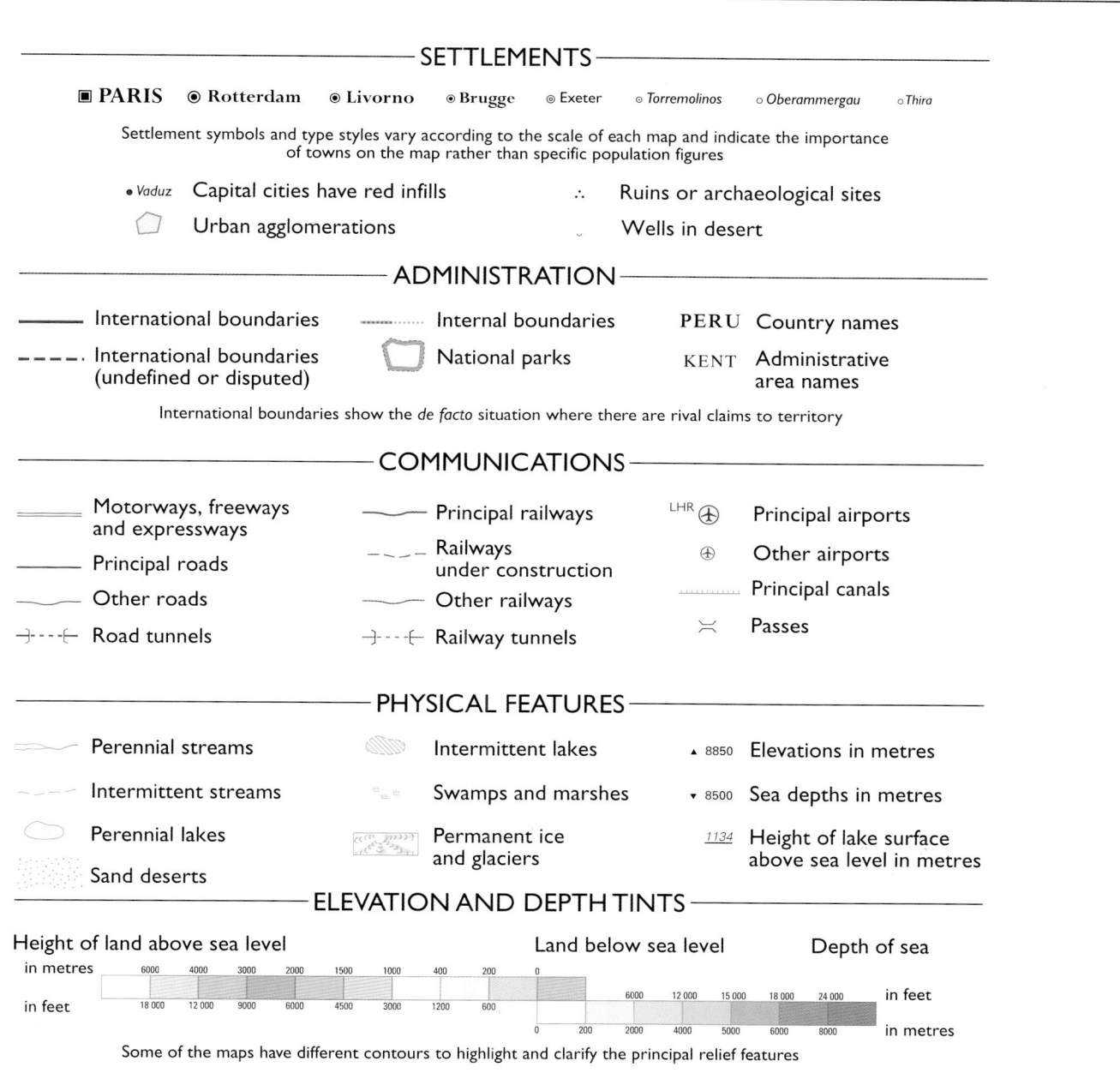

Height of land above sea level

| in metres | 6000 | 4000 | 3000 | 2000 | 1500 | 1000 | 400 | 200 | 0 |

Land below sea level

| | | 6000 | 12 000 | 15 000 | 18 000 | 24 000 | in feet |

| in feet | 18 000 | 12 000 | 9000 | 6000 | 4500 | 3000 | 1200 | 600 |

Depth of sea

| 0 | 200 | 2000 | 4000 | 5000 | 6000 | 8000 | in metres |

Some of the maps have different contours to highlight and clarify the principal relief features

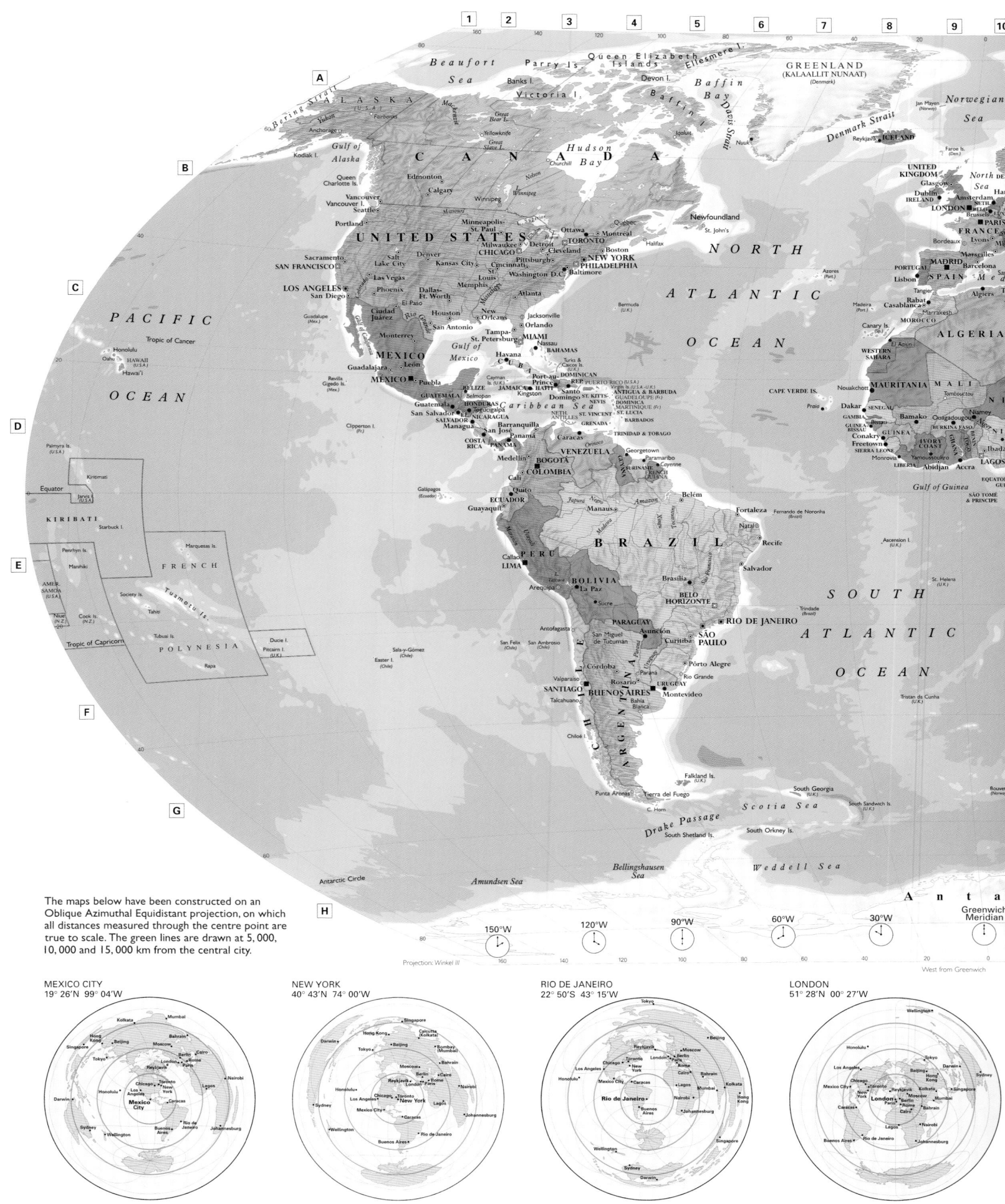

The maps below have been constructed on an Oblique Azimuthal Equidistant projection, on which all distances measured through the centre point are true to scale. The green lines are drawn at 5,000, 10,000 and 15,000 km from the central city.

MEXICO CITY
19° 26'N 99° 04'W

NEW YORK
40° 43'N 74° 00'W

RIO DE JANEIRO
22° 50'S 43° 15'W

LONDON
51° 28'N 00° 27'W

Projection: Winkel III

West from Greenwich

Greenwich
Meridian

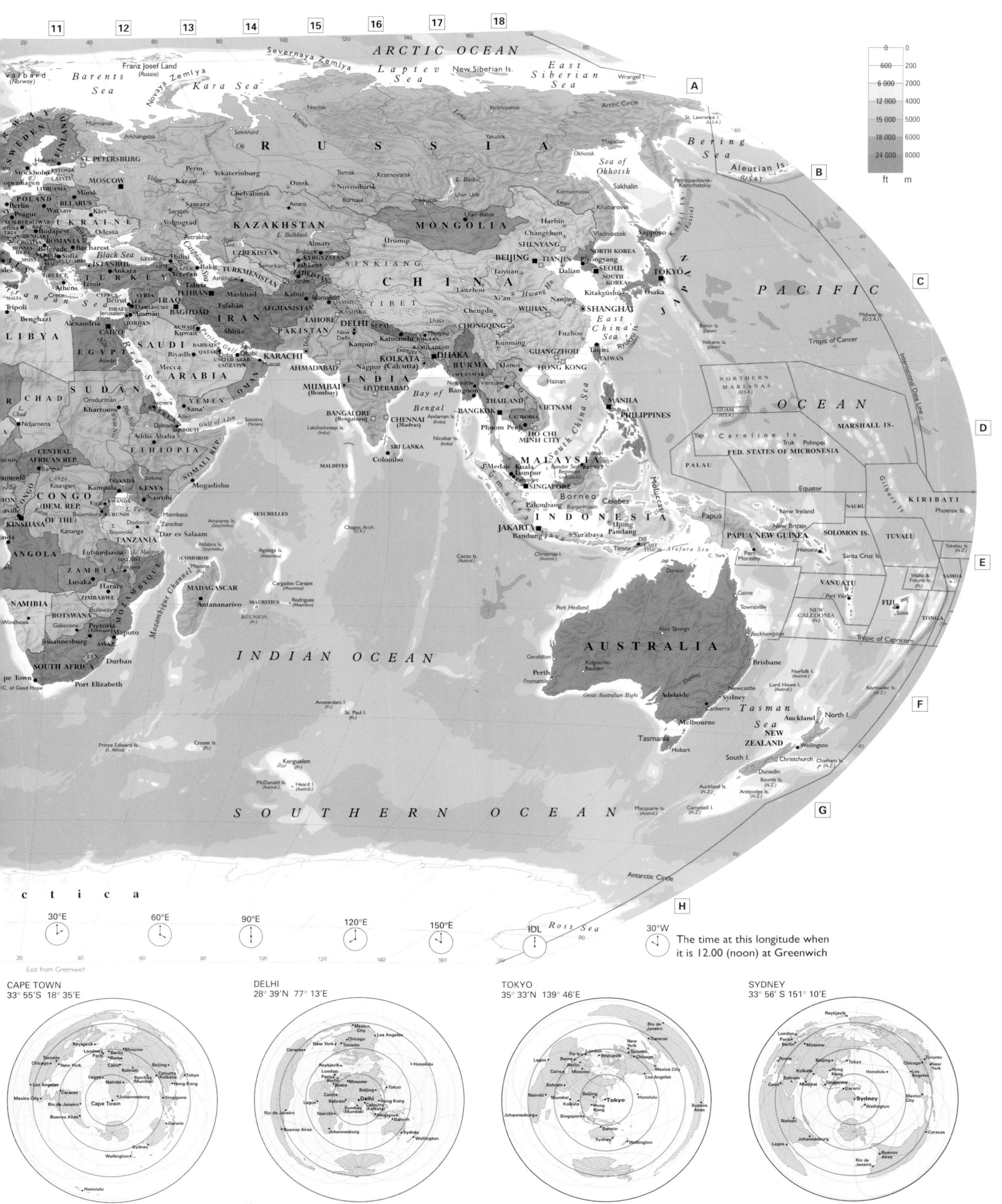

11 12 13 14 15 16 17 18

ARCTIC OCEAN

Severnaya Zemlya
Franz Josef Land
(Russia)
Laptev
Sea
New Siberian Is.
East
Siberian
Sea
Wrangel I.

Barents
Sea
Novaya Zemlya
Kara Sea

A

Murmansk
Norilsk
Verkhoyansk
Arctic Circle
St. Lawrence I.
(U.S.A.)

Arkhangelsk
Salekhard
Ob
Yenisey
Yakutsk
Lena

ST. PETERSBURG
Perm
Yekaterinburg
Tomsk
Krasnoyarsk
Magadan
Sea of
Okhotsk

MOSCOW
Volga
Kazan
Omsk
Novosibirsk
L. Baikal
Irkutsk
Ulan Ude
Okhotsk
Amur
Khabarovsk
Petropavlovsk-
Kamchatskiy

Bering
Sea

B

Aleutian Is.
(U.S.A.)

RUSSIA

Samara
Saratov
Astana
Barnaul
Ulan Bator
Harbin
Vladivostok
Sapporo

KAZAKHSTAN
L. Balkhash
Almaty
MONGOLIA
Changchun
SHENYANG
NORTH
KOREA
Pyongyang
SEOUL
TOKYO

Astrakhan
Aral Sea
UZBEKISTAN
Bishkek
KYRGYZSTAN
BEIJING
TIANJIN
SOUTH
KOREA

PACIFIC

C

Tbilisi
Baku
Samarkand
Tashkent
SINKIANG
Urumqi
Taiyuan
Dalian
Kitakyushu
Osaka

TURKMENISTAN
Ashkhabad
CHINA
Lanzhou
Xi'an
Hwang Ho

TURKEY
Ankara
TEHRAN
Mashhad
Kabul
Islamabad
TIBET
Lhasa
Chengdu
Nanjing
SHANGHAI

Izmir
IRAN
AFGHANISTAN
KASHMIR
WUHAN
East
China's
Sea

Athens
CYPRUS
SYRIA
Damascus
IRAQ
BAGHDAD
Isfahan
LAHORE
DELHI
NEPAL
Katmandu
BHUTAN
CHONGQING

D

Tripoli
Beirut
ISRAEL
Jerusalem
AMMAN
JORDAN
KUWAIT
Kuwait
Shiraz
PAKISTAN
New
Delhi
Kanpur
Ganges
Kunming
GUANGZHOU

Benghazi
Alexandria
CAIRO
EGYPT
SAUDI
Riyadh
QATAR
Abu Dhabi
UNITED ARAB
EMIRATES
KARACHI
AHMADABAD
Nagpur
KOLKATA
(Calcutta)
DHAKA
BURMA
MYANMAR
Hanoi
HONG KONG
Hainan

LIBYA
BAHRAIN
Aswan
Red Sea
Mecca
ARABIA
Muscat
OMAN
MUMBAI
(Bombay)
HYDERABAD
INDIA
Bay of
Bengal
Rangoon
THAILAND
VIETNAM
MANILA

SUDAN
CHAD
L. Chad
Omdurman
Khartoum
YEMEN
Sana'a
Aden
Gulf of Aden
Socotra
(Yemen)
BANGALORE
(Bengaluru)
CHENNAI
(Madras)
Andaman Is.
(India)
BANGKOK
CAMBODIA
Phnom Penh
PHILIPPINES

NORTHERN
MARIANAS
(USA)
GUAM
(USA)
Caroline Is.
MARSHALL IS.

Ndjamena
CENTRAL
AFRICAN REP.
ERITREA
DJIBOUTI
Addis Ababa
ETHIOPIA
SRI LANKA
Colombo
MALDIVES
Lakshadweep Is.
(India)
Nicobar Is.
(India)
HO CHI
MINH CITY
MALAYSIA
S.Medan
Kuala
Lumpur
Bandar Seri
Begawan
BRUNEI
Yap
PALAU
FED. STATES OF MICRONESIA
Truk
Pohnpei

Bangui
CONGO
(DEM. REP.
OF THE)
UGANDA
KENYA
Nairobi
Mombasa
SEYCHELLES
Amirante Is.
(Seychelles)
SINGAPORE
Palembang
Borneo
Celebes
New Ireland
KIRIBATI

KINSHASA
RWANDA
BURUNDI
TANZANIA
Dodoma
Zanzibar
Dar es Salaam
Aldabra Is.
(Seychelles)
Banjarmasin
Moluccas
New Britain
NAURU
Phoenix Is.

ANGOLA
Lubumbashi
MALAWI
L. Malawi
COMOROS
Mayotte
(Fr.)
JAKARTA
Bandung
Java
Surabaya
Ujung
Pandang
INDONESIA
Papua
PAPUA NEW GUINEA
SOLOMON IS.
Honiara
Santa Cruz Is.
TUVALU

E

ZAMBIA
Lusaka
Harare
ZIMBABWE
MADAGASCAR
Antananarivo
MAURITIUS
Rodrigues
(Mauritius)
Christmas I.
(Austral.)
Cocos Is.
(Austral.)
Timor
EAST
TIMOR
Dili
Arafura Sea
C. York
Darwin
Port
Moresby
VANUATU
Port Vila
Wallis &
Futuna Is.
(Fr.)
SAMOA

NAMIBIA
BOTSWANA
Bulawayo
Gaborone
Pretoria
Maputo
SWAZILAND
Agalega Is.
(Mauritius)
Cargados Carajos
(Mauritius)
RÉUNION
(Fr.)
Port Hedland
Cairns
Townsville
NEW
CALEDONIA
FIJI
Suva
TONGA

Windhoek
SOUTH AFRICA
Johannesburg
LESOTHO
Durban
Prince Edward Is.
(S. African)
Amsterdam I.
(Fr.)
St. Paul I.
(Fr.)
Crozet Is.
(Fr.)
AUSTRALIA
Geraldton
Alice Springs
Rockhampton
Brisbane
Norfolk I.
(Austral.)
Lord Howe I.
(Austral.)
Kermadec Is.
(N.Z.)

F

Cape Town
C. of Good Hope
Port Elizabeth
Kerguelen
(Fr.)
INDIAN OCEAN
Perth
Fremantle
Kalgoorlie
Boulder
Darling
Newcastle
Sydney
Canberra
Auckland
North I.

McDonald Is.
(Austral.)
Heard I.
(Austral.)
Great Australian Bight
Adelaide
Melbourne
Tasman
Sea
NEW
ZEALAND
Wellington

Tasmania
Hobart
South I.
Dunedin
Christchurch
Chatham Is.
(N.Z.)

G

SOUTHERN OCEAN
Macquarie I.
(Austral.)
Campbell I.
(N.Z.)
Auckland Is.
(N.Z.)
Bounty Is.
(N.Z.)
Antipodes Is.
(N.Z.)

Antarctic Circle

c t i c a
Ross Sea

H

30°E   60°E   90°E   120°E   150°E   IDL   30°W
The time at this longitude when
it is 12.00 (noon) at Greenwich

East from Greenwich

CAPE TOWN
33° 55'S 18° 35'E

DELHI
28° 39'N 77° 13'E

TOKYO
35° 33'N 139° 46'E

SYDNEY
33° 56'S 151° 10'E

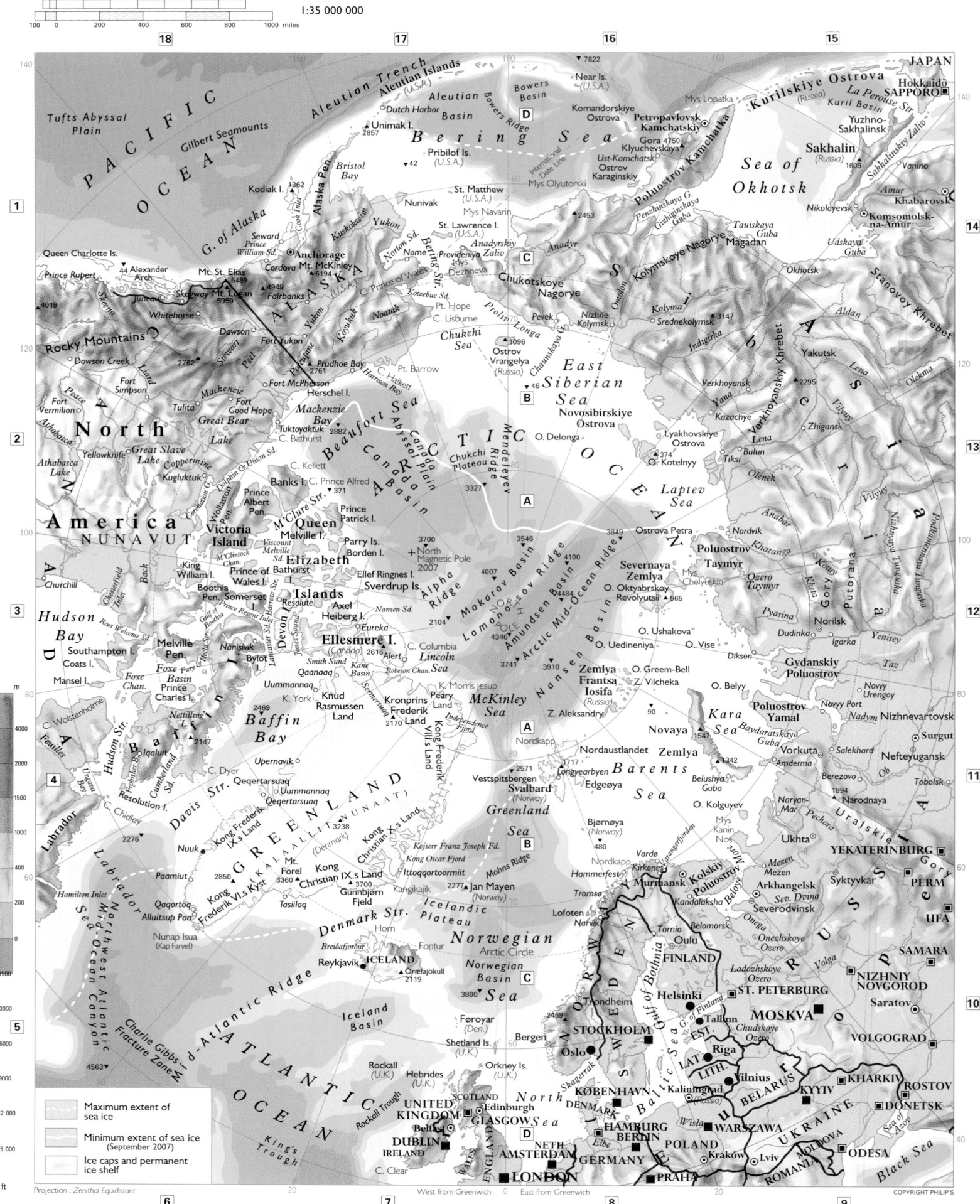

1:35 000 000

Projection : Zenithal Equidistant

West from Greenwich   East from Greenwich

COPYRIGHT PHILIP'S

Maximum extent of sea ice

Minimum extent of sea ice (September 2007)

Ice caps and permanent ice shelf

1:35 000 000

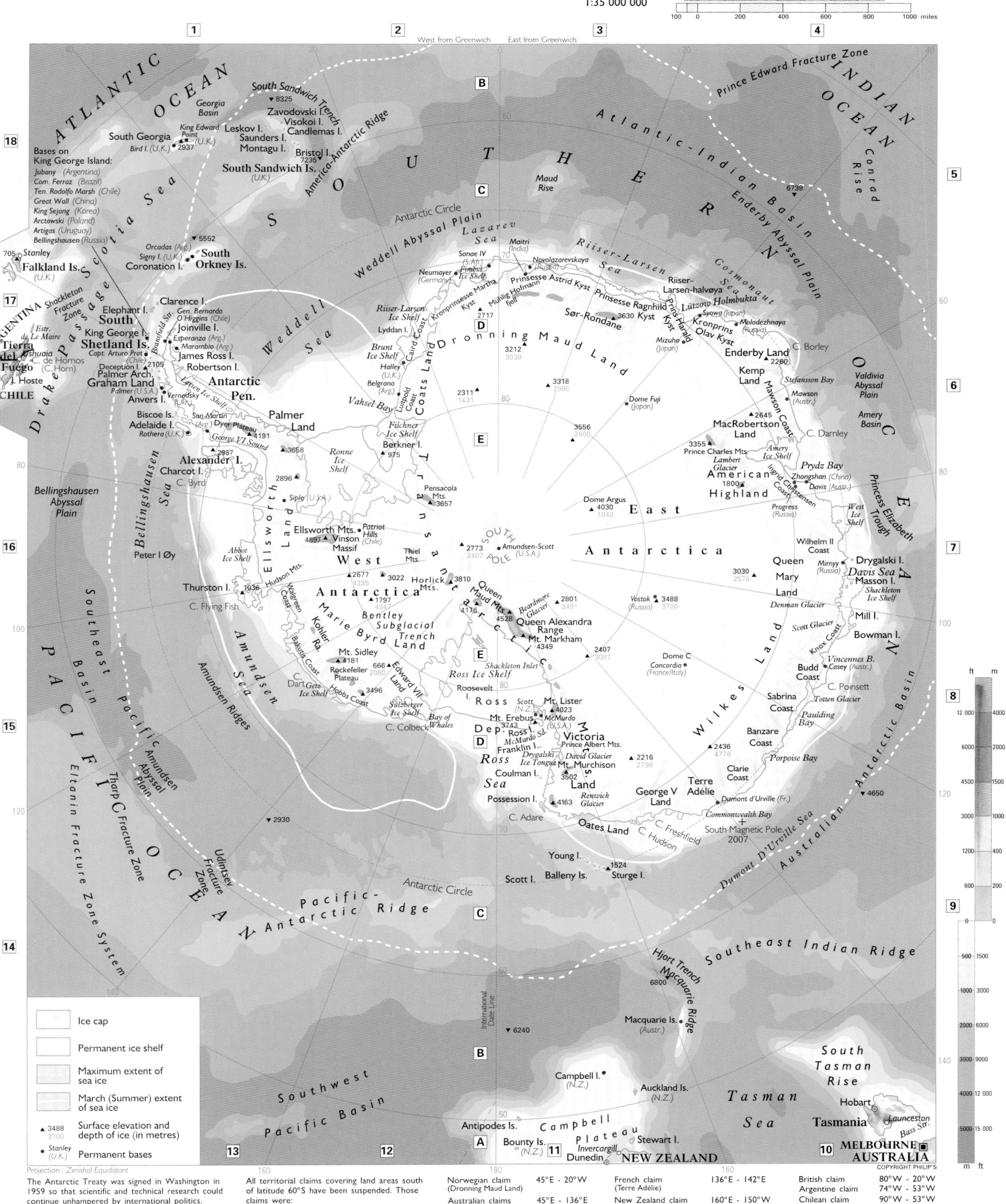

ANTARCTICA

ATLANTIC OCEAN

SOUTHERN

INDIAN OCEAN

Prince Edward Fracture Zone

Atlantic-Indian Basin

Enderby Abyssal Plain

Cosmonaut Sea

Conrad Rise

6739

South Sandwich Trench
Georgia Basin
8325
King Edward Point (U.K.)
Bird I. (U.K.) 2937
Leskov I.
Saunders I.
Montagu I.
Candlemas I.
Visokoi I.
Zavodovski I.
South Sandwich Is. (U.K.)
Bristol I. 7235

South Georgia

Bases on King George Island:
Jubany (Argentina)
Com. Ferraz (Brazil)
Ten. Rodolfo Marsh (Chile)
Great Wall (China)
King Sejong (Korea)
Arctowski (Poland)
Artigas (Uruguay)
Bellingshausen (Russia)

Maud Rise

America-Antarctic Ridge

Scotia Sea

Antarctic Circle

Weddell Abyssal Plain

Lazarev Sea

Riiser-Larsen Sea

705 Stanley
Falkland Is. (U.K.)

5552

Orcadas (Arg.)
Signy I. (U.K.)
Coronation I.

South Orkney Is.

Maitri (India)
Sanae IV (S. Afr.)
Neumayer (Germany)
Fimbul Ice Shelf
Novolazarevskaya (Russia)

Prinsesse Astrid Kyst

Prinsesse Ragnhild Kyst

Sør-Rondane

Riiser-Larsen-halvøya

Lützow-Holmbukta

Syowa (Japan)

Molodezhnaya (Russia)

ARGENTINA
Shackleton Fracture Zone

Clarence I.
Elephant I.
Gen. Bernardo O'Higgins (Chile)
Joinville I.
Esperanza (Arg.)
Marambio (Arg.)
Capt. Arturo Prat (Chile)
James Ross I.
Robertson I.

South Shetland Is.
King George I.
Bransfield Str.

Dronning Maud Land

Riiser-Larsen Ice Shelf

Kronprinsesse Martha Kyst

Mühlig Hofmann fjell

3630

2717

3212
3039

Enderby Land

Kemp Land

C. Borley

Kronprins Olav Kyst

Mizuho (Japan)

Stefansson Bay

Valdivia Abyssal Plain

Tierra del Fuego
Ushuaia
Estr. de Le Maire
C. de Hornos (C. Horn)
I. Hoste
CHILE

Palmer Arch.
Graham Land
Palmer (U.S.A.)
Anvers I.
Vernadsky (U.K.)
Deception I. (Chile)
2105

Antarctic Pen.

Larsen Ice Shelf

Coats Land
Caird Coast
Lyddan I.
Brunt Ice Shelf
Halley (U.K.)

3318
2990

Dome Fuji (Japan)

Mawson (Austr.)

2645

MacRobertson Land

C. Darnley

Amery Basin

Biscoe Is.
Adelaide I.
Rothera (U.K.)

Palmer Land

San Martin (Arg.)
Dyer Plateau

Vahsel Bay

Belgrano (Arg.)

Filchner Ice Shelf

2311
1431

3656
2600

3355
Prince Charles Mts.

Lambert Glacier

Amery Ice Shelf

Prydz Bay
Zhongshan (China)
Davis (Austr.)

Princess Elizabeth Trough

Alexander I.
Charcot I.
C. Byrd

George VI Sound
4191
2987
3658
Ronne Ice Shelf
Berkner I.
975

Ellsworth Land

2896

Siple (U.S.A.)

Pensacola Mts. 3657

American Highland
1800

4030
1040

East Antarctica

West Ice Shelf

Bellingshausen Abyssal Plain

Peter I Øy

Bellingshausen Sea

Thurston I.
1936

Hudson Mts.
Abbot Ice Shelf

Ellsworth Mts.
Vinson Massif 4897
Patriot Hills (Chile)
Thiel Mts.
2773
Amundsen-Scott (U.S.A.)
2407
SOUTH POLE

Wilhelm II Coast

3030
2570

Queen Mary Land

Drygalski I.
Mirnyy (Russia)
Davis Sea
Masson I.
Shackleton Ice Shelf

Southeast Pacific Basin

Amundsen Sea

2677
4335

3022

Horlick Mts.
3810

2801
3491

West Antarctica
1797

4116
4528
4349

Queen Maud Mts.

Beardmore Glacier

Vostok (Russia)
3488
3700

Denman Glacier
Scott Glacier

Mill I.
Bowman I.

Tharp Fracture Zone

Marie Byrd Land

Bentley Subglacial Trench
4344

Queen Alexandra Range
Mt. Markham 4349

2407
3087

Dome C
Concordia (France/Italy)

Wilkes Land

Knox Coast
Vincennes B.
Casey (Austr.)

Budd Coast

Eltanin Fracture Zone System

Amundsen Ridges

Kohler Ra.
Bakutis Coast

Mt. Sidley 4181
Rockefeller Plateau 2080
666

Edward VII Land

Shackleton Inlet

Ross Ice Shelf

C. Poinsett

Sabrina Coast
Totten Glacier

Paulding Bay

C. Flying Fish

Dart Gets Ice Shelf
Hobbs Coast
Sulzberger Ice Shelf
3496
C. Colbeck

Roosevelt I.
800
Bay of Whales
Ross Sea
Scott (N.Z.)
McMurdo (U.S.A.)
Mt. Erebus 3743
Ross I.
McMurdo Sd.

Mt. Lister 4023

Banzare Coast

Ross Dep.

Victoria Land

Prince Albert Mts.
Franklin I.
Drygalski Ice Tongue
David Glacier
Mt. Murchison 3502
Coulman I.

2216
2798

2436
4776

Clarie Coast
Porpoise Bay

Terre Adélie

Possession I.
4163

Renwick Glacier

George V Land

Dumont d'Urville (Fr.)

Commonwealth Bay

South Magnetic Pole 2007

Dumont D'Urville Sea

Australian-Antarctic Basin

C. Adare
Oates Land
C. Freshfield
C. Hudson

Young I.

4650

Antarctic Circle

Scott I.

Balleny Is.
1524
Sturge I.

International Date Line

Southeast Indian Ridge

Hjort Trench
Macquarie Ridge
6800

6240

Macquarie Is. (Austr.)

Pacific-Antarctic Ridge

Southwest Pacific Basin

Campbell I. (N.Z.)
Auckland Is. (N.Z.)

Tasman Sea

South Tasman Rise

Hobart

Tasmania

Launceston
Bass Str.

Antipodes Is.
Bounty Is. (N.Z.)
Campbell Plateau
Invercargill
Dunedin
Stewart I.
NEW ZEALAND

MELBOURNE
AUSTRALIA

COPYRIGHT PHILIP'S

Projection: Zenithal Equidistant

Legend:
Ice cap
Permanent ice shelf
Maximum extent of sea ice
March (Summer) extent of sea ice
3488 / 3700 Surface elevation and depth of ice (in metres)
Stanley (U.K.) Permanent bases

ft / m
12 000 / 4000
6000 / 2000
4500 / 1500
3000 / 1000
1200 / 400
600 / 200
0 / 0
500 / 1500
1000 / 3000
2000 / 6000
3000 / 9000
4000 / 12 000
5000 / 15 000
m / ft

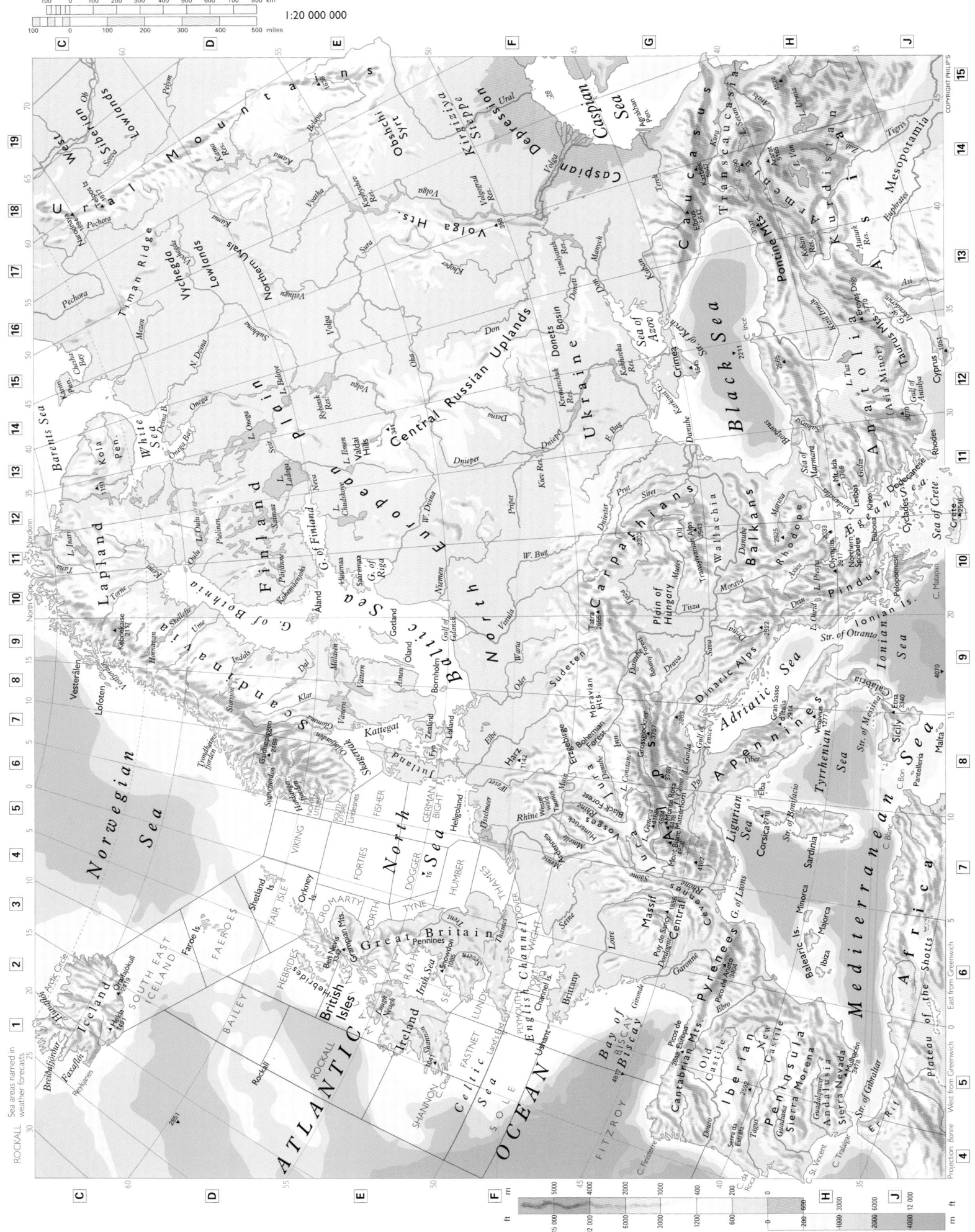

1:20 000 000

COPYRIGHT PHILIP'S

Projection: Bonne   West from Greenwich   East from Greenwich

1:20 000 000

100 0 100 200 300 400 500 600 700 800 km
100 0 100 200 300 400 500 miles

COPYRIGHT PHILIP'S

ATLANTIC OCEAN

Norwegian Sea

North Sea

White Sea

Baltic Sea

Gulf of Bothnia

Black Sea

Caspian Sea

Mediterranean Sea

Adriatic Sea

Tyrrhenian Sea

Ionian Sea

Aegean Sea

ICELAND — Reykjavik

Faroe Is. (Den.)
Torshavn

Shetland Is.
Lerwick

Orkney Is.
Kirkwall

UNITED KINGDOM
SCOTLAND
Stornoway, Hebrides, Aberdeen, Dundee, Glasgow, Edinburgh, Newcastle-upon-Tyne, Carlisle, Leeds, Sheffield, Manchester, Liverpool, ENGLAND, WALES, Birmingham, Cardiff, Bristol, Southampton, Plymouth, London

IRELAND — Dublin, Belfast, Cork

NORWAY — Oslo, Bergen, Stavanger, Trondheim, Tromsø, Narvik, Hammerfest

SWEDEN — Stockholm, Göteborg, Malmö, Uppsala, Örebro, Gävle, Jönköping, Luleå

FINLAND — Helsinki, Turku, Tampere, Vaasa, Oulu

DENMARK — Copenhagen, Aalborg, Århus, Kiel

Kattegat
Skagerrak

ESTONIA — Tallinn
LATVIA — Riga
LITHUANIA — Vilnius, Kaunas
Kaliningrad (Russia)

RUSSIA — MOSCOW, ST. PETERSBURG, Murmansk, Arkhangelsk, Vologda, Yaroslavl, Kostroma, Ivanovo, Smolensk, Tula, Orel, Kursk, Voronezh, Tambov, Penza, Saratov, Volgograd, Astrakhan, Rostov, Kirov, Perm, Ufa, Samara, Saransk, Nizhniy Novgorod

KARELIA, KOMI, UDMURTIA, BASHKORTOSTAN, TATARSTAN, CHUVASHIA, MARI EL, MORDVINIA, KALMYKIA

BELARUS — Minsk, Mahilyow, Vitebsk, Gomel, Brest

POLAND — Warsaw, Łódź, Kraków, Gdańsk, Szczecin, Poznań, Wrocław, Katowice, Bydgoszcz, Białystok, Lublin

GERMANY — Berlin, Hamburg, Bremen, Hannover, Magdeburg, Leipzig, Dresden, Cologne, Dortmund, Essen, Düsseldorf, Bonn, Frankfurt am Main, Nürnberg, München, Stuttgart, Halle, Chemnitz

NETHERLANDS — Amsterdam, The Hague, Rotterdam
BELGIUM — Brussels, Antwerp
LUX. — Luxembourg

CZECH REP. — Prague, Ostrava
SLOVAK REP. — Bratislava
AUSTRIA — Vienna, Linz, Graz, Salzburg, Innsbruck
SWITZERLAND — Zürich, Bern, Geneva, Basel
HUNGARY — Budapest, Miskolc, Debrecen

FRANCE — PARIS, Lille, Rouen, Le Havre, Nantes, Brest, Bordeaux, Toulouse, Lyons, St-Étienne, Marseilles, Nice, Strasbourg, Dijon, Limoges, Grenoble, Toulon

SPAIN — Madrid, Barcelona, Valencia, Sevilla, Málaga, Zaragoza, Bilbao, Córdoba, Murcia, Granada, Valladolid, La Coruña, Alicante, Cádiz, Vigo

PORTUGAL — Lisbon, Porto

ITALY — Rome, Milan, Turin, Genoa, Venice, Bologna, Florence, Naples, Bari, Palermo, Messina, Catania, Taranto, Cagliari
Sardinia, Sicily, Corsica

SLOVENIA — Ljubljana
CROATIA — Zagreb, Split, Rijeka
BOSNIA-HERZ. — Sarajevo
MONTENEGRO — Podgorica
SERBIA — Belgrade, Niš
ALBANIA — Tirana
MACEDONIA — Skopje

ROMANIA — Bucharest, Cluj-Napoca, Timișoara, Brașov, Ploiești
MOLDOVA — Kishinev
BULGARIA — Sofia, Plovdiv, Varna

GREECE — Athens, Thessaloníki, Pátra
Crete

UKRAINE — Kiev, Kharkov, Donetsk, Odessa, Dnepropetrovsk, Zaporozhye, Krivoy Rog, Nikolayev, Kherson, Lvov, Zhytomyr, Chernigov, Gomel
CRIMEA — Sevastopol, Simferopol

TURKEY — Ankara, Istanbul, Izmir, Bursa, Konya, Adana, Antalya, Samsun, Kayseri, Erzurum, Diyarbakir
CYPRUS — Nicosia

GEORGIA — Tbilisi
ARMENIA — Yerevan
AZERBAIJAN — Baku
DAGESTAN, CHECHNIA, NORTH OSSETIA, KABARDINO-BALKARIA, KARACHAI-CHERKESSIA, INGUSHETIA

SYRIA — Aleppo
IRAQ — Baghdad, Mosul
IRAN — Tabriz

KAZAKHSTAN

MALTA — Valletta
Pantelleria (Italy)

ALGERIA — Algiers, Annaba, Constantine
TUNISIA — Tunis
MOROCCO — Melilla, Ceuta

Africa

Arctic Circle

Bay of Biscay
English Channel

Ob, Ural, Volga, Don, Dnieper, Dniester, Danube, Vistula, Oder, Elbe, Rhine, Loire, Seine, Garonne, Rhône, Tiber, Ebro, Tagus

Gibraltar (U.K.), Str. of Gibraltar
Balearic Is. — Majorca, Minorca, Ibiza, Palma

Bosporus

LONDON Capital Cities

Projection: Bonne

West from Greenwich 0 East from Greenwich

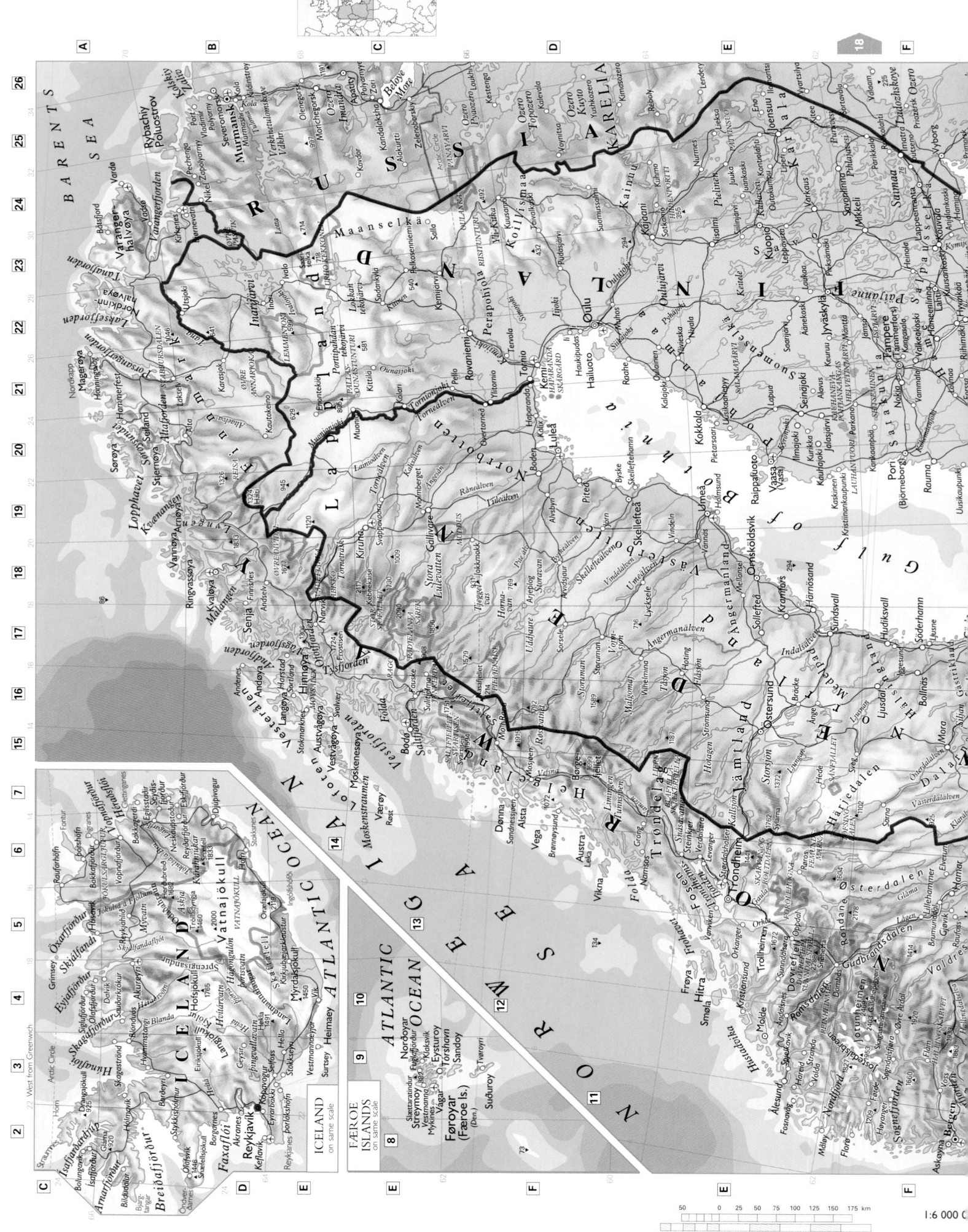

ICELAND
on same scale

FÆROE
ISLANDS
on same scale

1:6 000 0

50   0   25   50   75   100   125   150   175 km

50   0   25   50   75   100   125 miles

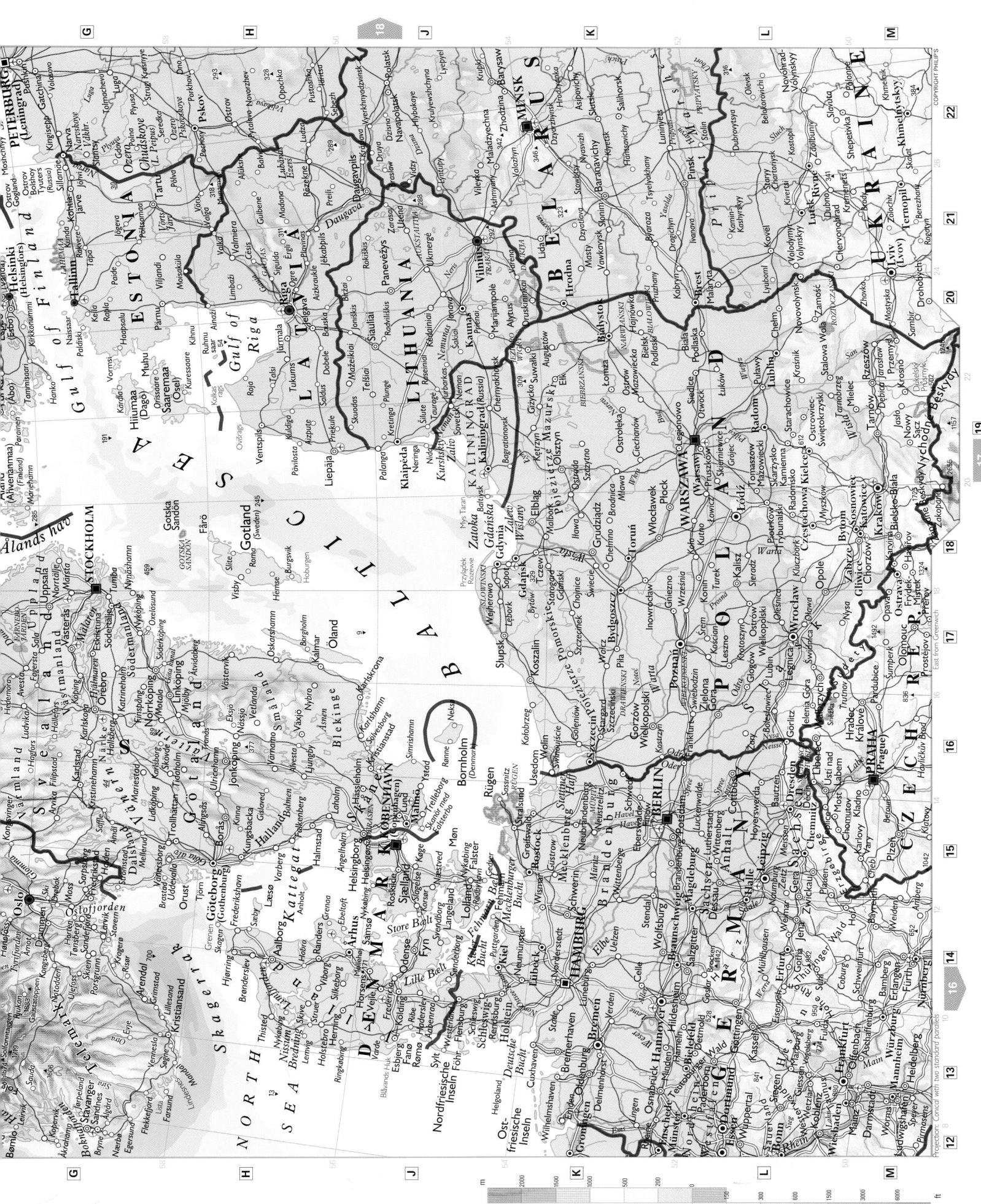

1:2 000 000

West from Greenwich
COPYRIGHT PHILIP'S

1:2 000 000

10 0 10 20 30 40 50 60 70 80 km
10 0 10 20 30 40 50 miles

Key to Scottish unitary
authorities on map
1 CITY OF ABERDEEN   8 EAST RENFREWSHIRE
2 DUNDEE CITY   9 NORTH LANARKSHIRE
3 WEST DUNBARTONSHIRE   10 FALKIRK
4 EAST DUNBARTONSHIRE   11 CLACKMANNANSHIRE
5 CITY OF GLASGOW   12 WEST LOTHIAN
6 INVERCLYDE   13 CITY OF EDINBURGH
7 RENFREWSHIRE   14 MIDLOTHIAN

ORKNEY IS.
on same scale

ORKNEY

SHETLAND IS.
on same scale

SHETLAND
Lerwick

Projection : Lambert's Conformal Conic

West from Greenwich

COPYRIGHT PHILIP'S

1:2 000 000

10 0 10 20 30 40 50 60 70 80 km
10 0 10 20 30 40 50 miles

Key to English unitary authorities on map

25 HARTLEPOOL
26 DARLINGTON
27 STOCKTON-ON-TEES
28 MIDDLESBROUGH
29 REDCAR AND CLEVELAND
30 BLACKPOOL
31 BLACKBURN WITH DARWEN
32 HALTON
33 WARRINGTON
34 KINGSTON UPON HULL
35 NORTH EAST LINCOLNSHIRE
36 STOKE-ON-TRENT
37 TELFORD AND WREKIN
38 DERBY CITY
39 CITY OF NOTTINGHAM
40 LEICESTER CITY
41 RUTLAND
42 PETERBOROUGH
43 MILTON KEYNES
44 LUTON
45 NORTH SOMERSET
46 CITY OF BRISTOL
47 BATH AND NORTH EAST SOMERSET
48 SWINDON
49 READING
50 WOKINGHAM
51 WINDSOR AND MAIDENHEAD
52 SLOUGH
53 BRACKNELL FOREST
54 THURROCK
55 SOUTHEND-ON-SEA
56 MEDWAY
57 TORBAY
58 PLYMOUTH
59 POOLE
60 BOURNEMOUTH
61 SOUTHAMPTON
62 PORTSMOUTH
63 BRIGHTON AND HOVE

Key to Welsh unitary authorities on map

15 SWANSEA
16 NEATH PORT TALBOT
17 BRIDGEND
18 RHONDDA CYNON TAFF
19 MERTHYR TYDFIL
20 CAERPHILLY
21 BLAENAU GWENT
22 TORFAEN
23 CARDIFF
24 NEWPORT

NORTH SEA

IRISH SEA

North Channel

SCOTLAND

NORTHUMBERLAND

NORTHERN IRELAND

ISLE OF MAN

CUMBRIA

LANCASHIRE

NORTH YORKSHIRE

EAST RIDING OF YORKSHIRE

LINCOLNSHIRE

The Wash

Newcastle-upon-Tyne
Sunderland
Hartlepool
Middlesbrough
Darlington
York
Leeds
Bradford
MANCHESTER
Sheffield
Liverpool
LIVERPOOL
Stoke-on-Trent
Derby
Nottingham
Lincoln

Edinburgh
Glasgow
STIRLING
FIFE
SCOTTISH BORDERS
DUMFRIES & GALLOWAY
SOUTH AYRSHIRE
NORTH AYRSHIRE
EAST AYRSHIRE
SOUTH LANARKSHIRE

Belfast

GWYNEDD
ANGLESEY
DENBIGH
WREXHAM

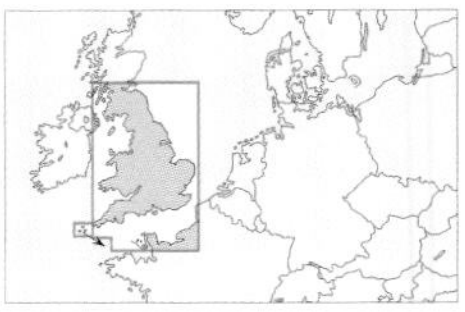

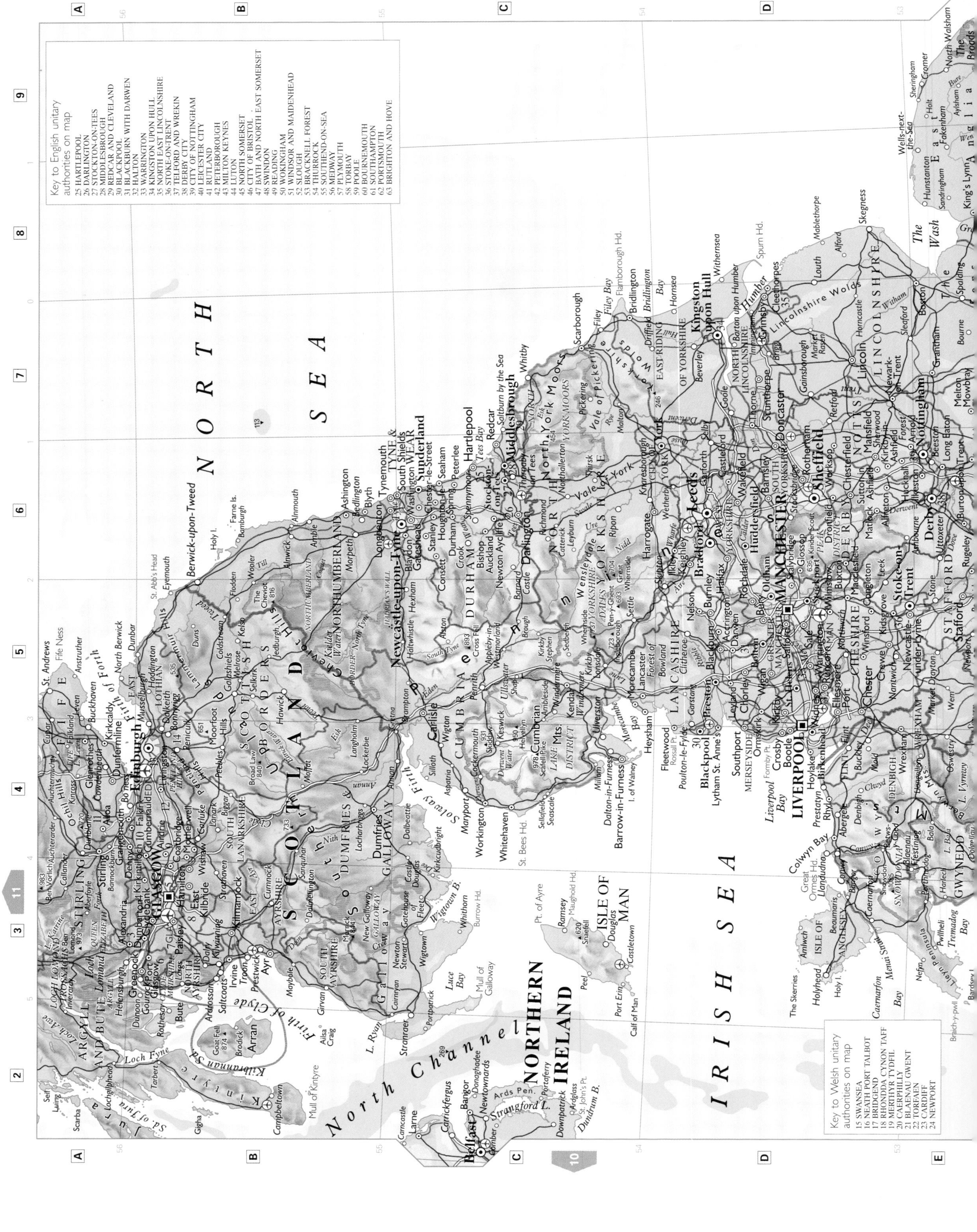

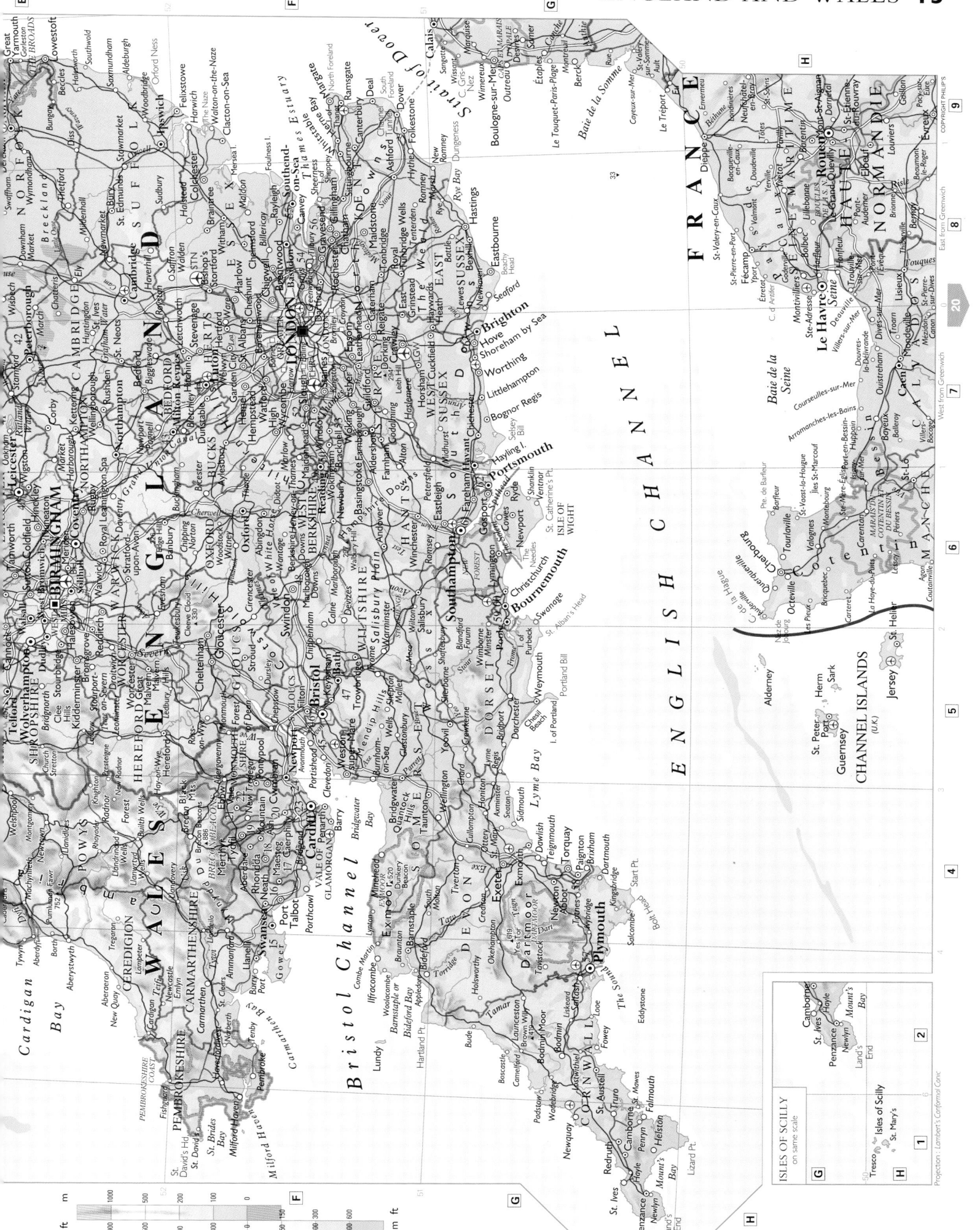

1:5 000 000

50   0   25   50   75   100   125   150   175 km
50   0   25   50   75   100   125 miles

1   2   3   4   5   6   7   8   9

ATLANTIC OCEAN

NORTH SEA

IRISH SEA

CELTIC SEA

English Channel

St. George's Channel

Bristol Channel

Cardigan Bay

North Channel

Firth of Clyde

Sea of the Hebrides

North Minch

Moray Firth

Pentland Firth

Galway B.

Bantry

1224
316
789
1182
1242
1311
1214
1041
953
99
618
978
893
816
640
636
926
886
1085
238
16
36
33

NORWAY
Bergen
Osøyro
Stord
Bømlo
Leirvik
Haugesund
Kopervik
Åkrahamn
Stavanger
Sandnes
Bryne
Nærbø
Boknafj.

Shetland Is. (U.K.)
Unst
Fetlar
Yell
Mainland
Lerwick
Foula
Fair Isle

Orkney Is.
Westray
Sanday
Stronsay
Mainland
Kirkwall
Hoy
South Ronaldsay

C. Wrath
Thurso
Wick
Helmsdale
Golspie
Lairg
Tain
Dingwall
Ullapool
Stornoway
Lewis
Harris
St. Kilda (U.K.)
North Uist
Benbecula
South Uist
Barra
Skye
Rhum
Eigg
Coll
Tiree
Tobermory
Mull
Colonsay
Jura
Islay
Oban
Campbeltown
Arran

North West Highlands
Grampian Mts.
Glen More
L. Ness
Inverness
Aviemore
CAIRNGORMS
Ben Nevis
Fort William
Nairn
Elgin
Buckie
Banff
Fraserburgh
Peterhead
Huntly
Inverurie
Aberdeen
Stonehaven
Deeside
Don
Ballater
Forfar
Arbroath
Montrose
Dundee
St. Andrews
Perth
Stirling
L. Lomond
L. Awe
L. Fyne
Dumbarton
Greenock
Paisley
GLASGOW
East Kilbride
Motherwell
Hamilton
Edinburgh
Dunfermline
Kirkcaldy
Glenrothes
Dunbar
Kilmarnock
Ayr
Irvine
Berwick-upon-Tweed

SCOTLAND

Southern Uplands
Cheviot Hills
Galashiels
Jedburgh
Hawick
Girvan
Dumfries
Alnwick
NORTHUMBERLAND

Malin Hd.
Buncrana
Letterkenny
Coleraine
Ballymena
Larne
Londonderry
Strabane
Bangor
Omagh
Lough Neagh
Belfast
Lisburn
Lurgan
Armagh
Newry
Enniskillen
Lower L. Erne
Donegal
Bundoran
Sligo
Leitrim
Cavan
Monaghan
Dundalk
Drogheda

NORTHERN IRELAND
Ulster

Douglas
I. of Man

Stranraer
Kirkcudbright
Mull of Galloway
Workington
Whitehaven
Carlisle
Hexham
Gateshead
Durham
Newcastle-upon-Tyne
South Shields
Sunderland
Hartlepool
Redcar
Middlesbrough
Darlington
Stockton-on-Tees
N. YORK MOORS
Scarborough
Bridlington
Cumbrian Mts.
LAKE DISTRICT
Barrow-in-Furness
Lancaster
Harrogate
York
Beverley
Kingston upon Hull
YORKSHIRE DALES
Pennines

Achill I.
Ballina
Castlebar
Westport
Lough Mask
Connemara
Lough Corrib
Galway
Aran Is.
BURREN
Ennis
Kilrush
Listowel
Tralee
Dingle
Carrantoohill
Valencia
Macgillycuddy's Reeks
Killarney
Mallow
Cork
Bandon
Kinsale
Cóbh
Youghal
C. Clear
Roscommon
Athlone
Lough Ree
Ballinasloe
Tullamore
Mullingar
Ceanannus Mor
Longford
Birr
Nenagh
Thurles
Limerick
Tipperary
Clonmel
Carrick-on-Suir
Waterford
Dungarvan
Blackwater
Shannon
Kilkenny
Carlow
Port Laoise
Pembroke
DUBLIN
Dun Laoghaire
Bray
Arklow
Wexford
Rosslare
Wicklow Mts.
Boyne
Liffey

IRELAND
UNITED KINGDOM

Anglesey
Holyhead
Bangor
Colwyn Bay
Conway
Chester
Crewe
Wrexham
Snowdon
SNOWDONIA
Pwllheli
Cambrian Mts.
Aberystwyth
Welshpool
Shrewsbury
Telford
Stafford
Stoke-on-Trent
PEAK DISTRICT
Derby
Nottingham
Grantham
Trent

WALES
BRECON BEACONS
Carmarthen
Brecon
Merthyr Tydfil
Llanelli
Swansea
Neath
Port Talbot
Rhondda
Cwmbran
Newport
Cardiff
Barry
Weston-super-Mare
Haverfordwest
Milford Haven
PEMBROKESHIRE COAST
Fishguard

Blackpool
Preston
Blackburn
Burnley
Keighley
Leeds
Bradford
Halifax
Huddersfield
Bolton
Oldham
MANCHESTER
LIVERPOOL
Warrington
Stockport
Sheffield
Barnsley
Rotherham
Doncaster
Grimsby
Scunthorpe
Lincoln
Louth
Skegness
Chesterfield
Mansfield
Boston
THE WASH
Cromer
THE BROADS
Great Yarmouth
Lowestoft
Norwich
King's Lynn
Peterborough
Corby
Leicester
Nuneaton
Coventry
Rugby
BIRMINGHAM
Wolverhampton
Worcester
Redditch
Royal Leamington Spa
Northampton
Bedford
Cambridge
Bury St. Edmunds
Ipswich
Felixstowe
Harwich
Colchester
Chelmsford
Hereford
Gloucester
Cheltenham
COTSWOLD HILLS
Oxford
High Wycombe
Hemel Hempstead
Milton Keynes
Luton
Harlow
Stevenage
Watford
Slough
Basildon
Southend-on-Sea
Margate
Canterbury
Dover
Maidstone
Chatham
LONDON
Reading
Newbury
Swindon
Bristol
Bath
Salisbury
Winchester
Southampton
Portsmouth
Isle of Wight
Newport
Weymouth
Poole
Bournemouth
NEW FOREST
Fareham
Havant
Worthing
Brighton
Eastbourne
Hastings
Folkestone
Ashford
Crawley
Guildford
Basingstoke
Woking

ENGLAND

Yeovil
Taunton
EXMOOR
Barnstaple
Bude
Newquay
Truro
St. Austell
Penzance
Land's End
Isles of Scilly
Falmouth
Plymouth
Torbay
Exeter
DARTMOOR
Dartmoor
Exmouth

Str. of Dover
C. Gris Nez

FRANCE
Calais
Dunkerque
Boulogne-sur-Mer
Le Touquet-Paris-Plage
Le Tréport
Dieppe
Abbeville
Amiens
St. Quentin
Rouen
Fécamp
Le Havre
Trouville-sur-Mer
Caen
Lisieux
Elbeuf
Bayeux
Pays de Caux
Picardie
Laon
Cambrai
Valenciennes

BELGIUM
BRUSSELS (Bruxelles)
Antwerp
Gent
Brugge
Oostende
Zeebrugge
Mechelen
LILLE
Tourcoing
Roubaix
Tournai
Mons
St-Omer
Béthune
Bruay-la-Buissière
Lens

NETHERLANDS
's-Gravenhage (Den Haag)
ROTTERDAM
Dordrecht
Hoek van Holland
Haarlem
Vlissingen
Den Helder
Alkmaar
Texel

Alderney
C. de la Hague
Pte. de Barfleur
Cherbourg
St. Peter Port
Guernsey
Sark
Jersey
St. Helier
Channel Is. (U.K.)
Cotentin
Valognes

ft   m
3000   1000
1500   500
600   200
300   100
150   50
0   0
50   150
100   300
200   600
500   1500
1000   3000
2000   6000
m   ft

Projection: Conical with two standard parallels

East from Greenwich
COPYRIGHT PHILIP'S
West from Greenwich

1:2 500 000

10 0 10 20 30 40 50 60 70 80 90 km
10 0 10 20 30 40 50 60 miles

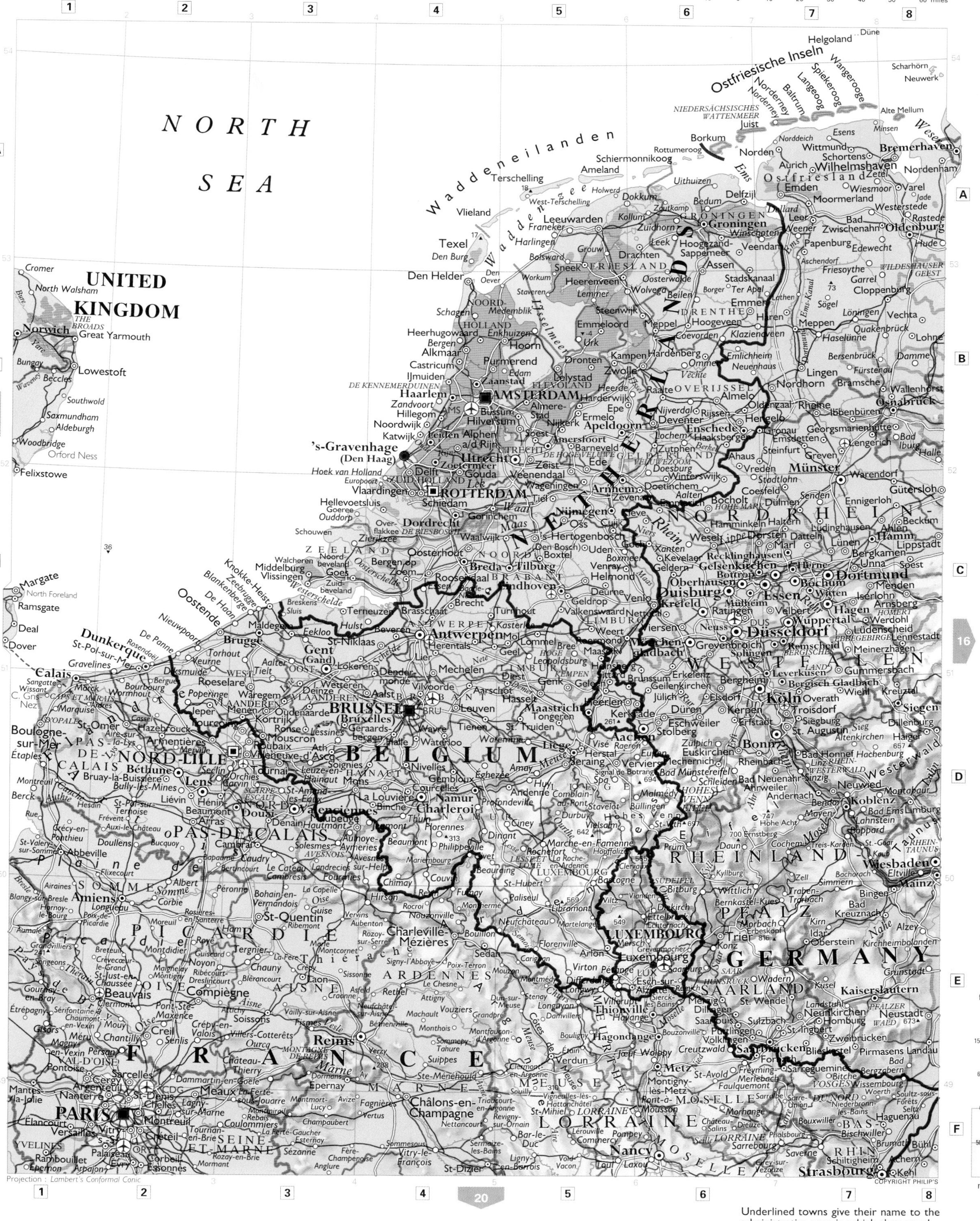

NORTH SEA

UNITED KINGDOM

Cromer
North Walsham
THE BROADS
Great Yarmouth
Norwich
Lowestoft
Southwold
Saxmundham
Aldeburgh
Woodbridge
Orford Ness
Felixstowe
Margate
North Foreland
Ramsgate
Deal
Dover
Calais
Boulogne-sur-Mer
Étaples

NETHERLANDS

Waddeneilanden
Terschelling
Vlieland
Texel
Den Burg
Den Helder
Den Oever
Leeuwarden
Franeker
Harlingen
Bolsward
Sneek
Heerenveen
Workum
Staveren
Lemmer
FRIESLAND
Dokkum
Kollum
Zoutkamp
Groningen
Winschoten
Veendam
Hoogezand-Sappemeer
Assen
Stadskanaal
DRENTHE
Hoogeveen
Emmen
Coevorden
Meppel
Steenwijk
OVERIJSSEL
Zwolle
Kampen
Almelo
Enschede
Deventer
Apeldoorn
AMSTERDAM
Haarlem
Zaanstad
Hilversum
Utrecht
's-Gravenhage (Den Haag)
Hoek van Holland
Delft
ROTTERDAM
Schiedam
Vlaardingen
Dordrecht
ZEELAND
Middelburg
Vlissingen
Goes
Breda
Tilburg
NOORD-BRABANT
Eindhoven
Helmond
Venlo
Nijmegen
Arnhem
LIMBURG
Roermond
Maastricht

BELGIUM

Oostende
Brugge
Gent (Gand)
Antwerpen
St-Niklaas
Mechelen
BRUSSEL / Bruxelles
Leuven
Hasselt
Genk
Namur
Charleroi
Liège
Mons
Tournai
Kortrijk
LUXEMBOURG

LUXEMBOURG

Luxembourg
Esch-sur-Alzette
Diekirch

GERMANY

Bremerhaven
Nordenham
Oldenburg
Wilhelmshaven
OSTFRIESLAND
Emden
Leer
Papenburg
Lingen
Nordhorn
Rheine
Osnabrück
Münster
NORDRHEIN-WESTFALEN
Dortmund
Essen
Duisburg
Düsseldorf
Köln
Bonn
Aachen
Koblenz
RHEINLAND-PFALZ
Wiesbaden
Mainz
Trier
SAARLAND
Saarbrücken
Kaiserslautern

FRANCE

PARIS
Versailles
Amiens
Beauvais
Compiègne
Reims
Charleville-Mézières
ARDENNES
Sedan
PICARDIE
NORD-LILLE
Arras
Lens
Douai
Cambrai
St-Quentin
LORRAINE
Metz
Verdun
Thionville
Nancy
Strasbourg

Projection: Lambert's Conformal Conic

COPYRIGHT PHILIP'S

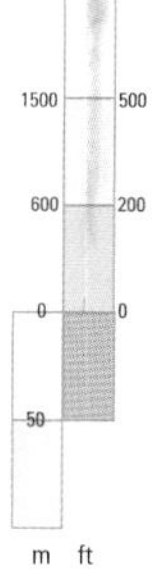

Underlined towns give their name to the administrative area in which they stand.

ft m
1500 500
600 200
0 0
50
m ft

Projection: Conical with two standard parallels

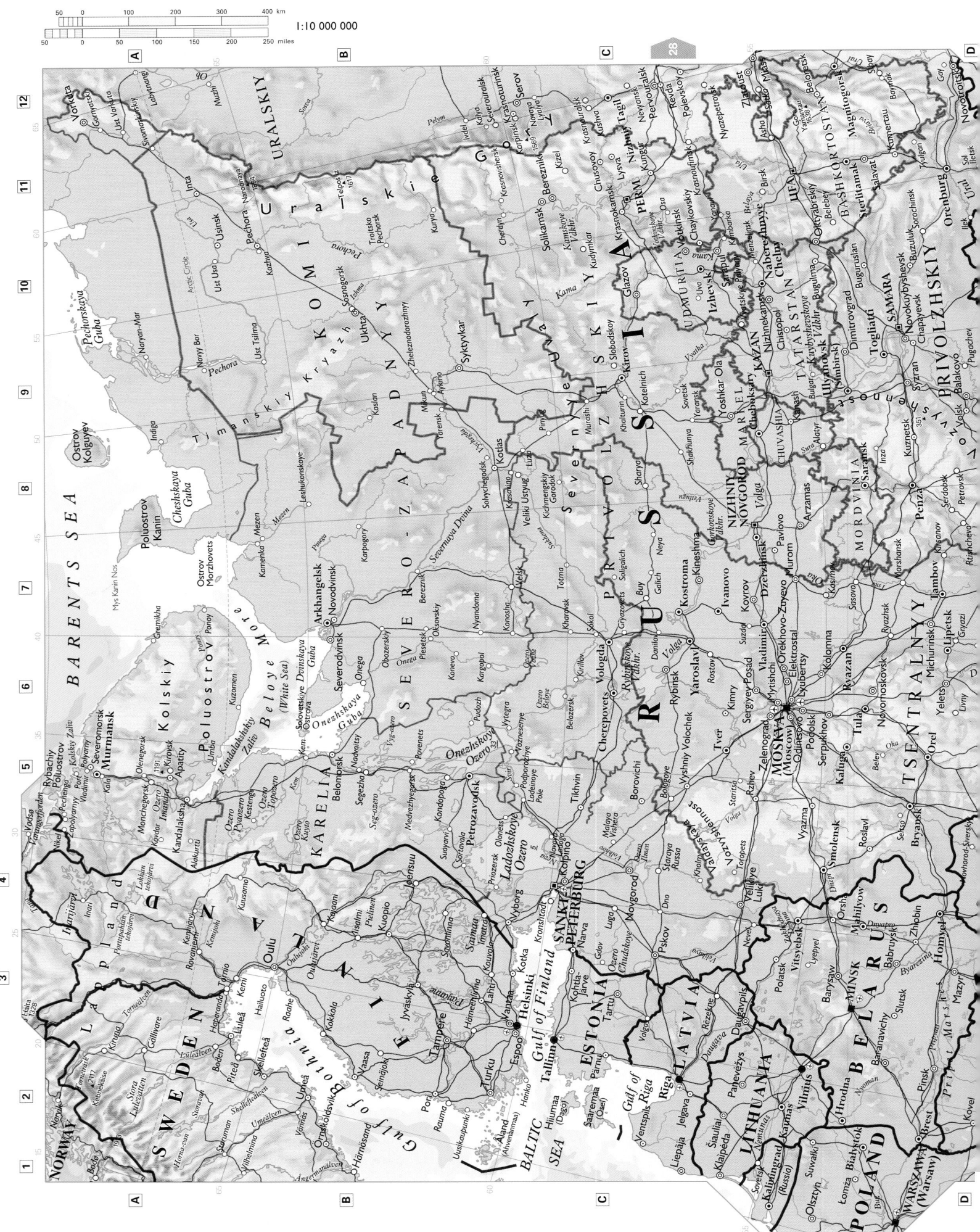

BLACK SEA
CASPIAN SEA
Sea of Azov
MEDITERRANEAN SEA
UKRAINE
KAZAKHSTAN
TURKMENISTAN
AZERBAIJAN
ARMENIA
GEORGIA
TURKEY
SYRIA
IRAQ
IRAN
LEBANON
CYPRUS
ROMANIA
BULGARIA
MOLDOVA
CRIMEA
Caspian Depression
Kirgiz Steppe
Ustyurt Plateau
Caucasus Mountains
Anadolu
Kuzey Anadolu Dağları
Toros Dağları
Kurdistan
Zagros
Dasht-e Kavīr
Bādiyat ash Shām
KYYIV (Kiev)
KHARKIV
DNIPROPETROVSK
DONETSK
ODESA
VOLGOGRAD
ROSTOV
Astrakhan
Krasnodar
Sevastopol
Simferopol
Makhachkala
Groznyy
TBILISI
YEREVAN
BAKI (Baku)
TEHRĀN
Tabrīz
ANKARA
İSTANBUL
İZMİR (Smyrna)
BURSA
ADANA
Samsun
Trabzon
Erzurum
Konya
Kayseri
HALAB (Aleppo)
DIMASHQ
BAYRŪT (Beirut)
AL MAWṢIL (Mosul)
BUCUREŞTI (Bucharest)
CHIŞINĂU
Nicosia
Projection: Conical with two standard parallels
East from Greenwich
COPYRIGHT PHILIP'S

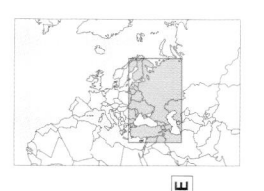

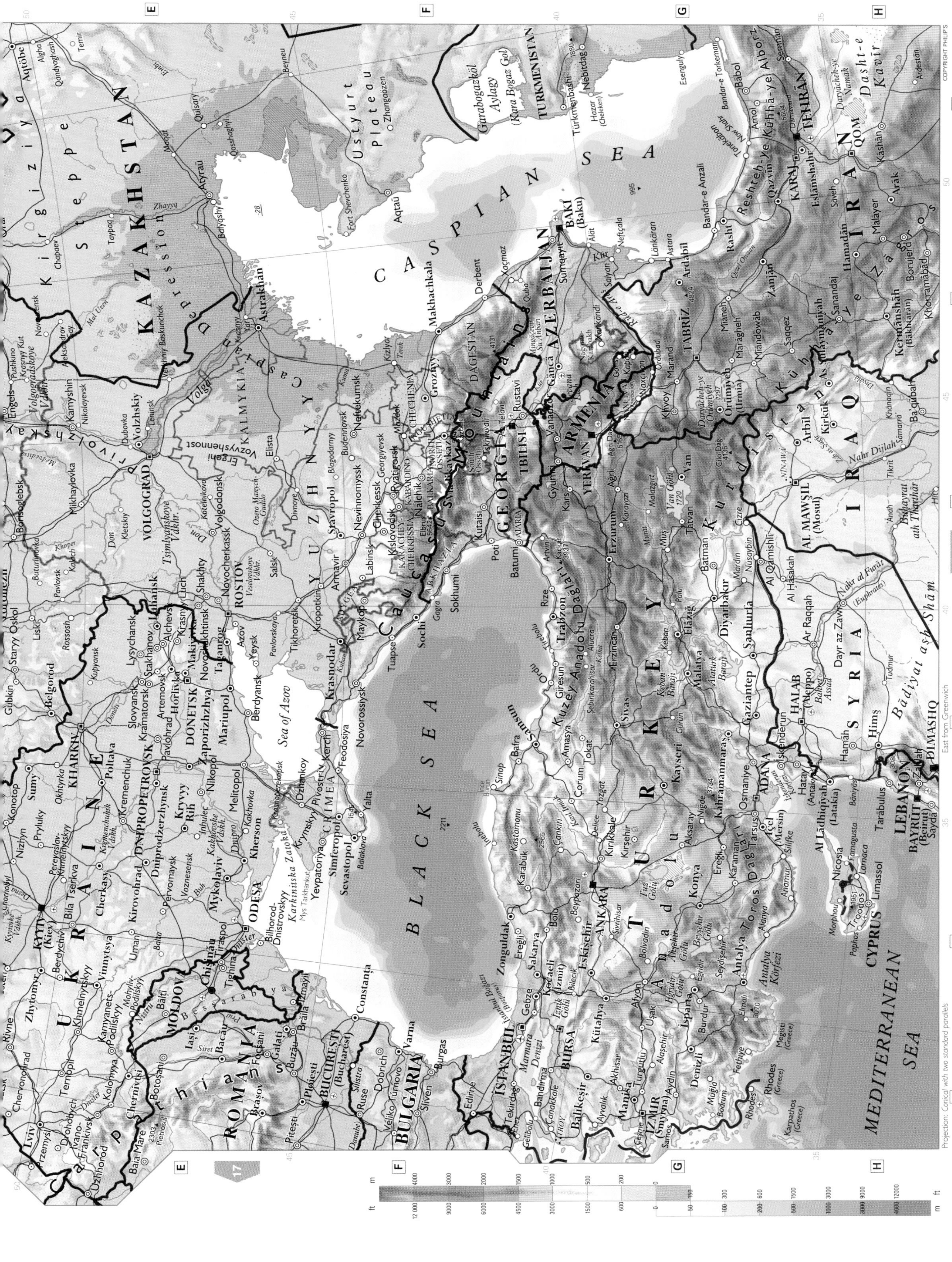

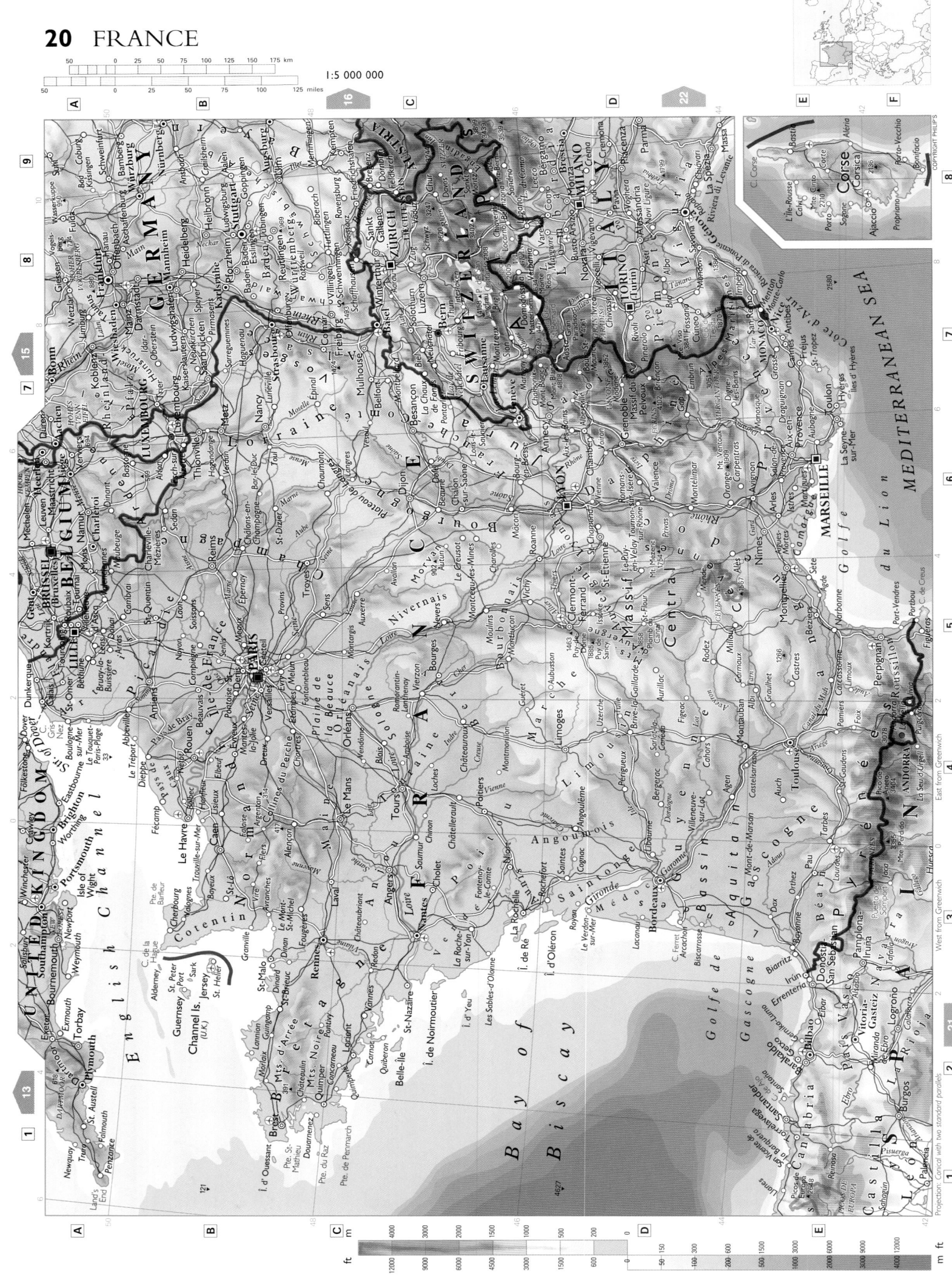

1:5 000 000

Corse
(Corsica)

MEDITERRANEAN SEA

English Channel

Bay of Biscay

UNITED KINGDOM

GERMANY

BELGIUM

LUXEMBOURG

SWITZERLAND

ITALY

AUSTRIA

SPAIN

ANDORRA

MONACO

FRANCE

Projection: Conical with two standard parallels

COPYRIGHT PHILIP'S

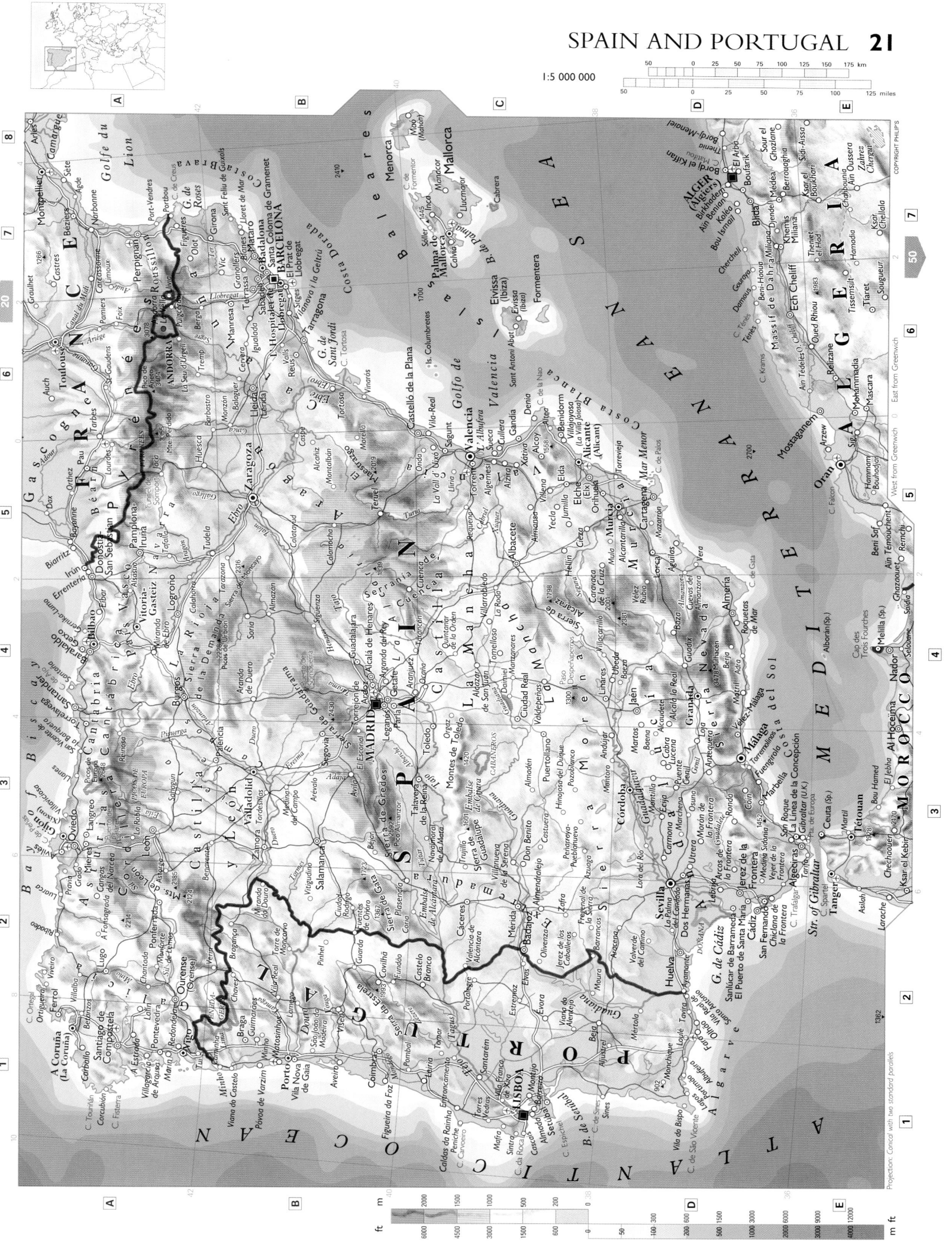

1:5 000 000

50   0   25   50   75   100   125   150   175 km
50   0   25   50   75   100   125 miles

COPYRIGHT PHILIP'S

Projection: Conical with two standard parallels

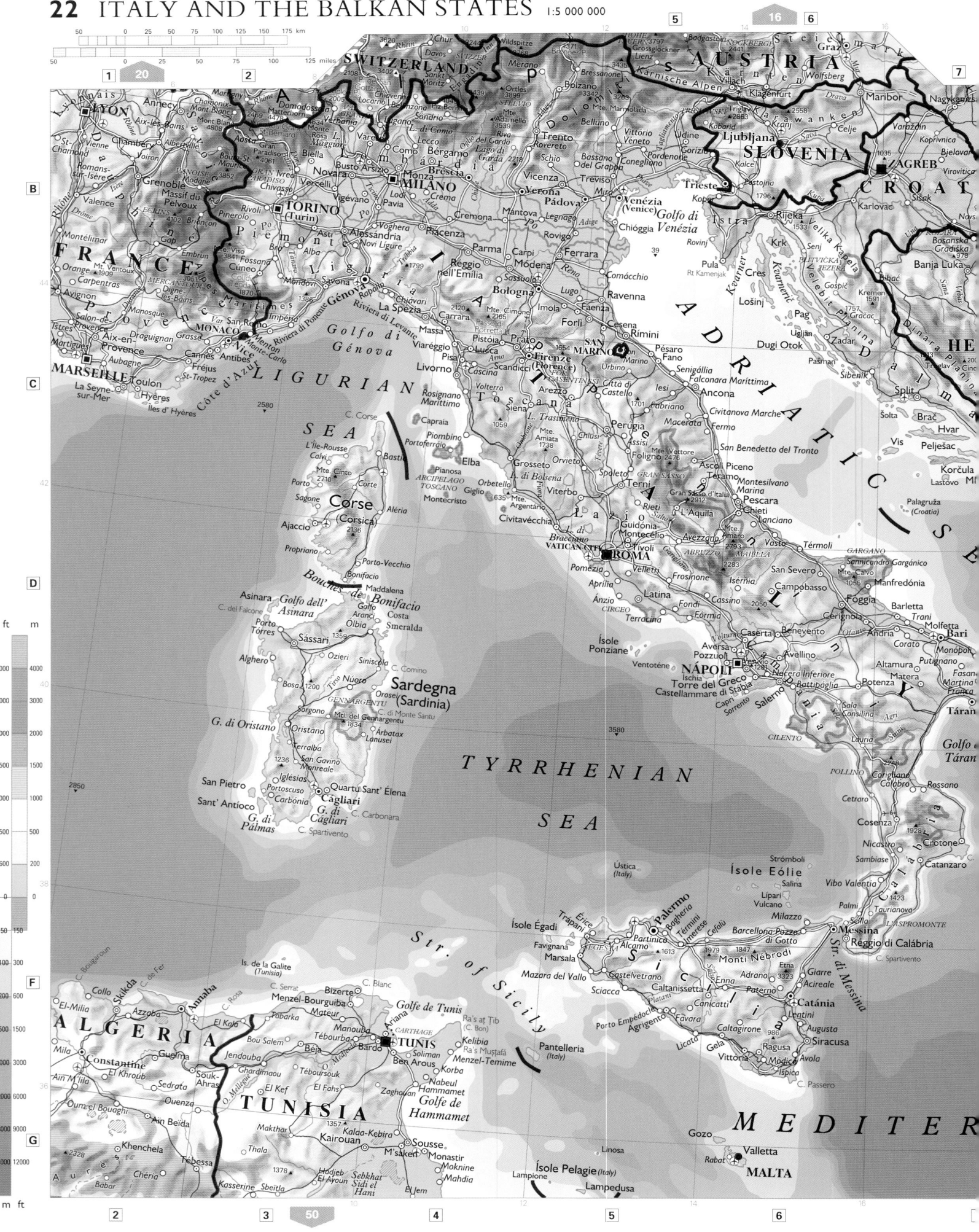

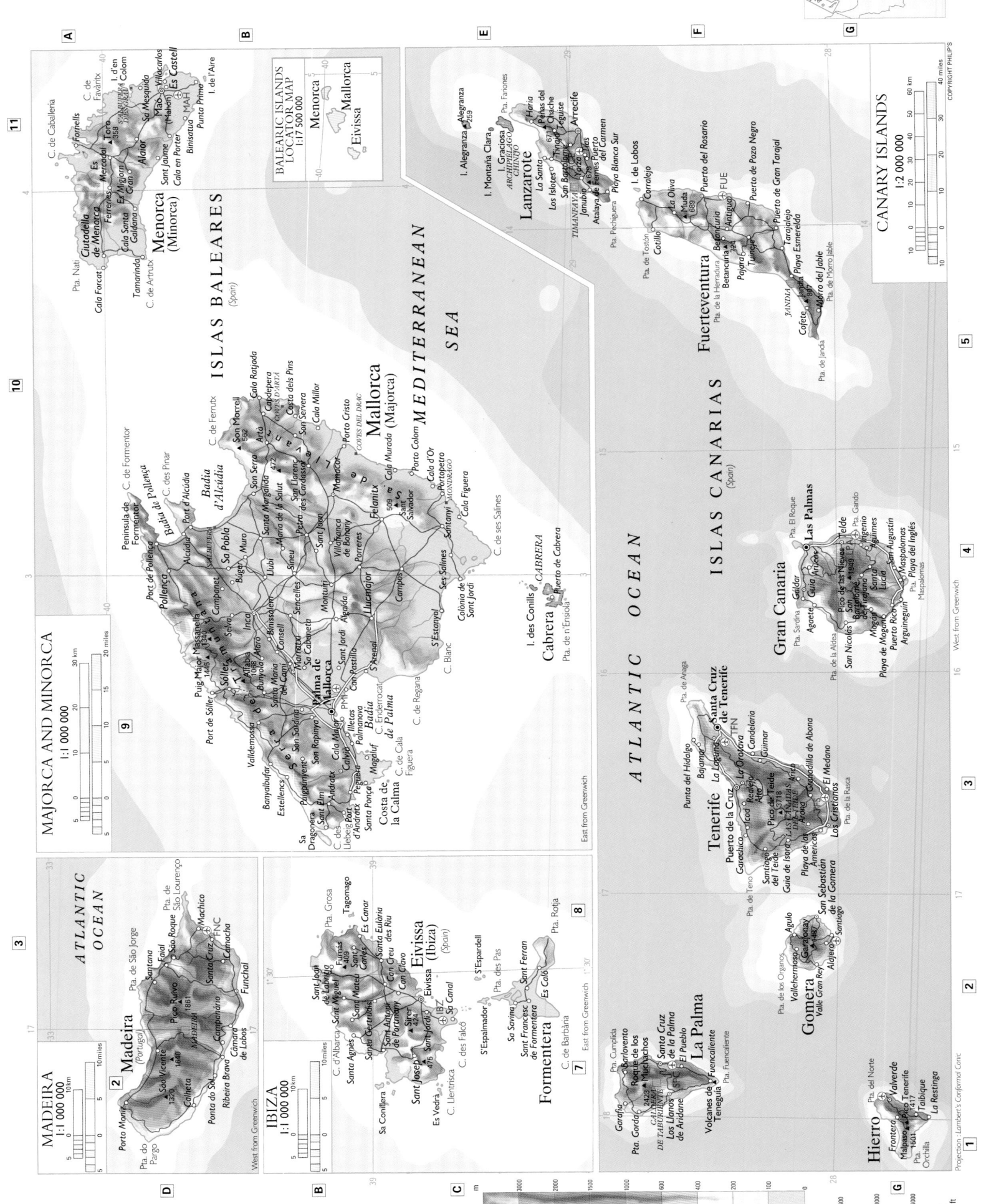

ISLAS BALEARES *(Spain)*

Menorca (Minorca)

MEDITERRANEAN SEA

Mallorca (Majorca)

BALEARIC ISLANDS LOCATOR MAP 1:7 500 000

CABRERA

ATLANTIC OCEAN

ISLAS CANARIAS *(Spain)*

Lanzarote

Fuerteventura

Gran Canaria

Tenerife

Gomera

La Palma

Hierro

MADEIRA 1:1 000 000

ATLANTIC OCEAN

Madeira *(Portugal)*

IBIZA 1:1 000 000

Eivissa (Ibiza) *(Spain)*

Formentera

MAJORCA AND MINORCA 1:1 000 000

CANARY ISLANDS 1:2 000 000

Projection: Lambert's Conformal Conic

COPYRIGHT PHILIP'S

Corfu
Rhodes
Malta
Crete
Cyprus

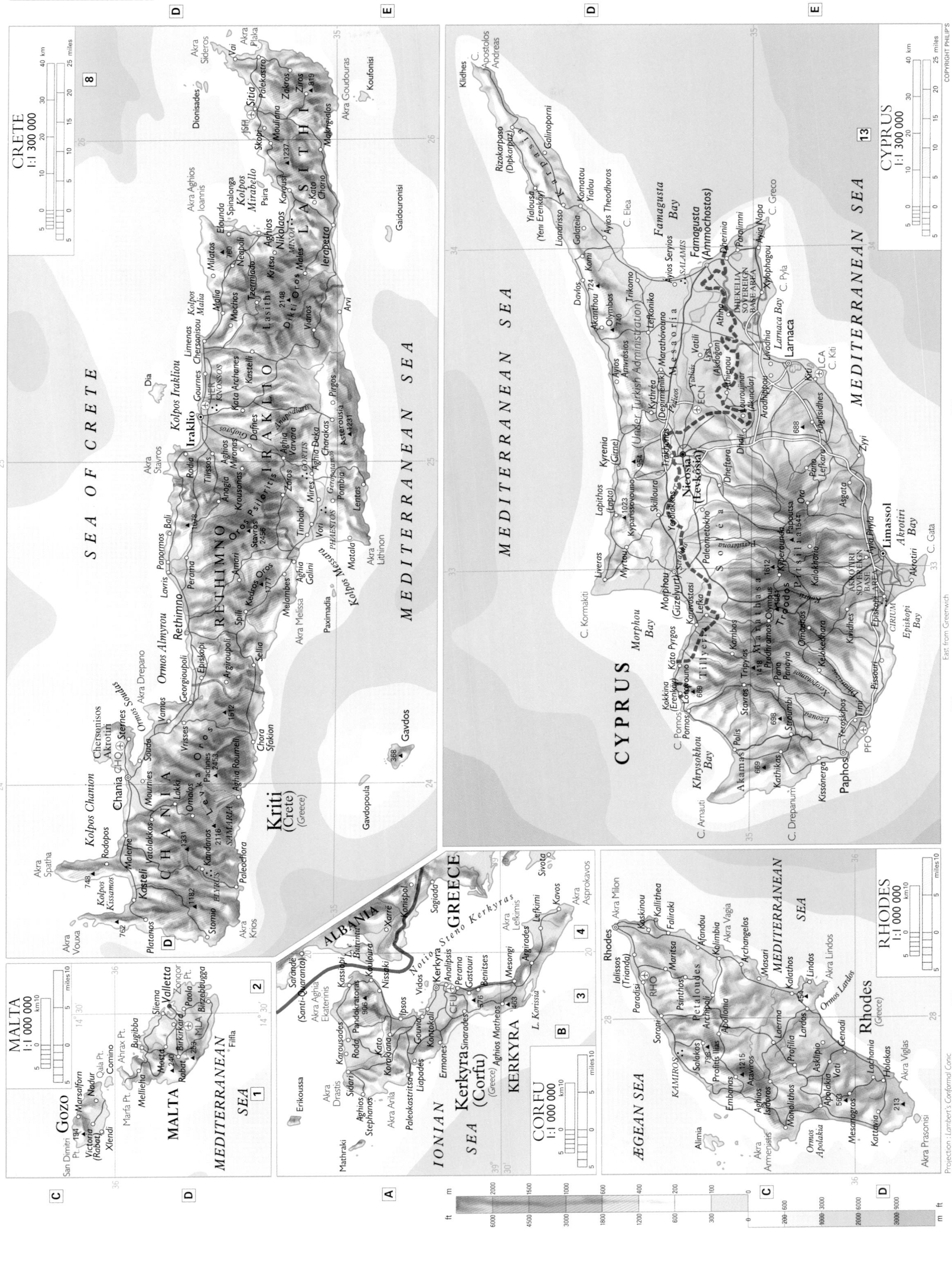

CRETE
1:1 300 000

SEA OF CRETE

MEDITERRANEAN SEA

Akra Sideros
Akra Plaka
Vai
Palekastro
Zakros
Ziros
Sitia
Skopi
Mouliano
Maghrela
Akra Goudouras
Koufonisi
Dionisades
LASITHI
Kalo Chorio
Psira
Kritsa
Agios Nikolaos
Neapoli
Kolpos Mirabello
Spinalonga
Elounda
Ierapetra
Dikti Oros 2148
Males
Kato
Mochos
Vianos
Arvi
Malia
Milatos
Limenas Chersonisou
Kolpos Malia
Kastelli
Gournes
Kata Archanes
IRAKLIO
Iraklio
Kolpos Irakliou
Akra Stavros
Dia
Akra Aghios Ioannis
Gazi
Rodia
Tilissos
Aghios Mironas
Krousonas
Anogia
Profitis Ilias 2456
Gerapetrou
Psiloritis Oros
Timbaki
Vori
Mires
PHAESTOS
Melambes
Aghia Galini
Kolpos Messara
Akra Lithinon
Matala
Lentas
Pombia
Asterousia
Pirgos
Charakas
Aghia Varvara
Gortys
Dafnes
Knossos
Zaros
RETHIMNO
Rethimno
Ormos Almyrou
Akra Drepano
Panormos
Lavris
Perama
Spili
Kedros 1777
Aghia
Amari
Episkopi
Georgioupoli
Argiroupoli
Vrisses
Chania
Akrotiri
Chersonisos
Sternes
Ormos Soudas
Souda
CHO
Vamos
Kal, Mournies
CHANIA
Lakki
Omalos
Samaria
Lefka Oros
Pachnes 2453
Kandanos
1116
Paleochora
Aghia Roumeli
Chora Sfakion
Akra Krios
Akra Vouxa
Akra Spatha
Kolpos Chanion
Rodopos
Maleme
Kasteli
748
Kolpos Kissamos
Platanos
Stomio
Gavdos
888
Gavdopoula

Kriti
(Crete)
(Greece)

MALTA
1:1 000 000

GOZO
San Dimitri Pt.
Victoria (Rabat)
Xlendi
Marsalforn
Nadur
Qala Pt.
Comino
Mellieha
Bugibba
St Paul's
Marfa Pt.
Ahrax Pt.
Mosta
Rabat
Mdina
Mellieha
Birkirkara
Sliema
Valletta
Zejtun
Paola
Zabbar
Birzebbuga
Mesta
Filfla

MALTA

MEDITERRANEAN SEA

KERKYRA
Kerkyra (Corfu)
(Greece)

CORFU
1:1 000 000

ALBANIA
GREECE
Sarandë (Santi-Quaranta)
Akra Aghia Ekaterinis
Kassiopi
Roda
Sidari
Karousades
Aghios Stephanos
Mathraki
Erikoussa
Paleokastritsa
Liapades
Ermones
Kontokali
Gouvia
Kerkyra
Vidos
Perama
Benitses
Gastouri
Messongi
Analipsis
Sinarades
Aghios Matheos
Argirades
Kavos
Lefkimi
Akra Asprokavos
L. Korissia
Sagiada
Igoumenitsa
Plataria
Konispol
Stena Kerkyras
Sivota

IONIAN SEA

RHODES
1:1 000 000

Rhodes
Ialissos (Trianda)
Kremasti
Paradisi
Kalithea
Faliraki
Afandou
Archangelos
Masari
Kalimbia
Akra Vagia
Arhipoli
Lindos
Akra Lindos
Ormos Lardos
Lardos
Asklipio
Laerma
Genadi
Profilia
Apolakkia
Kattavia
Akra Prasonisi
Katagros
213
Monolithos
Embonas
Kamiros
Soroni

AEGEAN SEA
MEDITERRANEAN SEA

Rhodes
(Greece)

CYPRUS
1:1 300 000

MEDITERRANEAN SEA

CYPRUS

C. Kormakiti
Kyrenia (Girne)
Lapithos (Lapta)
Morphou (Güzelyurt)
Morphou Bay
Kato Pyrgos
Kokkina (Erenköy)
C. Pomos
Pomos
Polis
Khrysokhou Bay
C. Arnauti
Akamas
Paphos
C. Drepanum
Kouklia
Episkopi
Episkopi Bay
AKROTIRI SOVEREIGN BASE AREA
Akrotiri
Akrotiri Bay
C. Gata
Limassol
Zyyi
DHEKELIA SOVEREIGN BASE AREA
Larnaca
Larnaca Bay
C. Kiti
C. Pyla
Ayia Napa
C. Greco
Xylophagou
Paralimni
Dherinia
Famagusta (Ammochostos)
Famagusta Bay
Trikomo
Yialousa (Yeni Erenköy)
Rizokarpaso (Dipkarpaz)
C. Apostolos Andreas
Klidhes
Galinoporni
Komatou Yialou
Ayios Theodhoros
Lionarisso
Galateia
Akanthou
Olymbos
Kythrea
Nicosia (Lefkosia)
Troodos
Mt Olympus 1951
Pano Lefkara
Dhali
Dhiorios
Skilloura
Kyrenia
Peristerona
Pentadaktylos
Mesaoria (Mesarya)
Athna
Liopetri
Lefka
Kambos
Tripylos
Stavros
Kykko
Panayia
Pedhoulas
Prodhromos
Platres
Mandria
Pissouri
Kolossi

(Under Turkish Administration)

Nicosia (Lefkosia)

East from Greenwich

Projection: Lambert's Conformal Conic

COPYRIGHT PHILIP'S

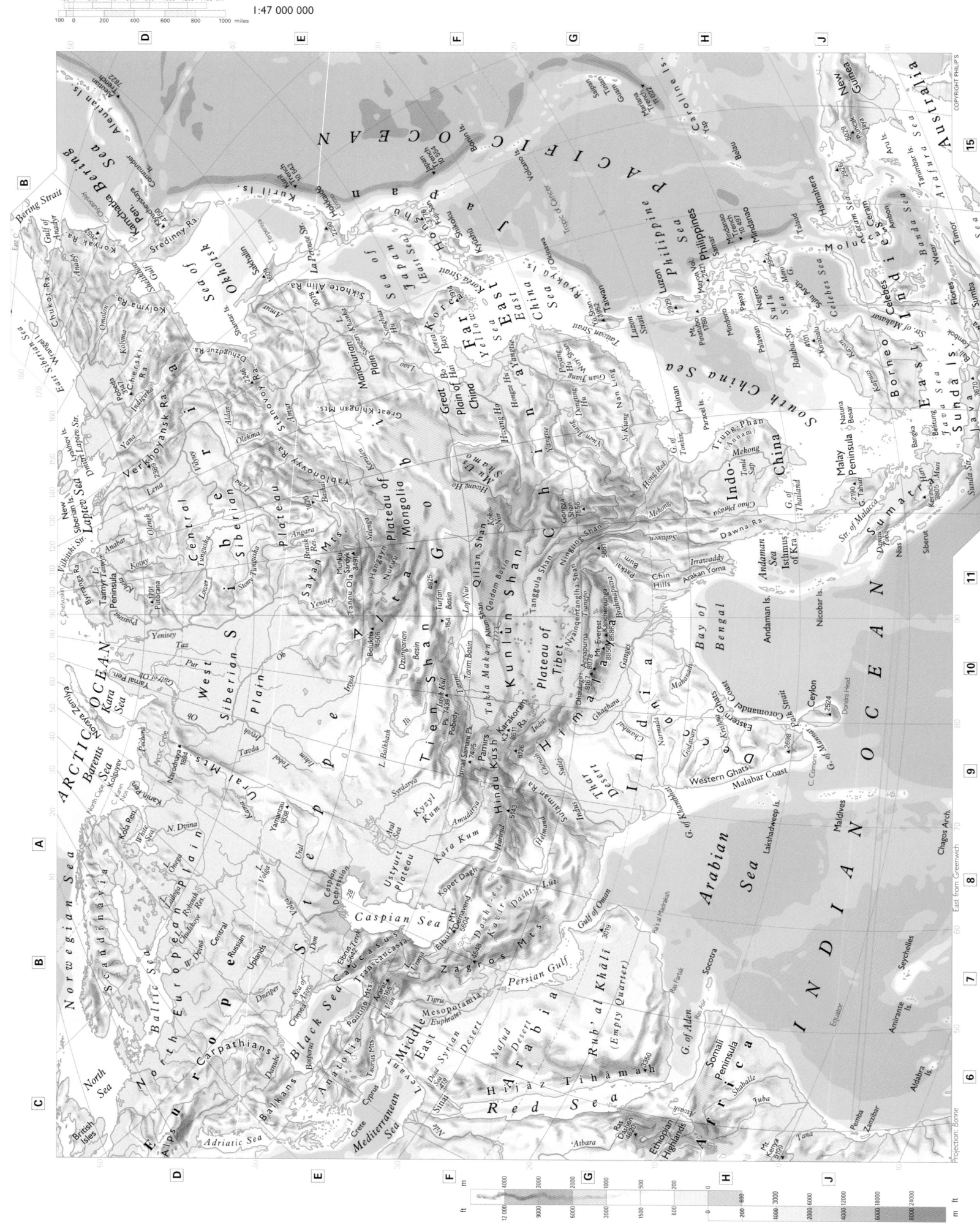

1:47 000 000

1:47 000 000

Projection: Conical Orthomorphic with two standard parallels

East from Greenwich

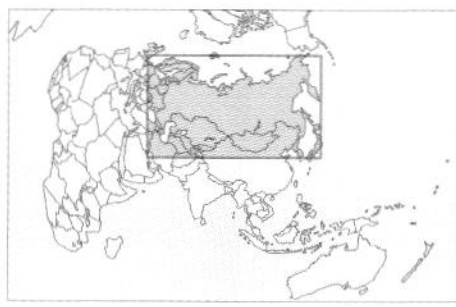

O C E A N

Severnaya Zemlya

Poluostrov Taymyr
Byrranga Gory

East Siberian Sea

Laptev Sea

Chukchi Sea

Bering Str.

Bering Sea

Ostrov Vrangelya

St. Lawrence I. (U.S.A.)

Poluostrov Kamchatka

Sea of Okhotsk

Sakhalin

Kurilskiye Ostrova

R U S S I A

Arctic Circle

K H R E B E T C H E R S K O G O

V E R K H O Y A N S K I Y K H R E B E T

S R E D I N N Y Y

Koryakskoye Nagorye

Kolymskoye Nagorye

D A L N E V O S T O C H N Y Y

Yakutsk

Lena

Stanovoy Khrebet

Sikhote Alin

Hokkaidō

SAPPORO

Hakodate

Irkutsk

Bratsk

Krasnoyarsk

Abakan

Ulan Ude

Ulaanbaatar

M O N G O L I A

(Aerhtai Shan)

Hangayn Nuruu

Gobi

HARBIN

QIQIHAR

DAQING

JIAMUSI

MUDANJIANG

JILIN

CHANGCHUN

Vladivostok

C H I N A
(Manchuria)

Khabarovsk

Komsomolsk-na-Amur

Yuzhno-Sakhalinsk

SHENYANG

ANSHAN

FUSHUN

CHIFENG

BEIJING

HOHHOT

BAOTOU

ZHANGJIAKOU

TANGSHAN

DALIAN

NORTH KOREA

PYONGYANG

NAMPO

Hamhŭng

Wŏnsan

SEOUL

INCHEON

SOUTH KOREA

DAEJEON

DAEGU

BUSAN

GWANGJU

JAPAN

KYOTO

OSAKA

KOBE

Honshū

Sea of Japan
(East Sea)

Hami

COPYRIGHT PHILIP'S

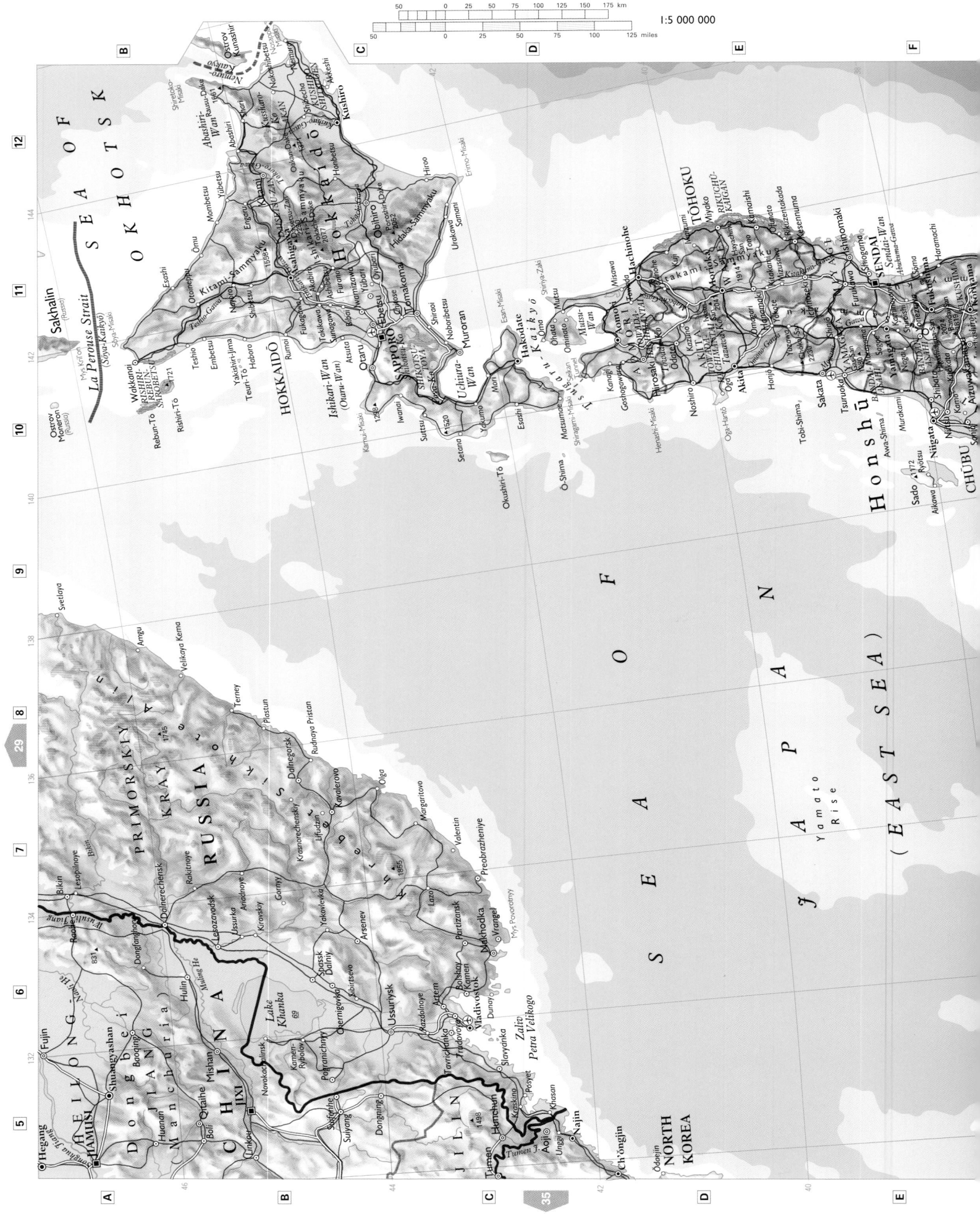

50   0   25   50   75   100 125 150 175 km

50   0   25   50   75   100 125 miles

1:5 000 000

B

C

D

E

F

12

11

10

9

8

29

7

6

5

A   B   C   35   D   E

S E A   O F

O K H O T S K

La Perouse Strait

Sakhalin
(Russia)

Ostrov
Moneron
(Russia)

HOKKAIDŌ

SAPPORO

Hakodate

RISHIRI-
REBUN-
SAROBETSU

Wakkanai

Kushiro

PRIMORSKY

KRAY

RUSSIA

CHINA

Manchuria

HEILONGJIANG

Dongbei

JILIN

NORTH
KOREA

Vladivostok

Ussuriysk

Lake
Khanka

Najin

Ch'ŏngjin

S E A   O F   J A P A N

(E A S T   S E A)

Yamato
Rise

TŌHOKU

Honshū

SENDAI

CHŪBU

Sado

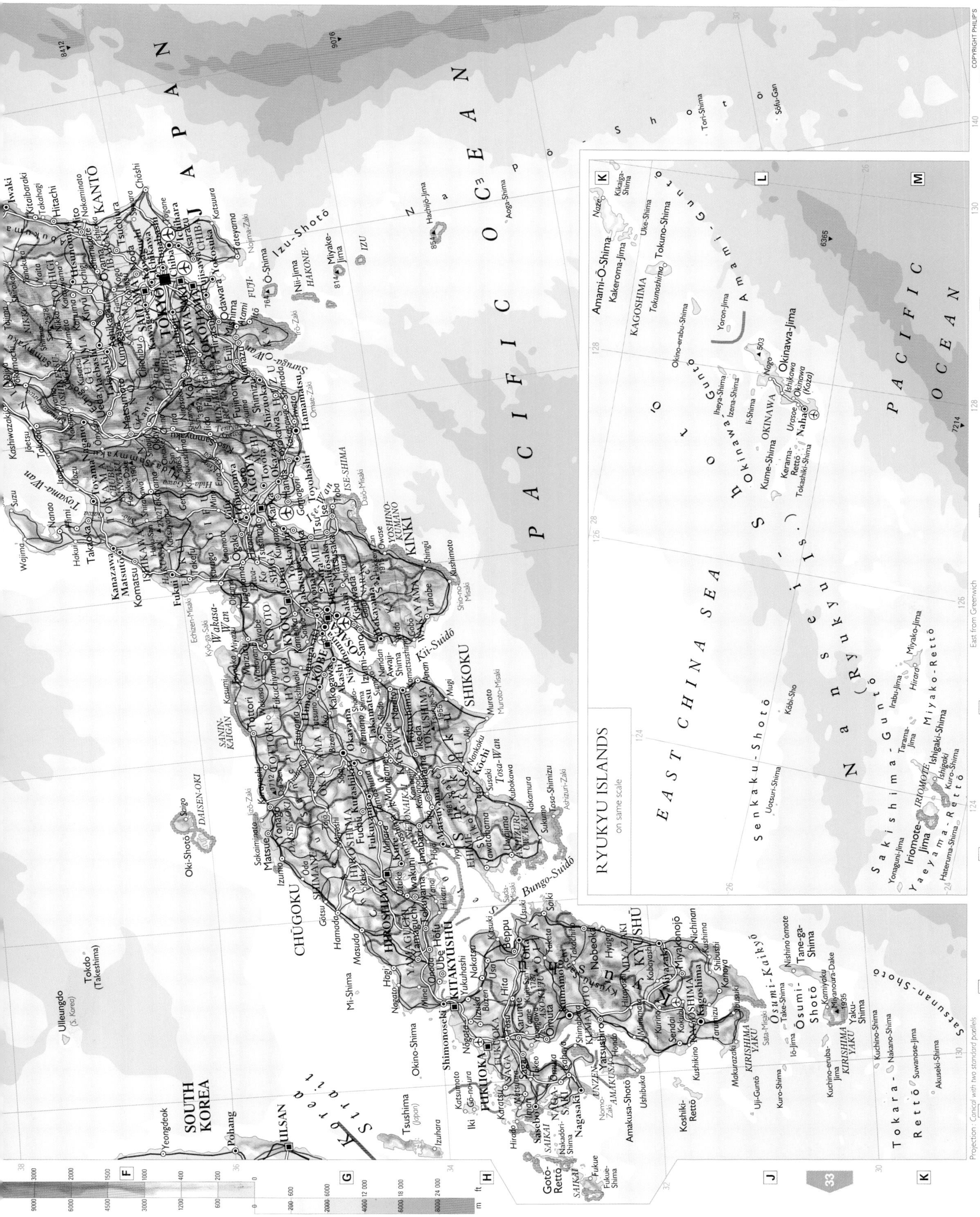

J A P A N

PACIFIC OCEAN

EAST CHINA SEA

SOUTH KOREA

RYUKYU ISLANDS
on same scale

Nansei-shotō (Ryukyu Is.)

KANTŌ

TOKYO

CHŪGOKU

SHIKOKU

KYŪSHŪ

KINKI

Tsushima (Japan)

Ullŭngdo (S Korea)

Tokdo (Takeshima)

Amami-Ō-Shima

KAGOSHIMA

Okinawa-Jima

OKINAWA

Naha

Sakishima-Guntō

Miyako-Rettō

Yaeyama-Rettō

Iriomote-Jima

Ishigaki-Shima

Senkaku-Shotō

Tokara-Rettō

Satsunan-Shotō

Ōsumi-Shotō

Tane-ga-Shima

Yaku-Shima

Izu-Shotō

Hachijō-Jima

KIRISHIMA-YAKU

UNZEN-AMAKUSA

ASO

SAIKAI

Goto-Rettō

Nagasaki

FUKUOKA

KITAKYUSHU

Shimonoseki

YAMAGUCHI

HIROSHIMA

OKAYAMA

KOBE

KYOTO

OSAKA

NAGOYA

Projection: Conical with two standard parallels

East from Greenwich

ft
9000 3000
6000 2000
4500 1500
3000 1000
1500 600
1200 400
600   200
0   0
m   -200 -600
      2000 6000
      4000 12 000
      6000 18 000
      8000 24 000

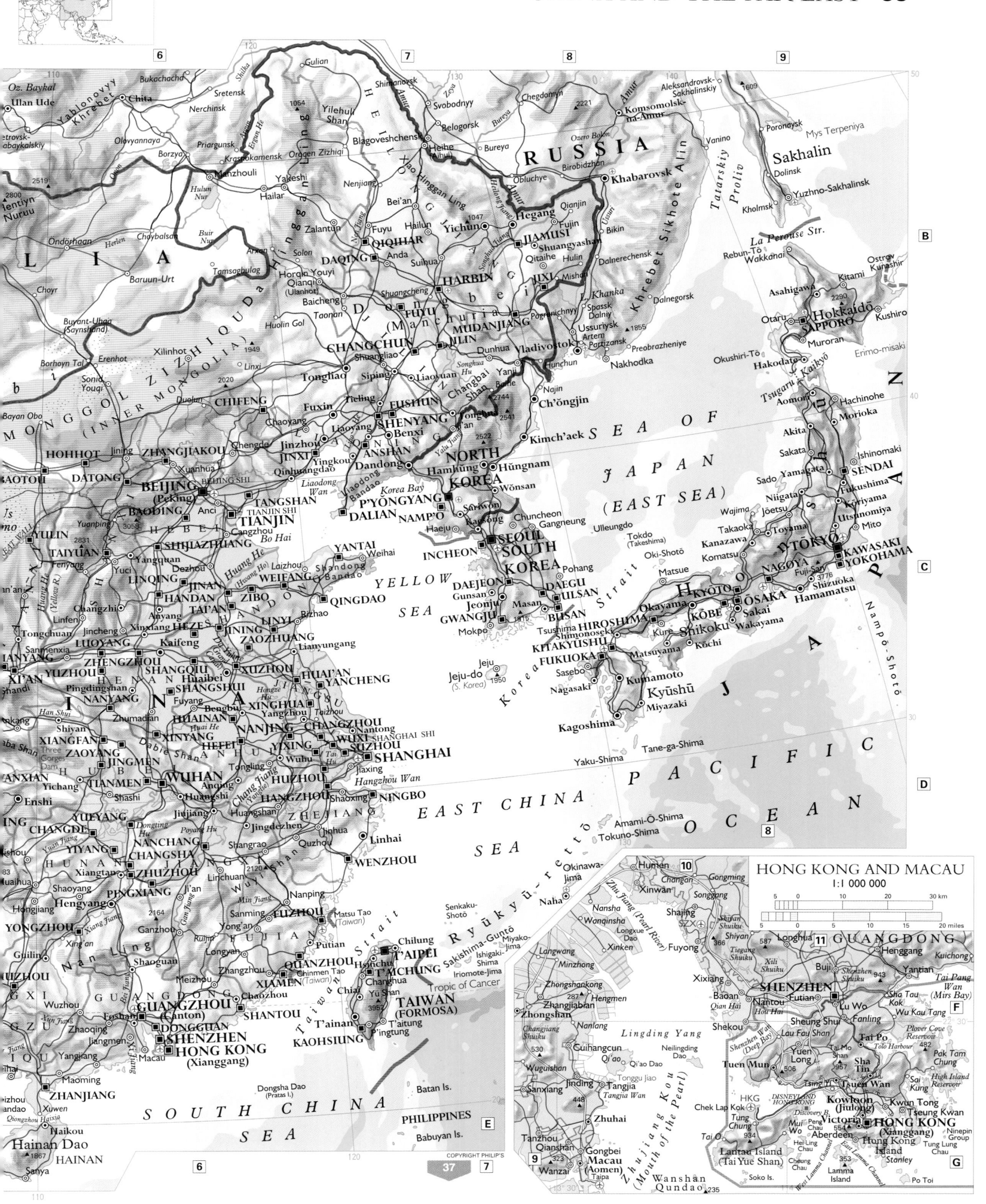

HONG KONG AND MACAU
1:1 000 000

COPYRIGHT PHILIP'S

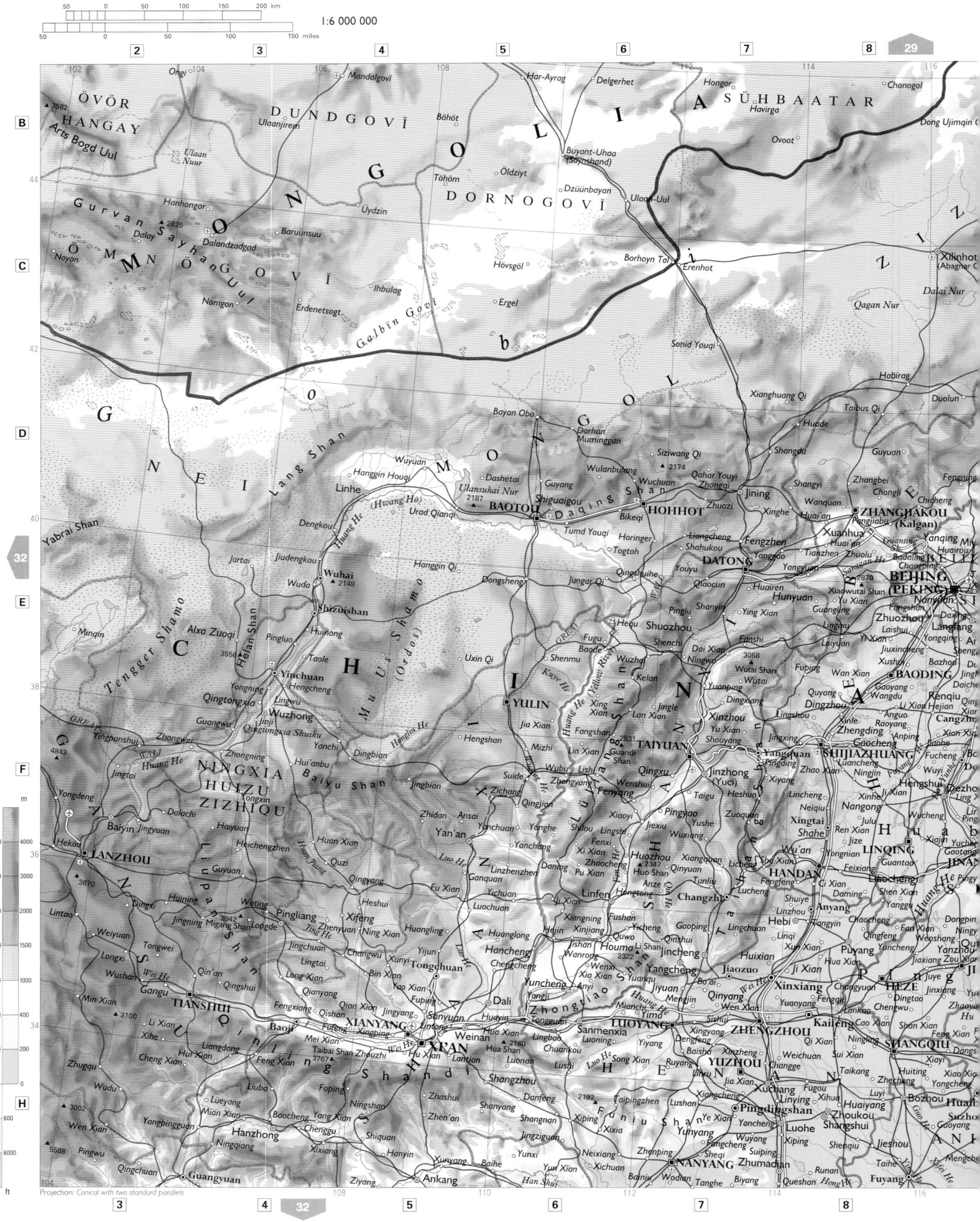

HIXING AN

Horqin Youyi Qianqi
(Ulanhot)

Zhenlai   Nen   **HARBIN**   Bin Xian

Baicheng   Da'an   Maoxing   Zhaoyuan   Shuangcheng   Acheng   Yanshou   Linkou   **JIXI**   Lake
Khanka   69

Tuquan   Qagan   Songhua   Changchunling   Shangzhi   H E I L O N G J I A N G   Hengdaohezi   Maqiaohe   Xiaochengzi   Pogranichnyy

Anguang   **FUYU**   Beitaolaizhao   Sanchahe   Wuchang   Hailin   Muling   Suiyang   Sufenhe   44

Tongyu   Qian'an   Kaoshan   Yushu   Shanhetun   **MUDANJIANG**   Ning'an   Dongning   Ussuriysk

Huolin Gol   Gorlos   Shenjingzi   Nong'an   Dehui   Shulan   Jingpo   Hu   Dongjingcheng   Luozigou   Golenki

Jarud Qi   Horqin Zuoyi   Fulongquan   Jiutai   Gangyao   Wulajie   Xinzhan   Emu   Chunyang   Wangqing   Shixian   **Vladivostok**

Changling   Zhongqi   Maqin   **CHANGCHUN**   **JILIN**   Jiaohe   Dunhua   Daxinggou   Mingyuegue   Yanji   Hunchun   Slavyanka   C

Xinkai He   Huaidezhen   Fanjiatun   Songhua   Jiang   Wangqing   Longjing   Helong   Namyang

2029▲   Linxi   Bairin   Zuoqi   Kailu   Tongliao   Dongliao He   Gongzhuling   Shuangyang   Huadian   Quanyang   Baihe   Antu   Changbai Shan   Aoji   Unggi   Najin

dexigtep Qi   Bairin Youqi   Xar Moron He   Shuangliao   Lishu   Siping   Yitong   Liaoyuan   Panshi   Huinan   Baishan   Jingyu   Fusong   Songjianghe   Musan   Pugdong   42

CHIFENG   (Ulanhad)   Xiawa   Hure Qi   Kangping   Bamianchang   Xifeng   Dongfeng   Jiangyuan   Shiren   Changbai   Puryong   Nanam   **Ch'ŏngjin**   Kyŏngsŏng

1:12 500 000

Projection: Mercator

East from Greenwich

1:6 000 000

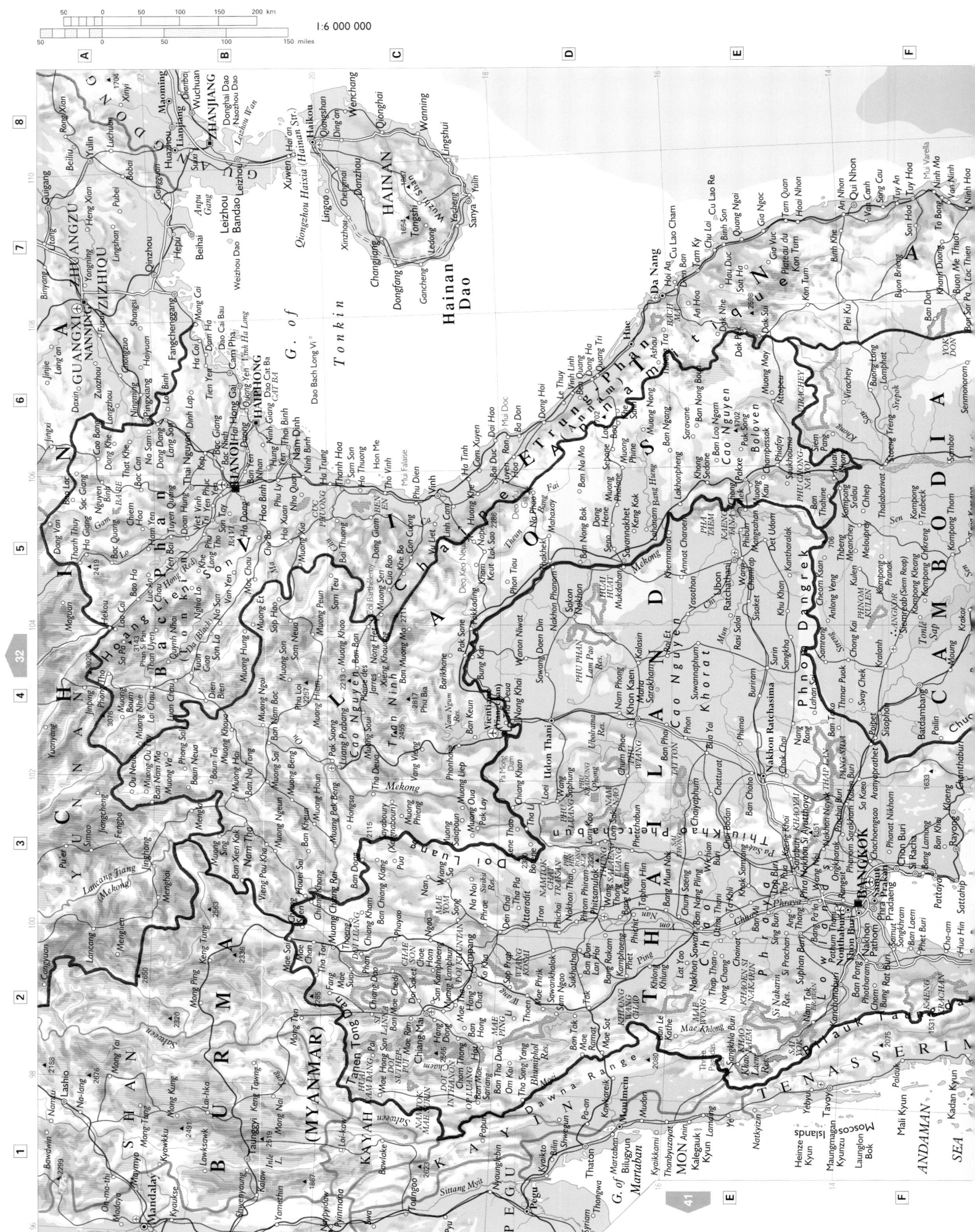

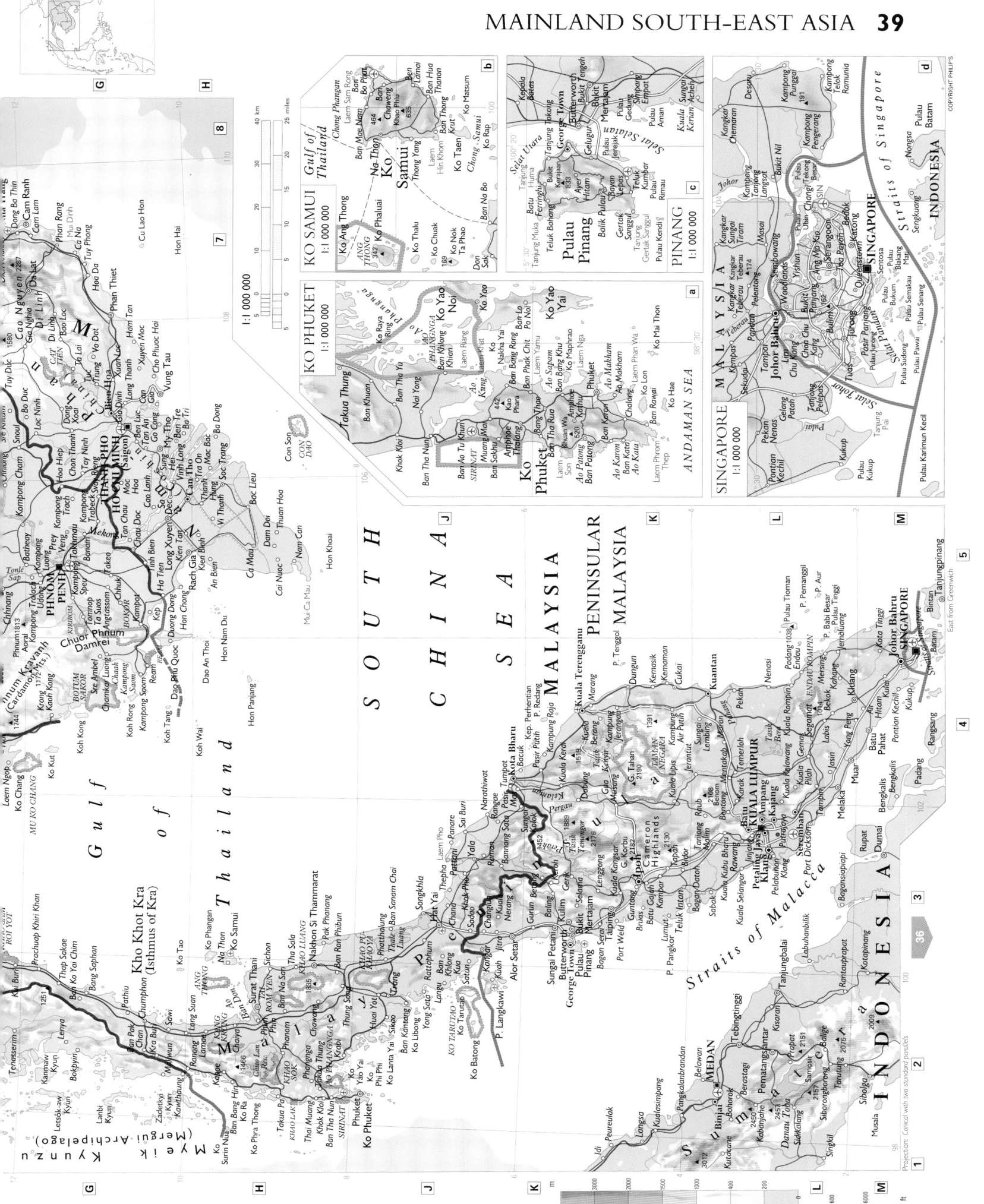

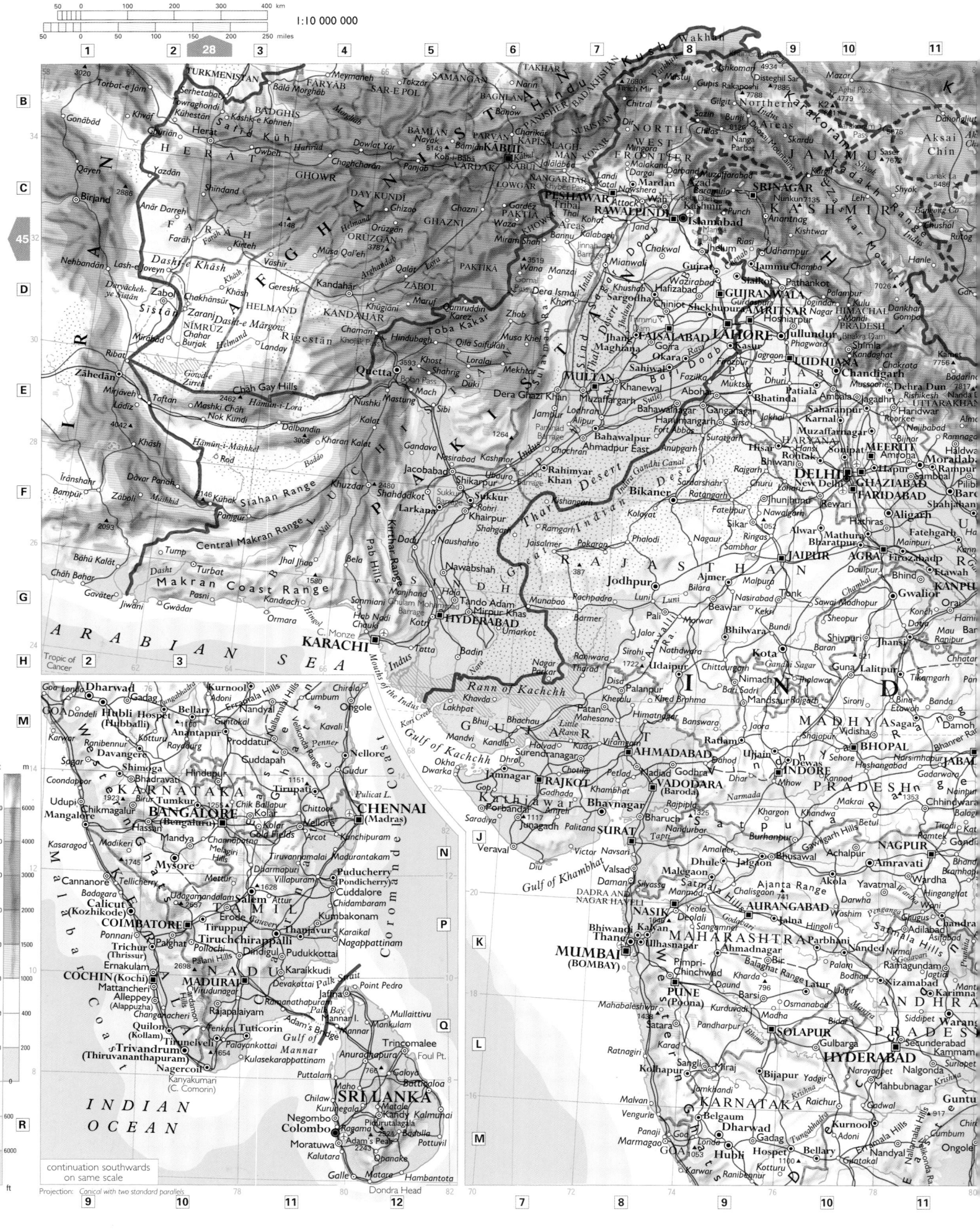

1:10 000 000

continuation southwards
on same scale

Projection: Conical with two standard parallels

B
C
D
E
F
G
H
J
K
L
38
M

NJIANG UYGUR ZIZHIQU Muz Tag 7723

Hoh Xil Shan

Q I N G H A I

Gyaring Hu 4237 Ngoring Hu
6094
Huang He
Huang He

Dogai Coring

XIZANG
ZIZHIQU

T a n g g u l a

C H I (Dangla) N A
5180 Tanggula Shankou Shan

Amdo

Baqên

Nangqên

Dêngqên

Qamdo

Baiyu
Garzê

Ngangla Ringco 6590

(T o n g I T i b e t)

Dongco

4495 Siling Co

Nagqu

Lhorong

Zhaxizê
Markam

Xinlong

SICHUAN

Yidun
Litang
Yajiang

Kangri

Ombu

Coqên

Xainza

Nam Co

Lhari

Nu Jiang

Gongbo'gyamda

Yushu

Dainkog

N i n g j i n g S h a n

Markam

Zhongdian

Kangrinboqe Feng (Kailash) 6714

Tangra Yumco

Gyaring Co

4627

Lhünzub

Namcha
Barwa 7756
Riga

Zayu
588
6740

Zhixixian

Muli Zangzu
Zizhixian

Weixi
5596
Lijiang

Simikot Mugu 7059 Namche
Shankou

Maquan He (Tsangpo)

Lhasa

Yarlung Zangbo Jiang

Jido
Nizamghat

Gogên

Z u S h a n

Jianchuan

NEPAL

Mustang

Zhongba

Saga

Xainza

Lhazê

Xigazê

Gyangzê

Nang Xian

Cona

7090 Kangto

ARUNACHAL PRADESH

Minutang (Thala La) 3072 Putao

Chaukan Pass 2432

Jinsha Jiang (Yangtze)

Zhongdian

Dhaulagiri 8167 Annapurna 8078

Mt Everest 8850 Kanchenjunga 8598 SIKKIM

7314

Thimphu BHUTAN

Punakha Tongsa Dzong

Rupa

Dibrugarh Tinsukia

Hukawng Valley 3411

Bumhpa Bum

YUNNAN

Yunlong

KATHMANDU Bhaktapur

Gangtok Darjiling

North Lakhimpur

Sibsagar

KACHIN

Singkaling Hkamti

Myitkyina

Tengchong
Longling

Changning

Dali

1:6 000 000

Projection: Conical with two standard parallels

JAMMU AND KASHMIR
on same scale

1:7 000 000

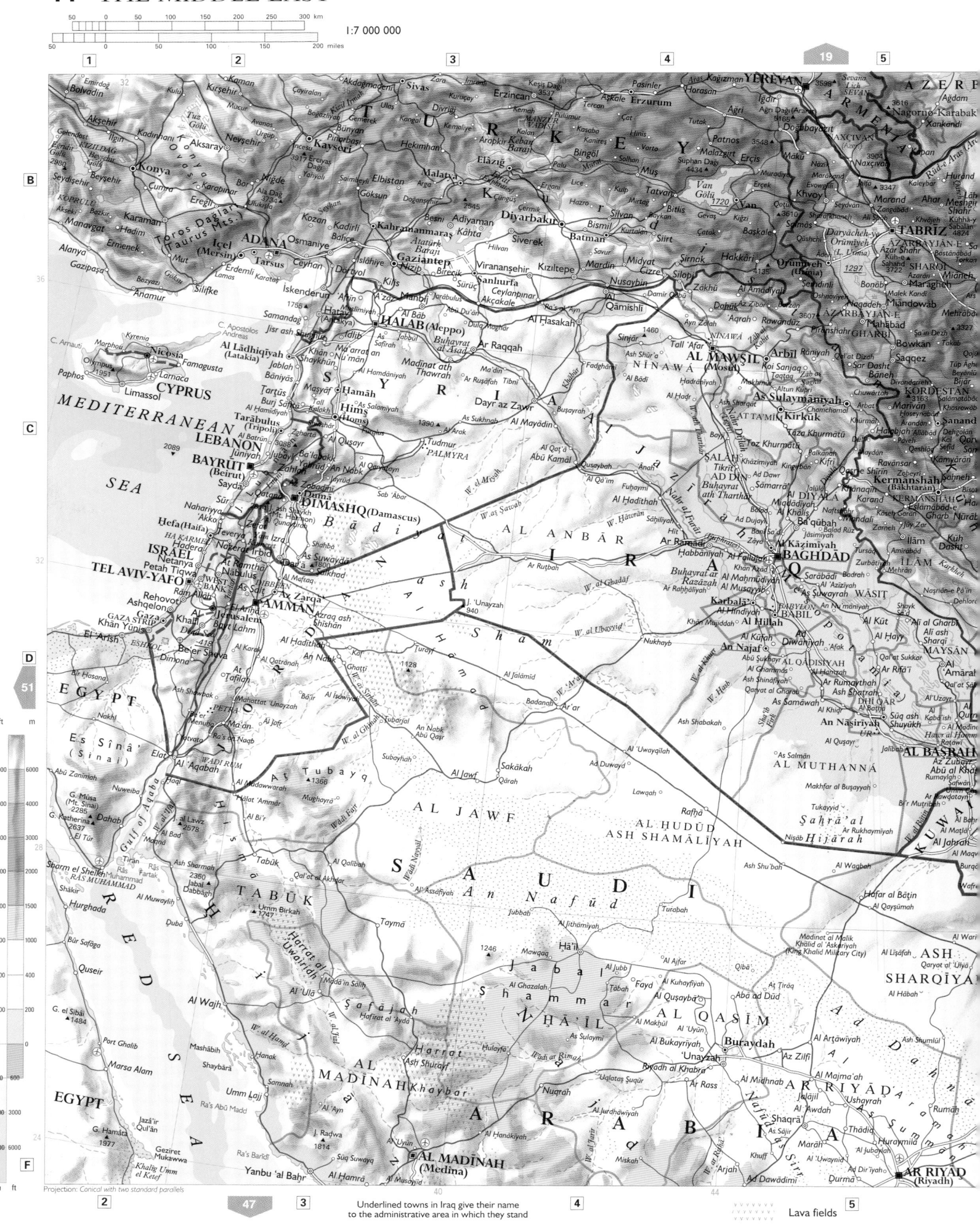

Underlined towns in Iraq give their name
to the administrative area in which they stand

Lava fields

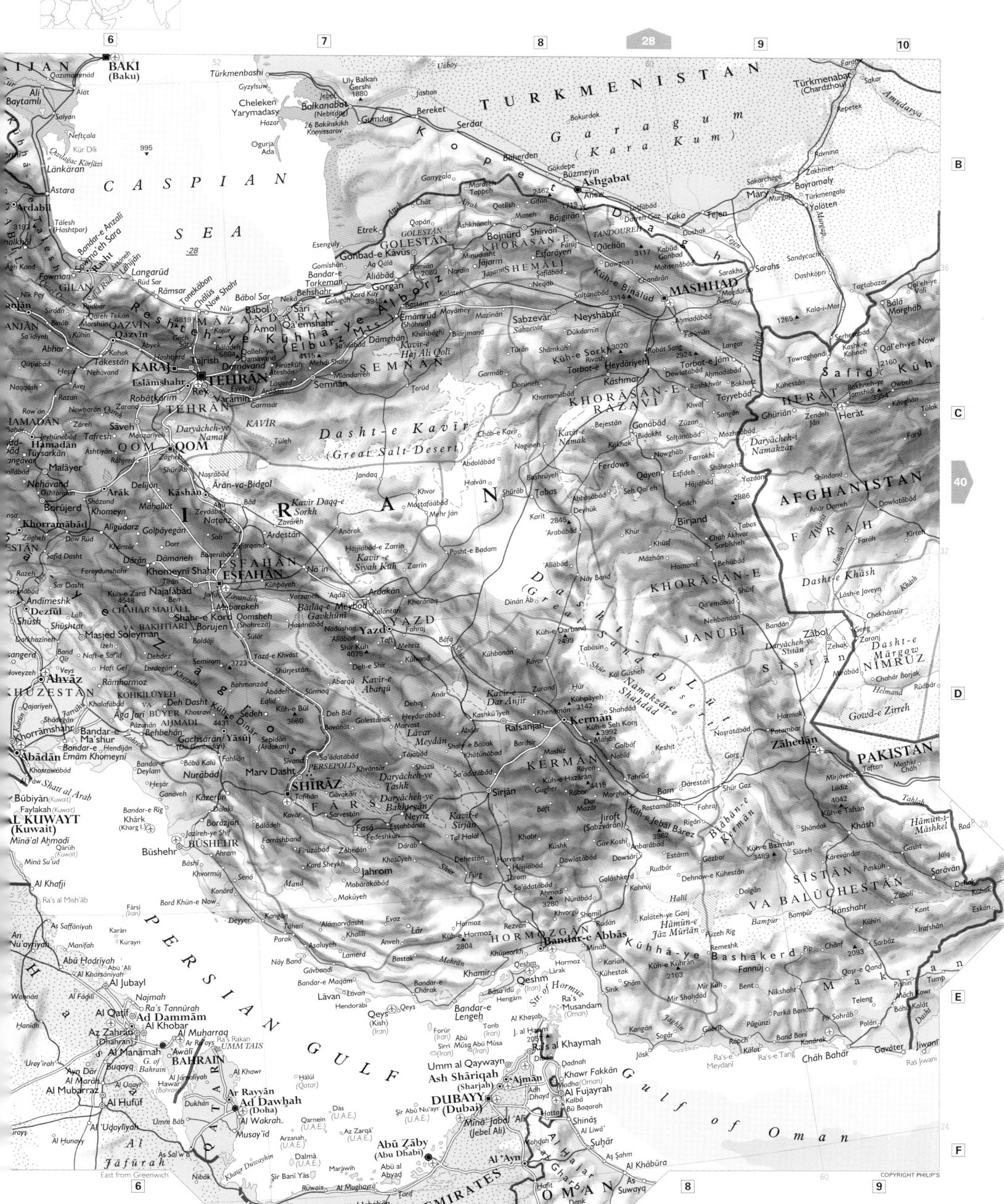

1:2 500 000

10 0 10 20 30 40 50 60 70 80 100 km
10 0 10 20 30 40 50 60 miles

| 1 | 2 | 3 | 4 | 44 | 5 | 6 |

Paphos Kivides Zyyi
Episkopi Limassol **CYPRUS**
Episkopi Akrotiri C. Gata
Bay Bay

Hims (Homs) Shinshar Furqlus

Al Hamidiyah

Al Mina' Al Hirmil Al Qusayr
ASH Kalakh
Tal
Halba

A

2775 ▼

M E D I T E R R A N E A N

SHAMAL **H I M S**
Tarabulus Zgharta Qurnat as Sawda 3088 Al Buwayj
(Tripoli) ▲2464
Al Batrun Al Labwa Al Qaryatayn

Jubayl Qartaba An Nabk
Ibrahim 2618 Ba'labakk Yabrud Bi'r Ghadir

S E A Juniyah 2089 ▼ ▲2628 J. Sannin **S Y R I A**
BAYRUT Bikfayya
(Beirut) Zahlah Sirghaya Jayrud
Ash Shuwayfat 'Alayh Dumayr
Ad Damur **JABAL** Az Zabadani Al Qutayfah Khan Abu Shamat
LEBANON **LUBNAN** Hawsh **D I M A S H Q**
1942 Mussa
J. al Barak Dumayr

B Sayda 1sh Shayhn Qatana Jaramanah Al Hajanah **DIMASHQ** (Damascus)
(Sidon) Jazzin 2814 Darayya DAM
An Nabatiyah Marj 'Uyun Al Kiswah
at Tahta **AL** Al 'Uyun
Sur **JANUB** 2
(Tyre) Qiryat (Mt. Hermon) Buraq Safa
Shemona 1197 Al Qunaytirah As Sanamayn

Nahariyya Hagalil Ar Rafid **D A R ' A** Shahba
'Akko (Acre) 1208▲ (Galilee) Zefat Yam Kinneret Izra 1800▲ Salah
Mifraz (Sea of Galilee) Shaykh Miskin **A S U W A Y D A**
Hefa Qiryat Karmi'el Saham al As Suwayda

C **Hefa** Qiryat Ata Teverya (Tiberias) -210 Jawlan Dar'a Malah
(Haifa) Nazerat Yarmuk Umm al Qittayn
Daliyat el Karmel **HEFA** (Nazareth) 'AJLUN Al Mafraq
KARMEL Afula Talbut **IRBID**
Umm el Fahm **KARKUR** Jenin 'Ajlun **A L   M A F R A Q**
TEL MEGIDDO ▲1247 Irbid ad Dar'a Umm al Qittayn
CAESAREA Shomron **JARASH**
Hadera Tulkarm Tubas **SAMARIA** Jarash
ISRAEL Netanya Nabulus N. az Zarqa Az Zarqa
HAMERKAZ Ra'ananna
Herzliyya Kefar Sava **AL BALQA**
Bene Beraq Petah Tiqwa **SHILOH** As Salt **AMMAN**
TEL AVIV-YAFO Ramat Gan Wadi as Sir
Bat Yam TLV **WEST** Karama
Holon Lod **BANK** -289
D Rishon le Ziyyon Ramla Ram El Ariha Na'ur At Tunayb
Yavne Rehovot Allah (Jericho) AMM **' A M M A N**
Ashdod Jerusalem Ma'daba
Qiryat Malakhi (Yerushalayim) (Al Quds) **MA'DABA** Azraq ash Shishan
Ashqelon Qiryat Bet Shemesh Bayt Lahm W. al Haydan **A Z   Z A R Q A**
Gat (Bethlehem) Dhiban
GAZA Gaza N. Shiqma Al Khalil Al
STRIP Sederot (Hebron) Dead W. al Mujib Hadithah
Khan Yunis Az Zahiriyah 'En Gedi Sea
Rafah Besor -418 W. al Ghadaf Al Qatranah
Bur Sa'id (Port Said) El Daheir Be'er -333 **AL KARAK**
Bur Fu'ad Bor Mashash Sheva Arad 1305▲ Al Karak
BUR SA'ID (Beersheba) **MASADA** Al Mazar
Khalig el Tina Sabkhet el El 'Arish Dimona 'En Boqeq
Ras Burun Bardawil Sedom

E Ramani Bir Qatia Bir Lahfan **HADAROM** W. al Hasa **J O R D A N**
El Qantara Bir el Duweidar Bir el Gararat Abu Aweigila Qezi'ot -121▼ At Tafilah W. Ba'ir
Wahid Bir Madkur 'Arish Birein Sede **AT TAFILAH** Ba'ir
Boqer Dana Shawmari
SHAMAL 892▲ Abu Aweigila Muweilih Nijil
Isma'iliya Talata Al Quseima Mizpe Ramon Mahattat 'Unayzah
ISMA'ILIYA **SINI** Rujm Tal'at Al Jafr
Khamsa Bir el Malhi **Hanegev** al Jama'ah Qa'el Jafr
El Buheirat (Negev Desert) 1730▲ **M A ' A N**
el Murrat G. Yi 'Allaq Bir Beida PETRA
el Kubra 1094 Wadi Mahattat ash Shidiyah
(Great Bitter L.) Musa **M A ' A N**

F Gineifa Bir el Thamada W. el Bruk N. Paran Ma'an
Mamarr Bir Gebeil Hisn El 'Agrud El Quntilla Ras an Naqb
Mitla El Suntilla 1435▲
E G Y P T **Es S i n a** N. Hiyyon Yotvata **AL AQABAH** Ras an Naqb
El Suweis Bur Taufiq (Sinai) Nakhl 'En Yahav
(Suez) Adabiya Ain Sudr W. el Giddi RUM 1592 1754▲ Batn al Ghul
'Uyun Musa W. el Brugi Bir Abu Muhammad El Thamad **WADI RUM** **S A U D I**
948▲ Rum
Ras Sudr G. el Kabrit Bir el Biarat Elat
Ghubbet Ras W. Janub Al 'Aqabah At Tubayq
el Bus Matarma 1272 **Sini** Haql Al Mudawwarah **A R A B I A**
Abu Sandul Bir el Heisi
Bir Wuseit 1165
EL SUWEIS

Projection: Polyconic East from Greenwich COPYRIGHT PHILIP'S

| 1 | 2 | 51 | 3 | 4 | 5 | 6 |

═ ═ ═ 1974 Cease Fire Lines

ft m
9000 3000
6000 2000
4500 1500
3000 1000
1500 400
600 200
0 0
200 600
500 1500
1000 3000
2000 6000
m ft

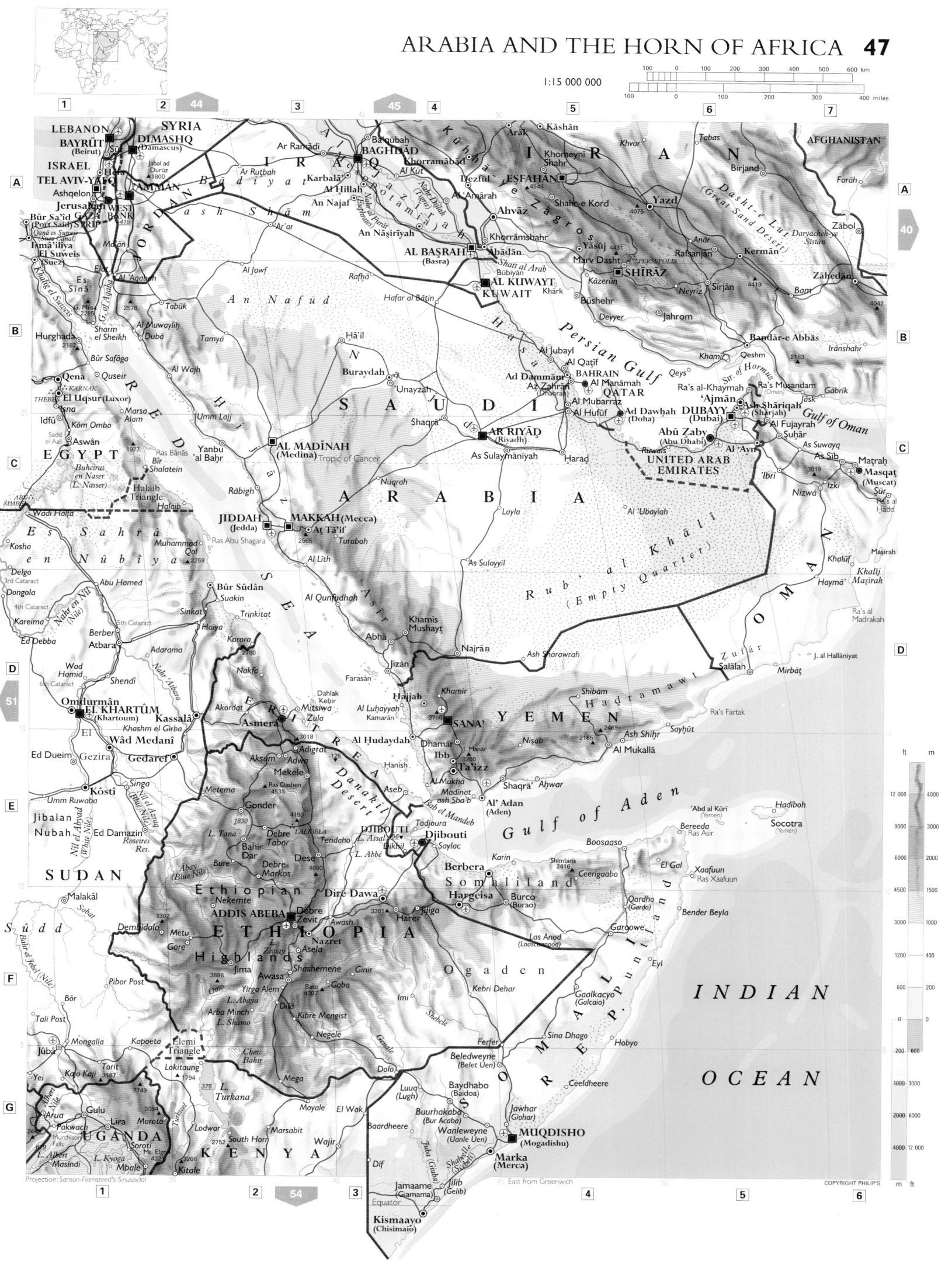

200 0 200 400 600 800 1000 1200 1400 1600 1800 km

200 0 200 400 600 800 1000 1200 miles

1:42 000 000

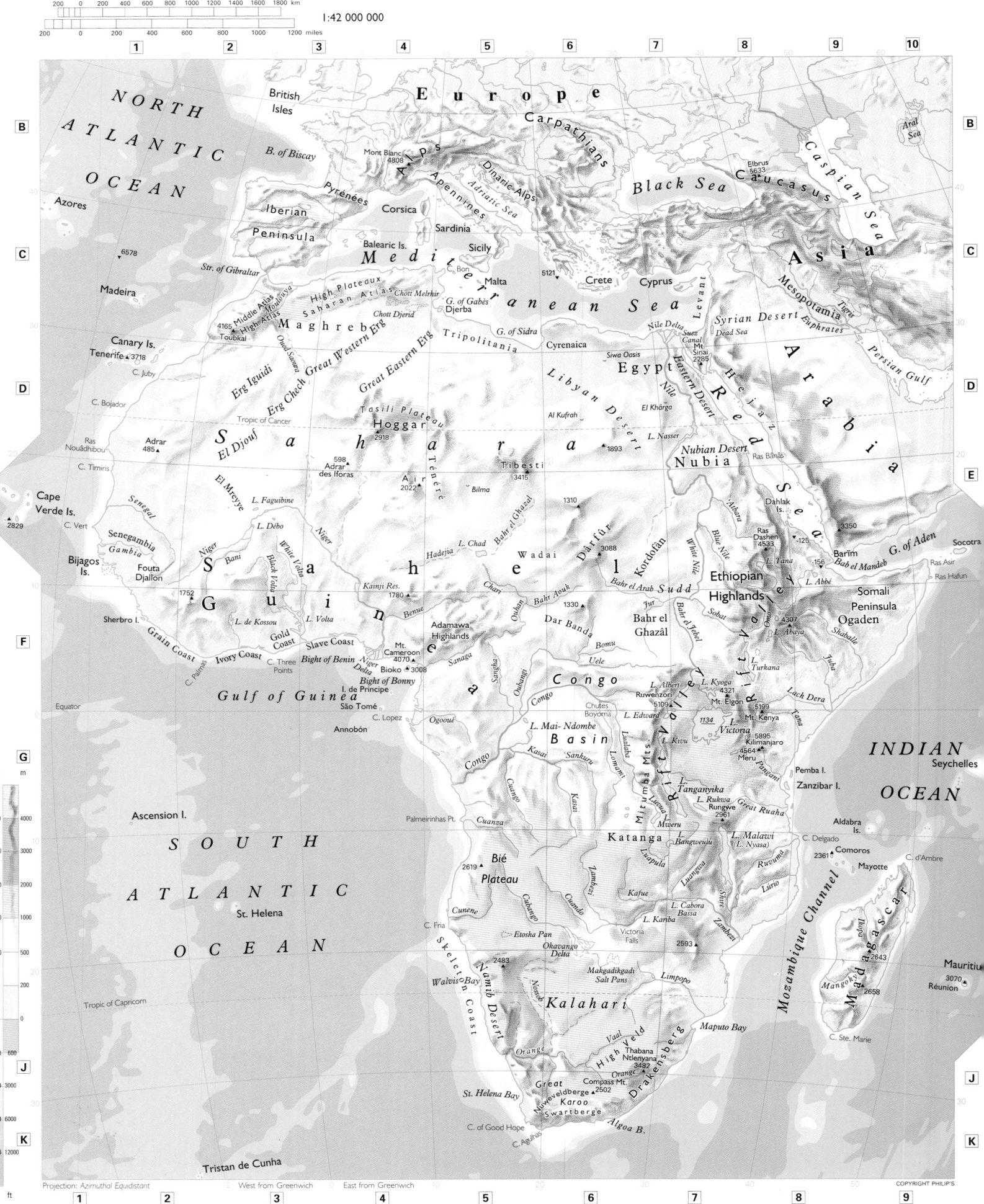

NORTH ATLANTIC OCEAN

British Isles

Europe

Carpathians

Aral Sea

B. of Biscay

Mont Blanc 4808

Alps

Dinaric Alps

Adriatic Sea

Apennines

Black Sea

Caucasus

Elbrus 5633

Caspian Sea

Azores

Pyrénées

Corsica

Asia

Iberian Peninsula

Sardinia

Str. of Gibraltar

Balearic Is.

Sicily

Mediterranean Sea

Mesopotamia

Tigris

6578

Madeira

C. Bon

Malta

5121

Crete

Cyprus

Levant

Euphrates

Persian Gulf

Middle Atlas

High Plateaux

Saharan Atlas

Chott Melrhir

G. of Gabès

Djerba

Syrian Desert

Dead Sea

Arabia

Canary Is.

4165

Toubkal

High Atlas

Oued Moulouya

Maghreb

Chott Djerid

G. of Sidra

Tripolitania

Cyrenaica

Nile Delta

Siwa Oasis

Suez Canal

Mt. Sinai 2285

Egypt

Hejaz

Tenerife 3718

C. Juby

Erg Iguidi

Erg Chech

Great Western Erg

Great Eastern Erg

Tropic of Cancer

Tasili Plateau

Libyan Desert

Al Kufrah

El Khârga

Eastern Desert

Nile

Red Sea

C. Bojador

S

a

h

a

r

a

Hoggar 2918

Ténéré

1893

L. Nasser

Nubian Desert

Ras Bânâs

Ras Nouâdhibou

Adrar 485

El Djouf

598 Adrar des Iforas

Aïr 2022

Tibesti 3415

Nubia

Dahlak Is.

3350

C. Timiris

El Mreyye

Bilma

1310

Darfûr

Ras Dashen 4533

-125

Barim

G. of Aden

Socotra

Cape Verde Is.

Senegal

L. Faguibine

Niger

Hadejia

L. Chad

Bahr el Ghazal

3088

Kordofan

White Nile

Blue Nile

Albara

L. Tana

156

Bab el Mandeb

Ras Asir

2829

C. Vert

Senegambia

Gambia

L. Débo

Niger

White Volta

Bani

S

a

h

Wadai

e

l

Bahr el Arab

Sudd

Ethiopian Highlands

Somali Peninsula

Ogaden

Ras Hafun

Bijagos Is.

Fouta Djallon

1752

Black Volta

Kainji Res. 1780

Chari

Benue

Adamawa Highlands

Bahr Aouk

1330

Dar Banda

Jur

Bahr el Ghazâl

Sobat

Omo

4307

L. Abaya

Shabelle

Sherbro I.

Grain Coast

Ivory Coast

L. de Kossou

Gold Coast

L. Volta

Slave Coast

C. Three Points

Bight of Benin

Niger Delta

Mt. Cameroon 4070

Bioko 3008

Sanaga

Oubangi

Bomu

Uele

Congo

Congo

Chutes Boyoma

1134

L. Albert

Ruwenzori 5109

L. Edward

L. Kyoga 4321

Mt. Elgon

L. Turkana

Lach Dera

Juba

C. Palmas

Bight of Bonny

I. de Principe

São Tomé

Gulf of Guinea

Equator

C. Lopez

Ogooué

Annobón

Guinea

L. Mai-Ndombe

Kasai

Sankuru

Lomami

Lualaba

Mitumba Mts.

Rift Valley

L. Kivu

L. Victoria

5199

Mt. Kenya

Kilimanjaro 5895

Meru 4564

Pangani

INDIAN OCEAN

Seychelles

Pemba I.

Zanzibar I.

Ascension I.

SOUTH ATLANTIC OCEAN

St. Helena

Palmeirinhas Pt.

Cuango

Congo

Cuanza

Basin

Lulua

Kasai

Katanga

L. Tanganyika

L. Rukwa

Rungwe 2961

Great Ruaha

L. Mweru

L. Bangweulu

L. Malawi

L. Nyasa

Ruvuma

Lurio

C. Delgado

Aldabra Is.

2361

Comoros

C. d'Ambre

Mayotte

2619

Bié Plateau

Cunene

C. Fria

Luapula

Zambezi

Kafue

Luangwa

Shire

Madagascar

Theona 2643

Mauritius

3070 Réunion

Etosha Pan

Okavango Delta

L. Cabora Bassa

L. Kariba

Victoria Falls

2593

Mozambique Channel

Mangoky

Tropic of Capricorn

Skeleton Coast

Namib Desert

Walvis Bay

2483

Noscob

Makgadikgadi Salt Pans

Kalahari

Limpopo

Maputo Bay

Mangoro 2658

Ianoro

C. Ste. Marie

St. Helena Bay

Orange

Vaal

High Veld

Thabana Ntlenyana 3492

Orange

Compass Mt. 2502

Drakensberg

Great Nuweveldberge

Karoo

Swartberge

Algoa B.

C. of Good Hope

C. Agulhas

Tristan de Cunha

West from Greenwich

East from Greenwich

COPYRIGHT PHILIP'S

ft m

12000 4000

9000 3000

6000 2000

3000 1000

1500 500

600 200

0 0

200 600

1000 3000

2000 6000

4000 12000

m ft

1:42 000 000

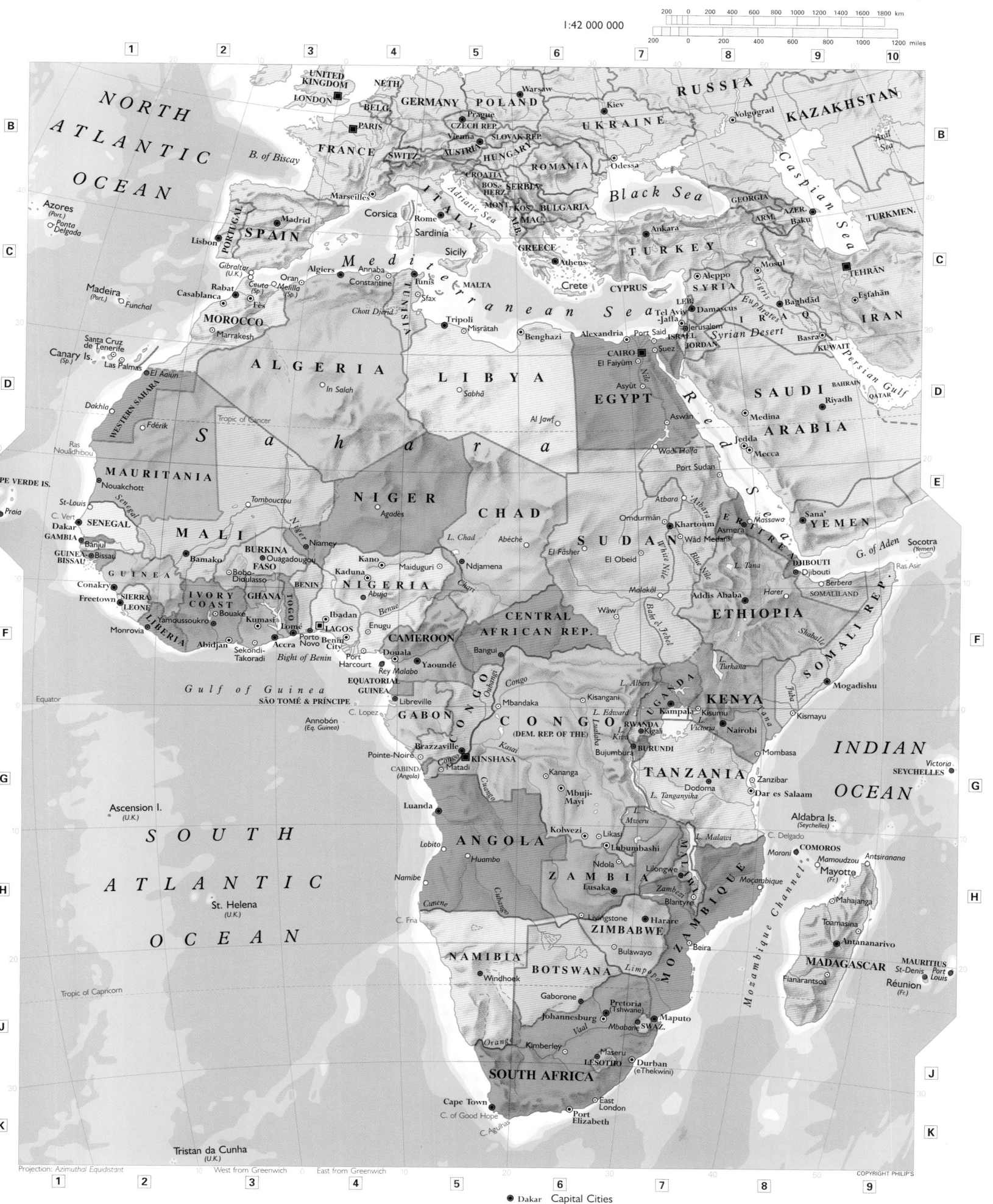

● Dakar   Capital Cities

Projection: Azimuthal Equidistant

COPYRIGHT PHILIP'S

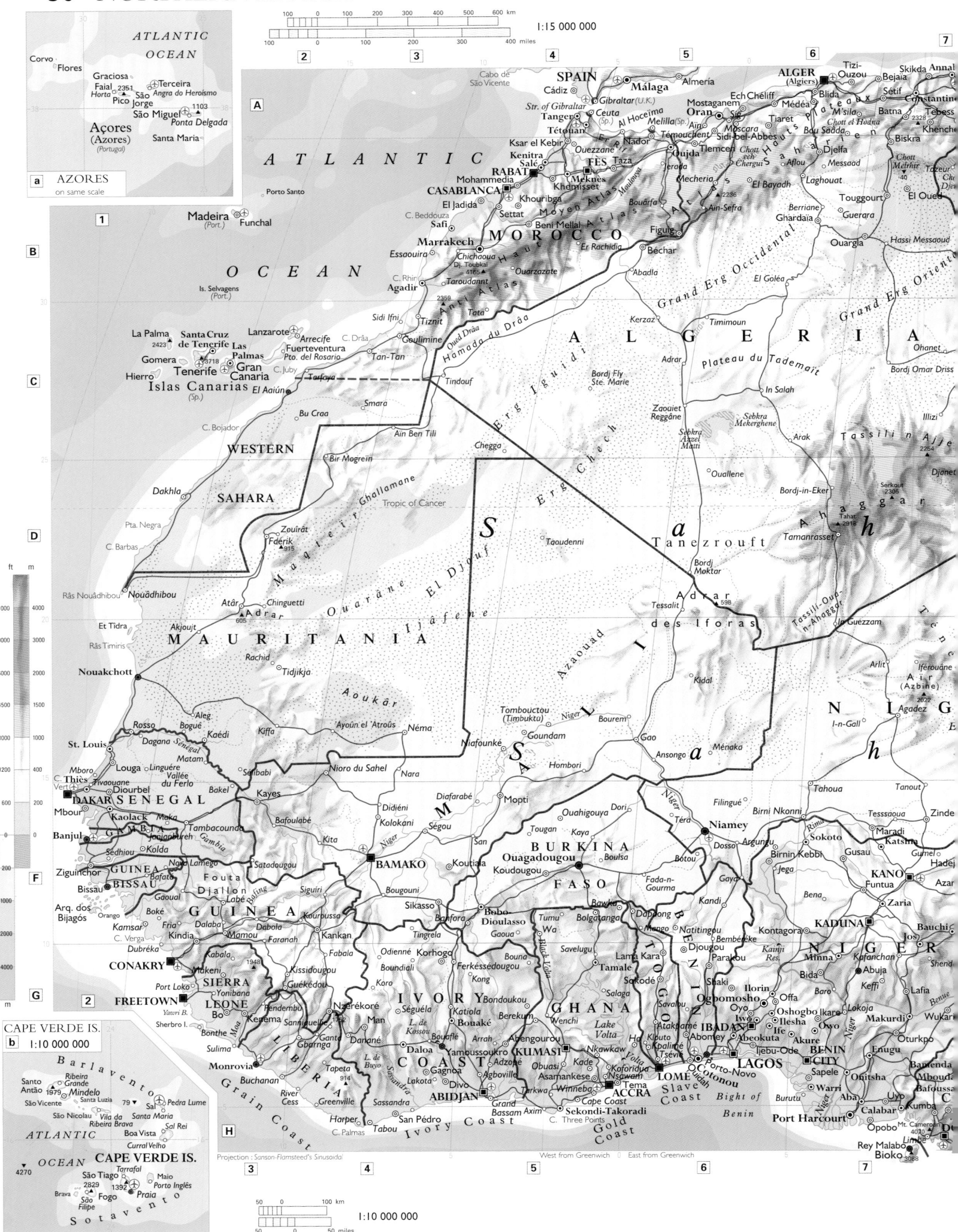

1:15 000 000

a AZORES
on same scale

ATLANTIC OCEAN

Corvo
Flores
Graciosa
Faial 2351 Terceira
Horta São Angra do Heroismo
Pico Jorge
São Miguel 1103
Ponta Delgada

Açores
(Azores)
(Portugal)
Santa Maria

b CAPE VERDE IS. 1:10 000 000

Barlavento
Santo Ribeira
Antão Grande 1979 Mindelo
São Vicente Santa Luzia
São Nicolau 79 Sal
Santa Maria Sal Rei
Vila da Boa Vista
Ribeira Brava Curral Velho

ATLANTIC OCEAN CAPE VERDE IS.
4270
Tarrafal
São Tiago
2829 Maio
Brava Fogo Porto Inglês
São Praia
Filipe 1392
Sotavento

1:10 000 000

a
b

8
9
10
11
12
13
14
A
B
C
D
E
F
G
H
47
52
MEDITERRANEAN SEA
Bizerte
CARTHAGE
Ra's at Tib (C. Bon)
TUNIS
Ariana
Béja
Nabeul
Pantelleria (It.)
Sicilia
ITALY
MALTA
Valletta
Sousse
Monastir
Mahdia
Lampedusa (It.)
Îles Kerkenna
Sfax
Golfe de Gabès
Gabès
Djerba
Zarzis
Médenine
Ben Gardane
Zuwārah
Az Zāwiyah
TARĀBULUS (Tripoli)
Al Khums
LEPTIS MAGNA
Misrātah
Gharyān
968
Mizdah
Tarābulus (Tripolitania)
Daraj
Ghadāmis
Al Hamādah al Hamrā'
Peloponnese
Cyclades
GREECE
Chania
Iraklio
Kriti
Rhodes
TURKEY
Antalya
Alanya
Anamur
İçel
ADANA
Hatay
HALAB (Aleppo)
Nahr al Furāt (Euphrates)
Al Lādhiqīyah
Hamāh
SYRIA
Hims
CYPRUS
Nicosia
Paphos
Limassol
Tarābulus
LEBANON
BAYRŪT (Beirut)
DIMASHQ (Damascus)
IRAQ
Ar Rutbah
Bādiyat ash Shām
Jabal ad Durūz 1800
Sūr
Hefa
ISRAEL
TEL AVIV-YAFO
Ashqelon
Jerusalem
WEST BANK
'AMMĀN
JORDAN
GAZA STRIP
CYRENE
Marsā Sūsah
Al Bayḍā
Darnah
Khalīj Bumbah
BANGHĀZĪ
Al Marj
Suluq
Tubruq
Bardīyah
Salûm
Surt
Khalīj Surt
Ajdābiya
Barqa (Cyrenaica)
Al Jaghbûb
Dahra
Hūn
Marādah
Awjilah
Zillah
Birāk
LIBYA
Sabhā
Idehan Awbārī
Awbārī
Al Harūj al Aswad
1200
Sarīr Calanscio
Sahrā' Lîbîya
Tazerbo
W. Barjūj
Marzūq
Fezzan
Wāw al Kabīr
Ghāt
1428
Al Qatrūn
Idehan Marzūq
Sahrā' Rebiana
Al Jawf
Al Kufrah
El Maḥalla el Kubra
Damanhûr
EL ISKANDARÎYA (Alexandria)
Marsâ Matrûh
El Alamein
Dumyât
Bûr Sa'îd (Port Said)
El Mansûra
Ismâ'ilîya
Qanâ es Suweis (Suez Canal)
Tanta
Zagazig
EL GÎZA
PYRAMIDS
EL QÂHIRA (Cairo)
El Suweis (Suez)
Helwân
Ed Déffa
Munkhafed el Qattâra
-133
Sîwa
Es Sahrâ' el Gharbîya
El Faiyûm
Beni Suef
Maghâgha
El Minyâ
Mallawi
Nahr en Nîl (Nile)
Es Sahrâ' esh Sharqîya
Es Sînâ'
Elat
Al 'Aqabah
G. Mûsa 2285
G. of Aqaba
Khalig el Suweis
Sharm el Sheikh
EGYPT
Manfalût
Asyût
Qasr Farâfra
Hurghada
2187
Bûr Safâga
Tahta
Sohâg
Girga
Qena
Quseir
THEBES
KARNAK
El Uqsur (Luxor)
El Khârga
Isna
Idfû
Kôm Ombo
Marsa Alam
Mût
El Wâhât el Dakhla
El Wâhât el Khârga
Sadd el Aali (Aswan High Dam)
Aswân
1977
Ras Bânâs
Bîr Shalatein
Halaib Triangle
Halaib
Ras Hadarba
Buheirat en Toshka
Buheirat en Naser (L. Nasser)
ABU SIMBEL
Wadi Halfa
Hadabat el Gilf el Kebîr
1082
J. Uweinat 1893
RED SEA
SAUDI ARABIA
Tabūk
2578
Al Muwaylih
Al Wajh
Al Jawf
Hijaz
Umm Lajj
Yanbu 'al Baḥr
Rābigh
Toummo
Madama
Chirfa
Aozou Strip
Sarīr Tibastī
Bikkū Bitti 2286
Bardai
Aozou
Pic Toussidé 3265
3376 Tarso Emissi
2910
Tibesti
Zouar
Emi Koussi 3415
Ma'tan as Sarra
Sahara
Ouniange Kébir
Borkou
Dépression du Mourdi
Faya-Largeau
Fachi
Bilma
Grand Erg de Bilma
Ténéré
Dépression du Bodéle
Fada
Ennedi
1310
Erg du Djourab
Zagaoua
Oum Chalouba
W. Howar (Shau)
CHAD
Ziguéy
Bahr el Ghazal
Mao
Moussoro
Biltine
Al Junaynah
Kutum
Malha
1954
Abéché
Nguigmi
Bosso
Lac Tchad
346
Massakory
Ati
Oum Hadjer
El Fâsher
Umm Keddada
Zalingei
J. Marrah 3088
Dârfûr
Nyâlâ
Ndjamena
Kousseri
Maiduguri
Geidam
Gashua
Titiwa
Potiskum
Bokoro
Mongo
Goz Beida
Massenya
Bitkine
Abou-Deïa
Am Timan
Chari
Bousso
Bongor
Bama
Goniri
Chibuk
Bajoga
Maroua
Biu
Kumo
Mubi
Guider
Birao
Numan
Jimeta
Garoua
Jalingo
Pala
Kélo
Laï
Logone
Harazé
Sarh
Koumra
Moundou
Doba
Goré
2042
Lac de Lagdo
1960
Baïbokoum
Ngaoundéré
Gashaka
Banyo
Lac de Mbakou
Meiganga
Tibati
Bétaré Oya
Yoko
Foumban
Paoua
Batangafo
Bossangoa
Bozoum
Bouar
Baboua
Carnot
Bossembélé
Bertoua
Nanga-Eboko
Batouri
Berbérati
YAOUNDÉ
Abong-Mbang
Bangui
Bimbo
Mbaïki
Zongo
Libenge
Bosobolo
Mobaye
Gbadolite
Bondo
Bangassou
Bakouma
Bambari
Sibut
Ippy
Bria
Yalinga
Kotto
Chinko
Ouarra
Bomu
Ubangi
CONGO
Uele
Ango
Dungu
CENTRAL AFRICAN REPUBLIC
Kaga Bandoro
Ndélé
Mt. Toussoro 1330
Massif des Bongos
Sa'id Bundas
Bahr el Ghazâl
Râgâ
Bahr el 'Arab
Ed Da'ein
El Odaiya
En Nahud
Kordofân
El Obeid
Abû Zabad
Er Rahad
Jibalan Nubah
1325
Kâdugli
Umm Ruwaba
Kôstî
Ed Dueim
Sodiri
El Wuz
SUDAN
Selîma
Es Sahrâ en Nûbîya
Kosha
Delgo
3rd Cataract
Dongola
Abu Hamed
Bir 'Atrun
Kareima
4th Cataract
5th Cataract
Ed Debba
Nahr en Nîl (Nile)
Berber
Atbara
Ed Dâmer
Wad Hamid
Shendî
6th Cataract
Nahr 'Atbara
Adarama
El Khartûm Bahrî
Omdurmân
EL KHARTÛM (Khartoum)
Kassalâ
Khashm el Girba
Wâd Medanî
Gedaref
El Gezira
Singa
Nil el Azraq (Blue Nile)
Nil el Abyad (White Nile)
Ed Damazin
Roseires Res.
Muhammad Qol
2259
Ras Abu Shagara
Bûr Sûdân
Suakin
Sinkat
Trinkitat
Haiya
Karora
2180
Nakfa
ERITREA
Akordat
Metema
Gonder
1830
L. Tana
Bahir Dar
Abay (Blue Nile)
Bure
Debre Markos
Nekemte
ETHIOPIA
3202
Dembidolo
Metu
Gore
Jima
3686
Omo
L. Abaya
Arba Minch
L. Shamo
Chew Bahir
Malakâl
Sobat
Bahr el Ghazâl
Jur
Sûdd
Bahr el Jebel (Nile)
Gogriál
Wâw
Tonj
Rumbêk
Pibor Post
Bôr
Toinya
Amadi
Tali Post
El Istwâ'îya
Yambio
Mongalla
Kapoeta
Elemi Triangle
Lokitaung
Jûbâ
Torit
Kajo Kaji
3187
Faradje
Yei
L. Turkana
375
15
20
25
30
35
40
10
5

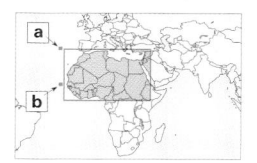

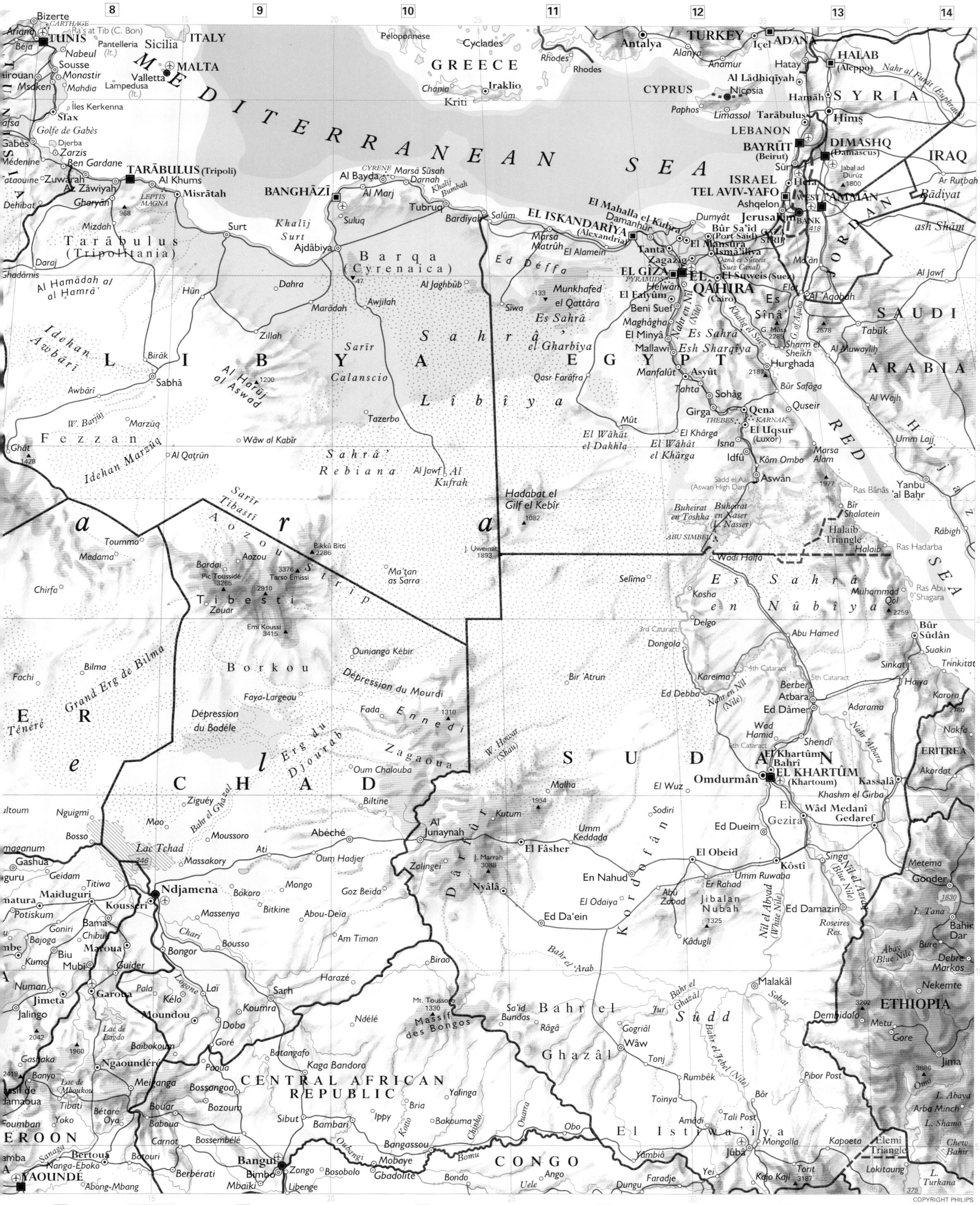

1:15 000 000

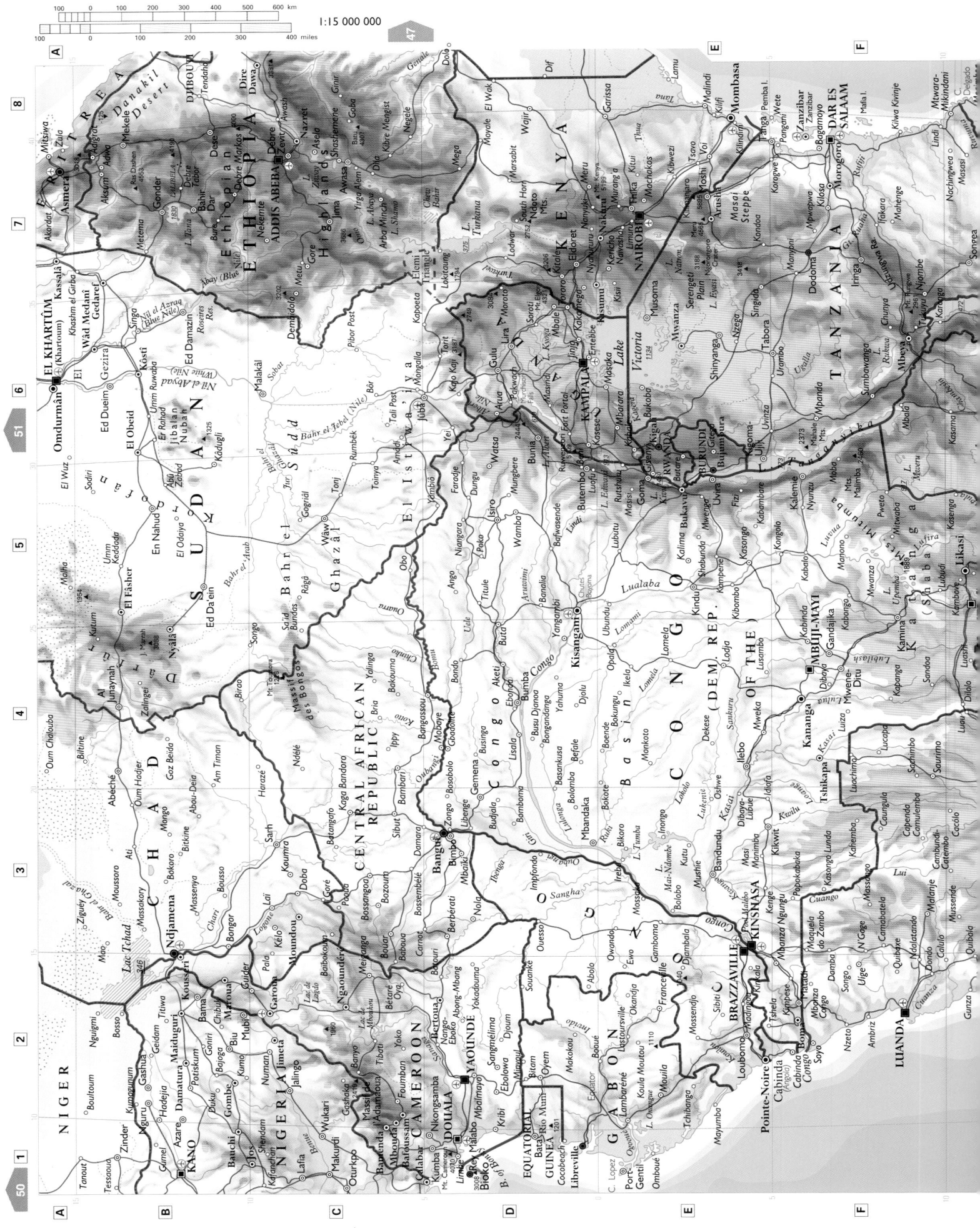

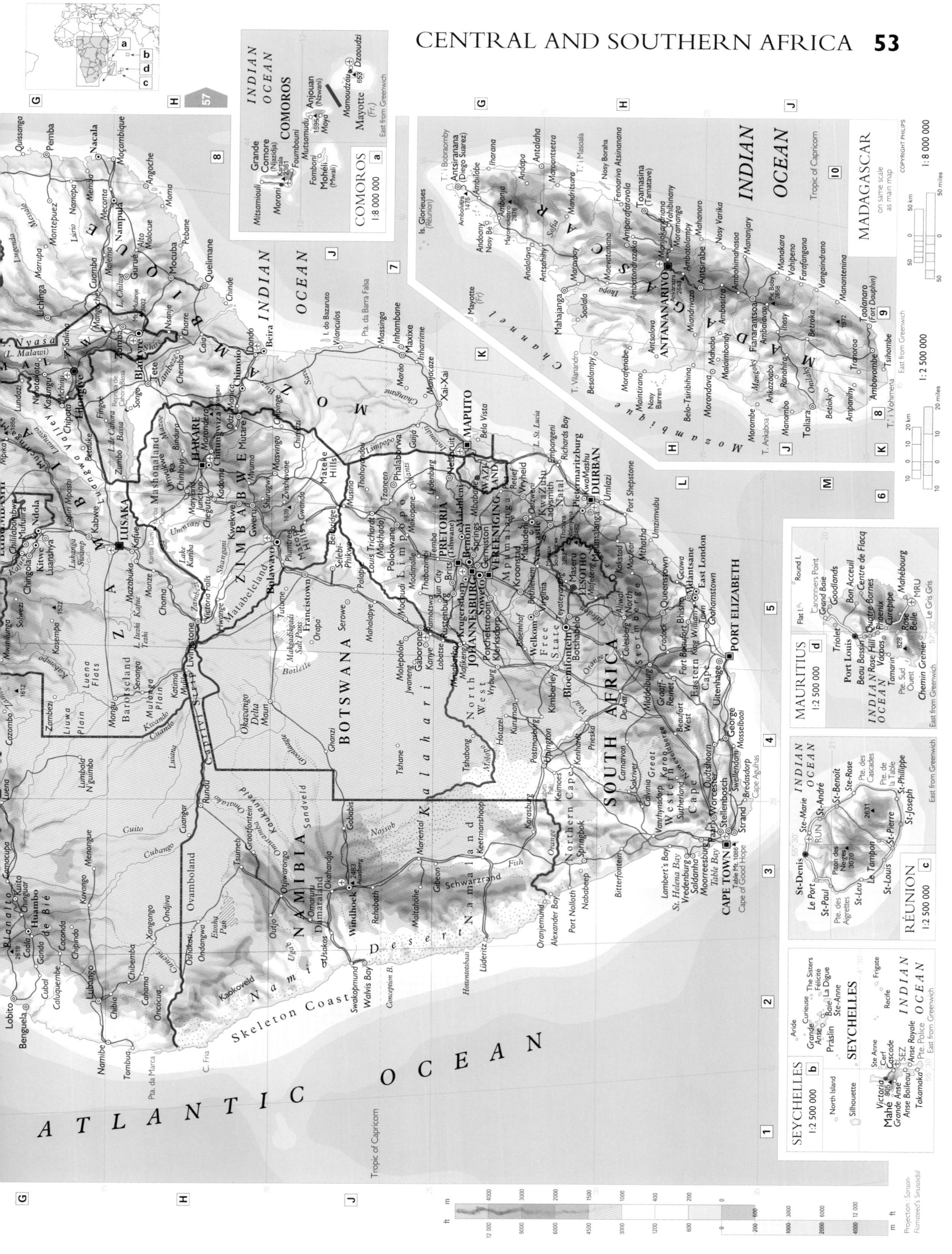

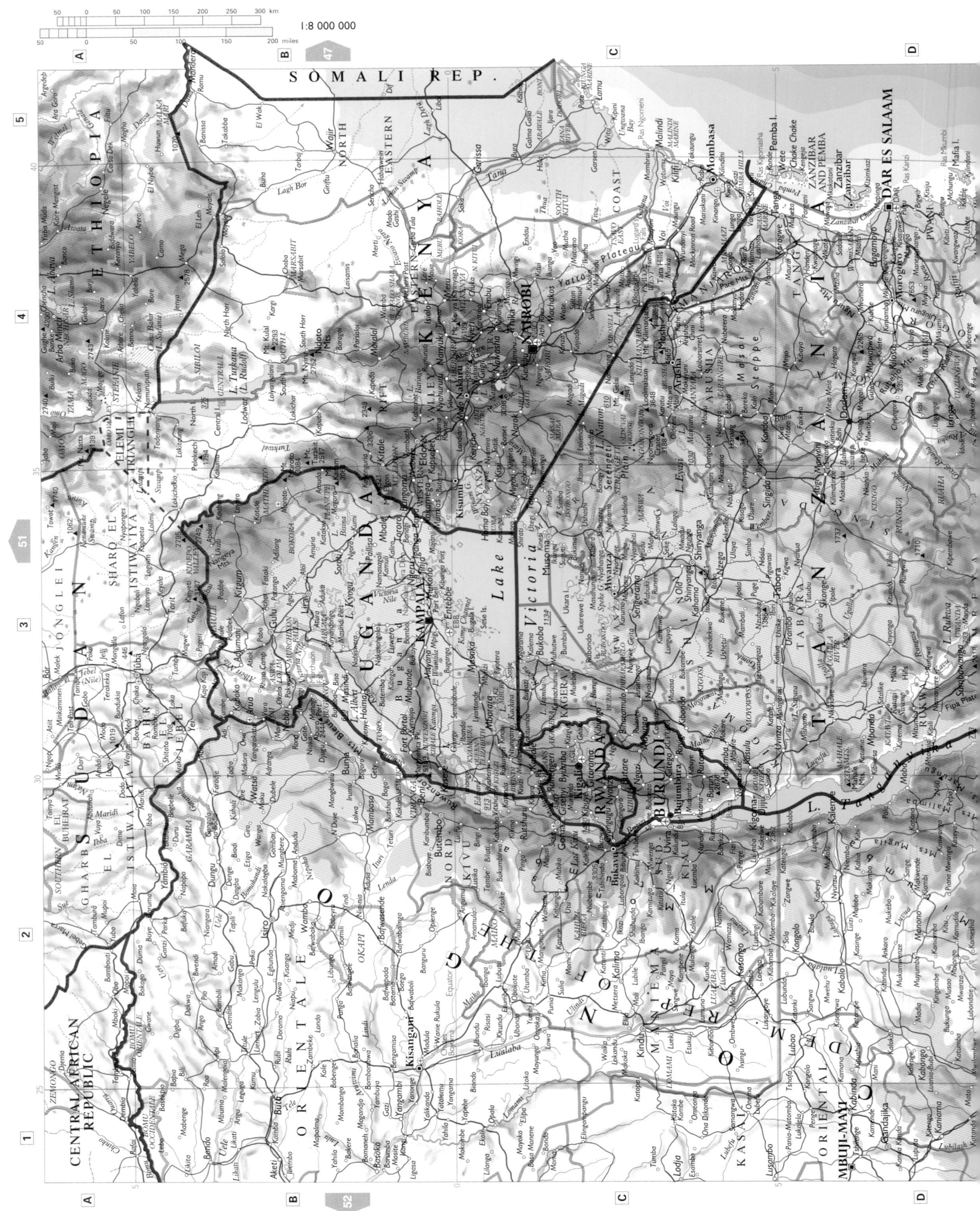

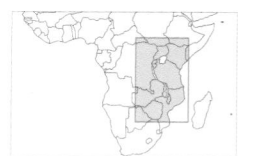

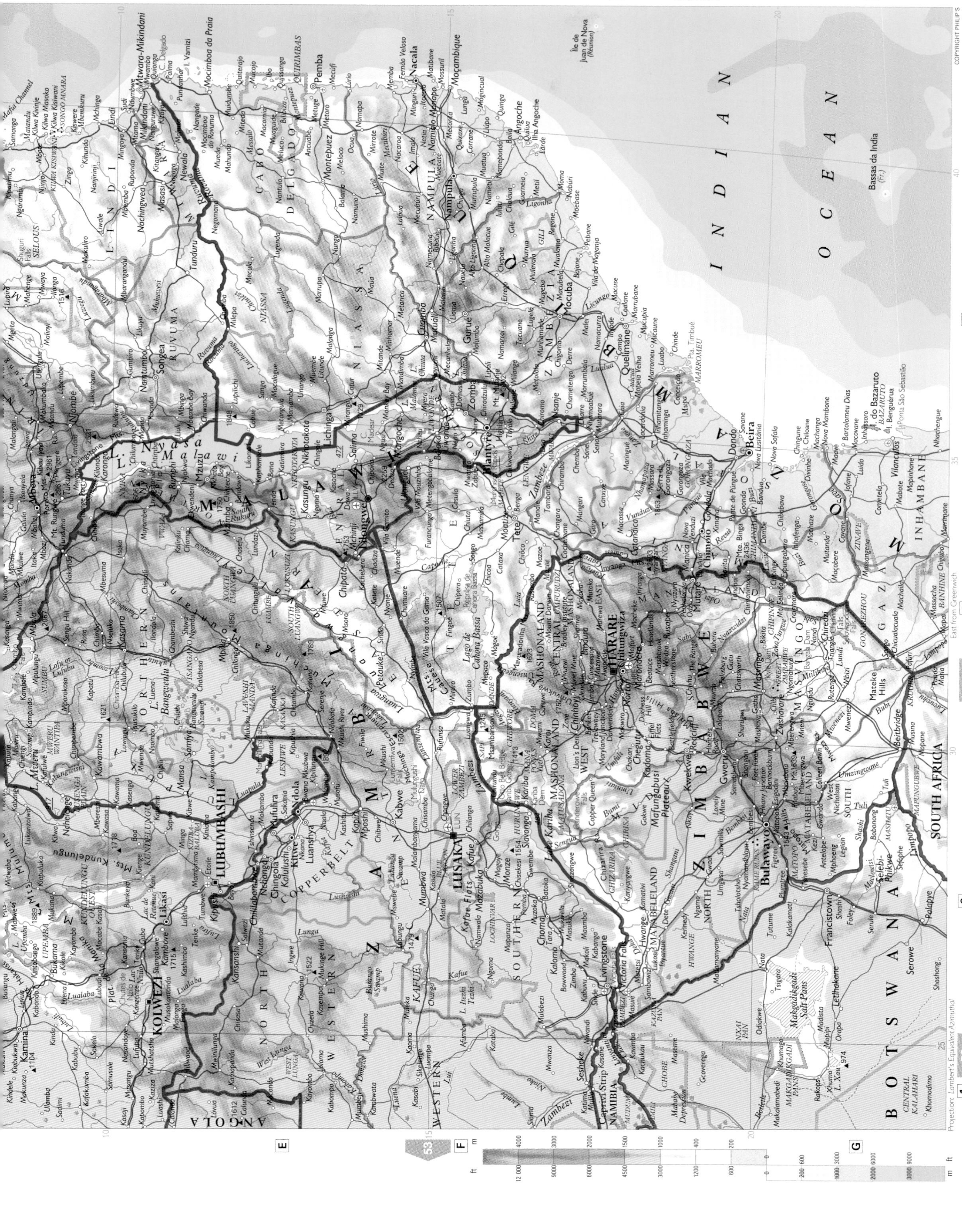
INDIAN
OCEAN
ZIMBABWE
BOTSWANA
LUSAKA
HARARE
SOUTH AFRICA
ANGOLA
COPYRIGHT PHILIP'S
Projection: Lambert's Equivalent Azimuthal

1:8 000 000

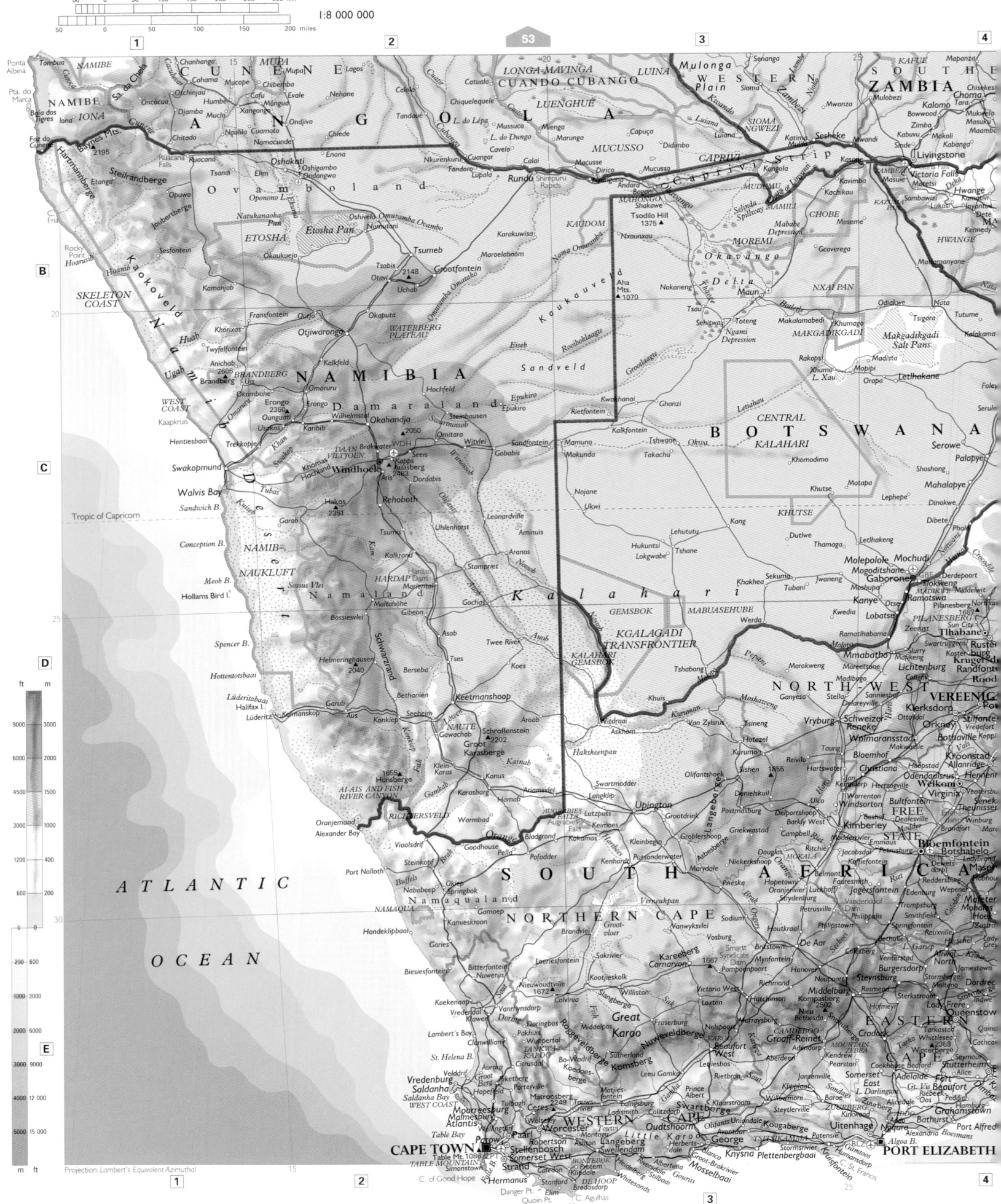

MADAGASCAR
1:8 000 000

INDIAN OCEAN

MOZAMBIQUE CHANNEL

MOZAMBIQUE

CHANNEL

INDIAN

OCEAN

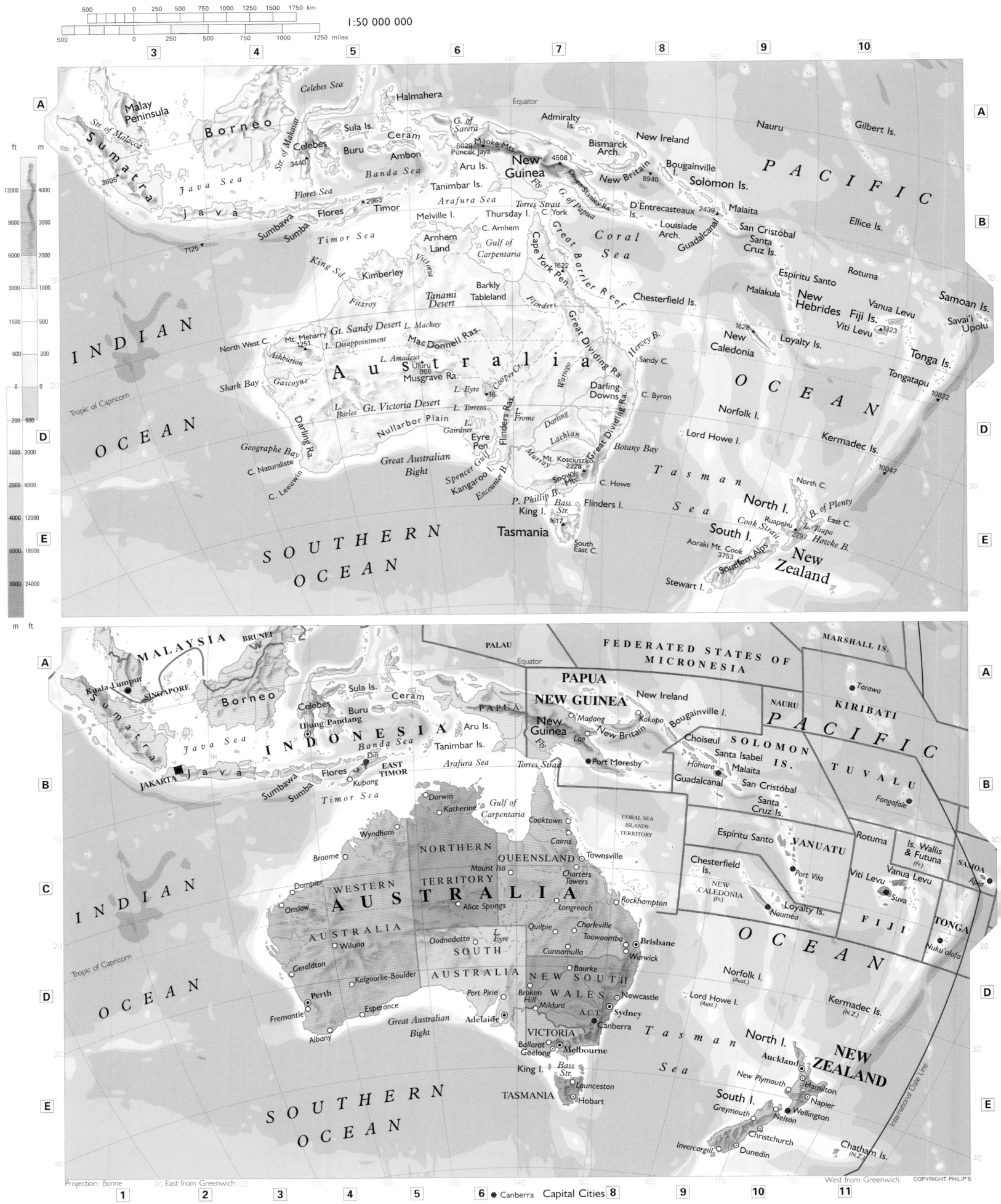

1:6 000 000

50 0 50 100 150 200 km
50 0 50 100 150 miles

FIJI a
on same scale

PACIFIC OCEAN

Great Sea Reef
Kia
Udu Pt.
Ringgold Is.
Yaqaga
Yasawa Group
Vanua Levu ▲1031
Labasa
Naduri Bay
Buca
Rabi
Yadua
Nacula
Somosomo
Qamea
Naviti
Savusavu
SAVUSAVU Bay
Taveuni
Vomo
Tavua
Rakiraki
Namenalala
Naitaba
Waya
Viwa
Nasau
Koro
Vacata
Vanua Balavu
Lomaloma
Mamanuca Group
Malolo
Tamanui ▲323
KORO Yani
Lawaki
Levuka
Koro
Vatu Vara
Mago
Cicia
Northern Lau Group
Lautoka
Nadi
Naval
KORO-NI-TU
Ovalau
Yunidawa
SEA
Batiki
Makogai
Nairai
Cicia
Tuvuca
Sigatoka
Koroley
Navua
Suva
Yanuca
Beqa
Nayau
Lakeba Passage
Tubou
Vanua Vatu
Lakeba
Oneata
Moala
Moce
Ono
Southern Lau Group
Namuka-i-Lau
Yagasa Cluster
Ogea Levu
Kadavu
Tavuki
Vunisea
Kadavu Passage
Totoya
Fulaga
Ogea Driki
Matuku

178 E 180 West from Greenwich Ogea Driki
East from Greenwich

SAMOA
Savai'i ▲1858
Falelima
Safune
Pu'apu'a
Saleloioga
Taga
Matautu
Salea'aula
Mulifanua
Falefa
Manono
'Upolu
Apia
OLE PUPU PU'E
Salani Bay
Amaile
Safata Bay

AMERICAN SAMOA (U.S.A.)
Ofu Olosega
Tau
AMERICAN SAMOA
Tutuila
Pago Pago
Leone
Vaitogi
Manu'a Is.

SAMOAN ISLANDS b
on same scale

West from Greenwich

TONGA c
on same scale

PACIFIC OCEAN

Fonualei
Toku
Vava'u
Neiafu
Late
Vava'u Group
Home Reef
Disney Reef
Ofolanga
Ha'ano
Tofua
Kao
Foa
Ha'apai
Lifuka
Uiha Ha'apai Group
Kotu Group
Fonuafo'ou
Nomuka
Oto Tolu Group
Hunga Ha'apai
Nomuka Group
Mango
Tonumea

TONGA
Nuku'alofa
Tongatapu
Tongatapu Group
Eua

West from Greenwich

TASMAN SEA

PACIFIC OCEAN

C. Reinga
North C.
C. Maria van Diemen
Houhora Heads
Rangaunu B.
Ahipara B.
Kaitaia
Okaihau
Waitangi
C. Brett
Tauroa Pt.
Rawene
Kaikohe
Opua
B. of Islands
Hokianga Harbour
Hikurangi
WHANGAREI
Waipoua Forest
Whangarei Harb.
Dargaville
Bream Hd.
Bream B.
C. Rodney
Little Barrier I.
Kaipara Harbour
Warkworth
Great Barrier I.
Helensville
Hauraki Gulf
C. Colville
Cuvier I.
Takapuna
Coromandel
Whitianga
AUCKLAND
Papakura
Thames
Manukau
Pukekohe
Waiuku
Mercer
Waihi
Whangamata
Mayor I.
Waikato
Morrinsville
Paeroa
Tauranga Harb.
Raglan
Huntly
Te Aroha
Mount Maunganui
Whakatane
Whakaari (White I.)
East C.
HAMILTON
Cambridge
Te Puke
Bay of Plenty
Runaway
Te Awamutu
Putaruru
Rotorua
Opotiki
Hikurangi ▲1753
Kawhia Harbour
Otorohanga
L. Rotorua
Matatua
Raukumara Ra.
Te Kuiti
Kihikihi
L. Tarawera
Murupara
Motu
Waitomo Caves
Mokai
Wairakei
UREWERA
Tolaga Bay
North Taranaki Bight
Mokau
Taupo
Rangitaiki
Waipiro
New Plymouth
Ongarue
L. Taupo
Waikaremoana
Gisborne
Inglewood
Taumarunui
Kaimai Mts.
Ormond
Mt. Taranaki or Mt. Egmont
WHANGANUI
Turangi
Tarawera
Poverty Bay
C. Egmont
Whangamomona
TONGARIRO
Ruahine Mts.
Wairoa
Opunake
2518 EGMONT
Ohakune
Waiouru
Mahia Pen.
Kapuni
Stratford
Raetihi
2197
Bay View
Hawke Bay
South Taranaki Bight
Eltham
Hawera
Taihape
Napier
Patea
Waverley
Mangaweka
C. Kidnappers
Wanganui
Bulls
Hunterville
Hastings
Halcombe
Waipawa
Marton
Feilding
Dannevirke
Waipukurau
Palmerston North
Woodville
Foxton
Shannon
Pahiatua
Paraparaumu
Levin
Otaki
Eketahuna
C. Turnagain
C. Farewell
Kapiti I.
Masterton
Golden B.
D'Urville I.
Pelorus
Carterton
Collingwood
ABEL TASMAN
Tasman B.
Featherston
Greytown
Takaka
Motueka
Upper Hutt
Martinborough
KAHURANGI
Tasman Mts.
Nelson
Havelock
Petone
Wairarapa
Karamea
Tadmor
Richmond
Lower Hutt
Karamea Bight
Motueka
Wakefield
Wellington
Seddonville
Matiri Ra.
NELSON LAKES
Picton
Cook Strait
Granity
Lyell
Murchison
Blenheim
Ward
Westport
Inangahua
L. Rotoroa
Seddon
Mt. Travers ▲2337
Spenser Mts.
PAPAROA
Punakaiki
Reefton
Kaikoura
Blackball
Grey
Hanmer Springs
Clarence
Runanga
Stillwater
Kumara
Waiau
Kaikoura
Greymouth
L. Brunner Jacksons
Hokitika
ARTHUR'S PASS
Waikari
Hurunui
Ross
Arthur's
Waipara
Pegasus Bay
Whitecliffs
Rangiora
Kaiapoi
Springfield
Oxford
Amberley
New Brighton
Westland
WESTLAND
Mt. Cook
Coleridge
Darfield
Riccarton
CHRISTCHURCH
Aoraki/Mt. Cook ▲3753
Waimakariri
Lyttelton
Akaroa
Mount Cook
Methven
Rakaia
Banks Pen.
Jackson B.
Okuru
Staveley
Selwyn
L. Ellesmere
Fairlie
Ashburton
Little River
MOUNT ASPIRING
Tekapo
Rakaia
Mt. Aspiring ▲3033
Canterbury Plains
Ohau
Rangitata
Temuka
Mt. Earnslaw ▲2819
L. Wanaka
Twizel
Timaru
Milford Sd.
Milford Sound
Wanaka
St. Andrews
Sutherland Falls
Arrowtown
Cromwell
Kurow
Waimate
Bligh Sound
Queenstown
Clyde
Naseby
Oamaru
George Sound
Otago
Maheno
Secretary I.
Wakatipu
Garvie Mts.
Alexandra
Hampden
Doubtful Sd.
FIORDLAND
Manapouri
Lumsden
Roxburgh
Dunback
Palmerston
Resolution I.
Dusky Sd.
Eyre Mts.
Ranfurly
Waikouaiti
Breaksea Sd.
L. Manapouri
Mossburn
Clinton
Port Chalmers
Southern
Edievale
Kelso
Waihola
Otago Harbour
Challis Inlet
Te Waewae B.
Orepuki
Pukerau
Milton
C. Saunders
Te Anau
Winton
Balclutha
DUNEDIN
Tuatapere
Heddon Bush
Mataura
Kaitangata
Nugget Pt.
Riverton
Gore
Wyndham
Owaka
Tahakopa
Invercargill
Bluff
Tokanui
Solander I.
Foveaux Str.
Ruapuke I.
South West C.
Halfmoon Bay
Stewart I. (Rakiura)
RAKIURA
Port Pegasus

North Island

South Island

Projection: Conical with two standard parallels

East from Greenwich

TAHITI & MOOREA d
1:1 000 000

Moorea (France)
Pte. Aroa
B. de Matavai
Pte. Vénus
Papetoai
Paopao
Mahina
Papeete
Arue
Pirae
Papenoo
Tiarei
Mt. Tohiea ▲1207
Faaa
Afareaitu
Pte. Nuupere
Haapiti
Punaauia
Faaone
Punaauia
Mt. Aorai ▲2060
Mt. Orohena ▲2241
Tahiti (France)
Hitiaa
Paea
Mt. Terufera ▲1799
Lac Vaihiria
Faaone
Tahiti
Maraa
Papara
Taravao
Isthme de Taravao
Atimaono
Mataiea
Afaahiti
Pte. Tatutua
Teahupoo
Mt. Rooniu ▲1332
Vairao
Tautira
Presqu'île de Taiarapu
Taravao

PACIFIC OCEAN

COPYRIGHT PHILIP'S

10 0 10 km
10 0 10 miles
1:1 000 000

ft m
9000 3000
6000 2000
3000 1000
1200 400
600 200
0 0
200 600
2000 6000
4000 12000
6000 18000
m ft

1:8 000 000

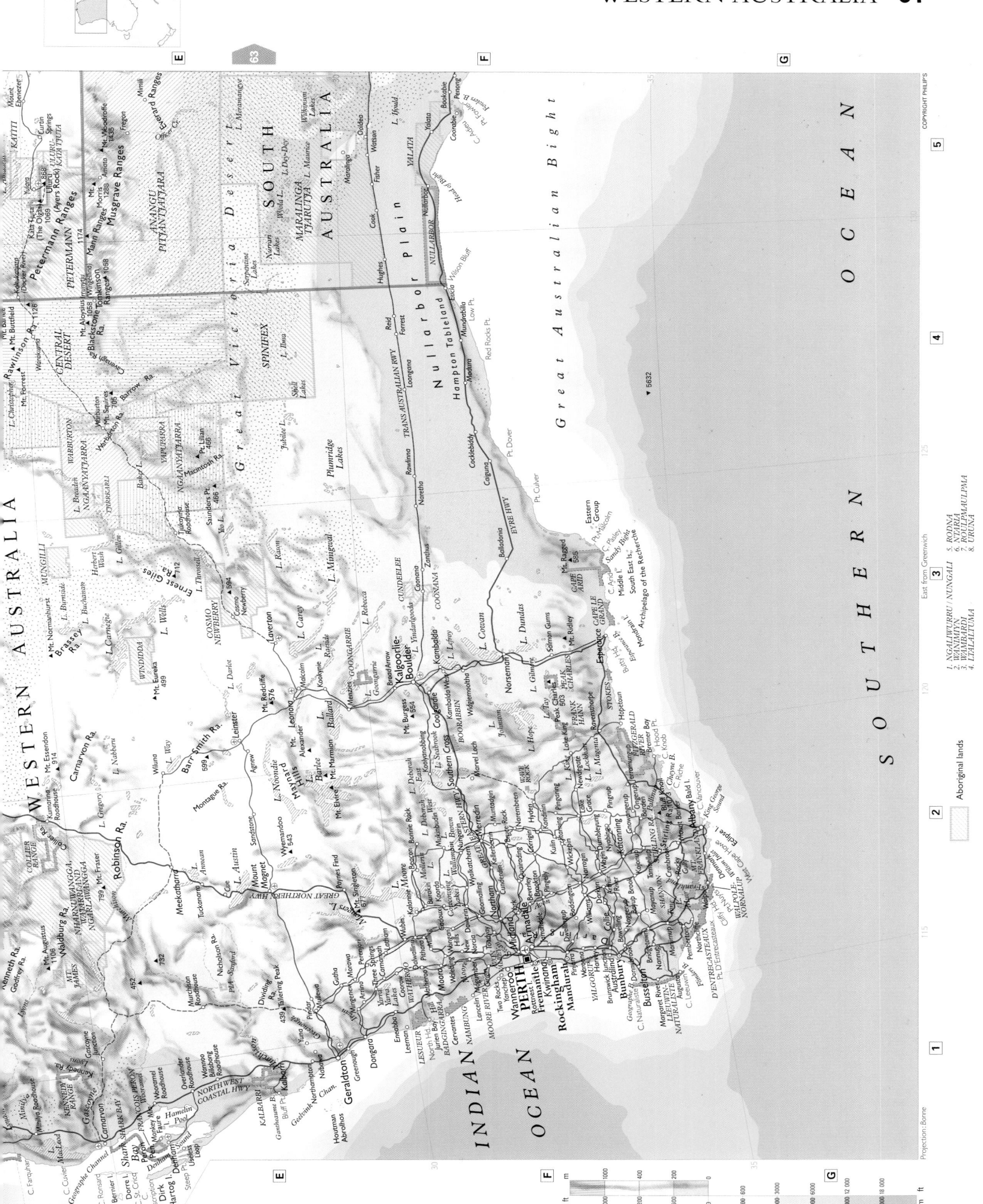

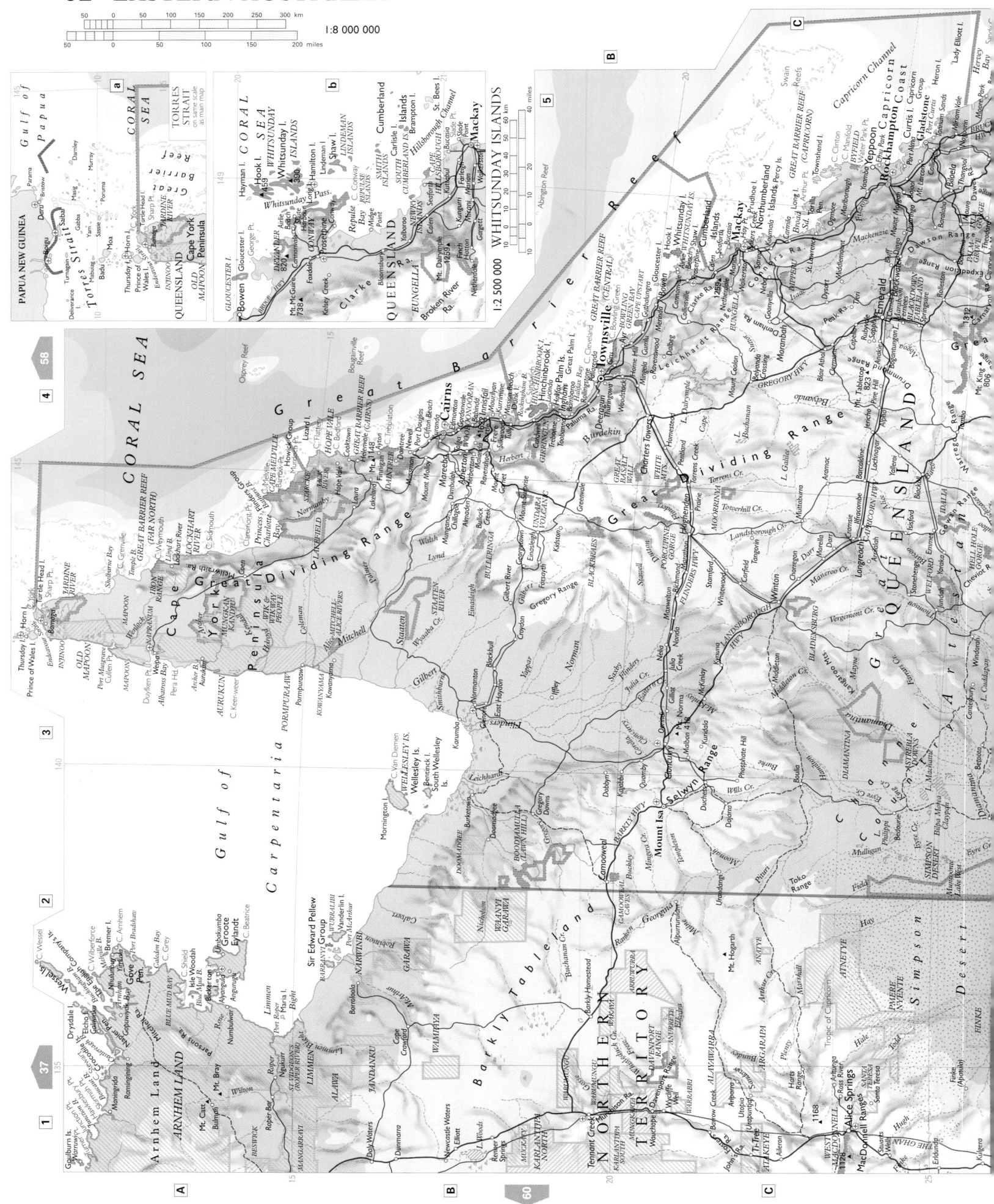

1:8 000 000

PAPUA NEW GUINEA

a

Gulf of Papua

CORAL SEA

TORRES STRAIT
on same scale
as main map

QUEENSLAND

OLD MAIPOON
Cape York Peninsula

Torres Strait

b

CORAL SEA

WHITSUNDAY
ISLANDS

Cumberland
ISLANDS

SMITH
ISLANDS

CUMBERLAND IS.

Mackay

QUEENSLAND

EUNGELLA

1:2 500 000

WHITSUNDAY ISLANDS

1:2 500 000

CORAL SEA

Gulf of Carpentaria

ARNHEM LAND

Arnhem Land

NORTHERN TERRITORY

Barkly Tableland

Alice Springs

MacDonnell Ranges

Simpson Desert

Cape York Peninsula

Great Dividing Range

GREAT BARRIER REEF
(FAR NORTH)

Cairns

Townsville

GREAT BARRIER REEF
(CENTRAL)

Mackay

Rockhampton

Gladstone

Capricorn Channel

Capricorn Coast

QUEENSLAND

Great Dividing Range

Mount Isa

Emerald

Longreach

Winton

SIMPSON DESERT

QUEENSLAND

NEW SOUTH WALES

SOUTH AUSTRALIA

VICTORIA

TASMANIA

TASMAN SEA

BRISBANE
SYDNEY
Canberra
MELBOURNE
ADELAIDE
Hobart
Newcastle
Wollongong

Bass Strait

COPYRIGHT PHILIP'S

Projection: Bonne

on same scale

Aboriginal lands

East from Greenwich

RUSSIA

Moskva
Volga
Yekaterinburg
Ob'
Tomsk
Novosibirsk
Irkutsk
Lena
Oz. Baykal
Chita
Astana (Aqmola)
Semey
Okhotsk
Sea of Okhotsk
Komandorskiye Ostrova (Russia)
Bering Sea
Near Is. (U.S.A.)
Andreanof Is. (U.S.A.)
Aleutian Basin

KAZAKHSTAN
Aral Sea
Balqash Köl
Altai
Blagoveshchensk
Sakhalin
Khabarovsk
Petropavlovsk-Kamchatskiy
Poluostrov Kamchatka
Shirshov Ridge (Russia)
Aleutian Trench
7822

MONGOLIA
Ulaanbaatar
Harbin
Changchun
Vladivostok
Sapporo
Hakodate
La Perouse Str.
Kurilskiye Ostrova
Kuril-Kamchatka Trench (Russia)
10,542
Northwest
Emperor Trough
Chinook Trough

Almaty
Ürümqi
KYRGYZSTAN
Shenyang
Sea of Japan
Emperor Seamount Chain
Pacific

Toshkent
TAJIKISTAN
Beijing
NORTH KOREA
Sendai
Shatsky Rise
Basin

Afghanistan
Kābul
Srinagar
Kunlun Shan
XIZANG
Lanzhou
Tianjin
Taiyuan
Dalian
Seoul
SOUTH KOREA
Nagoya
Kyōto
Fuji-San 3776
Tōkyō
Yokohama
Ozima-Ridge
Hō

PAKISTAN
Lahore
Delhi
Himalaya
Mt. Everest 8850
Lhasa
Xi'an
Qingdao
Kitakyūshū
Osaka JAPAN
Shikoku
Kyūshū
10,554
Japan Trench
Midway Is. (U.S.A.)

Kanpur
Ganga
NEPAL
Brahmaputra
Chongqing
Wuhan
Nanjing
Shanghai
East China Sea
Okinawa
Ryūkyū-rettō (Japan)
Iwo-Jima (Japan)
Kazan-Rettō (Japan)
Minami-Tori-Shima (Japan)
Wake I. (U.S.A.)
Lisianski I. (U.S.A.)

Kolkata (Calcutta)
Dhaka
BANGLADESH
Changsha
Hangzhou
Fuzhou
Taipei
TAIWAN
Philippine Sea
West Mariana Basin
NORTHERN MARIANAS (U.S.A.)
East Mariana Basin
Mid-Pacific Mountain
PA

INDIA
BURMA
Mandalay
Kunming
Guangzhou
Hong Kong
Macau
Hanoi
Hainan
Luzon
C. Engano
Philippine Basin
Kyushu-Palau Ridge
West Mariana Basin
Tinian
Saipan
MARSHALL IS.
Bikini Atoll

Hyderabad
Bay of Bengal
Rangoon
LAOS
Paracel Is.
Manila
PHILIPPINES
GUAM (U.S.A.)
Challenger Deep 11,022
Mariana Trench
Micronesia
Enewetak Atoll
Ratak Chain
Ralik Chain

Chennai (Madras)
Andaman Is. (India)
THAILAND
Bangkok
CAMBODIA
Phnom Penh
VIETNAM
Mekong
South China Sea
Mindoro
Samar
10,497
Yap
Caroline Is.
Chuuk
FED. STATES OF MICRONESIA
Pohnpei
Palikir
Jaluit I.
Majuro
Kwajalein

SRI LANKA
Colombo
Nicobar Is. (India)
G. of Thailand
Thanh Pho Ho Chi Minh
Palawan
Sulu Sea
Mindanao
Davao
Mindanao Trench
Melekeok
PALAU
West Caroline Basin
Eauripik Rise
East Caroline Basin
Solomon Rise
Melanesian Basin
Butaritari
Tarawa
Pacific

MALAYSIA
Kuala Lumpur
PEN. MALAYSIA
Singapore
SARAWAK
BRUNEI
SABAH
4101
Celebes Sea
Maluku
Halmahera
Seram
Melanesia
PAPUA NEW GUINEA
Admiralty Is.
New Ireland
NAURU
Banaba
Gilbert Is.
Phoenix Is.
Abariringa
Enderbury
Howland I. (U.S.A.)
Baker I. (U.S.A.)

Sumatera
Sunda Islands
Palembang
Java Sea
Jakarta
Jawa
Surabaya
Bali
Borneo
Ujung Pandang
Sulawesi
Buru
INDONESIA
Banda Sea
7440
Flores
Flores Sea
Dili
EAST TIMOR
Timor
Puncak Jaya 5029
PAPUA
New Guinea
Lae
Bismarck Arch.
Kokopo
8940
Bougainville
SOLOMON IS.
Honiara
Guadalcanal
Santa Cruz I.
9165
Tarawa
KIRIBATI
Fongafale
TUVALU
Tokelau Is. (N.Z.)

INDIAN OCEAN
Ninetyeast Ridge
Cocos Is. (Austral.)
Christmas I. (Austral.)
Selat Sunda
Java Trench
Sumbawa
Sumba
North Australian Basin
Arafura Sea
Torres Strait
C. York
Port Moresby
Louisiade Arch.
New Britain
Coral Sea Basin
Espiritu Santo
Rotuma
Is. Wallis & Futuna (Fr.)
SAMOA
Apia

ft m
12 000 4000
9000 3000
6000 2000
3000 1000
1500 500
600 200
0 0
200 600
1000 3000
2000 6000
4000 12 000
6000 18 000
8000 24 000
m ft

C. Arnhem
Darwin
Gulf of Carpentaria
Cairns
Townsville
Coral Sea
Ìs. Chesterfield
VANUATU
Port Vila
West Fiji Basin
Vanua Levu
Viti Levu
Suva
FIJI
Nuku'alofa
TONGA

Wharton Basin
Exmouth Plateau
Broome
North West C.
Mount Isa
Alice Springs
AUSTRALIA
Rockhampton
NEW CALEDONIA (Fr.)
Nouméa
Is. Loyauté
7570
South Fiji Basin
10,822
Tonga Trench

Geraldton
Perth Basin
Perth
L. Eyre
Brisbane
Middleton Basin
Lord Howe Rise
Norfolk I. (Austral.)
Kermadec Is. (N.Z.)
Kermadec Trench
10,047

Naturaliste Plateau
Albany
Great Australian Bight
Adelaide
Murray
Darling
Lord Howe I. (Austral.)
Sydney
Canberra
Mt. Kosciuszko 2228
Tasman Sea
New Caledonia Trough
South Fiji Basin
NEW ZEALAND
Auckland

Nouvelle Amsterdam (Fr.)
I. St. Paul (Fr.)
Melbourne
Bass Str.
Tasmania
Hobart
East Tasman Plateau
Tasman Basin
Aoraki Mt. Cook 3753
Christchurch
Chatham Rise
Chatham Is. (N.Z.)
Wellington
Cook Strait

Mid-Indian Ridge
SOUTHERN
South Australian Basin
South Tasman Rise
Dunedin
Bounty Trough
Bounty Is. (N.Z.)
Invercargill
Antipodes Is. (N.Z.)
Campbell Plateau

Is. Crozet (Fr.)
Kerguelen (Fr.)
Heard I. (Austral.)
OCEAN
Auckland Is. (N.Z.)
Macquarie Is. (Austral.)
Campbell I. (N.Z.)

Projection: Mollweide's Homolographic
East from Greenwich

1:35 000 000

Projection: Bonne

West from Greenwich

COPYRIGHT PHILIP'S

1:35 000 000

100 0   200 400 600 800 1000 1200 1400 km

100 0   200   400   600   800   1000 miles

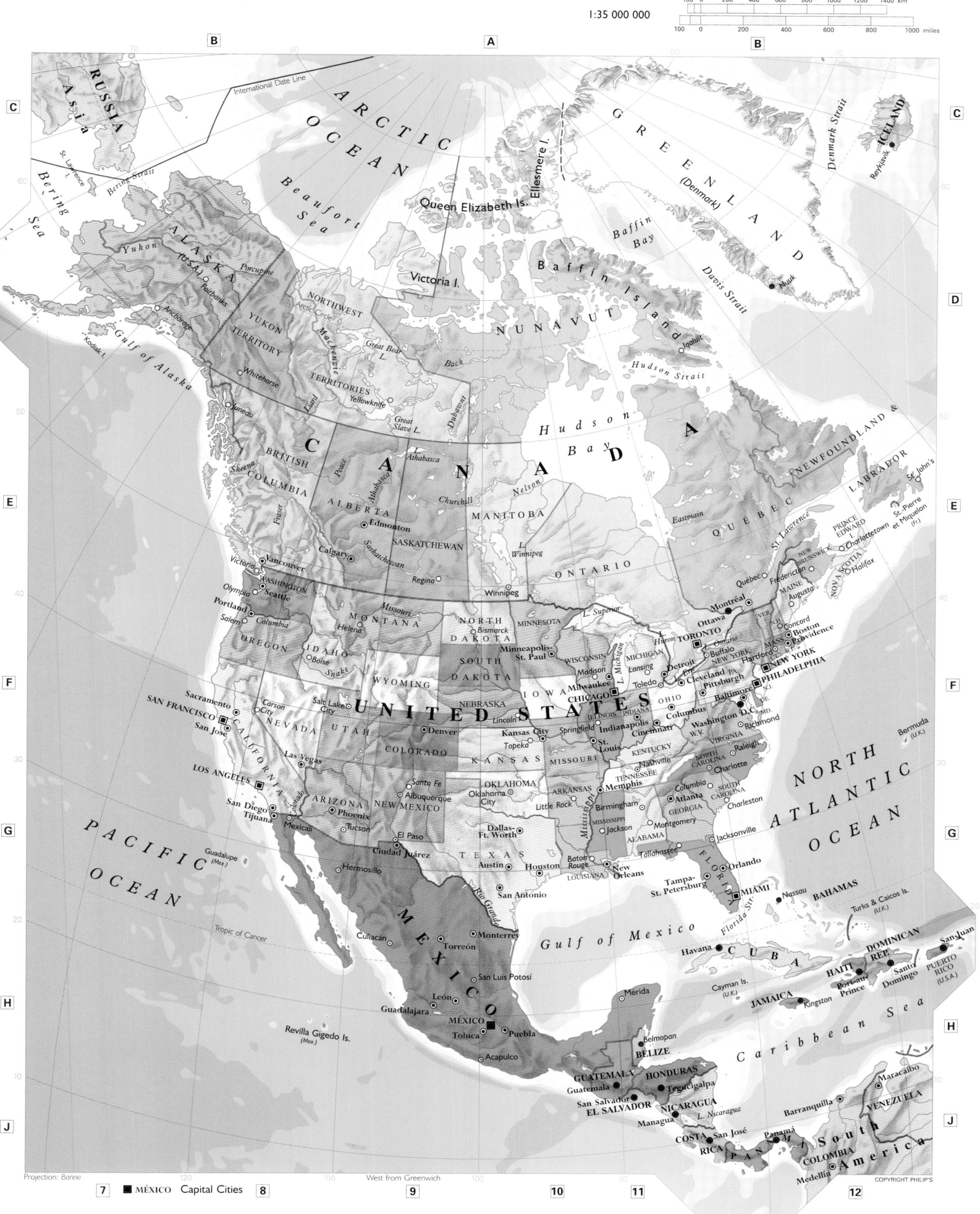

Projection: Bonne

West from Greenwich

COPYRIGHT PHILIP'S

7   ■ MÉXICO Capital Cities   8   9   10   11   12

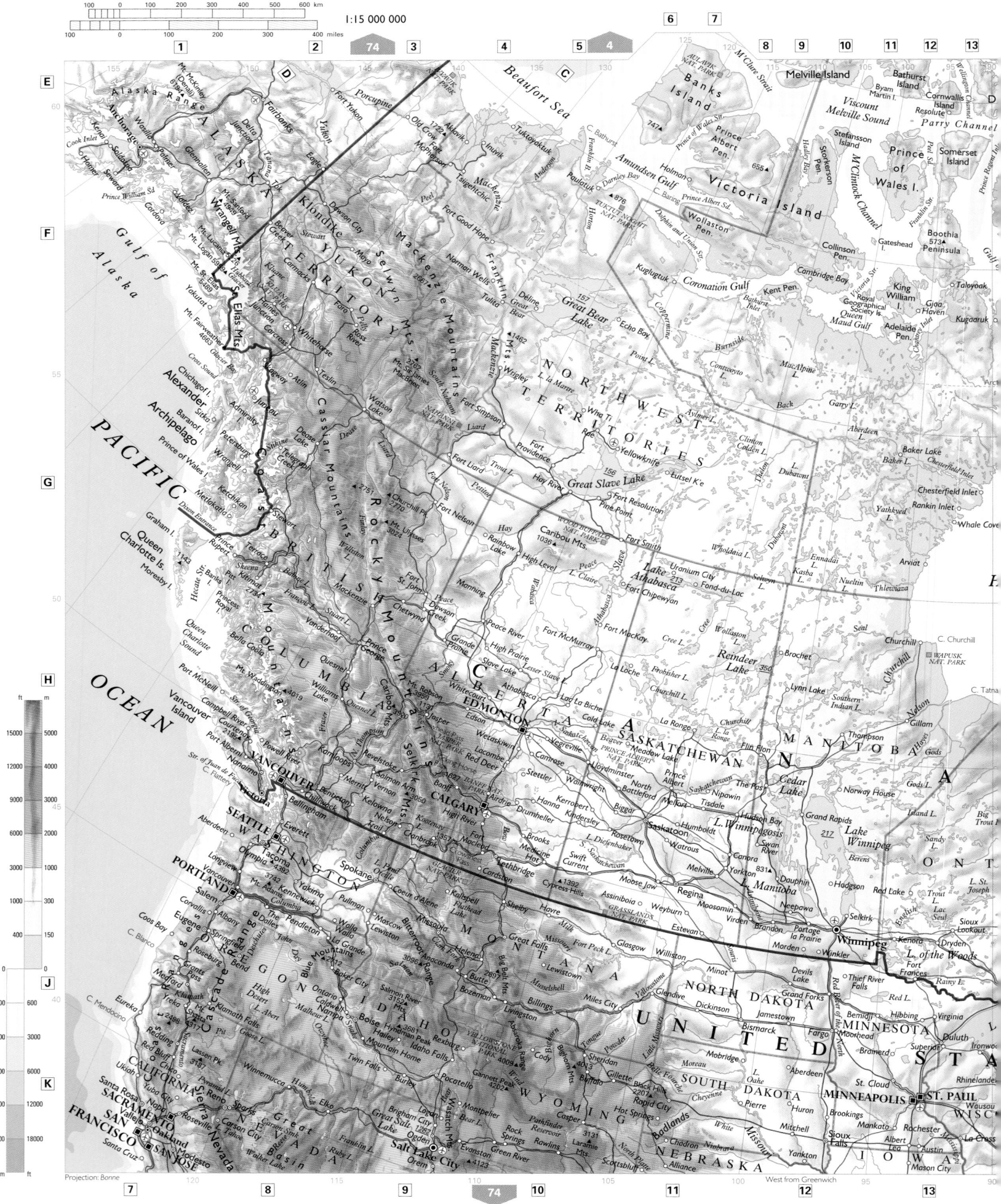

Projection: Bonne

1:15 000 000

West from Greenwich

NORTHERN CANADA
continuation northwards on same
scale as main map

ARCTIC OCEAN

GREENLAND (KALAALLIT NUNAAT)

Kronprins Frederik Land

Knud Rasmussen Land

Ellesmere Island

Queen Elizabeth Islands

NUNAVUT

N.W.T.

Parry Islands

Melville Island

Devon Island

Prince of Wales I.

Somerset Island

Baffin Bay

Baffin Bay

Lancaster Sound

Nunavik

Davis Strait

Baffin Island

Cumberland Peninsula

Foxe Basin

NUNAVUT

Hudson Strait

Southampton I.

Foxe Channel

Hudson Bay

Péninsule d'Ungava

Ungava Bay

Labrador Sea

ATLANTIC OCEAN

James Bay

Labrador

NEWFOUNDLAND & LABRADOR

Newfoundland

QUÉBEC

Gulf of St. Lawrence

PRINCE EDWARD I.

NEW BRUNSWICK

NOVA SCOTIA

ONTARIO

MONTRÉAL

OTTAWA

Québec

TORONTO

Lake Huron

Lake Ontario

Lake Erie

DETROIT

CLEVELAND

MAINE

NEW HAMPSHIRE

VERMONT

NEW YORK

MASS.

BOSTON

PROVIDENCE

CONN.

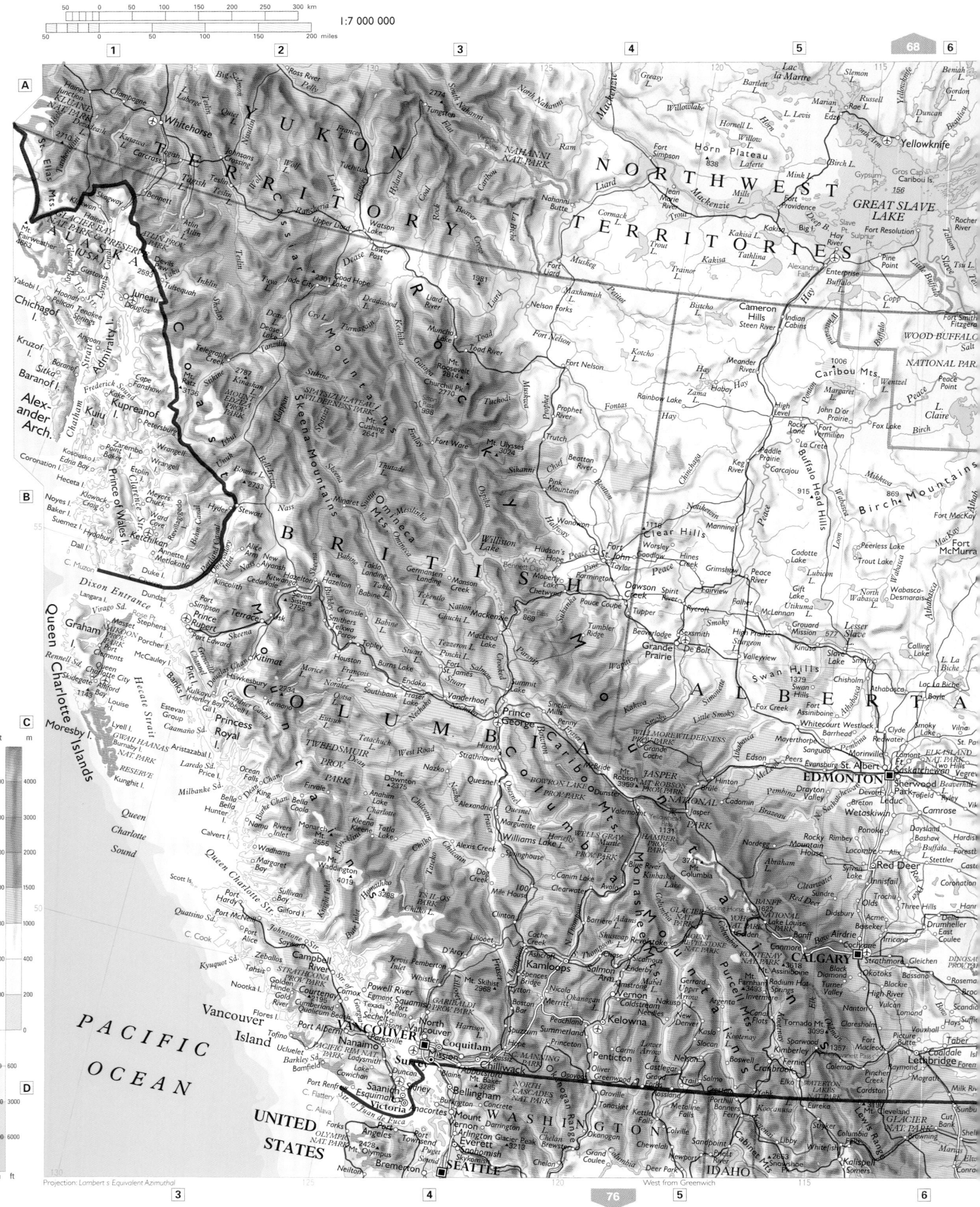

50   0   50   100   150   200   250   300 km

1:7 000 000

50   0   50   100   150   200 miles

Projection: Lambert's Equivalent Azimuthal

West from Greenwich

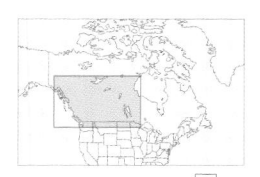

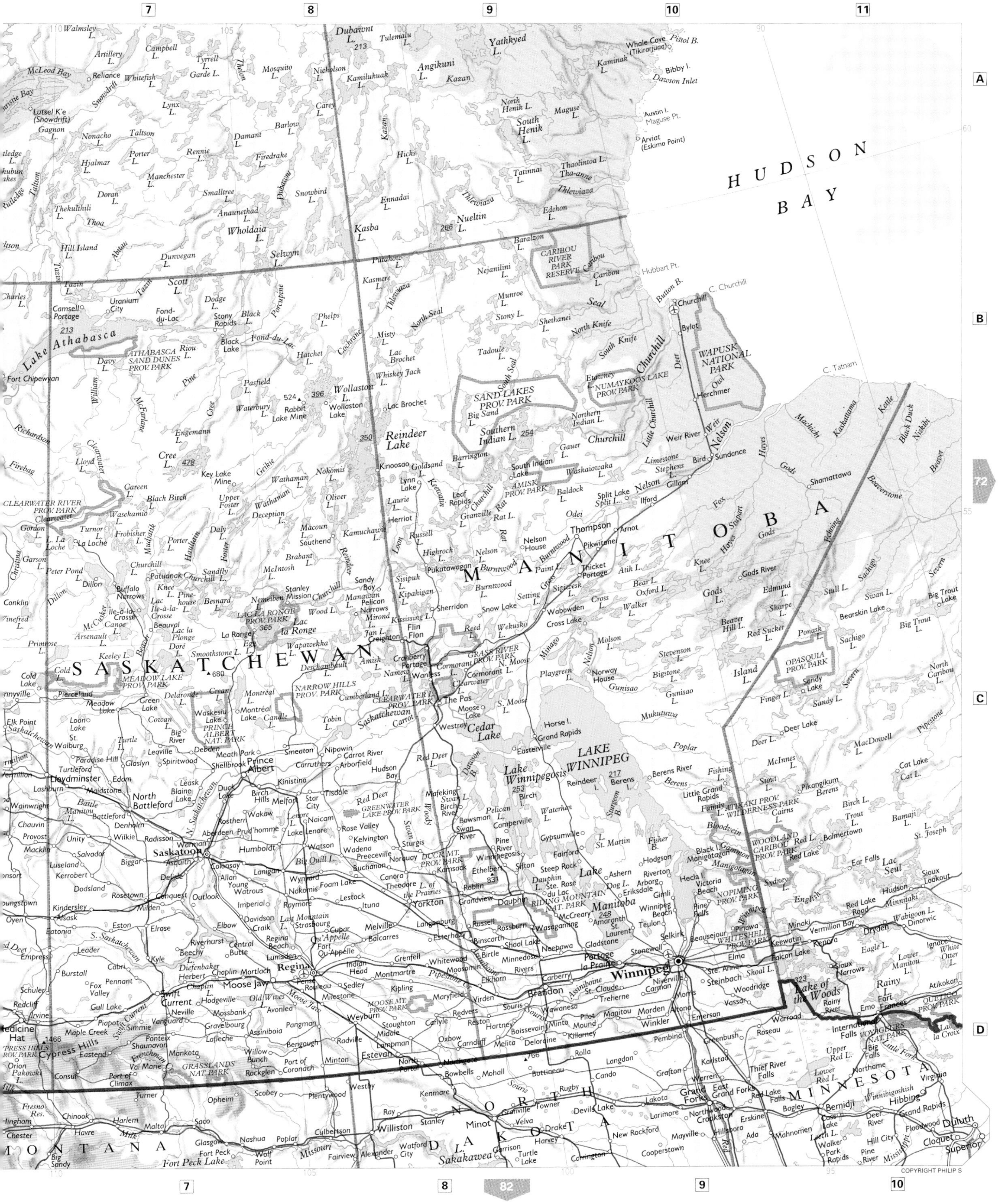
HUDSON BAY
SASKATCHEWAN
MANITOBA
NORTH DAKOTA
MINNESOTA
MONTANA
Lake Athabasca
Reindeer Lake
Wollaston L.
LAKE WINNIPEG
Lake Winnipegosis
Lake Manitoba
Cedar Lake
Lake of the Woods
Churchill
Thompson
Flin Flon
The Pas
Prince Albert
Saskatoon
Regina
Moose Jaw
Swift Current
Yorkton
Brandon
Winnipeg
Portage la Prairie
Kenora
Dryden
Medicine Hat
Lloydminster
North Battleford
Minot
Grand Forks
Bemidji
Duluth
Superior
International Falls
Fort Frances
Arviat (Eskimo Point)
Whale Cove (Tikirarjuaq)
WAPUSK NATIONAL PARK
PRINCE ALBERT NAT. PARK
RIDING MOUNTAIN NAT. PARK
GRASSLANDS NAT. PARK
VOYAGEURS NAT. PARK
Cypress Hills
COPYRIGHT PHILIP S

72
82

1:7 000 000

Projection: Lambert's Equivalent Azimuthal

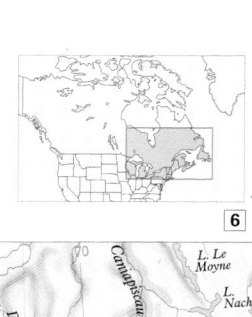

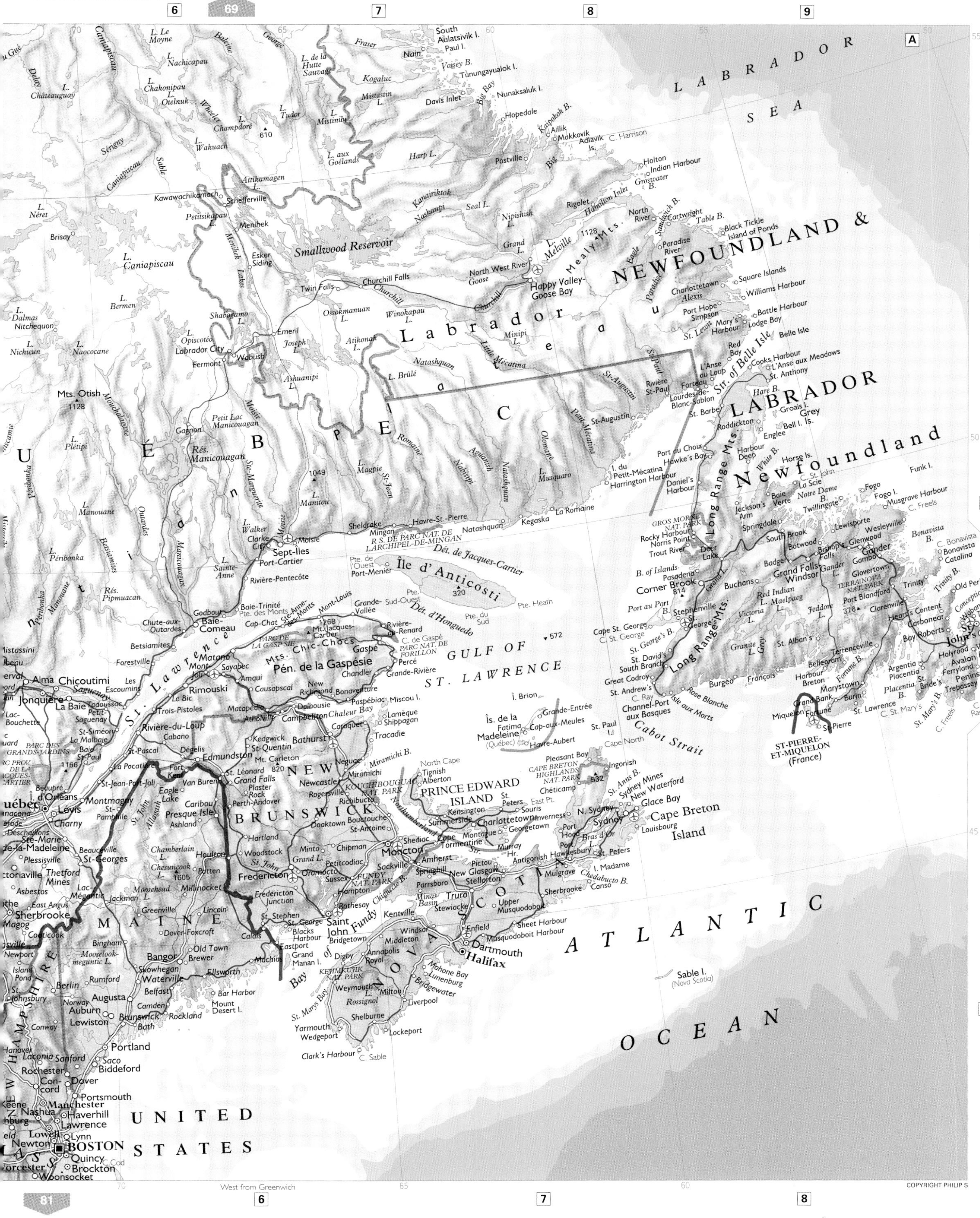

6
69
7
8
9
A
B
C
D
LABRADOR SEA
NEWFOUNDLAND & LABRADOR
Labrador
Newfoundland
QUÉBEC
NEW BRUNSWICK
NOVA SCOTIA
PRINCE EDWARD ISLAND
MAINE
UNITED STATES
GULF OF ST. LAWRENCE
ATLANTIC OCEAN
ST-PIERRE-ET-MIQUELON (France)
Île d' Anticosti
Cabot Strait
Str. of Belle Isle
Bay of Fundy
Chaleur Bay
Northumberland Str.
Smallwood Reservoir
Mealy Mts.
Long Range Mts.
Mts. Chic-Chocs
Pén. de la Gaspésie
Cape Breton Island
Sable I. (Nova Scotia)
Îs. de la Madeleine (Québec)
Mts. Otish 1128
Rés. Manicouagan
St. Lawrence
Nain
Hopedale
Postville
Rigolet
Cartwright
Happy Valley-Goose Bay
North West River
Churchill Falls
Labrador City
Wabush
Fermont
Schefferville
Sept-Îles
Port-Cartier
Baie-Comeau
Havre-St.-Pierre
Natashquan
Kegaska
La Romaine
St-Augustin
Blanc-Sablon
L'Anse aux Meadows
St. Anthony
Corner Brook
Deer Lake
Stephenville
Grand Falls-Windsor
Gander
Lewisporte
Clarenville
St. John's
Mt Pearl
Channel-Port aux Basques
Burgeo
St-Pierre
Miquelon
Gaspé
Matane
Rimouski
Rivière-du-Loup
Chicoutimi
Jonquière
Québec
Lévis
Sherbrooke
Campbellton
Bathurst
Edmundston
Fredericton
Moncton
Saint John
Miramichi
Charlottetown
Summerside
Sydney
Glace Bay
Halifax
Dartmouth
Truro
Yarmouth
Digby
Kentville
Bangor
Augusta
Portland
Lewiston
Auburn
Manchester
Nashua
Lowell
Lawrence
Haverhill
BOSTON
Quincy
Brockton
Woonsocket
West from Greenwich
70
65
60
55
50
45
81
6
7
8

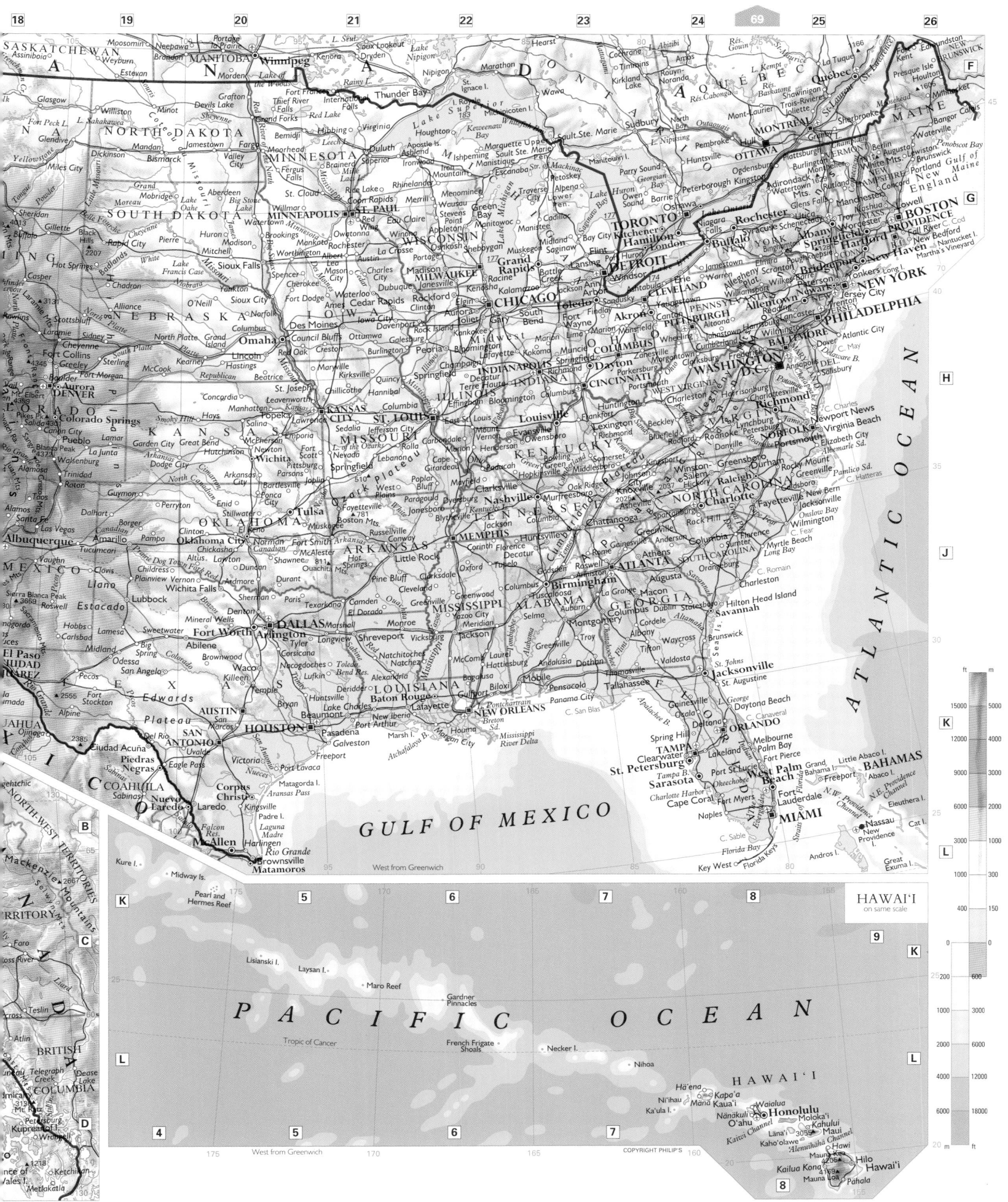

Projection: Albers' Equal Area with two standard parallels

West from Greenwich

Lava fields

1:2 500 000

WESTERN WASHINGTON REGION
on same scale

PACIFIC OCEAN

1:6 700 000

Projection: Albers' Equal Area with two standard parallels

West from Greenwich

ATLANTIC OCEAN
Gulf of Maine
LAKE ONTARIO
LAKE ERIE
LAKE HURON
Georgian Bay
Manitoulin I.
QUEBEC
ONTARIO
CANADA
MAINE
NEW HAMPSHIRE
VERMONT
NEW YORK
PENNSYLVANIA
NEW JERSEY
DELAWARE
MARYLAND
VIRGINIA
WEST VIRGINIA
OHIO
NORTH CAROLINA
SOUTH CAROLINA
GEORGIA
MA.
CT.
R.I.
NEW BRUNS.
Allegheny Plateau
Allegheny Mountains
Appalachian Mountains
Cumberland Plateau
Blue Ridge
Adirondack Mts.
ADIRONDACK PARK
Catskill Mts.
Chesapeake Bay
Delaware Bay
Pamlico Sound
Albemarle Sd.
Long Island
Long Island Sound
Cape Cod
C. Hatteras
C. Lookout
C. Fear
CAPE HATTERAS NAT. SEASHORE
CAPE LOOKOUT NAT. SEASHORE
CAPE COD NAT. SEASHORE
ASSATEAGUE ISLAND NAT. SEASHORE
SHENANDOAH NAT. PARK
GREAT SMOKY MTS. NAT. PARK
ACADIA NAT. PARK
ALGONQUIN PROV. PARK
LAKE SUPERIOR PROV. PARK
BRUCE PEN. NAT. PARK
BAXTER STATE PARK
St. Lawrence
Ottawa
Hudson
Susquehanna
Potomac
James
Roanoke
OTTAWA
MONTREAL
Québec
TORONTO
Hamilton
Buffalo
Rochester
Syracuse
Albany
Sudbury
Sault Ste. Marie
DETROIT
Windsor
Toledo
CLEVELAND
Akron
COLUMBUS
Dayton
CINCINNATI
PITTSBURGH
PHILADELPHIA
NEW YORK
Newark
Trenton
BALTIMORE
WASHINGTON D.C.
Richmond
NORFOLK
Virginia Beach
Raleigh
Durham
Greensboro
Winston-Salem
Charlotte
Columbia
Knoxville
Asheville
Chattanooga
ATLANTA
Lexington
BOSTON
PROVIDENCE
Hartford
Springfield
Worcester
Portland
Bangor
Augusta
Manchester
Concord
Burlington
Montpelier
Wilmington
Dover
Annapolis
Harrisburg
Scranton
Erie
Charleston
Grand Rapids
Lansing
Flint
Saginaw
Kingston
London
Sherbrooke
Trois-Rivières

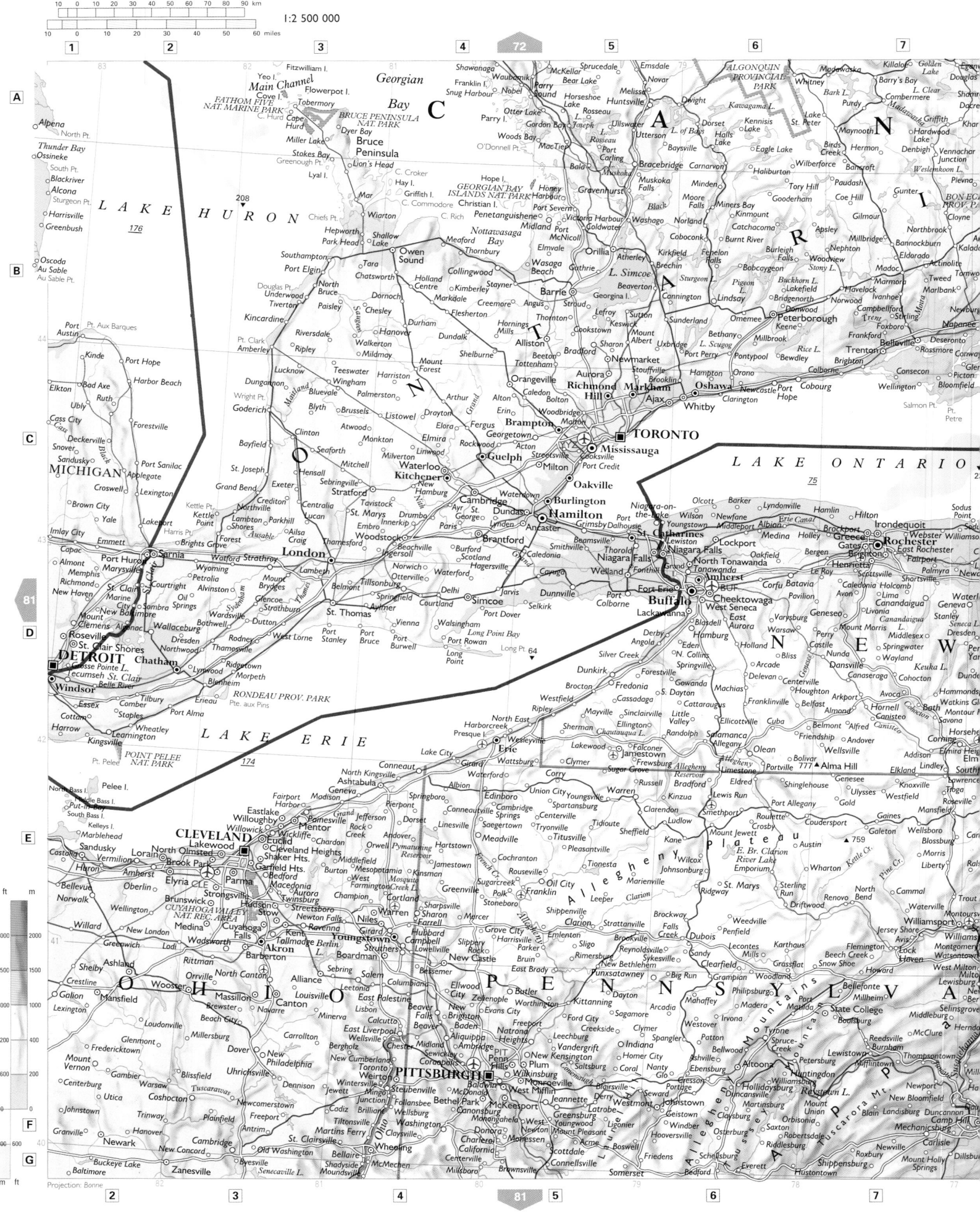

1:2 500 000

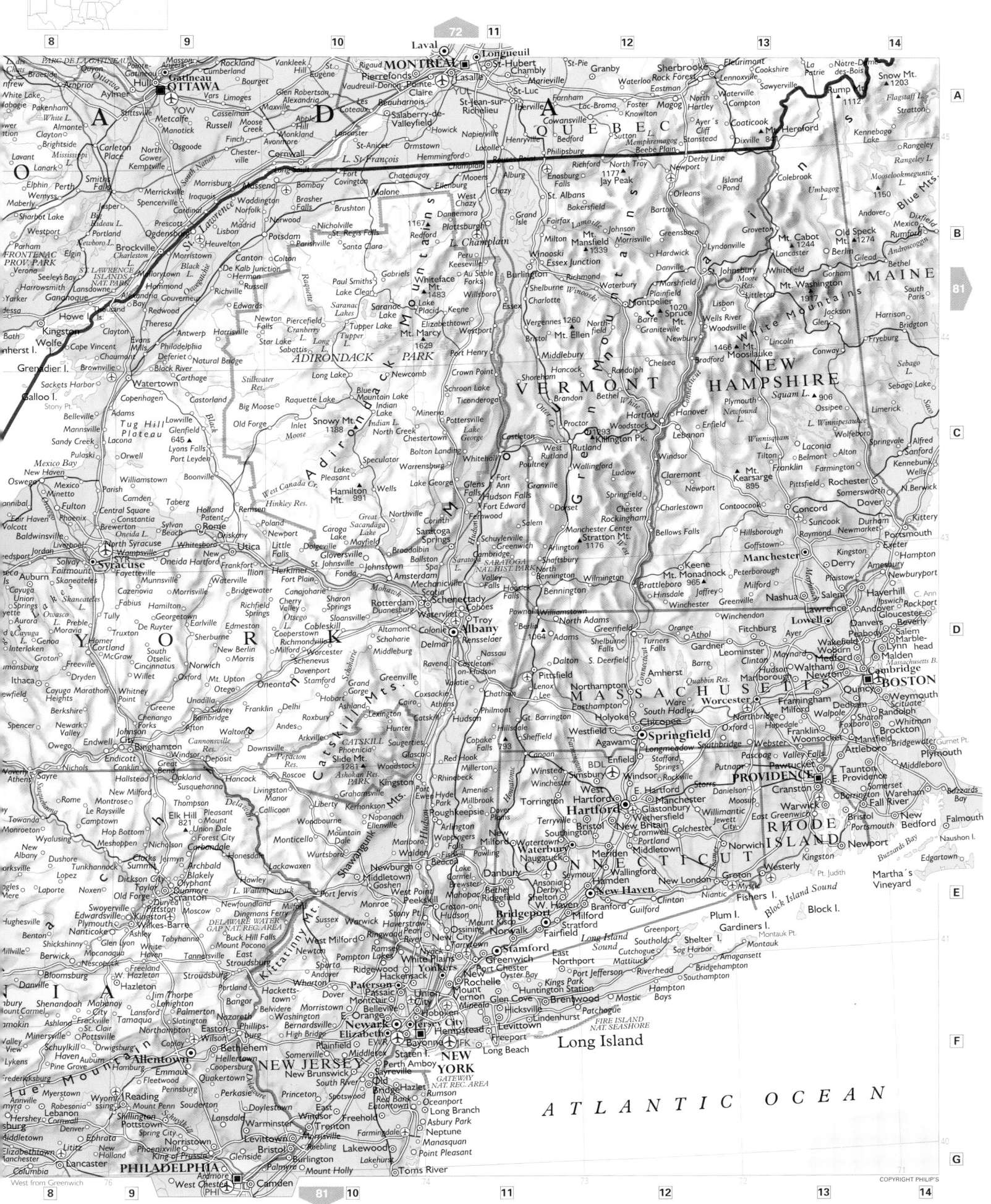

1:8 000 000

Projection: Bi-polar oblique Conical Orthomorphic

West from Greenwich

State names in Central Mexico

1 DISTRITO FEDERAL   3 GUANAJUATO   5 MÉXICO   7 QUERÉTARO
2 AGUASCALIENTES   4 HIDALGO   6 MORELOS   8 TLAXCALA

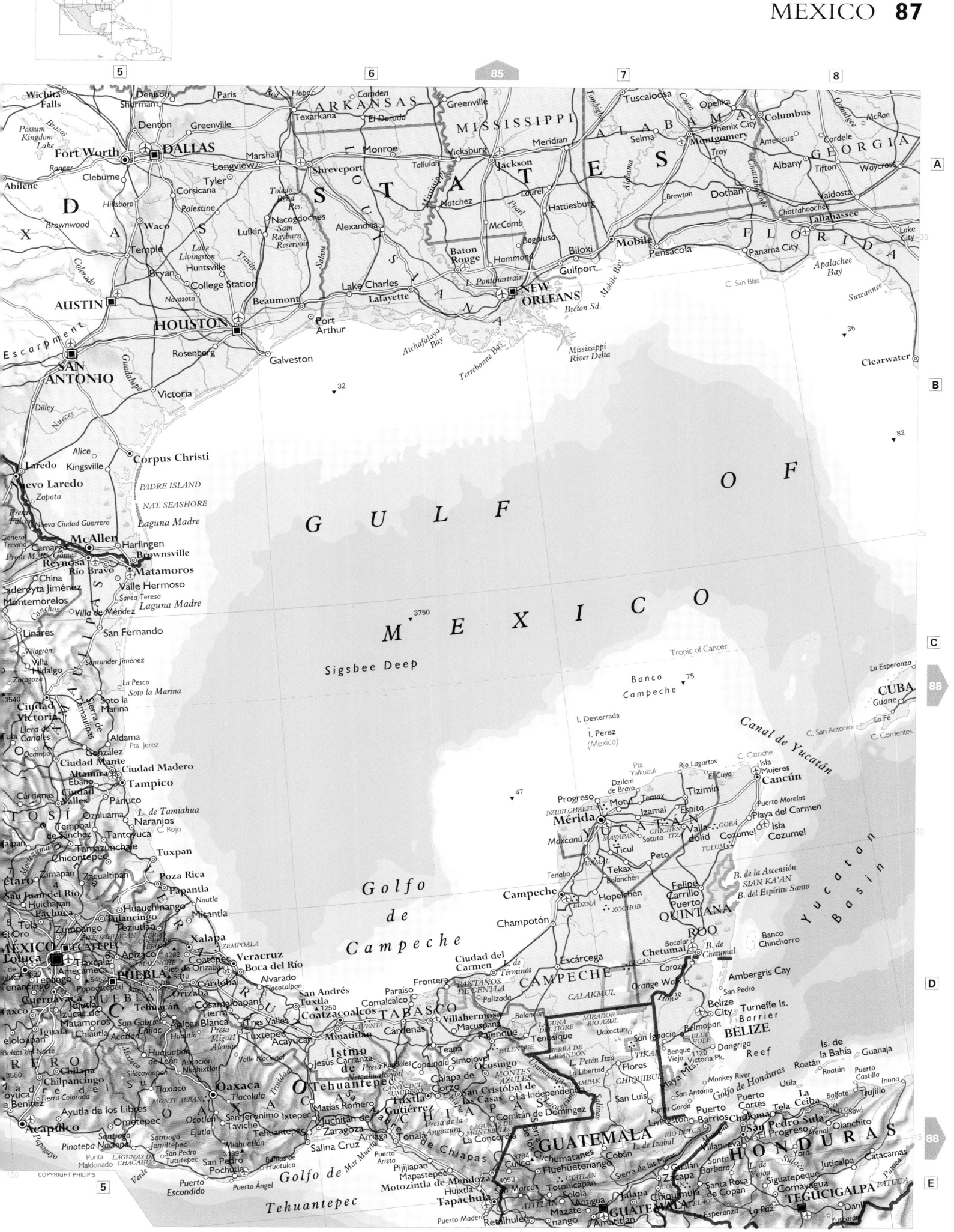

5 6 85 7 8

Wichita Falls
Denison
Sherman
Paris
Camden
Greenville
Tuscaloosa
Opelika
McRae

Fort Worth
DALLAS
Longview
Texarkana
El Dorado
MISSISSIPPI
Meridian
Phenix City
Columbus
Cordele

Abilene
Cleburne
Ranger
Tyler
Corsicana
Marshall
Monroe
Vicksburg
Jackson
Montgomery
Troy
Selma
Americus
Tifton
Waycross

A

Brownwood
Hillsboro
Waco
Palestine
Lufkin
Nacogdoches
Alexandria
Natchez
Hattiesburg
Dothan
Valdosta

Temple
Bryan
Huntsville
College Station
Navasota
Lake Charles
Lafayette
Baton Rouge
Hammond
Biloxi
Mobile
Pensacola
Panama City
FLORIDA
Lake City

AUSTIN
HOUSTON
Beaumont
Port Arthur
NEW ORLEANS
Gulfport
Apalachee Bay

SAN ANTONIO
Rosenberg
Galveston
Mississippi River Delta
Clearwater

B

Corpus Christi
GULF OF

Laredo
Nuevo Laredo
PADRE ISLAND
McAllen
Harlingen
Brownsville
Matamoros
MEXICO

Ciudad Victoria
Tampico
Mérida
Cancún
CUBA

Tropic of Cancer
Banco Campeche
Canal de Yucatán

C

Sigsbee Deep

Golfo de Campeche
YUCATÁN
QUINTANA ROO

MÉXICO
PUEBLA
Veracruz
Campeche
CAMPECHE
Chetumal
BELIZE

D

Oaxaca
OAXACA
Tuxtla Gutiérrez
CHIAPAS
GUATEMALA
HONDURAS

Acapulco
TEGUCIGALPA

E

COPYRIGHT PHILIP'S

5

Tehuantepec
GUATEMALA

1:8 000 00

JAMAICA
1:3 000 000

GUADELOUPE AND MARTINIQUE
1:2 000 000

Projection: Bi-polar oblique Conical Orthomorphic

ATLANTIC OCEAN

PUERTO RICO (U.S.A.)

PUERTO RICO d
1:3 000 000
10   0   10   20   30 40 50 km
10   0   10   20   30 miles

Pta. Aguijereada
Isabela
Aguadilla
Arecibo   Barceloneta
Manati   Vega   Rio Grande
San   Baja   Bayamón   Carolina   Dewey
Sebastian   Caguas   Fajardo   Culebra
Mayagüez   Adjuntas   Cayey   Sierra de   Puerca   Vieques
Cordillera Central   Luquillo   Naguabo
San German   1338 Cerro   Humacao   Esperanza
Uroyan   de Punta
Yauco   Coamo   Yabucoa
Pta. Aguila   Guanica   Ponce   Guayama
I. Caja de Muertos

VIRGIN ISLANDS e
1:2 000 000
10   0   10   20   30 km
10   0   10   20 miles

Rufling Pt.   The Settlement
Anegada   East Pt.
Virgin Islands (U.K.)
Great Camanoe
Jost Van   Guana I.
Dyke I.   521   Beef I.   Virgin Gorda
Virgin Is.   Hans   Tortola   Road Town   Spanish Town
(U.S.A.)   Lollik I.   Cruz   Peter I.
Charlotte   Bay   St.   St. John I.
Amalie   Thomas I.   VIRGIN IS.

ST. LUCIA f
1:1 000 000
5   0   10 km
5   0   10 miles

Cap Point
Pte. Hardy
Gros Islet   Esperance Bay
Castries   Marquis
Girard
Anse la Raye   Dennery
Canaries   Millet
Soufrière   Mt. Gimie   Trou Gras Pt.
Bay   950   Micoud
Soufrière   750
Petit Piton   Vierge Pt.
Gros Piton Pt.   796
Gros Piton
Choiseul   **ST. LUCIA**
Laborie   Vieux Fort
C. Moule à Chique

ATLANTIC OCEAN
Crab Hill   North Point
Spring Hall
Fustic   Boscobelle
Portland   245 Belleplaine
Speightstown   **BARBADOS**
Westmoreland   Bathsheba   Hillcrest
Alleynes Bay   840   Martin's Bay
Holetown   Mt. Hillaby
Jackson   Bridgefield   Massiah
Black Rock   Ellerton   Street   Six Cross Roads
Bridgetown   Edey   The Crane
Carlisle Bay   St. Martins
Worthing   Oistins   Chancery Lane
Bay   South Point   BGI

BARBADOS g
1:1 000 000
5   0   10 km
5   0   10 miles

ATLANTIC OCEAN

MAS

arthur's Town
New Bight
Cat I.
San Salvador I.
Conception I.
Rum Cay
Long I.   Samana Cay
Clarence Town
Crooked I. Passage
Crooked I.
Plana Cays
Albert   Snug
Town   Corner   Mayaguana I.
Acklins I.
Cay Verde   Mira or vos Cay
Caicos Passage
Hogsty Reef   Turks & Caicos Is. (U.K.)
Little Inagua I.   Caicos Is.
Cockburn Town
INAGUA   Caicos Is.   Turks Is.
Lake Rose   Caicos Island Passage
Great   Matthew   Silver Bank Passage
Inagua I.   Town   Mouchoir Bank   Silver Bank
Navidad Bank

C. Lucrecia
Moa
Mayari   Baracoa
Pta. de Maisi
Maisi
GUANTANAMO
BAY (U.S.A.)   Cap-Haitien   Monte Cristi   LA ISABELA
Jean Rabel   Port-de-   Puerto   Santiago de   San Francisco de Macoris
Paix   Plata   los Caballeros   Milwaukee
Cap-à-   Fort Liberté   La Vega   Nagua   Deep   Puerto Rico Trench
Foux   Gonaïves   3175   Samana   9200
G. de la   Hinche   Cord.   Sánchez
Gonâve   ARMAND   Central   Sabana de la Mar   Bayamón   SAN JUAN
Jérémie   BRITISH   Pico Duarte   Hato Mayor   Aguadilla   Arecibo   Carolina
Île de la Gonâve   HAITI   DOMINICAN   C. Engaño   Fajardo
PORT-   San Juan   REP.   San Pedro   Higüey   1338   Culebra
AU-PRINCE   L. Enriquillo   de Macoris   Ponce   St. Thomas   Virgin Gorda   Sombrero (U.K.)
Massif de la Hotte   Petit   SANTO   La Romana   Caguas   Tortola   Road Town   Anguilla (U.K.)
Les Cayes   Goave   Jacmel   DOMINGO   ESTE   Mayagüez   Vieques   Virgin Is.   St.-Martin (Fr.)
Pointe-à- Gravois   Aquin   San Cristóbal   B. de   Guayama   (U.S.A.)   Christiansted   St. Maarten
Île à Vache   Bani   Yuma   PUERTO   Frederiksted   (Neth.)   Saba (Neth.)   Barbuda
Sierra de   Compostela   I. Saona   RICO   St. Croix   St. Eustatius   ANTIGUA
Barahona   (U.S.A.)   (Neth.)   1156   ST. KITTS   & BARBUDA
Pedernales   Isla   & NEVIS   St. John's
Mona   Nevis   Antigua
C. Beata   (U.S.A.)   Redonda   Soufrière   Guadeloupe Passage
I. Beata   Montserrat   914   Ste -Rose   Le Moule   La Désirade
Hispaniola   (U.K.)   Hills   GUADELOUPE   Pointe-à-Pitre
Antilles   Basse-Terre   1467   Marie-Galante (Fr.)
Beata Ridge   (Fr.)   Grand-Bourg
I. des Saintes   Dominica Passage
Portsmouth   1447   DOMINICA
Morne   Diablotin   Roseau   MORNE TROIS PITONS
Martinique Passage
Mt. Pelée   Ste -Marie
1397   Le François
Fort-de-   Rivière-Pilote
France   MARTINIQUE (Fr.)
St. Lucia Channel
Castries   ST. LUCIA
Soufrière
St. Vincent Passage
Soufrière 1234   St. Vincent
Speightstown 340
Kingstown   Bridgetown
Bequia   BARBADOS
ST. VINCENT & THE GRENADINES

CARIBBEAN SEA
Venezuelan Basin
I. de Aves (Venezuela)
Lesser Antilles

Columbian Basin

ABC Islands   Lesser   Antilles
Aruba (Neth.)
Oranjestad   Curaçao   Bonaire
Willemstad   NETH. ANTILLES
Pta. Gallinas   ARC. LOS ROQUES
MACURIA   Is. Las Aves (Ven.)   Is. Los Roques (Ven.)
C. San Román   I. Orchila (Ven.)
Pen. de la   Pta. Espada   I. Blanquilla (Ven.)
COLOMBIA   Guajira   Paraguaná   NUEVA   Is. Los Hermanos (Ven.)
Punto Fijo   ESPARTA   Is. Los Testigos (Ven.)
Ríohacha   Uribia   Punta   I. de Margarita   Tobago
Santa   GUAJIRA   Cardón   MÉDANOS DE CORO   La Asunción   Scarborough
Marta   ISLA DE   Golfo de   Puerto Cumarebo   Porlamar   Port of   940 Point
BARRAN-   Ciénaga   STA. MARTA   Venezuela   Coro   CUEVA DE LA   La Tortuga   Pen. de Paria   Spain
QUILLA   Cardón   La Vela   QUEBRADA   (Ven.)   Trinidad
Soledad   Santa Marta   San   FALCON   Maiquetía   I. La Tortuga   Carúpano   Güiria   Río Claro
ATLANTICO   6275   Rafael   CERRO EL COPEY   La Guaira   Guaira   TRINIDAD
Baranoa   Santa Rita   LARA   Tucacas   MARACAY   CARACAS   & TOBAGO
Sabanalarga   Villa del   Carora   Puerto   Maiquetía   Cumaná   Río Claro
Calamar   MARACAIBO   Rosario   Cabello   MIRANDA   San   Serpent's Mouth
Fundación   La Concepción   Baragua   San Felipe   Los Teques   SUCRE
Ciudad   Mene de Mauroa   YARACUY   Ocumare del Tuy   Caripito   Maturin
Valledupar   Ojeda   BARQUISIMETO   VALENCIA   Villa   MONAGAS   MARIUSA
MAGDALENA   Machiques   Lago de   Mene   Yaritagua   de Cura   San Juan   Barcelona   DELTA
Agustín   Maracaibo   Grande   de   Aragua de   Anaco   AMACURO
Codazzi   CESAR   Baruta   CARABOBO   los Morros   Barcelona   Tucupita
Magangué   ZULIA   PERIJA   Betijoque   El Tocuyo   San Carlos   El Tigre
CIENAGAS DEL   Trujillo   COJEDES   Valle de   El Pao
CATATUMBO   TRUJILLO   PORTUGUESA   la Pascua   GUARICO   Los Barrancos
Mompós   San Carlos   GUARICO   Ciudad Guayana
BOLIVAR   Valera   del Zulia   Guanare   Portuguesa   Calabozo   Santa María   Soledad
El Banco   Encontrados   de Ipire
Ocaña   MÉRIDA   San Fernando   Ciudad
CATATUMBO-BARI   NORTE   Barinas   AGUARO-GUARIQUITO   de Apure   El Pao   Bolívar
DE   Mérida   BARINAS   ANZOÁTEGUI   Sierra Imataca
SANTANDER   5007   Ciudad de Nutrias   Embalse de Guri
TACHIRA   Cord. Mérida   Libertad   San Fernando   Guasipati
Cúcuta   Barbara   **VENEZUELA**   Bruzual   de Apure   Calcara   Guasipati   Tumeremo
OBA   Simití   Achaguas   Apure   Orinoco   El Callao

West from Greenwich

COPYRIGHT PHILIP'S

ft   4000   3000   2000   1500   1000   400   200   0
6000   12 000   18 000   24 000
12 000   9000   6000   4500   3000   1200   600   0
m   200   2000   4000   6000   8000

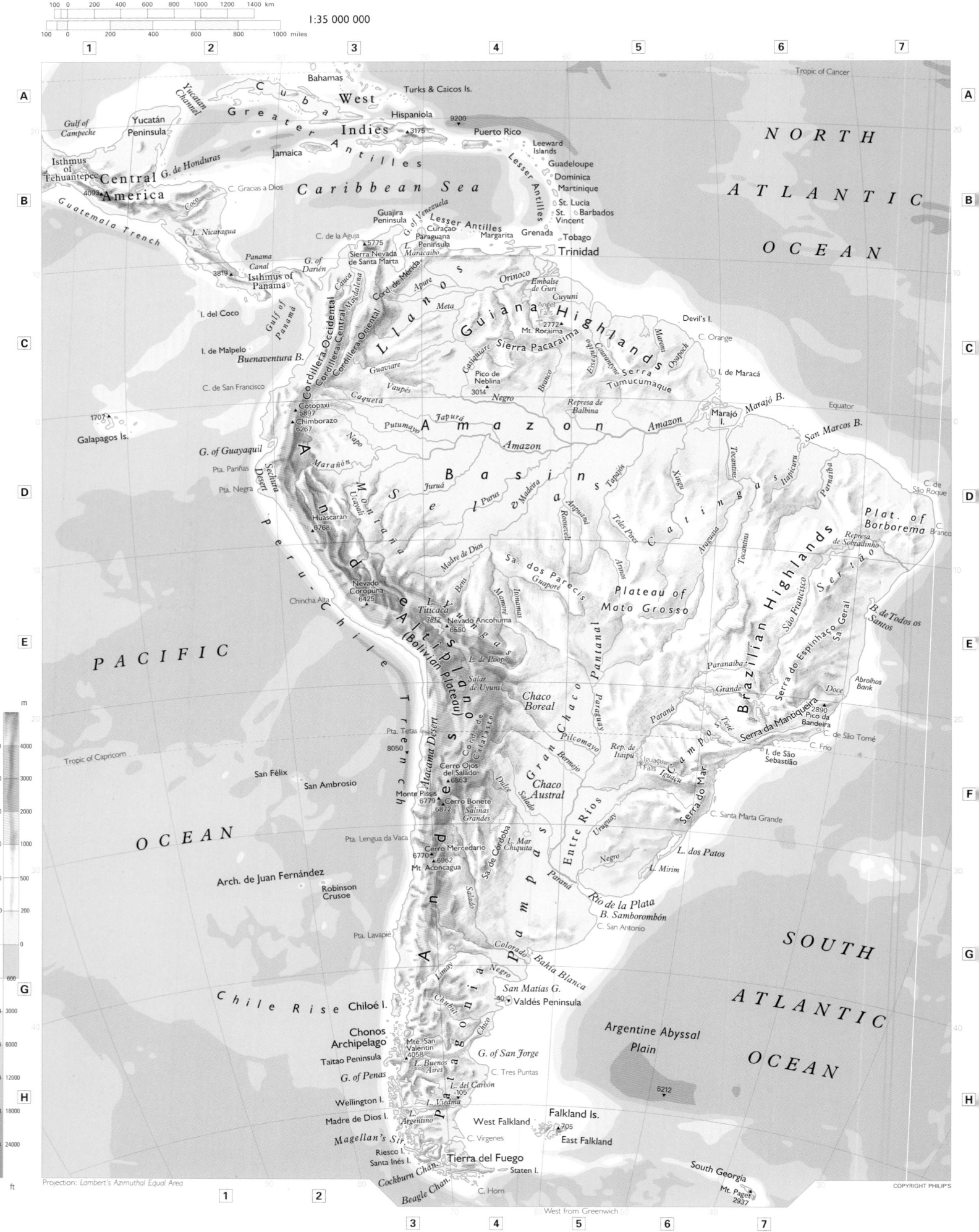

1:35 000 000

Projection: Lambert's Azimuthal Equal Area

COPYRIGHT PHILIP'S

1:35 000 000

100 0   200   400   600   800   1000   1200   1400 km

100 0   200   400   600   800   1000 miles

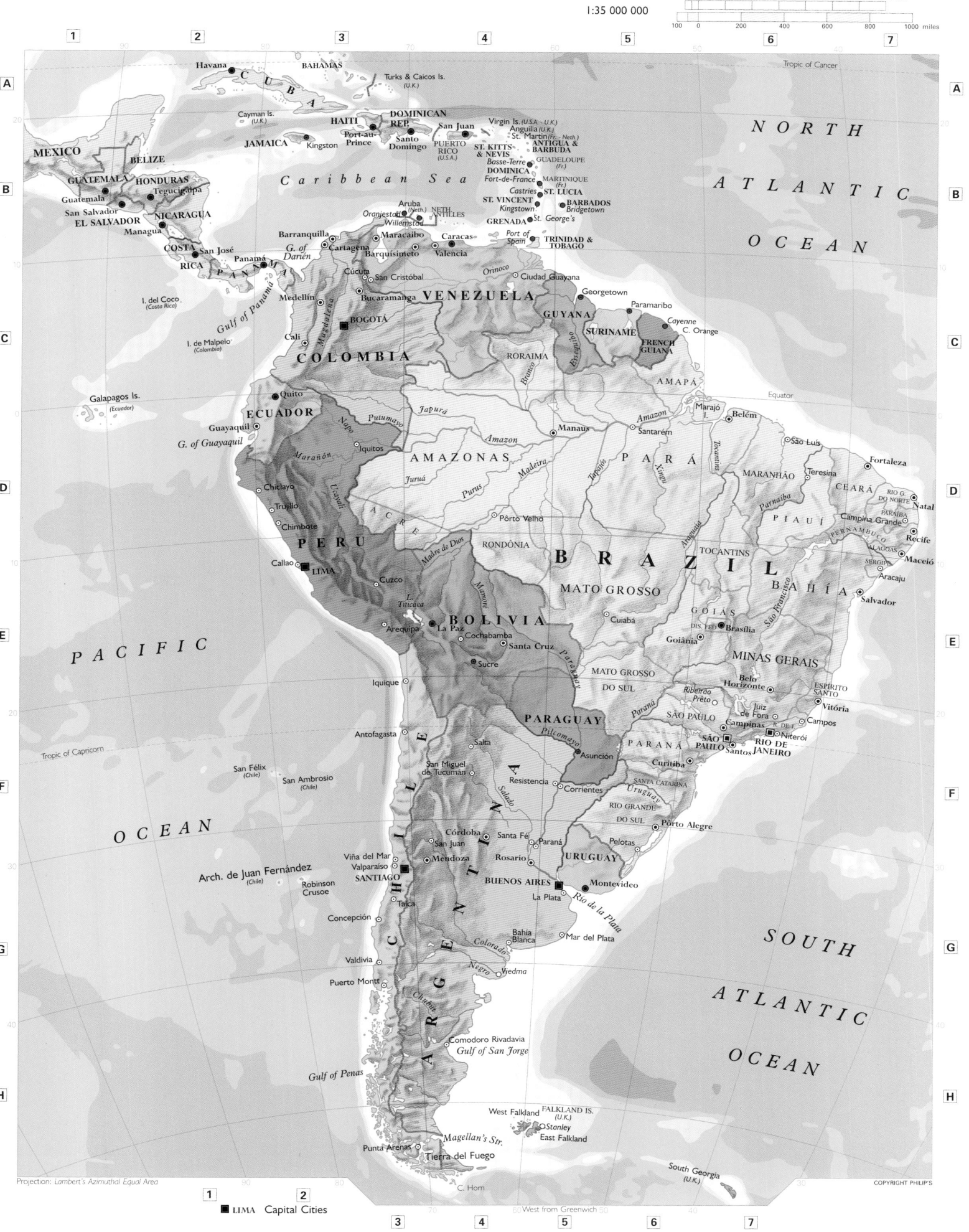

NORTH

ATLANTIC

OCEAN

Tropic of Cancer

Havana
BAHAMAS
Turks & Caicos Is.
(U.K.)
C U B A

Cayman Is.
(U.K.)

MEXICO

HAITI
DOMINICAN
REP.
San Juan
Virgin Is. (U.S.A. – U.K.)
Anguilla (U.K.)
St. Martin (Fr. – Neth.)
ANTIGUA &
BARBUDA

BELIZE
JAMAICA
Kingston
Port-au-
Prince
Santo
Domingo
PUERTO
RICO
(U.S.A.)
ST. KITTS
& NEVIS
GUADELOUPE
(Fr.)

GUATEMALA
HONDURAS
Tegucigalpa
Basse-Terre
DOMINICA
Fort-de-France
MARTINIQUE
(Fr.)

Guatemala
San Salvador
EL SALVADOR
NICARAGUA
Managua
Castries
ST. VINCENT
ST. LUCIA

Aruba
(Neth.)
Oranjestad
NETH.
ANTILLES
Willemstad
Kingstown
GRENADA
St. George's
BARBADOS
Bridgetown

COSTA
RICA
San José
Panamá
PANAMA
Barranquilla
Cartagena
Maracaibo
Caracas
Valencia
Port of
Spain
TRINIDAD &
TOBAGO

Caribbean Sea

I. del Coco
(Costa Rica)
G. of
Darién
Gulf of Panamá
Cúcuta
San Cristóbal
Barquísimeto
Orinoco
Ciudad Guayana

I. de Malpelo
(Colombia)
Medellín
Bucaramanga
VENEZUELA
Georgetown
Paramaribo

BOGOTÁ
GUYANA
SURINAME
Cayenne
C. Orange

Cali
Magdalena
FRENCH
GUIANA

COLOMBIA
RORAIMA
AMAPÁ

Galapagos Is.
(Ecuador)
Quito
Japurá
Equator

ECUADOR
Putumayo
Napo
Amazon
Marajó
I.
Belém

Guayaquil
Marañón
Iquitos
Manaus
Santarém
São Luís

G. of Guayaquil
AMAZONAS
Amazon
Tapajós
Madeira
MARANHÃO
Fortaleza
Teresina

Chiclayo
Furuá
Purus
PARÁ
Teresina
CEARÁ

Trujillo
ACRE
Xingu
RIO G.
DO NORTE
Natal

Chimbote
Pôrto Velho
PIAUÍ
PARAÍBA
Campina Grande

PERU
RONDÔNIA
TOCANTINS
PERNAMBUCO
Recife

Callao
LIMA
Madre de Dios
BRAZIL
ALAGOAS
Maceió

Cuzco
MATO GROSSO
SERGIPE
Aracaju

L.
Titicaca
Mamoré
BAHÍA
Salvador

PACIFIC
BOLIVIA
Cuiabá
GOIÁS
DIS. FED.
São Francisco

Arequipa
La Paz
Cochabamba
Brasília

Sucre
Santa Cruz
Goiânia
MINAS GERAIS

Iquique
MATO GROSSO
DO SUL
Belo
Horizonte
ESPÍRITO
SANTO

Ribeirão
Prêto
Vitória

Antofagasta
PARAGUAY
Paraná
SÃO PAULO
Juiz
de Fora
Campos

Salta
Pilcomayo
Asunción
Campinas
R. DE J.

San Miguel
de Tucumán
PARANÁ
SÃO
PAULO
RIO DE
JANEIRO

Tropic of Capricorn
San Félix
(Chile)
San Ambrosio
(Chile)
Resistencia
Corrientes
Curitiba
Santos
Niterói

Arch. de Juan Fernández
(Chile)
Robinson
Crusoe
Salado
Uruguay
SANTA CATARINA

OCEAN
Córdoba
Santa Fé
RIO GRANDE
DO SUL
Pôrto Alegre

Viña del Mar
San Juan
Paraná
URUGUAY
Pelotas

Valparaíso
SANTIAGO
Mendoza
Rosario

Talca
BUENOS AIRES
Montevideo

CHILE
ARGENTINA
La Plata
Rio de la Plata

Concepción
Bahía
Blanca
Mar del Plata

Valdivia
Colorado
Negro
Viedma

Puerto Montt
SOUTH

Comodoro Rivadavia
Gulf of San Jorge
ATLANTIC

Chubut
OCEAN

Gulf of Penas

West Falkland
FALKLAND IS.
(U.K.)

Punta Arenas
Magellan's Str.
Stanley
East Falkland

Tierra del Fuego

C. Horn
South Georgia
(U.K.)

Projection: Lambert's Azimuthal Equal Area

COPYRIGHT PHILIP'S

West from Greenwich

■ LIMA Capital Cities

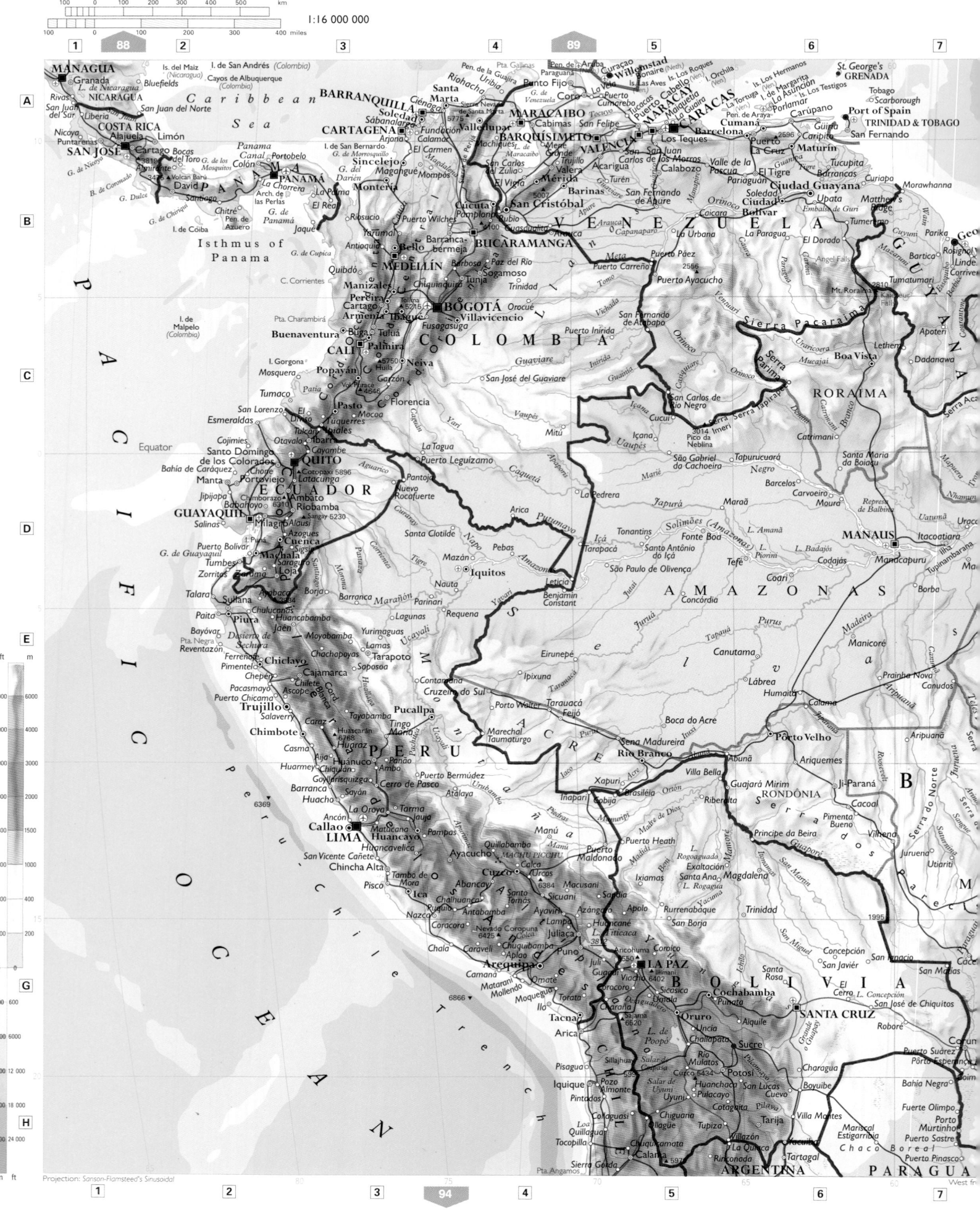

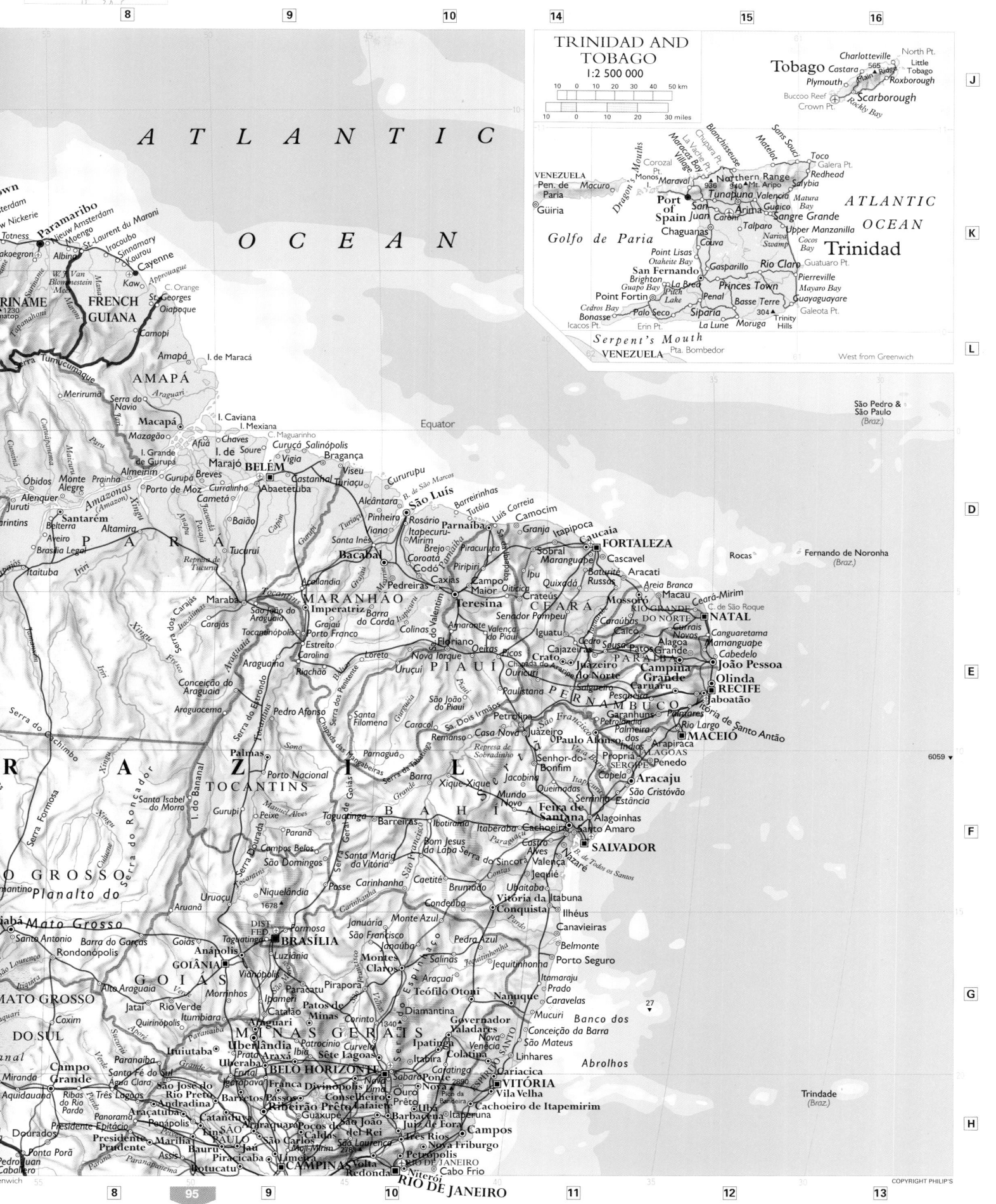

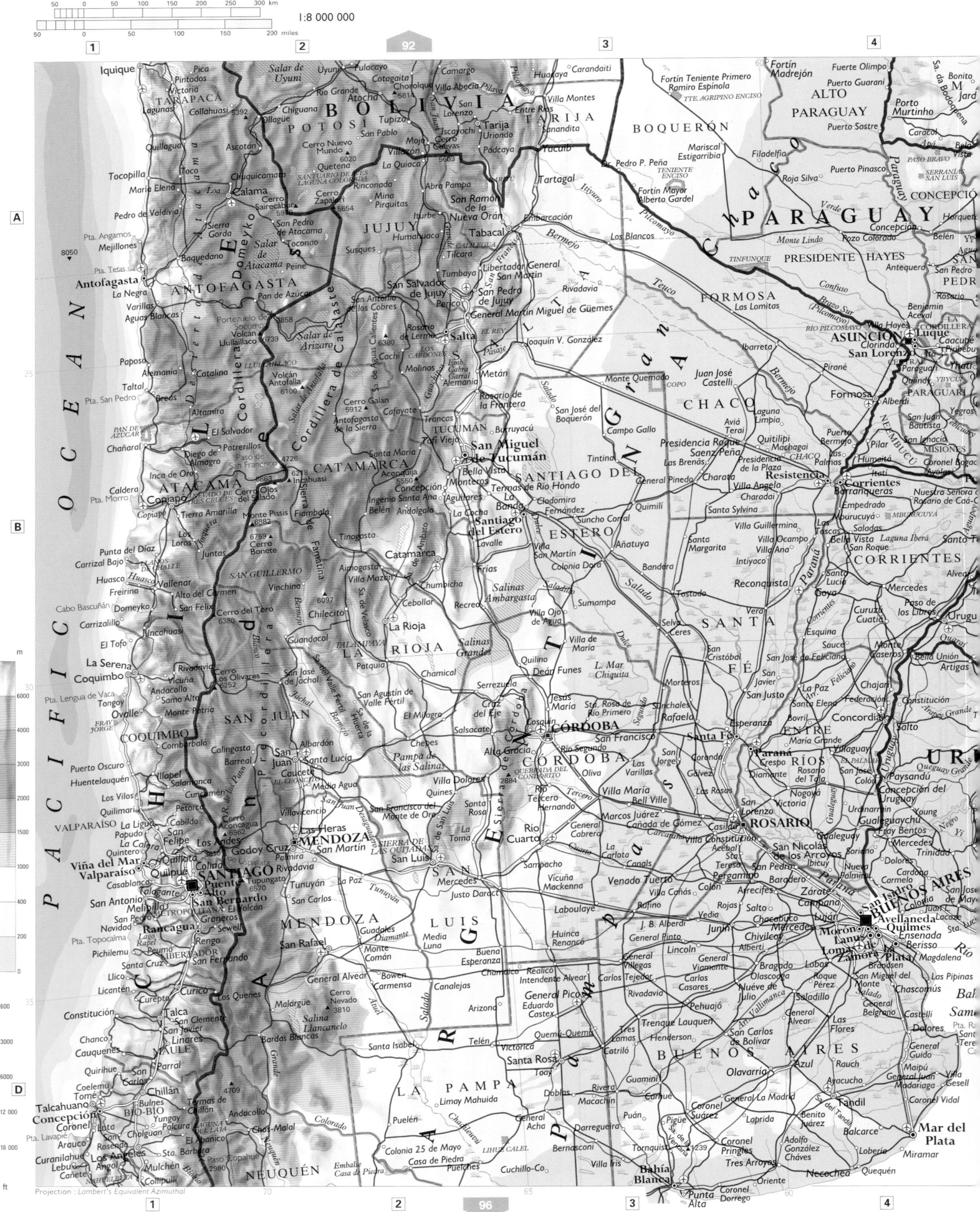

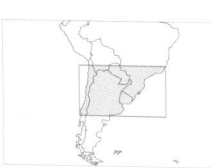

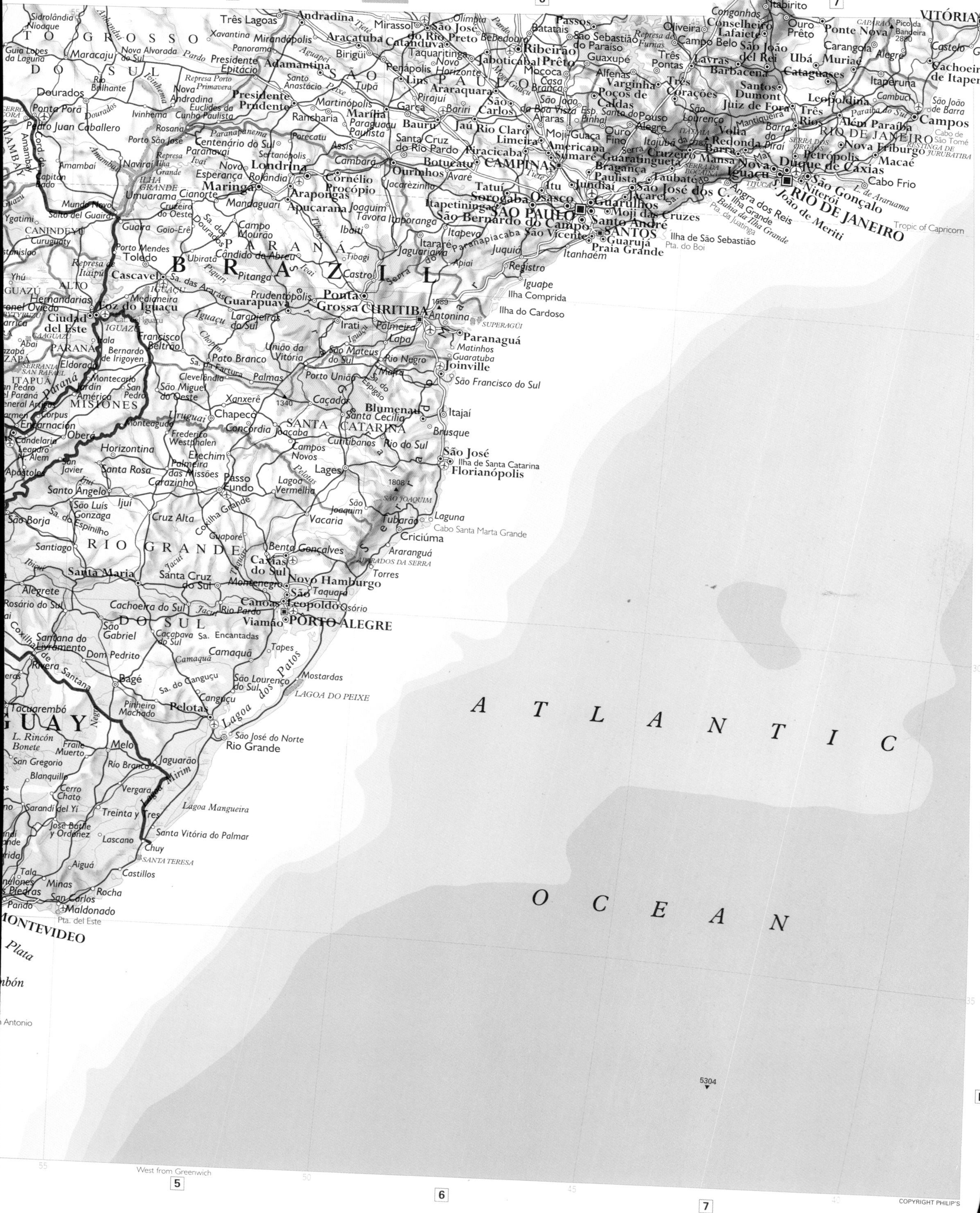
93
5
6
7
A
B
C
D
ATLANTIC
OCEAN
B R A Z I L
MATO GROSSO DO SUL
SÃO PAULO
PARANÁ
SANTA CATARINA
RIO GRANDE DO SUL
RIO DE JANEIRO
URUGUAY
MISIONES
BELO HORIZONTE
Betim
Contagem
Itabirito
VITÓRIA
Vila Velha
Guarapari
Cachoeiro de Itapemirim
Campos
Macaé
Cabo Frio
RIO DE JANEIRO
Niterói
São Gonçalo
Duque de Caxias
Petrópolis
Nova Friburgo
Volta Redonda
Juiz de Fora
Barbacena
São João del Rei
Campinas
SÃO PAULO
Guarulhos
Santo André
São Bernardo do Campo
Osasco
Sorocaba
Jundiaí
SANTOS
Guarujá
Praia Grande
São Vicente
Ilha de São Sebastião
Ribeirão Prêto
São José do Rio Preto
Araraquara
São Carlos
Bauru
Marília
Presidente Prudente
Londrina
Maringá
Ponta Grossa
CURITIBA
Paranaguá
Joinville
Blumenau
Itajaí
São José
Florianópolis
Lages
Criciúma
Tubarão
Caxias do Sul
Novo Hamburgo
São Leopoldo
Canoas
PORTO ALEGRE
Viamão
Santa Maria
Passo Fundo
Pelotas
Rio Grande
Lagoa dos Patos
Lagoa Mirim
Chuy
Foz do Iguaçu
Cascavel
Ciudad del Este
Encarnación
Dourados
Ponta Porã
Pedro Juan Caballero
Maldonado
MONTEVIDEO
Tropic of Capricorn
Cabo Santa Marta Grande
Ilha de Santa Catarina
Ilha do Cardoso
Ilha Comprida
5304
West from Greenwich
COPYRIGHT PHILIP'S

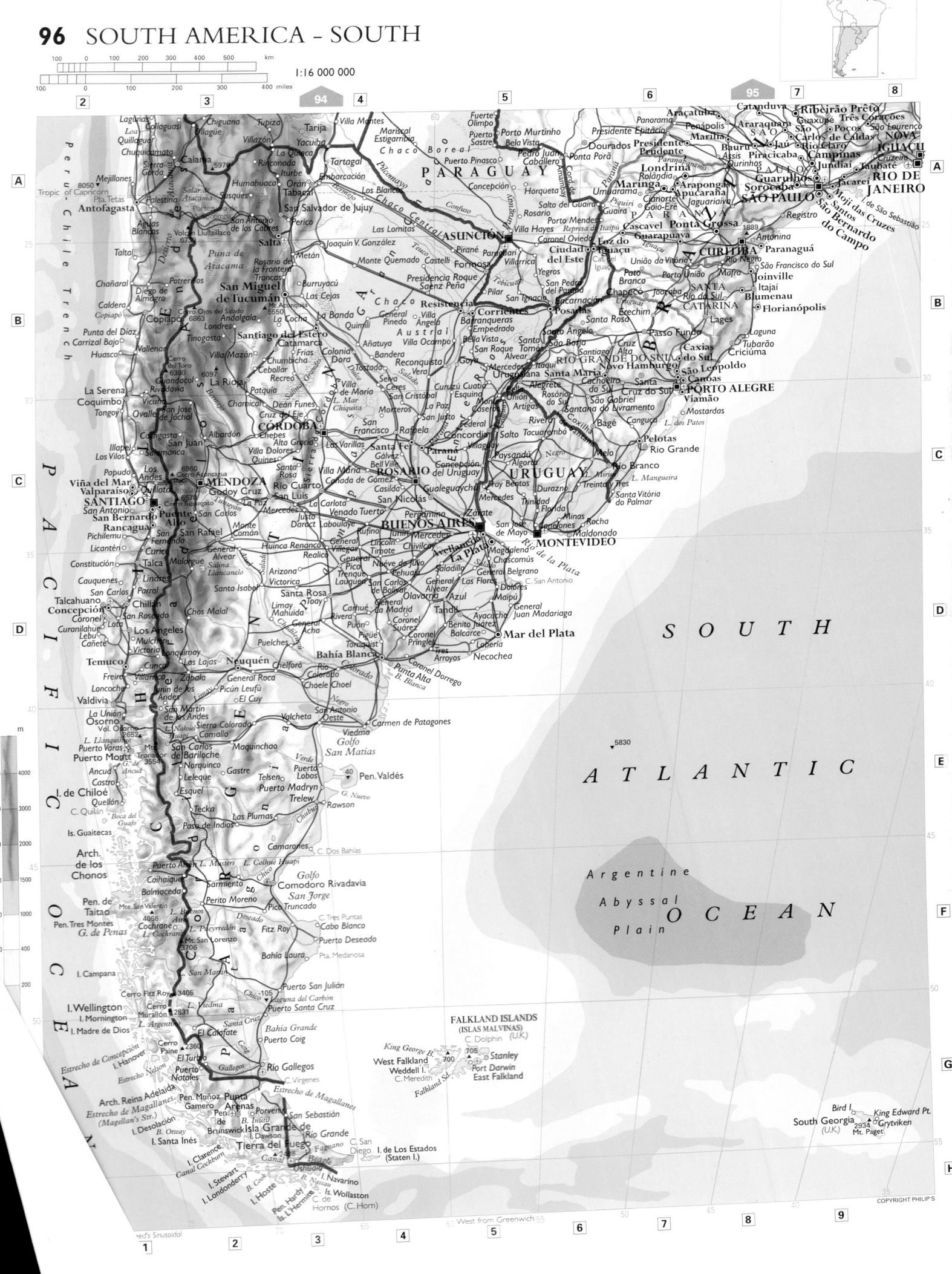

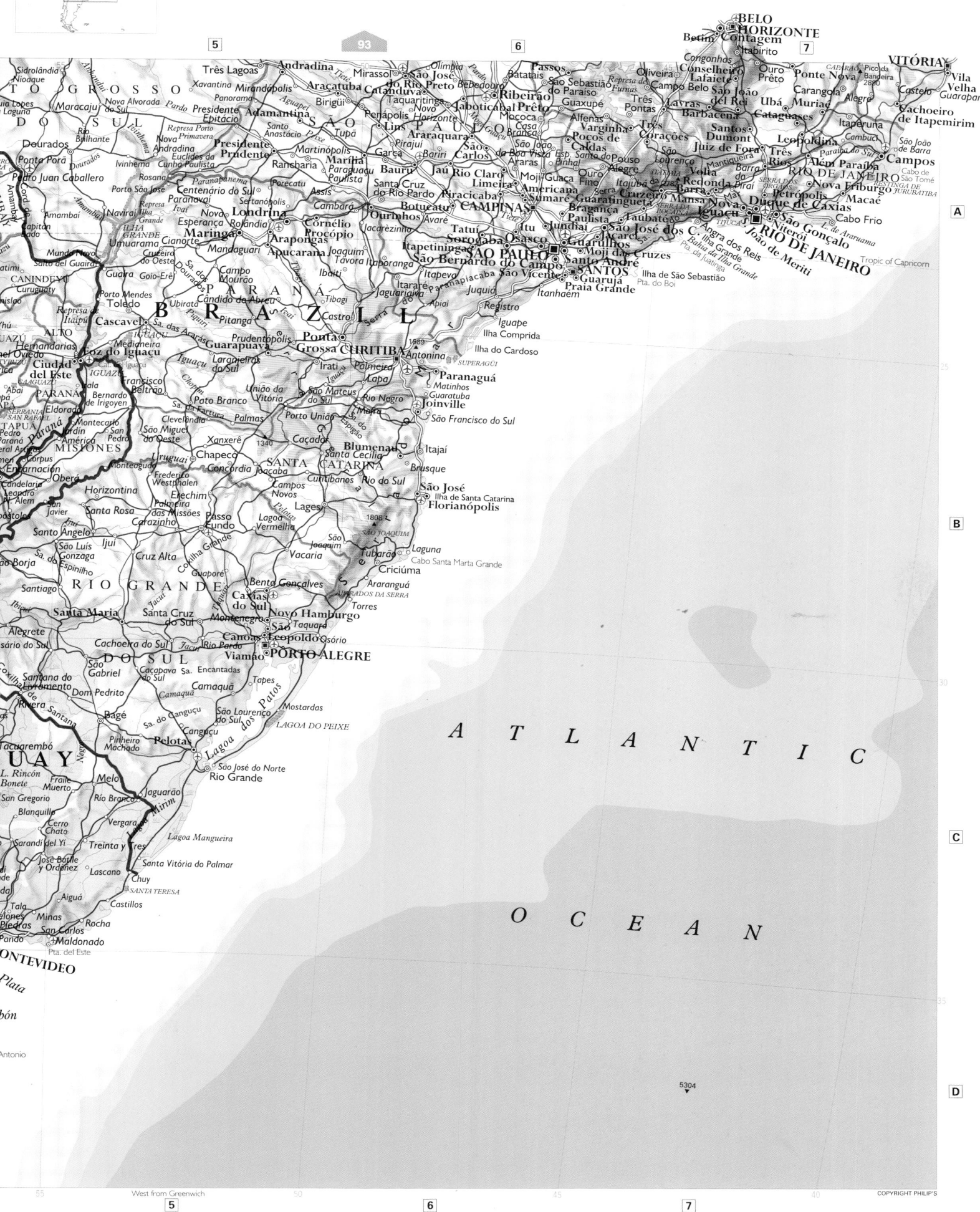

BELO HORIZONTE
Betim Contagem
Itabirito

VITÓRIA
Vila
Velha

A

Tropic of Capricorn

B

A T L A N T I C

O C E A N

5304
▼

C

D

1:16 000 000

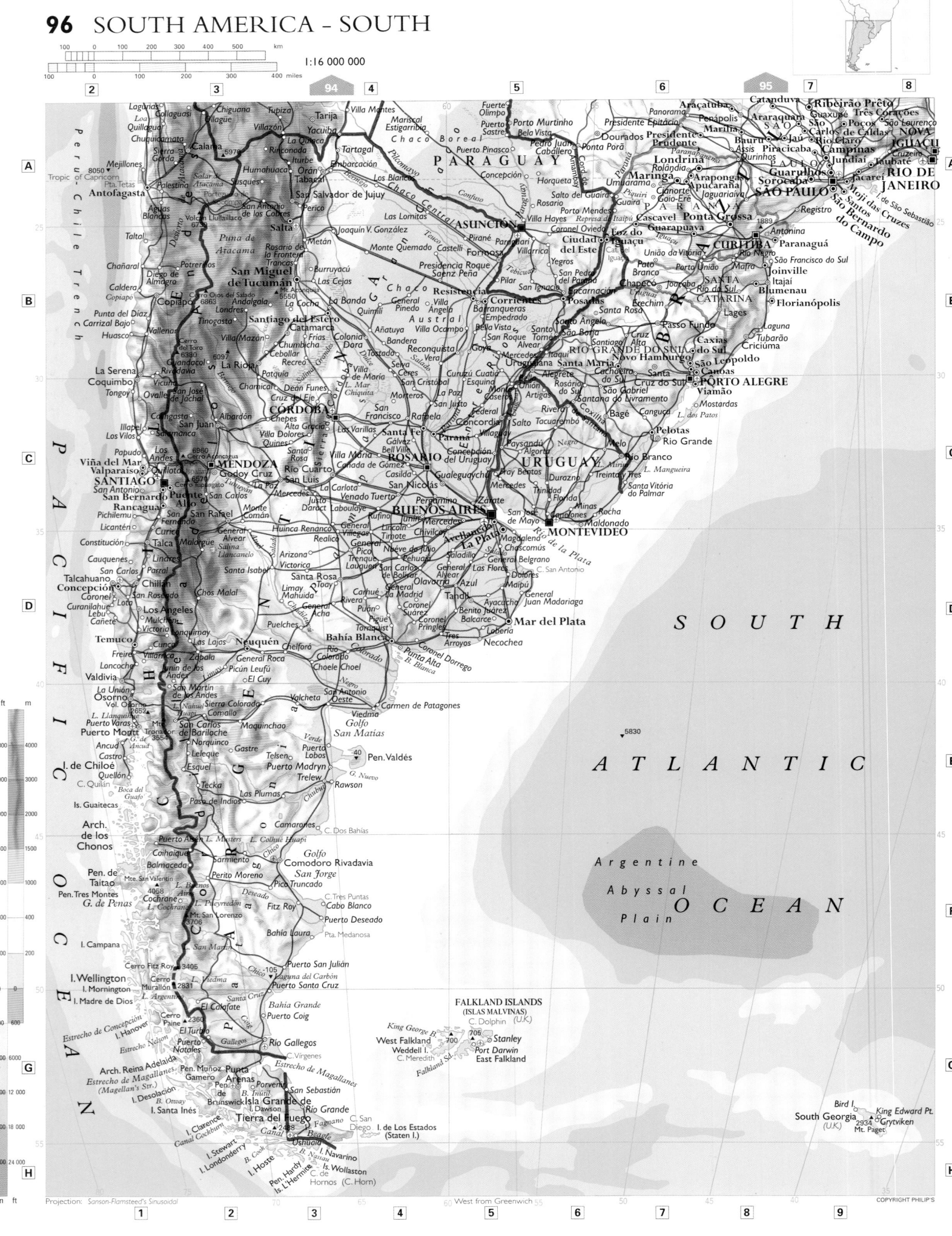

Projection: Sanson-Flamsteed's Sinusoidal

West from Greenwich

COPYRIGHT PHILIP'S

INDEX TO WORLD MAPS

The index contains the names of all the principal places and features shown on the World Maps. Each name is followed by an additional entry in italics giving the country or region within which it is located. The alphabetical order of names composed of two or more words is governed primarily by the first word, then by the second, and then by the country or region name that follows. This is an example of the rule:

Mīr Kūh *Iran*	26°22N 58°55E	**45** E8
Mīr Shahdād *Iran*	26°15N 58°29E	**45** E8
Mira *Italy*	45°26N 12°8E	**22** B5
Mira por vos Cay *Bahamas*	22°9N 74°30W	**89** B5

Physical features composed of a proper name (Erie) and a description (Lake) are positioned alphabetically by the proper name. The description is positioned after the proper name and is usually abbreviated:

Erie, L. *N. Amer.*	42°15N 81°0W	**82** D4

Where a description forms part of a settlement or administrative name, however, it is always written in full and put in its true alphabetical position:

Mount Morris *U.S.A.*	42°44N 77°52W	**82** D7

Names beginning with M' and Mc are indexed as if they were spelled Mac. Names beginning St. are alphabetized under Saint, but Sankt, Sint, Sant', Santa and San are all spelt in full and are alphabetized accordingly. If the same place name occurs two or more times in the index and all are in the same country, each is followed by the name of the administrative subdivision in which it is located.

The geographical co-ordinates which follow each name in the index give the latitude and longitude of each place. The first co-ordinate indicates latitude – the distance north or south of the Equator. The second co-ordinate indicates longitude – the distance east or west of the Greenwich Meridian. Both latitude and longitude are measured in degrees and minutes (there are 60 minutes in a degree).

The latitude is followed by N(orth) or S(outh) and the longitude by E(ast) or W(est).

The number in bold type which follows the geographical co-ordinates refers to the number of the map page where that feature or place will be found. This is usually the largest scale at which the place or feature appears.

The letter and figure that are immediately after the page number give the grid square on the map page, within which the feature is situated. The letter represents the latitude and the figure the longitude. A lower-case letter immediately after the page number refers to an inset map on that page.

In some cases the feature itself may fall within the specified square, while the name is outside. This is usually the case only with features that are larger than a grid square.

Rivers are indexed to their mouths or confluences, and carry the symbol ➔ after their names. The following symbols are also used in the index: ■ country, ☑ overseas territory or dependency, □ first-order administrative area, △ national park, ⌒ other park (provincial park, nature reserve or game reserve), ✕ (LHR) principal airport (and location identifier), ⊙ Australian aboriginal land.

Abbreviations used in the index

A.C.T. – Australian Capital Territory
A.R. – Autonomous Region
Afghan. – Afghanistan
Afr. – Africa
Ala. – Alabama
Alta. – Alberta
Amer. – America(n)
Ant. – Antilles
Arch. – Archipelago
Ariz. – Arizona
Ark. – Arkansas
Atl. Oc. – Atlantic Ocean
B. – Baie, Bahía, Bay, Bucht, Bugt
B.C. – British Columbia
Bangla. – Bangladesh
Barr. – Barrage
Bos.-H. – Bosnia-Herzegovina
C. – Cabo, Cap, Cape, Coast
C.A.R. – Central African Republic
C. Prov. – Cape Province
Calif. – California
Cat. – Catarata
Cent. – Central
Chan. – Channel
Colo. – Colorado
Conn. – Connecticut
Cord. – Cordillera
Cr. – Creek
Czech. – Czech Republic
D.C. – District of Columbia
Del. – Delaware
Dem. – Democratic
Dep. – Dependency
Des. – Desert
Dét. – Détroit
Dist. – District
Dj. – Djebel
Dom. Rep. – Dominican Republic

E. – East
El Salv. – El Salvador
Eq. Guin. – Equatorial Guinea
Est. – Estrecho
Falk. Is. – Falkland Is.
Fd. – Fjord
Fla. – Florida
Fr. – French
G. – Golfe, Golfo, Gulf, Guba, Gebel
Ga. – Georgia
Gt. – Great, Greater
Guinea-Biss. – Guinea-Bissau
H.K. – Hong Kong
H.P. – Himachal Pradesh
Hants. – Hampshire
Harb. – Harbor, Harbour
Hd. – Head
Hts. – Heights
I.(s). – Île, Ilha, Insel, Isla, Island, Isle
Ill. – Illinois
Ind. – Indiana
Ind. Oc. – Indian Ocean
Ivory C. – Ivory Coast
J. – Jabal, Jebel
Jaz. – Jazīrah
Junc. – Junction
K. – Kap, Kapp
Kans. – Kansas
Kep. – Kepulauan
Ky. – Kentucky
L. – Lac, Lacul, Lago, Lagoa, Lake, Limni, Loch, Lough
La. – Louisiana
Ld. – Land
Liech. – Liechtenstein
Lux. – Luxembourg
Mad. P. – Madhya Pradesh
Madag. – Madagascar
Man. – Manitoba
Mass. – Massachusetts

Md. – Maryland
Me. – Maine
Medit. S. – Mediterranean Sea
Mich. – Michigan
Minn. – Minnesota
Miss. – Mississippi
Mo. – Missouri
Mont. – Montana
Mozam. – Mozambique
Mt.(s) – Mont, Montaña, Mountain
Mte. – Monte
Mti. – Monti
N. – Nord, Norte, North, Northern, Nouveau, Nahal, Nahr
N.B. – New Brunswick
N.C. – North Carolina
N. Cal. – New Caledonia
N. Dak. – North Dakota
N.H. – New Hampshire
N.I. – North Island
N.J. – New Jersey
N. Mex. – New Mexico
N.S. – Nova Scotia
N.S.W. – New South Wales
N.W.T. – North West Territory
N.Y. – New York
N.Z. – New Zealand
Nac. – Nacional
Nat. – National
Nebr. – Nebraska
Neths. – Netherlands
Nev. – Nevada
Nfld & L. – Newfoundland and Labrador
Nic. – Nicaragua
O. – Oued, Ouadi
Occ. – Occidentale
Okla. – Oklahoma
Ont. – Ontario
Or. – Orientale

Oreg. – Oregon
Os. – Ostrov
Oz. – Ozero
P. – Pass, Passo, Pasul, Pulau
P.E.I. – Prince Edward Island
Pa. – Pennsylvania
Pac. Oc. – Pacific Ocean
Papua N.G. – Papua New Guinea
Pass. – Passage
Peg. – Pegunungan
Pen. – Peninsula, Péninsule
Phil. – Philippines
Pk. – Peak
Plat. – Plateau
Prov. – Province, Provincial
Pt. – Point
Pta. – Ponta, Punta
Pte. – Pointe
Qué. – Québec
Queens. – Queensland
R. – Rio, River
R.I. – Rhode Island
Ra. – Range
Raj. – Rajasthan
Recr. – Recreational, Récréatif
Reg. – Region
Rep. – Republic
Res. – Reserve, Reservoir
Rhld-Pfz. – Rheinland-Pfalz
S. – South, Southern, Sur
Si. Arabia – Saudi Arabia
S.C. – South Carolina
S. Dak. – South Dakota
S.I. – South Island
S. Leone – Sierra Leone
Sa. – Serra, Sierra
Sask. – Saskatchewan
Scot. – Scotland
Sd. – Sound
Sev. – Severnaya
Sib. – Siberia

Sprs. – Springs
St. – Saint
Sta. – Santa
Ste. – Sainte
Sto. – Santo
Str. – Strait, Stretto
Switz. – Switzerland
Tas. – Tasmania
Tenn. – Tennessee
Terr. – Territory, Territoire
Tex. – Texas
Tg. – Tanjung
Trin. & Tob. – Trinidad & Tobago
U.A.E. – United Arab Emirates
U.K. – United Kingdom
U.S.A. – United States of America
Ut. P. – Uttar Pradesh
Va. – Virginia
Vdkhr. – Vodokhranilishche
Vdskh. – Vodoskhovyshche
Vf. – Vîrful
Vic. – Victoria
Vol. – Volcano
Vt. – Vermont
W. – Wadi, West
W. Va. – West Virginia
Wall. & F. Is. – Wallis and Futuna Is.
Wash. – Washington
Wis. – Wisconsin
Wlkp. – Wielkopolski
Wyo. – Wyoming
Yorks. – Yorkshire

A

A Coruña Spain 43°20N 8°25W 21 A1
A Estrada Spain 42°43N 8°27W 21 A1
A Fonsagrada Spain 43°8N 7°4W 21 A2
Aabenraa Denmark 55°3N 9°25E 9 J13
Aachen Germany 50°45N 6°6E 16 C4
Aalborg Denmark 57°2N 9°54E 9 H13
Aalen Germany 48°51N 10°6E 16 D6
Aalst Belgium 50°56N 4°2E 15 D4
Aalten Neths. 51°56N 6°35E 15 C6
Aalter Belgium 51°5N 3°28E 15 C3
Äänekoski Finland 62°36N 25°44E 8 E21
Aarau Switz. 47°23N 8°4E 20 C8
Aare → Switz. 47°33N 8°14E 20 C8
Aarhus = Århus Denmark 56°8N 10°11E 9 H14
Aarschot Belgium 50°59N 4°49E 15 D4
Aba Dem. Rep. of the Congo 3°58N 30°17E 54 B3
Aba Nigeria 5°10N 7°19E 50 G7
Abaco I. Bahamas 26°25N 77°10W 88 A4
Ābādān Iran 30°22N 48°20E 45 D6
Ābādeh Iran 31°8N 52°40E 45 D7
Abadla Algeria 31°2N 2°45W 50 B5
Abaetetuba Brazil 1°40S 48°50W 93 D9
Abagnar Qi = Xilinhot China 43°52N 116°2E 34 C9
Abah, Tanjung Indonesia 8°46S 115°38E 37 K18
Abai Paraguay 25°58S 55°54W 95 B4
Abakan Russia 53°40N 91°10E 29 D10
Abancay Peru 13°35S 72°55W 92 F4
Abariringa Kiribati 2°50S 171°40W 64 H10
Abarqū Iran 31°10N 53°20E 45 D7
Abashiri Japan 44°0N 144°15E 30 B12
Abashiri-Wan Japan 44°0N 144°30E 30 C12
Ābay = Nîl el Azraq → Sudan 15°38N 32°31E 51 E12
Abay Kazakhstan 49°38N 72°53E 28 E8
Abaya, L. Ethiopia 6°30N 37°50E 47 F2
Abaza Russia 52°39N 90°6E 28 D9
'Abbāsābād Iran 33°34N 58°23E 45 C8
Abbay = Nîl el Azraq → Sudan 15°38N 32°31E 51 E12
Abbaye, Pt. U.S.A. 46°58N 88°8W 80 B9
Abbé, L. Ethiopia 11°8N 41°47E 47 E3
Abbeville France 50°6N 1°49E 20 A4
Abbeville Ala., U.S.A. 31°34N 85°15W 85 F12
Abbeville La., U.S.A. 29°58N 92°8W 84 G8
Abbeville S.C., U.S.A. 34°11N 82°23W 85 D13
Abbeyfeale Ireland 52°23N 9°18W 10 D2
Abbot Ice Shelf Antarctica 73°0S 92°0W 5 D16
Abbotsford Canada 49°5N 122°20W 70 D4
Abbottabad Pakistan 34°10N 73°15E 42 B5
ABC Islands = Netherlands Antilles ☑ W. Indies 12°15N 69°0W 92 A5
Abd al Kūrī Yemen 12°5N 52°20E 47 E5
Ābdar Iran 30°16N 55°19E 45 D7
'Abdolābād Iran 34°12N 56°30E 45 C8
Abdulpur Bangla. 24°15N 88°59E 43 G13
Abéché Chad 13°50N 20°35E 51 F10
Abel Tasman △ N.Z. 40°59S 173°3E 59 D4
Abengourou Ivory C. 6°42N 3°27W 50 G5
Åbenrå = Aabenraa Denmark 55°3N 9°25E 9 J13
Abeokuta Nigeria 7°3N 3°19E 50 G6
Aberaeron U.K. 52°15N 4°15W 13 E3
Aberayron = Aberaeron U.K. 52°15N 4°15W 13 E3
Aberchirder U.K. 57°34N 2°37W 11 D6
Abercorn Australia 25°12S 151°5E 63 D5
Aberdare U.K. 51°43N 3°27W 13 F4
Aberdare △ Kenya 0°22S 36°44E 54 C4
Aberdare Ra. Kenya 0°15S 36°50E 54 C4
Aberdeen Australia 32°9S 150°56E 63 E5
Aberdeen Canada 52°20N 106°8W 71 C7
Aberdeen China 22°14N 114°8E 33 G11
Aberdeen S. Africa 32°28S 24°2E 56 E3
Aberdeen U.K. 57°9N 2°5W 11 D6
Aberdeen Idaho, U.S.A. 42°57N 112°50W 76 E7
Aberdeen Md., U.S.A. 39°31N 76°10W 81 F15
Aberdeen Miss., U.S.A. 33°49N 88°33W 85 E10
Aberdeen S. Dak., U.S.A. 45°28N 98°29W 80 C4
Aberdeen Wash., U.S.A. 46°59N 123°50W 78 D3
Aberdeen, City of ☑ U.K. 57°10N 2°10W 11 D6
Aberdeen L. Canada 64°30N 99°0W 68 E12
Aberdeenshire ☑ U.K. 57°17N 2°36W 11 D6
Aberdovey = Aberdyfi U.K. 52°33N 4°3W 13 E3
Aberdyfi U.K. 52°33N 4°3W 13 E3
Aberfeldy U.K. 56°37N 3°51W 11 E5
Aberfoyle U.K. 56°11N 4°23W 11 E4
Abergavenny U.K. 51°49N 3°1W 13 F4
Abergele U.K. 53°17N 3°35W 12 D4
Abernathy U.S.A. 33°50N 101°51W 84 E4
Abert, L. U.S.A. 42°38N 120°14W 76 E3
Aberystwyth U.K. 52°25N 4°5W 13 E3
Abhā Si. Arabia 18°0N 42°34E 47 D3
Abhar Iran 36°9N 49°13E 45 B6
Abhayapuri India 26°24N 90°38E 43 F14
Abidjan Ivory C. 5°26N 3°58W 50 G5
Abilene Kans., U.S.A. 38°55N 97°13W 80 F5
Abilene Tex., U.S.A. 32°28N 99°43W 84 E5
Abingdon U.K. 51°40N 1°17W 13 F6
Abingdon U.S.A. 36°43N 81°59W 81 G13
Abington Reef Australia 18°0S 149°35E 62 B4
Abitau → Canada 59°53N 109°3W 71 B7
Abitibi → Canada 51°3N 80°55W 72 B3
Abitibi, L. Canada 48°40N 79°40W 72 C4
Abkhaz Republic = Abkhazia ☑ Georgia 43°12N 41°5E 19 F7
Abkhazia ☑ Georgia 43°12N 41°5E 19 F7
Abminga Australia 26°8S 134°51E 63 D1
Åbo = Turku Finland 60°30N 22°19E 9 F20
Abohar India 30°10N 74°10E 42 D6
Abomey Benin 7°10N 2°5E 50 G6
Abong-Mbang Cameroon 4°0N 13°8E 52 D2
Abou-Deïa Chad 11°20N 19°20E 51 F9

Aboyne U.K. 57°4N 2°47W 11 D6
Abra Pampa Argentina 22°43S 65°42W 94 A2
Abraham L. Canada 52°15N 116°35W 70 C5
Abreojos, Pta. Mexico 26°50N 113°40W 86 B2
Abrolhos, Banco dos Brazil 18°0S 38°0W 93 F11
Abrud Romania 46°19N 23°5E 17 E12
Absaroka Range U.S.A. 44°45N 109°50W 76 D9
Abu India 24°41N 72°50E 42 G5
Abū al Abyad U.A.E. 24°11N 53°50E 45 E7
Abū al Khaşīb Iraq 30°25N 48°0E 44 D5
Abū 'Alī Si. Arabia 27°20N 49°27E 45 E6
Abū 'Alī → Lebanon 34°25N 35°50E 46 A4
Abu Dhabi = Abū Ȥāby U.A.E. 24°28N 54°22E 45 E7
Abu Du'ān Syria 36°25N 38°15E 44 B3
Abu el Gaïn, W. → Egypt 29°35N 33°30E 46 F2
Abu Ga'da, W. → Egypt 29°15N 32°53E 46 F1
Abū Ḥadrīyah Si. Arabia 27°20N 48°58E 45 E6
Abu Hamed Sudan 19°32N 33°13E 51 E12
Abū Kamāl Syria 34°30N 41°0E 44 C4
Abū Madd, Ra's Si. Arabia 24°50N 37°7E 44 E3
Abū Mūsā U.A.E. 25°52N 55°3E 45 E7
Abū Qaşr Si. Arabia 30°24N 38°10E 44 D3
Abu Shagara, Ras Sudan 21°4N 37°19E 51 D13
Abu Simbel Egypt 22°18N 31°40E 51 D12
Abū Şukhayr Iraq 31°54N 44°30E 44 D5
Abū Zabad Sudan 12°25N 29°10E 51 F11
Abū Ȥāby U.A.E. 24°28N 54°22E 45 E7
Abū Zeydābād Iran 33°54N 51°45E 45 C6
Abuja Nigeria 9°5N 7°32E 50 G7
Abukuma-Gawa → Japan 38°6N 140°52E 30 E10
Abukuma-Sammyaku Japan 37°30N 140°45E 30 F10
Abunā Brazil 9°40S 65°20W 92 E5
Abunā → Brazil 9°41S 65°20W 92 E5
Aburo Dem. Rep. of the Congo 2°4N 30°53E 54 B3
Abut Hd. N.Z. 43°7S 170°15E 59 E3
Åbyek Iran 36°4N 50°33E 45 B6
Acadia △ U.S.A. 44°20N 68°13W 81 C19
Açailândia Brazil 4°57S 47°0W 93 D9
Acajutla El Salv. 13°36N 89°50W 88 D2
Acámbaro Mexico 20°2N 100°44W 86 D4
Acaponeta Mexico 22°30N 105°22W 86 C3
Acapulco Mexico 16°51N 99°55W 87 D5
Acaraí, Serra Brazil 1°50N 57°50W 92 C7
Acarigua Venezuela 9°33N 69°12W 92 B5
Acatlán Mexico 18°12N 98°3W 87 D5
Acayucán Mexico 17°57N 94°55W 87 D6
Accomac U.S.A. 37°43N 75°40W 81 G16
Accra Ghana 5°35N 0°6W 50 G5
Accrington U.K. 53°45N 2°22W 12 D5
Acebal Argentina 33°20S 60°50W 94 C3
Aceh ☐ Indonesia 4°15N 97°30E 36 D1
Achalpur India 21°22N 77°32E 40 J10
Acharnes Greece 38°5N 23°44E 23 E9
Acheloos → Greece 38°19N 21°7E 23 E9
Acheng China 45°30N 126°58E 35 B14
Acher India 23°10N 72°32E 42 H5
Achill Hd. Ireland 53°58N 10°15W 10 C1
Achill I. Ireland 53°58N 10°1W 10 C1
Achinsk Russia 56°20N 90°20E 29 D10
Acireale Italy 37°37N 15°10E 22 F6
Ackerman U.S.A. 33°19N 89°11W 85 E10
Acklins I. Bahamas 22°30N 74°0W 89 B5
Acme Canada 51°33N 113°30W 70 C6
Acme U.S.A. 40°8N 79°26W 82 F5
Aconcagua, Cerro Argentina 32°39S 70°0W 94 C2
Aconquija, Mt. Argentina 27°0S 66°0W 94 B2
Açores, Is. dos Atl. Oc. 38°0N 27°0W 50 a
Acornhoek S. Africa 24°37S 31°2E 57 C5
Acraman, L. Australia 32°2S 135°23E 63 E2
Acre = 'Akko Israel 32°55N 35°4E 46 C4
Acre ☐ Brazil 9°1S 71°0W 92 E4
Acre → Brazil 8°45S 67°22W 92 E5
Actinolite Canada 44°32N 77°19W 82 B7
Acton Canada 43°38N 80°3W 82 C4
Ad Dammām Si. Arabia 26°20N 50°5E 45 E6
Ad Dāmūr Lebanon 33°43N 35°27E 46 B4
Ad Dawādimī Si. Arabia 24°35N 44°15E 44 E5
Ad Dawḥah Qatar 25°15N 51°35E 45 E6
Ad Dawr Iraq 34°27N 43°47E 44 C4
Ad Dir'īyah Si. Arabia 24°44N 46°35E 44 E5
Ad Dīwānīyah Iraq 32°0N 45°0E 44 D5
Ad Dujayl Iraq 33°51N 44°14E 44 C5
Ad Duwayd Si. Arabia 30°15N 42°17E 44 D4
Ada Minn., U.S.A. 47°18N 96°31W 80 B5
Ada Okla., U.S.A. 34°46N 96°41W 84 D6
Adair, C. Canada 71°30N 71°34W 69 C17
Adaja → Spain 41°32N 4°52W 21 B3
Adak U.S.A. 51°45N 176°45W 74 E4
Adak I. U.S.A. 51°45N 176°45W 74 E4
Adamaoua, Massif de l' Cameroon 7°20N 12°20E 51 G8
Adamawa Highlands = Adamaoua, Massif de l' Cameroon 7°20N 12°20E 51 G8
Adamello, Mte. Italy 46°9N 10°30E 20 C9
Adaminaby Australia 36°0S 148°45E 63 F4
Adams Mass., U.S.A. 42°38N 73°7W 83 D11
Adams N.Y., U.S.A. 43°49N 76°1W 83 C8
Adams Wis., U.S.A. 43°57N 89°49W 80 D9
Adams, Mt. U.S.A. 46°12N 121°30W 78 D5
Adam's Bridge Sri Lanka 9°15N 79°40E 40 Q11
Adams L. Canada 51°10N 119°40W 70 C5
Adam's Peak Sri Lanka 6°48N 80°30E 40 R12
Adana Turkey 37°0N 35°16E 44 B2
Adapazarı = Sakarya Turkey 40°48N 30°25E 19 F5
Adarama Sudan 17°10N 34°52E 51 E12
Adare, C. Antarctica 71°0S 171°0E 5 D11
Adaut Indonesia 8°8S 131°7E 37 F8
Adavale Australia 25°52S 144°32E 63 D3

Adda → Italy 45°8N 9°53E 20 B8
Addis Ababa = Addis Abeba Ethiopia 9°2N 38°42E 47 F2
Addis Abeba Ethiopia 9°2N 38°42E 47 F2
Addison U.S.A. 42°1N 77°14W 82 D7
Addo S. Africa 33°32S 25°45E 56 E4
Addo △ S. Africa 33°30S 25°50E 56 E4
Ādeh Iran 37°42N 45°11E 44 B5
Adel U.S.A. 31°8N 83°25W 85 F13
Adelaide Australia 34°52S 138°30E 63 E2
Adelaide S. Africa 32°42S 26°20E 56 E4
Adelaide I. Antarctica 67°15S 68°30W 5 C17
Adelaide Pen. Canada 68°15N 97°30W 68 D12
Adelaide River Australia 13°15S 131°7E 60 B5
Adelaide Village Bahamas 25°0N 77°31W 88 A4
Adelanto U.S.A. 34°35N 117°22W 79 L9
Adele I. Australia 15°32S 123°9E 60 C3
Adélie, Terre Antarctica 68°0S 140°0E 5 C10
Adelie Land = Adélie, Terre Antarctica 68°0S 140°0E 5 C10
Aden = Al 'Adan Yemen 12°45N 45°0E 47 E4
Aden, G. of Ind. Oc. 12°30N 47°30E 47 E4
Adendorp S. Africa 32°15S 24°30E 56 E3
Adh Dhayd U.A.E. 25°17N 55°53E 45 E7
Adhoi India 23°26N 70°32E 42 H4
Adi Indonesia 4°15S 133°30E 37 E8
Adieu, C. Australia 32°0S 132°10E 61 F5
Adieu Pt. Australia 15°14S 124°35E 60 C3
Adige → Italy 45°9N 12°20E 22 B5
Adigrat Ethiopia 14°20N 39°26E 47 E2
Adilabad India 19°33N 78°20E 40 K11
Adirondack → U.S.A. 44°0N 74°20W 83 C10
Adirondack Mts. U.S.A. 44°0N 74°0W 83 C10
Adis Abeba = Addis Abeba Ethiopia 9°2N 38°42E 47 F2
Adjumani Uganda 3°20N 31°50E 54 B3
Adjuntas Puerto Rico 18°10N 66°43W 89 d
Adlavik Is. Canada 55°0N 58°40W 73 B8
Admiralty G. Australia 14°20S 125°55E 60 B4
Admiralty Gulf ☼ Australia 14°16S 125°52E 60 B4
Admiralty I. U.S.A. 57°30N 134°30W 70 B2
Admiralty Inlet Canada 72°30N 86°0W 69 C14
Admiralty Is. Papua N. G. 2°0S 147°0E 58 B7
Adolfo González Chaves Argentina 38°2S 60°5W 94 D3
Adolfo Ruiz Cortines, Presa Mexico 27°15N 109°6W 86 B3
Adonara Indonesia 8°15S 123°5E 37 F6
Adoni India 15°33N 77°18E 40 M10
Adour → France 43°32N 1°32W 20 E3
Adra India 23°30N 86°42E 43 H12
Adra Spain 36°43N 3°3W 21 D4
Adrano Italy 37°40N 14°50E 22 F6
Adrar Algeria 27°51N 0°11E 50 C6
Adrar Mauritania 20°30N 7°30W 50 D3
Adrar des Iforas Africa 19°40N 1°40E 50 E6
Adrian Mich., U.S.A. 41°54N 84°2W 81 E11
Adrian Tex., U.S.A. 35°16N 102°40W 84 D3
Adriatic Sea Medit. S. 43°0N 16°0E 22 C6
Adua Indonesia 1°45S 129°50E 37 E7
Adwa Ethiopia 14°15N 38°52E 47 E2
Adygea ☐ Russia 45°0N 40°0E 19 F7
Adzhar Republic = Ajaria ☐ Georgia 41°30N 42°0E 19 F7
Adzopé Ivory C. 6°7N 3°49W 50 G5
Ægean Sea Medit. S. 38°30N 25°0E 23 E11
Aerhtai Shan Mongolia 46°40N 92°45E 32 B4
Afaahiti Tahiti 17°45S 149°17W 59 d
'Afak Iraq 32°4N 45°15E 44 C5
Afandou Greece 36°18N 28°12E 25 C10
Afareaitu Moorea 17°33S 149°47W 59 d
Afghanistan ■ Asia 33°0N 65°0E 40 C4
Afognak I. U.S.A. 58°15N 152°30W 74 D9
Africa 10°0N 20°0E 48 E6
'Afrīn Syria 36°32N 36°50E 44 B3
Afton N.Y., U.S.A. 42°14N 75°32W 83 D9
Afton Wyo., U.S.A. 42°44N 110°56W 76 E8
Afuá Brazil 0°15S 50°20W 93 D8
'Afula Israel 32°37N 35°17E 46 C4
Afyon Turkey 38°45N 30°33E 19 G5
Afyonkarahisar = Afyon Turkey 38°45N 30°33E 19 G5
Ağa Jari Iran 30°42N 49°50E 45 D6
Agadés = Agadez Niger 16°58N 7°59E 50 E7
Agadez Niger 16°58N 7°59E 50 E7
Agadir Morocco 30°28N 9°55W 50 B4
Agaete Canary Is. 28°6N 15°43W 24 F4
Agalega Is. Mauritius 11°0S 57°0E 3 E12
Agar India 23°40N 76°2E 42 H7
Agartala India 23°50N 91°23E 41 H17
Agassiz Canada 49°14N 121°46W 70 D4
Agassiz Icecap Canada 80°15N 76°0W 69 A16
Agats Indonesia 5°33S 138°0E 37 F9
Agattu I. U.S.A. 52°25N 173°35E 74 E2
Agawam U.S.A. 42°5N 72°37W 83 D12
Agboville Ivory C. 5°55N 4°15W 50 G5
Ağdam Azerbaijan 40°0N 46°58E 44 B5
Agde France 43°19N 3°28E 20 E5
Agde, C. France 43°16N 3°28E 20 E5
Agen France 44°12N 0°38E 20 D4
Āgh Kand Iran 37°15N 48°4E 45 B6
Aghia Deka Greece 35°3N 24°58E 25 D6
Aghia Ekaterinis, Akra Greece 39°50N 19°50E 25 A3
Aghia Galini Greece 35°6N 24°41E 25 D6
Aghia Varvara Greece 35°8N 25°1E 25 D7
Aghios Efstratios Greece 39°34N 24°58E 23 E11
Aghios Ioannis, Akra Greece 35°20N 25°40E 25 D7
Aghios Isidoros Greece 36°9N 27°51E 25 C9
Aghios Matheos Greece 39°30N 19°47E 25 B3
Aghios Nikolaos Greece 35°11N 25°41E 25 D7
Aghios Stephanos Greece 39°34N 19°39E 25 A3
Aghiou Orous, Kolpos Greece 40°6N 24°0E 23 D11
Aginskoye Russia 51°6N 114°32E 29 D12
Agnew Australia 28°1S 120°31E 61 E3
Agori India 24°33N 82°57E 43 G10

Agra India 27°17N 77°58E 42 F7
Ağri Turkey 39°44N 43°3E 19 G7
Agri → Italy 40°13N 16°44E 22 D7
Ağrı Dağı Turkey 39°50N 44°15E 44 B5
Ağri Karakose = Ağri Turkey 39°44N 43°3E 19 G7
Agrigento Italy 37°19N 13°34E 22 F5
Agrinio Greece 38°37N 21°27E 23 E9
Agua Caliente Mexico 32°29N 116°59W 79 N10
Agua Caliente Springs U.S.A. 32°56N 116°19W 79 N10
Água Clara Brazil 20°25S 52°45W 93 H8
Agua Fria △ U.S.A. 34°14N 112°0W 77 J8
Agua Hechicera Mexico 32°28N 116°15W 79 N10
Agua Prieta Mexico 31°18N 109°34W 86 A3
Aguadilla Puerto Rico 18°26N 67°10W 89 d
Aguadulce Panama 8°15N 80°32W 88 E3
Aguanga U.S.A. 33°27N 116°51W 79 M10
Aguanish Canada 50°14N 62°2W 73 B7
Aguanus → Canada 50°13N 62°5W 73 B7
Aguapey → Argentina 29°7S 56°36W 94 B4
Aguaray Guazú → Paraguay 24°47S 57°19W 94 A4
Aguarico → Ecuador 0°59S 75°11W 92 D3
Aguaro-Guariquito △ Venezuela 8°20N 66°35W 89 E6
Aguas Blancas Chile 24°15S 69°55W 94 A2
Aguas Calientes, Sierra de Argentina 25°26S 66°40W 94 B2
Aguascalientes Mexico 21°53N 102°18W 86 C4
Aguascalientes ☐ Mexico 22°0N 102°20W 86 C4
Aguila, Punta Puerto Rico 17°57N 67°13W 89 d
Aguilares Argentina 27°26N 65°35W 94 B2
Águilas Spain 37°23N 1°35W 21 D5
Agüimes Canary Is. 27°58N 15°27W 24 G4
Aguja, C. de la Colombia 11°18N 74°12W 90 A4
Agujereada, Pta. Puerto Rico 18°30N 67°8W 89 d
Agulhas, C. S. Africa 34°52S 20°0E 56 E3
Agulo Canary Is. 28°11N 17°12W 24 F2
Agung, Gunung Indonesia 8°20S 115°28E 37 J18
Agur Uganda 2°28N 32°55E 54 B3
Agusan → Phil. 9°0N 125°30E 37 C7
Aha Mts. Botswana 19°45S 21°0E 56 B3
Ahaggar Algeria 23°0N 6°30E 50 D7
Ahar Iran 38°35N 47°0E 44 B5
Ahipara B. N.Z. 35°5S 173°5E 59 A4
Ahiri India 19°30N 80°0E 40 K12
Ahmad Wal Pakistan 29°18N 65°58E 42 E1
Ahmadabad India 23°0N 72°40E 42 H5
Aḥmadābād Khorāsān, Iran 35°3N 60°50E 45 C9
Aḥmadābād Khorāsān, Iran 35°49N 59°42E 45 C8
Aḥmadī Iran 27°56N 56°42E 45 E8
Ahmadnagar India 19°7N 74°46E 40 K9
Ahmadpur East Pakistan 29°12N 71°10E 42 E4
Ahmadpur Lamma Pakistan 28°19N 70°3E 42 E4
Ahmedabad = Ahmadabad India 23°0N 72°40E 42 H5
Ahmednagar = Ahmadnagar India 19°7N 74°46E 40 K9
Ahome Mexico 25°55N 109°11W 86 B3
Ahoskie U.S.A. 36°17N 76°59W 85 C16
Ahram Iran 28°52N 51°16E 45 D6
Ahrax Pt. Malta 35°59N 14°22E 25 C1
Ahuachapán El Salv. 13°54N 89°52W 88 D2
Ahvāz Iran 31°20N 48°40E 45 D6
Ahvenanmaa = Åland Finland 60°15N 20°0E 9 F19
Aḥwar Yemen 13°30N 46°40E 47 E4
Ai → India 26°26N 90°44E 43 F14
Ai-Ais Namibia 27°54S 17°59E 56 D2
Ai-Ais and Fish River Canyon △ Namibia 24°45S 17°15E 56 C2
Aichi ☐ Japan 35°0N 137°15E 31 G8
Aigrettes, Pte. des Réunion 21°3S 55°13E 53 c
Aiguá Uruguay 34°13S 54°46W 95 C5
Aigues-Mortes France 43°35N 4°12E 20 E6
Aihui = Heihe China 50°10N 127°30E 33 A7
Aija Peru 9°50S 77°45W 92 E3
Aikawa Japan 38°2N 138°15E 30 E9
Aiken U.S.A. 33°34N 81°43W 85 E14
Aileron Australia 22°39S 133°20E 62 C1
Aillik Canada 55°11N 59°18W 73 A8
Ailsa Craig Canada 43°8N 81°33W 82 C3
Ailsa Craig U.K. 55°15N 5°6W 11 F3
Aim Russia 59°0N 133°55E 29 D14
Aimere Indonesia 8°45S 121°3E 37 F6
Aimogasta Argentina 28°33S 66°50W 94 B2
Aïn Ben Tili Mauritania 25°59N 9°27W 50 C4
Aïn Sefra Algeria 32°47N 0°37W 50 B5
Ain Sudr Egypt 29°50N 33°6E 46 F2
Aïn Témouchent Algeria 35°16N 1°8W 50 A5
Ainaži Latvia 57°50N 24°24E 9 H21
Ainsworth U.S.A. 42°33N 99°52W 80 D4
Aiquile Bolivia 18°10S 65°10W 92 G5
Aïr Niger 18°30N 8°0E 50 E7
Air Force I. Canada 67°58N 74°5W 69 D17
Air Hitam Malaysia 1°55N 103°11E 39 M4
Airdrie Canada 51°18N 114°2W 70 C6
Airdrie U.K. 55°52N 3°57W 11 F5
Aire → U.K. 53°43N 0°55W 12 D7
Aire, I. de l' Spain 39°48N 4°16E 24 B11
Airlie Beach Australia 20°16S 148°43E 62 b
Aisne → France 49°26N 2°50E 20 B5
Ait India 25°54N 79°14E 43 G8
Aitkin U.S.A. 46°32N 93°42W 80 B7
Aitutaki Cook Is. 18°52S 159°45W 65 J12
Aiud Romania 46°19N 23°44E 17 E12
Aix-en-Provence France 43°32N 5°27E 20 E6
Aix-la-Chapelle = Aachen Germany 50°45N 6°6E 16 C4
Aix-les-Bains France 45°41N 5°53E 20 D6

Aizkraukle Latvia 56°36N 25°11E 9 H21
Aizpute Latvia 56°43N 21°40E 9 H19
Aizuwakamatsu Japan 37°30N 139°56E 30 F9
Ajaccio France 41°55N 8°40E 20 F8
Ajai △ Uganda 2°52N 31°16E 54 B3
Ajaigarh India 24°52N 80°16E 43 G9
Ajalpan Mexico 18°22N 97°15W 87 D5
Ajanta Ra. India 20°28N 75°50E 40 J9
Ajari Rep. = Ajaria ☐ Georgia 41°30N 42°0E 19 F7
Ajaria ☐ Georgia 41°30N 42°0E 19 F7
Ajax Canada 43°50N 79°1W 82 C5
Ajdābiyā Libya 30°54N 20°4E 51 B10
Ajka Hungary 47°4N 17°31E 17 E9
'Ajlūn Jordan 32°18N 35°47E 46 C4
'Ajlūn ☐ Jordan 32°18N 35°47E 46 C4
'Ajmān U.A.E. 25°25N 55°30E 45 E7
Ajmer India 26°28N 74°37E 42 F6
Ajnala India 31°50N 74°48E 42 D6
Ajo U.S.A. 32°22N 112°52W 77 K7
Ajo, C. de Spain 43°31N 3°35W 21 A4
Akabira Japan 43°33N 142°5E 30 C11
Akamas Cyprus 35°3N 32°18E 25 D11
Akan △ Japan 43°30N 144°20E 30 C12
Akanthou Cyprus 35°22N 33°45E 25 D12
Akaroa N.Z. 43°49S 172°59E 59 E4
Akashi Japan 34°45N 134°58E 31 G7
Akbarpur Bihar, India 26°18N 83°58E 43 G10
Akbarpur Ut. P., India 26°25N 82°32E 43 F10
Akçakale Turkey 36°41N 38°56E 44 B3
Akdoğan = Lysi Cyprus 35°6N 33°41E 25 D12
Akelamo Indonesia 1°35N 129°40E 37 D7
Aketi Dem. Rep. of the Congo 2°38N 23°47E 52 D4
Akhisar Turkey 38°56N 27°48E 23 E12
Akhnur India 32°52N 74°45E 43 C6
Akhtyrka = Okhtyrka Ukraine 50°25N 35°0E 19 D5
Aki Japan 33°30N 133°54E 31 H6
Akimiski I. Canada 52°50N 81°30W 72 B3
Akincilar = Louroujina Cyprus 35°0N 33°28E 25 E12
Akita Japan 39°45N 140°7E 30 E10
Akita ☐ Japan 39°40N 140°30E 30 E10
Akjoujt Mauritania 19°45N 14°15W 50 E3
Akkeshi Japan 43°2N 144°51E 30 C12
'Akko Israel 32°55N 35°4E 46 C4
Aklavik Canada 68°12N 135°0W 68 D4
Aklera India 24°26N 76°32E 42 G7
Akō Japan 34°45N 134°24E 31 G7
Akola India 20°42N 77°2E 40 J10
Akordat Eritrea 15°30N 37°40E 47 D2
Akpatok I. Canada 60°25N 68°8W 69 E18
Åkrahamn Norway 59°15N 5°10E 9 G11
Akranes Iceland 64°19N 22°5W 8 D2
Akron Colo., U.S.A. 40°10N 103°13W 76 F12
Akron Ohio, U.S.A. 41°5N 81°31W 82 E3
Akrotiri Cyprus 34°36N 32°57E 25 E11
Akrotiri Bay Cyprus 34°35N 33°10E 25 E12
Aksai Chin China 35°15N 79°55E 43 B8
Aksaray Turkey 38°25N 34°2E 44 B2
Aksay = Aqsay Kazakhstan 51°11N 53°0E 19 D9
Akşehir Turkey 38°18N 31°30E 44 B1
Akşehir Gölü Turkey 38°30N 31°25E 19 G5
Aksu China 41°5N 80°10E 32 B3
Aksum Ethiopia 14°5N 38°40E 47 E2
Aktsyabrski Belarus 52°38N 28°53E 17 B15
Aktyubinsk = Aqtöbe Kazakhstan 50°17N 57°10E 19 D10
Akure Nigeria 7°15N 5°5E 50 G7
Akureyri Iceland 65°40N 18°6W 8 D4
Akuseki-Shima Japan 29°27N 129°37E 31 K4
Akyab = Sittwe Burma 20°18N 92°45E 41 J18
Al 'Adan Yemen 12°45N 45°0E 47 E4
Al Aḥsā = Hasa Si. Arabia 25°50N 49°0E 45 E6
Al Ajfar Si. Arabia 27°26N 43°0E 44 E4
Al Amādīyah Iraq 37°5N 43°30E 44 B4
Al 'Amārah Iraq 31°55N 47°15E 44 D5
Al Anbār ☐ Iraq 33°25N 42°0E 44 C4
Al 'Aqabah Jordan 29°31N 35°0E 46 F4
Al 'Aqabah ☐ Jordan 29°30N 35°0E 46 F4
Al Arak Syria 34°38N 38°35E 44 C3
Al 'Aramah Si. Arabia 25°30N 46°0E 44 E5
Al Arţāwīyah Si. Arabia 26°31N 45°20E 44 E5
Al 'Āşimah = 'Ammān ☐ Jordan 31°40N 36°30E 46 D5
Al 'Assāfiyah Si. Arabia 28°17N 38°59E 44 D3
Al 'Awdah Si. Arabia 25°32N 45°41E 44 E5
Al 'Ayn Si. Arabia 25°4N 38°6W 44 E3
Al 'Ayn U.A.E. 24°15N 55°45E 45 E7
Al 'Azīzīyah Iraq 32°54N 45°4E 44 C5
Al Bāb Syria 36°23N 37°29E 44 B3
Al Bad' Si. Arabia 28°28N 35°1E 44 D2
Al Bādī Iraq 35°56N 41°32E 44 C4
Al Baḥrah Kuwait 29°40N 47°52E 44 D5
Al Baḥr Mayyit = Dead Sea Asia 31°30N 35°30E 46 D4
Al Balqā' ☐ Jordan 32°5N 35°45E 46 C4
Al Bārūk, J. Lebanon 33°39N 35°40E 46 B4
Al Başrah Iraq 30°30N 47°50E 44 D5
Al Baṭḥā Iraq 31°6N 45°53E 44 D5
Al Batrūn Lebanon 34°15N 35°40E 46 A4
Al Baydā Libya 32°50N 21°44E 51 B10
Al Biqā Lebanon 34°10N 36°10E 46 A5
Al Bi'r Si. Arabia 28°51N 36°16E 44 D3
Al Bukayrīyah Si. Arabia 26°9N 43°40E 44 E4
Al Burayj Syria 34°15N 36°46E 46 A5
Al Faḍilī Si. Arabia 26°58N 49°10E 45 E6
Al Fallūjah Iraq 33°20N 43°55E 44 C4
Al Fāw Iraq 30°0N 48°30E 45 D6
Al Fujayrah U.A.E. 25°7N 56°18E 45 E8
Al Ghadaf, W. → Jordan 31°26N 36°43E 46 D5
Al Ghammās Iraq 31°45N 44°37E 44 D5
Al Ghazālah Si. Arabia 26°48N 41°19E 44 E4
Al Ḥadīthah Iraq 34°0N 41°13E 44 C4
Al Ḥadīthah Si. Arabia 31°28N 37°8E 44 D3
Al Ḥadr Iraq 35°35N 42°44E 44 C4

Al Ḥājānah Syria 33°20N 36°33E 46 B5
Al Ḥajar al Gharbī Oman 24°10N 56°15E 45 E8
Al Ḥamad S. Arabia 31°30N 39°30E 44 D3
Al Ḥamdānīyah Syria 35°25N 36°50E 44 C3
Al Ḥamīdīyah Syria 34°42N 35°57E 46 A4
Al Ḥammām Iraq 30°57N 46°51E 44 D5
Al Ḥamrā' S. Arabia 24°2N 38°55E 44 E3
Al Ḥamzah Iraq 31°43N 44°58E 44 D5
Al Ḥanākīyah S. Arabia 24°51N 40°31E 44 E4
Al Harūj al Aswad Libya 27°0N 17°10E 51 C9
Al Ḥasakah Syria 36°35N 40°45E 44 B4
Al Ḥayy Iraq 32°5N 46°5E 44 C5
Al Ḥijarah Asia 30°0N 44°0E 44 D4
Al Ḥillah Iraq 32°30N 44°25E 44 C5
Al Ḥillah Si. Arabia 23°35N 46°50E 47 B4
Al Hindīyah Iraq 32°30N 44°10E 44 C5
Al Hirmil Lebanon 34°26N 36°24E 46 A5
Al Hoceïma Morocco 35°8N 3°58W 50 A5
Al Ḥudaydah Yemen 14°50N 43°0E 47 E3
Al Ḥudūd ash Shamālīyah □
 Si. Arabia 29°10N 42°30E 44 D4
Al Hufūf Si. Arabia 25°25N 49°45E 45 E6
Al Ḥumaydah Si. Arabia 29°14N 34°56E 44 D2
Al Ḥunayy Si. Arabia 25°58N 48°45E 45 E6
Al Īsāwīyah Si. Arabia 30°43N 37°59E 44 D3
Al Jafr Jordan 30°18N 36°14E 46 E5
Al Jāfūrah Si. Arabia 25°0N 50°15E 45 E7
Al Jaghbūb Libya 29°42N 24°38E 51 C10
Al Jahrah Kuwait 29°25N 47°40E 44 D5
Al Jalāmīd Si. Arabia 31°20N 40°6E 44 D3
Al Jamalīyah Qatar 25°37N 51°5E 45 E6
Al Janūb □ Lebanon 33°20N 35°20E 46 B4
Al Jawf Libya 24°10N 23°24E 51 D10
Al Jawf Si. Arabia 29°55N 39°40E 44 D3
Al Jawf □ Si. Arabia 29°30N 39°30E 44 D3
Al Jazair = Algeria ■
 Africa 28°30N 2°0E 50 C6
Al Jazirah Iraq 33°30N 44°0E 44 C5
Al Jithāmīyah Si. Arabia 27°41N 41°43E 44 E4
Al Jubayl Si. Arabia 27°0N 49°50E 45 E6
Al Jubaylah Si. Arabia 24°55N 46°25E 44 E5
Al Jubb Si. Arabia 27°11N 42°17E 44 E4
Al Junaynah Sudan 13°27N 22°45E 51 F10
Al Kabā'ish Iraq 30°58N 47°0E 44 D5
Al Karak Jordan 31°11N 35°42E 46 D4
Al Karak □ Jordan 31°0N 36°0E 46 E5
Al Kāẓimīyah Iraq 33°22N 44°18E 44 C5
Al Khābūrah Oman 23°57N 57°5E 45 F8
Al Khafji Si. Arabia 28°24N 48°29E 45 E6
Al Khalīl West Bank 31°32N 35°6E 46 D4
Al Khāliṣ Iraq 33°49N 44°32E 44 C5
Al Kharsānīyah
 Si. Arabia 27°13N 49°18E 45 E6
Al Khaṣab Oman 26°14N 56°15E 45 E8
Al Khawr Qatar 25°41N 51°30E 45 E6
Al Khiḍr Iraq 31°12N 45°33E 44 D5
Al Khiyām Lebanon 33°20N 35°36E 46 B4
Al Khobar Si. Arabia 26°17N 50°12E 45 E6
Al Khums Libya 32°40N 14°17E 51 B8
Al Kiswah Syria 33°23N 36°14E 46 B5
Al Kūfah Iraq 32°2N 44°24E 44 C4
Al Kufrah Libya 24°17N 23°15E 51 D10
Al Kuhayfiyah Si. Arabia 27°12N 43°3E 44 E4
Al Kūt Iraq 32°30N 46°0E 44 C5
Al Kuwayt Kuwait 29°30N 48°0E 44 D5
Al Labwah Lebanon 34°11N 36°20E 46 A5
Al Lādhiqīyah Syria 35°30N 35°45E 44 C2
Al Līth Si. Arabia 20°9N 40°15E 47 C3
Al Liwā' Oman 24°31N 56°36E 45 E8
Al Luḥayyah Yemen 15°45N 42°40E 47 D3
Al Madīnah Iraq 30°57N 47°16E 44 D5
Al Madīnah Si. Arabia 24°35N 39°52E 44 E3
Al Mafraq Jordan 32°17N 36°14E 46 C5
Al Mafraq □ Jordan 32°17N 36°15E 46 C5
Al Maghreb = Morocco ■
 N. Afr. 32°0N 5°50W 50 B4
Al Maḥmūdīyah Iraq 33°3N 44°21E 44 C5
Al Majma'ah Si. Arabia 25°57N 45°22E 44 E5
Al Makhruq, W. →
 Jordan 31°28N 37°0E 46 D6
Al Makḥūl Si. Arabia 26°37N 42°39E 44 E4
Al Manāmah Bahrain 26°10N 50°30E 45 E6
Al Maqwa' Kuwait 29°10N 47°59E 44 D5
Al Marāḥ Si. Arabia 25°35N 49°35E 45 E6
Al Marj Libya 32°25N 20°30E 51 B10
Al Maṭla Kuwait 29°24N 47°40E 44 D5
Al Mawṣil Iraq 36°15N 43°5E 44 B4
Al Mayādin Syria 35°1N 40°27E 44 C4
Al Mazār Jordan 31°4N 35°41E 46 D4
Al Midhnab Si. Arabia 25°50N 44°18E 44 E5
Al Minā' Lebanon 34°24N 35°49E 46 A4
Al Miqdādīyah Iraq 34°0N 45°0E 44 C5
Al Mubarraz Si. Arabia 25°30N 49°40E 45 E6
Al Mudawwarah Jordan 29°19N 36°0E 46 F5
Al Mughayrā' U.A.E. 24°5N 53°32E 45 E7
Al Muḥarraq Bahrain 26°15N 50°40E 45 E6
Al Mukallā Yemen 14°33N 49°2E 47 E4
Al Mukhā Yemen 13°18N 43°15E 47 E3
Al Musayjīd Si. Arabia 24°5N 39°5E 44 E3
Al Musayyib Iraq 32°49N 44°20E 44 C5
Al Muthanná □ Iraq 30°30N 45°15E 44 D5
Al Muwayliḥ Si. Arabia 27°40N 35°30E 44 E2
Al Qādisīyah □ Iraq 32°0N 45°0E 44 D5
Al Qā'im Iraq 34°21N 41°7E 44 C4
Al Qalībah Si. Arabia 28°24N 37°42E 44 D3
Al Qāmishlī Syria 37°2N 41°14E 44 B4
Al Qaryatayn Syria 34°12N 37°13E 44 A6
Al Qaṣīm □ Si. Arabia 26°0N 43°0E 44 E4
Al Qaṭ'ā Syria 34°40N 40°48E 44 C4
Al Qaṭīf Si. Arabia 26°35N 50°0E 45 E6
Al Qaṭrānah Jordan 31°12N 36°6E 46 D5
Al Qaṭrūn Libya 24°56N 15°3E 51 D9
Al Qayṣūmah Si. Arabia 28°20N 46°7E 44 D5
Al Quds = Jerusalem
 Israel/West Bank 31°47N 35°10E 46 D4
Al Qunayṭirah Syria 32°55N 35°45E 46 B4
Al Qunfudhah Si. Arabia 19°3N 41°4E 47 D3
Al Qurnah Iraq 31°1N 47°25E 44 D5
Al Quṣayr Iraq 30°39N 45°50E 44 D5

Al Quṣayr Syria 34°31N 36°34E 46 A5
Al Qutayfah Syria 33°44N 36°36E 46 B5
Al 'Ubaylah Si. Arabia 21°59N 50°57E 47 C5
Al 'Udaylīyah Si. Arabia 25°8N 49°18E 45 E6
Al 'Ulā Si. Arabia 26°35N 38°0E 44 E3
Al 'Uqayr Si. Arabia 25°40N 50°15E 45 E6
Al 'Uwaynid Si. Arabia 24°50N 46°0E 44 E5
Al 'Uwayqīlah Si. Arabia 30°30N 42°10E 44 D4
Al 'Uyūn Ḥijāz, Si. Arabia 24°33N 39°35E 44 E3
Al 'Uyūn Najd, Si. Arabia 26°30N 43°50E 44 E4
Al 'Uzayr Iraq 31°19N 47°25E 44 D5
Al Wajh Si. Arabia 26°10N 36°30E 44 E3
Al Wakrah Qatar 25°10N 51°40E 45 E6
Al Waqbah Si. Arabia 28°48N 45°33E 44 D5
Al Wari'āh Si. Arabia 27°51N 47°25E 44 E5
Al Yaman = Yemen ■
 Asia 15°0N 44°0E 47 E3
Ala Dağ Turkey 37°44N 35°9E 44 B2
Ala Tau Asia 45°30N 80°40E 28 E9
Ala Tau Shankou = Dzungarian
 Gate Asia 45°10N 82°0E 32 B3
Alabama □ U.S.A. 33°0N 87°0W 85 E11
Alabama → U.S.A. 31°8N 87°57W 85 F11
Alabaster U.S.A. 33°15N 86°49W 85 E11
Alaçam Dağları Turkey 39°18N 28°49E 23 E13
Alacant = Alicante Spain 38°23N 0°30W 21 C5
Alachua U.S.A. 29°47N 82°30W 85 G13
Alagoa Grande Brazil 7°3S 35°35W 93 E11
Alagoas □ Brazil 9°0S 36°0W 93 E11
Alagoinhas Brazil 12°7S 38°20W 93 F11
Alaior Spain 39°57N 4°8E 24 B11
Alajero Canary Is. 28°3N 17°13W 24 F2
Alajuela Costa Rica 10°2N 84°8W 88 D3
Alakamisy Madag. 21°19S 47°14E 57 C8
Alaknanda → India 30°8N 78°36E 43 D8
Alakurtti Russia 66°58N 30°25E 8 C24
Alamarvdasht Iran 27°37N 52°59E 45 E7
Alameda Calif., U.S.A. 37°46N 122°15W 78 H4
Alameda N. Mex.,
 U.S.A. 35°11N 106°37W 77 J10
Alamo U.S.A. 37°22N 115°10W 79 H11
Alamogordo U.S.A. 32°54N 105°57W 77 K11
Alamos Mexico 27°1N 108°56W 86 B3
Alamosa U.S.A. 37°28N 105°52W 77 H11
Åland Finland 60°15N 20°0E 9 F19
Ålands hav Europe 60°0N 19°30E 9 G18
Alania = North Ossetia □
 Russia 43°30N 44°30E 19 F7
Alanya Turkey 36°38N 32°0E 44 B1
Alaotra, Farihin' Madag. 17°30S 48°30E 57 B8
Alapayevsk Russia 57°52N 61°42E 28 D7
Alappuzha = Alleppey
 India 9°30N 76°28E 40 Q10
Alaró Spain 39°42N 2°47E 24 B9
Alarobia-Vohiposa
 Madag. 20°59S 47°9E 57 C8
Alaşehir Turkey 38°23N 28°30E 23 E13
Alaska □ U.S.A. 64°0N 154°0W 74 C9
Alaska, G. of Pac. Oc. 58°0N 145°0W 68 F3
Alaska Peninsula U.S.A. 56°0N 159°0W 74 D8
Alaska Range U.S.A. 62°50N 151°0W 68 E1
Älät Azerbaijan 39°58N 49°25E 45 B6
Alatau Shan = Ala Tau
 Asia 45°30N 80°40E 28 E9
Alatyr Russia 54°55N 46°35E 18 D8
Alausi Ecuador 2°0S 78°50W 92 D3
Alava, C. U.S.A. 48°10N 124°44W 76 B1
Alavo = Alavus Finland 62°35N 23°36E 8 E20
Alavus Finland 62°35N 23°36E 8 E20
Alawa ⌖ Australia 15°42S 134°39E 62 B1
Alawoona Australia 34°45S 140°30E 63 E3
Alayawarra ⌖ Australia 22°0S 134°30E 62 C1
'Alayh Lebanon 33°46N 35°33E 46 B4
Alba Italy 44°42N 8°2E 20 D8
Alba-Iulia Romania 46°8N 23°39E 17 E12
Albacete Spain 39°0N 1°50W 21 C5
Albacutya, L. Australia 35°45S 141°58E 63 F3
Albanel, L. Canada 50°55N 73°12W 72 B5
Albania ■ Europe 41°0N 20°0E 23 D9
Albany Australia 35°1S 117°58E 61 G2
Albany Ga., U.S.A. 31°35N 84°10W 85 F12
Albany N.Y., U.S.A. 42°39N 73°45W 83 D11
Albany Oreg., U.S.A. 44°38N 123°6W 76 D2
Albany Tex., U.S.A. 32°44N 99°18W 84 E5
Albany → Canada 52°17N 81°31W 72 B3
Albarca, C. d' Spain 39°4N 1°22E 24 B7
Albardón Argentina 31°20S 68°30W 94 C2
Albatross B. Australia 12°45S 141°30E 62 A3
Albemarle U.S.A. 35°21N 80°12W 85 D14
Albemarle Sd. U.S.A. 36°5N 76°0W 85 C16
Alberche → Spain 39°58N 4°46E 21 C3
Alberdi Paraguay 26°14S 58°20W 94 B4
Alberga → Australia 27°6S 135°33E 63 D2
Albert, L. Africa 1°30N 31°0E 54 B3
Albert, L. Australia 35°30S 139°10E 63 F2
Albert Edward Ra.
 Australia 18°17S 127°57E 60 C4
Albert Lea U.S.A. 43°39N 93°22W 80 D7
Albert Nile → Uganda 3°36N 32°2E 54 B3
Albert Town Bahamas 22°37N 74°33W 89 B5
Alberta □ Canada 54°40N 115°0W 70 C6
Alberti Argentina 35°1S 60°16W 94 D3
Albertinia S. Africa 34°11S 21°34E 56 E3
Alberton Canada 46°50N 64°0W 73 C7
Albertville France 45°40N 6°22E 20 D7
Albertville U.S.A. 34°16N 86°13W 85 D11
Albi France 43°56N 2°9E 20 E5
Albia U.S.A. 41°2N 92°48W 80 E7
Albina Suriname 5°37N 54°15W 93 B8
Albina, Ponta Angola 15°52S 11°44E 56 B1
Albion Mich., U.S.A. 42°15N 84°45W 81 D11
Albion Nebr., U.S.A. 41°42N 98°0W 80 E4
Albion Pa., U.S.A. 41°53N 80°22W 82 E4
Alborán Medit. S. 35°57N 3°0W 21 E4
Ålborg = Aalborg Denmark 57°2N 9°54E 9 H13
Alborz, Reshteh-ye Kūhhā-ye
 Iran 36°0N 52°0E 45 C7
Albufeira Portugal 37°5N 8°15W 21 D1
Albuquerque U.S.A. 35°5N 106°39W 77 J10

Albuquerque, Cayos de
 Caribbean 12°10N 81°50W 88 D3
Alburg U.S.A. 44°59N 73°18W 83 B11
Albury Australia 36°3S 146°56E 63 F4
Alcalá de Henares Spain 40°28N 3°22W 21 B4
Alcalá la Real Spain 37°27N 3°57W 21 D4
Álcamo Italy 37°59N 12°55E 22 F5
Alcañiz Spain 41°2N 0°8W 21 B5
Alcântara Brazil 2°0S 44°30W 93 D10
Alcántara, Embalse de
 Spain 39°44N 6°50W 21 C2
Alcantarilla Spain 37°59N 1°12W 21 D5
Alcaraz, Sierra de Spain 38°40N 2°20W 21 C4
Alcaudete Spain 37°35N 4°5W 21 D3
Alcázar de San Juan
 Spain 39°24N 3°12W 21 C4
Alchevsk Ukraine 48°30N 38°45E 19 E6
Alcira = Alzira Spain 39°9N 0°30W 21 C5
Alcova U.S.A. 42°34N 106°43W 76 E10
Alcoy Spain 38°43N 0°30W 21 C5
Alcúdia Spain 39°51N 3°7E 24 B10
Alcúdia, B. d' Spain 39°47N 3°15E 24 B10
Aldabra Is. Seychelles 9°22S 46°28E 49 G8
Aldama Mexico 22°55N 98°4W 87 C5
Aldan Russia 58°40N 125°30E 29 D13
Aldan → Russia 63°28N 129°35E 29 C13
Aldea, Pta. de la
 Canary Is. 28°0N 15°50W 24 G4
Aldeburgh U.K. 52°10N 1°37E 13 E9
Alder Pk. U.S.A. 35°53N 121°22W 78 K5
Alderney U.K. 49°42N 2°11W 13 H5
Aldershot U.K. 51°15N 0°44W 13 F7
Aledo U.S.A. 41°12N 90°45W 80 E8
Aleg Mauritania 17°3N 13°55W 50 E3
Alegranza Canary Is. 29°23N 13°32W 24 E6
Alegranza, I. Canary Is. 29°23N 13°32W 24 E6
Alegre Brazil 20°50S 41°30W 95 A7
Alegrete Brazil 29°40S 56°0W 95 B4
Aleksandriya = Oleksandriya
 Ukraine 50°37N 26°19E 17 C14
Aleksandrov Gay Russia 50°9N 48°34E 19 D8
Aleksandrovsk-Sakhalinskiy
 Russia 50°50N 142°20E 29 D15
Aleksandry, Zemlya
 Russia 80°25N 48°0E 28 A5
Além Paraíba Brazil 21°52S 42°41W 95 A7
Alemania Argentina 25°40S 65°30W 94 B2
Alemania Chile 25°10S 69°55W 94 B2
Alençon France 48°27N 0°4E 20 B4
Alenquer Brazil 1°56S 54°46W 93 D8
'Alenuihāhā Channel
 U.S.A. 20°30N 156°0W 75 L8
Aleppo = Ḥalab Syria 36°10N 37°15E 44 B3
Aléria France 42°5N 9°26E 20 E9
Alert Canada 83°2N 60°0W 69 A20
Alert Bay Canada 50°30N 126°55W 70 C3
Alès France 44°9N 4°5E 20 D6
Alessándria Italy 44°54N 8°37E 20 D8
Ålesund Norway 62°28N 6°12E 8 E12
Aleutian Basin Pac. Oc. 57°0N 177°0E 64 B9
Aleutian Is. Pac. Oc. 52°0N 175°0W 74 E5
Aleutian Range U.S.A. 60°0N 154°0W 74 D9
Aleutian Trench Pac. Oc. 48°0N 180°0E 4 D17
Alexander U.S.A. 47°51N 103°39W 80 B2
Alexander, Mt.
 Australia 28°58S 120°16E 61 E3
Alexander Arch. U.S.A. 56°0N 136°0W 68 F4
Alexander Bay S. Africa 28°40S 16°30E 56 D2
Alexander City U.S.A. 32°56N 85°58W 85 E12
Alexander I. Antarctica 69°0S 70°0W 5 C17
Alexandra Australia 37°8S 145°40E 63 F4
Alexandra N.Z. 45°14S 169°25E 59 F2
Alexandra Falls Canada 60°29N 116°18W 70 A5
Alexandria = El Iskandarîya
 Egypt 31°13N 29°58E 51 B11
Alexandria B.C.,
 Canada 52°35N 122°27W 70 C4
Alexandria Ont.,
 Canada 45°19N 74°38W 83 A10
Alexandria Romania 43°57N 25°24E 17 G13
Alexandria S. Africa 33°38S 26°28E 56 E4
Alexandria U.K. 55°59N 4°35W 11 F4
Alexandria La., U.S.A. 31°18N 92°27W 84 F8
Alexandria Minn.,
 U.S.A. 45°53N 95°22W 80 C6
Alexandria S. Dak.,
 U.S.A. 43°39N 97°47W 80 D5
Alexandria Va., U.S.A. 38°49N 77°5W 81 F15
Alexandria Bay U.S.A. 44°20N 75°55W 83 B9
Alexandrina, L.
 Australia 35°25S 139°10E 63 F2
Alexandroupoli Greece 40°50N 25°54E 23 D11
Alexis → Canada 52°33N 56°8W 73 B8
Alexis Creek Canada 52°10N 123°20W 70 C4
Aleysk Russia 52°40N 83°0E 28 D9
Alfabia Spain 39°44N 2°44E 24 B9
Alfenas Brazil 21°20S 46°10W 95 A6
Alford Aberds., U.K. 57°14N 2°41W 11 D6
Alford Lincs., U.K. 53°15N 0°10E 12 D8
Alfred Maine, U.S.A. 43°29N 70°43W 83 C14
Alfred N.Y., U.S.A. 42°16N 77°48W 82 D7
Alfreton U.K. 53°6N 1°24W 12 D6
Algaida Spain 39°33N 2°53E 24 B9
Ålgård Norway 58°46N 5°53E 9 G11
Algarve Portugal 36°58N 8°20W 21 E1
Algeciras Spain 36°9N 5°28E 21 D3
Algemesí Spain 39°11N 0°27W 21 C5
Alger Algeria 36°42N 3°8E 50 A6
Algeria ■ Africa 28°30N 2°0E 50 C6
Algha Kazakhstan 49°53N 57°20E 19 E10
Alghero Italy 40°33N 8°19E 22 D3
Algiers = Alger Algeria 36°42N 3°8E 50 A6
Algoa B. S. Africa 33°50S 25°45E 56 E4
Algoma U.S.A. 44°36N 87°26W 80 C10
Algona U.S.A. 43°4N 94°14W 80 D6
Algonac U.S.A. 42°37N 82°32W 82 D2
Algonquin □ Canada 45°50N 78°30W 72 C4
Algorta Uruguay 32°25S 57°23W 96 C5
Alhambra U.S.A. 34°5N 118°7W 79 L8
Alhucemas = Al Hoceïma
 Morocco 35°8N 3°58W 50 A5

'Alī al Gharbī Iraq 32°30N 46°45E 44 C5
'Alī ash Sharqī Iraq 32°7N 46°44E 44 C5
Äli Bayramli Azerbaijan 39°59N 48°52E 45 B6
Äli Khēl Afghan. 33°57N 69°43E 42 C3
Alī Shāh Iran 38°9N 45°50E 44 B5
'Alīābād Golestān, Iran 36°40N 54°33E 45 B7
'Alīābād Khorāsān, Iran 35°4N 46°58E 44 C5
'Alīābād Kordestān, Iran 35°4N 46°58E 44 C5
'Alīābād Yazd, Iran 31°41N 53°49E 45 D7
Aliağa Turkey 38°47N 26°59E 23 E12
Aliakmonas → Greece 40°30N 22°36E 23 D10
Alicante Spain 38°23N 0°30W 21 C5
Alice S. Africa 32°48S 26°55E 56 E4
Alice U.S.A. 27°45N 98°5W 84 H5
Alice → Queens.,
 Australia 24°2S 144°50E 62 C3
Alice → Queens.,
 Australia 15°35S 142°20E 62 B3
Alice Arm Canada 55°29N 129°31W 70 B3
Alice Springs Australia 23°40S 133°50E 62 C1
Alicedale S. Africa 33°15S 26°4E 56 E4
Aliceville U.S.A. 33°8N 88°9W 85 E10
Aligani India 27°30N 79°10E 43 F8
Aligarh Raj., India 25°55N 76°15E 42 G7
Aligarh Ut. P., India 27°55N 78°10E 42 F7
Alīgūdarz Iran 33°25N 49°45E 45 C6
Alimia Greece 36°16N 27°43E 25 C9
Alims → Russia 63°28N 129°35E 29 C13
Alingsås Sweden 57°56N 12°31E 9 H15
Alipur Pakistan 29°25N 70°55E 42 E4
Alipur Duar India 26°30N 89°35E 41 F16
Aliquippa U.S.A. 40°37N 80°15W 82 F4
Alitus = Alytus Lithuania 54°24N 24°3E 9 J21
Aliwal North S. Africa 30°45S 26°45E 56 E4
Alix Canada 52°24N 113°11W 70 C6
Aljustrel Portugal 37°55N 8°10W 21 D1
Alkmaar Neths. 52°37N 4°45E 15 B4
All American Canal
 U.S.A. 32°45N 115°15W 77 K6
Allagash → U.S.A. 47°5N 69°3W 81 B19
Allah Dad Pakistan 25°38N 67°34E 42 G2
Allahabad India 25°25N 81°58E 43 G9
Allan Canada 51°53N 106°4W 71 C7
Allanridge S. Africa 27°45S 26°40E 56 D4
Allanwater Canada 50°14N 90°10W 72 B2
Allegany U.S.A. 42°6N 78°30W 82 D6
Allegheny → U.S.A. 40°27N 80°1W 82 F5
Allegheny Mts. U.S.A. 38°15N 80°10W 81 F13
Allegheny Plateau
 U.S.A. 41°30N 78°30W 81 E14
Allegheny Res. U.S.A. 41°50N 79°0W 82 E6
Allen, Bog of Ireland 53°15N 7°0W 10 C5
Allen, L. Ireland 54°8N 8°4W 10 B3
Allende Mexico 28°20N 100°51W 86 B4
Allentown U.S.A. 40°37N 75°29W 83 F9
Alleppey India 9°30N 76°28E 40 Q10
Aller → Germany 52°56N 9°12E 16 B5
Alleynes B. Barbados 13°13N 59°39W 89 g
Alliance Nebr., U.S.A. 42°6N 102°52W 80 D2
Alliance Ohio, U.S.A. 40°55N 81°6W 82 F3
Allier → France 46°57N 3°4E 20 C5
Alliford Bay Canada 53°12N 131°58W 70 C2
Alligator Pond Jamaica 17°52N 77°34W 88 a
Alliston Canada 44°9N 79°52W 82 B5
Alloa U.K. 56°7N 3°47W 11 E5
Allora Australia 28°2S 152°0E 63 D5
Alluitsup Paa Greenland 60°30N 45°35W 4 C5
Alma Canada 48°35N 71°40W 73 C5
Alma Ga., U.S.A. 31°33N 82°28W 85 F13
Alma Kans., U.S.A. 39°1N 96°17W 80 F5
Alma Mich., U.S.A. 43°23N 84°39W 81 D11
Alma Nebr., U.S.A. 40°6N 99°22W 80 E4
Alma Wis., U.S.A. 44°20N 91°55W 80 C8
Alma Ata = Almaty
 Kazakhstan 43°15N 76°57E 28 E8
Alma Hill U.S.A. 42°2N 78°0W 82 D7
Almada Portugal 38°41N 9°8W 21 C1
Almaden Australia 17°22S 144°40E 62 B3
Almadén Spain 38°49N 4°52W 21 C3
Almalyk = Olmaliq
 Uzbekistan 40°50N 69°35E 28 E7
Almanor, L. U.S.A. 40°14N 121°9W 76 F3
Almansa Spain 38°51N 1°5E 21 C5
Almanzor, Pico Spain 40°15N 5°18W 21 B3
Almanzora → Spain 37°14N 1°46W 21 D5
Almaty Kazakhstan 43°15N 76°57E 28 E8
Almazán Spain 41°30N 2°30W 21 B4
Almeirim Brazil 1°30S 52°34W 93 D8
Almelo Neths. 52°22N 6°42E 15 B6
Almendralejo Spain 38°41N 6°26W 21 C2
Almere-Stad Neths. 52°20N 5°15E 15 B5
Almería Spain 36°52N 2°27W 21 D4
Almirante Panama 9°10N 82°30W 88 E3
Almond U.S.A. 42°19N 77°44W 82 D7
Almont U.S.A. 42°55N 83°3W 82 D1
Almonte Canada 45°14N 76°12W 83 A8
Almora India 29°38N 79°40E 43 E8
Almyrou, Ormos Greece 35°23N 24°20E 25 D6
Alness U.K. 57°41N 4°16W 11 D4
Alnmouth U.K. 55°24N 1°37W 12 B6
Alnwick U.K. 55°24N 1°42W 12 B6
Aloi Uganda 2°16N 33°10E 54 B3
Alon Burma 22°12N 95°5E 41 H19
Alon → Indonesia 8°15S 124°30E 37 F6
Alor Setar Malaysia 6°7N 100°22E 39 J3
Alot India 23°56N 75°40E 42 H6
Aloysius, Mt. Australia 26°0S 128°38E 61 E4
Alpaugh U.S.A. 35°53N 119°29W 78 K7
Alpena U.S.A. 45°4N 83°27W 81 C12
Alpercatas → Brazil 6°8S 43°53W 93 E10
Alpha Australia 23°39S 146°37E 62 C4
Alpha Ridge Arctic 84°0N 118°0W 4 A1
Alphen aan den Rijn
 Neths. 52°7N 4°40E 15 B4
Alpine Ariz., U.S.A. 33°51N 109°9W 77 K9
Alpine Calif., U.S.A. 32°50N 116°46W 79 N10
Alpine Tex., U.S.A. 30°22N 103°40W 84 F3
Alps Europe 46°30N 9°30E 16 E5
Alpurrulam Australia 20°59S 137°50E 62 C2
Alsace □ France 48°15N 7°25E 20 B7

Alsask Canada 51°21N 109°59W 71 C7
Alsasua Spain 42°54N 2°10W 21 A4
Alsek → U.S.A. 59°10N 138°12W 70 B1
Alsta Norway 65°58N 12°40E 8 D15
Alston U.K. 54°49N 2°25W 12 C5
Alta Norway 69°57N 23°10E 8 B20
Alta Gracia Argentina 31°40S 64°30W 94 C3
Alta Sierra U.S.A. 35°42N 118°33W 79 K8
Altaelva → Norway 69°54N 23°17E 8 B20
Altafjorden Norway 70°5N 23°5E 8 A20
Altai = Aerhtai Shan
 Mongolia 46°40N 92°45E 32 B4
Altai = Gorno-Altay □
 Russia 51°0N 86°0E 28 D9
Altamaha → U.S.A. 31°20N 81°20W 85 F14
Altamira Brazil 3°12S 52°10W 93 D8
Altamira Chile 25°47S 69°51W 94 B2
Altamira Mexico 22°24N 97°55W 87 C5
Altamont U.S.A. 42°42N 74°2W 83 D10
Altamura Italy 40°49N 16°33E 22 D7
Altanbulag Mongolia 50°16N 106°30E 32 A5
Altar Mexico 30°43N 111°44W 86 A2
Altar, Gran Desierto de
 Mexico 31°50N 114°10W 86 B2
Altata Mexico 24°40N 107°55W 86 C3
Altavista U.S.A. 37°6N 79°17W 81 G14
Altay China 47°48N 88°10E 32 B3
Altea Spain 38°38N 0°2W 21 C5
Altiplano Bolivia 17°0S 68°0W 92 G5
Alto Araguaia Brazil 17°15S 53°20W 93 G8
Alto Cuchumatanes =
 Cuchumatanes, Sierra de los
 Guatemala 15°35N 91°25W 88 C1
Alto del Carmen Chile 28°46S 70°30W 94 B1
Alto Ligonha Mozam. 15°30S 38°11E 55 F4
Alto Molocue Mozam. 15°50S 37°35E 55 F4
Alto Paraguay □
 Paraguay 21°0S 58°30W 94 A4
Alto Paraná □ Paraguay 25°30S 54°50W 95 B5
Alton Canada 43°54N 80°5W 82 C4
Alton U.K. 51°9N 0°59W 13 F7
Alton Ill., U.S.A. 38°53N 90°11W 80 F8
Alton N.H., U.S.A. 43°27N 71°13W 83 C13
Altona Canada 49°6N 97°33W 71 D9
Altoona U.S.A. 40°31N 78°24W 82 F6
Altun Kupri Iraq 35°45N 44°9E 44 C5
Altun Shan China 38°30N 88°0E 32 C3
Alturas U.S.A. 41°29N 120°32W 76 F3
Altus U.S.A. 34°38N 99°20W 84 D5
Alucra Turkey 40°22N 38°47E 19 F6
Alūksne Latvia 57°24N 27°3E 9 H22
Alunite U.S.A. 35°59N 114°55W 79 K12
Alusi Indonesia 7°35S 131°40E 37 F8
Alva U.S.A. 36°48N 98°40W 84 C5
Alvarado Mexico 18°46N 95°46W 87 D5
Alvarado U.S.A. 32°24N 97°13W 84 E6
Alvaro Obregón, Presa
 Mexico 27°52N 109°52W 86 B3
Alvear Argentina 29°5S 56°30W 94 B4
Alvesta Sweden 56°54N 14°35E 9 H16
Alvin U.S.A. 29°26N 95°15W 84 G7
Alvinston Canada 42°49N 81°52W 82 D3
Älvkarleby Sweden 60°34N 17°26E 9 F17
Alvord Desert U.S.A. 42°30N 118°25W 76 E4
Älvsbyn Sweden 65°40N 21°0E 8 D19
Alwar India 27°38N 76°34E 42 F7
Alxa Zuoqi China 38°50N 105°40E 34 E3
Alyangula Australia 13°55S 136°30E 62 A2
Alyata = Älät Azerbaijan 39°58N 49°25E 45 B6
Alyth U.K. 56°38N 3°13W 11 E5
Alytus Lithuania 54°24N 24°3E 9 J21
Alzada U.S.A. 45°2N 104°25W 76 D11
Alzamay Russia 55°33N 98°39E 29 D10
Alzira Spain 39°9N 0°30W 21 C5
Am Timan Chad 11°0N 20°10E 51 F10
Amadeus, L. Australia 24°54S 131°0E 61 D5
Amadi
 Dem. Rep. of the Congo 3°40N 26°40E 54 B2
Amâdi Sudan 5°29N 30°25E 51 G12
Amadjuak L. Canada 65°0N 71°8W 69 E17
Amagansett U.S.A. 40°59N 72°9W 83 F12
Amagasaki Japan 34°42N 135°23E 31 G7
Amahai Indonesia 3°20S 128°55E 37 E7
Amaile Samoa 13°59S 171°22W 59 b
Amakusa-Shotō Japan 32°15N 130°10E 31 H5
Åmål Sweden 59°3N 12°42E 9 G15
Amaliada Greece 37°47N 21°22E 23 F9
Amalner India 21°5N 75°5E 40 J9
Amamapare Indonesia 4°53S 136°38E 37 E9
Amambaí Brazil 23°5S 55°13W 95 A4
Amambaí → Brazil 23°22S 53°56W 95 A5
Amambay □ Paraguay 23°0S 56°0W 95 A4
Amambay, Cordillera de
 S. Amer. 23°0S 55°45W 95 A4
Amami-Guntō Japan 27°16N 129°21E 31 L4
Amami-Ō-Shima Japan 28°16N 129°21E 31 K4
Aman, Pulau Malaysia 5°16N 100°24E 39 c
Amaná, L. Brazil 2°35S 64°40W 92 D6
Amanat → India 24°7N 84°4E 43 G11
Amanda Park U.S.A. 47°28N 123°55W 78 C3
Amankeldi Kazakhstan 50°10N 65°10E 28 D7
Amapá Brazil 2°5N 50°50W 93 C8
Amapá □ Brazil 1°40N 52°0W 93 C8
Amarante Brazil 6°14S 42°50W 93 E10
Amaranth Canada 50°36N 98°43W 71 C9
Amargosa → U.S.A. 36°14N 116°51W 79 J10
Amargosa Desert
 U.S.A. 36°40N 116°30W 79 J10
Amargosa Range
 U.S.A. 36°20N 116°45W 79 J10
Amari Greece 35°13N 24°40E 25 D6
Amarillo U.S.A. 35°13N 101°50W 84 D4
Amarkantak India 22°40N 81°45E 43 H9
Amaro, Mte. Italy 42°5N 14°5E 22 C6
Amarpur India 25°5N 87°0E 43 G12
Amarwara India 22°18N 79°10E 43 H8
Amasya Turkey 40°40N 35°50E 19 F6
Amata Australia 26°9S 131°9E 61 E5
Amatikulu S. Africa 29°3S 31°33E 57 D5

Amatitlán *Guatemala* 14°29N 90°38W **88** D1
Amay *Belgium* 50°33N 5°19E **15** D5
Amazon = Amazonas →
 S. Amer. 0°5S 50°0W **93** D8
Amazonas □ *Brazil* 5°0S 65°0W **92** E6
Amazonas → *S. Amer.* 0°5S 50°0W **93** D8
Ambah *India* 26°43N 78°13E **42** F8
Ambahikily *Madag.* 21°36S 43°41E **57** C7
Ambahita *Madag.* 24°1S 45°16E **57** C8
Ambala *India* 30°23N 76°56E **42** D7
Ambalavao *Madag.* 21°50S 46°56E **57** C8
Ambanja *Madag.* 13°40S 48°27E **57** A8
Ambararata *Russia* 15°3S 48°33E **57** B8
Ambarchik *Russia* 69°40N 162°20E **29** C17
Ambarijeby *Madag.* 14°56S 47°41E **57** A8
Ambaro, Helodranon'
 Madag. 13°23S 48°38E **57** A8
Ambato *Ecuador* 1°5S 78°42W **92** D3
Ambato *Madag.* 13°24S 48°29E **57** A8
Ambato, Sierra de
 Argentina 28°25S 66°10W **94** B2
Ambato Boeny *Madag.* 16°28S 46°43E **57** B8
Ambatofinandrahana
 Madag. 20°33S 46°48E **57** C8
Ambatolampy *Madag.* 19°20S 47°35E **57** B8
Ambatomainty *Madag.* 17°41S 45°40E **57** B8
Ambatomanoina *Madag.* 18°18S 47°37E **57** B8
Ambatondrazaka
 Madag. 17°55S 48°28E **57** B8
Ambatosoratra *Madag.* 17°37S 48°31E **57** B8
Ambenja *Madag.* 15°17S 46°58E **57** B8
Amberg *Germany* 49°26N 11°52E **16** D6
Ambergris Cay *Belize* 18°0N 87°55W **87** D7
Amberley *Canada* 44°2N 81°42W **82** B3
Amberley *N.Z.* 43°9S 172°44E **59** E4
Ambikapur *India* 23°15N 83°15E **43** H10
Ambilobé *Madag.* 13°10S 49°3E **57** A8
Ambinanindrano *Madag.* 20°5S 48°23E **57** C8
Ambinanitelo *Madag.* 15°21S 49°35E **57** B8
Ambinda *Madag.* 16°25S 45°52E **57** B8
Amble *U.K.* 55°20N 1°36W **12** B6
Ambleside *U.K.* 54°26N 2°58W **12** C5
Ambo *Peru* 10°5S 76°10W **92** F3
Amboahangy *Madag.* 24°15S 46°22E **57** C8
Ambodifototra *Madag.* 16°59S 49°52E **57** B8
Ambodilazana *Madag.* 18°6S 49°10E **57** B8
Ambodiriana *Madag.* 17°55S 49°18E **57** B8
Ambohidratrimo *Madag.* 18°50S 47°26E **57** B8
Ambohidray *Madag.* 18°36S 48°18E **57** B8
Ambohimahamasina
 Madag. 21°56S 47°11E **57** C8
Ambohimahasoa *Madag.* 21°7S 47°13E **57** C8
Ambohimanga *Madag.* 20°52S 47°36E **57** C8
Ambohimitombo *Madag.* 20°43S 47°26E **57** C8
Ambohitra *Madag.* 12°30S 49°10E **57** A8
Amboise *France* 47°24N 1°2E **20** C4
Ambon *Indonesia* 3°43S 128°12E **37** E7
Ambondro *Madag.* 25°13S 45°44E **57** D8
Amboseli, L. *Kenya* 2°40S 37°10E **54** C4
Amboseli △ *Kenya* 2°37S 37°13E **54** C4
Ambositra *Madag.* 20°31S 47°25E **57** C8
Ambovombe *Madag.* 25°11S 46°5E **57** D8
Amboy *U.S.A.* 34°33N 115°45W **79** L11
Amboyna Cay
 S. China Sea 7°50N 112°50E **36** C4
Ambridge *U.S.A.* 40°36N 80°14W **82** F4
Ambriz *Angola* 7°48S 13°8E **52** F2
Amchitka I. *U.S.A.* 51°32N 179°0E **74** E3
Amderma *Russia* 69°45N 61°30E **28** C7
Amdhi *India* 23°51N 81°27E **43** H9
Ameca *Mexico* 20°33N 104°2W **86** C4
Ameca → *Mexico* 20°41N 105°18W **86** C3
Amecameca de Juárez
 Mexico 19°8N 98°46W **87** D5
Ameland *Neths.* 53°27N 5°45E **15** A5
Amenia *U.S.A.* 41°51N 73°33W **83** E11
America-Antarctica Ridge
 S. Ocean 58°0S 16°0W **5** B2
American Falls *U.S.A.* 42°47N 112°51W **76** E7
American Falls Res.
 U.S.A. 42°47N 112°52W **76** E7
American Fork *U.S.A.* 40°23N 111°48W **76** F8
American Highland
 Antarctica 73°0S 75°0E **5** D6
American Samoa ☑
 Pac. Oc. 14°20S 170°0W **59** b
American Samoa △
 Amer. Samoa 14°15S 170°28W **59** b
Americana *Brazil* 22°45S 47°20W **95** A6
Americus *U.S.A.* 32°4N 84°14W **85** E12
Amersfoort *Neths.* 52°9N 5°23E **15** B5
Amersfoort *S. Africa* 26°59S 29°53E **57** D4
Ames *U.S.A.* 42°2N 93°37W **80** D7
Amesbury *U.S.A.* 42°51N 70°56W **83** D14
Amet *India* 25°18N 73°56E **42** G5
Amga *Russia* 60°50N 132°0E **29** C14
Amga → *Russia* 62°38N 134°32E **29** C14
Amgu *Russia* 45°45N 137°15E **30** B8
Amgun → *Russia* 52°56N 139°38E **29** D14
Amherst *Canada* 45°48N 64°8W **73** C7
Amherst *Mass., U.S.A.* 42°23N 72°31W **83** D12
Amherst *N.Y., U.S.A.* 42°59N 78°48W **82** D6
Amherst *Ohio, U.S.A.* 41°24N 82°14W **82** E2
Amherst I. *Canada* 44°8N 76°43W **83** B8
Amherstburg *Canada* 42°6N 83°6W **72** D3
Amiata, Mte. *Italy* 42°53N 11°37E **22** C4
Amidon *U.S.A.* 46°29N 103°19W **80** B2
Amiens *France* 49°54N 2°16E **20** B5
Aminuis *Namibia* 23°43S 19°21E **56** C2
Amīrābād *Iran* 33°20N 46°1E **44** C5
Amirante Is. *Seychelles* 6°0S 53°0E **26** J7
Amisk L. *Canada* 54°35N 102°15W **71** C8
Amisk → *Canada* 56°43N 98°0W **71** B9
Amistad, Presa de la
 Mexico 29°26N 101°3W **86** B4
Amistad △ *U.S.A.* 29°32N 101°12W **84** G4
Amite *U.S.A.* 30°44N 90°30W **85** F9

Amla *India* 21°56N 78°7E **42** J8
Amlapura = Karangasem
 Indonesia 8°27S 115°37E **37** J18
Amlia I. *U.S.A.* 52°4N 173°30W **74** E5
Amlwch *U.K.* 53°24N 4°20W **12** D3
'Ammān *Jordan* 31°57N 35°52E **46** D4
'Ammān □ *Jordan* 31°40N 36°30E **46** D5
'Ammān ✈ (AMM)
 Jordan 31°45N 36°2E **46** D5
Ammanford *U.K.* 51°48N 3°59W **13** F4
Ammassalik = Tasiilaq
 Greenland 65°40N 37°20W **4** C6
Ammochostos = Famagusta
 Cyprus 35°8N 33°55E **25** D12
Ammon *U.S.A.* 43°28N 111°58W **76** E8
Amnat Charoen
 Thailand 15°51N 104°38E **38** E5
Amnura *Bangla.* 24°37N 88°25E **43** G13
Āmol *Iran* 36°23N 52°0E **45** B7
Amorgós *Greece* 36°50N 25°57E **23** F11
Amory *U.S.A.* 33°59N 88°29W **85** E10
Amos *Canada* 48°35N 78°5W **72** C4
Amoy = Xiamen *China* 24°25N 118°4E **33** D6
Ampanavoana *Madag.* 15°41S 50°22E **57** B9
Ampang *Malaysia* 3°8N 101°45E **39** L3
Ampangalana, Lakandranon'
 Madag. 22°48S 47°50E **57** C8
Ampanihy *Madag.* 24°40S 44°45E **57** C7
Amparafaravola *Madag.* 17°35S 48°13E **57** B8
Ampasinambo *Madag.* 20°31S 48°0E **57** C8
Ampasindava, Helodranon'
 Madag. 13°40S 48°15E **57** A8
Ampasindava, Saikanosy
 Madag. 13°42S 47°55E **57** A8
Ampenan *Indonesia* 8°34S 116°4E **37** K18
Amper → *Germany* 48°29N 11°57E **16** D6
Amphoe Kathu *Thailand* 7°55N 98°21E **39** a
Amphoe Thalang *Thailand* 8°1N 98°20E **39** a
Ampitsikinana *Madag.* 12°57S 49°49E **57** A8
Ampombiantambo
 Madag. 12°42S 48°57E **57** A8
Ampotaka *Madag.* 25°3S 44°41E **57** D7
Ampoza *Madag.* 22°20S 44°44E **57** C7
Amqui *Canada* 48°28N 67°27W **73** C6
Amravati *India* 20°55N 77°45E **40** J10
Amreli *India* 21°35N 71°17E **42** J4
Amritsar *India* 31°35N 74°57E **42** D6
Amroha *India* 28°53N 78°30E **43** E8
Amsterdam *Neths.* 52°23N 4°54E **15** B4
Amsterdam *U.S.A.* 42°56N 74°11W **83** D10
Amsterdam ✈ (AMS)
 Neths. 52°18N 4°45E **15** B4
Amsterdam, I. = Nouvelle
 Amsterdam, Î. *Ind. Oc.* 38°30S 77°30E **3** F13
Amstetten *Austria* 48°7N 14°51E **16** D8
Amudarya → *Uzbekistan* 43°58N 59°34E **28** E6
Amund Ringnes I.
 Canada 78°20N 96°25W **69** B12
Amundsen Abyssal Plain
 S. Ocean 65°0S 125°0W **5** C14
Amundsen Basin *Arctic* 87°30N 80°0E **4** A
Amundsen Gulf *Canada* 71°0N 124°0W **68** C7
Amundsen Ridges
 S. Ocean 69°15S 123°0W **5** C14
Amundsen-Scott *Antarctica* 90°0S 166°0E **5** E
Amundsen Sea *Antarctica* 72°0S 115°0W **5** D15
Amuntai *Indonesia* 2°28S 115°25E **36** E5
Amur → *Russia* 52°56N 141°10E **29** D15
Amurang *Indonesia* 1°5N 124°40E **37** D6
Amursk *Russia* 50°14N 136°54E **29** D14
Amyderya = Amudarya →
 Uzbekistan 43°58N 59°34E **28** E6
An Bien *Vietnam* 9°45N 105°0E **39** H5
An Cabhán = Cavan
 Ireland 54°0N 7°22W **10** B4
An Cóbh = Cóbh *Ireland* 51°51N 8°17W **10** E3
An Daingean = Dingle
 Ireland 52°9N 10°17W **10** D1
An Hoa *Vietnam* 15°40N 108°5E **38** E7
An Longfort = Longford
 Ireland 53°43N 7°49W **10** C4
An Muileann gCearr = Mullingar
 Ireland 53°31N 7°21W **10** C4
An Nabatīyah at Tahta
 Lebanon 33°23N 35°27E **46** B4
An Nabk *Si. Arabia* 31°20N 37°20E **44** D3
An Nabk *Syria* 34°2N 36°44E **46** A5
An Nafūd *Si. Arabia* 28°15N 41°0E **44** D4
An Najaf *Iraq* 32°3N 44°15E **44** C5
An Nás = Naas *Ireland* 53°12N 6°40W **10** C5
An Nāşirīyah *Iraq* 31°0N 46°15E **44** D5
An Nhon *Vietnam* 13°55N 109°7E **38** F7
An Nu'ayrīyah *Si. Arabia* 27°30N 48°30E **45** E6
An Nu'mānīyah *Iraq* 32°32N 45°25E **44** C5
An Ros = Rush *Ireland* 53°31N 6°6W **10** C5
An tAonach = Nenagh
 Ireland 52°52N 8°11W **10** D3
An Thoi, Dao *Vietnam* 9°58N 104°0E **39** H5
An tInbhear Mór = Arklow
 Ireland 52°48N 6°10W **10** D5
An Uaimh *Ireland* 53°39N 6°41W **10** C5
Anabar → *Russia* 73°8N 113°36E **29** B12
'Anabtā *West Bank* 32°19N 35°7E **46** C4
Anaconda *U.S.A.* 46°8N 112°57W **76** C7
Anacortes *U.S.A.* 48°30N 122°37W **78** B4
Anadarko *U.S.A.* 35°4N 98°15W **84** D5
Anadolu *Turkey* 39°0N 30°0E **19** G5
Anadyr *Russia* 64°35N 177°20E **29** C18
Anadyr → *Russia* 64°55N 176°5E **29** C18
Anadyrskiy Zaliv *Russia* 64°0N 180°0E **29** C19
Anaga, Pta. de *Canary Is.* 28°34N 16°9W **24** F3
'Ānah *Iraq* 34°25N 42°0E **44** C4
Anaheim *U.S.A.* 33°50N 117°55W **79** M9
Anahim Lake *Canada* 52°28N 125°18W **70** C3
Anakapalle *India* 17°42N 83°6E **41** L13
Anakie *Australia* 23°32S 147°45E **62** C4
Analalava *Madag.* 14°35S 48°0E **57** A8
Analavoka *Madag.* 22°23S 46°30E **57** C8

Analipsis *Greece* 39°36N 19°55E **25** A3
Anambar → *Pakistan* 30°15N 68°50E **42** D3
Anambas, Kepulauan
 Indonesia 3°20N 106°30E **36** D3
Anambas Is. = Anambas,
 Kepulauan *Indonesia* 3°20N 106°30E **36** D3
Anamosa *U.S.A.* 42°7N 91°17W **80** D8
Anamur *Turkey* 36°8N 32°58E **44** B2
Anan *Japan* 33°54N 134°40E **31** H7
Anand *India* 22°32N 72°59E **42** H5
Anangu Pitjantjatjara ☼
 Australia 27°0S 132°0E **61** E5
Anantapur *India* 14°39N 77°42E **40** M10
Anantnag *India* 33°45N 75°10E **43** C6
Ananyiv *Ukraine* 47°44N 29°58E **17** E15
Anapodiaris → *Greece* 34°59N 25°20E **25** E7
Anápolis *Brazil* 16°15S 48°50W **93** G9
Anapu → *Brazil* 1°53S 50°53W **93** D8
Anār *Iran* 30°55N 55°13E **45** D7
Anārak *Iran* 33°25N 53°40E **45** C7
Anas → *India* 23°26N 74°0E **42** H5
Anatolia = Anadolu
 Turkey 39°0N 30°0E **19** G5
Anatsogno *Madag.* 23°33S 43°46E **57** C7
Añatuya *Argentina* 28°20S 62°50W **94** B3
Anaye ☼ *Australia* 22°29S 137°3E **62** C2
Anaunethad L. *Canada* 60°55N 104°25W **71** A8
Anbyŏn *N. Korea* 39°1N 127°35E **35** E14
Ancaster *Canada* 43°13N 79°59W **82** C5
Anchor Bay *U.S.A.* 38°48N 123°34W **78** G3
Anchorage *U.S.A.* 61°13N 149°54W **68** E2
Anci *China* 39°20N 116°40E **34** E9
Ancohuma, Nevado
 Bolivia 16°0S 68°50W **92** G5
Ancón *Peru* 11°50S 77°10W **92** F3
Ancona *Italy* 43°38N 13°30E **22** C5
Ancud *Chile* 42°0S 73°50W **96** E2
Ancud, G. de *Chile* 42°0S 73°0W **96** E2
Anda *China* 46°24N 125°19E **33** B7
Andacollo *Argentina* 37°10S 70°42W **94** D1
Andacollo *Chile* 30°14S 71°6W **94** C1
Andado *Madag.* 13°25S 48°17E **57** B8
Andalgalá *Argentina* 27°40S 66°30W **94** B2
Åndalsnes *Norway* 62°35N 7°43E **8** E12
Andalucía □ *Spain* 37°35N 5°0W **21** D3
Andalusia = Andalucía □
 Spain 37°35N 5°0W **21** D3
Andalusia *U.S.A.* 31°18N 86°29W **85** F11
Andaman Is. *Ind. Oc.* 12°30N 92°45E **27** G11
Andaman Sea *Ind. Oc.* 13°0N 96°0E **36** B1
Andamooka *Australia* 30°27S 137°9E **63** E2
Andapa *Madag.* 14°39S 49°39E **57** A8
Andara *Namibia* 18°2S 21°9E **56** B3
Andenes *Norway* 69°19N 16°18E **8** B17
Andenne *Belgium* 50°28N 5°5E **15** D5
Anderson *Alaska,*
 U.S.A. 64°25N 149°15W **74** C10
Anderson *Calif., U.S.A.* 40°27N 122°18W **76** F2
Anderson *Ind., U.S.A.* 40°10N 85°41W **81** F11
Anderson *Mo., U.S.A.* 36°39N 94°27W **80** G6
Anderson *S.C., U.S.A.* 34°31N 82°39W **85** D13
Anderson → *Canada* 69°42N 129°0W **68** D6
Andes *U.S.A.* 42°12N 74°47W **83** D10
Andes, Cord. de los
 S. Amer. 20°0S 68°0W **92** H5
Andfjorden *Norway* 69°10N 16°20E **8** B17
Andhra Pradesh □ *India* 18°0N 79°0E **40** L11
Andijon *Uzbekistan* 41°10N 72°15E **28** E8
Andikíthira = Antikythira
 Greece 35°52N 23°15E **23** G10
Andilamena *Madag.* 17°1S 48°35E **57** B8
Andīmeshk *Iran* 32°27N 48°21E **45** C6
Andizhan = Andijon
 Uzbekistan 41°10N 72°15E **28** E8
Andoany *Madag.* 13°25S 48°16E **57** A8
Andohahela △ *Madag.* 24°45S 46°45E **57** D8
Andong *S. Korea* 36°40N 128°43E **35** F15
Andongwei *China* 35°6N 119°20E **35** G10
Andorra ■ *Europe* 42°30N 1°30E **20** E4
Andorra La Vella *Andorra* 42°31N 1°32E **20** E4
Andover *U.K.* 51°12N 1°29W **13** F6
Andover *Maine, U.S.A.* 44°38N 70°45W **83** B14
Andover *Mass., U.S.A.* 42°40N 71°8W **83** D13
Andover *N.J., U.S.A.* 40°59N 74°45W **83** F10
Andover *N.Y., U.S.A.* 42°10N 77°48W **82** D7
Andover *Ohio, U.S.A.* 41°36N 80°34W **82** E4
Andøya *Norway* 69°10N 15°50E **8** B16
Andradina *Brazil* 20°54S 51°23W **93** H8
Andrahary *Madag.* 13°37S 49°17E **57** A8
Andramasina *Madag.* 19°11S 47°35E **57** B8
Andranopasy *Madag.* 21°17S 43°44E **57** C7
Andranovory *Madag.* 23°8S 44°10E **57** C7
Andratx *Spain* 39°39N 2°25E **24** B9
Andreanof Is. *U.S.A.* 51°30N 176°0W **74** E4
Andrews *S.C., U.S.A.* 33°27N 79°34W **85** E15
Andrews *Tex., U.S.A.* 32°19N 102°33W **84** E3
Ándria *Italy* 41°13N 16°17E **22** D7
Andriamena *Madag.* 17°26S 47°30E **57** B8
Andriandampy *Madag.* 22°45S 45°41E **57** C8
Andriba *Madag.* 17°30S 46°58E **57** B8
Andringitra △ *Madag.* 22°13S 46°55E **57** C8
Androka *Madag.* 24°58S 44°2E **57** C7
Ándros *Greece* 37°50N 24°57E **23** F11
Andros I. *Bahamas* 24°30N 78°0W **88** B4
Andros Town *Bahamas* 24°43N 77°47W **88** B4
Androscoggin →
 U.S.A. 43°58N 69°52W **83** C14
Andselv *Norway* 69°4N 18°34E **8** B18
Andújar *Spain* 38°3N 4°5W **21** C3
Andulo *Angola* 11°25S 16°45E **52** G3
Anegada *Br. Virgin Is.* 18°45N 64°20W **89** e
Anegada Passage
 W. Indies 18°15N 63°45W **89** D7
Aneto, Pico de *Spain* 42°37N 0°40E **21** A6
Ang Mo Kio *Singapore* 1°23N 103°50E **39** d
Ang Thong *Thailand* 14°35N 100°31E **38** E3
Ang Thong *Thailand* 9°37N 99°41E **39** b
Ang Thong △ *Thailand* 9°40N 99°43E **39** H2
Angamos, Punta *Chile* 23°1S 70°32W **94** A1

Angara → *Russia* 58°5N 94°20E **29** D10
Angarsk *Russia* 52°30N 104°0E **29** D11
Angas Hills *Australia* 23°0S 127°50E **60** D4
Angaston *Australia* 34°30S 139°8E **63** E2
Ånge *Sweden* 62°31N 15°35E **8** E16
Ángel, Salto = Angel Falls
 Venezuela 5°57N 62°30W **92** B6
Ángel de la Guarda, I.
 Mexico 29°20N 113°25W **86** B2
Angel Falls *Venezuela* 5°57N 62°30W **92** B6
Ángeles *Phil.* 15°9N 120°33E **37** A6
Ängelholm *Sweden* 56°15N 12°58E **9** H15
Angels Camp *U.S.A.* 38°4N 120°32W **78** G6
Ångermanälven →
 Sweden 64°0N 17°20E **8** E17
Ångermanland *Sweden* 63°36N 17°45E **8** E17
Angers *Canada* 45°31N 75°29W **83** A9
Angers *France* 47°30N 0°35W **20** C3
Ängesån → *Sweden* 66°16N 22°47E **8** C20
Angikuni L. *Canada* 62°12N 99°59W **71** A9
Angkor *Cambodia* 13°22N 103°50E **38** F4
Anglesey *U.K.* 53°17N 4°20W **12** D3
Anglesey, Isle of □ *U.K.* 53°16N 4°18W **12** D3
Angleton *U.S.A.* 29°10N 95°26W **84** G7
Anglisidhes *Cyprus* 34°51N 33°27E **25** E12
Angmagssalik = Tasiilaq
 Greenland 65°40N 37°20W **4** C6
Ango *Dem. Rep. of the Congo* 4°10N 26°5E **54** B2
Angoche *Mozam.* 16°8S 39°55E **55** F4
Angoche, I. *Mozam.* 16°20S 39°50E **55** F4
Angol *Chile* 37°56S 72°45W **94** D1
Angola *Ind., U.S.A.* 41°38N 85°0W **81** E11
Angola *N.Y., U.S.A.* 42°38N 79°2W **82** D5
Angola ■ *Africa* 12°0S 18°0E **53** G3
Angoulême *France* 45°39N 0°10E **20** D4
Angoumois *France* 45°50N 0°25E **20** D3
Angra do Heroismo
 Azores 38°39N 27°13W **50** a
Angra dos Reis *Brazil* 23°0S 44°10W **95** A7
Angtassom *Cambodia* 11°1N 104°41E **39** G5
Angu
 Dem. Rep. of the Congo 3°23N 24°30E **54** B1
Anguang *China* 45°15N 123°45E **35** B12
Anguilla ■ *W. Indies* 18°14N 63°5W **89** C7
Anguo *China* 38°28N 115°15E **34** E8
Angurugu *Australia* 14°0S 136°25E **62** A2
Angus *Canada* 44°19N 79°53W **82** B5
Angus □ *U.K.* 56°46N 2°56W **11** E6
Angwa → *Zimbabwe* 16°0S 30°23E **55** F3
Anhandui → *Brazil* 21°46S 52°9W **95** A5
Anholt *Denmark* 56°42N 11°33E **9** H14
Anhui □ *China* 32°0N 117°0E **33** C6
Anhwei = Anhui □ *China* 32°0N 117°0E **33** C6
Anichab *Namibia* 21°14S 14°46E **56** C1
Animas → *U.S.A.* 36°43N 108°13W **77** H9
Anivorano *Madag.* 18°44S 48°58E **57** B8
Anjalankoski *Finland* 60°45N 26°51E **8** F22
Anjar *India* 23°6N 70°10E **42** H4
Anjou *France* 47°20N 0°15W **20** C3
Anjouan *Comoros Is.* 12°15S 44°20E **53** a
Anjozorobe *Madag.* 18°22S 47°52E **57** B8
Anju *N. Korea* 39°36N 125°40E **35** E13
Ankaboa, Tanjona
 Madag. 21°58S 43°20E **57** C7
Ankang *China* 32°40N 109°1E **34** H5
Ankara *Turkey* 39°57N 32°54E **19** G5
Ankarafantsika △ *Madag.* 16°8S 47°5E **57** B8
Ankaramena *Madag.* 21°57S 46°39E **57** C8
Ankaratra *Madag.* 19°25S 47°12E **53** H9
Ankasakasa *Madag.* 16°21S 44°52E **57** B7
Ankavandra *Madag.* 18°46S 45°18E **57** B8
Ankazoabo *Madag.* 22°18S 44°31E **57** C7
Ankazobe *Madag.* 18°20S 47°10E **57** B8
Ankeny *U.S.A.* 41°44N 93°36W **80** E7
Ankilimalinika *Madag.* 22°58S 43°45E **57** C7
Ankilizato *Madag.* 20°25S 45°1E **57** C8
Ankisabe *Madag.* 19°17S 46°29E **57** B8
Ankoro
 Dem. Rep. of the Congo 6°45S 26°55E **54** D2
Ankororoka *Madag.* 25°30S 45°11E **57** D8
Anlong *China* 25°2N 105°27E **34** E5
Anlong Veng *Cambodia* 14°14N 104°5E **38** E5
Anmyeondo *S. Korea* 36°25N 126°25E **35** F14
Ann, C. *U.S.A.* 42°38N 70°35W **83** D14
Ann Arbor *U.S.A.* 42°17N 83°45W **81** D12
Anna *U.S.A.* 37°28N 89°15W **80** G9
Annaba *Algeria* 36°50N 7°46E **50** A7
Annalee → *Ireland* 54°2N 7°24W **10** B4
Annam *Vietnam* 16°0N 108°0E **38** D7
Annamitique, Chaîne
 Asia 17°0N 106°0E **38** D6
Annan *U.K.* 54°59N 3°16W **11** G5
Annan → *U.K.* 54°58N 3°16W **11** G5
Annapolis *U.S.A.* 38°59N 76°30W **81** F15
Annapolis Royal *Canada* 44°44N 65°32W **73** D6
Annapurna *Nepal* 28°34N 83°50E **43** E10
Annean, L. *Australia* 26°54S 118°14E **61** E2
Annecy *France* 45°55N 6°8E **20** D7
Annette *U.S.A.* 55°1N 131°28W **70** B2
Anning *China* 24°55N 102°26E **34** E4
Anniston *U.S.A.* 33°39N 85°50W **85** E12
Annobón *Atl. Oc.* 1°25S 5°36E **49** G4
Annotto B. *Jamaica* 18°17N 76°45W **88** a
Annville *U.S.A.* 40°20N 76°31W **83** F8
Anogia *Greece* 35°16N 24°52E **25** D6
Anorotsangana *Madag.* 13°56S 47°55E **57** A8
Anosibe *Madag.* 19°26S 48°13E **57** B8
Anping *Hebei, China* 38°15N 115°30E **34** E8
Anping *Liaoning, China* 41°5N 123°30E **35** D12
Anqing *China* 30°30N 117°3E **33** C6
Anqiu *China* 36°25N 119°10E **35** F10
Ansai *China* 36°50N 109°20E **34** F5
Ansan *S. Korea* 37°21N 126°52E **35** F14
Ansbach *Germany* 49°28N 10°34E **16** D6
Anseba → *Eritrea* 16°0N 38°30E **47** D2
Anse Boileau *Seychelles* 4°43S 55°29E **53** b
Anse Royale *Seychelles* 4°44S 55°31E **53** b

Anson *U.S.A.* 32°45N 99°54W **84** E5
Anson B. *Australia* 13°20S 130°6E **60** B5
Ansonge *Mali* 15°25N 0°35E **50** E6
Ansonia *U.S.A.* 41°21N 73°5W **83** E11
Anstruther *U.K.* 56°14N 2°41W **11** E6
Ansudu *Indonesia* 2°11S 139°22E **37** E9
Antabamba *Peru* 14°40S 73°0W **92** F4
Antakya = Hatay *Turkey* 36°14N 36°10E **44** B3
Antalaha *Madag.* 14°57S 50°20E **57** A9
Antalya *Turkey* 36°52N 30°45E **19** G5
Antalya Körfezi *Turkey* 36°15N 31°30E **19** G5
Antambohobe *Madag.* 22°20S 46°47E **57** C8
Antanambao-Manampotsy
 Madag. 19°29S 48°34E **57** B8
Antanambe *Madag.* 16°26S 49°52E **57** B8
Antananarivo *Madag.* 18°55S 47°31E **57** B8
Antananarivo □ *Madag.* 19°0S 47°0E **57** B8
Antanifotsy *Madag.* 19°39S 47°19E **57** B8
Antanimbaribe *Madag.* 21°30S 44°48E **57** C7
Antanimora *Madag.* 24°49S 45°40E **57** C8
Antarctic Pen. *Antarctica* 67°0S 60°0W **5** C18
Antarctica 90°0S 0°0 **5** E3
Antelope *Zimbabwe* 21°2S 28°31E **55** G2
Antequera *Paraguay* 24°8S 57°7W **94** A4
Antequera *Spain* 37°5N 4°33W **21** D3
Antero, Mt. *U.S.A.* 38°41N 106°15W **76** G10
Antevamena *Madag.* 21°2S 44°8E **57** C7
Antgila, Helodrano
 Madag. 15°30S 49°50E **57** B8
Antibé *Madag.* 15°7S 47°24E **57** B8
Antibes *France* 43°34N 7°6E **20** E7
Anticosti, Î. d' *Canada* 49°30N 63°0W **73** C7
Antigo *U.S.A.* 45°9N 89°9W **80** C9
Antigonish *Canada* 45°38N 61°58W **73** C7
Antigua *Canary Is.* 28°24N 14°1W **24** F5
Antigua *Guatemala* 14°34N 90°41W **88** D1
Antigua *W. Indies* 17°0N 61°50W **89** C7
Antigua & Barbuda ■
 W. Indies 17°20N 61°48W **89** C7
Antikythira *Greece* 35°52N 23°15E **23** G10
Antilla *Cuba* 20°40N 75°50W **88** B4
Antilles = West Indies
 Cent. Amer. 15°0N 65°0W **89** D7
Antioch *U.S.A.* 38°1N 121°48W **78** G5
Antioquia *Colombia* 6°40N 75°55W **92** B3
Antipodes Is. *Pac. Oc.* 49°45S 178°40E **64** M9
Antlers *U.S.A.* 34°14N 95°37W **84** D7
Antoetra *Madag.* 20°46S 47°20E **57** C8
Antofagasta *Chile* 23°50S 70°30W **94** A1
Antofagasta □ *Chile* 24°0S 69°0W **94** A2
Antofagasta de la Sierra
 Argentina 26°5S 67°20W **94** B2
Antofalla *Argentina* 25°30S 68°5W **94** B2
Antofalla, Salar de
 Argentina 25°40S 67°45W **94** B2
Anton *U.S.A.* 33°49N 102°10W **84** E3
Antongila, Helodrano
 Madag. 15°30S 49°50E **57** B8
Antonibé *Madag.* 15°7S 47°24E **57** B8
Antonibé, Presqu'île d'
 Madag. 14°55S 47°20E **57** A8
Antonina *Brazil* 25°26S 48°42W **95** B6
Antrim *U.K.* 54°43N 6°14W **10** B5
Antrim *U.S.A.* 40°7N 81°21W **82** F3
Antrim □ *U.K.* 54°56N 6°25W **10** B5
Antrim, Mts. of *U.K.* 55°3N 6°14W **10** A5
Antrim Plateau *Australia* 18°8S 128°20E **60** C4
Antsakabary *Madag.* 15°3S 48°56E **57** B8
Antsalova *Madag.* 18°40S 44°37E **57** B7
Antsenavolo *Madag.* 21°24S 48°3E **57** C8
Antsiafabositra *Madag.* 17°18S 46°57E **57** B8
Antsirabe *Antananarivo,*
 Madag. 19°55S 47°2E **57** B8
Antsirabe *Antsiranana,*
 Madag. 14°0S 49°59E **57** A8
Antsirabe *Mahajanga,*
 Madag. 15°57S 48°58E **57** B8
Antsiranana *Madag.* 12°25S 49°20E **57** A8
Antsiranana □ *Madag.* 12°16S 49°17E **57** A8
Antsohihy *Madag.* 14°50S 47°59E **57** A8
Antsohimbondrona Seranana
 Madag. 13°7S 48°48E **57** A8
Antu *China* 42°30N 128°20E **35** C15
Antwerp = Antwerpen
 Belgium 51°13N 4°25E **15** C4
Antwerp *U.S.A.* 44°12N 75°37W **83** B9
Antwerpen *Belgium* 51°13N 4°25E **15** C4
Antwerpen □ *Belgium* 51°15N 4°40E **15** C4
Anupgarh *India* 29°10N 73°10E **42** E5
Anuppur *India* 23°6N 81°41E **43** H9
Anuradhapura *Sri Lanka* 8°22N 80°28E **40** Q12
Anurrete ☼ *Australia* 20°50S 135°38E **62** C2
Anveh *Iran* 27°23N 54°11E **45** E7
Anvers = Antwerpen
 Belgium 51°13N 4°25E **15** C4
Anvers I. *Antarctica* 64°30S 63°40W **5** C17
Anxi *China* 40°30N 95°43E **32** B4
Anxious B. *Australia* 33°24S 134°45E **63** E1
Anyang *China* 36°5N 114°21E **34** F8
Anyang *S. Korea* 37°23N 126°55E **35** F14
Anyer *Indonesia* 6°4S 105°53E **37** G11
Anyi *China* 35°2N 111°2E **34** G6
Anza *U.S.A.* 33°35N 116°39W **79** M10
Anze *China* 36°10N 112°12E **34** F7
Anzhero-Sudzhensk
 Russia 56°10N 86°0E **28** D9
Anzio *Italy* 41°27N 12°37E **22** D5
Ao Makham *Thailand* 7°50N 98°24E **39** a
Ao Phangnga △ *Thailand* 8°10N 98°32E **39** a
Aoga-Shima *Japan* 32°28N 139°46E **31** H9
Aoji *N. Korea* 42°31N 130°23E **35** C16
Aomen = Macau
 China 22°12N 113°33E **33** G10
Aomori *Japan* 40°45N 140°45E **30** D10
Aomori □ *Japan* 40°45N 140°40E **30** D10
Aonla *India* 28°16N 79°11E **43** E8

Aorai, Mt. *Tahiti* 17°34S 149°30W **59** d
Aoraki Mount Cook *N.Z.* 43°36S 170°9E **59** E3
Aosta *Italy* 45°45N 7°20E **20** D7
Aotearoa = New Zealand ■ *Oceania* 40°0S 176°0E **59** D6
Aoukâr *Mauritania* 17°40N 10°0W **50** E4
Aozou Strip *Chad* 22°0N 19°0E **51** D9
Apá → *S. Amer.* 22°6S 58°2W **94** A4
Apache *U.S.A.* 34°54N 98°22W **84** D5
Apache Junction *U.S.A.* 33°25N 111°33W **77** K8
Apalachee B. *U.S.A.* 30°0N 84°0W **85** G13
Apalachicola *U.S.A.* 29°43N 84°59W **85** G12
Apalachicola → *U.S.A.* 29°43N 84°58W **85** G12
Apaporis → *Colombia* 1°23S 69°25W **92** D5
Aparados da Serra △ *Brazil* 29°10S 50°8W **95** B5
Aparri *Phil.* 18°22N 121°38E **37** A6
Apatity *Russia* 67°34N 33°22E **8** C5
Apatula = Finke *Australia* 25°34S 134°35E **62** D1
Apatzingán *Mexico* 19°5N 102°21W **86** D4
Apeldoorn *Neths.* 52°13N 5°57E **15** B5
Apennines = Appennini *Italy* 44°30N 10°0E **22** B4
Api *Nepal* 30°0N 80°57E **32** C3
Apia *Samoa* 13°50S 171°50W **59** b
Apiacás, Serra dos *Brazil* 9°50S 57°0W **92** E7
Apies → *S. Africa* 25°15S 28°8E **57** D4
Apizaco *Mexico* 19°25N 98°8W **87** D5
Aplao *Peru* 16°0S 72°40W **92** G4
Apo, Mt. *Phil.* 6°53N 125°14E **37** C7
Apolakia *Greece* 36°5N 27°48E **25** C9
Apolakia, Ormos *Greece* 36°5N 27°45E **25** C9
Apollonia = Sûsah *Libya* 32°52N 21°59E **51** B10
Apollonia *Greece* 36°15N 27°58E **25** C9
Apolo *Bolivia* 14°30S 68°30W **92** F5
Apopa *El Salv.* 13°48N 89°10W **88** D2
Aporé → *Brazil* 19°27S 50°57W **93** G8
Apostle Is. *U.S.A.* 47°0N 90°40W **80** B8
Apostle Islands △ *U.S.A.* 46°55N 91°0W **80** B8
Apóstoles *Argentina* 28°0S 56°0W **95** B4
Apostolos Andreas, C. *Cyprus* 35°42N 34°35E **25** D13
Apoteri *Guyana* 4°2N 58°32W **92** C7
Appalachian Mts. *U.S.A.* 38°0N 80°0W **81** G14
Apple Hill *Canada* 45°13N 74°46W **83** A10
Apple Valley *U.S.A.* 34°32N 117°14W **79** L9
Appleby-in-Westmorland *U.K.* 54°35N 2°29W **12** C5
Appledore *U.K.* 51°3N 4°13W **13** F3
Appleton *U.S.A.* 44°16N 88°25W **80** C9
Approuague → *Fr. Guiana* 4°30N 51°57W **93** C8
Aprília *Italy* 41°36N 12°39E **22** D5
Apsley *Canada* 44°45N 78°6W **82** B6
Apucarana *Brazil* 23°55S 51°33W **95** A5
Apure → *Venezuela* 7°37N 66°25W **92** B5
Apurimac → *Peru* 12°17S 73°56W **92** F4
Āq Qālā *Iran* 37°10N 54°30E **45** B7
Aqaba = Al 'Aqabah *Jordan* 29°31N 35°0E **46** F4
Aqaba, G. of *Red Sea* 29°0N 34°40E **44** D2
'Aqabah, Khalij al = Aqaba, G. of *Red Sea* 29°0N 34°40E **44** D2
'Aqdā *Iran* 32°26N 53°37E **45** C7
'Aqrah *Iraq* 36°46N 43°45E **44** B4
Aqsay *Kazakhstan* 51°11N 53°0E **19** D9
Aqtaū *Kazakhstan* 43°39N 51°12E **19** F9
Aqtöbe *Kazakhstan* 50°17N 57°10E **19** D10
Aqtoghay *Kazakhstan* 46°57N 79°40E **28** E8
Aquidauana *Brazil* 20°30S 55°50W **93** H7
Aquila *Mexico* 18°36N 103°30W **86** D4
Aquiles Serdán *Mexico* 28°36N 105°53W **86** B3
Aquin *Haiti* 18°16N 73°24W **89** C5
Aquitain, Bassin *France* 44°0N 0°30W **20** D3
Ar Rafid *Syria* 32°57N 35°52E **46** C4
Ar Raḥḥālīyah *Iraq* 32°44N 43°23E **44** C4
Ar Ramādī *Iraq* 33°25N 43°20E **44** C4
Ar Ramthā *Jordan* 32°34N 36°0E **46** C5
Ar Raqqah *Syria* 35°59N 39°8E **44** C3
Ar Rashidiya = Er Rachidia *Morocco* 31°58N 4°20W **50** B5
Ar Rass *Si. Arabia* 25°50N 43°40E **44** E4
Ar Rayyan *Qatar* 25°17N 51°25E **45** E6
Ar Rifā'ī *Iraq* 31°50N 46°10E **44** D5
Ar Riyāḍ *Si. Arabia* 24°41N 46°42E **44** E5
Ar Ru'ays *Qatar* 26°8N 51°12E **45** E6
Ar Rukhaymīyah *Iraq* 29°22N 45°38E **44** D5
Ar Rumaythah *Iraq* 31°31N 45°12E **44** D5
Ar Ruṣāfah *Syria* 35°45N 38°49E **44** C3
Ar Ruṭbah *Iraq* 33°0N 40°15E **44** C4
Ara *India* 25°35N 84°32E **43** G11
Arab, Bahr el → *Sudan* 9°0N 29°30E **51** G11
'Arab, Shatt al → *Asia* 29°57N 48°34E **45** D6
'Arabābād *Iran* 33°2N 57°41E **45** C8
Arabia *Asia* 25°0N 45°0E **26** F6
Arabian Desert = Es Sahrâ' Esh Sharqiya *Egypt* 27°30N 32°30E **51** C12
Arabian Gulf = Persian Gulf *Asia* 27°0N 50°0E **45** E6
Arabian Sea *Ind. Oc.* 16°0N 65°0E **26** G8
Aracaju *Brazil* 10°55S 37°4W **93** F11
Aracati *Brazil* 4°30S 37°44W **93** D11
Araçatuba *Brazil* 21°10S 50°30W **95** A5
Aracena *Spain* 37°53N 6°38W **21** D2
Araçuaí *Brazil* 16°52S 42°4W **93** G10
'Arad *Israel* 31°15N 35°12E **46** D4
Arad *Romania* 46°10N 21°20E **17** E11
Arādān *Iran* 35°21N 52°30E **45** C7
Aradhippou *Cyprus* 34°57N 33°36E **25** E12
Arafura Sea *E. Indies* 9°0S 135°0E **58** B6
Aragón □ *Spain* 41°25N 0°40W **21** B5

Aragón → *Spain* 42°13N 1°44W **21** A5
Araguacema *Brazil* 8°50S 49°20W **93** E9
Araguaia → *Brazil* 5°21S 48°41W **93** E9
Araguaína *Brazil* 7°12S 48°12W **93** E9
Araguari *Brazil* 18°38S 48°11W **93** G9
Araguari → *Brazil* 1°15N 49°55W **93** C9
Araín *India* 26°27N 75°2E **42** F6
Arak *Algeria* 25°20N 3°45E **50** C6
Arāk *Iran* 34°0N 49°40E **45** C6
Araks = Aras, Rüd-e → *Asia* 40°5N 48°29E **44** B5
Aral *Kazakhstan* 46°41N 61°45E **28** E7
Aral Sea *Asia* 44°30N 60°0E **28** E7
Aral Tengizi = Aral Sea *Asia* 44°30N 60°0E **28** E7
Aralsk = Aral *Kazakhstan* 46°41N 61°45E **28** E7
Aralskoye More = Aral Sea *Asia* 44°30N 60°0E **28** E7
Aramac *Australia* 22°58S 145°14E **62** C4
Aran I. *Ireland* 55°0N 8°30W **10** A3
Aran Is. *Ireland* 53°6N 9°38W **10** C2
Aranda de Duero *Spain* 41°39N 3°42W **21** B4
Arandān *Iran* 35°23N 46°55E **44** C5
Aranjuez *Spain* 40°1N 3°40W **21** B4
Aranos *Namibia* 24°9S 19°7E **56** C2
Aransas Pass *U.S.A.* 27°55N 97°9W **84** H6
Aranyaprathet *Thailand* 13°41N 102°30E **38** F4
Arapahoe *U.S.A.* 40°18N 99°54W **80** E4
Arapey Grande → *Uruguay* 30°55S 57°49W **94** C4
Arapgir *Turkey* 39°5N 38°30E **44** B3
Arapiraca *Brazil* 9°45S 36°39W **93** E11
Arapongas *Brazil* 23°29S 51°28W **95** A5
Ar'ar *Si. Arabia* 30°59N 41°2E **44** D4
Araranguá *Brazil* 29°0S 49°30W **95** B6
Araraquara *Brazil* 21°50S 48°0W **93** H9
Araras, Serra das *Brazil* 25°0S 53°10W **95** B5
Ararat *Australia* 37°16S 142°58E **63** F3
Ararat, Mt. = Ağrı Dağı *Turkey* 39°50N 44°15E **44** B5
Araria *India* 26°9N 87°33E **43** F12
Araripe, Chapada do *Brazil* 7°20S 40°0W **93** E11
Araruama, L. de *Brazil* 22°53S 42°12W **95** A7
Aras = Aras, Rüd-e → *Asia* 40°5N 48°29E **44** B5
Aras, Rüd-e → *Asia* 40°5N 48°29E **44** B5
Arauca *Colombia* 7°0N 70°40W **92** B4
Arauca → *Venezuela* 7°24N 66°35W **92** B5
Arauco *Chile* 37°16S 73°25W **94** D1
Aravalli Range *India* 25°0N 73°30E **42** G5
Arawale △ *Kenya* 1°24S 40°9E **54** C5
Araxá *Brazil* 19°35S 46°55W **93** G9
Araxes = Aras, Rüd-e → *Asia* 40°5N 48°29E **44** B5
Araya, Pen. de *Venezuela* 10°40N 64°0W **92** A6
Araz = Aras, Rüd-e → *Asia* 40°5N 48°29E **44** B5
Arba Minch *Ethiopia* 6°0N 37°30E **47** F2
Arbat *Iraq* 35°25N 45°35E **44** C5
Árbatax *Italy* 39°56N 9°42E **22** E3
Arbīl *Iraq* 36°15N 44°5E **44** B5
Arborfield *Canada* 53°6N 103°39W **71** C8
Arborg *Canada* 50°54N 97°13W **71** C9
Arbroath *U.K.* 56°34N 2°35W **11** E6
Arbuckle *U.S.A.* 39°1N 122°3W **78** F4
Arcachon *France* 44°40N 1°10W **20** D3
Arcade *U.S.A.* 42°32N 78°25W **82** D6
Arcadia *Fla., U.S.A.* 27°13N 81°52W **85** H14
Arcadia *La., U.S.A.* 32°33N 92°55W **84** E8
Arcadia *Pa., U.S.A.* 40°47N 78°51W **82** F6
Arcata *U.S.A.* 40°52N 124°5W **76** F1
Archangel = Arkhangelsk *Russia* 64°38N 40°36E **18** B7
Archangelos *Greece* 36°13N 28°7E **25** C10
Archbald *U.S.A.* 41°30N 75°32W **83** E9
Archer → *Australia* 13°28S 141°41E **62** A3
Archer B. *Australia* 13°20S 141°30E **62** A3
Archer Bend = Mungkan Kandju △ *Australia* 13°35S 142°52E **62** A3
Archers Post *Kenya* 0°35N 37°35E **54** B4
Arches △ *U.S.A.* 38°45N 109°25W **76** G9
Archipel-de-Mingan △ *Canada* 50°13N 63°10W **73** B7
Archipiélago Chinijo △ *Canary Is.* 29°20N 13°30W **24** E6
Archipiélago Los Roques △ *Venezuela* 11°50N 66°44W **89** D6
Arckaringa Cr. → *Australia* 28°10S 135°22E **63** D2
Arco *U.S.A.* 43°38N 113°18W **76** E7
Arcos de la Frontera *Spain* 36°45N 5°49W **21** D3
Arcot *India* 12°53N 79°20E **40** N11
Arctic Bay *Canada* 73°1N 85°7W **69** C14
Arctic Mid-Ocean Ridge *Arctic* 87°0N 90°0E **4** A
Arctic Ocean *Arctic* 78°0N 160°0W **4** B18
Arctic Red River = Tsiigehtchic *Canada* 67°15N 134°0W **68** D5
Arctowski *Antarctica* 62°30S 58°0W **5** C18
Arda → *Bulgaria* 41°40N 26°30E **23** D12
Ardabīl *Iran* 38°15N 48°18E **45** B6
Ardabīl □ *Iran* 38°15N 48°20E **45** B6
Ardakān = Sepīdān *Iran* 30°20N 52°5E **45** D7
Ardakān *Iran* 32°19N 53°59E **45** C7
Ardara *Ireland* 54°46N 8°25W **10** B3
Ardee *Ireland* 53°52N 6°33W **10** C5
Arden *Canada* 44°43N 76°56W **82** B8
Arden *Calif., U.S.A.* 38°36N 121°33W **78** G5
Arden *Nev., U.S.A.* 36°1N 115°14W **79** J11
Ardenne *Belgium* 49°50N 5°5E **15** E5
Ardennes = Ardenne *Belgium* 49°50N 5°5E **15** E5
Arderin *Ireland* 53°2N 7°39W **10** C4
Ardestān *Iran* 33°20N 52°25E **45** C7
Ardfert *Ireland* 52°20N 9°47W **10** D2

Ardglass *U.K.* 54°17N 5°36W **10** B6
Ardivachar Pt. *U.K.* 57°23N 7°26W **11** D1
Ardlethan *Australia* 34°22S 146°53E **63** E4
Ardmore *Okla., U.S.A.* 34°10N 97°8W **84** D6
Ardmore *Pa., U.S.A.* 40°2N 75°17W **83** F9
Ardnamurchan, Pt. of *U.K.* 56°43N 6°14W **11** E2
Ardnave Pt. *U.K.* 55°53N 6°20W **11** F2
Ardrossan *Australia* 34°26S 137°53E **63** E2
Ardrossan *U.K.* 55°39N 4°49W **11** F4
Ards Pen. *U.K.* 54°33N 5°34W **10** B6
Arecibo *Puerto Rico* 18°29N 66°43W **89** d
Areia Branca *Brazil* 5°0S 37°0W **93** E11
Arena, Pt. *U.S.A.* 38°57N 123°44W **78** G3
Arenal *Honduras* 15°21N 86°50W **88** C2
Arendal *Norway* 58°28N 8°46E **9** G13
Arequipa *Peru* 16°20S 71°30W **92** G4
Arévalo *Spain* 41°3N 4°43W **21** B3
Arezzo *Italy* 43°25N 11°53E **22** C4
Arga *Turkey* 38°21N 37°59E **44** B3
Arganda del Rey *Spain* 40°19N 3°26W **21** B4
Argarapa ○ *Australia* 22°5S 131°42E **62** C1
Argenta *Canada* 50°11N 116°56W **70** C5
Argentan *France* 48°45N 0°1W **20** B3
Argentário, Mte. *Italy* 42°24N 11°9E **22** C4
Argentia *Canada* 47°18N 53°58W **73** C9
Argentina ■ *S. Amer.* 35°0S 66°0W **96** D3
Argentine Basin *Atl. Oc.* 45°0S 45°0W **96** F6
Argentino, L. *Argentina* 50°10S 73°0W **96** G2
Argeş → *Romania* 44°5N 26°38E **17** F14
Arghandab → *Afghan.* 31°30N 64°15E **42** D1
Argirades *Greece* 39°27N 19°58E **25** B3
Argiroupoli *Greece* 35°17N 24°20E **25** D6
Argolikos Kolpos *Greece* 37°20N 22°52E **23** F10
Argos *Greece* 37°40N 22°43E **23** F10
Argostoli *Greece* 38°11N 20°29E **23** E9
Arguello, Pt. *U.S.A.* 34°35N 120°39W **79** L6
Arguineguín *Canary Is.* 27°46N 15°41W **24** G4
Argun → *Russia* 53°20N 121°28E **29** D13
Argungu *Nigeria* 12°40N 4°31E **50** F6
Argus Pk. *U.S.A.* 35°52N 117°26W **79** K9
Argyle, L. *Australia* 16°20S 128°40E **60** C4
Argyll △ *U.K.* 56°6N 5°10W **11** E3
Argyll & Bute □ *U.K.* 56°13N 5°28W **11** E3
Århus *Denmark* 56°8N 10°11E **9** H14
Ariadnoye *Russia* 45°8N 134°25E **30** B7
Ariamsvlei *Namibia* 28°9S 19°51E **56** D2
Ariana *Tunisia* 36°52N 10°12E **51** A8
Arica *Chile* 18°32S 70°20W **92** G4
Arica *Colombia* 2°0S 71°50W **92** D4
Arico *Canary Is.* 28°9N 16°29W **24** F3
Arid, C. *Australia* 34°1S 123°10E **61** F3
Arida *Japan* 34°5N 135°8E **31** G7
Aride *Seychelles* 4°13S 55°40E **53** b
Ariège → *France* 43°30N 1°25E **20** E4
Arila, Akra *Greece* 39°43N 19°39E **25** A3
Arima *Trin. & Tob.* 10°38N 61°17W **93** K15
Arinos → *Brazil* 10°25S 58°20W **92** F7
Ario de Rosales *Mexico* 19°12N 101°43W **86** D4
Aripo, Mt. *Trin. & Tob.* 10°45N 61°15W **93** K15
Aripuanã *Brazil* 9°25S 60°30W **92** E6
Aripuanã → *Brazil* 5°7S 60°25W **92** E6
Ariquemes *Brazil* 9°55S 63°6W **92** E6
Arisaig *U.K.* 56°55N 5°51W **11** E3
Aristazabal I. *Canada* 52°40N 129°10W **70** C3
Arivonimamo *Madag.* 19°1S 47°11E **57** B8
Arizaro, Salar de *Argentina* 24°40S 67°50W **94** A2
Arizona *Argentina* 35°45S 65°25W **94** D2
Arizona □ *U.S.A.* 34°0N 112°0W **77** J8
Arizpe *Mexico* 30°20N 110°10W **86** A2
'Arjah *Si. Arabia* 24°43N 44°17E **44** E5
Arjeplog *Sweden* 66°3N 17°54E **8** C17
Arjepluovve = Arjeplog *Sweden* 66°3N 17°54E **8** C17
Arjona *Colombia* 10°14N 75°22W **92** A3
Arjuna *Indonesia* 7°49S 112°34E **37** G15
Arka *Russia* 60°15N 142°0E **29** C15
Arkadelphia *U.S.A.* 34°7N 93°4W **84** D8
Arkaig, L. *U.K.* 56°59N 5°10W **11** E3
Arkalyk = Arqalyk *Kazakhstan* 50°13N 66°50E **28** D7
Arkansas □ *U.S.A.* 35°0N 92°30W **84** D8
Arkansas → *U.S.A.* 33°47N 91°4W **84** E9
Arkansas City *U.S.A.* 37°4N 97°2W **80** G5
Arkaroola *Australia* 30°20S 139°22E **63** E2
Arkhangelsk *Russia* 64°38N 40°36E **18** B7
Arki *India* 31°9N 76°58E **42** D7
Arklow *Ireland* 52°48N 6°10W **10** D5
Arkport *U.S.A.* 42°24N 77°42W **82** D7
Arkticheskiy, Mys *Russia* 81°10N 95°0E **29** A10
Arkville *U.S.A.* 42°9N 74°37W **83** D10
Arlanzón → *Spain* 42°3N 4°17W **21** A3
Arlbergpass *Austria* 47°9N 10°12E **16** E6
Arlbergtunnel *Austria* 47°9N 10°12E **16** E6
Arles *France* 43°41N 4°40E **20** E6
Arlington *S. Africa* 28°1S 27°53E **57** D4
Arlington *N.Y., U.S.A.* 41°42N 73°54W **83** E11
Arlington *Oreg., U.S.A.* 45°43N 120°12W **76** D3
Arlington *S. Dak., U.S.A.* 44°22N 97°8W **80** C5
Arlington *Tex., U.S.A.* 32°44N 97°6W **84** E6
Arlington *Va., U.S.A.* 38°53N 77°7W **81** F15
Arlington *Vt., U.S.A.* 43°5N 73°9W **83** C11
Arlington *Wash., U.S.A.* 48°12N 122°8W **78** B4
Arlington Heights *U.S.A.* 42°5N 87°59W **80** D10
Arlit *Niger* 19°0N 7°38E **50** E7
Arlon *Belgium* 49°42N 5°49E **15** E5
Arltunga *Australia* 23°26S 134°41E **62** C1
Armadale *Australia* 32°9S 116°0E **61** F2
Armagh *U.K.* 54°21N 6°39W **10** B5
Armagh □ *U.K.* 54°18N 6°37W **10** B5
Armando Bermudez △ *Dom. Rep.* 19°3N 71°0W **89** C5
Armavir *Russia* 45°2N 41°7E **19** E7
Armenia *Colombia* 4°35N 75°45W **92** C3
Armenia ■ *Asia* 40°20N 45°0E **19** F7

Armenistis, Akra *Greece* 36°8N 27°42E **25** C9
Armidale *Australia* 30°30S 151°40E **63** E5
Armour *U.S.A.* 43°19N 98°21W **80** D4
Armstrong *B.C., Canada* 50°25N 119°10W **70** C5
Armstrong *Ont., Canada* 50°18N 89°4W **72** B2
Arnarfjörður *Iceland* 65°48N 23°40W **8** D2
Arnaud → *Canada* 59°59N 69°46W **69** F18
Arnauti, C. *Cyprus* 35°6N 32°17E **25** D11
Arnett *U.S.A.* 36°8N 99°46W **84** C5
Arnhem *Neths.* 51°58N 5°55E **15** C5
Arnhem, C. *Australia* 12°20S 137°30E **62** A2
Arnhem B. *Australia* 12°20S 136°10E **62** A2
Arnhem Land *Australia* 13°10S 134°30E **62** A1
Arnhem Land ○ *Australia* 12°50S 134°50E **62** A1
Arno → *Italy* 43°41N 10°17E **22** C4
Arno Bay *Australia* 33°54S 136°34E **63** E2
Arnold *U.K.* 53°1N 1°7W **12** D6
Arnold *U.S.A.* 38°15N 120°21W **78** G6
Arnot *Canada* 55°56N 96°41W **71** B9
Arnoya *Norway* 70°9N 20°40E **8** A19
Arnprior *Canada* 45°26N 76°21W **83** A8
Arnsberg *Germany* 51°24N 8°5E **16** C5
Aroa, Pte. *Moorea* 17°28S 149°46W **59** d
Aroab *Namibia* 26°41S 19°39E **56** D2
Aron *India* 25°57N 77°56E **42** G6
Arona *Canary Is.* 28°6N 16°40W **24** F3
Aros → *Mexico* 29°9N 107°57W **86** B3
Arqalyk *Kazakhstan* 50°13N 66°50E **28** D7
Arrah = Ara *India* 25°35N 84°32E **43** G11
Arrah *Ivory C.* 6°40N 3°58W **50** G5
Arran *U.K.* 55°34N 5°12W **11** F3
Arras *France* 50°17N 2°46E **20** A5
Arrecife *Canary Is.* 28°57N 13°37W **24** F6
Arrecifes *Argentina* 34°6S 60°9W **94** C3
Arrée, Mts. d' *France* 48°26N 3°55W **20** B2
Arriaga *Mexico* 16°14N 93°54W **87** D6
Arrilalah *Australia* 23°43S 143°54E **62** C3
Arrino *Australia* 29°30S 115°40E **61** E2
Arrow, L. *Ireland* 54°3N 8°19W **10** B3
Arrowtown *N.Z.* 44°57S 168°50E **59** F2
Arroyo Grande *U.S.A.* 35°7N 120°35W **79** K6
Ars *Iran* 37°9N 47°46E **44** B5
Arsenault L. *Canada* 55°6N 108°32W **71** B7
Arsenev *Russia* 44°10N 133°15E **30** B6
Arta *Greece* 39°8N 21°2E **23** E9
Artà *Spain* 39°41N 3°21E **24** B10
Artà, Coves d *Spain* 39°40N 3°24E **24** B10
Arteaga *Mexico* 18°28N 102°25W **86** D4
Artem *Russia* 43°22N 132°13E **30** C6
Artemovsk *Russia* 54°45N 93°35E **29** D10
Artemovsk *Ukraine* 48°35N 38°0E **19** E6
Artesia = Mosomane *Botswana* 24°2S 26°19E **56** C4
Artesia *U.S.A.* 32°51N 104°24W **77** K11
Arthur *Canada* 43°50N 80°32W **82** C4
Arthur → *Australia* 41°2S 144°40E **63** G3
Arthur Cr. → *Australia* 22°30S 136°25E **62** C2
Arthur Pt. *Australia* 22°7S 150°3E **62** C5
Arthur River *Australia* 33°20S 117°2E **61** F2
Arthur's Pass *N.Z.* 42°54S 171°35E **59** E3
Arthur's Pass △ *N.Z.* 42°53S 171°42E **59** E3
Arthur's Town *Bahamas* 24°38N 75°42W **89** B4
Artigas *Antarctica* 62°30S 58°0W **5** C18
Artigas *Uruguay* 30°20S 56°30W **94** C4
Artillery L. *Canada* 63°9N 107°52W **71** A7
Artois *France* 50°20N 2°30E **20** A5
Artrutx, C. de *Spain* 39°55N 3°49E **24** B10
Artux *China* 39°40N 76°10E **32** C2
Artvin *Turkey* 41°14N 41°44E **19** F7
Artyk *Russia* 64°12N 145°6E **29** C15
Aru, Kepulauan *Indonesia* 6°0S 134°30E **37** F8
Aru Is. = Aru, Kepulauan *Indonesia* 6°0S 134°30E **37** F8
Arua *Uganda* 3°1N 30°58E **54** B3
Aruanã *Brazil* 14°54S 51°10W **93** F8
Aruba ☑ *W. Indies* 12°30N 70°0W **89** D6
Arucas *Canary Is.* 28°7N 15°32W **24** F4
Arué *Tahiti* 17°31S 149°30W **59** d
Arun → *Nepal* 26°55N 87°10E **43** F12
Arun → *U.K.* 50°49N 0°33W **13** G7
Arunachal Pradesh □ *India* 28°0N 95°0E **41** F19
Arusha *Tanzania* 3°20S 36°40E **54** C4
Arusha □ *Tanzania* 4°0S 36°30E **54** C4
Arusha △ *Tanzania* 3°16S 36°47E **54** C4
Arusha Chini *Tanzania* 3°32S 37°20E **54** C4
Aruwimi → *Dem. Rep. of the Congo* 1°13N 23°36E **54** B1
Arvada *Colo., U.S.A.* 39°48N 105°5W **76** G11
Arvada *Wyo., U.S.A.* 44°39N 106°8W **76** D10
Arvayheer *Mongolia* 46°15N 102°48E **32** B5
Arvi *Greece* 34°59N 25°28E **25** E7
Arviat *Canada* 61°6N 93°59W **71** A10
Arvidsjaur *Sweden* 65°35N 19°10E **8** D18
Arvika *Sweden* 59°40N 12°36E **9** G15
Arvin *U.S.A.* 35°12N 118°50W **79** K8
Arwal *India* 25°15N 84°41E **43** G11
Arxan *China* 47°11N 119°57E **33** B6
Arys *Kazakhstan* 42°26N 68°48E **28** E7
Arzamas *Russia* 55°27N 43°55E **18** C7
Arzanah *U.A.E.* 24°47N 52°34E **45** E7
Aş Şafā *Syria* 33°10N 37°0E **46** B6
As Saffānīyah *Si. Arabia* 27°55N 48°50E **45** E6
As Safirah *Syria* 36°5N 37°21E **44** B3

As Sulayyil *Si. Arabia* 20°27N 45°34E **47** C4
As Summān *Si. Arabia* 25°0N 47°0E **44** E5
As Suwaydā' *Syria* 32°40N 36°30E **46** C5
As Suwaydā' □ *Syria* 32°45N 36°45E **46** C5
As Suwayq *Oman* 23°51N 57°26E **45** F8
Aş Şuwayrah *Iraq* 32°55N 45°0E **44** C5
Asab *Namibia* 25°30S 18°0E **56** D2
Asad, Buḥayrat al *Syria* 36°0N 38°15E **44** C3
Asahi-Gawa → *Japan* 34°36N 133°58E **31** G6
Asahigawa *Japan* 43°46N 142°22E **30** C11
Asaluyeh *Iran* 27°29N 52°37E **45** E7
Asamankese *Ghana* 5°50N 0°40W **50** G5
Asan → *India* 26°37N 78°24E **43** F8
Asansol *India* 23°40N 87°1E **43** H12
Asau *Samoa* 13°27S 172°33W **59** b
Asbesberge *S. Africa* 29°0S 23°0E **56** D3
Asbestos *Canada* 45°47N 71°58W **73** C5
Asbury Park *U.S.A.* 40°13N 74°1W **83** F10
Ascensión *Mexico* 31°6N 107°59W **86** A3
Ascensión, B. de la *Mexico* 19°40N 87°30W **87** D7
Ascension ■ *Atl. Oc.* 7°57S 14°23W **49** G2
Aschaffenburg *Germany* 49°58N 9°6E **16** D5
Aschersleben *Germany* 51°45N 11°29E **16** C6
Áscoli Piceno *Italy* 42°51N 13°34E **22** C5
Ascope *Peru* 7°46S 79°8W **92** E3
Ascotán *Chile* 21°45S 68°17W **94** A2
Aseb *Eritrea* 13°0N 42°40E **47** E3
Asela *Ethiopia* 8°0N 39°0E **47** F2
Asenovgrad *Bulgaria* 42°1N 24°51E **23** C11
Aşgabat = Ashgabat *Turkmenistan* 38°0N 57°50E **45** B8
Asgata *Cyprus* 34°46N 33°15E **25** E12
Ash Fork *U.S.A.* 35°13N 112°29W **77** J7
Ash Grove *U.S.A.* 37°19N 93°35W **80** G7
Ash Shabakah *Iraq* 30°49N 43°39E **44** D4
Ash Shamāl □ *Lebanon* 34°25N 36°0E **46** A5
Ash Shāmīyah *Iraq* 31°55N 44°35E **44** D5
Ash Shāriqah *U.A.E.* 25°23N 55°26E **45** E7
Ash Sharmah *Si. Arabia* 28°1N 35°16E **44** D2
Ash Sharqāt *Iraq* 35°27N 43°16E **44** C4
Ash Shaṭrah *Iraq* 31°30N 46°10E **44** D5
Ash Shawbak *Jordan* 30°32N 35°34E **44** D2
Ash Shiḥr *Yemen* 14°45N 49°36E **47** E4
Ash Shināfiyah *Iraq* 31°35N 44°39E **44** D5
Ash Shu'bah *Si. Arabia* 28°54N 44°44E **44** D5
Ash Shumlūl *Si. Arabia* 26°31N 47°20E **44** E5
Ash Shūr'a *Iraq* 35°58N 43°13E **44** C4
Ash Shurayf *Si. Arabia* 25°43N 39°14E **44** E3
Ash Shuwayfāt *Lebanon* 33°45N 35°30E **46** B4
Asha *Russia* 55°0N 57°16E **18** D10
Ashau *Vietnam* 16°6N 107°22E **38** D6
Ashbourne *U.K.* 53°2N 1°43W **12** D6
Ashburn *U.S.A.* 31°43N 83°39W **85** F13
Ashburton *N.Z.* 43°53S 171°48E **59** E3
Ashburton → *Australia* 21°40S 114°56E **60** D1
Ashcroft *Canada* 50°40N 121°20W **70** C4
Ashdod *Israel* 31°49N 34°35E **46** D3
Ashdown *U.S.A.* 33°40N 94°8W **84** E7
Asheboro *U.S.A.* 35°43N 79°49W **85** D15
Ashern *Canada* 51°11N 98°21W **71** C9
Asherton *U.S.A.* 28°27N 99°46W **84** G5
Asheville *U.S.A.* 35°36N 82°33W **85** D13
Asheweig → *Canada* 54°17N 87°12W **72** B2
Ashford *Australia* 29°15S 151°3E **63** D5
Ashford *U.K.* 51°8N 0°53E **13** F8
Ashgabat *Turkmenistan* 38°0N 57°50E **45** B8
Ashibetsu *Japan* 43°31N 142°11E **30** C11
Ashikaga *Japan* 36°28N 139°29E **31** F9
Ashizuri-Uwakai △ *Japan* 32°56N 132°32E **31** H6
Ashizuri-Zaki *Japan* 32°44N 133°0E **31** H6
Ashkarkot *Afghan.* 33°3N 67°58E **42** C2
Ashkhabad = Ashgabat *Turkmenistan* 38°0N 57°50E **45** B8
Āshkhāneh *Iran* 37°26N 56°55E **45** B8
Ashland *Kans., U.S.A.* 37°11N 99°46W **80** G4
Ashland *Ky., U.S.A.* 38°28N 82°38W **81** F12
Ashland *Maine, U.S.A.* 46°38N 68°24W **81** B19
Ashland *Mont., U.S.A.* 45°36N 106°16W **76** D10
Ashland *Ohio, U.S.A.* 40°52N 82°19W **82** F2
Ashland *Oreg., U.S.A.* 42°12N 122°43W **76** E2
Ashland *Pa., U.S.A.* 40°45N 76°22W **83** F8
Ashland *Va., U.S.A.* 37°46N 77°29W **81** G15
Ashland *Wis., U.S.A.* 46°35N 90°53W **80** B8
Ashley *N. Dak., U.S.A.* 46°2N 99°22W **80** B4
Ashley *Pa., U.S.A.* 41°12N 75°55W **83** E9
Ashmore and Cartier Is. *Ind. Oc.* 12°15S 123°0E **60** B3
Ashmore Reef *Australia* 12°14S 123°5E **60** B3
Ashmyany *Belarus* 54°26N 25°52E **17** A13
Ashoknagar *India* 24°34N 77°43E **42** G7
Ashqelon *Israel* 31°42N 34°35E **46** D3
Ashta *India* 23°1N 76°43E **42** H7
Ashtabula *U.S.A.* 41°52N 80°47W **82** E4
Āshtiyān *Iran* 34°31N 50°0E **45** C6
Ashton *S. Africa* 33°50S 20°5E **56** E3
Ashton *U.S.A.* 44°4N 111°27W **76** D8
Ashuanipi, L. *Canada* 52°45N 66°15W **73** B6
Ashuapmushuan → *Canada* 48°37N 72°20W **72** C5
Ashville *U.S.A.* 40°34N 78°33W **82** F6
Asia 45°0N 75°0E **26** E9
Asia, Kepulauan *Indonesia* 1°0N 131°13E **37** D8
Asifabad *India* 19°20N 79°24E **40** K11
Asinara *Italy* 41°4N 8°16E **22** D3
Asinara, G. dell' *Italy* 41°0N 8°30E **22** D3
Asino *Russia* 57°0N 86°0E **28** D9
Asipovichy *Belarus* 53°19N 28°33E **17** B15
'Asir *Si. Arabia* 18°40N 42°30E **47** D3
Asir, Ras *Somali Rep.* 11°55N 51°10E **47** E5
Askham *S. Africa* 26°59S 20°47E **56** D3
Askim *Norway* 59°35N 11°10E **9** G14
Askja *Iceland* 65°3N 16°48W **8** D5
Asklipio *Greece* 36°4N 27°56E **25** C9

Askøyna Norway 60°29N 5°10E 8 F11
Asmara = Asmera
  Eritrea 15°19N 38°55E 47 D2
Asmara Eritrea 15°19N 38°55E 47 D2
Åsnen Sweden 56°37N 14°45E 9 H16
Aso Kuju △ Japan 32°53N 131°6E 31 H5
Aspatria U.K. 54°47N 3°19W 12 C4
Aspen U.S.A. 39°11N 106°49W 76 G10
Aspermont U.S.A. 33°8N 100°14W 84 E4
Aspiring, Mt. N.Z. 44°23S 168°46E 59 F2
Asprokavos, Akra Greece 39°21N 20°6E 25 B4
Aspur India 23°58N 74°7E 42 H6
Asquith Canada 52°8N 107°13W 71 C7
Assab = Aseb Eritrea 13°0N 42°40E 47 E3
Assal, L. Djibouti 11°40N 42°26E 47 E3
Assam □ India 26°0N 93°0E 41 G18
Assateague Island ○
  U.S.A. 38°15N 75°10W 81 F16
Asse Belgium 50°24N 4°10E 15 D4
Assen Neths. 53°0N 6°35E 15 A6
Assiniboia Canada 49°40N 105°59W 71 D7
Assiniboine → Canada 49°53N 97°8W 71 D9
Assiniboine, Mt.
  Canada 50°52N 115°39W 70 C5
Assis Brazil 22°40S 50°20W 95 A5
Assisi Italy 43°4N 12°37E 22 C5
Assynt, L. U.K. 58°10N 5°3W 11 C3
Astana Kazakhstan 51°10N 71°30E 32 A2
Āstāneh Iran 37°17N 49°59E 45 B6
Astara Azerbaijan 38°30N 48°50E 45 B6
Astarabad = Gorgān
  Iran 36°55N 54°30E 45 B7
Asterousia Greece 34°59N 25°3E 25 E7
Asti Italy 44°54N 8°12E 20 D8
Astipalea Greece 36°32N 26°22E 23 F12
Astorga Spain 42°29N 6°8W 21 A2
Astoria U.S.A. 46°11N 123°50W 78 D3
Astrakhan Russia 46°25N 48°5E 19 E8
Astrebla Downs
  Australia 24°12S 140°34E 62 C3
Asturias □ Spain 43°15N 6°0W 21 A3
Asunción Paraguay 25°10S 57°30W 94 B4
Asunción Nochixtlán
  Mexico 17°28N 97°14W 87 D5
Aswa → Uganda 3°43N 31°55E 54 B3
Aswa-Lolim ○ Uganda 2°43N 31°35E 54 B3
Aswân Egypt 24°4N 32°57E 51 D12
Aswan High Dam = Sadd el Aali
  Egypt 23°54N 32°54E 51 D12
Asyût Egypt 27°11N 31°4E 51 C12
Aţ Ţafilah Jordan 30°45N 35°30E 46 E4
Aţ Ţafilah □ Jordan 30°45N 35°30E 46 E4
Aţ Ţā'if Si. Arabia 21°5N 40°27E 47 C3
Aţ Ţa'mīm □ Iraq 35°30N 44°20E 44 C5
Aţ Ţirāq Si. Arabia 27°19N 44°33E 44 E5
Aţ Ţubayq Si. Arabia 29°30N 37°0E 44 D3
Aţ Ţunayb Jordan 31°48N 35°57E 46 D4
Atacama □ Chile 27°30S 70°0W 94 B2
Atacama, Desierto de
  Chile 24°0S 69°20W 94 A2
Atacama, Salar de Chile 23°30S 68°20W 94 A2
Atakeye ○ Australia 22°30S 133°45E 60 D5
Atakpamé Togo 7°31N 1°13E 50 G6
Atalaya Peru 10°45S 73°50W 92 F4
Atalaya de Femes
  Canary Is. 28°56N 13°47W 24 F6
Atami Japan 35°5N 139°4E 31 G9
Atamyrat Turkmenistan 37°50N 65°12E 28 F7
Atapupu Indonesia 9°0S 124°51E 37 F6
Atâr Mauritania 20°30N 13°5W 50 D3
Atari Pakistan 30°56N 74°2E 42 D6
Atascadero U.S.A. 35°29N 120°40W 78 K6
Atasū Kazakhstan 48°30N 71°0E 28 E8
Atatürk Baraji Turkey 37°28N 38°30E 19 G6
Atauro E. Timor 8°10S 125°30E 37 F7
Ataviros Greece 36°12N 27°50E 25 C9
Atbara Sudan 17°42N 33°59E 51 E12
'Atbara, Nahr → Sudan 17°40N 33°56E 51 E12
Atbasar Kazakhstan 51°48N 68°20E 28 D7
Atchafalaya B. U.S.A. 29°25N 91°25W 84 G9
Atchison U.S.A. 39°34N 95°7W 80 F6
Āteshān Iran 35°35N 52°37E 45 C7
Ath Belgium 50°38N 3°47E 15 D3
Athabasca Canada 54°45N 113°20W 70 C6
Athabasca → Canada 58°40N 110°50W 71 B6
Athabasca, L. Canada 59°15N 109°15W 71 B7
Athabasca Sand Dunes ○
  Canada 59°4N 108°43W 71 B7
Athboy Ireland 53°37N 6°56W 10 C5
Athenry Ireland 53°18N 8°44W 10 C3
Athens = Athina Greece 37°58N 23°43E 23 F10
Athens Ala., U.S.A. 34°48N 86°58W 85 D11
Athens Ga., U.S.A. 33°57N 83°23W 85 E13
Athens N.Y., U.S.A. 42°16N 73°49W 83 D11
Athens Ohio, U.S.A. 39°20N 82°6W 81 F12
Athens Pa., U.S.A. 41°57N 76°31W 83 E8
Athens Tenn., U.S.A. 35°27N 84°36W 85 D12
Athens Tex., U.S.A. 32°12N 95°51W 84 E7
Atherley Canada 44°37N 79°20W 82 B5
Atherton Australia 17°17S 145°30E 62 B4
Athi River Kenya 1°28S 36°58E 54 C4
Athienou Cyprus 35°3N 33°32E 25 D12
Athina Greece 37°58N 23°43E 23 F10
Athínai = Athina
  Greece 37°58N 23°43E 23 F10
Athlone Ireland 53°25N 7°56W 10 C4
Athna Cyprus 35°3N 33°47E 25 D12
Athol U.S.A. 42°36N 72°14W 83 D12
Atholl, Forest of U.K. 56°51N 3°50W 11 E5
Atholville Canada 47°59N 66°43W 73 C6
Athos Greece 40°9N 24°22E 23 D11
Athy Ireland 53°0N 7°0W 10 C5
Ati Chad 13°13N 18°20E 51 F9
Atiak Uganda 3°12N 32°2E 54 B3
Atik L. Canada 55°15N 96°0W 71 B9
Atikaki ○ Canada 51°30N 95°31W 71 C9
Atikameg → Canada 52°30N 82°46W 72 B3
Atikokan Canada 48°45N 91°37W 72 C1
Atikonak L. Canada 52°40N 64°32W 73 B7

Atimaono Tahiti 17°46S 149°28W 59 d
Atitlán ○ Cent. Amer. 14°38N 91°10W 87 E6
Atiu Cook Is. 20°0S 158°10W 65 J12
Atka Russia 60°50N 151°48E 29 C16
Atka I. U.S.A. 52°7N 174°30W 74 E4
Atkinson U.S.A. 42°32N 98°59W 80 D4
Atlanta Ga., U.S.A. 33°45N 84°23W 85 E12
Atlanta Tex., U.S.A. 33°7N 94°10W 84 E7
Atlantic U.S.A. 41°24N 95°1W 80 E6
Atlantic City U.S.A. 39°21N 74°27W 81 F16
Atlantic-Indian Basin
  Antarctica 60°0S 30°0E 5 B4
Atlantic Ocean 0°0 20°0W 2 D8
Atlas Mts. = Haut Atlas
  Morocco 32°30N 5°0W 50 B4
Atlin Canada 59°31N 133°41W 70 B2
Atlin, L. Canada 59°26N 133°45W 70 B2
Atlin ○ Canada 59°10N 134°30W 70 B2
Atmore U.S.A. 31°2N 87°29W 85 F11
Atoka U.S.A. 34°23N 96°8W 84 D6
Atolia U.S.A. 35°19N 117°37W 79 K9
Atqasuk U.S.A. 70°28N 157°24W 74 A8
Atrai → Bangla. 24°7N 89°22E 43 G13
Atrak = Atrek →
  Turkmenistan 37°35N 53°58E 45 B8
Atrauli India 28°2N 78°20E 42 E8
Atrek → Turkmenistan 37°35N 53°58E 45 B8
Atsuta Japan 43°24N 141°26E 30 C10
Attalla U.S.A. 34°1N 86°6W 85 D11
Attapu Laos 14°48N 106°50E 38 E6
Attawapiskat Canada 52°56N 82°24W 72 B3
Attawapiskat →
  Canada 52°57N 82°18W 72 B3
Attawapiskat L. Canada 52°18N 87°54W 72 B2
Attica Ind., U.S.A. 40°18N 87°15W 80 E10
Attica Ohio, U.S.A. 41°4N 82°53W 82 E2
Attikamagen L. Canada 55°0N 66°30W 73 B6
Attleboro U.S.A. 41°57N 71°17W 83 E13
Attock Pakistan 33°52N 72°20E 42 C5
Attopeu = Attapu Laos 14°48N 106°50E 38 E6
Attur India 11°35N 78°30E 40 P11
Atuel → Argentina 36°17S 66°50W 94 D2
Atura Uganda 2°7N 32°2E 54 B3
Atwater Canada 37°21N 120°37W 78 H6
Atwater U.S.A. 39°48N 101°3W 80 F3
Atwood Canada 43°40N 81°1W 82 C3
Atyraū Kazakhstan 47°5N 52°0E 19 E9
Au Sable U.S.A. 44°25N 83°20W 82 B1
Au Sable → U.S.A. 44°25N 83°20W 82 B1
Au Sable Forks U.S.A. 44°27N 73°41W 83 B11
Au Sable Pt. U.S.A. 44°20N 83°20W 82 B1
Auas Honduras 15°29N 84°20W 88 C3
Auasberg Namibia 22°37S 17°13E 56 C2
Aubagne France 43°17N 5°37E 20 E6
Aube → France 48°34N 3°43E 20 B5
Auberry U.S.A. 37°7N 119°29W 78 H7
Auburn Ala., U.S.A. 32°36N 85°29W 85 E12
Auburn Calif., U.S.A. 38°54N 121°4W 78 G5
Auburn Ind., U.S.A. 41°22N 85°4W 81 E11
Auburn Maine, U.S.A. 44°6N 70°14W 81 C18
Auburn N.Y., U.S.A. 42°56N 76°34W 83 D8
Auburn Nebr., U.S.A. 40°23N 95°51W 80 E6
Auburn Pa., U.S.A. 40°36N 76°6W 83 F8
Auburn Wash., U.S.A. 47°18N 122°14W 78 C4
Auburn Ra. Australia 25°15S 150°30E 63 D5
Auburndale U.S.A. 28°4N 81°48W 85 G14
Aubusson France 45°57N 2°11E 20 D5
Auch France 43°39N 0°36E 20 E4
Auchterarder U.K. 56°18N 3°41W 11 E5
Auchtermuchty U.K. 56°18N 3°13W 11 E5
Auckland N.Z. 36°52S 174°46E 59 B5
Auckland Is. Pac. Oc. 50°40S 166°5E 64 N8
Aude → France 43°13N 3°14E 20 E5
Auden Canada 50°14N 87°53W 72 B2
Audubon U.S.A. 41°43N 94°56W 80 E6
Augathella Australia 25°48S 146°35E 63 D4
Aughnacloy U.K. 54°25N 6°59W 10 B5
Aughrim Ireland 53°18N 8°19W 10 C3
Augrabies Falls S. Africa 28°35S 20°20E 56 D3
Augrabies Falls △
  S. Africa 28°40S 20°22E 56 D3
Augsburg Germany 48°25N 10°52E 16 D6
Augusta Australia 34°19S 115°9E 61 F2
Augusta Italy 37°13N 15°13E 22 F6
Augusta Ark., U.S.A. 35°17N 91°22W 84 D9
Augusta Ga., U.S.A. 33°28N 81°58W 85 E14
Augusta Kans., U.S.A. 37°41N 96°59W 80 G5
Augusta Maine, U.S.A. 44°19N 69°47W 81 C19
Augusta Mont., U.S.A. 47°30N 112°24W 76 C7
Augustów Poland 53°51N 23°0E 17 B12
Augustus, Mt. Australia 24°20S 116°50E 61 D2
Augustus I. Australia 15°20S 124°30E 60 C3
Aujuittuq = Grise Fiord
  Canada 76°25N 82°57W 69 B15
Aukštaitija △ Lithuania 55°15N 26°0E 9 J22
Aukum U.S.A. 38°34N 120°43W 78 G6
Auld, L. Australia 22°25S 123°50E 60 D3
Aulavik △ Canada 73°42N 119°55W 68 C8
Ault U.S.A. 40°35N 104°44W 76 F11
Aulnay France 46°2N 0°22W 20 C3
Aunis France 46°5N 0°50W 20 C3
Aunu'u Amer. Samoa 14°20S 170°31W 59 b
Auponhia Indonesia 1°58S 125°27E 37 E7
Aur, Pulau Malaysia 2°35N 104°10E 39 L5
Auraiya India 26°28N 79°33E 43 F8
Aurangabad Bihar,
  India 24°45N 84°18E 43 G11
Aurangabad Maharashtra,
  India 19°50N 75°23E 40 K9
Aurich Germany 53°28N 7°28E 16 B4
Aurillac France 44°55N 2°26E 20 D5
Aurora Canada 44°0N 79°28W 82 C5
Aurora S. Africa 32°40S 18°29E 56 E2
Aurora Colo., U.S.A. 39°43N 104°49W 76 G11
Aurora Ill., U.S.A. 41°45N 88°19W 80 E9
Aurora Mo., U.S.A. 36°58N 93°43W 80 G7
Aurora N.Y., U.S.A. 42°45N 76°42W 83 D8
Aurora Nebr., U.S.A. 40°52N 98°0W 80 E5

Aurora Ohio, U.S.A. 41°21N 81°20W 82 E3
Aurukun Australia 13°20S 141°45E 62 A3
Aurukun ○ Australia 13°36S 141°48E 62 A3
Aus Namibia 26°35S 16°12E 56 D2
Ausable → Canada 43°19N 81°46W 82 C3
Auschwitz = Oświęcim
  Poland 50°2N 19°11E 17 C10
Auski Roadhouse
  Australia 22°22S 118°41E 60 D2
Austin Minn., U.S.A. 43°40N 92°58W 80 D7
Austin Nev., U.S.A. 39°30N 117°4W 76 G5
Austin Pa., U.S.A. 41°38N 78°6W 82 E6
Austin Tex., U.S.A. 30°17N 97°45W 84 F6
Austin, L. Australia 27°40S 118°0E 61 E2
Austin I. Canada 61°10N 94°0W 71 A10
Austra Norway 65°8N 11°55E 8 D14
Austral Is. = Tubuaï, Îs.
  French Polynesia 25°0S 150°0W 65 K13
Austral Seamount Chain
  Pac. Oc. 24°0S 150°0W 65 K13
Australia ■ Oceania 23°0S 135°0E 58 D6
Australian-Antarctic Basin
  S. Ocean 60°0S 120°0E 5 C9
Australian Capital Territory □
  Australia 35°30S 149°0E 63 F4
Australind Australia 33°17S 115°42E 61 F2
Austria ■ Europe 47°0N 14°0E 16 E8
Autlán de Navarro
  Mexico 19°46N 104°22W 86 D4
Autun France 46°58N 4°17E 20 C6
Auvergne □ France 45°20N 3°15E 20 D5
Auvergne, Mts. d' France 45°20N 2°55E 20 D5
Auxerre France 47°48N 3°32E 20 C5
Auyuittuq △ Canada 67°30N 66°0W 69 D18
Av-Dovurak Russia 51°17N 91°35E 29 D10
Ava U.S.A. 36°57N 92°40W 80 G7
Avallon France 47°30N 3°53E 20 C5
Avalon U.S.A. 33°21N 118°20W 79 M8
Avalon Pen. Canada 47°30N 53°20W 73 C9
Avanos Turkey 38°43N 34°51E 44 B2
Avaré Brazil 23°4S 48°58W 95 A6
Avawatz Mts. U.S.A. 35°40N 116°30W 79 K10
Aveiro Brazil 3°10S 55°5W 93 D7
Aveiro Portugal 40°37N 8°38W 21 B1
Āvej Iran 35°40N 49°15E 45 C6
Avellaneda Argentina 34°50S 58°10W 94 C4
Avellino Italy 40°54N 14°47E 22 D6
Avenal U.S.A. 36°0N 120°8W 78 K6
Aversa Italy 40°58N 14°12E 22 D6
Avery U.S.A. 47°15N 115°49W 76 C6
Aves, I. de W. Indies 15°45N 63°55W 89 C7
Aves, Is. las Venezuela 12°0N 67°30W 89 D6
Avesta Sweden 60°9N 16°10E 9 F17
Aveyron □ France 44°5N 1°16E 20 D4
Avezzano Italy 42°2N 13°25E 22 C5
Aviá Terai Argentina 26°45S 60°50W 94 B3
Aviemore U.K. 57°12N 3°50W 11 D5
Avignon France 43°57N 4°50E 20 E6
Ávila Spain 40°39N 4°43W 21 B3
Avila Beach U.S.A. 35°11N 120°44W 79 K6
Avilés Spain 43°35N 5°57W 21 A3
Avis U.S.A. 41°11N 77°19W 82 E7
Avoca → Australia 35°40S 143°43E 63 F3
Avoca → Ireland 52°48N 6°10W 10 D5
Avola Canada 51°45N 119°19W 70 C5
Avola Italy 36°56N 15°7E 22 F6
Avon U.S.A. 42°55N 77°45W 82 D7
Avon → Australia 31°40S 116°7E 61 F2
Avon → Bristol, U.K. 51°29N 2°41W 13 F5
Avon → Dorset, U.K. 50°44N 1°46W 13 G6
Avon → Warks., U.K. 52°0N 2°8W 13 E5
Avon Park U.S.A. 27°36N 81°31W 85 H14
Avondale Zimbabwe 17°43S 30°58E 55 F3
Avonlea Canada 50°0N 105°0W 71 D8
Avonmore Canada 45°10N 74°58W 83 A10
Avonmouth U.K. 51°30N 2°42W 13 F5
Avranches France 48°40N 1°20W 20 B3
Awa-Shima Japan 38°27N 139°14E 30 E9
A'waj → Syria 33°23N 36°20E 46 B5
Awaji-Shima Japan 34°30N 134°50E 31 G7
'Awālī Bahrain 26°0N 50°30E 45 E6
Awantipur India 33°55N 75°3E 43 C6
Awasa Ethiopia 7°2N 38°28E 47 F2
Awash Ethiopia 9°1N 40°10E 47 F3
Awatere → N.Z. 41°37S 174°10E 59 D5
Awbārī Libya 26°46N 12°57E 51 C8
Awbārī, Idehan Libya 27°10N 11°30E 51 C8
Awe, L. U.K. 56°17N 5°16W 11 E3
Awjilah Libya 29°8N 21°7E 51 C10
Axe → U.K. 50°42N 3°4W 13 G4
Axel Heiberg I. Canada 80°0N 90°0W 69 B14
Axim Ghana 4°51N 2°15W 50 H5
Axios → Greece 40°57N 22°35E 23 D10
Axminster U.K. 50°46N 3°0W 13 G4
Ayabaca Peru 4°40S 79°53W 92 D3
Ayabe Japan 35°20N 135°20E 31 G7
Ayacucho Argentina 37°5S 58°20W 94 D4
Ayacucho Peru 13°0S 74°0W 92 F4
Ayaguz = Ayaköz
  Kazakhstan 48°10N 80°10E 32 B3
Ayaköz Kazakhstan 48°10N 80°10E 32 B3
Ayamonte Spain 37°12N 7°24W 21 D2
Ayan Russia 56°30N 138°16E 29 D14
Ayaviri Peru 14°50S 70°35W 92 F4
Aydın Turkey 37°51N 27°51E 23 F12
Aydıngkol Hu China 42°40N 89°15E 32 B3
Ayer U.S.A. 42°34N 71°35W 83 D13
Ayer Hitam Malaysia 5°24N 100°16E 39 c
Ayer's Cliff Canada 45°10N 72°3W 83 A12
Ayers Rock = Uluru
  Australia 25°23S 131°5E 61 E5
Ayeyarwady = Irrawaddy →
  Burma 15°50N 95°6E 41 M19
Áyia Napa Cyprus 34°59N 34°0E 25 E13
Áyia Phyla Cyprus 34°43N 33°1E 25 E12
Áyios Amvrósios
  Cyprus 35°20N 33°35E 25 D12

Áyios Seryios Cyprus 35°12N 33°53E 25 D12
Áyios Theodhoros
  Cyprus 35°22N 34°1E 25 D13
Aykhal Russia 66°0N 111°30E 29 C12
Aykino Russia 62°15N 49°56E 18 B8
Aylesbury U.K. 51°49N 0°49W 13 F7
Aylmer Canada 42°46N 80°59W 82 D4
Aylmer, L. Canada 64°5N 108°30W 68 E10
'Ayn, Wādī al Oman 22°15N 55°28E 45 F7
Ayn Dār Si. Arabia 25°55N 49°10E 45 E7
Ayn Zālah Iraq 36°45N 42°35E 44 B4
Ayolas Paraguay 27°10S 56°59W 94 B4
Ayon, Ostrov Russia 69°50N 169°0E 29 C17
Ayr Australia 19°35S 147°25E 62 B4
Ayr Canada 43°17N 80°27W 82 C4
Ayr U.K. 55°28N 4°38W 11 F4
Ayr → U.K. 55°28N 4°38W 11 F4
Ayre, Pt. of I. of Man 54°25N 4°21W 12 C3
Ayton Australia 15°56S 145°22E 62 B4
Aytos Bulgaria 42°42N 27°16E 23 C12
Ayu, Kepulauan
  Indonesia 0°35N 131°5E 37 D8
Ayutla Guatemala 14°40N 92°10W 88 D1
Ayutla de los Libres
  Mexico 16°54N 99°13W 87 D5
Ayvacık Turkey 39°36N 26°24E 23 E12
Ayvalık Turkey 39°20N 26°46E 23 E12
Az Zabadānī Syria 33°43N 36°5E 46 B5
Az Zāhirīyah West Bank 31°25N 34°58E 46 D3
Az Zahrān Si. Arabia 26°10N 50°7E 45 E6
Az Zarqā Jordan 32°5N 36°4E 46 C5
Az Zarqā U.A.E. 24°53N 53°4E 45 E7
Az Zarqā □ Jordan 32°5N 36°4E 46 C5
Az Zāwiyah Libya 32°52N 12°56E 51 B8
Az Zībār Iraq 36°52N 44°4E 44 B5
Az Zilfī Si. Arabia 26°12N 44°52E 44 E5
Az Zubayr Iraq 30°26N 47°40E 44 D5
Azad Kashmir □
  Pakistan 33°50N 73°50E 43 C5
Azamgarh India 26°5N 83°13E 43 F10
Azangaro Peru 14°55S 70°13W 92 F4
Azaouad Mali 19°0N 3°0W 50 E5
Azar Shahr Iran 37°45N 45°59E 44 B5
Azarān Iran 37°25N 47°16E 44 B5
Azārbāyjan = Azerbaijan ■
  Asia 40°20N 48°0E 19 F8
Āzārbāyjān-e Gharbī □
  Iran 37°0N 44°30E 44 B5
Āzārbāyjān-e Sharqī □
  Iran 37°20N 47°0E 44 B5
Azare Nigeria 11°55N 10°10E 50 F8
A'zāz Syria 36°36N 37°4E 44 B3
Azbine = Aïr Niger 18°30N 8°0E 50 E7
Azerbaijan ■ Asia 40°20N 48°0E 19 F8
Azimganj India 24°14N 88°16E 43 G13
Azogues Ecuador 2°35S 78°0W 92 D3
Azores = Açores, Is. dos
  Atl. Oc. 38°0N 27°0W 50 a
Azov Russia 47°3N 39°25E 19 E6
Azov, Sea of Europe 46°0N 36°30E 19 E6
Azovskoye More = Azov, Sea of
  Europe 46°0N 36°30E 19 E6
Azraq ash Shīshān
  Jordan 31°50N 36°49E 46 D5
Aztec U.S.A. 36°49N 107°59W 77 H10
Azúa de Compostela
  Dom. Rep. 18°25N 70°44W 89 C5
Azuaga Spain 38°16N 5°39W 21 C3
Azuero, Pen. de Panama 7°30N 80°30W 88 E3
Azul Argentina 36°42S 59°43W 94 D4
Azusa U.S.A. 34°8N 117°52W 79 L9
Azzel Matti, Sebkra
  Algeria 26°10N 0°43E 50 C6

B

Ba Be △ Vietnam 22°25N 105°37E 38 A5
Ba Don Vietnam 17°45N 106°26E 38 D6
Ba Dong Vietnam 9°40N 106°33E 39 H6
Ba Ngoi = Cam Lam
  Vietnam 11°54N 109°10E 39 G7
Ba Tri Vietnam 10°2N 106°36E 39 G6
Ba Vi △ Vietnam 21°1N 105°22E 38 B5
Ba Xian = Bazhou China 39°8N 116°22E 34 E9
Baa Indonesia 10°50S 123°0E 60 B3
Baardheere Somali Rep. 2°20N 42°27E 47 G3
Baarle-Nassau Belgium 51°27N 4°56E 15 C4
Bab el Mandeb Red Sea 12°35N 43°25E 47 E3
Bābā, Koh-i- Afghan. 34°30N 67°0E 40 B5
Baba Burnu Turkey 39°29N 26°2E 23 E12
Bābā Kalū Iran 30°7N 50°49E 45 D6
Babadag Romania 44°53N 28°44E 17 F15
Babaeski Turkey 41°26N 27°6E 23 D12
Babahoyo Ecuador 1°40S 79°30W 92 D3
Babai = Sarju → India 27°21N 81°23E 43 F9
Babar Indonesia 8°0S 129°30E 37 F7
Babar Pakistan 31°7N 69°32E 42 D3
Babarkach Pakistan 29°45N 68°0E 42 E3
Babb U.S.A. 48°51N 113°27W 76 B7
Baberu India 25°33N 80°43E 43 G9
Babi Besar, Pulau
  Malaysia 2°25N 103°59E 39 L4
Babinda Australia 17°20S 145°56E 62 B4
Babine Canada 55°22N 126°37W 70 B3
Babine → Canada 55°45N 127°44W 70 B3
Babine L. Canada 54°48N 126°0W 70 C3
Babo Indonesia 2°30S 133°30E 37 E8
Bābol Iran 36°40N 52°50E 45 B7
Bābol Sar Iran 36°45N 52°45E 45 B7
Baboua C.A.R. 5°49N 14°58E 52 C2
Babruysk Belarus 53°10N 29°15E 17 B15
Babuhri India 26°49N 69°43E 42 F3
Babusar Pass Pakistan 35°12N 73°59E 43 B5
Babuyan Chan. Phil. 18°40N 121°30E 37 A6
Babylon Iraq 32°34N 44°22E 44 C5

Bac Can Vietnam 22°8N 105°49E 38 A5
Bac Giang Vietnam 21°16N 106°11E 38 B6
Bac Lieu Vietnam 9°17N 105°43E 39 H5
Bac Phan Vietnam 22°0N 105°0E 38 B5
Bac Ninh Vietnam 21°13N 106°4E 38 B6
Bac Quang Vietnam 22°30N 104°48E 38 A5
Bacabal Brazil 4°15S 44°45W 93 D10
Bacalar Mexico 18°43N 88°27W 87 D7
Bacan, Kepulauan
  Indonesia 0°35S 127°30E 37 E7
Bacarra Phil. 18°15N 120°37E 37 A6
Bacău Romania 46°35N 26°55E 17 E14
Bacerac Mexico 30°18N 108°50W 86 A3
Bach Long Vi, Dao
  Vietnam 20°10N 107°40E 38 B6
Bach Ma △ Vietnam 16°11N 107°49E 38 D6
Bachhwara India 25°35N 85°54E 43 G11
Back → Canada 65°10N 104°0W 68 D11
Bacolod Phil. 10°40N 122°57E 37 B6
Bacuk Malaysia 6°4N 102°25E 39 J4
Bácum Mexico 27°33N 110°5W 86 B2
Bād Iran 33°41N 52°1E 45 C7
Bad → U.S.A. 44°21N 100°22W 80 C3
Bad Axe U.S.A. 43°48N 83°0W 82 C2
Bad Ischl Austria 47°44N 13°38E 16 E7
Bad Kissingen Germany 50°11N 10°4E 16 C6
Bad Lands U.S.A. 43°40N 102°10W 80 D2
Badagara India 11°35N 75°40E 40 P9
Badain Jaran Shamo
  China 40°23N 102°0E 32 B5
Badajós, L. Brazil 3°15S 62°50W 92 D6
Badajoz Spain 38°50N 6°59W 21 C2
Badakhshān □ Afghan. 36°30N 71°0E 40 A7
Badaling China 40°21N 116°0E 33 B6
Badalona Spain 41°26N 2°15E 21 B7
Badalzai Afghan. 29°50N 65°35E 42 E1
Badampahar India 22°10N 86°10E 41 H15
Badanah Si. Arabia 30°58N 41°30E 44 D4
Badarinath India 30°45N 79°30E 43 D8
Badas, Kepulauan
  Indonesia 0°45N 107°5E 36 D3
Baddo → Pakistan 28°0N 64°20E 40 F4
Bade Indonesia 7°10S 139°35E 37 F9
Baden Austria 48°1N 16°13E 16 D9
Baden U.S.A. 40°38N 80°14W 82 F4
Baden-Baden Germany 48°44N 8°13E 16 D5
Baden-Württemberg □
  Germany 48°20N 8°40E 16 D5
Badgam India 34°1N 74°45E 43 B6
Badgastein Austria 47°7N 13°9E 16 E7
Badger Canada 49°0N 56°4W 73 C8
Badger U.S.A. 36°38N 119°1W 78 J7
Bādghīs □ Afghan. 35°0N 63°0E 40 B3
Badgingarra △
  Australia 30°23S 115°22E 61 F2
Badin Pakistan 24°38N 68°54E 42 G3
Badlands U.S.A. 43°55N 102°30W 80 D2
Badlands △ U.S.A. 43°38N 102°56W 80 D2
Badrah Iraq 33°6N 45°58E 44 C5
Badrinath India 30°44N 79°29E 43 D8
Badu Australia 10°7S 142°11E 62 a
Badulla Sri Lanka 7°1N 81°7E 40 R12
Badung, Selat Indonesia 8°40S 115°22E 37 K18
Baena Spain 37°37N 4°20W 21 D3
Baengnyeongdo
  S. Korea 37°57N 124°40E 35 F13
Baeza Spain 37°57N 3°25W 21 D4
Bafatá Guinea-Biss. 12°8N 14°40W 50 F3
Baffin B. N. Amer. 72°0N 64°0W 69 C19
Baffin I. Canada 68°0N 75°0W 69 D17
Bafing → Mali 13°49N 10°50W 50 F3
Bafliyūn Syria 36°37N 36°59E 44 B3
Bafoulabé Mali 13°50N 10°55W 50 F3
Bafoussam Cameroon 5°28N 10°25E 52 C2
Bāfq Iran 31°40N 55°25E 45 D7
Bafra Turkey 41°34N 35°54E 19 F6
Bāft Iran 29°15N 56°38E 45 D8
Bafwasende
  Dem. Rep. of the Congo 1°3N 27°5E 54 B2
Bagaha India 27°6N 84°5E 43 F11
Bagamoyo Tanzania 6°28S 38°55E 54 D4
Bagan Datoh Malaysia 3°59N 100°47E 39 L3
Bagan Serai Malaysia 5°1N 100°32E 39 K3
Baganga Phil. 7°34N 126°33E 37 C7
Bagani Namibia 18°7S 21°41E 56 B3
Bagansiapiapi Indonesia 2°12N 100°50E 36 D2
Bagasra India 21°30N 71°0E 42 J4
Bagaud India 22°19N 75°53E 42 H6
Bagdad U.S.A. 34°35N 115°53W 79 L11
Bagdarin Russia 54°26N 113°36E 29 D12
Bagé Brazil 31°20S 54°15W 95 C5
Bagenalstown = Muine Bheag
  Ireland 52°42N 6°58W 10 D5
Baggs U.S.A. 41°2N 107°39W 76 F10
Bagh Pakistan 33°59N 73°45E 43 C5
Baghain → India 25°32N 81°1E 43 G9
Baghdād Iraq 33°20N 44°23E 44 C5
Bagheria Italy 38°5N 13°30E 22 E5
Baghlān Afghan. 32°12N 68°46E 40 A6
Baghlān □ Afghan. 36°0N 68°30E 40 B6
Bagley U.S.A. 47°32N 95°24W 80 B6
Bago = Pegu Burma 17°20N 96°29E 41 L20
Bagodar India 24°5N 85°52E 43 G11
Bagrationovsk Russia 54°23N 20°39E 9 J19
Baguio Phil. 16°26N 120°34E 37 A6
Bah India 26°53N 78°36E 43 E8
Bahadurganj India 26°16N 87°49E 43 F12
Bahadurgarh India 28°40N 76°57E 42 E7
Bahama, Canal Viejo de
  W. Indies 22°10N 77°30W 88 B4
Bahamas ■ N. Amer. 24°0N 75°0W 89 B5
Bahār Iran 34°54N 48°26E 45 C6
Baharampur India 24°2N 88°27E 43 G13
Baharu Pandan = Pandan
  Malaysia 1°32N 103°46E 39 d
Bahawalnagar Pakistan 30°0N 73°15E 42 E5
Bahawalpur Pakistan 29°24N 71°40E 42 E4
Bäherden Turkmenistan 38°5N 57°26E 45 B8
Baheri India 28°45N 79°34E 43 E8

Bahgul → India 27°45N 79°36E **43** F8
Bahi Tanzania 5°58S 35°21E **54** D4
Bahi Swamp Tanzania 6°10S 35°0E **54** D4
Bahía = Salvador Brazil 13°0S 38°30W **93** F11
Bahía □ Brazil 12°0S 42°0W **93** F10
Bahía, Is. de la Honduras 16°45N 86°15W **88** C2
Bahía Blanca Argentina 38°35S 62°13W **94** D3
Bahía de Caráquez
   Ecuador 0°40S 80°27W **92** D2
Bahía Kino Mexico 28°47N 111°58W **86** B2
Bahía Laura Argentina 48°10S 66°30W **94** F3
Bahía Negra Paraguay 20°5S 58°5W **92** H7
Bahir Dar Ethiopia 11°37N 37°10E **47** E2
Bahmanzād Iran 31°15N 51°47E **45** D6
Bahraich India 27°38N 81°37E **43** F9
Bahrain ■ Asia 26°0N 50°35E **45** E6
Bahror India 27°51N 76°20E **42** F7
Bāhū Kalāt Iran 25°43N 61°25E **45** E9
Bai Bung, Mui = Ca Mau, Mui
   Vietnam 8°38N 104°44E **39** H5
Bai Duc Vietnam 18°3N 105°49E **38** C5
Bai Thuong Vietnam 19°54N 105°23E **38** C5
Baia Mare Romania 47°40N 23°35E **17** E12
Baião Brazil 2°40S 49°40W **93** D9
Baïbokoum Chad 7°46N 15°43E **51** G9
Baicheng China 45°38N 122°42E **35** B12
Baidoa = Baydhabo
   Somali Rep. 3°8N 43°30E **47** G3
Baie-Comeau Canada 49°12N 68°10W **73** C6
Baie-St-Paul Canada 47°28N 70°32W **73** C5
Baie Ste-Anne Seychelles 4°18S 55°45E **53** b
Baie-Trinité Canada 49°25N 67°20W **73** C6
Baie Verte Canada 49°55N 56°12W **73** C8
Baihar India 22°6N 80°33E **43** H9
Baihe China 32°50N 110°5E **34** H6
Ba'ījī Iraq 35°0N 43°30E **44** C4
Baijnath India 29°55N 79°37E **43** E8
Baikal, L. = Baykal, Oz.
   Russia 53°0N 108°0E **29** D11
Baikonur = Bayqongyr
   Kazakhstan 45°40N 63°20E **28** E7
Baikunthpur India 23°15N 82°33E **43** H10
Baile Átha Cliath = Dublin
   Ireland 53°21N 6°15W **10** C5
Baile Átha Fhirdhia = Ardee
   Ireland 53°52N 6°33W **10** C5
Baile Átha I = Athy Ireland 53°0N 7°0W **10** C5
Baile Átha Luain = Athlone
   Ireland 53°25N 7°56W **10** C4
Baile Átha Troim = Trim
   Ireland 53°33N 6°48W **10** C5
Baile Brigín = Balbriggan
   Ireland 53°37N 6°11W **10** C5
Băilești Romania 44°1N 23°20E **17** F12
Bainbridge Ga., U.S.A. 30°55N 84°35W **85** F12
Bainbridge N.Y., U.S.A. 42°18N 75°29W **83** D9
Bainbridge Island
   U.S.A. 47°38N 122°32W **78** C4
Baing Indonesia 10°14S 120°34E **37** F6
Bainiu China 32°50N 112°15E **34** H7
Bā'ir Jordan 30°45N 36°55E **46** E5
Baird Mts. U.S.A. 67°0N 160°0W **74** B8
Bairiki = Tarawa Kiribati 1°30N 173°0E **64** G9
Bairin Youqi China 43°30N 118°35E **35** C10
Bairin Zuoqi China 43°58N 119°15E **35** C10
Bairnsdale Australia 37°48S 147°36E **63** F4
Baisha China 34°20N 112°32E **34** G7
Baitadi Nepal 29°35N 80°25E **43** E9
Baiyin China 36°45N 104°14E **34** F3
Baiyu Shan China 37°15N 107°30E **34** F4
Baj Baj India 22°30N 88°5E **43** H13
Baja Hungary 46°12N 18°59E **17** E10
Baja, Pta. Mexico 29°58N 115°49W **86** B1
Baja California Mexico 31°10N 115°12W **86** A1
Baja California □ Mexico 30°0N 115°0W **86** B2
Baja California Sur □
   Mexico 25°50N 111°50W **86** B2
Bajag India 22°40N 81°21E **43** H9
Bajamar Canary Is. 28°33N 16°20W **24** F3
Bajana India 23°7N 71°49E **42** H4
Bajatrejo Indonesia 8°29S 114°19E **37** J17
Bajera Indonesia 8°31S 115°2E **37** J18
Bājgīrān Iran 37°36N 58°24E **45** B8
Bajimba, Mt. Australia 29°17S 152°6E **63** D5
Bajo Boquete Panama 8°46N 82°27W **88** E3
Bajo Nuevo Caribbean 15°40N 78°50W **88** C4
Bajoga Nigeria 10°57N 11°20E **51** F8
Bajool Australia 23°40S 150°35E **62** C5
Bakel Senegal 14°56N 12°20W **50** F3
Baker Calif., U.S.A. 35°16N 116°4W **79** K10
Baker Mont., U.S.A. 46°22N 104°17W **76** C11
Baker, L. Canada 64°0N 96°0W **68** E12
Baker, Mt. U.S.A. 48°50N 121°49W **76** B3
Baker City U.S.A. 44°47N 117°50W **76** D5
Baker I. Pac. Oc. 0°10N 176°35W **64** G10
Baker I. U.S.A. 55°20N 133°40W **70** B2
Baker L. Australia 26°54S 126°5E **61** E4
Baker Lake Canada 64°20N 96°3W **68** E12
Bakers Creek Australia 21°13S 149°7E **62** C4
Bakers Dozen Is. Canada 56°45N 78°45W **72** A4
Bakersfield Calif., U.S.A. 35°23N 119°1W **79** K8
Bakersfield Vt., U.S.A. 44°45N 72°48W **83** B12
Bakharden = Bäherden
   Turkmenistan 38°35N 57°26E **45** B8
Bākhtarān = Kermānshāh
   Iran 34°23N 47°0E **44** C5
Bākhtarān = Kermānshāh □
   Iran 34°0N 46°30E **44** C5
Bakı Azerbaijan 40°29N 49°56E **45** A6
Bakkafjörður Iceland 66°2N 14°48W **8** C6
Bakouma C.A.R. 5°40N 22°56E **52** C4
Bakswaho India 24°15N 79°18E **43** G8
Baku = Bakı Azerbaijan 40°29N 49°56E **45** A6
Bakutis Coast Antarctica 74°0S 120°0W **5** D15
Baky = Bakı Azerbaijan 40°29N 49°56E **45** A6
Bala Canada 45°1N 79°37W **82** A5
Bala U.K. 52°54N 3°36W **12** E4
Bala, L. U.K. 52°53N 3°37W **12** E4
Balabac I. Phil. 8°0N 117°0E **36** C5

Balabac Str. E. Indies 7°53N 117°5E **36** C5
Balabagh Afghan. 34°25N 70°12E **42** B4
Ba'labakk Lebanon 34°0N 36°10E **46** B5
Balabalangan, Kepulauan
   Indonesia 2°20S 117°30E **36** E5
Balad Iraq 34°0N 44°9E **44** C5
Balad Rūz Iraq 33°42N 45°5E **44** C5
Bālādeh Fārs, Iran 29°17N 51°56E **45** D6
Bālādeh Māzandaran, Iran 36°12N 51°48E **45** B6
Balaghat India 21°49N 80°12E **40** J12
Balaghat Ra. India 18°50N 76°30E **40** K10
Balaguer Spain 41°50N 0°50E **21** B6
Balaklava Ukraine 44°30N 33°30E **19** F5
Balakovo Russia 52°4N 47°55E **18** D8
Balamau India 27°10N 80°21E **43** F9
Balancán Mexico 17°48N 91°32W **87** D6
Balashov Russia 51°30N 43°10E **19** D7
Balasinor India 22°57N 73°23E **42** H5
Balasore = Baleshwar
   India 21°35N 87°3E **41** J15
Balaton Hungary 46°50N 17°40E **17** E9
Balbina, Represa de Brazil 2°0S 59°30W **92** D7
Balboa Panama 8°57N 79°34W **88** E4
Balbriggan Ireland 53°37N 6°11W **10** C5
Balcarce Argentina 38°0S 58°10W **94** D4
Balcarres Canada 50°50N 103°35W **71** C8
Balchik Bulgaria 43°28N 28°11E **23** C13
Balclutha N.Z. 46°15S 169°45E **59** G2
Balcones Escarpment
   U.S.A. 29°30N 99°15W **84** G5
Bald I. Australia 34°57S 118°27E **61** F2
Bald Knob U.S.A. 35°19N 91°34W **84** D9
Baldock L. Canada 56°33N 97°57W **71** B9
Baldwin Mich., U.S.A. 43°54N 85°51W **81** D11
Baldwin Pa., U.S.A. 40°22N 79°58W **82** F5
Baldwinsville U.S.A. 43°10N 76°20W **83** C8
Baldy Peak U.S.A. 33°54N 109°34W **77** K9
Baleares, Is. Spain 39°30N 3°0E **24** B10
Balearic Is. = Baleares, Is.
   Spain 39°30N 3°0E **24** B10
Baleine → Canada 58°15N 67°40W **73** A6
Baleine, Petite R. de la →
   Canada 56°0N 76°45W **72** A4
Baler Phil. 15°46N 121°34E **37** A6
Baleshare U.K. 57°31N 7°22W **11** D1
Baleshwar India 21°35N 87°3E **41** J15
Baley Russia 51°36N 116°37E **29** D12
Balfate Honduras 15°48N 86°25W **88** C2
Balgo Australia 20°9S 127°58E **60** D4
Bali Greece 35°25N 24°47E **25** D6
Bali India 25°11N 73°17E **42** G5
Bali Indonesia 8°20S 115°0E **37** J18
Bali □ Indonesia 8°20S 115°0E **37** J18
Bali, Selat Indonesia 8°18S 114°25E **37** J17
Bali Sea Indonesia 8°0S 115°0E **37** J17
Baliapal India 21°40N 87°17E **43** J12
Balige Indonesia 2°14N 99°7E **39** L2
Balik Pulau Malaysia 5°21N 100°14E **39** c
Balıkesir Turkey 39°39N 27°53E **23** E12
Balikpapan Indonesia 1°10S 116°55E **36** E5
Balimbing Phil. 5°5N 119°58E **37** C5
Baling Malaysia 5°41N 100°55E **39** K3
Balkan Mts. = Stara Planina
   Bulgaria 43°15N 23°0E **23** C10
Balkanabat Turkmenistan 39°30N 54°22E **45** B7
Balkh Afghan. 36°44N 66°47E **42** A4
Balkhash = Balqash
   Kazakhstan 46°50N 74°50E **28** E8
Balkhash, Ozero = Balqash Köli
   Kazakhstan 46°0N 74°50E **28** E8
Ballachulish U.K. 56°41N 5°8W **11** E3
Balladonia Australia 32°27S 123°51E **61** F3
Ballaghaderreen Ireland 53°55N 8°34W **10** C3
Ballarat Australia 37°33S 143°50E **63** F3
Ballard, L. Australia 29°20S 120°40E **61** E3
Ballater U.K. 57°3N 3°3W **11** D5
Ballenas, Canal de
   Mexico 29°10N 113°29W **86** B2
Balleny Is. Antarctica 66°30S 163°0E **5** C11
Ballia India 25°46N 84°12E **43** G11
Ballina Australia 28°50S 153°31E **63** D5
Ballina Ireland 54°7N 9°9W **10** B2
Ballinasloe Ireland 53°20N 8°13W **10** C3
Ballinger U.S.A. 31°45N 99°57W **84** F5
Ballinrobe Ireland 53°38N 9°13W **10** C2
Ballinskelligs B. Ireland 51°48N 10°13W **10** E1
Ballston Spa U.S.A. 43°0N 73°51W **83** D11
Ballyboghil Ireland 53°32N 6°16W **10** C5
Ballybunion Ireland 52°31N 9°40W **10** D2
Ballycanew Ireland 52°37N 6°19W **10** D5
Ballycastle U.K. 55°12N 6°15W **10** A5
Ballyclare U.K. 54°46N 6°0W **10** B5
Ballydehob Ireland 51°34N 9°28W **10** E2
Ballygawley U.K. 54°27N 7°2W **10** B4
Ballyhaunis Ireland 53°46N 8°46W **10** C3
Ballyheige Ireland 52°23N 9°49W **10** D2
Ballymena U.K. 54°52N 6°17W **10** B5
Ballymoney U.K. 55°5N 6°31W **10** A5
Ballymote Ireland 54°5N 8°31W **10** B3
Ballynahinch U.K. 54°24N 5°54W **10** B6
Ballyquintin Pt. U.K. 54°20N 5°30W **10** B6
Ballyshannon Ireland 54°30N 8°11W **10** B3
Balmaceda Chile 46°0S 71°50W **94** F2
Balmertown Canada 51°4N 93°41W **71** C10
Balmoral Australia 37°15S 141°48E **63** F3
Balmorhea U.S.A. 30°59N 103°45W **84** F3
Balochistan = Baluchistan □
   Pakistan 27°30N 65°0E **40** F4
Balonne → Australia 28°47S 147°56E **63** D4
Balotra India 25°50N 72°14E **42** G5
Balqash Kazakhstan 46°50N 74°50E **28** E8
Balqash Köli Kazakhstan 46°0N 74°50E **28** E8
Balrampur India 27°30N 82°20E **43** F10
Balranald Australia 34°38S 143°33E **63** E3
Balsas → Brazil 7°15S 44°35W **93** E10
Balsas Mexico 18°0N 99°46W **87** D5
Balsas → Mexico 18°0N 99°46W **87** D5
Balta Ukraine 48°2N 29°45E **17** D15
Bălți Moldova 47°48N 27°58E **17** E14
Baltic Sea Europe 57°0N 19°0E **9** H18

Baltimore Ireland 51°29N 9°22W **10** E2
Baltimore Md., U.S.A. 39°17N 76°36W **81** F15
Baltimore Ohio, U.S.A. 39°51N 82°36W **82** G2
Baltinglass Ireland 52°56N 6°43W **10** D5
Baltit Pakistan 36°15N 74°40E **43** A6
Baltiysk Russia 54°41N 19°58E **9** J18
Balurghat India 25°15N 88°44E **43** G13
Balvi Latvia 57°8N 27°15E **9** H22
Balya Turkey 39°44N 27°35E **23** E12
Balykchy Kyrgyzstan 42°26N 76°12E **32** B2
Balyqshy Kazakhstan 47°4N 51°52E **19** E9
Bam Iran 29°7N 58°14E **45** D8
Bama Nigeria 11°33N 13°41E **51** F8
Bamaga Australia 10°50S 142°25E **62** A3
Bamaji L. Canada 51°9N 91°25W **72** B1
Bamako Mali 12°34N 7°55W **50** F4
Bambari C.A.R. 5°40N 20°35E **52** C4
Bambaroo Australia 18°50S 146°10E **62** B4
Bamberg Germany 49°54N 10°54E **16** D6
Bamberg U.S.A. 33°18N 81°2W **85** E14
Bamberg
   Dem. Rep. of the Congo 3°40N 26°0E **54** B2
Bamburgh U.K. 55°37N 1°43W **12** B6
Bamenda Cameroon 5°57N 10°11E **52** C2
Bamfield Canada 48°45N 125°10W **70** D3
Bāmiān □ Afghan. 35°0N 67°0E **40** B5
Bamiancheng China 43°15N 124°2E **35** C13
Bampūr Iran 27°15N 60°21E **45** E9
Bampūr → Iran 27°24N 59°0E **45** E9
Ban Ao Tu Khun Thailand 8°9N 98°20E **39** a
Ban Ban Laos 19°31N 103°30E **38** C4
Ban Bang Hin Thailand 9°32N 98°35E **39** H2
Ban Bang Khu Thailand 7°57N 98°23E **39** a
Ban Bang Rong Thailand 8°3N 98°25E **39** a
Ban Bo Phut Thailand 9°33N 100°2E **39** b
Ban Chaweng Thailand 9°32N 100°3E **39** b
Ban Chiang Klang
   Thailand 19°25N 100°55E **38** C3
Ban Choho Thailand 15°2N 102°9E **38** E4
Ban Dan Lan Hoi Thailand 17°0N 99°35E **38** D2
Ban Don = Surat Thani
   Thailand 9°6N 99°20E **39** H2
Ban Don Vietnam 12°53N 107°48E **38** F6
Ban Don, Ao → Thailand 9°20N 99°25E **39** H2
Ban Dong Thailand 19°30N 100°59E **38** C3
Ban Hong Thailand 18°18N 98°50E **38** C2
Ban Hua Thanon Thailand 9°26N 100°1E **39** b
Ban Kantang Thailand 7°25N 99°31E **39** J2
Ban Karon Thailand 7°51N 98°18E **39** a
Ban Kata Thailand 7°50N 98°18E **39** a
Ban Keun Laos 18°22N 102°35E **38** C4
Ban Khai Thailand 12°46N 101°18E **38** F3
Ban Kheun Laos 20°13N 101°7E **38** B3
Ban Khlong Khian
   Thailand 8°10N 98°26E **39** a
Ban Khlong Kua Thailand 6°57N 100°8E **39** J3
Ban Khuan Thailand 8°3N 98°32E **39** a
Ban Khuan Mao Thailand 7°50N 99°37E **39** J2
Ban Ko Yai Chim
   Thailand 11°17N 99°26E **39** G2
Ban Laem Thailand 13°13N 99°59E **38** F2
Ban Lamai Thailand 9°28N 100°3E **39** b
Ban Lao Ngam Laos 15°28N 106°10E **38** E6
Ban Le Kathe Thailand 15°49N 98°53E **38** E2
Ban Lo Po Noi Thailand 8°1N 98°34E **39** a
Ban Mae Chedi Thailand 19°11N 99°31E **38** C2
Ban Mae Nam Thailand 9°34N 100°0E **39** b
Ban Mae Sariang
   Thailand 18°10N 97°56E **38** C1
Ban Mê Thuot = Buon Ma Thuot
   Vietnam 12°40N 108°3E **38** F7
Ban Mi Thailand 15°3N 100°32E **38** E3
Ban Muong Mo Laos 19°4N 103°58E **38** C4
Ban Na Bo Thailand 9°19N 99°41E **39** b
Ban Na Mo Laos 17°7N 105°40E **38** D5
Ban Na San Thailand 8°53N 99°52E **39** H2
Ban Na Tong Laos 20°56N 101°47E **38** B3
Ban Nam Bac Laos 20°38N 102°20E **38** B4
Ban Nam Ma Laos 22°2N 101°37E **38** A3
Ban Ngang Laos 15°59N 106°11E **38** E6
Ban Nong Bok Laos 17°5N 104°48E **38** D5
Ban Nong Boua Laos 15°40N 106°33E **38** E6
Ban Nong Pling
   Thailand 15°40N 100°10E **38** E3
Ban Pak Chan Thailand 10°32N 98°51E **39** G2
Ban Patong Thailand 7°54N 98°18E **39** a
Ban Phai Thailand 16°4N 102°44E **38** D4
Ban Phak Chit Thailand 18°0N 98°24E **39** a
Ban Pong Thailand 13°50N 99°55E **38** F2
Ban Rawai Thailand 7°47N 98°20E **39** a
Ban Ron Phibun Thailand 8°9N 99°51E **39** H2
Ban Sakhu Thailand 8°4N 98°18E **39** a
Ban Sanam Chai
   Thailand 7°33N 100°25E **39** J3
Ban Sangkha Thailand 14°37N 103°52E **38** E4
Ban Tak Thailand 17°2N 99°4E **38** D2
Ban Tako Thailand 14°5N 102°40E **38** E4
Ban Tha Dua Thailand 17°59N 98°39E **38** D2
Ban Tha Nun Thailand 8°12N 98°18E **39** a
Ban Tha Rua Thailand 7°59N 98°22E **39** a
Ban Tha Yu Thailand 8°3N 98°18E **39** a
Ban Thahine Laos 14°12N 105°33E **38** E5
Ban Xien Kok Laos 20°54N 100°39E **38** B3
Ban Yen Nhan Vietnam 20°57N 106°2E **38** B6
Banaba Kiribati 0°45S 169°50E **64** H8
Banalia
   Dem. Rep. of the Congo 1°32N 25°5E **54** B2
Banam Cambodia 11°20N 105°17E **39** G5
Bananal, I. do Brazil 11°30S 50°30W **93** F8
Banaras = Varanasi
   India 25°22N 83°0E **43** G10
Banas → Gujarat, India 23°45N 71°25E **42** H4
Banas → Mad. P., India 24°15N 81°30E **43** G9
Bânâs, Ras Egypt 23°57N 35°59E **51** D13
Banbridge U.K. 54°22N 6°16W **10** B5
Banbury U.K. 52°4N 1°20W **13** E6
Banchory U.K. 57°3N 2°29W **11** D6

Bancroft Canada 45°3N 77°51W **82** A7
Band Bonī Iran 25°30N 59°33E **45** E8
Band Qīr Iran 31°39N 48°53E **45** D6
Banda Mad. P., India 24°3N 78°57E **43** G8
Banda Ut. P., India 25°30N 80°26E **43** G9
Banda, Kepulauan
   Indonesia 4°37S 129°50E **37** E7
Banda Aceh Indonesia 5°35N 95°20E **36** C1
Banda Banda, Mt.
   Australia 31°10S 152°28E **63** E5
Banda Elat Indonesia 5°40S 133°5E **37** F8
Banda Is. = Banda, Kepulauan
   Indonesia 4°37S 129°50E **37** E7
Banda Sea Indonesia 6°0S 130°0E **37** F7
Bandai-Asahi △ Japan 37°38N 140°5E **30** F10
Bandai-San Japan 37°36N 140°4E **30** F10
Bandān Iran 31°23N 60°44E **45** D9
Bandanaira Indonesia 4°32S 129°54E **37** E7
Bandanwara India 26°9N 74°38E **42** F6
Bandar = Machilipatnam
   India 16°12N 81°8E **41** L12
Bandar-e Abbās Iran 27°15N 56°15E **45** E8
Bandar-e Anzalī Iran 37°30N 49°30E **45** B6
Bandar-e Bushehr = Būshehr
   Iran 28°55N 50°55E **45** D6
Bandar-e Chārak Iran 26°45N 54°20E **45** E7
Bandar-e Deylam Iran 30°5N 50°10E **45** D6
Bandar-e Emām Khomeynī
   Iran 30°30N 49°5E **45** D6
Bandar-e Lengeh Iran 26°35N 54°58E **45** E7
Bandar-e Maqām Iran 26°56N 53°29E **45** E7
Bandar-e Ma'shur Iran 30°35N 49°10E **45** D6
Bandar-e Rīg Iran 29°29N 50°38E **45** D6
Bandar-e Torkeman Iran 37°0N 54°10E **45** B7
Bandar Lampung
   Indonesia 5°20S 105°10E **36** F3
Bandar Maharani = Muar
   Malaysia 2°3N 102°34E **39** L4
Bandar Penggaram = Batu Pahat
   Malaysia 1°50N 102°56E **39** M4
Bandar Seri Begawan
   Brunei 4°52N 115°0E **36** D5
Bandar Sri Aman = Sri Aman
   Malaysia 1°15N 111°32E **36** D4
Bandawe Malawi 11°58S 34°5E **55** E3
Bandeira, Pico da Brazil 20°26S 41°47W **95** A7
Bandera Argentina 28°55S 62°20W **94** B3
Banderas, B. de Mexico 20°40N 105°25W **86** C3
Bandhavgarh India 23°40N 81°2E **43** H9
Bandi → India 26°12N 75°47E **42** F6
Bandikui India 27°3N 76°34E **42** F7
Bandırma Turkey 40°20N 28°0E **23** D13
Bandjarmasin = Banjarmasin
   Indonesia 3°20S 114°35E **36** E4
Bandon Ireland 51°44N 8°44W **10** E3
Bandon → Ireland 51°43N 8°37W **10** E3
Bandula Mozam. 19°0S 33°7E **55** F3
Bandundu
   Dem. Rep. of the Congo 3°15S 17°22E **52** E3
Bandung Indonesia 6°54S 107°36E **37** G12
Bāneh Iran 35°59N 45°53E **44** C5
Banes Cuba 21°0N 75°42W **89** B4
Banff Canada 51°10N 115°34W **70** C5
Banff U.K. 57°40N 2°33W **11** D6
Banff △ Canada 51°30N 116°15W **70** C5
Bang Fai → Laos 16°57N 104°45E **38** D5
Bang Hieng → Laos 16°10N 105°10E **38** D5
Bang Krathum Thailand 16°34N 100°18E **38** D3
Bang Lamung Thailand 13°3N 100°56E **38** F3
Bang Mun Nak Thailand 16°2N 100°23E **38** D3
Bang Pa In Thailand 14°14N 100°35E **38** E3
Bang Rakam Thailand 16°45N 100°7E **38** D3
Bang Saphan Thailand 11°14N 99°28E **39** G2
Bang Thao Thailand 7°59N 98°18E **39** a
Bangaduni I. India 21°34N 88°52E **43** J13
Bangala Dam Zimbabwe 21°7S 31°25E **55** G3
Bangalore India 12°59N 77°40E **40** N10
Banganga → India 27°6N 77°25E **42** F6
Bangaon India 23°0N 88°47E **43** H13
Bangassou C.A.R. 4°55N 23°7E **52** D4
Banggai Indonesia 1°34S 123°30E **37** E6
Banggai, Kepulauan
   Indonesia 1°40S 123°30E **37** E6
Banggai Arch. = Banggai,
   Kepulauan Indonesia 1°40S 123°30E **37** E6
Banggi, Pulau Malaysia 7°17N 117°12E **36** C5
Banghāzī Libya 32°11N 20°3E **51** B10
Bangka Sulawesi, Indonesia 1°50N 125°5E **37** D7
Bangka Sumatera,
   Indonesia 2°0S 105°50E **36** E3
Bangka, Selat Indonesia 2°30S 105°30E **36** E3
Bangka-Belitung □
   Indonesia 2°30S 107°0E **36** E3
Bangkalan Indonesia 7°2S 112°46E **37** G15
Bangkinang Indonesia 0°18N 101°5E **36** D2
Bangko Indonesia 2°5S 102°9E **36** E2
Bangkok Thailand 13°45N 100°35E **38** F3
Bangla = West Bengal □
   India 23°0N 88°0E **43** H13
Bangladesh ■ Asia 24°0N 90°0E **41** H17
Bangli Indonesia 8°27S 115°21E **37** J18
Bangong Co China 33°45N 78°43E **43** C8
Bangor Down, U.K. 54°40N 5°40W **10** B6
Bangor Gwynedd, U.K. 53°14N 4°8W **12** D3
Bangor Maine, U.S.A. 44°48N 68°46W **81** C19
Bangor Pa., U.S.A. 40°52N 75°13W **83** F9
Bangued Phil. 17°40N 120°37E **37** A6
Bangui C.A.R. 4°23N 18°35E **52** D3
Banguru
   Dem. Rep. of the Congo 0°30N 27°10E **54** B2
Bangweulu, L. Zambia 11°0S 30°0E **55** E3
Bangweulu Swamp
   Zambia 11°20S 30°15E **55** E3
Banhine △ Mozam. 22°49S 32°55E **57** C5
Banhol → Iran 28°16N 70°22E **45** D8
Baní Dom. Rep. 18°16N 70°22W **89** C5
Banī Sa'd Iraq 33°34N 44°32E **44** C5
Banihal Pass India 33°30N 75°12E **43** C6
Banissa Kenya 3°55N 40°19E **54** B4
Bāniyās Syria 35°10N 36°0E **44** C3

Banja Luka Bos.-H. 44°49N 17°11E **22** B7
Banjar India 31°38N 77°21E **42** D7
Banjar → India 22°36N 80°22E **43** H9
Banjarmasin Indonesia 3°20S 114°35E **36** E4
Banjul Gambia 13°28N 16°40W **50** F2
Banka India 24°53N 86°55E **43** G12
Banket Zimbabwe 17°27S 30°19E **55** F3
Bankipore India 25°35N 85°10E **41** G14
Banks I. = Moa Australia 10°11S 142°16E **62** a
Banks I. B.C., Canada 53°20N 130°0W **70** C3
Banks I. N.W.T., Canada 73°15N 121°30W **68** C7
Banks Pen. N.Z. 43°45S 173°15E **59** E4
Banks Str. Australia 40°40S 148°10E **63** G4
Bankura India 23°11N 87°18E **43** H12
Bann → Armagh, U.K. 54°30N 6°31W **10** B5
Bann → L'derry., U.K. 55°8N 6°41W **10** A5
Bannang Sata Thailand 6°16N 101°16E **39** J3
Banning U.S.A. 33°56N 116°53W **79** M10
Bannockburn Canada 44°39N 77°33W **82** B7
Bannockburn U.K. 56°5N 3°55W **11** E5
Bannockburn Zimbabwe 20°17S 29°48E **55** G2
Bannu Pakistan 33°0N 70°18E **40** C7
Bano India 22°40N 84°55E **43** H11
Bansgaon India 26°33N 83°21E **43** F10
Banská Bystrica
   Slovak Rep. 48°46N 19°14E **17** D10
Banswara India 23°32N 74°24E **42** H6
Bantaeng Indonesia 5°32S 119°56E **37** F5
Banten □ Indonesia 6°30S 106°0E **37** G11
Bantry Ireland 51°41N 9°27W **10** E2
Bantry B. Ireland 51°37N 9°44W **10** E2
Bantul Indonesia 7°55S 110°19E **37** G14
Bantva India 21°29N 70°12E **42** J4
Banyak, Kepulauan
   Indonesia 2°10N 97°10E **36** D1
Banyalbufar Spain 39°42N 2°31E **24** B9
Banyo Cameroon 6°52N 11°45E **52** C2
Banyumas Indonesia 7°32S 109°18E **37** G13
Banyuwangi Indonesia 8°13S 114°21E **37** J17
Banzare Coast Antarctica 68°0S 125°0E **5** C9
Bao Ha Vietnam 22°11N 104°21E **38** A5
Bao Lac Vietnam 22°57N 105°40E **38** A5
Bao Loc Vietnam 11°32N 107°48E **39** G6
Bao'an = Shenzhen
   China 22°32N 114°5E **33** F10
Baocheng China 33°12N 106°56E **34** H4
Baode China 39°1N 111°5E **34** E6
Baodi China 39°38N 117°20E **35** E9
Baoding China 38°50N 115°28E **34** E8
Baoji China 34°20N 107°5E **34** G4
Baoshan China 25°10N 99°5E **32** D4
Baotou China 40°32N 110°2E **34** D6
Baoying China 33°17N 119°20E **35** H10
Baoyou = Ledong China 18°41N 109°5E **38** C7
Bap India 27°23N 72°18E **42** F5
Bapatla India 15°55N 80°30E **41** M12
Bāqerābād Iran 33°2N 51°58E **45** C6
Ba'qūbah Iraq 33°45N 44°50E **44** C5
Baquedano Chile 23°20S 69°52W **94** A2
Bar Montenegro 42°8N 19°6E **23** C8
Bar Ukraine 49°4N 27°40E **17** D14
Bar Bigha India 25°21N 85°47E **43** G11
Bar Harbor U.S.A. 44°23N 68°13W **81** C19
Bar-le-Duc France 48°47N 5°10E **20** B6
Bara India 25°16N 81°43E **43** G9
Bara Banki India 26°55N 81°12E **43** F9
Barabai Indonesia 2°32S 115°34E **36** E5
Baraboo U.S.A. 43°28N 89°45W **80** D9
Baracoa Cuba 20°20N 74°30W **89** B5
Baradā → Syria 33°33N 36°34E **46** B5
Baradero Argentina 33°52S 59°29W **94** C4
Baraga U.S.A. 46°47N 88°30W **80** B9
Baragoi Kenya 1°47N 36°47E **54** B4
Barah → India 27°42N 77°5E **42** F6
Barahona Dom. Rep. 18°13N 71°7W **89** C5
Barail Range India 25°15N 93°20E **41** G18
Barakaldo Spain 43°18N 2°59W **21** A4
Barakar → India 24°7N 86°14E **43** G12
Barakot India 21°33N 84°59E **43** J11
Barakpur India 22°47N 88°21E **43** H13
Baralaba Australia 24°13S 149°50E **62** C4
Baramati India 60°0N 98°3W **71** B9
Baramula India 34°15N 74°20E **43** B6
Baran India 25°9N 76°40E **42** G7
Baran → Pakistan 25°13N 68°17E **42** G3
Baranavichy Belarus 53°10N 26°0E **17** B14
Baranof U.S.A. 57°5N 134°50W **70** B2
Baranof I. U.S.A. 57°0N 135°0W **68** F4
Barapasi Indonesia 2°15S 137°5E **37** E9
Barasat India 22°46N 88°31E **43** H13
Barat Daya, Kepulauan
   Indonesia 7°30S 128°0E **37** F7
Barataria B. U.S.A. 29°20N 89°55W **85** G10
Barauda India 23°33N 75°15E **42** H6
Baraut India 29°13N 77°7E **42** E7
Barbacena Brazil 21°15S 43°56W **95** A7
Barbados ■ W. Indies 13°10N 59°30W **89** g
Bàrbaria, C. de Spain 38°39N 1°24E **24** C7
Barbas, C. W. Sahara 22°20N 16°42W **50** D2
Barbastro Spain 42°2N 0°5E **21** A6
Barberton S. Africa 25°42S 31°2E **57** D5
Barberton U.S.A. 41°1N 81°39W **82** E3
Barbosa Colombia 5°57N 73°37W **92** B4
Barbuda W. Indies 17°30N 61°40W **89** C7
Barcaldine Australia 23°43S 145°6E **62** C4
Barcellona Pozzo di Gotto
   Italy 38°9N 15°13E **22** E6
Barcelona Spain 41°22N 2°10E **21** B7
Barcelona Venezuela 10°10N 64°40W **92** A6
Barceloneta Puerto Rico 18°27N 66°32W **89** d
Barcelos Brazil 1°0S 63°0W **92** D6
Barcoo → Australia 25°30S 142°50E **62** D3
Bardaï Chad 21°25N 17°0E **51** D9
Bardas Blancas
   Argentina 35°49S 69°45W **94** D2
Bardawîl, Sabkhet el
   Egypt 31°10N 33°15E **46** D2

Barddhaman *India* 23°14N 87°39E **43** H12
Bardejov *Slovak Rep.* 49°18N 21°15E **17** D11
Bardera = Baardheere
  Somali Rep. 2°20N 42°27E **47** G3
Bardīyah *Libya* 31°45N 25°5E **51** B10
Bardsey I. *U.K.* 52°45N 4°47W **12** E3
Bardstown *U.S.A.* 37°49N 85°28W **81** G11
Bareilly *India* 28°22N 79°27E **43** E8
Barela *India* 23°6N 80°3E **43** H9
Barents Sea *Arctic* 73°0N 39°0E **4** B9
Barfleur, Pte. de *France* 49°42N 1°16W **20** B3
Bargara *Australia* 24°50S 152°25E **62** C5
Bargi Dam *India* 22°59N 80°0E **43** H9
Barguzin *Russia* 53°37N 109°37E **29** D11
Barh *India* 25°29N 85°46E **43** G11
Barhaj *India* 26°18N 83°44E **43** F10
Barharwa *India* 24°52N 87°47E **43** G12
Barhi *India* 24°15N 85°25E **43** G11
Bari *India* 26°39N 77°39E **42** F7
Bari *Italy* 41°8N 16°51E **22** D7
Bari Doab *Pakistan* 30°20N 73°0E **42** D5
Bari Sadri *India* 24°28N 74°30E **42** G5
Barīdī, Ra's *Si. Arabia* 24°17N 37°31E **44** E3
Barīm *Yemen* 12°39N 43°25E **48** E8
Barinas *Venezuela* 8°36N 70°15W **92** B4
Baring, C. *Canada* 70°0N 117°30W **68** D8
Baringo, L. *Kenya* 0°47N 36°16E **54** B4
Barisal *Bangla.* 22°45N 90°20E **41** H17
Barisal □ *Bangla.* 22°45N 90°20E **41** H17
Barisan, Pegunungan
  Indonesia 3°30S 102°15E **36** E2
Barito → *Indonesia* 4°0S 114°50E **36** E4
Baritú △ *Argentina* 23°43S 64°40W **94** A3
Barjūj, Wadi → *Libya* 25°26N 12°12E **51** C8
Bark L. *Canada* 45°27N 77°51W **82** A7
Barkakana *India* 23°37N 85°29E **43** H11
Barker *U.S.A.* 43°20N 78°33W **82** C6
Barkley, L. *U.S.A.* 37°1N 88°14W **85** C10
Barkley Sound *Canada* 48°50N 125°10W **70** D3
Barkly East *S. Africa* 30°58S 27°33E **56** E4
Barkly Homestead
  Australia 19°52S 135°50E **62** B2
Barkly Tableland
  Australia 17°50S 136°40E **62** B2
Barkly West *S. Africa* 28°5S 24°31E **56** D3
Barkol Kazak Zizhixian
  China 43°37N 93°2E **32** B4
Bârlad *Romania* 46°15N 27°38E **17** E14
Bârlad → *Romania* 45°38N 27°32E **17** F14
Barlee, L. *Australia* 29°15S 119°30E **61** E2
Barlee, Mt. *Australia* 24°38S 128°13E **61** D4
Barletta *Italy* 41°19N 16°17E **22** D7
Barlovento *Canary Is.* 28°48N 17°48W **24** F2
Barlovento *C. Verde Is.* 17°0N 25°0W **50** b
Barlow L. *Canada* 62°0N 103°0W **71** A8
Barmedman *Australia* 34°9S 147°21E **63** E4
Barmer *India* 25°45N 71°20E **42** G4
Barmera *Australia* 34°15S 140°28E **63** E3
Barmouth *U.K.* 52°44N 4°4W **12** E3
Barna → *India* 25°21N 83°3E **43** G10
Barnagar *India* 23°7N 75°19E **42** H6
Barnala *India* 30°23N 75°33E **42** D6
Barnard Castle *U.K.* 54°33N 1°55W **12** C6
Barnaul *Russia* 53°20N 83°40E **28** D9
Barnesville *Ga., U.S.A.* 33°3N 84°9W **85** E12
Barnesville *Minn.,*
  U.S.A. 46°43N 96°28W **80** B5
Barnet □ *U.K.* 51°38N 0°9W **13** F7
Barneveld *Neths.* 52°7N 5°36E **15** B5
Barnhart *U.S.A.* 31°8N 101°10W **84** F4
Barnsley *U.K.* 53°34N 1°27W **12** D6
Barnstable *U.S.A.* 41°42N 70°18W **81** E18
Barnstaple *U.K.* 51°5N 4°4W **13** F3
Barnstaple Bay = Bideford Bay
  U.K. 51°5N 4°20W **13** F3
Barnwell *U.S.A.* 33°15N 81°23W **85** E14
Baro → *Nigeria* 8°35N 6°18E **50** G7
Baroda = Vadodara
  India 22°20N 73°10E **42** H5
Baroda *India* 25°29N 76°35E **42** G7
Baroe *S. Africa* 33°13S 24°33E **56** E3
Baron Ra. *Australia* 23°30S 127°45E **60** D4
Barotseland *Zambia* 15°0S 24°0E **53** H4
Barpeta *India* 26°20N 91°10E **41** F17
Barqa *Libya* 27°0N 23°0E **51** C10
Barques, Pt. Aux *U.S.A.* 44°4N 82°58W **82** B2
Barquísimeto *Venezuela* 10°4N 69°19W **92** A5
Barr Smith Range
  Australia 27°4S 120°20E **61** E3
Barra *Brazil* 11°5S 43°10W **93** F10
Barra *U.K.* 57°0N 7°29W **11** E1
Barra, Sd. of *U.K.* 57°4N 7°25W **11** E1
Barra de Navidad
  Mexico 19°12N 104°41W **86** D4
Barra do Corda *Brazil* 5°30S 45°10W **93** E9
Barra do Garças *Brazil* 15°54S 52°16W **93** G8
Barra do Piraí *Brazil* 22°30S 43°50W **95** A7
Barra Falsa, Pta. da
  Mozam. 22°58S 35°37E **57** C6
Barra Hd. *U.K.* 56°47N 7°40W **11** E1
Barra Mansa *Brazil* 22°35S 44°12W **95** A7
Barraba *Australia* 30°21S 150°35E **63** E5
Barrackpur = Barakpur
  India 22°47N 88°21E **43** H13
Barraigh = Barra *U.K.* 57°0N 7°29W **11** E1
Barranca *Lima, Peru* 10°45S 77°50W **92** F3
Barranca *Loreto, Peru* 4°50S 76°50W **92** D3
Barranca del Cobre △
  Mexico 27°18N 107°40W **86** B3
Barrancabermeja
  Colombia 7°0N 73°50W **92** B4
Barrancas *Venezuela* 8°55N 62°5W **92** B6
Barrancos *Portugal* 38°10N 6°58W **21** C2
Barranqueras *Argentina* 27°30S 59°0W **94** B4
Barranquilla *Colombia* 11°0N 74°50W **92** A4
Barraute *Canada* 48°26N 77°38W **72** C4
Barre *Mass., U.S.A.* 42°25N 72°6W **83** D12
Barre *Vt., U.S.A.* 44°12N 72°30W **83** B12
Barreal *Argentina* 31°33S 69°28W **94** C2

Barreiras *Brazil* 12°8S 45°0W **93** F10
Barreirinhas *Brazil* 2°30S 42°50W **93** D10
Barreiro *Portugal* 38°39N 9°5W **21** C1
Barren, Nosy *Madag.* 18°25S 43°40E **57** B7
Barretos *Brazil* 20°30S 48°35W **93** H9
Barrie *Canada* 44°24N 79°40W **82** B5
Barrier Ra. *Australia* 31°0S 141°30E **63** E3
Barrier Reef *Belize* 17°9N 88°3W **87** D7
Barrière *Canada* 51°12N 120°7W **70** C4
Barrington *U.S.A.* 41°44N 71°18W **83** E13
Barrington L. *Canada* 56°55N 100°15W **71** B8
Barrington Tops
  Australia 32°6S 151°28E **63** E5
Barringun *Australia* 29°1S 145°41E **63** D4
Barron *U.S.A.* 45°24N 91°51W **80** C8
Barrow *U.S.A.* 71°18N 156°47W **74** A8
Barrow → *Ireland* 52°25N 6°58W **10** D5
Barrow Creek *Australia* 21°30S 133°55E **62** C1
Barrow I. *Australia* 20°45S 115°20E **60** D2
Barrow-in-Furness *U.K.* 54°7N 3°14W **12** C4
Barrow Pt. *Australia* 14°20S 144°40E **62** A3
Barrow Ra. *Australia* 26°0S 127°40E **61** E4
Barrow Str. *Canada* 74°20N 95°0W **4** B3
Barry *U.K.* 51°24N 3°16W **13** F4
Barry's Bay *Canada* 45°29N 77°41W **82** A7
Barsat *Pakistan* 36°10N 72°45E **43** A5
Barsi *India* 18°10N 75°50E **40** K9
Barsoi *India* 25°48N 87°57E **41** G15
Barstow *U.S.A.* 34°54N 117°1W **79** L9
Barthélemy, Col *Vietnam* 19°26N 104°6E **38** C5
Bartica *Guyana* 6°25N 58°40W **92** B7
Bartle Frere *Australia* 17°27S 145°50E **62** B4
Bartlesville *U.S.A.* 36°45N 95°59W **84** C7
Bartlett *Calif., U.S.A.* 36°29N 118°2W **78** J8
Bartlett *Tenn., U.S.A.* 35°12N 89°52W **85** D10
Bartlett, L. *Canada* 63°5N 118°20W **70** A5
Bartolomeu Dias *Mozam.* 21°10S 35°8E **55** G4
Barton *U.S.A.* 44°45N 72°11W **83** B12
Barton upon Humber
  U.K. 53°41N 0°25W **12** D7
Bartow *U.S.A.* 27°54N 81°50W **85** H14
Barú, Volcan *Panama* 8°55N 82°35W **88** E3
Barumba
  Dem. Rep. of the Congo 1°3N 23°37E **54** B1
Baruun Urt *Mongolia* 46°46N 113°15E **29** E12
Baruunsuu *Mongolia* 43°43N 105°35E **34** C3
Barwani *India* 22°2N 74°57E **42** H6
Barysaw *Belarus* 54°17N 28°28E **17** A15
Barzân *Iraq* 36°55N 44°3E **44** B5
Bāsa'idū *Iran* 26°35N 55°20E **45** E7
Basal *Pakistan* 33°33N 72°13E **42** C5
Basankusa
  Dem. Rep. of the Congo 1°5N 19°50E **52** D3
Basarabeasca *Moldova* 46°21N 28°58E **17** E15
Basarabia = Bessarabiya
  Moldova 47°0N 28°10E **17** E15
Basawa *Afghan.* 34°15N 70°50E **42** B4
Basel *Switz.* 47°35N 7°35E **20** C7
Bashākerd, Kūhhā-ye
  Iran 26°42N 58°35E **45** E8
Bashaw *Canada* 52°35N 112°58W **70** C6
Bāshī *Iran* 28°41N 51°4E **45** D6
Bashkir Republic =
  Bashkortostan □
  Russia 54°0N 57°0E **18** D10
Bashkortostan □ *Russia* 54°0N 57°0E **18** D10
Basibasy *Madag.* 22°10S 43°40E **57** C7
Basilan *Phil.* 6°35N 122°0E **37** C6
Basilan Str. *Phil.* 6°50N 122°0E **37** C6
Basildon *U.K.* 51°34N 0°28E **13** F8
Basim = Washim *India* 20°3N 77°0E **40** J10
Basin *U.S.A.* 44°23N 108°2W **76** D9
Basingstoke *U.K.* 51°15N 1°5W **13** F6
Baskatong, Rés. *Canada* 46°46N 75°50W **72** C4
Basle = Basel *Switz.* 47°35N 7°35E **20** C7
Basoda *India* 23°52N 77°54E **42** H7
Basoko
  Dem. Rep. of the Congo 1°16N 23°40E **54** B1
Basque Provinces = País Vasco □
  Spain 42°50N 2°45W **21** A4
Basra = Al Baṣrah *Iraq* 30°30N 47°50E **44** D5
Bass Str. *Australia* 39°15S 146°30E **63** F4
Bassano *Canada* 50°48N 112°20W **70** C6
Bassano del Grappa *Italy* 45°46N 11°44E **22** B4
Bassas da India *Ind. Oc.* 22°0S 39°0E **55** G4
Basse-Pointe *Martinique* 14°52N 61°8W **88** c
Basse-Terre *Guadeloupe* 16°0N 61°44W **88** b
Basse Terre *Trin. & Tob.* 10°7N 61°19W **93** K15
Bassein *Burma* 16°45N 94°30E **41** L19
Basses, Pte. des
  Guadeloupe 15°52N 61°17W **88** b
Basseterre
  St. Kitts & Nevis 17°17N 62°43W **89** C7
Bassett *U.S.A.* 42°35N 99°32W **80** D4
Bassi *India* 30°44N 76°21E **42** D7
Bastak *Iran* 27°15N 54°25E **45** E7
Bastām *Iran* 36°29N 55°4E **45** B7
Bastar *India* 19°15N 81°40E **41** K12
Basti *India* 26°52N 82°55E **43** F10
Bastia *France* 42°40N 9°30E **20** E8
Bastogne *Belgium* 50°1N 5°43E **15** D5
Bastrop *La., U.S.A.* 32°47N 91°55W **84** E9
Bastrop *Tex., U.S.A.* 30°7N 97°19W **84** F6
Basuo = Dongfang
  China 18°50N 108°33E **38** C7
Bat Yam *Israel* 32°2N 34°44E **46** C3
Bata *Eq. Guin.* 1°57N 9°50E **52** D1
Bataan □ *Phil.* 14°40N 120°25E **37** B6
Batabanó *Cuba* 22°41N 82°18W **88** B3
Batabanó, G. de *Cuba* 22°30N 82°30W **88** B3
Batac *Phil.* 18°3N 120°34E **37** A6
Batagai *Russia* 67°38N 134°38E **29** C14
Batala *India* 31°48N 75°12E **42** D6
Batama
  Dem. Rep. of the Congo 0°58N 26°33E **54** B2
Batamay *Russia* 63°30N 129°15E **29** C13

Batang *Indonesia* 6°55S 109°45E **37** G13
Batangafo *C.A.R.* 7°25N 18°20E **52** C3
Batangas *Phil.* 13°35N 121°10E **37** B6
Batanta *Indonesia* 0°55S 130°40E **37** E8
Batatais *Brazil* 20°54S 47°37W **95** A6
Batavia *U.S.A.* 43°0N 78°11W **82** D6
Batchelor *Australia* 13°4S 131°1E **60** B5
Batdambang *Cambodia* 13°7N 103°12E **38** F4
Batemans Bay *Australia* 35°44S 150°11E **63** F5
Batesburg-Leesville
  U.S.A. 33°54N 81°33W **85** E14
Batesville *Ark., U.S.A.* 35°46N 91°39W **84** D9
Batesville *Miss., U.S.A.* 34°19N 89°57W **85** D10
Batesville *Tex., U.S.A.* 28°58N 99°37W **84** G5
Bath *Canada* 44°11N 76°47W **83** B8
Bath *U.K.* 51°23N 2°22W **13** F5
Bath *Maine, U.S.A.* 43°55N 69°49W **81** D19
Bath *N.Y., U.S.A.* 42°20N 77°19W **82** D7
Bath & North East Somerset □
  U.K. 51°21N 2°27W **13** F5
Batheay *Cambodia* 11°59N 104°57E **39** G5
Bathsheba *Barbados* 13°13N 59°32W **89** g
Bathurst *Australia* 33°25S 149°31E **63** E4
Bathurst *Canada* 47°37N 65°43W **73** C6
Bathurst *S. Africa* 33°30S 26°50E **56** E4
Bathurst, C. *Canada* 70°34N 128°0W **68** B7
Bathurst B. *Australia* 14°16S 144°25E **62** A3
Bathurst Harb.
  Australia 43°15S 146°10E **63** G4
Bathurst I. *Australia* 11°30S 130°10E **60** B5
Bathurst I. *Canada* 76°0N 100°30W **69** B11
Bathurst Inlet *Canada* 66°50N 108°1W **68** D10
Batiki *Fiji* 17°48S 179°10E **59** a
Batlow *Australia* 35°31S 148°9E **63** F4
Batman *Turkey* 37°55N 41°5E **44** B4
Baṭn al Ghūl *Jordan* 29°36N 35°56E **46** F4
Batna *Algeria* 35°34N 6°15E **50** A7
Batoka *Zambia* 16°45S 27°15E **55** F2
Baton Rouge *U.S.A.* 30°27N 91°11W **84** F9
Batong, Ko *Thailand* 6°32N 99°12E **39** J2
Batopilas *Mexico* 27°1N 107°44W **86** B3
Batouri *Cameroon* 4°30N 14°25E **52** D2
Båtsfjord *Norway* 70°38N 29°39E **8** A23
Battambang = Batdambang
  Cambodia 13°7N 103°12E **38** F4
Batticaloa *Sri Lanka* 7°43N 81°45E **40** R12
Battipáglia *Italy* 40°37N 14°58E **22** D6
Battle *U.K.* 50°55N 0°30E **13** G8
Battle → *Canada* 52°43N 108°15W **71** C7
Battle Creek *U.S.A.* 42°19N 85°11W **81** D11
Battle Ground *U.S.A.* 45°47N 122°32W **78** E4
Battle Harbour *Canada* 52°16N 55°35W **73** B8
Battle Lake *U.S.A.* 46°17N 95°43W **80** B6
Battle Mountain
  U.S.A. 40°38N 116°56W **76** F5
Battlefields *Zimbabwe* 18°37S 29°47E **55** F2
Battleford *Canada* 52°45N 108°15W **71** C7
Batu *Ethiopia* 6°55N 39°45E **47** F2
Batu *Malaysia* 3°15N 101°40E **39** L3
Batu, Kepulauan
  Indonesia 0°30S 98°25E **36** E1
Batu Ferringhi *Malaysia* 5°28N 100°15E **39** c
Batu Gajah *Malaysia* 4°28N 101°3E **39** K3
Batu Is. = Batu, Kepulauan
  Indonesia 0°30S 98°25E **36** E1
Batu Pahat *Malaysia* 1°50N 102°56E **39** M4
Batuata *Indonesia* 6°12S 122°42E **37** F6
Batugondang, Tanjung
  Indonesia 8°6S 114°29E **37** J17
Batukau, Gunung
  Indonesia 8°20S 115°5E **37** J18
Batumi *Georgia* 41°39N 41°44E **19** F7
Batur *Indonesia* 8°15S 115°22E **37** J18
Batur, Danau *Indonesia* 8°15S 115°24E **37** J18
Batur, Gunung
  Indonesia 8°14S 115°23E **37** J18
Batura Sar *Pakistan* 36°30N 74°31E **43** A6
Baturaja *Indonesia* 4°11S 104°15E **36** E2
Baturité *Brazil* 4°28S 38°45W **93** D11
Baturiti *Indonesia* 8°19S 115°11E **37** J18
Bau *Malaysia* 1°25N 110°9E **36** D4
Baubau *Indonesia* 5°25S 122°38E **37** F6
Baucau *E. Timor* 8°27S 126°27E **37** F7
Bauchi *Nigeria* 10°22N 9°48E **50** F7
Baudette *U.S.A.* 48°43N 94°36W **80** A6
Bauer, C. *Australia* 32°44S 134°4E **63** E1
Bauhinia *Australia* 24°35S 149°18E **62** C4
Baukau = Baucau
  E. Timor 8°27S 126°27E **37** F7
Bauld, C. *Canada* 51°38N 55°26W **69** G20
Bauru *Brazil* 22°10S 49°0W **95** A6
Bausi *India* 24°48N 87°1E **43** G12
Bauska *Latvia* 56°24N 24°15E **9** H21
Bautzen *Germany* 51°10N 14°26E **16** C8
Bavānāt *Iran* 30°28N 53°27E **45** D7
Bavaria = Bayern □
  Germany 48°50N 12°0E **16** D6
Bavispe → *Mexico* 29°15N 109°11W **86** B3
Bawdwin *Burma* 23°5N 97°20E **41** H20
Bawean *Indonesia* 5°46S 112°35E **36** F4
Bawku *Ghana* 11°3N 0°19W **50** F5
Bawlake *Burma* 19°11N 97°21E **41** K20
Baxley *U.S.A.* 31°47N 82°21W **85** F13
Baxter *U.S.A.* 46°21N 94°17W **80** B6
Baxter Springs *U.S.A.* 37°2N 94°44W **80** G6
Baxter State △ *U.S.A.* 45°55N 68°45W **81** C19
Bay City *Mich., U.S.A.* 43°36N 83°54W **81** D12
Bay City *Tex., U.S.A.* 28°59N 95°58W **84** G7
Bay Minette *U.S.A.* 30°53N 87°46W **85** F11
Bay Roberts *Canada* 47°36N 53°16W **73** C9
Bay St. Louis *U.S.A.* 30°19N 89°20W **85** F10
Bay Springs *U.S.A.* 31°59N 89°17W **85** F10
Bay View *N.Z.* 39°25S 176°50E **59** C6
Baya
  Dem. Rep. of the Congo 11°53S 27°25E **55** E2
Bayamo *Cuba* 20°20N 76°40W **88** B4
Bayamón *Puerto Rico* 18°24N 66°9W **89** d
Bayan Har Shan *China* 34°0N 98°0E **32** C4

Bayan Hot = Alxa Zuoqi
  China 38°50N 105°40E **34** E3
Bayan Lepas *Malaysia* 5°17N 100°16E **39** c
Bayan Obo *China* 41°52N 109°59E **34** D5
Bayan-Ovoo = Erdenetsogt
  Mongolia 42°55N 106°5E **34** C4
Bayana *India* 26°55N 77°18E **42** F7
Bayanaūyl *Kazakhstan* 50°45N 75°45E **28** D8
Bayandalay *Mongolia* 43°30N 103°29E **34** C2
Bayanhongor *Mongolia* 46°8N 102°43E **32** B5
Bayard *N. Mex., U.S.A.* 32°46N 108°8W **77** K9
Bayard *Nebr., U.S.A.* 41°45N 103°20W **80** E2
Baybay *Phil.* 10°40N 124°55E **37** B6
Baydaratskaya Guba
  Russia 69°0N 67°30E **28** C7
Baydhabo *Somali Rep.* 3°8N 43°30E **47** G3
Bayern □ *Germany* 48°50N 12°0E **16** D6
Bayeux *France* 49°17N 0°42W **20** B3
Bayfield *Canada* 43°34N 81°42W **82** C3
Bayfield *U.S.A.* 46°49N 90°49W **80** B8
Bayındır *Turkey* 38°13N 27°39E **23** E12
Baykal, Oz. *Russia* 53°0N 108°0E **29** D11
Baykan *Turkey* 38°7N 41°44E **44** B4
Baymak *Russia* 52°36N 58°19E **18** D10
Baynes Mts. *Namibia* 17°15S 13°0E **56** B1
Bayombong *Phil.* 16°30N 121°10E **37** A6
Bayonne *France* 43°30N 1°28W **20** E3
Bayonne *U.S.A.* 40°40N 74°6W **83** F10
Bayovar *Peru* 5°50S 81°0W **92** E2
Bayqongyr *Kazakhstan* 45°40N 63°20E **28** E7
Bayram-Ali = Baýramaly
  Turkmenistan 37°37N 62°10E **45** B9
Baýramaly *Turkmenistan* 37°37N 62°10E **45** B9
Bayramiç *Turkey* 39°48N 26°36E **23** E12
Bayreuth *Germany* 49°56N 11°35E **16** D6
Bayrūt *Lebanon* 33°53N 35°31E **46** B4
Bays, L. of *Canada* 45°15N 79°4W **82** A5
Baysville *Canada* 45°9N 79°7W **82** A5
Bayt Lahm *West Bank* 31°43N 35°12E **46** D4
Baytown *U.S.A.* 29°43N 94°59W **84** G7
Bayun *Indonesia* 8°11S 115°16E **37** J18
Baza *Spain* 37°30N 2°47W **21** D4
Bazaruto, I. do *Mozam.* 21°40S 35°28E **57** C6
Bazaruto △ *Mozam.* 21°42S 35°26E **57** C6
Bazhou *China* 39°8N 116°22E **34** E9
Bazmān, Kūh-e *Iran* 28°4N 60°1E **45** D9
Beach *U.S.A.* 46°58N 104°0W **80** B2
Beach City *U.S.A.* 40°39N 81°35W **82** F3
Beachport *Australia* 37°29S 140°0E **63** F3
Beachville *Canada* 43°5N 80°49W **82** C4
Beachy Hd. *U.K.* 50°44N 0°15E **13** G8
Beacon *Australia* 30°26S 117°52E **61** F2
Beacon *U.S.A.* 41°30N 73°58W **83** E11
Beaconsfield *Australia* 41°11S 146°48E **63** G4
Beagle, Canal *S. Amer.* 55°0S 68°30W **96** H3
Beagle Bay *Australia* 16°58S 122°40E **60** C3
Beagle Bay ○ *Australia* 16°53S 122°40E **60** C3
Beagle G. *Australia* 12°15S 130°25E **60** B5
Béal an Átha = Ballina
  Ireland 54°7N 9°9W **10** B2
Béal Átha na Sluaighe =
  Ballinasloe *Ireland* 53°20N 8°13W **10** C3
Bealanana *Madag.* 14°33S 48°44E **57** A8
Beals Cr. → *U.S.A.* 32°10N 100°51W **84** E4
Beamsville *Canada* 43°12N 79°28W **82** C5
Bear → *Calif., U.S.A.* 38°56N 121°36W **78** G5
Bear → *Utah, U.S.A.* 41°30N 112°8W **74** G17
Bear I. *Ireland* 51°38N 9°50W **10** E2
Bear L. *Canada* 55°8N 96°0W **71** B9
Bear L. *U.S.A.* 41°59N 111°21W **76** F8
Bear Lake *Canada* 55°27N 79°35W **82** A5
Beardmore *Canada* 49°36N 87°57W **72** C2
Beardmore Glacier
  Antarctica 84°30S 170°0E **5** E11
Beardstown *U.S.A.* 40°1N 90°26W **80** E8
Bearma → *India* 24°20N 79°51E **43** G8
Béarn *France* 43°20N 0°30W **20** E3
Bearpaw Mts. *U.S.A.* 48°12N 109°30W **76** B9
Bearskin Lake *Canada* 53°58N 91°2W **72** B1
Beas → *India* 31°10N 74°59E **42** D6
Beata, C. *Dom. Rep.* 17°40N 71°30W **89** C5
Beata, I. *Dom. Rep.* 17°34N 71°31W **89** C5
Beatrice *U.S.A.* 40°16N 96°45W **80** E6
Beatrice *Zimbabwe* 18°15S 30°55E **55** F3
Beatrice, C. *Australia* 14°20S 136°55E **62** A2
Beatton → *Canada* 56°15N 120°45W **70** B4
Beatton River *Canada* 57°26N 121°20W **70** B4
Beatty *U.S.A.* 36°54N 116°46W **78** J10
Beau Bassin *Mauritius* 20°13S 57°27E **53** d
Beauce, Plaine de la
  France 48°10N 1°45E **20** B4
Beauceville *Canada* 46°13N 70°46W **73** C5
Beaudesert *Australia* 27°59S 153°0E **63** D5
Beaufort *Malaysia* 5°30N 115°40E **36** C5
Beaufort *N.C., U.S.A.* 34°43N 76°40W **85** D16
Beaufort *S.C., U.S.A.* 32°26N 80°40W **85** E14
Beaufort Sea *Arctic* 72°0N 140°0W **66** B5
Beaufort West *S. Africa* 32°18S 22°36E **56** E3
Beauharnois *Canada* 45°20N 73°52W **83** A11
Beaulieu → *Canada* 62°3N 113°11W **70** A6
Beauly *U.K.* 57°30N 4°28W **11** D4
Beauly → *U.K.* 57°29N 4°27W **11** D4
Beaumaris *U.K.* 53°16N 4°6W **12** D3
Beaumont *Belgium* 50°15N 4°14E **15** D4
Beaumont *U.S.A.* 30°5N 94°6W **84** F7
Beaune *France* 47°2N 4°50E **20** C6
Beaupré *Canada* 47°3N 70°54W **73** C5
Beauraing *Belgium* 50°7N 4°57E **15** D4
Beausejour *Canada* 50°5N 96°35W **71** C9
Beauvais *France* 49°25N 2°8E **20** B5
Beauval *Canada* 55°9N 107°37W **71** B7
Beaver *Okla., U.S.A.* 36°49N 100°31W **84** C4
Beaver *Pa., U.S.A.* 40°42N 80°19W **82** F4
Beaver *Utah, U.S.A.* 38°17N 112°38W **76** G7
Beaver → *B.C., Canada* 59°52N 124°20W **70** B4
Beaver → *Ont., Canada* 55°55N 87°48W **72** A2
Beaver → *Sask., Canada* 55°26N 107°45W **71** B7
Beaver City *U.S.A.* 40°8N 99°50W **80** E4

Beaver Creek *Canada* 63°0N 141°0W **68** E3
Beaver Dam *U.S.A.* 43°28N 88°50W **80** D9
Beaver Falls *U.S.A.* 40°46N 80°20W **82** F4
Beaver Hill L. *Canada* 54°5N 94°50W **71** C10
Beaver I. *U.S.A.* 45°40N 85°33W **81** C11
Beavercreek *U.S.A.* 39°43N 84°11W **81** F11
Beaverhill L. *Canada* 53°27N 112°32W **70** C6
Beaverlodge *Canada* 55°11N 119°29W **70** B5
Beaverstone → *Canada* 54°59N 89°25W **72** B2
Beaverton *Canada* 44°26N 79°9W **82** B5
Beaverton *U.S.A.* 45°29N 122°48W **78** E4
Beawar *India* 26°3N 74°18E **42** F6
Bebedouro *Brazil* 21°0S 48°25W **95** A6
Bebera, Tanjung
  Indonesia 8°44S 115°51E **37** K18
Beboa *Madag.* 17°22S 44°33E **57** B7
Becán *Mexico* 18°34N 89°31W **87** D7
Bécancour *Canada* 46°20N 72°26W **81** B17
Beccles *U.K.* 52°27N 1°35E **13** E9
Bečej *Serbia* 45°36N 20°3E **23** B9
Béchar *Algeria* 31°38N 2°18W **50** B5
Becharof L. *U.S.A.* 57°56N 156°23W **74** D8
Beckley *U.S.A.* 37°47N 81°11W **81** G13
Beddouza, C. *Morocco* 32°33N 9°9W **50** B4
Bedford *Canada* 45°7N 72°59W **83** A12
Bedford *S. Africa* 32°40S 26°10E **56** E4
Bedford *U.K.* 52°8N 0°28W **13** E7
Bedford *Ind., U.S.A.* 38°52N 86°29W **80** F10
Bedford *Iowa, U.S.A.* 40°40N 94°44W **80** E6
Bedford *Ohio, U.S.A.* 41°23N 81°32W **82** E3
Bedford *Pa., U.S.A.* 40°1N 78°30W **82** F6
Bedford *Va., U.S.A.* 37°20N 79°31W **81** G14
Bedford, C. *Australia* 15°14S 145°21E **62** B4
Bedfordshire □ *U.K.* 52°4N 0°28W **13** E7
Bedok *Singapore* 1°19N 103°56E **39** d
Bedourie *Australia* 24°30S 139°30E **62** C2
Bedum *Neths.* 53°18N 6°36E **15** A6
Beebe Plain *Canada* 45°1N 72°9W **83** A12
Beech Creek *U.S.A.* 41°5N 77°36W **82** E7
Beechy *Canada* 50°53N 107°24W **71** C7
Beed = Bir *India* 19°4N 75°46E **40** K9
Beef I. *Br. Virgin Is.* 18°26N 64°30W **89** e
Beenleigh *Australia* 27°43S 153°10E **63** D5
Be'er Menuha *Israel* 30°19N 35°8E **46** E4
Be'er Sheva *Israel* 31°15N 34°48E **46** D3
Beersheba = Be'er Sheva
  Israel 31°15N 34°48E **46** D3
Beestekraal *S. Africa* 25°23S 27°38E **57** D4
Beeston *U.K.* 52°56N 1°14W **12** E6
Beeton *Canada* 44°5N 79°47W **82** B5
Beeville *U.S.A.* 28°24N 97°45W **84** G6
Befale
  Dem. Rep. of the Congo 0°25N 20°45E **52** D4
Befandriana *Mahajanga,*
  Madag. 15°16S 48°32E **57** B8
Befandriana *Toliara,*
  Madag. 21°55S 44°0E **57** C7
Befasy *Madag.* 20°33S 44°23E **57** C7
Befotaka *Antsiranana,*
  Madag. 13°15S 48°16E **57** A8
Befotaka *Fianarantsoa,*
  Madag. 23°49S 47°0E **57** C8
Bega *Australia* 36°41S 149°51E **63** F4
Begusarai *India* 25°24N 86°9E **43** G12
Behābād *Iran* 32°24N 59°47E **45** C8
Behala *India* 22°30N 88°18E **43** H13
Behara *Madag.* 24°55S 46°20E **57** C8
Behbehān *Iran* 30°30N 50°15E **45** D6
Behm Canal *U.S.A.* 55°10N 131°0W **70** B2
Behshahr *Iran* 36°45N 53°35E **45** B7
Bei Jiang → *China* 23°2N 112°58E **33** D6
Bei Shan *China* 41°30N 96°0E **32** B4
Bei'an *China* 48°10N 126°20E **33** B7
Beihai *China* 21°28N 109°6E **33** D5
Beijing *China* 39°53N 116°21E **34** E9
Beijing □ *China* 39°55N 116°20E **34** E9
Beilen *Neths.* 52°52N 6°27E **15** B6
Beilpajah *Australia* 32°54S 143°52E **63** E3
Beinn na Faoghla = Benbecula
  U.K. 57°26N 7°21W **11** D1
Beipiao *China* 41°52N 120°32E **35** D11
Beira *Mozam.* 19°50S 34°52E **55** F3
Beirut = Bayrūt *Lebanon* 33°53N 35°31E **46** B4
Beiseker *Canada* 51°23N 113°32W **70** C6
Beit Lekhem = Bayt Lahm
  West Bank 31°43N 35°12E **46** D4
Beitaolaizhao *China* 44°58N 125°58E **35** B13
Beitbridge *Zimbabwe* 22°12S 30°0E **55** G3
Beizhen = Binzhou
  China 37°20N 118°2E **35** F10
Beizhen *China* 41°38N 121°54E **35** D11
Beizhengzhen *China* 44°31N 123°30E **35** B12
Beja *Portugal* 38°2N 7°53W **21** C2
Béja *Tunisia* 36°43N 9°12E **51** A7
Bejaïa *Algeria* 36°42N 5°2E **50** A7
Béjar *Spain* 40°23N 5°46W **21** B3
Bejestān *Iran* 34°30N 58°5E **45** C8
Bekaa Valley = Al Biqā
  Lebanon 34°10N 36°10E **46** A5
Békéscsaba *Hungary* 46°40N 21°5E **17** E11
Bekily *Madag.* 24°13S 45°19E **57** C8
Bekisopa *Madag.* 21°40S 45°54E **57** C8
Bekitro *Madag.* 24°33S 45°18E **57** C8
Bekodoka *Madag.* 16°58S 45°7E **57** B8
Bekok *Malaysia* 2°20N 103°7E **39** L4
Bekopaka *Madag.* 19°9S 44°48E **57** B7
Bekuli *Indonesia* 8°22S 114°13E **37** J17
Bela *India* 25°50N 82°0E **43** G10
Bela *Pakistan* 26°12N 66°20E **42** F2
Bela Bela *S. Africa* 24°51S 28°19E **57** C4
Bela Crkva *Serbia* 44°55N 21°27E **23** B9
Bela Vista *Brazil* 22°12S 56°20E **94** A4
Bela Vista *Mozam.* 26°10S 32°44E **57** D5
Belan → *India* 24°2N 81°45E **43** G9
Belarus ■ *Europe* 53°30N 27°0E **17** B14
Belau = Palau ■ *Palau* 7°30N 134°30E **58** A6
Belavenona *Madag.* 24°50S 47°4E **57** C8
Belawan *Indonesia* 3°33N 98°32E **36** D1
Belaya → *Russia* 54°40N 56°0E **18** C9

Belaya Tserkov = Bila Tserkva
 Ukraine 49°45N 30°10E **17** D16
Belaya Zemlya, Ostrova
 Russia 81°36N 62°18E **28** A7
Belcher Is. Canada 56°15N 78°45W **72** A3
Belden U.S.A. 40°2N 121°17W **78** E5
Belebey Russia 54°7N 54°7E **18** D9
Beledweyne Somali Rep. 4°30N 45°5E **47** G4
Belém Brazil 1°20S 48°30W **93** D9
Belén Argentina 27°40S 67°5W **94** B2
Belén Paraguay 23°30S 57°6W **94** A4
Belen U.S.A. 34°40N 106°46W **77** J10
Belet Uen = Beledweyne
 Somali Rep. 4°30N 45°5E **47** G4
Belev Russia 53°50N 36°5E **18** D6
Belfair U.S.A. 47°27N 122°50W **78** C4
Belfast S. Africa 25°42S 30°2E **57** D5
Belfast U.K. 54°37N 5°56W **10** B6
Belfast Maine, U.S.A. 44°26N 69°1W **81** C19
Belfast N.Y., U.S.A. 42°21N 78°7W **82** D6
Belfast L. U.K. 54°40N 5°50W **10** B6
Belfield U.S.A. 46°53N 103°12W **80** B2
Belfort France 47°38N 6°50E **20** C7
Belfry U.S.A. 45°9N 109°1W **76** D9
Belgaum India 15°55N 74°35E **40** M9
Belgavi = Belgaum India 15°55N 74°35E **40** M9
Belgium ■ Europe 50°30N 5°0E **15** D4
Belgorod Russia 50°35N 36°35E **19** D6
Belgorod-Dnestrovskiy =
 Bilhorod-Dnistrovskyy
 Ukraine 46°11N 30°23E **19** E5
Belgrade = Beograd
 Serbia 44°50N 20°37E **23** B9
Belgrade U.S.A. 45°47N 111°11W **76** D8
Belgrano Antarctica 77°52S 34°37W **5** D1
Belhaven U.S.A. 35°33N 76°37W **85** D16
Beli Drim → Europe 42°6N 20°25E **23** C9
Belimbing Indonesia 8°24S 115°2E **37** J18
Belinyu Indonesia 1°35S 105°50E **36** E3
Beliton Is. = Belitung
 Indonesia 3°10S 107°50E **36** E3
Belitung Indonesia 3°10S 107°50E **36** E3
Belize ■ Cent. Amer. 17°0N 88°30W **87** D7
Belize City Belize 17°25N 88°10W **87** D7
Belkovskiy, Ostrov
 Russia 75°32N 135°44E **29** B14
Bell → Canada 49°48N 77°38W **72** C4
Bell I. Canada 50°46N 55°35W **73** B8
Bell-Irving → Canada 56°12N 129°5W **70** B3
Bell Peninsula Canada 63°50N 82°0W **69** E15
Bell Ville Argentina 32°40S 62°40W **94** C3
Bella Bella Canada 52°10N 128°10W **70** C3
Bella Coola Canada 52°25N 126°40W **70** C3
Bella Unión Uruguay 30°15S 57°40W **94** C4
Bella Vista Corrientes,
 Argentina 28°33S 59°0W **94** B4
Bella Vista Tucuman,
 Argentina 27°10S 65°25W **94** B2
Bellaire U.S.A. 40°1N 80°45W **82** F4
Bellary India 15°10N 76°56E **40** M10
Bellata Australia 29°53S 149°46E **63** D4
Belle Fourche U.S.A. 44°40N 103°51W **80** C2
Belle Fourche →
 U.S.A. 44°26N 102°18W **75** G19
Belle Glade U.S.A. 26°41N 80°40W **85** H14
Belle-Île France 47°20N 3°10W **20** C2
Belle Isle Canada 51°57N 55°25W **73** B8
Belle Isle, Str. of Canada 51°30N 56°30W **73** B8
Belle Plaine U.S.A. 41°54N 92°17W **80** E7
Belle River Canada 42°18N 82°43W **82** D2
Bellefontaine U.S.A. 40°22N 83°46W **81** E12
Bellefonte U.S.A. 40°55N 77°47W **82** F7
Belleoram Canada 47°31N 55°25W **73** C8
Belleplaine Barbados 13°15N 59°34W **89** g
Belleville Canada 44°10N 77°23W **82** B7
Belleville Ill., U.S.A. 38°31N 89°59W **80** F9
Belleville Kans., U.S.A. 39°50N 97°38W **80** F5
Belleville N.J., U.S.A. 40°47N 74°9W **83** F10
Belleville N.Y., U.S.A. 43°46N 76°10W **83** C8
Bellevue Idaho, U.S.A. 43°28N 114°16W **76** E6
Bellevue Nebr., U.S.A. 41°9N 95°54W **80** E6
Bellevue Ohio, U.S.A. 41°17N 82°51W **82** E2
Bellevue Wash., U.S.A. 47°37N 122°12W **78** C4
Bellin = Kangirsuk
 Canada 60°0N 70°0W **69** F18
Bellingen Australia 30°25S 152°50E **63** E5
Bellingham U.S.A. 48°46N 122°29W **78** B4
Bellingshausen Abyssal Plain
 S. Ocean 64°0S 90°0W **5** C16
Bellingshausen Sea
 Antarctica 66°0S 80°0W **5** C17
Bellinzona Switz. 46°11N 9°1E **20** C8
Bello Colombia 6°20N 75°33W **92** B3
Bellows Falls U.S.A. 43°8N 72°27W **83** C12
Bellpat Pakistan 29°0N 68°5E **42** E3
Bellwood U.S.A. 40°36N 78°20W **82** F6
Belmont Canada 42°53N 81°5W **82** D3
Belmont S. Africa 29°28S 24°22E **56** D3
Belmont U.S.A. 42°14N 78°2W **82** D6
Belmonte Brazil 16°0S 39°0W **93** G11
Belmopan Belize 17°18N 88°30W **87** D7
Belmullet Ireland 54°14N 9°58W **10** B2
Belo Horizonte Brazil 19°55S 43°56W **93** G10
Belo-sur-Mer Madag. 20°42S 44°0E **57** C7
Belo-Tsiribihina Madag. 19°40S 44°30E **57** B7
Belogorsk Russia 51°0N 128°20E **29** D13
Beloha Madag. 25°10S 45°3E **57** D8
Beloit Kans., U.S.A. 39°28N 98°6W **80** F4
Beloit Wis., U.S.A. 42°31N 89°2W **80** D9
Belokorovichi Ukraine 51°7N 28°2E **17** C15
Belomorsk Russia 64°35N 34°54E **18** B5
Belonia India 23°15N 91°30E **41** H17
Beloretsk Russia 53°58N 58°24E **18** D10
Belorussia = Belarus ■
 Europe 53°30N 27°0E **17** B14
Belovo Russia 54°30N 86°0E **28** D9
Beloyarskiy Russia 63°42N 66°40E **28** C7
Beloye, Ozero Russia 60°10N 37°35E **18** B6

Beloye More Russia 66°30N 38°0E **8** C25
Belozersk Russia 60°1N 37°45E **18** B6
Belpre U.S.A. 39°17N 81°34W **81** F13
Belrain India 28°23N 80°55E **43** E9
Beltana Australia 30°48S 138°25E **63** E2
Belterra Brazil 2°45S 55°0W **93** D8
Belton U.S.A. 31°3N 97°28W **84** F6
Belton L. U.S.A. 31°8N 97°32W **84** F6
Beltsy = Bălţi Moldova 47°48N 27°58E **17** E14
Belturbet Ireland 54°6N 7°26W **10** B4
Belukha Russia 49°50N 86°50E **28** E9
Belushya Guba Russia 71°32N 52°19E **28** B6
Belvidere Ill., U.S.A. 42°15N 88°50W **80** D9
Belvidere N.J., U.S.A. 40°50N 75°5W **83** F9
Belyando → Australia 21°38S 146°50E **62** C4
Belyando Crossing
 Australia 21°32S 146°51E **62** C4
Belyuen Australia 12°34S 130°42E **60** B5
Belyy, Ostrov Russia 73°30N 71°0E **28** B8
Belyy Yar Russia 58°26N 84°39E **28** D9
Belzoni U.S.A. 33°11N 90°29W **85** E9
Bemaraha, Lembalemban' i
 Madag. 18°40S 44°45E **57** B7
Bemarivo Madag. 21°45S 44°45E **57** C7
Bemarivo → Antsiranana,
 Madag. 14°9S 50°9E **57** A9
Bemarivo → Mahajanga,
 Madag. 15°27S 47°40E **57** B8
Bemavo Madag. 21°33S 45°25E **57** C8
Bembéréke Benin 10°11N 2°43E **50** F6
Bembesi Zimbabwe 20°0S 28°58E **55** G2
Bembesi → Zimbabwe 18°57S 27°47E **55** F2
Bemetara India 21°42N 81°32E **43** J9
Bemidji U.S.A. 47°28N 94°53W **80** B6
Bemolanga Madag. 17°44S 45°6E **57** B8
Ben Iran 32°32N 50°45E **45** C6
Ben Cruachan U.K. 56°26N 5°8W **11** E3
Ben Dearg U.K. 57°47N 4°56W **11** D4
Ben En △ Vietnam 19°37N 105°30E **38** C5
Ben Gardane Tunisia 33°11N 11°11E **51** B8
Ben Hope U.K. 58°25N 4°36W **11** C4
Ben Lawers U.K. 56°32N 4°14W **11** E4
Ben Lomond N.S.W.,
 Australia 30°1S 151°43E **63** E5
Ben Lomond Tas.,
 Australia 41°38S 147°42E **63** G4
Ben Lomond U.K. 56°11N 4°38W **11** E4
Ben Lomond △
 Australia 41°33S 147°39E **63** G4
Ben Luc Vietnam 10°39N 106°29E **39** G6
Ben Macdhui U.K. 57°4N 3°40W **11** D5
Ben Mhor U.K. 57°15N 7°18W **11** D1
Ben More Argyll & Bute,
 U.K. 56°26N 6°1W **11** E2
Ben More Stirling, U.K. 56°23N 4°32W **11** E4
Ben More Assynt U.K. 58°8N 4°52W **11** C4
Ben Nevis U.K. 56°48N 5°1W **11** E3
Ben Quang Vietnam 17°3N 106°55E **38** D5
Ben Tre Vietnam 10°14N 106°23E **39** G6
Ben Vorlich U.K. 56°21N 4°14W **11** E4
Ben Wyvis U.K. 57°40N 4°35W **11** D4
Bena Nigeria 11°20N 5°50E **50** F7
Benalla Australia 36°30S 146°0E **63** F4
Benares = Varanasi
 India 25°22N 83°0E **43** G10
Benavente Spain 42°2N 5°43W **21** A3
Benavides U.S.A. 27°36N 98°25W **84** H5
Benbecula U.K. 57°26N 7°21W **11** D1
Benbonyathe Hill
 Australia 30°25S 139°11E **63** E2
Bend U.S.A. 44°4N 121°19W **76** D3
Bender Beyla Somali Rep. 9°30N 50°48E **47** F5
Bendery = Tighina
 Moldova 46°50N 29°30E **17** E15
Bendigo Australia 36°40S 144°15E **63** F3
Benē Beraq Israel 32°6N 34°51E **46** C3
Benenitra Madag. 23°27S 45°5E **57** C8
Benevento Italy 41°8N 14°45E **22** D6
Benga Mozam. 16°11S 33°40E **55** F3
Bengal, Bay of Ind. Oc. 15°0N 90°0E **41** M17
Bengaluru = Bangalore
 India 12°59N 77°40E **40** N10
Bengbu China 32°58N 117°20E **35** H9
Benghazi = Banghāzī
 Libya 32°11N 20°3E **51** B10
Bengkalis Indonesia 1°30N 102°10E **39** M4
Bengkinang Indonesia 3°50S 102°12E **36** E2
Bengkulu Indonesia 3°48S 102°16E **36** E2
Bengkulu □ Indonesia 3°48S 102°16E **36** E2
Bengough Canada 49°25N 105°10W **71** D7
Benguela Angola 12°37S 13°25E **53** G2
Benguérua, I. Mozam. 21°58S 35°28E **57** C6
Beni Dem. Rep. of the Congo 0°30N 29°27E **54** B2
Beni → Bolivia 10°23S 65°24W **92** F5
Beni Mellal Morocco 32°21N 6°21W **50** B4
Beni Suef Egypt 29°5N 31°6E **51** C12
Beniah L. Canada 63°23N 112°17W **70** A6
Benidorm Spain 38°33N 0°9W **21** C5
Benin ■ Africa 10°0N 2°0E **50** G6
Benin, Bight of W. Afr. 5°0N 3°0E **50** H6
Benin City Nigeria 6°20N 5°31E **50** G7
Benito Juárez Argentina 37°40S 59°43W **94** D4
Benitses Greece 39°32N 19°55E **25** A3
Benjamin Aceval
 Paraguay 24°58S 57°34W **94** A4
Benjamin Constant
 Brazil 4°40S 70°15W **92** D4
Benjamín Hill Mexico 30°9N 111°7W **86** A2
Benkelman U.S.A. 40°3N 101°32W **80** E3
Bennett Canada 59°51N 135°0W **70** B2
Bennett, L. Australia 22°50S 131°2E **60** D5
Bennetta, Ostrov
 Russia 76°21N 148°56E **29** B15
Bennettsville U.S.A. 34°37N 79°41W **85** D15
Bennington N.H., U.S.A. 43°0N 71°55W **83** D11
Bennington Vt., U.S.A. 42°53N 73°12W **83** D11
Benom Malaysia 3°50N 102°6E **39** L4
Benoni S. Africa 26°11S 28°18E **57** D4

Benque Viejo Belize 17°5N 89°8W **87** D7
Benson Ariz., U.S.A. 31°58N 110°18W **77** L8
Benson Minn., U.S.A. 45°19N 95°36W **80** C6
Bent Iran 26°20N 59°31E **45** E8
Benteng Indonesia 6°10S 120°30E **37** F6
Bentinck I. Australia 17°3S 139°35E **62** B2
Bentley Subglacial Trench
 Antarctica 80°0S 115°0W **5** E15
Bento Gonçalves Brazil 29°10S 51°31W **95** B5
Benton Ark., U.S.A. 34°34N 92°35W **84** D8
Benton Calif., U.S.A. 37°48N 118°32W **78** H8
Benton Ill., U.S.A. 38°0N 88°55W **80** G10
Benton Pa., U.S.A. 41°12N 76°23W **83** E8
Benton Harbor U.S.A. 42°6N 86°27W **80** D10
Bentong Malaysia 3°31N 101°55E **39** L3
Bentonville U.S.A. 36°22N 94°13W **84** C7
Benue → Nigeria 7°48N 6°46E **50** G7
Benxi China 41°20N 123°48E **35** D12
Beo Indonesia 4°25N 126°50E **37** D7
Beograd Serbia 44°50N 20°37E **23** B9
Beolgyo S. Korea 34°51N 127°21E **35** G14
Beppu Japan 33°15N 131°30E **31** H5
Beqa Fiji 18°23S 178°8E **59** a
Beqaa Valley = Al Biqā
 Lebanon 34°10N 36°10E **46** A5
Ber Mota India 23°27N 68°34E **42** H3
Bera, Tasik Malaysia 3°5N 102°38E **39** L4
Berach → India 25°15N 75°2E **42** G6
Beraketa Madag. 23°7S 44°25E **57** C7
Berastagi Indonesia 3°11N 98°31E **39** L2
Berat Albania 40°43N 19°59E **23** D8
Berau = Tanjungredeb
 Indonesia 2°9N 117°29E **36** D5
Berau, Teluk Indonesia 2°30S 132°30E **37** E8
Beravina Madag. 18°10S 45°14E **57** B8
Berber Sudan 18°0N 34°0E **51** E12
Berbera Somali Rep. 10°30N 45°2E **47** E4
Berbérati C.A.R. 4°15N 15°40E **52** D3
Berbice → Guyana 6°20N 57°32W **92** B7
Berdichev = Berdychiv
 Ukraine 49°57N 28°30E **17** D15
Berdsk Russia 54°47N 83°2E **28** D9
Berdyansk Ukraine 46°45N 36°50E **19** E6
Berdychiv Ukraine 49°57N 28°30E **17** D15
Berea U.S.A. 37°34N 84°17W **81** G11
Berebere Indonesia 2°25N 128°45E **37** D7
Bereeda Somali Rep. 11°45N 51°0E **47** E5
Berehove Ukraine 48°15N 22°35E **17** D12
Bereket Turkmenistan 39°16N 55°32E **45** B7
Berekum Ghana 7°29N 2°34W **50** G5
Berens → Canada 52°25N 97°2W **71** C9
Berens I. Canada 52°18N 97°18W **71** C9
Berens River Canada 52°25N 97°0W **71** C9
Beresford U.S.A. 43°5N 96°47W **80** D5
Berestechko Ukraine 50°22N 25°5E **17** C13
Berevo Mahajanga,
 Madag. 17°14S 44°17E **57** B7
Berevo Toliara, Madag. 19°44S 44°58E **57** B7
Berezhany Ukraine 49°26N 24°58E **17** D13
Berezina = Byarezina →
 Belarus 52°33N 30°14E **17** B16
Berezniki Russia 62°51N 42°40E **18** B7
Berezniki Russia 59°24N 56°46E **18** C10
Berezovo Russia 64°0N 65°0E **28** C7
Berga Spain 42°6N 1°48E **21** A6
Bergama Turkey 39°8N 27°11E **23** E12
Bérgamo Italy 45°41N 9°43E **20** D8
Bergen Neths. 52°40N 4°43E **15** B4
Bergen Norway 60°20N 5°20E **8** F11
Bergen U.S.A. 43°5N 77°57W **82** C7
Bergen op Zoom Neths. 51°28N 4°18E **15** C4
Bergerac France 44°51N 0°30E **20** D4
Bergholz U.S.A. 40°31N 80°53W **82** F4
Bergisch Gladbach
 Germany 50°59N 7°8E **15** D7
Bergville S. Africa 28°52S 29°18E **57** D4
Berhala, Selat Indonesia 1°0S 104°15E **36** E2
Berhampore = Baharampur
 India 24°2N 88°27E **43** G13
Berhampur = Brahmapur
 India 19°15N 84°54E **41** K14
Bering Glacier U.S.A. 60°20N 143°30W **74** C11
Bering Sea Pac. Oc. 58°0N 171°0W **66** D1
Bering Strait Pac. Oc. 65°30N 169°0W **74** B6
Beringovskiy Russia 63°3N 179°19E **29** C18
Berisso Argentina 34°56S 57°50W **94** C4
Berja Spain 36°50N 2°56W **21** D4
Berkeley U.S.A. 37°51N 122°16W **78** H4
Berkner I. Antarctica 79°30S 50°0W **5** D18
Berkshire U.S.A. 42°19N 76°11W **83** D8
Berkshire Downs U.K. 51°33N 1°29W **13** F6
Berlin Germany 52°31N 13°23E **16** B7
Berlin Md., U.S.A. 38°20N 75°13W **81** F16
Berlin N.H., U.S.A. 44°28N 71°11W **83** B13
Berlin N.Y., U.S.A. 42°42N 73°23W **83** D11
Berlin Wis., U.S.A. 43°58N 88°57W **80** D9
Berlin L. U.S.A. 41°3N 81°0W **82** E4
Bermejo → Formosa,
 Argentina 26°51S 58°23W **94** B4
Bermejo → San Juan,
 Argentina 32°30S 67°30W **94** C2
Bermejo, Paso = Uspallata, P. de
 Argentina 32°37S 69°22W **94** C2
Bermen, L. Canada 53°35N 68°55W **73** B6
Bermuda ☑ Atl. Oc. 32°18N 64°45W **67** F13
Bern Switz. 46°57N 7°28E **20** C7
Bernalillo U.S.A. 35°18N 106°33W **77** J10
Bernardo de Irigoyen
 Argentina 26°15S 53°40W **95** B5
Bernardsville U.S.A. 40°43N 74°34W **83** F10
Bernasconi Argentina 37°55S 63°44W **94** D3
Bernburg Germany 51°47N 11°44E **16** C6
Berne = Bern Switz. 46°57N 7°28E **20** C7
Berner Ra. Australia 20°15N 130°8E **58** C4
Berneray U.K. 57°43N 7°11W **11** D1
Bernier I. Australia 24°50S 113°12E **61** D1
Bernina, Piz Switz. 46°20N 9°54E **20** C8
Beroroha Madag. 21°40S 45°10E **57** C8
Beroun Czech Rep. 49°57N 14°5E **16** D8
Berri Australia 34°14S 140°35E **63** E3

Berriane Algeria 32°50N 3°46E **50** B6
Berry Australia 34°46S 150°43E **63** E5
Berry France 46°50N 2°0E **20** C5
Berry Is. Bahamas 25°40N 77°50W **88** A4
Berryessa, L. U.S.A. 38°31N 122°6W **78** G4
Berryville U.S.A. 36°22N 93°34W **84** C8
Berseba Namibia 26°0S 17°46E **56** D2
Bershad Ukraine 48°22N 29°31E **17** D15
Berthold U.S.A. 48°19N 101°44W **80** A3
Berthoud U.S.A. 40°19N 105°5W **76** F11
Bertoua Cameroon 4°30N 13°45E **52** D2
Bertraghboy B. Ireland 53°22N 9°54W **10** C2
Berwick U.S.A. 41°3N 76°14W **83** E8
Berwick-upon-Tweed
 U.K. 55°46N 2°0W **12** B6
Berwyn Mts. U.K. 52°54N 3°26W **12** E4
Besal Pakistan 35°4N 73°56E **43** B5
Besalampy Madag. 16°43S 44°29E **57** B7
Besançon France 47°15N 6°2E **20** C7
Besar Indonesia 2°40S 116°0E **36** E5
Benxi China 41°20N 123°48E **35** D12
Beshamm Pakistan 32°59N 74°3E **43** A6
Besni Turkey 37°41N 37°52E **44** B3
Besnard L. Canada 55°25N 106°0W **71** B7
Besor, N. → Egypt 31°28N 34°22E **46** D3
Bessarabiya Moldova 47°0N 28°10E **17** E15
Bessarabka = Basarabeasca
 Moldova 46°21N 28°58E **17** E15
Bessemer Ala., U.S.A. 33°24N 86°58W **85** E11
Bessemer Mich., U.S.A. 46°29N 90°3W **80** B8
Bessemer Pa., U.S.A. 40°59N 80°30W **82** F4
Beswick ☉ Australia 14°34S 132°53E **60** B5
Beswick Australia 14°31S 132°51E **60** B5
Bet She'an Israel 32°30N 35°30E **46** C4
Bet Shemesh Israel 31°44N 35°0E **46** D4
Betafo Madag. 19°50S 46°51E **57** B8
Betancuria Canary Is. 28°25N 14°3W **24** F5
Betanzos Spain 43°15N 8°12W **21** A1
Bétaré Oya Cameroon 5°40N 14°5E **52** C2
Betatao Madag. 18°11S 47°52E **57** B8
Bethal S. Africa 26°27S 29°28E **57** D4
Bethanien Namibia 26°31S 17°8E **56** D2
Bethany Canada 44°11N 78°34W **82** B6
Bethany Mo., U.S.A. 40°16N 94°2W **80** E6
Bethany Okla., U.S.A. 35°31N 97°38W **84** D6
Bethel Alaska, U.S.A. 60°48N 161°45W **74** C7
Bethel Conn., U.S.A. 41°22N 73°25W **83** E11
Bethel Maine, U.S.A. 44°25N 70°47W **83** B14
Bethel Vt., U.S.A. 43°50N 72°38W **83** C12
Bethel Park U.S.A. 40°19N 80°2W **82** F4
Bethlehem = Bayt Lahm
 West Bank 31°43N 35°12E **46** D4
Bethlehem S. Africa 28°14S 28°18E **57** D4
Bethlehem U.S.A. 40°37N 75°23W **83** F9
Bethulie S. Africa 30°30S 25°59E **56** E4
Béthune France 50°30N 2°38E **20** A5
Betioky Madag. 23°48S 44°20E **57** C7
Betong Thailand 5°45N 101°5E **39** K3
Betoota Australia 25°45S 140°42E **62** D3
Betpaqdala Kazakhstan 45°45N 70°30E **32** B2
Betroka Madag. 23°16S 46°0E **57** C8
Betsiamites Canada 48°56N 68°40W **73** C6
Betsiamites → Canada 48°56N 68°38W **73** C6
Betsiboka → Madag. 16°3S 46°36E **57** B8
Bettendorf U.S.A. 41°32N 90°30W **80** E8
Bettiah India 26°48N 84°33E **43** F11
Betul India 21°58N 77°59E **40** J10
Betws-y-Coed U.K. 53°5N 3°48W **12** D4
Beulah Mich., U.S.A. 44°38N 86°6W **80** C10
Beulah N. Dak., U.S.A. 47°16N 101°47W **80** B3
Beveren Belgium 51°12N 4°16E **15** C4
Beverley Australia 32°9S 116°56E **61** F2
Beverley U.K. 53°51N 0°26W **12** D7
Beverly U.S.A. 42°33N 70°53W **83** D14
Beverly Hills Calif.,
 U.S.A. 34°5N 118°24W **79** L8
Beverly Hills Fla.,
 U.S.A. 28°55N 82°28W **85** G13
Bevoalavo Madag. 25°13S 45°26E **57** D7
Bewas → India 23°59N 79°21E **43** H8
Bewdley Canada 44°5N 78°19W **82** B6
Bexhill U.K. 50°51N 0°29E **13** G8
Beyānlū Iran 36°0N 47°51E **44** C5
Beyneu Kazakhstan 45°18N 55°9E **19** E10
Beypazarı Turkey 40°10N 31°56E **19** F5
Beyşehir Gölü Turkey 37°41N 31°33E **44** B1
Béziers France 43°20N 3°12E **20** E5
Bezwada = Vijayawada
 India 16°31N 80°39E **41** L12
Bhabua India 25°3N 83°37E **43** G10
Bhachau India 23°20N 70°16E **42** H4
Bhadar → Gujarat, India 22°17N 72°20E **42** H5
Bhadar → Gujarat, India 21°27N 69°47E **42** J3
Bhadarwah India 32°58N 75°46E **43** C6
Bhadgaon = Bhaktapur
 Nepal 27°38N 85°24E **43** F11
Bhadohi India 25°25N 82°34E **43** G10
Bhadra India 29°8N 75°14E **42** E6
Bhadrakh India 21°10N 86°30E **41** J15
Bhadran India 22°19N 72°6E **42** H5
Bhadravati India 13°49N 75°40E **40** N9
Bhag Pakistan 29°2N 67°49E **42** E2
Bhagalpur India 25°10N 87°0E **43** G12
Bhagirathi → Uttarakhand,
 India 30°8N 78°35E **43** D8
Bhagirathi → W. Bengal,
 India 23°25N 88°23E **43** H13
Bhakkar Pakistan 31°40N 71°5E **42** D4
Bhakra Dam India 31°30N 76°45E **42** D7
Bhaktapur Nepal 27°38N 85°24E **43** F11
Bhamo Burma 24°15N 97°15E **41** G20
Bhandara India 21°5N 79°42E **40** J11
Bhanpura India 24°31N 75°44E **42** G6
Bhanrer Ra. India 23°40N 79°45E **43** H8
Bhaptiahi India 26°19N 86°44E **43** F12
Bharat = India ■ Asia 20°0N 78°0E **40** K11
Bharatpur Chhattisgarh,
 India 23°44N 81°46E **43** H9
Bharatpur Raj., India 27°15N 77°30E **42** F7
Bharatpur Nepal 27°34N 84°10E **43** F11

Bharno India 23°14N 84°53E **43** H11
Bharuch India 21°47N 73°0E **40** J8
Bhatinda India 30°15N 74°57E **42** D6
Bhatpara India 22°50N 88°25E **43** H13
Bhattu India 29°36N 75°19E **42** E6
Bhaun Pakistan 32°55N 72°40E **42** C5
Bhaunagar = Bhavnagar
 India 21°45N 72°10E **40** J8
Bhavnagar India 21°45N 72°10E **40** J8
Bhawari India 25°42N 73°4E **42** G5
Bhayavadar India 21°51N 70°15E **42** J4
Bhera Pakistan 32°29N 72°57E **42** C5
Bhikangaon India 21°52N 75°57E **42** J6
Bhilai = Bhilainagar-Durg
 India 21°13N 81°26E **41** J12
Bhilainagar-Durg India 21°13N 81°26E **41** J12
Bhilsa = Vidisha India 23°28N 77°53E **42** H7
Bhilwara India 25°25N 74°38E **42** G6
Bhima → India 16°25N 77°17E **40** L10
Bhimbar Pakistan 32°59N 74°3E **43** C6
Bhind India 26°30N 78°46E **43** F8
Bhinga India 27°43N 81°56E **43** F9
Bhinmal India 25°0N 72°15E **42** G5
Bhisho S. Africa 32°50S 27°23E **57** E4
Bhiwandi India 19°20N 73°0E **40** K8
Bhiwani India 28°50N 76°9E **42** E7
Bhogava → India 22°26N 72°20E **42** H5
Bhola Bangla. 22°45N 90°35E **41** H17
Bholari Pakistan 25°19N 68°13E **42** G3
Bhopal India 23°20N 77°30E **42** H7
Bhubaneshwar India 20°15N 85°50E **41** J14
Bhuj India 23°15N 69°49E **42** H3
Bhumiphol Res. Thailand 17°20N 98°40E **38** D2
Bhusawal India 21°3N 75°46E **40** J9
Bhutan ■ Asia 27°25N 90°30E **41** F17
Biafra, B. of = Bonny, Bight of
 Africa 3°30N 9°20E **52** D1
Biak Indonesia 1°10S 136°6E **37** E9
Biala Podlaska Poland 52°4N 23°6E **17** B12
Białogard Poland 54°2N 15°58E **16** A8
Białystok Poland 53°10N 23°10E **17** B12
Biaora India 23°56N 76°56E **42** H7
Bīārjmand Iran 36°6N 55°53E **45** B7
Biaro Indonesia 2°5N 125°26E **37** D7
Biarritz France 43°29N 1°33W **20** E3
Bias Indonesia 8°24S 115°36E **37** J18
Bibai Japan 43°19N 141°52E **30** C10
Bibby I. Canada 61°55N 93°0W **71** A10
Biberach Germany 48°5N 9°47E **16** D5
Bibungwa
 Dem. Rep. of the Congo 2°40S 28°15E **54** C2
Bicester U.K. 51°54N 1°9W **13** F6
Bicheno Australia 41°52S 148°18E **63** G4
Bichia India 22°27N 80°42E **43** H9
Bickerton I. Australia 13°45S 136°10E **62** A2
Bid = Bir India 19°4N 75°46E **40** K9
Bida Nigeria 9°3N 5°58E **50** G7
Bidar India 17°55N 77°35E **40** L10
Biddeford U.S.A. 43°30N 70°28W **81** D18
Bideford U.K. 51°1N 4°13W **13** F3
Bideford Bay U.K. 51°5N 4°20W **13** F3
Bidhuna India 26°49N 79°31E **43** F8
Bidokht Iran 34°20N 58°46E **45** C8
Bidor Malaysia 4°6N 101°15E **39** K3
Bidyadanga Australia 18°45S 121°43E **60** C3
Bié, Planalto de Angola 12°0S 16°0E **53** G3
Bieber U.S.A. 41°7N 121°8W **76** F3
Biel Switz. 47°8N 7°14E **20** C7
Bielefeld Germany 52°1N 8°33E **16** B5
Biella Italy 45°34N 8°3E **20** D8
Bielsk Podlaski Poland 52°47N 23°12E **17** B12
Bielsko-Biała Poland 49°50N 19°2E **17** D10
Bien Hoa Vietnam 10°57N 106°49E **39** G6
Bienne = Biel Switz. 47°8N 7°14E **20** C7
Bienville, L. Canada 55°5N 72°40W **72** A5
Biesiesfontein S. Africa 30°57S 17°58E **56** E2
Big → Canada 54°50N 58°55W **73** B8
Big B. Canada 55°43N 60°35W **73** A7
Big Bear Lake U.S.A. 34°16N 116°51W **79** L10
Big Belt Mts. U.S.A. 46°30N 111°25W **76** C8
Big Bend Swaziland 26°50S 31°58E **57** D5
Big Bend △ U.S.A. 29°20N 103°5W **84** G3
Big Black → U.S.A. 32°3N 91°4W **85** F9
Big Blue → U.S.A. 39°35N 96°34W **80** F5
Big Creek U.S.A. 37°11N 119°14W **78** H7
Big Cypress △ U.S.A. 26°0N 81°10W **85** H14
Big Desert Australia 35°45S 141°10E **63** F3
Big Falls U.S.A. 48°12N 93°48W **80** A7
Big Fork → U.S.A. 48°31N 93°43W **80** A7
Big Horn Mts. = Bighorn Mts.
 U.S.A. 44°25N 107°0W **76** D10
Big I. Canada 61°7N 116°45W **70** A5
Big Lake U.S.A. 31°12N 101°28W **84** F4
Big Moose U.S.A. 43°49N 74°58W **83** C10
Big Muddy Cr. →
 U.S.A. 48°8N 104°36W **76** B11
Big Pine U.S.A. 37°10N 118°17W **78** H8
Big Piney U.S.A. 42°32N 110°7W **76** E8
Big Quill L. Canada 51°55N 104°30W **71** C8
Big Rapids U.S.A. 43°42N 85°29W **81** D11
Big Rideau L. Canada 44°40N 76°15W **83** B8
Big River Canada 53°50N 107°0W **71** C7
Big Run U.S.A. 40°57N 78°55W **82** F6
Big Sable Pt. U.S.A. 44°3N 86°1W **80** C10
Big Salmon → Canada 61°52N 134°55W **70** A2
Big Sand L. Canada 57°45N 99°45W **71** B9
Big Sandy U.S.A. 48°11N 110°7W **76** B8
Big Sandy → U.S.A. 38°25N 82°36W **81** F12
Big Sandy Cr. = Sandy Cr. →
 U.S.A. 41°51N 109°47W **76** F9
Big Sandy Cr. →
 U.S.A. 38°7N 102°29W **76** G12
Big Sioux → U.S.A. 42°29N 96°27W **80** D5
Big South Fork △
 U.S.A. 36°27N 84°47W **85** C12
Big Spring U.S.A. 32°15N 101°28W **84** E4
Big Stone City U.S.A. 45°18N 96°28W **80** C5
Big Stone Gap U.S.A. 36°52N 82°47W **81** G12

Big Stone L. U.S.A. 45°18N 96°27W 80 C5
Big Sur U.S.A. 36°15N 121°48W 78 J5
Big Timber U.S.A. 45°50N 109°57W 76 D9
Big Trout L. Canada 53°40N 90°0W 72 B2
Big Trout Lake Canada 53°45N 90°0W 72 B2
Biğa Turkey 40°13N 27°14E 23 D12
Bigadiç Turkey 39°22N 28°7E 23 E13
Biggar Canada 52°4N 108°0W 71 C7
Biggar U.K. 55°38N 3°32W 11 F5
Bigge I. Australia 14°35S 125°10E 60 B4
Biggenden Australia 25°31S 152°4E 63 D5
Biggleswade U.K. 52°5N 0°14W 13 E7
Biggs U.S.A. 39°25N 121°43W 78 F5
Bighorn U.S.A. 46°10N 107°27W 76 C10
Bighorn → U.S.A. 46°10N 107°28W 76 C10
Bighorn Canyon △
U.S.A. 45°10N 108°0W 76 D10
Bighorn L. U.S.A. 44°55N 108°15W 76 D9
Bighorn Mts. U.S.A. 44°30N 107°30W 76 D10
Bigstone L. Canada 53°42N 95°44W 71 C9
Bigwa Tanzania 7°10S 39°10E 54 D4
Bihać Bos.-H. 44°49N 15°57E 16 F8
Bihar India 25°5N 85°40E 43 G11
Bihar □ India 25°0N 86°0E 43 G12
Biharamulo Tanzania 2°25S 31°25E 54 C3
Biharamulo △ Tanzania 2°24S 31°26E 54 C3
Bihariganj India 25°44N 86°59E 43 G12
Bihor, Munţii Romania 46°29N 22°47E 17 E12
Bijagós, Arquipélago dos
Guinea-Biss. 11°15N 16°10W 50 F2
Bijaipur India 26°2N 77°20E 42 F7
Bijapur Chhattisgarh,
India 18°50N 80°50E 41 K12
Bijapur Karnataka, India 16°50N 75°55E 40 L9
Bījār Iran 35°52N 47°35E 44 C5
Bijawar India 24°38N 79°30E 43 G8
Bijeljina Bos.-H. 44°46N 19°14E 23 B8
Bijnor India 29°27N 78°11E 42 E8
Bikaner India 28°2N 73°18E 42 E5
Bikapur India 26°30N 82°7E 43 F10
Bikeqi China 40°43N 111°20E 34 D6
Bikfayyā Lebanon 33°55N 35°41E 46 B4
Bikin Russia 46°50N 134°20E 30 A7
Bikin → Russia 46°51N 134°2E 30 A7
Bikini Atoll Marshall Is. 12°0N 167°30E 64 F8
Bikita Zimbabwe 20°6S 31°41E 57 C5
Bikku Bītū Libya 22°0N 19°12E 51 D9
Bila Tserkva Ukraine 49°45N 30°10E 17 D16
Bilara India 26°14N 73°53E 42 F5
Bilaspur Chhattisgarh,
India 22°2N 82°15E 43 H10
Bilaspur Punjab, India 31°19N 76°50E 42 D7
Bilauk Taungdan Thailand 13°0N 99°0E 38 F2
Bilbao Spain 43°16N 2°56W 21 A4
Bilbo = Bilbao Spain 43°16N 2°56W 21 A4
Bíldudalur Iceland 65°41N 23°36W 8 D2
Bílé Karpaty Europe 49°5N 18°0E 17 D9
Bilecik Turkey 40°5N 30°5E 19 F5
Bilgram India 27°11N 80°2E 43 F9
Bilhaur India 26°51N 80°5E 43 F9
Bilhorod-Dnistrovskyy
Ukraine 46°11N 30°23E 19 E5
Bilibino Russia 68°3N 166°20E 29 C17
Bilibiza Mozam. 12°30S 40°20E 55 E5
Billiluna Australia 19°37S 127°41E 60 C4
Billings U.S.A. 45°47N 108°30W 76 D9
Billiton Is. = Belitung
Indonesia 3°10S 107°50E 36 E3
Bilma Niger 18°50N 13°30E 51 E8
Biloela Australia 24°24S 150°31E 62 C5
Biloxi U.S.A. 30°24N 88°53W 85 F10
Bilpa Morea Claypan
Australia 25°0S 140°0E 62 D3
Biltine Chad 14°40N 20°50E 51 F10
Bima Indonesia 8°22S 118°49E 37 F5
Bimbo C.A.R. 4°15N 18°33E 52 D3
Bimini Is. Bahamas 25°42N 79°25W 88 A4
Bin Xian Heilongjiang,
China 45°42N 127°32E 35 B14
Bin Xian Shaanxi, China 35°2N 108°4E 34 G5
Bina-Etawah India 24°13N 78°14E 42 G8
Binalbagan Phil. 10°12N 122°50E 37 B6
Binalong Australia 34°40S 148°39E 63 E4
Bīnālūd, Kūh-e Iran 36°30N 58°30E 45 B8
Binatang = Bintangau
Malaysia 2°10N 111°40E 36 D4
Binche Belgium 50°26N 4°10E 15 D4
Bindki India 26°2N 80°36E 43 F9
Bindura Zimbabwe 17°18S 31°18E 55 F3
Bingara Australia 29°52S 150°36E 63 D5
Bingham U.S.A. 45°3N 69°53W 81 C19
Binghamton U.S.A. 42°6N 75°55W 83 D9
Bingöl Turkey 38°53N 40°29E 44 B4
Binh Dinh = An Nhon
Vietnam 13°55N 109°7E 38 F7
Binh Khe Vietnam 13°57N 108°51E 38 F7
Binh Son Vietnam 15°20N 108°40E 38 E7
Binhai China 34°2N 119°49E 35 G10
Binisatua Spain 39°50N 4°11E 24 B11
Binissalem Spain 39°41N 2°50E 24 B9
Binjai Indonesia 3°20N 98°30E 36 D1
Binnaway Australia 31°28S 149°24E 63 E4
Binongko Indonesia 5°57S 124°2E 37 F6
Binscarth Canada 50°37N 101°17W 71 C8
Bintan Indonesia 1°0N 104°0E 36 D2
Bintangau Malaysia 2°10N 111°40E 36 D4
Bintulu Malaysia 3°10N 113°0E 36 D4
Bintuni Indonesia 2°7S 133°32E 37 E8
Binzert = Bizerte Tunisia 37°15N 9°50E 51 A7
Binzhou China 37°20N 118°2E 35 F10
Bío Bío □ Chile 37°35S 72°0W 94 D1
Bíobío → Chile 36°49S 73°10W 94 D1
Bioko Eq. Guin. 3°30N 8°40E 52 D1
Bir India 19°4N 75°46E 40 K9
Bîr Abu Muḩammad
Egypt 29°44N 34°14E 46 F3
Bi'r ad Dabbāghāt Jordan 30°26N 35°32E 46 E4
Bi'r al Butayyihāt Jordan 29°47N 35°20E 46 F4
Bi'r al Mārī Jordan 30°4N 35°33E 46 E4

Bi'r al Qattār Jordan 29°47N 35°32E 46 F4
Bîr Atrun Sudan 18°15N 26°40E 51 E11
Bîr Beiḑa Egypt 30°25N 34°29E 46 E3
Bir el 'Abd Egypt 31°2N 33°0E 46 D2
Bir el Biarât Egypt 29°30N 34°43E 46 F3
Bir el Duweidar Egypt 30°56N 32°32E 46 E1
Bir el Garârât Egypt 31°3N 33°34E 46 D2
Bir el Heisi Egypt 29°22N 34°36E 46 F3
Bir el Jafir Egypt 30°50N 32°41E 46 E1
Bir el Mâlḩi Egypt 30°38N 33°19E 46 E2
Bir el Thamâda Egypt 30°12N 33°27E 46 E2
Bir Gebeil Ḩiṣn Egypt 30°2N 33°18E 46 E2
Bi'r Ghadir Syria 34°6N 37°3E 46 A6
Bîr Ḩasana Egypt 30°29N 33°46E 46 E2
Bîr Kaseiba Egypt 31°0N 33°17E 46 E2
Bîr Lahfân Egypt 31°0N 33°51E 46 E2
Bîr Madkûr Egypt 30°44N 32°33E 46 E1
Bîr Mogreïn Mauritania 25°10N 11°25W 50 C3
Bi'r Muṭribah Kuwait 29°54N 47°17E 44 D5
Bîr Qaţia Egypt 30°58N 32°45E 46 E1
Bîr Shalatein Egypt 23°5N 35°25E 51 D13
Birāk Libya 27°31N 14°20E 51 C8
Biratnagar Nepal 26°27N 87°17E 43 F12
Birawa
Dem. Rep. of the Congo 2°20S 28°48E 54 C2
Birch → Canada 58°28N 112°17W 70 B6
Birch Hills Canada 52°59N 105°25W 71 C7
Birch I. Canada 52°26N 99°54W 71 C9
Birch L. N.W.T., Canada 62°4N 116°33W 70 A5
Birch L. Ont., Canada 51°23N 92°18W 72 B1
Birch Mts. Canada 57°30N 113°10W 70 B6
Birch River Canada 52°24N 101°6W 71 C8
Birchip Australia 35°56S 142°55E 63 F3
Bird Canada 56°30N 94°13W 71 B10
Bird I. = Aves, I. de
W. Indies 15°45N 63°55W 89 C7
Bird I. S. Georgia 54°0S 38°3W 96 G9
Birds Creek Canada 45°6N 77°52W 82 A7
Birdsville Australia 25°51S 139°20E 62 D2
Birdum Cr. → Australia 15°14S 133°0E 60 C5
Birecik Turkey 37°2N 38°0E 44 B3
Birein Israel 30°50N 34°28E 46 E3
Bireuen Indonesia 5°14N 96°39E 36 C1
Birigüi Brazil 21°18S 50°16W 95 A5
Birjand Iran 32°53N 59°13E 45 C8
Birkenhead U.K. 53°23N 3°2W 12 D4
Bîrlad = Bârlad
Romania 46°15N 27°38E 17 E14
Birmingham U.K. 52°29N 1°52W 13 E6
Birmingham U.S.A. 33°31N 86°48W 85 E11
Birmingham Int. ✈ (BHX)
U.K. 52°26N 1°45W 13 E6
Birmitrapur India 22°24N 84°46E 41 H14
Birni Nkonni Niger 13°55N 5°15E 50 F7
Birnin Kebbi Nigeria 12°32N 4°12E 50 F6
Birobidzhan Russia 48°50N 132°50E 29 E14
Birr Ireland 53°6N 7°54W 10 C4
Birrie → Australia 29°43S 146°37E 63 D4
Birsilpur India 28°11N 72°15E 42 E5
Birsk Russia 55°25N 55°30E 18 C10
Birtle Canada 50°30N 101°5W 71 C8
Birur India 13°30N 75°55E 40 N9
Biržai Lithuania 56°11N 24°45E 9 H21
Birzebbugga Malta 35°50N 14°32E 25 D2
Bisa Indonesia 1°15S 127°28E 37 E7
Bisalpur India 28°14N 79°48E 43 E8
Bisbee U.S.A. 31°27N 109°55W 77 L9
Biscarrosse France 44°22N 1°20W 20 D1
Biscay, B. of Atl. Oc. 45°0N 2°0W 20 D1
Biscayne B. U.S.A. 25°40N 80°12W 85 J14
Biscoe Is. Antarctica 66°0S 67°0W 5 C17
Biscotasing Canada 47°18N 82°9W 72 C3
Bishkek Kyrgyzstan 42°54N 74°46E 28 E8
Bishnupur India 23°8N 87°20E 43 H12
Bisho = Bhisho S. Africa 32°50S 27°23E 57 E4
Bishop Calif., U.S.A. 37°22N 118°24W 78 H8
Bishop Tex., U.S.A. 27°35N 97°48W 84 H6
Bishop Auckland U.K. 54°39N 1°40W 12 C6
Bishop's Falls Canada 49°2N 55°30W 73 C8
Bishop's Stortford U.K. 51°52N 0°10E 13 F8
Bisina, L. Uganda 1°38N 33°56E 54 B3
Biskra Algeria 34°50N 5°44E 50 B7
Bismarck U.S.A. 46°48N 100°47W 80 B3
Bismarck Arch.
Papua N. G. 2°30S 150°0E 58 B7
Biso Uganda 1°44N 31°26E 54 B3
Bison U.S.A. 45°31N 102°28W 80 C2
Bisotūn Iran 34°23N 47°26E 44 C5
Bissagos = Bijagós, Arquipélago
dos Guinea-Biss. 11°15N 16°10W 50 F2
Bissau Guinea-Biss. 11°45N 15°45W 50 F2
Bistcho L. Canada 59°45N 118°50W 70 B5
Bistriţa Romania 47°9N 24°35E 17 E13
Bistriţa → Romania 46°30N 26°57E 17 E14
Biswan India 27°29N 81°2E 43 F9
Bitam Gabon 2°5N 11°25E 52 D2
Bitkine Chad 11°59N 18°13E 51 F9
Bitlis Turkey 38°20N 42°3E 44 B4
Bitola Macedonia 41°1N 21°20E 23 D9
Bitolj = Bitola Macedonia 41°1N 21°20E 23 D9
Bitter Creek U.S.A. 41°33N 108°33W 76 F9
Bitterfontein S. Africa 31°1S 18°32E 56 E2
Bitterroot → U.S.A. 46°52N 114°7W 76 C6
Bitterroot Range U.S.A. 46°0N 114°20W 76 C6
Bitterwater U.S.A. 36°23N 121°0W 78 J6
Biu Nigeria 10°40N 12°3E 51 F8
Biwa-Ko Japan 35°15N 136°10E 31 G8
Biwabik U.S.A. 47°32N 92°21W 80 B7
Bixby U.S.A. 35°57N 95°53W 84 D7
Biyang China 32°38N 113°21E 34 H7
Biysk Russia 52°40N 85°0E 28 D9
Bizana S. Africa 30°50S 29°52E 57 E4
Bizen Japan 34°43N 134°8E 31 G7
Bizerte Tunisia 37°15N 9°50E 51 A7
Bjargtangar Iceland 65°30N 24°30W 8 D1
Bjelovar Croatia 45°56N 16°49E 22 B7
Björneborg = Pori
Finland 61°29N 21°48E 8 F19
Bjørnevatn Norway 69°40N 30°0E 8 B24

Bjørnøya Arctic 74°30N 19°0E 4 B8
Black = Da → Vietnam 21°15N 105°20E 38 B5
Black → Canada 44°42N 79°19W 82 B5
Black → Ariz., U.S.A. 33°44N 110°13W 77 K8
Black → Ark., U.S.A. 35°38N 91°20W 84 D9
Black → La., U.S.A. 31°16N 91°50W 84 F9
Black → Mich., U.S.A. 42°59N 82°27W 82 D2
Black → N.Y., U.S.A. 43°59N 76°4W 83 C8
Black → Wis., U.S.A. 43°57N 91°22W 80 D8
Black Bay Pen. Canada 48°38N 88°21W 72 C2
Black Birch L. Canada 56°53N 107°45W 71 B7
Black Canyon of the Gunnison △
U.S.A. 38°40N 107°35W 76 G10
Black Diamond Canada 50°45N 114°14W 70 C6
Black Duck → Canada 56°51N 89°2W 72 A2
Black Forest = Schwarzwald
Germany 48°30N 8°20E 16 D5
Black Forest U.S.A. 39°0N 104°43W 76 G11
Black Hd. Ireland 53°9N 9°16W 10 C2
Black Hills U.S.A. 44°0N 103°45W 80 D2
Black I. Canada 51°12N 96°30W 71 C9
Black L. Canada 59°12N 105°15W 71 B7
Black L. Mich., U.S.A. 45°28N 84°16W 81 C11
Black L. N.Y., U.S.A. 44°31N 75°36W 83 B9
Black Lake Canada 59°11N 105°20W 71 B7
Black Mesa U.S.A. 36°58N 102°58W 84 C3
Black Mt. = Mynydd Du
U.K. 51°52N 3°50W 13 F4
Black Mts. U.K. 51°55N 3°7W 13 F4
Black Range U.S.A. 33°15N 107°50W 77 K10
Black River Jamaica 18°0N 77°50W 88 a
Black River U.S.A. 44°0N 75°47W 83 C9
Black River Falls U.S.A. 44°18N 90°51W 80 C8
Black Rock Barbados 13°7N 59°37W 89 g
Black Rock Desert
U.S.A. 41°10N 118°50W 76 F4
Black Sea Eurasia 43°30N 35°0E 19 F6
Black Tickle Canada 53°28N 55°45W 73 B8
Black Volta → Africa 8°41N 1°33W 50 G5
Black Warrior →
U.S.A. 32°32N 87°51W 85 E11
Blackall Australia 24°25S 145°45E 62 C4
Blackball N.Z. 42°22S 171°26E 59 E3
Blackbull Australia 17°55S 141°45E 62 B3
Blackburn U.K. 53°45N 2°29W 12 D5
Blackburn, Mt. U.S.A. 61°44N 143°26W 74 C11
Blackburn with Darwen □
U.K. 53°45N 2°29W 12 D5
Blackdown Tableland △
Australia 23°52S 149°8E 62 C4
Blackfoot U.S.A. 43°11N 112°21W 76 E7
Blackfoot → U.S.A. 46°52N 113°53W 76 C7
Blackfoot Res. U.S.A. 42°55N 111°39W 76 E8
Blackpool U.K. 53°49N 3°3W 12 D4
Blackpool □ U.K. 53°49N 3°3W 12 D4
Blackriver U.S.A. 44°46N 83°17W 82 B1
Blacks Harbour Canada 45°3N 66°49W 73 C6
Blacksburg U.S.A. 37°14N 80°25W 81 G13
Blacksod B. Ireland 54°6N 10°0W 10 B1
Blackstairs Mt. Ireland 52°33N 6°48W 10 D5
Blackstone U.S.A. 37°5N 78°0W 81 G14
Blackstone Ra. Australia 26°0S 128°30E 61 E4
Blackwater = West Road →
Canada 53°18N 122°53W 70 C4
Blackwater Australia 23°35S 148°53E 62 C4
Blackwater → Meath.
Ireland 53°39N 6°41W 10 C4
Blackwater → Waterford.
Ireland 52°4N 7°52W 10 D4
Blackwater → U.K. 54°31N 6°35W 10 B5
Blackwell U.S.A. 36°48N 97°17W 84 C6
Blackwells Corner
U.S.A. 35°37N 119°47W 79 K7
Bladensburg △
Australia 22°30S 142°59E 62 C3
Bladworth Canada 51°19N 106°8W 71 C7
Blaenau Ffestiniog U.K. 53°0N 3°56W 12 E4
Blaenau Gwent □ U.K. 51°48N 3°12W 13 F4
Blagodarnoye = Blagodarnyy
Russia 45°7N 43°37E 19 E7
Blagodarnyy Russia 45°7N 43°37E 19 E7
Blagoevgrad Bulgaria 42°2N 23°5E 23 C10
Blagoveshchensk
Russia 50°20N 127°30E 29 D13
Blahkiuh Indonesia 8°31S 115°12E 37 J18
Blain U.S.A. 40°20N 77°31W 82 F7
Blaine Minn., U.S.A. 45°10N 93°13W 80 C7
Blaine Wash., U.S.A. 48°59N 122°45W 78 B4
Blaine Lake Canada 52°51N 106°52W 71 C7
Blair U.S.A. 41°33N 96°8W 80 E5
Blair Athol Australia 22°42S 147°31E 62 C4
Blair Atholl U.K. 56°46N 3°50W 11 E5
Blairgowrie U.K. 56°35N 3°21W 11 E5
Blairsden U.S.A. 39°47N 120°37W 78 F6
Blairsville U.S.A. 40°26N 79°16W 82 F5
Blakang Mati, Pulau
Singapore 1°15N 103°50E 39 d
Blake Pt. U.S.A. 48°11N 88°25W 80 A9
Blakely Ga., U.S.A. 31°23N 84°56W 85 F12
Blakely Pa., U.S.A. 41°28N 75°37W 83 E9
Blanc, C. Spain 39°21N 2°51E 24 B9
Blanc, Mont Europe 45°48N 6°50E 20 D7
Blanca, B. Argentina 39°10S 61°30W 96 D4
Blanca, Cord. Peru 9°10S 77°35W 92 E3
Blanca Peak U.S.A. 37°35N 105°29W 77 H11
Blanche, C. Australia 33°1S 134°9E 63 E1
Blanche, L. S. Austral.,
Australia 29°15S 139°40E 63 D2
Blanche, L. W. Austral.,
Australia 22°25S 123°17E 60 D3
Blanchisseuse
Trin. & Tob. 10°48N 61°18W 93 K15
Blanco S. Africa 33°55S 22°23E 56 E3
Blanco U.S.A. 30°6N 98°25W 84 F5
Blanco → Argentina 30°20S 68°42W 94 C2
Blanco, C. Costa Rica 9°34N 85°8W 88 E2
Blanco, C. U.S.A. 42°51N 124°34W 76 E1
Blanda → Iceland 65°37N 20°9W 8 D3
Blandford Forum U.K. 50°51N 2°9W 13 G5

Blanding U.S.A. 37°37N 109°29W 77 H9
Blanes Spain 41°40N 2°48E 21 B7
Blankenberge Belgium 51°20N 3°9E 15 C3
Blanquilla Venezuela 11°51N 64°37W 89 D7
Blanquillo Uruguay 32°53S 55°37W 95 C4
Blantyre Malawi 15°45S 35°0E 55 F4
Blarney Ireland 51°56N 8°33W 10 E3
Blasdell U.S.A. 42°48N 78°50W 82 D6
Blaydon U.K. 54°58N 1°42W 12 C6
Blayney Australia 33°32S 149°14E 63 E4
Blaze, Pt. Australia 12°56S 130°11E 60 B5
Blekinge Sweden 56°25N 15°20E 9 H16
Blenheim Canada 42°20N 82°0W 82 D3
Blenheim N.Z. 41°38S 173°57E 59 D4
Bletchley U.K. 51°59N 0°44W 13 F7
Bleus, Monts
Dem. Rep. of the Congo 1°30N 30°30E 54 B3
Blida Algeria 36°30N 2°49E 50 A6
Bligh Sound N.Z. 44°47S 167°32E 59 F1
Bligh Water Fiji 17°0S 178°0E 59 a
Blind River Canada 46°10N 82°58W 72 C3
Bliss Idaho, U.S.A. 42°56N 114°57W 76 E6
Bliss N.Y., U.S.A. 42°34N 78°15W 82 D6
Blissfield U.S.A. 40°24N 81°58W 82 F3
Blitar Indonesia 8°5S 112°11E 37 H15
Block I. U.S.A. 41°11N 71°35W 83 E13
Block Island Sd. U.S.A. 41°15N 71°40W 83 E13
Bloemfontein S. Africa 29°6S 26°7E 56 D4
Bloemhof S. Africa 27°38S 25°32E 56 D4
Blois France 47°35N 1°20E 20 C4
Blönduós Iceland 65°40N 20°12W 8 D3
Blongas Indonesia 8°53S 116°2E 37 K19
Bloodvein → Canada 51°47N 96°43W 71 C9
Bloody Foreland Ireland 55°10N 8°17W 10 A3
Bloomer U.S.A. 45°6N 91°29W 80 C8
Bloomfield Canada 43°59N 77°14W 82 C7
Bloomfield Iowa, U.S.A. 40°45N 92°25W 80 E7
Bloomfield N. Mex.,
U.S.A. 36°43N 107°59W 77 H10
Bloomfield Nebr., U.S.A. 42°36N 97°39W 80 D5
Bloomington Ill., U.S.A. 40°28N 89°0W 80 E9
Bloomington Ind.,
U.S.A. 39°10N 86°32W 81 F10
Bloomington Minn.,
U.S.A. 44°50N 93°17W 80 C7
Bloomsburg U.S.A. 41°0N 76°27W 83 F8
Bloomsbury Australia 20°48S 148°38E 62 b
Blora Indonesia 6°57S 111°25E 37 G14
Blossburg U.S.A. 41°41N 77°4W 82 E7
Blouberg S. Africa 23°8S 28°59E 57 C4
Blountstown U.S.A. 30°27N 85°3W 85 F12
Blue Earth U.S.A. 43°38N 94°6W 80 D7
Blue Hole △ Belize 17°24N 88°30W 88 C2
Blue Lagoon △ Zambia 15°28S 27°26E 55 F2
Blue Mesa Res. U.S.A. 38°28N 107°20W 76 G10
Blue Mountain Lake
U.S.A. 43°51N 74°27W 83 C10
Blue Mountain Pk.
Jamaica 18°3N 76°36W 88 a
Blue Mt. U.S.A. 40°30N 76°30W 83 F8
Blue Mts. Jamaica 18°3N 76°36W 88 a
Blue Mts. Maine, U.S.A. 44°50N 70°35W 83 B14
Blue Mts. Oreg., U.S.A. 45°0N 118°20W 76 D4
Blue Mud B. Australia 13°30S 136°0E 62 A2
Blue Mud Bay ☼
Australia 13°25S 136°2E 62 A2
Blue Nile = Nîl el Azraq →
Sudan 15°38N 32°31E 51 E12
Blue Rapids U.S.A. 39°41N 96°39W 80 F5
Blue Ridge U.S.A. 36°40N 80°50W 81 G13
Blue River Canada 52°6N 119°18W 70 C5
Bluefield U.S.A. 37°15N 81°17W 81 G13
Bluefields Nic. 12°20N 83°50W 88 D3
Bluevale Canada 43°51N 81°15W 82 C3
Bluff Australia 23°35S 149°4E 62 C4
Bluff N.Z. 46°37S 168°20E 59 G2
Bluff U.S.A. 37°17N 109°33W 77 H9
Bluff Knoll Australia 34°24S 118°15E 61 F2
Bluff Pt. Australia 27°50S 114°5E 61 E1
Bluffton U.S.A. 40°44N 85°11W 81 E11
Blumenau Brazil 27°0S 49°0W 95 B6
Blunt U.S.A. 44°31N 99°59W 80 C4
Bly U.S.A. 42°24N 121°3W 76 E3
Blyde River Canyon △
S. Africa 24°37S 31°2E 57 C5
Blyth Canada 43°44N 81°26W 82 C3
Blyth U.K. 55°8N 1°31W 12 B6
Blythe U.S.A. 33°37N 114°36W 79 M12
Blytheville U.S.A. 35°56N 89°55W 85 D10
Bo S. Leone 7°55N 11°50W 50 G3
Bo Duc Vietnam 11°58N 106°50E 39 G6
Bo Hai China 39°0N 119°0E 35 E10
Bo Xian = Bozhou
China 33°55N 115°41E 34 H8
Boa Vista Brazil 2°48N 60°30W 92 C6
Boa Vista C. Verde Is. 16°0N 22°49W 50 b
Boaco Nic. 12°29N 85°35W 88 D2
Bo'ai China 35°10N 113°3E 34 G7
Boalsburg U.S.A. 40°47N 77°49W 82 F7
Boane Mozam. 26°6S 32°19E 57 D5
Boardman U.S.A. 41°2N 80°40W 82 E4
Bobadah Australia 32°19S 146°41E 63 E4
Bobbili India 18°35N 83°30E 41 K13
Bobcaygeon Canada 44°33N 78°33W 82 B6
Bobo-Dioulasso
Burkina Faso 11°8N 4°13W 50 F5
Bobonong Botswana 21°58S 28°20E 55 G2
Bóbr → Poland 52°4N 15°4E 16 B8
Bobraomby, Tanjon' i
Madag. 12°40S 49°10E 57 A8
Bobruysk = Babruysk
Belarus 53°10N 29°15E 17 B15
Boby, Pic Madag. 22°12S 46°55E 53 J9
Boca del Río Mexico 19°5N 96°4W 87 D5
Boca do Acre Brazil 8°50S 67°27W 92 E5
Boca Raton U.S.A. 26°21N 80°5W 85 H14
Bocas del Dragón = Dragon's
Mouths Venezuela 11°0N 61°50W 93 K15

Bocas del Toro Panama 9°15N 82°20W 88 E3
Bochnia Poland 49°58N 20°27E 17 D11
Bochum Germany 51°28N 7°13E 16 C4
Bocoyna Mexico 27°52N 107°35W 86 B3
Bodaybo Russia 57°50N 114°0E 29 D12
Boddam U.K. 59°56N 1°17W 11 B7
Boddington Australia 32°50S 116°30E 61 F2
Bodega Bay U.S.A. 38°20N 123°3W 78 G3
Boden Sweden 65°50N 21°42E 8 D19
Bodensee Europe 47°35N 9°25E 20 C8
Bodhan India 18°40N 77°44E 40 K10
Bodmin U.K. 50°28N 4°43W 13 G3
Bodmin Moor U.K. 50°33N 4°36W 13 G3
Bodø Norway 67°17N 14°24E 8 C16
Bodrog → Hungary 48°11N 21°22E 17 D11
Bodrum Turkey 37°3N 27°30E 23 F12
Boende
Dem. Rep. of the Congo 0°24S 21°12E 52 E4
Boerne U.S.A. 29°47N 98°44W 84 G5
Boesmans → S. Africa 33°42S 26°39E 56 E4
Bogalusa U.S.A. 30°47N 89°52W 85 F10
Bogan → Australia 30°20S 146°55E 63 D4
Bogan Gate Australia 33°7S 147°49E 63 E4
Bogantungan Australia 23°41S 147°17E 62 C4
Bogata U.S.A. 33°28N 95°13W 84 E7
Bogda Shan China 43°35N 89°40E 32 B3
Boggabilla Australia 28°36S 150°24E 63 D5
Boggabri Australia 30°45S 150°5E 63 E5
Boggeragh Mts. Ireland 52°2N 8°55N 10 D3
Boglan = Solhan Turkey 38°57N 41°3E 44 B4
Bognor Regis U.K. 50°47N 0°40W 13 G7
Bogo Phil. 11°3N 124°0E 37 B6
Bogong, Mt. Australia 36°47S 147°17E 63 F4
Bogor Indonesia 6°36S 106°48E 37 G12
Bogotá Colombia 4°34N 74°0W 92 C4
Bogotol Russia 56°15N 89°50E 28 D9
Bogra Bangla. 24°51N 89°22E 41 G16
Boguchany Russia 58°40N 97°30E 29 D10
Bogué Mauritania 16°45N 14°10W 50 E3
Bohemian Forest = Böhmerwald
Germany 49°8N 13°14E 16 D7
Böhmerwald Germany 49°8N 13°14E 16 D7
Bohol □ Phil. 9°50N 124°10E 37 C6
Bohol Sea Phil. 9°0N 124°0E 37 C6
Bohorok Indonesia 3°30N 98°12E 39 L2
Bohuslän Sweden 58°25N 12°0E 9 G15
Boi, Pta. do Brazil 23°55S 45°15W 95 A6
Boiaçu Brazil 0°27S 61°46W 92 D6
Boigu Australia 9°16S 142°13E 62 a
Boileau, C. Australia 17°40S 122°7E 60 C3
Boise U.S.A. 43°37N 116°13W 76 E5
Boise City U.S.A. 36°44N 102°31W 84 C3
Boissevain Canada 49°15N 100°5W 71 D8
Bojador, C. W. Sahara 26°0N 14°30W 50 C3
Bojana → Albania 41°52N 19°22E 23 D8
Bojnūrd Iran 37°30N 57°20E 45 B8
Bojonegoro Indonesia 7°11S 111°54E 37 G14
Bokaro India 23°46N 85°55E 43 H11
Boké Guinea 10°56N 14°17W 50 F3
Bokhara → Australia 29°55S 146°42E 63 D4
Boknafjorden Norway 59°14N 5°40E 9 G11
Bokor △ Cambodia 10°50N 104°1E 39 G5
Bokoro Chad 12°25N 17°14E 51 F9
Bokpyin Burma 11°18N 98°42E 39 G2
Bokungu
Dem. Rep. of the Congo 0°35S 22°50E 52 E4
Bolan → Pakistan 28°38N 67°42E 42 E2
Bolan Pass Pakistan 29°50N 67°20E 40 E5
Bolaños → Mexico 21°12N 104°5W 86 C4
Bolbec France 49°30N 0°30E 20 B4
Boldājī Iran 31°56N 51°3E 45 D6
Bole China 45°11N 81°37E 32 B3
Bolekhiv Ukraine 49°0N 23°57E 17 D12
Bolesławiec Poland 51°17N 15°37E 16 C8
Bolgatanga Ghana 10°44N 0°53W 50 F5
Bolgrad = Bolhrad
Ukraine 45°40N 28°32E 17 F15
Bolhrad Ukraine 45°40N 28°32E 17 F15
Bolivar Mo., U.S.A. 37°37N 93°25W 80 G7
Bolivar N.Y., U.S.A. 42°4N 78°10W 82 D6
Bolivar Tenn., U.S.A. 35°12N 89°0W 85 D10
Bolivia ■ S. Amer. 17°6S 64°0W 92 G6
Bolivian Plateau = Altiplano
Bolivia 17°0S 68°0W 92 G5
Bollnäs Sweden 61°21N 16°24E 8 F17
Bollon Australia 28°2S 147°29E 63 D4
Bolmen Sweden 56°55N 13°40E 9 H15
Bolobo
Dem. Rep. of the Congo 2°6S 16°20E 52 E3
Bologna Italy 44°29N 11°20E 22 B4
Bologoye Russia 57°55N 34°5E 18 C5
Bolomba
Dem. Rep. of the Congo 0°35N 19°0E 52 D3
Bolonchén Mexico 20°1N 89°45W 87 D7
Boloven, Cao Nguyen
Laos 15°10N 106°30E 38 E6
Bolpur India 23°40N 87°45E 43 H12
Bolsena, L. di Italy 42°36N 11°56E 22 C4
Bolshevik, Ostrov
Russia 78°30N 102°0E 29 B11
Bolshoy Anyuy →
Russia 68°30N 160°49E 29 C17
Bolshoy Begichev, Ostrov
Russia 74°20N 112°30E 29 B12
Bolshoy Kamen Russia 43°7N 132°19E 30 C6
Bolshoy Kavkas = Caucasus
Mountains Eurasia 42°50N 44°0E 19 F7
Bolshoy Lyakhovskiy, Ostrov
Russia 73°35N 142°0E 29 B15
Bolshoy Tyuters, Ostrov
Russia 59°51N 27°13E 9 G22
Bolsward Neths. 53°3N 5°32E 15 A5
Bolt Head U.K. 50°12N 3°48W 13 G4
Bolton Canada 43°54N 79°45W 82 C5
Bolton U.K. 53°35N 2°26W 12 D5
Bolton Landing U.S.A. 43°32N 73°35W 83 C11
Bolu Turkey 40°45N 31°35E 19 F5
Bolungavík Iceland 66°9N 23°15W 8 C2

Bolvadin *Turkey* 38°45N 31°4E **44** B1
Bolzano *Italy* 46°31N 11°22E **22** A4
Bom Jesus da Lapa
  Brazil 13°15S 43°25W **93** F10
Boma *Dem. Rep. of the Congo* 5°50S 13°4E **52** F2
Bombala *Australia* 36°56S 149°15E **63** F4
Bombay = Mumbai
  India 18°56N 72°50E **40** K8
Bombay *U.S.A.* 44°56N 74°34W **83** B10
Bombedor, Pta.
  Venezuela 9°53N 61°37W **93** L15
Bomboma
  Dem. Rep. of the Congo 2°25N 18°55E **52** D3
Bombombwa
  Dem. Rep. of the Congo 1°40N 25°40E **54** B2
Bomili
  Dem. Rep. of the Congo 1°45N 27°5E **54** B2
Bømlo *Norway* 59°37N 5°13E **9** G11
Bomokandi →
  Dem. Rep. of the Congo 3°39N 26°8E **54** B2
Bomu → *C.A.R.* 4°40N 22°30E **52** D4
Bon, C. = Ra's aţ Tib
  Tunisia 37°1N 11°2E **22** F4
Bon Accueil *Mauritius* 20°10S 57°39E **53** d
Bon Echo △ *Canada* 44°55N 77°16W **82** B7
Bon Sar Pa *Vietnam* 12°24N 107°35E **38** F6
Bonāb *Iran* 36°35N 48°41E **45** B6
Bonaigarh *India* 21°50N 84°57E **43** J11
Bonaire *Neth. Ant.* 12°10N 68°15W **89** D6
Bonampak *Mexico* 16°4N 91°5W **87** D6
Bonang *Australia* 37°11S 148°41E **63** F4
Bonanza *Nic.* 13°54N 84°35W **88** D3
Bonaparte Arch.
  Australia 14°0S 124°30E **60** B3
Bonar Bridge *U.K.* 57°54N 4°20W **11** D4
Bonasse *Trin. & Tob.* 10°5N 61°54W **93** K15
Bonaventure *Canada* 48°5N 65°32W **73** C6
Bonavista *Canada* 48°40N 53°5W **73** C9
Bonavista, C. *Canada* 48°42N 53°5W **73** C9
Bonavista B. *Canada* 48°45N 53°25W **73** C9
Bondo
  Dem. Rep. of the Congo 3°55N 23°53E **54** B1
Bondoukou *Ivory C.* 8°2N 2°47W **50** G5
Bondowoso *Indonesia* 7°55S 113°49E **37** G15
Bone, Teluk *Indonesia* 4°10S 120°50E **37** E6
Bonerate *Indonesia* 7°25S 121°5E **37** F6
Bonerate, Kepulauan
  Indonesia 6°30S 121°10E **37** F6
Bo'ness *U.K.* 56°1N 3°37W **11** E5
Bonete, Cerro *Argentina* 27°55S 68°40W **94** B2
Bong Son = Hoai Nhon
  Vietnam 14°28N 109°1E **38** E7
Bongaigaon *India* 26°28N 90°34E **32** D4
Bongandanga
  Dem. Rep. of the Congo 1°24N 21°3E **52** D4
Bongor *Chad* 10°35N 15°20E **51** F9
Bongos, Massif des *C.A.R.* 8°40N 22°25E **52** C4
Bonham *U.S.A.* 33°35N 96°11W **84** E6
Boni △ *Kenya* 1°35S 41°18E **54** C5
Bonifacio *France* 41°24N 9°10E **20** F8
Bonifacio, Bouches de
  Medit. S. 41°12N 9°15E **22** D3
Bonin Is. = Ogasawara Gunto
  Pac. Oc. 27°0N 142°0E **27** F16
Bonn *Germany* 50°46N 7°6E **16** C4
Bonne Terre *U.S.A.* 37°55N 90°33W **80** G8
Bonners Ferry *U.S.A.* 48°42N 116°19W **76** B5
Bonney, L. *Australia* 37°50S 140°20E **63** F3
Bonnie Rock *Australia* 30°29S 118°22E **61** F2
Bonnyrigg *U.K.* 55°53N 3°6W **11** F5
Bonnyville *Canada* 54°20N 110°45W **71** C6
Bonoi *Indonesia* 1°45S 137°41E **37** E9
Bonsall *U.S.A.* 33°16N 117°14W **79** M9
Bontang *Indonesia* 0°10N 117°30E **36** D5
Bontebok △ *S. Africa* 34°5S 20°28E **56** E3
Bonthe *S. Leone* 7°30N 12°33W **50** G3
Bontoc *Phil.* 17°7N 120°58E **37** A6
Bonython Ra. *Australia* 23°40S 128°45E **60** D4
Boodjamulla △ *Australia* 18°15S 138°6E **62** B2
Bookabie *Australia* 31°50S 132°41E **61** F5
Booker *U.S.A.* 36°27N 100°32W **84** C4
Booligal *Australia* 33°58S 144°53E **63** E3
Böön Tsagaan Nuur
  Mongolia 45°35N 99°9E **32** B4
Boonah *Australia* 27°58S 152°41E **63** D5
Boone *Iowa, U.S.A.* 42°4N 93°53W **80** D7
Boone *N.C., U.S.A.* 36°13N 81°41W **85** C14
Booneville *Ark., U.S.A.* 35°8N 93°55W **84** D8
Booneville *Miss., U.S.A.* 34°39N 88°34W **85** D10
Boonville *Calif., U.S.A.* 39°1N 123°22W **78** F3
Boonville *Ind., U.S.A.* 38°3N 87°16W **80** F10
Boonville *Mo., U.S.A.* 38°58N 92°44W **80** F7
Boonville *N.Y., U.S.A.* 43°29N 75°20W **83** C9
Boorabbin △ *Australia* 31°30S 120°10E **61** F3
Boorindal *Australia* 30°22S 146°11E **63** E4
Boorowa *Australia* 34°28S 148°44E **63** E4
Boosaaso *Somali Rep.* 11°12N 49°18E **47** E4
Boothia, Gulf of *Canada* 71°0N 90°0W **68** C14
Boothia Pen. *Canada* 71°0N 94°0W **68** C13
Bootle *U.K.* 53°28N 3°1W **12** D4
Booué *Gabon* 0°5S 11°55E **52** E2
Boquilla, Presa de la
  Mexico 27°31N 105°30W **86** B3
Boquillas del Carmen
  Mexico 29°11N 102°58W **86** B4
Bor *Serbia* 44°5N 22°7E **23** B9
Bôr *Sudan* 6°10N 31°40E **51** G12
Bor Mashash *Israel* 31°7N 34°50E **46** D3
Bora Bora
  French Polynesia 16°30S 151°45W **65** J12
Borah Peak *U.S.A.* 44°8N 113°47W **76** D7
Borås *Sweden* 57°43N 12°56E **9** H15
Borāzjān *Iran* 29°22N 51°10E **45** D6
Borba *Brazil* 4°12S 59°34W **92** D7
Borborema, Planalto da
  Brazil 7°0S 37°0W **90** D7
Bord Khūn-e Now *Iran* 28°3N 51°28E **45** D6
Borda, C. *Australia* 35°45S 136°34E **63** F2

Bordeaux *France* 44°50N 0°36W **20** D3
Borden *Australia* 34°3S 118°12E **61** F2
Borden-Carleton *Canada* 46°18N 63°47W **73** C7
Borden I. *Canada* 78°30N 111°30W **69** B9
Borden Pen. *Canada* 73°0N 83°0W **69** C15
Border Ranges △
  Australia 28°24S 152°56E **63** D5
Borders = Scottish Borders □
  U.K. 55°35N 2°50W **11** F6
Bordertown *Australia* 36°19S 140°45E **63** F3
Borðeyri *Iceland* 65°12N 21°6W **8** D3
Bordj Fly Ste. Marie
  Algeria 27°19N 2°32W **50** C5
Bordj-in-Eker *Algeria* 24°9N 5°3E **50** D7
Bordj Mokhtar *Algeria* 21°20N 0°56E **50** D6
Bordj Omar Driss *Algeria* 28°10N 6°40E **50** C7
Borehamwood *U.K.* 51°40N 0°15W **13** F7
Borgarfjörður *Iceland* 65°33N 13°47W **8** D7
Borgarnes *Iceland* 64°32N 21°55W **8** D3
Børgefjellet *Norway* 65°20N 13°45E **8** D15
Borger *Neths.* 52°54N 6°44E **15** B6
Borger *U.S.A.* 35°39N 101°24W **84** D4
Borgholm *Sweden* 56°52N 16°39E **9** H17
Borhoyn Tal *Mongolia* 43°50N 111°58E **34** C6
Borikhane *Laos* 18°33N 103°43E **38** C4
Borisoglebsk *Russia* 51°27N 42°5E **19** D7
Borisov = Barysaw
  Belarus 54°17N 28°28E **17** A15
Borja *Peru* 4°20S 77°40W **92** D3
Borkou *Chad* 18°15N 18°50E **51** E9
Borkum *Germany* 53°34N 6°40E **16** B4
Borlänge *Sweden* 60°29N 15°26E **9** F16
Borley, C. *Antarctica* 66°15S 52°30E **5** C5
Borneo *E. Indies* 1°0N 115°0E **36** D5
Bornholm *Denmark* 55°10N 15°0E **9** J16
Borogontsy *Russia* 62°42N 131°8E **29** C14
Borohoro Shan *China* 44°6N 83°10E **32** B3
Boron *U.S.A.* 35°0N 117°39W **79** L9
Borongan *Phil.* 11°37N 125°26E **37** B7
Borovichi *Russia* 58°25N 33°55E **18** C5
Borrego Springs
  U.S.A. 33°15N 116°23W **79** M10
Borrisokane *Ireland* 53°0N 8°7W **10** D3
Borroloola *Australia* 16°4S 136°17E **62** B2
Borşa *Romania* 47°41N 24°50E **17** E13
Borsad *India* 22°25N 72°54E **42** H5
Borth *U.K.* 52°29N 4°2W **13** E3
Borūjerd *Iran* 33°55N 48°50E **45** C6
Boryeong *S. Korea* 36°21N 126°36E **35** F14
Boryslav *Ukraine* 49°18N 23°28E **17** D12
Borzya *Russia* 50°24N 116°31E **29** D12
Bosa *Italy* 40°18N 8°30E **22** D3
Bosanska Gradiška
  Bos.-H. 45°10N 17°15E **22** B7
Boscastle *U.K.* 50°41N 4°42W **13** G3
Boscobelle *Barbados* 13°17N 59°35W **89** g
Bose *China* 23°53N 106°35E **32** D5
Boseong *S. Korea* 34°46N 127°5E **35** G14
Boshan *China* 36°28N 117°49E **35** F9
Boshof *S. Africa* 28°31S 25°13E **56** D4
Boshrūyeh *Iran* 33°50N 57°30E **45** C8
Bosna → *Bos.-H.* 45°4N 18°29E **23** B8
Bosna i Hercegovina = Bosnia-
  Herzegovina ■ *Europe* 44°0N 18°0E **22** B7
Bosnia-Herzegovina ■
  Europe 44°0N 18°0E **22** B7
Bosnik *Indonesia* 1°5S 136°10E **37** E9
Bosobolo
  Dem. Rep. of the Congo 4°15N 19°50E **52** D3
Bosporus = İstanbul Boğazı
  Turkey 41°5N 29°3E **23** D13
Bosque Farms *U.S.A.* 35°51N 106°42W **77** J10
Bossangoa *C.A.R.* 6°35N 17°30E **52** C3
Bossier City *U.S.A.* 32°31N 93°44W **84** E8
Bosso *Niger* 13°43N 13°19E **51** F8
Bostan *Pakistan* 30°26N 67°2E **42** D2
Bostānābād *Iran* 37°50N 46°50E **44** B5
Bosten Hu *China* 41°55N 87°40E **32** B3
Boston *U.K.* 52°59N 0°2W **12** E7
Boston *U.S.A.* 42°22N 71°3W **83** D13
Boston Bar *Canada* 49°52N 121°30W **70** D4
Boston Mts. *U.S.A.* 35°42N 93°15W **84** D8
Boswell *Canada* 49°28N 116°45W **70** D5
Boswell *U.S.A.* 40°10N 79°2W **82** F5
Botad *India* 22°15N 71°40E **42** H4
Botany B. *Australia* 33°58S 151°11E **63** E5
Botene *Laos* 17°35N 101°12E **38** D3
Bothaville *S. Africa* 27°23S 26°34E **56** D4
Bothnia, G. of *Europe* 62°0N 20°0E **8** E19
Bothwell *Australia* 42°20S 147°1E **63** G4
Bothwell *Canada* 42°38N 81°52W **82** D3
Botletle → *Botswana* 20°10S 23°15E **56** C3
Botoşani *Romania* 47°42N 26°41E **17** E14
Botou *Burkina Faso* 12°42N 1°59E **50** F6
Botshabelo *S. Africa* 29°14S 26°44E **56** D4
Botswana ■ *Africa* 22°0S 24°0E **56** C3
Bottineau *U.S.A.* 48°50N 100°27W **80** A3
Bottrop *Germany* 51°31N 6°58E **15** C6
Botucatu *Brazil* 22°55S 48°30W **95** A6
Botum Sakor △
  Cambodia 11°5N 103°15E **39** G4
Botwood *Canada* 49°6N 55°23W **73** C8
Bou Saâda *Algeria* 35°11N 4°9E **50** A6
Bouaflé *Ivory C.* 7°1N 5°47W **50** G4
Bouaké *Ivory C.* 7°40N 5°2W **50** G4
Bouar *C.A.R.* 6°0N 15°40E **52** C3
Bouârfa *Morocco* 32°32N 1°58W **50** B5
Boucaut B. *Australia* 12°0S 134°25E **62** A1
Bouctouche *Canada* 46°30N 64°45W **73** C7
Bougainville, C. *Australia* 13°57S 126°4E **60** B4
Bougainville I. *Papua N. G.* 6°0S 155°0E **58** B8
Bougainville Reef
  Australia 15°30S 147°5E **62** B4
Bougie = Bejaïa *Algeria* 36°42N 5°2E **50** A7
Bougouni *Mali* 11°30N 7°20W **50** F4
Bouillon *Belgium* 49°44N 5°3E **15** E5
Boulder *Colo., U.S.A.* 40°1N 105°17W **76** F11
Boulder *Mont., U.S.A.* 46°14N 112°7W **76** C7
Boulder City *U.S.A.* 35°58N 114°49W **79** K12

Boulder Creek *U.S.A.* 37°7N 122°7W **78** H4
Boulder Dam = Hoover Dam
  U.S.A. 36°1N 114°44W **79** K12
Boulia *Australia* 22°52S 139°51E **62** C2
Boulogne-sur-Mer *France* 50°42N 1°36E **20** A4
Boulsa *Burkina Faso* 12°39N 0°34W **50** F5
Boultoum *Niger* 14°45N 10°25E **51** F8
Bouma △ *Fiji* 16°50S 179°52E **59** a
Boun Neua *Laos* 21°38N 101°54E **38** B3
Boun Tai *Laos* 21°23N 101°58E **38** B3
Bouna *Ivory C.* 9°10N 3°0W **50** G5
Boundary Peak *U.S.A.* 37°51N 118°21W **78** H8
Boundiali *Ivory C.* 9°30N 6°20W **50** G4
Bountiful *U.S.A.* 40°53N 111°52W **76** F8
Bounty Is. *Pac. Oc.* 48°0S 178°30E **64** M9
Bounty Trough *Pac. Oc.* 46°0S 178°0E **64** M9
Bourbonnais *France* 46°28N 3°0E **20** C5
Bourdel L. *Canada* 56°43N 74°10W **72** A5
Bourem *Mali* 17°0N 0°24W **50** E5
Bourg-en-Bresse *France* 46°13N 5°12E **20** C6
Bourg-St-Maurice *France* 45°35N 6°46E **20** D7
Bourgas = Burgas
  Bulgaria 42°33N 27°29E **23** C12
Bourges *France* 47°9N 2°25E **20** C5
Bourget *Canada* 45°26N 75°9W **83** A9
Bourgogne □ *France* 47°0N 4°50E **20** C6
Bourke *Australia* 30°8S 145°55E **63** E4
Bourne *U.S.A.* 52°47N 0°22W **12** E7
Bournemouth *U.K.* 50°43N 1°52E **13** G6
Bournemouth □ *U.K.* 50°43N 1°52W **13** G6
Bouse *U.S.A.* 33°56N 114°0W **79** M13
Bousso *Chad* 10°34N 16°52E **51** F9
Bouvet I. = Bouvetøya
  Antarctica 54°26S 3°24E **2** G10
Bouvetøya *Antarctica* 54°26S 3°24E **2** G10
Bovill *U.S.A.* 46°51N 116°24W **76** C5
Bovril *Argentina* 31°21S 59°26W **94** C4
Bow → *Canada* 49°57N 111°41W **76** C6
Bow Island *Canada* 49°50N 111°23W **76** B8
Bowbells *U.S.A.* 48°48N 102°15W **80** A3
Bowdle *U.S.A.* 45°27N 99°39W **80** C4
Bowelling *Australia* 33°25S 116°30E **61** F2
Bowen *Argentina* 35°0S 67°31W **94** D2
Bowen *Australia* 20°0S 148°16E **62** J6
Bowen Mts. *Australia* 37°0S 147°50E **63** F4
Bowers Basin *Pac. Oc.* 53°45N 176°0E **4** D16
Bowers Ridge *Pac. Oc.* 54°0N 180°0E **4** D17
Bowie *Ariz., U.S.A.* 32°19N 109°29W **77** K9
Bowie *Tex., U.S.A.* 33°34N 97°51W **84** E6
Bowkān *Iran* 36°31N 46°12E **44** B5
Bowland, Forest of *U.K.* 54°0N 2°30W **12** D5
Bowling Green *Ky.,
  U.S.A.* 36°59N 86°27W **80** G10
Bowling Green *Ohio,
  U.S.A.* 41°23N 83°39W **81** E12
Bowling Green, C.
  Australia 19°19S 147°25E **62** B4
Bowling Green Bay △
  Australia 19°26S 146°57E **62** B4
Bowman *U.S.A.* 46°11N 103°24W **80** B2
Bowman I. *Antarctica* 65°0S 104°0E **5** C8
Bowmanville = Clarington
  Canada 43°55N 78°41W **82** C6
Bowmore *U.K.* 55°45N 6°17W **11** F2
Bowral *Australia* 34°26S 150°27E **63** E5
Bowraville *Australia* 30°37S 152°52E **63** E5
Bowron → *Canada* 54°3N 121°50W **70** C4
Bowron Lake △ *Canada* 53°10N 121°5W **70** C4
Bowser L. *Canada* 56°30N 129°30W **70** B3
Bowsman *Canada* 52°14N 101°12W **71** C8
Bowwood *Zambia* 17°5S 26°20E **55** F2
Box Cr. → *Australia* 34°10S 143°50E **63** E3
Boxmeer *Neths.* 51°38N 5°56E **15** C5
Boxtel *Neths.* 51°36N 5°20E **15** C5
Boyce *U.S.A.* 31°23N 92°40W **84** F8
Boyd L. *Canada* 52°46N 76°42E **72** B4
Boyle *Canada* 54°35N 112°49W **70** C6
Boyle *Ireland* 53°59N 8°18W **10** C3
Boyne → *Ireland* 53°43N 6°15W **10** C5
Boyne City *U.S.A.* 45°13N 85°1W **81** C11
Boynton Beach *U.S.A.* 26°32N 80°4W **85** H14
Boyolali *Indonesia* 7°32S 110°35E **37** G14
Boyoma, Chutes
  Dem. Rep. of the Congo 0°35N 25°23E **54** B2
Boysen Res. *U.S.A.* 43°25N 108°11W **76** E9
Boyuibe *Bolivia* 20°25S 63°17W **92** G6
Boyup Brook *Australia* 33°50S 116°23E **61** F2
Boz Dağları *Turkey* 38°20N 28°0E **23** E13
Bozburun *Turkey* 36°43N 28°4E **23** F13
Bozcaada *Turkey* 39°49N 26°3E **23** E12
Bozdoğan *Turkey* 37°40N 28°17E **23** F13
Bozeman *U.S.A.* 45°41N 111°2W **76** D8
Bozen = Bolzano *Italy* 46°31N 11°22E **22** A4
Bozhou *China* 33°55N 115°41E **34** H8
Bozoum *C.A.R.* 6°25N 16°35E **52** C3
Bozyazı *Turkey* 36°6N 33°0E **44** B2
Bra *Italy* 44°42N 7°51E **20** D7
Brabant □ *Belgium* 50°46N 4°30E **15** D4
Brabant L. *Canada* 55°58N 103°43E **71** B8
Brač *Croatia* 43°20N 16°40E **22** C7
Bracadale, L. *U.K.* 57°20N 6°30W **11** D2
Bracciano, L. di *Italy* 42°7N 12°14E **22** C5
Bracebridge *Canada* 45°2N 79°19W **82** A5
Bräcke *Sweden* 62°45N 15°26E **8** E16
Brackettville *U.S.A.* 29°19N 100°25W **84** G4
Bracknell *U.K.* 51°25N 0°43W **13** F7
Bracknell Forest □ *U.K.* 51°25N 0°44W **13** F7
Brad *Romania* 46°10N 22°50E **17** E12
Bradenton *U.S.A.* 27°30N 82°34W **85** H13
Bradford *Canada* 44°7N 79°34W **82** B5
Bradford *U.K.* 53°47N 1°45W **12** D6
Bradford *Pa., U.S.A.* 41°58N 78°38W **82** E6
Bradford *Vt., U.S.A.* 43°59N 72°9W **83** C12
Bradley *Ark., U.S.A.* 33°6N 93°39W **84** E8
Bradley *Calif., U.S.A.* 35°52N 120°48W **78** K6
Bradley Institute
  Zimbabwe 17°7S 31°25E **55** F3
Brady *U.S.A.* 31°9N 99°20W **84** F5
Braeside *Canada* 45°28N 76°24W **83** A8

Braga *Portugal* 41°35N 8°25W **21** B1
Bragado *Argentina* 35°2S 60°27W **94** D3
Bragança *Brazil* 1°0S 47°2W **93** D9
Bragança *Portugal* 41°48N 6°50W **21** B2
Bragança Paulista
  Brazil 22°55S 46°32W **95** A6
Brahestad = Raahe
  Finland 64°40N 24°28E **8** D21
Brahmanbaria *Bangla.* 23°58N 91°15E **41** H17
Brahmani → *India* 20°39N 86°46E **41** J15
Brahmapur *India* 19°15N 84°54E **41** K14
Brahmaputra → *Asia* 23°40N 90°35E **43** H13
Braich-y-pwll *U.K.* 52°47N 4°46W **12** E3
Braidwood *Australia* 35°27S 149°49E **63** F4
Bräila *Romania* 45°19N 27°59E **17** F14
Brainerd *U.S.A.* 46°22N 94°12W **80** B6
Braintree *U.K.* 51°53N 0°34E **13** F8
Braintree *U.S.A.* 42°13N 71°0W **83** D14
Brak → *S. Africa* 29°35S 22°55E **56** D3
Brakwater *Namibia* 22°28S 17°3E **56** C2
Brampton *Canada* 43°45N 79°45W **82** C5
Brampton *U.K.* 54°57N 2°44W **12** C5
Brampton I. *Australia* 20°49S 149°16E **62** b
Branco → *Brazil* 1°20S 61°50W **92** D6
Brandberg *Namibia* 21°10S 14°33E **56** C1
Brandberg △ *Namibia* 21°10S 14°30E **56** C1
Brandenburg = Neubrandenburg
  Germany 53°33N 13°15E **16** B7
Brandenburg *Germany* 52°25N 12°33E **16** B7
Brandenburg □ *Germany* 52°50N 13°0E **16** B6
Brandfort *S. Africa* 28°40S 26°30E **56** D4
Brandon *Canada* 49°50N 99°57W **71** D9
Brandon *U.S.A.* 43°48N 73°6W **83** C11
Brandon B. *Ireland* 52°17N 10°8W **10** D1
Brandon Mt. *Ireland* 52°15N 10°15W **10** D1
Brandsen *Argentina* 35°10S 58°15W **94** D4
Brandvlei *S. Africa* 30°25S 20°30E **56** E3
Branford *U.S.A.* 41°17N 72°49W **83** E12
Braniewo *Poland* 54°25N 19°50E **17** A10
Bransfield Str. *Antarctica* 63°0S 59°0W **5** C18
Branson *U.S.A.* 36°39N 93°13W **80** G7
Brantford *Canada* 43°10N 80°15W **82** C4
Bras d'Or L. *Canada* 45°50N 60°50W **73** C7
Brasher Falls *U.S.A.* 44°49N 74°47W **83** B10
Brasil = Brazil ■ *S. Amer.* 12°0S 50°0W **93** F9
Brasil, Planalto *Brazil* 18°0S 46°30W **90** E6
Brasiléia *Brazil* 11°0S 68°45W **92** F5
Brasília *Brazil* 15°47S 47°55W **93** G9
Brasília Legal *Brazil* 3°49S 55°36W **93** D7
Braslaw *Belarus* 55°38N 27°0E **9** J22
Braşov *Romania* 45°38N 25°35E **17** F13
Brasschaat *Belgium* 51°19N 4°27E **15** C4
Brassey, Banjaran
  Malaysia 5°0N 117°15E **36** D5
Brassey Ra. *Australia* 25°8S 122°15E **61** E3
Brasstown Bald *U.S.A.* 34°53N 83°49W **85** D13
Brastad *Sweden* 58°23N 11°30E **9** G14
Bratislava *Slovak Rep.* 48°10N 17°7E **17** D9
Bratsk *Russia* 56°10N 101°30E **29** D11
Brattleboro *U.S.A.* 42°51N 72°34W **83** D12
Braunau *Austria* 48°15N 13°3E **16** D7
Braunschweig *Germany* 52°15N 10°31E **16** B6
Braunton *U.K.* 51°7N 4°10W **13** F3
Brava *C. Verde Is.* 15°0N 24°40W **50** b
Bravo del Norte, Rio = Grande,
  Rio → *N. Amer.* 25°58N 97°9W **84** J6
Brawley *U.S.A.* 32°59N 115°31W **79** N11
Bray *Ireland* 53°13N 6°7W **10** C5
Bray, Mt. *Australia* 14°0S 134°30E **62** A1
Bray, Pays de *France* 49°46N 1°26E **20** B4
Brazeau → *Canada* 52°55N 115°14W **70** C5
Brazil *U.S.A.* 39°32N 87°8W **80** F10
Brazil ■ *S. Amer.* 12°0S 50°0W **93** F9
Brazilian Highlands = Brasil,
  Planalto *Brazil* 18°0S 46°30W **90** E6
Brazo Sur → *S. Amer.* 25°21S 57°42W **94** B4
Brazos → *U.S.A.* 28°53N 95°23W **84** G7
Brazzaville *Congo* 4°9S 15°12E **52** E3
Brčko *Bos.-H.* 44°54N 18°46E **23** B8
Bré = Bray *Ireland* 53°13N 6°7W **10** C5
Breaden, L. *Australia* 25°51S 125°28E **61** E4
Breaksea Sd. *N.Z.* 45°35S 166°35E **59** F1
Bream B. *N.Z.* 35°56S 174°28E **59** A5
Bream Hd. *N.Z.* 35°51S 174°36E **59** A5
Breas *Chile* 25°29S 70°24W **94** B1
Brebes *Indonesia* 6°52S 109°3E **37** G13
Brechin *Canada* 44°32N 79°10W **82** B5
Brechin *U.K.* 56°44N 2°39W **11** E6
Brecht *Belgium* 51°21N 4°38E **15** C4
Breckenridge *Colo.,
  U.S.A.* 39°29N 106°3W **76** G10
Breckenridge *Minn.,
  U.S.A.* 46°16N 96°35W **80** B5
Breckenridge *Tex.,
  U.S.A.* 32°45N 98°54W **84** E5
Breckland *U.K.* 52°30N 0°40E **13** E8
Brecon *U.K.* 51°57N 3°23W **13** F4
Brecon Beacons *U.K.* 51°53N 3°26W **13** F4
Brecon Beacons △ *U.K.* 51°50N 3°30W **13** F4
Breda *Neths.* 51°35N 4°45E **15** C4
Bredasdorp *S. Africa* 34°33S 20°2E **56** E3
Bree *Belgium* 51°8N 5°35E **15** C5
Bregenz *Austria* 47°30N 9°45E **16** E5
Breiðafjörður *Iceland* 65°15N 23°15W **8** D2
Brejo *Brazil* 3°41S 42°47W **93** D10
Bremen *Germany* 53°4N 8°47E **16** B5
Bremer Bay *Australia* 34°21S 119°20E **61** F2
Bremer I. *Australia* 12°5S 136°45E **62** A2
Bremerhaven *Germany* 53°33N 8°36E **16** B5
Bremerton *U.S.A.* 47°34N 122°37W **78** C4
Brenham *U.S.A.* 30°10N 96°24W **84** F6
Brennerpass *Austria* 47°2N 11°30E **16** E6
Brent *U.S.A.* 32°56N 87°10W **85** E11
Brentwood *U.K.* 51°37N 0°19E **13** F8
Brentwood *Calif.,
  U.S.A.* 37°56N 121°42W **78** H5
Brentwood *N.Y., U.S.A.* 40°47N 73°15W **83** F11
Bréscia *Italy* 45°33N 10°15E **20** D9
Breskens *Neths.* 51°23N 3°33E **15** C3

Breslau = Wrocław *Poland* 51°5N 17°5E **17** C9
Bressanone *Italy* 46°43N 11°39E **22** A4
Bressay *U.K.* 60°9N 1°6W **11** A7
Brest *Belarus* 52°10N 23°40E **17** B12
Brest *France* 48°24N 4°31W **20** B1
Brest-Litovsk = Brest
  Belarus 52°10N 23°40E **17** B12
Bretagne □ *France* 48°10N 3°0W **20** B2
Breton *Canada* 53°7N 114°28W **70** C6
Breton Sd. *U.S.A.* 29°35N 89°15W **85** G10
Brett, C. *N.Z.* 35°10S 174°20E **59** A5
Brevard *U.S.A.* 35°14N 82°44W **85** D13
Breves *Brazil* 1°40S 50°29W **93** D8
Brewarrina *Australia* 30°0S 146°51E **63** E4
Brewer *U.S.A.* 44°48N 68°46W **81** C19
Brewer, Mt. *U.S.A.* 36°44N 118°28W **78** J8
Brewster *N.Y., U.S.A.* 41°24N 73°36W **83** E11
Brewster *Ohio, U.S.A.* 40°43N 81°36W **82** F3
Brewster *Wash., U.S.A.* 48°6N 119°47W **76** B4
Brewster, Kap = Kangikajik
  Greenland 70°7N 22°0W **4** B6
Brewton *U.S.A.* 31°7N 87°4W **85** F11
Breyten *S. Africa* 26°16S 30°0E **57** D5
Bria *C.A.R.* 6°30N 21°58E **52** C4
Briançon *France* 44°54N 6°39E **20** D7
Bribie I. *Australia* 27°0S 153°10E **63** D5
Bribri *Costa Rica* 9°38N 82°50E **88** E3
Bridgefield *Barbados* 13°9N 59°36W **89** g
Bridgehampton *U.S.A.* 40°56N 72°19W **83** F12
Bridgend *U.K.* 51°30N 3°34W **13** F4
Bridgend □ *U.K.* 51°36N 3°36W **13** F4
Bridgenorth *Canada* 44°23N 78°23W **82** B6
Bridgeport *Calif., U.S.A.* 38°15N 119°14W **78** G7
Bridgeport *Conn.,
  U.S.A.* 41°11N 73°12W **83** E11
Bridgeport *N.Y., U.S.A.* 43°9N 75°58W **83** C9
Bridgeport *Nebr., U.S.A.* 41°40N 103°6W **80** E2
Bridgeport *Tex., U.S.A.* 33°13N 97°45W **84** E6
Bridger *U.S.A.* 45°18N 108°55W **76** D9
Bridgeton *U.S.A.* 39°26N 75°14W **81** F16
Bridgetown *Australia* 33°58S 116°7E **61** F2
Bridgetown *Barbados* 13°6N 59°37W **89** g
Bridgetown *Canada* 44°55N 65°18W **73** D6
Bridgewater *Australia* 42°44S 147°14E **63** G4
Bridgewater *Canada* 44°25N 64°31W **73** D7
Bridgewater *Mass.,
  U.S.A.* 41°59N 70°58W **83** E14
Bridgewater *N.Y.,
  U.S.A.* 42°53N 75°15W **83** D9
Bridgewater, C.
  Australia 38°23S 141°23E **63** F3
Bridgnorth *U.K.* 52°32N 2°25W **13** E5
Bridgton *U.S.A.* 44°3N 70°42W **83** B14
Bridgwater *U.K.* 51°8N 2°59W **13** F5
Bridgwater B. *U.K.* 51°15N 3°15W **13** F4
Bridlington *U.K.* 54°5N 0°12W **12** C7
Bridlington B. *U.K.* 54°4N 0°10W **12** C7
Bridport *Australia* 40°59S 147°23E **63** G4
Bridport *U.K.* 50°44N 2°45W **13** G5
Brig *Switz.* 46°18N 7°59E **20** C7
Brigg *U.K.* 53°34N 0°28W **12** D7
Brigham City *U.S.A.* 41°31N 112°1W **76** F7
Bright *Australia* 36°42S 146°56E **63** F4
Brighton *Australia* 35°5S 138°30E **63** F2
Brighton *Canada* 44°2N 77°44W **82** B7
Brighton *Trin. & Tob.* 10°13N 61°39W **93** K15
Brighton *U.K.* 50°49N 0°7W **13** G7
Brighton *U.S.A.* 43°8N 77°34W **82** C7
Brightside *Canada* 45°7N 76°29W **83** A8
Brilliant *U.S.A.* 40°15N 80°39W **82** F4
Bríndisi *Italy* 40°39N 17°55E **23** D7
Brinkley *U.S.A.* 34°53N 91°12W **84** D9
Brinnon *U.S.A.* 47°41N 122°54W **78** C4
Brion, Î. *Canada* 47°46N 61°26W **73** C7
Brisay *Canada* 54°26N 70°31W **73** B5
Brisbane *Australia* 27°25S 153°2E **63** D5
Brisbane → *Australia* 27°24S 153°9E **63** D5
Bristol *U.K.* 51°26N 2°35W **13** F5
Bristol *Conn., U.S.A.* 41°40N 72°57W **83** E12
Bristol *Pa., U.S.A.* 40°6N 74°51W **83** F10
Bristol *R.I., U.S.A.* 41°40N 71°16W **83** E13
Bristol *Tenn., U.S.A.* 36°36N 82°11W **85** C13
Bristol *Vt., U.S.A.* 44°8N 73°4W **83** B11
Bristol, City of □ *U.K.* 51°27N 2°36W **13** F5
Bristol B. *U.S.A.* 58°0N 160°0W **74** D8
Bristol Channel *U.K.* 51°18N 4°30W **13** F3
Bristol I. *Antarctica* 58°45S 28°0W **5** B1
Bristol L. *U.S.A.* 34°28N 115°41W **77** J6
Bristow *U.S.A.* 35°50N 96°23W **84** D6
Britain = Great Britain
  Europe 54°0N 2°15W **6** E5
British Columbia □
  Canada 55°0N 125°15W **70** C3
British Indian Ocean Terr. =
  Chagos Arch. ☑ *Ind. Oc.* 6°0S 72°0E **26** J9
British Isles *Europe* 54°0N 4°0W **14** D5
British Mts. *N. Amer.* 68°50N 140°0W **74** B12
British Virgin Is. ☑
  W. Indies 18°30N 64°30W **89** e
Brits *S. Africa* 25°37S 27°48E **57** D4
Britstown *S. Africa* 30°37S 23°30E **56** E3
Britt *Canada* 45°46N 80°34W **72** C3
Brittany = Bretagne □
  France 48°10N 3°0W **20** B2
Britton *U.S.A.* 45°48N 97°45W **80** C5
Brive-la-Gaillarde *France* 45°10N 1°32E **20** D4
Brixen = Bressanone
  Italy 46°43N 11°39E **22** A4
Brixham *U.K.* 50°23N 3°31W **13** G4
Brno *Czech Rep.* 49°10N 16°35E **17** D9
Broach = Bharuch *India* 21°47N 73°0E **40** J8
Broad → *U.S.A.* 34°1N 81°4W **85** D14
Broad Arrow *Australia* 30°23S 121°15E **61** F3
Broad B. *U.K.* 58°14N 6°18W **11** C2
Broad Haven *Ireland* 54°20N 9°55W **10** B2
Broad Law *U.K.* 55°30N 3°21W **11** F5
Broad Pk. = Faichan Kangri
  India 35°48N 76°34E **43** B7
Broad Sd. *Australia* 22°0S 149°45E **62** C4

Broadalbin *U.S.A.* 43°4N 74°12W **83** C10
Broadback → *Canada* 51°21N 78°52W **72** B4
Broadhurst Ra.
 Australia 22°30S 122°30E **60** D3
Broads, The *U.K.* 52°45N 1°30E **12** E9
Broadus *U.S.A.* 45°27N 105°25W **76** D11
Brochet *Canada* 57°53N 101°40W **71** B8
Brochet, L. *Canada* 58°36N 101°35W **71** B8
Brock I. *Canada* 77°52N 114°19W **69** B9
Brocken *Germany* 51°47N 10°37E **16** C6
Brockport *U.S.A.* 43°13N 77°56W **82** C7
Brockton *U.S.A.* 42°5N 71°1W **83** D13
Brockville *Canada* 44°35N 75°41W **83** B9
Brockway *Mont.*,
 U.S.A. 47°18N 105°45W **76** C11
Brockway *Pa.*, *U.S.A.* 41°15N 78°47W **82** E6
Brocton *U.S.A.* 42°23N 79°26W **82** D5
Brodeur Pen. *Canada* 72°30N 88°10W **69** C14
Brodick *U.K.* 55°35N 5°9W **11** F3
Brodnica *Poland* 53°15N 19°25E **17** B10
Brody *Ukraine* 50°5N 25°10E **17** C13
Brogan *U.S.A.* 44°15N 117°31W **76** D5
Broken Arrow *U.S.A.* 36°3N 95°48W **84** C7
Broken Bow *Nebr.*,
 U.S.A. 41°24N 99°38W **80** E4
Broken Bow *Okla.*, *U.S.A.* 34°2N 94°44W **84** D7
Broken Bow Lake *U.S.A.* 34°9N 94°40W **84** D7
Broken Hill *Australia* 31°58S 141°29E **63** E3
Broken Ridge *Ind. Oc.* 30°0S 94°0E **64** L1
Broken River Ra.
 Australia 21°0S 148°22E **62** b
Bromley □ *U.K.* 51°24N 0°2E **13** F8
Bromo *Indonesia* 7°55S 112°55E **37** G15
Bromsgrove *U.K.* 52°21N 2°2W **13** E5
Brønderslev *Denmark* 57°16N 9°57E **9** H13
Bronkhorstspruit
 S. Africa 25°46S 28°45E **57** D4
Brønnøysund *Norway* 65°28N 12°14E **8** D15
Brook Park *U.S.A.* 41°23N 81°48W **82** E4
Brookhaven *U.S.A.* 31°35N 90°26W **85** F9
Brookings *Oreg.*, *U.S.A.* 42°3N 124°17W **76** E1
Brookings *S. Dak.*,
 U.S.A. 44°19N 96°48W **80** C5
Brooklin *Canada* 43°55N 78°55W **82** C6
Brooklyn Park *U.S.A.* 45°6N 93°23W **80** C7
Brooks *Canada* 50°35N 111°55W **70** C6
Brooks Range *U.S.A.* 68°0N 152°0W **74** B9
Brooksville *U.S.A.* 28°33N 82°23W **85** G13
Brookton *Australia* 32°22S 117°0E **61** F2
Brookville *U.S.A.* 41°10N 79°5W **82** E5
Broom, L. *U.K.* 57°55N 5°15W **11** D3
Broome *Australia* 18°0S 122°15E **60** C3
Brora *U.K.* 58°0N 3°52W **11** C5
Brora → *U.K.* 58°0N 3°51W **11** C5
Brosna → *Ireland* 53°14N 7°58W **10** C4
Brothers *U.S.A.* 43°49N 120°36W **76** E3
Brough *U.K.* 54°32N 2°18W **12** C5
Brough Hd. *U.K.* 59°8N 3°20W **11** B5
Broughton Island = Qikiqtarjuaq
 Canada 67°33N 63°0W **69** D19
Brown, L. *Australia* 31°5S 118°15E **61** F2
Brown, Pt. *Australia* 32°32S 133°50E **63** E1
Brown City *U.S.A.* 43°13N 82°59W **82** C2
Brown Willy *U.K.* 50°35N 4°37W **13** G3
Brownfield *U.S.A.* 33°11N 102°17W **84** E3
Browning *U.S.A.* 48°34N 113°1W **76** B7
Brownsville *Oreg.*,
 U.S.A. 44°24N 122°59W **76** D2
Brownsville *Pa.*, *U.S.A.* 40°1N 79°53W **82** F5
Brownsville *Tenn.*,
 U.S.A. 35°36N 89°16W **85** D10
Brownsville *Tex.*, *U.S.A.* 25°54N 97°30W **84** J6
Brownville *U.S.A.* 44°0N 75°59W **83** C9
Brownwood *U.S.A.* 31°43N 98°59W **84** F5
Browse I. *Australia* 14°7S 123°33E **60** B3
Bruas *Malaysia* 4°30N 100°47E **39** K3
Bruay-la-Buissière *France* 50°29N 2°33E **20** A5
Bruce, Mt. *Australia* 22°37S 118°8E **60** D2
Bruce Pen. *Canada* 45°0N 81°30W **82** A3
Bruce Peninsula △
 Canada 45°14N 81°36W **82** A3
Bruce Rock *Australia* 31°52S 118°8E **61** F2
Bruck an der Leitha
 Austria 48°1N 16°47E **17** D9
Bruck an der Mur
 Austria 47°24N 15°16E **16** E8
Brue → *U.K.* 51°13N 2°59W **13** F5
Bruges = Brugge *Belgium* 51°13N 3°13E **15** C3
Brugge *Belgium* 51°13N 3°13E **15** C3
Bruin *U.S.A.* 41°3N 79°43W **82** E5
Brûk, W. el → *Egypt* 30°15N 33°50E **46** E2
Brûlé *Canada* 53°15N 117°58W **70** C5
Brûlé, L. *Canada* 53°35N 64°4W **73** B7
Brumado *Brazil* 14°14S 41°40W **93** F10
Brumunddal *Norway* 60°53N 10°56E **8** F14
Bruneau *U.S.A.* 42°53N 115°48W **76** E6
Bruneau → *U.S.A.* 42°56N 115°57W **76** E6
Brunei = Bandar Seri Begawan
 Brunei 4°52N 115°0E **36** D5
Brunei ■ *Asia* 4°50N 115°0E **36** D5
Brunner, L. *N.Z.* 42°37S 171°27E **59** E3
Brunssum *Neths.* 50°57N 5°59E **15** D5
Brunswick = Braunschweig
 Germany 52°15N 10°31E **16** B6
Brunswick *Ga.*, *U.S.A.* 31°10N 81°30W **85** F14
Brunswick *Maine*,
 U.S.A. 43°55N 69°58W **81** D19
Brunswick *Md.*, *U.S.A.* 39°19N 77°38W **81** F15
Brunswick *Mo.*, *U.S.A.* 39°26N 93°8W **80** F7
Brunswick *Ohio*, *U.S.A.* 41°14N 81°51W **82** E3
Brunswick, Pen. de
 Chile 53°30S 71°30W **96** G2
Brunswick B. *Australia* 15°15S 124°50E **60** C3
Brunswick Junction
 Australia 33°15S 115°50E **61** F2
Brunt Ice Shelf *Antarctica* 75°30S 25°0W **5** D2
Brus Laguna *Honduras* 15°47N 84°35W **88** C3
Brush *U.S.A.* 40°15N 103°37W **76** F12
Brushton *U.S.A.* 44°50N 74°31W **83** B10

Brusque *Brazil* 27°5S 49°0W **95** B6
Brussel *Belgium* 50°51N 4°21E **15** D4
Brussel ✈ (BRU) *Belgium* 50°54N 4°29E **15** D5
Brussels = Brussel
 Belgium 50°51N 4°21E **15** D4
Brussels *Canada* 43°44N 81°15W **82** C3
Bruthen *Australia* 37°42S 147°50E **63** F4
Bryan *Ohio*, *U.S.A.* 41°28N 84°33W **81** E11
Bryan *Tex.*, *U.S.A.* 30°40N 96°22W **84** F6
Bryan, Mt. *Australia* 33°30S 139°5E **63** E2
Bryansk *Russia* 53°13N 34°25E **18** D4
Bryce Canyon △
 U.S.A. 37°30N 112°10W **77** H7
Bryne *Norway* 58°44N 5°38E **9** G11
Bryson City *U.S.A.* 35°26N 83°27W **85** D13
Bsharri *Lebanon* 34°15N 36°0E **46** A5
Bū Baqarah *U.A.E.* 25°35N 56°25E **45** E8
Bu Craa *W. Sahara* 26°45N 12°50W **50** C3
Bū Ḥasā *U.A.E.* 23°30N 53°20E **45** F7
Bua *Fiji* 16°48S 178°37E **59** a
Bua → *Malaysia* 12°45S 34°16E **55** E3
Bua Yai *Thailand* 15°33N 102°26E **38** E4
Buan *S. Korea* 35°44N 126°44E **35** G14
Buapinang *Indonesia* 4°40S 121°30E **37** E6
Bubanza *Burundi* 3°6S 29°23E **54** C2
Bubi → *Zimbabwe* 22°20S 31°7E **55** G3
Būbiyān *Kuwait* 29°45N 48°15E **45** D6
Buca *Fiji* 16°38S 179°52E **59** a
Bucaramanga *Colombia* 7°0N 73°0W **92** B4
Bucasia *Australia* 21°2S 149°10E **62** b
Buccaneer Arch.
 Australia 16°7S 123°20E **60** C3
Buccoo Reef
 Trin. & Tob. 11°10N 60°51W **93** J16
Buchach *Ukraine* 49°5N 25°25E **17** D13
Buchan *U.K.* 57°32N 2°21W **11** D6
Buchan Ness *U.K.* 57°29N 1°46W **11** D7
Buchanan *Canada* 51°40N 102°45W **71** C8
Buchanan *Liberia* 5°57N 10°2W **50** G3
Buchanan, L. *Queens.*,
 Australia 21°35S 145°52E **62** C4
Buchanan, L. *W. Austral.*,
 Australia 25°33S 123°2E **61** E3
Buchanan, L. *U.S.A.* 30°45N 98°25W **84** F5
Buchanan Cr. →
 Australia 19°13S 136°33E **62** B2
Buchans *Canada* 48°50N 56°52W **73** C8
Bucharest = București
 Romania 44°27N 26°10E **17** F14
Bucheon *S. Korea* 37°28N 126°45E **35** F14
Buchon, Pt. *U.S.A.* 35°15N 120°54W **78** K6
Buck Hill Falls *U.S.A.* 41°11N 75°16W **83** E9
Buckeye Lake *U.S.A.* 39°55N 82°29W **82** G2
Buckhannon *U.S.A.* 39°0N 80°8W **81** F13
Buckhaven *U.K.* 56°11N 3°3W **11** E5
Buckhorn L. *Canada* 44°29N 78°23W **82** B6
Buckie *U.K.* 57°41N 2°58W **11** D6
Buckingham *Canada* 45°37N 75°24W **72** C4
Buckingham *U.K.* 51°59N 0°57W **13** F7
Buckingham B.
 Australia 12°10S 135°40E **62** A2
Buckinghamshire □
 U.K. 51°53N 0°55W **13** F7
Buckle Hd. *Australia* 14°26S 127°52E **60** B4
Buckleboo *Australia* 32°54S 136°12E **63** E2
Buckley *U.S.A.* 53°10N 3°5W **12** D4
Buckley → *Australia* 20°10S 138°49E **62** C2
Bucklin *U.S.A.* 37°33N 99°38W **80** G4
Bucks L. *U.S.A.* 39°54N 121°12W **78** F5
București *Romania* 44°27N 26°10E **17** F14
Bucyrus *U.S.A.* 40°48N 82°59W **81** E12
Budalin *Burma* 22°20N 95°10E **41** H19
Budapest *Hungary* 47°29N 19°3E **17** E10
Budaun *India* 28°5N 79°10E **43** E8
Budd Coast *Antarctica* 68°0S 112°0E **5** C8
Bude *U.K.* 50°49N 4°34W **13** G3
Budennovsk *Russia* 44°50N 44°10E **19** F7
Budge Budge = Baj Baj
 India 22°30N 88°5E **43** H13
Budgewoi *Australia* 33°13S 151°34E **63** E5
Budjala
 Dem. Rep. of the Congo 2°50N 19°40E **52** D3
Buellton *U.S.A.* 34°37N 120°12W **79** L6
Buena Esperanza
 Argentina 34°45S 65°15W **94** C2
Buena Park *U.S.A.* 33°52N 117°59W **79** M9
Buena Vista *Colo.*,
 U.S.A. 38°51N 106°8W **76** G10
Buena Vista *Va.*, *U.S.A.* 37°44N 79°21W **81** G14
Buena Vista Lake Bed
 U.S.A. 35°12N 119°18W **79** K7
Buenaventura *Colombia* 3°53N 77°4W **92** C3
Buenaventura *Mexico* 29°51N 107°29W **86** B3
Buenos Aires *Argentina* 34°36S 58°22W **94** C4
Buenos Aires *Costa Rica* 9°10N 83°20W **88** E3
Buenos Aires □ *Argentina* 36°30S 60°0W **94** D4
Buenos Aires, L.
 Argentina 46°35S 72°30W **96** F2
Buffalo *Mo.*, *U.S.A.* 37°39N 93°6W **80** G7
Buffalo *N.Y.*, *U.S.A.* 42°53N 78°53W **82** D6
Buffalo *Okla.*, *U.S.A.* 36°50N 99°38W **84** C5
Buffalo *S. Dak.*, *U.S.A.* 45°35N 103°33W **80** C2
Buffalo *Wyo.*, *U.S.A.* 44°21N 106°42W **76** D10
Buffalo → *Canada* 60°5N 115°5W **70** A5
Buffalo → *S. Africa* 28°43S 30°37E **57** D5
Buffalo → *U.S.A.* 36°14N 92°36W **84** C8
Buffalo Head Hills
 Canada 57°25N 115°55W **70** B5
Buffalo L. *Alta.*, *Canada* 52°27N 112°54W **70** C6
Buffalo L. *N.W.T.*,
 Canada 60°12N 115°25W **70** A5
Buffalo Narrows
 Canada 55°51N 108°29W **71** B7
Buffalo Springs △ *Kenya* 0°32N 37°35E **54** B4
Buffels → *S. Africa* 29°36S 17°3E **56** D2
Buford *U.S.A.* 34°10N 84°0W **85** D12
Bug → = Buh → *Ukraine* 46°59N 31°58E **19** E5

Bug → *Poland* 52°31N 21°5E **17** B11
Buga *Colombia* 4°0N 76°15W **92** C3
Bugala I. *Uganda* 0°40S 32°20E **54** C3
Buganda *Uganda* 0°0 31°30E **54** C3
Buganga *Uganda* 0°3S 32°0E **54** C3
Bugel, Tanjung *Indonesia* 6°26S 111°3E **37** G14
Búger *Spain* 39°45N 2°59E **24** B9
Bugibba *Malta* 35°57N 14°25E **25** D1
Bugsuk I. *Phil.* 8°12N 117°18E **36** C5
Bugulma *Russia* 54°33N 52°48E **18** D9
Bugungu → *Uganda* 2°17N 31°50E **54** B3
Buguruslan *Russia* 53°39N 52°26E **18** D9
Buh → *Ukraine* 46°59N 31°58E **19** E5
Buhera *Zimbabwe* 19°18S 31°29E **55** B5
Buhl *U.S.A.* 42°36N 114°46W **76** E6
Builth Wells *U.K.* 52°9N 3°25W **13** E4
Buir Nur *Mongolia* 47°50N 117°42E **33** B6
Buji *China* 22°37N 114°5E **33** F11
Bujumbura *Burundi* 3°16S 29°18E **54** C2
Bukachacha *Russia* 52°55N 116°50E **29** D12
Bukama
 Dem. Rep. of the Congo 9°10S 25°50E **55** D2
Bukavu
 Dem. Rep. of the Congo 2°20S 28°52E **54** C2
Bukene *Tanzania* 4°15S 32°48E **54** C3
Bukhara = Buxoro
 Uzbekistan 39°48N 64°25E **28** F7
Bukhoro = Buxoro
 Uzbekistan 39°48N 64°25E **28** F7
Bukima *Tanzania* 1°50S 33°25E **54** C3
Bukit Badung *Indonesia* 8°49S 115°10E **37** K18
Bukit Kerajaan *Malaysia* 5°25N 100°15E **39** c
Bukit Mertajam *Malaysia* 5°22N 100°28E **39** c
Bukit Ni *Malaysia* 1°22N 104°12E **39** d
Bukit Panjang *Singapore* 1°23N 103°46E **39** d
Bukit Tengah *Malaysia* 5°22N 100°25E **39** c
Bukittinggi *Indonesia* 0°20S 100°20E **36** E2
Bukoba *Tanzania* 1°20S 31°49E **54** C3
Bukum, Pulau *Singapore* 1°14N 103°46E **39** d
Bukuya *Uganda* 0°40N 31°52E **54** B3
Bula *Indonesia* 3°6S 130°30E **37** E8
Bulahdelah *Australia* 32°23S 152°13E **63** E5
Bulan *Phil.* 12°40N 123°52E **37** B6
Bulandshahr *India* 28°28N 77°51E **42** E7
Bulawayo *Zimbabwe* 20°7S 28°32E **55** G2
Buldan *Turkey* 38°2N 28°50E **23** E13
Buldir I. *U.S.A.* 52°21N 175°56E **74** E3
Bulgan *Mongolia* 48°45N 103°34E **32** B5
Bulgar *Russia* 54°57N 49°4E **18** D8
Bulgaria ■ *Europe* 42°35N 25°30E **23** C11
Buli, Teluk *Indonesia* 0°48N 128°25E **37** D7
Buliluyan, C. *Phil.* 8°20N 117°15E **36** C5
Bulim *Singapore* 1°22N 103°43E **39** d
Bulkley → *Canada* 55°15N 127°40W **70** B3
Bull Shoals L. *U.S.A.* 36°22N 92°35W **84** C8
Bulleringa △ *Australia* 17°39S 143°56E **62** B3
Bullhead City *U.S.A.* 35°8N 114°32W **79** K12
Büllingen *Belgium* 50°25N 6°16E **15** D6
Bullock Creek *Australia* 17°43S 144°31E **62** B3
Bulloo → *Australia* 28°43S 142°30E **63** D3
Bulloo L. *Australia* 28°43S 142°25E **63** D3
Bulls *N.Z.* 40°10S 175°24E **59** D5
Bulman *Australia* 13°39S 134°20E **62** A1
Bulnes *Chile* 36°42S 72°19W **94** D1
Bulsar = Valsad *India* 20°40N 72°58E **40** J8
Bultfontein *S. Africa* 28°18S 26°10E **56** D4
Bulukumba *Indonesia* 5°33S 120°11E **37** F6
Bulun *Russia* 70°37N 127°30E **29** B13
Bumba
 Dem. Rep. of the Congo 2°13N 22°30E **52** D4
Bumbah, Khalīj *Libya* 32°20N 23°15E **51** B10
Bumbiri I. *Tanzania* 1°40S 31°55E **54** C3
Bumhpa Bum *Burma* 26°51N 97°14E **41** F20
Bumi → *Zimbabwe* 17°0S 28°20E **55** F2
Buna *Kenya* 2°58N 39°30E **54** B4
Bunaken *Indonesia* 1°37N 124°46E **37** D6
Bunazi *Tanzania* 1°3S 31°23E **54** C3
Bunbury *Australia* 33°20S 115°35E **61** F2
Bunclody *Ireland* 52°39N 6°40W **10** D5
Buncrana *Ireland* 55°8N 7°27W **10** A4
Bundaberg *Australia* 24°54S 152°22E **63** C5
Bundey → *Australia* 21°46S 135°37E **62** C2
Bundi *India* 25°30N 75°35E **42** G6
Bundjalung △ *Australia* 29°16S 153°21E **63** D5
Bundoran *Ireland* 54°28N 8°16W **10** B3
Bung Kan *Thailand* 18°23N 103°37E **38** C4
Bungay *U.K.* 52°27N 1°28E **13** E9
Bungil Cr. → *Australia* 27°5S 149°5E **63** D4
Bungle Bungle = Purnululu △
 Australia 17°20S 128°20E **60** C4
Bungo-Suidō *Japan* 33°0N 132°15E **31** H6
Bungoma *Kenya* 0°34N 34°34E **54** B3
Bungotakada *Japan* 33°35N 131°25E **31** H5
Bungu *Tanzania* 7°35S 39°0E **54** D4
Bunia
 Dem. Rep. of the Congo 1°35N 30°20E **54** B3
Bunji *Pakistan* 35°45N 74°40E **43** B6
Bunkie *U.S.A.* 30°57N 92°11W **84** F8
Bunnell *U.S.A.* 29°28N 81°16W **85** G14
Bunya Mts. △ *Australia* 26°51S 151°34E **63** D5
Bunyola *Spain* 39°41N 2°42E **24** B9
Bunyu *Indonesia* 3°35N 117°50E **36** D5
Buol *Indonesia* 1°15N 121°32E **37** D6
Buon Brieng *Vietnam* 13°9N 108°12E **38** F7
Buon Ma Thuot *Vietnam* 12°40N 108°3E **38** F7
Buong Long *Cambodia* 13°44N 106°59E **38** F6
Buorkhaya, Mys
 Russia 71°50N 132°40E **29** B14
Buqayq *Si. Arabia* 26°0N 49°45E **45** E6
Bur Acaba = Buurhakaba
 Somali Rep. 3°12N 44°20E **47** G3
Bûr Safâga *Egypt* 26°43N 33°57E **44** E2
Bûr Sa'îd *Egypt* 31°16N 32°18E **51** B12
Bûr Sûdân *Sudan* 19°32N 37°9E **51** E13
Bura *Kenya* 1°4S 39°58E **54** C4
Burakin *Australia* 30°31S 117°10E **61** F2
Burao = Burco *Somali Rep.* 9°32N 45°32E **47** F4

Burāq *Syria* 33°11N 36°29E **46** B5
Buraydah *Si. Arabia* 26°20N 43°59E **44** E4
Burbank *U.S.A.* 34°12N 118°18W **79** L8
Burco *Somali Rep.* 9°32N 45°32E **47** F4
Burda *India* 25°50N 77°35E **42** G6
Burdekin → *Australia* 19°38S 147°25E **62** B4
Burdur *Turkey* 37°45N 30°17E **19** G5
Burdwan = Barddhaman
 India 23°14N 87°39E **43** H12
Bure *Ethiopia* 10°40N 37°4E **47** E2
Bure → *U.K.* 52°38N 1°43E **12** E9
Bureya → *Russia* 49°27N 129°30E **29** E13
Burford *Canada* 43°7N 80°27W **82** C4
Burgas *Bulgaria* 42°33N 27°29E **23** C12
Burgeo *Canada* 47°37N 57°38W **73** C8
Burgersdorp *S. Africa* 31°0S 26°20E **56** E4
Burgess, Mt. *Australia* 30°50S 121°5E **61** F3
Burghead *U.K.* 57°43N 3°30W **11** D5
Burgos *Spain* 42°21N 3°41W **21** A4
Burgsvik *Sweden* 57°3N 18°19E **9** H18
Burgundy = Bourgogne □
 France 47°0N 4°50E **20** C6
Burhaniye *Turkey* 39°30N 26°58E **23** E12
Burhanpur *India* 21°18N 76°14E **40** J10
Burhi Gandak → *India* 25°20N 86°37E **43** G12
Burhner → *India* 22°43N 80°31E **43** H9
Burias I. *Phil.* 12°55N 123°5E **37** B6
Burica, Pta. *Costa Rica* 8°3N 82°51W **88** E3
Burien *U.S.A.* 47°28N 122°20W **78** C4
Burigi, L. *Tanzania* 2°2S 31°22E **54** C3
Burigi △ *Tanzania* 2°20S 31°6E **54** C3
Burin *Canada* 47°1N 55°14W **73** C8
Buriram *Thailand* 15°0N 103°0E **38** E4
Burkburnett *U.S.A.* 34°6N 98°34W **84** D5
Burke → *Australia* 23°12S 139°33E **62** C2
Burke Chan. *Canada* 52°10N 127°30W **70** C3
Burketown *Australia* 17°45S 139°33E **62** B2
Burkina Faso ■ *Africa* 12°0N 1°0W **50** F5
Burk's Falls *Canada* 45°37N 79°24W **72** C4
Burleigh Falls *Canada* 44°33N 78°12W **82** B6
Burley *U.S.A.* 42°32N 113°48W **76** E7
Burlingame *U.S.A.* 37°35N 122°21W **78** H4
Burlington *Canada* 43°18N 79°45W **82** C5
Burlington *Colo.*,
 U.S.A. 39°18N 102°16W **76** G12
Burlington *Iowa*, *U.S.A.* 40°49N 91°14W **80** E8
Burlington *Kans.*, *U.S.A.* 38°12N 95°45W **80** F6
Burlington *N.C.*, *U.S.A.* 36°6N 79°26W **85** C15
Burlington *N.J.*, *U.S.A.* 40°4N 74°51W **83** F10
Burlington *Vt.*, *U.S.A.* 44°29N 73°12W **83** B11
Burlington *Wash.*,
 U.S.A. 48°28N 122°20W **78** B4
Burlington *Wis.*, *U.S.A.* 42°41N 88°17W **80** D9
Burma ■ *Asia* 21°0N 96°30E **41** J20
Burnaby I. *Canada* 52°25N 131°19W **70** C2
Burnet *U.S.A.* 30°45N 98°14W **84** F5
Burney *U.S.A.* 40°53N 121°40W **76** F3
Burnham *U.S.A.* 40°38N 77°34W **82** F7
Burnham-on-Sea *U.K.* 51°14N 3°0W **13** F5
Burnie *Australia* 41°4S 145°56E **63** G4
Burnley *U.K.* 53°47N 2°14W **12** D5
Burns *U.S.A.* 43°35N 119°3W **76** E4
Burns Junction *U.S.A.* 42°47N 117°51W **76** E5
Burns Lake *Canada* 54°14N 125°45W **70** C3
Burnside → *Canada* 66°51N 108°4W **68** D10
Burnside, L. *Australia* 25°22S 123°0E **61** E3
Burnsville *U.S.A.* 44°47N 93°17W **80** C7
Burnt River *Canada* 44°41N 78°42W **82** B6
Burntwood → *Canada* 56°8N 96°34W **71** B9
Burntwood L. *Canada* 55°22N 100°26W **71** B8
Burqān *Kuwait* 29°0N 47°57E **44** D5
Burqin *China* 47°43N 87°0E **32** B3
Burra *Australia* 33°40S 138°55E **63** E2
Burray *U.K.* 58°51N 2°54W **11** C6
Burren *Ireland* 53°9N 9°5W **10** C2
Burren △ *Ireland* 53°1N 8°58W **10** C3
Burren Junction
 Australia 30°7S 148°58E **63** E4
Burrinjuck, L. *Australia* 35°0S 148°36E **63** F4
Burro, Serranías del
 Mexico 28°56N 102°5W **86** B4
Burrow Hd. *U.K.* 54°41N 4°24W **11** G4
Burrum Coast △
 Australia 25°13S 152°36E **63** D5
Burruyacú *Argentina* 26°30S 64°40W **94** B3
Burry Port *U.K.* 51°41N 4°15W **13** F3
Bursa *Turkey* 40°15N 29°5E **23** D13
Burstall *Canada* 50°39N 109°54W **71** C7
Burton *Ohio*, *U.S.A.* 41°28N 81°8W **82** E3
Burton, L. *Canada* 54°45N 78°20W **72** B4
Burton S.C., *U.S.A.* 32°26N 80°43W **85** E14
Burton upon Trent *U.K.* 52°48N 1°38W **12** E6
Buru *Indonesia* 3°30S 126°30E **37** E7
Burûn, Râs *Egypt* 31°14N 33°7E **46** D2
Burundi ■ *Africa* 3°15S 30°0E **54** C3
Bururi *Burundi* 3°57S 29°37E **54** C2
Burutu *Nigeria* 5°20N 5°29E **50** G7
Burwell *U.S.A.* 41°47N 99°8W **80** E4
Burwick *U.K.* 58°45N 2°58W **11** C6
Bury *U.K.* 53°35N 2°17W **12** D5
Bury St. Edmunds *U.K.* 52°15N 0°43E **13** E8
Buryatia □ *Russia* 53°0N 110°0E **29** D12
Busan *S. Korea* 35°5N 129°0E **35** G15
Busango Swamp *Zambia* 14°15S 25°45E **55** E2
Busaso = Boosaaso
 Somali Rep. 11°12N 49°18E **47** E4
Buşayrah *Syria* 35°9N 40°26E **44** C4
Būshehr *Iran* 28°55N 50°55E **45** D6
Būshehr □ *Iran* 28°20N 51°45E **45** D6
Bushenyi *Uganda* 0°35S 30°10E **54** C3
Bushire = Būshehr *Iran* 28°55N 50°55E **45** D6
Businga
 Dem. Rep. of the Congo 3°16N 20°59E **52** D4
Buso → *India* 26°51N 89°35E **43** F13
Busra ash Shām *Syria* 32°30N 36°25E **46** C5
Busselton *Australia* 33°42S 115°15E **61** F2
Bussum *Neths.* 52°16N 5°10E **15** B5
Busto Arsízio *Italy* 45°37N 8°51E **20** D8
Busu Djanoa
 Dem. Rep. of the Congo 1°43N 21°23E **52** D4

Busuanga I. *Phil.* 12°10N 120°0E **37** B6
Busungbiu *Indonesia* 8°16S 114°58E **37** J17
Buta *Dem. Rep. of the Congo* 2°50N 24°53E **54** B1
Butare *Rwanda* 2°31S 29°52E **54** C2
Butaritari *Kiribati* 3°30N 174°0E **64** G9
Bute *U.K.* 55°48N 5°2W **11** F3
Bute Inlet *Canada* 50°40N 124°53W **70** C4
Butemba *Uganda* 1°9N 31°37E **54** B3
Butembo
 Dem. Rep. of the Congo 0°9N 29°18E **54** B2
Butere *Kenya* 0°13N 34°30E **54** B3
Butha Qi *China* 48°0N 122°32E **33** B7
Butiaba *Uganda* 1°50N 31°20E **54** B3
Butler *Mo.*, *U.S.A.* 38°16N 94°20W **80** F6
Butler *Pa.*, *U.S.A.* 40°52N 79°54W **82** F5
Buton *Indonesia* 5°0S 122°45E **37** F6
Butte *Mont.*, *U.S.A.* 46°0N 112°32W **76** C7
Butte *Nebr.*, *U.S.A.* 42°58N 98°51W **80** D4
Butte Creek → *U.S.A.* 39°12N 121°56W **78** F5
Butterworth = Gcuwa
 S. Africa 32°20S 28°11E **57** E4
Butterworth *Malaysia* 5°24N 100°23E **39** c
Buttevant *Ireland* 52°14N 8°40W **10** D3
Buttfield, Mt. *Australia* 24°45S 128°9E **61** D4
Button B. *Canada* 58°45N 94°23W **71** B10
Buttonwillow *U.S.A.* 35°24N 119°28W **79** K7
Butty Hd. *Australia* 33°54S 121°39E **61** F3
Butuan *Phil.* 8°57N 125°33E **37** C7
Butung = Buton *Indonesia* 5°0S 122°45E **37** F6
Buturlinovka *Russia* 50°50N 40°35E **19** D7
Buurhakaba *Somali Rep.* 3°12N 44°20E **47** G3
Buxa Duar *India* 27°45N 89°35E **43** F13
Buxar *India* 25°34N 83°58E **43** G10
Buxoro *Uzbekistan* 39°48N 64°25E **28** F7
Buxtehude *Germany* 53°28N 9°39E **16** B5
Buxton *U.K.* 53°16N 1°54W **12** D6
Buy *Russia* 58°28N 41°28E **18** C7
Buyant-Uhaa *Mongolia* 44°55N 110°11E **33** B6
Buyo, L. de *Ivory C.* 6°16N 7°10W **50** G4
Büyük Menderes →
 Turkey 37°28N 27°11E **23** F12
Büyükçekmece *Turkey* 41°2N 28°35E **23** D13
Büzău *Romania* 45°10N 26°50E **17** F14
Büzău → *Romania* 45°26N 27°44E **17** F14
Buzen *Japan* 33°35N 131°5E **31** H5
Buzi → *Mozam.* 19°50S 34°43E **55** F3
Büzméyin *Turkmenistan* 38°3N 58°12E **45** B8
Buzuluk *Russia* 52°48N 52°12E **18** D9
Buzzards Bay *U.S.A.* 41°45N 70°37W **83** E14
Bwana Mkubwe
 Dem. Rep. of the Congo 13°8S 28°38E **55** E2
Bwindi △ *Uganda* 1°2S 29°42E **54** C2
Byam Martin I.
 Canada 75°15N 104°15W **69** B11
Byarezina → *Belarus* 52°33N 30°14E **17** B16
Bydgoszcz *Poland* 53°10N 18°0E **17** B9
Byelorussia = Belarus ■
 Europe 53°30N 27°0E **17** B14
Byers *U.S.A.* 39°43N 104°14W **76** G11
Byesville *U.S.A.* 39°58N 81°32W **82** G3
Byfield △ *Australia* 22°52S 150°45E **62** C5
Bykhaw *Belarus* 53°31N 30°14E **17** B16
Bykhov = Bykhaw
 Belarus 53°31N 30°14E **17** B16
Bylas *U.S.A.* 33°8N 110°7W **77** K8
Bylot *Canada* 58°25N 94°8W **71** B10
Bylot I. *Canada* 73°13N 78°34W **69** C16
Byrd, C. *Antarctica* 69°38S 76°7W **5** C17
Byrock *Australia* 30°40S 146°27E **63** E4
Byron, C. *Australia* 28°43S 153°37E **63** D5
Byron Bay *Australia* 28°43S 153°37E **63** D5
Byrranga, Gory *Russia* 75°0N 100°0E **29** B11
Byrranga Mts. = Byrranga, Gory
 Russia 75°0N 100°0E **29** B11
Byske *Sweden* 64°57N 21°11E **8** D19
Byskeälven → *Sweden* 64°57N 21°13E **8** D19
Bytom *Poland* 50°25N 18°54E **17** C10
Bytów *Poland* 54°10N 17°30E **17** A9
Byumba *Rwanda* 1°35S 30°4E **54** C3

C

C.W. McConaughy, L.
 U.S.A. 41°14N 101°40W **80** E3
Ca → *Vietnam* 18°45N 105°45E **38** C5
Ca Mau *Vietnam* 9°7N 105°8E **39** H5
Ca Mau, Mui *Vietnam* 8°38N 104°44E **39** H5
Ca Na *Vietnam* 11°20N 108°54E **39** G7
Caacupé *Paraguay* 25°23S 57°5W **94** B4
Caaguazú □ *Paraguay* 26°5S 55°31W **95** B4
Caála *Angola* 12°46S 15°30E **53** G3
Caamaño Sd. *Canada* 52°55N 129°25W **70** C3
Caazapá *Paraguay* 26°8S 56°19W **94** B4
Caazapá □ *Paraguay* 26°10S 56°0W **95** B4
Caballeria, C. de *Spain* 40°5N 4°5E **24** A11
Cabanatuan *Phil.* 15°30N 120°58E **37** A6
Cabano *Canada* 47°40N 68°56W **73** C6
Cabazon *U.S.A.* 33°55N 116°47W **79** M10
Cabedelo *Brazil* 7°0S 34°50W **93** E12
Cabildo *Chile* 32°30S 71°5W **94** C1
Cabimas *Venezuela* 10°23N 71°25W **92** A4
Cabinda *Angola* 5°33S 12°11E **52** F2
Cabinda □ *Angola* 5°0S 12°30E **52** F2
Cabinet Mts. *U.S.A.* 48°10N 115°50W **76** B6
Cabo Blanco *Argentina* 47°15S 65°47W **96** F3
Cabo Frio *Brazil* 22°51S 42°3W **95** A7
Cabo Pantoja *Peru* 1°0S 75°10W **92** D3
Cabo San Lucas *Mexico* 22°53N 109°54W **86** C3
Cabo Verde = Cape Verde Is. ■
 Atl. Oc. 16°0N 24°0W **50** b
Cabonga, Réservoir
 Canada 47°20N 76°40W **72** C4
Cabool *U.S.A.* 37°7N 92°6W **80** G8
Cabooltura *Australia* 27°5S 152°58E **63** D5
Cabora Bassa Dam = Cahora
 Bassa, Lago de *Mozam.* 15°20S 32°50E **55** F3
Caborca *Mexico* 30°37N 112°6W **86** A2
Cabot, Mt. *U.S.A.* 44°30N 71°25W **83** B13

Cabot Hd. *Canada* 45°14N 81°17W **82 A3**
Cabot Str. *Canada* 47°15N 59°40W **73 C8**
Cabra *Spain* 37°30N 4°28W **21 D3**
Cabrera *Spain* 39°8N 2°57E **24 B9**
Cabri *Canada* 50°35N 108°25W **71 C7**
Cabriel → *Spain* 39°14N 1°3W **21 C5**
Caçador *Brazil* 26°47S 51°0W **95 B5**
Čačak *Serbia* 43°54N 20°20E **23 C9**
Caçapava do Sul *Brazil* 30°30S 53°30W **95 C5**
Cáceres *Brazil* 16°5S 57°40W **92 G7**
Cáceres *Spain* 39°26N 6°23W **21 C2**
Cache Bay *Canada* 46°22N 80°0W **72 C4**
Cache Cr. → *U.S.A.* 38°42N 121°42W **78 G5**
Cache Creek *Canada* 50°48N 121°19W **70 C4**
Cachi *Argentina* 25°5S 66°10W **94 B2**
Cachimbo, Serra do
 Brazil 9°30S 55°30W **93 E7**
Cachinal de la Sierra
 Chile 24°58S 69°32W **94 A2**
Cachoeira *Brazil* 12°30S 39°0W **93 F11**
Cachoeira do Sul *Brazil* 30°3S 52°53W **95 C5**
Cachoeiro de Itapemirim
 Brazil 20°51S 41°7W **95 A7**
Cacoal *Brazil* 11°32S 61°18W **92 F6**
Cacólo *Angola* 10°9S 19°21E **52 G3**
Caconda *Angola* 13°48S 15°8E **53 G3**
Caddo *U.S.A.* 34°7N 96°16W **84 D6**
Cader Idris *U.K.* 52°42N 3°53W **13 E4**
Cadereyta de Jiménez
 Mexico 25°36N 100°0W **86 B5**
Cadibarrawirracanna, L.
 Australia 28°52S 135°27E **63 D2**
Cadillac *U.S.A.* 44°15N 85°24W **81 C11**
Cadiz *Phil.* 10°57N 123°15E **37 B6**
Cádiz *Spain* 36°30N 6°20W **21 D2**
Cadiz *Calif., U.S.A.* 34°30N 115°28W **79 L11**
Cadiz *Ohio, U.S.A.* 40°22N 81°0W **82 F4**
Cádiz, G. de *Spain* 36°40N 7°0W **21 D2**
Cadiz L. *U.S.A.* 34°18N 115°24W **77 J6**
Cadney Park *Australia* 27°55S 134°3E **63 D1**
Cadomin *Canada* 53°2N 117°20W **70 C5**
Cadotte Lake *Canada* 56°26N 116°23W **70 B5**
Cadoux *Australia* 30°46S 117°7E **61 F2**
Caen *France* 49°10N 0°22W **20 B3**
Caernarfon *U.K.* 53°8N 4°16W **12 D3**
Caernarfon B. *U.K.* 53°4N 4°40W **12 D3**
Caernarvon = Caernarfon
 U.K. 53°8N 4°16W **12 D3**
Caerphilly *U.K.* 51°35N 3°13W **13 F4**
Caerphilly □ *U.K.* 51°37N 3°12W **13 F4**
Caesarea *Israel* 32°30N 34°53E **46 C3**
Caetité *Brazil* 13°50S 42°32W **93 F10**
Cafayate *Argentina* 26°2S 66°0W **94 B2**
Cafu *Angola* 16°30S 15°8E **56 B2**
Cagayan de Oro *Phil.* 8°30N 124°40E **37 C6**
Cagayan Is. *Phil.* 9°40N 121°16E **37 C5**
Cágliari *Italy* 39°13N 9°7E **22 E3**
Cágliari, G. di *Italy* 39°8N 9°11E **22 E3**
Caguán → *Colombia* 0°8S 74°18W **92 D4**
Caguas *Puerto Rico* 18°14N 66°2W **89 d**
Caha Mts. *Ireland* 51°45N 9°40W **10 E2**
Cahama *Angola* 16°17S 14°19E **56 B1**
Caher *Ireland* 52°22N 7°56W **10 D4**
Cahersiveen *Ireland* 51°56N 10°14W **10 E1**
Cahora Bassa, Lago de
 Mozam. 15°20S 32°50E **55 F3**
Cahore Pt. *Ireland* 52°33N 6°12W **10 D5**
Cahors *France* 44°27N 1°27E **20 D4**
Cahul *Moldova* 45°50N 28°15E **17 F15**
Cai Bau, Dao *Vietnam* 21°10N 107°27E **38 B6**
Cai Nuoc *Vietnam* 8°56N 105°1E **39 H5**
Caia *Mozam.* 17°51S 35°24E **55 F4**
Caianda *Angola* 11°2S 23°31E **55 E1**
Caibarién *Cuba* 22°30N 79°30W **88 B4**
Caicara *Venezuela* 7°38N 66°10W **92 B5**
Caicó *Brazil* 6°20S 37°0W **93 E11**
Caicos Is. *Turks & Caicos* 21°40N 71°40W **89 B5**
Caicos Passage *W. Indies* 22°45N 72°45W **89 B5**
Caiguna *Australia* 32°16S 125°29E **61 F4**
Caird Coast *Antarctica* 75°0S 25°0W **5 D1**
Cairn Gorm *U.K.* 57°7N 3°39W **11 D5**
Cairngorm Mts. *U.K.* 57°6N 3°42W **11 D5**
Cairngorms △ *U.K.* 57°10N 3°50N **11 D5**
Cairnryan *U.K.* 54°59N 5°1W **11 G3**
Cairns *Australia* 16°57S 145°45E **62 B4**
Cairns L. *Canada* 51°42N 94°30W **71 C10**
Cairo = El Qâhira *Egypt* 30°2N 31°13E **51 B12**
Cairo *Ga., U.S.A.* 30°52N 84°13W **85 F12**
Cairo *Ill., U.S.A.* 37°0N 89°11W **80 G9**
Cairo *N.Y., U.S.A.* 42°18N 74°0W **83 D10**
Caiseal = Cashel *Ireland* 52°33N 7°53W **10 D4**
Caisleán an Bharraigh = Castlebar
 Ireland 53°52N 9°18W **10 C2**
Caithness *U.K.* 58°25N 3°35W **11 C5**
Caithness, Ord of *U.K.* 58°8N 3°36W **11 C5**
Caja de Muertos, I.
 Puerto Rico 17°54N 66°32W **89 d**
Cajamarca *Peru* 7°5S 78°28W **92 E3**
Cajàzeiras *Brazil* 6°52S 38°30W **93 E11**
Cala d'Or *Spain* 39°23N 3°14E **24 B10**
Cala en Porter *Spain* 39°52N 4°8E **24 B11**
Cala Figuera *Spain* 39°20N 3°4E **24 B10**
Cala Figuera, C. de *Spain* 39°27N 2°31E **24 B9**
Cala Forcat *Spain* 40°0N 3°47E **24 B10**
Cala Major *Spain* 39°33N 2°37E **24 B9**
Cala Mezquida = Sa Mesquida
 Spain 39°55N 4°16E **24 B11**
Cala Millor *Spain* 39°35N 3°22E **24 B10**
Cala Murada *Spain* 39°27N 3°17E **24 B10**
Cala Ratjada *Spain* 39°43N 3°27E **24 B10**
Cala Santa Galdana
 Spain 39°56N 3°58E **24 B10**
Calabar *Nigeria* 4°57N 8°20E **50 H7**
Calabogie *Canada* 45°18N 76°43W **83 A8**
Calabozo *Venezuela* 9°0N 67°28W **92 B5**
Calàbria □ *Italy* 39°0N 16°30E **22 E7**
Calaforra *Spain* 42°18N 1°59W **21 A5**
Calais *France* 50°57N 1°56E **20 A4**
Calais *U.S.A.* 45°11N 67°17W **81 C20**

Calakmul ◠ *Mexico* 18°14N 89°48W **87 D7**
Calalaste, Cord. de
 Argentina 25°0S 67°0W **94 B2**
Calama *Brazil* 8°0S 62°50W **92 E6**
Calama *Chile* 22°30S 68°55W **94 A2**
Calamar *Colombia* 10°15N 74°55W **92 A4**
Calamian Group *Phil.* 11°50N 119°55E **37 B5**
Calamocha *Spain* 40°50N 1°17W **21 B5**
Calang *Indonesia* 4°37N 95°37E **36 D1**
Calanscio, Sarīr *Libya* 27°30N 21°30E **51 C10**
Calapan *Phil.* 13°25N 121°7E **37 B6**
Călăraşi *Romania* 44°12N 27°20E **17 F14**
Calatayud *Spain* 41°20N 1°40W **21 B5**
Calauag *Phil.* 13°55N 122°15E **37 B6**
Calavite, C. *Phil.* 13°26N 120°20E **37 B6**
Calbayog *Phil.* 12°4N 124°38E **37 B6**
Calca *Peru* 13°22S 72°0W **92 F4**
Calcasieu L. *U.S.A.* 29°55N 93°18W **84 G8**
Calcium *U.S.A.* 44°1N 75°50W **83 B9**
Calcutta = Kolkata
 India 22°34N 88°21E **43 H13**
Calcutta *U.S.A.* 40°40N 80°34W **82 F4**
Caldas da Rainha *Portugal* 39°24N 9°8W **21 C1**
Calder → *U.K.* 53°44N 1°22W **12 D6**
Caldera *Chile* 27°5S 70°55W **94 B1**
Caldera de Taburiente ◠
 Canary Is. 28°43N 17°52W **24 F2**
Caldwell *Idaho, U.S.A.* 43°40N 116°41W **76 E5**
Caldwell *Kans., U.S.A.* 37°2N 97°37W **80 G5**
Caldwell *Tex., U.S.A.* 30°32N 96°42W **84 F6**
Caledon *Canada* 43°51N 79°51W **82 C5**
Caledon *S. Africa* 34°14S 19°26E **56 E2**
Caledon → *S. Africa* 30°31S 26°5E **56 E4**
Caledon B. *Australia* 12°45S 137°0E **62 A2**
Caledonia *Canada* 43°7N 79°58W **82 C5**
Caledonia *U.S.A.* 42°58N 77°51W **82 D7**
Calemba *Angola* 16°0S 15°44E **56 B2**
Calen *Australia* 20°56S 148°48E **62 b**
Caletones *Chile* 34°6S 70°27W **94 C1**
Calexico *U.S.A.* 32°40N 115°30W **79 N11**
Calf of Man *I. of Man* 54°3N 4°48W **12 C3**
Calgary *Canada* 51°0N 114°10W **70 C6**
Calheta *Madeira* 32°44N 17°11W **24 D2**
Calhoun *U.S.A.* 34°30N 84°57W **85 D12**
Cali *Colombia* 3°25N 76°35W **92 C3**
Caliente *U.S.A.* 37°37N 114°31W **77 H6**
California *Mo., U.S.A.* 38°38N 92°34W **80 F7**
California *Pa., U.S.A.* 40°4N 79°54W **82 F5**
California □ *U.S.A.* 37°30N 119°30W **78 H7**
California, Baja, T.N. = Baja
 California □ *Mexico* 30°0N 115°0W **86 B2**
California, Baja, T.S. = Baja
 California Sur □
 Mexico 25°50N 111°50W **86 B2**
California, G. de *Mexico* 27°0N 111°0W **86 B2**
California City *U.S.A.* 35°10N 117°55W **79 K9**
California Hot Springs
 U.S.A. 35°51N 118°41W **79 K8**
Calilegua △ *Argentina* 25°36S 64°50W **94 B3**
Calingasta *Argentina* 31°15S 69°30W **94 C2**
Calipatria *U.S.A.* 33°8N 115°31W **79 M11**
Calistoga *U.S.A.* 38°35N 122°35W **78 G4**
Callabonna, L. *Australia* 29°40S 140°5E **63 D3**
Callan *Ireland* 52°32N 7°24W **10 D4**
Callander *U.K.* 56°15N 4°13W **11 E4**
Callao *Peru* 12°3S 77°8W **92 F3**
Callicoon *U.S.A.* 41°46N 75°3W **83 E9**
Calling Lake *Canada* 55°15N 113°12W **70 B6**
Calliope *Australia* 24°0S 151°16E **62 C5**
Calma, Costa de la *Spain* 39°28N 2°26E **24 B9**
Calne *U.K.* 51°26N 2°0W **13 F6**
Calola *Angola* 16°25S 17°48E **56 B2**
Caloundra *Australia* 26°45S 153°10E **63 D5**
Calpella *U.S.A.* 39°14N 123°12W **78 F3**
Calpine *U.S.A.* 39°40N 120°27W **78 F6**
Calstock *Canada* 49°47N 84°9W **72 C3**
Caltagirone *Italy* 37°14N 14°31E **22 F6**
Caltanissetta *Italy* 37°29N 14°4E **22 F6**
Calulo *Angola* 10°1S 14°56E **52 G2**
Calvert → *Australia* 16°17S 137°44E **62 B2**
Calvert I. *Canada* 51°30N 128°0W **70 C3**
Calvert Ra. *Australia* 24°0S 122°30E **60 D3**
Calvi *France* 42°34N 8°45E **20 E8**
Calvià *Spain* 39°34N 2°31E **24 B9**
Calvillo *Mexico* 21°51N 102°43W **86 C4**
Calvinia *S. Africa* 31°28S 19°45E **56 E2**
Calwa *U.S.A.* 36°42N 119°46W **78 J7**
Cam → *U.K.* 52°21N 0°16E **13 E8**
Cam Lam *Vietnam* 11°54N 109°10E **39 G7**
Cam Pha *Vietnam* 21°7N 107°18E **38 B6**
Cam Ranh *Vietnam* 11°54N 109°12E **39 G7**
Cam Xuyen *Vietnam* 18°15N 106°0E **38 C6**
Camabatela *Angola* 8°20S 15°26E **52 F3**
Camacha *Madeira* 32°41N 16°49W **24 D3**
Camacupa *Angola* 11°58S 17°22E **53 G3**
Camagüey *Cuba* 21°20N 77°55W **88 B4**
Camaná *Peru* 16°30S 72°50W **92 G4**
Camanche Res. *U.S.A.* 38°14N 121°1W **78 G6**
Camaquã *Brazil* 30°51S 51°49W **95 C5**
Camaquã → *Brazil* 31°17S 51°47W **95 C5**
Câmara de Lobos
 Madeira 32°39N 16°59W **24 D3**
Camargo *Mexico* 26°19N 98°50W **87 B5**
Camarillo *U.S.A.* 34°13N 119°2W **79 L7**
Camarón, C. *Honduras* 16°0N 85°5W **88 C2**
Camarones *Argentina* 44°50S 65°40W **96 E3**
Camas *U.S.A.* 45°35N 122°24W **78 E4**
Camas Valley *U.S.A.* 43°2N 123°40W **76 E2**
Camballin *Australia* 17°59S 124°12E **60 C3**
Cambará *Brazil* 23°2S 50°5W **95 A6**
Cambay = Khambhat
 India 22°23N 72°33E **42 H5**
Cambay, G. of = Khambhat, G. of
 India 20°45N 72°30E **40 J8**
Cambodia ■ *Asia* 12°15N 105°0E **38 F5**
Camborne *U.K.* 50°12N 5°19W **13 G2**
Cambrai *France* 50°11N 3°14E **20 A5**

Cambria *U.S.A.* 35°34N 121°5W **78 K5**
Cambrian Mts. *U.K.* 52°3N 3°57W **13 E4**
Cambridge *Canada* 43°23N 80°15W **82 C4**
Cambridge *Jamaica* 18°18N 77°54W **88 a**
Cambridge *N.Z.* 37°54S 175°29E **59 B5**
Cambridge *U.K.* 52°12N 0°8E **13 E8**
Cambridge *Mass., U.S.A.* 42°23N 71°7W **83 D13**
Cambridge *Minn., U.S.A.* 45°34N 93°13W **80 C7**
Cambridge *N.Y., U.S.A.* 43°2N 73°22W **83 C11**
Cambridge *Nebr..*
 U.S.A. 40°17N 100°10W **80 E3**
Cambridge *Ohio, U.S.A.* 40°2N 81°35W **82 F3**
Cambridge Bay *Canada* 69°10N 105°0W **68 D11**
Cambridge G. *Australia* 14°55S 128°15E **60 B4**
Cambridge Springs
 U.S.A. 41°48N 80°4W **82 E4**
Cambridgeshire □ *U.K.* 52°25N 0°7W **13 E7**
Cambuci *Brazil* 21°35S 41°55W **95 A7**
Cambundi-Catembo
 Angola 10°10S 17°35E **52 G3**
Camden *Australia* 34°1S 150°43E **63 B5**
Camden *Ala., U.S.A.* 31°59N 87°17W **85 F11**
Camden *Ark., U.S.A.* 33°35N 92°50W **84 E8**
Camden *Maine, U.S.A.* 44°13N 69°4W **81 C19**
Camden *N.J., U.S.A.* 39°55N 75°7W **83 G9**
Camden *N.Y., U.S.A.* 43°20N 75°45W **83 C9**
Camden *S.C., U.S.A.* 34°16N 80°36W **85 D14**
Camden Sd. *Australia* 15°27S 124°25E **60 C3**
Camdenton *U.S.A.* 38°1N 92°45W **80 F7**
Camelford *U.K.* 50°37N 4°42W **13 G3**
Cameron *Ariz., U.S.A.* 35°53N 111°25W **77 J8**
Cameron *La., U.S.A.* 29°48N 93°20W **84 G8**
Cameron *Mo., U.S.A.* 39°44N 94°14W **80 F7**
Cameron *Tex., U.S.A.* 30°51N 96°59W **84 F6**
Cameron Highlands
 Malaysia 4°27N 101°22E **39 K3**
Cameron Hills *Canada* 59°48N 118°0W **70 B5**
Cameroon ■ *Africa* 6°0N 12°30E **51 G7**
Cameroun, Mt. *Cameroon* 4°13N 9°10E **52 D1**
Cametá *Brazil* 2°12S 49°30W **93 D9**
Camiguin I. *Phil.* 18°56N 121°55E **37 C6**
Camilla *U.S.A.* 31°14N 84°12W **85 F12**
Caminha *Portugal* 41°50N 8°50W **21 B1**
Camino *U.S.A.* 38°44N 120°41W **78 G6**
Cammal *U.S.A.* 41°24N 77°28W **82 E7**
Camocim *Brazil* 2°55S 40°50W **93 D10**
Camooweal *Australia* 19°56S 138°7E **62 B2**
Camooweal Caves △
 Australia 20°1S 138°11E **62 C2**
Camopi *Fr. Guiana* 3°12N 52°17W **93 C8**
Camp Hill *U.S.A.* 40°14N 76°55W **82 F8**
Camp Nelson *U.S.A.* 36°8N 118°39W **79 J8**
Camp Pendleton
 U.S.A. 33°13N 117°24W **79 M9**
Camp Verde *U.S.A.* 34°34N 111°51W **77 J8**
Camp Wood *U.S.A.* 29°40N 100°1W **84 G4**
Campana *Argentina* 34°10S 58°55W **94 C4**
Campana, I. *Chile* 48°20S 75°20W **96 F1**
Campanário *Madeira* 32°39N 17°2W **24 D2**
Campanet *Spain* 39°46N 2°58E **24 B9**
Campánia □ *Italy* 41°0N 14°30E **22 D6**
Campbell *S. Africa* 28°48S 23°44E **56 D3**
Campbell *Calif., U.S.A.* 37°17N 121°57W **78 H5**
Campbell *Ohio, U.S.A.* 41°5N 80°37W **82 E4**
Campbell I. *Pac. Oc.* 52°30S 169°0E **64 N8**
Campbell L. *Canada* 63°14N 106°55W **71 A7**
Campbell Plateau *S. Ocean* 50°0S 170°0E **5 A11**
Campbell River *Canada* 50°5N 125°20W **70 C3**
Campbellford *Canada* 44°18N 77°48W **82 B7**
Campbellpur *Pakistan* 33°46N 72°26E **42 C5**
Campbellsville *U.S.A.* 37°21N 85°20W **81 G11**
Campbellton *Canada* 47°57N 66°43W **73 C6**
Campbelltown *Australia* 34°4S 150°49E **63 B5**
Campbeltown *U.K.* 55°26N 5°36W **11 F3**
Campeche *Mexico* 19°51N 90°32W **87 D6**
Campeche □ *Mexico* 19°0N 90°30W **87 D6**
Campeche, Golfo de
 Mexico 19°30N 93°0W **87 D6**
Camperdown *Australia* 38°14S 143°9E **63 F3**
Camperville *Canada* 51°59N 100°9W **71 C8**
Câmpina *Romania* 45°10N 25°45E **17 F13**
Campina Grande *Brazil* 7°20S 35°47W **93 E11**
Campinas *Brazil* 22°50S 47°0W **95 A6**
Campo Grande *Brazil* 20°25S 54°40W **93 H8**
Campo Maior *Brazil* 4°50S 42°12W **93 D10**
Campo Mourão *Brazil* 24°3S 52°22W **95 A5**
Campobasso *Italy* 41°34N 14°39E **22 D6**
Campos *Brazil* 21°50S 41°20W **95 A7**
Campos Belos *Brazil* 13°10S 47°3W **93 F9**
Campos Novos *Brazil* 27°21S 51°50W **95 B5**
Camptonville *U.S.A.* 39°27N 121°3W **78 F5**
Camptown *U.S.A.* 41°44N 76°14W **83 E8**
Câmpulung *Romania* 45°17N 25°3E **17 F13**
Camrose *Canada* 53°0N 112°50W **70 C6**
Camsell Portage
 Canada 59°37N 109°15W **71 B7**
Çan *Turkey* 40°2N 27°3E **23 D12**
Can Clavo *Spain* 38°57N 1°27E **24 C7**
Can Creu *Spain* 38°58N 1°28E **24 C7**
Can Gio *Vietnam* 10°25N 106°58E **39 G6**
Can Pastilla *Spain* 39°32N 2°42E **24 B9**
Can Tho *Vietnam* 10°2N 105°46E **39 G5**
Canaan *U.S.A.* 42°2N 73°20W **83 D11**
Canada ■ *N. Amer.* 60°0N 100°0W **68 C11**
Canada Abyssal Plain
 Arctic 80°0N 140°0W **4 B18**
Canada Basin *Arctic* 80°0N 145°0W **4 B18**
Canadian *U.S.A.* 35°55N 100°23W **84 D4**
Canadian → *U.S.A.* 35°28N 95°3W **84 D7**
Canadian Shield *Canada* 53°0N 75°0W **66 D12**
Canajoharie *U.S.A.* 42°54N 74°35W **83 D10**
Çanakkale *Turkey* 40°8N 26°24E **23 D12**
Çanakkale Boğazı
 Turkey 40°17N 26°32E **23 D12**
Canal Flats *Canada* 50°10N 115°48W **70 C5**
Canalejas *Argentina* 35°15S 66°34W **94 D2**

Canals *Argentina* 33°35S 62°53W **94 C3**
Canandaigua *U.S.A.* 42°54N 77°17W **82 D7**
Canandaigua L. *U.S.A.* 42°47N 77°19W **82 D7**
Cananea *Mexico* 31°0N 110°18W **86 A2**
Canarias, Is. *Atl. Oc.* 28°30N 16°0W **24 F4**
Canaries *St. Lucia* 13°55N 61°4W **89 f**
Canarreos, Arch. de los
 Cuba 21°35N 81°40W **88 B3**
Canary Is. = Canarias, Is.
 Atl. Oc. 28°30N 16°0W **24 F4**
Canaseraga *U.S.A.* 42°27N 77°45W **82 D7**
Canatlán *Mexico* 24°31N 104°47W **86 C4**
Canaveral, C. *U.S.A.* 28°27N 80°32W **85 G14**
Canaveral *U.S.A.* 28°28N 80°34W **85 G14**
Canavieiras *Brazil* 15°39S 39°0W **93 G11**
Canberra *Australia* 35°15S 149°8E **63 F4**
Canby *Calif., U.S.A.* 41°27N 120°52W **76 F3**
Canby *Minn., U.S.A.* 44°43N 96°16W **80 C5**
Canby *Oreg., U.S.A.* 45°16N 122°42W **78 E4**
Cancún *Mexico* 21°8N 86°44W **87 C7**
Candelaria *Argentina* 27°29S 55°44W **95 B4**
Candelaria *Canary Is.* 28°22N 16°22W **24 F3**
Candelo *Australia* 36°47S 149°43E **63 F4**
Candi Dasa *Indonesia* 8°30S 115°34E **37 J18**
Candia = Iraklio *Greece* 35°20N 25°12E **25 D7**
Candle L. *Canada* 53°50N 105°18W **71 C7**
Candlemas I. *Antarctica* 57°3S 26°40W **5 B1**
Cando *U.S.A.* 48°32N 99°12W **80 A4**
Canea = Chania *Greece* 35°30N 24°4E **25 D6**
Canelones *Uruguay* 34°32S 56°17W **95 C4**
Cangas del Narcea *Spain* 43°10N 6°32W **21 A2**
Canguaretama *Brazil* 6°20S 35°5W **93 E11**
Canguçu *Brazil* 31°22S 52°43W **95 C5**
Canguçu, Serra do
 Brazil 31°20S 52°40W **95 C5**
Cangzhou *China* 38°19N 116°52E **34 E9**
Caniapiscau → *Canada* 56°40N 69°30W **73 A6**
Caniapiscau, L. *Canada* 54°10N 69°55W **73 B6**
Canicattì *Italy* 37°21N 13°51E **22 F5**
Canim Lake *Canada* 51°47N 120°54W **70 C4**
Canindeyu □ *Paraguay* 24°10S 55°0W **95 A5**
Canisteo *U.S.A.* 42°16N 77°36W **82 D7**
Canisteo → *U.S.A.* 42°7N 77°8W **82 D7**
Cañitas de Felipe Pescador
 Mexico 23°36N 102°43W **86 C4**
Çankırı *Turkey* 40°40N 33°37E **19 F5**
Cankuzo *Burundi* 3°10S 30°31E **54 C3**
Canmore *Canada* 51°7N 115°18W **70 C5**
Cann River *Australia* 37°35S 149°7E **63 F4**
Canna *U.K.* 57°3N 6°33W **11 D2**
Cannanore *India* 11°53N 75°27E **40 P9**
Cannes *France* 43°32N 7°1E **20 E7**
Canning Town = Port Canning
 India 22°23N 88°40E **43 H13**
Cannington *Canada* 44°20N 79°2W **82 B5**
Cannock *U.K.* 52°41N 2°1W **13 E5**
Cannonball → *U.S.A.* 46°26N 100°35W **80 B3**
Cannondale Mt.
 Australia 25°13S 148°57E **62 D4**
Cannonsville Res. *U.S.A.* 42°4N 75°22W **83 D9**
Cannonvale *Australia* 20°17S 148°43E **62 b**
Canoas *Brazil* 29°56S 51°11W **95 B5**
Canoe L. *Canada* 55°10N 108°15W **71 B7**
Cañon City *U.S.A.* 38°27N 105°14W **76 G11**
Cañon de Río Blanco △
 Mexico 18°43N 97°15W **87 D5**
Cañón del Sumidero △
 Mexico 19°22N 96°24W **87 D5**
Canonniers Pt. *Mauritius* 20°2S 57°32E **53 d**
Canora *Canada* 51°40N 102°30W **71 C8**
Canowindra *Australia* 33°35S 148°38E **63 E4**
Canso *Canada* 45°20N 61°0W **73 C7**
Cantabria □ *Spain* 43°10N 4°0W **21 A4**
Cantabrian Mts. = Cantábrica,
 Cordillera *Spain* 43°0N 5°10W **21 A3**
Cantábrica, Cordillera
 Spain 43°0N 5°10W **21 A3**
Cantal, Plomb du *France* 45°3N 2°45E **20 D5**
Cantanhede *Portugal* 40°20N 8°36W **21 B1**
Canterbury *Australia* 25°23S 141°53E **62 D3**
Canterbury *U.K.* 51°16N 1°6E **13 F9**
Canterbury Bight *N.Z.* 44°16S 171°55E **59 F3**
Canterbury Plains *N.Z.* 43°55S 171°22E **59 E3**
Cantil *U.S.A.* 35°18N 117°58W **79 K9**
Canton = Guangzhou
 China 23°6N 113°13E **33 D6**
Canton *Ga., U.S.A.* 34°14N 84°29W **85 D12**
Canton *Ill., U.S.A.* 40°33N 90°2W **80 E8**
Canton *Miss., U.S.A.* 32°37N 90°2W **85 E9**
Canton *Mo., U.S.A.* 40°8N 91°32W **80 E8**
Canton *N.Y., U.S.A.* 44°36N 75°10W **83 B9**
Canton *Ohio, U.S.A.* 40°48N 81°23W **82 F3**
Canton *Pa., U.S.A.* 41°39N 76°51W **82 E8**
Canton *S. Dak., U.S.A.* 43°18N 96°35W **80 D6**
Canton L. *U.S.A.* 36°6N 98°35W **84 C5**
Canudos *Brazil* 7°13S 58°5W **92 E7**
Canumã → *Brazil* 3°55S 59°10W **92 D7**
Canutama *Brazil* 6°30S 64°20W **92 E6**
Canutillo *U.S.A.* 31°55N 106°36W **84 A1**
Canvey *U.K.* 51°31N 0°37E **13 F8**
Canyon *U.S.A.* 34°59N 101°55W **84 D4**
Canyon De Chelly △
 U.S.A. 36°10N 109°20W **77 H9**
Canyonlands △ *U.S.A.* 38°15N 110°0W **77 G9**
Canyons of the Ancients ◠
 U.S.A. 37°30N 108°55W **77 H9**
Canyonville *U.S.A.* 42°56N 123°17W **76 E2**
Cao Bang *Vietnam* 22°40N 106°15E **38 A6**
Cao He → *China* 40°10N 124°32E **35 D13**
Cao Lanh *Vietnam* 10°27N 105°38E **39 G5**
Cao Xian *China* 34°50N 115°35E **34 G8**
Cap-aux-Meules *Canada* 47°23N 61°52W **73 C7**
Cap-Chat *Canada* 49°6N 66°40W **73 C6**
Cap-de-la-Madeleine
 Canada 46°22N 72°31W **72 C5**
Cap-Haïtien *Haiti* 19°40N 72°20W **89 C5**
Cap Pt. *St. Lucia* 14°7N 60°57W **89 f**
Capac *U.S.A.* 43°1N 82°56W **82 C2**
Capanaparo → *Venezuela* 7°1N 67°7W **92 B5**

Cape → *Australia* 20°59S 146°51E **62 C4**
Cape Arid △ *Australia* 33°58S 123°13E **61 F3**
Cape Barren I. *Australia* 40°25S 148°15E **63 G4**
Cape Breton Highlands
 Canada 46°50N 60°40W **73 C7**
Cape Breton I. *Canada* 46°0N 60°30W **73 C7**
Cape Charles *U.S.A.* 37°16N 76°1W **81 G15**
Cape Coast *Ghana* 5°5N 1°15W **50 G5**
Cape Cod △ *U.S.A.* 41°56N 70°6W **81 E18**
Cape Coral *U.S.A.* 26°33N 81°57W **85 H14**
Cape Crawford *Australia* 16°41S 135°43E **62 B2**
Cape Dorset = Kinngait
 Canada 64°14N 76°32W **69 E16**
Cape Fear → *U.S.A.* 33°53N 78°1W **85 D15**
Cape Girardeau *U.S.A.* 37°19N 89°32W **80 G9**
Cape Hatteras △
 U.S.A. 35°30N 75°28W **85 D17**
Cape Hillsborough △
 Australia 20°54S 149°2E **62 b**
Cape Le Grand △
 Australia 33°54S 122°26E **61 F3**
Cape Lookout ◠
 U.S.A. 35°45N 76°25W **85 D16**
Cape May *U.S.A.* 38°56N 74°56W **81 F16**
Cape May Point *U.S.A.* 38°56N 74°58W **81 F16**
Cape Melville △
 Australia 14°26S 144°28E **62 A3**
Cape Range △ *Australia* 22°3S 114°0E **60 D1**
Cape St. George *Canada* 48°28N 59°14W **73 C8**
Cape Tormentine *Canada* 46°8N 63°47W **73 C7**
Cape Town *S. Africa* 33°55S 18°22E **56 E2**
Cape Upstart △
 Australia 19°45S 147°48E **62 B4**
Cape Verde Is. ■ *Atl. Oc.* 16°0N 24°0W **50 b**
Cape Vincent *U.S.A.* 44°8N 76°20W **83 B8**
Cape York Peninsula
 Australia 12°0S 142°30E **62 A3**
Capela *Brazil* 10°30S 37°0W **93 F11**
Capella *Australia* 23°2S 148°1E **62 C4**
Capesterre-Belle-Eau
 Guadeloupe 16°4N 61°36W **88 b**
Capesterre-de-Marie-Galante
 Guadeloupe 15°53N 61°14W **88 b**
Capim → *Brazil* 1°40S 47°47W **93 D9**
Capitán *U.S.A.* 33°35N 105°35W **77 K11**
Capitán Arturo Prat
 Antarctica 63°0S 61°0W **5 C17**
Capitol Reef △ *U.S.A.* 38°15N 111°10W **77 G8**
Capitola *U.S.A.* 36°59N 121°57W **78 J5**
Capoche → *Mozam.* 15°35S 33°0E **55 F3**
Capraia *Italy* 43°2N 9°50E **20 E8**
Capreol *Canada* 46°43N 80°56W **72 C3**
Capri *Italy* 40°33N 14°14E **22 D6**
Capricorn Coast
 Australia 23°16S 150°49E **62 C5**
Capricorn Group
 Australia 23°30S 151°55E **62 C5**
Capricorn Ra. *Australia* 23°20S 116°50E **60 D2**
Caprivi Game △ *Namibia* 17°55S 22°37E **56 B3**
Caprivi Strip *Namibia* 18°0S 23°0E **56 B3**
Captains Flat *Australia* 35°35S 149°27E **63 F4**
Capulin Volcano ◠
 U.S.A. 36°47N 103°58W **84 C3**
Caquetá → *Colombia* 1°15S 69°15W **92 D5**
Caracal *Romania* 44°8N 24°22E **17 F13**
Caracas *Venezuela* 10°30N 66°55W **92 A5**
Caracol *Belize* 16°45N 89°6W **88 C2**
Caracol *Mato Grosso do Sul,*
 Brazil 22°18S 57°1W **94 A4**
Caracol *Piauí, Brazil* 9°15S 43°22W **93 E10**
Carajás *Brazil* 6°5S 50°23W **93 E8**
Carajás, Serra dos *Brazil* 6°0S 51°30W **93 E8**
Carangola *Brazil* 20°44S 42°5W **95 A7**
Caransebeş *Romania* 45°28N 22°18E **17 F12**
Caraquet *Canada* 47°48N 64°57W **73 C6**
Caratasca, L. de
 Honduras 15°20N 83°40W **88 C3**
Caratinga *Brazil* 19°50S 42°10W **93 G10**
Caraúbas *Brazil* 5°43S 37°33W **93 E11**
Caravaca de la Cruz *Spain* 38°8N 1°52W **21 C5**
Caravelas *Brazil* 17°45S 39°15W **93 G11**
Caraveli *Peru* 15°45S 73°25W **92 G4**
Caravelle, Presqu'île de la
 Martinique 14°46N 60°48W **88 c**
Caraz *Peru* 9°3S 77°47W **92 E3**
Carazinho *Brazil* 28°16S 52°46W **95 B5**
Carballo *Spain* 43°13N 8°41W **21 A1**
Carberry *Canada* 49°50N 99°25W **71 D9**
Carbó *Mexico* 29°42N 110°58W **86 B2**
Carbón, L. del *Argentina* 49°35S 68°21W **90 G3**
Carbonara, C. *Italy* 39°6N 9°31E **22 E3**
Carbondale *Colo.,*
 U.S.A. 39°24N 107°13W **76 G10**
Carbondale *Ill., U.S.A.* 37°44N 89°13W **80 G9**
Carbondale *Pa., U.S.A.* 41°35N 75°30W **83 E9**
Carbonear *Canada* 47°42N 53°13W **73 C9**
Carbónia *Italy* 39°10N 8°30E **22 E3**
Carcajou *Canada* 57°47N 117°6W **70 B5**
Carcarana → *Argentina* 32°27S 60°48W **94 C3**
Carcasse, C. *Haiti* 18°30N 74°28W **89 C5**
Carcassonne *France* 43°13N 2°20E **20 E5**
Carcross *Canada* 60°13N 134°45W **70 A2**
Cardamon Hills *India* 9°30N 77°15E **40 Q10**
Cardamon Mts. = Kravanh,
 Chuor Phnum
 Cambodia 12°0N 103°32E **39 G4**
Cárdenas *Cuba* 23°0N 81°30W **88 B3**
Cárdenas *San Luis Potosí,*
 Mexico 22°0N 99°38W **87 C5**
Cárdenas *Tabasco,*
 Mexico 17°59N 93°22W **87 D6**
Cardiff *U.K.* 51°29N 3°10W **13 F4**
Cardiff □ *U.K.* 51°31N 3°12W **13 F4**
Cardiff-by-the-Sea
 U.S.A. 33°1N 117°17W **79 M9**
Cardigan *U.K.* 52°5N 4°40W **13 E3**
Cardigan B. *U.K.* 52°30N 4°30W **13 E3**
Cardinal *Canada* 44°47N 75°23W **83 B9**
Cardona *Uruguay* 33°53S 57°18W **94 C4**

Cardoso, Ilha do Brazil 25°8S 47°58W **95 B5**
Cardston Canada 49°15N 113°20W **70 D6**
Cardwell Australia 18°14S 146°2E **62 B4**
Careen L. Canada 57°0N 108°11W **71 B7**
Carei Romania 47°40N 22°29E **17 E12**
Careme = Ciremay Indonesia 6°55S 108°27E **37 G13**
Carey U.S.A. 43°19N 113°57W **76 E7**
Carey, L. Australia 29°0S 122°15E **61 E3**
Carey L. Canada 62°12N 102°55W **71 A8**
Carhué Argentina 37°10S 62°50W **94 D3**
Caria Turkey 37°20N 28°10E **23 F13**
Cariacica Brazil 20°16S 40°25W **93 H10**
Caribbean Sea W. Indies 15°0N 75°0W **89 D5**
Cariboo Mts. Canada 53°0N 121°0W **70 C4**
Caribou U.S.A. 46°52N 68°1W **81 B19**
Caribou → Man., Canada 59°20N 94°44W **71 B10**
Caribou → N.W.T., Canada 61°27N 125°45W **70 A3**
Caribou I. Canada 47°22N 85°49W **72 C2**
Caribou Is. Canada 61°55N 113°15W **70 A6**
Caribou L. Man., Canada 59°21N 96°10W **71 B9**
Caribou L. Ont., Canada 50°25N 89°5W **72 B2**
Caribou Mts. Canada 59°12N 115°40W **70 B5**
Caribou River △ Canada 59°35N 96°35W **71 B9**
Carichíc Mexico 27°56N 107°3W **86 B3**
Carinda Australia 30°28S 147°41E **63 E4**
Carinhanha Brazil 14°15S 44°46W **93 F10**
Carinhanha → Brazil 14°20S 43°47W **93 F10**
Carinthia = Kärnten □ Austria 46°52N 13°30E **16 E8**
Caripito Venezuela 10°8N 63°6W **92 A6**
Carleton, Mt. Canada 47°23N 66°53W **73 C6**
Carleton Place Canada 45°8N 76°9W **83 A8**
Carletonville S. Africa 26°23S 27°22E **56 D4**
Carlin U.S.A. 40°43N 116°7W **76 F5**
Carlingford L. U.K. 54°3N 6°9W **10 B5**
Carlinville U.S.A. 39°17N 89°53W **80 F9**
Carlisle U.K. 54°54N 2°56W **12 C5**
Carlisle U.S.A. 40°12N 77°12W **82 F7**
Carlisle B. Barbados 13°5N 59°37W **89 g**
Carlisle I. Australia 20°49S 149°18E **62 b**
Carlos Casares Argentina 35°32S 61°20W **94 D3**
Carlos Tejedor Argentina 35°25S 62°25W **94 D3**
Carlow Ireland 52°50N 6°56W **10 D5**
Carlow □ Ireland 52°43N 6°50W **10 D5**
Carlsbad Calif., U.S.A. 33°10N 117°21W **79 M9**
Carlsbad N. Mex., U.S.A. 32°25N 104°14W **77 K11**
Carlsbad Caverns △ U.S.A. 32°10N 104°35W **77 K11**
Carluke U.K. 55°45N 3°50W **11 F5**
Carlyle Canada 49°40N 102°20W **71 D8**
Carmacks Canada 62°5N 136°16W **68 E4**
Carman Canada 49°30N 98°0W **71 D9**
Carmarthen U.K. 51°52N 4°19W **13 F3**
Carmarthen B. U.K. 51°40N 4°30W **13 F3**
Carmarthenshire □ U.K. 51°55N 4°13W **13 F3**
Carmaux France 44°3N 2°10E **20 D5**
Carmel U.S.A. 41°26N 73°41W **83 E11**
Carmel-by-the-Sea U.S.A. 36°33N 121°55W **78 J5**
Carmel Valley U.S.A. 36°29N 121°43W **78 J5**
Carmelo Uruguay 34°0S 58°20W **94 C4**
Carmen Paraguay 27°13S 56°12W **95 B4**
Carmen → Mexico 30°42N 106°29W **86 A3**
Carmen, I. Mexico 25°57N 111°12W **86 B2**
Carmen de Patagones Argentina 40°50S 63°0W **96 E4**
Carmensa Argentina 35°15S 67°40W **94 D2**
Carmi Canada 49°36N 119°8W **70 D5**
Carmi U.S.A. 38°5N 88°10W **80 F9**
Carmichael U.S.A. 38°38N 121°19W **78 G5**
Carmila Australia 21°55S 149°24E **62 C4**
Carmona Costa Rica 10°0N 85°15W **88 E2**
Carmona Spain 37°28N 5°42W **21 D3**
Carn Ban U.K. 57°7N 4°15W **11 D4**
Carn Eige U.K. 57°17N 5°8W **11 D3**
Carnamah Australia 29°41S 115°53E **61 E2**
Carnarvon Australia 24°51S 113°42E **61 D1**
Carnarvon S. Africa 30°56S 22°8E **56 E3**
Carnarvon △ Australia 24°54S 148°2E **62 C4**
Carnarvon Ra. Queens., Australia 25°15S 148°30E **62 D4**
Carnarvon Ra. W. Austral., Australia 25°20S 120°45E **61 E3**
Carnation U.S.A. 47°39N 121°55W **78 C5**
Carncastle U.K. 54°54N 5°53W **10 B6**
Carndonagh Ireland 55°16N 7°15W **10 A4**
Carnduff Canada 49°10N 101°50W **71 D8**
Carnegie U.S.A. 40°24N 80°5W **82 F4**
Carnegie, L. Australia 26°5S 122°30E **61 E3**
Carnegie Ridge Pac. Oc. 1°0S 87°0W **65 H19**
Carnic Alps = Karnische Alpen Europe 46°36N 13°0E **16 E7**
Carniche Alpi = Karnische Alpen Europe 46°36N 13°0E **16 E7**
Carnot C.A.R. 4°59N 15°56E **52 D3**
Carnot, C. Australia 34°57S 135°38E **63 E2**
Carnot B. Australia 17°20S 122°15E **60 C3**
Carnoustie U.K. 56°30N 2°42W **11 E6**
Carnsore Pt. Ireland 52°10N 6°22W **10 D5**
Caro U.S.A. 43°29N 83°24W **81 D12**
Caroga Lake U.S.A. 43°8N 74°28W **83 C10**
Carol City U.S.A. 25°56N 80°14W **85 J14**
Carolina Brazil 7°10S 47°30W **93 E9**
Carolina Puerto Rico 18°23N 65°58W **89 d**
Carolina S. Africa 26°5S 30°6E **57 D5**
Caroline I. Kiribati 9°58S 150°13W **65 H12**
Caroline Is. Micronesia 8°0N 150°0E **64 G6**
Caroni Trin. & Tob. 10°34N 61°23W **93 K15**
Caroní → Venezuela 8°21N 62°43W **92 B6**
Caronie = Nébrodi, Monti Italy 37°54N 14°35E **22 F6**
Caroona Australia 31°24S 150°26E **63 E5**
Carpathians Europe 49°30N 21°0E **17 D11**
Carpații Meridionali Romania 45°30N 25°0E **17 F13**

Carpentaria, G. of Australia 14°0S 139°0E **62 A2**
Carpentras France 44°3N 5°2E **20 D6**
Carpi Italy 44°47N 10°53E **22 B4**
Carpinteria U.S.A. 34°24N 119°31W **79 L7**
Carr Boyd Ra. Australia 16°15S 128°35E **60 C4**
Carra, L. Ireland 53°41N 9°14W **10 C2**
Carrabelle U.S.A. 29°51N 84°40W **85 G12**
Carraig Mhachdire Rois = Carrickmacross Ireland 53°59N 6°43W **10 C5**
Carraig na Siúire = Carrick-on-Suir Ireland 52°21N 7°24W **10 D4**
Carranya ☼ Australia 19°13S 127°46E **60 C4**
Carranza, Presa V. Mexico 27°20N 100°50W **86 B4**
Carrara Italy 44°5N 10°6E **20 D9**
Carrauntoohill Ireland 52°0N 9°45W **10 D2**
Carrick-on-Shannon Ireland 53°57N 8°5W **10 C3**
Carrick-on-Suir Ireland 52°21N 7°24W **10 D4**
Carrickfergus U.K. 54°43N 5°49W **10 B6**
Carrickmacross Ireland 53°59N 6°43W **10 C5**
Carrieton Australia 32°25S 138°31E **63 E2**
Carrillo Mexico 26°54N 103°55W **86 B4**
Carrington U.S.A. 47°27N 99°8W **80 B4**
Carrizal Bajo Chile 28°5S 71°20W **94 B1**
Carrizalillo Chile 29°5S 71°30W **94 B1**
Carrizo Cr. → U.S.A. 36°55N 103°55W **77 H12**
Carrizo Plain △ U.S.A. 35°11N 119°47W **78 K7**
Carrizo Springs U.S.A. 28°31N 99°52W **84 G5**
Carrizozo U.S.A. 33°38N 105°53W **77 K11**
Carroll U.S.A. 42°4N 94°52W **80 D6**
Carrollton Ga., U.S.A. 33°35N 85°5W **85 E12**
Carrollton Ill., U.S.A. 39°18N 90°24W **80 F8**
Carrollton Ky., U.S.A. 38°41N 85°11W **81 F11**
Carrollton Mo., U.S.A. 39°22N 93°30W **80 F7**
Carrollton Ohio, U.S.A. 40°34N 81°5W **82 F3**
Carron → U.K. 57°53N 4°22W **11 D4**
Carron, L. U.K. 57°22N 5°35W **11 D3**
Carrot → Canada 53°50N 101°17W **71 C8**
Carrot River Canada 53°17N 103°35W **71 C8**
Carruthers Canada 52°52N 109°16W **71 C7**
Carson Calif., U.S.A. 33°49N 118°16W **79 M8**
Carson N. Dak., U.S.A. 46°25N 101°34W **80 B3**
Carson → U.S.A. 39°10N 119°46W **78 F7**
Carson City U.S.A. 39°10N 119°46W **78 F7**
Carson Sink U.S.A. 39°50N 118°25W **76 G4**
Cartagena Colombia 10°25N 75°33W **92 A3**
Cartagena Spain 37°38N 0°59W **21 D5**
Cartago Colombia 4°45N 75°55W **92 C3**
Cartago Costa Rica 9°50N 83°55W **88 E3**
Cartersville U.S.A. 34°10N 84°48W **85 D12**
Carterton N.Z. 41°2S 175°31E **59 D5**
Carthage Tunisia 36°52N 10°20E **22 F4**
Carthage Ill., U.S.A. 40°25N 91°8W **80 E8**
Carthage Mo., U.S.A. 37°11N 94°19W **80 G6**
Carthage N.Y., U.S.A. 43°59N 75°37W **81 D16**
Carthage Tex., U.S.A. 32°9N 94°20W **84 E7**
Cartier I. Australia 12°31S 123°29E **60 B3**
Cartwright Canada 53°41N 56°58W **73 B8**
Caruaru Brazil 8°15S 35°55W **93 E11**
Carúpano Venezuela 10°39N 63°15W **92 A6**
Caruthersville U.S.A. 36°11N 89°39W **80 G9**
Carvoeiro Brazil 1°30S 61°59W **92 D6**
Carvoeiro, C. Portugal 39°21N 9°24W **21 C1**
Cary U.S.A. 35°47N 78°46W **85 D15**
Casa de Piedra Argentina 38°5S 67°28W **94 D2**
Casa de Piedra, Embalse Argentina 38°5S 67°32W **94 D2**
Casa Grande U.S.A. 32°53N 111°45W **77 K8**
Casa Nova Brazil 9°25S 41°5W **93 E10**
Casablanca Chile 33°20S 71°25W **94 C1**
Casablanca Morocco 33°36N 7°36W **50 B4**
Cascada de Basaseachic △ Mexico 28°9N 108°15W **86 B3**
Cascade Seychelles 4°39S 55°29E **53 b**
Cascade Idaho, U.S.A. 44°31N 116°2W **76 D5**
Cascade Mont., U.S.A. 47°16N 111°42W **76 C8**
Cascade Locks U.S.A. 45°40N 121°54W **78 E5**
Cascade Ra. U.S.A. 47°0N 121°30W **78 D5**
Cascade Res. U.S.A. 44°32N 116°3W **76 D5**
Cascades, Pte. des Réunion 21°9S 55°51E **53 c**
Cascais Portugal 38°41N 9°25W **21 C1**
Cascavel Brazil 24°57S 53°28W **95 A5**
Cáscina Italy 43°41N 10°33E **22 C4**
Casco B. U.S.A. 43°45N 70°0W **81 D19**
Caserta Italy 41°4N 14°20E **22 D6**
Casey Antarctica 66°0S 76°0E **5 C8**
Caseyr, Raas = Asir, Ras Somali Rep. 11°55N 51°10E **47 E5**
Cashel Ireland 52°30N 7°53W **10 D4**
Casiguran Phil. 16°22N 122°7E **37 A6**
Casilda Argentina 33°10S 61°10W **94 C3**
Casino Australia 28°52S 153°3E **63 D5**
Casiquiare → Venezuela 2°1N 67°7W **92 C5**
Casma Peru 9°30S 78°20W **92 E3**
Casmalia U.S.A. 34°50N 120°32W **79 L6**
Caspe Spain 41°14N 0°1W **21 B5**
Casper U.S.A. 42°51N 106°19W **76 E10**
Caspian Depression Eurasia 47°0N 48°0E **19 E8**
Caspian Sea Eurasia 43°0N 50°0E **19 F9**
Cass City U.S.A. 43°36N 83°10W **82 C1**
Cass Lake U.S.A. 47°23N 94°37W **80 B6**
Cassadaga U.S.A. 42°20N 79°19W **82 D5**
Casselman Canada 45°19N 75°5W **83 A9**
Casselton U.S.A. 46°54N 97°13W **80 B5**
Cassiar Mts. Canada 59°30N 130°30W **70 B2**
Cassino Italy 41°30N 13°49E **22 D5**
Cassville U.S.A. 36°41N 93°52W **80 G7**
Castaic U.S.A. 34°30N 118°38W **79 L8**
Castalia U.S.A. 41°24N 82°49W **82 E2**
Castanhal Brazil 1°18S 47°55W **93 D9**
Castara Trin. & Tob. 11°17N 60°42W **93 J16**
Castellammare di Stábia Italy 40°42N 14°29E **22 D6**
Castelli Argentina 36°7S 57°47W **94 D4**
Castelló de la Plana Spain 39°58N 0°3W **21 C5**

Castelo Brazil 20°33S 41°14W **95 A7**
Castelo Branco Portugal 39°50N 7°31W **21 C2**
Castelsarrasin France 44°2N 1°7E **20 E4**
Castelvetrano Italy 37°41N 12°47E **22 F5**
Castile U.S.A. 42°38N 78°3W **82 D6**
Castilla-La Mancha □ Spain 39°30N 3°30W **21 C4**
Castilla y Leon □ Spain 42°0N 5°0W **21 B3**
Castillos Uruguay 34°12S 53°52W **95 C5**
Castle Dale U.S.A. 39°13N 111°1W **76 G8**
Castle Douglas U.K. 54°56N 3°56W **11 G5**
Castle Rock Colo., U.S.A. 39°22N 104°51W **76 G11**
Castle Rock Wash., U.S.A. 46°17N 122°54W **78 D4**
Castlebar Ireland 53°52N 9°18W **10 C2**
Castlebay U.K. 56°57N 7°31W **11 E1**
Castleblaney Ireland 54°7N 6°44W **10 B5**
Castlederg U.K. 54°42N 7°35W **10 B4**
Castleford U.K. 53°43N 1°21W **12 D6**
Castlegar Canada 49°20N 117°40W **70 D5**
Castlemaine Australia 37°2S 144°12E **63 F3**
Castlemaine Ireland 52°10N 9°42W **10 D2**
Castlepollard Ireland 53°41N 7°19W **10 C4**
Castlerea Ireland 53°46N 8°29W **10 C3**
Castlereagh = Carlow Ireland 52°50N 6°56W **10 D5**
Castlereagh Australia 30°12S 147°32E **63 E4**
Castlereagh B. Australia 12°10S 135°10E **62 A2**
Castleton U.S.A. 43°37N 73°11W **83 C11**
Castleton-on-Hudson U.S.A. 42°31N 73°45W **83 D11**
Castletown I. of Man 54°5N 4°38W **12 C3**
Castletown Bearhaven Ireland 51°39N 9°55W **10 E2**
Castor Canada 52°15N 111°50W **70 C6**
Castor → Canada 53°24N 78°58W **72 B4**
Castorland U.S.A. 43°53N 75°31W **83 C9**
Castres France 43°37N 2°13E **20 E5**
Castricum Neths. 52°33N 4°40E **15 B4**
Castries St. Lucia 14°2N 60°58W **89 f**
Castro Brazil 24°45S 50°0W **95 A6**
Castro Chile 42°30S 73°50W **96 E2**
Castro Alves Brazil 12°46S 39°33W **93 F11**
Castro Valley U.S.A. 37°41N 122°5W **78 H4**
Castroville U.S.A. 36°46N 121°45W **78 J5**
Castuera Spain 38°43N 5°37W **21 C3**
Cat Ba, Dao Vietnam 20°50N 107°0E **38 B6**
Cat Ba △ Vietnam 20°47N 107°3E **38 B6**
Cat I. Bahamas 24°30N 75°30W **89 B4**
Cat L. Canada 51°40N 91°50W **72 B1**
Cat Lake Canada 51°40N 91°50W **72 B1**
Cat Tien △ Vietnam 11°25N 107°17E **39 G6**
Catacamas Honduras 14°54N 85°56W **88 D2**
Cataguases Brazil 21°23S 42°39W **95 A7**
Catalão Brazil 18°10S 47°57W **93 G9**
Çatalca Turkey 41°8N 28°27E **23 D13**
Catalina Canada 48°31N 53°4W **73 C9**
Catalina Chile 25°13S 69°43W **94 B2**
Catalina U.S.A. 32°30N 110°50W **77 K8**
Catalonia = Cataluña □ Spain 41°40N 1°15E **21 B6**
Cataluña □ Spain 41°40N 1°15E **21 B6**
Catamarca Argentina 28°30S 65°50W **94 B2**
Catamarca □ Argentina 27°0S 65°50W **94 B2**
Catanduanes □ Phil. 13°50N 124°20E **37 B6**
Catanduva Brazil 21°5S 48°58W **95 A6**
Catánia Italy 37°30N 15°6E **22 F6**
Catanzaro Italy 38°54N 16°35E **22 E7**
Catarman Phil. 12°28N 124°35E **37 B6**
Catatumbo-Bari △ Colombia 9°3N 73°12W **89 E5**
Catchacoma Canada 44°44N 78°19W **82 B6**
Cateel Phil. 7°47N 126°24E **37 C7**
Catembe Mozam. 26°0S 32°33E **57 D5**
Caterham U.K. 51°15N 0°4W **13 F7**
Cathair Mart = Westport Ireland 53°48N 9°31W **10 C2**
Cathair Saidhbhín = Cahersiveen Ireland 51°56N 10°14W **10 E1**
Cathcart S. Africa 32°18S 27°10E **56 E4**
Cathedral City U.S.A. 33°47N 116°28W **79 M10**
Cathlamet U.S.A. 46°12N 123°23W **78 D3**
Catlettsburg U.S.A. 38°25N 82°36W **81 F12**
Catoche, C. Mexico 21°35N 87°5W **87 C7**
Catril Argentina 36°26S 63°24W **94 D3**
Catrimani Brazil 0°27N 61°41W **92 C6**
Catrimani → Brazil 0°28N 61°44W **92 C6**
Catskill U.S.A. 42°14N 73°52W **83 D11**
Catskill △ U.S.A. 42°8N 74°39W **83 D10**
Catskill Mts. U.S.A. 42°10N 74°25W **83 D10**
Catt, Mt. Australia 13°49S 134°23E **62 A1**
Cattaraugus U.S.A. 42°20N 78°52W **82 D6**
Catterick U.K. 54°23N 1°37W **12 C6**
Catuala Angola 16°25S 19°2E **56 B2**
Catuane Mozam. 26°48S 32°18E **57 D5**
Catur Mozam. 13°45S 35°30E **55 E4**
Caubvick, Mt. = Iberville, Mt. d' Canada 58°50N 63°50W **69 F19**
Cauca → Colombia 8°54N 74°28W **92 B4**
Caucaia Brazil 3°40S 38°35W **93 D11**
Caucasus Mountains Eurasia 42°50N 44°0E **19 F7**
Caucete Argentina 31°38S 68°20W **94 C2**
Cauese Mts. Mozam. 15°14S 30°33E **55 F3**
Caungula Angola 8°26S 18°38E **52 F3**
Cauquenes Chile 36°0S 72°22W **94 D1**
Caura → Venezuela 7°38N 64°53W **92 B6**
Cauresi → Mozam. 17°8S 33°0E **55 F3**
Causapscal Canada 48°19N 67°12W **73 C6**
Cauvery → India 11°9N 78°52E **40 P11**
Caux, Pays de France 49°38N 0°35E **20 B4**
Cavalier U.S.A. 48°48N 97°37W **80 A5**
Cavan Ireland 54°0N 7°22W **10 B4**
Cavan □ Ireland 54°1N 7°16W **10 C4**
Cave Creek U.S.A. 33°50N 111°57W **77 K8**
Cavenagh Ra. Australia 26°12S 127°55E **61 E4**
Cavendish Australia 37°31S 142°2E **63 F3**
Caviana, I. Brazil 0°10N 50°10W **93 C8**

Cavite Phil. 14°29N 120°54E **37 B6**
Cawndilla L. Australia 32°30S 142°15E **63 E3**
Cawnpore = Kanpur India 26°28N 80°20E **43 F9**
Caxias Brazil 4°55S 43°20W **93 D10**
Caxias do Sul Brazil 29°10S 51°10W **95 B5**
Cay Sal Bank Bahamas 23°45N 80°0W **88 B4**
Cayambe Ecuador 0°3N 78°8W **92 C3**
Cayenne Fr. Guiana 5°5N 52°18W **93 B8**
Cayey Puerto Rico 18°7N 66°10W **89 d**
Cayman Brac Cayman Is. 19°43N 79°49W **88 C4**
Cayman Is. ☑ W. Indies 19°40N 80°30W **88 C3**
Cayman Trough Caribbean 19°0N 81°0W **66 H11**
Cayuga Canada 42°59N 79°50W **82 D5**
Cayuga U.S.A. 42°54N 76°44W **83 D8**
Cayuga Heights U.S.A. 42°27N 76°29W **83 D8**
Cayuga L. U.S.A. 42°41N 76°41W **83 D8**
Cazenovia U.S.A. 42°56N 75°51W **83 D9**
Cazombo Angola 11°54S 22°56E **53 G4**
Ceanannus Mor Ireland 53°44N 6°53W **10 C5**
Ceará = Fortaleza Brazil 3°45S 38°35W **93 D11**
Ceará □ Brazil 5°0S 40°0W **93 E11**
Ceará-Mirim Brazil 5°38S 35°25W **93 E11**
Ceatharlach = Carlow Ireland 52°50N 6°56W **10 D5**
Cébaco, I. de Panama 7°33N 81°9W **88 E3**
Cebollar Argentina 29°10S 66°35W **94 B2**
Cebu Phil. 10°18N 123°54E **37 B6**
Cecil Plains Australia 27°30S 151°11E **63 D5**
Cedar → U.S.A. 41°17N 91°21W **80 E8**
Cedar City U.S.A. 37°41N 113°4W **77 H7**
Cedar Creek Res. U.S.A. 32°11N 96°4W **84 E6**
Cedar Falls Iowa, U.S.A. 42°32N 92°27W **80 D7**
Cedar Falls Wash., U.S.A. 47°25N 121°45W **78 C5**
Cedar Key U.S.A. 29°8N 83°2W **85 G13**
Cedar L. Canada 53°10N 100°0W **71 C9**
Cedar Park U.S.A. 30°30N 97°49W **84 F6**
Cedar Rapids U.S.A. 41°59N 91°40W **80 E8**
Cedartown U.S.A. 34°1N 85°15W **85 D12**
Cedarvale Canada 55°1N 128°22W **70 B3**
Cedarville S. Africa 30°23S 29°3E **57 E4**
Cedral Mexico 23°50N 100°45W **86 C4**
Cedro Brazil 6°34S 39°3W **93 E11**
Cedros, I. Mexico 28°12N 115°15W **86 B1**
Cedros B. Trin. & Tob. 10°16N 61°54W **93 K15**
Ceduna Australia 32°7S 133°46E **63 E1**
Ceel Gaal Somali Rep. 10°58N 50°20E **47 E5**
Ceel Waaq Kenya 2°49N 40°56E **54 B5**
Ceeldheere Somali Rep. 3°50N 47°8E **47 G4**
Ceerigaabo Somali Rep. 10°35N 47°20E **47 E4**
Cefalù Italy 38°2N 14°1E **22 E6**
Cegléd Hungary 47°11N 19°47E **17 E10**
Celaque △ Honduras 14°30N 88°43W **88 D2**
Celaya Mexico 20°31N 100°37W **86 C4**
Celebes = Sulawesi Indonesia 2°0S 120°0E **37 E6**
Celebes Sea Indonesia 3°0N 123°0E **37 D6**
Celina U.S.A. 40°33N 84°35W **81 E11**
Celje Slovenia 46°16N 15°18E **16 E8**
Celle Germany 52°37N 10°4E **16 B6**
Celtic Sea Atl. Oc. 50°9N 9°34W **14 F2**
Cenderwasih, Teluk Indonesia 3°0S 135°20E **37 E9**
Center N. Dak., U.S.A. 47°7N 101°18W **80 B3**
Center Tex., U.S.A. 31°48N 94°11W **84 F7**
Centerburg U.S.A. 40°18N 82°42W **82 F2**
Centerville Calif., U.S.A. 36°44N 119°30W **78 J7**
Centerville Iowa, U.S.A. 40°44N 92°52W **80 E7**
Centerville Pa., U.S.A. 40°3N 79°59W **82 F5**
Centerville Tenn., U.S.A. 35°47N 87°28W **85 D11**
Centerville Tex., U.S.A. 31°16N 95°59W **84 F7**
Central = Tsentralnyy Russia 52°0N 40°0E **28 C4**
Central □ Kenya 0°30S 37°30E **54 C4**
Central □ Malawi 13°30S 33°30E **55 E3**
Central □ Zambia 14°25S 28°50E **55 E2**
Central, Cordillera Colombia 5°0N 75°0W **92 C3**
Central, Cordillera Costa Rica 10°10N 84°5W **88 D3**
Central, Cordillera Dom. Rep. 19°15N 71°0W **89 C5**
Central, Cordillera Puerto Rico 18°8N 66°35W **89 d**
Central African Rep. ■ Africa 7°0N 20°0E **51 G9**
Central America America 12°0N 85°0W **66 H11**
Central Australia ☼ Australia 22°30S 128°30E **60 D4**
Central Butte Canada 50°48N 106°31W **71 C7**
Central City Colo., U.S.A. 39°48N 105°31W **76 G11**
Central City Ky., U.S.A. 37°18N 87°7W **80 G10**
Central City Nebr., U.S.A. 41°7N 98°0W **80 E4**
Central Desert ☼ Australia 19°56S 130°46E **60 C5**
Central I. Kenya 3°30N 36°0E **54 B4**
Central Island △ Kenya 2°33N 36°1E **54 B4**
Central Kalahari △ Botswana 22°36S 23°58E **56 C3**
Central Makran Range Pakistan 26°30N 64°15E **40 F4**
Central Pacific Basin Pac. Oc. 8°0N 175°0W **64 G10**
Central Patricia Canada 51°30N 90°9W **72 B1**
Central Point U.S.A. 42°23N 122°55W **76 E2**
Central Russian Uplands Europe 54°0N 36°0E **6 E13**
Central Siberian Plateau Russia 65°0N 105°0E **26 B12**
Central Square U.S.A. 43°17N 76°9W **83 C8**
Centralia Canada 43°17N 81°28W **82 C3**
Centralia Ill., U.S.A. 38°32N 89°8W **80 F9**
Centralia Mo., U.S.A. 39°13N 92°8W **80 F7**

Centralia Wash., U.S.A. 46°43N 122°58W **78 D4**
Centre de Flacq Mauritius 20°12S 57°43E **53 d**
Centreville N.Y., U.S.A. 42°28N 78°14W **82 D6**
Centreville Pa., U.S.A. 41°44N 79°45W **82 E5**
Cephalonia = Kefalonia Greece 38°15N 20°30E **23 E9**
Cepu Indonesia 7°9S 111°35E **37 G14**
Ceram = Seram Indonesia 3°10S 129°0E **37 E7**
Ceram Sea = Seram Sea Indonesia 2°30S 128°30E **37 E7**
Ceredigion □ U.K. 52°16N 4°15W **13 E3**
Ceres Argentina 29°55S 61°55W **94 B3**
Ceres S. Africa 33°21S 19°18E **56 E2**
Ceres U.S.A. 37°35N 120°57W **78 H6**
Cerf Seychelles 4°38S 55°40E **53 b**
Cerignola Italy 41°17N 15°53E **22 D6**
Cerigo = Kythira Greece 36°8N 23°0E **23 F10**
Çerkezköy Turkey 41°17N 28°0E **23 D12**
Cerralvo I. Mexico 24°15N 109°55W **86 C3**
Cerritos Mexico 22°25N 100°16W **86 C4**
Cerro Chato Uruguay 33°6S 55°8W **95 C4**
Cerro Cofre de Perote △ Mexico 19°29N 97°8W **87 D5**
Cerro Corá △ Paraguay 22°35S 56°29W **95 A4**
Cerro de Pasco Peru 10°45S 76°10W **92 F3**
Cerro el Copey △ Venezuela 10°59N 63°53W **89 D7**
Cerro Hoya △ Panama 7°17N 80°45W **88 E3**
Cerro Saroche △ Venezuela 10°8N 69°38W **89 D6**
Cerventes Australia 30°31S 115°3E **61 F2**
Cervera Spain 41°40N 1°16E **21 B6**
Cesena Italy 44°8N 12°15E **22 B5**
Cēsis Latvia 57°18N 25°15E **9 H21**
Česká Rep. = Czech Rep. ■ Europe 50°0N 15°0E **16 D8**
České Budějovice Czech Rep. 48°55N 14°25E **16 D8**
Českomoravská Vrchovina Czech Rep. 49°30N 15°40E **16 D8**
Çeşme Turkey 38°20N 26°23E **23 E12**
Cessnock Australia 32°50S 151°21E **63 E5**
Cetinje Montenegro 42°23N 18°59E **23 C8**
Cetraro Italy 39°31N 15°55E **22 E6**
Ceuta N. Afr. 35°52N 5°18E **21 E3**
Cévennes France 44°10N 3°50E **20 D5**
Ceyhan Turkey 37°4N 35°47E **44 B2**
Ceylanpınar Turkey 36°50N 40°2E **44 B4**
Ceylon = Sri Lanka ■ Asia 7°30N 80°50E **40 R12**
Cha-am Thailand 12°48N 99°58E **38 F2**
Chacabuco Argentina 34°40S 60°27W **94 C3**
Chachapoyas Peru 6°15S 77°50W **92 E3**
Chachoengsao Thailand 13°42N 101°5E **38 F3**
Chachran Pakistan 28°55N 70°30E **42 E4**
Chachro Pakistan 25°5N 70°15E **42 G4**
Chaco □ Argentina 26°30S 61°0W **94 B3**
Chaco □ Paraguay 26°0S 60°0W **94 B4**
Chaco → U.S.A. 36°46N 108°39W **77 H9**
Chaco Austral S. Amer. 27°0S 59°30W **94 B4**
Chaco Boreal S. Amer. 22°0S 60°0W **92 H6**
Chaco Central S. Amer. 24°0S 61°0W **94 B4**
Chaco Culture △ U.S.A. 36°3N 107°58W **77 H10**
Chacon, C. U.S.A. 54°42N 132°0W **70 C2**
Chad ■ Africa 15°0N 17°15E **51 F8**
Chad, L. = Tchad, L. Chad 13°30N 14°30E **51 F8**
Chadileuvú → Argentina 37°46S 66°0W **94 D2**
Chadiza Zambia 14°45S 32°27E **55 E3**
Chadron U.S.A. 42°50N 103°0W **80 D2**
Chadyr-Lunga = Ciadâr-Lunga Moldova 46°3N 28°51E **17 E15**
Chae Hom Thailand 18°43N 99°35E **38 C2**
Chae Son △ Thailand 18°42N 99°20E **38 C2**
Chaem → Thailand 18°11N 98°38E **38 C2**
Chaeryŏng N. Korea 38°24N 125°36E **35 E13**
Chagai Hills = Chāh Gay Hills Afghan. 29°30N 64°0E **40 E3**
Chagda Russia 58°45N 130°38E **29 D14**
Chaghcharān Afghan. 34°31N 65°15E **40 B4**
Chagos Arch. ☑ Ind. Oc. 6°0S 72°0E **26 J9**
Chagres △ Panama 9°23N 79°37W **88 E4**
Chaguanas Trin. & Tob. 10°30N 61°26W **93 K15**
Chāh Ākhvor Iran 32°41N 59°40E **45 C8**
Chāh Bahar Iran 25°20N 60°40E **45 E9**
Chāh-e Kavīr Iran 34°29N 56°52E **45 C8**
Chāh Gay Hills Afghan. 29°30N 64°0E **40 E3**
Chahār Borjak Afghan. 30°17N 62°3E **40 D3**
Chahār Mahāll va Bakhtīarī □ Iran 32°0N 49°0E **45 C6**
Chai Badan Thailand 15°12N 101°8E **38 E3**
Chai Wan China 22°16N 114°14E **33 G11**
Chaibasa India 22°42N 85°49E **43 H11**
Chainat Thailand 15°11N 100°8E **38 E3**
Chaiya Thailand 9°23N 99°14E **39 H2**
Chaiyaphum Thailand 15°48N 102°2E **38 E4**
Chaj Doab Pakistan 32°15N 73°0E **42 C5**
Chajari Argentina 30°42S 58°0W **94 C4**
Chak Amru Pakistan 32°22N 75°11E **42 C6**
Chakar → Pakistan 29°29N 68°2E **42 E3**
Chakari Zimbabwe 18°5S 29°51E **57 B4**
Chake Chake Tanzania 5°15S 39°45E **54 D4**
Chakhānsūr Afghan. 31°10N 62°0E **40 D3**
Chakonipau, L. Canada 56°18N 68°30W **73 A6**
Chakradharpur India 22°45N 85°40E **43 H11**
Chakrata India 30°42N 77°51E **42 D7**
Chakwal Pakistan 32°56N 72°53E **42 C5**
Chala Peru 15°48S 74°20W **92 G4**
Chalchihuites Mexico 23°29N 103°53W **86 C4**
Chalcis = Halkida Greece 38°27N 23°42E **23 E10**
Chaleur B. Canada 47°55N 65°30W **73 C6**
Chalfant U.S.A. 37°32N 118°21W **78 H8**
Chalhuanca Peru 14°15S 73°15W **92 F4**
Chalisgaon India 20°30N 75°10E **40 J9**
Chalk River Canada 46°1N 77°27W **72 C4**
Chalky Inlet N.Z. 46°3S 166°31E **59 G1**

Challapata Bolivia 18°53S 66°50W 92 G5
Challenger Deep Pac. Oc. 11°30N 142°0E 64 F6
Challenger Fracture Zone Pac. Oc. 35°0S 105°0W 65 L17
Challis U.S.A. 44°30N 114°14W 76 D6
Chalmette U.S.A. 29°56N 89°57W 85 G10
Chalon-sur-Saône France 46°48N 4°50E 20 C6
Chalong Thailand 7°50N 98°22E 39 a
Châlons-en-Champagne France 48°58N 4°20E 20 B6
Chálten, Cerro = Fitz Roy, Cerro Argentina 49°17S 73°5W 96 F2
Chālūs Iran 36°38N 51°26E 45 B6
Cham, Cu Lao Vietnam 15°57N 108°30E 38 E7
Chama U.S.A. 36°54N 106°35W 77 H10
Chamaicó Argentina 35°3S 64°58W 94 D3
Chaman Pakistan 30°58N 66°25E 40 D5
Chamba India 32°35N 76°10E 42 C7
Chamba Tanzania 11°37S 37°0E 55 E4
Chambal → India 26°29N 79°15E 43 F8
Chamberlain U.S.A. 43°49N 99°20W 80 D4
Chamberlain → Australia 15°30S 127°54E 60 C4
Chamberlain L. U.S.A. 46°14N 69°19W 81 B19
Chambers U.S.A. 35°11N 109°26W 77 J9
Chambersburg U.S.A. 39°56N 77°40W 81 F15
Chambéry France 45°34N 5°55E 20 D6
Chambeshi → Zambia 11°53S 29°48E 52 G6
Chambly Canada 45°27N 73°17W 83 A11
Chambord Canada 48°25N 72°6W 73 C5
Chamchamal Iraq 35°32N 44°50E 44 C5
Chamela Mexico 19°32N 105°5W 86 D3
Chamical Argentina 30°22S 66°27W 94 C2
Chamkar Luong Cambodia 11°0N 103°45E 39 G4
Chamoli India 30°24N 79°21E 43 D8
Chamonix-Mont Blanc France 45°55N 6°51E 20 D7
Chamouchuane = Ashuapmushuan → Canada 48°37N 72°20W 72 C5
Champa India 22°2N 82°43E 43 H10
Champagne Canada 60°49N 136°30W 70 A1
Champagne France 48°40N 4°20E 20 B6
Champaign U.S.A. 40°7N 88°15W 80 E9
Champassak Laos 14°53N 105°52E 38 E5
Champawat India 29°20N 80°6E 43 E9
Champdoré, L. Canada 55°55N 65°49W 73 A6
Champion U.S.A. 41°19N 80°51W 82 E4
Champlain U.S.A. 44°59N 73°27W 83 B11
Champlain, L. U.S.A. 44°40N 73°20W 83 B11
Champotón Mexico 19°21N 90°43W 87 D6
Champua India 22°5N 85°40E 43 H11
Chana Thailand 6°55N 100°44E 39 J3
Chañaral Chile 26°23S 70°40W 94 B1
Chanārān Iran 36°39N 59°6E 45 B8
Chanasma India 23°44N 72°5E 42 H5
Chancery Lane Barbados 13°3N 59°30W 89 g
Chanco Chile 35°44S 72°32W 94 D1
Chand India 21°57N 79°7E 43 J8
Chandan India 24°38N 86°40E 43 G12
Chandan Chauki India 28°33N 80°47E 43 E9
Chandannagar India 22°52N 88°24E 43 H13
Chandausi India 28°27N 78°49E 43 E8
Chandeleur Is. U.S.A. 29°55N 88°57W 85 G10
Chandeleur Sd. U.S.A. 29°55N 89°0W 85 G10
Chandigarh India 30°43N 76°47E 42 D7
Chandil India 22°58N 86°3E 43 H12
Chandler Australia 27°0S 133°19E 63 D1
Chandler Canada 48°18N 64°46W 73 C7
Chandler Ariz., U.S.A. 33°18N 111°50W 77 K8
Chandler Okla., U.S.A. 35°42N 96°53W 84 D6
Chandod India 21°59N 73°28E 42 J5
Chandpur Bangla. 23°8N 90°45E 41 H17
Chandrapur India 19°57N 79°25E 40 K11
Chānf Iran 26°38N 60°29E 45 E9
Chang Pakistan 26°59N 68°30E 42 F3
Chang, Ko Thailand 12°0N 102°23E 39 G4
Ch'ang Chiang = Chang Jiang → China 31°48N 121°10E 33 C7
Chang Jiang → China 31°48N 121°10E 33 C7
Chang-won S. Korea 35°16N 128°37E 35 G15
Changa India 33°53N 77°35E 43 C7
Changan China 22°48N 113°48E 33 F10
Changanacheri India 9°25N 76°31E 40 Q10
Changanassery = Changanacheri India 9°25N 76°31E 40 Q10
Changane → Mozam. 24°30S 33°30E 57 C5
Changbai China 41°25N 128°5E 35 D15
Changbai Shan China 42°20N 129°0E 35 C15
Changchiak'ou = Zhangjiakou China 40°48N 114°55E 34 D8
Ch'angchou = Changzhou China 31°47N 119°58E 33 C6
Changchun China 43°57N 125°17E 35 C13
Changchunling China 45°18N 125°27E 35 B13
Changde China 29°4N 111°35E 33 D6
Chango-ri N. Korea 38°30N 127°40E 35 E14
Changhai = Shanghai China 31°15N 121°26E 33 C7
Changhua Taiwan 24°2N 120°30E 33 D7
Changhŭngni N. Korea 40°24N 128°19E 35 D15
Changi Singapore 1°23N 103°59E 39 d
Changi, Singapore ✈ (SIN) Singapore 1°23N 103°59E 39 M4
Changji China 44°1N 87°19E 32 B3
Changjiang China 19°20N 108°55E 38 C7
Changjiang Shuiku China 22°29N 113°27E 33 G10
Changjin N. Korea 40°23N 127°15E 35 D14
Changjin-ho N. Korea 40°30N 127°15E 35 D14
Changli China 39°40N 119°13E 35 E10
Changling China 44°20N 123°58E 35 B12
Changlun Malaysia 6°25N 100°26E 39 J3
Changping China 40°14N 116°12E 34 D9
Changsha China 28°12N 113°0E 33 D6
Changshan Qundao China 39°11N 122°32E 35 E12
Changuinola Panama 9°26N 82°31W 88 E3
Changwu China 35°10N 107°45E 34 G4
Changyi China 36°40N 119°30E 35 F10
Changyŏn N. Korea 38°15N 125°6E 35 E13
Changyuan China 35°15N 114°42E 34 G8
Changzhi China 36°10N 113°6E 34 F7
Changzhou China 31°47N 119°58E 33 C6
Chanhanga Angola 16°0S 14°8E 56 B1
Chania Greece 35°30N 24°4E 25 D6
Chania □ Greece 35°30N 24°0E 25 D6
Chanion, Kolpos Greece 35°33N 23°55E 25 D5
Channapatna India 12°40N 77°15E 40 N10
Channel Is. U.K. 49°19N 2°24W 13 H5
Channel Is. U.S.A. 33°40N 119°15W 79 M7
Channel Islands △ U.S.A. 34°0N 119°24W 79 L7
Channel-Port aux Basques Canada 47°30N 59°9W 73 C8
Channel Tunnel Europe 51°0N 1°30E 13 F9
Channing U.S.A. 35°41N 102°20W 84 D3
Chantada Spain 42°36N 7°46W 21 A2
Chanthaburi Thailand 12°38N 102°12E 38 F4
Chantrey Inlet Canada 67°48N 96°20W 68 D12
Chanute U.S.A. 37°41N 95°27W 80 G6
Chao Phraya → Thailand 13°40N 100°31E 38 F3
Chao Phraya Lowlands Thailand 15°30N 100°0E 38 E3
Chaocheng China 36°4N 115°37E 34 F8
Chaoyang China 41°35N 120°22E 35 D11
Chaozhou China 23°42N 116°32E 33 D6
Chapaev Kazakhstan 50°25N 51°10E 19 D9
Chapais Canada 49°47N 74°51W 72 C5
Chapala Mozam. 15°50S 37°35E 55 F4
Chapala, L. de Mexico 20°15N 103°0W 86 C4
Chapayevsk Russia 53°0N 49°40E 18 D8
Chapecó Brazil 27°14S 52°41W 95 B5
Chapel Hill U.S.A. 35°55N 79°4W 85 D15
Chapleau Canada 47°50N 83°24W 72 C3
Chaplin Canada 50°28N 106°40W 71 C7
Chaplin L. Canada 50°22N 106°36W 71 C7
Chappell U.S.A. 41°6N 102°28W 80 E2
Chapra = Chhapra India 25°48N 84°44E 43 G11
Chara Russia 56°54N 118°20E 29 D12
Charadai Argentina 27°35S 59°55W 94 B4
Charagua Bolivia 19°45S 63°10W 92 G6
Charakas Greece 35°1N 25°7E 25 D7
Charambirá, Punta Colombia 4°16N 77°32W 92 C3
Charaña Bolivia 17°30S 69°25W 92 G5
Charanwala India 27°51N 72°10E 42 F5
Charata Argentina 27°13S 61°14W 94 B3
Charcas Mexico 23°8N 101°7W 86 C4
Charcot I. Antarctica 70°0S 70°0W 5 C17
Chard U.K. 50°52N 2°58W 13 G5
Chardon U.S.A. 41°35N 81°12W 82 E3
Chardzhou = Türkmenabat Turkmenistan 39°6N 63°34E 45 B9
Charente → France 45°57N 1°5W 20 D3
Chari → Chad 12°58N 14°31E 51 F8
Chārīkār Afghan. 35°0N 69°10E 40 B6
Chariton U.S.A. 41°1N 93°19W 80 E7
Chariton → U.S.A. 39°19N 92°58W 80 F7
Chärjew = Türkmenabat Turkmenistan 39°6N 63°34E 45 B9
Charkhari India 25°24N 79°45E 43 G8
Charkhi Dadri India 28°37N 76°17E 42 E7
Charleroi Belgium 50°24N 4°27E 15 D4
Charleroi U.S.A. 40°9N 79°57W 82 F5
Charles, C. U.S.A. 37°7N 75°58W 81 G16
Charles, Peak Australia 32°52S 121°11E 61 F3
Charles City U.S.A. 43°4N 92°41W 80 D7
Charles I. Canada 62°39N 74°15W 69 E17
Charles L. Canada 59°50N 110°33W 71 B6
Charles Town U.S.A. 39°17N 77°52W 81 F15
Charlesbourg Canada 46°51N 71°16W 81 B18
Charleston Ill., U.S.A. 39°30N 88°10W 80 F9
Charleston Miss., U.S.A. 34°1N 90°4W 85 D9
Charleston Mo., U.S.A. 36°55N 89°21W 80 G9
Charleston S.C., U.S.A. 32°46N 79°56W 85 E15
Charleston W. Va., U.S.A. 38°21N 81°38W 81 F13
Charleston L. Canada 44°32N 76°0W 83 B9
Charleston Peak U.S.A. 36°16N 115°42W 79 J11
Charlestown Ireland 53°58N 8°48W 10 C3
Charlestown S. Africa 27°26S 29°53E 57 D4
Charlestown Ind., U.S.A. 38°27N 85°40W 81 F11
Charlestown N.H., U.S.A. 43°14N 72°25W 83 C12
Charlestown of Aberlour U.K. 57°28N 3°14W 11 D5
Charleville = Rath Luirc Ireland 52°21N 8°40W 10 D3
Charleville Australia 26°24S 146°15E 63 D4
Charleville-Mézières France 49°44N 4°40E 20 B6
Charlevoix U.S.A. 45°19N 85°16W 81 C11
Charlotte Mich., U.S.A. 42°34N 84°50W 81 D11
Charlotte N.C., U.S.A. 35°13N 80°50W 85 D14
Charlotte Vt., U.S.A. 44°19N 73°16W 83 B11
Charlotte Amalie U.S. Virgin Is. 18°21N 64°56W 89 e
Charlotte Harbor U.S.A. 26°57N 82°4W 85 H13
Charlotte L. Canada 52°12N 125°19W 70 C3
Charlottesville U.S.A. 38°2N 78°30W 81 F14
Charlottetown Nfld. & L., Canada 52°46N 56°7W 73 B8
Charlottetown P.E.I., Canada 46°14N 63°8W 73 C7
Charlotteville Trin. & Tob. 11°20N 60°33W 93 J16
Charlton Australia 36°16S 143°24E 63 F3
Charlton I. Canada 52°0N 79°20W 72 B4
Charny Canada 46°43N 71°15W 73 C5
Charolles France 46°27N 4°16E 20 C6
Charre Mozam. 17°13S 35°10E 55 F4
Charsadda Pakistan 34°7N 71°45E 42 B4
Charters Towers Australia 20°5S 146°13E 62 C4
Chartres France 48°29N 1°30E 20 B4
Chascomús Argentina 35°30S 58°0W 94 D4
Chase Canada 50°50N 119°41W 70 C5
Chasefu Zambia 11°55S 33°8E 55 E3
Chashma Barrage Pakistan 32°27N 71°20E 42 C4
Chāt Iran 37°59N 55°16E 45 B7
Châteaubriant France 47°43N 1°23W 20 C3
Chateaugay U.S.A. 44°56N 74°5W 83 B10
Châteauguay, L. Canada 56°26N 70°3W 73 A5
Châteaulin France 48°11N 4°8W 20 B1
Châteauroux France 46°50N 1°40E 20 C4
Châteaux, Pte. des Guadeloupe 16°15N 61°10W 88 b
Châtellerault France 46°50N 0°30E 20 C4
Chatham = Miramichi Canada 47°2N 65°28W 73 C6
Chatham Canada 42°24N 82°11W 82 D2
Chatham U.K. 51°22N 0°32E 13 F8
Chatham U.S.A. 42°21N 73°36W 83 D11
Chatham Is. Pac. Oc. 44°0S 176°40W 64 M10
Chatham Rise Pac. Oc. 43°30S 180°0E 64 M10
Chatmohar Bangla. 24°15N 89°15E 43 G13
Chatra India 24°12N 84°56E 43 G11
Chatrapur India 19°22N 85°2E 41 K14
Chats, L. des Canada 45°30N 76°20W 83 A8
Chatsu India 26°36N 75°57E 42 F6
Chatsworth Canada 44°27N 80°54W 82 B4
Chatsworth Zimbabwe 19°38S 31°13E 55 F3
Châttagâm = Chittagong Bangla. 22°19N 91°48E 41 H17
Chattahoochee U.S.A. 30°42N 84°51W 85 F12
Chattahoochee → U.S.A. 30°54N 84°57W 85 F12
Chattanooga U.S.A. 35°3N 85°19W 85 D12
Chatteris U.K. 52°28N 0°2E 13 E8
Chatturat Thailand 15°40N 101°51E 38 E3
Chau Doc Vietnam 10°42N 105°7E 39 G5
Chaukan Pass Burma 27°8N 97°10E 41 F20
Chaumont France 48°7N 5°8E 20 B6
Chaumont U.S.A. 44°4N 76°8W 83 B8
Chaunskaya G. Russia 69°0N 169°0E 29 C17
Chautauqua L. U.S.A. 42°10N 79°24W 82 D5
Chauvin Canada 52°45N 110°10W 71 C6
Chaves Brazil 0°15S 49°55W 93 D9
Chaves Portugal 41°45N 7°32W 21 B2
Chawang Thailand 8°25N 99°30E 39 H2
Chaykovskiy Russia 56°47N 54°9E 18 C9
Chazy U.S.A. 44°53N 73°26W 83 B11
Cheb Czech Rep. 50°9N 12°28E 16 C7
Cheboksary Russia 56°8N 47°12E 18 C8
Cheboygan U.S.A. 45°39N 84°29W 81 C11
Chech, Erg Africa 25°0N 2°15W 50 D5
Chechenia □ Russia 43°30N 45°29E 19 F8
Checheno-Ingush Republic = Chechenia □ Russia 43°30N 45°29E 19 F8
Chechnya = Chechenia □ Russia 43°30N 45°29E 19 F8
Checotah U.S.A. 35°28N 95°31W 84 D7
Chedabucto B. Canada 45°25N 61°8W 73 C7
Cheduba I. Burma 18°45N 93°40E 41 K18
Cheektowaga U.S.A. 42°54N 78°45W 82 D6
Cheepie Australia 26°33S 145°0E 63 D4
Chegdomyn Russia 51°7N 133°1E 29 D14
Chegga Mauritania 25°27N 5°40W 50 C4
Chegutu Zimbabwe 18°10S 30°14E 55 F3
Chehalis U.S.A. 46°40N 122°58W 78 D4
Chehalis → U.S.A. 46°57N 123°50W 78 D3
Cheju = Jeju S. Korea 33°31N 126°32E 35 H14
Cheju-do = Jeju-do S. Korea 33°29N 126°34E 35 H14
Chekiang = Zhejiang □ China 29°0N 120°0E 33 D7
Chela, Sa. da Angola 16°20S 13°20E 56 B1
Chelan U.S.A. 47°51N 120°1W 76 C3
Chelan, L. U.S.A. 48°11N 120°30W 76 B3
Cheleken = Hazar Turkmenistan 39°34N 53°16E 19 G9
Cheleken Yarymadasy Turkmenistan 39°30N 53°15E 45 B7
Chelforó Argentina 39°0S 66°33W 96 D3
Chelkar = Shalqar Kazakhstan 47°48N 59°39E 28 E6
Chelm Poland 51°8N 23°30E 17 C12
Chelmno Poland 53°20N 18°30E 17 B10
Chelmsford U.K. 51°44N 0°29E 13 F8
Chelsea Australia 38°5S 145°8E 63 F4
Chelsea U.S.A. 43°59N 72°27W 83 C12
Cheltenham U.K. 51°54N 2°4W 13 F5
Chelyabinsk Russia 55°10N 61°24E 28 D7
Chelyuskin, C. = Chelyuskin, Mys Russia 77°30N 103°0E 29 B11
Chelyuskin, Mys Russia 77°30N 103°0E 29 B11
Chemainus Canada 48°55N 123°42W 78 B3
Chemba Mozam. 17°9S 34°53E 53 H6
Chemin Grenier Mauritius 20°29S 57°28E 53 d
Chemnitz Germany 50°51N 12°54E 16 C7
Chemult U.S.A. 43°14N 121°47W 76 E3
Chen, Gora Russia 65°16N 141°50E 29 C15
Chenab → Pakistan 30°23N 71°2E 42 D4
Chenab Nagar Pakistan 31°45N 72°55E 42 D5
Chenango Forks U.S.A. 42°15N 75°51W 83 D9
Cheney U.S.A. 47°30N 117°35W 76 C5
Cheng Xian China 33°43N 105°42E 34 H3
Chengcheng China 35°8N 109°56E 34 G5
Chengchou = Zhengzhou China 34°45N 113°34E 34 G7
Chengde China 40°59N 117°58E 35 D9
Chengdu China 30°38N 104°2E 32 C5
Chenggu China 33°10N 107°21E 34 H4
Chengjiang China 24°39N 103°0E 32 D5
Chengmai China 19°50N 109°58E 38 C7
Ch'engtu = Chengdu China 30°38N 104°2E 32 C5
Chengwu China 34°58N 115°50E 34 G8
Chengyang China 36°18N 120°21E 35 F11
Chenjiagang China 34°23N 119°47E 35 G10
Chennai India 13°8N 80°19E 40 N12
Cheò, Eilean a' = Skye U.K. 57°15N 6°10W 11 D2
Cheom Ksan Cambodia 14°13N 104°56E 38 E5
Cheonan S. Korea 36°48N 127°9E 35 F14
Cheongdo S. Korea 35°38N 128°42E 35 G15
Cheongju S. Korea 36°39N 127°27E 35 F14
Cheorwon S. Korea 38°15N 127°10E 35 E14
Chepén Peru 7°15S 79°23W 92 E3
Chepes Argentina 31°20S 66°35W 94 C2
Chepo Panama 9°10N 79°6W 88 E4
Chepstow U.K. 51°38N 2°41W 13 F5
Chequamegon B. U.S.A. 46°39N 90°51W 80 B8
Cher → France 47°21N 0°29E 20 C4
Cheraw U.S.A. 34°42N 79°53W 85 D15
Cherbourg France 49°39N 1°40W 20 B3
Cherdyn Russia 60°24N 56°29E 18 B10
Cheremkhovo Russia 53°8N 103°1E 29 D11
Cherepovets Russia 59°5N 37°55E 18 C6
Chergui, Chott ech Algeria 34°21N 0°25E 50 B6
Cherikov = Cherykaw Belarus 53°32N 31°20E 17 B16
Cherkasy Ukraine 49°27N 32°4E 19 E5
Cherkessk Russia 44°15N 42°5E 19 F7
Cherlak Russia 54°15N 74°55E 28 D8
Chernaya Russia 70°30N 89°10E 29 B9
Chernigov = Chernihiv Ukraine 51°28N 31°20E 18 D5
Chernigovka Russia 44°19N 132°34E 30 B6
Chernihiv Ukraine 51°28N 31°20E 18 D5
Chernivtsi Ukraine 48°15N 25°52E 17 D13
Chernobyl = Chornobyl Ukraine 51°20N 30°15E 17 C16
Chernogorsk Russia 53°49N 91°18E 29 D10
Chernovtsy = Chernivtsi Ukraine 48°15N 25°52E 17 D13
Chernyakhovsk Russia 54°36N 21°48E 9 J19
Chernysheyskiy Russia 63°0N 112°30E 29 C12
Cherokee Iowa, U.S.A. 42°45N 95°33W 80 D6
Cherokee Okla., U.S.A. 36°45N 98°21W 84 C5
Cherokee Village U.S.A. 36°18N 91°31W 84 C9
Cherokees, Grand Lake O' The U.S.A. 36°28N 94°55W 84 C7
Cherrapunji India 25°17N 91°47E 41 G17
Cherry Valley U.S.A. 42°48N 74°45W 83 D10
Cherskiy Russia 68°45N 161°18E 29 C17
Cherskogo Khrebet Russia 65°0N 143°0E 29 C15
Chersonisos Greece 35°18N 25°22E 25 D7
Chersonisos Akrotiri Greece 35°30N 24°10E 25 D6
Cherven Belarus 53°45N 28°28E 17 B15
Chervonohrad Ukraine 50°25N 24°10E 17 C13
Cherwell → U.K. 51°44N 1°14W 13 F6
Cherykaw Belarus 53°32N 31°20E 17 B16
Chesapeake U.S.A. 36°49N 76°16W 81 G15
Chesapeake B. U.S.A. 38°0N 76°10W 81 F14
Cheshire □ U.K. 53°14N 2°30W 12 D5
Cheshskaya Guba Russia 67°20N 47°0E 18 A8
Cheshunt U.K. 51°43N 0°1W 13 F7
Chesil Beach U.K. 50°37N 2°33W 13 G5
Chesley Canada 44°17N 81°5W 82 B3
Chester U.K. 53°12N 2°53W 12 D5
Chester Calif., U.S.A. 40°19N 121°14W 76 F3
Chester Ill., U.S.A. 37°55N 89°49W 80 G9
Chester Mont., U.S.A. 48°31N 110°58W 76 B8
Chester Pa., U.S.A. 39°51N 75°22W 81 F16
Chester S.C., U.S.A. 34°43N 81°12W 85 D14
Chester Vt., U.S.A. 43°16N 72°36W 83 C12
Chester W. Va., U.S.A. 40°37N 80°34W 82 F4
Chester-le-Street U.K. 54°51N 1°34W 12 C6
Chesterfield U.K. 53°15N 1°25W 12 D6
Chesterfield, Îs. N. Cal. 19°52S 158°15E 58 C8
Chesterfield Inlet Canada 63°30N 90°45W 68 E13
Chesterton Ra. Australia 25°30S 147°27E 63 D4
Chesterton Range △ Australia 26°16S 147°22E 63 D4
Chestertown U.S.A. 43°40N 73°48W 83 C11
Chesterville Canada 45°6N 75°14W 83 A9
Chesuncook L. U.S.A. 46°0N 69°21W 81 C19
Chéticamp Canada 46°37N 60°59W 73 C7
Chetumal Mexico 18°30N 88°20W 87 D7
Chetumal, B. de Cent. Amer. 18°40N 88°10W 87 D7
Chetwynd Canada 55°45N 121°36W 70 B4
Cheviot, The U.K. 55°29N 2°9W 12 B5
Cheviot Hills U.K. 55°20N 2°30W 12 B5
Cheviot Ra. Australia 25°20S 143°45E 62 D3
Chew Bahir Ethiopia 4°40N 36°50E 47 G2
Chewelah U.S.A. 48°17N 117°43W 76 B5
Chewore ⌓ Zimbabwe 16°0S 29°52E 55 F2
Cheyenne Okla., U.S.A. 35°37N 99°40W 84 D5
Cheyenne Wyo., U.S.A. 41°8N 104°49W 76 F11
Cheyenne → U.S.A. 44°41N 101°18W 80 C3
Cheyenne Wells U.S.A. 38°49N 102°21W 76 G12
Cheyne B. Australia 34°35S 118°50E 61 F2
Chhabra India 24°40N 76°54E 42 G7
Chhaktala India 22°6N 74°11E 42 H6
Chhapra India 25°48N 84°44E 43 G11
Chhata India 27°42N 77°30E 42 F7
Chhatarpur Jharkhand, India 24°23N 84°11E 43 G11
Chhatarpur Mad. P., India 24°55N 79°35E 43 G8
Chhattisgarh □ India 22°0N 82°0E 43 J10
Chhep Cambodia 13°45N 105°24E 38 F5
Chhindwara Mad. P., India 23°3N 79°29E 43 H8
Chhindwara Mad. P., India 22°2N 78°59E 43 H8
Chhlong Cambodia 12°15N 105°58E 39 F5
Chhota Tawa → India 22°14N 76°36E 42 H7
Chhoti Kali Sindh → India 24°2N 75°31E 42 G6
Chhuikhadan India 21°32N 80°59E 43 J9
Chhuk Cambodia 10°46N 104°28E 39 G5
Chi → Thailand 15°11N 104°43E 38 E5
Chiai Taiwan 23°29N 120°25E 33 D7
Chiamboni Somali Rep. 1°39S 41°35E 52 E8
Chiang Dao Thailand 19°22N 98°58E 38 C2
Chiang Kham Thailand 19°32N 100°18E 38 C3
Chiang Khan Thailand 17°52N 101°36E 38 D3
Chiang Khong Thailand 20°17N 100°24E 38 B3
Chiang Mai Thailand 18°47N 98°59E 38 C2
Chiang Rai Thailand 19°52N 99°50E 38 C2
Chiang Saen Thailand 20°16N 100°5E 38 B3
Chiapa → Mexico 16°42N 93°0W 87 D6
Chiapa de Corzo Mexico 16°42N 93°0W 87 D6
Chiapas □ Mexico 16°30N 92°30W 87 D6
Chiapas, Sa. Madre de Mexico 15°40N 93°0W 87 D6
Chiautla de Tapia Mexico 18°18N 98°36W 87 D5
Chiávari Italy 44°19N 9°19E 20 D8
Chiavenna Italy 46°19N 9°24E 20 C8
Chiba Japan 35°30N 140°7E 31 G10
Chiba □ Japan 35°30N 140°20E 31 G10
Chibabava Mozam. 20°17S 33°35E 57 C5
Chibemba Cunene, Angola 15°48S 14°8E 53 H2
Chibemba Huila, Angola 16°20S 15°20E 56 B2
Chibi Zimbabwe 20°18S 30°25E 57 C5
Chibia Angola 15°10S 13°42E 53 H2
Chibougamau Canada 49°56N 74°24W 72 C5
Chibougamau, L. Canada 49°50N 74°20W 72 C5
Chibuk Nigeria 10°52N 12°50E 51 F8
Chibuto Mozam. 24°40S 33°33E 57 C5
Chic-Chocs, Mts. Canada 48°55N 66°0W 73 C6
Chicacole = Srikakulam India 18°14N 83°58E 41 K13
Chicago U.S.A. 41°52N 87°38W 80 E10
Chicago Heights U.S.A. 41°30N 87°38W 80 E10
Chichagof I. U.S.A. 57°30N 135°30W 68 F4
Chichaoua Morocco 31°32N 8°44W 50 B4
Chichawatni Pakistan 30°32N 72°42E 42 D5
Chichén-Itzá Mexico 20°37N 88°35W 87 C7
Chicheng China 40°55N 115°55E 34 D8
Chichester U.K. 50°50N 0°47W 13 G7
Chichester Ra. Australia 22°12S 119°15E 60 D2
Chichibu Japan 35°59N 139°10E 31 F9
Chichibu-Tama △ Japan 35°52N 138°42E 31 G9
Ch'ich'ihaerh = Qiqihar China 47°26N 124°0E 33 B7
Chicholi India 22°1N 77°40E 42 H8
Chickasaw ⌓ U.S.A. 34°26N 97°0W 84 D6
Chickasha U.S.A. 35°3N 97°58W 84 D6
Chiclana de la Frontera Spain 36°26N 6°9W 21 D2
Chiclayo Peru 6°42S 79°50W 92 E3
Chico U.S.A. 39°44N 121°50W 78 F5
Chico → Chubut, Argentina 44°0S 67°0W 96 E3
Chico → Santa Cruz, Argentina 50°0S 68°30W 96 G3
Chicoa Mozam. 15°36S 32°20E 55 F3
Chicomo Mozam. 24°31S 34°6E 57 C5
Chicomostoc Mexico 22°28N 102°46W 86 C4
Chicontepec Mexico 20°58N 98°10W 87 C5
Chicopee U.S.A. 42°9N 72°37W 83 D12
Chicoutimi Canada 48°28N 71°5W 73 C5
Chicualacuala Mozam. 22°6S 31°42E 57 C5
Chidambaram India 11°20N 79°45E 40 P11
Chidenguele Mozam. 24°55S 34°11E 57 C5
Chidley, C. Canada 60°23N 64°26W 69 E19
Chiducuane Mozam. 24°35S 34°25E 57 C5
Chiede Angola 17°15S 16°22E 56 B2
Chiefs Pt. Canada 44°41N 81°18W 82 B3
Chiem Hoa Vietnam 22°12N 105°17E 38 A5
Chiemsee Germany 47°53N 12°28E 16 E7
Chiengi Zambia 8°45S 29°10E 55 D2
Chiengmai = Chiang Mai Thailand 18°47N 98°59E 38 C2
Chiese → Italy 45°8N 10°25E 20 D9
Chieti Italy 42°21N 14°10E 22 C6
Chifeng China 42°18N 118°58E 35 C10
Chignecto B. Canada 45°30N 64°40W 73 C7
Chiguana Bolivia 21°0S 67°58W 94 A2
Chigwell U.K. 51°37N 0°6E 13 F8
Chihli, G. of = Bo Hai China 39°0N 119°0E 35 E10
Chihuahua Mexico 28°38N 106°5W 86 B3
Chihuahua □ Mexico 28°30N 106°0W 86 B3
Chiili = Shīeli Kazakhstan 44°20N 66°15E 28 E7
Chik Bollapur India 13°25N 77°45E 40 N10
Chikmagalur India 13°15N 75°45E 40 N9
Chikwawa Malawi 16°2S 34°50E 55 F3
Chilanga Zambia 15°33S 28°16E 55 F2
Chilapa Mexico 17°36N 99°10W 87 D5
Chilas Pakistan 35°25N 74°5E 43 B6
Chilaw Sri Lanka 7°30N 79°50E 40 R11
Chilcotin → Canada 51°44N 122°23W 70 C4
Childers Australia 25°15S 152°17E 63 D5
Childress U.S.A. 34°25N 100°13W 84 D4
Chile ■ S. Amer. 35°0S 72°0W 96 D2
Chile Rise Pac. Oc. 38°0S 92°0W 65 L18
Chilecito Argentina 29°10S 67°30W 94 B2
Chilete Peru 7°10S 78°50W 92 E3
Chililabombwe Zambia 12°18S 27°43E 55 E2
Chilim Pakistan 35°5N 75°5E 43 B6
Chilin = Jilin China 43°44N 126°30E 35 C14
Chilka L. India 19°40N 85°25E 41 K14
Chilko → Canada 52°0N 123°40W 70 C4
Chilko L. Canada 51°20N 124°10W 70 C4
Chillagoe Australia 17°7S 144°33E 62 B3
Chillán Chile 36°40S 72°10W 94 D1
Chillicothe Ill., U.S.A. 40°55N 89°29W 80 E9
Chillicothe Mo., U.S.A. 39°48N 93°33W 80 F7
Chillicothe Ohio, U.S.A. 39°20N 82°59W 81 F12
Chilliwack Canada 49°10N 121°54W 70 D4
Chilo India 27°25N 73°32E 42 F5
Chiloane, I. Mozam. 20°40S 34°55E 57 C5
Chiloé, I. de Chile 42°30S 73°50W 96 E2
Chilpancingo Mexico 17°33N 99°30W 87 D5

Chiltern Hills U.K. 51°40N 0°53W 13 F7
Chilton U.S.A. 44°2N 88°10W 80 C9
Chilubi Zambia 11°5S 29°58E 55 E2
Chilubula Zambia 10°14S 30°51E 55 E3
Chilumba Malawi 10°28S 34°12E 55 E3
Chilung Taiwan 25°3N 121°45E 33 D7
Chilwa, L. Malawi 15°15S 35°40E 55 F4
Chimaltitán Mexico 21°35N 103°50W 86 C4
Chimán Panama 8°45N 78°40W 88 E4
Chimanimani Zimbabwe 19°48S 32°52E 57 B5
Chimay Belgium 50°3N 4°20E 15 D4
Chimayo U.S.A. 36°0N 105°56W 77 J11
Chimba Zambia 9°54S 31°28E 55 D3
Chimbay Uzbekistan 42°57N 59°47E 28 E6
Chimborazo Ecuador 1°29S 78°55W 92 D3
Chimbote Peru 9°0S 78°35W 92 E3
Chimkent = Shymkent
  Kazakhstan 42°18N 69°36E 28 E7
Chimoio Mozam. 19°4S 33°30E 55 F3
Chimpembe Zambia 9°31S 29°33E 55 D2
Chin □ Burma 22°0N 93°0E 41 J18
Chin Hills Burma 22°30N 93°30E 41 H18
Chin Ling Shan = Qinling Shandi
  China 33°50N 108°10E 34 H5
China Mexico 25°42N 99°14W 87 B5
China ■ Asia 30°0N 110°0E 33 C6
China, Great Plain of
  Asia 35°0N 115°0E 26 E13
China Lake U.S.A. 35°44N 117°37W 79 K9
Chinan = Jinan China 36°38N 117°1E 34 F9
Chinandega Nic. 12°35N 87°12W 88 D2
Chinati Peak U.S.A. 29°57N 104°29W 84 G2
Chincha Alta Peru 13°25S 76°7W 92 F3
Chinchaga → Canada 58°53N 118°20W 70 B5
Chinchilla Australia 26°45S 150°38E 63 D5
Chinchorro, Banco
  Mexico 18°35N 87°22W 87 D7
Chinchou = Jinzhou
  China 41°5N 121°3E 35 D11
Chincoteague U.S.A. 37°56N 75°23W 81 G16
Chinde Mozam. 18°35S 36°30E 55 F4
Chindwin → Burma 21°26N 95°15E 41 J19
Chineni India 33°2N 75°15E 43 C6
Chinga Mozam. 15°13S 38°35E 55 F4
Chingola Zambia 12°31S 27°53E 55 E2
Chingole Malawi 13°4S 34°17E 55 E3
Ch'ingtao = Qingdao
  China 36°5N 120°20E 35 F11
Chinguetti Mauritania 20°25N 12°24W 50 D3
Chingune Mozam. 20°33S 34°58E 57 C5
Chinhanguanine
  Mozam. 25°21S 32°30E 57 D5
Chinhoyi Zimbabwe 17°20S 30°8E 55 F3
Chini India 31°32N 78°15E 42 D8
Chiniot Pakistan 31°45N 73°0E 42 D5
Chínipas Mexico 27°23N 108°32W 86 B3
Chinji Pakistan 32°42N 72°22E 42 C5
Chinju = Jinju S. Korea 35°12N 128°2E 35 G15
Chinko → C.A.R. 4°50N 23°53E 52 D4
Chinle U.S.A. 36°9N 109°33W 77 H9
Chinnampo = Namp'o
  N. Korea 38°52N 125°10E 35 E13
Chino Japan 35°59N 138°9E 31 G9
Chino U.S.A. 34°1N 117°41W 79 L9
Chino Valley U.S.A. 34°45N 112°27W 77 J7
Chinon France 47°10N 0°15E 20 C4
Chinook U.S.A. 48°35N 109°14W 76 B9
Chinook Trough
  Pac. Oc. 44°0N 175°0W 64 C10
Chinsali Zambia 10°30S 32°2E 55 E3
Chinsura = Chunchura
  India 22°53N 88°27E 43 H13
Chióggia Italy 45°13N 12°17E 22 B5
Chíos = Hios Greece 38°27N 26°9E 23 E12
Chipata Zambia 13°38S 32°28E 55 E3
Chipindo Angola 13°49S 15°48E 53 G3
Chipinge Zimbabwe 20°13S 32°28E 55 G3
Chipinge △ Zimbabwe 20°14S 33°0E 55 G3
Chipley U.S.A. 30°47N 85°32W 85 F12
Chipman Canada 46°6N 65°53W 73 C6
Chipoka Malawi 13°57S 34°28E 55 E3
Chippenham U.K. 51°27N 2°6W 13 F5
Chippewa → U.S.A. 44°25N 92°5W 80 C7
Chippewa Falls U.S.A. 44°56N 91°24W 80 C8
Chipping Norton U.K. 51°56N 1°32W 13 F6
Chiputneticook Lakes
  N. Amer. 45°35N 67°35W 81 C20
Chiquián Peru 10°10S 77°0W 92 F3
Chiquibul △ Belize 16°49N 88°52W 88 C2
Chiquimula Guatemala 14°51N 89°37W 88 D2
Chiquinquira Colombia 5°37N 73°50W 92 B4
Chirala India 15°50N 80°26E 40 M12
Chiramba Mozam. 16°55S 34°39E 55 F3
Chirawa India 28°14N 75°42E 42 E6
Chirchiq Uzbekistan 41°29N 69°35E 28 E7
Chiredzi Zimbabwe 21°0S 31°38E 57 C5
Chiricahua △ U.S.A. 32°0N 109°20W 77 K9
Chiricahua Peak
  U.S.A. 31°51N 109°18W 77 L9
Chirikof I. U.S.A. 55°50N 155°40W 74 D8
Chiriquí, G. de Panama 8°0N 82°10W 88 E3
Chiriquí, L. de Panama 9°10N 82°0W 88 E3
Chirisa △ Zimbabwe 17°53S 28°15E 55 F2
Chirivira Falls Zimbabwe 21°10S 32°12E 55 G3
Chirmiri India 23°15N 82°20E 43 H10
Chirripó Grande, Cerro
  Costa Rica 9°29N 83°29W 88 E3
Chisamba Zambia 14°55S 28°20E 55 E2
Chisapani Nepal 28°37N 81°16E 43 E9
Chisasibi Canada 53°50N 79°0W 72 B4
Chisholm Canada 54°55N 114°10W 70 C6
Chisholm U.S.A. 47°29N 92°53W 80 B7
Chishtian Mandi
  Pakistan 29°50N 72°55E 42 E5
Chisimaio = Kismaayo
  Somali Rep. 0°22S 42°32E 47 H3
Chisimba Falls Zambia 10°12S 31°5E 55 E3
Chişinău Moldova 47°2N 28°50E 17 E15

Chisos Mts. U.S.A. 29°5N 103°15W 84 G3
Chistopol Russia 55°25N 50°38E 18 C9
Chita Russia 52°0N 113°35E 29 D12
Chitipa Malawi 9°41S 33°19E 55 D3
Chitose Japan 42°49N 141°39E 30 C10
Chitral Pakistan 35°50N 71°56E 40 B7
Chitré Panama 7°59N 80°27W 88 E3
Chittagong Bangla. 22°19N 91°48E 41 H17
Chittagong □ Bangla. 24°5N 91°0E 41 G17
Chittaurgarh India 24°52N 74°38E 42 G6
Chittoor India 13°15N 79°5E 40 N11
Chitungwiza Zimbabwe 18°0S 31°6E 55 F3
Chiusi Italy 43°1N 11°57E 22 C4
Chivasso Italy 45°11N 7°53E 20 D7
Chivhu Zimbabwe 19°2S 30°52E 55 F3
Chivilcoy Argentina 34°55S 60°0W 94 C4
Chiwanda Tanzania 11°23S 34°55E 55 E3
Chizarira Zimbabwe 17°36S 27°45E 55 F2
Chizarira △ Zimbabwe 17°44S 27°7E 55 F2
Chizela Zambia 13°8S 25°0E 55 E2
Chkalov = Orenburg
  Russia 51°45N 55°6E 18 D10
Chloride U.S.A. 35°25N 114°12W 79 K12
Cho Bo Vietnam 20°46N 105°10E 38 B5
Cho-do N. Korea 38°30N 124°40E 35 E13
Cho Phuoc Hai Vietnam 10°26N 107°18E 39 G6
Choa Chu Kang Singapore 1°22N 103°41E 39 d
Choba Kenya 2°30N 38°5E 54 B4
Chobe → Botswana 18°37S 24°23E 56 B4
Chocolate Mts.
  U.S.A. 33°15N 115°15W 79 M11
Choctawhatchee →
  U.S.A. 30°25N 86°8W 85 F11
Choele Choel Argentina 39°11S 65°40W 96 D3
Choiseul St. Lucia 13°47N 61°3W 89 f
Choiseul Solomon Is. 7°0S 156°40E 58 B8
Choix Mexico 26°43N 108°17W 86 B3
Chojnice Poland 53°42N 17°32E 17 B9
Chok Chai Thailand 14°44N 102°10E 38 E4
Chōkai-San Japan 39°6N 140°3E 30 E10
Choke Canyon Res.
  U.S.A. 28°30N 98°20W 84 G5
Chokurdakh Russia 70°38N 147°55E 29 B15
Cholame U.S.A. 35°44N 120°18W 78 K6
Cholet France 47°4N 0°52W 20 C3
Cholguan Chile 37°10S 72°3W 94 D1
Choloma Honduras 15°37N 87°57W 88 C2
Choluteca Honduras 13°20N 87°14W 88 D2
Choluteca → Honduras 13°0N 87°20W 88 D2
Chom Bung Thailand 13°37N 99°36E 38 F2
Chom Thong Thailand 18°25N 98°41E 38 C2
Choma Zambia 16°48S 26°59E 55 F2
Chomolungma = Everest, Mt.
  Nepal 28°5N 86°58E 43 E12
Chomun India 27°15N 75°40E 42 F6
Chomutov Czech Rep. 50°28N 13°23E 16 C7
Chon Buri Thailand 13°21N 101°1E 38 F3
Chon Thanh Vietnam 11°24N 106°36E 39 G6
Chone Ecuador 0°40S 80°0W 92 D3
Chong Kai Cambodia 13°57N 103°35E 38 F4
Chong Mek Thailand 15°10N 105°27E 38 E5
Chong Phangan Thailand 9°39N 100°0E 39 b
Chong Samui Thailand 9°21N 99°50E 39 b
Ch'ŏngjin N. Korea 41°47N 129°50E 35 D15
Chŏngju N. Korea 39°40N 125°5E 35 E13
Chongli China 40°58N 115°15E 34 D8
Chongqing China 29°35N 106°25E 32 D5
Chongqing Shi □ China 30°0N 108°0E 32 C5
Chonguene Mozam. 25°3S 33°49E 57 C5
Chongwe Zambia 15°15S 28°42E 55 F2
Chonos, Arch. de los Chile 45°0S 75°0W 96 F2
Chop Ukraine 48°26N 22°12E 17 D12
Chopim → Brazil 25°35S 53°5W 95 B5
Chor Pakistan 25°31N 69°46E 42 G3
Chora Sfakion Greece 35°15N 24°9E 25 D6
Chorbat La India 34°42N 76°37E 43 B7
Chorley U.K. 53°39N 2°38W 12 D5
Chornobyl Ukraine 51°20N 30°15E 17 C16
Chorolque, Cerro Bolivia 20°59S 66°5W 94 A2
Chorregon Australia 22°40S 143°32E 62 C3
Chorro el Indio △
  Venezuela 7°43N 72°9W 89 E5
Chortkiv Ukraine 49°2N 25°46E 17 D13
Chorzów Poland 50°18N 18°57E 17 C10
Chos-Malal Argentina 37°20S 70°15W 94 D1
Ch'osan N. Korea 40°50N 125°47E 35 D13
Choszczno Poland 53°7N 15°25E 16 B8
Choteau U.S.A. 47°49N 112°11W 76 C7
Chotila India 22°23N 71°15E 42 H4
Chotta Udepur India 22°19N 74°1E 42 H6
Chowchilla U.S.A. 37°7N 120°16W 78 H6
Choybalsan Mongolia 48°4N 114°30E 33 B6
Choyr Mongolia 46°24N 108°30E 29 F12
Christchurch N.Z. 43°33S 172°47E 59 E4
Christchurch U.K. 50°44N 1°47W 13 G6
Christian I. Canada 44°50N 80°12W 82 B4
Christian Sd. U.S.A. 55°56N 134°40W 70 D13
Christiana S. Africa 27°52S 25°8E 56 D4
Christiansted
  U.S. Virgin Is. 17°45N 64°42W 89 C7
Christie B. Canada 62°32N 111°10W 71 A6
Christina → Canada 56°40N 111°3W 71 B6
Christmas Cr. →
  Australia 18°29S 125°23E 60 C4
Christmas I. = Kiritimati
  Kiribati 1°58N 157°27W 65 G12
Christmas I. Ind. Oc. 10°30S 105°40E 64 J2
Christopher, L.
  Australia 24°49S 127°42E 61 D4
Chtimba Malawi 10°35S 34°13E 55 E3
Chū = Shū Kazakhstan 43°36N 73°42E 28 E8
Chu → Vietnam 19°53N 105°45E 38 C5
Chu Lai Vietnam 15°28N 108°45E 38 E7
Chuadanga Bangla. 23°38N 88°51E 43 H13
Chuak, Ko Thailand 9°38N 99°41E 39 b
Ch'uanchou = Quanzhou
  China 24°55N 118°34E 33 D6
Chuankou China 34°20N 110°59E 34 G6
Chubbuck U.S.A. 42°55N 112°28W 76 E7

Chūbu □ Japan 36°45N 137°30E 31 F8
Chubu-Sangaku △
  Japan 36°30N 137°40E 31 F8
Chubut → Argentina 43°20S 65°5W 96 E3
Chuchi L. Canada 55°12N 124°30W 70 B4
Chuda India 22°29N 71°41E 42 H4
Chudskoye, Ozero
  Russia 58°13N 27°30E 9 G22
Chugach Mts. U.S.A. 60°45N 147°0W 74 C10
Chūgoku □ Japan 35°0N 133°0E 31 G6
Chūgoku-Sanchi Japan 35°0N 133°0E 31 G6
Chugwater U.S.A. 41°46N 104°50W 76 F11
Chuka Kenya 0°20S 37°39E 54 C4
Chukchi Plateau Arctic 78°0N 165°0W 4 B17
Chukchi Sea Russia 68°0N 175°0W 29 C19
Chukotskiy Mys Russia 66°14N 173°8W 74 C5
Chukotskiy Poluostrov
  Russia 66°0N 174°0W 74 B5
Chukotskoye Nagorye
  Russia 68°0N 175°0E 29 C18
Chula Vista U.S.A. 32°38N 117°5W 79 N9
Chulucanas Peru 5°8S 80°10W 92 E2
Chulym → Russia 57°43N 83°51E 28 D9
Chum Phae Thailand 16°40N 102°6E 38 D4
Chum Saeng Thailand 15°55N 100°15E 38 E3
Chumar India 32°40N 78°35E 43 C8
Chumbicha Argentina 29°0S 66°10W 94 B2
Chumikan Russia 54°40N 135°10E 29 D14
Chumphon Thailand 10°35N 99°14E 39 G2
Chumuare Mozam. 14°31S 31°50E 55 E3
Chuna → Russia 57°47N 94°37E 29 D10
Chuncheon S. Korea 37°58N 127°44E 35 F14
Chunchura India 22°53N 88°27E 43 H13
Chunggang-ŭp
  N. Korea 41°48N 126°48E 35 D14
Chunghwa N. Korea 38°52N 125°47E 35 E13
Chungju S. Korea 36°58N 127°58E 35 F14
Chungking = Chongqing
  China 29°35N 106°25E 32 D5
Chungt'iaoshan = Zhongtiao
  Shan China 35°0N 111°10E 34 G6
Chunian Pakistan 30°57N 74°0E 42 D6
Chunya Tanzania 8°30S 33°27E 55 D3
Chunyang China 43°38N 129°23E 35 C15
Chupara Pt.
  Trin. & Tob. 10°49N 61°22W 93 K15
Chuquibamba Peru 15°47S 72°44W 92 G4
Chuquicamata Chile 22°15S 69°0W 94 A2
Chur Switz. 46°52N 9°32E 20 C8
Churachandpur India 24°20N 93°40E 41 G18
Church Stretton U.K. 52°32N 2°48W 13 E5
Churchill Canada 58°47N 94°11W 71 B10
Churchill → Man.,
  Canada 58°47N 94°12W 71 B10
Churchill → Nfld. & L.,
  Canada 53°19N 60°10W 73 B7
Churchill, C. Canada 58°46N 93°12W 71 B10
Churchill Falls Canada 53°36N 64°19W 73 B7
Churchill L. Canada 55°55N 108°20W 71 B7
Churchill Pk. Canada 58°10N 125°10W 70 B3
Churki India 23°50N 83°12E 43 H10
Churu India 28°20N 74°50E 42 E6
Churún Merú = Angel Falls
  Venezuela 5°57N 62°30W 92 B6
Chushal India 33°40N 78°40E 43 C8
Chuska Mts. U.S.A. 36°15N 108°50W 77 H9
Chusovoy Russia 58°22N 57°50E 18 C10
Chute-aux-Outardes
  Canada 49°7N 68°24W 73 C6
Chuuk = Truk
  Micronesia 7°25N 151°46E 64 G7
Chuvash Republic = Chuvashia □
  Russia 55°30N 47°0E 18 C8
Chuvashia □ Russia 55°30N 47°0E 18 C8
Chuwārtah Iraq 35°43N 45°34E 44 C5
Chuy Uruguay 33°41S 53°27W 95 C5
Ci Xian China 36°20N 114°25E 34 F8
Ciadâr-Lunga Moldova 46°3N 28°51E 17 E15
Ciamis Indonesia 7°20S 108°21E 37 G13
Cianjur Indonesia 6°49S 107°8E 37 G12
Cianorte Brazil 23°37S 52°37W 95 A5
Cibola U.S.A. 33°17N 114°42W 79 M12
Cicero U.S.A. 41°51N 87°44W 80 E10
Cicia Fiji 17°45S 179°18W 59 a
Ciénagas del Catatumbo △
  Venezuela 9°25N 71°54W 89 E5
Ciechanów Poland 52°52N 20°38E 17 B11
Ciego de Ávila Cuba 21°50N 78°50W 88 B4
Ciénaga Colombia 11°1N 74°15W 92 A4
Cienfuegos Cuba 22°10N 80°30W 88 B3
Cieszyn Poland 49°45N 18°35E 17 D10
Cieza Spain 38°17N 1°23W 21 C5
Cihuatlán Mexico 19°14N 104°35W 86 D4
Cijara, Embalse de Spain 39°18N 4°52W 21 C3
Cijulang Indonesia 7°42S 108°27E 37 G13
Cilacap Indonesia 7°43S 109°0E 37 G13
Cill Airne = Killarney
  Ireland 52°4N 9°30W 10 D2
Cill Chainnigh = Kilkenny
  Ireland 52°39N 7°15W 10 D4
Cill Dara = Kildare Ireland 53°9N 6°55W 10 C5
Cill Mhantáin = Wicklow
  Ireland 52°59N 6°3W 10 D5
Cilo Dağı Turkey 37°28N 43°55E 19 G7
Cimarron Kans., U.S.A. 37°48N 100°21W 80 G4
Cimarron N. Mex.,
  U.S.A. 36°31N 104°55W 77 H11
Cimarron → U.S.A. 36°10N 96°16W 84 C6
Cimișlia Moldova 46°34N 28°44E 17 E15
Cimone, Mte. Italy 44°12N 10°42E 22 B4
Cinca → Spain 41°26N 0°21E 21 B6
Cincar Bos.-H. 43°55N 17°5E 22 C7
Cincinnati U.S.A. 39°9N 84°27W 81 F11
Cincinnatus U.S.A. 42°33N 75°54W 83 D9
Çine Turkey 37°37N 28°2E 23 F13
Ciney Belgium 50°18N 5°5E 15 D5
Cinto, Mte. France 42°24N 8°54E 20 E8

Circle Alaska, U.S.A. 65°50N 144°4W 74 B11
Circle Mont., U.S.A. 47°25N 105°35W 76 C11
Circleville U.S.A. 39°36N 82°57W 81 F12
Cirebon Indonesia 6°45S 108°32E 37 G13
Ciremay Indonesia 6°55S 108°27E 37 G13
Cirencester U.K. 51°43N 1°57W 13 F6
Cirium Cyprus 34°40N 32°53E 25 E11
Cisco U.S.A. 32°23N 98°59W 84 E5
Citlaltépetl = Orizaba, Pico de
  Mexico 18°58N 97°15W 87 D5
Citrus Heights U.S.A. 38°42N 121°17W 78 G5
Citrusdal S. Africa 32°35S 19°0E 56 E2
Città del Vaticano = Vatican
  City ■ Europe 41°54N 12°27E 22 D5
Città di Castello Italy 43°27N 12°14E 22 C5
Ciudad Acuña Mexico 29°18N 100°55W 86 B4
Ciudad Altamirano
  Mexico 18°20N 100°40W 86 D4
Ciudad Anáhuac
  Mexico 27°14N 100°7W 86 B4
Ciudad Bolívar Venezuela 8°5N 63°36W 92 B6
Ciudad Camargo
  Mexico 27°40N 105°10W 86 B3
Ciudad Cortés Costa Rica 8°55N 84°0W 88 E3
Ciudad de México Mexico 19°24N 99°9W 87 D5
Ciudad de Valles Mexico 22°0N 99°0W 87 C5
Ciudad del Carmen
  Mexico 18°38N 91°50W 87 D6
Ciudad del Este Paraguay 25°30S 54°50W 95 B5
Ciudad Delicias = Delicias
  Mexico 28°13N 105°28W 86 B3
Ciudad Frontera
  Mexico 26°56N 101°27W 86 B4
Ciudad Guayana
  Venezuela 8°0N 62°30W 92 B6
Ciudad Guerrero
  Mexico 28°33N 107°30W 86 B3
Ciudad Guzmán
  Mexico 19°41N 103°29W 86 D4
Ciudad Juárez Mexico 31°44N 106°29W 86 A3
Ciudad Lerdo Mexico 25°32N 103°32W 86 B4
Ciudad Madero Mexico 22°19N 97°50W 87 C5
Ciudad Mante Mexico 22°44N 98°59W 87 C5
Ciudad Obregón
  Mexico 27°29N 109°56W 86 B3
Ciudad Real Spain 38°59N 3°55W 21 C4
Ciudad Rodrigo Spain 40°35N 6°32W 21 B2
Ciudad Victoria Mexico 23°44N 99°8W 87 C5
Ciudadela Spain 40°0N 3°50E 24 B10
Civitanova Marche Italy 43°18N 13°44E 22 C5
Civitavécchia Italy 42°6N 11°48E 22 C4
Cizre Turkey 37°19N 42°10E 44 B4
Clackmannanshire □
  U.K. 56°10N 3°43W 11 E5
Clacton-on-Sea U.K. 51°47N 1°11E 13 F9
Claire, L. Canada 58°35N 112°5W 70 B6
Clairton U.S.A. 40°18N 79°53W 82 F5
Clallam Bay U.S.A. 48°15N 124°16W 78 B2
Clanton U.S.A. 32°51N 86°38W 85 E11
Clanwilliam S. Africa 32°11S 18°52E 56 E2
Clara Ireland 53°21N 7°37W 10 C4
Claraville U.S.A. 35°24N 118°20W 79 K8
Clare Australia 33°50S 138°37E 63 E2
Clare U.S.A. 43°49N 84°46W 81 D11
Clare □ Ireland 52°45N 9°0W 10 D3
Clare → Ireland 53°20N 9°2W 10 C2
Clare I. Ireland 53°49N 10°0W 10 C1
Claremont Calif., U.S.A. 34°6N 117°43W 79 L9
Claremont N.H., U.S.A. 43°23N 72°20W 83 C12
Claremont Pt. Australia 14°1S 143°41E 62 A3
Claremore U.S.A. 36°19N 95°36W 84 C7
Claremorris Ireland 53°45N 9°0W 10 C3
Clarence → Australia 29°25S 153°22E 63 D5
Clarence → N.Z. 42°10S 173°56E 59 E4
Clarence, I. Chile 54°0S 72°0W 96 G2
Clarence I. Antarctica 61°10S 54°0W 5 C18
Clarence Str. Australia 12°0S 131°0E 60 B5
Clarence Town Bahamas 23°6N 74°59W 89 B5
Clarendon Pa., U.S.A. 41°47N 79°6W 82 E5
Clarendon Tex., U.S.A. 34°56N 100°53W 84 D4
Clarenville Canada 48°10N 54°1W 73 C9
Claresholm Canada 50°2N 113°33W 70 C6
Clarie Coast Antarctica 68°0S 135°0E 5 C9
Clarinda U.S.A. 40°44N 95°2W 80 E6
Clarington Canada 43°55N 78°41W 82 C6
Clarion Iowa, U.S.A. 42°44N 93°44W 80 D7
Clarion Pa., U.S.A. 41°13N 79°23W 82 E5
Clarion → U.S.A. 41°7N 79°41W 82 E5
Clarion Fracture Zone
  Pac. Oc. 20°0N 120°0W 66 H7
Clark U.S.A. 44°53N 97°44W 80 C5
Clark, Pt. Canada 44°4N 81°45W 82 B3
Clark Fork U.S.A. 48°9N 116°11W 76 B5
Clark Fork → U.S.A. 48°9N 116°15W 76 B5
Clarkdale U.S.A. 34°46N 112°3W 77 J7
Clarke City Canada 50°12N 66°38W 73 B6
Clarke I. Australia 40°32S 148°10E 63 G4
Clarke Ra. Australia 20°40S 148°30E 62 b
Clarks Fork Yellowstone →
  U.S.A. 45°32N 108°50W 76 D9
Clark's Harbour Canada 43°25N 65°38W 73 D6
Clarks Hill L. = J. Strom
  Thurmond L. U.S.A. 33°40N 82°12W 85 E13
Clarks Summit U.S.A. 41°30N 75°42W 83 E9
Clarksburg U.S.A. 39°17N 80°30W 81 F13
Clarksdale U.S.A. 34°12N 90°35W 85 D9
Clarkston U.S.A. 46°25N 117°3W 76 C5
Clarksville Ark., U.S.A. 35°28N 93°28W 84 D8
Clarksville Tenn.,
  U.S.A. 36°32N 87°21W 85 C11
Clarksville Tex., U.S.A. 33°37N 95°3W 84 E7
Clatskanie U.S.A. 46°6N 123°12W 78 D3
Claude U.S.A. 35°7N 101°22W 84 D4
Claveria Phil. 18°37N 121°10W 37 A6
Clay U.S.A. 38°17N 121°10W 78 G5
Clay Center U.S.A. 39°23N 97°8W 80 F5
Claypool U.S.A. 33°25N 110°51W 77 K8
Claysburg U.S.A. 40°18N 78°27W 82 F6
Claysville U.S.A. 40°7N 80°25W 82 F4

Clayton Canada 45°11N 76°19W 83 A8
Clayton N. Mex.,
  U.S.A. 36°27N 103°11W 77 H12
Clayton N.Y., U.S.A. 44°14N 76°5W 83 B8
Clear, C. Ireland 51°25N 9°32W 10 E2
Clear, L. Canada 45°26N 77°12W 82 A7
Clear Hills Canada 56°40N 119°30W 70 B5
Clear I. Ireland 51°26N 9°30W 10 E2
Clear L. U.S.A. 39°2N 122°47W 78 F4
Clear Lake Iowa, U.S.A. 43°8N 93°23W 80 D7
Clear Lake S. Dak.,
  U.S.A. 44°45N 96°41W 80 C5
Clear Lake Res. U.S.A. 41°56N 121°5W 76 F3
Clearfield Pa., U.S.A. 41°2N 78°27W 82 E6
Clearfield Utah, U.S.A. 41°7N 112°2W 76 F7
Clearlake U.S.A. 38°57N 122°38W 78 G4
Clearwater Canada 51°38N 120°2W 70 C4
Clearwater U.S.A. 27°59N 82°48W 85 H13
Clearwater → Alta.,
  Canada 52°22N 114°57W 70 C6
Clearwater → Alta.,
  Canada 56°44N 111°23W 71 B6
Clearwater L. Canada 53°34N 99°49W 71 C9
Clearwater Lake △
  Canada 54°0N 101°0W 71 C8
Clearwater Mts. U.S.A. 46°5N 115°20W 76 C6
Clearwater River △
  Canada 56°55N 109°10W 71 B7
Cleburne U.S.A. 32°21N 97°23W 84 E6
Clee Hills U.K. 52°26N 2°35W 13 E5
Cleethorpes U.K. 53°33N 0°3W 12 D7
Cleeve Cloud U.K. 51°56N 2°0W 13 F6
Clemson U.S.A. 34°41N 82°50W 85 D13
Clerke Reef Australia 17°22S 119°20E 60 C2
Clermont Australia 22°49S 147°39E 62 C4
Clermont U.S.A. 28°33N 81°46W 85 G14
Clermont-Ferrand France 45°46N 3°4E 20 D5
Clervaux Lux. 50°4N 6°2E 15 D6
Clevedon U.K. 51°26N 2°52W 13 F5
Cleveland Miss., U.S.A. 33°45N 90°43W 85 E9
Cleveland Ohio, U.S.A. 41°29N 81°41W 82 E3
Cleveland Okla., U.S.A. 36°19N 96°28W 84 C6
Cleveland Tenn., U.S.A. 35°10N 84°53W 85 D12
Cleveland Tex., U.S.A. 30°21N 95°5W 84 F7
Cleveland, C. Australia 19°11S 147°1E 62 B4
Cleveland, Mt. U.S.A. 48°56N 113°51W 76 B7
Cleveland Heights
  U.S.A. 41°31N 81°33W 82 E3
Clevelândia Brazil 26°24S 52°23W 95 B5
Clew B. Ireland 53°50N 9°49W 10 C2
Clewiston U.S.A. 26°45N 80°56W 85 H14
Clifden Ireland 53°29N 10°1W 10 C1
Clifden N.Z. 46°1S 167°42E 59 G1
Cliffdell U.S.A. 46°56N 121°5W 78 D5
Cliffy Hd. Australia 35°1S 116°29E 61 G2
Clifton Australia 27°59S 151°53E 63 D5
Clifton Ariz., U.S.A. 33°3N 109°18W 77 K9
Clifton Colo., U.S.A. 39°7N 108°25W 76 G9
Clifton Tex., U.S.A. 31°47N 97°35W 84 F6
Clifton Beach Australia 16°46S 145°39E 62 B4
Clinch → U.S.A. 35°53N 84°29W 85 D12
Clingmans Dome
  U.S.A. 35°34N 83°30W 85 D13
Clint U.S.A. 31°35N 106°14W 84 F1
Clinton B.C., Canada 51°6N 121°35W 70 C4
Clinton Ont., Canada 43°37N 81°32W 82 C3
Clinton N.Z. 46°12S 169°23E 59 G2
Clinton Ark., U.S.A. 35°36N 92°28W 84 D8
Clinton Conn., U.S.A. 41°17N 72°32W 83 E12
Clinton Ill., U.S.A. 40°9N 88°57W 80 E9
Clinton Ind., U.S.A. 39°40N 87°24W 80 F10
Clinton Iowa, U.S.A. 41°51N 90°12W 80 E8
Clinton Mass., U.S.A. 42°25N 71°41W 83 D13
Clinton Miss., U.S.A. 32°20N 90°20W 85 E9
Clinton Mo., U.S.A. 38°22N 93°46W 80 F7
Clinton N.C., U.S.A. 35°0N 78°22W 85 D15
Clinton Okla., U.S.A. 35°31N 98°58W 84 D5
Clinton Tenn., U.S.A. 36°6N 84°8W 85 C12
Clinton Wash., U.S.A. 47°59N 122°22W 78 C4
Clinton, C. Australia 22°30S 150°45E 62 C5
Clinton Colden L.
  Canada 63°58N 107°27W 68 E10
Clintonville U.S.A. 44°37N 88°46W 80 C9
Clipperton, I. Pac. Oc. 10°18N 109°13W 65 F17
Clipperton Fracture Zone
  Pac. Oc. 19°0N 122°0W 65 G16
Clisham U.K. 57°58N 6°49W 11 D2
Clitheroe U.K. 53°53N 2°22W 12 D5
Clo-oose Canada 48°39N 124°49W 78 B2
Cloates, Pt. Australia 22°43S 113°40E 60 D1
Clocolan S. Africa 28°55S 27°34E 57 D4
Clodomira Argentina 27°35S 64°14W 94 B3
Clogher Hd. Ireland 53°48N 6°14W 10 C5
Clonakilty Ireland 51°37N 8°53W 10 E3
Clonakilty B. Ireland 51°35N 8°51W 10 E3
Cloncurry Australia 20°40S 140°28E 62 C3
Cloncurry → Australia 18°37S 140°40E 62 B3
Clondalkin Ireland 53°19N 6°25W 10 C5
Clones Ireland 54°11N 7°15W 10 B4
Clonmel Ireland 52°21N 7°42W 10 D4
Cloquet U.S.A. 46°43N 92°28W 80 B7
Clorinda Argentina 25°16S 57°45W 94 B4
Cloud Bay Canada 48°5N 89°26W 72 C2
Cloud Peak U.S.A. 44°23N 107°11W 76 D10
Cloudcroft U.S.A. 32°58N 105°45W 77 K11
Cloverdale U.S.A. 38°48N 123°1W 78 G4
Clovis Calif., U.S.A. 36°49N 119°42W 78 J7
Clovis N. Mex., U.S.A. 34°24N 103°12W 77 J12
Cloyne Canada 44°49N 77°11W 82 B7
Cluain Meala = Clonmel
  Ireland 52°21N 7°42W 10 D4
Cluj-Napoca Romania 46°47N 23°38E 17 E12
Clunes Australia 37°20S 143°45E 63 F3
Clutha → N.Z. 46°20S 169°49E 59 G2
Clwyd → U.K. 53°19N 3°31W 12 D4
Clyde Canada 54°9N 113°39W 70 C6
Clyde N.Z. 45°12S 169°20E 59 F2

Clyde U.S.A. 43°5N 76°52W 82 C8
Clyde → U.K. 55°55N 4°30W 11 F4
Clyde, Firth of U.K. 55°22N 5°1W 11 F3
Clyde Muirshiel △ U.K. 55°50N 4°40W 11 F4
Clyde River Canada 70°30N 68°30W 69 C18
Clydebank U.K. 55°54N 4°23W 11 F4
Clymer N.Y., U.S.A. 42°1N 79°37W 82 D5
Clymer Pa., U.S.A. 40°40N 79°1W 82 D5
Coachella U.S.A. 33°41N 116°10W 79 M10
Coachella Canal
    U.S.A. 32°43N 114°57W 79 N12
Coahoma U.S.A. 32°18N 101°18W 84 E4
Coahuayana →
    Mexico 18°41N 103°45W 86 D4
Coahuila □ Mexico 27°20N 102°0W 86 B4
Coal → Canada 59°39N 126°57W 70 B3
Coalane Mozam. 17°48S 37°2E 55 F4
Coalcomán Mexico 18°47N 103°9W 86 D4
Coaldale Canada 49°45N 112°35W 70 D6
Coalgate U.S.A. 34°32N 96°13W 84 D6
Coalinga U.S.A. 36°9N 120°21W 78 J6
Coalisland U.K. 54°33N 6°42W 10 B5
Coalville U.K. 52°44N 1°23W 12 E6
Coalville U.S.A. 40°55N 111°24W 76 F8
Coamo Puerto Rico 18°5N 66°22W 89 d
Coari Brazil 4°8S 63°7W 92 D6
Coast □ Kenya 2°40S 39°45E 54 C4
Coast Mts. Canada 55°0N 129°20W 70 C3
Coast Ranges U.S.A. 39°0N 123°0W 78 G4
Coatbridge U.K. 55°52N 4°6W 11 F4
Coatepec Mexico 19°27N 96°58W 87 D5
Coatepeque Guatemala 14°46N 91°55W 88 D1
Coatesville U.S.A. 39°59N 75°50W 81 F16
Coaticook Canada 45°10N 71°46W 83 A13
Coats I. Canada 62°30N 83°0W 69 E15
Coats Land Antarctica 77°0S 25°0W 5 D1
Coatzacoalcos Mexico 18°7N 94°25W 87 D6
Cobá Mexico 20°31N 87°45W 87 C7
Cobalt Canada 47°25N 79°42W 72 C4
Cobán Guatemala 15°30N 90°21W 88 C1
Cobar Australia 31°27S 145°48E 63 E4
Cóbh Ireland 51°51N 8°17W 10 E3
Cobija Bolivia 11°0S 68°50W 92 F5
Cobleskill U.S.A. 42°41N 74°29W 83 D10
Coboconk Canada 44°39N 78°48W 82 B6
Cobourg Canada 43°58N 78°10W 82 C6
Cobourg Pen. Australia 11°20S 132°15E 60 B5
Cobram Australia 35°54S 145°40E 63 F4
Cóbué Mozam. 12°0S 34°58E 55 E3
Coburg Germany 50°15N 10°58E 16 C6
Coburg I. Canada 75°57N 79°26W 69 B16
Cocanada = Kakinada
    India 16°57N 82°11E 41 L13
Cochabamba Bolivia 17°26S 66°10W 92 G5
Cochemane Mozam. 17°0S 32°54E 55 F3
Cochin India 9°58N 76°20E 40 Q10
Cochin China = Nam-Phan
    Vietnam 10°30N 106°0E 39 G6
Cochran U.S.A. 32°23N 83°21W 85 E13
Cochrane Alta., Canada 51°11N 114°30W 70 C6
Cochrane Ont., Canada 49°0N 81°0W 72 C3
Cochrane Chile 47°15S 72°33W 96 F2
Cochrane → Canada 59°0N 103°40W 71 B8
Cochrane, L. Chile 47°10S 72°0W 96 F2
Cochranton U.S.A. 41°31N 80°3W 82 E4
Cockburn Australia 32°5S 141°0E 63 E3
Cockburn, Canal Chile 54°30S 72°0W 96 G2
Cockburn I. Canada 45°55N 83°22W 72 C3
Cockburn Ra. Australia 15°46S 128°0E 60 C4
Cockermouth U.K. 54°40N 3°22W 12 C4
Cocklebiddy Australia 32°0S 126°3E 61 F4
Cockpit Country, The
    Jamaica 18°15N 77°45W 88 a
Coco → Cent. Amer. 15°0N 83°8W 88 D3
Coco, I. del Pac. Oc. 5°25N 87°55W 65 G19
Cocoa U.S.A. 28°21N 80°44W 85 G14
Cocobeach Gabon 0°59N 9°34E 52 D1
Cocos B. Trin. & Tob. 10°25N 61°2W 93 K15
Cocos Is. Ind. Oc. 12°10S 96°55E 64 J1
Cocos Ridge Pac. Oc. 4°0N 88°0W 65 G19
Cod, C. U.S.A. 42°5N 70°10W 81 D18
Codajás Brazil 3°55S 62°0W 92 D6
Codó Brazil 4°30S 43°55W 93 D10
Cody U.S.A. 44°32N 109°3W 76 D9
Coe Hill Canada 44°52N 77°50W 82 B7
Coelemu Chile 36°30S 72°48W 94 D1
Coen Australia 13°52S 143°12E 62 A3
Coeur d'Alene U.S.A. 47°41N 116°46W 76 C5
Coeur d'Alene L.
    U.S.A. 47°32N 116°49W 76 C5
Coevorden Neths. 52°40N 6°44E 15 B6
Cofete Canary Is. 28°6N 14°23W 24 F5
Coffeyville U.S.A. 37°2N 95°37W 80 G6
Coffin B. Australia 34°38S 135°28E 63 E2
Coffin Bay Australia 34°37S 135°29E 63 E2
Coffin Bay △ Australia 34°34S 135°19E 63 E2
Coffin Bay Peninsula
    Australia 34°32S 135°15E 63 E2
Coffs Harbour Australia 30°16S 153°5E 63 E5
Cognac France 45°41N 0°20W 20 D3
Cohocton U.S.A. 42°30N 77°30W 82 D7
Cohocton → U.S.A. 42°9N 77°6W 82 D7
Cohoes U.S.A. 42°46N 73°42W 83 D11
Cohuna Australia 35°45S 144°15E 63 F3
Coiba, I. de Panama 7°30N 81°40W 88 E3
Coig → Argentina 51°0S 69°10W 96 G3
Coigeach, Rubha U.K. 58°6N 5°26W 11 C3
Coihaique Chile 45°30S 71°45W 96 F2
Coimbatore India 11°2N 76°59E 40 P10
Coimbra Brazil 19°55S 57°48W 92 G7
Coimbra Portugal 40°15N 8°27W 21 B1
Coín Spain 36°40N 4°48W 21 D3
Coipasa, Salar de Bolivia 19°26S 68°9W 92 G5
Cojimies Ecuador 0°20N 80°0W 92 C3
Cojutepeque El Salv. 13°41N 88°54W 88 D2
Cokeville U.S.A. 42°5N 110°57W 76 E8
Colac Australia 38°21S 143°35E 63 F3
Colatina Brazil 19°32S 40°37W 93 G10
Colbeck, C. Antarctica 77°6S 157°48W 5 D13

Colborne Canada 44°0N 77°53W 82 C7
Colby U.S.A. 39°24N 101°3W 80 F3
Colca → Peru 15°55S 72°43W 92 G4
Colchester U.K. 51°54N 0°55E 13 F8
Colchester U.S.A. 41°35N 72°20W 83 E12
Cold L. Canada 54°33N 110°5W 71 C7
Cold Lake Canada 54°27N 110°10W 71 C6
Coldstream Canada 50°13N 119°11W 70 C5
Coldstream U.K. 55°39N 2°15W 11 F6
Coldwater Canada 44°42N 79°40W 82 B5
Coldwater Kans., U.S.A. 37°16N 99°20W 80 G4
Coldwater Mich., U.S.A. 41°57N 85°0W 81 E11
Colebrook U.S.A. 44°54N 71°30W 83 B13
Coleman Canada 49°40N 114°30W 70 D6
Coleman U.S.A. 31°50N 99°26W 84 F5
Coleman → Australia 15°6S 141°38E 62 B3
Colenso S. Africa 28°44S 29°50E 57 D4
Coleraine Australia 37°36S 141°40E 63 F3
Coleraine U.K. 55°8N 6°41W 10 A5
Coleridge, L. N.Z. 43°17S 171°30E 59 E3
Colesberg S. Africa 30°45S 25°5E 56 E4
Coleville U.S.A. 38°34N 119°30W 78 G7
Colfax Calif., U.S.A. 39°6N 120°57W 78 F6
Colfax La., U.S.A. 31°31N 92°42W 84 F8
Colfax Wash., U.S.A. 46°53N 117°22W 76 C5
Colhué Huapi, L.
    Argentina 45°30S 69°0W 96 F3
Coligny S. Africa 26°17S 26°15E 57 D4
Colima Mexico 19°14N 103°43W 86 D4
Colima □ Mexico 19°10N 104°0W 86 D4
Colima, Nevado de
    Mexico 19°33N 103°38W 86 D4
Colina Chile 33°13S 70°45W 94 C1
Colinas Brazil 6°0S 44°10W 93 E10
Collahuasi Chile 21°5S 68°45W 94 A2
Collarenebri Australia 29°33S 148°34E 63 D4
Colleen Bawn Zimbabwe 21°0S 29°12E 55 G2
College U.S.A. 64°52N 147°49W 74 C10
College Park U.S.A. 33°39N 84°27W 85 E12
College Station U.S.A. 30°37N 96°21W 84 F6
Collie Australia 33°22S 116°8E 61 F2
Collier B. Australia 16°10S 124°15E 60 C3
Collier Ra. Australia 24°45S 119°10E 61 D2
Collier Range △
    Australia 24°39S 119°7E 61 D2
Collierville U.S.A. 35°3N 89°40W 85 D10
Collina, Passo di Italy 44°2N 10°56E 22 B4
Collingwood Canada 44°29N 80°13W 82 B4
Collingwood N.Z. 40°41S 172°40E 59 D4
Collins Canada 50°17N 89°27W 72 B2
Collins Bay Canada 44°14N 76°36W 83 B8
Collinson Pen. Canada 69°58N 101°24W 68 D11
Collinsville Australia 20°30S 147°56E 62 C4
Collipulli Chile 37°55S 72°30W 94 D1
Collooney Ireland 54°11N 8°29W 10 B3
Colmar France 48°5N 7°20E 20 B7
Colo → Australia 33°25S 150°52E 63 E5
Cologne = Köln Germany 50°56N 6°57E 16 C4
Colom, I. d'en Spain 39°58N 4°16E 24 B11
Coloma U.S.A. 38°48N 120°53W 78 G6
Colomb-Béchar = Béchar
    Algeria 31°38N 2°18W 50 B5
Colombia ■ S. Amer. 3°45N 73°0W 92 C4
Colombian Basin
    S. Amer. 14°0N 76°0W 66 H12
Colombo Sri Lanka 6°56N 79°58E 40 R11
Colón B. Aires, Argentina 33°53S 61°7W 94 C3
Colón Entre Ríos,
    Argentina 32°12S 58°10W 94 C4
Colón Cuba 22°42N 80°54W 88 B3
Colón Panama 9°20N 79°54W 88 E4
Colón, Arch. de Ecuador 0°0 91°0W 90 D1
Colònia de Sant Jordi
    Spain 39°19N 2°59E 24 B9
Colonia del Sacramento
    Uruguay 34°25S 57°50W 94 C4
Colonia Dora Argentina 28°34S 62°59W 94 B3
Colonial Beach U.S.A. 38°15N 76°58W 81 F15
Colonie U.S.A. 42°43N 73°50W 83 D11
Colonsay Canada 51°59N 105°52W 71 C7
Colonsay U.K. 56°5N 6°12W 11 E2
Colorado □ U.S.A. 39°30N 105°30W 76 G11
Colorado → Argentina 39°50S 62°8W 96 D4
Colorado → N. Amer. 31°45N 114°40W 77 L6
Colorado → U.S.A. 28°36N 95°59W 84 G7
Colorado City U.S.A. 32°24N 100°52W 84 E4
Colorado Plateau U.S.A. 37°0N 111°0W 77 H8
Colorado River Aqueduct
    U.S.A. 33°50N 117°23W 79 L12
Colorado Springs
    U.S.A. 38°50N 104°49W 76 G11
Colotlán Mexico 22°6N 103°16W 86 C4
Colstrip U.S.A. 45°53N 106°38W 76 D10
Colton U.S.A. 44°33N 74°56W 83 B10
Columbia Ky., U.S.A. 37°6N 85°18W 81 G11
Columbia La., U.S.A. 32°6N 92°5W 84 E8
Columbia Miss., U.S.A. 31°15N 89°50W 85 F10
Columbia Mo., U.S.A. 38°57N 92°20W 80 F7
Columbia Pa., U.S.A. 40°2N 76°30W 83 F8
Columbia S.C., U.S.A. 34°0N 81°2W 85 D14
Columbia Tenn., U.S.A. 35°37N 87°2W 85 D11
Columbia → N. Amer. 46°15N 124°5W 78 D2
Columbia, C. Canada 83°6N 69°57W 69 A18
Columbia, District of □
    U.S.A. 38°55N 77°0W 81 F15
Columbia, Mt. Canada 52°8N 117°20W 70 C5
Columbia Falls U.S.A. 48°23N 114°11W 76 B6
Columbia Mts. Canada 52°0N 119°0W 70 C5
Columbia Plateau
    U.S.A. 44°0N 117°30W 76 E5
Columbiana U.S.A. 40°53N 80°42W 82 F4
Columbretes, Is. Spain 39°50N 0°50E 21 C6
Columbus Ga., U.S.A. 32°28N 84°59W 85 E12
Columbus Ind., U.S.A. 39°13N 85°55W 81 F11
Columbus Kans., U.S.A. 37°10N 94°50W 80 G6
Columbus Miss., U.S.A. 33°30N 88°25W 85 E10
Columbus Mont.,
    U.S.A. 45°38N 109°15W 76 D9

Columbus N. Mex.,
    U.S.A. 31°50N 107°38W 77 L10
Columbus Nebr., U.S.A. 41°26N 97°22W 80 E5
Columbus Ohio, U.S.A. 39°58N 83°0W 81 F12
Columbus Tex., U.S.A. 29°42N 96°33W 84 G6
Colusa U.S.A. 39°13N 122°1W 78 F4
Colville U.S.A. 48°33N 117°54W 76 B5
Colville → U.S.A. 70°25N 150°30W 74 A9
Colville, C. N.Z. 36°29S 175°21E 59 B5
Colwood Canada 48°26N 123°29W 78 B3
Colwyn Bay U.K. 53°18N 3°44W 12 D4
Comácchio Italy 44°42N 12°11E 22 B5
Comalcalco Mexico 18°16N 93°13W 87 D6
Comallo Argentina 41°0S 70°5W 96 E2
Comanche U.S.A. 31°54N 98°36W 84 F5
Comandante Ferraz
    Antarctica 62°30S 58°0W 5 C18
Comayagua Honduras 14°25N 87°37W 88 D2
Combahee → U.S.A. 32°31N 80°31W 85 E14
Combarbalá Chile 31°11S 71°2W 94 C1
Combe Martin U.K. 51°12N 4°3W 13 F3
Comber Canada 42°14N 82°33W 82 D2
Comber U.K. 54°33N 5°45W 10 B6
Combermere Canada 45°22N 77°37W 82 A7
Comblain-au-Pont
    Belgium 50°29N 5°35E 15 D5
Comeragh Mts. Ireland 52°18N 7°34E 10 D4
Comet Australia 23°36S 148°38E 62 C4
Comilla Bangla. 23°28N 91°10E 41 H17
Comino Malta 36°1N 14°20E 25 C1
Comino, C. Italy 40°32N 9°49E 22 D3
Comitán de Domínguez
    Mexico 16°15N 92°8W 87 D6
Commerce Ga., U.S.A. 34°12N 83°28W 85 D13
Commerce Tex., U.S.A. 33°15N 95°54W 84 E7
Committee B. Canada 68°30N 86°30W 69 D14
Commodore, C. Canada 44°47N 80°54W 82 B4
Commonwealth B.
    Antarctica 67°0S 144°0E 5 C10
Commoron Cr. →
    Australia 28°22S 150°8E 63 D5
Communism Pk. = imeni Ismail
    Samani, Pik Tajikistan 39°0N 72°2E 28 F8
Como Italy 45°47N 9°5E 20 D8
Como, Lago di Italy 46°0N 9°11E 20 D8
Comodoro Rivadavia
    Argentina 45°50S 67°40W 96 F3
Comorin, C. = Kannyakumari
    India 8°3N 77°40E 40 Q10
Comoros ■ Ind. Oc. 12°10S 44°15E 53 a
Comox Canada 49°42N 124°55W 70 D4
Compiègne France 49°24N 2°50E 20 B5
Compostela Mexico 21°14N 104°55W 86 C4
Comprida, I. Brazil 24°50S 47°42W 95 A6
Compton Canada 45°14N 71°49W 83 A13
Compton U.S.A. 33°53N 118°13W 79 M8
Comrat Moldova 46°18N 28°40E 17 E15
Con Cuong Vietnam 19°2N 104°54E 38 C5
Con Dao △ Vietnam 8°42N 106°35E 39 H6
Con Son Vietnam 8°41N 106°37E 39 H6
Conakry Guinea 9°29N 13°49W 50 G3
Conara Australia 41°50S 147°26E 63 G4
Concarneau France 47°52N 3°56W 20 C2
Conceição Mozam. 18°47S 36°7E 55 F4
Conceição da Barra
    Brazil 18°35S 39°45W 93 G11
Conceição do Araguaia
    Brazil 8°0S 49°2W 93 E9
Concepción Argentina 27°20S 65°35W 94 B2
Concepción Bolivia 16°15S 62°8W 92 G6
Concepción Chile 36°50S 73°0W 94 D1
Concepción Mexico 18°15N 90°5W 87 D6
Concepción Paraguay 23°22S 57°26W 94 A4
Concepción □ Chile 37°0S 72°30W 94 D1
Concepción → Mexico 30°32N 113°2W 86 A2
Concepción, Est. de
    Chile 50°30S 74°55W 96 G2
Concepción, L. Bolivia 17°20S 61°20W 92 G6
Concepción, Pta.
    Mexico 26°53N 111°50W 86 B2
Concepción del Oro
    Mexico 24°38N 101°25W 86 C4
Concepción del Uruguay
    Argentina 32°35S 58°20W 94 C4
Conception, Pt. U.S.A. 34°27N 120°28W 79 L6
Conception B. Canada 47°45S 53°0W 73 C9
Conception B. Namibia 23°55S 14°22E 56 C1
Conception I. Bahamas 23°52N 75°9W 89 B4
Concession Zimbabwe 17°27S 30°56E 55 F3
Conchas Dam U.S.A. 35°22N 104°11W 77 J11
Concho U.S.A. 34°28N 109°36W 77 J9
Concho → U.S.A. 31°34N 99°43W 84 F5
Conchos → Chihuahua,
    Mexico 29°35N 104°25W 86 B4
Conchos → Chihuahua,
    Mexico 27°29N 106°45W 86 B3
Conchos → Tamaulipas,
    Mexico 24°55N 97°38W 87 B5
Concord Calif., U.S.A. 37°59N 122°2W 78 H4
Concord N.C., U.S.A. 35°25N 80°35W 85 D14
Concord N.H., U.S.A. 43°12N 71°32W 83 C13
Concordia Antarctica 75°6S 123°23E 5 D17
Concordia Argentina 31°20S 58°2W 94 C4
Concórdia Amazonas,
    Brazil 4°36S 66°36W 92 D5
Concórdia Sta. Catarina,
    Brazil 27°14S 52°1W 95 B5
Concordia Mexico 23°17N 106°4W 86 C3
Concordia U.S.A. 39°34N 97°40W 80 F5
Concrete U.S.A. 48°32N 121°45W 76 B3
Condamine Australia 26°56S 150°9E 63 D5
Conde U.S.A. 45°9N 98°6W 80 C4
Condeúba Brazil 14°52S 42°0W 93 F10
Condobolin Australia 33°4S 147°6E 63 E4
Condon U.S.A. 45°14N 120°11W 76 D3
Conegliano Italy 45°53N 12°18E 22 B5
Conejera, I. = Conills, I. des
    Spain 39°11N 2°58E 24 B9
Conejos Mexico 26°14N 103°53W 86 B4

Conemaugh → U.S.A. 40°28N 79°19W 82 F5
Confuso → Paraguay 25°9S 57°34W 94 B4
Congleton U.K. 53°10N 2°13W 12 D5
Congo (Brazzaville) = Congo ■
    Africa 1°0S 16°0E 52 E3
Congo (Kinshasa) = Congo, Dem.
    Rep. of the ■ Africa 3°0S 23°0E 52 E4
Congo ■ Africa 1°0S 16°0E 52 E3
Congo → Africa 6°4S 12°24E 52 F2
Congo, Dem. Rep. of the ■
    Africa 3°0S 23°0E 52 E4
Congo Basin Africa 0°10S 24°30E 52 E4
Congonhas Brazil 20°30S 43°52W 95 A7
Congress U.S.A. 34°9N 112°51W 77 J7
Coniston Canada 46°29N 80°51W 72 C3
Conjeeveram = Kanchipuram
    India 12°52N 79°45E 40 N11
Conklin Canada 55°38N 111°5W 71 B6
Conklin U.S.A. 42°2N 75°49W 83 D9
Conn, L. Ireland 54°3N 9°15W 10 B2
Connacht □ Ireland 53°43N 9°12W 10 C2
Conneaut U.S.A. 41°57N 80°34W 82 E4
Conneautville U.S.A. 41°45N 80°22W 82 E4
Connecticut □ U.S.A. 41°30N 72°45W 83 E12
Connecticut → U.S.A. 41°16N 72°20W 83 E12
Connell U.S.A. 46°40N 118°52W 76 C4
Connellsville U.S.A. 40°1N 79°35W 82 F5
Connemara △ Ireland 53°29N 9°45W 10 C2
Connemara △ Ireland 53°32N 9°52W 10 C2
Connersville U.S.A. 39°39N 85°8W 81 F11
Connors Ra. Australia 21°40S 149°10E 62 C4
Conoename → Suriname 5°48N 55°55W 93 B7
Conquest Canada 51°32N 107°14W 71 C7
Conrad U.S.A. 48°10N 111°57W 76 B8
Conran, C. Australia 37°49S 148°44E 63 F4
Conroe U.S.A. 30°19N 95°27W 84 F7
Consecon Canada 44°0N 77°31W 82 C7
Conselheiro Lafaiete
    Brazil 20°40S 43°48W 95 A7
Consell Spain 39°40N 2°49E 24 B9
Consett U.K. 54°51N 1°50W 12 C6
Consort Canada 52°1N 110°46W 71 C6
Constance = Konstanz
    Germany 47°40N 9°10E 16 E5
Constance, L. = Bodensee
    Europe 47°35N 9°25E 20 C8
Constanţa Romania 44°14N 28°38E 17 F15
Constantine Algeria 36°25N 6°42E 50 A7
Constitución Chile 35°20S 72°30W 94 D1
Constitución Uruguay 31°0S 57°50W 94 C4
Constitución de 1857 △
    Mexico 32°4N 115°55W 86 A1
Consul Canada 49°20N 109°30W 71 D7
Contact U.S.A. 41°46N 114°45W 76 F6
Contai India 21°54N 87°46E 43 J12
Contamana Peru 7°19S 74°55W 92 E4
Contas → Brazil 14°17S 39°1W 93 F11
Contoocook U.S.A. 43°13N 71°45W 83 C13
Contra Costa Mozam. 25°9S 33°30E 57 D5
Contwoyto L. Canada 65°42N 110°50W 68 D9
Conway = Conwy U.K. 53°17N 3°50W 12 D4
Conway = Conwy →
    U.K. 53°17N 3°50W 12 D4
Conway Australia 20°24S 148°41E 62 b
Conway Canada 44°6N 76°54W 82 B8
Conway Ark., U.S.A. 35°5N 92°26W 84 D8
Conway N.H., U.S.A. 43°59N 71°7W 83 C13
Conway S.C., U.S.A. 33°51N 79°3W 85 E15
Conway, C. Australia 20°34S 148°46E 62 b
Conwy U.K. 53°17N 3°50W 12 D4
Conwy □ U.K. 53°10N 3°44W 12 D4
Conwy → U.K. 53°17N 3°50W 12 D4
Coober Pedy Australia 29°1S 134°43E 63 D1
Cooch Behar = Koch Bihar
    India 26°22N 89°29E 41 F16
Cooinda Australia 13°15S 130°5E 60 B5
Cook Australia 30°37S 130°25E 61 F5
Cook U.S.A. 47°51N 92°41W 80 B7
Cook, B. Chile 55°10S 70°0W 96 H3
Cook, C. Canada 50°8N 127°55W 70 C3
Cook, Mt. = Aoraki Mount Cook
    N.Z. 43°36S 170°9E 59 E3
Cook Inlet U.S.A. 60°0N 152°0W 68 F1
Cook Is. Pac. Oc. 17°0S 160°0W 65 J12
Cook Strait N.Z. 41°15S 174°29E 59 D5
Cookeville U.S.A. 36°10N 85°30W 85 C12
Cookhouse S. Africa 32°44S 25°47E 56 E4
Cooks Harbour Canada 51°36N 55°52W 73 B8
Cookshire Canada 45°25N 71°38W 83 A13
Cookstown Canada 44°11N 79°42W 82 B5
Cookstown U.K. 54°39N 6°45W 10 B5
Cooksville Canada 43°35N 79°38W 82 C5
Cooktown Australia 15°30S 145°16E 62 B4
Coolabah Australia 31°1S 146°43E 63 E4
Cooladdi Australia 26°37S 145°23E 63 D4
Coolah Australia 31°48S 149°41E 63 E4
Coolamon Australia 34°46S 147°8E 63 E4
Coolgardie Australia 30°55S 121°8E 61 F3
Coolidge U.S.A. 32°59N 111°31W 77 K8
Coolidge Dam U.S.A. 33°10N 110°32W 77 K8
Cooma Australia 36°12S 149°8E 63 F4
Coon Rapids U.S.A. 45°9N 93°19W 80 C7
Coonabarabran
    Australia 31°14S 149°18E 63 E4
Coonamble Australia 30°56S 148°27E 63 E4
Coonana Australia 31°0S 123°0E 61 F3
Coonana ◎ Australia 30°51S 122°53E 61 F3
Coondapoor India 13°42N 74°40E 40 N9
Cooninnie, L. Australia 26°4S 139°59E 63 D2
Cooper U.S.A. 33°23N 95°42W 84 E7
Cooper Cr. → Australia 28°29S 137°46E 63 D2
Cooper Ridge Pac. Oc. 10°0N 150°30W 65 G12
Cooperstown N. Dak.,
    U.S.A. 47°27N 98°8W 80 B4
Cooperstown N.Y.,
    U.S.A. 42°42N 74°56W 83 D10

Coorabie Australia 31°54S 132°18E 61 F5
Coorong, The Australia 35°50S 139°20E 63 F2
Coorow Australia 29°53S 116°2E 61 E2
Cooroy Australia 26°22S 152°54E 63 D5
Coos Bay U.S.A. 43°22N 124°13W 76 E1
Coosa → U.S.A. 32°30N 86°16W 85 E11
Cootamundra Australia 34°36S 148°1E 63 E4
Cootehill Ireland 54°4N 7°5W 10 B4
Copahue Paso Argentina 37°49S 71°8W 94 D1
Copainalá Mexico 17°4N 93°18W 87 D6
Copake U.S.A. 42°7N 73°31W 83 D11
Copán Honduras 14°50N 89°9W 88 D2
Cope U.S.A. 39°40N 102°51W 76 G12
Copenhagen = København
    Denmark 55°40N 12°26E 9 J15
Copenhagen U.S.A. 43°54N 75°41W 83 C9
Copiapó Chile 27°30S 70°20W 94 B1
Copiapó → Chile 27°19S 70°56W 94 B1
Coplay U.S.A. 40°44N 75°29W 83 F9
Copo △ Argentina 25°53S 61°41W 94 B3
Copp L. Canada 60°14N 114°40W 70 A6
Copper Canyon = Barranca del
    Cobre △ Mexico 27°18N 107°40W 86 B3
Copper Center U.S.A. 61°58N 145°18W 74 C10
Copper Harbor U.S.A. 47°28N 87°53W 80 B10
Copper Queen Zimbabwe 17°29S 29°18E 55 F2
Copperas Cove U.S.A. 31°8N 97°54W 84 F6
Copperbelt □ Zambia 13°15S 27°30E 55 E2
Coppermine = Kugluktuk
    Canada 67°50N 115°5W 68 D8
Coppermine → Canada 67°49N 116°4W 68 D8
Copperopolis U.S.A. 37°58N 120°38W 78 H6
Coquet → U.K. 55°20N 1°32W 12 B6
Coquille U.S.A. 43°11N 124°11W 76 E1
Coquimbo Chile 30°0S 71°20W 94 C1
Coquimbo □ Chile 31°0S 71°0W 94 C1
Coquitlam Canada 49°17N 122°45W 70 D4
Corabia Romania 43°48N 24°30E 17 G13
Coracora Peru 15°5S 73°45W 92 G4
Coraki Australia 28°59S 153°17E 63 D5
Coral U.S.A. 40°29N 79°10W 82 F5
Coral Bay Australia 23°8S 113°46E 60 D1
Coral Gables U.S.A. 25°43N 80°16W 85 J14
Coral Harbour Canada 64°8N 83°10W 69 E15
Coral Sea Pac. Oc. 15°0S 150°0E 64 J7
Coral Sea Basin Pac. Oc. 14°0S 152°0E 64 J7
Coral Sea Islands Terr. ■
    Australia 20°0S 155°0E 58 C8
Coral Springs U.S.A. 26°16N 80°16W 85 H14
Coraopolis U.S.A. 40°31N 80°10W 82 F4
Corato Italy 41°9N 16°25E 22 D7
Corbett △ India 29°20N 79°0E 43 E8
Corbin U.S.A. 36°57N 84°6W 81 G11
Corby U.K. 52°30N 0°41W 13 E7
Corcaigh = Cork Ireland 51°54N 8°29W 10 E3
Corcoran U.S.A. 36°6N 119°33W 78 J7
Corcovado △ Costa Rica 8°33N 83°35W 88 E3
Corcubión Spain 42°56N 9°12W 21 A1
Cordele U.S.A. 31°58N 83°47W 85 F13
Cordell U.S.A. 35°17N 98°59W 84 D5
Córdoba Argentina 31°20S 64°10W 94 C3
Córdoba Mexico 18°53N 96°56W 87 D5
Córdoba Spain 37°50N 4°50W 21 D3
Córdoba □ Argentina 31°22S 64°15W 94 C3
Córdoba, Sierra de
    Argentina 31°10S 64°25W 94 C3
Cordova U.S.A. 60°33N 145°45W 68 E2
Corella △ Australia 19°34S 140°47E 62 B3
Corfield Australia 21°40S 143°21E 62 C3
Corfu = Kerkyra Greece 39°38N 19°50E 25 A3
Corfu, Str. of U.K. 42°57N 78°24W 82 D6
Corfu, Str. of = Kerkyras, Notio
    Steno Greece 39°34N 20°0E 25 A4
Coria Spain 39°58N 6°33W 21 C2
Corigliano Cálabro Italy 39°36N 16°31E 22 E7
Coringa Is. Australia 16°58S 149°58E 62 B4
Corinth = Korinthos
    Greece 37°56N 22°55E 23 F10
Corinth Miss., U.S.A. 34°56N 88°31W 85 D10
Corinth N.Y., U.S.A. 43°15N 73°49W 83 C11
Corinth, G. of = Korinthiakos
    Kolpos Greece 38°16N 22°30E 23 E10
Corinto Brazil 18°20S 44°30W 93 G10
Corinto Nic. 12°30N 87°10W 88 D2
Cork Ireland 51°54N 8°29W 10 E3
Cork □ Ireland 51°57N 8°40W 10 E3
Cork Harbour Ireland 51°47N 8°16W 10 E3
Çorlu Turkey 41°11N 27°49E 23 D12
Cormack L. Canada 54°14N 74°0W 71 B10
Cormorant Canada 54°14N 100°35W 71 C8
Cormorant L. Canada 54°15N 100°50W 71 C8
Corn Is. = Maíz, Is. del
    Nic. 12°15N 83°4W 88 D3
Cornélio Procópio Brazil 23°7S 50°40W 95 A5
Corner Brook Canada 48°57N 57°58W 73 C8
Corneşti Moldova 47°21N 28°1E 17 E15
Corning Ark., U.S.A. 36°25N 90°35W 84 C9
Corning Calif., U.S.A. 39°56N 122°11W 76 G2
Corning Iowa, U.S.A. 40°59N 94°44W 80 E6
Corning N.Y., U.S.A. 42°9N 77°3W 82 D7
Cornwall Canada 45°2N 74°44W 83 A10
Cornwall U.S.A. 40°17N 76°25W 83 F8
Cornwall □ U.K. 50°26N 4°40W 13 G3
Cornwall I. Canada 77°37N 94°38W 69 B13
Cornwallis I. Canada 75°8N 95°0W 69 B13
Corny Pt. Australia 34°55S 137°0E 63 E2
Coro Venezuela 11°25N 69°41W 92 A5
Coroatá Brazil 4°8S 44°0W 93 D10
Corocoro Bolivia 17°15S 68°28W 92 G5
Coroico Bolivia 16°0S 67°50W 92 G5
Coromandel N.Z. 36°45S 175°31E 59 B5
Coromandel Coast India 12°30N 81°0E 40 N12
Corona Calif., U.S.A. 33°53N 117°34W 79 M9
Corona N. Mex., U.S.A. 34°15N 105°36W 77 J11
Coronado U.S.A. 32°41N 117°11W 79 N9
Coronado, B. de Costa Rica 9°0N 83°40W 88 E3
Coronados, Is. Los
    Mexico 32°26N 117°19W 79 N9
Coronation Canada 52°5N 111°27W 70 C6

Coronation Gulf
  Canada 68°25N 110°0W **68** D10
Coronation I. *Antarctica* 60°45S 46°0W **5** C18
Coronation Is. *Australia* 14°57S 124°55E **60** B3
Coronda *Argentina* 31°58S 60°56W **94** C3
Coronel *Chile* 37°0S 73°10W **94** D1
Coronel Bogado
  Paraguay 27°11S 56°18W **94** B4
Coronel Dorrego
  Argentina 38°40S 61°10W **94** D3
Coronel Oviedo
  Paraguay 25°24S 56°30W **94** B4
Coronel Pringles
  Argentina 37°30S 61°52W **94** D3
Coronel Suárez
  Argentina 37°30S 61°52W **94** D3
Coronel Vidal *Argentina* 37°28S 57°45W **94** D4
Coropuna, Nevado *Peru* 15°30S 72°41W **92** G4
Corowa *Australia* 35°58S 146°21E **63** F4
Corozal □ *Belize* 18°23N 88°23W **87** D7
Corozal Pt. *Trin. & Tob.* 10°45N 61°37W **93** K15
Corpus *Argentina* 27°10S 55°30W **95** B4
Corpus Christi *U.S.A.* 27°47N 97°24W **84** H6
Corpus Christi, L. *U.S.A.* 28°2N 97°52W **84** G6
Corralejo *Canary Is.* 28°43N 13°53W **24** F6
Corraun Pen. *Ireland* 53°54N 9°54W **10** C2
Corrientes, C. das *Mozam.* 24°6S 35°34E **57** C6
Corrib, L. *Ireland* 53°27N 9°16W **10** C2
Corrientes *Argentina* 27°30S 58°45W **94** B4
Corrientes □ *Argentina* 28°0S 57°0W **94** B4
Corrientes → *Argentina* 30°42S 59°38W **94** C4
Corrientes → *Peru* 3°43S 74°35W **92** D4
Corrientes, C. *Colombia* 5°30N 77°34W **92** B3
Corrientes, C. *Cuba* 21°43N 84°30W **88** B3
Corrientes, C. *Mexico* 20°25N 105°42W **86** C3
Corrigan *U.S.A.* 31°0N 94°52W **84** F7
Corrigin *Australia* 32°20S 117°53E **61** F2
Corriverton *Guyana* 5°55N 57°20W **92** B7
Corry *U.S.A.* 41°55N 79°39W **82** E5
Corse □ *France* 42°0N 9°0E **20** F8
Corse, C. *France* 43°1N 9°25E **20** E8
Corsica = Corse □ *France* 42°0N 9°0E **20** F8
Corsicana *U.S.A.* 32°6N 96°28W **84** E6
Corte *France* 42°19N 9°11E **20** E8
Cortés, Mar de = California, G. de
  Mexico 27°0N 111°0W **86** B2
Cortez *U.S.A.* 37°21N 108°35W **77** H9
Cortland *N.Y., U.S.A.* 42°36N 76°11W **83** D8
Cortland *Ohio, U.S.A.* 41°20N 80°44W **82** E4
Çorum *Turkey* 40°30N 34°57E **19** F5
Corumbá *Brazil* 19°0S 57°30W **92** G7
Corunna = A Coruña
  Spain 43°20N 8°25W **21** A1
Corvallis *U.S.A.* 44°34N 123°16W **76** D2
Corvette, L. de la *Canada* 53°25N 74°3W **72** B5
Corvo *Azores* 39°43N 31°8W **50** a
Corydon *U.S.A.* 40°46N 93°19W **80** E7
Cosalá *Mexico* 24°23N 106°41W **86** C3
Cosamaloapan de Carpio
  Mexico 18°22N 95°48W **87** D5
Cosenza *Italy* 39°18N 16°15E **22** E7
Coshocton *U.S.A.* 40°16N 81°51W **82** F3
Cosmo Newberry
  Australia 28°0S 122°54E **61** E3
Cosmo Newberry ◌
  Australia 27°59S 122°53E **61** E3
Cosmonaut Sea *S. Ocean* 66°30S 40°0E **5** C5
Coso Junction *U.S.A.* 36°3N 117°57W **79** J9
Coso Pk. *U.S.A.* 36°13N 117°44W **79** J9
Cosquín *Argentina* 31°15S 64°30W **94** C3
Costa Blanca *Spain* 38°25N 0°10W **21** C5
Costa Brava *Spain* 41°30N 3°0E **21** B7
Costa Daurada *Spain* 41°12N 1°15E **21** B6
Costa del Sol *Spain* 36°30N 4°30W **21** D3
Costa dels Pins *Spain* 39°38N 3°26E **24** B10
Costa Mesa *U.S.A.* 33°38N 117°55W **79** M9
Costa Rica ■ *Cent. Amer.* 10°0N 84°0W **88** D3
Costa Smeralda *Italy* 41°5N 9°35E **22** D3
Cosumnes → *U.S.A.* 38°16N 121°26W **78** G5
Cotabato *Phil.* 7°14N 124°15E **37** C6
Cotagaita *Bolivia* 20°45S 65°40W **94** A2
Côte d'Azur *France* 43°25N 7°10E **20** E7
Côte-d'Ivoire = Ivory Coast ■
  Africa 7°30N 5°0W **50** G4
Coteau des Prairies
  U.S.A. 45°20N 97°50W **80** C5
Coteau du Missouri
  U.S.A. 47°0N 100°0W **80** B4
Cotentin *France* 49°15N 1°30W **20** B3
Cotillo *Canary Is.* 28°41N 14°1W **24** F5
Cotonou *Benin* 6°20N 2°25E **50** G6
Cotopaxi *Ecuador* 0°40S 78°30W **92** D3
Cotswold Hills *U.K.* 51°42N 2°10W **13** F5
Cottage Grove *U.S.A.* 43°48N 123°3W **76** E2
Cottam *Canada* 42°8N 82°45W **82** D2
Cottbus *Germany* 51°45N 14°20E **16** C8
Cottonwood *U.S.A.* 34°45N 112°1W **77** J7
Cotulla *U.S.A.* 28°26N 99°14W **84** G5
Coudersport *U.S.A.* 41°46N 78°1W **82** E6
Couedic, C. du *Australia* 36°5S 136°40E **63** F2
Coulee City *U.S.A.* 47°37N 119°17W **76** C4
Coulee Dam Nat. Recr. Area =
  Lake Roosevelt =
  U.S.A. 48°5N 118°14W **76** B4
Coulman I. *Antarctica* 73°35S 170°0E **5** D11
Coulonge → *Canada* 45°52N 76°46W **72** C4
Coulterville *U.S.A.* 37°43N 120°12W **78** H6
Council *Alaska, U.S.A.* 64°53N 163°41W **74** C7
Council *Idaho, U.S.A.* 44°44N 116°26W **76** D5
Council Bluffs *U.S.A.* 41°16N 95°52W **80** E6
Council Grove *U.S.A.* 38°40N 96°29W **80** F5
Coupeville *U.S.A.* 48°13N 122°41W **78** B4
Courantyne → *S. Amer.* 5°55N 57°5W **92** B7
Courcelles *Belgium* 50°28N 4°22E **15** D4
Courtenay *Canada* 49°45N 125°0W **70** D4
Courtland *Canada* 42°51N 80°38W **82** D4
Courtland *U.S.A.* 38°20N 121°34W **78** G5
Courtrai = Kortrijk
  Belgium 50°50N 3°17E **15** D3

Courtright *Canada* 42°49N 82°28W **82** D2
Coushatta *U.S.A.* 32°1N 93°21W **84** E8
Coutts Crossing
  Australia 29°49S 152°55E **63** D5
Couva *Trin. & Tob.* 10°25N 61°27W **93** K15
Couvin *Belgium* 50°3N 4°29E **15** D4
Cove I. *Canada* 45°17N 81°44W **82** A3
Coventry *U.K.* 52°25N 1°28W **13** E6
Covilhã *Portugal* 40°17N 7°31W **21** B2
Covington *Ga., U.S.A.* 33°36N 83°51W **85** E13
Covington *Ky., U.S.A.* 39°5N 84°30W **81** F11
Covington *Tenn., U.S.A.* 35°34N 89°39W **85** D10
Covington *Va., U.S.A.* 37°47N 79°59W **81** G14
Cowal, L. *Australia* 33°40S 147°25E **63** E4
Cowan, L. *Australia* 31°45S 121°45E **61** F3
Cowan L. *Canada* 54°0N 107°15W **71** C7
Cowangie *Australia* 35°12S 141°26E **63** F3
Cowansville *Canada* 45°14N 72°46W **83** A12
Coward Springs
  Australia 29°24S 136°49E **63** D2
Cowcowing Lakes
  Australia 30°55S 117°20E **61** F2
Cowdenbeath *U.K.* 56°7N 3°21W **11** E5
Cowell *Australia* 33°39S 136°56E **63** E2
Cowes *U.K.* 50°45N 1°18W **13** G6
Cowichan L. *Canada* 48°53N 124°17W **78** B2
Cowlitz → *U.S.A.* 46°6N 122°55W **78** D4
Cowra *Australia* 33°49S 148°42E **63** E4
Coxilha Grande *Brazil* 28°18S 51°30W **95** B5
Coxim *Brazil* 18°30S 54°55W **93** G8
Cox's Bazar *Bangla.* 21°26N 91°59E **41** J17
Coyote Wells *U.S.A.* 32°44N 115°58W **79** N11
Coyuca de Benitez
  Mexico 17°2N 100°4W **87** D4
Coyuca de Catalán
  Mexico 18°20N 100°39W **86** D4
Cozad *U.S.A.* 40°52N 99°59W **80** E4
Cozumel *Mexico* 20°31N 86°55W **87** C7
Cozumel, Isla *Mexico* 20°30N 86°40W **87** C7
Crab Hill *Barbados* 13°19N 59°38W **89** g
Cracow = Kraków
  Poland 50°4N 19°57E **17** C10
Cracow *Australia* 25°17S 150°17E **63** D5
Cradle Mt.-Lake St. Clair △
  Australia 41°43S 147°56E **63** G4
Cradock *Australia* 32°6S 138°31E **63** E2
Cradock *S. Africa* 32°8S 25°36E **56** E4
Craig *U.S.A.* 40°31N 107°33W **76** F10
Craigavon *U.K.* 54°27N 6°23W **10** B5
Craigmore *Zimbabwe* 20°28S 32°50E **55** G3
Craik *Canada* 51°3N 105°49W **71** C7
Crailsheim *Germany* 49°8N 10°5E **16** D6
Craiova *Romania* 44°21N 23°48E **17** F12
Cramsie *Australia* 23°20S 144°15E **62** C3
Cranberry L. *U.S.A.* 44°11N 74°50W **83** B10
Cranberry Portage
  Canada 54°35N 101°23W **71** C8
Cranbrook *Australia* 34°18S 117°33E **61** F2
Cranbrook *Canada* 49°30N 115°46W **70** D5
Crandon *U.S.A.* 45°34N 88°54W **80** C9
Crane *Oreg., U.S.A.* 43°25N 118°35W **76** E4
Crane *Tex., U.S.A.* 31°24N 102°21W **84** F3
Crane, The *Barbados* 13°6N 59°27W **89** g
Cranston *U.S.A.* 41°47N 71°26W **83** E13
Crater L. *U.S.A.* 42°56N 122°6W **76** E2
Crater Lake △ *U.S.A.* 42°55N 122°10W **76** E2
Craters of the Moon △
  U.S.A. 43°25N 113°30W **76** E7
Crateús *Brazil* 5°10S 40°39W **93** E10
Crato *Brazil* 7°10S 39°25W **93** E11
Craven, L. *Canada* 54°20N 76°56W **72** B4
Crawford *U.S.A.* 42°41N 103°25W **80** D3
Crawfordsville *U.S.A.* 40°2N 86°54W **81** E10
Crawley *U.K.* 51°7N 0°11W **13** F7
Crazy Mts. *U.S.A.* 46°12N 110°20W **76** C8
Crean L. *Canada* 54°5N 106°9W **71** C7
Crediton *Canada* 43°17N 81°33W **82** C3
Crediton *U.K.* 50°47N 3°40W **13** G4
Cree → *Canada* 58°57N 105°47W **71** B7
Cree → *U.K.* 54°55N 4°25W **11** G4
Cree L. *Canada* 57°30N 106°30W **71** B7
Creede *U.S.A.* 37°51N 106°56W **77** H10
Creekside *U.S.A.* 40°40N 79°11W **82** F5
Creel *Mexico* 27°45N 107°38W **86** B3
Creemore *Canada* 44°19N 80°6W **82** B4
Creighton *Canada* 54°45N 101°54W **71** C8
Creighton *U.S.A.* 42°28N 97°54W **80** D5
Crema *Italy* 45°22N 9°41E **20** D8
Cremona *Italy* 45°7N 10°2E **20** D9
Cres *Croatia* 44°58N 14°25E **16** F8
Crescent City *U.S.A.* 41°45N 124°12W **76** F1
Crespo *Argentina* 32°2S 60°19W **94** C3
Cresson *U.S.A.* 40°28N 78°36W **82** F6
Crestline *Calif., U.S.A.* 34°14N 117°18W **79** L9
Crestline *Ohio, U.S.A.* 40°47N 82°44W **82** F2
Creston *Canada* 49°10N 116°31W **70** D5
Creston *Calif., U.S.A.* 35°32N 120°33W **78** K6
Creston *Iowa, U.S.A.* 41°4N 94°22W **80** E6
Crestview *Calif., U.S.A.* 37°46N 118°58W **78** H8
Crestview *Fla., U.S.A.* 30°46N 86°34W **85** F11
Crete = Kriti *Greece* 35°15N 25°0E **25** D7
Crete *U.S.A.* 40°38N 96°58W **80** E5
Créteil *France* 48°47N 2°27E **20** B5
Creus, C. de *Spain* 42°20N 3°19E **21** A7
Creuse → *France* 47°0N 0°34E **20** C4
Crewe *U.K.* 53°6N 2°26W **12** D5
Crewkerne *U.K.* 50°53N 2°48W **13** G5
Crianlarich *U.K.* 56°24N 4°37W **11** E4
Criciúma *Brazil* 28°40S 49°23W **95** B6
Crieff *U.K.* 56°22N 3°50W **11** E5
Crimea □ *Ukraine* 45°30N 33°10E **19** E5
Crimean Pen. = Krymskyy
  Pivostriv *Ukraine* 45°0N 34°0E **19** F5
Crişul Alb → *Romania* 46°42N 21°17E **17** E11
Crişul Negru →
  Romania 46°42N 21°16E **17** E11
Crna → *Macedonia* 41°33N 21°59E **23** D9
Crna Gora = Montenegro ■
  Europe 42°40N 19°20E **23** C8

Crna Gora *Macedonia* 42°10N 21°30E **23** C9
Crna Reka = Crna →
  Macedonia 41°33N 21°59E **23** D9
Croagh Patrick *Ireland* 53°46N 9°40W **10** C1
Croatia ■ *Europe* 45°20N 16°0E **16** F9
Crocker, Banjaran
  Malaysia 5°40N 116°30E **36** C5
Crockett *U.S.A.* 31°19N 95°27W **84** F7
Crocodile = Umgwenya →
  Mozam. 25°14S 32°18E **57** D5
Crocodile Is. *Australia* 12°3S 134°58E **62** A1
Crohy Hd. *Ireland* 54°55N 8°26W **10** B3
Croix, L. la *Canada* 48°20N 92°15W **72** C1
Croker, C. *Australia* 10°58S 132°35E **60** B5
Croker, C. *Canada* 44°58N 80°59W **82** B4
Croker I. *Australia* 11°12S 132°32E **60** B5
Croker Islands Seas ◌
  Australia 11°20S 132°30E **60** B5
Cromarty *U.K.* 57°40N 4°2W **11** D4
Cromer *U.K.* 52°56N 1°17E **12** E9
Cromwell *N.Z.* 45°3S 169°14E **59** F2
Cromwell *U.S.A.* 41°36N 72°39W **83** E12
Crook *U.K.* 54°43N 1°45W **12** C6
Crooked → *Canada* 54°50N 122°54W **70** C4
Crooked → *U.S.A.* 44°32N 121°16W **76** D3
Crooked I. *Bahamas* 22°50N 74°10W **89** B5
Crooked Island Passage
  Bahamas 22°55N 74°35W **89** B5
Crookston *Minn., U.S.A.* 47°47N 96°37W **80** B5
Crookston *Nebr., U.S.A.* 42°56N 100°45W **80** D3
Crookwell *Australia* 34°28S 149°24E **63** E4
Crosby *U.K.* 53°30N 3°3W **12** D4
Crosby *N. Dak., U.S.A.* 48°55N 103°18W **80** A2
Crosby *Pa., U.S.A.* 41°45N 78°23W **82** E6
Crosbyton *U.S.A.* 33°40N 101°14W **84** E4
Cross City *U.S.A.* 29°38N 83°7W **85** G13
Cross Fell *U.K.* 54°43N 2°28W **12** C5
Cross L. *Canada* 54°45N 97°30W **71** C9
Cross Sound *U.S.A.* 58°0N 135°0W **68** F4
Crossett *U.S.A.* 33°8N 91°58W **84** E9
Crosshaven *Ireland* 51°47N 8°17W **10** E3
Crossmaglen *Ireland* 54°5N 6°36W **10** B5
Crossmolina *Ireland* 54°6N 9°20W **10** B2
Crossville *U.S.A.* 35°57N 85°2W **85** D12
Croswell *U.S.A.* 43°16N 82°37W **82** C2
Croton-on-Hudson
  U.S.A. 41°12N 73°55W **83** E11
Crotone *Italy* 39°5N 17°8E **22** E7
Crow → *Canada* 59°41N 124°20W **70** B4
Crow Agency *U.S.A.* 45°36N 107°28W **76** D10
Crow Hd. *Ireland* 51°35N 10°9W **10** E1
Crowell *U.S.A.* 33°59N 99°43W **84** E5
Crowley *U.S.A.* 30°13N 92°22W **84** F8
Crowley, L. *U.S.A.* 37°35N 118°42W **78** H8
Crown Point *Ind.*
  U.S.A. 41°25N 87°22W **80** E10
Crown Point *N.Y.,*
  U.S.A. 43°57N 73°26W **83** C11
Crown Pt. *Trin. & Tob.* 11°18N 60°51W **93** J16
Crownpoint *U.S.A.* 35°41N 108°9W **77** J9
Crows Landing *U.S.A.* 37°23N 121°6W **78** H5
Crows Nest *Australia* 27°16S 152°4E **63** D5
Crowsnest Pass *Canada* 49°40N 114°40W **70** D6
Croydon *Australia* 18°13S 142°14E **62** B3
Croydon □ *U.K.* 51°22N 0°5W **13** F7
Crozet, Is. *Ind. Oc.* 46°27S 52°0E **3** G12
Crusheen *Ireland* 52°57N 8°53W **10** D3
Cruz, C. *Cuba* 19°50N 77°50W **88** C4
Cruz Alta *Brazil* 28°45S 53°40W **95** B5
Cruz Bay *U.S. Virgin Is.* 18°20N 64°48W **89** e
Cruz del Eje *Argentina* 30°45S 64°50W **94** C3
Cruzeiro *Brazil* 22°33S 45°0W **95** A7
Cruzeiro do Oeste *Brazil* 23°46S 53°4W **95** A5
Cruzeiro do Sul *Brazil* 7°35S 72°35W **92** E4
Cry L. *Canada* 58°45N 129°0W **70** B3
Crystal Bay *U.S.A.* 39°15N 120°0W **78** F7
Crystal Brook *Australia* 33°21S 138°12E **63** E2
Crystal City *U.S.A.* 28°41N 99°50W **84** G5
Crystal Falls *U.S.A.* 46°5N 88°20W **80** B9
Crystal River *U.S.A.* 28°54N 82°35W **85** G13
Crystal Springs *U.S.A.* 31°59N 90°21W **85** F9
Csongrád *Hungary* 46°43N 20°12E **17** E11
Cu Lao Hon *Vietnam* 10°54N 108°18E **39** G7
Cua Rao *Vietnam* 19°16N 104°27E **38** C5
Cuácua → *Mozam.* 17°54S 37°0E **55** F4
Cuamato *Angola* 17°2S 15°7E **56** B2
Cuamba *Mozam.* 14°45S 36°22E **55** E4
Cuando → *Angola* 17°30S 23°15E **53** H4
Cuando Cubango □
  Angola 16°25S 20°0E **56** B3
Cuangar *Angola* 17°36S 18°39E **56** B2
Cuango = Kwango →
  Dem. Rep. of the Congo 3°14S 17°22E **52** E3
Cuanza → *Angola* 9°21S 13°9E **52** F2
Cuarto → *Argentina* 33°25S 63°2W **94** C3
Cuatrociénegas *Mexico* 26°59N 102°5W **86** B4
Cuauhtémoc *Mexico* 28°25N 106°52W **86** B3
Cuba *N. Mex., U.S.A.* 36°1N 107°4W **77** H10
Cuba *N.Y., U.S.A.* 42°13N 78°17W **82** D6
Cuba ■ *W. Indies* 22°0N 79°0W **88** B4
Cubango → *Africa* 18°50S 22°25E **56** B3
Cuc Phuong △ *Vietnam* 20°17N 105°38E **38** B5
Cuchumatanes, Sierra de los
  Guatemala 15°35N 91°25W **88** C1
Cuckfield *U.K.* 51°1N 0°8W **13** F7
Cucuí *Brazil* 1°12N 66°50W **92** C5
Cucurpé *Mexico* 30°20N 110°43W **86** A2
Cúcuta *Colombia* 7°54N 72°31W **92** B4
Cuddalore *India* 11°46N 79°45E **40** P11
Cuddapah *India* 14°30N 78°47E **40** M11
Cuddapan, L. *Australia* 25°45S 141°26E **62** D3
Cue *Australia* 27°25S 117°54E **61** E2
Cuenca *Ecuador* 2°50S 79°9W **92** D3
Cuenca *Spain* 40°5N 2°10W **21** B4
Cuenca, Serranía de
  Spain 39°55N 1°50W **21** C5
Cuernavaca *Mexico* 18°55N 99°15W **87** D5
Cuero *U.S.A.* 29°6N 97°17W **84** G6

Cueva de la Quebrada del Toro △
  Venezuela 10°46N 69°3W **89** D6
Cuevas del Almanzora
  Spain 37°18N 1°58W **21** D5
Cuevo *Bolivia* 20°15S 63°30W **92** H6
Cuiabá *Brazil* 15°30S 56°0W **93** G7
Cuiabá → *Brazil* 17°5S 56°36W **93** G7
Cuihangcun *China* 22°27N 113°32E **33** G10
Cuijk *Neths.* 51°44N 5°50E **15** C5
Cuilco *Guatemala* 15°24N 91°58W **88** C1
Cuillin Hills *U.K.* 57°13N 6°15W **11** D2
Cuillin Sd. *U.K.* 57°4N 6°20W **11** D2
Cuilo = Kwilu →
  Dem. Rep. of the Congo 3°22S 17°22E **52** E3
Cuito → *Angola* 18°1S 20°48E **56** B3
Cuitzeo, L. de *Mexico* 19°55N 101°5W **86** D4
Cukai *Malaysia* 4°13N 103°25E **39** K4
Culbertson *U.S.A.* 48°9N 104°31W **76** B11
Culcairn *Australia* 35°41S 147°3E **63** F4
Culebra *Puerto Rico* 18°19N 65°18W **89** d
Culgoa → *Australia* 29°56S 146°20E **63** D4
Culgoa Flood Plain △
  Australia 28°58S 147°5E **63** D4
Culiacán *Mexico* 24°50N 107°23W **86** C3
Culiacán → *Mexico* 24°30N 107°42W **86** C3
Culik *Indonesia* 8°21S 115°37E **37** J18
Culion *Phil.* 11°54N 119°58E **37** B6
Cullarin Ra. *Australia* 34°30S 149°30E **63** E4
Cullen *U.K.* 57°42N 2°49W **11** D6
Cullen Pt. *Australia* 11°57S 141°54E **62** A3
Cullera *Spain* 39°9N 0°17W **21** C5
Cullman *U.S.A.* 34°11N 86°51W **85** E11
Cullompton *U.K.* 50°51N 3°24W **13** G4
Culpeper *U.S.A.* 38°30N 78°0W **81** F14
Culuene → *Brazil* 12°56S 52°51W **93** F8
Culver, Pt. *Australia* 32°54S 124°43E **61** F3
Culverden *N.Z.* 42°47S 172°49E **59** E4
Cumaná *Venezuela* 10°30N 64°5W **92** A6
Cumberland *B.C.,*
  Canada 49°40N 125°0W **70** D4
Cumberland *Ont.,*
  Canada 45°29N 75°24W **83** A9
Cumberland *U.S.A.* 39°39N 78°46W **81** F14
Cumberland → *U.S.A.* 37°9N 88°25W **80** G9
Cumberland, L. *U.S.A.* 36°52N 85°9W **81** G11
Cumberland Gap △
  U.S.A. 36°36N 83°40W **81** G12
Cumberland I. *U.S.A.* 30°50N 81°25W **85** F14
Cumberland Is. *Australia* 20°35S 149°10E **62** b
Cumberland Island △
  U.S.A. 30°12N 81°24W **85** F14
Cumberland L. *Canada* 54°3N 102°18W **71** C8
Cumberland Pen. *Canada* 67°0N 64°0W **69** D19
Cumberland Plateau
  U.S.A. 36°0N 85°0W **85** D12
Cumberland Sd. *Canada* 65°30N 66°0W **69** D18
Cumbernauld *U.K.* 55°57N 3°58W **11** F5
Cumborah *Australia* 29°40S 147°45E **63** D4
Cumbres de Majalca △
  Mexico 28°48N 106°30W **86** B3
Cumbres de Monterrey △
  Mexico 25°26N 100°25W **86** B4
Cumbria □ *U.K.* 54°42N 2°52W **12** C5
Cumbrian Mts. *U.K.* 54°30N 3°0W **12** C5
Cumbum *India* 15°40N 79°10E **40** M11
Cuminá → *Brazil* 1°30S 56°0W **93** D7
Cummings Mt. *U.S.A.* 35°2N 118°34W **79** K8
Cummins *Australia* 34°16S 135°43E **63** E2
Cumnock *Australia* 32°59S 148°46E **63** E4
Cumnock *U.K.* 55°28N 4°17W **11** F4
Cumpas *Mexico* 30°2N 109°48W **86** B3
Cumplida, Pta.
  Canary Is. 28°50N 17°48W **24** F2
Cunco *Chile* 38°55S 72°2W **96** D2
Cuncumén *Chile* 31°53S 70°38W **94** C1
Cundeelee ◌ *Australia* 30°43S 123°25E **61** F3
Cunderdin *Australia* 31°37S 117°12E **61** F2
Cunene → *Angola* 17°20S 11°50E **56** B1
Cúneo *Italy* 44°23N 7°32E **20** D7
Çüngüş *Turkey* 38°13N 39°17E **44** B3
Cunillera, I. = Sa Conillera
  Spain 38°59N 1°13E **24** C7
Cunnamulla *Australia* 28°2S 145°38E **63** D4
Cupar *Canada* 50°57N 104°10W **71** C8
Cupar *U.K.* 56°19N 3°1W **11** E5
Cupertino *U.S.A.* 37°19N 122°2W **78** H4
Cupica, G. de *Colombia* 6°25N 77°30W **92** B3
Curaçao *Neth. Ant.* 12°10N 69°0W **89** D6
Curanilahue *Chile* 37°29S 73°28W **94** D1
Curaray → *Peru* 2°20S 74°5W **92** D4
Curepipe *Mauritius* 20°19S 57°31E **53** d
Curepto *Chile* 35°8S 72°1W **94** D1
Curiapo *Venezuela* 8°33N 61°5W **92** B6
Curicó *Chile* 34°55S 71°20W **94** C1
Curitiba *Brazil* 25°20S 49°10W **95** B6
Curitibanos *Brazil* 27°18S 50°36W **95** B5
Currabubula *Australia* 31°16S 150°44E **63** E5
Currais Novos *Brazil* 6°13S 36°30W **93** E11
Curral Velho *C. Verde Is.* 16°8N 22°48W **50** b
Curralinho *Brazil* 1°45S 49°46W **93** D9
Currane, L. *Ireland* 51°49N 10°4W **10** E1
Currant *U.S.A.* 38°44N 115°28W **76** G6
Currarong *Australia* 35°0S 150°49E **63** F5
Current → *U.S.A.* 36°15N 90°55W **84** C9
Currie *Australia* 39°56S 143°53E **63** F3
Currie *U.S.A.* 40°16N 114°45W **76** F6
Curtea de Argeş
  Romania 45°12N 24°42E **17** F13
Curtin Springs *Australia* 25°20S 131°45E **61** E5
Curtis *U.S.A.* 40°38N 100°31W **80** E3
Curtis Group *Australia* 39°30S 146°37E **63** F4
Curtis I. *Australia* 23°35S 151°10E **62** C5
Curuápanema → *Brazil* 2°25S 55°2W **93** D7
Curuçá *Brazil* 0°43S 47°50W **93** D9
Curuguaty *Paraguay* 24°31S 55°42W **95** A4
Çürüksu Çayi = Büyük
  Menderes → *Turkey* 37°28N 27°11E **23** F12
Curup *Indonesia* 4°26S 102°13E **36** E2

Cururupu *Brazil* 1°50S 44°50W **93** D10
Curuzú Cuatiá *Argentina* 29°50S 58°5W **94** B4
Curvelo *Brazil* 18°45S 44°27W **93** G10
Cusco = Cuzco *Peru* 13°32S 72°0W **92** F4
Cushendall *U.K.* 55°5N 6°4W **10** A5
Cushing *U.S.A.* 35°59N 96°46W **84** D6
Cushing, Mt. *Canada* 57°35N 126°57W **70** B3
Cusihuiríachic *Mexico* 28°14N 106°50W **86** B3
Custer *U.S.A.* 43°46N 103°36W **80** D2
Cut Bank *U.S.A.* 48°38N 112°20W **76** B7
Cutchogue *U.S.A.* 41°1N 72°30W **83** E12
Cuthbert *U.S.A.* 31°46N 84°48W **85** F12
Cutler *U.S.A.* 36°31N 119°17W **78** J7
Cuttaburra → *Australia* 29°43S 144°22E **63** D3
Cuttack *India* 20°25N 85°57E **41** J14
Cuvier, C. *Australia* 23°14S 113°22E **61** D1
Cuvier I. *N.Z.* 36°27S 175°50E **59** B5
Cuxhaven *Germany* 53°51N 8°41E **16** B5
Cuyahoga Falls *U.S.A.* 41°8N 81°29W **82** E3
Cuyahoga Valley △
  U.S.A. 41°24N 81°33W **82** E3
Cuyo *Phil.* 10°51N 121°2E **37** B6
Cuyuni → *Guyana* 6°23N 58°41W **92** B7
Cuzco *Bolivia* 20°0S 66°50W **92** H5
Cuzco *Peru* 13°32S 72°0W **92** F4
Cwmbran *U.K.* 51°39N 3°2W **13** F4
Cyangugu *Rwanda* 2°29S 28°54E **54** C2
Cyclades *Greece* 37°0N 24°30E **23** F11
Cygnet *Australia* 43°8S 147°1E **63** G4
Cynthiana *U.S.A.* 38°23N 84°18W **81** F11
Cypress Hills *Canada* 49°40N 109°30W **71** D7
Cypress Hills △ *Canada* 49°40N 109°30W **71** D7
Cyprus ■ *Asia* 35°0N 33°0E **25** E12
Cyrenaica = Barqa *Libya* 27°0N 23°0E **51** C10
Cyrene *Libya* 32°53N 21°52E **51** B10
Czar *Canada* 52°27N 110°50W **71** C6
Czech Rep. ■ *Europe* 50°0N 15°0E **16** D8
Częstochowa *Poland* 50°49N 19°7E **17** C10

D

Da → *Vietnam* 21°15N 105°20E **38** B5
Da Hinggan Ling *China* 48°0N 121°0E **33** B7
Da Lat *Vietnam* 11°56N 108°25E **39** G7
Da Nang *Vietnam* 16°4N 108°13E **38** D7
Da Qaidam *China* 37°50N 95°15E **32** C4
Da Yunhe → *Hopei,*
  China 39°10N 117°10E **35** E9
Da Yunhe → *Jiangsu,*
  China 34°25N 120°5E **35** G11
Da'an *China* 45°30N 124°7E **35** B13
Daan Viljoen ◌ *Namibia* 22°2S 16°45E **56** C2
Daba Shan *China* 32°0N 109°0E **33** C5
Dabbagh, Jabal *Si. Arabia* 27°52N 35°45E **44** E2
Dabhoi *India* 22°10N 73°20E **42** H5
Dabo = Pasirkuning
  Indonesia 0°30S 104°33E **36** E2
Dabola *Guinea* 10°50N 11°5W **50** F3
Dabung *Malaysia* 5°23N 102°1E **39** K4
Dacca = Dhaka *Bangla.* 23°43N 90°26E **43** H14
Dacca = Dhaka □
  Bangla. 24°25N 90°25E **43** G14
Dachau *Germany* 48°15N 11°26E **16** D6
Dachigam △ *India* 34°10N 75°0E **42** B6
Dacre *Canada* 45°22N 76°57W **82** A8
Dadanawa *Guyana* 2°50N 59°30W **92** C7
Dade City *U.S.A.* 28°22N 82°11W **85** G13
Dadhar *Pakistan* 29°28N 67°39E **42** E2
Dadnah *U.A.E.* 25°32N 56°22E **45** E8
Dadra & Nagar Haveli □
  India 20°5N 73°0E **40** J8
Dadri = Charkhi Dadri
  India 28°37N 76°17E **42** E7
Dadu *Pakistan* 26°45N 67°45E **42** F2
Daegu *S. Korea* 35°50N 128°37E **35** G15
Daejeon *S. Korea* 36°20N 127°28E **35** F14
Daejeong *S. Korea* 33°18N 126°17E **35** H14
Daet *Phil.* 14°2N 122°55E **37** B6
Dafnes *Greece* 35°13N 25°3E **25** D7
Dagana *Senegal* 16°30N 15°35W **50** E2
Dagestan □ *Russia* 42°30N 47°0E **19** F8
Daggett *U.S.A.* 34°52N 116°52W **79** L10
Daghestan Republic =
  Dagestan □ *Russia* 42°30N 47°0E **19** F8
Dağlıq Qarabağ =
  Nagorno-Karabakh □
  Azerbaijan 39°55N 46°45E **44** B5
Dagö = Hiiumaa *Estonia* 58°50N 22°45E **9** G20
Dagu *China* 38°59N 117°40E **35** E9
Dagupan *Phil.* 16°3N 120°20E **37** A6
Daguragu *Australia* 17°33S 130°30E **60** C5
Daguragu ◌ *Australia* 17°24S 130°48E **60** C5
Dahab *Egypt* 28°31N 34°31E **44** D2
Dahlak Kebir *Eritrea* 15°50N 40°10E **47** D3
Dahlonega *U.S.A.* 34°32N 83°59W **85** D13
Dahod *India* 22°50N 74°15E **42** H6
Dahongliutan *China* 35°45N 79°20E **43** B8
Dahra *Libya* 29°30N 17°50E **51** C9
Dahūk *Iraq* 36°50N 43°1E **44** B3
Dai Hao *Vietnam* 18°1N 106°25E **38** C6
Dai-Sen *Japan* 35°22N 133°32E **31** G6
Dai Xian *China* 39°4N 112°58E **34** E7
Daicheng *China* 38°42N 116°38E **34** E9
Daikondi = Day Kundī □
  Afghan. 34°0N 66°0E **40** C5
Daingean *Ireland* 53°18N 7°17W **10** C4
Daintree *Australia* 16°20S 145°20E **62** B4
Daintree → *Australia* 16°8S 145°2E **62** B4
Daiō-Misaki *Japan* 34°15N 136°45E **31** G8
Daisen-Oki △ *Japan* 35°23N 133°24E **31** G6
Daisetsu-Zan *Japan* 43°30N 142°57E **30** C11
Daisetsu-Zan △ *Japan* 43°30N 142°55E **30** C11
Dajarra *Australia* 21°42S 139°30E **62** C2
Dajiawa *China* 37°9N 119°0E **35** F10
Dak Dam *Cambodia* 12°20N 107°21E **38** F6
Dak Nhe *Vietnam* 15°28N 107°48E **38** E6
Dak Pek *Vietnam* 15°4N 107°44E **38** E6
Dak Song *Vietnam* 12°19N 107°35E **39** F6

Dak Sui *Vietnam* 14°55N 107°43E **38 E6**
Dakar *Senegal* 14°34N 17°29W **50 F2**
Dakhla *W. Sahara* 23°50N 15°53W **50 D2**
Dakhla, El Wâhât el
  Egypt 25°30N 28°50E **51 C11**
Dakor *India* 22°45N 73°11E **42 H5**
Dakota City *U.S.A.* 42°25N 96°25W **80 D5**
Đakovica *Kosovo* 42°22N 20°26E **23 C9**
Dalachi *China* 36°48N 105°00E **34 F3**
Dalai Nur *China* 43°20N 116°45E **34 C9**
Dālakī *Iran* 29°26N 51°17E **45 D6**
Dälälven → *Sweden* 60°12N 16°43E **9 F17**
Dalaman *Turkey* 36°41N 28°43E **23 F13**
Dalandzadgad *Mongolia* 43°27N 104°30E **34 C3**
Dalap-Uliga-Darrit = Majuro
  Marshall Is. 7°9N 171°12E **64 G9**
Dalarna *Sweden* 61°0N 14°0E **8 F16**
Dälbandin *Pakistan* 29°0N 64°23E **40 E4**
Dalbeattie *U.K.* 54°56N 3°50W **11 G5**
Dalby *Australia* 27°10S 151°17E **63 D5**
Dale City *U.S.A.* 38°38N 77°19W **81 F15**
Dale Hollow L. *U.S.A.* 36°32N 85°27W **85 C12**
Dalgān *Iran* 27°31N 59°19E **45 E8**
Dalhart *U.S.A.* 36°4N 102°31W **84 C3**
Dalhousie *Canada* 48°5N 66°26W **73 C6**
Dalhousie *India* 32°38N 75°58E **42 C6**
Dali *Shaanxi, China* 34°48N 109°58E **34 G5**
Dali *Yunnan, China* 25°40N 100°10E **41 G22**
Dalian *China* 38°50N 121°40E **35 E11**
Daliang Shan *China* 28°0N 102°45E **32 D5**
Daling He → *China* 40°55N 121°40E **35 D11**
Dāliyat el Karmel *Israel* 32°43N 35°2E **46 C4**
Dalkeith *U.K.* 55°54N 3°4W **11 F5**
Dallas *Oreg., U.S.A.* 44°55N 123°19W **76 D2**
Dallas *Tex., U.S.A.* 32°47N 96°48W **84 E6**
Dalles, The *U.S.A.* 45°36N 121°10W **76 D3**
Dalmã *U.A.E.* 24°30N 52°20E **45 E7**
Dalmacija *Croatia* 43°20N 17°0E **22 C7**
Dalmas, L. *Canada* 53°30N 71°50W **73 B5**
Dalmatia = Dalmacija
  Croatia 43°20N 17°0E **22 C7**
Dalmau *India* 26°4N 81°2E **43 F9**
Dalmellington *U.K.* 55°19N 4°23W **11 F4**
Dalnegorsk *Russia* 44°32N 135°33E **30 B7**
Dalnerechensk *Russia* 45°50N 133°40E **30 B6**
Dalnevostochnyy □
  Russia 67°0N 140°0E **29 C14**
Daloa *Ivory C.* 7°0N 6°30W **50 G4**
Dalry *U.K.* 55°42N 4°43W **11 F4**
Dalrymple, L. *Australia* 20°40S 147°0E **62 C4**
Dalrymple, Mt. *Australia* 21°1S 148°39E **62 b**
Dalsland *Sweden* 58°50N 12°15E **9 G15**
Daltenganj *India* 24°0N 84°4E **43 H11**
Dalton *Ga., U.S.A.* 34°46N 84°58W **85 D12**
Dalton *Mass., U.S.A.* 42°28N 73°11W **83 D11**
Dalton *Nebr., U.S.A.* 41°25N 102°58W **80 E2**
Dalton-in-Furness *U.K.* 54°10N 3°11W **12 C4**
Dalvík *Iceland* 65°58N 18°32W **8 D4**
Dálvvadis = Jokkmokk
  Sweden 66°35N 19°50E **8 C18**
Dalwallinu *Australia* 30°17S 116°40E **61 F2**
Daly → *Australia* 13°35S 130°19E **60 B5**
Daly City *U.S.A.* 37°42N 122°27W **78 H4**
Daly L. *Canada* 56°32N 105°39W **71 B7**
Daly River *Australia* 13°46S 130°42E **60 B5**
Daly River-Port Keats ◇
  Australia 14°13S 129°36E **60 B4**
Daly Waters *Australia* 16°15S 133°24E **62 B1**
Dam Doi *Vietnam* 8°50N 105°12E **39 H5**
Dam Ha *Vietnam* 21°21N 107°36E **38 B6**
Daman *India* 20°25N 72°57E **40 J8**
Dāmaneh *Iran* 33°1N 50°29E **45 C6**
Damanhûr *Egypt* 31°0N 30°30E **51 B12**
Damant L. *Canada* 61°45N 105°5W **71 A7**
Damanzhuang *China* 38°5N 116°35E **34 E9**
Damar *Indonesia* 7°7S 128°40E **37 F7**
Damara *C.A.R.* 4°58N 18°42E **52 D3**
Damaraland *Namibia* 20°0S 15°0E **56 C2**
Damascus = Dimashq
  Syria 33°30N 36°18E **46 B5**
Damaturu *Nigeria* 11°45N 11°55E **52 B2**
Damāvand *Iran* 35°47N 52°0E **45 C7**
Damāvand, Qolleh-ye
  Iran 35°56N 52°10E **45 C7**
Damba *Angola* 6°44S 15°20E **52 F3**
Dâmboviţa → *Romania* 44°12N 26°26E **17 F14**
Dame Marie *Haiti* 18°36N 74°26W **89 C5**
Dāmghān *Iran* 36°10N 54°17E **45 B7**
Damiel *Spain* 39°4N 3°37W **21 C4**
Damietta = Dumyât
  Egypt 31°24N 31°48E **51 B12**
Daming *China* 36°15N 115°6E **34 F8**
Damīr Qābū *Syria* 36°58N 41°51E **44 B4**
Dammam = Ad Dammām
  Si. Arabia 26°20N 50°5E **45 E6**
Damodar → *India* 23°17N 87°35E **43 H12**
Damoh *India* 23°50N 79°28E **43 H8**
Dampier *Australia* 20°41S 116°42E **60 D2**
Dampier, Selat *Indonesia* 0°40S 131°0E **37 E8**
Dampier Arch.
  Australia 20°38S 116°32E **60 D2**
Damrei, Chuor Phnum
  Cambodia 11°30N 103°0E **39 G4**
Damyang *S. Korea* 35°19N 126°59E **35 G14**
Dana *Indonesia* 11°0S 122°52E **37 F6**
Dana *Jordan* 30°41N 35°37E **46 E4**
Dana, L. *Canada* 50°53N 77°20W **72 B4**
Dana, Mt. *U.S.A.* 37°54N 119°12W **78 H7**
Danakil Desert *Ethiopia* 12°45N 41°0E **47 E3**
Danané *Ivory C.* 7°16N 8°9W **50 G4**
Danau Poso *Indonesia* 1°52S 120°35E **37 E6**
Danbury *U.S.A.* 41°24N 73°28W **83 E11**
Danby L. *U.S.A.* 34°13N 115°7W **77 J6**
Dand *Afghan.* 31°28N 65°32E **42 D1**
Dande → *Zimbabwe* 15°56S 30°16E **55 F3**
Dandeli *India* 15°5N 74°30E **40 M9**
Dandenong *Australia* 38°0S 145°15E **63 F4**

Dandong *China* 40°10N 124°20E **35 D13**
Danfeng *China* 33°45N 110°25E **34 H6**
Danger Is. = Pukapuka
  Cook Is. 10°53S 165°49W **65 J11**
Danger Pt. *S. Africa* 34°40S 19°17E **56 E2**
Danginpuri *Indonesia* 8°40S 115°13E **37 K18**
Dangla Shan = Tanggula Shan
  China 32°40N 92°10E **32 C4**
Dangrek, Mts. = Dangrek, Phnom
  Thailand 14°20N 104°0E **38 E5**
Dangrek, Phnom
  Thailand 14°20N 104°0E **38 E5**
Dangriga *Belize* 17°0N 88°13W **87 D7**
Dangshan *China* 34°27N 116°22E **34 G9**
Daniel *U.S.A.* 42°52N 110°4W **76 E8**
Daniel's Harbour
  Canada 50°13N 57°35W **73 B8**
Danielskuil *S. Africa* 28°11S 23°33E **56 D3**
Danielson *U.S.A.* 41°48N 71°53W **83 E13**
Danilov *Russia* 58°16N 40°13E **18 C7**
Daning *China* 36°28N 110°45E **34 F6**
Dank *Oman* 23°33N 56°16E **45 F8**
Dankhar Gompa *India* 32°10N 78°10E **42 C8**
Danli *Honduras* 14°4N 86°35W **88 D2**
Danmark = Denmark ■
  Europe 55°45N 10°0E **9 J14**
Dannemora *U.S.A.* 44°43N 73°44W **83 B11**
Dannevirke *N.Z.* 40°12S 176°8E **59 D6**
Dannhauser *S. Africa* 28°0S 30°3E **57 D5**
Dansville *U.S.A.* 42°34N 77°42W **82 D7**
Danta *India* 24°11N 72°46E **42 G5**
Dantan *India* 21°57N 87°20E **43 J12**
Dante = Xaafuun
  Somali Rep. 10°25N 51°16E **47 E5**
Danube = Dunărea →
  Europe 45°20N 29°40E **17 F15**
Danvers *U.S.A.* 42°34N 70°56W **83 D14**
Danville *Ill., U.S.A.* 40°8N 87°37W **80 E10**
Danville *Ky., U.S.A.* 37°39N 84°46W **81 G11**
Danville *Pa., U.S.A.* 40°58N 76°37W **83 F8**
Danville *Va., U.S.A.* 36°36N 79°23W **81 G14**
Danville *Vt., U.S.A.* 44°25N 72°9W **83 B12**
Danzhou *China* 19°31N 109°33E **38 C7**
Danzig = Gdańsk
  Poland 54°22N 18°40E **17 A10**
Dapaong *Togo* 10°55N 0°16E **50 F6**
Daqing Shan *China* 40°40N 111°0E **34 D6**
Daqq-e Sorkh, Kavīr
  Iran 33°45N 52°50E **45 C7**
Dar Banda *Africa* 8°0N 23°0E **48 F6**
Dar el Beida = Casablanca
  Morocco 33°36N 7°36W **50 B4**
Dar es Salaam *Tanzania* 6°50S 39°12E **54 D4**
Dar Mazār *Iran* 29°14N 57°20E **45 D8**
Dar'ā *Syria* 32°36N 36°7E **46 C5**
Dar'ā □ *Syria* 32°55N 36°10E **46 C5**
Dārāb *Iran* 28°50N 54°30E **45 D7**
Daraban *Pakistan* 31°44N 70°20E **42 D4**
Daraina *Madag.* 13°12S 49°40E **57 A8**
Daraj *Libya* 30°10N 10°28E **51 B8**
Dārān *Iran* 32°59N 50°24E **45 C6**
Dārayyā *Syria* 33°28N 36°15E **46 B5**
Darband *Pakistan* 34°20N 72°50E **42 B5**
Darband, Kūh-e *Iran* 31°34N 57°8E **45 D8**
Darbhanga *India* 26°15N 85°55E **43 F11**
D'Arcy *Canada* 50°33N 122°29W **70 C4**
Dardanelle *Ark., U.S.A.* 35°13N 93°9W **84 D8**
Dardanelle *Calif.,
  U.S.A.* 38°20N 119°50W **78 G7**
Dardanelles = Çanakkale Boğazı
  Turkey 40°17N 26°32E **23 D12**
Dārestān *Iran* 29°9N 58°42E **45 D8**
Dārfūr *Sudan* 13°40N 24°0E **51 F10**
Dargai *Pakistan* 34°25N 71°55E **42 B4**
Dargaville *N.Z.* 35°57S 173°52E **59 A4**
Darhan *Mongolia* 49°37N 106°21E **32 B5**
Darhan Muminggan Lianheqi
  China 41°40N 110°28E **34 D6**
Darıca *Turkey* 40°45N 29°23E **23 D13**
Darién, G. del *Colombia* 9°0N 77°0W **92 B3**
Darién □ *Panama* 7°36N 77°57W **88 E4**
Dariganga = Ovoot
  Mongolia 45°21N 113°45E **34 B7**
Darjeeling = Darjiling
  India 27°3N 88°18E **43 F13**
Darjiling *India* 27°3N 88°18E **43 F13**
Darkan *Australia* 33°20S 116°43E **61 F2**
Darkhana *Pakistan* 30°39N 72°11E **42 D5**
Darkhazīneh *Iran* 31°54N 48°39E **45 D6**
Darkot Pass *Pakistan* 36°45N 73°26E **43 A5**
Darling → *Australia* 34°4S 141°54E **63 E3**
Darling Downs
  Australia 27°30S 150°30E **63 D5**
Darling Ra. *Australia* 32°30S 116°20E **61 F2**
Darlington *U.K.* 54°32N 1°33W **12 C6**
Darlington *U.S.A.* 34°18N 79°52W **85 D15**
Darlington □ *U.K.* 54°32N 1°33W **12 C6**
Darlington, L. *S. Africa* 33°10S 25°9E **56 E4**
Darlot, L. *Australia* 27°48S 121°35E **61 E3**
Darłowo *Poland* 54°25N 16°25E **16 A9**
Darmstadt *Germany* 49°51N 8°39E **16 D5**
Darnah *Libya* 32°45N 22°45E **51 B10**
Darnall *S. Africa* 29°23S 31°18E **57 D5**
Darnley *Australia* 9°35S 143°46E **62 a**
Darnley, C. *Antarctica* 68°0S 69°0E **5 C6**
Darnley B. *Canada* 69°30N 123°30W **68 D7**
Darr → *Australia* 23°39S 143°50E **62 C3**
Darra Pezu *Pakistan* 32°19N 70°44E **42 C4**
Darrequerira *Argentina* 37°42S 63°10W **94 D3**
Darrington *U.S.A.* 48°15N 121°36W **76 B3**
Dart → *U.K.* 50°24N 3°39W **13 G4**
Dart, C. *Antarctica* 73°6S 126°20W **5 D14**
Dartford *U.K.* 51°26N 0°13E **13 F8**
Dartmoor *U.K.* 50°38N 3°57W **13 G4**
Dartmoor △ *U.K.* 50°37N 3°59W **13 G4**
Dartmouth *Canada* 44°40N 63°30W **73 D7**
Dartmouth *U.K.* 50°21N 3°36W **13 G4**
Dartmouth Res.
  Australia 26°4S 145°18E **63 D4**

Dartuch, C. = Artrutx, C. de
  Spain 39°55N 3°49E **24 B10**
Darvaza *Turkmenistan* 40°11N 58°24E **28 E6**
Darvel, Teluk = Lahad Datu,
  Telok *Malaysia* 4°50N 118°20E **37 D5**
Darwen *U.K.* 53°42N 2°29W **12 D5**
Darwendale *Zimbabwe* 17°41S 30°33E **57 B5**
Darwha *India* 20°15N 77°45E **40 J10**
Darwin *Australia* 12°25S 130°51E **60 B5**
Darwin *U.S.A.* 36°15N 117°35W **79 J9**
Darya Khan *Pakistan* 31°48N 71°6E **42 D4**
Daryāateh-ye Bakhtegān
  Iran 29°40N 53°50E **45 D7**
Daryoi Amu = Amudarya →
  Uzbekistan 43°58N 59°34E **28 E6**
Dās *U.A.E.* 25°20N 53°30E **45 E7**
Dashen, Ras *Ethiopia* 13°8N 38°26E **47 E2**
Dashetai *China* 41°0N 109°5E **34 D5**
Dashköpri *Turkmenistan* 36°16N 62°8E **45 B9**
Dashoguz *Turkmenistan* 41°49N 59°58E **28 E6**
Dasht → *Pakistan* 25°10N 61°40E **40 G2**
Daska *Pakistan* 32°20N 74°20E **42 C6**
Dasuya *India* 31°49N 75°38E **42 C6**
Datça *Turkey* 36°46N 27°40E **23 F12**
Datia *India* 25°39N 78°27E **43 G8**
Datong *China* 40°6N 113°18E **34 D7**
Dattakhel *Pakistan* 32°54N 69°46E **42 C3**
Datu, Tanjung *Indonesia* 2°5N 109°39E **36 D3**
Datu Piang *Phil.* 7°2N 124°30E **37 C6**
Datuk, Tanjong = Datu, Tanjung
  Indonesia 2°5N 109°39E **36 D3**
Daud Khel *Pakistan* 32°53N 71°34E **42 C4**
Daudnagar *India* 25°2N 84°24E **43 G11**
Daugava → *Latvia* 57°4N 24°3E **9 H21**
Daugavpils *Latvia* 55°53N 26°32E **9 J22**
Daulpur *India* 26°45N 77°59E **42 F7**
Dauphin *Canada* 51°9N 100°5W **71 C8**
Dauphin *U.S.A.* 40°22N 76°56W **82 F8**
Dauphin L. *Canada* 51°20N 99°45W **71 C9**
Dauphiné *France* 45°15N 5°25E **20 D6**
Dausa *India* 26°52N 76°20E **42 F7**
Davangere *India* 14°25N 75°55E **40 M9**
Davao *Phil.* 7°0N 125°40E **37 C7**
Davao G. *Phil.* 6°30N 125°48E **37 C7**
Dāvar Panāh = Sarāvān
  Iran 27°25N 62°15E **45 E9**
Davenport *Calif., U.S.A.* 37°1N 122°12W **78 H4**
Davenport *Iowa, U.S.A.* 41°32N 90°35W **80 E8**
Davenport *Wash., U.S.A.* 47°39N 118°9W **76 C4**
Davenport Ra. *Australia* 20°28S 134°0E **62 C1**
Davenport Range △
  Australia 20°36S 134°22E **62 C1**
Daventry *U.K.* 52°16N 1°10W **13 E6**
David *Panama* 8°30N 82°30W **88 E3**
David City *U.S.A.* 41°15N 97°8W **80 E5**
David Glacier *Antarctica* 75°20S 162°0E **5 D21**
David Gorodok = Davyd Haradok
  Belarus 52°4N 27°8E **17 B14**
Davidson *Canada* 51°16N 105°59W **71 C7**
Davidson Mts. *U.S.A.* 68°41N 142°22W **74 B11**
Davis *Antarctica* 68°34S 77°55E **5 C6**
Davis *U.S.A.* 38°33N 121°44W **78 G5**
Davis Dam *U.S.A.* 35°12N 114°34W **79 K12**
Davis Inlet *Canada* 55°50N 60°59W **73 A7**
Davis Mts. *U.S.A.* 30°50N 103°55W **84 F3**
Davis Sea *Antarctica* 66°0S 92°0E **5 C7**
Davis Str. *N. Amer.* 65°0N 58°0W **69 D19**
Davlos *Cyprus* 35°25N 33°54E **25 D12**
Davos *Switz.* 46°48N 9°49E **20 C8**
Davy L. *Canada* 58°53N 108°18W **71 B7**
Davyd Haradok *Belarus* 52°4N 27°8E **17 B14**
Dawei = Tavoy *Burma* 14°2N 98°12E **38 E2**
Dawes Ra. *Australia* 24°40S 150°40E **62 C5**
Dawlish *U.K.* 50°35N 3°28W **13 G4**
Dawna Ra. *Burma* 16°30N 98°30E **38 D2**
Dawros Hd. *Ireland* 54°50N 8°33W **10 B3**
Dawson *U.S.A.* 31°46N 84°27W **85 F12**
Dawson, I. *Chile* 53°50S 70°50W **96 G2**
Dawson B. *Canada* 52°53N 100°49W **71 C8**
Dawson City *Canada* 64°10N 139°30W **68 E4**
Dawson Creek *Canada* 55°45N 120°15W **70 B4**
Dawson Inlet *Canada* 61°50N 93°25W **71 A10**
Dawson Ra. *Australia* 24°30S 149°48E **62 C4**
Dax *France* 43°44N 1°3W **20 E3**
Daxian *China* 31°15N 107°23E **32 C5**
Daxindian *China* 37°30N 120°50E **35 F11**
Daxinggou *China* 43°25N 129°40E **35 C15**
Daxue Shan *China* 30°30N 101°30E **32 C5**
Day Kundī □ *Afghan.* 34°0N 66°0E **40 C5**
Daylesford *Australia* 37°21S 144°9E **63 F3**
Dayr az Zawr *Syria* 35°20N 40°5E **44 C4**
Daysland *Canada* 52°50N 112°20W **70 C6**
Dayton *Nev., U.S.A.* 39°14N 119°36W **78 F7**
Dayton *Ohio, U.S.A.* 39°45N 84°12W **81 F11**
Dayton *Pa., U.S.A.* 40°53N 79°15W **82 F5**
Dayton *Tenn., U.S.A.* 35°30N 85°1W **85 D12**
Dayton *Wash., U.S.A.* 46°19N 117°59W **76 C5**
Dayton *Wyo., U.S.A.* 44°53N 107°16W **76 D10**
Daytona Beach *U.S.A.* 29°13N 81°1W **85 G14**
Dayville *U.S.A.* 44°28N 119°32W **76 D4**
De Aar *S. Africa* 30°39S 24°0E **56 E3**
De Biesbosch △ *Neths.* 51°45N 4°48E **15 C4**
De Funiak Springs
  U.S.A. 30°43N 86°7W **85 F11**
De Grey → *Australia* 20°12S 119°13E **60 D2**
De Haan *Belgium* 51°16N 3°2E **15 C3**
De Hoge Veluwe △ *Neths.* 52°5N 5°46E **15 B5**
De Hoop *S. Africa* 34°30S 20°28E **56 E3**
De Kalb Junction *U.S.A.* 44°30N 75°16W **83 B9**
De Kennemerduinen △
  Neths. 52°27N 4°33E **15 B4**
De Land *U.S.A.* 29°2N 81°18W **85 G14**
De Leon *U.S.A.* 32°7N 98°32W **84 E5**
De Long Mts. *U.S.A.* 68°10N 163°30W **74 B7**
De Panne *Belgium* 51°6N 2°34E **15 C2**
De Pere *U.S.A.* 44°27N 88°4W **80 C9**
De Queen *U.S.A.* 34°2N 94°21W **84 D7**
De Quincy *U.S.A.* 30°27N 93°26W **84 F8**
De Ruyters *U.S.A.* 42°45N 75°53W **83 D9**

De Smet *U.S.A.* 44°23N 97°33W **80 C5**
De Soto *U.S.A.* 38°8N 90°34W **80 F8**
De Tour Village *U.S.A.* 46°0N 83°56W **81 B12**
De Witt *U.S.A.* 34°18N 91°20W **84 D9**
Dead Sea *Asia* 31°30N 35°30E **46 D4**
Deadwood *U.S.A.* 44°23N 103°44W **80 C2**
Deadwood L. *Canada* 59°10N 128°30W **70 B3**
Deal *U.K.* 51°13N 1°25E **13 F9**
Deal I. *Australia* 39°30S 147°20E **63 F4**
Dealesville *S. Africa* 28°41S 25°44E **56 D4**
Dean → *Canada* 52°49N 126°58W **70 C3**
Dean, Forest of *U.K.* 51°45N 2°33W **13 F5**
Dean Chan. *Canada* 52°30N 127°15W **70 C3**
Deán Funes *Argentina* 30°20S 64°20W **94 C3**
Dease → *Canada* 59°56N 128°32W **70 B3**
Dease L. *Canada* 58°40N 130°5W **70 B2**
Dease Lake *Canada* 58°25N 130°6W **70 B2**
Death Valley *U.S.A.* 36°15N 116°50W **79 J10**
Death Valley △ *U.S.A.* 36°29N 117°6W **79 J9**
Death Valley Junction
  U.S.A. 36°20N 116°25W **79 J10**
Debagram *India* 23°51N 90°33E **43 H14**
Debar *Macedonia* 41°31N 20°30E **23 D9**
Debden *Canada* 53°30N 106°50W **71 C7**
Dębica *Poland* 50°2N 21°25E **17 C11**
DeBolt *Canada* 55°12N 118°1W **70 B5**
Deborah East, L.
  Australia 30°45S 119°30E **61 F2**
Deborah West, L.
  Australia 30°45S 119°5E **61 F2**
Debre Markos *Ethiopia* 10°20N 37°40E **47 E2**
Debre Tabor *Ethiopia* 11°50N 38°26E **47 E2**
Debre Zebit *Ethiopia* 11°48N 38°30E **47 E2**
Debrecen *Hungary* 47°33N 21°42E **17 E11**
Decatur *Ala., U.S.A.* 34°36N 86°59W **85 D11**
Decatur *Ga., U.S.A.* 33°46N 84°16W **85 D12**
Decatur *Ill., U.S.A.* 39°51N 88°57W **80 F9**
Decatur *Ind., U.S.A.* 40°50N 84°56W **81 E11**
Decatur *Tex., U.S.A.* 33°14N 97°35W **84 E6**
Deccan *India* 18°0N 79°0E **40 L11**
Deception Bay *Australia* 27°10S 153°5E **63 D5**
Deception I. *Antarctica* 63°0S 60°15W **5 C17**
Deception L. *Canada* 56°33N 104°13W **71 B8**
Dechhu *India* 26°46N 72°20E **42 F5**
Děčín *Czech Rep.* 50°47N 14°12E **16 C8**
Deckerville *U.S.A.* 43°32N 82°44W **82 C2**
Decorah *U.S.A.* 43°18N 91°48W **80 D8**
Dedéagach = Alexandroupoli
  Greece 40°50N 25°54E **23 D11**
Dedham *U.S.A.* 42°15N 71°10W **83 D13**
Dee → *Aberds., U.K.* 57°9N 2°5W **11 D6**
Dee → *Dumf. & Gall., U.K.* 54°51N 4°3W **11 G4**
Dee → *Wales, U.K.* 53°22N 3°17W **12 D4**
Deep B. *Canada* 61°15N 116°35W **70 A5**
Deep Bay = Shenzhen Wan
  China 22°27N 113°55E **33 G10**
Deepwater *Australia* 29°25S 151°51E **63 D5**
Deer → *Canada* 58°23N 94°13W **71 B10**
Deer L. *Canada* 52°40N 94°20W **71 C10**
Deer Lake *Nfld. & L.,*
  Canada 49°11N 57°27W **73 C8**
Deer Lake *Ont., Canada* 52°36N 94°20W **71 C10**
Deer Lodge *U.S.A.* 46°24N 112°44W **76 C7**
Deer Park *U.S.A.* 47°57N 117°28W **76 C5**
Deer River *U.S.A.* 47°20N 93°48W **80 B7**
Deeragun *Australia* 19°16S 146°33E **62 B4**
Deerdepoort *S. Africa* 24°37S 26°27E **56 C4**
Defiance *U.S.A.* 41°17N 84°22W **81 E11**
Degana *India* 26°50N 74°20E **42 F6**
Dégelis *Canada* 47°30N 68°35W **73 C6**
Deggendorf *Germany* 48°50N 12°57E **16 D7**
Degh → *Pakistan* 31°3N 73°21E **42 D5**
Degirmenlik = Kythréa
  Cyprus 35°15N 33°29E **25 D12**
Deh Bīd *Iran* 30°39N 53°11E **45 D7**
Deh Dasht *Iran* 30°47N 50°33E **45 D6**
Deh-e Shīr *Iran* 31°29N 53°45E **45 D7**
Dehaj *Iran* 30°42N 54°53E **45 D7**
Dehak *Iran* 27°11N 62°37E **45 E9**
Dehdez *Iran* 31°43N 50°17E **45 D6**
Dehej *India* 21°44N 72°40E **42 J5**
Dehestān *Iran* 28°30N 55°35E **45 D7**
Dehgolān *Iran* 35°17N 47°25E **44 C5**
Dehibat *Tunisia* 32°0N 10°47E **51 B8**
Dehlorān *Iran* 32°41N 47°16E **44 C5**
Dehnow-e Kūhestān
  Iran 27°58N 58°32E **45 E8**
Dehra Dun *India* 30°20N 78°4E **42 D8**
Dehri *India* 24°50N 84°15E **43 G11**
Dehui *China* 44°30N 125°40E **35 B13**
Deinze *Belgium* 50°59N 3°32E **15 D3**
Dej *Romania* 47°10N 23°52E **17 E12**
Deka → *Zimbabwe* 18°4S 26°42E **55 F2**
DeKalb *U.S.A.* 41°56N 88°46W **80 E9**
Dekese
  Dem. Rep. of the Congo 3°24S 21°24E **52 E4**
Del Mar *U.S.A.* 32°58N 117°16W **79 N9**
Del Norte *U.S.A.* 37°41N 106°21W **77 H10**
Del Rio *U.S.A.* 29°22N 100°54W **84 G4**
Delambre I. *Australia* 20°26S 117°5E **60 D2**
Delano *U.S.A.* 35°46N 119°15W **79 K7**
Delano Peak *U.S.A.* 38°22N 112°22W **76 G7**
Delareyville *S. Africa* 26°41S 25°26E **56 D4**
Delaronde L. *Canada* 54°3N 107°3W **71 C7**
Delavan *U.S.A.* 42°38N 88°39W **80 D9**
Delaware *U.S.A.* 40°18N 83°4W **81 E12**
Delaware □ *U.S.A.* 39°0N 75°20W **81 F8**
Delaware → *U.S.A.* 39°15N 75°20W **83 G9**
Delaware Water Gap △
  U.S.A. 41°10N 74°55W **83 F10**
Delay → *Canada* 56°56N 71°28W **73 A5**
Delegate *Australia* 37°4S 148°56E **63 F4**
Delevan *U.S.A.* 42°29N 78°29W **82 D6**
Delft *Neths.* 52°1N 4°22E **15 B4**
Delfzijl *Neths.* 53°20N 6°55E **15 A6**
Delgado, C. *Mozam.* 10°45S 40°40E **55 E5**
Delgerhet *Mongolia* 45°50N 110°30E **34 B6**

Delgo *Sudan* 20°6N 30°40E **51 D12**
Delhi *Canada* 42°51N 80°30W **82 D4**
Delhi *India* 28°39N 77°13E **42 E7**
Delhi *La., U.S.A.* 32°28N 91°30W **84 E9**
Delhi *N.Y., U.S.A.* 42°17N 74°55W **83 D10**
Delia *Canada* 51°38N 112°23W **70 C6**
Delice *Turkey* 39°54N 34°2E **19 G5**
Delicias *Mexico* 28°13N 105°28W **86 B3**
Delījān *Iran* 33°59N 50°40E **45 C6**
Déline *Canada* 65°11N 123°25W **68 C7**
Delisle *Canada* 51°55N 107°8W **71 C7**
Deliverance I. *Australia* 9°31S 141°34E **62 a**
Dell City *U.S.A.* 31°56N 105°12W **84 F2**
Dell Rapids *U.S.A.* 43°50N 96°43W **80 D5**
Delmar *U.S.A.* 42°37N 73°47W **83 D11**
Delmenhorst *Germany* 53°3N 8°37E **16 B5**
Delonga, Ostrova
  Russia 76°40N 149°20E **29 B15**
Deloraine *Australia* 41°30S 146°40E **63 G4**
Deloraine *Canada* 49°15N 100°29W **71 D8**
Delphi *U.S.A.* 40°36N 86°41W **80 E10**
Delphos *U.S.A.* 40°51N 84°21W **81 E11**
Delportshoop *S. Africa* 28°22S 24°20E **56 D3**
Delray Beach *U.S.A.* 26°28N 80°4W **85 H14**
Delta *Colo., U.S.A.* 38°44N 108°4W **76 G9**
Delta *Utah, U.S.A.* 39°21N 112°35W **76 G7**
Delta Dunărea □
  Romania 45°15N 29°25E **17 F15**
Delta Junction *U.S.A.* 64°2N 145°44W **68 C2**
Deltona *U.S.A.* 28°54N 81°16W **85 G14**
Delungra *Australia* 29°39S 150°51E **63 D5**
Delvada *India* 20°46N 71°2E **42 J4**
Delvinë *Albania* 39°59N 20°6E **23 E9**
Demak *Indonesia* 6°53S 110°38E **37 G14**
Demanda, Sierra de la
  Spain 42°15N 3°0W **21 A4**
Demavend = Damāvand,
  Qolleh-ye *Iran* 35°56N 52°10E **45 C7**
Dembia *C.A.R.* 4°56N 23°53E **54 B1**
Dembia
  Dem. Rep. of the Congo 3°33N 25°48E **54 B2**
Dembidolo *Ethiopia* 8°34N 34°50E **47 F1**
Demchok *India* 32°42N 79°29E **43 C8**
Demer → *Belgium* 50°57N 4°42E **15 D4**
Deming *N. Mex.,*
  U.S.A. 32°16N 107°46W **77 K10**
Deming *Wash., U.S.A.* 48°50N 122°13W **78 B4**
Demini → *Brazil* 0°46S 62°56W **92 D6**
Demirci *Turkey* 39°2N 28°38E **23 E13**
Demirköy *Turkey* 41°49N 27°45E **23 D12**
Demopolis *U.S.A.* 32°31N 87°50W **85 E11**
Dempo *Indonesia* 4°2S 103°15E **36 E2**
Den Bosch = 's-Hertogenbosch
  Neths. 51°42N 5°17E **15 C5**
Den Burg *Neths.* 53°3N 4°47E **15 A4**
Den Chai *Thailand* 17°59N 100°4E **38 D3**
Den Haag = 's-Gravenhage
  Neths. 52°7N 4°17E **15 B4**
Den Helder *Neths.* 52°57N 4°45E **15 B4**
Den Oever *Neths.* 52°56N 5°2E **15 B5**
Denair *U.S.A.* 37°32N 120°48W **78 H6**
Denali = McKinley, Mt.
  U.S.A. 63°4N 151°0W **68 E1**
Denau *Uzbekistan* 38°16N 67°54E **28 F7**
Denbigh *Canada* 45°8N 77°15W **82 A7**
Denbigh *U.K.* 53°12N 3°25W **12 D4**
Denbighshire □ *U.K.* 53°8N 3°22W **12 D4**
Dendang *Indonesia* 3°7S 107°56E **36 E3**
Dendermonde *Belgium* 51°2N 4°5E **15 C4**
Dengfeng *China* 34°25N 113°2E **34 G7**
Dengkou *China* 40°18N 106°55E **34 D4**
Denham *Australia* 25°56S 113°31E **61 E1**
Denham, Mt. *Jamaica* 18°13N 77°32W **88 a**
Denham Ra. *Australia* 21°55S 147°46E **62 C4**
Denham Sd. *Australia* 25°45S 113°15E **61 E1**
Denholm *Canada* 52°39N 108°1W **71 C7**
Denia *Spain* 38°49N 0°8E **21 C6**
Denial B. *Australia* 32°14S 133°32E **63 E1**
Deniliquin *Australia* 35°30S 144°58E **63 F3**
Denimoo = Fort Resolution
  Canada 61°10N 113°40W **70 A6**
Denison *Iowa, U.S.A.* 42°1N 95°21W **80 D6**
Denison *Tex., U.S.A.* 33°45N 96°33W **84 E6**
Denison Plains *Australia* 18°35S 128°0E **60 C4**
Denizli *Turkey* 37°42N 29°2E **19 G4**
Denman Glacier
  Antarctica 66°45S 99°25E **5 C7**
Denmark *Australia* 34°59S 117°25E **61 F2**
Denmark ■ *Europe* 55°45N 10°0E **9 J14**
Denmark Str. *Atl. Oc.* 66°0N 30°0W **66 C17**
Dennery *St. Lucia* 13°55N 60°54W **89 f**
Dennison *U.S.A.* 40°24N 81°19W **82 F3**
Denny *U.K.* 56°1N 3°55W **11 E5**
Denpasar *Indonesia* 8°45S 115°14E **37 K18**
Denpasar ✈ (DPS)
  Indonesia 8°44S 115°10E **37 K18**
Denton *Mont., U.S.A.* 47°19N 109°57W **76 C9**
Denton *Tex., U.S.A.* 33°13N 97°8W **84 E6**
D'Entrecasteaux, Pt.
  Australia 34°50S 115°57E **61 F2**
D'Entrecasteaux △
  Australia 34°20S 115°33E **61 F2**
D'Entrecasteaux Is.
  Papua N. G. 9°0S 151°0E **58 B8**
Denver *Colo., U.S.A.* 39°42N 104°59W **76 G11**
Denver *Pa., U.S.A.* 40°14N 76°8W **83 F8**
Denver City *U.S.A.* 32°58N 102°50W **84 E3**
Deoband *India* 29°42N 77°43E **42 E7**
Deogarh *India* 25°32N 73°54E **42 G5**
Deoghar *India* 24°30N 86°42E **43 G12**
Deolali *India* 19°58N 73°50E **40 K8**
Deoli = Devli *India* 25°50N 75°20E **42 G6**
Deora *India* 26°22N 70°55E **42 F4**
Deori *India* 23°24N 79°1E **43 H8**
Deoria *India* 26°31N 83°48E **43 F10**
Deosai Mts. *Pakistan* 35°40N 75°0E **43 B6**
Deosri *India* 26°46N 90°29E **43 F14**
Depalpur *India* 22°51N 75°33E **42 H6**
Deping *China* 37°25N 116°58E **35 F9**

Deposit *U.S.A.* 42°4N 75°25W **83 D9**
Depuch I. *Australia* 20°37S 117°44E **60 D2**
Deputatskiy *Russia* 69°18N 139°54E **29 C14**
Dera Ghazi Khan
  Pakistan 30°5N 70°43E **42 D4**
Dera Ismail Khan
  Pakistan 31°50N 70°50E **42 D4**
Derabugti *Pakistan* 29°2N 69°9E **42 E3**
Derawar Fort *Pakistan* 28°46N 71°20E **42 E4**
Derbent *Russia* 42°5N 48°15E **19 F8**
Derby *Australia* 17°18S 123°38E **60 C3**
Derby *U.K.* 52°56N 1°28W **12 E6**
Derby *Conn., U.S.A.* 41°19N 73°5W **83 E11**
Derby *Kans., U.S.A.* 37°33N 97°16W **80 G5**
Derby *N.Y., U.S.A.* 42°41N 78°58W **82 D6**
Derby City □ *U.K.* 52°56N 1°28W **12 E6**
Derby Line *U.S.A.* 45°0N 72°6W **83 B12**
Derbyshire □ *U.K.* 53°11N 1°38W **12 D6**
Derdepoort *S. Africa* 24°38S 26°24E **56 C4**
Dereham *U.K.* 52°41N 0°57E **13 E8**
Derg → *U.K.* 54°44N 7°26W **10 B4**
Derg, L. *Ireland* 53°0N 8°20W **10 D3**
Deridder *U.S.A.* 30°51N 93°17W **84 F8**
Dermott *U.S.A.* 33°32N 91°26W **84 E9**
Derry = Londonderry
  U.K. 55°0N 7°20W **10 B4**
Derry = Londonderry □
  U.K. 55°0N 7°20W **10 B4**
Derry *N.H., U.S.A.* 42°53N 71°19W **83 D13**
Derry *Pa., U.S.A.* 40°20N 79°18W **82 F5**
Derryveagh Mts. *Ireland* 54°56N 8°11W **10 B3**
Derwent → *Cumb., U.K.* 54°39N 3°33W **12 C4**
Derwent → *Derby, U.K.* 52°57N 1°28W **12 E6**
Derwent → *N. Yorks.,*
  U.K. 53°45N 0°58W **12 D7**
Derwent Water *U.K.* 54°35N 3°9W **12 C4**
Des Moines *Iowa, U.S.A.* 41°35N 93°37W **80 E7**
Des Moines *N. Mex.,*
  U.S.A. 36°46N 103°50W **77 H12**
Des Moines *Wash.,*
  U.S.A. 47°24N 122°19W **78 C4**
Des Moines → *U.S.A.* 40°23N 91°25W **80 E8**
Desaguadero →
  Argentina 34°30S 66°46W **94 C2**
Desaguadero → *Bolivia* 16°35S 69°5W **92 G5**
Desar *Malaysia* 1°31N 104°17E **39 d**
Descanso, Pta. *Mexico* 32°21N 117°3W **79 N9**
Deschaillons-sur-St-Laurent
  Canada 46°32N 72°7W **73 C5**
Deschambault L.
  Canada 54°50N 103°30W **71 C8**
Deschutes → *U.S.A.* 45°38N 120°55W **76 D3**
Dese *Ethiopia* 11°5N 39°40E **47 E2**
Deseado → *Argentina* 47°45S 65°54W **96 F3**
Deseronto *Canada* 44°12N 77°3W **82 B7**
Desert Center *U.S.A.* 33°43N 115°24W **79 M11**
Desert Hot Springs
  U.S.A. 33°58N 116°30W **79 M10**
Deshnok *India* 27°48N 73°21E **42 F5**
Desierto Central de Baja
  California △ *Mexico* 29°40N 114°50W **86 B2**
Desna → *Ukraine* 50°33N 30°32E **17 C16**
Desolación, I. *Chile* 53°0S 74°0W **96 G2**
Despeñaperros, Paso
  Spain 38°24N 3°30W **21 C4**
Dessau *Germany* 51°51N 12°14E **16 C7**
Dessye = Dese *Ethiopia* 11°5N 39°40E **47 E2**
D'Estrees B. *Australia* 35°55S 137°45E **63 F2**
Desuri *India* 25°18N 73°35E **42 G5**
Det Udom *Thailand* 14°54N 105°5E **38 E5**
Dete *Zimbabwe* 18°38S 26°50E **56 B4**
Detmold *Germany* 51°56N 8°52E **16 C5**
Detour, Pt. *U.S.A.* 45°40N 86°40W **80 C10**
Detroit *U.S.A.* 42°19N 83°12W **82 D1**
Detroit Lakes *U.S.A.* 46°49N 95°51W **80 B6**
Deua △ *Australia* 35°32S 149°46E **63 F4**
Deurne *Neths.* 51°27N 5°49E **15 C5**
Deutsche Bucht *Germany* 54°15N 8°0E **16 A5**
Deutschland = Germany ■
  Europe 51°0N 10°0E **16 C6**
Deva *Romania* 45°53N 22°55E **17 F12**
Devakottai *India* 9°55N 78°45E **40 Q11**
Devaprayag *India* 30°13N 78°35E **43 D8**
Deventer *Neths.* 52°15N 6°10E **15 B6**
Deveron → *U.K.* 57°41N 2°32W **11 D6**
Devgadh Bariya *India* 22°40N 73°55E **42 H5**
Devikot *India* 26°42N 71°12E **42 F4**
Devils Den *U.S.A.* 35°46N 119°58W **78 K7**
Devils Hole = Death Valley △
  U.S.A. 36°29N 117°6W **79 J9**
Devils Lake *U.S.A.* 48°7N 98°52W **80 A4**
Devils Paw *Canada* 58°47N 134°0W **70 B2**
Devils Postpile △ *U.S.A.* 37°37N 119°5W **78 H7**
Devils Tower *U.S.A.* 44°35N 104°42W **76 D11**
Devils Tower △
  U.S.A. 44°48N 104°55W **76 D11**
Devine *U.S.A.* 29°8N 98°54W **84 G5**
Devizes *U.K.* 51°22N 1°58W **13 F6**
Devli *India* 25°50N 75°20E **42 G6**
Devon *Canada* 53°24N 113°44W **70 C6**
Devon □ *U.K.* 50°50N 3°40W **13 G4**
Devon I. *Canada* 75°10N 85°0W **69 B15**
Devonport *Australia* 41°10S 146°22E **63 G4**
Devonport *N.Z.* 36°49S 174°49E **59 B5**
Dewas *India* 22°59N 76°3E **42 H7**
Dewetsdorp *S. Africa* 29°33S 26°39E **56 D4**
Dewey *Puerto Rico* 18°18N 65°18W **89 d**
Dexter *Maine, U.S.A.* 45°1N 69°18W **81 C19**
Dexter *Mo., U.S.A.* 36°48N 89°57W **80 G9**
Dexter *N. Mex., U.S.A.* 33°12N 104°22W **77 K11**
Dey-Dey, L. *Australia* 29°12S 131°4E **61 E5**
Deyang *China* 31°3N 104°27E **32 C5**
Deyhūk *Iran* 33°15N 57°30E **45 C8**
Deyyer *Iran* 27°55N 51°55E **45 E6**
Dez → *Iran* 31°39N 48°52E **45 D6**
Dezadeash L. *Canada* 60°28N 136°58W **70 A1**
Dezhneva, Mys *Russia* 66°5N 169°40W **29 C19**
Dezhou *China* 37°26N 116°18E **34 F9**

Dhadhar → *India* 24°56N 85°24E **43 G11**
Dhahiriya = Az Zāhirīyah
  West Bank 31°25N 34°58E **46 D3**
Dhahran = Az Zahrān
  Si. Arabia 26°10N 50°7E **45 E6**
Dhak *Pakistan* 32°25N 72°33E **42 C5**
Dhaka *Bangla.* 23°43N 90°26E **43 H14**
Dhaka □ *Bangla.* 24°25N 90°25E **43 G14**
Dhali *Cyprus* 35°1N 33°25E **25 D12**
Dhamār *Yemen* 14°30N 44°20E **47 E3**
Dhampur *India* 29°19N 78°33E **43 E8**
Dhamtari *India* 20°42N 81°35E **41 J12**
Dhanbad *India* 23°50N 86°30E **43 H12**
Dhangarhi *Nepal* 28°55N 80°40E **43 E9**
Dhankuta *Nepal* 26°55N 87°40E **43 F12**
Dhanpuri *India* 23°13N 81°30E **43 H9**
Dhar *India* 22°35N 75°26E **42 H6**
Dharampur *India* 22°13N 75°18E **42 H6**
Dharamsala = Dharmsala
  India 32°16N 76°23E **42 C7**
Dharan *Nepal* 26°49N 87°17E **43 F12**
Dhariwal *India* 31°57N 75°19E **42 D6**
Dharla → *Bangla.* 25°46N 89°42E **43 G13**
Dharmapuri *India* 12°10N 78°10E **40 N11**
Dharmjaygarh *India* 22°28N 83°13E **43 H10**
Dharmsala *India* 32°16N 76°23E **42 C7**
Dharni *India* 21°33N 76°53E **42 J7**
Dharwad *India* 15°30N 75°4E **40 M9**
Dhasan → *India* 25°48N 79°24E **43 G8**
Dhaulagiri *Nepal* 28°39N 83°28E **43 E10**
Dhebar, L. *India* 24°10N 74°0E **42 G6**
Dheftera *Cyprus* 35°5N 33°16E **25 D12**
Dhenkanal *India* 20°45N 85°35E **41 J14**
Dherinia *Cyprus* 35°3N 33°57E **25 D12**
Dhī Qār □ *Iraq* 31°0N 46°15E **44 D5**
Dhībān *Jordan* 31°30N 35°46E **46 D4**
Dhilwan *India* 31°31N 75°21E **42 D6**
Dhimarkhera *India* 23°28N 80°22E **43 H9**
Dhodhekánisos = Dodecanese
  Greece 36°35N 27°0E **23 F12**
Dholka *India* 22°44N 72°29E **42 H5**
Dhoraji *India* 21°45N 70°37E **42 J4**
Dhrangadhra *India* 22°59N 71°31E **42 H4**
Dhrol *India* 22°33N 70°25E **42 H4**
Dhuburi *India* 26°2N 89°59E **41 F16**
Dhule *India* 20°58N 74°50E **40 J9**
Di Linh *Vietnam* 11°35N 108°4E **39 G7**
Di Linh, Cao Nguyen
  Vietnam 11°30N 108°0E **39 G7**
Dia *Greece* 35°28N 25°14E **25 D7**
Diablo Range *U.S.A.* 37°20N 121°25W **78 J5**
Diafarabé *Mali* 14°9N 4°57W **50 F5**
Diamante *Argentina* 32°5S 60°40W **94 C3**
Diamante → *Argentina* 34°30S 66°46W **94 C2**
Diamantina *Brazil* 18°17S 43°40W **93 G10**
Diamantina →
  Australia 26°45S 139°10E **63 D2**
Diamantina △ *Australia* 23°33S 141°23E **62 C3**
Diamantino *Brazil* 14°30S 56°30W **93 F7**
Diamond Bar *U.S.A.* 34°1N 117°48W **79 L9**
Diamond Harbour
  India 22°11N 88°14E **43 H13**
Diamond Is. *Australia* 17°25S 151°5E **62 B5**
Diamond Mts. *U.S.A.* 39°40N 115°50W **76 G6**
Diamond Springs
  U.S.A. 38°42N 120°49W **78 G6**
Diaoyu Tai = Senkaku-Shotō
  E. China Sea 25°45N 123°30E **31 M1**
Dībā *U.A.E.* 25°45N 56°16E **45 E8**
Dibai *India* 28°13N 78°15E **42 E8**
Dibaya
  Dem. Rep. of the Congo 6°30S 22°57E **52 F4**
Dibaya-Lubue
  Dem. Rep. of the Congo 4°12S 19°54E **52 E3**
Dibbeen △ *Jordan* 32°20N 35°45E **46 C4**
D'Iberville, Lac *Canada* 55°55N 73°15W **72 A5**
Dibete *Botswana* 23°45S 26°32E **56 C4**
Dibrugarh *India* 27°29N 94°55E **41 F19**
Dickens *U.S.A.* 33°37N 100°50W **84 E4**
Dickinson *U.S.A.* 46°53N 102°47W **80 B2**
Dickson *U.S.A.* 36°5N 87°23W **85 C11**
Dickson City *U.S.A.* 41°28N 75°36W **83 E9**
Didiéni *Mali* 13°53N 8°6W **50 F4**
Didsbury *Canada* 51°35N 114°10W **70 C6**
Didwana *India* 27°23N 74°36E **42 F6**
Diefenbaker, L. *Canada* 51°0N 106°55W **71 C7**
Diego de Almagro *Chile* 26°22S 70°3W **94 B1**
Diego Suarez = Antsiranana
  Madag. 12°25S 49°20E **57 A8**
Diekirch *Lux.* 49°52N 6°10E **15 E6**
Dien Ban *Vietnam* 15°53N 108°16E **38 E7**
Dien Bien *Vietnam* 21°20N 103°0E **38 B4**
Dien Khanh *Vietnam* 12°15N 109°6E **39 F7**
Dieppe *France* 49°54N 1°4E **20 B4**
Dierks *U.S.A.* 34°7N 94°1W **84 D7**
Diest *Belgium* 50°58N 5°4E **15 D5**
Dif *Somali Rep.* 0°59N 40°58E **47 G3**
Differdange *Lux.* 49°31N 5°54E **15 E5**
Dig *India* 27°28N 77°20E **42 F7**
Digba
  Dem. Rep. of the Congo 4°25N 25°48E **54 D2**
Digby *Canada* 44°38N 65°50W **73 D6**
Digges Is. *Canada* 62°40N 77°50W **69 E16**
Diggi *India* 26°22N 75°26E **42 F6**
Dighinala *Bangla.* 23°15N 92°5E **41 H18**
Dighton *U.S.A.* 38°29N 100°28W **80 F3**
Digne-les-Bains *France* 44°5N 6°12E **20 D7**
Digos *Phil.* 6°45N 125°20E **37 C7**
Digranes *Iceland* 66°4N 14°44W **8 C6**
Digul → *Indonesia* 7°7S 138°42E **37 F9**
Dihang = Brahmaputra →
  Asia 23°40N 90°35E **43 H13**
Dijlah, Nahr → *Asia* 31°0N 47°25E **44 D5**
Dijon *France* 47°20N 5°3E **20 C6**
Dikhil *Djibouti* 11°8N 42°20E **47 E3**
Dikkil = Dikhil *Djibouti* 11°8N 42°20E **47 E3**
Diksmuide *Belgium* 51°2N 2°52E **15 C2**
Dikson *Russia* 73°40N 80°5E **28 B9**

Dikti Oros *Greece* 35°8N 25°30E **25 D7**
Dila *Ethiopia* 6°21N 38°22E **47 F2**
Dili *E. Timor* 8°39S 125°34E **37 F7**
Dilli = Delhi *India* 28°39N 77°13E **42 E7**
Dillingham *U.S.A.* 59°3N 158°28W **74 D8**
Dillon *Canada* 55°56N 108°35W **71 B7**
Dillon *Mont., U.S.A.* 45°13N 112°38W **76 D7**
Dillon *S.C., U.S.A.* 34°25N 79°22W **85 D15**
Dillon → *Canada* 55°56N 108°56W **71 B7**
Dillsburg *U.S.A.* 40°7N 77°2W **82 F7**
Dilolo
  Dem. Rep. of the Congo 10°28S 22°18E **52 G4**
Dimapur *India* 25°54N 93°45E **32 D4**
Dimas *Mexico* 23°43N 106°47W **86 C3**
Dimashq *Syria* 33°30N 36°18E **46 B5**
Dimashq □ *Syria* 33°30N 36°30E **46 B5**
Dimbaza *S. Africa* 32°50S 27°14E **57 E4**
Dimboola *Australia* 36°28S 142°7E **63 F3**
Dîmbovița = Dâmbovița →
  Romania 44°12N 26°26E **17 F14**
Dimbulah *Australia* 17°8S 145°4E **62 B4**
Dimitrovgrad *Bulgaria* 42°5N 25°35E **23 C11**
Dimitrovgrad *Russia* 54°14N 49°39E **18 D8**
Dimitrovo = Pernik
  Bulgaria 42°35N 23°2E **23 C10**
Dimmitt *U.S.A.* 34°33N 102°19W **84 D3**
Dimona *Israel* 31°2N 35°1E **46 D4**
Dinagat *Phil.* 10°10N 125°40E **37 B7**
Dinajpur *Bangla.* 25°33N 88°43E **41 G16**
Dinan *France* 48°28N 2°2W **20 B2**
Dīnān Āb *Iran* 32°4N 56°49E **45 C8**
Dinant *Belgium* 50°16N 4°55E **15 D4**
Dinapur *India* 25°38N 85°5E **43 G11**
Dīnār, Kūh-e *Iran* 30°42N 51°46E **45 D6**
Dinara Planina *Croatia* 44°0N 16°30E **22 C7**
Dinard *France* 48°38N 2°6W **20 B2**
Dinaric Alps = Dinara Planina
  Croatia 44°0N 16°30E **22 C7**
Dindigul *India* 10°25N 78°0E **40 P11**
Dindori *India* 22°57N 81°5E **43 H9**
Ding Xian = Dingzhou
  China 38°30N 114°59E **34 E8**
Dinga *Pakistan* 25°26N 67°10E **42 G2**
Ding'an *China* 19°42N 110°19E **38 C8**
Dingbian *China* 37°35N 107°32E **34 F4**
Dingle *Ireland* 52°9N 10°17W **10 D1**
Dingle B. *Ireland* 52°3N 10°20W **10 D1**
Dingmans Ferry *U.S.A.* 41°13N 74°55W **83 E10**
Dingo *Australia* 23°38S 149°19E **62 C4**
Dingtao *China* 35°5N 115°35E **34 G8**
Dingwall *U.K.* 57°36N 4°26W **11 D4**
Dingxi *China* 35°30N 104°33E **34 G3**
Dingxiang *China* 38°30N 112°58E **34 E7**
Dingzhou *China* 38°30N 114°59E **34 E8**
Dinh, Mui *Vietnam* 11°22N 109°1E **39 G7**
Dinh Lap *Vietnam* 21°33N 107°6E **38 B6**
Dinin → *Ireland* 52°43N 7°18W **10 D4**
Dinira △ *Venezuela* 9°57N 70°6W **89 E6**
Dinokwe *Botswana* 23°29S 26°37E **56 C4**
Dinorwic *Canada* 49°41N 92°30W **71 D10**
Dinosaur △ *Canada* 50°47N 111°30W **70 C6**
Dinosaur △ *U.S.A.* 40°30N 108°45W **76 F9**
Dinuba *U.S.A.* 36°32N 119°23W **78 J7**
Dionisades *Greece* 35°20N 26°10E **25 D8**
Diourbel *Senegal* 14°39N 16°12W **50 F2**
Dipalpur *India* 30°40N 73°39E **42 D5**
Dipkarpaz = Rizokarpaso
  Cyprus 35°36N 34°23E **25 D13**
Diplo *Pakistan* 24°35N 69°35E **42 G3**
Dipolog *Phil.* 8°36N 123°20E **37 C6**
Dipperu △ *Australia* 21°56S 148°42E **62 C4**
Dir *Pakistan* 35°8N 71°59E **40 B7**
Dire Dawa *Ethiopia* 9°35N 41°45E **47 F3**
Dirfis Oros *Greece* 38°40N 23°54E **23 E10**
Diriamba *Nic.* 11°51N 86°19W **88 D2**
Dirk Hartog I. *Australia* 25°50S 113°5E **61 E1**
Dirranbandi *Australia* 28°33S 148°17E **63 D4**
Disa *India* 24°18N 72°10E **42 G5**
Disappointment, C.
  U.S.A. 46°18N 124°5W **76 C1**
Disappointment, L.
  Australia 23°20S 122°40E **60 D3**
Disaster B. *Australia* 37°15S 149°58E **63 F4**
Discovery B. *Australia* 38°10S 140°40E **63 F3**
Discovery B. *China* 22°18N 114°1E **33 G11**
Disko = Qeqertarsuaq
  Greenland 69°45N 53°30W **66 C14**
Disney Reef *Tonga* 19°17S 174°7W **59 c**
Diss *U.K.* 52°23N 1°7E **13 E9**
Disteghil Sar *Pakistan* 36°20N 75°12E **43 A6**
District of Columbia □
  U.S.A. 38°55N 77°0W **81 F15**
Distrito Federal □ *Brazil* 15°45S 47°45W **93 G9**
Distrito Federal □
  Mexico 19°15N 99°10W **87 D5**
Diu *India* 20°45N 70°58E **42 J4**
Dīvāndarreh *Iran* 35°55N 47°2E **44 C5**
Divide *U.S.A.* 45°45N 112°45W **76 D7**
Dividing Ra. *Australia* 27°45S 116°0E **61 E2**
Divinópolis *Brazil* 20°10S 44°54W **93 H10**
Divnoye *Russia* 45°55N 43°21E **19 E7**
Divo *Ivory C.* 5°48N 5°15W **50 G4**
Dīwāl Kol *Afghan.* 34°30N 67°52E **42 B2**
Dixie Mt. *U.S.A.* 39°55N 120°16W **78 F6**
Dixon *Calif., U.S.A.* 38°27N 121°49W **78 G5**
Dixon *Ill., U.S.A.* 41°50N 89°29W **80 E9**
Dixon Entrance *U.S.A.* 54°30N 132°0W **68 G5**
Dixville *Canada* 45°4N 71°46W **83 A13**
Diyālā □ *Iraq* 33°45N 44°50E **44 C5**
Diyālā → *Iraq* 33°13N 44°30E **44 C5**
Diyarbakır *Turkey* 37°55N 40°18E **44 B4**
Diyodar *India* 24°8N 71°50E **42 G4**
Djakarta = Jakarta
  Indonesia 6°9S 106°52E **37 G12**
Djamba *Angola* 16°45S 13°58E **56 B1**
Djambala *Congo* 2°32S 14°30E **52 E2**
Djanet *Algeria* 24°35N 9°32E **50 D7**
Djawa = Jawa *Indonesia* 7°0S 110°0E **36 F3**

Djelfa *Algeria* 34°40N 3°15E **50 B6**
Djema *C.A.R.* 6°3N 25°15E **54 A2**
Djerba, Î. de *Tunisia* 33°50N 10°48E **51 B8**
Djerid, Chott *Tunisia* 33°42N 8°30E **50 B7**
Djibouti *Djibouti* 11°30N 43°5E **47 E3**
Djibouti ■ *Africa* 12°0N 43°0E **47 E3**
Djolu *Dem. Rep. of the Congo* 0°35N 22°5E **52 D4**
Djougou *Benin* 9°40N 1°45E **50 G6**
Djoum *Cameroon* 2°41N 12°35E **52 D2**
Djourab, Erg du *Chad* 16°40N 18°50E **51 E9**
Djugu
  Dem. Rep. of the Congo 1°55N 30°35E **54 B3**
Djukbinj △ *Australia* 12°11S 131°2E **60 B5**
Djúpivogur *Iceland* 64°39N 14°17W **8 D6**
Dmitriya Lapteva, Proliv
  Russia 73°0N 140°0E **29 B15**
Dnepr = Dnipro →
  Ukraine 46°30N 32°18E **19 E5**
Dneprodzerzhinsk =
  Dniprodzerzhynsk
  Ukraine 48°32N 34°37E **19 E5**
Dnepropetrovsk =
  Dnipropetrovsk
  Ukraine 48°30N 35°0E **19 E6**
Dnestr = Dnister →
  Europe 46°18N 30°17E **17 E16**
Dnieper = Dnipro →
  Ukraine 46°30N 32°18E **19 E5**
Dniester = Dnister →
  Europe 46°18N 30°17E **17 E16**
Dnipro → *Ukraine* 46°30N 32°18E **19 E5**
Dniprodzerzhynsk
  Ukraine 48°32N 34°37E **19 E5**
Dnipropetrovsk *Ukraine* 48°30N 35°0E **19 E6**
Dnister → *Europe* 46°18N 30°17E **17 E16**
Dno *Russia* 57°50N 29°58E **9 H23**
Dnyapro = Dnipro →
  Ukraine 46°30N 32°18E **19 E5**
Do Gonbadān = Gachsārān
  Iran 30°15N 50°45E **45 D6**
Doaktown *Canada* 46°33N 66°8W **73 C6**
Doan Hung *Vietnam* 21°30N 105°10E **38 B5**
Doany *Madag.* 14°21S 49°30E **57 A8**
Doba *Chad* 8°40N 16°50E **51 G9**
Dobandi *Pakistan* 31°13N 66°50E **42 D2**
Dobbyn *Australia* 19°44S 140°2E **62 B3**
Dobele *Latvia* 56°37N 23°16E **9 H20**
Doberai, Jazirah *Indonesia* 1°25S 133°0E **37 E8**
Doblas *Argentina* 37°5S 64°0W **94 D3**
Dobo *Indonesia* 5°45S 134°15E **37 F8**
Doboj *Bos.-H.* 44°46N 18°4E **23 B8**
Dobrich *Bulgaria* 43°37N 27°49E **23 C12**
Dobruja *Europe* 44°30N 28°15E **17 F15**
Dobrush *Belarus* 52°25N 31°22E **17 B16**
Doc, Mui *Vietnam* 17°58N 106°30E **38 D6**
Docker River = Kaltukatjara
  Australia 24°52S 129°5E **61 D4**
Doctor Arroyo *Mexico* 23°40N 100°11W **86 C4**
Doctor Pedro P. Peña
  Paraguay 22°27S 62°21W **94 A3**
Doda *India* 33°10N 75°34E **43 C6**
Doda, L. *Canada* 49°25N 75°13W **72 C4**
Dodecanese *Greece* 36°35N 27°0E **23 F12**
Dodekanisa = Dodecanese
  Greece 36°35N 27°0E **23 F12**
Dodge City *U.S.A.* 37°45N 100°1W **80 G4**
Dodge L. *Canada* 59°50N 105°36W **71 B7**
Dodgeville *U.S.A.* 42°58N 90°8W **80 D8**
Dodoma *Tanzania* 6°8S 35°45E **54 D4**
Dodoma □ *Tanzania* 6°0S 36°0E **54 D4**
Dodori *Kenya* 1°55S 41°7E **54 C5**
Dodsland *Canada* 51°50N 108°45W **71 C7**
Dodson *U.S.A.* 48°24N 108°15W **76 B9**
Doesburg *Neths.* 52°1N 6°9E **15 B6**
Doetinchem *Neths.* 51°59N 6°18E **15 C6**
Dog Creek *Canada* 51°35N 122°14W **70 C4**
Dog L. *Man., Canada* 51°2N 98°31W **71 C9**
Dog L. *Ont., Canada* 48°48N 89°30W **72 C2**
Dogran *Pakistan* 31°48N 73°35E **42 D5**
Doğubayazıt *Turkey* 39°31N 44°5E **44 B5**
Doha = Ad Dawḩah
  Qatar 25°15N 51°35E **45 E6**
Dohazari *Bangla.* 22°10N 92°5E **41 H18**
Dohrighat *India* 26°16N 83°31E **43 F10**
Doi *Indonesia* 2°14N 127°49E **37 D7**
Doi Inthanon △ *Thailand* 18°33N 98°34E **38 C2**
Doi Khuntan △ *Thailand* 18°33N 99°14E **38 C2**
Doi Luang *Thailand* 18°30N 101°0E **38 C3**
Doi Luang △ *Thailand* 19°22N 99°35E **38 C2**
Doi Saket *Thailand* 18°52N 99°9E **38 C2**
Doi Suthep △ *Thailand* 18°49N 98°53E **38 C2**
Dois Irmãos, Sa. *Brazil* 9°0S 42°30W **93 E10**
Dokkum *Neths.* 53°20N 5°59E **15 A5**
Dokri *Pakistan* 27°25N 68°7E **42 F3**
Dolak, Pulau *Indonesia* 8°0S 138°30E **37 F9**
Dolbeau-Mistassini
  Canada 48°53N 72°14W **73 C5**
Dole *France* 47°7N 5°31E **20 C6**
Dolgellau *U.K.* 52°45N 3°53W **12 E4**
Dolgelley = Dolgellau
  U.K. 52°45N 3°53W **12 E4**
Dolinsk *Russia* 47°21N 142°48E **29 E15**
Dollard *Neths.* 53°20N 7°10E **15 A7**
Dolo *Ethiopia* 4°11N 42°3E **47 G3**
Dolomites = Dolomiti
  Italy 46°23N 11°51E **22 A4**
Dolomiti *Italy* 46°23N 11°51E **22 A4**
Dolores *Argentina* 36°20S 57°40W **94 D4**
Dolores *Uruguay* 33°34S 58°15W **94 C4**
Dolores *U.S.A.* 37°28N 108°30W **77 H9**
Dolores → *U.S.A.* 38°49N 109°17W **76 G9**
Dolphin, C. *Falk. Is.* 51°10S 59°0W **96 G5**
Dolphin and Union Str.
  Canada 69°5N 114°45W **68 D7**
Dom Pedrito *Brazil* 31°0S 54°40W **95 C5**
Doma *Zimbabwe* 16°28S 30°12E **55 F3**
Domariaganj → *India* 26°17N 83°44E **43 F10**
Domasi *Malawi* 15°15S 35°22E **55 F4**
Dombarovskiy *Russia* 50°46N 59°32E **28 D6**

Dombås *Norway* 62°4N 9°8E **8 E13**
Dome Argus *Antarctica* 80°50S 76°30E **5 E12**
Dome C. *Antarctica* 75°12S 123°37E **5 D17**
Dome Fuji *Antarctica* 77°20S 39°45E **5 D5**
Domel I. = Letsôk-aw Kyun
  Burma 11°30N 98°25E **39 G2**
Domeyko *Chile* 29°0S 71°0W **94 B1**
Domeyko, Cordillera
  Chile 24°30S 69°0W **94 A2**
Dominador *Chile* 24°21S 69°20W **94 A2**
Dominica ■ *W. Indies* 15°20N 61°20W **89 C7**
Dominica Passage
  W. Indies 15°10N 61°20W **89 C7**
Dominican Rep. ■
  W. Indies 19°0N 70°30W **89 C5**
Domodóssola *Italy* 46°7N 8°17E **20 C8**
Domville, Mt. *Australia* 28°1S 151°15E **63 D5**
Don → *Russia* 47°4N 39°18E **19 E6**
Don → *Aberds., U.K.* 57°11N 2°5W **11 D6**
Don → *S. Yorks., U.K.* 53°41N 0°52W **12 D7**
Don, C. *Australia* 11°18S 131°46E **60 B5**
Don Benito *Spain* 38°53N 5°51W **21 C3**
Don Figuero Mts.
  Jamaica 18°5N 77°36W **88 a**
Don Sak *Thailand* 9°18N 99°41E **39 b**
Dona Ana = Nhamaubué
  Mozam. 17°25S 35°5E **55 F4**
Donaghadee *U.K.* 54°39N 5°33W **10 B6**
Donaghmore *Ireland* 52°52N 7°36W **10 D4**
Donald *Australia* 36°23S 143°0E **63 F3**
Donaldsonville *U.S.A.* 30°6N 90°59W **84 F9**
Donalsonville *U.S.A.* 31°3N 84°53W **85 F12**
Donau = Dunărea →
  Europe 45°20N 29°40E **17 F15**
Donauwörth *Germany* 48°43N 10°47E **16 D6**
Doncaster *U.K.* 53°32N 1°6W **12 D6**
Dondo *Angola* 9°45S 14°25E **52 F2**
Dondo *Mozam.* 19°33S 34°46E **55 F3**
Dondo, Teluk *Indonesia* 0°50N 120°30E **37 D6**
Dondra Head *Sri Lanka* 5°55N 80°40E **40 S12**
Donegal *Ireland* 54°39N 8°5W **10 B3**
Donegal □ *Ireland* 54°53N 8°0W **10 B4**
Donegal B. *Ireland* 54°31N 8°49W **10 B3**
Donets → *Russia* 47°33N 40°55E **19 E7**
Donets Basin *Ukraine* 49°0N 38°0E **6 F13**
Donetsk *Ukraine* 48°0N 37°45E **19 E6**
Dong Ba Thin *Vietnam* 12°8N 109°13E **39 F7**
Dong Dang *Vietnam* 21°54N 106°42E **38 B6**
Dong Giam *Vietnam* 19°25N 105°31E **38 C5**
Dong Ha *Vietnam* 16°55N 107°8E **38 D6**
Dong Hene *Laos* 16°40N 105°18E **38 D5**
Dong Hoi *Vietnam* 17°29N 106°36E **38 D6**
Dong Ujimqin Qi *China* 45°32N 116°55E **34 B9**
Dong Van *Vietnam* 23°16N 105°22E **38 A5**
Dong Xoai *Vietnam* 11°32N 106°55E **39 G6**
Dongara *Australia* 29°14S 114°57E **61 E1**
Dongbei *China* 45°0N 125°0E **30 A5**
Dongchuan *China* 26°8N 103°1E **32 D5**
Dongfang *China* 18°50N 108°33E **38 C7**
Dongfeng *China* 42°40N 125°34E **35 C13**
Donggala *Indonesia* 0°30S 119°40E **37 E5**
Donggang *China* 39°52N 124°10E **35 E13**
Dongguan *China* 22°58N 113°44E **33 G10**
Dongguang *China* 37°50N 116°30E **34 F9**
Donghae *S. Korea* 37°29N 129°7E **35 F15**
Dongjingcheng *China* 44°5N 129°10E **35 B15**
Dongnae *S. Korea* 35°12N 129°5E **35 G15**
Dongning *China* 44°2N 131°5E **35 B16**
Dongola *Sudan* 19°9N 30°22E **51 E12**
Dongou *Congo* 2°0N 18°5E **52 D3**
Dongsheng *China* 39°50N 110°0E **34 E6**
Dongtai *China* 32°51N 120°21E **35 H11**
Dongting Hu *China* 29°18N 112°45E **33 D6**
Donington, C. *Australia* 34°45S 136°0E **63 E2**
Doniphan *U.S.A.* 36°37N 90°50W **80 G8**
Dønna *Norway* 66°6N 12°30E **8 C15**
Donna *U.S.A.* 26°9N 98°4W **84 H5**
Donnaconda *Canada* 46°41N 71°41W **73 C5**
Donnelly's Crossing
  N.Z. 35°42S 173°38E **59 A4**
Donnybrook *Australia* 33°34S 115°48E **61 F2**
Donnybrook *S. Africa* 29°59S 29°48E **57 D4**
Donora *U.S.A.* 40°11N 79°52W **82 F5**
Donostia = Donostia-San
  Sebastián *Spain* 43°17N 1°58W **21 A5**
Donostia-San Sebastián
  Spain 43°17N 1°58W **21 A5**
Donwood *Canada* 44°9N 78°16W **82 B6**
Doomadgee *Australia* 17°56S 138°49E **62 B2**
Doomadgee ✪ *Australia* 17°56S 138°49E **62 B2**
Doon → *U.K.* 55°27N 4°39W **11 F4**
Doon Doon ✪ *Australia* 16°18S 128°14E **60 C4**
Dora, L. *Australia* 22°0S 123°0E **60 D3**
Dora Báltea → *Italy* 45°11N 8°3E **20 D8**
Doran L. *Canada* 61°13N 108°6W **71 A7**
Dorchester *U.K.* 50°42N 2°27W **13 G5**
Dorchester, C. *Canada* 65°27N 77°27W **69 D16**
Dordabis *Namibia* 22°52S 17°38E **56 C2**
Dordogne → *France* 45°2N 0°36W **20 D3**
Dordrecht *Neths.* 51°48N 4°39E **15 C4**
Dordrecht *S. Africa* 31°54S 18°39E **56 E4**
Doré L. *Canada* 54°46N 107°17W **71 C7**
Dori *Burkina Faso* 14°3N 0°2W **50 F5**
Doring → *S. Africa* 31°54S 18°16E **56 E2**
Doringbos *S. Africa* 31°59S 19°16E **56 E2**
Dorking *U.K.* 51°14N 0°19W **13 F7**
Dornbirn *Austria* 47°25N 9°45E **16 E5**
Dornie *U.K.* 57°17N 5°31W **11 D3**
Dornoch *U.K.* 44°18N 80°51W **82 D4**
Dornoch Firth *U.K.* 57°53N 4°2W **11 D4**
Dornogovĭ □ *Mongolia* 44°0N 110°0E **34 C6**
Doro *Kavo Greece* 38°9N 24°38E **23 E11**
Dorohoi *Romania* 47°56N 26°23E **17 E14**
Döröö Nuur *Mongolia* 48°0N 93°0E **32 B4**
Dorr *Iran* 33°17N 50°38E **45 C6**
Dorre I. *Australia* 25°13S 113°12E **61 E1**
Dorrigo *Australia* 30°20S 152°44E **63 E5**

Dorris *U.S.A.* 41°58N 121°55W **76** F3
Dorset *Canada* 45°14N 78°54W **82** A6
Dorset *Ohio, U.S.A.* 41°40N 80°40W **82** E4
Dorset *Vt., U.S.A.* 43°15N 73°5W **83** C11
Dorset □ *U.K.* 50°45N 2°26W **13** G5
Dortmund *Germany* 51°30N 7°28E **16** C4
Dörtyol *Turkey* 36°50N 36°13E **44** B3
Doruma
 Dem. Rep. of the Congo 4°42N 27°33E **54** B2
Dorüneh *Iran* 35°10N 57°18E **45** C8
Dos Bahías, C. *Argentina* 44°58S 65°32W **96** E3
Dos Hermanas *Spain* 37°16N 5°55W **21** D3
Dos Palos *U.S.A.* 36°59N 120°37W **78** J6
Dosso *Niger* 13°0N 3°13E **50** F6
Dothan *U.S.A.* 31°13N 85°24W **85** F12
Doty *U.S.A.* 46°38N 123°17W **78** D3
Douai *France* 50°21N 3°4E **20** A5
Douala *Cameroon* 4°0N 9°45E **52** D1
Douarnenez *France* 48°6N 4°21W **20** B1
Double Island Pt.
 Australia 25°56S 153°11E **63** D5
Double Mountain Fork ➤
 U.S.A. 33°16N 100°0W **84** E4
Doubs ➤ *France* 46°53N 5°1E **20** C6
Doubtful Sd. *N.Z.* 45°20S 166°49E **59** F1
Doubtless B. *N.Z.* 34°55S 173°26E **59** A4
Douglas *Canada* 45°31N 76°56W **82** A8
Douglas *I. of Man* 54°10N 4°28W **12** C3
Douglas *S. Africa* 29°4S 23°46E **56** D3
Douglas *Ariz., U.S.A.* 31°21N 109°33W **77** L9
Douglas *Ga., U.S.A.* 31°31N 82°51W **85** F13
Douglas *Wyo., U.S.A.* 42°45N 105°24W **76** E11
Douglas Apsley △
 Australia 41°45S 148°11E **63** G4
Douglas Chan. *Canada* 53°40N 129°20W **70** C3
Douglas Pt. *Canada* 44°19N 81°37W **82** B3
Douglasville *U.S.A.* 33°45N 84°45W **85** E12
Dounreay *U.K.* 58°35N 3°44W **11** C5
Dourada, Serra *Brazil* 13°10N 49°45W **93** F9
Dourados *Brazil* 22°9S 54°50W **95** A5
Dourados ➤ *Brazil* 21°58S 54°18W **95** A5
Dourados, Serra dos
 Brazil 23°30S 53°30W **95** A5
Douro ➤ *Europe* 41°8N 8°40W **21** B1
Dove ➤ *U.K.* 52°51N 1°36W **12** E6
Dove Creek *U.S.A.* 37°46N 108°54W **77** H9
Dover *Australia* 43°18S 147°2E **63** G4
Dover *U.K.* 51°7N 1°19E **13** F9
Dover *Del., U.S.A.* 39°10N 75°32W **81** F16
Dover *N.H., U.S.A.* 43°12N 70°56W **83** C14
Dover *N.J., U.S.A.* 40°53N 74°34W **83** F10
Dover *Ohio, U.S.A.* 40°32N 81°29W **82** F3
Dover, Pt. *Australia* 32°32S 125°32E **61** F4
Dover, Str. of *Europe* 51°0N 1°30E **13** G9
Dover-Foxcroft *U.S.A.* 45°11N 69°13W **81** C19
Dover Plains *U.S.A.* 41°43N 73°35W **83** E11
Dovey = Dyfi ➤ *U.K.* 52°32N 4°3W **13** E3
Dovrefjell *Norway* 62°15N 9°33E **8** E13
Dow Rūd *Iran* 33°28N 49°4E **45** C6
Dowa *Malawi* 13°38S 33°58E **55** E3
Dowagiac *U.S.A.* 41°59N 86°6W **80** E10
Dowerin *Australia* 31°12S 117°2E **61** F2
Dowgha'i *Iran* 36°54N 58°32E **45** B8
Dowlatābād *Kermān,*
 Iran 28°20N 56°40E **45** D8
Dowlatābād *Khorāsān,*
 Iran 35°16N 59°29E **45** C8
Down □ *U.K.* 54°23N 6°2W **10** B5
Downey *Calif., U.S.A.* 33°56N 118°9W **79** M8
Downey *Idaho, U.S.A.* 42°26N 112°7W **76** E7
Downham Market *U.K.* 52°37N 0°23E **13** E8
Downieville *U.S.A.* 39°34N 120°50W **78** F6
Downpatrick *U.K.* 54°20N 5°43W **10** B6
Downpatrick Hd. *Ireland* 54°20N 9°21W **10** B2
Downsville *U.S.A.* 42°5N 75°0W **83** D10
Downton, Mt. *Canada* 52°42N 124°52W **70** C4
Dowsārī *Iran* 28°25N 57°59E **45** D8
Doyle *U.S.A.* 40°2N 120°6W **78** E6
Doylestown *U.S.A.* 40°21N 75°10W **83** F9
Dozois, Rés. *Canada* 47°30N 77°5W **72** C4
Dra Khel *Pakistan* 27°58N 66°45E **42** F2
Drâa, C. *Morocco* 28°47N 11°0W **50** C3
Drâa, Hamada du *Algeria* 28°0N 7°0W **50** C4
Drâa, Oued ➤ *Morocco* 28°40N 11°10W **50** C3
Drac, Coves del *Spain* 39°31N 3°19E **24** B10
Drachten *Neths.* 53°7N 6°5E **15** A6
Drăgășani *Romania* 44°39N 24°17E **17** F13
Dragichyn *Belarus* 52°15N 25°8E **17** B13
Dragoman, Prokhod
 Bulgaria 42°58N 22°53E **23** C10
Dragon's Mouths
 Venezuela 11°0N 61°50W **93** K15
Draguignan *France* 43°32N 6°27E **20** E7
Drain *U.S.A.* 43°40N 123°19W **76** E2
Drake *U.S.A.* 47°55N 100°23W **80** B3
Drake Passage *S. Ocean* 58°0S 68°0W **5** B17
Drakensberg *S. Africa* 31°0S 28°0E **57** D4
Drama *Greece* 41°9N 24°10E **23** D11
Drammen *Norway* 59°42N 10°12E **9** G14
Drangajökull *Iceland* 66°9N 22°15W **8** C2
Dras *India* 34°25N 75°48E **43** B6
Drastis, Akra *Greece* 39°48N 19°40E **25** A3
Drau = Drava ➤
 Croatia 45°33N 18°55E **23** B8
Drava ➤ *Croatia* 45°33N 18°55E **23** B8
Drayton *Canada* 43°46N 80°40W **82** C4
Drayton Valley *Canada* 53°12N 114°58W **70** C6
Drenthe □ *Neths.* 52°52N 6°40E **15** B6
Drepano, Akra *Greece* 35°28N 24°14E **25** D6
Drepanum, C. *Cyprus* 34°54N 32°19E **25** E11
Dresden *Canada* 42°35N 82°11W **82** D2
Dresden *Germany* 51°3N 13°44E **16** C7
Dresden *U.S.A.* 42°41N 76°57W **82** D8
Dreux *France* 48°44N 1°23E **20** B4
Driffield *U.K.* 54°0N 0°26W **12** C7
Driftwood *U.S.A.* 41°20N 78°8W **82** E6
Driggs *U.S.A.* 43°44N 111°6W **76** E8
Drin ➤ *Albania* 42°1N 19°38E **23** C8
Drina ➤ *Bos.-H.* 44°53N 19°21E **23** B8
Drøbak *Norway* 59°39N 10°39E **9** G14

Drobeta-Turnu Severin
 Romania 44°39N 22°41E **17** F12
Drochia *Moldova* 48°2N 27°48E **17** D14
Drogheda *Ireland* 53°43N 6°22W **10** C5
Drogichin = Dragichyn
 Belarus 52°15N 25°8E **17** B13
Drogobych = Drohobych
 Ukraine 49°20N 23°30E **17** D12
Drohobych *Ukraine* 49°20N 23°30E **17** D12
Droichead Atha = Drogheda
 Ireland 53°43N 6°22W **10** C5
Droichead na Bandan = Bandon
 Ireland 51°44N 8°44W **10** E3
Droichead Nua *Ireland* 53°11N 6°48W **10** C5
Droitwich *U.K.* 52°16N 2°8W **13** E5
Drôme ➤ *France* 44°46N 4°46E **20** D6
Dromedary, C. *Australia* 36°17S 150°10E **63** F5
Dromore *U.K.* 54°31N 7°28W **10** B4
Dromore West *Ireland* 54°15N 8°52W **10** B3
Dronfield *U.K.* 53°19N 1°27W **12** D6
Dronning Maud Land
 Antarctica 72°30S 12°0E **5** D3
Dronten *Neths.* 52°32N 5°43E **15** B5
Druk Yul = Bhutan ■
 Asia 27°25N 90°30E **41** F17
Drumbo *Canada* 43°16N 80°35W **82** C4
Drumcliff *Ireland* 54°20N 8°29W **10** B3
Drumheller *Canada* 51°25N 112°40W **70** C6
Drummond *U.S.A.* 46°40N 113°9W **76** C7
Drummond I. *U.S.A.* 46°1N 83°39W **81** B12
Drummond Pt. *Australia* 34°9S 135°16E **63** E2
Drummond Ra.
 Australia 23°45S 147°10E **62** C4
Drummondville *Canada* 45°55N 72°25W **72** C5
Drumright *U.S.A.* 35°59N 96°36W **84** D6
Druskininkai *Lithuania* 54°3N 23°58E **9** J20
Drut ➤ *Belarus* 53°8N 30°5E **17** B16
Druzhina *Russia* 68°14N 145°18E **29** C15
Dry Harbour Mts.
 Jamaica 18°19N 77°24W **88** a
Dry Tortugas *U.S.A.* 24°38N 82°55W **85** F13
Dryander △ *Australia* 20°13S 148°34E **62** b
Dryden *Canada* 49°47N 92°50W **71** D10
Dryden *U.S.A.* 42°30N 76°18W **83** D8
Drygalski I. *Antarctica* 66°0S 92°0E **5** C7
Drygalski Ice Tongue
 Antarctica 75°24S 163°30E **5** D21
Drysdale ➤ *Australia* 13°59S 126°51E **60** B4
Drysdale I. *Australia* 11°41S 136°0E **62** A2
Drysdale River △
 Australia 14°56S 127°2E **60** B4
Du Gué ➤ *Canada* 57°21N 70°45W **72** A5
Du Quoin *U.S.A.* 38°1N 89°14W **80** F9
Duanesburg *U.S.A.* 42°45N 74°11W **83** D10
Duaringa *Australia* 23°42S 149°42E **62** C4
Duarte, Pico *Dom. Rep.* 19°2N 70°59W **89** D5
Dubai = Dubayy *U.A.E.* 25°18N 55°20E **45** E7
Dubăsari *Moldova* 47°15N 29°10E **17** E15
Dubăsari Vdkhr. =
 Dubăsari Vdkhr.
 Moldova 47°30N 29°0E **17** E15
Dubawnt ➤ *Canada* 64°33N 100°6W **71** A8
Dubawnt L. *Canada* 63°8N 101°28W **71** A8
Dubayy *U.A.E.* 25°18N 55°20E **45** E7
Dubbo *Australia* 32°11S 148°35E **63** E4
Dubele
 Dem. Rep. of the Congo 2°56N 29°35E **54** B2
Dublin *Ireland* 53°21N 6°15W **10** C5
Dublin *Ga., U.S.A.* 32°32N 82°54W **85** E13
Dublin *Tex., U.S.A.* 32°5N 98°21W **84** E5
Dublin □ *Ireland* 53°24N 6°20W **10** C5
Dublin ✈ (DUB) *Ireland* 53°26N 6°15W **10** C5
Dubno *Ukraine* 50°25N 25°45E **17** C13
Dubois *Idaho, U.S.A.* 44°10N 112°14W **76** D7
DuBois *Pa., U.S.A.* 41°7N 78°46W **82** E6
Dubossary = Dubăsari
 Moldova 47°15N 29°10E **17** E15
Dubossary Vdkhr. = Dubăsari
 Vdkhr. *Moldova* 47°30N 29°0E **17** E15
Dubovka *Russia* 49°5N 44°50E **19** E7
Dubrajpur *India* 23°48N 87°25E **43** H12
Dubréka *Guinea* 9°46N 13°31W **50** G3
Dubrovitsa = Dubrovytsya
 Ukraine 51°31N 26°35E **17** C14
Dubrovnik *Croatia* 42°39N 18°6E **23** C8
Dubrovytsya *Ukraine* 51°31N 26°35E **17** C14
Dubuque *U.S.A.* 42°30N 90°41W **80** D8
Duchesne *U.S.A.* 40°10N 110°24W **76** F8
Duchess *Australia* 21°20S 139°50E **62** C2
Ducie I. *Pac. Oc.* 24°40S 124°48W **65** K15
Duck ➤ *U.S.A.* 36°2N 87°52W **85** C11
Duck Cr. ➤ *Australia* 22°37S 116°53E **60** D2
Duck Lake *Canada* 52°50N 106°16W **71** C7
Duck Mountain △
 Canada 51°45N 101°0W **71** C8
Duckwall, Mt. *U.S.A.* 37°58N 120°7W **78** H6
Dudhi *India* 24°15N 83°10E **43** G10
Dudinka *Russia* 69°30N 86°13E **29** C9
Dudley *U.K.* 52°31N 2°5W **13** E5
Dudwa *India* 28°30N 80°41E **43** E9
Dudwa △ *India* 28°30N 80°40E **43** E9
Duero = Douro ➤ *Europe* 41°8N 8°40W **21** B1
Dufftown *U.K.* 57°27N 3°8W **11** D5
Dugi Otok *Croatia* 44°0N 15°3E **16** G8
Duisburg *Germany* 51°26N 6°45E **16** C4
Duiwelskloof = Modjadjiskloof
 S. Africa 23°42S 30°10E **57** C5
Dükdamīn *Iran* 35°59N 57°43E **45** C8
Dukelský Průsmyk
 Slovak Rep. 49°25N 21°42E **17** D11
Dukhān *Qatar* 25°25N 50°50E **45** E6
Duki *Pakistan* 30°14N 68°25E **40** D6
Duku *Nigeria* 10°43N 10°43E **51** F8
Dulce *U.S.A.* 36°56N 107°0W **77** H10
Dulce ➤ *Argentina* 30°32S 62°33W **94** C3
Dulce, G. *Costa Rica* 8°40N 83°20W **88** E3
Dulf *Iraq* 35°7N 45°51E **44** C5
Duliu *China* 39°2N 116°55E **34** E9
Dullewala *Pakistan* 31°50N 71°25E **42** D4
Dullstroom *S. Africa* 25°27S 30°7E **57** D5
Dulq Maghār *Syria* 36°22N 38°39E **44** B3

Duluth *U.S.A.* 46°47N 92°6W **80** B7
Dum Dum *India* 22°39N 88°26E **43** H13
Dum Duma *India* 27°40N 95°40E **41** F19
Dūmā *Syria* 33°34N 36°24E **46** B5
Dumaguete *Phil.* 9°17N 123°15E **37** C6
Dumai *Indonesia* 1°35N 101°28E **36** D2
Dumaran *Phil.* 10°33N 119°50E **37** B5
Dumas *Ark., U.S.A.* 33°53N 91°29W **84** E9
Dumas *Tex., U.S.A.* 35°52N 101°58W **84** D4
Dumayr *Syria* 33°39N 36°42E **46** B5
Dumbarton *U.K.* 55°57N 4°33W **11** F4
Dumbleyung *Australia* 33°17S 117°42E **61** F2
Dumfries *U.K.* 55°4N 3°37W **11** F5
Dumfries & Galloway □
 U.K. 55°9N 3°58W **11** F5
Dumka *India* 24°12N 87°15E **43** G12
Dumoine ➤ *Canada* 46°13N 77°51W **72** C4
Dumoine, L. *Canada* 46°55N 77°55W **72** C4
Dumont d'Urville
 Antarctica 67°0S 110°0E **5** C10
Dumont d'Urville Sea
 S. Ocean 63°30S 138°0E **5** C9
Dumraon *India* 25°33N 84°8E **43** G11
Dumyât *Egypt* 31°24N 31°48E **51** B12
Dún Dealgan = Dundalk
 Ireland 54°1N 6°24W **10** B5
Dún Garbhán = Dungarvan
 Ireland 52°5N 7°37W **10** D4
Dún Laoghaire *Ireland* 53°17N 6°8W **10** C5
Duna = Dunărea ➤
 Europe 45°20N 29°40E **17** F15
Dunagiri *India* 30°31N 79°52E **43** D8
Dunaj = Dunărea ➤
 Europe 45°20N 29°40E **17** F15
Dunakeszi *Hungary* 47°37N 19°8E **17** E10
Dunărea ➤ *Europe* 45°20N 29°40E **17** F15
Dunaújváros *Hungary* 46°58N 18°57E **17** E10
Dunav = Dunărea ➤
 Europe 45°20N 29°40E **17** F15
Dunay *Russia* 42°52N 132°22E **30** C6
Dunback *N.Z.* 45°23S 170°36E **59** F3
Dunbar *U.K.* 56°0N 2°31W **11** E6
Dunblane *U.K.* 56°11N 3°58W **11** E5
Duncan *Canada* 48°45N 123°40W **78** B3
Duncan *Ariz., U.S.A.* 32°43N 109°6W **77** K9
Duncan *Okla., U.S.A.* 34°30N 97°57W **84** D6
Duncan, L. *Canada* 53°29N 77°58W **72** B4
Duncan L. *Canada* 62°51N 113°58W **70** A6
Duncan Town *Bahamas* 22°15N 75°45W **88** B4
Duncannon *U.S.A.* 40°23N 77°2W **82** F7
Duncansby Head *U.K.* 58°38N 3°1W **11** C5
Duncansville *U.S.A.* 40°25N 78°26W **82** F6
Dundalk *Canada* 44°10N 80°24W **82** B4
Dundalk *Ireland* 54°1N 6°24W **10** B5
Dundalk *U.S.A.* 39°15N 76°31W **81** F15
Dundalk Bay *Ireland* 53°55N 6°15W **10** C5
Dundas = Uummannaq
 Greenland 77°33N 68°52W **69** B18
Dundas *Canada* 43°17N 79°59W **82** C5
Dundas, L. *Australia* 32°35S 121°50E **61** F3
Dundas I. *Canada* 54°30N 130°50W **70** C2
Dundas Str. *Australia* 11°15S 131°35E **60** B5
Dundee *S. Africa* 28°11S 30°15E **57** D5
Dundee *U.K.* 56°28N 2°59W **11** E6
Dundee *U.S.A.* 42°32N 76°59W **82** D8
Dundee City □ *U.K.* 56°30N 2°58W **11** E6
Dundgovĭ □ *Mongolia* 45°10N 106°0E **34** B4
Dundrum *U.K.* 54°16N 5°52W **10** B6
Dundrum B. *U.K.* 54°13N 5°47W **10** B6
Dunedin *N.Z.* 45°50S 170°33E **59** F3
Dunedin *U.S.A.* 28°1N 82°46W **85** G13
Dunfanaghy *Ireland* 55°11N 7°58W **10** A4
Dunfermline *U.K.* 56°5N 3°27W **11** E5
Dungannon *Canada* 43°51N 81°36W **82** C3
Dungannon *U.K.* 54°31N 6°46W **10** B5
Dungarpur *India* 23°52N 73°45E **42** H5
Dungarvan *Ireland* 52°5N 7°37W **10** D4
Dungarvan Harbour
 Ireland 52°4N 7°35W **10** D4
Dungeness *U.K.* 50°54N 0°59E **13** G8
Dunglow *Ireland* 54°57N 8°21W **10** B3
Dungo, L. do *Angola* 17°15S 19°0E **56** B2
Dungog *Australia* 32°22S 151°46E **63** E5
Dungu
 Dem. Rep. of the Congo 3°40N 28°32E **54** B2
Dungun *Malaysia* 4°45N 103°25E **39** K4
Dunhua *China* 43°20N 128°14E **35** C15
Dunhuang *China* 40°8N 94°36E **32** B4
Dunk I. *Australia* 17°59S 146°29E **62** B4
Dunkeld *Australia* 33°25S 149°29E **63** E4
Dunkeld *U.K.* 56°34N 3°35W **11** E5
Dunkerque *France* 51°2N 2°20E **20** A5
Dunkery Beacon *U.K.* 51°9N 3°36W **13** F4
Dunkirk = Dunkerque
 France 51°2N 2°20E **20** A5
Dunkirk *U.S.A.* 42°29N 79°20W **82** D5
Dúnleary = Dún Laoghaire
 Ireland 53°17N 6°8W **10** C5
Dunleer *Ireland* 53°50N 6°24W **10** C5
Dunmanus B. *Ireland* 51°31N 9°50W **10** E2
Dunmanway *Ireland* 51°43N 9°6W **10** E2
Dunmarra *Australia* 16°42S 133°25E **62** B1
Dunmore *U.S.A.* 41°25N 75°38W **83** E9
Dunmore East *Ireland* 52°9N 7°0W **10** D5
Dunmore Hd. *Ireland* 52°10N 10°35W **10** D1
Dunmore Town
 Bahamas 25°30N 76°39W **88** A4
Dunn *U.S.A.* 35°19N 78°37W **85** D15
Dunnellon *U.S.A.* 29°3N 82°28W **85** G13
Dunnet Hd. *U.K.* 58°40N 3°21W **11** C5
Dunning *U.S.A.* 41°50N 100°6W **80** E3
Dunnville *Canada* 42°54N 79°36W **82** D5
Dunolly *Australia* 36°51S 143°44E **63** F3
Dunoon *U.K.* 55°57N 4°56W **11** F4
Duns *U.K.* 55°47N 2°20W **11** F6
Dunseith *U.S.A.* 48°50N 100°3W **80** A3
Dunshaughlin *Ireland* 53°31N 6°33W **10** C5
Dunsmuir *U.S.A.* 41°13N 122°16W **76** F2
Dunstable *U.K.* 51°53N 0°32W **13** F7
Dunstan Mts. *N.Z.* 44°53S 169°35E **59** F2

Dunster *Canada* 53°8N 119°50W **70** C5
Dunvegan *U.K.* 57°27N 6°35W **11** D2
Dunvegan L. *Canada* 60°8N 107°10W **71** A7
Duolun *China* 42°12N 116°28E **34** C9
Duong Dong *Vietnam* 10°13N 103°58E **39** G4
Dupree *U.S.A.* 45°4N 101°35W **80** C3
Dupuyer *U.S.A.* 48°13N 112°30W **76** B7
Duque de Caxias *Brazil* 22°46S 43°18W **95** A7
Durack ➤ *Australia* 15°33S 127°52E **60** C4
Durack Ra. *Australia* 16°50S 127°40E **60** C4
Durack River *Australia* 15°32S 127°39E **60** C4
Durance ➤ *France* 43°55N 4°45E **20** E6
Durand *U.S.A.* 44°38N 91°58W **80** C8
Durango *Mexico* 24°3N 104°39W **86** C4
Durango *U.S.A.* 37°16N 107°53W **77** H10
Durango □ *Mexico* 24°50N 105°20W **86** C4
Durazno *Uruguay* 33°25S 56°31W **94** C4
Durazzo = Durrës
 Albania 41°19N 19°28E **23** D8
Durban *S. Africa* 29°49S 31°1E **57** D5
Durbuy *Belgium* 50°21N 5°28E **15** D5
Düren *Germany* 50°48N 6°29E **16** C4
Durg = Bhilainagar-Durg
 India 21°13N 81°26E **41** J12
Durgapur *India* 23°30N 87°20E **43** H12
Durham *Canada* 44°10N 80°49W **82** B4
Durham *U.K.* 54°47N 1°34W **12** C6
Durham *Calif., U.S.A.* 39°39N 121°48W **78** F5
Durham *N.C., U.S.A.* 35°59N 78°54W **85** D15
Durham *N.H., U.S.A.* 43°8N 70°56W **83** C14
Durham □ *U.K.* 54°42N 1°45W **12** C6
Durlas = Thurles *Ireland* 52°41N 7°49W **10** D4
Durmă *Si. Arabia* 24°37N 46°8E **44** E5
Durmitor *Montenegro* 43°10N 19°0E **23** C8
Durness *U.K.* 58°34N 4°45W **11** C4
Durrës *Albania* 41°19N 19°28E **23** D8
Durrow *Ireland* 52°51N 7°24W **10** D4
Dursey I. *Ireland* 51°36N 10°12W **10** E1
Dursley *U.K.* 51°40N 2°21W **13** F5
Dursunbey *Turkey* 39°35N 28°37E **23** E13
Duru
 Dem. Rep. of the Congo 4°14N 28°50E **54** B2
Durūz, Jabal ad *Jordan* 32°35N 36°40E **46** C5
D'Urville, Tanjung
 Indonesia 1°28S 137°54E **37** E9
D'Urville I. *N.Z.* 40°50S 173°55E **59** D4
Duryea *U.S.A.* 41°20N 75°45W **83** E9
Dushak *Turkmenistan* 37°13N 60°1E **45** B9
Dushanbe *Tajikistan* 38°33N 68°48E **28** F7
Dushore *U.S.A.* 41°31N 76°24W **83** E8
Dusky Sd. *N.Z.* 45°47S 166°30E **59** F1
Dussejour, C. *Australia* 14°45S 128°13E **60** B4
Düsseldorf *Germany* 51°14N 6°47E **16** C4
Dutch Harbor *U.S.A.* 53°53N 166°32W **74** E6
Dutlwe *Botswana* 23°58S 23°46E **56** C3
Dutton *Canada* 42°39N 81°30W **82** D3
Dutton ➤ *Australia* 20°44S 143°10E **62** C3
Dutywa *S. Africa* 32°8S 28°18E **57** E4
Duwayhin, Khawr
 U.A.E. 24°20N 51°25E **45** E6
Duyfken Pt. *Australia* 12°33S 141°38E **62** A3
Duyun *China* 26°18N 107°29E **32** D5
Dvina, Severnaya ➤
 Russia 64°32N 40°30E **18** B7
Dvinsk = Daugavpils
 Latvia 55°53N 26°32E **9** J22
Dvinskaya Guba *Russia* 65°0N 39°0E **18** B6
Dwarka *India* 22°18N 69°8E **42** H3
Dwellingup *Australia* 32°43S 116°4E **61** F2
Dwight *Canada* 45°20N 79°1W **82** A5
Dwight *U.S.A.* 41°5N 88°26W **80** E9
Dyatlovo = Dzyatlava
 Belarus 53°28N 25°28E **17** B13
Dyce *U.K.* 57°13N 2°12W **11** D6
Dyer, C. *Canada* 66°37N 61°16W **69** D19
Dyer Bay *Canada* 45°10N 81°20W **82** A3
Dyer Plateau *Antarctica* 70°45S 65°30W **5** D17
Dyersburg *U.S.A.* 36°3N 89°23W **85** C10
Dyfi ➤ *U.K.* 52°32N 4°3W **13** E3
Dymer *Ukraine* 50°47N 30°18E **17** C16
Dysart *Australia* 22°32S 148°23E **62** C4
Dzaoudzi *Mayotte* 12°47S 45°16E **53** a
Dzavhan Gol ➤ *Mongolia* 48°54N 93°23E **32** B4
Dzerzhinsk *Russia* 56°14N 43°30E **18** C7
Dzhalinda *Russia* 53°26N 124°0E **29** D13
Dzhambul = Taraz
 Kazakhstan 42°54N 71°22E **28** E8
Dzhankoy *Ukraine* 45°40N 34°20E **19** E5
Dzhezkazgan = Zhezqazghan
 Kazakhstan 47°44N 67°40E **28** E7
Dzhizak = Jizzax
 Uzbekistan 40°6N 67°50E **28** E7
Dzhugdzur, Khrebet
 Russia 57°30N 138°0E **29** D14
Dzhungarskiye Vorota =
 Dzungarian Gate *Asia* 45°10N 82°0E **32** B3
Działdowo *Poland* 53°15N 20°15E **17** B11
Dzibilchaltún *Mexico* 21°10N 89°35W **87** C7
Dzilam de Bravo *Mexico* 21°24N 88°53W **87** C7
Dzirzoniów *Poland* 50°45N 16°39E **17** C9
Dzūkija △ *Lithuania* 54°10N 24°30E **9** J21
Dzungaria = Junggar
 Pendi *China* 44°30N 86°0E **32** B3
Dzungarian Gate *Asia* 45°10N 82°0E **32** B3
Dzüünbulag *Mongolia* 46°58N 115°30E **34** B5
Dzüünmod *Mongolia* 47°45N 106°58E **32** B5
Dzyarzhynsk *Belarus* 53°40N 27°1E **17** B14
Dzyatlava *Belarus* 53°28N 25°28E **17** B13

E

E.C. Manning △ *Canada* 49°5N 120°45W **70** D4
Eabamet L. *Canada* 51°30N 87°46W **72** B2
Eabametoong *Canada* 51°30N 88°0W **72** B2
Éadan Doire = Edenderry
 Ireland 53°21N 7°4W **10** C4
Eads *U.S.A.* 38°29N 102°47W **76** G12

Eagar *U.S.A.* 34°6N 109°17W **77** J9
Eagle *Alaska, U.S.A.* 64°47N 141°12W **68** E3
Eagle *Colo., U.S.A.* 39°39N 106°50W **76** G10
Eagle ➤ *Canada* 53°36N 57°26W **73** B8
Eagle Butte *U.S.A.* 45°0N 101°10W **80** C3
Eagle Grove *U.S.A.* 42°40N 93°54W **80** D7
Eagle L. *Canada* 49°42N 93°13W **71** D10
Eagle L. *Calif., U.S.A.* 40°39N 120°45W **76** F3
Eagle L. *Maine, U.S.A.* 46°20N 69°22W **81** B19
Eagle Lake *Canada* 45°8N 78°29W **82** A6
Eagle Lake *Maine, U.S.A.* 47°3N 68°36W **81** B19
Eagle Lake *Tex., U.S.A.* 29°35N 96°20W **84** G6
Eagle Mountain
 U.S.A. 33°49N 115°27W **79** M11
Eagle Nest *U.S.A.* 36°33N 105°16W **77** H11
Eagle Pass *U.S.A.* 28°43N 100°30W **84** G4
Eagle Pk. *U.S.A.* 38°10N 119°25W **78** G7
Eagle Pt. *Australia* 16°11S 124°23E **60** C3
Eagle River *Mich., U.S.A.* 47°25N 88°18W **80** B9
Eagle River *Wis., U.S.A.* 45°55N 89°15W **80** C9
Eaglehawk *Australia* 36°44S 144°15E **63** F3
Eagles Mere *U.S.A.* 41°25N 76°33W **83** E8
Ealing □ *U.K.* 51°31N 0°20W **13** F7
Ear Falls *Canada* 50°38N 93°13W **71** C10
Earle *U.S.A.* 35°16N 90°28W **85** D9
Earlimart *U.S.A.* 35°53N 119°16W **79** K7
Earlville *U.S.A.* 42°44N 75°32W **83** D9
Earn ➤ *U.K.* 56°21N 3°18W **11** E5
Earn, L. *U.K.* 56°23N 4°13W **11** E4
Earnslaw, Mt. *N.Z.* 44°32S 168°27E **59** F2
Earth *U.S.A.* 34°14N 102°24W **84** D3
Easley *U.S.A.* 34°50N 82°36W **85** D13
East Anglia *U.K.* 52°30N 1°0E **12** E9
East Angus *Canada* 45°30N 71°40W **73** C5
East Antarctica *Antarctica* 80°0S 90°0E **5** D7
East Aurora *U.S.A.* 42°46N 78°37W **82** D6
East Ayrshire □ *U.K.* 55°26N 4°11W **11** F4
East Bengal *Bangla.* 24°0N 90°0E **41** G17
East Beskids = Vychodné Beskydy
 Europe 49°20N 22°0E **17** D11
East Brady *U.S.A.* 40°59N 79°37W **82** F5
East Branch Clarion River L.
 U.S.A. 41°35N 78°35W **82** E6
East C. = Dezhneva, Mys
 Russia 66°5N 169°40W **29** C19
East C. *N.Z.* 37°42S 178°35E **59** B7
East Caroline Basin
 Pac. Oc. 4°0N 146°45E **64** G6
East Chicago *U.S.A.* 41°38N 87°27W **80** E10
East China Sea *Asia* 30°0N 126°0E **33** D7
East Coulee *Canada* 51°23N 112°27W **70** C6
East Dereham = Dereham
 U.K. 52°41N 0°57E **13** E8
East Dunbartonshire □
 U.K. 55°57N 4°13W **11** F4
East Falkland *Falk. Is.* 51°30S 58°30W **96** G5
East Grand Forks *U.S.A.* 47°56N 97°1W **80** B5
East Greenwich *U.S.A.* 41°40N 71°27W **83** E13
East Grinstead *U.K.* 51°7N 0°0 **13** F8
East Hartford *U.S.A.* 41°46N 72°39W **83** E12
East Haydon *Australia* 18°0S 141°30E **62** B3
East Helena *U.S.A.* 46°35N 111°56W **76** C8
East Indies *Asia* 0°0 120°0E **26** E14
East Kilbride *U.K.* 55°47N 4°11W **11** F4
East Lamma Channel
 China 22°14N 114°9E **33** G11
East Lansing *U.S.A.* 42°44N 84°29W **81** D11
East Liverpool *U.S.A.* 40°37N 80°35W **82** F4
East London *S. Africa* 33°0S 27°55E **57** E4
East Lothian □ *U.K.* 55°58N 2°44W **11** F6
East Main = Eastmain
 Canada 52°10N 78°30W **72** B4
East Mariana Basin
 Pac. Oc. 12°0N 153°0E **64** F7
East Northport *U.S.A.* 40°53N 73°20W **83** F11
East Orange *U.S.A.* 40°46N 74°12W **83** F10
East Pacific Rise *Pac. Oc.* 15°0S 110°0W **65** J17
East Palestine *U.S.A.* 40°50N 80°33W **82** F4
East Pine *Canada* 55°48N 120°12W **70** B4
East Point *U.S.A.* 33°41N 84°27W **85** E12
East Providence *U.S.A.* 41°49N 71°23W **83** E13
East Pt. *Br. Virgin Is.* 18°40N 64°18W **89** e
East Pt. *Canada* 46°27N 61°58W **73** C7
East Renfrewshire □
 U.K. 55°46N 4°21W **11** F4
East Retford = Retford
 U.K. 53°19N 0°56W **12** D7
East Riding of Yorkshire □
 U.K. 53°55N 0°30W **12** D7
East Rochester *U.S.A.* 43°7N 77°29W **82** C7
East St. Louis *U.S.A.* 38°37N 90°9W **80** F8
East Schelde = Oosterschelde
 Neths. 51°33N 4°0E **15** C4
East Sea = Japan, Sea of
 Asia 40°0N 135°0E **30** E7
East Siberian Sea *Russia* 73°0N 160°0E **29** B17
East Stroudsburg *U.S.A.* 41°1N 75°11W **83** E9
East Sussex □ *U.K.* 50°56N 0°19E **13** G8
East Tasman Plateau
 Pac. Oc. 43°30S 152°0E **64** M7
East Tawas *U.S.A.* 44°17N 83°29W **81** C12
East Timor ■ *Asia* 8°50S 126°0E **37** F7
East Toorale *Australia* 30°27S 145°28E **63** E4
East Walker ➤ *U.S.A.* 38°52N 119°10W **78** G7
East Windsor *U.S.A.* 40°17N 74°34W **83** F10
Eastbourne *N.Z.* 41°19S 174°55E **59** D5
Eastbourne *U.K.* 50°46N 0°18E **13** G8
Eastend *Canada* 49°32N 108°50W **71** D7
Easter Fracture Zone
 Pac. Oc. 25°0S 115°0W **65** K16
Easter I. = Pascua, I. de
 Chile 27°7S 109°23W **65** K17
Eastern □ *Kenya* 0°0 38°30E **54** C4
Eastern □ *S. Africa* 29°0S 26°0E **56** D4
Eastern Cr. ➤ *Australia* 20°40S 141°35E **62** C3
Eastern Desert = Es Sahrâ' Esh
 Sharqîya *Egypt* 27°30N 32°30E **51** C12
Eastern Ghats *India* 14°0N 78°50E **40** N11
Eastern Group = Lau Group
 Fiji 17°0S 178°30W **59** a

Eastern Group *Australia* 33°30S 124°30E **61** F3
Eastern Guruma ☉
  Australia 22°0S 117°30E **60** D2
Eastern Transvaal =
  Mpumalanga □
  S. Africa 26°0S 30°0E **57** D5
Easterville *Canada* 53°8N 99°49W **71** C9
Easthampton *U.S.A.* 42°16N 72°40W **83** D12
Eastlake *U.S.A.* 41°40N 81°26W **82** E3
Eastland *U.S.A.* 32°24N 98°49W **84** E5
Eastleigh *U.K.* 50°58N 1°21W **13** G6
Eastmain *Canada* 52°10N 78°30W **72** B4
Eastmain → *Canada* 52°27N 78°26W **72** B4
Eastman *Canada* 45°18N 72°19W **83** A12
Eastman *U.S.A.* 32°12N 83°11W **85** E13
Easton *Md., U.S.A.* 38°47N 76°5W **81** F15
Easton *Pa., U.S.A.* 40°41N 75°13W **83** F9
Easton *Wash., U.S.A.* 47°14N 121°11W **78** C5
Eastport *U.S.A.* 44°56N 67°0W **81** C14
Eastsound *U.S.A.* 48°42N 122°55W **78** B4
Eaton *U.S.A.* 40°32N 104°42W **76** F11
Eatonia *Canada* 51°13N 109°25W **71** C7
Eatonton *U.S.A.* 33°20N 83°23W **85** E13
Eatontown *U.S.A.* 40°19N 74°4W **83** F10
Eatonville *U.S.A.* 46°52N 122°16W **78** D4
Eau Claire *U.S.A.* 44°49N 91°30W **80** C8
Eau Claire, L. à l' *Canada* 56°10N 74°25W **72** A5
Eauripik Rise *Pac. Oc.* 2°0N 142°0E **64** G6
Ebano *Mexico* 22°13N 98°24W **87** C5
Ebbw Vale *U.K.* 51°46N 3°12W **13** F4
Ebeltoft *Denmark* 56°12N 10°41E **9** H14
Ebensburg *U.S.A.* 40°29N 78°44W **82** F6
Eberswalde-Finow
  Germany 52°50N 13°49E **16** B7
Ebetsu *Japan* 43°7N 141°34E **30** C10
Ebey's Landing △
  U.S.A. 48°12N 122°41W **78** B4
Ebinur Hu *China* 44°55N 82°55E **32** B3
Ebolowa *Cameroon* 2°55N 11°10E **52** D2
Ebonda
  Dem. Rep. of the Congo 2°12N 22°21E **52** D4
Ebre = Ebro → *Spain* 40°43N 0°54E **21** B6
Ebro → *Spain* 40°43N 0°54E **21** B6
Ecatepec de Morelos
  Mexico 19°36N 99°3W **87** D5
Ecbatana = Hamadān
  Iran 34°52N 48°32E **45** C6
Eceabat *Turkey* 40°11N 26°21E **23** D12
Ech Chéliff *Algeria* 36°10N 1°20E **50** A6
Echigo-Sammyaku
  Japan 36°50N 139°50E **31** F9
Echizen-Misaki *Japan* 35°59N 135°57E **31** G7
Echo Bay *N.W.T., Canada* 66°5N 117°55W **68** D8
Echo Bay *Ont., Canada* 46°29N 84°4W **72** C3
Echoing → *Canada* 55°51N 92°5W **72** B1
Echternach *Lux.* 49°49N 6°25E **15** E6
Echuca *Australia* 36°10S 144°45E **63** F3
Écija *Spain* 37°30N 5°10W **21** D3
Eclipse I. *Australia* 35°5S 117°58E **61** G2
Eclipse Is. *Australia* 13°54S 126°19E **60** B4
Eclipse Sd. *Canada* 72°38N 79°0W **69** C16
Ecuador ■ *S. Amer.* 2°0S 78°0W **92** D3
Ed Da'ein *Sudan* 11°26N 26°9E **52** B5
Ed Damazin *Sudan* 11°46N 34°21E **51** F12
Ed Dâmer *Sudan* 17°27N 34°0E **51** E12
Ed Dar el Beida = Casablanca
  Morocco 33°36N 7°36W **50** B4
Ed Debba *Sudan* 18°0N 30°51E **51** E12
Ed Déffa *Egypt* 30°40N 26°30E **51** B11
Ed Dueim *Sudan* 14°0N 32°10E **51** F12
Edam *Canada* 53°11N 108°46W **71** C7
Edam *Neths.* 52°31N 5°3E **15** B5
Eday *U.K.* 59°11N 2°47W **11** B6
Eddrachillis B. *U.K.* 58°17N 5°14W **11** C3
Eddystone *U.K.* 50°11N 4°16W **13** G3
Eddystone Pt. *Australia* 40°59S 148°20E **63** G4
Ede *Neths.* 52°4N 5°40E **15** B5
Edehon L. *Canada* 60°25N 97°15W **71** A9
Eden *Australia* 37°3S 149°55E **63** F4
Eden *N.C., U.S.A.* 36°29N 79°53W **85** C15
Eden *N.Y., U.S.A.* 42°39N 78°55W **82** D6
Eden *Tex., U.S.A.* 31°13N 99°51W **84** F5
Eden → *U.K.* 54°57N 3°1W **12** C4
Edenburg *S. Africa* 29°43S 25°58E **56** D4
Edendale *S. Africa* 29°39S 30°18E **57** D5
Edenderry *Ireland* 53°21N 7°4W **10** C4
Edenton *U.S.A.* 36°4N 76°39W **85** C16
Edenville *S. Africa* 27°37S 27°34E **57** D4
Eder → *Germany* 51°12N 9°28E **16** C5
Edessa *Greece* 40°48N 22°5E **23** D10
Edfu = Idfû *Egypt* 24°55N 32°49E **51** D12
Edgar *U.S.A.* 40°22N 97°58W **80** E5
Edgartown *U.S.A.* 41°23N 70°31W **83** E14
Edge Hill *U.K.* 52°8N 1°26W **13** E6
Edgefield *U.S.A.* 33°47N 81°56W **85** E14
Edgeley *U.S.A.* 46°22N 98°43W **80** B4
Edgemont *U.S.A.* 43°18N 103°50W **80** D2
Edgeøya *Svalbard* 77°45N 22°30E **4** B9
Édhessa = Edessa *Greece* 40°48N 22°5E **23** D10
Edievale *N.Z.* 45°49S 169°22E **59** F2
Edina *U.S.A.* 40°10N 92°11W **80** E7
Edinboro *U.S.A.* 41°52N 80°8W **82** E4
Edinburg *U.S.A.* 26°18N 98°10W **84** H5
Edinburgh *U.K.* 55°57N 3°13W **11** F5
Edinburgh ✈ (EDI) *U.K.* 55°54N 3°22W **11** F5
Edinburgh, City of □
  U.K. 55°57N 3°17W **11** F5
Edineț *Moldova* 48°9N 27°18E **17** D14
Edirne *Turkey* 41°40N 26°34E **23** D12
Edison *U.S.A.* 48°33N 122°27W **78** B4
Edithburgh *Australia* 35°5S 137°43E **63** F2
Edmond *U.S.A.* 35°39N 97°29W **84** D6
Edmonds *U.S.A.* 47°48N 122°22W **78** C4
Edmonton *Australia* 17°2S 145°46E **62** B4
Edmonton *Canada* 53°30N 113°30W **70** C6
Edmund L. *Canada* 54°45N 93°17W **72** B1
Edmundston *Canada* 47°23N 68°20W **73** C6
Edna *U.S.A.* 28°59N 96°39W **84** G6

Edremit *Turkey* 39°34N 27°0E **23** E12
Edremit Körfezi *Turkey* 39°30N 26°45E **23** E12
Edson *Canada* 53°35N 116°28W **70** C5
Eduardo Castex
  Argentina 35°50S 64°18W **94** D3
Edward → *Australia* 35°5S 143°30E **63** F3
Edward, L. *Africa* 0°25S 29°40E **54** C2
Edward VII Land
  Antarctica 80°0S 150°0W **5** E13
Edwards *Calif., U.S.A.* 34°50N 117°40W **79** L9
Edwards *N.Y., U.S.A.* 44°20N 75°15W **83** B9
Edwards Plateau
  U.S.A. 30°45N 101°20W **84** F4
Edwardsville *U.S.A.* 41°15N 75°56W **83** E9
Edzná *Mexico* 19°39N 90°19W **87** D6
Edzo *Canada* 62°49N 116°4W **70** A5
Eeklo *Belgium* 51°11N 3°33E **15** C3
Eesti = Estonia ■ *Europe* 58°30N 25°30E **9** G21
Effigy Mounds △ *U.S.A.* 43°5N 91°11W **80** D8
Effingham *U.S.A.* 39°7N 88°33W **80** F9
Égadi, Ísole *Italy* 37°55N 12°16E **22** F5
Egan Range *U.S.A.* 39°35N 114°55W **76** G6
Eganville *Canada* 45°32N 77°5W **82** A7
Eger = Cheb *Czech Rep.* 50°9N 12°28E **16** C7
Eger *Hungary* 47°53N 20°27E **17** E11
Egersund *Norway* 58°26N 6°1E **9** G12
Egg L. *Canada* 55°5N 105°30W **71** B7
Éghezée *Belgium* 50°35N 4°55E **15** D4
Egio *Greece* 38°15N 22°5E **23** E10
Eglinton I. *Canada* 75°48N 118°30W **69** B8
Egmont *Canada* 49°45N 123°56W **70** D4
Egmont, C. *N.Z.* 39°16S 173°45E **59** C4
Egmont, Mt. = Taranaki, Mt.
  N.Z. 39°17S 174°5E **59** C5
Egmont △ *N.Z.* 39°17S 174°4E **59** C5
Egra *India* 21°54N 87°32E **43** J12
Eğridir *Turkey* 37°52N 30°51E **19** G5
Eğridir Gölü *Turkey* 37°53N 30°50E **44** B1
Egvekinot *Russia* 66°19N 179°50W **29** C19
Egypt ■ *Africa* 28°0N 31°0E **51** C12
Ehime □ *Japan* 33°30N 132°40E **31** H6
Ehrenberg *U.S.A.* 33°36N 114°31W **79** M12
Eibar *Spain* 43°11N 2°28W **21** A4
Eidsvold *Australia* 25°25S 151°12E **63** D5
Eidsvoll *Norway* 60°19N 11°14E **9** F14
Eielson *U.S.A.* 64°40N 147°4W **74** C10
Eifel *Germany* 50°15N 6°50E **16** C4
Eiffel Flats *Zimbabwe* 18°20S 30°0E **55** F3
Eigg *U.K.* 56°54N 6°10W **11** E2
Eighty Mile Beach
  Australia 19°30S 120°40E **60** C3
Eil, L. *U.K.* 56°51N 5°16W **11** E3
Eildon, L. *Australia* 37°10S 146°0E **63** F4
Eilean Sar = Western Isles □
  U.K. 57°30N 7°10W **11** D1
Einasleigh *Australia* 18°32S 144°5E **62** B3
Einasleigh → *Australia* 17°30S 142°17E **62** B3
Eindhoven *Neths.* 51°26N 5°28E **15** C5
Eire = Ireland ■ *Europe* 53°50N 7°52W **10** C4
Eiríksjökull *Iceland* 64°46N 20°24W **8** D3
Eirunepé *Brazil* 6°35S 69°53W **92** E5
Eisenb → *Namibia* 20°33S 20°59E **56** C2
Eisenach *Germany* 50°58N 10°19E **16** C6
Eisenerz *Austria* 47°32N 14°54E **16** E8
Eivissa *Spain* 38°54N 1°26E **24** C7
Ejeda *Madag.* 24°0S 44°31E **57** C7
Ejutla *Mexico* 16°34N 96°44W **87** D5
Ekalaka *U.S.A.* 45°53N 104°33W **76** D11
Ekaterinburg = Yekaterinburg
  Russia 56°50N 60°30E **28** D7
Ekenäs = Tammisaari
  Finland 60°0N 23°26E **9** G20
Eketahuna *N.Z.* 40°38S 175°43E **59** D5
Ekibastuz *Kazakhstan* 51°50N 75°10E **28** D8
Ekoli *Dem. Rep. of the Congo* 0°23S 24°13E **54** C1
Eksjö *Sweden* 57°40N 14°58E **9** H16
Ekuma → *Namibia* 18°40S 16°2E **56** B2
Ekwan → *Canada* 53°12N 82°15W **72** B3
Ekwan Pt. *Canada* 53°16N 82°7W **72** B3
El Aaiún *W. Sahara* 27°9N 13°12W **50** C3
El Abanico *Chile* 37°20S 71°31W **94** D1
El Alamein *Egypt* 30°48N 28°58E **51** B11
El 'Aqaba, W. → *Egypt* 30°7N 33°54E **46** E2
El Arīḥā *West Bank* 31°52N 35°27E **46** D4
El 'Arīsh *Egypt* 31°8N 33°50E **46** D2
El 'Arīsh, W. → *Egypt* 31°8N 33°47E **46** D2
El Asnam = Ech Chéliff
  Algeria 36°10N 1°20E **50** A6
El Bayadh *Algeria* 33°40N 1°1E **50** B6
El Bluff *Nic.* 11°59N 83°40W **88** D3
El Cajon *U.S.A.* 32°48N 116°58W **79** N10
El Calafate *Argentina* 50°19S 72°15W **96** G2
El Campo *U.S.A.* 29°12N 96°16W **84** G6
El Capitan *U.S.A.* 37°44N 119°38E **78** H7
El Carbón *Honduras* 15°25N 85°32W **88** C2
El Carmen *Colombia* 9°43N 75°8W **92** B3
El Centro *U.S.A.* 32°48N 115°34W **79** N11
El Cerro *Bolivia* 17°30S 61°40W **92** G6
El Compadre *Mexico* 32°20N 116°14W **79** N10
El Cuy *Argentina* 39°55S 68°25W **96** D3
El Cuyo *Mexico* 21°31N 87°41W **87** C7
El Daheir *Egypt* 31°13N 34°10E **46** D3
El Descanso *Mexico* 32°12N 116°58W **79** N10
El Desemboque *Mexico* 30°33N 113°1W **86** A2
El Diviso *Colombia* 1°22N 78°14W **92** C3
El Djouf *Mauritania* 20°0N 9°0W **50** D4
El Dorado *Ark., U.S.A.* 33°12N 92°40W **84** E8
El Dorado *Kans., U.S.A.* 37°49N 96°52W **80** G6
El Dorado *Venezuela* 6°55N 61°37W **92** B6
El Dorado Springs *U.S.A.* 37°52N 94°1W **80** G6
El Escorial *Spain* 40°35N 4°7W **21** B3
El Faiyûm *Egypt* 29°19N 30°50E **51** C12
El Fâsher *Sudan* 13°33N 25°26E **51** F11
El Ferrol = Ferrol *Spain* 43°29N 8°15W **21** A1
El Fuerte *Mexico* 26°25N 108°39W **86** B3
El Geneina = Al Junaynah
  Sudan 13°27N 22°45E **51** F10

El Gezira □ *Sudan* 15°0N 33°0E **51** F12
El Gîza *Egypt* 30°0N 31°12E **51** C12
El Gogorrón △ *Mexico* 21°49N 100°57W **86** C4
El Goléa *Algeria* 30°30N 2°50E **50** B6
El Golfo de Santa Clara
  Mexico 31°42N 114°30W **86** A2
El Guácharo △ *Venezuela* 10°8N 63°21W **89** D7
El Guache △ *Venezuela* 9°45N 69°30W **89** E6
El Iskandarîya *Egypt* 31°13N 29°58E **51** B11
El Istiwa'iya *Sudan* 5°0N 28°0E **51** G11
El Jadida *Morocco* 33°11N 8°17W **50** B4
El Jardal *Honduras* 14°54N 88°50W **88** D2
El Kef □ *Tunisia* 36°0N 9°0E **51** A7
El Khârga *Egypt* 25°30N 30°33E **51** C12
El Khartûm *Sudan* 15°31N 32°35E **51** E12
El Khartûm Bahrî
  Sudan 15°40N 32°31E **51** E12
El Kuntilla *Egypt* 30°1N 34°45E **46** E3
El Leoncito △ *Argentina* 31°58S 69°10W **94** C2
El Lucero *Mexico* 30°37N 106°31W **86** A3
El Maestrazgo *Spain* 40°30N 0°25W **21** B5
El Mahalla el Kubra
  Egypt 31°0N 31°0E **51** B12
El Malpais △ *U.S.A.* 34°53N 108°0W **77** J10
El Mansûra *Egypt* 31°0N 31°19E **51** B12
El Medano *Canary Is.* 28°3N 16°32W **24** F3
El Ménia = El Goléa
  Algeria 30°30N 2°50E **50** B6
El Milagro *Argentina* 30°59S 65°59W **94** C2
El Minyâ *Egypt* 28°7N 30°33E **51** C12
El Monte *U.S.A.* 34°4N 118°1W **79** L8
El Obeid *Sudan* 13°8N 30°10E **51** F12
El Odaiya *Sudan* 12°8N 28°12E **51** F11
El Oro *Mexico* 19°51N 100°7W **87** D4
El Oued *Algeria* 33°20N 6°58E **50** B7
El Palmar △ *Argentina* 32°10S 58°31W **94** C4
El Palmito, Presa
  Mexico 25°40N 105°30W **86** B3
El Paso *U.S.A.* 31°45N 106°29W **84** F1
El Pinacate y Gran Desierto de
  Altar = Gran Desierto del
  Pinacate △ *Mexico* 31°51N 113°32W **86** A2
El Portal *U.S.A.* 37°41N 119°47W **78** H7
El Porvenir *Mexico* 31°15N 105°51W **86** A3
El Prat de Llobregat *Spain* 41°19N 2°5E **21** B7
El Progreso *Honduras* 15°26N 87°51W **88** C2
El Pueblito *Mexico* 29°6N 105°7W **86** B3
El Pueblo *Canary Is.* 27°47N 17°59W **24** F2
El Puerto de Santa María
  Spain 36°36N 6°13W **21** D2
El Qâhira *Egypt* 30°2N 31°13E **51** B12
El Qantara *Egypt* 30°51N 32°20E **46** E1
El Quseima *Egypt* 30°40N 34°15E **46** E3
El Real de Santa María
  Panama 8°0N 77°40W **92** B3
El Reno *U.S.A.* 35°32N 97°57W **75** H20
El Rey △ *Argentina* 24°40S 64°34W **94** A3
El Rio *U.S.A.* 34°14N 119°10W **79** L7
El Roque, Pta. *Canary Is.* 28°10N 15°25W **24** F4
El Rosarito *Mexico* 28°38N 114°4W **86** B2
El Salto *Mexico* 23°47N 105°22W **86** C3
El Salvador ■ *Cent. Amer.* 13°50N 89°0W **88** D2
El Sauce *Nic.* 13°0N 86°40W **88** D2
El Sueco *Mexico* 29°54N 106°24W **86** B3
El Suweis *Egypt* 29°58N 32°31E **51** C12
El Tamarāni, W. → *Egypt* 30°7N 34°43E **46** E3
El Thamad *Egypt* 29°40N 34°28E **46** F3
El Tigre *Venezuela* 8°44N 64°15W **92** B6
El Tîh, Gebel *Egypt* 29°40N 33°50E **46** F2
El Tofo *Chile* 29°22S 71°18W **94** B1
El Tránsito *Chile* 28°52S 70°17W **94** B1
El Tûr *Egypt* 28°14N 33°36E **44** D2
El Turbio *Argentina* 51°45S 72°5W **96** G2
El Uqsur *Egypt* 25°41N 32°38E **51** C12
El Vergel *Mexico* 26°28N 106°22W **86** B3
El Vigía *Venezuela* 8°38N 71°39W **92** B4
El Wabeira *Egypt* 29°34N 33°6E **46** F2
El Wuz *Sudan* 15°5N 30°7E **51** E12
Elat *Israel* 29°30N 34°56E **46** F3
Elâzığ *Turkey* 38°37N 39°14E **44** B3
Elba *Italy* 42°46N 10°17E **22** C4
Elba *U.S.A.* 31°25N 86°4W **85** F11
Elbasan *Albania* 41°9N 20°9E **23** D9
Elbe *U.S.A.* 46°45N 122°10W **78** D4
Elbe → *Europe* 53°50N 9°0E **16** B5
Elbert, Mt. *U.S.A.* 39°7N 106°27W **76** G10
Elberton *U.S.A.* 34°7N 82°52W **85** D13
Elbeuf *France* 49°17N 1°2E **20** B4
Elbing = Elbląg *Poland* 54°10N 19°25E **17** A10
Elbistan *Turkey* 38°13N 37°15E **44** B3
Elbląg *Poland* 54°10N 19°25E **17** A10
Elbow *Canada* 51°7N 106°35W **71** C7
Elbrus *Russia* 43°21N 42°30E **19** F7
Elburz Mts. = Alborz, Reshteh-ye
  Kūhhā-ye *Iran* 36°0N 52°0E **45** C7
Elche *Spain* 38°15N 0°42W **21** C5
Elcho I. *Australia* 11°55S 135°45E **62** A2
Elda *Spain* 38°29N 0°47W **21** C5
Eldama Ravine *Kenya* 0°3N 35°43E **54** B4
Elde → *Germany* 53°7N 11°15E **16** B6
Eldon *Mo., U.S.A.* 38°21N 92°35W **80** F7
Eldon *Wash., U.S.A.* 47°33N 123°3W **78** C3
Eldora *U.S.A.* 42°22N 93°5W **80** D7
Eldorado *Argentina* 26°28S 54°43W **95** B5
Eldorado *Canada* 59°35N 108°30W **71** B7
Eldorado *Ill., U.S.A.* 37°49N 88°26W **80** G9
Eldorado *Tex., U.S.A.* 30°52N 100°36W **84** F4
Eldoret *Kenya* 0°30N 35°17E **54** B4
Eldred *U.S.A.* 41°58N 78°23W **82** E6
Elea, C. *Cyprus* 35°19N 34°4E **25** D13
Eleanora, Pk. *Australia* 32°57S 121°9E **61** F3
Elefantes → *Africa* 24°10S 32°40E **57** C5
Elektrostal *Russia* 55°41N 38°32E **18** C6
Elemi Triangle *Africa* 5°0N 35°20E **54** B4
Elephant Butte Res.
  U.S.A. 33°9N 107°11W **77** K10
Elephant I. *Antarctica* 61°0S 55°0W **5** C18
Eleuthera *Bahamas* 25°0N 76°20W **88** B4
Elgin *Canada* 44°36N 76°13W **83** B8

Elgin *U.K.* 57°39N 3°19W **11** D5
Elgin *Ill., U.S.A.* 42°2N 88°17W **80** D9
Elgin *N. Dak., U.S.A.* 46°24N 101°51W **80** B3
Elgin *Oreg., U.S.A.* 45°34N 117°55W **76** D5
Elgin *Tex., U.S.A.* 30°21N 97°22W **84** F6
Elgon, Mt. *Africa* 1°10N 34°30E **54** B3
Eliase *Indonesia* 8°21S 130°48E **37** F8
Elim *Namibia* 17°48S 15°31E **56** B2
Elim *S. Africa* 34°35S 19°45E **56** E2
Elista *Russia* 46°16N 44°14E **19** E7
Elizabeth *Australia* 34°42S 138°41E **63** E2
Elizabeth *U.S.A.* 40°39N 74°12W **83** F10
Elizabeth City *U.S.A.* 36°18N 76°14W **85** C16
Elizabethton *U.S.A.* 36°21N 82°13W **85** C13
Elizabethtown *Ky.,
  U.S.A.* 37°42N 85°52W **81** G11
Elizabethtown *N.Y.,
  U.S.A.* 44°13N 73°36W **83** B11
Elizabethtown *Pa., U.S.A.* 40°9N 76°36W **83** F8
Elk *Poland* 53°50N 22°21E **17** B12
Elk → *Canada* 49°11N 115°14W **70** D5
Elk → *U.S.A.* 34°46N 87°16W **85** D11
Elk City *U.S.A.* 35°25N 99°25W **84** D5
Elk Creek *U.S.A.* 39°36N 122°32W **78** F4
Elk Grove *U.S.A.* 38°25N 121°22W **78** G5
Elk Island △ *Canada* 53°35N 112°59W **70** C6
Elk Lake *Canada* 47°40N 80°25W **72** C3
Elk Point *Canada* 53°54N 110°55W **71** C6
Elk River *Idaho, U.S.A.* 46°47N 116°11W **76** C5
Elk River *Minn., U.S.A.* 45°18N 93°35W **80** C7
Elkedra → *Australia* 21°8S 136°22E **62** C2
Elkhart *Ind., U.S.A.* 41°41N 85°58W **81** E11
Elkhart *Kans., U.S.A.* 37°0N 101°54W **80** G3
Elkhorn *Canada* 49°59N 101°14W **71** D8
Elkhorn → *U.S.A.* 41°8N 96°19W **80** E5
Elkhovo *Bulgaria* 42°10N 26°35E **23** C12
Elkin *U.S.A.* 36°15N 80°51W **85** C14
Elkins *U.S.A.* 38°55N 79°51W **81** F14
Elkland *U.S.A.* 41°59N 77°19W **82** E7
Elko *Canada* 49°20N 115°10W **70** D5
Elko *U.S.A.* 40°50N 115°46W **76** F6
Elkton *U.S.A.* 43°49N 83°11W **82** C2
Ellas = Greece ■ *Europe* 40°0N 23°0E **23** E9
Ellef Ringnes I. *Canada* 78°30N 102°2W **69** B11
Ellen, Mt. *U.S.A.* 44°9N 72°56W **83** B12
Ellenburg *U.S.A.* 44°54N 73°48W **83** B11
Ellendale *U.S.A.* 46°0N 98°32W **80** B4
Ellensburg *U.S.A.* 46°59N 120°34W **76** C3
Ellenville *U.S.A.* 41°43N 74°24W **83** E10
Ellerton *Barbados* 13°7N 59°33W **89** g
Ellery, Mt. *Australia* 37°28S 148°47E **63** F4
Ellesmere, L. *N.Z.* 43°47S 172°28E **59** G4
Ellesmere I. *Canada* 79°30N 80°0E **69** B16
Ellesmere Island = Quttinirpaaq △
  Canada 82°13N 72°13W **69** A17
Ellesmere Port *U.K.* 53°17N 2°54W **12** D5
Ellice Is. = Tuvalu ■
  Pac. Oc. 8°0S 178°0E **58** B10
Ellicottville *U.S.A.* 42°17N 78°40W **82** D6
Ellington *U.S.A.* 42°13N 79°6W **82** D5
Elliot *Australia* 17°33S 133°32E **62** B1
Elliot *S. Africa* 31°22S 27°48E **57** E4
Elliot Lake *Canada* 46°25N 82°35W **72** C3
Elliotdale = Xhora
  S. Africa 31°55S 28°38E **57** E4
Ellis *U.S.A.* 38°56N 99°34W **80** F4
Elliston *Australia* 33°39S 134°53E **63** E1
Ellisville *U.S.A.* 31°36N 89°12W **85** F10
Ellon *U.K.* 57°22N 2°4W **11** D6
Ellore = Eluru *India* 16°48N 81°8E **41** L12
Ellsworth *Kans., U.S.A.* 38°44N 98°14W **80** F4
Ellsworth *Maine, U.S.A.* 44°33N 68°25W **81** C19
Ellsworth Land *Antarctica* 76°0S 89°0W **5** D16
Ellsworth Mts. *Antarctica* 78°30S 85°0W **5** D16
Ellwood City *U.S.A.* 40°52N 80°17W **82** F4
Elma *Canada* 49°52N 95°55W **71** D9
Elma *U.S.A.* 47°0N 123°25W **78** D3
Elmalı *Turkey* 36°44N 29°56E **19** G4
Elmhurst *U.S.A.* 41°53N 87°56W **80** E10
Elmira *Canada* 43°36N 80°33W **82** C4
Elmira *U.S.A.* 42°6N 76°48W **82** D8
Elmira Heights *U.S.A.* 42°8N 76°50W **82** D8
Elmore *Australia* 36°30S 144°37E **63** F3
Elmshorn *Germany* 53°43N 9°40E **16** B5
Elmvale *Canada* 44°35N 79°52W **82** B5
Elora *Canada* 43°41N 80°26W **82** C4
Elounda *Greece* 35°16N 25°42E **25** D7
Eloy *U.S.A.* 32°45N 111°33W **77** K8
Elphin *Canada* 44°55N 76°37W **83** B8
Elrose *Canada* 51°12N 108°0W **71** C7
Elsby △ *Australia* 14°55S 133°10E **60** B5
Elsie *U.S.A.* 45°52N 123°36W **78** E3
Elsinore = Helsingør
  Denmark 56°2N 12°35E **9** H15
Eltanin Fracture Zone System
  S. Ocean 54°0S 130°0W **5** B14
Eltham *N.Z.* 39°26S 174°19E **59** C5
Eluru *India* 16°48N 81°8E **41** L12
Elvas *Portugal* 38°50N 7°10W **21** C2
Elverum *Norway* 60°53N 11°34E **8** F14
Elvire → *Australia* 17°51S 128°11E **60** C4
Elvire, Mt. *Australia* 29°22S 119°36E **61** E2
Elwell, L. = Tiber Res.
  U.S.A. 48°19N 111°6W **76** B8
Elwood *Ind., U.S.A.* 40°17N 85°50W **81** E11
Elwood *Nebr., U.S.A.* 40°36N 99°52W **80** E4
Elx = Elche *Spain* 38°15N 0°42W **21** C5
Ely *U.K.* 52°24N 0°16E **13** E8
Ely *Minn., U.S.A.* 47°55N 91°51W **80** B8
Ely *Nev., U.S.A.* 39°15N 114°54W **76** G6
Elyria *U.S.A.* 41°22N 82°6W **82** E2
eMalahleni *S. Africa* 25°51S 29°14E **57** D4
Emāmrūd *Iran* 36°30N 55°0E **45** B7
Embarcación *Argentina* 23°10S 64°0W **94** A3
Embetsu *Japan* 44°44N 141°47E **30** B10
Embi *Kazakhstan* 48°50N 58°8E **28** E6
Embi → *Kazakhstan* 46°55N 53°28E **19** E9
Embonas *Greece* 36°13N 27°51E **25** C9
Embro *Canada* 43°9N 80°54W **82** C4

Embrun *France* 44°34N 6°30E **20** D7
Embu *Kenya* 0°32S 37°38E **54** C4
Emden *Germany* 53°21N 7°12E **16** B4
Emerald *Australia* 23°32S 148°10E **62** C4
Emerald I. *Canada* 76°48N 114°10W **69** B9
Emerson *Canada* 49°0N 97°10W **71** D9
Emet *Turkey* 39°20N 29°15E **23** E13
Emi Koussi *Chad* 19°45N 18°55E **51** E9
Eminabad *Pakistan* 32°2N 74°8E **42** C6
Emine, Nos *Bulgaria* 42°40N 27°56E **23** C12
Emissi, Tarso *Chad* 21°27N 18°36E **51** D9
Emlenton *U.S.A.* 41°11N 79°43W **82** E5
Emmaus *S. Africa* 29°2S 25°15E **56** D4
Emmaus *U.S.A.* 40°32N 75°30W **83** F9
Emmeloord *Neths.* 52°44N 5°46E **15** B5
Emmen *Neths.* 52°48N 6°57E **15** B6
Emmet *Australia* 24°45S 144°30E **62** C3
Emmetsburg *U.S.A.* 43°7N 94°41W **80** D6
Emmett *Idaho, U.S.A.* 43°52N 116°30W **76** E5
Emmett *Mich., U.S.A.* 42°59N 82°46W **82** D2
Emmonak *U.S.A.* 62°47N 164°31W **74** C7
Emo *Canada* 48°38N 93°50W **71** D10
Empalme *Mexico* 27°58N 110°51W **86** B2
Empangeni *S. Africa* 28°50S 31°52E **57** D5
Empedrado *Argentina* 28°0S 58°46W **94** B4
Emperor Seamount Chain
  Pac. Oc. 40°0N 170°0E **64** D9
Emperor Trough *Pac. Oc.* 43°0N 175°30E **64** C9
Emporia *Kans., U.S.A.* 38°25N 96°11W **80** F5
Emporia *Va., U.S.A.* 36°42N 77°32W **81** G15
Emporium *U.S.A.* 41°31N 78°14W **82** E6
Empress *Canada* 50°57N 110°0W **71** C7
Empty Quarter = Rub' al Khālī
  Si. Arabia 19°0N 48°0E **47** D4
Ems → *Germany* 53°20N 7°12E **16** B4
Emsdale *Canada* 45°32N 79°19W **82** A5
Emu *China* 43°40N 128°6E **35** C15
Emu Park *Australia* 23°13S 150°50E **62** C5
eMuziwezinto *S. Africa* 30°15S 30°45E **57** E5
'En 'Avrona *Israel* 29°43N 35°0E **46** F3
'En Boqeq *Israel* 31°12N 35°21E **45** D4
'En Gedi *Israel* 31°28N 35°25E **45** D4
En Nahud *Sudan* 12°45N 28°25E **51** F11
Ena *Japan* 35°25N 137°25E **31** G8
Enana *Namibia* 17°30S 16°23E **56** B2
Enard B. *U.K.* 58°5N 5°20W **11** C3
Enare = Inarijärvi *Finland* 69°0N 28°0E **8** B23
Enarotali *Indonesia* 3°55S 136°21E **37** E9
Encampment *U.S.A.* 41°12N 106°47W **76** F10
Encantadas, Serra *Brazil* 30°40S 53°0W **95** C5
Encarnación *Paraguay* 27°15S 55°50W **95** B4
Encarnación de Díaz
  Mexico 21°31N 102°14W **86** C4
Encinitas *U.S.A.* 33°3N 117°17W **79** M9
Encounter B. *Australia* 35°45S 138°45E **63** F2
Endako *Canada* 54°6N 125°2W **70** C3
Endau Rompin △
  Malaysia 2°27N 103°45E **39** L4
Ende *Indonesia* 8°45S 121°40E **37** F6
Endeavour Str. *Australia* 10°45S 142°0E **62** A3
Enderbury I. *Kiribati* 3°8S 171°5E **64** H10
Enderby *Canada* 50°35N 119°10W **70** C5
Enderby Abyssal Plain
  S. Ocean 60°0S 40°0E **5** C5
Enderby I. *Australia* 20°35S 116°30E **60** D2
Enderby Land *Antarctica* 66°0S 53°0E **5** C5
Enderlin *U.S.A.* 46°38N 97°36W **80** B5
Enderrocat, C. *Spain* 39°28N 2°43E **24** B9
Endicott *U.S.A.* 42°6N 76°4W **83** D8
Endicott Mts. *U.S.A.* 68°0N 152°0W **74** B9
Endwell *U.S.A.* 42°6N 76°2W **83** D8
Endyalgout I. *Australia* 11°40S 132°35E **60** B5
Eneabba *Australia* 29°49S 115°16E **61** E2
Enewetak Atoll
  Marshall Is. 11°30N 162°15E **64** F8
Enez *Turkey* 40°45N 26°5E **23** D12
Enfer, Pte. d' *Martinique* 14°22N 60°54W **88** c
Enfield *Canada* 44°56N 63°32W **73** D7
Enfield *Conn., U.S.A.* 41°58N 72°36W **83** E12
Enfield *N.C., U.S.A.* 36°11N 77°41W **85** C16
Enfield *N.H., U.S.A.* 43°39N 72°9W **83** C12
Engadin *Switz.* 46°45N 10°10E **20** C9
Engaño, C. *Dom. Rep.* 18°30N 68°20W **89** C6
Engaño, C. *Phil.* 18°35N 122°23E **37** A6
Engaru *Japan* 44°3N 143°31E **30** B11
Engcobo = Ngcobo
  S. Africa 31°37S 28°0E **57** E4
Engels *Russia* 51°28N 46°6E **19** D8
Engemann L. *Canada* 58°0N 106°55W **71** B7
Enggano *Indonesia* 5°20S 102°40E **36** F2
England *U.S.A.* 34°33N 91°58W **84** D9
England □ *U.K.* 53°0N 2°0W **13** E5
Englee *Canada* 50°45N 56°5W **73** B8
Englehart *Canada* 47°49N 79°52W **72** C4
Englewood *U.S.A.* 39°38N 104°59W **76** G11
English → *Canada* 49°12N 91°5W **71** C10
English Bazar = Ingraj Bazar
  India 24°58N 88°10E **43** G13
English Channel *Europe* 50°0N 2°0W **13** G6
English Company's Is., The
  Australia 11°50S 136°32E **62** A2
English River *Canada* 49°14N 91°0W **72** C1
Enid *U.S.A.* 36°24N 97°53W **84** C6
Enkhuizen *Neths.* 52°42N 5°17E **15** B5
Enna *Italy* 37°34N 14°16E **22** F6
Ennadai L. *Canada* 60°58N 101°20W **71** A8
Ennedi *Chad* 17°15N 22°0E **51** E10
Enngonia *Australia* 29°21S 145°50E **63** D4
Ennis *Ireland* 52°51N 8°59W **10** D3
Ennis *Mont., U.S.A.* 45°21N 111°44W **76** D8
Ennis *Tex., U.S.A.* 32°20N 96°38W **84** E6
Enniscorthy *Ireland* 52°30N 6°34W **10** D5
Enniskillen *U.K.* 54°21N 7°39W **10** B4
Ennistimon *Ireland* 52°57N 9°17W **10** D2
Enns → *Austria* 48°14N 14°32E **16** D8
Eno *Finland* 62°47N 30°10E **8** E24
Enontekiö *Finland* 68°23N 23°37E **8** B20

Enosburg Falls U.S.A. 44°55N 72°48W **83** B12
Enriquillo, L. Dom. Rep. 18°20N 72°5W **89** C5
Enschede Neths. 52°13N 6°53E **15** B6
Ensenada Argentina 34°55S 57°55W **94** C4
Ensenada Mexico 31°52N 116°37W **86** A1
Ensenada de los Muertos
  Mexico 23°59N 109°51W **86** C2
Ensiola, Pta. de n' Spain 39°7N 2°55E **24** B9
Entebbe Uganda 0°4N 32°28E **54** B3
Enterprise Canada 60°47N 115°45W **70** A5
Enterprise Ala., U.S.A. 31°19N 85°51W **85** F12
Enterprise Oreg., U.S.A. 45°25N 117°17W **76** D5
Entre Ríos Bolivia 21°30S 64°25W **94** A3
Entre Ríos □ Argentina 30°30S 58°30W **94** C4
Entroncamento Portugal 39°28N 8°28W **21** C1
Enugu Nigeria 6°30N 7°30E **50** G7
Enumclaw U.S.A. 47°12N 121°59W **78** C5
Eochaill = Youghal
  Ireland 51°56N 7°52W **10** E4
Eólie, Ís. Italy 38°30N 14°57E **22** E6
Epe Neths. 52°21N 5°59E **15** B5
Épernay France 49°3N 3°56E **20** B5
Ephesus Turkey 37°55N 27°22E **23** F12
Ephraim U.S.A. 39°22N 111°35W **76** G8
Ephrata Pa., U.S.A. 40°11N 76°11W **83** F8
Ephrata Wash., U.S.A. 47°19N 119°33W **76** C4
Épinal France 48°10N 6°27E **20** B7
Episkopi Cyprus 34°40N 32°54E **25** E11
Episkopi Greece 35°20N 24°20E **25** D6
Episkopi Bay Cyprus 34°35N 32°50E **25** E11
Epsom U.K. 51°19N 0°16W **13** F7
Epukiro Namibia 21°40S 19°9E **56** C2
Equatoria = El Istiwa'iya
  Sudan 5°0N 28°0E **51** G11
Equatorial Guinea ■ Africa 2°0N 8°0E **52** D1
Er Hai China 25°48N 100°11E **41** G22
Er Rachidia Morocco 31°58N 4°20W **50** B5
Er Rahad Sudan 12°45N 30°32E **51** F12
Er Rif Morocco 35°1N 4°1W **50** A5
Eráwadī Myit = Irrawaddy ~
  Burma 15°50N 95°6E **41** M19
Eráwadī Myitwanya = Irrawaddy,
  Mouths of the Burma 15°30N 95°0E **41** M19
Erawan △ Thailand 14°25N 98°58E **38** E2
Erbil = Arbīl Iraq 36°15N 44°5E **44** B5
Erçek Turkey 38°39N 43°36E **44** B4
Erciyas Daği Turkey 38°30N 35°30E **44** B2
Érd Hungary 47°22N 18°56E **17** E10
Erdao Jiang ~ China 42°37N 128°0E **35** C14
Erdek Turkey 40°23N 27°47E **23** D12
Erdene = Ulaan-Uul
  Mongolia 44°13N 111°10E **34** B6
Erdenet Mongolia 49°2N 104°5E **32** B5
Erdenetsogt Mongolia 42°55N 106°5E **34** C4
Erebus, Mt. Antarctica 77°35S 167°0E **5** D11
Erechim Brazil 27°35S 52°15W **95** B5
Ereğli Konya, Turkey 37°31N 34°4E **44** B2
Ereğli Zonguldak, Turkey 41°15N 31°24E **19** F5
Erenhot China 43°48N 112°2E **34** C7
Eresma ~ Spain 41°26N 4°45W **21** B3
Erfenisdam S. Africa 28°30S 26°50E **56** D4
Erfurt Germany 50°58N 11°2E **16** C6
Ergani Turkey 38°17N 39°49E **44** B3
Ergel Mongolia 43°8N 109°5E **34** C5
Ergeni Vozvyshennost
  Russia 47°0N 44°0E **19** E7
Ērgli Latvia 56°54N 25°38E **9** H21
Eriboll, L. U.K. 58°30N 4°42W **11** C4
Érice Italy 38°2N 12°35E **22** E5
Erie U.S.A. 42°8N 80°5W **82** D4
Erie, L. N. Amer. 42°15N 81°0W **82** D4
Erie Canal U.S.A. 43°5N 78°43W **82** C7
Erieau Canada 42°16N 81°57W **82** D3
Erigavo = Ceerigaabo
  Somali Rep. 10°35N 47°20E **47** E4
Erikoussa Greece 39°53N 19°34E **25** A3
Eriksdale Canada 50°52N 98°7W **71** C9
Erimanthos Greece 37°57N 21°50E **23** F9
Erimo-misaki Japan 41°50N 143°15E **30** D11
Erin Canada 43°45N 80°7W **82** C4
Erin Pt. Trin. & Tob. 10°3N 61°39W **93** K15
Erinpura India 25°9N 73°3E **42** G5
Eriskay U.K. 57°4N 7°18W **11** D1
Erne ~ Ireland 54°30N 8°16W **10** B3
Erne, Lower L. U.K. 54°28N 7°47W **10** B4
Erne, Upper L. U.K. 54°14N 7°32W **10** B4
Ernest Giles Ra. Australia 27°0S 123°45E **61** E3
Erode India 11°24N 77°45E **40** P10
Eromanga Australia 26°40S 143°11E **63** D3
Erongo Namibia 21°39S 15°58E **56** C2
Erramala Hills India 15°30N 78°15E **40** M11
Errentería Spain 43°19N 1°54W **21** A5
Erri-Nundra △ Australia 37°28S 148°5E **63** F4
Errigal Ireland 55°2N 8°6W **10** A3
Erris Hd. Ireland 54°19N 10°0W **10** B1
Erskine U.S.A. 47°40N 96°0W **80** B6
Ertis = Irtysh ~ Russia 61°4N 68°52E **28** C7
Erwin U.S.A. 36°9N 82°25W **85** G13
Erzgebirge Germany 50°27N 12°55E **16** C7
Erzin Russia 50°15N 95°10E **29** D10
Erzincan Turkey 39°46N 39°30E **44** B3
Erzurum Turkey 39°57N 41°15E **44** B4
Es Caló Spain 38°40N 1°30E **24** C8
Es Canar Spain 39°2N 1°36E **24** B8
Es Mercadal Spain 39°59N 4°5E **24** B11
Es Migjorn Gran Spain 39°57N 4°3E **24** B11
Es Sahrâ' Esh Sharqîya
  Egypt 27°30N 32°30E **51** C12
Es Sînâ' Egypt 29°0N 34°0E **46** F3
Es Vedrà Spain 38°52N 1°12E **24** C7

Esambo
  Dem. Rep. of the Congo 3°48S 23°30E **54** C1
Esan-Misaki Japan 41°40N 141°10E **30** D10
Esashi Hokkaidō, Japan 44°56N 142°35E **30** B11
Esashi Hokkaidō, Japan 41°52N 140°7E **30** D10
Esbjerg Denmark 55°29N 8°29E **9** J13
Esbo = Espoo Finland 60°12N 24°40E **9** F21
Escalante U.S.A. 37°47N 111°36W **77** H8
Escalante ~ U.S.A. 37°24N 110°57W **77** H8
Escalón Mexico 26°45N 104°20W **86** B4
Escambia ~ U.S.A. 30°32N 87°11W **85** F11
Escanaba U.S.A. 45°45N 87°4W **80** C10
Esch-sur-Alzette Lux. 49°32N 6°0E **15** E6
Escondido U.S.A. 33°7N 117°5W **79** M9
Escuinapa de Hidalgo
  Mexico 22°50N 105°50W **86** C3
Escuintla Guatemala 14°20N 90°48W **88** D1
Esenguly Turkmenistan 37°37N 53°59E **28** F6
Eşfahān Iran 32°39N 51°43E **45** C6
Eşfahān □ Iran 32°50N 51°50E **45** C6
Esfarāyen Iran 37°4N 57°30E **45** B8
Esfideh Iran 33°39N 59°46E **45** C8
Esh Sham = Dimashq
  Syria 33°30N 36°18E **46** B5
Esha Ness U.K. 60°29N 1°38W **11** A7
Esher U.K. 51°21N 0°20W **13** F7
Eshkol △ Israel 31°20N 34°30E **46** D3
Eshowe S. Africa 28°50S 31°30E **57** D5
Esigodini Zimbabwe 20°18S 28°56E **57** C4
Esil = Ishim ~ Russia 57°45N 71°10E **28** D8
Esira Madag. 24°20S 46°42E **57** C8
Esk ~ Dumf. & Gall., U.K. 54°58N 3°2W **11** G5
Esk ~ N. Yorks., U.K. 54°30N 0°37W **12** C7
Eskān Iran 26°48N 63°9E **45** E9
Esker Siding Canada 53°53N 66°25W **73** B6
Eskifjörður Iceland 65°3N 13°55W **8** D7
Eskilstuna Sweden 59°22N 16°32E **9** G17
Eskimo Point = Arviat
  Canada 61°6N 93°59W **71** A10
Eskişehir Turkey 39°50N 30°30E **19** G5
Esla ~ Spain 41°29N 6°3W **21** B2
Eslāmābād-e Gharb Iran 34°10N 46°30E **44** C5
Eslāmshahr Iran 35°40N 51°10E **45** C6
Eşme Turkey 38°23N 28°58E **23** E13
Esmeraldas Ecuador 1°0N 79°40W **92** C3
Esna = Isna Egypt 25°17N 32°30E **51** C12
Esnagi L. Canada 48°36N 84°33W **72** C3
España = Spain ■ Europe 39°0N 4°0W **21** B4
Espanola Canada 46°15N 81°46W **72** C3
Espanola U.S.A. 35°59N 106°5W **77** J10
Esparza Costa Rica 9°59N 84°40W **88** E3
Esperance Australia 33°45S 121°55E **61** F3
Esperance B. Australia 33°48S 121°55E **61** F3
Esperance Harbour
  St. Lucia 14°4N 60°55W **89** f
Esperanza Antarctica 65°0S 55°0W **5** C18
Esperanza Argentina 31°29S 61°3W **94** C3
Esperanza Puerto Rico 18°6N 65°28W **89** d
Espichel, C. Portugal 38°22N 9°16W **21** C1
Espigão, Serra do Brazil 26°35S 50°30W **95** B5
Espinal, Sierra del = Espinhaço,
  Serra do Brazil 17°30S 43°30W **93** G10
Espinhaço, Serra do
  Brazil 17°30S 43°30W **93** G10
Espinilho, Serra do Brazil 28°30S 55°0W **95** B5
Espírito Santo □ Brazil 20°0S 40°45W **93** H10
Espírito Santo do Pinhal
  Brazil 22°10S 46°46W **95** A6
Espíritu Santo Vanuatu 15°15S 166°50E **58** C9
Espíritu Santo, B. del
  Mexico 19°20N 87°35W **87** D7
Espíritu Santo, I.
  Mexico 24°30N 110°22W **86** C2
Espita Mexico 21°1N 88°19W **87** C7
Espoo Finland 60°12N 24°40E **9** F21
Espungabera Mozam. 20°29S 32°45E **57** C5
Esquel Argentina 42°55S 71°20W **96** E2
Esquimalt Canada 48°26N 123°25W **78** B3
Esquina Argentina 30°0S 59°30W **94** C4
Essaouira Morocco 31°32N 9°42W **50** B4
Essebie
  Dem. Rep. of the Congo 2°58N 30°40E **54** B3
Essen Belgium 51°28N 4°28E **15** C4
Essen Germany 51°28N 7°2E **16** C4
Essendon, Mt. Australia 25°0S 120°29E **61** E3
Essequibo ~ Guyana 6°50N 58°30W **92** B7
Essex Canada 42°10N 82°49W **82** D2
Essex Calif., U.S.A. 34°44N 115°15W **79** L11
Essex N.Y., U.S.A. 44°19N 73°21W **83** B11
Essex □ U.K. 51°54N 0°27E **13** F8
Essex Junction U.S.A. 44°29N 73°7W **83** B11
Esslingen Germany 48°44N 9°18E **16** D5
Estación Camacho
  Mexico 24°25N 102°18W **86** C4
Estación Simón Mexico 24°42N 102°35W **86** C4
Estados, I. de Los
  Argentina 54°40S 64°30W **96** G4
Eştahbānāt Iran 29°8N 54°4E **45** D7
Estância Brazil 11°16S 37°26W **93** F11
Estancia U.S.A. 34°46N 106°4W **77** J10
Estärm Iran 28°21N 58°21E **45** D8
Estcourt S. Africa 29°0S 29°53E **57** D4
Este △ Dom. Rep. 18°14N 68°42W **89** C6
Estelí Nic. 13°9N 86°22W **88** D2
Estellencs Spain 39°39N 2°29E **24** B9
Estevan Canada 49°10N 102°59W **71** D8
Estevan Group Canada 53°3N 129°38W **70** C3
Estherville U.S.A. 43°24N 94°50W **80** D6
Eston Canada 51°8N 108°40W **71** C7
Estonia ■ Europe 58°30N 25°30E **9** G21
Estreito Brazil 6°32S 47°25W **93** E9
Estrela, Serra da Portugal 40°10N 7°45W **21** B2
Estremoz Portugal 38°51N 7°39W **21** C2
Estrondo, Serra do Brazil 7°20S 48°0W **93** E9
Esztergom Hungary 47°47N 18°44E **17** E10
Et Tidra Mauritania 19°45N 16°20W **50** E2
Etah India 27°35N 78°40E **43** F8
Étampes France 48°26N 2°10E **20** B5

Etanga Namibia 17°55S 13°0E **56** B1
Etawah India 26°48N 79°6E **43** F8
Etawney L. Canada 57°50N 96°50W **71** B9
Etchojoa Mexico 26°55N 109°38W **86** B3
eThekwini = Durban
  S. Africa 29°49S 31°1E **57** D5
Ethel U.S.A. 46°32N 122°46W **78** D4
Ethelbert Canada 51°32N 100°25W **71** C8
Ethiopia ■ Africa 8°0N 40°0E **47** F3
Ethiopian Highlands
  Ethiopia 10°0N 37°0E **47** F2
Etive, L. U.K. 56°29N 5°10W **11** E3
Etna Italy 37°50N 14°55E **22** F6
Etoile
  Dem. Rep. of the Congo 11°33S 27°30E **55** E2
Etolin Strait U.S.A. 60°20N 165°15W **74** C6
Etosha △ Namibia 19°0S 16°0E **56** B2
Etosha Pan Namibia 18°40S 16°30E **56** B2
Etowah U.S.A. 35°20N 84°32W **85** D12
Etrek Turkmenistan 37°36N 54°46E **45** B7
Ettelbruck Lux. 49°51N 6°5E **15** E6
Ettrick Water ~ U.K. 55°31N 2°55W **11** F6
Etuku
  Dem. Rep. of the Congo 3°42S 25°45E **54** C2
Etzná-Tixmucuy = Edzná
  Mexico 19°39N 90°19W **87** D6
Eua Tonga 21°22S 174°56W **59** c
Euboea = Evia Greece 38°30N 24°0E **23** E11
Eucla Australia 31°41S 128°52E **61** F4
Euclid U.S.A. 41°34N 81°32W **82** E3
Eucumbene, L. Australia 36°2S 148°40E **63** F4
Eudora U.S.A. 33°7N 91°16W **84** E9
Eufaula Ala., U.S.A. 31°54N 85°9W **85** F12
Eufaula Okla., U.S.A. 35°17N 95°35W **84** D7
Eufaula L. U.S.A. 35°18N 95°21W **84** D7
Eugene U.S.A. 44°5N 123°4W **76** D2
Eugowra Australia 33°22S 148°24E **63** E4
Eulo Australia 28°10S 145°3E **63** D4
Eungella △ Australia 20°57S 148°40E **62** b
Eunice La., U.S.A. 30°30N 92°25W **84** F8
Eunice N. Mex., U.S.A. 32°26N 103°10W **77** K12
Eupen Belgium 50°37N 6°3E **15** D6
Euphrates = Furāt, Nahr al ~
  Asia 31°0N 47°25E **44** D5
Eureka Canada 80°0N 85°56W **69** B14
Eureka Calif., U.S.A. 40°47N 124°9W **76** F1
Eureka Kans., U.S.A. 37°49N 96°17W **80** G5
Eureka Mont., U.S.A. 48°53N 115°3W **76** B6
Eureka Nev., U.S.A. 39°31N 115°58W **76** G6
Eureka S. Dak., U.S.A. 45°46N 99°38W **80** C4
Eureka, Mt. Australia 26°35S 121°35E **61** E3
Eureka Sd. Canada 79°0N 85°0W **69** B15
Euroa Australia 36°44S 145°35E **63** F4
Europa, Île Ind. Oc. 22°20S 40°22E **53** J8
Europa, Picos de Spain 43°10N 4°49W **21** A3
Europa, Pt. Gib. 36°3N 5°21W **21** D3
Europe 50°0N 20°0E **6** E10
Europoort Neths. 51°57N 4°10E **15** C4
Eustis U.S.A. 28°51N 81°41W **85** G14
Eutsuk L. Canada 53°20N 126°45W **70** C3
Evale Angola 16°33S 15°44E **56** B2
Evans Canada 40°23N 104°41W **76** F11
Evans, L. Canada 50°50N 77°0W **72** B4
Evans City U.S.A. 40°46N 80°4W **82** F4
Evansburg Canada 53°36N 114°59W **70** C5
Evanston Ill., U.S.A. 42°3N 87°40W **80** E9
Evanston Wyo., U.S.A. 41°16N 110°58W **76** F8
Evansville U.S.A. 37°58N 87°35W **80** G10
Evaz Iran 27°46N 53°59E **45** E7
Eveleth U.S.A. 47°28N 92°32W **80** B7
Evensk Russia 62°12N 159°30E **29** C16
Everard, L. Australia 31°30S 135°0E **63** E2
Everard Ranges Australia 27°5S 132°28E **61** E5
Everest, Mt. Nepal 28°5N 86°58E **43** E12
Everett Pa., U.S.A. 40°1N 78°23W **82** F6
Everett Wash., U.S.A. 47°59N 122°12W **78** C4
Everglades, The U.S.A. 25°50N 81°0W **85** J14
Everglades △ U.S.A. 25°30N 81°0W **85** J14
Everglades City U.S.A. 25°52N 81°23W **85** J14
Evergreen Ala., U.S.A. 31°26N 86°57W **85** F11
Evergreen Mont.,
  U.S.A. 48°14N 114°17W **76** B6
Evesham U.K. 52°6N 1°56W **13** E6
Evia Greece 38°30N 24°0E **23** E11
Evje Norway 58°36N 7°51E **9** G12
Évora Portugal 38°33N 7°57W **21** C2
Evowghli Iran 38°43N 45°13E **44** B5
Évreux France 49°3N 1°8E **20** B4
Évros ~ Greece 41°40N 26°34E **23** D12
Évry France 48°38N 2°27E **20** B5
Évvoia = Evia Greece 38°30N 24°0E **23** E11
Ewe, L. U.K. 57°49N 5°38W **11** D3
Ewing U.S.A. 42°16N 98°21W **80** D4
Ewo Congo 0°48S 14°45E **52** E2
Exaltación Bolivia 13°10S 65°20W **92** F5
Excelsior Springs U.S.A. 39°20N 94°13W **80** F6
Exe ~ U.K. 50°41N 3°29W **13** G4
Exeter Canada 43°21N 81°29W **82** C3
Exeter U.K. 50°43N 3°31W **13** G4
Exeter Calif., U.S.A. 36°18N 119°9W **78** J7
Exeter N.H., U.S.A. 42°59N 70°57W **83** D14
Exmoor U.K. 51°12N 3°45W **13** F4
Exmoor △ U.K. 51°8N 3°42W **13** F4
Exmouth Australia 21°54S 114°10E **60** D1
Exmouth U.K. 50°37N 3°25W **13** G4
Exmouth G. Australia 22°15S 114°15E **60** D1
Exmouth Plateau Ind. Oc. 19°0S 114°0E **64** J3
Expedition △ Australia 25°41S 149°7E **63** D4
Expedition Ra. Australia 24°30S 149°12E **62** C4
Extremadura □ Spain 39°30N 6°5W **21** C2
Exuma Sound Bahamas 24°30N 76°20W **88** B4
Eyasi, L. Tanzania 3°30S 35°0E **54** C4
Eye Pen. U.K. 58°13N 6°10W **11** C2
Eyemouth U.K. 55°52N 2°5W **11** F6
Eyjafjörður Iceland 66°15N 18°30W **8** C4
Eyl Somali Rep. 8°0N 49°50E **47** F4
Eyre (North), L.
  Australia 28°30S 137°20E **63** D2

Eyre (South), L.
  Australia 29°18S 137°25E **63** D2
Eyre, L. Australia 29°30S 137°26E **58** D6
Eyre Mts. N.Z. 45°25S 168°25E **59** F2
Eyre Pen. Australia 33°30S 136°17E **63** E2
Eysturoy Færoe Is. 62°13N 6°54W **8** E9
Eyvän = Jūy Zar Iran 33°50N 46°18E **44** C5
Eyvānkī Iran 35°24N 51°56E **45** C6
Ezine Turkey 39°48N 26°20E **23** E12
Ezouza ~ Cyprus 34°44N 32°27E **25** E11

F

F.Y.R.O.M. = Macedonia ■
  Europe 41°53N 21°40E **23** D9
Faaa Tahiti 17°34S 149°35W **59** d
Faaone Tahiti 17°40S 149°21W **59** d
Fabala Guinea 9°44N 9°5W **50** G4
Fabens U.S.A. 31°30N 106°10W **84** F1
Fabius U.S.A. 42°50N 75°59W **83** D9
Fabriano Italy 43°20N 12°54E **22** C5
Fachi Niger 18°6N 11°34E **51** E8
Fada Chad 17°13N 21°34E **51** E10
Fada-n-Gourma
  Burkina Faso 12°10N 0°30E **50** F6
Faddeyevskiy, Ostrov
  Russia 76°0N 144°0E **29** B15
Fadghāmī Syria 35°53N 40°52E **44** C4
Faenza Italy 44°17N 11°53E **22** B4
Færoe Is. = Føroyar ☑
  Atl. Oc. 62°0N 7°0W **8** F9
Făgăraş Romania 45°48N 24°58E **17** F13
Fagersta Sweden 60°1N 15°46E **9** F16
Fagnano, L. Argentina 54°30S 68°0W **96** G3
Fahlīān Iran 30°11N 51°28E **45** D6
Fahraj Kermān, Iran 29°0N 59°0E **45** D8
Fahraj Yazd, Iran 31°46N 54°36E **45** D7
Faial Azores 38°34N 28°42W **50** a
Faial Madeira 32°47N 16°53W **24** D3
Faichan Kangri India 35°48N 76°34E **43** B7
Fair Haven N.Y., U.S.A. 43°18N 76°42W **83** C8
Fair Haven Vt., U.S.A. 43°36N 73°16W **83** D17
Fair Hd. U.K. 55°14N 6°9W **10** A5
Fair Isle U.K. 59°32N 1°38W **14** B6
Fair Oaks U.S.A. 38°39N 121°16W **78** G5
Fairbanks U.S.A. 64°51N 147°43W **68** E2
Fairbury U.S.A. 40°8N 97°11W **80** E5
Fairfax U.S.A. 44°40N 73°1W **83** B11
Fairfield Ala., U.S.A. 33°29N 86°55W **85** E11
Fairfield Calif., U.S.A. 38°15N 122°3W **78** G4
Fairfield Conn., U.S.A. 41°9N 73°16W **83** E11
Fairfield Idaho, U.S.A. 43°21N 114°44W **76** E6
Fairfield Ill., U.S.A. 38°23N 88°22W **80** F9
Fairfield Iowa, U.S.A. 40°56N 91°57W **80** E8
Fairfield Tex., U.S.A. 31°44N 96°10W **84** F6
Fairford Canada 51°37N 98°38W **71** C9
Fairhope U.S.A. 30°31N 87°54W **85** F11
Fairlie N.Z. 44°5S 170°49E **59** F3
Fairmead U.S.A. 37°5N 120°10W **78** H6
Fairmont Minn., U.S.A. 43°39N 94°28W **80** D6
Fairmont W. Va., U.S.A. 39°29N 80°9W **81** F13
Fairmount Calif., U.S.A. 34°45N 118°27W **79** L8
Fairmount N.Y., U.S.A. 43°5N 76°12W **83** C8
Fairplay U.S.A. 39°15N 106°2W **76** G10
Fairport U.S.A. 43°6N 77°27W **82** C7
Fairport Harbor U.S.A. 41°45N 81°17W **82** E3
Fairview Canada 56°5N 118°25W **70** B5
Fairview Mont., U.S.A. 47°51N 104°3W **76** C11
Fairview Okla., U.S.A. 36°16N 98°29W **84** C5
Fairweather, Mt.
  U.S.A. 58°55N 137°32W **70** B1
Faisalabad Pakistan 31°30N 73°5E **42** D5
Faith U.S.A. 45°2N 102°2W **80** C2
Faizabad India 26°45N 82°10E **43** F10
Fajardo Puerto Rico 18°20N 65°39W **89** d
Fajr, W. ~ Si. Arabia 29°10N 38°10E **44** D3
Fakenham U.K. 52°51N 0°51E **12** E8
Fakfak Indonesia 2°55S 132°18E **37** E8
Faku China 42°32N 123°21E **35** C12
Falaise France 48°54N 0°12W **20** B3
Falaise, Mui Vietnam 19°6N 105°45E **38** C5
Falam Burma 23°0N 93°45E **41** H18
Falcó, C. des Spain 38°50N 1°23E **24** C7
Falcón, Presa Mexico 26°35N 99°10W **87** B5
Falcon Lake Canada 49°42N 95°15W **71** D9
Falcon Res. U.S.A. 26°34N 99°10W **84** H5
Falconara Maríttima
  Italy 43°37N 13°24E **22** C5
Falcone, C. del Italy 40°58N 8°12E **22** D3
Falconer U.S.A. 42°7N 79°13W **82** D5
Falefa Samoa 13°54S 171°31W **59** b
Falelatai Samoa 13°55S 171°59W **59** b
Falelima Samoa 13°32S 172°41W **59** b
Faleshty = Fălești
  Moldova 47°32N 27°44E **17** E14
Fălești Moldova 47°32N 27°44E **17** E14
Falfurrias U.S.A. 27°14N 98°9W **84** H5
Falher Canada 55°44N 117°15W **70** B5
Faliraki Greece 36°22N 28°12E **25** C10
Falkenberg Sweden 56°54N 12°30E **9** H15
Falkirk U.K. 56°0N 3°47W **11** F5
Falkirk □ U.K. 55°58N 3°49W **11** F5
Falkland U.K. 56°16N 3°12W **11** E5
Falkland Is. ☑ Atl. Oc. 51°30S 59°0W **96** G5
Falkland Sd. Falk. Is. 52°0S 60°0W **96** G5
Fall River U.S.A. 41°43N 71°10W **83** E13
Fallbrook U.S.A. 33°23N 117°15W **79** M9
Fallon U.S.A. 39°28N 118°47W **76** G4
Falls City U.S.A. 40°3N 95°36W **80** E6
Falls Creek U.S.A. 41°9N 78°48W **82** E6
Falmouth Jamaica 18°30N 77°40W **88** a
Falmouth U.K. 50°9N 5°5W **13** G2
Falmouth U.S.A. 41°33N 70°37W **83** E14
Falsa, Pta. Mexico 27°51N 115°3W **86** B1
False B. S. Africa 34°15S 18°40E **56** E2
Falso, C. Honduras 15°12N 83°21W **88** C3
Falster Denmark 54°45N 11°55E **9** J14
Falsterbo Sweden 55°23N 12°50E **9** J15

Fălticeni Romania 47°21N 26°20E **17** E14
Falun Sweden 60°37N 15°37E **8** F16
Famagusta Cyprus 35°8N 33°55E **25** D12
Famagusta Bay Cyprus 35°15N 34°0E **25** D13
Famatina, Sierra de
  Argentina 27°30S 68°0W **94** B2
Family L. Canada 51°54N 95°27W **71** C9
Famoso U.S.A. 35°37N 119°12W **79** K7
Fan Xian China 35°55N 115°38E **34** G8
Fanad Hd. Ireland 55°17N 7°38W **10** A4
Fandriana Madag. 20°14S 47°21E **57** C8
Fang Thailand 19°55N 99°13E **38** C2
Fangcheng China 33°18N 112°59E **34** H7
Fangshan China 38°3N 111°25E **34** E6
Fangzi China 36°33N 119°10E **35** F10
Fanjakana Madag. 21°10S 46°53E **57** C8
Fanjiatun China 43°40N 125°15E **35** C13
Fanling China 22°30N 114°8E **33** F11
Fannich, L. U.K. 57°38N 4°59W **11** D4
Fannūj Iran 26°35N 59°38E **45** E8
Fanø Denmark 55°25N 8°25E **9** J13
Fano Italy 43°50N 13°1E **22** C5
Fanshi China 39°12N 113°20E **34** E7
Fao = Al Fāw Iraq 30°0N 48°30E **45** D6
Faqirwali Pakistan 29°27N 73°0E **42** E5
Far East = Dalnevostochnyy □
  Russia 67°0N 140°0E **29** C14
Far East Asia 40°0N 130°0E **26** E14
Faradje
  Dem. Rep. of the Congo 3°50N 29°45E **54** B2
Farafangana Madag. 22°49S 47°50E **57** C8
Farāh Afghan. 32°20N 62°7E **40** C3
Farāh □ Afghan. 32°25N 62°10E **40** C3
Farahalana Madag. 14°26S 50°10E **57** A9
Faranah Guinea 10°3N 10°45W **50** F3
Farasān, Jazā'ir
  Si. Arabia 16°45N 41°55E **47** D3
Farasan Is. = Farasān, Jazā'ir
  Si. Arabia 16°45N 41°55E **47** D3
Faratsiho Madag. 19°24S 46°57E **57** B8
Fareham U.K. 50°51N 1°11W **13** G6
Farewell, C. N.Z. 40°29S 172°43E **59** D4
Farewell C. = Nunap Isua
  Greenland 59°48N 43°55W **66** D15
Farghona Uzbekistan 40°23N 71°19E **28** E8
Fargo U.S.A. 46°53N 96°48W **80** B5
Fār'iah, W. al ~
  West Bank 32°12N 35°27E **46** C4
Faribault U.S.A. 44°18N 93°16W **80** C7
Faridabad India 28°26N 77°19E **42** E6
Faridkot India 30°44N 74°45E **42** D6
Faridpur Bangla. 23°15N 89°55E **43** H13
Faridpur India 28°13N 79°33E **43** E8
Farīmān Iran 35°40N 59°49E **45** C8
Fariones, Pta. Canary Is. 29°13N 13°28W **24** E6
Farleigh Australia 21°4S 149°8E **62** b
Farmerville U.S.A. 32°47N 92°24W **84** E8
Farmingdale U.S.A. 40°12N 74°10W **83** F10
Farmington Canada 55°54N 120°30W **70** B4
Farmington Calif.,
  U.S.A. 37°55N 120°59W **78** H6
Farmington Maine,
  U.S.A. 44°40N 70°9W **81** C18
Farmington Mo., U.S.A. 37°47N 90°25W **80** G8
Farmington N.H., U.S.A. 43°24N 71°4W **83** C13
Farmington N. Mex.,
  U.S.A. 36°44N 108°12W **77** H9
Farmington Utah,
  U.S.A. 40°59N 111°53W **76** F8
Farmington ~ U.S.A. 41°51N 72°38W **83** E12
Farmville U.S.A. 37°18N 78°24W **81** G14
Farne Is. U.K. 55°38N 1°37W **12** B6
Farnham Canada 45°17N 72°59W **83** A12
Farnham, Mt. Canada 50°29N 116°30W **70** C5
Faro Brazil 2°10S 56°39W **93** D7
Faro Canada 62°11N 133°22W **68** E5
Faro Portugal 37°2N 7°55W **21** D2
Fårö Sweden 57°55N 19°5E **9** H18
Farquhar, C. Australia 23°50S 113°36E **61** D1
Farrars Cr. ~ Australia 25°35S 140°43E **62** D3
Farräshband Iran 28°57N 52°5E **45** D7
Farrell U.S.A. 41°13N 80°30W **82** E4
Farrokhī Iran 33°50N 59°31E **45** C8
Farruch, C. = Ferrutx, C. de
  Spain 39°47N 3°21E **24** B10
Farrukhabad India 27°24N 79°34E **43** F8
Fārs □ Iran 29°30N 55°0E **45** D7
Farsala Greece 39°17N 22°23E **23** E10
Fārsī Iran 27°58N 50°11E **45** E6
Farson U.S.A. 42°7N 109°26W **76** E9
Farsund Norway 58°5N 6°55E **9** G12
Fartak, Râs Si. Arabia 28°5N 34°34E **44** D2
Fartak, Ra's Yemen 15°38N 52°15E **47** D5
Fartura, Serra da Brazil 26°21S 52°52W **95** B5
Fārūj Iran 37°14N 58°14E **45** B8
Farvel, Kap = Nunap Isua
  Greenland 59°48N 43°55W **66** D15
Farwell U.S.A. 34°23N 103°2W **84** D3
Fāryāb □ Afghan. 36°0N 65°0E **40** B4
Fasā Iran 29°0N 53°39E **45** D7
Fasano Italy 40°50N 17°22E **22** D7
Fastiv Ukraine 50°7N 29°57E **17** C15
Fastnet Rock Ireland 51°22N 9°37W **10** E2
Fastov = Fastiv Ukraine 50°7N 29°57E **17** C15
Fatagar, Tanjung
  Indonesia 2°46S 131°57E **37** E8
Fatehabad Haryana, India 29°31N 75°27E **42** E6
Fatehabad Ut. P., India 27°1N 78°19E **42** F8
Fatehgarh India 27°25N 79°35E **43** F8
Fatehpur Bihar, India 24°38N 85°14E **43** G11
Fatehpur Raj., India 28°0N 74°40E **42** F6
Fatehpur Ut. P., India 25°56N 81°13E **43** G9
Fatehpur Ut. P., India 27°10N 81°13E **43** F9
Fatehpur Sikri India 27°6N 77°40E **42** F6
Fathom Five △ Canada 45°17N 81°40W **82** A3
Fatima Canada 47°24N 61°53W **73** C7
Faulkton U.S.A. 45°2N 99°8W **80** C4
Faure I. Australia 25°52S 113°50E **61** E1
Fauresmith S. Africa 29°44S 25°17E **56** D4

Fauske Norway 67°17N 15°25E 8 C16
Favara Italy 37°19N 13°39E 22 F5
Faváritx, C. de Spain 40°0N 4°15E 24 B11
Favignana Italy 37°56N 12°20E 22 F5
Fawcett, Pt. Australia 11°46S 130°2E 60 B5
Fawn → Canada 55°20N 87°35W 72 A2
Fawnskin U.S.A. 34°16N 116°56W 79 L10
Faxaflói Iceland 64°29N 23°0W 8 D2
Faya-Largeau Chad 17°58N 19°6E 51 E9
Fayd Si. Arabia 27°1N 42°52E 44 E4
Fayette Ala., U.S.A. 33°41N 87°50W 85 E11
Fayette Mo., U.S.A. 39°9N 92°41W 80 F8
Fayette N.Y., U.S.A. 42°48N 76°48W 83 D8
Fayetteville Ark., U.S.A. 36°4N 94°10W 84 C7
Fayetteville N.C., U.S.A. 35°3N 78°53W 85 D15
Fayetteville N.Y., U.S.A. 43°1N 76°0W 83 C9
Fayetteville Tenn., U.S.A. 35°9N 86°34W 85 D11
Faylakah Kuwait 29°27N 48°20E 45 D6
Fazilka India 30°27N 74°2E 42 D6
Fazilpur Pakistan 29°18N 70°29E 42 E4
Fdérik Mauritania 22°40N 12°45W 50 D3
Feakle Ireland 52°56N 8°40W 10 D3
Feale → Ireland 52°27N 9°37W 10 D2
Fear, C. U.S.A. 33°50N 77°58W 85 E16
Feather → U.S.A. 38°47N 121°36W 76 G3
Feather Falls U.S.A. 39°36N 121°16W 78 F5
Featherston N.Z. 41°6S 175°20E 59 D5
Featherstone Zimbabwe 18°42S 30°55E 55 F3
Fécamp France 49°45N 0°22E 20 B4
Fedala = Mohammedia Morocco 33°44N 7°21W 50 B4
Federación Argentina 31°0S 57°55W 94 C4
Féderal Argentina 30°57S 58°48W 96 C5
Federal Way U.S.A. 47°18N 122°19W 78 C4
Fedeshkūh Iran 28°49N 53°50E 45 D7
Fehmarn Germany 54°27N 11°7E 16 A6
Fehmarn Bælt Europe 54°35N 11°20E 9 J14
Fehmarn Belt = Fehmarn Bælt Europe 54°35N 11°20E 9 J14
Fei Xian China 35°18N 117°59E 35 G9
Feijó Brazil 8°9S 70°21W 92 E4
Feilding N.Z. 40°13S 175°35E 59 D5
Feira de Santana Brazil 12°15S 38°57W 93 F11
Feixiang China 36°30N 114°45E 34 F8
Felanitx Spain 39°28N 3°9E 24 B10
Feldkirch Austria 47°15N 9°37E 16 E5
Félicité Seychelles 4°19S 55°52E 53 b
Felipe Carrillo Puerto Mexico 19°38N 88°3W 87 D7
Felixburg Zimbabwe 19°29S 30°51E 57 B5
Felixstowe U.K. 51°58N 1°23E 13 F9
Felton U.S.A. 37°3N 122°4W 78 H4
Femer Bælt = Fehmarn Bælt Europe 54°35N 11°20E 9 J14
Femunden Norway 62°10N 11°53E 8 E14
Fen He → China 35°36N 110°42E 34 G6
Fenelon Falls Canada 44°32N 78°45W 82 B6
Feng Xian Jiangsu, China 34°43N 116°35E 34 G9
Feng Xian Shaanxi, China 33°54N 106°40E 34 H4
Fengcheng China 40°28N 124°5E 35 D13
Fengfeng China 36°28N 114°8E 34 F8
Fengning China 41°10N 116°33E 34 D9
Fengqiu China 35°2N 114°25E 34 G8
Fengrun China 39°48N 118°8E 35 E10
Fengtai China 39°49N 116°14E 34 E9
Fengxiang China 34°29N 107°25E 34 G4
Fengyang China 32°51N 117°29E 35 H9
Fengzhen China 40°25N 113°2E 34 D7
Fenoarivo Fianarantsoa, Madag. 21°43S 46°24E 57 C8
Fenoarivo Fianarantsoa, Madag. 20°52S 46°53E 57 C8
Fenoarivo Afovoany Madag. 18°26S 46°34E 57 B8
Fenoarivo Atsinanana Madag. 17°22S 49°25E 57 B8
Fens, The U.K. 52°38N 0°2W 12 E7
Fenton U.S.A. 42°48N 83°42W 81 D12
Fenxi China 36°40N 111°31E 34 F6
Fenyang China 37°18N 111°48E 34 F6
Feodosiya Ukraine 45°2N 35°16E 19 E6
Ferbane Ireland 53°16N 7°50W 10 C4
Ferdows Iran 33°58N 58°2E 45 C8
Ferfer Somali Rep. 5°4N 45°9E 47 F4
Fergana = Farghona Uzbekistan 40°23N 71°19E 28 E8
Fergus Canada 43°43N 80°24W 82 C4
Fergus Falls U.S.A. 46°17N 96°4W 80 B5
Ferkéssédougou Ivory C. 9°35N 5°6W 50 G4
Ferland Canada 50°19N 88°27W 72 B2
Ferlo, Vallée du Senegal 15°15N 14°15W 50 E3
Fermanagh □ U.K. 54°21N 7°40W 10 B4
Fermo Italy 43°9N 13°43E 22 C5
Fermont Canada 52°47N 67°5W 73 B6
Fermoy Ireland 52°9N 8°16W 10 D3
Fernández Argentina 27°55S 63°50W 94 B3
Fernandina Beach U.S.A. 30°40N 81°27W 85 F14
Fernando de Noronha Brazil 4°0S 33°10W 93 D12
Fernando Póo = Bioko Eq. Guin. 3°30N 8°40E 52 D1
Ferndale Canada 44°58N 81°17W 82 B3
Ferndale U.S.A. 48°51N 122°36W 78 B4
Fernie Canada 49°30N 115°5W 70 D5
Fernlees Australia 23°51S 148°7E 62 C4
Fernley U.S.A. 39°36N 119°15W 76 G4
Fernwood U.S.A. 43°16N 73°38W 83 C11
Ferozepore = Firozpur India 30°55N 74°40E 42 D6
Ferrara Italy 44°50N 11°35E 22 B4
Ferreñafe Peru 6°42S 79°50W 92 E3
Ferrerías Spain 39°59N 4°1E 24 B11
Ferret, C. France 44°38N 1°15W 20 D3
Ferriday U.S.A. 31°38N 91°33W 84 F9
Ferrol Spain 43°29N 8°15W 21 A1
Ferron U.S.A. 39°5N 111°8W 76 G8
Ferrutx, C. de Spain 39°47N 3°21E 24 B10

Ferryland Canada 47°2N 52°53W 73 C9
Fertile U.S.A. 47°32N 96°17W 80 B5
Fès Morocco 34°0N 5°0W 50 B5
Fessenden U.S.A. 47°39N 99°38W 80 B4
Festus U.S.A. 38°13N 90°24W 80 F8
Feteşti Romania 44°22N 27°51E 17 F14
Fethiye Turkey 36°36N 29°6E 19 G4
Feuilles → Canada 58°47N 70°4W 69 F17
Fez = Fès Morocco 34°0N 5°0W 50 B5
Fezzan Libya 27°0N 13°0E 51 C8
Fiambalá Argentina 27°45S 67°37W 94 B2
Fianarantsoa Madag. 21°26S 47°5E 57 C8
Fianarantsoa □ Madag. 19°30S 47°0E 57 B8
Ficksburg S. Africa 28°51S 27°53E 57 D4
Field → Australia 23°48S 138°0E 62 C2
Field I. Australia 12°5S 132°23E 60 B5
Fier Albania 40°43N 19°33E 23 D8
Fife □ U.K. 56°16N 3°1W 11 E5
Fife → U.K. 56°15N 3°15W 11 E5
Fife Ness U.K. 56°17N 2°35W 11 E6
Fifth Cataract Sudan 18°22N 33°50E 51 E12
Figeac France 44°37N 2°2E 20 D5
Figtree Zimbabwe 20°22S 28°20E 55 G2
Figueira da Foz Portugal 40°7N 8°54W 21 B1
Figueres Spain 42°18N 2°58E 21 A7
Figuig Morocco 32°5N 1°11W 50 B5
Fihaonana Madag. 18°36S 47°12E 57 B8
Fiherenana Madag. 18°29S 48°24E 57 B8
Fiherenana → Madag. 23°19S 43°37E 57 C7
Fiji ■ Pac. Oc. 17°20S 179°0E 59 a
Filabusi Zimbabwe 20°34S 29°20E 57 C5
Filadelfia Paraguay 22°21S 60°2W 94 A3
Filchner Ice Shelf Antarctica 79°0S 40°0W 5 D1
Filey U.K. 54°12N 0°18W 12 C7
Filey B. U.K. 54°12N 0°15W 12 C7
Filfla Malta 35°47N 14°24E 25 D1
Filiatra Greece 37°9N 21°35E 23 F9
Filingué Niger 14°21N 3°22E 50 F6
Filipstad Sweden 59°43N 14°9E 9 G16
Fillmore Calif., U.S.A. 34°24N 118°55W 79 L8
Fillmore Utah, U.S.A. 38°58N 112°20W 76 G7
Fimbul Ice Shelf S. Ocean 69°30S 1°0W 5 C2
Finch Canada 45°11N 75°7W 83 A9
Finch Hatton Australia 20°25S 148°35E 62 C4
Findhorn → U.K. 57°38N 3°38W 11 D5
Findlay U.S.A. 41°2N 83°39W 81 E12
Fine U.S.A. 44°14N 75°8W 83 B9
Finger L. Canada 53°33N 93°30W 72 B1
Finger Lakes U.S.A. 42°40N 76°30W 83 D8
Fíngoè Mozam. 14°55S 31°50E 55 E3
Finisterre, C. = Fisterra, C. Spain 42°50N 9°19W 21 A1
Finke Australia 25°34S 134°35E 62 D1
Finke Gorge △ Australia 24°8S 132°49E 60 D5
Finland ■ Europe 63°0N 27°0E 8 E22
Finland, G. of Europe 60°0N 26°0E 9 G22
Finlay → Canada 57°0N 125°10W 70 B3
Finley Australia 35°38S 145°35E 63 F4
Finley U.S.A. 47°31N 97°50W 80 B5
Finn → Ireland 54°51N 7°28W 10 B4
Finnigan, Mt. Australia 15°49S 145°17E 62 B4
Finniss, C. Australia 33°8S 134°51E 63 E1
Finnmark Norway 69°37N 23°57E 8 B20
Finnsnes Norway 69°14N 18°0E 8 B18
Finspång Sweden 58°43N 15°47E 9 G16
Fiora → Italy 42°20N 11°34E 22 C4
Fiordland △ N.Z. 45°46S 167°0E 59 F1
Fīq Syria 32°46N 35°41E 46 C4
Firat = Furāt, Nahr al → Asia 31°0N 47°25E 44 D5
Fire Island △ U.S.A. 40°38N 73°8W 83 F11
Firebag → Canada 57°45N 111°21W 71 B6
Firebaugh U.S.A. 36°52N 120°27W 78 J6
Firedrake L. Canada 61°25N 104°30W 71 A8
Firenze Italy 43°46N 11°15E 22 C4
Firk, Sha'ib → Iraq 30°59N 44°34E 44 D5
Firozabad India 27°10N 78°25E 43 F8
Firozpur India 30°55N 74°40E 42 D6
Firozpur-Jhirka India 27°48N 76°57E 42 F7
Fīrūzābād Iran 28°52N 52°35E 45 D7
Fīrūzkūh Iran 35°50N 52°50E 45 C7
Firvale Canada 52°27N 126°13W 70 C3
Fish → Namibia 28°7S 17°10E 56 D2
Fish → Namibia 31°30S 20°16E 56 E3
Fish River Canyon Namibia 27°40S 17°35E 56 D2
Fisher B. Canada 51°35N 97°13W 71 C9
Fishers I. U.S.A. 41°15N 72°0W 83 E13
Fishguard U.K. 52°0N 4°58W 13 E3
Fishing L. Canada 52°10N 95°24W 71 C9
Fishkill U.S.A. 41°32N 73°54W 83 E11
Fisterra, C. Spain 42°50N 9°19W 21 A1
Fitchburg Mass., U.S.A. 42°35N 71°48W 83 D13
Fitchburg Wis., U.S.A. 42°58N 89°28W 80 D9
Fitz Roy Argentina 47°0S 67°0W 96 F3
Fitz Roy, Cerro Argentina 49°17S 73°5W 96 F2
Fitzgerald Canada 59°51N 111°36W 70 B6
Fitzgerald U.S.A. 31°43N 83°15W 85 F13
Fitzgerald River △ Australia 33°53S 119°55E 61 F3
Fitzmaurice → Australia 14°45S 130°5E 60 B5
Fitzroy → Queens., Australia 23°32S 150°52E 62 C5
Fitzroy → W. Austral., Australia 17°31S 123°35E 60 C3
Fitzroy Crossing Australia 18°9S 125°38E 60 C4
Fitzwilliam I. Canada 45°30N 81°45W 82 A3
Fiume = Rijeka Croatia 45°20N 14°21E 16 F8
Five Points U.S.A. 36°26N 120°6W 78 J6
Fizi Dem. Rep. of the Congo 4°17S 28°55E 54 C2
Flagstaff U.S.A. 35°12N 111°39W 77 J8
Flagstaff L. U.S.A. 45°12N 70°18W 83 A14
Flaherty I. Canada 56°15N 79°15W 72 A4
Flåm Norway 60°50N 7°7E 8 F12
Flambeau → U.S.A. 45°18N 91°14W 80 C8
Flamborough Hd. U.K. 54°7N 0°5W 12 C7
Flaming Gorge → U.S.A. 41°10N 109°25W 76 F9

Flaming Gorge Res. U.S.A. 41°10N 109°25W 76 F9
Flamingo, Teluk Indonesia 5°30S 138°0E 37 F9
Flanders = Flandre Europe 50°50N 2°30E 15 B9
Flandre Belgium 50°50N 2°30E 15 B9
Flandre-Occidentale = West-Vlaanderen □ Belgium 51°0N 3°0E 15 D2
Flandre-Orientale = Oost-Vlaanderen □ Belgium 51°5N 3°50E 15 C3
Flandreau U.S.A. 44°3N 96°36W 80 C5
Flanigan U.S.A. 40°10N 119°53W 78 E7
Flannan Is. U.K. 58°9N 7°52W 11 C1
Flåsjön Sweden 64°5N 15°40E 8 D16
Flat → Canada 61°33N 125°18W 70 A3
Flat I. Mauritius 19°53S 57°35E 53 d
Flathead L. U.S.A. 47°51N 114°8W 76 C6
Flattery, C. Australia 14°58S 145°21E 62 A4
Flattery, C. U.S.A. 48°23N 124°29W 78 B2
Flatwoods U.S.A. 38°31N 82°43W 81 F12
Fleetwood U.K. 53°55N 3°1W 12 D4
Fleetwood U.S.A. 40°27N 75°49W 83 F9
Flekkefjord Norway 58°18N 6°39E 9 G12
Flemington U.S.A. 41°7N 77°28W 82 E7
Flensburg Germany 54°47N 9°27E 16 A5
Flers France 48°47N 0°33W 20 B3
Flesherton Canada 44°16N 80°33W 82 B4
Flesko, Tanjung Indonesia 0°29N 124°30E 37 D6
Fleurieu Pen. Australia 35°40S 138°5E 63 F2
Flevoland □ Neths. 52°30N 5°30E 15 B5
Flin Flon Canada 54°46N 101°53W 71 C8
Flinders → Australia 17°36S 140°36E 62 B3
Flinders B. Australia 34°19S 115°19E 61 F2
Flinders Group Australia 14°11S 144°15E 62 A3
Flinders I. S. Austral., Australia 33°44S 134°41E 63 E1
Flinders I. Tas., Australia 40°0S 148°0E 63 G4
Flinders Ranges Australia 31°30S 138°30E 63 E2
Flinders Reefs Australia 17°37S 148°31E 62 B4
Florø Italy 44°13N 12°3E 22 B5
Flint U.K. 53°15N 3°8W 12 D4
Flint U.S.A. 43°1N 83°41W 81 D12
Flint → U.S.A. 30°57N 84°34W 85 F12
Flint I. Kiribati 11°26S 151°48W 65 J12
Flintshire □ U.K. 53°17N 3°17W 12 D4
Flodden U.K. 55°37N 2°8W 12 B5
Floodwood U.S.A. 46°56N 92°55W 80 B7
Flora U.S.A. 38°40N 88°29W 80 F9
Florala U.S.A. 31°0N 86°20W 85 F11
Florence = Firenze Italy 43°46N 11°15E 22 C4
Florence Ala., U.S.A. 34°48N 87°41W 85 D11
Florence Ariz., U.S.A. 33°2N 111°23W 77 K8
Florence Colo., U.S.A. 38°23N 105°8W 76 G2
Florence Oreg., U.S.A. 43°58N 124°7W 76 D1
Florence S.C., U.S.A. 34°12N 79°46W 85 D15
Florence, L. Australia 28°53S 138°9E 63 D2
Florencia Colombia 1°36N 75°36W 92 C3
Florennes Belgium 50°15N 4°35E 15 D4
Florenville Belgium 49°40N 5°19E 15 E5
Flores Azores 39°26N 31°13W 50 a
Flores Guatemala 16°59N 89°50W 88 C2
Flores Indonesia 8°35S 121°0E 37 F6
Flores I. Canada 49°20N 126°10W 70 D3
Flores Sea Indonesia 6°30S 120°0E 37 F6
Floreşti Moldova 47°53N 28°17E 17 E15
Floresville U.S.A. 29°8N 98°10W 84 G5
Floriano Brazil 6°50S 43°0W 93 E10
Florianópolis Brazil 27°30S 48°30W 95 B6
Florida Cuba 21°32N 78°14W 88 B4
Florida Uruguay 34°7S 56°10W 95 C4
Florida □ U.S.A. 28°0N 82°0W 85 G14
Florida, Straits of U.S.A. 25°0N 80°0W 88 B4
Florida B. U.S.A. 25°0N 80°45W 88 B3
Florida Keys U.S.A. 24°40N 81°0W 85 J14
Florin U.S.A. 38°30N 121°24W 78 G5
Florina Greece 40°48N 21°26E 23 D9
Florissant U.S.A. 38°47N 90°19W 80 F8
Florø Norway 61°35N 5°1E 8 F11
Flower Station Canada 45°10N 76°41W 83 A8
Flowerpot I. Canada 45°18N 81°38W 82 A3
Floydada U.S.A. 33°59N 101°20W 84 E4
Fluk Indonesia 1°42S 127°44E 37 E7
Flushing = Vlissingen Neths. 51°26N 3°34E 15 C3
Fly → Papua N. G. 8°25S 143°0E 58 B7
Flying Fish, C. Antarctica 72°6S 102°29W 5 D15
Foa Tonga 19°45S 174°18W 59 c
Foam Lake Canada 51°40N 103°32W 71 C8
Foça Turkey 38°39N 26°46E 23 E12
Fochabers U.K. 57°37N 3°6W 11 D5
Focşani Romania 45°41N 27°15E 17 F14
Fóggia Italy 41°27N 15°34E 22 D6
Fogo Canada 49°43N 54°17W 73 C9
Fogo C. Verde Is. 15°5N 24°20W 50 b
Fogo I. Canada 49°40N 54°5W 73 C9
Föhr Germany 54°43N 8°30E 16 A5
Foix France 42°58N 1°38E 20 E4
Folda Nord-Trøndelag, Norway 64°32N 10°30E 8 D14
Folda Nordland, Norway 67°38N 14°50E 8 C16
Foley Botswana 21°34S 27°21E 57 C4
Foley U.S.A. 30°24N 87°41W 85 F11
Foleyet Canada 48°15N 82°25W 72 C3
Folgefonna Norway 60°3N 6°23E 9 F12
Foligno Italy 42°57N 12°42E 22 C5
Folkestone U.K. 51°5N 1°12E 13 F9
Folkston U.S.A. 30°50N 82°0W 85 F13
Follansbee U.S.A. 40°19N 80°35W 82 F4
Folsom U.S.A. 38°42N 121°9W 78 G5
Fomboni Comoros Is. 12°18S 43°46E 53 a
Fond-du-Lac Canada 59°19N 107°12W 71 B7
Fond du Lac U.S.A. 43°47N 88°27W 80 D9
Fond-du-Lac → Canada 59°17N 106°0W 71 B7
Fonda U.S.A. 42°57N 74°22W 83 D10
Fondi Italy 41°21N 13°25E 22 D5
Fongafale Tuvalu 8°31S 179°13E 58 B10
Fonsagrada = A Fonsagrada Spain 43°8N 7°4W 21 A2

Fonseca, G. de Cent. Amer. 13°10N 87°40W 88 D2
Fontainebleau France 48°24N 2°40E 20 B5
Fontana U.S.A. 34°6N 117°26W 79 L9
Fontas → Canada 58°14N 121°48W 70 B4
Fontenay-le-Comte France 46°28N 0°48W 20 C3
Fontenelle Res. U.S.A. 42°1N 110°3E 78 E8
Fontur Iceland 66°23N 14°32W 8 C6
Fonualei Tonga 18°1S 174°19W 59 c
Foochow = Fuzhou China 26°5N 119°16E 33 D6
Foping China 33°41N 108°0E 34 H5
Foraker, Mt. U.S.A. 62°58N 151°24W 74 C9
Forbes Australia 33°22S 148°5E 63 E4
Forbesganj India 26°17N 87°18E 43 F12
Ford City Calif., U.S.A. 35°9N 119°27W 79 K7
Ford City Pa., U.S.A. 40°46N 79°32W 82 F5
Førde Norway 61°27N 5°53E 8 F11
Fords Bridge Australia 29°41S 145°29E 63 D4
Fordyce U.S.A. 33°49N 92°25W 84 E8
Forel, Mt. Greenland 66°52N 36°55W 66 C16
Foremost Canada 49°26N 111°34W 70 D6
Forest Canada 43°6N 82°0W 82 C2
Forest U.S.A. 32°22N 89°29W 85 E10
Forest City Iowa, U.S.A. 43°16N 93°39W 80 D7
Forest City N.C., U.S.A. 35°20N 81°52W 85 D14
Forest City Pa., U.S.A. 41°39N 75°28W 83 E9
Forest Grove U.S.A. 45°31N 123°7W 78 E3
Forestburg Canada 52°35N 112°1W 70 C6
Foresthill U.S.A. 39°1N 120°49W 78 F6
Forestier Pen. Australia 43°0S 148°0E 63 G4
Forestville Canada 48°48N 69°2W 73 C6
Forestville Calif., U.S.A. 38°28N 122°54W 78 G4
Forestville N.Y., U.S.A. 42°28N 79°10W 82 D5
Forfar U.K. 56°39N 2°53W 11 E6
Forillon △ Canada 48°46N 64°12W 73 C7
Forks U.S.A. 47°57N 124°23W 78 C2
Forksville U.S.A. 41°29N 76°35W 83 E8
Forlì Italy 44°13N 12°3E 22 B5
Forman U.S.A. 46°7N 97°38W 80 B5
Formby Pt. U.K. 53°33N 3°6W 12 D4
Formentera Spain 38°43N 1°27E 24 C7
Formentor, C. de Spain 39°58N 3°13E 24 B10
Formentor, Pen. de Spain 39°56N 3°11E 24 B10
Former Yugoslav Republic of Macedonia = Macedonia ■ Europe 41°53N 21°40E 23 D9
Fórmia Italy 41°15N 13°37E 22 D5
Formosa = Taiwan ■ Asia 23°30N 121°0E 33 D7
Formosa Argentina 26°15S 58°10W 94 B4
Formosa Brazil 15°32S 47°20W 93 G9
Formosa □ Argentina 25°0S 60°0W 94 B4
Formosa, Serra Brazil 12°0S 55°0W 93 F8
Formosa B. = Ungwana B. Kenya 2°45S 40°20E 54 C5
Fornells Spain 40°3N 4°7E 24 A11
Føroyar ☑ Atl. Oc. 62°0N 7°0W 8 F9
Forres U.K. 57°37N 3°37W 11 D5
Forrest Australia 30°51S 128°6E 61 F4
Forrest, Mt. Australia 24°48S 127°45E 61 D4
Forrest City U.S.A. 35°1N 90°47W 85 D9
Forsayth Australia 18°33S 143°34E 62 B3
Forssa Finland 60°49N 23°38E 8 F20
Forst Germany 51°45N 14°37E 16 C8
Forster Australia 32°12S 152°31E 63 E5
Forsyth U.S.A. 46°16N 106°41W 76 C10
Fort Abbas Pakistan 29°12N 72°52E 42 E5
Fort Albany Canada 52°15N 81°35W 72 B3
Fort Assiniboine Canada 54°20N 114°45W 70 C6
Fort Augustus U.K. 57°9N 4°42W 11 D4
Fort Beaufort S. Africa 32°46S 26°40E 56 E4
Fort Benton U.S.A. 47°49N 110°40W 76 C8
Fort Bragg U.S.A. 39°26N 123°48W 76 G2
Fort Bridger U.S.A. 41°19N 110°23W 76 F8
Fort Chipewyan Canada 58°42N 111°8W 71 B6
Fort Clatsop = Lewis and Clark △ U.S.A. 46°8N 123°53W 78 D3
Fort Collins U.S.A. 40°35N 105°5W 76 F11
Fort-Coulonge Canada 45°50N 76°45W 72 C4
Fort Covington U.S.A. 44°59N 74°29W 83 B10
Fort Dauphin = Taolanaro Madag. 25°2S 47°0E 57 D8
Fort Davis U.S.A. 30°35N 103°54W 84 F3
Fort-de-France Martinique 14°36N 61°2W 88 c
Fort Defiance U.S.A. 35°45N 109°5W 77 J9
Fort Dodge U.S.A. 42°30N 94°11W 80 D6
Fort Edward U.S.A. 43°16N 73°35W 83 C11
Fort Erie Canada 42°54N 78°56W 82 D6
Fort Fairfield U.S.A. 46°46N 67°50W 81 B20
Fort Frances Canada 48°36N 93°24W 71 D10
Fort Franklin = Déline Canada 65°11N 123°25W 68 C7
Fort Garland U.S.A. 37°26N 105°26W 77 H11
Fort George = Chisasibi Canada 53°50N 79°0W 72 B4
Fort Good Hope Canada 66°14N 128°40W 68 C7
Fort Hancock U.S.A. 31°18N 105°51W 84 F2
Fort Hope = Eabametoong Canada 51°30N 88°0W 72 B2
Fort Irwin U.S.A. 35°16N 116°41W 79 K10
Fort Kent U.S.A. 47°15N 68°36W 81 B19
Fort Klamath U.S.A. 42°42N 122°0W 76 D3
Fort Laramie U.S.A. 42°13N 104°31W 76 E11
Fort Lauderdale U.S.A. 26°7N 80°8W 85 H14
Fort Liard Canada 60°14N 123°30W 70 A4
Fort Liberté Haiti 19°42N 71°51W 89 C5
Fort Lupton U.S.A. 40°5N 104°49W 76 F11
Fort MacKay Canada 57°12N 111°41W 70 B6
Fort Macleod Canada 49°45N 113°30W 70 D6
Fort McMurray Canada 56°44N 111°7W 70 B6
Fort McPherson Canada 67°30N 134°55W 68 C5
Fort Madison U.S.A. 40°38N 91°27W 80 E8

Fort Meade U.S.A. 27°45N 81°48W 85 H14
Fort Morgan U.S.A. 40°15N 103°48W 76 F12
Fort Myers U.S.A. 26°39N 81°52W 85 H14
Fort Nelson Canada 58°50N 122°44W 70 B4
Fort Nelson → Canada 59°32N 124°0W 70 B4
Fort Norman = Tulita Canada 64°57N 125°30W 68 E6
Fort Payne U.S.A. 34°26N 85°43W 85 D12
Fort Peck U.S.A. 48°1N 106°27W 76 B10
Fort Peck Dam U.S.A. 48°0N 106°26W 76 C10
Fort Peck L. U.S.A. 48°0N 106°26W 76 C10
Fort Pierce U.S.A. 27°27N 80°20W 85 H14
Fort Pierre U.S.A. 44°21N 100°22W 80 C3
Fort Plain U.S.A. 42°56N 74°37W 83 D10
Fort Portal Uganda 0°40N 30°20E 54 B3
Fort Providence Canada 61°3N 117°40W 70 A5
Fort Qu'Appelle Canada 50°45N 103°50W 71 C8
Fort Resolution Canada 61°10N 113°40W 70 A6
Fort Rixon Zimbabwe 20°2S 29°17E 55 G2
Fort Ross U.S.A. 38°32N 123°13W 78 G3
Fort Rupert = Waskaganish Canada 51°30N 78°40W 72 B4
Fort St. James Canada 54°30N 124°10W 70 C4
Fort St. John Canada 56°15N 120°50W 70 B4
Fort Saskatchewan Canada 53°40N 113°15W 70 C6
Fort Scott U.S.A. 37°50N 94°42W 80 G6
Fort Severn Canada 56°0N 87°40W 72 A2
Fort Shevchenko Kazakhstan 44°35N 50°23E 19 F9
Fort Simpson Canada 61°45N 121°15W 70 A4
Fort Smith Canada 60°0N 111°51W 70 B6
Fort Smith U.S.A. 35°23N 94°25W 84 D7
Fort Stockton U.S.A. 30°53N 102°53W 84 F3
Fort Sumner U.S.A. 34°28N 104°15W 77 J11
Fort Thompson U.S.A. 44°3N 99°26W 80 C4
Fort Union △ U.S.A. 35°54N 105°1W 77 J11
Fort Valley U.S.A. 32°33N 83°53W 85 E13
Fort Vermilion Canada 58°24N 116°0W 70 B5
Fort Walton Beach U.S.A. 30°25N 86°36W 85 F11
Fort Ware Canada 57°26N 125°41W 70 B3
Fort Wayne U.S.A. 41°4N 85°9W 81 E11
Fort William U.K. 56°49N 5°7W 11 E3
Fort Worth U.S.A. 32°43N 97°19W 84 E6
Fort Yates U.S.A. 46°5N 100°38W 80 B3
Fort Yukon U.S.A. 66°34N 145°16W 68 D2
Fortaleza Brazil 3°45S 38°35W 93 D11
Forteau Canada 51°28N 56°58W 73 B8
Fortescue → Australia 21°0S 116°4E 60 D2
Fortescue River Roadhouse Australia 21°17S 116°8E 60 D2
Forth → U.K. 56°9N 3°50W 11 E5
Forth, Firth of U.K. 56°5N 2°55W 11 E6
Fortrose U.K. 57°35N 4°9W 11 D4
Fortuna Calif., U.S.A. 40°36N 124°9W 76 F1
Fortuna N. Dak., U.S.A. 48°55N 103°47W 80 A2
Fortune B. Canada 47°30N 55°22W 73 C8
Forūr Iran 26°17N 54°32E 45 E7
Fosen Norway 63°50N 10°20E 8 E14
Foshan China 23°6N 113°9E 33 D6
Fosnavåg Norway 62°22N 5°38E 8 E11
Fossano Italy 44°33N 7°43E 20 D7
Fossil U.S.A. 45°0N 120°9W 76 D3
Fossil Butte △ U.S.A. 41°50N 110°27W 76 F8
Foster Canada 45°17N 72°30W 83 A12
Foster → Canada 55°47N 105°49W 71 B7
Fosters Ra. Australia 21°35S 133°48E 62 C1
Fostoria U.S.A. 41°10N 83°25W 81 E12
Fotadrevo Madag. 24°3S 45°1E 57 C8
Fougères France 48°21N 1°14W 20 B3
Foul Pt. Sri Lanka 8°35N 81°18E 40 Q12
Foula U.K. 60°10N 2°5W 11 A6
Foulness I. U.K. 51°36N 0°55E 13 F8
Foulpointe Madag. 17°41S 49°31E 57 B8
Foumban Cameroon 5°45N 10°50E 52 C2
Foumbouni Comoros Is. 11°51S 43°29E 53 a
Fountain U.S.A. 38°41N 104°42W 76 G11
Fountain Hills U.S.A. 33°37N 111°43W 77 K8
Fountain Springs U.S.A. 35°54N 118°51W 79 K8
Four Mountains, Is. of U.S.A. 53°0N 170°0W 74 E5
Fouriesburg S. Africa 28°38S 28°14E 56 D4
Fourni Greece 37°36N 26°32E 23 F12
Fourth Cataract Sudan 18°47N 32°3E 51 E12
Fouta Djallon Guinea 11°20N 12°10W 50 F3
Foux, Cap-à- Haiti 19°43N 73°27W 89 C5
Foveaux Str. N.Z. 46°42S 168°10E 59 G2
Fowey U.K. 50°20N 4°39W 13 G3
Fowler Calif., U.S.A. 36°38N 119°41W 78 J7
Fowler Colo., U.S.A. 38°8N 104°2W 76 G11
Fowler, Pt. Australia 32°2S 132°3E 61 F5
Fowlers B. Australia 31°59S 132°34E 61 F5
Fowman Iran 37°13N 49°19E 45 B6
Fox → Canada 56°3N 93°18W 71 B10
Fox Creek Canada 54°24N 116°48W 70 C5
Fox Is. U.S.A. 53°0N 168°0W 74 E4
Fox Valley Canada 50°30N 109°25W 71 C7
Foxboro Canada 44°14N 77°26W 82 B7
Foxboro U.S.A. 42°4N 71°16W 83 D13
Foxdale Australia 20°22S 148°35E 62 b
Foxe Basin Canada 66°0N 77°0W 69 B12
Foxe Chan. Canada 65°0N 80°0W 69 B11
Foxe Pen. Canada 65°0N 76°0W 69 B12
Foxford Ireland 53°59N 9°7W 10 C2
Foxton N.Z. 40°29S 175°18E 59 D5
Foyle, Lough U.K. 55°7N 7°4W 10 A4
Foynes Ireland 52°37N 9°7W 10 D2
Foz do Cunene Angola 17°15S 11°48E 56 B1
Foz do Iguaçu Brazil 25°30S 54°30W 95 B5
Frackville U.S.A. 40°47N 76°14W 83 F8
Fraile Muerto Uruguay 32°31S 54°32E 95 C5
Framingham U.S.A. 42°18N 71°24W 83 D13
Franca Brazil 20°33S 47°30W 93 H9
Francavilla Fontana Italy 40°32N 17°35E 23 D7

France ■ Europe 47°N 3°0E 20 C5
Frances Australia 36°41S 140°55E 63 F3
Frances → Canada 60°16N 129°10W 70 A3
Frances L. Canada 61°23N 129°30W 70 A3
Franceville Gabon 1°40S 13°32E 52 E2
Francis Case, L. U.S.A. 43°4N 98°34W 80 D4
Francisco Beltrão Brazil 26°5S 53°4W 95 B5
Francisco Ignacio Madero
 Coahuila, Mexico 25°48N 103°18W 86 B4
Francisco Ignacio Madero Durango,
 Mexico 24°26N 104°18W 86 C4
Francisco Ignacio Madero, Presa
 Mexico 28°10N 105°37W 86 B3
Francistown Botswana 21°7S 27°33E 57 C4
François Canada 47°35N 56°45W 73 C8
François L. Canada 54°0N 125°30W 70 C3
François Peron △
 Australia 25°42S 113°33E 61 E1
Francs Pk. U.S.A. 43°58N 109°20W 76 E9
Franeker Neths. 53°12N 5°33E 15 A5
Frank Hann △ Australia 32°52S 120°19E 61 F3
Frankford Canada 44°12N 77°36W 82 B7
Frankford S. Africa 27°17S 28°30E 57 D4
Frankfort Ind., U.S.A. 40°17N 86°31W 80 E10
Frankfort Kans., U.S.A. 39°42N 96°25W 80 F5
Frankfort Ky., U.S.A. 38°12N 84°52W 81 F11
Frankfort N.Y., U.S.A. 43°2N 75°4W 83 C9
Frankfurt Brandenburg,
 Germany 52°20N 14°32E 16 B8
Frankfurt Hessen, Germany 50°7N 8°41E 16 C5
Fränkische Alb Germany 49°10N 11°23E 16 D6
Frankland → Australia 35°0S 116°48E 61 G2
Franklin Ky., U.S.A. 36°43N 86°35W 80 G10
Franklin La., U.S.A. 29°48N 91°30W 84 G9
Franklin Mass., U.S.A. 42°5N 71°24W 83 D13
Franklin N.H., U.S.A. 43°27N 71°39W 83 C13
Franklin N.Y., U.S.A. 42°20N 75°9W 83 D9
Franklin Nebr., U.S.A. 40°6N 98°57W 80 E4
Franklin Pa., U.S.A. 41°24N 79°50W 82 E5
Franklin Va., U.S.A. 36°41N 76°56W 81 G15
Franklin W. Va., U.S.A. 38°39N 79°20W 81 F14
Franklin B. Canada 69°45N 126°0W 68 D6
Franklin D. Roosevelt L.
 U.S.A. 48°18N 118°9W 76 B4
Franklin-Gordon Wild Rivers △
 Australia 42°19S 145°51E 63 G4
Franklin I. Antarctica 76°10S 168°30E 5 D11
Franklin I. Canada 45°24N 80°20W 82 A4
Franklin L. U.S.A. 40°25N 115°22W 76 F6
Franklin Mts. Canada 65°0N 125°0W 68 D6
Franklin Str. Canada 72°0N 96°0W 68 C12
Franklinton U.S.A. 30°51N 90°9W 85 F9
Franklinville U.S.A. 42°20N 78°27W 82 D6
Frankston Australia 38°8S 145°8E 63 F4
Fransfontein Namibia 20°12S 15°1E 56 C2
Frantsa Iosifa, Zemlya
 Russia 82°0N 55°0E 28 A6
Franz Canada 48°25N 84°30W 72 C3
Franz Josef Land = Frantsa Iosifa,
 Zemlya Russia 82°0N 55°0E 28 A6
Fraser U.S.A. 42°32N 82°57W 82 D2
Fraser → B.C., Canada 49°7N 123°11W 78 A3
Fraser → Nfld. & L.,
 Canada 56°39N 62°10W 73 A7
Fraser, Mt. Australia 25°35S 118°20E 61 E2
Fraser I. Australia 25°15S 153°10E 63 D5
Fraser Lake Canada 54°0N 124°50W 70 C4
Fraserburg S. Africa 31°55S 21°30E 56 E3
Fraserburgh U.K. 57°42N 2°1W 11 D6
Fraserdale Canada 49°55N 81°37W 72 C3
Fray Bentos Uruguay 33°10S 58°15W 94 C4
Fray Jorge △ Chile 30°42S 71°40W 94 C1
Frazier Downs ○
 Australia 18°48S 121°42E 60 C3
Fredericia Denmark 55°34N 9°45E 9 J13
Frederick Md., U.S.A. 39°25N 77°25W 81 F15
Frederick Okla., U.S.A. 34°23N 99°1W 84 D5
Frederick S. Dak., U.S.A. 45°50N 98°31W 80 C4
Fredericksburg Pa.,
 U.S.A. 40°27N 76°26W 83 F8
Fredericksburg Tex.,
 U.S.A. 30°16N 98°52W 84 F5
Fredericksburg Va.,
 U.S.A. 38°18N 77°28W 81 F15
Fredericktown Mo.,
 U.S.A. 37°34N 90°18W 80 G8
Fredericktown Ohio,
 U.S.A. 40°29N 82°33W 82 F2
Frederico Westphalen
 Brazil 27°22S 53°24W 95 B5
Fredericton Canada 45°57N 66°40W 73 C6
Fredericton Junction
 Canada 45°41N 66°40W 73 C6
Frederikshåb = Paamiut
 Greenland 62°0N 49°43W 4 C5
Frederikshamn = Hamina
 Finland 60°34N 27°12E 8 F22
Frederikshavn Denmark 57°28N 10°31E 9 H14
Frederiksted
 U.S. Virgin Is. 17°43N 64°53W 89 C7
Fredonia Ariz., U.S.A. 36°57N 112°32W 77 H7
Fredonia Kans., U.S.A. 37°32N 95°49W 80 G6
Fredonia N.Y., U.S.A. 42°26N 79°20W 82 D5
Fredrikstad Norway 59°13N 10°57E 9 G14
Free State □ S. Africa 28°30S 27°0E 56 D4
Freehold U.S.A. 40°16N 74°17W 83 F10
Freeland U.S.A. 41°1N 75°54W 83 E9
Freels, C. Nfld. & L.,
 Canada 49°15N 53°29W 73 C9
Freels, C. Nfld. & L.,
 Canada 46°37N 53°32W 73 C9
Freeman Calif., U.S.A. 35°35N 117°53W 79 K9
Freeman S. Dak., U.S.A. 43°21N 97°26W 80 D5
Freeport Bahamas 26°30N 78°47W 88 A4
Freeport Ill., U.S.A. 42°17N 89°36W 80 D9
Freeport N.Y., U.S.A. 40°39N 73°35W 83 F11
Freeport Ohio, U.S.A. 40°12N 81°15W 82 F3
Freeport Pa., U.S.A. 40°41N 79°41W 82 F5

Freeport Tex., U.S.A. 28°57N 95°21W 84 G7
Freetown S. Leone 8°30N 13°17W 50 G3
Freeville U.S.A. 42°30N 76°20W 83 D8
Frégate, L. de la Canada 53°15N 74°45W 72 B5
Fregenal de la Sierra
 Spain 38°10N 6°39W 21 C2
Fregon Australia 26°45S 132°1E 61 E5
Freibourg = Fribourg
 Switz. 46°49N 7°9E 20 C7
Freiburg Germany 47°59N 7°51E 16 E4
Freire Chile 38°54S 72°38W 96 D2
Freirina Chile 28°30S 71°10W 94 B1
Freising Germany 48°24N 11°45E 16 D6
Freistadt Austria 48°30N 14°30E 16 D8
Fréjus France 43°25N 6°44E 20 E7
Fremantle Australia 32°7S 115°47E 61 F2
Fremont Calif., U.S.A. 37°32N 121°57W 78 H4
Fremont Mich., U.S.A. 43°28N 85°57W 81 D11
Fremont Nebr., U.S.A. 41°26N 96°30W 80 E5
Fremont Ohio, U.S.A. 41°21N 83°7W 81 E12
Fremont → U.S.A. 38°24N 110°42W 76 G8
French Camp U.S.A. 37°53N 121°16W 78 H5
French Cays = Plana Cays
 Bahamas 22°38N 73°30W 89 B5
French Creek → U.S.A. 41°24N 79°50W 82 E5
French Frigate Shoals
 U.S.A. 23°45N 166°10W 75 L6
French Guiana ☑ S. Amer. 4°0N 53°0W 93 C8
French Polynesia ☑
 Pac. Oc. 20°0S 145°0W 65 J13
Frenchman Cr. →
 N. Amer. 48°31N 107°10W 76 B10
Frenchman Cr. →
 U.S.A. 40°14N 100°50W 80 E3
Fresco → Brazil 7°15S 51°30W 93 E8
Freshfield, C. Antarctica 68°25S 151°10E 5 C10
Fresnillo Mexico 23°10N 102°53W 86 C4
Fresno U.S.A. 36°44N 119°47W 78 J7
Fresno Res. U.S.A. 48°36N 109°57W 76 B9
Frew → Australia 20°0S 135°38E 62 C2
Frewsburg U.S.A. 42°3N 79°10W 82 D5
Freycinet △ Australia 42°11S 148°19E 63 G4
Freycinet Pen. Australia 42°10S 148°25E 63 G4
Fria Guinea 10°27N 13°38W 50 F3
Fria, C. Namibia 18°0S 12°0E 56 B1
Friant U.S.A. 36°59N 119°43W 78 J7
Frías Argentina 28°40S 65°5W 94 B2
Fribourg Switz. 46°49N 7°9E 20 C7
Friday Harbor U.S.A. 48°32N 123°1W 78 B3
Friedens U.S.A. 40°3N 78°59W 82 F6
Friedrichshafen Germany 47°39N 9°30E 16 E5
Friendship U.S.A. 42°12N 78°8W 82 D6
Friesland □ Neths. 53°5N 5°50E 15 A5
Frigate Seychelles 4°35S 55°56E 53 b
Frio → U.S.A. 28°26N 98°11W 84 G5
Frio, C. Brazil 22°50S 41°50W 90 F6
Friona U.S.A. 34°38N 102°43W 84 D3
Fritch U.S.A. 35°38N 101°36W 84 D4
Frobisher B. Canada 62°30N 66°0W 69 E18
Frobisher Bay = Iqaluit
 Canada 63°44N 68°31W 69 E18
Frobisher L. Canada 56°20N 108°15W 71 B7
Frohavet Norway 64°0N 9°30E 8 E13
Frome U.K. 51°14N 2°19W 13 F5
Frome → U.K. 50°41N 2°6W 13 G5
Frome, L. Australia 30°45S 139°45E 63 E2
Front Range U.S.A. 40°25N 105°45W 75 G18
Front Royal U.S.A. 38°55N 78°12W 81 F14
Frontenac △ Canada 44°32N 76°30W 83 B8
Frontera Canary Is. 27°47N 17°59W 24 G2
Frontera Mexico 18°32N 92°38W 87 D6
Fronteras Mexico 30°56N 109°31W 86 A3
Frosinone Italy 41°38N 13°19E 22 D5
Frostburg U.S.A. 39°39N 78°56W 81 F14
Frostisen Norway 68°14N 17°10E 8 B17
Froya Norway 63°43N 8°40E 8 E13
Frunze = Bishkek
 Kyrgyzstan 42°54N 74°46E 28 E8
Frutal Brazil 20°0S 49°0W 93 H9
Frýdek-Místek
 Czech Rep. 49°40N 18°20E 17 D10
Fryeburg U.S.A. 44°1N 70°59W 83 B14
Fu Xian = Wafangdian
 China 39°38N 121°58E 35 E11
Fu Xian China 36°0N 109°20E 34 G5
Fucheng China 37°50N 116°10E 34 F9
Fuchou = Fuzhou China 26°5N 119°16E 33 D6
Fuchū Japan 34°34N 133°14E 31 G6
Fuencaliente Canary Is. 28°28N 17°50W 24 F2
Fuencaliente, Pta.
 Canary Is. 28°27N 17°51W 24 F2
Fuengirola Spain 36°32N 4°41W 21 D3
Fuentes de Oñoro Spain 40°33N 6°52W 21 B2
Fuerte → Mexico 25°54N 109°22W 86 B3
Fuerte Olimpo Paraguay 21°0S 57°51W 94 A4
Fuerteventura Canary Is. 28°30N 14°0W 24 F6
Fuerteventura ✈ (FUE)
 Canary Is. 28°24N 13°52W 24 F6
Fufeng China 34°22N 108°0E 34 G5
Fugou China 34°3N 114°25E 34 G8
Fugu China 39°2N 111°3E 34 E6
Fuhai China 47°2N 87°25E 32 B3
Fuḩaymī Iraq 34°16N 42°10E 44 C4
Fuji Japan 35°9N 138°39E 31 G9
Fuji-Hakone-Izu △
 Japan 35°15N 138°45E 31 G9
Fuji-San Japan 35°22N 138°44E 31 G9
Fuji-Yoshida Japan 35°30N 138°46E 31 G9
Fujian □ China 26°0N 118°0E 33 D6
Fujinomiya Japan 35°10N 138°40E 31 G9
Fujisawa Japan 35°22N 139°29E 31 G9
Fujiyama, Mt. = Fuji-San
 Japan 35°22N 138°44E 31 G9
Fukagawa Japan 43°43N 142°2E 30 C11
Fukien = Fujian □ China 26°0N 118°0E 33 D6
Fukuchiyama Japan 35°19N 135°9E 31 G7
Fukue-Shima Japan 32°40N 128°45E 31 H4
Fukui Japan 36°5N 136°10E 31 F8
Fukui □ Japan 36°0N 136°12E 31 G8

Fukuoka Japan 33°39N 130°21E 31 H5
Fukuoka □ Japan 33°30N 131°0E 31 H5
Fukushima Japan 37°44N 140°28E 30 F10
Fukushima □ Japan 37°30N 140°15E 30 F10
Fukuyama Japan 34°35N 133°20E 31 G6
Fulaga Fiji 19°8S 178°33W 59 a
Fulda Germany 50°32N 9°40E 16 C5
Fulda → Germany 51°25N 9°39E 16 C5
Fulford Harbour
 Canada 48°47N 123°27W 78 B3
Fullerton Calif., U.S.A. 33°53N 117°56W 79 M9
Fullerton Nebr., U.S.A. 41°22N 97°58W 80 E5
Fulongquan China 44°20N 124°42E 35 B13
Fulton Mo., U.S.A. 38°52N 91°57W 80 F8
Fulton N.Y., U.S.A. 43°19N 76°25W 83 C8
Funabashi Japan 35°45N 140°0E 31 G10
Funafuti = Fongafale
 Tuvalu 8°31S 179°13E 58 B10
Funchal Madeira 32°38N 16°54W 24 D3
Funchal ✈ (FNC)
 Madeira 32°42N 16°45W 24 D3
Fundación Colombia 10°31N 74°11W 92 A4
Fundão Portugal 40°8N 7°30W 21 B2
Fundy, B. of Canada 45°0N 66°0W 73 D6
Fundy △ Canada 45°35N 65°10W 73 C6
Funhalouro Mozam. 23°3S 34°25E 57 C5
Funing Hebei, China 39°53N 119°12E 35 E10
Funing Jiangsu, China 33°45N 119°50E 35 H10
Funiu Shan China 33°30N 112°20E 34 H7
Funtua Nigeria 11°30N 7°18E 50 F7
Fuping Hebei, China 38°48N 114°12E 34 E8
Fuping Shaanxi, China 34°42N 109°10E 34 G5
Furano Japan 43°21N 142°23E 30 C11
Furāt, Nahr al → Asia 31°0N 47°25E 44 D5
Furbero Mexico 20°22N 97°45W 87 C5
Fürg Iran 28°18N 55°13E 45 D7
Furnás Spain 39°3N 1°32E 24 B8
Furnas, Represa de
 Brazil 20°50S 45°30W 95 A6
Furneaux Group
 Australia 40°10S 147°50E 63 G4
Furqlus Syria 34°36N 37°8E 46 A6
Fürstenwalde Germany 52°22N 14°3E 16 B8
Fürth Germany 49°28N 10°59E 16 D6
Furukawa Japan 38°34N 140°58E 30 E10
Fury and Hecla Str.
 Canada 69°56N 84°0W 69 D15
Fusagasugá Colombia 4°21N 74°22W 92 C4
Fushan Shandong,
 China 37°30N 121°15E 35 F11
Fushan Shanxi, China 35°58N 111°51E 34 G6
Fushun China 41°50N 123°56E 35 D12
Fusong China 42°20N 127°15E 35 C14
Fustic Barbados 13°16N 59°38W 89 g
Futian China 22°32N 114°4E 33 F11
Fuxin China 42°5N 121°48E 35 C11
Fuyang China 33°0N 115°48E 34 H8
Fuyang He → China 38°12N 117°0E 34 E9
Fuyong China 22°40N 113°49E 33 F10
Fuyu Heilongjiang, China 47°49N 124°27E 33 B7
Fuyu Jilin, China 45°12N 124°43E 35 B13
Fuyun China 47°0N 89°28E 32 B3
Fuzhou China 26°5N 119°16E 33 D6
Fylde U.K. 53°50N 2°58W 12 D5
Fyn Denmark 55°20N 10°30E 9 J14
Fyne, L. U.K. 55°59N 5°23W 11 F3

G

Gaalkacyo Somali Rep. 6°30N 47°30E 47 F4
Gabba Australia 9°45S 142°38E 62 a
Gabela Angola 11°0S 14°24E 52 G2
Gabès Tunisia 33°53N 10°2E 51 B8
Gabès, G. de Tunisia 34°0N 10°30E 51 B8
Gabon ■ Africa 0°10S 10°0E 52 E2
Gaborone Botswana 24°45S 25°57E 56 C4
Gabriels U.S.A. 44°26N 74°12W 83 B10
Gābrīk Iran 25°44N 58°28E 45 E8
Gabrovo Bulgaria 42°52N 25°19E 23 C11
Gāch Sār Iran 36°7N 51°19E 45 B6
Gachsārān Iran 30°15N 50°45E 45 D6
Gadag India 15°30N 75°45E 40 M9
Gadap Pakistan 25°5N 67°28E 42 G2
Gadarwara India 22°50N 78°50E 43 H8
Gadhada India 22°0N 71°35E 42 J4
Gadra Pakistan 25°40N 70°38E 42 G4
Gadsden U.S.A. 34°1N 86°1W 85 D11
Gadwal India 16°10N 77°50E 40 L10
Gaffney U.S.A. 35°5N 81°39W 85 D14
Gafsa Tunisia 34°24N 8°43E 50 B7
Gagaria India 25°43N 70°46E 42 G4
Găgăuzia □ Moldova 46°10N 28°40E 17 E15
Gagnoa Ivory C. 6°56N 5°16W 50 G4
Gagnon Canada 51°50N 68°5W 73 B6
Gagnon, L. Canada 62°3N 110°27W 71 A6
Gahini Rwanda 1°50S 30°30E 54 C3
Gahmar India 25°27N 83°49E 43 G10
Gai Xian = Gaizhou
 China 40°22N 122°20E 35 D12
Gaidouronisi Greece 34°53N 25°41E 25 E7
Gail → U.S.A. 32°46N 101°27W 84 E4
Gaillimh = Galway Ireland 53°17N 9°3W 10 C2
Gaines U.S.A. 41°46N 77°35W 82 E7
Gainesville Fla., U.S.A. 29°40N 82°20W 85 G13
Gainesville Ga., U.S.A. 34°18N 83°50W 85 D13
Gainesville Mo., U.S.A. 36°36N 92°26W 80 G7
Gainesville Tex., U.S.A. 33°38N 97°8W 84 E6
Gainsborough U.K. 53°24N 0°46W 12 D7
Gairdner, L. Australia 31°30S 136°0E 63 E2
Gairloch U.K. 57°43N 5°41W 11 D3
Gairloch, L. U.K. 57°43N 5°45W 11 D3
Gaizhou China 40°22N 122°20E 35 D12
Gaj → Pakistan 26°26N 67°21E 42 F2
Gakuch Pakistan 36°7N 73°45E 43 A5
Galán, Cerro Argentina 25°55S 66°52W 94 B2
Galana → Kenya 3°9S 40°8E 54 C5
Galápagos = Colón, Arch. de
 Ecuador 0°0 91°0W 90 D1
Galapagos Fracture Zone
 Pac. Oc. 3°0N 110°0W 65 G17

Galapagos Rise Pac. Oc. 15°0S 95°0W 65 J18
Galashiels U.K. 55°37N 2°49W 11 F6
Galatea Cyprus 35°25N 34°4E 25 D13
Galați Romania 45°27N 28°2E 17 F15
Galatina Italy 40°10N 18°10E 23 D8
Galax U.S.A. 36°40N 80°56W 81 G13
Galcaio = Gaalkacyo
 Somali Rep. 6°30N 47°30E 47 F4
Galdhøpiggen Norway 61°38N 8°18E 8 F13
Galeana Chihuahua,
 Mexico 30°7N 107°38W 86 A3
Galeana Nuevo León,
 Mexico 24°50N 100°4W 86 B4
Galela Indonesia 1°50N 127°49E 37 D7
Galeota Pt. Trin. & Tob. 10°8N 60°59W 93 K16
Galera Pt. Trin. & Tob. 10°49N 60°54W 93 K16
Galesburg U.S.A. 40°57N 90°22W 80 E8
Galeton U.S.A. 41°44N 77°39W 82 E7
Galich Russia 58°22N 42°24E 18 C7
Galicia □ Spain 42°43N 7°45W 21 A2
Galilee = Hagalil Israel 32°53N 35°18E 46 C4
Galilee, L. Australia 22°20S 145°50E 62 C4
Galilee, Sea of = Yam Kinneret
 Israel 32°45N 35°35E 46 C4
Galina Pt. Jamaica 18°24N 76°58W 88 a
Galinoporni Cyprus 35°31N 34°18E 25 D13
Galion U.S.A. 40°44N 82°47W 82 F2
Galiuro Mts. U.S.A. 32°30N 110°20W 77 K8
Galiwinku Australia 12°2S 135°34E 62 A2
Gallan Hd. U.K. 58°15N 7°2W 11 C1
Gallatin U.S.A. 36°24N 86°27W 85 C11
Galle Sri Lanka 6°5N 80°10E 40 R12
Gállego → Spain 41°39N 0°51W 21 B5
Gallegos → Argentina 51°35S 69°0W 96 G3
Galley Hd. Ireland 51°32N 8°55W 10 E3
Gallinas, Pta. Colombia 12°28N 71°40W 92 A4
Gallipoli = Gelibolu
 Turkey 40°28N 26°43E 23 D12
Gallipoli Italy 40°3N 17°58E 23 D8
Gallipolis U.S.A. 38°49N 82°12W 81 F12
Gällivare Sweden 67°9N 20°40E 8 C19
Galloo I. U.S.A. 43°55N 76°25W 83 C8
Galloway U.K. 55°1N 4°29W 11 F4
Galloway, Mull of U.K. 54°39N 4°52W 11 G4
Galloway △ U.K. 55°0N 4°0W 11 F4
Gallup U.S.A. 35°32N 108°45W 77 J9
Galoya Sri Lanka 8°10N 80°55E 40 Q12
Galt U.S.A. 38°15N 121°18W 78 G5
Galty Mts. Ireland 52°22N 8°10W 10 D3
Galtymore Ireland 52°21N 8°11W 10 D3
Galugāh Iran 36°43N 53°48E 45 B7
Galva U.S.A. 41°10N 90°3W 80 E8
Galveston U.S.A. 29°18N 94°48W 84 G7
Galveston B. U.S.A. 29°36N 94°50W 84 G7
Gálvez Argentina 32°0S 61°14W 94 C3
Galway Ireland 53°17N 9°3W 10 C2
Galway □ Ireland 53°22N 9°1W 10 C2
Galway B. Ireland 53°13N 9°10W 10 C2
Gam → Vietnam 21°55N 105°12E 38 B5
Gamagōri Japan 34°50N 137°14E 31 G8
Gambat Pakistan 27°17N 68°26E 42 F3
Gambhir → India 26°58N 77°27E 42 F6
Gambia ■ W. Afr. 13°25N 16°0W 50 F2
Gambia → W. Afr. 13°28N 16°34W 50 F2
Gambier, C. Australia 11°56S 130°57E 60 B5
Gambier, Îs.
 French Polynesia 23°8S 134°58W 65 K14
Gambier Is. Australia 35°3S 136°30E 63 F2
Gambo Canada 48°47N 54°13W 73 C9
Gamboli Pakistan 29°53N 68°24E 42 E3
Gamboma Congo 1°55S 15°52E 52 E3
Gamka → S. Africa 33°18S 21°39E 56 E3
Gamkab → Namibia 28°4S 17°54E 56 D2
Gamlakarleby = Kokkola
 Finland 63°50N 23°8E 8 E20
Gammon → Canada 51°24N 95°44W 71 C9
Gammon Ranges △
 Australia 30°38S 139°8E 63 E2
Gamtoos → S. Africa 33°58S 25°1E 56 E4
Gan Jiang → China 29°15N 116°0E 33 D6
Ganado U.S.A. 35°43N 109°33W 77 J9
Gananoque Canada 44°20N 76°10W 83 B8
Ganāveh Iran 29°35N 50°35E 45 D6
Gäncä Azerbaijan 40°45N 46°20E 19 F8
Gancheng China 18°51N 108°37E 38 C7
Gand = Gent Belgium 51°2N 3°42E 15 C3
Ganda Angola 13°3S 14°35E 53 G2
Gandajika
 Dem. Rep. of the Congo 6°46S 23°58E 52 F4
Gandak → India 25°39N 85°13E 43 G11
Gandava Pakistan 28°32N 67°32E 42 E2
Gander Canada 48°58N 54°35W 73 C9
Gander L. Canada 48°58N 54°35W 73 C9
Ganderowe Falls
 Zimbabwe 17°20S 29°10E 55 F2
Gandhi Sagar India 24°40N 75°40E 42 G6
Gandhinagar India 23°15N 72°45E 42 H5
Gandia Spain 38°58N 0°9W 21 C5
Gando, Pta. Canary Is. 27°55N 15°22W 24 G4
Ganedidalem = Gani
 Indonesia 0°48S 128°14E 37 E7
Ganga → India 23°20N 90°30E 43 H14
Ganga Sagar India 21°38N 88°5E 43 J13
Gangan → India 28°38N 78°58E 43 E8
Ganganagar India 29°56N 73°56E 42 E5
Gangapur India 26°32N 76°49E 42 F7
Gangaw Burma 22°5N 94°5E 41 H19
Gangdisê Shan China 31°20N 81°0E 43 D9
Ganges = Ganga →
 India 23°20N 90°30E 43 H14
Ganges Canada 48°51N 123°31W 70 D4
Ganges, Mouths of the
 India 21°30N 90°0E 43 J14
Ganggyeong S. Korea 36°10N 127°0E 35 F14
Ganghwa S. Korea 37°45N 126°30E 35 F14
Gangneung S. Korea 37°45N 128°54E 35 F15
Gangoh India 29°46N 77°18E 42 E7

Gangotri India 30°50N 79°10E 43 D8
Gangotri △ India 30°50N 79°10E 43 D8
Gangseong S. Korea 38°24N 128°30E 35 E15
Gangtok India 27°20N 88°37E 41 F16
Gangu China 34°40N 105°15E 34 G3
Gangyao China 44°12N 126°37E 35 B14
Gani Indonesia 0°48S 128°14E 37 E7
Ganj India 27°45N 78°57E 43 F8
Gannett Peak U.S.A. 43°11N 109°39W 76 E9
Ganquan China 36°20N 109°20E 34 F5
Gansu □ China 36°0N 104°0E 34 G3
Ganta Liberia 7°15N 8°59W 50 G4
Gantheaume, C.
 Australia 36°4S 137°32E 63 F2
Gantheaume B.
 Australia 27°40S 114°10E 61 E1
Gantsevichi = Hantsavichy
 Belarus 52°49N 26°30E 17 B14
Ganyem = Genyem
 Indonesia 2°46S 140°12E 37 E10
Ganyu China 34°50N 119°8E 35 G10
Ganzhou China 25°51N 114°56E 33 D6
Gao Mali 16°15N 0°5W 50 E5
Gaomi China 36°20N 119°42E 35 F10
Gaoping China 35°45N 112°55E 34 G7
Gaotang China 36°50N 116°15E 34 F9
Gaoua Burkina Faso 10°20N 3°8W 50 F5
Gaoual Guinea 11°45N 13°25W 50 F3
Gaoxiong = Kaohsiung
 Taiwan 22°35N 120°16E 33 D7
Gaoyang China 38°40N 115°45E 34 E8
Gaoyou Hu China 32°45N 119°20E 35 H10
Gaoyuan China 37°8N 117°58E 35 F9
Gap France 44°33N 6°5E 20 D7
Gapat → India 24°30N 82°28E 43 G10
Gapuwiyak Australia 12°25S 135°43E 62 A2
Gar China 32°10N 79°58E 32 C2
Gara, L. Ireland 53°57N 8°26W 10 C3
Garabogazköl Aylagy
 Turkmenistan 41°0N 53°30E 19 F9
Garachico Canary Is. 28°22N 16°46W 24 F3
Garachiné Panama 8°0N 78°12W 88 E4
Garafia Canary Is. 28°48N 17°57W 24 F2
Garagum Turkmenistan 39°30N 60°0E 45 B8
Garah Australia 29°5S 149°38E 63 D4
Garajonay Canary Is. 28°7N 17°14W 24 F2
Garamba △
 Dem. Rep. of the Congo 4°10N 29°40E 54 B3
Garanhuns Brazil 8°50S 36°30W 93 E11
Garautha India 25°34N 79°18E 43 G8
Garawa ◎ Australia 16°43S 136°51E 62 B2
Garba Tula Kenya 0°30N 38°32E 54 B4
Garberville U.S.A. 40°6N 123°48W 76 F2
Garbiyang India 30°8N 80°54E 43 D9
Gard → France 43°51N 4°37E 20 E6
Garda, L. di Italy 45°40N 10°41E 22 B4
Garde L. Canada 62°50N 106°13W 71 A7
Garden City Ga., U.S.A. 32°6N 81°9W 85 E14
Garden City Kans.,
 U.S.A. 37°58N 100°53W 80 G3
Garden City Tex.,
 U.S.A. 31°52N 101°29W 84 F4
Garden Grove U.S.A. 33°47N 117°55W 79 M9
Gardēz Afghan. 33°37N 69°9E 42 C3
Gardiner Maine, U.S.A. 44°14N 69°47W 81 C19
Gardiner Mont., U.S.A. 45°2N 110°22W 76 D8
Gardiners I. U.S.A. 41°6N 72°6W 83 E12
Gardner U.S.A. 42°34N 71°59W 83 D13
Gardner Canal Canada 53°27N 128°8W 70 C3
Gardner Pinnacles
 U.S.A. 25°0N 167°55W 75 L6
Gardnerville U.S.A. 38°56N 119°45W 78 G7
Gardo = Qardho
 Somali Rep. 9°30N 49°6E 47 F4
Garey U.S.A. 34°53N 120°19W 79 L6
Garfield U.S.A. 47°1N 117°9W 76 C5
Garforth U.K. 53°47N 1°24W 12 D6
Gargantua, C. Canada 47°36N 85°2W 81 B11
Gargett Australia 21°9S 148°46E 62 b
Garibaldi △ Canada 49°50N 122°40W 70 D4
Gariep, L. S. Africa 30°40S 25°40E 56 E4
Garies S. Africa 30°32S 17°59E 56 E2
Garig Gunak Barlu △
 Australia 11°26S 131°58E 60 B5
Garigliano → Italy 41°13N 13°45E 22 D5
Garissa Kenya 0°25S 39°40E 54 C4
Garland Tex., U.S.A. 32°54N 96°38W 84 E6
Garland Utah, U.S.A. 41°45N 112°10W 76 F7
Garmāb Iran 35°25N 56°45E 45 C8
Garmisch-Partenkirchen
 Germany 47°30N 11°6E 16 E6
Garmsār Iran 35°20N 52°25E 45 C7
Garner U.S.A. 43°6N 93°36W 80 D7
Garnett U.S.A. 38°17N 95°14W 80 F6
Garo Hills India 25°30N 90°30E 43 G14
Garoe = Garoowe
 Somali Rep. 8°25N 48°33E 47 F4
Garoowe Somali Rep. 8°25N 48°33E 47 F4
Garot India 24°19N 75°41E 42 G6
Garoua Cameroon 9°19N 13°21E 51 G8
Garrauli India 25°5N 79°22E 43 G8
Garrison Mont., U.S.A. 46°31N 112°49W 76 C7
Garrison N. Dak., U.S.A. 47°40N 101°25W 80 B3
Garrison Res. = Sakakawea, L.
 U.S.A. 47°30N 101°25W 80 B3
Garron Pt. U.K. 55°3N 5°59W 11 A6
Garry → U.K. 56°44N 3°47W 11 E5
Garry, L. Canada 65°58N 100°18W 68 D11
Garryaga Turkmenistan 38°31N 56°29E 45 B8
Garsen Kenya 2°20S 40°5E 54 C5
Garson L. Canada 56°19N 110°2W 71 B6
Garstang U.K. 53°55N 2°46W 12 D5
Garu India 23°40N 84°14E 43 H11
Garub Namibia 26°37S 16°0E 56 D2
Garut Indonesia 7°14S 107°53E 37 G12
Garwa = Garoua
 Cameroon 9°19N 13°21E 51 G8

Garwa *India* 24°11N 83°47E **43** G10
Gary *U.S.A.* 41°36N 87°20W **80** E10
Garzê *China* 31°38N 100°1E **32** C5
Garzón *Colombia* 2°10N 75°40W **92** C3
Gas-San *Japan* 38°32N 140°1E **30** E10
Gasan Kuli = Esenguly
  Turkmenistan 37°37N 53°59E **28** F6
Gascogne *France* 43°45N 0°20E **20** E4
Gascogne, G. de *Europe* 44°0N 2°0W **20** D2
Gascony = Gascogne
  France 43°45N 0°20E **20** E4
Gascoyne ⇌ *Australia* 24°52S 113°37E **61** D1
Gascoyne Junction
  Australia 25°2S 115°17E **61** E2
Gashaka *Nigeria* 7°20N 11°29E **51** G8
Gasherbrum *Pakistan* 35°40N 76°40E **43** B7
Gashua *Nigeria* 12°54N 11°0E **51** F8
Gasparillo *Trin. & Tob.* 10°18N 61°26W **93** K15
Gaspé *Canada* 48°52N 64°30W **73** C7
Gaspé, C. de *Canada* 48°48N 64°7W **73** C7
Gaspé Pen. = Gaspésie, Pén. de la
  Canada 48°45N 65°40W **73** C6
Gaspésie, Pén. de la
  Canada 48°45N 65°40W **73** C6
Gaspésie △ *Canada* 48°55N 66°10W **73** C6
Gasteiz = Vitoria-Gasteiz
  Spain 42°50N 2°41W **21** A4
Gastonia *U.S.A.* 35°16N 81°11W **85** D14
Gastre *Argentina* 42°20S 69°15W **96** E3
Gata, C. *Cyprus* 34°34N 33°2E **25** E12
Gata, C. de *Spain* 36°41N 2°13W **21** D4
Gata, Sierra de *Spain* 40°20N 6°45W **21** B2
Gataga ⇌ *Canada* 58°35N 126°59W **70** B3
Gatchina *Russia* 59°35N 30°9E **9** G24
Gatehouse of Fleet *U.K.* 54°53N 4°12W **11** G4
Gates *U.S.A.* 43°9N 77°42W **82** C7
Gateshead *U.K.* 54°57N 1°35W **12** C6
Gateshead I. *Canada* 70°36N 100°26W **68** C11
Gatesville *U.S.A.* 31°26N 97°45W **84** F6
Gateway ⇌ *U.S.A.* 40°38N 73°51W **83** F11
Gaths *Zimbabwe* 20°2S 30°32E **55** G3
Gatineau *Canada* 45°29N 75°39W **83** A9
Gatineau ⇌ *Canada* 45°27N 75°42W **72** C4
Gatineau △ *Canada* 45°40N 76°0W **72** C4
Gatton *Australia* 27°32S 152°17E **63** D5
Gatún, L. *Panama* 9°7N 79°56W **88** E4
Gatwick, London ✈ (LGW)
  U.K. 51°10N 0°11W **13** F7
Gatyana *S. Africa* 32°16S 28°31E **57** E4
Gau *Fiji* 18°2S 179°18E **59** a
Gauer L. *Canada* 57°0N 97°50W **71** B9
Gauhati = Guwahati
  India 26°10N 91°45E **41** F17
Gauja ⇌ *Latvia* 57°10N 24°16E **9** H21
Gaujas △ *Latvia* 57°10N 24°50E **9** H21
Gaula ⇌ *Norway* 63°21N 10°14E **8** E14
Gauri Phanta *India* 28°41N 80°36E **43** E9
Gaustatoppen *Norway* 59°48N 8°40E **9** G13
Gauteng □ *S. Africa* 26°0S 28°0E **57** D4
Gāv Koshī *Iran* 28°38N 57°12E **45** D8
Gāvakān *Iran* 29°37N 53°10E **45** D7
Gavāter *Iran* 25°10N 61°31E **45** E9
Gāvbandī *Iran* 27°12N 53°4E **45** E7
Gavdopoula *Greece* 34°56N 24°0E **25** E6
Gavdos *Greece* 34°50N 24°5E **25** E6
Gaviota *U.S.A.* 34°29N 120°13W **79** L6
Gāvkhūnī, Bāṭlāq-e *Iran* 32°6N 52°52E **45** C7
Gävle *Sweden* 60°40N 17°9E **8** F17
Gawachab *Namibia* 27°4S 17°55E **56** D2
Gawilgarh Hills *India* 21°15N 76°45E **40** J10
Gawler *Australia* 34°30S 138°42E **63** E2
Gawler Ranges
  Australia 32°30S 135°45E **63** E2
Gaxun Nur *China* 42°22N 100°30E **32** B5
Gay *Russia* 51°27N 58°27E **18** D10
Gaya *India* 24°47N 85°4E **43** G11
Gaya *Niger* 11°52N 3°28E **50** F6
Gaylord *U.S.A.* 45°2N 84°41W **81** C11
Gayndah *Australia* 25°35S 151°32E **63** D5
Gaysin = Haysyn
  Ukraine 48°57N 29°25E **17** D15
Gayvoron = Hayvoron
  Ukraine 48°22N 29°52E **17** D15
Gaza *Gaza Strip* 31°30N 34°28E **46** D3
Gaza □ *Mozam.* 23°10S 32°45E **57** C5
Gaza Strip □ *Asia* 31°29N 34°25E **46** D3
Gazanjyk = Bereket
  Turkmenistan 39°16N 55°32E **45** B7
Gāzbor *Iran* 28°5N 58°51E **45** D8
Gazi *Dem. Rep. of the Congo* 1°3N 24°30E **54** B1
Gaziantep *Turkey* 37°6N 37°23E **44** B3
Gazimağusa = Famagusta
  Cyprus 35°8N 33°55E **25** D12
Gbadolite
  Dem. Rep. of the Congo 4°17N 21°1E **52** D4
Gbarnga *Liberia* 7°19N 9°13W **50** G4
Gcoverega *Botswana* 19°8S 24°18E **56** B3
Gcuwa *S. Africa* 32°20S 28°11E **57** E4
Gdańsk *Poland* 54°22N 18°40E **17** A10
Gdańska, Zatoka
  Poland 54°30N 19°20E **17** A10
Gdov *Russia* 58°48N 27°55E **9** G22
Gdynia *Poland* 54°35N 18°33E **17** A10
Gebe *Indonesia* 0°5N 129°25E **37** D7
Gebze *Turkey* 40°47N 29°25E **23** D13
Gedaref *Sudan* 14°2N 35°28E **51** F13
Gediz ⇌ *Turkey* 38°35N 26°48E **23** E12
Gedser *Denmark* 54°35N 11°55E **9** J14
Gedung, Pulau *Malaysia* 5°17N 100°23E **39** c
Geegully Cr. ⇌
  Australia 18°32S 123°41E **60** C3
Geel *Belgium* 51°10N 4°59E **15** C4
Geelong *Australia* 38°10S 144°22E **63** F3
Geelvink B. = Cenderawasih, Teluk
  Indonesia 3°0S 135°20E **37** E9
Geelvink Chan. *Australia* 28°30S 114°0E **61** E1
Geesthacht *Germany* 53°26N 10°22E **16** B6
Geidam *Nigeria* 12°57N 11°57E **51** F8
Geikie ⇌ *Canada* 57°45N 103°52W **71** B8

Geikie Gorge △ *Australia* 18°3S 125°41E **60** C4
Geistown *U.S.A.* 40°18N 78°52W **82** F6
Geita *Tanzania* 2°48S 32°12E **54** C3
Gejiu *China* 23°20N 103°10E **32** D5
Gel, Meydān-e *Iran* 29°4N 54°50E **45** D7
Gela *Italy* 37°4N 14°15E **22** F6
Gelang Patah *Malaysia* 1°27N 103°35E **39** d
Gelderland □ *Neths.* 52°5N 6°10E **15** B6
Geldrop *Neths.* 51°25N 5°32E **15** C5
Geleen *Neths.* 50°57N 5°49E **15** D5
Gelib = Jilib *Somali Rep.* 0°29N 42°46E **47** G3
Gelibolu *Turkey* 40°28N 26°43E **23** D12
Gelsenkirchen *Germany* 51°32N 7°6E **16** C4
Gelugur *Malaysia* 5°22N 100°18E **39** c
Gemas *Malaysia* 2°37N 102°36E **39** L4
Gembloux *Belgium* 50°34N 4°43E **15** D4
Gemena
  Dem. Rep. of the Congo 3°13N 19°48E **52** D3
Gemerek *Turkey* 39°15N 36°10E **44** B3
Gemlik *Turkey* 40°26N 29°9E **23** D13
Gemsbok △ *Botswana* 25°5S 21°1E **56** D3
Genadi *Greece* 36°2N 27°56E **25** C9
Genale ⇌ *Ethiopia* 6°2N 39°1E **47** F2
General Acha *Argentina* 37°20S 64°38W **94** D3
General Alvear *B. Aires,*
  Argentina 36°0S 60°0W **94** D4
General Alvear *Mendoza,*
  Argentina 35°0S 67°40W **94** D2
General Artigas
  Paraguay 26°52S 56°16W **94** B4
General Belgrano
  Argentina 36°35S 58°47W **94** D4
General Bernardo O'Higgins
  Antarctica 63°0S 58°3W **5** C18
General Cabrera
  Argentina 32°53S 63°52W **94** C3
General Cepeda *Mexico* 25°21N 101°22W **86** B4
General Guido *Argentina* 36°40S 57°50W **94** D4
General Juan Madariaga
  Argentina 37°0S 57°0W **94** D4
General La Madrid
  Argentina 37°17S 61°20W **94** D3
General MacArthur
  Phil. 11°18N 125°28E **37** B7
General Martín Miguel de Güemes
  Argentina 24°50S 65°0W **94** A3
General Pico *Argentina* 35°45S 63°50W **94** D3
General Pinedo
  Argentina 27°15S 61°20W **94** B3
General Pinto *Argentina* 34°45S 61°50W **94** C3
General Roca *Argentina* 39°2S 67°35W **96** D3
General Santos *Phil.* 6°5N 125°14E **37** C7
General Treviño *Mexico* 26°14N 99°29W **87** B5
General Trías *Mexico* 28°21N 106°22W **86** B3
General Viamonte
  Argentina 35°1S 61°3W **94** D3
General Villegas *Argentina* 35°5S 63°0W **94** D3
Genesee *Idaho, U.S.A.* 46°33N 116°56W **76** C5
Genesee *Pa., U.S.A.* 41°59N 77°54W **82** E7
Genesee ⇌ *U.S.A.* 43°16N 77°36W **82** C7
Geneseo *Ill., U.S.A.* 41°27N 90°9W **80** E8
Geneseo *N.Y., U.S.A.* 42°48N 77°49W **82** D7
Geneva = Genève *Switz.* 46°12N 6°9E **20** C7
Geneva *Ala., U.S.A.* 31°2N 85°52W **85** F12
Geneva *N.Y., U.S.A.* 42°52N 76°59W **82** D8
Geneva *Nebr., U.S.A.* 40°32N 97°36W **80** E5
Geneva *Ohio, U.S.A.* 41°48N 80°57W **82** E4
Geneva, L. = Léman, L.
  Europe 46°26N 6°30E **20** C7
Genève *Switz.* 46°12N 6°9E **20** C7
Genil ⇌ *Spain* 37°42N 5°19W **21** D3
Genk *Belgium* 50°58N 5°32E **15** D5
Gennargentu, Mti. del
  Italy 40°1N 9°19E **22** D3
Genoa = Génova *Italy* 44°25N 8°57E **20** D8
Genoa *Australia* 37°29S 149°35E **63** F4
Genoa *N.Y., U.S.A.* 42°40N 76°32W **83** D8
Genoa *Nebr., U.S.A.* 41°27N 97°44W **80** E5
Genoa *Nev., U.S.A.* 39°2N 119°50W **78** F7
Génova *Italy* 44°25N 8°57E **20** D8
Génova, G. di *Italy* 44°0N 9°0E **22** C3
Genriyetty, Ostrov
  Russia 77°6N 156°30E **29** B16
Gent *Belgium* 51°2N 3°42E **15** C3
Genteng *Bali, Indonesia* 8°22S 114°9E **37** J17
Genteng *Jawa Barat,*
  Indonesia 7°22S 106°24E **37** G12
Genyem *Indonesia* 2°46S 140°12E **37** E10
Geochang *S. Korea* 35°41N 127°55E **35** G14
Geographe B. *Australia* 33°30S 115°15E **61** F2
Geographe Chan.
  Australia 24°30S 113°0E **61** D1
Georga, Zemlya *Russia* 80°30N 49°0E **28** A5
George *S. Africa* 33°58S 22°29E **56** E3
George ⇌ *Canada* 58°49N 66°10W **73** A6
George, L. *N.S.W.,*
  Australia 35°10S 149°25E **63** F4
George, L. *S. Austral.,*
  Australia 37°25S 140°0E **63** F3
George, L. *W. Austral.,*
  Australia 22°45S 123°40E **60** D3
George, L. *Uganda* 0°5N 30°10E **54** B3
George, L. *Fla., U.S.A.* 29°17N 81°36W **85** G14
George, L. *N.Y., U.S.A.* 43°37N 73°33W **83** C11
George Gill Ra.
  Australia 24°22S 131°45E **60** D5
George Pt. *Australia* 20°6S 148°36E **62** b
George River = Kangiqsualujjuaq
  Canada 58°30N 65°59W **69** F18
George Sound *N.Z.* 44°52S 167°25E **59** F1
George Town *Australia* 41°6S 146°49E **63** G4
George Town *Bahamas* 23°33N 75°47W **88** B4
George Town *Cayman Is.* 19°20N 81°24W **88** C3
George Town *Malaysia* 5°25N 100°20E **39** c
George V Land *Antarctica* 69°0S 148°0E **5** C10
George VI Sound
  Antarctica 71°0S 68°0W **5** D17
George West *U.S.A.* 28°20N 98°7W **84** G5
Georgetown = Janjanbureh
  Gambia 13°30N 14°47W **50** F3

Georgetown *Australia* 18°17S 143°33E **62** B3
Georgetown *Ont.,*
  Canada 43°40N 79°56W **82** C5
Georgetown *P.E.I.,*
  Canada 46°13N 62°24W **73** C7
Georgetown *Guyana* 6°50N 58°12W **92** B7
Georgetown *Calif.,*
  U.S.A. 38°54N 120°50W **78** G6
Georgetown *Colo.,*
  U.S.A. 39°42N 105°42W **76** G11
Georgetown *Ky., U.S.A.* 38°13N 84°33W **81** F11
Georgetown *N.Y.,*
  U.S.A. 42°46N 75°44W **83** D9
Georgetown *Ohio,*
  U.S.A. 38°52N 83°54W **81** F12
Georgetown *S.C.,*
  U.S.A. 33°23N 79°17W **85** E15
Georgetown *Tex., U.S.A.* 30°38N 97°41W **84** F6
Georgia □ *U.S.A.* 32°50N 83°15W **85** E13
Georgia ■ *Asia* 42°0N 43°0E **19** F7
Georgia, Str. of *N. Amer.* 49°25N 124°0W **78** A3
Georgia Basin *S. Ocean* 50°45S 35°30W **5** B1
Georgian B. *Canada* 45°15N 81°0W **82** A4
Georgian Bay Islands △
  Canada 44°53N 79°52W **82** B5
Georgievka *Kazakhstan* 49°19N 84°34E **28** E9
Georgina ⇌ *Australia* 23°30S 139°47E **62** C2
Georgina I. *Canada* 44°22N 79°17W **82** B5
Georgioupoli *Greece* 35°20N 24°15E **25** D6
Georgiyevsk *Russia* 44°12N 43°28E **19** F7
Gera *Germany* 50°53N 12°4E **16** C7
Geraardsbergen *Belgium* 50°45N 3°53E **15** D3
Geral, Serra *Brazil* 26°25S 50°0W **95** B6
Geral de Goiás, Serra
  Brazil 12°0S 46°0W **93** F9
Geraldine *U.S.A.* 47°36N 110°16W **76** C8
Geraldton *Australia* 28°48S 114°32E **61** E1
Geraldton *Canada* 49°44N 87°10W **72** C2
Gereshk *Afghan.* 31°47N 64°35E **40** D4
Gerdine, Mt. *U.S.A.* 61°35N 152°27W **74** C9
Gerik *Malaysia* 5°50N 101°15E **39** K3
Gering *U.S.A.* 41°50N 103°40W **80** E2
Gerlach *U.S.A.* 40°39N 119°21W **76** F4
German Bight = Deutsche Bucht
  Germany 54°15N 8°0E **16** A5
Germantown *U.S.A.* 35°5N 89°49W **85** D10
Germany ■ *Europe* 51°0N 10°0E **16** C6
Germí *Iran* 39°1N 48°3E **45** B6
Germiston *S. Africa* 26°13S 28°10E **57** D4
Gernika-Lumo *Spain* 43°19N 2°40W **21** A4
Gero *Japan* 35°48N 137°14E **31** G8
Gerokgak *Indonesia* 8°11S 114°27E **37** J17
Gerona = Girona *Spain* 41°58N 2°46E **21** B7
Geropotamos ⇌ *Greece* 35°3N 24°50E **25** D6
Gerrard *Canada* 50°30N 117°17W **70** C5
Gertak Sanggul *Malaysia* 5°17N 100°12E **39** c
Gertak Sanggul, Tanjung
  Malaysia 5°16N 100°11E **39** c
Gerung *Indonesia* 8°43S 116°7E **37** K19
Geser *Indonesia* 3°50S 130°54E **37** E8
Getafe *Spain* 40°18N 3°43W **21** B4
Gettysburg *Pa., U.S.A.* 39°50N 77°14W **81** F15
Gettysburg *S. Dak., U.S.A.* 45°1N 99°57W **80** C4
Getxo *Spain* 43°21N 2°59W **21** A4
Getz Ice Shelf *Antarctica* 75°0S 130°0W **5** D14
Geyser *U.S.A.* 47°16N 110°30W **76** C8
Geyserville *U.S.A.* 38°42N 122°54W **78** G4
Ghadāf, W. al ⇌ *Iraq* 32°56N 43°30E **44** C4
Ghadāmis *Libya* 30°11N 9°29E **51** B8
Ghaggar ⇌ *India* 29°30N 74°53E **42** E6
Ghaghara ⇌ *India* 25°45N 84°40E **43** G11
Ghaghat ⇌ *Bangla.* 25°19N 89°38E **43** G13
Ghagra *India* 23°17N 84°33E **43** H11
Ghagra ⇌ *India* 27°29N 81°9E **43** F9
Ghallamane *Mauritania* 23°15N 10°0W **50** D4
Ghana ■ *W. Afr.* 8°0N 1°0W **50** G5
Ghansor *India* 22°39N 80°1E **43** H9
Ghanzi *Botswana* 21°50S 21°34E **56** C3
Gharb Bahr el Ghazâl □
  Sudan 7°30N 27°30E **48** F5
Ghardaïa *Algeria* 32°20N 3°37E **50** B6
Gharm *Tajikistan* 39°0N 70°20E **28** F8
Gharyān *Libya* 32°10N 13°0E **51** B8
Ghat *Libya* 24°59N 10°11E **51** D8
Ghatal *India* 22°40N 87°46E **43** H12
Ghatampur *India* 26°8N 80°13E **43** F9
Ghats, Eastern *India* 14°0N 78°50E **40** N11
Ghats, Western *India* 14°0N 75°0E **40** N9
Ghatsila *India* 22°36N 86°29E **43** H12
Ghaṭṭī *Si. Arabia* 31°16N 37°31E **44** D3
Ghawdex = Gozo *Malta* 36°3N 14°15E **25** C1
Ghazal, Bahr el ⇌ *Chad* 13°0N 15°47E **51** F9
Ghazâl, Bahr el ⇌
  Sudan 9°31N 30°25E **51** G12
Ghaziabad *India* 28°42N 77°26E **42** E7
Ghazipur *India* 25°38N 83°35E **43** G10
Ghazni *Afghan.* 33°30N 68°28E **42** C3
Ghaznī □ *Afghan.* 32°10N 68°20E **40** C6
Ghent = Gent *Belgium* 51°2N 3°42E **15** C3
Gheorghe Gheorghiu-Dej = Oneşti
  Romania 46°17N 26°47E **17** E14
Ghīnah, Wādī al ⇌
  Si. Arabia 30°27N 38°14E **44** D3
Ghizar ⇌ *Pakistan* 36°15N 73°43E **43** A5
Ghotaru *India* 27°20N 70°1E **42** F4
Ghotki *Pakistan* 28°5N 69°21E **42** E3
Ghowr □ *Afghan.* 34°0N 64°20E **40** C4
Ghughri *India* 22°39N 80°41E **43** H9
Ghugus *India* 19°58N 79°12E **40** K11
Ghulam Mohammad Barrage
  Pakistan 25°30N 68°20E **42** G3
Ghūrīān *Afghan.* 34°17N 61°25E **40** B2
Gia Dinh *Vietnam* 10°49N 106°42E **39** G6
Gia Lai = Plei Ku
  Vietnam 13°57N 108°0E **38** F7
Gia Nghia *Vietnam* 11°58N 107°42E **39** G6
Gia Ngoc *Vietnam* 14°50N 108°58E **38** E7

Gia Vuc *Vietnam* 14°42N 108°34E **38** E7
Giamama = Jamaame
  Somali Rep. 0°4N 42°44E **47** G3
Gianitsa *Greece* 40°46N 22°24E **23** D10
Giant Forest *U.S.A.* 36°36N 118°43W **78** J8
Giant Sequoia △
  U.S.A. 36°10N 118°35W **78** K8
Giants Causeway *U.K.* 55°16N 6°29W **10** A5
Gianyar *Indonesia* 8°32S 115°20E **37** K18
Giarabub = Al Jaghbūb
  Libya 29°42N 24°38E **51** C10
Giarre *Italy* 37°43N 15°11E **22** F6
Gibara *Cuba* 21°9N 76°11W **88** B4
Gibbon *U.S.A.* 40°45N 98°51W **80** E4
Gibeon *Namibia* 25°9S 17°43E **56** D2
Gibraltar ☒ *Europe* 36°7N 5°22W **21** D3
Gibraltar, Str. of *Medit.* 35°55N 5°40W **21** E3
Gibraltar Range △
  Australia 29°31S 152°19E **63** D5
Gibson Desert *Australia* 24°0S 126°0E **60** D4
Gibsons *Canada* 49°24N 123°32W **70** D4
Gibsonville *U.S.A.* 39°46N 120°54W **78** F6
Giddings *U.S.A.* 30°11N 96°56W **84** F6
Giebnegáisi = Kebnekaise
  Sweden 67°53N 18°33E **8** C18
Giessen *Germany* 50°34N 8°41E **16** C5
Gīfān *Iran* 37°54N 57°28E **45** B8
Gift Lake *Canada* 55°53N 115°49W **70** B5
Gifu *Japan* 35°30N 136°45E **31** G8
Gifu □ *Japan* 35°40N 137°0E **31** G8
Giganta, Sa. de la
  Mexico 26°0N 111°39W **86** B2
Gigha *U.K.* 55°42N 5°44W **11** F3
Gíglio *Italy* 42°20N 10°52E **22** C4
Gijón *Spain* 43°32N 5°42W **21** A3
Gikongoro *Rwanda* 2°28S 29°34E **54** C2
Gil I. *Canada* 53°12N 129°15W **70** C3
Gila ⇌ *U.S.A.* 32°43N 114°33W **77** K6
Gila Bend *U.S.A.* 32°57N 112°43W **77** K7
Gila Bend Mts. *U.S.A.* 33°10N 113°0W **77** K7
Gila Cliff Dwellings △
  U.S.A. 33°12N 108°16W **77** K9
Gīlān □ *Iran* 37°0N 50°0E **45** B6
Gilbert ⇌ *Australia* 16°35S 141°15E **62** B3
Gilbert Is. *Kiribati* 1°0N 172°0E **58** A10
Gilbert River *Australia* 18°9S 142°52E **62** B3
Gilbert Seamounts
  Pac. Oc. 52°50N 150°10W **4** D18
Gilead *U.S.A.* 44°24N 70°59W **83** B14
Gilford I. *Canada* 50°40N 126°30W **70** C3
Gilgandra *Australia* 31°43S 148°39E **63** E4
Gilgil *Kenya* 0°30S 36°20E **54** C4
Gilgit *India* 35°50N 74°15E **43** B6
Gilgit ⇌ *Pakistan* 35°44N 74°37E **43** B6
Gili △ *Mozam.* 16°39S 38°27E **55** F4
Gilimanuk *Indonesia* 8°10S 114°26E **37** J17
Gillam *Canada* 56°20N 94°40W **71** B10
Gillen, L. *Australia* 26°11S 124°38E **61** E3
Gilles, L. *Australia* 32°50S 136°45E **63** E2
Gillette *U.S.A.* 44°18N 105°30W **76** D11
Gilliat *Australia* 20°40S 141°28E **62** C3
Gillingham *U.K.* 51°23N 0°33E **13** F8
Gilmer *U.S.A.* 32°44N 94°57W **84** E7
Gilmore, L. *Australia* 32°29S 121°37E **61** F3
Gilmour *Canada* 44°48N 77°37W **82** B7
Gilroy *U.S.A.* 37°1N 121°34W **78** H5
Gimcheon *S. Korea* 36°11N 128°4E **35** F15
Gimhae *S. Korea* 35°14N 128°53E **35** G15
Gimhwa *S. Korea* 38°17N 127°28E **35** E14
Gimie, Mt. *St. Lucia* 13°54N 61°0W **89** f
Gimje *S. Korea* 35°48N 126°45E **35** G14
Gimli *Canada* 50°40N 97°0W **71** C9
Gin Gin *Australia* 25°0S 151°58E **63** D5
Gingin *Australia* 31°22S 115°54E **61** F2
Gingindlovu *S. Africa* 29°2S 31°30E **57** D5
Ginir *Ethiopia* 7°6N 40°40E **47** F3
Giofyros ⇌ *Greece* 35°20N 25°6E **25** D7
Giohar = Jawhar
  Somali Rep. 2°48N 45°30E **47** G4
Giona, Oros *Greece* 38°38N 22°14E **23** E10
Gir □ *India* 21°0N 71°0E **42** J4
Gir Hills *India* 21°0N 71°0E **42** J4
Girab *India* 26°2N 70°38E **42** F4
Girāfi, W. ⇌ *Egypt* 29°58N 34°39E **46** F3
Girard *St. Lucia* 13°59N 60°57W **89** D7
Girard *Kans., U.S.A.* 37°31N 94°51W **80** G6
Girard *Ohio, U.S.A.* 41°9N 80°42W **82** E4
Girard *Pa., U.S.A.* 42°0N 80°19W **82** E4
Girdle Ness *U.K.* 57°9N 2°3W **11** D6
Giresun *Turkey* 40°55N 38°30E **19** F6
Girga *Egypt* 26°17N 31°55E **51** C12
Giri ⇌ *India* 30°28N 77°41E **42** D7
Giridih *India* 24°10N 86°21E **43** G12
Giriftu *Kenya* 1°59N 39°46E **54** B4
Giriyondo *S. Africa* 23°15S 31°40E **57** C5
Girne = Kyrenia *Cyprus* 35°20N 33°20E **25** D12
Giron = Kiruna *Sweden* 67°52N 20°15E **8** C19
Girona *Spain* 41°58N 2°46E **21** B7
Gironde ⇌ *France* 45°32N 1°7W **20** D3
Girvan *U.K.* 55°14N 4°51W **11** F4
Gisborne *N.Z.* 38°39S 178°5E **59** C7
Gisenyi *Rwanda* 1°41S 29°15E **54** C2
Gislaved *Sweden* 57°19N 13°32E **9** H15
Gitarama *Rwanda* 2°4S 29°45E **54** C2
Gitega *Burundi* 3°26S 29°56E **54** C2
Githio *Greece* 36°46N 22°34E **23** F10
Giuba = Juba ⇌
  Somali Rep. 1°30N 42°35E **47** G3
Giurgiu *Romania* 43°52N 25°57E **17** G13
Giza = El Giza *Egypt* 30°0N 31°12E **51** C12
Giza Pyramids *Egypt* 29°58N 31°9E **51** C12
Gīzab *Afghan.* 33°22N 66°17E **42** C1
Gizhiga *Russia* 62°3N 160°30E **29** C17
Gizhiginskaya Guba
  Russia 61°0N 158°0E **29** C16

Giżycko *Poland* 54°2N 21°48E **17** A11
Gjirokastër *Albania* 40°7N 20°10E **23** D9
Gjoa Haven *Canada* 68°38N 95°53W **68** D12
Gjøvik *Norway* 60°47N 10°43E **8** F14
Glace Bay *Canada* 46°11N 59°58W **73** C8
Glacier △ *U.S.A.* 51°15N 117°30W **70** C5
Glacier △ *U.S.A.* 48°42N 113°48W **76** B7
Glacier Bay *U.S.A.* 58°40N 136°0W **68** F4
Glacier Bay △ *U.S.A.* 58°45N 136°30W **70** B1
Glacier Peak *U.S.A.* 48°7N 121°7W **76** B3
Gladewater *U.S.A.* 32°33N 94°56W **84** E7
Gladstone *Queens.,*
  Australia 23°52S 151°16E **62** C5
Gladstone *S. Austral.,*
  Australia 33°15S 138°22E **63** E2
Gladstone *Canada* 50°13N 98°57W **71** C9
Gladstone *U.S.A.* 45°51N 87°1W **80** C10
Gladwin *U.S.A.* 43°59N 84°29W **81** D11
Glagah *Indonesia* 8°13S 114°18E **37** J17
Glåma = Glomma ⇌
  Norway 59°12N 10°57E **9** G14
Gláma *Iceland* 65°48N 23°0W **8** D2
Glamis *U.S.A.* 32°55N 115°5W **79** N11
Glamorgan, Vale of □
  U.K. 51°28N 3°25W **13** F4
Glasco *Kans., U.S.A.* 39°22N 97°50W **80** F5
Glasco *N.Y., U.S.A.* 42°3N 73°57W **83** D11
Glasgow *U.K.* 55°51N 4°15W **11** F4
Glasgow *Ky., U.S.A.* 37°0N 85°55W **81** G11
Glasgow *Mont., U.S.A.* 48°12N 106°38W **76** B10
Glasgow, City of □ *U.K.* 55°51N 4°12W **11** F4
Glasgow Int. ✈ (GLA)
  U.K. 55°51N 4°21W **11** F4
Glaslyn *Canada* 53°22N 108°21W **71** C7
Glastonbury *U.K.* 51°9N 2°43W **13** F5
Glastonbury *U.S.A.* 41°43N 72°37W **83** E12
Glazov *Russia* 58°9N 52°40E **18** C9
Gleichen *Canada* 50°52N 113°3W **70** C6
Gleiwitz = Gliwice
  Poland 50°22N 18°41E **17** C10
Glen *U.S.A.* 44°7N 71°11W **83** B13
Glen Affric *U.K.* 57°17N 5°1W **11** D3
Glen Canyon *U.S.A.* 37°30N 110°40W **77** H8
Glen Canyon △ *U.S.A.* 37°15N 111°0W **77** H8
Glen Canyon Dam
  U.S.A. 36°57N 111°29W **77** H8
Glen Coe *U.K.* 56°40N 5°0W **11** E3
Glen Cove *U.S.A.* 40°51N 73°38W **83** F11
Glen Garry *U.K.* 57°3N 5°7W **11** D3
Glen Innes *Australia* 29°44S 151°44E **63** D5
Glen Lyon *U.S.A.* 41°10N 76°5W **83** E8
Glen Mor *U.K.* 57°9N 4°37W **11** D4
Glen More △ *U.K.* 57°8N 3°40W **11** D5
Glen Moriston *U.K.* 57°11N 4°52W **11** D4
Glen Robertson *Canada* 45°22N 74°30W **83** A10
Glen Spean *U.K.* 56°53N 4°40W **11** E4
Glen Ullin *U.S.A.* 46°49N 101°50W **80** B3
Glenariff △ *Ireland* 55°2N 6°10W **10** A5
Glenbeigh *Ireland* 52°3N 9°58W **10** D2
Glencoe *Canada* 42°45N 81°43W **82** D3
Glencoe *S. Africa* 28°11S 30°11E **57** D5
Glencoe *U.S.A.* 44°46N 94°9W **80** C6
Glencolumbkille *Ireland* 54°43N 8°42W **10** B3
Glendale *Ariz., U.S.A.* 33°32N 112°11W **77** K7
Glendale *Calif., U.S.A.* 34°9N 118°15W **79** L8
Glendale *Zimbabwe* 17°22S 31°5E **55** F3
Glendive *U.S.A.* 47°7N 104°43W **76** C11
Glendo *U.S.A.* 42°30N 105°2W **76** E11
Glenelg ⇌ *Australia* 38°4S 140°59E **63** F3
Glenfield *U.S.A.* 43°43N 75°24W **83** C9
Glengad Hd. *Ireland* 55°20N 7°10W **10** A4
Glengarriff *Ireland* 51°45N 9°34W **10** E2
Glenmont *U.S.A.* 40°31N 82°6W **82** F2
Glenmorgan *Australia* 27°14S 149°42E **63** D4
Glenn *U.S.A.* 39°31N 122°1W **78** F4
Glennallen *U.S.A.* 62°7N 145°33W **68** E2
Glennamaddy *Ireland* 53°37N 8°33E **10** C3
Glenns Ferry *U.S.A.* 42°57N 115°18W **76** E6
Glenorchy *Australia* 42°49S 147°18E **63** G4
Glenore *Australia* 17°50S 141°12E **62** B3
Glenreagh *Australia* 30°2S 153°1E **63** E5
Glenrock *U.S.A.* 42°52N 105°52W **76** E11
Glenrothes *U.K.* 56°12N 3°10W **11** E5
Glens Falls *U.S.A.* 43°19N 73°39W **83** C11
Glenside *U.S.A.* 40°6N 75°9W **83** F9
Glenties *Ireland* 54°49N 8°16W **10** B3
Glenveagh △ *Ireland* 55°3N 8°1W **10** A3
Glenville *U.S.A.* 38°56N 80°50W **81** F13
Glenwood *Canada* 49°0N 54°58W **73** C9
Glenwood *Ark., U.S.A.* 34°20N 93°33W **84** D8
Glenwood *Iowa, U.S.A.* 41°3N 95°45W **80** E6
Glenwood *Minn., U.S.A.* 45°39N 95°23W **80** C6
Glenwood *Wash., U.S.A.* 46°1N 121°17W **78** D5
Glenwood Springs
  U.S.A. 39°33N 107°19W **76** G10
Glettinganes *Iceland* 65°30N 13°37W **8** D7
Glin *Ireland* 52°34N 9°17W **10** D2
Gliwice *Poland* 50°22N 18°41E **17** C10
Globe *U.S.A.* 33°24N 110°47W **77** K8
Głogów *Poland* 51°37N 16°5E **16** C9
Glomma ⇌ *Norway* 59°12N 10°57E **9** G14
Glorieuses, Îs. *Ind. Oc.* 11°30S 47°20E **57** A8
Glossop *U.K.* 53°27N 1°56W **12** D6
Gloucester *Australia* 32°0S 151°59E **63** E5
Gloucester *U.K.* 51°53N 2°15W **13** F5
Gloucester *U.S.A.* 42°37N 70°40W **83** D14
Gloucester I. *Australia* 20°0S 148°30E **62** b
Gloucester Island △
  Australia 20°2S 148°30E **62** b
Gloucester Point
  U.S.A. 37°15N 76°30W **81** G15
Gloucestershire □ *U.K.* 51°46N 1°59W **13** F5
Gloversville *U.S.A.* 43°3N 74°21W **83** C10
Glovertown *Canada* 48°40N 54°3W **73** C9
Glusk *Belarus* 52°53N 28°41E **17** B15
Gmünd *Austria* 48°45N 15°0E **16** D8
Gmunden *Austria* 47°55N 13°48E **16** E7
Gniezno *Poland* 52°30N 17°35E **17** B9

Gnowangerup *Australia* 33°58S 117°59E **61** F2
Go Cong *Vietnam* 10°22N 106°40E **39** G6
Gō-no-ura *Japan* 33°44N 129°40E **31** H4
Goa *India* 15°33N 73°59E **40** M8
Goa □ *India* 15°33N 73°59E **40** M8
Goalen Hd. *Australia* 36°33S 150°4E **63** F5
Goalpara *India* 26°10N 90°40E **41** F17
Goaltor *India* 22°43N 87°10E **43** H12
Goalundo Ghat *Bangla.* 23°50N 89°47E **43** H13
Goat Fell *U.K.* 55°38N 5°11W **11** F3
Goba *Ethiopia* 7°1N 39°59E **47** F2
Goba *Mozam.* 26°15S 32°13E **57** D5
Gobabis *Namibia* 22°30S 19°0E **56** C2
Gobi *Asia* 44°0N 110°0E **34** C6
Gobō *Japan* 33°53N 135°10E **31** H7
Gochas *Namibia* 24°59S 18°55E **56** C2
Godalming *U.K.* 51°11N 0°36W **13** F7
Godavari → *India* 16°25N 82°18E **41** L13
Godavari Pt. *India* 17°0N 82°20E **41** L13
Godbout *Canada* 49°20N 67°38W **73** C6
Godda *India* 24°50N 87°13E **43** G12
Goderich *Canada* 43°45N 81°41W **82** C3
Godfrey Ra. *Australia* 24°0S 117°0E **61** D2
Godhavn = Qeqertarsuaq
    Greenland 69°15N 53°38W **4** C5
Godhra *India* 22°49N 73°40E **42** H5
Godoy Cruz *Argentina* 32°56S 68°52W **94** C2
Gods → *Canada* 56°22N 92°51W **72** A1
Gods L. *Canada* 54°40N 94°15W **72** B1
Gods River *Canada* 54°50N 94°5W **71** C10
Godthåb = Nuuk
    Greenland 64°10N 51°35W **67** C14
Goeie Hoop, Kaap die = Good
    Hope, C. of *S. Africa* 34°24S 18°30E **56** E2
Goéland, L. au *Canada* 49°50N 76°48W **72** C4
Goélands, L. aux *Canada* 55°27N 64°17W **73** A7
Goeree *Neths.* 51°50N 4°0E **15** C3
Goes *Neths.* 51°30N 3°55E **15** C3
Goffstown *U.S.A.* 43°1N 71°36W **83** C13
Gogama *Canada* 47°35N 81°43W **72** C3
Gogebic, L. *U.S.A.* 46°30N 89°35W **80** B9
Gogra = Ghaghara →
    India 25°45N 84°40E **43** G11
Gogriâl *Sudan* 8°30N 28°8E **51** G11
Gohana *India* 29°8N 76°42E **42** E7
Goharganj *India* 23°1N 77°41E **42** H7
Goi → *India* 22°4N 74°46E **42** H6
Goiânia *Brazil* 16°43S 49°20W **93** G9
Goiás *Brazil* 15°55S 50°10W **93** G8
Goiás □ *Brazil* 12°10S 48°0W **93** F9
Goio-Erê *Brazil* 24°12S 53°1W **95** A5
Gojō *Japan* 34°21N 135°42E **31** G7
Gojra *Pakistan* 31°10N 72°40E **42** D5
Gökçeada *Turkey* 40°10N 25°50E **23** D11
Gökova Körfezi *Turkey* 36°55N 27°50E **23** F12
Göksu → *Turkey* 36°19N 34°5E **44** B2
Gokteik *Burma* 22°26N 97°0E **41** H20
Gokurt *Pakistan* 29°40N 67°26E **42** E2
Gokwe *Zimbabwe* 18°7S 28°58E **57** B4
Gola *India* 28°3N 80°32E **43** E9
Golakganj *India* 26°8N 89°52E **43** F13
Golan Heights = Hagolan
    Syria 33°0N 35°45E **46** C4
Golāshkerd *Iran* 27°59N 57°16E **45** E8
Golchikha *Russia* 71°45N 83°30E **4** B12
Golconda *U.S.A.* 40°58N 117°30W **76** F5
Gold *U.S.A.* 41°52N 77°50W **82** E7
Gold Beach *U.S.A.* 42°25N 124°25W **76** E1
Gold Coast *W. Afr.* 4°0N 1°40W **50** H5
Gold Hill *U.S.A.* 42°26N 123°3W **76** E2
Gold River *Canada* 49°46N 126°3W **70** D3
Golden *Canada* 51°20N 116°59W **70** C5
Golden B. *N.Z.* 40°40S 172°50E **59** D4
Golden Gate *U.S.A.* 37°48N 122°29W **77** H2
Golden Gate Highlands △
    S. Africa 28°40S 28°40E **57** D4
Golden Hinde *Canada* 49°40N 125°44W **70** D3
Golden Lake *Canada* 45°34N 77°21W **82** A7
Golden Spike △ *U.S.A.* 41°37N 112°33W **76** F7
Golden Vale *Ireland* 52°33N 8°17W **10** D3
Goldendale *U.S.A.* 45°49N 120°50W **76** D3
Goldfield *U.S.A.* 37°42N 117°14W **77** H5
Goldsand L. *Canada* 57°2N 101°8W **71** B8
Goldsboro *U.S.A.* 35°23N 77°59W **85** D16
Goldsmith *U.S.A.* 31°59N 102°37W **84** F3
Goldthwaite *U.S.A.* 31°27N 98°34W **84** F5
Goleniów *Poland* 53°35N 14°50E **16** B8
Golestān □ *Iran* 37°20N 55°25E **45** B7
Golestānak *Iran* 30°36N 54°14E **45** D7
Goleta *U.S.A.* 34°27N 119°50W **79** L7
Golfito *Costa Rica* 8°41N 83°5W **88** E3
Golfo Aranci *Italy* 40°59N 9°38E **22** D3
Goliad *U.S.A.* 28°40N 97°23W **84** G6
Golpāyegān *Iran* 33°27N 50°18E **45** C6
Golra *Pakistan* 33°37N 72°56E **42** C5
Golspie *U.K.* 57°58N 3°59W **11** D5
Goma
    Dem. Rep. of the Congo 1°37S 29°10E **54** C2
Gomal Pass *Pakistan* 31°56N 69°20E **42** D3
Gomati → *India* 25°32N 83°11E **43** G10
Gombari
    Dem. Rep. of the Congo 2°45N 29°3E **54** B2
Gombe *Nigeria* 10°19N 11°2E **51** F8
Gombe → *Tanzania* 4°38S 31°40E **54** C3
Gombe Stream △
    Tanzania 4°42S 29°37E **54** C2
Gomel = Homyel *Belarus* 52°28N 31°0E **17** B16
Gomera *Canary Is.* 28°7N 17°14W **24** F2
Gómez Palacio *Mexico* 25°34N 103°30W **86** B4
Gomīshān *Iran* 37°4N 54°6E **45** B7
Gomogomo *Indonesia* 6°39S 134°43E **37** F8
Gomoh *India* 23°52N 86°10E **43** H12
Gompa = Ganta *Liberia* 7°15N 8°59W **50** G4
Gonābād *Iran* 34°15N 58°45E **45** C8
Gonaïves *Haiti* 19°20N 72°42W **89** C5
Gonarezhou △ *Zimbabwe* 21°32S 31°55E **55** G3
Gonâve, G. de la *Haiti* 19°29N 72°42W **89** C5
Gonâve, Île de la *Haiti* 18°51N 73°3W **89** C5
Gonbad-e Kāvūs *Iran* 37°20N 55°25E **45** B7

Gonda *India* 27°9N 81°58E **43** F9
Gondal *India* 21°58N 70°52E **42** J4
Gonder *Ethiopia* 12°39N 37°30E **47** E2
Gondia *India* 21°23N 80°10E **40** J12
Gondola *Mozam.* 19°10S 33°37E **55** F3
Gönen *Turkey* 40°6N 27°39E **23** D12
Gongbei *China* 22°12N 113°32E **33** G10
Gonghe *China* 36°18N 100°32E **32** C5
Gongju *S. Korea* 36°37N 127°7E **35** F14
Gongming *China* 22°47N 113°53E **33** F10
Gongolgon *Australia* 30°21S 146°54E **63** E4
Gongzhuling *China* 43°30N 124°40E **35** C13
Goniri *Nigeria* 11°30N 12°15E **51** F8
Gonzales *Calif., U.S.A.* 36°30N 121°26W **78** J5
Gonzales *Tex., U.S.A.* 29°30N 97°27W **84** G6
González *Mexico* 22°50N 98°25W **87** C5
Good Hope, C. of *S. Africa* 34°24S 18°30E **56** E2
Good Hope Lake
    Canada 59°16N 129°18W **70** B3
Gooderham *Canada* 44°54N 78°21W **82** B6
Goodhouse *S. Africa* 28°57S 18°13E **56** D2
Gooding *U.S.A.* 42°56N 114°43W **76** E6
Goodland *U.S.A.* 39°21N 101°43W **80** F3
Goodlands *Mauritius* 20°2S 57°39E **53** d
Goodlow *Canada* 56°20N 120°8W **70** B4
Goodooga *Australia* 29°3S 147°28E **63** D4
Goodsprings *U.S.A.* 35°49N 115°27W **79** K11
Goole *U.K.* 53°42N 0°53W **12** D7
Goolgowi *Australia* 33°58S 145°41E **63** E4
Goomalling *Australia* 31°15S 116°49E **61** F2
Goomeri *Australia* 26°12S 152°6E **63** D5
Goonda *Mozam.* 19°48S 33°57E **55** F3
Goondiwindi *Australia* 28°30S 150°21E **63** D5
Goongarrie, L. *Australia* 30°3S 121°9E **61** F3
Goongarrie △ *Australia* 30°7S 121°30E **61** F3
Goonyella *Australia* 21°47S 147°58E **62** C4
Goose → *Canada* 53°20N 60°35W **73** B7
Goose Creek *U.S.A.* 32°59N 80°2W **85** E14
Goose L. *U.S.A.* 41°56N 120°26W **76** F3
Gop *India* 22°5N 69°50E **42** H3
Gopalganj *India* 26°28N 84°30E **43** F11
Göppingen *Germany* 48°42N 9°39E **16** D5
Gorakhpur *India* 26°47N 83°23E **43** F10
Goražde *Bos.-H.* 43°38N 18°58E **23** C8
Gorda, Pta. *Canada* 28°45N 18°0W **24** F2
Gorda, Pta. *Nic.* 14°20N 83°10W **88** D3
Gordan B. *Australia* 11°35S 130°10E **60** B5
Gordon *U.S.A.* 42°48N 102°12W **80** D2
Gordon → *Australia* 42°27S 145°30E **63** G4
Gordon Bay *Canada* 45°12N 79°47W **82** A5
Gordon L., *Alta., Canada* 56°30N 110°25W **71** B6
Gordon L. *N.W.T.,*
    Canada 63°5N 113°11W **70** A6
Gordonvale *Australia* 17°5S 145°50E **62** B4
Goré *Chad* 7°59N 16°31E **51** G9
Gore *Ethiopia* 8°12N 35°32E **47** F2
Gore *N.Z.* 46°5S 168°58E **59** G2
Gore Bay *Canada* 45°57N 82°28W **72** C3
Gorey *Ireland* 52°41N 6°18W **10** D5
Gorg *Iran* 29°29N 59°43E **45** D8
Gorgān *Iran* 36°55N 54°30E **45** B7
Gorgona, I. *Colombia* 3°0N 78°10W **92** C3
Gorham *U.S.A.* 44°23N 71°10W **83** B13
Goriganga → *India* 29°45N 80°23E **43** E9
Gorinchem *Neths.* 51°50N 4°59E **15** C4
Goris *Armenia* 39°31N 46°22E **19** G8
Gorízia *Italy* 45°56N 13°37E **22** B5
Gorkiy = Nizhniy Novgorod
    Russia 56°20N 44°0E **18** C7
Gorkovskoye Vdkhr.
    Russia 57°2N 43°4E **18** C7
Gorleston *U.K.* 52°35N 1°44E **13** E9
Görlitz *Germany* 51°9N 14°58E **16** C8
Gorlovka = Horlivka
    Ukraine 48°19N 38°5E **19** E6
Gorman *U.S.A.* 34°47N 118°51W **79** L8
Gorna Dzhumayo = Blagoevgrad
    Bulgaria 42°2N 23°5E **23** C10
Gorna Oryakhovitsa
    Bulgaria 43°7N 25°40E **23** C11
Gorno-Altay □ *Russia* 51°0N 86°0E **28** D9
Gorno-Altaysk *Russia* 51°50N 86°5E **28** D9
Gornozavodsk *Russia* 46°33N 141°50E **29** E15
Gornyatskiy *Russia* 67°32N 64°3E **18** A11
Gornyy *Russia* 44°57N 133°59E **30** B6
Gorodenka = Horodenka
    Ukraine 48°41N 25°29E **17** D13
Gorodok = Horodok
    Ukraine 49°46N 23°32E **17** D12
Gorokhov = Horokhiv
    Ukraine 50°30N 24°45E **17** C13
Goromonzi *Zimbabwe* 17°52S 31°22E **55** F3
Gorong, Kepulauan
    Indonesia 3°59S 131°25E **37** E8
Gorongosa △ *Mozam.* 18°50S 34°29E **57** B5
Gorongose → *Mozam.* 20°30S 34°40E **57** C5
Gorongoza *Mozam.* 18°44S 34°2E **55** F3
Gorongoza, Sa. da *Mozam.* 18°27S 34°2E **55** F3
Gorontalo *Indonesia* 0°35N 123°5E **37** D6
Gorontalo □ *Indonesia* 0°30N 123°0E **37** D6
Gort *Ireland* 53°3N 8°49W **10** C3
Gortis *Greece* 35°4N 24°58E **25** D6
Goryeong *S. Korea* 35°44N 128°15E **35** G15
Gorzów Wielkopolski
    Poland 52°43N 15°15E **16** B8
Gosford *Australia* 33°23S 151°18E **63** E5
Goshen *Calif., U.S.A.* 36°21N 119°25W **78** J7
Goshen *Ind., U.S.A.* 41°35N 85°50W **81** E11
Goshen *N.Y., U.S.A.* 41°24N 74°20W **83** E10
Goshogawara *Japan* 40°48N 140°27E **30** D10
Goslar *Germany* 51°54N 10°25E **16** C6
Gospić *Croatia* 44°35N 15°23E **16** F8
Gosport *U.K.* 50°48N 1°9W **13** G6
Gosse → *Australia* 19°32S 134°37E **62** B1
Göta älv → *Sweden* 57°42N 11°54E **9** H14
Göta kanal *Sweden* 58°30N 15°58E **9** G16
Götaland *Sweden* 57°30N 14°30E **9** H15
Göteborg *Sweden* 57°43N 11°59E **9** H14
Gotha *Germany* 50°56N 10°42E **16** C6

Gothenburg = Göteborg
    Sweden 57°43N 11°59E **9** H14
Gothenburg *U.S.A.* 40°56N 100°10W **80** E3
Gotland *Sweden* 57°30N 18°33E **9** H18
Gotō-Rettō *Japan* 32°55N 129°5E **31** H4
Göttingen *Germany* 51°31N 9°55E **16** C5
Gottwaldov = Zlin
    Czech Rep. 49°14N 17°40E **17** D9
Goubangzi *China* 41°20N 121°52E **35** D11
Gouda *Neths.* 52°1N 4°42E **15** B4
Goudouras, Akra *Greece* 34°59N 26°6E **25** E8
Gough I. *S. Ocean* 40°10S 9°45W **2** G9
Gouin, Rés. *Canada* 48°35N 74°40W **72** C5
Goulburn *Australia* 34°44S 149°44E **63** E4
Goulburn Is. *Australia* 11°40S 133°20E **62** A1
Goulimine *Morocco* 28°56N 10°0W **50** C3
Goundam *Mali* 16°27N 3°40W **50** E5
Gourits → *S. Africa* 34°21S 21°52E **56** E3
Gourock *U.K.* 55°57N 4°49W **11** F4
Gouverneur *U.S.A.* 44°20N 75°28W **83** B9
Gouvia *Greece* 39°39N 19°50E **25** A3
Gove Peninsula
    Australia 12°17S 136°49E **62** A2
Governador Valadares
    Brazil 18°15S 41°57W **93** G10
Governor's Harbour
    Bahamas 25°10N 76°14W **88** A4
Govindgarh *India* 24°23N 81°18E **43** G9
Gowan Ra. *Australia* 25°0S 145°0E **62** D4
Gowanda *U.S.A.* 42°28N 78°56W **82** D6
Gower *U.K.* 51°35N 4°10W **13** F3
Gowna, L. *Ireland* 53°51N 7°34W **10** C4
Goya *Argentina* 29°10S 59°10W **94** B4
Goyang *S. Korea* 37°39N 126°50E **33** C7
Goyder Lagoon *Australia* 27°3S 138°58E **63** D2
Goyllarisquizga *Peru* 10°31S 76°24W **92** F3
Goz Beïda *Chad* 12°10N 21°20E **51** F10
Gozo *Malta* 36°3N 14°15E **25** C1
Graaff-Reinet *S. Africa* 32°13S 24°32E **56** E3
Gračac *Croatia* 44°18N 15°57E **16** F8
Gracias a Dios, C.
    Honduras 15°0N 83°10W **88** D3
Graciosa *Azores* 39°4N 28°0W **50** a
Graciosa, I. *Canary Is.* 29°15N 13°32W **24** E6
Grado *Spain* 43°23N 6°4W **21** A2
Grady *U.S.A.* 34°49N 103°19W **77** J12
Grafham Water *U.K.* 52°19N 0°18W **13** E7
Grafton *Australia* 29°38S 152°58E **63** D5
Grafton *N. Dak., U.S.A.* 48°25N 97°25W **80** A5
Grafton *W. Va., U.S.A.* 39°21N 80°2W **81** F13
Graham *Canada* 49°20N 90°30W **72** C1
Graham *U.S.A.* 33°6N 98°35W **84** E5
Graham, Mt. *U.S.A.* 32°42N 109°52W **77** K9
Graham Bell, Ostrov = Greem-
    Bell, Ostrov *Russia* 81°0N 62°0E **28** A7
Graham I., *B.C., Canada* 53°40N 132°30W **70** C2
Graham I. *Nunavut,*
    Canada 77°25N 90°30W **69** B13
Graham Land *Antarctica* 65°0S 64°0W **5** C17
Grahamstown *S. Africa* 33°19S 26°31E **56** E4
Grahamsville *U.S.A.* 41°51N 74°33W **83** E10
Grain Coast *W. Afr.* 4°20N 10°0W **50** H3
Grajagan *Indonesia* 8°35S 114°13E **37** K17
Grajagan, Teluk
    Indonesia 8°40S 114°18E **37** K17
Grajaú *Brazil* 5°50S 46°4W **93** E9
Grajaú → *Brazil* 3°41S 44°48W **93** D10
Grampian *U.S.A.* 40°58N 78°37W **82** F6
Grampian Highlands = Grampian
    Mts. *U.K.* 56°50N 4°0W **11** E5
Grampian Mts. *U.K.* 56°50N 4°0W **11** E5
Grampians, The
    Australia 37°15S 142°20E **63** F3
Gran Canaria *Canary Is.* 27°55N 15°35W **24** G4
Gran Chaco *S. Amer.* 25°0S 61°0W **94** B3
Gran Desierto del Pinacate △
    Mexico 31°51N 113°32W **86** A2
Gran Paradiso *Italy* 45°33N 7°17E **20** D7
Gran Sasso d'Itália *Italy* 42°27N 13°42E **22** C5
Granada *Nic.* 11°58N 86°0W **88** D2
Granada *Spain* 37°10N 3°35W **21** D4
Granada *U.S.A.* 38°4N 102°19W **76** G12
Granadilla de Abona
    Canary Is. 28°7N 16°33W **24** F3
Granard *Ireland* 53°47N 7°30W **10** C4
Granbury *U.S.A.* 32°27N 97°47W **84** E6
Granby *Canada* 45°25N 72°45W **83** A12
Granby *U.S.A.* 40°5N 105°56W **76** F11
Grand → *Canada* 42°51N 79°34W **82** D5
Grand → *Mo., U.S.A.* 39°23N 93°7W **80** F7
Grand → *S. Dak.,*
    U.S.A. 45°40N 100°45W **80** C3
Grand Bahama I.
    Bahamas 26°40N 78°30W **88** A4
Grand Baie *Mauritius* 20°0S 57°35E **53** d
Grand Bank *Canada* 47°6N 55°48W **73** C8
Grand Bassam *Ivory C.* 5°10N 3°49W **50** G5
Grand Bend *Canada* 43°18N 81°45W **82** C3
Grand-Bourg *Guadeloupe* 15°53N 61°19W **88** b
Grand Canal = Da Yunhe →
    China 39°10N 117°10E **35** E9
Grand Canyon *U.S.A.* 36°3N 112°9W **77** H7
Grand Canyon △
    U.S.A. 36°15N 112°30W **77** H7
Grand Canyon-Parashant △
    U.S.A. 36°30N 113°45W **77** H7
Grand Cayman
    Cayman Is. 19°20N 81°20W **88** C3
Grand Coulee *U.S.A.* 47°57N 119°0W **76** C4
Grand Coulee Dam
    U.S.A. 47°57N 118°59W **76** C4
Grand Erg de Bilma *Niger* 18°30N 14°0E **51** E8
Grand Falls *Canada* 47°3N 67°44W **73** C6
Grand Falls-Windsor
    Canada 48°56N 55°40W **73** C8
Grand Forks *Canada* 49°0N 118°30W **70** D5
Grand Forks *U.S.A.* 47°55N 97°3W **80** B5

Grand Gorge *U.S.A.* 42°21N 74°29W **83** D10
Grand Haven *U.S.A.* 43°4N 86°13W **80** D10
Grand I. *Mich., U.S.A.* 46°31N 86°40W **80** B10
Grand I. *N.Y., U.S.A.* 43°0N 78°58W **82** D6
Grand Island *U.S.A.* 40°55N 98°21W **80** E4
Grand Isle *La., U.S.A.* 29°14N 90°0W **85** G9
Grand Isle *Vt., U.S.A.* 44°43N 73°18W **83** B11
Grand Junction *U.S.A.* 39°4N 108°33W **76** G9
Grand L. *N.B., Canada* 45°57N 66°7W **73** C6
Grand L. *Nfld. & L.,*
    Canada 49°0N 57°30W **73** C8
Grand L. *Nfld. & L.,*
    Canada 53°40N 60°30W **73** B7
Grand L. *U.S.A.* 29°55N 92°47W **84** G8
Grand Lake *U.S.A.* 40°15N 105°49W **76** F11
Grand Manan I. *Canada* 44°45N 66°52W **73** D6
Grand Marais *Mich.,*
    U.S.A. 46°40N 85°59W **81** B11
Grand Marais *Minn.,*
    U.S.A. 47°45N 90°25W **72** C1
Grand-Mère *Canada* 46°36N 72°40W **72** C5
Grand Portage *U.S.A.* 47°58N 89°41W **80** B9
Grand Prairie *U.S.A.* 32°44N 96°59W **84** E6
Grand Rapids *Canada* 53°12N 99°19W **71** C9
Grand Rapids *Mich.,*
    U.S.A. 42°58N 85°40W **81** D11
Grand Rapids *Minn.,*
    U.S.A. 47°14N 93°31W **80** B7
Grand St-Bernard, Col du
    Europe 45°50N 7°10E **20** D7
Grand Staircase-Escalante △
    U.S.A. 37°25N 111°33W **77** H8
Grand Teton *U.S.A.* 43°54N 110°50W **76** E8
Grand Teton △ *U.S.A.* 43°50N 110°50W **76** E8
Grand Union Canal *U.K.* 52°7N 0°53W **13** E7
Grande → *Jujuy,*
    Argentina 24°20S 65°2W **94** A2
Grande → *Mendoza,*
    Argentina 36°52S 69°45W **94** D2
Grande → *Bolivia* 15°51S 64°39W **92** G6
Grande → *Bahia, Brazil* 11°30S 44°30W **93** F10
Grande → *Minas Gerais,*
    Brazil 20°6S 51°4W **93** H8
Grande, B. *Argentina* 50°30S 68°20W **96** G3
Grande, Rio → *N. Amer.* 25°58N 97°9W **84** H6
Grande Anse *Seychelles* 4°18S 55°45E **53** b
Grande Baleine →
    Canada 55°16N 77°47W **72** A4
Grande Cache *Canada* 53°53N 119°8W **70** C5
Grande Comore
    Comoros Is. 11°35S 43°20E **53** a
Grande-Entrée *Canada* 47°30N 61°40W **73** C7
Grande Prairie *Canada* 55°10N 118°50W **70** B5
Grande-Rivière *Canada* 48°26N 64°30W **73** C7
Grande-Terre *Guadeloupe* 16°20N 61°25W **88** b
Grande-Vallée *Canada* 49°14N 65°8W **73** C6
Grande Vigie, Pte. de la
    Guadeloupe 16°32N 61°27W **88** b
Grandfalls *U.S.A.* 31°20N 102°51W **84** F3
Grands-Jardins △
    Canada 47°41N 70°51W **73** C5
Grandview *Canada* 51°10N 100°42W **71** C8
Grandview *U.S.A.* 46°15N 119°54W **76** C4
Graneros *Chile* 34°5S 70°45W **94** C1
Grangemouth *U.K.* 56°1N 3°42W **11** E5
Granger *U.S.A.* 41°35N 109°58W **76** F9
Grangeville *U.S.A.* 45°56N 116°7W **76** D5
Granisle *Canada* 54°53N 126°13W **70** C3
Granite City *U.S.A.* 38°42N 90°8W **80** F8
Granite Falls *U.S.A.* 44°49N 95°33W **80** C6
Granite L. *Canada* 48°8N 57°5W **73** C8
Granite Mt. *U.S.A.* 33°5N 116°28W **79** M10
Granite Pk. *U.S.A.* 45°10N 109°48W **76** D9
Graniteville *U.S.A.* 44°8N 72°29W **83** B12
Granity *N.Z.* 41°39S 171°51E **59** D3
Granja *Brazil* 3°7S 40°50W **93** D10
Granollers *Spain* 41°39N 2°18E **21** B7
Grant *U.S.A.* 40°53N 101°42W **80** E3
Grant, Mt. *U.S.A.* 38°34N 118°48W **76** G4
Grant City *U.S.A.* 40°29N 94°25W **80** E6
Grant I. *Australia* 11°10S 132°52E **60** B5
Grant Range *U.S.A.* 38°30N 115°25W **76** G6
Grantham *U.K.* 52°55N 0°38W **12** E7
Grantown-on-Spey *U.K.* 57°20N 3°36W **11** D5
Grants *U.S.A.* 35°9N 107°52W **77** J10
Grants Pass *U.S.A.* 42°26N 123°19W **76** E2
Grantsville *U.S.A.* 40°36N 112°28W **76** F7
Granville *France* 48°50N 1°35W **20** B3
Granville *N. Dak.,*
    U.S.A. 48°16N 100°47W **80** A3
Granville *N.Y., U.S.A.* 43°24N 73°16W **83** C11
Granville *Ohio, U.S.A.* 40°4N 82°31W **82** F2
Granville L. *Canada* 56°18N 100°30W **71** B8
Graskop *S. Africa* 24°56S 30°49E **57** C5
Grass → *Canada* 56°3N 96°33W **71** B9
Grass Range *U.S.A.* 47°2N 108°48W **76** C9
Grass River △ *Canada* 54°40N 100°50W **71** C8
Grass Valley *Calif.,*
    U.S.A. 39°13N 121°4W **78** F6
Grass Valley *Oreg.,*
    U.S.A. 45°22N 120°47W **76** D3
Grasse *France* 43°38N 6°56E **20** E7
Grassflat *U.S.A.* 41°0N 78°6W **82** F6
Grasslands △ *Canada* 49°11N 107°38W **71** D7
Grassy *Australia* 40°3S 144°5E **63** G3
Graulhet *France* 43°45N 1°59E **20** E4
Gravelbourg *Canada* 49°50N 106°35W **71** D7
's-Gravenhage *Neths.* 52°7N 4°17E **15** B4
Gravenhurst *Canada* 44°52N 79°20W **82** B5
Gravesend *Australia* 29°35S 150°20E **63** D5
Gravesend *U.K.* 51°26N 0°22E **13** F8
Gravois, Pointe-à- *Haiti* 16°15N 73°56W **89** C5
Grayling *U.S.A.* 44°40N 84°43W **81** C11
Grays *U.K.* 51°28N 0°21E **13** F8
Grays Harbor *U.S.A.* 46°59N 124°1W **76** C1
Grays L. *U.S.A.* 43°4N 111°26W **76** E8
Grays River *U.S.A.* 46°21N 123°37W **78** D3
Graz *Austria* 47°4N 15°27E **16** E8
Greasy L. *Canada* 62°55N 122°12W **70** A4

Great Abaco I. = Abaco I.
    Bahamas 26°25N 77°10W **88** A4
Great Artesian Basin
    Australia 23°0S 144°0E **62** C3
Great Australian Bight
    Australia 33°30S 130°0E **61** F5
Great Bahama Bank
    Bahamas 23°15N 78°0W **88** B4
Great Barrier I. *N.Z.* 36°11S 175°25E **59** B5
Great Barrier Reef
    Australia 18°0S 146°50E **62** B4
Great Barrier Reef △
    Australia 20°0S 150°0E **62** B4
Great Barrington
    U.S.A. 42°12N 73°22W **83** D11
Great Basalt Wall △
    Australia 19°52S 145°43E **62** B4
Great Basin *U.S.A.* 40°0N 117°0W **76** G5
Great Basin △ *U.S.A.* 38°56N 114°15W **76** G6
Great Bear → *Canada* 65°0N 126°0W **68** C7
Great Bear L. *Canada* 65°30N 120°0W **68** D8
Great Belt = Store Bælt
    Denmark 55°20N 11°0E **9** J14
Great Bend *Kans., U.S.A.* 38°22N 98°46W **80** F4
Great Bend *Pa., U.S.A.* 41°58N 75°45W **83** E9
Great Blasket I. *Ireland* 52°6N 10°32W **10** D1
Great Britain *Europe* 54°0N 2°15W **6** E5
Great Camanoe
    Br. Virgin Is. 18°30N 64°35W **89** e
Great Coco I. = Koko Kyunzu
    Burma 14°7N 93°22E **41** M18
Great Codroy *Canada* 47°51N 59°16W **73** C8
Great Divide, The = Great
    Dividing Ra. *Australia* 23°0S 146°0E **62** C4
Great Divide Basin
    U.S.A. 42°0N 108°0W **76** E9
Great Dividing Ra.
    Australia 23°0S 146°0E **62** C4
Great Driffield = Driffield
    U.K. 54°0N 0°26W **12** C7
Great Exuma I. *Bahamas* 23°30N 75°50W **88** B4
Great Falls *U.S.A.* 47°30N 111°17W **76** C8
Great Fish = Groot-Vis →
    S. Africa 33°28S 27°5E **56** E4
Great Guana Cay
    Bahamas 24°0N 76°20W **88** B4
Great Himalayan △
    India 31°30N 77°30E **42** D7
Great Inagua I. *Bahamas* 21°0N 73°20W **89** B5
Great Indian Desert = Thar Desert
    India 28°0N 72°0E **42** F5
Great Karoo *S. Africa* 31°55S 21°0E **56** E3
Great Khingan Mts. = Da
    Hinggan Ling *China* 48°0N 121°0E **33** B7
Great Lake *Australia* 41°50S 146°40E **63** G4
Great Lakes *N. Amer.* 46°0N 84°0W **66** E11
Great Limpopo Transfrontier △
    Africa 23°0S 31°45E **57** C5
Great Malvern *U.K.* 52°7N 2°18W **13** E5
Great Miami → *U.S.A.* 39°7N 84°49W **81** F11
Great Ormes Head *U.K.* 53°20N 3°52W **12** D4
Great Ouse → *U.K.* 52°48N 0°21E **12** E8
Great Palm I. *Australia* 18°45S 146°40E **62** B4
Great Pedro Bluff *Jamaica* 17°51N 77°44W **88** a
Great Pee Dee →
    U.S.A. 33°21N 79°10W **85** E15
Great Plains *N. Amer.* 47°0N 105°0W **66** E9
Great Ruaha → *Tanzania* 7°56S 37°52E **54** D4
Great Sacandaga L.
    U.S.A. 43°6N 74°16W **83** C10
Great Saint Bernard Pass = Grand
    St-Bernard, Col du
    Europe 45°50N 7°10E **20** D7
Great Salt Desert = Kavīr, Dasht-e
    Iran 34°30N 55°0E **45** C7
Great Salt Desert = Lūt, Dasht-e
    Iran 31°30N 58°0E **45** D8
Great Salt L. *U.S.A.* 41°15N 112°40W **76** F7
Great Salt Lake Desert
    U.S.A. 40°50N 113°30W **76** F7
Great Salt Plains L.
    U.S.A. 36°45N 98°8W **84** C5
Great Sand Dunes △
    U.S.A. 37°48N 105°45W **77** H11
Great Sandy △ *Australia* 26°13S 153°2E **63** D5
Great Sandy Desert
    Australia 21°0S 124°0E **60** D3
Great Sangi = Sangihe, Pulau
    Indonesia 3°35N 125°30E **37** D7
Great Sea Reef *Fiji* 16°15S 179°0E **59** a
Great Sitkin I. *U.S.A.* 52°3N 176°6W **74** E4
Great Skellig *Ireland* 51°47N 10°33W **10** E1
Great Slave L. *Canada* 61°23N 115°38W **70** A5
Great Smoky Mts. △
    U.S.A. 35°40N 83°40W **85** D13
Great Stour = Stour →
    U.K. 51°18N 1°22E **13** F9
Great Victoria Desert
    Australia 29°30S 126°30E **61** E4
Great Wall *Antarctica* 62°30S 58°0W **5** C18
Great Wall *China* 38°30N 109°30E **34** E5
Great Whernside *U.K.* 54°10N 1°58W **12** C6
Great Yarmouth *U.K.* 52°37N 1°44E **13** E9
Great Zab = Zāb al Kabīr →
    Iraq 36°1N 43°24E **44** B4
Great Zimbabwe
    Zimbabwe 20°16S 30°54E **55** G3
Greater Antilles *W. Indies* 17°40N 74°0W **89** C5
Greater London □ *U.K.* 51°31N 0°6W **13** F7
Greater Manchester □
    U.K. 53°30N 2°15W **12** D5
Greater St. Lucia Wetlands △
    S. Africa 28°6S 32°27E **57** D5
Greater Sudbury = Sudbury
    Canada 46°30N 81°0W **72** C3
Greater Sunda Is. *Indonesia* 7°0S 112°0E **36** F4
Greco, C. *Cyprus* 34°57N 34°5E **25** E13
Gredos, Sierra de *Spain* 40°20N 5°0W **21** B3
Greece *U.S.A.* 43°13N 77°41W **82** C7

Greece ■ *Europe* 40°0N 23°0E 23 E9
Greeley *Colo., U.S.A.* 40°25N 104°42W 76 F11
Greeley *Nebr., U.S.A.* 41°33N 98°32W 80 E4
Greely Fd. *Canada* 80°30N 85°0W 69 A15
Greem-Bell, Ostrov *Russia* 81°0N 62°0E 28 A7
Green → *Ky., U.S.A.* 37°54N 87°30W 80 G10
Green → *Utah, U.S.A.* 38°11N 109°53W 76 G9
Green B. *U.S.A.* 45°0N 87°30W 80 C10
Green Bay *U.S.A.* 44°31N 88°0W 80 C9
Green C. *Australia* 37°13S 150°1E 63 F5
Green Cove Springs *U.S.A.* 29°59N 81°42W 85 G14
Green Lake *Canada* 54°17N 107°47W 71 C7
Green Mts. *U.S.A.* 43°45N 72°45W 83 C12
Green River *Utah, U.S.A.* 38°59N 110°10W 76 G8
Green River *Wyo., U.S.A.* 41°32N 109°28W 76 F9
Green Valley *U.S.A.* 31°52N 110°56W 77 L8
Greenbank *U.S.A.* 48°6N 122°34W 78 B4
Greenbush *Mich., U.S.A.* 44°35N 83°19W 82 B1
Greenbush *Minn., U.S.A.* 48°42N 96°11W 80 A5
Greencastle *U.S.A.* 39°38N 86°52W 80 F10
Greene *U.S.A.* 42°20N 75°46W 83 D9
Greeneville *U.S.A.* 36°10N 82°50W 85 C13
Greenfield *Calif., U.S.A.* 36°19N 121°15W 78 J5
Greenfield *Calif., U.S.A.* 35°15N 119°0W 79 K8
Greenfield *Ind., U.S.A.* 39°47N 85°46W 81 F11
Greenfield *Iowa, U.S.A.* 41°18N 94°28W 80 E6
Greenfield *Mass., U.S.A.* 42°35N 72°36W 83 D12
Greenfield *Mo., U.S.A.* 37°25N 93°51W 80 G7
Greenfield Park *Canada* 45°29N 73°28W 83 A11
Greenland ⊠ *N. Amer.* 66°0N 45°0W 67 C15
Greenland Sea *Arctic* 73°0N 10°0W 4 B7
Greenock *U.K.* 55°57N 4°46W 11 F4
Greenore *Ireland* 54°2N 6°8W 10 B5
Greenore Pt. *Ireland* 52°14N 6°19W 10 D5
Greenough *Australia* 28°58S 114°43E 61 E1
Greenough → *Australia* 28°51S 114°38E 61 E1
Greenough Pt. *Canada* 44°58N 81°26W 82 B3
Greenport *U.S.A.* 41°6N 72°22W 83 E12
Greensboro *Ga., U.S.A.* 33°35N 83°11W 85 E13
Greensboro *N.C., U.S.A.* 36°4N 79°48W 85 C15
Greensboro *Vt., U.S.A.* 44°36N 72°18W 83 B12
Greensburg *Ind., U.S.A.* 39°20N 85°29W 81 F11
Greensburg *Kans., U.S.A.* 37°36N 99°18W 80 G4
Greensburg *Pa., U.S.A.* 40°18N 79°33W 82 F5
Greenstone = Geraldton *Canada* 49°44N 87°10W 72 C2
Greenstone Pt. *U.K.* 57°55N 5°37W 11 D3
Greenvale *Australia* 18°59S 145°7E 62 B4
Greenville *Liberia* 5°1N 9°6W 50 G4
Greenville *Ala., U.S.A.* 31°50N 86°38W 85 F11
Greenville *Calif., U.S.A.* 40°8N 120°57W 78 E6
Greenville *Maine, U.S.A.* 45°28N 69°35W 81 C19
Greenville *Mich., U.S.A.* 43°11N 85°15W 81 D11
Greenville *Miss., U.S.A.* 33°24N 91°4W 85 E9
Greenville *Mo., U.S.A.* 37°8N 90°27W 80 G8
Greenville *N.C., U.S.A.* 35°37N 77°23W 85 D16
Greenville *N.H., U.S.A.* 42°46N 71°49W 83 D13
Greenville *N.Y., U.S.A.* 42°25N 74°1W 83 D10
Greenville *Ohio, U.S.A.* 40°6N 84°38W 81 E11
Greenville *Pa., U.S.A.* 41°24N 80°23W 82 E4
Greenville *S.C., U.S.A.* 34°51N 82°24W 85 D13
Greenville *Tex., U.S.A.* 33°8N 96°7W 84 E6
Greenwater Lake ⌓ *Canada* 52°32N 103°30W 71 C8
Greenwich *Conn., U.S.A.* 41°2N 73°38W 83 E11
Greenwich *N.Y., U.S.A.* 43°5N 73°30W 83 C11
Greenwich *Ohio, U.S.A.* 41°2N 82°31W 82 E2
Greenwich □ *U.K.* 51°29N 0°1E 13 F8
Greenwood *Canada* 49°10N 118°40W 70 D5
Greenwood *Ark., U.S.A.* 35°13N 94°16W 84 D7
Greenwood *Ind., U.S.A.* 39°37N 86°7W 80 F10
Greenwood *Miss., U.S.A.* 33°31N 90°11W 85 E9
Greenwood *S.C., U.S.A.* 34°12N 82°10W 85 D13
Greenwood, Mt. *Australia* 13°48S 130°4E 60 B5
Gregory *U.S.A.* 43°14N 99°26W 80 D4
Gregory → *Australia* 17°53S 139°17E 62 B2
Gregory, L. *S. Austral., Australia* 28°55S 139°0E 63 D2
Gregory, L. *W. Austral., Australia* 20°0S 127°40E 60 D4
Gregory, L. *W. Austral., Australia* 25°38S 119°58E 61 E2
Gregory △ *Australia* 15°38S 131°15E 60 C5
Gregory Downs *Australia* 18°35S 138°45E 62 B2
Gregory Ra. *Queens., Australia* 19°30S 143°40E 62 B3
Gregory Ra. *W. Austral., Australia* 21°20S 121°12E 60 D3
Greifswald *Germany* 54°5N 13°23E 16 A7
Greiz *Germany* 50°39N 12°10E 16 C7
Gremikha *Russia* 67°59N 39°47E 18 A6
Grenaa *Denmark* 56°25N 10°53E 9 H14
Grenada *U.S.A.* 33°47N 89°49W 85 E10
Grenada ■ *W. Indies* 12°10N 61°40W 89 D7
Grenadier I. *U.S.A.* 44°3N 76°22W 83 B8
Grenadines, The *St. Vincent* 12°40N 61°20W 89 D7
Grenen *Denmark* 57°44N 10°40E 9 H14
Grenfell *Australia* 33°52S 148°8E 63 E4
Grenfell *Canada* 50°30N 102°56W 71 C8
Grenoble *France* 45°12N 5°42E 20 D6
Grenville, C. *Australia* 12°0S 143°13E 62 A3
Grenville Chan. *Canada* 53°40N 129°46W 70 C3
Gresham *U.S.A.* 45°30N 122°25W 78 E4
Gresik *Indonesia* 7°13S 112°38E 37 G15
Gretna *U.K.* 55°0N 3°3W 11 F5
Gretna *U.S.A.* 29°54N 90°3W 85 G9
Grevenmacher *Lux.* 49°41N 6°26E 15 E6
Grey → *Canada* 47°34N 57°6W 73 C8
Grey → *N.Z.* 42°27S 171°12E 59 E3
Grey, C. *Australia* 13°0S 136°35E 62 A2
Grey Is. *Canada* 50°50N 55°35W 69 G20
Grey Ra. *Australia* 27°0S 143°30E 63 D3
Greybull *U.S.A.* 44°30N 108°3W 76 D9
Greymouth *N.Z.* 42°29S 171°13E 59 E3
Greystones *Ireland* 53°9N 6°5W 10 C5
Greytown *N.Z.* 41°5S 175°29E 59 D5
Greytown *S. Africa* 29°1S 30°36E 57 D5
Gribbell I. *Canada* 53°23N 129°0W 70 C3
Gridley *U.S.A.* 39°22N 121°42W 78 F5
Griekwastad *S. Africa* 28°49S 23°15E 56 D3
Griffin *U.S.A.* 33°15N 84°16W 85 E12
Griffith *Australia* 34°18S 146°2E 63 E4
Griffith *Canada* 45°15N 77°10W 82 A7
Griffith I. *Canada* 44°50N 80°55W 82 B4
Grimaylov = Hrymayliv *Ukraine* 49°20N 26°5E 17 D14
Grimes *U.S.A.* 39°4N 121°54W 78 F5
Grimsay *U.K.* 57°29N 7°14W 11 D1
Grimsby *Canada* 43°12N 79°34W 82 C5
Grimsby *U.K.* 53°34N 0°5W 12 D7
Grímsey *Iceland* 66°33N 17°58W 8 C5
Grimshaw *Canada* 56°10N 117°40W 70 B5
Grimstad *Norway* 58°20N 8°35E 9 G13
Grinnell *U.S.A.* 41°45N 92°43W 80 E7
Grinnell Pen. *Canada* 76°40N 95°0W 69 B13
Gris-Nez, C. *France* 50°52N 1°35E 20 A4
Grise Fiord *Canada* 76°25N 82°57W 69 B15
Groais I. *Canada* 50°55N 55°35W 73 B8
Groblersdal *S. Africa* 25°15S 29°25E 57 D4
Grodno = Hrodna *Belarus* 53°42N 23°52E 17 B12
Grodzyanka = Hrodzyanka *Belarus* 53°31N 28°42E 17 B15
Groesbeck *U.S.A.* 31°31N 96°32W 84 F6
Grójec *Poland* 51°50N 20°58E 17 C11
Grong *Norway* 64°25N 12°8E 8 D15
Groningen *Neths.* 53°15N 6°35E 15 A6
Groningen □ *Neths.* 53°16N 6°40E 15 A6
Groom *U.S.A.* 35°12N 101°6W 84 D4
Groot → *S. Africa* 33°45S 24°36E 56 E3
Groot-Berg → *S. Africa* 32°47S 18°8E 56 E2
Groot-Brakrivier *S. Africa* 34°2S 22°18E 56 E3
Groot Karasberge *Namibia* 27°20S 18°40E 56 D2
Groot-Kei → *S. Africa* 32°41S 28°22E 57 E4
Groot-Vis → *S. Africa* 33°28S 27°5E 56 E4
Grootdrink *S. Africa* 28°33S 21°42E 56 D3
Groote Eylandt *Australia* 14°0S 136°40E 62 A2
Grootfontein *Namibia* 19°31S 18°6E 56 B2
Grootlaagte → *Africa* 20°55S 21°27E 56 C3
Grootvloer → *S. Africa* 30°0S 20°40E 56 E3
Gros C. *Canada* 61°59N 113°32W 70 A6
Gros Islet *St. Lucia* 14°5N 60°58W 89 f
Gros Morne △ *Canada* 49°40N 57°50W 73 C8
Gros Piton *St. Lucia* 13°49N 61°5W 89 f
Gros Piton Pt. *St. Lucia* 13°49N 61°5W 89 f
Grossa, Pta. *Spain* 39°6N 1°36E 24 B8
Grosse Point *U.S.A.* 42°23N 82°54W 82 D2
Grosser Arber *Germany* 49°6N 13°8E 16 D7
Grosseto *Italy* 42°46N 11°8E 22 C4
Grossglockner *Austria* 47°5N 12°40E 16 E7
Groswater B. *Canada* 54°20N 57°40W 73 B8
Groton *Conn., U.S.A.* 41°21N 72°5W 83 E12
Groton *N.Y., U.S.A.* 42°36N 76°22W 83 D8
Groton *S. Dak., U.S.A.* 45°27N 98°6W 80 C4
Grouard Mission *Canada* 55°33N 116°9W 70 B5
Groundhog → *Canada* 48°45N 82°58W 72 C3
Grouw *Neths.* 53°5N 5°51E 15 A5
Grove City *U.S.A.* 41°10N 80°5W 82 E4
Grove Hill *U.S.A.* 31°42N 87°47W 85 F11
Groveland *U.S.A.* 37°50N 120°14W 78 H6
Grover Beach *U.S.A.* 35°7N 120°37W 79 K6
Groves *U.S.A.* 29°57N 93°54W 84 G8
Groveton *U.S.A.* 44°36N 71°31W 83 B13
Groznyy *Russia* 43°20N 45°45E 19 F8
Grudziądz *Poland* 53°30N 18°47E 17 B10
Gruinard B. *U.K.* 57°56N 5°35W 11 D3
Grundy Center *U.S.A.* 42°22N 92°47W 80 D7
Gruver *U.S.A.* 36°16N 101°24W 84 C4
Gryazi *Russia* 52°30N 39°58E 18 D6
Gryazovets *Russia* 58°50N 40°10E 18 C7
Grytviken *S. Georgia* 54°19S 36°33W 96 G9
Gua *India* 22°18N 85°20E 43 H11
Gua Musang *Malaysia* 4°53N 101°58E 39 K3
Guacanayabo, G. de *Cuba* 20°40N 77°20W 88 B4
Guachípas → *Argentina* 25°40S 65°30W 94 B2
Guadalajara *Mexico* 20°40N 103°20W 86 C4
Guadalajara *Spain* 40°37N 3°12W 21 B4
Guadalcanal *Solomon Is.* 9°32S 160°12E 58 B9
Guadales *Argentina* 34°30S 67°55W 94 C2
Guadalete → *Spain* 36°35N 6°13W 21 D2
Guadalquivir → *Spain* 36°47N 6°22W 21 D2
Guadalupe = Guadeloupe ⊠ *W. Indies* 16°20N 61°40W 88 b
Guadalupe *Mexico* 22°45N 102°31W 86 C4
Guadalupe *U.S.A.* 34°58N 120°34W 79 L6
Guadalupe → *U.S.A.* 28°27N 96°47W 84 G6
Guadalupe, Sierra de *Spain* 39°28N 5°30W 21 C3
Guadalupe Bravos *Mexico* 31°20N 106°10W 86 A3
Guadalupe I. *Pac. Oc.* 29°0N 118°50W 66 G8
Guadalupe Mts. △ *U.S.A.* 31°40N 104°30W 84 F2
Guadalupe Peak *U.S.A.* 31°50N 104°52W 84 F2
Guadalupe y Calvo *Mexico* 26°6N 106°58W 86 B3
Guadarrama, Sierra de *Spain* 41°0N 4°0W 21 B4
Guadeloupe ⊠ *W. Indies* 16°20N 61°40W 88 b
Guadeloupe △ *Guadeloupe* 16°10N 61°40W 88 b
Guadeloupe Passage *W. Indies* 16°50N 62°15W 89 C7
Guadiana → *Portugal* 37°14N 7°22W 21 D2
Guadix *Spain* 37°18N 3°11W 21 D4
Guafo, Boca del *Chile* 43°35S 74°0W 96 E2
Guaico *Trin. & Tob.* 10°35N 61°9W 93 K15
Guainía → *Colombia* 2°1N 67°7W 92 C5
Guaíra *Brazil* 24°5S 54°10W 95 A5
Guaíra □ *Paraguay* 25°45S 56°30W 94 B4
Guaire = Gorey *Ireland* 52°41N 6°18W 10 D5
Guaitecas, Is. *Chile* 44°0S 74°30W 96 E2
Guajará-Mirim *Brazil* 10°50S 65°20W 92 F5
Guajira, Pen. de la *Colombia* 12°0N 72°0W 92 A4
Gualán *Guatemala* 15°8N 89°22W 88 C2
Gualeguay *Argentina* 33°10S 59°14W 94 C4
Gualeguaychú *Argentina* 33°3S 59°31W 94 C4
Gualequay → *Argentina* 33°19S 59°39W 94 C4
Guam ⊠ *Pac. Oc.* 13°27N 144°45E 64 F6
Guaminí *Argentina* 37°1S 62°28W 94 D3
Guamúchil *Mexico* 25°28N 108°6W 86 B3
Guana I. *Br. Virgin Is.* 18°30N 64°30W 89 e
Guanabacoa *Cuba* 23°8N 82°18W 88 B3
Guanacaste, Cordillera de *Costa Rica* 10°40N 85°4W 88 D2
Guanacaste △ *Costa Rica* 10°57N 85°30W 88 D2
Guanaceví *Mexico* 25°56N 105°57W 86 B3
Guanahani = San Salvador I. *Bahamas* 24°0N 74°40W 89 B5
Guanaja *Honduras* 16°30N 85°55W 88 C2
Guanajay *Cuba* 22°56N 82°42W 88 B3
Guanajuato *Mexico* 21°1N 101°15W 86 C4
Guanajuato □ *Mexico* 21°0N 101°0W 86 C4
Guandacol *Argentina* 29°30S 68°40W 94 B2
Guane *Cuba* 22°10N 84°7W 88 B3
Guangdong □ *China* 23°0N 113°0E 33 D6
Guangling *China* 39°47N 114°22E 34 E8
Guangrao *China* 37°5N 118°25E 35 F10
Guangwu *China* 37°48N 105°57E 34 F3
Guangxi Zhuangzu Zizhiqu □ *China* 24°0N 109°0E 33 D5
Guangzhou *China* 23°6N 113°13E 33 D6
Guanica *Puerto Rico* 17°58N 66°55W 89 d
Guanipa → *Venezuela* 9°56N 62°26W 92 B6
Guannan *China* 34°8N 119°21E 35 G10
Guantánamo *Cuba* 20°10N 75°14W 89 B4
Guantánamo B. *Cuba* 19°59N 75°10W 89 C4
Guantao *China* 36°42N 115°25E 34 F8
Guanyun *China* 34°20N 119°18E 35 G10
Guapay = Grande → *Bolivia* 15°51S 64°39W 92 G6
Guápiles *Costa Rica* 10°10N 83°46W 88 D3
Guapo B. *Trin. & Tob.* 10°12N 61°41W 93 K15
Guaporé *Brazil* 28°51S 51°54W 95 B5
Guaporé → *Brazil* 11°55S 65°4W 92 F5
Guaqui *Bolivia* 16°41S 68°54W 92 G5
Guaramacal △ *Venezuela* 9°13N 70°12W 89 E5
Guarapari *Brazil* 20°40S 40°30W 95 A7
Guarapuava *Brazil* 25°20S 51°30W 95 B5
Guaratinguetá *Brazil* 22°49S 45°9W 95 A6
Guaratuba *Brazil* 25°53S 48°38W 95 B6
Guarda *Portugal* 40°32N 7°20W 21 B2
Guardafui, C. = Asir, Ras *Somali Rep.* 11°55N 51°10E 47 E5
Guárico □ *Venezuela* 8°40N 66°35W 92 B5
Guarujá *Brazil* 24°2S 46°25W 95 A6
Guarulhos *Brazil* 23°29S 46°33W 95 A6
Guasave *Mexico* 25°34N 108°27W 86 B3
Guasdualito *Venezuela* 7°15N 70°44W 92 B4
Guatemala *Guatemala* 14°40N 90°22W 88 D1
Guatemala ■ *Cent. Amer.* 15°40N 90°30W 88 C1
Guatemala Basin *Pac. Oc.* 11°0N 95°0W 65 F18
Guatemala Trench *Pac. Oc.* 14°0N 95°0W 66 H10
Guatopo △ *Venezuela* 10°5N 66°30W 89 D6
Guatuaro Pt. *Trin. & Tob.* 10°19N 60°59W 93 K16
Guaviare → *Colombia* 4°3N 67°44W 92 C5
Guaxupé *Brazil* 21°10S 47°5W 95 A6
Guayaguayare *Trin. & Tob.* 10°8N 61°2W 93 K15
Guayama *Puerto Rico* 17°59N 66°7W 89 d
Guayaquil *Ecuador* 2°15S 79°52W 92 D3
Guayaquil *Mexico* 29°59N 115°4W 86 B1
Guayaquil, G. de *Ecuador* 3°10S 81°0W 92 D2
Guaymas *Mexico* 27°56N 110°54W 86 B2
Guba *Dem. Rep. of the Congo* 10°38S 26°27E 55 E2
Gubkin *Russia* 51°17N 37°32E 19 D6
Gubkinskiy *Russia* 64°27N 76°36E 28 C8
Gudbrandsdalen *Norway* 61°33N 10°10E 8 F14
Guddu Barrage *Pakistan* 28°30N 69°50E 42 E3
Gudur *India* 14°12N 79°55E 40 M11
Guecho = Getxo *Spain* 43°21N 2°59W 21 A4
Guékédou *Guinea* 8°40N 10°5W 50 G3
Guelmine = Goulimine *Morocco* 28°56N 10°0W 50 C3
Guelph *Canada* 43°35N 80°20W 82 C4
Guerara *Algeria* 32°51N 4°22E 50 B6
Guéret *France* 46°11N 1°51E 20 C4
Guerneville *U.S.A.* 38°30N 123°0W 78 G4
Guernica = Gernika-Lumo *Spain* 43°19N 2°40W 21 A4
Guernsey *U.K.* 49°26N 2°35W 13 H5
Guernsey *U.S.A.* 42°16N 104°45W 76 E11
Guerrero □ *Mexico* 17°40N 100°0W 87 D5
Gügher *Iran* 29°28N 56°27E 45 D8
Guhakolak, Tanjung *Indonesia* 6°50S 105°14E 37 G11
Guia *Canary Is.* 28°8N 15°38W 24 F4
Guia de Isora *Canary Is.* 28°12N 16°46W 24 F3
Guia Lopes da Laguna *Brazil* 21°26S 56°7W 95 A4
Guiana Highlands *S. Amer.* 5°10N 60°40W 90 C4
Guidónia-Montecélio *Italy* 42°1N 12°45E 22 C5
Guijá *Mozam.* 24°27S 33°0E 57 C5
Guildford *U.K.* 51°14N 0°34W 13 F7
Guilford *U.S.A.* 41°17N 72°41W 83 E12
Guilin *China* 25°18N 110°15E 33 D6
Guillaume-Delisle, L. *Canada* 56°15N 76°17W 72 A4
Güímar *Canary Is.* 28°18N 16°24W 24 F3
Guimarães *Portugal* 41°28N 8°24W 21 B1
Guimaras □ *Phil.* 10°35N 122°37E 37 B6
Guinda *U.S.A.* 38°50N 122°12W 78 G4
Guinea *Africa* 8°0N 8°0E 48 F4
Guinea ■ *W. Afr.* 10°20N 11°30W 50 F3
Guinea, Gulf of *Atl. Oc.* 3°0N 2°30E 49 F4
Guinea-Bissau ■ *Africa* 12°0N 15°0W 50 F3
Güines *Cuba* 22°50N 82°0W 88 B3
Guingamp *France* 48°34N 3°10W 20 B2
Güiria *Venezuela* 10°32N 62°18W 93 K14
Guiuan *Phil.* 11°5N 125°55E 37 B7
Guiyang *China* 26°32N 106°40E 32 D5
Guizhou □ *China* 27°0N 107°0E 32 D5
Gujar Khan *Pakistan* 33°16N 73°19E 42 C5
Gujarat □ *India* 23°20N 71°0E 42 H4
Gujranwala *Pakistan* 32°10N 74°12E 42 C6
Gujrat *Pakistan* 32°40N 74°2E 42 C6
Gulbarga *India* 17°20N 76°50E 40 L10
Gulbene *Latvia* 57°8N 26°52E 9 H22
Gulf, The = Persian Gulf *Asia* 27°0N 50°0E 45 E6
Gulf Islands ⌓ *U.S.A.* 30°10N 87°10W 85 F11
Gulfport *U.S.A.* 30°22N 89°6W 85 F10
Gulgong *Australia* 32°20S 149°49E 63 E4
Gulistan *Pakistan* 30°30N 66°35E 42 D2
Gulja = Yining *China* 43°58N 81°10E 32 B3
Gull Lake *Canada* 50°10N 108°29W 71 C7
Güllük *Turkey* 37°14N 27°35E 23 F12
Gulmarg *India* 34°3N 74°25E 43 B6
Gülshat *Kazakhstan* 46°38N 74°21E 28 C8
Gulu *Uganda* 2°48N 32°17E 54 B3
Gulwe *Tanzania* 6°30S 36°25E 54 D4
Gumal → *Pakistan* 31°40N 71°50E 42 D4
Gumbaz *Pakistan* 30°2N 69°0E 42 D3
Gumel *Nigeria* 12°39N 9°22E 50 F7
Gumi *S. Korea* 36°10N 128°12E 35 F15
Gumla *India* 23°3N 84°33E 43 H11
Gumlu *Australia* 19°53S 147°41E 62 B4
Gumma □ *Japan* 36°30N 138°20E 31 F9
Gumzai *Indonesia* 5°28S 134°42E 37 F8
Guna *India* 24°40N 77°19E 42 G7
Gunbalanya *Australia* 12°20S 133°4E 60 B5
Gundabooka △ *Australia* 30°30S 145°20E 63 E4
Gunisao → *Canada* 53°56N 97°53W 71 C9
Gunisao L. *Canada* 53°33N 96°15W 71 C9
Gunjyal *Pakistan* 32°20N 71°55E 42 C4
Gunnbjørn Fjeld *Greenland* 68°55N 29°47W 4 C6
Gunnedah *Australia* 30°59S 150°15E 63 E5
Gunnewin *Australia* 25°59S 148°33E 63 D4
Gunningbar Cr. → *Australia* 31°14S 147°6E 63 E4
Gunnison *Colo., U.S.A.* 38°33N 106°56W 76 G10
Gunnison *Utah, U.S.A.* 39°9N 111°49W 76 G8
Gunnison → *U.S.A.* 39°4N 108°35W 76 G9
Gunsan *S. Korea* 35°59N 126°45E 35 G14
Guntakal *India* 15°11N 77°27E 40 M10
Gunter *Canada* 44°52N 77°32W 82 B7
Guntersville *U.S.A.* 34°21N 86°18W 85 D11
Guntong *Malaysia* 4°36N 101°3E 39 K3
Guntur *India* 16°23N 80°30E 41 L12
Gunungapi *Indonesia* 6°45S 126°30E 37 F7
Gunungsitoli *Indonesia* 1°15N 97°30E 36 D1
Gunza *Angola* 10°50S 13°50E 52 G2
Guo He → *China* 32°59N 117°10E 35 H9
Guoyang *China* 33°32N 116°12E 34 H9
Gupis *Pakistan* 36°15N 73°20E 43 A5
Gurbantünggüt Shamo *China* 45°8N 87°20E 32 B3
Gurdaspur *India* 32°5N 75°31E 42 C6
Gurdon *U.S.A.* 33°55N 93°9W 84 E8
Gurgaon *India* 28°27N 77°1E 42 E7
Gurgueia → *Brazil* 6°50S 43°24W 93 E10
Gurha *India* 25°12N 71°39E 42 G4
Guri, Embalse de *Venezuela* 7°50N 62°52W 92 B6
Gurkha *Nepal* 28°5N 84°40E 43 E11
Gurla Mandhata = Naimona'nyi Feng *Nepal* 30°26N 81°18E 43 D9
Gurley *Australia* 29°45S 149°48E 63 D4
Gurnet Point *U.S.A.* 42°1N 70°34W 83 D14
Guro *Mozam.* 17°26S 32°30E 55 F3
Gurué *Mozam.* 15°25S 36°58E 55 F4
Gurun *Malaysia* 5°49N 100°27E 39 K3
Gürün *Turkey* 38°43N 37°15E 19 G6
Gurupá *Brazil* 1°25S 51°35W 93 D8
Gurupá, I. Grande de *Brazil* 1°25S 51°45W 93 D8
Gurupi *Brazil* 11°43S 49°4W 93 F9
Gurupi → *Brazil* 1°13S 46°6W 93 D9
Guruwe *Zimbabwe* 16°40S 30°42E 57 B5
Gurvan Sayhan Uul *Mongolia* 43°50N 104°0E 32 B5
Guryev = Atyraū *Kazakhstan* 47°5N 52°0E 19 E9
Gusau *Nigeria* 12°12N 6°40E 50 F7
Gushan *China* 39°50N 123°35E 35 E12
Gushgy = Serhetabat *Turkmenistan* 35°20N 62°18E 45 C9
Gusinoozersk *Russia* 51°16N 106°27E 29 D11
Gustavus *U.S.A.* 58°25N 135°44W 70 B1
Gustine *U.S.A.* 37°16N 121°0W 78 H6
Güstrow *Germany* 53°47N 12°10E 16 B7
Gütersloh *Germany* 51°54N 8°24E 16 C5
Gutha *Australia* 28°58S 115°55E 61 E2
Guthalungra *Australia* 19°52S 147°50E 62 B4
Guthrie *Canada* 44°28N 79°32W 82 B5
Guthrie *Okla., U.S.A.* 35°53N 97°25W 84 D6
Guthrie *Tex., U.S.A.* 33°37N 100°19W 84 E4
Guttenberg *U.S.A.* 42°47N 91°6W 80 D8
Gutu *Zimbabwe* 19°41S 31°9E 57 B5
Guwahati *India* 26°10N 91°45E 41 F17
Guy Fawkes River △ *Australia* 30°0S 152°20E 63 D5
Guyana ■ *S. Amer.* 5°0N 59°0W 92 C7
Guyane française = French Guiana ⊠ *S. Amer.* 4°0N 53°0W 93 C8
Guyang *China* 41°0N 110°5E 34 D6
Guyenne *France* 44°30N 0°40E 20 D4
Guymon *U.S.A.* 36°41N 101°29W 84 C4
Guyra *Australia* 30°15S 151°40E 63 E5
Guyuan *Hebei, China* 41°37N 115°40E 34 D8
Guyuan *Ningxia Huizu, China* 36°0N 106°20E 34 F4
Güzelyurt = Morphou *Cyprus* 35°12N 32°59E 25 D11
Guzhen *China* 33°22N 117°18E 35 H9
Guzmán, L. de *Mexico* 31°20N 107°30W 86 A3
Gwa *Burma* 17°36N 94°34E 41 L19
Gwaai *Zimbabwe* 19°15S 27°45E 55 F2
Gwaai → *Zimbabwe* 17°59S 26°52E 55 F2
Gwabegar *Australia* 30°37S 148°59E 63 E4
Gwādar *Pakistan* 25°10N 62°18E 40 G3
Gwaii Haanas △ *Canada* 52°21N 131°26W 70 C2
Gwalior *India* 26°12N 78°10E 42 F8
Gwanda *Zimbabwe* 20°55S 29°0E 55 G2
Gwane *Dem. Rep. of the Congo* 4°45N 25°48E 54 B2
Gwangju *S. Korea* 35°9N 126°54E 35 G14
Gwanju = Gwangju *S. Korea* 35°9N 126°54E 35 G14
Gweebarra B. *Ireland* 54°51N 8°23W 10 B3
Gweedore *Ireland* 55°3N 8°13W 10 A3
Gweru *Zimbabwe* 19°28S 29°45E 55 F2
Gwinn *U.S.A.* 46°19N 87°27W 80 B10
Gwydir → *Australia* 29°27S 149°48E 63 D4
Gwynedd □ *U.K.* 52°52N 4°10W 12 E3
Gyandzha = Gäncä *Azerbaijan* 40°45N 46°20E 19 F8
Gyaring Hu *China* 34°50N 97°40E 32 C4
Gydanskiy Poluostrov *Russia* 70°0N 78°0E 28 C8
Gyeongju *S. Korea* 35°51N 129°14E 35 G15
Gympie *Australia* 26°11S 152°38E 63 D5
Gyöngyös *Hungary* 47°48N 19°56E 17 E10
Győr *Hungary* 47°41N 17°40E 17 E9
Gypsum Pt. *Canada* 61°53N 114°35W 70 A6
Gypsumville *Canada* 51°45N 98°40W 71 C9
Gyula *Hungary* 46°38N 21°17E 17 E11
Gyumri *Armenia* 40°47N 43°50E 19 F7
Gyzylarbat = Serdar *Turkmenistan* 39°4N 56°23E 45 B8
Gyzyletrek = Etrek *Turkmenistan* 37°36N 54°46E 45 B7

H

Ha 'Arava → *Israel* 30°50N 35°20E 46 E4
Ha Coi *Vietnam* 21°26N 107°46E 38 B6
Ha Dong *Vietnam* 20°58N 105°46E 38 B5
Ha Giang *Vietnam* 22°50N 104°59E 38 A5
Ha Karmel △ *Israel* 32°45N 35°5E 46 C4
Ha Long, Vinh *Vietnam* 20°56N 107°3E 38 B6
Ha Tien *Vietnam* 10°23N 104°29E 39 G5
Ha Tinh *Vietnam* 18°20N 105°54E 38 C5
Ha Trung *Vietnam* 19°58N 105°50E 38 C5
Haaksbergen *Neths.* 52°9N 6°45E 15 B6
Ha'ano *Tonga* 19°41S 174°18W 59 c
Ha'apai Group *Tonga* 19°47S 174°27W 59 c
Haapiti *Moorea* 17°34S 149°52W 59 d
Haapsalu *Estonia* 58°56N 23°30E 9 G20
Haarlem *Neths.* 52°23N 4°39E 15 B4
Haast → *N.Z.* 43°50S 169°2E 59 E2
Haasts Bluff *Australia* 23°22S 132°0E 60 D5
Haasts Bluff ✪ *Australia* 23°39S 130°34E 60 D5
Hab → *Pakistan* 24°53N 66°41E 42 G3
Hab Nadi Chauki *Pakistan* 25°0N 66°50E 42 G2
Habahe *China* 48°3N 86°23E 32 B3
Habaswein *Kenya* 1°2N 39°30E 54 B4
Habay *Canada* 58°50N 118°44W 70 B5
Ḩabbānīyah *Iraq* 33°17N 43°29E 44 C4
Haboro *Japan* 44°22N 141°42E 30 B10
Ḩabshān *U.A.E.* 23°50N 53°37E 45 F7
Hachijō-Jima *Japan* 33°5N 139°45E 31 H9
Hachinohe *Japan* 40°30N 141°29E 30 D10
Hachiōji *Japan* 35°40N 139°20E 31 G9
Hackensack *U.S.A.* 40°52N 74°4W 83 F10
Hackettstown *U.S.A.* 40°51N 74°50W 83 F10
Hadali *Pakistan* 32°16N 72°11E 42 C5
Hadarba, Ras *Sudan* 22°4N 36°51E 51 D13
Hadarom □ *Israel* 31°0N 35°0E 46 E4
Ḩadd, Ra's al *Oman* 22°35N 59°50E 47 C6
Haddington *U.K.* 55°57N 2°47W 11 F6
Hadejia *Nigeria* 12°30N 10°5E 50 F7
Ḩadera *Israel* 32°27N 34°55E 46 C3
Ḩadera, N. → *Israel* 32°28N 34°52E 46 C3
Haderslev *Denmark* 55°15N 9°30E 9 J13
Hadhramaut = Ḩadramawt *Yemen* 15°30N 49°30E 47 D4
Hadībοh *Yemen* 12°39N 54°2E 47 E5
Hadley B. *Canada* 72°31N 108°12W 68 C10
Hadong *S. Korea* 35°5N 127°44E 35 G14
Ḩadramawt *Yemen* 15°30N 49°30E 47 D4
Ḩadrānīyah *Iraq* 35°38N 43°14E 44 C4
Hadrian's Wall *U.K.* 55°0N 2°30W 12 B5
Hae, Ko *Thailand* 7°44N 98°22E 39 a
Haeju *N. Korea* 38°3N 125°45E 35 E13
Hä'ena *U.S.A.* 22°14N 159°34W 75 L8
Haenam *S. Korea* 34°34N 126°35E 35 G14
Haenertsburg *S. Africa* 24°0S 29°50E 57 C4
Haerhpin = Harbin *China* 45°48N 126°40E 35 B14
Hafar al Bāţin *Si. Arabia* 28°32N 45°52E 44 D5
Ḩafirat al 'Aydā *Si. Arabia* 26°26N 39°12E 44 E3
Ḩafit *Oman* 23°59N 55°49E 45 F7
Hafizabad *Pakistan* 32°5N 73°40E 42 C5
Haflong *India* 25°10N 93°5E 41 G18
Haft Gel *Iran* 31°30N 49°32E 45 D6
Hagalil *Israel* 32°53N 35°18E 46 C4
Hagemeister I. *U.S.A.* 58°39N 160°54W 74 D7
Hagen *Germany* 51°21N 7°27E 16 C4
Hagerman *U.S.A.* 33°7N 104°20W 77 K11

Hagerman Fossil Beds △
  U.S.A. 42°48N 114°57W **76** E6
Hagerstown U.S.A. 39°39N 77°43W **81** F15
Hagersville Canada 42°58N 80°3W **82** D4
Hagfors Sweden 60°3N 13°45E **9** F15
Hagi Japan 34°30N 131°22E **31** G5
Hagolan Syria 33°0N 35°45E **46** C4
Hagondange France 49°16N 6°11E **20** B7
Hags Hd. Ireland 52°57N 9°28W **10** D2
Hague, C. de la France 49°44N 1°56W **20** B3
Hague, The = 's-Gravenhage
  Neths. 52°7N 4°17E **15** B4
Haguenau France 48°49N 7°47E **20** B7
Haicheng China 40°50N 122°45E **35** D12
Haidar Khel Afghan. 33°58N 68°38E **42** C3
Haidarābād = Hyderabad
  India 17°22N 78°29E **40** L11
Haidargarh India 26°37N 81°22E **43** F9
Haifa = Ḥefa Israel 32°46N 35°0E **46** C4
Haikou China 20°1N 110°16E **38** B8
Ḥāʾil □ Si. Arabia 26°40N 41°40E **44** E4
Hailar China 49°10N 119°38E **33** B6
Hailey U.S.A. 43°31N 114°19W **76** E6
Haileybury Canada 47°30N 79°38W **72** C4
Hailin China 44°37N 129°30E **35** B15
Hailuoto Finland 65°3N 24°45E **8** D21
Hainan □ China 19°0N 109°30E **38** C7
Hainan Dao China 19°0N 109°30E **38** C7
Hainan Str. = Qiongzhou Haixia
  China 20°10N 110°15E **38** B8
Hainaut □ Belgium 50°30N 4°0E **15** D4
Haines Alaska, U.S.A. 59°14N 135°26W **70** B1
Haines Oreg., U.S.A. 44°55N 117°56W **76** D5
Haines City U.S.A. 28°7N 81°38W **85** G14
Haines Junction
  Canada 60°45N 137°30W **70** A1
Haiphong Vietnam 20°47N 106°41E **38** B6
Haiti ■ W. Indies 19°0N 72°30W **89** C5
Haiya Sudan 18°20N 36°21E **51** E13
Haiyan China 36°53N 100°59E **32** C5
Haiyang China 36°47N 121°9E **35** F11
Haiyuan China 36°35N 105°52E **34** F3
Haizhou China 34°37N 119°7E **35** G10
Haizhou Wan China 34°50N 119°20E **35** G10
Haj Ali Qoli, Kavīr Iran 35°55N 54°50E **45** C7
Hajdúböszörmény
  Hungary 47°40N 21°30E **17** E11
Haji Ibrahim Iraq 36°40N 44°30E **44** B5
Hājjiābād Iran 33°37N 60°0E **45** C9
Hajipur India 25°45N 85°13E **43** G11
Hajjah Yemen 15°42N 43°36E **47** D3
Ḥājjiābād Iran 28°19N 55°55E **45** D7
Ḥājjiābād-e Zarrīn Iran 33°9N 54°51E **45** C7
Hajnówka Poland 52°47N 23°35E **17** B12
Hakansson, Mts.
  Dem. Rep. of the Congo 8°40S 25°45E **55** D2
Hakkâri Turkey 37°34N 43°44E **44** B4
Hakken-Zan Japan 34°10N 135°54E **31** G7
Hakodate Japan 41°45N 140°44E **30** D10
Hakos Namibia 23°13S 16°21E **56** C2
Haku-San Japan 36°9N 136°46E **31** F8
Haku-San △ Japan 36°15N 136°45E **31** F8
Hakui Japan 36°53N 136°47E **31** F8
Hala Pakistan 25°43N 68°20E **42** G6
Ḥalab Syria 36°10N 37°15E **44** B3
Ḥalabjah Iraq 35°10N 45°58E **44** C5
Halaib Sudan 22°12N 36°30E **51** D13
Halaib Triangle Africa 22°30N 35°20E **51** D13
Ḥalāt ʿAmmār Si. Arabia 29°10N 36°4E **44** D3
Halba Lebanon 34°34N 36°6E **46** A5
Halberstadt Germany 51°54N 11°3E **16** C6
Halcombe N.Z. 40°8S 175°30E **59** D5
Halcon Phil. 13°0N 121°30E **37** B6
Halde Fjäll = Haltiatunturi
  Finland 69°17N 21°18E **8** B19
Halden Norway 59°9N 11°23E **9** G14
Haldia Bangla. 22°1N 88°3E **43** H13
Haldwani India 29°31N 79°30E **43** E8
Hale → U.S.A. 24°56S 135°53E **62** C2
Halesowen U.K. 52°27N 2°3W **13** E5
Halesworth U.K. 52°20N 1°31E **13** E9
Haleyville U.S.A. 34°14N 87°37W **85** D11
Half Dome U.S.A. 37°44N 119°32E **78** H7
Halfmoon Bay N.Z. 46°50S 168°5E **59** G2
Halfway → Canada 56°12N 121°32W **70** B4
Halia India 24°50N 82°19E **43** G10
Haliburton Canada 45°3N 78°30W **82** A6
Halifax Australia 18°32S 146°22E **62** B4
Halifax Canada 44°38N 63°35W **73** D7
Halifax U.K. 53°43N 1°52W **12** D6
Halifax U.S.A. 40°25N 76°55W **82** F8
Halifax B. Australia 18°50S 147°0E **62** B4
Halifax I. Namibia 26°38S 15°4E **56** D2
Ḥalīl → Iran 27°40N 58°30E **45** E8
Halkida Greece 38°27N 23°42E **23** E10
Halkirk U.K. 58°30N 3°29W **11** C5
Hall Beach Canada 68°46N 81°12W **69** D15
Hall Pen. Canada 63°30N 66°0W **69** E18
Hall Pt. Australia 15°40S 124°23E **60** C3
Halland Sweden 57°8N 12°47E **9** H15
Hallāniyat, Jazā'ir al
  Oman 17°30N 55°58E **47** D6
Hallasan △ S. Korea 33°22N 126°32E **35** H14
Halle Belgium 50°44N 4°13E **15** D4
Halle Germany 51°30N 11°56E **16** C6
Hällefors Sweden 59°47N 14°31E **9** G16
Hallett Australia 33°25S 138°55E **63** E2
Hallettsville U.S.A. 29°27N 96°57W **84** G6
Halley Antarctica 75°35S 26°39W **5** D1
Hallim S. Korea 33°24N 126°15E **35** H14
Hallingdalselva →
  Norway 60°23N 9°35E **8** F13
Hallock U.S.A. 48°47N 96°57W **80** A5
Halls Creek Australia 18°16S 127°38E **60** C4
Halls Gap Australia 37°8S 142°34E **63** F3
Halls Lake Canada 45°7N 78°45W **82** A6
Hallsberg Sweden 59°5N 15°7E **9** G16
Hallstead U.S.A. 41°58N 75°45W **83** E9

Halmahera Indonesia 0°40N 128°0E **37** D7
Halmstad Sweden 56°41N 12°52E **9** H15
Hälsingborg = Helsingborg
  Sweden 56°3N 12°42E **9** H15
Hälsingland Sweden 61°40N 16°5E **8** F17
Haltiatunturi Finland 69°17N 21°18E **8** B19
Halton □ U.K. 53°22N 2°45W **12** D5
Haltwhistle U.K. 54°58N 2°26W **12** C5
Ḥālūl Qatar 25°40N 52°40E **45** E7
Halvad India 23°1N 71°11E **42** H4
Ḥalvān Iran 33°57N 56°15E **45** C8
Ham Tan Vietnam 10°40N 107°45E **39** G6
Ham Yen Vietnam 22°4N 105°3E **38** A5
Hamab Namibia 28°7S 19°16E **56** D2
Hamada Japan 34°56N 132°4E **31** G6
Hamadān Iran 34°52N 48°32E **45** C6
Hamadān □ Iran 35°0N 49°0E **45** C6
Ḥamāh Syria 35°5N 36°40E **44** C3
Hamamatsu Japan 34°45N 137°45E **31** G8
Hamar Norway 60°48N 11°7E **8** F14
Hamâta, Gebel Egypt 24°17N 35°0E **44** E2
Hambantota Sri Lanka 6°10N 81°10E **40** R12
Hamber △ Canada 52°20N 118°0W **70** C5
Hamburg Germany 53°33N 9°59E **16** B5
Hamburg Ark., U.S.A. 33°14N 91°48W **84** E9
Hamburg N.Y., U.S.A. 42°43N 78°50W **82** D6
Hamburg Pa., U.S.A. 40°33N 75°59W **83** F9
Ḥamd, W. al →
  Si. Arabia 24°55N 36°20E **44** E3
Hamden U.S.A. 41°23N 72°54W **83** E12
Häme Finland 61°38N 25°10E **8** F21
Hämeenlinna Finland 61°0N 24°28E **8** F21
Hamelin Pool Australia 26°22S 114°20E **61** E1
Hameln Germany 52°6N 9°21E **16** B5
Hamerkaz □ Israel 32°15N 34°55E **46** C3
Hamersley Ra. Australia 22°0S 117°45E **60** D2
Hamhŭng N. Korea 39°54N 127°30E **35** E14
Hami China 42°55N 93°25E **32** B4
Hamilton Australia 37°45S 142°2E **63** F3
Hamilton Canada 43°15N 79°50W **82** C5
Hamilton N.Z. 37°47S 175°19E **59** B5
Hamilton U.K. 55°46N 4°2W **11** F4
Hamilton Ala., U.S.A. 34°9N 87°59W **85** D11
Hamilton Mont., U.S.A. 46°15N 114°10W **76** C6
Hamilton N.Y., U.S.A. 42°50N 75°33W **83** D9
Hamilton Ohio, U.S.A. 39°24N 84°34W **81** F11
Hamilton Tex., U.S.A. 31°42N 98°7W **84** F5
Hamilton → Queens.,
  Australia 23°30S 139°47E **62** C2
Hamilton → S. Austral.,
  Australia 26°40S 135°19E **63** D2
Hamilton City U.S.A. 39°45N 122°1W **78** F4
Hamilton Inlet Canada 54°0N 57°30W **73** B8
Hamilton Mt. U.S.A. 43°25N 74°22W **83** C10
Hamina Finland 60°34N 27°12E **8** F22
Hamipur H.P., India 31°41N 76°31E **42** D7
Hamirpur Ut. P., India 25°57N 80°9E **43** G9
Hamju N. Korea 39°51N 127°26E **35** E14
Hamlet U.S.A. 34°53N 79°42W **85** D15
Hamley Bridge Australia 34°17S 138°35E **63** E2
Hamlin = Hameln
  Germany 52°6N 9°21E **16** B5
Hamlin N.Y., U.S.A. 43°17N 77°55W **82** C7
Hamlin Tex., U.S.A. 32°53N 100°8W **84** E4
Hamm Germany 51°40N 7°50E **16** C4
Hammār, Hawr al Iraq 30°50N 47°10E **44** D5
Hammerfest Norway 70°39N 23°41E **8** A20
Hammond Ind., U.S.A. 41°38N 87°30W **80** E10
Hammond La., U.S.A. 30°30N 90°28W **85** F9
Hammond N.Y., U.S.A. 44°27N 75°42W **83** B9
Hammondsport U.S.A. 42°25N 77°13W **82** D7
Hammonton U.S.A. 39°39N 74°48W **81** F16
Hampden N.Z. 45°18S 170°50E **59** F3
Hampshire □ U.K. 51°7N 1°23W **13** F6
Hampshire Downs U.K. 51°15N 1°10W **13** F6
Hampton N.B., Canada 45°32N 65°51W **73** C6
Hampton Ont., Canada 43°58N 78°45W **82** C6
Hampton Ark., U.S.A. 33°32N 92°28W **84** E8
Hampton Iowa, U.S.A. 42°45N 93°13W **80** D7
Hampton N.H., U.S.A. 42°57N 70°50W **83** D14
Hampton S.C., U.S.A. 32°52N 81°7W **85** E14
Hampton Va., U.S.A. 37°2N 76°21W **81** G15
Hampton Bays U.S.A. 40°53N 72°30W **83** F12
Hampton Tableland
  Australia 32°0S 127°0E **61** F4
Hamyang S. Korea 35°32N 127°42E **35** G14
Han Pijesak Bos.-H. 44°5N 18°57E **23** B8
Hanak Si. Arabia 25°32N 37°0E **44** E3
Hanamaki Japan 39°23N 141°7E **30** E10
Hanang Tanzania 4°30S 35°25E **54** C4
Hanau Germany 50°7N 8°56E **16** C5
Hanbogd = Ihbulag
  Mongolia 43°11N 107°10E **34** C4
Hancheng China 35°31N 110°25E **34** G6
Hancock Mich., U.S.A. 47°8N 88°35W **80** B9
Hancock N.Y., U.S.A. 41°57N 75°17W **83** E9
Hancock Vt., U.S.A. 43°55N 72°50W **83** C12
Handa Japan 34°53N 136°55E **31** G8
Handa I. U.K. 58°23N 5°11W **11** C3
Handan China 36°35N 114°28E **34** F8
Handeni Tanzania 5°25S 38°2E **54** D4
Handwara India 34°21N 74°20E **43** B6
Hanegev Israel 30°50N 35°0E **46** E4
Hanford U.S.A. 36°20N 119°39W **78** J7
Hanford Reach △
  U.S.A. 46°40N 119°30W **76** C4
Hang Chat Thailand 18°20N 99°21E **38** C2
Hang Dong Thailand 18°41N 98°55E **38** C2
Hangang → S. Korea 37°50N 126°30E **35** F14
Hangayn Nuruu Mongolia 47°30N 99°0E **32** B4
Hangchou = Hangzhou
  China 30°18N 120°11E **33** C7
Hanggin Houqi China 40°58N 107°4E **34** D4
Hanggin Qi China 39°52N 108°50E **34** E5
Hangu China 39°18N 117°53E **35** E9
Hangzhou China 30°18N 120°11E **33** C7
Hangzhou Wan China 30°15N 120°45E **33** C7

Hanh Mongolia 51°32N 100°35E **32** A5
Hanhongor Mongolia 43°55N 104°28E **34** C3
Hania = Chania Greece 35°30N 24°4E **25** D6
Ḥanīdh Si. Arabia 26°35N 48°38E **45** E6
Hanish Yemen 13°45N 42°46E **47** E3
Hankinson U.S.A. 46°4N 96°54W **80** B5
Hankö Finland 59°50N 22°57E **9** G20
Hanksville U.S.A. 38°22N 110°43W **76** G8
Hanle India 32°42N 79°4E **43** C8
Hanmer Springs N.Z. 42°32S 172°50E **59** E4
Hann → Australia 17°26S 126°17E **60** C4
Hann, Mt. Australia 15°45S 126°0E **60** C4
Hanna Canada 51°40N 111°54W **70** C6
Hanna U.S.A. 41°52N 106°34W **76** F10
Hannah B. Canada 51°40N 80°0W **72** B4
Hannibal Mo., U.S.A. 39°42N 91°22W **80** F8
Hannibal N.Y., U.S.A. 43°19N 76°35W **83** C8
Hannover Germany 52°22N 9°46E **16** B5
Hanoi Vietnam 21°5N 105°55E **38** B5
Hanover = Hannover
  Germany 52°22N 9°46E **16** B5
Hanover Canada 44°9N 81°2W **82** B3
Hanover S. Africa 31°4S 24°29E **56** E3
Hanover N.H., U.S.A. 43°42N 72°17W **83** C12
Hanover Ohio, U.S.A. 40°4N 82°16W **82** F2
Hanover Pa., U.S.A. 39°48N 76°59W **81** F15
Hanover, I. Chile 51°0S 74°50W **96** G2
Hans Lollik I.
  U.S. Virgin Is. 18°24N 64°53W **89** e
Hansdiha India 24°36N 87°5E **43** G12
Hansi H.P., India 32°27N 77°50E **42** C7
Hansi Haryana, India 29°10N 75°57E **42** E6
Hanson, L. Australia 31°0S 136°15E **63** E2
Hantsavichy Belarus 52°49N 26°30E **17** B14
Hanumangarh India 29°35N 74°19E **42** E6
Hanzhong China 33°10N 107°1E **34** H4
Hanzhuang China 34°33N 117°23E **35** G9
Haora India 22°34N 88°18E **43** H13
Haparanda Sweden 65°52N 24°8E **8** D21
Happy U.S.A. 34°45N 101°52W **84** D4
Happy Camp U.S.A. 41°48N 123°23W **76** F2
Happy Valley-Goose Bay
  Canada 53°15N 60°20W **73** B7
Hapsu N. Korea 41°13N 128°51E **35** D15
Hapur India 28°45N 77°45E **42** E7
Ḥaql Si. Arabia 29°10N 34°58E **46** F3
Har Indonesia 5°16S 133°14E **37** F8
Har-Ayrag Mongolia 45°47N 109°16E **34** B5
Har Hu China 38°20N 97°38E **32** C4
Har Us Nuur Mongolia 48°0N 92°0E **32** B4
Har Yehuda Israel 31°35N 34°57E **46** D3
Ḥaraḍ Si. Arabia 24°22N 49°0E **47** C4
Haramosh Pakistan 35°50N 74°54E **43** B6
Haranomachi Japan 37°38N 140°58E **30** F10
Harare Zimbabwe 17°43S 31°2E **55** F3
Harazé Chad 9°57N 20°48E **51** G10
Harbin China 45°48N 126°40E **35** B14
Harbor Beach U.S.A. 43°51N 82°39W **82** C2
Harborcreek U.S.A. 42°9N 79°57W **82** D5
Harbour Breton Canada 47°29N 55°50W **73** C8
Harbour Deep Canada 50°25N 56°32W **73** B8
Harda India 22°27N 77°5E **42** H7
Hardangerfjorden Norway 60°5N 6°0E **9** F12
Hardangervidda Norway 60°7N 7°20E **8** F12
Hardap □ Namibia 24°29S 17°45E **56** C2
Hardap Dam Namibia 24°32S 17°50E **56** C2
Hardenberg Neths. 52°34N 6°37E **15** B6
Harderwijk Neths. 52°21N 5°38E **15** B5
Hardey → Australia 22°45S 116°8E **60** D2
Hardin U.S.A. 45°44N 107°37W **76** D10
Harding S. Africa 30°35S 29°55E **57** E4
Harding Ra. Australia 16°17S 124°55E **60** C3
Hardisty Canada 52°40N 111°18W **70** C6
Hardoi India 27°26N 80°6E **43** F9
Hardwar = Haridwar
  India 29°58N 78°9E **42** E8
Hardwick U.S.A. 44°30N 72°22W **83** B12
Hardwood Lake Canada 45°12N 77°26W **82** A7
Hardy, Pen. Chile 55°30S 68°20W **96** H3
Hardy, Pte. St. Lucia 14°6N 60°56W **89** f
Hare B. Canada 51°15N 55°45W **73** B8
Hareid Norway 62°22N 6°1E **8** E12
Harer Ethiopia 9°20N 42°8E **47** F3
Hargeisa Somali Rep. 9°30N 44°2E **47** F3
Hari → Indonesia 1°16S 104°5E **36** E2
Haria Canary Is. 29°8N 13°32W **24** E6
Haridwar India 29°58N 78°9E **42** E8
Harim, Jabal al Oman 25°58N 56°14E **45** E8
Haringhata → Bangla. 22°0N 89°58E **41** J16
Ḥarīr, W. al → Syria 32°44N 35°59E **46** C4
Ḥarīrūd → Asia 37°24N 60°38E **45** B9
Härjedalen Sweden 62°22N 13°5E **8** E15
Harlan Iowa, U.S.A. 41°39N 95°19W **80** E6
Harlan Ky., U.S.A. 36°51N 83°19W **81** G12
Harlech U.K. 52°52N 4°6W **12** E3
Harlem U.S.A. 48°32N 108°47W **76** B9
Harlingen Neths. 53°11N 5°25E **15** A5
Harlingen U.S.A. 26°12N 97°42W **84** H6
Harlow U.K. 51°46N 0°8E **13** F8
Harlowton U.S.A. 46°26N 109°50W **76** C9
Harnai Pakistan 30°6N 67°56E **42** D2
Harney Basin U.S.A. 43°30N 119°0W **76** E4
Harney L. U.S.A. 43°14N 119°8W **76** E4
Harney Peak U.S.A. 43°52N 103°32W **80** D2
Härnösand Sweden 62°38N 17°55E **8** E17
Haroldswick U.K. 60°48N 0°50W **11** A8
Harp L. Canada 55°5N 61°50W **73** A7
Harper Liberia 4°25N 7°43W **50** H4
Harper, Mt. U.S.A. 64°14N 143°51W **74** C11
Harrai India 22°37N 79°13E **43** H8
Harrand Pakistan 29°28N 70°3E **42** E4
Harricana → Canada 50°56N 79°32W **72** B4
Harriman U.S.A. 35°56N 84°33W **85** D12
Harrington Harbour
  Canada 50°31N 59°30W **73** B8
Harris U.K. 57°50N 6°55W **11** D2
Harris, L. Australia 31°10S 135°10E **63** E2
Harris, Sd. of U.K. 57°44N 7°6W **11** D1
Harris Pt. Canada 43°6N 82°9W **82** C2

Harrisburg Ill., U.S.A. 37°44N 88°32W **80** G9
Harrisburg Nebr.,
  U.S.A. 41°33N 103°44W **80** E2
Harrisburg Pa., U.S.A. 40°16N 76°53W **82** F8
Harrismith S. Africa 28°15S 29°8E **57** D4
Harrison Ark., U.S.A. 36°14N 93°7W **84** C8
Harrison Maine, U.S.A. 44°7N 70°39W **83** B14
Harrison Nebr., U.S.A. 42°41N 103°53W **80** D2
Harrison, C. Canada 54°55N 57°55W **73** B8
Harrison Bay U.S.A. 70°40N 151°0W **74** A9
Harrison L. Canada 49°33N 121°50W **70** D4
Harrisonburg U.S.A. 38°27N 78°52W **81** F14
Harrisonville U.S.A. 38°39N 94°21W **80** F6
Harriston Canada 43°57N 80°53W **82** C4
Harrisville Mich., U.S.A. 44°39N 83°17W **82** B1
Harrisville N.Y., U.S.A. 44°9N 75°19W **83** B9
Harrisville Pa., U.S.A. 41°8N 80°0W **82** E5
Harrodsburg U.S.A. 37°46N 84°51W **81** G11
Harrogate U.K. 54°0N 1°33W **12** C6
Harrow Canada 42°2N 82°55W **82** D2
Harrow □ U.K. 51°35N 0°21W **13** F7
Harrowsmith Canada 44°24N 76°40W **83** B8
Harry S. Truman Res.
  U.S.A. 38°16N 93°24W **80** F7
Harsīn Iran 34°18N 47°33E **44** C5
Harstad Norway 68°48N 16°30E **8** B17
Harsud India 22°6N 76°44E **42** H7
Hart U.S.A. 43°42N 86°22W **80** D10
Hart, L. Australia 31°10S 136°25E **63** E2
Hartbees → S. Africa 28°45S 20°32E **56** D3
Hartford Conn., U.S.A. 41°46N 72°41W **83** E12
Hartford Ky., U.S.A. 37°27N 86°55W **80** G10
Hartford S. Dak., U.S.A. 43°38N 96°57W **80** D5
Hartford Vt., U.S.A. 43°40N 72°20W **83** C12
Hartford Wis., U.S.A. 43°19N 88°22W **80** D9
Hartford City U.S.A. 40°27N 85°22W **81** E11
Hartland Canada 46°20N 67°32W **73** C6
Hartland Pt. U.K. 51°1N 4°32W **13** F3
Hartlepool U.K. 54°42N 1°13W **12** C6
Hartlepool □ U.K. 54°42N 1°17W **12** C6
Hartley Bay Canada 53°25N 129°15W **70** C3
Hartmannberge Namibia 17°0S 13°0E **56** B1
Hartney Canada 49°30N 100°35W **71** D8
Harts → S. Africa 28°24S 24°17E **56** D3
Harts Range Australia 23°6S 134°55E **62** C1
Hartselle U.S.A. 34°27N 86°56W **85** D11
Hartshorne U.S.A. 34°51N 95°34W **84** D7
Hartstown U.S.A. 41°33N 80°23W **82** E4
Hartsville U.S.A. 34°23N 80°4W **85** D14
Hartswater S. Africa 27°34S 24°43E **56** D3
Hartwell U.S.A. 34°21N 82°56W **85** D13
Harunabad Pakistan 29°35N 73°8E **42** E5
Harvand Iran 28°25N 55°43E **45** D7
Harvey Australia 33°5S 115°54E **61** F2
Harvey Ill., U.S.A. 41°36N 87°50W **80** E10
Harvey N. Dak., U.S.A. 47°47N 99°56W **80** B4
Harwich U.K. 51°56N 1°17E **13** F9
Haryana □ India 29°0N 76°10E **42** E7
Haryn → Belarus 52°7N 27°17E **17** B14
Harz Germany 51°38N 10°44E **16** C6
Hasa Si. Arabia 25°50N 49°0E **45** E6
Ḥasā, W. al → Jordan 31°4N 35°29E **46** D4
Ḥasanābād Iran 32°8N 52°44E **45** C7
Ḥasb, W. → Iraq 31°45N 44°17E **44** D5
Hasdo → India 21°44N 82°44E **43** J10
Hashimoto Japan 34°19N 135°37E **31** G7
Hashtjerd Iran 35°52N 50°40E **45** C6
Hashtpur = Tālesh Iran 37°58N 48°58E **45** B6
Haskell U.S.A. 33°10N 99°44W **84** E5
Haskovo = Khaskovo
  Bulgaria 41°56N 25°30E **23** D11
Haslemere U.K. 51°5N 0°43W **13** F7
Hasselt Belgium 50°56N 5°21E **15** D5
Hassi Messaoud Algeria 31°51N 6°1E **50** B7
Hässleholm Sweden 56°10N 13°46E **9** H15
Hastings N.Z. 39°39S 176°52E **59** C6
Hastings U.K. 50°51N 0°35E **13** G8
Hastings Mich., U.S.A. 42°39N 85°17W **81** D11
Hastings Minn., U.S.A. 44°44N 92°51W **80** C7
Hastings Nebr., U.S.A. 40°35N 98°23W **80** E4
Hastings Ra. Australia 31°15S 152°14E **63** E5
Hat Yai Thailand 7°1N 100°27E **39** J3
Hatanbulag = Ergel
  Mongolia 43°8N 109°5E **34** C5
Hatay Turkey 36°14N 36°10E **44** B3
Hatch U.S.A. 32°40N 107°9W **77** K10
Hatchet L. Canada 58°36N 103°40W **71** B8
Hateruma-Shima Japan 24°3N 123°47E **31** M1
Hatfield Australia 33°54S 143°49E **63** E3
Hatgal Mongolia 50°26N 100°9E **32** A5
Hathras India 27°36N 78°6E **42** F8
Hatia Bangla. 22°30N 91°5E **41** H17
Hato Mayor Dom. Rep. 18°46N 69°15W **89** C6
Hatta India 24°7N 79°36E **43** G8
Hatta U.A.E. 24°45N 56°4E **45** E8
Hattah Australia 34°48S 142°17E **63** E3
Hattah Kulkyne △
  Australia 34°16S 142°33E **63** E3
Hatteras, C. U.S.A. 35°14N 75°32W **85** D17
Hattiesburg U.S.A. 31°20N 89°17W **85** F10
Hatvan Hungary 47°40N 19°45E **17** E10
Hau Duc Vietnam 15°20N 108°13E **38** E7
Haugesund Norway 59°23N 5°13E **9** G11
Haukipudas Finland 65°12N 25°20E **8** D21
Haultain → Canada 55°51N 106°46W **71** B7
Hauraki G. N.Z. 36°35S 175°5E **59** B5
Haut Atlas Morocco 32°30N 5°0W **50** B4
Hautes Fagnes = Hohes Venn
  Belgium 50°30N 6°5E **15** D6
Hauts Plateaux Algeria 35°0N 1°0E **50** B6
Havana = La Habana
  Cuba 23°8N 82°22W **88** B3
Havana U.S.A. 40°18N 90°4W **80** E8
Havant U.K. 50°51N 0°58W **13** G7
Havasu, L. U.S.A. 34°18N 114°28W **79** L12
Havel → Germany 52°50N 12°3E **16** B7
Havelian Pakistan 34°2N 73°10E **42** B5
Havelock Canada 44°26N 77°53W **82** B7

Havelock N.Z. 41°17S 173°48E **59** D4
Havelock U.S.A. 34°53N 76°54W **85** D16
Haverfordwest U.K. 51°48N 4°58W **13** F3
Haverhill U.K. 52°5N 0°28E **13** E8
Haverhill U.S.A. 42°47N 71°5W **83** D13
Haverstraw U.S.A. 41°12N 73°58W **83** E11
Havirga Mongolia 45°41N 113°5E **34** B7
Havířov Czech Rep. 49°46N 18°20E **17** D10
Havlíčkův Brod
  Czech Rep. 49°36N 15°33E **16** D8
Havre U.S.A. 48°33N 109°41W **76** B9
Havre-Aubert Canada 47°12N 61°56W **73** C7
Havre-St.-Pierre Canada 50°18N 63°33W **73** B7
Haw → U.S.A. 35°36N 79°3W **85** D15
Hawai'i U.S.A. 19°30N 155°30W **75** M8
Hawai'i □ U.S.A. 19°30N 156°30W **75** M8
Hawaiian Is. Pac. Oc. 20°30N 156°0W **65** E12
Hawaiian Ridge Pac. Oc. 24°0N 165°0W **65** E11
Hawarden U.S.A. 43°0N 96°29W **80** D5
Hawea, L. N.Z. 44°28S 169°19E **59** F2
Hawera N.Z. 39°35S 174°19E **59** C5
Hawi U.S.A. 20°14N 155°50W **75** L8
Hawick U.K. 55°26N 2°47W **11** F6
Hawk Junction Canada 48°5N 84°38W **72** C3
Hawke B. N.Z. 39°25S 177°20E **59** C6
Hawker Australia 31°59S 138°22E **63** E2
Hawke's Bay Canada 50°36N 57°10W **73** B8
Hawkesbury Canada 45°37N 74°37W **72** C5
Hawkesbury → Australia 33°30S 151°10E **63** E5
Hawkesbury I. Canada 53°37N 129°3W **70** C3
Hawkesbury Pt.
  Australia 11°55S 134°5E **62** A1
Hawkinsville U.S.A. 32°17N 83°28W **85** D13
Hawley Minn., U.S.A. 46°53N 96°19W **80** B5
Hawley Pa., U.S.A. 41°28N 75°11W **83** E9
Ḥawrān, W. → Iraq 33°58N 42°34E **44** C4
Hawsh Mūssá Lebanon 33°45N 35°55E **46** B4
Hawthorne U.S.A. 38°32N 118°38W **76** G4
Hay Australia 34°30S 144°51E **63** E3
Hay → Australia 24°50S 138°0E **62** C2
Hay → Canada 60°50N 116°26W **70** A5
Hay, C. Australia 14°5S 129°29E **60** B4
Hay L. Canada 44°53N 80°58W **82** B4
Hay L. Canada 58°50N 118°50W **70** B5
Hay-on-Wye U.K. 52°5N 3°8W **13** E4
Hay Point Australia 21°18S 149°17E **62** C4
Hay River Canada 60°51N 115°44W **70** A5
Hay Springs U.S.A. 42°41N 102°41W **80** D2
Haya = Tehoru Indonesia 3°23S 129°30E **37** E7
Hayachine-San Japan 39°34N 141°29E **30** E10
Hayastan = Armenia ■
  Asia 40°20N 45°0E **19** F7
Haydān, W. al → Jordan 31°29N 35°34E **46** D4
Hayden U.S.A. 40°30N 107°16W **76** F10
Hayes U.S.A. 44°23N 101°1W **80** C3
Hayes → Canada 57°3N 92°12W **72** A1
Hayes, Mt. U.S.A. 63°37N 146°43W **74** C10
Hayes Creek Australia 13°43S 131°22E **60** B5
Hayle U.K. 50°11N 5°26W **13** G2
Hayman I. Australia 20°4S 148°53E **62** b
Hayrabolu Turkey 41°12N 27°5E **23** D12
Hays Canada 50°6N 111°48W **70** C6
Hays U.S.A. 38°53N 99°20W **80** F4
Haysyn Ukraine 48°57N 29°25E **17** D15
Hayvoron Ukraine 48°22N 29°52E **17** D15
Hayward Calif., U.S.A. 37°40N 122°4W **78** H4
Hayward Wis., U.S.A. 46°1N 91°29W **80** B8
Haywards Heath U.K. 51°0N 0°5W **13** G7
Hazafon □ Israel 32°40N 35°20E **46** C4
Hazar Turkmenistan 39°34N 53°16E **19** G9
Hazārān, Kūh-e Iran 29°35N 57°20E **45** D8
Hazard U.S.A. 37°15N 83°12W **81** G12
Hazaribag India 23°58N 85°26E **43** H11
Hazaribag Road India 24°12N 85°57E **43** G11
Hazelton Canada 55°20N 127°42W **70** B3
Hazelton U.S.A. 46°29N 100°17W **80** B3
Hazen U.S.A. 47°18N 101°38W **80** B3
Hazen, L. Canada 81°47N 71°1W **69** A17
Hazenmore Canada 49°42N 107°35W **71** D7
Hazerswoude Neths. 52°6N 4°36E **15** B4
Hazlehurst Ga., U.S.A. 31°52N 82°36W **85** F13
Hazlehurst Miss., U.S.A. 31°52N 90°24W **85** F9
Hazleton U.S.A. 40°57N 75°59W **83** F9
Hazlett, L. Australia 21°30S 128°48E **60** D4
Hazro Turkey 38°15N 40°47E **44** B4
Head of Bight Australia 31°30S 131°25E **61** F5
Headlands Zimbabwe 18°15S 32°2E **55** F3
Healdsburg U.S.A. 38°37N 122°52W **78** G4
Healdton U.S.A. 34°14N 97°29W **84** D6
Healesville Australia 37°35S 145°30E **63** F4
Healy U.S.A. 63°52N 148°58W **74** C10
Heany Junction Zimbabwe 20°6S 28°54E **57** C4
Heard I. Ind. Oc. 53°6S 72°36E **3** G13
Hearne U.S.A. 30°53N 96°36W **84** F6
Hearst Canada 49°40N 83°41W **72** C3
Heart → U.S.A. 46°46N 100°50W **80** B3
Heart's Content Canada 47°54N 53°27W **73** C9
Heath, Pte. Canada 49°8N 61°40W **73** C7
Heathrow, London ✈ (LHR)
  U.K. 51°28N 0°27W **13** F7
Heavener U.S.A. 34°53N 94°36W **84** D7
Hebbronville U.S.A. 27°18N 98°41W **84** H5
Hebei □ China 39°0N 116°0E **34** E9
Hebel Australia 28°58S 147°47E **63** D4
Heber U.S.A. 34°4N 115°32W **79** N11
Heber Springs U.S.A. 35°30N 92°2W **84** D8
Hebgen L. U.S.A. 44°52N 111°20W **76** D8
Hebi China 35°57N 114°7E **34** G8
Hebrides U.K. 57°30N 7°0W **11** D2
Hebrides, Sea of the U.K. 57°5N 7°0W **11** D2
Hebron = Al Khalīl
  West Bank 31°32N 35°6E **46** D4
Hebron Canada 58°5N 62°30W **69** F19
Hebron N. Dak., U.S.A. 46°54N 102°3W **80** B2
Hebron Nebr., U.S.A. 40°10N 97°35W **80** E5
Hecate Str. Canada 53°10N 130°30W **70** C2
Heceta I. Canada 55°46N 133°40W **70** B2
Hechi China 24°40N 108°2E **32** D5
Hechuan China 30°2N 106°12E **32** C5
Hecla U.S.A. 45°53N 98°9W **80** C4

Hecla I. *Canada* 51°10N 96°43W **71** C9
Hede *Sweden* 62°23N 13°30E **8** E15
Hedemora *Sweden* 60°18N 15°58E **9** F16
Heerde *Neths.* 52°24N 6°2E **15** B6
Heerenveen *Neths.* 52°57N 5°55E **15** B5
Heerhugowaard *Neths.* 52°40N 4°51E **15** B4
Heerlen *Neths.* 50°55N 5°58E **15** D5
Hefa *Israel* 32°46N 35°0E **46** C4
Ḥefa □ *Israel* 32°40N 35°0E **46** C4
Hefei *China* 31°52N 117°18E **33** C6
Hegang *China* 47°20N 130°19E **33** B8
Hei Ling Chau *China* 22°15N 114°2E **33** G11
Heichengzhen *China* 36°24N 106°3E **34** F4
Heidelberg *Germany* 49°24N 8°42E **16** D5
Heidelberg *S. Africa* 34°6S 20°59E **56** E3
Heihe *China* 50°10N 127°30E **33** A7
Heilbron *S. Africa* 27°16S 27°59E **57** D4
Heilbronn *Germany* 49°9N 9°13E **16** D5
Heilongjiang □ *China* 48°0N 126°0E **33** B7
Heilunkiang = Heilongjiang □
  China 48°0N 126°0E **33** B7
Heimaey *Iceland* 63°26N 20°17W **8** E3
Heinola *Finland* 61°13N 26°2E **8** F22
Heinze Kyun *Burma* 14°25N 97°45E **38** E1
Heishan *China* 41°40N 122°5E **35** D12
Heishui *China* 42°8N 119°30E **35** C10
Hejaz = Ḥijāz *Si. Arabia* 24°0N 40°0E **44** E3
Hejian *China* 38°25N 116°5E **34** E9
Hejin *China* 35°35N 110°42E **34** G6
Hekimhan *Turkey* 38°50N 37°58E **44** B3
Hekla *Iceland* 63°56N 19°35W **8** E4
Hekou *China* 22°30N 103°59E **32** D5
Helan Shan *China* 38°30N 105°55E **34** E3
Helen Atoll *Pac. Oc.* 2°40N 132°0E **37** D8
Helena *Ark., U.S.A.* 34°32N 90°36W **85** D9
Helena *Mont., U.S.A.* 46°36N 112°2W **76** C7
Helendale *U.S.A.* 34°44N 117°19W **79** L9
Helensburgh *U.K.* 56°1N 4°43W **11** E4
Helensville *N.Z.* 36°41S 174°29E **59** B5
Helenvale *Australia* 15°43S 145°14E **62** B4
Helgeland *Norway* 66°7N 13°29E **8** C15
Helgoland *Germany* 54°10N 7°53E **16** A4
Heligoland = Helgoland
  Germany 54°10N 7°53E **16** A4
Heligoland B. = Deutsche Bucht
  Germany 54°15N 8°0E **16** A5
Hell Hole Gorge △
  Australia 25°31S 144°12E **62** D3
Hella *Iceland* 63°50N 20°24W **8** E3
Hellas = Greece ■ *Europe* 40°0N 23°0E **23** E9
Hellertown *U.S.A.* 40°35N 75°21W **83** F9
Hellespont = Çanakkale Boğazı
  Turkey 40°17N 26°32E **23** D12
Hellevoetsluis *Neths.* 51°50N 4°8E **15** C4
Hellín *Spain* 38°31N 1°40W **21** C5
Hells Canyon △ *U.S.A.* 45°30N 117°45W **76** D5
Hell's Gate △ *Kenya* 0°54S 36°19E **54** C4
Helmand □ *Afghan.* 31°20N 64°0E **40** D4
Helmand → *Afghan.* 31°12N 61°34E **40** D2
Helmeringhausen
  Namibia 25°54S 16°57E **56** D2
Helmond *Neths.* 51°29N 5°41E **15** C5
Helmsdale *U.K.* 58°7N 3°39W **11** C5
Helmsdale → *U.K.* 58°8N 3°43W **11** C5
Helong *China* 42°40N 129°0E **35** C15
Helper *U.S.A.* 39°41N 110°51W **76** G8
Helsingborg *Sweden* 56°3N 12°42E **9** H15
Helsingfors = Helsinki
  Finland 60°10N 24°55E **9** F21
Helsingør *Denmark* 56°2N 12°35E **9** H15
Helsinki *Finland* 60°10N 24°55E **9** F21
Helston *U.K.* 50°6N 5°17W **13** G2
Helvellyn *U.K.* 54°32N 3°1W **12** C4
Helwân *Egypt* 29°50N 31°20E **51** C12
Hemel Hempstead *U.K.* 51°44N 0°28W **13** F7
Hemet *U.S.A.* 33°45N 116°58W **79** M10
Hemingford *U.S.A.* 42°19N 103°4W **80** D2
Hemis △ *India* 34°10N 77°15E **42** B7
Hemmingford *Canada* 45°3N 73°35W **83** A11
Hempstead *N.Y., U.S.A.* 40°42N 73°37W **83** F11
Hempstead *Tex., U.S.A.* 30°6N 96°5W **84** F6
Hemse *Sweden* 57°15N 18°22E **9** H18
Henan □ *China* 34°0N 114°0E **34** H8
Henares → *Spain* 40°24N 3°30W **21** B4
Henashi-Misaki *Japan* 40°37N 139°51E **30** D9
Henderson *Argentina* 36°18S 61°43W **94** D3
Henderson *Ky., U.S.A.* 37°50N 87°35W **80** G10
Henderson *N.C., U.S.A.* 36°20N 78°25W **85** G15
Henderson *N.Y., U.S.A.* 43°50N 76°10W **83** C8
Henderson *Nev., U.S.A.* 36°2N 114°58W **79** J12
Henderson *Tenn.,*
  U.S.A. 35°26N 88°38W **85** D10
Henderson *Tex., U.S.A.* 32°9N 94°48W **84** E7
Henderson I. *Pac. Oc.* 24°22S 128°19W **65** K15
Hendersonville *N.C.,*
  U.S.A. 35°19N 82°28W **85** D13
Hendersonville *Tenn.,*
  U.S.A. 36°18N 86°37W **85** C11
Hendījān *Iran* 30°14N 49°43E **45** D6
Hendorābī *Iran* 26°40N 53°37E **45** E7
Hengcheng *China* 38°18N 106°28E **34** E4
Hengdaohezi *China* 44°52N 129°0E **35** B15
Hengduan Shan *China* 27°30N 99°0E **32** D4
Hengelo *Neths.* 52°16N 6°48E **15** B6
Henggang *China* 22°39N 114°12E **33** F11
Hengmen *China* 22°33N 113°35E **33** F10
Hengqin Dao *China* 22°13N 113°34E **33** G10
Hengshan *China* 37°58N 109°5E **34** F5
Hengshui *China* 37°41N 115°40E **34** F8
Hengyang *China* 26°59N 112°22E **33** D6
Henley-on-Thames *U.K.* 51°32N 0°54W **13** F7
Henlopen, C. *U.S.A.* 38°48N 75°6W **81** F16
Hennenman *S. Africa* 27°59S 27°1E **56** D4
Hennessey *U.S.A.* 36°6N 97°54W **84** C6
Henri Pittier △
  Venezuela 10°26N 67°37W **89** D6
Henrietta *N.Y., U.S.A.* 43°4N 77°37W **82** C7
Henrietta *Tex., U.S.A.* 33°49N 98°12W **84** E5
Henrietta, Ostrov = Genriyetty,
  Ostrov *Russia* 77°6N 156°30E **29** B16

Henrietta Maria, C.
  Canada 55°9N 82°20W **72** A3
Henry *U.S.A.* 41°7N 89°22W **80** E9
Henryetta *U.S.A.* 35°27N 95°59W **84** D7
Henryville *Canada* 45°8N 73°11W **83** A11
Hensall *Canada* 43°26N 81°30W **82** C3
Hentiesbaai *Namibia* 22°8S 14°18E **56** C1
Hentiyn Nuruu
  Mongolia 48°30N 108°30E **33** B5
Henty *Australia* 35°30S 147°3E **63** F4
Henzada *Burma* 17°38N 95°26E **41** L19
Heppner *U.S.A.* 45°21N 119°33W **76** D4
Hepworth *Canada* 44°37N 81°9W **82** B3
Hequ *China* 39°20N 111°15E **34** E6
Hérault □ *France* 43°34N 3°15E **20** E5
Héraðsflói *Iceland* 65°42N 14°12W **8** D6
Héraðsvötn → *Iceland* 65°45N 19°25W **8** D4
Heraklion = Iraklio
  Greece 35°20N 25°12E **25** D7
Herald Cays *Australia* 16°58S 149°9E **62** B4
Herāt *Afghan.* 34°20N 62°7E **40** B3
Herāt □ *Afghan.* 35°0N 62°0E **40** B3
Herbert *Canada* 50°30N 107°10W **71** C7
Herbert → *Australia* 18°31S 146°17E **62** B4
Herberton *Australia* 17°20S 145°25E **62** B4
Herbertsdale *S. Africa* 34°1S 21°46E **56** E3
Herceg-Novi *Montenegro* 42°30N 18°33E **23** C8
Herchmer *Canada* 57°22N 94°10W **71** B10
Herðubreið *Iceland* 65°11N 16°21W **8** D5
Hereford *U.K.* 52°4N 2°43W **13** E5
Hereford *U.S.A.* 34°49N 102°24W **84** D3
Herefordshire □ *U.K.* 52°8N 2°40W **13** E5
Herentals *Belgium* 51°12N 4°51E **15** C4
Herford *Germany* 52°7N 8°39E **16** B5
Herington *U.S.A.* 38°40N 96°57W **80** F5
Herkimer *U.S.A.* 43°2N 74°59W **83** D10
Herlong *U.S.A.* 40°8N 120°8W **78** E6
Herm *U.K.* 49°30N 2°28W **13** H5
Hermann *U.S.A.* 38°42N 91°27W **80** F8
Hermannsburg
  Australia 23°57S 132°45E **60** D5
Hermanus *S. Africa* 34°27S 19°12E **56** E2
Hermidale *Australia* 31°30S 146°42E **63** E4
Hermiston *U.S.A.* 45°51N 119°17W **76** D4
Hermon *Canada* 45°6N 77°37W **82** A7
Hermon *U.S.A.* 44°28N 75°14W **83** B9
Hermon, Mt. = Shaykh, J. ash
  Lebanon 33°25N 35°50E **46** B4
Hermosillo *Mexico* 29°10N 111°0W **86** B2
Hernád → *Hungary* 47°56N 21°8E **17** D11
Hernandarias *Paraguay* 25°20S 54°40W **95** B5
Hernandez *U.S.A.* 36°24N 120°46W **78** J6
Hernando *Argentina* 32°28S 63°40W **94** C3
Hernando *U.S.A.* 34°50N 90°0W **85** D9
Herndon *U.S.A.* 40°43N 76°51W **82** F8
Herne *Germany* 51°32N 7°14E **15** C7
Herne Bay *U.K.* 51°21N 1°8E **13** F9
Herning *Denmark* 56°8N 8°58E **9** H13
Heroica Caborca = Caborca
  Mexico 30°37N 112°6W **86** A2
Heroica Nogales = Nogales
  Mexico 31°19N 110°56W **86** A2
Heron Bay *Canada* 48°40N 86°25W **72** C2
Heron I. *Australia* 23°27S 151°55E **62** C5
Herradura, Pta. de la
  Canary Is. 28°26N 14°8W **24** F5
Herreid *U.S.A.* 45°50N 100°4W **80** C3
Herrin *U.S.A.* 37°48N 89°2W **80** G9
Herriot *Canada* 56°22N 101°16W **71** B8
Hershey *U.S.A.* 40°17N 76°39W **83** F8
Herstal *Belgium* 50°40N 5°38E **15** D5
Hertford *U.K.* 51°48N 0°4W **13** F7
Hertfordshire □ *U.K.* 51°51N 0°5W **13** F7
's-Hertogenbosch *Neths.* 51°42N 5°17E **15** C5
Hertzogville *S. Africa* 28°9S 25°30E **56** D4
Hervey B. *Australia* 25°0S 152°52E **62** C5
Herzliyya *Israel* 32°10N 34°50E **46** C3
Ḥeşār *Fārs, Iran* 29°52N 50°16E **45** D6
Ḥeşār *Markazī, Iran* 35°50N 49°12E **45** C6
Heshui *China* 35°48N 108°0E **34** G5
Heshun *China* 37°22N 113°32E **34** F7
Hesperia *U.S.A.* 34°25N 117°18W **79** L9
Hesse = Hessen □
  Germany 50°30N 9°0E **16** C5
Hessen □ *Germany* 50°30N 9°0E **16** C5
Hetauda *Nepal* 27°25N 85°2E **43** F11
Hetch Hetchy Aqueduct
  U.S.A. 37°29N 122°19W **78** H5
Hettinger *U.S.A.* 46°0N 102°42W **80** B2
Heuksando *S. Korea* 34°40N 125°30E **35** G13
Heunghae *S. Korea* 36°12N 129°21E **35** F15
Heuvelton *U.S.A.* 44°37N 75°25W **83** B9
Hewitt *U.S.A.* 31°28N 97°12W **84** F6
Hexham *U.K.* 54°58N 2°4W **12** C5
Hexigten Qi *China* 43°18N 117°30E **35** C9
Heydarābād *Iran* 30°33N 55°38E **45** D7
Heysham *U.K.* 54°3N 2°53W **12** C5
Heywood *Australia* 38°8S 141°37E **63** F3
Heze *China* 35°14N 115°20E **34** G8
Hi Vista *U.S.A.* 34°45N 117°46W **79** L9
Hialeah *U.S.A.* 25°51N 80°16W **85** J14
Hiawatha *U.S.A.* 39°51N 95°32W **80** F6
Hibbing *U.S.A.* 47°25N 92°56W **80** B7
Hibernia Reef *Australia* 12°0S 123°23E **60** B3
Hickman *U.S.A.* 36°34N 89°11W **80** G9
Hickory *U.S.A.* 35°44N 81°21W **85** D14
Hicks, Pt. *Australia* 37°49S 149°17E **63** F4
Hicks L. *Canada* 61°25N 100°0W **71** A9
Hicksville *U.S.A.* 40°46N 73°32W **83** F11
Hida-Gawa → *Japan* 35°26N 137°3E **31** G8
Hida-Sammyaku *Japan* 36°30N 137°40E **31** F8
Hidaka-Sammyaku
  Japan 42°35N 142°45E **30** C11
Hidalgo □ *Mexico* 20°30N 99°0W **87** C5
Hidalgo, Presa M.
  Mexico 26°30N 108°35W **86** B3
Hidalgo del Parral
  Mexico 26°56N 105°40W **86** B3
Hierro *Canary Is.* 27°44N 18°0W **24** G1

Higashiajima-San
  Japan 37°40N 140°10E **30** F10
Higashiōsaka *Japan* 34°39N 135°37E **31** G7
Higgins *U.S.A.* 36°7N 100°2W **84** C4
Higgins Corner *U.S.A.* 39°2N 121°5W **78** F5
High Bridge *U.S.A.* 40°40N 74°54W **83** F10
High Desert *U.S.A.* 43°40N 120°20W **74** G15
High Island Res. *China* 22°22N 114°21E **33** G11
High Level *Canada* 58°31N 117°8W **70** B5
High Point *U.S.A.* 35°57N 80°0W **85** D15
High Prairie *Canada* 55°30N 116°30W **70** B5
High River *Canada* 50°30N 113°50W **70** C6
High Tatra = Tatry
  Slovak Rep. 49°20N 20°0E **17** D11
High Veld *Africa* 27°0S 27°0E **48** J6
High Wycombe *U.K.* 51°37N 0°45W **13** F7
Highland □ *U.K.* 57°17N 4°21W **11** D4
Highland Park *U.S.A.* 42°11N 87°48W **80** D10
Highmore *U.S.A.* 44°31N 99°27W **80** C4
Highrock L. *Canada* 55°45N 100°30W **71** B8
Higüey *Dom. Rep.* 18°37N 68°42W **89** C6
Hiiumaa *Estonia* 58°50N 22°45E **9** G20
Ḥijārah, Şaḥrā' al *Iraq* 30°25N 44°30E **44** D5
Ḥijāz *Si. Arabia* 24°0N 40°0E **44** E3
Hijo = Tagum *Phil.* 7°33N 125°53E **37** C7
Hikari *Japan* 33°58N 131°58E **31** H5
Hiko *U.S.A.* 37°32N 115°14W **78** H11
Hikone *Japan* 35°15N 136°10E **31** G8
Hikurangi *Gisborne, N.Z.* 37°55S 178°4E **59** C6
Hikurangi *Northland,*
  N.Z. 35°36S 174°17E **59** A5
Hildesheim *Germany* 52°9N 9°56E **16** B5
Hill → *Australia* 30°23S 115°3E **61** F2
Hill City *Idaho, U.S.A.* 43°18N 115°3W **76** E6
Hill City *Kans., U.S.A.* 39°22N 99°51W **80** F4
Hill City *Minn., U.S.A.* 46°59N 93°36W **80** B7
Hill City *S. Dak., U.S.A.* 43°56N 103°35W **80** D2
Hill Island L. *Canada* 60°30N 109°50W **71** A7
Hillaby, Mt. *Barbados* 13°12N 59°35W **89** g
Hillcrest *Barbados* 13°13N 59°31W **89** g
Hillcrest Center *U.S.A.* 35°23N 118°57W **79** K8
Hillegom *Neths.* 52°18N 4°35E **15** B4
Hillsboro *Kans., U.S.A.* 38°21N 97°12W **80** F5
Hillsboro *N. Dak., U.S.A.* 47°26N 97°3W **80** B5
Hillsboro *Ohio, U.S.A.* 39°12N 83°37W **81** F12
Hillsboro *Oreg., U.S.A.* 45°31N 122°59W **78** E4
Hillsboro *Tex., U.S.A.* 32°1N 97°8W **84** E6
Hillsborough *Grenada* 12°28N 61°28W **89** D7
Hillsborough *U.S.A.* 43°7N 71°54W **83** C13
Hillsborough Channel
  Australia 20°56S 149°15E **62** b
Hillsdale *Mich., U.S.A.* 41°56N 84°38W **81** E11
Hillsdale *N.Y., U.S.A.* 42°11N 73°32W **83** D11
Hillsport *Canada* 49°27N 85°34W **72** C2
Hillston *Australia* 33°30S 145°31E **63** E4
Hilo *U.S.A.* 19°44N 155°5W **75** M8
Hilton *U.S.A.* 43°17N 77°48W **82** C7
Hilton Head Island
  U.S.A. 32°13N 80°45W **85** E14
Hilversum *Neths.* 52°14N 5°10E **15** B5
Himachal Pradesh □
  India 31°30N 77°0E **42** D7
Himalaya *Asia* 29°0N 84°0E **43** E11
Himalchuli *Nepal* 28°27N 84°38E **43** E11
Himatnagar *India* 23°37N 72°57E **42** H5
Himeji *Japan* 34°50N 134°40E **31** G7
Himi *Japan* 36°50N 136°55E **31** F8
Ḥimṣ *Syria* 34°40N 36°45E **46** A5
Ḥimṣ □ *Syria* 34°30N 37°0E **46** A6
Hinche *Haiti* 19°9N 72°1W **89** C5
Hinchinbrook I.
  Australia 18°20S 146°15E **62** B4
Hinchinbrook Island △
  Australia 18°14S 146°6E **62** B4
Hinckley *U.K.* 52°33N 1°22W **13** E6
Hinckley *U.S.A.* 46°1N 92°56W **80** B7
Hindaun *India* 26°44N 77°5E **42** F7
Hindmarsh, L. *Australia* 36°5S 141°55E **63** F3
Hindu Bagh *Pakistan* 30°56N 67°50E **42** D2
Hindu Kush *Asia* 36°0N 71°0E **40** B7
Hindupur *India* 13°49N 77°32E **40** N10
Hines Creek *Canada* 56°20N 118°40W **70** B5
Hinesville *U.S.A.* 31°51N 81°36W **85** F14
Hinganghat *India* 20°30N 78°52E **40** J11
Hingir *India* 21°57N 83°41E **43** J10
Hingoli *India* 19°41N 77°15E **40** K10
Hinna = Imi *Ethiopia* 6°28N 42°10E **47** F3
Hinnøya *Norway* 68°35N 15°50E **8** B16
Hinojosa del Duque *Spain* 38°30N 5°9W **21** C3
Hinsdale *U.S.A.* 42°47N 72°29W **83** D12
Hinthada = Henzada
  Burma 17°38N 95°26E **41** L19
Hinton *Canada* 53°26N 117°34W **70** C5
Hinton *U.S.A.* 37°40N 80°54W **81** G13
Hios *Greece* 38°27N 26°9E **23** E12
Hirado *Japan* 33°22N 129°33E **31** H4
Hirakud Dam *India* 21°32N 83°45E **41** J13
Hiran → *India* 23°6N 79°21E **43** H8
Hirapur *India* 24°22N 79°13E **43** G8
Hirara *Japan* 24°48N 125°17E **31** M2
Hiratsuka *Japan* 35°19N 139°21E **31** G9
Hiroo *Japan* 42°17N 143°19E **30** C11
Hirosaki *Japan* 40°34N 140°28E **30** D10
Hiroshima *Japan* 34°24N 132°30E **31** G6
Hiroshima □ *Japan* 34°50N 133°0E **31** G6
Hisar *India* 29°12N 75°45E **42** E6
Ḥisb, Sha'ib → = Ḥasb, W. →
  Iraq 31°45N 44°17E **44** D5
Ḥismā *Si. Arabia* 28°30N 36°0E **44** D3
Hispaniola *W. Indies* 19°0N 71°0W **89** C5
Ḥīt *Iraq* 33°38N 42°49E **44** C4
Hita *Japan* 33°20N 130°58E **31** H5
Hitachi *Japan* 36°36N 140°39E **31** F10
Hitchin *U.K.* 51°58N 0°16W **13** F7
Hitiaa *Tahiti* 17°36S 149°18W **59** d
Hitoyoshi *Japan* 32°13N 130°45E **31** H5
Hitra *Norway* 63°30N 8°45E **8** E13
Hiva Oa *French Polynesia* 9°45S 139°0W **65** H14

Hixon *Canada* 53°25N 122°35W **70** C4
Ḥiyyon, N. → *Israel* 30°25N 35°10E **46** E4
Hjalmar L. *Canada* 61°33N 109°25W **71** A7
Hjälmaren *Sweden* 59°18N 15°40E **9** G16
Hjørring *Denmark* 57°29N 9°59E **9** H13
Hjort Trench *S. Ocean* 58°0S 157°30E **5** A10
Hkakabo Razi *Burma* 28°25N 97°23E **41** E20
Hkamti = Singkaling Hkamti
  Burma 26°0N 95°39E **41** G19
Hlobane *S. Africa* 27°42S 31°0E **57** D5
Hluhluwe *S. Africa* 28°1S 32°15E **57** D5
Hluhluwe → *S. Africa* 22°10S 32°5E **57** C5
Hlyboka *Ukraine* 48°5N 25°56E **17** D13
Ho *Ghana* 6°37N 0°27E **50** G6
Ho Chi Minh City = Thanh Pho
  Ho Chi Minh *Vietnam* 10°58N 106°40E **39** G6
Ho Thuong *Vietnam* 19°32N 105°48E **38** C5
Hoa Binh *Vietnam* 20°50N 105°20E **38** B5
Hoa Da *Vietnam* 11°16N 108°40E **39** G7
Hoa Hiep *Vietnam* 11°34N 105°51E **39** G5
Hoai Nhon *Vietnam* 14°28N 109°1E **38** E7
Hoang Lien Son *Vietnam* 22°0N 104°0E **38** A4
Hoare B. *Canada* 65°17N 62°30W **69** D19
Hoarusib → *Namibia* 19°3S 12°36E **56** B2
Hobart *Australia* 42°50S 147°21E **63** G4
Hobart *U.S.A.* 35°1N 99°6W **84** D5
Hobbs *U.S.A.* 32°42N 103°8W **77** K12
Hobbs Coast *Antarctica* 74°50S 131°0W **5** D14
Hobe Sound *U.S.A.* 27°4N 80°8W **85** H14
Hoboken *U.S.A.* 40°44N 74°3W **83** F10
Hobro *Denmark* 56°39N 9°46E **9** H13
Hoburgen *Sweden* 56°55N 18°7E **9** H18
Hobyo *Somali Rep.* 5°25N 48°30E **47** F4
Hochfeld *Namibia* 21°28S 17°58E **56** C2
Hodaka-Dake *Japan* 36°17N 137°39E **31** F8
Hodeida = Al Ḥudaydah
  Yemen 14°50N 43°0E **47** E3
Hodgeville *Canada* 50°7N 106°58W **71** C7
Hodgson *Canada* 51°13N 97°36W **71** C9
Hódmezővásárhely
  Hungary 46°28N 20°22E **17** E11
Hodna, Chott el *Algeria* 35°26N 4°43E **50** A6
Hodonín *Czech Rep.* 48°50N 17°10E **17** D9
Hoek van Holland *Neths.* 52°0N 4°7E **15** C4
Hoengseong *S. Korea* 37°29N 127°59E **35** F14
Hoeryong *N. Korea* 42°30N 129°45E **35** C15
Hoeyang *N. Korea* 38°43N 127°36E **35** E14
Hof *Germany* 50°19N 11°55E **16** C6
Hofmeyr *S. Africa* 31°39S 25°50E **56** E4
Höfn *Iceland* 64°15N 15°13W **8** D6
Hofors *Sweden* 60°31N 16°15E **9** F17
Hofsjökull *Iceland* 64°49N 18°48W **8** D4
Hōfu *Japan* 34°3N 131°34E **31** G5
Hogan Group *Australia* 39°13S 147°1E **63** F4
Hogarth, Mt. *Australia* 21°48S 136°58E **62** C2
Hoge Kempen △ *Belgium* 51°6N 5°35E **15** C5
Hoggar = Ahaggar *Algeria* 23°0N 6°30E **50** D7
Hoh → *U.S.A.* 47°45N 124°29W **78** C2
Hoh Xil Shan *China* 35°0N 89°0E **32** C3
Hohenwald *U.S.A.* 35°33N 87°33W **85** D11
Hoher Rhön = Rhön
  Germany 50°24N 9°58E **16** C5
Hohes Venn *Belgium* 50°30N 6°5E **15** D6
Hohhot *China* 40°52N 111°40E **34** D6
Hoi An *Vietnam* 15°30N 108°19E **38** E7
Hoi Xuan *Vietnam* 20°25N 105°9E **38** B5
Hoisington *U.S.A.* 38°31N 98°47W **80** F4
Hōjō *Japan* 33°58N 132°46E **31** H6
Hokianga Harbour
  N.Z. 35°31S 173°22E **59** A4
Hokitika *N.Z.* 42°42S 171°0E **59** E3
Hokkaidō □ *Japan* 43°30N 143°0E **30** C11
Hola *Kenya* 1°29S 40°2E **54** B4
Holakas *Greece* 35°57N 27°53E **25** D9
Holbrook *Australia* 35°42S 147°18E **63** F4
Holbrook *U.S.A.* 34°54N 110°10W **77** J8
Holcomb *U.S.A.* 42°54N 77°25W **82** D7
Holden *U.S.A.* 39°6N 112°16W **76** G7
Holdenville *U.S.A.* 35°5N 96°24W **84** D6
Holdrege *U.S.A.* 40°26N 99°23W **80** E4
Holetown *Barbados* 13°11N 59°38W **89** g
Holguín *Cuba* 20°50N 76°20W **88** B4
Hollams Bird I. *Namibia* 24°40S 14°30E **56** C1
Holland = Netherlands ■
  Europe 52°0N 5°30E **15** C5
Holland *Mich., U.S.A.* 42°47N 86°7W **80** D10
Holland *N.Y., U.S.A.* 42°38N 78°32W **82** D6
Holland Centre *Canada* 44°23N 80°47W **82** B4
Holland Patent *U.S.A.* 43°14N 75°15W **83** C9
Hollandale *U.S.A.* 33°10N 90°51W **85** E9
Holley *U.S.A.* 43°14N 78°2W **82** C6
Hollidaysburg *U.S.A.* 40°26N 78°24W **82** F6
Hollis *U.S.A.* 34°41N 99°55W **84** D5
Hollister *Calif., U.S.A.* 36°51N 121°24W **78** J5
Hollister *Idaho, U.S.A.* 42°21N 114°35W **76** E6
Holly Hill *U.S.A.* 29°16N 81°3W **85** G14
Holly Springs *U.S.A.* 34°46N 89°27W **85** D10
Hollywood *U.S.A.* 26°0N 80°8W **85** J14
Holman *Canada* 70°44N 117°44W **68** C8
Hólmavík *Iceland* 65°42N 21°40W **8** D3
Holmen *U.S.A.* 43°58N 91°15W **80** D8
Holmes Reefs *Australia* 16°27S 148°0E **62** B4
Holmsund *Sweden* 63°41N 20°20E **8** E19
Holroyd → *Australia* 14°10S 141°36E **62** A3
Holstebro *Denmark* 56°22N 8°37E **9** H13
Holsworthy *U.K.* 50°48N 4°22W **13** G3
Holton *Canada* 54°31N 57°12W **73** B8
Holton *U.S.A.* 39°28N 95°44W **80** F6
Holtville *U.S.A.* 32°49N 115°23W **79** N11
Holwerd *Neths.* 53°22N 5°54E **15** A5
Holy Cross *U.S.A.* 62°12N 159°46W **74** C8
Holy I. *Anglesey, U.K.* 53°17N 4°37W **12** D3
Holy I. *Northumberland,*
  U.K. 55°40N 1°47W **12** B6
Holyhead *U.K.* 53°18N 4°38W **12** D3
Holyoke *Colo., U.S.A.* 40°35N 102°18W **76** F12
Holyoke *Mass., U.S.A.* 42°12N 72°37W **83** D12

Holyrood *Canada* 47°27N 53°8W **73** C9
Homa Bay *Kenya* 0°36S 34°30E **54** C3
Homalin *Burma* 24°55N 95°0E **41** G19
Homand *Iran* 32°28N 59°37E **45** C8
Homathko → *Canada* 51°0N 124°56W **70** C4
Hombori *Mali* 15°20N 1°38W **50** E5
Home B. *Canada* 68°40N 67°10W **69** D18
Home Hill *Australia* 19°43S 147°25E **62** B4
Home Reef *Tonga* 18°59S 174°47W **59** c
Homedale *U.S.A.* 43°37N 116°56W **76** E5
Homer *Alaska, U.S.A.* 59°39N 151°33W **68** F1
Homer *N.Y., U.S.A.* 42°38N 76°10W **83** D8
Homer City *U.S.A.* 40°32N 79°10W **82** F5
Homestead *Australia* 20°20S 145°40E **62** C4
Homestead *U.S.A.* 25°28N 80°29W **85** J14
Homestead △ *U.S.A.* 40°17N 96°50W **80** E5
Homoine *Mozam.* 23°55S 35°8E **57** C6
Homs = Ḥimṣ *Syria* 34°40N 36°45E **46** A5
Homyel *Belarus* 52°28N 31°0E **17** B16
Hon Chong *Vietnam* 10°25N 104°30E **39** G5
Hon Hai *Vietnam* 10°0N 109°0E **39** H7
Hon Me *Vietnam* 19°23N 105°56E **38** C5
Honan = Henan □ *China* 34°0N 114°0E **34** H8
Honbetsu *Japan* 43°7N 143°37E **30** C11
Honcut *U.S.A.* 39°20N 121°32W **78** F5
Honda, Bahía *Cuba* 22°54N 83°10W **88** B3
Hondeklipbaai *S. Africa* 30°19S 17°17E **56** E2
Hondo *Japan* 32°27N 130°12E **31** H5
Hondo *U.S.A.* 29°21N 99°9W **84** G5
Hondo, Río → *Belize* 18°25N 88°21W **87** D7
Honduras ■ *Cent. Amer.* 14°40N 86°30W **88** D2
Honduras, G. de
  Caribbean 16°50N 87°0W **88** C2
Hønefoss *Norway* 60°10N 10°18E **9** F14
Honesdale *U.S.A.* 41°34N 75°16W **83** E9
Honey Harbour *Canada* 44°52N 79°49W **82** B5
Honey L. *U.S.A.* 40°15N 120°19W **78** E6
Honfleur *France* 49°25N 0°13E **20** B4
Hong Gai *Vietnam* 20°57N 107°5E **38** B6
Hong He → *China* 32°25N 115°35E **34** H8
Hong Kong □ *China* 22°11N 114°14E **33** G11
Hong Kong I. *China* 22°16N 114°12E **33** G11
Hong Kong Int. ✈ (HKG)
  China 22°19N 113°57E **33** G10
Hongcheon *S. Korea* 37°44N 127°53E **35** F14
Hongjiang *China* 27°7N 109°59E **33** D5
Hongliu He → *China* 38°0N 109°50E **34** F5
Hongor *Mongolia* 45°45N 112°50E **34** B7
Hongsa *Laos* 19°43N 101°20E **38** C3
Hongseong *S. Korea* 36°37N 126°38E **35** F14
Hongshui He → *China* 23°48N 109°30E **33** D5
Hongtong *China* 36°16N 111°40E **34** F6
Honguedo, Détroit d'
  Canada 49°15N 64°0W **73** C7
Hongwon *N. Korea* 40°0N 127°56E **35** E14
Hongze Hu *China* 33°15N 118°35E **35** H10
Honiara *Solomon Is.* 9°27S 159°57E **58** B8
Honiton *U.K.* 50°47N 3°11W **13** G4
Honjō *Japan* 39°23N 140°3E **30** E10
Honningsvåg *Norway* 70°59N 25°59E **8** A21
Honolulu *U.S.A.* 21°19N 157°52W **75** L8
Honshū *Japan* 36°0N 138°0E **30** F9
Hood, Mt. *U.S.A.* 45°23N 121°42W **78** D4
Hood, Pt. *Australia* 34°23S 119°34E **61** F2
Hood River *U.S.A.* 45°43N 121°31W **78** E5
Hoodsport *U.S.A.* 47°24N 123°9W **78** C3
Hoogeveen *Neths.* 52°44N 6°28E **15** B6
Hoogezand-Sappemeer
  Neths. 53°9N 6°45E **15** A6
Hooghly = Hugli →
  India 21°56N 88°4E **43** J13
Hooghly-Chinsura = Chunchura
  India 22°53N 88°27E **43** H13
Hook Hd. *Ireland* 52°7N 6°56W **10** D5
Hook I. *Australia* 20°4S 149°0E **62** b
Hook of Holland = Hoek van
  Holland *Neths.* 52°0N 4°7E **15** C4
Hooker *U.S.A.* 36°52N 101°13W **84** C4
Hooker Creek = Lajamanu
  Australia 18°23S 130°38E **60** C5
Hooker Creek ⊙
  Australia 18°6S 130°23E **60** C5
Hoonah *U.S.A.* 58°7N 135°27W **70** B1
Hooper Bay *U.S.A.* 61°32N 166°6W **74** C6
Hoopeston *U.S.A.* 40°28N 87°40W **80** E10
Hoopstad *S. Africa* 27°50S 25°55E **56** D4
Hoorn *Neths.* 52°38N 5°4E **15** B5
Hoover *U.S.A.* 33°24N 86°49W **85** E11
Hoover Dam *U.S.A.* 36°1N 114°44W **79** K12
Hooversville *U.S.A.* 40°9N 78°55W **82** F6
Hop Bottom *U.S.A.* 41°42N 75°46W **83** E9
Hope *Canada* 49°25N 121°25W **70** D4
Hope *Ariz., U.S.A.* 33°43N 113°42W **79** M13
Hope *Ark., U.S.A.* 33°40N 93°36W **84** E8
Hope, L. *S. Austral.,*
  Australia 28°24S 139°18E **63** D2
Hope, L. *W. Austral.,*
  Australia 32°35S 120°15E **61** F3
Hope, Pt. *U.S.A.* 68°21N 166°47W **66** C3
Hope I. *Canada* 44°55N 80°11W **82** B4
Hope Town *Bahamas* 26°35N 76°57W **88** A4
Hope Vale *Australia* 15°16S 145°20E **62** B4
Hope Vale ⊙ *Australia* 15°16S 145°20E **62** B4
Hopedale *Canada* 55°28N 60°13W **73** A7
Hopedale *U.S.A.* 42°8N 71°33W **83** D13
Hopefield *S. Africa* 33°3S 18°22E **56** E2
Hopei = Hebei □ *China* 39°0N 116°0E **34** E9
Hopelchén *Mexico* 19°46N 89°51W **87** D7
Hopetoun *Vic., Australia* 35°42S 142°22E **63** F3
Hopetoun *W. Austral.,*
  Australia 33°57S 120°7E **61** F3
Hopetown *S. Africa* 29°34S 24°3E **56** D3
Hopevale ⊙ *Australia* 15°16S 145°20E **62** B4
Hopewell *U.S.A.* 37°18N 77°17W **81** G15
Hopkins, L. *Australia* 24°15S 128°35E **60** D4
Hopkinsville *U.S.A.* 36°52N 87°29W **80** G10
Hopland *U.S.A.* 38°58N 123°7W **78** G3
Hoquiam *U.S.A.* 46°59N 123°53W **78** D3
Hordern Hills *Australia* 20°15S 130°0E **60** D5

Horinger *China* 40°28N 111°48E **34** D6
Horizontina *Brazil* 27°37S 54°19W **95** B5
Horlick Mts. *Antarctica* 84°0S 102°0W **5** E15
Hormak *Iran* 29°58N 60°51E **45** D9
Hormoz *Iran* 27°35N 55°0E **45** E7
Hormoz, Jaz.-ye *Iran* 27°8N 56°28E **45** E8
Hormozgān □ *Iran* 27°30N 56°0E **45** E8
Hormoz, Kūh-e *Iran* 27°27N 55°10E **45** E7
Hormuz, Str. of *The Gulf* 26°30N 56°30E **45** E8
Horn *Austria* 48°39N 15°40E **16** D8
Horn → *Canada* 61°30N 118°1W **70** A5
Horn, Cape = Hornos, C. de
  Chile 55°50S 67°30W **96** H3
Horn Head *Ireland* 55°14N 8°0W **10** A3
Horn I. *Australia* 10°37S 142°17E **62** A3
Horn Plateau *Canada* 62°15N 119°15W **70** A5
Hornavan *Sweden* 66°15N 17°30E **8** C17
Hornbeck *U.S.A.* 31°20N 93°24W **84** F8
Hornbrook *U.S.A.* 41°55N 122°33W **76** F2
Horncastle *U.K.* 53°13N 0°7W **12** D7
Hornell *U.S.A.* 42°20N 77°40W **82** D7
Hornell L. *Canada* 62°20N 119°25W **70** A5
Hornepayne *Canada* 49°14N 84°48W **72** C3
Hornings Mills *Canada* 44°9N 80°12W **82** B4
Hornitos *U.S.A.* 37°30N 120°14W **78** H6
Hornos, C. de *Chile* 55°50S 67°30W **96** H3
Hornsby *Australia* 33°42S 151°2E **63** B5
Hornsea *U.K.* 53°55N 0°11W **12** D7
Horobetsu = Noboribetsu
  Japan 42°24N 141°6E **30** C10
Horodenka *Ukraine* 48°41N 25°29E **17** D13
Horodok *Khmelnytskyy,*
  Ukraine 49°10N 26°34E **17** D14
Horodok *Lviv, Ukraine* 49°46N 23°32E **17** D12
Horokhiv *Ukraine* 50°30N 24°45E **17** C13
Horqin Youyi Qianqi
  China 46°5N 122°3E **35** A12
Horqueta *Paraguay* 23°15S 56°55W **94** A4
Horse Cr. → *U.S.A.* 41°57N 103°58W **76** E12
Horse I. *Canada* 53°20N 99°6W **71** C9
Horse Is. *Canada* 50°15N 55°50W **73** B8
Horsefly L. *Canada* 52°25N 121°0W **70** C4
Horseheads *U.S.A.* 42°10N 76°49W **82** D8
Horseshoe Lake *Canada* 45°17N 79°51W **82** A5
Horsham *Australia* 36°44S 142°13E **63** F3
Horsham *U.K.* 51°4N 0°20W **13** F7
Horta *Azores* 38°32N 28°38W **50** a
Horten *Norway* 59°25N 10°32E **9** G14
Horton *U.S.A.* 39°40N 95°32W **80** F6
Horton → *Canada* 69°56N 126°52W **68** C6
Horwood L. *Canada* 48°5N 82°20W **72** C3
Hosapete = Hospet
  India 15°15N 76°20E **40** M10
Hoseynābād *Khuzestan,*
  Iran 32°45N 48°20E **45** C6
Hoseynābād *Kordestän,*
  Iran 35°33N 47°8E **44** C5
Hoshangabad *India* 22°45N 77°45E **42** H7
Hoshiarpur *India* 31°30N 75°58E **42** D6
Hospet *India* 15°15N 76°20E **40** M10
Hoste, I. *Chile* 55°0S 69°0W **96** H3
Hot *Thailand* 18°8N 98°29E **38** C2
Hot Creek Range
  U.S.A. 38°40N 116°20W **76** G5
Hot Springs *Ark., U.S.A.* 34°31N 93°3W **84** D8
Hot Springs *S. Dak.,*
  U.S.A. 43°26N 103°29W **80** D2
Hot Springs △ *U.S.A.* 34°31N 93°3W **84** D8
Hotagen *Sweden* 63°59N 14°12E **8** E16
Hotan *China* 37°25N 79°55E **32** C2
Hotan He → *China* 40°22N 80°56E **32** B3
Hotazel *S. Africa* 27°17S 22°58E **56** D3
Hotchkiss *U.S.A.* 38°48N 107°43W **76** G10
Hotham, C. *Australia* 12°2S 131°18E **60** B5
Hoting *Sweden* 64°8N 16°15E **8** D17
Hotte, Massif de la *Haiti* 18°30N 73°45W **89** C5
Hottentotsbaai *Namibia* 26°8S 14°59E **56** D1
Hou Hai *China* 22°32N 113°56E **33** F10
Houei Sai *Laos* 20°18N 100°26E **38** B3
Houffalize *Belgium* 50°8N 5°48E **15** D5
Houghton *Mich., U.S.A.* 47°7N 88°34W **80** B9
Houghton *N.Y., U.S.A.* 42°25N 78°10W **82** D6
Houghton L. *U.S.A.* 44°21N 84°44W **81** C11
Houghton-le-Spring
  U.K. 54°51N 1°28W **12** C6
Houhora Heads *N.Z.* 34°49S 173°9E **59** A4
Houlton *U.S.A.* 46°8N 67°51W **81** B20
Houma *U.S.A.* 29°36N 90°43W **85** G9
Housatonic → *U.S.A.* 41°10N 73°7W **83** E11
Houston *Canada* 54°25N 126°39W **70** C3
Houston *Mo., U.S.A.* 37°22N 91°58W **80** G8
Houston *Tex., U.S.A.* 29°45N 95°21W **84** G7
Hout = Mogwadi →
  S. Africa 23°4S 29°36E **57** C4
Houtkraal *S. Africa* 30°23S 24°5E **56** E3
Houtman Abrolhos
  Australia 28°43S 113°48E **61** E1
Hovd □ *Mongolia* 48°2N 91°37E **32** B4
Hove *U.K.* 50°50N 0°10W **13** G7
Hovenweep △ *U.S.A.* 37°20N 109°0W **77** H9
Hoveyzeh *Iran* 31°27N 48°4E **45** D6
Hövsgöl *Mongolia* 43°37N 109°2E **34** C5
Hövsgöl Nuur *Mongolia* 51°0N 100°30E **32** A5
Howar, Wadi → *Sudan* 17°30N 27°8E **51** E11
Howard *Australia* 25°16S 152°32E **63** D5
Howard *Pa., U.S.A.* 41°1N 77°40W **82** F7
Howard *S. Dak., U.S.A.* 44°1N 97°32W **80** C5
Howe *U.S.A.* 43°48N 113°0W **76** E7
Howe, C. *Australia* 37°30S 150°0E **63** F5
Howe, West Cape
  Australia 35°8S 117°36E **61** G2
Howe I. *Canada* 44°16N 76°17W **83** B8
Howell *U.S.A.* 42°36N 83°56W **81** D12
Howick *Canada* 45°11N 73°51W **83** A11
Howick *S. Africa* 29°28S 30°14E **57** D5
Howick Group *Australia* 14°20S 145°30E **62** A4
Howitt, L. *Australia* 27°40S 138°40E **63** D2

Howland I. *Pac. Oc.* 0°48N 176°38W **64** G10
Howrah = Haora *India* 22°34N 88°18E **43** H13
Howth *Ireland* 53°23N 6°6W **10** C5
Howth Hd. *Ireland* 53°22N 6°4W **10** C5
Höxter *Germany* 51°46N 9°22E **16** C5
Hoy *U.K.* 58°50N 3°15W **11** C5
Høyanger *Norway* 61°13N 6°4E **8** F12
Hoyerswerda *Germany* 51°26N 14°14E **16** C8
Hoylake *U.K.* 53°24N 3°10W **12** D4
Hpa-an = Pa-an *Burma* 16°51N 97°40E **41** L20
Hpunan Pass *Burma* 27°30N 96°55E **41** F20
Hradec Králové
  Czech Rep. 50°15N 15°50E **16** C8
Hrodna *Belarus* 53°42N 23°52E **17** B12
Hrodzyanka *Belarus* 53°31N 28°42E **17** B15
Hron → *Slovak Rep.* 47°49N 18°45E **17** E10
Hrvatska = Croatia ■
  Europe 45°20N 16°0E **16** F9
Hrymayliv *Ukraine* 49°20N 26°5E **17** D14
Hsenwi *Burma* 23°22N 97°55E **41** H20
Hsiamen = Xiamen
  China 24°25N 118°4E **33** D6
Hsian = Xi'an *China* 34°15N 109°0E **34** G5
Hsinchu *Taiwan* 24°48N 120°58E **33** D7
Hsinhailien = Lianyungang
  China 34°40N 119°11E **35** G10
Hsüchou = Xuzhou
  China 34°18N 117°10E **35** G9
Hu Xian *China* 34°8N 108°42E **34** G5
Hua Hin *Thailand* 12°34N 99°58E **38** F2
Hua Xian *Henan, China* 35°30N 114°30E **34** G8
Hua Xian *Shaanxi, China* 34°30N 109°48E **34** G5
Huab → *Namibia* 20°52S 13°25E **56** B2
Huachinera *Mexico* 30°9N 108°55W **86** A3
Huacho *Peru* 11°10S 77°35W **92** F3
Huade *China* 41°55N 113°59E **34** D7
Huadian *China* 43°0N 126°40E **35** C14
Huahine, Î.
  French Polynesia 16°46S 150°58W **65** J12
Huai Hat △ *Thailand* 16°52N 104°17E **38** D5
Huai He → *China* 33°0N 118°30E **33** C6
Huai Nam Dang △
  Thailand 19°30N 98°30E **38** C2
Huai Yot *Thailand* 7°45N 99°37E **39** J2
Huai'an *Hebei, China* 40°30N 114°20E **34** D8
Huai'an *Jiangsu, China* 33°30N 119°10E **35** H10
Huaibei *China* 34°0N 116°48E **34** G9
Huaide = Gongzhuling
  China 43°30N 124°40E **35** C13
Huaidezhen *China* 43°48N 124°50E **35** C13
Huainan *China* 32°38N 116°58E **33** C6
Huairen *China* 39°48N 113°20E **34** E7
Huairou *China* 40°20N 116°35E **34** D9
Huaiyang *China* 33°40N 114°52E **34** H8
Huaiyin *China* 33°30N 119°2E **35** H10
Huaiyuan *China* 32°55N 117°10E **35** H9
Huajuapán de León
  Mexico 17°48N 97°46W **87** D5
Hualapai Peak *U.S.A.* 35°5N 113°54W **77** J7
Huallaga → *Peru* 5°15S 75°30W **92** E3
Huambo *Angola* 12°42S 15°54E **53** G3
Huan Jiang → *China* 34°28N 109°0E **34** G5
Huan Xian *China* 36°33N 107°7E **34** F4
Huancabamba *Peru* 5°10S 79°15W **92** E3
Huancane *Peru* 15°10S 69°44W **92** G5
Huancavelica *Peru* 12°50S 75°5W **92** F3
Huancayo *Peru* 12°5S 75°12W **92** F3
Huanchaca *Bolivia* 20°15S 66°40W **92** H5
Huang Hai = Yellow Sea
  China 35°0N 123°0E **35** G12
Huang He → *China* 37°55N 118°50E **35** F10
Huang Xian *China* 37°38N 120°30E **35** F11
Huangling *China* 35°34N 109°15E **34** G5
Huanglong *China* 35°30N 109°59E **34** G5
Huangshan *China* 29°42N 118°25E **33** D6
Huangshi *China* 30°10N 115°3E **33** C6
Huangsongdian *China* 43°45N 127°25E **35** C14
Huanren *China* 41°23N 125°20E **35** D13
Huantai *China* 36°58N 117°56E **35** F9
Huánuco *Peru* 9°55S 76°15W **92** E3
Huaraz *Peru* 9°30S 77°32W **92** E3
Huarmey *Peru* 10°5S 78°5W **92** F3
Huascarán, Nevado *Peru* 9°7S 77°37W **92** E3
Huasco *Chile* 28°30S 71°15W **94** B1
Huasco → *Chile* 28°27S 71°13W **94** B1
Huasna *U.S.A.* 35°6N 120°24W **79** K6
Huatabampo *Mexico* 26°50N 109°38W **86** B3
Huauchinango *Mexico* 20°12N 98°3W **87** C5
Huautla de Jiménez
  Mexico 18°8N 96°51W **87** D5
Huayin *China* 34°35N 110°5E **34** G6
Hubballi = Hubli *India* 15°22N 75°15E **40** M9
Hubbard *Ohio, U.S.A.* 41°9N 80°34W **82** E4
Hubbard *Tex., U.S.A.* 31°51N 96°48W **84** F6
Hubbard Glacier
  Canada 60°18N 139°22W **68** E4
Hubbart Pt. *Canada* 59°21N 94°41W **71** B10
Hubei □ *China* 31°0N 112°0E **33** C6
Hubli *India* 15°22N 75°15E **40** M9
Huch'ang *N. Korea* 41°25N 127°2E **35** D14
Hucknall *U.K.* 53°3N 1°13W **12** D6
Huddersfield *U.K.* 53°39N 1°47W **12** D6
Hudiksvall *Sweden* 61°43N 17°10E **8** F17
Hudson *Canada* 50°6N 92°9W **72** B1
Hudson *Mass., U.S.A.* 42°23N 71°34W **83** D13
Hudson *N.Y., U.S.A.* 42°15N 73°46W **83** D11
Hudson *Wis., U.S.A.* 44°58N 92°45W **80** C7
Hudson *Wyo., U.S.A.* 42°54N 108°35W **76** E9
Hudson → *U.S.A.* 40°42N 74°2W **83** F10
Hudson, C. *Antarctica* 68°21S 153°45E **5** C20
Hudson Bay *Nunavut,*
  Canada 60°0N 86°0W **69** F14
Hudson Bay *Sask.,*
  Canada 52°51N 102°23W **71** C8
Hudson Falls *U.S.A.* 43°18N 73°35W **83** C11
Hudson Mts. *Antarctica* 74°32S 99°20W **5** D16
Hudson Str. *Canada* 62°0N 70°0W **69** E18
Hudson's Hope *Canada* 56°0N 121°54W **70** B4
Hue *Vietnam* 16°30N 107°35E **38** D6

Huehuetenango
  Guatemala 15°20N 91°28W **88** C1
Huejúcar *Mexico* 22°21N 103°13W **86** C4
Huelva *Spain* 37°18N 6°57W **21** D2
Huentelauquén *Chile* 31°38S 71°33W **94** C1
Huerta, Sa. de la
  Argentina 31°10S 67°30W **94** C2
Huesca *Spain* 42°8N 0°25W **21** A5
Huetamo *Mexico* 18°35N 100°53W **86** D4
Hugh → *Australia* 25°1S 134°1E **62** D1
Hughenden *Australia* 20°52S 144°10E **62** C3
Hughesville *U.S.A.* 41°14N 76°44W **83** E8
Hugli → *India* 21°56N 88°4E **43** J13
Hugo *Colo., U.S.A.* 39°8N 103°28W **76** G12
Hugo *Okla., U.S.A.* 34°1N 95°31W **84** D7
Hugoton *U.S.A.* 37°11N 101°21W **80** G3
Hui Xian = Huixian
  China 35°27N 113°12E **34** G7
Hui Xian *China* 33°50N 106°4E **34** H4
Hui'anbu *China* 37°28N 106°38E **34** F4
Huichapan *Mexico* 20°23N 99°39W **87** C5
Huichon *N. Korea* 40°10N 126°16E **35** D14
Huifa He → *China* 43°0N 127°50E **35** C14
Huila, Nevado del *Colombia* 3°0N 76°0W **92** C3
Huimin *China* 37°27N 117°28E **35** F9
Huinan *China* 42°40N 126°2E **35** C14
Huinca Renancó
  Argentina 34°51S 64°22W **94** C3
Huining *China* 35°38N 105°0E **34** G3
Huinong *China* 39°5N 106°35E **34** E4
Huiting *China* 34°5N 116°5E **34** G9
Huixian *China* 35°27N 113°12E **34** G7
Huixtla *Mexico* 15°9N 92°28W **87** D6
Huize *China* 26°24N 103°15E **32** D5
Hukawng Valley
  Burma 26°30N 96°30E **41** F20
Hukuntsi *Botswana* 23°58S 21°45E **56** C3
Hulayfā' *Si. Arabia* 25°58N 40°45E **44** E4
Hulin He → *China* 45°0N 122°10E **35** B12
Hull = Kingston upon Hull
  U.K. 53°45N 0°21W **12** D7
Hull *Canada* 45°26N 75°43W **83** A9
Hull → *U.K.* 53°44N 0°20W **12** D7
Hulst *Neths.* 51°17N 4°2E **15** C4
Hulun Nur *China* 49°0N 117°30E **33** B6
Huma, Tanjung *Malaysia* 5°29N 100°16E **39** c
Humacao *Puerto Rico* 18°9N 65°50W **89** d
Humahuaca *Argentina* 23°10S 65°25W **94** A2
Humaitá *Brazil* 7°35S 63°1W **92** E6
Humaitá *Paraguay* 27°2S 58°31W **94** B4
Humansdorp *S. Africa* 34°2S 24°46E **56** E3
Humbe *Angola* 16°40S 14°55E **56** B1
Humber → *U.K.* 53°42N 0°27W **12** D7
Humboldt *Canada* 52°15N 105°9W **71** C7
Humboldt *Iowa, U.S.A.* 42°44N 94°13W **80** D6
Humboldt *Tenn., U.S.A.* 35°50N 88°55W **85** D10
Humboldt → *U.S.A.* 39°59N 118°36W **76** G4
Humboldt Gletscher =
  Sermersuaq *Greenland* 79°30N 62°0W **69** B19
Hume *U.S.A.* 36°48N 118°54W **78** J8
Hume, L. *Australia* 36°0S 147°5E **63** F4
Humen *China* 22°49N 113°40E **33** F10
Humenné *Slovak Rep.* 48°55N 21°50E **17** D11
Humphreys, Mt.
  U.S.A. 37°17N 118°40W **78** H8
Humphreys Peak
  U.S.A. 35°21N 111°41W **77** J8
Humptulips *U.S.A.* 47°14N 123°57W **78** C3
Hūn *Libya* 29°2N 16°0E **51** C9
Hun Jiang → *China* 40°50N 125°38E **35** D13
Húnaflói *Iceland* 65°50N 20°50W **8** D3
Hunan □ *China* 27°30N 112°0E **33** D6
Hunchun *China* 42°52N 130°28E **35** C16
Hundewali *Pakistan* 31°55N 72°38E **42** D5
Hundred Mile House
  Canada 51°38N 121°18W **70** C4
Hunedoara *Romania* 45°40N 22°50E **17** F12
Hung Yen *Vietnam* 20°39N 106°4E **38** B6
Hunga Ha'apai *Tonga* 20°41S 175°7W **59** c
Hungary ■ *Europe* 47°20N 19°20E **17** E10
Hungary, Plain of *Europe* 47°0N 20°0E **6** F10
Hungerford *Australia* 28°58S 144°24E **63** D3
Hŭngnam *N. Korea* 39°49N 127°45E **35** E14
Hunjiang *China* 41°54N 126°26E **35** D14
Hunsberge *Namibia* 27°45S 17°12E **56** D2
Hunsrück *Germany* 49°56N 7°27E **16** D4
Hunstanton *U.K.* 52°56N 0°29E **12** E8
Hunter *U.S.A.* 42°13N 74°13W **83** D10
Hunter I. *Australia* 40°30S 144°45E **63** G3
Hunter I. *Canada* 51°55N 128°0W **70** C3
Hunter Ra. *Australia* 32°45S 150°15E **63** E5
Hunters Road *Zimbabwe* 19°9S 29°49E **55** F2
Hunterville *N.Z.* 39°56S 175°35E **59** C5
Huntingburg *U.S.A.* 38°18N 86°57W **80** F10
Huntingdon *U.K.* 52°20N 0°11W **13** E7
Huntingdon *U.S.A.* 40°30N 78°1W **82** F6
Huntington *Ind., U.S.A.* 40°53N 85°30W **81** E11
Huntington *N.Y.,*
  U.S.A. 40°52N 73°26W **83** F11
Huntington *Oreg.,*
  U.S.A. 44°21N 117°16W **76** D5
Huntington *Utah,*
  U.S.A. 39°20N 110°58W **76** G8
Huntington *W. Va.,*
  U.S.A. 38°25N 82°27W **81** F12
Huntington Beach
  U.S.A. 33°40N 118°5W **79** M9
Huntly *N.Z.* 37°34S 175°11E **59** B5
Huntly *U.K.* 57°27N 2°47W **11** D6
Huntsville *Canada* 45°20N 79°14W **82** A5
Huntsville *Ala., U.S.A.* 34°44N 86°35W **85** D11
Huntsville *Tex., U.S.A.* 30°43N 95°33W **84** F7
Hunyani → *Zimbabwe* 15°57S 30°39E **55** F3
Hunyuan *China* 39°42N 113°42E **34** E7
Hunza → *India* 35°54N 74°20E **43** B6
Huo Xian = Huozhou
  China 36°36N 111°42E **34** F6
Huong Khe *Vietnam* 18°13N 105°41E **38** C5
Huonville *Australia* 43°0S 147°5E **63** G4

Huozhou *China* 36°36N 111°42E **34** F6
Hupeh = Hubei □ *China* 31°0N 112°0E **33** C6
Ḩūr *Iran* 30°50N 57°7E **45** D8
Hurānd *Iran* 38°51N 47°22E **44** B5
Ḩuraymīla *Si. Arabia* 25°8N 46°8E **44** E5
Hurghada *Egypt* 27°15N 33°50E **51** C12
Hurley *N. Mex., U.S.A.* 32°42N 108°8W **77** K9
Hurley *Wis., U.S.A.* 46°27N 90°11W **80** B8
Huron *Calif., U.S.A.* 36°12N 120°6W **78** J6
Huron *Ohio, U.S.A.* 41°24N 82°33W **82** E2
Huron *S. Dak., U.S.A.* 44°22N 98°13W **80** C4
Huron, L. *U.S.A.* 44°30N 82°40W **82** B2
Huron East *Canada* 43°37N 81°18W **82** C3
Hurricane *U.S.A.* 37°11N 113°17W **77** H7
Hurungwe △ *Zimbabwe* 16°7S 29°5E **55** F2
Hurunui → *N.Z.* 42°54S 173°18E **59** E4
Húsavík *Iceland* 66°3N 17°21W **8** C5
Huşi *Romania* 46°41N 28°7E **17** E15
Hustadvika *Norway* 63°0N 7°0E **8** E12
Hustontown *U.S.A.* 40°3N 78°2W **82** F6
Hutchinson *Kans., U.S.A.* 38°5N 97°56W **80** F5
Hutchinson *Minn.,*
  U.S.A. 44°54N 94°22W **80** C6
Hutte Sauvage, L. de la
  Canada 56°15N 64°45W **73** A7
Hutton, Mt. *Australia* 25°51S 148°20E **63** D4
Huy *Belgium* 50°31N 5°15E **15** D5
Huzhou *China* 30°51N 120°8E **33** C7
Hvammstangi *Iceland* 65°24N 20°57W **8** D3
Hvar *Croatia* 43°11N 16°28E **22** C7
Hvítá → *Iceland* 64°30N 21°58W **8** D3
Hwacheon-Cheosuji
  S. Korea 38°5N 127°50E **35** E14
Hwang Ho = Huang He →
  China 37°55N 118°50E **35** F10
Hwange *Zimbabwe* 18°18S 26°30E **55** F2
Hwange △ *Zimbabwe* 19°0S 26°30E **56** B4
Hyannis *Mass., U.S.A.* 41°39N 70°17W **81** E18
Hyannis *Nebr., U.S.A.* 42°0N 101°46W **80** E3
Hyargas Nuur *Mongolia* 49°0N 93°0E **32** B4
Hydaburg *U.S.A.* 55°15N 132°50W **70** B2
Hyde Park *U.S.A.* 41°47N 73°56W **83** E11
Hyden *Australia* 32°24S 118°53E **61** F2
Hyder *U.S.A.* 55°55N 130°5W **70** B2
Hyderabad *India* 17°22N 78°29E **40** L11
Hyderabad *Pakistan* 25°23N 68°24E **42** G3
Hydra *Greece* 37°20N 23°28E **23** F10
Hyères *France* 43°8N 6°9E **20** E7
Hyères, Îs. d' *France* 43°0N 6°20E **20** E7
Hyesan *N. Korea* 41°20N 128°10E **35** D15
Hyland → *Canada* 59°52N 128°12W **70** B3
Hymia *India* 33°40N 78°2E **43** C8
Hyndman Peak *U.S.A.* 43°45N 114°8W **76** E6
Hyōgo □ *Japan* 35°15N 134°50E **31** G7
Hyrum *U.S.A.* 41°38N 111°51W **76** F8
Hysham *U.S.A.* 46°18N 107°14W **76** C10
Hythe *U.K.* 51°4N 1°5E **13** F9
Hyūga *Japan* 32°25N 131°35E **31** H5
Hyvinge = Hyvinkää
  Finland 60°38N 24°50E **8** F21
Hyvinkää *Finland* 60°38N 24°50E **8** F21

I

I-n-Gall *Niger* 16°51N 7°1E **50** E7
Iaco → *Brazil* 9°3S 68°34W **92** E5
Iakora *Madag.* 23°6S 46°40E **57** C8
Ialissos *Greece* 36°24N 28°10E **25** C10
Ialomiţa → *Romania* 44°42N 27°51E **17** F14
Iaşi *Romania* 47°10N 27°40E **17** E14
Ib → *India* 21°34N 83°48E **43** J10
Iba *Phil.* 15°22N 120°0E **37** A6
Ibadan *Nigeria* 7°22N 3°58E **50** G6
Ibagué *Colombia* 4°20N 75°20W **92** C3
Ibar → *Serbia* 43°43N 20°45E **23** C9
Ibaraki □ *Japan* 36°10N 140°10E **31** F10
Ibarra *Ecuador* 0°21N 78°7W **92** C3
Ibb *Yemen* 14°2N 44°10E **47** E3
Ibembo
  Dem. Rep. of the Congo 2°35N 23°35E **54** B1
Ibenga → *Congo* 2°19N 18°9E **52** D3
Ibera, L. *Argentina* 28°30S 57°9W **94** B4
Iberian Peninsula *Europe* 40°0N 5°0W **6** H5
Iberville *Canada* 45°19N 73°17W **83** A11
Iberville, Mt. d' *Canada* 58°50N 63°50W **69** F19
Ibiá *Brazil* 19°30S 46°30W **93** G9
Ibiapaba, Sa. da *Brazil* 4°0S 41°30W **93** D10
Ibicuí → *Brazil* 29°25S 56°47W **95** B4
Ibicuy *Argentina* 33°55S 59°10W **94** C4
Ibiza = Eivissa *Spain* 38°54N 1°26E **24** C7
Ibo *Mozam.* 12°22S 40°40E **55** E5
Ibonma *Indonesia* 3°29S 133°31E **37** E8
Ibotirama *Brazil* 12°13S 43°12W **93** F10
Ibrāhīm → *Lebanon* 34°4N 35°38E **46** A4
'Ibrī *Oman* 23°14N 56°30E **45** F8
Ibu *Indonesia* 1°35N 127°33E **37** D7
Ibusuki *Japan* 31°12N 130°40E **31** J5
Ica *Peru* 14°0S 75°48W **92** F3
Iça → *Brazil* 2°55S 67°58W **92** D5
Içana *Brazil* 0°21N 67°19W **92** C5
Içana → *Brazil* 0°26N 67°19W **92** C5
İçel *Turkey* 36°51N 34°36E **44** B2
Iceland ■ *Europe* 64°45N 19°0W **8** D4
Iceland Basin *Atl. Oc.* 61°0N 19°0W **4** C7
Icelandic Plateau *Arctic* 64°0N 10°0W **4** C7
Ich'ang = Yichang
  China 30°40N 111°20E **33** C6
Ichchapuram *India* 19°10N 84°40E **41** K14
Icheon *S. Korea* 37°17N 127°27E **35** F14
Ichhawar *India* 23°1N 77°1E **42** H7
Ichihara *Japan* 35°28N 140°5E **31** G10
Ichikawa *Japan* 35°43N 139°54E **31** G9
Ichilo → *Bolivia* 15°57S 64°50W **92** G6
Ichinohe *Japan* 40°13N 141°17E **30** D10
Ichinomiya *Japan* 35°18N 136°48E **31** G8

Ichinoseki *Japan* 38°55N 141°8E **30** E10
Icod *Canary Is.* 28°22N 16°43W **24** F3
Icy C. *U.S.A.* 70°20N 161°52W **66** B3
Ida Grove *U.S.A.* 42°21N 95°28W **80** D6
Idabel *U.S.A.* 33°54N 94°50W **84** E7
Idaho □ *U.S.A.* 45°0N 115°0W **76** D6
Idaho City *U.S.A.* 43°50N 115°50W **76** E6
Idaho Falls *U.S.A.* 43°30N 112°2W **76** E7
Idalia △ *Australia* 24°49S 144°36E **62** C3
Idar-Oberstein *Germany* 49°43N 7°16E **16** D4
Idensalmi = Iisalmi
  Finland 63°32N 27°10E **8** E22
Idfû *Egypt* 24°55N 32°49E **51** D12
Ídhra = Hydra *Greece* 37°20N 23°28E **23** F10
Idi *Indonesia* 5°2N 97°37E **36** C1
Idi, Oros = Psiloritis, Oros
  Greece 35°15N 24°45E **25** D6
Idiofa
  Dem. Rep. of the Congo 4°55S 19°42E **52** E3
Idlib *Syria* 35°55N 36°36E **44** C3
Idria *U.S.A.* 36°25N 120°41W **78** J6
Idutywa = Dutywa
  S. Africa 32°8S 28°18E **57** E4
Ieper *Belgium* 50°51N 2°53E **15** D2
Ierapetra *Greece* 35°1N 25°44E **25** E7
Iesi *Italy* 43°31N 13°14E **22** C5
Ifakara *Tanzania* 8°8S 36°41E **54** D4
'Ifāl, W. al → *Si. Arabia* 28°7N 35°3E **44** D2
Ifanadiana *Madag.* 21°19S 47°39E **57** C8
Ife *Nigeria* 7°30N 4°31E **50** G6
Iffley *Australia* 18°53S 141°12E **62** B3
Iforas, Adrar des *Africa* 19°40N 1°40E **50** E6
Ifould, L. *Australia* 30°52S 132°6E **61** F5
Iganga *Uganda* 0°37N 33°28E **54** B3
Igarapava *Brazil* 20°3S 47°47W **93** H9
Igarka *Russia* 67°30N 86°33E **28** C9
Iggesund *Sweden* 61°39N 17°10E **8** F17
Iglésias *Italy* 39°19N 8°32E **22** E3
Igloolik = Iglulik
  Canada 69°20N 81°49W **69** D15
Igluligaarjuk = Chesterfield Inlet
  Canada 63°30N 90°45W **68** E13
Iglulik *Canada* 69°20N 81°49W **69** D15
Ignace *Canada* 49°30N 91°40W **72** C1
İğneada Burnu *Turkey* 41°53N 28°2E **23** D13
Igoumenitsa *Greece* 39°32N 20°18E **23** E9
Igrim *Russia* 63°12N 64°30E **28** C7
Iguaçu → *Brazil* 25°36S 54°36W **95** B5
Iguaçu, Cat. del *Brazil* 25°41S 54°26W **95** B5
Iguaçu → *Brazil* 25°36S 54°36W **95** B5
Iguaçu Falls = Iguaçu, Cat. del
  Brazil 25°41S 54°26W **95** B5
Iguala *Mexico* 18°21N 99°32W **87** D5
Igualada *Spain* 41°37N 1°37E **21** B6
Iguassu = Iguaçu →
  Brazil 25°36S 54°36W **95** B5
Iguatu *Brazil* 6°20S 39°18W **93** E11
Iguazú △ *Argentina* 25°42S 54°22W **95** B5
Iguidi, Erg *Africa* 27°0N 7°0W **50** C4
Iharana *Madag.* 13°25S 50°0E **57** A9
Ihbulag *Mongolia* 43°11N 107°10E **34** C4
Iheya-Shima *Japan* 27°4N 127°58E **31** L3
Ihosy *Madag.* 22°24S 46°8E **57** C8
Ihotry, Farihy *Madag.* 21°56S 43°41E **57** C7
Ii *Finland* 65°19N 25°22E **8** D21
Ii-Shima *Japan* 26°43N 127°47E **31** L3
Iida *Japan* 35°35N 137°50E **31** G8
Iijoki → *Finland* 65°20N 25°20E **8** D21
Iisalmi *Finland* 63°32N 27°10E **8** E22
Iiyama *Japan* 36°51N 138°22E **31** F9
Iizuka *Japan* 33°38N 130°42E **31** H5
Ijâfene *Mauritania* 20°40N 8°0W **50** D4
Ijebu-Ode *Nigeria* 6°47N 3°58E **50** G6
IJmuiden *Neths.* 52°28N 4°35E **15** B4
Ijo älv = Iijoki →
  Finland 65°20N 25°20E **8** D21
IJssel → *Neths.* 52°35N 5°50E **15** B5
IJsselmeer *Neths.* 52°45N 5°20E **15** B5
Ijuí *Brazil* 28°23S 53°55W **95** B5
Ijuí → *Brazil* 27°58S 55°20W **95** B4
Ikalamavony *Madag.* 21°9S 46°35E **57** C8
Ikanga *Kenya* 1°42S 38°4E **54** C4
Ikare *Nigeria* 7°32N 5°40E **50** G7
Ikaria *Greece* 37°35N 26°10E **23** F12
Ikeda *Japan* 34°1N 133°48E **31** G6
Ikela *Dem. Rep. of the Congo* 1°6S 23°6E **52** E4
Iki *Japan* 33°45N 129°42E **31** H4
Ikimba L. *Tanzania* 1°30S 31°20E **54** C3
Ikongo *Madag.* 21°52S 47°27E **57** C8
Ikopa → *Madag.* 16°45S 46°40E **57** B8
Ikorongo △ *Tanzania* 1°50S 34°53E **54** C3
Ikparjuk = Arctic Bay
  Canada 73°1N 85°7W **69** C14
Iksan *S. Korea* 35°59N 127°0E **35** G14
Ikungu *Tanzania* 1°33S 33°42E **54** C3
Ikuntji = Haasts Bluff
  Australia 23°22S 132°0E **60** D5
Ilagan *Phil.* 17°7N 121°53E **37** A6
Ilaka *Madag.* 19°33S 48°52E **57** B8
Ilām *Iran* 33°36N 46°36E **44** C5
Ilam *Nepal* 26°58N 87°58E **43** F12
Īlām □ *Iran* 33°0N 47°0E **44** C5
Ilanskiy *Russia* 56°14N 96°3E **29** D10
Iława *Poland* 53°36N 19°34E **17** B10
Ile → *Kazakhstan* 45°53N 77°10E **28** E8
Île-à-la-Crosse *Canada* 55°27N 107°53W **71** B7
Île-à-la-Crosse, Lac
  Canada 55°40N 107°45W **71** B7
Île-de-France □ *France* 49°0N 2°20E **20** B5
Ilebo *Dem. Rep. of the Congo* 4°17S 20°55E **52** E4
Ilek *Russia* 51°32N 53°21E **28** D6
Ilek → *Russia* 51°30N 53°22E **28** D6
Ilesha *Nigeria* 7°37N 4°40E **50** G6
Ilford *Canada* 56°4N 95°35W **71** B9
Ilfracombe *Australia* 23°30S 144°30E **62** C3
Ilfracombe *U.K.* 51°12N 4°8W **13** F3
Ilha Grande, Represa
  Brazil 23°10S 53°5W **95** A5
Ilha Grande △ *Brazil* 23°10S 53°20W **95** A5

Ilhéus *Brazil* 14°49S 39°2W **93** F11
Ili = Ile → *Kazakhstan* 45°53N 77°10E **28** E8
Iliamna L. *U.S.A.* 59°30N 155°0W **74** D8
Ilias, Profítis *Greece* 36°17N 27°56E **25** C9
Iligan *Phil.* 8°12N 124°13E **37** C6
Ilion *U.S.A.* 43°1N 75°2W **83** D9
Ilkeston *U.K.* 52°58N 1°19W **12** E6
Ilkley *U.K.* 53°56N 1°48W **12** D6
Illampu = Ancohuma, Nevado
  Bolivia 16°0S 68°50W **92** G5
Illana B. *Phil.* 7°35N 123°45E **37** C6
Illapel *Chile* 32°0S 71°10W **94** C1
Iller → *Germany* 48°23N 9°58E **16** D6
Illetas *Spain* 39°32N 2°35E **24** B9
Illimani, Nevado *Bolivia* 16°30S 67°50W **92** G5
Illinois □ *U.S.A.* 40°15N 89°30W **80** E9
Illinois → *U.S.A.* 38°58N 90°28W **80** F8
Illizi *Algeria* 26°31N 8°32E **50** C7
Ilma, L. *Australia* 29°13S 127°46E **61** E4
Ilmajoki *Finland* 62°44N 22°34E **8** E20
Ilmen, Ozero *Russia* 58°15N 31°10E **18** C5
Ilo *Peru* 17°40S 71°20W **92** G4
Iloilo *Phil.* 10°45N 122°33E **37** B6
Ilomantsi *Finland* 62°38N 30°57E **8** E24
Ilorin *Nigeria* 8°30N 4°35E **50** G6
Ilwaco *U.S.A.* 46°19N 124°3W **78** D2
Ilwaki *Indonesia* 7°55S 126°30E **37** F7
Imabari *Japan* 34°4N 133°0E **31** G6
Imaloto → *Madag.* 23°27S 45°13E **57** C8
Imandra, Ozero *Russia* 67°30N 33°0E **8** C25
Imanombo *Madag.* 24°26S 45°49E **57** C8
Imari *Japan* 33°15N 129°52E **31** H4
Imatra *Finland* 61°12N 28°48E **8** F23
imeni 26 Bakinskikh Komissarov
  = Neftçala *Azerbaijan* 39°19N 49°12E **45** B6
imeni 26 Bakinskikh Komissarov
  Turkmenistan 39°22N 54°10E **45** B7
imeni Ismail Samani, Pik
  Tajikistan 39°0N 72°2E **28** F8
Imeri, Serra *Brazil* 0°50N 65°25W **92** C5
Imerimandroso *Madag.* 17°26S 48°35E **57** B8
Imfolozi → *S. Africa* 28°18S 31°50E **57** D5
Imi *Ethiopia* 6°28N 42°10E **47** F3
Imlay *U.S.A.* 40°40N 118°9W **76** F4
Imlay City *U.S.A.* 43°2N 83°5W **82** D1
Immingham *U.K.* 53°37N 0°13W **12** D7
Immokalee *U.S.A.* 26°25N 81°25W **85** H14
Ímola *Italy* 44°20N 11°42E **22** B4
Imperatriz *Brazil* 5°30S 47°29W **93** E9
Impéria *Italy* 43°53N 8°3E **20** E8
Imperial *Canada* 51°21N 105°28W **71** C7
Imperial *Calif., U.S.A.* 32°51N 115°34W **79** N11
Imperial *Nebr., U.S.A.* 40°31N 101°39W **80** E3
Imperial Beach *U.S.A.* 32°35N 117°6W **79** N9
Imperial Dam *U.S.A.* 32°55N 114°25W **79** N12
Imperial Res. *U.S.A.* 32°53N 114°28W **79** N12
Imperial Valley *U.S.A.* 33°0N 115°30W **79** N11
Imperieuse Reef
  Australia 17°36S 118°50E **60** C2
Impfondo *Congo* 1°40N 18°0E **52** D3
Imphal *India* 24°48N 93°56E **41** G18
İmroz = Gökçeada
  Turkey 40°10N 25°50E **23** D11
Imuris *Mexico* 30°47N 110°52W **86** A2
Imuruan B. *Phil.* 10°40N 119°10E **37** B5
In Guezzam *Algeria* 19°37N 5°52E **50** E7
In Salah *Algeria* 27°10N 2°32E **50** C6
Ina *Japan* 35°50N 137°55E **31** G8
Inagua △ *Bahamas* 21°5N 73°24W **89** B5
Inangahua *N.Z.* 41°52S 171°59E **59** D3
Inanwatan *Indonesia* 2°8S 132°10E **37** E8
Iñapari *Peru* 11°0S 69°40W **92** F5
Inari *Finland* 68°54N 27°1E **8** B22
Inarijärvi *Finland* 69°0N 28°0E **8** B23
Inawashiro-Ko *Japan* 37°29N 140°6E **30** F10
Inca *Spain* 39°43N 2°54E **24** B9
Inca de Oro *Chile* 26°45S 69°54W **94** B2
Incahuasi *Argentina* 27°2S 68°18W **94** B2
Incahuasi *Chile* 29°12S 71°5W **94** B1
İnce Burun *Turkey* 42°7N 34°56E **19** F5
İncesu *Turkey* 38°38N 35°11E **44** B2
Incheon *S. Korea* 37°27N 126°40E **35** F14
İncirliova *Turkey* 37°50N 27°41E **23** F12
Incline Village *U.S.A.* 39°10N 119°58W **76** G4
Incomáti → *Mozam.* 25°46S 32°43E **57** D5
Indalsälven → *Sweden* 62°36N 17°30E **8** E17
Indaw *Burma* 24°15N 96°5E **41** G20
Independence *Calif.,*
  U.S.A. 36°48N 118°12W **78** J8
Independence *Iowa,*
  U.S.A. 42°28N 91°54W **80** D9
Independence *Kans.,*
  U.S.A. 37°14N 95°42W **80** G6
Independence *Ky.,*
  U.S.A. 38°57N 84°33W **81** F11
Independence *Mo., U.S.A.* 39°6N 94°25W **80** F6
Independence Fjord
  Greenland 82°10N 29°0W **4** A6
Independence Mts.
  U.S.A. 41°20N 116°0W **76** F5
Index *U.S.A.* 47°50N 121°33W **78** C5
India ■ *Asia* 20°0N 78°0E **40** K11
Indian → *U.S.A.* 27°59N 80°34W **85** H14
Indian Cabins *Canada* 59°52N 117°40W **70** B5
Indian Harbour *Canada* 54°27N 57°13W **73** B8
Indian Head *Canada* 50°30N 103°41W **71** C8
Indian L. *U.S.A.* 43°47N 74°16W **83** C10
Indian Lake *U.S.A.* 43°47N 74°16W **83** C10
Indian Springs *U.S.A.* 36°35N 115°40W **79** J11
Indiana *U.S.A.* 40°37N 79°9W **82** F5
Indiana □ *U.S.A.* 40°0N 86°0W **81** F11
Indianapolis *U.S.A.* 39°46N 86°9W **81** F11
Indianola *Iowa, U.S.A.* 41°22N 93°34W **80** E7
Indianola *Miss., U.S.A.* 33°27N 90°39W **85** E9
Indiga *Russia* 67°38N 49°9E **18** A8
Indigirka → *Russia* 70°48N 148°54E **29** B15
Indio *U.S.A.* 33°43N 116°13W **79** M10
Indira Gandhi Canal *India* 28°0N 72°0E **42** F5
Indira Sagar *India* 22°15N 76°40E **42** H7

Indo-China *Asia* 15°0N 102°0E **26** G12
Indonesia ■ *Asia* 5°0S 115°0E **36** F5
Indore *India* 22°42N 75°53E **42** H6
Indramayu *Indonesia* 6°20S 108°19E **37** G13
Indravati → *India* 19°20N 80°20E **41** K12
Indre □ *France* 47°16N 0°11E **20** C4
Indulkana *Australia* 26°58S 133°5E **63** D1
Indus → *Pakistan* 24°20N 67°47E **42** G2
Indus, Mouths of the
  Pakistan 24°0N 68°0E **42** H3
İnebolu *Turkey* 41°55N 33°40E **19** F5
Infiernillo, Presa del
  Mexico 18°35N 101°50W **86** D4
Ingenio *Canary Is.* 27°55N 15°26W **24** G4
Ingenio Santa Ana
  Argentina 27°25S 65°40W **94** B2
Ingersoll *Canada* 43°4N 80°55W **82** C4
Ingham *Australia* 18°43S 146°10E **62** B4
Ingleborough *U.K.* 54°10N 2°22W **12** C5
Inglewood *Queens.,*
  Australia 28°25S 151°2E **63** D5
Inglewood *Vic., Australia* 36°29S 143°53E **63** F3
Inglewood *N.Z.* 39°9S 174°14E **59** C5
Inglewood *U.S.A.* 33°58N 118°21W **79** M8
Ingólfshöfði *Iceland* 63°48N 16°39W **8** E5
Ingomar *U.S.A.* 46°35N 107°23W **76** C10
Ingonish *Canada* 46°42N 60°18W **73** C7
Ingraj Bazar *India* 24°58N 88°10E **43** G13
Ingrid Christensen Coast
  Antarctica 69°30S 76°0E **5** C6
Ingulec = Inhulec
  Ukraine 47°42N 33°14E **19** E5
Ingushetia □ *Russia* 43°20N 44°50E **19** F8
Ingwavuma *S. Africa* 27°9S 31°59E **57** D5
Inhafenga *Mozam.* 20°36S 33°53E **57** C5
Inhambane *Mozam.* 23°54S 35°30E **57** C6
Inhambane □ *Mozam.* 22°30S 34°20E **57** C5
Inhaminga *Mozam.* 18°26S 35°0E **55** F4
Inharrime *Mozam.* 24°30S 35°0E **57** C6
Inharrime → *Mozam.* 24°30S 35°0E **57** C6
Inhulec *Ukraine* 47°42N 33°14E **19** E5
Ining = Yining *China* 43°58N 81°10E **32** B3
Inírida → *Colombia* 3°55N 67°52W **92** C5
Inis = Ennis *Ireland* 52°51N 8°59W **10** D3
Inis Córthaidh = Enniscorthy
  Ireland 52°30N 6°34W **10** D5
Inishbofin *Ireland* 53°37N 10°13W **10** C1
Inisheer *Ireland* 53°3N 9°32W **10** C2
Inishfree B. *Ireland* 55°4N 8°23W **10** A3
Inishkea North *Ireland* 54°9N 10°11W **10** B1
Inishkea South *Ireland* 54°7N 10°12W **10** B1
Inishmaan *Ireland* 53°5N 9°35W **10** C2
Inishmore *Ireland* 53°8N 9°45W **10** C2
Inishmurray I. *Ireland* 54°26N 8°39W **10** B3
Inishshark *Ireland* 53°37N 10°16W **10** C1
Inishturk *Ireland* 53°42N 10°7W **10** C1
Inishvickillane *Ireland* 52°3N 10°37W **10** D1
Injinoo ◎ *Australia* 10°56S 142°15E **62** A3
Injune *Australia* 25°53S 148°32E **63** D4
Inklin → *N. Amer.* 58°50N 133°10W **70** B2
Inland Kaikoura Ra.
  N.Z. 41°59S 173°41E **59** D4
Inland Sea = Setonaikai
  Japan 34°20N 133°30E **31** G6
Inle L. *Burma* 20°30N 96°58E **41** J20
Inlet *U.S.A.* 43°45N 74°48W **83** C10
Inn → *Austria* 48°35N 13°28E **16** D7
Innamincka *Australia* 27°44S 140°46E **63** D3
Inner Hebrides *U.K.* 57°0N 6°30W **11** E2
Inner Mongolia = Nei Monggol
  Zizhiqu □ China 42°0N 112°0E **34** D7
Inner Sound *U.K.* 57°30N 5°55W **11** D3
Innerkip *Canada* 43°13N 80°42W **82** C4
Innetalling I. *Canada* 56°0N 79°0W **72** A4
Innisfail *Australia* 17°33S 146°5E **62** B4
Innisfail *Canada* 52°2N 113°57W **70** C6
In'noshima *Japan* 34°19N 133°10E **31** G6
Innsbruck *Austria* 47°16N 11°23E **16** E6
Inny → *Ireland* 53°30N 7°50W **10** C4
Inongo
  Dem. Rep. of the Congo 1°55S 18°30E **52** E3
Inoucdjouac = Inukjuak
  Canada 58°25N 78°15W **69** F16
Inowrocław *Poland* 52°50N 18°12E **17** B10
Inscription, C. *Australia* 25°29S 112°59E **61** E1
Insein *Burma* 16°50N 96°5E **41** L20
Inta *Russia* 66°5N 60°8E **18** A11
Intendente Alvear
  Argentina 35°12S 63°32W **94** D3
Interlaken *Switz.* 46°41N 7°50E **20** C7
Interlaken *U.S.A.* 42°37N 76°44W **83** D8
International Falls
  U.S.A. 48°36N 93°25W **80** A7
Intiyaco *Argentina* 28°43S 60°5W **94** B3
Inukjuak *Canada* 58°25N 78°15W **69** F16
Inútil, B. *Chile* 53°30S 70°15W **96** G2
Inuvik *Canada* 68°16N 133°40W **68** D5
Inveraray *U.K.* 56°14N 5°5W **11** E3
Inverbervie *U.K.* 56°51N 2°17W **11** E6
Invercargill *N.Z.* 46°24S 168°24E **59** G2
Inverclyde □ *U.K.* 55°55N 4°49W **11** F4
Inverell *Australia* 29°45S 151°8E **63** D5
Invergordon *U.K.* 57°41N 4°10W **11** D4
Inverloch *Australia* 38°38S 145°45E **63** F4
Invermere *Canada* 50°30N 116°2W **70** C5
Inverness *Canada* 46°15N 61°19W **73** C7
Inverness *U.K.* 57°29N 4°13W **11** D4
Inverness *Calif., U.S.A.* 38°6N 122°51W **78** G4
Inverness *Fla., U.S.A.* 28°50N 82°20W **85** G13
Inverurie *U.K.* 57°17N 2°23W **11** D6
Investigator Group
  Australia 34°45S 134°20E **63** E1
Investigator Str.
  Australia 35°30S 137°0E **63** F2
Inya *Russia* 50°28N 86°37E **28** D9
Inyanga *Zimbabwe* 18°12S 32°40E **55** F3
Inyangani *Zimbabwe* 18°5S 32°50E **55** F3

Inyantue *Zimbabwe* 18°33S 26°39E **56** B4
Inyo Mts. *U.S.A.* 36°40N 118°0W **78** J9
Inyokern *U.S.A.* 35°39N 117°49W **79** K9
Inyonga *Tanzania* 6°45S 32°2E **54** D3
Inza *Russia* 53°55N 46°25E **18** D8
Iō-Jima *Japan* 30°48N 130°18E **31** J5
Ioannina *Greece* 39°42N 20°47E **23** E9
Iola *U.S.A.* 37°55N 95°24W **80** G6
Ione *U.S.A.* 38°21N 120°56W **78** G6
Ionia *U.S.A.* 42°59N 85°4W **81** D11
Ionian Is. = Iónioi Nísoi
  Greece 38°40N 20°0E **23** E9
Ionian Sea *Medit. S.* 37°30N 17°30E **23** E7
Iónioi Nísoi *Greece* 38°40N 20°0E **23** E9
Ios *Greece* 36°41N 25°20E **23** F11
Iowa □ *U.S.A.* 42°18N 93°30W **80** D7
Iowa → *U.S.A.* 41°10N 91°1W **80** E8
Iowa City *U.S.A.* 41°40N 91°32W **80** E9
Iowa Falls *U.S.A.* 42°31N 93°16W **80** D7
Iowa Park *U.S.A.* 33°57N 98°40W **84** E5
Ipala *Tanzania* 4°30S 32°52E **54** C3
Ipameri *Brazil* 17°44S 48°9W **93** G9
Ipatinga *Brazil* 19°32S 42°30W **93** G10
Ipiales *Colombia* 0°50N 77°37W **92** C3
Ipin = Yibin *China* 28°45N 104°32E **32** D5
Ipixuna *Brazil* 7°0S 71°40W **92** E4
Ipoh *Malaysia* 4°35N 101°5E **39** K3
Ippy *C.A.R.* 6°5N 21°7E **52** C4
Ipsala *Turkey* 40°55N 26°23E **23** D12
Ipswich *Australia* 27°35S 152°40E **63** D5
Ipswich *U.K.* 52°4N 1°10E **13** E9
Ipswich *Mass., U.S.A.* 42°41N 70°50W **83** D14
Ipswich *S. Dak., U.S.A.* 45°27N 99°2W **80** C4
Ipu *Brazil* 4°23S 40°44W **93** D10
Iqaluit *Canada* 63°44N 68°31W **69** E18
Iqaluktuutiaq = Cambridge Bay
  Canada 69°10N 105°0W **68** D11
Iquique *Chile* 20°19S 70°5W **92** H4
Iquitos *Peru* 3°45S 73°10W **92** D4
Irabu-Jima *Japan* 24°50N 125°10E **31** M2
Iracoubo *Fr. Guiana* 5°30N 53°10W **93** B8
Írafshán *Iran* 26°42N 61°56E **45** E9
Iráklio *Greece* 35°20N 25°12E **25** D7
Iráklio □ *Greece* 35°10N 25°10E **25** D7
Iráklion = Iráklio *Greece* 35°20N 25°12E **25** D7
Iráklion, Kólpos *Greece* 35°23N 25°8E **25** D7
Irala *Paraguay* 25°55S 54°35W **95** B5
Iran ■ *Asia* 33°0N 53°0E **45** C7
Iran, Pegunungan
  Malaysia 2°20N 114°50E **36** D4
Iran Ra. = Iran, Pegunungan
  Malaysia 2°20N 114°50E **36** D4
Īrānshahr *Iran* 27°15N 60°40E **45** E9
Irapuato *Mexico* 20°41N 101°28W **86** C4
Iraq ■ *Asia* 33°0N 44°0E **44** C5
Irati *Brazil* 25°25S 50°38W **95** B5
Irbid *Jordan* 32°35N 35°48E **46** C4
Irbid □ *Jordan* 32°30N 35°0E **46** C5
Irebu *Dem. Rep. of the Congo* 0°40S 17°46E **52** E3
Ireland ■ *Europe* 53°50N 7°52W **10** C4
Iri = Iksan *S. Korea* 35°59N 127°0E **35** G14
Irian Jaya = Papua □
  Indonesia 4°0S 137°0E **37** E9
Irian Jaya Barat □
  Indonesia 2°5S 132°50E **37** E8
Iringa *Tanzania* 7°48S 35°43E **54** D4
Iringa □ *Tanzania* 7°48S 35°43E **54** D4
Iriomote △ *Japan* 24°29N 123°53E **31** M1
Iriomote-Jima *Japan* 24°19N 123°48E **31** M1
Iriona *Honduras* 15°57N 85°11W **88** C2
Iriri → *Brazil* 3°52S 52°37W **93** D8
Irish Republic ■ *Europe* 53°50N 7°52W **10** C4
Irish Sea *Europe* 53°38N 4°48W **12** D3
Irkutsk *Russia* 52°18N 104°20E **29** D11
Irma *Canada* 52°55N 111°14W **71** C6
Irō-Zaki *Japan* 34°36N 138°51E **31** G9
Iron Baron *Australia* 32°58S 137°11E **63** E2
Iron Gate = Portile de Fier
  Europe 44°44N 22°30E **17** F12
Iron Knob *Australia* 32°46S 137°8E **63** E2
Iron Mountain *U.S.A.* 45°49N 88°4W **80** C9
Iron Range △ *Australia* 12°34S 143°18E **62** A3
Iron River *U.S.A.* 46°6N 88°39W **80** B9
Irondequoit *U.S.A.* 43°13N 77°35W **82** C7
Ironton *Mo., U.S.A.* 37°36N 90°38W **80** G8
Ironton *Ohio, U.S.A.* 38°32N 82°41W **81** F12
Ironwood *U.S.A.* 46°27N 90°9W **80** B8
Ironwood Forest △
  U.S.A. 32°32N 111°28W **77** K8
Iroquois *Canada* 44°51N 75°19W **83** B9
Iroquois Falls *Canada* 48°46N 80°41W **72** C3
Irpin *Ukraine* 50°30N 30°15E **17** C16
Irrara Cr. → *Australia* 29°35S 145°31E **63** D4
Irrawaddy □ *Burma* 17°0N 95°0E **41** L19
Irrawaddy → *Burma* 15°50N 95°6E **41** M19
Irrawaddy, Mouths of the
  Burma 15°30N 95°0E **41** M19
Irricana *Canada* 51°19N 113°37W **70** C6
Irrunytju *Australia* 26°3S 128°56E **61** E4
Irtysh → *Russia* 61°4N 68°52E **28** C7
Irumu
  Dem. Rep. of the Congo 1°32N 29°53E **54** B2
Irún *Spain* 43°20N 1°52W **21** A5
Irunea = Pamplona-Iruña
  Spain 42°48N 1°38W **21** A5
Irvine *Canada* 49°57N 110°16W **71** D6
Irvine *U.K.* 55°37N 4°41W **11** F4
Irvine *Calif., U.S.A.* 33°41N 117°46W **79** M9
Irvine *Ky., U.S.A.* 37°42N 83°58W **81** G12
Irving *U.S.A.* 32°48N 96°56W **84** E6
Irvona *U.S.A.* 40°46N 78°33W **82** F6
Irwin → *Australia* 29°15S 114°54E **61** E1
Irymple *Australia* 34°14S 142°8E **63** E3
Isa Khel *Pakistan* 32°41N 71°17E **42** C4
Isaac → *Australia* 22°55S 149°20E **62** C4
Isabel *U.S.A.* 45°24N 101°26W **80** C3
Isabel, I. *Mexico* 21°51N 105°55W **86** C3

Isabela *Phil.* 6°40N 121°59E **37** C6
Isabela *Puerto Rico* 18°30N 67°2W **89** d
Isabela, Cord. *Nic.* 13°30N 85°25W **88** D2
Isabella B. *Australia* 21°0S 121°4E **60** D3
Isabella, Cord. = Isabela,
  Cord. *Nic.* 13°30N 85°25W **88** D2
Ísachsen, C. *Canada* 79°20N 105°28W **69** B10
Ísafjarðardjúp *Iceland* 66°10N 23°0W **8** C2
Ísafjörður *Iceland* 66°5N 23°9W **8** C2
Isagarh *India* 24°48N 77°51E **42** G7
Isahaya *Japan* 32°52N 130°2E **31** H5
Isaka *Tanzania* 3°56S 32°59E **54** C3
Isalo △ *Madag.* 22°23S 45°16E **57** C8
Isan → *India* 26°51N 80°7E **43** F9
Isana = Içana → *Brazil* 0°26N 67°19W **92** C5
Isangano △ *Zambia* 11°8S 30°35E **55** E3
Isar → *Germany* 48°48N 12°57E **16** D7
Ischia *Italy* 40°44N 13°57E **22** D6
Isdell → *Australia* 16°27S 124°51E **60** C3
Ise *Japan* 34°25N 136°45E **31** G8
Ise-Shima △ *Japan* 34°25N 136°48E **31** G8
Ise-Wan *Japan* 34°43N 136°43E **31** G8
Iseramagazi *Tanzania* 4°37S 32°10E **54** C3
Isère □ *France* 44°59N 4°51E **20** D6
Isérnia *Italy* 41°36N 14°14E **22** D6
Isfahan = Eşfahān *Iran* 32°39N 51°43E **45** C6
Ishigaki *Japan* 24°26N 124°10E **31** M2
Ishigaki-Shima *Japan* 24°20N 124°10E **31** M2
Ishikari-Gawa →
  Japan 43°15N 141°23E **30** C10
Ishikari-Sammyaku
  Japan 43°30N 143°0E **30** C11
Ishikari-Wan *Japan* 43°25N 141°1E **30** C10
Ishikawa □ *Japan* 26°25N 127°49E **31** L3
Ishikawa □ *Japan* 36°30N 136°30E **31** F8
Ishim *Russia* 56°10N 69°30E **28** D7
Ishim → *Russia* 57°45N 71°10E **28** D8
Ishinomaki *Japan* 38°32N 141°20E **30** E10
Ishioka *Japan* 36°11N 140°16E **31** F10
Ishkoman *Pakistan* 36°30N 73°50E **43** A5
Ishpeming *U.S.A.* 46°29N 87°40W **80** B10
Isil Kul *Russia* 54°55N 71°16E **28** D8
Isiolo *Kenya* 0°24N 37°33E **54** B4
Isiro *Dem. Rep. of the Congo* 2°53N 27°40E **54** B2
Isisford *Australia* 24°15S 144°21E **62** C3
İskenderun *Turkey* 36°32N 36°10E **44** B3
İskenderun Körfezi
  Turkey 36°40N 35°50E **19** G6
Iskŭr → *Bulgaria* 43°45N 24°25E **23** C11
Iskut → *Canada* 56°45N 131°49W **70** B2
Isla → *U.K.* 56°32N 3°20W **11** E5
Isla Coiba △ *Panama* 7°33N 81°36W **88** E3
Isla de Salamanca △
  Colombia 10°59N 74°40W **89** D5
Isla Gorge △ *Australia* 25°10S 149°57E **62** D4
Isla Isabel △ *Mexico* 21°54N 105°58W **86** C3
Isla Tiburón y San Estéban △
  Mexico 29°0N 112°27W **86** B2
Isla Vista *U.S.A.* 34°25N 119°53W **79** L7
Islam Headworks
  Pakistan 29°49N 72°33E **42** E5
Islamabad *Pakistan* 33°40N 73°10E **42** C5
Islamgarh *Pakistan* 27°51N 70°48E **42** F4
Islamkot *Pakistan* 24°42N 70°13E **42** G4
Islampur *Bihar, India* 25°9N 85°12E **43** G11
Islampur *W. Bengal,*
  India 26°16N 88°12E **43** F13
Island = Iceland ■ *Europe* 64°45N 19°0W **8** D4
Island L. *Canada* 53°47N 94°25W **71** C10
Island Lagoon *Australia* 31°30S 136°40E **63** E2
Island Pond *U.S.A.* 44°49N 71°53W **83** B13
Islands, B. of *Canada* 49°11N 58°15W **73** C8
Islands, B. of *N.Z.* 35°15S 174°6E **59** A5
Islay *U.K.* 55°46N 6°10W **11** F2
Isle → *France* 44°55N 0°15W **20** D3
Isle aux Morts *Canada* 47°35N 59°0W **73** C8
Isle of Wight □ *U.K.* 50°41N 1°17W **13** G6
Isle Royale △ *U.S.A.* 48°0N 88°55W **80** B9
Isleton *U.S.A.* 38°10N 121°37W **78** G5
Ismail = Izmayil
  Ukraine 45°22N 28°46E **17** F15
Ismâ'ilîya *Egypt* 30°37N 32°18E **51** B12
Isna *Egypt* 25°17N 32°30E **51** C12
Isoanala *Madag.* 23°50S 45°44E **57** C8
Isparta *Turkey* 37°47N 30°30E **19** G5
Íspica *Italy* 36°47N 14°55E **22** F6
Israel ■ *Asia* 32°0N 34°50E **46** D3
Issoire *France* 45°32N 3°15E **20** D5
Issyk-Kul = Balykchy
  Kyrgyzstan 42°26N 76°12E **32** B2
Issyk-Kul, Ozero = Ysyk-Köl
  Kyrgyzstan 42°25N 77°15E **28** E8
İstanbul *Turkey* 41°0N 28°58E **23** D13
İstanbul Boğazı *Turkey* 41°5N 29°3E **23** D13
Istiea *Greece* 38°57N 23°9E **23** E10
Isto, Mt. *U.S.A.* 69°12N 143°48W **74** B11
Istokpoga, L. *U.S.A.* 27°23N 81°17W **85** H14
Istra *Russia* 55°55N 36°50E **18** C6
Istra *Croatia* 45°10N 14°0E **16** F7
Istres *France* 43°31N 4°59E **20** E6
Istria = Istra *Croatia* 45°10N 14°0E **16** F7
Itá *Paraguay* 25°29S 57°21W **94** B4
Itaberaba *Brazil* 12°32S 40°18W **93** F10
Itabira *Brazil* 19°37S 43°13W **93** G10
Itabirito *Brazil* 20°15S 43°48W **95** A7
Itabuna *Brazil* 14°48S 39°16W **93** F11
Itacaunas → *Brazil* 5°21S 49°8W **93** E9
Itacoatiara *Brazil* 3°8S 58°25W **92** D7
Itaipú, Represa de *Brazil* 25°30S 54°30W **95** B5
Itaituba *Brazil* 4°10S 55°50W **93** D7
Itajaí *Brazil* 27°50S 48°39W **95** B6
Itajubá *Brazil* 22°24S 45°30W **95** A6
Itaka *Tanzania* 8°50S 32°49E **55** D3
Itala △ *S. Africa* 27°30S 31°7E **57** D5
Italy ■ *Europe* 42°0N 13°0E **22** C5
Itamaraju *Brazil* 17°5S 39°32W **93** G11
Itampolo *Madag.* 24°41S 43°57E **57** C7
Itandrano *Madag.* 21°47S 45°17E **57** C8
Itapecuru Mirim *Brazil* 3°24S 44°20W **93** D10
Itaperuna *Brazil* 21°10S 41°54W **95** A7
Itapetininga *Brazil* 23°36S 48°7W **95** A6
Itapeva *Brazil* 23°59S 48°59W **95** A6

Itapicuru → *Bahia,*
  Brazil 11°47S 37°32W **93** F11
Itapicuru → *Maranhão,*
  Brazil 2°52S 44°12W **93** D10
Itapipoca *Brazil* 3°30S 39°35W **93** D11
Itapuá □ *Paraguay* 26°40S 55°40W **95** B4
Itaqui *Brazil* 29°8S 56°30W **94** B4
Itararé *Brazil* 24°6S 49°23W **95** A6
Itarsi *India* 22°36N 77°51E **42** H7
Itatí *Argentina* 27°16S 58°15W **94** B4
Itatiaia △ *Brazil* 22°22S 44°38W **95** A7
Itchen → *U.K.* 50°55N 1°22W **13** G6
Itezhi Tezhi, L. *Zambia* 15°30S 25°30E **55** F2
Ithaca = Itháki *Greece* 38°25N 20°40E **23** E9
Ithaca *U.S.A.* 42°27N 76°30W **83** D8
Itháki *Greece* 38°25N 20°40E **23** E9
Itiquira → *Brazil* 17°18S 56°44W **93** G7
Itiyuro → *Argentina* 22°40S 63°50W **94** A3
Itō *Japan* 34°58N 139°5E **31** G9
Itoigawa *Japan* 37°2N 137°51E **31** F8
Itonamas → *Bolivia* 12°28S 64°24W **92** F6
Ittoqqortoormiit *Greenland* 70°20N 23°0W **4** B6
Itu *Brazil* 23°17S 47°15W **95** A6
Itu Aba I. *S. China Sea* 10°23N 114°21E **36** B4
Ituiutaba *Brazil* 19°0S 49°25W **93** G9
Itumbiara *Brazil* 18°20S 49°10W **93** G9
Ituna *Canada* 51°10N 103°24W **71** C8
Itunge Port *Tanzania* 9°40S 33°55E **55** D3
Iturbe *Argentina* 23°0S 65°25W **94** A2
Ituri →
  Dem. Rep. of the Congo 1°40N 27°1E **54** B2
Iturup, Ostrov *Russia* 45°0N 148°0E **29** E15
Ituxí → *Brazil* 7°18S 64°51W **92** E6
Itzehoe *Germany* 53°55N 9°31E **16** B5
Ivahona *Madag.* 23°27S 46°10E **57** C8
Ivaí → *Brazil* 23°18S 53°42W **95** A5
Ivalo *Finland* 68°38N 27°35E **8** B22
Ivalojoki → *Finland* 68°40N 27°40E **8** B22
Ivanava *Belarus* 52°7N 25°29E **17** B13
Ivanhoe *Australia* 32°56S 144°20E **63** E3
Ivanhoe *Canada* 44°23N 77°28W **82** B7
Ivanhoe *Calif., U.S.A.* 36°23N 119°13W **78** J7
Ivanhoe *Minn., U.S.A.* 44°28N 96°15W **80** C5
Ivano-Frankivsk
  Ukraine 48°40N 24°40E **17** D13
Ivanovo = Ivanava
  Belarus 52°7N 25°29E **17** B13
Ivanovo *Russia* 57°5N 41°0E **18** C7
Ivato *Madag.* 20°37S 47°10E **57** C8
Ivatsevichy *Belarus* 52°43N 25°21E **17** B13
Ivdel *Russia* 60°42N 60°24E **18** B11
Ivinheima → *Brazil* 23°14S 53°42W **95** A5
Ivinhema *Brazil* 22°10S 53°37W **95** A5
Ivohibe *Madag.* 22°31S 46°57E **57** C8
Ivory Coast *W. Afr.* 4°20N 5°0W **50** H4
Ivory Coast ■ *Africa* 7°30N 5°0W **50** G4
Ivrea *Italy* 45°28N 7°52E **20** D7
Ivujivik *Canada* 62°24N 77°55W **69** E16
Ivvavik △ *Canada* 69°6N 139°30W **68** D4
Ivybridge *U.K.* 50°23N 3°56W **13** G4
Iwaizumi *Japan* 39°50N 141°45E **30** E10
Iwaki *Japan* 37°3N 140°55E **31** F10
Iwakuni *Japan* 34°15N 132°8E **31** G6
Iwamizawa *Japan* 43°12N 141°46E **30** C10
Iwanai *Japan* 42°58N 140°30E **30** C10
Iwata *Japan* 34°42N 137°51E **31** G8
Iwate □ *Japan* 39°30N 141°30E **30** E10
Iwate-San *Japan* 39°51N 141°0E **30** E10
Iwo *Nigeria* 7°39N 4°9E **50** G6
Iwŏn *N. Korea* 40°19N 128°39E **35** D15
Ixiamas *Bolivia* 13°50S 68°5W **92** F5
Ixopo *S. Africa* 30°11S 30°5E **57** E5
Ixtepec *Mexico* 16°34N 95°6W **87** D5
Ixtlán del Río *Mexico* 21°2N 104°22W **86** C4
Iyo *Japan* 33°45N 132°45E **31** H6
Izabal, L. de *Guatemala* 15°30N 89°10W **88** C2
Izamal *Mexico* 20°56N 89°1W **87** C7
Izena-Shima *Japan* 26°56N 127°56E **31** L3
Izhevsk *Russia* 56°51N 53°14E **18** C9
Izhma → *Russia* 65°19N 52°54E **18** A9
Izmayil *Ukraine* 45°22N 28°46E **17** F15
İzmir *Turkey* 38°25N 27°8E **23** E12
İzmit = Kocaeli *Turkey* 40°45N 29°50E **19** F4
İznik Gölü *Turkey* 40°27N 29°30E **23** D13
Izra *Syria* 32°51N 36°15E **46** C5
Izu-Shotō *Japan* 34°30N 140°0E **31** G10
Izúcar de Matamoros
  Mexico 18°36N 98°28W **87** D5
Izumi-Sano *Japan* 34°23N 135°18E **31** G7
Izumo *Japan* 35°20N 132°46E **31** G6
Izyaslav *Ukraine* 50°5N 26°50E **17** C14

J

J.F.K. Int. ✈ (JFK)
  U.S.A. 40°38N 73°47W **83** F11
J. Strom Thurmond L.
  U.S.A. 33°40N 82°12W **85** E13
Jabalpur *India* 23°9N 79°58E **43** H8
Jabbūl *Syria* 36°4N 37°30E **44** B3
Jabiru *Australia* 12°40S 132°53E **60** B5
Jablah *Syria* 35°20N 36°0E **44** C3
Jablonec nad Nisou
  Czech Rep. 50°43N 15°10E **16** C8
Jaboatão *Brazil* 8°7S 35°1W **93** E11
Jaboticabal *Brazil* 21°15S 48°17W **95** A6
Jaca *Spain* 42°35N 0°33W **21** A5
Jacareí *Brazil* 23°20S 46°0W **95** A6
Jacarèzinho *Brazil* 23°5S 49°58W **95** A6
Jack River △ *Australia* 14°58S 144°19E **62** A3
Jackman *U.S.A.* 45°37N 70°15W **81** C18
Jacksboro *U.S.A.* 33°13N 98°10W **84** E5
Jackson *Barbados* 13°7N 59°36W **89** g
Jackson *Ala., U.S.A.* 31°31N 87°53W **85** F11
Jackson *Calif., U.S.A.* 38°21N 120°46W **78** G6
Jackson *Ky., U.S.A.* 37°33N 83°23W **81** G12
Jackson *Mich., U.S.A.* 42°15N 84°24W **81** D11
Jackson *Minn., U.S.A.* 43°37N 95°1W **80** D6

Jackson *Miss., U.S.A.* 32°18N 90°12W **85** E9
Jackson *Mo., U.S.A.* 37°23N 89°40W **80** G9
Jackson *N.H., U.S.A.* 44°10N 71°11W **83** B13
Jackson *Ohio, U.S.A.* 39°3N 82°39W **81** F12
Jackson *Tenn., U.S.A.* 35°37N 88°49W **85** D10
Jackson *Wyo., U.S.A.* 43°29N 110°46W **76** E8
Jackson B. *N.Z.* 43°58S 168°42E **59** E2
Jackson L. *U.S.A.* 43°52N 110°36W **76** E8
Jacksons *N.Z.* 42°46S 171°32E **59** E3
Jackson's Arm *Canada* 49°52N 56°47W **73** C8
Jacksonville *Ala., U.S.A.* 33°49N 85°46W **85** E12
Jacksonville *Ark., U.S.A.* 34°52N 92°7W **84** D8
Jacksonville *Calif., U.S.A.* 37°52N 120°24W **78** H6
Jacksonville *Fla., U.S.A.* 30°20N 81°39W **85** F14
Jacksonville *Ill., U.S.A.* 39°44N 90°14W **80** F8
Jacksonville *N.C., U.S.A.* 34°45N 77°26W **85** D16
Jacksonville *Tex., U.S.A.* 31°58N 95°17W **84** F7
Jacksonville Beach *U.S.A.* 30°17N 81°24W **85** F14
Jacmel *Haiti* 18°14N 72°32W **89** C5
Jacob Lake *U.S.A.* 36°43N 112°13W **77** H7
Jacobabad *Pakistan* 28°20N 68°29E **42** E3
Jacobina *Brazil* 11°11S 40°30W **93** F10
Jacques-Cartier, Dét. de *Canada* 50°0N 63°30W **73** C7
Jacques-Cartier, Mt. *Canada* 48°57N 66°0W **73** C6
Jacques-Cartier △ *Canada* 47°15N 71°33W **73** C5
Jacuí → *Brazil* 30°2S 51°15W **95** C5
Jacumba *U.S.A.* 32°37N 116°11W **79** N10
Jacundá → *Brazil* 1°57S 50°26W **93** D9
Jade City *Canada* 59°15N 129°37W **70** B3
Jaén *Peru* 5°25S 78°40W **92** E3
Jaén *Spain* 37°44N 3°43W **21** D7
Jafarabad *India* 20°52N 71°22E **42** J4
Jaffa = Tel Aviv-Yafo *Israel* 32°4N 34°48E **46** C3
Jaffa, C. *Australia* 36°58S 139°40E **63** F2
Jaffna *Sri Lanka* 9°45N 80°2E **40** Q12
Jaffrey *U.S.A.* 42°49N 72°2W **83** D12
Jagadhri *India* 30°10N 77°20E **42** D7
Jagadishpur *India* 25°30N 84°21E **43** G11
Jagdalpur *India* 19°3N 82°0E **41** K13
Jagersfontein *S. Africa* 29°44S 25°27E **56** D4
Jaghīn → *Iran* 27°17N 57°13E **45** E8
Jagraon *India* 30°50N 75°25E **42** D6
Jagtial *India* 18°50N 79°0E **40** K11
Jaguariaíva *Brazil* 24°10S 49°50W **95** A6
Jaguaribe → *Brazil* 4°25S 37°45W **93** D11
Jagüey Grande *Cuba* 22°35N 81°7W **88** B3
Jahanabad *India* 25°13N 84°59E **43** G11
Jahazpur *India* 25°37N 75°17E **42** G6
Jahrom *Iran* 28°30N 53°31E **45** D7
Jaijon *India* 31°21N 76°9E **42** D7
Jailolo *Indonesia* 1°5N 127°30E **37** D7
Jailolo, Selat *Indonesia* 0°5N 129°5E **37** D7
Jaipur *India* 27°0N 75°50E **42** F6
Jais *India* 26°15N 81°32E **43** F9
Jaisalmer *India* 26°55N 70°54E **42** F4
Jaisinghnagar *India* 23°38N 80°30E **43** H8
Jaitaran *India* 26°12N 73°56E **42** G5
Jaithari *India* 23°14N 78°37E **43** H8
Jājarm *Iran* 36°58N 56°27E **45** B8
Jakam → *India* 23°54N 74°13E **42** H6
Jakarta *Indonesia* 6°9S 106°52E **37** G12
Jakhal *India* 29°48N 75°50E **42** E6
Jakhau *India* 23°13N 68°43E **42** H3
Jakobstad = Pietarsaari *Finland* 63°40N 22°43E **8** E20
Jal *U.S.A.* 32°7N 103°12W **77** K12
Jalājil *Si. Arabia* 25°40N 45°27E **44** E5
Jalalabad *Afghan.* 34°30N 70°29E **42** B4
Jalalabad *India* 27°41N 79°42E **43** F8
Jalalpur Jattan *Pakistan* 32°38N 74°11E **42** C6
Jalama *U.S.A.* 34°29N 120°29W **79** L6
Jalandhar = Jullundur *India* 31°20N 75°40E **42** D6
Jalapa *Guatemala* 14°39N 89°59W **88** D2
Jalapa Enríquez = Xalapa *Mexico* 19°32N 96°55W **87** D5
Jalasjärvi *Finland* 62°29N 22°47E **8** E20
Jalaun *India* 26°8N 79°25E **43** F8
Jaldhaka → *Bangla.* 26°16N 89°16E **43** F13
Jalesar *India* 27°29N 78°19E **42** F8
Jaleswar *Nepal* 26°38N 85°48E **43** F11
Jalgaon *India* 21°0N 75°42E **40** J9
Jalībah *Iraq* 30°35N 46°32E **44** D5
Jalingo *Nigeria* 8°55N 11°25E **51** G8
Jalisco □ *Mexico* 20°20N 103°40W **86** D4
Jalkot *Pakistan* 35°14N 73°24E **43** B5
Jalna *India* 19°48N 75°38E **40** K9
Jalón → *Spain* 41°47N 1°4W **21** B5
Jalor *India* 25°21N 72°37E **42** G5
Jalpa *Mexico* 21°38N 102°58W **86** C4
Jalpaiguri *India* 26°32N 88°46E **41** F16
Jalpan *Mexico* 21°14N 99°29W **87** C5
Jaluit I. *Marshall Is.* 6°0N 169°30E **64** G8
Jalūlā' *Iraq* 34°16N 45°10E **44** C5
Jamaame *Somali Rep.* 0°4N 42°44E **47** G3
Jamaica ■ *W. Indies* 18°10N 77°30W **88** a
Jamalpur *Bangla.* 24°52N 89°56E **41** G16
Jamalpur *India* 25°18N 86°28E **43** G12
Jamalpurganj *India* 23°2N 87°59E **43** H13
Jamanxim → *Brazil* 4°43S 56°18W **93** D7
Jambewangi *Indonesia* 8°17S 114°7E **37** J17
Jambi *Indonesia* 1°38S 103°30E **36** E2
Jambi □ *Indonesia* 1°30S 102°30E **36** E2
Jambongan, Pulau *Malaysia* 6°45N 117°20E **36** C5
Jambusar *India* 22°3N 72°51E **42** H5
James → *S. Dak., U.S.A.* 42°52N 97°18W **80** D5
James → *Va., U.S.A.* 36°56N 76°27W **81** G15
James B. *Canada* 54°0N 80°0W **72** B3

James Ranges *Australia* 24°10S 132°30E **60** D5
James Ross I. *Antarctica* 63°58S 57°50W **5** C18
Jamesabad *Pakistan* 25°17N 69°15E **42** G3
Jamestown *Australia* 33°10S 138°32E **63** E2
Jamestown *S. Africa* 31°6S 26°45E **56** E4
Jamestown *N. Dak., U.S.A.* 46°54N 98°42W **80** B4
Jamestown *N.Y., U.S.A.* 42°6N 79°14W **82** D5
Jamestown *Pa., U.S.A.* 41°29N 80°27W **82** E4
Jamīlābād *Iran* 34°24N 48°28E **45** C6
Jamira → *India* 21°35N 88°28E **43** J13
Jammu *India* 32°43N 74°54E **42** C6
Jammu & Kashmir □ *India* 34°25N 77°0E **43** B7
Jamnagar *India* 22°30N 70°6E **42** H4
Jamni → *India* 25°13N 78°35E **43** G8
Jampur *Pakistan* 29°39N 70°40E **42** E4
Jamrud *Pakistan* 33°59N 71°24E **42** C4
Jämsä *Finland* 61°53N 25°10E **8** F21
Jamshedpur *India* 22°44N 86°12E **43** H12
Jamtara *India* 23°59N 86°49E **43** H12
Jämtland *Sweden* 63°31N 14°0E **8** E16
Jan L. *Canada* 54°56N 102°55W **71** C8
Jan Mayen *Arctic* 71°0N 9°0W **4** B7
Janakpur *India* 26°42N 85°55E **43** F11
Janaúba *Brazil* 15°48S 43°19W **93** G10
Jand *Pakistan* 33°30N 72°6E **42** C5
Jandanku ۞ *Australia* 16°20S 135°45E **62** B2
Jandaq *Iran* 34°3N 54°22E **45** C7
Jandia *Canary Is.* 28°6N 14°21W **24** F5
Jandía, Pta. de *Canary Is.* 28°3N 14°31W **24** F5
Jandía △ *Canary Is.* 28°4N 14°19W **24** F5
Jandola *Pakistan* 32°20N 70°9E **42** C4
Jandowae *Australia* 26°45S 151°7E **63** D5
Janesville *U.S.A.* 42°41N 89°1W **80** D9
Jangamo *Mozam.* 24°6S 35°21E **57** C6
Janghai *India* 25°33N 82°19E **43** G10
Jangheung *S. Korea* 34°41N 126°52E **35** G14
Janjanbureh *Gambia* 13°30N 14°47W **50** F3
Janjgir *India* 22°1N 82°34E **43** J10
Janjina *Madag.* 20°30S 45°50E **57** C8
Janos *Mexico* 30°54N 108°10W **86** A3
Januária *Brazil* 15°25S 44°25W **93** G10
Janûb Sînî □ *Egypt* 29°30N 33°50E **46** F2
Janubio *Canary Is.* 28°56N 13°50W **24** F6
Jaora *India* 23°40N 75°10E **42** H6
Japan ■ *Asia* 36°0N 136°0E **31** G8
Japan, Sea of *Asia* 40°0N 135°0E **30** E7
Japen = Yapen *Indonesia* 1°50S 136°0E **37** E9
Japla *India* 24°33N 84°1E **43** G11
Japurá → *Brazil* 3°8S 65°46W **92** D5
Jaquarão *Brazil* 32°34S 53°23W **95** C5
Jaqué *Panama* 7°27N 78°8W **88** E4
Jarābulus *Syria* 36°49N 38°1E **44** B3
Jarama → *Spain* 40°24N 3°32W **21** B4
Jaranwala *Pakistan* 31°15N 73°26E **42** D5
Jarash *Jordan* 32°17N 35°54E **46** C4
Jarash □ *Jordan* 32°17N 35°54E **46** C4
Jardim *Brazil* 21°28S 56°2W **94** A4
Jardín América *Argentina* 27°3S 55°14W **95** B4
Jardine River △ *Australia* 11°9S 142°21E **62** A3
Jardines de la Reina, Arch. de los *Cuba* 20°50N 78°50W **88** B4
Jargalang *China* 43°5N 122°55E **35** C12
Jari → *Brazil* 1°9S 51°54W **93** D8
Jarīr, W. al → *Si. Arabia* 25°38N 42°30E **44** E4
Jarosław *Poland* 50°2N 22°42E **17** C12
Jarrahdale *Australia* 32°24S 116°5E **61** F2
Jarres, Plaine des *Laos* 19°27N 103°10E **38** C4
Jartai *China* 39°45N 105°48E **34** E3
Jarud Qi *China* 44°28N 120°50E **35** B11
Järvenpää *Finland* 60°29N 25°5E **8** F21
Jarvis *Canada* 42°53N 80°6W **82** D4
Jarvis I. *Pac. Oc.* 0°15S 160°5W **65** H12
Jarwa *India* 27°38N 82°30E **43** F10
Jasdan *India* 22°2N 71°12E **42** H4
Jashpurnagar *India* 22°54N 84°9E **43** H11
Jasidih *India* 24°31N 86°39E **43** G12
Jāsimīyah *Iraq* 33°45N 44°41E **44** C5
Jasin *Malaysia* 2°20N 102°26E **39** L4
Jāsk *Iran* 25°38N 57°45E **45** E8
Jasło *Poland* 49°45N 21°30E **17** D11
Jaso *India* 24°30N 80°29E **43** G9
Jasper *Alta., Canada* 52°55N 118°5W **70** C5
Jasper *Ont., Canada* 44°52N 75°57W **83** B9
Jasper *Ala., U.S.A.* 33°50N 87°17W **85** E11
Jasper *Fla., U.S.A.* 30°31N 82°57W **85** F13
Jasper *Ind., U.S.A.* 38°24N 86°56W **80** F10
Jasper *Tex., U.S.A.* 30°56N 94°1W **84** F7
Jasper △ *Canada* 52°50N 118°8W **70** C5
Jasrasar *India* 27°43N 73°49E **42** F5
Jászberény *Hungary* 47°30N 19°55E **17** E10
Jataí *Brazil* 17°58S 51°48W **93** G8
Jatibarang *Indonesia* 6°28S 108°18E **37** G13
Jatiluwih *Indonesia* 8°23S 115°8E **37** J18
Jatinegara *Indonesia* 6°13S 106°52E **37** G12
Játiva = Xàtiva *Spain* 38°59N 0°32W **21** C5
Jaú *Brazil* 22°10S 48°30W **95** A6
Jaú → *Brazil* 1°54S 61°26W **92** D6
Jauja *Peru* 11°45S 75°15W **92** F3
Jaunpur *India* 25°46N 82°44E **43** G10
Java = Jawa *Indonesia* 7°0S 110°0E **36** F3
Java Sea *Indonesia* 4°35S 107°15E **36** E3
Java Trench *Ind. Oc.* 9°0S 105°0E **36** F3
Jawa *Indonesia* 7°0S 110°0E **36** F3
Jawa Barat □ *Indonesia* 7°0S 107°0E **37** G12
Jawa Tengah □ *Indonesia* 7°0S 110°0E **37** G14
Jawa Timur □ *Indonesia* 8°0S 113°0E **37** G15
Jawad *India* 24°36N 74°51E **42** G6
Jawhar *Somali Rep.* 2°48N 45°30E **47** G4
Jawoyn ۞ *Australia* 14°16S 132°28E **60** B5
Jay Peak *U.S.A.* 44°55N 72°32W **83** B12
Jayanti *India* 26°45N 89°40E **41** F16
Jayapura *Indonesia* 2°28S 140°38E **37** E10
Jayawijaya, Pegunungan *Indonesia* 5°0S 139°0E **37** F9

Jaynagar *India* 26°43N 86°9E **43** F12
Jaypur = Jeypore *India* 18°50N 82°38E **41** K13
Jayrūd *Syria* 33°49N 36°44E **44** C3
Jayton *U.S.A.* 33°15N 100°34W **84** E4
Jāz Mūrīān, Hāmūn-e *Iran* 27°20N 58°55E **45** E8
Jazīreh-ye Shīf *Iran* 29°4N 50°54E **45** D6
Jazminal *Mexico* 24°52N 101°24W **86** C4
Jazzīn *Lebanon* 33°31N 35°35E **46** B4
Jean *U.S.A.* 35°47N 115°20W **79** K11
Jean Marie River *Canada* 61°32N 120°38W **70** A4
Jean-Rabel *Haiti* 19°50N 73°5W **89** C5
Jeanerette *U.S.A.* 29°55N 91°40W **84** G9
Jeanette, Ostrov = Zhannetty, Ostrov *Russia* 76°43N 158°0E **29** B16
Jeannette *U.S.A.* 40°20N 79°36W **82** F5
Jebāl Bārez, Kūh-e *Iran* 28°30N 58°20E **45** D8
Jebel, Bahr el → *Sudan* 9°30N 30°25E **51** G12
Jebel Ali = Minā' Jabal 'Alī *U.A.E.* 25°2N 55°8E **45** E7
Jecheon *S. Korea* 37°8N 128°12E **35** F15
Jedburgh *U.K.* 55°29N 2°33W **11** F6
Jedda = Jiddah *Si. Arabia* 21°29N 39°10E **47** C2
Jeddore L. *Canada* 48°3N 55°55W **73** C8
Jędrzejów *Poland* 50°35N 20°15E **17** C11
Jefferson *Iowa, U.S.A.* 42°1N 94°23W **80** D6
Jefferson *Ohio, U.S.A.* 41°44N 80°46W **82** E4
Jefferson *Tex., U.S.A.* 32°46N 94°21W **84** E7
Jefferson, Mt. *Nev., U.S.A.* 38°47N 116°56W **76** G5
Jefferson, Mt. *Oreg., U.S.A.* 44°41N 121°48W **76** D3
Jefferson City *Mo., U.S.A.* 38°34N 92°10W **80** F7
Jefferson City *Tenn., U.S.A.* 36°7N 83°30W **85** C13
Jeffersontown *U.S.A.* 38°12N 85°35W **81** F11
Jeffersonville *U.S.A.* 38°17N 85°44W **81** F11
Jeffrey City *U.S.A.* 42°30N 107°49W **76** E10
Jega *Nigeria* 12°15N 4°23E **50** F6
Jeju *S. Korea* 33°31N 126°32E **35** H14
Jeju-do *S. Korea* 33°29N 126°34E **35** H14
Jēkabpils *Latvia* 56°29N 25°57E **9** H21
Jekyll I. *U.S.A.* 31°4N 81°25W **85** F14
Jelenia Góra *Poland* 50°50N 15°45E **16** C8
Jelgava *Latvia* 56°41N 23°49E **9** H20
Jemaja *Indonesia* 3°5N 105°45E **39** L5
Jember *Indonesia* 8°11S 113°41E **37** H15
Jemaluang *Malaysia* 2°16N 103°52E **39** L4
Jena *Germany* 50°54N 11°35E **16** C6
Jena *U.S.A.* 31°41N 92°8W **84** F8
Jenīn *West Bank* 32°28N 35°18E **46** C4
Jenkins *U.S.A.* 37°10N 82°38W **81** G12
Jenner *U.S.A.* 38°27N 123°7W **78** G3
Jennings *U.S.A.* 30°13N 92°40W **84** F8
Jeong-eup *S. Korea* 35°35N 126°50E **35** G14
Jeonju *S. Korea* 35°50N 127°4E **35** G14
Jepara *Indonesia* 7°40S 109°14E **37** G14
Jeparit *Australia* 36°8S 142°1E **63** F3
Jequié *Brazil* 13°51S 40°5W **93** F10
Jequitinhonha *Brazil* 16°30S 41°0W **93** G10
Jequitinhonha → *Brazil* 15°51S 38°53W **93** G11
Jerada *Morocco* 34°17N 2°10W **50** B5
Jerantut *Malaysia* 3°56N 102°22E **39** L4
Jerejak, Pulau *Malaysia* 5°19N 100°19E **39** c
Jérémie *Haiti* 18°40N 74°10W **89** C5
Jerez, Pta. *Mexico* 22°58N 97°40W **87** C5
Jerez de García Salinas *Mexico* 22°39N 103°0W **86** C4
Jerez de la Frontera *Spain* 36°41N 6°7W **21** D2
Jerez de los Caballeros *Spain* 38°20N 6°45W **21** C2
Jericho = El Arīḥā *West Bank* 31°52N 35°27E **46** D4
Jericho *Australia* 23°38S 146°6E **62** C4
Jerid, Chott el = Djerid, Chott *Tunisia* 33°42N 8°30E **50** B7
Jerilderie *Australia* 35°20S 145°41E **63** F4
Jermyn *U.S.A.* 41°32N 75°31E **83** E9
Jerome *U.S.A.* 42°44N 114°31W **76** E6
Jerramungup *Australia* 33°55S 118°55E **61** F2
Jersey *U.K.* 49°11N 2°7W **13** H5
Jersey City *U.S.A.* 40°42N 74°4W **83** F10
Jersey Shore *U.S.A.* 41°12N 77°15W **82** E7
Jerseyville *U.S.A.* 39°7N 90°20W **80** F8
Jerusalem *Israel/West Bank* 31°47N 35°10E **46** D4
Jervis B. *Australia* 35°8S 150°46E **63** F5
Jervis Inlet *Canada* 50°0N 123°57W **70** C4
Jesi = Iesi *Italy* 43°31N 13°14E **22** C5
Jessore *Bangla.* 23°10N 89°10E **41** H16
Jesup *U.S.A.* 31°36N 81°53W **85** F14
Jesús Carranza *Mexico* 17°26N 95°2W **87** D5
Jesús María *Argentina* 30°59S 64°5W **94** C3
Jetmore *U.S.A.* 38°4N 99°54W **80** F4
Jetpur *India* 21°45N 70°10E **42** J4
Jevnaker *Norway* 60°15N 10°26E **9** F14
Jewett *U.S.A.* 40°22N 81°2W **82** F3
Jewett City *U.S.A.* 41°36N 71°59W **83** E13
Jeyḥūnābād *Iran* 34°58N 48°59E **45** C6
Jeypore *India* 18°50N 82°38E **41** K13
Jha Jha *India* 24°46N 86°22E **43** G12
Jhaarkand = Jharkhand □ *India* 24°0N 85°50E **43** H11
Jhabua *India* 22°46N 74°36E **42** H6
Jhajjar *India* 28°37N 76°42E **42** E7
Jhal *Pakistan* 28°17N 67°27E **42** E2
Jhal Jhao *Pakistan* 26°20N 65°35E **40** F4
Jhalawar *India* 24°40N 76°10E **42** G7
Jhalida *India* 23°22N 85°58E **43** H11
Jhalrapatan *India* 24°33N 76°10E **42** G7
Jhang Maghiana *Pakistan* 31°15N 72°22E **42** D5
Jhansi *India* 25°30N 78°36E **43** G8
Jhargram *India* 22°27N 86°59E **43** H12
Jharia *India* 23°45N 86°26E **43** H12
Jharkhand □ *India* 24°0N 85°50E **43** H11

Jharsuguda *India* 21°56N 84°5E **41** J14
Jhelum *Pakistan* 33°0N 73°45E **42** C5
Jhelum → *Pakistan* 31°20N 72°10E **42** D5
Jhilmilli *India* 23°24N 82°51E **43** H10
Jhudo *Pakistan* 24°58N 69°18E **42** G3
Jhunjhunu *India* 28°10N 75°30E **42** E6
Ji-Paraná *Brazil* 10°52S 62°57W **92** F6
Ji Xian *Hebei, China* 37°35N 115°30E **34** F8
Ji Xian *Henan, China* 35°22N 114°5E **34** G8
Ji Xian *Shanxi, China* 36°7N 110°40E **34** F6
Jia Xian *Henan, China* 33°59N 113°12E **34** H7
Jia Xian *Shaanxi, China* 38°12N 110°28E **34** E6
Jiaji = Qionghai *China* 19°15N 110°26E **38** C8
Jiamusi *China* 46°40N 130°26E **33** B8
Ji'an *Jiangxi, China* 27°6N 114°59E **33** D6
Ji'an *Jilin, China* 41°5N 126°10E **35** D14
Jianchang *China* 40°55N 120°35E **35** D11
Jianchangying *China* 40°10N 118°50E **35** D10
Jiangcheng *China* 22°36N 101°52E **32** D5
Jiangmen *China* 22°32N 113°0E **33** D6
Jiangsu □ *China* 33°0N 120°0E **35** H11
Jiangxi □ *China* 27°30N 116°0E **33** D6
Jiao Xian = Jiaozhou *China* 36°18N 120°1E **35** F11
Jiaohe *Hebei, China* 38°2N 116°20E **34** E9
Jiaohe *Jilin, China* 43°40N 127°22E **35** C14
Jiaozhou *China* 36°18N 120°1E **35** F11
Jiaozhou Wan *China* 36°5N 120°10E **35** F11
Jiaozuo *China* 35°16N 113°12E **34** G7
Jiawang *China* 34°28N 117°26E **35** G9
Jiaxiang *China* 35°25N 116°20E **34** G9
Jiaxing *China* 30°49N 120°45E **33** C7
Jiayi = Chiai *Taiwan* 23°29N 120°25E **33** D7
Jibuti = Djibouti ■ *Africa* 12°0N 43°0E **47** E3
Jicarón, I. *Panama* 7°10N 81°50W **88** E3
Jiddah *Si. Arabia* 21°29N 39°10E **47** C2
Jido *India* 29°2N 94°58E **41** E19
Jieshou *China* 33°18N 115°22E **34** H8
Jiexiu *China* 37°2N 111°55E **34** F6
Jigalong *Australia* 23°21S 120°47E **60** D3
Jigalong ۞ *Australia* 23°21S 120°46E **60** D3
Jigni *India* 25°45N 79°25E **43** G8
Jihlava *Czech Rep.* 49°28N 15°35E **16** D8
Jihlava → *Czech Rep.* 48°55N 16°36E **17** D9
Jijiga *Ethiopia* 9°20N 42°50E **47** F3
Jilib *Somali Rep.* 0°29N 42°46E **47** G3
Jilin *China* 43°44N 126°30E **35** C14
Jilin □ *China* 44°0N 127°0E **35** C14
Jilong = Chilung *Taiwan* 25°3N 121°45E **33** D7
Jima *Ethiopia* 7°40N 36°47E **47** F2
Jimbaran, Teluk *Indonesia* 8°46S 115°9E **37** K18
Jiménez *Mexico* 27°8N 104°54W **86** B4
Jimeta *Nigeria* 9°17N 12°28E **52** C2
Jimo *China* 36°23N 120°30E **35** F11
Jin Xian = Jinzhou *Hebei, China* 38°2N 115°2E **34** E8
Jin Xian = Jinzhou *Liaoning, China* 38°55N 121°42E **35** E11
Jinan *China* 36°38N 117°1E **34** F9
Jinchang *China* 38°30N 102°10E **32** C5
Jincheng *China* 35°29N 112°50E **34** G7
Jind *India* 29°19N 76°22E **42** E7
Jindabyne *Australia* 36°25S 148°35E **63** F4
Jinding *China* 22°22N 113°33E **33** G10
Jindo *S. Korea* 34°28N 126°15E **35** G14
Jindřichův Hradec *Czech Rep.* 49°10N 15°2E **16** D8
Jing He → *China* 34°27N 109°4E **34** G5
Jingbian *China* 37°20N 108°30E **34** F5
Jingchuan *China* 35°20N 107°20E **34** G4
Jingdezhen *China* 29°20N 117°11E **33** D6
Jinggu *China* 23°35N 100°41E **32** D5
Jinghai *China* 38°55N 116°55E **34** E9
Jingle *China* 38°20N 111°55E **34** E6
Jingning *China* 35°30N 105°43E **34** G3
Jingpo Hu *China* 43°55N 128°55E **35** C15
Jingtai *China* 37°10N 104°6E **34** F3
Jingxing *China* 38°2N 114°8E **34** E8
Jingyang *China* 34°30N 108°50E **34** G5
Jingyu *China* 42°25N 126°45E **35** C14
Jingyuan *China* 36°30N 104°40E **34** F3
Jingziguan *China* 33°15N 111°0E **34** H6
Jinhua *China* 29°8N 119°38E **33** D6
Jining *Nei Monggol Zizhiqu, China* 41°5N 113°0E **34** D7
Jining *Shandong, China* 35°22N 116°34E **34** G9
Jinja *Uganda* 0°25N 33°12E **54** B3
Jinjang *Malaysia* 3°13N 101°39E **39** L3
Jinji *China* 37°58N 106°8E **34** F4
Jinju *S. Korea* 35°12N 128°2E **35** G15
Jinnah Barrage *Pakistan* 32°58N 71°33E **42** C4
Jinotega *Nic.* 13°6N 85°59W **88** D2
Jinotepe *Nic.* 11°50N 86°10W **88** D2
Jinsha Jiang → *China* 28°50N 104°36E **32** C5
Jinxi *China* 40°52N 120°50E **35** D11
Jinxiang *China* 35°5N 116°22E **34** G9
Jinzhong *China* 37°42N 112°46E **34** F7
Jinzhou *Hebei, China* 38°2N 115°2E **34** E8
Jinzhou *Liaoning, China* 38°55N 121°42E **35** E11
Jiparaná → *Brazil* 8°3S 62°52W **92** E6
Jipijapa *Ecuador* 1°0S 80°40W **92** D2
Jiquilpan *Mexico* 19°59N 102°43W **86** D4
Jirisan *S. Korea* 35°20N 127°44E **35** G14
Jiroft *Iran* 28°45N 57°50E **45** D8
Jishan *China* 35°34N 110°58E **34** G6
Jisr ash Shughūr *Syria* 35°49N 36°18E **44** C3
Jitarning *Australia* 32°48S 117°57E **61** F2
Jitra *Malaysia* 6°16N 100°25E **39** J3
Jiu → *Romania* 43°47N 23°48E **17** F12
Jiudengkou *China* 39°56N 106°40E **34** E4
Jiujiang *China* 29°42N 115°58E **33** D6
Jiulong = Kowloon *China* 22°19N 114°11E **33** G11
Jiuquan *China* 39°50N 98°20E **32** C4
Jiutai *China* 44°10N 125°50E **35** B13
Jiuxincheng *China* 39°17N 115°59E **34** E8

Jiwani *Pakistan* 25°1N 61°44E **40** G2
Jixi *China* 45°20N 130°50E **35** B16
Jiyang *China* 37°0N 117°12E **35** F9
Jiyuan *China* 35°7N 112°57E **34** G7
Jīzan *Si. Arabia* 17°0N 42°20E **47** D3
Jize *China* 36°54N 114°56E **34** F8
Jizl, Wādī al → *Si. Arabia* 25°39N 38°25E **44** E3
Jizo-Zaki *Japan* 35°34N 133°20E **31** G6
Jizzax *Uzbekistan* 40°6N 67°50E **28** E7
Joaçaba *Brazil* 27°5S 51°31W **95** B5
João Pessoa *Brazil* 7°10S 34°52W **93** E12
Joaquín V. González *Argentina* 25°10S 64°0W **94** B3
Jodhpur *India* 26°23N 73°8E **42** F5
Jodiya *India* 22°42N 70°18E **42** H4
Joensuu *Finland* 62°37N 29°49E **8** E23
Jōetsu *Japan* 37°12N 138°10E **31** F9
Jofane *Mozam.* 21°15S 34°18E **57** C5
Jogbani *India* 26°25N 87°15E **43** F12
Jõgeva *Estonia* 58°45N 26°24E **9** G22
Jogjakarta = Yogyakarta *Indonesia* 7°49S 110°22E **37** G14
Johannesburg *S. Africa* 26°11S 28°2E **57** D4
Johannesburg *U.S.A.* 35°22N 117°38W **79** K9
Johilla → *India* 23°37N 81°14E **43** H9
John Crow Mts. *Jamaica* 18°5N 76°25W **88** a
John Day *U.S.A.* 44°25N 118°57W **76** D4
John Day → *U.S.A.* 45°44N 120°39W **76** D3
John Day Fossil Beds △ *U.S.A.* 44°33N 119°38W **76** D4
John D'or Prairie *Canada* 58°30N 115°8W **70** B5
John H. Kerr Res. *U.S.A.* 36°36N 78°18W **85** C15
John o' Groats *U.K.* 58°38N 3°4W **11** C5
Johnnie *U.S.A.* 36°25N 116°5W **79** J10
John's Ra. *Australia* 21°55S 133°23E **62** C1
Johnson *Kans., U.S.A.* 37°34N 101°45W **80** G3
Johnson City *N.Y., U.S.A.* 42°7N 75°58W **83** D9
Johnson City *Tenn., U.S.A.* 36°19N 82°21W **85** C13
Johnson City *Tex., U.S.A.* 30°17N 98°25W **84** F5
Johnsonburg *U.S.A.* 41°29N 78°41W **82** E6
Johnsondale *U.S.A.* 35°58N 118°32W **79** K8
Johnsons Crossing *Canada* 60°29N 133°18W **70** A2
Johnston, L. *Australia* 32°25S 120°30E **61** F3
Johnston Falls = Mambilima Falls *Zambia* 10°31S 28°45E **55** E2
Johnston I. *Pac. Oc.* 17°10N 169°8W **65** F11
Johnstone Str. *Canada* 50°28N 126°0W **70** C3
Johnstown *Ireland* 52°45N 7°33W **10** D4
Johnstown *N.Y., U.S.A.* 43°0N 74°22W **83** C10
Johnstown *Ohio, U.S.A.* 40°9N 82°41W **82** F2
Johnstown *Pa., U.S.A.* 40°20N 78°55W **82** F6
Johor, Selat *Asia* 1°28N 103°47E **39** d
Johor Bahru *Malaysia* 1°28N 103°46E **39** d
Jõhvi *Estonia* 59°22N 27°27E **9** G22
Joinville *Brazil* 26°15S 48°55W **95** B6
Joinville I. *Antarctica* 65°0S 55°30W **5** C18
Jojutla *Mexico* 18°37N 99°11W **87** D5
Jokkmokk *Sweden* 66°35N 19°50E **8** C18
Jökulsá á Bru → *Iceland* 65°40N 14°16W **8** D6
Jökulsá á Fjöllum → *Iceland* 66°10N 16°30W **8** C5
Jolfa *Āzarbājān-e Sharqī, Iran* 38°57N 45°38E **44** B5
Jolfa *Eşfahan, Iran* 32°58N 51°37E **45** C6
Joliet *U.S.A.* 41°32N 88°5W **80** E9
Joliette *Canada* 46°3N 73°24W **72** C5
Jolo *Phil.* 6°0N 121°0E **37** C6
Jolon *U.S.A.* 35°58N 121°9W **78** K5
Jombang *Indonesia* 7°33S 112°14E **37** G15
Jonava *Lithuania* 55°8N 24°12E **9** J21
Jones Sound *Canada* 76°0N 85°0W **69** B15
Jonesboro *Ark., U.S.A.* 35°50N 90°42W **85** D9
Jonesboro *La., U.S.A.* 32°15N 92°43W **84** E8
Joniškis *Lithuania* 56°13N 23°35E **9** H20
Jönköping *Sweden* 57°45N 14°8E **9** H16
Jonquière *Canada* 48°27N 71°14W **73** C5
Joplin *U.S.A.* 37°6N 94°31W **80** G6
Jora *India* 26°20N 77°49E **42** F6
Jordan *Mont., U.S.A.* 47°19N 106°55W **76** C10
Jordan *N.Y., U.S.A.* 43°4N 76°29W **83** C8
Jordan ■ *Asia* 31°0N 36°0E **46** E5
Jordan → *Asia* 31°48N 35°32E **46** D4
Jordan Valley *U.S.A.* 42°59N 117°3W **76** E5
Jorhat *India* 26°45N 94°12E **41** F19
Jörn *Sweden* 65°4N 20°1E **8** D19
Jorong *Indonesia* 3°58S 114°56E **36** E4
Jørpeland *Norway* 59°3N 6°1E **9** G12
Jorquera → *Chile* 28°3S 69°58W **94** B2
Jos *Nigeria* 9°53N 8°51E **50** G7
José Batlle y Ordóñez *Uruguay* 33°20S 55°10W **95** C4
Joseph, L. *Canada* 45°10N 79°44W **82** A5
Joseph Bonaparte G. *Australia* 14°35S 128°50E **60** B4
Joseph L. *Canada* 52°45N 65°18W **73** B6
Joshinath *India* 30°34N 79°34E **43** D8
Joshinetsu-Kōgen △ *Japan* 36°42N 138°32E **31** F9
Joshua Tree *U.S.A.* 34°8N 116°19W **79** L10
Joshua Tree △ *U.S.A.* 33°55N 116°0W **79** M10
Jost Van Dyke I. *Br. Virgin Is.* 18°29N 64°47W **89** e
Jostedalsbreen *Norway* 61°40N 6°59E **8** F12
Jotunheimen *Norway* 61°35N 8°25E **8** F13
Joubertberge *Namibia* 18°30S 14°0E **56** B1
Jourdanton *U.S.A.* 28°55N 98°33W **84** G5
Jovellanos *Cuba* 22°40N 81°10W **88** B3
Ju Xian *China* 36°35N 118°20E **35** F10
Juan Aldama *Mexico* 24°19N 103°21W **86** C4
Juan Bautista Alberdi *Argentina* 34°26S 61°48W **94** C3
Juan de Fuca, Str. of. *N. Amer.* 48°15N 124°0W **78** B3

130 Juán de Nova INDEX TO WORLD MAPS

Juán de Nova Ind. Oc. 17°3S 43°45E 57 B7
Juan Fernández, Arch. de Pac. Oc. 33°50S 80°0W 90 G2
Juan José Castelli Argentina 25°27S 60°57W 94 B3
Juan L. Lacaze Uruguay 34°26S 57°25W 94 C4
Juankoski Finland 63°3N 28°19E 8 E23
Juárez Mexico 27°37N 100°44W 86 B4
Juárez, Sierra de Mexico 32°0N 116°0W 86 A1
Juàzeiro Brazil 9°30S 40°30W 93 E10
Juàzeiro do Norte Brazil 7°10S 39°18W 93 E11
Jûbâ Sudan 4°50N 31°35E 51 H12
Juba → Somali Rep. 1°30N 42°35E 47 G3
Jubany Antarctica 62°30S 58°0W 5 C18
Jubayl Lebanon 34°5N 35°39E 46 A4
Jubbah Si. Arabia 28°2N 40°56E 44 D4
Jubbal India 31°5N 77°40E 42 D7
Jubbulpore = Jabalpur India 23°9N 79°58E 43 H8
Jubilee L. Australia 29°0S 126°50E 61 E4
Juby, C. Morocco 28°0N 12°59W 50 C3
Júcar = Xúquer → Spain 39°5N 0°10W 21 C5
Júcaro Cuba 21°37N 78°51W 88 B4
Juchitán de Zaragoza Mexico 16°26N 95°1W 87 D5
Judea = Har Yehuda Israel 31°35N 34°57E 46 D3
Judith → U.S.A. 47°44N 109°39W 76 C9
Judith, Pt. U.S.A. 41°22N 71°29W 83 E13
Judith Gap U.S.A. 46°41N 109°45W 76 C9
Juigalpa Nic. 12°6N 85°26W 88 D2
Juiz de Fora Brazil 21°43S 43°19W 95 A7
Jujuy □ Argentina 23°20S 65°40W 94 A2
Julesburg U.S.A. 40°59N 102°16W 76 F12
Juli Peru 16°10S 69°25W 92 G5
Julia Cr. → Australia 20°0S 141°11E 62 C3
Julia Creek Australia 20°39S 141°44E 62 C3
Juliaca Peru 15°25S 70°10W 92 G4
Julian U.S.A. 33°4N 116°38W 79 M10
Julian, L. Canada 54°25N 77°57W 72 B4
Julianatop Suriname 3°40N 56°30W 93 C7
Julianehåb = Qaqortoq Greenland 60°43N 46°0W 4 C5
Julimes Mexico 28°25N 105°27W 86 B3
Jullundur India 31°20N 75°40E 42 D6
Julu China 37°15N 115°2E 34 F8
Jumbo Zimbabwe 17°30S 30°58E 55 F3
Jumbo Pk. U.S.A. 36°12N 114°11W 79 J12
Jumentos Cays Bahamas 23°0N 75°40W 88 B4
Jumilla Spain 38°28N 1°19W 21 C5
Jumla Nepal 29°15N 82°13E 43 E10
Jumna = Yamuna → India 25°30N 81°53E 43 G9
Jumunjin S. Korea 37°55N 128°54E 35 F15
Junagadh India 21°30N 70°30E 42 J4
Junction Tex., U.S.A. 30°29N 99°46W 84 F5
Junction Utah, U.S.A. 38°14N 112°13W 77 G7
Junction B. Australia 11°52S 133°55E 62 A1
Junction City Kans., U.S.A. 39°2N 96°50W 80 F5
Junction City Oreg., U.S.A. 44°13N 123°12W 76 D2
Junction Pt. Australia 11°45S 133°50E 62 A1
Jundah Australia 24°46S 143°2E 62 C3
Jundiaí Brazil 24°30S 47°0W 95 A6
Juneau U.S.A. 58°18N 134°25W 70 B2
Junee Australia 34°53S 147°35E 63 E4
Jungfrau Switz. 46°32N 7°58E 20 C7
Junggar Pendi China 44°30N 86°0E 32 B3
Jungshahi Pakistan 24°52N 67°44E 42 G2
Juniata → U.S.A. 40°24N 77°1W 82 F7
Junín Argentina 34°33S 60°57W 94 C3
Junín de los Andes Argentina 39°45S 71°0W 96 D2
Jūniyah Lebanon 33°59N 35°38E 46 B4
Juntas Chile 28°24S 69°58W 94 B2
Juntura U.S.A. 43°45N 118°5W 76 E4
Jur, Nahr el → Sudan 8°45N 29°15E 51 G11
Jura = Jura, Mts. du Europe 46°40N 6°5E 20 C7
Jura = Schwäbische Alb Germany 48°20N 9°30E 16 D5
Jura U.K. 56°0N 5°50W 11 F3
Jura, Mts. du Europe 46°40N 6°5E 20 C7
Jura, Sd. of U.K. 55°57N 5°45W 11 F3
Jurbarkas Lithuania 55°4N 22°46E 9 J20
Jurien Bay Australia 30°18S 115°2E 61 F2
Jūrmala Latvia 56°58N 23°34E 9 H20
Jurong Singapore 1°19N 103°42E 39 d
Juruá → Brazil 2°37S 65°44W 92 D5
Juruena Brazil 13°0S 58°10W 92 F7
Juruena → Brazil 7°20S 58°3W 92 E7
Juruti Brazil 2°9S 56°4W 93 D7
Justo Daract Argentina 33°52S 65°12W 94 C2
Jutaí → Brazil 2°43S 66°57W 92 D5
Juticalpa Honduras 14°40N 86°12W 88 D2
Jutland = Jylland Denmark 56°25N 9°30E 9 H13
Juuka Finland 63°13N 29°17E 8 E23
Juventud, I. de la Cuba 21°40N 82°40W 88 B3
Jūy Zar Iran 33°50N 46°18E 44 C5
Juye China 35°22N 116°5E 34 G9
Jwaneng Botswana 24°45S 24°50E 53 J4
Jylland Denmark 56°25N 9°30E 9 H13
Jyväskylä Finland 62°14N 25°50E 8 E21

K

K2 Pakistan 35°58N 76°32E 43 B7
Kaakha = Kaka Turkmenistan 37°21N 59°36E 45 B8
Kaap Plateau S. Africa 28°30S 24°0E 56 D3
Kaapkruis Namibia 21°55S 13°57E 56 C1
Kaapstad = Cape Town S. Africa 33°55S 18°22E 56 E2
Kabaena Indonesia 5°15S 122°0E 37 F6
Kabala S. Leone 9°38N 11°37W 50 G3
Kabale Uganda 1°15S 30°0E 54 C3
Kabalo Dem. Rep. of the Congo 6°0S 27°0E 54 D2
Kabambare Dem. Rep. of the Congo 4°41S 27°39E 54 C2
Kabango Dem. Rep. of the Congo 8°35S 28°30E 55 D2
Kabanjahe Indonesia 3°6N 98°30E 36 D1
Kabara Fiji 18°59S 178°56W 59 a
Kabardino-Balkaria □ Russia 43°30N 43°30E 19 F7
Kabarega Falls = Murchison Falls Uganda 2°15N 31°30E 54 B3
Kabarnet Kenya 0°30N 35°45E 54 B4
Kabasalan Phil. 7°47N 122°44E 37 C6
Kabat Indonesia 8°16S 114°19E 37 J17
Kabin Buri Thailand 13°57N 101°43E 38 F3
Kabinakagami L. Canada 48°54N 84°25W 72 C3
Kabinda Dem. Rep. of the Congo 6°19S 24°20E 52 F4
Kabompo Zambia 13°36S 24°14E 55 E1
Kabompo → Zambia 14°11S 23°11E 53 G4
Kabondo Dem. Rep. of the Congo 8°58S 25°40E 55 D2
Kabongo Dem. Rep. of the Congo 7°22S 25°33E 54 D2
Kabrît, G. el Egypt 29°42N 33°16E 46 F2
Kabūd Gonbad Iran 37°5N 59°45E 45 B8
Kābul Afghan. 34°28N 69°11E 42 B3
Kābul □ Afghan. 34°30N 69°0E 40 B6
Kābul → Pakistan 33°55N 72°14E 42 C5
Kabunga Dem. Rep. of the Congo 1°38S 28°3E 54 C2
Kaburuang Indonesia 3°50N 126°30E 37 D7
Kabwe Zambia 14°30S 28°29E 55 E2
Kachchh, Gulf of India 22°50N 69°15E 42 H3
Kachchh, Rann of India 24°0N 70°0E 42 H4
Kachchhidhana India 21°44N 78°46E 43 J8
Kachebera Zambia 13°50S 32°50E 55 E3
Kachikau Botswana 18°8S 24°26E 56 B3
Kachin □ Burma 26°0N 97°30E 41 G20
Kachira, L. Uganda 0°40S 31°7E 54 C3
Kachiry Kazakhstan 53°10N 75°50E 28 D8
Kachnara India 23°50N 75°6E 42 H6
Kachot Cambodia 11°30N 103°3E 39 G4
Kaçkar Turkey 40°45N 41°10E 19 F7
Kadam, Mt. Uganda 1°45N 34°45E 54 B3
Kadan Kyun Burma 12°30N 98°20E 38 F2
Kadanai → Afghan. 31°22N 65°45E 42 D1
Kadavu Fiji 19°0S 178°15E 59 a
Kadavu Passage Fiji 18°45S 178°0E 59 a
Kade Ghana 6°7N 0°56W 50 G5
Kadhimain = Al Kāẓimīyah Iraq 33°22N 44°18E 44 C5
Kadi India 23°18N 72°23E 42 H5
Kadina Australia 33°55S 137°43E 63 E2
Kadipur India 26°10N 82°23E 43 F10
Kadirli Turkey 37°23N 36°5E 44 B3
Kadiyevka = Stakhanov Ukraine 48°35N 38°40E 19 E6
Kadoka U.S.A. 43°50N 101°31W 80 D3
Kadoma Zimbabwe 18°20S 29°52E 55 F2
Kâdugli Sudan 11°0N 29°45E 51 F11
Kaduna Nigeria 10°30N 7°21E 50 F7
Kaédi Mauritania 16°9N 13°28W 50 E3
Kaeng Khoï Thailand 14°35N 101°0E 38 E3
Kaeng Krachan △ Thailand 12°57N 99°23E 38 F2
Kaeng Tana △ Thailand 15°25N 105°32E 38 E5
Kaesŏng N. Korea 37°58N 126°35E 35 F14
Kāf Si. Arabia 31°25N 37°29E 44 D3
Kafan = Kapan Armenia 39°18N 46°27E 44 B5
Kafanchan Nigeria 9°40N 8°20E 50 G7
Kafinda Zambia 12°32S 30°20E 55 E3
Kafue Zambia 15°46S 28°9E 55 F2
Kafue → Zambia 15°30S 29°0E 53 H5
Kafue △ Zambia 15°12S 25°38E 55 F2
Kafue Flats Zambia 15°40S 27°25E 55 F2
Kafulwe Zambia 9°0S 29°1E 55 D2
Kaga Afghan. 34°14N 70°10E 42 B4
Kaga Bandoro C.A.R. 7°0N 19°10E 52 C3
Kagawa □ Japan 34°15N 134°0E 31 G7
Kagera □ Tanzania 2°0S 31°30E 54 C3
Kagera → Uganda 0°57S 31°47E 54 C3
Kağızman Turkey 40°5N 43°10E 44 B4
Kagoshima Japan 31°35N 130°33E 31 J5
Kagoshima □ Japan 31°30N 130°30E 31 J5
Kagul = Cahul Moldova 45°50N 28°15E 17 F15
Kahak Iran 36°6N 49°46E 45 B6
Kahama Tanzania 4°8S 32°30E 54 C3
Kahan Pakistan 29°18N 68°54E 42 E3
Kahang Malaysia 2°12N 103°32E 39 L4
Kahayan → Indonesia 3°40S 114°0E 36 E4
Kahe Tanzania 3°30S 37°25E 54 C4
Kahemba Dem. Rep. of the Congo 7°18S 18°55E 52 F3
Kahnūj Iran 27°55N 57°40E 45 E8
Kahoka U.S.A. 40°25N 91°44W 80 E8
Kaho'olawe U.S.A. 20°33N 156°37W 75 L8
Kahramanmaraş Turkey 37°37N 36°53E 44 B3
Kâhta Turkey 37°46N 38°36E 44 B3
Kahului U.S.A. 20°54N 156°28W 75 L8
Kahurangi △ N.Z. 41°10S 172°32E 59 D4
Kahuta Pakistan 33°35N 73°24E 42 C5
Kahuzi-Biega △ Dem. Rep. of the Congo 1°50S 27°55E 54 C2
Kai, Kepulauan Indonesia 5°55S 132°45E 37 F8
Kai Besar Indonesia 5°35S 133°0E 37 F8
Kai Is. = Kai, Kepulauan Indonesia 5°55S 132°45E 37 F8
Kai Kecil Indonesia 5°45S 132°40E 37 F8
Kaiapoi N.Z. 43°24S 172°40E 59 E4
Kaidu He → China 41°46N 86°31E 32 B3
Kaieteur Falls Guyana 5°1N 59°10W 92 B7
Kaifeng China 34°48N 114°21E 34 G8
Kaikohe N.Z. 35°25S 173°49E 59 A4
Kaikoura N.Z. 42°25S 173°43E 59 E4
Kailash = Kangrinboqe Feng China 31°0N 81°25E 43 D9
Kailu China 43°38N 121°18E 35 C11
Kailua Kona U.S.A. 19°39N 155°59W 75 M8
Kaimana Indonesia 3°39S 133°45E 37 E8
Kaimanawa Mts. N.Z. 39°15S 175°56E 59 C5
Kaimganj India 27°33N 79°24E 43 F8
Kaimur Hills India 24°30N 82°0E 43 G10
Kainab → Namibia 28°32S 19°34E 56 D2
Kainji Res. Nigeria 10°1N 4°40E 50 F6
Kainuu Finland 64°30N 29°7E 8 D23
Kaipara Harbour N.Z. 36°25S 174°14E 59 B5
Kaipokok B. Canada 54°54N 59°47W 73 B8
Kaira India 22°45N 72°50E 42 H5
Kairana India 29°24N 77°15E 42 E7
Kaironi Indonesia 0°47S 133°40E 37 E8
Kairouan Tunisia 35°45N 10°5E 51 A8
Kaiserslautern Germany 49°26N 7°45E 16 D4
Kaitaia N.Z. 35°8S 173°17E 59 A4
Kaitangata N.Z. 46°17S 169°51E 59 G2
Kaithal India 29°48N 76°26E 42 E7
Kaitu → Pakistan 33°10N 70°30E 42 C4
Kaiwi Channel U.S.A. 21°15N 157°30W 75 L8
Kaiyuan Liaoning, China 42°28N 124°1E 35 C13
Kaiyuan Yunnan, China 23°40N 103°12E 32 D5
Kaiyuh Mts. U.S.A. 64°30N 158°0W 74 C8
Kajaani Finland 64°17N 27°46E 8 D22
Kajabbi Australia 20°0S 140°1E 62 C3
Kajana = Kajaani Finland 64°17N 27°46E 8 D22
Kajang Malaysia 2°59N 101°48E 39 L3
Kajiado Kenya 1°53S 36°48E 54 C4
Kajo Kaji Sudan 3°58N 31°40E 51 H12
Kaka Turkmenistan 37°21N 59°36E 45 B8
Kakabeka Falls Canada 48°24N 89°37W 72 C2
Kakadu △ Australia 12°0S 132°3E 60 B5
Kakamas S. Africa 28°45S 20°33E 56 D3
Kakamega Kenya 0°20N 34°46E 54 B3
Kakanui Mts. N.Z. 45°10S 170°30E 59 F3
Kakdwip India 21°53N 88°11E 43 J13
Kake Japan 34°36N 132°19E 31 G6
Kake U.S.A. 56°59N 133°57W 70 B2
Kakegawa Japan 34°45N 138°1E 31 G9
Kakeroma-Jima Japan 28°8N 129°14E 31 K4
Kākhak Iran 34°9N 58°38E 45 C8
Kakhovka Ukraine 46°45N 33°30E 19 E5
Kakhovske Vdskh. Ukraine 47°5N 34°0E 19 E5
Kakinada India 16°57N 82°11E 41 L13
Kakisa Canada 60°56N 117°25W 70 A5
Kakisa → Canada 61°3N 118°10W 70 A5
Kakisa L. Canada 60°56N 117°43W 70 A5
Kakogawa Japan 34°46N 134°51E 31 G7
Kakuma Kenya 3°43N 34°52E 54 B3
Kakwa → Canada 54°37N 118°28W 70 C5
Kāl Gūsheh Iran 30°59N 58°12E 45 D8
Kal Sefīd Iran 34°52N 47°23E 44 C5
Kalaallit Nunaat = Greenland ⊘ N. Amer. 66°0N 45°0W 67 C15
Kalabagh Pakistan 33°0N 71°28E 42 C4
Kalabahi Indonesia 8°13S 124°31E 37 F6
Kalach Russia 50°22N 41°0E 19 D7
Kaladan → Burma 20°20N 93°5E 41 J18
Kaladar Canada 44°37N 77°5W 82 B7
Kalahari Africa 24°0S 21°30E 56 C3
Kalahari Gemsbok △ S. Africa 25°30S 20°30E 56 D3
Kalajoki Finland 64°12N 24°10E 8 D21
Kalakamati Botswana 20°40S 27°25E 57 C4
Kalakan Russia 55°15N 116°45E 29 D12
K'alak'unlun Shank'ou = Karakoram Pass Asia 35°33N 77°50E 43 B7
Kalam Pakistan 35°34N 72°30E 43 B5
Kalama Dem. Rep. of the Congo 2°52S 28°35E 54 C2
Kalama U.S.A. 46°1N 122°51W 78 E4
Kalamata Greece 37°3N 22°10E 23 F10
Kalamazoo U.S.A. 42°17N 85°35W 81 D11
Kalamazoo → U.S.A. 42°40N 86°10W 80 D10
Kalambo Falls Tanzania 8°37S 31°35E 55 D3
Kalan Turkey 39°7N 39°32E 44 B3
Kalannie Australia 30°22S 117°5E 61 F2
Kalāntarī Iran 32°10N 54°8E 45 C7
Kalao Indonesia 7°21S 121°0E 37 F6
Kalaotoa Indonesia 7°20S 121°50E 37 F6
Kalasin Thailand 16°26N 103°30E 38 D4
Kalāt Iran 25°29N 59°22E 45 E8
Kalat Pakistan 29°8N 66°31E 40 E5
Kalāteh Iran 36°33N 55°41E 45 B7
Kalāteh-ye Ganj Iran 27°31N 57°55E 45 E8
Kalbā U.A.E. 25°5N 56°22E 45 E8
Kalbarri Australia 27°40S 114°10E 61 E1
Kalbarri △ Australia 27°51S 114°30E 61 E1
Kalburgi = Gulbarga India 17°20N 76°50E 40 L10
Kalce Slovenia 45°54N 14°13E 16 F8
Kale Turkey 37°27N 28°49E 23 F13
Kalegauk Kyun Burma 15°33N 97°35E 38 E1
Kalehe Dem. Rep. of the Congo 2°6S 28°50E 54 C2
Kalema Tanzania 1°12S 31°55E 54 C3
Kalemie Dem. Rep. of the Congo 5°55S 29°9E 54 D2
Kalewa Burma 23°10N 94°15E 41 H19
Kaleybar Iran 38°47N 47°2E 44 B5
Kalgoorlie-Boulder Australia 30°40S 121°22E 61 F3
Kali → India 27°6N 79°55E 43 F8
Kali Sindh → India 25°32N 76°17E 42 G6
Kaliakra, Nos Bulgaria 43°21N 28°30E 23 C13
Kalianda Indonesia 5°50S 105°45E 36 F3
Kalibo Phil. 11°43N 122°22E 37 B6
Kalima Dem. Rep. of the Congo 2°33S 26°32E 54 C2
Kalimantan Indonesia 0°0 114°0E 36 E4
Kalimantan Barat □ Indonesia 0°0 110°30E 36 E4
Kalimantan Selatan □ Indonesia 2°30S 115°30E 36 E5
Kalimantan Tengah □ Indonesia 2°0S 113°30E 36 E4
Kalimantan Timur □ Indonesia 1°30N 116°30E 36 D5
Kálimnos Greece 37°0N 27°0E 23 F12
Kalimpong India 27°4N 88°35E 43 F13
Kaliningrad Russia 54°42N 20°32E 9 J19
Kalinkavichy Belarus 52°12N 29°20E 17 B15
Kalinkovichi = Kalinkavichy Belarus 52°12N 29°20E 17 B15
Kaliro Uganda 0°56N 33°30E 54 B3
Kalispell U.S.A. 48°12N 114°19W 76 B6
Kalisz Poland 51°45N 18°8E 17 C10
Kaliua Tanzania 5°5S 31°48E 54 D3
Kalix = Kalixälven → Sweden 65°50N 23°11E 8 D20
Kalix Sweden 65°53N 23°12E 8 D20
Kalixälven → Sweden 65°50N 23°11E 8 D20
Kalka India 30°46N 76°57E 42 D7
Kalkarindji Australia 17°30S 130°47E 60 C5
Kalkaska U.S.A. 44°44N 85°11W 81 C11
Kalkfeld Namibia 20°57S 16°14E 56 C2
Kalkfontein Botswana 22°4S 20°57E 56 C3
Kalkrand Namibia 24°1S 17°35E 56 C2
Kallavesi Finland 62°58N 27°30E 8 E22
Kallsjön Sweden 63°38N 13°0E 8 E15
Kalmar Sweden 56°40N 16°20E 9 H17
Kalmykia □ Russia 46°5N 46°1E 19 E8
Kalna India 23°13N 88°25E 43 H13
Kalnai India 22°46N 83°30E 43 H10
Kalocsa Hungary 46°32N 19°0E 17 E10
Kalokhorio Cyprus 34°51N 33°2E 25 E12
Kaloko Dem. Rep. of the Congo 6°47S 25°48E 54 D2
Kalol Gujarat, India 22°37N 73°31E 42 H5
Kalol Gujarat, India 23°15N 72°33E 42 H5
Kalomo Zambia 17°0S 26°30E 55 F2
Kalpi India 26°8N 79°47E 43 F8
Kaltag U.S.A. 64°20N 158°43W 74 C8
Kaltukatjara Australia 24°52S 129°5E 61 D4
Kalu Pakistan 25°5N 67°39E 42 G2
Kaluga Russia 54°35N 36°10E 18 D6
Kalulushi Zambia 12°50S 28°3E 55 E2
Kalumburu Australia 13°55S 126°35E 60 B4
Kalumburu ✪ Australia 14°17S 126°38E 60 B4
Kalush Ukraine 49°3N 24°23E 17 D13
Kalutara Sri Lanka 6°35N 80°0E 40 R12
Kalya Russia 60°15N 59°59E 18 B10
Kalyan India 19°15N 73°9E 40 K8
Kama Dem. Rep. of the Congo 3°30S 27°5E 54 C2
Kama → Russia 55°45N 52°0E 18 C9
Kamachumu Tanzania 1°37S 31°37E 54 C3
Kamaishi Japan 39°16N 141°53E 30 E10
Kamalia Pakistan 30°44N 72°42E 42 D5
Kaman India 27°39N 77°16E 42 F6
Kamanjab Namibia 19°35S 14°51E 56 B2
Kamapanda Zambia 12°5S 24°0E 55 E1
Kamarān Yemen 15°21N 42°35E 47 D3
Kamativi Zimbabwe 18°20S 27°6E 56 B4
Kambalda West Australia 31°10S 121°37E 61 F3
Kambar Pakistan 27°37N 68°1E 42 F3
Kambarka Russia 56°15N 54°11E 18 C9
Kambolé Zambia 8°47S 30°48E 55 D3
Kambos Cyprus 35°2N 32°44E 25 D11
Kambove Dem. Rep. of the Congo 10°51S 26°33E 55 E2
Kamchatka, Poluostrov Russia 57°0N 160°0E 29 D17
Kamchatka Pen. = Kamchatka, Poluostrov Russia 57°0N 160°0E 29 D17
Kamchiya → Bulgaria 43°4N 27°44E 23 C12
Kame Ruins Zimbabwe 20°7S 28°25E 55 G2
Kamen Russia 53°50N 81°30E 28 D9
Kamen-Rybolov Russia 44°46N 132°2E 30 B6
Kamenjak, Rt Croatia 44°47N 13°55E 16 F7
Kamenka Russia 65°58N 44°0E 18 A7
Kamenka Bugskaya = Kamyanka-Buzka Ukraine 50°8N 24°16E 17 C13
Kamensk Uralskiy Russia 56°25N 62°2E 28 D7
Kamenskoye Russia 62°45N 165°30E 29 C17
Kameoka Japan 35°0N 135°35E 31 G7
Kamet India 30°55N 79°35E 43 D8
Kamiah U.S.A. 46°14N 116°2W 76 C5
Kamieskroon S. Africa 30°9S 17°56E 56 E2
Kamilukuak L. Canada 62°22N 101°40W 71 A8
Kamin-Kashyrskyy Ukraine 51°39N 24°56E 17 C13
Kamina Dem. Rep. of the Congo 8°45S 25°0E 55 D2
Kaminak L. Canada 62°10N 95°0W 71 A10
Kaministiquia Canada 48°32N 89°35W 72 C1
Kaminoyama Japan 38°9N 140°17E 30 E10
Kamiros Greece 36°20N 27°56E 25 C9
Kamituga Dem. Rep. of the Congo 3°2S 28°10E 54 C2
Kamla → India 25°35N 86°36E 43 G12
Kamloops Canada 50°40N 120°20W 70 C4
Kamo Japan 37°39N 139°3E 30 F9
Kamoke Pakistan 32°4N 74°4E 42 C6
Kampala Uganda 0°20N 32°30E 54 B3
Kampar Malaysia 4°18N 101°9E 39 K3
Kampar → Indonesia 0°30N 103°8E 36 D2
Kampen Neths. 52°33N 5°53E 15 B5
Kampene Dem. Rep. of the Congo 3°36S 26°40E 52 E5
Kamphaeng Phet Thailand 16°28N 99°30E 38 D2
Kampolombo, L. Zambia 11°37S 29°42E 55 E2
Kampong Chhnang Cambodia 12°20N 104°35E 39 F5
Kampong Pengerang Malaysia 1°22N 104°7E 39 d
Kampong Punggai Malaysia 1°27N 104°18E 39 d
Kampong Saom Cambodia 10°38N 103°30E 39 G4
Kampong Saom, Chaak Cambodia 10°50N 103°32E 39 G4
Kampong Tanjong Langsat Malaysia 1°28N 104°1E 39 d
Kampong Telok Ramunia Malaysia 1°22N 104°15E 39 d
Kampot Cambodia 10°36N 104°10E 39 G5
Kampuchea = Cambodia ■ Asia 12°15N 105°0E 38 F5
Kampung Air Putih Malaysia 4°15N 103°10E 39 K4
Kampung Jerangau Malaysia 4°50N 103°10E 39 K4
Kampung Raja Malaysia 5°45N 102°35E 39 K4
Kampungbaru = Tolitoli Indonesia 1°5N 120°50E 37 D6
Kamrau, Teluk Indonesia 3°30S 133°36E 37 E8
Kamsack Canada 51°34N 101°54W 71 C8
Kamsar Guinea 10°40N 14°36W 50 F3
Kamskoye Vdkhr. Russia 58°41N 56°7E 18 C10
Kamuchawie L. Canada 56°18N 101°59W 71 B8
Kamui-Misaki Japan 43°20N 140°21E 30 C10
Kamyanets-Podilskyy Ukraine 48°45N 26°40E 17 D14
Kamyanka-Buzka Ukraine 50°8N 24°16E 17 C13
Kāmyārān Iran 34°47N 46°56E 44 C5
Kamyshin Russia 50°10N 45°24E 19 D8
Kanaaupscow → Canada 54°2N 76°30W 72 B4
Kanab U.S.A. 37°3N 112°32W 77 H7
Kanab Cr. → U.S.A. 36°24N 112°38W 77 H7
Kanacea Lau Group, Fiji 17°15S 179°6W 59 a
Kanacea Taveuni, Fiji 16°59S 179°56E 59 a
Kanaga I. U.S.A. 51°45N 177°22W 74 E4
Kanagi Japan 40°54N 140°27E 30 D10
Kanairiktok → Canada 55°2N 60°18W 73 A7
Kananga Dem. Rep. of the Congo 5°55S 22°18E 52 F4
Kanash Russia 55°30N 47°32E 18 C8
Kanaskat U.S.A. 47°19N 121°54W 78 C5
Kanastraíon, Ákra = Paliouri, Akra Greece 39°57N 23°45E 23 E10
Kanawha → U.S.A. 38°50N 82°9W 81 F12
Kanazawa Japan 36°30N 136°38E 31 F8
Kanchanaburi Thailand 14°2N 99°31E 38 E2
Kanchenjunga Nepal 27°50N 88°10E 43 F13
Kanchipuram India 12°52N 79°45E 40 N11
Kandaghat India 30°59N 77°7E 42 D7
Kandahār Afghan. 31°32N 65°43E 40 D4
Kandahār □ Afghan. 31°0N 65°0E 40 D4
Kandalaksha Russia 67°9N 32°30E 8 C25
Kandalakshskiy Zaliv Russia 66°0N 35°0E 18 A6
Kandangan Indonesia 2°50S 115°20E 36 E5
Kandanghaur Indonesia 6°21S 108°6E 37 G13
Kandanos Greece 35°19N 23°44E 25 D5
Kandavu = Kadavu Fiji 19°0S 178°15E 59 a
Kandavu Passage = Kadavu Passage Fiji 18°45S 178°0E 59 a
Kandhkot Pakistan 28°16N 69°8E 42 E3
Kandhla India 29°18N 77°19E 42 E7
Kandi Benin 11°7N 2°55E 50 F6
Kandi India 23°58N 88°5E 43 H13
Kandiaro Pakistan 27°4N 68°13E 42 F3
Kandla India 23°0N 70°10E 42 H4
Kandos Australia 32°45S 149°58E 63 E4
Kandreho Madag. 17°29S 46°6E 57 B8
Kandy Sri Lanka 7°18N 80°43E 40 R12
Kane U.S.A. 41°40N 78°49W 82 E6
Kane Basin Greenland 79°1N 70°0W 69 B18
Kang Botswana 23°41S 22°50E 56 C3
Kang Krung △ Thailand 9°30N 98°50E 39 H2
Kangān Fārs, Iran 27°50N 52°3E 45 E7
Kangān Hormozgān, Iran 25°48N 57°28E 45 E8
Kangar Malaysia 6°27N 100°12E 39 J3
Kangaroo I. Australia 35°45S 137°0E 63 F2
Kangaroo Mts. Australia 23°29S 141°51E 62 C3
Kangasala Finland 61°28N 24°4E 8 F21
Kangāvar Iran 34°40N 48°0E 45 C6
Kangdong N. Korea 39°9N 126°5E 35 E14
Kangean, Kepulauan Indonesia 6°55S 115°23E 36 F5
Kangean Is. = Kangean, Kepulauan Indonesia 6°55S 115°23E 36 F5
Kanggye N. Korea 41°0N 126°35E 35 D14
Kangikajik Greenland 70°7N 22°0W 4 B6
Kangiqliniq = Rankin Inlet Canada 62°30N 93°0W 68 E13
Kangiqsualujjuaq Canada 58°30N 65°59W 69 F18
Kangiqsujuaq Canada 61°30N 72°0W 69 E17
Kangiqtugaapik = Clyde River Canada 70°30N 68°30W 69 C18
Kangirsuk Canada 60°0N 70°0W 69 F18
Kangkar Chemaran Malaysia 1°34N 104°12E 39 d
Kangkar Sungai Tiram Malaysia 1°35N 103°55E 39 d
Kangkar Teberau Malaysia 1°32N 103°51E 39 d
Kangping China 42°43N 123°18E 35 C12
Kangra India 32°6N 76°16E 42 C7
Kangrinboqe Feng China 31°0N 81°25E 43 D9
Kangto China 27°50N 92°35E 41 F18
Kanha △ India 22°15N 80°40E 43 H9
Kanhar → India 24°28N 83°8E 43 G10
Kaniama Dem. Rep. of the Congo 7°30S 24°12E 54 D1
Kaniapiskau = Caniapiscau → Canada 56°40N 69°30W 73 A6
Kaniapiskau, L. = Caniapiscau, L. Canada 54°10N 69°55W 73 B6
Kanin, Poluostrov Russia 68°0N 45°0E 18 A8
Kanin Nos, Mys Russia 68°39N 43°32E 18 A7
Kanin Pen. = Kanin, Poluostrov Russia 68°0N 45°0E 18 A8
Kaniva Australia 36°22S 141°18E 63 F3
Kanjut Sar Pakistan 36°7N 75°25E 43 A6
Kankaanpää Finland 61°44N 22°50E 8 F20
Kankakee U.S.A. 41°7N 87°52W 80 E10
Kankakee → U.S.A. 41°23N 88°15W 80 E9
Kankan Guinea 10°23N 9°15W 50 F4

Kankendy = Xankändi
  Azerbaijan 39°52N 46°49E **44** B5
Kanker India 20°10N 81°40E **41** J12
Kankroli India 25°4N 73°53E **42** G5
Kannapolis U.S.A. 35°30N 80°37W **85** D14
Kannauj India 27°3N 79°56E **43** F8
Kannod India 22°45N 76°40E **40** H10
Kannur = Cannanore
  India 11°53N 75°27E **40** P9
Kannyakumari India 8°3N 77°40E **40** Q10
Kano Nigeria 12°2N 8°30E **50** F7
Kan'onji Japan 34°7N 133°39E **31** G6
Kanowit Malaysia 2°14N 112°20E **36** D4
Kanoya Japan 31°25N 130°50E **31** J5
Kanpetlet Burma 21°10N 93°59E **41** J18
Kanpur India 26°28N 80°20E **43** F9
Kansas □ U.S.A. 38°30N 99°00W **80** F4
Kansas → U.S.A. 39°7N 94°37W **80** F6
Kansas City Kans., U.S.A. 39°7N 94°38W **80** F6
Kansas City Mo., U.S.A. 39°6N 94°35W **80** F6
Kansenia
  Dem. Rep. of the Congo 10°20S 26°0E **55** E2
Kansk Russia 56°20N 95°37E **29** D10
Kansu = Gansu □ China 36°0N 104°0E **34** G8
Kantaphor India 22°35N 76°34E **42** H7
Kantharalak Thailand 14°39N 104°39E **38** E5
Kanthi = Contai India 21°54N 87°46E **43** J12
Kantō □ Japan 36°15N 139°30E **31** F9
Kantō-Sanchi Japan 35°59N 138°50E **31** G9
Kanturk Ireland 52°11N 8°54W **10** D3
Kanuma Japan 36°34N 139°42E **31** F9
Kanus Namibia 27°50S 18°39E **56** D2
Kanye Botswana 24°55S 25°28E **56** C4
Kanzenze
  Dem. Rep. of the Congo 10°30S 25°12E **55** E2
Kanzi, Ras Tanzania 7°1S 39°33E **54** D4
Kao Tonga 19°40S 175°1W **59** c
Kao Phara Thailand 8°3N 98°22E **39** a
Kaohsiung Taiwan 22°35N 120°16E **33** D7
Kaokoveld Namibia 19°15S 14°30E **56** B1
Kaolack Senegal 14°5N 16°8W **50** F2
Kaoshan China 44°38N 124°50E **35** B13
Kapa'a U.S.A. 22°5N 159°19W **75** L8
Kapadvanj India 23°5N 73°0E **42** H5
Kapan Armenia 39°18N 46°27E **44** B5
Kapanga
  Dem. Rep. of the Congo 8°30S 22°40E **52** F4
Kapchagai = Qapshaghay
  Kazakhstan 43°51N 77°14E **28** E8
Kapedo Kenya 1°10N 36°6E **54** B4
Kapela = Velika Kapela
  Croatia 45°10N 15°5E **16** F8
Kapema
  Dem. Rep. of the Congo 10°45S 28°22E **55** E2
Kapenguria Kenya 1°14N 35°7E **54** B4
Kapfenberg Austria 47°26N 15°18E **16** E8
Kapiri Mposhi Zambia 13°59S 28°43E **55** E2
Kāpīsā □ Afghan. 35°0N 69°20E **40** B6
Kapiskau → Canada 52°47N 81°55W **72** B3
Kapiti I. N.Z. 40°50S 174°56E **59** D5
Kaplan U.S.A. 30°0N 92°17W **84** F8
Kapoe Thailand 9°34N 98°32E **39** H2
Kapoeta Sudan 4°50N 33°35E **51** H12
Kaposvár Hungary 46°25N 17°47E **17** E9
Kapowsin U.S.A. 46°59N 122°13W **78** D4
Kapps Namibia 22°32S 17°18E **56** C2
Kapsabet Kenya 0°12N 35°6E **54** B4
Kapsan N. Korea 41°4N 128°19E **35** D15
Kapsukas = Marijampolė
  Lithuania 54°33N 23°19E **9** J20
Kaptai L. Bangla. 22°40N 92°20E **41** H18
Kapuas → Indonesia 0°25S 109°20E **36** E3
Kapuas Hulu, Pegunungan
  Malaysia 1°30N 113°30E **36** D4
Kapuas Hulu Ra. = Kapuas Hulu,
  Pegunungan Malaysia 1°30N 113°30E **36** D4
Kapulo
  Dem. Rep. of the Congo 8°18S 29°15E **55** D2
Kapunda Australia 34°20S 138°56E **63** E2
Kapuni N.Z. 39°29S 174°8E **59** D5
Kapurthala India 31°23N 75°25E **42** D6
Kapuskasing Canada 49°25N 82°30W **72** C3
Kapuskasing → Canada 49°49N 82°0W **72** C3
Kaputar, Mt. Australia 30°15S 150°10E **63** E5
Kaputir Kenya 2°5N 35°28E **54** B4
Kara → Russia 69°10N 65°0E **28** C7
Kara Bogaz Gol, Zaliv =
  Garabogazköl Aylagy
  Turkmenistan 41°0N 53°30E **19** F9
Kara-Kala = Garrygala
  Turkmenistan 38°31N 56°29E **45** B8
Kara Kalpak Republic =
  Qoraqalpoghiston □
  Uzbekistan 43°0N 58°0E **28** E6
Kara Kum = Garagum
  Turkmenistan 39°30N 60°0E **45** B8
Kara Sea Russia 75°0N 70°0E **28** B8
Karabiğa Turkey 40°23N 27°17E **23** D12
Karabük Turkey 41°12N 32°37E **19** F5
Karaburun Turkey 38°41N 26°28E **23** E12
Karabutak = Qarabutaq
  Kazakhstan 49°59N 60°14E **28** E7
Karacabey Turkey 40°12N 28°21E **23** D13
Karacasu Turkey 37°43N 28°35E **23** F13
Karachey-Cherkessia □
  Russia 43°40N 41°30E **19** F7
Karachi Pakistan 24°50N 67°0E **42** G2
Karad India 17°15N 74°10E **40** L9
Karaganda = Qaraghandy
  Kazakhstan 49°50N 73°10E **28** E8
Karagayly = Qaraghayly
  Kazakhstan 49°26N 76°0E **28** E8
Karaginskiy, Ostrov
  Russia 58°45N 164°0E **29** D17
Karagiye, Vpadina
  Kazakhstan 43°27N 51°45E **19** F9
Karagiye Depression = Karagiye,
  Vpadina Kazakhstan 43°27N 51°45E **19** F9

Karagola Road India 25°29N 87°23E **43** G12
Karaikal India 10°59N 79°50E **40** P11
Karaikkudi India 10°5N 78°45E **40** P11
Karaj Iran 35°48N 51°0E **45** C6
Karajarri ☉ Australia 19°0S 122°30E **60** C3
Karak Malaysia 3°25N 102°2E **39** L4
Karakalpakstan =
  Qoraqalpoghiston □
  Uzbekistan 43°0N 58°0E **28** E6
Karakelong Indonesia 4°35N 126°50E **37** D7
Karakitang Indonesia 3°14N 125°28E **37** D7
Karakol Kyrgyzstan 42°30N 78°20E **32** B2
Karakoram Pass Asia 35°33N 77°50E **43** B7
Karakoram Ra. Pakistan 35°30N 77°0E **43** B7
Karakuwisa Namibia 18°56S 19°40E **56** B2
Karalon Russia 57°5N 115°50E **29** D12
Karama Jordan 31°57N 35°35E **46** D4
Karaman Turkey 37°14N 33°13E **44** B2
Karamay China 45°30N 84°58E **32** B3
Karambu Indonesia 3°53S 116°6E **36** E5
Karamea Bight N.Z. 41°22S 171°40E **59** D3
Karamnasa → India 25°31N 83°52E **43** G10
Karān Si. Arabia 27°43N 49°49E **45** E6
Karand Iran 34°16N 46°15E **44** C5
Karanganyar Indonesia 7°38S 109°37E **37** G13
Karangasem Indonesia 8°27S 115°37E **37** J18
Karanjia India 21°47N 85°58E **43** J11
Karasburg Namibia 28°0S 18°44E **56** D2
Karasino Russia 66°50N 86°50E **28** C9
Karasjok Norway 69°27N 25°30E **8** B21
Karasuk Russia 53°44N 78°2E **28** D8
Karasuyama Japan 36°39N 140°9E **31** F10
Karatau, Khrebet = Qarataū
  Kazakhstan 43°30N 69°30E **28** E7
Karatax Shan China 35°57N 81°0E **32** C3
Karatsu Japan 33°26N 129°58E **31** H5
Karaul Russia 70°6N 82°15E **28** B9
Karauli India 26°30N 77°4E **42** F7
Karavostasi Cyprus 35°8N 32°50E **25** D11
Karawang Indonesia 6°30S 107°15E **37** G12
Karawanken Europe 46°30N 14°40E **16** E8
Karayazı Turkey 39°41N 42°9E **19** G7
Karazhal = Qarazhal
  Kazakhstan 48°2N 70°49E **28** E8
Karbalā' Iraq 32°36N 44°3E **44** C5
Karcag Hungary 47°19N 20°57E **17** E11
Karcha → Pakistan 34°45N 76°10E **43** B7
Karchana India 25°17N 81°56E **43** G9
Karditsa Greece 39°23N 21°54E **23** E9
Kärdla Estonia 59°0N 22°45E **9** G20
Kareeberge S. Africa 30°59S 21°50E **56** E3
Kareha → India 25°44N 86°21E **43** G12
Kareima Sudan 18°30N 31°49E **51** E12
Karelia □ Russia 65°30N 32°30E **8** D25
Karelian Republic = Karelia □
  Russia 65°30N 32°30E **8** D25
Karera India 25°32N 78°9E **42** G8
Kārevāndar Iran 27°53N 60°44E **45** E9
Kargasok Russia 59°3N 80°53E **28** D9
Kargat Russia 55°10N 80°15E **28** D9
Kargi Kenya 2°31N 37°34E **54** B4
Kargil India 34°32N 76°12E **43** B7
Kargopol Russia 61°30N 38°58E **18** B6
Karhal India 27°1N 78°57E **43** F8
Kariān Iran 26°57N 57°14E **45** E8
Karianga Madag. 22°25S 47°22E **57** C8
Kariba Zimbabwe 16°28S 28°50E **55** F2
Kariba, L. Zimbabwe 16°40S 28°25E **55** F2
Kariba Dam Zimbabwe 16°30S 28°35E **55** F2
Kariba Gorge Zambia 16°30S 28°50E **55** F2
Karibib Namibia 22°0S 15°56E **56** C2
Kariijini △ Australia 23°8S 118°15E **60** D2
Karimata, Kepulauan
  Indonesia 1°25S 109°0E **36** E3
Karimata, Selat Indonesia 2°0S 108°40E **36** E3
Karimata Is. = Karimata,
  Kepulauan Indonesia 1°25S 109°0E **36** E3
Karimnagar India 18°26N 79°10E **40** K11
Karimun Kecil, Pulau
  Indonesia 1°8N 103°22E **39** d
Karimunjawa, Kepulauan
  Indonesia 5°50S 110°30E **36** F4
Karin Somali Rep. 10°50N 45°52E **47** E4
Karīt Iran 33°29N 56°55E **45** C8
Kariya Japan 34°58N 137°1E **31** G8
Kariyangwe Zimbabwe 18°0S 27°38E **57** B4
Karjala Finland 62°0N 30°25E **8** F24
Karkaralinsk = Qarqaraly
  Kazakhstan 49°26N 75°30E **28** E8
Karkheh → Iran 31°2N 47°29E **44** D5
Karkinitska Zatoka
  Ukraine 45°56N 33°0E **19** E5
Karkinitskiy Zaliv = Karkinitska
  Zatoka Ukraine 45°56N 33°0E **19** E5
Karkuk = Kirkūk Iraq 35°30N 44°21E **44** C5
Karlantijpa North ☉
  Australia 19°27S 133°33E **60** C5
Karlantijpa South ☉
  Australia 20°31S 133°9E **60** D5
Karleby = Kokkola
  Finland 63°50N 23°8E **8** E20
Karlovac Croatia 45°31N 15°36E **16** F8
Karlovo Bulgaria 42°38N 24°47E **23** C11
Karlovy Vary Czech Rep. 50°13N 12°51E **16** C7
Karlsbad = Karlovy Vary
  Czech Rep. 50°13N 12°51E **16** C7
Karlsena, Mys Russia 77°0N 67°42E **28** B7
Karlshamn Sweden 56°10N 14°51E **9** H16
Karlskoga Sweden 59°28N 14°33E **9** G16
Karlskrona Sweden 56°10N 15°35E **9** H16
Karlsruhe Germany 49°0N 8°23E **16** D5
Karlstad Sweden 59°23N 13°30E **9** G15
Karlstad U.S.A. 48°35N 96°31W **80** A5
Karmi'el Israel 32°55N 35°18E **46** C4
Karnak Egypt 25°43N 32°39E **51** C12
Karnal India 29°42N 77°2E **42** E7
Karnali → Nepal 28°45N 81°16E **43** E9
Karnaphuli Res. = Kaptai L.
  Bangla. 22°40N 92°20E **41** H18

Karnaprayag India 30°16N 79°15E **43** D8
Karnataka □ India 13°15N 77°0E **40** N10
Karnes City U.S.A. 28°53N 97°54W **84** G6
Karnische Alpen Europe 46°36N 13°0E **16** E7
Kärnten □ Austria 46°52N 13°30E **16** E8
Karoi Zimbabwe 16°48S 29°45E **55** F2
Karon, Ao Thailand 7°51N 98°17E **39** a
Karonga Malawi 9°57S 33°55E **55** D3
Karoo □ S. Africa 32°18S 22°27E **56** E3
Karoonda Australia 35°1S 139°59E **63** F2
Karor Pakistan 31°15N 70°59E **42** D4
Karora Sudan 17°44N 38°15E **51** E13
Karpasia Cyprus 35°32N 34°15E **25** D13
Karpathos Greece 35°37N 27°10E **23** G12
Karpinsk Russia 59°45N 60°1E **18** C11
Karpogory Russia 64°0N 44°27E **18** B7
Karpuz Burnu = Apostolos
  Andreas, C. Cyprus 35°42N 34°35E **25** D13
Karratha Australia 20°44S 116°52E **60** D2
Kars Turkey 40°40N 43°5E **19** F7
Karsakpay Kazakhstan 47°55N 66°40E **28** E7
Karshi = Qarshi
  Uzbekistan 38°53N 65°48E **28** F7
Karsiyang India 26°56N 88°18E **43** F13
Karsog India 31°23N 77°12E **42** D7
Kartala Comoros Is. 11°45S 43°21E **53** a
Kartaly Russia 53°3N 60°40E **28** D7
Kartapur India 31°27N 75°32E **42** D6
Karthaus U.S.A. 41°8N 78°9W **82** E6
Karufa Indonesia 3°50S 133°20E **37** E8
Karuma △ Uganda 2°5N 32°15E **54** B3
Karumba Australia 17°31S 140°50E **62** B3
Karumo Tanzania 2°25S 32°50E **54** C3
Karumwa Tanzania 3°12S 32°38E **54** C3
Kārūn → Iran 30°26N 48°10E **45** D6
Karungu Kenya 0°50S 34°10E **54** C3
Karviná Czech Rep. 49°53N 18°31E **17** D10
Karwan → India 27°26N 78°4E **42** F8
Karwar India 14°55N 74°13E **40** M9
Karwi India 25°12N 80°57E **43** G9
Karymskoye Russia 51°36N 114°21E **29** D12
Kasache Malawi 13°25S 34°20E **55** E3
Kasai →
  Dem. Rep. of the Congo 3°30S 16°10E **52** E3
Kasai-Oriental □
  Dem. Rep. of the Congo 5°0S 24°30E **54** D1
Kasaji
  Dem. Rep. of the Congo 10°25S 23°27E **55** E1
Kasama Zambia 10°16S 31°9E **55** E3
Kasan N. Korea 41°18N 126°55E **35** D14
Kasandra Kolpos Greece 40°5N 23°30E **23** D10
Kasane Namibia 17°34S 24°50E **56** B3
Kasanga Tanzania 8°30S 31°10E **55** D3
Kasanka △ Zambia 11°34S 30°15E **55** E3
Kasaragod India 12°30N 74°58E **40** N9
Kasba L. Canada 60°20N 102°10W **71** A9
Kāseh Garān Iran 34°5N 46°2E **44** C5
Kasempa Zambia 13°30S 25°44E **55** E2
Kasenga
  Dem. Rep. of the Congo 10°20S 28°45E **55** E2
Kasese Uganda 0°13N 30°3E **54** B3
Kasewa Zambia 14°28S 28°53E **55** E2
Kasganj India 27°48N 78°42E **43** F8
Kashabowie Canada 48°40N 90°26W **72** C1
Kashaf → Iran 35°58N 61°7E **45** C9
Kāshān Iran 34°5N 51°30E **45** C6
Kashechewan Canada 52°18N 81°37W **72** B3
Kashgar = Kashi China 39°30N 76°2E **32** C2
Kashi China 39°30N 76°2E **32** C2
Kashimbo
  Dem. Rep. of the Congo 11°12S 26°19E **55** E2
Kashipur India 29°15N 79°0E **43** E8
Kashiwazaki Japan 37°22N 138°33E **31** F9
Kashk-e Kohneh
  Afghan. 34°55N 62°30E **40** B3
Kashkūʿīyeh Iran 30°31N 55°40E **45** D7
Kāshmar Iran 35°16N 58°26E **45** C8
Kashmir Asia 34°0N 76°0E **43** C7
Kashmor Pakistan 28°28N 69°32E **42** E3
Kashun Noerh = Gaxun Nur
  China 42°22N 100°30E **32** B5
Kasiari India 22°8N 87°14E **43** H12
Kasimov Russia 54°55N 41°20E **18** D7
Kasinge
  Dem. Rep. of the Congo 6°15S 26°58E **54** D2
Kasiruta Indonesia 0°25S 127°12E **37** E7
Kaskaskia → U.S.A. 37°58N 89°57W **80** G10
Kaskattama → Canada 57°3N 90°4W **71** B10
Kaskinen Finland 62°22N 21°15E **8** E19
Kaskö = Kaskinen
  Finland 62°22N 21°15E **8** E19
Kaslo Canada 49°55N 116°55W **70** D5
Kasmere L. Canada 59°34N 101°10W **71** B8
Kasongo
  Dem. Rep. of the Congo 4°30S 26°33E **54** C2
Kasongo Lunda
  Dem. Rep. of the Congo 6°35S 16°49E **52** F3
Kasos Greece 35°20N 26°55E **23** G12
Kassalâ Sudan 15°30N 36°0E **51** E13
Kassel Germany 51°18N 9°26E **16** C5
Kassiopi Greece 39°48N 19°53E **25** A3
Kasson U.S.A. 44°2N 92°45W **80** C7
Kastamonu Turkey 41°25N 33°43E **19** F5
Kastéli Greece 35°29N 23°38E **25** D5
Kastelli Greece 35°12N 25°20E **25** D7
Kasterlee Belgium 51°15N 4°59E **15** C4
Kastoria Greece 40°30N 21°19E **23** D9
Kasulu Tanzania 4°37S 30°5E **54** C3
Kasumi Japan 35°38N 134°38E **31** G7
Kasungu Malawi 13°0S 33°29E **55** E3
Kasungu △ Malawi 12°53S 33°9E **55** E3
Kasur Pakistan 31°5N 74°25E **42** D6
Kata, Ao Thailand 7°48N 98°18E **39** J2
Kata Archanes Greece 35°15N 25°10E **25** D7
Kata Tjuta Australia 25°20S 130°50E **61** E5
Kataba Zambia 16°5S 25°10E **55** F2
Katahdin, Mt. U.S.A. 45°54N 68°56W **81** C19
Katako Kombe
  Dem. Rep. of the Congo 3°25S 24°20E **54** C1

Katale Tanzania 4°52S 31°7E **54** C3
Katanda Katanga,
  Dem. Rep. of the Congo 7°52S 24°13E **54** D1
Katanda Nord-Kivu,
  Dem. Rep. of the Congo 0°55S 29°21E **54** C2
Katanga □
  Dem. Rep. of the Congo 8°0S 25°0E **54** D2
Katangi India 21°56N 79°50E **40** J11
Katanning Australia 33°40S 117°33E **61** F2
Katavi △ Tanzania 6°51S 31°3E **54** D3
Katavi Swamp Tanzania 6°50S 31°10E **54** D3
Katerini Greece 40°18N 22°37E **23** D10
Katghora India 22°30N 82°33E **43** H10
Katha Burma 24°10N 96°30E **41** G20
Katherine Australia 14°27S 132°20E **60** B5
Katherine Gorge = Nitmiluk △
  Australia 14°6S 132°15E **60** B5
Kathi India 21°47N 74°3E **42** J6
Kathiawar India 22°20N 71°0E **42** H4
Kathikas Cyprus 34°55N 32°25E **25** E11
Kathmandu Nepal 27°45N 85°20E **43** F11
Kathua India 32°23N 75°34E **42** C6
Katihar India 25°34N 87°36E **43** G12
Katima Mulilo Namibia 17°28S 24°13E **56** B3
Katimbira Malawi 12°40S 34°0E **55** E3
Katingan = Mendawai →
  Indonesia 3°30S 113°0E **36** E4
Katiola Ivory C. 8°10N 5°10W **50** G4
Katiti ☉ Australia 25°1S 131°11E **61** E5
Katmandu = Kathmandu
  Nepal 27°45N 85°20E **43** F11
Katni = Murwara India 23°46N 80°28E **43** H9
Katni India 23°51N 80°24E **43** H9
Kato Chorio Greece 35°3N 25°47E **25** D7
Kato Korakiana Greece 39°42N 19°45E **25** A3
Káto Pyrgos Cyprus 35°11N 32°41E **25** D11
Katompe
  Dem. Rep. of the Congo 6°2S 26°23E **54** D2
Katong Singapore 1°18N 103°53E **39** d
Katonga → Uganda 0°34N 31°50E **54** B3
Katoomba Australia 33°41S 150°19E **63** E5
Katowice Poland 50°17N 19°5E **17** C10
Katrine, L. U.K. 56°15N 4°30W **11** E4
Katrineholm Sweden 59°9N 16°12E **9** G17
Katsepe Madag. 15°45S 46°15E **57** B8
Katsina Nigeria 13°0N 7°32E **50** F7
Katsumoto Japan 33°51N 129°42E **31** H4
Katsuura Japan 35°10N 140°20E **31** G10
Katsuyama Japan 36°3N 136°30E **31** F8
Kattavia Greece 35°57N 27°46E **25** D9
Kattegat Denmark 56°40N 11°20E **9** H14
Katumba
  Dem. Rep. of the Congo 7°40S 25°17E **54** D2
Katwa India 23°30N 88°5E **43** H13
Katwijk Neths. 52°12N 4°24E **15** B4
Kaua'i U.S.A. 22°3N 159°30W **75** L8
Kaudom △ Namibia 18°45S 20°51E **56** B3
Kaufman U.S.A. 32°35N 96°19W **84** E6
Kauhajoki Finland 62°25N 22°10E **8** E20
Kaukauna U.S.A. 44°17N 88°17W **80** C9
Kaukauveld Namibia 20°0S 20°15E **56** C3
Ka'ula I. U.S.A. 21°40N 160°33W **75** L7
Kaunas Lithuania 54°54N 23°54E **9** J20
Kaunia Bangla. 25°46N 89°26E **43** G13
Kautokeino Norway 69°0N 23°4E **8** B20
Kauwapur India 27°31N 82°18E **43** F10
Kavacha Russia 60°16N 169°51E **29** C17
Kavala Greece 40°57N 24°28E **23** D11
Kavalerovo Russia 44°15N 135°4E **30** B7
Kavali India 14°55N 80°1E **40** M12
Kavār Iran 29°11N 52°44E **45** D7
Kavi India 22°12N 72°38E **42** H5
Kavimba Botswana 18°2S 24°38E **56** B3
Kavīr, Dasht-e Iran 34°30N 55°0E **45** C7
Kavīr △ Iran 34°40N 52°0E **45** C7
Kavos Greece 39°23N 20°3E **25** B4
Kaw Fr. Guiana 4°30N 52°15W **93** C8
Kawagama L. Canada 45°18N 78°45W **82** A6
Kawagoe Japan 35°55N 139°29E **31** G9
Kawaguchi Japan 35°52N 139°45E **31** G9
Kawambwa Zambia 9°48S 29°3E **55** D2
Kawanoe Japan 34°1N 133°34E **31** G6
Kawardha India 22°0N 81°17E **43** J9
Kawasaki Japan 35°31N 139°43E **31** G9
Kawasi Indonesia 1°38S 127°28E **37** E7
Kawawachikamach
  Canada 54°48N 66°50W **73** B6
Kawerau N.Z. 38°7S 176°42E **59** C6
Kawhia N.Z. 38°4S 174°49E **59** C5
Kawhia Harbour N.Z. 38°5S 174°51E **59** C5
Kawio, Kepulauan
  Indonesia 4°30N 125°30E **37** D7
Kawthaung Burma 10°5N 98°36E **39** H2
Kawthoolei = Kayin □
  Burma 18°0N 97°30E **41** L20
Kawthule = Kayin □
  Burma 18°0N 97°30E **41** L20
Kaya Burkina Faso 13°4N 1°10W **50** F5
Kayah □ Burma 19°15N 97°15E **41** K20
Kayak I. U.S.A. 59°56N 144°23W **74** D11
Kayan → Indonesia 2°55S 117°35E **36** D5
Kaycee U.S.A. 43°43N 106°38W **76** E10
Kayeli Indonesia 3°20S 127°10E **37** E7
Kayenta U.S.A. 36°44N 110°17W **77** H8
Kayes Mali 14°25N 11°30W **50** F3
Kayin □ Burma 18°0N 97°30E **41** L20
Kayoa Indonesia 0°1N 127°28E **37** D7
Kayomba Zambia 13°11S 24°2E **55** E1
Kayseri Turkey 38°45N 35°30E **44** B2
Kaysville U.S.A. 41°2N 111°56W **76** F8
Kazachye Russia 70°52N 135°58E **29** B14
Kazakhstan ■ Asia 50°0N 70°0E **28** E8
Kazan Russia 55°50N 49°10E **18** C8
Kazan → Canada 64°2N 95°29W **71** A9
Kazan-Rettō Pac. Oc. 25°0N 141°0E **64** E6
Kazanlŭk Bulgaria 42°38N 25°20E **23** C11
Kazatin = Kozyatyn
  Ukraine 49°45N 28°50E **17** D15

Kāzerūn Iran 29°38N 51°40E **45** D6
Kazi Magomed = Qazımämmäd
  Azerbaijan 40°3N 49°0E **45** A6
Kazuma Pan △
  Zimbabwe 18°20S 25°48E **55** F2
Kazuno Japan 40°10N 140°45E **30** D10
Kazym → Russia 63°54N 65°50E **28** C7
Kea Greece 37°35N 24°22E **23** F11
Keady U.K. 54°15N 6°42W **10** B5
Kearney U.S.A. 40°42N 99°5W **80** E4
Kearney ☉ Australia 20°10S 128°4E **60** D4
Kearny U.S.A. 33°3N 110°55W **77** K8
Kearsarge, Mt. U.S.A. 43°22N 71°50W **83** C13
Keban Turkey 38°50N 38°50E **19** G6
Keban Baraji Turkey 38°41N 38°33E **44** B3
Kebnekaise Sweden 67°53N 18°33E **8** C18
Kebri Dehar Ethiopia 6°45N 44°17E **47** F3
Kebumen Indonesia 7°42S 109°40E **37** G13
Kechika → Canada 59°41N 127°12W **70** B3
Kecskemét Hungary 46°57N 19°42E **17** E10
Kėdainiai Lithuania 55°15N 24°2E **9** J21
Kedarnath India 30°44N 79°4E **43** D8
Kedgwick Canada 47°40N 67°20W **73** C6
Kediri Indonesia 7°51S 112°1E **37** G15
Kedros Oros Greece 35°11N 24°37E **25** D6
Keeler U.S.A. 36°29N 117°52W **78** J9
Keeley L. Canada 54°54N 108°8W **71** C7
Keeling Is. = Cocos Is.
  Ind. Oc. 12°10S 96°55E **64** J1
Keelung = Chilung
  Taiwan 25°3N 121°45E **33** D7
Keene Canada 44°15N 78°10W **82** B6
Keene Calif., U.S.A. 35°13N 118°33E **79** K8
Keene N.H., U.S.A. 42°56N 72°17W **83** D11
Keene N.Y., U.S.A. 44°16N 73°46W **83** B11
Keep River △ Australia 15°49S 129°8E **60** B4
Keeper Hill Ireland 52°45N 8°16W **10** D3
Keerweer, C. Australia 14°0S 141°32E **62** A3
Keeseville U.S.A. 44°29N 73°30W **83** B11
Keetmanshoop Namibia 26°35S 18°8E **56** D2
Keewatin U.S.A. 49°46N 94°34W **71** D10
Keewatin → Canada 56°29N 100°46W **71** B8
Kefalonia Greece 38°15N 20°30E **23** E9
Kefamenanu Indonesia 9°28S 124°29E **37** F6
Kefar Sava Israel 32°11N 34°54E **46** C3
Keffi Nigeria 8°55N 7°43E **50** G7
Keflavík Iceland 64°2N 22°35W **8** D2
Keg River Canada 57°54N 117°55W **70** B5
Kegaska Canada 50°9N 61°18W **73** B7
Kehancha Kenya 1°11S 34°37E **54** C3
Keighley U.K. 53°52N 1°54W **12** D6
Keila Estonia 59°18N 24°25E **9** G21
Keimoes S. Africa 28°41S 20°59E **56** D3
Keitele Finland 63°10N 26°20E **8** E22
Keith Australia 36°6S 140°20E **63** F3
Keith U.K. 57°32N 2°57W **11** D6
Keiyasi Fiji 17°53S 177°46E **59** a
Keizer U.S.A. 44°57N 123°1W **76** D2
Kejimkujik △ Canada 44°25N 65°25W **73** D6
Kejserr Franz Joseph Fd.
  Greenland 73°30N 24°30E **4** B6
Kekri India 26°0N 75°10E **42** G6
Kelan China 38°43N 111°31E **34** E6
Kelang = Klang Malaysia 3°2N 101°26E **39** L3
Kelantan → Malaysia 6°13N 102°14E **39** J4
Kelkit → Turkey 40°45N 36°32E **19** F6
Kellerberrin Australia 31°36S 117°38E **61** F2
Kellett, C. Canada 72°0N 126°0W **4** B1
Kelleys I. U.S.A. 41°36N 82°42W **82** E2
Kellogg U.S.A. 47°32N 116°7W **76** C5
Kells = Ceanannus Mor
  Ireland 53°44N 6°53W **10** C5
Kélo Chad 9°10N 15°45E **51** G9
Kelokedhara Cyprus 34°48N 32°39E **25** E11
Kelowna Canada 49°50N 119°25W **70** D5
Kelsey Creek Australia 20°26S 148°31E **62** b
Kelseyville U.S.A. 38°59N 122°50W **78** G4
Kelso N.Z. 45°54S 169°15E **59** F2
Kelso U.K. 55°36N 2°26W **11** F6
Kelso U.S.A. 46°9N 122°54W **78** D4
Keluang = Kluang
  Malaysia 2°3N 103°18E **39** L4
Kelvington Canada 52°10N 103°30W **71** C8
Kem Russia 65°0N 34°38E **18** B5
Kem → Russia 64°57N 34°41E **18** B5
Kema Indonesia 1°22N 125°8E **37** D7
Kemah Turkey 39°32N 39°5E **44** B3
Kemaman Malaysia 4°12N 103°18E **39** K4
Kemano Canada 53°35N 128°0W **70** C3
Kemasik Malaysia 4°25N 103°27E **39** K4
Kemerovo Russia 55°20N 86°5E **28** D9
Kemi Finland 65°44N 24°34E **8** D21
Kemi älv = Kemijoki →
  Finland 65°47N 24°32E **8** D21
Kemi träsk = Kemijärvi
  Finland 66°43N 27°22E **8** C22
Kemijärvi Finland 66°43N 27°22E **8** C22
Kemijoki → Finland 65°47N 24°32E **8** D21
Kemmerer U.S.A. 41°48N 110°32W **76** F8
Kemmuna = Comino
  Malta 36°1N 14°20E **25** C1
Kemp, L. U.S.A. 33°46N 99°9W **84** E5
Kemp Land Antarctica 69°0S 55°0E **5** C5
Kempas Malaysia 1°33N 103°42E **39** d
Kempsey Australia 31°1S 152°50E **63** E5
Kempt, L. Canada 47°25N 74°22W **72** C5
Kempten Germany 47°45N 10°17E **16** E6
Kempton Australia 42°31S 147°12E **63** G4
Kemptville Canada 45°0N 75°38W **83** B9
Ken → India 25°13N 80°27E **43** G9
Kenai U.S.A. 60°33N 151°16W **68** C4
Kenai Mts. U.S.A. 60°0N 150°0W **74** D9
Kenamuke Swamp Sudan 5°55N 33°48E **51** G12
Kendai India 22°45N 82°37E **43** H10
Kendal Indonesia 6°56S 110°14E **37** G14
Kendal U.K. 54°20N 2°44E **12** C5
Kendall Australia 31°35S 152°44E **63** E5
Kendall U.S.A. 25°40N 80°19W **85** J14
Kendall → Australia 14°4S 141°35E **62** A3

Kendallville U.S.A. 41°27N 85°16W **81** E11
Kendari Indonesia 3°50S 122°30E **37** E6
Kendawangan Indonesia 2°32S 110°17E **36** E4
Kendrapara India 20°35N 86°30E **41** J15
Kendrew S. Africa 32°32S 24°30E **56** E3
Kene Thao Laos 17°44N 101°10E **38** D3
Kenedy U.S.A. 28°49N 97°51W **84** G6
Kenema S. Leone 7°50N 11°14W **50** G3
Keng Kok Laos 16°26N 105°12E **38** D5
Keng Tawng Burma 20°45N 98°18E **41** J21
Keng Tung Burma 21°0N 99°30E **41** J21
Kengeja Tanzania 5°26S 39°45E **54** D4
Kenhardt S. Africa 29°19S 21°12E **56** D3
Kenitra Morocco 34°15N 6°40W **50** B4
Kenli China 37°30N 118°20E **35** F10
Kenmare Ireland 51°53N 9°36W **10** E2
Kenmare U.S.A. 48°41N 102°5W **80** A2
Kenmare River Ireland 51°48N 9°51W **10** E2
Kennebago Lake U.S.A. 45°4N 70°40W **83** A14
Kennebec U.S.A. 43°54N 99°52W **80** D4
Kennebec → U.S.A. 43°45N 69°46W **81** D19
Kennebunk U.S.A. 43°23N 70°33W **83** C14
Kennedy Zimbabwe 18°52S 27°10E **56** B4
Kennedy Channel
  Arctic 80°50N 66°0W **69** A18
Kennedy Ra. Australia 24°45S 115°10E **61** D2
Kennedy Range △
  Australia 24°34S 115°2E **61** D2
Kenner U.S.A. 29°59N 90°14W **85** G9
Kennet → U.K. 51°27N 0°57W **13** F7
Kenneth Ra. Australia 23°50S 117°8E **61** D2
Kennett U.S.A. 36°14N 90°3W **80** G9
Kennewick U.S.A. 46°12N 119°7W **76** C4
Kennisis Lake Canada 45°13N 78°36W **82** A6
Kenogami → Canada 51°6N 84°28W **72** B3
Kenora Canada 49°47N 94°29W **71** D10
Kenosha U.S.A. 42°35N 87°49W **80** D10
Kensington Canada 46°28N 63°34W **73** C7
Kent Ohio, U.S.A. 41°9N 81°22W **82** E3
Kent Tex., U.S.A. 31°4N 104°13W **84** F2
Kent Wash., U.S.A. 47°22N 122°14W **78** C4
Kent □ U.K. 51°12N 0°40E **13** F8
Kent Group Australia 39°30S 147°20E **63** F4
Kent Pen. Canada 68°30N 107°0W **68** D10
Kentaū Kazakhstan 43°32N 68°36E **28** E7
Kentland U.S.A. 40°46N 87°27W **80** E10
Kenton U.S.A. 40°39N 83°37W **81** E12
Kentucky □ U.S.A. 37°0N 84°0W **81** G11
Kentucky → U.S.A. 38°41N 85°11W **81** F11
Kentucky L. U.S.A. 37°1N 88°16W **80** G9
Kentville Canada 45°6N 64°29W **73** C7
Kentwood U.S.A. 30°56N 90°31W **85** F9
Kenya ■ Africa 1°0N 38°0E **54** B4
Kenya, Mt. Kenya 0°10S 37°18E **54** C4
Kenyir, Tasik Malaysia 5°1N 102°54E **39** K4
Keo Neua, Deo Vietnam 18°23N 105°10E **38** C5
Keokuk U.S.A. 40°24N 91°24W **80** E8
Keoladeo △ India 27°0N 77°20E **42** F7
Keonjhargarh India 21°28N 85°35E **43** J11
Kep Cambodia 10°29N 104°19E **39** G5
Kep Vietnam 21°24N 106°16E **38** B6
Kepala Batas Malaysia 5°31N 100°26E **39** c
Kepi Indonesia 6°32S 139°19E **37** F9
Kerala □ India 11°0N 76°15E **40** P10
Kerama-Rettō Japan 26°5N 127°15E **31** L3
Keran Pakistan 34°35N 73°59E **43** B5
Kerang Australia 35°40S 143°55E **63** F3
Keraudren, C. Australia 19°58S 119°45E **60** C2
Kerch Ukraine 45°20N 36°20E **19** E6
Kerguelen Ind. Oc. 49°15S 69°10E **3** G13
Kericho Kenya 0°22S 35°15E **54** C4
Kerinci Indonesia 1°40S 101°15E **36** E2
Kerki = Atamyrat
  Turkmenistan 37°50N 65°12E **28** F7
Kerkrade Neths. 50°53N 6°4E **15** D6
Kerkyra Greece 39°38N 19°50E **25** A3
Kerkyras, Notio Steno
  Greece 39°34N 20°0E **25** A4
Kermadec Is. Pac. Oc. 30°0S 178°15W **58** E11
Kermadec Trench
  Pac. Oc. 30°30S 176°0W **64** L10
Kermān Iran 30°15N 57°1E **45** D8
Kermān □ Iran 36°43N 100°4W **78** J6
Kermān □ Iran 30°0N 57°0E **45** D8
Kermān, Bīābān-e Iran 28°45N 59°45E **45** D8
Kermānshāh Iran 34°23N 47°0E **44** C5
Kermānshāh □ Iran 34°0N 46°30E **44** C5
Kermit U.S.A. 31°52N 103°6W **84** F3
Kern → U.S.A. 35°16N 119°18W **79** K7
Kernow = Cornwall □
  U.K. 50°26N 4°40W **13** G3
Kernville U.S.A. 35°45N 118°26W **79** K8
Keroh Malaysia 5°43N 101°1E **39** K3
Kerrera U.K. 56°24N 5°33W **11** E3
Kerrobert Canada 51°56N 109°8W **71** C7
Kerrville U.S.A. 30°3N 99°8W **84** F5
Kerry □ Ireland 52°7N 9°35W **10** D2
Kerry Hd. Ireland 52°25N 9°56W **10** D2
Kerulen → Asia 48°48N 117°0E **33** B6
Kerzaz Algeria 29°29N 1°37W **50** C5
Kesagami → Canada 51°40N 79°45W **72** B4
Kesagami L. Canada 50°23N 80°15W **72** B3
Keşan Turkey 40°49N 26°38E **23** D12
Kesennuma Japan 38°54N 141°35E **30** E10
Keshit Iran 29°43N 58°17E **45** D8
Kestell S. Africa 28°17S 28°42E **57** D4
Kestenga Russia 65°50N 31°45E **8** D5
Keswick U.K. 54°36N 3°8W **12** C4
Ket → Russia 58°55N 81°32E **28** D9
Ketapang Bali, Indonesia 8°9S 114°27E **37** J17
Ketapang Kalimantan,
  Indonesia 1°55S 110°0E **36** E4
Ketchikan U.S.A. 55°21N 131°39W **70** B2
Ketchum U.S.A. 43°41N 114°22W **76** E6
Ketef, Khalig Umm el
  Egypt 23°40N 35°35E **44** F2
Keti Bandar Pakistan 24°8N 67°27E **42** G2
Ketri India 28°1N 75°50E **42** E6

Kętrzyn Poland 54°7N 21°22E **17** A11
Kettering U.K. 52°24N 0°43W **13** E7
Kettering U.S.A. 39°41N 84°10W **81** F11
Kettle → Canada 56°40N 89°34W **71** B11
Kettle Falls U.S.A. 48°37N 118°3W **76** B4
Kettle Point Canada 43°10N 82°1W **82** C2
Kettle Pt. Canada 43°13N 82°1W **82** D7
Kettleman City U.S.A. 36°1N 119°58W **78** J7
Keuka L. U.S.A. 42°30N 77°9W **82** D7
Keurimg Finland 62°16N 24°41E **8** E21
Kewanee U.S.A. 41°14N 89°56W **80** E9
Kewaunee U.S.A. 44°27N 87°31W **80** C10
Keweenaw B. U.S.A. 47°0N 88°15W **80** B9
Keweenaw Pen. U.S.A. 47°15N 88°15W **80** B9
Keweenaw Pt. U.S.A. 47°25N 87°43W **80** B10
Key, L. Ireland 54°0N 8°15W **10** C3
Key Lake Mine Canada 57°5N 105°32W **71** B7
Key Largo U.S.A. 25°5N 80°27W **85** J14
Key West U.S.A. 24°33N 81°48W **88** B3
Keynsham U.K. 51°24N 2°29W **13** F5
Keyser U.S.A. 39°26N 78°59W **81** F14
Kezhma Russia 58°59N 101°9E **29** D11
Kezi Zimbabwe 20°58S 28°32E **57** C4
Kgalagadi Transfrontier △
  Africa 25°10S 21°0E **56** D3
Khabarovsk Russia 48°30N 135°5E **29** E14
Khabr Iran 28°51N 56°22E **45** D8
Khābūr → Syria 35°17N 40°35E **44** C4
Khachmas = Xaçmaz
  Azerbaijan 41°31N 48°42E **19** F8
Khachrod India 23°25N 75°20E **42** H6
Khadro Pakistan 26°11N 68°50E **42** F3
Khadzhilyangar = Dahongliutan
  China 35°45N 79°20E **43** B8
Khaga India 25°47N 81°7E **43** G9
Khagaria India 25°30N 86°32E **43** G12
Khaipur Pakistan 29°34N 72°17E **42** E5
Khair India 27°57N 77°46E **42** F7
Khairabad India 27°33N 80°47E **43** F9
Khairagarh India 21°27N 81°2E **43** J9
Khairpur Pakistan 27°32N 68°49E **42** F3
Khairpur Nathan Shah
  Pakistan 27°6N 67°44E **42** F2
Khairwara India 23°58N 73°38E **42** H5
Khaisor → Pakistan 31°17N 68°59E **42** D3
Khajuri Kach Pakistan 32°4N 69°51E **42** C3
Khakassia □ Russia 53°0N 90°0E **28** D9
Khakhea Botswana 24°48S 23°22E **56** C3
Khalafābād Iran 30°54N 49°24E **45** D6
Khalilabad India 26°48N 83°5E **43** F10
Khalīlī Iran 27°38N 53°17E **45** E7
Khalkhāl Iran 37°37N 48°32E **45** B6
Khalkís = Halkida
  Greece 38°27N 23°42E **23** E10
Khalmer Yu Russia 67°58N 65°1E **28** C7
Khalturin Russia 58°40N 48°50E **18** C8
Khalūf Oman 20°30N 58°13E **47** C6
Kham Keut Laos 18°15N 104°43E **38** C5
Khamaria India 23°5N 80°48E **43** H9
Khambhaliya India 22°14N 69°41E **42** H3
Khambhat India 22°23N 72°33E **42** H5
Khambhat, G. of India 20°45N 72°30E **40** J8
Khamir Iran 26°57N 55°36E **45** E7
Khamir Yemen 16°2N 44°0E **47** D3
Khamis Mushayt
  Si. Arabia 18°18N 42°44E **47** D3
Khamsa Egypt 30°27N 32°23E **46** E1
Khan → Namibia 22°37S 14°56E **56** C2
Khān Abū Shāmat Syria 33°39N 36°53E **46** B5
Khān Azād Iraq 33°7N 44°22E **44** C5
Khān Mujiddah Iraq 32°21N 43°48E **44** C4
Khān Shaykhūn Syria 35°26N 36°38E **44** C3
Khan Tengri, Pik Asia 42°12N 80°10E **32** B3
Khān Yūnis Gaza Strip 31°21N 34°18E **46** D3
Khanai Pakistan 30°30N 67°8E **42** D2
Khānaqīn Iraq 34°23N 45°25E **44** C5
Khānbāghī Iran 36°10N 55°25E **45** B7
Khandwa India 21°49N 76°22E **40** J10
Khandyga Russia 62°42N 135°35E **29** C14
Khanewal Pakistan 30°20N 71°55E **42** D4
Khangah Dogran
  Pakistan 31°50N 73°37E **42** D5
Khanh Duong Vietnam 12°44N 108°44E **38** F7
Khaniá = Chania Greece 35°30N 24°4E **25** D6
Khaniadhana India 25°1N 78°8E **42** G8
Khanka, L. Asia 45°0N 132°24E **30** B6
Khankendy = Xankändi
  Azerbaijan 39°52N 46°49E **44** B5
Khanna India 30°42N 76°16E **42** D7
Khanozai Pakistan 30°37N 67°19E **42** D2
Khanpur Pakistan 28°42N 70°35E **42** E4
Khanty-Mansiysk Russia 61°0N 69°0E **28** C7
Khao Laem △ Thailand 14°56N 98°31E **38** E2
Khao Laem Res. Thailand 14°50N 98°30E **38** E2
Khao Lak △ Malaysia 8°38N 98°18E **39** H2
Khao Luang △ Thailand 8°34N 99°42E **39** H2
Khao Phlu Thailand 9°29N 99°59E **39** b
Khao Pu-Khao Ya △
  Thailand 7°6N 99°57E **39** J2
Khao Sam Roi Yot △
  Thailand 12°13N 99°57E **39** F2
Khao Sok △ Thailand 8°55N 98°38E **39** H2
Khao Yai △ Thailand 14°21N 101°29E **38** E3
Khaoen Si Nakarin △
  Thailand 14°47N 99°0E **38** E2
Khapalu Pakistan 35°10N 76°20E **43** B7
Khapcheranga Russia 49°42N 112°24E **29** E12
Khaptao △ Nepal 29°20N 81°10E **43** E9
Kharaghoda India 23°11N 71°46E **42** H4
Kharagpur India 22°20N 87°25E **43** H12
Kharan Kalat Pakistan 28°34N 65°21E **40** E4
Kharānaq Iran 32°20N 54°45E **45** C7
Kharda India 18°40N 75°34E **40** K9
Khardung La India 34°20N 77°43E **43** B7
Kharg = Khārk, Jazīreh-ye
  Iran 29°15N 50°28E **45** D6
Khārga, El Wâhât el
  Egypt 25°10N 30°35E **51** C12
Khargon India 21°45N 75°40E **40** J9

Khari → India 25°54N 74°31E **42** G6
Kharian Pakistan 32°49N 73°52E **42** C5
Khārk, Jazīreh-ye Iran 29°15N 50°28E **45** D6
Kharkiv Ukraine 49°58N 36°20E **19** E6
Kharkov = Kharkiv
  Ukraine 49°58N 36°20E **19** E6
Kharovsk Russia 59°56N 40°13E **18** C7
Kharsawangarh India 22°48N 85°50E **43** H11
Kharta Turkey 40°55N 29°7E **23** D13
Khartoum = El Khartûm
  Sudan 15°31N 32°35E **51** E12
Khartum Canada 45°15N 77°5W **82** A7
Khasan Russia 42°25N 130°40E **30** C5
Khāsh Iran 28°15N 61°15E **45** D9
Khashm el Girba Sudan 14°59N 35°58E **51** F13
Khaskovo Bulgaria 41°56N 25°30E **23** D11
Khatanga Russia 72°0N 102°20E **29** B11
Khatanga → Russia 72°55N 106°0E **29** B11
Khatauli India 29°17N 77°43E **42** E7
Khatra India 22°59N 86°51E **43** H12
Khātūnābād Iran 30°1N 55°25E **45** D7
Khatyrka Russia 62°3N 175°15E **29** C18
Khavda India 23°51N 69°43E **42** H3
Khawr Fakkān U.A.E. 25°21N 56°22E **45** E8
Khaybar, Ḥarrat
  Si. Arabia 25°45N 40°0E **44** E4
Khāzimiyah Iraq 34°46N 43°37E **44** C4
Khe Bo Vietnam 19°8N 104°41E **38** C5
Khe Long Vietnam 21°29N 104°46E **38** B5
Khe Sanh Vietnam 16°37N 106°45E **38** D6
Khed Brahma India 24°7N 73°5E **42** G5
Khekra India 28°52N 77°20E **42** E7
Khemarak Phouminville = Krong
  Kaoh Kong Cambodia 11°37N 102°59E **39** G4
Khemisset Morocco 33°50N 6°1W **50** B4
Khemmarat Thailand 16°10N 105°15E **38** D5
Khenāmān Iran 30°27N 56°29E **45** D8
Khenchela Algeria 35°28N 7°11E **50** A7
Khersān → Iran 31°33N 50°22E **45** D6
Kherson Ukraine 46°35N 32°35E **19** E5
Kheta → Russia 71°54N 102°6E **29** B11
Khewari Pakistan 26°36N 68°52E **42** F3
Khilchipur India 24°2N 76°34E **42** G7
Khilok Russia 51°30N 110°45E **29** D12
Khíos = Hios Greece 38°27N 26°9E **23** E12
Khirsadoh India 22°11N 78°47E **43** H8
Khiuma = Hiiumaa
  Estonia 58°50N 22°45E **9** G20
Khiva Uzbekistan 41°30N 60°18E **28** E7
Khlong Khlung Thailand 16°12N 99°43E **38** D2
Khmelnik Ukraine 49°33N 27°58E **17** D14
Khmelnytskyy Ukraine 49°23N 27°0E **17** D14
Khmer Rep. = Cambodia ■
  Asia 12°15N 105°0E **38** F5
Khoai, Hon Vietnam 8°26N 104°50E **39** H5
Khodoriv Ukraine 49°24N 24°19E **17** D13
Khodzent = Khŭjand
  Tajikistan 40°17N 69°37E **28** E7
Khojak Pass Afghan. 30°51N 66°34E **42** D2
Khok Kloi Thailand 8°17N 98°19E **39** a
Khok Pho Thailand 6°43N 101°6E **39** J3
Khok Samrong Thailand 15°3N 100°43E **38** E3
Kholm Russia 57°10N 31°15E **18** C5
Kholmsk Russia 47°40N 142°5E **29** E15
Khomas Hochland
  Namibia 22°40S 16°0E **56** C2
Khomeyn Iran 33°40N 50°7E **45** C6
Khomeynī Shahr Iran 32°41N 51°31E **45** C6
Khomodino Botswana 22°46S 23°52E **56** C3
Khon Kaen Thailand 16°30N 102°47E **38** D4
Khong → Cambodia 13°32N 105°58E **38** F5
Khong Sedone Laos 15°34N 105°49E **38** E5
Khonuu Russia 66°30N 143°12E **29** C15
Khoper → Russia 49°30N 42°20E **19** D6
Khorāsān □ Iran 34°0N 58°0E **45** C8
Khorat = Nakhon Ratchasima
  Thailand 14°59N 102°12E **38** E4
Khorat, Cao Nguyen
  Thailand 15°30N 102°50E **38** E4
Khorixas Namibia 20°16S 14°59E **56** C1
Khorramābād Khorāsān,
  Iran 35°6N 57°57E **45** C8
Khorramābād Lorestān,
  Iran 33°30N 48°25E **45** C6
Khorrāmshahr Iran 30°29N 48°15E **45** D6
Khorugh Tajikistan 37°30N 71°36E **28** F8
Khosravī Iran 30°48N 51°28E **45** D6
Khosrowābād Khuzestān,
  Iran 30°10N 48°25E **45** D6
Khosrowābād Kordestān,
  Iran 35°31N 47°38E **44** C5
Khost Pakistan 30°13N 67°35E **42** D2
Khosūyeh Iran 28°32N 54°26E **45** D7
Khotyn Ukraine 48°31N 26°27E **17** D14
Khouribga Morocco 32°58N 6°57W **50** B4
Khowst Afghan. 33°22N 69°58E **42** C3
Khowst □ Afghan. 33°20N 70°0E **40** C6
Khoyniki Belarus 51°54N 29°55E **17** C15
Khrysokhou B. Cyprus 35°6N 32°25E **25** D11
Khu Khan Thailand 14°42N 104°12E **38** E5
Khuan Wa Thailand 7°53N 98°17E **39** a
Khudzhand = Khŭjand
  Tajikistan 40°17N 69°37E **28** E7
Khuff Si. Arabia 24°55N 44°53E **44** E5
Khūgīānī Afghan. 31°34N 66°32E **42** D2
Khuis Botswana 26°40S 21°49E **56** D3
Khuiyala India 27°9N 70°25E **42** F4
Khujner India 23°47N 76°36E **42** H7
Khulna Bangla. 22°45N 89°34E **41** H16
Khulna □ Bangla. 22°25N 89°35E **41** H16
Khumago Botswana 20°26S 24°32E **56** C3
Khunjerab Pass = Kinjirap Daban
  Asia 36°40N 75°25E **40** A9
Khūnsorkh Iran 27°9N 56°7E **45** E8
Khunti India 23°5N 85°17E **43** H11
Khūr Iran 32°55N 58°18E **45** C8
Khurai India 24°3N 78°23E **42** G8

Khurayş Si. Arabia 25°6N 48°2E **45** E6
Khurja India 28°15N 77°58E **42** E7
Khūrmāl Iraq 35°18N 46°2E **44** C5
Khurr, Wādī al Iraq 32°3N 43°52E **44** C4
Khūsf Iran 32°46N 58°53E **45** C8
Khushab Pakistan 32°20N 72°20E **42** C5
Khust Ukraine 48°10N 23°18E **17** D12
Khutse △ Botswana 23°31S 24°12E **56** C3
Khuzdar Pakistan 27°52N 66°30E **42** F2
Khūzestān □ Iran 31°0N 49°0E **45** D6
Khvāf Iran 34°33N 60°8E **45** C9
Khvājeh Iran 38°9N 46°35E **44** B5
Khvānsār Iran 29°56N 54°8E **45** D7
Khvor Iran 33°45N 55°0E **45** C7
Khvorgū Iran 27°34N 56°27E **45** E8
Khvormūj Iran 28°40N 51°30E **45** D6
Khvoy Iran 38°35N 45°0E **44** B5
Khyber Pass Afghan. 34°10N 71°8E **42** B4
Kia Fiji 16°16S 179°8E **59** a
Kiabukwa
  Dem. Rep. of the Congo 8°40S 24°48E **55** D1
Kiama Australia 34°40S 150°50E **63** E5
Kiamba Phil. 6°2N 124°46E **37** C6
Kiambi
  Dem. Rep. of the Congo 7°15S 28°0E **54** D2
Kiambu Kenya 1°8S 36°50E **54** C4
Kiangara Madag. 17°58S 47°2E **57** B8
Kiangsi = Jiangxi □
  China 27°30N 116°0E **33** D6
Kiangsu = Jiangsu □
  China 33°0N 120°0E **35** H11
Kibale △ Uganda 0°16N 30°18E **54** B3
Kibanga Port Uganda 0°10N 32°58E **54** B3
Kibara Tanzania 2°8S 33°30E **54** C3
Kibare, Mts.
  Dem. Rep. of the Congo 8°25S 27°10E **54** D2
Kibira △ Burundi 3°6S 30°24E **54** C2
Kiboga Uganda 0°58N 31°45E **54** B3
Kibombo
  Dem. Rep. of the Congo 3°57S 25°53E **54** C2
Kibondo Tanzania 3°35S 30°45E **54** C3
Kibre Mengist Ethiopia 5°54N 38°59E **47** F2
Kıbrıs = Cyprus ■ Asia 35°0N 33°0E **25** E12
Kibumbu Burundi 3°32S 29°45E **54** C2
Kibungo Rwanda 2°10S 30°32E **54** C3
Kibuye Burundi 3°39S 29°59E **54** C2
Kibuye Rwanda 2°3S 29°21E **54** C2
Kibwesa Tanzania 6°30S 29°58E **54** D2
Kibwezi Kenya 2°27S 37°57E **54** C4
Kichha India 28°53N 79°30E **43** E8
Kichha → India 28°41N 79°18E **43** E8
Kichmengskiy Gorodok
  Russia 59°59N 45°48E **18** B8
Kicking Horse Pass
  Canada 51°28N 116°16W **70** C5
Kidal Mali 18°26N 1°22E **50** E6
Kidderminster U.K. 52°24N 2°15W **13** E5
Kidepo Valley △ Uganda 3°52N 33°50E **54** B3
Kidete Tanzania 6°25S 37°17E **54** D4
Kidnappers, C. N.Z. 39°38S 177°5E **59** C6
Kidsgrove U.K. 53°5N 2°14W **12** D5
Kidston Australia 18°52S 144°8E **62** B3
Kidugallo Tanzania 6°49S 38°15E **54** D4
Kiel Germany 54°19N 10°8E **16** A6
Kiel Canal = Nord-Ostsee-Kanal
  Germany 54°12N 9°32E **16** A5
Kielce Poland 50°52N 20°42E **17** C11
Kielder Water U.K. 55°11N 2°31W **12** B5
Kieler Bucht Germany 54°35N 10°25E **16** A6
Kien Binh Vietnam 9°55N 105°19E **39** H5
Kien Tan Vietnam 10°7N 105°17E **39** G5
Kienge
  Dem. Rep. of the Congo 10°30S 27°30E **55** E2
Kiev = Kyyiv Ukraine 50°30N 30°28E **17** C16
Kiffa Mauritania 16°37N 11°24W **50** E3
Kifrī Iraq 34°45N 45°0E **44** C5
Kigali Rwanda 1°59S 30°4E **54** C3
Kigarama Tanzania 1°1S 31°50E **54** C3
Kigezi □ Tanzania 0°34S 29°55E **54** C2
Kigoma □ Tanzania 5°0S 30°0E **54** D2
Kigoma-Ujiji Tanzania 4°55S 29°36E **54** C2
Kigomasha, Ras Tanzania 4°58S 38°58E **54** C4
Kigosi □ Tanzania 4°10S 31°45E **54** C3
Kiğzı Turkey 38°18N 43°25E **44** B4
Kihnu Estonia 58°9N 24°1E **9** G21
Kii-Sanchi Japan 34°20N 136°0E **31** G8
Kii-Suidō Japan 33°40N 134°45E **31** H7
Kiira Dam Uganda 0°25N 33°0E **54** B3
Kikaiga-Shima Japan 28°19N 129°59E **31** K4
Kikiak = Rigolet Canada 54°10N 58°23W **73** B8
Kikinda Serbia 45°50N 20°30E **23** B9
Kikládhes = Cyclades
  Greece 37°0N 24°30E **23** F11
Kikwit
  Dem. Rep. of the Congo 5°0S 18°45E **52** F3
Kilar India 33°6N 76°25E **42** C7
Kilbeggan Ireland 53°22N 7°30E **10** C4
Kilbrannan Sd. U.K. 55°37N 5°26W **11** F3
Kilbuck Mts. U.S.A. 60°36N 159°53W **74** C7
Kilchu N. Korea 40°57N 129°25E **35** D15
Kilcoy Australia 26°59S 152°30E **63** D5
Kildare Ireland 53°9N 6°55W **10** C5
Kildare □ Ireland 53°10N 6°50W **10** C5
Kildinstroy Russia 68°48N 33°6E **8** B25
Kilfinnane Ireland 52°21N 8°28W **10** D3
Kilgarvan Ireland 51°54N 9°27W **10** E2
Kilgore U.S.A. 32°23N 94°53W **84** E7
Kilifi Kenya 3°40S 39°48E **54** C4
Kilimanjaro □ Tanzania 3°7S 37°20E **54** C4
Kilimanjaro △ Tanzania 3°2S 37°19E **54** C4
Kilindini Kenya 4°4S 39°40E **54** C4
Kilis Turkey 36°42N 37°6E **44** B3
Kiliya Ukraine 45°28N 29°16E **17** F15
Kilkee Ireland 52°41N 9°39W **10** D2
Kilkeel U.K. 54°4N 6°0W **10** B5
Kilkenny Ireland 52°39N 7°15W **10** D4
Kilkenny □ Ireland 52°35N 7°15W **10** D4

Kilkieran B. Ireland 53°20N 9°41W **10** C2
Kilkis Greece 40°58N 22°57E **23** D10
Killala Ireland 54°13N 9°12W **10** B2
Killala B. Ireland 54°16N 9°8W **10** B2
Killaloe Canada 45°33N 77°25W **82** A7
Killaloe Ireland 52°48N 8°28W **10** D3
Killarney Australia 28°20S 152°18E **63** D5
Killarney Canada 49°10N 99°40W **71** D9
Killarney Ireland 52°4N 9°30W **10** D2
Killarney △ Ireland 52°0N 9°33W **10** D2
Killary Harbour Ireland 53°38N 9°52W **10** C2
Killdeer U.S.A. 47°22N 102°45W **80** B2
Killeen U.S.A. 31°7N 97°44W **84** F6
Killin U.K. 56°28N 4°19W **11** E4
Killiney Ireland 53°15N 6°7W **10** C5
Killington Pk. U.S.A. 43°36N 72°49W **83** C12
Killini Greece 37°54N 22°25E **23** F10
Killorglin Ireland 52°6N 9°47W **10** D2
Killybegs Ireland 54°38N 8°26W **10** B3
Kilmarnock U.K. 55°37N 4°29W **11** F4
Kilmore Australia 37°25S 144°53E **63** F3
Kilmore Quay Ireland 52°10N 6°36W **10** D5
Kilondo Tanzania 9°45S 34°20E **55** D3
Kilosa Tanzania 6°48S 37°0E **54** D4
Kilrush Ireland 52°38N 9°29W **10** D2
Kilwa Kisiwani Tanzania 8°58S 39°32E **55** D4
Kilwa Kivinje Tanzania 8°45S 39°25E **55** D4
Kilwa Masoko Tanzania 8°55S 39°30E **55** D4
Kilwinning U.K. 55°39N 4°43W **11** F4
Kim U.S.A. 37°15N 103°21W **77** H12
Kimaam Indonesia 7°58S 138°53E **37** F9
Kimamba Tanzania 6°45S 37°10E **54** D4
Kimba Australia 33°8S 136°23E **63** E2
Kimball Nebr., U.S.A. 41°14N 103°40W **80** E2
Kimball S. Dak., U.S.A. 43°45N 98°57W **80** D4
Kimberley Australia 16°20S 127°0E **60** C4
Kimberley Canada 49°40N 115°59W **70** D5
Kimberley Ont., Canada 44°23N 80°32W **82** B4
Kimberley S. Africa 28°43S 24°46E **56** D3
Kimberly U.S.A. 42°32N 114°22W **76** E6
Kimch'aek N. Korea 40°40N 129°10E **35** D15
Kimhae = Gimhae
  S. Korea 35°14N 128°53E **35** G15
Kimmirut Canada 62°50N 69°50W **69** E18
Kimpese
  Dem. Rep. of the Congo 5°35S 14°26E **52** F2
Kimry Russia 56°55N 37°15E **18** C6
Kinabalu, Gunung
  Malaysia 6°3N 116°14E **36** C5
Kinango Kenya 4°8S 39°19E **54** C4
Kinaskan L. Canada 57°38N 130°8W **70** B2
Kinbasket L. Canada 52°0N 118°10W **70** C5
Kincardine Canada 44°10N 81°40W **82** B3
Kincolith Canada 55°0N 129°57W **70** C3
Kinda Dem. Rep. of the Congo 9°18S 25°4E **55** D2
Kinde U.S.A. 43°56N 83°0W **82** C2
Kinder Scout U.K. 53°24N 1°52W **12** D6
Kindersley Canada 51°30N 109°10W **71** C7
Kindia Guinea 10°0N 12°52W **50** F3
Kindu
  Dem. Rep. of the Congo 2°55S 25°50E **54** C2
Kineshma Russia 57°30N 42°5E **18** C7
Kinesi Tanzania 1°25S 33°50E **54** C3
King, L. Australia 33°10S 119°35E **61** F2
King, Mt. Australia 25°10S 147°30E **62** D4
King Christian I.
  Canada 77°48N 101°40W **69** B11
King City U.S.A. 36°13N 121°8W **78** J5
King Cr. → Australia 24°35S 139°30E **62** C2
King Edward →
  Australia 14°14S 126°35E **60** B4
King Edward Point
  S. Georgia 54°17S 36°30W **96** G9
King Frederick VI Land = Kong
  Frederik VI Kyst
  Greenland 63°0N 43°0W **4** C5
King George B. Falk. Is. 51°30S 60°30W **96** G4
King George I. Antarctica 60°0S 60°0W **5** C18
King George Is. Canada 57°20N 80°30W **69** F15
King George Sd. Australia 35°5S 118°0E **61** G2
King I. = Kadan Kyun
  Burma 12°30N 98°20E **38** F2
King I. Australia 39°50S 144°0E **63** F3
King I. Canada 52°10N 127°40W **70** C3
King Khalid Military City =
  Madinat al Malik Khālid al
  Askarīyah Si. Arabia 27°54N 45°31E **44** E5
King Leopold Ranges
  Australia 17°30S 125°45E **60** C4
King of Prussia U.S.A. 40°5N 75°23W **83** F9
King Sd. Australia 16°50S 123°20E **60** C3
King Sejong Antarctica 62°30S 58°0W **5** C18
King William I. Canada 69°10N 97°25W **68** D12
King William's Town
  S. Africa 32°51S 27°22E **56** E4
Kingaok = Bathurst Inlet
  Canada 66°50N 108°1W **68** D10
Kingaroy Australia 26°32S 151°51E **63** D5
Kingfisher U.S.A. 35°52N 97°56W **84** D6
Kingirbân Iraq 34°40N 44°54E **44** C5
King's Lynn U.K. 52°45N 0°24E **12** E8
Kings Park U.S.A. 40°53N 73°16W **83** F11
Kings Peak U.S.A. 40°46N 110°23W **76** F8
Kingsbridge U.K. 50°17N 3°47W **13** G4
Kingsburg U.S.A. 36°31N 119°33W **78** J7
Kingscote Australia 35°40S 137°38E **63** F2
Kingscourt Ireland 53°55N 6°48W **10** C5
Kingsford U.S.A. 45°48N 88°4W **80** C9

Kingsland *U.S.A.* 30°48N 81°41W **85** F14
Kingsport *U.S.A.* 36°33N 82°33W **85** C13
Kingston *Canada* 44°14N 76°30W **83** B8
Kingston *Jamaica* 18°0N 76°50W **88** a
Kingston *N.Z.* 45°20S 168°43E **59** F2
Kingston *N.H., U.S.A.* 42°56N 71°3W **83** D13
Kingston *N.Y., U.S.A.* 41°56N 73°59W **83** E11
Kingston *Pa., U.S.A.* 41°16N 75°54W **83** E9
Kingston *R.I., U.S.A.* 41°29N 71°30W **83** E13
Kingston Pk. *U.S.A.* 35°44N 115°55W **79** K11
Kingston South East
  Australia 36°51S 139°55E **63** F2
Kingston upon Hull *U.K.* 53°45N 0°21W **12** D7
Kingston upon Hull □
  U.K. 53°45N 0°21W **12** D7
Kingston-upon-Thames □
  U.K. 51°24N 0°17W **13** F7
Kingstown *St. Vincent* 13°10N 61°10W **89** D7
Kingstree *U.S.A.* 33°40N 79°50W **85** E15
Kingsville *Canada* 42°2N 82°45W **82** D2
Kingsville *U.S.A.* 27°31N 97°52W **84** H6
Kingussie *U.K.* 57°6N 4°2W **11** D4
Kingwood *U.S.A.* 30°2N 95°54W **84** A9
Kınık *Turkey* 39°6N 27°24E **23** E12
Kinistino *Canada* 52°57N 105°2W **71** C7
Kinjirap Daban *Asia* 36°40N 75°25E **40** A9
Kinkala *Congo* 4°18S 14°49E **52** E2
Kinki □ *Japan* 33°45N 136°0E **31** H8
Kinleith *N.Z.* 38°20S 175°56E **59** C5
Kinlochleven *U.K.* 56°43N 5°0W **11** E4
Kinmount *Canada* 44°48N 78°45W **82** B6
Kinna *Sweden* 57°32N 12°42E **9** H15
Kinnairds Hd. *U.K.* 57°43N 2°1W **11** D6
Kinngait *Canada* 64°14N 76°32W **69** L16
Kino Nuevo *Mexico* 28°52N 112°3W **86** B2
Kinoje → *Canada* 52°8N 81°25W **72** B3
Kinomoto *Japan* 35°30N 136°13E **31** G8
Kinoni *Uganda* 0°41S 30°28E **54** C3
Kinoosao *Canada* 57°5N 102°1W **71** B8
Kinross *U.K.* 56°13N 3°25W **11** E5
Kinsale *Ireland* 51°42N 8°31W **10** E3
Kinsale, Old Hd. of
  Ireland 51°37N 8°33W **10** E3
Kinsha = Chang Jiang →
  China 31°48N 121°10E **33** C7
Kinshasa
  Dem. Rep. of the Congo 4°20S 15°15E **52** E3
Kinsley *U.S.A.* 37°55N 99°25W **80** G4
Kinsman *U.S.A.* 41°26N 80°35W **82** E4
Kinston *U.S.A.* 35°16N 77°35W **85** D16
Kintamani *Indonesia* 8°14S 115°19E **37** J18
Kintore *U.K.* 57°14N 2°20W **11** D6
Kintore Ra. *Australia* 23°15S 128°47E **60** D4
Kintyre *U.K.* 55°30N 5°35W **11** F3
Kintyre, Mull of *U.K.* 55°17N 5°47W **11** F3
Kinushseo → *Canada* 55°15N 83°45W **72** A3
Kinuso *Canada* 55°20N 115°25W **70** B5
Kinvarra *Ireland* 53°8N 8°56W **10** C3
Kinyangiri *Tanzania* 4°25S 34°37E **54** C3
Kinyeti *Sudan* 3°57N 32°54E **54** B3
Kinzua *U.S.A.* 41°52N 78°58W **82** E6
Kiosk *Canada* 46°6N 78°53W **72** C4
Kiowa *Kans., U.S.A.* 37°1N 98°29W **80** G4
Kiowa *Okla., U.S.A.* 34°43N 95°54W **84** D7
Kipahigan L. *Canada* 55°20N 101°55W **71** B8
Kipanga *Tanzania* 6°15S 35°20E **54** D4
Kiparissia *Greece* 37°15N 21°40E **23** F9
Kiparissiakos Kolpos
  Greece 37°25N 21°25E **23** F9
Kipawa, L. *Canada* 46°50N 79°0W **72** C4
Kipembawe *Tanzania* 7°38S 33°27E **54** D3
Kipengere Ra. *Tanzania* 9°12S 34°15E **55** D3
Kipili *Tanzania* 7°28S 30°32E **54** D3
Kipini *Kenya* 2°30S 40°32E **54** C5
Kipling *Canada* 50°6N 102°38W **71** C8
Kippure *Ireland* 53°11N 6°21W **10** C5
Kipushi
  Dem. Rep. of the Congo 11°48S 27°12E **55** E2
Kiranomena *Madag.* 18°17S 46°2E **57** B8
Kirensk *Russia* 57°50N 107°55E **29** D11
Kirghiz Range *Asia* 42°40N 73°40E **32** B2
Kirghizia = Kyrgyzstan ■
  Asia 42°0N 75°0E **28** E8
Kirgiziya Steppe *Eurasia* 50°0N 55°0E **19** E10
Kiribati ■ *Pac. Oc.* 3°0S 180°0E **58** B10
Kırıkkale *Turkey* 39°51N 33°32E **19** G5
Kirillov *Russia* 59°49N 38°24E **18** C6
Kirin = Jilin *China* 43°44N 126°30E **35** C14
Kirinyaga = Kenya, Mt.
  Kenya 0°10S 37°18E **54** C4
Kirirom △ *Cambodia* 11°18N 104°5E **39** G5
Kirishima Yaku △
  Japan 31°24N 130°50E **31** J5
Kiritimati *Kiribati* 1°58N 157°27W **65** G12
Kirkby *U.K.* 53°30N 2°54W **12** D5
Kirkby-in-Ashfield *U.K.* 53°6N 1°14W **12** D6
Kirkby Lonsdale *U.K.* 54°12N 2°36W **12** C5
Kirkby Stephen *U.K.* 54°29N 2°21W **12** C5
Kirkcaldy *U.K.* 56°7N 3°9W **11** E5
Kirkcudbright *U.K.* 54°50N 4°2W **11** G4
Kirkenes *Norway* 69°40N 30°5E **8** B24
Kirkfield *Canada* 44°34N 78°59W **82** B6
Kirkintilloch *U.K.* 55°56N 4°8W **11** F4
Kirkjubæjarklaustur
  Iceland 63°47N 18°4W **8** E4
Kirkkonummi *Finland* 60°8N 24°26E **9** F21
Kirkland *U.S.A.* 47°40N 122°12W **78** C4
Kirkland Lake *Canada* 48°9N 80°2W **72** C3
Kırklareli *Turkey* 41°44N 27°15E **23** D12
Kirksville *U.S.A.* 40°12N 92°35W **80** E7
Kirkük *Iraq* 35°30N 44°21E **44** C5
Kirkwall *U.K.* 58°59N 2°58W **11** C6
Kirkwood *S. Africa* 33°22S 25°15E **56** E4
Kirov *Russia* 58°35N 49°40E **18** C8
Kirovabad = Gäncä
  Azerbaijan 40°45N 46°20E **19** F8
Kirovograd = Kirovohrad
  Ukraine 48°35N 32°20E **19** E5
Kirovohrad *Ukraine* 48°35N 32°20E **19** E5

Kirovsk *Russia* 67°32N 33°41E **18** A5
Kirovskiy *Kamchatka,
  Russia* 54°27N 155°42E **29** D16
Kirovskiy *Primorsk,
  Russia* 45°7N 133°30E **30** B6
Kirriemuir *U.K.* 56°41N 3°1W **11** E5
Kirsanov *Russia* 52°35N 42°40E **18** D7
Kırşehir *Turkey* 39°14N 34°5E **44** B2
Kirthar △ *Pakistan* 25°45N 67°30E **42** F2
Kirthar Range *Pakistan* 27°0N 67°0E **42** F2
Kirtland *U.S.A.* 36°44N 108°21W **77** H9
Kiruna *Sweden* 67°52N 20°15E **8** C19
Kirundu
  Dem. Rep. of the Congo 0°50S 25°35E **54** C2
Kiryū *Japan* 36°24N 139°20E **31** F9
Kisaga *Tanzania* 4°30S 34°23E **54** C3
Kisanga
  Dem. Rep. of the Congo 2°30N 26°35E **54** B2
Kisangani
  Dem. Rep. of the Congo 0°35N 25°15E **54** B2
Kisar *Indonesia* 8°5S 127°10E **37** F7
Kisarawe *Tanzania* 6°53S 39°0E **54** D4
Kisarazu *Japan* 35°23N 139°55E **31** G9
Kiselevsk *Russia* 54°0N 86°39E **28** D9
Kish = Qeys *Iran* 26°32N 53°58E **45** E7
Kishanganga →
  Pakistan 34°18N 73°28E **43** B5
Kishanganj *India* 26°3N 88°14E **43** F13
Kishangarh *Raj., India* 26°34N 74°52E **42** F6
Kishangarh *Raj., India* 27°50N 70°30E **42** F4
Kishinev = Chişinău
  Moldova 47°2N 28°50E **17** E15
Kishiwada *Japan* 34°28N 135°22E **31** G7
Kishtwar *India* 33°20N 75°48E **42** C6
Kisigo → *Tanzania* 6°27S 34°17E **54** D3
Kisii *Kenya* 0°40S 34°45E **54** C3
Kisiju *Tanzania* 7°23S 39°19E **54** D4
Kisizi *Uganda* 1°0S 29°58E **54** C2
Kiska I. *U.S.A.* 51°59N 177°30E **74** E3
Kiskőrös *Hungary* 46°37N 19°20E **17** E10
Kiskunfélegyháza
  Hungary 46°42N 19°53E **17** E10
Kiskunhalas *Hungary* 46°28N 19°37E **17** E10
Kislovodsk *Russia* 43°50N 42°45E **19** F7
Kismaayo *Somali Rep.* 0°22S 42°32E **47** H3
Kiso-Gawa → *Japan* 35°20N 136°45E **31** G8
Kiso-Sammyaku *Japan* 35°45N 137°45E **31** G8
Kisofukushima *Japan* 35°52N 137°43E **31** G8
Kisoro *Uganda* 1°17S 29°48E **54** C2
Kissamos = Kasteli
  Greece 35°29N 23°38E **25** D5
Kissamos, Kolpos *Greece* 35°30N 23°38E **25** D5
Kissidougou *Guinea* 9°5N 10°5W **50** G3
Kissimmee *U.S.A.* 28°18N 81°24W **85** G14
Kissimmee → *U.S.A.* 27°9N 80°52W **85** H14
Kississing L. *Canada* 55°10N 101°20W **71** B8
Kissónerga *Cyprus* 34°49N 32°24E **25** E11
Kisumu *Kenya* 0°3S 34°45E **54** C3
Kiswani *Tanzania* 4°5S 37°57E **54** C4
Kiswere *Tanzania* 9°27S 39°30E **55** D4
Kit Carson *U.S.A.* 38°46N 102°48W **76** G12
Kita *Mali* 13°5N 9°25W **50** F4
Kitaibaraki *Japan* 36°50N 140°45E **31** F10
Kitakami *Japan* 39°20N 141°10E **30** E10
Kitakami-Gawa →
  Japan 38°25N 141°19E **30** E10
Kitakami-Sammyaku
  Japan 39°30N 141°30E **30** E10
Kitakata *Japan* 37°39N 139°52E **30** F9
Kitakyūshū *Japan* 33°50N 130°50E **31** H5
Kitale *Kenya* 1°0N 35°0E **54** B4
Kitami *Japan* 43°48N 143°54E **30** C11
Kitami-Sammyaku
  Japan 44°22N 142°43E **30** B11
Kitangiri, L. *Tanzania* 4°5S 34°20E **54** C3
Kitaya *Tanzania* 10°38S 40°8E **55** E5
Kitchener *Canada* 43°27N 80°29W **82** C4
Kitee *Finland* 62°5N 30°8E **8** E24
Kitega = Gitega *Burundi* 3°26S 29°56E **54** C2
Kitengo
  Dem. Rep. of the Congo 7°26S 24°8E **54** D1
Kitgum *Uganda* 3°17N 32°52E **54** B3
Kíthira *Greece* 36°8N 23°0E **23** F10
Kithnos *Greece* 37°26N 24°27E **23** F11
Kiti *Cyprus* 34°50N 33°34E **25** E12
Kiti, C. *Cyprus* 34°48N 33°36E **25** E12
Kitimat *Canada* 54°3N 128°38W **70** C3
Kitinen → *Finland* 67°14N 27°27E **8** C22
Kitsuki *Japan* 33°25N 131°37E **31** H5
Kittakittaooloo, L.
  Australia 28°3S 138°14E **63** D2
Kittanning *U.S.A.* 40°49N 79°31W **82** F5
Kittatinny Mt. *U.S.A.* 41°19N 74°39W **83** F10
Kittery *U.S.A.* 43°5N 70°45W **83** C14
Kittilä *Finland* 67°40N 24°51E **8** C21
Kitui *Kenya* 1°17S 38°0E **54** C4
Kitwanga *Canada* 55°6N 128°4W **70** B3
Kitwe *Zambia* 12°54S 28°13E **55** E2
Kiunga Marine △ *Kenya* 2°1S 41°14E **54** C5
Kivarli *India* 24°33N 72°46E **42** G5
Kivertsi *Ukraine* 50°50N 25°28E **17** C13
Kividhes *Cyprus* 34°46N 32°51E **25** E11
Kivu, L.
  Dem. Rep. of the Congo 1°48S 29°0E **54** C2
Kiwirrkurra *Australia* 22°49S 127°45E **60** D4
Kiwirrkurra ◎
  Australia 22°49S 127°45E **60** D4
Kiyev = Kyyiv *Ukraine* 50°30N 30°28E **17** C16
Kiyevskoye Vdkhr. = Kyyivske
  Vdskh. *Ukraine* 51°0N 30°25E **17** C16
Kizel *Russia* 59°3N 57°40E **18** C10
Kiziba-Baluba ○ *Congo* 11°50S 28°0E **55** E2
Kiziguru *Rwanda* 1°46S 30°23E **54** C3
Kızıl Irmak → *Turkey* 41°44N 35°58E **19** F6
Kızıl Jilga *China* 35°26N 78°50E **43** B8
Kızıltepe *Turkey* 37°12N 40°35E **44** B4
Kizimkazi *Tanzania* 6°28S 39°30E **54** D4
Kizlyar *Russia* 43°51N 46°40E **19** F8

Kizyl-Arvat = Serdar
  Turkmenistan 39°4N 56°23E **45** B8
Kjölur *Iceland* 64°50N 19°25E **8** D4
Kladno *Czech Rep.* 50°10N 14°7E **16** C8
Klaeng *Thailand* 12°47N 101°39E **38** F3
Klagenfurt *Austria* 46°38N 14°20E **16** E8
Klaipėda *Lithuania* 55°43N 21°10E **9** J19
Klaksvík *Faeroe Is.* 62°14N 6°35W **8** E9
Klamath → *U.S.A.* 41°33N 124°5W **76** F1
Klamath Falls *U.S.A.* 42°13N 121°46W **76** E3
Klamath Mts. *U.S.A.* 41°50N 123°20W **76** F2
Klamono *Indonesia* 1°8S 131°30E **37** E8
Klang *Malaysia* 3°2N 101°26E **39** L3
Klappan → *Canada* 58°0N 129°43W **70** B3
Klarälven → *Sweden* 59°23N 13°32E **9** G15
Klatovy *Czech Rep.* 49°23N 13°18E **16** D7
Klawer *S. Africa* 31°44S 18°36E **56** E2
Klazienaveen *Neths.* 52°44N 7°0E **15** B6
Kleena Kleene *Canada* 52°0N 124°59W **70** C4
Klein-Karas *Namibia* 27°33S 18°7E **56** D2
Klerksdorp *S. Africa* 26°53S 26°38E **56** D4
Kletsk = Klyetsk *Belarus* 53°5N 26°45E **17** B14
Kletskiy *Russia* 49°16N 43°11E **19** E7
Klickitat *U.S.A.* 45°49N 121°9W **78** E5
Klickitat → *U.S.A.* 45°42N 121°17W **78** E5
Klidhes *Cyprus* 35°42N 34°36E **25** D13
Klinaklini → *Canada* 51°21N 125°40W **70** C3
Klip → *S. Africa* 27°3S 29°3E **57** D4
Klipdale *S. Africa* 34°19S 19°57E **56** E2
Klipplaat *S. Africa* 33°1S 24°22E **56** E3
Kłodzko *Poland* 50°28N 16°38E **17** C9
Klondike *Canada* 64°0N 139°26W **68** E4
Klong Wang Chao △
  Thailand 16°20N 99°9E **38** D2
Klouto *Togo* 6°57N 0°44E **50** G6
Kluane △ *Canada* 60°45N 139°30W **70** A1
Kluane L. *Canada* 61°15N 138°40W **68** E4
Kluang *Malaysia* 2°3N 103°18E **39** L4
Kluczbork *Poland* 50°58N 18°12E **17** C10
Klukwan *U.S.A.* 59°24N 135°54W **70** B1
Klungkung *Indonesia* 8°32S 115°24E **37** K18
Klyetsk *Belarus* 53°5N 26°45E **17** B14
Klyuchevskaya, Gora
  Russia 55°50N 160°30E **29** D17
Klyuchi *Russia* 56°18N 160°51E **29** D17
Knaresborough *U.K.* 54°1N 1°28W **12** C6
Knee L., *Man., Canada* 55°3N 94°45W **72** A1
Knee L., *Sask., Canada* 55°51N 107°0W **71** B7
Knight Inlet *Canada* 50°45N 125°40W **70** C3
Knighton *U.K.* 52°21N 3°3W **13** E4
Knights Ferry *U.S.A.* 37°50N 120°40W **78** H6
Knights Landing
  U.S.A. 38°48N 121°43W **78** G5
Knob, C. *Australia* 34°32S 119°16E **61** F2
Knock *Ireland* 53°48N 8°55W **10** C3
Knockmealdown Mts.
  Ireland 52°14N 7°56W **10** D4
Knokke-Heist *Belgium* 51°21N 3°17E **15** C3
Knossos *Greece* 35°16N 25°10E **25** D7
Knowlton *Canada* 45°13N 72°31W **83** A12
Knox *U.S.A.* 41°18N 86°37W **80** E10
Knox Coast *Antarctica* 66°30S 108°0E **5** C8
Knoxville *Iowa, U.S.A.* 41°19N 93°6W **80** E7
Knoxville *Pa., U.S.A.* 41°57N 77°27W **82** E7
Knoxville *Tenn., U.S.A.* 35°58N 83°55W **85** D13
Knud Rasmussen Land
  Greenland 78°0N 60°0W **69** B20
Knysna *S. Africa* 34°2S 23°2E **56** E3
Ko Kha *Thailand* 18°11N 99°24E **38** C2
Ko Tarutao △ *Thailand* 6°31N 99°26E **39** J2
Ko Yao *Thailand* 8°7N 98°35E **39** a
Koba *Indonesia* 6°37S 134°37E **37** F8
Kobarid *Slovenia* 46°15N 13°30E **16** E7
Kobayashi *Japan* 31°56N 130°59E **31** J5
Kōbe *Japan* 34°41N 135°13E **31** G7
København *Denmark* 55°40N 12°26E **9** J15
Kōbi-Sho *Japan* 25°56N 123°41E **31** M1
Koblenz *Germany* 50°21N 7°36E **16** C4
Kobryn *Belarus* 52°15N 24°22E **17** B13
Kobuk → *U.S.A.* 66°54N 160°38W **74** B7
Kocaeli *Turkey* 40°45N 29°50E **19** F4
Kočani *Macedonia* 41°55N 22°25E **23** D10
Koch Bihar *India* 26°22N 89°29E **41** F16
Kochas *India* 25°15N 83°56E **43** G10
Kochi = Cochin *India* 9°58N 76°20E **40** Q10
Kōchi *Japan* 33°30N 133°35E **31** H6
Kōchi □ *Japan* 33°40N 133°30E **31** H6
Kochiu = Gejiu *China* 23°20N 103°10E **32** D5
Kodarma *India* 24°28N 85°36E **43** G11
Kodi *Indonesia* 9°33S 119°0E **60** A2
Kodiak *U.S.A.* 57°47N 152°24W **74** D9
Kodiak I. *U.S.A.* 57°30N 152°45W **74** D9
Kodinar *India* 20°46N 70°46E **42** J4
Kodinsk *Russia* 58°40N 99°10E **29** D10
Koedoesberg *S. Africa* 32°40S 20°11E **56** E3
Koes *Namibia* 26°0S 19°15E **56** D2
Koffiefontein *S. Africa* 29°30S 25°0E **56** D4
Kofiau *Indonesia* 1°11S 129°50E **37** E7
Koforidua *Ghana* 6°3N 0°17W **50** G5
Kōfu *Japan* 35°40N 138°30E **31** G9
Koga *Japan* 36°11N 139°43E **31** F9
Kogaluc → *Canada* 56°12N 61°44W **73** A7
Køge *Denmark* 55°27N 12°11E **9** J15
Kogon *Uzbekistan* 39°43N 64°33E **28** F7
Koh-i-Khurd *Afghan.* 33°30N 65°59E **42** C1
Koh-i-Maran *Pakistan* 29°18N 66°50E **42** E2
Kohat *Pakistan* 33°40N 71°29E **42** C4
Kohima *India* 25°35N 94°10E **41** G19
Kohkīlūyeh va Būyer Aḥmadī □
  Iran 31°30N 50°30E **45** D6
Kohler Ra. *Antarctica* 77°0S 110°0W **5** D15
Kohtla-Järve *Estonia* 59°20N 27°20E **9** G22
Koi Sanjaq *Iraq* 36°5N 44°38E **44** B5
Koillismaa *Finland* 65°44N 28°36E **8** D23
Koin *N. Korea* 40°28N 126°18E **35** D14
Kojŏ *N. Korea* 38°58N 127°58E **35** E14

Kojonup *Australia* 33°48S 117°10E **61** F2
Kojūr *Iran* 36°23N 51°43E **45** B6
Kokand = Qŭqon
  Uzbekistan 40°31N 70°56E **28** E8
Kokas *Indonesia* 2°42S 132°26E **37** E8
Kokchetav = Kökshetaū
  Kazakhstan 53°20N 69°25E **28** D7
Kokemäenjoki →
  Finland 61°32N 21°44E **8** F19
Kokkola *Finland* 63°50N 23°8E **8** E20
Koko Kyunzu *Burma* 14°7N 93°22E **41** M18
Kokomo *U.S.A.* 40°29N 86°8W **80** E10
Koksan *N. Korea* 38°46N 126°40E **35** E14
Koksoak → *Canada* 58°30N 68°10W **69** F18
Kokstad *S. Africa* 30°32S 29°29E **57** E4
Kokubu *Japan* 31°44N 130°46E **31** J5
Kola *Indonesia* 5°35S 134°30E **37** F8
Kola *Russia* 68°45N 33°8E **8** B25
Kola Pen. = Kolskiy Poluostrov
  Russia 67°30N 38°0E **18** A6
Kolachi → *Pakistan* 27°8N 67°2E **42** F2
Kolahoi *India* 34°12N 75°22E **43** B6
Kolaka *Indonesia* 4°3S 121°46E **37** E6
Kolar *India* 13°12N 78°15E **40** N11
Kolar Gold Fields *India* 12°58N 78°16E **40** N11
Kolaras *India* 25°14N 77°36E **42** G6
Kolari *Finland* 67°20N 23°48E **8** C20
Kolayat *India* 27°50N 72°50E **42** F5
Kolda *Senegal* 12°55N 14°57W **50** F3
Kolding *Denmark* 55°30N 9°29E **9** J13
Kolepom = Dolak, Pulau
  Indonesia 8°0S 138°30E **37** F9
Kolguyev, Ostrov *Russia* 69°20N 48°30E **18** A8
Kolhapur *India* 16°43N 74°15E **40** L9
Kolimbia *Greece* 36°15N 28°10E **25** C10
Kolín *Czech Rep.* 50°2N 15°9E **16** C8
Kolka *Latvia* 57°46N 22°37E **9** H20
Kolkata *India* 22°34N 88°21E **43** H13
Kollam = Quilon *India* 8°50N 76°38E **40** Q10
Kollum *Neths.* 53°17N 6°10E **15** A6
Kolmanskop *Namibia* 26°45S 15°14E **56** D2
Köln *Germany* 50°56N 6°57E **16** C4
Kolo *Poland* 52°14N 18°40E **17** B10
Kołobrzeg *Poland* 54°10N 15°35E **16** A8
Kolokani *Mali* 13°35N 7°45W **50** F4
Kolomna *Russia* 55°8N 38°45E **18** C6
Kolomyya *Ukraine* 48°31N 25°2E **17** D13
Kolonodale *Indonesia* 2°0S 121°19E **37** E6
Kolosib *India* 24°15N 92°45E **41** G18
Kolpashevo *Russia* 58°20N 83°5E **28** D9
Kolpino *Russia* 59°44N 30°39E **18** C5
Kolskiy Poluostrov
  Russia 67°30N 38°0E **18** A6
Kolskiy Zaliv *Russia* 69°23N 34°0E **8** B26
Kolwezi
  Dem. Rep. of the Congo 10°40S 25°25E **55** E2
Kolyma → *Russia* 69°30N 161°0E **29** C17
Kolymskoye Nagorye
  Russia 63°0N 157°0E **29** C16
Kôm Ombo *Egypt* 24°25N 32°52E **51** D12
Komandorskiye Is. =
  Komandorskiye Ostrova
  Russia 55°0N 167°0E **29** D17
Komandorskiye Ostrova
  Russia 55°0N 167°0E **29** D17
Komárno *Slovak Rep.* 47°49N 18°5E **17** E10
Komatipoort *S. Africa* 25°25S 31°55E **57** D5
Komatou Yialou *Cyprus* 35°25N 34°8E **25** D13
Komatsu *Japan* 36°25N 136°30E **31** F8
Komatsushima *Japan* 34°0N 134°35E **31** H7
Kome Channel *Uganda* 0°10S 32°55E **54** C3
Komi □ *Russia* 64°0N 55°0E **18** B10
Kommunarsk = Alchevsk
  Ukraine 48°30N 38°45E **19** E6
Kommunizma, Pik = imeni Ismail
  Samani, Pik *Tajikistan* 39°0N 72°2E **28** F8
Komodo *Indonesia* 8°37S 119°20E **37** F5
Komoran, Pulau
  Indonesia 8°18S 138°45E **37** F9
Komoro *Japan* 36°19N 138°26E **31** F9
Komotini *Greece* 41°9N 25°26E **23** D11
Kompasberg *S. Africa* 31°45S 24°32E **56** E3
Kompong Cham
  Cambodia 12°0N 105°30E **39** G5
Kompong Chhnang = Kampong
  Chhnang *Cambodia* 12°20N 104°35E **39** F5
Kompong Chikreng
  Cambodia 13°5N 104°18E **38** F5
Kompong Kleang
  Cambodia 13°6N 104°8E **38** F5
Kompong Luong
  Cambodia 11°49N 104°48E **39** G5
Kompong Pranak
  Cambodia 13°35N 104°55E **38** F5
Kompong Som = Kampong Saom
  Cambodia 10°38N 103°30E **39** G4
Kompong Som, Chhung =
  Kampong Saom, Chaak
  Cambodia 10°50N 103°32E **39** G4
Kompong Speu
  Cambodia 11°26N 104°32E **39** G5
Kompong Sralau
  Cambodia 14°5N 105°46E **38** E5
Kompong Thom
  Cambodia 12°35N 104°51E **38** F5
Kompong Trabeck
  Cambodia 13°6N 105°14E **38** F5
Kompong Trabeck
  Cambodia 11°9N 105°28E **39** G5
Kompong Trach
  Cambodia 11°25N 105°48E **39** G5
Kompong Tralach
  Cambodia 11°54N 104°47E **39** G5
Komrat = Comrat
  Moldova 46°18N 28°40E **17** E15
Komsberg *S. Africa* 32°40S 20°45E **56** E3
Komsomolets, Ostrov
  Russia 80°30N 95°0E **29** A10

Komsomolsk-na-Amur
  Russia 50°30N 137°0E **33** A8
Kon Tum *Vietnam* 14°24N 108°0E **38** E7
Kon Tum, Plateau du
  Vietnam 14°30N 108°30E **38** E7
Konar □ *Afghan.* 34°30N 71°3E **40** B7
Konārī *Iran* 28°13N 51°36E **45** D6
Konch *India* 26°0N 79°10E **43** G8
Konde *Tanzania* 4°57S 39°45E **54** C4
Kondinin *Australia* 32°34S 118°8E **61** F2
Kondoa *Tanzania* 4°55S 35°50E **54** C4
Kondopoga *Russia* 62°12N 34°17E **18** B5
Kondratyevo *Russia* 57°22N 98°15E **29** D10
Köneürgench
  Turkmenistan 42°19N 59°10E **28** E6
Konevo *Russia* 62°8N 39°20E **18** B6
Kong = Khong →
  Cambodia 13°32N 105°58E **38** F5
Kong *Ivory C.* 8°54N 4°36W **50** G5
Kong, Koh *Cambodia* 11°20N 103°0E **39** G4
Kong Christian IX Land
  Greenland 68°0N 36°0W **4** C6
Kong Christian X Land
  Greenland 74°0N 29°0W **4** B6
Kong Frederik IX Land
  Greenland 67°0N 52°0W **4** C5
Kong Frederik VI Kyst
  Greenland 63°0N 43°0W **4** C5
Kong Frederik VIII Land
  Greenland 78°30N 26°0W **4** B6
Kong Oscar Fjord
  Greenland 72°20N 24°0W **4** B6
Konglu *Burma* 27°13N 97°57E **41** F20
Kongola *Namibia* 17°45S 23°20E **56** B3
Kongolo *Kasai-Or.,
  Dem. Rep. of the Congo* 5°26S 24°49E **54** D1
Kongolo *Katanga,
  Dem. Rep. of the Congo* 5°22S 27°0E **54** D2
Kongsberg *Norway* 59°39N 9°39E **9** G13
Kongsvinger *Norway* 60°12N 12°2E **9** F15
Kongur Shan *China* 38°34N 75°18E **32** C2
Kongwa *Tanzania* 6°11S 36°26E **54** D4
Koni
  Dem. Rep. of the Congo 10°40S 27°11E **55** E2
Koni, Mts.
  Dem. Rep. of the Congo 10°36S 27°10E **55** E2
Konin *Poland* 52°12N 18°15E **17** B10
Konjic *Bos.-H.* 43°42N 17°58E **23** C7
Konkiep *Namibia* 26°49S 17°15E **56** D2
Konosha *Russia* 61°0N 40°5E **18** B7
Kōnosu *Japan* 36°3N 139°31E **31** F9
Konotop *Ukraine* 51°12N 33°7E **19** D5
Konqi He → *China* 41°0N 86°0E **32** B3
Końskie *Poland* 51°15N 20°23E **17** C11
Konstanz *Germany* 47°40N 9°10E **16** E5
Kont *Iran* 26°55N 61°50E **45** E9
Kontagora *Nigeria* 10°23N 5°27E **50** F7
Kontiolahti *Finland* 62°46N 29°50E **8** E23
Kontokali *Greece* 39°38N 19°51E **25** A3
Konya *Turkey* 37°52N 32°35E **44** B2
Konza *Kenya* 1°45S 37°7E **54** C4
Koocanusa, L. *Canada* 49°20N 115°15W **76** B6
Kookynie *Australia* 29°17S 121°22E **61** E3
Koolyanobbing
  Australia 30°48S 119°36E **61** F2
Koonibba *Australia* 31°54S 133°25E **63** E1
Koorawatha *Australia* 34°2S 148°33E **63** E4
Koorda *Australia* 30°48S 117°35E **61** F2
Kooskia *U.S.A.* 46°9N 115°59W **76** C6
Kootenay → *U.S.A.* 49°19N 117°39W **70** D5
Kootenay L. *Canada* 51°0N 116°0W **70** C5
Kootenay L. *Canada* 49°45N 116°50W **76** B5
Kootjieskolk *S. Africa* 31°15S 20°21E **56** E3
Kopaonik *Serbia* 43°10N 20°50E **23** C9
Kópavogur *Iceland* 64°6N 21°55W **8** D3
Koper *Slovenia* 45°31N 13°44E **16** F7
Kopervik *Norway* 59°17N 5°17E **9** G11
Kopet Dagh *Asia* 38°0N 58°0E **45** B8
Kopi *Australia* 33°24S 135°40E **63** E2
Köping *Sweden* 59°31N 16°3E **9** G17
Koppeh Dāgh = Kopet Dagh
  Asia 38°0N 58°0E **45** B8
Koppies *S. Africa* 27°20S 27°30E **57** D4
Koprivnica *Croatia* 46°12N 16°45E **16** E9
Köprülü △ *Turkey* 37°20N 31°5E **44** B1
Kopychyntsi *Ukraine* 49°7N 25°58E **17** D13
Kora △ *Kenya* 0°14S 38°44E **54** C4
Korab *Macedonia* 41°44N 20°40E **23** D9
Koral *India* 21°50N 73°12E **42** J5
Korba *India* 22°20N 82°45E **43** H10
Korbu, G. *Malaysia* 4°41N 101°18E **39** K3
Korçë *Albania* 40°37N 20°50E **23** D9
Korčula *Croatia* 42°56N 16°57E **22** C7
Kord Kūy *Iran* 36°48N 54°7E **45** B7
Kord Sheykh *Iran* 28°31N 52°53E **45** D7
Kordestān □ *Iran* 36°0N 47°0E **44** C5
Kordofân □ *Sudan* 13°0N 29°0E **51** F11
Korea, North ■ *Asia* 40°0N 127°0E **35** E14
Korea, South ■ *Asia* 36°0N 128°0E **35** G15
Korea Bay *Korea* 39°0N 124°0E **35** E13
Korea Strait *Asia* 34°0N 129°30E **35** H15
Korets *Ukraine* 50°40N 27°5E **17** C14
Korhogo *Ivory C.* 9°29N 5°28W **50** G4
Korinthiakos Kolpos
  Greece 38°16N 22°30E **23** E10
Korinthos *Greece* 37°56N 22°55E **23** F10
Korissia, L. *Greece* 39°27N 19°53E **25** B3
Kōriyama *Japan* 37°24N 140°23E **30** F10
Korla *China* 41°45N 86°4E **32** B3
Kormakiti, C. *Cyprus* 35°23N 32°56E **25** D11
Korneshty = Corneşti
  Moldova 47°21N 28°1E **17** E15
Koro *Fiji* 17°19S 179°23E **59** a
Koro *Ivory C.* 8°32N 7°30W **50** G4
Koro Sea *Fiji* 17°30S 179°45W **59** a
Korogwe *Tanzania* 5°5S 38°25E **54** D4
Korolevu *Fiji* 18°12S 177°46E **59** a
Koronadal *Phil.* 6°12N 125°1E **37** C6
Koror *Palau* 7°20N 134°28E **64** G5

Körös → Hungary 46°43N 20°12E **17** E11
Korosten Ukraine 50°54N 28°36E **17** C15
Korostyshev Ukraine 50°19N 29°4E **17** C15
Korovou Fiji 17°47S 178°32E **59** a
Koroyanitu △ Fiji 17°40S 177°35E **59** a
Korraraika, Helodranon' i
Madag. 17°45S 43°57E **57** B7
Korsakov Russia 46°36N 142°42E **29** E15
Korshunovo Russia 58°37N 110°10E **29** D12
Korsør Denmark 55°20N 11°9E **9** J14
Kortrijk Belgium 50°50N 3°17E **15** D3
Korwai India 24°7N 78°5E **42** G8
Koryakskoye Nagorye
Russia 61°0N 171°0E **29** C18
Kos Greece 36°50N 27°15E **23** F12
Kosan N. Korea 38°52N 127°25E **35** E14
Kościan Poland 52°5N 16°40E **17** B9
Kosciusko U.S.A. 33°4N 89°35W **85** E10
Kosciuszko, Mt.
Australia 36°27S 148°16E **63** F4
Kosha Sudan 20°50N 30°30E **51** D12
K'oshih = Kashi China 39°30N 76°2E **32** C2
Koshiki-Rettō Japan 31°45N 129°49E **31** J4
Kosi India 27°48N 77°29E **42** F7
Kosi → India 28°41N 78°57E **43** E8
Košice Slovak Rep. 48°42N 21°15E **17** D11
Koskinou Greece 36°23N 28°13E **25** C10
Koslan Russia 63°34N 49°14E **18** B8
Kosŏng N. Korea 38°40N 128°22E **35** E15
Kosovo □ Europe 42°30N 21°0E **23** C9
Kosovska Mitrovica
Kosovo 42°54N 20°52E **23** C9
Kossou, L. de Ivory C. 6°59N 5°31W **50** G4
Koster S. Africa 25°52S 26°54E **56** D4
Kôsti Sudan 13°8N 32°43E **51** F12
Kostopil Ukraine 50°51N 26°22E **17** C14
Kostroma Russia 57°50N 40°58E **18** C7
Kostrzyn Poland 52°35N 14°39E **16** B8
Koszalin Poland 54°11N 16°8E **16** A9
Kot Addu Pakistan 30°30N 71°0E **42** D4
Kot Kapura India 30°35N 74°50E **42** D6
Kot Moman Pakistan 32°13N 73°0E **42** C5
Kot Sultan Pakistan 30°46N 70°56E **42** D4
Kota India 25°14N 75°49E **42** G6
Kota Barrage India 25°6N 75°51E **42** G6
Kota Belud Malaysia 6°21N 116°26E **36** C5
Kota Bharu Malaysia 6°7N 102°14E **39** J4
Kota Kinabalu Malaysia 6°0N 116°4E **36** C5
Kota Tinggi Malaysia 1°44N 103°53E **39** M4
Kotaagung Indonesia 5°38S 104°29E **36** F2
Kotabaru Indonesia 3°20S 116°20E **36** E5
Kotabumi Indonesia 4°49S 104°54E **36** E2
Kotamobagu Indonesia 0°57N 124°31E **37** D6
Kotapinang Indonesia 1°53N 100°5E **39** M3
Kotcho L. Canada 59°7N 121°12W **70** B4
Kotdwara India 29°45N 78°32E **43** E8
Kotelnich Russia 58°22N 48°24E **18** C8
Kotelnikovo Russia 47°38N 43°8E **19** E7
Kotelnyy, Ostrov
Russia 75°10N 139°0E **29** B14
Kothari → India 25°20N 75°49E **42** G6
Kothi Chhattisgarh, India 23°21N 82°3E **43** H10
Kothi Mad. P., India 24°45N 80°40E **43** G9
Kotiro Pakistan 26°17N 67°13E **42** F2
Kotka Finland 60°28N 26°58E **8** F22
Kotlas Russia 61°17N 46°43E **18** B8
Kotli Pakistan 33°30N 73°55E **42** C5
Kotma India 23°12N 81°58E **43** H9
Kotor Montenegro 42°25N 18°47E **23** C8
Kotovsk Ukraine 47°45N 29°35E **17** E15
Kotputli India 27°43N 76°12E **42** F7
Kotri Pakistan 25°22N 68°22E **42** G3
Kotto → C.A.R. 4°14N 22°2E **52** D4
Kotturu India 14°45N 76°10E **40** M10
Kotu Group Tonga 20°0S 174°45W **59** c
Kotuy → Russia 71°54N 102°6E **29** B11
Kotzebue U.S.A. 66°53N 162°39W **74** B7
Kotzebue Sound U.S.A. 66°20N 163°0W **74** B7
Kouchibouguac △
Canada 46°50N 65°0W **73** C6
Koudougou Burkina Faso 12°10N 2°20W **50** F5
Koufonisi Greece 34°56N 26°8E **25** E8
Kougaberge S. Africa 33°48S 23°50E **56** E3
Kouilou → Congo 4°10S 12°5E **52** E2
Koukdjuak → Canada 66°43N 73°0W **69** D17
Koula Moutou Gabon 1°15S 12°25E **52** E2
Koulen = Kulen
Cambodia 13°50N 104°40E **38** F5
Kouloura Greece 39°42N 19°54E **25** A3
Koumala Australia 21°38S 149°15E **62** C4
Koumra Chad 8°50N 17°35E **51** G9
Kountze U.S.A. 30°22N 94°19W **84** F7
Kouris → Cyprus 34°38N 32°54E **25** E11
Kourou Fr. Guiana 5°9N 52°39W **93** B8
Kouroussa Guinea 10°45N 9°45W **50** F4
Kousséri Cameroon 12°0N 14°55E **51** F8
Koutiala Mali 12°25N 5°23W **50** F4
Kouvola Finland 60°52N 26°43E **8** F22
Kovdor Russia 67°34N 30°24E **8** C24
Kovel Ukraine 51°11N 24°38E **17** C13
Kovrov Russia 56°25N 41°25E **18** C7
Kowanyama Australia 15°29S 141°44E **62** B3
Kowanyama ◌
Australia 15°20S 141°47E **62** B3
Kowloon China 22°19N 114°11E **33** G11
Kowŏn N. Korea 39°26N 127°14E **35** E14
Koyampattur = Coimbatore
India 11°2N 76°59E **40** P10
Köyceğiz Turkey 36°57N 28°40E **23** F13
Koyukuk → U.S.A. 64°55N 157°32W **74** C8
Koza = Okinawa Japan 26°19N 127°46E **31** L3
Kozan Turkey 37°26N 35°50E **44** B6
Kozani Greece 40°19N 21°47E **23** D9
Kozhikode = Calicut
India 11°15N 75°43E **40** P9
Kozhva Russia 65°10N 57°0E **18** A10
Kozyatyn Ukraine 49°45N 28°50E **17** D15
Kozyrevsk Russia 56°3N 159°51E **29** D16

Kpalimé Togo 6°57N 0°44E **50** G6
Kra, Isthmus of = Kra, Kho Khot
Thailand 10°15N 99°30E **39** G2
Kra, Kho Khot Thailand 10°15N 99°30E **39** G2
Kra Buri Thailand 10°22N 98°46E **39** G2
Kraai → S. Africa 30°40S 26°45E **56** E4
Krabi Thailand 8°4N 98°55E **39** H2
Kracheh Cambodia 12°32N 106°10E **38** F6
Kragan Indonesia 6°43S 111°38E **37** G14
Kragerø Norway 58°52N 9°25E **9** G13
Kragujevac Serbia 44°2N 20°56E **23** B9
Krakatau = Rakata, Pulau
Indonesia 6°10S 105°20E **36** F3
Krakatoa = Rakata, Pulau
Indonesia 6°10S 105°20E **36** F3
Krakor Cambodia 12°32N 104°12E **38** F5
Kraków Poland 50°4N 19°57E **17** C10
Kralanh Cambodia 13°35N 103°25E **38** F4
Kraljevo Serbia 43°44N 20°41E **23** C9
Kramatorsk Ukraine 48°50N 37°30E **19** E6
Kramfors Sweden 62°55N 17°48E **8** E17
Kranj Slovenia 46°16N 14°22E **16** E8
Krankskop S. Africa 28°0S 30°47E **57** D5
Krasavino Russia 60°58N 46°29E **18** B8
Kraskino Russia 42°44N 130°48E **30** C5
Kraśnik Poland 50°55N 22°15E **17** C12
Krasnoarmeysk Russia 51°0N 45°42E **28** D5
Krasnodar Russia 45°5N 39°0E **19** E6
Krasnokamensk Russia 50°3N 118°0E **29** D12
Krasnokamsk Russia 58°4N 55°48E **18** C10
Krasnoperekopsk Ukraine 46°0N 33°54E **19** E5
Krasnorechenskiy
Russia 44°41N 135°14E **30** B7
Krasnoselkup Russia 65°20N 82°10E **28** C9
Krasnoturinsk Russia 59°46N 60°12E **18** C11
Krasnoufimsk Russia 56°36N 57°38E **18** C10
Krasnouralsk Russia 58°21N 60°3E **18** C11
Krasnovishersk Russia 60°23N 57°3E **18** B10
Krasnyy Kut Russia 50°50N 47°0E **19** D8
Krasnyy Luch Ukraine 48°13N 39°0E **19** E6
Krasnyy Yar Russia 46°43N 48°23E **19** E8
Kratie = Kracheh
Cambodia 12°32N 106°10E **38** F6
Krau Indonesia 3°19S 140°5E **37** E10
Kravanh, Chuor Phnum
Cambodia 12°0N 103°32E **39** G4
Krefeld Germany 51°20N 6°33E **16** C4
Kremenchuk Ukraine 49°5N 33°25E **19** E5
Kremenchuksk Vdskh.
Ukraine 49°20N 32°30E **19** E5
Kremenets Ukraine 50°8N 25°43E **17** C13
Kremmling U.S.A. 40°4N 106°24W **76** F10
Krems Austria 48°25N 15°36E **16** D8
Kretinga Lithuania 55°53N 21°15E **9** J19
Krichev = Krychaw
Belarus 53°40N 31°41E **17** B16
Kril'on, Mys Russia 45°53N 142°5E **30** B11
Krios, Akra Greece 35°13N 23°34E **25** D5
Krishna → India 15°57N 80°59E **41** M12
Krishnanagar India 23°24N 88°33E **43** H13
Kristiansand Norway 58°8N 8°1E **9** G13
Kristianstad Sweden 56°2N 14°9E **9** H16
Kristiansund Norway 63°7N 7°45E **8** E12
Kristiinankaupunki
Finland 62°16N 21°21E **8** E19
Kristinehamn Sweden 59°18N 14°7E **9** G16
Kristinestad =
Kristiinankaupunki
Finland 62°16N 21°21E **8** E19
Kriti Greece 35°15N 25°0E **25** D7
Kritsa Greece 35°10N 25°41E **25** D7
Krivoy Rog = Kryvyy Rih
Ukraine 47°51N 33°20E **19** E5
Krk Croatia 45°8N 14°40E **16** F8
Krokodil = Umgwenya →
Mozam. 25°14S 32°18E **57** D5
Krong Kaoh Kong
Cambodia 11°37N 102°59E **39** G4
Kronprins Frederik Land
Greenland 81°0N 45°0W **4** B5
Kronprins Olav Kyst
Antarctica 69°0S 42°0E **5** C5
Kronprinsesse Märtha Kyst
Antarctica 73°30S 10°0W **5** D2
Kronshtadt Russia 59°57N 29°51E **18** B4
Kroonstad S. Africa 27°43S 27°19E **56** D4
Kropotkin Russia 45°28N 40°28E **19** E7
Krosno Poland 49°42N 21°46E **17** D11
Krotoszyn Poland 51°42N 17°23E **17** C9
Krousonas Greece 35°13N 24°59E **25** D6
Kruger △ S. Africa 24°50S 26°10E **57** C5
Krugersdorp S. Africa 26°5S 27°46E **57** D4
Kruisfontein S. Africa 33°59S 24°43E **56** E3
Krung Thep = Bangkok
Thailand 13°45N 100°35E **38** F3
Krupki Belarus 54°19N 29°8E **17** A15
Kruševac Serbia 43°35N 21°28E **23** C9
Krychaw Belarus 53°40N 31°41E **17** B16
Krymskiy Poluostrov = Krymskyy
Pivostriv Ukraine 45°0N 34°0E **19** F5
Krymskyy Pivostriv
Ukraine 45°0N 34°0E **19** F5
Kryvyy Rih Ukraine 47°51N 33°20E **19** E5
Ksar el Kebir Morocco 35°0N 6°0W **50** B4
Ksar es Souk = Er Rachidia
Morocco 31°58N 4°20W **50** B5
Kuah Malaysia 6°19N 99°51E **39** J2
Kuala Belait Malaysia 4°35N 114°11E **36** D4
Kuala Berang Malaysia 5°5N 103°1E **39** K4
Kuala Dungun = Dungun
Malaysia 4°45N 103°25E **39** K4
Kuala Kangsar Malaysia 4°46N 100°56E **39** K3
Kuala Kelawang Malaysia 2°56N 102°5E **39** L4
Kuala Kerai Malaysia 5°30N 102°12E **39** K4
Kuala Kerian Malaysia 5°10N 100°25E **39** c
Kuala Kubu Bharu
Malaysia 3°34N 101°39E **39** L3

Kuala Lipis Malaysia 4°10N 102°3E **39** K4
Kuala Lumpur Malaysia 3°9N 101°41E **39** L3
Kuala Nerang Malaysia 6°16N 100°37E **39** J3
Kuala Pilah Malaysia 2°45N 102°15E **39** L4
Kuala Rompin Malaysia 2°49N 103°29E **39** L4
Kuala Selangor Malaysia 3°20N 101°15E **39** L3
Kuala Sepetang
Malaysia 4°49N 100°28E **39** K3
Kuala Terengganu
Malaysia 5°20N 103°8E **39** K4
Kualajelai Indonesia 2°58S 110°46E **36** E4
Kualakapuas Indonesia 2°55S 114°20E **36** E4
Kualakurun Indonesia 1°10S 113°50E **36** E4
Kualapembuang
Indonesia 3°14S 112°38E **36** E4
Kualasimpang Indonesia 4°17N 98°3E **36** D1
Kuancheng China 40°37N 118°30E **35** D10
Kuandang Indonesia 0°56N 123°1E **37** D6
Kuandian China 40°45N 124°45E **35** D13
Kuangchou = Guangzhou
China 23°6N 113°13E **33** D6
Kuantan Malaysia 3°49N 103°20E **39** L4
Kuba = Quba Azerbaijan 41°21N 48°32E **19** F8
Kuban → Russia 45°20N 37°30E **19** E6
Kubokawa Japan 33°12N 133°8E **31** H6
Kubu Indonesia 8°16S 115°35E **37** J18
Kubutambahan
Indonesia 8°5S 115°10E **37** J18
Kucar, Tanjung
Indonesia 8°39S 114°34E **37** K18
Kuchaman India 27°13N 74°47E **42** F6
Kuchinda India 21°44N 84°21E **43** J11
Kuching Malaysia 1°33N 110°25E **36** D4
Kuchino-eruba-Jima
Japan 30°28N 130°12E **31** J5
Kuchino-Shima Japan 29°57N 129°55E **31** K4
Kuchinotsu Japan 32°36N 130°11E **31** H5
Kucing = Kuching
Malaysia 1°33N 110°25E **36** D4
Kud → Pakistan 26°5N 66°20E **42** F2
Kuda India 23°10N 71°15E **42** H4
Kudat Malaysia 6°55N 116°55E **36** C5
Kudus Indonesia 6°48S 110°51E **37** G14
Kudymkar Russia 59°1N 54°39E **18** C9
Kueiyang = Guiyang
China 26°32N 106°40E **32** D5
Kufra Oasis = Al Kufrah
Libya 24°17N 23°15E **51** D10
Kufstein Austria 47°35N 12°11E **16** E7
Kugaaruk = Pelly Bay
Canada 68°38N 89°50W **69** D14
Kugluktuk Canada 67°50N 115°5W **68** D8
Kugong I. Canada 56°18N 79°50W **72** A4
Kühak Iran 27°12N 63°10E **45** E9
Kühbonän Iran 31°23N 56°19E **45** D8
Kühestak Iran 26°47N 57°2E **45** E8
Kuhin Iran 36°22N 49°40E **45** B6
Kūhīrī Iran 26°55N 61°2E **45** E9
Kuhmo Finland 64°7N 29°31E **8** D23
Kühpāyeh Esfahan, Iran 32°44N 52°20E **45** C7
Kühpāyeh Kermān, Iran 30°35N 57°15E **45** D8
Kührān, Küh-e Iran 26°46N 58°12E **45** E8
Kui Buri Thailand 12°3N 99°52E **39** F2
Kuichong China 22°38N 114°25E **33** F11
Kuiseb → Namibia 22°59S 14°31E **56** C1
Kuito Angola 12°22S 16°55E **53** G3
Kuiu I. U.S.A. 57°45N 134°10W **70** B2
Kujang N. Korea 39°57N 126°1E **35** E14
Kuji Japan 40°11N 141°46E **30** D10
Kujū-San Japan 33°5N 131°15E **31** H5
Kukës Albania 42°5N 20°27E **23** C9
Kukup Malaysia 1°20N 103°27E **39** d
Kukup, Pulau Malaysia 1°18N 103°25E **39** d
Kula Turkey 38°32N 28°40E **23** E13
K'ula Shan Bhutan 28°14N 90°36E **32** C4
Kulachi Pakistan 31°56N 70°27E **42** D4
Kulai Malaysia 1°44N 103°35E **39** M4
Kulasekarappattinam
India 8°20N 78°5E **40** Q11
Kuldiga Latvia 56°58N 21°59E **9** H19
Kulen Cambodia 13°50N 104°40E **38** F5
Kulgam India 33°36N 75°2E **43** C6
Kulgera Australia 25°50S 133°18E **62** D1
Kulim Malaysia 5°22N 100°34E **39** K3
Kulin Australia 32°40S 118°2E **61** F2
Kulkayu = Hartley Bay
Canada 53°25N 129°15W **70** C3
Kullu India 31°58N 77°6E **42** D7
Külob Tajikistan 37°55N 69°50E **28** F7
Kulsary = Qulsary
Kazakhstan 46°59N 54°1E **19** E9
Kulti India 23°43N 86°50E **43** H12
Kulunda Russia 52°35N 78°57E **28** D8
Kulungar Afghan. 34°0N 69°2E **42** C3
Külvand Iran 31°21N 54°35E **45** D7
Kulwin Australia 35°2S 142°42E **63** F3
Kulyab = Külob
Tajikistan 37°55N 69°50E **28** F7
Kuma → Russia 44°55N 47°0E **19** F8
Kumaganum Nigeria 13°8N 10°38E **51** F8
Kumagaya Japan 36°9N 139°22E **31** F9
Kumai Indonesia 2°44S 111°43E **36** E4
Kumamba, Kepulauan
Indonesia 1°36S 138°45E **37** E9
Kumamoto Japan 32°45N 130°45E **31** H5
Kumamoto □ Japan 32°55N 130°55E **31** H5
Kumanovo Macedonia 42°9N 21°42E **23** C9
Kumara N.Z. 42°37S 171°12E **59** E3
Kumarina Roadhouse
Australia 24°41S 119°32E **61** D2
Kumasi Ghana 6°41N 1°38W **50** G5
Kumba Cameroon 4°36N 9°24E **52** D1
Kumbakonam India 10°58N 79°25E **40** P11
Kumbarilla Australia 27°15S 150°55E **63** D5
Kumbhraj India 24°22N 77°3E **42** G7
Kumbia Australia 26°41S 151°39E **63** D5

Kümch'ŏn N. Korea 38°10N 126°29E **35** E14
Kumdok India 33°32N 78°10E **43** C8
Kume-Shima Japan 26°20N 126°47E **31** L3
Kumertau Russia 52°45N 55°57E **18** D10
Kumharsain India 31°19N 77°27E **42** D7
Kumi Uganda 1°30N 33°58E **54** B3
Kumo Nigeria 10°1N 11°12E **51** F8
Kumo älv = Kokemäenjoki →
Finland 61°32N 21°44E **8** F19
Kumon Bum Burma 26°30N 97°15E **41** F20
Kumtag Shamo China 39°40N 92°0E **32** C4
Kunashir, Ostrov Russia 44°0N 146°0E **29** E15
Kunda Estonia 59°30N 26°34E **9** G22
Kunda India 25°43N 81°31E **43** G9
Kundar → Pakistan 31°56N 69°19E **42** D3
Kundelungu △
Dem. Rep. of the Congo 10°30S 27°40E **55** E2
Kundelungu Ouest △
Dem. Rep. of the Congo 9°55S 27°17E **55** D2
Kundian Pakistan 32°27N 71°28E **42** C4
Kundla India 21°21N 71°25E **42** J4
Kung, Ao Thailand 8°5N 98°24E **39** a
Kunga → Bangla. 21°46N 89°30E **43** J13
Kunghit I. Canada 52°6N 131°3W **70** C2
Kungrad = Qŭnghirot
Uzbekistan 43°2N 58°50E **28** E6
Kungsbacka Sweden 57°30N 12°5E **9** H15
Kungur Russia 57°25N 56°57E **18** C10
Kungurri Australia 21°4S 148°45E **62** b
Kuningan Indonesia 6°59S 108°29E **37** G13
Kunlong Burma 23°20N 98°50E **41** F21
Kunlun Shan Asia 36°0N 86°30E **32** C3
Kunming China 25°1N 102°41E **32** D5
Kununnya ◌ Australia 15°28S 124°42E **60** C3
Kununurra Australia 15°40S 128°50E **60** C4
Kunwari → India 26°26N 79°11E **43** F8
Kunya-Urgench = Köneürgench
Turkmenistan 42°19N 59°10E **28** E6
Kuopio Finland 62°53N 27°35E **8** E22
Kupa → Croatia 45°28N 16°24E **16** F9
Kupang Indonesia 10°19S 123°39E **37** F6
Kupreanof I. U.S.A. 56°50N 133°30W **70** B2
Kupyansk-Uzlovoi
Ukraine 49°40N 37°43E **19** E6
Kuqa China 41°35N 82°30E **32** B3
Kür → Azerbaijan 39°29N 49°15E **19** G8
Kür Dili Azerbaijan 39°3N 49°13E **45** B6
Kura = Kür →
Azerbaijan 39°29N 49°15E **19** G8
Kuranda Australia 16°48S 145°35E **62** B4
Kuranga India 22°4N 69°10E **42** H3
Kurashiki Japan 34°40N 133°50E **31** G6
Kurayn Si. Arabia 27°39N 49°50E **45** E6
Kurayoshi Japan 35°26N 133°50E **31** G6
Kürchatov Kazakhstan 50°45N 78°32E **28** D8
Kürdzhali Bulgaria 41°38N 25°21E **23** D11
Kure Japan 34°14N 132°32E **31** G6
Kure I. U.S.A. 28°25N 178°25W **75** K4
Kuressaare Estonia 58°15N 22°30E **9** G20
Kurgan Russia 55°26N 65°18E **28** D7
Kuri India 26°37N 70°43E **42** F4
Kuria Maria Is. = Hallāniyat,
Jazā'ir al Oman 17°30N 55°58E **47** D6
Kuridala Australia 21°16S 140°29E **62** C3
Kurigram Bangla. 25°49N 89°39E **41** G16
Kurikka Finland 62°36N 22°24E **8** E20
Kuril Basin Pac. Oc. 47°0N 150°0E **4** E15
Kuril Is. = Kurilskiye Ostrova
Russia 45°0N 150°0E **29** E16
Kuril-Kamchatka Trench
Pac. Oc. 44°0N 153°0E **64** C7
Kurilsk Russia 45°14N 147°53E **29** E16
Kurilskiye Ostrova
Russia 45°0N 150°0E **29** E16
Kurino Japan 31°57N 130°43E **31** J5
Kurinskaya Kosa = Kür Dili
Azerbaijan 39°3N 49°13E **45** B6
Kurnool India 15°45N 78°0E **40** M11
Kuro-Shima Kagoshima,
Japan 30°50N 129°57E **31** J4
Kuro-Shima Okinawa,
Japan 24°14N 124°1E **31** M2
Kurow N.Z. 44°44S 170°29E **59** F3
Kurram → Pakistan 32°36N 71°20E **42** C4
Kurri Kurri Australia 32°50S 151°28E **63** E5
Kurrimine Australia 17°47S 146°6E **62** B4
Kurseong = Karsiyang
India 26°56N 88°18E **43** F13
Kurshskiy Zaliv Russia 55°9N 21°6E **9** J19
Kursk Russia 51°42N 36°11E **18** D6
Kuruçay Turkey 39°39N 38°29E **44** B3
Kurukshetra = Thanesar
India 30°1N 76°52E **42** D7
Kuruktag China 41°0N 89°0E **32** B3
Kurum S. Africa 27°28S 23°28E **56** D3
Kuruman → S. Africa 26°56S 20°39E **56** D3
Kurume Japan 33°15N 130°30E **31** H5
Kurunegala Sri Lanka 7°30N 80°23E **40** R12
Kurya Russia 61°42N 57°9E **18** B10
Kus Gölü Turkey 40°10N 27°55E **23** D12
Kuşadası Turkey 37°52N 27°15E **23** F12
Kusamba Indonesia 8°34S 115°27E **37** K18
Kusatsu Japan 35°3N 138°34E **31** F9
Kusawa L. Canada 60°20N 136°13W **70** A1
Kushalgarh India 23°10N 74°27E **42** H6
Kushikino Japan 31°44N 130°16E **31** J5
Kushima Japan 31°29N 131°14E **31** J5
Kushimoto Japan 33°28N 135°47E **31** H7
Kushiro Japan 43°0N 144°25E **30** C12
Kushiro-Gawa →
Japan 42°59N 144°23E **30** C12
Kushk Iran 28°46N 56°51E **45** D8
Kushiro Shitsugen △
Japan 43°9N 144°26E **30** C12
Kushka = Serhetabat
Turkmenistan 35°20N 62°18E **45** C9
Kushol India 33°40N 76°36E **43** C7

Kushtia Bangla. 23°55N 89°5E **41** H16
Kushva Russia 58°18N 59°45E **18** C10
Kuskokwim → U.S.A. 60°5N 162°25W **74** C7
Kuskokwim B. U.S.A. 59°45N 162°25W **74** D7
Kuskokwim Mts.
U.S.A. 62°30N 156°0W **74** C8
Kusmi India 23°17N 83°55E **43** H10
Kusŏng N. Korea 39°59N 125°15E **35** E13
Kussharo-Ko Japan 43°38N 144°21E **30** C12
Kustanay = Qostanay
Kazakhstan 53°10N 63°35E **28** D7
Kut, Ko Thailand 11°40N 102°35E **39** G4
Kuta Indonesia 8°43S 115°11E **37** K18
Kütahya Turkey 39°30N 30°2E **19** G5
Kutaisi Georgia 42°19N 42°40E **19** F7
Kutaraja = Banda Aceh
Indonesia 5°35N 95°20E **36** C1
Kutch, Gulf of = Kachchh, Gulf of
India 22°50N 69°15E **42** H3
Kutch, Rann of = Kachchh, Rann
of India 24°0N 70°0E **42** H4
Kutiyana India 21°36N 70°2E **42** J4
Kutno Poland 52°15N 19°23E **17** B10
Kutse Botswana 21°7S 22°16E **56** C3
Kuttabul Australia 21°1S 148°54E **62** b
Kutu Dem. Rep. of the Congo 2°40S 18°11E **52** E3
Kutum Sudan 14°10N 24°40E **51** F10
Kuujjuaq Canada 58°6N 68°15W **69** F18
Kuujjuarapik Canada 55°20N 77°35W **72** A4
Kuusamo Finland 65°57N 29°8E **8** D23
Kuusankoski Finland 60°55N 26°38E **8** F22
Kuwait = Al Kuwayt
Kuwait 29°30N 48°0E **44** D5
Kuwait ■ Asia 29°30N 47°30E **44** D5
Kuwana Japan 35°5N 136°43E **31** G8
Kuwana → India 26°25N 83°15E **43** F10
Kuybyshev = Samara
Russia 53°8N 50°6E **18** D9
Kuybyshev Russia 55°27N 78°19E **28** D8
Kuybyshevskoye Vdkhr.
Russia 55°2N 49°30E **18** C8
Küyeh Iran 38°23N 110°46E **34** E6
Küye He → China 38°23N 110°46E **34** E6
Kuyto, Ozero Russia 65°6N 31°20E **8** D24
Kuyumba Russia 60°58N 96°59E **29** C10
Kuzey Anadolu Dağları
Turkey 41°30N 35°0E **19** F6
Kuznetsk Russia 53°12N 46°40E **18** D8
Kuzomen Russia 66°22N 36°50E **18** A6
Kvænangen Norway 70°5N 21°15E **8** A19
Kvaløya Norway 69°40N 18°30E **8** B18
Kvarner Croatia 44°50N 14°10E **16** F8
Kvarnerič Croatia 44°43N 14°37E **16** F8
Kwabhaca S. Africa 30°51S 29°0E **57** E4
Kwajalein Marshall Is. 9°5N 167°20E **64** G8
Kwakhanai Botswana 21°39S 21°16E **56** C3
Kwakoegron Suriname 5°12N 55°25W **93** B7
Kwale Kenya 4°15S 39°31E **54** C4
KwaMashu S. Africa 29°45S 30°58E **57** D5
Kwando → Africa 18°27S 23°32E **56** B3
Kwangchow = Guangzhou
China 23°6N 113°13E **33** D6
Kwango →
Dem. Rep. of the Congo 3°14S 17°22E **52** E3
Kwangsi-Chuang = Guangxi
Zhuangzu Zizhiqu □
China 24°0N 109°0E **33** D5
Kwangtung = Guangdong □
China 23°0N 113°0E **33** D6
Kwataboahegan →
Canada 51°9N 80°50W **72** B3
Kwatisore Indonesia 3°18S 134°50E **37** E8
KwaZulu Natal □ S. Africa 29°0S 30°0E **57** D5
Kweichow = Guizhou □
China 27°0N 107°0E **32** D5
Kwekwe Zimbabwe 18°58S 29°48E **55** F2
Kwidzyn Poland 53°44N 18°55E **17** B10
Kwilu →
Dem. Rep. of the Congo 3°22S 17°22E **52** E3
Kwinana Australia 32°15S 115°47E **61** F2
Kwoka Indonesia 0°31S 132°27E **37** E8
Kwun Tong China 22°19N 114°13E **33** G11
Kyabra Cr. → Australia 25°36S 142°55E **63** D3
Kyabram Australia 36°19S 145°4E **63** F4
Kyaikto Burma 17°20N 97°3E **38** D1
Kyakhta Russia 50°30N 106°25E **29** D11
Kyambura ◌ Uganda 0°7S 30°9E **54** C3
Kyaukpadaung Burma 20°52N 95°8E **41** J19
Kyaukpyu Burma 19°28N 93°30E **41** K18
Kyaukse Burma 21°36N 96°10E **41** J20
Kyburz U.S.A. 38°47N 120°18W **78** G6
Kyelang India 32°35N 77°2E **42** C7
Kyenjojo Uganda 0°40N 30°37E **54** B3
Kyle Canada 50°50N 108°2W **71** C7
Kyle Dam Zimbabwe 20°15S 31°0E **55** G3
Kyle of Lochalsh U.K. 57°17N 5°44W **11** D3
Kymijoki → Finland 60°30N 26°55E **8** F22
Kymmene älv = Kymijoki →
Finland 60°30N 26°55E **8** F22
Kyneton Australia 37°10S 144°29E **63** F3
Kynuna Australia 21°37S 141°55E **62** C3
Kyō-ga-Saki Japan 35°45N 135°15E **31** G7
Kyogle Australia 28°40S 153°0E **63** D5
Kyŏngju = Gyeongju
S. Korea 35°51N 129°14E **35** G15
Kyongpyaw Burma 17°12N 95°10E **41** L19
Kyŏngsŏng N. Korea 41°35N 129°36E **35** D15
Kyōto Japan 35°0N 135°45E **31** G7
Kyōto □ Japan 35°15N 135°45E **31** G7
Kyparissovouno Cyprus 35°19N 33°10E **25** D12
Kyperounda Cyprus 34°56N 32°58E **25** E11
Kyrenia = Girne Cyprus 35°20N 33°19E **25** D12
Kyrenia Cyprus 35°20N 33°20E **25** D12
Kyrgyzstan ■ Asia 42°0N 75°0E **28** E8
Kyro älv = Kyrönjoki →
Finland 63°14N 21°45E **8** E19
Kyrönjoki → Finland 63°14N 21°45E **8** E19

Kystatyam *Russia* 67°20N 123°10E **29 C13**
Kythira *Greece* 36°8N 23°0E **23 F10**
Kythréa *Cyprus* 35°15N 33°29E **25 D12**
Kyunhla *Burma* 23°25N 95°15E **41 H19**
Kyuquot Sound *Canada* 50°2N 127°22W **70 D3**
Kyūshū *Japan* 33°0N 131°0E **31 H5**
Kyūshū □ *Japan* 33°0N 131°0E **31 H5**
Kyūshū-Palau Ridge
  Pac. Oc. 20°0N 136°0E **64 E5**
Kyūshū-Sanchi *Japan* 32°35N 131°17E **31 H5**
Kyustendil *Bulgaria* 42°16N 22°41E **23 C10**
Kyusyur *Russia* 70°19N 127°30E **29 B13**
Kyyiv *Ukraine* 50°30N 30°28E **17 C16**
Kyyivske Vdskh.
  Ukraine 51°0N 30°25E **17 C16**
Kyzyl *Russia* 51°50N 94°30E **32 A4**
Kyzyl Kum *Uzbekistan* 42°30N 65°0E **28 E7**
Kyzyl Kyya *Kyrgyzstan* 40°16N 72°8E **28 E8**
Kyzyl Orda = Qyzylorda
  Kazakhstan 44°48N 65°28E **28 E7**

L

La Alcarria *Spain* 40°31N 2°45W **21 B4**
La Amistad △ *Cent. Amer.* 9°28N 83°18W **88 E3**
La Asunción *Venezuela* 11°2N 63°53W **92 A6**
La Baie *Canada* 48°19N 70°53W **73 C5**
La Banda *Argentina* 27°45S 64°10W **94 B3**
La Barca *Mexico* 20°17N 102°34W **86 C4**
La Barge *U.S.A.* 42°16N 110°12W **76 E8**
La Barra *Nic.* 12°54N 83°33W **88 D3**
La Belle *U.S.A.* 26°46N 81°26W **85 H14**
La Biche → *Canada* 59°57N 123°50W **70 B4**
La Biche, L. *Canada* 54°50N 112°3W **70 C6**
La Brea *Trin. & Tob.* 10°15N 61°37W **93 K15**
La Calera *Chile* 32°50S 71°10W **94 C1**
La Campana △ *Chile* 32°58S 71°14W **94 C1**
La Canal = Sa Canal
  Spain 38°51N 1°23E **24 C7**
La Carlota *Argentina* 33°30S 63°20W **94 C3**
La Ceiba *Honduras* 15°40N 86°50W **88 C2**
La Chaux-de-Fonds *Switz.* 47°7N 6°50E **20 C7**
La Chorrera *Panama* 8°53N 79°47W **88 E4**
La Cocha *Argentina* 27°50S 65°40W **94 B2**
La Concepción *Panama* 8°31N 82°37W **88 E3**
La Concordia *Mexico* 16°8N 92°38W **87 D6**
La Coruña = A Coruña
  Spain 43°20N 8°25W **21 A1**
La Crescent *U.S.A.* 43°50N 91°18W **80 D8**
La Crete *Canada* 58°11N 116°24W **70 B5**
La Crosse *Kans., U.S.A.* 38°32N 99°18W **80 F4**
La Crosse *Wis., U.S.A.* 43°48N 91°15W **80 D8**
La Cruz *Costa Rica* 11°4N 85°39W **88 D2**
La Cruz *Mexico* 23°55N 106°54W **86 C3**
La Désirade *Guadeloupe* 16°18N 61°3W **88 b**
La Digue *Seychelles* 4°20S 55°51E **53 b**
La Esperanza *Cuba* 22°46N 83°44W **88 B3**
La Esperanza *Honduras* 14°15N 88°10W **88 D2**
La Estrada = A Estrada
  Spain 42°43N 8°27W **21 A1**
La Fayette *U.S.A.* 34°42N 85°17W **85 D12**
La Fé *Cuba* 22°2N 84°15W **88 B3**
La Follette *U.S.A.* 36°23N 84°7W **85 C12**
La Grande *U.S.A.* 45°20N 118°5W **76 D4**
La Grande → *Canada* 53°50N 79°0W **72 B5**
La Grande 3, Rés.
  Canada 53°40N 75°10W **72 B5**
La Grande 4, Rés. *Canada* 54°0N 73°15W **72 B5**
La Grange *Calif., U.S.A.* 37°42N 120°27W **78 H6**
La Grange *Ga., U.S.A.* 33°2N 85°2W **85 E12**
La Grange *Ky., U.S.A.* 38°24N 85°22W **81 F11**
La Grange *Tex., U.S.A.* 29°54N 96°52W **84 G6**
La Guaira *Venezuela* 10°36N 66°56W **92 A5**
La Habana *Cuba* 23°8N 82°22W **88 B3**
La Independencia *Mexico* 16°15N 92°1W **87 D6**
La Isabela *Dom. Rep.* 19°58N 71°2W **89 C5**
La Junta *U.S.A.* 37°59N 103°33W **76 H12**
La Laguna *Canary Is.* 28°28N 16°18W **24 F3**
La Libertad = Puerto Libertad
  Mexico 29°55N 112°43W **86 B2**
La Libertad *Guatemala* 16°47N 90°7W **88 C1**
La Ligua *Chile* 32°30S 71°16W **94 C1**
La Línea de la Concepción
  Spain 36°15N 5°23W **21 D3**
La Loche *Canada* 56°29N 109°26W **71 B7**
La Louvière *Belgium* 50°27N 4°10E **15 D4**
La Lune *Trin. & Tob.* 10°3N 61°22W **93 K15**
La Malbaie *Canada* 47°40N 70°10W **73 C5**
La Mancha *Spain* 39°10N 2°54W **21 C4**
La Martre, L. *Canada* 63°15N 117°55W **70 A5**
La Mesa *Mexico* 32°30N 116°57W **79 N10**
La Mesa *U.S.A.* 32°46N 117°1W **79 N9**
La Mesilla *U.S.A.* 32°16N 106°48W **77 K10**
La Misión *Mexico* 32°6N 116°53W **86 A1**
La Moure *U.S.A.* 46°21N 98°18W **80 B4**
La Negra *Chile* 23°46S 70°18W **94 A1**
La Oliva *Canary Is.* 28°36N 13°57W **24 F6**
La Orotava *Canary Is.* 28°22N 16°32W **24 F3**
La Oroya *Peru* 11°32S 75°54W **92 F3**
La Palma *Canary Is.* 28°40N 17°50W **24 F2**
La Palma *Panama* 8°15N 78°0W **88 E4**
La Palma del Condado
  Spain 37°21N 6°38W **21 D2**
La Paloma *Chile* 30°35S 71°0W **94 C1**
La Pampa □ *Argentina* 36°50S 66°0W **94 D2**
La Paragua *Venezuela* 6°50N 63°20W **92 B6**
La Paz *Entre Ríos,*
  Argentina 30°50S 59°45W **94 C4**
La Paz *San Luis,*
  Argentina 33°30S 67°20W **94 C2**
La Paz *Bolivia* 16°20S 68°10W **92 G5**
La Paz *Honduras* 14°20N 87°47W **88 D2**
La Paz *Mexico* 24°10N 110°18W **86 C2**
La Paz Centro *Nic.* 12°20N 86°41W **88 D2**
La Pedrera *Colombia* 1°18S 69°43W **92 D5**
La Pérade *Canada* 46°35N 72°12W **73 C5**
La Perla *Mexico* 28°18N 104°32W **86 B4**

La Perouse Str. *Asia* 45°40N 142°0E **30 B11**
La Pesca *Mexico* 23°46N 97°47W **87 C5**
La Piedad *Mexico* 20°21N 102°0W **86 C4**
La Pine *U.S.A.* 43°40N 121°30W **76 E3**
La Plata *Argentina* 35°0S 57°55W **94 C4**
La Pocatière *Canada* 47°22N 70°2W **73 C5**
La Porte *U.S.A.* 29°40N 95°1W **84 G7**
La Purísima *Mexico* 26°10N 112°4W **86 B2**
La Push *U.S.A.* 47°55N 124°38W **78 C2**
La Quiaca *Argentina* 22°5S 65°35W **94 A2**
La Restinga *Canary Is.* 27°38N 17°59W **24 G2**
La Rioja *Argentina* 29°20S 67°0W **94 B2**
La Rioja □ *Argentina* 29°30S 67°0W **94 B2**
La Rioja □ *Spain* 42°20N 2°20W **21 A4**
La Robla *Spain* 42°50N 5°41W **21 A3**
La Roche-en-Ardenne
  Belgium 50°11N 5°35E **15 D5**
La Roche-sur-Yon *France* 46°40N 1°25W **20 C3**
La Rochelle *France* 46°10N 1°9W **20 C3**
La Roda *Spain* 39°13N 2°15W **21 C4**
La Romaine *Canada* 50°13N 60°40W **73 B7**
La Romana *Dom. Rep.* 18°27N 68°57W **89 C6**
La Ronge *Canada* 55°5N 105°20W **71 B7**
La Rumorosa *Mexico* 32°34N 116°6W **79 N10**
La Sabina = Sa Savina
  Spain 38°44N 1°25E **24 C7**
La Salle *U.S.A.* 41°20N 89°6W **80 E9**
La Santa *Canary Is.* 29°5N 13°40W **24 E6**
La Sarre *Canada* 48°45N 79°15W **72 C4**
La Scie *Canada* 49°57N 55°36W **73 C8**
La Selva Beach *U.S.A.* 36°56N 121°51W **78 J5**
La Serena *Chile* 29°55S 71°10W **94 B1**
La Seu d'Urgell *Spain* 42°22N 1°23E **21 A6**
La Seyne-sur-Mer *France* 43°7N 5°52E **20 E6**
La Soufrière *St. Vincent* 13°20N 61°11W **89 D7**
La Spézia *Italy* 44°7N 9°50E **20 D8**
La Tagua *Colombia* 0°3N 74°40W **92 C4**
La Tortuga *Venezuela* 11°0N 65°22W **89 D6**
La Trinité *Martinique* 14°43N 60°58W **88 c**
La Tuque *Canada* 47°30N 72°50W **72 C5**
La Unión *Chile* 40°10S 73°0W **96 E2**
La Unión *El Salv.* 13°20N 87°50W **88 D2**
La Unión *Mexico* 17°58N 101°49W **86 D4**
La Urbana *Venezuela* 7°8N 66°56W **92 B5**
La Vache Pt.
  Trin. & Tob. 10°47N 61°28W **93 K15**
La Vall d'Uixó *Spain* 39°49N 0°15W **21 C5**
La Vega *Dom. Rep.* 19°20N 70°30W **89 C5**
La Vela de Coro
  Venezuela 11°27N 69°34W **92 A5**
La Venta *Mexico* 18°5N 94°3W **87 D6**
La Vergne *U.S.A.* 36°1N 86°35W **85 C11**
La Villa Joiosa = Villajoyosa
  Spain 38°30N 0°12W **21 C5**
Laascaanood = Las Anod
  Somali Rep. 8°26N 47°19E **47 F4**
Labasa *Fiji* 16°30S 179°27E **59 a**
Labdah = Leptis Magna
  Libya 32°40N 14°12E **51 B8**
Labe = Elbe → *Europe* 53°50N 9°0E **16 B5**
Labé *Guinea* 11°24N 12°16W **50 F3**
Laberge, L. *Canada* 61°11N 135°12W **70 A1**
Labinsk *Russia* 44°40N 40°48E **19 F7**
Labis *Malaysia* 2°22N 103°2E **39 L4**
Laborie *St. Lucia* 13°45N 61°2W **89 f**
Laboulaye *Argentina* 34°10S 63°30W **94 C3**
Labrador *Canada* 53°20N 61°0W **73 B7**
Labrador City *Canada* 52°57N 66°55W **73 B6**
Labrador Sea *Atl. Oc.* 57°0N 54°0W **69 F21**
Lábrea *Brazil* 7°15S 64°51W **92 E6**
Labuan *Malaysia* 5°20N 115°14E **36 C5**
Labuan, Pulau *Malaysia* 5°21N 115°13E **36 C5**
Labuha *Indonesia* 0°30S 127°30E **37 E7**
Labuhan *Indonesia* 6°22S 105°50E **37 G11**
Labuhanbajo *Indonesia* 8°28S 119°54E **37 F6**
Labuhanbilik *Indonesia* 2°31N 100°10E **39 L3**
Labuk, Telok *Malaysia* 6°10N 117°50E **36 C5**
Labyrinth, L. *Australia* 30°40S 135°11E **63 E2**
Labytnangi *Russia* 66°39N 66°21E **18 A12**
Lac-Bouchette *Canada* 48°16N 72°11W **73 C5**
Lac Édouard *Canada* 47°40N 72°16W **72 C5**
Lac La Biche *Canada* 54°45N 111°58W **70 C6**
Lac la Martre = Wha Ti
  Canada 63°8N 117°16W **68 E8**
Lac La Ronge △ *Canada* 55°9N 104°41W **71 B7**
Lac-Mégantic *Canada* 45°35N 70°53W **73 C5**
Lac Thien *Vietnam* 12°25N 108°11E **38 F7**
Lacanau *France* 44°58N 1°5W **20 D3**
Lacantún → *Mexico* 16°36N 90°39W **87 D6**
Laccadive Is. = Lakshadweep Is.
  India 10°0N 72°30E **3 D13**
Lacepede B. *Australia* 36°40S 139°40E **63 F2**
Lacepede Is. *Australia* 16°55S 122°0E **60 C3**
Lacerdónia *Mozam.* 18°3S 35°35E **55 F4**
Lacey *U.S.A.* 47°7N 122°49W **78 C4**
Lachania *Greece* 35°58N 27°54E **25 D9**
Lachhmangarh *India* 27°50N 75°4E **42 F6**
Lachine *Canada* 45°26N 73°42W **72 C5**
Lachlan → *Australia* 34°22S 143°55E **63 E3**
Lachute *Canada* 45°39N 74°21W **72 C5**
Lackagh Hills *Ireland* 54°16N 8°10W **10 B3**
Lackawanna *U.S.A.* 42°50N 78°50W **82 D6**
Lackawaxen *U.S.A.* 41°29N 74°59W **83 E10**
Lacolle *Canada* 45°5N 73°22W **83 A11**
Lacona *U.S.A.* 43°32N 71°28W **83 C13**
Laconia *U.S.A.* 43°32N 71°28W **83 C13**
Ladakh Ra. *India* 34°0N 78°0E **43 C8**
Ladismith *S. Africa* 33°28S 21°15E **56 E3**
Lādīz *Iran* 28°55N 61°15E **45 D9**
Ladnun *India* 27°38N 74°25E **42 F6**
Ladoga, L. = Ladozhskoye Ozero
  Russia 61°15N 30°30E **8 F24**
Ladozhskoye Ozero
  Russia 61°15N 30°30E **8 F24**
Lady Elliott I. *Australia* 24°7S 152°42E **62 C5**
Lady Grey *S. Africa* 30°43S 27°13E **56 E4**
Ladybrand *S. Africa* 29°9S 27°29E **56 D4**

Ladysmith *Canada* 49°0N 123°49W **78 B3**
Ladysmith *S. Africa* 28°32S 29°46E **57 D4**
Ladysmith *U.S.A.* 45°28N 91°12W **80 C8**
Lae *Papua N. G.* 6°40S 147°2E **58 B7**
Laem Hin Khom *Thailand* 9°25N 99°56E **39 b**
Laem Khat *Thailand* 8°6N 98°26E **39 a**
Laem Nga *Thailand* 7°55N 98°27E **39 a**
Laem Ngop *Thailand* 12°10N 102°26E **39 F4**
Laem Phan Wa *Thailand* 7°47N 98°25E **39 a**
Laem Pho *Thailand* 6°55N 101°19E **39 J3**
Laem Phrom Thep *Thailand* 7°45N 98°19E **39 a**
Laem Riang *Thailand* 8°7N 98°27E **39 a**
Laem Sam Rong *Thailand* 9°35N 100°4E **39 b**
Laem Son *Thailand* 7°59N 98°18E **39 a**
Laem Yamu *Thailand* 7°59N 98°26E **39 a**
Laerma *Greece* 36°9N 27°57E **25 C9**
Lafayette *Ind., U.S.A.* 40°25N 86°54W **80 E10**
Lafayette *La., U.S.A.* 30°14N 92°1W **84 F8**
Lafayette *Tenn., U.S.A.* 36°31N 86°2W **85 C11**
Laferte → *Canada* 61°53N 117°44W **70 A5**
Lafia *Nigeria* 8°30N 8°34E **50 G7**
Lafleche *Canada* 49°45N 106°40W **71 D7**
Lagan → *U.S.A.* 54°36N 5°55W **10 B6**
Lagarfljót → *Iceland* 65°40N 14°18W **8 D6**
Lagdo, L. de *Cameroon* 8°40N 14°0E **51 G8**
Lågen → *Oppland, Norway* 61°8N 10°25E **8 F14**
Lågen → *Vestfold, Norway* 59°3N 10°3E **9 G14**
Lages *Brazil* 27°48S 50°20W **95 B5**
Laghouat *Algeria* 33°50N 2°59E **50 B6**
Lagoa do Peixe △ *Brazil* 31°12S 50°55W **95 C5**
Lagoa Vermelha *Brazil* 28°13S 51°32W **95 B5**
Lagonoy G. *Phil.* 13°35N 123°50E **37 B6**
Lagos *Nigeria* 6°25N 3°27E **50 G6**
Lagos *Portugal* 37°5N 8°41W **21 D1**
Lagos de Moreno
  Mexico 21°21N 101°55W **86 C4**
Lagrange = Bidyadanga
  Australia 18°45S 121°43E **60 C3**
Lagrange B. *Australia* 18°38S 121°42E **60 C3**
Laguna *Brazil* 28°30S 48°50W **95 B6**
Laguna *U.S.A.* 35°2N 107°25W **77 J10**
Laguna, Sa. de la
  Mexico 23°35N 109°55W **86 C3**
Laguna Beach *U.S.A.* 33°33N 117°47W **79 M9**
Laguna de la Restinga △
  Venezuela 10°58N 64°0W **89 D6**
Laguna de Lachuá △
  Guatemala 15°55N 90°40W **88 C1**
Laguna del Laja △ *Chile* 37°27S 71°20W **94 D1**
Laguna del Tigre △
  Guatemala 17°32N 90°56W **88 C1**
Laguna Limpia
  Argentina 26°32S 59°45W **94 B4**
Lagunas *Chile* 21°0S 69°45W **94 A2**
Lagunas *Peru* 5°10S 75°35W **92 E3**
Lagunas de Chacahua △
  Mexico 16°0N 97°43W **87 D5**
Lagunas de Montebello △
  Mexico 16°4N 91°42W **87 D6**
Lahad Datu *Malaysia* 5°0N 118°20E **37 D5**
Lahad Datu, Telok
  Malaysia 4°50N 118°20E **37 D5**
Lahan Sai *Thailand* 14°25N 102°52E **38 E4**
Lahanam *Laos* 16°16N 105°16E **38 D5**
Lahar *India* 26°12N 78°57E **43 F8**
Laharpur *India* 27°43N 80°56E **43 F9**
Lahat *Indonesia* 3°45S 103°30E **36 E2**
Lahewa *Indonesia* 1°22N 97°12E **36 D1**
Lāhījān *Iran* 37°10N 50°6E **45 B6**
Lahn → *Germany* 50°19N 7°37E **16 C4**
Laholm *Sweden* 56°30N 13°2E **9 H15**
Lahore *Pakistan* 31°32N 74°22E **42 D6**
Lahri *Pakistan* 29°11N 68°13E **42 E3**
Lāhrūd *Iran* 38°30N 47°52E **44 B5**
Lahti *Finland* 60°58N 25°40E **8 F21**
Lahtis = Lahti *Finland* 60°58N 25°40E **8 F21**
Laï *Chad* 9°25N 16°18E **51 G9**
Lai Chau *Vietnam* 22°5N 103°3E **38 A4**
Laila = Layla *Si. Arabia* 22°10N 46°40E **47 C4**
Laingsburg *S. Africa* 33°9S 20°52E **56 E3**
Lainioälven → *Sweden* 67°35N 22°40E **8 C20**
Lairg *U.K.* 58°2N 4°24W **11 C4**
Laisamis *Kenya* 1°36N 37°48E **54 B4**
Laishui *China* 39°23N 115°45E **34 E8**
Laiwu *China* 36°15N 117°40E **35 F9**
Laixi *China* 36°50N 120°31E **35 F11**
Laiyang *China* 36°59N 120°45E **35 F11**
Laiyuan *China* 39°20N 114°40E **34 E8**
Laizhou *China* 37°8N 119°57E **35 F10**
Laizhou Wan *China* 37°30N 119°30E **35 F10**
Laja → *Mexico* 20°55N 100°46W **86 C4**
Lajamanu *Australia* 18°23S 130°38E **60 C5**
Lak Sao *Laos* 18°11N 104°59E **38 C5**
Lakaband *Pakistan* 31°2N 69°15E **42 D3**
Lake *U.S.A.* 44°33N 110°24W **76 D8**
Lake Alpine *U.S.A.* 38°29N 120°0W **78 G7**
Lake Andes *U.S.A.* 43°9N 98°32W **80 D4**
Lake Arthur *U.S.A.* 30°5N 92°41W **84 F8**
Lake Bindegolly △
  Australia 28°0S 144°12E **63 D3**
Lake Cargelligo
  Australia 33°15S 146°22E **63 E4**
Lake Charles *U.S.A.* 30°14N 93°13W **84 F8**
Lake City *Colo., U.S.A.* 38°2N 107°19W **76 G10**
Lake City *Fla., U.S.A.* 30°11N 82°38W **85 F13**
Lake City *Mich., U.S.A.* 44°20N 85°13W **81 C11**
Lake City *Minn., U.S.A.* 44°27N 92°16W **80 C7**
Lake City *Pa., U.S.A.* 42°1N 80°21W **82 D4**
Lake City *S.C., U.S.A.* 33°52N 79°45W **85 E15**
Lake Cowichan *Canada* 48°49N 124°3W **78 D4**
Lake District △ *U.K.* 54°30N 3°21W **12 C4**
Lake Elsinore *U.S.A.* 33°38N 117°20W **79 M9**
Lake Eyre △ *Australia* 28°40S 137°31E **63 D2**
Lake Gairdner △
  Australia 31°41S 135°51E **63 E2**
Lake George *U.S.A.* 43°26N 73°43W **83 C11**
Lake Grace *Australia* 33°7S 118°28E **61 F2**
Lake Gregory ○
  Australia 20°12S 127°27E **60 D4**

Lake Harbour = Kimmirut
  Canada 62°50N 69°50W **69 E18**
Lake Havasu City
  U.S.A. 34°27N 114°22W **79 L12**
Lake Hughes *U.S.A.* 34°41N 118°26W **79 L8**
Lake Isabella *U.S.A.* 35°38N 118°28W **79 K8**
Lake Jackson *U.S.A.* 29°3N 95°27W **84 G7**
Lake King *Australia* 33°5S 119°45E **61 F2**
Lake Lenore *Canada* 52°24N 104°59W **71 C8**
Lake Louise *Canada* 51°30N 116°10W **70 C5**
Lake Mackay ○
  Australia 21°48S 129°46E **60 D4**
Lake Mburo △ *Uganda* 0°33S 30°56E **54 C3**
Lake Mead △ *U.S.A.* 36°30N 114°22W **79 K12**
Lake Meredith ○
  U.S.A. 35°50N 101°50W **84 D4**
Lake Mills *U.S.A.* 43°25N 93°32W **80 D7**
Lake Nakuru △ *Kenya* 0°21S 36°8E **54 C4**
Lake Placid *U.S.A.* 44°17N 73°59W **83 B11**
Lake Pleasant *U.S.A.* 43°28N 74°25W **83 C10**
Lake Providence *U.S.A.* 32°48N 91°10W **84 E9**
Lake Roosevelt ○
  U.S.A. 48°5N 118°14W **76 B4**
Lake St. Peter *Canada* 45°18N 78°2W **82 A6**
Lake Superior ○ *Canada* 47°45N 84°45W **72 C3**
Lake Torrens △
  Australia 30°55S 137°40E **63 E2**
Lake Village *U.S.A.* 33°20N 91°17W **84 E9**
Lake Wales *U.S.A.* 27°54N 81°35W **85 H14**
Lake Worth *U.S.A.* 26°37N 80°3W **85 H14**
Lakeba *Fiji* 18°13S 178°47W **59 a**
Lakeba Passage *Fiji* 18°0S 178°45W **59 a**
Lakefield *Canada* 44°25N 78°16W **82 B6**
Lakefield △ *Australia* 15°24S 144°26E **62 B3**
Lakehurst *U.S.A.* 40°1N 74°19W **83 F10**
Lakeland *Australia* 15°49S 144°57E **62 B3**
Lakeland *U.S.A.* 28°3N 81°57W **85 G14**
Lakemba = Lakeba *Fiji* 18°13S 178°47W **59 a**
Lakeport *Calif., U.S.A.* 39°3N 122°55W **78 F4**
Lakeport *Mich., U.S.A.* 43°7N 82°30W **82 C2**
Lakes Entrance *Australia* 37°50S 148°0E **63 F4**
Lakeside *Calif., U.S.A.* 32°52N 116°55W **79 N10**
Lakeside *Nebr., U.S.A.* 42°3N 102°26W **80 D2**
Lakeview *U.S.A.* 42°11N 120°21W **76 E3**
Lakeville *U.S.A.* 44°39N 93°14W **80 C7**
Lakewood *Colo., U.S.A.* 39°42N 105°4W **76 G11**
Lakewood *N.J., U.S.A.* 40°6N 74°13W **83 F10**
Lakewood *N.Y., U.S.A.* 42°6N 79°19W **82 D5**
Lakewood *Ohio, U.S.A.* 41°28N 81°47W **82 E3**
Lakewood *Wash.,*
  U.S.A. 47°11N 122°32W **78 C4**
Lakha *India* 26°9N 70°54E **42 F4**
Lakhimpur *India* 27°57N 80°46E **43 F9**
Lakhisarai *India* 25°11N 86°5E **43 G12**
Lakhnau = Lucknow
  India 26°50N 81°0E **43 F9**
Lakhonpheng *Laos* 15°54N 105°34E **38 E5**
Lakhpat *India* 23°48N 68°47E **42 H3**
Lakin *U.S.A.* 37°57N 101°15W **80 G3**
Lakitusaki → *Canada* 54°21N 82°25W **72 B3**
Lakki *Greece* 35°24N 23°57E **25 D5**
Lakki *Pakistan* 32°36N 70°55E **42 C4**
Lakonikos Kolpos
  Greece 36°40N 22°40E **23 F10**
Lakor *Indonesia* 8°15S 128°17E **37 F7**
Lakota *Ivory C.* 5°50N 5°30W **50 G4**
Lakota *U.S.A.* 48°2N 98°21W **80 A4**
Laksar *India* 29°46N 78°3E **42 E8**
Laksefjorden *Norway* 70°45N 26°50E **8 A22**
Lakselv *Norway* 70°2N 25°0E **8 A21**
Lakshadweep Is. *India* 10°0N 72°30E **3 D13**
Lakshmanpur *India* 22°58N 83°3E **43 H10**
Lakshmikantapur *India* 22°5N 88°20E **43 H13**
Lala Musa *Pakistan* 32°40N 73°57E **42 C5**
Lalaghat *India* 24°30N 92°40E **41 B18**
Lalago *Tanzania* 3°28S 33°58E **54 C3**
Lalapanzi *Zimbabwe* 19°20S 30°15E **55 F3**
Lalganj *India* 25°52N 85°13E **43 G11**
Lalgola *India* 24°25N 88°15E **43 G13**
Lālī *Iran* 32°21N 49°6E **45 C6**
Lalibela *Ethiopia* 12°3N 39°0E **47 E2**
Lalin *China* 45°12N 127°0E **35 B14**
Lalín *Spain* 42°40N 8°5W **21 A1**
Lalin He → *China* 45°32N 125°40E **35 B13**
Lalitapur *Nepal* 27°40N 85°20E **43 F11**
Lalitpur *India* 24°42N 78°28E **43 G8**
Lalkua *India* 29°5N 79°31E **43 E8**
Lalsot *India* 26°34N 76°20E **42 F7**
Lam Pao Res. *Thailand* 16°50N 103°15E **38 D4**
Lama Kara *Togo* 9°30N 1°15E **50 G6**
Lamae *Thailand* 9°51N 99°5E **39 H2**
Lamaing *Burma* 15°25N 97°53E **38 E1**
Lamar *Colo., U.S.A.* 38°5N 102°37W **76 G12**
Lamar *Mo., U.S.A.* 37°30N 94°16W **80 G6**
Lamas *Peru* 6°28S 76°31W **92 E3**
Lamayuru *India* 34°25N 76°56E **43 B7**
Lambaréné *Gabon* 0°41S 10°12E **52 E2**
Lambasa = Labasa *Fiji* 16°30S 179°27E **59 a**
Lambay I. *Ireland* 53°29N 6°1W **10 C5**
Lambert's Bay *S. Africa* 32°5S 18°17E **56 E2**
Lambeth *Canada* 42°54N 81°18W **82 D3**
Lambomakondro
  Madag. 22°41S 44°44E **57 C7**
Lame Deer *U.S.A.* 45°37N 106°40W **76 D10**
Lamego *Portugal* 41°5N 7°52W **21 B2**
Lamèque *Canada* 47°45N 64°38W **73 C7**
Lameroo *Australia* 35°19S 140°33E **63 F3**
Lamesa *U.S.A.* 32°44N 101°58W **84 E4**
Lamia *Greece* 38°55N 22°26E **23 E10**
Lamington △ *Australia* 28°13S 153°12E **63 D5**
Lamma I. *China* 22°12N 114°7E **33 G11**
Lamon B. *Phil.* 14°30N 122°20E **37 B6**
Lamont *Canada* 53°46N 112°50W **70 C6**
Lamont *Calif., U.S.A.* 35°15N 118°55W **79 K8**
Lamont *Wyo., U.S.A.* 42°13N 107°29W **76 E10**

Lampa *Peru* 15°22S 70°22W **92 G4**
Lampang *Thailand* 18°16N 99°32E **38 C2**
Lampasas *U.S.A.* 31°4N 98°11W **84 F5**
Lampazos de Naranjo
  Mexico 27°1N 100°31W **86 B4**
Lampedusa *Medit. S.* 35°36N 12°40E **22 G5**
Lampeter *U.K.* 52°7N 4°4W **13 E3**
Lampione *Medit. S.* 35°33N 12°20E **22 G5**
Lampman *Canada* 49°25N 102°50W **71 D8**
Lampung □ *Indonesia* 5°30S 104°30E **36 F2**
Lamta *India* 22°8N 80°7E **43 H9**
Lamu *Kenya* 2°16S 40°55E **54 C5**
Lamy *U.S.A.* 35°29N 105°53W **77 J11**
Lan Xian *China* 38°15N 111°35E **34 E6**
Lāna'i *U.S.A.* 20°50N 156°55W **75 L8**
Lanak La *China* 34°27N 79°32E **43 B8**
Lanak'o Shank'ou = Lanak La
  China 34°27N 79°32E **43 B8**
Lanark *Canada* 45°1N 76°22W **83 A8**
Lanark *U.K.* 55°40N 3°47W **11 F5**
Lanbi Kyun *Burma* 10°50N 98°20E **39 G2**
Lancang Jiang →
  China 21°40N 101°10E **32 D5**
Lancashire □ *U.K.* 53°50N 2°48W **12 D5**
Lancaster *Canada* 45°10N 74°30W **83 A10**
Lancaster *U.K.* 54°3N 2°48W **12 C5**
Lancaster *Calif., U.S.A.* 34°42N 118°8W **79 L8**
Lancaster *Ky., U.S.A.* 37°37N 84°35W **81 G11**
Lancaster *N.H., U.S.A.* 44°29N 71°34W **83 B13**
Lancaster *Ohio, U.S.A.* 39°43N 82°36W **81 F12**
Lancaster *Pa., U.S.A.* 40°2N 76°19W **83 F8**
Lancaster *S.C., U.S.A.* 34°43N 80°46W **85 D14**
Lancaster *Wis., U.S.A.* 42°51N 90°43W **80 D8**
Lancaster Sd. *Canada* 74°13N 84°0W **69 C15**
Lancelin *Australia* 31°0S 115°18E **61 F2**
Lanchow = Lanzhou
  China 36°1N 103°52E **34 F2**
Lanciano *Italy* 42°14N 14°23E **22 C6**
Lancun *China* 36°25N 120°10E **35 F11**
Land Between the Lakes ○
  U.S.A. 36°25N 88°0W **85 C11**
Landeck *Austria* 47°9N 10°34E **16 E6**
Lander *U.S.A.* 42°50N 108°44W **76 E9**
Lander → *Australia* 22°0S 132°0E **60 D5**
Landes *France* 44°0N 1°0W **20 D3**
Landi Kotal *Pakistan* 34°7N 71°6E **42 B4**
Landisburg *U.S.A.* 40°21N 77°19W **82 F7**
Landmannalaugar *Iceland* 63°59N 19°4W **8 E4**
Land's End *U.K.* 50°4N 5°44W **13 G2**
Landsborough Cr. →
  Australia 22°28S 144°35E **62 C3**
Landshut *Germany* 48°34N 12°8E **16 D7**
Lanesboro *U.S.A.* 41°57N 75°34W **83 E9**
Lanett *U.S.A.* 32°52N 85°12W **85 E12**
Lang Shan *China* 41°0N 106°30E **34 D4**
Lang Son *Vietnam* 21°52N 106°42E **38 B6**
Lang Suan *Thailand* 9°57N 99°4E **39 H2**
La'nga Co *China* 30°45N 81°15E **43 D9**
Langar *Iran* 35°23N 60°25E **45 C9**
Langara I. *Canada* 54°14N 133°1W **70 C2**
Langarūd *Iran* 37°11N 50°8E **45 B6**
Langdon *U.S.A.* 48°45N 98°22W **80 A4**
Langeberg *S. Africa* 33°55S 21°0E **56 E3**
Langeberg *S. Africa* 28°15S 22°33E **56 D3**
Langeland *Denmark* 54°56N 10°48E **9 J14**
Langenburg *Canada* 50°51N 101°43W **71 C8**
Langholm *U.K.* 55°9N 3°0W **11 F5**
Langjökull *Iceland* 64°39N 20°12W **8 D3**
Langkawi, Pulau
  Malaysia 6°25N 99°45E **39 J2**
Langklip *S. Africa* 28°12S 20°20E **56 D3**
Langkon *Malaysia* 6°30N 116°40E **36 C5**
Langley *Canada* 49°7N 122°39W **78 A4**
Langøya *Norway* 68°45N 14°50E **8 B16**
Langreo *Spain* 43°18N 5°40W **21 A3**
Langres *France* 47°52N 5°20E **20 C6**
Langres, Plateau de *France* 47°45N 5°3E **20 C6**
Langsa *Indonesia* 4°30N 97°57E **36 D1**
Langtang △ *Nepal* 28°0N 85°30E **43 E11**
Langtry *U.S.A.* 29°49N 101°34W **84 G4**
Langu *Thailand* 6°53N 99°47E **39 J2**
Languedoc *France* 43°58N 3°55E **20 E5**
Langwang *China* 22°38N 113°27E **33 F9**
Langxiangzhen *China* 39°43N 116°8E **34 E9**
Lanigan *Canada* 51°51N 105°2W **71 C7**
Lankao *China* 34°48N 114°50E **34 G8**
Länkäran *Azerbaijan* 38°48N 48°52E **45 B6**
Lannion *France* 48°46N 3°29W **20 B2**
L'Annonciation *Canada* 46°25N 74°55W **72 C5**
Lansdale *U.S.A.* 40°14N 75°17W **83 F9**
Lansdowne *Australia* 31°48S 152°30E **63 E5**
Lansdowne *Canada* 44°24N 76°1W **83 B8**
Lansdowne *India* 29°50N 78°41E **43 E8**
Lansdowne House = Neskantaga
  Canada 52°14N 87°53W **72 B2**
L'Anse *U.S.A.* 46°45N 88°27W **80 B9**
L'Anse au Loup *Canada* 51°32N 56°50W **73 B8**
L'Anse aux Meadows
  Canada 51°36N 55°32W **73 B8**
L'Anse la Raye *St. Lucia* 13°55N 61°3W **89 f**
Lansford *U.S.A.* 40°50N 75°53W **83 F9**
Lansing *U.S.A.* 42°44N 84°33W **81 D11**
Lanta Yai, Ko *Thailand* 7°35N 99°3E **39 J2**
Lantau I. *China* 22°15N 113°56E **33 G10**
Lantian *China* 34°11N 109°20E **34 G5**
Lanus *Argentina* 34°42S 58°23W **94 C4**
Lanusei *Italy* 39°52N 9°34E **22 E3**
Lanzarote *Canary Is.* 29°0N 13°40W **24 F6**
Lanzarote ✈ (ACE)
  Canary Is. 28°57N 13°40W **24 F6**
Lanzhou *China* 36°1N 103°52E **34 F2**
Lao Bao *Laos* 16°35N 106°30E **38 D6**
Lao Cai *Vietnam* 22°30N 103°57E **38 A4**
Laoag *Phil.* 18°7N 120°34E **37 A6**
Laoha He → *China* 43°25N 120°35E **35 C11**
Laois □ *Ireland* 52°57N 7°36W **10 D4**
Laon *France* 49°33N 3°35E **20 B5**
Laona *U.S.A.* 45°34N 88°40W **80 C9**

Laos ■ Asia 17°45N 105°0E **38** D5
Lapa Brazil 25°46S 49°44W **95** B6
Lapeer U.S.A. 43°3N 83°19W **81** D12
Lapithos Cyprus 35°21N 33°11E **25** D12
Lapland = Lappland Europe 68°7N 24°0E **8** B21
LaPorte Ind., U.S.A. 41°36N 86°43W **80** E10
Laporte Pa., U.S.A. 41°25N 76°30W **83** E8
Lappeenranta Finland 61°3N 28°12E **8** F23
Lappland Europe 68°7N 24°0E **8** B21
Lappo = Lapua Finland 62°58N 23°0E **8** E20
Laprida Argentina 37°34S 60°45W **94** D3
Lâpseki Turkey 40°20N 26°41E **23** D12
Laptev Sea Russia 76°0N 125°0E **29** B13
Lapua Finland 62°58N 23°0E **8** E20
L'Áquila Italy 42°22N 13°22E **22** C5
Lār Iran 27°40N 54°14E **45** E7
Laramie U.S.A. 41°19N 105°35W **76** F11
Laramie Mts. U.S.A. 42°0N 105°30W **76** F11
Laranjeiras do Sul Brazil 25°23S 52°23W **95** B5
Larantuka Indonesia 8°21S 122°55E **37** F6
Larat Indonesia 7°0S 132°0E **37** F8
Larde Mozam. 16°28S 39°43E **55** F4
Larder Lake Canada 48°5N 79°40W **72** C4
Lardos Greece 36°6N 28°1E **25** C10
Lardos, Akra = Lindos, Akra Greece 36°4N 28°10E **25** C10
Lardos, Ormos Greece 36°4N 28°2E **25** C10
Lare Kenya 0°20N 37°56E **54** C4
Laredo U.S.A. 27°30N 99°30W **84** H5
Laredo Sd. Canada 52°30N 128°53W **70** C3
Largo U.S.A. 27°54N 82°47W **85** H13
Largs U.K. 55°47N 4°52W **11** F4
Lariang Indonesia 1°26S 119°17E **37** E5
Larimore U.S.A. 47°54N 97°38W **80** B5
Larisa Greece 39°36N 22°27E **23** E10
Larkana Pakistan 27°32N 68°18E **42** F3
Larnaca Cyprus 34°55N 33°38E **25** E12
Larnaca Bay Cyprus 34°53N 33°45E **25** E12
Larne U.K. 54°51N 5°51W **10** B6
Larned U.S.A. 38°11N 99°6W **80** F4
Larose U.S.A. 29°34N 90°23W **85** G9
Larrimah Australia 15°35S 133°12E **60** C5
Larsen Ice Shelf Antarctica 67°0S 62°0W **5** C17
Larvik Norway 59°4N 10°2E **9** G14
Las Animas U.S.A. 38°4N 103°13W **76** G12
Las Anod Somali Rep. 8°26N 47°19E **47** F4
Las Brenãs Argentina 27°5S 61°7W **94** B3
Las Cañadas del Teide △ Canary Is. 28°15N 16°37W **24** F3
Las Cejas Argentina 26°53S 64°44W **96** B4
Las Chimeneas Mexico 32°8N 116°5W **79** N10
Las Cruces U.S.A. 32°19N 106°47W **77** K10
Las Flores Argentina 36°10S 59°7W **94** D4
Las Heras Argentina 32°51S 68°49W **94** C2
Las Lajas Argentina 38°30S 70°25W **96** D2
Las Lomitas Argentina 24°43S 60°35W **94** A3
Las Palmas Argentina 27°8S 58°45W **94** B4
Las Palmas Canary Is. 28°7N 15°26W **24** F4
Las Palmas ➤ Mexico 32°31N 116°58W **79** N10
Las Palmas ✈ (LPA) Canary Is. 27°55N 15°25W **24** G4
Las Piedras Uruguay 34°44S 56°14W **95** C4
Las Pipinas Argentina 35°30S 57°19W **94** D4
Las Plumas Argentina 43°40S 67°15W **96** E3
Las Rosas Argentina 32°30S 61°35W **94** C3
Las Tablas Panama 7°49N 80°14W **88** E3
Las Toscas Argentina 28°21S 59°18W **94** B4
Las Truchas Mexico 17°57N 102°13W **86** D4
Las Tunas Cuba 20°58N 76°59W **88** B4
Las Varillas Argentina 31°50S 62°50W **94** C3
Las Vegas N. Mex., U.S.A. 35°36N 105°13W **77** J11
Las Vegas Nev., U.S.A. 36°10N 115°8W **79** J11
Las Vegas McCarran Int. ✈ (LAS) U.S.A. 36°5N 115°9W **79** J11
Lascano Uruguay 33°35S 54°12W **95** C5
Lashburn Canada 53°10N 109°40W **71** C7
Lashio Burma 22°56N 97°45E **41** H20
Lashkar India 26°10N 78°10E **42** F8
Lasithi Greece 35°11N 25°31E **25** D7
Lasithi □ Greece 35°5N 25°50E **25** D7
Lāsjerd Iran 35°24N 53°4E **45** C7
Lassen Pk. U.S.A. 40°29N 121°30W **76** F3
Lassen Volcanic △ U.S.A. 40°30N 121°20W **76** F3
Last Mountain L. Canada 51°5N 105°14W **71** C7
Lastchance Cr. ➤ U.S.A. 40°2N 121°15W **78** E5
Lastoursville Gabon 0°55S 12°38E **52** E2
Lastovo Croatia 42°46N 16°55E **22** C7
Lat Yao Thailand 15°45N 99°48E **38** E2
Latacunga Ecuador 0°50S 78°35W **92** D3
Latakia = Al Lādhiqīyah Syria 35°30N 35°45E **44** C2
Latchford Canada 47°20N 79°50W **72** C4
Late Tonga 18°48S 174°39W **59** c
Latehar India 23°45N 84°30E **43** H11
Latham Australia 29°44S 116°20E **61** E2
Lathi India 27°43N 71°23E **42** F4
Lathrop Wells U.S.A. 36°39N 116°24W **79** J10
Latina Italy 41°28N 12°52E **22** D5
Latium = Lazio □ Italy 42°10N 12°30E **22** C5
Laton U.S.A. 36°26N 119°41W **78** J7
Latouche Treville, C. Australia 18°27S 121°49E **60** C3
Latrobe Australia 41°14S 146°30E **63** G4
Latrobe U.S.A. 40°19N 79°23W **82** F5
Latvia ■ Europe 56°50N 24°0E **9** H21
Lau Fau Shan China 22°28N 113°59E **33** G10
Lau Group Fiji 17°0S 178°30W **59** a
Lauchhammer Germany 51°29N 13°47E **16** C7
Lauge Koch Kyst Greenland 75°45N 57°45W **69** B20
Laughlin U.S.A. 35°10N 114°34W **77** J6
Laukaa Finland 62°24N 25°56E **8** E21
Launceston Australia 41°24S 147°8E **63** G4
Launceston U.K. 50°38N 4°22W **13** G3
Laune ➤ Ireland 52°7N 9°47W **10** D2
Launglon Bok Burma 13°50N 97°54E **38** F1
Laura Australia 15°32S 144°32E **62** B3
Laurel Miss., U.S.A. 31°41N 89°8W **85** F10
Laurel Mont., U.S.A. 45°40N 108°46W **76** D9
Laurel Hill U.S.A. 40°14N 79°6W **82** F5
Laurencekirk U.K. 56°50N 2°28W **11** E6
Laurens U.S.A. 34°30N 82°1W **85** D13
Laurentian Plateau Canada 52°0N 70°0W **73** B6
Lauria Italy 40°2N 15°50E **22** E6
Laurie L. Canada 56°35N 101°57W **71** B8
Laurinburg U.S.A. 34°47N 79°28W **85** D15
Laurium U.S.A. 47°14N 88°27W **80** B9
Laut Indonesia 4°45N 108°0E **36** D3
Laut, Pulau Indonesia 3°40S 116°10E **36** E5
Laut Kecil, Kepulauan Indonesia 4°45S 115°40E **36** E5
Lautoka Fiji 17°37S 177°27E **59** a
Lava Beds △ U.S.A. 41°40N 121°30W **76** F3
Lavagh More Ireland 54°46N 8°6W **10** B3
Laval France 48°4N 0°48W **20** B3
Laval-des-Rapides Canada 45°33N 73°42W **72** C5
Lavalle Argentina 28°15S 65°15W **94** B2
Lāvān Iran 26°48N 53°22E **45** E7
Lavant Canada 45°3N 76°42W **83** A8
Lāvar Meydān Iran 30°20N 54°30E **45** D7
Laverton Australia 28°44S 122°29E **61** E3
Lavras Brazil 21°20S 45°0W **95** A7
Lavrio Greece 37°40N 24°4E **23** F11
Lavris Greece 35°25N 24°40E **25** D6
Lavumisa Swaziland 27°20S 31°55E **57** D5
Lavushi Manda △ Zambia 12°46S 31°0E **55** E3
Lawaki Fiji 17°40S 178°35E **59** a
Lawas Malaysia 4°55N 115°25E **36** D5
Lawele Indonesia 5°13S 122°57E **37** F6
Lawn Hill = Boodjamulla △ Australia 18°15S 138°6E **62** B2
Lawqah Si. Arabia 29°49N 42°45E **44** D4
Lawrence N.Z. 45°55S 169°41E **59** F2
Lawrence Ind., U.S.A. 39°50N 86°2W **81** F10
Lawrence Kans., U.S.A. 38°58N 95°14W **80** F6
Lawrence Mass., U.S.A. 42°43N 71°10W **83** D13
Lawrenceburg Ind., U.S.A. 39°6N 84°52W **81** F11
Lawrenceburg Tenn., U.S.A. 35°14N 87°20W **85** D11
Lawrenceville Ga., U.S.A. 33°57N 83°59W **85** E13
Lawrenceville Pa., U.S.A. 41°59N 77°8W **82** E7
Laws U.S.A. 37°24N 118°20W **78** H8
Lawton U.S.A. 34°37N 98°25W **84** D5
Lawu Indonesia 7°40S 111°13E **37** G14
Laxford, L. U.K. 58°24N 5°6W **11** C3
Layla Si. Arabia 22°10N 46°40E **47** C4
Laylān Iraq 35°18N 44°31E **44** C5
Laysan I. U.S.A. 25°50N 171°50W **75** K5
Layton U.S.A. 41°4N 111°58W **76** F8
Laytonville U.S.A. 39°41N 123°29W **76** G2
Lazarev Russia 52°13N 141°32E **29** D15
Lazarev Sea S. Ocean 67°30S 3°0W **5** C2
Lazarivo Madag. 23°54S 44°59E **57** C8
Lázaro Cárdenas Mexico 17°55N 102°11W **86** D4
Lazio □ Italy 42°10N 12°30E **22** C5
Lazo Russia 43°25N 133°55E **30** C6
Le Bic Canada 48°20N 68°41W **73** C6
Le Creusot France 46°48N 4°24E **20** C6
Le François Martinique 14°38N 60°57W **88** c
Le Gosier Guadeloupe 16°14N 61°29W **88** b
Le Gris Gris Mauritius 20°31S 57°32E **53** d
Le Havre France 49°30N 0°5E **20** B4
Le Lamentin Martinique 14°35N 61°2W **88** c
Le Mans France 48°0N 0°10E **20** C4
Le Marin Martinique 14°27N 60°55W **88** c
Le Mars U.S.A. 42°47N 96°10W **80** D5
Le Mont-St-Michel France 48°40N 1°30W **20** B3
Le Moule Guadeloupe 16°20N 61°22W **88** b
Le Moyne, L. Canada 56°45N 68°47W **73** A6
Le Port Réunion 20°55S 55°18E **53** c
Le Prêcheur Martinique 14°50N 61°12W **88** c
Le Puy-en-Velay France 45°3N 3°52E **20** D5
Le Raysville U.S.A. 41°50N 76°10W **83** E8
Le Robert Martinique 14°40N 60°56W **88** c
Le Roy U.S.A. 42°58N 77°59W **82** D7
Le St-Esprit Martinique 14°34N 60°56W **88** c
Le Sueur U.S.A. 44°28N 93°55W **80** C7
Le Tampon Réunion 21°16S 55°32E **53** c
Le Thuy Vietnam 17°14N 106°49E **38** D6
Le Touquet-Paris-Plage France 50°30N 1°36E **20** A4
Le Tréport France 50°3N 1°20E **20** A4
Le Verdon-sur-Mer France 45°33N 1°4W **20** D3
Lea ➤ U.K. 51°31N 0°1E **13** F8
Leach Cambodia 12°21N 103°46E **39** F4
Lead U.S.A. 44°21N 103°46W **80** C2
Leader Canada 50°50N 109°30W **71** C7
Leadville U.S.A. 39°15N 106°18W **76** G10
Leaf ➤ U.S.A. 30°59N 88°44W **85** F10
Leaf Rapids Canada 56°30N 99°59W **71** B9
Leamington Canada 42°3N 82°36W **82** D2
Leamington U.S.A. 39°32N 112°17W **76** G7
Leamington Spa = Royal Leamington Spa U.K. 52°18N 1°31W **13** E6
Leandro Norte Alem Argentina 27°34S 55°15W **95** B4
Leane, L. Ireland 52°2N 9°32W **10** D2
Learmonth Australia 22°13S 114°10E **60** D1
Leask Canada 53°5N 106°45W **71** C7
Leatherhead U.K. 51°18N 0°20W **13** F7
Leavenworth Kans., U.S.A. 39°19N 94°55W **80** F6
Leavenworth Wash., U.S.A. 47°36N 120°40W **76** C3
Leawood U.S.A. 38°58N 94°37W **80** F6
Lebak Phil. 6°32N 124°5E **37** C6
Lebam U.S.A. 46°34N 123°33W **78** D3
Lebanon Ind., U.S.A. 40°3N 86°28W **80** E10
Lebanon Kans., U.S.A. 39°49N 98°33W **80** F4
Lebanon Ky., U.S.A. 37°34N 85°15W **81** G11
Lebanon Mo., U.S.A. 37°41N 92°40W **80** G7
Lebanon N.H., U.S.A. 43°39N 72°15W **83** C12
Lebanon Oreg., U.S.A. 44°32N 122°55W **76** D2
Lebanon Pa., U.S.A. 40°20N 76°26W **83** F8
Lebanon Tenn., U.S.A. 36°12N 86°18W **85** C11
Lebanon ■ Asia 34°0N 36°0E **46** B5
Lebec U.S.A. 34°51N 118°52W **79** L8
Lebel-sur-Quévillon Canada 49°3N 76°59W **72** C4
Lebomboberge S. Africa 24°30S 32°0E **57** C5
Lebork Poland 54°33N 17°46E **17** A9
Lebrija Spain 36°53N 6°5W **21** D2
Lebu Chile 37°40S 73°47W **94** D1
Lecce Italy 40°23N 18°11E **23** D8
Lecco Italy 45°51N 9°23E **20** D8
Lech ➤ Germany 48°43N 10°56E **16** D6
Lecontes Mills U.S.A. 41°5N 78°17W **82** E6
Ledong China 18°41N 109°5E **38** C7
Leduc Canada 53°15N 113°30W **70** C6
Lee U.S.A. 42°19N 73°15W **83** D11
Lee ➤ Ireland 51°53N 8°56W **10** E3
Lee Vining U.S.A. 37°58N 119°7W **78** H7
Leech L. U.S.A. 47°10N 94°24W **80** B7
Leechburg U.S.A. 40°37N 79°36W **82** F5
Leeds U.K. 53°48N 1°33W **12** D6
Leeds U.S.A. 33°33N 86°33W **85** E11
Leek Neths. 53°10N 6°24E **15** A6
Leek U.K. 53°7N 2°1W **12** D5
Leeman Australia 29°57S 114°58E **61** E1
Leeper U.S.A. 41°22N 79°18W **82** E5
Leer Germany 53°13N 7°26E **16** B4
Leesburg U.S.A. 28°49N 81°53W **85** G14
Leesville U.S.A. 31°8N 93°16W **84** F8
Leeton Australia 34°33S 146°23E **63** E4
Leetonia U.S.A. 40°53N 80°45W **82** F4
Leeu Gamka S. Africa 32°47S 21°59E **56** E3
Leeuwarden Neths. 53°15N 5°48E **15** A5
Leeuwin, C. Australia 34°20S 115°9E **61** F2
Leeuwin Naturaliste △ Australia 34°6S 115°3E **61** F2
Leeward Is. Atl. Oc. 16°30N 63°30W **89** C7
Lefka Cyprus 35°6N 32°51E **25** D11
Lefkada Greece 38°40N 20°43E **23** E9
Lefkimi Greece 39°25N 20°3E **25** B4
Lefkimis, Akra Greece 39°29N 20°4E **25** B4
Lefkoniko Cyprus 35°18N 33°44E **25** D12
Lefroy U.S.A. 44°16N 79°34W **82** B5
Lefroy, L. Australia 31°21S 121°40E **61** F3
Leganés Spain 40°19N 3°45W **21** B4
Legazpi Phil. 13°10N 123°45E **37** B6
Legendre I. Australia 20°22S 116°55E **60** D2
Leghorn = Livorno Italy 43°33N 10°19E **22** C4
Legionowo Poland 52°25N 20°50E **17** B11
Legnago Italy 45°11N 11°18E **22** B4
Legnica Poland 51°12N 16°10E **16** C9
Leh India 34°9N 77°35E **43** B7
Lehigh Acres U.S.A. 26°36N 81°39W **85** H14
Leighton U.S.A. 40°50N 75°43W **83** F9
Lehututu Botswana 23°54S 21°55E **56** C3
Leiah Pakistan 30°58N 70°58E **42** D4
Leicester U.K. 52°38N 1°8W **13** E6
Leicester City □ U.K. 52°38N 1°8W **13** E6
Leicestershire □ U.K. 52°41N 1°17W **13** E6
Leichhardt ➤ Australia 17°35S 139°48E **62** B2
Leichhardt Ra. Australia 20°46S 147°40E **62** C4
Leiden Neths. 52°9N 4°30E **15** B4
Leie ➤ Belgium 51°2N 3°45E **15** C3
Leimus Nic. 14°40N 84°3W **88** D3
Leine ➤ Germany 52°43N 9°36E **16** B5
Leinster Australia 27°51S 120°36E **61** E3
Leinster Ireland 53°3N 7°8W **10** C4
Leinster, Mt. Ireland 52°37N 6°46W **10** D5
Leipzig Germany 51°18N 12°22E **16** C7
Leiria Portugal 39°46N 8°53W **21** C1
Leirvik Norway 59°47N 5°28E **9** G11
Leisler, Mt. Australia 23°23S 129°20E **60** D4
Leith U.K. 55°59N 3°11W **11** F5
Leith Hill U.K. 51°11N 0°22W **13** F7
Leitir Ceanainn = Letterkenny Ireland 54°57N 7°45W **10** B4
Leitrim Ireland 54°0N 8°5W **10** B3
Leitrim □ Ireland 54°8N 8°0W **10** B4
Leizhou Bandao China 21°0N 110°0E **33** D6
Lek ➤ Neths. 51°54N 4°35E **15** C4
Leka Norway 65°5N 11°35E **8** D14
Leland Mich., U.S.A. 45°1N 85°45W **81** C11
Leland Miss., U.S.A. 33°24N 90°54W **85** E9
Leleque Argentina 42°28S 71°0W **96** E2
Lelystad Neths. 52°30N 5°25E **15** B5
Léman, L. Europe 46°26N 6°30E **20** C7
Lembar Indonesia 8°45S 116°4E **37** K19
Lembuak Indonesia 8°36S 116°11E **37** K19
Lemera Dem. Rep. of the Congo 3°0S 28°55E **54** C2
Lemhi Ra. U.S.A. 44°0N 113°0W **76** D7
Lemmer Neths. 52°51N 5°43E **15** B5
Lemmon U.S.A. 45°57N 102°10W **80** C2
Lemon Grove U.S.A. 32°43N 117°1W **79** N9
Lemoore U.S.A. 36°18N 119°46W **78** J7
Lemvig Denmark 56°33N 8°20E **9** H13
Lena ➤ Russia 72°52N 126°40E **29** B13
Lenadoon Pt. Ireland 54°18N 9°3W **10** B2
Lenggong Malaysia 5°6N 100°58E **39** K3
Lengua de Vaca, Pta. Chile 30°14S 71°38W **94** C1
Lengwe △ Malawi 16°14S 34°45E **55** F3
Leninogorsk Kazakhstan 50°20N 83°30E **28** D9
Leninsk Russia 48°40N 45°15E **19** E8
Leninsk-Kuznetskiy Russia 54°44N 86°10E **28** D9
Lenkoran = Länkäran Azerbaijan 38°48N 48°52E **45** B6
Lenmalu Indonesia 1°45S 130°15E **37** E8
Lennox U.S.A. 43°21N 96°53W **80** D5
Lennoxville Canada 45°22N 71°51W **83** A13
Lenoir U.S.A. 35°55N 81°32W **85** D14
Lenoir City U.S.A. 35°48N 84°16W **85** D12
Lenore L. Canada 52°30N 104°59W **71** C8
Lenox U.S.A. 42°22N 73°17W **83** D11
Lens France 50°26N 2°50E **20** A5
Lensk Russia 60°48N 114°55E **29** C12
Lentas Greece 34°56N 24°56E **25** E6
Lentini Italy 37°17N 15°0E **22** F6
Lenwood U.S.A. 34°53N 117°7W **79** L9
Lenya Burma 11°33N 98°57E **39** G2
Leoben Austria 47°22N 15°5E **16** E8
Leodhas = Lewis U.K. 58°9N 6°40W **11** C2
Leola U.S.A. 45°43N 98°56W **80** C4
Leominster U.K. 52°14N 2°43E **13** E5
Leominster U.S.A. 42°32N 71°46W **83** D13
León Mexico 21°6N 101°41W **86** C4
León Nic. 12°20N 86°51W **88** D2
León Spain 42°38N 5°34W **21** A3
Leon U.S.A. 40°44N 93°45W **80** E7
Leon ➤ U.S.A. 31°14N 97°28W **84** F6
León, Montes de Spain 42°30N 6°18W **21** A2
Leonardtown U.S.A. 38°17N 76°38W **81** F15
Leonardville Namibia 23°29S 18°49E **56** C2
Leone, Amer. Samoa 14°23S 170°48W **59** b
Leongatha Australia 38°30S 145°58E **63** F4
Leonora Australia 28°49S 121°19E **61** E3
Leopoldina Brazil 21°28S 42°40W **95** A7
Leopoldsburg Belgium 51°7N 5°13E **15** C5
Leoti U.S.A. 38°29N 101°21W **80** F3
Leova Moldova 46°28N 28°15E **17** E15
Leoville Canada 53°39N 107°33W **71** C7
Lepel = Lyepyel Belarus 54°50N 28°40E **9** J23
Lépo, L. do Angola 17°0S 19°0E **56** B2
Leppävirta Finland 62°29N 27°46E **8** E22
Leptis Magna Libya 32°40N 14°12E **51** B8
Léribe Lesotho 28°51S 28°3E **57** D4
Lérida = Lleida Spain 41°37N 0°39E **21** B6
Lerwick U.K. 60°9N 1°9W **11** A7
Les Cayes Haiti 18°15N 73°46W **89** C5
Les Coteaux Canada 45°15N 74°13W **83** A10
Les Escoumins Canada 48°21N 69°24W **73** C6
Les Sables-d'Olonne France 46°30N 1°45W **20** C3
Lesbos Greece 39°10N 26°20E **23** E12
Leshan China 29°33N 103°41E **32** D5
Leshukonskoye Russia 64°54N 45°46E **18** B8
Leshwe Dem. Rep. of the Congo 12°45S 29°30E **55** E2
Leskov I. Antarctica 56°0S 28°0W **5** B1
Leskovac Serbia 43°0N 21°58E **23** C9
Lesopilnoye Russia 46°44N 134°20E **30** A7
Lesotho ■ Africa 29°40S 28°0E **57** D4
Lesozavodsk Russia 45°30N 133°29E **30** B6
Lesse ➤ Belgium 50°15N 4°54E **15** D4
Lesse et Lomme ○ Belgium 50°8N 5°9E **15** D5
Lesser Antilles W. Indies 15°0N 61°0W **89** D7
Lesser Slave L. Canada 55°30N 115°25W **70** B5
Lesser Sunda Is. Indonesia 8°0S 120°0E **37** F6
Lessines Belgium 50°42N 3°50E **15** D3
Lester B. Pearson Int., Toronto ✈ (YYZ) Canada 43°46N 79°35W **82** C5
Lestock Canada 51°19N 103°59W **71** C8
Lesuer I. Australia 13°50S 127°17E **60** B4
Lesueur △ Australia 30°11S 115°10E **61** F2
Lésvos = Lesbos Greece 39°10N 26°20E **23** E12
Leszno Poland 51°50N 16°30E **17** C9
Letaba S. Africa 23°59S 31°50E **57** C5
Letchworth U.K. 51°59N 0°13W **13** F7
Lethbridge Canada 49°45N 112°45W **70** D6
Lethem Guyana 3°20N 59°50W **92** C7
Leti, Kepulauan Indonesia 8°10S 128°0E **37** F7
Leti Is. = Leti, Kepulauan Indonesia 8°10S 128°0E **37** F7
Letiahau ➤ Botswana 21°16S 24°0E **56** C3
Leticia Colombia 4°9S 70°0W **92** D5
Leting China 39°23N 118°55E **35** E10
Letjiesbos S. Africa 32°34S 22°16E **56** E3
Letlhakane Botswana 21°27S 25°30E **56** C4
Letlhakeng Botswana 24°0S 24°59E **56** C3
Letpadan Burma 17°45N 95°45E **41** L19
Letpan Burma 19°28N 94°10E **41** K19
Letsôk-aw Kyun Burma 11°30N 98°25E **39** G2
Letterkenny Ireland 54°57N 7°45W **10** B4
Leucadia U.S.A. 33°4N 117°18W **79** M9
Leuchars U.K. 56°24N 2°53W **11** E6
Leuser, G. Indonesia 3°46N 97°12E **36** D1
Leuven Belgium 50°52N 4°42E **15** D4
Leuze-en-Hainaut Belgium 50°36N 3°37E **15** D3
Levanger Norway 63°45N 11°19E **8** E14
Levelland U.S.A. 33°35N 102°23W **84** E3
Leven U.K. 56°12N 3°0W **11** E6
Leven, L. U.K. 56°12N 3°22W **11** E5
Leven, Toraka Madag. 12°30S 47°45E **57** A8
Leveque C. Australia 16°20S 123°0E **60** C3
Levice Slovak Rep. 48°13N 18°35E **17** D10
Levin N.Z. 40°37S 175°18E **59** D5
Lévis Canada 46°48N 71°9W **73** C5
Levis, L. Canada 62°37N 117°58W **70** A5
Levittown N.Y., U.S.A. 40°44N 73°31W **83** F11
Levittown Pa., U.S.A. 40°9N 74°51W **83** F10
Levkás = Lefkada Greece 38°40N 20°43E **23** E9
Levkôsia = Nicosia Cyprus 35°10N 33°25E **25** D12
Levskigrad = Karlovo Bulgaria 42°38N 24°47E **23** C11
Levuka Fiji 17°34S 179°0E **59** a
Lewes U.K. 50°52N 0°1E **13** G8
Lewes U.S.A. 38°46N 75°9W **81** F16
Lewis ➤ U.S.A. 45°51N 122°48W **78** E4
Lewis U.K. 58°9N 6°40W **11** C2
Lewis, Butt of U.K. 58°31N 6°16W **11** C2
Lewis and Clark △ U.S.A. 46°8N 123°53W **78** D3
Lewis Ra. Australia 20°3S 128°50E **60** D4
Lewis Range U.S.A. 48°5N 113°5W **76** B7
Lewis Run U.S.A. 41°52N 78°40W **82** E6
Lewisburg Pa., U.S.A. 40°58N 76°54W **82** F8
Lewisburg Tenn., U.S.A. 35°27N 86°48W **85** D11
Lewisburg W. Va., U.S.A. 37°48N 80°27W **81** G13
Lewisporte Canada 49°15N 55°3W **73** C8
Lewiston Idaho, U.S.A. 46°25N 117°1W **76** C5
Lewiston Maine, U.S.A. 44°6N 70°13W **81** C18
Lewiston N.Y., U.S.A. 43°11N 79°3W **82** C5
Lewistown Mont., U.S.A. 47°4N 109°26W **76** C9
Lewistown Pa., U.S.A. 40°36N 77°34W **82** F7
Lewisville U.S.A. 33°2N 96°59W **84** E6
Lexington Ill., U.S.A. 40°39N 88°47W **80** E9
Lexington Ky., U.S.A. 38°3N 84°30W **81** F11
Lexington Mich., U.S.A. 43°16N 82°32W **82** C2
Lexington Mo., U.S.A. 39°11N 93°52W **80** F7
Lexington N.C., U.S.A. 35°49N 80°15W **85** D14
Lexington Nebr., U.S.A. 40°47N 99°45W **80** E4
Lexington Ohio, U.S.A. 40°41N 82°35W **82** F2
Lexington Tenn., U.S.A. 35°39N 88°24W **85** D10
Lexington Va., U.S.A. 37°47N 79°27W **81** G14
Lexington Park U.S.A. 38°16N 76°27W **81** F15
Leyburn U.K. 54°19N 1°48W **12** C6
Leyland U.K. 53°42N 2°43W **12** D5
Leyte □ Phil. 11°0N 125°0E **37** B7
Lezhë Albania 41°47N 19°39E **23** D8
Lhasa China 29°25N 90°58E **32** D4
Lhazê China 29°5N 87°38E **32** D3
L'Hermite, I. Chile 55°50S 68°0W **96** H3
Lhokkruet Indonesia 4°55N 95°24E **36** D1
Lhokseumawe Indonesia 5°10N 97°10E **36** C1
L'Hospitalet de Llobregat Spain 41°21N 2°6E **21** B7
Li Thailand 17°48N 98°57E **38** D2
Li Xian Gansu, China 34°10N 105°5E **34** G3
Li Xian Hebei, China 38°30N 115°35E **34** E8
Liancourt Rocks = Tokdo Asia 37°15N 131°52E **31** F5
Lianga Phil. 8°38N 126°6E **37** C7
Liangcheng Nei Monggol Zizhiqu, China 40°28N 112°25E **34** D7
Liangcheng Shandong, China 35°32N 119°37E **35** G10
Liangdang China 33°56N 106°18E **34** H4
Liangpran Indonesia 1°4N 114°23E **36** D4
Lianhua China 27°3N 113°54E **35** D9
Lianjiang Fujian, China 26°12N 119°27E **35** D12
Lianjiang Guangdong, China 21°40N 110°8E **35** H8
Lianping China 24°26N 114°30E **35** E10
Lianshan China 24°38N 112°8E **35** E9
Lianshanguan China 40°53N 123°43E **35** D12
Lianshui China 33°42N 119°20E **35** H10
Lianyungang China 34°40N 119°11E **35** G10
Liao He ➤ China 41°0N 121°50E **35** D11
Liaocheng China 36°28N 115°58E **34** F8
Liaodong Bandao China 40°0N 123°0E **35** E12
Liaodong Wan China 40°20N 121°10E **35** D11
Liaoning □ China 41°40N 122°30E **35** D12
Liaotung, G. of = Liaodong Wan China 40°20N 121°10E **35** D11
Liaoyang China 41°15N 122°58E **35** D12
Liaoyuan China 42°58N 125°2E **35** C13
Liaozhong China 41°23N 122°50E **35** D12
Liapades Greece 39°42N 19°40E **25** A3
Liard ➤ Canada 61°51N 121°18W **70** A4
Liard River Canada 59°25N 126°5W **70** B3
Liari Pakistan 25°37N 66°30E **42** G2
Libau = Liepāja Latvia 56°30N 21°0E **9** H19
Libby U.S.A. 48°23N 115°33W **76** B6
Libenge Dem. Rep. of the Congo 3°40N 18°55E **52** D3
Liberal U.S.A. 37°3N 100°55W **80** G3
Liberec Czech Rep. 50°47N 15°7E **16** C8
Liberia Costa Rica 10°40N 85°30W **88** D2
Liberia ■ W. Afr. 6°30N 9°30W **50** G4
Libertador □ Chile 34°15S 70°45W **94** C1
Liberty Mo., U.S.A. 39°15N 94°25W **80** F6
Liberty N.Y., U.S.A. 41°48N 74°45W **83** E10
Liberty Pa., U.S.A. 41°34N 77°6W **82** E7
Liberty Tex., U.S.A. 30°3N 94°48W **84** F7
Liberty-Newark Int. ✈ (EWR) U.S.A. 40°40N 74°10W **83** F10
Lîbiya, Sahrâ' Africa 25°0N 25°0E **51** C10
Libobo, Tanjung Indonesia 0°54S 128°28E **37** E7
Libode S. Africa 31°33S 29°2E **57** E4
Libong, Ko Thailand 7°15N 99°23E **39** J2
Libourne France 44°55N 0°14W **20** D3
Libramont Belgium 49°55N 5°23E **15** E5
Libreville Gabon 0°25N 9°26E **52** D1
Libya ■ N. Afr. 27°0N 17°0E **51** C9
Libyan Desert = Lîbiya, Sahrâ' Africa 25°0N 25°0E **51** C10
Libyan Plateau = Ed Dêffa Egypt 30°40N 26°30E **51** B11
Licantén Chile 35°55S 72°0W **94** D1
Licata Italy 37°6N 13°56E **22** F5
Licheng China 36°28N 113°20E **34** F7
Lichfield U.K. 52°41N 1°49W **13** E6
Lichinga Mozam. 13°13S 35°11E **55** E4
Lichtenburg S. Africa 26°8S 26°8E **56** D4
Licking ➤ U.S.A. 39°6N 84°30W **81** F11
Licungo ➤ Mozam. 17°40S 37°15E **55** F4
Lida Belarus 53°53N 25°15E **17** B13
Lidköping Sweden 58°31N 13°7E **9** G15
Liebig, Mt. Australia 23°18S 131°22E **60** D5
Liechtenstein ■ Europe 47°8N 9°35E **20** C8
Liège Belgium 50°38N 5°35E **15** D5
Liège □ Belgium 50°32N 5°35E **15** D5
Liegnitz = Legnica Poland 51°12N 16°10E **16** C9
Lieksa Finland 63°18N 30°2E **8** E24
Lienart Dem. Rep. of the Congo 3°3N 25°31E **54** B2
Lienyünchiangshih = Lianyünkang China 34°40N 119°11E **35** G10
Lienz Austria 46°50N 12°46E **16** E7
Liepāja Latvia 56°30N 21°0E **9** H19
Lier Belgium 51°7N 4°34E **15** C4
Lietuva = Lithuania ■ Europe 55°30N 24°0E **9** J21
Lièvre ➤ Canada 45°31N 75°26W **72** C4
Liffey ➤ Ireland 53°21N 6°13W **10** C5
Lifford Ireland 54°51N 7°29W **10** B4

Lifudzin *Russia* 44°21N 134°58E **30** B7
Lightning Ridge
　Australia 29°22S 148°0E **63** D4
Ligonha → *Mozam.* 16°54S 39°9E **55** F4
Ligonier *U.S.A.* 40°15N 79°14W **82** F5
Liguria □ *Italy* 44°30N 8°50E **20** D8
Ligurian Sea *Medit. S.* 43°20N 9°0E **22** C3
Lihou Reefs and Cays
　Australia 17°25S 151°40E **62** B5
Lihué Calel △ *Argentina* 38°0S 65°10W **94** D2
Lijiang *China* 26°55N 100°20E **32** D5
Likasi
　Dem. Rep. of the Congo 10°55S 26°48E **55** E2
Likoma I. *Malawi* 12°3S 34°45E **55** E3
Likumburu *Tanzania* 9°43S 35°8E **55** D4
L'Île-Rousse *France* 42°38N 8°57E **20** E8
Lille *France* 50°38N 3°3E **20** A5
Lille Bælt *Denmark* 55°20N 9°45E **9** J13
Lillehammer *Norway* 61°8N 10°30E **8** F14
Lillesand *Norway* 58°15N 8°23E **9** G13
Lillian Pt. *Australia* 27°40S 126°6E **61** E4
Lillooet *Canada* 50°44N 121°57W **70** C4
Lillooet → *Canada* 49°15N 121°57W **70** D4
Lilongwe *Malawi* 14°0S 33°48E **55** E3
Liloy *Phil.* 8°4N 122°39E **37** C6
Lim → *Europe* 43°45N 19°15E **23** C8
Lim Chu Kang *Singapore* 1°26N 103°43E **39** d
Lima *Indonesia* 3°39S 127°58E **37** E7
Lima *Peru* 12°3S 77°2W **92** F3
Lima *Mont., U.S.A.* 44°38N 112°36W **76** D7
Lima *N.Y., U.S.A.* 42°54N 77°36W **82** D7
Lima *Ohio, U.S.A.* 40°44N 84°6W **81** E11
Lima → *Portugal* 41°41N 8°50W **21** B1
Liman *Indonesia* 7°48S 111°45E **37** G14
Limassol *Cyprus* 34°42N 33°1E **25** E12
Limavady *U.K.* 55°3N 6°56W **10** A5
Limay → *Argentina* 39°0S 68°0W **96** D3
Limay Mahuida
　Argentina 37°10S 66°45W **94** D2
Limbang *Brunei* 4°42N 115°6E **36** D5
Limbaži *Latvia* 57°31N 24°42E **9** H21
Limbdi *India* 22°34N 71°51E **42** H4
Limbe *Cameroon* 4°1N 9°10E **52** D1
Limburg *Germany* 50°22N 8°4E **16** C5
Limburg □ *Belgium* 51°2N 5°25E **15** C5
Limburg □ *Neths.* 51°20N 5°55E **15** C5
Limeira *Brazil* 22°35S 47°28W **95** A6
Limerick *Ireland* 52°40N 8°37W **10** D3
Limerick *U.S.A.* 43°41N 70°48W **83** C14
Limerick □ *Ireland* 52°30N 8°50W **10** D3
Limestone *U.S.A.* 42°2N 78°38W **82** D6
Limestone → *Canada* 56°31N 94°7W **71** B10
Limfjorden *Denmark* 56°55N 9°0E **9** H13
Limia = Lima → *Portugal* 41°41N 8°50W **21** B1
Limingen *Norway* 64°48N 13°35E **8** D15
Limmen △ *Australia* 15°15S 135°30E **62** B2
Limmen Bight *Australia* 14°40S 135°35E **62** A2
Limmen Bight →
　Australia 15°7S 135°44E **62** B2
Limnos *Greece* 39°50N 25°5E **23** E11
Limoges *Canada* 45°20N 75°16W **83** A9
Limoges *France* 45°50N 1°15E **20** D4
Limón *Costa Rica* 10°0N 83°2W **88** E3
Limon *U.S.A.* 39°16N 103°41W **76** G12
Limousin □ *France* 45°30N 1°30E **20** D4
Limoux *France* 43°4N 2°12E **20** E5
Limpopo □ *S. Africa* 24°5S 29°0E **57** C4
Limpopo → *Africa* 25°5S 33°30E **57** D5
Limuru *Kenya* 1°2S 36°35E **54** C4
Lin Xian *China* 37°57N 110°58E **34** F6
Linares *Chile* 35°50S 71°40W **94** D1
Linares *Mexico* 24°52N 99°34W **87** C5
Linares *Spain* 38°10N 3°40W **21** C4
Lincang *China* 23°58N 100°1E **32** D5
Lincheng *China* 37°25N 114°30E **34** F8
Lincoln = Beamsville
　Canada 43°12N 79°28W **82** C5
Lincoln *Argentina* 34°55S 61°30W **94** C3
Lincoln *N.Z.* 43°38S 172°30E **59** E4
Lincoln *U.K.* 53°14N 0°32W **12** D7
Lincoln *Calif., U.S.A.* 38°54N 121°17W **78** G5
Lincoln *Ill., U.S.A.* 40°9N 89°22W **80** E9
Lincoln *Kans., U.S.A.* 39°3N 98°9W **80** F4
Lincoln *Maine, U.S.A.* 45°22N 68°30W **81** C19
Lincoln *N.H., U.S.A.* 44°3N 71°40W **83** B13
Lincoln *N. Mex.,
　U.S.A.* 33°30N 105°23W **77** K11
Lincoln *Nebr., U.S.A.* 40°49N 96°41W **80** E5
Lincoln City *U.S.A.* 44°57N 124°1W **76** D1
Lincoln Hav = Lincoln Sea
　Arctic 84°0N 55°0W **69** A21
Lincoln Sea *Arctic* 84°0N 55°0W **69** A21
Lincolnshire □ *U.K.* 53°14N 0°32W **12** D7
Lincolnshire Wolds *U.K.* 53°26N 0°13W **12** D7
Lincolnton *U.S.A.* 35°29N 81°16W **85** D14
Lind *U.S.A.* 46°58N 118°37W **76** C4
Linda *U.S.A.* 39°8N 121°34W **78** F5
Lindeman I. *Australia* 20°27S 149°3E **62** b
Lindeman Islands △
　Australia 20°28S 149°5E **62** b
Linden *Guyana* 6°0N 58°10W **92** B7
Linden *Ala., U.S.A.* 32°18N 87°48W **85** E11
Linden *Calif., U.S.A.* 38°1N 121°5W **78** G5
Linden *Tex., U.S.A.* 33°1N 94°22W **84** E7
Lindenhurst *U.S.A.* 40°41N 73°23W **83** F11
Lindesnes *Norway* 57°58N 7°3E **9** H12
Lindi *Tanzania* 9°58S 39°38E **54** D4
Lindi □ *Tanzania* 9°40S 38°30E **55** D4
Lindi →
　Dem. Rep. of the Congo 0°33N 25°5E **54** B2
Lindley *U.S.A.* 42°1N 77°8W **82** D7
Lindos *Greece* 36°6N 28°4E **25** C10
Lindos, Akra *Greece* 36°4N 28°10E **25** C10
Lindsay *Canada* 44°22N 78°43W **82** B6
Lindsay *Calif., U.S.A.* 36°12N 119°5W **78** J7
Lindsay *Okla., U.S.A.* 34°50N 97°38W **84** D6
Lindsborg *U.S.A.* 38°35N 97°40W **80** F5
Line Islands *Pac. Oc.* 7°0N 160°0W **65** H12
Linesville *U.S.A.* 41°39N 80°26W **82** E4

Linfen *China* 36°3N 111°30E **34** F6
Ling Xian *China* 37°22N 116°30E **34** F9
Lingao *China* 19°56N 109°42E **38** C7
Lingayen *Phil.* 16°1N 120°14E **37** A6
Lingayen G. *Phil.* 16°10N 120°15E **37** A6
Lingbi *China* 33°33N 117°33E **35** H9
Lingchuan *China* 35°45N 113°12E **34** G7
Lingding Yang *China* 22°25N 113°44E **33** G10
Lingen *Germany* 52°31N 7°19E **16** B4
Lingga *Indonesia* 0°12S 104°37E **36** E2
Lingga, Kepulauan
　Indonesia 0°10S 104°30E **36** E2
Lingga Arch. = Lingga,
　Kepulauan *Indonesia* 0°10S 104°30E **36** E2
Lingle *U.S.A.* 42°8N 104°21W **76** E11
Lingqiu *China* 39°28N 114°22E **34** E8
Lingshi *China* 36°48N 111°48E **34** F6
Lingshou *China* 38°20N 114°20E **34** E8
Lingshui *China* 18°27N 110°0E **38** C8
Lingtai *China* 35°0N 107°40E **34** G4
Linguère *Senegal* 15°25N 15°5W **50** E2
Lingwu *China* 38°6N 106°20E **34** E4
Lingyuan *China* 41°10N 119°15E **35** D10
Linhai *China* 28°50N 121°8E **33** D7
Linhares *Brazil* 19°25S 40°4W **93** G10
Linhe *China* 40°48N 107°20E **34** D4
Linjiang *China* 41°50N 127°0E **35** D14
Linköping *Sweden* 58°28N 15°36E **9** G16
Linkou *China* 45°15N 130°18E **35** B16
Linnhe, L. *U.K.* 56°36N 5°25W **11** E3
Linosa *Medit. S.* 35°51N 12°50E **22** G5
Linqi *China* 35°45N 113°52E **34** G7
Linqing *China* 36°50N 115°42E **34** F8
Linqu *China* 36°25N 118°30E **35** F10
Linru *China* 34°11N 112°52E **34** G7
Lins *Brazil* 21°40S 49°44W **95** A6
Linstead *Jamaica* 18°8N 77°2W **88** a
Linta → *Madag.* 25°2S 44°5E **57** D7
Linton *U.S.A.* 39°2N 87°10W **80** F10
Linton *N. Dak., U.S.A.* 46°16N 100°14W **80** B3
Lintong *China* 34°20N 109°10E **34** G5
Linwood *Canada* 43°35N 80°43W **82** C4
Linxi *China* 43°36N 118°2E **35** C10
Linxia *China* 35°36N 103°10E **32** C5
Linyanti → *Africa* 17°50S 25°5E **56** B4
Linyi *China* 35°5N 118°21E **35** G10
Linz *Austria* 48°18N 14°18E **16** D8
Linzhenzhen *China* 36°30N 109°59E **34** F5
Linzi *China* 36°50N 118°20E **35** F10
Lion, G. du *France* 43°10N 4°0E **20** E6
Lionárisso *Cyprus* 35°28N 34°8E **25** D13
Lions, G. of = Lion, G. du
　France 43°10N 4°0E **20** E6
Lion's Den *Zimbabwe* 17°15S 30°5E **55** F3
Lion's Head *Canada* 44°58N 81°15W **82** B3
Lipa *Phil.* 13°57N 121°10E **37** B6
Lipali *Mozam.* 15°50S 35°50E **55** F4
Lípari *Italy* 38°26N 14°58E **22** E6
Lípari, Is. = Eólie, Ís.
　Italy 38°30N 14°57E **22** E6
Lipcani *Moldova* 48°14N 26°48E **17** D14
Liperi *Finland* 62°31N 29°24E **8** E23
Lipetsk *Russia* 52°37N 39°35E **18** D6
Lipkany = Lipcani
　Moldova 48°14N 26°48E **17** D14
Lipovets *Ukraine* 49°12N 29°1E **17** D15
Lippe → *Germany* 51°39N 6°36E **16** C4
Lipscomb *U.S.A.* 36°14N 100°16W **84** C4
Liptrap, C. *Australia* 38°50S 145°55E **63** F4
Lira *Uganda* 2°17N 32°57E **54** B3
Liria = Lliria *Spain* 39°37N 0°35W **21** C5
Lisala
　Dem. Rep. of the Congo 2°12N 21°38E **52** D4
Lisboa *Portugal* 38°42N 9°8W **21** C1
Lisbon = Lisboa *Portugal* 38°42N 9°8W **21** C1
Lisbon *N. Dak., U.S.A.* 46°27N 97°41W **80** B5
Lisbon *N.H., U.S.A.* 44°13N 71°55W **83** B13
Lisbon *N.Y., U.S.A.* 44°43N 75°19W **83** B9
Lisbon *Ohio, U.S.A.* 40°46N 80°46W **82** F4
Lisbon Falls *U.S.A.* 44°0N 70°4W **81** D18
Lisburn *U.K.* 54°31N 6°3W **10** B5
Lisburne, C. *U.S.A.* 68°53N 166°13W **74** B6
Liscannor B. *Ireland* 52°55N 9°24W **10** D2
Lisdoonvarna *Ireland* 53°2N 9°18W **10** C2
Lishi *China* 37°31N 111°8E **34** F6
Lishu *China* 43°20N 124°18E **35** C13
Lisianski I. *U.S.A.* 26°2N 174°0W **75** K5
Lisichansk = Lysychansk
　Ukraine 48°55N 38°30E **19** E6
Lisieux *France* 49°10N 0°12E **20** B4
Liski *Russia* 51°3N 39°30E **19** D6
Lismore *Australia* 28°44S 153°21E **63** D5
Lismore *Ireland* 52°8N 7°55W **10** D4
Lista *Norway* 58°7N 6°39E **9** G12
Lister, Mt. *Antarctica* 78°0S 162°0E **5** D11
Liston *Australia* 28°39S 152°6E **63** D5
Listowel *Canada* 43°44N 80°58W **82** C4
Listowel *Ireland* 52°27N 9°29W **10** D2
Litani → *Lebanon* 33°20N 35°15E **46** B4
Litchfield *Calif., U.S.A.* 40°24N 120°23W **78** E6
Litchfield *Conn., U.S.A.* 41°45N 73°11W **83** E11
Litchfield *Ill., U.S.A.* 39°11N 89°39W **80** F9
Litchfield *Minn., U.S.A.* 45°8N 94°32W **80** C6
Litchfield △ *Australia* 13°14S 131°1E **60** B5
Lithgow *Australia* 33°25S 150°8E **63** E5
Lithino, Akra *Greece* 34°55N 24°44E **25** E6
Lithuania ■ *Europe* 55°30N 24°0E **9** J21
Litití *U.S.A.* 40°9N 76°18W **83** F8
Litoměřice *Czech Rep.* 50°33N 14°10E **16** C8
Little Abaco *Bahamas* 26°50N 77°30W **88** A4
Little Barrier I. *N.Z.* 36°12S 175°8E **59** B5
Little Belt Mts. *U.S.A.* 46°40N 110°45W **76** C8
Little Bighorn Battlefield △
　U.S.A. 45°34N 107°25W **76** D10
Little Blue → *U.S.A.* 39°42N 96°41W **80** F5
Little Buffalo → *Canada* 61°0N 113°46W **70** A6
Little Cayman *Cayman Is.* 19°41N 80°3W **88** C3
Little Churchill →
　Canada 57°30N 95°22W **71** B9

Little Colorado →
　U.S.A. 36°12N 111°48W **77** H8
Little Current *Canada* 45°55N 82°0W **72** C3
Little Current → *Canada* 50°57N 84°36W **72** B3
Little Diomede I.
　U.S.A. 65°45N 168°56W **74** B6
Little Falls *Minn., U.S.A.* 45°59N 94°22W **80** C6
Little Falls *N.Y., U.S.A.* 43°3N 74°51W **83** D10
Little Fork → *U.S.A.* 48°31N 93°35W **80** A7
Little Grand Rapids
　Canada 52°0N 95°29W **71** C9
Little Humboldt →
　U.S.A. 41°1N 117°43W **76** F5
Little Inagua I. *Bahamas* 21°40N 73°50W **89** B5
Little Karoo *S. Africa* 33°45S 21°0E **56** E3
Little Khingan Mts. = Xiao
　Hinggan Ling *China* 49°0N 127°0E **33** B7
Little Lake *U.S.A.* 35°56N 117°55W **79** K9
Little Laut Is. = Laut Kecil,
　Kepulauan *Indonesia* 4°45S 115°40E **36** E5
Little Mecatina = Petit-
　Mécatina → *Canada* 50°40N 59°30W **73** B8
Little Minch *U.K.* 57°35N 6°45W **11** D2
Little Missouri →
　U.S.A. 47°36N 102°25W **80** B2
Little Ouse → *U.K.* 52°22N 1°12E **13** E9
Little Rann *India* 23°25N 71°25E **42** H4
Little Red → *U.S.A.* 35°11N 91°27W **84** D9
Little River *N.Z.* 43°45S 172°49E **59** E4
Little Rock *U.S.A.* 34°45N 92°17W **84** D8
Little Ruaha → *Tanzania* 7°57S 37°53E **54** D4
Little Sable Pt. *U.S.A.* 43°38N 86°33W **80** D10
Little Sioux → *U.S.A.* 41°48N 96°4W **80** E5
Little Smoky →
　Canada 54°44N 117°11W **70** C5
Little Snake → *U.S.A.* 40°27N 108°26W **76** F9
Little Tobago
　Trin. & Tob. 11°18N 60°30W **93** J16
Little Valley *U.S.A.* 42°15N 78°48W **82** D6
Little Wabash → *U.S.A.* 37°55N 88°5W **80** G9
Little White → *U.S.A.* 43°40N 100°40W **80** D3
Little Zab = Zāb aş Şaghīr →
　Iraq 35°17N 43°29E **44** C4
Littlefield *U.S.A.* 33°55N 102°20W **84** E3
Littlehampton *U.K.* 50°49N 0°32W **13** G7
Littleton *U.S.A.* 44°18N 71°46W **83** B13
Liu He → *China* 40°55N 121°35E **35** D11
Liuba *China* 33°38N 106°55E **34** H4
Liugou *China* 40°57N 118°15E **35** D10
Liuhe *China* 42°17N 125°43E **35** C13
Liukang Tenggaja = Sabalana,
　Kepulauan *Indonesia* 6°45S 118°50E **37** F5
Liuli *Tanzania* 11°3S 34°38E **55** E3
Liupanshui *China* 26°38N 104°48E **32** D5
Liuwa Plain *Zambia* 14°20S 22°30E **53** G4
Liuzhou *China* 24°22N 109°22E **33** D5
Liuzhuang *China* 33°12N 120°18E **35** H11
Livadhia *Cyprus* 34°57N 33°38E **25** E12
Livadia *Greece* 38°27N 22°54E **23** E10
Live Oak *Calif., U.S.A.* 39°17N 121°40W **78** F5
Live Oak *Fla., U.S.A.* 30°18N 82°59W **85** F13
Lively *Canada* 46°26N 81°9W **81** B13
Liveras *Cyprus* 35°23N 32°57E **25** D11
Livermore *U.S.A.* 37°41N 121°47W **78** H5
Livermore, Mt. *U.S.A.* 30°38N 104°11W **84** F2
Livermore Falls *U.S.A.* 44°29N 70°11W **81** C18
Liverpool *Australia* 33°54S 150°58E **63** B5
Liverpool *Canada* 44°5N 64°41W **73** D7
Liverpool *U.K.* 53°25N 3°0W **12** D4
Liverpool *U.S.A.* 43°6N 76°13W **83** C8
Liverpool Bay *U.K.* 53°30N 3°20W **12** D4
Liverpool Ra. *Australia* 31°50S 150°30E **63** E5
Livingston *Guatemala* 15°50N 88°50W **88** C2
Livingston *U.K.* 55°54N 3°30W **11** F5
Livingston *Ala., U.S.A.* 32°35N 88°11W **85** E10
Livingston *Calif., U.S.A.* 37°23N 120°43W **78** H6
Livingston *Mont.,
　U.S.A.* 45°40N 110°34W **76** D8
Livingston *S.C., U.S.A.* 33°38N 81°7W **85** E14
Livingston *Tenn.,
　U.S.A.* 36°23N 85°19W **85** C12
Livingston *Tex., U.S.A.* 30°43N 94°56W **84** F7
Livingston, L. *U.S.A.* 30°50N 95°10W **84** F7
Livingston Manor
　U.S.A. 41°54N 74°50W **83** E10
Livingstone *Zambia* 17°46S 25°52E **55** F2
Livingstone Mts. *Tanzania* 9°40S 34°20E **55** D3
Livingstonia *Malawi* 10°38S 34°5E **55** E3
Livny *Russia* 52°30N 37°30E **18** D6
Livonia *Mich., U.S.A.* 42°23N 83°23W **81** D12
Livonia *N.Y., U.S.A.* 42°49N 77°40W **82** D7
Livorno *Italy* 43°33N 10°19E **22** C4
Livramento *Brazil* 30°55S 55°30W **95** C4
Liwale *Tanzania* 9°48S 37°58E **55** D4
Liwonde △ *Malawi* 15°4S 35°20E **55** F4
Lizard I. *Australia* 14°42S 145°30E **62** A4
Lizard Pt. *U.K.* 49°57N 5°13W **13** H2
Ljubljana *Slovenia* 46°4N 14°33E **16** E8
Ljungan → *Sweden* 62°18N 17°23E **8** E17
Ljungby *Sweden* 56°49N 13°55E **9** H15
Ljusdal *Sweden* 61°46N 16°3E **8** F17
Ljusnan → *Sweden* 61°12N 17°8E **8** F17
Ljusne *Sweden* 61°13N 17°7E **8** F17
Llancanelo, Salina
　Argentina 35°40S 69°8W **94** D2
Llandeilo *U.K.* 51°53N 3°59W **13** F4
Llandovery *U.K.* 51°59N 3°48W **13** F4
Llandrindod Wells *U.K.* 52°14N 3°22E **13** E4
Llandudno *U.K.* 53°19N 3°50W **12** D4
Llanelli *U.K.* 51°41N 4°10W **13** F3
Llanes *Spain* 43°25N 4°50W **21** A3
Llangollen *U.K.* 52°58N 3°11W **12** E4
Llanidloes *U.K.* 52°27N 3°31W **13** E4
Llano *U.S.A.* 30°45N 98°41W **84** F5
Llano → *U.S.A.* 30°39N 98°26W **84** F5
Llano Estacado *U.S.A.* 33°30N 103°0W **84** E3
Llanos *S. Amer.* 5°0N 71°35W **92** C4
Llanos de Challe △ *Chile* 28°8S 71°1W **94** B1

Llanquihue, L. *Chile* 41°10S 72°50W **96** E1
Llanwrtyd Wells *U.K.* 52°7N 3°38W **13** E4
Llebeig, C. des *Spain* 39°33N 2°18E **24** B9
Lleida *Spain* 41°37N 0°39E **21** B6
Llera de Canales *Mexico* 23°19N 99°1W **87** C5
Llico *Chile* 34°46S 72°5W **94** C1
Lliria *Spain* 39°37N 0°35W **21** C5
Llobregat → *Spain* 41°19N 2°5E **21** B7
Lloret de Mar *Spain* 41°41N 2°53E **21** B7
Lloseta *Spain* 39°43N 2°52E **24** B9
Lloyd B. *Australia* 12°45S 143°27E **62** A3
Lloyd L. *Canada* 57°22N 108°57W **71** B7
Lloydminster *Canada* 53°17N 110°0W **71** C7
Llubí *Spain* 39°42N 3°0E **24** B10
Llucmajor *Spain* 39°29N 2°53E **24** B9
Llullaillaco, Volcán
　S. Amer. 24°43S 68°30W **94** A2
Llullaillaco △ *Chile* 24°50S 68°51W **94** A2
Lo → *Vietnam* 21°18N 105°25E **38** B5
Loa *U.S.A.* 38°24N 111°39W **76** G8
Loa → *Chile* 21°26S 70°41W **94** A1
Loaita I. *S. China Sea* 10°41N 114°25E **36** B4
Loange →
　Dem. Rep. of the Congo 4°17S 20°2E **52** E4
Lobatse *Botswana* 25°12S 25°40E **56** D4
Lobería *Argentina* 38°10S 58°40W **94** D4
Lobito *Angola* 12°18S 13°35E **53** G2
Lobos *Argentina* 35°10S 59°0W **94** D4
Lobos, I. *Mexico* 27°20N 110°36W **86** B2
Lobos, I. de *Canary Is.* 28°45N 13°50W **24** F6
Loc Binh *Vietnam* 21°46N 106°54E **38** B6
Loc Ninh *Vietnam* 11°50N 106°34E **39** G6
Locarno *Switz.* 46°10N 8°47E **20** C8
Loch Baghasdail = Lochboisdale
　U.K. 57°9N 7°20W **11** D1
Loch Garman = Wexford
　Ireland 52°20N 6°28W **10** D5
Loch Lomond and the
　Trossachs △ *U.K.* 56°10N 4°40W **11** E4
Loch Nam Madadh = Lochmaddy
　U.K. 57°36N 7°10W **11** D1
Lochaber *U.K.* 56°59N 5°1W **11** E3
Locharbriggs *U.K.* 55°7N 3°35W **11** F5
Lochboisdale *U.K.* 57°9N 7°20W **11** D1
Loche, L. La *Canada* 56°30N 109°30W **71** B7
Lochem *Neths.* 52°9N 6°26E **15** B6
Loches *France* 47°7N 1°0E **20** C4
Lochgilphead *U.K.* 56°2N 5°26W **11** E3
Lochinvar △ *Zambia* 15°55S 27°15E **55** F2
Lochinver *U.K.* 58°9N 5°14W **11** C3
Lochmaddy *U.K.* 57°36N 7°10W **11** D1
Lochnagar *Australia* 23°33S 145°38E **62** C4
Lochnagar *U.K.* 56°57N 3°15W **11** E5
Lochy, L. *U.K.* 57°0N 4°53W **11** E4
Lock *Australia* 33°34S 135°46E **63** E2
Lock Haven *U.S.A.* 41°8N 77°28W **82** E7
Lockeford *U.S.A.* 38°10N 121°9W **78** G5
Lockeport *Canada* 43°47N 65°4W **73** D6
Lockerbie *U.K.* 55°7N 3°21W **11** F5
Lockhart *U.S.A.* 29°53N 97°40W **84** G6
Lockhart, L. *Australia* 33°15S 119°3E **61** F2
Lockhart River
　Australia 12°58S 143°30E **62** A3
Lockhart River ○
　Australia 12°47S 143°20E **62** A3
Lockney *U.S.A.* 34°7N 101°27W **84** D4
Lockport *U.S.A.* 43°10N 78°42W **82** C6
Lod *Israel* 31°57N 34°54E **46** D3
Lodeinoye Pole *Russia* 60°44N 33°33E **18** B5
Lodge Bay *Canada* 52°14N 55°51W **73** B8
Lodge Grass *U.S.A.* 45°19N 107°22W **76** D10
Lodhran *Pakistan* 29°32N 71°30E **42** E4
Lodi *Italy* 45°19N 9°30E **20** D8
Lodi *Calif., U.S.A.* 38°8N 121°16W **78** G5
Lodi *Ohio, U.S.A.* 41°2N 82°1W **82** E3
Lodja
　Dem. Rep. of the Congo 3°30S 23°23E **54** C1
Lodwar *Kenya* 3°7N 35°36E **54** B4
Łódź *Poland* 51°45N 19°27E **17** C10
Loei *Thailand* 17°29N 101°35E **38** D3
Loengo
　Dem. Rep. of the Congo 4°48S 26°30E **54** C2
Loeriesfontein *S. Africa* 31°0S 19°26E **56** E2
Lofoten *Norway* 68°30N 13°59E **8** B16
Logan *Iowa, U.S.A.* 41°39N 95°47W **80** E6
Logan *Ohio, U.S.A.* 39°32N 82°25W **81** F12
Logan *Utah, U.S.A.* 41°44N 111°50W **76** F8
Logan, Mt. *Canada* 60°34N 140°23W **68** E3
Logandale *U.S.A.* 36°36N 114°29W **79** J12
Logansport *Ind., U.S.A.* 40°45N 86°22W **80** E10
Logansport *La., U.S.A.* 31°58N 94°0W **84** F8
Logone → *Chad* 12°6N 15°2E **51** F9
Logroño *Spain* 42°28N 2°27E **21** A4
Lohardaga *India* 23°27N 84°45E **43** H11
Loharia *India* 23°45N 74°14E **42** H6
Loharu *India* 28°27N 75°49E **42** E6
Lohri Wah → *Pakistan* 27°27N 67°37E **42** F2
Loi-kaw *Burma* 19°40N 97°17E **41** K20
Loimaa *Finland* 60°50N 23°5E **8** F20
Loir → *France* 47°33N 0°32W **20** C3
Loire → *France* 47°16N 2°10W **20** C2
Loja *Ecuador* 3°59S 79°16W **92** D3
Loja *Spain* 37°10N 4°10W **21** D3
Loji = Kawasi *Indonesia* 1°38S 127°28E **37** E7
Lokandu
　Dem. Rep. of the Congo 2°30S 25°45E **54** C2
Lokeren *Belgium* 51°6N 3°59E **15** C3
Lokgwabe *Botswana* 24°10S 21°50E **56** C3
Lokichar *Kenya* 2°23N 35°39E **54** B4
Lokichokio *Kenya* 4°19N 34°13E **54** B3
Lokitaung *Kenya* 4°12N 35°48E **54** B4
Lokkan tekojärvi
　Finland 67°55N 27°35E **8** C22
Lokoja *Nigeria* 7°47N 6°45E **50** G7
Lokolo →
　Dem. Rep. of the Congo 1°43S 18°23E **52** E3

Lola, Mt. *U.S.A.* 39°26N 120°22W **78** F6
Lolgorien *Kenya* 1°14S 34°48E **54** C3
Loliondo *Tanzania* 2°2S 35°39E **54** C4
Lolland *Denmark* 54°45N 11°30E **9** J14
Lolo *U.S.A.* 46°45N 114°5W **76** C6
Lom *Bulgaria* 43°48N 23°12E **23** C10
Lom Kao *Thailand* 16°53N 101°14E **38** D3
Lom Sak *Thailand* 16°47N 101°15E **38** D3
Loma *U.S.A.* 47°56N 110°30W **76** C8
Loma Linda *U.S.A.* 34°3N 117°16W **79** L9
Lomaloma *Fiji* 17°17S 178°59W **59** a
Lomami →
　Dem. Rep. of the Congo 0°46N 24°16E **54** B1
Lomas de Zamora
　Argentina 34°45S 58°24W **94** C4
Lombadina *Australia* 16°31S 122°54E **60** C3
Lombardia □ *Italy* 45°40N 9°30E **20** D8
Lombardy = Lombárdia □
　Italy 45°40N 9°30E **20** D8
Lomblen *Indonesia* 8°30S 123°32E **37** F6
Lombok *Indonesia* 8°45S 116°30E **36** F5
Lombok, Selat *Indonesia* 8°30S 115°50E **37** K18
Lomé *Togo* 6°9N 1°20E **50** G6
Lomela
　Dem. Rep. of the Congo 2°19S 23°15E **52** E4
Lomela →
　Dem. Rep. of the Congo 0°15S 20°40E **52** E4
Lommel *Belgium* 51°14N 5°19E **15** C5
Lomond *Canada* 50°24N 112°36W **70** C6
Lomond, L. *U.K.* 56°8N 4°38W **11** E4
Lomonosov Ridge *Arctic* 88°0N 140°0E **4** A
Lomphat *Cambodia* 13°30N 106°59E **38** F6
Lompobatang *Indonesia* 5°24S 119°56E **37** F5
Lompoc *U.S.A.* 34°38N 120°28W **79** L6
Łomża *Poland* 53°10N 22°2E **17** B12
Lon, Ko *Thailand* 7°47N 98°23E **39** a
Loncoche *Chile* 39°20S 72°50W **96** D2
Londa *India* 15°30N 74°30E **40** M9
Londiani *Kenya* 0°10S 35°33E **54** C4
London *Canada* 42°59N 81°15W **82** D3
London *U.K.* 51°30N 0°3W **13** F7
London *Ky., U.S.A.* 37°8N 84°5W **81** G11
London *Ohio, U.S.A.* 39°53N 83°27W **81** F12
London, Greater □ *U.K.* 51°36N 0°5W **13** F7
London Gatwick ✈ (LGW)
　U.K. 51°10N 0°11W **13** F7
London Heathrow ✈ (LHR)
　U.K. 51°28N 0°27W **13** F7
London Stansted ✈ (STN)
　U.K. 51°54N 0°14E **13** F8
Londonderry *U.K.* 55°0N 7°20W **10** B4
Londonderry □ *U.K.* 55°0N 7°20W **10** B4
Londonderry, C.
　Australia 13°45S 126°55E **60** B4
Londonderry, I. *Chile* 55°0S 71°0W **96** H2
Londres *Argentina* 27°43S 67°7W **96** B3
Londrina *Brazil* 23°18S 51°10W **95** A5
Lone Pine *U.S.A.* 36°36N 118°4W **78** J8
Lonely Mine *Zimbabwe* 19°30S 28°49E **57** B4
Long B. *U.S.A.* 33°35N 78°45W **85** E15
Long Beach *Calif.,
　U.S.A.* 33°46N 118°11W **79** M8
Long Beach *N.Y.,
　U.S.A.* 40°35N 73°39W **83** F11
Long Beach *Wash.,
　U.S.A.* 46°21N 124°3W **78** D2
Long Branch *U.S.A.* 40°18N 74°0W **83** F11
Long Creek *U.S.A.* 44°43N 119°6W **76** D4
Long Eaton *U.K.* 52°53N 1°15W **12** E6
Long I. *Australia* 20°22S 148°51E **62** b
Long I. *Bahamas* 23°20N 75°10W **89** B4
Long I. *Canada* 54°50N 79°20W **72** B4
Long I. *Ireland* 51°30N 9°34W **10** E2
Long I. *U.S.A.* 40°45N 73°30W **83** F11
Long Island Sd. *U.S.A.* 41°10N 73°0W **83** E12
Long L. *Canada* 49°30N 86°50W **72** C2
Long L. *U.S.A.* 44°0N 74°23W **83** C10
Long Lake *U.S.A.* 43°58N 74°25W **83** C10
Long Point *Canada* 42°34N 80°25W **82** D4
Long Point B. *Canada* 42°40N 80°10W **82** D4
Long Prairie *U.S.A.* 45°59N 94°52W **80** C6
Long Prairie → *U.S.A.* 46°20N 94°36W **80** B6
Long Pt. *Ont., Canada* 42°35N 80°2W **82** D4
Long Pt. *Ont., Canada* 43°56N 76°53W **83** C8
Long Range Mts.
　Canada 49°30N 57°30W **73** C8
Long Reef *Australia* 14°1S 125°48E **60** B4
Long Sault *Canada* 45°2N 74°53W **83** A10
Long Str. = Longa, Proliv
　Russia 70°0N 175°0E **29** C18
Long Thanh *Vietnam* 10°47N 106°57E **39** G6
Long Xian *China* 34°55N 106°55E **34** G4
Long Xuyen *Vietnam* 10°19N 105°28E **39** G5
Longa, Proliv *Russia* 70°0N 175°0E **29** C18
Longbenton *U.K.* 55°1N 1°31W **12** B6
Longboat Key *U.S.A.* 27°23N 82°39W **85** H13
Longde *China* 35°30N 106°20E **34** G4
Longford *Australia* 41°32S 147°3E **63** G4
Longford *Ireland* 53°43N 7°49W **10** C4
Longford □ *Ireland* 53°42N 7°45W **10** C4
Longhua *Guangdong,
　China* 22°39N 114°0E **33** F11
Longhua *Hebei, China* 41°18N 117°45E **35** D9
Longido *Tanzania* 2°43S 36°42E **54** C4
Longiram *Indonesia* 0°5S 115°45E **36** E5
Longkou *China* 37°40N 120°18E **35** F11
Longlac *Canada* 49°45N 86°25W **72** C2
Longmeadow *U.S.A.* 42°3N 72°34W **83** D12
Longmont *U.S.A.* 40°10N 105°6W **76** F11
Longnawan *Indonesia* 1°51N 114°55E **36** D4
Longreach *Australia* 23°28S 144°14E **62** C3
Longueuil *Canada* 45°31N 73°29W **83** A11
Longview *Tex., U.S.A.* 32°30N 94°44W **84** E7
Longview *Wash., U.S.A.* 46°8N 122°57W **78** D4
Longxi *China* 34°53N 104°40E **34** G3
Longxue Dao *China* 22°41N 113°38E **33** F10
Longyearbyen *Svalbard* 78°13N 15°40E **4** B8
Lonoke *U.S.A.* 34°47N 91°54W **84** D9
Lonquimay *Chile* 38°26S 71°14W **96** D2

Lons-le-Saunier *France* 46°40N 5°31E **20** C6
Looe *U.K.* 50°22N 4°28W **13** G3
Lookout, C. *Canada* 55°18N 83°56W **72** A3
Lookout, C. *U.S.A.* 34°35N 76°32W **85** D16
Loolmalasin *Tanzania* 3°0S 35°53E **54** C4
Loon → *Alta., Canada* 57°8N 115°3W **70** B5
Loon → *Man., Canada* 55°53N 101°59W **71** B8
Loon Lake *Canada* 54°2N 109°10W **71** C7
Loongana *Australia* 30°52S 127°5E **61** F4
Loop Hd. *Ireland* 52°34N 9°56W **10** D2
Lop *China* 37°3N 80°11E **32** C3
Lop Buri *Thailand* 14°48N 100°37E **38** E3
Lop Nor = Lop Nur
China 40°20N 90°10E **32** B4
Lop Nur *China* 40°20N 90°10E **32** B4
Lopatina, Gora *Russia* 50°47N 143°10E **29** D15
Lopatka, Mys *Russia* 50°52N 156°40E **29** D16
Lopez *U.S.A.* 41°27N 76°20W **83** E8
Lopez, C. *Gabon* 0°47S 8°40E **52** E1
Lopphavet *Norway* 70°27N 21°15E **8** A19
Lora → *Afghan.* 31°35N 66°32E **40** D4
Lora, Hāmūn-i- *Pakistan* 29°38N 64°58E **40** E4
Lora Cr. → *Australia* 28°10S 135°22E **63** D2
Lora del Río *Spain* 37°39N 5°33W **21** D3
Lorain *U.S.A.* 41°28N 82°11W **82** E2
Loralai *Pakistan* 30°20N 68°41E **42** D3
Lorca *Spain* 37°41N 1°42W **21** D5
Lord Howe I. *Pac. Oc.* 31°33S 159°6E **58** E8
Lord Howe Rise *Pac. Oc.* 30°0S 162°30E **64** L8
Lordsburg *U.S.A.* 32°21N 108°43W **77** K9
Lorestän □ *Iran* 33°30N 48°40E **45** C6
Loreto *Brazil* 7°5S 45°10W **93** E9
Loreto *Mexico* 26°0N 111°21W **86** B2
Lorient *France* 47°45N 3°23W **20** C2
Lormi *India* 22°17N 81°41E **43** H9
Lorn *U.K.* 56°26N 5°10W **11** E3
Lorn, Firth of *U.K.* 56°20N 5°40W **11** E3
Lorne *Australia* 38°33S 143°59E **63** F3
Lorovouno *Cyprus* 35°8N 32°36E **25** D11
Lorraine □ *France* 48°53N 6°0E **20** B7
Los Alamos *Calif.,*
U.S.A. 34°44N 120°17W **79** L6
Los Alamos *N. Mex.,*
U.S.A. 35°53N 106°19W **77** J10
Los Altos *U.S.A.* 37°23N 122°7W **78** H4
Los Andes *Chile* 32°50S 70°40W **94** C1
Los Angeles *Chile* 37°28S 72°23W **94** D1
Los Angeles *U.S.A.* 34°4N 118°15W **79** M8
Los Angeles, Bahia de
Mexico 28°56N 113°34W **86** B2
Los Angeles Aqueduct
U.S.A. 35°22N 118°5W **79** K9
Los Angeles Int. ✈ **(LAX)**
U.S.A. 33°57N 118°25W **79** M8
Los Banos *U.S.A.* 37°4N 120°51W **78** H6
Los Blancos *Argentina* 23°40S 62°30W **94** A3
Los Cardones △ *Argentina* 25°8S 65°55W **94** B2
Los Chiles *Costa Rica* 11°2N 84°43W **88** D3
Los Cristianos *Canary Is.* 28°3N 16°42W **24** F3
Los Gatos *U.S.A.* 37°14N 121°59W **78** H5
Los Haïtises △ *Dom. Rep.* 19°4N 69°36W **89** C6
Los Hermanos Is.
Venezuela 11°45N 64°25W **89** D7
Los Islotes *Canary Is.* 29°4N 13°44W **24** E6
Los Llanos de Aridane
Canary Is. 28°38N 17°54W **24** F2
Los Loros *Chile* 27°50S 70°6W **94** B1
Los Lunas *U.S.A.* 34°48N 106°44W **77** J10
Los Mochis *Mexico* 25°45N 108°57W **86** B3
Los Olivos *U.S.A.* 34°40N 120°7W **79** L6
Los Palacios *Cuba* 22°35N 83°15W **88** B3
Los Queñes *Chile* 35°1S 70°48W **94** D1
Los Reyes de Salgado
Mexico 19°35N 102°29W **86** D4
Los Roques Is. *Venezuela* 11°50N 66°45W **89** D6
Los Teques *Venezuela* 10°21N 67°2W **92** A5
Los Testigos, Is. *Venezuela* 11°23N 63°6W **92** A6
Los Vilos *Chile* 32°10S 71°30W **94** C1
Lošinj *Croatia* 44°30N 14°30E **16** F8
Loskop Dam *S. Africa* 25°23S 29°20E **57** D4
Lossiemouth *U.K.* 57°42N 3°17W **11** D5
Lostwithiel *U.K.* 50°24N 4°41W **13** G3
Lot → *France* 44°18N 0°20E **20** D4
Lota *Chile* 37°5S 73°10W **94** D1
Loţfābād *Iran* 37°32N 59°20E **45** B8
Lothair *S. Africa* 26°22S 30°27E **57** D5
Lotta → *Europe* 68°42N 31°6E **8** B24
Loubomo *Congo* 4°9S 12°47E **52** E2
Loudonville *U.S.A.* 40°38N 82°14W **82** F2
Louga *Senegal* 15°45N 16°5W **50** E2
Loughborough *U.K.* 52°47N 1°11W **12** E6
Lougheed I. *Canada* 77°26N 105°6W **69** B10
Loughrea *Ireland* 53°12N 8°33W **10** C3
Loughros More B. *Ireland* 54°48N 8°32W **10** B3
Louis Trichardt *S. Africa* 23°1S 29°43E **57** C4
Louis XIV, Pte. *Canada* 54°37N 79°45W **72** B4
Louisa *U.S.A.* 38°7N 82°36W **81** F12
Louisburg *Canada* 45°55N 60°0W **73** C8
Louisburgh *Ireland* 53°46N 9°49W **10** C2
Louise I. *Canada* 52°55N 131°50W **70** C2
Louiseville *Canada* 46°20N 72°56W **72** C5
Louisiade Arch.
Papua N. G. 11°10S 153°0E **58** C8
Louisiana *U.S.A.* 39°27N 91°3W **80** F8
Louisiana □ *U.S.A.* 30°50N 92°0W **84** F9
Louisville *Ky., U.S.A.* 38°15N 85°46W **81** F11
Louisville *Miss., U.S.A.* 33°7N 89°3W **85** E10
Louisville *Ohio, U.S.A.* 40°50N 81°16W **82** F3
Louisville Ridge
Pac. Oc. 31°0S 172°30W **64** L10
Loulé *Portugal* 37°9N 8°0W **21** D1
Loup City *U.S.A.* 41°17N 98°58W **80** E4
Loups Marins, Lacs des
Canada 56°30N 73°45W **72** A5
Lourdes *France* 43°6N 0°3W **20** E3
Lourdes-de-Blanc-Sablon
Canada 51°24N 57°12W **73** B8
Louroujina *Cyprus* 35°0N 33°28E **25** E12
Louth *Australia* 30°30S 145°8E **63** E4

Louth *Ireland* 53°58N 6°32W **10** C5
Louth *U.K.* 53°22N 0°1W **12** D7
Louth □ *Ireland* 53°56N 6°34W **10** C5
Louvain = Leuven
Belgium 50°52N 4°42E **15** D4
Louwsburg *S. Africa* 27°37S 31°7E **57** D5
Lovech *Bulgaria* 43°8N 24°42E **23** C11
Loveland *U.S.A.* 40°24N 105°5W **76** F11
Lovell *U.S.A.* 44°50N 108°24W **76** D9
Lovelock *U.S.A.* 40°11N 118°28W **76** F4
Loviisa *Finland* 60°28N 26°12E **8** F22
Lovington *U.S.A.* 32°57N 103°21W **77** K12
Lovisa = Loviisa *Finland* 60°28N 26°12E **8** F22
Low, L. *Canada* 52°29N 76°17W **72** B4
Low Pt. *Australia* 32°25S 127°25E **61** F4
Low Tatra = Nízké Tatry
Slovak Rep. 48°55N 19°30E **17** D10
Lowa
Dem. Rep. of the Congo 1°25S 25°47E **54** C2
Lowa →
Dem. Rep. of the Congo 1°24S 25°51E **54** C2
Lowell *U.S.A.* 42°38N 71°19W **83** D13
Lowellville *U.S.A.* 41°2N 80°32W **82** E4
Löwen → *Namibia* 26°51S 18°17E **56** D2
Lower Alkali L. *U.S.A.* 41°16N 120°2W **76** F3
Lower Arrow L. *Canada* 49°40N 118°5W **70** D5
Lower California = Baja California
Mexico 31°10N 115°12W **86** A1
Lower Hutt *N.Z.* 41°10S 174°55E **59** D5
Lower Lake *U.S.A.* 38°55N 122°37W **78** G4
Lower Manitou L.
Canada 49°15N 93°0W **71** D10
Lower Post *Canada* 59°58N 128°30W **70** B3
Lower Red L. *U.S.A.* 47°58N 95°0W **80** B6
Lower Saxony = Niedersachsen □
Germany 52°50N 9°0E **16** B5
Lower Tunguska = Tunguska, Nizhnyaya → *Russia* 65°48N 88°4E **29** C9
Lower Zambezi △ *Zambia* 15°25S 29°40E **55** F2
Lowestoft *U.K.* 52°29N 1°45E **13** E9
Lowgar □ *Afghan.* 34°0N 69°0E **40** B6
Łowicz *Poland* 52°6N 19°55E **17** B10
Lowther I. *Canada* 74°33N 97°30W **69** C12
Lowville *U.S.A.* 43°47N 75°29W **83** C9
Loxton *Australia* 34°28S 140°31E **63** E3
Loxton *S. Africa* 31°30S 22°22E **56** E3
Loyalton *U.S.A.* 39°41N 120°14W **78** F6
Loyalty Is. = Loyauté, Îs.
N. Cal. 20°50S 166°30E **58** D9
Loyang = Luoyang
China 34°40N 112°26E **34** G7
Loyauté, Îs. *N. Cal.* 20°50S 166°30E **58** D9
Loyev = Loyew *Belarus* 51°56N 30°46E **17** C16
Loyew *Belarus* 51°56N 30°46E **17** C16
Loyoro *Uganda* 3°22N 34°14E **54** B3
Ltalaltuma ◎ *Australia* 23°57S 132°25E **60** D5
Lu Wo *China* 22°33N 114°6E **33** F11
Luachimo *Angola* 7°23S 20°48E **52** F4
Luajan → *India* 24°44N 85°1E **43** G11
Lualaba →
Dem. Rep. of the Congo 0°26N 25°20E **54** B2
Luambe △ *Zambia* 12°30S 32°15E **55** E3
Luampa *Zambia* 15°4S 24°20E **55** F1
Luan Chau *Vietnam* 21°38N 103°24E **38** B4
Luan He → *China* 39°20N 119°5E **35** E10
Luan Xian *China* 39°40N 118°40E **35** E10
Luancheng *China* 37°53N 114°40E **34** F8
Luanda *Angola* 8°50S 13°15E **52** F2
Luang, Thale *Thailand* 7°30N 100°15E **39** J3
Luang Prabang *Laos* 19°52N 102°10E **38** C4
Luangwa *Zambia* 15°35S 30°16E **55** F3
Luangwa → *Zambia* 14°25S 30°25E **55** E3
Luangwa Valley *Zambia* 13°30S 31°30E **55** E3
Luangwe = Loange →
Dem. Rep. of the Congo 4°17S 20°2E **52** E4
Luanne *China* 40°55N 117°40E **35** D9
Luanping *China* 40°53N 117°23E **35** D9
Luanshya *Zambia* 13°3S 28°28E **55** E2
Luapula □ *Zambia* 11°0S 29°0E **55** E2
Luapula → *Africa* 9°26S 28°33E **55** D2
Luarca *Spain* 43°32N 6°32W **21** A2
Luashi
Dem. Rep. of the Congo 10°50S 23°36E **55** E1
Luau *Angola* 10°40S 22°10E **52** G4
Lubana, Ozero = Lubānas Ezers
Latvia 56°45N 27°0E **9** H22
Lubānas Ezers *Latvia* 56°45N 27°0E **9** H22
Lubang Is. *Phil.* 13°50N 120°12E **37** B6
Lubango *Angola* 14°55S 13°30E **53** G2
Lubao
Dem. Rep. of the Congo 5°17S 25°42E **54** D2
Lubbock *U.S.A.* 33°35N 101°51W **84** E4
Lübeck *Germany* 53°52N 10°40E **16** B6
Lubefu
Dem. Rep. of the Congo 4°47S 24°27E **54** C1
Lubefu →
Dem. Rep. of the Congo 4°10S 23°0E **54** C1
Lubero = Luofu
Dem. Rep. of the Congo 0°10S 29°15E **54** C2
Lubicon L. *Canada* 56°23N 115°56W **70** B5
Lubilash →
Dem. Rep. of the Congo 6°2S 23°45E **52** F4
Lubin *Poland* 51°24N 16°11E **16** C9
Lublin *Poland* 51°12N 22°38E **17** C12
Lubnān = Lebanon ■ *Asia* 34°0N 36°0E **46** B5
Lubnān, Jabal *Lebanon* 33°45N 35°45E **46** B4
Lubny *Ukraine* 50°3N 32°58E **28** D4
Lubongola
Dem. Rep. of the Congo 2°35S 27°50E **54** C2
Lubudi
Dem. Rep. of the Congo 9°57S 25°58E **52** F5
Lubudi →
Dem. Rep. of the Congo 9°0S 25°35E **55** D2
Lubuklinggau *Indonesia* 3°15S 102°55E **36** E2
Lubuksikaping *Indonesia* 0°10N 100°15E **36** D2
Lubumbashi
Dem. Rep. of the Congo 11°40S 27°28E **55** E2

Lubunda
Dem. Rep. of the Congo 5°12S 26°41E **54** D2
Lubungu *Zambia* 14°35S 26°24E **55** E2
Lubutu
Dem. Rep. of the Congo 0°45S 26°30E **54** C2
Luc An Chau *Vietnam* 22°6N 104°43E **38** A5
Lucan *Canada* 43°11N 81°24W **82** C3
Lucania, Mt. *Canada* 61°1N 140°27W **68** C3
Lucas Channel = Main Channel
Canada 45°21N 81°45W **82** A3
Lucca *Italy* 43°50N 10°29E **22** C4
Luce Bay *U.K.* 54°45N 4°48W **11** G4
Lucea *Jamaica* 18°27N 78°10W **88** a
Lucedale *U.S.A.* 30°56N 88°35W **85** F10
Lucena *Phil.* 13°56N 121°37E **37** B6
Lucena *Spain* 37°27N 4°31W **21** D3
Lučenec *Slovak Rep.* 48°18N 19°42E **17** D10
Lucerne = Luzern *Switz.* 47°3N 8°18E **20** C8
Lucerne *U.S.A.* 39°6N 122°48W **78** F4
Lucerne Valley *U.S.A.* 34°27N 116°57W **79** L10
Lucero *Mexico* 30°49N 106°30W **86** A3
Lucheng *China* 36°20N 121°33W **78** J5
Lucheringo → *Mozam.* 11°43S 36°17E **55** E4
Lucia *U.S.A.* 36°2N 121°33W **78** J5
Lucinda *Australia* 18°32S 146°20E **62** B4
Luckenwalde *Germany* 52°5N 13°10E **16** B7
Luckhoff *S. Africa* 29°44S 24°43E **56** D3
Lucknow *Canada* 43°57N 81°31W **82** C3
Lucknow *India* 26°50N 81°0E **43** F9
Lüda = Dalian *China* 38°50N 121°40E **35** E11
Lüderitz *Namibia* 26°41S 15°8E **56** D2
Lüderitzbaai *Namibia* 26°36S 15°8E **56** D2
Ludhiana *India* 30°57N 75°56E **42** D6
Ludington *U.S.A.* 43°57N 86°27W **80** D10
Ludlow *U.K.* 52°22N 2°42W **13** E5
Ludlow *Calif., U.S.A.* 34°43N 116°10W **79** L10
Ludlow *Pa., U.S.A.* 41°43N 78°56W **82** E6
Ludlow *Vt., U.S.A.* 43°24N 72°42W **83** C12
Ludvika *Sweden* 60°8N 15°14E **9** F16
Ludwigsburg *Germany* 48°53N 9°11E **16** D5
Ludwigshafen *Germany* 49°29N 8°26E **16** D5
Lueki
Dem. Rep. of the Congo 3°20S 25°48E **54** C2
Luena
Dem. Rep. of the Congo 9°28S 25°43E **55** D2
Luena *Zambia* 10°40S 30°25E **55** E3
Luena Flats *Zambia* 14°47S 23°17E **53** G4
Luenha = Ruenya →
Africa 16°24S 33°48E **55** F3
Lüeyang *China* 33°22N 106°10E **34** H4
Lufira →
Dem. Rep. of the Congo 9°30S 27°0E **55** D2
Lufkin *U.S.A.* 31°21N 94°44W **84** F7
Lufupa
Dem. Rep. of the Congo 10°37S 24°56E **55** E1
Luga *Russia* 58°40N 29°55E **9** G23
Lugano *Switz.* 46°1N 8°57E **20** C8
Lugansk = Luhansk
Ukraine 48°38N 39°15E **19** E6
Lugard's Falls *Kenya* 3°6S 38°41E **54** C4
Lugela *Mozam.* 16°25S 36°43E **55** F4
Lugenda → *Mozam.* 11°25S 38°33E **55** E4
Lugh Ganana = Luuq
Somali Rep. 3°48N 42°34E **47** G3
Lugnaquillia *Ireland* 52°58N 6°28W **10** D5
Lugo *Italy* 44°25N 11°54E **22** B4
Lugo *Spain* 43°2N 7°35W **21** A2
Lugoj *Romania* 45°42N 21°57E **17** F11
Lugovoy = Qulan
Kazakhstan 42°55N 72°43E **28** E8
Luhansk *Ukraine* 48°38N 39°15E **19** E6
Lui → *Angola* 8°21S 17°33E **52** F3
Luiana *Angola* 17°25S 22°59E **56** B3
Luiana → *Angola* 17°24S 23°3E **53** H4
Luichow Pen. = Leizhou Bandao
China 21°0N 110°0E **33** D6
Luimneach = Limerick
Ireland 52°40N 8°37W **10** D3
Luing *U.K.* 56°14N 5°39W **11** E3
Luís Correia *Brazil* 3°0S 41°35W **93** D10
Luitpold Coast *Antarctica* 78°30S 32°0W **5** D1
Luiza *Dem. Rep. of the Congo* 7°40S 22°30E **52** F4
Luizi *Dem. Rep. of the Congo* 6°0S 27°25E **54** D2
Luján *Argentina* 34°45S 59°5W **94** C4
Lukanga Swamp *Zambia* 14°30S 27°40E **55** E2
Lukenie →
Dem. Rep. of the Congo 3°0S 18°50E **52** E3
Lukolela
Dem. Rep. of the Congo 5°23S 24°32E **54** D1
Lukosi *Zimbabwe* 18°30S 26°30E **55** F2
Łuków *Poland* 51°55N 22°23E **17** C12
Lukusuzi △ *Zambia* 12°43S 32°36E **55** E3
Luleå *Sweden* 65°35N 22°10E **8** D20
Luleälven → *Sweden* 65°35N 22°10E **8** D20
Lüleburgaz *Turkey* 41°23N 27°22E **23** D12
Lulima
Dem. Rep. of the Congo 4°12S 25°36E **54** C2
Luling *U.S.A.* 29°41N 97°39W **84** G6
Lulong *China* 39°53N 118°51E **35** E10
Lulonga →
Dem. Rep. of the Congo 1°0N 18°10E **52** D3
Lulua →
Dem. Rep. of the Congo 4°30S 20°30E **52** E4
Luma *Amer. Samoa* 14°16S 169°33W **59** b
Lumajang *Indonesia* 8°8S 113°13E **37** H15
Lumbala N'guimbo
Angola 14°18S 21°18E **53** G4
Lumberton *U.S.A.* 34°37N 79°0W **85** D15
Lumsden *Canada* 50°39N 104°52W **71** C8
Lumsden *N.Z.* 45°44S 168°27E **59** F2
Lumut *Malaysia* 4°13N 100°37E **39** K3
Lumut, Tanjung
Indonesia 3°50S 105°58E **36** E3
Luna *India* 23°43N 69°16E **42** H3
Lunavada *India* 23°8N 73°37E **42** H5
Lund *Sweden* 55°44N 13°12E **9** J15
Lundazi *Zambia* 12°20S 33°7E **55** E3
Lundi → *Zimbabwe* 21°43S 32°34E **55** G3
Lundu *Malaysia* 1°40N 109°50E **36** D3

Lundy *U.K.* 51°10N 4°41W **13** F3
Lune → *U.K.* 54°0N 2°51W **12** C5
Lüneburg *Germany* 53°10N 10°24E **16** B6
Lüneburg Heath = Lüneburger Heide *Germany* 53°10N 10°12E **16** B6
Lüneburger Heide
Germany 53°10N 10°12E **16** B6
Lunenburg *Canada* 44°22N 64°18W **73** D7
Lunéville *France* 48°36N 6°30E **20** B7
Lunga → *Zambia* 14°34S 26°25E **55** E2
Lunga Lunga *Kenya* 4°33S 39°7E **54** C4
Lunglei *India* 22°55N 92°45E **41** H18
Luni *India* 26°0N 73°6E **42** G5
Luni → *India* 24°41N 71°14E **42** G4
Luninets = Luninyets
Belarus 52°15N 26°50E **17** B14
Luning *U.S.A.* 38°30N 118°11W **76** G4
Luninyets *Belarus* 52°15N 26°50E **17** B14
Lunkaransar *India* 28°29N 73°44E **42** E5
Lunsemfwa → *Zambia* 14°54S 30°12E **55** E3
Lunsemfwa Falls *Zambia* 14°30S 29°6E **55** E2
Luo He → *China* 34°35N 110°20E **34** G6
Luochuan *China* 35°45N 109°26E **34** G5
Luofu
Dem. Rep. of the Congo 0°10S 29°15E **54** C2
Luohe *China* 33°32N 114°2E **34** H8
Luonan *China* 34°5N 110°10E **34** G6
Luoning *China* 34°35N 111°40E **34** G6
Luoyang *China* 34°40N 112°26E **34** G7
Luozigou *China* 43°42N 130°18E **35** C16
Lupanshui = Liupanshui *China* 26°38N 104°48E **34** D5
Lupilichi *Mozam.* 11°47S 35°13E **55** E4
Luque *Paraguay* 25°19S 57°25W **94** B4
Luquillo, Sierra de
Puerto Rico 18°20N 65°47W **89** d
Luray *U.S.A.* 38°40N 78°28W **81** F14
Lurgan *U.K.* 54°28N 6°19W **10** B5
Lúrio *Mozam.* 13°32S 40°30E **55** E5
Lúrio → *Mozam.* 13°32S 40°30E **55** E5
Lusaka *Zambia* 15°28S 28°16E **55** F2
Lusaka □ *Zambia* 15°30S 29°0E **55** F2
Lusambo
Dem. Rep. of the Congo 4°58S 23°28E **54** C1
Lusangaye
Dem. Rep. of the Congo 4°54S 26°0E **54** C2
Luseland *Canada* 52°5N 109°24W **71** C7
Lusenga Plain △ *Zambia* 9°22S 29°14E **55** D2
Lushan *China* 33°45N 112°55E **34** H7
Lushi *China* 34°3N 111°3E **34** G6
Lushnjë *Albania* 40°55N 19°41E **23** D8
Lushoto *Tanzania* 4°47S 38°20E **54** C4
Lüshun *China* 38°45N 121°15E **35** F11
Lusk *U.S.A.* 42°46N 104°27W **76** E11
Lūt, Dasht-e *Iran* 31°30N 58°0E **45** D8
Luta = Dalian *China* 38°50N 121°40E **35** E11
Lutherstadt Wittenberg
Germany 51°53N 12°39E **16** C7
Luton *U.K.* 51°53N 0°24W **13** F7
Luton □ *U.K.* 51°53N 0°24W **13** F7
Lutsel K'e *Canada* 62°24N 110°44W **71** A6
Lutsk *Ukraine* 50°50N 25°15E **17** C13
Lutto = Lotta → *Europe* 68°42N 31°6E **8** B24
Lützow Holmbukta
Antarctica 69°10S 37°30E **5** C4
Lutzputs *S. Africa* 28°3S 20°40E **56** D3
Luuq *Somali Rep.* 3°48N 42°34E **47** G3
Luverne *Ala., U.S.A.* 31°43N 86°16W **85** F11
Luverne *Minn., U.S.A.* 43°39N 96°13W **80** D5
Luvua
Dem. Rep. of the Congo 8°48S 25°17E **55** D2
Luvua →
Dem. Rep. of the Congo 6°50S 27°30E **54** D2
Luvuvhu → *S. Africa* 22°25S 31°18E **57** C5
Luwegu → *Tanzania* 8°31S 37°23E **55** D4
Luwero *Uganda* 0°50N 32°28E **54** B3
Luwuk *Indonesia* 0°56S 122°47E **37** E6
Luxembourg *Lux.* 49°37N 6°9E **15** E6
Luxembourg □ *Belgium* 49°58N 5°30E **15** E5
Luxembourg ■ *Europe* 49°45N 6°0E **15** E5
Luxembourg ✈ **(LUX)**
Lux. 49°37N 6°10E **15** E6
Luxi *China* 24°27N 98°36E **32** D4
Luxor = El Uqsur *Egypt* 25°41N 32°38E **51** C12
Luyi *China* 33°50N 115°35E **34** H8
Luza *Russia* 60°39N 47°10E **18** B8
Luzern *Switz.* 47°3N 8°18E **20** C8
Luziânia *Brazil* 16°20S 48°0W **93** G9
Luzon *Phil.* 16°0N 121°0E **37** A6
Lviv *Ukraine* 49°50N 24°0E **17** D13
Lvov = Lviv *Ukraine* 49°50N 24°0E **17** D13
Lyakhavichy *Belarus* 53°2N 26°32E **17** B14
Lyakhovskiye, Ostrova
Russia 73°40N 141°0E **29** B15
Lyal I. *Canada* 44°57N 81°24W **82** B3
Lybster *U.K.* 58°18N 3°15W **11** C5
Lydda = Lod *Israel* 31°57N 34°54E **46** D3
Lyddan I. *Antarctica* 74°0S 21°0W **5** D2
Lydenburg *S. Africa* 25°10S 30°29E **57** D5
Lydia *Turkey* 38°48N 28°19E **23** E13
Lyell *N.Z.* 41°48S 172°4E **59** D4
Lyell I. *Canada* 52°40N 131°35W **70** C2
Lyepyel *Belarus* 54°50N 28°40E **9** J23
Lykens *U.S.A.* 40°34N 76°42W **83** F8
Lyman *U.S.A.* 41°20N 110°18W **76** F8
Lyme B. *U.K.* 50°42N 2°53W **13** G4
Lyme Regis *U.K.* 50°43N 2°57W **13** G5
Lymington *U.K.* 50°45N 1°32W **13** G6
Łyna → *Poland* 54°37N 21°14E **17** A11
Lynchburg *U.S.A.* 37°25N 79°9W **81** G14
Lynd → *Australia* 16°28S 143°18E **62** B3
Lynd Ra. *Australia* 25°30S 149°20E **63** D4
Lynden *Canada* 43°14N 80°9W **82** C4
Lynden *U.S.A.* 48°57N 122°27W **78** B4
Lyndhurst *Australia* 30°15S 138°18E **63** E2
Lyndon → *Australia* 23°29S 114°6E **61** D1
Lyndonville *N.Y., U.S.A.* 43°20N 78°23W **82** C6
Lyndonville *Vt., U.S.A.* 44°31N 72°1W **83** B12
Lyngen *Norway* 69°45N 20°30E **8** B19
Lynher Reef *Australia* 15°27S 121°55E **60** C3

Lynn *U.S.A.* 42°28N 70°57W **83** D14
Lynn Canal *U.S.A.* 58°50N 135°15W **74** D12
Lynn Haven *U.S.A.* 30°15N 85°39W **85** F12
Lynn Lake *Canada* 56°51N 101°3W **71** B8
Lynnwood *U.S.A.* 47°49N 122°18W **78** C4
Lynton *U.K.* 51°13N 3°50W **13** F4
Lyntupy *Belarus* 55°4N 26°23E **9** J22
Lynx L. *Canada* 62°25N 106°15W **71** A7
Lyon *France* 45°46N 4°50E **20** D6
Lyonnais *France* 45°45N 4°15E **20** D6
Lyons = Lyon *France* 45°46N 4°50E **20** D6
Lyons *Ga., U.S.A.* 32°12N 82°19W **85** E13
Lyons *Kans., U.S.A.* 38°21N 98°12W **80** F4
Lyons *N.Y., U.S.A.* 43°5N 77°0W **82** C7
Lyons → *Australia* 25°2S 115°9E **61** E2
Lyons Falls *U.S.A.* 43°37N 75°22W **83** C9
Lys = Leie → *Belgium* 51°2N 3°45E **15** C3
Lysi *Cyprus* 35°6N 33°41E **25** D12
Lysva *Russia* 58°7N 57°49E **18** C10
Lysychansk *Ukraine* 48°55N 38°30E **19** E6
Lytham St. Anne's *U.K.* 53°45N 3°0W **12** D4
Lyttelton *N.Z.* 43°35S 172°44E **59** E4
Lytton *Canada* 50°13N 121°31W **70** C4
Lyubertsy *Russia* 55°40N 37°51E **18** C6
Lyuboml *Ukraine* 51°11N 24°4E **17** C13**

M

Ma → *Vietnam* 19°47N 105°56E **38** C5
Ma'adaba *Jordan* 30°43N 35°47E **46** E4
Maamba *Zambia* 17°17S 26°28E **56** B4
Ma'ān *Jordan* 30°12N 35°44E **46** E4
Ma'ān □ *Jordan* 30°0N 36°0E **46** F5
Maanselkä *Finland* 63°52N 28°32E **8** E23
Ma'anshan *China* 31°44N 118°29E **33** C6
Maarianhamina = Mariehamn
Finland 60°5N 19°55E **9** F18
Ma'arrat an Nu'mān
Syria 35°43N 36°43E **44** C3
Maas → *Neths.* 51°45N 4°32E **15** C4
Maaseik *Belgium* 51°6N 5°45E **15** C5
Maasin *Phil.* 10°8N 124°50E **37** B6
Maastricht *Neths.* 50°50N 5°40E **15** D5
Maave *Mozam.* 21°4S 34°47E **57** C5
Mababe Depression
Botswana 18°50S 24°15E **56** B3
Mabalane *Mozam.* 23°37S 32°31E **57** C5
Mabel L. *Canada* 50°35N 118°43W **70** C5
Mabenge
Dem. Rep. of the Congo 4°15N 24°12E **54** B1
Maberly *Canada* 44°50N 76°32W **83** B8
Mablethorpe *U.K.* 53°20N 0°15E **12** D8
Maboma
Dem. Rep. of the Congo 2°30N 28°10E **54** B2
Mabuasehube △
Botswana 25°5S 21°10E **56** D3
Mabuiag *Australia* 9°57S 142°11E **62** a
Mac Bac *Vietnam* 9°46N 106°7E **39** H6
Macachín *Argentina* 37°10S 63°43W **94** D3
Macaé *Brazil* 22°20S 41°43W **95** A7
McAlester *U.S.A.* 34°56N 95°46W **84** D7
MacAlpine L. *Canada* 66°32N 102°45W **68** D11
Macamic *Canada* 48°45N 79°0W **72** C4
Macao = Macau *China* 22°12N 113°33E **33** G10
Macapá *Brazil* 0°5N 51°4W **93** C8
Macarao △ *Venezuela* 10°22N 67°9W **89** D6
McArthur → *Australia* 15°54S 136°40E **62** B2
McArthur, Port *Australia* 16°4S 136°23E **62** B2
Macau *Brazil* 5°15S 36°40W **93** E11
Macau *China* 22°12N 113°33E **33** G10
McBride *Canada* 53°20N 120°19W **70** C4
McCall *U.S.A.* 44°55N 116°6W **76** D5
McCamey *U.S.A.* 31°8N 102°14W **84** F3
McCammon *U.S.A.* 42°39N 112°12W **76** E7
McCarran Int., Las Vegas ✈ **(LAS)**
U.S.A. 36°5N 115°9W **79** J11
McCauley I. *Canada* 53°40N 130°15W **70** C2
McCleary *U.S.A.* 47°3N 123°16W **78** C3
Macclenny *U.S.A.* 30°17N 82°7W **85** F13
Macclesfield *U.K.* 53°15N 2°8W **12** D5
M'Clintock Chan.
Canada 72°0N 102°0W **68** A10
M'Clintock Ra.
Australia 18°44S 127°38E **60** C4
McCloud *U.S.A.* 41°15N 122°8W **76** F2
McCluer I. *Australia* 11°5S 133°0E **60** B5
McClure *U.S.A.* 40°42N 77°19W **82** F7
McClure, L. *U.S.A.* 37°35N 120°16W **78** H6
M'Clure Str. *Canada* 75°0N 119°0W **69** C8
McClusky *U.S.A.* 47°29N 100°27W **80** B4
McComb *U.S.A.* 31°15N 90°27W **85** F9
McCook *U.S.A.* 40°12N 100°38W **80** E3
McCreary *Canada* 50°47N 99°29W **71** C9
McCullough Mt.
U.S.A. 35°35N 115°13W **79** K11
McCusker → *Canada* 55°32N 108°39W **71** B7
McDermitt *U.S.A.* 41°59N 117°43W **76** F5
McDonald *U.S.A.* 40°22N 80°14W **82** F4
Macdonald, L. *Australia* 23°30S 129°0E **60** D4
Macdonald Is. *Ind. Oc.* 53°0S 73°0E **3** G13
MacDonnell Ranges
Australia 23°40S 133°0E **60** D5
MacDowell L. *Canada* 52°15N 92°45W **72** B1
Macduff *U.K.* 57°40N 2°31W **11** D6
Macedonia *U.S.A.* 41°19N 81°31W **82** E3
Macedonia □ *Greece* 40°39N 22°0E **23** D10
Macedonia ■ *Europe* 41°53N 21°40E **23** D9
Maceió *Brazil* 9°40S 35°41W **93** E11
Macerata *Italy* 43°18N 13°27E **22** C5
McFarland *U.S.A.* 35°41N 119°14W **79** K7
McFarlane → *Canada* 59°12N 107°58W **71** B7
Macfarlane, L. *Australia* 32°0S 136°40E **63** E2
McGehee *U.S.A.* 33°38N 91°24W **84** E9
McGill *U.S.A.* 39°23N 114°47W **76** G6
Macgillycuddy's Reeks
Ireland 51°58N 9°45W **10** E2
McGraw *U.S.A.* 42°36N 76°8W **83** D8

McGregor *U.S.A.* 43°1N 91°11W **80 D8**
McGregor Ra. *Australia* 27°0S 142°45E **63 D3**
McGuire, Mt. *Australia* 20°18S 148°23E **62 b**
Mach *Pakistan* 29°50N 67°20E **42 E2**
Mâch Kowr *Iran* 25°48N 61°28E **45 E9**
Machado = Jiparaná →
  Brazil 8°3S 62°52W **92 E6**
Machagai *Argentina* 26°56S 60°2W **94 B3**
Machakos *Kenya* 1°30S 37°15E **54 C4**
Machala *Ecuador* 3°20S 79°57W **92 D3**
Machanga *Mozam.* 20°59S 35°0E **57 C6**
Machattie, L. *Australia* 24°50S 139°48E **62 C2**
Machava *Mozam.* 25°54S 32°28E **57 D5**
Machece *Mozam.* 19°15S 35°32E **55 F4**
Macheke *Zimbabwe* 18°5S 31°51E **57 B5**
Machhu → *India* 23°6N 70°46E **42 H4**
Machiara △ *Pakistan* 34°40N 73°30E **42 B5**
Machias *Maine, U.S.A.* 44°43N 67°28W **81 C20**
Machias *N.Y., U.S.A.* 42°25N 78°29W **82 D6**
Machichi → *Canada* 57°3N 92°6W **71 B10**
Machico *Madeira* 32°43N 16°44W **24 D3**
Machilipatnam *India* 16°12N 81°8E **41 L12**
Machiques *Venezuela* 10°4N 72°34W **92 A4**
Machu Picchu *Peru* 13°8S 72°30W **92 F4**
Machynlleth *U.K.* 52°35N 3°50W **13 E4**
Macia *Mozam.* 25°2S 33°8E **57 D5**
McIlwraith Ra.
  Australia 13°50S 143°20E **62 A3**
McInnes L. *Canada* 52°13N 93°45W **71 C10**
McIntosh *U.S.A.* 45°55N 101°21W **80 C3**
McIntosh L. *Canada* 55°45N 105°0W **71 B8**
Macintosh Ra. *Australia* 27°39S 125°32E **61 E4**
Macintyre → *Australia* 28°37S 150°47E **63 D5**
Mackay *Australia* 21°8S 149°11E **62 K7**
Mackay *U.S.A.* 43°55N 113°37W **76 E7**
MacKay → *Canada* 57°10N 111°38W **70 B6**
Mackay, L. *Australia* 22°30S 129°0E **60 D4**
McKay Ra. *Australia* 23°0S 122°30E **60 D3**
McKeesport *U.S.A.* 40°20N 79°51W **82 F5**
McKellar *Canada* 45°30N 79°55W **82 A5**
McKenna *U.S.A.* 46°56N 122°33W **78 D4**
Mackenzie *Canada* 55°20N 123°5W **70 B4**
Mackenzie → *Australia* 23°38S 149°46E **62 C4**
Mackenzie → *Canada* 69°10N 134°20W **68 D5**
McKenzie → *U.S.A.* 44°7N 123°6W **76 D2**
Mackenzie Bay *Canada* 69°0N 137°30W **66 C6**
Mackenzie City = Linden
  Guyana 6°0N 58°10W **92 B7**
Mackenzie King I.
  Canada 77°45N 111°0W **69 B9**
Mackenzie Mts. *Canada* 64°0N 130°0W **68 E6**
Mackinac, Straits of
  U.S.A. 45°50N 84°40W **75 F23**
Mackinaw City *U.S.A.* 45°47N 84°44W **81 C11**
McKinlay *Australia* 21°16S 141°18E **62 C3**
McKinlay → *Australia* 20°50S 141°28E **62 C3**
McKinley, Mt. *U.S.A.* 63°4N 151°0W **68 E1**
McKinney *U.S.A.* 33°12N 96°37W **84 E6**
Mackinnon Road *Kenya* 3°40S 39°1E **54 C4**
McKittrick *U.S.A.* 35°18N 119°37W **79 K7**
Macklin *Canada* 52°20N 109°56W **71 C7**
Macksville *Australia* 30°40S 152°56E **63 E5**
McLaughlin *U.S.A.* 45°49N 100°49W **80 C3**
Maclean *Australia* 29°26S 153°16E **63 D5**
McLean *U.S.A.* 35°14N 100°36W **84 D4**
McLeansboro *U.S.A.* 38°6N 88°32W **80 F9**
Maclear *S. Africa* 31°2S 28°23E **57 E4**
Maclear, C. *Malawi* 13°58S 34°49E **55 E3**
Macleay → *Australia* 30°56S 153°0E **63 E5**
McLennan *Canada* 55°42N 116°50W **70 B5**
McLeod → *Canada* 54°9N 115°44W **70 C5**
MacLeod, L. *Australia* 24°9S 113°47E **61 D1**
MacLeod B. *Canada* 62°53N 110°0W **71 A7**
MacLeod Lake *Canada* 54°58N 123°0W **70 C4**
McLoughlin, Mt.
  U.S.A. 42°27N 122°19W **76 E2**
McMechen *U.S.A.* 39°57N 80°44W **82 G4**
McMinnville *Oreg.,*
  U.S.A. 45°13N 123°12W **76 D2**
McMinnville *Tenn.,*
  U.S.A. 35°41N 85°46W **85 D12**
McMurdo *Antarctica* 77°0S 140°0E **5 D11**
McMurdo Sd. *Antarctica* 77°0S 170°0E **5 D11**
McMurray = Fort McMurray
  Canada 56°44N 111°7W **70 B6**
McMurray *U.S.A.* 48°19N 122°14W **78 B4**
Maçobere *Mozam.* 21°13S 32°47E **55 G3**
Macodoene *Mozam.* 23°32S 35°5E **57 C6**
Macomb *U.S.A.* 40°27N 90°40W **80 E8**
Mâcon *France* 46°19N 4°50E **20 C6**
Macon *Ga., U.S.A.* 32°51N 83°38W **85 J4**
Macon *Miss., U.S.A.* 33°7N 88°34W **85 E10**
Macon *Mo., U.S.A.* 39°44N 92°28W **80 F7**
Macossa *Mozam.* 17°55S 33°56E **55 F3**
Macoun L. *Canada* 56°32N 103°40W **71 B8**
Macovane *Mozam.* 21°30S 35°2E **57 C6**
McPherson *U.S.A.* 38°22N 97°40W **80 F6**
McPherson Pk. *U.S.A.* 34°53N 119°53W **79 L7**
McPherson Ra.
  Australia 28°15S 153°15E **63 D5**
Macquarie → *Australia* 30°7S 147°24E **63 E4**
Macquarie Harbour
  Australia 42°15S 145°23E **63 G4**
Macquarie Is. *S. Pac. Oc.* 54°36S 158°55E **64 N7**
Macquarie Ridge *S. Ocean* 57°0S 159°0E **5 B10**
MacRobertson Land
  Antarctica 71°0S 64°0E **5 D6**
Macroom *Ireland* 51°54N 8°57W **10 E3**
MacTier *Canada* 45°8N 79°47W **82 A5**
Macubela *Mozam.* 16°53S 37°49E **55 F4**
Macuira △ *Colombia* 12°9N 71°21W **89 D5**
Macuiza *Mozam.* 18°7S 34°29E **55 F3**
Macumba → *Australia* 27°52S 137°12E **63 D2**
Macusani *Peru* 14°4S 70°29W **92 F4**
Macuse *Mozam.* 17°45S 37°10E **55 F4**
Macuspana *Mexico* 17°46N 92°36W **87 D6**

Macusse *Angola* 17°48S 20°23E **56 B3**
Ma'dabā □ *Jordan* 31°43N 35°47E **46 D4**
Madadeni *S. Africa* 27°43S 30°3E **57 D5**
Madā'in Şālih *Si. Arabia* 26°46N 37°57E **44 E3**
Madama *Niger* 22°0N 13°40E **51 D8**
Madame, I. *Canada* 45°30N 60°58W **73 C7**
Madang *Papua N. G.* 5°12S 145°49E **58 B7**
Madaripur *Bangla.* 23°19N 90°15E **41 H17**
Madawaska *Canada* 45°30N 78°0W **82 A7**
Madawaska → *Canada* 45°27N 76°21W **82 A7**
Madaya *Burma* 22°12N 96°10E **41 H20**
Maddalena *Italy* 41°16N 9°23E **22 D3**
Madeira *Atl. Oc.* 32°50N 17°0W **24 D3**
Madeira → *Brazil* 3°22S 58°45W **92 D7**
Madeleine, Îs. de la
  Canada 47°30N 61°40W **73 C7**
Madera *Mexico* 29°12N 108°7W **86 B3**
Madera *Calif., U.S.A.* 36°57N 120°3W **78 J6**
Madera *Pa., U.S.A.* 40°49N 78°26W **82 F6**
Madha *India* 18°0N 75°30E **40 L9**
Madhavpur *India* 21°15N 69°58E **42 J3**
Madhepura *India* 26°11N 86°23E **43 F12**
Madhubani *India* 26°21N 86°7E **43 F12**
Madhupur *India* 24°16N 86°39E **43 G12**
Madhya Pradesh □ *India* 22°50N 78°0E **42 J8**
Madidi → *Bolivia* 12°32S 66°52W **92 F5**
Madikeri *India* 12°30N 75°45E **40 N9**
Madikwe △ *S. Africa* 27°38S 32°15E **57 D5**
Madill *U.S.A.* 34°6N 96°46W **84 D6**
Madimba
  Dem. Rep. of the Congo 4°58S 15°5E **52 E3**
Ma'din *Syria* 35°45N 39°36E **44 C3**
Madinat al Malik Khālid al
  Askarīyah *Si. Arabia* 27°54N 45°31E **44 E5**
Madingou *Congo* 4°10S 13°33E **52 E2**
Madirovalo *Madag.* 16°26S 46°32E **57 B8**
Madison *Calif., U.S.A.* 38°41N 121°59W **78 G5**
Madison *Fla., U.S.A.* 30°28N 83°25W **85 F13**
Madison *Ind., U.S.A.* 38°44N 85°23W **81 F11**
Madison *Nebr., U.S.A.* 41°50N 97°27W **80 E5**
Madison *Ohio, U.S.A.* 41°46N 81°3W **82 E3**
Madison *S. Dak., U.S.A.* 44°0N 97°7W **80 C5**
Madison *Wis., U.S.A.* 43°4N 89°24W **80 D9**
Madison → *U.S.A.* 45°56N 111°31W **76 D8**
Madison Heights *U.S.A.* 37°25N 79°8W **81 G14**
Madisonville *Ky.,*
  U.S.A. 37°20N 87°30W **80 G10**
Madisonville *Tex.,*
  U.S.A. 30°57N 95°55W **84 F7**
Madista *Botswana* 21°15S 25°6E **56 C4**
Madiun *Indonesia* 7°38S 111°32E **37 G14**
Mado Gashi *Kenya* 0°44N 39°10E **54 B4**
Madoc *Canada* 44°30N 77°28W **82 B7**
Madona *Latvia* 56°53N 26°5E **9 H22**
Madrakah, Ra's al *Oman* 19°0N 57°50E **47 D6**
Madras = Chennai *India* 13°8N 80°19E **40 N12**
Madras = Tamil Nadu □
  India 11°0N 77°0E **40 P10**
Madras *U.S.A.* 44°38N 121°8W **76 D3**
Madre, L. *U.S.A.* 25°15N 97°30W **84 J6**
Madre, Sierra *Phil.* 17°0N 122°0E **37 A6**
Madre de Dios → *Bolivia* 10°59S 66°8W **92 F5**
Madre de Dios, I. *Chile* 50°20S 75°10W **96 G1**
Madre del Sur, Sierra
  Mexico 17°30N 100°0W **87 D5**
Madre Occidental, Sierra
  Mexico 27°0N 107°0W **86 B3**
Madre Oriental, Sierra
  Mexico 25°0N 100°0W **86 C5**
Madri *India* 24°16N 73°32E **42 G5**
Madrid *Spain* 40°24N 3°42W **21 B4**
Madrid *U.S.A.* 44°45N 75°8W **83 B9**
Madula
  Dem. Rep. of the Congo 0°27N 25°22E **54 B2**
Madura *Australia* 31°55S 127°0E **61 F4**
Madura *Indonesia* 7°30S 114°0E **37 G15**
Madura, Selat *Indonesia* 7°30S 113°20E **37 G15**
Madurai *India* 9°55N 78°10E **40 Q11**
Madurantakam *India* 12°30N 79°50E **40 N11**
Mae Chan *Thailand* 20°9N 99°52E **38 B2**
Mae Hong Son *Thailand* 19°16N 97°56E **38 C2**
Mae Khlong → *Thailand* 13°24N 100°0E **38 F3**
Mae Phrik *Thailand* 17°27N 99°7E **38 D2**
Mae Ping △ *Thailand* 17°37N 98°51E **38 D2**
Mae Ramat *Thailand* 16°58N 98°31E **38 D2**
Mae Rim *Thailand* 18°54N 98°57E **38 C2**
Mae Sai *Thailand* 20°20N 99°55E **38 B2**
Mae Sot *Thailand* 16°43N 98°34E **38 D2**
Mae Suai *Thailand* 19°39N 99°33E **38 C2**
Mae Tha *Thailand* 18°28N 99°8E **38 C2**
Mae Wong △ *Thailand* 15°54N 99°12E **38 E2**
Mae Yom △ *Thailand* 18°43N 100°15E **38 C3**
Maebashi *Japan* 36°24N 139°4E **31 F9**
Maelpaeg L. *Canada* 48°20N 56°30W **73 C8**
Maesteg *U.K.* 51°36N 3°40W **13 F4**
Maestra, Sierra *Cuba* 20°15N 77°0W **88 B4**
Maevatanana *Madag.* 16°56S 46°49E **57 B8**
Mafeking = Mafikeng
  S. Africa 25°50S 25°38E **56 D4**
Mafeking *Canada* 52°40N 101°10W **71 C8**
Mafeteng *Lesotho* 29°51S 27°15E **56 D4**
Maffra *Australia* 37°53S 146°58E **63 F4**
Mafia I. *Tanzania* 7°45S 39°50E **54 D4**
Mafikeng *S. Africa* 25°50S 25°38E **56 D4**
Mafra *Brazil* 26°10S 49°55W **95 B6**
Mafra *Portugal* 38°55N 9°20W **21 C1**
Mafungabusi Plateau
  Zimbabwe 18°30S 29°8E **55 F2**
Magadan *Russia* 59°38N 150°50E **29 D16**
Magadi *Kenya* 1°54S 36°19E **54 C4**
Magadi, L. *Kenya* 1°54S 36°19E **54 C4**
Magaliesburg *S. Africa* 26°0S 27°32E **57 D4**
Magallanes, Estrecho de
  Chile 52°30S 75°0W **96 G2**
Magangué *Colombia* 9°14N 74°45W **92 B4**
Magdagachi *Russia* 53°27N 125°48E **29 D13**

Magdalen Is. = Madeleine, Îs. de la
  Canada 47°30N 61°40W **73 C7**
Magdalena *Argentina* 35°5S 57°30W **94 D4**
Magdalena *Bolivia* 13°13S 63°57W **92 F6**
Magdalena *U.S.A.* 34°7N 107°15W **77 J10**
Magdalena → *Colombia* 11°6N 74°51W **92 A4**
Magdalena → *Mexico* 30°40N 112°25W **86 A2**
Magdalena, B. *Mexico* 24°35N 112°0W **86 C2**
Magdalena, I. *Mexico* 24°40N 112°15W **86 C2**
Magdalena, Llano de
  Mexico 25°0N 111°25W **86 C2**
Magdalena de Kino
  Mexico 30°38N 110°57W **86 A2**
Magdeburg *Germany* 52°7N 11°38E **16 B6**
Magdelaine Cays
  Australia 16°33S 150°18E **62 B5**
Magee *U.S.A.* 31°52N 89°44W **85 F10**
Magelang *Indonesia* 7°29S 110°13E **37 G14**
Magellan's Str. = Magallanes,
  Estrecho de *Chile* 52°30S 75°0W **96 G2**
Magenta, L. *Australia* 33°30S 119°2E **61 F2**
Magerøya *Norway* 71°3N 25°40E **8 A21**
Maggiore, Lago *Italy* 45°57N 8°39E **20 D8**
Maggotty *Jamaica* 18°9N 77°46W **88 a**
Maghâgha *Egypt* 28°38N 30°50E **51 C12**
Magherafelt *U.K.* 54°45N 6°37W **10 B5**
Maghreb *N. Afr.* 32°0N 4°0W **50 B5**
Magistralnyy *Russia* 56°16N 107°36E **29 D11**
Magnetic Pole (North)
  Canada 82°42N 114°24W **4 A2**
Magnetic Pole (South)
  Antarctica 64°8S 138°8E **5 C9**
Magnitogorsk *Russia* 53°27N 59°4E **18 D10**
Magnolia *Ark., U.S.A.* 33°16N 93°14W **84 E8**
Magnolia *Miss., U.S.A.* 31°9N 90°28W **85 F9**
Mago *Fiji* 17°26S 179°8W **59 a**
Magog *Canada* 45°18N 72°9W **83 A12**
Magoro *Uganda* 1°45N 34°12E **54 B3**
Magoša = Famagusta
  Cyprus 35°8N 33°55E **25 D12**
Magoulades *Greece* 39°45N 19°42E **25 A3**
Magoye *Zambia* 16°1S 27°30E **55 F2**
Magpie, L. *Canada* 51°0N 64°41W **73 B7**
Magrath *Canada* 49°25N 112°50W **70 D6**
Magu *Tanzania* 2°30S 33°30E **54 C3**
Maguarinho, C. *Brazil* 0°15S 48°30W **93 D9**
Magude *Mozam.* 25°2S 32°40E **57 D5**
Magusa = Famagusta
  Cyprus 35°8N 33°55E **25 D12**
Maguse L. *Canada* 61°37N 95°10W **71 A9**
Maguse Pt. *Canada* 61°20N 93°50W **71 A10**
Magvana *India* 23°13N 69°22E **42 H3**
Magwe *Burma* 20°10N 95°0E **41 J19**
Magyarország = Hungary ■
  Europe 47°20N 19°20E **17 E10**
Maha Sarakham
  Thailand 16°12N 103°16E **38 D4**
Mahābād *Iran* 36°50N 45°45E **44 B5**
Mahabharat Lekh *Nepal* 28°30N 82°0E **43 E10**
Mahabo *Madag.* 20°23S 44°40E **57 C7**
Mahadeo Hills *India* 22°20N 78°30E **43 H8**
Mahaffey *U.S.A.* 40°53N 78°44W **82 F6**
Mahagi
  Dem. Rep. of the Congo 2°20N 31°0E **54 B3**
Mahajamba → *Madag.* 15°33S 47°8E **57 B8**
Mahajamba, Helodranon' i
  Madag. 15°24S 47°5E **57 B8**
Mahajan *India* 28°48N 73°56E **42 E5**
Mahajanga *Madag.* 15°40S 46°25E **57 B8**
Mahajanga □ *Madag.* 17°0S 47°0E **57 B8**
Mahajilo → *Madag.* 19°42S 45°22E **57 B8**
Mahakam → *Indonesia* 0°35S 117°17E **36 E5**
Mahalapye *Botswana* 23°1S 26°51E **56 C4**
Mahale Mts. *Tanzania* 6°20S 30°0E **54 D2**
Mahale Mts. △ *Tanzania* 6°10S 29°50E **54 D2**
Maḥallāt *Iran* 33°55N 50°30E **45 C6**
Māhān *Iran* 30°5N 57°18E **45 D8**
Mahan → *India* 23°30N 82°50E **43 H10**
Mahanadi → *India* 20°20N 86°25E **41 J15**
Mahananda → *India* 25°12N 87°52E **43 G12**
Mahanoro *Madag.* 19°54S 48°48E **57 B8**
Mahanoy City *U.S.A.* 40°49N 76°9W **83 F8**
Maharashtra □ *India* 20°30N 75°30E **40 J9**
Mahasham, W. →
  Egypt 30°15N 34°10E **46 E3**
Mahasoa *Madag.* 22°12S 46°6E **57 C8**
Mahasolo *Madag.* 19°7S 46°22E **57 B8**
Mahattat ash Shīdīyah
  Jordan 29°55N 35°55E **46 F4**
Mahattat 'Unayzah
  Jordan 30°30N 35°47E **46 E4**
Mahavavy → *Madag.* 15°57S 45°54E **57 B8**
Mahaxay *Laos* 17°22N 105°12E **38 D5**
Mahbubnagar *India* 16°45N 77°59E **40 L10**
Mahda *U.A.E.* 25°20N 56°15E **45 E8**
Maḥḏah *Oman* 24°24N 55°59E **45 E7**
Mahdia *Tunisia* 35°28N 11°0E **51 A8**
Mahe *India* 33°10N 78°32E **43 C8**
Mahé *Seychelles* 5°0S 55°30E **53 b**
Mahébourg *Mauritius* 20°24S 57°42E **53 d**
Mahendragarh *India* 28°17N 76°14E **42 E7**
Mahendranagar *Nepal* 28°55N 80°20E **43 E9**
Mahenge *Tanzania* 8°45S 36°41E **55 D4**
Maheno *N.Z.* 45°10S 170°50E **59 F3**
Mahesana *India* 23°39N 72°26E **42 H5**
Maheshwar *India* 22°11N 75°35E **42 H6**
Mahgawan *India* 26°29N 78°37E **43 F8**
Mahi → *India* 22°15N 72°55E **42 H5**
Mahia Pen. *N.Z.* 39°9S 177°55E **59 C6**
Mahilyow *Belarus* 53°55N 30°18E **17 B16**
Mahina *Tahiti* 17°30S 149°27W **59 d**
Mahinerangi, L. *N.Z.* 45°50S 169°56E **59 F2**
Mahmud Kot *Pakistan* 30°16N 71°0E **42 D4**
Mahnomen *U.S.A.* 47°19N 95°58W **80 B6**
Mahoba *India* 25°15N 79°55E **43 G8**
Mahón = Maó *Spain* 39°53N 4°16E **24 B11**
Mahone Bay *Canada* 44°27N 64°23W **73 D7**
Mahopac *U.S.A.* 41°22N 73°45W **83 E11**

Mahuva *India* 21°5N 71°48E **42 J4**
Mai-Ndombe, L.
  Dem. Rep. of the Congo 2°0S 18°20E **52 E3**
Mai Thon, Ko *Thailand* 7°40N 98°28E **39 a**
Maicuru → *Brazil* 2°14S 54°17W **93 D8**
Maidan Khula *Afghan.* 33°36N 69°50E **42 C3**
Maidenhead *U.K.* 51°31N 0°42W **13 F7**
Maidstone *Canada* 53°5N 109°20W **71 C7**
Maidstone *U.K.* 51°16N 0°32E **13 F8**
Maiduguri *Nigeria* 12°0N 13°20E **51 F8**
Maigh Nuad = Maynooth
  Ireland 53°23N 6°34W **10 C5**
Maihar *India* 24°16N 80°45E **43 G9**
Maikala Ra. *India* 22°0N 81°0E **41 J12**
Maiko △
  Dem. Rep. of the Congo 0°30S 27°50E **54 C2**
Mailani *India* 28°17N 80°21E **43 E9**
Mailsi *Pakistan* 29°48N 72°15E **42 E5**
Main → *Germany* 50°0N 8°18E **16 C5**
Main → *U.K.* 54°48N 6°18W **10 B5**
Main Channel *Canada* 45°21N 81°45W **82 A3**
Main Range △
  Australia 28°11S 152°27E **63 D5**
Main Ridge *Trin. & Tob.* 11°16N 60°40W **93 J16**
Maine *France* 48°20N 0°15W **20 C3**
Maine □ *U.S.A.* 45°20N 69°0W **81 C19**
Maine → *Ireland* 52°9N 9°45W **10 D2**
Maine, G. of *U.S.A.* 43°0N 68°30W **81 D19**
Maingkwan *Burma* 26°15N 96°37E **41 F20**
Mainistir an Corann = Midleton
  Ireland 51°55N 8°10W **10 E3**
Mainit, L. *Phil.* 9°31N 125°30E **37 C7**
Mainland *Orkney, U.K.* 58°59N 3°8W **11 C5**
Mainland *Shet., U.K.* 60°15N 1°22W **11 A7**
Mainpuri *India* 27°18N 79°4E **43 F8**
Maintirano *Madag.* 18°3S 44°1E **57 B7**
Mainz *Germany* 50°1N 8°14E **16 C5**
Maio *C. Verde Is.* 15°10N 23°10W **50 b**
Maipú *Argentina* 36°52S 57°50W **94 D4**
Maiquetía *Venezuela* 10°36N 66°57W **92 A5**
Mairabari *India* 26°30N 92°22E **41 F18**
Maisí *Cuba* 20°17N 74°9W **89 B5**
Maisi, Pta. de *Cuba* 20°10N 74°10W **89 B5**
Maitland *N.S.W.,*
  Australia 32°33S 151°36E **63 E5**
Maitland *S. Austral.,*
  Australia 34°23S 137°40E **63 E2**
Maitland → *Canada* 43°45N 81°43W **82 C3**
Maitri *Antarctica* 70°0S 3°0W **5 D3**
Maíz, Is. del *Nic.* 12°15N 83°4W **88 D3**
Maizuru *Japan* 35°25N 135°22E **31 G7**
Majalengka *Indonesia* 6°50S 108°13E **37 G13**
Majene *Indonesia* 3°38S 118°57E **37 E5**
Majete △ *Malawi* 15°54S 34°34E **55 F3**
Majorca = Mallorca
  Spain 39°30N 3°0E **24 B10**
Majuro *Marshall Is.* 7°9N 171°12E **64 G9**
Maka *Senegal* 13°40N 14°10W **50 F3**
Makaha *Zimbabwe* 17°20S 32°39E **57 B5**
Makalamabedi *Botswana* 20°19S 23°51E **56 C3**
Makale *Indonesia* 3°6S 119°51E **37 E5**
Makalu-Barun △ *Nepal* 27°45N 87°10E **43 F12**
Makamba *Burundi* 4°8S 29°49E **54 C2**
Makarikari = Makgadikgadi Salt
  Pans *Botswana* 20°40S 25°45E **56 C4**
Makarov Basin *Arctic* 87°0N 150°0W **4 A**
Makarovo *Russia* 57°40N 107°45E **29 D11**
Makasar = Ujung Pandang
  Indonesia 5°10S 119°20E **37 F5**
Makasar, Selat *Indonesia* 1°0S 118°20E **37 E5**
Makasar, Str. of = Makasar, Selat
  Indonesia 1°0S 118°20E **37 E5**
Makat = Maqat
  Kazakhstan 47°39N 53°19E **19 E9**
Makedonija = Macedonia ■
  Europe 41°53N 21°40E **23 D9**
Makeni *S. Leone* 8°55N 12°5W **50 G3**
Makeyevka = Makiyivka
  Ukraine 48°0N 38°0E **19 E6**
Makgadikgadi △
  Botswana 20°27S 24°47E **56 C3**
Makgadikgadi Salt Pans
  Botswana 20°40S 25°45E **56 C4**
Makhachkala *Russia* 43°0N 47°30E **19 F8**
Makhado = Louis Trichardt
  S. Africa 23°1S 29°43E **57 C4**
Makham, Ao *Thailand* 7°51N 98°25E **39 a**
Makhfar al Buşayyah
  Iraq 30°0N 46°10E **44 D5**
Makhmūr *Iraq* 35°46N 43°35E **44 C4**
Makian *Indonesia* 0°20N 127°20E **37 D7**
Makindu *Kenya* 2°18S 37°50E **54 C4**
Makīnsk *Kazakhstan* 52°37N 70°26E **28 D8**
Makira = San Cristóbal
  Solomon Is. 10°30S 161°0E **58 C9**
Makiyivka *Ukraine* 48°0N 38°0E **19 E6**
Makkah *Si. Arabia* 21°30N 39°54E **47 C2**
Makkovik *Canada* 55°10N 59°10W **73 A8**
Makó *Hungary* 46°14N 20°33E **17 E11**
Makogai *Fiji* 17°28S 179°0E **59 a**
Makokou *Gabon* 0°40N 12°50E **52 D2**
Makongo
  Dem. Rep. of the Congo 3°25N 26°17E **54 B2**
Makoro
  Dem. Rep. of the Congo 3°10N 29°59E **54 B2**
Makrai *India* 22°2N 77°0E **42 H7**
Makran Coast Range
  Pakistan 25°40N 64°0E **40 G4**
Makrana *India* 27°2N 74°46E **42 F6**
Makrigialos *Greece* 35°2N 25°59E **25 D7**
Mākū *Iran* 39°15N 44°31E **44 B5**
Makunda *Botswana* 22°30S 20°7E **56 C3**
Makurazaki *Japan* 31°15N 130°20E **31 J5**
Makurdi *Nigeria* 7°43N 8°35E **50 G7**
Makushin Volcano
  U.S.A. 53°53N 166°55W **74 E6**
Makūyeh *Iran* 28°7N 53°9E **45 D7**
Makwassie *S. Africa* 27°17S 26°0E **56 D4**

Makwiro *Zimbabwe* 17°58S 30°25E **57 B5**
Mal B. *Ireland* 52°50N 9°30W **10 D2**
Mala = Mallow *Ireland* 52°8N 8°39W **10 D3**
Mala ○ *Australia* 21°39S 130°45E **60 D5**
Malabar Coast *India* 11°0N 75°0E **40 P9**
Malacca, Straits of
  Indonesia 3°0N 101°0E **39 L3**
Malad City *U.S.A.* 42°12N 112°15W **76 E7**
Maladzyechna *Belarus* 54°20N 26°50E **17 A14**
Málaga *Spain* 36°43N 4°23W **21 D3**
Malagarasi *Tanzania* 5°5S 30°50E **54 D3**
Malagarasi → *Tanzania* 5°12S 29°47E **54 D2**
Malagasy Rep. = Madagascar ■
  Africa 20°0S 47°0E **57 C8**
Malahide *Ireland* 53°26N 6°9E **10 C5**
Malaimbandy *Madag.* 20°35S 45°36E **57 C8**
Malaita *Solomon Is.* 9°0S 161°0E **58 B9**
Malakâl *Sudan* 9°33N 31°40E **51 G12**
Malakand *Pakistan* 34°40N 71°55E **42 B4**
Malakula *Vanuatu* 16°15S 167°30E **58 C9**
Malakwal *Pakistan* 32°34N 73°13E **42 C5**
Malamala *Indonesia* 3°21S 120°55E **37 E6**
Malanda *Australia* 17°22S 145°35E **62 B4**
Malang *Indonesia* 7°59S 112°45E **37 G15**
Malanga *Mozam.* 13°28S 36°7E **55 E4**
Malangen *Norway* 69°24N 18°37E **8 B18**
Malanje *Angola* 9°36S 16°17E **52 F3**
Mälaren *Sweden* 59°30N 17°10E **9 G17**
Malargüe *Argentina* 35°32S 69°30W **94 D2**
Malartic *Canada* 48°9N 78°9W **72 C4**
Malaryta *Belarus* 51°50N 24°3E **17 C13**
Malaspina Glacier
  U.S.A. 59°50N 140°30W **74 D11**
Malatya *Turkey* 38°25N 38°20E **44 B3**
Malawi ■ *Africa* 11°55S 34°0E **55 E3**
Malawi, L. *Africa* 12°30S 34°30E **55 E3**
Malay Pen. *Asia* 7°25N 100°0E **39 J3**
Malaya Vishera *Russia* 58°55N 32°25E **18 C5**
Malaybalay *Phil.* 8°5N 125°7E **37 C7**
Malāyer *Iran* 34°19N 48°51E **45 C6**
Malaysia ■ *Asia* 5°0N 110°0E **39 K4**
Malazgirt *Turkey* 39°10N 42°33E **44 B4**
Malbon *Australia* 21°5S 140°17E **62 C3**
Malbooma *Australia* 30°41S 134°11E **63 E1**
Malbork *Poland* 54°3N 19°1E **17 B10**
Malcolm *Australia* 28°51S 121°25E **61 E3**
Malcolm, Pt. *Australia* 33°48S 123°45E **61 F3**
Maldah *India* 25°2N 88°9E **43 G13**
Maldegem *Belgium* 51°14N 3°26E **15 C3**
Malden *Mass., U.S.A.* 42°26N 71°3W **83 D13**
Malden *Mo., U.S.A.* 36°34N 89°57W **80 G9**
Malden I. *Kiribati* 4°3S 155°1W **65 H12**
Maldives ■ *Ind. Oc.* 5°0N 73°0E **26 H9**
Maldon *U.K.* 51°44N 0°42E **13 F8**
Maldonado *Uruguay* 34°59S 55°0W **95 C5**
Maldonado, Pta. *Mexico* 16°20N 98°33W **87 D5**
Malé Karpaty *Slovak Rep.* 48°30N 17°20E **17 D9**
Malé Karpaty *Slovak Rep.* 48°30N 17°20E **17 D9**
Maleas, Akra *Greece* 36°28N 23°7E **23 F10**
Malebo, Pool *Africa* 4°17S 15°20E **52 E3**
Malegaon *India* 20°30N 74°38E **40 J9**
Malei *Mozam.* 17°12S 36°58E **55 F4**
Malek Kandī *Iran* 37°9N 46°6E **44 B5**
Malela
  Dem. Rep. of the Congo 4°22S 26°8E **54 C2**
Malema *Mozam.* 14°57S 37°20E **55 E4**
Maleme *Greece* 35°31N 23°49E **25 D5**
Malerkotla *India* 30°32N 75°58E **42 D6**
Males *Greece* 35°6N 25°35E **25 D7**
Malgomaj *Sweden* 64°40N 16°30E **8 D17**
Malha *Sudan* 15°8N 25°10E **51 E11**
Malhargarh *India* 24°17N 74°59E **42 G6**
Malheur → *U.S.A.* 44°4N 116°59W **76 D5**
Malheur L. *U.S.A.* 43°20N 118°48W **76 E4**
Mali ■ *Africa* 17°0N 3°0W **50 E5**
Mali → *Burma* 25°42N 97°30E **41 G20**
Mali Kyun *Burma* 13°0N 98°20E **38 F2**
Malia *Greece* 35°17N 25°32E **25 D7**
Malia, Kolpos *Greece* 35°19N 25°27E **25 D7**
Malibu *U.S.A.* 34°2N 118°41W **79 L8**
Maliku *Indonesia* 0°39S 123°16E **37 E6**
Malili *Indonesia* 2°42S 121°6E **37 E6**
Malimba, Mts.
  Dem. Rep. of the Congo 7°30S 29°30E **54 D2**
Malin Hd. *Ireland* 55°23N 7°23W **10 A4**
Malin Pen. *Ireland* 55°20N 7°17W **10 A4**
Malindi *Kenya* 3°12S 40°5E **54 C5**
Malindi Marine △ *Kenya* 3°15S 40°7E **54 C5**
Malines = Mechelen
  Belgium 51°2N 4°29E **15 C4**
Malino *Indonesia* 1°0N 121°0E **37 D6**
Malinyi *Tanzania* 8°56S 36°0E **55 D4**
Malita *Phil.* 6°19N 125°39E **37 C7**
Maliwun *Burma* 10°17N 98°40E **38 G2**
Maliya *India* 23°5N 70°46E **42 H4**
Malka Mari △ *Kenya* 4°11N 40°46E **54 B5**
Malkara *Turkey* 40°53N 26°53E **23 D12**
Mallacoota Inlet
  Australia 37°34S 149°40E **63 F4**
Mallaig *U.K.* 57°0N 5°50W **11 D3**
Mallawan *India* 27°4N 80°12E **43 F9**
Mallawi *Egypt* 27°44N 30°44E **51 C12**
Mallicolo = Malakula
  Vanuatu 16°15S 167°30E **58 C9**
Mallorca *Spain* 39°30N 3°0E **24 B10**
Mallorytown *Canada* 44°29N 75°53W **83 B9**
Mallow *Ireland* 52°8N 8°39W **10 D3**
Malmberget *Sweden* 67°11N 20°40E **8 C19**
Malmédy *Belgium* 50°25N 6°2E **15 D6**
Malmesbury *S. Africa* 33°28S 18°41E **56 E2**
Malmivaara = Malmberget
  Sweden 67°11N 20°40E **8 C19**
Malmö *Sweden* 55°36N 12°59E **9 J15**
Malolo *Fiji* 17°45S 177°11E **59 a**
Malolos *Phil.* 14°50N 120°49E **37 B6**
Malolotja △ *Swaziland* 26°4S 31°6E **57 D5**
Malombe L. *Malawi* 14°40S 35°15E **55 E4**
Malone *U.S.A.* 44°51N 74°18W **83 B10**
Måløy *Norway* 61°57N 5°6E **8 F11**

Malpaso Canary Is. 27°43N 18°3W 24 G1
Malpaso, Presa =
Netzahualcóyotl, Presa
Mexico 17°8N 93°35W 87 D6
Malpelo, I. de Colombia 4°3N 81°35W 92 C2
Malpur India 23°21N 73°27E 42 H5
Malpura India 26°17N 75°23E 42 F6
Malta Idaho, U.S.A. 42°18N 113°22W 76 E7
Malta Mont., U.S.A. 48°21N 107°52W 76 B10
Malta ■ Europe 35°55N 14°26E 25 D2
Maltahöhe Namibia 24°55S 17°0E 56 C2
Malton Canada 43°42N 79°38W 82 C5
Malton U.K. 54°8N 0°49W 12 C7
Maluku Indonesia 1°0S 127°0E 37 E7
Maluku □ Indonesia 3°0S 128°0E 37 E7
Maluku Sea = Molucca Sea
Indonesia 0°0 125°0E 37 E6
Malvan India 16°2N 73°30E 40 L8
Malvern U.S.A. 34°22N 92°49W 84 D7
Malvern Hills U.K. 52°0N 2°19W 13 E5
Malvinas, Is. = Falkland Is. ☒
Atl. Oc. 51°30S 59°0W 96 G5
Malya Tanzania 3°5S 33°38E 54 C3
Malyn Ukraine 50°46N 29°3E 17 C15
Malyy Lyakhovskiy, Ostrov
Russia 74°7N 140°36E 29 B15
Malyy Taymyr, Ostrov
Russia 78°6N 107°15E 29 B11
Mama Russia 58°18N 112°54E 29 D12
Mamanguape Brazil 6°50S 35°4W 93 E11
Mamanuca Group Fiji 17°35S 177°5E 59 a
Mamarr Mitlā Egypt 30°2N 32°54E 46 E1
Mamasa Indonesia 2°55S 119°20E 37 E5
Mambasa
Dem. Rep. of the Congo 1°22N 29°3E 54 B2
Mamberamo → Indonesia 2°0S 137°50E 37 E9
Mambilima Falls Zambia 10°31S 28°45E 55 E2
Mambirima
Dem. Rep. of the Congo 11°25S 27°33E 55 E2
Mambo Tanzania 4°52S 38°22E 54 C4
Mambrui Kenya 3°5S 40°5E 54 C5
Mamburao Phil. 13°13N 120°39E 37 B6
Mameigwess L. Canada 52°35N 87°50W 72 B2
Mammoth U.S.A. 32°43N 110°39W 77 K8
Mammoth Cave △
U.S.A. 37°8N 86°13W 80 G10
Mamoré → Bolivia 10°23S 65°53W 92 F5
Mamou Guinea 10°15N 12°0W 50 F3
Mamoudzou Mayotte 12°48S 45°14E 53 a
Mampikony Madag. 16°6S 47°38E 57 B8
Mamuju Indonesia 2°41S 118°50E 37 E5
Mamuno Botswana 22°16S 20°1E 56 C3
Man Ivory C. 7°30N 7°40W 50 G4
Man, I. of U.K. 54°15N 4°30W 12 C3
Man-Bazar India 23°4N 86°39E 43 H12
Man Na Burma 23°27N 97°19E 41 H20
Mänä U.S.A. 22°2N 159°47W 75 L8
Mana → Fr. Guiana 5°45N 53°55W 93 B8
Mana Pools △ Zimbabwe 15°56S 29°25E 55 F2
Manaar, G. of = Mannar, G. of
Asia 8°30N 79°0E 40 Q11
Manacapuru Brazil 3°16S 60°37W 92 D6
Manacor Spain 39°34N 3°13E 24 B10
Manado Indonesia 1°29N 124°51E 37 D6
Managua Nic. 12°6N 86°20W 88 D2
Managua, L. de Nic. 12°20N 86°30W 88 D2
Manakara Madag. 22°8S 48°1E 57 C8
Manali India 32°16N 77°10E 42 C7
Manama = Al Manāmah
Bahrain 26°10N 50°30E 45 E6
Manambao → Madag. 17°35S 44°0E 57 B7
Manambato Madag. 13°43S 49°7E 57 A8
Manambolo → Madag. 19°18S 44°22E 57 B7
Manambolosy Madag. 16°2S 49°40E 57 B8
Mananara → Madag. 23°21S 47°42E 57 C8
Mananara Madag. 16°10S 49°46E 57 B8
Mananara △ Madag. 16°14S 49°45E 57 B8
Mananjary Madag. 21°13S 48°20E 57 C8
Manantenina Madag. 24°17S 47°19E 57 C8
Manaos = Manaus Brazil 3°0S 60°0W 92 D7
Manapire → Venezuela 7°42N 66°7W 92 B5
Manapouri N.Z. 45°34S 167°39E 59 F1
Manapouri, L. N.Z. 45°32S 167°32E 59 F1
Manār, Jabal Yemen 14°2N 44°17E 47 E3
Manaravolo Madag. 23°59S 45°39E 57 C8
Manas China 44°17N 85°56E 32 B3
Manas → India 26°12N 90°40E 41 F17
Manas He → China 45°38N 85°12E 32 B3
Manaslu Nepal 28°33N 84°33E 43 E11
Manasquan U.S.A. 40°8N 74°3W 83 F10
Manassa U.S.A. 37°11N 105°56W 77 H11
Manaung Burma 18°45N 93°40E 41 K18
Manaus Brazil 3°0S 60°0W 92 D7
Manawan L. Canada 55°24N 103°14W 71 B8
Manbij Syria 36°31N 37°57E 44 B3
Manchegorsk Russia 67°54N 32°58E 28 C4
Manchester U.K. 53°29N 2°12W 12 D5
Manchester Calif.,
U.S.A. 38°58N 123°41W 78 G3
Manchester Conn.,
U.S.A. 41°47N 72°31W 83 E12
Manchester Ga., U.S.A. 32°51N 84°37W 85 E12
Manchester Ky., U.S.A. 37°9N 83°46W 81 G12
Manchester N.H.,
U.S.A. 42°59N 71°28W 83 D13
Manchester N.Y., U.S.A. 42°56N 77°16W 82 D7
Manchester Pa., U.S.A. 40°4N 76°43W 83 F8
Manchester Tenn.,
U.S.A. 35°29N 86°5W 85 D11
Manchester Vt., U.S.A. 43°10N 73°5W 83 C11
Manchester Int. ✈ (MAN)
U.K. 53°21N 2°17W 12 D5
Manchester L. Canada 61°28N 107°29W 71 A7
Manchhar L. Pakistan 26°25N 67°39E 42 F2
Manchuria = Dongbei
China 45°0N 125°0E 30 A5
Manchurian Plain China 47°0N 124°0E 26 D14

Mand → India 21°42N 83°15E 43 J10
Mand → Iran 28°20N 52°30E 45 D7
Manda Ludewe, Tanzania 10°30S 34°40E 55 E3
Manda Mbeya, Tanzania 7°58S 32°29E 54 D3
Manda Mbeya, Tanzania 8°30S 32°49E 55 D3
Mandabé Madag. 21°0S 44°55E 57 C7
Mandaguari Brazil 23°32S 51°42W 95 A5
Mandah = Töhöm
Mongolia 44°27N 108°2E 34 B5
Mandal Norway 58°2N 7°25E 9 G12
Mandala, Puncak
Indonesia 4°44S 140°20E 37 E10
Mandalay Burma 22°0N 96°4E 41 J20
Mandale = Mandalay
Burma 22°0N 96°4E 41 J20
Mandalgarh India 25°12N 75°6E 42 G6
Mandalgovĭ Mongolia 45°45N 106°10E 34 B4
Mandalī Iraq 33°43N 45°28E 44 C5
Mandan U.S.A. 46°50N 100°54W 80 B3
Mandar, Teluk Indonesia 3°35S 119°15E 37 E5
Mandaue Phil. 10°20N 123°56E 37 B6
Mandera Kenya 3°55N 41°53E 54 B5
Mandi India 31°39N 76°58E 42 D7
Mandi Burewala Pakistan 30°9N 72°41E 42 D5
Mandi Dabwali India 29°58N 74°42E 42 E6
Mandimba Mozam. 14°20S 35°40E 55 E4
Mandioli Indonesia 0°40S 127°20E 37 E7
Mandla India 22°39N 80°30E 43 H9
Mandorah Australia 12°32S 130°42E 60 B5
Mandra Pakistan 33°23N 73°12E 42 C5
Mandrare → Madag. 25°10S 46°30E 57 D8
Mandritsara Madag. 15°50S 48°49E 57 B8
Mandronarivo Madag. 21°7S 45°38E 57 C8
Mandsaur India 24°3N 75°8E 42 G6
Mandurah Australia 32°36S 115°48E 61 F2
Mandvi India 22°51N 69°22E 42 H3
Mandya India 12°30N 77°0E 40 N10
Mandzai Pakistan 30°55N 67°6E 42 D2
Maneh Iran 37°39N 57°7E 45 B8
Manera Madag. 22°55S 44°20E 57 C7
Maneroo Cr. →
Australia 23°21S 143°53E 62 C3
Manfalût Egypt 27°20N 30°52E 51 C12
Manfredónia Italy 41°38N 15°55E 22 D6
Mangabeiras, Chapada das
Brazil 10°0S 46°30W 93 F9
Mangaia Cook Is. 21°55S 157°55W 65 K12
Mangalia Romania 43°50N 28°35E 17 G15
Mangalore India 12°55N 74°47E 40 N9
Mangaluru = Mangalore
India 12°55N 74°47E 40 N9
Mangan India 27°31N 88°32E 43 F13
Mangawan India 24°41N 81°33E 43 G9
Mangaweka N.Z. 39°48S 175°47E 59 C5
Manggar Indonesia 2°50S 108°10E 36 E3
Manggawitu Indonesia 4°8S 133°32E 37 E8
Mangghystaŭ Tübegi
Kazakhstan 44°30N 52°30E 28 E6
Manggis Indonesia 8°29S 115°31E 37 J18
Mangindrano Madag. 14°17S 48°58E 57 A8
Mangkalihat, Tanjung
Indonesia 1°2N 118°59E 37 D5
Mangkururrpa ◎
Australia 20°35S 129°43E 60 D4
Mangla Pakistan 33°7N 73°39E 42 C5
Mangla Dam Pakistan 33°9N 73°44E 43 C5
Manglaur India 29°44N 77°49E 42 E7
Mangnai China 37°52N 91°43E 32 C4
Mangnai Zhen China 38°24N 90°14E 32 C4
Mango Togo 10°20N 0°30E 50 F6
Mango Tonga 20°17S 174°29W 59 c
Mangoche Malawi 14°25S 35°16E 55 E4
Mangoky → Madag. 21°29S 43°41E 57 C7
Mangole Indonesia 1°50S 125°55E 37 E6
Mangombe
Dem. Rep. of the Congo 1°20S 26°48E 54 C2
Mangonui N.Z. 35°1S 173°32E 59 A4
Mangoro → Madag. 20°0S 48°45E 57 B8
Mangrol Mad. P., India 21°7N 70°7E 42 J4
Mangrol Raj., India 25°20N 76°31E 42 G6
Mangueira, L. da Brazil 33°0S 52°50W 95 C5
Mangum U.S.A. 34°53N 99°30W 84 D5
Manguri Australia 28°58S 134°22E 63 A1
Mangyshlak, Poluostrov =
Mangghystaŭ Tübegi
Kazakhstan 44°30N 52°30E 28 E6
Manhattan U.S.A. 39°11N 96°35W 80 F5
Manhiça Mozam. 25°23S 32°49E 57 D5
Mania → Madag. 19°42S 45°22E 57 B8
Manica Mozam. 18°58S 32°59E 57 B5
Manica □ Mozam. 19°10S 33°45E 57 B5
Manicaland □ Zimbabwe 19°0S 32°30E 55 F3
Manicoré Brazil 5°48S 61°16W 92 E6
Manicouagan →
Canada 49°30N 68°30W 73 C6
Manicouagan, Rés.
Canada 51°5N 68°40W 73 B6
Maniema □
Dem. Rep. of the Congo 3°0S 26°0E 54 C2
Manifah Si. Arabia 27°44N 49°0E 45 E6
Manifold, C. Australia 22°41S 150°50E 62 C5
Manigotagan Canada 51°6N 96°18W 71 C9
Manigotagan → Canada 51°7N 96°20W 71 C9
Manihari India 25°21N 87°38E 43 G12
Manihiki Cook Is. 10°24S 161°1W 65 J11
Manihiki Plateau
Pac. Oc. 11°0S 164°0W 65 J11
Manika, Plateau de la
Dem. Rep. of the Congo 10°0S 25°5E 55 E2
Manikpur India 25°4N 81°7E 43 G9
Manila Phil. 14°35N 120°58E 37 B6
Manila U.S.A. 40°59N 109°43W 76 F9
Manila B. Phil. 14°40N 120°35E 37 B6
Manilla Australia 30°45S 150°43E 63 E5
Maningrida Australia 12°3S 134°13E 62 A1
Manipur □ India 25°0N 94°0E 41 G19
Manipur → Burma 23°45N 94°20E 41 H19

Manisa Turkey 38°38N 27°30E 23 E12
Manistee U.S.A. 44°15N 86°19W 80 C10
Manistee → U.S.A. 44°15N 86°21W 80 C10
Manistique U.S.A. 45°57N 86°15W 80 C10
Manitoba □ Canada 53°30N 97°0W 71 B9
Manitoba, L. Canada 51°0N 98°45W 71 C9
Manitou Canada 49°15N 98°32W 71 D9
Manitou, L. Canada 50°55N 65°17W 73 B6
Manitou L. Canada 45°8N 86°0W 80 C10
Manitou L. Canada 52°43N 109°43W 71 C7
Manitou Springs
U.S.A. 38°52N 104°55W 76 G11
Manitoulin I. Canada 45°40N 82°30W 72 C3
Manitouwadge Canada 49°8N 85°48W 72 C2
Manitowoc U.S.A. 44°5N 87°40W 80 C10
Manizales Colombia 5°5N 75°32W 92 B3
Manja Madag. 21°26S 44°20E 57 C7
Manjacaze Mozam. 24°45S 34°0E 57 C5
Manjakandriana Madag. 18°55S 47°47E 57 B8
Manjhand Pakistan 25°50N 68°10E 42 G3
Manjimup Australia 34°15S 116°6E 61 F2
Manjra → India 18°49N 77°52E 40 K10
Mankato Kans., U.S.A. 39°47N 98°13W 80 F4
Mankato Minn., U.S.A. 44°10N 94°0W 80 C6
Mankayane Swaziland 26°40S 31°4E 57 D5
Mankota Canada 49°25N 107°5W 71 D7
Manlay = Üydzin
Mongolia 44°9N 107°0E 34 B4
Manmad India 20°18N 74°28E 40 J9
Mann Ranges Australia 26°6S 130°5E 61 E5
Manna Indonesia 4°25S 102°55E 36 E2
Mannahill Australia 32°25S 140°0E 63 E3
Mannar Sri Lanka 9°1N 79°54E 40 Q11
Mannar, G. of Asia 8°30N 79°0E 40 Q11
Mannar I. Sri Lanka 9°5N 79°45E 40 Q11
Mannheim Germany 49°29N 8°29E 16 D5
Manning Canada 56°53N 117°39W 70 B5
Manning Oreg., U.S.A. 45°45N 123°13W 78 E3
Manning S.C., U.S.A. 33°42N 80°13W 85 E14
Mannum Australia 34°50S 139°20E 63 E2
Manohorpur India 22°23N 85°12E 43 H11
Manokwari Indonesia 0°54S 134°0E 37 E8
Manombo Madag. 22°57S 43°28E 57 C7
Manono
Dem. Rep. of the Congo 7°15S 27°25E 54 D2
Manono Samoa 13°50S 172°5W 59 b
Manorhamilton Ireland 54°18N 8°9W 10 B3
Manosque France 43°49N 5°47E 20 E6
Manotick Canada 45°13N 75°41W 83 A9
Manouane → Canada 49°30N 71°10W 73 C5
Manouane, L. Canada 50°45N 70°45W 73 B5
Manp'o N. Korea 41°6N 126°24E 35 D14
Manpojin = Manp'o
N. Korea 41°6N 126°24E 35 D14
Manpur Chhattisgarh,
India 23°17N 83°35E 43 H10
Manpur Mad. P., India 22°26N 75°37E 42 H6
Manresa Spain 41°48N 1°50E 21 B6
Mansa Gujarat, India 23°27N 72°45E 42 H5
Mansa Punjab, India 30°0N 75°27E 42 E6
Mansa Zambia 11°13S 28°55E 55 E2
Mansehra Pakistan 34°20N 73°15E 42 B5
Mansel I. Canada 62°0N 80°0W 69 E15
Mansfield Australia 37°4S 146°6E 63 F4
Mansfield U.K. 53°9N 1°11W 12 D6
Mansfield La., U.S.A. 32°2N 93°43W 84 E8
Mansfield Mass., U.S.A. 42°2N 71°13W 83 D13
Mansfield Ohio, U.S.A. 40°45N 82°31W 82 F2
Mansfield Pa., U.S.A. 41°48N 77°5W 82 E7
Mansfield Tex., U.S.A. 32°34N 97°8W 84 E6
Mansfield, Mt. U.S.A. 44°33N 72°49W 83 B12
Manson Creek Canada 55°37N 124°32W 70 B4
Manta Ecuador 1°0S 80°40W 92 D2
Mantadia △ Madag. 18°54S 48°21E 57 B8
Mantare Tanzania 2°42S 33°13E 54 C3
Manteca U.S.A. 37°48N 121°13W 78 H5
Manteo U.S.A. 35°55N 75°40W 85 D17
Mantes-la-Jolie France 48°58N 1°41E 20 B4
Manthani India 18°40N 79°35E 40 K11
Manti U.S.A. 39°16N 111°38W 76 G8
Mantiqueira, Serra da
Brazil 22°0S 44°0W 95 A7
Manton U.S.A. 44°25N 85°24W 81 C11
Mántova Italy 45°9N 10°48E 22 B4
Mänttä Finland 62°3N 24°40E 8 E21
Mantua = Mántova Italy 45°9N 10°48E 22 B4
Manú Peru 12°10S 70°51W 92 F4
Manú → Peru 12°16S 70°55W 92 F4
Manu'a Is. Amer. Samoa 14°13S 169°35W 59 b
Manuel Alves → Brazil 11°19S 48°28W 93 F9
Manui Indonesia 3°35S 123°5E 37 E6
Manukau N.Z. 37°0S 174°52E 59 B5
Manuripi → Bolivia 11°6S 67°36W 92 F5
Many U.S.A. 31°34N 93°29W 84 F8
Manyallaluk ◎
Australia 14°16S 132°49E 60 B5
Manyani Kenya 3°5S 38°30E 54 C4
Manyara, L. Tanzania 3°40S 35°50E 54 C4
Manyara △ Tanzania 3°35S 35°50E 54 C4
Manych-Gudilo, Ozero
Russia 46°24N 42°38E 19 E7
Manyonga → Tanzania 4°10S 34°15E 54 C3
Manyoni Tanzania 5°45S 34°55E 54 D3
Manzai Pakistan 32°12N 70°15E 42 C4
Manzanares Spain 39°2N 3°22E 21 C4
Manzanillo Cuba 20°20N 77°31W 88 B4
Manzanillo Mexico 19°3N 104°20W 86 D4
Manzanillo, Pta. Panama 9°30N 79°40W 88 E4
Manzano Mts. U.S.A. 34°40N 106°20W 77 J10
Manzariyeh Iran 34°53N 50°50E 45 C6
Manzhouli China 49°35N 117°25E 33 B6
Manzini Swaziland 26°30S 31°4E 57 D5
Manzur Vadisi △ Turkey 39°10N 39°38E 44 B3
Mao Chad 14°4N 15°19E 51 F9
Maó Spain 39°53N 4°16E 24 B11

Maoke, Pegunungan
Indonesia 3°40S 137°30E 37 E9
Maolin China 43°58N 123°30E 35 C12
Maoming China 21°50N 110°54E 33 D6
Maoxing China 45°28N 124°40E 35 B13
Mapam Yumco China 30°45N 81°28E 43 D9
Mapastepec Mexico 15°26N 92°54W 87 D6
Maphrao, Ko Thailand 7°56N 98°26E 39 a
Mapia, Kepulauan
Indonesia 0°50N 134°20E 37 D8
Mapimí Mexico 25°49N 103°51W 86 B4
Mapimí, Bolsón de
Mexico 27°0N 104°15W 86 B4
Mapinga Tanzania 6°40S 39°12E 54 D4
Mapinhane Mozam. 22°20S 35°0E 57 C6
Maple Creek Canada 49°55N 109°29W 71 D7
Maple Valley U.S.A. 47°25N 122°3W 78 C4
Mapleton U.S.A. 44°2N 123°52W 76 D2
Mapoon ◎ Australia 11°4S 142°8E 62 A3
Mapuera → Brazil 1°5S 57°2W 92 D7
Mapulanguene Mozam. 24°29S 32°6E 57 C5
Mapungubwe △
S. Africa 22°12S 29°22E 55 G2
Maputo Mozam. 25°58S 32°32E 57 D5
Maputo □ Mozam. 26°0S 32°25E 57 D5
Maputo, B. de Mozam. 25°50S 32°45E 57 D5
Maputo → Mozam. 26°23S 32°48E 57 D5
Maqat Kazakhstan 47°39N 53°19E 19 E9
Maqên China 34°24N 100°6E 32 C5
Maqiaohe China 44°40N 130°30E 35 B16
Maqnā Si. Arabia 28°25N 34°50E 44 D2
Maqteïr Mauritania 21°50N 11°40W 50 D3
Maquan He = Brahmaputra →
Asia 23°40N 90°35E 43 H13
Maquela do Zombo Angola 6°0S 15°15E 52 F3
Maquinchao Argentina 41°15S 68°50W 96 E3
Maquoketa U.S.A. 42°4N 90°40W 80 D8
Mar Canada 44°49N 81°12W 82 B3
Mar, Serra do Brazil 25°30S 49°0W 95 B6
Mar Chiquita, L.
Argentina 30°40S 62°50W 94 C3
Mar del Plata Argentina 38°0S 57°30W 94 D4
Mar Menor Spain 37°40N 0°45W 21 D5
Mara Tanzania 1°30S 34°32E 54 C3
Mara □ Tanzania 1°45S 34°20E 54 C3
Maraã Brazil 1°52S 65°25W 92 D5
Maraa Tahiti 17°46S 149°34W 59 d
Marabá Brazil 5°20S 49°5W 93 E9
Maraboon, L. Australia 23°41S 148°0E 62 C4
Maracá, I. de Brazil 2°10N 50°30W 93 C8
Maracaibo Venezuela 10°40N 71°37W 92 A4
Maracaibo, L. de
Venezuela 9°40N 71°30W 92 B4
Maracaju Brazil 21°38S 55°9W 95 A4
Maracas Bay Village
Trin. & Tob. 10°46N 61°28W 93 K15
Maracay Venezuela 10°15N 67°28W 92 A5
Marādah Libya 29°15N 19°15E 51 C9
Maradi Niger 13°29N 7°20E 50 F7
Marāgheh Iran 37°30N 46°12E 44 B5
Marāh Si. Arabia 25°0N 45°35E 44 E5
Marajo, I. de Brazil 1°0S 49°30W 93 D9
Marākand Iran 38°51N 45°16E 44 B5
Marakele △ S. Africa 32°14S 25°27E 57 E4
Maralal Kenya 1°0N 36°38E 54 B4
Maralinga Australia 30°13S 131°32E 61 F5
Maralinga Tjarutja ◎
Australia 29°30S 131°0E 61 E5
Marambio Antarctica 64°0S 56°0W 5 C18
Marampa S. Leone 8°45N 12°28W 50 G3
Marana U.S.A. 32°27N 111°13W 77 K8
Maranboy Australia 14°40S 132°39E 60 B5
Marand Iran 38°30N 45°45E 44 B5
Marang Malaysia 5°12N 103°13E 39 K4
Maranguape Brazil 3°55S 38°50W 93 D11
Maranhão = São Luís
Brazil 2°39S 44°15W 93 D10
Maranhão □ Brazil 5°0S 46°0W 93 E9
Maranoa → Australia 27°50S 148°37E 63 D4
Marañón → Peru 4°30S 73°35W 92 D4
Marão Mozam. 24°18S 34°2E 57 C5
Maras = Kahramanmaraş
Turkey 37°37N 36°53E 44 B3
Marathasa Cyprus 34°59N 32°51E 25 E11
Marathon Australia 20°51S 143°32E 62 C3
Marathon Canada 48°44N 86°23W 72 C2
Marathon N.Y., U.S.A. 42°27N 76°2W 83 D8
Marathon Tex., U.S.A. 30°12N 103°15W 84 F3
Marathóvouno Cyprus 35°13N 33°37E 25 D12
Maratua Indonesia 2°10N 118°35E 37 D5
Maraval Trin. & Tob. 10°42N 61°31W 93 K15
Maravatío Mexico 19°54N 100°27W 86 D4
Marāwih U.A.E. 24°18N 53°18E 45 E7
Marbella Spain 36°30N 4°57W 21 D3
Marble Bar Australia 21°9S 119°44E 60 D2
Marble Falls U.S.A. 30°35N 98°16W 84 F5
Marblehead Mass.,
U.S.A. 42°29N 70°51W 83 D14
Marblehead Ohio, U.S.A. 41°32N 82°44W 82 E2
Marburg Germany 50°47N 8°46E 16 C5
Marca, Pta. do Angola 16°31S 11°43E 53 H2
March U.K. 52°33N 0°5E 13 E8
Marche France 46°5N 1°20E 20 C4
Marche-en-Famenne
Belgium 50°14N 5°19E 15 D5
Marchena Spain 37°18N 5°23W 21 D3
Marco Island U.S.A. 25°58N 81°44W 85 H14
Marcos Juárez Argentina 32°42S 62°5W 94 C3
Marcus Baker, Mt.
U.S.A. 61°26N 147°45W 74 C10
Marcus I. = Minami-Tori-Shima
Pac. Oc. 24°20N 153°58E 64 E7
Marcy, Mt. U.S.A. 44°7N 73°56W 83 B11
Mardan Pakistan 34°20N 72°0E 42 B5
Mardie Australia 21°12S 115°59E 60 D2
Mardin Turkey 37°20N 40°43E 44 B4
Maree, L. U.K. 57°40N 5°26W 11 D3
Mareeba Australia 16°59S 145°28E 62 B4
Mareetsane S. Africa 26°9S 25°25E 56 D4

Marek = Stanke Dimitrov
Bulgaria 42°17N 23°9E 23 C10
Marengo U.S.A. 41°48N 92°4W 80 E7
Marerano Madag. 21°23S 44°52E 57 C7
Marfa U.S.A. 30°19N 104°1W 84 F2
Marfa Pt. Malta 35°59N 14°19E 25 D1
Margaret → Australia 18°9S 125°41E 60 C4
Margaret Bay Canada 51°20N 127°35W 70 C3
Margaret L. Canada 58°56N 115°25W 70 B5
Margaret River Australia 33°57S 115°4E 61 F2
Margarita, I. de Venezuela 11°0N 64°0W 92 A6
Margaritovo Russia 43°25N 134°45E 30 C7
Margate S. Africa 30°50S 30°20E 57 E5
Margate U.K. 51°23N 1°23E 13 F9
Margherita Pk. Uganda 0°22N 29°51E 54 B3
Marghilon Uzbekistan 40°27N 71°42E 28 E8
Mārgow, Dasht-e
Afghan. 30°40N 62°30E 40 D3
Marguerite Canada 52°30N 122°25W 70 C4
Mari El □ Russia 56°30N 48°0E 18 C8
Mari Indus Pakistan 32°57N 71°34E 42 C4
Mari Republic = Mari El □
Russia 56°30N 48°0E 18 C8
María de la Salut Spain 39°39N 3°5E 24 B10
María Elena Chile 22°18S 69°40W 94 A2
María Grande Argentina 31°45S 59°55W 94 C4
Maria I. N. Terr.,
Australia 14°52S 135°45E 62 A2
Maria I. Tas., Australia 42°35S 148°0E 63 G4
Maria Island △ Australia 42°38S 148°5E 63 G4
Maria van Diemen, C.
N.Z. 34°29S 172°40E 59 A4
Mariakani Kenya 3°50S 39°27E 54 C4
Mariala △ Australia 25°57S 145°2E 63 D4
Marian Australia 21°9S 148°57E 62 b
Marian L. Canada 63°0N 116°15W 70 A5
Mariana Trench Pac. Oc. 13°0N 145°0E 64 F6
Marianna Ark., U.S.A. 34°46N 90°46W 85 D9
Marianna Fla., U.S.A. 30°46N 85°14W 85 F12
Marias → U.S.A. 47°56N 110°30W 76 C8
Marías, Islas Mexico 21°25N 106°28W 86 C3
Mariato, Punta Panama 7°12N 80°52W 88 E3
Maribor Slovenia 46°36N 15°40E 16 E8
Marico → Africa 23°35S 26°57E 56 C4
Maricopa Ariz., U.S.A. 33°4N 112°3W 77 K7
Maricopa Calif., U.S.A. 35°4N 119°24W 79 K7
Marié → Brazil 0°27S 66°26W 92 D5
Marie Byrd Land
Antarctica 79°30S 125°0W 5 D14
Marie-Galante
Guadeloupe 15°56N 61°16W 88 b
Mariecourt = Kangiqsujuaq
Canada 61°30N 72°0W 69 E17
Mariehamn Finland 60°5N 19°55E 9 F18
Mariembourg Belgium 50°6N 4°31E 15 D4
Mariental Namibia 24°36S 18°0E 56 C2
Marienville U.S.A. 41°28N 79°8W 82 E5
Mariestad Sweden 58°43N 13°50E 9 G15
Marietta Ga., U.S.A. 33°57N 84°33W 85 E12
Marietta Ohio, U.S.A. 39°25N 81°27W 81 F13
Marieville Canada 45°26N 73°10W 83 A11
Mariinsk Russia 56°10N 87°20E 28 D9
Marijampolė Lithuania 54°33N 23°19E 9 J20
Marília Brazil 22°13S 50°0W 95 A6
Marín Spain 42°23N 8°42W 21 A1
Marina U.S.A. 36°41N 121°48W 78 J5
Marinduque Phil. 13°25N 122°0E 37 B6
Marine City U.S.A. 42°43N 82°30W 82 D2
Marinette U.S.A. 45°6N 87°38W 80 C10
Maringá Brazil 23°26S 52°2W 95 A5
Marion Ala., U.S.A. 32°38N 87°19W 85 E11
Marion Ill., U.S.A. 37°44N 88°56W 80 G9
Marion Ind., U.S.A. 40°32N 85°40W 81 E11
Marion Iowa, U.S.A. 42°2N 91°36W 80 D8
Marion Kans., U.S.A. 38°21N 97°1W 80 F5
Marion N.C., U.S.A. 35°41N 82°1W 85 D13
Marion Ohio, U.S.A. 40°35N 83°8W 81 E12
Marion S.C., U.S.A. 34°11N 79°24W 85 D15
Marion Va., U.S.A. 36°50N 81°31W 81 G13
Marion, L. U.S.A. 33°28N 80°10W 85 E14
Mariposa U.S.A. 37°29N 119°58W 78 H7
Mariscal Estigarribia
Paraguay 22°3S 60°40W 94 A3
Maritime Alps = Maritimes, Alpes
Europe 44°10N 7°10E 20 D7
Maritimes, Alpes Europe 44°10N 7°10E 20 D7
Maritsa = Évros →
Greece 41°40N 26°34E 23 D12
Maritsa Greece 36°22N 28°8E 25 C10
Mariupol Ukraine 47°5N 37°31E 19 E6
Mariusa △ Venezuela 9°24N 61°27W 89 E7
Marīvān Iran 35°30N 46°25E 44 C5
Marj 'Uyūn Lebanon 33°21N 35°34E 46 B4
Marka Somali Rep. 1°48N 44°50E 47 G3
Markam China 29°42N 98°38E 41 E21
Markdale Canada 44°19N 80°39W 82 B4
Marked Tree U.S.A. 35°32N 90°25W 85 D9
Market Drayton U.K. 52°54N 2°29W 12 E5
Market Harborough
U.K. 52°29N 0°55W 13 E7
Market Rasen U.K. 53°24N 0°20W 12 D7
Markham Canada 43°52N 79°16W 82 C5
Markham, Mt. Antarctica 83°0S 164°0E 5 E11
Markleeville U.S.A. 38°42N 119°47W 78 G7
Markovo Russia 64°40N 170°24E 29 C17
Marks Russia 51°45N 46°50E 18 D8
Marksville U.S.A. 31°8N 92°4W 84 F8
Marla Australia 27°19S 133°33E 63 D1
Marlbank Canada 44°26N 77°6W 82 B7
Marlboro N.Y., U.S.A. 41°36N 73°59W 83 E11
Marlborough Australia 22°46S 149°52E 62 C4
Marlborough U.K. 51°25N 1°43W 13 F6
Marlborough U.S.A. 42°21N 71°33W 83 D13
Marlborough Downs
U.K. 51°27N 1°53W 13 F6
Marlin U.S.A. 31°18N 96°54W 84 F6
Marlow U.K. 51°34N 0°46W 13 F7
Marlow U.S.A. 34°39N 97°58W 84 D6
Marmagao India 15°25N 73°56E 40 M8

Marmara *Turkey* 40°35N 27°34E **23** D12
Marmara, Sea of = Marmara
Denizi *Turkey* 40°45N 28°15E **23** D13
Marmara Denizi *Turkey* 40°45N 28°15E **23** D13
Marmaris *Turkey* 36°50N 28°14E **23** F13
Marmion, Mt. *Australia* 29°16S 119°50E **61** E2
Marmion L. *Canada* 48°55N 91°20W **72** C1
Marmolada, Mte. *Italy* 46°26N 11°51E **22** A4
Marmora *Canada* 44°28N 77°41W **82** B7
Marmugao = Marmagao
India 15°25N 73°56E **40** M8
Marne → *France* 48°47N 2°29E **20** B5
Maro Reef *U.S.A.* 25°25N 170°35W **75** K5
Maroala *Madag.* 15°23S 47°59E **57** B8
Maroantsetra *Madag.* 15°26S 49°44E **57** B8
Maroelaboom *Namibia* 19°15S 18°53E **56** B2
Marofandilia *Madag.* 20°7S 44°34E **57** C7
Marojejy △ *Madag.* 14°26S 49°21E **57** A8
Marolambo *Madag.* 20°2S 48°7E **57** C8
Maromandia *Madag.* 14°13S 48°5E **57** A8
Maromokotro *Madag.* 14°0S 49°0E **57** A8
Marondera *Zimbabwe* 18°5S 31°42E **55** F3
Maroni → *Fr. Guiana* 5°30N 54°0W **93** B8
Maroochydore *Australia* 26°29S 153°5E **63** D5
Maroona *Australia* 37°27S 142°54E **63** F3
Marosakoa *Madag.* 15°26S 46°38E **57** B8
Maroseranana *Madag.* 18°32S 48°51E **57** B8
Marotandrano *Madag.* 16°10S 48°50E **57** B8
Marotaolano *Madag.* 12°47S 49°15E **57** A8
Maroua *Cameroon* 10°40N 14°20E **51** F8
Marovato *Madag.* 15°48S 48°5E **57** B8
Marovoay *Madag.* 16°6S 46°39E **57** B8
Marquard *S. Africa* 28°40S 27°28E **56** D4
Marquesas Fracture Zone
Pac. Oc. 9°0S 125°0W **65** H15
Marquesas Is. = Marquises, Îs.
French Polynesia 9°30S 140°0W **65** H14
Marquette *U.S.A.* 46°33N 87°24W **80** B10
Marquis *St. Lucia* 14°2N 60°54W **89** f
Marquises, Îs.
French Polynesia 9°30S 140°0W **65** H14
Marra, Djebel *Sudan* 13°10N 24°22E **51** F10
Marracuene *Mozam.* 25°45S 32°35E **57** D5
Marrakech *Morocco* 31°9N 8°0W **50** B4
Marrawah *Australia* 40°55S 144°42E **63** G3
Marree *Australia* 29°39S 138°1E **63** D2
Marrero *U.S.A.* 29°53N 90°6W **85** G9
Marrimane *Mozam.* 22°58S 33°34E **57** C5
Marromeu *Mozam.* 18°15S 36°25E **57** B6
Marromeu △ *Mozam.* 19°0S 36°0E **57** B6
Marrowie Cr. →
Australia 33°23S 145°40E **63** E4
Marrubane *Mozam.* 18°0S 37°0E **55** F4
Marrupa *Mozam.* 13°8S 37°30E **55** E4
Mars Hill *U.S.A.* 46°31N 67°52W **81** B20
Marsá 'Alam *Egypt* 25°5N 34°54E **47** B1
Marsá Matrûh *Egypt* 31°19N 27°9E **51** B11
Marsabit *Kenya* 2°18N 38°0E **54** B4
Marsabit △ *Kenya* 2°23N 37°56E **54** B4
Marsala *Italy* 37°48N 12°26E **22** F5
Marsalforn *Malta* 36°4N 14°16E **25** C1
Marsden *Australia* 33°47S 147°32E **63** E4
Marseille *France* 43°18N 5°23E **20** E6
Marseilles = Marseille
France 43°18N 5°23E **20** E6
Marsh I. *U.S.A.* 29°34N 91°53W **84** G9
Marshall *Ark., U.S.A.* 35°55N 92°38W **84** D8
Marshall *Mich., U.S.A.* 42°16N 84°58W **81** D11
Marshall *Minn., U.S.A.* 44°27N 95°47W **80** C6
Marshall *Mo., U.S.A.* 39°7N 93°12W **80** F7
Marshall *Tex., U.S.A.* 32°33N 94°23W **84** E7
Marshall → *Australia* 22°59S 136°59E **62** C2
Marshall Is. ■ *Pac. Oc.* 9°0N 171°0E **58** A10
Marshalltown *U.S.A.* 42°3N 92°55W **80** D7
Marshbrook *Zimbabwe* 18°33S 31°9E **57** B5
Marshfield *Mo., U.S.A.* 37°15N 92°54W **80** G7
Marshfield *Vt., U.S.A.* 44°20N 72°20W **83** B12
Marshfield *Wis., U.S.A.* 44°40N 90°10W **80** C8
Marshün *Iran* 36°19N 49°23E **45** B6
Märsta *Sweden* 59°37N 17°52E **9** G17
Mart *U.S.A.* 31°33N 96°50W **84** F6
Martaban *Burma* 16°30N 97°35E **41** L20
Martaban, G. of *Burma* 16°5N 96°30E **41** L20
Martapura *Kalimantan,*
Indonesia 3°22S 114°47E **36** E4
Martapura *Sumatera,*
Indonesia 4°19S 104°22E **36** E2
Marte R. Gómez, Presa
Mexico 26°10N 99°0W **87** B5
Martelange *Belgium* 49°49N 5°43E **15** E5
Martha's Vineyard
U.S.A. 41°25N 70°38W **83** E14
Martigny *Switz.* 46°6N 7°3E **20** C7
Martigues *France* 43°24N 5°4E **20** E6
Martin *Slovak Rep.* 49°6N 18°58E **17** D10
Martin *S. Dak., U.S.A.* 43°11N 101°44W **80** D3
Martin *Tenn., U.S.A.* 36°21N 88°51W **85** C10
Martin L. *U.S.A.* 32°41N 85°55W **85** E12
Martina Franca *Italy* 40°42N 17°20E **22** D7
Martinborough *N.Z.* 41°14S 175°29E **59** D5
Martinez *Calif., U.S.A.* 38°1N 122°8W **78** G4
Martinez *Ga., U.S.A.* 33°31N 82°5W **85** E13
Martinique ☑ *W. Indies* 14°40N 61°0W **88** c
Martinique Passage
W. Indies 15°15N 61°0W **89** C7
Martinópolis *Brazil* 22°11S 51°12W **95** A5
Martin's Bay *Barbados* 13°12N 59°29W **89** g
Martins Ferry *U.S.A.* 40°6N 80°44W **82** F4
Martinsburg *Pa., U.S.A.* 40°19N 78°20W **82** F6
Martinsburg *W. Va.,*
U.S.A. 39°27N 77°58W **81** F15
Martinsville *Ind.,*
U.S.A. 39°26N 86°25W **80** F10
Martinsville *Va., U.S.A.* 36°41N 79°52W **81** G14
Marton *N.Z.* 40°4S 175°23E **59** D5
Martos *Spain* 37°44N 3°58W **21** D4
Martu ☑ *Australia* 22°30S 122°0E **60** D3
Marudi *Malaysia* 4°11N 114°19E **36** D4
Maruf *Afghan.* 31°30N 67°6E **40** D5

Marugame *Japan* 34°15N 133°40E **31** G6
Marunga *Angola* 17°28S 20°2E **56** B3
Marungu, Mts.
Dem. Rep. of the Congo 7°30S 30°0E **54** D3
Maruwa ☑ *Australia* 22°30S 127°30E **60** D4
Marv Dasht *Iran* 29°50N 52°40E **45** D7
Marvast *Iran* 30°30N 54°15E **45** D7
Marvel Loch *Australia* 31°28S 119°29E **61** F2
Marwar *India* 25°43N 73°45E **42** G5
Mary *Turkmenistan* 37°40N 61°50E **45** B9
Maryborough = Port Laoise
Ireland 53°2N 7°18W **10** C4
Maryborough *Queens.,*
Australia 25°31S 152°37E **63** D5
Maryborough *Vic.,*
Australia 37°3S 143°44E **63** F3
Maryfield *Canada* 49°50N 101°35W **71** D8
Maryland ☐ *U.S.A.* 39°0N 76°30W **81** F15
Maryland Junction
Zimbabwe 17°45S 30°31E **55** F3
Maryport *U.K.* 54°44N 3°28W **12** C4
Mary's Harbour *Canada* 52°18N 55°51W **73** B8
Marystown *Canada* 47°10N 55°10W **73** C8
Marysville *Calif., U.S.A.* 39°9N 121°35W **78** F5
Marysville *Kans., U.S.A.* 39°51N 96°39W **80** F5
Marysville *Mich., U.S.A.* 42°54N 82°29W **82** D2
Marysville *Ohio, U.S.A.* 40°14N 83°22W **81** E12
Marysville *Wash., U.S.A.* 48°3N 122°11W **78** B4
Maryville *Mo., U.S.A.* 40°21N 94°52W **80** E6
Maryville *Tenn., U.S.A.* 35°46N 83°58W **85** D13
Marzūq *Libya* 25°53N 13°57E **51** C8
Marzūq, Idehân *Libya* 24°50N 13°51E **51** D8
Masada *Israel* 31°15N 35°20E **46** D4
Masahunga *Tanzania* 2°6S 33°18E **54** C3
Masai *Malaysia* 1°29N 103°55E **39** d
Masai Mara △ *Kenya* 1°25S 35°5E **54** C4
Masai Steppe *Tanzania* 4°30S 36°30E **54** C4
Masaka *Uganda* 0°21S 31°45E **54** C3
Masalembo, Kepulauan
Indonesia 5°35S 114°30E **36** F4
Masalima, Kepulauan
Indonesia 5°4S 117°5E **36** F5
Masamba *Indonesia* 2°30S 120°15E **37** E6
Masan *S. Korea* 35°11N 128°32E **35** G15
Masandam, Ra's *Oman* 26°30N 56°30E **45** E8
Masasi *Tanzania* 10°45S 38°52E **55** E4
Masaya *Nic.* 12°0N 86°7W **88** D2
Masbate *Phil.* 12°21N 123°36E **37** B6
Mascara *Algeria* 35°26N 0°6E **50** A6
Mascota *Mexico* 20°32N 104°49W **86** C4
Masela *Indonesia* 8°9S 129°51E **37** F7
Maseru *Lesotho* 29°18S 27°30E **56** D4
Mashaba *Zimbabwe* 20°2S 30°29E **55** G3
Mashatu △ *Botswana* 22°45S 29°5E **57** C4
Masherbrum *Pakistan* 35°38N 76°18E **43** B7
Mashhad *Iran* 36°20N 59°35E **45** B8
Mashiz *Iran* 29°56N 56°37E **45** D8
Mäshkel, Hämün-i-
Pakistan 28°20N 62°56E **45** D9
Mashki Chāh *Pakistan* 29°5N 62°30E **40** E3
Mashonaland *Zimbabwe* 16°30S 31°0E **53** H6
Mashonaland Central ☐
Zimbabwe 17°30S 31°0E **57** B5
Mashonaland East ☐
Zimbabwe 18°0S 32°0E **57** B5
Mashonaland West ☐
Zimbabwe 17°30S 29°30E **57** B4
Mashrakh *India* 26°7N 84°48E **43** F11
Masi Manimba
Dem. Rep. of the Congo 4°40S 17°54E **52** E3
Masig *Australia* 9°45S 143°24E **62** a
Masindi *Uganda* 1°40N 31°43E **54** B3
Masindi Port *Uganda* 1°43N 32°2E **54** B3
Masinga Res. *Kenya* 0°58S 37°38E **54** C4
Masisi
Dem. Rep. of the Congo 1°23S 28°49E **54** C2
Masjed Soleyman *Iran* 31°55N 49°18E **45** D6
Mask, L. *Ireland* 53°36N 9°22W **10** C2
Maskin *Oman* 23°44N 56°52E **45** F8
Masoala, Tanjon' i
Madag. 15°59S 50°13E **57** B9
Masoala △ *Madag.* 15°30S 50°12E **57** B9
Masoarivo *Madag.* 19°3S 44°19E **57** B7
Masohi = Amahai
Indonesia 3°20S 128°55E **37** E7
Masomeloka *Madag.* 20°17S 48°37E **57** C8
Mason *Nev., U.S.A.* 38°56N 119°8W **78** G7
Mason *Tex., U.S.A.* 30°45N 99°14W **84** F5
Mason City *U.S.A.* 43°9N 93°12W **80** D7
Maspalomas *Canary Is.* 27°46N 15°35W **24** G4
Maspalomas, Pta.
Canary Is. 27°43N 15°36W **24** G4
Masqaṭ *Oman* 23°37N 58°36E **47** C6
Massa *Italy* 44°1N 10°9E **20** D9
Massachusetts ☐ *U.S.A.* 42°30N 72°0W **83** D13
Massachusetts B.
U.S.A. 42°25N 70°50W **83** D14
Massakory *Chad* 13°0N 15°49E **51** F9
Massamba *Mozam.* 15°58S 33°31E **55** F3
Massanella *Spain* 39°48N 2°51E **24** B9
Massangena *Mozam.* 21°34S 33°0E **57** C5
Massango *Angola* 8°2S 16°21E **52** F3
Massawa = Mitsiwa
Eritrea 15°35N 39°25E **47** D2
Massena *U.S.A.* 44°56N 74°54W **83** B10
Massenya *Chad* 11°21N 16°9E **51** F9
Masset *Canada* 54°2N 132°10W **70** C2
Massiah Street *Barbados* 13°9N 59°29W **89** g
Massif Central *France* 44°55N 3°0E **20** D5
Massillon *U.S.A.* 40°48N 81°32W **82** F3
Massinga *Mozam.* 23°15S 35°22E **57** C6
Massingir *Mozam.* 23°51S 32°4E **57** C5
Masson-Angers *Canada* 45°32N 75°25W **83** A9
Masson I. *Antarctica* 66°10S 93°20E **5** C7
Mastanli = Momchilgrad
Bulgaria 41°33N 25°23E **23** D11

Masterton *N.Z.* 40°56S 175°39E **59** D5
Mastic *U.S.A.* 40°47N 72°54W **83** F12
Mastuj *Pakistan* 36°20N 72°36E **43** A5
Mastung *Pakistan* 29°50N 66°56E **40** E5
Masty *Belarus* 53°27N 24°38E **17** B13
Masuda *Japan* 34°40N 131°51E **31** G5
Masuku = Franceville
Gabon 1°40S 13°32E **52** E2
Masurian Lakes = Mazurski,
Pojezierze *Poland* 53°50N 21°0E **17** B11
Masvingo *Zimbabwe* 20°8S 30°49E **55** G3
Masvingo ☐ *Zimbabwe* 21°0S 31°30E **55** G3
Maswa △ *Tanzania* 2°58S 34°19E **54** C3
Maşyāf *Syria* 35°4N 36°20E **44** C3
Mata-au = Clutha →
N.Z. 46°20S 169°49E **59** G2
Matabeleland *Zimbabwe* 18°0S 27°0E **53** H5
Matabeleland North ☐
Zimbabwe 19°0S 28°0E **55** F2
Matabeleland South ☐
Zimbabwe 21°0S 29°0E **55** G2
Matachewan *Canada* 47°56N 80°39W **72** C3
Matadi
Dem. Rep. of the Congo 5°52S 13°31E **52** F2
Matagalpa *Nic.* 13°0N 85°58W **88** D2
Matagami *Canada* 49°45N 77°34W **72** C4
Matagami, L. *Canada* 49°50N 77°40W **72** C4
Matagorda B. *U.S.A.* 28°40N 96°12W **84** G6
Matagorda I. *U.S.A.* 28°15N 96°30W **84** G6
Mataiea *Tahiti* 17°46S 149°25W **59** d
Matak *Indonesia* 3°18N 106°16E **36** D3
Matala *Greece* 34°59N 24°45E **25** E6
Matam *Senegal* 15°34N 13°17W **50** E3
Matamoros *Campeche,*
Mexico 18°50N 90°50W **87** D6
Matamoros *Coahuila,*
Mexico 25°32N 103°15W **86** B4
Matamoros *Tamaulipas,*
Mexico 25°53N 97°30W **87** B5
Ma'ṭan as Sarra *Libya* 21°45N 22°0E **51** D10
Matandu → *Tanzania* 8°45S 34°19E **55** D3
Matane *Canada* 48°50N 67°33W **73** C6
Matanomadh *India* 23°33N 68°57E **42** H3
Matanzas *Cuba* 23°0N 81°40W **88** B3
Matapa *Botswana* 23°11S 24°39E **56** C3
Matapan, C. = Ténaro, Akra
Greece 36°22N 22°27E **23** F10
Matapédia *Canada* 48°0N 66°59W **73** C6
Matapo △ *Zimbabwe* 20°30S 29°40E **55** G2
Matara *Sri Lanka* 5°58N 80°30E **40** S12
Mataram *Indonesia* 8°35S 116°7E **37** K18
Matarani *Peru* 17°0S 72°10W **92** G4
Mataranka *Australia* 14°55S 133°4E **60** B5
Matarma, Râs *Egypt* 30°27N 32°44E **46** E1
Mataró *Spain* 41°32N 2°29E **21** B7
Matatiele *S. Africa* 30°20S 28°49E **57** E4
Mataura *N.Z.* 46°11S 168°51E **59** G2
Matavai, B. de *Tahiti* 17°30S 149°23W **59** d
Matehuala *Mexico* 23°39N 100°39W **86** C4
Mateke Hills *Zimbabwe* 21°48S 31°0E **55** G3
Matelot *Trin. & Tob.* 10°50N 61°7W **93** K15
Matera *Italy* 40°40N 16°36E **22** D7
Matetsi *Zimbabwe* 18°12S 26°0E **55** F2
Mathis *U.S.A.* 28°6N 97°50W **84** G6
Mathraki *Greece* 39°48N 19°31E **25** A3
Mathura *India* 27°30N 77°40E **42** F7
Mati *Phil.* 6°55N 126°15E **37** C7
Matiali *India* 26°56N 88°49E **43** F13
Matías Romero *Mexico* 16°53N 95°2W **87** D5
Matibane *Mozam.* 14°49S 40°45E **55** E5
Matiri Ra. *N.Z.* 41°38S 172°20E **59** D4
Matjiesfontein *S. Africa* 33°14S 20°35E **56** E3
Matla → *India* 21°40N 88°40E **43** J13
Matlamanyane
Botswana 19°33S 25°57E **56** B4
Matli *Pakistan* 25°2N 68°39E **42** G3
Matlock *U.K.* 53°9N 1°33W **12** D6
Mato Grosso ☐ *Brazil* 14°0S 55°0W **93** F8
Mato Grosso, Planalto do
Brazil 15°0S 55°0W **93** G8
Mato Grosso do Sul ☐
Brazil 18°0S 55°0W **93** G8
Matobo = Matapo △
Zimbabwe 20°36S 28°20E **55** G2
Matochkin Shar, Proliv
Russia 73°23N 55°12E **28** B6
Matopo Hills *Zimbabwe* 20°36S 28°20E **55** G2
Matopos *Zimbabwe* 20°20S 28°29E **55** G2
Matosinhos *Portugal* 41°11N 8°42W **21** B1
Matroosberg *S. Africa* 33°23S 19°40E **56** E2
Maṭruḥ *Oman* 23°37N 58°30E **47** C6
Matsue *Japan* 35°25N 133°10E **31** G6
Matsumae *Japan* 41°26N 140°7E **30** D10
Matsumoto *Japan* 36°15N 138°0E **31** F9
Matsusaka *Japan* 34°34N 136°32E **31** G8
Matsuura *Japan* 33°20N 129°49E **31** H4
Matsuyama *Japan* 33°45N 132°45E **31** H6
Mattagami → *Canada* 50°43N 81°29W **72** B3
Mattancheri *India* 9°50N 76°15E **40** Q10
Mattawa *Canada* 46°20N 78°45W **72** C4
Matterhorn *Switz.* 45°58N 7°39E **20** D7
Matthew Town
Bahamas 20°57N 73°40W **89** B5
Matthews Ridge *Guyana* 7°37N 60°10W **92** B6
Mattice *Canada* 49°40N 83°20E **72** C3
Mattituck *U.S.A.* 40°59N 72°32W **83** F12
Mattō *Japan* 36°31N 136°34E **31** F8
Mattoon *U.S.A.* 39°29N 88°23W **80** F9
Matuba *Mozam.* 24°28S 32°49E **57** C5
Matucana *Peru* 11°55S 76°25W **92** F3
Matuku *Fiji* 19°10S 179°44E **59** a
Matūn = Khowst
Afghan. 33°22N 69°58E **42** C3
Matura B. *Trin. & Tob.* 10°39N 61°1W **93** K15
Matúrin *Venezuela* 9°45N 63°11W **92** B6
Matusadona △ *Zimbabwe* 16°58S 28°42E **55** F2
Mau *Mad. P., India* 26°17N 78°41E **43** F8

Mau *Ut. P., India* 25°56N 83°33E **43** G10
Mau *Ut. P., India* 25°17N 81°23E **43** G9
Mau Escarpment *Kenya* 0°40S 36°0E **54** C4
Mau Ranipur *India* 25°16N 79°8E **43** G8
Maua *Kenya* 0°14N 37°56E **54** C4
Maua *Mozam.* 13°53S 37°10E **55** E4
Maubeuge *France* 50°17N 3°57E **20** A6
Maubin *Burma* 16°44N 95°39E **41** L19
Maud, Pt. *Australia* 23°6S 113°45E **60** D1
Maude *Australia* 34°29S 144°18E **63** E3
Maud Rise *S. Ocean* 66°0S 3°0E **5** C3
Maudin Sun *Burma* 16°0N 94°30E **41** M19
Maués *Brazil* 3°20S 57°45W **92** D7
Mauganj *India* 24°50N 81°55E **43** G9
Maughold Hd. *I. of Man* 54°18N 4°18W **12** C3
Maui *U.S.A.* 20°48N 156°20W **75** L8
Maulamyaing = Moulmein
Burma 16°30N 97°40E **41** L20
Maule ☐ *Chile* 36°5S 72°30W **94** D1
Maumee *U.S.A.* 41°34N 83°39W **81** E12
Maumee → *U.S.A.* 41°42N 83°28W **81** E12
Maumere *Indonesia* 8°38S 122°13E **37** F6
Maun *Botswana* 20°0S 23°26E **56** C3
Mauna Kea *U.S.A.* 19°50N 155°28W **75** M8
Mauna Loa *U.S.A.* 19°30N 155°35W **75** M8
Maunath Bhanjan = Mau
India 25°56N 83°33E **43** G10
Maungmagan Kyunzu
Burma 14°0N 97°48E **38** E1
Maungu *Kenya* 3°33S 38°45E **54** C4
Maupin *U.S.A.* 45°11N 121°5W **76** D3
Maurepas, L. *U.S.A.* 30°15N 90°30W **85** F9
Maurice, L. *Australia* 29°30S 131°0E **61** E5
Mauricie △ *Canada* 46°45N 73°0W **72** C5
Mauritania ■ *Africa* 20°50N 10°0W **50** E3
Mauritius ■ *Ind. Oc.* 20°0S 57°0E **53** d
Mauston *U.S.A.* 43°48N 90°5W **80** D8
Mavli *India* 24°45N 73°55E **42** G5
Mavuradonha Mts.
Zimbabwe 16°30S 31°30E **55** F3
Mawa
Dem. Rep. of the Congo 2°45N 26°40E **54** B2
Mawai *India* 22°30N 81°4E **43** H9
Mawana *India* 29°6N 77°58E **42** E7
Mawand *Pakistan* 29°33N 68°38E **42** E3
Mawjib, W. al → *Jordan* 31°28N 35°36E **46** D4
Mawk Mai *Burma* 20°14N 97°37E **41** J20
Mawlaik *Burma* 23°40N 94°26E **41** H19
Mawlamyine = Moulmein
Burma 16°30N 97°40E **41** L20
Mawqaq *Si. Arabia* 27°25N 41°8E **44** E4
Mawson Base *Antarctica* 67°30S 62°53E **5** C6
Mawson Coast *Antarctica* 68°30S 63°0E **5** C6
Max *U.S.A.* 47°49N 101°18W **80** B3
Maxcanú *Mexico* 20°35N 90°0W **87** C6
Maxesibeni *S. Africa* 30°49S 29°23E **57** E4
Maxixe *Mozam.* 23°54S 35°17E **57** C6
Maxville *Canada* 45°17N 74°51W **83** A10
Maxwell *U.S.A.* 39°17N 122°11W **78** F4
Maxwelton *Australia* 20°43S 142°41E **62** C3
May, C. *U.S.A.* 38°56N 74°58W **81** F16
May Pen *Jamaica* 17°58N 77°15W **88** a
Maya → *Russia* 60°28N 134°28E **29** D14
Maya Mts. *Belize* 16°30N 89°0W **87** D7
Mayaguana *Bahamas* 22°30N 72°44W **89** B5
Mayagüez *Puerto Rico* 18°12N 67°9W **89** d
Mayāmey *Iran* 36°24N 55°42E **45** B7
Mayanup *Australia* 33°57S 116°27E **61** F2
Mayapán *Mexico* 20°29N 89°11W **87** C7
Mayari *Cuba* 20°40N 75°41W **88** B4
Mayaro B. *Trin. & Tob.* 10°14N 60°59W **93** K16
Maybell *U.S.A.* 40°31N 108°5W **76** F9
Maybole *U.K.* 55°21N 4°42W **11** F4
Maydān *Iraq* 34°55N 45°37E **44** C5
Mayenne *France* 47°30N 0°32W **20** C3
Mayenne → *France* 47°30N 0°32W **20** C3
Mayer *U.S.A.* 34°24N 112°14W **77** J7
Mayerthorpe *Canada* 53°57N 115°8W **70** C5
Mayfield *Ky., U.S.A.* 36°44N 88°38W **80** G9
Mayfield *N.Y., U.S.A.* 43°6N 74°16W **83** D10
Mayhill *U.S.A.* 32°53N 105°29W **77** K11
Maykop *Russia* 44°35N 40°10E **19** F7
Maymyo *Burma* 22°2N 96°28E **38** A1
Maynard *Mass., U.S.A.* 42°26N 71°27W **83** D13
Maynard *Wash., U.S.A.* 47°59N 122°55W **78** C4
Maynard Hills *Australia* 28°28S 119°49E **61** E2
Mayne → *Australia* 23°40S 141°55E **62** C3
Maynooth *Canada* 45°13N 77°56W **82** A7
Maynooth *Ireland* 53°23N 6°34W **10** C5
Mayo *Canada* 63°38N 135°57W **68** E4
Mayo ☐ *Ireland* 53°53N 9°3W **10** C2
Mayon Volcano *Phil.* 13°15N 123°41E **37** B6
Mayor I. *N.Z.* 37°16S 176°17E **59** B6
Mayotte ☑ *Ind. Oc.* 12°50S 45°10E **53** a
Maysān ☐ *Iraq* 31°55N 47°15E **44** D5
Maysville *U.S.A.* 38°39N 83°46W **81** F12
Mayu *Indonesia* 1°30N 126°30E **37** D7
Mayville *N. Dak., U.S.A.* 47°30N 97°20W **80** B5
Mayville *N.Y., U.S.A.* 42°15N 79°30W **82** D5
Mazabuka *Zambia* 15°52S 27°44E **55** F2
Mazagán = El Jadida
Morocco 33°11N 8°17W **50** B4
Mazagão *Brazil* 0°7S 51°16W **93** D8
Mazán *Peru* 3°30S 73°0W **92** D4
Māzandarān ☐ *Iran* 36°30N 52°0E **45** B7
Mazapil *Mexico* 24°39N 101°34W **86** C4
Mazar *China* 36°32N 77°1E **42** B5
Mazara del Vallo *Italy* 37°39N 12°35E **22** F5
Mazarrón *Spain* 37°38N 1°19W **21** D5
Mazaruni → *Guyana* 6°25N 58°35W **92** B7
Mazatán *Mexico* 29°0N 110°8W **86** B2
Mazatenango *Guatemala* 14°35N 91°30W **88** D1
Mazatlán *Mexico* 23°13N 106°25W **86** C3
Mažeikiai *Lithuania* 56°20N 22°20E **9** H20
Māzhān *Iran* 32°30N 59°0E **45** C8
Mazīnān *Iran* 36°19N 56°56E **45** B8
Mazoe *Mozam.* 16°42S 33°7E **55** F3
Mazoe → *Mozam.* 16°20S 33°30E **55** F3
Mazowe *Zimbabwe* 17°28S 30°58E **55** F3

Mazurski, Pojezierze
Poland 53°50N 21°0E **17** B11
Mazyr *Belarus* 51°59N 29°15E **17** B15
Mba *Fiji* 17°33S 177°41E **59** a
Mbabane *Swaziland* 26°18S 31°6E **57** D5
Mbaïki *C.A.R.* 3°53N 18°1E **52** D3
Mbala *Zambia* 8°46S 31°24E **55** D3
Mbale *Uganda* 1°8N 34°12E **54** B3
Mbalmayo *Cameroon* 3°33N 11°33E **52** D2
Mbamba Bay *Tanzania* 11°13S 34°49E **55** E3
Mbandaka
Dem. Rep. of the Congo 0°1N 18°18E **52** D3
Mbanza Congo *Angola* 6°18S 14°16E **52** F2
Mbanza Ngungu
Dem. Rep. of the Congo 5°12S 14°53E **52** F2
Mbarangandu *Tanzania* 10°11S 36°48E **55** D4
Mbarara *Uganda* 0°35S 30°40E **54** C3
Mbengga = Beqa *Fiji* 18°23S 178°8E **59** a
Mbenkuru → *Tanzania* 9°25S 39°50E **55** D4
Mberengwa *Zimbabwe* 20°29S 29°57E **55** G2
Mberengwa, Mt.
Zimbabwe 20°37S 29°55E **55** G2
Mbesuma *Zambia* 10°0S 32°2E **55** E3
Mbeya *Tanzania* 8°54S 33°29E **55** D3
Mbeya ☐ *Tanzania* 8°15S 33°30E **55** D3
Mbhashe → *S. Africa* 32°15S 28°54E **57** E4
Mbinga *Tanzania* 10°50S 35°0E **55** E4
Mbini = Río Muni ☐
Eq. Guin. 1°30N 10°0E **52** D2
Mbizi *Zimbabwe* 21°23S 31°1E **55** G3
Mbouda *Cameroon* 5°38N 10°15E **50** G8
M'bouk'ou, L. de
Cameroon 6°23N 12°50E **52** C2
Mbour *Senegal* 14°22N 16°54W **50** F2
Mbuji-Mayi
Dem. Rep. of the Congo 6°9S 23°40E **54** D1
Mbulu *Tanzania* 3°45S 35°30E **54** C4
Mburucuyá *Argentina* 28°1S 58°14W **94** B4
Mburucuyá △ *Argentina* 28°1S 58°12W **94** B4
Mchinja *Tanzania* 9°44S 39°45E **55** D4
Mchinji *Malawi* 13°47S 32°58E **55** E3
Mdantsane *S. Africa* 32°56S 27°46E **57** E4
Mead, L. *U.S.A.* 36°0N 114°44W **79** J12
Meadow Lake *Canada* 54°10N 108°26W **71** C7
Meadow Lake △ *Canada* 54°27N 109°0W **71** C7
Meadow Valley Wash →
U.S.A. 36°40N 114°34W **79** J12
Meadville *U.S.A.* 41°39N 80°9W **82** E4
Meaford *Canada* 44°36N 80°35W **82** B4
Mealy Mts. *Canada* 53°10N 58°0W **73** B8
Meander River *Canada* 59°2N 117°42W **70** B5
Meares, C. *U.S.A.* 45°37N 124°0W **76** D1
Mearim → *Brazil* 3°4S 44°35W **93** D10
Meath ☐ *Ireland* 53°40N 6°57W **10** C5
Meath Park *Canada* 53°27N 105°22W **71** C7
Meaux *France* 48°58N 2°50E **20** B5
Mebechi-Gawa →
Japan 40°31N 141°31E **30** D10
Mebulu, Tanjung
Indonesia 8°50S 115°5E **37** K18
Mecanhelas *Mozam.* 15°12S 35°54E **55** F4
Mecca = Makkah
Si. Arabia 21°30N 39°54E **47** C2
Mecca *U.S.A.* 33°34N 116°5W **79** M10
Mechanicsburg *U.S.A.* 40°13N 77°1W **82** F8
Mechanicville *U.S.A.* 42°54N 73°41W **83** D11
Mechelen *Belgium* 51°2N 4°29E **15** C4
Mecheria *Algeria* 33°35N 0°18W **50** B5
Mecklenburg *Germany* 53°33N 11°40E **16** B7
Mecklenburger Bucht
Germany 54°20N 11°40E **16** A6
Meconta *Mozam.* 14°59S 39°50E **55** E4
Mecubúri *Mozam.* 14°39S 38°54E **55** E4
Mecubúri → *Mozam.* 14°10S 40°30E **55** E5
Mecúfi *Mozam.* 13°20S 40°32E **55** E5
Medan *Indonesia* 3°40N 98°38E **36** D1
Médanos de Coro △
Venezuela 11°35N 69°44W **89** D6
Medanosa, Pta. *Argentina* 48°8S 66°0W **96** F3
Médéa *Algeria* 36°12N 2°50E **50** A6
Medellín *Colombia* 6°15N 75°35W **92** B3
Medelpad *Sweden* 62°33N 16°30E **8** E17
Medemblik *Neths.* 52°46N 5°8E **15** B5
Medford *Mass., U.S.A.* 42°25N 71°7W **83** D13
Medford *Oreg., U.S.A.* 42°19N 122°52W **76** E2
Medford *Wis., U.S.A.* 45°9N 90°20W **80** C8
Medgidia *Romania* 44°15N 28°19E **17** F15
Media Agua *Argentina* 31°58S 68°25W **94** C2
Media Luna *Argentina* 34°45S 66°44W **94** C2
Medianeira *Brazil* 25°17S 54°5W **95** B5
Mediaş *Romania* 46°9N 24°22E **17** E13
Medicine Bow *U.S.A.* 41°54N 106°12W **76** F10
Medicine Bow Mts.
U.S.A. 40°40N 106°0W **76** F10
Medicine Bow Pk.
U.S.A. 41°21N 106°19W **76** F10
Medicine Hat *Canada* 50°0N 110°45W **71** D6
Medicine Lake *U.S.A.* 48°30N 104°30W **76** B11
Medicine Lodge *U.S.A.* 37°17N 98°35W **80** G4
Medina = Al Madīnah
Si. Arabia 24°35N 39°52E **44** E3
Medina *N. Dak., U.S.A.* 46°54N 99°18W **80** B4
Medina *N.Y., U.S.A.* 43°13N 78°23W **82** C6
Medina *Ohio, U.S.A.* 41°8N 81°52W **82** E3
Medina → *U.S.A.* 29°16N 98°29W **84** G5
Medina del Campo *Spain* 41°18N 4°55W **21** B3
Medina L. *U.S.A.* 29°32N 98°56W **84** G5
Medina Sidonia *Spain* 36°28N 5°57W **21** D3
Medinipur *India* 22°25N 87°21E **43** H12
Mediterranean Sea *Europe* 35°0N 15°0E **6** H7
Médoc *France* 45°10N 0°50W **20** D3
Medveditsa → *Russia* 49°35N 42°41E **19** E7
Medvezhi, Ostrava
Russia 71°0N 161°0E **29** B17
Medvezhyegorsk *Russia* 63°0N 34°25E **18** B5

Medway □ U.K. 51°25N 0°32E 13 F8
Medway ➤ U.K. 51°27N 0°46E 13 F8
Meekatharra Australia 26°32S 118°29E 61 E2
Meeker U.S.A. 40°2N 107°55W 76 F10
Meerut India 29°1N 77°42E 42 E7
Meeteetse U.S.A. 44°9N 108°52W 76 D9
Mega Ethiopia 3°57N 38°19E 47 G2
Megara Greece 37°58N 23°22E 23 F10
Megasini India 21°38N 86°21E 43 J12
Meghalaya □ India 25°50N 91°0E 41 G17
Meghna ➤ Bangla. 22°50N 90°50E 41 H17
Megion Russia 61°3N 76°6E 28 C8
Mégiscane, L. Canada 48°35N 75°55W 72 C4
Meharry, Mt. Australia 22°59S 118°35E 60 D2
Mehlville U.S.A. 38°31N 90°19W 80 F8
Mehndawal India 26°58N 83°5E 43 F10
Mehr Jān Iran 33°50N 55°6E 45 C7
Mehrābād Iran 36°53N 47°55E 44 B5
Mehrān Iran 33°7N 46°10E 44 C5
Mehrān ➤ Iran 26°45N 55°26E 45 E7
Mehrgarh Pakistan 29°30N 67°30E 42 E2
Mehriz Iran 31°35N 54°28E 45 D7
Mei Xian China 34°18N 107°55E 34 G4
Meighen I. Canada 80°0N 99°30W 69 B12
Meihekou China 42°32N 125°40E 35 C13
Meiktila Burma 20°53N 95°54E 41 J19
Meissen Germany 51°9N 13°29E 16 C7
Meizhou China 24°16N 116°6E 33 D6
Meja India 25°9N 82°7E 43 G10
Mejillones Chile 23°10S 70°30W 94 A1
Mekele Ethiopia 13°33N 39°30E 47 E2
Mekerghene, Sebkra Algeria 26°21N 1°30E 50 C6
Mekhtar Pakistan 30°30N 69°15E 40 D6
Meknès Morocco 33°57N 5°33W 50 B4
Mekong ➤ Asia 9°30N 106°15E 39 H6
Mekongga Indonesia 3°39S 121°15E 37 E6
Mekvari = Kür ➤ Azerbaijan 39°29N 49°15E 19 G8
Melagiri Hills India 12°20N 77°30E 40 N10
Melaka Malaysia 2°15N 102°15E 39 L4
Melalap Malaysia 5°10N 116°5E 36 C5
Melambes Greece 35°8N 24°40E 25 D6
Melanesia Pac. Oc. 4°0S 155°0E 64 H7
Melanesian Basin Pac. Oc. 0°5N 160°35E 64 G8
Melaya Indonesia 8°17S 114°30E 37 J17
Melbourne Australia 37°48S 144°58E 63 F4
Melbourne U.S.A. 28°5N 80°37W 85 G14
Melchor Múzquiz Mexico 27°53N 101°31W 86 B4
Melchor Ocampo Mexico 24°51N 101°39W 86 C4
Mélèzes ➤ Canada 57°40N 69°29W 72 A5
Melfort Canada 52°50N 104°37W 71 C8
Melfort Zimbabwe 18°0S 31°25E 55 F3
Melhus Norway 63°17N 10°18E 8 E14
Melilla N. Afr. 35°21N 2°57W 21 E4
Melipilla Chile 33°42S 71°15W 94 C1
Melissa Canada 45°24N 79°14W 82 A5
Melissa, Akra Greece 35°6N 24°33E 25 D6
Melita Canada 49°15N 101°0W 71 D8
Melitopol Ukraine 46°50N 35°22E 19 E6
Melk Austria 48°13N 15°20E 16 D8
Mellansel Sweden 63°26N 18°19E 8 E18
Mellen U.S.A. 46°20N 90°40W 80 B8
Mellerud Sweden 58°41N 12°28E 9 G15
Mellette U.S.A. 45°9N 98°30W 80 C4
Mellieha Malta 35°57N 14°22E 25 D1
Melo Uruguay 32°20S 54°10W 95 C5
Melolo Indonesia 9°53S 120°40E 37 F6
Melouprey Cambodia 13°48N 105°16E 38 F5
Melrhir, Chott Algeria 34°13N 6°30E 50 B7
Melrose Australia 32°42S 146°57E 63 E4
Melrose U.K. 55°36N 2°43W 11 F6
Melrose Minn., U.S.A. 45°40N 94°49W 80 C6
Melrose N. Mex., U.S.A. 34°26N 103°38W 77 J12
Melstone U.S.A. 46°36N 107°52W 76 C10
Melton Mowbray U.K. 52°47N 0°54W 12 E7
Melun France 48°32N 2°39E 20 B5
Melville Canada 50°55N 102°50W 71 C8
Melville, C. Australia 14°11S 144°30E 62 A3
Melville, L. Canada 53°30N 60°0W 73 B8
Melville B. Australia 12°0S 136°45E 62 A2
Melville B. Greenland 75°30N 63°0W 69 B19
Melville I. Australia 11°30S 131°0E 60 B5
Melville I. Canada 75°30N 112°0W 69 B9
Melville Pen. Canada 68°0N 84°0W 69 D15
Melvin, Lough Ireland 54°26N 8°10W 10 B3
Memba Mozam. 14°11S 40°30E 55 E5
Memboro Indonesia 9°30S 119°30E 60 A2
Memel = Klaipėda Lithuania 55°43N 21°10E 9 J19
Memel S. Africa 27°38S 29°36E 57 D4
Memmingen Germany 47°58N 10°10E 16 E6
Mempawah Indonesia 0°30N 109°5E 36 D3
Memphis Mich., U.S.A. 42°54N 82°46W 82 D2
Memphis Tenn., U.S.A. 35°8N 90°2W 85 D9
Memphis Tex., U.S.A. 34°44N 100°33W 84 D4
Memphrémagog, L. N. Amer. 45°8N 72°17W 83 B12
Mena U.S.A. 34°35N 94°15W 84 D7
Menai Strait U.K. 53°11N 4°13W 12 D3
Ménaka Mali 15°59N 2°18E 50 E6
Menan = Chao Phraya ➤ Thailand 13°40N 100°31E 38 F3
Menarandra ➤ Madag. 25°17S 44°30E 57 D7
Menard U.S.A. 30°55N 99°47W 84 F5
Menard Fracture Zone Pac. Oc. 43°0S 97°0W 65 M18
Mendaña Fracture Zone Pac. Oc. 16°0S 91°0W 65 J18
Mendawai ➤ Indonesia 3°30S 113°0E 36 E4
Mende France 44°31N 3°30E 20 D5
Mendeleyev Ridge Arctic 80°0N 178°0W 4 B17
Mendhar India 33°35N 74°10E 43 C6
Mendip Hills U.K. 51°17N 2°40W 13 F5
Mendocino U.S.A. 39°19N 123°48W 76 G2
Mendocino, C. U.S.A. 40°26N 124°25W 76 F1

Mendocino Fracture Zone Pac. Oc. 40°0N 142°0W 65 D13
Mendota Calif., U.S.A. 36°45N 120°23W 78 J6
Mendota Ill., U.S.A. 41°33N 89°7W 80 E9
Mendoyo Indonesia 8°23S 114°42E 37 J17
Mendoza Argentina 32°50S 68°52W 94 C2
Mendoza □ Argentina 33°0S 69°0W 94 C2
Mene Grande Venezuela 9°49N 70°56W 92 B4
Menemen Turkey 38°34N 27°3E 23 E12
Menen Belgium 50°47N 3°7E 15 D3
Menggala Indonesia 4°30S 105°15E 36 E3
Mengjin China 34°55N 112°45E 34 G7
Mengyin China 35°40N 117°58E 35 G9
Mengzi China 23°20N 103°22E 32 D5
Menihek Canada 54°28N 56°36W 73 B6
Menihek L. Canada 54°0N 67°0W 73 B6
Menin = Menen Belgium 50°47N 3°7E 15 D3
Menindee Australia 32°20S 142°25E 63 E3
Menindee L. Australia 32°20S 142°25E 63 E3
Meningie Australia 35°50S 139°18E 63 F2
Menjangan, Pulau Indonesia 8°7S 114°31E 37 J17
Menlo Park U.S.A. 37°27N 122°12W 78 H4
Menngen ⊙ Australia 15°21S 131°16E 60 C5
Menominee U.S.A. 45°6N 87°37W 80 C10
Menominee ➤ U.S.A. 45°6N 87°35W 80 C10
Menomonie U.S.A. 44°53N 91°55W 80 C8
Menongue Angola 14°48S 17°52E 53 G3
Menorca Spain 40°0N 4°0E 24 B11
Mentawai, Kepulauan Indonesia 2°0S 99°0E 36 E1
Menton France 43°50N 7°29E 20 E7
Mentor U.S.A. 41°40N 81°21W 82 E3
Menzelinsk Russia 55°47N 53°11E 18 C9
Menzies Australia 29°40S 121°2E 61 E3
Meob B. Namibia 24°25S 14°34E 56 C1
Me'ona Israel 33°1N 35°15E 46 B4
Meoqui Mexico 28°17N 105°29W 86 B3
Mepaco Mozam. 15°57S 30°48E 55 F3
Meppel Neths. 52°42N 6°12E 15 B6
Merak Indonesia 6°10N 106°26E 37 F12
Meramangye, L. Australia 28°25S 132°13E 61 E5
Meran = Merano Italy 46°40N 11°9E 22 A4
Merano Italy 46°40N 11°9E 22 A4
Merauke Indonesia 8°29S 140°24E 37 F10
Merbein Australia 34°10S 142°2E 63 E3
Merbuk, Gunung Indonesia 8°13S 114°39E 37 J17
Merca = Marka Somali Rep. 1°48N 44°50E 47 G3
Merced U.S.A. 37°18N 120°29W 78 H6
Merced ➤ U.S.A. 37°21N 120°59W 78 H6
Merced Pk. U.S.A. 37°36N 119°24W 78 H7
Mercedes B. Aires, Argentina 34°40S 59°30W 94 C4
Mercedes Corrientes, Argentina 29°10S 58°5W 94 B4
Mercedes San Luis, Argentina 33°40S 65°21W 94 C2
Mercedes Uruguay 33°12S 58°0W 94 C4
Merceditas Chile 28°20S 70°35W 94 B1
Mercer N.Z. 37°16S 175°5E 59 B5
Mercer U.S.A. 41°14N 80°15W 82 E4
Mercer Island U.S.A. 47°34N 122°13W 78 C4
Mercy, C. Canada 65°0N 63°30W 69 E19
Mere U.K. 51°6N 2°16W 13 F5
Meredith, C. Falk. Is. 52°15S 60°40W 96 G4
Meredith, L. U.S.A. 35°43N 101°33W 84 D4
Mergui Burma 12°26N 98°34E 38 F2
Mergui Arch. = Myeik Kyunzu Burma 11°30N 97°30E 39 G1
Mérida Mexico 20°58N 89°37W 87 C7
Mérida Spain 38°55N 6°25W 21 C2
Mérida Venezuela 8°24N 71°8W 92 B4
Mérida, Cord. de Venezuela 9°0N 71°0W 92 B4
Meriden U.K. 52°26N 1°38W 13 E6
Meriden U.S.A. 41°32N 72°48W 83 E12
Meridian Calif., U.S.A. 39°9N 121°55W 78 F5
Meridian Idaho, U.S.A. 43°37N 116°24W 76 E5
Meridian Miss., U.S.A. 32°22N 88°42W 85 E10
Merinda Australia 20°2S 148°11E 62 C4
Merir Pac. Oc. 4°10N 132°30E 37 D8
Merirumã Brazil 1°15N 54°50W 93 C8
Merkel U.S.A. 32°28N 100°1W 84 E4
Mermaid Reef Australia 17°6S 119°36E 60 C2
Merredin Australia 31°28S 118°18E 61 F2
Merrick U.K. 55°8N 4°28W 11 F4
Merrickville Canada 44°55N 75°50W 83 B9
Merrill Oreg., U.S.A. 42°1N 121°36W 76 E3
Merrill Wis., U.S.A. 45°11N 89°41W 80 C9
Merrimack ➤ U.S.A. 42°49N 70°49W 83 D14
Merriman U.S.A. 42°55N 101°42W 80 D3
Merriwa Australia 32°6S 150°22E 63 E5
Merry I. Canada 55°29N 77°31W 72 A4
Merryville U.S.A. 30°45N 93°33W 84 F8
Mersch Lux. 49°44N 6°7E 15 E6
Mersea I. U.K. 51°47N 0°58E 13 F8
Merseburg Germany 51°22N 11°59E 16 C6
Mersey ➤ U.K. 53°25N 3°1W 12 D4
Merseyside □ U.K. 53°31N 3°2W 12 D4
Mersin = İçel Turkey 36°51N 34°36E 44 B2
Mersing Malaysia 2°25N 103°50E 39 L4
Merta India 26°39N 74°4E 42 F6
Merta Road India 26°43N 73°55E 42 F5
Merthyr Tydfil U.K. 51°45N 3°23W 13 F4
Merthyr Tydfil □ U.K. 51°46N 3°21W 13 F4
Merti Kenya 1°4N 38°40E 54 B4
Mértola Portugal 37°40N 7°40W 21 D2
Mertzon U.S.A. 31°16N 100°49W 84 F4
Meru Kenya 0°3N 37°40E 54 B4
Meru Tanzania 3°15S 36°46E 54 C4
Meru △ Kenya 0°5N 38°10E 54 B4
Mesa U.S.A. 33°25N 111°50W 77 K8
Mesa Verde △ U.S.A. 37°11N 108°29W 77 H9

Mesanagros Greece 36°1N 27°49E 25 C9
Mesaoría Cyprus 35°12N 33°14E 25 D12
Mesgouez, L. Canada 51°20N 75°0W 72 B5
Meshed = Mashhad Iran 36°20N 59°35E 45 B8
Meshgīn Shahr Iran 38°30N 47°45E 44 B5
Meshoppen U.S.A. 41°36N 76°3W 83 E8
Mesilinka ➤ Canada 56°6N 124°30W 70 B4
Mesologi Greece 38°21N 21°28E 23 E9
Mesongi Greece 39°29N 19°56E 25 B3
Mesopotamia = Al Jazirah Iraq 33°30N 44°0E 44 C5
Mesopotamia U.S.A. 41°27N 80°57W 82 E4
Mesquite U.S.A. 36°48N 114°4W 77 H6
Messaad Algeria 34°8N 3°30E 50 B6
Messalo ➤ Mozam. 12°25S 39°15E 55 E4
Messara, Kolpos Greece 35°6N 24°47E 25 D6
Messina = Musina S. Africa 22°20S 30°5E 57 C5
Messina Italy 38°11N 15°34E 22 E6
Messina, Str. di Italy 38°15N 15°35E 22 F6
Messini Greece 37°4N 22°1E 23 F10
Messiniakos Kolpos Greece 36°45N 22°5E 23 F10
Mesta = Nestos ➤ Europe 40°54N 24°49E 23 D11
Meta ➤ S. Amer. 6°12N 67°28W 92 B5
Meta Incognita Pen. Canada 62°45N 68°30W 69 E18
Metabetchouan Canada 48°26N 71°52W 73 C5
Metairie U.S.A. 29°59N 90°9W 85 G9
Metaline Falls U.S.A. 48°52N 117°22W 76 B5
Metán Argentina 25°30S 65°0W 94 B3
Metangula Mozam. 12°40S 34°50E 55 E3
Metcalfe Canada 45°14N 75°28W 83 A9
Metema Ethiopia 12°58N 36°12E 47 E2
Metengobalame Mozam. 14°49S 34°30E 55 E3
Methven N.Z. 43°38S 171°40E 59 E3
Metil Mozam. 16°24S 39°0E 55 F4
Metlakatla U.S.A. 55°8N 131°35W 68 F5
Metropolis U.S.A. 37°9N 88°44W 80 G9
Metropolitana □ Chile 33°30S 70°50W 94 C1
Metu Ethiopia 8°18N 35°35E 47 F2
Metz France 49°8N 6°10E 20 B7
Meulaboh Indonesia 4°11N 96°3E 36 D1
Meureudu Indonesia 5°19N 96°10E 36 C1
Meuse ➤ Europe 50°45N 5°41E 15 D5
Mexia U.S.A. 31°41N 96°29W 84 F6
Mexiana, I. Brazil 0°0 49°30W 93 D9
Mexicali Mexico 32°40N 115°30W 79 N11
Mexican Plateau Mexico 25°0N 105°0W 66 G9
Mexican Water U.S.A. 36°57N 109°32W 77 H9
México Mexico 19°24N 99°9W 87 D5
Mexico Maine, U.S.A. 44°34N 70°33W 83 B14
Mexico Mo., U.S.A. 39°10N 91°53W 80 F8
Mexico N.Y., U.S.A. 43°28N 76°14W 83 C8
México □ Mexico 19°20N 99°30W 87 D5
Mexico ■ Cent. Amer. 25°0N 105°0W 86 C4
México, Ciudad de Mexico 19°24N 99°9W 87 D5
Mexico, G. of Cent. Amer. 25°0N 90°0W 87 C7
Mexico B. U.S.A. 43°35N 76°20W 83 C8
Meydān-e Naftūn Iran 31°56N 49°18E 45 D6
Meydani, Ra's-e Iran 25°24N 59°6E 45 E8
Meyers Chuck U.S.A. 55°45N 132°15W 70 B2
Meymaneh Afghan. 35°53N 64°38E 40 B4
Mezen Russia 65°50N 44°20E 18 A7
Mezen ➤ Russia 65°44N 44°22E 18 A7
Mézenc, Mt. France 44°54N 4°11E 20 D6
Mezhdurechensk Russia 53°41N 88°3E 28 D9
Mezhdurechenskiy Russia 59°36N 65°56E 28 D7
Mezőkövesd Hungary 47°49N 20°35E 17 E11
Mezőtúr Hungary 47°1N 20°41E 17 E11
Mezquital Mexico 23°29N 104°23W 86 C4
Mfolozi ➤ S. Africa 28°25S 32°26E 57 D5
Mgeta Tanzania 8°22S 36°6E 55 D4
Mhlaba Hills Zimbabwe 18°30S 30°30E 55 F3
Mhow India 22°33N 75°50E 42 H6
Miahuatlán Mexico 16°20N 96°36W 87 D5
Miami Fla., U.S.A. 25°46N 80°11W 85 J14
Miami Okla., U.S.A. 36°53N 94°53W 84 C7
Miami Tex., U.S.A. 35°42N 100°38W 84 D4
Miami Beach U.S.A. 25°47N 80°7W 85 J14
Mian Xian China 33°10N 106°32E 34 H4
Mianchi China 34°48N 111°48E 34 G6
Miāndarreh Iran 35°37N 53°39E 45 C7
Miāndowāb Iran 37°0N 46°5E 44 B5
Miandrivazo Madag. 19°31S 45°29E 57 B8
Miāneh Iran 37°30N 47°40E 44 B5
Mianwali Pakistan 32°38N 71°28E 42 C4
Mianyang China 31°22N 104°47E 32 C5
Miarinarivo Antananarivo, Madag. 18°57S 46°55E 57 B8
Miarinarivo Toamasina, Madag. 16°38S 48°15E 57 B8
Miariravaratra Madag. 20°13S 47°31E 57 C8
Miass Russia 54°59N 60°6E 18 D11
Mica S. Africa 24°10S 30°48E 57 C5
Michalovce Slovak Rep. 48°47N 21°58E 17 D11
Michigan □ U.S.A. 44°0N 85°0W 81 C11
Michigan, L. U.S.A. 44°0N 87°0W 80 D10
Michigan City U.S.A. 41°43N 86°54W 80 E10
Michipicoten I. Canada 47°40N 85°40W 72 C2
Michoacán □ Mexico 19°10N 101°50W 86 D4
Michurin Bulgaria 42°9N 27°51E 23 C12
Michurinsk Russia 52°58N 40°27E 18 D7
Micoud St. Lucia 13°49N 60°54W 89 f
Micronesia Pac. Oc. 11°0N 160°0E 64 G7
Micronesia, Federated States of ■ Pac. Oc. 9°0N 150°0E 58 A8
Mid-Pacific Seamounts Pac. Oc. 18°0N 170°0W 64 F9
Midai Indonesia 3°0N 107°47E 36 D3
Midale Canada 49°25N 103°20W 71 D8
Middelburg Neths. 51°30N 3°36E 15 C3
Middelburg Eastern Cape, S. Africa 31°30S 25°0E 56 E4
Middelburg Mpumalanga, S. Africa 25°49S 29°28E 57 D4

Middelpos S. Africa 31°55S 20°13E 56 E3
Middelwit S. Africa 24°51S 27°3E 56 C4
Middle Alkali L. U.S.A. 41°27N 120°5W 76 F3
Middle America Trench = Guatemala Trench Pac. Oc. 14°0N 95°0W 66 H10
Middle Bass I. U.S.A. 41°41N 82°48W 82 E2
Middle East Asia 35°0N 40°0E 26 C5
Middle Fork Feather ➤ U.S.A. 38°33N 121°30W 78 F5
Middle I. Australia 34°6S 123°11E 61 F3
Middle Loup ➤ U.S.A. 41°17N 98°24W 80 E4
Middleboro U.S.A. 41°54N 70°55W 83 E14
Middleburg Fla., U.S.A. 30°4N 81°52W 85 F14
Middleburg Pa., U.S.A. 40°47N 77°3W 82 F7
Middleburgh U.S.A. 42°36N 74°20W 83 D10
Middlebury U.S.A. 44°1N 73°10W 83 B11
Middlefield U.S.A. 41°27N 81°4W 82 E3
Middlemount Australia 22°50S 148°40E 62 C4
Middleport N.Y., U.S.A. 43°13N 78°29W 82 C6
Middleport Ohio, U.S.A. 39°0N 82°3W 81 F12
Middlesboro U.S.A. 36°36N 83°43W 81 G12
Middlesbrough U.K. 54°35N 1°13W 12 C6
Middlesbrough □ U.K. 54°28N 1°13W 12 C6
Middlesex Belize 17°2N 88°31W 88 C2
Middlesex N.J., U.S.A. 40°36N 74°30W 83 F10
Middlesex N.Y., U.S.A. 42°42N 77°16W 82 D7
Middleton Australia 22°22S 141°32E 62 C3
Middleton Canada 44°57N 65°4W 73 D6
Middleton Cr. ➤ Australia 22°35S 141°51E 62 C3
Middleton I. U.S.A. 59°26N 146°20W 74 D10
Middletown U.K. 54°17N 6°51W 10 B5
Middletown Calif., U.S.A. 38°45N 122°37W 78 G4
Middletown Conn., U.S.A. 41°34N 72°39W 83 E12
Middletown N.Y., U.S.A. 41°27N 74°25W 83 E10
Middletown Ohio, U.S.A. 39°31N 84°24W 81 F11
Middletown Pa., U.S.A. 40°12N 76°44W 83 F8
Midge Point Australia 20°39S 148°43E 62 b
Midhurst Canada 44°26N 79°43W 82 B5
Midhurst U.K. 50°59N 0°44W 13 G7
Midi, Canal du ➤ France 43°45N 1°21E 20 E4
Midland Australia 31°54S 116°1E 61 F2
Midland Canada 44°45N 79°50W 82 B5
Midland Calif., U.S.A. 33°52N 114°48W 79 M12
Midland Mich., U.S.A. 43°37N 84°14W 81 D11
Midland Pa., U.S.A. 40°39N 80°27W 82 F4
Midland Tex., U.S.A. 32°0N 102°3W 84 F3
Midlands □ Zimbabwe 19°40S 29°0E 55 F2
Midleton Ireland 51°55N 8°10W 10 E3
Midlothian U.S.A. 32°30N 97°0W 84 E6
Midlothian □ U.K. 55°51N 3°5W 11 F5
Midnapore = Medinipur India 22°25N 87°21E 43 H12
Midongy, Tangorombohitr' i Madag. 23°35S 47°1E 57 C8
Midongy Atsimo Madag. 23°35S 47°1E 57 C8
Midway Is. Pac. Oc. 28°13N 177°22W 75 K4
Midway Wells U.S.A. 32°41N 115°7W 79 N11
Midwest Wyo., U.S.A. 43°25N 106°16W 76 E10
Midwest City U.S.A. 35°27N 97°24W 84 D6
Midyat Turkey 37°25N 41°23E 44 B4
Midžor Bulgaria 43°24N 22°40E 23 C10
Mie □ Japan 34°30N 136°10E 31 G8
Międzychód Poland 52°35N 15°53E 16 B8
Międzyrzec Podlaski Poland 51°58N 22°45E 17 C12
Mielec Poland 50°15N 21°25E 17 C11
Mienga Angola 17°12S 19°48E 56 B2
Miercurea-Ciuc Romania 46°21N 25°48E 17 E13
Mieres Spain 43°18N 5°48W 21 A3
Mifflintown U.S.A. 40°34N 77°24W 82 F7
Mifraz Hefa Israel 32°52N 35°0E 46 C4
Migori Kenya 1°4S 34°28E 54 C3
Miguel Alemán, Presa Mexico 18°15N 96°32W 87 D5
Mihara Japan 34°24N 133°5E 31 G6
Mikese Tanzania 6°48S 37°55E 54 D4
Mikhaylovgrad = Montana Bulgaria 43°27N 23°16E 23 C10
Mikhaylovka Russia 50°3N 43°5E 19 D7
Mikines Greece 37°43N 22°46E 23 F10
Mikkeli Finland 61°43N 27°15E 8 F22
Mikkwa ➤ Canada 58°25N 114°46W 70 B6
Mikonos = Mykonos Greece 37°30N 25°25E 23 F11
Mikumi Tanzania 7°26S 37°0E 54 D4
Mikumi △ Tanzania 7°35S 37°15E 54 D4
Mikun Russia 62°20N 50°0E 18 B9
Milaca U.S.A. 45°45N 93°39W 80 C7
Milagro Ecuador 2°11S 79°36W 92 D3
Milan = Milano Italy 45°28N 9°10E 20 D8
Milan Mo., U.S.A. 40°12N 93°7W 80 E7
Milan Tenn., U.S.A. 35°55N 88°46W 85 D10
Milange Mozam. 16°3S 35°45E 55 F4
Milano Italy 45°28N 9°10E 20 D8
Milanoa Madag. 13°35S 49°47E 57 A8
Milas Turkey 37°20N 27°50E 23 F12
Milatos Greece 35°18N 25°34E 25 D7
Milazzo Italy 38°13N 15°15E 22 E6
Milbank U.S.A. 45°13N 96°38W 80 C5
Milbanke Sd. Canada 52°15N 128°35W 70 C3
Milden Canada 51°29N 107°32W 71 C7
Mildenhall U.K. 52°21N 0°32E 13 E8
Mildmay Canada 44°3N 81°7W 82 B3
Mildura Australia 34°13S 142°9E 63 E3
Miles Australia 26°40S 150°9E 63 D5
Miles City U.S.A. 46°25N 105°51W 76 C11
Milestone Canada 49°59N 104°31W 71 D8
Miletus Turkey 37°30N 27°18E 23 F12
Milford Calif., U.S.A. 40°10N 120°22W 78 E6
Milford Conn., U.S.A. 41°14N 73°3W 83 E11
Milford Del., U.S.A. 38°55N 75°26W 81 F16
Milford Mass., U.S.A. 42°8N 71°31W 83 D13

Milford N.H., U.S.A. 42°50N 71°39W 83 D13
Milford N.Y., U.S.A. 42°35N 74°56W 83 D10
Milford Pa., U.S.A. 41°19N 74°48W 83 E10
Milford Utah, U.S.A. 38°24N 113°1W 76 G7
Milford Haven U.K. 51°42N 5°7W 13 F2
Milford Sd. N.Z. 44°41S 167°47E 59 F1
Milford Sound N.Z. 44°41S 167°55E 59 F1
Milh, Bahr al = Razāzah, Buhayrat ar Iraq 32°40N 43°35E 44 C4
Milikapiti Australia 11°26S 130°40E 60 B5
Miling Australia 30°30S 116°17E 61 F2
Milk River Canada 49°10N 112°5W 70 D6
Mill ➤ U.S.A. 42°57N 83°23W 82 D1
Mill I. Antarctica 65°30S 138°42E 5 C8
Mill I. Canada 63°58N 77°47W 69 E16
Mill Valley U.S.A. 37°54N 122°32W 78 H4
Millau France 44°8N 3°4E 20 D5
Millbridge Canada 44°41N 77°36W 82 B7
Millbrook Canada 44°10N 78°29W 82 B6
Millbrook Ala., U.S.A. 32°29N 86°22W 85 E11
Millbrook N.Y., U.S.A. 41°47N 73°42W 83 E11
Mille Lacs, L. des Canada 48°45N 90°35W 72 C1
Mille Lacs L. U.S.A. 46°15N 93°39W 80 B7
Milledgeville U.S.A. 33°5N 83°14W 85 E13
Millen U.S.A. 32°48N 81°57W 85 E14
Millennium I. = Caroline I. Kiribati 9°58S 150°13W 65 H12
Miller U.S.A. 44°31N 98°59W 80 C4
Miller Lake Canada 45°6N 81°26W 82 A3
Millersburg Ohio, U.S.A. 40°33N 81°55W 82 F3
Millersburg Pa., U.S.A. 40°32N 76°58W 82 F8
Millerton U.S.A. 41°57N 73°31W 83 E11
Millerton L. U.S.A. 37°1N 119°41W 78 J7
Millet St. Lucia 13°55N 60°59W 89 f
Millheim U.S.A. 40°54N 77°29W 82 F7
Millicent Australia 37°34S 140°21E 63 F3
Millington U.S.A. 35°20N 89°53W 85 D10
Millinocket U.S.A. 45°39N 68°43W 81 C19
Millmerran Australia 27°53S 151°16E 63 D5
Millom U.K. 54°13N 3°16W 12 C4
Mills L. Canada 61°30N 118°20W 70 A5
Millsboro U.S.A. 40°0N 80°0W 82 G5
Millstream Chichester △ Australia 21°35S 117°6E 60 D2
Millstreet Ireland 52°4N 9°4W 10 D2
Milltown Malbay Ireland 52°52N 9°24W 10 D2
Millville N.J., U.S.A. 39°24N 75°2W 81 F16
Millville Pa., U.S.A. 41°7N 76°32W 83 E8
Millwood L. U.S.A. 33°42N 93°58W 84 E8
Milne ➤ Australia 21°10S 137°33E 62 C2
Milo U.S.A. 45°15N 68°59W 81 C19
Milon, Akra Greece 36°15N 28°11E 25 C10
Milos Greece 36°44N 24°25E 23 F11
Milparinka Australia 29°46S 141°57E 63 D3
Milpitas U.S.A. 37°26N 121°55W 78 H5
Milton N.S., Canada 44°4N 64°45W 73 D7
Milton Ont., Canada 43°31N 79°53W 82 C5
Milton N.Z. 46°7S 169°59E 59 G2
Milton Calif., U.S.A. 38°3N 120°51W 78 G6
Milton Fla., U.S.A. 30°38N 87°3W 85 F11
Milton Pa., U.S.A. 41°1N 76°51W 82 F8
Milton Vt., U.S.A. 44°38N 73°7W 83 B11
Milton-Freewater U.S.A. 45°56N 118°23W 76 D4
Milton Keynes U.K. 52°1N 0°44W 13 E7
Milton Keynes □ U.K. 52°1N 0°44W 13 E7
Milverton Canada 43°34N 80°55W 82 C4
Milwaukee U.S.A. 43°2N 87°54W 80 D10
Milwaukee Deep Atl. Oc. 19°50N 68°0W 89 C6
Milwaukie U.S.A. 45°26N 122°38W 78 E4
Mimili Australia 27°0S 132°42E 61 E5
Min Jiang ➤ Fujian, China 26°0N 119°35E 33 D6
Min Jiang ➤ Sichuan, China 28°45N 104°40E 32 D5
Min Xian China 34°25N 104°5E 34 G3
Mina Pirquitas Argentina 22°40S 66°30W 94 A2
Mina' Jabal 'Alī U.A.E. 25°2N 55°8E 45 E7
Mina Pirquitas Argentina 22°40S 66°30W 94 A2
Mīnā Su'ud Si. Arabia 28°45N 48°28E 45 D6
Mīnā' al Ahmadī Kuwait 29°5N 48°10E 45 D6
Minago ➤ Canada 54°33N 98°59W 71 C9
Minaki Canada 49°59N 94°40W 71 D10
Minamata Japan 32°10N 130°30E 31 H5
Minami-Arapusa △ Japan 35°30N 138°9E 31 G9
Minami-Tori-Shima Pac. Oc. 24°20N 153°58E 64 E7
Minas Uruguay 34°20S 55°10W 95 C4
Minas, Sierra de las Guatemala 15°9N 89°31W 88 C2
Minas Basin Canada 45°20N 64°12W 73 C7
Minas Gerais □ Brazil 18°50S 46°0W 93 G9
Minatitlán Mexico 17°59N 94°31W 87 D6
Minbu Burma 20°10N 94°52E 41 J19
Minchinabad Pakistan 30°10N 73°34E 42 D5
Mindanao Phil. 8°0N 125°0E 37 C6
Mindanao Sea = Bohol Sea Phil. 9°0N 124°0E 37 C6
Mindanao Trench Pac. Oc. 12°0N 126°6E 37 B7
Mindelo C. Verde Is. 16°44N 25°0W 50 b
Minden Canada 44°55N 78°43W 82 B6
Minden Germany 52°17N 8°55E 16 B5
Minden La., U.S.A. 32°37N 93°17W 84 E8
Minden Nev., U.S.A. 38°57N 119°46W 78 G7
Mindibungu = Billiluna Australia 19°37S 127°41E 60 C4
Mindiptana Indonesia 5°55S 140°22E 37 F10
Mindoro Phil. 13°0N 121°0E 37 B6
Mindoro Str. Phil. 12°30N 120°30E 37 B6
Mine Japan 34°12N 131°7E 31 G5
Minehead U.K. 51°12N 3°29W 13 F4
Mineola N.Y., U.S.A. 40°44N 73°38W 83 F11
Mineola Tex., U.S.A. 32°40N 95°29W 84 E7
Mineral King U.S.A. 36°27N 118°36W 78 J8
Mineral Wells U.S.A. 32°48N 98°7W 84 E5
Miners Bay Canada 44°49N 78°46W 82 B6
Minersville U.S.A. 40°41N 76°16W 83 F8

Minerva *N.Y., U.S.A.*   43°47N 73°59W **83 C11**
Minerva *Ohio, U.S.A.*   40°44N 81°6W **82 F3**
Minetto *U.S.A.*   43°24N 76°28W **83 C8**
Minfeng *China*   37°4N 82°46E **32 C3**
Mingäçevir Su Anbarı
  Azerbaijan   40°57N 46°50E **19 F8**
Mingan *Canada*   50°20N 64°0W **73 B7**
Mingechaurskoye Vdkhr. =
  Mingäçevir Su Anbarı
  Azerbaijan   40°57N 46°50E **19 F8**
Mingela *Australia*   19°52S 146°38E **62 B4**
Mingenew *Australia*   29°12S 115°21E **61 E2**
Mingera Cr. =
  Australia   20°38S 137°45E **62 C2**
Mingin *Burma*   22°50N 94°30E **41 H19**
Mingo Junction *U.S.A.*   40°19N 80°37W **82 F4**
Mingora *Pakistan*   34°48N 72°22E **43 B5**
Mingteke Daban = Mintaka Pass
  Pakistan   37°0N 74°58E **43 A6**
Mingyuegue *China*   43°2N 128°50E **35 C15**
Minho = Miño → *Spain*   41°52N 8°40W **21 A2**
Minho *Portugal*   41°25N 8°20W **21 B1**
Minidoka *U.S.A.*   42°45N 113°29W **76 E7**
Minigwal, L. *Australia*   29°31S 123°14E **61 E3**
Minilya → *Australia*   23°45S 114°0E **61 D1**
Minilya Roadhouse
  Australia   23°55S 114°0E **61 D1**
Minipi L. *Canada*   52°25N 60°45W **73 B7**
Minjilang *Australia*   11°8S 132°33E **60 B5**
Mink L. *Canada*   61°54N 117°40W **70 A5**
Minna *Nigeria*   9°37N 6°30E **50 G7**
Minneapolis *Kans., U.S.A.*   39°8N 97°42W **80 F5**
Minneapolis *Minn.,*
  U.S.A.   44°57N 93°16W **80 C7**
Minnedosa *Canada*   50°14N 99°50W **71 C9**
Minnesota □ *U.S.A.*   46°0N 94°15W **80 B6**
Minnesota → *U.S.A.*   44°54N 93°9W **80 C7**
Minnewaukan *U.S.A.*   48°4N 99°15W **80 A4**
Minnipa *Australia*   32°51S 135°9E **63 E2**
Minnitaki L. *Canada*   49°57N 92°10W **72 C1**
Mino *Japan*   35°32N 136°55E **31 G8**
Miño → *Spain*   41°52N 8°40W **21 A2**
Minorca = Menorca *Spain*   40°0N 4°0E **24 B11**
Minot *U.S.A.*   48°14N 101°18W **80 A3**
Minqin *China*   38°38N 103°20E **34 E2**
Minsk *Belarus*   53°52N 27°30E **17 B14**
Mińsk Mazowiecki
  Poland   52°10N 21°33E **17 B11**
Mintabie *Australia*   27°15S 133°7E **63 D1**
Mintaka Pass *Pakistan*   37°0N 74°58E **43 A6**
Minto *Canada*   46°5N 66°5W **73 C6**
Minto, L. *Canada*   57°13N 75°0W **72 A5**
Minton *Canada*   49°10N 104°35W **71 D8**
Minturn *U.S.A.*   39°35N 106°26W **76 G10**
Minudasht *Iran*   37°17N 56°7E **45 B8**
Minusinsk *Russia*   53°43N 91°20E **29 D10**
Minutang *India*   28°15N 96°30E **41 E10**
Minvoul *Gabon*   2°9N 12°8E **52 D2**
Minzhong *China*   22°37N 113°30E **33 F10**
Miquelon *Canada*   49°25N 76°27W **72 C4**
Miquelon *St-P. & M.*   47°8N 56°22W **73 C8**
Mīr Kūh *Iran*   26°22N 58°55E **45 E8**
Mīr Shahdād *Iran*   26°15N 58°29E **45 E8**
Mira *Italy*   45°26N 12°8E **22 B5**
Mira por vos Cay
  Bahamas   22°9N 74°30W **89 B5**
Mirabela, Kolpos *Greece*   35°10N 25°50E **25 D7**
Mirador-Río Azul △
  Guatemala   17°45N 89°50W **88 C2**
Miraj *India*   16°50N 74°45E **40 L9**
Miram Shah *Pakistan*   33°0N 70°2E **42 C4**
Miramar *Argentina*   38°15S 57°50W **94 D4**
Miramar *Mozam.*   23°50S 35°35E **57 C6**
Miramichi *Canada*   47°2N 65°28W **73 C6**
Miramichi B. *Canada*   47°15N 65°0W **73 C7**
Miranda *Brazil*   20°10S 56°15W **93 H7**
Miranda → *Brazil*   19°25S 57°20W **92 G7**
Miranda de Ebro *Spain*   42°41N 2°57W **21 A4**
Miranda do Douro
  Portugal   41°30N 6°16W **21 B2**
Mirandópolis *Brazil*   21°9S 51°6W **95 A5**
Mirango *Malawi*   13°32S 34°58E **55 E3**
Mirani *Australia*   21°9S 148°53E **62 b**
Mirassol *Brazil*   20°46S 49°28W **95 A6**
Mirbāt *Oman*   17°0N 54°45E **47 D5**
Mires *Greece*   35°4N 24°56E **25 D6**
Miri *Malaysia*   4°23N 113°59E **36 D4**
Miriam Vale *Australia*   24°20S 151°33E **62 C5**
Mirim, L. *S. Amer.*   32°45S 52°50W **95 C5**
Miriuwung Gajerrong ⬡
  Australia   15°0S 128°45E **60 C4**
Mīrjāveh *Iran*   29°1N 61°30E **45 D9**
Mirnyy *Antarctica*   66°50S 92°30E **5 C14**
Mirnyy *Russia*   62°33N 113°53E **29 C12**
Mirokhan *Pakistan*   27°46N 68°6E **42 F3**
Mirond L. *Canada*   55°6N 102°47W **71 B8**
Mirpur *Pakistan*   33°32N 73°56E **43 C5**
Mirpur Batoro *Pakistan*   24°44N 68°16E **42 G3**
Mirpur Bibiwari *Pakistan*   28°33N 67°44E **42 E2**
Mirpur Khas *Pakistan*   25°30N 69°0E **42 G3**
Mirpur Sakro *Pakistan*   24°33N 67°41E **42 G2**
Mirs Bay = Tai Pang Wan
  China   22°33N 114°24E **33 F11**
Mirtağ *Turkey*   38°23N 41°56E **44 B4**
Mirtoo Sea *Greece*   37°0N 23°20E **23 F10**
Miryang *S. Korea*   35°31N 128°44E **35 G15**
Mirzapur *India*   25°10N 82°34E **43 G10**
Mirzapur-cum-Vindhyachal =
  Mirzapur *India*   25°10N 82°34E **43 G10**
Misantla *Mexico*   19°56N 96°50W **87 D5**
Misawa *Japan*   40°41N 141°24E **30 D10**
Miscou I. *Canada*   47°57N 64°31W **73 C7**
Mish'āb, Ra's al
  Si. Arabia   28°15N 48°43E **45 D6**
Mishamo *Tanzania*   5°41S 30°41E **54 D3**
Mishan *China*   45°37N 131°48E **30 B5**
Mishawaka *U.S.A.*   41°40N 86°11W **80 E10**
Mishima *Japan*   35°10N 138°52E **31 G9**
Misión *Mexico*   32°6N 116°53W **79 N10**

Misiones □ *Argentina*   27°0S 55°0W **95 B5**
Misiones □ *Paraguay*   27°0S 56°0W **94 B4**
Miskah *Si. Arabia*   24°49N 42°56E **44 E4**
Miskitos, Cayos *Nic.*   14°26N 82°50W **88 D3**
Miskolc *Hungary*   48°7N 20°50E **17 D11**
Misoke
  Dem. Rep. of the Congo   0°42S 28°2E **54 C2**
Misool *Indonesia*   1°52S 130°10E **37 E8**
Misr = Egypt ■ *Africa*   28°0N 31°0E **51 C12**
Misrātah *Libya*   32°24N 15°3E **51 B9**
Missanabie *Canada*   48°20N 84°6W **72 C3**
Missinaibi → *Canada*   50°43N 81°29W **72 B3**
Missinaibi L. *Canada*   48°23N 83°40W **72 C3**
Mission *Canada*   49°10N 122°15W **70 D4**
Mission *S. Dak., U.S.A.*   43°18N 100°39W **80 D3**
Mission *Tex., U.S.A.*   26°13N 98°20W **84 H5**
Mission Beach *Australia*   17°53S 146°6E **62 B4**
Mission Viejo *U.S.A.*   33°36N 117°40W **79 M9**
Missisa L. *Canada*   52°20N 85°7W **72 B2**
Missisicabi → *Canada*   51°14N 79°31W **72 B4**
Mississagi → *Canada*   46°15N 83°9W **72 C3**
Mississauga *Canada*   43°32N 79°35W **82 C5**
Mississippi □ *U.S.A.*   33°0N 90°0W **85 E10**
Mississippi → *U.S.A.*   29°9N 89°15W **85 G10**
Mississippi L. *Canada*   45°5N 76°10W **83 A8**
Mississippi River Delta
  U.S.A.   29°10N 89°15W **85 G10**
Mississippi Sd. *U.S.A.*   30°20N 89°0W **85 F10**
Missoula *U.S.A.*   46°52N 114°1W **76 C6**
Missouri □ *U.S.A.*   38°25N 92°30W **80 F7**
Missouri → *U.S.A.*   38°49N 90°7W **80 F8**
Missouri City *U.S.A.*   29°37N 95°32W **84 G7**
Missouri Valley *U.S.A.*   41°34N 95°53W **80 E6**
Mist *U.S.A.*   45°59N 123°15W **78 E3**
Mistassibi → *Canada*   48°53N 72°13W **73 B5**
Mistassini *Canada*   48°53N 72°12W **73 C5**
Mistassini → *Canada*   48°42N 72°20W **73 C5**
Mistassini, L. *Canada*   51°0N 73°30W **72 B5**
Mistastin L. *Canada*   55°57N 63°20W **73 A7**
Mistinibi, L. *Canada*   55°56N 64°17W **73 A7**
Mistissini *Canada*   48°53N 72°12W **73 C5**
Misty L. *Canada*   58°53N 101°40W **71 B8**
Misurata = Misrātah
  Libya   32°24N 15°3E **51 B9**
Mitande *Mozam.*   14°6S 35°58E **54 D4**
Mitchell *Australia*   26°29S 147°58E **63 D4**
Mitchell *Canada*   43°28N 81°12W **82 C3**
Mitchell *Nebr., U.S.A.*   41°57N 103°49W **80 E2**
Mitchell *Oreg., U.S.A.*   44°34N 120°9W **76 D3**
Mitchell *S. Dak., U.S.A.*   43°43N 98°2W **80 D4**
Mitchell → *Australia*   15°12S 141°35E **62 B3**
Mitchell, Mt. *U.S.A.*   35°46N 82°16W **85 D13**
Mitchell-Alice Rivers △
  Australia   15°28S 142°5E **62 B3**
Mitchell Ra. *Australia*   12°49S 135°36E **62 A2**
Mitchelstown *Ireland*   52°15N 8°16W **10 D3**
Mitha Tiwana *Pakistan*   32°13N 72°6E **42 C5**
Mithi *Pakistan*   24°44N 69°48E **42 G3**
Mithrao *Pakistan*   27°28N 69°40E **42 F3**
Mitilini *Greece*   39°6N 26°35E **23 E12**
Mitla Pass = Mamarr Mitlā
  Egypt   30°2N 32°54E **46 E1**
Mito *Japan*   36°20N 140°30E **31 F10**
Mitrovica = Kosovska Mitrovica
  Kosovo   42°54N 20°52E **23 C9**
Mitsamiouli *Comoros Is.*   11°20S 43°16E **53 a**
Mitsinjo *Madag.*   16°1S 45°52E **57 B8**
Mitsiwa *Eritrea*   15°35N 39°25E **47 D2**
Mitsukaidō *Japan*   36°1N 139°59E **31 F9**
Mittagong *Australia*   34°28S 150°29E **63 E5**
Mittimatalik = Pond Inlet
  Canada   72°40N 77°0W **69 C16**
Mitú *Colombia*   1°15N 70°13W **92 C4**
Mitumba *Tanzania*   7°8S 31°2E **54 D3**
Mitumba, Mts.
  Dem. Rep. of the Congo   7°0S 27°30E **54 D2**
Mitwaba
  Dem. Rep. of the Congo   8°2S 27°17E **55 D2**
Mityana *Uganda*   0°23N 32°2E **54 B3**
Mixteco → *Mexico*   18°11N 98°30W **87 D5**
Miyagi □ *Japan*   38°15N 140°45E **30 E10**
Miyāh, W. el → *Syria*   34°44N 39°57E **44 C3**
Miyake-Jima *Japan*   34°5N 139°30E **31 G9**
Miyako *Japan*   39°40N 141°59E **30 E10**
Miyako-Jima *Japan*   24°45N 125°20E **31 M2**
Miyako-Rettō *Japan*   24°24N 125°0E **31 M2**
Miyakonojō *Japan*   31°40N 131°5E **31 J5**
Miyani *India*   21°50N 69°26E **42 J3**
Miyanoura-Dake *Japan*   30°20N 130°31E **31 J5**
Miyazaki *Japan*   31°56N 131°30E **31 J5**
Miyazaki □ *Japan*   32°30N 131°30E **31 H5**
Miyazu *Japan*   35°35N 135°10E **31 G7**
Miyet, Bahr el = Dead Sea
  Asia   31°30N 35°30E **46 D4**
Miyoshi *Japan*   34°48N 132°51E **31 G6**
Miyun *China*   40°28N 116°50E **34 D9**
Miyun Shuiku *China*   40°30N 117°0E **35 D9**
Mizdah *Libya*   31°30N 13°0E **51 B8**
Mizen Hd. *Cork, Ireland*   51°27N 9°50W **10 E2**
Mizen Hd. *Wicklow, Ireland*   52°51N 6°4W **10 D5**
Mizhi *China*   37°47N 110°12E **34 F6**
Mizoram □ *India*   23°30N 92°40E **41 H18**
Mizpe Ramon *Israel*   30°34N 34°49E **46 E3**
Mizusawa *Japan*   39°8N 141°8E **30 E10**
Mjøsa *Norway*   60°40N 11°0E **8 F14**
Mkata *Tanzania*   5°45S 38°20E **54 D4**
Mkhaya △ *Swaziland*   26°34S 31°45E **57 D5**
Mkhuze → *S. Africa*   29°25S 29°30E **57 D5**
Mkokotoni *Tanzania*   5°55S 39°15E **54 D4**
Mkomazi *Tanzania*   4°40S 38°7E **54 C4**
Mkomazi → *S. Africa*   30°12S 30°50E **57 E5**
Mkomazi △ *Tanzania*   4°4S 38°0E **54 C4**
Mkulwe *Tanzania*   8°37S 32°20E **55 D3**
Mkumbi, Ras *Tanzania*   7°38S 39°55E **54 D4**
Mkushi *Zambia*   14°25S 29°15E **55 E2**
Mkushi River *Zambia*   13°32S 29°45E **55 E2**
Mkuze *S. Africa*   27°10S 32°0E **57 D5**

Mladá Boleslav
  Czech Rep.   50°27N 14°53E **16 C8**
Mlala Hills *Tanzania*   6°50S 31°40E **54 D3**
Mlange = Mulanje, Mt.
  Malawi   16°2S 35°33E **55 F4**
Mława *Poland*   53°9N 20°25E **17 B11**
Mlawula △ *Swaziland*   26°12S 32°2E **57 D5**
Mljet *Croatia*   42°43N 17°30E **22 C7**
Mmabatho *S. Africa*   25°49S 25°30E **56 D4**
Mo i Rana *Norway*   66°20N 14°7E **8 C16**
Moa *Australia*   10°11S 142°16E **62 a**
Moa *Cuba*   20°40N 74°56W **89 B4**
Moa *Indonesia*   8°0S 128°0E **37 F7**
Moa → *S. Leone*   6°59N 11°36W **50 G3**
Moab *U.S.A.*   38°35N 109°33W **76 G9**
Moala *Fiji*   18°36S 179°53E **59 a**
Moama *Australia*   36°7S 144°46E **63 F3**
Moamba *Mozam.*   25°36S 32°15E **57 D5**
Moapa *U.S.A.*   36°40N 114°37W **79 J12**
Moate *Ireland*   53°24N 7°44W **10 C4**
Moba *Dem. Rep. of the Congo*   7°0S 29°48E **54 D2**
Mobārakābād *Iran*   28°24N 53°20E **45 D7**
Mobaye *C.A.R.*   4°25N 21°5E **52 D4**
Moberly *U.S.A.*   39°25N 92°26W **80 F7**
Moberly Lake *Canada*   55°50N 121°44W **70 B4**
Mobile *U.S.A.*   30°41N 88°3W **85 F10**
Mobile B. *U.S.A.*   30°30N 88°0W **85 F11**
Mobridge *U.S.A.*   45°32N 100°26W **80 C3**
Moc Chau *Vietnam*   20°50N 104°38E **38 B5**
Moc Hoa *Vietnam*   10°46N 105°56E **39 G5**
Mocabe Kasari
  Dem. Rep. of the Congo   9°58S 26°12E **55 D2**
Moçambique = Mozambique ■
  Africa   19°0S 35°0E **55 F4**
Moçambique *Mozam.*   15°3S 40°42E **55 F5**
Mocanaqua *U.S.A.*   41°9N 76°8W **83 E8**
Moce *Fiji*   18°40S 178°29W **59 a**
Mochima △ *Venezuela*   10°30N 64°5W **89 D7**
Mochos *Greece*   35°16N 25°27E **25 D7**
Mochudi *Botswana*   24°27S 26°7E **56 C4**
Moclips *U.S.A.*   47°14N 124°13W **78 C2**
Mocoa *Colombia*   1°7N 76°35W **92 C3**
Mococa *Brazil*   21°28S 47°0W **95 A6**
Mocorito *Mexico*   25°29N 107°55W **86 B3**
Moctezuma *Mexico*   29°48N 109°42W **86 B3**
Moctezuma → *Mexico*   21°59N 98°34W **87 C5**
Mocuba *Mozam.*   16°54S 36°57E **55 F4**
Modane *France*   45°12N 6°40E **20 D7**
Modasa *India*   23°30N 73°21E **42 H5**
Modder → *S. Africa*   29°2S 24°37E **56 D3**
Modderrivier *S. Africa*   29°2S 24°38E **56 D3**
Módena *Italy*   44°40N 10°55E **22 B4**
Modena *U.S.A.*   37°48N 113°56W **77 H7**
Modesto *U.S.A.*   37°39N 121°0W **78 H6**
Módica *Italy*   36°52N 14°46E **22 F6**
Modimolle *S. Africa*   24°42S 28°22E **57 C4**
Modjadjiskloof *S. Africa*   23°42S 30°10E **57 C5**
Moe *Australia*   38°12S 146°19E **63 F4**
Moebase *Mozam.*   17°3S 38°41E **55 F4**
Moengo *Suriname*   5°45N 54°20W **93 B8**
Moffat *U.K.*   55°21N 3°27W **11 F5**
Moga *India*   30°48N 75°8E **42 D6**
Mogadisho = Muqdisho
  Somali Rep.   2°2N 45°25E **47 G4**
Mogador = Essaouira
  Morocco   31°32N 9°42W **50 B4**
Mogalakwena →
  S. Africa   22°38S 28°40E **57 C4**
Mogami-Gawa →
  Japan   38°45N 140°0E **30 E10**
Mogán *Canary Is.*   27°53N 15°43W **24 G4**
Mogaung *Burma*   25°20N 97°0E **41 G20**
Mogi das Cruzes *Brazil*   23°31S 46°11W **95 A6**
Mogi-Guaçu → *Brazil*   20°53S 48°10W **95 A6**
Mogi-Mirim *Brazil*   22°29S 47°0W **95 A6**
Mogilev = Mahilyow
  Belarus   53°55N 30°18E **17 B16**
Mogilev-Podolskiy = Mohyliv-
  Podilskyy *Ukraine*   48°26N 27°48E **17 D14**
Mogincual *Mozam.*   15°35S 40°25E **55 F5**
Mogocha *Russia*   53°40N 119°50E **29 D12**
Mogok *Burma*   23°0N 96°40E **41 H20**
Mogollon Rim *U.S.A.*   34°10N 110°50W **77 J8**
Mogumber *Australia*   31°2S 116°3E **61 F2**
Mogwadi → *S. Africa*   23°4S 29°36E **57 C4**
Mohács *Hungary*   45°58N 18°41E **17 F10**
Mohales Hoek *Lesotho*   30°7S 27°26E **56 E4**
Mohall *U.S.A.*   48°46N 101°31W **80 A3**
Mohammadābād *Iran*   37°52N 59°5E **45 B8**
Mohammedia *Morocco*   33°44N 7°21W **50 B4**
Mohana → *India*   24°43N 85°0E **43 G11**
Mohanlalganj *India*   26°41N 80°58E **43 F9**
Mohave, L. *U.S.A.*   35°12N 114°34W **79 K12**
Mohawk → *U.S.A.*   42°47N 73°41W **83 D11**
Mohéli *Comoros Is.*   12°20S 43°40E **53 a**
Mohenjodaro *Pakistan*   27°19N 68°7E **42 F3**
Moher, Cliffs of *Ireland*   52°58N 9°27W **10 D2**
Mohicanville Res. *U.S.A.*   40°45N 82°9W **82 F2**
Mohns Ridge *Arctic*   72°30N 5°0E **4 B7**
Mohoro *Tanzania*   8°6S 39°8E **54 D4**
Mohsenābād *Iran*   36°40N 59°35E **45 B8**
Mohyliv-Podilskyy
  Ukraine   48°26N 27°48E **17 D14**
Moidart, L. *U.K.*   56°47N 5°52W **11 E3**
Moira → *Canada*   44°21N 77°24W **82 B7**
Moisaküla *Estonia*   58°3N 25°12E **9 G21**
Moisie *Canada*   50°12N 66°1W **73 B6**
Moisie → *Canada*   50°14N 66°5W **73 B6**
Mojave *U.S.A.*   35°3N 118°10W **79 K8**
Mojave → *U.S.A.*   35°7N 115°30W **79 J11**
Mojave Desert *U.S.A.*   35°0N 116°30W **79 L10**
Mojo *Bolivia*   21°48S 65°33W **94 A2**
Mojokerto *Indonesia*   7°28S 112°26E **37 G15**
Mokai *N.Z.*   38°32S 175°56E **59 C5**
Mokameh *India*   25°24N 85°55E **43 G11**

Mokau *N.Z.*   38°42S 174°39E **59 C5**
Mokelumne → *U.S.A.*   38°13N 121°28W **78 G5**
Mokelumne Hill
  U.S.A.   38°18N 120°43W **78 G6**
Mokhotlong *Lesotho*   29°22S 29°2E **57 D4**
Mokoan, L. *Australia*   36°27S 146°5E **63 C4**
Mokokchung *India*   26°15N 94°30E **41 F19**
Mokolo → *S. Africa*   23°14S 27°43E **57 C4**
Mokopane *S. Africa*   24°10S 28°55E **57 C4**
Mokpo *S. Korea*   34°50N 126°25E **35 G14**
Mokra Gora *Europe*   42°50N 20°30E **23 C9**
Mol *Belgium*   51°11N 5°5E **15 C5**
Molchanovo *Russia*   57°40N 83°50E **28 D9**
Mold *U.K.*   53°9N 3°8W **12 D4**
Moldavia = Moldova ■
  Europe   47°0N 28°0E **17 E15**
Moldavia *Romania*   46°30N 27°0E **17 E14**
Molde *Norway*   62°45N 7°9E **8 E12**
Moldova ■ *Europe*   47°0N 28°0E **17 E15**
Moldoveanu, Vf.
  Romania   45°36N 24°45E **17 F13**
Mole → *U.K.*   51°24N 0°21W **13 F7**
Molepolole *Botswana*   24°28S 25°28E **56 C4**
Molfetta *Italy*   41°12N 16°36E **22 D7**
Moline *U.S.A.*   41°30N 90°31W **80 E8**
Molinos *Argentina*   25°28S 66°15W **94 B2**
Moliro
  Dem. Rep. of the Congo   8°12S 30°30E **54 D3**
Mollendo *Peru*   17°0S 72°0W **92 G4**
Mollerin, L. *Australia*   30°30S 117°35E **61 F2**
Molo *Kenya*   0°15S 35°44E **54 C4**
Molodechno = Maladzyechna
  Belarus   54°20N 26°50E **17 A14**
Molodezhnaya *Antarctica*   67°40S 45°51E **5 C9**
Moloka'i *U.S.A.*   21°8N 157°0W **75 L8**
Molokai Fracture Zone
  Pac. Oc.   28°0N 125°0W **65 E15**
Molong *Australia*   33°5S 148°54E **63 E4**
Molopo → *Africa*   28°30S 20°12E **56 D3**
Molson L. *Canada*   54°22N 96°40W **71 C9**
Molteno *S. Africa*   31°22S 26°22E **56 E4**
Molu *Indonesia*   6°45S 131°40E **37 F8**
Molucca Sea *Indonesia*   0°0 125°0E **37 E6**
Moluccas = Maluku
  Indonesia   1°0S 127°0E **37 E7**
Moma
  Dem. Rep. of the Congo   1°35S 23°52E **54 C1**
Moma *Mozam.*   16°47S 39°4E **55 F4**
Mombasa *Kenya*   4°3S 39°40E **54 C4**
Mombetsu *Japan*   44°21N 143°22E **30 B11**
Momchilgrad *Bulgaria*   41°33N 25°23E **23 D11**
Momi *Dem. Rep. of the Congo*   1°42S 27°0E **54 C2**
Mompós *Colombia*   9°14N 74°26W **92 B4**
Mon □ *Burma*   16°0N 97°30E **41 L20**
Mon *Denmark*   54°57N 12°20E **9 J15**
Mon □ *Burma*   16°0N 97°30E **41 L20**
Mona, Canal de la = Mona
  Passage *W. Indies*   18°30N 67°45W **89 C6**
Mona, Isla *Puerto Rico*   18°5N 67°54W **89 C6**
Mona, Pta. *Costa Rica*   9°37N 82°36W **88 E3**
Mona Passage *W. Indies*   18°30N 67°45W **89 C6**
Monaca *U.S.A.*   40°41N 80°17W **82 F4**
Monaco ■ *Europe*   43°46N 7°23E **20 E7**
Monadhliath Mts. *U.K.*   57°10N 4°4W **11 D4**
Monadnock, Mt. *U.S.A.*   42°52N 72°7W **83 D12**
Monaghan *Ireland*   54°15N 6°57W **10 B5**
Monaghan □ *Ireland*   54°11N 6°56W **10 B5**
Monahans *U.S.A.*   31°36N 102°54W **84 F3**
Monapo *Mozam.*   14°56S 40°19E **55 E5**
Monar, L. *U.K.*   57°26N 5°8W **11 D3**
Monarch Mt. *Canada*   51°55N 125°57W **70 C3**
Monashee Mts. *Canada*   51°0N 118°43W **70 C5**
Monasterevin *Ireland*   53°8N 7°4W **10 C4**
Monastir = Bitola
  Macedonia   41°1N 21°20E **23 D9**
Monastir *Tunisia*   35°50N 10°49E **51 A8**
Moncayo, Sierra del
  Spain   41°48N 1°50W **21 B5**
Monchegorsk *Russia*   67°54N 32°58E **8 C25**
Mönchengladbach
  Germany   51°11N 6°27E **16 C4**
Monchique *Portugal*   37°19N 8°38W **21 D1**
Moncks Corner *U.S.A.*   33°12N 80°1W **85 E14**
Monclova *Mexico*   26°54N 101°25W **86 B4**
Moncton *Canada*   46°7N 64°51W **73 C7**
Mondego → *Portugal*   40°9N 8°52W **21 B1**
Mondeodo *Indonesia*   3°34S 122°9E **37 E6**
Mondovì *Italy*   44°23N 7°49E **20 D7**
Mondrain I. *Australia*   34°9S 122°14E **61 F3**
Moneague *Jamaica*   18°16N 77°7W **88 a**
Moneron, Ostrov
  Russia   46°15N 141°16E **30 A10**
Monessen *U.S.A.*   40°9N 79°54W **82 F5**
Monett *U.S.A.*   36°55N 93°55W **80 G7**
Moneymore *U.K.*   54°41N 6°40W **10 B5**
Monforte de Lemos *Spain*   42°31N 7°33W **21 A2**
Mong Cai *Vietnam*   21°27N 107°54E **38 B6**
Mong Hsu *Burma*   21°54N 98°30E **41 J21**
Mong Kung *Burma*   21°35N 97°35E **41 J20**
Mong Nai *Burma*   20°32N 97°46E **41 J20**
Mong Pawk *Burma*   22°4N 99°16E **41 H21**
Mong Ton *Burma*   20°17N 98°45E **41 J21**
Mong Wa *Burma*   21°26N 100°27E **41 J22**
Mong Yai *Burma*   22°21N 98°3E **41 H21**
Mongalla *Sudan*   5°8N 31°42E **51 G12**
Mongers, L. *Australia*   29°25S 117°5E **61 E2**
Monghyr = Munger
  India   25°23N 86°30E **43 G12**
Mongibello = Etna *Italy*   37°50N 14°55E **22 F6**
Mongo *Chad*   12°14N 18°43E **51 F9**
Mongolia ■ *Asia*   47°0N 103°0E **32 B5**
Mongolia, Plateau of
  Asia   45°0N 105°0E **26 D12**
Mongu *Zambia*   15°16S 23°12E **53 H4**
Môngua *Angola*   16°43S 15°20E **56 B2**
Monifieth *U.K.*   56°30N 2°48W **11 E6**
Monkey Bay *Malawi*   14°7S 35°1E **55 E4**
Monkey Mia *Australia*   25°48S 113°43E **61 E1**
Monkey River *Belize*   16°22N 88°29W **87 D7**
Monkland *Canada*   45°11N 74°52W **83 A10**

Monkoto
  Dem. Rep. of the Congo   1°38S 20°35E **52 E4**
Monkton *Canada*   43°35N 81°5W **82 C3**
Monmouth *U.K.*   51°48N 2°42W **13 F5**
Monmouth *Ill., U.S.A.*   40°55N 90°39W **80 E8**
Monmouth *Oreg.,*
  U.S.A.   44°51N 123°14W **76 D2**
Monmouthshire □ *U.K.*   51°48N 2°54W **13 F5**
Mono, Pta. *Nic.*   12°0N 83°30W **88 D3**
Mono L. *U.S.A.*   38°1N 119°1W **78 H7**
Monolith *U.S.A.*   35°7N 118°22W **79 K8**
Monolithos *Greece*   36°7N 27°45E **25 C9**
Monongahela *U.S.A.*   40°12N 79°56W **82 F5**
Monópoli *Italy*   40°57N 17°18E **22 D7**
Monos I. *Trin. & Tob.*   10°42N 61°44W **93 K15**
Monroe *La., U.S.A.*   32°30N 92°7W **84 E8**
Monroe *Mich., U.S.A.*   41°55N 83°24W **81 E12**
Monroe *N.C., U.S.A.*   34°59N 80°33W **85 D14**
Monroe *N.Y., U.S.A.*   41°20N 74°11W **83 E10**
Monroe *Utah, U.S.A.*   38°38N 112°7W **76 G7**
Monroe *Wash., U.S.A.*   47°51N 121°58W **78 C5**
Monroe *Wis., U.S.A.*   42°36N 89°38W **80 D9**
Monroe City *U.S.A.*   39°39N 91°44W **80 F8**
Monrovia *U.S.A.*   41°43N 76°29W **83 E8**
Monroeville *Ala.,*
  U.S.A.   31°31N 87°20W **85 F11**
Monroeville *Pa., U.S.A.*   40°26N 79°45W **82 F5**
Monrovia *Liberia*   6°18N 10°47W **50 G3**
Mons *Belgium*   50°27N 3°58E **15 D3**
Monse *Indonesia*   4°7S 123°15E **37 E6**
Mont-de-Marsan *France*   43°54N 0°31W **20 E3**
Mont-Joli *Canada*   48°37N 68°10W **73 C6**
Mont-Laurier *Canada*   46°35N 75°30W **72 C4**
Mont-Louis *Canada*   49°15N 65°44W **73 C6**
Mont-St-Michel, Le
  France   48°40N 1°30W **20 B3**
Mont-Tremblant △
  Canada   46°30N 74°30W **72 C5**
Montagne d'Ambre △
  Madag.   12°37S 49°8E **57 A8**
Montagu *S. Africa*   33°45S 20°8E **56 E3**
Montagu I. *Antarctica*   58°25S 26°20W **5 B1**
Montague *Canada*   46°10N 62°39W **73 C7**
Montague, I. *Mexico*   31°45N 114°48W **86 A2**
Montague I. *U.S.A.*   60°0N 147°30W **74 D10**
Montague Ra. *Australia*   27°15S 119°30E **61 E2**
Montague Sd. *Australia*   14°28S 125°20E **60 B4**
Montalbán *Spain*   40°50N 0°45W **21 B5**
Montalvo *U.S.A.*   34°15N 119°12W **79 L7**
Montana *Bulgaria*   43°27N 23°16E **23 C10**
Montaña *Peru*   6°0S 73°0W **92 E4**
Montana □ *U.S.A.*   47°0N 110°0W **76 C9**
Montaña Clara, I.
  Canary Is.   29°17N 13°33W **24 E6**
Montargis *France*   47°59N 2°43E **20 C5**
Montauban *France*   44°2N 1°21E **20 D4**
Montauk *U.S.A.*   41°3N 71°57W **83 E13**
Montauk Pt. *U.S.A.*   41°4N 71°51W **83 E13**
Montbéliard *France*   47°31N 6°48E **20 C7**
Montceau-les-Mines
  France   46°40N 4°23E **20 C6**
Montclair *U.S.A.*   40°49N 74°12W **83 F10**
Monte Albán *Mexico*   17°2N 96°46W **87 D5**
Monte Alegre *Brazil*   2°0S 54°0W **93 D8**
Monte Azul *Brazil*   15°9S 42°53W **93 G10**
Monte-Carlo *Monaco*   43°44N 7°25E **20 E7**
Monte Caseros
  Argentina   30°10S 57°50W **94 C4**
Monte Comán *Argentina*   34°40S 67°53W **94 C2**
Monte Cristi *Dom. Rep.*   19°52N 71°39W **89 C5**
Monte Lindo →
  Paraguay   23°56S 57°12W **94 A4**
Monte Patria *Chile*   30°42S 70°58W **94 C1**
Monte Quemado
  Argentina   25°53S 62°41W **94 B3**
Monte Rio *U.S.A.*   38°28N 123°0W **78 G4**
Monte Santu, C. di *Italy*   40°5N 9°44E **22 D3**
Monte Vista *U.S.A.*   37°35N 106°9W **77 H10**
Monteagudo *Argentina*   27°14S 54°8W **95 B5**
Montebello *Canada*   45°40N 74°55W **72 C5**
Montebello Is. *Australia*   20°30S 115°45E **60 D2**
Montecarlo *Argentina*   26°34S 54°47W **95 B5**
Montecito *U.S.A.*   34°26N 119°40W **79 L7**
Montecristo *Italy*   42°20N 10°19E **22 C4**
Montego Bay *Jamaica*   18°28N 77°55W **88 a**
Montélimar *France*   44°33N 4°45E **20 D6**
Montello *U.S.A.*   43°48N 89°20W **80 D9**
Montemorelos *Mexico*   25°12N 99°49W **87 B5**
Montenegro *Brazil*   29°39S 51°29W **95 B5**
Montenegro ■ *Europe*   42°40N 19°20E **23 C8**
Montepuez *Mozam.*   13°8S 38°59E **55 E4**
Montepuez → *Mozam.*   12°32S 40°27E **55 E5**
Monterey *U.S.A.*   36°37N 121°55W **78 J5**
Monterey B. *U.S.A.*   36°45N 122°0W **78 J5**
Montería *Colombia*   8°46N 75°53W **92 B3**
Monteros *Argentina*   27°11S 65°30W **94 B2**
Monterrey *Mexico*   25°40N 100°19W **86 B4**
Montes Azules △ *Mexico*   16°21N 91°3W **87 D6**
Montes Claros *Brazil*   16°30S 43°50W **93 G10**
Montesano *U.S.A.*   46°59N 123°36W **78 D3**
Montesilvano *Italy*   42°29N 14°8E **22 C6**
Montevideo *Uruguay*   34°50S 56°11W **95 C4**
Montevideo *U.S.A.*   44°57N 95°43W **80 C6**
Montezuma *U.S.A.*   41°35N 92°32W **80 E7**
Montezuma Castle △
  U.S.A.   34°39N 111°45W **77 J8**
Montgomery *U.K.*   52°34N 3°8W **13 E4**
Montgomery *Ala.,*
  U.S.A.   32°23N 86°19W **85 E11**
Montgomery *Pa., U.S.A.*   41°10N 76°53W **82 E8**
Montgomery *W. Va.,*
  U.S.A.   38°11N 81°19W **81 F13**
Montgomery City
  U.S.A.   38°59N 91°30W **80 F8**
Monticello *Ark., U.S.A.*   33°38N 91°47W **84 E9**
Monticello *Fla., U.S.A.*   30°33N 83°52W **85 F13**
Monticello *Ind., U.S.A.*   40°45N 86°46W **80 E10**
Monticello *Iowa, U.S.A.*   42°15N 91°12W **80 D8**

Monticello *Ky., U.S.A.* 36°50N 84°51W **81** G11
Monticello *Minn., U.S.A.* 45°18N 93°48W **80** C7
Monticello *Miss., U.S.A.* 31°33N 90°7W **85** F9
Monticello *N.Y., U.S.A.* 41°39N 74°42W **83** E10
Monticello *Utah, U.S.A.* 37°52N 109°21W **77** H9
Montijo *Portugal* 38°41N 8°54W **21** C1
Montilla *Spain* 37°36N 4°40W **21** D3
Montluçon *France* 46°22N 2°36E **20** C5
Montmagny *Canada* 46°58N 70°34W **73** C5
Montmartre *Canada* 50°14N 103°27W **71** C8
Montmorillon *France* 46°26N 0°50E **20** C4
Monto *Australia* 24°52S 151°6E **62** C5
Montongbuwoh
Indonesia 8°33S 116°4E **37** K19
Montoro *Spain* 38°1N 4°27W **21** C3
Montour Falls *U.S.A.* 42°21N 76°51W **82** D8
Montoursville *U.S.A.* 41°15N 76°55W **82** E8
Montpelier *Idaho,*
U.S.A. 42°19N 111°18W **76** E8
Montpelier *Vt., U.S.A.* 44°16N 72°35W **83** B12
Montpellier *France* 43°37N 3°52E **20** E5
Montréal *Canada* 45°30N 73°33W **83** A11
Montreal → *Canada* 47°14N 84°39W **72** C3
Montréal L. *Canada* 54°20N 105°45W **71** C7
Montreal Lake *Canada* 54°3N 105°46W **71** C7
Montreux *Switz.* 46°26N 6°55E **20** C7
Montrose *U.K.* 56°44N 2°27W **11** E6
Montrose *Colo., U.S.A.* 38°29N 107°53W **76** G10
Montrose *Pa., U.S.A.* 41°50N 75°53W **83** E9
Monts, Pte. des *Canada* 49°20N 67°12W **73** C6
Montserrat ☒ *W. Indies* 16°40N 62°10W **89** C7
Montuiri *Spain* 39°34N 2°59E **24** B9
Monywa *Burma* 22°7N 95°11E **41** H19
Monza *Italy* 45°35N 9°16E **20** D8
Monze *Zambia* 16°17S 27°29E **55** F2
Monze, C. *Pakistan* 24°47N 66°37E **42** G2
Monzón *Spain* 41°52N 0°10E **21** B6
Mooers *U.S.A.* 44°58N 73°35W **83** B11
Mooi → *S. Africa* 28°45S 30°34E **57** D5
Mooi River *S. Africa* 29°13S 29°50E **57** D4
Moomba *Australia* 28°6S 140°12E **63** A3
Moonah → *Australia* 22°3S 138°33E **62** C2
Moonda, L. *Australia* 25°52S 140°25E **62** D3
Moonie *Australia* 27°46S 150°20E **63** D5
Moonie → *Australia* 29°19S 148°43E **63** D4
Moonta *Australia* 34°6S 137°32E **63** E2
Moora *Australia* 30°37S 115°58E **61** F2
Moorcroft *U.S.A.* 44°16N 104°57W **76** D11
Moore → *Australia* 31°22S 115°30E **61** F2
Moore, L. *Australia* 29°50S 117°35E **61** E2
Moore Falls *Canada* 44°48N 78°48W **82** B6
Moore Park *Australia* 24°43S 152°17E **62** C5
Moore Res. *U.S.A.* 44°20N 71°53W **83** B13
Moore River △ *Australia* 31°7S 115°39E **61** F2
Moorea *French Polynesia* 17°30S 149°50W **59** d
Moorefield *U.S.A.* 39°4N 78°58W **81** F14
Moorfoot Hills *U.K.* 55°44N 3°8W **11** F5
Moorhead *U.S.A.* 46°53N 96°45W **80** B6
Moorpark *U.S.A.* 34°17N 118°53W **79** L8
Moorreesburg *S. Africa* 33°6S 18°38E **56** E2
Moorrinya △ *Australia* 21°42S 144°58E **62** C3
Moose → *Canada* 51°20N 80°25W **72** B3
Moose → *U.S.A.* 43°38N 75°24W **83** C9
Moose Creek *Canada* 45°15N 74°58W **83** A10
Moose Factory *Canada* 51°16N 80°32W **72** B3
Moose Jaw *Canada* 50°24N 105°30W **71** C7
Moose Jaw → *Canada* 50°34N 105°18W **71** C7
Moose Lake *Canada* 53°46N 100°8W **71** C8
Moose Lake *U.S.A.* 46°27N 92°46W **80** B7
Moose Mountain △
Canada 49°48N 102°25W **71** D8
Moosehead L. *U.S.A.* 45°38N 69°40W **81** C19
Mooselookmeguntic L.
U.S.A. 44°55N 70°49W **83** B14
Moosilauke, Mt. *U.S.A.* 44°3N 71°40W **83** B13
Moosomin *Canada* 50°9N 101°40W **71** C8
Moosonee *Canada* 51°17N 80°39W **72** B3
Moosup *U.S.A.* 41°43N 71°53W **83** E13
Mopane *S. Africa* 22°37S 29°52E **57** C4
Mopeia Velha *Mozam.* 17°30S 35°40E **55** F4
Mopipi *Botswana* 21°6S 24°55E **56** C3
Mopoi *C.A.R.* 5°6N 26°54E **54** A2
Mopti *Mali* 14°30N 4°0W **50** F5
Moqor *Afghan.* 32°50N 67°42E **42** C2
Moquegua *Peru* 17°15S 70°46W **92** G4
Mora *Sweden* 61°2N 14°38E **8** F16
Mora *Minn., U.S.A.* 45°53N 93°18W **80** C7
Mora *N. Mex., U.S.A.* 35°58N 105°20W **77** J11
Moradabad *India* 28°50N 78°50E **43** E8
Morafenobe *Madag.* 17°50S 44°53E **57** B7
Moramanga *Madag.* 18°56S 48°12E **57** B8
Moran *Kans., U.S.A.* 37°55N 95°10W **80** G6
Moran *Wyo., U.S.A.* 43°50N 110°31W **76** E8
Moranbah *Australia* 22°1S 148°6E **62** C4
Morang = Biratnagar
Nepal 26°27N 87°17E **43** F12
Morant Bay *Jamaica* 17°53N 76°25W **88** a
Morant Cays *Jamaica* 17°22N 76°0W **88** C4
Morant Pt. *Jamaica* 17°55N 76°12W **88** a
Morar *India* 26°14N 78°14E **42** F8
Morar, L. *U.K.* 56°57N 5°40W **11** E3
Moratuwa *Sri Lanka* 6°45N 79°55E **40** R11
Morava → *Serbia* 44°36N 21°4E **23** B9
Morava → *Slovak Rep.* 48°10N 16°59E **17** D9
Moravia *U.S.A.* 42°43N 76°25W **83** D8
Moravian Hts. = Českomoravská
Vrchovina *Czech Rep.* 49°30N 15°40E **16** D8
Morawa *Australia* 29°13S 116°0E **61** E2
Morawhanna *Guyana* 8°30N 59°40W **92** B7
Moray □ *U.K.* 57°31N 3°18W **11** D5
Moray Firth *U.K.* 57°40N 3°52W **11** D5
Morbi *India* 22°50N 70°42E **42** H4
Morden *Canada* 49°15N 98°10W **71** D9
Mordovian Republic =
Mordvinia □ *Russia* 54°20N 44°30E **18** D7
Mordvinia □ *Russia* 54°20N 44°30E **18** D7
Moreau → *U.S.A.* 45°18N 100°43W **80** C3
Morebeng *S. Africa* 23°30S 29°55E **57** C4
Morecambe *U.K.* 54°5N 2°52W **12** C5

Morecambe B. *U.K.* 54°7N 3°0W **12** C5
Moree *Australia* 29°28S 149°54E **63** D4
Morehead *Australia* 38°11N 83°26W **81** F12
Morehead City *U.S.A.* 34°43N 76°43W **85** D16
Morel → *India* 26°13N 76°36E **42** F7
Morelia *Mexico* 19°42N 101°7W **86** D4
Morella *Australia* 23°0S 143°52E **62** C3
Morella *Spain* 40°35N 0°5W **21** B5
Morelos *Mexico* 26°42N 107°40W **86** B3
Morelos □ *Mexico* 18°45N 99°0W **87** D5
Moremi △ *Botswana* 19°18S 23°10E **56** B3
Morena *India* 26°30N 78°4E **42** F8
Morena, Sierra *Spain* 38°20N 4°0W **21** C3
Moreno Valley *U.S.A.* 33°56N 117°14W **79** M10
Moresby I. *Canada* 52°30N 131°40W **70** C2
Moreton I. *Australia* 27°10S 153°25E **63** D5
Moreton Island △
Australia 27°2S 153°24E **63** D5
Morgan *U.S.A.* 41°2N 111°41W **76** F8
Morgan City *U.S.A.* 29°42N 91°12W **84** G9
Morgan Hill *U.S.A.* 37°8N 121°39W **78** H5
Morganfield *U.S.A.* 37°41N 87°55W **80** G10
Morganton *U.S.A.* 35°45N 81°41W **85** D14
Morgantown *U.S.A.* 39°38N 79°57W **81** F14
Morgenzon *S. Africa* 26°45S 29°36E **57** D4
Morghak *Iran* 29°7N 57°54E **45** D8
Morhar → *India* 25°29N 85°11E **43** G11
Mori *Japan* 42°6N 140°35E **30** C10
Moriarty *U.S.A.* 34°59N 106°3W **77** J10
Morice L. *Canada* 53°50N 127°40W **70** C3
Morinville *Canada* 53°49N 113°41W **70** C6
Morioka *Japan* 39°45N 141°8E **30** E10
Moris *Mexico* 28°10N 108°32W **86** B3
Morlaix *France* 48°36N 3°52W **20** B2
Mornington *Australia* 38°15S 145°5E **63** F4
Mornington, I. *Chile* 49°50S 75°30W **96** F1
Mornington, I. *Australia* 16°30S 139°30E **62** B2
Moro *Pakistan* 26°40N 68°0E **42** F2
Moro → *Pakistan* 29°42N 67°22E **42** E2
Moro G. *Phil.* 6°30N 123°0E **37** C6
Morocco ■ *N. Afr.* 32°0N 5°50W **50** B4
Morogoro *Tanzania* 6°50S 37°40E **54** D4
Morogoro □ *Tanzania* 8°0S 37°0E **54** D4
Moroleón *Mexico* 20°8N 101°12W **86** C4
Morombe *Madag.* 21°45S 43°22E **57** C7
Moron *Argentina* 34°39S 58°37W **94** C4
Morón *Cuba* 22°8N 78°39W **88** B4
Mörön *Mongolia* 49°38N 100°9E **32** B4
Morón de la Frontera
Spain 37°6N 5°28W **21** D3
Morona → *Peru* 4°40S 77°10W **92** D3
Morondava *Madag.* 20°17S 44°17E **57** C7
Morongo Valley *U.S.A.* 34°3N 116°37W **79** L10
Moroni *Comoros Is.* 11°40S 43°16E **53** a
Moroni *U.S.A.* 39°32N 111°35W **76** G8
Morotai *Indonesia* 2°10N 128°30E **37** D7
Moroto *Uganda* 2°28N 34°42E **54** B3
Moroto, Mt. *Uganda* 2°30N 34°43E **54** B3
Morpeth *Canada* 42°23N 81°50W **82** D3
Morpeth *U.K.* 55°10N 1°41W **12** B6
Morphou *Cyprus* 35°12N 32°59E **25** D11
Morphou Bay *Cyprus* 35°15N 32°50E **25** D11
Morrilton *U.S.A.* 35°9N 92°44W **84** D8
Morrinhos *Brazil* 17°45S 49°10W **93** G9
Morrinsville *N.Z.* 37°40S 175°32E **59** B5
Morris *Canada* 49°25N 97°22W **71** D9
Morris *Ill., U.S.A.* 41°22N 88°26W **80** E9
Morris *Minn., U.S.A.* 45°35N 95°55W **80** C6
Morris *N.Y., U.S.A.* 42°33N 75°15W **83** D9
Morris *Pa., U.S.A.* 41°35N 77°17W **82** E7
Morris, Mt. *Australia* 26°9S 131°4E **61** E5
Morris Jesup, Kap
Greenland 83°40N 34°0W **66** A16
Morrisburg *Canada* 44°55N 75°7W **83** B9
Morristown *Ariz.,*
U.S.A. 33°51N 112°37W **77** K7
Morristown *N.J., U.S.A.* 40°48N 74°29W **83** F10
Morristown *N.Y., U.S.A.* 44°35N 75°39W **83** B9
Morristown *Tenn.,*
U.S.A. 36°13N 83°18W **85** C13
Morrisville *N.Y., U.S.A.* 42°53N 75°35W **83** D9
Morrisville *Pa., U.S.A.* 40°13N 74°47W **83** F10
Morrisville *Vt., U.S.A.* 44°34N 72°36W **83** B12
Morro, Pta. *Chile* 27°6S 71°0W **94** B1
Morro Bay *U.S.A.* 35°22N 120°51W **78** K6
Morro del Jable *Canary Is.* 28°3N 14°23W **24** F5
Morro Jable, Pta. de
Canary Is. 28°2N 14°20W **24** F5
Morrocoy △ *Venezuela* 10°48N 68°13W **89** D6
Morrosquillo, G. de
Colombia 9°35N 75°40W **88** E4
Morrumbene *Mozam.* 23°31S 35°16E **57** C6
Morshansk *Russia* 53°28N 41°50E **18** D7
Morteros *Argentina* 30°50S 62°0W **94** C3
Mortlach *Canada* 50°27N 106°4W **71** C7
Mortlake *Australia* 38°5S 142°50E **63** F3
Morton *Tex., U.S.A.* 33°44N 102°46W **84** E3
Morton *Wash., U.S.A.* 46°34N 122°17W **78** D4
Moruga *Trin. & Tob.* 10°4N 61°16W **93** K15
Morundah *Australia* 34°57S 146°19E **63** E4
Moruya *Australia* 35°58S 150°3E **63** F5
Morvan *France* 47°5N 4°3E **20** C6
Morven *Australia* 26°22S 147°5E **63** D4
Morvern *U.K.* 56°38N 5°44W **11** E3
Morwell *Australia* 38°10S 146°22E **63** F4
Morzhovets, Ostrov
Russia 66°44N 42°35E **18** A7
Mosakahiken = Moose Lake
Canada 53°46N 100°8W **71** C8
Moscos Is. *Burma* 14°0N 97°30E **38** F1
Moscow = Moskva
Russia 55°45N 37°37E **18** C6
Moscow *Idaho, U.S.A.* 46°44N 117°0W **76** C5
Moscow *Pa., U.S.A.* 41°20N 75°31W **83** E9
Mosel → *Europe* 50°22N 7°36E **20** A4
Moselle = Mosel →
Europe 50°22N 7°36E **20** A4
Moses Lake *U.S.A.* 47°8N 119°17W **76** C4
Mosgiel *N.Z.* 45°53S 170°21E **59** F3

Moshaweng → *S. Africa* 26°35S 22°50E **56** D3
Moshchnyy, Ostrov
Russia 60°1N 27°50E **9** F22
Moshi *Tanzania* 3°22S 37°18E **54** C4
Moshupa *Botswana* 24°46S 25°29E **56** C4
Mosjøen *Norway* 65°51N 13°12E **8** D15
Moskenesøya *Norway* 67°58N 13°0E **8** C15
Moskenstraumen
Norway 67°47N 12°45E **8** C15
Moskva *Russia* 55°45N 37°37E **18** C6
Mosomane *Botswana* 24°2S 26°19E **56** C4
Mosonmagyaróvár
Hungary 47°52N 17°18E **17** E9
Mosquera *Colombia* 2°35N 78°24W **92** C3
Mosquero *U.S.A.* 35°47N 103°58W **77** J12
Mosquitia *Honduras* 15°20N 84°10W **88** C3
Mosquito Coast = Mosquitia
Honduras 15°20N 84°10W **88** C3
Mosquito Creek L.
U.S.A. 41°18N 80°46W **82** E4
Mosquito L. *Canada* 62°35N 103°20W **71** A8
Mosquitos, G. de los
Panama 9°15N 81°10W **88** E3
Moss *Norway* 59°27N 10°40E **9** G14
Moss Vale *Australia* 34°32S 150°25E **63** E5
Mossaka *Congo* 1°15S 16°45E **52** E3
Mossbank *Canada* 49°56N 105°56W **71** D7
Mossburn *N.Z.* 45°41S 168°15E **59** F2
Mosselbaai *S. Africa* 34°11S 22°8E **56** E3
Mossendjo *Congo* 2°55S 12°42E **52** E2
Mossgiel *Australia* 33°15S 144°5E **63** E3
Mossman *Australia* 16°21S 145°15E **62** B4
Mossoró *Brazil* 5°10S 37°15W **93** E11
Mossuril *Mozam.* 14°58S 40°42E **55** E5
Most *Czech Rep.* 50°31N 13°38E **16** C7
Mosta *Malta* 35°55N 14°26E **25** D1
Mostaganem *Algeria* 35°54N 0°5E **50** A6
Mostar *Bos.-H.* 43°22N 17°50E **23** C7
Mostardas *Brazil* 31°2S 50°51W **95** C5
Mostiska = Mostyska
Ukraine 49°48N 23°4E **17** D12
Mosty = Masty *Belarus* 53°27N 24°38E **17** B13
Mostyska *Ukraine* 49°48N 23°4E **17** D12
Mosul = Al Mawşil *Iraq* 36°15N 43°5E **44** B4
Motagua → *Guatemala* 15°44N 88°14W **88** C2
Motala *Sweden* 58°32N 15°1E **9** G16
Motaze *Mozam.* 24°48S 32°52E **57** C5
Moth *India* 25°43N 78°57E **43** G8
Motherwell *U.K.* 55°47N 3°58W **11** F5
Motihari *India* 26°30N 84°55E **43** F11
Motozintla de Mendoza
Mexico 15°22N 92°14W **87** D6
Motril *Spain* 36°31N 3°37W **21** D4
Mott *U.S.A.* 46°23N 102°20W **80** B2
Motueka *N.Z.* 41°7S 173°1E **59** D4
Motueka → *N.Z.* 41°5S 173°1E **59** D4
Motul *Mexico* 21°6N 89°17W **87** C7
Mouchalagane →
Canada 50°56N 68°41W **73** B6
Moudros *Greece* 39°50N 25°18E **23** E11
Mouhoun = Black Volta →
Africa 8°41N 1°33W **50** G5
Mouila *Gabon* 1°50S 11°0E **52** E2
Moulamein *Australia* 35°3S 144°1E **63** F3
Moule à Chique, C.
St. Lucia 13°43N 60°57W **89** f
Mouliana *Greece* 35°10N 25°59E **25** D7
Moulins *France* 46°35N 3°19E **20** C5
Moulmein *Burma* 16°30N 97°40E **41** L20
Moulouya, O. → *Morocco* 35°5N 2°25W **50** B5
Moultrie *U.S.A.* 31°11N 83°47W **85** F13
Moultrie, L. *U.S.A.* 33°20N 80°5W **85** E14
Mound City *Mo., U.S.A.* 40°7N 95°14W **80** E6
Mound City *S. Dak.,*
U.S.A. 45°44N 100°4W **80** C3
Moundou *Chad* 8°40N 16°10E **51** G9
Moundsville *U.S.A.* 39°55N 80°44W **82** G4
Moung *Cambodia* 12°46N 103°27E **38** F4
Mount Airy *U.S.A.* 36°31N 80°37W **85** C14
Mount Albert *Canada* 44°8N 79°19W **82** B5
Mount Aspiring △ *N.Z.* 44°19S 168°47E **59** F2
Mount Barker *S. Austral.,*
Australia 35°5S 138°52E **63** F2
Mount Barker *W. Austral.,*
Australia 34°38S 117°40E **61** F2
Mount Barnett Roadhouse
Australia 16°39S 125°57E **60** C4
Mount Bellew Bridge
Ireland 53°28N 8°31W **10** C3
Mount Brydges *Canada* 42°54N 81°29W **82** D3
Mount Burr *Australia* 37°34S 140°26E **63** F3
Mount Carmel = Ha Karmel △
Israel 32°45N 35°5E **46** C4
Mount Carmel *Ill.,*
U.S.A. 38°25N 87°46W **80** F10
Mount Carmel *Pa.,*
U.S.A. 40°47N 76°26W **83** F8
Mount Clemens *U.S.A.* 42°35N 82°53W **82** D2
Mount Coolon *Australia* 21°25S 147°25E **62** C4
Mount Darwin *Zimbabwe* 16°47S 31°38E **55** F3
Mount Desert I. *U.S.A.* 44°21N 68°20W **81** C19
Mount Dora *U.S.A.* 28°48N 81°38W **85** G14
Mount Ebenezer
Australia 25°6S 132°34E **61** E5
Mount Edziza △
Canada 57°30N 130°45W **70** B2
Mount Elgon △ *E. Afr.* 1°0N 34°42E **54** B3
Mount Field △ *Australia* 42°39S 146°35E **63** G4
Mount Fletcher *S. Africa* 30°40S 28°30E **57** E4
Mount Forest *Canada* 43°59N 80°43W **82** C4
Mount Frankland △
Australia 31°47S 116°37E **61** F2
Mount Frederick ☒
Australia 19°39S 129°18E **60** D4
Mount Gambier
Australia 37°50S 140°46E **63** F3
Mount Garnet *Australia* 17°37S 145°6E **62** B4
Mount Holly *U.S.A.* 39°59N 74°47W **83** G10

Mount Holly Springs
U.S.A. 40°7N 77°12W **82** F7
Mount Hope *N.S.W.,*
Australia 32°51S 145°51E **63** E4
Mount Hope *S. Austral.,*
Australia 34°7S 135°23E **63** E2
Mount Isa *Australia* 20°42S 139°26E **62** C2
Mount James ☒
Australia 24°51S 116°54E **61** D2
Mount Jewett *U.S.A.* 41°44N 78°39W **82** E6
Mount Kaputar △
Australia 30°16S 150°10E **63** E5
Mount Kenya △ *Kenya* 0°7S 37°21E **54** C4
Mount Kisco *U.S.A.* 41°12N 73°44W **83** E11
Mount Laguna *U.S.A.* 32°52N 116°25W **79** N10
Mount Larcom
Australia 23°48S 150°59E **62** C5
Mount Lofty Ranges
Australia 34°35S 139°5E **63** E2
Mount Magnet *Australia* 28°2S 117°47E **61** E2
Mount Maunganui
N.Z. 37°40S 176°14E **59** B6
Mount Molloy *Australia* 16°42S 145°20E **62** B4
Mount Morgan
Australia 23°40S 150°25E **62** C5
Mount Morris *U.S.A.* 42°44N 77°52W **82** D7
Mount Pearl *Canada* 47°31N 52°47W **73** C9
Mount Penn *U.S.A.* 40°20N 75°54W **83** F9
Mount Perry *Australia* 25°13S 151°42E **63** D5
Mount Pleasant *Iowa,*
U.S.A. 40°58N 91°33W **80** E8
Mount Pleasant *Mich.,*
U.S.A. 43°36N 84°46W **81** D11
Mount Pleasant *Pa.,*
U.S.A. 40°9N 79°33W **82** F5
Mount Pleasant *S.C.,*
U.S.A. 32°47N 79°52W **85** E15
Mount Pleasant *Tenn.,*
U.S.A. 35°32N 87°12W **85** D11
Mount Pleasant *Tex.,*
U.S.A. 33°9N 94°58W **84** E7
Mount Pleasant *Utah,*
U.S.A. 39°33N 111°27W **76** G8
Mount Pocono *U.S.A.* 41°7N 75°22W **83** E9
Mount Rainier *U.S.A.*
 46°55N 121°50W **78** D5
Mount Revelstoke △
Canada 51°5N 118°30W **70** C5
Mount Robson △ *Canada* 53°0N 119°0W **70** C5
Mount St. Helens △
U.S.A. 46°14N 122°11W **78** D4
Mount Selinda *Zimbabwe* 20°24S 32°43E **57** C5
Mount Shasta *U.S.A.* 41°19N 122°19W **76** F2
Mount Signal *U.S.A.* 32°39N 115°37W **79** N11
Mount Sterling *Ill.,*
U.S.A. 39°59N 90°45W **80** F8
Mount Sterling *Ky.,*
U.S.A. 38°4N 83°56W **81** F12
Mount Surprise
Australia 18°10S 144°17E **62** B3
Mount Union *U.S.A.* 40°23N 77°53W **82** F7
Mount Upton *U.S.A.* 42°26N 75°23W **83** D9
Mount Vernon *Ill.,*
U.S.A. 38°19N 88°55W **80** F9
Mount Vernon *Ind.,*
U.S.A. 37°56N 87°54W **80** G10
Mount Vernon *N.Y.,*
U.S.A. 40°54N 73°49W **83** F11
Mount Vernon *Ohio,*
U.S.A. 40°23N 82°29W **82** F2
Mount Vernon *Wash.,*
U.S.A. 48°25N 122°20W **78** B4
Mount William △
Australia 40°56S 148°14E **63** G4
Mountain Ash *U.K.* 51°40N 3°23W **13** F4
Mountain Center
U.S.A. 33°42N 116°44W **79** M10
Mountain City *Nev.,*
U.S.A. 41°50N 115°58W **76** F6
Mountain City *Tenn.,*
U.S.A. 36°29N 81°48W **85** C14
Mountain Dale *U.S.A.* 41°41N 74°32W **83** E10
Mountain Grove *U.S.A.* 37°8N 92°16W **80** G7
Mountain Home *Ark.,*
U.S.A. 36°20N 92°23W **84** C8
Mountain Home *Idaho,*
U.S.A. 43°8N 115°41W **76** E6
Mountain Iron *U.S.A.* 47°32N 92°37W **80** B7
Mountain Pass *U.S.A.* 35°29N 115°35W **79** K11
Mountain View *Ark.,*
U.S.A. 35°52N 92°7W **84** D8
Mountain View *Calif.,*
U.S.A. 37°23N 122°5W **78** H4
Mountain Zebra △
S. Africa 32°14S 25°27E **56** E4
Mountainair *U.S.A.* 34°31N 106°15W **77** J10
Mountlake Terrace
U.S.A. 47°47N 122°18W **78** C4
Mountmellick *Ireland* 53°7N 7°20W **10** C4
Mountrath *Ireland* 53°0N 7°28W **10** C4
Moura *Australia* 24°35S 149°58E **62** C4
Moura *Brazil* 1°32S 61°38W **92** D6
Moura *Portugal* 38°7N 7°30W **21** C2
Mourdi, Dépression du
Chad 18°10N 23°0E **51** E10
Mourilyan *Australia* 17°35S 146°3E **62** B4
Mourne → *U.K.* 54°52N 7°26W **10** B4
Mourne Mts. *U.K.* 54°10N 6°0W **10** B5
Mournies *Greece* 35°29N 24°1E **25** D6
Mouscron *Belgium* 50°45N 3°12E **15** D3
Moussoro *Chad* 13°41N 16°35E **51** F9
Moutong *Indonesia* 0°28N 121°13E **37** D6
Movas *Mexico* 28°10N 109°25W **86** B3
Moville *Ireland* 55°11N 7°3W **10** A4
Mowandjum *Australia* 17°22S 123°40E **60** C3
Moy → *Ireland* 54°8N 9°8W **10** B2
Moya *Comoros Is.* 12°18S 44°18E **53** a
Moyale *Kenya* 3°30N 39°0E **54** B4

Moyen Atlas *Morocco* 33°0N 5°0W **50** B4
Moyo *Indonesia* 8°10S 117°40E **36** F5
Moyobamba *Peru* 6°0S 77°0W **92** E3
Moyowosi △ *Tanzania* 3°50S 31°0E **54** C3
Moyyero → *Russia* 68°44N 103°42E **29** C11
Moyynqum *Kazakhstan* 44°12N 71°0E **32** B2
Moyynty *Kazakhstan* 47°10N 73°18E **28** E8
Mozambique = Moçambique
Mozam. 15°3S 40°42E **55** F5
Mozambique ■ *Africa* 19°0S 35°0E **55** F4
Mozambique Chan.
Africa 17°30S 42°30E **57** B7
Mozdok *Russia* 43°45N 44°48E **19** F7
Mozdūrān *Iran* 36°9N 60°35E **45** B9
Mozhnābād *Iran* 34°7N 60°6E **45** C9
Mozyr = Mazyr *Belarus* 51°59N 29°15E **17** B15
Mpanda *Tanzania* 6°23S 31°1E **54** D3
Mphoeng *Zimbabwe* 21°10S 27°51E **55** G2
Mpika *Zambia* 11°51S 31°25E **55** E3
Mpulungu *Zambia* 8°51S 31°5E **55** D3
Mpumalanga *S. Africa* 29°50S 30°33E **57** D5
Mpumalanga □ *S. Africa* 26°0S 30°0E **57** D5
Mpwapwa *Tanzania* 6°23S 36°30E **54** D4
Mqanduli *S. Africa* 31°49S 28°45E **57** E4
Msaken *Tunisia* 35°49N 10°33E **51** A8
Msambansovu *Zimbabwe* 15°50S 30°3E **55** F3
M'sila → *Algeria* 35°30N 4°29E **50** A6
Msoro *Zambia* 13°35S 31°50E **55** E3
Mstislavl = Mstsislaw
Belarus 54°0N 31°50E **17** A16
Mstsislaw *Belarus* 54°0N 31°50E **17** A16
Mtama *Tanzania* 10°17S 39°21E **55** E4
Mtamvuna = Mthamvuna →
S. Africa 31°6S 30°12E **57** E5
Mthamvuna → *S. Africa* 31°6S 30°12E **57** E5
Mthatha *S. Africa* 31°36S 28°49E **57** E4
Mtilikwe → *Zimbabwe* 21°9S 31°30E **55** G3
Mtito Andei *Kenya* 2°41S 38°10E **54** C4
Mtubatuba *S. Africa* 28°30S 32°8E **57** D5
Mtwalume *S. Africa* 30°30S 30°38E **57** E5
Mtwara-Mikindani
Tanzania 10°20S 40°20E **55** E5
Mu Gia, Deo *Vietnam* 17°40N 105°47E **38** D5
Mu Ko Chang △
Thailand 11°59N 102°22E **39** G4
Mu Us Shamo *China* 39°0N 109°0E **34** E5
Muang Chiang Rai = Chiang Rai
Thailand 19°52N 99°50E **38** C2
Muang Khong *Laos* 14°7N 105°51E **38** E5
Muang Lamphun
Thailand 18°40N 99°2E **38** C2
Muang Mai *Thailand* 8°5N 98°21E **39** a
Muang Pak Beng *Laos* 19°54N 101°8E **38** C3
Muar *Malaysia* 2°3N 102°34E **39** L4
Muarabungo *Indonesia* 1°28S 102°52E **36** E2
Muaraenim *Indonesia* 3°40S 103°50E **36** E2
Muarajuloi *Indonesia* 0°12S 114°3E **36** E4
Muarakaman *Indonesia* 0°2S 116°45E **36** E5
Muaratebo *Indonesia* 1°30S 102°26E **36** E2
Muaratembesi *Indonesia* 1°42S 103°8E **36** E2
Muaratewe *Indonesia* 0°58S 114°52E **36** E4
Mubarakpur *India* 26°6N 83°18E **43** F10
Mubarraz = Al Mubarraz
Si. Arabia 25°30N 49°40E **45** E6
Mubende *Uganda* 0°33N 31°22E **54** B3
Mubi *Nigeria* 10°18N 13°16E **51** F8
Mucajaí → *Brazil* 2°25N 60°52W **92** C6
Muchachos, Roque de los
Canary Is. 28°44N 17°52W **24** F2
Muchinga Mts. *Zambia* 11°30S 31°30E **55** E3
Muck *U.K.* 56°50N 6°15W **11** E2
Muckadilla *Australia* 26°35S 148°23E **63** D4
Muckaty ☒ *Australia* 18°37S 133°52E **62** B1
Muckle Flugga *U.K.* 60°51N 0°54W **11** A8
Mucori *Brazil* 18°0S 39°36W **93** G11
Mucusso *Angola* 18°1S 21°25E **56** B3
Muda *Canary Is.* 28°34N 13°57W **24** F6
Mudanjiang *China* 44°38N 129°30E **35** B15
Mudanya *Turkey* 40°25N 28°50E **23** D13
Muddy Cr. → *U.S.A.* 38°24N 110°42W **76** G8
Mudgee *Australia* 32°32S 149°31E **63** E4
Mudjatik → *Canada* 56°1N 107°36W **71** B7
Muecate *Mozam.* 14°55S 39°40E **55** E4
Mueda *Mozam.* 11°36S 39°28E **55** E4
Mueller Ranges
Australia 18°18S 126°46E **60** C4
Muende *Mozam.* 14°28S 33°0E **55** E3
Muerto, Mar *Mexico* 16°10N 94°10W **87** D6
Mufulira *Zambia* 12°32S 28°15E **55** E2
Mufumbiro Range *Africa* 1°25S 29°30E **54** C2
Mughal Sarai *India* 25°18N 83°7E **43** G10
Mughayrā' *Si. Arabia* 29°17N 37°41E **44** D3
Mugi *Japan* 33°40N 134°25E **31** H7
Mugila, Mts.
Dem. Rep. of the Congo 7°0S 28°50E **54** D2
Muğla *Turkey* 37°15N 28°22E **23** F13
Mugu *Nepal* 29°45N 82°30E **43** E10
Muhala *Congo* 5°40S 28°43E **54** D2
Muhammad, Râs *Egypt* 27°44N 34°16E **44** E2
Muhammadabad *India* 26°4N 83°25E **43** F10
Muhesi → *Tanzania* 7°0S 35°20E **54** D4
Mühlhausen *Germany* 51°12N 10°27E **16** C6
Mühlig Hofmann fjell
Antarctica 72°30S 5°0E **5** D3
Muhos *Finland* 64°47N 25°59E **8** D21
Muhu *Estonia* 58°36N 23°11E **9** G20
Muhutwe *Tanzania* 1°35S 31°45E **54** C3
Mui Wo *China* 22°16N 113°59E **33** G10
Muine Bheag *Ireland* 52°42N 6°58W **10** D5
Muineachán = Monaghan
Ireland 54°15N 6°57W **10** B5
Muir, L. *Australia* 34°30S 116°40E **61** F2
Muir of Ord *U.K.* 57°32N 4°28W **11** D4
Mujeres, I. *Mexico* 21°13N 86°43W **88** B2
Mujnak = Muynak
Uzbekistan 43°44N 59°10E **28** E6
Muka, Tanjung *Malaysia* 5°28N 100°11E **39** c
Mukacheve *Ukraine* 48°27N 22°45E **17** D12

Mukachevo = Mukacheve
 Ukraine   48°27N 22°45E 17 D12
Mukah Malaysia   2°55N 112°5E 36 D4
Mukandwara India   24°49N 75°59E 42 G6
Mukawwa, Geziret
 Egypt   23°55N 35°53E 44 F2
Mukdahan Thailand   16°32N 104°43E 38 D5
Mukden = Shenyang
 China   41°48N 123°27E 35 D12
Mukerian India   31°57N 75°37E 42 D6
Mukinbudin Australia   30°55S 118°5E 61 F2
Mukishi
 Dem. Rep. of the Congo   8°30S 24°44E 55 D1
Mukomuko Indonesia   2°30S 101°10E 36 E2
Mukomwenze
 Dem. Rep. of the Congo   6°49S 27°15E 54 D2
Mukono Uganda   0°21N 32°45E 54 B3
Muktsar India   30°30N 74°30E 42 D6
Mukur = Moqor Afghan.   32°50N 67°42E 42 C2
Mukutuwa → Canada   53°10N 97°24W 71 C9
Mukwela Zambia   17°0S 26°40E 55 F2
Mula Spain   38°3N 1°33W 21 C5
Mula → Pakistan   27°57N 67°36E 42 F2
Mulange
 Dem. Rep. of the Congo   3°40S 27°10E 54 C2
Mulanje, Mt. Malawi   15°50S 35°33E 55 F4
Mulchatna → U.S.A.   59°40N 157°7W 74 D8
Mulchén Chile   37°45S 72°20W 94 D1
Mulde → Germany   51°53N 12°15E 16 C7
Mule Creek Junction
 U.S.A.   43°23N 104°13W 76 E11
Muleba Tanzania   1°50S 31°37E 54 C3
Mulegé Mexico   26°53N 111°59W 86 B2
Muleshoe U.S.A.   34°13N 102°43W 84 D3
Mulgrave Canada   45°38N 61°31W 73 C7
Mulgrave I. = Badu
 Australia   10°7S 142°11E 62 a
Mulhacén Spain   37°4N 3°20W 21 D4
Mulhouse France   47°40N 7°20E 20 C7
Mulifanua Samoa   13°50S 171°59W 59 b
Muling China   44°35N 130°10E 35 B16
Mull U.K.   56°25N 5°56W 11 E3
Mull, Sound of U.K.   56°30N 5°50W 11 E3
Mullach Íde = Malahide
 Ireland   53°26N 6°9W 10 C5
Mullaittivu Sri Lanka   9°15N 80°49E 40 Q12
Mullen U.S.A.   42°3N 101°1W 80 D3
Mullengudgery
 Australia   31°43S 147°23E 63 B4
Mullens U.S.A.   37°35N 81°23W 81 G13
Muller, Pegunungan
 Indonesia   0°30N 113°30E 36 D4
Mullet Pen. Ireland   54°13N 10°2W 10 B1
Mullewa Australia   28°29S 115°30E 61 E2
Mulligan → Australia   25°0S 139°0E 62 D2
Mullingar Ireland   53°31N 7°21W 10 C4
Mullins U.S.A.   34°12N 79°15W 85 D15
Mullumbimby Australia   28°30S 153°30E 63 D5
Mulobezi Zambia   16°45S 25°7E 55 F2
Mulonga Plain Zambia   16°20S 22°40E 53 H4
Mulroy B. Ireland   55°15N 7°46W 10 A4
Multan Pakistan   30°15N 71°36E 42 D4
Mulumbe, Mts.
 Dem. Rep. of the Congo   8°40S 27°30E 55 D2
Mulungushi Dam
 Zambia   14°48S 28°48E 55 E2
Mulvane U.S.A.   37°29N 97°15W 80 G5
Mulwala, L. Australia   35°59S 146°1E 63 C4
Mumbai India   18°56N 72°50E 40 K8
Mumbwa Zambia   15°0S 27°0E 55 F2
Mumias Kenya   0°20N 34°29E 54 C4
Mun → Thailand   15°19N 105°30E 38 E5
Muna Indonesia   5°0S 122°30E 37 F6
Munabao India   25°45N 70°17E 42 G4
Munamagi Estonia   57°43N 27°4E 9 H22
Muncan Indonesia   8°34S 115°11E 37 K18
Muncar Indonesia   8°26S 114°20E 37 J17
München = Munich
 Germany   48°8N 11°34E 16 D6
Munchen-Gladbach =
 Mönchengladbach
 Germany   51°11N 6°27E 16 C4
Muncho Lake Canada   59°0N 125°50W 70 B3
Munch'ŏn N. Korea   39°14N 127°19E 35 E14
Muncie U.S.A.   40°12N 85°23W 81 E11
Muncoonie L. West
 Australia   25°12S 138°40E 62 D2
Mundabbera Australia   25°36S 151°18E 63 D5
Munday U.S.A.   33°27N 99°38W 84 E5
Münden Germany   51°25N 9°38E 16 C5
Mundiwindi Australia   23°47S 120°9E 60 D3
Mundo Novo Brazil   11°50S 40°29W 93 F10
Mundra India   22°54N 69°48E 42 H3
Mundrabilla Australia   31°52S 127°51E 61 F4
Mungallala Australia   26°28S 147°34E 63 D4
Mungallala Cr. →
 Australia   28°53S 147°5E 63 D4
Mungana Australia   17°8S 144°27E 62 B3
Mungaoli India   24°24N 78°7E 42 G8
Mungari Mozam.   17°12S 33°30E 55 F3
Mungbere
 Dem. Rep. of the Congo   2°36N 28°28E 54 B2
Mungeli India   22°4N 81°41E 43 H9
Munger India   25°23N 86°30E 43 G12
Mungilli ☉ Australia   25°14S 124°17E 61 E3
Mungkan Kandju △
 Australia   13°35S 142°52E 62 A3
Mungkarta ☉ Australia   20°22S 134°2E 62 C1
Munich = München
 Germany   48°8N 11°34E 16 D6
Munising U.S.A.   46°25N 86°40W 80 B10
Munku-Sardyk Russia   51°45N 100°20E 29 D11
Munnsville U.S.A.   42°58N 75°35W 83 D9
Muñoz Gamero, Pen.
 Chile   52°30S 73°5W 96 G2
Munroe L. Canada   59°13N 98°35W 71 B9
Munsan S. Korea   37°51N 126°48E 35 F14
Münster Germany   51°58N 7°37E 16 C4
Munster □ Ireland   52°18N 8°44W 10 D3

Muntadgin Australia   31°45S 118°33E 61 F2
Muntok Indonesia   2°5S 105°10E 36 E3
Muong Beng Laos   20°23N 101°46E 38 B3
Muong Boum Vietnam   22°24N 102°49E 38 A4
Muong Et Laos   20°49N 104°1E 38 B5
Muong Hai Laos   21°3N 101°49E 38 B3
Muong Hiem Laos   20°5N 103°22E 38 B4
Muong Houn Laos   20°8N 101°23E 38 B3
Muong Hung Vietnam   20°56N 103°53E 38 B4
Muong Kau Laos   15°6N 105°47E 38 E5
Muong Khao Laos   19°38N 103°32E 38 C4
Muong Khoua Laos   21°5N 102°31E 38 B4
Muong Liep Laos   18°29N 101°40E 38 C3
Muong May Laos   14°49N 106°56E 38 E6
Muong Ngeun Laos   20°36N 101°3E 38 B3
Muong Ngoi Laos   20°43N 102°41E 38 B4
Muong Nhie Vietnam   22°12N 102°28E 38 A4
Muong Nong Laos   16°22N 106°30E 38 D6
Muong Ou Tay Laos   22°7N 101°48E 38 A3
Muong Oua Laos   18°18N 101°20E 38 C3
Muong Peun Laos   19°33N 103°52E 38 B4
Muong Phalane Laos   16°39N 105°34E 38 D5
Muong Phieng Laos   19°6N 101°32E 38 C3
Muong Phine Laos   16°32N 106°2E 38 D6
Muong Sai Laos   20°42N 101°59E 38 B3
Muong Saiapoun Laos   18°24N 101°31E 38 C3
Muong Sen Vietnam   19°24N 104°8E 38 C5
Muong Sing Laos   21°11N 101°9E 38 B3
Muong Son Laos   20°27N 103°19E 38 B4
Muong Soui Laos   19°33N 102°52E 38 C4
Muong Va Laos   21°53N 102°19E 38 B4
Muong Xia Vietnam   20°19N 104°50E 38 B4
Muonio Finland   67°57N 23°40E 8 C20
Muonio älv = Muonionjoki →
 Finland   67°11N 23°34E 8 C20
Muonioälven = Muonionjoki →
 Finland   67°11N 23°34E 8 C20
Muonionjoki → Finland   67°11N 23°34E 8 C20
Mupa → Mozam.   18°58S 35°54E 55 F4
Muping China   37°22N 121°36E 35 F11
Muqdisho Somali Rep.   2°2N 45°25E 47 G4
Mur → Austria   46°18N 16°52E 17 E9
Murakami Japan   38°14N 139°29E 30 E9
Muralag = Prince of Wales I.
 Australia   10°40S 142°10E 62 A3
Murallón, Cerro Chile   49°48S 73°30W 96 F2
Muranda Rwanda   1°52S 29°20E 54 C2
Murang'a Kenya   0°45S 37°9E 54 C4
Murashi Russia   59°30N 49°0E 18 C8
Murat → Turkey   38°46N 40°0E 19 G7
Muratlı Turkey   41°10N 27°29E 23 D12
Murayama Japan   38°30N 140°25E 30 E10
Murchison → Australia   27°45S 114°0E 61 E1
Murchison, Mt.
 Antarctica   73°25S 166°20E 5 D11
Murchison Falls Uganda   2°15N 31°30E 54 B3
Murchison Falls △
 Uganda   2°1N 31°48E 54 B3
Murchison Ra. Australia   20°0S 134°10E 62 C1
Murchison Rapids
 Malawi   15°55S 34°35E 55 F3
Murchison Roadhouse
 Australia   27°39S 114°14E 61 E1
Murcia Spain   38°5N 1°10W 21 D5
Murcia □ Spain   37°50N 1°30W 21 D5
Murdo U.S.A.   43°53N 100°43W 80 D3
Murdoch Pt. Australia   14°37S 144°55E 62 A3
Mureş → Romania   46°15N 20°13E 17 E11
Mureşul = Mureş →
 Romania   46°15N 20°13E 17 E11
Murewa Zimbabwe   17°39S 31°47E 57 B5
Murfreesboro N.C.,
 U.S.A.   36°27N 77°6W 85 C16
Murfreesboro Tenn.,
 U.S.A.   35°51N 86°24W 85 D11
Murgap = Murghob
 Tajikistan   38°10N 74°2E 28 F8
Murgap → Turkmenistan   38°18N 61°12E 45 B9
Murgenella Australia   11°34S 132°56E 60 B5
Murgha Kibzai Pakistan   30°44N 69°25E 42 D3
Murghob Tajikistan   38°10N 74°2E 28 F8
Murgon Australia   26°15S 151°54E 63 D5
Muri India   23°22N 85°52E 43 H11
Muria Indonesia   6°36S 110°53E 37 G14
Muriaé Brazil   21°8S 42°23W 95 A7
Muriel Mine Zimbabwe   17°14S 30°40E 55 F3
Müritz Germany   53°25N 12°42E 16 B7
Murliganj India   25°54N 86°59E 43 G12
Murmansk Russia   68°57N 33°10E 8 B25
Murmashi Russia   68°47N 32°42E 8 B25
Muro Spain   39°44N 3°3E 24 B10
Murom Russia   55°35N 42°3E 18 C7
Muroran Japan   42°25N 141°0E 30 C10
Muroto Japan   33°18N 134°9E 31 H7
Muroto-Misaki Japan   33°15N 134°10E 31 H7
Murphy U.S.A.   43°13N 116°33W 76 E5
Murphys U.S.A.   38°8N 120°28W 78 G6
Murray Australia   9°56S 144°2E 62 a
Murray Ky., U.S.A.   36°37N 88°19W 80 G9
Murray Utah, U.S.A.   40°40N 111°53W 76 F8
Murray → Australia   35°20S 139°22E 63 F2
Murray, L. U.S.A.   34°3N 81°13W 85 D14
Murray Bridge Australia   35°6S 139°14E 63 F2
Murray Fracture Zone
 Pac. Oc.   35°0N 130°0W 65 D14
Murray River →
 Australia   34°23S 140°32E 63 E3
Murraysburg S. Africa   31°58S 23°47E 56 E3
Murree Pakistan   33°56N 73°28E 42 C5
Murrieta U.S.A.   33°33N 117°13W 79 M9
Murrumbidgee →
 Australia   34°43S 143°12E 63 E3
Murrumburrah
 Australia   34°32S 148°22E 63 E4
Murrurundi Australia   31°42S 150°51E 63 E5
Murshidabad India   24°11N 88°19E 43 G13
Murtle L. Canada   52°8N 119°38W 70 C5
Murtoa Australia   36°35S 142°28E 63 F3

Murungu Tanzania   4°12S 31°10E 54 C3
Mururoa
 French Polynesia   21°52S 138°55W 65 K14
Murwara India   23°46N 80°28E 43 H9
Murwillumbah
 Australia   28°18S 153°27E 63 D5
Mürzzuschlag Austria   47°36N 15°41E 16 E8
Muş Turkey   38°45N 41°30E 44 B4
Mûsa, Gebel Egypt   28°33N 33°59E 44 D2
Musa Khel Pakistan   30°59N 69°52E 42 D3
Mûsa Qal'eh Afghan.   32°20N 64°50E 40 C4
Musafirkhana India   26°22N 81°48E 43 F9
Musala Bulgaria   42°13N 23°37E 23 C10
Musala Indonesia   1°41N 98°28E 36 D1
Musan N. Korea   42°12N 129°12E 35 C15
Musangu
 Dem. Rep. of the Congo   10°28S 23°55E 55 E1
Musasa Tanzania   3°25S 31°30E 54 C3
Musay'īd Qatar   25°0N 51°33E 45 E6
Muscat = Masqat Oman   23°37N 58°36E 47 C6
Muscatine U.S.A.   41°25N 91°3W 80 E8
Muscle Shoals U.S.A.   34°45N 87°40W 85 D11
Musengezi = Unsengedsi →
 Zimbabwe   15°43S 31°14E 55 F3
Musgrave Harbour
 Canada   49°27N 53°58W 73 C9
Musgrave Ranges
 Australia   26°0S 132°0E 61 E5
Mushie
 Dem. Rep. of the Congo   2°56S 16°55E 52 E3
Musi → Indonesia   2°20S 104°56E 36 E2
Musina S. Africa   22°20S 30°5E 57 C5
Muskeg → Canada   60°20N 123°20W 70 A4
Muskegon U.S.A.   43°14N 86°16W 80 D10
Muskegon → U.S.A.   43°14N 86°21W 80 D10
Muskegon Heights
 U.S.A.   43°12N 86°16W 80 D10
Muskoka, L. Canada   45°0N 79°25W 82 B5
Muskoka Falls Canada   44°59N 79°17W 82 B5
Muskwa → Canada   58°47N 122°48W 70 B4
Muslīmiyah Syria   36°19N 37°12E 44 B3
Musofu Zambia   13°30S 29°0E 55 E2
Musoma Tanzania   1°30S 33°48E 54 C3
Musquaro, L. Canada   50°38N 61°5W 73 B7
Musquodoboit Harbour
 Canada   44°50N 63°9W 73 D7
Musselburgh U.K.   55°57N 3°2W 11 F5
Musselshell → U.S.A.   47°21N 107°57W 76 C10
Mussende Angola   10°32S 16°5E 52 G3
Mussoorie India   30°27N 78°6E 42 D8
Mussuco Angola   17°2S 19°3E 56 B2
Mustafakemalpaşa
 Turkey   40°2N 28°24E 23 D13
Mustang Nepal   29°10N 83°55E 43 E10
Musters, L. Argentina   45°20S 69°25W 96 F3
Musudan N. Korea   40°50N 129°43E 35 D15
Muswellbrook Australia   32°16S 150°56E 63 E5
Mût Egypt   25°28N 28°58E 51 C11
Mut Turkey   36°40N 33°28E 44 B2
Mutanda Mozam.   21°0S 33°34E 57 C5
Mutanda Zambia   12°24S 26°13E 55 E2
Mutare Zimbabwe   18°58S 32°38E 55 F3
Mutawintji △ Australia   31°10S 142°30E 63 E3
Mutha Kenya   1°48S 38°26E 54 C4
Muting Indonesia   7°23S 140°20E 37 F10
Mutki = Mirtağ Turkey   38°23N 41°56E 44 B4
Mutoko Zimbabwe   17°24S 32°13E 57 B5
Mutomo Kenya   1°51S 38°12E 54 C4
Mutoray Russia   60°56N 101°0E 29 C11
Mutsamudu Comoros Is.   12°10S 44°25E 53 a
Mutshatsha
 Dem. Rep. of the Congo   10°35S 24°20E 55 E1
Mutsu Japan   41°5N 140°55E 30 D10
Mutsu-Wan Japan   41°5N 140°55E 30 D10
Muttaburra Australia   22°38S 144°29E 62 C3
Mutton I. Ireland   52°49N 9°32W 10 D2
Mutuáli Mozam.   14°55S 37°0E 55 E4
Mutumba Burundi   3°25S 29°21E 54 C2
Mutumbo
 Dem. Rep. of the Congo   8°40S 26°27E 55 D2
Muweilih Egypt   30°42N 34°19E 46 E3
Muy Muy Nic.   12°39N 85°36W 88 D2
Muyinga Burundi   3°14S 30°33E 54 C3
Muynak Uzbekistan   43°44N 59°10E 28 E6
Muyunkum, Peski = Moyynqum
 Kazakhstan   44°12N 71°0E 32 B2
Muz Tag China   36°25N 87°25E 32 C3
Muzaffarabad Pakistan   34°25N 73°30E 43 B5
Muzaffargarh Pakistan   30°5N 71°14E 42 D4
Muzaffarnagar India   29°26N 77°40E 42 E7
Muzaffarpur India   26°7N 85°23E 43 F11
Muzafirpur Pakistan   30°58N 69°9E 42 D3
Muzhi Russia   65°25N 64°40E 18 A11
Muztagh-Ata China   38°17N 75°7E 32 C2
Mvuma Zimbabwe   19°16S 30°30E 55 F3
Mvurwi Zimbabwe   17°0S 30°57E 55 F3
Mwabvi △ Malawi   16°42S 35°0E 55 F4
Mwadui Tanzania   3°26S 33°32E 54 C3
Mwali = Mohéli
 Comoros Is.   12°20S 43°40E 53 a
Mwambo Tanzania   10°30S 40°22E 55 E5
Mwandi Zambia   17°30S 24°51E 55 F1
Mwanza
 Dem. Rep. of the Congo   7°55S 26°43E 54 D2
Mwanza Tanzania   2°30S 32°58E 54 C3
Mwanza Zambia   16°58S 24°28E 55 F1
Mwanza □ Tanzania   2°0S 33°0E 54 C3
Mwaya Tanzania   9°32S 33°55E 55 D3
Mweelrea Ireland   53°39N 9°49W 10 C2
Mweka
 Dem. Rep. of the Congo   4°50S 21°34E 52 E4
Mwenezi Zimbabwe   21°15S 30°48E 55 G3
Mwenezi → Mozam.   22°40S 31°50E 55 G3
Mwenga
 Dem. Rep. of the Congo   3°1S 28°28E 54 C2
Mweru, L. Zambia   9°0S 28°40E 55 D2
Mweru Wantipa △
 Zambia   8°39S 29°25E 55 D2

Mweza Range Zimbabwe   21°0S 30°0E 55 G3
Mwilambwe
 Dem. Rep. of the Congo   8°7S 25°5E 54 D2
Mwimbi Tanzania   8°38S 31°39E 55 D3
Mwingi Kenya   0°56S 38°4E 54 C4
Mwinilunga Zambia   11°43S 24°25E 55 E1
My Tho Vietnam   10°29N 106°23E 39 G6
Myajlar India   26°15N 70°20E 42 F4
Myanaung Burma   18°18N 95°22E 41 K19
Myanmar = Burma ■
 Asia   21°0N 96°30E 41 J20
Myaungmya Burma   16°30N 94°40E 41 L19
Mycenæ = Mikines
 Greece   37°43N 22°46E 23 F10
Myeik Kyunzu Burma   11°30N 97°30E 39 G1
Myerstown U.S.A.   40°22N 76°19W 83 F8
Myingyan Burma   21°30N 95°20E 41 J19
Myitkyina Burma   25°24N 97°26E 41 G20
Mykines Greece   37°43N 22°46E 23 F10
Mykolayiv Ukraine   46°58N 32°0E 19 E5
Mykonos Greece   37°30N 25°25E 23 F11
Mymensingh Bangla.   24°45N 90°24E 41 G17
Mynydd Du U.K.   51°52N 3°50W 13 F4
Mýrdalsjökull Iceland   63°40N 19°6W 8 E4
Myrtle Beach U.S.A.   33°42N 78°53E 85 D15
Myrtle Creek U.S.A.   43°1N 123°17W 76 E2
Myrtle Point U.S.A.   43°4N 124°8W 76 E1
Myrtou Cyprus   35°18N 33°4E 25 D12
Mysia Turkey   39°50N 27°0E 23 E12
Mysore = Karnataka □
 India   13°15N 77°0E 40 N10
Mysore India   12°17N 76°41E 40 N10
Mystic U.S.A.   41°21N 71°58W 83 E13
Mysuru = Mysore India   12°17N 76°41E 40 N10
Myszków Poland   50°45N 19°22E 17 C10
Mytishchi Russia   55°50N 37°50E 18 C6
Mývatn Iceland   65°36N 17°0W 8 D5
Mzimba Malawi   11°55S 33°39E 55 E3
Mzimkulu → S. Africa   30°44S 30°28E 57 E5
Mzimvubu → S. Africa   31°38S 29°33E 57 E4
Mzuzu Malawi   11°30S 33°55E 55 E3

N

Na Clocha Liatha = Greystones
 Ireland   53°9N 6°5W 10 C5
Na Hearadh = Harris
 U.K.   57°50N 6°55W 11 D2
Na Noi Thailand   18°19N 100°43E 38 C3
Na Phao Laos   17°35N 105°44E 38 D5
Na Sam Vietnam   22°3N 106°37E 38 A6
Na San Vietnam   21°12N 104°2E 38 B5
Na Thon Thailand   9°32N 99°56E 39 b
Naab → Germany   49°1N 12°2E 16 D6
Naantali Finland   60°29N 22°2E 9 F20
Naas Ireland   53°12N 6°40W 10 C5
Nababeep S. Africa   29°36S 17°46E 56 D2
Nabadwip = Navadwip
 India   23°34N 88°20E 43 H13
Nabawa Australia   28°30S 114°48E 61 E1
Nabberu, L. Australia   25°50S 120°30E 61 E3
Naberezhnyye Chelny
 Russia   55°42N 52°19E 18 C9
Nabeul Tunisia   36°30N 10°44E 51 A8
Nabha India   30°26N 76°14E 42 D7
Nabīd Iran   29°40N 57°38E 45 D8
Nabire Indonesia   3°15S 135°26E 37 E9
Nabisar Pakistan   25°8N 69°40E 42 G3
Nabisipi → Canada   50°14N 62°13W 73 B7
Nabiswera Uganda   1°27N 32°15E 54 B3
Nablus = Nābulus
 West Bank   32°14N 35°15E 46 C4
Naboomspruit S. Africa   24°32S 28°40E 57 C4
Nabouwalu Fiji   17°0S 178°45E 59 a
Nābulus West Bank   32°14N 35°15E 46 C4
Nacala Mozam.   14°32S 40°34E 55 E5
Nacaome Honduras   13°31N 87°30W 88 D2
Nacaroa Mozam.   14°22S 39°56E 55 E4
Naches U.S.A.   46°44N 120°42W 76 C3
Naches → U.S.A.   46°38N 120°31W 78 D6
Nachicapau, L. Canada   56°40N 68°5W 73 A6
Nachingwea Tanzania   10°23S 38°49E 55 E4
Nachna India   27°34N 71°41E 42 F4
Nacimiento, L. U.S.A.   35°46N 120°53W 78 K6
Naco Mexico   31°19N 109°56W 86 A3
Nacogdoches U.S.A.   31°36N 94°39W 84 F7
Nácori Chico Mexico   29°40N 108°57W 86 B3
Nacozari de García
 Mexico   30°25N 109°38W 86 A3
Nacula Fiji   16°54S 177°27E 59 a
Nadendal = Naantali
 Finland   60°29N 22°2E 9 F20
Nadi Fiji   17°42S 177°20E 59 a
Nadiad India   22°41N 72°56E 42 H5
Nador Morocco   35°14N 2°58W 50 B5
Nadur Malta   36°2N 14°18E 25 C1
Nadūshan Iran   32°2N 53°35E 45 C7
Nadvirna Ukraine   48°37N 24°30E 17 D13
Nadvoitsy Russia   63°52N 34°14E 18 B5
Nadvornaya = Nadvirna
 Ukraine   48°37N 24°30E 17 D13
Nadym Russia   65°35N 72°42E 28 C8
Nadym → Russia   66°12N 72°0E 28 C8
Nærbø Norway   58°40N 5°39E 9 G11
Næstved Denmark   55°13N 11°44E 9 J14
Nafarroa □ Spain   42°40N 1°40W 21 A5
Nafplio Greece   37°33N 22°50E 23 F10
Naft-e Safīd Iran   31°40N 49°17E 45 D6
Naftshahr Iran   34°0N 45°30E 44 C5
Nafud Desert = An Nafūd
 Si. Arabia   28°15N 41°0E 44 D4
Naga Phil.   13°38N 123°15E 37 B6
Nagagami → Canada   50°23N 84°20W 72 B3
Nagahama Japan   35°23N 136°16E 31 G8
Nagai Japan   38°6N 140°2E 30 E10
Nagaland □ India   26°0N 94°30E 41 G19
Nagano Japan   36°40N 138°10E 31 F9
Nagano □ Japan   36°15N 138°0E 31 F9

Nagaoka Japan   37°27N 138°51E 31 F9
Nagaon = Nowgong
 India   26°20N 92°50E 41 F18
Nagappattinam India   10°46N 79°51E 40 P11
Nagar → Bangla.   24°27N 89°12E 43 G13
Nagar Parkar Pakistan   24°28N 70°46E 42 G4
Nagasaki Japan   32°47N 129°50E 31 H4
Nagasaki □ Japan   32°50N 129°40E 31 H4
Nagato Japan   34°19N 131°5E 31 G5
Nagaur India   27°15N 73°45E 42 F5
Nagda India   23°27N 75°25E 42 H6
Nagercoil India   8°12N 77°26E 40 Q10
Nagina India   29°30N 78°30E 43 E8
Nagīneh Iran   34°20N 57°15E 45 C8
Nagir Pakistan   36°12N 74°42E 43 A6
Nagles Mts. Ireland   52°8N 8°30W 10 D3
Nagod India   24°34N 80°36E 43 G9
Nagoorin Australia   24°17S 151°15E 62 C5
Nagorno-Karabakh □
 Azerbaijan   39°55N 46°45E 44 B5
Nagornyy Russia   55°58N 124°57E 29 D13
Nagoya Japan   35°10N 136°50E 31 G8
Nagpur India   21°8N 79°10E 40 J11
Nagua Dom. Rep.   19°23N 69°50W 89 C6
Naguabo Puerto Rico   18°13N 65°44W 89 d
Nagurunguru ☉
 Australia   16°45S 129°45E 60 C4
Nagykanizsa Hungary   46°28N 17°0E 17 E9
Nagykőrös Hungary   47°5N 19°48E 17 E10
Naha Japan   26°13N 127°42E 31 L3
Nahan India   30°33N 77°18E 42 D7
Nahanni △ Canada   61°36N 125°41W 70 A4
Nahanni Butte Canada   61°2N 123°31W 70 A4
Nahargarh Mad. P., India   24°10N 75°14E 42 G6
Nahargarh Raj., India   24°55N 76°50E 42 G7
Nahariyya Israel   33°1N 35°5E 44 C2
Nahāvand Iran   34°10N 48°22E 45 C6
Nahuel Huapí, L.
 Argentina   41°0S 71°32W 96 E2
Nahuelbuta △ Chile   37°44S 72°57W 94 D1
Nai Yong Thailand   8°14N 98°22E 39 a
Naicá Mexico   27°53N 105°31W 86 B3
Naicam Canada   52°30N 104°30W 71 C8
Naikoon △ Canada   53°55N 131°55W 70 C2
Naimisharanya India   27°21N 80°30E 43 F9
Naimona'nyi Feng Nepal   30°26N 81°18E 43 D9
Nain Canada   56°34N 61°40W 73 A7
Nā'īn Iran   32°54N 53°0E 45 C7
Naini Tal India   29°30N 79°30E 43 E8
Nainpur India   22°30N 80°10E 43 H9
Nainwa India   25°46N 75°51E 42 G6
Nairai Fiji   17°49S 179°15E 59 a
Nairn U.K.   57°35N 3°53W 11 D5
Nairobi Kenya   1°17S 36°48E 54 C4
Nairobi △ Kenya   1°22S 36°50E 54 C4
Naissaar Estonia   59°34N 24°29E 9 G21
Naitaba Fiji   17°0S 179°16W 59 a
Naivasha Kenya   0°40S 36°30E 54 C4
Naivasha, L. Kenya   0°48S 36°20E 54 C4
Najaf = An Najaf Iraq   32°3N 44°15E 44 C5
Najafābād Iran   32°40N 51°15E 45 C6
Najibabad India   29°40N 78°20E 42 E8
Najin N. Korea   42°12N 130°15E 35 C16
Najmah Si. Arabia   26°42N 50°6E 45 E6
Najrān Si. Arabia   17°34N 44°18E 47 D3
Naju S. Korea   35°3N 126°43E 35 G14
Nakadōri-Shima Japan   32°57N 129°4E 31 H4
Nakalagba
 Dem. Rep. of the Congo   2°50N 27°58E 54 B2
Nakaminato Japan   36°21N 140°36E 31 F10
Nakamura Japan   32°59N 132°56E 31 H6
Nakano Japan   36°45N 138°22E 31 F9
Nakano-Shima Japan   29°51N 129°52E 31 K4
Nakashibetsu Japan   43°33N 144°59E 30 C12
Nakfa Eritrea   16°40N 38°32E 47 D2
Nakha Yai, Ko Thailand   8°3N 98°28E 39 a
Nakhichevan = Naxçıvan
 Azerbaijan   39°12N 45°15E 44 B5
Nakhichevan Rep. = Naxçıvan □
 Azerbaijan   39°25N 45°26E 44 B5
Nakhl Egypt   29°55N 33°43E 46 F3
Nakhl-e Taqī Iran   27°28N 52°36E 45 E7
Nakhodka Russia   42°53N 132°54E 30 C6
Nakhon Nayok
 Thailand   14°12N 101°13E 38 E4
Nakhon Pathom
 Thailand   13°49N 100°3E 38 F3
Nakhon Phanom
 Thailand   17°23N 104°43E 38 D5
Nakhon Ratchasima
 Thailand   14°59N 102°12E 38 E4
Nakhon Sawan
 Thailand   15°35N 100°10E 38 E3
Nakhon Si Thammarat
 Thailand   8°29N 100°0E 39 H3
Nakhon Thai Thailand   17°5N 100°44E 38 D3
Nakina Canada   50°10N 86°40W 72 B2
Nakodar India   31°8N 75°31E 42 D6
Naktong → S. Korea   35°7N 128°57E 35 G15
Nakuru Kenya   0°15S 36°4E 54 C4
Nakuru, L. Kenya   0°23S 36°5E 54 C4
Nakusp Canada   50°20N 117°45W 70 C5
Nal Pakistan   27°40N 66°12E 42 F2
Nal → Pakistan   25°20N 65°30E 42 G1
Nalázi Mozam.   24°3S 33°20E 57 C5
Nalchik Russia   43°30N 43°33E 19 F7
Nalgonda India   17°6N 79°15E 40 L11
Nalhati India   24°17N 87°52E 43 G12
Naliya India   23°16N 68°50E 42 H3
Nallamalai Hills India   15°30N 78°50E 40 M11
Nalubaale Dam Uganda   0°30N 33°5E 54 B3
Nam Can Vietnam   8°46N 104°59E 39 H5
Nam-ch'on N. Korea   38°15N 126°26E 35 E14
Nam Co China   30°30N 90°45E 32 C4
Nam Dinh Vietnam   20°25N 106°5E 38 B6
Nam Du, Hon Vietnam   9°41N 104°21E 39 H5
Nam Nao △ Thailand   16°44N 101°32E 38 D3

Nam Ngum Res. *Laos* 18°35N 102°34E **38 C4**
Nam-Phan *Vietnam* 10°30N 106°0E **39 G6**
Nam Phong *Thailand* 16°42N 102°52E **38 D4**
Nam Tha *Laos* 20°58N 101°30E **38 B3**
Nam Tok *Thailand* 14°21N 99°4E **38 E2**
Namacunde *Angola* 17°18S 15°50E **56 B2**
Namacurra *Mozam.* 17°30S 36°50E **57 B6**
Namak, Daryācheh-ye
  Iran 34°30N 52°0E **45 C7**
Namak, Kavir-e *Iran* 34°30N 57°30E **45 C8**
Namakzār, Daryācheh-ye
  Iran 34°0N 60°30E **45 C9**
Namaland *Namibia* 26°0S 17°0E **56 C2**
Namanga *Kenya* 2°33S 36°47E **54 C4**
Namangan *Uzbekistan* 41°0N 71°40E **28 E8**
Namapa *Mozam.* 13°43S 39°50E **55 E4**
Namaqualand *S. Africa* 30°0S 17°25E **56 E2**
Namasagali *Uganda* 1°2N 33°0E **54 B3**
Namber *Indonesia* 1°2S 134°49E **37 E8**
Nambour *Australia* 26°32S 152°58E **63 D5**
Nambouwalu = Nabouwalu
  Fiji 17°0S 178°45E **59 a**
Nambucca Heads
  Australia 30°37S 153°0E **63 E5**
Nambung △ *Australia* 30°30S 115°5E **61 F2**
Namcha Barwa *China* 29°40N 95°10E **32 D4**
Namche Bazar *Nepal* 27°51N 86°47E **43 F12**
Namchonjöm = Nam-ch'on
  N. Korea 38°15N 126°26E **35 E14**
Namecunda *Mozam.* 14°54S 37°37E **55 E4**
Namenalala *Fiji* 17°8S 179°9E **59 a**
Nameponda *Mozam.* 15°50S 39°50E **55 F4**
Nametil *Mozam.* 15°40S 39°21E **55 F4**
Namew L. *Canada* 54°14N 101°56W **71 C8**
Namgia *India* 31°48N 78°40E **43 D8**
Namialo *Mozam.* 14°55S 39°59E **55 E4**
Namib Desert *Namibia* 22°30S 15°0E **56 C2**
Namib-Naukluft △
  Namibia 24°40S 15°16E **56 C2**
Namibe *Angola* 15°7S 12°11E **53 H2**
Namibe □ *Angola* 16°35S 12°30E **56 B1**
Namibia ■ *Africa* 22°0S 18°9E **56 C2**
Namibwoestyn = Namib Desert
  Namibia 22°30S 15°0E **56 C2**
Namlea *Indonesia* 3°18S 127°5E **37 E7**
Namoi → *Australia* 30°12S 149°30E **63 E4**
Nampa *U.S.A.* 43°34N 116°34W **76 E5**
Namp'o *N. Korea* 38°52N 125°10E **35 E13**
Nampō-Shotō *Japan* 32°0N 140°0E **31 J10**
Nampula *Mozam.* 15°6S 39°15E **55 F4**
Namrole *Indonesia* 3°46S 126°46E **37 E7**
Namse Shankou *China* 30°0N 82°25E **43 E10**
Namsen → *Norway* 64°28N 11°37E **8 D14**
Namsos *Norway* 64°29N 11°30E **8 D14**
Namtok Chat Trakan △
  Thailand 17°17N 100°40E **38 D3**
Namtok Mae Surin △
  Thailand 18°55N 98°2E **38 C2**
Namtsy *Russia* 62°43N 129°37E **29 C13**
Namtu *Burma* 23°5N 97°28E **41 H20**
Namtumbo *Tanzania* 10°30S 36°4E **55 E4**
Namu *Canada* 51°52N 127°50W **70 C3**
Namuka-i-Lau *Fiji* 18°53S 178°37W **59 a**
Namur *Belgium* 50°27N 4°52E **15 D4**
Namur □ *Belgium* 50°17N 5°0E **15 D4**
Namuruputh *Kenya* 4°34N 35°57E **54 B4**
Namutoni *Namibia* 18°49S 16°55E **56 B2**
Namwala *Zambia* 15°44S 26°30E **55 F2**
Namwon *S. Korea* 35°23N 127°23E **35 G14**
Namyang *N. Korea* 42°57N 129°52E **35 C15**
Nan *Thailand* 18°48N 100°46E **38 C3**
Nan → *Thailand* 15°42N 100°9E **38 E3**
Nan-ch'ang = Nanchang
  China 28°42N 115°55E **33 D6**
Nanaimo *Canada* 49°10N 124°0W **70 D4**
Nänäkuli *U.S.A.* 21°24N 158°9W **75 L8**
Nanam *N. Korea* 41°44N 129°40E **35 D15**
Nanango *Australia* 26°40S 152°0E **63 D5**
Nanao *Japan* 37°0N 137°0E **31 F8**
Nanchang *China* 28°42N 115°55E **33 D6**
Nanching = Nanjing
  China 32°2N 118°47E **33 C6**
Nanchong *China* 30°43N 106°2E **32 C5**
Nancy *France* 48°42N 6°12E **20 B7**
Nanda Devi *India* 30°23N 79°59E **43 D8**
Nanda Devi △ *India* 30°30N 79°50E **43 D8**
Nanda Kot *India* 30°17N 80°5E **43 D9**
Nandan *Japan* 34°10N 134°42E **31 G7**
Nanded *India* 19°10N 77°20E **40 K10**
Nandewar Ra. *Australia* 30°15S 150°35E **63 E5**
Nandi = Nadi *Fiji* 17°42S 177°20E **59 a**
Nandi *Zimbabwe* 20°58S 31°44E **55 G3**
Nandigram *India* 22°1N 87°58E **43 H12**
Nandurbar *India* 21°20N 74°15E **40 J9**
Nandyal *India* 15°30N 78°30E **40 M11**
Nang Rong *Thailand* 14°50N 102°48E **38 E4**
Nanga-Eboko *Cameroon* 4°41N 12°22E **52 D2**
Nanga Parbat *Pakistan* 35°10N 74°35E **43 B6**
Nangade *Mozam.* 11°5S 39°36E **55 E4**
Nangapinoh *Indonesia* 0°20S 111°44E **36 E4**
Nangarhār □ *Afghan.* 34°20N 70°0E **40 B7**
Nangatayap *Indonesia* 1°32S 110°34E **36 E4**
Nangeya Mts. *Uganda* 3°30N 33°30E **54 B3**
Nangong *China* 37°23N 115°22E **34 F8**
Nanhuang *China* 36°58N 121°48E **35 F11**
Nanisivik *Canada* 73°2N 84°33W **69 C15**
Nanjeko *Zambia* 15°31S 23°30E **55 F1**
Nanjing *China* 32°2N 118°47E **33 C6**
Nanjirinji *Tanzania* 9°41S 39°5E **55 D4**
Nankana Sahib *Pakistan* 31°27N 73°38E **42 D5**
Nanking = Nanjing
  China 32°2N 118°47E **33 C6**
Nankoku *Japan* 33°39N 133°44E **31 H6**
Nanlang *China* 22°30N 113°32E **33 G10**
Nanning *China* 22°48N 108°20E **32 D5**
Nanpara *India* 27°52N 81°33E **43 F9**
Nanpi *China* 38°2N 116°45E **34 E9**
Nanping *China* 26°38N 118°10E **33 D6**

Nanripe *Mozam.* 13°52S 38°52E **55 E4**
Nansei-Shotō = Ryūkyū-rettō
  Japan 26°0N 126°0E **31 M3**
Nansen Basin *Arctic* 84°0N 50°0E **4 A11**
Nansen Sd. *Canada* 81°0N 91°0W **69 A13**
Nansha *China* 22°45N 113°34E **33 F10**
Nanshan I. *S. China Sea* 10°45N 115°49E **36 B5**
Nansio *Tanzania* 2°3S 33°4E **54 C3**
Nantawarrinna ☉
  Australia 30°49S 138°58E **63 B2**
Nantes *France* 47°12N 1°33W **20 C3**
Nanticoke *U.S.A.* 41°12N 76°0W **83 E8**
Nanton *Canada* 50°21N 113°46W **70 C6**
Nantong *China* 32°1N 120°52E **33 C7**
Nantou *China* 22°32N 113°55E **33 F10**
Nantucket *U.S.A.* 41°17N 70°6W **81 E18**
Nantucket I. *U.S.A.* 41°16N 70°5W **81 E18**
Nantulo *Mozam.* 12°32S 38°45E **55 E4**
Nantwich *U.K.* 53°4N 2°31W **12 D5**
Nanty Glo *U.S.A.* 40°28N 78°50W **82 F6**
Nanuku Passage *Fiji* 16°45S 179°15W **59 a**
Nanuque *Brazil* 17°50S 40°21W **93 G10**
Nanusa, Kepulauan
  Indonesia 4°45N 127°1E **37 D7**
Nanutarra Roadhouse
  Australia 22°32S 115°30E **60 D2**
Nanyang *China* 33°11N 112°30E **34 H7**
Nanyuki *Kenya* 0°2N 37°4E **54 B4**
Nao, C. de la *Spain* 38°44N 0°14E **21 C6**
Naococane, L. *Canada* 52°50N 70°45W **73 B5**
Napa *U.S.A.* 38°18N 122°17W **78 G4**
Napa → *U.S.A.* 38°10N 122°19W **78 G4**
Napanee *Canada* 44°15N 77°0W **82 B8**
Napanoch *U.S.A.* 41°44N 74°22W **83 E10**
Nape *Laos* 18°18N 105°6E **38 C5**
Nape Pass = Keo Neua, Deo
  Vietnam 18°23N 105°10E **38 C5**
Napier *N.Z.* 39°30S 176°56E **59 C6**
Napier Broome B.
  Australia 14°2S 126°37E **60 B4**
Napier Pen. *Australia* 12°4S 135°43E **62 A2**
Napierville *Canada* 45°11N 73°25W **83 A11**
Naples = Nápoli *Italy* 40°50N 14°15E **22 D6**
Naples *U.S.A.* 26°8N 81°48W **85 H14**
Napo → *Peru* 3°20S 72°40W **92 D4**
Napoleon *N. Dak., U.S.A.* 46°30N 99°46W **80 B4**
Napoleon *Ohio, U.S.A.* 41°23N 84°8W **81 E11**
Nápoli *Italy* 40°50N 14°15E **22 D6**
Napopo
  Dem. Rep. of the Congo 4°15N 28°0E **54 B2**
Naqadeh *Iran* 36°57N 45°23E **44 B5**
Naqb, Ra's an *Jordan* 29°48N 35°44E **46 F4**
Naqqāsh *Iran* 35°40N 49°6E **45 C6**
Nara *Japan* 34°40N 135°49E **31 G7**
Nara *Mali* 15°10N 7°20W **50 E4**
Nara → *Japan* 34°30N 136°0E **31 G8**
Nara Canal *Pakistan* 24°30N 69°20E **42 G3**
Nara Visa *U.S.A.* 35°37N 103°6W **77 J12**
Naracoorte *Australia* 36°58S 140°45E **63 F3**
Naradhan *Australia* 33°34S 146°17E **63 E4**
Naraini *India* 25°11N 80°29E **43 G9**
Naranjos *Mexico* 21°21N 97°41W **87 C5**
Narasapur *India* 16°26N 81°40E **41 L12**
Narathiwat *Thailand* 6°30N 101°48E **39 J3**
Narayangadh = Bharatpur
  Nepal 27°34N 84°10E **43 F11**
Narayanganj *Bangla.* 23°40N 90°33E **41 H17**
Narayanpet *India* 16°45N 77°30E **40 L10**
Narberth *U.K.* 51°47N 4°44W **13 F3**
Narbonne *France* 43°11N 3°0E **20 E5**
Nardin *Iran* 37°3N 55°59E **45 B7**
Nardò *Italy* 40°11N 18°2E **23 D8**
Narembeen *Australia* 32°7S 118°24E **61 F2**
Narendranagar *India* 30°10N 78°18E **42 D8**
Nares Str. *Arctic* 80°0N 70°0W **69 B18**
Naretha *Australia* 31°0S 124°45E **61 F3**
Narew → *Poland* 52°26N 20°41E **17 B11**
Nari → *Pakistan* 28°0N 67°40E **42 F2**
Narin *Afghan.* 36°5N 69°0E **40 A6**
Narindra, Helodranon' i
  Madag. 14°55S 47°30E **57 A8**
Narita *Japan* 35°47N 140°19E **31 G10**
Nariva Swamp
  Trin. & Tob. 10°26N 61°4W **93 K15**
Narmada → *India* 21°38N 72°36E **42 J5**
Narnaul *India* 28°5N 76°11E **42 E7**
Narodnaya *Russia* 65°5N 59°58E **18 A10**
Narok *Kenya* 1°55S 35°52E **54 C4**
Narooma *Australia* 36°14S 150°4E **63 F5**
Narowal *Pakistan* 32°6N 74°52E **42 C6**
Narrabri *Australia* 30°19S 149°46E **63 E4**
Narran → *Australia* 28°37S 148°12E **63 D4**
Narrandera *Australia* 34°42S 146°31E **63 E4**
Narrogin *Australia* 32°58S 117°14E **61 F2**
Narromine *Australia* 32°12S 148°12E **63 E4**
Narrow Hills △ *Canada* 54°0N 104°37W **71 C8**
Narsimhapur *India* 22°54N 79°14E **43 H8**
Narsinghgarh *India* 23°45N 76°40E **42 H7**
Naruto *Japan* 34°11N 134°37E **31 G7**
Narva *Estonia* 59°23N 28°12E **18 C4**
Narva → *Russia* 59°27N 28°2E **9 G23**
Narva Bay = Narva Laht
  Estonia 59°35N 27°35E **9 G22**
Narva Laht *Estonia* 59°35N 27°35E **9 G22**
Narvik *Norway* 68°28N 17°26E **8 B17**
Narwana *India* 29°39N 76°6E **42 E7**
Narwinbi ☉ *Australia* 16°7S 136°17E **62 B2**
Naryan-Mar *Russia* 67°42N 53°12E **18 A9**
Narym *Russia* 59°0N 81°30E **28 D9**
Naryn *Kyrgyzstan* 41°26N 75°58E **28 E8**
Naryn Qum *Kazakhstan* 47°30N 49°0E **28 E5**
Nasa *Norway* 66°29N 15°23E **8 C16**
Nasau *Fiji* 17°19S 179°27E **59 a**
Nasca = Nazca *Peru* 14°50S 74°57W **92 F4**
Naseby *N.Z.* 45°1S 170°10E **59 F3**
Naselle *U.S.A.* 46°22N 123°49W **78 D3**
Naser, Buheirat en
  Egypt 23°0N 32°30E **51 D12**
Nashik = Nasik *India* 19°58N 73°50E **40 K8**

Nashua *Mont., U.S.A.* 48°8N 106°22W **76 B10**
Nashua *N.H., U.S.A.* 42°45N 71°28W **83 D13**
Nashville *Ark., U.S.A.* 33°57N 93°51W **84 E8**
Nashville *Ga., U.S.A.* 31°12N 83°15W **85 F13**
Nashville *Tenn., U.S.A.* 36°10N 86°47W **85 C11**
Nasik *India* 19°58N 73°50E **40 K8**
Nasirabad *India* 26°15N 74°45E **42 F6**
Nasirabad *Pakistan* 28°23N 68°24E **42 E3**
Nasiri = Ahvāz *Iran* 31°20N 48°40E **45 D6**
Nasiriyah = An Nāşirīyah
  Iraq 31°0N 46°15E **44 D5**
Naskaupi → *Canada* 53°47N 60°51W **73 B7**
Naşrābād *Iran* 34°8N 51°26E **45 C6**
Naşrīān-e Pā'īn *Iran* 32°52N 46°52E **45 C5**
Nass → *Canada* 55°0N 129°40W **70 C3**
Nassau *Bahamas* 25°5N 77°20W **88 A4**
Nassau *U.S.A.* 42°31N 73°37W **83 D11**
Nassau, B. *Chile* 55°20S 68°0W **96 H3**
Nasser, L. = Naser, Buheirat en
  Egypt 23°0N 32°30E **51 D12**
Nässjö *Sweden* 57°39N 14°42E **9 H16**
Nastapoka → *Canada* 56°55N 76°33W **72 A4**
Nastapoka, Is. *Canada* 56°55N 76°50W **72 A4**
Nata *Botswana* 20°12S 26°12E **56 C4**
Nata → *Botswana* 20°14S 26°10E **56 C4**
Natal *Brazil* 5°47S 35°13W **93 E11**
Natal *Indonesia* 0°35N 99°7E **36 D1**
Natal Drakensberg △
  S. Africa 29°27S 29°30E **57 D4**
Natanz *Iran* 33°30N 51°55E **45 C6**
Natashquan *Canada* 50°14N 61°46W **73 B7**
Natashquan → *Canada* 50°7N 61°50W **73 B7**
Natchez *U.S.A.* 31°34N 91°24W **84 F9**
Natchitoches *U.S.A.* 31°46N 93°5W **84 F8**
Natewa B. *Fiji* 16°35S 179°40E **59 a**
Nathalia *Australia* 36°1S 145°13E **63 F4**
Nathdwara *India* 24°55N 73°50E **42 G5**
Nati, Pta. *Spain* 40°3N 3°50E **24 A10**
Natimuk *Australia* 36°42S 142°0E **63 F3**
Nation → *Canada* 55°30N 123°32W **70 B4**
National City *U.S.A.* 32°40N 117°5W **79 N9**
Natitingou *Benin* 10°20N 1°26E **50 F6**
Natividad, I. *Mexico* 27°52N 115°11W **86 B1**
Natkyizin *Burma* 14°57N 97°59E **38 E1**
Natron, L. *Tanzania* 2°20S 36°0E **54 C4**
Natrona Heights *U.S.A.* 40°37N 79°44W **82 F5**
Natukanaoka Pan
  Namibia 18°40S 15°45E **56 B2**
Natuna Besar, Kepulauan
  Indonesia 4°0N 108°15E **36 D3**
Natuna Is. = Natuna Besar,
  Kepulauan *Indonesia* 4°0N 108°15E **36 D3**
Natuna Selatan, Kepulauan
  Indonesia 2°45N 109°0E **36 D3**
Natural Bridge *U.S.A.* 44°5N 75°30W **83 B9**
Natural Bridges △
  U.S.A. 37°36N 110°0W **77 H9**
Naturaliste, C. *Tas.,*
  Australia 40°50S 148°15E **63 G4**
Naturaliste, C. *W. Austral.,*
  Australia 33°32S 115°0E **61 F2**
Naturaliste Plateau
  Ind. Oc. 34°0S 112°0E **64 L3**
Nau Qala *Afghan.* 34°5N 68°5E **42 B3**
Naugatuck *U.S.A.* 41°30N 73°3W **83 E11**
Naujaat = Repulse Bay
  Canada 66°30N 86°30W **69 D14**
Naumburg *Germany* 51°9N 11°47E **16 C6**
Nauru ■ *Pac. Oc.* 1°0S 166°0E **58 B9**
Naushahra = Nowshera
  Pakistan 34°0N 72°0E **40 C8**
Naushahro *Pakistan* 26°50N 68°7E **42 F3**
Naushon I. *U.S.A.* 41°29N 70°45W **83 E14**
Nausori *Fiji* 18°2S 178°32E **59 a**
Nauta *Peru* 4°31S 73°35W **92 D4**
Nautanwa *India* 27°20N 83°25E **43 F10**
Naute → *Namibia* 26°55S 17°57E **56 D2**
Nautla *Mexico* 20°13N 96°47W **87 C5**
Nava *Mexico* 28°25N 100°45W **86 B4**
Navadwip *India* 23°34N 88°20E **43 H13**
Navahrudak *Belarus* 53°40N 25°50E **17 B13**
Navajo Res. *U.S.A.* 36°48N 107°36W **77 H10**
Navalmoral de la Mata
  Spain 39°52N 5°33W **21 C3**
Navan = An Uaimh
  Ireland 53°39N 6°41W **10 C5**
Navarin, Mys *Russia* 62°15N 179°5E **29 C18**
Navarino, I. *Chile* 55°0S 67°40W **96 H3**
Navarra □ *Spain* 42°40N 1°40W **21 A5**
Navarre *U.S.A.* 40°43N 81°31W **82 F3**
Navarro → *U.S.A.* 39°11N 123°45W **78 F3**
Navasota *U.S.A.* 30°23N 96°5W **84 F6**
Navassa I. *W. Indies* 18°30N 75°0W **89 C5**
Naver → *U.K.* 58°32N 4°14W **11 C4**
Navibandar *India* 21°26N 69°48E **42 J3**
Navidad *Chile* 33°57S 71°50W **94 C1**
Naviraí *Brazil* 23°8S 54°13W **95 A5**
Naviti *Fiji* 17°7S 177°15E **59 a**
Navlakhi *India* 22°58N 70°28E **42 H4**
Navodari *Romania* 44°19N 28°36E **17 F15**
Navoiy *Uzbekistan* 40°9N 65°22E **28 E7**
Navojoa *Mexico* 27°6N 109°26W **86 B3**
Navolato *Mexico* 24°47N 107°42W **86 C3**
Navsari *India* 20°57N 72°59E **40 J8**
Navua *Fiji* 18°12S 178°11E **59 a**
Nawa Kot *Pakistan* 28°21N 71°24E **42 E4**
Nawab Khan *Pakistan* 30°17N 69°12E **42 D3**
Nawabganj *Ut. P., India* 26°56N 81°14E **43 F9**
Nawabganj *Ut. P., India* 28°32N 79°40E **43 E8**
Nawabshah *Pakistan* 26°15N 68°25E **42 F3**
Nawada *India* 24°50N 85°33E **43 G11**
Nawakot *Nepal* 27°55N 85°10E **43 F11**
Nawalgarh *India* 27°50N 75°15E **42 F6**
Nawanshahr *India* 32°33N 74°48E **43 C6**
Nawar, Dasht-i- *Afghan.* 33°52N 68°0E **40 C5**
Nawoiy = Navoiy
  Uzbekistan 40°9N 65°22E **28 E7**
Naxçıvan *Azerbaijan* 39°12N 45°15E **44 B5**
Naxçıvan □ *Azerbaijan* 39°25N 45°26E **44 B5**

Naxos *Greece* 37°8N 25°25E **23 F11**
Nay, Mui = Varella, Mui
  Vietnam 12°54N 109°26E **38 F7**
Nãy Band *Būshehr, Iran* 27°20N 52°40E **45 E7**
Nãy Band *Khorāsān, Iran* 32°20N 57°34E **45 C8**
Nayakhan *Russia* 61°56N 159°0E **29 C16**
Nayarit □ *Mexico* 22°0N 105°0W **86 C4**
Nayau *Fiji* 18°6S 178°10E **59 a**
Nayoro *Japan* 44°21N 142°28E **30 B11**
Naypyidaw *Burma* 19°44N 96°12E **38 C1**
Nayyāl, W. → *Si. Arabia* 28°35N 39°4E **44 D3**
Nazaré *Brazil* 13°2S 39°0W **93 F11**
Nazareth = Nazerat
  Israel 32°42N 35°17E **46 C4**
Nazareth *U.S.A.* 40°44N 75°19W **83 F9**
Nazarovo *Russia* 57°2N 90°40E **29 D10**
Nazas *Mexico* 25°14N 104°8W **86 B4**
Nazas → *Mexico* 25°12N 104°12W **86 B4**
Nazca *Peru* 14°50S 74°57W **92 F4**
Nazca Ridge *Pac. Oc.* 20°0S 80°0W **65 K19**
Naze *Japan* 28°22N 129°27E **31 K4**
Naze, The *U.K.* 51°53N 1°18E **13 F9**
Nazerat *Israel* 32°42N 35°17E **46 C4**
Nāzik *Iran* 39°1N 45°4E **44 B5**
Nazilli *Turkey* 37°55N 28°15E **23 F13**
Nazko *Canada* 53°1N 123°37W **70 C4**
Nazko → *Canada* 53°7N 123°34W **70 C4**
Nazret *Ethiopia* 8°32N 39°22E **47 F2**
Nchanga *Zambia* 12°30S 27°49E **55 E2**
Ncheu *Malawi* 14°50S 34°47E **55 E3**
Ndala *Tanzania* 4°45S 33°15E **54 C3**
Ndalatando *Angola* 9°12S 14°48E **52 F2**
Ndareda *Tanzania* 4°12S 35°30E **54 C4**
Ndélé *C.A.R.* 8°25N 20°36E **52 C4**
Ndjamena *Chad* 12°10N 14°59E **51 F8**
Ndola *Zambia* 13°0S 28°34E **55 E2**
Ndomo → *S. Africa* 26°52S 32°15E **57 D5**
Ndoto Mts. *Kenya* 2°0N 37°0E **54 B4**
Nduguti *Tanzania* 4°18S 34°41E **54 C3**
Neagh, Lough *U.K.* 54°37N 6°25W **10 B5**
Neah Bay *U.S.A.* 48°22N 124°37W **78 B2**
Neale, L. *Australia* 24°15S 130°0E **60 D5**
Neales → *Australia* 28°8S 136°47E **63 D2**
Neapoli *Greece* 35°15N 25°37E **25 D7**
Near Is. *U.S.A.* 52°30N 174°0E **74 E2**
Neath *U.K.* 51°39N 3°48W **13 F4**
Neath Port Talbot □
  U.K. 51°42N 3°45W **13 F4**
Nebbi *Uganda* 2°28N 31°6E **54 B3**
Nebine Cr. → *Australia* 29°27S 146°56E **63 D4**
Nebitdag = Balkanabat
  Turkmenistan 39°30N 54°22E **45 B7**
Nebo *Australia* 21°42S 148°42E **62 C4**
Nebraska □ *U.S.A.* 41°30N 99°30W **80 E4**
Nebraska City *U.S.A.* 40°41N 95°52W **80 E6**
Nébrodi, Monti *Italy* 37°54N 14°35E **22 F6**
Necedah *U.S.A.* 44°2N 90°4W **80 C8**
Nechako → *Canada* 53°55N 122°42W **70 C4**
Neches → *U.S.A.* 29°58N 93°51W **84 G8**
Neckar → *Germany* 49°27N 8°29E **16 D5**
Necker I. *U.S.A.* 23°35N 164°42W **75 L7**
Necochea *Argentina* 38°30S 58°50W **94 D4**
Needles *Canada* 49°53N 118°7W **70 D5**
Needles *U.S.A.* 34°51N 114°37W **79 L12**
Needles, The *U.K.* 50°39N 1°35W **13 G6**
Neembucú □ *Paraguay* 27°0S 58°0W **94 B4**
Neemuch = Nimach
  India 24°30N 74°56E **42 G6**
Neenah *U.S.A.* 44°11N 88°28W **80 C9**
Neepawa *Canada* 50°15N 99°30W **71 C9**
Neftçala *Azerbaijan* 39°19N 49°12E **45 B6**
Neftegorsk *Russia* 53°1N 142°58E **29 D15**
Neftekumsk *Russia* 44°46N 44°50E **19 F7**
Nefteyugansk *Russia* 61°5N 72°42E **28 C8**
Nefyn *U.K.* 52°56N 4°31W **12 E3**
Negapatam = Nagappattinam
  India 10°46N 79°51E **40 P11**
Negara *Indonesia* 8°22S 114°37E **37 J17**
Negaunee *U.S.A.* 46°30N 87°36W **80 B10**
Negele *Ethiopia* 5°20N 39°36E **47 F2**
Negev Desert = Hanegev
  Israel 30°50N 35°0E **46 E4**
Negombo *Sri Lanka* 7°12N 79°50E **40 R11**
Negotin *Serbia* 44°16N 22°37E **23 B10**
Negra, Pta. *Mauritania* 22°54N 16°18W **50 D2**
Negra, Pta. *Peru* 6°6S 81°10W **92 E2**
Negrais, C. = Maudin Sun
  Burma 16°0N 94°30E **41 M19**
Negril *Jamaica* 18°22N 78°20W **88 a**
Negro → *Argentina* 41°2S 62°47W **96 E4**
Negro → *Brazil* 3°0S 60°0W **92 D7**
Negro → *Uruguay* 33°24S 58°22W **94 C4**
Negros *Phil.* 9°30N 122°40E **37 C6**
Neguac *Canada* 47°15N 65°5W **73 C6**
Nehalem → *U.S.A.* 45°40N 123°56W **78 E3**
Nehāvand *Iran* 35°56N 49°31E **45 C6**
Nehbandān *Iran* 31°35N 60°5E **45 D9**
Nei Monggol Zizhiqu □
  China 42°0N 112°0E **34 D7**
Neiafu *Tonga* 18°39S 173°59W **59 c**
Neiges, Piton des *Réunion* 21°5S 55°29E **53 c**
Neijiang *China* 29°35N 104°55E **32 D5**
Neilingding Dao *China* 22°25N 113°48E **33 G10**
Neillsville *U.S.A.* 44°34N 90°36W **80 C8**
Neilton *U.S.A.* 47°25N 123°53W **78 C3**
Neiqiu *China* 37°15N 114°30E **34 F8**
Neiva *Colombia* 2°56N 75°18W **92 C3**
Neixiang *China* 33°10N 111°52E **34 H6**
Nejanilini L. *Canada* 59°33N 97°48W **71 B9**
Nejd = Najd *Si. Arabia* 26°30N 42°0E **44 E4**
Nekā *Iran* 36°39N 53°19E **45 B7**
Nekemte *Ethiopia* 9°4N 36°30E **47 F2**
Neksø *Denmark* 55°4N 15°8E **9 J16**
Nelia *Australia* 20°39S 142°12E **62 C3**
Neligh *U.S.A.* 42°8N 98°2W **80 D4**
Nelkan *Russia* 57°40N 136°4E **29 D14**
Nellore *India* 14°27N 79°59E **40 M11**

Nelson *Canada* 49°30N 117°20W **70 D5**
Nelson *N.Z.* 41°18S 173°16E **59 D4**
Nelson *U.K.* 53°50N 2°13W **12 D5**
Nelson *Ariz., U.S.A.* 35°31N 113°19W **77 J7**
Nelson *Nev., U.S.A.* 35°42N 114°49W **79 K12**
Nelson → *Canada* 54°33N 98°2W **71 C9**
Nelson, C. *Australia* 38°26S 141°32E **63 F3**
Nelson, Estrecho *Chile* 51°30S 75°0W **96 G2**
Nelson Forks *Canada* 59°30N 124°0W **70 B4**
Nelson House *Canada* 55°47N 98°51W **71 B9**
Nelson L. *Canada* 55°48N 100°7W **71 B8**
Nelson Lakes △ *N.Z.* 41°55S 172°44E **59 D4**
Nelspoort *S. Africa* 32°7S 23°0E **56 E3**
Nelspruit *S. Africa* 25°29S 30°59E **57 D5**
Néma *Mauritania* 16°40N 7°15W **50 E4**
Neman = Nemunas →
  Lithuania 55°25N 21°10E **9 J19**
Nembrala *Indonesia* 10°53S 122°50E **60 B3**
Nemeiben L. *Canada* 55°20N 105°20W **71 B7**
Nemiscau *Canada* 51°18N 76°54W **72 B4**
Nemiscau, L. *Canada* 51°25N 76°40W **72 B4**
Nemunas → *Lithuania* 55°25N 21°10E **9 J19**
Nemuro *Japan* 43°20N 145°35E **30 C12**
Nemuro-Kaikyō *Japan* 43°30N 145°30E **30 C12**
Nen Jiang → *China* 45°28N 124°30E **35 B13**
Nenagh *Ireland* 52°52N 8°11W **10 D3**
Nenana *U.S.A.* 64°34N 149°5W **74 C10**
Nene → *U.K.* 52°49N 0°11E **13 E8**
Nenjiang *China* 49°10N 125°10E **33 B7**
Neno *Malawi* 15°25S 34°40E **55 F3**
Neodesha *U.S.A.* 37°25N 95°41W **80 G6**
Neora Valley △ *India* 27°0N 88°45E **43 F13**
Neosho *U.S.A.* 36°52N 94°22W **80 G6**
Neosho → *U.S.A.* 36°48N 95°18W **84 C7**
Nepal ■ *Asia* 28°0N 84°30E **43 F11**
Nepalganj *Nepal* 28°5N 81°40E **43 E9**
Nepalganj Road *India* 28°1N 81°41E **43 E9**
Nephi *U.S.A.* 39°43N 111°50W **76 G8**
Nephin *Ireland* 54°1N 9°22W **10 B2**
Nephin Beg Range *Ireland* 54°0N 9°40W **10 C2**
Neptune *U.S.A.* 40°13N 74°2W **83 F10**
Neqāb *Iran* 36°42N 57°25E **45 B8**
Nerang *Australia* 27°58S 153°20E **63 D5**
Nerastro, Sarīr *Libya* 24°20N 20°37E **51 D10**
Nerchinsk *Russia* 52°0N 116°39E **29 D12**
Néret, L. *Canada* 54°45N 70°44W **73 B5**
Neretva → *Croatia* 43°1N 17°27E **23 C7**
Neringa *Lithuania* 55°20N 21°5E **9 J19**
Neris → *Lithuania* 55°8N 24°16E **9 J21**
Neryungri *Russia* 57°38N 124°28E **29 D13**
Nescopeck *U.S.A.* 41°3N 76°12W **83 E8**
Neskantaga *Canada* 52°14N 87°53W **72 B2**
Ness, L. *U.K.* 57°15N 4°32W **11 D4**
Ness City *U.S.A.* 38°27N 99°54W **80 F4**
Nesterov *Ukraine* 50°4N 23°58E **17 C12**
Nestos → *Europe* 40°54N 24°49E **23 D11**
Nesvizh = Nyasvizh
  Belarus 53°14N 26°38E **17 B14**
Netanya *Israel* 32°20N 34°51E **46 C3**
Netarhat *India* 23°29N 84°16E **43 H11**
Nete → *Belgium* 51°7N 4°14E **15 C4**
Netherdale *Australia* 21°10S 148°33E **62 b**
Netherlands ■ *Europe* 52°0N 5°30E **15 C5**
Netherlands Antilles ☑
  W. Indies 12°15N 69°0W **92 A5**
Netrang *India* 21°39N 73°21E **42 J5**
Nettilling L. *Canada* 66°30N 71°0W **69 C17**
Netzahualcóyotl, Presa
  Mexico 17°8N 93°35W **87 D6**
Neubrandenburg
  Germany 53°33N 13°15E **16 B7**
Neuchâtel *Switz.* 47°0N 6°55E **20 C7**
Neuchâtel, Lac de *Switz.* 46°53N 6°50E **20 C7**
Neufchâteau *Belgium* 49°50N 5°25E **15 E5**
Neumayer *Antarctica* 71°0S 68°30W **5 D17**
Neumünster *Germany* 54°4N 9°58E **16 A5**
Neunkirchen *Germany* 49°20N 7°9E **16 D4**
Neuquén *Argentina* 38°55S 68°0W **96 D3**
Neuquén □ *Argentina* 38°0S 69°50W **94 D2**
Neuruppin *Germany* 52°55N 12°48E **16 B7**
Neuse → *U.S.A.* 35°6N 76°29W **85 D16**
Neusiedler See *Austria* 47°50N 16°47E **17 E9**
Neustrelitz *Germany* 53°21N 13°4E **16 B7**
Neva → *Russia* 59°56N 30°20E **18 C5**
Nevada *Iowa, U.S.A.* 42°1N 93°27W **80 D7**
Nevada *Mo., U.S.A.* 37°51N 94°22W **80 G6**
Nevada □ *U.S.A.* 39°0N 117°0W **76 G5**
Nevada City *U.S.A.* 39°16N 121°1W **78 F6**
Nevado, Cerro *Argentina* 35°30S 68°32W **94 D2**
Nevado de Colima = Volcán de
  Colima △ *Mexico* 19°30N 103°40W **86 D4**
Nevado de Tres Cruces △
  Chile 27°13S 69°5W **94 B2**
Nevel *Russia* 56°0N 29°55E **18 C4**
Nevelsk *Russia* 46°40N 141°51E **29 E15**
Nevers *France* 47°0N 3°9E **20 C5**
Nevertire *Australia* 31°50S 147°44E **63 E4**
Neville *Canada* 49°58N 107°39W **71 D7**
Nevinnomyssk *Russia* 44°40N 42°0E **19 F7**
Nevis *St. Kitts & Nevis* 17°0N 62°30W **89 C7**
Nevşehir *Turkey* 38°33N 34°40E **44 B2**
Nevyansk *Russia* 57°30N 60°13E **18 C11**
New Aiyansh *Canada* 55°12N 129°4W **70 B3**
New Albany *Ind.,*
  U.S.A. 38°18N 85°49W **81 F11**
New Albany *Miss.,*
  U.S.A. 34°29N 89°0W **85 D10**
New Albany *Pa., U.S.A.* 41°36N 76°27W **83 E8**
New Amsterdam *Guyana* 6°15N 57°36W **92 B7**
New Baltimore *U.S.A.* 42°41N 82°44W **82 D2**
New Bedford *U.S.A.* 41°38N 70°56W **83 E14**
New Berlin *N.Y., U.S.A.* 42°37N 75°20W **83 D9**
New Berlin *Pa., U.S.A.* 40°50N 76°57W **82 F8**
New Bern *U.S.A.* 35°7N 77°3W **85 D16**
New Bethlehem *U.S.A.* 41°0N 79°20W **82 F5**
New Bight *Bahamas* 24°19N 75°24W **89 B4**
New Bloomfield *U.S.A.* 40°25N 77°11W **82 F7**

New Boston U.S.A. 33°28N 94°25W 84 E7
New Braunfels U.S.A. 29°42N 98°8W 84 G5
New Brighton N.Z. 43°29S 172°43E 59 E4
New Brighton U.K. 40°42N 80°19W 82 F4
New Britain Papua N. G. 5°50S 150°20E 58 B8
New Britain U.S.A. 41°40N 72°47W 83 E12
New Brunswick U.S.A. 40°30N 74°27W 83 F10
New Brunswick □ Canada 46°50N 66°30W 73 C6
New Caledonia ☑ Pac. Oc. 21°0S 165°0E 58 D9
New Caledonia Trough Pac. Oc. 30°0S 165°0E 64 L8
New Castle = Castilla-La Mancha □ Spain 39°30N 3°30W 21 C4
New Castle Ind., U.S.A. 39°55N 85°22W 81 F11
New Castle Pa., U.S.A. 41°0N 80°21W 82 F4
New City U.S.A. 41°9N 73°59W 83 E11
New Concord U.S.A. 39°59N 81°54W 82 G3
New Cumberland U.S.A. 40°30N 80°36W 82 F4
New Cuyama U.S.A. 34°57N 119°38W 79 L7
New Delhi India 28°36N 77°11E 42 E7
New Denver Canada 50°0N 117°25W 70 D5
New Don Pedro Res. U.S.A. 37°43N 120°24W 78 H6
New England U.S.A. 43°0N 71°0W 75 G25
New England N. Dak., U.S.A. 46°32N 102°52W 80 B2
New England Ra. Australia 30°20S 151°45E 63 E5
New Forest △ U.K. 50°53N 1°34W 13 G6
New Galloway U.K. 55°5N 4°9W 11 F4
New Glasgow Canada 45°35N 62°36W 73 C7
New Guinea Oceania 4°0S 136°0E 58 B6
New Hamburg Canada 43°23N 80°42W 82 C4
New Hampshire □ U.S.A. 44°0N 71°30W 83 C13
New Hampton U.S.A. 43°3N 92°19W 80 D7
New Hanover S. Africa 29°22S 30°31E 57 D5
New Hartford U.S.A. 43°4N 75°18W 83 C9
New Haven Conn., U.S.A. 41°18N 72°55W 83 E12
New Haven Mich., U.S.A. 42°44N 82°48W 82 D2
New Haven N.Y., U.S.A. 43°28N 76°18W 83 C8
New Hazelton Canada 55°20N 127°30W 70 B3
New Hebrides = Vanuatu ■ Pac. Oc. 15°0S 168°0E 58 C9
New Holland U.S.A. 40°6N 76°5W 83 F8
New Iberia U.S.A. 30°1N 91°49W 84 F9
New Ireland Papua N. G. 3°20S 151°50E 58 B8
New Jersey □ U.S.A. 40°0N 74°30W 81 F16
New Kensington U.S.A. 40°34N 79°46W 82 F5
New Lexington U.S.A. 39°43N 82°13W 81 F12
New Liskeard Canada 47°31N 79°41W 72 C4
New London Conn., U.S.A. 41°22N 72°6W 83 E12
New London Ohio, U.S.A. 41°5N 82°24W 82 E2
New London Wis., U.S.A. 44°23N 88°45W 80 C9
New Madrid U.S.A. 36°36N 89°32W 80 G9
New Martinsville U.S.A. 39°39N 80°52W 81 F13
New Meadows U.S.A. 44°58N 116°18W 76 D5
New Melones L. U.S.A. 37°57N 120°31W 78 H6
New Mexico □ U.S.A. 34°30N 106°0W 77 J11
New Milford Conn., U.S.A. 41°35N 73°25W 83 E11
New Milford Pa., U.S.A. 41°52N 75°44W 83 E9
New Moore I. Ind. Oc. 21°37N 89°12E 43 J13
New Norcia Australia 30°57S 116°13E 61 F2
New Norfolk Australia 42°46S 147°2E 63 G4
New Orleans U.S.A. 29°57N 90°4W 85 G9
New Philadelphia U.S.A. 40°30N 81°27W 82 F3
New Plymouth N.Z. 39°4S 174°5E 59 C5
New Plymouth U.S.A. 43°58N 116°49W 76 E5
New Port Richey U.S.A. 28°16N 82°43W 85 G13
New Providence Bahamas 25°25N 78°35W 88 A4
New Quay U.K. 52°13N 4°21W 13 E3
New Radnor U.K. 52°15N 3°9W 13 E4
New Richmond Canada 48°15N 65°45W 73 C6
New Richmond U.S.A. 45°7N 92°32W 80 C7
New River Gorge △ U.S.A. 37°53N 81°5W 81 G13
New Roads U.S.A. 30°42N 91°26W 84 F9
New Rochelle U.S.A. 40°55N 73°46W 83 F11
New Rockford U.S.A. 47°41N 99°8W 80 B4
New Romney U.K. 50°59N 0°57E 13 G8
New Ross Ireland 52°23N 6°57W 10 D5
New Salem U.S.A. 46°51N 101°25W 80 B4
New Scone = Scone U.K. 56°25N 3°24W 11 E5
New Siberian I. = Novaya Sibir, Ostrov Russia 75°10N 150°0E 29 B16
New Siberian Is. = Novosibirskiye Ostrova Russia 75°0N 142°0E 29 B15
New Smyrna Beach U.S.A. 29°1N 80°56W 85 G14
New South Wales □ Australia 33°0S 146°0E 63 E4
New Tecumseth = Alliston Canada 44°9N 79°52W 82 B5
New Town U.S.A. 47°59N 102°30W 80 B2
New Tredegar U.K. 51°44N 3°16W 13 F4
New Ulm U.S.A. 44°19N 94°28W 80 C7
New Waterford Canada 46°13N 60°4W 73 C7
New Westminster Canada 49°13N 122°55W 78 A4
New York U.S.A. 40°43N 74°0W 83 F11
New York □ U.S.A. 43°0N 75°0W 83 D9
New York J.F. Kennedy Int. ✈ (JFK) U.S.A. 40°38N 73°47W 83 F11
New Zealand ■ Oceania 40°0S 176°0E 59 D6
Newaj → India 24°24N 76°49E 42 G7
Newala Tanzania 10°58S 39°18E 54 E4
Newark Del., U.S.A. 39°41N 75°46W 81 F16
Newark N.J., U.S.A. 40°44N 74°10W 83 F10

Newark N.Y., U.S.A. 43°3N 77°6W 82 C7
Newark Ohio, U.S.A. 40°3N 82°24W 82 F2
Newark Liberty Int. ✈ (EWR) U.S.A. 40°42N 74°10W 83 F10
Newark-on-Trent U.K. 53°5N 0°48W 12 D7
Newark Valley U.S.A. 42°14N 76°11W 83 D8
Newberg U.S.A. 45°18N 122°58W 76 D2
Newberry Mich., U.S.A. 46°21N 85°30W 81 B11
Newberry S.C., U.S.A. 34°17N 81°37W 85 D14
Newberry Springs U.S.A. 34°50N 116°41W 79 L10
Newboro L. Canada 44°38N 76°20W 83 B8
Newbridge = Droichead Nua Ireland 53°11N 6°48W 10 C5
Newburgh Canada 44°19N 76°52W 82 B8
Newburgh U.S.A. 41°30N 74°1W 83 E10
Newbury U.K. 51°24N 1°20W 13 F6
Newbury N.H., U.S.A. 43°19N 72°3W 83 C12
Newbury Vt., U.S.A. 44°5N 72°4W 83 B12
Newburyport U.S.A. 42°49N 70°53W 83 D14
Newcastle Australia 33°0S 151°46E 63 E5
Newcastle N.B., Canada 47°1N 65°38W 73 C6
Newcastle Ont., Canada 43°55N 78°35W 72 D4
Newcastle S. Africa 27°45S 29°58E 57 D4
Newcastle Calif., U.S.A. 38°53N 121°8W 78 G5
Newcastle Wyo., U.S.A. 43°50N 104°11W 76 E11
Newcastle Emlyn U.K. 52°2N 4°28W 13 E3
Newcastle-under-Lyme U.K. 53°1N 2°14W 12 D5
Newcastle-upon-Tyne U.K. 54°58N 1°36W 12 C6
Newcastle Waters Australia 17°30S 133°28E 62 B1
Newcastle West Ireland 52°27N 9°3W 10 D2
Newcomb U.S.A. 43°58N 74°10W 83 C10
Newcomerstown U.S.A. 40°16N 81°36W 82 F3
Newdegate Australia 33°6S 119°0E 61 F2
Newell Australia 16°20S 145°16E 62 B4
Newell U.S.A. 44°43N 103°25W 80 C2
Newenham, C. U.S.A. 58°39N 162°11W 74 D7
Newfane U.S.A. 43°17N 78°43W 82 C6
Newfield U.S.A. 42°18N 76°33W 83 D8
Newfound L. U.S.A. 43°40N 71°47W 83 C13
Newfoundland Canada 49°0N 55°0W 73 C8
Newfoundland U.S.A. 41°18N 75°19W 83 E9
Newfoundland & Labrador □ Canada 53°0N 58°0W 73 B8
Newhaven U.K. 50°47N 0°3E 13 G8
Newkirk U.S.A. 36°53N 97°3W 84 C6
Newlyn U.K. 50°6N 5°34W 13 G2
Newman Australia 23°18S 119°45E 60 D2
Newman U.S.A. 37°19N 121°1W 78 H5
Newmarket Canada 44°3N 79°28W 82 B5
Newmarket Ireland 52°13N 9°0W 10 D2
Newmarket U.K. 52°15N 0°25E 13 E8
Newman U.S.A. 43°5N 70°56W 83 C14
Newnan U.S.A. 33°23N 84°48W 85 E12
Newport Ireland 53°53N 9°33W 10 C2
Newport I. of W., U.K. 50°42N 1°17W 13 G6
Newport Newport, U.K. 51°35N 3°0W 13 F5
Newport Ark., U.S.A. 35°37N 91°16W 84 D9
Newport Ky., U.S.A. 39°5N 84°29W 81 F11
Newport N.H., U.S.A. 43°22N 72°10W 83 C12
Newport N.Y., U.S.A. 43°11N 75°1W 83 C9
Newport Oreg., U.S.A. 44°39N 124°3W 76 D1
Newport Pa., U.S.A. 40°29N 77°8W 82 F7
Newport R.I., U.S.A. 41°29N 71°19W 83 E13
Newport Tenn., U.S.A. 35°58N 83°11W 85 D13
Newport Vt., U.S.A. 44°56N 72°13W 83 B12
Newport □ U.K. 51°33N 3°1W 13 F4
Newport Beach U.S.A. 33°37N 117°56W 79 M9
Newport News U.S.A. 36°58N 76°25W 81 G15
Newport Pagnell U.K. 52°5N 0°43W 13 E7
Newquay U.K. 50°25N 5°6W 13 G2
Newry U.K. 54°11N 6°21W 10 B5
Newry Islands △ Australia 20°51S 148°56E 62 b
Newton Ill., U.S.A. 38°59N 88°10W 80 F9
Newton Iowa, U.S.A. 41°42N 93°3W 80 E7
Newton Kans., U.S.A. 38°3N 97°21W 80 F5
Newton Mass., U.S.A. 42°21N 71°12W 83 D13
Newton Miss., U.S.A. 32°19N 89°10W 85 E10
Newton N.C., U.S.A. 35°40N 81°13W 85 D14
Newton N.J., U.S.A. 41°3N 74°45W 83 E10
Newton Tex., U.S.A. 30°51N 93°46W 84 F8
Newton Abbot U.K. 50°32N 3°37W 13 G4
Newton Aycliffe U.K. 54°37N 1°34W 12 C6
Newton Falls N.Y., U.S.A. 44°12N 74°59W 83 B10
Newton Falls Ohio, U.S.A. 41°11N 80°59W 82 E4
Newton Stewart U.K. 54°57N 4°30W 11 G4
Newtonmore U.K. 57°4N 4°8W 11 D4
Newtown U.K. 52°31N 3°19W 13 E4
Newtownabbey U.K. 54°40N 5°56W 10 B6
Newtownards U.K. 54°36N 5°42W 10 B6
Newtownbarry = Bunclody Ireland 52°39N 6°40W 10 D5
Newtownstewart U.K. 54°43N 7°23W 10 B4
Newville U.S.A. 40°10N 77°24W 82 F7
Neya Russia 58°21N 43°49E 18 C7
Neyriz Iran 29°15N 54°19E 45 D7
Neyshābūr Iran 36°10N 58°50E 45 B8
Nezhin = Nizhyn Ukraine 51°5N 31°55E 19 D5
Nezperce U.S.A. 46°14N 116°14W 76 C5
Ngaanyatjarra ◎ Australia 22°40S 127°0E 60 D4
Ngabang Indonesia 0°23N 109°55E 36 D3
Ngabordamlu, Tanjung Indonesia 6°56S 134°11E 37 F8
N'Gage Angola 7°46S 15°15E 52 F3
Ngalurrtju ◎ Australia 22°44S 132°55E 60 D5

Ngami Depression Botswana 20°30S 22°46E 56 C3
Ngamo Zimbabwe 19°3S 27°32E 55 F2
Nganglong Kangri China 33°0N 81°0E 43 C9
Ngao Thailand 18°46N 99°59E 38 C2
Ngaoundéré Cameroon 7°15N 13°35E 52 C2
Ngapara N.Z. 44°57S 170°46E 59 F3
Ngara Tanzania 2°29S 30°40E 54 C3
Ngarluma ◎ Australia 21°29S 117°5E 60 D2
Ngawi Indonesia 7°24S 111°26E 37 G14
Ngcobo S. Africa 31°37S 28°0E 57 E4
Ngeru Uganda 0°27N 33°54E 54 B3
Ngoma Malawi 13°8S 33°45E 55 E3
Ngomahura Zimbabwe 20°26S 30°43E 55 G3
Ngomba Tanzania 8°20S 32°53E 55 D3
Ngomeni, Ras Kenya 2°59S 40°14E 54 C5
Ngong Kenya 1°22S 36°39E 54 C4
Ngoring Hu China 34°55N 97°5E 32 C4
Ngorongoro Tanzania 3°11S 35°32E 54 C4
Ngorongoro △ Tanzania 2°40S 35°30E 54 C4
Ngozi Burundi 2°54S 29°50E 54 C2
Ngudu Tanzania 2°58S 33°25E 54 C3
Nguigmi Niger 14°20N 13°20E 51 F8
Nguiu Australia 11°46S 130°38E 60 B5
Ngukurr Australia 14°44S 134°44E 62 A1
Ngundu Zimbabwe 18°11S 31°15E 55 F3
Ngunga Tanzania 3°37S 33°37E 54 C3
Nguru Nigeria 12°56N 10°29E 51 F8
Nguru Mts. Tanzania 6°0S 37°30E 54 D4
Ngusi Malawi 14°0S 34°50E 55 E3
Nguyen Binh Vietnam 22°39N 105°56E 38 A5
Nha Trang Vietnam 12°16N 109°10E 39 F7
Nhacoongo Mozam. 24°18S 35°14E 57 C6
Nhamaabué Mozam. 17°25S 35°5E 55 F4
Nhamundá → Brazil 2°12S 56°41W 93 D7
Nhangulaze, L. Mozam. 24°0S 34°30E 57 C5
Nharnuwangga, Wajarri and Ngarlawangga ◎ Australia 24°50S 118°0E 61 D2
Nhill Australia 36°18S 141°40E 63 F3
Nho Quan Vietnam 20°18N 105°45E 38 B5
Nhulunbuy Australia 12°10S 137°20E 62 A2
Nia-nia Dem. Rep. of the Congo 1°30N 27°40E 54 B2
Niafounké Mali 16°0N 4°5W 50 E5
Niagara Falls Canada 43°7N 79°5W 82 C5
Niagara Falls U.S.A. 43°5N 79°4W 82 C6
Niagara-on-the-Lake Canada 43°15N 79°4W 82 C5
Niah Malaysia 3°58N 113°46E 36 D4
Niamey Niger 13°27N 2°6E 50 F6
Niangara Dem. Rep. of the Congo 3°42N 27°50E 54 B2
Niantic U.S.A. 41°20N 72°11W 83 E12
Nias Indonesia 1°0N 97°30E 36 D1
Niassa □ Mozam. 13°30S 36°0E 55 E4
Niassa △ Mozam. 12°45S 36°57E 55 E4
Nibāk Si. Arabia 24°25N 50°50E 45 E7
Nicaragua ■ Cent. Amer. 11°40N 85°30W 88 D2
Nicaragua, L. de Nic. 12°0N 85°30W 88 D2
Nicastro Italy 38°59N 16°19E 22 E7
Nice France 43°42N 7°14E 20 E7
Niceville U.S.A. 30°31N 86°30W 85 F11
Nichicun, L. Canada 53°5N 71°0W 73 B5
Nichinan Japan 31°38N 131°23E 31 J5
Nicholás, Canal W. Indies 23°30N 80°5W 88 B3
Nicholasville U.S.A. 37°53N 84°34W 81 G11
Nichols U.S.A. 42°1N 76°22W 83 D8
Nicholson Australia 18°2S 128°54E 60 C4
Nicholson U.S.A. 41°37N 75°47W 83 E9
Nicholson → Australia 17°31S 139°36E 62 B2
Nicholson L. Canada 62°40N 102°40W 71 A8
Nicholson Ra. Australia 27°15S 116°45E 61 E2
Nicholville U.S.A. 44°41N 74°39W 83 B10
Nicobar Is. Ind. Oc. 8°0N 93°30E 27 H11
Nicola Canada 50°12N 120°40W 70 C4
Nicolls Town Bahamas 25°8N 78°0W 88 A4
Nicosia Cyprus 35°10N 33°25E 25 D12
Nicoya Costa Rica 10°9N 85°27W 88 D2
Nicoya, G. de Costa Rica 10°0N 85°0W 88 E3
Nicoya, Pen. de Costa Rica 9°45N 85°40W 88 E2
Nidd → U.K. 53°59N 1°23W 12 D6
Niedersachsen □ Germany 52°50N 9°0E 16 B5
Niekerkshoop S. Africa 29°19S 22°51E 56 D3
Niemba Dem. Rep. of the Congo 5°58S 28°24E 54 D2
Niemen = Nemunas → Lithuania 55°25N 21°10E 9 J19
Nienburg Germany 52°39N 9°13E 16 B5
Nieu Bethesda S. Africa 31°51S 24°34E 56 E3
Nieuw Amsterdam Suriname 5°53N 55°5W 93 B7
Nieuw Nickerie Suriname 6°0N 56°59W 93 B7
Nieuwoudtville S. Africa 31°23S 19°7E 56 E2
Nieuwpoort Belgium 51°8N 2°45E 15 C2
Nieves, Pico de las Canary Is. 27°57N 15°35W 24 G4
Niğde Turkey 37°58N 34°40E 44 B2
Nigel S. Africa 26°27S 28°25E 57 D4
Niger □ W. Afr. 17°30N 10°0E 50 E7
Niger → W. Afr. 5°33N 6°33E 50 G7
Nigeria ■ W. Afr. 8°30N 8°0E 50 G7
Nighasin India 28°14N 80°52E 43 E9
Nightcaps N.Z. 45°57S 168°2E 59 F2
Nihoa U.S.A. 23°6N 161°58W 75 L7
Nihon = Japan ■ Asia 36°0N 136°0E 31 G8
Nii-Jima Japan 34°20N 139°15E 31 G9
Niigata Japan 37°58N 139°0E 31 F9
Niigata □ Japan 37°15N 138°45E 31 F9
Niihama Japan 33°55N 133°16E 31 H6
Ni'ihau U.S.A. 21°54N 160°9W 75 L7
Niimi Japan 34°59N 133°28E 31 G6
Niitsu Japan 37°48N 139°7E 30 F9
Nijil Jordan 30°32N 35°33E 46 E4
Nijkerk Neths. 52°13N 5°30E 15 B5
Nijmegen Neths. 51°50N 5°52E 15 C5

Nijverdal Neths. 52°22N 6°28E 15 B6
Nīk Pey Iran 36°50N 48°10E 45 B6
Nikel Russia 69°24N 30°13E 8 B24
Nikiniki Indonesia 9°49S 124°30E 60 b
Nikkō Japan 36°45N 139°35E 31 F9
Nikkō △ Japan 36°56N 139°37E 31 F9
Nikolayev = Mykolayiv Ukraine 46°58N 32°0E 19 E5
Nikolayevsk Russia 50°0N 45°35E 19 E8
Nikolayevsk-na-Amur Russia 53°8N 140°44E 29 D15
Nikolskoye Russia 55°12N 166°0E 29 D17
Nikopol Ukraine 47°35N 34°25E 19 E5
Nikshahr Iran 26°15N 60°10E 45 E9
Nikšić Montenegro 42°50N 18°57E 23 C8
Nīl, Nahr en → Africa 30°10N 31°6E 51 B12
Nīl el Abyad → Sudan 15°38N 32°31E 51 E12
Nīl el Azraq → Sudan 15°38N 32°31E 51 E12
Nila Indonesia 6°44S 129°31E 37 F7
Niland U.S.A. 33°14N 115°31W 79 M11
Nile = Nīl, Nahr en → Africa 30°10N 31°6E 51 B12
Niles Mich., U.S.A. 41°50N 86°15W 80 E10
Niles Ohio, U.S.A. 41°11N 80°46W 82 E4
Nim Ka Thana India 27°44N 75°48E 42 F6
Nimach India 24°30N 74°56E 42 G6
Nimbahera India 24°37N 74°45E 42 G6
Nîmes France 43°50N 4°23E 20 E6
Nimfaíon, Ákra = Pines, Akra Greece 40°5N 24°20E 23 D11
Nimmitabel Australia 36°29S 149°15E 63 F4
Nīnawá Iraq 36°25N 43°10E 44 B4
Nīnawá □ Iraq 36°15N 43°0E 44 B4
Nindigully Australia 28°21S 148°50E 63 D4
Ninepin Group China 22°16N 114°21E 33 G11
Nineveh = Nīnawá Iraq 36°25N 43°10E 44 B4
Ning Xian China 35°30N 107°58E 34 G4
Ningaloo Marine △ Australia 22°23S 113°32E 60 D1
Ning'an China 44°22N 129°20E 35 B15
Ningbo China 29°51N 121°28E 33 D7
Ningcheng China 41°32N 119°53E 35 D10
Ningjin China 37°35N 114°57E 34 F8
Ningjing Shan China 30°0N 98°20E 41 E12
Ningling China 34°25N 115°22E 34 G8
Ningpo = Ningbo China 29°51N 121°28E 33 D7
Ningqiang China 32°47N 106°15E 34 H4
Ningshan China 33°21N 108°21E 34 H5
Ningsia Hui A.R. = Ningxia Huizu Zizhiqu □ China 38°0N 106°0E 34 F4
Ningwu China 39°0N 112°18E 34 E7
Ningxia Huizu Zizhiqu □ China 38°0N 106°0E 34 F4
Ningyang China 35°47N 116°45E 34 G9
Ninh Binh Vietnam 20°15N 105°55E 38 B5
Ninh Giang Vietnam 20°44N 106°24E 38 B6
Ninh Hoa Vietnam 12°30N 109°7E 38 F7
Ninh Ma Vietnam 12°48N 109°21E 38 F7
Ninove Belgium 50°51N 4°2E 15 D4
Nioaque Brazil 21°5S 55°50W 95 A4
Niobrara U.S.A. 42°45N 98°2W 80 D4
Niobrara → U.S.A. 42°46N 98°3W 80 D4
Nioro du Sahel Mali 15°15N 9°30W 50 E4
Niort France 46°19N 0°29W 20 C3
Nipawin Canada 53°20N 104°0W 71 C8
Nipigon Canada 49°0N 88°17W 72 C2
Nipigon, L. Canada 49°50N 88°30W 72 C2
Nipishish L. Canada 54°12N 60°45W 73 B7
Nipissing, L. Canada 46°20N 80°0W 72 C4
Nipomo U.S.A. 35°3N 120°29W 79 K6
Nippon = Japan ■ Asia 36°0N 136°0E 31 G8
Nipton U.S.A. 35°28N 115°16W 79 K11
Niquelândia Brazil 14°33S 48°23W 93 F9
Nīr Iran 38°2N 47°59E 44 B5
Nirasaki Japan 35°42N 138°27E 31 G9
Nirmal India 19°3N 78°20E 40 K11
Nirmali India 26°20N 86°35E 43 F12
Niš Serbia 43°19N 21°58E 23 C9
Nişāb Si. Arabia 29°11N 44°43E 44 D5
Nişāb Yemen 14°25N 46°29E 47 E4
Nishinomiya Japan 34°45N 135°20E 31 G7
Nishino'omote Japan 30°43N 130°59E 31 J5
Nishiwaki Japan 34°59N 134°58E 31 G7
Niskibi → Canada 56°29N 88°9W 72 A2
Nisqually → U.S.A. 47°7N 122°42W 78 C4
Nissaki Greece 39°43N 19°52E 25 A3
Nissum Bredning Denmark 56°40N 8°20E 9 H13
Nistru = Dnister → Europe 46°18N 30°17E 17 E16
Nisutlin → Canada 60°14N 132°34W 70 A2
Nitchequon Canada 53°10N 70°58W 73 B5
Niterói Brazil 22°53S 43°7W 95 A7
Nith → Canada 43°12N 80°23W 82 C4
Nith → U.K. 55°14N 3°33W 11 F5
Nitmiluk △ Australia 14°6S 132°15E 60 B5
Nitra Slovak Rep. 48°19N 18°4E 17 D10
Nitra → Slovak Rep. 47°46N 18°10E 17 E10
Niue Pac. Oc. 19°2S 169°54W 65 J11
Niut Indonesia 0°55N 110°6E 36 D4
Niuzhuang China 40°58N 122°28E 35 D12
Nivala Finland 63°56N 24°57E 8 E21
Nivelles Belgium 50°35N 4°20E 15 D4
Nivernais France 47°15N 3°30E 20 C5
Niverville Canada 49°36N 97°3W 71 D9
Niwas India 23°3N 80°26E 43 H9
Nixa U.S.A. 37°3N 93°18W 80 G7
Nixon U.S.A. 29°16N 97°46W 84 G6
Nizamabad India 18°45N 78°7E 40 K11
Nizamghat India 28°20N 95°45E 41 E19
Nizhne Kolymsk Russia 68°34N 160°55E 29 C17
Nizhnekamsk Russia 55°38N 51°49E 18 C9
Nizhneudinsk Russia 54°54N 99°3E 29 D10
Nizhnevartovsk Russia 60°56N 76°38E 28 C8
Nizhniy Bestyakh Russia 61°57N 129°54E 29 C13
Nizhniy Novgorod Russia 56°20N 44°0E 18 C7
Nizhniy Tagil Russia 57°55N 59°57E 18 C10

Nizhyn Ukraine 51°5N 31°55E 19 D5
Nizip Turkey 37°5N 37°50E 44 B3
Nízké Tatry Slovak Rep. 48°55N 19°30E 17 D10
Nizwá Oman 22°56N 57°32E 47 C6
Njakwa Malawi 11°1S 33°56E 55 E3
Njanji Zambia 14°25S 31°46E 55 E3
Njazidja = Grande Comore Comoros Is. 11°35S 43°20E 53 a
Njinjo Tanzania 8°48S 38°54E 55 D4
Njombe Tanzania 9°20S 34°50E 55 D3
Njombe → Tanzania 6°56S 35°6E 54 D4
Nkana Zambia 12°50S 28°8E 55 E2
Nkandla S. Africa 28°37S 31°5E 57 D5
Nkawkaw Ghana 6°36N 0°49W 50 G5
Nkayi Zimbabwe 19°41S 29°20E 55 F2
Nkhotakota Malawi 12°56S 34°15E 55 E3
Nkhotakota △ Malawi 12°50S 34°0E 55 E3
Nkondwe Tanzania 5°51S 30°51E 54 D3
Nkurenkuru Namibia 17°42S 18°32E 56 B2
Nmai → Burma 25°30N 97°25E 41 G20
Noakhali Bangla. 22°48N 91°10E 41 H17
Nobel Canada 45°25N 80°6W 82 A4
Nobeoka Japan 32°36N 131°41E 31 H5
Noblesville U.S.A. 40°3N 86°1W 81 E11
Noboribetsu Japan 42°24N 141°6E 30 C10
Noccundra Australia 27°50S 142°36E 63 D3
Nocera Inferiore Italy 40°44N 14°38E 22 D6
Nocona U.S.A. 33°47N 97°44W 84 E6
Noda Japan 35°56N 139°52E 31 G9
Nogales Mexico 31°19N 110°56W 86 A2
Nogales U.S.A. 31°21N 110°56W 77 L8
Nōgata Japan 33°48N 130°44E 31 H5
Noggerup Australia 33°32S 116°5E 61 F2
Noginsk Russia 64°30N 90°50E 29 C10
Nogliki Russia 51°50N 143°10E 29 D15
Nogoa → Australia 23°40S 147°55E 62 C4
Nogoyá Argentina 32°24S 59°48W 94 C4
Nohar India 29°11N 74°49E 42 E6
Nohta India 23°40N 79°34E 43 H8
Noires, Mts. France 48°11N 3°40W 20 B2
Noirmoutier, Î. de France 46°58N 2°10W 20 C2
Nojane Botswana 23°15S 20°14E 56 C3
Nojima-Zaki Japan 34°54N 139°53E 31 G9
Nok Kundi Pakistan 28°50N 62°45E 40 E3
Nok Ta Phao, Ko Thailand 9°23N 99°40E 39 b
Nokaneng Botswana 19°40S 22°17E 56 B3
Nokia Finland 61°30N 23°30E 8 F20
Nokomis Canada 51°35N 105°0W 71 C8
Nokomis L. Canada 57°0N 103°0W 71 B8
Nola C.A.R. 3°35N 16°4E 52 D3
Noma Omuramba → Namibia 18°52S 20°53E 56 B3
Nombre de Dios Panama 9°34N 79°28W 88 E4
Nome U.S.A. 64°30N 165°25W 74 C6
Nomo-Zaki Japan 32°35N 129°44E 31 H4
Nomuka Tonga 20°17S 174°48W 59 c
Nomuka Group Tonga 20°20S 174°48W 59 c
Nonacho L. Canada 61°42N 109°40W 71 A7
Nonda Australia 20°40S 142°28E 62 C3
Nong Chang Thailand 15°23N 99°51E 38 E2
Nong Het Laos 19°29N 103°59E 38 C4
Nong Khai Thailand 17°50N 102°46E 38 D4
Nong'an China 44°25N 125°5E 35 B13
Nongoma S. Africa 27°58S 31°35E 57 D5
Nongsa Indonesia 1°11N 104°8E 39 d
Nonoava Mexico 27°28N 106°44W 86 B3
Nonsan S. Korea 36°12N 127°5E 35 F14
Nonthaburi Thailand 13°50N 100°29E 38 F3
Noonamah Australia 12°40S 131°4E 60 B5
Noonkanbah ◎ Australia 18°30S 124°50E 60 C3
Noord Brabant □ Neths. 51°40N 5°0E 15 C5
Noord Holland □ Neths. 52°30N 4°45E 15 B4
Noordbeveland Neths. 51°35N 3°50E 15 C3
Noordoostpolder Neths. 52°45N 5°45E 15 B5
Noordwijk Neths. 52°14N 4°26E 15 B4
Noosa Heads Australia 26°25S 153°6E 63 D5
Nootka I. Canada 49°32N 126°42W 70 D3
Nopiming △ Canada 50°30N 95°37W 71 C9
Noralee Canada 53°59N 126°26W 70 C3
Noranda = Rouyn-Noranda Canada 48°20N 79°0W 72 C4
Norco U.S.A. 33°56N 117°33W 79 M9
Nord-Kivu □ Dem. Rep. of the Congo 1°0S 29°0E 54 C2
Nord-Ostsee-Kanal Germany 54°12N 9°32E 16 A5
Nordaustlandet Svalbard 79°14N 23°0E 4 B9
Nordegg Canada 52°29N 116°5W 70 C5
Norderney Germany 53°42N 7°9E 16 B4
Norderstedt Germany 53°42N 10°1E 16 B5
Nordfjord Norway 61°55N 5°30E 8 F11
Nordfriesische Inseln Germany 54°40N 8°20E 16 A5
Nordhausen Germany 51°30N 10°47E 16 C6
Norðoyar Faroe Is. 62°17N 6°35W 8 E9
Nordkapp Norway 71°10N 25°50E 8 A21
Nordkapp Svalbard 80°31N 20°0E 4 A9
Nordkinnhalvøya Norway 70°55N 27°40E 8 A22
Nordrhein-Westfalen □ Germany 51°45N 7°30E 16 C4
Nordvik Russia 74°2N 111°32E 29 B12
Nore → Ireland 52°25N 6°58W 10 D3
Noreland Canada 44°43N 78°48W 82 B6
Norfolk = Simcoe Canada 42°50N 80°23W 82 D4
Norfolk N.Y., U.S.A. 44°48N 74°59W 83 B10
Norfolk Nebr., U.S.A. 42°2N 97°25W 80 D5
Norfolk Va., U.S.A. 36°50N 76°17W 81 G15
Norfolk □ U.K. 52°39N 0°54E 13 E8
Norfolk Broads △ U.K. 52°45N 1°30E 13 E9
Norfolk I. Pac. Oc. 28°58S 168°3E 58 D7
Norfolk Ridge Pac. Oc. 30°0S 168°0E 64 K8
Norfolk L. U.S.A. 36°15N 92°14W 84 C8
Norge = Norway ■ Europe 63°0N 11°0E 8 E14
Norilsk Russia 69°20N 88°6E 29 C9

Norma, Mt. Australia 20°55S 140°42E 62 C3
Normal U.S.A. 40°31N 88°59W 80 E9
Norman U.S.A. 35°13N 97°26W 84 D6
Norman → Australia 19°18S 141°51E 62 B3
Norman Wells Canada 65°17N 126°51W 68 D6
Normanby → Australia 14°23S 144°10E 62 A3
Normandie France 48°45N 0°10E 20 B4
Normandin Canada 48°49N 72°31W 72 C5
Normandy = Normandie France 48°45N 0°10E 20 B4
Normanhurst, Mt. Australia 25°4S 122°30E 61 E3
Normanton Australia 17°40S 141°10E 62 B3
Normétal Canada 49°0N 79°22W 72 C4
Norquay Canada 51°53N 102°5W 71 C8
Norquinco Argentina 41°51S 70°55W 96 E2
Norrbottens län □ Sweden 66°50N 20°0E 8 C19
Norris Point Canada 49°31N 57°53W 73 C8
Norristown U.S.A. 40°7N 75°21W 83 F9
Norrköping Sweden 58°37N 16°11E 9 G17
Norrland Sweden 62°15N 15°45E 8 E16
Norrtälje Sweden 59°46N 18°42E 9 G18
Norseman Australia 32°8S 121°43E 61 F3
Norsk Russia 52°30N 130°5E 29 D14
Norte, Pta. del Canary Is. 27°51N 17°57W 24 G2
Norte, Serra do Brazil 11°20S 59°0W 92 F7
North, C. Canada 47°2N 60°24W 73 C7
North Adams U.S.A. 42°42N 73°7W 83 D11
North America 40°0N 100°0W 66 F10
North Arm Canada 62°0N 114°30W 70 A5
North Augusta U.S.A. 33°30N 81°59W 85 E14
North Australian Basin Ind. Oc. 14°30S 116°30E 60 B2
North Ayrshire □ U.K. 55°45N 4°44W 11 F4
North Bass I. U.S.A. 41°40N 82°56W 82 E2
North Battleford Canada 52°50N 108°17W 71 C7
North Bay Canada 46°20N 79°30W 72 C4
North Belcher Is. Canada 56°50N 79°50W 72 A4
North Bend Oreg., U.S.A. 43°24N 124°14W 76 E1
North Bend Pa., U.S.A. 41°20N 77°42W 82 E7
North Bend Wash., U.S.A. 47°30N 121°47W 78 C5
North Bennington U.S.A. 42°56N 73°15W 83 D11
North Berwick U.K. 56°4N 2°42W 11 E6
North Berwick U.S.A. 43°18N 70°44W 83 C14
North Bruce Canada 44°22N 81°26W 82 B3
North C. Canada 47°5N 64°0W 73 C7
North C. N.Z. 34°23S 173°4E 59 A4
North Canadian → U.S.A. 35°22N 95°37W 84 D7
North Canton U.S.A. 40°53N 81°24W 82 F3
North Cape = Nordkapp Norway 71°10N 25°50E 8 A21
North Caribou L. Canada 52°50N 90°40W 72 B1
North Carolina □ U.S.A. 35°30N 80°0W 85 D15
North Cascades △ U.S.A. 48°45N 121°10W 76 B3
North Channel Canada 46°0N 83°0W 72 C3
North Channel U.K. 55°13N 5°52W 11 F3
North Charleston U.S.A. 32°53N 79°58W 85 E15
North Chicago U.S.A. 42°19N 87°51W 80 D10
North Collins U.S.A. 42°35N 78°56W 82 D6
North Creek U.S.A. 43°42N 73°59W 83 C11
North Dakota □ U.S.A. 47°30N 100°15W 80 B3
North Downs U.K. 51°19N 0°21E 13 F8
North East U.S.A. 42°13N 79°50W 82 D5
North East Frontier Agency = Arunachal Pradesh □ India 28°0N 95°0E 41 F19
North East Lincolnshire □ U.K. 53°34N 0°2W 12 D7
North Eastern □ Kenya 1°30N 40°0E 54 B5
North Esk → U.K. 56°46N 2°24W 11 E6
North European Plain Europe 55°0N 25°0E 6 E10
North Foreland U.K. 51°22N 1°28E 13 F9
North Fork U.S.A. 37°14N 119°21W 78 H7
North Fork American → U.S.A. 38°57N 120°59W 78 G5
North Fork Feather → U.S.A. 38°33N 121°30W 78 F5
North Fork Grand → U.S.A. 45°47N 102°16W 80 C2
North Fork Red → U.S.A. 34°24N 99°14W 84 D5
North Frisian Is. = Nordfriesische Inseln Germany 54°40N 8°20E 16 A5
North Gower Canada 45°8N 75°43W 83 A9
North Hd. Australia 30°14S 114°59E 61 F1
North Henik L. Canada 61°45N 97°40W 71 A9
North Highlands U.S.A. 38°40N 121°23W 78 G5
North Horr Kenya 3°20N 37°8E 54 B4
North I. Kenya 4°5N 36°5E 54 B4
North I. N.Z. 38°0S 175°0E 59 C5
North I. Seychelles 4°25S 55°13E 53 b
North Kingsville U.S.A. 41°54N 80°42W 82 E4
North Kitui ⌂ Kenya 0°15S 38°29E 54 C4
North Knife → Canada 58°53N 94°45W 71 B10
North Koel → India 24°45N 83°50E 43 G10
North Korea ■ Asia 40°0N 127°0E 35 E14
North Lakhimpur India 27°14N 94°7E 41 F19
North Lanarkshire □ U.K. 55°52N 3°56W 11 F5
North Las Vegas U.S.A. 36°11N 115°7W 79 J11
North Lincolnshire □ U.K. 53°36N 0°30W 12 D7
North Little Rock U.S.A. 34°45N 92°16W 84 D8
North Loup → U.S.A. 41°17N 98°24W 80 E4
North Luangwa △ Zambia 11°49S 32°9E 55 E3
North Magnetic Pole Canada 82°42N 114°24W 4 A2
North Mankato U.S.A. 44°10N 94°2W 80 C6
North Minch U.K. 58°5N 5°55W 11 C3
North Moose L. Canada 54°4N 100°12W 71 C8
North Myrtle Beach U.S.A. 33°48N 78°42W 85 E15
North Nahanni → Canada 62°15N 123°20W 70 A4
North Olmsted U.S.A. 41°25N 81°56W 82 E3
North Ossetia □ Russia 43°30N 44°30E 19 F7
North Pagai, I. = Pagai Utara, Pulau Indonesia 2°35S 100°0E 36 E2
North Palisade U.S.A. 37°6N 118°31W 78 H8
North Platte U.S.A. 41°8N 100°46W 80 E3
North Platte → U.S.A. 41°7N 100°42W 80 E3
North Pole Arctic 90°0N 0°0 4 A
North Portal Canada 49°0N 102°33W 71 D8
North Powder U.S.A. 45°2N 117°55W 76 D5
North Pt. Barbados 13°20N 59°37W 89 g
North Pt. Trin. & Tob. 11°21N 60°31W 93 J16
North Pt. U.S.A. 45°2N 83°16W 82 A1
North Rhine Westphalia = Nordrhein-Westfalen □ Germany 51°45N 7°30E 16 C4
North River Canada 53°49N 57°6W 73 B8
North Ronaldsay U.K. 59°22N 2°26W 11 B6
North Saskatchewan → Canada 53°15N 105°5W 71 C7
North Sea Europe 56°0N 4°0E 6 D6
North Seal → Canada 58°50N 98°7W 71 B9
North Slope ☆ U.S.A. 69°15N 152°0W 74 B9
North Somerset □ U.K. 51°24N 2°45W 13 F5
North Sydney Canada 46°12N 60°15W 73 C7
North Syracuse U.S.A. 43°8N 76°7W 83 C8
North Taranaki Bight N.Z. 38°50S 174°15E 59 C5
North Thompson → Canada 50°40N 120°20W 70 C4
North Tonawanda U.S.A. 43°2N 78°53W 82 C6
North Troy U.S.A. 45°0N 72°24W 83 B12
North Twin I. Canada 53°20N 80°0W 72 B4
North Tyne → U.K. 55°0N 2°8W 12 B5
North Uist U.K. 57°40N 7°15W 11 D1
North Vancouver Canada 49°19N 123°4W 78 A3
North Vernon U.S.A. 39°0N 85°38W 81 F11
North Wabasca L. Canada 56°0N 113°55W 70 B6
North Walsham U.K. 52°50N 1°22E 12 E9
North West = Severo-Zapadnyy □ Russia 65°0N 40°0E 28 C4
North-West □ S. Africa 27°0S 25°0E 56 D4
North West C. Australia 21°45S 114°9E 60 D1
North West Frontier □ Pakistan 34°0N 72°0E 42 C4
North West Highlands U.K. 57°33N 4°58W 11 D4
North West River Canada 53°30N 60°10W 73 B7
North Western □ Zambia 13°30S 25°30E 55 E2
North Wildwood U.S.A. 39°0N 74°48W 81 F16
North York Moors U.K. 54°23N 0°53W 12 C7
North York Moors △ U.K. 54°27N 0°51W 12 C7
North Yorkshire □ U.K. 54°15N 1°25W 12 C6
Northallerton U.K. 54°20N 1°26W 12 C6
Northam Australia 31°35S 116°42E 61 F2
Northam S. Africa 24°56S 27°18E 56 C4
Northampton Australia 28°27S 114°33E 61 E1
Northampton U.K. 52°15N 0°53W 13 E7
Northampton Mass., U.S.A. 42°19N 72°38W 83 D12
Northampton Pa., U.S.A. 40°41N 75°30W 83 F9
Northamptonshire □ U.K. 52°16N 0°55W 13 E7
Northbridge U.S.A. 42°9N 71°39W 83 D13
Northbrook Canada 44°44N 77°9W 82 B7
Northcliffe Australia 34°39S 116°7E 61 F2
Northeast Pacific Basin Pac. Oc. 32°0N 145°0W 65 D13
Northeast Providence Chan. W. Indies 26°0N 76°0W 88 A4
Northern = Limpopo □ S. Africa 24°5S 29°0E 57 C4
Northern □ Malawi 11°0S 34°0E 55 E3
Northern □ Zambia 10°30S 31°0E 55 E3
Northern Areas □ Pakistan 36°30N 73°0E 43 A5
Northern Cape □ S. Africa 30°0S 20°0E 56 D3
Northern Circars India 17°30N 82°30E 41 L13
Northern Indian L. Canada 57°20N 97°20W 71 B9
Northern Ireland □ U.K. 54°45N 7°0W 10 B5
Northern Lau Group Fiji 17°30S 178°59W 59 a
Northern Light L. Canada 48°15N 90°39W 72 C1
Northern Marianas ⊠ Pac. Oc. 17°0N 145°0E 64 F6
Northern Province □ S. Africa 24°0S 29°0E 57 C4
Northern Range Trin. & Tob. 10°46N 61°15W 93 K15
Northern Sporades Greece 39°15N 23°30E 23 E10
Northern Territory □ Australia 20°0S 133°0E 60 D5
Northfield Minn., U.S.A. 44°27N 93°9W 80 C7
Northfield Vt., U.S.A. 44°9N 72°40W 83 B12
Northgate Canada 49°0N 102°16W 71 D8
Northland □ N.Z. 35°30S 173°30E 59 A4
Northome U.S.A. 47°52N 94°17W 80 B6
Northport Ala., U.S.A. 33°14N 87°35W 85 E11
Northport Wash., U.S.A. 48°55N 117°48W 76 B5
Northumberland □ U.K. 55°12N 2°0W 12 B6
Northumberland, C. Australia 38°5S 140°40E 63 F3
Northumberland Is. Australia 21°30S 149°50E 62 C4
Northumberland Str. Canada 46°20N 64°0W 73 C7
Northville Canada 43°10N 81°56W 82 C3
Northville U.S.A. 43°13N 74°11W 83 C10
Northwest Pacific Basin Pac. Oc. 32°0N 165°0E 64 D8
Northwest Providence Channel W. Indies 26°0N 78°0W 88 A4
Northwest Territories □ Canada 63°0N 118°0W 68 E8
Northwich U.K. 53°15N 2°31W 12 D5
Northwood Iowa, U.S.A. 43°27N 93°13W 80 D7
Northwood N. Dak., U.S.A. 47°44N 97°34W 80 B5
Norton U.S.A. 39°50N 99°53W 80 F4
Norton Zimbabwe 17°52S 30°40E 55 F3
Norton Sd. U.S.A. 63°50N 164°0W 74 C7
Norwalk Calif., U.S.A. 33°54N 118°4W 79 M8
Norwalk Conn., U.S.A. 41°7N 73°22W 83 E11
Norwalk Iowa, U.S.A. 41°29N 93°41W 80 E7
Norwalk Ohio, U.S.A. 41°15N 82°37W 82 E2
Norway Maine, U.S.A. 44°13N 70°32W 81 C18
Norway Mich., U.S.A. 45°47N 87°55W 80 C10
Norway ■ Europe 63°0N 11°0E 8 E14
Norway House Canada 53°59N 97°50W 71 C9
Norwegian B. Canada 77°30N 90°0W 69 B14
Norwegian Basin Atl. Oc. 68°0N 2°0W 4 C7
Norwegian Sea Atl. Oc. 66°0N 1°0E 6 B6
Norwich Canada 42°59N 80°36W 82 D4
Norwich U.K. 52°38N 1°18E 13 E9
Norwich Conn., U.S.A. 41°31N 72°5W 83 E12
Norwich N.Y., U.S.A. 42°32N 75°32W 83 D9
Norwood Canada 44°23N 77°59W 82 B7
Norwood U.S.A. 44°45N 75°0W 83 B10
Nosappu-Misaki Japan 45°26N 141°39E 30 C12
Noshiro Japan 40°12N 140°0E 30 D10
Noşratābād Iran 29°55N 60°0E 45 D8
Noss Hd. U.K. 58°28N 3°3W 11 C5
Nossob → S. Africa 26°55S 20°45E 56 D3
Nosy Barren Madag. 18°25S 43°40E 53 H8
Nosy Bé Madag. 13°25S 48°15E 53 G9
Nosy Boraha Madag. 16°50S 49°55E 57 B8
Nosy Lava Madag. 14°33S 47°36E 57 A8
Nosy Varika Madag. 20°35S 48°32E 57 C8
Noteć → Poland 52°44N 15°26E 16 B8
Notikewin → Canada 57°2N 117°38W 70 B5
Notodden Norway 59°35N 9°17E 9 G13
Notre Dame B. Canada 49°45N 55°30W 73 C8
Notre-Dame-de-Koartac = Quaqtaq Canada 60°55N 69°40W 69 E18
Notre-Dame-des-Bois Canada 45°24N 71°4W 83 A13
Notre-Dame-d'Ivugivic = Ivujivik Canada 62°24N 77°55W 69 E16
Notre-Dame-du-Nord Canada 47°36N 79°30W 72 C4
Nottawasaga B. Canada 44°35N 80°15W 82 B4
Nottaway → Canada 51°22N 78°55W 72 B4
Nottingham U.K. 52°58N 1°10W 12 E6
Nottingham, City of □ U.K. 52°58N 1°10W 12 E6
Nottingham I. Canada 63°20N 77°55W 69 E16
Nottinghamshire □ U.K. 53°10N 1°3W 12 D6
Nottoway → U.S.A. 36°33N 76°55W 81 G15
Notwane → Botswana 23°35S 26°58E 56 C4
Nouâdhibou Mauritania 20°54N 17°0W 50 D2
Nouâdhibou, Râs Mauritania 20°50N 17°0W 50 D2
Nouakchott Mauritania 18°9N 15°58W 50 E2
Nouméa N. Cal. 22°17S 166°30E 58 D9
Noupoort S. Africa 31°10S 24°57E 56 E3
Nouveau Comptoir = Wemindji Canada 53°0N 78°49W 72 B4
Nouvelle Amsterdam, Î. Ind. Oc. 38°30S 77°30E 3 F13
Nouvelle-Calédonie = New Caledonia ⊠ Pac. Oc. 21°0S 165°0E 58 D9
Nova Esperança Brazil 23°8S 52°24W 95 A5
Nova Friburgo Brazil 22°16S 42°30W 95 A7
Nova Iguaçu Brazil 22°45S 43°28W 95 A7
Nova Iorque Brazil 7°0S 44°5W 93 E10
Nova Lamego Guinea-Biss. 12°19N 14°11W 50 F3
Nova Lusitânia Mozam. 19°50S 34°34E 55 F3
Nova Mambone Mozam. 21°0S 35°3E 57 C6
Nova Scotia □ Canada 45°10N 63°0W 73 C7
Nova Sofala Mozam. 20°7S 34°42E 57 C5
Nova Venécia Brazil 18°45S 40°24W 93 G10
Nova Zagora Bulgaria 42°32N 26°1E 23 C11
Novar Canada 45°27N 79°15W 82 A5
Novara Italy 45°28N 8°38E 20 D8
Novato U.S.A. 38°6N 122°35W 78 G4
Novaya Ladoga Russia 60°7N 32°16E 18 B5
Novaya Lyalya Russia 59°4N 60°45E 18 C11
Novaya Sibir, Ostrov Russia 75°10N 150°0E 29 B16
Novaya Zemlya Russia 75°0N 56°0E 28 B6
Nové Zámky Slovak Rep. 48°2N 18°8E 17 D10
Novgorod Russia 58°30N 31°25E 18 C5
Novgorod-Severskiy = Novhorod-Siverskyy Ukraine 52°2N 33°10E 18 D5
Novhorod-Siverskyy Ukraine 52°2N 33°10E 18 D5
Novi Lígure Italy 44°46N 8°47E 20 D8
Novi Pazar Serbia 43°12N 20°28E 23 C9
Novi Sad Serbia 45°18N 19°52E 23 B8
Novo Hamburgo Brazil 29°37S 51°7W 95 B5
Novo Mesto Slovenia 45°47N 15°12E 22 B6
Novoaltaysk Russia 53°30N 84°0E 28 D9
Novocherkassk Russia 47°27N 40°15E 19 E7
Novodvinsk Russia 64°25N 40°42E 18 B7
Novogrudok = Navahrudak Belarus 53°40N 25°50E 17 B13
Novohrad-Volynskyy Ukraine 50°34N 27°35E 17 C14
Novokachalinsk Russia 45°5N 132°0E 30 B5
Novokuybyshevsk Russia 53°7N 49°58E 18 D8
Novokuznetsk Russia 53°45N 87°10E 28 D9
Novolazarevskaya Antarctica 71°0S 12°0E 5 D3
Novomoskovsk Russia 54°5N 38°15E 18 D6
Novorossiysk Russia 44°43N 37°46E 19 F6
Novorybnoye Russia 72°50N 105°50E 29 B11
Novoselytsya Ukraine 48°14N 26°15E 17 D14
Novoshakhtinsk Russia 47°46N 39°58E 19 E6
Novosibirsk Russia 55°0N 83°5E 28 D9
Novosibirskiye Ostrova Russia 75°0N 142°0E 29 B15
Novotroitsk Russia 51°10N 58°15E 18 D10
Novouzensk Russia 50°32N 48°17E 19 D8
Novovolynsk Ukraine 50°45N 24°4E 17 C13
Novska Croatia 45°19N 17°0E 22 B7
Novyy Bor Russia 66°43N 52°19E 18 A9
Novyy Port Russia 67°40N 72°30E 28 C8
Novyy Urengoy Russia 65°48N 76°52E 28 C8
Nowa Sól Poland 51°48N 15°44E 16 C8
Nowata U.S.A. 36°42N 95°38W 84 C7
Nowbarān Iran 35°8N 49°42E 45 C6
Nowghāb Iran 33°53N 59°4E 45 C8
Nowgong Assam, India 26°20N 92°50E 41 F18
Nowgong Mad. P., India 25°4N 79°27E 43 G8
Nowra Australia 34°53S 150°35E 63 E5
Nowshera Pakistan 34°0N 72°0E 40 C8
Nowy Sącz Poland 49°40N 20°41E 17 D11
Nowy Targ Poland 49°29N 20°2E 17 D11
Nowy Tomyśl Poland 52°19N 16°10E 16 B9
Noxen U.S.A. 41°25N 76°4W 83 E8
Noyab'rsk Russia 64°34N 76°21E 28 C8
Noyon France 49°34N 2°59E 20 B5
Noyon Mongolia 43°2N 102°4E 34 C2
Nqutu S. Africa 28°13S 30°32E 57 D5
Nsanje Malawi 16°55S 35°12E 55 F4
Nsawam Ghana 5°50N 0°24W 50 G5
Nseluka Zambia 9°58S 31°16E 55 D3
Nsomba Zambia 10°45S 29°51E 55 E2
Ntaria ☼ Australia 24°0S 132°41E 60 D5
Ntungamo Uganda 0°56S 30°17E 54 C3
Nu Jiang → China 29°58N 97°25E 32 D4
Nu Shan China 26°0N 99°20E 41 G21
Nuba Mts. = Nubah, Jibalan Sudan 12°0N 31°0E 51 F12
Nubah, Jibalan Sudan 12°0N 31°0E 51 F12
Nubia Africa 21°0N 32°0E 48 D7
Nubian Desert = Nûbîya, Es Sahrâ en Sudan 21°30N 33°30E 51 D12
Nûbîya, Es Sahrâ en Sudan 21°30N 33°30E 51 D12
Nuboai Indonesia 2°10S 136°30E 37 E9
Nubra → India 34°35N 77°35E 43 B7
Nueces → U.S.A. 27°51N 97°30W 84 H6
Nueltin L. Canada 60°30N 99°30W 71 A9
Nuestra Señora del Rosario de Caá-Catí Argentina 27°45S 57°36W 94 B4
Nueva Ciudad Guerrero Mexico 26°34N 99°12W 87 B5
Nueva Gerona Cuba 21°53N 82°49W 88 B3
Nueva Palmira Uruguay 33°52S 58°20W 94 C4
Nueva Rosita Mexico 27°57N 101°13W 86 B4
Nueva San Salvador El Salv. 13°40N 89°18W 88 D2
Nuéve de Julio Argentina 35°30S 61°0W 94 D3
Nuevitas Cuba 21°30N 77°20W 88 B4
Nuevo, G. Argentina 43°0S 64°30W 96 E4
Nuevo Casas Grandes Mexico 30°25N 107°55W 86 A3
Nuevo Laredo Mexico 27°30N 99°31W 87 B5
Nuevo León □ Mexico 25°20N 100°0W 86 C5
Nuevo Rocafuerte Ecuador 0°55S 75°27W 92 D3
Nugget Pt. N.Z. 46°27S 169°50E 59 G2
Nuhaka N.Z. 39°3S 177°45E 59 C6
Nukey Bluff Australia 32°26S 135°29E 63 E2
Nukhayb Iraq 32°4N 42°3E 44 C4
Nuku Hiva French Polynesia 8°54S 140°6W 65 H13
Nuku'alofa Tonga 21°10S 175°12W 59 c
Nukus Uzbekistan 42°27N 59°41E 28 E6
Nulato U.S.A. 64°43N 158°6W 74 C8
Nullagine Australia 21°53S 120°7E 60 D3
Nullagine → Australia 21°20S 120°20E 60 D3
Nullarbor Australia 31°28S 130°55E 61 F5
Nullarbor △ Australia 32°39S 130°0E 61 F5
Nullarbor Plain Australia 31°10S 129°0E 61 F4
Numalla, L. Australia 28°43S 144°20E 63 D3
Numan Nigeria 9°29N 12°3E 51 G8
Numata Japan 36°45N 139°4E 31 F9
Numaykoos Lake ⌂ Canada 57°52N 95°58W 71 B9
Numazu Japan 35°7N 138°51E 31 G9
Numbulwar Australia 14°15S 135°45E 62 A2
Numfoor Indonesia 1°0S 134°50E 37 E8
Numurkah Australia 36°5S 145°26E 63 F4
Nunaksaluk I. Canada 55°49N 60°20W 73 A7
Nunap Isua Greenland 59°48N 43°55W 66 D15
Nunavik Greenland 71°50N 54°25W 69 C21
Nunavut □ Canada 66°0N 85°0W 69 D15
Nunda U.S.A. 42°35N 77°56W 82 D7
Nuneaton U.K. 52°32N 1°27W 13 E6
Nungarin Australia 31°12S 118°6E 61 F2
Nungo Mozam. 13°23S 37°43E 55 E4
Nungwe Tanzania 2°48S 32°2E 54 C3
Nunivak I. U.S.A. 60°10N 166°30W 74 C6
Nunkun India 33°57N 76°2E 43 C7
Núoro Italy 40°20N 9°20E 22 D3
Nūr Iran 36°33N 52°1E 45 B7
Nūrābād Hormozgān, Iran 27°47N 57°12E 45 E8
Nūrābād Lorestān, Iran 34°4N 47°58E 44 C5
Nuremberg = Nürnberg Germany 49°27N 11°3E 16 D6
Nuri Mexico 28°5N 109°22W 86 B3
Nuriootpa Australia 34°27S 139°0E 63 E2
Nuristān □ Afghan. 35°20N 71°0E 40 B7
Nurmes Finland 63°33N 29°10E 8 E23
Nürnberg Germany 49°27N 11°3E 16 D6
Nurpur Pakistan 31°53N 71°54E 42 D4
Nurran, L. = Terewah, L. Australia 29°52S 147°35E 63 D4
Nurrari Lakes Australia 29°1S 130°5E 61 E5
Nusa Barung Indonesia 8°30S 113°30E 37 H15
Nusa Dua Indonesia 8°48S 115°14E 37 K18
Nusa Kambangan Indonesia 7°40S 108°10E 37 G13
Nusa Tenggara Barat □ Indonesia 8°50S 117°30E 36 F5
Nusa Tenggara Timur □ Indonesia 9°30S 122°0E 37 F6
Nusaybin Turkey 37°3N 41°10E 19 G7
Nushki Pakistan 29°35N 66°0E 42 E2
Nuuk Greenland 64°10N 51°35W 67 C14
Nuupere, Pte. Moorea 17°36S 149°47W 59 d
Nuwakot Nepal 28°10N 83°55E 43 E10
Nuwayb'ī, W. an → Si. Arabia 29°18N 34°57E 46 F3
Nuweiba' Egypt 28°59N 34°39E 44 D2
Nuwerus S. Africa 31°8S 18°24E 56 E2
Nuweveldberge S. Africa 32°10S 21°45E 56 E3
Nuyts, Pt. Australia 35°4S 116°38E 61 G2
Nuyts Arch. Australia 32°35S 133°20E 63 E1
Nxai Pan △ Botswana 19°50S 24°46E 56 B3
Nxaunxau Botswana 18°57S 21°4E 56 B3
Nyabing Australia 33°33S 118°9E 61 F2
Nyack U.S.A. 41°5N 73°55W 83 E11
Nyagan Russia 62°30N 65°38E 28 C7
Nyahanga Tanzania 2°20S 33°37E 54 C3
Nyahua Tanzania 5°25S 33°23E 54 D3
Nyahururu Kenya 0°2N 36°27E 54 B4
Nyainqêntanglha Shan China 30°0N 90°0E 32 D3
Nyakanazi Tanzania 3°2S 31°10E 54 C3
Nyâlâ Sudan 12°2N 24°58E 51 F10
Nyamandhlovu Zimbabwe 19°55S 28°16E 55 F2
Nyambiti Tanzania 2°48S 33°27E 54 C3
Nyamira Kenya 0°36S 34°52E 54 B4
Nyamwaga Tanzania 1°27S 34°33E 54 C3
Nyandekwa Tanzania 3°57S 32°32E 54 C3
Nyandoma Russia 61°40N 40°12E 18 B7
Nyanga △ Zimbabwe 18°17S 32°46E 55 F3
Nyangana Namibia 18°0S 20°40E 56 B3
Nyanguge Tanzania 2°30S 33°12E 54 C3
Nyanza Rwanda 2°20S 29°42E 54 C2
Nyanza □ Kenya 0°10S 34°15E 54 C3
Nyanza-Lac Burundi 4°21S 29°36E 54 C2
Nyasa, L. = Malawi, L. Africa 12°30S 34°30E 55 E3
Nyasvizh Belarus 53°14N 26°38E 17 B14
Nyazepetrovsk Russia 56°3N 59°36E 18 C10
Nyazura Zimbabwe 18°40S 32°16E 55 F3
Nyazwidzi → Zimbabwe 20°0S 31°17E 55 G3
Nybro Sweden 56°44N 15°55E 9 H16
Nyda Russia 66°40N 72°58E 28 C8
Nyeboe Land Greenland 82°0N 57°0W 69 A20
Nyeri Kenya 0°23S 36°56E 54 C4
Nyika △ Malawi 10°30S 33°53E 55 E3
Nyimba Zambia 14°33S 30°50E 55 E3
Nyíregyháza Hungary 47°58N 21°47E 17 E11
Nyiru, Mt. Kenya 2°8N 36°50E 54 B4
Nykarleby = Uusikaarlepyy Finland 63°32N 22°31E 8 E20
Nykøbing Nordjylland, Denmark 56°48N 8°51E 9 H13
Nykøbing Sjælland, Denmark 54°56N 11°52E 9 J14
Nykøbing Sjælland, Denmark 55°55N 11°40E 9 J14
Nyköping Sweden 58°45N 17°1E 9 G17
Nylstroom = Modimolle S. Africa 24°42S 28°22E 57 C4
Nymagee Australia 32°7S 146°20E 63 E4
Nymboida △ Australia 29°38S 152°26E 63 D5
Nynäshamn Sweden 58°54N 17°57E 9 G17
Nyngan Australia 31°30S 147°8E 63 E4
Nyoma Rap India 33°10N 78°40E 43 C8
Nyoman = Nemunas → Lithuania 55°25N 21°10E 9 J19
Nysa Poland 50°30N 17°22E 17 C9
Nysa → Europe 52°4N 14°46E 16 B8
Nyslott = Savonlinna Finland 61°52N 28°53E 8 F23
Nyssa U.S.A. 43°53N 117°0W 76 E5
Nystad = Uusikaupunki Finland 60°47N 21°25E 8 F19
Nyunzu Dem. Rep. of the Congo 5°57S 27°58E 54 D2
Nyurba Russia 63°17N 118°28E 29 C12
Nzega Tanzania 4°10S 33°12E 54 C3
Nzérékoré Guinea 7°49N 8°48W 50 G4
Nzeto Angola 7°10S 12°52E 52 F2
Nzilo, Chutes de Dem. Rep. of the Congo 10°18S 25°27E 55 E2
Nzubuka Tanzania 4°45S 32°50E 54 C3
Nzwani = Anjouan Comoros Is. 12°15S 44°20E 53 a

O

O Le Pupū Pu'e △ Samoa 13°59S 171°43W 59 b
Ō-Shima Hokkaidō, Japan 41°30N 139°22E 30 D9
Ō-Shima Shizuoka, Japan 34°44N 139°24E 31 G9
Oa, Mull of U.K. 55°35N 6°20W 11 F2
Oacoma U.S.A. 43°48N 99°24W 80 D4
Oahe, L. U.S.A. 44°27N 100°24W 80 C3
Oahe Dam U.S.A. 44°27N 100°24W 80 C3
O'ahu U.S.A. 21°28N 157°58W 75 L8
Oak Harbor U.S.A. 48°18N 122°39W 78 B4
Oak Hill U.S.A. 37°59N 81°9W 81 G13
Oak Island U.S.A. 33°55N 78°10W 85 E15
Oak Ridge U.S.A. 36°1N 84°16W 85 C12
Oak View U.S.A. 34°24N 119°18W 79 L7
Oakan-Dake Japan 43°27N 144°10E 30 C12

Oakdale *Calif., U.S.A.* 37°46N 120°51W **78** H6
Oakdale *La., U.S.A.* 30°49N 92°40W **84** F8
Oakes *U.S.A.* 46°8N 98°6W **80** B4
Oakesdale *U.S.A.* 47°8N 117°15W **76** C5
Oakey *Australia* 27°25S 151°43E **63** D5
Oakfield *U.S.A.* 43°4N 78°16W **82** C6
Oakham *U.K.* 52°40N 0°43W **13** E7
Oakhurst *U.S.A.* 37°19N 119°40W **78** H7
Oakland *Calif., U.S.A.* 37°48N 122°18W **78** H4
Oakland *Pa., U.S.A.* 41°57N 75°36W **83** E9
Oakley *Idaho, U.S.A.* 42°15N 113°53W **76** E7
Oakley *Kans., U.S.A.* 39°8N 100°51W **80** F3
Oakover → *Australia* 21°0S 120°40E **60** D3
Oakridge *U.S.A.* 43°45N 122°28W **76** E2
Oakville *Canada* 43°27N 79°41W **82** C5
Oakville *U.S.A.* 46°51N 123°14W **78** D3
Oamaru *N.Z.* 45°5S 170°59E **59** F3
Oasis *Calif., U.S.A.* 37°29N 117°55W **78** H9
Oasis *Calif., U.S.A.* 33°28N 116°6W **79** M10
Oates Land *Antarctica* 69°0S 160°0E **5** C11
Oatman *U.S.A.* 35°1N 114°19W **79** K12
Oaxaca *Mexico* 17°3N 96°43W **87** D5
Oaxaca □ *Mexico* 17°0N 96°30W **87** D5
Ob → *Russia* 66°45N 69°30E **28** C7
Oba *Canada* 49°4N 84°7W **72** C3
Obama *Japan* 35°30N 135°45E **31** G7
Oban *U.K.* 56°25N 5°29W **11** E3
Obbia = Hobyo
  Somali Rep. 5°25N 48°30E **47** F4
Oberá *Argentina* 27°21S 55°2W **95** B4
Oberhausen *Germany* 51°28N 6°51E **16** C4
Oberlin *Kans., U.S.A.* 39°49N 100°32W **80** F3
Oberlin *La., U.S.A.* 30°37N 92°46W **84** F8
Oberlin *Ohio, U.S.A.* 41°18N 82°13W **82** E2
Oberon *Australia* 33°45S 149°52E **63** E4
Obi, Kepulauan *Indonesia* 1°23S 127°45E **37** E7
Óbidos *Brazil* 1°50S 55°30W **93** D7
Obihiro *Japan* 42°56N 143°12E **30** C11
Obilatu *Indonesia* 1°25S 127°20E **37** E7
Obluchye *Russia* 49°1N 131°4E **29** E14
Obo *C.A.R.* 5°20N 26°32E **54** A2
Oboyan *Russia* 51°15N 36°21E **28** D4
Obozerskaya = Obozerskiy
  Russia 63°34N 40°21E **18** B7
Obozerskiy *Russia* 63°34N 40°21E **18** B7
Observatory Inlet
  Canada 55°10N 129°54W **70** B3
Obshchi Syrt *Russia* 52°0N 53°0E **6** E16
Obskaya Guba *Russia* 69°0N 73°0E **28** C8
Obuasi *Ghana* 6°17N 1°40W **50** G5
Ocala *U.S.A.* 29°11N 82°8W **85** G13
Ocampo *Chihuahua,*
  Mexico 28°11N 108°23W **86** B3
Ocampo *Tamaulipas,*
  Mexico 22°50N 99°20W **87** C5
Ocaña *Spain* 39°55N 3°30W **21** C4
Occidental, Cordillera
  Colombia 5°0N 76°0W **92** C3
Occidental, Grand Erg
  Algeria 30°20N 1°0E **50** B6
Ocean City *Md., U.S.A.* 38°20N 75°5W **81** F16
Ocean City *N.J., U.S.A.* 39°17N 74°35W **81** F16
Ocean City *Wash.,*
  U.S.A. 47°4N 124°10W **78** C2
Ocean Falls *Canada* 52°18N 127°48W **70** C3
Ocean I. = Banaba
  Kiribati 0°45S 169°50E **64** H8
Ocean Park *U.S.A.* 46°30N 124°3W **78** D2
Oceano *U.S.A.* 35°6N 120°37W **79** K6
Oceanport *U.S.A.* 40°19N 74°3W **83** F10
Oceanside *U.S.A.* 33°12N 117°23W **79** M9
Ochil Hills *U.K.* 56°14N 3°40W **11** E5
Ocho Rios *Jamaica* 18°24N 77°6W **88** a
Ocilla *U.S.A.* 31°36N 83°15W **85** F13
Ocmulgee → *U.S.A.* 31°58N 82°33W **85** F13
Ocniţa *Moldova* 48°25N 27°30E **17** D14
Oconee → *U.S.A.* 31°58N 82°33W **85** F13
Oconomowoc *U.S.A.* 43°7N 88°30W **80** D9
Oconto *U.S.A.* 44°53N 87°52W **80** C10
Oconto Falls *U.S.A.* 44°52N 88°9W **80** C9
Ocosingo *Mexico* 16°53N 92°6W **87** D6
Ocotal *Nic.* 13°41N 86°31W **88** D2
Ocotlán *Jalisco, Mexico* 20°21N 102°42W **86** C4
Ocotlán *Oaxaca, Mexico* 16°48N 96°40W **87** D5
Ōda *Japan* 35°11N 132°30E **31** G6
Ódáðahraun *Iceland* 65°5N 17°0W **8** D5
Ōdaejin *N. Korea* 41°34N 129°40E **30** D4
Odate *Japan* 40°16N 140°34E **30** D10
Odawara *Japan* 35°20N 139°6E **31** G9
Odda *Norway* 60°3N 6°35E **9** F12
Odei → *Canada* 56°6N 96°54W **71** B9
Ödemiş *Turkey* 38°15N 28°0E **23** E13
Odendaalsrus *S. Africa* 27°48S 26°45E **56** D4
Odense *Denmark* 55°22N 10°23E **9** J14
Oder → *Europe* 53°33N 14°38E **16** B8
Odesa *Ukraine* 46°30N 30°45E **19** E5
Odessa = Odesa *Ukraine* 46°30N 30°45E **19** E5
Odessa *Canada* 44°17N 76°43W **83** B8
Odessa *Tex., U.S.A.* 31°52N 102°23W **84** F3
Odessa *Wash., U.S.A.* 47°20N 118°41W **76** C4
Odiakwe *Botswana* 20°12S 25°17E **56** C4
Odienné *Ivory C.* 9°30N 7°34W **50** G4
Odintsovo *Russia* 55°40N 37°16E **18** C6
Odiongan *U.S.A.* 32°58N 101°50W **84** E4
O'Donnell *U.S.A.* 45°5N 80°5W **82** A4
Odorheiu Secuiesc
  Romania 46°21N 25°21E **17** E13
Odra = Oder → *Europe* 53°33N 14°38E **16** B8
Odzi *Zimbabwe* 19°0S 32°20E **57** B5
Odzi → *Zimbabwe* 19°45S 32°23E **57** B5
Oeiras *Brazil* 7°0S 42°8W **93** E10
Oelrichs *U.S.A.* 43°11N 103°14W **80** D2
Oelwein *U.S.A.* 42°41N 91°55W **80** D8
Oeno I. *Pac. Oc.* 24°0S 131°0W **65** K14
Oenpelli = Gunbalanya
  Australia 12°20S 133°4E **60** B5
Ofanto → *Italy* 41°22N 16°13E **22** D7
Offa *Nigeria* 8°13N 4°42E **50** G6
Offaly □ *Ireland* 53°15N 7°30W **10** C4

Offenbach *Germany* 50°6N 8°44E **16** C5
Offenburg *Germany* 48°28N 7°56E **16** D4
Officer Cr. → *Australia* 27°46S 132°30E **61** E5
Ofolanga *Tonga* 19°38S 174°27W **59** c
Ofotfjorden *Norway* 68°27N 17°0E **8** B17
Ofu *Amer. Samoa* 14°11S 169°41W **59** b
Ōfunato *Japan* 39°4N 141°43E **30** E10
Oga *Japan* 39°55N 139°50E **30** E9
Oga-Hantō *Japan* 39°58N 139°47E **30** E9
Ogaden *Ethiopia* 7°30N 45°30E **47** F3
Ōgaki *Japan* 35°21N 136°37E **31** G8
Ogallala *U.S.A.* 41°8N 101°43W **80** E3
Ogasawara Gunto
  Pac. Oc. 27°0N 142°0E **27** F16
Ogbomosho *Nigeria* 8°1N 4°11E **50** G6
Ogden *U.S.A.* 41°13N 111°58W **76** F8
Ogdensburg *U.S.A.* 44°42N 75°30W **83** B9
Ogea Driki *Fiji* 19°12S 178°27W **59** a
Ogea Levu *Fiji* 19°8S 178°24W **59** a
Ogeechee → *U.S.A.* 31°50N 81°3W **85** F14
Ogilby *U.S.A.* 32°49N 114°50W **79** N12
Óglio → *Italy* 45°2N 10°39E **22** B4
Ogmore *Australia* 22°37S 149°35E **62** C4
Ogoki *Canada* 51°38N 85°58W **72** B2
Ogoki → *Canada* 51°38N 85°57W **72** B2
Ogoki L. *Canada* 50°50N 87°10W **72** B2
Ogoki Res. *Canada* 50°45N 88°15W **72** B2
Ogoouė → *Gabon* 1°0S 9°0E **52** E1
Ogowe = Ogooué → *Gabon* 1°0S 9°0E **52** E1
Ogre *Latvia* 56°49N 24°36E **9** H21
Ogurchinskiy, Ostrov
  Turkmenistan 38°55N 53°2E **45** B7
Ohai *N.Z.* 45°55S 168°0E **59** F2
Ohakune *N.Z.* 39°24S 175°24E **59** C5
Ohata *Japan* 41°24N 141°10E **30** D10
Ohau, L. *N.Z.* 44°15S 169°53E **59** F2
Ohio □ *U.S.A.* 40°15N 82°45W **82** F2
Ohio → *U.S.A.* 36°59N 89°8W **80** G9
Ohře → *Czech Rep.* 50°30N 14°10E **16** C8
Ohrid *Macedonia* 41°8N 20°52E **23** D9
Ohridsko Jezero
  Macedonia 41°8N 20°52E **23** D9
Ohrigstad *S. Africa* 24°39S 30°36E **57** C5
Oiapoque *Brazil* 3°50N 51°50W **93** C8
Oikou *China* 38°35N 117°42E **35** E9
Oil City *U.S.A.* 41°26N 79°42W **82** E5
Oil Springs *Canada* 42°47N 82°7W **82** D2
Oildale *U.S.A.* 35°25N 119°1W **79** K7
Oise → *France* 49°0N 2°4E **20** B5
Oistins *Barbados* 13°4N 59°33W **89** g
Oistins B. *Barbados* 13°4N 59°33W **89** g
Ōita *Japan* 33°14N 131°36E **31** H5
Ōita □ *Japan* 33°15N 131°30E **31** H5
Oiticica *Brazil* 5°3S 41°5W **93** E10
Ojai *U.S.A.* 34°27N 119°15W **79** L7
Ojinaga *Mexico* 29°34N 104°25W **86** B4
Ojiya *Japan* 37°18N 138°48E **31** F9
Ojo Caliente *Mexico* 21°53N 102°15W **86** C4
Ojo de Liebre, L.
  Mexico 27°45N 114°15W **86** B2
Ojos del Salado, Cerro
  Argentina 27°0S 68°40W **94** B2
Oka → *Russia* 56°20N 43°59E **18** C7
Okaba *Indonesia* 8°6S 139°42E **37** F9
Okahandja *Namibia* 22°0S 16°59E **56** C2
Okanagan L. *Canada* 50°0N 119°30W **70** D5
Okandja *Gabon* 0°35S 13°45E **52** E2
Okanogan *U.S.A.* 48°22N 119°35W **76** B4
Okanogan → *U.S.A.* 48°6N 119°44W **76** B4
Okanogan Range
  N. Amer. 49°0N 119°55W **70** D5
Okapi △
  Dem. Rep. of the Congo 2°30N 27°20E **54** B2
Okaputa *Namibia* 20°5S 17°0E **56** C2
Okara *Pakistan* 30°50N 73°31E **42** D5
Okaukuejo *Namibia* 19°10S 16°0E **56** B2
Okavango Delta
  Botswana 18°45S 22°45E **56** B3
Okavango Swamp = Okavango
  Delta *Botswana* 18°45S 22°45E **56** B3
Okaya *Japan* 36°5N 138°10E **31** F9
Okayama *Japan* 34°40N 133°54E **31** G6
Okayama □ *Japan* 35°0N 133°50E **31** G6
Okazaki *Japan* 34°57N 137°10E **31** G8
Okeechobee *U.S.A.* 27°15N 80°50W **85** H14
Okeechobee, L. *U.S.A.* 27°0N 80°50W **85** H14
Okefenokee △ *U.S.A.* 30°45N 82°18W **85** F13
Okefenokee Swamp
  U.S.A. 30°40N 82°20W **85** F13
Okehampton *U.K.* 50°44N 4°0W **13** G3
Okha *India* 22°27N 69°4E **42** H3
Okha *Russia* 53°40N 143°0E **29** D15
Okhotsk *Russia* 59°20N 143°10E **29** D15
Okhotsk, Sea of *Asia* 55°0N 145°0E **29** D15
Okhotskiy Perevoz
  Russia 61°52N 135°35E **29** C14
Okhtyrka *Ukraine* 50°25N 35°0E **19** D5
Oki-Shotō *Japan* 36°5N 133°15E **31** F6
Okiep *S. Africa* 29°39S 17°53E **56** D2
Okinawa *Japan* 26°19N 127°46E **31** L3
Okinawa □ *Japan* 26°40N 128°0E **31** L4
Okinawa-Guntō *Japan* 26°40N 128°0E **31** L4
Okinawa-Jima *Japan* 26°32N 128°0E **31** L4
Okino-erabu-Shima
  Japan 27°21N 128°33E **31** L4
Oklahoma □ *U.S.A.* 35°20N 97°30W **84** D6
Oklahoma City *U.S.A.* 35°30N 97°30W **84** D6
Okmulgee *U.S.A.* 35°37N 95°58W **84** D7
Oknitsa = Ocniţa
  Moldova 48°25N 27°30E **17** D14
Okolo *Uganda* 2°37N 31°8E **54** B3
Okolona *U.S.A.* 34°0N 88°45W **85** E10
Okombahe *Namibia* 21°23S 15°22E **56** C2
Okotoks *Canada* 50°43N 113°58W **70** C6
Oksibil *Indonesia* 4°59S 140°35E **37** E10
Oksovskiy *Russia* 62°33N 39°57E **18** B6
Oktyabrsk = Qandyaghash
  Kazakhstan 49°28N 57°25E **19** E10

Oktyabrskiy = Aktsyabrski
  Belarus 52°38N 28°53E **17** B15
Oktyabrskiy *Bashkortostan,*
  Russia 54°28N 53°28E **18** D9
Oktyabrskiy *Kamchatka,*
  Russia 52°39N 156°14E **29** D16
Oktyabrskoy Revolyutsii, Ostrov
  Russia 79°30N 97°0E **29** B10
Okuru *N.Z.* 43°55S 168°55E **59** E2
Okushiri-Tō *Japan* 42°15N 139°30E **30** C9
Okwa → *Botswana* 22°30S 23°0E **56** C3
Ola *Russia* 59°35N 151°17E **29** D16
Ola *U.S.A.* 35°2N 93°13W **84** D8
Ólafsfjörður *Iceland* 66°4N 18°39W **8** C4
Ólafsvík *Iceland* 64°53N 23°43W **8** D2
Olancha *U.S.A.* 36°17N 118°1W **79** J8
Olancha Pk. *U.S.A.* 36°16N 118°7W **79** J8
Olanchito *Honduras* 15°30N 86°30W **88** C2
Öland *Sweden* 56°45N 16°38E **9** H17
Olary *Australia* 32°18S 140°19E **63** E3
Olascoaga *Argentina* 35°15S 60°39W **94** D3
Olathe *U.S.A.* 38°53N 94°49W **80** F6
Olavarría *Argentina* 36°55S 60°20W **94** D3
Oława *Poland* 50°57N 17°20E **17** C9
Ólbia *Italy* 40°55N 9°31E **22** D3
Olcott *U.S.A.* 43°20N 78°42W **82** C6
Old Bahama Chan. = Bahama,
  Canal Viejo de
  W. Indies 22°10N 77°30W **88** B4
Old Baldy Pk. = San Antonio, Mt.
  U.S.A. 34°17N 117°38W **79** L9
Old Bridge *U.S.A.* 40°25N 74°22W **83** F10
Old Castile = Castilla y Leon □
  Spain 42°0N 5°0W **21** B3
Old Crow *Canada* 67°30N 139°55W **68** D4
Old Dale *U.S.A.* 34°8N 115°47W **79** L11
Old Forge *N.Y., U.S.A.* 43°43N 74°58W **83** C10
Old Forge *Pa., U.S.A.* 41°22N 75°45W **83** E9
Old Mapoon ⊙ *Australia* 11°5S 142°22E **62** A3
Old Perlican *Canada* 48°5N 53°1W **73** C9
Old Shinyanga *Tanzania* 3°33S 33°27E **54** C3
Old Speck Mt. *U.S.A.* 44°34N 70°57W **83** B14
Old Town *U.S.A.* 44°56N 68°39W **81** C19
Old Washington *U.S.A.* 40°2N 81°27W **82** F3
Old Wives L. *Canada* 50°5N 106°0W **71** C7
Oldbury *U.K.* 51°38N 2°33W **13** F5
Oldcastle *Ireland* 53°46N 7°10W **10** C4
Oldeani *Tanzania* 3°22S 35°35E **54** C4
Oldenburg *Germany* 53°9N 8°13E **16** B5
Oldenzaal *Neths.* 52°19N 6°53E **15** B6
Oldham *U.K.* 53°33N 2°7W **12** D5
Oldman → *Canada* 49°57N 111°42W **70** D6
Oldmeldrum *U.K.* 57°20N 2°19W **11** D6
Olds *Canada* 51°50N 114°10W **70** C6
Olduvai Gorge *Tanzania* 2°57S 35°23E **54** C4
Oldziyt *Mongolia* 44°40N 109°1E **34** B5
Olean *U.S.A.* 42°5N 78°26W **82** D6
Olekma → *Russia* 60°22N 120°42E **29** C13
Olekminsk *Russia* 60°25N 120°30E **29** C13
Oleksandriya *Ukraine* 50°37N 26°19E **17** C14
Olema *U.S.A.* 38°3N 122°47W **78** G4
Olenegorsk *Russia* 68°9N 33°18E **8** B25
Olenek *Russia* 68°28N 112°18E **29** C12
Olenek → *Russia* 73°0N 120°10E **29** B13
Oléron, Î. d' *France* 45°55N 1°15W **20** D3
Oleśnica *Poland* 51°13N 17°22E **17** C9
Olevsk *Ukraine* 51°12N 27°39E **17** C14
Olga, L. *Canada* 49°47N 77°15W **72** C4
Olgas, The = Kata Tjuta
  Australia 25°20S 130°50E **61** E5
Ölgiy *Mongolia* 48°56N 89°57E **32** B3
Olhão *Portugal* 37°3N 7°48W **21** D2
Olifants = Elefantes →
  Africa 24°10S 32°40E **57** C5
Olifants → *Namibia* 25°30S 19°30E **56** C2
Olifantshoek *S. Africa* 27°57S 22°42E **56** D3
Ólimbos, Óros = Olymbos Oros
  Greece 40°6N 22°23E **23** D10
Olímpia *Brazil* 20°44S 48°54W **95** A6
Olinda *Brazil* 8°1S 34°51W **93** E12
Oliva *Argentina* 32°0S 63°38W **94** C3
Olivares, Cerro los
  Argentina 30°18S 69°55W **94** C2
Olive Branch *U.S.A.* 34°57N 89°49W **85** D10
Olivehurst *U.S.A.* 39°6N 121°34W **78** F5
Olivenza *Spain* 38°41N 7°9W **21** C2
Oliver *Canada* 49°13N 119°37W **70** D5
Oliver L. *Canada* 56°56N 103°22W **71** B8
Ollagüe *Chile* 21°15S 68°10W **94** A2
Olmaliq *Uzbekistan* 40°50N 69°35E **28** E7
Olney *Ill., U.S.A.* 38°44N 88°5W **80** F9
Olney *Tex., U.S.A.* 33°22N 98°45W **84** E5
Oloitokitok *Kenya* 2°56S 37°30E **54** C4
Olomane → *Canada* 50°14N 60°37W **73** B7
Olomouc *Czech Rep.* 49°38N 17°12E **17** D9
Olonets *Russia* 61°0N 32°54E **18** B5
Olongapo *Phil.* 14°50N 120°18E **37** B6
Olosega *Amer. Samoa* 14°10S 169°37W **59** b
Olosenga = Swains I.
  Amer. Samoa 11°11S 171°4W **65** J11
Olot *Spain* 42°11N 2°30E **21** A7
Olovyannaya *Russia* 50°58N 115°35E **29** D12
Oloy → *Russia* 66°29N 159°29E **29** C16
Olsztyn *Poland* 53°48N 20°29E **17** B11
Olt → *Romania* 43°43N 24°51E **17** G13
Olteniţa *Romania* 44°7N 26°42E **17** F14
Oltu *Turkey* 40°35N 41°50E **19** F7
Olymbos *Cyprus* 35°21N 33°45E **25** D12
Olymbos Oros *Greece* 40°6N 22°23E **23** D10
Olympia *Greece* 37°39N 21°39E **23** F9
Olympia *U.S.A.* 47°3N 122°53W **78** D4
Olympic △ *U.S.A.* 47°48N 123°43W **78** C3
Olympic Dam *Australia* 30°30S 136°55E **63** E2
Olympic Mts. *U.S.A.* 47°55N 123°45W **78** C3
Olympus *Cyprus* 34°56N 32°52E **25** E11
Olympus, Mt. = Olymbos Oros
  Greece 40°6N 22°23E **23** D10
Olympus, Mt. = Uludağ
  Turkey 40°4N 29°13E **23** D13

Olympus, Mt. *U.S.A.* 47°48N 123°43W **78** C3
Olyphant *U.S.A.* 41°27N 75°36W **83** E9
Olyutorskiy, Mys
  Russia 59°55N 170°27E **29** D18
Om → *Russia* 54°59N 73°22E **28** D8
Om Koi *Thailand* 17°48N 98°22E **38** D2
Ōma *Japan* 41°45N 141°5E **30** D10
Ōmachi *Japan* 36°30N 137°50E **31** F8
Omae-Zaki *Japan* 34°36N 138°14E **31** G9
Ōmagari *Japan* 39°27N 140°29E **30** E10
Omagh *U.K.* 54°36N 7°19W **10** B4
Omagh □ *U.K.* 54°35N 7°15W **10** B4
Omaha *U.S.A.* 41°17N 95°58W **80** E6
Omak *U.S.A.* 48°25N 119°31W **76** B4
Omalos *Greece* 35°19N 23°55E **25** D5
Oman ■ *Asia* 23°0N 58°0E **47** C6
Oman, G. of *Asia* 24°30N 58°30E **45** E8
Omaruru *Namibia* 21°26S 16°0E **56** C2
Omaruru → *Namibia* 22°7S 14°15E **56** C1
Omate *Peru* 16°45S 71°0W **92** G4
Ombai, Selat *Indonesia* 8°30S 124°50E **37** F6
Omboué *Gabon* 1°35S 9°15E **52** E1
Ombrone → *Italy* 42°42N 11°5E **22** C4
Omdurmân *Sudan* 15°40N 32°28E **51** E12
Omemee *Canada* 44°18N 78°33W **82** B6
Omeonga
  Dem. Rep. of the Congo 3°40S 24°22E **54** C1
Ometepe, I. de *Nic.* 11°32N 85°35W **88** D2
Ometepec *Mexico* 16°41N 98°25W **87** D5
Ominato *Japan* 41°17N 141°10E **30** D10
Omineca → *Canada* 56°3N 124°16W **70** B4
Omineca Mts. *Canada* 56°30N 125°30W **70** B3
Omitara *Namibia* 22°16S 18°2E **56** C2
Ōmiya = Saitama *Japan* 35°54N 139°38E **31** G9
Ommen *Neths.* 52°31N 6°26E **15** B6
Ömnögovĭ □ *Mongolia* 43°15N 104°0E **34** C3
Omo → *Ethiopia* 6°25N 36°10E **47** F2
Omodhos *Cyprus* 34°51N 32°48E **25** E11
Omolon → *Russia* 68°42N 158°36E **29** C16
Omono-Gawa → *Japan* 39°46N 140°3E **30** E10
Ompha *Canada* 45°0N 76°50W **83** B8
Omsk *Russia* 55°0N 73°12E **28** D8
Omsukchan *Russia* 62°32N 155°48E **29** C16
Ōmu *Japan* 44°34N 142°58E **30** B11
Omul, Vf. *Romania* 45°27N 25°29E **17** F13
Ōmura *Japan* 32°56N 129°57E **31** H4
Omuramba Omatako →
  Namibia 17°45S 20°25E **56** B2
Omuramba Ovambo →
  Namibia 18°45S 16°59E **56** B2
Ōmuta *Japan* 33°5N 130°26E **31** H5
Onaga *U.S.A.* 39°29N 96°10W **80** F5
Onalaska *U.S.A.* 43°53N 91°14W **80** D8
Onancock *U.S.A.* 37°43N 75°45W **81** G16
Onang *Indonesia* 3°2S 118°49E **37** E5
Onangue, L. *Gabon* 0°57S 10°4E **52** E2
Onaping L. *Canada* 47°3N 81°30W **72** C3
Onavas *Mexico* 28°31N 109°35W **86** B3
Onawa *U.S.A.* 42°2N 96°6W **80** D5
Oncócua *Angola* 16°30S 13°25E **56** B1
Onda *Spain* 39°55N 0°17W **21** C5
Ondangwa *Namibia* 17°57S 16°4E **56** B2
Ondjiva *Angola* 16°48S 15°50E **56** B2
Öndörshil *Mongolia* 45°13N 108°5E **34** B5
Öndverðarnes *Iceland* 64°52N 24°0W **8** D2
One Arm Point *Australia* 16°26S 123°3E **60** C3
One Arm Point ⊙
  Australia 16°31S 122°53E **60** C3
One Tree *Australia* 34°11S 144°43E **63** E3
Oneata *Fiji* 18°26S 178°25W **59** a
Onega *Russia* 64°0N 38°10E **18** B6
Onega → *Russia* 63°58N 38°2E **18** B6
Onega, G. of = Onezhskaya Guba
  Russia 64°24N 36°38E **18** B6
Onega, L. = Onezhskoye Ozero
  Russia 61°44N 35°22E **18** B6
Oneida *U.S.A.* 43°6N 75°39W **83** C9
Oneida L. *U.S.A.* 43°12N 75°54W **83** C9
O'Neill *U.S.A.* 42°27N 98°39W **80** D4
Onekotan, Ostrov
  Russia 49°25N 154°45E **29** E16
Onema
  Dem. Rep. of the Congo 4°35S 24°30E **54** C1
Oneonta *U.S.A.* 42°27N 75°4W **83** D9
Oneşti *Romania* 46°17N 26°47E **17** E14
Onezhskaya Guba
  Russia 64°24N 36°38E **18** B6
Onezhskoye Ozero
  Russia 61°44N 35°22E **18** B6
Ongarue *N.Z.* 38°42S 175°19E **59** C5
Ongea Levu = Ogea Levu
  Fiji 19°8S 178°24W **59** a
Ongers → *S. Africa* 31°4S 23°13E **56** E3
Ongerup *Australia* 33°58S 118°28E **61** F2
Ongjin *N. Korea* 37°56N 125°21E **35** F13
Ongkharak *Thailand* 14°8N 101°1E **38** E3
Ongniud Qi *China* 43°0N 118°38E **35** C10
Ongoka
  Dem. Rep. of the Congo 1°20S 26°0E **54** C2
Ongole *India* 15°33N 80°2E **40** M12
Ongon = Havirga
  Mongolia 45°41N 113°5E **34** B7
Onida *U.S.A.* 44°42N 100°4W **80** C3
Onilahy → *Madag.* 23°34S 43°45E **57** C7
Onitsha *Nigeria* 6°6N 6°42E **50** G7
Ono *Fiji* 18°55S 178°29E **59** a
Onoda *Japan* 33°59N 131°11E **31** G5
Onslow *Australia* 21°40S 115°12E **60** D2
Onslow B. *U.S.A.* 34°20N 77°15W **85** D16
Ontake-San *Japan* 35°53N 137°29E **31** G8
Ontario *Calif., U.S.A.* 34°4N 117°39W **79** L9
Ontario *Oreg., U.S.A.* 44°2N 116°58W **76** D5
Ontario □ *Canada* 48°0N 83°0W **72** B2
Ontario, L. *N. Amer.* 43°20N 78°0W **82** C7
Ontonagon *U.S.A.* 46°52N 89°19W **80** B9
Onyx *U.S.A.* 35°41N 118°14W **79** K8
Oodnadatta *Australia* 27°33S 135°30E **63** D2
Ooldea *Australia* 30°27S 131°50E **61** F5

Oombulgurri *Australia* 15°15S 127°45E **60** C4
Oombulgurri ⊙
  Australia 15°10S 127°50E **60** C4
Oorindi *Australia* 20°40S 141°1E **62** C3
Oost-Vlaanderen □
  Belgium 51°5N 3°50E **15** C3
Oostende *Belgium* 51°15N 2°54E **15** C2
Oosterhout *Neths.* 51°39N 4°47E **15** C4
Oosterschelde → *Neths.* 51°33N 4°0E **15** C4
Oosterwolde *Neths.* 53°0N 6°17E **15** B6
Ootacamund = Udagamandalam
  India 11°30N 76°44E **40** P10
Ootsa L. *Canada* 53°50N 126°2W **70** C3
Ooty = Udagamandalam
  India 11°30N 76°44E **40** P10
Op Luang △ *Thailand* 18°12N 98°32E **38** C2
Opala
  Dem. Rep. of the Congo 0°40S 24°20E **54** C1
Opanake *Sri Lanka* 6°35N 80°40E **40** R12
Opasatika *Canada* 49°30N 82°50W **72** C3
Opasquia △ *Canada* 53°33N 93°5W **72** B1
Opava *Czech Rep.* 49°57N 17°58E **17** D9
Opelika *U.S.A.* 32°39N 85°23W **85** E12
Opelousas *U.S.A.* 30°32N 92°5W **84** F8
Opémisca, L. *Canada* 49°56N 74°52W **72** C5
Opheim *U.S.A.* 48°51N 106°24W **76** B10
Ophthalmia Ra.
  Australia 23°15S 119°30E **60** D2
Opinaca → *Canada* 52°15N 78°2W **72** B4
Opinaca, Rés. *Canada* 52°39N 76°20W **72** B4
Opinnagau → *Canada* 54°12N 82°25W **72** B3
Opiscotéo, L. *Canada* 53°10N 68°10W **73** B6
Opobo *Nigeria* 4°35N 7°34E **50** H7
Opole *Poland* 50°42N 17°58E **17** C9
Oponono L. *Namibia* 18°8S 15°45E **56** B2
Oporto = Porto *Portugal* 41°8N 8°40W **21** B1
Opotiki *N.Z.* 38°1S 177°19E **59** C6
Opp *U.S.A.* 31°17N 86°16W **85** F11
Oppdal *Norway* 62°35N 9°41E **8** E13
Opportunity *U.S.A.* 47°39N 117°15W **76** C5
Opua *N.Z.* 35°19S 174°9E **59** A5
Opunake *N.Z.* 39°26S 173°52E **59** C4
Opuwo *Namibia* 18°3S 13°45E **56** B1
Ora *Cyprus* 34°51N 33°12E **25** E12
Oracle *U.S.A.* 32°37N 110°46W **77** K8
Oradea *Romania* 47°2N 21°58E **17** E11
Öræfajökull *Iceland* 64°2N 16°39W **8** D5
Orai *India* 25°58N 79°30E **43** G8
Oral = Zhayyq →
  Kazakhstan 47°0N 51°48E **19** E9
Oral *Kazakhstan* 51°20N 51°20E **19** D9
Oran *Algeria* 35°45N 0°39W **50** A5
Orange *Australia* 33°15S 149°7E **63** E4
Orange *France* 44°8N 4°47E **20** D6
Orange *Calif., U.S.A.* 33°47N 117°51W **79** M9
Orange *Mass., U.S.A.* 42°35N 72°19W **83** D12
Orange *Tex., U.S.A.* 30°6N 93°44W **84** F8
Orange *Va., U.S.A.* 38°15N 78°7W **81** F14
Orange → *S. Africa* 28°41S 16°28E **56** D2
Orange, C. *Brazil* 4°20N 51°30W **93** C8
Orange Cove *U.S.A.* 36°38N 119°19W **78** J7
Orange Free State = Free State □
  S. Africa 28°30S 27°0E **56** D4
Orange Grove *U.S.A.* 27°58N 97°56W **84** H6
Orange Walk *Belize* 18°6N 88°33W **87** D7
Orangeburg *U.S.A.* 33°30N 80°52W **85** E14
Orangeville *Canada* 43°55N 80°5W **82** C4
Orango *Guinea-Biss.* 11°5N 16°0W **50** F2
Oranienburg *Germany* 52°45N 13°14E **16** B7
Oranje = Orange →
  S. Africa 28°41S 16°28E **56** D2
Oranjemund *Namibia* 28°38S 16°29E **56** D2
Oranjerivier *S. Africa* 29°40S 24°12E **56** D3
Oranjestad *Aruba* 12°32N 70°2W **89** D5
Orapa *Botswana* 21°15S 25°30E **53** J5
Oras *Phil.* 12°9N 125°28E **37** B7
Orbetello *Italy* 42°27N 11°13E **22** C4
Orbisonia *U.S.A.* 40°15N 77°54W **82** F7
Orbost *Australia* 37°40S 148°29E **63** F4
Orcadas *Antarctica* 60°44S 44°37W **5** C18
Orcas I. *U.S.A.* 48°42N 122°56W **78** B4
Orchard City *U.S.A.* 38°50N 107°58W **76** G10
Orchard Homes *U.S.A.* 46°55N 114°4W **76** C6
Orchila, I. *Venezuela* 11°48N 66°10W **89** D6
Orchila, Pta. *Canary Is.* 27°42N 18°10W **24** G1
Orcutt *U.S.A.* 34°52N 120°27W **79** L6
Ord *U.S.A.* 41°36N 98°56W **80** E4
Ord → *Australia* 15°33S 128°15E **60** C4
Ord, Mt. *Australia* 17°20S 125°34E **60** C4
Ord Mts. *U.S.A.* 34°39N 116°45W **79** L10
Orderville *U.S.A.* 37°17N 112°38W **77** H7
Ordos = Mu Us Shamo
  China 39°0N 109°0E **34** E5
Ordu *Turkey* 40°55N 37°53E **19** F6
Ordway *U.S.A.* 38°13N 103°46W **76** G12
Ore *Dem. Rep. of the Congo* 3°17N 29°30E **54** B2
Ore Mts. = Erzgebirge
  Germany 50°27N 12°55E **16** C7
Örebro *Sweden* 59°20N 15°18E **9** G16
Oregon *U.S.A.* 42°1N 89°20W **80** D9
Oregon □ *U.S.A.* 44°0N 121°0W **76** E3
Oregon City *U.S.A.* 45°21N 122°36W **78** E4
Oregon Dunes △ *U.S.A.* 43°40N 124°10W **76** E1
Orekhovo-Zuyevo
  Russia 55°50N 38°55E **18** C6
Orel *Russia* 52°57N 36°3E **18** D6
Orem *U.S.A.* 40°19N 111°42W **76** F8
Ören *Turkey* 37°3N 27°57E **23** F12
Orenburg *Russia* 51°45N 55°6E **18** D10
Orense = Ourense *Spain* 42°19N 7°55W **21** A2
Orepuki *N.Z.* 46°19S 167°46E **59** G1
Orestes Pereyra *Mexico* 26°30N 105°39W **86** B3
Orestiada *Greece* 41°30N 26°33E **23** D12
Orfanos Kolpos *Greece* 40°33N 24°0E **23** D11
Orford Ness *U.K.* 52°5N 1°35E **13** E9
Organ Pipe Cactus △
  U.S.A. 32°0N 112°52W **77** K7

Organos, Pta. de los
  Canary Is. 28°12N 17°17W 24 F2
Orgaz Spain 39°39N 3°53W 21 C4
Orgeyev = Orhei
  Moldova 47°24N 28°50E 17 E15
Orhaneli Turkey 39°54N 28°59E 23 E13
Orhangazi Turkey 40°29N 29°18E 23 D13
Orhei Moldova 47°24N 28°50E 17 E15
Orhon Gol → Mongolia 50°21N 106°0E 32 A5
Oriental, Cordillera
  Colombia 6°0N 73°0W 92 B4
Oriental, Grand Erg Algeria 30°0N 6°30E 50 B7
Orientale □
  Dem. Rep. of the Congo 2°20N 26°0E 54 B2
Oriente Argentina 38°44S 60°37W 94 D3
Orihuela Spain 38°7N 0°55W 21 C5
Orillia Canada 44°40N 79°24W 82 B5
Orinoco → Venezuela 9°15N 61°30W 92 B6
Orion Canada 49°27N 110°49W 71 D6
Oriskany U.S.A. 43°10N 75°20W 83 C9
Orissa □ India 20°0N 84°0E 41 K14
Orissaare Estonia 58°34N 23°5E 9 G20
Oristano Italy 39°54N 8°36E 22 E3
Oristano, G. di Italy 39°50N 8°29E 22 E3
Orizaba Mexico 18°51N 97°6W 87 D5
Orizaba, Pico de Mexico 18°58N 97°15W 87 D5
Orkanger Norway 63°18N 9°52E 8 E13
Orkla → Norway 63°18N 9°51E 8 E13
Orkney S. Africa 26°58S 26°40E 56 D4
Orkney □ U.K. 59°2N 3°13W 11 B5
Orkney Is. U.K. 59°0N 3°0W 11 B6
Orland U.S.A. 39°45N 122°12W 78 F4
Orlando U.S.A. 28°32N 81°22W 85 G14
Orléanais France 48°0N 2°0E 20 C5
Orléans France 47°54N 1°52E 20 C4
Orleans U.S.A. 44°49N 72°12W 83 B12
Orléans, Î. d' Canada 46°54N 70°58W 73 C5
Ormara Pakistan 25°16N 64°33E 40 G4
Ormoc Phil. 11°0N 124°37E 37 B6
Ormond N.Z. 38°33S 177°56E 59 C6
Ormond Beach U.S.A. 29°17N 81°3W 85 G14
Ormskirk U.K. 53°35N 2°54W 12 D5
Ormstown Canada 45°8N 74°0W 83 A11
Örnsköldsvik Sweden 63°17N 18°40E 8 E18
Oro N. Korea 40°1N 127°27E 35 D14
Oro → Mexico 25°35N 105°2W 86 B3
Oro Grande U.S.A. 34°36N 117°20W 79 L9
Oro Valley U.S.A. 32°26N 110°58W 77 K8
Orocué Colombia 4°48N 71°20W 92 C4
Orofino U.S.A. 46°29N 116°15W 76 C5
Orohena, Mt. Tahiti 17°37S 149°28W 59 d
Orol Dengizi = Aral Sea
  Asia 44°30N 60°0E 28 E7
Oromocto Canada 45°54N 66°29W 73 C6
Orono Canada 43°59N 78°37W 82 C6
Orono U.S.A. 44°53N 68°40W 81 C19
Oronsay U.K. 56°1N 6°15W 11 E2
Oroqen Zizhiqi China 50°34N 123°43E 33 A7
Oroquieta Phil. 8°32N 123°44E 37 C6
Orosei Italy 40°23N 9°42E 22 D3
Orosháza Hungary 46°32N 20°42E 17 E11
Orotukan Russia 62°16N 151°42E 29 C16
Oroville Calif., U.S.A. 39°31N 121°33W 78 F5
Oroville Wash., U.S.A. 48°56N 119°26W 76 B4
Oroville, L. U.S.A. 39°33N 121°29W 78 F5
Ororoo Australia 32°43S 138°38E 63 E2
Orrville U.S.A. 40°50N 81°46W 82 F3
Orsha Belarus 54°30N 30°25E 18 D5
Orsk Russia 51°12N 58°34E 28 D6
Orşova Romania 44°41N 22°25E 17 F12
Ortaca Turkey 36°49N 28°45E 23 F13
Ortegal, C. Spain 43°43N 7°52W 21 A2
Orthez France 43°29N 0°48W 20 E3
Ortigueira Spain 43°40N 7°50W 21 A2
Orting U.S.A. 47°6N 122°12W 78 C4
Ortles Italy 46°31N 10°33E 20 C9
Ortón → Bolivia 10°50S 67°0W 92 F5
Ortonville U.S.A. 45°19N 96°27W 80 C5
Orūmīyeh Iran 37°40N 45°0E 44 B5
Orūmīyeh, Daryācheh-ye
  Iran 37°50N 45°30E 44 B5
Oruro Bolivia 18°0S 67°9W 92 G5
Orust Sweden 58°10N 11°40E 9 G14
Oruzgān □ Afghan. 33°0N 66°0E 40 C5
Orvieto Italy 42°43N 12°7E 22 C5
Orwell N.Y., U.S.A. 43°35N 75°50W 83 C9
Orwell Ohio, U.S.A. 41°32N 80°52W 82 E4
Orwell → U.K. 51°59N 1°18E 13 F9
Orwigsburg U.S.A. 40°38N 76°6W 83 F8
Oryakhovo Bulgaria 43°40N 23°57E 23 C10
Oryol = Orel Russia 52°57N 36°3E 18 D6
Osa Russia 57°17N 55°26E 18 C10
Osa, Pen. de Costa Rica 8°0N 84°0W 88 E3
Osage U.S.A. 43°17N 92°49W 80 D7
Osage → U.S.A. 38°36N 91°57W 80 F8
Osage City U.S.A. 38°38N 95°50W 80 F6
Ōsaka Japan 34°42N 135°30E 31 G7
Osan S. Korea 37°11N 127°4E 35 F14
Osawatomie U.S.A. 38°31N 94°57W 80 F6
Osborne U.S.A. 39°26N 98°42W 80 F4
Osceola Ark., U.S.A. 35°42N 89°58W 85 D10
Osceola Iowa, U.S.A. 41°2N 93°46W 80 E7
Oscoda U.S.A. 44°26N 83°20W 81 C4
Ösel = Saaremaa Estonia 58°30N 22°30E 9 G20
Osgoode Canada 45°8N 75°36W 83 A9
Osh Kyrgyzstan 40°37N 72°49E 32 B2
Oshakati Namibia 17°45S 15°40E 53 H3
Oshawa Canada 43°50N 78°50W 82 C6
Oshigambo Namibia 17°45S 16°5E 56 B2
Oshkosh Nebr., U.S.A. 41°24N 102°21W 80 E2
Oshkosh Wis., U.S.A. 44°1N 88°33W 80 C9
Oshmyany = Ashmyany
  Belarus 54°26N 25°52E 17 A13
Oshnovīyeh Iran 37°2N 45°6E 44 B5
Oshogbo Nigeria 7°48N 4°37E 50 G6
Oshtorīnān Iran 34°1N 48°38E 45 C6
Oshwe
  Dem. Rep. of the Congo 3°25N 19°28E 52 E3

Osijek Croatia 45°34N 18°41E 23 B8
Osipovichi = Asipovichy
  Belarus 53°19N 28°33E 17 B15
Osiyan India 26°43N 72°55E 42 F5
Osizweni S. Africa 27°49S 30°7E 57 D5
Oskaloosa U.S.A. 41°18N 92°39W 80 E7
Oskarshamn Sweden 57°15N 16°27E 9 H17
Öskemen Kazakhstan 50°0N 82°36E 28 E9
Oslo Norway 59°54N 10°43E 9 G14
Oslofjorden Norway 59°20N 10°35E 9 G14
Osmanabad India 18°5N 76°10E 40 K10
Osmaniye Turkey 37°5N 36°10E 44 B3
Osnabrück Germany 52°17N 8°3E 16 B5
Osório Brazil 29°53S 50°17W 95 B5
Osorno Chile 40°25S 73°0W 96 E2
Osorno, Vol. Chile 41°0S 72°30W 96 E2
Osoyoos Canada 49°0N 119°30W 70 D5
Osøyro Norway 60°9N 5°30E 8 F11
Ospika → Canada 56°20N 124°0W 70 B4
Osprey Reef Australia 13°52S 146°36E 62 A4
Oss Neths. 51°46N 5°32E 15 C5
Ossa, Mt. Australia 41°52S 146°3E 63 G4
Ossa, Oros Greece 39°47N 22°42E 23 E10
Ossabaw I. U.S.A. 31°50N 81°5W 85 F14
Ossining U.S.A. 41°10N 73°55W 83 E11
Ossipee U.S.A. 43°41N 71°7W 83 C13
Ossokmanuan L. Canada 53°25N 65°0W 73 B7
Ossora Russia 59°20N 163°13E 29 D17
Ostend = Oostende
  Belgium 51°15N 2°54E 15 C2
Oster Ukraine 50°57N 30°53E 17 C16
Österbotten = Pohjanmaa
  Finland 62°58N 22°50E 8 E20
Osterburg U.S.A. 40°16N 78°31W 82 F6
Österdalälven Sweden 61°30N 13°45E 8 F15
Østerdalen Norway 61°40N 10°50E 8 F14
Östermyra = Seinäjoki
  Finland 62°40N 22°51E 8 E20
Österreich = Austria ■
  Europe 47°0N 14°0E 16 E8
Östersund Sweden 63°10N 14°38E 8 E16
Ostfriesische Inseln
  Germany 53°42N 7°0E 16 B4
Ostrava Czech Rep. 49°51N 18°18E 17 D10
Ostróda Poland 53°42N 19°58E 17 B10
Ostroh Ukraine 50°20N 26°30E 17 C14
Ostrołęka Poland 53°4N 21°32E 17 B11
Ostrów Mazowiecka
  Poland 52°50N 21°51E 17 B11
Ostrów Wielkopolski
  Poland 51°36N 17°44E 17 C9
Ostrowiec-Świętokrzyski
  Poland 50°55N 21°22E 17 C11
Ostuni Italy 40°44N 17°35E 23 D7
Ōsumi-Kaikyō Japan 30°55N 131°0E 31 J5
Ōsumi-Shotō Japan 30°30N 130°0E 31 J5
Osuna Spain 37°14N 5°8W 21 D3
Oswegatchie → U.S.A. 44°42N 75°30W 83 B9
Oswego U.S.A. 43°27N 76°31W 83 C8
Oswego → U.S.A. 43°27N 76°30W 83 C8
Oswestry U.K. 52°52N 3°3W 12 E4
Oświęcim Poland 50°2N 19°11E 17 C10
Otago □ N.Z. 45°15S 170°0E 59 F2
Otago Harbour N.Z. 45°47S 170°42E 59 F3
Otaheite B. Trin. & Tob. 10°15N 61°30W 93 K15
Ōtake Japan 34°12N 132°13E 31 G6
Otaki N.Z. 40°45S 175°10E 59 D5
Otaru Japan 43°10N 141°0E 30 C10
Otaru-Wan = Ishikari-Wan
  Japan 43°25N 141°1E 30 C10
Otavalo Ecuador 0°13N 78°20W 92 C3
Otavi Namibia 19°40S 17°24E 56 B2
Otchinjau Angola 16°30S 13°56E 56 B1
Otego U.S.A. 42°23N 75°10W 83 D9
Otelnuk, L. Canada 56°9N 68°12W 73 A6
Othello U.S.A. 46°50N 119°10W 76 C4
Otish, Mts. Canada 52°22N 70°30W 73 B5
Otjiwarongo Namibia 20°30S 16°33E 56 C2
Oto Tolu Group Tonga 20°21S 174°32W 59 c
Otoineppu Japan 44°44N 142°16E 30 B11
Otorohanga N.Z. 38°12S 175°14E 59 C5
Otoskwin → Canada 52°13N 88°6W 72 B2
Otra → Norway 58°9N 8°1E 9 G13
Otranto Italy 40°9N 18°28E 23 D8
Otranto, C. d' Italy 40°7N 18°30E 23 D8
Otranto, Str. of Italy 40°15N 18°40E 23 D8
Otse S. Africa 25°2S 25°45E 56 D4
Otsego L. U.S.A. 42°45N 74°53W 83 D10
Ōtsu Japan 35°0N 135°50E 31 G7
Ōtsuki Japan 35°36N 138°57E 31 G9
Ottawa = Outaouais →
  Canada 45°27N 74°8W 72 C5
Ottawa Canada 45°26N 75°42W 83 A9
Ottawa Ill., U.S.A. 41°21N 88°51W 80 E9
Ottawa Kans., U.S.A. 38°37N 95°16W 80 F6
Ottawa Is. Canada 59°35N 80°10W 69 F15
Otter Cr. → U.S.A. 44°13N 73°17W 83 B11
Otter Lake Canada 45°17N 76°26W 82 A5
Otterville Canada 42°55N 80°36W 82 D4
Ottery St. Mary U.K. 50°44N 3°17W 13 G4
Otto Beit Bridge
  Zimbabwe 15°59S 28°56E 55 F2
Ottosdal S. Africa 26°46S 25°59E 56 D4
Ottumwa U.S.A. 41°1N 92°25W 80 E7
Oturkpo Nigeria 7°16N 8°8E 50 G7
Otway, B. Chile 53°30S 74°0W 96 G2
Otway, C. Australia 38°52S 143°30E 63 F3
Otwock Poland 52°5N 21°20E 17 B11
Ou → Laos 20°4N 102°13E 38 B4
Ou Neua Laos 22°18N 101°48E 38 A3
Ou-Sammyaku Japan 39°20N 140°35E 30 E10
Ouachita → U.S.A. 31°38N 91°49W 84 F9
Ouachita, L. U.S.A. 34°34N 93°12W 84 D8
Ouachita Mts. U.S.A. 34°30N 94°30W 84 D7
Ouagadougou
  Burkina Faso 12°25N 1°30W 50 F5
Ouahigouya Burkina Faso 13°31N 2°25W 50 F5

Ouahran = Oran Algeria 35°45N 0°39W 50 A5
Ouallene Algeria 24°41N 1°11E 50 D6
Ouarâne Mauritania 21°0N 10°30W 50 D3
Ouargla Algeria 31°59N 5°16E 50 B7
Ouarra → C.A.R. 5°0N 24°26E 52 C4
Ouarzazate Morocco 30°55N 6°50W 50 B4
Oubangi →
  Dem. Rep. of the Congo 0°30S 17°50E 52 E3
Ouddorp Neths. 51°50N 3°57E 15 C3
Oude Rijn → Neths. 52°12N 4°24E 15 B4
Oudenaarde Belgium 50°50N 3°37E 15 D3
Oudtshoorn S. Africa 33°35S 22°14E 56 E3
Ouessant, Î. d' France 48°28N 5°6W 20 B1
Ouesso Congo 1°37N 16°5E 52 D3
Ouest, Pte. de l' Canada 49°52N 64°40W 73 C7
Ouezzane Morocco 34°51N 5°35W 50 B4
Ouidah Benin 6°25N 2°0E 50 G6
Oujda Morocco 34°41N 1°55W 50 B5
Oulainen Finland 64°17N 24°47E 8 D21
Oulu Finland 65°1N 25°29E 8 D21
Oulujärvi Finland 64°25N 27°15E 8 D22
Oulujoki → Finland 65°1N 25°30E 8 D21
Oum Chalouba Chad 15°48N 20°46E 51 E10
Oum Hadjer Chad 13°18N 19°41E 51 F9
Ounasjoki → Finland 66°31N 25°40E 8 C21
Ounguati Namibia 22°0S 15°46E 56 C2
Ounianga Kébir Chad 19°4N 20°29E 51 E10
Our → Lux. 49°55N 6°5E 15 E6
Ouray U.S.A. 38°1N 107°40W 77 G10
Ourense Spain 42°19N 7°55W 21 A2
Ouricuri Brazil 7°53S 40°5W 93 E10
Ourinhos Brazil 23°0S 49°54W 95 A6
Ouro Fino Brazil 22°16S 46°25W 95 A6
Ouro Prêto Brazil 20°20S 43°30W 95 A7
Ourthe → Belgium 50°29N 5°35E 15 D5
Ouse → E. Sussex, U.K. 50°47N 0°4E 13 G8
Ouse → N. Yorks., U.K. 53°44N 0°55W 12 D7
Outaouais → Canada 45°27N 74°8W 72 C5
Outardes → Canada 49°24N 69°30W 73 C6
Outer Hebrides U.K. 57°30N 7°40W 11 D1
Outjo Namibia 20°5S 16°7E 56 C2
Outlook Canada 51°30N 107°0W 71 C7
Outokumpu Finland 62°43N 29°1E 8 E23
Ouyen Australia 35°1S 142°22E 63 F3
Ovalau Fiji 17°40S 178°48E 59 a
Ovalle Chile 30°33S 71°18W 94 C1
Ovamboland Namibia 18°30S 16°0E 56 B2
Overflakkee Neths. 51°44N 4°10E 15 C4
Overijssel □ Neths. 52°25N 6°35E 15 B6
Overland Park U.S.A. 38°58N 94°40W 80 F6
Overlander Roadhouse
  Australia 26°19S 114°28E 61 E1
Overton U.S.A. 36°33N 114°27W 79 J12
Övertorneå Sweden 66°23N 23°38E 8 C20
Ovid U.S.A. 42°41N 76°49W 83 D8
Oviedo Spain 43°25N 5°50W 21 A3
Oviši Latvia 57°33N 21°44E 9 H19
Ovoot Mongolia 45°21N 113°45E 34 B7
Övör Hangay □
  Mongolia 45°0N 102°30E 34 B2
Øvre Årdal Norway 61°19N 7°48E 8 F12
Ovruch Ukraine 51°25N 28°45E 17 C15
Owaka N.Z. 46°27S 169°40E 59 G2
Owambo = Ovamboland
  Namibia 18°30S 16°0E 56 B2
Owasco L. U.S.A. 42°50N 76°31W 83 D8
Owase Japan 34°7N 136°12E 31 G8
Owatonna U.S.A. 44°5N 93°14W 80 C7
Owbeh Afghan. 34°28N 63°10E 40 B3
Owego U.S.A. 42°6N 76°16W 83 D8
Owen Falls Dam = Nalubaale
  Dam Uganda 0°30N 33°5E 54 B3
Owen Sound Canada 44°35N 80°55W 82 B4
Owen Stanley Ra.
  Papua N. G. 8°30S 147°0E 58 B7
Oweniny → Ireland 54°8N 9°34W 10 B2
Owens → U.S.A. 36°33N 117°59W 78 J9
Owens L. U.S.A. 36°26N 117°57W 79 J9
Owensboro U.S.A. 37°46N 87°7W 80 G10
Owl → Canada 57°51N 92°44W 71 B10
Owo Nigeria 7°10N 5°39E 50 G7
Owosso U.S.A. 43°0N 84°10W 81 D11
Owyhee U.S.A. 41°57N 116°6W 76 F5
Owyhee → U.S.A. 43°49N 117°2W 76 E5
Owyhee, L. U.S.A. 43°38N 117°14W 76 E5
Ox Mts. = Slieve Gamph
  Ireland 54°6N 9°0W 10 B3
Öxarfjörður Iceland 66°15N 16°45W 8 C5
Oxbow Canada 49°14N 102°10W 71 D8
Oxelösund Sweden 58°43N 17°5E 9 G17
Oxford N.Z. 43°18S 172°11E 59 E4
Oxford U.K. 51°46N 1°15W 13 F6
Oxford Mass., U.S.A. 42°7N 71°52W 83 D13
Oxford Miss., U.S.A. 34°22N 89°31W 85 D10
Oxford N.C., U.S.A. 36°19N 78°35W 85 G15
Oxford N.Y., U.S.A. 42°27N 75°36W 83 D9
Oxford Ohio, U.S.A. 39°31N 84°45W 81 F11
Oxford L. Canada 54°51N 95°37W 71 C9
Oxfordshire □ U.K. 51°48N 1°16W 13 F6
Oxnard U.S.A. 34°12N 119°11W 79 L7
Oxus = Amudarya →
  Uzbekistan 43°58N 59°34E 28 E6
Oya Malaysia 2°55N 111°55E 36 D4
Oyama Japan 36°18N 139°48E 31 F9
Oyem Gabon 1°34N 11°31E 52 D2
Oyen Canada 51°22N 110°28W 71 C6
Oykel → U.K. 57°56N 4°26W 11 D4
Oymyakon Russia 63°25N 142°44E 29 C15
Oyo Nigeria 7°46N 3°56E 50 G6
Oyster Bay U.S.A. 40°52N 73°32W 83 F11
Öyübari Japan 43°1N 142°5E 30 C11
Ozamiz Phil. 8°15N 123°50E 37 C6
Ozark Ala., U.S.A. 31°28N 85°39W 85 F12
Ozark Ark., U.S.A. 35°29N 93°50W 84 D8
Ozark Mo., U.S.A. 37°1N 93°12W 80 G7
Ozark Plateau U.S.A. 37°20N 91°40W 80 G8

Ozarks, L. of the U.S.A. 38°12N 92°38W 80 F7
Ózd Hungary 48°14N 20°15E 17 D11
Ozernovskiy Russia 51°30N 156°31E 29 D16
Ozette, L. U.S.A. 48°6N 124°38W 78 B2
Ozieri Italy 40°35N 9°0E 22 D3
Ozona U.S.A. 30°43N 101°12W 84 F4
Ozuluama Mexico 21°40N 97°51W 87 C5

P

Pa-an Burma 16°51N 97°40E 41 L20
Pa Mong Dam Thailand 18°0N 102°22E 38 D4
Pa Sak → Thailand 15°30N 101°0E 38 E3
Paamiut Greenland 62°0N 49°43W 4 C5
Paarl S. Africa 33°45S 18°56E 56 E2
Pab Hills Pakistan 26°30N 66°45E 42 F2
Pabbay U.K. 57°46N 7°14W 11 D1
Pabianice Poland 51°40N 19°20E 17 C10
Pabna Bangla. 24°1N 89°18E 41 G16
Pabo Uganda 3°1N 32°10E 54 B3
Pacaja → Brazil 1°56S 50°50W 93 D8
Pacaraima, Sa. S. Amer. 4°0N 62°30W 92 C6
Pacasmayo Peru 7°20S 79°35W 92 E3
Pachitea → Peru 8°46S 74°33W 92 E4
Pachmarhi India 22°28N 78°26E 43 H8
Pachnes Greece 35°16N 24°4E 25 D6
Pachpadra India 25°58N 72°10E 42 G5
Pachuca Mexico 20°7N 98°44W 87 C5
Pacific Antarctic Ridge
  Pac. Oc. 43°0S 115°0W 5 B13
Pacific Grove U.S.A. 36°38N 121°56W 78 J5
Pacific Ocean 10°0N 140°0W 65 G14
Pacific Rim △ Canada 48°40N 124°45W 78 B2
Pacifica U.S.A. 37°37N 122°27W 78 H4
Pacitan Indonesia 8°12S 111°7E 37 H14
Packwood U.S.A. 46°36N 121°40W 78 D5
Padaido, Kepulauan
  Indonesia 1°15S 136°30E 37 E9
Padang Riau, Indonesia 1°3N 102°30E 39 M4
Padang Sumatera Barat,
  Indonesia 1°0S 100°20E 36 E2
Padang Endau Malaysia 2°40N 103°38E 39 L4
Padangpanjang
  Indonesia 0°40S 100°20E 36 E2
Padangsidempuan
  Indonesia 1°30N 99°15E 36 D1
Paddle Prairie Canada 57°57N 117°29W 70 B5
Paderborn Germany 51°42N 8°45E 16 C5
Padma India 24°12N 85°22E 43 G11
Pádova Italy 45°25N 11°53E 22 B4
Padra India 22°15N 73°7E 42 H5
Padrauna India 26°54N 83°59E 43 F10
Padre I. U.S.A. 27°10N 97°25W 84 H6
Padre Island △ U.S.A. 27°0N 97°25W 84 H6
Padstow U.K. 50°33N 4°58W 13 G3
Padua = Pádova Italy 45°25N 11°53E 22 B4
Paducah Ky., U.S.A. 37°5N 88°37W 80 G9
Paducah Tex., U.S.A. 34°1N 100°18W 84 D4
Paea Tahiti 17°41S 149°35W 59 d
Paeroa N.Z. 37°23S 175°41E 59 B5
Pafúri Mozam. 22°28S 31°17E 57 C5
Pag Croatia 44°25N 15°3E 16 F8
Pagadian Phil. 7°55N 123°30E 37 C6
Pagai Selatan, Pulau
  Indonesia 3°0S 100°15E 36 E2
Pagai Utara, Pulau
  Indonesia 2°35S 100°0E 36 E2
Pagalu = Annobón Atl. Oc. 1°25S 5°36E 49 G4
Pagara India 24°22N 80°1E 43 G9
Pagastikos Kolpos
  Greece 39°15N 23°0E 23 E10
Pagatan Indonesia 3°33S 115°59E 36 E5
Page U.S.A. 36°57N 111°27W 77 H8
Paget, Mt. S. Georgia 54°26N 36°31W 96 G9
Pago Pago Amer. Samoa 14°16S 170°43W 59 b
Pagosa Springs U.S.A. 37°16N 107°1W 77 H10
Pagwa River Canada 50°2N 85°14W 72 B2
Pāhala U.S.A. 19°12N 155°29W 75 M8
Pahang → Malaysia 3°30N 103°9E 39 L4
Pahiatua N.Z. 40°27S 175°50E 59 D5
Pahokee U.S.A. 26°50N 80°40W 85 H14
Pahrump U.S.A. 36°12N 115°59W 79 J11
Pahute Mesa U.S.A. 37°20N 116°45W 78 H10
Pai Thailand 19°19N 98°27E 38 C2
Paicines U.S.A. 36°44N 121°17W 78 J5
Paide Estonia 58°53N 25°33E 9 G21
Paignton U.K. 50°26N 3°35W 13 G4
Päijänne Finland 61°30N 25°30E 8 F21
Pailani India 25°45N 80°26E 43 G9
Pailin Cambodia 12°46N 102°36E 38 F4
Painan Indonesia 1°21S 100°34E 36 E2
Painesville U.S.A. 41°43N 81°15W 82 E3
Paint Hills = Wemindji
  Canada 53°0N 78°49W 72 B4
Paint L. Canada 55°28N 97°57W 71 B9
Painted Desert U.S.A. 36°0N 111°0W 77 H8
Paintsville U.S.A. 37°49N 82°48W 81 G12
País Vasco □ Spain 42°50N 2°45W 21 A4
Paisley Canada 44°18N 81°16W 82 B3
Paisley U.K. 55°50N 4°25W 11 F4
Paisley U.S.A. 42°42N 120°32W 76 E3
Paita Peru 5°11S 81°9W 92 E2
Pajares, Puerto de Spain 43°0N 5°46W 21 A3
Pak Lay Laos 18°15N 101°27E 38 C3
Pak Phanang Thailand 8°21N 100°12E 39 H3
Pak Sane Laos 18°22N 103°39E 38 C4
Pak Song Laos 15°11N 106°14E 38 E6
Pak Suong Laos 19°58N 102°15E 38 C4
Pak Tam Chung China 22°24N 114°19E 33 G11
Pakaur India 24°38N 87°51E 43 G12
Pakch'ŏn N. Korea 39°55N 125°35E 35 E13
Pakenham Canada 45°18N 76°18W 83 A8
Pakhuis S. Africa 32°9S 19°5E 56 E2
Pakistan ■ Asia 30°0N 70°0E 42 E4
Pakkading Laos 18°19N 103°59E 38 C4
Pakokku Burma 21°20N 95°0E 41 J19
Pakowki L. Canada 49°20N 111°0W 71 D6
Pakpattan Pakistan 30°25N 73°27E 42 D5

Paktīā □ Afghan. 33°30N 69°15E 40 C6
Paktīkā □ Afghan. 32°30N 69°0E 40 C6
Pakwach Uganda 2°28N 31°27E 54 B3
Pakxe Laos 15°5N 105°52E 38 E5
Pal Lahara India 21°27N 85°11E 43 J11
Pala Chad 9°25N 15°5E 51 G9
Pala Dem. Rep. of the Congo 6°45S 29°30E 54 D2
Pala U.S.A. 33°22N 117°5W 79 M9
Palabek Uganda 3°22N 32°33E 54 B3
Palacios U.S.A. 28°42N 96°13W 84 G6
Palagruža Croatia 42°24N 16°15E 22 C7
Palakkad = Palghat
  India 10°46N 76°42E 40 P10
Palam India 19°0N 77°0E 40 K10
Palampur India 32°10N 76°30E 42 C7
Palana Australia 39°45S 147°55E 63 F4
Palana Russia 59°10N 159°59E 29 D16
Palanan Phil. 17°8N 122°29E 37 A6
Palanan Pt. Phil. 17°17N 122°30E 37 A6
Palandri Pakistan 33°42N 73°40E 43 C5
Palanga Lithuania 55°58N 21°3E 9 J19
Palangkaraya Indonesia 2°16S 113°56E 36 E4
Palani Hills India 10°14N 77°33E 40 P10
Palanpur India 24°10N 72°25E 42 G5
Palapye Botswana 22°30S 27°7E 56 C4
Palas Pakistan 35°4N 73°14E 43 B5
Palasponga India 21°47N 85°34E 43 J11
Palatka Russia 60°6N 150°54E 29 C16
Palatka U.S.A. 29°39N 81°38W 85 G14
Palau ■ Palau 7°30N 134°30E 58 A6
Palauk Burma 13°10N 98°40E 38 F2
Palawan Phil. 9°30N 118°30E 36 C5
Palayankottai India 8°45N 77°45E 40 Q10
Paldiski Estonia 59°23N 24°9E 9 G21
Palekastro Greece 35°12N 26°15E 25 D8
Paleleh Indonesia 1°10N 121°50E 37 D6
Palembang Indonesia 3°0S 104°50E 36 E2
Palencia Spain 42°1N 4°34W 21 A3
Palenque Mexico 17°29N 92°1W 87 D6
Paleochora Greece 35°16N 23°39E 25 D5
Paleokastritsa Greece 39°40N 19°41E 25 A3
Paleometokho Cyprus 35°7N 33°11E 25 D12
Palermo Italy 38°7N 13°22E 22 E5
Palermo U.S.A. 39°26N 121°33W 76 G3
Palestina Chile 23°50S 69°47W 96 A3
Palestine Asia 32°0N 35°0E 46 D4
Palestine U.S.A. 31°46N 95°38W 84 F7
Paletwa Burma 21°10N 92°50E 41 J18
Palghat India 10°46N 76°42E 40 P10
Palgrave, Mt. Australia 23°22S 115°58E 60 D2
Pali India 25°50N 73°20E 42 G5
Palikir Micronesia 6°55N 158°9E 64 G7
Paliouri, Akra Greece 39°57N 23°45E 23 E10
Palisades Res. U.S.A. 43°20N 111°12W 76 E8
Paliseul Belgium 49°54N 5°8E 15 E5
Palitana India 21°32N 71°49E 42 J4
Palizada Mexico 18°15N 92°5W 87 D6
Palk Bay Asia 9°30N 79°15E 40 Q11
Palk Strait Asia 10°0N 79°45E 40 Q11
Palkānah Iraq 35°49N 44°26E 44 C5
Palkot India 22°52N 84°39E 43 H11
Pallanza = Verbánia Italy 45°56N 8°33E 20 D8
Pallarenda Australia 19°12S 146°46E 62 B4
Pallinup → Australia 34°27S 118°50E 61 F2
Pallisa Uganda 1°12N 33°43E 54 B3
Pallu India 28°59N 74°14E 42 E6
Palm Bay U.S.A. 28°2N 80°35W 85 G14
Palm Beach U.S.A. 26°43N 80°2W 85 H14
Palm Coast U.S.A. 29°35N 81°12W 85 G14
Palm Desert U.S.A. 33°43N 116°22W 79 M10
Palm-Grove △ Australia 24°59S 149°21E 62 C4
Palm Is. Australia 18°40S 146°35E 62 B4
Palm Springs U.S.A. 33°50N 116°33W 79 M10
Palma Mozam. 10°46S 40°29E 55 E5
Palma, B. de Spain 39°30N 2°39E 24 B9
Palma de Mallorca Spain 39°35N 2°39E 24 B9
Palma Nova = Palmanova
  Spain 39°32N 2°34E 24 B9
Palma Soriano Cuba 20°15N 76°0W 88 B4
Palmanova Spain 39°32N 2°34E 24 B9
Palmares Brazil 8°41S 35°28W 93 E11
Palmas Brazil 26°29S 52°0W 95 B5
Palmas, C. Liberia 4°27N 7°46W 50 H4
Pálmas, G. di Italy 39°0N 8°30E 22 E3
Palmdale U.S.A. 34°35N 118°7W 79 L8
Palmeira das Missões
  Brazil 27°55S 53°17W 95 B5
Palmeira dos Índios
  Brazil 9°25S 36°37W 93 E11
Palmer Antarctica 64°35S 65°0W 5 C17
Palmer U.S.A. 61°36N 149°7W 68 E2
Palmer → Australia 16°0S 142°26E 62 B3
Palmer Arch. Antarctica 64°15S 65°0W 5 C17
Palmer Lake U.S.A. 39°7N 104°55W 76 G11
Palmer Land Antarctica 73°0S 63°0W 5 D18
Palmerston Australia 12°31S 130°59E 60 B5
Palmerston Canada 43°50N 80°51W 82 C4
Palmerston N.Z. 45°29S 170°43E 59 F3
Palmerston North N.Z. 40°21S 175°39E 59 D5
Palmerton U.S.A. 40°48N 75°37W 83 F9
Palmetto U.S.A. 27°31N 82°34W 85 H13
Palmi Italy 38°21N 15°51E 22 E6
Palmira Argentina 32°59S 68°34W 94 C2
Palmira Colombia 3°32N 76°16W 92 C3
Palmyra = Tudmur
  Syria 34°36N 38°15E 44 C3
Palmyra Mo., U.S.A. 39°48N 91°32W 80 F8
Palmyra N.J., U.S.A. 40°0N 75°1W 83 F9
Palmyra N.Y., U.S.A. 43°5N 77°18W 82 C7
Palmyra Pa., U.S.A. 40°18N 76°36W 83 F8
Palmyra Is. Pac. Oc. 5°52N 162°5W 65 G11
Palo Alto U.S.A. 37°27N 122°10W 78 H4
Palo Seco Trin. & Tob. 10°4N 61°36W 93 K15
Palo Verde U.S.A. 33°26N 114°44W 79 M12
Palo Verde △ Costa Rica 10°21N 85°21W 88 D2
Palomar Mt. U.S.A. 33°22N 116°50W 79 M10
Palopo Indonesia 3°0S 120°16E 37 E6
Palos, C. de Spain 37°38N 0°40W 21 D5

Palos Verdes, Pt.
  U.S.A. 33°46N 118°25W **79 M8**
Palos Verdes Estates
  U.S.A. 33°48N 118°23W **79 M8**
Palu Indonesia 1°0S 119°52E **37 E5**
Palu Turkey 38°45N 40°0E **44 B3**
Paluma Ra. Australia 19°9S 146°22E **62 B4**
Palwal India 28°8N 77°19E **42 E7**
Pamanukan Indonesia 6°16S 107°49E **37 G12**
Pamekasan Indonesia 7°10S 113°28E **37 G15**
Pamenang Indonesia 8°24S 116°6E **37 J19**
Pamiers France 43°7N 1°39E **20 E4**
Pamir Tajikistan 37°40N 73°0E **28 F8**
Pamlico → U.S.A. 35°20N 76°28W **85 D16**
Pamlico Sd. U.S.A. 35°20N 76°0W **85 D17**
Pampa U.S.A. 35°32N 100°58W **84 D4**
Pampa de las Salinas
  Argentina 32°1S 66°58W **94 C2**
Pampanua Indonesia 4°16S 120°8E **37 E6**
Pampas Argentina 35°0S 63°0W **94 D3**
Pampas Peru 12°20S 74°50W **92 F4**
Pamplona Colombia 7°23N 72°39W **92 B4**
Pamplona-Iruña Spain 42°48N 1°38W **21 A5**
Pampoenpoort S. Africa 31°3S 22°40E **56 E3**
Pan de Azúcar Chile 24°5S 68°10W **94 A2**
Pan de Azúcar △ Chile 26°0S 70°40W **94 B1**
Pana U.S.A. 39°23N 89°5W **80 F9**
Panaca U.S.A. 37°47N 114°23W **77 H6**
Panaitan Indonesia 6°36S 105°12E **37 G12**
Panaji India 15°25N 73°50E **40 M8**
Panamá Panama 9°0N 79°25W **88 E4**
Panama ■ Cent. Amer. 8°48N 79°55W **88 E4**
Panamá, G. de Panama 8°4N 79°20W **88 E4**
Panama, Isthmus of
  Cent. Amer. 9°0N 79°0W **66 J12**
Panama Basin Pac. Oc. 5°0N 83°30W **65 G19**
Panama Canal Panama 9°10N 79°37W **88 E4**
Panama City U.S.A. 30°10N 85°40W **85 F12**
Panamint Range
  U.S.A. 36°20N 117°20W **79 J9**
Panamint Springs
  U.S.A. 36°20N 117°28W **79 J9**
Panão Peru 9°55S 75°55W **92 E3**
Panare Thailand 6°51N 101°30E **39 J3**
Panay Phil. 11°10N 122°30E **37 B6**
Panay G. Phil. 11°0N 122°30E **37 B6**
Panayarvi → Russia 66°16N 30°10E **8 C24**
Pančevo Serbia 44°52N 20°41E **23 B9**
Panda Mozam. 24°2S 34°45E **57 C5**
Pandan Malaysia 1°32N 103°46E **39 d**
Pandan Phil. 11°45N 122°10E **37 B6**
Pandan, Selat Singapore 1°15N 103°44E **39 d**
Pandan Tampoi = Tampoi
  Malaysia 1°31N 103°39E **39 d**
Pandegelang Indonesia 6°25S 106°5E **37 G12**
Pandhana India 21°42N 76°13E **42 J7**
Pandharpur India 17°41N 75°20E **40 L9**
Pando Uruguay 34°44S 56°0W **95 C4**
Pando, L. = Hope, L.
  Australia 28°24S 139°18E **63 D2**
Pandokratoras Greece 39°45N 19°50E **25 A3**
Pandora Costa Rica 9°43N 83°3W **88 E3**
Panevėžys Lithuania 55°42N 24°25E **9 J21**
Pang-Long Burma 23°11N 98°45E **41 H21**
Pang Sida △ Thailand 14°5N 102°17E **38 F4**
Pang-Yang Burma 22°7N 98°48E **41 H21**
Panga
  Dem. Rep. of the Congo 1°52N 26°18E **54 B2**
Pangalanes, Canal des =
  Ampangalana, Lakandranon'
  Madag. 22°48S 47°50E **57 C8**
Pangani Tanzania 5°25S 38°58E **54 D4**
Pangani → Tanzania 5°26S 38°58E **54 D4**
Pangfou = Bengbu
  China 32°58N 117°20E **35 H9**
Pangil
  Dem. Rep. of the Congo 3°10S 26°35E **54 C2**
Pangkah, Tanjung
  Indonesia 6°51S 112°33E **37 G15**
Pangkajene Indonesia 4°46S 119°34E **37 E5**
Pangkalanbrandan
  Indonesia 4°1N 98°20E **36 D1**
Pangkalanbuun
  Indonesia 2°41S 111°37E **36 E4**
Pangkalpinang Indonesia 2°0S 106°0E **36 E3**
Pangkor, P. Malaysia 4°13N 100°34E **39 K3**
Pangniqtuuq = Pangnirtung
  Canada 66°8N 65°43W **69 D18**
Pangnirtung Canada 66°8N 65°43W **69 D18**
Pangody Russia 65°52N 74°27E **28 C8**
Pangong Tso = Bangong Co
  China 33°45N 78°43E **43 C8**
Panguitch U.S.A. 37°50N 112°26W **77 H7**
Pangutaran Group Phil. 6°18N 120°34E **37 C6**
Panhandle U.S.A. 35°21N 101°23W **84 D4**
Pani Mines India 22°29N 73°50E **42 H5**
Pania-Mutombo
  Dem. Rep. of the Congo 5°11S 23°51E **54 D1**
Panikota I. India 20°46N 71°21E **42 J4**
Panipat India 29°25N 77°2E **42 E7**
Panjal Range = Pir Panjal Range
  India 32°30N 76°50E **42 C7**
Panjang, Hon Vietnam 9°20N 103°28E **39 H4**
Panjgur Pakistan 27°0N 64°5E **40 F4**
Panjim = Panaji India 15°25N 73°50E **40 M8**
Panjin China 41°3N 122°2E **35 D12**
Panjnad → Pakistan 28°57N 70°30E **42 E4**
Panjnad Barrage
  Pakistan 29°22N 71°15E **42 E4**
Panjwai Afghan. 31°26N 65°27E **42 D1**
Panmunjŏm N. Korea 37°59N 126°38E **35 F14**
Panna India 24°40N 80°15E **43 G9**
Panna △ India 24°40N 80°0E **43 G8**
Panna Hills India 24°40N 81°15E **43 G9**
Pannawonica Australia 21°39S 116°19E **60 D2**
Pannga, Tanjung
  Indonesia 8°54S 116°2E **37 K19**
Pano Akil Pakistan 27°51N 69°7E **42 F3**
Pano Lefkara Cyprus 34°53N 33°20E **25 E12**

Pano Panayia Cyprus 34°55N 32°38E **25 E11**
Panorama Brazil 21°21S 51°51W **95 A5**
Panormos Greece 35°25N 24°41E **25 D6**
Pansemal India 21°39N 74°42E **42 J6**
Panshan = Panjin China 41°3N 122°2E **35 D12**
Panshi China 42°58N 126°5E **35 C14**
Pantanal Brazil 17°30S 57°40W **92 H7**
Pantanos de Centla △
  Mexico 18°25N 92°25W **87 D6**
Pantar Indonesia 8°28S 124°10E **37 F6**
Pante Macassar E. Timor 9°30S 123°58E **37 F6**
Pantelleria Italy 36°50N 11°57E **22 F4**
Pánuco Mexico 22°3N 98°10W **87 C5**
Panzhihua China 26°33N 101°44E **32 D5**
Paola Malta 35°52N 14°30E **25 D2**
Paola U.S.A. 38°35N 94°53W **80 F6**
Paonia U.S.A. 38°52N 107°36W **76 G10**
Paopao Moorea 17°30S 149°49W **59 d**
Paoting = Baoding
  China 38°50N 115°28E **34 E8**
Paot'ou = Baotou China 40°32N 110°2E **34 D6**
Paoua C.A.R. 7°9N 16°20E **52 C3**
Pápa Hungary 47°22N 17°30E **17 E9**
Papa Stour U.K. 60°20N 1°42W **11 A7**
Papa Westray U.K. 59°20N 2°55W **11 B6**
Papagayo → Mexico 16°46N 99°43W **87 D5**
Papagayo, G. de
  Costa Rica 10°30N 85°50W **88 D2**
Papakura N.Z. 37°4S 174°59E **59 B5**
Papantla Mexico 20°27N 97°19W **87 C5**
Papar Malaysia 5°45N 116°0E **36 C5**
Papara Tahiti 17°43S 149°31W **59 d**
Paparoa △ N.Z. 42°7S 171°26E **59 E3**
Papeete Tahiti 17°32S 149°34W **59 d**
Papenoo Tahiti 17°30S 149°25W **59 d**
Papenoo → Tahiti 17°30S 149°25W **59 d**
Papetoai Moorea 17°29S 149°52W **59 d**
Paphos Cyprus 34°46N 32°25E **25 E11**
Paposo Chile 25°0S 70°30W **94 B1**
Papoutsa Cyprus 34°54N 33°4E **25 E12**
Papua □ Indonesia 4°0S 137°0E **37 E9**
Papua, G. of Papua N. G. 9°0S 144°50E **58 B7**
Papua New Guinea ■
  Oceania 8°0S 145°0E **58 B7**
Papudo Chile 32°29S 71°27W **94 C1**
Papun Burma 18°2N 97°30E **41 K20**
Papunya Australia 23°15S 131°54E **60 D5**
Pará = Belém Brazil 1°20S 48°30W **93 D9**
Pará □ Brazil 3°20S 52°0W **93 D8**
Paraburdoo Australia 23°14S 117°32E **60 D2**
Paracel Is. S. China Sea 15°50N 112°0E **36 A4**
Parachilna Australia 31°10S 138°21E **63 E2**
Parachinar Pakistan 33°55N 70°5E **42 C4**
Paradip India 20°15N 86°35E **41 J15**
Paradise Calif., U.S.A. 39°46N 121°37W **78 F5**
Paradise Nev., U.S.A. 36°5N 115°8W **79 J11**
Paradise → Canada 53°27N 57°19W **73 B8**
Paradise Hill Canada 53°32N 109°28W **71 C7**
Paradise River Canada 53°27N 57°17W **73 B8**
Paradise Valley U.S.A. 41°30N 117°32W **76 F5**
Paradisi Greece 36°18N 28°7E **25 C10**
Parado Indonesia 8°42S 118°30E **37 F5**
Paragould U.S.A. 36°3N 90°29W **85 C9**
Paragua → Venezuela 6°55N 62°55W **92 B6**
Paraguaçu → Brazil 12°45S 38°54W **93 F11**
Paraguaçu Paulista
  Brazil 22°22S 50°35W **95 A5**
Paraguaná, Pen. de
  Venezuela 12°0N 70°0W **92 A5**
Paraguarí Paraguay 25°36S 57°0W **94 B4**
Paraguarí □ Paraguay 26°0S 57°10W **94 B4**
Paraguay ■ S. Amer. 23°0S 57°0W **94 A4**
Paraguay → Paraguay 27°18S 58°38W **94 B4**
Paraíba = João Pessoa
  Brazil 7°10S 34°52W **93 E12**
Paraíba □ Brazil 7°0S 36°0W **93 E11**
Paraíba do Sul → Brazil 21°37S 41°3W **95 A7**
Parainen Finland 60°18N 22°18E **9 F20**
Paraíso Mexico 18°24N 93°14W **87 D6**
Parak Iran 27°38N 52°25E **45 E7**
Parakou Benin 9°25N 2°40E **50 G6**
Paralimni Cyprus 35°2N 33°58E **25 D12**
Paramaribo Suriname 5°50N 55°10W **93 B7**
Páramos del Batallón y La
  Negra △ Venezuela 8°2N 71°55W **89 E5**
Paramushir, Ostrov
  Russia 50°24N 156°0E **29 D16**
Paran → Israel 30°20N 35°10E **46 E4**
Paraná Argentina 31°45S 60°30W **94 C3**
Paraná Brazil 12°30S 47°48W **93 F9**
Paraná □ Brazil 24°30S 51°0W **95 A5**
Paraná → Argentina 33°43S 59°15W **94 C4**
Paranaguá Brazil 25°30S 48°30W **95 B6**
Paranaíba Brazil 19°40S 51°11W **93 G8**
Paranaíba → Brazil 20°6S 51°4W **93 H8**
Paranapanema → Brazil 22°40S 53°9W **95 A5**
Paranapiacaba, Serra do
  Brazil 24°31S 48°35W **95 A6**
Paranavaí Brazil 23°4S 52°56W **95 A5**
Parang Maguindanao,
  Phil. 7°23N 124°16E **37 C6**
Parang Sulu, Phil. 5°55N 120°54E **37 C6**
Parângul Mare, Vf.
  Romania 45°20N 23°37E **17 F12**
Paraparaumu N.Z. 40°57S 175°3E **59 D5**
Parbati → Mad. P., India 25°50N 76°30E **42 G7**
Parbati → Raj., India 26°54N 77°53E **42 F7**
Parbhani India 19°8N 76°52E **40 K10**
Parchim Germany 53°26N 11°52E **16 B6**
Pardes Hanna-Karkur
  Israel 32°28N 34°57E **46 C3**
Pardo → Bahia, Brazil 15°40S 39°0W **93 G11**
Pardo → Mato Grosso,
  Brazil 21°46S 52°9W **95 A5**
Pardoo Roadhouse
  Australia 20°6S 119°3E **60 D2**
Pardubice Czech Rep. 50°3N 15°45E **16 C8**
Pare Indonesia 7°43S 112°12E **37 G15**

Pare Mts. Tanzania 4°0S 37°45E **54 C4**
Parecis, Serra dos Brazil 13°0S 60°0W **92 F7**
Paren Russia 62°30N 163°15E **29 C17**
Parent Canada 47°55N 74°35W **72 C5**
Parent, L. Canada 48°31N 77°1W **72 C4**
Parepare Indonesia 4°0S 119°40E **37 E5**
Parga Greece 39°15N 20°29E **23 E9**
Pargas = Parainen
  Finland 60°18N 22°18E **9 F20**
Pargo, Pta. do Madeira 32°49N 17°17W **24 D2**
Parham Canada 44°39N 76°43W **83 B8**
Paria → U.S.A. 36°52N 111°36W **77 H8**
Paria, G. de Venezuela 10°20N 62°0W **93 K14**
Pariaguán Venezuela 8°51N 64°34W **92 B6**
Paricutín, Cerro
  Mexico 19°28N 102°15W **86 D4**
Parigi Indonesia 0°50S 120°5E **37 E6**
Parika Guyana 6°50N 58°20W **92 B7**
Parikkala Finland 61°33N 29°31E **8 F23**
Parima, Serra Brazil 2°30N 64°0W **92 C6**
Parinari Peru 4°35S 74°25W **92 D4**
Pariñas, Pta. Peru 4°30S 82°0W **90 D2**
Parintins Brazil 2°40S 56°50W **93 D7**
Pariparit Kyun Burma 14°52N 93°41E **41 M18**
Paris Canada 43°12N 80°25W **82 C4**
Paris France 48°53N 2°20E **20 B5**
Paris Idaho, U.S.A. 42°14N 111°24W **76 E8**
Paris Ky., U.S.A. 38°13N 84°15W **81 F11**
Paris Tenn., U.S.A. 36°18N 88°19W **85 C10**
Paris Tex., U.S.A. 33°40N 95°33W **84 E7**
Parish U.S.A. 43°25N 76°8W **83 C8**
Parishville U.S.A. 44°38N 74°49W **83 B10**
Pariti Indonesia 10°1S 123°45E **60 B3**
Park U.S.A. 48°45N 122°18W **78 B4**
Park City U.S.A. 37°48N 97°20W **80 G5**
Park Falls U.S.A. 45°56N 90°27W **80 C8**
Park Head Canada 44°36N 81°9W **82 B3**
Park Hills U.S.A. 37°51N 90°51W **80 G8**
Park Range U.S.A. 40°41N 106°41W **76 F10**
Park Rapids U.S.A. 46°55N 95°4W **80 B6**
Park River U.S.A. 48°24N 97°45W **80 A5**
Park Rynie S. Africa 30°25S 30°45E **57 E5**
Parkā Bandar Iran 25°55N 59°35E **45 E8**
Parkano Finland 62°1N 23°0E **8 E20**
Parker Ariz., U.S.A. 34°9N 114°17W **79 L12**
Parker Pa., U.S.A. 41°5N 79°41W **82 E5**
Parker Dam U.S.A. 34°18N 114°8W **79 L12**
Parkersburg U.S.A. 39°16N 81°34W **81 F13**
Parkes Australia 33°9S 148°11E **63 E4**
Parkfield U.S.A. 35°54N 120°26W **78 K6**
Parkhill Canada 43°15N 81°38W **82 C3**
Parkland U.S.A. 47°9N 122°26W **78 C4**
Parkston U.S.A. 43°24N 97°59W **80 D5**
Parksville Canada 49°20N 124°21W **70 D4**
Parkway U.S.A. 38°32N 121°26W **78 G5**
Parla Spain 40°14N 3°46W **21 B4**
Parma Italy 44°48N 10°20E **20 D9**
Parma Idaho, U.S.A. 43°47N 116°57W **76 E5**
Parma Ohio, U.S.A. 41°24N 81°43W **82 E3**
Parnaguá Brazil 10°10S 44°38W **93 F10**
Parnaíba Brazil 2°54S 41°47W **93 D10**
Parnaíba → Brazil 3°0S 41°50W **93 D10**
Parnassos Greece 38°35N 22°30E **23 E10**
Pärnu Estonia 58°28N 24°33E **9 G21**
Paro Dzong Bhutan 27°32N 89°53E **43 F13**
Paroo → Australia 31°28S 143°32E **63 E3**
Paros Greece 37°5N 25°12E **23 F11**
Parowan U.S.A. 37°51N 112°50W **77 H7**
Parral Chile 36°10S 71°52W **94 D1**
Parramatta Australia 33°48S 151°1E **63 B5**
Parras Mexico 25°30N 102°11W **86 B4**
Parrett → U.K. 51°12N 3°1W **13 F4**
Parris I. U.S.A. 32°20N 80°41W **85 E14**
Parrsboro Canada 45°30N 64°25W **73 C7**
Parry Channel Canada 74°15N 94°0W **69 C13**
Parry I. Canada 45°18N 80°10W **82 A4**
Parry Is. Canada 77°0N 110°0W **69 B10**
Parry Sound Canada 45°20N 80°0W **82 A5**
Parsnip → Canada 55°10N 123°2W **70 B4**
Parsons U.S.A. 37°20N 95°16W **80 G6**
Parsons Ra. Australia 13°30S 135°15E **62 A2**
Partinico Italy 38°3N 13°7E **22 E5**
Partizansk Russia 43°8N 133°9E **30 C6**
Partridge I. Canada 55°59N 87°37W **72 A2**
Partry Mts. Ireland 53°40N 9°28W **10 C2**
Paru → Brazil 1°33S 52°38W **93 D8**
Parvān □ Afghan. 35°0N 69°0E **40 B6**
Parvatipuram India 18°50N 83°25E **41 K13**
Parvatsar India 26°52N 74°49E **42 F6**
Parys S. Africa 26°54S 27°32E **56 D4**
Pas, Pta. des Spain 38°46N 1°26E **24 C7**
Pas, The Canada 53°45N 101°15W **71 C8**
Pasadena Calif., U.S.A. 34°9N 118°8W **79 L8**
Pasadena Tex., U.S.A. 29°43N 95°13W **84 G7**
Pasaje → Argentina 25°39S 63°56W **94 B3**
Pasar Indonesia 8°27S 114°54E **37 J17**
Pascagoula U.S.A. 30°21N 88°33W **85 F10**
Pascagoula → U.S.A. 30°23N 88°37W **85 F10**
Pașcani Romania 47°14N 26°45E **17 E14**
Pasco U.S.A. 46°14N 119°6W **76 C4**
Pasco I. Australia 20°57S 115°20E **60 D2**
Pascoag U.S.A. 41°57N 71°42W **83 E13**
Pascua, I. de Chile 27°7S 109°23W **65 K17**
Pasfield L. Canada 58°24N 105°20W **71 B7**
Pasir Mas Malaysia 6°2N 102°8E **39 J4**
Pasir Panjang Singapore 1°18N 103°46E **39 d**
Pasir Putih Malaysia 5°50N 102°24E **39 K4**
Pasirian Indonesia 8°13S 113°8E **37 H15**
Pasirkuning Indonesia 0°30S 104°33E **36 E2**
Paskūh Iran 27°34N 61°39E **45 E9**
Pasley, C. Australia 33°52S 123°35E **61 F3**
Pašman Croatia 43°58N 15°20E **16 G8**
Pasni Pakistan 25°15N 63°27E **40 G3**
Paso Bravo △ Paraguay 22°32S 57°55W **94 A4**
Paso Cantinela
  Mexico 32°33N 115°47W **79 N11**
Paso de Indios Argentina 43°55S 69°0W **96 E3**

Paso de los Libres
  Argentina 29°44S 57°10W **94 B4**
Paso de los Toros
  Uruguay 32°45S 56°30W **94 C4**
Paso Robles U.S.A. 35°38N 120°41W **78 K6**
Paspébiac Canada 48°3N 65°17W **73 C6**
Pasrur Pakistan 32°16N 74°43E **42 C6**
Passage East Ireland 52°14N 7°0W **10 D5**
Passage West Ireland 51°52N 8°21W **10 E3**
Passaic U.S.A. 40°51N 74°7W **83 F10**
Passau Germany 48°34N 13°28E **16 D7**
Passero, C. Italy 36°41N 15°10E **22 F6**
Passo Fundo Brazil 28°10S 52°20W **95 B5**
Passos Brazil 20°45S 46°37W **93 H9**
Pastavy Belarus 55°4N 26°50E **9 J22**
Pastaza → Peru 4°50S 76°52W **92 D3**
Pasto Colombia 1°13N 77°17W **92 C3**
Pasuruan Indonesia 7°40S 112°44E **37 G15**
Patagonia Argentina 45°0S 69°0W **96 F3**
Patagonia U.S.A. 31°33N 110°45W **77 L8**
Patambar Iran 29°45N 60°17E **45 D9**
Patan = Lalitapur Nepal 27°40N 85°20E **43 F11**
Patan = Somnath India 20°53N 70°22E **42 J4**
Patan India 23°54N 72°14E **42 H5**
Patani Indonesia 0°20N 128°50E **37 D7**
Pataudi India 28°18N 76°48E **42 E7**
Patchewollock Australia 35°22S 142°12E **63 F3**
Patchogue U.S.A. 40°46N 73°1W **83 F11**
Pate Kenya 2°10S 41°0E **54 C5**
Patea N.Z. 39°45S 174°30E **59 C5**
Patensie S. Africa 33°46S 24°49E **56 E3**
Paternò Italy 37°34N 14°54E **22 F6**
Pateros U.S.A. 48°3N 119°54W **76 B4**
Paterson U.S.A. 40°54N 74°9W **83 F10**
Paterson Ra. Australia 21°45S 122°10E **60 D3**
Pathankot India 32°18N 75°45E **42 C6**
Pathein = Bassein
  Burma 16°45N 94°30E **41 L19**
Pathfinder Res. U.S.A. 42°28N 106°51W **76 E10**
Pathiu Thailand 10°42N 99°19E **39 G2**
Pathum Thani Thailand 14°1N 100°32E **38 E3**
Pati Indonesia 6°45S 111°1E **37 G14**
Patía → Colombia 2°13N 78°40W **92 C3**
Patiala Punjab, India 30°23N 76°26E **42 D7**
Patiala Ut. P., India 27°43N 79°1E **43 F8**
Patkai Bum India 27°0N 95°30E **41 F19**
Patmos Greece 37°21N 26°36E **23 F12**
Patna India 25°35N 85°12E **43 G11**
Pato Branco Brazil 26°13S 52°40W **95 B5**
Patong, Ao Thailand 7°54N 98°17E **39 a**
Patonga Uganda 2°45N 33°15E **54 B3**
Patos Brazil 6°55S 37°16W **93 E11**
Patos, L. dos Brazil 31°20S 51°0W **95 C5**
Patos, Río de los →
  Argentina 31°18S 69°25W **94 C2**
Patos de Minas Brazil 18°35S 46°32W **93 G9**
Patquía Argentina 30°2S 66°55W **94 C2**
Patra Greece 38°14N 21°47E **23 E9**
Patraikos Kolpos Greece 38°17N 21°30E **23 E9**
Patras = Patra Greece 38°14N 21°47E **23 E9**
Patriot Hills Antarctica 82°20S 81°25W **5 E16**
Patrocínio Brazil 18°57S 47°0W **93 G9**
Pattani Thailand 6°48N 101°15E **39 J3**
Pattaya Thailand 12°52N 100°55E **38 F3**
Patten U.S.A. 46°0N 68°38W **81 B19**
Patterson Calif., U.S.A. 37°28N 121°8W **78 H5**
Patterson La., U.S.A. 29°42N 91°18W **84 G9**
Patterson, Mt. U.S.A. 38°29N 119°20W **78 G7**
Patti Punjab, India 31°17N 74°54E **42 D6**
Patti Ut. P., India 25°55N 82°12E **43 G10**
Pattoki Pakistan 31°5N 73°52E **42 D5**
Patton U.S.A. 40°38N 78°39W **82 F6**
Patuakhali Bangla. 22°20N 90°25E **41 H17**
Patuanak Canada 55°55N 107°43W **71 B7**
Patuca → Honduras 15°50N 84°18W **88 C3**
Patuca, Punta Honduras 15°49N 84°14W **88 C3**
Patuca △ Honduras 14°30N 85°30W **88 D2**
Patvinsuo △ Finland 63°7N 30°45E **8 E24**
Pátzcuaro Mexico 19°31N 101°38W **86 D4**
Pau France 43°19N 0°25W **20 E3**
Paudash Canada 44°59N 77°58W **82 B7**
Pauk Burma 21°27N 94°30E **41 J19**
Paul I. Canada 56°30N 61°20W **73 A7**
Paul Smiths U.S.A. 44°26N 74°15W **83 B10**
Paulatuk Canada 69°25N 124°0W **68 D7**
Paulding Bay S. Ocean 66°0S 118°0E **5 C8**
Paulistana Brazil 8°9S 41°9W **93 E10**
Paulo Afonso Brazil 9°21S 38°15W **93 E11**
Paulpietersburg S. Africa 27°23S 30°50E **57 D5**
Pauls Valley U.S.A. 34°44N 97°13W **84 D6**
Pauma Valley U.S.A. 33°16N 116°58W **79 M10**
Pauri India 30°9N 78°47E **43 D8**
Pāveh Iran 35°3N 46°22E **44 C5**
Pavia Italy 45°7N 9°8E **20 D8**
Pavilion U.S.A. 42°52N 78°1W **82 D6**
Pāvilosta Latvia 56°53N 21°14E **9 H19**
Pavlodar Kazakhstan 52°33N 77°0E **28 D8**
Pavlograd = Pavlohrad
  Ukraine 48°30N 35°52E **19 E6**
Pavlohrad Ukraine 48°30N 35°52E **19 E6**
Pavlovo Russia 55°58N 43°5E **18 C7**
Pavlovsk Russia 50°26N 40°5E **19 E6**
Pavlovskaya Russia 46°17N 39°47E **19 E6**
Pawai, Pulau Singapore 1°11N 103°44E **39 d**
Pawayan India 28°4N 80°6E **43 E9**
Pawhuska U.S.A. 36°40N 96°20W **84 C6**
Pawnee U.S.A. 36°20N 96°48W **84 C6**
Pawnee City U.S.A. 40°7N 96°9W **80 E5**
Pawtucket U.S.A. 41°53N 71°23W **83 E13**
Paxi Greece 39°14N 20°12E **23 E9**
Paximadia Greece 35°0N 24°35E **25 E6**
Paxton U.S.A. 40°27N 88°6W **80 E9**
Payakumbuh Indonesia 0°20S 100°35E **36 E2**
Payette U.S.A. 44°5N 116°56W **76 D5**
Payne Bay = Kangirsuk
  Canada 60°0N 70°0W **69 F17**
Payne L. Canada 59°30N 74°30W **69 F17**
Paynes Find Australia 29°15S 117°42E **61 E2**

Paynesville U.S.A. 45°23N 94°43W **80 C6**
Paysandú Uruguay 32°19S 58°8W **94 C4**
Payson Ariz., U.S.A. 34°14N 111°20W **77 J8**
Payson Utah, U.S.A. 40°3N 111°44W **76 F8**
Paz → Guatemala 13°44N 90°10W **88 D1**
Paz, B. de la Mexico 24°9N 110°25W **86 C2**
Pāzanān Iran 30°35N 49°59E **45 D6**
Pazardzhik Bulgaria 42°12N 24°20E **23 C11**
Pe Ell U.S.A. 46°34N 123°18W **78 D3**
Peabody U.S.A. 42°31N 70°56W **83 D14**
Peace → Canada 59°0N 111°25W **70 B6**
Peace Point Canada 59°7N 112°27W **70 B6**
Peace River Canada 56°15N 117°18W **70 B5**
Peach Springs U.S.A. 35°32N 113°25W **77 J7**
Peachland Canada 49°47N 119°45W **70 D5**
Peachtree City U.S.A. 33°25N 84°35W **85 E12**
Peak, The = Kinder Scout
  U.K. 53°24N 1°52W **12 D6**
Peak Charles △
  Australia 32°42S 121°10E **61 F3**
Peak District △ U.K. 53°24N 1°46W **12 D6**
Peak Hill Australia 32°47S 148°11E **63 E4**
Peak Ra. Australia 22°50S 148°20E **62 C4**
Peake Cr. → Australia 28°2S 136°7E **63 D2**
Pearblossom U.S.A. 34°30N 117°55W **79 L9**
Pearl → U.S.A. 30°11N 89°32W **85 F10**
Pearl and Hermes Reef
  U.S.A. 27°55N 175°45W **75 K4**
Pearl River U.S.A. 41°4N 74°2W **83 E10**
Pearsall U.S.A. 28°54N 99°6W **84 G5**
Pearson Int. Toronto ✈ (YYZ)
  Canada 43°46N 79°35W **82 C5**
Peary Land Greenland 82°40N 33°0W **4 A6**
Pease → U.S.A. 34°12N 99°2W **84 D5**
Peawanuck Canada 55°15N 85°12W **72 A2**
Pebane Mozam. 17°10S 38°8E **55 F4**
Pebas Peru 3°10S 71°46W **92 D4**
Pebble Beach U.S.A. 36°34N 121°57W **78 J5**
Peć Kosovo 42°40N 20°17E **23 C9**
Pechenga Russia 69°29N 31°4E **8 B24**
Pechenizhyn Ukraine 48°30N 24°48E **17 D13**
Pechiguera, Pta.
  Canary Is. 28°51N 13°53W **24 F6**
Pechora Russia 65°10N 57°11E **18 A10**
Pechora → Russia 68°13N 54°15E **18 A9**
Pechorskaya Guba Russia 68°40N 54°0E **18 A9**
Pechory Russia 57°48N 27°40E **9 H22**
Pecos N. Mex., U.S.A. 35°35N 105°41W **77 J11**
Pecos Tex., U.S.A. 31°26N 103°30W **84 F3**
Pecos → U.S.A. 29°42N 101°22W **84 G4**
Pécs Hungary 46°5N 18°15E **17 E10**
Pedasí Panama 7°32N 80°2E **88 E3**
Pedder, L. Australia 42°55S 146°10E **63 G4**
Peddie S. Africa 33°14S 27°7E **57 E4**
Pedernales Dom. Rep. 18°2N 71°44W **89 C5**
Pedieos → Cyprus 35°10N 33°54E **25 D12**
Pedirka Desert Australia 26°47S 134°11E **63 A1**
Pedra Azul Brazil 16°2S 41°17W **93 G10**
Pedra Lume C. Verde Is. 16°40N 22°52W **50 b**
Pedreiras Brazil 4°32S 44°40W **93 D10**
Pedro Afonso Brazil 9°0S 48°10W **93 E9**
Pedro Cays Jamaica 17°5N 77°48W **88 C4**
Pedro de Valdivia Chile 22°55S 69°38W **94 A2**
Pedro Juan Caballero
  Paraguay 22°30S 55°40W **95 A4**
Pee Dee = Great Pee Dee →
  U.S.A. 33°21N 79°10W **85 E15**
Peebinga Australia 34°52S 140°57E **63 E3**
Peebles U.K. 55°40N 3°11W **11 F5**
Peekskill U.S.A. 41°17N 73°55W **83 E11**
Peel I. of Man 54°13N 4°40W **12 C3**
Peel → Australia 30°50S 150°29E **63 E5**
Peel → Canada 67°0N 135°0W **68 D5**
Peel Sd. Canada 73°0N 96°0W **68 C12**
Peera Peera Poolanna L.
  Australia 26°30S 138°0E **63 D2**
Peerless Lake Canada 56°37N 114°40W **70 B6**
Peers Canada 53°40N 116°0W **70 C5**
Pegasus Bay N.Z. 43°20S 173°10E **59 E4**
Pegu Burma 17°20N 96°29E **41 L20**
Pegu Yoma Burma 19°0N 96°0E **41 K20**
Pehuajó Argentina 35°45S 62°0W **94 D3**
Pei Xian = Pizhou
  China 34°44N 116°55E **34 G9**
Peine Chile 23°45S 68°8W **94 A2**
Peine Germany 52°19N 10°14E **16 B6**
Peip'ing = Beijing China 39°53N 116°21E **34 E9**
Peipus, L. = Chudskoye, Ozero
  Russia 58°13N 27°30E **9 G22**
Peixe Brazil 12°0S 48°40W **93 F9**
Peixe → Brazil 21°31S 51°58W **93 H8**
Pekalongan Indonesia 6°53S 109°40E **37 G13**
Pekan Malaysia 3°30N 103°25E **39 L4**
Pekan Nenas Malaysia 1°31N 103°31E **39 d**
Pekanbaru Indonesia 0°30N 101°15E **36 D2**
Pekin U.S.A. 40°35N 89°40W **80 E9**
Peking = Beijing China 39°53N 116°21E **34 E9**
Pekutatan Indonesia 8°25S 114°49E **37 J17**
Pelabuhan Klang
  Malaysia 3°0N 101°23E **39 L3**
Pelabuhan Ratu, Teluk
  Indonesia 7°5S 106°30E **37 G12**
Pelabuhanratu Indonesia 7°0S 106°32E **37 G12**
Pelagie, Is. Italy 35°39N 12°33E **22 G5**
Pelaihari Indonesia 3°55S 114°45E **36 E4**
Pelée, Mt. Martinique 14°48N 61°10W **88 c**
Pelee, Pt. Canada 41°54N 82°31W **72 D3**
Pelee I. Canada 41°47N 82°40W **82 E2**
Pelekech Kenya 3°52N 35°8E **54 B4**
Peleng Indonesia 1°20S 123°30E **37 E6**
Pelentong Malaysia 1°32N 103°49E **39 d**
Pelican U.S.A. 57°58N 136°14W **70 B1**
Pelican Narrows
  Canada 55°10N 102°56W **71 B8**
Peljesac Croatia 42°55N 17°25E **22 C7**
Pelkosenniemi Finland 67°6N 27°28E **8 C22**

Pella _S. Africa_ 29°1S 19°6E **56** D2
Pella _U.S.A._ 41°25N 92°55W **80** E7
Pello _Finland_ 66°47N 23°59E **8** C20
Pelly → _Canada_ 62°47N 137°19W **70** A1
Pelly Bay _Canada_ 68°38N 89°50W **69** D14
Peloponnese □ _Greece_ 37°10N 22°0E **23** F9
Pelorus Sd. _N.Z._ 40°59S 173°59E **59** D4
Pelotas _Brazil_ 31°42S 52°23W **95** C5
Pelotas → _Brazil_ 27°28S 51°55W **95** B5
Pelvoux, Massif du
  France 44°52N 6°20E **20** D7
Pemalang _Indonesia_ 6°53S 109°23E **37** G13
Pemanggil, Pulau
  Malaysia 2°37N 104°21E **39** L5
Pematangsiantar _Indonesia_ 2°57N 99°5E **36** D1
Pemba _Mozam._ 12°58S 40°30E **55** E5
Pemba _Zambia_ 16°30S 27°28E **55** F2
Pemba Channel _Tanzania_ 5°0S 39°37E **54** D4
Pemba I. _Tanzania_ 5°0S 39°45E **54** D4
Pemberton _Australia_ 34°30S 116°0E **61** F2
Pemberton _Canada_ 50°25N 122°50W **70** C4
Pembina → _Canada_ 54°45N 114°17W **70** C6
Pembroke _Canada_ 45°50N 77°7W **72** C4
Pembroke _U.K._ 51°41N 4°55W **13** F3
Pembrokeshire □ _U.K._ 51°52N 4°56W **13** F3
Pembrokeshire Coast △
  _U.K._ 51°50N 5°2W **13** F2
Pen-y-Ghent _U.K._ 54°10N 2°14W **12** C5
Penal _Trin. & Tob._ 10°9N 61°29W **93** K15
Penang = Pinang
  Malaysia 5°25N 100°15E **39** c
Penápolis _Brazil_ 21°30S 50°0W **95** A6
Peñarroya-Pueblonuevo
  Spain 38°19N 5°16W **21** C3
Penarth _U.K._ 51°26N 3°11W **13** F4
Peñas, C. de _Spain_ 43°42N 5°52W **21** A3
Peñas, G. de _Chile_ 47°0S 75°0W **96** F2
Peñas del Chache
  Canary Is. 29°6N 13°33W **24** E6
Pench △ _India_ 21°45N 79°20E **43** J8
Pench'i = Benxi _China_ 41°20N 123°48E **35** D12
Pend Oreille → _U.S.A._ 49°4N 117°37W **76** B5
Pend Oreille, L. _U.S.A._ 48°10N 116°21W **76** B5
Pendembu _S. Leone_ 9°7N 11°14W **50** G3
Pender B. _Australia_ 16°45S 122°42E **60** C3
Pendleton _U.S.A._ 45°40N 118°47W **76** D4
Pendra _India_ 22°46N 81°57E **43** H9
Penedo _Brazil_ 10°15S 36°36W **93** F11
Penelokan _Indonesia_ 8°17S 115°22E **37** J18
Penetanguishene
  Canada 44°50N 79°55W **82** B5
Penfield _U.S.A._ 41°13N 78°35W **82** E6
Peng Chau _China_ 22°17N 114°2E **33** G11
Pengalengan _Indonesia_ 7°9S 107°30E **37** G12
Penge _Kasai-Or.,_
  Dem. Rep. of the Congo 5°30S 24°33E **54** D1
Penge _Sud-Kivu,_
  Dem. Rep. of the Congo 4°27S 28°25E **54** C2
Penglai _China_ 37°48N 120°42E **35** F11
Penguin _Australia_ 41°8S 146°6E **63** G4
Penhalonga _Zimbabwe_ 18°52S 32°40E **55** F3
Peniche _Portugal_ 39°19N 9°22W **21** C1
Penicuik _U.K._ 55°50N 3°13W **11** F5
Penida, Nusa _Indonesia_ 8°45S 115°30E **37** K18
Peninsular Malaysia □
  Malaysia 4°0N 102°0E **39** L4
Penitente, Serra do _Brazil_ 8°45S 46°20W **93** E9
Penkridge _U.K._ 52°44N 2°6W **12** E5
Penmarch, Pte. de _France_ 47°48N 4°22W **20** C1
Penn Hills _U.S.A._ 40°28N 79°52W **82** F5
Penn Yan _U.S.A._ 42°40N 77°3W **82** D7
Pennant _Canada_ 50°32N 108°14W **71** C7
Penner → _India_ 14°35N 80°10E **40** M12
Pennines _U.K._ 54°45N 2°27W **12** C5
Pennington _U.S.A._ 39°15N 121°47W **78** F5
Pennsburg _U.S.A._ 40°23N 75°29W **83** F9
Pennsylvania □ _U.S.A._ 40°45N 77°30W **81** E15
Penny _Canada_ 53°51N 121°20W **70** C4
Penobscot → _U.S.A._ 44°30N 68°48W **81** C19
Penobscot B. _U.S.A._ 44°35N 68°50W **81** C19
Penola _Australia_ 37°25S 140°48E **63** F3
Penong _Australia_ 31°56S 133°1E **61** F5
Penonomé _Panama_ 8°31N 80°21W **88** E3
Penrhyn _Cook Is._ 9°0S 158°0W **65** H12
Penrith _Australia_ 33°43S 150°38E **63** E5
Penrith _U.K._ 54°40N 2°45W **12** C5
Penryn _U.K._ 50°9N 5°7W **13** G2
Penza _Russia_ 53°15N 45°5E **18** D8
Penzance _U.K._ 50°7N 5°33W **13** G2
Penzhino _Russia_ 63°30N 167°55E **29** C17
Penzhinskaya Guba
  Russia 61°30N 163°0E **29** C17
Peoria _Ariz., U.S.A._ 33°43N 112°14W **77** K7
Peoria _Ill., U.S.A._ 40°42N 89°36W **80** E9
Pepacton Res. _U.S.A._ 42°5N 74°58W **83** D10
Pepani → _S. Africa_ 25°49S 22°47E **56** D3
Pera Hd. _Australia_ 12°55S 141°37E **62** A3
Perabumulih _Indonesia_ 3°27S 104°15E **36** E2
Perak → _Malaysia_ 4°0N 100°50E **39** K3
Perama _Kerkyra, Greece_ 39°34N 19°54E **25** A3
Perama _Kriti, Greece_ 35°20N 24°40E **25** D6
Perancak _Indonesia_ 8°24S 114°37E **37** J17
Peräpohjola _Finland_ 66°16N 26°10E **8** C22
Percé _Canada_ 48°31N 64°13W **73** C7
Perche, Collines du
  France 48°30N 0°40E **20** B4
Percival Lakes _Australia_ 21°25S 125°0E **60** D4
Percy Is. _Australia_ 21°39S 150°16E **62** C5
Perdido, Mte. _Spain_ 42°40N 0°5E **21** A6

Perdu, Mt. = Perdido, Mte.
  Spain 42°40N 0°5E **21** A6
Pereira _Colombia_ 4°49N 75°43W **92** C3
Perenjori _Australia_ 29°26S 116°16E **61** E2
Pereyaslav-Khmelnytskyy
  Ukraine 50°3N 31°28E **19** D5
Pérez, I. _Mexico_ 22°24N 89°42W **87** C7
Pergamino _Argentina_ 33°52S 60°30W **94** C3
Pergau → _Malaysia_ 5°23N 102°2E **39** K3
Perham _U.S.A._ 46°36N 95°34W **80** B6
Perhentian, Kepulauan
  Malaysia 5°54N 102°42E **39** K4
Péribonka → _Canada_ 48°45N 72°5W **73** C5
Péribonka, L. _Canada_ 50°1N 71°10W **73** B5
Perico _Argentina_ 24°20S 65°5W **94** A2
Pericos _Mexico_ 25°3N 107°42W **86** B3
Périgueux _France_ 45°10N 0°42E **20** D4
Perijá, Sierra de _Colombia_ 9°30N 73°3W **92** B4
Perijá △ _Venezuela_ 9°30N 72°55W **89** E5
Peristerona → _Cyprus_ 35°8N 33°5E **25** D12
Perito Moreno _Argentina_ 46°36S 70°56W **96** F2
Perkasie _U.S.A._ 40°22N 75°18W **83** F9
Perlas, Arch. de las
  Panama 8°41N 79°7W **88** E4
Perlas, Punta de _Nic._ 12°30N 83°30W **88** D3
Perm _Russia_ 58°0N 56°10E **18** C10
Pernambuco = Recife
  Brazil 8°0S 35°0W **93** E12
Pernambuco □ _Brazil_ 8°0S 37°0W **93** E11
Pernatty Lagoon
  Australia 31°30S 137°12E **63** E2
Pernik _Bulgaria_ 42°35N 23°2E **23** C10
Peron Is. _Australia_ 13°9S 130°4E **60** B5
Peron Pen. _Australia_ 26°0S 113°10E **61** E1
Perow _Canada_ 54°35N 126°10W **70** C3
Perpignan _France_ 42°42N 2°53E **20** E5
Perris _U.S.A._ 33°47N 117°14W **79** M9
Perry _Fla., U.S.A._ 30°7N 83°35W **85** F13
Perry _Ga., U.S.A._ 32°28N 83°44W **85** E13
Perry _Iowa, U.S.A._ 41°51N 94°6W **80** E6
Perry _N.Y., U.S.A._ 42°42N 78°0W **82** D7
Perry _Okla., U.S.A._ 36°17N 97°14W **84** C6
Perryton _U.S.A._ 36°24N 100°48W **84** C4
Perryville _U.S.A._ 37°43N 89°52W **80** G9
Persepolis _Iran_ 29°55N 52°50E **45** D7
Pershotravensk _Ukraine_ 50°13N 27°40E **17** C14
Persia = Iran ■ _Asia_ 33°0N 53°0E **45** C7
Persian Gulf _Asia_ 27°0N 50°0E **45** E6
Perth _Australia_ 31°57S 115°52E **61** F2
Perth _Canada_ 44°55N 76°15W **83** B8
Perth _U.K._ 56°24N 3°26W **11** E5
Perth & Kinross □ _U.K._ 56°45N 3°55W **11** E5
Perth Amboy _U.S.A._ 40°30N 74°15W **83** F10
Perth-Andover _Canada_ 46°44N 67°42W **73** C6
Perth Basin _Ind. Oc._ 30°0S 108°0E **64** L2
Peru _Ind., U.S.A._ 40°45N 86°4W **80** E10
Peru _N.Y., U.S.A._ 44°35N 73°32W **83** B11
Peru ■ _S. Amer._ 4°0S 75°0W **92** D4
Peru Basin _Pac. Oc._ 20°0S 95°0W **65** J18
Peru-Chile Trench
  Pac. Oc. 20°0S 72°0W **92** G3
Perúgia _Italy_ 43°7N 12°23E **22** C5
Pervomaysk _Ukraine_ 48°10N 30°46E **19** E5
Pervouralsk _Russia_ 56°59N 59°59E **18** C10
Pésaro _Italy_ 43°54N 12°55E **22** C5
Pescara _Italy_ 42°28N 14°13E **22** C6
Peshawar _Pakistan_ 34°2N 71°37E **42** B4
Peshkopi _Albania_ 41°41N 20°25E **23** D9
Peshtigo _U.S.A._ 45°3N 87°45W **80** C10
Pesqueira _Brazil_ 8°20S 36°42W **93** E11
Petah Tiqwa _Israel_ 32°6N 34°53E **46** C3
Petaling Jaya _Malaysia_ 3°4N 101°42E **39** L3
Petaloudes _Greece_ 36°18N 28°5E **25** C10
Petaluma _U.S.A._ 38°14N 122°39W **78** G4
Pétange _Lux._ 49°33N 5°55E **15** E5
Petaro _Pakistan_ 25°31N 68°18E **42** G3
Petatlán _Mexico_ 17°31N 101°16W **86** D4
Petauke _Zambia_ 14°14S 31°20E **55** E3
Petawawa _Canada_ 45°54N 77°17W **72** C4
Petén Itzá, L. _Guatemala_ 16°58N 89°50W **88** C2
Peter I. _Br. Virgin Is._ 18°22N 64°35W **89** e
Peter I. Øy _Antarctica_ 69°0S 91°0W **5** C16
Peter Pond L. _Canada_ 55°55N 108°44W **71** B7
Peterbell _Canada_ 48°36N 83°21W **72** C3
Peterborough _Australia_ 32°58S 138°51E **63** E2
Peterborough _Canada_ 44°20N 78°20W **82** B6
Peterborough _U.K._ 52°35N 0°15W **13** E7
Peterborough _U.S.A._ 42°53N 71°57W **83** D13
Peterborough □ _U.K._ 52°35N 0°15W **13** E7
Peterculter _U.K._ 57°6N 2°16W **11** D6
Peterhead _U.K._ 57°31N 1°48W **11** D7
Peterlee _U.K._ 54°47N 1°20W **12** C6
Petermann ♦ _Australia_ 24°58S 130°0E **61** E4
Petermann Gletscher
  Greenland 80°30N 60°0W **69** A20
Petermann Ranges
  Australia 26°0S 130°30E **61** E5
Petersburg _Alaska,_
  _U.S.A._ 56°48N 132°58W **68** F5
Petersburg _Pa., U.S.A._ 40°34N 78°3W **82** F6
Petersburg _Va., U.S.A._ 37°14N 77°24W **81** G15
Petersburg _W. Va., U.S.A._ 39°1N 79°5W **81** F14
Petersfield _U.K._ 51°1N 0°56W **13** F7
Petit-Canal _Guadeloupe_ 16°25N 61°31W **88** b
Petit Goâve _Haiti_ 18°27N 72°51W **89** C5
Petit Lac Manicouagan
  Canada 51°25N 67°40W **73** B6
Petit-Mécatina →
  Canada 50°40N 59°30W **73** B8
Petit-Mécatina, Î. du
  Canada 50°30N 59°25W **73** B8
Petit Piton _St. Lucia_ 13°51N 61°5W **89** f
Petit-Saguenay _Canada_ 48°15N 70°4W **73** C5
Petitcodiac _Canada_ 45°57N 65°11W **73** C6
Petite Terre, Îles de la
  Guadeloupe 16°13N 61°9W **88** b
Petitot → _Canada_ 60°14N 123°29W **70** A4
Petitsikapau L. _Canada_ 54°37N 66°18W **73** B6
Petlad _India_ 22°30N 72°45E **42** H5

Peto _Mexico_ 20°8N 88°55W **87** C7
Petone _N.Z._ 41°13S 174°53E **59** D5
Petorca _Chile_ 32°15S 70°56W **94** C1
Petoskey _U.S.A._ 45°22N 84°57W **81** C11
Petra _Jordan_ 30°20N 35°22E **46** E4
Petra _Spain_ 39°37N 3°6E **24** B10
Petra, Ostrova _Russia_ 76°15N 118°30E **29** B12
Petra Velikogo, Zaliv
  Russia 42°40N 132°0E **30** C6
Petre, Pt. _Canada_ 43°50N 77°9W **82** C7
Petrich _Bulgaria_ 41°24N 23°13E **23** D10
Petrified Forest △ _U.S.A._ 35°0N 109°30W **77** J9
Petrolândia _Brazil_ 9°5S 38°20W **93** E11
Petrolia _Canada_ 42°54N 82°9W **82** D2
Petrolina _Brazil_ 9°24S 40°30W **93** E10
Petropavl _Kazakhstan_ 54°53N 69°13E **28** D7
Petropavlovsk = Petropavl
  Kazakhstan 54°53N 69°13E **28** D7
Petropavlovsk-Kamchatskiy
  Russia 53°3N 158°43E **29** D16
Petrópolis _Brazil_ 22°33S 43°9W **95** A7
Petroşani _Romania_ 45°28N 23°20E **17** F12
Petrovaradin _Serbia_ 45°16N 19°55E **23** B8
Petrovsk _Russia_ 52°22N 45°19E **18** D8
Petrovsk-Zabaykalskiy
  Russia 51°20N 108°55E **29** D11
Petrozavodsk _Russia_ 61°41N 34°20E **18** B5
Petrus Steyn _S. Africa_ 27°38S 28°8E **57** D4
Petrusburg _S. Africa_ 29°4S 25°26E **56** D4
Peumo _Chile_ 34°21S 71°12W **94** C1
Peureulak _Indonesia_ 4°48N 97°45E **36** D1
Pevek _Russia_ 69°41N 171°19E **29** C18
Pforzheim _Germany_ 48°52N 8°41E **16** D5
Pha Taem △ _Thailand_ 15°32N 105°30E **38** E5
Phaestos _Greece_ 35°2N 24°50E **25** D6
Phagwara _India_ 31°10N 75°40E **42** D6
Phala _Botswana_ 23°45S 26°50E **56** C4
Phalera = Phulera _India_ 26°52N 75°16E **42** F6
Phalodi _India_ 27°12N 72°24E **42** F5
Phaluai, Ko _Thailand_ 9°32N 99°41E **39** b
Phan _Thailand_ 19°28N 99°43E **38** C2
Phan Rang _Vietnam_ 11°34N 109°0E **39** G7
Phan Ri = Hoa Da
  Vietnam 11°16N 108°40E **39** G7
Phan Si Pan _Vietnam_ 22°18N 103°46E **38** A4
Phan Thiet _Vietnam_ 11°1N 108°9E **39** G7
Phanat Nikhom
  Thailand 13°27N 101°11E **38** F3
Phangan, Ko _Thailand_ 9°45N 100°0E **39** H3
Phangnga _Thailand_ 8°28N 98°30E **39** H2
Phangnga, Ao _Thailand_ 8°16N 98°33E **39** a
Phanom Sarakham
  Thailand 13°45N 101°21E **38** F3
Phaphund _India_ 26°36N 79°28E **43** F8
Pharenda _India_ 27°5N 83°17E **43** F10
Pharr _U.S.A._ 26°12N 98°11W **84** H5
Phatthalung _Thailand_ 7°39N 100°6E **39** J3
Phayao _Thailand_ 19°11N 99°55E **38** C2
Phelps _U.S.A._ 42°58N 77°3W **82** D7
Phelps L. _Canada_ 59°15N 103°15W **71** B8
Phenix City _U.S.A._ 32°28N 85°0W **85** E12
Phet Buri _Thailand_ 13°1N 99°55E **38** F2
Phetchabun _Thailand_ 16°25N 101°8E **38** D3
Phetchabun, Thiu Khao
  Thailand 16°0N 101°20E **38** E3
Phetchaburi = Phet Buri
  Thailand 13°1N 99°55E **38** F2
Phi Phi, Ko _Thailand_ 7°45N 98°46E **39** J2
Phiafay _Laos_ 14°48N 106°0E **38** E6
Phibun Mangsahan
  Thailand 15°14N 105°14E **38** E5
Phichai _Thailand_ 17°22N 100°10E **38** D3
Phichit _Thailand_ 16°26N 100°22E **38** D3
Philadelphia _Miss.,_
  _U.S.A._ 32°46N 89°7W **85** E10
Philadelphia _N.Y., U.S.A._ 44°9N 75°43W **83** B9
Philadelphia _Pa., U.S.A._ 39°57N 75°9W **83** G9
Philip _U.S.A._ 44°2N 101°40W **80** C3
Philip Smith Mts. _U.S.A._ 68°0N 148°0W **74** B10
Philippeville _Belgium_ 50°12N 4°33E **15** D4
Philippi _U.S.A._ 39°9N 80°3W **81** F13
Philippi L. _Australia_ 24°20S 138°55E **62** C2
Philippine Basin _Pac. Oc._ 17°0N 132°0E **64** F5
Philippine Sea _Pac. Oc._ 18°0N 125°0E **64** F4
Philippine Trench = Mindanao
  Trench _Pac. Oc._ 12°0N 126°6E **37** B7
Philippines ■ _Asia_ 12°0N 123°0E **37** B6
Philippolis _S. Africa_ 30°15S 25°16E **56** E4
Philippopolis = Plovdiv
  Bulgaria 42°8N 24°44E **23** C11
Philipsburg _Canada_ 45°2N 73°5W **83** A11
Philipsburg _Mont.,_
  _U.S.A._ 46°20N 113°18W **76** C7
Philipsburg _Pa., U.S.A._ 40°54N 78°13W **82** F6
Philipstown = Daingean
  Ireland 53°18N 7°17W **10** C4
Philipstown _S. Africa_ 30°28S 24°30E **56** E3
Phillip I. _Australia_ 38°30S 145°12E **63** F4
Phillips _U.S.A._ 45°42N 90°24W **80** C8
Phillipsburg _Kans.,_
  _U.S.A._ 39°45N 99°19W **80** F4
Phillipsburg _N.J., U.S.A._ 40°42N 75°12W **83** F9
Philmont _U.S.A._ 42°15N 73°39W **83** D11
Philomath _U.S.A._ 44°32N 123°22W **76** D2
Phimai _Thailand_ 15°13N 102°30E **38** E4
Phitsanulok _Thailand_ 16°50N 100°12E **38** D3
Phnom Kulen △
  Cambodia 13°38N 104°15E **38** F5
Phnom Penh _Cambodia_ 11°33N 104°55E **39** G5
Phnom Penh = Phnom Penh
  Cambodia 11°33N 104°55E **39** G5
Phoenicia _U.S.A._ 42°5N 74°14W **83** D10
Phoenix _Mauritius_ 20°17S 57°30E **53** d
Phoenix _Ariz., U.S.A._ 33°26N 112°4W **77** K7
Phoenix _N.Y., U.S.A._ 43°14N 76°18W **83** C8
Phoenix Is. _Kiribati_ 3°30S 172°0W **64** H10
Phoenixville _U.S.A._ 40°8N 75°31W **83** F9

Phon _Thailand_ 15°49N 102°36E **38** E4
Phon Tiou _Laos_ 17°53N 104°37E **38** D5
Phong → _Thailand_ 16°23N 102°56E **38** D4
Phong Saly _Laos_ 21°42N 102°9E **38** A4
Phong Tho _Vietnam_ 22°32N 103°21E **38** A4
Phonhong _Laos_ 18°30N 102°25E **38** C4
Phonum _Thailand_ 8°49N 98°48E **39** H2
Phophtaram _Thailand_ 13°41N 99°51E **38** F2
Phra Nakhon Si Ayutthaya
  Thailand 14°25N 100°30E **38** E3
Phra Pradaeng _Thailand_ 13°39N 100°33E **38** F3
Phra Thong, Ko _Thailand_ 9°5N 98°17E **39** H2
Phrae _Thailand_ 18°7N 100°9E **38** C3
Phrom Phiram _Thailand_ 17°2N 100°12E **38** D3
Phu Bia _Laos_ 19°10N 103°0E **38** C4
Phu Chong-Na Yoi △
  Thailand 14°25N 105°30E **38** E5
Phu Dien _Vietnam_ 18°58N 105°31E **38** C5
Phu Hin Rang Kla △
  Thailand 17°0N 100°59E **38** D3
Phu Kradung △ _Thailand_ 17°2N 101°44E **38** D3
Phu Loi _Laos_ 20°14N 103°14E **38** B4
Phu Luang △ _Thailand_ 17°15N 101°29E **38** D3
Phu Ly _Vietnam_ 20°35N 105°50E **38** B5
Phu Phan △ _Thailand_ 17°0N 103°56E **38** D4
Phu Quoc, Dao _Vietnam_ 10°20N 104°0E **39** G4
Phu Wiang △ _Thailand_ 16°39N 102°23E **38** D4
Phuc Yen _Vietnam_ 21°16N 105°45E **38** B5
Phuket _Thailand_ 7°53N 98°24E **39** a
Phuket, Ko _Thailand_ 8°0N 98°22E **39** a
Phul _India_ 30°19N 75°14E **42** D6
Phulad _India_ 25°38N 73°49E **42** G5
Phulchari _Bangla._ 25°11N 89°37E **43** G13
Phulera _India_ 26°52N 75°16E **42** F6
Phulpur _India_ 25°31N 82°49E **43** G10
Phun Phin _Thailand_ 9°7N 99°12E **39** H2
Phuntsholing _Bhutan_ 26°51N 89°23E **43** F13
Pia ♦ _Australia_ 27°7S 116°23E **61** E2
Piacenza _Italy_ 45°1N 9°40E **20** D8
Piai, Tanjung _Malaysia_ 1°17N 103°30E **39** d
Pian Cr. → _Australia_ 30°2S 148°12E **63** E4
Pian-Upe △ _Uganda_ 1°44N 34°20E **54** B3
Pianosa _Italy_ 42°35N 10°5E **22** C4
Piapot _Canada_ 49°59N 109°8W **71** D7
Piatra Neamţ _Romania_ 46°56N 26°21E **17** E14
Piauí □ _Brazil_ 7°0S 43°0W **93** E10
Piauí → _Brazil_ 6°38S 42°42W **93** E10
Piave → _Italy_ 45°32N 12°44E **22** B5
Pibor Post _Sudan_ 6°47N 33°3E **51** G12
Picardie □ _France_ 49°50N 3°0E **20** B5
Picardy = Picardie □
  France 49°50N 3°0E **20** B5
Picayune _U.S.A._ 30°32N 89°41W **85** F10
Pichhor _India_ 25°58N 78°20E **43** G8
Pichilemu _Chile_ 34°22S 72°0W **94** C1
Pichor _India_ 25°11N 78°11E **42** G8
Pickerel L. _Canada_ 48°40N 91°25W **72** C1
Pickering _U.K._ 54°15N 0°46W **12** C7
Pickering, Vale of _U.K._ 54°14N 0°45W **12** C7
Pickle Lake _Canada_ 51°30N 90°12W **72** B1
Pickwick L. _U.S.A._ 35°4N 88°15W **85** D11
Pico _Azores_ 38°28N 28°20W **50** a
Pico Bonito △ _Honduras_ 15°34N 86°48W **88** C2
Pico Truncado _Argentina_ 46°40S 68°0W **96** F3
Picos _Brazil_ 7°5S 41°28W **93** E10
Picton _Canada_ 44°1N 77°9W **82** B7
Picton _N.Z._ 41°18S 174°3E **59** D5
Pictou _Canada_ 45°41N 62°42W **73** C7
Picture Butte _Canada_ 49°55N 112°45W **70** D6
Pictured Rocks △
  _U.S.A._ 46°30N 86°30W **80** B10
Picún Leufú _Argentina_ 39°30S 69°5W **96** D3
Pidurutalagala _Sri Lanka_ 7°10N 80°50E **40** R12
Piedmont = Piemonte □
  Italy 45°0N 8°0E **20** D7
Piedmont _Ala., U.S.A._ 33°55N 85°37W **85** E12
Piedmont _S.C., U.S.A._ 34°42N 82°28W **66** F11
Piedras Negras _Mexico_ 28°42N 100°31W **86** B4
Pieksämäki _Finland_ 62°18N 27°10E **8** E22
Pielinen _Finland_ 63°15N 29°40E **8** E23
Piemonte □ _Italy_ 45°0N 8°0E **20** D7
Pienaarsrivier _S. Africa_ 25°15S 28°18E **57** D4
Piercefield _U.S.A._ 44°13N 74°35W **83** B10
Pierceland _Canada_ 54°20N 109°46W **71** C7
Pierpont _U.S.A._ 41°45N 80°34W **82** E4
Pierre _U.S.A._ 44°22N 100°21W **80** C3
Pierrefonds _Canada_ 45°29N 73°51W **83** A11
Pierreville _Trin. & Tob._ 10°16N 61°0W **93** K16
Piet Retief _S. Africa_ 27°1S 30°50E **57** D5
Pietarsaari _Finland_ 63°40N 22°43E **8** E20
Pietermaritzburg
  S. Africa 29°35S 30°25E **57** D5
Pietersburg = Polokwane
  S. Africa 23°54S 29°25E **57** C4
Pietrosul, Vf. _Maramureş,_
  Romania 47°35N 24°43E **17** E13
Pietrosul, Vf. _Suceava,_
  Romania 47°12N 25°18E **17** E13
Pigeon L. _Canada_ 44°27N 78°30W **82** B6
Piggott _U.S.A._ 36°23N 90°11W **85** C9
Pigüe _Argentina_ 37°36S 62°25W **94** D3
Pihani _India_ 27°36N 80°15E **43** F9
Pihlajavesi _Finland_ 61°45N 28°45E **8** F23
Pijijiapan _Mexico_ 15°42N 93°14W **87** D6
Pikangikum _Canada_ 51°49N 94°0W **71** C10
Pikes Peak _U.S.A._ 38°50N 105°3W **76** G11
Piketberg _S. Africa_ 32°55S 18°40E **56** E2
Pikeville _U.S.A._ 37°29N 82°31W **81** G12
Pikou _China_ 39°18N 122°22E **35** E12
Pikwitonei _Canada_ 55°35N 97°9W **71** B9
Pila _Poland_ 53°10N 16°48E **17** B9
Pilanesberg △ _S. Africa_ 25°15S 27°4E **56** D4
Pilani _India_ 28°22N 75°33E **42** E6
Pilar _Paraguay_ 26°50S 58°20W **94** B4
Pilaya → _Bolivia_ 20°55S 64°4W **94** A3
Pilbara _Australia_ 21°15S 118°16E **60** D2
Pilcomayo → _Paraguay_ 25°21S 57°42W **94** B4

Pilgrim's Rest _S. Africa_ 24°55S 30°44E **57** C5
Pilibhit _India_ 28°40N 79°50E **43** E8
Pilica → _Poland_ 51°52N 21°17E **17** C11
Pilipinas = Philippines ■
  Asia 12°0N 123°0E **37** B6
Pilkhawa _India_ 28°43N 77°42E **42** E7
Pilliga _Australia_ 30°21S 148°54E **63** E4
Pilos _Greece_ 36°55N 21°42E **23** F9
Pilot Mound _Canada_ 49°15N 98°54W **71** D9
Pilot Point _U.S.A._ 33°24N 96°58W **84** E6
Pilot Rock _U.S.A._ 45°29N 118°50W **76** D4
Pima _U.S.A._ 32°54N 109°50W **77** K9
Pimba _Australia_ 31°18S 136°46E **63** E2
Pimenta Bueno _Brazil_ 11°35S 61°10W **92** F6
Pimentel _Peru_ 6°45S 79°55W **92** E2
Pin Valley △ _India_ 31°50N 77°50E **42** D7
Pinang _Malaysia_ 5°25N 100°15E **39** c
Pinar, C. des _Spain_ 39°53N 3°12E **24** B10
Pinar del Río _Cuba_ 22°26N 83°40W **88** B3
Pnarhisar _Turkey_ 41°37N 27°30E **23** D12
Pinatubo, Mt. _Phil._ 15°8N 120°21E **37** A6
Pinawa _Canada_ 50°9N 95°50W **71** C9
Pincher Creek _Canada_ 49°30N 113°57W **70** D6
Pinchi L. _Canada_ 54°38N 124°30W **70** C4
Pinckneyville _U.S.A._ 38°5N 89°23W **80** F9
Pińczów _Poland_ 50°32N 20°32E **17** C11
Pindar _Australia_ 28°30S 115°47E **61** E2
Pindera Downs ☆
  Australia 29°24S 142°37E **63** A3
Pindi Gheb _Pakistan_ 33°14N 72°21E **42** C5
Pindos Oros _Greece_ 40°0N 21°0E **23** E9
Pindus Mts. = Pindos Oros
  Greece 40°0N 21°0E **23** E9
Pine → _B.C., Canada_ 56°8N 120°43W **70** B4
Pine → _Sask., Canada_ 58°50N 105°38W **71** B7
Pine Bluff _U.S.A._ 34°13N 92°1W **84** D8
Pine Bluffs _U.S.A._ 41°11N 104°4W **76** F11
Pine City _U.S.A._ 45°50N 92°59W **80** C7
Pine Cr. → _U.S.A._ 41°10N 77°16W **82** E7
Pine Creek _Australia_ 13°50S 131°50E **60** B5
Pine Falls _Canada_ 50°34N 96°11W **71** C9
Pine Flat L. _U.S.A._ 36°50N 119°20W **78** J7
Pine Grove _U.S.A._ 40°33N 76°23W **83** F8
Pine Hill _Australia_ 23°38S 146°57E **62** C4
Pine Pass _Canada_ 55°25N 122°42W **70** B4
Pine Point _Canada_ 60°50N 114°28W **70** A6
Pine Ridge _U.S.A._ 43°2N 102°33W **80** D2
Pine River _Canada_ 51°45N 100°30W **71** C8
Pine River _U.S.A._ 46°43N 94°24W **80** B6
Pine Valley _U.S.A._ 32°50N 116°32W **79** N10
Pinecrest _U.S.A._ 38°12N 120°1W **78** G6
Pinedale _Calif., U.S.A._ 36°50N 119°48W **78** J7
Pinedale _Wyo., U.S.A._ 42°52N 109°52W **76** E9
Pinega → _Russia_ 64°30N 44°19E **18** B8
Pinehouse L. _Canada_ 55°32N 106°35W **71** B7
Pineimuta → _Canada_ 52°8N 88°33W **72** B1
Pinerolo _Italy_ 44°53N 7°21E **20** D7
Pines, Akra _Greece_ 40°5N 24°20E **23** D11
Pinetop-Lakeside _U.S.A._ 34°9N 109°58W **77** J9
Pinetown _S. Africa_ 29°48S 30°54E **57** D5
Pineville _U.S.A._ 31°19N 92°26W **84** F8
Ping → _Thailand_ 15°42N 100°9E **38** E3
Pingaring _Australia_ 32°40S 118°32E **61** F2
Pingding _China_ 37°47N 113°38E **34** F7
Pingdingshan _China_ 33°43N 113°27E **34** H7
Pingdong _Taiwan_ 22°39N 120°30E **33** F13
Pingdu _China_ 36°42N 119°59E **35** F10
Pingelly _Australia_ 32°32S 117°5E **61** F2
Pingliang _China_ 35°35N 106°31E **34** G4
Pinglu _China_ 39°31N 112°30E **34** E7
Pingluo _China_ 38°52N 106°30E **34** E4
Pingquan _China_ 41°1N 118°37E **35** D10
Pingrup _Australia_ 33°32S 118°29E **61** F2
P'ingtung _Taiwan_ 22°38N 120°30E **33** D7
Pingwu _China_ 32°25N 104°30E **34** H3
Pingxiang _China_ 22°6N 106°46E **32** D5
Pingyao _China_ 37°12N 112°10E **34** F7
Pingyi _China_ 35°30N 117°35E **35** G9
Pingyin _China_ 36°20N 116°25E **34** F9
Pingyuan _China_ 37°10N 116°22E **34** F9
Pinheiro _Brazil_ 2°31S 45°5W **93** D9
Pinheiro Machado
  Brazil 31°34S 53°23W **95** C5
Pinhel _Portugal_ 40°50N 7°1W **21** B2
Pini _Indonesia_ 0°10N 98°40E **36** D1
Pinios → _Greece_ 39°55S 22°41E **23** E10
Pinjarra _Australia_ 32°37S 115°52E **61** F2
Pink Mountain _Canada_ 57°3N 122°52W **70** B4
Pinnacles △ _U.S.A._ 36°25N 121°12W **78** J5
Pinnaroo _Australia_ 35°17S 140°53E **63** F3
Pinon Hills _U.S.A._ 34°26N 117°39W **79** L9
Pinos _Mexico_ 22°18N 101°34W **86** C4
Pinos, Mt. _U.S.A._ 34°49N 119°8W **79** L7
Pinos Pt. _U.S.A._ 36°38N 121°57W **77** H3
Pinrang _Indonesia_ 3°46S 119°41E **37** E5
Pins, Pte. aux _Canada_ 42°15N 81°51W **82** D3
Pinsk _Belarus_ 52°10N 26°1E **17** B14
Pintados _Chile_ 20°35S 69°40W **92** H5
Pinyug _Russia_ 60°5N 48°0E **18** B8
Pioche _U.S.A._ 37°56N 114°27W **77** H6
Piombino _Italy_ 42°55N 10°32E **22** C4
Pioner, Ostrov _Russia_ 79°50N 92°0E **29** B10
Piopiotaki = Milford Sd.
  _N.Z._ 44°41S 167°47E **59** F1
Piorini, L. _Brazil_ 3°15S 62°35W **92** D6
Piotrków Trybunalski
  Poland 51°23N 19°43E **17** C10
Pip _Iran_ 26°45N 60°10E **45** E9
Pipar _India_ 26°25N 73°31E **42** F5
Pipar Road _India_ 26°27N 73°27E **42** F5
Piparia _Mad. P., India_ 22°45N 78°23E **42** H8
Piparia _Mad. P., India_ 21°49N 77°37E **42** J7
Pipestone _U.S.A._ 44°0N 96°19W **80** D5
Pipestone → _Canada_ 52°53N 89°23W **72** B2
Pipestone Cr. →
  Canada 49°38N 100°15W **71** D8
Piplan _Pakistan_ 32°17N 71°21E **42** C4
Piploda _India_ 23°37N 74°56E **42** H6
Pipmuacan, Rés. _Canada_ 49°45N 70°30W **73** C5

Pippingarra *Australia* 20°27S 118°42E **60** D2
Piqua *U.S.A.* 40°9N 84°15W **81** E11
Piquiri → *Brazil* 24°3S 54°14W **95** A5
Pir Panjal Range *India* 32°30N 76°50E **42** C7
Pīr Sohrāb *Iran* 25°44N 60°54E **45** E9
Piracicaba *Brazil* 22°45S 47°40W **95** A6
Piracuruca *Brazil* 3°50S 41°50W **93** D10
Pirae *Tahiti* 17°31S 149°32W **59** d
Piræus = Peiraías *Greece* 37°57N 23°42E **23** F10
Piraiévs = Peiraías *Greece* 37°57N 23°42E **23** F10
Pirajuí *Brazil* 21°59S 49°29W **95** A6
Piram I. *India* 21°36N 72°21E **42** J5
Pirané *Argentina* 25°42S 59°6W **94** B4
Pīrānshahr *Iran* 36°41N 45°8E **44** B5
Pirapora *Brazil* 17°20S 44°56W **93** G10
Pirawa *India* 24°10N 76°2E **42** G7
Pireas *Greece* 37°57N 23°42E **23** F10
Pirgos *Greece* 37°40N 21°27E **23** F9
Piribebuy *Paraguay* 25°26S 57°2W **94** B4
Pirimapun *Indonesia* 6°20S 138°24E **37** F9
Pirin Planina *Bulgaria* 41°40N 23°30E **23** D10
Pirineos = Pyrénées
  Europe 42°45N 0°18E **20** E4
Piripiri *Brazil* 4°15S 41°46W **93** D10
Pirlangimpi *Australia* 11°24S 130°26E **60** B5
Pirmasens *Germany* 49°12N 7°36E **16** D4
Pirot *Serbia* 43°9N 22°33E **23** C10
Piru *Indonesia* 3°4S 128°12E **37** E7
Piru *U.S.A.* 34°25N 118°48W **79** L8
Pisa *Italy* 43°43N 10°23E **22** C4
Pisagua *Chile* 19°40S 70°15W **92** G4
Pisco *Peru* 13°50S 76°12W **92** F3
Pisek *Czech Rep.* 49°19N 14°10E **16** D8
Pishan *China* 37°30N 78°33E **32** C2
Pīshīn *Iran* 26°6N 61°47E **45** E9
Pishin *Pakistan* 30°35N 67°0E **42** D2
Pishin Lora → *Pakistan* 29°9N 64°5E **42** E1
Pising *Indonesia* 5°8S 121°53E **37** F6
Pismo Beach *U.S.A.* 35°9N 120°38W **79** K6
Pissis, Cerro *Argentina* 27°45S 68°48W **94** B2
Pissouri *Cyprus* 34°40N 32°42E **25** E11
Pistóia *Italy* 43°55N 10°54E **22** C4
Pistol B. *Canada* 62°25N 92°37W **71** A10
Pisuerga → *Spain* 41°33N 4°52W **21** B3
Pit → *U.S.A.* 40°47N 122°6W **76** F2
Pitarpunga L. *Australia* 34°24S 143°30E **63** E3
Pitcairn I. *Pac. Oc.* 25°5S 130°5W **65** K14
Pitch L. *Trin. & Tob.* 10°12N 61°39W **93** K15
Piteå *Sweden* 65°20N 21°25E **8** D19
Piteälven → *Sweden* 65°20N 21°25E **8** D19
Pitesti *Romania* 44°52N 24°54E **17** F13
Pithapuram *India* 17°10N 82°15E **41** L13
Pithara *Australia* 30°20S 116°35E **61** F2
Pithoragarh *India* 29°35N 80°13E **43** E9
Pithoro *Pakistan* 25°31N 69°23E **42** G3
Pitlochry *U.K.* 56°42N 3°44W **11** E5
Pitsilia *Cyprus* 34°55N 33°0E **25** E12
Pitt I. *Canada* 53°30N 129°50W **70** C3
Pittsburg *Calif., U.S.A.* 38°2N 121°53W **78** G5
Pittsburg *Kans., U.S.A.* 37°25N 94°42W **80** G6
Pittsburg *Tex., U.S.A.* 33°0N 94°59W **84** E7
Pittsburgh *U.S.A.* 40°26N 79°58W **82** F5
Pittsfield *Ill., U.S.A.* 39°36N 90°49W **80** F9
Pittsfield *Maine, U.S.A.* 44°47N 69°23W **81** C19
Pittsfield *Mass., U.S.A.* 42°27N 73°15W **83** D11
Pittsfield *N.H., U.S.A.* 43°18N 71°20W **83** C13
Pittston *U.S.A.* 41°19N 75°47W **83** E9
Pittsworth *Australia* 27°41S 151°37E **63** D5
Pituri → *Australia* 22°35S 138°30E **62** C2
Piura *Peru* 5°15S 80°38W **92** E2
Pixley *U.S.A.* 35°58N 119°18W **78** K7
Pizhou *China* 34°44N 116°55E **34** G9
Placentia *Canada* 47°20N 54°0W **73** C9
Placentia B. *Canada* 47°0N 54°40W **73** C9
Placerville *U.S.A.* 38°44N 120°48W **78** G6
Placetas *Cuba* 22°15N 79°44W **88** B4
Plainfield *N.J., U.S.A.* 40°37N 74°25W **83** F10
Plainfield *Ohio, U.S.A.* 40°13N 81°43W **82** F3
Plainfield *Vt., U.S.A.* 44°17N 72°26W **83** B12
Plains *Mont., U.S.A.* 47°28N 114°53W **76** C6
Plains *Tex., U.S.A.* 33°11N 102°50W **84** E3
Plainview *Nebr., U.S.A.* 42°21N 97°47W **80** D5
Plainview *Tex., U.S.A.* 34°11N 101°43W **84** D4
Plainwell *U.S.A.* 42°27N 85°38W **81** D11
Plaistow *U.S.A.* 42°50N 71°6W **83** D13
Plaka, Ákra *Greece* 35°11N 26°19E **25** D8
Plana Cays *Bahamas* 22°38N 73°30W **89** B5
Planada *U.S.A.* 37°16N 120°19W **78** H6
Plano *U.S.A.* 33°1N 96°42W **84** E6
Plant City *U.S.A.* 28°1N 82°7W **85** G13
Plaquemine *U.S.A.* 30°17N 91°14W **84** F9
Plasencia *Spain* 40°3N 6°8W **21** B2
Plaster City *U.S.A.* 32°47N 115°51W **79** N11
Plaster Rock *Canada* 46°53N 67°22W **73** C6
Plastun *Russia* 44°45N 136°19E **30** B8
Plata, Río de la →
  S. Amer. 34°45S 57°30W **94** C4
Plátani → *Italy* 37°23N 13°16E **22** F5
Plátanos *Greece* 35°28N 23°33E **25** D5
Platte *U.S.A.* 43°23N 98°51W **80** D4
Platte → *Mo., U.S.A.* 39°16N 94°50W **80** F6
Platte → *Nebr., U.S.A.* 41°4N 95°53W **80** E6
Platteville *U.S.A.* 42°44N 90°29W **80** D8
Plattsburgh *U.S.A.* 44°42N 73°28W **83** B11
Plattsmouth *U.S.A.* 41°1N 95°53W **80** E6
Plauen *Germany* 50°30N 12°8E **16** C7
Plavinas *Latvia* 56°35N 25°46E **9** H21
Playa Blanca *Canary Is.* 28°55N 13°37W **24** F6
Playa Blanca Sur
  Canary Is. 28°51N 13°50W **24** F6
Playa de las Americas
  Canary Is. 28°5N 16°43W **24** F3
Playa de Mogán
  Canary Is. 27°48N 15°47W **24** G4
Playa del Carmen *Mexico* 20°37N 87°4W **87** C7
Playa del Inglés
  Canary Is. 27°45N 15°33W **24** G4
Playa Esmeralda
  Canary Is. 28°8N 14°16W **24** F5

Playgreen L. *Canada* 54°0N 98°15W **71** C9
Pleasant Bay *Canada* 46°51N 60°48W **73** C7
Pleasant Hill *U.S.A.* 37°57N 122°4W **78** H4
Pleasant Mount *U.S.A.* 41°44N 75°26W **83** E9
Pleasanton *Calif.,*
  U.S.A. 37°39N 121°52W **78** H5
Pleasanton *Tex., U.S.A.* 28°58N 98°29W **84** G5
Pleasantville *N.J.,*
  U.S.A. 39°24N 74°32W **81** F16
Pleasantville *Pa., U.S.A.* 41°35N 79°34W **82** E5
Plei Ku *Vietnam* 13°57N 108°0E **38** F7
Plenty → *Australia* 23°25S 136°31E **62** C2
Plenty, B. of *N.Z.* 37°45S 177°0E **59** B6
Plentywood *U.S.A.* 48°47N 104°34W **76** B11
Plesetsk *Russia* 62°43N 40°20E **18** B7
Plessisville *Canada* 46°14N 71°47W **73** C5
Plétipi, L. *Canada* 51°44N 70°6W **73** B5
Pleven *Bulgaria* 43°26N 24°37E **23** C11
Plevlja *Montenegro* 43°21N 19°21E **23** C8
Plevna *Canada* 44°58N 76°59W **82** B8
Plock *Poland* 52°32N 19°40E **17** B10
Plöckenstein *Germany* 48°46N 13°51E **16** D7
Ploiesti *Romania* 44°57N 26°5E **17** F14
Plonge, Lac la *Canada* 55°8N 107°20W **71** B7
Plovdiv *Bulgaria* 42°8N 24°44E **23** C11
Plover Cove Res. *China* 22°28N 114°15E **33** G11
Plum *U.S.A.* 40°29N 79°47W **82** F5
Plum I. *U.S.A.* 41°11N 72°12W **83** E12
Plumas *U.S.A.* 39°45N 120°4W **78** F6
Plummer *U.S.A.* 47°20N 116°53W **76** C5
Plumridge Lakes
  Australia 29°26S 125°16E **61** E4
Plumtree *Zimbabwe* 20°27S 27°55E **55** G2
Plunge *Lithuania* 55°53N 21°59E **9** J19
Plymouth *Trin. & Tob.* 11°14N 60°48W **93** J16
Plymouth *U.K.* 50°22N 4°10W **13** G3
Plymouth *Calif., U.S.A.* 38°29N 120°51W **78** G6
Plymouth *Ind., U.S.A.* 41°21N 86°19W **80** E10
Plymouth *Mass., U.S.A.* 41°57N 70°40W **83** E14
Plymouth *N.C., U.S.A.* 35°52N 76°43W **85** D16
Plymouth *N.H., U.S.A.* 43°46N 71°41W **83** C13
Plymouth *Pa., U.S.A.* 41°14N 75°57W **83** E9
Plymouth *Wis., U.S.A.* 43°45N 87°59W **80** D10
Plympton-Wyoming = Wyoming
  Canada 42°57N 82°7W **82** D2
Plynlimon = Pumlumon Fawr
  U.K. 52°28N 3°46W **13** E4
Plyusa *Russia* 58°28N 29°27E **9** G23
Plzeň *Czech Rep.* 49°45N 13°22E **16** D7
Pmere Nyente ◊
  Australia 24°15S 136°10E **62** C2
Po → *Italy* 44°57N 12°4E **22** B5
Po Hai = Bo Hai *China* 39°0N 119°0E **35** E10
Po Toi *China* 22°10N 114°16E **33** G11
Pobeda *Russia* 65°12N 146°12E **29** C15
Pobedy, Pik *Kyrgyzstan* 42°0N 79°58E **32** B2
Pocahontas *Ark., U.S.A.* 36°16N 90°58W **85** C9
Pocahontas *Iowa, U.S.A.* 42°44N 94°40W **80** D6
Pocatello *U.S.A.* 42°52N 112°27W **76** E7
Pocomoke City *U.S.A.* 38°5N 75°34W **81** F16
Poços de Caldas *Brazil* 21°50S 46°33W **95** A6
Podgorica *Montenegro* 42°30N 19°19E **23** C8
Podilska Vysochyna
  Ukraine 49°0N 28°0E **17** D14
Podolsk *Russia* 55°25N 37°30E **18** C6
Podporozhye *Russia* 60°55N 34°2E **18** B5
Pofadder *S. Africa* 29°10S 19°22E **56** D2
Pogranichnyy *Russia* 44°25N 131°24E **30** B5
Poh *Indonesia* 0°46S 122°51E **37** E6
Pohang *S. Korea* 36°1N 129°23E **35** F15
Pohjanmaa *Finland* 62°58N 22°50E **8** E20
Pohnpei *Micronesia* 6°55N 158°10E **64** G7
Pohri *India* 25°32N 77°22E **42** G6
Poinsett, C. *Antarctica* 65°42S 113°18E **5** C8
Point Arena *U.S.A.* 38°55N 123°41W **78** G3
Point Baker *U.S.A.* 56°21N 133°37W **70** B2
Point Fortin
  Trin. & Tob. 10°10N 61°42W **93** K15
Point Hope *U.S.A.* 68°21N 166°47W **74** B6
Point L. *Canada* 65°15N 113°4W **68** D9
Point Lisas *Trin. & Tob.* 10°24N 61°29W **93** K15
Point Pedro *Sri Lanka* 9°50N 80°15E **40** Q12
Point Pelee △ *Canada* 41°57N 82°31W **82** E2
Point Pleasant *N.J.,*
  U.S.A. 40°5N 74°4W **83** F10
Point Pleasant *W. Va.,*
  U.S.A. 38°51N 82°8W **81** F12
Point Reyes *U.S.A.* 38°5N 123°0W **78** G4
Pointe-à-Pitre *Guadeloupe* 16°10N 61°32W **88** b
Pointe-au-Pic = La Malbaie
  Canada 47°40N 70°10W **73** C5
Pointe-Claire *Canada* 45°26N 73°50W **83** A11
Pointe-Gatineau *Canada* 45°27N 75°41W **83** A9
Pointe-Noire *Congo* 4°48S 11°53E **52** E2
Pointe-Noire *Guadeloupe* 16°14N 61°47W **88** b
Poipet *Cambodia* 13°39N 102°33E **38** F4
Poisonbush Ra.
  Australia 22°30S 121°30E **60** D3
Poissonnier Pt.
  Australia 19°57S 119°10E **60** C2
Poitiers *France* 46°35N 0°20E **20** C4
Poitou *France* 46°40N 0°10W **20** C3
Pojoaque *U.S.A.* 35°54N 106°1W **77** J10
Pokaran *India* 27°0N 71°50E **42** F4
Pokataroo *Australia* 29°30S 148°36E **63** D4
Pokhara *Nepal* 28°14N 83°58E **43** E10
Poko *Dem. Rep. of the Congo* 3°7N 26°52E **54** B2
Pokrovsk *Russia* 61°29N 129°0E **29** C13
Pola = Pula *Croatia* 44°54N 13°57E **16** F7
Polacca *U.S.A.* 35°50N 110°23W **77** J8
Polan *Iran* 25°30N 61°10E **45** E9
Poland ■ *Europe* 52°0N 20°0E **17** C10
Polar Bear △ *Canada* 55°0N 83°45W **72** A2
Polatsk *Belarus* 55°30N 28°50E **9** J23
Polcura *Chile* 37°17S 71°43W **94** D1
Polesye = Pripet Marshes
  Europe 52°10N 28°10E **17** B15
Polevskoy *Russia* 56°26N 60°11E **18** C11

Police *Poland* 53°33N 14°33E **16** B8
Police, Pte. *Seychelles* 4°51S 55°32E **53** b
Poligiros *Greece* 40°23N 23°25E **23** D10
Polillo Is. *Phil.* 14°56N 122°0E **37** B6
Polis *Cyprus* 35°2N 32°26E **25** D11
Polk *U.S.A.* 41°22N 79°56W **82** E5
Pollachi *India* 10°35N 77°0E **40** P10
Pollença *Spain* 39°54N 3°1E **24** B10
Pollença, B. de *Spain* 39°53N 3°8E **24** B10
Polnovat *Russia* 63°50N 65°54E **28** C7
Polokwane *S. Africa* 23°54S 29°25E **57** C4
Polokwane → *S. Africa* 22°25S 30°5E **57** C5
Polonne *Ukraine* 50°6N 27°30E **17** C14
Polonnoye = Polonne
  Ukraine 50°6N 27°30E **17** C14
Polson *U.S.A.* 47°41N 114°9W **76** C6
Poltava *Ukraine* 49°35N 34°35E **19** E5
Põltsamaa *Estonia* 58°39N 25°58E **9** G21
Polunochnoye *Russia* 60°52N 60°25E **28** C7
Põlva *Estonia* 58°3N 27°3E **9** G22
Polyarny *Russia* 69°8N 33°20E **8** B25
Polyarnyye Zori *Russia* 67°22N 32°30E **8** C25
Polynesia *Pac. Oc.* 10°0S 162°0W **65** F11
Polynésie française = French
  Polynesia ☑ *Pac. Oc.* 20°0S 145°0W **65** J13
Pombal *Portugal* 39°55N 8°40W **21** C1
Pombia *Greece* 35°0N 24°51E **25** E6
Pomene *Mozam.* 22°53S 35°33E **57** C6
Pomeroy *Ohio, U.S.A.* 39°2N 82°2W **81** F12
Pomeroy *Wash., U.S.A.* 46°28N 117°36W **76** C5
Pomézia *Italy* 41°40N 12°30E **22** D5
Pomona *Australia* 26°22S 152°52E **63** D5
Pomona *U.S.A.* 34°4N 117°45W **79** L9
Pomorskie, Pojezierze
  Poland 53°40N 16°37E **17** B9
Pomos *Cyprus* 35°9N 32°33E **25** D11
Pomos, C. *Cyprus* 35°10N 32°33E **25** D11
Pompano Beach *U.S.A.* 26°14N 80°7W **85** H14
Pompeys Pillar *U.S.A.* 45°59N 107°57W **76** D10
Pompeys Pillar △
  U.S.A. 46°0N 108°0W **76** D10
Pompton Lakes *U.S.A.* 41°0N 74°17W **83** F10
Ponape = Pohnpei
  Micronesia 6°55N 158°10E **64** G7
Ponask L. *Canada* 54°0N 92°41W **72** B1
Ponca *U.S.A.* 42°34N 96°43W **80** D5
Ponca City *U.S.A.* 36°42N 97°5W **84** C6
Ponce *Puerto Rico* 18°1N 66°37W **89** d
Ponchatoula *U.S.A.* 30°26N 90°26W **85** F9
Poncheville, L. *Canada* 50°10N 76°55W **72** B4
Pond *U.S.A.* 35°43N 119°20W **79** K7
Pond Inlet *Canada* 72°40N 77°0W **69** C16
Pondicherry = Puducherry
  India 11°59N 79°50E **40** P11
Ponds, I. of *Canada* 53°27N 55°52W **73** B8
Ponferrada *Spain* 42°32N 6°35W **21** A2
Ponnani *India* 10°45N 75°59E **40** P9
Ponoka *Canada* 52°42N 113°40W **70** C6
Ponorogo *Indonesia* 7°52S 111°27E **37** G14
Ponoy *Russia* 67°0N 41°13E **18** A7
Ponoy → *Russia* 66°59N 41°17E **18** A7
Ponta Delgada *Azores* 37°44N 25°40W **50** a
Ponta do Sol *Madeira* 32°42N 17°7W **24** D2
Ponta Grossa *Brazil* 25°7S 50°10W **95** B5
Ponta Porã *Brazil* 22°20S 55°35W **95** A4
Pontarlier *France* 46°54N 6°20E **20** C7
Pontchartrain, L. *U.S.A.* 30°5N 90°5W **85** F9
Ponte do Pungué
  Mozam. 19°30S 34°33E **55** F3
Ponte Nova *Brazil* 20°25S 42°54W **95** A7
Ponteix *Canada* 49°46N 107°29W **71** D7
Pontevedra *Spain* 42°26N 8°40W **21** A1
Pontiac *Ill., U.S.A.* 40°53N 88°38W **80** E9
Pontiac *Mich., U.S.A.* 42°38N 83°18W **81** D12
Pontian Kechil *Malaysia* 1°29N 103°23E **39** d
Pontianak *Indonesia* 0°3S 109°15E **36** E3
Pontine Is. = Ponziane, Ísole
  Italy 40°55N 12°57E **22** D5
Pontine Mts. = Kuzey Anadolu
  Dağları *Turkey* 41°0N 36°45E **19** F6
Pontivy *France* 48°5N 2°58W **20** B2
Pontoise *France* 49°3N 2°5E **20** B5
Ponton → *Canada* 58°27N 116°11W **70** B5
Pontypool *Canada* 44°6N 78°38W **82** B6
Pontypool *U.K.* 51°42N 3°2W **13** F4
Ponziane, Ísole *Italy* 40°55N 12°57E **22** D5
Poochera *Australia* 32°43S 134°51E **63** E1
Poole *U.K.* 50°43N 1°59W **13** G6
Poole □ *U.K.* 50°43N 1°59W **13** G6
Poona = Pune *India* 18°29N 73°57E **40** K8
Pooncarie *Australia* 33°22S 142°31E **63** E3
Poopelloe L. *Australia* 31°40S 144°0E **63** E3
Poopó, L. de *Bolivia* 18°30S 67°35W **92** G5
Popayán *Colombia* 2°27N 76°36W **92** C3
Poperinge *Belgium* 50°51N 2°42E **15** D2
Popiltah L. *Australia* 33°10S 141°42E **63** E3
Popio L. *Australia* 33°10S 141°52E **63** D5
Poplar *U.S.A.* 48°7N 105°12W **76** B11
Poplar → *Canada* 53°0N 97°19W **71** C9
Poplar Bluff *U.S.A.* 36°46N 90°24W **80** G8
Poplarville *U.S.A.* 30°51N 89°32W **85** F10
Popocatépetl, Volcán
  Mexico 19°2N 98°38W **87** D5
Popokabaka
  Dem. Rep. of the Congo 5°41S 16°40E **52** F3
Poprad *Slovak Rep.* 49°3N 20°18E **17** D11
Porali → *Pakistan* 25°58N 66°26E **42** G2
Porbandar *India* 21°44N 69°43E **42** J3
Porcher I. *Canada* 53°50N 130°30W **70** C2
Porcupine → *Canada* 59°11N 104°46W **71** B8
Porcupine → *U.S.A.* 66°34N 145°19W **68** D2
Porcupine Gorge △
  Australia 20°22S 144°26E **62** C3
Pordenone *Italy* 45°57N 12°39E **22** B5
Pori *Finland* 61°29N 21°48E **8** F19
Porkhov *Russia* 57°45N 29°38E **9** H23
Porlamar *Venezuela* 10°57N 63°51W **92** A6
Pormpuraaw *Australia* 14°59S 141°26E **62** A3

Pormpuraaw ◊
  Australia 14°55S 141°47E **62** A3
Poronaysk *Russia* 49°13N 143°0E **29** E15
Poroshiri-Dake *Japan* 42°41N 142°52E **30** C11
Poroto Mts. *Tanzania* 9°0S 33°30E **55** D3
Porpoise B. *Antarctica* 66°0S 127°0E **5** C9
Porreres *Spain* 39°31N 3°2E **24** B10
Porsangerfjorden
  Norway 70°40N 25°40E **8** A21
Porsgrunn *Norway* 59°10N 9°40E **9** G13
Port Alberni *Canada* 49°14N 124°50W **70** D4
Port Alfred *S. Africa* 33°36S 26°55E **56** E4
Port Alice *Canada* 50°20N 127°25W **70** C3
Port Allegany *U.S.A.* 41°48N 78°17W **82** E6
Port Allen *U.S.A.* 30°27N 91°12W **84** F9
Port Alma *Australia* 23°38S 150°53E **62** C5
Port Alma *Canada* 42°10N 82°14W **82** D2
Port Angeles *U.S.A.* 48°7N 123°27W **78** B3
Port Antonio *Jamaica* 18°10N 76°26W **88** a
Port Aransas *U.S.A.* 27°50N 97°4W **84** H6
Port Arthur *Australia* 43°7S 147°50E **63** G4
Port Arthur *U.S.A.* 29°54N 93°56W **84** H8
Port au Choix *Canada* 50°43N 57°22W **73** B8
Port au Port B. *Canada* 48°40N 58°50W **73** C8
Port-au-Prince *Haiti* 18°40N 72°20W **89** C5
Port Augusta *Australia* 32°30S 137°50E **63** E2
Port Austin *U.S.A.* 44°3N 83°1W **82** B2
Port Bell *Uganda* 0°18N 32°35E **54** B3
Port Bergé Vaovao
  Madag. 15°33S 47°40E **57** B8
Port Blandford *Canada* 48°20N 54°10W **73** C9
Port Bradshaw
  Australia 12°30S 137°20E **62** A2
Port Broughton
  Australia 33°37S 137°56E **63** E2
Port Bruce *Canada* 42°39N 81°0W **82** D4
Port Burwell *Canada* 42°40N 80°48W **82** D4
Port Canning *India* 22°23N 88°40E **43** H13
Port Carling *Canada* 45°7N 79°35W **82** A5
Port-Cartier *Canada* 50°2N 66°50W **73** B6
Port Chalmers *N.Z.* 45°49S 170°30E **59** F3
Port Charlotte *U.S.A.* 26°59N 82°6W **85** H13
Port Chester *U.S.A.* 41°0N 73°40W **83** F11
Port Clements *Canada* 53°40N 132°10W **70** C2
Port Clinton *U.S.A.* 41°31N 82°56W **81** E12
Port Colborne *Canada* 42°50N 79°10W **82** D5
Port Coquitlam *Canada* 49°15N 122°45W **78** A4
Port Credit *Canada* 43°33N 79°35W **82** C5
Port Curtis *Australia* 23°57S 151°20E **62** C5
Port d'Alcúdia *Spain* 39°50N 3°7E **24** B10
Port Dalhousie *Canada* 43°13N 79°16W **82** C5
Port d'Andratx *Spain* 39°32N 2°23E **24** B9
Port Darwin *Australia* 12°24S 130°45E **60** B5
Port Darwin *Falk. Is.* 51°50S 59°0W **96** G5
Port Davey *Australia* 43°16S 145°55E **63** G4
Port-de-Paix *Haiti* 19°50N 72°50W **89** C5
Port de Pollença *Spain* 39°54N 3°4E **24** B10
Port de Sóller *Spain* 39°48N 2°42E **24** B9
Port Dickson *Malaysia* 2°30N 101°49E **39** L3
Port Douglas *Australia* 16°30S 145°30E **62** B4
Port Dover *Canada* 42°47N 80°12W **82** D4
Port Edward *Canada* 54°12N 130°10W **70** C2
Port Elgin *Canada* 44°25N 81°25W **82** B3
Port Elizabeth *S. Africa* 33°58S 25°40E **56** E4
Port Ellen *U.K.* 55°38N 6°11W **11** F2
Port Erin *I. of Man* 54°5N 4°45W **12** C3
Port Essington *Australia* 11°15S 132°10E **60** B5
Port Ewen *U.S.A.* 41°54N 73°59W **83** E11
Port Fairy *Australia* 38°22S 142°12E **63** F3
Port Gamble *U.S.A.* 47°51N 122°34W **78** C4
Port-Gentil *Gabon* 0°40S 8°50E **52** E1
Port Germein *Australia* 33°1S 138°1E **63** E2
Port Ghalib *Egypt* 25°20N 34°50E **44** E2
Port Gibson *U.S.A.* 31°58N 90°59W **84** F9
Port Glasgow *U.K.* 55°56N 4°41W **11** F4
Port Harcourt *Nigeria* 4°40N 7°10E **50** H7
Port Hardy *Canada* 50°41N 127°30W **70** C3
Port Harrison = Inukjuak
  Canada 58°25N 78°15W **69** F16
Port Hawkesbury
  Canada 45°36N 61°22W **73** C7
Port Hedland *Australia* 20°25S 118°35E **60** D2
Port Henry *U.S.A.* 44°3N 73°28W **83** B11
Port Hood *Canada* 46°0N 61°32W **73** C7
Port Hope *Canada* 43°56N 78°20W **82** C6
Port Hope *U.S.A.* 43°57N 82°43W **82** C2
Port Hope Simpson
  Canada 52°33N 56°18W **73** B8
Port Hueneme *U.S.A.* 34°7N 119°12W **79** L7
Port Huron *U.S.A.* 42°58N 82°26W **82** D2
Port Jefferson *U.S.A.* 40°57N 73°3W **83** F11
Port Jervis *U.S.A.* 41°22N 74°41W **83** E10
Port Kelang = Pelabuhan Klang
  Malaysia 3°0N 101°23E **39** L3
Port Kenny *Australia* 33°10S 134°41E **63** E1
Port Lairge = Waterford
  Ireland 52°15N 7°8W **10** D4
Port Laoise *Ireland* 53°2N 7°18W **10** C4
Port Lavaca *U.S.A.* 28°37N 96°38W **84** G6
Port Leyden *U.S.A.* 43°35N 75°21W **83** C9
Port Lincoln *Australia* 34°42S 135°52E **63** E2
Port Loko *S. Leone* 8°48N 12°46W **50** G3
Port-Louis *Guadeloupe* 16°28N 61°32W **88** b
Port Louis *Mauritius* 20°10S 57°30E **53** d
Port MacDonnell
  Australia 38°5S 140°48E **63** F3
Port McNeill *Canada* 50°35N 127°6W **70** C3
Port Macquarie
  Australia 31°25S 152°25E **63** E5
Port Maria *Jamaica* 18°22N 76°54W **88** a
Port Matilda *U.S.A.* 40°48N 78°3W **82** F6
Port Mellon *Canada* 49°32N 123°31W **70** D4
Port-Menier *Canada* 49°51N 64°15W **73** C7
Port Moody *Canada* 49°17N 122°51W **78** A4
Port Morant *Jamaica* 17°54N 76°19W **88** a
Port Moresby *Papua N. G.* 9°24S 147°8E **58** B7
Port Musgrave
  Australia 11°55S 141°50E **62** A3

Port Neches *U.S.A.* 30°0N 93°59W **84** G8
Port Nolloth *S. Africa* 29°17S 16°52E **56** D2
Port Nouveau-Québec =
  Kangiqsualujjuaq
  Canada 58°30N 65°59W **69** F18
Port of Climax *Canada* 49°10N 108°20W **71** D7
Port of Coronach
  Canada 49°7N 105°31W **71** D7
Port of Spain
  Trin. & Tob. 10°40N 61°31W **93** K15
Port Orange *U.S.A.* 29°9N 80°59W **85** G14
Port Orchard *U.S.A.* 47°32N 122°38W **78** C4
Port Orford *U.S.A.* 42°45N 124°30W **76** E1
Port Pegasus *N.Z.* 47°12S 167°41E **59** G1
Port Perry *Canada* 44°6N 78°56W **82** B6
Port Phillip B. *Australia* 38°10S 144°50E **63** F3
Port Pirie *Australia* 33°10S 138°1E **63** E2
Port Renfrew *Canada* 48°30N 124°20W **78** B2
Port Roper *Australia* 14°45S 135°25E **62** A2
Port Rowan *Canada* 42°40N 80°30W **82** D4
Port Safaga = Bûr Safâga
  Egypt 26°43N 33°57E **44** E2
Port Said = Bûr Sa'îd
  Egypt 31°16N 32°18E **51** B12
Port St. Joe *U.S.A.* 29°49N 85°18W **85** G12
Port St. Johns = Umzimvubu
  S. Africa 31°38S 29°33E **57** E4
Port St. Lucie *U.S.A.* 27°18N 80°21W **85** H14
Port Sanilac *U.S.A.* 43°26N 82°33W **82** C2
Port Severn *Canada* 44°48N 79°43W **82** B5
Port Shepstone *S. Africa* 30°44S 30°28E **57** E5
Port Simpson *Canada* 54°30N 130°20W **70** C2
Port Stanley = Stanley
  Falk. Is. 51°40S 59°51W **96** G5
Port Stanley *Canada* 42°40N 81°10W **82** D3
Port Sudan = Bûr Sûdân
  Sudan 19°32N 37°9E **51** E13
Port Sulphur *U.S.A.* 29°29N 89°42W **85** G10
Port Talbot *U.K.* 51°35N 3°47W **13** F4
Port Townsend *U.S.A.* 48°7N 122°45W **78** B4
Port-Vendres *France* 42°32N 3°8E **20** E5
Port Vila *Vanuatu* 17°45S 168°18E **58** C9
Port Vladimir *Russia* 69°25N 33°6E **8** B25
Port Wakefield *Australia* 34°12S 138°10E **63** E2
Port Washington
  U.S.A. 43°23N 87°53W **80** D10
Porta Orientalis *Romania* 45°6N 22°18E **17** F12
Portacloy *Ireland* 54°20N 9°46W **10** B2
Portadown *U.K.* 54°25N 6°27W **10** B5
Portaferry *U.K.* 54°23N 5°33W **10** B6
Portage *Pa., U.S.A.* 40°23N 78°41W **82** F6
Portage *Wis., U.S.A.* 43°33N 89°28W **80** D9
Portage la Prairie
  Canada 49°58N 98°18W **71** D9
Portageville *U.S.A.* 36°26N 89°42W **80** G10
Portalegre *Portugal* 39°19N 7°25W **21** C2
Portales *U.S.A.* 34°11N 103°20W **77** J12
Portarlington *Ireland* 53°9N 7°14W **10** C4
Portbou *Spain* 42°25N 3°9E **21** A7
Porter L. *N.W.T., Canada* 61°41N 108°5W **71** A7
Porter L. *Sask., Canada* 56°20N 107°20W **71** B7
Porterville *S. Africa* 33°0S 19°0E **56** E2
Porterville *U.S.A.* 36°4N 119°1W **78** J8
Porthcawl *U.K.* 51°29N 3°42W **13** F4
Porthill *U.S.A.* 48°59N 116°30W **76** B5
Porthmadog *U.K.* 52°55N 4°8W **12** E3
Portile de Fier *Europe* 44°44N 22°30E **17** F12
Portimão *Portugal* 37°8N 8°32W **21** D1
Portishead *U.K.* 51°29N 2°46W **13** F5
Portknockie *U.K.* 57°42N 2°51W **11** D6
Portland *N.S.W.,*
  Australia 33°20S 150°0E **63** E5
Portland *Vic., Australia* 38°20S 141°35E **63** F3
Portland *Canada* 44°42N 76°12W **83** B8
Portland *Conn., U.S.A.* 41°34N 72°38W **83** E12
Portland *Maine, U.S.A.* 43°39N 70°16W **81** D18
Portland *Mich., U.S.A.* 42°52N 84°54W **81** D11
Portland *Oreg., U.S.A.* 45°32N 122°37W **78** E4
Portland *Pa., U.S.A.* 40°55N 75°6W **83** F9
Portland *Tex., U.S.A.* 27°53N 97°20W **84** H6
Portland, I. of *U.K.* 50°33N 2°26E **13** G5
Portland Bight *Jamaica* 17°52N 77°5W **88** a
Portland Bill *U.K.* 50°31N 2°28E **13** G5
Portland Canal *U.S.A.* 55°56N 130°0W **70** B2
Portland Int. ✈ (PDX)
  U.S.A. 45°35N 122°36W **78** E4
Portland Pt. *Jamaica* 17°42N 77°11W **88** a
Portmadoc = Porthmadog
  U.K. 52°55N 4°8W **12** E3
Portmore *Jamaica* 17°53N 76°53W **88** a
Porto *France* 42°16N 8°42E **20** E8
Porto *Portugal* 41°8N 8°40W **21** B1
Pôrto Alegre *Brazil* 30°5S 51°10W **95** C5
Porto Colom *Spain* 39°26N 3°15E **24** B10
Porto Cristo *Spain* 39°33N 3°20E **24** B10
Porto de Moz *Brazil* 1°41S 52°13W **93** D8
Pôrto Empédocle *Italy* 37°17N 13°32E **22** F5
Pôrto Esperança *Brazil* 19°37S 57°29W **92** G7
Pôrto Franco *Brazil* 6°20S 47°24W **93** E9
Porto Inglês = C. Verde Is. 15°21N 23°10W **50** b
Pôrto Mendes *Brazil* 24°30S 54°15W **95** A5
Porto Moniz *Madeira* 32°52N 17°11W **24** D2
Pôrto Murtinho *Brazil* 21°45S 57°55W **92** H7
Pôrto Nacional *Brazil* 10°40S 48°30W **93** F9
Porto-Novo *Benin* 6°23N 2°42E **50** G6
Porto Primavera, Represa
  Brazil 22°10S 52°45W **95** A5
Porto Santo, I. de
  Madeira 33°45N 16°25W **50** B2
Pôrto São José *Brazil* 22°43S 53°10W **95** A5
Porto Seguro *Brazil* 16°26S 39°5W **93** G11
Pôrto Tôrres *Italy* 40°50N 8°24E **22** D3
Pôrto União *Brazil* 26°10S 51°10W **95** B5
Pôrto-Vecchio *France* 41°35N 9°16E **20** F8
Pôrto Velho *Brazil* 8°46S 63°54W **92** E6
Port Walter *Brazil* 8°15S 72°40W **92** E4
Portobelo *Panama* 9°35N 79°42W **88** E4
Portoferráio *Italy* 42°48N 10°20E **22** C4

Portola *U.S.A.* 39°49N 120°28W **78 F6**
Portopetro *Spain* 39°22N 3°13E **24 B10**
Portoscuso *Italy* 39°12N 8°24E **22 E3**
Portoviejo *Ecuador* 1°7S 80°28W **92** D2
Portpatrick *U.K.* 54°51N 5°7W **11 G3**
Portree *U.K.* 57°25N 6°12W **11 D2**
Portrush *U.K.* 55°12N 6°40W **10** A5
Portsmouth *Dominica* 15°34N 61°27W **89** C7
Portsmouth *U.K.* 50°48N 1°6W **13 G6**
Portsmouth *N.H., U.S.A.* 43°5N 70°45W **83** C14
Portsmouth *Ohio,*
  U.S.A. 38°44N 82°57W **81** F12
Portsmouth *R.I., U.S.A.* 41°36N 71°15W **83** E13
Portsmouth *Va., U.S.A.* 36°58N 76°23W **81** G15
Portsmouth □ *U.K.* 50°48N 1°6W **13 G6**
Portsoy *U.K.* 57°41N 2°41W **11** D6
Portstewart *U.K.* 55°11N 6°43W **10** A5
Porttipahdan tekojärvi
  Finland 68°5N 26°40E **8 B22**
Portugal ■ *Europe* 40°0N 8°0W **21** C1
Portumna *Ireland* 53°6N 8°14W **10** C3
Portville *U.S.A.* 42°3N 78°20W **82** D6
Poruma *Australia* 10°2S 143°4E **62** a
Porvenir *Chile* 53°10S 70°16W **96** G2
Posadas *Argentina* 27°30S 55°50W **95** B4
Posht-e Badam *Iran* 33°2N 55°23E **45** C7
Poso *Indonesia* 1°20S 120°55E **37** E6
Posse *Brazil* 14°4S 46°18W **93** F9
Possession I. *Antarctica* 72°4S 172°0E **5** D11
Possum Kingdom L.
  U.S.A. 32°52N 98°26W **84** E5
Post *U.S.A.* 33°12N 101°23W **84** E4
Post Falls *U.S.A.* 47°43N 116°57W **76** C5
Postavy = Pastavy
  Belarus 55°4N 26°50E **9 J22**
Poste-de-la-Baleine =
  Kuujjuarapik *Canada* 55°20N 77°35W **72** A4
Postmasburg *S. Africa* 28°18S 23°5E **56** D3
Postojna *Slovenia* 45°46N 14°12E **16** F8
Poston *U.S.A.* 34°0N 114°24W **79** J7
Postville *Canada* 54°54N 59°47W **73** B8
Posyet *Russia* 42°39N 130°48E **30** C5
Potchefstroom *S. Africa* 26°41S 27°7E **56** D4
Poteau *U.S.A.* 35°3N 94°37W **84** D7
Poteet *U.S.A.* 29°2N 98°35W **84** G5
Potenza *Italy* 40°38N 15°48E **22** D6
Poteriteri, L. *N.Z.* 46°5S 167°10E **59** G1
Potgietersrus = Mokopane
  S. Africa 24°10S 28°55E **57** C4
Poti *Georgia* 42°10N 41°38E **19** F7
Potiskum *Nigeria* 11°39N 11°2E **51** F8
Potomac → *U.S.A.* 38°0N 76°23W **81** F14
Potosí *Bolivia* 19°38S 65°50W **92** G5
Potosí Mt. *U.S.A.* 35°57N 115°29W **79** K11
Pototan *Phil.* 10°54N 122°38E **37** B6
Potrerillos *Chile* 26°30S 69°30W **94** B2
Potsdam *Germany* 52°23N 13°3E **16** B7
Potsdam *U.S.A.* 44°40N 74°59W **83** B10
Pottersville *U.S.A.* 43°43N 73°50W **83** C11
Pottstown *U.S.A.* 40°15N 75°39W **83** F9
Pottsville *U.S.A.* 40°41N 76°12W **83** F8
Pottuvil *Sri Lanka* 6°55N 81°50E **40** R12
Pouce Coupé *Canada* 55°40N 120°10W **70** B4
Poughkeepsie *U.S.A.* 41°42N 73°56W **83** E11
Poulaphouca Res. *Ireland* 53°8N 6°30W **10** C5
Poulsbo *U.S.A.* 47°44N 122°38W **78** C4
Poultney *U.S.A.* 43°31N 73°14W **83** C11
Poulton-le-Fylde *U.K.* 53°51N 2°58W **12** D5
Pouso Alegre *Brazil* 22°14S 45°57W **95** A6
Pouthisat *Cambodia* 12°34N 103°50E **38** F4
Považská Bystrica
  Slovak Rep. 49°8N 18°27E **17** D10
Povenets *Russia* 62°50N 34°50E **18** B5
Poverty B. *N.Z.* 38°43S 178°2E **59** C7
Póvoa de Varzim
  Portugal 41°25N 8°46W **21** B1
Povorotnyy, Mys *Russia* 42°40N 133°2E **30** C6
Povungnituk = Puvirnituq
  Canada 60°2N 77°10W **69** E16
Powassan *Canada* 46°5N 79°25W **72** C4
Poway *U.S.A.* 32°58N 117°2W **79** N9
Powder → *U.S.A.* 46°45N 105°26W **76** C11
Powder River *U.S.A.* 43°2N 106°59W **76** E10
Powell *U.S.A.* 44°45N 108°46W **76** D9
Powell, L. *U.S.A.* 36°57N 111°29W **77** H8
Powell River *Canada* 49°50N 124°35W **70** D4
Powers *U.S.A.* 45°41N 87°32W **80** C10
Pownal *U.S.A.* 42°45N 73°14W **83** D11
Powys □ *U.K.* 52°20N 3°20W **13** E4
Poyang Hu *China* 29°5N 116°20E **33** D6
Poyarkovo *Russia* 49°36N 128°41E **29** E13
Poza Rica *Mexico* 20°33N 97°27W **87** C5
Požarevac *Serbia* 44°35N 21°18E **23** B9
Poznań *Poland* 52°25N 16°55E **17** B9
Pozo *U.S.A.* 35°20N 120°24W **79** K6
Pozo Almonte *Chile* 20°10S 69°50W **92** H5
Pozo Colorado *Paraguay* 23°30S 58°45W **94** A4
Pozoblanco *Spain* 38°23N 4°51W **21** C3
Pozzuoli *Italy* 40°49N 14°7E **22** D6
Prachin Buri *Thailand* 14°0N 101°25E **38** F3
Prachuap Khiri Khan
  Thailand 11°49N 99°48E **39** G2
Prado *Brazil* 17°20S 39°13W **93** G11
Prague = Praha
  Czech Rep. 50°4N 14°25E **16** C8
Praha *Czech Rep.* 50°4N 14°25E **16** C8
Praia *C. Verde Is.* 15°2N 23°34W **50** b
Prainha *Brazil* 1°45S 53°30W **93** D8
Prainha Nova *Brazil* 7°10S 60°30W **92** E6
Prairie *Australia* 20°50S 144°35E **62** C3
Prairie City *U.S.A.* 44°28N 118°43W **76** D4
Prairie Dog Town Fork Red →
  U.S.A. 34°34N 99°58W **84** D5
Prairie du Chien *U.S.A.* 43°3N 91°9W **80** D8
Prairies, L. of the
  Canada 51°16N 101°32W **71** C8
Pran Buri *Thailand* 12°23N 99°55E **38** F2
Prapat *Indonesia* 2°41N 98°58E **36** D1
Praslin *Seychelles* 4°18S 55°45E **53** b

Prasonisi, Akra *Greece* 35°42N 27°46E **25** D9
Prata *Brazil* 19°25S 48°54W **93** G9
Pratabpur *India* 23°28N 83°15E **43 H10**
Pratapgarh *Raj., India* 24°2N 74°40E **42** G6
Pratapgarh *Ut. P., India* 25°56N 81°59E **43** G9
Prato *Italy* 43°53N 11°6E **22** C4
Pratt *U.S.A.* 37°39N 98°44W **80** G4
Prattville *U.S.A.* 32°28N 86°29W **85** E11
Pravia *Spain* 43°30N 6°12W **21** A2
Praya *Indonesia* 8°39S 116°17E **36** F5
Prayag = Allahabad
  India 25°25N 81°58E **43** G9
Preble *U.S.A.* 42°44N 76°8W **83** D8
Precipice △ *Australia* 25°18S 150°5E **63** D5
Preeceville *Canada* 51°57N 102°40W **71** C8
Preili *Latvia* 56°18N 26°43E **9 H22**
Premont *U.S.A.* 27°22N 98°7W **84** H5
Prentice *U.S.A.* 45°33N 90°17W **80** C9
Preobrazheniye *Russia* 42°54N 133°54E **30** C6
Preparis I. = Pariparit Kyun
  Burma 14°52N 93°41E **41 M18**
Preparis North Channel
  Ind. Oc. 15°27N 94°5E **41 M18**
Preparis South Channel
  Ind. Oc. 14°33N 93°30E **41 M18**
Přerov *Czech Rep.* 49°28N 17°27E **17** D9
Prescott *Canada* 44°45N 75°30W **83** B9
Prescott *Ariz., U.S.A.* 34°33N 112°28W **77** J7
Prescott *Ark., U.S.A.* 33°48N 93°23W **84** E8
Prescott Valley *U.S.A.* 34°40N 112°18W **77** J7
Preservation Inlet *N.Z.* 46°8S 166°35E **59** G1
Presho *U.S.A.* 43°54N 100°3W **80** D3
Presidencia de la Plaza
  Argentina 27°0S 59°50W **94** B4
Presidencia Roque Saenz Peña
  Argentina 26°45S 60°30W **94** B3
Presidente Epitácio *Brazil* 21°56S 52°6W **93** H8
Presidente Hayes □
  Paraguay 24°0S 59°0W **94** A4
Presidente Prudente
  Brazil 22°5S 51°25W **95** A5
Presidio *Mexico* 29°29N 104°23W **86** B4
Presidio *U.S.A.* 29°34N 104°22W **84** G2
Prešov *Slovak Rep.* 49°0N 21°15E **17** D11
Prespa, L. = Prespansko Jezero
  Macedonia 40°55N 21°0E **23** D9
Prespansko Jezero
  Macedonia 40°55N 21°0E **23** D9
Presque I. *U.S.A.* 42°10N 80°6W **82** D4
Presque Isle *U.S.A.* 46°41N 68°1W **81** B19
Prestatyn *U.K.* 53°20N 3°24W **12** D4
Presteigne *U.K.* 52°17N 3°0W **13** E5
Preston *Canada* 43°23N 80°21W **82** C4
Preston *U.K.* 53°46N 2°42W **12** D5
Preston *Idaho, U.S.A.* 42°6N 111°53W **76** E8
Preston *Minn., U.S.A.* 43°40N 92°5W **80** D7
Preston, C. *Australia* 20°51S 116°12E **60** D2
Prestonsburg *U.S.A.* 37°40N 82°47W **81** G12
Prestwick *U.K.* 55°29N 4°37W **11** F4
Pretoria *S. Africa* 25°44S 28°12E **57** D4
Preveza *Greece* 38°57N 20°45E **23** E9
Prey Veng *Cambodia* 11°35N 105°29E **39** G5
Pribilof Is. *U.S.A.* 57°0N 170°0W **74** D6
Příbram *Czech Rep.* 49°41N 14°2E **16** D8
Price *U.S.A.* 39°36N 110°49W **76** G8
Price I. *Canada* 52°23N 128°41W **70** C3
Prichard *U.S.A.* 30°44N 88°5W **85** F10
Priekule *Latvia* 56°26N 21°35E **9 H19**
Prienai *Lithuania* 54°38N 23°57E **9 J20**
Prieska *S. Africa* 29°40S 22°42E **56** D3
Priest L. *U.S.A.* 48°35N 116°52W **76** B5
Priest River *U.S.A.* 48°11N 116°55W **76** B5
Priest Valley *U.S.A.* 36°10N 120°39W **78** J6
Prievidza *Slovak Rep.* 48°46N 18°36E **17** D10
Prikaspiyskaya Nizmennost =
  Caspian Depression
  Eurasia 47°0N 48°0E **19** E8
Prilep *Macedonia* 41°21N 21°32E **23** D9
Priluki = Pryluky
  Ukraine 50°30N 32°24E **19** D5
Prime Seal I. *Australia* 40°3S 147°43E **63** G4
Primo Tapia *Mexico* 32°16N 116°54W **79** N10
Primorskiy Kray □
  Russia 45°0N 135°0E **30** B7
Primrose L. *Canada* 54°55N 109°45W **71** C7
Prince Albert *Canada* 53°15N 105°50W **71** C7
Prince Albert *S. Africa* 33°12S 22°2E **56** E3
Prince Albert △ *Canada* 54°0N 106°25W **71** C7
Prince Albert Mts.
  Antarctica 76°0S 161°30E **5** D11
Prince Albert Pen.
  Canada 72°30N 116°0W **68** C8
Prince Albert Sd.
  Canada 70°25N 115°0W **68** C9
Prince Alfred, C. *Canada* 74°20N 124°40W **4** B1
Prince Charles I.
  Canada 67°47N 76°12W **69** D16
Prince Charles Mts.
  Antarctica 72°0S 67°0E **5** D6
Prince Edward Fracture Zone
  Ind. Oc. 46°0S 35°0E **5** A4
Prince Edward I. □
  Canada 46°20N 63°20W **73** C7
Prince Edward Is. *Ind. Oc.* 46°35S 38°0E **3** G11
Prince George *Canada* 53°55N 122°50W **70** C4
Prince of Wales, C.
  U.S.A. 65°36N 168°5W **74** B6
Prince of Wales I.
  Australia 10°40S 142°10E **62** A3
Prince of Wales I. *Canada* 73°0N 99°0W **68** C12
Prince of Wales I.
  U.S.A. 55°47N 132°50W **68** C6
Prince of Wales Icefield
  Canada 78°15N 79°0W **69** B16
Prince of Wales Str.
  Canada 73°0N 117°0W **68** C8
Prince Patrick I. *Canada* 77°0N 120°0W **69** B8

Prince Regent Inlet
  Canada 73°0N 90°0W **69** C14
Prince Rupert *Canada* 54°20N 130°20W **70** C2
Prince William Sd.
  U.S.A. 60°40N 147°0W **68** E2
Princes Town
  Trin. & Tob. 10°16N 61°23W **93** K15
Princess Charlotte B.
  Australia 14°25S 144°0E **62** A3
Princess Elizabeth Trough
  S. Ocean 64°10S 83°0E **5** C7
Princess May Ranges
  Australia 15°30S 125°30E **60** C4
Princess Royal I. *Canada* 53°0N 128°40W **70** C3
Princeton *Canada* 49°27N 120°30W **70** D4
Princeton *Calif., U.S.A.* 39°24N 122°1W **78** F4
Princeton *Ill., U.S.A.* 41°23N 89°28W **80** E9
Princeton *Ind., U.S.A.* 38°21N 87°34W **80** F10
Princeton *Ky., U.S.A.* 37°7N 87°53W **80** G10
Princeton *Mo., U.S.A.* 40°24N 93°35W **80** E7
Princeton *N.J., U.S.A.* 40°21N 74°39W **83** F10
Princeton *W. Va., U.S.A.* 37°22N 81°6W **81** G13
Príncipe *São Tomé & Príncipe* 1°37N 7°25E **48** F4
Principe da Beira *Brazil* 12°20S 64°30W **92** F6
Prineville *U.S.A.* 44°18N 120°51W **76** D3
Prins Harald Kyst *Antarctica* 70°0S 35°1E **5** D4
Prinsesse Astrid Kyst
  Antarctica 70°45S 12°30E **5** D3
Prinsesse Ragnhild Kyst
  Antarctica 70°15S 27°30E **5** D4
Prinzapolca *Nic.* 13°20N 83°35W **88** D3
Priozersk *Russia* 61°2N 30°7E **8 F24**
Pripet = Prypyat →
  Europe 51°20N 30°15E **17** C16
Pripet Marshes *Europe* 52°10N 28°10E **17** B15
Pripyat Marshes = Pripet Marshes
  Europe 52°10N 28°10E **17** B15
Pripyats = Prypyat →
  Europe 51°20N 30°15E **17** C16
Priština *Kosovo* 42°40N 21°13E **23** C9
Privas *France* 44°45N 4°37E **20** D6
Privolzhskaya Vozvyshennost
  Russia 51°0N 46°0E **19** D8
Privolzhskiy □ *Russia* 56°0N 50°0E **28** D6
Prizren *Kosovo* 42°13N 20°45E **23** C9
Probolinggo *Indonesia* 7°46S 113°13E **37** G15
Proctor *U.S.A.* 43°40N 73°2W **83** C11
Proddatur *India* 14°45N 78°30E **40** M11
Prodhromos *Cyprus* 34°57N 32°50E **25** E11
Profília *Greece* 36°5N 27°51E **25** C9
Profondeville *Belgium* 50°23N 4°52E **15** D4
Progreso *Coahuila,*
  Mexico 27°28N 100°59W **86** B4
Progreso *Yucatán,*
  Mexico 21°20N 89°40W **87** C7
Progress *Antarctica* 66°22S 76°22E **5** C12
Progress *Russia* 49°45N 129°37E **29** E13
Prokopyevsk *Russia* 54°0N 86°45E **28** D9
Prokuplje *Serbia* 43°16N 21°36E **23** C9
Prome *Burma* 18°49N 95°13E **41** K19
Prophet → *Canada* 58°48N 122°40W **70** B4
Prophet River *Canada* 58°6N 122°43W **70** B4
Propriá *Brazil* 10°13S 36°51W **93** F11
Propriano *France* 41°41N 8°52E **20** F8
Proserpine *Australia* 20°21S 148°36E **62** b
Prosna → *Poland* 52°6N 17°44E **17** B9
Prospect *U.S.A.* 43°18N 75°9W **83** C9
Prosser *U.S.A.* 46°12N 119°46W **76** C4
Prostějov *Czech Rep.* 49°30N 17°9E **17** D9
Proston *Australia* 26°8S 151°32E **63** D5
Provence *France* 43°40N 5°46E **20** E6
Providence *Ky., U.S.A.* 37°24N 87°46W **80** G10
Providence *R.I., U.S.A.* 41°49N 71°24W **83** E13
Providence Bay *Canada* 45°41N 82°15W **72** C3
Providence Mts.
  U.S.A. 35°10N 115°15W **79** K11
Providencia, I. de
  Colombia 13°25N 81°26W **88** D3
Provideniya *Russia* 64°23N 173°18W **29** C19
Provincetown *U.S.A.* 42°3N 70°11W **81** D18
Provins *France* 48°33N 3°15E **20** B5
Provo *U.S.A.* 40°14N 111°39W **76** F8
Provost *Canada* 52°25N 110°20W **71** C6
Prudhoe Bay *U.S.A.* 70°18N 148°22W **74** A10
Prudhoe I. *Australia* 21°19S 149°41E **62** C4
Prud'homme *Canada* 52°20N 105°54W **71** C7
Pruszków *Poland* 52°9N 20°49E **17** B11
Prut → *Romania* 45°28N 28°10E **17** F15
Pruzhany *Belarus* 52°33N 24°28E **17** B13
Prydz B. *Antarctica* 69°0S 74°0E **5** C6
Pryluky *Ukraine* 50°30N 32°24E **19** D5
Pryor *U.S.A.* 36°19N 95°19W **84** C7
Prypyat → *Europe* 51°20N 30°15E **17** C16
Przemyśl *Poland* 49°50N 22°45E **17** D12
Przhevalsk = Karakol
  Kyrgyzstan 42°30N 78°20E **32** B2
Psara *Greece* 38°37N 25°38E **23** E11
Psiloritis, Oros *Greece* 35°15N 24°45E **25** D6
Psira *Greece* 35°12N 25°52E **25** D7
Pskov *Russia* 57°50N 28°25E **9 H23**
Ptich → *Belarus* 52°9N 28°52E **17** B15
Ptichia = Vidos *Greece* 39°38N 19°55E **25** A3
Ptolemaida *Greece* 40°30N 21°43E **23** D9
Ptsich → *Belarus* 52°9N 28°52E **17** B15
Pu Xian *China* 36°24N 111°6E **34** F6
Pua *Thailand* 19°11N 100°55E **38** C3
Puán *Argentina* 37°30S 62°45W **94** D3
Pu'apu'a *Samoa* 13°34S 172°9W **59** b
Pucallpa *Peru* 8°25S 74°30W **92** E4
Puch'on = Bucheon
  S. Korea 37°28N 126°45E **35** F14
Pudozh *Russia* 61°48N 36°32E **18** B6
Puducherry *India* 11°59N 79°50E **40** P11
Pudukkottai *India* 10°28N 78°47E **40** P11
Puebla *Mexico* 19°3N 98°12W **87** D5
Puebla □ *Mexico* 18°50N 98°0W **87** D5
Pueblo *U.S.A.* 38°16N 104°37W **76** G11

Puelches *Argentina* 38°5S 65°51W **94** D2
Puelén *Argentina* 37°32S 67°38W **94** D2
Puente Alto *Chile* 33°32S 70°35W **94** C1
Puente-Genil *Spain* 37°22N 4°47W **21** D3
Puerca, Pta. *Puerto Rico* 18°13N 65°36W **89** d
Puerco → *U.S.A.* 34°22N 107°50W **77** J10
Puerto Aisén *Chile* 45°27S 73°0W **96** F2
Puerto Ángel *Mexico* 15°40N 96°29W **87** D5
Puerto Arista *Mexico* 15°56N 93°48W **87** D6
Puerto Armuelles
  Panama 8°20N 82°51W **88** E3
Puerto Ayacucho
  Venezuela 5°40N 67°35W **92** B5
Puerto Barrios
  Guatemala 15°40N 88°32W **88** C2
Puerto Bermejo
  Argentina 26°55S 58°34W **94** B4
Puerto Bermúdez *Peru* 10°20S 74°58W **92** F4
Puerto Bolívar *Ecuador* 3°19S 79°55W **92** D3
Puerto Cabello *Venezuela* 10°28N 68°1W **92** A5
Puerto Cabezas *Nic.* 14°0N 83°30W **88** D3
Puerto Cabo Gracias á Dios
  Nic. 15°0N 83°10W **88** D3
Puerto Carreño *Colombia* 6°12N 67°22W **92** B5
Puerto Castilla *Honduras* 16°0N 86°0W **88** C2
Puerto Chicama *Peru* 7°45S 79°20W **92** E3
Puerto Coig *Argentina* 50°54S 69°15W **96** G3
Puerto Cortés *Honduras* 15°51N 88°0W **88** C2
Puerto Cumarebo
  Venezuela 11°29N 69°30W **92** A5
Puerto de Alcudia = Port
  d'Alcúdia *Spain* 39°50N 3°7E **24** B10
Puerto de Cabrera *Spain* 39°8N 2°56E **24** B9
Puerto de Gran Tarajal
  Canary Is. 28°13N 14°1W **24** F5
Puerto de la Cruz
  Canary Is. 28°24N 16°32W **24** F3
Puerto de los Angeles △
  Mexico 23°39N 105°45W **86** C3
Puerto de Pozo Negro
  Canary Is. 28°19N 13°55W **24** F6
Puerto de Sóller = Port de Sóller
  Spain 39°48N 2°42E **24** B9
Puerto del Carmen
  Canary Is. 28°55N 13°38W **24** F6
Puerto del Rosario
  Canary Is. 28°30N 13°52W **24** F6
Puerto Deseado *Argentina* 47°55S 66°0W **96** F3
Puerto Escondido *Mexico* 15°50N 97°3W **87** D5
Puerto Heath *Bolivia* 12°34S 68°39W **92** F5
Puerto Inírida *Colombia* 3°53N 67°52W **92** C5
Puerto Juárez *Mexico* 21°11N 86°49W **87** C7
Puerto La Cruz
  Venezuela 10°13N 64°38W **92** A6
Puerto Leguízamo
  Colombia 0°12S 74°46W **92** D4
Puerto Lempira
  Honduras 15°16N 83°46W **88** C3
Puerto Libertad *Mexico* 29°55N 112°43W **86** B2
Puerto Limón *Colombia* 3°23N 73°30W **92** C4
Puerto Lobos *Argentina* 42°0S 65°3W **96** E3
Puerto Madryn *Argentina* 42°48S 65°4W **96** E3
Puerto Maldonado *Peru* 12°30S 69°10W **92** F5
Puerto Manatí *Cuba* 21°22N 76°50W **88** B4
Puerto Montt *Chile* 41°28S 73°0W **96** E2
Puerto Morazán *Nic.* 12°51N 87°11W **88** D2
Puerto Morelos *Mexico* 20°50N 86°52W **87** C7
Puerto Natales *Chile* 51°45S 72°15W **96** G2
Puerto Oscuro *Chile* 31°24S 71°35W **94** C1
Puerto Padre *Cuba* 21°13N 76°35W **88** B4
Puerto Páez *Venezuela* 6°13N 67°28W **92** B5
Puerto Peñasco *Mexico* 31°20N 113°33W **86** A2
Puerto Pinasco
  Paraguay 22°36S 57°50W **94** A4
Puerto Plata *Dom. Rep.* 19°48N 70°45W **89** C5
Puerto Pollensa = Port de
  Pollença *Spain* 39°54N 3°4E **24** B10
Puerto Princesa *Phil.* 9°46N 118°45E **37** C5
Puerto Quepos *Costa Rica* 9°29N 84°6W **88** E3
Puerto Rico *Canary Is.* 27°47N 15°42W **24** G4
Puerto Rico ☐ *W. Indies* 18°15N 66°45W **89** d
Puerto Rico Trench
  Atl. Oc. 19°50N 66°0W **89** C6
Puerto San Julián
  Argentina 49°18S 67°43W **96** F3
Puerto Santa Cruz
  Argentina 50°0S 68°32W **96** G3
Puerto Sastre *Paraguay* 22°2S 57°55W **94** A4
Puerto Suárez *Bolivia* 18°58S 57°52W **92** G7
Puerto Vallarta *Mexico* 20°37N 105°15W **86** C3
Puerto Varas *Chile* 41°19S 72°59W **96** E2
Puerto Wilches *Colombia* 7°21N 73°54W **92** B4
Puertollano *Spain* 38°43N 4°7W **21** C3
Pueu *Tahiti* 17°44S 149°13W **59** d
Pueyrredón, L. *Argentina* 47°20S 72°0W **96** F2
Puffin I. *Ireland* 51°50N 10°24W **10** E1
Pugachev *Russia* 52°0N 48°49E **18** D9
Pugal *India* 28°30N 72°48E **42** E5
Puge *Tanzania* 4°45S 33°11E **54** C3
Puget Sound *U.S.A.* 47°50N 122°30W **76** C2
Pugŏdong *N. Korea* 42°5N 130°0E **35** C16
Pugu *Tanzania* 6°55S 39°4E **54** D4
Pūgūnzī *Iran* 25°49N 59°10E **45** E8
Puig Major *Spain* 39°48N 2°28E **24** B9
Puigcerdà *Spain* 42°24N 1°50E **21** A6
Puigpunyent *Spain* 39°38N 2°32E **24** B9
Pujon-ho *N. Korea* 40°35N 127°35E **35** D14
Pukaki, L. *N.Z.* 44°4S 170°1E **59** F3
Pukapuka *Cook Is.* 10°53S 165°49W **65** J11
Pukaskwa △ *Canada* 48°20N 86°0W **72** C2
Pukatawagan *Canada* 55°45N 101°20W **71** B8
Pukchin *N. Korea* 40°12N 125°45E **35** D13
Pukch'ŏng *N. Korea* 40°14N 128°10E **35** D15
Pukekohe *N.Z.* 37°12S 174°55E **59** B5
Pukhrayan *India* 26°14N 79°51E **43** F8
Pula *Croatia* 44°54N 13°57E **16** F7
Pulacayo *Bolivia* 20°25S 66°41W **92** H5
Pulai *Malaysia* 1°20N 103°31E **39** d
Pulandian *China* 39°25N 121°58E **35** E11

Pulaski *N.Y., U.S.A.* 43°34N 76°8W **83** C8
Pulaski *Tenn., U.S.A.* 35°12N 87°2W **85** D11
Pulaski *Va., U.S.A.* 37°3N 80°47W **81** G13
Pulau → *Indonesia* 5°50S 138°15E **37** F9
Puławy *Poland* 51°23N 21°59E **17** C11
Pulga *U.S.A.* 39°48N 121°29W **78** F5
Pulicat L. *India* 13°40N 80°15E **40** N12
Pullman *U.S.A.* 46°44N 117°10W **76** C5
Pulog, Mt. *Phil.* 16°40N 120°50E **37** A6
Pułtusk *Poland* 52°43N 21°6E **17** B11
Pumlumon Fawr *U.K.* 52°28N 3°46W **13** E4
Puná, I. *Ecuador* 2°55S 80°5W **92** D2
Punaauia *Tahiti* 17°37S 149°34W **59** d
Punakaiki *N.Z.* 42°7S 171°20E **59** E3
Punakha Dzong *Bhutan* 27°42N 89°52E **41** F17
Punata *Bolivia* 17°32S 65°50W **92** G5
Punch *India* 33°48N 74°4E **43** C6
Punch → *Pakistan* 33°12N 73°40E **42** C5
Punda Maria *S. Africa* 22°40S 31°5E **57** C5
Pune *India* 18°29N 73°57E **40** K8
Pungue, Ponte de *Mozam.* 19°0S 34°0E **55** F3
Punjab □ *India* 31°0N 76°0E **42** D7
Punjab □ *Pakistan* 32°0N 72°30E **42** E6
Puno *Peru* 15°55S 70°3W **92** G4
Punpun → *India* 25°31N 85°18E **43** G11
Punta, Cerro de
  Puerto Rico 18°10N 66°37W **89** d
Punta Alta *Argentina* 38°53S 62°4W **96** D4
Punta Arenas *Chile* 53°10S 71°0W **96** G2
Punta del Díaz *Chile* 28°0S 70°45W **94** B1
Punta del Hidalgo
  Canary Is. 28°33N 16°19W **24** F3
Punta Gorda *Belize* 16°10N 88°45W **87** D7
Punta Gorda *U.S.A.* 26°56N 82°3W **85** H13
Punta Prieta *Mexico* 28°58N 114°17W **86** B2
Punta Prima *Spain* 39°48N 4°16E **24** B11
Puntarenas *Costa Rica* 10°0N 84°50W **88** E3
Puntland *Somali Rep.* 8°0N 49°0E **47** F4
Punto Fijo *Venezuela* 11°50N 70°13W **92** A4
Punxsutawney *U.S.A.* 40°57N 78°59W **82** F6
Pupuan *Indonesia* 8°19S 115°0E **37** J18
Puquio *Peru* 14°45S 74°10W **92** F4
Pur → *Russia* 67°31N 77°55E **28** C8
Puracé, Vol. *Colombia* 2°21N 76°23W **92** C3
Puralia = Puruliya
  India 23°17N 86°24E **43** H12
Puranpur *India* 28°31N 80°9E **43** E9
Purbeck, Isle of *U.K.* 50°39N 1°59W **13** G5
Purcell *U.S.A.* 35°1N 97°22W **84** D6
Purcell Mts. *Canada* 49°55N 116°15W **70** D5
Purdy *Canada* 45°19N 77°44W **82** A7
Puri *India* 19°50N 85°58E **41** K14
Purmerend *Neths.* 52°32N 4°58E **15** B4
Purnia *India* 25°45N 87°31E **43** G12
Purnululu △ *Australia* 17°20S 128°20E **60** C4
Pursat = Pouthisat
  Cambodia 12°34N 103°50E **38** F4
Purukcahu *Indonesia* 0°35S 114°35E **36** E4
Puruliya *India* 23°17N 86°24E **43** H12
Purus → *Brazil* 3°42S 61°28W **92** D6
Puruvesi *Finland* 61°50N 29°30E **8 F23**
Purvis *U.S.A.* 31°9N 89°25W **85** F10
Purwa *India* 26°28N 80°47E **43** F9
Purwakarta *Indonesia* 6°35S 107°29E **37** G12
Purwo, Tanjung
  Indonesia 8°44S 114°21E **37** K18
Purwodadi *Indonesia* 7°7S 110°55E **37** G14
Purwokerto *Indonesia* 7°25S 109°14E **37** G13
Puryŏng *N. Korea* 42°5N 129°43E **35** C15
Pusa *India* 25°59N 85°41E **43** G11
Pusan = Busan *S. Korea* 35°5N 129°0E **35** G15
Pushkin *Russia* 59°45N 30°25E **9 G24**
Pushkino *Russia* 51°16N 47°0E **19** D8
Put-in-Bay *U.S.A.* 41°39N 82°49W **82** E2
Putahow L. *Canada* 59°54N 100°40W **71** B8
Putao *Burma* 27°28N 97°30E **41** F20
Putaruru *N.Z.* 38°2S 175°50E **59** C5
Putignano *Italy* 40°51N 17°7E **22** D7
Puting, Tanjung
  Indonesia 3°31S 111°46E **36** E4
Putnam *U.S.A.* 41°55N 71°55W **83** E13
Putorana, Gory *Russia* 69°0N 95°0E **29** C10
Putrajaya *Malaysia* 2°55N 101°40E **39** L3
Puttalam *Sri Lanka* 8°1N 79°55E **40** Q11
Puttgarden *Germany* 54°30N 11°10E **16** A6
Putumayo → *S. Amer.* 3°7S 67°58W **92** D5
Putussibau *Indonesia* 0°50N 112°56E **36** D4
Puvirnituq *Canada* 60°2N 77°10W **69** E16
Puy-de-Dôme *France* 45°46N 2°57E **20** D5
Puyallup *U.S.A.* 47°12N 122°18W **78** C4
Puyang *China* 35°40N 115°1E **34** G8
Pūzeh Rīg *Iran* 27°20N 58°40E **45** E8
Pwani □ *Tanzania* 7°0S 39°0E **54** D4
Pweto
  Dem. Rep. of the Congo 8°25S 28°51E **55** D2
Pwllheli *U.K.* 52°53N 4°25W **12** E3
Pyaozero, Ozero *Russia* 66°5N 30°58E **8** C24
Pyapon *Burma* 16°20N 95°40E **41** L19
Pyasina → *Russia* 73°30N 87°0E **29** B9
Pyatigorsk *Russia* 44°2N 43°6E **19** F7
Pyè = Prome *Burma* 18°49N 95°13E **41** K19
Pyeongtaek *S. Korea* 37°1N 127°4E **35** F14
Pyetrikaw *Belarus* 52°11N 28°29E **17** B15
Pyinmana *Burma* 19°45N 96°12E **41** K20
Pyla, C. *Cyprus* 34°56N 33°51E **25** E12
Pymatuning Res. *U.S.A.* 41°30N 80°28W **82** E4
Pyŏktong *N. Korea* 40°50N 125°50E **35** D13
Pyŏnggang *N. Korea* 38°24N 127°17E **35** E14
P'yŏngsong *N. Korea* 39°14N 125°52E **35** E13
P'yŏngyang *N. Korea* 39°0N 125°30E **35** E13
Pyote *U.S.A.* 31°32N 103°8W **84** F3
Pyramid L. *U.S.A.* 40°1N 119°35W **76** F4
Pyramid Pk. *U.S.A.* 36°25N 116°37W **79** J10
Pyramids *Egypt* 29°58N 31°9E **51** C12
Pyrénées *Europe* 42°45N 0°18E **20** E4
Pyu *Burma* 18°30N 96°28E **41** K20

Q

Qaanaaq Greenland 77°30N 69°10W 69 B18
Qachasnek S. Africa 30°6S 28°42E 57 E4
Qa'el Jafr Jordan 30°20N 36°25E 46 E5
Qa'emābād Iran 31°44N 60°2E 45 D9
Qā'emshahr Iran 36°30N 52°53E 45 B7
Qagan Nur China 43°30N 114°55E 34 C8
Qahar Youyi Zhongqi China 41°12N 112°40E 34 D7
Qahremānshahr = Kermānshāh Iran 34°23N 47°0E 44 C5
Qaidam Pendi China 37°0N 95°0E 32 C4
Qajarīyeh Iran 31°1N 48°22E 45 D6
Qala, Ras il Malta 36°2N 14°20E 25 C1
Qala-i-Jadid = Spīn Būldak Afghan. 31°1N 66°25E 42 D2
Qala Point = Qala, Ras il Malta 36°2N 14°20E 25 C1
Qala Viala Pakistan 30°49N 67°17E 42 D2
Qala Yangi Afghan. 34°20N 66°30E 42 B2
Qal'at al Akhḍar Si. Arabia 28°4N 37°9E 44 E3
Qal'at Dīzah Iraq 36°11N 45°7E 44 B5
Qal'at Ṣāliḥ Iraq 31°31N 47°16E 44 D5
Qal'at Sukkar Iraq 31°51N 46°5E 44 D5
Qamani'tuaq = Baker Lake Canada 64°20N 96°3W 68 E12
Qamdo China 31°15N 97°6E 32 C4
Qamea Fiji 16°45S 179°45W 59 a
Qamruddin Karez Pakistan 31°45N 68°20E 42 D3
Qandahār = Kandahār Afghan. 31°32N 65°43E 40 D4
Qandahār = Kandahār □ Afghan. 31°0N 65°0E 40 D4
Qandyaghash Kazakhstan 49°28N 57°25E 19 E10
Qapān Iran 37°40N 55°47E 45 B7
Qapshaghay Kazakhstan 43°51N 77°14E 28 E8
Qaqortoq Greenland 60°43N 46°0W 4 C5
Qara Qash → China 35°0N 78°30E 43 B8
Qarabutaq Kazakhstan 49°59N 60°14E 28 E7
Qaraghandy Kazakhstan 49°50N 73°10E 28 E8
Qaraghayly Kazakhstan 49°26N 76°0E 28 E8
Qārah Si. Arabia 29°55N 40°3E 44 D4
Qarataū Ongtüstik Qazaqstan, Kazakhstan 43°30N 69°30E 28 E7
Qarataū Zhambyl, Kazakhstan 43°10N 70°28E 28 E8
Qarazhal Kazakhstan 48°2N 70°49E 28 E8
Qardho Somali Rep. 9°30N 49°6E 47 F4
Qareh → Iran 39°25N 47°22E 44 B5
Qareh Tekān Iran 36°38N 49°29E 45 B6
Qarnein U.A.E. 24°56N 52°52E 45 E7
Qarqan He → China 39°30N 88°30E 32 C3
Qarqaraly Kazakhstan 49°26N 75°30E 28 E8
Qarshi Uzbekistan 38°53N 65°48E 28 F7
Qartabā Lebanon 34°4N 35°50E 46 A4
Qārūh Kuwait 28°49N 48°46E 45 D6
Qaryat al Gharab Iraq 31°27N 44°48E 44 D5
Qaryat al 'Ulyā Si. Arabia 27°33N 47°42E 44 E5
Qasr 'Amra Jordan 31°48N 36°35E 44 D3
Qaṣr-e Qand Iran 26°15N 60°45E 45 E9
Qaṣr-e Shīrīn Iran 34°31N 45°35E 44 C5
Qasr Farâfra Egypt 27°0N 28°1E 51 C11
Qasuittuq = Resolute Canada 74°42N 94°54W 69 C13
Qatanā Syria 33°26N 36°4E 46 B5
Qatar ■ Asia 25°30N 51°15E 45 E6
Qatlīsh Iran 37°50N 57°19E 45 B8
Qattâra, Munkhafed el Egypt 29°30N 27°30E 51 C11
Qattâra Depression = Qattâra, Munkhafed el Egypt 29°30N 27°30E 51 C11
Qawām al Ḥamzah = Al Ḥamzah Iraq 31°43N 44°58E 44 D5
Qāyen Iran 33°40N 59°10E 45 C8
Qazaqstan = Kazakhstan ■ Asia 50°0N 70°0E 28 E8
Qazımämmäd Azerbaijan 40°3N 49°0E 45 A6
Qazvīn Iran 36°15N 50°0E 45 B6
Qazvīn □ Iran 36°20N 50°0E 45 B6
Qena Egypt 26°10N 32°43E 51 C12
Qeqertarsuaq Greenland 69°15N 53°38W 4 C5
Qeqertarsuaq Greenland 69°45N 53°30W 66 C14
Qeshlāq Iran 34°55N 46°28E 44 C5
Qeshm Iran 26°55N 56°10E 45 E8
Qeys Iran 26°32N 53°58E 45 E7
Qezel Owzen → Iran 36°45N 49°22E 45 B6
Qezi'ot Israel 30°52N 34°26E 46 E3
Qi Xian China 34°40N 114°48E 34 G8
Qian Gorlos China 45°5N 124°42E 35 B13
Qian Hai China 22°32N 113°54E 33 F10
Qian Xian China 34°31N 108°15E 34 G5
Qianshan China 22°15N 113°31E 33 G10
Qianyang China 34°40N 107°8E 34 G4
Qi'ao China 22°25N 113°39E 33 G10
Qi'ao Dao China 22°25N 113°38E 33 G10
Qiemo China 38°8N 85°32E 32 C3
Qijiaojing China 43°28N 91°36E 32 B4
Qikiqtarjuaq Canada 67°33N 63°0W 69 D19
Qila Saifullāh Pakistan 30°45N 68°17E 42 D3
Qilian Shan China 38°30N 96°0E 32 C4
Qin He → China 35°1N 113°22E 34 G7
Qin Ling = Qinling Shandi China 33°50N 108°10E 34 H5
Qin'an China 34°48N 105°40E 34 G3
Qing Xian China 38°35N 116°45E 34 E9
Qingcheng China 37°15N 117°40E 35 F9
Qingdao China 36°5N 120°20E 35 F11
Qingfeng China 35°52N 115°8E 34 G8
Qinghai □ China 36°0N 98°0E 32 C4
Qinghai Hu China 36°40N 100°10E 32 C5
Qinghecheng China 41°28N 124°15E 35 D13
Qinghemen China 41°48N 121°25E 35 D11
Qingjian China 37°8N 110°8E 34 F6
Qingjiang = Huaiyin China 33°30N 119°2E 35 H10
Qingshui China 34°48N 106°8E 34 G4
Qingshuihe China 39°55N 111°35E 34 E6
Qingtongxia Shuiku China 37°50N 105°58E 34 F3
Qingxu China 37°34N 112°22E 34 F7
Qingyang China 36°2N 107°55E 34 F4
Qingyuan China 42°10N 124°55E 35 C13
Qingyun China 37°45N 117°20E 35 F9
Qinhuangdao China 39°56N 119°30E 35 E10
Qinling Shandi China 33°50N 108°10E 34 H5
Qinshui China 35°40N 112°8E 34 G7
Qinyang = Jiyuan China 35°7N 112°57E 34 G7
Qinyuan China 36°29N 112°20E 34 F7
Qinzhou China 21°58N 108°38E 32 D5
Qionghai China 19°15N 110°26E 38 C8
Qiongzhou Haixia China 20°10N 110°15E 38 B8
Qiqihar China 47°26N 124°0E 33 B7
Qira China 37°0N 80°48E 32 C3
Qiraîya, W. → Egypt 30°27N 34°0E 46 E3
Qiryat Ata Israel 32°47N 35°6E 46 C4
Qiryat Gat Israel 31°32N 34°46E 46 D3
Qiryat Mal'akhi Israel 31°44N 34°44E 46 D3
Qiryat Shemona Israel 33°13N 35°35E 46 B4
Qiryat Yam Israel 32°51N 35°4E 46 C4
Qishan China 34°25N 107°38E 34 G4
Qitai China 44°2N 89°35E 32 B3
Qitaihe China 45°48N 130°51E 30 B5
Qixia China 37°17N 120°52E 35 F11
Qızılağac Körfäzi Azerbaijan 39°9N 49°0E 45 B6
Qojūr Iran 36°12N 47°55E 44 B5
Qom Iran 34°40N 51°0E 45 C6
Qom □ Iran 34°40N 51°0E 45 C6
Qomolangma Feng = Everest, Mt. Nepal 28°5N 86°58E 43 E12
Qomsheh Iran 32°0N 51°55E 45 D6
Qoqek = Tacheng China 46°40N 82°58E 32 B3
Qoqon = Qŭqon Uzbekistan 40°31N 70°56E 28 E8
Qoraqalpoghistan □ Uzbekistan 43°0N 58°0E 28 E6
Qorveh Iran 35°10N 47°48E 44 C5
Qosshaghyl Kazakhstan 46°40N 54°0E 19 E9
Qostanay Kazakhstan 53°10N 63°35E 28 D7
Quabbin Res. U.S.A. 42°20N 72°20W 83 D12
Quairading Australia 32°0S 117°21E 61 F2
Quakertown U.S.A. 40°26N 75°21W 83 F9
Qualicum Beach Canada 49°22N 124°26W 70 D4
Quambatook Australia 35°49S 143°34E 63 F3
Quambone Australia 30°57S 147°53E 63 E4
Quamby Australia 20°22S 140°17E 62 C3
Quan Long = Ca Mau Vietnam 9°7N 105°8E 39 H5
Quanah U.S.A. 34°18N 99°44W 84 D5
Quang Ngai Vietnam 15°13N 108°58E 38 E7
Quang Tri Vietnam 16°45N 107°13E 38 D6
Quang Yen Vietnam 20°56N 106°52E 38 B6
Quantock Hills U.K. 51°8N 3°10W 13 F4
Quanzhou China 24°55N 118°34E 33 D6
Qu'Appelle → Canada 50°33N 103°53W 71 C8
Quaqtaq Canada 60°55N 69°40W 69 E18
Quaraí Brazil 30°15S 56°20W 94 C4
Quartu Sant'Élena Italy 39°15N 9°10E 22 E3
Quartzsite U.S.A. 33°40N 114°13W 79 M12
Quatre Bornes Mauritius 20°15S 57°28E 53 d
Quatsino Sd. Canada 50°25N 127°58W 70 C3
Quba Azerbaijan 41°21N 48°32E 19 F8
Qūchān Iran 37°10N 58°27E 45 B8
Queanbeyan Australia 35°17S 149°14E 63 F4
Québec Canada 46°52N 71°13W 73 C5
Québec □ Canada 48°0N 74°0W 73 C6
Quebrada del Condorito △ Argentina 31°49S 64°40W 94 C3
Queen Alexandra Ra. Antarctica 85°0S 170°0E 5 E11
Queen Charlotte City Canada 53°15N 132°2W 70 C2
Queen Charlotte Is. Canada 53°20N 132°10W 70 C2
Queen Charlotte Sd. Canada 51°0N 128°0W 70 C3
Queen Charlotte Strait Canada 50°45N 127°10W 70 C3
Queen Elizabeth △ Uganda 0°0 30°0E 54 C3
Queen Elizabeth ⌂ U.K. 56°7N 4°30W 11 E4
Queen Elizabeth Is. Canada 76°0N 95°0W 69 B13
Queen Mary Land Antarctica 70°0S 95°0E 5 D7
Queen Maud G. Canada 68°15N 102°30W 68 D11
Queen Maud Land = Dronning Maud Land Antarctica 72°30S 12°0E 5 D3
Queen Maud Mts. Antarctica 86°0S 160°0W 5 E13
Queens Channel Australia 15°0S 129°30E 60 C4
Queenscliff Australia 38°16S 144°39E 63 F3
Queensland □ Australia 22°0S 142°0E 62 C3
Queenstown Australia 42°4S 145°35E 63 G4
Queenstown N.Z. 45°1S 168°40E 59 F2
Queenstown Singapore 1°18N 103°48E 39 d
Queenstown S. Africa 31°52S 26°52E 56 E4
Queets U.S.A. 47°32N 124°19W 78 C2
Queguay Grande → Uruguay 32°9S 58°9W 94 C4
Queimadas Brazil 11°0S 39°38W 93 F11
Quelimane Mozam. 17°53S 36°58E 55 F4
Quellón Chile 43°7S 73°37W 96 E2
Quelpart = Jeju-do S. Korea 33°29N 126°34E 35 H14
Quemado N. Mex., U.S.A. 34°20N 108°30W 77 J9
Quemado Tex., U.S.A. 28°56N 100°37W 84 G4
Quemú-Quemú Argentina 36°3S 63°36W 94 D3
Quequén Argentina 38°30S 58°30W 94 D4
Querétaro Mexico 20°36N 100°23W 86 C4
Querétaro □ Mexico 21°0N 99°55W 86 C5
Queshan China 32°55N 114°2E 34 H8
Quesnel Canada 53°0N 122°30W 70 C4
Quesnel → Canada 52°58N 122°29W 70 C4
Quesnel L. Canada 52°30N 121°20W 70 C4
Questa U.S.A. 36°42N 105°36W 77 H11
Quetico ⌂ Canada 48°30N 91°45W 72 C1
Quetta Pakistan 30°15N 66°55E 42 D2
Quezaltenango Guatemala 14°50N 91°30W 88 D1
Quezon City Phil. 14°37N 121°2E 37 B6
Qufār Si. Arabia 27°26N 41°37E 44 E4
Qui Nhon Vietnam 13°40N 109°13E 38 F7
Quibala Angola 10°46S 14°59E 52 G2
Quibaxe Angola 8°24S 14°27E 52 F2
Quibdó Colombia 5°42N 76°40W 92 B3
Quiberon France 47°29N 3°9W 20 C2
Quiet L. Canada 61°5N 133°5W 70 A2
Quiindy Paraguay 25°58S 57°14W 94 B4
Quilá Mexico 24°23N 107°13W 86 C3
Quilán, C. Chile 43°15S 74°30W 96 E2
Quilcene U.S.A. 47°49N 122°53W 78 C4
Quilimarí Chile 32°5S 71°30W 94 C1
Quilino Argentina 30°14S 64°29W 94 C3
Quillabamba Peru 12°50S 72°50W 92 F4
Quillagua Chile 21°40S 69°40W 94 A2
Quillota Chile 32°54S 71°16W 94 C1
Quilmes Argentina 34°43S 58°15W 94 C4
Quilon India 8°50N 76°38E 40 Q10
Quilpie Australia 26°35S 144°11E 63 D3
Quilpué Chile 33°5S 71°33W 94 C1
Quilua Mozam. 16°17S 39°54E 55 F4
Quimilí Argentina 27°40S 62°30W 94 B3
Quimper France 48°0N 4°9W 20 B1
Quimperlé France 47°53N 3°33W 20 C2
Quinault → U.S.A. 47°21N 124°18W 78 C2
Quincy Calif., U.S.A. 39°56N 120°57W 78 F6
Quincy Fla., U.S.A. 30°35N 84°34W 85 F12
Quincy Ill., U.S.A. 39°56N 91°23W 80 F8
Quincy Mass., U.S.A. 42°14N 71°0W 83 D14
Quincy Wash., U.S.A. 47°14N 119°51W 76 C4
Quines Argentina 32°13S 65°48W 94 C2
Quinga Mozam. 15°49S 40°15E 55 F5
Quintana Roo □ Mexico 19°40N 88°30W 87 D7
Quintanar de la Orden Spain 39°36N 3°5W 21 C4
Quintero Chile 32°45S 71°30W 94 C1
Quirihue Chile 36°15S 72°35W 94 D1
Quirimbas △ Mozam. 12°30S 40°15E 55 E5
Quirindi Australia 31°28S 150°40E 63 E5
Quirinópolis Brazil 18°32S 50°30W 93 G8
Quissanga Mozam. 12°24S 40°28E 55 E5
Quissico Mozam. 24°42S 34°44E 57 C5
Quitilipi Argentina 26°50S 60°13W 94 B3
Quitman U.S.A. 30°47N 83°34W 85 F13
Quito Ecuador 0°15S 78°35W 92 D3
Quixadá Brazil 4°55S 39°0W 93 D11
Quixaxe Mozam. 15°17S 40°4E 55 F5
Qulan Kazakhstan 42°55N 72°43E 28 E8
Qul'ân, Jazâ'ir Egypt 24°22N 35°31E 44 E2
Qulsary Kazakhstan 46°59N 54°1E 19 E9
Qumbu S. Africa 31°10S 28°48E 57 E4
Quneitra Syria 33°7N 35°48E 46 B4
Qŭnghirot Uzbekistan 43°2N 58°50E 28 E6
Quoin I. Australia 14°54S 129°32E 60 B4
Quoin Pt. S. Africa 34°46S 19°37E 56 E2
Quorn Australia 32°25S 138°5E 63 E2
Qŭqon Uzbekistan 40°31N 70°56E 28 E8
Qurimbas Mozam. 12°20S 40°10E 55 E5
Qurnat as Sawdā' Lebanon 34°18N 36°6E 46 A5
Quṣaybā' Si. Arabia 26°53N 43°35E 44 E4
Qusaybah Iraq 34°24N 40°59E 44 C4
Quseir Egypt 26°7N 34°16E 44 E2
Qūshchī Iran 37°59N 45°3E 44 B5
Quthing Lesotho 30°25S 27°36E 57 E4
Qūṭīābād Iran 35°47N 48°30E 45 C6
Quttinirpaaq △ Canada 82°13N 72°13W 69 A17
Quwo China 35°38N 111°25E 34 G6
Quyang China 38°35N 114°40E 34 E8
Quynh Nhai Vietnam 21°49N 103°33E 38 B4
Quyon Canada 45°31N 76°14W 83 A8
Quzhou China 28°57N 118°54E 33 D6
Quzi China 36°20N 107°20E 34 F4
Qyzylorda Kazakhstan 44°48N 65°28E 28 E7

R

Ra, Ko Thailand 9°13N 98°16E 39 H2
Raahe Finland 64°40N 24°28E 8 D21
Raalte Neths. 52°23N 6°16E 15 B6
Raasay U.K. 57°25N 6°4W 11 D2
Raasay, Sd. of U.K. 57°30N 6°8W 11 D2
Raba Indonesia 8°36S 118°55E 37 F5
Rába → Hungary 47°38N 17°38E 17 E9
Rabai Kenya 3°50S 39°31E 54 C4
Rabat = Victoria Malta 36°3N 14°14E 25 C1
Rabat Malta 35°53N 14°24E 25 D1
Rabat Morocco 34°2N 6°48W 50 B4
Rabaul Papua N. G. 4°24S 152°18E 58 B8
Rabbit Flat Australia 20°11S 130°1E 60 D5
Rabbit Lake Mine Canada 58°4N 104°5W 71 B8
Rabi Fiji 16°30S 179°59W 59 a
Rābigh Si. Arabia 22°50N 39°5E 47 C2
Râbniţa Moldova 47°45N 29°0E 17 E15
Rābor Iran 29°17N 56°55E 45 D8
Rabwah = Chenab Nagar Pakistan 31°45N 72°55E 42 D5
Race, C. Canada 46°40N 53°5W 73 C9
Rach Gia Vietnam 10°5N 105°5E 39 G5
Rachid Mauritania 18°45N 11°35W 50 E3
Racibórz Poland 50°7N 18°18E 17 C10
Racine U.S.A. 42°44N 87°47W 80 D10
Rackerby U.S.A. 39°26N 121°22W 78 F5
Radama, Nosy Madag. 14°0S 47°47E 57 A8
Radama, Saikanosy Madag. 14°16S 47°53E 57 A8
Rădăuţi Romania 47°50N 25°59E 17 E13
Radcliff U.S.A. 37°51N 85°57W 81 G11
Radekhiv Ukraine 50°25N 24°32E 17 C13
Radekhov = Radekhiv Ukraine 50°25N 24°32E 17 C13
Radford U.S.A. 37°8N 80°34W 81 G13
Radhanpur India 23°50N 71°38E 42 H4
Radhwa, Jabal Si. Arabia 24°34N 38°18E 44 E3
Radisson Qué., Canada 53°47N 77°37W 72 B4
Radisson Sask., Canada 52°30N 107°20W 71 C7
Radium Hot Springs Canada 50°35N 116°2W 70 C5
Radnor Forest U.K. 52°17N 3°10W 13 E4
Radom Poland 51°23N 21°12E 17 C11
Radomsko Poland 51°5N 19°28E 17 C10
Radomyshl Ukraine 50°30N 29°12E 17 C15
Radstock, C. Australia 33°12S 134°20E 63 E1
Raduzhnyy Russia 62°5N 77°28E 28 C8
Radviliškis Lithuania 55°49N 23°33E 9 J20
Radville Canada 49°30N 104°15W 71 D8
Rae Canada 62°50N 116°3W 70 A5
Rae Bareli India 26°18N 81°20E 43 F9
Rae Isthmus Canada 66°40N 87°30W 69 D14
Raeren Belgium 50°41N 6°7E 15 D6
Raeside, L. Australia 29°20S 122°0E 61 E3
Raetihi N.Z. 39°25S 175°17E 59 C5
Rafaela Argentina 31°10S 61°30W 94 C3
Rafah Gaza Strip 31°18N 34°14E 46 D3
Rafai C.A.R. 4°59N 23°58E 54 B1
Rafḥā Si. Arabia 29°35N 43°35E 44 D4
Rafsanjān Iran 30°30N 56°5E 45 D8
Raft Pt. Australia 16°4S 124°26E 60 C3
Rāgâ Sudan 8°28N 25°41E 51 G11
Ragachow Belarus 53°8N 30°5E 17 B16
Ragama Sri Lanka 7°0N 79°50E 40 R11
Ragged, Mt. Australia 33°27S 123°25E 61 F3
Ragged Pt. Barbados 13°10N 59°26W 89 g
Raghunathpalli India 22°14N 84°48E 43 H11
Raghunathpur India 23°33N 86°40E 43 H12
Raglan N.Z. 37°55S 174°55E 59 B5
Ragusa Italy 36°55N 14°44E 22 F6
Raha Indonesia 4°55S 123°0E 37 E6
Rahaeng = Tak Thailand 16°52N 99°8E 38 D2
Rahatgarh India 23°47N 78°22E 43 H8
Rahimyar Khan Pakistan 28°30N 70°25E 42 E4
Rāhjerd Iran 34°22N 50°22E 45 C6
Rahole ⌂ Kenya 0°5N 38°57E 54 B4
Rahon India 31°3N 76°7E 42 D7
Raiatéa, Î. French Polynesia 16°50S 151°25W 65 J12
Raichur India 16°10N 77°20E 40 L10
Raiganj India 25°37N 88°10E 43 G13
Raigarh India 21°56N 83°25E 41 J13
Raijua Indonesia 10°37S 121°36E 37 F6
Raikot India 30°41N 75°42E 42 D6
Railton Australia 41°25S 146°28E 63 G4
Rainbow Bridge ⌂ U.S.A. 37°5N 110°58W 77 H8
Rainbow Lake Canada 58°30N 119°23W 70 B5
Rainier U.S.A. 46°53N 122°41W 78 D4
Rainier, Mt. U.S.A. 46°52N 121°46W 78 D5
Rainy L. Canada 48°42N 93°10W 71 D10
Rainy River Canada 48°43N 94°29W 71 D10
Raippaluoto Finland 63°13N 21°14E 8 E19
Raipur India 21°17N 81°45E 41 J12
Raisen India 23°20N 77°48E 42 H8
Raisio Finland 60°28N 22°11E 9 F20
Raj Nandgaon India 21°5N 81°5E 41 J12
Raj Nilgiri India 21°28N 86°46E 43 J12
Raja, Ujung Indonesia 3°40N 96°25E 36 D1
Raja Ampat, Kepulauan Indonesia 0°30S 130°0E 37 E8
Rajahmundry India 17°1N 81°48E 41 L12
Rajaji △ India 30°10N 78°20E 42 D8
Rajang → Malaysia 2°30N 112°0E 36 D4
Rajanpur Pakistan 29°6N 70°19E 42 E4
Rajapalaiyam India 9°25N 77°35E 40 Q10
Rajasthan □ India 26°45N 73°30E 42 F5
Rajasthan Canal = Indira Gandhi Canal India 28°0N 72°0E 42 F5
Rajauri India 33°25N 74°21E 43 C6
Rajgarh Mad. P., India 24°2N 76°45E 42 G7
Rajgarh Raj., India 27°14N 76°38E 42 F7
Rajgarh Raj., India 28°40N 75°25E 42 E6
Rajgir India 25°2N 85°25E 43 G11
Rajkot India 22°15N 70°56E 42 H4
Rajmahal Hills India 24°30N 87°30E 43 G12
Rajpipla India 21°50N 73°30E 40 J8
Rajpur India 22°18N 74°21E 42 H6
Rajpura India 30°25N 76°32E 42 D7
Rajsamand = Kankroli India 25°4N 73°53E 42 G5
Rajshahi Bangla. 24°22N 88°39E 41 G16
Rajshahi □ Bangla. 25°0N 89°0E 43 G13
Rajula India 21°3N 71°26E 42 J4
Rakaia N.Z. 43°45S 172°1E 59 E4
Rakaia → N.Z. 43°36S 172°15E 59 E4
Rakan, Ra's Qatar 26°10N 51°20E 45 E6
Rakaposhi Pakistan 36°10N 74°25E 43 A6
Rakata, Pulau Indonesia 6°10S 105°20E 36 F3
Rakhiv Ukraine 48°3N 24°12E 17 D13
Rakhni Pakistan 30°4N 69°56E 42 D3
Rakhni → Pakistan 29°31N 69°36E 42 E3
Rakiraki Fiji 17°22S 178°11E 59 a
Rakitnoye Russia 45°36N 134°17E 30 B7
Rakiura = Stewart I. N.Z. 46°58S 167°54E 59 G1
Rakiura △ N.Z. 47°0S 167°50E 59 G1
Rakops Botswana 21°1S 24°28E 56 C3
Rakvere Estonia 59°20N 26°25E 9 G22
Raleigh U.S.A. 35°47N 78°39W 85 D15
Ralik Chain Pac. Oc. 8°0N 168°0E 64 G8
Ralls U.S.A. 33°41N 101°24W 84 E4
Ralston U.S.A. 41°30N 76°57W 82 E8
Ram → Canada 62°1N 123°41W 70 A4
Rām Allāh West Bank 31°55N 35°10E 46 D4
Rama Nic. 12°9N 84°15W 88 D3
Ramakona India 21°43N 78°50E 43 J8
Rāmallāh = Rām Allāh West Bank 31°55N 35°10E 46 D4
Raman Thailand 6°29N 101°18E 39 J3
Ramanathapuram India 9°25N 78°55E 40 Q11
Ramanetaka, B. de Madag. 14°13S 47°52E 57 A8
Ramanujganj India 23°48N 83°42E 43 H10
Ramat Gan Israel 32°4N 34°48E 46 C3
Ramatlhabama S. Africa 25°37S 25°33E 56 D4
Ramban India 33°14N 75°12E 43 C6
Rambi = Rabi Fiji 16°30S 179°59W 59 a
Rambipuji Indonesia 8°12S 113°37E 37 H15
Rame Hd. Australia 37°47S 149°30E 63 F4
Ramechhap Nepal 27°25N 86°10E 43 F12
Ramganga → India 27°5N 79°58E 43 F8
Ramgarh Jharkhand, India 23°40N 85°35E 43 H11
Ramgarh Raj., India 27°16N 75°14E 42 F6
Ramgarh Raj., India 27°30N 70°36E 42 F4
Rāmhormoz Iran 31°15N 49°35E 45 D6
Ramīān Iran 37°3N 55°16E 45 B7
Ramingining Australia 12°19S 135°3E 62 A2
Ramla Israel 31°55N 34°52E 46 D3
Ramm = Rum Jordan 29°39N 35°26E 46 F4
Ramm, Jabal Jordan 29°35N 35°24E 46 F4
Ramnad = Ramanathapuram India 9°25N 78°55E 40 Q11
Ramnagar Jammu & Kashmir, India 32°47N 75°18E 43 C6
Ramnagar Uttarakhand, India 29°24N 79°7E 43 E8
Râmnicu Sărat Romania 45°26N 27°3E 17 F14
Râmnicu Vâlcea Romania 45°9N 24°21E 17 F13
Ramona U.S.A. 33°2N 116°52W 79 M10
Ramore Canada 48°30N 80°25W 72 C3
Ramotswa Botswana 24°50S 25°52E 56 C4
Rampur H.P., India 31°26N 77°43E 42 D7
Rampur Mad. P., India 23°25N 73°53E 42 H5
Rampur Ut. P., India 28°50N 79°5E 43 E8
Rampur Hat India 24°10N 87°50E 43 G12
Rampura India 24°30N 75°27E 42 G6
Ramrama Tola India 21°52N 79°55E 43 J8
Ramree I. Burma 19°0N 93°40E 41 K19
Rāmsar Iran 36°53N 50°41E 45 B6
Ramsey I. of Man 54°20N 4°22W 12 C3
Ramsey U.S.A. 41°4N 74°9W 83 E10
Ramsey L. Canada 47°13N 82°15W 72 C3
Ramsgate U.K. 51°20N 1°25E 13 F9
Ramtek India 21°20N 79°15E 40 J11
Ramu Kenya 3°55N 41°10E 54 B5
Rana Pratap Sagar Dam India 24°58N 75°38E 42 G6
Ranaghat India 23°15N 88°35E 43 H13
Ranahu Pakistan 25°55N 69°45E 42 G3
Ranau Malaysia 6°2N 116°40E 36 C5
Rancagua Chile 34°10S 70°50W 94 C1
Rancheria → Canada 60°13N 129°7W 70 A3
Ranchester U.S.A. 44°54N 107°10W 76 D10
Ranchi India 23°19N 85°27E 43 H11
Rancho Cordova U.S.A. 38°36N 121°18W 78 G5
Rancho Cucamonga U.S.A. 34°10N 117°30W 79 L9
Randalstown U.K. 54°45N 6°19W 10 B5
Randers Denmark 56°29N 10°1E 9 H14
Randfontein S. Africa 26°8S 27°45E 57 D4
Randle U.S.A. 46°32N 121°57W 78 D5
Randolph Mass., U.S.A. 42°10N 71°2W 83 D13
Randolph N.Y., U.S.A. 42°10N 78°59W 82 D6
Randolph Utah, U.S.A. 41°40N 111°11W 76 F8
Randolph Vt., U.S.A. 43°55N 72°40W 83 C12
Randsburg U.S.A. 35°22N 117°39W 79 K9
Råneälven → Sweden 65°50N 22°20E 8 D20
Rangae Thailand 6°19N 101°44E 39 J3
Rangaunu B. N.Z. 34°51S 173°15E 59 A4
Range, The Zimbabwe 19°2S 31°2E 55 F3
Rangeley U.S.A. 44°58N 70°39W 83 B14
Rangeley L. U.S.A. 44°55N 70°43W 83 B14
Rangely U.S.A. 40°5N 108°48W 76 F9
Ranger U.S.A. 32°28N 98°41W 84 E5
Rangia India 26°28N 91°38E 41 F17
Rangiora N.Z. 43°19S 172°36E 59 E4
Rangitaiki → N.Z. 37°54S 176°49E 59 B6
Rangitata → N.Z. 43°45S 171°15E 59 E3
Rangitoto ke te tonga = D'Urville I. N.Z. 40°50S 173°55E 59 D4
Rangkasbitung Indonesia 6°21S 106°15E 37 G12
Rangon → Burma 16°28N 96°40E 41 L20
Rangoon Burma 16°45N 96°20E 41 L20
Rangpur Bangla. 25°42N 89°22E 41 G16
Rangsang Indonesia 1°20N 103°30E 39 M4
Rangsit Thailand 13°59N 100°37E 38 F3
Ranibennur India 14°35N 75°30E 40 M9
Raniganj Ut. P., India 27°3N 82°13E 43 F9
Raniganj W. Bengal, India 23°40N 87°5E 41 H15
Ranikhet India 29°39N 79°25E 43 E8
Raniwara India 24°50N 72°10E 42 G5
Rāniyah Iraq 36°15N 44°53E 44 B5
Ranka India 23°59N 83°47E 43 H10
Ranken → Australia 20°31S 137°36E 62 C2
Rankin U.S.A. 31°13N 101°56W 84 F4
Rankin Inlet Canada 62°30N 93°0W 68 E13
Rankins Springs Australia 33°49S 146°14E 63 E4
Rannoch, L. U.K. 56°41N 4°20W 11 E4
Rannoch Moor U.K. 56°38N 4°48W 11 E4
Ranobe, Helodranon' i Madag. 23°3S 43°33E 57 C7
Ranohira Madag. 22°29S 45°24E 57 C8
Ranomafana Toamasina, Madag. 18°57S 48°50E 57 B8
Ranomafana Toliara, Madag. 24°34S 47°0E 57 C8
Ranomafana △ Madag. 21°16S 47°25E 57 C8
Ranomena Madag. 23°25S 47°17E 57 C8

Ranong *Thailand* 9°56N 98°40E **39** H2
Ranotsara Nord *Madag.* 22°48S 46°36E **57** C8
Rānsa *Iran* 33°39N 48°18E **45** C6
Ransiki *Indonesia* 1°30S 134°10E **37** E8
Rantabe *Madag.* 15°42S 49°39E **57** B8
Rantauprapat *Indonesia* 2°15N 99°50E **36** D1
Rantemario *Indonesia* 3°15S 119°57E **37** E5
Ranthambore △ *India* 26°10N 76°30E **42** F7
Rantoul *U.S.A.* 40°19N 88°9W **80** E9
Raohe *China* 46°47N 134°0E **30** A7
Raoyang *China* 38°15N 115°45E **34** E8
Rap, Ko *Thailand* 9°19N 99°58E **39** b
Rapa *French Polynesia* 27°35S 144°20W **65** K13
Rapa Nui = Pascua, I. de
　　Chile 27°7S 109°23W **65** K17
Rapallo *Italy* 44°21N 9°14E **20** D8
Rapar *India* 23°34N 70°38E **42** H4
Rāpch *Iran* 25°40N 59°15E **45** E8
Rapel, Lago *Chile* 34°20S 71°14W **94** C1
Raper, C. *Canada* 69°44N 67°6W **69** D18
Rapid City *U.S.A.* 44°5N 103°14W **80** C2
Rapid River *U.S.A.* 45°55N 86°58W **80** C10
Rapla *Estonia* 59°1N 24°52E **9** G21
Rapti → *India* 26°18N 83°41E **43** F10
Raquette → *U.S.A.* 45°0N 74°42W **83** C10
Raquette Lake *U.S.A.* 43°49N 74°40W **83** C10
Rara △ *Nepal* 29°30N 82°10E **43** E10
Rarotonga *Cook Is.* 21°30S 160°0W **65** K12
Ra's al 'Ayn *Syria* 36°45N 40°12E **44** B4
Ra's al Khaymah *U.A.E.* 25°50N 55°59E **45** E7
Ra's aţ Ţib *Tunisia* 37°1N 11°2E **22** F4
Rasa, Pta. *Argentina* 36°20S 56°41W **94** D4
Rasca, Pta. de la
　　Canary Is. 27°59N 16°41W **24** G3
Raseiniai *Lithuania* 55°25N 23°5E **9** J20
Rashmi *India* 25°4N 74°22E **42** G6
Rasht *Iran* 37°20N 49°40E **45** B6
Rasi Salai *Thailand* 15°20N 104°9E **38** E5
Rason L. *Australia* 28°45S 124°25E **61** E3
Rasra *India* 25°50N 83°50E **43** G10
Rasul *Pakistan* 32°42N 73°34E **42** C5
Rat → *Canada* 49°35N 97°10W **71** D9
Rat Buri *Thailand* 13°30N 99°54E **38** F2
Rat Islands *U.S.A.* 52°0N 178°0E **74** E3
Rat L. *Canada* 56°10N 99°40W **71** B9
Ratak Chain *Pac. Oc.* 1°0N 170°0E **64** G8
Ratangarh *India* 28°5N 74°35E **42** E6
Raţāwī *Iraq* 30°38N 47°13E **44** D5
Rath *India* 25°36N 79°37E **43** G8
Rath Luirc *Ireland* 52°21N 8°40W **10** D3
Rathangan *Ireland* 53°13N 7°1W **10** C4
Rathdrum *Ireland* 52°56N 6°14W **10** D5
Rathenow *Germany* 52°37N 12°19E **16** B7
Rathkeale *Ireland* 52°32N 8°56W **10** D3
Rathlin I. *U.K.* 55°18N 6°14W **10** A5
Rathmelton *Ireland* 55°2N 7°38W **10** A4
Ratibor = Racibórz
　　Poland 50°7N 18°18E **17** C10
Ratlam *India* 23°20N 75°0E **42** H6
Ratmanova Ostrov
　　Russia 65°46N 169°6W **74** B6
Ratnagiri *India* 16°57N 73°18E **40** L8
Ratodero *Pakistan* 27°48N 68°18E **42** F3
Raton *U.S.A.* 36°54N 104°24W **77** H11
Rattaphum *Thailand* 7°8N 100°16E **39** J3
Rattray Hd. *U.K.* 57°38N 1°50W **11** D7
Ratz, Mt. *Canada* 57°23N 132°12W **70** B2
Raub *Malaysia* 3°47N 101°52E **39** L3
Rauch *Argentina* 36°45S 59°5W **94** D4
Raudales *Mexico* 17°27N 93°39W **87** D6
Raufarhöfn *Iceland* 66°27N 15°57W **8** C6
Raufoss *Norway* 60°44N 10°37E **8** F14
Raukumara Ra. *N.Z.* 38°5S 177°55E **59** C6
Rauma *Finland* 61°10N 21°30E **8** F19
Raumo = Rauma
　　Finland 61°10N 21°30E **8** F19
Raung, Gunung *Indonesia* 8°8S 114°3E **37** J17
Raurkela *India* 22°14N 84°50E **43** H11
Rausu-Dake *Japan* 44°4N 145°7E **30** B12
Rava-Ruska *Ukraine* 50°15N 23°42E **17** C12
Rava Russkaya = Rava-Ruska
　　Ukraine 50°15N 23°42E **17** C12
Ravalli *U.S.A.* 47°17N 114°11W **76** C6
Ravānsar *Iran* 34°43N 46°40E **44** C5
Rāvar *Iran* 31°20N 56°51E **45** D8
Ravena *U.S.A.* 42°28N 73°49W **83** D11
Ravenna *Italy* 44°25N 12°12E **22** B5
Ravenna *Nebr., U.S.A.* 41°1N 98°55W **80** E4
Ravenna *Ohio, U.S.A.* 41°9N 81°15W **82** E3
Ravensburg *Germany* 47°46N 9°36E **16** E5
Ravenshoe *Australia* 17°37S 145°29E **62** B4
Ravensthorpe *Australia* 33°35S 120°2E **61** F3
Ravenswood *Australia* 20°6S 146°54E **62** C4
Ravenswood *U.S.A.* 38°57N 81°46W **81** F13
Ravi → *Pakistan* 30°35N 71°49E **42** D4
Rawalpindi *Pakistan* 33°38N 73°8E **42** C5
Rawang *Malaysia* 3°20N 101°35E **39** L3
Rawene *N.Z.* 35°25S 173°32E **59** A4
Rawlinna *Australia* 30°58S 125°28E **61** F4
Rawlins *U.S.A.* 41°47N 107°14W **76** F10
Rawlinson Ra. *Australia* 24°40S 128°30E **61** D4
Rawson *Argentina* 43°15S 65°5W **96** E3
Raxaul *India* 26°59N 84°51E **43** F11
Ray *U.S.A.* 48°21N 103°10W **80** A2
Ray, C. *Canada* 47°33N 59°15W **73** C8
Ray Mts. *U.S.A.* 66°0N 152°0W **74** B9
Raya Ring, Ko *Thailand* 8°18N 98°29E **39** a
Rayadurg *India* 14°40N 76°50E **40** M10
Rayagada *India* 19°15N 83°20E **41** K13
Raychikhinsk *Russia* 49°46N 129°25E **29** E13
Rāyen *Iran* 29°34N 57°26E **45** D8
Rayleigh *U.K.* 51°36N 0°37E **13** F8
Raymond *Canada* 49°30N 112°35W **70** D6
Raymond *Calif., U.S.A.* 37°13N 119°54W **78** H7
Raymond *N.H., U.S.A.* 43°2N 71°11W **83** C13
Raymond *Wash.,*
　　U.S.A. 46°41N 123°44W **78** D3
Raymondville *U.S.A.* 26°29N 97°47W **84** H6
Raymore *Canada* 51°25N 104°31W **71** C8

Rayón *Mexico* 29°43N 110°35W **86** B2
Rayong *Thailand* 12°40N 101°20E **38** F3
Raystown L. *U.S.A.* 40°25N 78°5W **82** F6
Rayville *U.S.A.* 32°29N 91°46W **84** E9
Raz, Pte. du *France* 48°2N 4°47W **20** C1
Razan *Iran* 35°23N 49°2E **45** C6
Razāzah, Buḩayrat ar
　　Iraq 32°40N 43°35E **44** C4
Razāzah, L. = Razāzah, Buḩayrat
　　ar *Iraq* 32°40N 43°35E **44** C4
Razdel'naya = Rozdilna
　　Ukraine 46°50N 30°2E **17** E16
Razdolnoye *Russia* 43°30N 131°52E **30** C5
Razeh *Iran* 32°47N 48°9E **45** C6
Razgrad *Bulgaria* 43°33N 26°34E **23** C12
Razim, Lacul *Romania* 44°50N 29°0E **17** F15
Razmak *Pakistan* 32°45N 69°50E **42** C3
Re, Cu Lao *Vietnam* 15°22N 109°8E **38** E7
Ré, Î. de *France* 46°12N 1°30W **20** C3
Reading *U.K.* 51°27N 0°58W **13** F7
Reading *U.S.A.* 40°20N 75°56W **83** F9
Reading □ *U.K.* 51°27N 0°58W **13** F7
Realicó *Argentina* 35°0S 64°15W **94** D3
Ream *Cambodia* 10°34N 103°39E **39** G4
Ream △ *Cambodia* 10°30N 103°45E **39** G4
Reay Forest *U.K.* 58°22N 4°55W **11** C4
Rebecca, L. *Australia* 30°0S 122°15E **61** F3
Rebi *Indonesia* 6°23S 134°7E **37** F8
Rebiana *Libya* 24°12N 22°10E **51** D10
Rebiana, Sahrâ' *Libya* 24°30N 21°0E **51** D10
Reboly *Russia* 63°49N 30°47E **8** E24
Rebun-Tō *Japan* 45°23N 141°2E **30** B10
Recherche, Arch. of the
　　Australia 34°15S 122°50E **61** F3
Rechna Doab *Pakistan* 31°35N 73°30E **42** D5
Rechytsa *Belarus* 52°21N 30°24E **17** B16
Recife *Brazil* 8°0S 35°0W **93** E12
Recife *Seychelles* 4°36S 55°42E **53** b
Recklinghausen *Germany* 51°37N 7°12E **15** C7
Reconquista *Argentina* 29°10S 59°45W **94** B4
Recreo *Argentina* 29°25S 65°10W **94** B2
Red → *U.S.A.* 31°1N 91°45W **84** F9
Red Bank *U.S.A.* 40°21N 74°5W **83** F10
Red Bay *Canada* 51°44N 56°25W **73** B8
Red Bluff *U.S.A.* 40°11N 122°15W **76** F2
Red Bluff Res. *U.S.A.* 31°54N 103°55W **77** L12
Red Cliffs *Australia* 34°19S 142°11E **63** E3
Red Cloud *U.S.A.* 40°5N 98°32W **80** E4
Red Creek *U.S.A.* 43°14N 76°45W **83** C8
Red Deer *Canada* 52°20N 113°50W **70** C6
Red Deer → *Alta.,*
　　Canada 50°58N 110°0W **71** C7
Red Deer → *Man.,*
　　Canada 52°53N 101°1W **71** C8
Red Deer L. *Canada* 52°55N 101°20W **71** C8
Red Hook *U.S.A.* 41°55N 73°53W **83** E11
Red Indian L. *Canada* 48°35N 57°0W **73** C8
Red L. *Canada* 51°3N 93°49W **71** C10
Red Lake *Canada* 51°3N 93°49W **71** C10
Red Lake Falls *U.S.A.* 47°53N 96°16W **80** B5
Red Lake Road *Canada* 49°59N 93°25W **71** C10
Red Lodge *U.S.A.* 45°11N 109°15W **76** D9
Red Mountain *U.S.A.* 35°37N 117°38W **79** K9
Red Oak *U.S.A.* 41°1N 95°14W **80** E6
Red River of the North →
　　N. Amer. 49°0N 97°15W **80** A5
Red Rock *Canada* 48°55N 88°15W **72** C2
Red Rock, L. *U.S.A.* 41°22N 92°59W **80** E7
Red Rocks Pt. *Australia* 32°13S 127°32E **61** F4
Red Sea *Asia* 25°0N 36°0E **47** C2
Red Slate Mt. *U.S.A.* 37°31N 118°52W **78** H8
Red Sucker L. *Canada* 54°9N 93°40W **72** B1
Red Tower Pass = Turnu Roşu, P.
　　Romania 45°33N 24°17E **17** F13
Red Wing *U.S.A.* 44°34N 92°31W **80** C7
Redang *Malaysia* 5°49N 103°2E **39** K4
Redange *Lux.* 49°46N 5°52E **15** E5
Redcar *U.K.* 54°37N 1°4W **12** C6
Redcar & Cleveland □
　　U.K. 54°29N 1°0W **12** C7
Redcliff *Canada* 50°10N 110°50W **76** A8
Redcliffe *Australia* 27°12S 153°6E **63** D5
Redcliffe, Mt. *Australia* 28°30S 121°30E **61** E3
Reddersburg *S. Africa* 29°41S 26°10E **56** D4
Redding *U.S.A.* 40°35N 122°24W **76** F2
Redditch *U.K.* 52°18N 1°55W **13** E6
Redfield *U.S.A.* 44°53N 98°31W **80** C4
Redford *U.S.A.* 44°38N 73°48W **83** B11
Redhead *Trin. & Tob.* 10°44N 60°58W **93** K16
Redlands *U.S.A.* 34°4N 117°11W **79** M9
Redmond *Oreg., U.S.A.* 44°17N 121°11W **76** D3
Redmond *Wash., U.S.A.* 47°40N 122°7W **78** C4
Redon *France* 47°40N 2°6W **20** C2
Redonda *Antigua & B.* 16°58N 62°19W **89** C7
Redondela *Spain* 42°15N 8°38W **21** A1
Redondo Beach *U.S.A.* 33°50N 118°23W **79** M8
Redoubt Volcano
　　U.S.A. 60°29N 152°45W **74** C9
Redruth *U.K.* 50°14N 5°14W **13** G2
Redvers *Canada* 49°35N 101°40W **71** D8
Redwater *Canada* 53°55N 113°6W **70** C6
Redwood *U.S.A.* 44°18N 75°48W **83** B9
Redwood △ *U.S.A.* 41°40N 124°5W **76** F1
Redwood City *U.S.A.* 37°30N 122°15W **78** H4
Redwood Falls *U.S.A.* 44°32N 95°7W **80** C6
Ree, L. *Ireland* 53°35N 8°0W **10** C3
Reed City *U.S.A.* 43°53N 85°31W **81** D11
Reed L. *Canada* 54°38N 100°30W **71** C8
Reedley *U.S.A.* 36°36N 119°27W **78** J7
Reedsburg *U.S.A.* 43°32N 90°0W **80** D8
Reedsport *U.S.A.* 43°42N 124°6W **76** E1
Reedsville *U.S.A.* 40°39N 77°35W **82** F7
Reefton *N.Z.* 42°6S 171°51E **59** E3
Reese → *U.S.A.* 40°48N 117°4W **76** F5
Refugio *U.S.A.* 28°18N 97°17W **84** G6
Regana, C. de *Spain* 39°25N 2°43E **24** B9
Regensburg *Germany* 49°1N 12°6E **16** D7
Reggâne = Zaouiet Reggâne
　　Algeria 26°32N 0°3E **50** C6

Réggio di Calábria *Italy* 38°6N 15°39E **22** E6
Réggio nell'Emília *Italy* 44°43N 10°36E **22** B4
Reghin *Romania* 46°46N 24°42E **17** E13
Regina *Canada* 50°27N 104°35W **71** C8
Regina Beach *Canada* 50°47N 105°0W **71** C8
Registro *Brazil* 24°29S 47°49W **95** A6
Rehar → *India* 23°55N 82°40E **43** H10
Rehli *India* 23°38N 79°5E **43** H8
Rehoboth *Namibia* 23°15S 17°4E **56** C2
Rehovot *Israel* 31°54N 34°48E **46** D3
Reichenbach *Germany* 50°37N 12°17E **16** C7
Reid *Australia* 30°49S 128°26E **61** F4
Reidsville *U.S.A.* 36°21N 79°40W **85** C15
Reigate *U.K.* 51°14N 0°12W **13** F7
Reims *France* 49°15N 4°1E **20** B6
Reina Adelaida, Arch.
　　Chile 52°20S 74°0W **96** G2
Reina Sofia, Tenerife ✈ (TFS)
　　Canary Is. 28°3N 16°33W **24** F3
Reindeer → *Canada* 55°36N 103°11W **71** B8
Reindeer I. *Canada* 52°30N 98°0W **71** C9
Reindeer L. *Canada* 57°15N 102°15W **71** B8
Reinga, C. *N.Z.* 34°25S 172°43E **59** A4
Reinosa *Spain* 43°2N 4°15W **21** A3
Reitz *S. Africa* 27°48S 28°29E **57** D4
Reivilo *S. Africa* 27°36S 24°8E **56** D3
Reliance *Canada* 63°0N 109°20W **71** A7
Remanso *Brazil* 9°41S 42°4W **93** E10
Remarkable, Mt.
　　Australia 32°48S 138°10E **63** E2
Rembang *Indonesia* 6°42S 111°21E **37** G14
Remedios *Panama* 8°15N 81°50W **88** E3
Remeshk *Iran* 26°55N 58°50E **45** E8
Remich *Lux.* 49°32N 6°22E **15** E6
Remscheid *Germany* 51°11N 7°12E **15** C7
Ren Xian *China* 37°8N 114°40E **34** F8
Rendang *Indonesia* 8°26S 115°25E **37** J18
Rendsburg *Germany* 54°17N 9°39E **16** A5
Renfrew *Canada* 45°30N 76°40W **83** A8
Renfrewshire □ *U.K.* 55°49N 4°38W **11** F4
Rengat *Indonesia* 0°30S 102°45E **36** E2
Rengo *Chile* 34°24S 70°50W **94** C1
Reni = Taranagar *India* 28°43N 74°50E **42** E6
Reni *Ukraine* 45°28N 28°15E **17** F15
Renmark *Australia* 34°11S 140°43E **63** E3
Rennell Sd. *Canada* 53°23N 132°35W **70** C2
Renner Springs
　　Australia 18°20S 133°47E **62** B1
Rennes *France* 48°7N 1°41W **20** B3
Rennick Glacier
　　Antarctica 70°30S 161°45E **5** D21
Rennie L. *Canada* 61°32N 105°35W **71** A7
Reno *U.S.A.* 39°31N 119°48W **78** F7
Reno → *Italy* 44°38N 12°16E **22** B5
Renovo *U.S.A.* 41°20N 77°45W **82** E7
Renqiu *China* 38°43N 116°5E **34** E9
Rensselaer *Ind., U.S.A.* 40°57N 87°9W **80** E10
Rensselaer *N.Y., U.S.A.* 42°38N 73°45W **83** D11
Renton *U.S.A.* 47°28N 122°12W **78** C4
Renukoot *India* 24°12N 83°2E **43** G10
Reotipur *India* 25°33N 83°45E **43** G10
Republic *Mo., U.S.A.* 37°7N 93°29W **80** G7
Republic *Wash., U.S.A.* 48°39N 118°44W **76** B4
Republican → *U.S.A.* 39°4N 96°48W **80** F5
Repulse B. *Australia* 20°35S 148°46E **62** b
Repulse Bay *Canada* 66°30N 86°30W **69** D14
Requena *Peru* 5°5S 73°52W **92** E4
Requena *Spain* 39°30N 1°4W **21** C5
Reserve *U.S.A.* 33°43N 108°45W **77** K9
Resht = Rasht *Iran* 37°20N 49°40E **45** B6
Resistencia *Argentina* 27°30S 59°0W **94** B4
Reşiţa *Romania* 45°18N 21°53E **17** F11
Reso = Raisio *Finland* 60°28N 22°11E **9** F20
Resolute *Canada* 74°42N 94°54W **69** C13
Resolution I. *Canada* 61°30N 65°0W **69** E19
Resolution I. *N.Z.* 45°40S 166°40E **59** F1
Ressano Garcia *Mozam.* 25°25S 32°0E **57** D5
Reston *Canada* 49°33N 101°6W **71** D8
Retalhuleu *Guatemala* 14°33N 91°46W **88** D1
Retenue, L. de
　　Dem. Rep. of the Congo 11°0S 27°0E **55** E2
Retford *U.K.* 53°19N 0°56W **12** D7
Rethimno *Greece* 35°18N 24°30E **25** D6
Rethimno □ *Greece* 35°23N 24°28E **25** D6
Reti *Pakistan* 28°5N 69°48E **42** E3
Réunion ☑ *Ind. Oc.* 21°0S 56°0E **53** c
Reus *Spain* 41°10N 1°5E **21** B6
Reutlingen *Germany* 48°29N 9°12E **16** D5
Reval = Tallinn *Estonia* 59°22N 24°48E **9** G21
Revda *Russia* 56°48N 59°57E **18** C10
Revelganj *India* 25°50N 84°40E **43** G11
Revelstoke *Canada* 51°0N 118°10W **70** C5
Reventazón *Peru* 6°10S 80°58W **92** E2
Revillagigedo, Is. de
　　Pac. Oc. 18°40N 112°0W **86** D2
Revuè → *Mozam.* 19°50S 34°0E **55** F3
Rewa *India* 24°33N 81°25E **43** G9
Rewari *India* 28°15N 76°40E **42** E7
Rexburg *U.S.A.* 43°49N 111°47W **76** E8
Rey *Iran* 35°35N 51°25E **45** C6
Rey, I. del *Panama* 8°20N 78°30W **88** E4
Rey, L. del *Mexico* 27°1N 103°26W **86** B4
Rey Malabo *Eq. Guin.* 3°45N 8°50E **52** D1
Reyðarfjörður *Iceland* 65°2N 14°13W **8** D6
Reyes, Pt. *U.S.A.* 38°0N 123°0W **78** H3
Reykjahlíð *Iceland* 65°40N 16°55W **8** D5
Reykjanes *Iceland* 63°48N 22°40W **8** E2
Reykjavík *Iceland* 64°10N 21°57W **8** D3
Reynolds Ra. *Australia* 22°30S 133°0E **60** D5
Reynoldsville *U.S.A.* 41°5N 78°58W **82** E6
Reynosa *Mexico* 26°7N 98°18W **87** B5
Rēzekne *Latvia* 56°30N 27°17E **9** H22
Rezvan *Iran* 27°34N 56°6E **45** E8
Rhayader *U.K.* 52°18N 3°29E **13** E4
Rhein → *Europe* 51°52N 6°2E **15** C6
Rhein-Main-Donau-Kanal
　　Germany 49°1N 11°27E **16** D6
Rheine *Germany* 52°17N 7°26E **16** B4
Rheinland-Pfalz □ *Germany* 50°0N 7°0E **16** C4

Rhin = Rhein → *Europe* 51°52N 6°2E **15** C6
Rhine = Rhein → *Europe* 51°52N 6°2E **15** C6
Rhinebeck *U.S.A.* 41°56N 73°55W **83** E11
Rhineland-Palatinate =
　　Rheinland-Pfalz □
　　Germany 50°0N 7°0E **16** C4
Rhinelander *U.S.A.* 45°38N 89°25W **80** C9
Rhinns Pt. *U.K.* 55°40N 6°29W **11** F2
Rhino Camp *Uganda* 3°0N 31°22E **54** B3
Rhir, Cap *Morocco* 30°38N 9°54W **50** B4
Rhode Island □ *U.S.A.* 41°40N 71°30W **83** E13
Rhodes *Greece* 36°15N 28°10E **25** C10
Rhodope Mts. = Rhodopi Planina
　　Bulgaria 41°40N 24°20E **23** D11
Rhodopi Planina
　　Bulgaria 41°40N 24°20E **23** D11
Rhön *Germany* 50°24N 9°58E **16** C5
Rhondda *U.K.* 51°39N 3°31W **13** F4
Rhondda Cynon Taff □
　　U.K. 51°42N 3°27W **13** F4
Rhône → *France* 43°28N 4°42E **20** E6
Rhum *U.K.* 57°0N 6°20W **11** E2
Rhyl *U.K.* 53°20N 3°29W **12** D4
Riachão *Brazil* 7°20S 46°37W **93** E9
Riasi *India* 33°10N 74°50E **43** C6
Riau □ *Indonesia* 0°0 102°35E **36** E2
Riau, Kepulauan
　　Indonesia 0°30N 104°20E **36** D2
Riau Arch. = Riau, Kepulauan
　　Indonesia 0°30N 104°20E **36** D2
Ribadeo *Spain* 43°35N 7°5W **21** A2
Ribas do Rio Pardo
　　Brazil 20°27S 53°46W **93** H8
Ribauè *Mozam.* 14°57S 38°17E **55** E4
Ribble → *U.K.* 53°52N 2°25E **12** D5
Ribe *Denmark* 55°19N 8°44E **9** J13
Ribeira Brava *Madeira* 32°41N 17°4W **24** D2
Ribeira Grande *C. Verde Is.* 17°0N 25°4W **50** b
Ribeirão Prêto *Brazil* 21°10S 47°50W **95** A6
Riberalta *Bolivia* 11°0S 66°0W **92** F5
Riccarton *N.Z.* 43°32S 172°37E **59** E4
Rice *U.S.A.* 34°5N 114°51W **79** L12
Rice L. *Canada* 44°12N 78°10W **82** B6
Rice Lake *U.S.A.* 45°30N 91°44W **80** C8
Rich, C. *Canada* 44°43N 80°38W **82** B4
Richards Bay *S. Africa* 28°48S 32°6E **57** D5
Richardson → *Canada* 58°25N 111°14W **71** B6
Richardson Lakes
　　U.S.A. 44°46N 70°58W **81** C18
Richardson Springs
　　U.S.A. 39°51N 121°46W **78** F5
Riche, C. *Australia* 34°36S 118°47E **61** F2
Richey *U.S.A.* 47°39N 105°4W **76** C11
Richfield *U.S.A.* 38°46N 112°5W **76** G7
Richfield Springs
　　U.S.A. 42°51N 74°59W **83** D10
Richford *U.S.A.* 45°0N 72°40W **83** B12
Richibucto *Canada* 46°42N 64°54W **73** C7
Richland *Ga., U.S.A.* 32°5N 84°40W **85** E12
Richland *Wash., U.S.A.* 46°17N 119°18W **76** C4
Richland Center *U.S.A.* 43°21N 90°23W **80** D8
Richlands *U.S.A.* 37°6N 81°48W **81** G13
Richmond *Australia* 20°43S 143°8E **62** C3
Richmond *N.Z.* 41°20S 173°12E **59** D4
Richmond *U.K.* 54°25N 1°43W **12** C6
Richmond *Calif., U.S.A.* 37°56N 122°21W **78** H4
Richmond *Ind., U.S.A.* 39°50N 84°53W **81** F11
Richmond *Ky., U.S.A.* 37°45N 84°18W **81** G11
Richmond *Mich., U.S.A.* 42°49N 82°45W **82** D2
Richmond *Mo., U.S.A.* 39°17N 93°58W **80** F7
Richmond *Tex., U.S.A.* 29°35N 95°46W **84** G7
Richmond *Utah, U.S.A.* 41°56N 111°48W **76** F8
Richmond *Va., U.S.A.* 37°33N 77°27W **81** G15
Richmond *Vt., U.S.A.* 44°24N 72°59W **83** B12
Richmond Hill *Canada* 43°52N 79°27W **82** C5
Richmond Ra. *Australia* 29°0S 152°45E **63** D5
Richmondville *U.S.A.* 42°38N 74°33W **83** D10
Richtersveld △ *S. Africa* 28°15S 17°10E **56** D2
Richville *U.S.A.* 44°25N 75°23W **83** B9
Richwood *U.S.A.* 38°14N 80°32W **81** F13
Ridder = Leninogorsk
　　Kazakhstan 50°20N 83°30E **28** D9
Riddlesburg *U.S.A.* 40°9N 78°15W **82** F6
Ridgecrest *U.S.A.* 35°38N 117°40W **79** K9
Ridgefield *Conn., U.S.A.* 41°17N 73°30W **83** E11
Ridgefield *Wash.,*
　　U.S.A. 45°49N 122°45W **78** E4
Ridgeland *Miss., U.S.A.* 32°26N 90°8W **85** E9
Ridgeland *S.C., U.S.A.* 32°29N 80°59W **85** E14
Ridgetown *Canada* 42°26N 81°52W **82** D3
Ridgewood *U.S.A.* 40°59N 74°7W **83** F10
Ridgway *U.S.A.* 41°25N 78°44W **82** E6
Riding Mountain △
　　Canada 50°50N 100°0W **71** C9
Ridley, Mt. *Australia* 33°12S 122°7E **61** F3
Riebeek-Oos *S. Africa* 33°10S 26°10E **56** E4
Ried *Austria* 48°14N 13°30E **16** D7
Riesa *Germany* 51°17N 13°17E **16** C7
Riet → *S. Africa* 29°0S 23°54E **56** D3
Rietbron *S. Africa* 32°54S 23°10E **56** E3
Rietfontein *Namibia* 21°58S 20°58E **56** C3
Rieti *Italy* 42°24N 12°51E **22** C5
Rif = Er Rif *Morocco* 35°1N 4°1W **50** A5
Riffe L. *U.S.A.* 46°32N 122°26W **78** D4
Rifle *U.S.A.* 39°32N 107°47W **76** G10
Rift Valley *Africa* 7°0N 30°0E **48** G7
Rift Valley □ *Kenya* 0°20N 36°0E **54** B4
Rīga *Latvia* 56°53N 24°8E **9** H21
Riga, G. of *Latvia* 57°40N 23°45E **9** H20
Rīgān *Iran* 28°37N 58°58E **45** D8
Rīgas Jūras Līcis = Riga, G. of
　　Latvia 57°40N 23°45E **9** H20
Rigaud *Canada* 45°29N 74°18W **83** A10
Rigby *U.S.A.* 43°40N 111°55W **76** E8
Rīgestān *Afghan.* 30°15N 65°0E **40** D4
Riggins *U.S.A.* 45°25N 116°19W **76** D5
Rigolet *Canada* 54°10N 58°23W **73** B8
Rihand Dam *India* 24°9N 83°2E **43** G10
Riḩimäki *Finland* 60°45N 24°48E **8** F21

Riiser-Larsen-halvøya
　　Antarctica 68°0S 35°0E **5** C4
Riiser-Larsen Ice Shelf
　　S. Ocean 74°0S 19°0W **5** D2
Riiser-Larsen Sea *S. Ocean* 67°30S 22°0E **5** C4
Rijeka *Croatia* 45°20N 14°21E **16** F8
Rijssen *Neths.* 52°19N 6°31E **15** B6
Rikuchū-Kaigan △
　　Japan 39°20N 142°0E **30** E11
Rikuzentakada *Japan* 39°0N 141°40E **30** E10
Riley *U.S.A.* 43°32N 119°28W **76** E4
Rima → *Nigeria* 13°4N 5°10E **50** F7
Rimah, Wadi ar →
　　Si. Arabia 26°5N 41°30E **44** E4
Rimau, Pulau *Malaysia* 5°15N 100°16E **39** c
Rimbey *Canada* 52°35S 114°15W **70** C6
Rimersburg *U.S.A.* 41°3N 79°30W **82** E5
Rímini *Italy* 44°3N 12°33E **22** B5
Rimouski *Canada* 48°27N 68°30W **73** C6
Rimrock *U.S.A.* 46°40N 121°7W **78** D5
Rinca *Indonesia* 8°45S 119°35E **37** F5
Rincón de Romos
　　Mexico 22°14N 102°18W **86** C4
Rinconada *Argentina* 22°26S 66°10W **94** A2
Rind → *India* 25°53N 80°33E **43** G9
Ringas *India* 27°21N 75°34E **42** F6
Ringgold Is. *Fiji* 16°15S 179°25W **59** a
Ringkøbing *Denmark* 56°5N 8°15E **9** H13
Ringvassøya *Norway* 69°56N 19°15E **8** B18
Rinjani *Indonesia* 8°24S 116°28E **36** F5
Rinns Pt. *U.K.* 55°40N 6°29W **11** F2
Rio Branco *Brazil* 9°58S 67°49W **92** E5
Rio Branco *Uruguay* 32°40S 53°40W **95** C5
Río Bravo *Mexico* 25°59N 98°6W **87** B5
Río Bravo △ *N. Amer.* 29°20N 102°45W **86** B4
Río Bravo del Norte →
　　Mexico 25°57N 97°9W **87** B5
Rio Brilhante *Brazil* 21°48S 54°33W **95** A5
Rio Claro *Brazil* 22°19S 47°35W **95** A6
Rio Claro *Trin. & Tob.* 10°20N 61°25W **93** K15
Río Colorado *Argentina* 39°0S 64°0W **96** D4
Río Cuarto *Argentina* 33°10S 64°25W **94** C3
Rio das Pedras *Mozam.* 23°8S 35°28E **57** C6
Rio de Janeiro *Brazil* 22°54S 43°12W **95** A7
Rio de Janeiro □ *Brazil* 22°50S 43°0W **95** A7
Rio do Sul *Brazil* 27°13S 49°37W **95** B6
Río Dulce △ *Guatemala* 15°43N 88°50W **88** C2
Río Gallegos *Argentina* 51°35S 69°15W **96** G3
Río Grande *Argentina* 53°50S 67°45W **96** G3
Río Grande *Brazil* 32°0S 52°20W **95** C5
Río Grande *Mexico* 23°50N 103°2W **86** C4
Río Grande *Puerto Rico* 18°23N 65°50W **89** d
Río Grande △ *N. Amer.* 25°58N 97°9W **84** J6
Río Grande City *U.S.A.* 26°23N 98°49W **84** H5
Río Grande de Santiago →
　　Mexico 21°36N 105°26W **86** C3
Río Grande do Norte □
　　Brazil 5°40S 36°0W **93** E11
Río Grande do Sul □
　　Brazil 30°0S 53°0W **95** C5
Río Hato *Panama* 8°22N 80°10W **88** E3
Río Lagartos *Mexico* 21°36N 88°10W **87** C7
Río Largo *Brazil* 9°28S 35°50W **93** E11
Río Muni □ *Eq. Guin.* 1°30N 10°0E **52** D2
Rio Negro *Brazil* 26°0S 49°55W **95** B6
Rio Pardo *Brazil* 30°0S 52°30W **95** C5
Río Pilcomayo △
　　Argentina 25°5S 58°5W **94** B4
Río Platano △ *Honduras* 15°45N 85°0W **88** C3
Río Rancho *U.S.A.* 35°14N 106°41W **77** J10
Río Segundo *Argentina* 31°40S 63°59W **94** C3
Río Tercero *Argentina* 32°15S 64°8W **94** C3
Rio Verde *Brazil* 17°50S 51°0W **93** G8
Río Verde *Mexico* 21°56N 99°59W **87** C5
Río Vista *U.S.A.* 38°10N 121°42W **78** G5
Rīshā', W. ar → *Si. Arabia* 25°33N 44°5E **44** E5
Rishiri-Rebun-Sarobetsu △
　　Japan 45°26N 141°30E **30** B10
Rishiri-Tō *Japan* 45°11N 141°15E **30** B10
Rishon le Ziyyon *Israel* 31°58N 34°48E **46** D3
Rison *U.S.A.* 33°58N 92°11W **84** E8
Risør *Norway* 58°43N 9°13E **9** G13
Rita Blanca Cr. →
　　U.S.A. 35°40N 102°29W **84** D3
Ritter, Mt. *U.S.A.* 37°41N 119°12W **78** H7
Rittman *U.S.A.* 40°58N 81°47W **82** F3
Ritzville *U.S.A.* 47°8N 118°23W **76** C4
Riva del Garda *Italy* 45°53N 10°50E **22** B4
Rivadavia *B. Aires,*
　　Argentina 35°29S 62°59W **94** D3
Rivadavia *Mendoza,*
　　Argentina 33°13S 68°30W **94** C2
Rivadavia *Salta, Argentina* 24°5S 62°54W **94** A3
Rivadavia *Chile* 29°57S 70°35W **94** B1
Rivas *Nic.* 11°30N 85°50W **88** D2
Rivash *Iran* 35°28N 58°26E **45** C8
River Cess *Liberia* 5°30N 9°32W **50** G4
River Jordan *Canada* 48°26N 124°3W **78** B2
Rivera *Argentina* 37°12S 63°14W **94** D3
Riverbank *U.S.A.* 37°44N 120°56W **78** H6
Riverdale *U.S.A.* 36°26N 119°52W **78** J7
Riverhead *U.S.A.* 40°55N 72°40W **83** F12
Riverhurst *Canada* 50°55N 106°50W **71** C7
Rivers *Canada* 50°2N 100°14W **71** C8
Rivers Inlet *Canada* 51°42N 127°15W **70** C3

Riversdale *Canada* 44°5N 81°20W **82 B3**
Riversdale *S. Africa* 34°7S 21°15E **56 E3**
Riverside *U.S.A.* 33°59N 117°22W **79 M9**
Riverton *Australia* 34°10S 138°46E **63 E2**
Riverton *Canada* 51°1N 97°0W **71 C9**
Riverton *N.Z.* 46°21S 168°0E **59 G2**
Riverton *U.S.A.* 43°2N 108°23W **76 E9**
Riviera *U.S.A.* 35°4N 114°35W **79 K12**
Riviera di Levante *Italy* 44°15N 9°30E **20 D8**
Riviera di Ponente *Italy* 44°10N 8°20E **20 D8**
Rivière-au-Renard
  Canada 48°59N 64°23W **73 C7**
Rivière-du-Loup *Canada* 47°50N 69°30W **73 C6**
Rivière-Pentecôte *Canada* 49°57N 67°1W **73 C6**
Rivière-Pilote *Martinique* 14°26N 60°53W **88 c**
Rivière-St-Paul *Canada* 51°28N 57°45W **73 B8**
Rivière-Salée *Martinique* 14°31N 61°0W **88 c**
Rivne *Ukraine* 50°40N 26°10E **17 C14**
Rívoli *Italy* 45°3N 7°31E **20 D7**
Rivoli B. *Australia* 37°32S 140°3E **63 F3**
Riyadh = Ar Riyāḍ
  Si. Arabia 24°41N 46°42E **44 E5**
Riyadh al Khabrā'
  Si. Arabia 26°2N 43°33E **44 E4**
Rize *Turkey* 41°0N 40°30E **19 F7**
Rizhao *China* 35°25N 119°30E **35 G10**
Rizokarpaso *Cyprus* 35°36N 34°23E **25 D13**
Rizzuto, C. *Italy* 38°53N 17°5E **22 E7**
Rjukan *Norway* 59°54N 8°33E **9 G13**
Road Town *Br. Virgin Is.* 18°27N 64°37W **89 e**
Roan Plateau *U.S.A.* 39°20N 109°20W **76 G9**
Roanne *France* 46°3N 4°4E **20 C6**
Roanoke *Ala., U.S.A.* 33°9N 85°22W **85 E12**
Roanoke *Va., U.S.A.* 37°16N 79°56W **81 G14**
Roanoke → *U.S.A.* 35°57N 76°42W **85 D16**
Roanoke I. *U.S.A.* 35°53N 75°39W **85 D17**
Roanoke Rapids *U.S.A.* 36°28N 77°40W **85 C16**
Roatán *Honduras* 16°18N 86°35W **88 C2**
Robāt Sang *Iran* 35°35N 59°10E **45 C8**
Robāṭkarīm *Iran* 35°25N 50°59E **45 C6**
Robbins I. *Australia* 40°42S 145°0E **63 G4**
Robe → *Australia* 21°42S 116°15E **60 D2**
Robe
  Canada 53°40N 76°55W **72 B4**
Robert Lee *U.S.A.* 31°54N 100°29W **84 F4**
Robertsdale *U.S.A.* 40°11N 78°6W **82 F6**
Robertsganj *India* 24°44N 83°4E **43 G10**
Robertson *S. Africa* 33°46S 19°50E **56 E2**
Robertson I. *Antarctica* 65°15S 59°30W **5 C18**
Robertson Ra. *Australia* 23°15S 121°0E **60 D3**
Robertstown *Australia* 33°58S 139°5E **63 E2**
Roberval *Canada* 48°32N 72°15W **73 C5**
Robeson Chan. *N. Amer.* 82°0N 61°30W **69 A19**
Robinson *U.S.A.* 39°0N 87°44W **80 F10**
Robinson → *Australia* 16°3S 137°16E **62 B2**
Robinson Crusoe I.
  Pac. Oc. 33°38S 78°52W **90 F2**
Robinson Ra. *Australia* 25°40S 119°0E **61 E2**
Robinvale *Australia* 34°40S 142°45E **63 E3**
Roblin *Canada* 51°14N 101°21W **71 C8**
Roboré *Bolivia* 18°10S 59°45W **92 G7**
Robson, Mt. *Canada* 53°10N 119°10W **70 C5**
Robstown *U.S.A.* 27°47N 97°40W **84 H6**
Roca, C. de *Portugal* 38°40N 9°31W **21 C1**
Roca Partida, I. *Mexico* 19°1N 112°2W **86 D2**
Rocas, I. *Brazil* 4°0S 34°1W **93 D12**
Rocha *Uruguay* 34°30S 54°25W **95 C5**
Rochdale *U.K.* 53°38N 2°9W **12 D5**
Rochefort *Belgium* 50°9N 5°12E **15 D5**
Rochefort *France* 45°56N 0°57W **20 D3**
Rochelle *U.S.A.* 41°56N 89°4W **80 E9**
Rocher River *Canada* 61°23N 112°44W **70 A6**
Rochester *U.K.* 51°23N 0°31E **13 F8**
Rochester *Ind., U.S.A.* 41°4N 86°13W **80 E10**
Rochester *Minn., U.S.A.* 44°1N 92°28W **80 C8**
Rochester *N.H., U.S.A.* 43°18N 70°59W **83 C14**
Rochester *N.Y., U.S.A.* 43°10N 77°37W **82 C7**
Rock → *Canada* 60°7N 127°7W **70 A3**
Rock, The *Australia* 35°15S 147°2E **63 F4**
Rock Creek *U.S.A.* 41°40N 80°52W **82 E4**
Rock Falls *U.S.A.* 41°47N 89°41W **80 E9**
Rock Hill *U.S.A.* 34°56N 81°1W **85 D14**
Rock Island *U.S.A.* 41°30N 90°34W **80 E8**
Rock Port *U.S.A.* 40°25N 95°31W **80 E6**
Rock Rapids *U.S.A.* 43°26N 96°10W **80 D5**
Rock Sound *Bahamas* 24°54N 76°12W **88 B4**
Rock Springs *Mont.,*
  U.S.A. 46°49N 106°15W **76 C10**
Rock Springs *Wyo.,*
  U.S.A. 41°35N 109°14W **76 F9**
Rock Valley *U.S.A.* 43°12N 96°18W **80 D5**
Rockall *Atl. Oc.* 57°37N 13°42W **6 D3**
Rockdale *Tex., U.S.A.* 30°39N 97°0W **84 F6**
Rockdale *Wash., U.S.A.* 47°22N 121°28W **78 C5**
Rockeby = Mungkan Kandju △
  Australia 13°35S 142°52E **62 A3**
Rockefeller Plateau
  Antarctica 76°0S 130°0W **5 E14**
Rockford *U.S.A.* 42°16N 89°6W **80 D9**
Rockglen *Canada* 49°11N 105°57W **71 D7**
Rockhampton *Australia* 23°22S 150°32E **62 C5**
Rockingham *Australia* 32°15S 115°38E **61 F2**
Rockingham *N.C.,*
  U.S.A. 34°57N 79°46W **85 D15**
Rockingham *Vt.,*
  U.S.A. 43°11N 72°29W **83 C12**
Rockingham B. *Australia* 18°5S 146°10E **62 B4**
Rocklake *U.S.A.* 48°47N 99°15W **80 A4**
Rockland *Canada* 45°33N 75°17W **83 A9**
Rockland *Idaho, U.S.A.* 42°34N 112°53W **76 E7**
Rockland *Maine, U.S.A.* 44°6N 69°7W **81 C19**
Rockland *Mich., U.S.A.* 46°44N 89°11W **80 B9**
Rocklin *U.S.A.* 38°48N 121°14W **78 G5**
Rockly B. *Trin. & Tob.* 11°9N 60°46W **93 J16**
Rockmart *U.S.A.* 34°0N 85°3W **85 D12**
Rockport *Mass., U.S.A.* 42°39N 70°37W **83 D14**
Rockport *Tex., U.S.A.* 28°2N 97°3W **84 G6**
Rocksprings *U.S.A.* 30°1N 100°13W **84 F4**

Rockville *Conn., U.S.A.* 41°52N 72°28W **83 E12**
Rockville *Md., U.S.A.* 39°5N 77°9W **81 F15**
Rockwall *U.S.A.* 32°56N 96°28W **84 E6**
Rockwell City *U.S.A.* 42°24N 94°38W **80 D6**
Rockwood *Canada* 43°37N 80°8W **82 C4**
Rockwood *Maine,*
  U.S.A. 45°41N 69°45W **81 C19**
Rockwood *Tenn.,*
  U.S.A. 35°52N 84°41W **85 D12**
Rocky Ford *U.S.A.* 38°3N 103°43W **76 G12**
Rocky Gully *Australia* 34°30S 117°0E **61 F2**
Rocky Harbour *Canada* 49°36N 57°55W **73 C8**
Rocky Island L. *Canada* 46°55N 83°0W **72 C3**
Rocky Lane *Canada* 58°31N 116°22W **70 B5**
Rocky Mount *U.S.A.* 35°57N 77°48W **85 D16**
Rocky Mountain △
  U.S.A. 40°25N 105°45W **76 F11**
Rocky Mountain House
  Canada 52°22N 114°55W **70 C6**
Rocky Mts. *N. Amer.* 49°0N 115°0W **76 B6**
Rocky Point *Namibia* 19°3S 12°30E **56 B2**
Rod *Pakistan* 28°10N 63°5E **40 E3**
Roda *Greece* 39°48N 19°46E **25 A3**
Rødbyhavn *Denmark* 54°39N 11°22E **9 J14**
Roddickton *Canada* 50°51N 56°8W **73 B8**
Rodez *France* 44°21N 2°33E **20 D5**
Ródhos = Rhodes
  Greece 36°15N 28°10E **25 C10**
Rodia *Greece* 35°22N 25°1E **25 D7**
Rodna ◇ *Australia* 23°45S 132°4E **60 D5**
Rodney *Canada* 42°34N 81°41W **82 D3**
Rodney, C. *N.Z.* 36°17S 174°50E **59 B5**
Rodopos *Greece* 35°34N 23°45E **25 D5**
Rodrigues *Ind. Oc.* 19°45S 63°20E **3 E13**
Roe → *U.K.* 55°6N 6°59W **10 A5**
Roebling *U.S.A.* 40°7N 74°47W **83 F10**
Roebourne *Australia* 20°44S 117°9E **60 D2**
Roebuck B. *Australia* 18°5S 122°20E **60 C3**
Roebuck Roadhouse
  Australia 17°59S 122°36E **60 C3**
Roermond *Neths.* 51°12N 6°0E **15 C6**
Roes Welcome Sd.
  Canada 65°0N 87°0W **69 E14**
Roeselare *Belgium* 50°57N 3°7E **15 D3**
Rogachev = Ragachow
  Belarus 53°8N 30°5E **17 B16**
Rogagua, L. *Bolivia* 13°43S 66°50W **92 F5**
Rogatyn *Ukraine* 49°24N 24°36E **17 D13**
Rogers *U.S.A.* 36°20N 94°7W **84 C7**
Rogers City *U.S.A.* 45°25N 83°49W **81 C12**
Rogersville *Canada* 46°44N 65°26W **73 C6**
Roggan → *Canada* 54°24N 79°25W **72 B4**
Roggan L. *Canada* 54°8N 77°50W **72 B4**
Roggeveen Basin
  Pac. Oc. 31°30S 95°30W **65 L18**
Roggeveldberge *S. Africa* 32°10S 20°10E **56 E3**
Rogoaguado, L. *Bolivia* 13°0S 65°30W **92 F5**
Rogojampi *Indonesia* 8°19S 114°17E **37 J17**
Rogue → *U.S.A.* 42°26N 124°26W **76 E1**
Rohnert Park *U.S.A.* 38°16N 122°40W **78 G4**
Rohri *Pakistan* 27°45N 68°51E **42 F3**
Rohri Canal *Pakistan* 26°15N 68°27E **42 F3**
Rohtak *India* 28°55N 76°43E **42 E7**
Roi Et *Thailand* 16°4N 103°40E **38 D4**
Roja *Latvia* 57°29N 22°43E **9 H20**
Rojas *Argentina* 34°10S 60°45W **94 C3**
Rojo, C. *Mexico* 21°33N 97°20W **87 C5**
Rokan → *Indonesia* 2°0N 100°50E **36 D2**
Rokiškis *Lithuania* 55°55N 25°35E **9 J21**
Rolândia *Brazil* 23°18S 51°23W **95 A5**
Rolla *Mo., U.S.A.* 37°57N 91°46W **80 G8**
Rolla *N. Dak., U.S.A.* 48°52N 99°37W **80 A4**
Rolleston *Australia* 24°28S 148°35E **62 C4**
Rollingstone *Australia* 19°2S 146°24E **62 B4**
Roma *Italy* 41°54N 12°28E **22 D5**
Roma *Sweden* 57°32N 18°26E **9 H18**
Roma-Los Saenz *U.S.A.* 26°24N 99°1W **84 H5**
Romain → *Canada* 33°0N 79°22W **85 E15**
Romaine → *Canada* 50°18N 63°47W **73 B7**
Roman *Romania* 46°57N 26°55E **17 E14**
Romang *Indonesia* 7°30S 127°20E **37 F7**
Români *Egypt* 30°59N 32°38E **46 E1**
Romania ■ *Europe* 46°0N 25°0E **17 F12**
Romano, Cayo *Cuba* 22°0N 77°30W **88 B4**
Romans-sur-Isère *France* 45°3N 5°3E **20 D6**
Romanzof C. *U.S.A.* 61°49N 166°6W **74 C6**
Romblon *Phil.* 12°33N 122°17E **37 B6**
Rome = Roma *Italy* 41°54N 12°28E **22 D5**
Rome *Ga., U.S.A.* 34°15N 85°10W **85 D12**
Rome *N.Y., U.S.A.* 43°13N 75°27W **83 C9**
Rome *Pa., U.S.A.* 41°51N 76°21W **83 E8**
Romney *U.S.A.* 39°21N 78°45W **81 F14**
Romney Marsh *U.K.* 51°2N 0°54E **13 F8**
Rømø *Denmark* 55°10N 8°30E **9 J13**
Romorantin-Lanthenay
  France 47°21N 1°45E **20 C4**
Romsdalen *Norway* 62°25N 7°52E **8 E12**
Romsey *U.K.* 51°0N 1°29W **13 G6**
Ron *Vietnam* 17°53N 106°27E **38 D6**
Rona *U.K.* 57°34N 5°59W **11 D3**
Ronan *U.S.A.* 47°32N 114°6W **76 C6**
Roncador, Cayos
  Colombia 13°32N 80°4W **88 D3**
Roncador, Serra do
  Brazil 12°30S 52°30W **93 F8**
Ronda *Spain* 36°46N 5°12W **21 D3**
Rondane *Norway* 61°57N 9°50E **8 F13**
Rondônia □ *Brazil* 11°0S 63°0W **92 F6**
Rondonópolis *Brazil* 16°28S 54°38W **93 G8**
Rondu *Pakistan* 35°32N 75°10E **43 B6**
Rong, Koh *Cambodia* 10°45N 103°15E **39 G4**
Ronge, L. la *Canada* 55°6N 105°17W **71 B7**
Rønne *Denmark* 55°6N 14°43E **9 J15**
Ronne Ice Shelf
  Antarctica 77°30S 60°0W **5 D18**
Ronsard, C. *Australia* 24°46S 113°10E **61 D1**
Ronse *Belgium* 50°45N 3°35E **15 D3**
Roodepoort *S. Africa* 26°11S 27°54E **57 D4**

Roof Butte *U.S.A.* 36°28N 109°5W **77 H9**
Rooiboklaagte →
  Namibia 20°50S 21°0E **56 C3**
Rooiu, Mt. *Tahiti* 17°49S 149°12W **59 d**
Roorkee *India* 29°52N 77°59E **42 E7**
Roosendaal *Neths.* 51°32N 4°29E **15 C4**
Roosevelt *U.S.A.* 40°18N 109°59W **76 F9**
Roosevelt → *Brazil* 7°35S 60°20W **92 E6**
Roosevelt, Mt. *Canada* 58°26N 125°20W **70 B3**
Roosevelt I. *Antarctica* 79°30S 162°0W **5 D12**
Roper → *Australia* 14°43S 135°27E **62 A2**
Roper Bar *Australia* 14°44S 134°44E **62 A1**
Roper River = St. Vidgeon's ◇
  Australia 14°47S 134°53E **62 A1**
Roque Pérez *Argentina* 35°25S 59°24W **94 D4**
Roquetas de Mar *Spain* 36°46N 2°36W **21 D4**
Roraima □ *Brazil* 2°0N 61°30W **92 C6**
Roraima, Mt. *Venezuela* 5°10N 60°40W **92 B6**
Røros *Norway* 62°35N 11°23E **8 E14**
Ros Comáin = Roscommon
  Ireland 53°38N 8°11W **10 C3**
Rosa *Zambia* 9°33S 31°15E **55 D3**
Rosa, Monte *Europe* 45°57N 7°53E **20 D7**
Rosalia *U.S.A.* 47°14N 117°22W **76 C5**
Rosamond *U.S.A.* 34°52N 118°10W **79 L8**
Rosario *Argentina* 33°0S 60°40W **94 C3**
Rosário *Brazil* 3°0S 44°15W **93 D10**
Rosario *Baja Calif.,*
  Mexico 30°0N 115°50W **86 B1**
Rosario *Sinaloa, Mexico* 22°58N 105°53W **86 C3**
Rosario *Paraguay* 24°30S 57°35W **94 A4**
Rosario de la Frontera
  Argentina 25°50S 65°0W **94 B3**
Rosario de Lerma
  Argentina 24°59S 65°35W **94 A2**
Rosario del Tala
  Argentina 32°20S 59°10W **94 C4**
Rosário do Sul *Brazil* 30°15S 54°55W **95 C5**
Rosarito *Mexico* 32°20N 117°2W **79 N9**
Roscoe *U.S.A.* 41°56N 74°55W **83 E10**
Roscommon *Ireland* 53°38N 8°11W **10 C3**
Roscommon □ *Ireland* 53°49N 8°23W **10 C3**
Roscrea *Ireland* 52°57N 7°49W **10 D4**
Rose → *Australia* 14°16S 135°45E **62 A2**
Rose, L. *Bahamas* 21°0N 73°30W **89 B5**
Rose Belle *Mauritius* 20°24S 57°36E **53 d**
Rose Blanche *Canada* 47°38N 58°45W **73 C8**
Rose Hill *Mauritius* 20°14S 57°27E **53 d**
Rose Pt. *Canada* 54°11N 131°39W **70 C2**
Rose Valley *Canada* 52°19N 103°49W **71 C8**
Roseau *Dominica* 15°17N 61°24W **89 C7**
Roseau *U.S.A.* 48°51N 95°46W **80 A6**
Rosebery *Australia* 41°46S 145°33E **63 G4**
Rosebud *S. Dak., U.S.A.* 43°14N 100°51W **80 D3**
Rosebud *Tex., U.S.A.* 31°4N 96°59W **84 F6**
Roseburg *U.S.A.* 43°13N 123°20W **76 E2**
Rosedale *U.S.A.* 33°51N 91°2W **85 E9**
Rosehearty *U.K.* 57°42N 2°7W **11 D6**
Roseires Res. *Sudan* 11°51N 34°23E **51 F12**
Roseland *U.S.A.* 38°25N 122°43W **78 G4**
Rosemary *Canada* 50°46N 112°5W **70 C6**
Rosenberg *U.S.A.* 29°34N 95°49W **84 G7**
Rosenheim *Germany* 47°51N 12°7E **16 E7**
Roses, G. de *Spain* 42°10N 3°15E **21 A7**
Rosetown *Canada* 51°35N 107°59W **71 C7**
Roseville *Calif., U.S.A.* 38°45N 121°17W **78 G5**
Roseville *Mich., U.S.A.* 42°30N 82°56W **82 D2**
Roseville *Pa., U.S.A.* 41°51N 76°57W **83 E8**
Rosewood *Australia* 27°38S 152°36E **63 D5**
Roshkhvār *Iran* 34°58N 59°37E **45 C8**
Rosignano Maríttimo
  Italy 43°24N 10°28E **22 C4**
Rosignol *Guyana* 6°15N 57°30W **92 B7**
Roșiori de Vede *Romania* 44°9N 25°0E **17 F13**
Roskilde *Denmark* 55°38N 12°3E **9 J15**
Roslavl *Russia* 53°57N 32°55E **18 D5**
Roslyn *Australia* 34°29N 149°36E **63 E4**
Rosmead *S. Africa* 31°29S 25°8E **56 E4**
Ross *Australia* 42°2S 147°30E **63 G4**
Ross *N.Z.* 42°53S 170°49E **59 E3**
Ross Dependency
  Antarctica 76°0S 170°0W **5 D12**
Ross I. *Antarctica* 77°30S 168°0E **5 D11**
Ross Ice Shelf *Antarctica* 80°0S 180°0E **5 E12**
Ross Mhic Thriúin = New Ross
  Ireland 52°23N 6°57W **10 D5**
Ross-on-Wye *U.K.* 51°54N 2°34W **13 F5**
Ross River *Australia* 23°44S 134°30E **62 C1**
Ross River *Canada* 62°30N 131°30W **70 A2**
Ross Sea *Antarctica* 74°0S 178°0E **5 D11**
Rossall Pt. *U.K.* 53°55N 3°3W **12 D4**
Rossan Pt. *Ireland* 54°42N 8°47W **10 B3**
Rossano *Italy* 39°36N 16°39E **22 E7**
Rossburn *Canada* 50°40N 100°49W **71 C8**
Rosseau *Canada* 45°16N 79°39W **82 A5**
Rosseau, L. *Canada* 45°10N 79°35W **82 A5**
Rosses, The *Ireland* 55°2N 8°20W **10 A3**
Rossignol, L. *Canada* 52°43N 73°40W **72 B5**
Rossignol, L. *Canada* 44°12N 65°10W **73 D6**
Rossiya = Russia ■
  Eurasia 62°0N 105°0E **29 C11**
Rossland *Canada* 49°6N 117°50W **70 D5**
Rosslare *Ireland* 52°17N 6°24W **10 D5**
Rosslare Harbour *Ireland* 52°15N 6°20W **10 D5**
Rossmore *Canada* 44°8N 77°23W **82 B7**
Rosso *Mauritania* 16°40N 15°45W **50 E2**
Rossosh *Russia* 50°15N 39°28E **19 D6**
Røssvatnet *Norway* 65°45N 14°5E **8 D16**
Røst *Norway* 67°32N 12°0E **8 C15**
Rosthern *Canada* 52°40N 106°20W **71 C7**
Rostock *Germany* 54°5N 12°8E **16 A7**
Rostov *Don, Russia* 47°15N 39°45E **19 E6**
Rostov *Yaroslavl, Russia* 57°14N 39°25E **18 C6**
Roswell *Ga., U.S.A.* 34°2N 84°22W **85 D12**
Roswell *N. Mex.,*
  U.S.A. 33°24N 104°32W **77 K11**
Rotan *U.S.A.* 32°51N 100°28W **84 E4**
Rother → *U.K.* 50°59N 0°45E **13 G8**
Rothera *Antarctica* 67°34S 68°8W **5 C17**

Rotherham *U.K.* 53°26N 1°20W **12 D6**
Rothes *U.K.* 57°32N 3°13W **11 D5**
Rothesay *Canada* 45°23N 66°0W **73 C6**
Rothesay *U.K.* 55°50N 5°3W **11 F3**
Roti *Indonesia* 10°50S 123°0E **37 F6**
Roto *Australia* 33°0S 145°30E **63 E4**
Rotondo, Mte. *France* 42°14N 9°8E **20 E8**
Rotoroa, L. *N.Z.* 41°55S 172°39E **59 D4**
Rotorua *N.Z.* 38°9S 176°16E **59 C6**
Rotorua, L. *N.Z.* 38°5S 176°18E **59 C6**
Rotterdam *Neths.* 51°55N 4°30E **15 C4**
Rotterdam *U.S.A.* 42°48N 74°1W **83 D10**
Rottnest I. *Australia* 32°0S 115°27E **61 F2**
Rottumeroog *Neths.* 53°33N 6°34E **15 A6**
Rottweil *Germany* 48°9N 8°37E **16 D5**
Rotuma *Fiji* 12°25S 177°5E **58 C10**
Roubaix *France* 50°40N 3°10E **20 A5**
Rouen *France* 49°27N 1°4E **20 B4**
Rouleau *Canada* 50°10N 104°56W **71 C8**
Roulpmaulpma ◇
  Australia 23°52S 133°0E **60 D5**
Round I. *Mauritius* 19°51S 57°45E **53 d**
Round Mountain
  U.S.A. 38°43N 117°4W **76 G5**
Round Mt. *Australia* 30°26S 152°16E **63 E5**
Round Rock *U.S.A.* 30°31N 97°41W **84 F6**
Roundup *U.S.A.* 46°27N 108°33W **76 C9**
Rousay *U.K.* 59°10N 3°2W **11 B5**
Rouses Point *U.S.A.* 44°59N 73°22W **83 B11**
Rouseville *U.S.A.* 41°28N 79°42W **82 E5**
Rousse = Ruse *Bulgaria* 43°48N 25°59E **23 C12**
Roussillon *France* 42°30N 2°35E **20 E5**
Rouxville *S. Africa* 30°25S 26°50E **56 E4**
Rouyn-Noranda *Canada* 48°20N 79°0W **72 C4**
Rovaniemi *Finland* 66°29N 25°41E **8 C21**
Rovereto *Italy* 45°53N 11°3E **22 B4**
Rovigo *Italy* 45°4N 11°47E **22 B4**
Rovinj *Croatia* 45°5N 13°40E **16 F7**
Rovno = Rivne *Ukraine* 50°40N 26°10E **17 C14**
Rovuma = Ruvuma →
  Tanzania 10°29S 40°28E **55 E5**
Row'ān *Iran* 35°8N 48°51E **45 C6**
Rowena *Australia* 29°48S 148°55E **63 D4**
Rowley I. *Canada* 69°6N 77°52W **69 D16**
Rowley Shoals *Australia* 17°30S 119°0E **60 C2**
Roxas *Phil.* 11°36N 122°49E **37 B6**
Roxboro *U.S.A.* 36°24N 78°59W **85 C15**
Roxborough
  Trin. & Tob. 11°15N 60°35W **93 J16**
Roxburgh *N.Z.* 45°33S 169°19E **59 F2**
Roxbury *N.Y., U.S.A.* 42°17N 74°33W **83 D10**
Roxbury *Pa., U.S.A.* 40°6N 77°39W **82 F7**
Roxby Downs *Australia* 30°43S 136°46E **63 E2**
Roy *Mont., U.S.A.* 47°20N 108°58W **76 C9**
Roy *N. Mex., U.S.A.* 35°57N 104°12W **77 J11**
Roy *Utah, U.S.A.* 41°10N 112°2W **76 F7**
Royal Bardia △ *Nepal* 28°20N 81°20E **43 E9**
Royal Canal *Ireland* 53°30N 7°13W **10 C4**
Royal Chitawan △
  Nepal 26°30N 84°30E **43 F11**
Royal Geographical Society Is.
  Canada 68°56N 100°15W **68 D11**
Royal Leamington Spa
  U.K. 52°18N 1°31W **13 E6**
Royal Natal △ *S. Africa* 28°43S 28°51E **57 D4**
Royal Tunbridge Wells
  U.K. 51°7N 0°16E **13 F8**
Royale, Isle *U.S.A.* 48°0N 88°54W **80 B9**
Royan *France* 45°37N 1°2W **20 D3**
Royston *U.K.* 52°3N 0°0 **13 E7**
Rozdilna *Ukraine* 46°50N 30°2E **17 E16**
Rozhyshche *Ukraine* 50°54N 25°15E **17 C13**
Rtishchevo *Russia* 52°18N 43°46E **18 D7**
Ruacaná *Namibia* 17°27S 14°21E **56 B1**
Ruaha △ *Tanzania* 7°41S 34°30E **54 D3**
Ruahine Ra. *N.Z.* 39°55S 176°2E **59 C6**
Ruapehu *N.Z.* 39°17S 175°35E **59 C5**
Ruapuke I. *N.Z.* 46°46S 168°31E **59 G2**
Ruâq, W. → *Egypt* 30°0N 33°49E **46 F2**
Rub' al Khālī *Si. Arabia* 19°0N 48°0E **47 D4**
Rubeho Mts. *Tanzania* 6°50S 36°25E **54 D4**
Rubh a' Mhail *U.K.* 55°56N 6°8W **11 F2**
Rubha Hunish *U.K.* 57°42N 6°20W **11 D2**
Rubha Robhanais = Lewis, Butt of
  U.K. 58°31N 6°16W **11 C2**
Rubicon → *U.S.A.* 38°53N 121°4W **78 G5**
Rubio *Venezuela* 7°43N 72°22W **92 B4**
Rubondo △ *Tanzania* 2°18S 31°58E **54 C3**
Rubtsovsk *Russia* 51°30N 81°10E **28 D9**
Ruby L. *U.S.A.* 40°10N 115°28W **76 F6**
Ruby Mts. *U.S.A.* 40°30N 115°20W **76 F6**
Rubyvale *Australia* 23°25S 147°42E **62 C4**
Rūd Sar *Iran* 37°8N 50°18E **45 B6**
Rudall *Australia* 33°43S 136°17E **63 E2**
Rudall → *Australia* 22°34S 122°13E **60 D3**
Rudall River △
  Australia 22°38S 122°30E **60 D3**
Rudbar *Iran* 36°48N 49°23E **45 B6**
Rudewa *Tanzania* 10°7S 34°40E **55 E3**
Rudnyy *Kazakhstan* 52°57N 63°7E **28 D7**
Rudolfa, Ostrov *Russia* 81°45N 58°30E **28 A6**
Rudyard *U.S.A.* 46°14N 84°36W **81 B11**
Ruenya → *Africa* 16°24S 33°48E **55 F3**
Ruffling Pt. *Br. Virgin Is.* 18°44N 64°27W **89 e**
Rufiji → *Tanzania* 7°50S 39°15E **54 D4**
Rufino *Argentina* 34°20S 62°50W **94 C3**
Rufunsa *Zambia* 15°4S 29°34E **55 F2**
Rugby *U.K.* 52°23N 1°16W **13 E6**
Rugby *U.S.A.* 48°22N 100°0W **80 A4**
Rügen *Germany* 54°22N 13°24E **16 A7**
Ruhengeri *Rwanda* 1°30S 29°36E **54 C2**
Ruhnu *Estonia* 57°48N 23°15E **9 H21**
Ruhr → *Germany* 51°27N 6°43E **16 C4**
Ruhuhu → *Tanzania* 10°31S 34°34E **55 E3**
Ruidoso *U.S.A.* 33°20N 105°41W **77 K11**
Ruivo, Pico *Madeira* 32°45N 16°56W **24 D3**
Rujm Tal'at al Jamā'ah
  Jordan 30°24N 35°30E **46 E4**
Ruk *Pakistan* 27°50N 68°42E **42 F3**

Rukhla *Pakistan* 32°27N 71°57E **42 C4**
Ruki →
  Dem. Rep. of the Congo 0°5N 18°17E **52 E3**
Rukwa □ *Tanzania* 7°0S 31°30E **54 D3**
Rukwa, L. *Tanzania* 8°0S 32°20E **54 D3**
Rulenge *Burundi* 2°43S 30°37E **54 C3**
Rulhieres, C. *Australia* 13°56S 127°22E **60 B4**
Rum = Rhum *U.K.* 57°0N 6°20W **11 E2**
Rum *Jordan* 29°39N 35°26E **46 F4**
Rum Cay *Bahamas* 23°40N 74°58W **89 B5**
Rum Jungle *Australia* 13°0S 130°59E **60 B5**
Ruma △ *Kenya* 0°39S 34°18E **54 C3**
Rumāḥ *Si. Arabia* 25°29N 47°10E **44 E5**
Rumania = Romania ■
  Europe 46°0N 25°0E **17 F12**
Rumaylah *Iraq* 30°47N 47°37E **44 D5**
Rumbêk *Sudan* 6°54N 29°37E **51 G11**
Rumford *U.S.A.* 44°33N 70°33W **83 B14**
Rumia *Poland* 54°37N 18°25E **17 A10**
Rumoi *Japan* 43°56N 141°39E **30 C10**
Rumonge *Burundi* 3°59S 29°26E **54 C2**
Rumphi *Malawi* 11°1S 33°52E **55 E3**
Rumson *U.S.A.* 40°23N 74°0W **83 F11**
Rumuruti *Kenya* 0°17N 36°32E **54 B4**
Runan *China* 33°0N 114°30E **34 H8**
Runanga *N.Z.* 42°25S 171°15E **59 E3**
Runaway, C. *N.Z.* 37°32S 177°59E **59 B6**
Runaway Bay *Jamaica* 18°27N 77°20W **88 a**
Runcorn *U.K.* 53°21N 2°44W **12 D5**
Rundu *Namibia* 17°52S 19°43E **56 B2**
Rungwa *Tanzania* 6°55S 33°32E **54 D3**
Rungwa → *Tanzania* 7°36S 31°50E **54 D3**
Rungwa △ *Tanzania* 6°53S 34°2E **54 D3**
Rungwe *Tanzania* 9°11S 33°32E **55 D3**
Rungwe, Mt. *Tanzania* 9°8S 33°40E **52 F6**
Runton Ra. *Australia* 23°31S 123°6E **60 D3**
Ruo Shui → *China* 41°0N 100°16E **32 B5**
Ruokolahti *Finland* 61°17N 28°50E **8 F23**
Ruoqiang *China* 38°55N 88°10E **32 C3**
Rupa *India* 27°15N 92°21E **41 F18**
Rupar *India* 31°2N 76°38E **42 D7**
Rupat *Indonesia* 1°45N 101°40E **36 D2**
Rupen → *India* 23°28N 71°31E **42 H4**
Rupert *U.S.A.* 42°37N 113°41W **76 E7**
Rupert → *Canada* 51°29N 78°45W **72 B4**
Rupert B. *Canada* 51°35N 79°0W **72 B4**
Rupert House = Waskaganish
  Canada 51°30N 78°40W **72 B4**
Rupsa *India* 21°37N 87°1E **43 J12**
Rurrenabaque *Bolivia* 14°30S 67°32W **92 F5**
Rusambo *Zimbabwe* 16°30S 32°4E **55 F3**
Rusape *Zimbabwe* 18°35S 32°8E **55 F3**
Ruschuk = Ruse
  Bulgaria 43°48N 25°59E **23 C12**
Ruse *Bulgaria* 43°48N 25°59E **23 C12**
Rush *Ireland* 53°31N 6°6W **10 C5**
Rushan *China* 36°56N 121°30E **35 F11**
Rushden *U.K.* 52°18N 0°35W **13 E7**
Rushmore, Mt. *U.S.A.* 43°53N 103°28W **80 D2**
Rushville *Ill., U.S.A.* 40°7N 90°34W **80 E8**
Rushville *Ind., U.S.A.* 39°37N 85°27W **81 F11**
Rushville *Nebr., U.S.A.* 42°43N 102°28W **80 D2**
Russas *Brazil* 4°55S 37°50W **93 D11**
Russell *Canada* 50°50N 101°20W **71 C8**
Russell *Kans., U.S.A.* 38°54N 98°52W **80 F4**
Russell *N.Y., U.S.A.* 44°27N 75°9W **83 B9**
Russell *Pa., U.S.A.* 41°56N 79°8W **82 E5**
Russell Cave △ *U.S.A.* 34°59N 85°49W **85 D12**
Russell I. *Man., Canada* 51°56N 101°30W **71 B8**
Russell L. *N.W.T.,*
  Canada 63°5N 115°44W **70 A5**
Russellkonda *India* 19°57N 84°42E **41 K14**
Russellville *Ala., U.S.A.* 34°30N 87°44W **85 D11**
Russellville *Ark., U.S.A.* 35°17N 93°8W **84 D8**
Russellville *Ky., U.S.A.* 36°51N 86°53W **80 G10**
Russia ■ *Eurasia* 62°0N 105°0E **29 C11**
Russian → *U.S.A.* 38°27N 123°8W **78 G3**
Rustam Shahr *Pakistan* 26°58N 66°6E **42 F2**
Rustavi *Georgia* 41°30N 45°0E **19 F8**
Rustenburg *S. Africa* 25°41S 27°14E **56 D4**
Ruston *U.S.A.* 32°32N 92°38W **84 E8**
Rutana *Burundi* 3°55S 30°0E **54 C3**
Ruteng *Indonesia* 8°35S 120°30E **37 F6**
Rutenga *Zimbabwe* 21°15S 30°44E **55 G3**
Ruth *U.S.A.* 43°42N 82°45W **82 C2**
Rutherford *U.S.A.* 38°26N 122°24W **78 G4**
Rutland *U.S.A.* 43°37N 72°58W **83 C12**
Rutland □ *U.K.* 52°38N 0°40W **13 E7**
Rutland Water *U.K.* 52°39N 0°38W **13 E7**
Rutledge → *Canada* 61°4N 112°0W **71 A6**
Rutledge L. *Canada* 61°33N 110°47W **71 A6**
Rutog *China* 33°27N 79°42E **32 C2**
Rutshuru
  Dem. Rep. of the Congo 1°13S 29°25E **54 C2**
Ruvu *Tanzania* 6°49S 38°43E **54 D4**
Ruvu → *Tanzania* 6°23S 38°52E **54 D4**
Ruvuba △ *Burundi* 3°3S 29°33E **54 C2**
Ruvuma □ *Tanzania* 10°20S 36°0E **55 E4**
Ruvuma → *Tanzania* 10°29S 40°28E **55 E5**
Ruwais *U.A.E.* 24°5N 52°50E **45 E7**
Ruwenzori *Africa* 0°30N 29°55E **54 B2**
Ruwenzori △ *Uganda* 0°20N 30°0E **54 B2**
Ruya → *Zimbabwe* 16°27S 32°5E **57 B5**
Ruyigi *Burundi* 3°29S 30°15E **54 C3**
Ruzhou *China* 34°11N 112°52E **34 G7**
Ružomberok *Slovak Rep.* 49°3N 19°17E **17 D10**
Rwanda ■ *Africa* 2°0S 30°0E **54 C3**
Ryan, L. *U.K.* 55°0N 5°2W **11 G3**
Ryazan *Russia* 54°40N 39°40E **18 D6**
Ryazhsk *Russia* 53°45N 40°3E **18 D7**
Rybachiy Poluostrov
  Russia 69°43N 32°0E **8 B25**
Rybachye = Balykchy
  Kyrgyzstan 42°26N 76°12E **32 B2**
Rybinsk *Russia* 58°5N 38°50E **18 C6**
Rybinskoye Vdkhr.
  Russia 58°30N 38°25E **18 C6**
Rybnitsa = Rábnița
  Moldova 47°45N 29°0E **17 E15**
Rycroft *Canada* 55°45N 118°40W **70 B5**

Ryde U.K.	50°43N 1°9W	13 G6	
Ryderwood U.S.A.	46°23N 123°3W	78 D3	
Rye U.K.	50°57N 0°45E	13 G8	
Rye → U.K.	54°11N 0°44W	12 C7	
Rye Bay U.K.	50°52N 0°49E	13 G8	
Rye Patch Res. U.S.A.	40°28N 118°19W	76 F4	
Ryegate U.S.A.	46°18N 109°15W	76 C9	
Ryley Canada	53°17N 112°26W	70 C6	
Rylstone Australia	32°46S 149°58E	63 E4	
Ryn Peski = Naryn Qum Kazakhstan	47°30N 49°0E	28 E5	
Ryōtsu Japan	38°5N 138°26E	30 E9	
Rypin Poland	53°3N 19°25E	17 B10	
Ryūgasaki Japan	35°54N 140°11E	31 G10	
Ryukyu Is. = Ryūkyū-rettō Japan	26°0N 126°0E	31 M3	
Ryūkyū-rettō Japan	26°0N 126°0E	31 M3	
Rzeszów Poland	50°5N 21°58E	17 C11	
Rzhev Russia	56°20N 34°20E	18 C5	

S

Sa Thailand	18°34N 100°45E	38 C3	
Sa Cabaneta Spain	39°37N 2°45E	24 B9	
Sa Canal Spain	38°51N 1°23E	24 C7	
Sa Conillera Spain	38°59N 1°13E	24 C7	
Sa Dec Vietnam	10°20N 105°46E	39 G5	
Sa Dragonera Spain	39°35N 2°19E	24 B9	
Sa Kaeo Thailand	13°49N 102°4E	38 F4	
Sa Mesquida Spain	39°55N 4°16E	24 B11	
Sa Pa Vietnam	22°20N 103°47E	38 A4	
Sa Savina Spain	38°44N 1°25E	24 C7	
Sa'ādatābād Fārs, Iran	30°10N 53°5E	45 D7	
Sa'ādatābād Hormozgān, Iran	28°3N 55°53E	45 D7	
Sa'ādatābād Kermān, Iran	29°40N 55°51E	45 D7	
Saale → Germany	51°56N 11°54E	16 C6	
Saalfeld Germany	50°38N 11°21E	16 C6	
Saanich Canada	48°29N 123°26W	78 B3	
Saar → Europe	49°41N 6°32E	15 E6	
Saarbrücken Germany	49°14N 6°59E	16 D4	
Saaremaa Estonia	58°30N 22°30E	9 G20	
Saarijärvi Finland	62°43N 25°16E	8 E21	
Saariselkä Finland	68°16N 28°15E	8 B23	
Sab 'Ābar Syria	33°46N 37°41E	44 C3	
Saba W. Indies	17°38N 63°14W	89 C7	
Šabac Serbia	44°48N 19°42E	23 B8	
Sabadell Spain	41°28N 2°7E	21 B7	
Sabah □ Malaysia	6°0N 117°0E	36 C5	
Sabak Malaysia	3°46N 100°58E	39 L3	
Sabalana, Kepulauan Indonesia	6°45S 118°50E	37 F5	
Sábana de la Mar Dom. Rep.	19°7N 69°24W	89 C6	
Sábanalarga Colombia	10°38N 74°55W	92 A4	
Sabang Indonesia	5°50N 95°15E	36 C1	
Sabarmati → India	22°18N 72°22E	42 H5	
Sabattis U.S.A.	44°6N 74°40W	83 B10	
Saberania Indonesia	2°5S 138°18E	37 E9	
Sabhā Libya	27°9N 14°29E	51 C8	
Sabi → India	28°29N 76°44E	42 E7	
Sabie S. Africa	25°10S 30°48E	57 D5	
Sabinal Mexico	30°57N 107°30W	86 A3	
Sabinal U.S.A.	29°19N 99°28W	84 G5	
Sabinas Mexico	27°51N 101°7W	86 B4	
Sabinas → Mexico	27°37N 100°42W	86 B4	
Sabinas Hidalgo Mexico	26°30N 100°10W	86 B4	
Sabine → U.S.A.	29°59N 93°47W	84 G8	
Sabine L. U.S.A.	29°53N 93°51W	84 G8	
Sabine Pass U.S.A.	29°44N 93°54W	84 G8	
Sablayan Phil.	12°50N 120°50E	37 B6	
Sable Canada	55°30N 68°21W	73 A6	
Sable, C. Canada	43°29N 65°38W	73 D6	
Sable, C. U.S.A.	25°9N 81°8W	88 A3	
Sable I. Canada	44°0N 60°0W	73 D8	
Sabrina Coast Antarctica	68°0S 120°0E	5 C9	
Sabulubbek Indonesia	1°36S 98°40E	36 E1	
Sabzevār Iran	36°15N 57°40E	45 B8	
Sabzvārān = Jiroft Iran	28°45N 57°50E	45 D8	
Sac City U.S.A.	42°25N 95°0W	80 D6	
Săcele Romania	45°37N 25°41E	17 F13	
Sacheon S. Korea	35°0N 128°6E	35 G15	
Sachigo → Canada	55°6N 88°58W	72 A2	
Sachigo, L. Canada	53°50N 92°12W	72 B1	
Sachimbo Angola	9°14S 20°16E	52 F4	
Sachsen □ Germany	50°55N 13°10E	16 C7	
Sachsen-Anhalt □ Germany	52°0N 12°0E	16 C7	
Sackets Harbor U.S.A.	43°57N 76°7W	83 C8	
Sackville Canada	45°54N 64°22W	73 C7	
Saco Maine, U.S.A.	43°30N 70°27W	83 C14	
Saco Mont., U.S.A.	48°28N 107°21W	76 B10	
Sacramento U.S.A.	38°35N 121°29W	78 G5	
Sacramento → U.S.A.	38°3N 121°56W	78 G5	
Sacramento Mts. U.S.A.	32°30N 105°30W	77 K11	
Sacramento Valley U.S.A.	39°30N 122°0W	78 G5	
Sada-Misaki Japan	33°20N 132°5E	31 H6	
Sadabad India	27°27N 78°3E	42 F8	
Sadani Tanzania	5°58S 38°35E	54 D4	
Sadani □ Tanzania	6°3S 38°47E	54 D4	
Sadao Thailand	6°38N 100°26E	39 J3	
Sadd el Aali Egypt	23°54N 32°54E	51 D12	
Saddle Mt. U.S.A.	45°58N 123°41W	78 E3	
Sadimi Dem. Rep. of the Congo	9°25S 23°32E	55 D1	
Sado Japan	38°0N 138°25E	30 F9	
Sadra India	23°21N 72°43E	42 H5	
Sadri India	25°11N 73°26E	42 G5	
Sæby Denmark	57°21N 10°30E	9 H14	
Saegertown U.S.A.	41°43N 80°9W	82 E4	
Şafājah Si. Arabia	26°25N 39°0E	44 E3	
Safata B. Samoa	14°0S 171°50W	59 b	

Safford U.S.A.	32°50N 109°43W	77 K9	
Saffron Walden U.K.	52°1N 0°16E	13 E8	
Safi Morocco	32°18N 9°20W	50 B4	
Şafiābād Iran	36°45N 57°58E	45 B8	
Safid Dasht Iran	33°27N 48°11E	45 C6	
Safid Kūh Afghan.	34°45N 63°0E	40 B3	
Safid Rūd → Iran	37°23N 50°11E	45 B6	
Safipur India	26°44N 80°21E	43 F9	
Şafītā Syria	34°48N 36°7E	44 C3	
Safune Samoa	13°25S 172°21W	59 b	
Şafwān Iraq	30°7N 47°43E	44 D5	
Sag Harbor U.S.A.	41°0N 72°18W	83 F12	
Saga Japan	33°15N 130°16E	31 H5	
Saga □ Japan	33°15N 130°20E	31 H5	
Sagae Japan	38°22N 140°17E	30 E10	
Sagaing Burma	21°52N 95°59E	41 J19	
Sagamore U.S.A.	40°46N 79°14W	82 F5	
Saganaga L. Canada	48°14N 90°52W	80 A8	
Sagar Karnataka, India	14°14N 75°6E	40 M9	
Sagar Mad. P., India	23°50N 78°44E	43 H8	
Sagara, L. Tanzania	5°20S 31°0E	54 D3	
Sagarmatha = Everest, Mt. Nepal	28°5N 86°58E	43 E12	
Sagarmatha △ Nepal	27°55N 86°45E	43 F12	
Saginaw U.S.A.	43°26N 83°56W	81 D12	
Saginaw B. U.S.A.	43°50N 83°40W	81 D12	
Saglouc = Salluit Canada	62°14N 75°38W	69 E16	
Sagone France	42°7N 8°42E	20 E8	
Sagone, G. of France	42°4N 8°40E	20 E8	
Sagua la Grande Cuba	22°50N 80°10W	88 B3	
Saguache U.S.A.	38°5N 106°8W	76 G10	
Saguaro △ U.S.A.	32°12N 110°38W	77 K8	
Saguenay → Canada	48°22N 71°0W	73 C5	
Sagunt Spain	39°42N 0°18W	21 C5	
Sagunto = Sagunt Spain	39°42N 0°18W	21 C5	
Sagwara India	23°41N 74°1E	42 H6	
Sahagún Spain	42°18N 5°2W	21 A3	
Saham al Jawlān Syria	32°45N 35°55E	46 C4	
Sahamandrevo Madag.	23°15S 45°35E	57 C8	
Sahand, Kūh-e Iran	37°44N 46°27E	44 B5	
Sahara Africa	23°0N 5°0E	50 D6	
Saharan Atlas = Saharien, Atlas Algeria	33°30N 1°0E	50 B6	
Saharanpur India	29°58N 77°33E	42 E7	
Saharien, Atlas Algeria	33°30N 1°0E	50 B6	
Saharsa India	25°53N 86°36E	43 G12	
Sahasinaka Madag.	21°49S 47°49E	57 C8	
Sahaswan India	28°5N 78°45E	43 E8	
Sahibganj India	25°12N 87°40E	43 G12	
Sāhīlīyah Iraq	33°43N 42°42E	44 C4	
Sahiwal Pakistan	30°45N 73°8E	42 D5	
Sahneh Iran	34°29N 47°41E	44 C5	
Sahrawi = Western Sahara ■ Africa	25°0N 13°0W	50 D3	
Sahuaripa Mexico	29°3N 109°14W	86 B3	
Sahuarita U.S.A.	31°57N 110°58W	77 L8	
Sahuayo de Díaz Mexico	20°4N 102°43W	86 C4	
Sai → India	25°39N 82°47E	43 G10	
Sai Buri Thailand	6°43N 101°45E	39 J3	
Sai Kung China	22°23N 114°16E	33 G11	
Sai Twong △ Thailand	15°56N 101°10E	38 E3	
Sai Yok △ Thailand	14°25N 98°40E	38 E2	
Saibai I. Australia	9°25S 142°40E	62 a	
Sa'id Bundãs Sudan	8°24N 24°48E	51 G10	
Sa'īdābād = Sīrjān Iran	29°30N 55°45E	45 D7	
Sa'īdābād Iran	36°8N 54°11E	45 B7	
Sa'īdīyeh Iran	36°20N 48°55E	45 B6	
Saidpur Bangla.	25°48N 89°0E	41 G16	
Saidpur India	25°33N 83°11E	43 G10	
Saidu Sharif Pakistan	34°43N 72°24E	43 B5	
Saigō Japan	36°12N 133°20E	31 F6	
Saigon = Thanh Pho Ho Chi Minh Vietnam	10°58N 106°40E	39 G6	
Saijō Japan	33°55N 133°11E	31 H6	
Saikai △ Japan	33°11N 129°36E	31 H4	
Saikanosy Masoala Madag.	15°45S 50°10E	57 B9	
Saikhoa Ghat India	27°50N 95°40E	41 F19	
Saiki Japan	32°58N 131°51E	31 H5	
Sā'il Si. Arabia	27°28N 41°45E	44 E4	
Sailana India	23°28N 74°56E	42 H6	
Sailolof Indonesia	1°15S 130°46E	37 E8	
Saimaa Finland	61°15N 28°15E	8 F23	
Saimen = Saimaa Finland	61°15N 28°15E	8 F23	
Şa'in Dezh Iran	36°40N 46°25E	44 B5	
St. Abb's Head U.K.	55°55N 2°8W	11 F6	
St. Alban's Canada	47°51N 55°50W	73 C8	
St. Albans U.K.	51°45N 0°19W	13 F7	
St. Albans Vt., U.S.A.	44°49N 73°5W	83 B11	
St. Albans W. Va., U.S.A.	38°23N 81°50W	81 F13	
St. Alban's Head U.K.	50°34N 2°4W	13 G5	
St. Albert Canada	53°37N 113°32W	70 C6	
St-André Réunion	20°57S 55°39E	53 c	
St. Andrew's Canada	47°45N 59°15W	73 C8	
St. Andrews U.K.	56°20N 2°47W	11 E6	
St-Anicet Canada	45°8N 74°22W	83 A10	
St. Annes Canada	49°40N 96°39W	71 D9	
St. Anns B. Canada	46°22N 60°25W	73 C7	
St. Ann's Bay Jamaica	18°26N 77°12W	88 a	
St. Anthony Canada	51°22N 55°35W	73 B8	
St-Antoine Canada	46°22N 64°45W	73 C7	
St. Arnaud Australia	36°40S 143°16E	63 F3	
St-Augustin Canada	51°13N 58°38W	73 B8	
St-Augustin → Canada	51°16N 58°40W	73 B8	
St. Augustine U.S.A.	29°54N 81°19W	85 G14	
St. Austell U.K.	50°20N 4°47W	13 G3	
St-Barbe Canada	51°12N 56°46W	73 B8	
St-Barthélemy W. Indies	17°50N 62°50W	89 C7	
St. Bees Hd. U.K.	54°31N 3°38W	12 C4	
St. Bees I. Australia	20°56S 149°26E	62 b	
St-Benoît Réunion	21°2S 55°43E	53 c	
St. Bride's Canada	46°56N 54°10W	73 C9	
St. Brides B. U.K.	51°49N 5°9W	13 F2	
St-Brieuc France	48°30N 2°46W	20 B2	

St. Catharines Canada	43°10N 79°15W	82 C5	
St. Catherines I. U.S.A.	31°40N 81°10W	85 F14	
St. Catherine's Pt. U.K.	50°34N 1°18W	13 G6	
St-Chamond France	45°28N 4°31E	20 D6	
St. Charles Ill., U.S.A.	41°54N 88°19W	80 E9	
St. Charles Md., U.S.A.	38°36N 76°56W	81 F15	
St. Charles Mo., U.S.A.	38°47N 90°29W	80 F8	
St. Charles Va., U.S.A.	36°48N 83°4W	81 G12	
St. Christopher-Nevis = St. Kitts & Nevis ■ W. Indies	17°20N 62°40W	89 C7	
St. Clair Mich., U.S.A.	42°50N 82°30W	82 D2	
St. Clair Pa., U.S.A.	40°43N 76°12W	83 F8	
St. Clair → U.S.A.	42°38N 82°31W	82 D2	
St. Clair, L. N. Amer.	42°27N 82°39W	82 D2	
St. Clairsville U.S.A.	40°5N 80°54W	82 F4	
St. Claude Canada	49°40N 98°20W	71 D9	
St. Clears U.K.	51°49N 4°31W	13 F3	
St-Clet Canada	45°21N 74°13W	83 A10	
St. Cloud Fla., U.S.A.	28°15N 81°17W	85 G14	
St. Cloud Minn., U.S.A.	45°34N 94°10W	80 C6	
St. Cricq, C. Australia	25°17S 113°6E	61 E1	
St. Croix → U.S. Virgin Is.	17°45N 64°45W	89 C7	
St. Croix → U.S.A.	44°45N 92°48W	80 C7	
St. Croix Falls U.S.A.	45°24N 92°38W	80 C7	
St. David's Canada	48°12N 58°52W	73 C8	
St. David's U.K.	51°53N 5°16W	13 F2	
St. David's Head U.K.	51°54N 5°19W	13 F1	
St-Denis France	48°56N 2°20E	20 B5	
St-Denis Réunion	20°52S 55°27E	53 c	
St-Denis ✈ (RUN) Réunion	20°53S 55°32E	53 c	
St-Dizier France	48°38N 4°56E	20 B6	
St. Elias, Mt. U.S.A.	60°18N 140°56W	68 E3	
St. Elias Mts. N. Amer.	60°33N 139°28W	70 A1	
St-Étienne France	45°27N 4°22E	20 D6	
St. Eugène Canada	45°30N 74°28W	83 A10	
St. Eustatius W. Indies	17°20N 63°0W	89 C7	
St-Félicien Canada	48°40N 72°25W	72 C5	
St-Flour France	45°2N 3°6E	20 D5	
St. Francis U.S.A.	39°47N 101°48W	80 F3	
St. Francis → U.S.A.	34°38N 90°36W	85 D9	
St. Francis, C. S. Africa	34°14S 24°49E	56 E3	
St. Francisville U.S.A.	30°47N 91°23W	84 F9	
St-François, L. Canada	45°10N 74°22W	83 A10	
St-Gabriel Canada	46°17N 73°24W	72 C5	
St. Gallen = Sankt Gallen Switz.	47°26N 9°22E	20 C8	
St-Gaudens France	43°6N 0°44E	20 E4	
St. George Australia	28°1S 148°30E	63 D4	
St. George N.B., Canada	45°11N 66°50W	73 C6	
St. George Ont., Canada	43°15N 80°15W	82 C4	
St. George S.C., U.S.A.	33°11N 80°35W	85 E14	
St. George Utah, U.S.A.	37°6N 113°35W	77 H7	
St. George, C. Canada	48°30N 59°16W	73 C8	
St. George, C. U.S.A.	29°40N 85°5W	85 G12	
St. George I. U.S.A.	56°35N 169°35W	74 D6	
St. George Ra. Australia	18°40S 125°0E	60 C4	
St-Georges Canada	48°26N 58°31W	73 C8	
St-Georges Canada	46°8N 70°40W	73 C5	
St. George's Grenada	12°5N 61°43W	89 D7	
St. George's B. Canada	48°24N 58°53W	73 C8	
St. Georges Basin N.S.W., Australia	35°7S 150°36E	63 F5	
St. Georges Basin W. Austral., Australia	15°23S 125°2E	60 C4	
St. George's Channel Europe	52°0N 6°0W	10 E6	
St. Georges Hd. Australia	35°12S 150°42E	63 F5	
St. Gotthard P. = San Gottardo, P. del Switz.	46°33N 8°33E	20 C8	
St. Helena Atl. Oc.	15°58S 5°42W	48 H3	
St. Helena U.S.A.	38°30N 122°28W	76 G2	
St. Helena, Mt. U.S.A.	38°40N 122°36W	78 G4	
St. Helena B. S. Africa	32°40S 18°10E	56 E2	
St. Helens Australia	41°20S 148°15E	63 G4	
St. Helens U.K.	53°27N 2°44W	12 D5	
St. Helens U.S.A.	45°52N 122°48W	78 E4	
St. Helens, Mt. U.S.A.	46°12N 122°12W	78 D4	
St. Helier U.K.	49°10N 2°7W	13 H5	
St-Hubert Belgium	50°2N 5°23E	15 D5	
St-Hubert Canada	45°29N 73°25W	83 A11	
St-Hyacinthe Canada	45°40N 72°58W	72 C5	
St. Ignace Canada	45°8N 84°44W	81 C11	
St. Ignace I. Canada	48°45N 88°0W	72 C2	
St. Ignatius U.S.A.	47°19N 114°6W	76 C6	
St. Ives Cambs., U.K.	52°20N 0°4W	13 E7	
St. Ives Corn., U.K.	50°12N 5°30W	13 G2	
St. James U.S.A.	43°59N 94°38W	80 D6	
St-Jean → Canada	50°17N 64°20W	73 B7	
St-Jean, L. Canada	48°40N 72°0W	73 C5	
St-Jean-Port-Joli Canada	47°15N 70°13W	73 C5	
St-Jean-sur-Richelieu Canada	45°20N 73°20W	83 A11	
St-Jérôme Canada	45°47N 74°0W	72 C5	
St. John Canada	45°20N 66°8W	73 C6	
St. John U.S.A.	38°0N 98°46W	80 F4	
St. John → N. Amer.	45°12N 66°5W	81 C20	
St. John, C. Canada	50°0N 55°32W	73 C8	
St. John's Antigua & B.	17°6N 61°51W	89 C7	
St. John's Canada	47°35N 52°40W	73 C9	
St. Johns Ariz., U.S.A.	34°30N 109°22W	77 J9	
St. Johns Mich., U.S.A.	43°0N 84°33W	81 D11	
St. Johns → U.S.A.	30°24N 81°24W	85 F14	
St. John's Pt. Ireland	54°34N 8°27W	10 B3	
St. Johnsbury U.S.A.	44°25N 72°1W	83 B12	
St. Johnsville U.S.A.	43°0N 74°43W	83 D10	
St. Joseph Canada	43°24N 81°42W	82 C3	
St-Joseph Martinique	14°39N 61°4W	88 c	
St-Joseph Réunion	21°22S 55°37E	53 c	
St. Joseph La., U.S.A.	31°55N 91°14W	84 F9	
St. Joseph Mo., U.S.A.	39°46N 94°50W	80 F7	
St. Joseph → U.S.A.	42°7N 86°29W	80 D10	
St. Joseph, I. Canada	46°12N 83°58W	72 C3	
St. Joseph, L. Canada	51°10N 90°35W	72 B1	
St-Jovite Canada	46°8N 74°38W	72 C5	
St. Kilda U.K.	57°49N 8°34W	14 C2	
St. Kitts & Nevis ■ W. Indies	17°20N 62°40W	89 C7	

St. Laurent Canada	50°25N 97°58W	71 C9	
St-Laurent Australia	22°16S 149°31E	62 C4	
St. Lawrence Canada	46°54N 55°23W	73 C8	
St. Lawrence → Canada	49°30N 66°0W	73 C6	
St. Lawrence, Gulf of Canada	48°25N 62°0W	73 C7	
St. Lawrence I. U.S.A.	63°30N 170°30W	74 C5	
St. Lawrence Islands △ Canada	44°27N 75°52W	83 B9	
St-Léonard Canada	47°12N 67°58W	73 C6	
St-Leu Réunion	21°9S 55°18E	53 c	
St. Lewis → Canada	52°26N 56°11W	73 B8	
St-Lô France	49°7N 1°5W	20 B3	
St-Louis Guadeloupe	15°56N 61°19W	88 b	
St-Louis Réunion	21°16S 55°25E	53 c	
St. Louis Senegal	16°8N 16°27W	50 E2	
St. Louis U.S.A.	38°37N 90°11W	80 F8	
St. Louis → U.S.A.	46°44N 92°9W	80 B7	
St-Luc Canada	45°22N 73°18W	83 A11	
St. Lucia ■ W. Indies	14°0N 60°57W	89 f	
St. Lucia, L. S. Africa	28°5S 32°30E	57 D5	
St. Lucia Channel W. Indies	14°15N 61°0W	89 D7	
St-Maarten ☑ W. Indies	18°0N 63°5W	89 C7	
St. Magnus B. U.K.	60°25N 1°35W	11 A7	
St-Malo France	48°39N 2°1W	20 B2	
St-Marc Haiti	19°10N 72°41W	89 C5	
St. Maries U.S.A.	47°19N 116°35W	76 C5	
St-Martin ☑ W. Indies	18°0N 63°0W	89 C7	
St. Martin, C. Martinique	14°52N 61°14W	88 c	
St. Martin, L. Canada	51°40N 98°30W	71 C9	
St. Martins Barbados	13°5N 59°28W	89 g	
St. Mary Pk. Australia	31°32S 138°34E	63 E2	
St. Marys Australia	41°35S 148°11E	63 G4	
St. Marys Canada	43°20N 81°10W	82 C3	
St. Mary's Corn., U.K.	49°55N 6°18W	13 H1	
St. Mary's Orkney, U.K.	58°54N 2°54W	11 C6	
St. Marys Ga., U.S.A.	30°44N 81°33W	85 F14	
St. Marys Pa., U.S.A.	41°26N 78°34W	82 E6	
St. Mary's, C. Canada	46°50N 54°12W	73 C9	
St. Mary's B. Canada	46°50N 53°50W	73 C9	
St. Mary's Bay Canada	44°25N 66°10W	73 D6	
St-Mathieu, Pte. France	48°20N 4°45W	20 B1	
St. Matthew I. U.S.A.	60°24N 172°42W	74 C5	
St-Maurice → Canada	46°21N 72°31W	72 C5	
St. Mawes U.K.	50°10N 5°1W	13 G2	
St-Nazaire France	47°17N 2°12W	20 C2	
St. Neots U.K.	52°14N 0°15W	13 E7	
St-Niklaas Belgium	51°10N 4°8E	15 C4	
St-Omer France	50°45N 2°15E	20 A5	
St-Pamphile Canada	46°58N 69°48W	73 C6	
St-Pascal Canada	47°32N 69°48W	73 C6	
St. Paul Canada	54°0N 111°17W	70 C6	
St. Paul Réunion	20°59S 55°17E	53 c	
St. Paul Minn., U.S.A.	44°56N 93°5W	80 C7	
St. Paul Nebr., U.S.A.	41°13N 98°27W	80 E4	
St-Paul → Canada	51°27N 57°42W	73 B8	
St. Paul, I. Ind. Oc.	38°55S 77°34E	3 F13	
St. Paul I. Canada	47°12N 60°9W	73 C7	
St. Paul I. U.S.A.	57°10N 170°15W	74 D5	
St. Peter U.S.A.	44°20N 93°57W	80 C7	
St. Peter Port U.K.	49°26N 2°33W	13 H5	
St. Peters N.S., Canada	45°40N 60°53W	73 C7	
St. Peters P.E.I., Canada	46°25N 62°35W	73 C7	
St. Petersburg = Sankt-Peterburg Russia	59°55N 30°20E	9 G24	
St. Petersburg U.S.A.	27°46N 82°40W	85 H13	
St-Phillippe Réunion	21°21S 55°44E	53 c	
St-Pie Canada	45°30N 72°54W	83 A12	
St-Pierre Martinique	14°45N 61°10W	88 c	
St-Pierre Réunion	21°19S 55°28E	53 c	
St-Pierre St-P. & M.	46°46N 56°12W	73 C8	
St-Pierre, L. Canada	46°12N 72°52W	72 C5	
St-Pierre-et-Miquelon ☑ N. Amer.	46°55N 56°10W	73 C8	
St-Quentin Canada	47°30N 67°23W	73 C6	
St-Quentin France	49°50N 3°16E	20 B5	
St. Regis U.S.A.	47°18N 115°6W	76 C6	
St. Regis Falls U.S.A.	44°40N 74°32W	83 B10	
St. Sebastien, Tanjon' i Madag.	12°26S 48°44E	57 A8	
St-Siméon Canada	47°51N 69°54W	73 C6	
St. Simons I. U.S.A.	31°12N 81°15W	85 F14	
St. Simons Island U.S.A.	31°9N 81°22W	85 F14	
St. Stephen Canada	45°16N 67°17W	73 C6	
St. Thomas Canada	42°45N 81°10W	82 D3	
St. Thomas I. U.S. Virgin Is.	18°20N 64°55W	89 e	
St-Tite Canada	46°45N 72°34W	72 C5	
St-Tropez France	43°17N 6°38E	20 E7	
St-Troud = St. Truiden Belgium	50°48N 5°10E	15 D5	
St. Truiden Belgium	50°48N 5°10E	15 D5	
St. Vidgeon's ◎ Australia	14°47S 134°53E	62 A1	
St. Vincent = São Vicente C. Verde Is.	17°0N 25°0W	50 b	
St. Vincent, G. Australia	35°0S 138°0E	63 F2	
St. Vincent & the Grenadines ■ W. Indies	13°0N 61°10W	89 D7	
St. Vincent Passage W. Indies	13°30N 61°0W	89 D7	
St-Vith Belgium	50°17N 6°9E	15 D6	
St. Walburg Canada	53°39N 109°12W	71 C7	
Ste-Agathe-des-Monts Canada	46°3N 74°17W	72 C5	
Ste-Anne Guadeloupe	16°13N 61°24W	88 b	
Ste-Anne Seychelles	4°36S 55°31E	53 b	
Ste-Anne, L. Canada	50°0N 67°42W	73 B6	
Ste-Anne-des-Monts Canada	49°8N 66°30W	73 C6	
Ste. Genevieve U.S.A.	37°59N 90°2W	80 G8	
Ste-Marguerite → Canada	50°9N 66°36W	73 B6	
Ste-Marie Canada	46°26N 71°0W	73 C5	
Ste-Marie Martinique	14°48N 61°1W	88 c	
Ste-Marie, Ile = Nosy Boraha Madag.	16°50S 49°55E	57 B8	

Ste-Rose Guadeloupe	16°20N 61°45W	88 b	
Ste-Rose Réunion	21°8S 55°45E	53 c	
Ste. Rose du Lac Canada	51°4N 99°30W	71 C9	
Saintes France	45°45N 0°37W	20 D3	
Saintes, Îs. des Guadeloupe	15°50N 61°35W	88 b	
Saintfield U.K.	54°28N 5°49W	10 B6	
Saintonge France	45°40N 0°50W	20 D3	
Saipan N. Marianas	15°12N 145°45E	64 F6	
Sairang India	23°50N 92°45E	41 H18	
Sairecábur, Cerro Bolivia	22°43S 67°54W	94 A2	
Saitama Japan	35°54N 139°38E	31 G9	
Saitama □ Japan	36°25N 139°30E	31 F9	
Saiyid Pakistan	33°7N 73°2E	42 C5	
Sajama Bolivia	18°7S 69°0W	92 G5	
Sajószentpéter Hungary	48°12N 20°44E	17 D11	
Sajum India	33°20N 79°0E	43 C8	
Sak → S. Africa	30°52S 20°25E	56 E3	
Saka Kenya	0°9S 39°20E	54 C4	
Sakai Japan	34°34N 135°27E	31 G7	
Sakaide Japan	34°19N 133°50E	31 G6	
Sakaiminato Japan	35°38N 133°11E	31 G6	
Sakākah Si. Arabia	30°0N 40°8E	44 D4	
Sakakawea, L. U.S.A.	47°30N 101°25W	80 B3	
Sakami → Canada	53°40N 76°40W	72 B4	
Sakami, L. Canada	53°15N 77°0W	72 B4	
Sakania Dem. Rep. of the Congo	12°43S 28°30E	55 E2	
Sakaraha Madag.	22°55S 44°32E	57 C7	
Sakartvelo = Georgia ■ Asia	42°0N 43°0E	19 F7	
Sakarya Turkey	40°48N 30°25E	19 F5	
Sakashima-Guntō Japan	24°46N 124°0E	31 M2	
Sakata Japan	38°55N 139°50E	30 E9	
Sakchu N. Korea	40°23N 125°2E	35 D13	
Sakeny → Madag.	20°0S 45°25E	57 C8	
Sakha □ Russia	66°0N 130°0E	29 C14	
Sakhalin Russia	51°0N 143°0E	29 D15	
Sakhalinskiy Zaliv Russia	54°0N 141°0E	29 D15	
Šakiai Lithuania	54°59N 23°2E	9 J20	
Sakon Nakhon Thailand	17°10N 104°9E	38 D5	
Sakrand Pakistan	26°10N 68°15E	42 F3	
Sakri India	26°13N 86°5E	43 F12	
Sakrivier S. Africa	30°54S 20°28E	56 E3	
Sakti India	22°2N 82°58E	43 H10	
Sakurai Japan	35°3N 137°49E	31 G8	
Sakata Japan	34°30N 135°51E	31 G7	
Sal C. Verde Is.	16°45N 22°55W	50 b	
Sal Rei C. Verde Is.	16°11N 22°53W	50 b	
Sala Sweden	59°58N 16°35E	9 G17	
Sala Consilina Italy	40°23N 15°36E	22 D6	
Sala-y-Gómez Pac. Oc.	26°28S 105°28W	65 K17	
Sala y Gómez Ridge Pac. Oc.	25°0S 98°0W	65 K18	
Salaberry-de-Valleyfield Canada	45°15N 74°8W	83 A10	
Salada, L. Mexico	32°20N 115°40W	77 K6	
Saladas Argentina	28°15S 58°40W	94 B4	
Saladillo Argentina	35°40S 59°55W	94 D4	
Salado → B. Aires, Argentina	35°44S 57°22W	94 D4	
Salado → La Pampa, Argentina	37°30S 67°0W	96 D3	
Salado → Santa Fe, Argentina	31°40S 60°41W	94 C3	
Salado → Mexico	26°52N 99°19W	84 H5	
Salaga Ghana	8°31N 0°31W	50 G5	
Şalāḥ Syria	32°40N 36°45E	46 C5	
Şalāh ad Dīn □ Iraq	34°35N 43°35E	44 C4	
Salakos Greece	36°17N 27°57E	25 C9	
Salālah Oman	16°56N 53°59E	47 D5	
Salamanca Chile	31°46S 70°59W	94 C1	
Salamanca Spain	40°58N 5°39W	21 B3	
Salamanca U.S.A.	42°10N 78°43W	82 D6	
Salāmatābād Iran	35°39N 47°50E	44 C5	
Salamina Greece	37°56N 23°30E	23 F10	
Salamis Cyprus	35°11N 33°54E	25 D12	
Salar de Atacama Chile	23°30S 68°25W	94 A2	
Salar de Uyuni Bolivia	20°30S 67°45W	92 H5	
Salatiga Indonesia	7°19S 110°30E	37 G14	
Salavat Russia	53°21N 55°55E	18 D10	
Salaverry Peru	8°15S 79°0W	92 E3	
Salawati Indonesia	1°7S 130°52E	37 E8	
Salaya India	22°19N 69°35E	42 H3	
Salayar Indonesia	6°7S 120°30E	37 F6	
S'Albufera Spain	39°47N 3°7E	24 B10	
Salcombe U.K.	50°14N 3°47W	13 G4	
Saldanha S. Africa	33°0S 17°58E	56 E2	
Saldanha B. S. Africa	33°6S 18°0E	56 E2	
Saldus Latvia	56°38N 22°30E	9 H20	
Sale Australia	38°6S 147°6E	63 F4	
Salé Morocco	34°3N 6°48W	50 B4	
Sale U.K.	53°26N 2°19W	12 D5	
Salekhard Russia	66°30N 66°35E	28 C7	
Salelologa Samoa	13°41S 172°11W	59 b	
Salem India	11°40N 78°11E	40 P11	
Salem Ill., U.S.A.	38°38N 88°57W	80 F9	
Salem Ind., U.S.A.	38°36N 86°6W	80 F10	
Salem Mass., U.S.A.	42°31N 70°53W	83 D14	
Salem Mo., U.S.A.	37°39N 91°32W	80 G8	
Salem N.H., U.S.A.	42°45N 71°12W	83 D13	
Salem N.J., U.S.A.	39°34N 75°28W	81 F16	
Salem N.Y., U.S.A.	43°10N 73°20W	83 C11	
Salem Ohio, U.S.A.	40°54N 80°52W	82 F4	
Salem Oreg., U.S.A.	44°56N 123°2W	76 D2	
Salem Va., U.S.A.	37°18N 80°3W	81 G13	
Salerno Italy	40°41N 14°47E	22 D6	
Salford U.K.	53°30N 2°18W	12 D5	
Salgótarján Hungary	48°5N 19°47E	17 D10	
Salgueiro Brazil	8°4S 39°6W	93 E11	
Salibabu Indonesia	3°51N 126°40E	37 D7	
Salibea = Salybia Trin. & Tob.	10°43N 61°2W	93 K15	
Salida U.S.A.	38°32N 106°0W	75 H10	
Salihli Turkey	38°28N 28°8E	23 E13	
Salihorsk Belarus	52°51N 27°27E	17 B14	
Salima Malawi	13°47S 34°28E	53 G6	

Salina *Italy* 38°34N 14°50E **22** E6
Salina *Kans., U.S.A.* 38°50N 97°37W **80** F5
Salina *Utah, U.S.A.* 38°58N 111°51W **76** G8
Salina Cruz *Mexico* 16°10N 95°12W **87** D5
Salinas *Brazil* 16°10S 42°10W **93** G10
Salinas *Ecuador* 2°10S 80°58W **92** D2
Salinas *U.S.A.* 36°40N 121°39W **78** J5
Salinas → *Guatemala* 16°28N 90°31W **87** D6
Salinas → *U.S.A.* 36°45N 121°48W **78** J5
Salinas, B. de *Nic.* 11°4N 85°45W **88** D2
Salinas, Pampa de las
  Argentina 31°58S 66°42W **94** C2
Salinas Ambargasta
  Argentina 29°0S 65°0W **94** B3
Salinas de Hidalgo
  Mexico 22°38N 101°43W **86** C4
Salinas Grandes *Argentina* 30°0S 65°0W **94** C3
Salinas Pueblo Missions △
  U.S.A. 34°6N 106°4W **77** J10
Salinas Valley *U.S.A.* 36°15N 121°15W **78** J5
Saline → *Ark., U.S.A.* 33°10N 92°8W **84** E8
Saline → *Kans., U.S.A.* 38°52N 97°30W **80** F5
Salines, C. de ses *Spain* 39°16N 3°4E **24** B10
Salinópolis *Brazil* 0°40S 47°20W **93** D9
Salisbury *Australia* 34°46S 138°38E **63** E2
Salisbury *U.K.* 51°4N 1°47W **13** F6
Salisbury *Md., U.S.A.* 38°22N 75°36W **81** F16
Salisbury *N.C., U.S.A.* 35°40N 80°29W **85** D14
Salisbury I. *Canada* 63°30N 77°0W **69** E16
Salisbury Plain *U.K.* 51°14N 1°55W **13** F6
Şalkhad *Syria* 32°29N 36°43E **46** C5
Salla *Finland* 66°50N 28°49E **8** C23
Salliq = Coral Harbour
  Canada 64°8N 83°10W **69** E15
Sallisaw *U.S.A.* 35°28N 94°47W **84** D7
Salluit *Canada* 62°14N 75°38W **69** E16
Salmās *Iran* 38°11N 44°47E **44** B5
Salmo *Canada* 49°10N 117°20W **70** D5
Salmon *U.S.A.* 45°11N 113°54W **76** D7
Salmon → *Canada* 54°3N 122°40W **70** C4
Salmon → *U.S.A.* 45°51N 116°47W **76** D5
Salmon Arm *Canada* 50°40N 119°15W **70** C5
Salmon Gums *Australia* 32°59S 121°38E **61** F3
Salmon Pt. *Canada* 43°52N 77°15W **82** C7
Salmon River Mts.
  U.S.A. 44°50N 115°30W **76** D6
Salmon River Res.
  U.S.A. 43°32N 75°55W **83** C9
Salo *Finland* 60°22N 23°10E **9** F20
Salome *U.S.A.* 33°47N 113°37W **79** M13
Salon *India* 26°2N 81°27E **43** F9
Salon-de-Provence *France* 43°39N 5°6E **20** E6
Salonica = Thessaloniki
  Greece 40°38N 22°58E **23** D10
Salonta *Romania* 46°49N 21°42E **17** E11
Salpausselkä *Finland* 61°3N 26°15E **8** F22
Salsacate *Argentina* 31°20S 65°5W **94** C2
Salsk *Russia* 46°28N 41°30E **19** E7
Salso → *Italy* 37°6N 13°57E **22** F5
Salt → *Canada* 60°0N 112°25W **70** B6
Salt → *U.S.A.* 33°23N 112°19W **77** K7
Salt Fork Red → *U.S.A.* 34°27N 99°21W **84** D5
Salt L. *Australia* 30°6S 142°8E **63** E3
Salt Lake City *U.S.A.* 40°45N 111°53W **76** F8
Salt Range *Pakistan* 32°30N 72°25E **42** C5
Salta *Argentina* 24°57S 65°25W **94** A2
Salta □ *Argentina* 24°48S 65°30W **94** A2
Saltash *U.K.* 50°24N 4°14W **13** G3
Saltburn by the Sea *U.K.* 54°35N 0°58W **12** C7
Saltcoats *U.K.* 55°38N 4°47W **11** F4
Saltee Is. *Ireland* 52°7N 6°37W **10** D5
Saltfjellet *Norway* 66°40N 15°15E **8** C16
Saltfjorden *Norway* 67°15N 14°10E **8** C16
Saltillo *Mexico* 25°25N 101°0W **86** B4
Salto *Argentina* 34°20S 60°15W **94** C3
Salto *Uruguay* 31°27S 57°50W **94** C4
Salto → *Italy* 42°26N 12°25E **22** C5
Salto del Guairá *Paraguay* 24°3S 54°17W **95** A5
Salton City *U.S.A.* 33°18N 115°57W **79** M11
Salton Sea *U.S.A.* 33°15N 115°45W **79** M11
Saltsburg *U.S.A.* 40°29N 79°27W **82** F5
Saluda → *U.S.A.* 34°1N 81°4W **85** D14
Salûm *Egypt* 31°31N 25°7E **51** B11
Salur *India* 18°27N 83°18E **41** K13
Salvador *Brazil* 13°0S 38°30W **93** F11
Salvador *Canada* 52°10N 109°32W **71** C7
Salvador, El ■
  Cent. Amer. 13°50N 89°0W **88** D2
Salvador, L. *U.S.A.* 29°43N 90°15W **85** G9
Salween → *Burma* 16°31N 97°37E **41** L20
Salyan *Azerbaijan* 39°33N 48°59E **45** B6
Salybia *Trin. & Tob.* 10°43N 61°2W **93** K15
Salzach → *Austria* 48°12N 12°56E **16** D7
Salzburg *Austria* 47°48N 13°2E **16** E7
Salzgitter *Germany* 52°9N 10°19E **16** B6
Salzwedel *Germany* 52°52N 11°10E **16** B6
Sam *India* 26°50N 70°31E **42** F4
Sam Neua *Laos* 20°29N 104°5E **38** B5
Sam Ngao *Thailand* 17°18N 99°0E **38** D2
Sam Rayburn Res. *U.S.A.* 31°4N 94°5W **84** F7
Sam Son *Vietnam* 19°44N 105°54E **38** C5
Sam Teu *Laos* 19°59N 104°38E **38** C5
Sama de Langreo = Langreo
  Spain 43°18N 5°40W **21** A3
Samagaltay *Russia* 50°36N 95°3E **29** D10
Samales Group *Phil.* 6°0N 122°0E **37** C6
Samana *India* 30°10N 76°13E **42** D7
Samana Cay *Bahamas* 23°3N 73°45W **89** B5
Samanga *Tanzania* 8°20S 39°13E **55** D4
Samangān □ *Afghan.* 36°15N 68°3E **40** B5
Samangwa
  Dem. Rep. of the Congo 4°23S 24°10E **54** C1
Samani *Japan* 42°7N 142°56E **30** C11
Samar *Phil.* 12°0N 125°0E **37** B7
Samara *Russia* 53°8N 50°6E **18** D9
Samaria = Shōmrōn
  West Bank 32°15N 35°13E **46** C4
Samaria △ *Greece* 35°17N 23°58E **25** D5
Samarinda *Indonesia* 0°30S 117°9E **36** E5

Samarkand = Samarqand
  Uzbekistan 39°40N 66°55E **28** F7
Samarqand *Uzbekistan* 39°40N 66°55E **28** F7
Sāmarrā' *Iraq* 34°12N 43°52E **44** C4
Samastipur *India* 25°50N 85°50E **43** G11
Samba
  Dem. Rep. of the Congo 4°38S 26°22E **54** C2
Samba *India* 32°32N 75°10E **43** C6
Sambalpur *India* 21°28N 84°4E **41** J14
Sambar, Tanjung
  Indonesia 2°59S 110°19E **36** E4
Sambas *Indonesia* 1°20N 109°20E **36** D3
Sambava *Madag.* 14°16S 50°10E **57** A9
Sambawizi *Zimbabwe* 18°24S 26°13E **55** F2
Sambhajinagar = Aurangabad
  India 19°50N 75°23E **40** K9
Sambhal *India* 28°35N 78°37E **43** E8
Sambhar *India* 26°52N 75°6E **42** F6
Sambhar L. *India* 26°55N 75°12E **42** F6
Sambiase *Italy* 38°58N 16°17E **22** E7
Sambir *Ukraine* 49°30N 23°10E **17** D12
Sambor *Cambodia* 12°46N 106°0E **38** F6
Samborombón, B.
  Argentina 36°5S 57°20W **94** D4
Samburu △ *Kenya* 0°37N 37°31E **54** B4
Samcheok *S. Korea* 37°30N 129°10E **35** F15
Same *Tanzania* 4°2S 37°38E **54** C4
Samfya *Zambia* 11°22S 29°31E **55** E2
Samnah *Si. Arabia* 25°10N 37°15E **44** E3
Samo Alto *Chile* 30°22S 71°0W **94** C1
Samoa ■ *Pac. Oc.* 14°0S 172°0W **59** b
Samokov *Bulgaria* 42°18N 23°35E **23** C10
Samos *Greece* 37°45N 26°50E **23** F12
Samothráki = Mathraki
  Greece 39°48N 19°31E **25** A3
Samothraki *Greece* 40°28N 25°28E **23** D11
Sampacho *Argentina* 33°20S 64°50W **94** C3
Sampalan *Indonesia* 8°41S 115°34E **37** K18
Sampang *Indonesia* 7°11S 113°13E **37** G15
Sampit *Indonesia* 2°34S 113°0E **36** E4
Sampit, Teluk *Indonesia* 3°5S 113°3E **36** E4
Samrong *Cambodia* 14°15N 103°30E **38** E4
Samrong *Thailand* 15°10N 100°40E **38** E3
Samsø *Denmark* 55°50N 10°35E **9** J14
Samsun *Turkey* 41°15N 36°22E **19** F6
Samui, Ko *Thailand* 9°30N 100°0E **39** b
Samusole
  Dem. Rep. of the Congo 10°2S 24°0E **55** E1
Samut Prakan *Thailand* 13°40N 100°36E **38** F3
Samut Songkhram
  Thailand 13°24N 100°1E **38** F3
Samwari *Pakistan* 28°30N 66°46E **42** E2
San *Mali* 13°15N 4°57W **50** F5
San → *Cambodia* 13°32N 105°57E **38** F5
San → *Poland* 50°45N 21°51E **17** C11
San Agustin, C. *Phil.* 6°20N 126°13E **37** C7
San Agustín de Valle Fértil
  Argentina 30°35S 67°30W **94** C2
San Ambrosio *Pac. Oc.* 26°28S 79°53W **90** F3
San Andrés, I. de
  Caribbean 12°42N 81°46W **88** D3
San Andres Mts.
  U.S.A. 33°0N 106°30W **77** K10
San Andrés Tuxtla
  Mexico 18°27N 95°13W **87** D5
San Angelo *U.S.A.* 31°28N 100°26W **84** F4
San Anselmo *U.S.A.* 37°59N 122°34W **78** H4
San Antonio *Belize* 16°15N 89°2W **87** D7
San Antonio *Chile* 33°40S 71°40W **94** C1
San Antonio *N. Mex.,
  U.S.A.* 33°55N 106°52W **77** K10
San Antonio *Tex.,
  U.S.A.* 29°25N 98°29W **84** G5
San Antonio → *U.S.A.* 28°30N 96°54W **84** G6
San Antonio, C.
  Argentina 36°15S 56°40W **94** D4
San Antonio, C. de Cuba 21°50N 84°57W **88** B3
San Antonio, Mt.
  U.S.A. 34°17N 117°38W **79** L9
San Antonio de los Baños
  Cuba 22°54N 82°31W **88** B3
San Antonio de los Cobres
  Argentina 24°10S 66°17W **94** A2
San Antonio Oeste
  Argentina 40°40S 65°0W **96** E4
San Ardo *U.S.A.* 36°1N 120°54W **78** J6
San Augustín *Canary Is.* 27°47N 15°32W **24** G4
San Augustine *U.S.A.* 31°32N 94°7W **84** F7
San Bartolomé
  Canary Is. 28°59N 13°37W **24** F6
San Bartolomé de Tirajana
  Canary Is. 27°54N 15°34W **24** G4
San Benedetto del Tronto
  Italy 42°57N 13°53E **22** C5
San Benedicto, I.
  Mexico 19°18N 110°49W **86** D2
San Benito *U.S.A.* 26°8N 97°38W **84** H6
San Benito → *U.S.A.* 36°53N 121°34W **78** J5
San Benito Mt. *U.S.A.* 36°22N 120°37W **78** J6
San Bernardino *U.S.A.* 34°7N 117°19W **79** L9
San Bernardino Mts.
  U.S.A. 34°10N 116°45W **79** L10
San Bernardino Str. *Phil.* 13°0N 125°0E **37** B7
San Bernardo *Chile* 33°40S 70°50W **94** C1
San Bernardo, I. de
  Colombia 9°45N 75°50W **92** B3
San Blas *Mexico* 26°5N 108°46W **86** B3
San Blas, Arch. de
  Panama 9°50N 78°31W **88** E4
San Blas, C. *U.S.A.* 29°40N 85°21W **85** G12
San Borja *Bolivia* 14°50S 66°52W **92** F5
San Buenaventura = Ventura
  U.S.A. 34°17N 119°18W **79** L7
San Buenaventura
  Mexico 27°5N 101°32W **86** B4
San Carlos = Sant Carles
  Spain 39°3N 1°34E **24** B8
San Carlos *Argentina* 33°50S 69°0W **94** C2

San Carlos *Chile* 36°10S 72°0W **94** D1
San Carlos *Baja Calif. S.,
  Mexico* 24°47N 112°7W **86** C2
San Carlos *Coahuila,
  Mexico* 29°1N 100°51W **86** B4
San Carlos *Nic.* 11°12N 84°50W **88** D3
San Carlos *Phil.* 10°29N 123°25E **37** B6
San Carlos *Uruguay* 34°46S 54°58W **95** C5
San Carlos *Venezuela* 9°40N 68°36W **92** B5
San Carlos de Bariloche
  Argentina 41°10S 71°25W **96** E2
San Carlos de Bolívar
  Argentina 36°15S 61°6W **94** D3
San Carlos del Zulia
  Venezuela 9°1N 71°55W **92** B4
San Carlos L. *U.S.A.* 33°11N 110°32W **77** K8
San Clemente *Chile* 35°30S 71°29W **94** D1
San Clemente *U.S.A.* 33°26N 117°37W **79** M9
San Clemente I. *U.S.A.* 32°53N 118°29W **79** N8
San Cristóbal = Es Migjorn Gran
  Spain 39°57N 4°3E **24** B11
San Cristóbal *Argentina* 30°20S 61°10W **94** C3
San Cristóbal *Dom. Rep.* 18°25N 70°6W **89** C5
San Cristóbal *Solomon Is.* 10°30S 161°0E **58** C9
San Cristóbal *Venezuela* 7°46N 72°14W **92** B4
San Cristóbal de las Casas
  Mexico 16°45N 92°38W **87** D6
San Diego *Calif., U.S.A.* 32°42N 117°9W **79** N9
San Diego *Tex., U.S.A.* 27°46N 98°14W **84** H5
San Diego, C. *Argentina* 54°40S 65°10W **96** G3
San Diego de la Unión
  Mexico 21°28N 100°52W **86** C4
San Diego Int. ✈ (SAN)
  U.S.A. 32°44N 117°11W **79** N9
San Dimitri, Ras *Malta* 36°4N 14°11E **25** C1
San Dimitri Point = San Dimitri,
  Ras *Malta* 36°4N 14°11E **25** C1
San Estanislao *Paraguay* 24°39S 56°26W **94** A4
San Felipe *Chile* 32°43S 70°42W **94** C1
San Felipe *Mexico* 31°1N 114°52W **86** A2
San Felipe *Venezuela* 10°20N 68°44W **92** A5
San Felipe → *U.S.A.* 33°10N 115°49W **79** M11
San Félix *Chile* 28°56S 70°28W **94** B1
San Félix *Pac. Oc.* 26°23S 80°0W **90** F2
San Fernando = Sant Ferran
  Spain 38°42N 1°28E **24** C7
San Fernando *Chile* 34°30S 71°0W **94** C1
San Fernando *Mexico* 24°51N 98°10W **87** C5
San Fernando *La Union,
  Phil.* 16°40N 120°23E **37** A6
San Fernando *Pampanga,
  Phil.* 15°5N 120°37E **37** A6
San Fernando *Spain* 36°28N 6°17W **21** D2
San Fernando
  Trin. & Tob. 10°16N 61°28W **93** K15
San Fernando *U.S.A.* 34°17N 118°26W **79** L8
San Fernando de Apure
  Venezuela 7°54N 67°15W **92** B5
San Fernando de Atabapo
  Venezuela 4°3N 67°42W **92** C5
San Francisco *Argentina* 31°30S 62°5W **94** C3
San Francisco *U.S.A.* 37°46N 122°23W **78** H4
San Francisco →
  U.S.A. 32°59N 109°22W **77** K9
San Francisco, C. de
  Colombia 6°18N 77°29W **90** C3
San Francisco, Paso de
  S. Amer. 27°0S 68°0W **94** B2
San Francisco de Macorís
  Dom. Rep. 19°19N 70°15W **89** C5
San Francisco del Monte de Oro
  Argentina 32°36S 66°8W **94** C2
San Francisco del Oro
  Mexico 26°52N 105°51W **86** B3
San Francisco Int. ✈ (SFO)
  U.S.A. 37°37N 122°22W **78** H4
San Francisco Javier = Sant
  Francesc de Formentera
  Spain 38°42N 1°26E **24** C7
San Gabriel *Chile* 33°47S 70°15W **94** C1
San Gabriel Chilac
  Mexico 18°19N 97°21W **87** D5
San Gabriel Mts.
  U.S.A. 34°17N 117°38W **79** L9
San Gavino Monreale
  Italy 39°33N 8°47E **22** E3
San German *Puerto Rico* 18°4N 67°4W **89** d
San Gorgonio Mt.
  U.S.A. 34°6N 116°50W **79** L10
San Gottardo, P. del
  Switz. 46°33N 8°33E **20** C8
San Gregorio *Uruguay* 32°37S 55°40W **95** C4
San Gregorio *U.S.A.* 37°20N 122°23W **78** H4
San Guillermo △
  Argentina 27°50S 69°45W **94** B2
San Ignacio *Belize* 17°10N 89°5W **87** D7
San Ignacio *Bolivia* 16°20S 60°55W **92** G6
San Ignacio *Mexico* 27°27N 112°51W **86** B2
San Ignacio *Paraguay* 26°52S 57°3W **94** B4
San Ignacio, L. *Mexico* 26°54N 113°13W **86** B2
San Ildefonso, C. *Phil.* 16°0N 122°1E **37** A6
San Isidro *Argentina* 34°29S 58°31W **94** C4
San Jacinto *U.S.A.* 33°47N 116°57W **79** M10
San Jaime = Sant Jaume
  Spain 39°54N 4°4E **24** B11
San Javier *Misiones,
  Argentina* 27°55S 55°5W **95** B4
San Javier *Santa Fe,
  Argentina* 30°40S 59°55W **94** C4
San Javier *Bolivia* 16°18S 62°30W **92** G6
San Javier *Chile* 35°40S 71°45W **94** D1
San Jerónimo Taviche
  Mexico 16°44N 96°35W **87** D5
San Joaquin *U.S.A.* 36°36N 120°11W **78** J6
San Joaquin → *U.S.A.* 38°4N 121°51W **78** G5
San Joaquin Valley
  U.S.A. 37°20N 121°0W **78** J6
San Jon *U.S.A.* 35°6N 103°20W **77** J12

San Jordi = Sant Jordi
  Spain 39°33N 2°46E **24** B9
San Jorge *Argentina* 31°54S 61°50W **94** C3
San Jorge, B. *Mexico* 31°20N 113°20W **86** A2
San Jorge, G. *Argentina* 46°0S 66°0W **96** F3
San José = San Josep
  Spain 38°55N 1°18E **24** C7
San José *Argentina* 32°12S 58°15W **94** C4
San José *Costa Rica* 9°55N 84°2W **88** E3
San José *Guatemala* 14°0N 90°50W **88** D1
San Jose *Mind. Occ., Phil.* 12°27N 121°4E **37** B6
San Jose *Nueva Ecija,
  Phil.* 15°45N 120°55E **37** A6
San Jose *U.S.A.* 37°20N 121°53W **78** H5
San Jose → *U.S.A.* 34°25N 106°45W **77** J10
San José, I. *Mexico* 25°0N 110°38W **86** C2
San Jose de Buenavista
  Phil. 10°45N 121°56E **37** B6
San José de Chiquitos
  Bolivia 17°53S 60°50W **92** G6
San José de Feliciano
  Argentina 30°26S 58°46W **94** C4
San José de Jáchal
  Argentina 30°15S 68°46W **94** C2
San José de Mayo
  Uruguay 34°27S 56°40W **94** C4
San José del Cabo
  Mexico 23°3N 109°41W **86** C3
San José del Guaviare
  Colombia 2°35N 72°38W **92** C4
San Josep *Spain* 38°55N 1°18E **24** C7
San Juan *Argentina* 31°30S 68°30W **94** C2
San Juan *Puerto Rico* 18°28N 66°7W **89** d
San Juan *Trin. & Tob.* 10°39N 61°29W **93** K15
San Juan □ *Argentina* 31°9S 69°0W **94** C2
San Juan → *Argentina* 32°20S 67°25W **94** C2
San Juan → *Nic.* 10°56N 83°42W **88** D3
San Juan → *U.S.A.* 37°16N 110°26W **77** H8
San Juan Bautista = Sant Joan de
  Labritja *Spain* 39°5N 1°31E **24** B8
San Juan Bautista
  Paraguay 26°37S 57°6W **94** B4
San Juan Bautista
  U.S.A. 36°51N 121°32W **78** J5
San Juan Capistrano
  U.S.A. 33°30N 117°40W **79** M9
San Juan Cr. → *U.S.A.* 35°40N 120°22W **78** J5
San Juan de Guadalupe
  Mexico 24°38N 102°44W **86** C4
San Juan de la Costa
  Mexico 24°20N 110°41W **86** C2
San Juan de los Lagos
  Mexico 21°15N 102°18W **86** C4
San Juan de los Morros
  Venezuela 9°55N 67°21W **92** B5
San Juan del Norte *Nic.* 10°58N 83°40W **88** D3
San Juan del Norte, B. de
  Nic. 11°0N 83°40W **88** D3
San Juan del Río *Mexico* 20°23N 100°0W **87** C5
San Juan del Sur *Nic.* 11°20N 85°51W **88** D2
San Juan I. *U.S.A.* 48°32N 123°5W **78** B3
San Juan Island △
  U.S.A. 48°35N 123°8W **78** B4
San Juan Mts. *U.S.A.* 37°30N 107°0W **77** H10
San Justo *Argentina* 30°47S 60°30W **94** C3
San Kamphaeng *Thailand* 18°45N 99°8E **38** C2
San Lázaro, C. *Mexico* 24°50N 112°18W **86** C2
San Leandro *U.S.A.* 37°44N 122°9W **78** H4
San Lorenzo = Sant Llorenç des
  Cardassar *Spain* 39°37N 3°17E **24** B10
San Lorenzo *Argentina* 32°45S 60°45W **94** C3
San Lorenzo *Ecuador* 1°15N 78°50W **92** C3
San Lorenzo *Paraguay* 25°20S 57°32W **94** B4
San Lorenzo → *Mexico* 24°15N 107°24W **86** C3
San Lorenzo, I. *Mexico* 28°38N 112°51W **86** B2
San Lorenzo, Mte.
  Argentina 47°40S 72°20W **96** F2
San Lucas = Cabo San Lucas
  Mexico 22°53N 109°54W **86** C3
San Lucas *Bolivia* 20°5S 65°7W **92** H5
San Lucas *Mexico* 27°10N 112°14W **86** B2
San Lucas, C. *Mexico* 22°52N 109°53W **86** C3
San Lucas, C. *Mexico* 36°8N 121°1W **78** J5
San Luis *Argentina* 33°20S 66°20W **94** C2
San Luis *Cuba* 22°17N 83°46W **88** B3
San Luis *Guatemala* 16°14N 89°27W **88** C2
San Luis *Ariz., U.S.A.* 32°29N 114°47W **77** K6
San Luis *Colo., U.S.A.* 37°12N 105°25W **77** H11
San Luis □ *Argentina* 34°0S 66°0W **94** C2
San Luis, I. *Mexico* 29°58N 114°26W **86** B2
San Luis, Sierra de
  Argentina 32°30S 66°10W **94** C2
San Luis de la Paz
  Mexico 21°18N 100°31W **86** C4
San Luis Obispo *U.S.A.* 35°17N 120°40W **79** K6
San Luis Potosí *Mexico* 22°9N 100°59W **86** C4
San Luis Potosí □ *Mexico* 23°0N 101°0W **86** C4
San Luis Res. *U.S.A.* 37°4N 121°5W **78** H5
San Luis Río Colorado
  Mexico 32°29N 114°58W **86** A2
San Manuel *U.S.A.* 32°36N 110°38W **77** K8
San Marcos *Guatemala* 14°59N 91°52W **88** D1
San Marcos *Calif.,
  U.S.A.* 33°9N 117°10W **79** M9
San Marcos *Tex., U.S.A.* 29°53N 97°56W **84** G6
San Marcos, I. *Mexico* 27°13N 112°6W **86** B2
San Marino *Europe* 43°56N 12°25E **22** C5
San Marino ■ *Europe* 43°56N 12°25E **22** C5
San Martín *Antarctica* 68°11S 67°0W **5** C17
San Martín *Argentina* 33°5S 68°28W **94** C2
San Martín → *Bolivia* 13°8S 63°43W **92** F6
San Martín, L. *Argentina* 48°50S 72°50W **96** F2
San Martín de los Andes
  Argentina 40°10S 71°20W **96** E2
San Mateo = Sant Mateu
  Spain 39°3N 1°23E **24** B7
San Mateo *U.S.A.* 37°34N 122°19W **78** H4
San Matías *Bolivia* 16°25S 58°20W **92** G7
San Matías, G. *Argentina* 41°30S 64°0W **96** E4

San Miguel = Sant Miquel
  Spain 39°3N 1°26E **24** B7
San Miguel *El Salv.* 13°30N 88°12W **88** D2
San Miguel *Panama* 8°27N 78°55W **88** E4
San Miguel *U.S.A.* 35°45N 120°42W **78** K6
San Miguel → *Bolivia* 13°52S 63°56W **92** F6
San Miguel de Tucumán
  Argentina 26°50S 65°20W **94** B2
San Miguel del Monte
  Argentina 35°23S 58°50W **94** D4
San Miguel I. *U.S.A.* 34°2N 120°23W **79** L6
San Nicolás *Canary Is.* 27°58N 15°47W **24** G4
San Nicolás de los Arroyos
  Argentina 33°25S 60°10W **94** C3
San Nicolas I. *U.S.A.* 33°15N 119°30W **79** M7
San Onofre *U.S.A.* 33°22N 117°34W **79** M9
San Pablo *Bolivia* 21°43S 66°38W **94** A2
San Pablo *U.S.A.* 37°58N 122°21W **78** H4
San Pedro *B. Aires,
  Argentina* 33°40S 59°40W **94** C4
San Pedro *Chile* 33°54S 71°28W **94** C1
San Pedro *Ivory C.* 4°50N 6°33W **50** H4
San Pedro *Mexico* 23°55N 110°17W **86** C2
San Pedro □ *Paraguay* 24°0S 57°0W **94** A4
San Pedro → *Chihuahua,
  Mexico* 28°20N 106°10W **86** B3
San Pedro → *Nayarit,
  Mexico* 21°45N 105°30W **86** C3
San Pedro → *U.S.A.* 32°59N 110°47W **77** K8
San Pedro, Pta. *Chile* 25°30S 70°38W **94** B1
San Pedro Channel
  U.S.A. 33°30N 118°25W **79** M8
San Pedro de Atacama
  Chile 22°55S 68°15W **94** A2
San Pedro de Jujuy
  Argentina 24°12S 64°55W **94** A3
San Pedro de las Colonias
  Mexico 25°45N 102°59W **86** B4
San Pedro de Macorís
  Dom. Rep. 18°30N 69°18W **89** C6
San Pedro del Norte *Nic.* 13°4N 84°33W **88** D3
San Pedro del Paraná
  Paraguay 26°43S 56°13W **94** B4
San Pedro Mártir, Sierra
  Mexico 31°0N 115°30W **86** A1
San Pedro Mártir △
  Mexico 31°0N 115°21W **86** A1
San Pedro Ocampo = Melchor
  Ocampo *Mexico* 24°51N 101°39W **86** C4
San Pedro Pochutla
  Mexico 15°44N 96°28W **87** D5
San Pedro Sula *Honduras* 15°30N 88°0W **88** C2
San Pedro Tututepec
  Mexico 16°9N 97°38W **87** D5
San Pietro *Italy* 39°8N 8°17E **22** E3
San Rafael *Argentina* 34°40S 68°21W **94** C2
San Rafael *Calif., U.S.A.* 37°58N 122°32W **78** H4
San Rafael *N. Mex.,
  U.S.A.* 35°7N 107°53W **77** J10
San Rafael Mt. *U.S.A.* 34°41N 119°52W **79** L7
San Rafael Mts. *U.S.A.* 34°40N 119°50W **79** L7
San Ramón de la Nueva Orán
  Argentina 23°10S 64°20W **94** A3
San Remo *Italy* 43°49N 7°46E **20** E7
San Roque *Argentina* 28°25S 58°45W **94** B4
San Roque *Spain* 36°17N 5°21W **21** D3
San Rosendo *Chile* 37°16S 72°43W **94** D1
San Saba *U.S.A.* 31°12N 98°43W **84** F5
San Salvador *El Salv.* 13°40N 89°10W **88** D2
San Salvador de Jujuy
  Argentina 24°10S 64°48W **94** A3
San Salvador I. *Bahamas* 24°0N 74°40W **89** B5
San Sebastián = Donostia-San
  Sebastián *Spain* 43°17N 1°58W **21** A5
San Sebastián *Argentina* 53°10S 68°30W **96** G3
San Sebastián *Puerto Rico* 18°20N 66°59W **89** d
San Sebastián de la Gomera
  Canary Is. 28°5N 17°7W **24** F2
San Serra = Son Serra
  Spain 39°43N 3°13E **24** B10
San Severo *Italy* 41°41N 15°23E **22** D6
San Simeon *U.S.A.* 35°39N 121°11W **78** K5
San Simon *U.S.A.* 32°16N 109°14W **77** K9
San Telmo = Sant Elm
  Spain 39°35N 2°21E **24** B9
San Telmo *Mexico* 30°58N 116°6W **86** A1
San Tiburcio *Mexico* 24°8N 101°32W **86** C4
San Valentin, Mte. *Chile* 46°30S 73°30W **96** F2
San Vicente de Cañete
  Peru 13°8S 76°30W **92** F3
San Vicente de la Barquera
  Spain 43°23N 4°29W **21** A3
San Vito *Costa Rica* 8°50N 82°58W **88** E3
Sana' *Yemen* 15°27N 44°12E **47** D3
Sana → *Bos.-H.* 45°3N 16°23E **16** F9
Sanae IV *Antarctica* 70°20S 9°0W **5** D2
Sanaga → *Cameroon* 3°35N 9°38E **54** D1
Sanak I. *U.S.A.* 54°25N 162°40W **74** E7
Sanaloa, Presa *Mexico* 24°50N 107°20W **86** C3
Sanana *Indonesia* 2°4S 125°58E **37** E7
Sanand *India* 22°59N 72°25E **42** H5
Sanandaj *Iran* 35°18N 47°1E **44** C5
Sanandita *Bolivia* 21°40S 63°45W **94** A3
Sanawad *India* 22°11N 76°5E **42** H7
Sancellas = Sencelles
  Spain 39°39N 2°54E **24** B9
Sanchahe *China* 44°50N 126°2E **35** B14
Sánchez *Dom. Rep.* 19°15N 69°36W **89** C6
Sanchor *India* 24°45N 71°55E **42** G4
Sancti Spíritus *Cuba* 21°52N 79°33W **88** B4
Sancy, Puy de *France* 45°32N 2°50E **20** D5
Sand → Polokwane →
  S. Africa 22°25S 30°5E **57** C5
Sand Hills *U.S.A.* 42°10N 101°30W **80** D3
Sand Lakes △ *Canada* 57°51N 98°32W **71** B9
Sand Springs *U.S.A.* 36°9N 96°7W **84** C6
Sanda *Japan* 34°53N 135°14E **31** G7

Sandakan *Malaysia* 5°53N 118°4E **36 C5**
Sandan = Sambor
  Cambodia 12°46N 106°0E **38 F6**
Sandanski *Bulgaria* 41°35N 23°16E **23 D10**
Sanday *U.K.* 59°16N 2°31W **11 B6**
Sandefjord *Norway* 59°10N 10°15E **9 G14**
Sanders *U.S.A.* 35°13N 109°20W **77 J9**
Sandersville *U.S.A.* 32°59N 82°48W **85 E13**
Sandfire Roadhouse
  Australia 19°45S 121°15E **60 C3**
Sandfly L. *Canada* 55°43N 106°6W **71 B7**
Sandfontein *Namibia* 23°48S 19°1E **56 C2**
Sandheads, The *India* 21°10N 88°20E **43 J13**
Sandía *Peru* 14°10S 69°30W **92 F5**
Sandila *India* 27°5N 80°31E **43 F9**
Sandnes *Norway* 58°50N 5°45E **9 G11**
Sandnessjøen *Norway* 66°2N 12°38E **8 C15**
Sandoa
  Dem. Rep. of the Congo 9°41S 23°0E **52 F4**
Sandomierz *Poland* 50°40N 21°43E **17 C11**
Sandover → *Australia* 21°43S 136°32E **62 C2**
Sandoway = Thandwe
  Burma 18°20N 94°30E **41 K19**
Sandoy *Færoe Is.* 61°52N 6°46W **8 F9**
Sandpoint *U.S.A.* 48°17N 116°33W **76 B5**
Sandray *U.K.* 56°53N 7°31W **11 E1**
Sandringham *U.K.* 52°51N 0°31E **12 E8**
Sandstone *Australia* 27°59S 119°16E **61 E2**
Sandusky *Mich., U.S.A.* 43°25N 82°50W **82 C2**
Sandusky *Ohio, U.S.A.* 41°27N 82°42W **82 E2**
Sandveld *Namibia* 21°25S 20°0E **56 C3**
Sandviken *Sweden* 60°38N 16°46E **8 F17**
Sandwich, C. *Australia* 18°14S 146°18E **62 B4**
Sandwich B. *Canada* 53°40N 57°15W **73 B8**
Sandwich B. *Namibia* 23°25S 14°20E **56 C1**
Sandy *Oreg., U.S.A.* 45°24N 122°16E **78 E4**
Sandy *Pa., U.S.A.* 41°6N 78°46W **82 E6**
Sandy *Utah, U.S.A.* 40°32N 111°50W **76 F8**
Sandy Bay *Canada* 55°31N 102°19W **71 B8**
Sandy Bight *Australia* 33°50S 123°20E **61 F3**
Sandy C. *Queens.,*
  Australia 24°42S 153°15E **62 C5**
Sandy C. *Tas., Australia* 41°25S 144°45E **63 G3**
Sandy Cay *Bahamas* 23°13N 75°18W **89 B4**
Sandy Cr. → *Australia* 31°54S 145°18E **63 B4**
Sandy Cr. → *U.S.A.* 41°51N 109°47W **76 F9**
Sandy Creek *U.S.A.* 43°38N 76°5W **83 C8**
Sandy L. *Canada* 53°2N 93°0W **72 B1**
Sandy Lake *Canada* 53°0N 93°15W **72 B1**
Sandy Valley *U.S.A.* 35°49N 115°38W **79 K11**
Sanford *Fla., U.S.A.* 28°48N 81°16W **85 G14**
Sanford *Maine, U.S.A.* 43°27N 70°47W **83 C14**
Sanford *N.C., U.S.A.* 35°29N 79°10W **85 D15**
Sanford → *Australia* 27°22S 115°53E **61 E2**
Sanford, Mt. *U.S.A.* 62°13N 144°8W **68 E3**
Sang-i-Masha *Afghan.* 33°8N 67°27E **42 C2**
Sanga *Mozam.* 12°22S 35°21E **55 E4**
Sanga → *Congo* 1°5S 17°0E **52 E3**
Sangamner *India* 19°37N 74°15E **40 K9**
Sangān *Iran* 34°23N 60°15E **45 C9**
Sangar *Afghan.* 32°56N 65°30E **42 C1**
Sangar *Russia* 64°2N 127°31E **29 C13**
Sangar Sarai *Afghan.* 34°27N 70°35E **42 B4**
Sangarh → *Pakistan* 30°43N 70°44E **42 D4**
Sangay *Ecuador* 2°0S 78°20W **92 D3**
Sange
  Dem. Rep. of the Congo 6°58S 28°21E **54 D2**
Sangeang *Indonesia* 8°12S 119°6E **37 F5**
Sanger *U.S.A.* 36°42N 119°33W **78 J7**
Sangerhausen *Germany* 51°28N 11°18E **16 C6**
Sanggan He → *China* 38°12N 117°15E **34 E9**
Sanggau *Indonesia* 0°5N 110°30E **36 D4**
Sanghar *Pakistan* 26°2N 68°57E **42 F3**
Sangihe, Kepulauan
  Indonesia 3°0N 125°30E **37 D7**
Sangihe, Pulau *Indonesia* 3°35N 125°30E **37 D7**
Sangju *S. Korea* 36°25N 128°10E **35 F15**
Sangkapura *Indonesia* 5°52S 112°40E **36 F4**
Sangkhla Buri *Thailand* 14°57N 98°28E **38 E2**
Sangkulirang *Indonesia* 0°59N 117°58E **36 D5**
Sangla *Pakistan* 31°43N 73°23E **42 D5**
Sangli *India* 16°55N 74°33E **40 L9**
Sangmélima *Cameroon* 2°57N 12°1E **52 D2**
Sango *Zimbabwe* 18°44S 31°44E **55 F3**
Sangod *India* 24°55N 76°17E **42 G7**
Sangre de Cristo Mts.
  U.S.A. 37°30N 105°20W **77 H11**
Sangre Grande
  Trin. & Tob. 10°35N 61°8W **93 K15**
Sangrur *India* 30°14N 75°50E **42 D6**
Sangudo *Canada* 53°50N 114°54W **70 C6**
Sangue → *Brazil* 11°1S 58°39W **92 F7**
Sanibel *U.S.A.* 26°27N 82°1W **85 H13**
Sanikiluaq *Canada* 56°32N 79°14W **72 A4**
Sanin-Kaigan △ *Japan* 35°39N 134°37E **31 G7**
Sanirajak = Hall Beach
  Canada 68°46N 81°12W **69 D15**
Sanjawi *Pakistan* 30°17N 68°21E **42 D3**
Sanje *Uganda* 0°49S 31°30E **54 C3**
Sanjo *Japan* 37°37N 138°57E **30 F9**
Sankh → *India* 22°15N 84°48E **43 H11**
Sankt Gallen *Switz.* 47°26N 9°22E **20 C8**
Sankt Michel = Mikkeli
  Finland 61°43N 27°15E **8 F22**
Sankt Moritz *Switz.* 46°30N 9°51E **20 C8**
Sankt-Peterburg *Russia* 59°55N 30°20E **9 G24**
Sankt Pölten *Austria* 48°12N 15°38E **16 D8**
Sankuru →
  Dem. Rep. of the Congo 4°17S 20°25E **52 E4**
Sanliurfa *Turkey* 37°12N 38°50E **44 B3**
Sanlúcar de Barrameda
  Spain 36°46N 6°21W **21 D2**
Sanmenxia *China* 34°47N 111°12E **34 G6**
Sanming *China* 26°15N 117°40E **33 D6**
Sannicandro Gargánico
  Italy 41°50N 15°34E **22 D6**
Sânnicolau Mare
  Romania 46°5N 20°39E **17 E11**

Sannieshof *S. Africa* 26°30S 25°47E **56 D4**
Sannīn, J. *Lebanon* 33°57N 35°52E **46 B4**
Sanniquellie *Liberia* 7°19N 8°38W **50 G4**
Sanok *Poland* 49°35N 22°10E **17 D12**
Sanquhar *U.K.* 55°22N 3°54W **11 F5**
Sans Souci *Trin. & Tob.* 10°50N 61°0W **93 K16**
Sant Antoni de Portmany
  Spain 38°59N 1°19E **24 C7**
Sant Carles *Spain* 39°3N 1°34E **24 B8**
Sant Elm *Spain* 39°35N 2°21E **24 B9**
Sant Feliu de Guíxols *Spain* 41°45N 3°1E **21 B7**
Sant Ferran *Spain* 38°42N 1°28E **24 C7**
Sant Francesc de Formentera
  Spain 38°42N 1°26E **24 C7**
Sant Jaume *Spain* 39°54N 4°4E **24 B11**
Sant Joan *Spain* 39°36N 3°4E **24 B10**
Sant Joan de Labritja *Spain* 39°5N 1°31E **24 B8**
Sant Jordi *Ibiza, Spain* 38°53N 1°24E **24 C7**
Sant Jordi *Mallorca, Spain* 39°33N 2°46E **24 B9**
Sant Jordi, G. de *Spain* 40°53N 1°2E **21 B6**
Sant Llorenç des Cardassar
  Spain 39°37N 3°17E **24 B10**
Sant Mateu *Spain* 39°3N 1°23E **24 B7**
Sant Miquel *Spain* 39°3N 1°26E **24 B7**
Sant Salvador *Spain* 39°27N 3°11E **24 B10**
Sant Agnés *Spain* 39°3N 1°21E **24 B7**
Santa Ana *Bolivia* 13°50S 65°40W **92 F5**
Santa Ana *El Salv.* 14°0N 89°31W **88 D2**
Santa Ana *Mexico* 30°33N 111°7W **86 A2**
Santa Ana *U.S.A.* 33°46N 117°52W **79 M9**
Sant' Antíoco *Italy* 39°4N 8°27E **22 E3**
Santa Bárbara *Honduras* 14°53N 88°14W **88 D2**
Santa Bárbara *Mexico* 26°48N 105°49W **86 B3**
Santa Barbara *U.S.A.* 34°25N 119°42W **79 L7**
Santa Barbara Channel
  U.S.A. 34°15N 120°0W **79 L7**
Santa Barbara I. *U.S.A.* 33°29N 119°2W **79 M7**
Santa Catalina, Gulf of
  U.S.A. 33°10N 117°50W **79 N9**
Santa Catalina, I.
  Mexico 25°40N 110°47W **86 B2**
Santa Catalina I.
  U.S.A. 33°23N 118°25W **79 M8**
Santa Catarina □ *Brazil* 27°25S 48°30W **95 B6**
Santa Catarina, I. de
  Brazil 27°30S 48°40W **95 B6**
Santa Cecília *Brazil* 26°56S 50°18W **95 B5**
Santa Clara *Cuba* 22°20N 80°0W **88 B4**
Santa Clara *Calif.,*
  U.S.A. 37°21N 121°57W **78 H5**
Santa Clara *N.Y.,*
  U.S.A. 44°38N 74°27W **83 B10**
Santa Clara *Utah, U.S.A.* 37°8N 113°39W **77 H7**
Santa Clara de Olimar
  Uruguay 32°50S 54°54W **95 C5**
Santa Clara Valley
  U.S.A. 36°50N 121°30W **78 J5**
Santa Clarita *U.S.A.* 34°24N 118°33W **79 L8**
Santa Clotilde *Peru* 2°33S 73°45W **92 D4**
Santa Coloma de Gramenet
  Spain 41°27N 2°13E **21 B7**
Santa Cruz *Bolivia* 17°43S 63°10W **92 G6**
Santa Cruz *Chile* 34°38S 71°27W **94 C1**
Santa Cruz *Costa Rica* 10°15N 85°35W **88 D2**
Santa Cruz *Madeira* 32°42N 16°46W **24 D3**
Santa Cruz *Phil.* 14°20N 121°24E **37 B6**
Santa Cruz *U.S.A.* 36°58N 122°1W **78 J4**
Santa Cruz → *Argentina* 50°10S 68°20W **96 G3**
Santa Cruz de la Palma
  Canary Is. 28°41N 17°46W **24 F2**
Santa Cruz de la Palma ✈ (SPC)
  Canary Is. 28°40N 17°45W **24 F2**
Santa Cruz de Tenerife
  Canary Is. 28°28N 16°15W **24 F3**
Santa Cruz del Norte
  Cuba 23°9N 81°55W **88 B3**
Santa Cruz del Sur *Cuba* 20°44N 78°0W **88 B4**
Santa Cruz do Rio Pardo
  Brazil 22°54S 49°37W **95 A6**
Santa Cruz do Sul *Brazil* 29°42S 52°25W **95 B5**
Santa Cruz I. *U.S.A.* 34°1N 119°43W **79 M7**
Santa Cruz Is. *Solomon Is.* 10°30S 166°0E **58 C9**
Santa Cruz Mts. *Jamaica* 17°58N 77°43W **88 a**
Santa Domingo, Cay
  Bahamas 21°25N 75°15W **88 B4**
Santa Elena *Argentina* 30°58S 59°47W **94 C4**
Santa Elena, C.
  Costa Rica 10°54N 85°56W **88 D2**
Santa Eulària des Riu
  Spain 38°59N 1°32E **24 C8**
Santa Fé *Argentina* 31°35S 60°41W **94 C3**
Santa Fe *U.S.A.* 35°41N 105°57W **77 J11**
Santa Fé □ *Argentina* 31°50S 60°55W **94 C3**
Santa Fé do Sul *Brazil* 20°13S 50°56W **93 H8**
Santa Filomena *Brazil* 9°6S 45°50W **93 E9**
Santa Gertrudis *Spain* 39°0N 1°26E **24 C7**
Santa Inês *Brazil* 13°17S 39°48W **93 F11**
Santa Inés, I. *Chile* 54°0S 73°0W **96 G2**
Santa Isabel *Argentina* 36°10S 66°54W **94 D2**
Santa Isabel do Morro
  Brazil 11°34S 50°40W **93 F8**
Santa Lucía *Corrientes,*
  Argentina 28°58S 59°5W **94 B4**
Santa Lucía *San Juan,*
  Argentina 31°35S 68°30W **94 C2**
Santa Lucía *Uruguay* 34°27S 56°24W **94 C4**
Santa Lucia Range
  U.S.A. 36°0N 121°20W **78 K5**
Santa Luzia *C. Verde Is.* 16°50N 24°35W **50 b**
Santa Margalida *Spain* 39°42N 3°6E **24 B10**
Santa Margarita
  Argentina 38°28S 61°35W **94 D3**
Santa Margarita
  U.S.A. 35°23N 120°37W **78 K6**
Santa Margarita →
  U.S.A. 33°13N 117°23W **79 M9**
Santa Margarita, I.
  Mexico 24°27N 111°50W **86 C2**

Santa María *Argentina* 26°40S 66°0W **94 B2**
Santa Maria *Azores* 36°58N 25°6W **50 a**
Santa Maria *Brazil* 29°40S 53°48W **95 B5**
Santa Maria *C. Verde Is.* 16°31N 22°53W **50 b**
Santa Maria *U.S.A.* 34°57N 120°26W **79 L6**
Santa María → *Mexico* 31°0N 107°14W **86 A3**
Santa María, B. de
  Mexico 25°4N 108°6W **86 B3**
Santa Maria da Vitória
  Brazil 13°24S 44°12W **93 F10**
Santa María del Camí
  Spain 39°38N 2°47E **24 B9**
Santa Maria di Léuca, C.
  Italy 39°47N 18°22E **23 E8**
Santa Marta *Colombia* 11°15N 74°13W **92 A4**
Santa Marta, Sierra Nevada de
  Colombia 10°55N 73°50W **92 A4**
Santa Marta Grande, C.
  Brazil 28°43S 48°50W **95 B6**
Santa Maura = Lefkada
  Greece 38°40N 20°43E **23 E9**
Santa Monica *U.S.A.* 34°1N 118°29W **79 M8**
Santa Monica Mts. △
  U.S.A. 34°4N 118°44W **79 L8**
Santa Paula *U.S.A.* 34°21N 119°4W **79 L7**
Santa Ponça *Spain* 39°30N 2°28E **24 B9**
Santa Rosa *La Pampa,*
  Argentina 36°40S 64°17W **94 D3**
Santa Rosa *San Luis,*
  Argentina 32°21S 65°10W **94 C2**
Santa Rosa *Brazil* 27°52S 54°29W **95 B5**
Santa Rosa *Calif.,*
  U.S.A. 38°26N 122°43W **78 G4**
Santa Rosa *N. Mex.,*
  U.S.A. 34°57N 104°41W **77 J11**
Santa Rosa and San Jacinto
  Mts. △ *U.S.A.* 33°28N 116°20W **79 M10**
Santa Rosa de Copán
  Honduras 14°47N 88°46W **88 D2**
Santa Rosa de Río Primero
  Argentina 31°8S 63°20W **94 C3**
Santa Rosa del Sara
  Bolivia 17°7S 63°35W **92 G6**
Santa Rosa I. *Calif.,*
  U.S.A. 33°58N 120°6W **79 M6**
Santa Rosa I. *Fla.,*
  U.S.A. 30°20N 86°50W **85 F11**
Santa Rosa Range
  U.S.A. 41°45N 117°40W **76 F5**
Santa Rosalía *Mexico* 27°19N 112°17W **86 B2**
Santa Sylvina *Argentina* 27°50S 61°10W **94 B3**
Santa Tecla = Nueva San
  Salvador *El Salv.* 13°40N 89°18W **88 D2**
Santa Teresa *Argentina* 33°25S 60°47W **94 C3**
Santa Teresa *Australia* 24°8S 134°22E **62 C1**
Santa Teresa *Mexico* 25°17N 97°51W **87 B5**
Santa Teresa △ *Uruguay* 33°57S 53°31W **95 C5**
Santa Teresita *Argentina* 36°32S 56°41W **94 D4**
Santa Vitória do Palmar
  Brazil 33°32S 53°25W **95 C5**
Santa Ynez → *U.S.A.* 34°41N 120°36W **79 L6**
Santa Ynez Mts. *U.S.A.* 34°30N 120°0W **79 L6**
Santa Ysabel *U.S.A.* 33°7N 116°40W **79 M10**
Santai *China* 31°5N 104°58E **32 C5**
Santana *Madeira* 32°48N 16°52W **24 D3**
Santana, Coxilha de
  Brazil 30°50S 55°35W **95 C4**
Santana do Livramento
  Brazil 30°55S 55°30W **95 C4**
Santander *Spain* 43°27N 3°51W **21 A4**
Santander Jiménez
  Mexico 24°13N 98°28W **87 C5**
Santanilla, Is. *Honduras* 17°22N 83°57W **88 C3**
Santany *Spain* 39°20N 3°5E **24 B10**
Santaquin *U.S.A.* 39°59N 111°47W **76 G8**
Santarém *Brazil* 2°25S 54°42W **93 D8**
Santarém *Portugal* 39°12N 8°42W **21 C1**
Santaren Channel
  W. Indies 24°0N 79°30W **88 B4**
Santee *U.S.A.* 32°50N 116°58W **79 N10**
Santee → *U.S.A.* 33°7N 79°17W **85 E15**
Santiago = Río Grande de
  Santiago → *Mexico* 21°36N 105°26W **86 C3**
Santiago = São Tiago
  C. Verde Is. 15°0N 23°40W **50 b**
Santiago *Brazil* 29°11S 54°52W **95 B5**
Santiago *Canary Is.* 28°2N 17°12W **24 F2**
Santiago *Chile* 33°26S 70°40W **94 C1**
Santiago *Panama* 8°0N 81°0W **88 E3**
Santiago → *Peru* 4°27S 77°38W **92 D3**
Santiago de Compostela
  Spain 42°52N 8°37W **21 A1**
Santiago de Cuba *Cuba* 20°0N 75°49W **88 C4**
Santiago de los Caballeros
  Dom. Rep. 19°30N 70°40W **89 C5**
Santiago del Estero
  Argentina 27°50S 64°15W **94 B3**
Santiago del Estero □
  Argentina 27°40S 63°15W **94 B3**
Santiago del Teide
  Canary Is. 28°17N 16°48W **24 F3**
Santiago Ixcuintla
  Mexico 21°49N 105°13W **86 C3**
Santiago Jamiltepec
  Mexico 16°17N 97°49W **87 D5**
Santiago Papasquiaro
  Mexico 25°3N 105°25W **86 C3**
Santiago Pinotepa Nacional
  Mexico 16°19N 98°1W **87 D5**
Santiaguillo, L. de
  Mexico 24°48N 104°48W **86 C4**
Santo Amaro *Brazil* 12°30S 38°43W **93 F11**
Santo Anastácio *Brazil* 21°58S 51°39W **95 A5**
Santo André *Brazil* 23°39S 46°29W **95 A6**
Santo Ângelo *Brazil* 28°15S 54°15W **95 B5**
Santo Antão *C. Verde Is.* 16°52N 25°10W **50 b**
Santo Antônio do Içá
  Brazil 3°5S 67°57W **92 D5**

Santo Antônio do Leverger
  Brazil 15°52S 56°5W **93 G7**
Santo Domingo
  Dom. Rep. 18°30N 69°59W **89 C6**
Santo Domingo *Baja Calif.,*
  Mexico 30°43N 116°2W **86 A1**
Santo Domingo *Baja Calif. S.,*
  Mexico 25°29N 111°55W **86 B2**
Santo Domingo *Nic.* 12°14N 84°59W **88 D3**
Santo Domingo de los Colorados
  Ecuador 0°15S 79°9W **92 D3**
Santo Domingo Pueblo
  U.S.A. 35°31N 106°22W **77 J10**
Santo Tomás *Mexico* 31°33N 116°24W **86 A1**
Santo Tomás *Peru* 14°26S 72°8W **92 F4**
Santo Tomé *Argentina* 28°40S 56°5W **95 B4**
Santo Tomé de Guayana = Ciudad
  Guayana *Venezuela* 8°0N 62°30W **92 B6**
Santoña *Spain* 43°29N 3°27W **21 A4**
Santorini *Greece* 36°23N 25°27E **23 F11**
Santos *Brazil* 24°0S 46°20W **95 A6**
Santos Dumont *Brazil* 22°55S 43°10W **95 A7**
Santuario de Aves Laguna
  Colorada △ *Bolivia* 22°10S 67°45W **94 A2**
Sanur *Indonesia* 8°41S 115°15E **37 K18**
Sanwer *India* 22°59N 75°50E **42 H6**
Sanxia Shuiku *China* 30°10N 108°0E **33 C5**
Sanxiang *China* 22°21N 113°25E **33 G9**
Sanya *China* 18°14N 109°29E **38 C7**
Sanyuan *China* 34°35N 108°58E **34 G5**
São Bernardo do Campo
  Brazil 23°45S 46°34W **95 A6**
São Borja *Brazil* 28°39S 56°0W **95 B4**
São Carlos *Brazil* 22°0S 47°50W **95 A6**
São Cristóvão *Brazil* 11°1S 37°15W **93 F11**
São Domingos *Brazil* 13°25S 46°19W **93 F9**
São Filipe *C. Verde Is.* 15°2N 24°30W **50 b**
São Francisco *Brazil* 16°0S 44°50W **93 G10**
São Francisco →
  Brazil 10°30S 36°24W **93 F11**
São Francisco do Sul
  Brazil 26°15S 48°36W **95 B6**
São Gabriel *Brazil* 30°20S 54°20W **95 C4**
São Gonçalo *Brazil* 22°48S 43°5W **95 A7**
Sao Hill *Tanzania* 8°20S 35°12E **55 D4**
São João da Boa Vista
  Brazil 22°0S 46°52W **95 A6**
São João da Madeira
  Portugal 40°54N 8°30W **21 B1**
São João del Rei *Brazil* 21°8S 44°15W **95 A7**
São João do Araguaia
  Brazil 5°23S 48°46W **93 E9**
São João do Piauí *Brazil* 8°21S 42°15W **93 E10**
São Joaquim *Brazil* 28°18S 49°56W **95 B6**
São Joaquim △ *Brazil* 28°12S 49°37W **95 B6**
São Jorge *Azores* 38°38N 28°3W **50 a**
São Jorge, Pta. de
  Madeira 32°50N 16°53W **24 D3**
São José *Brazil* 27°38S 48°39W **95 B5**
São José do Norte *Brazil* 32°1S 52°3W **95 C5**
São José do Rio Preto
  Brazil 20°50S 49°20W **95 A6**
São José dos Campos
  Brazil 23°7S 45°52W **95 A6**
São Leopoldo *Brazil* 29°50S 51°10W **95 B5**
São Lourenço *Brazil* 22°7S 45°3W **95 A6**
São Lourenço → *Brazil* 17°53S 57°27W **93 G7**
São Lourenço, Pta. de
  Madeira 32°44N 16°39W **24 D3**
São Lourenço do Sul
  Brazil 31°22S 51°58W **95 C5**
São Luís *Brazil* 2°39S 44°15W **93 D10**
São Luís Gonzaga *Brazil* 28°25S 55°0W **95 B5**
São Marcos → *Brazil* 18°15S 47°37W **93 G9**
São Marcos, B. de *Brazil* 2°0S 44°0W **93 D10**
São Mateus *Brazil* 18°44S 39°50W **93 G11**
São Mateus do Sul
  Brazil 25°52S 50°23W **95 B5**
São Miguel *Azores* 37°47N 25°30W **50 a**
São Miguel do Oeste
  Brazil 26°45S 53°34W **95 B5**
São Nicolau *C. Verde Is.* 16°20N 24°20W **50 b**
São Paulo *Brazil* 23°32S 46°38W **95 A6**
São Paulo □ *Brazil* 22°0S 49°0W **95 A6**
São Paulo de Olivença
  Brazil 3°27S 68°48W **92 D5**
São Roque *Madeira* 32°46N 16°48W **24 D3**
São Roque, C. de *Brazil* 5°30S 35°16W **93 E11**
São Sebastião, I. de
  Brazil 23°50S 45°18W **95 A6**
São Sebastião do Paraíso
  Brazil 20°54S 46°59W **95 A6**
São Tiago *C. Verde Is.* 15°0N 23°40W **50 b**
São Tomé
  São Tomé & Príncipe 0°10N 6°39E **48 F4**
São Tomé *C. Verde Is.* 22°0S 40°59W **95 A7**
São Tomé & Príncipe ■
  Africa 0°12N 6°39E **49 F4**
São Vicente *Brazil* 23°57S 46°23W **95 A6**
São Vicente *C. Verde Is.* 17°0N 25°0W **50 b**
São Vicente *Madeira* 32°48N 17°3W **24 D2**
São Vicente, C. de *Portugal* 37°0N 9°0W **21 D1**
Saona, I. *Dom. Rep.* 18°10N 68°40W **89 C6**
Saône → *France* 45°44N 4°50E **20 D6**
Saonek *Indonesia* 0°22S 130°55E **37 E8**
Sapam, Ao *Thailand* 8°0N 98°26E **39 a**
Saparua *Indonesia* 3°33S 128°40E **37 E7**
Sapele *Nigeria* 5°50N 5°40E **50 G7**
Sapelo I. *U.S.A.* 31°25N 81°12W **85 F14**
Sapi → *Zimbabwe* 15°48S 29°42E **55 F2**
Saposoa *Peru* 6°55S 76°45W **92 E3**
Sapphire *Australia* 23°28S 147°43E **62 C4**
Sappho *U.S.A.* 48°4N 124°16W **78 B2**
Sapporo *Japan* 43°0N 141°21E **30 C10**
Sapulpa *U.S.A.* 35°59N 96°5W **84 D6**
Saqqez *Iran* 36°15N 46°20E **44 B5**
Sar Dasht *Āzarbāyjān-e Gharbī,*
  Iran 36°9N 45°28E **44 B5**
Sar Dasht *Khuzestān, Iran* 32°32N 48°52E **45 C6**

Sar-e Pol □ *Afghan.* 36°20N 65°50E **40 B4**
Sar Gachīneh = Yāsūj
  Iran 30°31N 51°31E **45 D6**
Sar Planina *Macedonia* 42°0N 21°0E **23 C9**
Sara Buri = Saraburi
  Thailand 14°30N 100°55E **38 E3**
Sarāb *Iran* 37°55N 47°40E **44 B5**
Sarābādī *Iraq* 33°1N 44°48E **44 C5**
Saraburi *Thailand* 14°30N 100°55E **38 E3**
Saradiya *India* 21°34N 70°2E **42 J4**
Saragossa = Zaragoza
  Spain 41°39N 0°53W **21 B5**
Saraguro *Ecuador* 3°35S 79°16W **92 D3**
Sarahs *Turkmenistan* 36°32N 61°13E **45 B9**
Sarai Naurang *Pakistan* 32°50N 70°47E **42 C4**
Saraikela *India* 22°42N 85°56E **43 H11**
Sarajevo *Bos.-H.* 43°52N 18°26E **23 C8**
Sarakhs *Turkmenistan* 36°32N 61°13E **45 B9**
Saran, Gunung *Indonesia* 0°30S 111°25E **36 E4**
Saranac Lake *U.S.A.* 44°20N 74°10W **83 B10**
Saranac Lakes *U.S.A.* 44°22N 74°28W **83 B10**
Saranda *Tanzania* 5°45S 34°59E **54 D3**
Sarandí del Yí *Uruguay* 33°18S 55°38W **95 C4**
Sarandí Grande
  Uruguay 33°44S 56°20W **94 C4**
Sarangani B. *Phil.* 6°0N 125°13E **37 C7**
Sarangani Is. *Phil.* 5°25N 125°25E **37 C7**
Sarangarh *India* 21°30N 83°5E **41 J12**
Saransk *Russia* 54°10N 45°10E **18 D8**
Sarapul *Russia* 56°28N 53°48E **18 C9**
Sarasota *U.S.A.* 27°20N 82°32W **85 H13**
Saratoga *Calif., U.S.A.* 37°16N 122°2W **78 H4**
Saratoga *Wyo., U.S.A.* 41°27N 106°49W **76 F10**
Saratoga △ *U.S.A.* 43°0N 73°38W **83 D11**
Saratoga L. *U.S.A.* 43°1N 73°44W **83 C11**
Saratoga Springs *U.S.A.* 43°5N 73°47W **83 C11**
Saratok *Malaysia* 1°55N 111°17E **36 D4**
Saratov *Russia* 51°30N 46°2E **19 D8**
Saravane *Laos* 15°43N 106°25E **38 E6**
Sarawak □ *Malaysia* 2°0N 113°0E **36 D4**
Saray *Turkey* 41°26N 27°55E **23 D12**
Sarayköy *Turkey* 37°55N 28°54E **23 F13**
Sarbāz *Iran* 26°38N 61°19E **45 E9**
Sarbīsheh *Iran* 32°30N 59°40E **45 C8**
Sarda → *India* 27°21N 81°23E **43 F9**
Sardarshahr *India* 28°30N 74°29E **42 E6**
Sardegna □ *Italy* 40°0N 9°0E **22 D3**
Sardhana *India* 29°9N 77°39E **42 E7**
Sardina, Pta. *Canary Is.* 28°9N 15°44W **24 F4**
Sardinia = Sardegna □
  Italy 40°0N 9°0E **22 D3**
Sardis *Turkey* 38°28N 27°58E **23 E12**
Sārdūīyeh = Dar Mazār
  Iran 29°14N 57°20E **45 D8**
Saren *Indonesia* 8°26S 115°34E **37 J18**
Sarera, G. of *Indonesia* 2°0S 135°0E **58 B6**
Sargasso Sea *Atl. Oc.* 27°0N 72°0W **66 G13**
Sargodha *Pakistan* 32°10N 72°40E **42 C5**
Sarh *Chad* 9°5N 18°23E **51 G9**
Sārī *Iran* 36°30N 53°4E **45 B7**
Saria *India* 21°38N 83°22E **43 J10**
Sariab *Pakistan* 30°6N 66°59E **42 D2**
Sarıgöl *Turkey* 38°14N 28°41E **23 E13**
Sarikei *Malaysia* 2°8N 111°30E **36 D4**
Sarila *India* 25°46N 79°41E **43 G8**
Sarina *Australia* 21°22S 149°13E **62 C4**
Sarita *U.S.A.* 27°13N 97°47W **84 H6**
Sariwŏn *N. Korea* 38°31N 125°46E **35 E13**
Sarju → *India* 27°21N 81°23E **43 F9**
Sark *U.K.* 49°25N 2°22E **13 H5**
Sarkari Tala *India* 27°39N 70°52E **42 F4**
Sarlat-la-Canéda *France* 44°54N 1°13E **20 D4**
Sarmi *Indonesia* 1°49S 138°44E **37 E9**
Sarmiento *Argentina* 45°35S 69°5W **96 F3**
Särna *Sweden* 61°41N 13°8E **8 F15**
Sarnia *Canada* 42°58N 82°23W **82 D2**
Sarolangun *Indonesia* 2°19S 102°42E **36 E2**
Saronikos Kolpos
  Greece 37°45N 23°45E **23 F10**
Saros Körfezi *Turkey* 40°30N 26°15E **23 D12**
Sarpsborg *Norway* 59°16N 11°7E **9 G14**
Sarqan *Kazakhstan* 45°24N 79°55E **32 B3**
Sarre = Saar → *Europe* 49°41N 6°32E **15 E6**
Sarreguemines *France* 49°5N 7°4E **20 B7**
Sarthe → *France* 47°33N 0°31W **20 C3**
Saruna → *Pakistan* 26°31N 67°7E **42 F2**
Sarvar *India* 26°4N 75°0E **42 F6**
Sarvestān *Iran* 29°20N 53°10E **45 D7**
Sary-Tash *Kyrgyzstan* 39°44N 73°15E **28 F8**
Saryshagan *Kazakhstan* 46°12N 73°38E **28 E8**
Sasan Gir *India* 21°10N 70°36E **42 J4**
Sasaram *India* 24°57N 84°5E **43 G11**
Sasebo *Japan* 33°10N 129°43E **31 H4**
Saskatchewan □
  Canada 54°40N 106°0W **71 C7**
Saskatchewan →
  Canada 53°37N 100°40W **71 C8**
Saskatoon *Canada* 52°10N 106°38W **71 C7**
Saskylakh *Russia* 71°55N 114°1E **29 B12**
Saslaya △ *Nic.* 13°45N 85°4W **88 D2**
Sasolburg *S. Africa* 26°46S 27°49E **56 D4**
Sasovo *Russia* 54°25N 41°55E **18 D7**
Sassandra *Ivory C.* 4°55N 6°8W **50 H4**
Sassandra → *Ivory C.* 4°58N 6°5W **50 H4**
Sássari *Italy* 40°43N 8°34E **22 D3**
Sassie *Australia* 10°25S 142°51E **62 a**
Sassnitz *Germany* 54°29N 13°39E **16 A7**
Sassuolo *Italy* 44°33N 10°47E **22 B4**
Sasyk, Ozero *Ukraine* 45°45N 29°20E **17 F15**
Sata-Misaki *Japan* 31°0N 130°40E **31 J5**
Satadougou *Mali* 12°25N 11°25W **50 F3**
Satakunda = Satakunta
  Finland 61°45N 23°0E **8 F20**
Satakunta *Finland* 61°45N 23°0E **8 F20**

Satara India 17°44N 73°58E 40 L8
Satara S. Africa 24°29S 31°47E 57 C5
Satbarwa India 23°55N 84°16E 43 H11
Satevó Mexico 27°57N 106°7W 86 B3
Satilla → U.S.A. 30°59N 81°29W 85 F14
Satka Russia 55°3N 59°1E 18 C10
Satmala Hills Andhra Pradesh,
India 19°45N 78°45E 40 K11
Satmala Hills Maharashtra,
India 20°15N 74°40E 40 J9
Satna India 24°35N 80°50E 43 G9
Sátoraljaújhely
Hungary 48°25N 21°41E 17 D11
Satpura △ India 22°40N 78°15E 42 H8
Satpura Ra. India 21°25N 76°10E 40 J10
Satsuna-Shotō Japan 30°0N 130°0E 31 K5
Sattahip Thailand 12°41N 100°54E 38 F3
Satui Indonesia 3°50S 115°27E 36 E5
Satun Thailand 6°43N 100°2E 39 J3
Satupa'itea Samoa 13°45S 172°18W 59 b
Saturnina → Brazil 12°15S 58°10W 92 F7
Sauce Argentina 30°5S 58°46W 94 C4
Sauceda Mexico 25°46N 101°19W 86 B4
Saucillo Mexico 28°1N 105°17W 86 B3
Sauda Norway 59°40N 6°20E 9 G12
Sauðarkrókur Iceland 65°45N 19°40W 8 D4
Saudi Arabia ■ Asia 26°0N 44°0E 44 B3
Sauerland Germany 51°12N 7°59E 16 C4
Saugeen → Canada 44°30N 81°22W 82 B3
Saugerties U.S.A. 42°5N 73°57W 83 D11
Saugus U.S.A. 34°25N 118°32W 79 L8
Sauk Centre U.S.A. 45°44N 94°57W 80 C6
Sauk Rapids U.S.A. 45°35N 94°10W 80 C6
Sault Ste. Marie Canada 46°30N 84°20W 72 C3
Sault Ste. Marie U.S.A. 46°30N 84°21W 81 B11
Saumlaki Indonesia 7°55S 131°20E 37 F8
Saumur France 47°15N 0°5W 20 C3
Saunders, C. N.Z. 45°53S 170°45E 59 F3
Saunders I. Antarctica 57°48S 26°57W 5 B1
Saunders Pt. Australia 27°52S 125°38E 61 E4
Saurimo Angola 9°40S 20°12E 52 F4
Sausalito U.S.A. 37°51N 122°29W 78 H4
Savá Honduras 15°32N 86°15W 88 C2
Sava → Serbia 44°50N 20°26E 23 B9
Savage U.S.A. 47°27N 104°21W 76 C11
Savage I. = Niue
Pac. Oc. 19°2S 169°54W 65 J11
Savage River Australia 41°31S 145°14E 63 G4
Savai'i Samoa 13°28S 172°24W 59 b
Savalou Benin 7°57N 1°58E 50 G6
Savane Mozam. 19°37S 35°8E 55 F4
Savanna U.S.A. 42°5N 90°8W 80 D8
Savanna-la-Mar Jamaica 18°10N 78°10W 88 a
Savannah Ga., U.S.A. 32°5N 81°6W 85 E14
Savannah Mo., U.S.A. 39°56N 94°50W 80 F6
Savannah Tenn., U.S.A. 35°14N 88°15W 85 D10
Savannah → U.S.A. 32°2N 80°53W 85 E14
Savannakhet Laos 16°30N 104°49E 38 D5
Savant L. Canada 50°16N 90°44W 72 B1
Savant Lake Canada 50°14N 90°40W 72 B1
Savarkundla = Kundla
India 21°21N 71°25E 42 J4
Sāve → Mozam. 21°16S 34°0E 57 C5
Säveh Iran 35°2N 50°20E 45 C6
Savelugu Ghana 9°38N 0°54W 50 G5
Savo Finland 62°45N 27°30E 8 E22
Savoie □ France 45°26N 6°25E 20 D7
Savolax = Savo Finland 62°45N 27°30E 8 E22
Savona Italy 44°17N 8°30E 20 D8
Savona U.S.A. 42°17N 77°13W 82 D7
Savonlinna Finland 61°52N 28°53E 8 F23
Savoy = Savoie □ France 45°26N 6°25E 20 D7
Savur Turkey 37°34N 40°53E 44 B4
Savusavu Fiji 16°34S 179°15E 59 a
Savusavu B. Fiji 16°45S 179°15E 59 a
Sawahlunto Indonesia 0°40S 100°52E 36 E2
Sawai Indonesia 3°0S 129°5E 37 E7
Sawai Madhopur India 26°0N 76°25E 42 G7
Sawaleke Fiji 17°59S 179°18E 59 a
Sawang Daen Din
Thailand 17°28N 103°28E 38 D4
Sawankhalok Thailand 17°19N 99°50E 38 D2
Sawara Japan 35°55N 140°30E 31 G10
Sawatch Range U.S.A. 39°0N 106°30W 76 G10
Sawel Mt. U.K. 54°50N 7°2W 10 B4
Sawi Thailand 10°14N 99°5E 39 G2
Sawmills Zimbabwe 19°30S 28°2E 55 F2
Sawtooth △ U.S.A. 44°0N 114°50W 76 D6
Sawtooth Range U.S.A. 44°3N 114°58W 76 D6
Sawu Indonesia 10°35S 121°50E 37 F6
Sawu Sea Indonesia 9°30S 121°50E 37 F6
Saxby → Australia 18°25S 140°53E 62 B3
Saxmundham U.K. 52°13N 1°30E 13 E9
Saxby → Australia 18°25S 140°53E 62 B3
Saxony = Sachsen □
Germany 50°55N 13°10E 16 C7
Saxony, Lower =
Niedersachsen □
Germany 52°50N 9°0E 16 B5
Saxton U.S.A. 40°13N 78°15W 82 F6
Sayabec Canada 48°35N 67°41W 73 C6
Sayaboury Laos 19°15N 101°45E 38 C3
Sayán Peru 11°8S 77°12W 92 F3
Sayan, Vostochnyy
Russia 54°0N 96°0E 29 D10
Sayan, Zapadnyy Russia 52°30N 94°0E 32 A4
Sayanogorsk Russia 53°5N 91°23E 29 D10
Saydā Lebanon 33°35N 35°25E 46 B4
Sayhandulaan = Oldziyt
Mongolia 44°40N 109°1E 34 B5
Sayḩūt Yemen 15°12N 51°10E 47 D5
Saylac Somali Rep. 11°21N 43°30E 47 E3
Saynshand = Buyant-Uhaa
Mongolia 44°55N 110°11E 33 B6
Sayre Okla., U.S.A. 35°18N 99°38W 84 D5
Sayre Pa., U.S.A. 41°59N 76°32W 83 E8
Sayreville U.S.A. 40°28N 74°22W 83 F10
Sayula Mexico 19°50N 103°36W 86 D4
Sayward Canada 50°21N 125°55W 70 C3

Sazanit Albania 40°30N 19°20E 23 D8
Sázava → Czech Rep. 49°53N 14°24E 16 D8
Sazin Pakistan 35°35N 73°30E 43 B5
Scafell Pike U.K. 54°27N 3°14W 12 C4
Scalloway U.K. 60°9N 1°17W 11 A7
Scalpay U.K. 57°18N 6°0W 11 D3
Scandia Canada 50°20N 112°2W 70 C6
Scandicci Italy 43°45N 11°11E 22 C4
Scandinavia Europe 64°0N 12°0E 6 C8
Scapa Flow U.K. 58°53N 3°3W 11 C5
Scappoose U.S.A. 45°45N 122°53W 78 E4
Scarba U.K. 56°11N 5°43W 11 E3
Scarborough
Trin. & Tob. 11°11N 60°42W 93 J16
Scarborough U.K. 54°17N 0°24W 12 C7
Scariff I. Ireland 51°44N 10°15W 10 E1
Scarp U.K. 58°1N 7°8W 11 C1
Scebeli = Shabeelle →
Somali Rep. 2°0N 44°0E 47 G3
Schaffhausen Switz. 47°42N 8°39E 20 C8
Schagen Neths. 52°49N 4°48E 15 B4
Schaghticoke U.S.A. 42°54N 73°35W 83 D11
Schefferville Canada 54°48N 66°50W 73 B6
Schelde → Belgium 51°15N 4°16E 15 C4
Schell Creek Ra. U.S.A. 39°25N 114°40W 76 G6
Schellsburg U.S.A. 40°3N 78°39W 82 F6
Schenectady U.S.A. 42°49N 73°57W 83 D11
Schenevus U.S.A. 42°33N 74°50W 83 D10
Schiedam Neths. 51°55N 4°25E 15 C4
Schiermonnikoog Neths. 53°30N 6°15E 15 A6
Schio Italy 45°43N 11°21E 22 B4
Schiphol, Amsterdam ✈ (AMS)
Neths. 52°18N 4°45E 15 B4
Schleswig Germany 54°31N 9°34E 16 A5
Schleswig-Holstein □
Germany 54°30N 9°30E 16 A5
Schœlcher Martinique 14°36N 61°7W 88 c
Schoharie U.S.A. 42°40N 74°19W 83 D10
Schoharie Cr. →
U.S.A. 42°57N 74°18W 83 D10
Scholls U.S.A. 45°24N 122°56W 78 E4
Schouten I. Australia 42°20S 148°20E 63 G4
Schouten Is. = Supiori
Indonesia 1°0S 136°0E 37 E9
Schouwen Neths. 51°43N 3°45E 15 C3
Schreiber Canada 48°45N 87°20W 72 C2
Schroffenstein Namibia 27°11S 18°42E 56 D2
Schroon Lake U.S.A. 43°50N 73°46W 83 C11
Schuler Canada 50°20N 110°6W 71 C6
Schumacher Canada 48°30N 81°16W 72 C3
Schurz U.S.A. 38°57N 118°49W 76 G4
Schuyler U.S.A. 41°27N 97°4W 80 E5
Schuylerville U.S.A. 43°6N 73°35W 83 C11
Schuylkill → U.S.A. 39°53N 75°12W 83 G9
Schuylkill Haven U.S.A. 40°37N 76°11W 83 F8
Schwäbische Alb
Germany 48°20N 9°30E 16 D5
Schwaner, Pegunungan
Indonesia 1°0S 112°30E 36 E4
Schwarzrand Namibia 25°37S 16°50E 56 D2
Schwarzwald Germany 48°30N 8°20E 16 D5
Schwatka Mts. U.S.A. 67°20N 156°30W 74 B8
Schwedt Germany 53°3N 14°16E 16 B8
Schweinfurt Germany 50°3N 10°14E 16 C6
Schweiz = Switzerland ■
Europe 46°30N 8°0E 20 C8
Schweizer-Reneke
S. Africa 27°11S 25°18E 56 D4
Schwenningen = Villingen-
Schwenningen Germany 48°3N 8°26E 16 D5
Schwerin Germany 53°36N 11°22E 16 B6
Schwyz Switz. 47°2N 8°39E 20 C8
Sciacca Italy 37°31N 13°3E 22 F5
Scilla Italy 38°15N 15°43E 22 E6
Scilly, Isles of U.K. 49°56N 6°22W 13 H1
Scioto → U.S.A. 38°44N 83°1W 81 F12
Scituate U.S.A. 42°12N 70°44W 83 D14
Scobey U.S.A. 48°47N 105°25W 76 B11
Scone Australia 32°5S 150°52E 63 E5
Scone U.K. 56°25N 3°24W 11 E5
Scoresbysund = Ittoqqortoormiit
Greenland 70°20N 23°0W 4 B6
Scotia Calif., U.S.A. 40°29N 124°6W 76 F1
Scotia N.Y., U.S.A. 42°50N 73°58W 83 D11
Scotia Sea Antarctica 56°5S 56°0W 5 B18
Scotland Canada 43°1N 80°22W 82 C4
Scotland □ U.K. 57°0N 4°0W 11 E5
Scott Antarctica 77°0S 165°0E 5 D11
Scott, C. Australia 13°30S 129°49E 60 B4
Scott City U.S.A. 38°29N 100°54W 80 F3
Scott Glacier Antarctica 66°15S 100°5E 5 C8
Scott I. Antarctica 67°0S 179°0E 5 C11
Scott Is. Canada 50°48N 128°40W 70 C3
Scott L. Canada 59°55N 106°18W 71 B7
Scott Reef Australia 14°0S 121°50E 60 B3
Scottburgh S. Africa 30°15S 30°47E 57 E5
Scottdale U.S.A. 40°6N 79°35W 82 F5
Scottish Borders □ U.K. 55°35N 2°50W 11 F6
Scotts Valley U.S.A. 37°3N 122°1W 78 H4
Scottsbluff U.S.A. 41°52N 103°40W 80 E2
Scottsboro U.S.A. 34°40N 86°2W 85 D11
Scottsburg U.S.A. 38°41N 85°47W 81 F11
Scottsdale Australia 41°9S 147°31E 63 G4
Scottsdale U.S.A. 33°40N 111°54W 77 K7
Scottsville Ky., U.S.A. 36°45N 86°11W 80 G10
Scottsville N.Y., U.S.A. 43°2N 77°47W 82 C7
Scottville U.S.A. 43°58N 86°17W 80 D10
Scranton U.S.A. 41°25N 75°40W 83 E9
Scugog, L. Canada 44°10N 78°55W 82 B6
Scunthorpe U.K. 53°36N 0°39W 12 D7
Scutari = Shkodër
Albania 42°4N 19°32E 23 C8
Sea Is. U.S.A. 31°30N 81°7W 85 F14
Seabrook, L. Australia 30°55S 119°40E 61 F2
Seaford Australia 20°55S 148°57E 62 b
Seaford U.S.A. 38°39N 75°37W 81 F16
Seaforth Australia 20°55S 148°57E 62 b
Seaforth Canada 43°35N 81°25W 82 C3
Seaforth, L. U.K. 57°52N 6°36W 11 D2

Seagraves U.S.A. 32°57N 102°34W 84 E3
Seaham U.K. 54°50N 1°20W 12 C6
Seal → Canada 59°4N 94°48W 71 B10
Seal L. Canada 54°20N 61°30W 73 B7
Sealy U.S.A. 29°47N 96°9W 84 G6
Searchlight U.S.A. 35°28N 114°55W 79 K12
Searcy U.S.A. 35°15N 91°44W 84 D9
Searles L. U.S.A. 35°44N 117°21W 79 K9
Seascale U.K. 54°24N 3°29W 12 C4
Seaside Calif., U.S.A. 36°37N 121°50W 78 J5
Seaside Oreg., U.S.A. 46°0N 123°56W 78 E3
Seaspray Australia 38°25S 147°15E 63 F4
Seattle U.S.A. 47°36N 122°19W 78 C4
Seattle-Tacoma Int. ✈ (SEA)
U.S.A. 47°27N 122°18W 78 C4
Seba Indonesia 10°29S 121°50E 60 B3
Sebago L. U.S.A. 43°52N 70°34W 83 C14
Sebago Lake U.S.A. 43°51N 70°34W 83 C14
Sebastián Vizcaíno, B.
Mexico 28°0N 114°30W 86 B2
Sebastopol = Sevastopol
Ukraine 44°35N 33°30E 19 F5
Sebastopol U.S.A. 38°24N 122°49W 78 G4
Sebewaing U.S.A. 43°44N 83°27W 81 D12
Sebha = Sabhā Libya 27°9N 14°29E 51 C8
Sebinkarahisar Turkey 40°22N 38°28E 19 F6
Sebring Fla., U.S.A. 27°30N 81°27W 85 H14
Sebring Ohio, U.S.A. 40°55N 81°2W 82 F3
Sebringville Canada 43°24N 81°4W 82 C3
Sebuku Indonesia 3°30S 116°25E 36 E5
Sebuku, Teluk Malaysia 4°0N 118°10E 36 D5
Sechelt Canada 49°25N 123°42W 70 D4
Sechura, Desierto de Peru 6°0S 80°30W 92 E2
Secretary I. N.Z. 45°15S 166°56E 59 F1
Secunderabad India 17°28N 78°30E 40 L11
Security U.S.A. 38°45N 104°45W 76 G11
Sedalia U.S.A. 38°42N 93°14W 80 F7
Sedan France 49°43N 4°57E 20 B6
Sedan U.S.A. 37°8N 96°11W 80 G5
Sedbergh U.K. 54°20N 2°31W 12 C5
Seddon N.Z. 41°40S 174°7E 59 D5
Seddonville N.Z. 41°33S 172°1E 59 D4
Sedé Boqér Israel 30°52N 34°47E 46 E3
Sedeh Fárs, Iran 30°45N 52°11E 45 D7
Sedeh Khorāsān, Iran 33°20N 59°14E 45 C8
Sederot Israel 31°32N 34°37E 46 D3
Sédhiou Senegal 12°44N 15°30W 50 F2
Sedley Canada 50°10N 104°0W 71 C8
Sedona U.S.A. 34°52N 111°46W 77 J8
Sedova, Pik Russia 73°29N 54°58E 28 B6
Sedro-Woolley U.S.A. 48°30N 122°14W 78 B4
Seeheim Namibia 26°50S 17°45E 56 D2
Seeis Namibia 22°29S 17°39E 56 C2
Seekoei → S. Africa 30°18S 25°1E 56 E4
Seeley's Bay Canada 44°29N 76°14W 83 B8
Seferihisar Turkey 38°10N 26°50E 23 E12
Sefophe Botswana 22°11S 27°58E 57 C4
Seg-ozero Russia 63°20N 33°46E 18 B5
Segamat Malaysia 2°30N 102°50E 39 L4
Segesta Italy 37°56N 12°50E 22 F5
Segezha Russia 63°44N 34°19E 18 B5
Ségou Mali 13°30N 6°16W 50 F4
Segovia = Coco →
Cent. Amer. 15°0N 83°8W 88 D3
Segovia Spain 40°57N 4°10W 21 B3
Segre → Spain 41°40N 0°43E 21 B6
Seguam I. U.S.A. 52°19N 172°30W 74 E5
Séguéla Ivory C. 7°55N 6°40W 50 G4
Seguin U.S.A. 29°34N 97°58W 84 G6
Segundo → Argentina 30°53S 62°44W 94 C3
Segura → Spain 38°3N 0°44E 21 C5
Seh Konj, Kūh-e Iran 30°6N 57°30E 45 D8
Seh Qal'eh Iran 33°40N 58°24E 45 C8
Sehithwa Botswana 20°30S 22°30E 56 C3
Sehlabathebe △ Lesotho 29°53S 29°7E 57 D4
Sehore India 23°10N 77°5E 42 H7
Sehwan Pakistan 26°28N 67°53E 42 F2
Seikan Tunnel Japan 41°28N 140°10E 30 D10
Seil U.K. 56°18N 5°38W 11 E3
Seiland Norway 70°25N 23°15E 8 A20
Seiling U.S.A. 36°9N 98°56W 84 C5
Seinäjoki Finland 62°40N 22°51E 8 E20
Seine → France 49°26N 0°26E 20 B4
Seistan = Sīstān Asia 30°50N 61°0E 45 D9
Seistan, Daryācheh-ye = Sīstān,
Daryācheh-ye Iran 31°0N 61°0E 45 D9
Sekayu Indonesia 2°51S 103°51E 36 E2
Seke Tanzania 3°20S 33°31E 54 C3
Sekenke Tanzania 4°18S 34°11E 54 C3
Sekondi-Takoradi Ghana 4°58N 1°45W 50 H5
Sekudai Malaysia 1°32N 103°39E 39 d
Sekuma Botswana 24°36S 23°50E 56 C3
Selah U.S.A. 46°39N 120°32W 76 C3
Selama Malaysia 5°12N 100°42E 39 K3
Selaru Indonesia 8°9S 131°0E 37 F8
Selby U.K. 53°47N 1°5W 12 D6
Selby U.S.A. 45°31N 100°2W 80 C3
Selçuk Turkey 37°56N 27°22E 23 F12
Selden U.S.A. 39°33N 100°34W 80 F3
Sele → Italy 40°29N 14°56E 22 D6
Selebi-Phikwe Botswana 21°58S 27°48E 57 C4
Selemdzha → Russia 51°42N 128°53E 29 D13
Selenga = Selenge Mörön →
Asia 52°16N 106°16E 32 A5
Selenge Mörön → Asia 52°16N 106°16E 32 A5
Seletan, Tanjung
Indonesia 4°10S 114°40E 36 E4
Sélibabi Mauritania 15°10N 12°15W 50 E3
Seligman U.S.A. 35°20N 112°53W 77 J7
Selīma Sudan 21°22N 29°19E 51 D11
Selinda Spillway
Botswana 18°35S 23°10E 56 B3
Selinsgrove U.S.A. 40°48N 76°52W 82 F8
Selkirk Canada 50°10N 96°55W 71 C9
Selkirk Man., Canada 50°10N 96°55W 71 C9
Selkirk Ont., Canada 42°49N 79°56W 82 D5

Selkirk U.K. 55°33N 2°50W 11 F6
Selkirk I. = Horse I.
Canada 53°20N 99°6W 71 C9
Selkirk Mts. Canada 51°15N 117°40W 68 G8
Sellafield U.K. 54°25N 3°29W 12 C4
Sellia Greece 35°12N 24°23E 25 D6
Sells U.S.A. 31°55N 111°53W 77 L8
Selma Ala., U.S.A. 32°25N 87°1W 85 E11
Selma Calif., U.S.A. 36°34N 119°37W 78 J7
Selma N.C., U.S.A. 35°32N 78°17W 85 D15
Selmer U.S.A. 35°10N 88°36W 85 D10
Selous ⌂ Tanzania 8°37S 37°42E 55 D4
Selowandoma Falls
Zimbabwe 21°15S 31°50E 55 G3
Selpele Indonesia 0°1S 130°5E 37 E8
Selsey Bill U.K. 50°43N 0°47W 13 G7
Seltso Russia 53°22N 34°4E 18 D5
Selu Indonesia 7°32S 130°55E 37 F8
Selva Argentina 29°50S 62°0W 94 B3
Selva Spain 39°46N 2°54E 24 B9
Selva Lancandona = Montes
Azules ⌂ Mexico 16°21N 91°3W 87 D6
Selvagens, Ilhas Madeira 30°5N 15°55W 50 B2
Selvas Brazil 6°30S 67°0W 92 E5
Selwyn L. Canada 60°0N 104°30W 71 B8
Selwyn Mts. Canada 63°0N 130°0W 68 E5
Selwyn Ra. Australia 21°10S 140°0E 62 C3
Seman → Albania 40°47N 19°30E 23 D8
Semarang Indonesia 7°0S 110°26E 37 G14
Sembabule Uganda 0°4S 31°25E 54 C3
Sembawang Singapore 1°27N 103°50E 39 d
Sembung Indonesia 8°28S 115°11E 37 J18
Semeru Indonesia 8°4S 112°55E 37 H15
Semey Kazakhstan 50°30N 80°10E 28 D9
Seminoe Res. U.S.A. 42°9N 106°55W 76 E10
Seminole Okla., U.S.A. 35°14N 96°41W 84 D6
Seminole Tex., U.S.A. 32°43N 102°39W 84 E3
Seminole Draw →
U.S.A. 32°27N 102°20W 84 E3
Semipalatinsk = Semey
Kazakhstan 50°30N 80°10E 28 D9
Semirara Is. Phil. 12°0N 121°20E 37 B6
Semisopochnoi I.
U.S.A. 51°55N 179°36E 74 E3
Semitau Indonesia 0°29N 111°57E 36 D4
Semiyarka Kazakhstan 50°55N 78°23E 28 D8
Semmering P. Austria 47°41N 15°45E 16 E8
Semnān Iran 35°40N 53°23E 45 C7
Semnān □ Iran 36°0N 54°0E 45 C7
Semporna Malaysia 4°30N 118°33E 37 D5
Semuda Indonesia 2°51S 112°58E 36 E4
Sen → Cambodia 12°32N 104°28E 38 F5
Senā Iran 28°27N 51°36E 45 D6
Sena Mozam. 17°25S 35°0E 55 F4
Sena Madureira Brazil 9°5S 68°45W 92 E5
Senador Pompeu Brazil 5°40S 39°20W 93 E11
Senang, Pulau Singapore 1°11N 103°52E 39 d
Senanga Zambia 16°7S 23°16E 53 H4
Senatobia U.S.A. 34°37N 89°58W 85 D10
Sencelles Spain 39°39N 2°54E 24 B9
Sendai Kagoshima, Japan 31°50N 130°20E 31 J5
Sendai Miyagi, Japan 38°15N 140°53E 30 E10
Sendai-Wan Japan 38°15N 141°0E 30 E10
Sendhwa India 21°41N 75°6E 42 J6
Seneca U.S.A. 34°41N 82°57W 85 D13
Seneca Falls U.S.A. 42°55N 76°48W 83 D8
Seneca L. U.S.A. 42°40N 76°54W 82 D8
Senecaville L. U.S.A. 39°55N 81°25W 82 G3
Senegal ■ W. Afr. 14°30N 14°30W 50 F3
Senegal → W. Afr. 15°48N 16°32W 50 E2
Senegambia Africa 12°45N 12°0W 48 E2
Senekal S. Africa 28°20S 27°36E 57 D4
Senga Hill Zambia 9°19S 31°11E 55 D3
Senge Khambab = Indus →
Pakistan 24°20N 67°47E 42 G2
Sengerema Tanzania 2°42S 32°35E 54 C3
Sengua → Zimbabwe 17°7S 28°5E 55 F2
Senhor-do-Bonfim
Brazil 10°30S 40°10W 93 F10
Senigállia Italy 43°43N 13°13E 22 C5
Senj Croatia 45°0N 14°58E 16 F8
Senja Norway 69°25N 17°30E 8 B17
Senkaku-Shotō
E. China Sea 25°45N 123°30E 31 M1
Senkuang Indonesia 1°11N 104°2E 39 d
Senlis France 49°13N 2°35E 20 B5
Senmonorom Cambodia 12°27N 107°12E 38 F6
Senneterre Canada 48°25N 77°15W 72 C4
Seno Laos 16°35N 104°50E 38 D5
Senqu = Orange →
S. Africa 28°41S 16°28E 56 D2
Sens France 48°11N 3°15E 20 B5
Senta Serbia 45°55N 20°3E 23 B9
Sentani Indonesia 2°36S 140°37E 37 E10
Sentery = Lubao
Dem. Rep. of the Congo 5°17S 25°42E 54 D2
Sentinel U.S.A. 32°52N 113°13W 77 K7
Sentosa Singapore 1°16N 103°50E 39 d
Seo de Urgel = La Seu d'Urgell
Spain 42°22N 1°23E 21 A6
Seogwipo S. Korea 33°13N 126°34E 35 H14
Seohara India 29°20N 78°35E 43 E8
Seonath → India 21°44N 82°28E 43 J10
Seongnam S. Korea 37°26N 127°6E 35 F14
Seoni India 22°5N 79°30E 43 H8
Seoni Malwa India 22°27N 77°28E 42 H8
Seosan S. Korea 36°47N 126°27E 35 F14
Seoul S. Korea 37°31N 126°58E 35 F14
Sepīdān Iran 30°20N 52°5E 45 D7
Sepo'o N. Korea 38°57N 127°25E 35 E14
Sepone Laos 16°45N 106°13E 38 D6
Sept-Îles Canada 50°13N 66°22W 73 B6
Sequim U.S.A. 48°5N 123°6W 78 B3
Sequoia △ U.S.A. 36°30N 118°30W 78 J8
Seraing Belgium 50°35N 5°32E 15 D5

Serakhis → Cyprus 35°13N 32°55E 25 D11
Seram Indonesia 3°10S 129°0E 37 E7
Seram Sea Indonesia 2°30S 128°30E 37 E7
Serampore = Shrirampur
India 22°44N 88°21E 43 H13
Serangtsara Madag. 18°30S 49°5E 57 B8
Serang Indonesia 6°8S 106°1E 37 G12
Serangoon Singapore 1°23N 103°54E 39 d
Serasan Indonesia 2°29N 109°4E 36 D3
Serbia ■ Europe 43°20N 20°0E 23 B9
Serdar Turkmenistan 39°4N 56°23E 45 B8
Serdobsk Russia 52°28N 44°10E 18 D7
Seremban Malaysia 2°43N 101°53E 39 L3
Serengeti △ Tanzania 2°11S 35°0E 54 C3
Serengeti Plain Tanzania 2°40S 35°0E 54 C4
Serenje Zambia 13°14S 30°15E 55 E3
Sereth = Siret →
Romania 45°24N 28°1E 17 F14
Sergeya Kirova, Ostrova
Russia 77°30N 90°0E 29 B10
Sergino Russia 62°25N 65°12E 28 C7
Sergipe □ Brazil 10°30S 37°30W 93 F11
Sergiyev Posad Russia 56°20N 38°10E 18 C6
Serhetabat Turkmenistan 35°20N 62°18E 45 C9
Seria Brunei 4°37N 114°23E 36 D4
Serian Malaysia 1°10N 110°31E 36 D4
Seribu, Kepulauan
Indonesia 5°36S 106°33E 36 F3
Sericho Kenya 1°5N 39°5E 54 B4
Serifos Greece 37°9N 24°30E 23 F6
Sérigny → Canada 56°47N 66°0W 73 A6
Seringapatam Reef
Australia 13°38S 122°5E 60 B3
Seririt Indonesia 8°12S 114°56E 37 J17
Serkout Algeria 23°56N 6°47E 50 D7
Sermata Indonesia 8°15S 128°50E 37 F7
Sermersuaq Greenland 79°30N 62°0W 69 B19
Serov Russia 59°29N 60°35E 18 C11
Serowe Botswana 22°25S 26°43E 56 C4
Serpentine Lakes
Australia 28°30S 129°10E 61 E4
Serpent's Mouth = Sierpe, Bocas
de la Venezuela 10°0N 61°30W 93 L15
Serpukhov Russia 54°55N 37°28E 18 D6
Serra do Navio Brazil 0°59N 52°3W 93 C8
Serranía San Luís △
Paraguay 22°35S 57°22W 94 A4
Serranía San Rafael △
Paraguay 26°30S 56°0W 95 B4
Serres Greece 41°5N 23°31E 23 D10
Serrezuela Argentina 30°40S 65°20W 94 C2
Serrinha Brazil 11°39S 39°0W 93 F11
Sertanópolis Brazil 23°4S 51°2W 95 A5
Serua Indonesia 6°18S 130°1E 37 F8
Serui Indonesia 1°53S 136°10E 37 E9
Serule Botswana 21°57S 27°20E 56 C4
Ses Salines Spain 39°21N 3°3E 24 B10
Sese Is. Uganda 0°20S 32°20E 54 C3
Sesepe Indonesia 1°30S 127°59E 37 E7
Sesfontein Namibia 19°7S 13°39E 56 B1
Sesheke Zambia 17°29S 24°13E 56 B3
S'Espalmador Spain 38°47N 1°26E 24 C7
S'Espardell Spain 38°48N 1°29E 24 C7
S'Estanyol Spain 39°22N 2°54E 24 B9
Setana Japan 42°26N 139°51E 30 C9
Sète France 43°25N 3°42E 20 E5
Sete Lagoas Brazil 19°27S 44°16W 93 G10
Sétif Algeria 36°9N 5°26E 50 A7
Seto Japan 35°14N 137°6E 31 G8
Setonaikai Japan 34°20N 133°30E 31 G6
Setonaikai △ Japan 34°15N 133°15E 31 G6
Settat Morocco 33°0N 7°40W 50 B4
Setting L. Canada 55°0N 98°38W 71 C9
Settle U.K. 54°5N 2°16W 12 C5
Settlement, The
Br. Virgin Is. 18°43N 64°22W 89 e
Settlers S. Africa 25°2S 28°30E 57 C4
Setúbal Portugal 38°30N 8°58E 21 C1
Setúbal, B. de Portugal 38°40N 8°56W 21 C1
Seul, Lac Canada 50°20N 92°30W 72 B1
Sevan, Ozero = Sevana Lich
Armenia 40°30N 45°20E 44 A5
Sevana Lich Armenia 40°30N 45°20E 44 A5
Sevastopol Ukraine 44°35N 33°30E 19 F5
Seven Sisters Canada 54°56N 128°10W 70 C3
Severn → Canada 56°2N 87°36W 72 A2
Severn → U.K. 51°35N 2°40W 13 F5
Severnaya Zemlya
Russia 79°0N 100°0E 29 B11
Severnyye Uvaly Russia 60°0N 50°0E 18 C8
Severo-Kurilsk Russia 50°40N 156°8E 29 D16
Severo-Yeniseyskiy
Russia 60°22N 93°1E 29 C10
Severo-Zapadnyy □ Russia 65°0N 40°0E 28 C4
Severobaykalsk
Russia 55°39N 109°19E 29 D11
Severodvinsk Russia 64°27N 39°58E 18 B6
Severomorsk Russia 69°5N 33°27E 8 B25
Severouralsk Russia 60°9N 59°57E 18 B10
Sevier → U.S.A. 39°4N 113°6W 76 G7
Sevier Desert U.S.A. 39°40N 112°45W 76 G7
Sevier L. U.S.A. 38°54N 113°9W 76 G7
Seville = Sevilla Spain 37°23N 5°58W 21 D2
Seville Spain 37°23N 5°58W 21 D2
Sevlievo Bulgaria 43°2N 25°6E 23 C11
Sevnica Slovenia 46°2N 15°19E 16 E8
Sewani India 28°58N 75°39E 42 E6
Seward Alaska, U.S.A. 60°7N 149°27W 68 F2
Seward Nebr., U.S.A. 40°55N 97°6W 80 E5
Seward Pa., U.S.A. 40°25N 79°1W 82 F5
Seward Peninsula
U.S.A. 65°30N 166°0W 74 B6
Sewell Chile 34°10S 70°23W 94 C1
Sewer Indonesia 5°53S 134°40E 37 F8
Sewickley U.S.A. 40°32N 80°12W 82 F4
Sexsmith Canada 55°21N 118°47W 70 B5
Seychelles ■ Ind. Oc. 5°0S 56°0E 53 b
Seyðisfjörður Iceland 65°16N 13°57W 8 D7
Seydişehir Turkey 37°25N 31°51E 19 G5

Seydvān Iran 38°34N 45°2E 44 B5
Seyhan → Turkey 36°43N 34°53E 44 B2
Seym → Ukraine 51°27N 32°34E 19 D5
Seymour Australia 37°2S 145°10E 63 F4
Seymour S. Africa 32°33S 26°46E 57 E4
Seymour Conn., U.S.A. 41°24N 73°4W 83 E11
Seymour Ind., U.S.A. 38°58N 85°53W 81 F11
Seymour Tex., U.S.A. 33°35N 99°16W 84 E5
Sfântu Gheorghe Romania 45°52N 25°48E 17 F13
Sfax Tunisia 34°49N 10°48E 51 B8
Sha Tau Kok China 22°33N 114°13E 33 F11
Sha Tin China 22°23N 114°12E 33 G11
Shaanxi □ China 35°0N 109°0E 34 G5
Shaba = Katanga □ Dem. Rep. of the Congo 8°0S 25°0E 54 D2
Shaba ⌂ Kenya 0°38N 37°48E 54 B4
Shabeelle → Somali Rep. 2°0N 44°0E 47 G3
Shabogamo L. Canada 53°15N 66°30W 73 B6
Shabunda Dem. Rep. of the Congo 2°40S 27°16E 54 C2
Shache China 38°20N 77°10E 32 C2
Shackleton Fracture Zone S. Ocean 60°0S 60°0W 5 B18
Shackleton Ice Shelf Antarctica 66°0S 100°0E 5 C8
Shackleton Inlet Antarctica 83°0S 160°0E 5 E11
Shādegān Iran 30°40N 48°38E 45 D6
Shadi India 33°24N 77°14E 43 C7
Shadrinsk Russia 56°5N 63°32E 28 D7
Shadyside U.S.A. 39°58N 80°45W 82 G4
Shafter U.S.A. 35°30N 119°16W 79 K7
Shaftesbury U.K. 51°0N 2°11W 13 F5
Shaftsbury U.S.A. 43°0N 73°11W 83 D11
Shagram Pakistan 36°24N 72°20E 43 A5
Shah Alam Malaysia 3°5N 101°32E 39 L3
Shah Alizai Pakistan 29°25N 66°33E 42 E2
Shah Bunder Pakistan 24°13N 67°56E 42 G2
Shahabad Punjab, India 30°10N 76°55E 42 D7
Shahabad Raj., India 25°15N 77°11E 42 G7
Shahabad Ut. P., India 27°36N 79°56E 43 F8
Shahadpur Pakistan 25°55N 68°35E 42 G3
Shahbā' Syria 32°52N 36°38E 46 C5
Shahdād Iran 30°30N 57°40E 45 D8
Shahdād, Namakzār-e Iran 30°20N 58°20E 45 D8
Shahdadkot Pakistan 27°50N 67°55E 42 F2
Shahdol India 23°19N 81°26E 43 H9
Shahe China 37°0N 114°32E 34 F8
Shahganj India 26°3N 82°44E 43 F10
Shahgarh India 27°15N 69°50E 42 F3
Shahjahanpur India 27°54N 79°57E 43 F8
Shahpur = Salmās Iran 38°11N 44°47E 44 B5
Shahpur India 22°12N 77°58E 42 H7
Shahpur Baluchistan, Pakistan 28°46N 68°27E 42 E3
Shahpur Punjab, Pakistan 32°17N 72°26E 42 C5
Shahpur Chakar Pakistan 26°9N 68°39E 42 F3
Shahpura Mad. P., India 23°10N 80°45E 43 H9
Shahpura Raj., India 25°38N 74°56E 42 G6
Shahr-e Bābak Iran 30°7N 55°9E 45 D7
Shahr-e Kord Iran 32°15N 50°55E 45 C6
Shāhrakht Iran 33°38N 60°16E 45 C9
Shahrezā = Qomsheh Iran 32°0N 51°55E 45 D6
Shahrig Pakistan 30°15N 67°40E 42 D2
Shāhrud = Emāmrūd Iran 36°30N 55°0E 45 B7
Shahukou China 40°20N 112°18E 34 D7
Shaikhabad Afghan. 34°2N 68°45E 42 B3
Shajapur India 23°27N 76°21E 42 H7
Shajing China 22°44N 113°48E 33 F10
Shakargarh Pakistan 32°17N 75°10E 42 C6
Shakawe Botswana 18°28S 21°49E 56 B3
Shaker Heights U.S.A. 41°28N 81°32W 82 E3
Shakhtersk Russia 49°10N 142°8E 29 E15
Shakhty Russia 47°40N 40°16E 19 E7
Shakhunya Russia 57°40N 46°46E 18 C8
Shaki Nigeria 8°41N 3°21E 50 G6
Shaksam Valley Asia 36°0N 76°20E 43 A7
Shallow Lake Canada 44°36N 81°5W 82 B3
Shalqar Kazakhstan 47°48N 59°39E 28 E6
Shaluli Shan China 30°40N 99°55E 41 D21
Shām Iran 26°39N 57°21E 45 E8
Shām, Bādiyat ash Asia 32°0N 40°0E 44 C3
Shamâl Sînî □ Egypt 30°30N 33°30E 46 E2
Shamattawa Canada 55°51N 92°5W 72 A1
Shamattawa → Canada 55°1N 85°23W 72 A2
Shamīl Iran 27°30N 56°55E 45 E8
Shāmkūh Iran 35°47N 57°50E 45 C8
Shamli India 29°32N 77°18E 42 E7
Shammar, Jabal Si. Arabia 27°40N 41°0E 44 E4
Shamo = Gobi Asia 44°0N 110°0E 34 C6
Shamo, L. Ethiopia 5°45N 37°30E 47 F2
Shamokin U.S.A. 40°47N 76°34W 83 F8
Shamrock Canada 45°23N 76°50W 83 A8
Shamrock U.S.A. 35°13N 100°15W 84 D4
Shamva Zimbabwe 17°20S 31°32E 55 F3
Shan □ Burma 21°30N 98°30E 41 J21
Shan Xian China 34°50N 116°5E 34 G9
Shanchengzhen China 42°20N 125°20E 35 C13
Shāndak Iran 28°28N 60°27E 45 D9
Shandon U.S.A. 35°39N 120°23W 78 K6
Shandong □ China 36°0N 118°0E 35 G10
Shandong Bandao China 37°0N 121°0E 35 F11
Shandur Pass Pakistan 36°4N 72°31E 43 A5
Shang Xian = Shangzhou China 33°50N 109°58E 34 H5
Shangalowe Dem. Rep. of the Congo 10°50S 26°30E 55 E2
Shangani Zimbabwe 19°41S 29°20E 57 B4
Shangani → Zimbabwe 18°41S 27°10E 55 F2
Shangbancheng China 40°50N 118°1E 35 D10
Shangdu China 41°30N 113°30E 34 D7
Shanghai China 31°15N 121°26E 33 C7
Shanghe China 37°20N 117°10E 35 F9
Shangnan China 33°32N 110°50E 34 H6
Shangqiu China 34°26N 115°36E 34 G8
Shangrao China 28°25N 117°59E 33 D6
Shangri-La = Zhongdian China 27°48N 99°42E 32 D4
Shangshui China 33°42N 114°35E 33 C6
Shangzhi China 45°22N 127°56E 35 B14
Shangzhou China 33°50N 109°58E 34 H5
Shanhetun China 44°33N 127°15E 35 B14
Shanklin U.K. 50°38N 1°11W 13 G6
Shannon N.Z. 40°33S 175°25E 59 D5
Shannon → Ireland 52°35N 9°30W 10 D2
Shannon ✕ (SNN) Ireland 52°42N 8°57W 10 D3
Shannon, Mouth of the Ireland 52°30N 9°55W 10 D2
Shannon △ Australia 34°35S 116°25E 61 F2
Shannonbridge Ireland 53°17N 8°3W 10 C3
Shansi = Shanxi □ China 37°0N 112°0E 34 F7
Shantar, Ostrov Bolshoy Russia 55°9N 137°40E 29 D14
Shantipur India 23°17N 88°25E 43 H13
Shantou China 23°18N 116°40E 33 D6
Shantung = Shandong □ China 36°0N 118°0E 35 G10
Shanxi □ China 37°0N 112°0E 34 F7
Shanyang China 33°31N 109°55E 34 H5
Shanyin China 39°25N 112°56E 34 E7
Shaoguan China 24°48N 113°35E 33 D6
Shaoxing China 30°0N 120°35E 33 D7
Shaoyang China 27°14N 111°25E 33 D6
Shap U.K. 54°32N 2°40W 12 C5
Shapinsay U.K. 59°3N 2°51W 11 B6
Shaqra' Si. Arabia 25°15N 45°16E 44 E5
Shaqrā' Yemen 13°22N 45°44E 47 E4
Sharafkhāneh Iran 38°11N 45°29E 44 B5
Sharbot Lake Canada 44°46N 76°41W 83 B8
Shari Japan 43°55N 144°40E 30 C12
Sharjah = Ash Shāriqah U.A.E. 25°23N 55°26E 45 E7
Shark B. Australia 25°30S 113°32E 61 E1
Shark Bay △ Australia 25°30S 113°30E 61 E1
Sharm el Sheikh Egypt 27°53N 34°18E 51 C12
Sharon Canada 44°6N 79°26W 82 B5
Sharon Mass., U.S.A. 42°7N 71°11W 83 D13
Sharon Pa., U.S.A. 41°14N 80°31W 82 E4
Sharon Springs Kans., U.S.A. 38°54N 101°45W 80 F3
Sharon Springs N.Y., U.S.A. 42°48N 74°37W 83 D10
Sharp Pt. Australia 10°58S 142°43E 62 A3
Sharpe L. Canada 54°24N 93°40W 72 B1
Sharpsville U.S.A. 41°15N 80°29W 82 E4
Sharqi, Al Jabal ash Lebanon 33°40N 36°10E 46 B5
Sharya Russia 58°22N 45°20E 18 C8
Shashemene Ethiopia 7°13N 38°33E 47 F2
Shashi Botswana 21°15S 27°27E 57 C4
Shashi China 30°25N 112°14E 33 C6
Shashi → Africa 21°14S 29°20E 55 G2
Shasta, Mt. U.S.A. 41°25N 122°12W 76 F2
Shasta L. U.S.A. 40°43N 122°25W 76 F2
Shatsky Rise Pac. Oc. 34°0N 157°0E 64 D7
Shatt al Arab Asia 29°57N 48°34E 45 D6
Shaunavon Canada 49°35N 108°25W 71 D7
Shaver L. U.S.A. 37°9N 119°18W 78 H7
Shaw → Australia 20°21S 119°17E 60 D2
Shaw I. Australia 20°30S 149°2E 62 b
Shawanaga Canada 45°31N 80°17W 82 A4
Shawangunk Mts. U.S.A. 41°35N 74°30W 83 E10
Shawano U.S.A. 44°47N 88°36W 80 C9
Shawinigan Canada 46°35N 72°50W 72 C5
Shawmari, J. ash Jordan 30°35N 36°35E 46 E5
Shawnee U.S.A. 35°20N 96°55W 84 D6
Shay Gap Australia 20°30S 120°10E 60 D3
Shaybārā Si. Arabia 25°26N 36°47E 44 E3
Shaykh, J. ash Lebanon 33°25N 35°50E 46 B4
Shaykh Miskīn Syria 32°49N 36°9E 46 C5
Shaykh Sa'd Iraq 32°34N 46°17E 44 C5
Shāzand Iran 33°56N 49°24E 45 C6
Shchūchīnsk Kazakhstan 52°56N 70°12E 28 D8
She Xian China 36°30N 113°40E 34 F7
Shebele = Shabeelle → Somali Rep. 2°0N 44°0E 47 G3
Sheboygan U.S.A. 43°46N 87°45W 80 D10
Shediac Canada 46°14N 64°32W 73 C7
Sheelin, L. Ireland 53°48N 7°20W 10 C4
Sheenjek → U.S.A. 66°45N 144°33W 74 B11
Sheep Haven Ireland 55°11N 7°52W 10 A4
Sheep Range U.S.A. 36°35N 115°15W 79 J11
Sheerness U.K. 51°26N 0°47E 13 F8
Sheet Harbour Canada 44°56N 62°31W 73 D7
Sheffield U.K. 53°23N 1°28W 12 D6
Sheffield Ala., U.S.A. 34°46N 87°41W 85 D11
Sheffield Mass., U.S.A. 42°5N 73°21W 83 D11
Sheffield Pa., U.S.A. 41°42N 79°3W 82 E5
Sheikhpura India 25°9N 85°53E 43 G11
Shekhupura Pakistan 31°42N 73°58E 42 D5
Shekou China 22°30N 113°55E 33 G10
Shelburne N.S., Canada 43°47N 65°20W 73 D6
Shelburne Ont., Canada 44°4N 80°15W 82 B4
Shelburne U.S.A. 44°23N 73°14W 83 B11
Shelburne B. Australia 11°50S 142°50E 62 A3
Shelburne Falls U.S.A. 42°36N 72°45W 83 D12
Shelby Mich., U.S.A. 43°37N 86°22W 80 D10
Shelby Miss., U.S.A. 33°57N 90°46W 85 E9
Shelby Mont., U.S.A. 48°30N 111°51W 76 B8
Shelby N.C., U.S.A. 35°17N 81°32W 85 D14
Shelby Ohio, U.S.A. 40°53N 82°40W 82 F2
Shelbyville Ill., U.S.A. 39°24N 88°48W 80 F9
Shelbyville Ind., U.S.A. 39°31N 85°47W 81 F11
Shelbyville Ky., U.S.A. 38°13N 85°14W 81 F11
Shelbyville Tenn., U.S.A. 35°29N 86°28W 85 D11
Sheldon U.S.A. 43°11N 95°51W 80 D6
Sheldrake Canada 50°20N 64°51W 73 B7
Shelikhova, Zaliv Russia 59°30N 157°0E 29 D16
Shelikof Strait U.S.A. 57°30N 155°0W 74 D9
Shell Lakes Australia 29°20S 127°30E 61 E4
Shellbrook Canada 53°13N 106°24W 71 C7
Shellharbour Australia 34°31S 150°51E 63 E5
Shelter I. U.S.A. 41°4N 72°20W 83 E12
Shelton Conn., U.S.A. 41°19N 73°5W 83 E11
Shelton Wash., U.S.A. 47°13N 123°6W 78 C3
Shen Xian China 36°15N 115°40E 34 F8
Shenandoah Iowa, U.S.A. 40°46N 95°22W 80 E6
Shenandoah Pa., U.S.A. 40°49N 76°12W 83 F8
Shenandoah Va., U.S.A. 38°29N 78°37W 81 F14
Shenandoah → U.S.A. 39°19N 77°44W 81 F15
Shenandoah △ U.S.A. 38°35N 78°22W 81 F14
Shenchi China 39°8N 112°10E 34 E7
Shendam Nigeria 8°49N 9°30E 50 G7
Shendî Sudan 16°46N 33°22E 51 E12
Shenfeng China 39°3N 116°42E 34 E9
Shenjingzi China 44°40N 124°30E 35 B13
Shenmu China 38°50N 110°29E 34 E6
Shenqiu China 33°25N 115°5E 34 H8
Shensi = Shaanxi □ China 35°0N 109°0E 34 G5
Shenyang China 41°48N 123°27E 35 D12
Shenzhen China 22°32N 114°5E 33 F10
Shenzhen ✕ (SZX) China 22°41N 113°49E 33 F10
Shenzhen Shuiku China 22°34N 114°8E 33 F11
Shenzhen Wan China 22°27N 113°55E 33 G10
Sheo India 26°11N 71°15E 42 F4
Sheopur Kalan India 25°40N 76°40E 42 G7
Shepetivka Ukraine 50°10N 27°10E 17 C14
Shepparton Australia 36°23S 145°26E 63 F4
Sheppey, I. of U.K. 51°25N 0°48E 13 F8
Shepton Mallet U.K. 51°11N 2°33W 13 F5
Sheqi China 33°12N 112°57E 34 H7
Sher Qila Pakistan 36°7N 74°2E 43 A6
Sherborne U.K. 50°57N 2°31W 13 G5
Sherbro I. S. Leone 7°30N 12°40W 50 G3
Sherbrooke N.S., Canada 45°8N 61°59W 73 C7
Sherbrooke Qué., Canada 45°28N 71°57W 83 A13
Sherburne U.S.A. 42°41N 75°30W 83 D9
Shergarh India 26°20N 72°18E 42 F5
Sherghati India 24°34N 84°47E 43 G11
Sheridan Ark., U.S.A. 34°19N 92°24W 84 D8
Sheridan Wyo., U.S.A. 44°48N 106°58W 76 D10
Sheringham U.K. 52°56N 1°13E 12 E9
Sherkin I. Ireland 51°28N 9°26W 10 E2
Sherkot India 29°22N 78°35E 43 E8
Sherlovaya Gora Russia 50°34N 116°15E 29 D12
Sherman N.Y., U.S.A. 42°9N 79°35W 82 D5
Sherman Tex., U.S.A. 33°38N 96°36W 84 E6
Sherpur India 25°34N 83°47E 43 G10
Sherridon Canada 55°8N 101°5W 71 B8
Sherwood Forest U.K. 53°6N 1°7W 12 D6
Sherwood Park Canada 53°31N 113°19W 70 C6
Sheslay → Canada 58°48N 132°5W 70 B2
Shethanei L. Canada 58°48N 97°50W 71 B9
Shetland □ U.K. 60°30N 1°30W 11 A7
Shetland Is. U.K. 60°30N 1°30W 11 A7
Shetrunji → India 21°19N 72°7E 42 J5
Sheung Shui China 22°31N 114°7E 33 F11
Shey-Phoksundo △ Nepal 29°30N 82°45E 43 E10
Sheyenne → U.S.A. 47°2N 96°50W 80 B5
Shiashkotan, Ostrov Russia 48°49N 154°6E 29 E16
Shibām Yemen 15°59N 48°36E 47 D4
Shibata Japan 37°57N 139°20E 30 F9
Shibecha Japan 43°17N 144°36E 30 C12
Shibetsu Japan 44°10N 142°23E 30 B11
Shibogama L. Canada 53°35N 88°15W 72 B2
Shibushi Japan 31°25N 131°8E 31 J5
Shickshinny U.S.A. 41°9N 76°9W 83 E8
Shickshock Mts. = Chic-Chocs, Mts. Canada 48°55N 66°0W 73 C6
Shidao China 36°50N 122°25E 35 F12
Shido Japan 34°19N 134°10E 31 G7
Shiel, L. U.K. 56°48N 5°34W 11 E3
Shield, C. Australia 13°20S 136°20E 62 A2
Shīeli Kazakhstan 44°20N 66°15E 28 E7
Shiga □ Japan 35°20N 136°0E 31 G8
Shiguaigou China 40°52N 110°15E 34 D6
Shihchiachuangi = Shijiazhuang China 38°2N 114°28E 34 E8
Shihezi China 44°15N 86°2E 32 B3
Shijiazhuang China 38°2N 114°28E 34 E8
Shikarpur India 28°17N 78°7E 42 E8
Shikarpur Pakistan 27°57N 68°39E 42 F3
Shikohabad India 27°6N 78°36E 43 F8
Shikoku □ Japan 33°30N 133°30E 31 H6
Shikoku-Sanchi Japan 33°30N 133°30E 31 H6
Shikotan, Ostrov Asia 43°47N 146°44E 29 E15
Shikotsu-Ko Japan 42°45N 141°25E 30 C10
Shikotsu-Tōya △ Japan 44°4N 145°8E 30 C10
Shiliguri India 26°45N 88°25E 41 F16
Shiliu = Changjiang China 19°20N 108°55E 38 C7
Shilka Russia 52°0N 115°55E 29 D12
Shilka → Russia 53°20N 121°26E 29 D13
Shillelagh Ireland 52°45N 6°32W 10 D5
Shillington U.S.A. 40°18N 75°58W 83 F9
Shillong India 25°35N 91°53E 41 G17
Shilo West Bank 32°4N 35°18E 46 C4
Shilou China 37°0N 110°48E 34 F6
Shimabara Japan 32°48N 130°20E 31 H5
Shimada Japan 34°49N 138°10E 31 G9
Shimane □ Japan 35°0N 132°30E 31 G6
Shimanovsk Russia 52°15N 127°30E 29 D13
Shimba Hills ⌂ Kenya 4°14S 39°25E 54 C4
Shimbiris Somali Rep. 10°44N 47°14E 47 E4
Shimizu Japan 35°0N 138°30E 31 G9
Shimla India 31°2N 77°9E 42 D7
Shimodate Japan 36°20N 139°55E 31 F9
Shimoga India 13°57N 75°32E 40 N9
Shimoni Kenya 4°38S 39°20E 54 C4
Shimonoseki Japan 33°58N 130°55E 31 H5
Shimpuru Rapids Namibia 17°45S 19°55E 56 B2
Shin, L. U.K. 58°5N 4°30W 11 C4
Shinano-Gawa → Japan 36°50N 138°30E 31 F9
Shināş Oman 24°46N 56°28E 45 E8
Shīndand Afghan. 33°12N 62°8E 40 C3
Shinglehouse U.S.A. 41°58N 78°12W 82 E6
Shingū Japan 33°40N 135°55E 31 H7
Shingwidzi S. Africa 23°5S 31°25E 57 C5
Shinjō Japan 38°46N 140°18E 30 E10
Shinkolobwe Dem. Rep. of the Congo 11°10S 26°40E 52 G5
Shinshār Syria 34°36N 36°43E 46 A5
Shinyanga Tanzania 3°45S 33°27E 54 C3
Shinyanga □ Tanzania 3°50S 34°0E 54 C3
Shio-no-Misaki Japan 33°25N 135°45E 31 H7
Shiogama Japan 38°19N 141°1E 30 E10
Shiojiri Japan 36°6N 137°58E 31 F8
Shipchenski Prokhod Bulgaria 42°45N 25°15E 23 C11
Shiping China 23°45N 102°23E 32 D5
Shippagan Canada 47°45N 64°45W 73 C7
Shippensburg U.S.A. 40°3N 77°31W 82 F7
Shippenville U.S.A. 41°15N 79°28W 82 E5
Shiprock U.S.A. 36°47N 108°41W 77 H9
Shiqma, N. → Israel 31°37N 34°30E 46 D3
Shiquan China 33°5N 108°15E 34 H5
Shiquan He = Indus → Pakistan 24°20N 67°47E 42 G2
Shīr Kūh Iran 31°39N 54°3E 45 D7
Shiragami-Misaki Japan 41°24N 140°12E 30 D10
Shirakawa Fukushima, Japan 37°7N 140°13E 31 F10
Shirakawa Gifu, Japan 36°17N 136°56E 31 F8
Shirane-San Gumma, Japan 36°48N 139°22E 31 F9
Shirane-San Yamanashi, Japan 35°42N 138°9E 31 G9
Shiraoi Japan 42°33N 141°21E 30 C10
Shīrāz Iran 29°42N 52°30E 45 D7
Shire → Africa 17°42S 35°19E 55 F4
Shiretoko-Misaki Japan 44°21N 145°20E 30 B12
Shirinab → Pakistan 30°15N 66°28E 42 D2
Shiriya-Zaki Japan 41°25N 141°30E 30 D10
Shiroishi Japan 38°0N 140°37E 30 F10
Shirshov Ridge Pac. Oc. 58°0N 170°0E 64 B8
Shīrvān Iran 37°30N 57°50E 45 B8
Shirwa, L. = Chilwa, L. Malawi 15°15S 35°40E 55 F4
Shishaldin Volcano U.S.A. 54°45N 163°58W 74 E7
Shivamogga = Shimoga India 13°57N 75°32E 40 N9
Shivpuri India 25°26N 77°42E 42 G7
Shixian China 43°5N 129°50E 35 C15
Shiyan China 22°42N 113°56E 33 F10
Shiyan Shuiku China 22°42N 113°54E 33 F10
Shizuishan China 39°15N 106°50E 34 E4
Shizuoka Japan 34°57N 138°24E 31 G9
Shizuoka □ Japan 35°15N 138°40E 31 G9
Shklov = Shklow Belarus 54°16N 30°15E 17 A16
Shklow Belarus 54°16N 30°15E 17 A16
Shkodër Albania 42°4N 19°32E 23 C8
Shkumbini → Albania 41°2N 19°31E 23 D8
Shmidta, Ostrov Russia 81°0N 91°0E 29 A10
Shō-Gawa → Japan 36°47N 137°4E 31 F8
Shoal L. Canada 49°33N 95°1W 71 D9
Shoal Lake Canada 50°30N 100°35W 71 C8
Shōdo-Shima Japan 34°30N 134°15E 31 G7
Sholapur = Solapur India 17°43N 75°56E 40 L9
Shōmrōn West Bank 32°15N 35°13E 46 C4
Shoreham U.S.A. 43°53N 73°18W 83 C11
Shoreham by Sea U.K. 50°50N 0°16W 13 G7
Shori → Pakistan 28°29N 69°44E 42 E3
Shorkot Pakistan 30°50N 72°0E 42 D4
Shorkot Road Pakistan 30°47N 72°15E 42 D5
Shoshone Calif., U.S.A. 35°58N 116°16W 79 K10
Shoshone Idaho, U.S.A. 42°56N 114°25W 76 E6
Shoshone L. U.S.A. 44°22N 110°43W 76 D8
Shoshone Mts. U.S.A. 39°20N 117°25W 76 G5
Shoshong Botswana 22°56S 26°31E 56 C4
Shoshoni U.S.A. 43°14N 108°7W 76 E9
Shouguang China 37°52N 118°45E 35 F10
Shouyang China 37°54N 113°8E 34 F7
Show Low U.S.A. 34°15N 110°2W 77 J8
Shqipëria = Albania ■ Europe 41°0N 20°0E 23 D9
Shreveport U.S.A. 32°31N 93°45W 84 E8
Shrewsbury U.K. 52°43N 2°45W 13 E5
Shri Mohangarh India 27°17N 71°18E 42 F4
Shrirampur India 22°44N 88°21E 43 H13
Shropshire □ U.K. 52°36N 2°45W 13 E5
Shū Kazakhstan 43°36N 73°42E 28 E8
Shuangcheng China 45°20N 126°15E 35 B14
Shuanggou China 34°2N 117°30E 35 G9
Shuangliao China 43°29N 123°30E 35 C12
Shuangshanzi China 40°20N 119°8E 35 D10
Shuangyang China 43°28N 125°40E 35 C13
Shuangyashan China 46°28N 131°5E 33 B8
Shuguri Falls Tanzania 8°33S 37°22E 55 D4
Shuiye China 36°7N 114°8E 34 F8
Shujalpur India 23°18N 76°46E 42 H7
Shukpa Kunzang India 34°22N 78°22E 43 B8
Shulan China 44°28N 127°0E 35 B14
Shule China 39°25N 76°3E 32 C2
Shule He → China 40°20N 92°50E 32 B4
Shumagin Is. U.S.A. 55°7N 160°30W 74 D7
Shumen Bulgaria 43°18N 26°55E 23 C12
Shumikha Russia 55°10N 63°15E 28 D7
Shungnak U.S.A. 66°52N 157°9W 74 B8
Shuo Xian = Shuozhou China 39°20N 112°33E 34 E7
Shuozhou China 39°20N 112°33E 34 E7
Shūr → Fārs, Iran 28°30N 55°0E 45 D7
Shūr → Kermān, Iran 30°52N 57°37E 45 D8
Shūr → Yazd, Iran 31°45N 55°15E 45 D7
Shūr Āb Iran 34°23N 51°11E 45 C6
Shūr Gaz Iran 29°10N 59°20E 45 D8
Shūrāb Iran 33°43N 56°29E 45 C8
Shūrjestān Iran 31°24N 52°25E 45 D7
Shurugwi Zimbabwe 19°40S 30°0E 55 F3
Shūsf Iran 31°50N 60°5E 45 D9
Shūshtar Iran 32°0N 48°50E 45 D6
Shuswap L. Canada 50°55N 119°3W 70 C5
Shute Harbour △ Australia 20°17S 148°47E 62 b
Shuyang China 34°10N 118°42E 35 G10
Shūzū Iran 29°52N 54°30E 45 D7
Shwebo Burma 22°30N 95°45E 41 H19
Shwegu Burma 24°15N 96°26E 41 G20
Shweli → Burma 23°45N 96°45E 41 H20
Shymkent Kazakhstan 42°18N 69°36E 28 E7
Shyok India 34°13N 78°12E 43 B8
Shyok → Pakistan 35°13N 75°53E 43 B6
Si Kiang = Xi Jiang → China 22°5N 113°20E 33 D6
Si Lanna △ Thailand 19°17N 99°12E 38 C2
Si Nakarin Res. Thailand 14°35N 99°0E 38 E2
Si-ngan = Xi'an China 34°15N 109°0E 34 G5
Si Prachan Thailand 14°37N 100°9E 38 E3
Si Racha Thailand 13°10N 100°48E 38 F3
Si Xian China 33°30N 117°50E 35 H9
Siachen Glacier Asia 35°20N 77°30E 43 B7
Siahaf → Pakistan 29°3N 68°57E 42 E3
Siahan Range Pakistan 27°30N 64°40E 40 F4
Siaksriindrapura Indonesia 0°51N 102°0E 36 D2
Sialkot Pakistan 32°32N 74°30E 42 C6
Siam = Thailand ■ Asia 16°0N 102°0E 38 E4
Sian = Xi'an China 34°15N 109°0E 34 G5
Sian Ka'an ⌂ Mexico 19°35N 87°40W 87 D7
Siantan Indonesia 3°10N 106°15E 36 D3
Sīāreh Iran 28°5N 60°14E 45 D9
Siargao I. Phil. 9°52N 126°3E 37 C7
Siari Pakistan 34°55N 76°40E 43 B7
Siasi Phil. 5°34N 120°50E 37 C6
Siau Indonesia 2°50N 125°25E 37 D7
Šiauliai Lithuania 55°56N 23°15E 9 J20
Sibâi, Gebel el Egypt 25°45N 34°10E 44 E2
Sibang Indonesia 8°34S 115°13E 37 K18
Sibay Russia 52°42N 58°39E 18 D10
Sibayi, L. S. Africa 27°20S 32°45E 57 D5
Šibenik Croatia 43°48N 15°54E 22 C6
Siberia = Sibirskiy □ Russia 58°0N 90°0E 29 D10
Siberia Russia 60°0N 100°0E 4 D13
Siberut Indonesia 1°30S 99°0E 36 E1
Sibi Pakistan 29°30N 67°54E 42 E2
Sibil = Oksibil Indonesia 4°59S 140°35E 37 E10
Sibiloi △ Kenya 4°0N 36°20E 54 B4
Sibirskiy □ Russia 58°0N 90°0E 29 D10
Sibirtsevo Russia 44°12N 132°26E 30 B5
Sibiti Congo 3°38S 13°19E 52 E2
Sibiu Romania 45°45N 24°9E 17 F13
Sibley U.S.A. 43°24N 95°45W 80 D6
Sibolga Indonesia 1°42N 98°45E 36 D1
Siborongborong Indonesia 2°13N 98°59E 39 L2
Sibsagar India 27°0N 94°36E 41 F19
Sibu Malaysia 2°18N 111°49E 36 D4
Sibuco Phil. 7°20N 122°10E 37 C6
Sibuguey B. Phil. 7°50N 122°45E 37 C6
Sibut C.A.R. 5°46N 19°10E 52 C3
Sibutu Phil. 4°45N 119°30E 37 D5
Sibutu Passage E. Indies 4°50N 120°0E 37 D6
Sibuyan I. Phil. 12°25N 122°40E 37 B6
Sibuyan Sea Phil. 12°30N 122°20E 37 B6
Sicamous Canada 50°49N 119°0W 70 C5
Siccus → Australia 31°55S 139°17E 63 E2
Sichon Thailand 9°0N 99°54E 39 H2
Sichuan □ China 30°30N 103°0E 32 C5
Sicilia Italy 37°30N 14°30E 22 F6
Sicily = Sicilia Italy 37°30N 14°30E 22 F6
Sicily, Str. of Medit. S. 37°35N 11°56E 22 F4
Sico → Honduras 15°58N 84°58W 88 C3
Sicuani Peru 14°21S 71°10W 92 F4
Sidari Greece 39°47N 19°41E 25 A3
Siddhapur India 23°56N 72°25E 42 H5
Siddipet India 18°5N 78°51E 40 K11
Sideros, Akra Greece 35°19N 26°19E 25 D8
Sidhauli India 27°17N 80°50E 43 F9
Sidhi India 24°25N 81°53E 43 G9
Sidi-bel-Abbès Algeria 35°13N 0°39W 50 A5
Sidi Ifni Morocco 29°29N 10°12W 50 C3
Sidikalang Indonesia 2°45N 98°19E 39 L2
Sidlaw Hills U.K. 56°32N 3°2W 11 E5
Sidley, Mt. Antarctica 77°2S 126°2W 5 D14
Sidmouth U.K. 50°40N 3°15W 13 G4
Sidmouth, C. Australia 13°25S 143°36E 62 A3
Sidney Canada 48°39N 123°24W 78 B3
Sidney Mont., U.S.A. 47°43N 104°9W 76 C11
Sidney N.Y., U.S.A. 42°19N 75°24W 83 D9
Sidney Nebr., U.S.A. 41°8N 102°59W 80 E2
Sidney Ohio, U.S.A. 40°17N 84°9W 81 E11
Sidney Lanier, L. U.S.A. 34°10N 84°4W 85 D12
Sidoarjo Indonesia 7°27S 112°43E 37 G15
Sidon = Saydā Lebanon 33°35N 35°25E 46 B4
Sidra, G. of = Surt, Khalīj Libya 31°40N 18°30E 51 B9
Siedlce Poland 52°10N 22°20E 17 B12
Sieg → Germany 50°46N 7°6E 16 C4
Siegen Germany 50°51N 8°0E 16 C5
Siem Pang Cambodia 14°7N 106°23E 38 E6
Siem Reap = Siemreab Cambodia 13°20N 103°52E 38 F4
Siemreab Cambodia 13°20N 103°52E 38 F4
Siena Italy 43°19N 11°21E 22 C4
Sieradz Poland 51°37N 18°41E 17 C10
Sierpe, Bocas de la Venezuela 10°0N 61°30W 93 L15
Sierra Blanca U.S.A. 31°11N 105°22W 84 F2
Sierra Blanca Peak U.S.A. 33°23N 105°49W 77 K11

Sierra City U.S.A. 39°34N 120°38W 78 F6
Sierra Colorada
  Argentina 40°35S 67°50W 96 E3
Sierra de Agalta △
  Honduras 15°1N 85°48W 88 C2
Sierra de Bahoruco △
  Dom. Rep. 18°10N 71°25W 89 C5
Sierra de La Culata △
  Venezuela 8°45N 71°10W 89 E5
Sierra de Lancandón △
  Guatemala 16°59N 90°23W 88 C1
Sierra de las Quijadas △
  Argentina 32°29S 67°55W 94 C2
Sierra de San Luis △
  Venezuela 11°20N 69°43W 89 D6
Sierra de San Pedro Mártir △
  Mexico 31°10N 115°30W 86 A1
Sierra Gorda Chile 22°50S 69°15W 94 A2
Sierra Leone ■ W. Afr. 9°0N 12°0W 50 G3
Sierra Madre Mexico 16°0N 93°0W 87 D6
Sierra Madre Occidental
  Mexico 27°0N 107°0W 86 B3
Sierra Madre Oriental
  Mexico 25°0N 100°0W 86 C5
Sierra Mojada Mexico 27°18N 103°41W 86 B4
Sierra Nevada Spain 37°3N 3°15W 21 D4
Sierra Nevada U.S.A. 39°0N 120°30W 78 H8
Sierra Nevada △
  Venezuela 8°35N 70°45W 89 E5
Sierra Nevada de Santa Marta △
  Colombia 10°56N 73°36W 89 D5
Sierra Vista U.S.A. 31°33N 110°18W 77 L8
Sierraville U.S.A. 39°36N 120°22W 78 F6
Sifnos Greece 37°0N 24°45E 23 F11
Sifton Canada 51°21N 100°8W 71 C8
Sifton Pass Canada 57°52N 126°15W 70 B3
Sig Algeria 35°32N 0°12W 50 A5
Sigatoka Fiji 18°8S 177°32E 59 a
Sighetu-Marmației
  Romania 47°57N 23°52E 17 E12
Sighișoara Romania 46°12N 24°50E 17 E13
Sigli Indonesia 5°25N 96°0E 36 C1
Siglufjörður Iceland 66°12N 18°55W 8 C4
Signal de Botrang Belgium 50°29N 6°4E 15 D6
Signal Pk. U.S.A. 33°20N 114°2W 79 M12
Signy I. Antarctica 60°43S 45°36W 5 C18
Sigsig Ecuador 3°0S 78°50W 92 D3
Sigüenza Spain 41°3N 2°40W 21 B4
Siguiri Guinea 11°31N 9°10W 50 F4
Sigulda Latvia 57°10N 24°55E 9 H21
Sihora India 23°29N 80°6E 43 H9
Siikajoki → Finland 64°50N 24°43E 8 D21
Siilinjärvi Finland 63°4N 27°39E 8 E22
Sijarira Ra. = Chizarira
  Zimbabwe 17°36S 27°45E 55 F2
Sika India 22°26N 69°47E 42 H3
Sikanni Chief →
  Canada 57°47N 122°15W 70 B4
Sikao Thailand 7°34N 99°21E 39 J2
Sikar India 27°33N 75°10E 42 F6
Sikasso Mali 11°18N 5°35W 50 F4
Sikeston U.S.A. 36°53N 89°35W 80 G9
Sikhote Alin, Khrebet
  Russia 45°0N 136°0E 30 B8
Sikhote Alin Ra. = Sikhote Alin,
  Khrebet Russia 45°0N 136°0E 30 B8
Sikinos Greece 36°40N 25°8E 23 F11
Sikkim □ India 27°50N 88°30E 41 F16
Sil → Spain 42°27N 7°43W 21 A2
Silacayoapan Mexico 17°30N 98°9W 87 D5
Silawad India 21°54N 74°54E 42 J6
Silchar India 24°49N 92°48E 41 G18
Siler City U.S.A. 35°44N 79°28W 85 D15
Silesia = Śląsk Poland 51°0N 16°30E 16 C9
Silgarhi Doti Nepal 29°15N 81°0E 43 E9
Silghat India 26°35N 93°0E 41 F18
Silhouette Seychelles 4°29S 55°12E 53 b
Silifke Turkey 36°22N 33°58E 44 B2
Siliguri = Shiliguri India 26°45N 88°25E 41 F16
Siling Co China 31°50N 89°20E 32 C3
Silistra Bulgaria 44°6N 27°19E 23 B12
Silivri Turkey 41°4N 28°14E 23 D13
Siljan Sweden 60°55N 14°45E 8 F16
Silkeborg Denmark 56°10N 9°32E 9 H13
Silkwood Australia 17°45S 146°2E 62 B4
Sillajhuay, Cordillera
  Chile 19°46S 68°40W 92 G5
Sillamäe Estonia 59°24N 27°45E 9 G22
Silloth U.K. 54°52N 3°23W 12 C4
Siloam Springs U.S.A. 36°11N 94°32W 84 C7
Silopi Turkey 37°15N 42°27E 44 B4
Silsbee U.S.A. 30°21N 94°11W 84 F7
Šilutė Lithuania 55°21N 21°33E 9 J19
Silvan Turkey 38°7N 41°2E 44 B4
Silvani India 23°18N 78°25E 43 H8
Silver City U.S.A. 32°46N 108°17W 77 K9
Silver Cr. → U.S.A. 43°16N 119°13W 76 E4
Silver Creek U.S.A. 42°33N 79°10W 82 D5
Silver L. U.S.A. 38°39N 120°6W 78 G6
Silver Lake Calif.,
  U.S.A. 35°21N 116°7W 79 K10
Silver Lake Oreg., U.S.A. 43°8N 121°3W 76 E3
Silvermine Mts. Ireland 52°47N 8°15W 10 D3
Silverton Colo., U.S.A. 37°49N 107°40W 77 H10
Silverton Tex., U.S.A. 34°28N 101°19W 84 D4
Silvies → U.S.A. 43°34N 119°2W 76 E4
Simaltala India 24°43N 86°33E 43 G12
Simanggang = Sri Aman
  Malaysia 1°15N 111°32E 36 D4
Simard, L. Canada 47°40N 78°40W 72 C4
Simav Turkey 39°4N 28°58E 23 E13
Simba Tanzania 2°10S 37°36E 54 C4
Simbirsk = Ulyanovsk
  Russia 54°20N 48°25E 18 D8
Simbo Tanzania 4°51S 29°41E 54 C2
Simcoe Canada 42°50N 80°20W 82 D4
Simcoe, L. Canada 44°25N 79°20W 82 B5
Simdega India 22°37N 84°31E 43 H11
Simeria Romania 45°51N 23°1E 17 F12

Simeulue Indonesia 2°45N 95°45E 36 D1
Simferopol Ukraine 44°55N 34°3E 19 F5
Simi Greece 36°35N 27°50E 23 F12
Simi Valley U.S.A. 34°16N 118°47W 79 L8
Simikot Nepal 30°0N 81°50E 43 E9
Simla = Shimla India 31°2N 77°9E 42 D7
Simlipal △ India 21°45N 86°30E 43 J12
Simmie Canada 49°56N 108°6W 71 D7
Simmler U.S.A. 35°21N 119°59W 79 K7
Simo älv = Simojoki →
  Finland 65°35N 25°1E 8 D21
Simojoki → Finland 65°35N 25°1E 8 D21
Simojovel Mexico 17°12N 92°38W 87 D6
Simonette → Canada 55°9N 118°15W 70 B5
Simonstown S. Africa 34°14S 18°26E 56 E2
Simpang Empat Malaysia 5°27N 100°29E 39 c
Simplonpass Switz. 46°15N 8°3E 20 C8
Simpson Desert Australia 25°0S 137°0E 62 D2
Simpson Desert △
  Australia 24°59S 138°21E 62 C2
Simpson Pen. Canada 68°34N 88°45W 69 D14
Simrishamn Sweden 55°33N 14°22E 9 J16
Simsbury U.S.A. 41°53N 72°48W 83 E12
Simushir, Ostrov
  Russia 46°50N 152°30E 29 E16
Sin Cowe I. S. China Sea 9°53N 114°19E 36 C4
Sina Dhago Somali Rep. 5°50N 47°0E 47 F4
Sinabang Indonesia 2°30N 96°24E 36 D1
Sinai = Es Sînâ' Egypt 29°0N 34°0E 46 F3
Sinai, Mt. = Mûsa, Gebel
  Egypt 28°33N 33°59E 44 D2
Sinaloa □ Mexico 25°0N 107°30W 86 C3
Sinaloa de Leyva
  Mexico 25°50N 108°14W 86 B3
Sinarades Greece 39°34N 19°51E 25 A3
Sincelejo Colombia 9°18N 75°24W 92 B3
Sinch'ang N. Korea 40°7N 128°28E 35 D15
Sinch'ŏn N. Korea 38°17N 125°21E 35 E13
Sinclair U.S.A. 41°47N 107°7W 76 F10
Sinclair Mills Canada 54°5N 121°40W 70 C4
Sinclair's B. U.K. 58°31N 3°5W 11 C5
Sinclairville U.S.A. 42°16N 79°16W 82 D5
Sincorá, Serra do Brazil 13°30S 41°0W 93 F10
Sind = Sindh □ Pakistan 26°0N 69°0E 42 G3
Sind → Jammu & Kashmir,
  India 34°18N 74°45E 43 B6
Sind → Mad. P., India 26°26N 79°13E 43 F8
Sind Sagar Doab Pakistan 32°0N 71°30E 42 D4
Sindangan Phil. 8°10N 123°5E 37 C6
Sindangbarang Indonesia 7°27S 107°1E 37 G12
Sinde Zambia 17°28S 25°51E 55 F2
Sindh □ Pakistan 24°20N 67°47E 42 G2
Sindh □ Pakistan 26°0N 69°0E 42 G3
Sindri India 23°45N 86°42E 43 H12
Sines Portugal 37°56N 8°51W 21 D1
Sines, C. de Portugal 37°58N 8°53W 21 D1
Sineu Spain 39°38N 3°1E 24 B10
Sing Buri Thailand 14°53N 100°25E 38 E3
Singa Sudan 13°10N 33°57E 51 F12
Singalila △ India 27°10N 88°5E 43 F13
Singapore ■ Asia 1°17N 103°51E 39 d
Singapore, Straits of Asia 1°15N 104°0E 39 d
Singapore Changi ✈ (SIN)
  Singapore 1°23N 103°59E 39 M4
Singaraja Indonesia 8°7S 115°6E 37 J18
Singatoka = Sigatoka Fiji 18°8S 177°32E 59 a
Singida Tanzania 4°49S 34°48E 54 C3
Singida □ Tanzania 6°0S 34°30E 54 D3
Singkaling Hkamti
  Burma 26°0N 95°39E 41 G19
Singkang Indonesia 4°8S 120°1E 37 E6
Singkawang Indonesia 1°0N 108°57E 36 D3
Singkep Indonesia 0°30S 104°25E 36 E2
Singkil Indonesia 2°17N 97°49E 39 L1
Singleton U.S.A. 32°33S 151°0E 63 E5
Singleton, Mt. N. Terr.,
  Australia 22°0S 130°46E 60 D5
Singleton, Mt. W. Austral.,
  Australia 29°27S 117°15E 61 E2
Singoli India 25°0N 75°22E 42 G6
Singora = Songkhla
  Thailand 7°13N 100°37E 39 J3
Sinhung N. Korea 40°11N 127°34E 35 D14
Siniscóla Italy 40°34N 9°41E 22 D3
Sinjai Indonesia 5°7S 120°20E 37 F6
Sinjár Iraq 36°19N 41°52E 44 B4
Sinkat Sudan 18°55N 36°49E 51 E13
Sinkiang = Xinjiang Uygur
  Zizhiqu □ China 42°0N 86°0E 32 C3
Sinmak N. Korea 38°25N 126°14E 35 E14
Sinmi-do N. Korea 39°33N 124°53E 35 E13
Sinnamary Fr. Guiana 5°25N 53°0W 93 B8
Sinni → Italy 40°8N 16°41E 22 D7
Sinop Turkey 42°1N 35°11E 19 F6
Sinor India 21°55N 73°20E 42 J5
Sinp'o N. Korea 40°0N 128°13E 35 E15
Sinsk Russia 61°8N 126°48E 29 C13
Sintang Indonesia 0°5N 111°35E 36 D4
Sinton U.S.A. 28°2N 97°31W 84 G6
Sintra Portugal 38°47N 9°25W 21 C1
Sinŭiju N. Korea 40°5N 124°24E 35 D13
Siocon Phil. 7°40N 122°10E 37 C6
Siófok Hungary 46°54N 18°3E 17 E10
Sion Switz. 46°14N 7°20E 20 C7
Sion Mills U.K. 54°48N 7°29W 10 B4
Sionainn = Shannon →
  Ireland 52°35N 9°30W 10 D2
Sioux Center U.S.A. 43°5N 96°11W 80 D5
Sioux City U.S.A. 42°30N 96°24W 80 D5
Sioux Falls U.S.A. 43°33N 96°44W 80 D5
Sioux Lookout Canada 50°10N 91°50W 72 B1
Sioux Narrows Canada 49°25N 94°10W 71 D10
Sipadan Malaysia 4°6N 118°38E 37 D5
Siparia Trin. & Tob. 10°8N 61°31W 93 K15
Siping China 43°8N 124°21E 35 C13
Sipiwesk L. Canada 55°5N 97°35W 71 B9
Siple Antarctica 75°0S 74°0W 5 D7
Sipra → India 23°55N 75°28E 42 H6

Sipura Indonesia 2°18S 99°40E 36 E1
Siquia → Nic. 12°10N 84°20W 88 D3
Siquijor Phil. 9°12N 123°35E 37 C6
Siquirres Costa Rica 10°6N 83°30W 88 D3
Şīr Abu Nu'ayr U.A.E. 25°20N 54°20E 45 E7
Şīr Banī Yās U.A.E. 24°19N 52°37E 45 E7
Sir Edward Pellew Group
  Australia 15°40S 137°10E 62 B2
Sir Graham Moore Is.
  Australia 13°53S 126°34E 60 B4
Sir James MacBrien, Mt.
  Canada 62°7N 127°41W 68 E6
Sira → Norway 58°23N 6°34E 9 G12
Siracusa Italy 37°4N 15°17E 22 F6
Sirajganj Bangla. 24°25N 89°47E 43 G13
Sirathu India 25°39N 81°19E 43 G9
Sīrdān Iran 36°39N 49°12E 45 B6
Siren U.S.A. 45°47N 92°24W 80 C7
Sirer Spain 38°56N 1°22E 24 C7
Siret → Romania 45°24N 28°1E 17 F14
Sirghāyā Syria 33°51N 36°8E 46 B5
Sirinat △ Thailand 8°6N 98°17E 39 a
Sīrjān Iran 29°30N 55°45E 45 D7
Sirmaur India 24°51N 81°23E 43 G9
Sirmilik △ Canada 72°50N 80°35W 69 C15
Sirohi India 24°52N 72°53E 42 G5
Sironj India 24°5N 77°39E 42 G7
Síros = Ermoupoli
  Greece 37°28N 24°57E 23 F11
Sirr, Nafud as Si. Arabia 25°33N 44°35E 44 E5
Sirretta Pk. U.S.A. 35°56N 118°19W 79 K8
Sīrrī Iran 25°55N 54°32E 45 E7
Sirsa India 29°33N 75°4E 42 E6
Sirsa → India 26°51N 79°4E 43 F8
Sisak Croatia 45°30N 16°21E 16 F9
Sisaket Thailand 15°8N 104°23E 38 E5
Sishen S. Africa 27°47S 22°59E 56 D3
Sishui Henan, China 34°48N 113°15E 34 G7
Sishui Shandong, China 35°42N 117°18E 35 G9
Sisipuk L. Canada 55°45N 101°50W 71 B8
Sisophon Cambodia 13°38N 102°59E 38 F4
Sisseton U.S.A. 45°40N 97°3W 80 C5
Sīstān Asia 30°50N 61°0E 45 D9
Sīstān, Daryācheh-ye Iran 31°0N 61°0E 45 D9
Sīstān va Balūchestān □
  Iran 27°0N 62°0E 45 E9
Sisters U.S.A. 44°18N 121°33W 76 D3
Sisters, The Seychelles 4°16S 55°52E 53 b
Siswa Bazar India 27°9N 83°46E 43 F10
Sitamarhi India 26°37N 85°30E 43 F11
Sitampiky Madag. 16°41S 46°6E 57 B8
Sitapur India 27°38N 80°45E 43 F9
Siteki Swaziland 26°32S 31°58E 57 D5
Sitges Spain 41°17N 1°47E 21 B6
Sitia Greece 35°13N 26°6E 25 D8
Sitito-Ozima Ridge
  Pac. Oc. 23°0N 143°0E 64 E6
Sitka U.S.A. 57°3N 135°20W 70 B1
Sitoti Botswana 23°15S 23°40E 56 C3
Sittang Myit → Burma 17°20N 96°45E 41 L20
Sittard Neths. 51°0N 5°52E 15 C5
Sittingbourne U.K. 51°21N 0°45E 13 F8
Sittoung = Sittang Myit →
  Burma 17°20N 96°45E 41 L20
Sittwe Burma 20°18N 92°45E 41 J18
Situbondo Indonesia 7°42S 114°0E 37 G16
Si'umu Samoa 14°1S 171°48W 59 b
Siuna Nic. 13°37N 84°45W 88 D3
Siuri India 23°50N 87°34E 43 H12
Sīvand Iran 30°5N 52°55E 45 D7
Sivas Turkey 39°43N 36°58E 44 B3
Siverek Turkey 37°50N 39°19E 44 B3
Sivomaskinskiy Russia 66°40N 62°35E 18 A11
Sivrihisar Turkey 39°30N 31°35E 19 G5
Sîwa Egypt 29°11N 25°31E 51 C11
Sîwa, El Wâhât es Egypt 29°10N 25°30E 48 D6
Siwa Oasis = Sîwa, El Wâhât es
  Egypt 29°10N 25°30E 48 D6
Siwalik Range Nepal 28°0N 83°0E 43 F10
Siwan India 26°13N 84°21E 43 F11
Siwana India 25°38N 72°25E 42 G6
Six Cross Roads Barbados 13°7N 59°28W 89 g
Sixmilebridge Ireland 52°44N 8°46W 10 D3
Sixth Cataract Sudan 16°20N 32°42E 51 E12
Siyah Kuh, Kavīr-e Iran 32°55N 53°55E 45 C7
Siziwang Qi China 41°25N 111°40E 34 D6
Sjælland Denmark 55°30N 11°30E 9 J14
Sjumen = Shumen
  Bulgaria 43°18N 26°55E 23 C12
Skadarsko Jezero Europe 42°10N 19°20E 23 C8
Skaftafell Iceland 64°1N 17°0W 8 D5
Skaftárós Iceland 63°46N 16°59W 8 D5
Skagafjörður Iceland 65°54N 19°35W 8 D4
Skagastølstindane
  Norway 61°28N 7°52E 8 F12
Skagen Denmark 57°43N 10°35E 9 H14
Skagerrak Denmark 57°30N 9°0E 9 H13
Skagit → U.S.A. 48°23N 122°22W 78 B4
Skagway U.S.A. 59°28N 135°19W 68 F4
Skala-Podilska Ukraine 48°50N 26°15E 17 D14
Skala Ukraine 48°50N 26°15E 17 D14
Skalat Ukraine 49°23N 25°55E 17 D13
Skåne Sweden 55°59N 13°30E 9 J15
Skantzoúra Greece 39°4N 24°3E 23 E11
Skardu Pakistan 35°20N 75°44E 43 B6
Skarżysko-Kamienna
  Poland 51°7N 20°52E 17 C11
Skeena → Canada 54°9N 130°5W 70 C2
Skeena Mts. Canada 56°40N 128°30W 70 B3
Skegness U.K. 53°9N 0°20E 12 D8
Skeldon = Corriverton
  Guyana 5°55N 57°20W 92 B7
Skeleton Coast Namibia 20°0S 13°0E 53 J2
Skeleton Coast △ Namibia 20°0S 13°0E 56 C1
Skellefteå Sweden 64°45N 20°50E 8 D19
Skellefteälven →
  Sweden 64°45N 21°10E 8 D19
Skelleftehamn Sweden 64°40N 21°9E 8 D19

Skerries, The U.K. 53°25N 4°36W 12 D3
Ski Norway 59°43N 10°52E 9 G14
Skiathos Greece 39°12N 23°30E 23 E10
Skibbereen Ireland 51°33N 9°16E 10 E2
Skiddaw U.K. 54°39N 3°9W 12 C4
Skien Norway 59°12N 9°35E 9 G13
Skierniewice Poland 51°58N 20°10E 17 C11
Skikda Algeria 36°50N 6°58E 50 A7
Skilloura Cyprus 35°14N 33°10E 25 D12
Skipton U.K. 53°58N 2°3W 12 D5
Skirmish Pt. Australia 11°59S 134°17E 62 A1
Skiros Greece 38°55N 24°34E 23 E11
Skive Denmark 56°33N 9°2E 9 H13
Skjálfandafljót → Iceland 65°59N 17°25W 8 D5
Skjálfandi Iceland 66°5N 17°30W 8 C5
Skole Ukraine 49°3N 23°30E 17 D12
Skopelos Greece 39°9N 23°47E 23 E10
Skopi Greece 35°11N 26°2E 25 D8
Skopje Macedonia 42°1N 21°26E 23 C9
Skövde Sweden 58°24N 13°50E 9 G15
Skovorodino Russia 54°0N 124°0E 29 D13
Skowhegan U.S.A. 44°46N 69°43W 81 C19
Skull Ireland 51°32N 9°34W 10 E2
Skunk → U.S.A. 40°42N 91°7W 80 E8
Skuodas Lithuania 56°16N 21°33E 9 H19
Skvyra Ukraine 49°44N 29°40E 17 D15
Skye U.K. 57°15N 6°10W 11 D2
Skykomish U.S.A. 47°42N 121°22W 76 C3
Skyros = Skiros Greece 38°55N 24°34E 23 E11
Slade Point Australia 21°4S 149°13E 62 b
Slade Pt. Australia 21°5S 149°13E 62 b
Slættaratindur Færoe Is. 62°18N 7°1W 8 E9
Slagelse Denmark 55°23N 11°19E 9 J14
Slamet Indonesia 7°16S 109°8E 37 G13
Slane Ireland 53°42N 6°33W 10 C5
Slaney → Ireland 52°26N 6°33W 10 D5
Slangberge S. Africa 31°32S 20°48E 56 E3
Śląsk Poland 51°0N 16°30E 16 C9
Slate Is. Canada 48°40N 87°0W 72 C2
Slatina Romania 44°28N 24°22E 17 F13
Slatington U.S.A. 40°45N 75°37W 83 F9
Slaton U.S.A. 33°26N 101°39W 84 E4
Slave → Canada 61°18N 113°39W 70 A6
Slave Coast W. Afr. 6°0N 2°30E 50 G6
Slave Lake Canada 55°17N 114°43W 70 B6
Slave Pt. Canada 61°11N 115°56W 70 A5
Slavgorod Russia 53°1N 78°37E 28 D8
Slavonski Brod Croatia 45°11N 18°1E 23 B8
Slavuta Ukraine 50°15N 27°2E 17 C14
Slavyanka Russia 42°53N 131°21E 30 C5
Slavyansk = Slovyansk
  Ukraine 48°55N 37°36E 19 E6
Slawharad Belarus 53°27N 31°0E 17 B16
Sleaford U.K. 53°0N 0°24E 12 D7
Sleaford B. Australia 34°55S 135°45E 63 E2
Sleat, Sd. of U.K. 57°5N 5°47W 11 D3
Sleeper Is. Canada 58°30N 81°0W 69 F15
Sleeping Bear Dunes △
  U.S.A. 44°50N 86°5W 80 C10
Sleepy Eye U.S.A. 44°18N 94°43W 80 C6
Slemon L. Canada 63°13N 116°4W 70 A5
Slide Mt. U.S.A. 42°0N 74°25W 83 E10
Slidell U.S.A. 30°17N 89°47W 85 F10
Sliema Malta 35°55N 14°30E 25 D2
Slieve Aughty Ireland 53°4N 8°30W 10 C3
Slieve Bloom Ireland 53°4N 7°40W 10 C4
Slieve Donard U.K. 54°11N 5°55W 10 B6
Slieve Gamph Ireland 54°6N 9°0W 10 B3
Slieve Gullion U.K. 54°7N 6°26W 10 B5
Slieve League Ireland 54°40N 8°42W 10 B3
Slieve Mish Ireland 52°12N 9°50W 10 D2
Slievenamon Ireland 52°25N 7°34W 10 D4
Sligeach = Sligo Ireland 54°16N 8°28W 10 B3
Sligo Ireland 54°16N 8°28W 10 B3
Sligo □ Ireland 54°8N 8°42W 10 B3
Sligo B. Ireland 54°18N 8°40W 10 B3
Slippery Rock U.S.A. 41°4N 80°3W 82 E4
Slite Sweden 57°42N 18°48E 9 H18
Sliven Bulgaria 42°42N 26°19E 23 C12
Sloan U.S.A. 35°57N 115°13W 79 K11
Sloansville U.S.A. 42°45N 74°22W 83 D10
Slobodskoy Russia 58°40N 50°6E 18 C9
Slobozia Romania 44°34N 27°23E 17 F14
Slocan Canada 49°48N 117°28W 70 D5
Slonim Belarus 53°4N 25°19E 17 B13
Slough U.K. 51°30N 0°36W 13 F7
Slough □ U.K. 51°30N 0°36W 13 F7
Sloughhouse U.S.A. 38°26N 121°12W 78 G5
Slovak Rep. ■ Europe 48°30N 20°0E 17 D10
Slovakia = Slovak Rep. ■
  Europe 48°30N 20°0E 17 D10
Slovakian Ore Mts. = Slovenské
  Rudohorie Slovak Rep. 48°45N 20°0E 17 D10
Slovenia ■ Europe 45°58N 14°30E 16 F8
Slovenija = Slovenia ■
  Europe 45°58N 14°30E 16 F8
Slovenská = Slovak Rep. ■
  Europe 48°30N 20°0E 17 D10
Slovenské Rudohorie
  Slovak Rep. 48°45N 20°0E 17 D10
Slovyansk Ukraine 48°55N 37°36E 19 E6
Sluch → Ukraine 51°37N 26°38E 17 C14
Sluis Neths. 51°18N 3°23E 15 C3
Słupsk Poland 54°30N 17°3E 17 A9
Slurry S. Africa 25°49S 25°42E 56 D4
Slutsk Belarus 53°2N 27°31E 17 B14
Slyne Hd. Ireland 53°25N 10°10W 10 C1
Slyudyanka Russia 51°40N 103°40E 29 D11
Småland Sweden 57°15N 15°25E 9 H16
Smalltree L. Canada 61°0N 105°0W 71 A8
Smallwood Res. Canada 54°5N 64°30W 73 B7
Smarhon Belarus 54°20N 26°24E 17 A14
Smartt Syndicate Dam
  S. Africa 30°45S 23°10E 56 E3
Smartville U.S.A. 39°13N 121°18W 78 F5
Smeaton Canada 53°30N 104°49W 71 C8

Smederevo Serbia 44°40N 20°57E 23 B9
Smerwick Harbour
  Ireland 52°12N 10°23W 10 D1
Smethport U.S.A. 41°49N 78°27W 82 E6
Smidovich Russia 48°36N 133°49E 29 E14
Smith Canada 55°10N 114°0W 70 B6
Smith Center U.S.A. 39°47N 98°47W 80 F4
Smith I. Canada 60°45N 78°25W 69 E16
Smith Islands △ Australia 20°40S 149°9E 62 b
Smith River → Canada 59°46N 126°7W 70 C3
Smithburne → Australia 17°3S 140°57E 62 B3
Smithers Canada 54°45N 127°10W 70 C3
Smithfield S. Africa 30°9S 26°30E 57 E4
Smithfield N.C., U.S.A. 35°31N 78°21W 85 D15
Smithfield Utah, U.S.A. 41°50N 111°50W 76 F8
Smiths Falls Canada 44°55N 76°0W 83 B9
Smithton Australia 40°53S 145°6E 63 G4
Smithville Canada 43°6N 79°33W 82 C5
Smithville U.S.A. 30°1N 97°10W 84 F6
Smoke Creek Desert
  U.S.A. 40°30N 119°40W 76 F4
Smoky → Canada 56°10N 117°21W 70 B5
Smoky Bay Australia 32°22S 134°13E 63 E1
Smoky Hill → U.S.A. 39°4N 96°48W 80 F5
Smoky Hills U.S.A. 39°15N 99°30W 80 F4
Smoky Lake Canada 54°10N 112°30W 70 C6
Smøla Norway 63°23N 8°3E 8 E13
Smolensk Russia 54°45N 32°5E 18 D4
Smolikas, Oros Greece 40°9N 20°58E 23 D9
Smolyan Bulgaria 41°36N 24°38E 23 D11
Smooth Rock Falls
  Canada 49°17N 81°37W 72 C3
Smoothstone L. Canada 54°40N 106°50W 71 C7
Smorgon = Smarhon
  Belarus 54°20N 26°24E 17 A14
Smyrna = İzmir Turkey 38°25N 27°8E 23 E12
Smyrna U.S.A. 39°18N 75°36W 81 F16
Snæfell Iceland 64°48N 15°34W 8 D6
Snaefell I. of Man 54°16N 4°27W 12 C3
Snæfellsjökull Iceland 64°49N 23°46W 8 D2
Snake → U.S.A. 46°12N 119°2W 76 C4
Snake I. Australia 38°47S 146°33E 63 F4
Snake Range U.S.A. 39°0N 114°20W 76 G6
Snake River Plain
  U.S.A. 42°50N 114°0W 76 E7
Snåsavatnet Norway 64°12N 12°0E 8 D15
Sneek Neths. 53°2N 5°40E 15 A5
Sneem Ireland 51°50N 9°54W 10 E2
Sneeuberge S. Africa 31°46S 24°20E 56 E3
Snelling U.S.A. 37°31N 120°26W 78 H6
Snežka Europe 50°41N 15°50E 16 C8
Snizort, L. U.K. 57°33N 6°28W 11 D2
Snøhetta Norway 62°19N 9°16E 8 E13
Snohomish U.S.A. 47°55N 122°6W 78 C4
Snoqualmie Pass
  U.S.A. 47°25N 121°25W 78 C5
Snoul Cambodia 12°4N 106°26E 39 F6
Snover U.S.A. 43°27N 82°58W 82 C2
Snow Hill U.S.A. 38°11N 75°24W 81 F16
Snow Lake Canada 54°52N 100°3W 71 C8
Snow Mt. Calif., U.S.A. 39°23N 122°45W 78 F4
Snow Mt. Maine, U.S.A. 45°18N 70°48W 83 A14
Snow Shoe U.S.A. 41°2N 77°57W 82 E7
Snowbird L. Canada 60°45N 103°0W 71 A8
Snowdon U.K. 53°4N 4°5W 12 D3
Snowdonia △ U.K. 53°7N 3°59W 12 D4
Snowdrift = Łutsel K'e
  Canada 62°24N 110°44W 71 A6
Snowdrift → Canada 62°24N 110°44W 71 A6
Snowflake U.S.A. 34°30N 110°5W 77 J8
Snowshoe Pk. U.S.A. 48°13N 115°41W 76 B6
Snowtown Australia 33°46S 138°14E 63 E2
Snowville U.S.A. 41°58N 112°43W 76 F7
Snowy → Australia 37°46S 148°30E 63 F4
Snowy Mt. U.S.A. 43°42N 74°23W 83 C10
Snowy Mts. Australia 36°30S 148°20E 63 F4
Snug Corner Bahamas 22°33N 73°52W 89 B5
Snug Harbour Canada 45°22N 80°17W 82 A4
Snyatyn Ukraine 48°27N 25°38E 17 D13
Snyder Okla., U.S.A. 34°40N 98°57W 84 D5
Snyder Tex., U.S.A. 32°44N 100°55W 84 E4
Soahanina Madag. 18°42S 44°13E 57 B7
Soalala Madag. 16°6S 45°20E 57 B8
Soaloka Madag. 18°32S 45°15E 57 B8
Soamanonga Madag. 23°52S 44°47E 57 C7
Soan → Pakistan 33°1N 71°44E 42 C4
Soanierana-Ivongo
  Madag. 16°55S 49°35E 57 B8
Soanindraniny Madag. 19°54S 47°14E 57 B8
Soavina Madag. 20°23S 46°56E 57 C8
Soavinandriana Madag. 19°9S 46°45E 57 B8
Sobat, Nahr → Sudan 9°22N 31°33E 51 G12
Sobhapur India 22°47N 78°17E 42 H8
Sobradinho, Represa de
  Brazil 9°30S 42°0W 93 E10
Sobral Brazil 3°50S 40°20W 93 D10
Soc Giang Vietnam 22°54N 106°1E 38 A6
Soc Trang Vietnam 9°37N 105°50E 39 H5
Socastee U.S.A. 33°41N 78°59W 85 E15
Soch'e = Shache China 38°20N 77°10E 32 C2
Sochi Russia 43°35N 39°40E 19 F6
Société, Îs. de la
  French Polynesia 17°0S 151°0W 65 J12
Society Is. = Société, Îs. de la
  French Polynesia 17°0S 151°0W 65 J12
Socompa, Portezuelo de
  Chile 24°27S 68°18W 94 A2
Socorro N. Mex., U.S.A. 34°4N 106°54W 77 J10
Socorro Tex., U.S.A. 31°39N 106°18W 84 F1
Socorro, I. Mexico 18°45N 110°58W 86 D2
Socotra Yemen 12°30N 54°0E 47 E5
Soda L. U.S.A. 35°10N 116°4W 77 J5
Soda Plains India 35°30N 79°0E 43 B8
Soda Springs U.S.A. 42°39N 111°36W 76 E8
Sodankylä Finland 67°29N 26°40E 8 C22
Soddy-Daisy U.S.A. 35°17N 85°10W 85 D12
Söderhamn Sweden 61°18N 17°10E 8 F17
Söderköping Sweden 58°31N 16°20E 9 G17
Södermanland Sweden 58°56N 16°55E 9 G17

Södertälje *Sweden* 59°12N 17°39E **9** G17
Sodiri *Sudan* 14°27N 29°0E **51** F11
Sodus *U.S.A.* 43°14N 77°4W **82** C7
Sodwana Bay △ *S. Africa* 27°35S 32°43E **57** D5
Soe *Indonesia* 9°52S 124°17E **60** A3
Soekmekaar = Morebeng
  S. Africa 23°30S 29°55E **57** C4
Soest *Neths.* 52°9N 5°19E **15** B5
Sofala □ *Mozam.* 19°30S 34°30E **57** B5
Sofia = Sofiya *Bulgaria* 42°45N 23°20E **23** C10
Sofia → *Madag.* 15°27S 47°23E **57** B8
Sofiya *Bulgaria* 42°45N 23°20E **23** C10
Söfu-Gan *Japan* 29°49N 140°21E **31** K10
Sogamoso *Colombia* 5°43N 72°56W **92** B4
Sogār *Iran* 25°53N 58°6E **45** E8
Sogndalsfjøra *Norway* 61°14N 7°5E **8** F12
Søgne *Norway* 58°5N 7°48E **9** G12
Sognefjorden *Norway* 61°10N 5°50E **8** F11
Soh *Iran* 33°26N 51°27E **45** C6
Sohâg *Egypt* 26°33N 31°42E **51** C12
Sohagpur *India* 22°42N 78°12E **42** H8
Soignies *Belgium* 50°35N 4°5E **15** D4
Soissons *France* 49°25N 3°19E **20** B5
Sōja *Japan* 34°40N 133°45E **31** G6
Sojat *India* 25°55N 73°45E **42** G5
Sokal *Ukraine* 50°31N 24°15E **17** C13
Sokcho *S. Korea* 38°12N 128°36E **35** E15
Söke *Turkey* 37°48N 27°28E **23** F12
Sokelo
  Dem. Rep. of the Congo 9°55S 24°36E **55** D1
Sokhumi *Georgia* 43°0N 41°0E **19** F7
Soko Is. *China* 22°10N 113°54E **33** G10
Sokodé *Togo* 9°0N 1°11E **50** G6
Sokol *Russia* 59°30N 40°5E **18** C7
Sokółka *Poland* 53°25N 23°30E **17** B12
Sokołów Podlaski
  Poland 52°25N 22°15E **17** B12
Sokoto *Nigeria* 13°2N 5°16E **50** F7
Sokoto *Russia* 51°10N 55°0E **18** D10
Solai *Kenya* 0°2N 36°12E **54** B4
Solan *India* 30°55N 77°7E **42** D7
Solana Beach *U.S.A.* 32°58N 117°16W **79** N9
Solander I. *N.Z.* 46°34S 166°54E **59** G1
Solano *Phil.* 16°31N 121°15E **37** A6
Solapur *India* 17°43N 75°56E **40** L9
Soldotna *U.S.A.* 60°29N 151°3W **68** E1
Soléa *Cyprus* 35°5N 33°4E **25** D12
Soledad *Colombia* 10°55N 74°46W **92** A4
Soledad *U.S.A.* 36°26N 121°20W **78** J5
Soledad *Venezuela* 8°10N 63°34W **92** B6
Solent, The *U.K.* 50°45N 1°25W **13** G6
Solfonntaggen *Norway* 60°2N 6°57E **9** F12
Solhan *Turkey* 38°57N 41°3E **44** B4
Soligalich *Russia* 59°5N 42°10E **18** C7
Soligorsk = Salihorsk
  Belarus 52°51N 27°27E **17** B14
Solihull *U.K.* 52°26N 1°47W **13** E6
Solikamsk *Russia* 59°38N 56°50E **18** C10
Solila *Madag.* 21°25S 46°37E **57** C8
Solimões = Amazonas →
  S. Amer. 0°5S 50°0W **93** D8
Solingen *Germany* 51°10N 7°5E **16** C4
Sollefteå *Sweden* 63°12N 17°20E **8** E17
Sóller *Spain* 39°46N 2°43E **24** B9
Solo → *Indonesia* 6°47S 112°22E **37** G15
Sologne *France* 47°40N 1°45E **20** C4
Solok *Indonesia* 0°45S 100°40E **36** E2
Sololá *Guatemala* 14°49N 91°10W **88** D1
Sololo *Kenya* 3°33N 38°39E **54** B4
Solomon, N. Fork →
  U.S.A. 39°29N 98°26W **80** F4
Solomon, S. Fork →
  U.S.A. 39°25N 99°12W **80** F4
Solomon Is. ■ *Pac. Oc.* 6°0S 155°0E **58** B8
Solomon Rise *Pac. Oc.* 1°0N 157°0E **64** G7
Solon *China* 46°32N 121°10E **33** B7
Solon Springs *U.S.A.* 46°22N 91°49W **80** B8
Solor *Indonesia* 8°27S 123°0E **37** F6
Solothurn *Switz.* 47°13N 7°32E **20** C7
Šolta *Croatia* 43°24N 16°15E **22** C7
Solţānābād *Khorāsān,*
  Iran 34°13N 59°58E **45** C8
Solţānābād *Khorāsān, Iran* 36°29N 58°5E **45** B8
Solunska Glava
  Macedonia 41°44N 21°31E **23** D9
Solvang *U.S.A.* 34°36N 120°8W **79** L6
Solvay *U.S.A.* 43°3N 76°13W **83** C8
Sölvesborg *Sweden* 56°5N 14°35E **9** H16
Solway Firth *U.K.* 54°49N 3°35W **12** C4
Solwezi *Zambia* 12°11S 26°21E **55** E2
Sōma *Japan* 37°40N 140°50E **30** F10
Soma *Turkey* 39°10N 27°35E **23** E12
Somabhula *Zimbabwe* 19°42S 29°40E **57** B4
Somali Pen. *Africa* 7°0N 46°0E **48** F8
Somali Rep. ■ *Africa* 7°0N 47°0E **47** F4
Somalia = Somali Rep. ■
  Africa 7°0N 47°0E **47** F4
Somaliland □ *Somali Rep.* 9°0N 46°0E **47** F4
Sombor *Serbia* 45°46N 19°9E **23** B8
Sombra *Canada* 42°43N 82°29W **82** D2
Sombrerete *Mexico* 23°38N 103°39W **86** C4
Sombrero *Anguilla* 18°37N 63°30W **89** C7
Somdari *India* 25°47N 72°38E **42** G5
Somers *U.S.A.* 48°5N 114°13W **76** B6
Somerset *Ky., U.S.A.* 37°5N 84°36W **81** G3
Somerset *Mass., U.S.A.* 41°47N 71°8W **83** E13
Somerset *Pa., U.S.A.* 40°1N 79°5W **82** F5
Somerset □ *U.K.* 51°9N 3°0W **13** F5
Somerset East *S. Africa* 32°42S 25°35E **56** E4
Somerset I. *Canada* 73°30S 93°0W **68** C13
Somerset West *S. Africa* 34°8S 18°50E **56** E2
Somerton *U.S.A.* 32°36N 114°43W **77** K6
Somerville *U.S.A.* 40°35N 74°38W **83** F10
Someş → *Romania* 47°49N 22°43E **17** D12
Somme → *France* 50°11N 1°38E **20** A4
Somnath *India* 20°53N 70°22E **42** J4

Somosierra, Puerto de
  Spain 41°4N 3°35W **21** B4
Somosomo *Fiji* 16°47S 179°58W **59** a
Somosomo Str. *Fiji* 16°0S 180°0E **59** a
Somoto *Nic.* 13°28N 86°37W **88** D2
Somport, Tunnel de
  Spain 42°48N 0°31W **20** E3
Son → *India* 25°42N 84°52E **43** G11
Son Ha *Vietnam* 15°3N 108°34E **38** E7
Son Hoa *Vietnam* 13°2N 108°58E **38** F7
Son La *Vietnam* 21°20N 103°50E **38** B5
Son Morrell *Spain* 39°44N 3°20E **24** B10
Son Rapinya *Spain* 39°35N 2°37E **24** B9
Son Sardina *Spain* 39°37N 2°40E **24** B9
Son Serra *Spain* 39°43N 3°13E **24** B10
Soná *Panama* 8°0N 81°20W **88** E3
Sonamarg *India* 34°18N 75°21E **43** B6
Sonamukhi *India* 23°18N 87°27E **43** H12
Sonar → *India* 24°24N 79°56E **43** G8
Sönch'ön *N. Korea* 39°48N 124°55E **35** E13
Sondags → *S. Africa* 33°44S 25°51E **56** E4
Sondar *India* 33°28N 75°56E **43** C6
Sóndrio *Italy* 46°10N 9°52E **20** C8
Sone *Mozam.* 17°23S 34°55E **55** F3
Sonepur *India* 20°55N 83°50E **41** J13
Song *Thailand* 18°28N 100°11E **38** C3
Song Cau *Vietnam* 13°27N 109°18E **38** F7
Song Hong → *Vietnam* 22°0N 104°0E **32** D5
Song Xian *China* 34°12N 112°8E **34** G7
Songan *Indonesia* 8°13S 115°21E **37** J18
Songea *Tanzania* 10°40S 35°40E **55** E4
Songgang *China* 22°46N 113°50E **33** F10
Songhua Hu *China* 43°35N 126°50E **35** C14
Songhua Jiang →
  China 47°45N 132°30E **33** B8
Songimvelo △ *S. Africa* 25°50S 31°2E **57** D5
Songjin = Kimch'aek
  N. Korea 40°40N 129°10E **35** D15
Songkhla *Thailand* 7°13N 100°37E **39** J3
Songnim *N. Korea* 38°45N 125°39E **35** E13
Songo *Mozam.* 15°34S 32°38E **55** F3
Songo *Sudan* 9°47N 24°21E **51** G10
Songpan *China* 32°40N 103°30E **32** C5
Songwe
  Dem. Rep. of the Congo 3°20S 26°16E **54** C2
Songwe → *Africa* 9°44S 33°58E **55** D3
Sonhat *India* 23°29N 82°31E **43** H10
Sonid Youqi *China* 42°45N 112°48E **34** C7
Sonipat *India* 29°0N 77°5E **42** E7
Sonkach *India* 22°59N 76°21E **42** H7
Sonmiani *Pakistan* 25°25N 66°40E **42** G2
Sonmiani B. *Pakistan* 25°15N 66°30E **42** G2
Sono → *Brazil* 9°58S 48°11W **93** E9
Sonoma *U.S.A.* 38°18N 122°28W **78** G4
Sonora *Calif., U.S.A.* 37°59N 120°23W **78** H6
Sonora *Tex., U.S.A.* 30°34N 100°39W **84** F4
Sonora □ *Mexico* 29°20N 110°40W **86** B2
Sonora → *Mexico* 29°5N 110°55W **86** B2
Sonoran Desert
  U.S.A. 33°40N 113°30W **79** L12
Sonoyta *Mexico* 31°51N 112°50W **86** A2
Sonsonate *El Salv.* 13°43N 89°44W **88** D2
Soochow = Suzhou
  China 31°19N 120°38E **33** C7
Sooke *Canada* 48°13N 123°43W **78** B3
Soomaaliya = Somali Rep. ■
  Africa 7°0N 47°0E **47** F4
Sop Hao *Laos* 20°33N 104°27E **38** B5
Sop Prap *Thailand* 17°53N 99°20E **38** D2
Sopi *Indonesia* 2°34N 128°28E **37** D7
Sopot *Poland* 54°27N 18°31E **17** A10
Sopron *Hungary* 47°45N 16°32E **17** E9
Sopur *India* 34°18N 74°27E **43** B6
Sør-Rondane *Antarctica* 72°0S 25°0E **5** D4
Sorah *Pakistan* 27°13N 68°56E **42** F3
Soraon *India* 25°37N 81°51E **43** G9
Sord = Swords *Ireland* 53°28N 6°13W **10** C5
Sorel-Tracy *Canada* 46°0N 73°10W **72** C5
Sórgono *Italy* 40°1N 9°6E **22** D3
Soria *Spain* 41°43N 2°32W **21** B4
Soriano *Uruguay* 33°24S 58°19W **94** C4
Sorkh, Kuh-e *Iran* 35°40N 58°30E **45** C8
Soroca *Moldova* 48°8N 28°12E **17** D15
Sorocaba *Brazil* 23°31S 47°27W **95** A6
Sorochinsk *Russia* 52°26N 53°10E **18** D9
Soroki = Soroca *Moldova* 48°8N 28°12E **17** D15
Sorong *Indonesia* 0°55S 131°15E **37** E8
Soroni *Greece* 36°21N 28°1E **25** C10
Soroti *Uganda* 1°43N 33°35E **54** B3
Sørøya *Norway* 70°40N 22°30E **8** A20
Sørøysundet *Norway* 70°25N 23°0E **8** A20
Sorrell *Australia* 42°47S 147°34E **63** G4
Sorrento *Italy* 40°37N 14°22E **22** D6
Sorsele *Sweden* 65°31N 17°30E **8** D17
Sorsogon *Phil.* 13°0N 124°0E **37** B6
Sortavala *Russia* 61°42N 30°41E **8** F24
Sortland *Norway* 68°42N 15°25E **8** B16
Soscumica, L. *Canada* 50°15N 77°27W **72** B4
Sosnogorsk *Russia* 63°37N 53°51E **18** B9
Sosnowiec *Poland* 50°20N 19°10E **17** C10
Sossus Vlei *Namibia* 24°40S 15°23E **56** C2
Sŏsura *N. Korea* 42°16N 130°36E **35** C16
Sot → *India* 27°27N 79°37E **43** F8
Sotavento *C. Verde Is.* 15°0N 25°0W **50** b
Sotik *Kenya* 0°41S 35°7E **54** C4
Sotkamo *Finland* 64°8N 28°23E **8** D23
Soto la Marina *Mexico* 23°46N 98°13W **87** C5
Soto la Marina →
  Mexico 23°45N 97°45W **87** C5
Sotuta *Mexico* 20°36N 89°1W **87** C7
Souanké *Congo* 2°10N 14°3E **52** D2
Souda *Greece* 35°29N 24°4E **25** D6
Soudas, Ormos *Greece* 35°25N 24°10E **25** D6
Souderton *U.S.A.* 40°19N 75°19W **83** F9
Soufrière *Guadeloupe* 16°5N 61°40W **88** b
Soufrière *St. Lucia* 13°51N 61°3W **89** f
Soufrière Bay *Dominica* 15°13N 61°22W **89** f

Soukhouma *Laos* 14°38N 105°48E **38** E5
Sŏul = Seoul *S. Korea* 37°31N 126°58E **35** F14
Sound, The *U.K.* 50°20N 4°10W **13** G3
Sources, Mt. aux *Lesotho* 28°45S 28°50E **57** D4
Soure *Brazil* 0°35S 48°30W **93** D9
Souris *Man., Canada* 49°40N 100°20W **71** D8
Souris *P.E.I., Canada* 46°21N 62°15W **73** C7
Souris → *N. Amer.* 49°40N 99°34W **80** A4
Sousa *Brazil* 6°45S 38°10W **93** E11
Sousse *Tunisia* 35°50N 10°38E **51** A8
Sout → *S. Africa* 31°35S 18°24E **56** E2
South Africa ■ *Africa* 32°0S 23°0E **56** E3
South America 10°0S 60°0W **90** E5
South Aulatsivik I.
  Canada 56°45N 61°30W **73** A7
South Australia □
  Australia 32°0S 139°0E **63** E2
South Australian Basin
  Ind. Oc. 38°0S 126°0E **64** L4
South Ayrshire □ *U.K.* 55°18N 4°41W **11** F4
South Baldy Pk. *U.S.A.* 34°6N 107°11W **77** J10
South Bass I. *U.S.A.* 41°39N 82°49W **82** E2
South Bend *Ind., U.S.A.* 41°41N 86°15W **80** E10
South Bend *Wash.,*
  U.S.A. 46°40N 123°48W **78** D3
South Boston *U.S.A.* 36°42N 78°54W **81** G14
South Branch *Canada* 47°55N 59°2W **73** C8
South Brook *Canada* 49°26N 56°5W **73** C8
South Bruny I. *Australia* 43°20S 147°15E **63** G4
South Carolina □ *U.S.A.* 34°0N 81°0W **85** E15
South Charleston
  U.S.A. 38°22N 81°44W **81** F13
South Cumberland Is. △
  Australia 20°42S 149°11E **62** b
South Dakota □ *U.S.A.* 44°15N 100°0W **80** C4
South Dayton *U.S.A.* 42°21N 79°3W **82** D5
South Deerfield *U.S.A.* 42°29N 72°37W **83** D12
South Downs *U.K.* 50°52N 0°25W **13** G7
South East C. *Australia* 43°40S 146°50E **63** G4
South East Is. *Australia* 34°17S 123°30E **61** F3
South Esk → *U.K.* 56°43N 2°31W **11** E6
South Fiji Basin *Pac. Oc.* 26°0S 175°0E **64** K9
South Foreland *U.K.* 51°8N 1°24E **13** F9
South Fork American →
  U.S.A. 38°57N 120°59W **78** G5
South Fork Feather →
  U.S.A. 39°17N 121°36W **78** F5
South Fork Grand →
  U.S.A. 45°43N 102°17W **80** C2
South Fork Milk →
  U.S.A. 48°4N 106°19W **76** B10
South Fork Republican →
  U.S.A. 40°3N 101°31W **80** E3
South Georgia *Antarctica* 54°30S 37°0W **96** G9
South Gloucestershire □
  U.K. 51°32N 2°28W **13** F5
South Hadley *U.S.A.* 42°16N 72°35W **83** D12
South Haven *U.S.A.* 42°24N 86°16W **80** D10
South Henik L. *Canada* 61°30N 97°20W **71** A9
South Horr *Kenya* 2°12N 36°56E **54** B4
South I. *Kenya* 2°35N 36°35E **54** B4
South I. *N.Z.* 44°0S 170°0E **59** F3
South Indian Lake
  Canada 56°47N 98°56W **71** B9
South Invercargill *N.Z.* 46°26S 168°23E **59** G2
South Island △ *Kenya* 2°39N 36°35E **54** B4
South Kitui △ *Kenya* 1°48S 38°46E **54** C4
South Knife → *Canada* 58°55N 94°37W **71** B10
South Koel → *India* 22°32N 85°14E **43** H11
South Korea ■ *Asia* 36°0N 128°0E **35** G15
South Lake Tahoe
  U.S.A. 38°57N 119°59W **78** G6
South Lanarkshire □
  U.K. 55°37N 3°53W **11** F5
South Loup → *U.S.A.* 41°4N 98°39W **80** E4
South Luangwa △ *Zambia* 13°0S 31°20E **55** E3
South Magnetic Pole
  Antarctica 64°8S 138°8E **5** C9
South Milwaukee
  U.S.A. 42°55N 87°52W **80** D10
South Molton *U.K.* 51°1N 3°51W **13** F4
South Moose L. *Canada* 53°49N 100°1W **71** C8
South Nahanni →
  Canada 61°3N 123°21W **70** A4
South Nation → *Canada* 45°34N 75°6W **83** A9
South Natuna Is. = Natuna
  Selatan, Kepulauan
  Indonesia 2°45N 109°0E **36** D3
South Negril Pt. *Jamaica* 18°16N 78°22W **88** a
South Orkney Is.
  Antarctica 63°0S 45°0W **5** C18
South Ossetia □ *Georgia* 42°21N 44°2E **19** F7
South Otselic *U.S.A.* 42°38N 75°46W **83** D9
South Pagai, I. = Pagai Selatan,
  Pulau *Indonesia* 3°0S 100°15E **36** E2
South Paris *U.S.A.* 44°14N 70°31W **83** B14
South Pittsburg *U.S.A.* 35°1N 85°42W **85** D12
South Platte → *U.S.A.* 41°7N 100°42W **80** E3
South Pole *Antarctica* 90°0S 0°0E **5** E
South Porcupine *Canada* 48°30N 81°12W **72** C3
South Portland *U.S.A.* 43°38N 70°15W **81** D18
South Pt. *Barbados* 13°2N 59°32W **89** g
South River *Canada* 45°52N 79°23W **72** C4
South River *U.S.A.* 40°27N 74°23W **83** F10
South Ronaldsay *U.K.* 58°48N 2°58W **11** C6
South Rukuru → *Malawi* 10°44S 34°14E **55** E3
South Sandwich Is.
  Antarctica 57°0S 27°0W **5** B1
South Sandwich Trench
  Atl. Oc. 56°0S 24°0W **5** B1
South Saskatchewan →
  Canada 53°15N 105°5W **71** C7
South Seal → *Canada* 58°48N 98°8W **71** B9
South Shetland Is.
  Antarctica 62°0S 59°0W **5** C18
South Shields *U.K.* 55°0N 1°25W **12** C6
South Sioux City *U.S.A.* 42°28N 96°24W **80** D5

South Sister *U.S.A.* 44°4N 121°51W **76** D3
South Talpatti = New Moore I.
  Ind. Oc. 21°37N 89°10E **43** J13
South Taranaki Bight
  N.Z. 39°40S 174°5E **59** C5
South Tasman Rise
  S. Ocean 48°0S 146°0E **5** A10
South Thompson →
  Canada 50°40N 120°20W **70** C4
South Twin I. *Canada* 53°7N 79°52W **72** B4
South Tyne → *U.K.* 54°59N 2°8W **12** C5
South Uist *U.K.* 57°20N 7°15W **11** D1
South Valley *U.S.A.* 35°1N 106°41W **77** J10
South Wellesley Is.
  Australia 16°58S 139°17E **62** B2
South West C. *Australia* 34°30N 81°25W **82** B3
South West C. *N.Z.* 47°17S 167°28E **59** G1
South Williamsport
  U.S.A. 41°13N 77°0W **82** E8
South Yorkshire □ *U.K.* 53°27N 1°36W **12** D6
Southampton *Canada* 44°30N 81°25W **82** B3
Southampton *U.K.* 50°54N 1°23W **13** G6
Southampton *U.S.A.* 40°53N 72°23W **83** F12
Southampton □ *U.K.* 50°54N 1°23W **13** G6
Southampton I. *Canada* 64°30N 84°0W **69** E15
Southaven *U.S.A.* 34°59N 90°0W **85** D9
Southbank *Canada* 54°2N 125°46W **70** C3
Southbridge *U.S.A.* 42°5N 72°2W **83** D12
Southbridge *N.Z.* 43°48S 172°16E **59** E4
Southend *Canada* 56°19N 103°22W **71** B8
Southend-on-Sea *U.K.* 51°32N 0°44E **13** F8
Southend-on-Sea □ *U.K.* 51°32N 0°44E **13** F8
Southern = Yuzhnyy □
  Russia 44°0N 40°0E **28** E5
Southern □ *Malawi* 15°0S 35°0E **55** F4
Southern □ *Zambia* 16°20S 26°20E **55** F2
Southern Alps *N.Z.* 43°41S 170°11E **59** E3
Southern Cross
  Australia 31°12S 119°15E **61** F2
Southern Indian L.
  Canada 57°10N 98°30W **71** B9
Southern Lau Group
  Fiji 18°40S 178°40W **59** a
Southern Ocean *Antarctica* 62°0S 60°0E **5** C6
Southern Pines *U.S.A.* 35°11N 79°24W **85** D15
Southern Uplands *U.K.* 55°28N 3°52W **11** F5
Southington *U.S.A.* 41°36N 72°53W **83** E12
Southland □ *N.Z.* 45°30S 168°0E **59** F1
Southold *U.S.A.* 41°4N 72°26W **83** E12
Southport *Australia* 27°58S 153°25E **63** D5
Southport *U.K.* 53°39N 3°0W **12** D4
Southport *U.S.A.* 42°3N 76°49W **82** D8
Southwest △ *Australia* 43°8S 146°5E **63** G4
Southwest Pacific Basin
  Pac. Oc. 40°0S 140°0W **5** A12
Southwold *U.K.* 52°20N 1°41E **13** E9
Southwood △ *Australia* 27°48S 150°8E **63** D5
Soutpansberg *S. Africa* 23°0S 29°30E **57** C4
Sovetsk *Kaliningrad, Russia* 55°6N 21°50E **9** J19
Sovetsk *Kirov, Russia* 57°38N 48°53E **18** C8
Sovetskaya Gavan
  Russia 48°58N 140°0E **29** E15
Soweto *S. Africa* 26°14S 27°52E **57** D4
Sowma'eh Sarā *Iran* 37°17N 49°18E **45** B6
Sōya-Kaikyō = La Perouse Str.
  Asia 45°40N 142°0E **30** B11
Sōya-Misaki *Japan* 45°30N 141°55E **30** B10
Soyo *Angola* 6°13S 12°20E **52** F2
Sozh → *Belarus* 51°57N 30°48E **17** B16
Spa *Belgium* 50°29N 5°53E **15** D5
Spain ■ *Europe* 39°0N 4°0W **21** B4
Spalding *Australia* 33°30S 138°37E **63** E2
Spalding *U.K.* 52°48N 0°9E **12** E7
Spanaway *U.S.A.* 47°6N 122°26W **78** C4
Spangler *U.S.A.* 40°39N 78°48W **82** F6
Spanish *Canada* 46°12N 82°20W **72** C3
Spanish Fork *U.S.A.* 40°7N 111°39W **76** F8
Spanish Town
  Br. Virgin Is. 17°43N 64°26W **89** e
Spanish Town *Jamaica* 18°0N 76°57W **88** a
Sparks *U.S.A.* 39°32N 119°45W **78** F7
Sparta = Sparti *Greece* 37°5N 22°25E **23** F10
Sparta *Mich., U.S.A.* 43°10N 85°42W **81** D11
Sparta *N.J., U.S.A.* 41°2N 74°38W **83** E10
Sparta *Wis., U.S.A.* 43°56N 90°49W **80** D8
Spartanburg *U.S.A.* 34°56N 81°57W **85** D14
Spartí *Greece* 37°5N 22°25E **23** F10
Spartivento, C. *Calabria,*
  Italy 37°55N 16°4E **22** F7
Spartivento, C. *Sard., Italy* 38°53N 8°50E **22** E3
Sparwood *Canada* 49°44N 114°53W **70** D6
Spassk Dalniy *Russia* 44°40N 132°48E **30** B6
Spatha, Akra *Greece* 35°42N 23°43E **25** D5
Spatsizi → *Canada* 57°42N 128°7W **70** B3
Spatsizi Plateau Wilderness △
  Canada 57°40N 128°0W **70** B3
Spean → *U.K.* 56°55N 4°59W **11** E4
Spearfish *U.S.A.* 44°30N 103°52W **80** C2
Spearman *U.S.A.* 36°12N 101°12W **84** C4
Speculator *U.S.A.* 43°30N 74°22W **83** C10
Speightstown *Barbados* 13°15N 59°39W **89** g
Speke Gulf *Tanzania* 2°20S 32°50E **54** C3
Spence Bay = Taloyoak
  Canada 69°32N 93°32W **68** D13
Spencer *Idaho, U.S.A.* 44°22N 112°11W **76** D7
Spencer *Iowa, U.S.A.* 43°9N 95°9W **80** D6
Spencer *N.Y., U.S.A.* 42°13N 76°30W **83** D8
Spencer *Nebr., U.S.A.* 42°53N 98°42W **80** D4
Spencer, C. *Australia* 35°20S 136°53E **63** F2
Spencer B. *Namibia* 25°30S 14°47E **56** D1
Spencer G. *Australia* 34°0S 137°20E **63** E2
Spencerville *Canada* 44°51N 75°33W **83** B9
Spences Bridge *Canada* 50°25N 121°20W **70** C4
Spennymoor *U.K.* 54°42N 1°36W **12** C6
Spenser Mts. *N.Z.* 42°15S 172°45E **59** E4
Sperrin Mts. *U.K.* 54°50N 7°0W **10** B5
Spey → *U.K.* 57°40N 3°6W **11** D5
Speyer *Germany* 49°29N 8°25E **16** D5
Spezand *Pakistan* 29°59N 67°0E **42** E2

Spiddle *Ireland* 53°15N 9°18W **10** C2
Spili *Greece* 35°13N 24°31E **25** D6
Spīn Būldak *Afghan.* 31°1N 66°25E **42** D2
Spinalonga *Greece* 35°18N 25°44E **25** D7
Spinifex ۞ *Australia* 28°30S 128°30E **61** E4
Spirit Lake *U.S.A.* 46°15N 122°9W **78** D4
Spirit River *Canada* 55°45N 118°50W **70** B5
Spiritwood *Canada* 53°24N 107°33W **71** C7
Spithead *U.K.* 50°45N 1°10W **13** G6
Spitzbergen = Svalbard
  Arctic 78°0N 17°0E **4** B8
Spjelkavik *Norway* 62°28N 6°22E **8** E12
Split *Croatia* 43°31N 16°26E **22** C7
Split L. *Canada* 56°8N 96°15W **71** B9
Split Lake *Canada* 56°8N 96°15W **71** B9
Spofford *U.S.A.* 29°10N 100°25W **84** G4
Spokane *U.S.A.* 47°40N 117°24W **76** C5
Spoleto *Italy* 42°44N 12°44E **22** C5
Spooner *U.S.A.* 45°50N 91°53W **80** C8
Sporyy Navolok, Mys
  Russia 75°50N 68°40E **28** B7
Sprague *U.S.A.* 47°18N 117°59W **76** C5
Spratly I. *S. China Sea* 8°38N 111°55E **36** C4
Spratly Is. *S. China Sea* 8°20N 112°0E **36** C4
Spray *U.S.A.* 44°50N 119°48W **76** D4
Spree → *Germany* 52°32N 13°12E **16** B7
Sprengisandur *Iceland* 64°52N 18°7W **8** D4
Spring City *U.S.A.* 40°11N 75°33W **83** F9
Spring Creek *U.S.A.* 40°44N 115°35W **76** F6
Spring Garden *U.S.A.* 39°52N 120°47W **78** F6
Spring Hall *Barbados* 13°18N 59°36W **89** g
Spring Hill *U.S.A.* 28°27N 82°41W **85** G13
Spring Mts. *U.S.A.* 36°0N 115°45W **79** J11
Spring Valley *Calif.,*
  U.S.A. 32°44N 116°59W **79** N10
Spring Valley *Nev.,*
  U.S.A. 36°6N 115°14W **79** J11
Springbok *S. Africa* 29°42S 17°54E **56** D2
Springboro *U.S.A.* 41°48N 80°22W **82** E4
Springdale *Canada* 49°30N 56°6W **73** C8
Springdale *U.S.A.* 36°11N 94°8W **84** C7
Springer *U.S.A.* 36°22N 104°36W **77** H11
Springerville *U.S.A.* 34°8N 109°17W **77** J9
Springfield *Canada* 42°50N 80°56W **82** D4
Springfield *N.Z.* 43°19S 171°56E **59** E3
Springfield *Colo.,*
  U.S.A. 37°24N 102°37W **77** H12
Springfield *Ill., U.S.A.* 39°48N 89°39W **80** F10
Springfield *Mass., U.S.A.* 42°6N 72°35W **83** D12
Springfield *Mo., U.S.A.* 37°13N 93°17W **80** G7
Springfield *Ohio, U.S.A.* 39°55N 83°49W **81** F12
Springfield *Oreg., U.S.A.* 44°3N 123°1W **76** D2
Springfield *Tenn.,*
  U.S.A. 36°31N 86°53W **85** C11
Springfield *Vt., U.S.A.* 43°18N 72°29W **83** C12
Springfontein *S. Africa* 30°15S 25°40E **56** E4
Springhill *Canada* 45°40N 64°4W **73** C7
Springhill *U.S.A.* 33°0N 93°28W **84** E8
Springhouse *Canada* 51°56N 122°7W **70** C4
Springs *S. Africa* 26°13S 28°25E **57** D4
Springsure *Australia* 24°8S 148°6E **62** C4
Springvale *U.S.A.* 43°28N 70°48W **83** C14
Springville *Calif., U.S.A.* 36°8N 118°49W **78** J8
Springville *N.Y., U.S.A.* 42°31N 78°40W **82** D6
Springville *Utah, U.S.A.* 40°10N 111°37W **76** F8
Springwater *U.S.A.* 42°38N 77°35W **82** D7
Spruce-Creek *U.S.A.* 40°36N 78°9W **82** F6
Spruce Knob-Seneca Rocks △
  U.S.A. 38°50N 79°30W **81** F14
Spruce Mt. *U.S.A.* 44°12N 72°19W **83** B12
Sprucedale *Canada* 45°29N 79°28W **82** A5
Spur *U.S.A.* 33°28N 100°52W **84** E4
Spurn Hd. *U.K.* 53°35N 0°8E **12** D8
Spuzzum *Canada* 49°37N 121°23W **70** D4
Squam L. *U.S.A.* 43°45N 71°32W **83** C13
Squamish *Canada* 49°45N 123°10W **70** D4
Square Islands *Canada* 52°47N 55°47W **73** B8
Squires, Mt. *Australia* 26°14S 127°28E **61** E4
Srbija = Serbia ■ *Europe* 43°20N 20°0E **23** B9
Sre Ambel *Cambodia* 11°8N 103°46E **39** G4
Sre Khtum *Cambodia* 12°10N 106°52E **39** F6
Sre Umbell = Sre Ambel
  Cambodia 11°8N 103°46E **39** G4
Srebrenica *Bos.-H.* 44°6N 19°18E **23** B8
Sredinny Ra. = Sredinnyy Khrebet
  Russia 57°0N 160°0E **29** D17
Sredinnyy Khrebet
  Russia 57°0N 160°0E **29** D17
Srednekolymsk *Russia* 67°27N 153°40E **29** C16
Śrem *Poland* 52°6N 17°2E **17** B9
Sremska Mitrovica
  Serbia 44°59N 19°38E **23** B8
Srepok → *Cambodia* 13°33N 106°16E **38** F6
Sretensk *Russia* 52°10N 117°40E **29** D12
Sri Aman *Malaysia* 1°15N 111°32E **36** D4
Sri Lanka ■ *Asia* 7°30N 80°50E **40** R12
Srikakulam *India* 18°14N 83°58E **41** K13
Srinagar *India* 34°5N 74°50E **43** B6
Srono *Indonesia* 8°24S 114°16E **37** J17
Ssese Is. = Sese Is. *Uganda* 0°20S 32°20E **54** C3
Staaten → *Australia* 16°24S 141°17E **62** B3
Staaten River △
  Australia 16°15S 142°40E **62** B3
Stade *Germany* 53°35N 9°29E **16** B5
Stadskanaal *Neths.* 53°4N 6°55E **15** A6
Staffa *U.K.* 56°27N 6°21W **11** E2
Stafford *U.K.* 52°49N 2°7W **12** E5
Stafford *U.S.A.* 37°58N 98°36W **80** G4
Stafford Springs *U.S.A.* 41°57N 72°18W **83** E12
Staffordshire □ *U.K.* 52°53N 2°10W **12** E5
Staines *U.K.* 51°26N 0°29W **13** F7
Stakhanov *Ukraine* 48°35N 38°40E **19** E6
Stalida *Greece* 35°17N 25°25E **25** D7
Stalowa Wola *Poland* 50°34N 22°3E **17** C12
Stalybridge *U.K.* 53°28N 2°3W **12** D5
Stamford *Australia* 21°15S 143°46E **62** C3
Stamford *U.K.* 52°39N 0°29W **12** E7
Stamford *Conn., U.S.A.* 41°3N 73°32W **83** E11
Stamford *N.Y., U.S.A.* 42°25N 74°38W **83** D10

Stamford *Tex., U.S.A.* 32°57N 99°48W **84** E5
Stampriet *Namibia* 24°20S 18°28E **56** C2
Stamps *U.S.A.* 33°22N 93°30W **84** E8
Standerton *S. Africa* 26°55S 29°7E **57** D4
Standish *U.S.A.* 43°59N 83°57W **81** D12
Stanford *S. Africa* 34°26S 19°29E **56** E2
Stanford *U.S.A.* 47°9N 110°13W **76** C8
Stanger *S. Africa* 29°27S 31°14E **57** D5
Stängselåsen = Salpausselkä
 Finland 61°3N 26°15E **8** F22
Stanislaus ⇀ *U.S.A.* 37°40N 121°14W **78** H5
Stanke Dimitrov
 Bulgaria 42°17N 23°9E **23** C10
Stanley *Australia* 40°46S 145°19E **63** G4
Stanley *China* 22°13N 114°12E **33** G11
Stanley *Falk. Is.* 51°40S 59°51W **96** G5
Stanley *U.K.* 54°53N 1°41W **12** C6
Stanley *Idaho, U.S.A.* 44°13N 114°56W **76** D6
Stanley *N. Dak., U.S.A.* 48°19N 102°23W **80** A2
Stanley *N.Y., U.S.A.* 42°48N 77°6W **82** D7
Stanley Mission
 Canada 55°25N 104°33W **71** B8
Stannards *U.S.A.* 42°5N 77°55W **82** D7
Stanovoy Khrebet
 Russia 55°0N 130°0E **29** D14
Stanovoy Ra. = Stanovoy Khrebet
 Russia 55°0N 130°0E **29** D14
Stansmore Ra. *Australia* 21°23S 128°33E **60** D4
Stansted, London ✈ (STN)
 U.K. 51°54N 0°14E **13** F8
Stanthorpe *Australia* 28°36S 151°59E **63** D5
Stanton *U.S.A.* 32°8N 101°48W **84** E4
Stanwood *U.S.A.* 48°15N 122°23W **78** B4
Staples *Canada* 42°10N 82°35W **82** D2
Staples *U.S.A.* 46°21N 94°48W **80** B6
Stapleton *U.S.A.* 41°29N 100°31W **80** E3
Star City *Canada* 52°50N 104°20W **71** C8
Star Lake *U.S.A.* 44°10N 75°2W **83** B9
Stara Planina *Bulgaria* 43°15N 23°0E **23** C10
Stara Zagora *Bulgaria* 42°26N 25°39E **23** C11
Starachowice *Poland* 51°3N 21°2E **17** C11
Staraya Russa *Russia* 57°58N 31°23E **18** C5
Starbuck I. *Kiribati* 5°37S 155°55W **65** H12
Starcke △ *Australia* 14°56S 145°2E **62** A4
Stargard Szczeciński
 Poland 53°20N 15°0E **16** B8
Staritsa *Russia* 56°33N 34°55E **18** C5
Starke *U.S.A.* 29°57N 82°7W **85** G13
Starkville *U.S.A.* 33°28N 88°49W **85** E10
Starogard Gdański
 Poland 53°59N 18°30E **17** B10
Starokonstantinov =
 Starokonstyantyniv
 Ukraine 49°48N 27°10E **17** D14
Starokonstyantyniv
 Ukraine 49°48N 27°10E **17** D14
Start Pt. *U.K.* 50°13N 3°39W **13** G4
Staryy Chartoriysk
 Ukraine 51°15N 25°54E **17** C13
Staryy Oskol *Russia* 51°19N 37°55E **19** D6
State College *U.S.A.* 40°48N 77°52W **82** F7
Stateline *U.S.A.* 38°57N 119°56W **78** G7
Staten, I. = Estados, I. de Los
 Argentina 54°40S 64°30W **96** G4
Staten I. *U.S.A.* 40°35N 74°9W **83** F10
Statesboro *U.S.A.* 32°27N 81°47W **85** E14
Statesville *U.S.A.* 35°47N 80°53W **85** D14
Statia = St. Eustatius
 W. Indies 17°20N 63°0W **89** C7
Stauffer *U.S.A.* 34°45N 119°3W **79** L7
Staunton *Ill., U.S.A.* 39°1N 89°47W **80** F9
Staunton *Va., U.S.A.* 38°9N 79°4W **81** F14
Stavanger *Norway* 58°57N 5°40E **9** G11
Staveley *N.Z.* 43°40S 171°32E **59** E3
Stavelot *Belgium* 50°23N 5°55E **15** D5
Stavern *Norway* 59°0N 10°1E **9** G14
Stavoren *Neths.* 52°53N 5°22E **15** B5
Stavropol *Russia* 45°5N 42°0E **19** E7
Stavros *Cyprus* 35°1N 32°38E **25** D11
Stavros *Greece* 35°12N 24°45E **25** D6
Stavros, Akra *Greece* 35°26N 24°58E **25** D6
Stawell *Australia* 37°5S 142°47E **63** F3
Stawell ⇀ *Australia* 20°20S 142°55E **62** C3
Stayner *Canada* 44°25N 80°5W **82** B4
Stayton *U.S.A.* 44°48N 122°48W **76** D2
Steamboat Springs
 U.S.A. 40°29N 106°50W **76** F10
Steele *U.S.A.* 46°51N 99°55W **80** B4
Steelton *U.S.A.* 40°14N 76°50W **82** F8
Steen River *Canada* 59°40N 117°12W **70** B5
Steens Mt. *U.S.A.* 42°35N 118°40W **76** E4
Steenwijk *Neths.* 52°47N 6°7E **15** B6
Steep Pt. *Australia* 26°8S 113°8E **61** E1
Steep Rock *Canada* 51°30N 98°48W **71** C9
Stefanie L. = Chew Bahir
 Ethiopia 4°40N 36°50E **47** G2
Stefansson Bay *Antarctica* 67°20S 59°8E **5** C5
Stefansson I. *Canada* 73°20N 105°45W **69** C10
Steiermark □ *Austria* 47°26N 15°0E **16** E8
Steilacoom *U.S.A.* 47°10N 122°36W **78** C4
Steilrandberge *Namibia* 17°45S 13°20E **56** B1
Steinbach *Canada* 49°32N 96°40W **71** D9
Steinhausen *Namibia* 21°49S 18°20E **56** C2
Steinkjer *Norway* 64°1N 11°31E **8** D14
Steinkopf *S. Africa* 29°18S 17°43E **56** D2
Stellarton *Canada* 45°32N 62°30W **73** C7
Stellenbosch *S. Africa* 33°58S 18°50E **56** E2
Stendal *Germany* 52°36N 11°53E **16** B6
Steornabhaigh = Stornoway
 U.K. 58°13N 6°23W **11** C2
Stepanakert = Xankändi
 Azerbaijan 39°52N 46°49E **44** B5
Stephens Creek
 Australia 31°50S 141°30E **63** E3
Stephens I. *Canada* 54°10N 130°45W **70** C2
Stephens L. *Canada* 56°32N 95°0W **71** B9
Stephenville *Canada* 48°31N 58°35W **73** C8
Stephenville *U.S.A.* 32°13N 98°12W **84** E5
Steppe *Asia* 50°0N 50°0E **26** C7

Sterkstroom *S. Africa* 31°32S 26°32E **56** E4
Sterling *Colo., U.S.A.* 40°37N 103°13W **76** F12
Sterling *Ill., U.S.A.* 41°48N 89°42W **80** E9
Sterling *Kans., U.S.A.* 38°13N 98°12W **80** F4
Sterling City *U.S.A.* 31°51N 101°0W **84** F4
Sterling Heights *U.S.A.* 42°35N 83°2W **81** D12
Sterling Run *U.S.A.* 41°25N 78°12W **82** E6
Sterlitamak *Russia* 53°40N 56°0E **18** D10
Sternes *Greece* 35°39N 24°9E **25** D6
Stettin = Szczecin *Poland* 53°27N 14°27E **16** B8
Stettiner Haff *Germany* 53°47N 14°15E **16** B8
Stettler *Canada* 52°19N 112°40W **70** C6
Steubenville *U.S.A.* 40°22N 80°37W **82** F4
Stevenage *U.K.* 51°55N 0°13W **13** F7
Stevens Point *U.S.A.* 44°31N 89°34W **80** C9
Stevenson *U.S.A.* 45°42N 121°53W **78** E5
Stevenson ⇀ *Australia* 27°6S 135°33E **63** D2
Stevenson L. *Canada* 53°55N 96°0W **71** C9
Stevensville *U.S.A.* 46°30N 114°5W **76** C6
Stewart *Canada* 55°56N 129°57W **70** B3
Stewart *U.S.A.* 39°5N 119°46W **78** F7
Stewart ⇀ *Canada* 63°19N 139°26W **68** E4
Stewart, C. *Australia* 11°57S 134°56E **62** A1
Stewart, I. *Chile* 54°50S 71°15W **96** G2
Stewart I. *N.Z.* 46°58S 167°54E **59** G1
Stewarts Point *U.S.A.* 38°39N 123°24W **78** G3
Stewartville *U.S.A.* 43°51N 92°29W **80** D7
Stewiacke *Canada* 45°9N 63°22W **73** C7
Steynsburg *S. Africa* 31°15S 25°49E **56** E4
Steytlerville *S. Africa* 33°17S 24°19E **56** E3
Stigler *U.S.A.* 35°15N 95°8W **84** D7
Stikine ⇀ *Canada* 56°40N 132°30W **70** B2
Stilfontein *S. Africa* 26°51S 26°50E **56** D4
Stillwater *N.Z.* 42°27S 171°20E **59** E3
Stillwater *N.Y., U.S.A.* 42°55N 73°41W **83** D11
Stillwater *Okla., U.S.A.* 36°7N 97°4W **84** C6
Stillwater Range *U.S.A.* 39°50N 118°5W **76** G4
Stillwater Res. *U.S.A.* 43°54N 75°3W **83** C9
Stilwell *U.S.A.* 35°49N 94°38W **84** D7
Stînga Nistrului □
 Moldova 47°20N 29°15E **17** E15
Stip *Macedonia* 41°42N 22°10E **23** D10
Stirling *Canada* 44°18N 77°33W **82** B7
Stirling *U.K.* 56°8N 3°57W **11** E5
Stirling □ *U.K.* 56°12N 4°18W **11** E4
Stirling Ra. *Australia* 34°23S 118°0E **61** F2
Stirling Range △
 Australia 34°26S 118°20E **61** F2
Stittsville *Canada* 45°15N 75°55W **83** A9
Stjernøya *Norway* 70°20N 22°40E **8** A20
Stjørdalshalsen *Norway* 63°29N 10°51E **8** E14
Stockerau *Austria* 48°24N 16°12E **16** D9
Stockholm *Sweden* 59°19N 18°4E **9** G18
Stockport *U.K.* 53°25N 2°9W **12** D5
Stocksbridge *U.K.* 53°29N 1°35W **12** D6
Stockton *Calif., U.S.A.* 37°58N 121°17W **78** H5
Stockton *Kans., U.S.A.* 39°26N 99°16W **80** F4
Stockton *Mo., U.S.A.* 37°42N 93°48W **80** G7
Stockton-on-Tees *U.K.* 54°35N 1°19W **12** C6
Stockton-on-Tees □
 U.K. 54°35N 1°19W **12** C6
Stockton Plateau
 U.S.A. 30°30N 102°30W **84** F3
Stoeng Treng *Cambodia* 13°31N 105°58E **38** F5
Stoer, Pt. of *U.K.* 58°16N 5°23W **11** C3
Stoke-on-Trent *U.K.* 53°1N 2°11W **12** D5
Stoke-on-Trent □ *U.K.* 53°1N 2°11W **12** D5
Stokes △ *Australia* 33°45S 121°11E **61** F3
Stokes Bay *Canada* 45°0N 81°28W **82** B3
Stokes Pt. *Australia* 40°10S 143°56E **63** G3
Stokes Ra. *Australia* 15°50S 130°50E **60** C5
Stokksnes *Iceland* 64°14N 14°58W **8** D6
Stokmarknes *Norway* 68°34N 14°54E **8** B16
Stolac *Bos.-H.* 43°5N 17°59E **23** C7
Stolbovoy, Ostrov
 Russia 74°44N 135°14E **29** B14
Stolbtsy = Stowbtsy
 Belarus 53°30N 26°43E **17** B14
Stolin *Belarus* 51°53N 26°50E **17** C14
Stomio *Greece* 35°21N 23°22E **25** D5
Stone *U.K.* 52°55N 2°9W **12** E5
Stoneboro *U.S.A.* 41°20N 80°7W **82** E4
Stonehaven *U.K.* 56°59N 2°12W **11** E6
Stonehenge *Australia* 24°22S 143°17E **62** C3
Stonehenge *U.K.* 51°9N 1°45W **13** F6
Stonewall *Canada* 50°10N 97°19W **71** C9
Stony I. *U.S.A.* 43°53N 76°19W **83** C8
Stony L. *Man., Canada* 58°51N 98°40W **71** B9
Stony L. *Ont., Canada* 44°30N 78°5W **82** B6
Stony Point *U.S.A.* 41°14N 73°59W **83** E11
Stony Pt. *U.S.A.* 43°50N 76°18W **83** C8
Stony Rapids *Canada* 59°16N 105°50W **71** B7
Stony Tunguska = Tunguska,
 Podkamennaya ⇀
 Russia 61°50N 90°13E **29** C10
Stonyford *U.S.A.* 39°23N 122°33W **78** F4
Stora Lulevatten *Sweden* 67°10N 19°30E **8** C18
Storavan *Sweden* 65°45N 18°10E **8** D18
Stord *Norway* 59°52N 5°23E **9** G11
Store Bælt *Denmark* 55°20N 11°0E **9** J14
Storkerson Pen.
 Canada 72°30N 106°30W **68** C10
Storm B. *Australia* 43°10S 147°30E **63** G4
Storm Lake *U.S.A.* 42°39N 95°13W **80** D6
Stormberge *S. Africa* 31°16S 26°17E **56** E4
Stormsrivier *S. Africa* 33°59S 23°52E **56** E3
Stornoway *U.K.* 58°13N 6°23W **11** C2
Storozhinets = Storozhynets
 Ukraine 48°14N 25°45E **17** D13
Storozhynets *Ukraine* 48°14N 25°45E **17** D13
Storrs *U.S.A.* 41°49N 72°15W **83** E12
Storsjön *Sweden* 63°9N 14°30E **8** E16
Storuman *Sweden* 65°5N 17°10E **8** D17
Storuman, L. *Sweden* 65°13N 16°50E **8** D17
Stouffville *Canada* 43°58N 79°15W **82** C5
Stoughton *Canada* 49°40N 103°0W **71** D8
Stour ⇀ *Dorset, U.K.* 50°43N 1°47W **13** G6
Stour ⇀ *Kent, U.K.* 51°18N 1°22E **13** F9

Stour ⇀ *Suffolk, U.K.* 51°57N 1°4E **13** F9
Stourbridge *U.K.* 52°28N 2°8W **13** E5
Stout L. *Canada* 52°0N 94°40W **71** C10
Stove Pipe Wells Village
 U.S.A. 36°35N 117°11W **79** J9
Stow *U.S.A.* 41°10N 81°27W **82** E3
Stowbtsy *Belarus* 53°30N 26°43E **17** B14
Stowmarket *U.K.* 52°12N 1°0E **13** E9
Strabane *U.K.* 54°50N 7°27W **10** B4
Strahan *Australia* 42°9S 145°20E **63** G4
Stralsund *Germany* 54°18N 13°4E **16** A7
Strand *S. Africa* 34°9S 18°48E **56** E2
Stranda *Møre og Romsdal,*
 Norway 62°19N 6°58E **8** E12
Stranda *Nord-Trøndelag,*
 Norway 63°33N 10°14E **8** E14
Strangford L. *U.K.* 54°30N 5°37W **10** B6
Stranorlar *Ireland* 54°48N 7°46W **10** B4
Stranraer *U.K.* 54°54N 5°1W **11** G3
Strasbourg *Canada* 51°4N 104°55W **71** C8
Strasbourg *France* 48°35N 7°42E **20** B7
Stratford *Canada* 43°23N 81°0W **82** D3
Stratford *N.Z.* 39°20S 174°19E **59** C5
Stratford *Calif., U.S.A.* 36°11N 119°49W **78** J7
Stratford *Conn., U.S.A.* 41°12N 73°8W **83** E11
Stratford *Tex., U.S.A.* 36°20N 102°4W **84** C3
Stratford-upon-Avon
 U.K. 52°12N 1°42W **13** E6
Strath Spey *U.K.* 57°9N 3°49W **11** D5
Strathalbyn *Australia* 35°13S 138°53E **63** F2
Strathaven *U.K.* 55°40N 4°5W **11** F4
Strathcona △ *Canada* 49°38N 125°40W **70** D3
Strathmore *Canada* 51°5N 113°18W **70** C6
Strathmore *U.K.* 56°37N 3°7W **11** E5
Strathmore *U.S.A.* 36°9N 119°4W **78** J7
Strathnaver *Canada* 53°20N 122°33W **70** C4
Strathpeffer *U.K.* 57°35N 4°32W **11** D4
Strathroy *Canada* 42°58N 81°38W **82** D3
Strathy Pt. *U.K.* 58°36N 4°1W **11** C4
Strattanville *U.S.A.* 41°12N 79°19W **82** E5
Stratton *U.S.A.* 45°8N 70°26W **83** A14
Stratton Mt. *U.S.A.* 43°4N 72°55W **83** C12
Straubing *Germany* 48°52N 12°34E **16** D7
Straumnes *Iceland* 66°26N 23°8W **8** C2
Strawberry ⇀ *U.S.A.* 40°10N 110°24W **76** F8
Streaky B. *Australia* 32°48S 134°13E **63** E1
Streaky Bay *Australia* 32°51S 134°18E **63** E1
Streator *U.S.A.* 41°8N 88°50W **80** E9
Streetsboro *U.S.A.* 41°14N 81°21W **82** E3
Streetsville *Canada* 43°35N 79°42W **82** C5
Streng ⇀ *Cambodia* 13°12N 103°37E **38** F4
Streymoy *Færoe Is.* 62°8N 7°5W **8** E9
Strezhevoy *Russia* 60°42N 77°34E **28** C8
Strimonas ⇀ *Greece* 40°46N 23°51E **23** D10
Strokestown *Ireland* 53°46N 8°7W **10** C3
Stroma *U.K.* 58°41N 3°7W **11** C5
Strómboli *Italy* 38°47N 15°13E **22** E6
Stromeferry *U.K.* 57°21N 5°33W **11** D3
Stromness *U.K.* 58°58N 3°17W **11** C5
Stromsburg *U.S.A.* 41°7N 97°36W **80** E5
Strömstad *Sweden* 58°56N 11°10E **9** G14
Strömsund *Sweden* 63°51N 15°33E **8** E16
Strongsville *U.S.A.* 41°19N 81°50W **82** E3
Stronsay *U.K.* 59°7N 2°35W **11** B6
Stroud *U.K.* 51°45N 2°13W **13** F5
Stroud Road *Australia* 32°18S 151°57E **63** E5
Stroudsburg *U.S.A.* 40°59N 75°12W **83** F9
Stroumbi *Cyprus* 34°53N 32°29E **25** E11
Struer *Denmark* 56°30N 8°35E **9** H13
Strugi Krasnyye *Russia* 58°21N 29°1E **9** G23
Strumica *Macedonia* 41°28N 22°41E **23** D10
Struthers *U.S.A.* 41°4N 80°39W **82** E4
Stryker *U.S.A.* 48°41N 114°46W **76** B6
Stryy *Ukraine* 49°16N 23°48E **17** D12
Strzelecki Cr. ⇀
 Australia 29°37S 139°59E **63** D2
Strzelecki Desert
 Australia 29°30S 140°0E **63** D3
Stuart *Fla., U.S.A.* 27°12N 80°15W **85** H14
Stuart *Nebr., U.S.A.* 42°36N 99°8W **80** D4
Stuart ⇀ *Canada* 54°0N 123°35W **70** C4
Stuart Bluff Ra.
 Australia 22°50S 131°52E **60** D5
Stuart I. *U.S.A.* 63°35N 162°30W **74** C7
Stuart L. *Canada* 54°30N 124°30W **70** C4
Stuart Ra. *Australia* 29°10S 134°56E **63** D1
Stull L. *Canada* 54°24N 92°34W **72** B1
Stung Treng = Stoeng Treng
 Cambodia 13°31N 105°58E **38** F5
Stupart ⇀ *Canada* 56°0N 93°25W **72** A1
Sturge I. *Antarctica* 67°26S 164°47E **5** C11
Sturgeon B. *Canada* 52°0N 97°50W **71** C9
Sturgeon Bay *U.S.A.* 44°50N 87°23W **80** C10
Sturgeon Falls *Canada* 46°25N 79°57W **72** C4
Sturgeon L. *Alta., Canada* 55°6N 117°32W **70** B5
Sturgeon L. *Ont., Canada* 50°0N 90°45W **72** C1
Sturgeon L. *Ont., Canada* 44°28N 78°43W **82** B6
Sturgis *Canada* 51°56N 102°36W **71** C8
Sturgis *Mich., U.S.A.* 41°48N 85°25W **81** E11
Sturgis *S. Dak., U.S.A.* 44°25N 103°31W **80** C2
Sturt ⇀ *Australia* 27°17S 141°37E **63** D3
Sturt Cr. ⇀ *Australia* 19°8S 127°50E **60** C4
Sturt Stony Desert
 Australia 28°30S 141°0E **63** D3
Stutterheim *S. Africa* 32°33S 27°28E **56** E4
Stuttgart *Germany* 48°48N 9°11E **16** D5
Stuttgart *U.S.A.* 34°30N 91°33W **84** D9
Stuyvesant *U.S.A.* 42°23N 73°45W **83** D11
Stykkishólmur *Iceland* 65°2N 22°40W **8** D2
Styria = Steiermark □
 Austria 47°26N 15°0E **16** E8
Su Xian = Suzhou
 China 33°41N 116°59E **34** H9
Suakin *Sudan* 19°8N 37°20E **51** E13
Suan *N. Korea* 38°42N 126°22E **35** E14
Suar *India* 29°2N 79°3E **43** E8
Subā *Si. Arabia* 27°10N 35°40E **44** E2
Subang *Indonesia* 6°34S 107°45E **37** G12
Subansiri ⇀ *India* 26°48N 93°50E **41** F18

Subarnarekha ⇀ *India* 22°34N 87°24E **43** H12
Subayhah *Si. Arabia* 30°2N 38°50E **44** D3
Subi *Indonesia* 2°58N 108°50E **36** D3
Subotica *Serbia* 46°6N 19°39E **23** A8
Suceava *Romania* 47°38N 26°16E **17** E14
Suchan = Partizansk
 Russia 43°8N 133°9E **30** C6
Suchil *Mexico* 23°39N 103°54W **86** C4
Suchou = Suzhou
 China 31°19N 120°38E **33** C7
Süchow = Xuzhou
 China 34°18N 117°10E **35** G9
Suck ⇀ *Ireland* 53°17N 8°3W **10** C3
Sucre *Bolivia* 19°0S 65°15W **92** G5
Sucuriú ⇀ *Brazil* 20°47S 51°38W **93** H8
Sud, Pte. du *Canada* 49°3N 62°14W **73** C7
Sud-Kivu □
 Dem. Rep. of the Congo 3°0S 28°30E **54** C2
Sud-Ouest, Pte. *Canada* 49°23N 63°36W **73** C7
Sud Ouest, Pte. *Mauritius* 20°28S 57°18E **53** d
Sudan *U.S.A.* 34°4N 102°31W **84** D3
Sudan ■ *Africa* 15°0N 30°0E **51** E11
Sudbury *Canada* 46°30N 81°0W **72** C3
Sudbury *U.K.* 52°2N 0°45E **13** E8
Sûdd *Sudan* 8°20N 30°0E **51** G12
Sudeten Mts. = Sudety
 Europe 50°20N 16°45E **17** C9
Sudety *Europe* 50°20N 16°45E **17** C9
Suðuroy *Færoe Is.* 61°32N 6°50W **8** F9
Sudi *Tanzania* 10°11S 39°57E **55** E4
Sudirman, Pegunungan
 Indonesia 4°30S 137°0E **37** E9
Sudong, Pulau *Singapore* 1°13N 103°44E **39** d
Sueca *Spain* 39°12N 0°21W **21** C5
Suemez I. *U.S.A.* 55°15N 133°20W **70** B2
Suez = El Suweis *Egypt* 29°58N 32°31E **51** C12
Suez, G. of = Suweis, Khalig el
 Egypt 28°40N 33°0E **51** C12
Suez Canal = Suweis, Qanâ es
 Egypt 31°0N 32°20E **51** B12
Suffield *Canada* 50°12N 111°10W **70** C6
Suffolk *U.S.A.* 36°44N 76°35W **81** G15
Suffolk □ *U.K.* 52°16N 1°0E **13** E9
Sugar Grove *U.S.A.* 41°59N 79°20W **82** E5
Sugarcreek *U.S.A.* 41°25N 79°52W **82** E5
Sugarive ⇀ *India* 26°16N 86°24E **43** F12
Sugluk = Salluit
 Canada 62°14N 75°38W **69** E16
Şuḥār *Oman* 24°20N 56°40E **45** E8
Sühbaatar *Mongolia* 50°17N 106°10E **32** A5
Sühbaatar □ *Mongolia* 45°30N 114°0E **34** B8
Suhl *Germany* 50°36N 10°42E **16** C6
Sui *Pakistan* 28°37N 69°19E **42** E3
Sui Xian *China* 34°25N 115°2E **34** G8
Suide *China* 37°30N 110°12E **34** F6
Suifenhe *China* 44°25N 131°10E **35** B16
Suihua *China* 46°32N 126°55E **33** B7
Suining *Jiangsu, China* 33°56N 117°58E **35** H9
Suining *Sichuan, China* 30°26N 105°35E **32** C5
Suiping *China* 33°10N 113°59E **34** H7
Suir ⇀ *Ireland* 52°16N 7°9W **10** D4
Suisse = Switzerland ■
 Europe 46°30N 8°0E **20** C8
Suisun City *U.S.A.* 38°15N 122°2W **78** G4
Suiyang *China* 44°30N 130°56E **35** B16
Suizhong *China* 40°21N 120°20E **35** D11
Sujangarh *India* 27°42N 74°31E **42** F6
Sukabumi *Indonesia* 6°56S 106°50E **37** G12
Sukadana *Indonesia* 1°10S 110°0E **36** E4
Sukagawa *Japan* 37°17N 140°23E **31** F10
Sukaraja *Indonesia* 2°28S 110°25E **36** E4
Sukarnapura = Jayapura
 Indonesia 2°28S 140°38E **37** E10
Sukawati *Indonesia* 8°35S 115°17E **37** K18
Sukch'ŏn *N. Korea* 39°22N 125°35E **35** E13
Sukhona ⇀ *Russia* 61°15N 46°39E **18** C6
Sukhothai *Thailand* 17°1N 99°49E **38** D2
Sukhumi = Sokhumi
 Georgia 43°0N 41°0E **19** F7
Sukkur *Pakistan* 27°42N 68°54E **42** F3
Sukkur Barrage *Pakistan* 27°40N 68°50E **42** F3
Sukri ⇀ *India* 25°4N 71°43E **42** G4
Sukumo *Japan* 32°56N 132°44E **31** H6
Sukunka ⇀ *Canada* 55°45N 121°15W **70** B4
Sula, Kepulauan *Indonesia* 1°45S 125°0E **37** E7
Sulaco ⇀ *Honduras* 15°2N 87°44W **88** C2
Sulaiman Range
 Pakistan 30°30N 69°50E **42** D3
Sūlār *Iran* 31°53N 51°54E **45** D6
Sulawesi □ *Indonesia* 2°0S 120°0E **37** E6
Sulawesi Barat □ *Indonesia* 3°0S 119°0E **37** E5
Sulawesi Sea = Celebes Sea
 Indonesia 3°0N 123°0E **37** D6
Sulawesi Selatan □
 Indonesia 2°30S 120°0E **37** E6
Sulawesi Tengah □
 Indonesia 1°0S 121°0E **37** E6
Sulawesi Tenggara □
 Indonesia 3°50S 122°0E **37** E6
Sulawesi Utara □ *Indonesia* 1°0N 124°0E **37** D6
Sulima *S. Leone* 6°58N 11°32W **52** G3
Sulina *Romania* 45°10N 29°40E **17** F15
Sulitjelma *Norway* 67°9N 16°3E **8** C17
Sullana *Peru* 4°52S 80°39W **92** D2
Sullivan *Ill., U.S.A.* 39°36N 88°37W **80** F9
Sullivan *Ind., U.S.A.* 39°6N 87°24W **80** F10
Sullivan *Mo., U.S.A.* 38°13N 91°10W **80** F8
Sullivan Bay *Canada* 50°55N 126°50W **70** C3
Sullivan I. = Lanbi Kyun
 Burma 10°50N 98°20E **39** G2
Sullom Voe *U.K.* 60°27N 1°20W **11** A7
Sulphur *La., U.S.A.* 30°14N 93°23W **84** F8
Sulphur *Okla., U.S.A.* 34°31N 96°58W **84** D6
Sulphur Pt. *Canada* 60°56N 114°48W **70** A6
Sulphur Springs *U.S.A.* 33°8N 95°36W **84** E7
Sultan *Canada* 47°36N 82°47W **72** C3
Sultan *U.S.A.* 47°52N 121°49W **78** C5
Sultan Hamud *Kenya* 2°1S 37°22E **54** C4
Sultanābād = Arāk *Iran* 34°0N 49°40E **45** C6
Sultanpur *Mad. P., India* 23°9N 77°56E **42** H8
Sultanpur *Punjab, India* 31°13N 75°11E **42** D6

Sultanpur *Ut. P., India* 26°18N 82°4E **43** F10
Sulu Arch. *Phil.* 6°0N 121°0E **37** C6
Sulu Sea *E. Indies* 8°0N 120°0E **37** C6
Sulūq *Libya* 31°44N 20°14E **51** B10
Sulzberger Ice Shelf
 Antarctica 78°0S 150°0W **5** E13
Sumalata *Indonesia* 1°0N 122°31E **37** D6
Sumampa *Argentina* 29°25S 63°29W **94** B3
Sumatera *Indonesia* 0°40N 100°20E **36** D2
Sumatera Barat □
 Indonesia 1°0S 101°0E **36** E2
Sumatera Utara □
 Indonesia 2°30N 98°0E **36** D1
Sumatra = Sumatera
 Indonesia 0°40N 100°20E **36** D2
Sumba *Indonesia* 9°45S 119°35E **37** F5
Sumba, Selat *Indonesia* 9°0S 118°40E **37** F5
Sumbawa *Indonesia* 8°26S 117°30E **36** F5
Sumbawa Besar
 Indonesia 8°30S 117°26E **36** F5
Sumbawanga □ *Tanzania* 8°0S 31°30E **52** F6
Sumbe *Angola* 11°10S 13°48E **52** G2
Sumburgh Hd. *U.K.* 59°52N 1°17W **11** B7
Sumdeo *India* 31°26N 78°44E **43** D8
Sumdo *China* 35°6N 78°41E **43** B8
Sumedang *Indonesia* 6°52S 107°55E **37** G12
Šumen = Shumen
 Bulgaria 43°18N 26°55E **23** C12
Sumenep *Indonesia* 7°1S 113°52E **37** G15
Sumgait = Sumqayıt
 Azerbaijan 40°34N 49°38E **19** F8
Summer L. *U.S.A.* 42°50N 120°45W **76** E3
Summerland *Canada* 49°32N 119°41W **70** D5
Summerside *Canada* 46°24N 63°47W **73** C7
Summersville *U.S.A.* 38°17N 80°51W **81** F13
Summerville *Ga.,*
 U.S.A. 34°29N 85°21W **85** D12
Summerville *S.C., U.S.A.* 33°1N 80°11W **85** E14
Summit Lake *Canada* 54°20N 122°40W **70** C4
Summit Peak *U.S.A.* 37°21N 106°42W **77** H10
Sumner *Iowa, U.S.A.* 42°51N 92°6W **80** D7
Sumner *Wash., U.S.A.* 47°12N 122°14W **78** C4
Sumoto *Japan* 34°21N 134°54E **31** G7
Šumperk *Czech Rep.* 49°59N 16°59E **17** D9
Sumqayıt *Azerbaijan* 40°34N 49°38E **19** F8
Sumter *U.S.A.* 33°55N 80°21W **85** E14
Sumy *Ukraine* 50°57N 34°50E **19** D5
Sun City *S. Africa* 25°17S 27°3E **56** D4
Sun City *Ariz., U.S.A.* 33°35N 112°16W **77** K7
Sun City *Calif., U.S.A.* 33°42N 117°11W **79** M9
Sun City Center *U.S.A.* 27°43N 82°21W **85** H13
Sun Lakes *U.S.A.* 33°10N 111°52W **77** K8
Sun Valley *U.S.A.* 43°42N 114°21W **76** E6
Sunagawa *Japan* 43°29N 141°55E **30** C10
Sunan *N. Korea* 39°15N 125°40E **35** E13
Sunart, L. *U.K.* 56°42N 5°43W **11** E3
Sunburst *U.S.A.* 48°53N 111°55W **76** B8
Sunbury *Australia* 37°35S 144°44E **63** F3
Sunbury *U.S.A.* 40°52N 76°48W **83** F8
Sunchales *Argentina* 30°58S 61°35W **94** C3
Suncheon *S. Korea* 34°52N 127°31E **35** G14
Suncho Corral *Argentina* 27°55S 63°27W **94** B3
Sunch'on *N. Korea* 39°25N 125°56E **35** E13
Suncook *U.S.A.* 43°8N 71°27W **83** C13
Sunda, Selat *Indonesia* 6°20S 105°30E **36** F3
Sunda Is. *Indonesia* 5°0S 105°0E **64** H2
Sunda Str. = Sunda, Selat
 Indonesia 6°20S 105°30E **36** F3
Sunda Trench = Java Trench
 Ind. Oc. 9°0S 105°0E **36** F3
Sundance *Canada* 56°32N 94°4W **71** B10
Sundance *U.S.A.* 44°24N 104°23W **76** D11
Sundar Nagar *India* 31°32N 76°53E **42** D7
Sundarbans *Asia* 22°0N 89°0E **41** J16
Sundarbans △ *India* 22°0N 88°45E **43** J13
Sundargarh *India* 22°4N 84°5E **41** H14
Sundays = Sondags ⇀
 S. Africa 33°44S 25°51E **56** E4
Sunderland *Canada* 44°16N 79°4W **82** B5
Sunderland *U.K.* 54°55N 1°23W **12** C6
Sundown △ *Australia* 28°49S 151°38E **63** D5
Sundre *Canada* 51°49N 114°38W **70** C6
Sundsvall *Sweden* 62°23N 17°17E **8** E17
Sung Hei *Vietnam* 10°20N 106°2E **39** G6
Sungai Acheh *Malaysia* 5°8N 100°30E **39** c
Sungai Kolok *Thailand* 6°2N 101°58E **39** J3
Sungai Lembing *Malaysia* 3°55N 103°3E **39** L4
Sungai Petani *Malaysia* 5°37N 100°30E **39** K3
Sungaigerong *Indonesia* 2°59S 104°52E **36** E2
Sungailiat *Indonesia* 1°51S 106°8E **36** E3
Sungaipenuh *Indonesia* 2°1S 101°20E **36** E2
Sungari = Songhua Jiang ⇀
 China 47°45N 132°30E **33** B8
Sunghua Chiang = Songhua
 Jiang ⇀ *China* 47°45N 132°30E **33** B8
Sunland Park *U.S.A.* 31°50N 106°40W **77** L10
Sunndalsøra *Norway* 62°40N 8°33E **8** E13
Sunnyside *U.S.A.* 46°20N 120°0W **76** C3
Sunnyvale *U.S.A.* 37°23N 122°2W **78** H4
Sunrise Manor *U.S.A.* 36°12N 115°4W **79** J11
Suntar *Russia* 62°15N 117°30E **29** C12
Suomenselkä *Finland* 62°52N 24°0E **8** E21
Suomi = Finland ■ *Europe* 63°0N 27°0E **8** E22
Suomussalmi *Finland* 64°54N 29°10E **8** D23
Suoyarvi *Russia* 62°3N 32°20E **18** B5
Supai *U.S.A.* 36°15N 112°41W **77** H7
Supaul *India* 26°10N 86°40E **43** F12
Superior *Ariz., U.S.A.* 33°18N 111°6W **77** K8
Superior *Mont., U.S.A.* 47°12N 114°53W **76** C6
Superior *Nebr., U.S.A.* 40°1N 98°4W **80** E4
Superior *Wis., U.S.A.* 46°44N 92°6W **80** B7
Superior, L. *N. Amer.* 47°0N 87°0W **72** C2
Suphan Buri *Thailand* 14°14N 100°10E **38** E3
Suphan Dağı *Turkey* 38°54N 42°48E **44** B4
Supiori *Indonesia* 1°0S 136°0E **37** E9
Supung Shuiku *China* 40°35N 124°50E **35** D13
Sūq ash Shuyūkh *Iraq* 30°53N 46°28E **44** D5
Sūq Suwayq *Si. Arabia* 24°23N 38°27E **44** E3

Suqian *China* 33°54N 118°8E **35** H10
Suquṭra = Socotra *Yemen* 12°30N 54°0E **47** E5
Şūr *Lebanon* 33°19N 35°16E **46** B4
Şūr *Oman* 22°34N 59°32E **47** D6
Sur, Pt. *U.S.A.* 36°18N 121°54W **78** J5
Sura *Russia* 56°6N 46°0E **18** D8
Surab *Pakistan* 28°25N 66°15E **42** E2
Surabaja = Surabaya
  Indonesia 7°17S 112°45E **37** G15
Surabaya *Indonesia* 7°17S 112°45E **37** G15
Surakarta *Indonesia* 7°35S 110°48E **37** G14
Surat *Australia* 27°10S 149°6E **63** D4
Surat *India* 21°12N 72°55E **40** J8
Surat Thani *Thailand* 9°6N 99°20E **39** H2
Surax *India* 29°18N 73°55E **42** E5
Şuraymilā *Si. Arabia* 25°7N 46°7E **44** E5
Surendranagar *India* 22°45N 71°40E **42** H4
Surf *U.S.A.* 34°41N 120°36W **79** L6
Surfers Paradise
  Australia 28°0S 153°25E **63** D5
Surgut *Russia* 61°14N 73°20E **28** C8
Suriapet *India* 17°10N 79°40E **40** L11
Surigao *Phil.* 9°47N 125°29E **37** C7
Surin *Thailand* 14°50N 103°34E **38** E4
Surin Nua, Ko *Thailand* 9°30N 97°55E **39** H1
Surinam = Suriname ■
  S. Amer. 4°0N 56°0W **93** C7
Suriname ■ *S. Amer.* 4°0N 56°0W **93** C7
Suriname → *Suriname* 5°50N 55°15W **93** B7
Sūrmaq *Iran* 31°3N 52°48E **45** D7
Surrey *Canada* 49°7N 122°45W **78** A4
Surrey □ *U.K.* 51°15N 0°31W **13** F7
Sursand *India* 26°39N 85°43E **43** F11
Sursar → *India* 26°14N 87°3E **43** F12
Surt *Libya* 31°11N 16°39E **51** B9
Surt, Khalīj *Libya* 31°40N 18°30E **51** B9
Surtanaha *Pakistan* 26°22N 70°0E **42** F4
Surtsey *Iceland* 63°20N 20°30W **8** E3
Suruga-Wan *Japan* 34°45N 138°30E **31** G9
Sūsah *Libya* 32°52N 21°59E **51** B10
Susaki *Japan* 33°22N 133°17E **31** H6
Süsangerd *Iran* 31°35N 48°6E **45** D6
Susanville *U.S.A.* 40°25N 120°39W **76** F3
Susner *India* 23°57N 76°5E **42** H7
Susquehanna *U.S.A.* 41°57N 75°36W **83** E9
Susquehanna → *U.S.A.* 39°33N 76°5W **83** G8
Susques *Argentina* 23°35S 66°25W **94** A2
Sussex *Canada* 45°45N 65°37W **73** C6
Sussex *U.S.A.* 41°13N 74°37W **83** E10
Sussex, E. □ *U.K.* 51°0N 0°20E **13** G8
Sussex, W. □ *U.K.* 51°0N 0°30W **13** G7
Sustut → *Canada* 56°20N 127°30W **70** B3
Susuman *Russia* 62°47N 148°10E **29** C15
Susunu *Indonesia* 3°7S 133°39E **37** E8
Susurluk *Turkey* 39°54N 28°8E **23** E13
Sutay Uul *Asia* 46°35N 93°38E **32** B4
Sutherland *S. Africa* 32°24S 20°40E **56** E3
Sutherland *U.K.* 58°12N 4°50W **11** C4
Sutherland *U.S.A.* 41°10N 101°8W **80** E3
Sutherland Falls *N.Z.* 44°48S 167°46E **59** F1
Sutherlin *U.S.A.* 43°23N 123°19W **76** E2
Suthri *India* 23°3N 68°55E **42** H3
Sutlej → *Pakistan* 29°23N 71°3E **42** E4
Sutter *U.S.A.* 39°10N 121°45W **78** F5
Sutter Buttes *U.S.A.* 39°12N 121°49W **78** F5
Sutter Creek *U.S.A.* 38°24N 120°48W **78** G6
Sutton *Canada* 45°6N 72°37W **83** A12
Sutton *Nebr., U.S.A.* 40°36N 97°52W **80** E5
Sutton *W. Va., U.S.A.* 38°40N 80°43W **81** F13
Sutton → *Canada* 55°15N 83°45W **72** A3
Sutton Coldfield *U.K.* 52°35N 1°49W **13** E6
Sutton in Ashfield *U.K.* 53°8N 1°16W **12** D6
Sutton L. *Canada* 54°15N 84°42W **72** B3
Suttor → *Australia* 21°36S 147°2E **62** C4
Suttsu *Japan* 42°48N 140°14E **30** C10
Sutwik I. *U.S.A.* 56°34N 157°12W **74** D8
Suva *Fiji* 18°6S 178°30E **59** a
Suva Planina *Serbia* 43°10N 22°5E **23** C10
Suvorov Is. = Suwarrow Is.
  Cook Is. 13°15S 163°5W **65** J11
Suwałki *Poland* 54°8N 22°59E **17** A12
Suwana *Indonesia* 8°44S 115°36E **37** K18
Suwannaphum
  Thailand 15°33N 103°47E **38** E4
Suwannee → *U.S.A.* 29°17N 83°10W **85** G13
Suwanose-Jima *Japan* 29°38N 129°43E **31** K4
Suwarrow Is. *Cook Is.* 13°15S 163°5W **65** J11
Suweis, Khalīg el *Egypt* 28°40N 33°0E **51** C12
Suweis, Qanâ es *Egypt* 31°0N 32°20E **51** B12
Suwŏn *S. Korea* 37°17N 127°1E **35** F14
Suzdal *Russia* 56°29N 40°26E **18** C7
Suzhou *Anhui, China* 33°41N 116°59E **34** H9
Suzhou *Jiangsu, China* 31°19N 120°38E **33** B13
Suzu *Japan* 37°25N 137°17E **31** F8
Suzu-Misaki *Japan* 37°31N 137°21E **31** F8
Suzuka *Japan* 34°55N 136°36E **31** G8
Svalbard *Arctic* 78°0N 17°0E **4** B8
Svalbard Radio = Longyearbyen
  Svalbard 78°13N 15°40E **4** B8
Svappavaara *Sweden* 67°40N 21°3E **8** C19
Svartisen *Norway* 66°40N 13°59E **8** C16
Svay Chek *Cambodia* 13°48N 102°58E **38** F4
Svay Rieng *Cambodia* 11°9N 105°45E **39** G5
Svealand □ *Sweden* 60°20N 15°0E **9** E16
Sveg *Sweden* 62°2N 14°21E **8** E16
Svendborg *Denmark* 55°4N 10°35E **9** J14
Sverdrup Chan. *Canada* 79°56N 96°25W **69** B12
Sverdrup Is. *Canada* 79°0N 97°0W **66** B10
Sverige = Sweden ■
  Europe 57°0N 15°0E **9** H16
Svetlaya *Russia* 46°33N 138°18E **30** A9
Svetlogorsk = Svyetlahorsk
  Belarus 52°38N 29°46E **17** B15
Svir → *Russia* 60°30N 32°48E **18** B5
Svishtov *Bulgaria* 43°36N 25°23E **23** C11
Svislach *Belarus* 53°3N 24°2E **17** B13
Svizzera = Switzerland ■
  Europe 46°30N 8°0E **20** C8
Svobodnyy *Russia* 51°20N 128°0E **29** D13

Svolvær *Norway* 68°15N 14°34E **8** B16
Svyetlahorsk *Belarus* 52°38N 29°46E **17** B15
Swabian Alps = Schwäbische Alb
  Germany 48°20N 9°30E **16** D5
Swaffham *U.K.* 52°39N 0°42E **13** E8
Swains I. *Amer. Samoa* 11°11S 171°4W **65** J11
Swainsboro *U.S.A.* 32°36N 82°20W **85** E13
Swakop → *Namibia* 22°38S 14°36E **56** C2
Swakopmund *Namibia* 22°37S 14°30E **56** C1
Swale → *U.K.* 54°5N 1°20W **12** C6
Swan → *Australia* 32°3S 115°45E **61** F2
Swan → *Canada* 52°30N 100°45W **71** C8
Swan Hill *Australia* 35°20S 143°33E **63** F3
Swan Hills *Canada* 54°43N 115°24W **70** C5
Swan Is. = Santanilla, Is.
  Honduras 17°22N 83°57W **88** C3
Swan L. *Man., Canada* 52°30N 100°40W **71** C8
Swan L. *Ont., Canada* 54°16N 91°11W **72** B1
Swan Ra. *U.S.A.* 48°0N 113°45W **76** C7
Swan River *Canada* 52°10N 101°16W **71** C8
Swanage *U.K.* 50°36N 1°58W **13** G6
Swansea *Australia* 42°8S 148°4E **63** G4
Swansea *Canada* 43°38N 79°28W **82** C5
Swansea *U.K.* 51°37N 3°57W **13** F4
Swansea □ *U.K.* 51°38N 4°3W **13** F3
Swartberge *S. Africa* 33°20S 22°0E **56** E3
Swartmodder *S. Africa* 28°1S 20°32E **56** D3
Swartnossob → *Namibia* 23°8S 18°42E **56** C2
Swartruggens *S. Africa* 25°39S 26°42E **56** D4
Swastika *Canada* 48°7N 80°6W **72** C3
Swat → *Pakistan* 34°40N 72°5E **43** B5
Swatow = Shantou
  China 23°18N 116°40E **33** D6
Swaziland ■ *Africa* 26°30S 31°30E **57** D5
Sweden ■ *Europe* 57°0N 15°0E **9** H16
Sweet Grass *U.S.A.* 48°59N 111°58W **76** B8
Sweet Home *U.S.A.* 44°24N 122°44W **76** D2
Sweetwater *Nev., U.S.A.* 38°27N 119°9W **78** G7
Sweetwater *Tenn.,
  U.S.A.* 35°36N 84°28W **85** D12
Sweetwater *Tex.,
  U.S.A.* 32°28N 100°25W **84** E4
Sweetwater → *U.S.A.* 42°31N 107°2W **76** E10
Swellendam *S. Africa* 34°1S 20°26E **56** E3
Świdnica *Poland* 50°50N 16°30E **17** C9
Świdnik *Poland* 51°13N 22°39E **17** C12
Świebodzin *Poland* 52°15N 15°31E **16** B8
Świecie *Poland* 53°25N 18°30E **17** B10
Swift Current *Canada* 50°20N 107°45W **71** C7
Swift Current →
  Canada 50°38N 107°44W **71** C7
Swilly, L. *Ireland* 55°12N 7°33W **10** A4
Swindon *U.K.* 51°34N 1°46W **13** F6
Swindon □ *U.K.* 51°34N 1°46W **13** F6
Swinemünde = Świnoujście
  Poland 53°54N 14°16E **16** B8
Swinford *Ireland* 53°57N 8°58W **10** C3
Świnoujście *Poland* 53°54N 14°16E **16** B8
Switzerland ■ *Europe* 46°30N 8°0E **20** C8
Swords *Ireland* 53°28N 6°13W **10** C5
Swoyerville *U.S.A.* 41°18N 75°33W **83** E9
Sydenham → *Canada* 42°33N 82°25W **82** D2
Sydney *Australia* 33°52S 151°12E **63** E5
Sydney *Canada* 46°7N 60°7W **73** C7
Sydney L. *Canada* 50°41N 94°25W **71** C10
Sydney Mines *Canada* 46°18N 60°15W **73** C7
Sydprøven = Alluitsup Paa
  Greenland 60°30N 45°35W **4** C5
Sydra, G. of = Surt, Khalīj
  Libya 31°40N 18°30E **51** B9
Sykesville *U.S.A.* 41°3N 78°50W **82** E6
Syktyvkar *Russia* 61°45N 50°40E **18** B9
Sylacauga *U.S.A.* 33°10N 86°15W **85** E11
Sylarna *Sweden* 63°2N 12°13E **8** E15
Sylhet *Bangla.* 24°54N 91°52E **41** G17
Sylhet □ *Bangla.* 24°50N 91°50E **41** G17
Sylt *Germany* 54°54N 8°22E **16** A5
Sylvan Beach *U.S.A.* 43°12N 75°44W **83** C9
Sylvan Lake *Canada* 52°20N 114°3W **70** C6
Sylvania *Ga., U.S.A.* 32°45N 81°38W **85** E14
Sylvania *Ohio, U.S.A.* 41°43N 83°42W **81** E12
Sylvester *U.S.A.* 31°32N 83°50W **85** F13
Sym *Russia* 60°20N 88°18E **28** C9
Synnot Ra. *Australia* 16°30S 125°20E **60** C4
Syowa *Antarctica* 68°50S 12°0E **5** C5
Syracuse *Kans., U.S.A.* 37°59N 101°45W **80** G3
Syracuse *N.Y., U.S.A.* 43°3N 76°9W **83** C8
Syracuse *Nebr., U.S.A.* 40°39N 96°11W **80** E5
Syrdarya → *Kazakhstan* 46°3N 61°0E **28** E7
Syria ■ *Asia* 35°0N 38°0E **44** C3
Syrian Desert = Shām, Bādiyat
  ash *Asia* 32°0N 40°0E **44** C3
Syros = Ermoupoli
  Greece 37°28N 24°57E **23** F11
Syzran *Russia* 53°12N 48°30E **18** D8
Szczecin *Poland* 53°27N 14°27E **16** B8
Szczecinek *Poland* 53°43N 16°41E **17** B9
Szczeciński, Zalew = Stettiner Haff
  Germany 53°47N 14°15E **16** B8
Szczytno *Poland* 53°33N 21°0E **17** B11
Szechwan = Sichuan □
  China 30°30N 103°0E **32** C5
Szeged *Hungary* 46°16N 20°10E **17** E11
Székesfehérvár *Hungary* 47°15N 18°25E **17** E10
Szekszárd *Hungary* 46°22N 18°42E **17** E10
Szentes *Hungary* 46°39N 20°21E **17** E11
Szolnok *Hungary* 47°10N 20°15E **17** E11
Szombathely *Hungary* 47°14N 16°38E **17** E9

T

Ta Khli *Thailand* 15°15N 100°21E **38** E3
Ta Khli Khok *Thailand* 15°18N 100°20E **38** E3
Ta Lai *Vietnam* 11°24N 107°23E **39** G6
Tabacal *Argentina* 23°15S 64°15W **94** A3
Tabaco *Phil.* 13°22N 123°44E **37** B6
Ṭabāh *Si. Arabia* 26°55N 42°38E **44** E4
Tabanan *Indonesia* 8°32S 115°8E **37** K18

Ṭabas *Khorāsān, Iran* 32°48N 60°12E **45** C9
Ṭabas *Yazd, Iran* 33°35N 56°55E **45** C8
Tabasará, Serranía de
  Panama 8°35N 81°40W **88** E3
Tabasco □ *Mexico* 18°0N 92°40W **87** D6
Ṭabāsīn *Iran* 31°12N 57°54E **45** D8
Tabatinga, Serra da
  Brazil 10°30S 44°0W **93** F10
Taber *Canada* 49°47N 112°8W **70** D6
Tablas *Phil.* 12°25N 122°2E **37** B6
Table, Pte. de la *Réunion* 21°14S 55°48E **53** c
Table B. *Canada* 53°40N 56°25W **73** B8
Table B. *S. Africa* 33°35S 18°25E **56** E2
Table Mountain △
  S. Africa 34°0S 18°28E **56** E2
Table Mt. *S. Africa* 34°0S 18°28E **56** E2
Table Rock L. *U.S.A.* 36°36N 93°19W **80** G7
Tabletop, Mt. *Australia* 23°24S 147°11E **62** C4
Tábor *Czech Rep.* 49°25N 14°39E **16** D8
Tabora *Tanzania* 5°2S 32°50E **54** D3
Tabora □ *Tanzania* 5°0S 33°0E **54** D3
Tabou *Ivory C.* 4°30N 7°20W **50** H4
Tabrīz *Iran* 38°7N 46°20E **44** B5
Tabuaeran *Kiribati* 3°51N 159°22W **65** G12
Tabūk *Si. Arabia* 28°23N 36°36E **44** D3
Tabūk □ *Si. Arabia* 27°40N 36°50E **44** E3
Tácacheo de Codallos
  Mexico 19°14N 101°28W **86** D4
Tacheng *China* 46°40N 82°58E **32** B3
Tach'ing Shan = Daqing Shan
  China 40°40N 111°0E **34** D6
Tacloban *Phil.* 11°15N 124°58E **37** B6
Tacna *Peru* 18°0S 70°20W **92** G4
Tacoma *U.S.A.* 47°14N 122°26W **78** C4
Tacuarembó *Uruguay* 31°45S 56°0W **95** C4
Tademaït, Plateau du
  Algeria 28°30N 2°30E **50** C6
Tadjoura *Djibouti* 11°50N 42°55E **47** E3
Tadmor *N.Z.* 41°27S 172°45E **59** D4
Tadoule L. *Canada* 58°36N 98°20W **71** B9
Tadoussac *Canada* 48°11N 69°42W **73** C6
Tadzhikistan = Tajikistan ■
  Asia 38°30N 70°0E **28** F8
Taegu = Daegu
  S. Korea 35°50N 128°37E **35** G15
Taegwan *N. Korea* 40°13N 125°12E **35** D13
Taejon = Daejeon
  S. Korea 36°20N 127°28E **35** F14
Taen, Ko *Thailand* 9°22N 99°57E **39** b
Tafalla *Spain* 42°30N 1°41W **21** A5
Tafelbaai = Table B.
  S. Africa 33°35S 18°25E **56** E2
Tafermaar *Indonesia* 6°47S 134°10E **37** F8
Tafí Viejo *Argentina* 26°43S 65°17W **94** B2
Tafihān *Iran* 29°25S 52°39E **45** D7
Tafresh *Iran* 34°45N 49°57E **45** C6
Taft *Iran* 31°45N 54°14E **45** D7
Taft *Phil.* 11°57N 125°30E **37** B7
Taft *U.S.A.* 35°8N 119°28W **79** K7
Taftan *Pakistan* 28°50N 61°0E **40** E2
Taftān, Kūh-e *Iran* 28°40N 61°0E **45** D9
Taga *Samoa* 13°46S 172°28W **59** b
Taga Dzong *Bhutan* 27°5N 89°55E **41** F16
Taganrog *Russia* 47°12N 38°50E **19** E6
Tagbilaran *Phil.* 9°39N 123°51E **37** C6
Tagish *Canada* 60°19N 134°16W **70** A2
Tagish L. *Canada* 60°10N 134°20W **70** A2
Tagliamento → *Italy* 45°38N 13°6E **22** B5
Tagomago *Spain* 39°2N 1°39E **24** B8
Taguatinga *Brazil* 12°27S 46°22W **93** F10
Tagum *Phil.* 7°33N 125°53E **37** C7
Tagus = Tejo → *Europe* 38°40N 9°24W **21** C1
Tahakopa *N.Z.* 46°30S 169°23E **59** G2
Tahan, Gunung
  Malaysia 4°34N 102°17E **39** K4
Tahat *Algeria* 23°18N 5°33E **50** D7
Tāherī *Iran* 27°43N 52°20E **45** E7
Tahiti *French Polynesia* 17°37S 149°27W **59** d
Tahiti, I. *Tahiti* 17°37S 149°27W **59** d
Tahlequah *U.S.A.* 35°55N 94°58W **84** D7
Tahoe, L. *U.S.A.* 39°6N 120°2W **78** G6
Tahoe City *U.S.A.* 39°10N 120°9W **78** F6
Tahoka *U.S.A.* 33°10N 101°48W **84** E4
Taholah *U.S.A.* 47°21N 124°17W **78** C2
Tahoua *Niger* 14°57N 5°16E **50** F7
Tahrūd *Iran* 29°26N 57°49E **45** D8
Tahsis *Canada* 49°55N 126°40W **70** D3
Tahta *Egypt* 26°44N 31°32E **51** C12
Tahulandang *Indonesia* 2°27N 125°23E **37** D7
Tahuna *Indonesia* 3°38N 125°30E **37** D7
Tai Au Mun *China* 22°18N 114°17E **33** G11
Tai Mo Shan *China* 22°25N 114°7E **33** G11
Tai O *China* 22°15N 113°52E **33** G10
Tai Pang Wan *China* 22°33N 114°24E **33** F11
Tai Po *China* 22°27N 114°10E **33** G11
Tai Rom Yen △ *Thailand* 8°45N 99°30E **39** H2
Tai Shan *China* 36°25N 117°20E **35** F9
Tai Yue Shan = Lantau I.
  China 22°15N 113°56E **33** G10
Tai'an *China* 36°12N 117°8E **35** F9
Taiarapu, Presqu'île de
  Tahiti 17°47S 149°14W **59** d
Taibei = T'aipei *Taiwan* 25°4N 121°29E **33** D7
Taibique *Canary Is.* 27°42N 17°58W **24** G2
Taibus Qi *China* 41°54N 115°22E **34** D8
T'aichung *Taiwan* 24°12N 120°35E **33** D7
Taieri → *N.Z.* 46°3S 170°12E **59** G3
Taigu *China* 37°28N 112°30E **34** F7
Taihang Shan *China* 36°0N 113°30E **34** G7
Taihape *N.Z.* 39°41S 175°48E **59** C5
Taihe *China* 33°20N 115°42E **34** H8
Taikang *China* 34°5N 114°50E **34** G8
Tailem Bend *Australia* 35°12S 139°29E **63** F2
Taimyr Peninsula = Taymyr,
  Poluostrov *Russia* 75°0N 100°0E **29** B11
Tain *U.K.* 57°49N 4°4W **11** D4
T'ainan *Taiwan* 23°0N 120°10E **33** D7
Taipa *China* 22°10N 113°35E **33** G10
T'aipei *Taiwan* 25°4N 121°29E **33** D7

Taiping *Malaysia* 4°51N 100°44E **39** K3
Taipingzhen *China* 33°35N 111°42E **34** H6
Tairbeart = Tarbert *U.K.* 57°54N 6°49W **11** D2
Taita Hills *Kenya* 3°25S 38°15E **54** C4
Taitao, Pen. de *Chile* 46°30S 75°0W **96** F2
Taitung *Taiwan* 22°43N 121°4E **33** D7
Taivalkoski *Finland* 65°33N 28°12E **8** D23
Taiwan ■ *Asia* 23°30N 121°0E **33** D7
Taiyiba *Israel* 32°36N 35°27E **46** C4
Taiyuan *China* 37°52N 112°33E **34** F7
Taizhong = T'aichung
  Taiwan 24°9N 120°37E **33** D7
Ta'izz *Yemen* 13°35N 44°2E **47** E3
Tājābād *Iran* 30°2N 54°24E **45** D7
Tajikistan ■ *Asia* 38°30N 70°0E **28** F8
Tajima *Japan* 37°12N 139°46E **31** F9
Tajo → *Spain* 38°40N 9°24W **21** C1
Tajrīsh *Iran* 35°48N 51°25E **45** C6
Tak *Thailand* 16°52N 99°8E **38** D2
Takāb *Iran* 36°24N 47°7E **44** B5
Takachiho *Japan* 32°42N 131°18E **31** H5
Takachu *Botswana* 22°37S 21°58E **56** C3
Takada *Japan* 37°7N 138°15E **31** F9
Takahagi *Japan* 36°43N 140°45E **31** F10
Takaka *N.Z.* 40°51S 172°50E **59** D4
Takamaka *Seychelles* 4°50S 55°30E **53** b
Takamatsu *Japan* 34°20N 134°5E **31** G7
Takaoka *Japan* 36°47N 137°0E **31** F8
Takapuna *N.Z.* 36°47S 174°47E **59** B5
Takasaki *Japan* 36°20N 139°0E **31** F9
Takatsuki *Japan* 34°51N 135°37E **31** G7
Takaungu *Kenya* 3°38S 39°52E **54** C4
Takayama *Japan* 36°18N 137°11E **31** F8
Take-Shima *Japan* 30°49N 130°26E **31** J5
Takefu *Japan* 35°50N 136°10E **31** G8
Takengon *Indonesia* 4°45N 96°50E **36** D1
Takeo *Japan* 33°12N 130°1E **31** H5
Takeshima = Tokdo
  Asia 37°15N 131°52E **31** F5
Tākestān *Iran* 36°0N 49°40E **45** C6
Taketa *Japan* 32°58N 131°24E **31** H5
Takev *Cambodia* 10°59N 104°47E **39** G5
Takh *India* 33°6N 77°32E **43** C7
Takhar □ *Afghan.* 36°40N 70°0E **40** A6
Takhmau *Cambodia* 11°29N 104°57E **39** G5
Takht-Sulaiman
  Pakistan 31°40N 69°58E **42** D3
Takikawa *Japan* 43°33N 141°54E **30** C10
Takla L. *Canada* 55°15N 125°45W **70** B3
Takla Landing *Canada* 55°30N 125°50W **70** B3
Takla Makan *China* 38°0N 83°0E **32** C3
Taklamakan Shamo = Takla
  Makan *China* 38°0N 83°0E **32** C3
Taksimo *Russia* 56°20N 114°52E **29** D12
Taku → *Canada* 58°30N 133°50W **70** B2
Takua Pa *Thailand* 8°52N 98°21E **39** H2
Takua Thung *Thailand* 8°24N 98°27E **39** a
Tal Ḥalāl *Iran* 34°35N 55°1E **45** D7
Tala *Uruguay* 34°21S 55°46W **95** C4
Talagang *Pakistan* 32°55N 72°25E **42** C5
Talagante *Chile* 33°40S 70°50W **94** C1
Talamanca, Cordillera de
  Cent. Amer. 9°20N 83°20W **88** E3
Talampaya △ *Argentina* 29°43S 67°42W **94** B2
Talara *Peru* 4°38S 81°18W **92** D2
Talas *Kyrgyzstan* 42°30N 72°13E **28** E8
Talâta *Egypt* 30°36N 32°20E **46** E1
Talaud, Kepulauan
  Indonesia 4°30N 126°50E **37** D7
Talaud Is. = Talaud, Kepulauan
  Indonesia 4°30N 126°50E **37** D7
Talavera de la Reina
  Spain 39°55N 4°46W **21** C3
Talayan *Phil.* 6°52N 124°24E **37** C6
Talbandh *India* 22°3N 86°20E **43** H12
Talbot, C. *Australia* 13°48S 126°43E **60** B4
Talbragar → *Australia* 32°12S 148°37E **63** E4
Talca *Chile* 35°28S 71°40W **94** D1
Talcahuano *Chile* 36°40S 73°10W **94** D1
Talcher *India* 21°0N 85°18E **41** J14
Taldy Kurgan = Taldyqorghan
  Kazakhstan 45°10N 78°45E **28** E8
Taldyqorghan
  Kazakhstan 45°10N 78°45E **28** E8
Tālesh *Iran* 37°58N 48°58E **45** B6
Tālesh, Kūhhā-ye *Iran* 37°42N 48°55E **45** B6
Tali Post *Sudan* 5°55N 30°44E **51** G12
Taliabu *Indonesia* 1°50S 125°0E **37** E6
Talibon *Phil.* 10°9N 124°20E **37** B6
Talihina *U.S.A.* 34°45N 95°3W **84** D7
Taliwang *Indonesia* 8°50S 116°55E **36** F5
Tall 'Afar *Iraq* 36°22N 42°27E **44** B4
Tall Kalakh *Syria* 34°41N 36°15E **46** A5
Talladega *U.S.A.* 33°26N 86°6E **85** E11
Tallahassee *U.S.A.* 30°27N 84°17W **85** F12
Tallangatta *Australia* 36°15S 147°19E **63** F4
Tallering Pk. *Australia* 28°6S 115°37E **61** E2
Talli *Pakistan* 29°32N 68°8E **42** E3
Tallinn *Estonia* 59°22N 24°48E **9** G21
Tallmadge *U.S.A.* 41°6N 81°27W **82** E3
Tallulah *U.S.A.* 32°25N 91°11W **84** E9
Talnakh *Russia* 69°29N 88°22E **29** C9
Taloyoak *Canada* 69°32N 93°32W **68** D13
Talpa de Allende
  Mexico 20°23N 104°51W **86** C4
Talparo *Trin. & Tob.* 10°30N 61°17W **93** K15
Talsi *Latvia* 57°10N 22°30E **9** H20
Taltal *Chile* 25°23S 70°33W **94** B1
Taltson → *Canada* 61°24N 112°46W **70** A6
Talwood *Australia* 28°29S 149°29E **63** D4
Talyawalka Cr. →
  Australia 32°15N 142°22E **63** E3
Tam Ky *Vietnam* 15°34N 108°29E **38** E7
Tam Quan *Vietnam* 14°35N 109°3E **38** E7
Tama *U.S.A.* 41°58N 92°35W **80** E7
Tama Abu, Banjaran
  Malaysia 3°10N 115°5E **36** D5
Tamale *Ghana* 9°22N 0°50W **50** G5
Taman Negara △
  Malaysia 4°38N 102°26E **39** K4

Tamano *Japan* 34°29N 133°59E **31** G6
Tamanrasset *Algeria* 22°50N 5°30E **50** D7
Tamaqua *U.S.A.* 40°48N 75°58W **83** F9
Tamar → *U.K.* 50°27N 4°15W **13** G3
Tamar → *Russia* 50°27N 4°15W **13** G3
Tamarin *Mauritius* 20°19S 57°20E **53** d
Tamarinda *Spain* 39°55N 3°49E **24** B10
Tamashima *Japan* 34°32N 133°40E **31** G6
Tamatave = Toamasina
  Madag. 18°10S 49°25E **57** B8
Tamaulipas □ *Mexico* 24°0N 98°45W **87** C5
Tamaulipas, Sierra de
  Mexico 23°30N 98°20W **87** C5
Tamazula *Mexico* 24°57N 106°57W **86** C3
Tamazunchale *Mexico* 21°16N 98°47W **87** C5
Tambach *Kenya* 0°36N 35°31E **54** B4
Tambacounda *Senegal* 13°45N 13°40W **50** F3
Tambelan, Kepulauan
  Indonesia 1°0N 107°30E **36** D3
Tambellup *Australia* 34°4S 117°37E **61** F2
Tambo *Australia* 24°54S 146°14E **62** C4
Tambo de Mora *Peru* 13°30S 76°8W **92** F3
Tambohorano *Madag.* 17°30S 43°58E **57** B7
Tambora *Indonesia* 8°12S 118°5E **36** F5
Tambora *C.A.R.* 5°10N 25°12E **54** A2
Tambov *Russia* 52°45N 41°28E **18** D7
Tambuku *Indonesia* 7°8S 113°40E **37** G15
Tâmega → *Portugal* 41°5N 8°21E **21** B1
Tamenglong *India* 25°0N 93°35E **41** G18
Tamiahua, L. de *Mexico* 21°35N 97°35W **87** C5
Tamil Nadu □ *India* 11°0N 77°0E **40** P10
Tamluk *India* 22°18N 87°58E **43** H12
Tammerfors = Tampere
  Finland 61°30N 23°50E **8** F20
Tammisaari *Finland* 60°0N 23°26E **9** G20
Tampa *U.S.A.* 27°56N 82°27W **85** H13
Tampa, Tanjung
  Indonesia 8°55S 116°12E **37** K19
Tampa B. *U.S.A.* 27°50N 82°30W **85** H13
Tampere *Finland* 61°30N 23°50E **8** F20
Tampico *Mexico* 22°13N 97°51W **87** C5
Tampin *Malaysia* 2°28N 102°13E **39** L4
Tampoi *Malaysia* 1°30N 103°39E **39** d
Tamu *Burma* 24°13N 94°12E **41** G19
Tamworth *Australia* 31°7S 150°58E **63** E5
Tamworth *Canada* 44°29N 77°0W **82** B8
Tamworth *U.K.* 52°39N 1°41W **13** E6
Tan An *Vietnam* 10°32N 106°25E **39** G6
Tan Chau *Vietnam* 10°48N 105°12E **39** G5
Tan-Tan *Morocco* 28°29N 11°1W **50** C3
Tana → *Kenya* 2°32S 40°31E **54** C5
Tana → *Norway* 70°30N 28°14E **8** A23
Tana, L. *Ethiopia* 13°5N 37°30E **47** E2
Tana River Primate △
  Kenya 1°55S 40°7E **54** C5
Tanabe *Japan* 33°44N 135°22E **31** H7
Tanafjorden *Norway* 70°45N 28°25E **8** A23
Tanaga I. *U.S.A.* 51°48N 177°53W **74** E4
Tanahbala *Indonesia* 0°30S 98°30E **36** E1
Tanahgrogot *Indonesia* 1°55S 116°15E **36** E5
Tanahmasa *Indonesia* 0°12S 98°39E **36** E1
Tanahmerah *Indonesia* 6°5S 140°16E **37** F10
Tanakpur *India* 29°5N 80°7E **43** E9
Tanakura *Japan* 37°10N 140°20E **31** F10
Tanami Desert *Australia* 18°50S 132°0E **60** C5
Tanana *U.S.A.* 65°10N 152°4W **74** B9
Tanana → *U.S.A.* 65°10N 151°58W **68** D1
Tananarive = Antananarivo
  Madag. 18°55S 47°31E **57** B8
Tánaro → *Italy* 44°55N 8°40E **20** D8
Tancheng *China* 34°25N 118°20E **35** G10
Tanch'ŏn *N. Korea* 40°27N 128°54E **35** D15
Tanda *Ut. P., India* 26°33N 82°35E **43** F10
Tanda *Ut. P., India* 28°57N 78°56E **43** E8
Tandag *Phil.* 9°4N 126°9E **37** C7
Tandaia *Tanzania* 9°25S 34°15E **55** D3
Tandaué *Angola* 16°58S 18°5E **56** B2
Tandil *Argentina* 37°15S 59°6W **94** D4
Tandil, Sa. del *Argentina* 37°30S 59°0W **94** D4
Tandlianwala *Pakistan* 31°3N 73°9E **42** D5
Tando Adam *Pakistan* 25°45N 68°40E **42** G3
Tando Allahyar *Pakistan* 25°28N 68°43E **42** G3
Tando Bago *Pakistan* 24°47N 68°58E **42** G3
Tando Mohammed Khan
  Pakistan 25°8N 68°32E **42** G3
Tandou L. *Australia* 32°40S 142°5E **63** E3
Tandoureh △ *Iran* 37°50N 59°0E **45** B8
Tandragee *U.K.* 54°21N 6°24W **10** B5
Tane-ga-Shima *Japan* 30°30N 131°0E **31** J5
Taneatua *N.Z.* 38°4S 177°1E **59** C6
Tanen Tong Dan = Dawna Ra.
  Burma 16°30N 98°30E **38** D2
Tanezrouft *Algeria* 23°9N 0°11E **50** D6
Tang, Koh *Cambodia* 10°16N 103°7E **39** G4
Tang, Ra's-e *Iran* 25°21N 59°52E **45** E8
Tang Krasang *Cambodia* 12°34N 105°3E **38** F5
Tanga *Tanzania* 5°5S 39°2E **54** D4
Tanga □ *Tanzania* 5°20S 38°0E **54** D4
Tanga *Morocco* — (see Tanger)
Tangerang *Indonesia* 6°11S 106°37E **37** G12
Tanggu *China* 39°2N 117°40E **35** E9
Tanggula Shan *China* 32°40N 92°10E **32** C4
Tanggula Shankou
  China 32°42N 92°27E **32** C4
Tanghe *China* 32°47N 112°50E **34** H7
Tanghla Range = Tanggula Shan
  China 32°40N 92°10E **32** C4
Tangier = Tanger
  Morocco 35°50N 5°49W **50** A4
Tangjia *China* 22°22N 113°35E **33** G10
Tangjia Wan *China* 22°21N 113°36E **33** G10
Tangorin *Australia* 21°47S 144°12E **62** C3
Tangorombohitr'i Makay
  Madag. 21°0S 45°15E **57** C8
Tangra Yumco *China* 31°0N 86°38E **32** C3
Tangshan *China* 39°38N 118°10E **35** E10
Tangtou *China* 35°28N 118°30E **35** G10

Tanimbar, Kepulauan
  Indonesia 7°30S 131°30E **37** F8
Tanimbar Is. = Tanimbar,
  Kepulauan Indonesia 7°30S 131°30E **37** F8
Taninthari = Tenasserim
  Burma 12°6N 99°3E **39** F2
Tanjay Phil. 9°30N 123°5E **37** C6
Tanjong Malim Malaysia 3°42N 101°31E **39** L3
Tanjong Pelepas Malaysia 1°21N 103°33E **39** d
Tanjore = Thanjavur
  India 10°48N 79°12E **40** P11
Tanjung Bali, Indonesia 8°21S 116°9E **37** J19
Tanjung Kalimantan,
  Indonesia 2°10S 115°25E **36** E5
Tanjung Tokong Malaysia 5°28N 100°18E **39** c
Tanjungbalai Indonesia 2°55N 99°44E **36** D1
Tanjungbatu Indonesia 2°23N 118°3E **36** D5
Tanjungkarang Telukbetung =
  Bandar Lampung
  Indonesia 5°20S 105°10E **36** F3
Tanjungpandan
  Indonesia 2°43S 107°38E **36** E3
Tanjungpinang Indonesia 1°5N 104°30E **36** D2
Tanjungredeb Indonesia 2°9N 117°29E **36** D5
Tanjungselor Indonesia 2°55N 117°25E **36** D5
Tank Pakistan 32°14N 70°25E **42** C4
Tankhala India 21°58N 73°47E **42** J5
Tankwa-Karoo △
  S. Africa 32°14S 19°50E **56** E2
Tannersville U.S.A. 41°3N 75°18W **83** E9
Tannu Ola Asia 51°0N 94°0E **29** D10
Tannum Sands
  Australia 23°57S 151°22E **62** C5
Tanout Niger 14°50N 8°55E **50** F7
Tanta Egypt 30°45N 30°57E **51** B12
Tantoyuca Mexico 21°21N 98°14W **87** C5
Tantung = Dandong
  China 40°10N 124°20E **35** D13
Tanunda Australia 34°30S 139°0E **63** E2
Tanzhou China 22°16N 113°28E **33** G10
Tanzilla → Canada 58°8N 130°43W **70** B2
Tao, Ko Thailand 10°5N 99°52E **39** G2
Tao'an = Taonan
  China 45°22N 122°40E **35** B12
Tao'er He → China 45°45N 124°5E **35** B13
Taolanaro Madag. 25°2S 47°0E **57** D8
Taole China 38°48N 106°40E **34** E4
Taonan China 45°22N 122°40E **35** B12
Taos U.S.A. 36°24N 105°35W **77** H11
Taoudenni Mali 22°40N 3°55W **50** D5
Tapa Estonia 59°15N 25°50E **9** G21
Tapa Shan = Daba Shan
  China 32°0N 109°0E **35** C5
Tapachula Mexico 14°54N 92°17W **87** E6
Tapah Malaysia 4°12N 101°15E **39** K3
Tapajós → Brazil 2°24S 54°41W **93** D8
Tapaktuan Indonesia 3°15N 97°10E **36** D1
Tapanahoni → Suriname 4°20N 54°25W **93** C8
Tapanui N.Z. 45°56S 169°18E **59** F2
Tapauá Brazil 5°40S 64°21W **92** E6
Tapes Brazil 30°40S 51°23W **95** C5
Tapeta Liberia 6°29N 8°52W **50** G4
Taphan Hin Thailand 16°13N 100°26E **38** D3
Tapirapecó, Serra
  Venezuela 1°10N 65°0W **92** C6
Tapo-Capara △ Venezuela 7°55N 71°15W **89** E5
Tapti → India 21°8N 72°41E **40** J8
Tapuae-o-Uenuku N.Z. 42°0S 173°39E **59** E4
Tapul Group Phil. 5°35N 120°50E **37** C6
Tapurucuará Brazil 0°24S 65°2W **92** D5
Taqtaq Iraq 35°53N 44°35E **44** C5
Taquara Brazil 29°36S 50°46W **95** B5
Taquari → Brazil 19°15S 57°17W **92** G7
Tara Australia 27°17S 150°31E **63** D5
Tara Canada 44°28N 81°9W **82** B3
Tara Russia 56°55N 74°24E **28** D8
Tara Zambia 16°58S 26°45E **55** F2
Tara → Montenegro 43°21N 18°51E **23** C8
Tarābulus Lebanon 34°31N 35°50E **46** A4
Tarābulus Libya 32°49N 13°7E **51** B8
Tarābulus N. Afr. 31°0N 13°0E **51** B8
Taradehi India 23°18N 79°21E **43** H8
Tarajalejo Canary Is. 28°12N 14°7W **24** F5
Tarakan Indonesia 3°20N 117°35E **36** D5
Tarakit, Mt. Kenya 2°2N 35°10E **54** B4
Tarama-Jima Japan 24°39N 124°42E **31** M2
Taran, Mys Russia 54°56N 19°59E **9** J18
Taranagar India 28°43N 74°50E **42** E6
Taranaki □ N.Z. 39°25S 174°30E **59** C5
Taranaki, Mt. N.Z. 39°17S 174°5E **59** C5
Tarancón Spain 40°1N 3°1W **21** B4
Tarangire △ Tanzania 4°21S 36°7E **54** C4
Taransay U.K. 57°54N 7°0W **11** D1
Táranto Italy 40°28N 17°14E **22** D7
Táranto, G. di Italy 40°8N 17°20E **22** D7
Tarapacá Colombia 2°56S 69°46W **92** D5
Tarapacá □ Chile 20°45S 69°30W **94** A2
Tarapoto Peru 6°30S 76°20W **92** E3
Tararua Ra. N.Z. 40°45S 175°25E **59** D5
Tarashcha Ukraine 49°30N 30°31E **17** D16
Tarauacá Brazil 8°6S 70°48W **92** E4
Tarauacá → Brazil 6°42S 69°48W **92** E5
Taravao Tahiti 17°43S 149°19W **59** d
Taravao, Isthme de
  Tahiti 17°43S 149°19W **59** d
Tarawa Kiribati 1°30N 173°0E **64** G9
Tarawera N.Z. 39°2S 176°36E **59** C6
Tarawera, L. N.Z. 38°13S 176°27E **59** C6
Taraz Kazakhstan 42°54N 71°22E **28** E8
Tarazona Spain 41°55N 1°43W **21** B5

Tarbes France 43°15N 0°3E **20** E4
Tarboro U.S.A. 35°54N 77°32W **85** D16
Tarcoola Australia 30°44S 134°36E **63** E1
Tarcoon Australia 30°15S 146°43E **63** E4
Taree Australia 31°50S 152°30E **63** E5
Tarfaya Morocco 27°55N 12°55W **50** C3
Târgovişte Romania 44°55N 25°27E **17** F13
Târgu Jiu Romania 45°5N 23°19E **17** F12
Târgu Mureş Romania 46°31N 24°38E **17** E13
Tarif U.A.E. 24°3N 53°46E **45** E7
Tarifa Spain 36°1N 5°36W **21** D3
Tarija Bolivia 21°30S 64°40W **94** A3
Tarija □ Bolivia 21°30S 63°30W **94** A3
Tariku → Indonesia 2°55S 138°26E **37** E9
Tarim Basin = Tarim Pendi
  China 40°0N 84°0E **32** B3
Tarim He → China 39°30N 88°30E **32** C3
Tarim Pendi China 40°0N 84°0E **32** B3
Taritatu → Indonesia 2°54S 138°27E **37** E9
Tarka → S. Africa 32°10S 26°0E **56** E4
Tarka La Bhutan 27°12N 89°44E **43** F13
Tarkastad S. Africa 32°0S 26°16E **56** E4
Tarkhankut, Mys
  Ukraine 45°25N 32°30E **19** E5
Tarko Sale Russia 64°55N 77°50E **28** C8
Tarkwa Ghana 5°20N 2°0W **50** G5
Tarlac Phil. 15°29N 120°35E **37** A6
Tarma Peru 11°25S 75°45W **92** F3
Tarn → France 44°5N 1°6E **20** E4
Târnăveni Romania 46°19N 24°13E **17** E13
Tarnobrzeg Poland 50°35N 21°41E **17** C11
Tarnów Poland 50°3N 21°0E **17** C11
Tarnowskie Góry
  Poland 50°27N 18°54E **17** C10
Tārom Iran 28°11N 55°46E **45** D7
Taroom Australia 25°36S 149°48E **63** D4
Taroudannt Morocco 30°30N 8°52W **50** B4
Tarpon Springs U.S.A. 28°9N 82°45W **85** G13
Tarrafal C. Verde Is. 15°18N 23°39W **50** b
Tarragona Spain 41°5N 1°17E **21** B6
Tarraleah Australia 42°17S 146°26E **63** G4
Tarrasa = Terrassa Spain 41°34N 2°1E **21** B7
Tarrytown U.S.A. 41°4N 73°52W **83** E11
Tarshiha = Me'ona Israel 33°1N 35°15E **46** B4
Tarsus Turkey 36°58N 34°55E **44** B2
Tartagal Argentina 22°30S 63°50W **94** A3
Tartu Estonia 58°20N 26°44E **9** G22
Tarțûs Syria 34°55N 35°55E **44** C2
Tarumizu Japan 31°29N 130°42E **31** J5
Tarutao = Ko Tarutao △
  Thailand 6°31N 99°26E **39** J2
Tarutao, Ko Thailand 6°33N 99°40E **39** J2
Tarutung Indonesia 2°0N 98°54E **36** D1
Taseko → Canada 52°8N 123°45W **70** C4
Tash-Kömür Kyrgyzstan 41°40N 72°10E **28** E8
Tash-Kumyr = Tash-Kömür
  Kyrgyzstan 41°40N 72°10E **28** E8
Tashauz = Dashoguz
  Turkmenistan 41°49N 59°58E **28** E6
Tashi Chho Dzong = Thimphu
  Bhutan 27°31N 89°45E **41** F16
Tashk, Daryācheh-ye
  Iran 29°45N 53°35E **45** D7
Tashkent = Toshkent
  Uzbekistan 41°20N 69°10E **28** E7
Tashtagol Russia 52°47N 87°53E **28** D9
Tasiilaq Greenland 65°40N 37°20W **4** C6
Tasik Kenyir Malaysia 5°5N 102°45E **39** K4
Tasikmalaya Indonesia 7°18S 108°12E **37** G13
Tåsjön Sweden 64°15N 15°40E **8** D16
Taskan Russia 62°59N 150°20E **29** C16
Tasman B. N.Z. 40°59S 173°25E **59** D4
Tasman Basin Pac. Oc. 46°0S 158°0E **64** M7
Tasman Mts. N.Z. 41°3S 172°25E **59** D4
Tasman Pen. Australia 43°10S 148°0E **63** G4
Tasman Sea Pac. Oc. 36°0S 160°0E **58** E9
Tasmania □ Australia 42°0S 146°30E **63** G4
Tasmanian Wilderness World
  Heritage Area △
  Australia 43°0S 146°0E **63** G4
Tassili n'Ajjer Algeria 25°47N 8°1E **50** C7
Tassili-Oua-n-Ahaggar
  Algeria 20°41N 5°30E **50** D7
Tat Ton △ Thailand 15°57N 102°2E **38** E4
Tata Morocco 29°46N 7°56W **50** C4
Tatabánya Hungary 47°32N 18°25E **17** E10
Tatahouine Tunisia 32°56N 10°27E **51** B8
Tataouine Tunisia 32°57N 10°29E **51** B8
Tatar Republic = Tatarstan □
  Russia 55°30N 51°30E **18** C9
Tatarbunary Ukraine 45°50N 29°39E **17** F15
Tatarsk Russia 55°14N 76°0E **28** D8
Tatarskiy Proliv Russia 50°0N 141°0E **29** E15
Tatarstan □ Russia 55°30N 51°30E **18** C9
Tatatua, Pte. Tahiti 17°44S 149°8W **59** d
Tateyama Japan 35°0N 139°50E **31** G9
Tathlina L. Canada 60°33N 117°39W **70** A5
Tathra Australia 36°44S 149°59E **63** F4
Tatinnai L. Canada 60°55N 97°40W **71** A9
Tatla Lake Canada 52°0N 124°20W **70** C4
Tatnam, C. Canada 57°16N 91°0W **71** B10
Tatra = Tatry Slovak Rep. 49°20N 20°0E **17** D11
Tatry Slovak Rep. 49°20N 20°0E **17** D11
Tatshenshini →
  Canada 59°28N 137°45W **70** B1
Tatsuno Japan 34°52N 134°33E **31** G7
Tatta Pakistan 24°42N 67°55E **42** G2
Tatuī Brazil 23°25S 47°53W **95** A6
Tatum U.S.A. 33°16N 103°19W **77** K12
Tat'ung = Datong China 40°6N 113°18E **34** D7
Tatvan Turkey 38°31N 42°15E **44** B4
Ta'ū Amer. Samoa 14°15S 169°30W **59** b
Taubaté Brazil 23°0S 45°36W **95** A6
Tauern Austria 47°15N 12°40E **16** E7
Taumarunui N.Z. 38°53S 175°15E **59** C5
Taumaturgo Brazil 8°54S 72°51W **92** E4
Taung S. Africa 27°33S 24°47E **56** D3
Taungdwingyi Burma 20°1N 95°40E **41** J19
Taunggyi Burma 20°50N 97°0E **41** J20

Taungup Burma 18°51N 94°14E **41** K19
Taunsa Pakistan 30°42N 70°39E **42** D4
Taunsa Barrage Pakistan 30°42N 70°50E **42** D4
Taunton U.K. 51°1N 3°5W **13** F4
Taunton U.S.A. 41°54N 71°6W **83** E13
Taunus Germany 50°13N 8°34E **16** C5
Taupo N.Z. 38°41S 176°7E **59** C6
Taupo, L. N.Z. 38°46S 175°55E **59** C5
Tauragė Lithuania 55°14N 22°16E **9** J20
Tauranga N.Z. 37°42S 176°11E **59** B6
Tauranga Harb. N.Z. 37°30S 176°5E **59** B6
Taureau, Rés. Canada 46°46N 73°50W **72** C5
Taurianova Italy 38°21N 16°1E **22** E7
Taurus Mts. = Toros Dağları
  Turkey 37°0N 32°30E **44** B2
Tautira Tahiti 17°44S 149°9W **59** d
Tauyskaya Guba
  Russia 59°20N 150°20E **29** D16
Tavan Bogd Uul
  Mongolia 49°10N 87°49E **32** B3
Tavastehus = Hämeenlinna
  Finland 61°0N 24°28E **8** F21
Tavda Russia 58°7N 65°8E **28** D7
Tavda → Russia 57°47N 67°18E **28** D7
Taverner B. Canada 67°12N 72°25W **69** D17
Taveta Kenya 3°23S 37°37E **54** C4
Taveuni Fiji 16°51S 179°58W **59** a
Tavira Portugal 37°8N 7°40W **21** D2
Tavistock Canada 43°19N 80°50W **82** C4
Tavistock U.K. 50°33N 4°9W **13** G3
Tavoy Burma 14°2N 98°12E **38** E2
Tavrichanka Russia 43°18N 131°59E **30** C5
Tavua Fiji 17°37S 177°5E **59** a
Tavuki Fiji 19°7S 178°8E **59** a
Taw → U.K. 51°4N 4°4W **13** F3
Tawa → India 22°48N 77°48E **42** H8
Tawas City U.S.A. 44°16N 83°31W **81** C12
Tawau Malaysia 4°20N 117°55E **36** D5
Tawi-Tawi Phil. 5°10N 120°15E **37** C6
Taxco Mexico 18°33N 99°36W **87** D5
Taxila Pakistan 33°42N 72°52E **42** C5
Taxkorgan Tajik Zizhixian
  China 37°49N 75°14E **32** C2
Tay → U.K. 56°37N 3°38W **11** E5
Tay, Firth of U.K. 56°25N 3°8W **11** E5
Tay, L. Australia 32°55S 120°48E **61** F3
Tay, L. U.K. 56°32N 4°8W **11** E4
Tay → U.K. 56°43N 3°59W **11** E5
Tay Ninh Vietnam 11°20N 106°5E **39** G6
Tayabamba Peru 8°15S 77°16W **92** E3
Taygetos Oros Greece 37°0N 22°23E **23** F10
Taylakova Russia 59°13N 74°0E **28** D8
Taylor Canada 56°13N 120°40W **70** B4
Taylor Nebr., U.S.A. 41°46N 99°23W **80** E4
Taylor Pa., U.S.A. 41°23N 75°43W **83** E9
Taylor Tex., U.S.A. 30°34N 97°25W **84** F6
Taylor, Mt. U.S.A. 35°14N 107°37W **77** J10
Taylorville U.S.A. 39°33N 89°18W **80** F9
Taymā Si. Arabia 27°35N 38°45E **44** E3
Taymyr, Oz. Russia 74°20N 102°0E **29** B11
Taymyr, Poluostrov
  Russia 75°0N 100°0E **29** B11
Taypaq Kazakhstan 49°0N 51°47E **19** E9
Tayport U.K. 56°27N 2°52W **11** E6
Tayrona △ Colombia 11°20N 74°2W **89** D5
Tayshet Russia 55°58N 98°1E **29** D10
Taytay Phil. 10°45N 119°30E **37** B5
Tāyyebād Iran 34°45N 60°45E **45** C9
Tāyyebād □ Iran 34°44N 60°44E **45** C9
Taz → Russia 67°32N 78°40E **28** C8
Taza Morocco 34°16N 4°6W **50** B5
Tāza Khurmātū Iraq 35°18N 44°20E **44** C5
Tazawa-Ko Japan 39°43N 140°40E **30** E10
Tazerbo Libya 25°45N 21°0E **51** C10
Tazin → Canada 59°48N 109°55W **71** B7
Tazin L. Canada 59°44N 108°42W **71** B7
Tazovskiy Russia 67°30N 78°44E **28** C8
Tbilisi Georgia 41°43N 44°50E **19** F7
Tchad = Chad ■ Africa 15°0N 17°15E **51** F8
Tchad, L. Chad 13°30N 14°30E **51** F8
Tch'eng-tou = Chengdu
  China 30°38N 104°2E **32** C5
Tchentlo L. Canada 55°15N 125°0W **70** B3
Tchibanga Gabon 2°45S 11°0E **52** E2
Tch'ong-k'ing = Chongqing
  China 29°35N 106°25E **32** D5
Tczew Poland 54°8N 18°50E **17** A10
Te Anau, L. N.Z. 45°15S 167°45E **59** F1
Te Aroha N.Z. 37°32S 175°44E **59** B5
Te Awamutu N.Z. 38°1S 175°20E **59** C5
Te Ika a Maui = North I.
  N.Z. 38°0S 175°0E **59** C5
Te Kuiti N.Z. 38°20S 175°11E **59** C5
Te Puke N.Z. 37°46S 176°22E **59** B6
Te Waewae B. N.Z. 46°13S 167°33E **59** G1
Te Wai Pounamu = South I.
  N.Z. 44°0S 170°0E **59** E3
Teague U.S.A. 31°38N 96°17W **84** F6
Teahupoo Tahiti 17°50S 149°16W **59** d
Teapa Mexico 17°33N 92°57W **87** D6
Tebakang Malaysia 1°6N 110°30E **36** D4
Teberu Malaysia 1°30N 103°42E **39** d
Tebessa Algeria 35°22N 8°8E **50** A7
Tebicuary → Paraguay 26°36S 58°16W **94** B4
Tebingtinggi Riau,
  Indonesia 1°0N 102°45E **36** E2
Tebingtinggi Sumatera Utara,
  Indonesia 3°20N 99°9E **36** D1
Tecate Mexico 32°34N 116°38W **79** N10
Tecka Argentina 43°29S 70°48W **96** E2
Tecomán Mexico 18°55N 103°53W **86** D4
Tecopa U.S.A. 35°51N 116°13W **79** K10
Tecoripa Mexico 28°37N 109°57W **86** B3
Tecuala Mexico 22°23N 105°27W **86** C3
Tecuci Romania 45°51N 27°27E **17** F14
Tecumseh Canada 42°19N 82°54W **82** D2
Tecumseh Mich., U.S.A. 42°0N 83°57W **81** D12
Tecumseh Okla., U.S.A. 35°15N 96°56W **84** D6

Tedzhen = Tejen
  Turkmenistan 37°23N 60°31E **28** F7
Tees → U.K. 54°37N 1°10W **12** C6
Tees B. U.K. 54°40N 1°9W **12** C6
Teesside Canada 43°59N 81°17W **82** C3
Tefé Brazil 3°25S 64°50W **92** D6
Tegal Indonesia 6°52S 109°8E **37** G13
Tegallalang Indonesia 8°27S 115°17E **37** J18
Tegalsari Indonesia 8°25S 114°8E **37** J17
Tegid, L. = Bala, L. U.K. 52°53N 3°37W **12** E4
Tegucigalpa Honduras 14°5N 87°14W **88** D2
Tehachapi U.S.A. 35°8N 118°27W **79** K8
Tehachapi Mts. U.S.A. 35°0N 118°30W **79** L8
Teheran = Tehrān Iran 35°41N 51°25E **45** C6
Tehoru Indonesia 3°23S 129°30E **37** E7
Tehrān Iran 35°41N 51°25E **45** C6
Tehrān □ Iran 35°30N 51°30E **45** C6
Tehri India 30°23N 78°29E **43** D8
Tehuacán Mexico 18°27N 97°23W **87** D5
Tehuantepec Mexico 16°21N 95°13W **87** D5
Tehuantepec, G. de
  Mexico 15°50N 95°12W **87** D5
Tehuantepec, Istmo de
  Mexico 17°15N 94°30W **87** D6
Teide, Pico de Canary Is. 28°15N 16°38W **24** F3
Teifi → U.K. 52°5N 4°41W **13** E3
Teign → U.K. 50°32N 3°32W **13** G4
Teignmouth U.K. 50°33N 3°31W **13** G4
Tejakula Indonesia 8°8S 115°20E **37** J18
Tejam India 29°57N 80°11E **43** E9
Tejen Turkmenistan 37°23N 60°31E **28** F7
Tejo → Europe 38°40N 9°24W **21** C1
Tejon Pass U.S.A. 34°49N 118°53W **79** L8
Tekamah U.S.A. 41°47N 96°13W **80** E5
Tekapo, L. N.Z. 43°53S 170°33E **59** E3
Tekax Mexico 20°12N 89°17W **87** C7
Tekeli Kazakhstan 44°50N 79°0E **28** E8
Tekirdağ Turkey 40°58N 27°30E **23** D12
Tekkali India 18°37N 84°15E **41** K14
Tekoa U.S.A. 47°14N 117°4W **76** C5
Tekong Besar, Pulau
  Singapore 1°25N 104°3E **39** d
Tel Aviv △ Israel 37°49N 75°14E **32** C2
Tel Aviv ✈ (TLV) Israel 32°5N 34°49E **46** C3
Tel Aviv-Yafo Israel 32°4N 34°48E **46** C3
Tel Lakhish Israel 31°34N 34°51E **46** D3
Tel Megiddo Israel 32°35N 35°11E **46** C4
Tela Honduras 15°40N 87°28W **88** C2
Telanaipura = Jambi
  Indonesia 1°38S 103°30E **36** E2
Telavi Georgia 42°0N 45°30E **19** F8
Telde Canary Is. 27°59N 15°25W **24** G4
Telegraph Creek Canada 58°0N 131°10W **70** B2
Telekhany = Tsyelyakhany
  Belarus 52°30N 25°46E **17** B13
Telemark Norway 59°15N 7°40E **9** G12
Telén Argentina 36°15S 65°31W **94** D2
Teleng Iran 25°47N 61°3E **45** E9
Teles Pires → Brazil 7°21S 58°3W **92** E7
Telescope Pk. U.S.A. 36°10N 117°5W **79** J9
Telford U.K. 52°40N 2°27W **13** E5
Telford and Wrekin □
  U.K. 52°45N 2°27W **12** E5
Telkwa Canada 54°41N 127°5W **70** C3
Tell City U.S.A. 37°57N 86°46W **80** G10
Teller U.S.A. 65°16N 166°22W **74** B6
Tellicherry India 11°45N 75°30E **40** P9
Telluride U.S.A. 37°56N 107°49W **77** H10
Teloloapán Mexico 18°21N 99°51W **87** D5
Telpos Iz Russia 63°16N 59°13E **18** B10
Telsen Argentina 42°30S 66°50W **96** E3
Telšiai Lithuania 55°59N 22°14E **9** J20
Teluk Anson = Teluk Intan
  Malaysia 4°3N 101°0E **39** K3
Teluk Bahang Malaysia 5°28N 100°13E **39** c
Teluk Betung = Bandar Lampung
  Indonesia 5°20S 105°10E **36** F3
Teluk Intan Malaysia 4°3N 101°0E **39** K3
Teluk Kumbar Malaysia 5°18N 100°14E **39** c
Telukbutun Indonesia 4°13N 108°12E **36** D3
Telukdalem Indonesia 0°33N 97°50E **36** D1
Tema Ghana 5°41N 0°0 **50** G5
Temagami, L. Canada 47°0N 80°10W **72** C3
Temax Mexico 21°9N 88°56W **87** C7
Temba S. Africa 25°20S 28°17E **57** D4
Tembagapura Indonesia 4°20S 137°0E **37** E9
Tembe
  Dem. Rep. of the Congo 0°16S 28°14E **54** C2
Tembe △ S. Africa 26°51S 32°24E **57** D5
Temblor Range U.S.A. 35°20N 119°50W **79** K7
Teme → U.K. 52°11N 2°13W **13** E5
Temecula U.S.A. 33°30N 117°9W **79** M9
Temengor, Tasik
  Malaysia 5°24N 101°18E **39** K3
Temerloh Malaysia 3°27N 102°25E **39** L4
Teminabuan Indonesia 1°26S 132°1E **37** E8
Temir Kazakhstan 49°1N 57°14E **19** E10
Temirtau Kazakhstan 50°5N 72°56E **32** A2
Temirtau Russia 53°10N 87°30E **28** D9
Témiscamie → Canada 50°59N 73°5W **73** B5
Témiscaming Canada 46°44N 79°5W **72** C4
Témiscamingue, L.
  Canada 47°10N 79°25W **72** C4
Temosachic Mexico 28°57N 107°51W **86** B3
Tempe U.S.A. 33°24N 111°54W **77** K8
Tempiute U.S.A. 37°39N 115°38W **78** H11
Temple U.S.A. 31°6N 97°21W **84** F6
Temple B. Australia 12°15S 143°3E **62** A3
Templemore Ireland 52°47N 7°51W **10** D4
Templeton U.S.A. 35°33N 120°42W **78** K6
Templeton → Australia 21°0S 138°40E **62** C2
Tempoal de Sánchez
  Mexico 21°31N 98°23W **87** C5
Temuco Chile 38°45S 72°40W **96** D2
Temuka N.Z. 44°14S 171°17E **59** F3
Tenabo Mexico 20°3N 90°14W **87** C6
Tenaha U.S.A. 31°57N 94°15W **84** F7
Tenakee Springs
  U.S.A. 57°47N 135°13W **70** B1

Tenali India 16°15N 80°35E **41** L12
Tenancingo de Degollado
  Mexico 18°58N 99°36W **87** D5
Tenango del Valle
  Mexico 19°7N 99°33W **87** D5
Tenaro, Akra Greece 36°22N 22°27E **23** F10
Tenasserim Burma 12°6N 99°3E **39** F2
Tenasserim □ Burma 14°0N 98°30E **38** F2
Tenby U.K. 51°40N 4°42E **13** F3
Tenda, Colle di France 44°7N 7°36E **20** D7
Tendaho Ethiopia 11°48N 40°54E **47** E3
Tendukhera India 23°24N 79°33E **43** H8
Teneguía, Volcanes de
  Canary Is. 28°28N 17°51W **24** F2
Ténéré, Erg du Niger 17°35N 10°55E **51** E8
Tenerife Canary Is. 28°15N 16°35W **24** F3
Tenerife, Pico Canary Is. 27°43N 18°1W **24** G1
Tenerife Norte ✈ (TFN)
  Canary Is. 28°28N 16°17W **24** F3
Tenerife Sur ✈ (TFS)
  Canary Is. 28°3N 16°33W **24** F3
Teng Xian China 35°5N 117°10E **35** G9
Tengah, Kepulauan
  Indonesia 7°5S 118°15E **36** F5
Tengchong China 25°0N 98°28E **32** D4
Tengchowfu = Penglai
  China 37°48N 120°42E **35** F11
Tenggarong Indonesia 0°24S 116°58E **36** E5
Tengger Shamo China 38°0N 104°0E **32** C5
Tenggol, Pulau Malaysia 4°48N 103°41E **39** K4
Tengiz Köli Kazakhstan 50°30N 69°0E **32** A2
Teniente Enciso △
  Paraguay 21°5S 61°8W **94** A3
Teniente Rodolfo Marsh
  Antarctica 62°30S 58°0W **5** C18
Tenino U.S.A. 46°51N 122°51W **78** D4
Tenkasi India 8°55N 77°20E **40** Q10
Tenke Katanga,
  Dem. Rep. of the Congo 11°22S 26°40E **55** E2
Tenke Katanga,
  Dem. Rep. of the Congo 10°32S 26°7E **55** E2
Tennant Creek
  Australia 19°30S 134°15E **62** B1
Tennessee □ U.S.A. 36°0N 86°30W **85** D11
Tennessee → U.S.A. 37°4N 88°34W **85** G10
Teno, Pta. de Canary Is. 28°21N 16°55W **24** F3
Tenom Malaysia 5°4N 115°57E **36** C5
Tenosique Mexico 17°29N 91°26W **87** D6
Tenryū-Gawa → Japan 35°39N 137°48E **31** G8
Tenterden U.K. 51°4N 0°42E **13** F8
Tenterfield Australia 29°0S 152°0E **63** D5
Teófilo Otoni Brazil 17°50S 41°30W **93** G10
Tepa Indonesia 7°52S 129°31E **37** F7
Tepalcatepec →
  Mexico 18°35N 101°59W **86** D4
Tepehuanes Mexico 25°21N 105°44W **86** B3
Tepetongo Mexico 22°28N 103°9W **86** C4
Tepic Mexico 21°30N 104°54W **86** C4
Teplice Czech Rep. 50°40N 13°48E **16** C7
Tepoca, C. Mexico 30°20N 112°25W **86** A2
Tequila Mexico 20°54N 103°47W **86** C4
Ter → Spain 42°2N 3°12E **21** A7
Ter Apel Neths. 52°53N 7°5E **15** B7
Téra Niger 14°0N 0°45E **50** F6
Teraina Kiribati 4°43N 160°25W **65** G12
Téramo Italy 42°39N 13°42E **22** C5
Terang Australia 38°15S 142°55E **63** F3
Terang, Teluk Indonesia 8°45S 116°0E **37** K19
Terceira Azores 38°43N 27°13W **50** a
Tercero → Argentina 32°58S 61°47W **94** C3
Terebovlya Ukraine 49°18N 25°44E **17** D13
Terek → Russia 44°0N 47°30E **19** F8
Terepaima △ Venezuela 9°58N 69°17W **89** E6
Teresina Brazil 5°9S 42°45W **93** E10
Terewah, L. Australia 29°52S 147°35E **63** D4
Teridgerie Cr. →
  Australia 30°25S 148°50E **63** E4
Termas de Río Hondo
  Argentina 27°29S 64°52W **94** B3
Termez = Termiz
  Uzbekistan 37°15N 67°15E **28** F7
Términi Imerese Italy 37°59N 13°42E **22** F5
Términos, L. de Mexico 18°37N 91°33W **87** D6
Termiz Uzbekistan 37°15N 67°15E **28** F7
Térmoli Italy 42°0N 15°0E **22** C6
Ternate Indonesia 0°45N 127°25E **37** D7
Terneuzen Neths. 51°20N 3°50E **15** C3
Terney Russia 45°3N 136°37E **30** B8
Terni Italy 42°34N 12°37E **22** C5
Ternopil Ukraine 49°30N 25°40E **17** D13
Ternopol = Ternopil
  Ukraine 49°30N 25°40E **17** D13
Terowie Australia 33°8S 138°55E **63** E2
Terra Bella U.S.A. 35°58N 119°3W **79** K7
Terra Nova △ Canada 48°33N 53°55W **73** C9
Terrace Canada 54°30N 128°35W **70** C3
Terrace Bay Canada 48°47N 87°5W **72** C2
Terracina Italy 41°17N 13°15E **22** D5
Terralba Italy 39°43N 8°39E **22** E3
Terrassa Spain 41°34N 2°1E **21** B7
Terre Haute U.S.A. 39°28N 87°25W **80** F10
Terrebonne B. U.S.A. 29°5N 90°35W **85** D9
Terrell U.S.A. 32°44N 96°17W **84** E6
Terrenceville Canada 47°40N 54°44W **73** C9
Terry U.S.A. 46°47N 105°19W **76** C11
Terryville U.S.A. 41°41N 73°3W **83** E11
Terschelling Neths. 53°25N 5°20E **15** A5
Teruel Spain 40°22N 1°8W **21** B5
Tervola Finland 66°6N 24°49E **8** C21
Teryaweynya L.
  Australia 32°18S 143°22E **63** E3
Teshio Japan 44°53N 141°44E **30** B10
Teshio-Gawa → Japan 44°53N 141°45E **30** B10
Tesiyn Gol → Mongolia 50°40N 93°20E **32** A4
Teslin Canada 60°10N 132°43E **70** A2
Teslin → Canada 61°34N 134°35W **70** A2
Teslin L. Canada 60°15N 132°57W **70** A2
Tessalit Mali 20°12N 1°0E **50** D6
Tessaoua Niger 13°47N 7°56E **50** F7

Test → U.K. 50°56N 1°29W 13 G6
Testigos, Is. Los Venezuela 11°23N 63°7W 89 D7
Tetachuck L. Canada 53°18N 125°55W 70 C3
Tetas, Pta. Chile 23°31S 70°38W 94 A1
Tete Mozam. 16°13S 33°33E 55 F3
Tete □ Mozam. 15°15S 32°40E 55 F3
Teterev → Ukraine 51°1N 30°5E 17 C16
Teteven Bulgaria 42°58N 24°17E 23 C11
Tethul → Canada 60°35N 112°12W 70 A6
Tetiyev Ukraine 49°22N 29°38E 17 D15
Tetlit Zheh = Fort McPherson Canada 67°30N 134°55W 68 D5
Teton → U.S.A. 47°56N 110°31W 76 C8
Tétouan Morocco 35°35N 5°21W 50 A4
Tetovo Macedonia 42°1N 20°59E 23 C9
Tetufera, Mt. Tahiti 17°40S 149°26W 59 d
Teuco → Argentina 25°35S 60°11W 94 B3
Teulon Canada 50°23N 97°16W 71 C9
Teun Indonesia 6°59S 129°8E 37 F7
Teuri-Tō Japan 44°26N 141°19E 30 B10
Teutoburger Wald Germany 52°5N 8°22E 16 B5
Tevere → Italy 41°44N 12°14E 22 D5
Teverya Israel 32°47N 35°32E 46 C4
Teviot → U.K. 55°29N 2°38W 11 F6
Tewantin Australia 26°27S 153°3E 63 D5
Tewkesbury U.K. 51°59N 2°9W 13 F5
Texada I. Canada 49°40N 124°25W 70 D4
Texarkana Ark., U.S.A. 33°26N 94°2W 84 E7
Texarkana Tex., U.S.A. 33°26N 94°3W 84 E7
Texas Australia 28°49S 151°9E 63 D5
Texas □ U.S.A. 31°40N 98°30W 84 F5
Texas City U.S.A. 29°24N 94°54W 84 G7
Texel Neths. 53°5N 4°50E 15 A4
Texline U.S.A. 36°23N 103°2W 84 C3
Texoma, L. U.S.A. 33°50N 96°34W 84 E6
Teyateyaneng Lesotho 29°7S 27°34E 53 K5
Tezin Afghan. 34°24N 69°30E 42 B3
Teziutlán Mexico 19°49N 97°21W 87 D5
Tezpur India 26°40N 92°45E 41 F18
Tezzeron L. Canada 54°43N 124°30W 70 C4
Tha-anne → Canada 60°31N 94°37W 71 A10
Tha Deua Laos 17°57N 102°53E 38 D4
Tha Deua Laos 19°26N 101°50E 38 C3
Tha Li Thailand 17°37N 101°25E 38 D3
Tha Pla Thailand 17°48N 100°32E 38 D3
Tha Rua Thailand 14°34N 100°44E 38 E3
Tha Sala Thailand 8°40N 99°56E 39 H2
Tha Song Yang Thailand 17°34N 97°55E 38 D1
Thaba Putsoa Lesotho 29°45S 28°0E 57 D4
Thabana Ntlenyana Lesotho 29°30S 29°16E 57 D4
Thabazimbi S. Africa 24°40S 27°21E 57 C4
Thādiq Si. Arabia 25°18N 45°52E 44 E5
Thai Binh Vietnam 20°35N 106°1E 38 B6
Thai Muang Thailand 8°24N 98°16E 39 H2
Thai Nguyen Vietnam 21°35N 105°55E 38 B5
Thailand ■ Asia 16°0N 102°0E 38 E4
Thailand, G. of Asia 11°30N 101°0E 39 G3
Thakhek Laos 17°25N 104°45E 38 D5
Thal Pakistan 33°28N 70°33E 42 C4
Thal Desert Pakistan 31°10N 71°30E 42 D4
Thala La = Hkakabo Razi Burma 28°25N 97°23E 41 E20
Thalabarivat Cambodia 13°33N 105°57E 38 F5
Thalassery = Tellicherry India 11°45N 75°30E 40 P9
Thallon Australia 28°39S 148°49E 63 D4
Thalu, Ko Thailand 9°26N 99°54E 39 b
Thames N.Z. 37°7S 175°34E 59 B5
Thames → Canada 42°20N 82°25W 82 D2
Thames → U.K. 51°29N 0°34E 13 F8
Thames → U.S.A. 41°18N 72°5W 83 E12
Thames Estuary U.K. 51°29N 0°52E 13 F8
Thamesford Canada 43°4N 81°0W 82 C4
Thamesville Canada 42°33N 81°59W 82 D3
Than India 22°34N 71°11E 42 H4
Than Uyen Vietnam 22°0N 103°54E 38 B4
Thana Gazi India 27°25N 76°19E 42 F7
Thandla India 23°0N 74°34E 42 H6
Thandwe Burma 18°20N 94°30E 41 K19
Thane India 19°12N 72°59E 40 K8
Thanesar India 30°1N 76°52E 42 D7
Thanet, I. of U.K. 51°21N 1°20E 13 F9
Thangool Australia 24°38S 150°42E 62 C5
Thanh Hoa Vietnam 19°48N 105°46E 38 C5
Thanh Hung Vietnam 9°55N 105°43E 39 H5
Thanh Pho Ho Chi Minh Vietnam 10°58N 106°40E 39 G6
Thanh Thuy Vietnam 22°55N 104°51E 38 A5
Thanjavur India 10°48N 79°12E 40 P11
Thanlwin = Salween → Burma 16°31N 97°37E 41 L20
Thano Bula Khan Pakistan 25°22N 67°50E 42 G2
Thaolintoa L. Canada 61°30N 96°25W 71 A9
Thap Lan △ Thailand 14°15N 102°16E 38 E4
Thap Sakae Thailand 11°30N 99°37E 39 G2
Thap Than Thailand 15°27N 99°54E 38 E2
Thar Desert India 28°0N 72°0E 42 F5
Tharad India 24°30N 71°44E 42 G4
Thargomindah Australia 27°58S 143°46E 63 D3
Tharp Fracture Zone S. Ocean 54°0S 135°0W 5 B14
Tharrawaddy Burma 17°38N 95°48E 41 L19
Tharthār, Buḩayrat ath Iraq 34°0N 43°15E 44 C4
Tharthār, L. = Tharthār, Buḩayrat ath Iraq 34°0N 43°15E 44 C4
Tharthār, W. ath → Iraq 34°32N 43°4E 44 C4
Thasos Greece 40°40N 24°40E 23 D11
That Khe Vietnam 22°16N 106°28E 38 A6
Thatcher Ariz., U.S.A. 32°51N 109°46W 77 K9
Thatcher Colo., U.S.A. 37°33N 104°7W 77 H11
Thaton Burma 16°55N 97°22E 41 L20
Thaungdut Burma 24°30N 94°40E 41 G19
Thayer U.S.A. 36°31N 91°33W 80 G8
Thayetmyo Burma 19°20N 95°10E 41 K19

Thazi Burma 21°0N 96°5E 41 J20
Thbeng Meanchey Cambodia 13°49N 104°58E 38 F5
The Broads U.K. 52°45N 1°30E 12 E9
The Everglades U.S.A. 25°50N 81°0W 85 J14
The Gulf = Persian Gulf Asia 27°0N 50°0E 45 E6
The Hague = 's-Gravenhage Neths. 52°7N 4°17E 15 B4
The Pas Canada 53°45N 101°15W 71 C8
The Wash U.K. 52°58N 0°20E 12 E8
The Weald U.K. 51°4N 0°20E 13 F8
Thebes = Thiva Greece 38°19N 23°19E 23 E10
Thebes Egypt 25°40N 32°35E 51 C12
Thedford U.S.A. 41°59N 100°35W 80 E3
Theebine Australia 25°57S 152°34E 63 D5
Thekulthili L. Canada 61°3N 110°0W 71 A7
Thelon → Canada 64°16N 96°4W 71 A8
Theodore Australia 24°55S 150°3E 62 C5
Theodore Canada 51°26N 102°55W 71 C8
Theodore U.S.A. 30°33N 88°10W 85 F10
Theodore Roosevelt △ U.S.A. 47°0N 103°25W 80 B2
Theodore Roosevelt L. U.S.A. 33°40N 111°10W 77 K8
Thepha Thailand 6°52N 100°58E 39 J3
Theresa U.S.A. 44°13N 75°48W 83 B9
Thermopolis U.S.A. 43°39N 108°13W 76 E9
Thermopylae Greece 38°48N 22°35E 23 E10
Thessalon Canada 46°20N 83°30W 72 C3
Thessalonica, Gulf of = Thessaloniki Kolpos Greece 40°15N 22°45E 23 D10
Thessaloniki Greece 40°38N 22°58E 23 D10
Thessaloniki Kolpos Greece 40°15N 22°45E 23 D10
Thetford U.K. 52°25N 0°45E 13 E8
Thetford Mines Canada 46°8N 71°18W 73 C5
Theun → Laos 18°19N 104°0E 38 C5
Theunissen S. Africa 28°26S 26°43E 56 D4
Thevenard Australia 32°9S 133°38E 63 E1
Thibodaux U.S.A. 29°48N 90°49W 85 G9
Thicket Portage Canada 55°19N 97°42W 71 B9
Thief River Falls U.S.A. 48°7N 96°10W 80 A5
Thiel Mts. Antarctica 85°15S 91°0W 5 E16
Thiers France 45°52N 3°33E 20 D5
Thiès Senegal 14°50N 16°51W 50 F2
Thika Kenya 1°1S 37°5E 54 C4
Thimphu Bhutan 27°31N 89°45E 41 F16
Thina → S. Africa 31°18S 29°13E 57 E4
Þingvallavatn Iceland 64°11N 21°9W 8 D3
Thionville France 49°20N 6°10E 20 B7
Thira = Santorini Greece 36°23N 25°27E 23 F11
Third Cataract Sudan 19°42N 30°20E 51 E12
Thirsk U.K. 54°14N 1°19W 12 C6
Thiruvananthapuram = Trivandrum India 8°41N 77°0E 40 Q10
Thisted Denmark 56°58N 8°40E 9 H13
Thistle I. Australia 35°0S 136°8E 63 F2
Thithia = Cicia Fiji 17°45S 179°18W 59 a
Thiva Greece 38°19N 23°19E 23 E10
Þjórsá → Iceland 63°47N 20°48W 8 E3
Thlewiaza → Canada 60°29N 94°40W 71 A10
Thmar Puok Cambodia 13°57N 103°4E 38 F4
Tho Vinh Vietnam 19°16N 105°42E 38 C5
Thoa → Canada 60°31N 109°47W 71 A7
Thoen Thailand 17°43N 99°12E 38 D2
Thoeng Thailand 19°41N 100°12E 38 C3
Thohoyandou S. Africa 22°58S 30°29E 53 J6
Tholdi Pakistan 35°5N 76°6E 43 B7
Thomas U.S.A. 35°45N 98°45W 84 D5
Thomas, L. Australia 26°4S 137°58E 63 D2
Thomas Hubbard, C. Canada 82°0N 94°25W 69 A13
Thomaston U.S.A. 32°53N 84°20W 85 E12
Thomasville Ala., U.S.A. 31°55N 87°44W 85 F11
Thomasville Ga., U.S.A. 30°50N 83°59W 85 F13
Thomasville N.C., U.S.A. 35°53N 80°5W 85 D14
Thompson Canada 55°45N 97°52W 71 B9
Thompson U.S.A. 41°52N 75°31W 83 E9
Thompson → Canada 50°15N 121°24W 70 C4
Thompson → U.S.A. 39°46N 93°37W 80 F7
Thompson Falls U.S.A. 47°36N 115°21W 76 C6
Thompson Pk. U.S.A. 41°0N 123°2W 76 F2
Thompson Springs U.S.A. 38°58N 109°43W 76 G9
Thompsontown U.S.A. 40°33N 77°14W 82 F7
Thomson U.S.A. 33°28N 82°30W 85 E13
Thomson → Australia 25°11S 142°53E 62 C3
Thong Yang Thailand 9°28N 99°56E 39 b
Thoothukudi = Tuticorin India 8°50N 78°12E 40 Q11
Thornaby on Tees U.K. 54°33N 1°18W 12 C6
Thornbury Canada 44°34N 80°26W 82 B4
Thorne U.K. 53°37N 0°57W 12 D7
Thornton Canada 44°16N 79°43W 82 B5
Thornton U.S.A. 39°52N 104°58W 76 G11
Thorold Canada 43°7N 79°12W 82 C5
Þórshöfn Iceland 66°12N 15°20W 8 C6
Thouin, C. Australia 20°20S 118°10E 60 D2
Thousand Islands Canada 44°20N 76°0W 83 B9
Thousand Oaks U.S.A. 34°10N 118°50W 79 L8
Thrace Turkey 41°0N 27°0E 23 D12
Three Forks U.S.A. 45°54N 111°33W 76 D8
Three Gorges Res. = Sanxia Shuiku China 30°10N 108°0E 33 C5
Three Hills Canada 51°43N 113°15W 70 C6
Three Hummock I. Australia 40°25S 144°55E 63 G3
Three Pagodas Pass Asia 15°20N 98°30E 38 E2
Three Points, C. Ghana 4°42N 2°6W 50 H5
Three Rivers Calif., U.S.A. 36°26N 118°54W 78 J8
Three Rivers Tex., U.S.A. 28°28N 98°11W 84 G5
Three Springs Australia 29°32S 115°45E 61 E2

Thrissur = Trichur India 10°30N 76°18E 40 P10
Throssell, L. Australia 27°33S 124°10E 61 E3
Throssell Ra. Australia 22°3S 121°43E 60 D3
Thrushton △ Australia 27°47S 147°40E 63 D4
Thua → Kenya 1°31S 39°30E 54 C4
Thuan Hoa Vietnam 8°58N 105°30E 39 H5
Thubun Lakes Canada 61°30N 112°0W 71 A6
Thuin Belgium 50°20N 4°17E 15 D4
Thule = Qaanaaq Greenland 77°30N 69°10W 69 B18
Thule Air Base = Uummannaq Greenland 77°33N 68°52W 69 B18
Thun Switz. 46°45N 7°38E 20 C7
Thunder B. U.S.A. 45°0N 83°20W 82 B1
Thunder Bay Canada 48°20N 89°15W 72 C2
Thung Salaeng Luang △ Thailand 16°43N 100°50E 38 D3
Thung Song Thailand 8°10N 99°40E 39 H2
Thunkar Bhutan 27°55N 91°0E 41 F17
Thuong Tra Vietnam 16°2N 107°42E 38 D6
Thüringer Wald Germany 50°35N 11°0E 16 C6
Thuringowa △ Australia 19°18S 146°43E 62 B4
Thurles Ireland 52°41N 7°49W 10 D4
Thurrock □ U.K. 51°31N 0°23E 13 F8
Thursday I. Australia 10°30S 142°3E 62 A3
Thurso Canada 45°36N 75°15W 72 C4
Thurso U.K. 58°36N 3°32W 11 C5
Thurso → U.K. 58°36N 3°32W 11 C5
Thurston I. Antarctica 72°0S 100°0W 5 D16
Thutade L. Canada 57°0N 126°55W 70 B3
Thyolo Malawi 16°7S 35°5E 55 F4
Ti-Tree Australia 22°5S 133°22E 62 C1
Tian Shan Asia 40°30N 76°0E 32 B3
Tianshifu China 41°17N 124°22E 35 D13
Tianshui China 34°32N 105°40E 34 G3
Tianyar Indonesia 8°12S 115°30E 37 J18
Tianzhen China 40°24N 114°5E 34 D8
Tianzhuangtai China 40°43N 122°5E 35 D12
Tiarei Tahiti 17°32S 149°20W 59 d
Tiaret Algeria 35°20N 1°21E 50 A6
Tibagi Brazil 24°30S 50°24W 95 A5
Tibagi → Brazil 22°47S 51°1W 95 A5
Tibastī, Sarīr Libya 22°50N 18°30E 51 D9
Tibati Cameroon 6°22N 12°30E 52 C2
Tiber = Tevere → Italy 41°44N 12°14E 22 D5
Tiber Res. U.S.A. 48°19N 111°6W 76 B8
Tiberias = Teverya Israel 32°47N 35°32E 46 C4
Tiberias, L. = Yam Kinneret Israel 32°45N 35°35E 46 C4
Tibesti Chad 21°0N 17°30E 51 D9
Tibet = Xizang Zizhiqu □ China 32°0N 88°0E 32 C3
Tibet, Plateau of Asia 32°0N 86°0E 26 E10
Tibnī Syria 35°36N 39°50E 44 C3
Tibooburra Australia 29°26S 142°1E 63 D3
Tiburón, I. Mexico 29°0N 112°25W 86 B2
Ticino → Italy 45°9N 9°14E 20 D8
Ticonderoga U.S.A. 43°51N 73°26W 83 C11
Ticul Mexico 20°24N 89°32W 87 C7
Tidaholm Sweden 58°12N 13°58E 9 G15
Tiddim Burma 23°28N 93°45E 41 H18
Tidioute U.S.A. 41°41N 79°24W 82 E5
Tidjikja Mauritania 18°29N 11°35W 50 E3
Tidore Indonesia 0°40N 127°25E 37 D7
Tiefa China 42°28N 123°32E 35 C12
Tiegang Shuiku China 22°37N 113°53E 33 F10
Tiel Neths. 51°53N 5°26E 15 C5
Tieling China 42°20N 123°55E 35 C12
Tielt Belgium 51°0N 3°20E 15 C3
Tien Shan = Tian Shan Asia 40°30N 76°0E 32 B3
Tien-tsin = Tianjin China 39°7N 117°12E 35 E9
Tien Yen Vietnam 21°20N 107°24E 38 B6
T'ienching = Tianjin China 39°7N 117°12E 35 E9
Tienen Belgium 50°48N 4°57E 15 D4
Tientsin = Tianjin China 39°7N 117°12E 35 E9
Tieri Australia 23°2S 148°21E 62 C4
Tierra Amarilla Chile 27°28S 70°18W 94 B1
Tierra Amarilla U.S.A. 36°42N 106°33W 77 H10
Tierra Colorada Mexico 17°11N 99°32W 87 D5
Tierra de Campos Spain 42°10N 4°50W 21 A3
Tierra del Fuego, I. Grande de Argentina 54°0S 69°0W 96 G3
Tiétar → Spain 39°50N 6°1W 21 C3
Tieté → Brazil 20°40S 51°35W 95 A5
Tiffin U.S.A. 41°7N 83°11W 81 E12
Tifton U.S.A. 31°27N 83°31W 85 F13
Tifu Indonesia 3°39S 126°24E 37 E7
Tighina Moldova 46°50N 29°30E 17 E15
Tigil Russia 57°49N 158°40E 29 D16
Tignish Canada 46°58N 64°2W 73 C7
Tigre → Peru 4°30S 74°10W 92 D4
Tigre → Venezuela 9°20N 62°30W 92 B6
Tigris = Dijlah, Nahr → Asia 31°0N 47°25E 44 D5
Tigyaing Burma 23°45N 96°10E 41 H20
Tīhāmah Asia 15°3N 41°55E 47 D3
Tijara India 27°56N 76°31E 42 F7
Tijuana Mexico 32°32N 117°1W 79 N9
Tikal Guatemala 17°13N 89°24W 88 C2
Tikamgarh India 24°44N 78°50E 43 G8
Tikhoretsk Russia 45°56N 40°5E 19 E7
Tikhvin Russia 59°35N 33°30E 18 C5
Tikirarjuaq = Whale Cove Canada 62°10N 92°34W 71 A10
Tikrīt Iraq 34°35N 43°37E 44 C4
Tiksi Russia 71°40N 128°45E 29 B13
Tilamuta Indonesia 0°32N 122°37E 37 D6
Tilbury Canada 42°17N 82°23W 82 D2
Tilbury U.K. 51°27N 0°22E 13 F8

Tilcara Argentina 23°36S 65°23W 94 A2
Tilden U.S.A. 42°3N 97°50W 80 D5
Tilhar India 28°0N 79°45E 43 F8
Tilichiki Russia 60°27N 166°5E 29 C17
Tilissos Greece 35°20N 25°1E 25 D7
Till → U.K. 55°41N 2°13W 12 B5
Tillamook U.S.A. 45°27N 123°51W 76 D2
Tillsonburg Canada 42°53N 80°44W 82 D4
Tillyeria Cyprus 35°6N 32°40E 25 D11
Tilos Greece 36°27N 27°27E 23 F12
Tilpa Australia 30°57S 144°24E 63 E3
Tilt → U.K. 56°46N 3°51W 11 E5
Tilton U.S.A. 43°27N 71°36W 83 C13
Tiltonsville U.S.A. 40°10N 80°41W 82 F4
Timanfaya △ Canary Is. 29°0N 13°46W 24 F6
Timanskiy Kryazh Russia 65°58N 50°5E 18 A9
Timaru N.Z. 44°23S 171°14E 59 F3
Timau Kenya 0°4N 37°15E 54 B4
Timbaki Greece 35°4N 24°45E 25 D6
Timber Creek Australia 15°40S 130°29E 60 C5
Timber Lake U.S.A. 45°26N 101°5W 80 C3
Timber Mt. U.S.A. 37°6N 116°28W 78 H10
Timbué, Ponta Mozam. 18°47S 36°22E 55 F4
Timbuktu = Tombouctou Mali 16°50N 3°0W 50 E5
Timi Cyprus 34°44N 32°31E 25 E11
Timimoun Algeria 29°14N 0°16E 50 C6
Timiris, Râs Mauritania 19°21N 16°30W 50 E2
Timiskaming, L. = Témiscamingue, L. Canada 47°10N 79°25W 72 C4
Timişoara Romania 45°43N 21°15E 17 F11
Timmins Canada 48°28N 81°25W 72 C3
Timok → Serbia 44°10N 22°40E 23 B10
Timoleague Ireland 51°39N 8°46W 10 E3
Timor Asia 9°0S 125°0E 37 F7
Timor Leste = East Timor ■ Asia 8°50S 126°0E 37 F7
Timor Sea Ind. Oc. 12°0S 127°0E 60 B4
Tin Can Bay Australia 25°56S 153°0E 63 D5
Tin Mt. U.S.A. 36°50N 117°10W 78 J9
Tina → S. Africa 31°18S 29°13E 57 E4
Tina, Khalîg el Egypt 31°10N 32°40E 46 D1
Tinaca Pt. Phil. 5°30N 125°25E 37 C7
Tinajo Canary Is. 29°4N 13°42W 24 E6
Tindal Australia 14°31S 132°22E 60 B5
Tindouf Algeria 27°42N 8°10W 50 C4
Tinfunque △ Paraguay 23°55S 60°17W 94 A3
Tinggi, Pulau Malaysia 2°18N 104°7E 39 L5
Tingo María Peru 9°10S 75°54W 92 E3
Tingrela Ivory C. 10°27N 6°25W 50 F4
Tinh Bien Vietnam 10°36N 104°57E 39 G5
Tinian N. Marianas 15°0N 145°38E 64 F6
Tinnevelly = Tirunelveli India 8°45N 77°45E 40 Q10
Tinogasta Argentina 28°5S 67°32W 94 B2
Tinos Greece 37°33N 25°8E 23 F11
Tinpahar India 24°59N 87°44E 43 G12
Tintina Argentina 27°2S 62°45W 94 B3
Tintinara Australia 35°48S 140°2E 63 F3
Tioga N. Dak., U.S.A. 48°24N 102°56W 80 A2
Tioga Pa., U.S.A. 41°55N 77°8W 82 E7
Tioman, Pulau Malaysia 2°50N 104°10E 39 L5
Tionesta U.S.A. 41°30N 79°28W 82 E5
Tiobraid Árann = Tipperary Ireland 52°28N 8°10W 10 D3
Tipperary Ireland 52°28N 8°10W 10 D3
Tipperary □ Ireland 52°37N 7°55W 10 D4
Tipton Calif., U.S.A. 36°4N 119°19W 78 J7
Tipton Iowa, U.S.A. 41°46N 91°8W 80 E8
Tipton Mt. U.S.A. 35°32N 114°12W 79 K12
Tiptonville U.S.A. 36°23N 89°29W 85 C10
Tīrān Iran 32°45N 51°8E 45 C6
Tiranë Albania 41°18N 19°49E 23 D8
Tirari Desert Australia 28°22S 138°7E 63 D2
Tiraspol Moldova 46°55N 29°35E 17 E15
Tire Turkey 38°5N 27°45E 23 E12
Tirebolu Turkey 40°58N 38°45E 19 F6
Tiree U.K. 56°31N 6°55W 11 E2
Tiree, Passage of U.K. 56°30N 6°30W 11 E2
Tîrgovişte = Târgovişte Romania 44°55N 25°27E 17 F13
Tîrgu Jiu = Târgu Jiu Romania 45°5N 23°19E 17 F12
Tîrgu Mureş = Târgu Mureş Romania 46°31N 24°38E 17 E13
Tirich Mir Pakistan 36°15N 71°55E 40 A7
Tiritiri o te Moana = Southern Alps N.Z. 43°41S 170°11E 59 E3
Tírnavos Greece 39°45N 22°18E 23 E10
Tirodi India 21°40N 79°44E 40 J11
Tirol □ Austria 47°3N 10°43E 16 E6
Tirso → Italy 39°53N 8°32E 22 E3
Tiruchchirappalli India 10°45N 78°45E 40 P11
Tirunelveli India 8°45N 77°45E 40 Q10
Tirupati India 13°39N 79°25E 40 N11
Tiruppur India 11°5N 77°22E 40 P10
Tiruvannamalai India 12°15N 79°5E 40 N11
Tisa → Serbia 45°15N 20°17E 23 B9
Tisdale Canada 52°50N 104°0W 71 C8
Tishomingo U.S.A. 34°14N 96°41W 84 D6
Tisza = Tisa → Serbia 45°15N 20°17E 23 B9
Tit-Ary Russia 71°55N 127°2E 29 B13
Tithwal Pakistan 34°21N 73°50E 43 B5
Titicaca, L. S. Amer. 15°30S 69°30W 92 G5
Titiwa Nigeria 12°14N 12°53E 51 F8
Titule Dem. Rep. of the Congo 3°15N 25°31E 54 B2
Titusville Fla., U.S.A. 28°37N 80°49W 85 G14
Titusville Pa., U.S.A. 41°38N 79°41W 82 E5
Tivaouane Senegal 14°56N 16°45W 50 F2
Tiverton Canada 44°16N 81°32W 82 B3
Tiverton U.K. 50°54N 3°29W 13 G4
Tívoli Italy 41°58N 12°45E 22 D5
Tiwi ۞ Australia 11°33S 130°42E 60 B5
Tizi-Ouzou Algeria 36°42N 4°3E 50 A6
Tizimín Mexico 21°9N 88°9W 87 C7
Tiznit Morocco 29°48N 9°45W 50 C4

Tjeggelvas Sweden 66°37N 17°45E 8 C17
Tjieggelvas = Tjeggelvas Sweden 66°37N 17°45E 8 C17
Tjirebon = Cirebon Indonesia 6°45S 108°32E 37 G13
Tjirrkarli ۞ Australia 26°0S 125°28E 61 E4
Tjluring Indonesia 8°25S 114°13E 37 J17
Tjörn Sweden 58°0N 11°35E 9 H14
Tjukayirla Roadhouse Australia 27°9S 124°34E 61 E3
Tjurabalan ۞ Australia 19°50S 128°0E 60 C4
Tlacotalpan Mexico 18°37N 95°40W 87 D5
Tlahualilo de Zaragoza Mexico 26°7N 103°27W 86 B4
Tlaquepaque Mexico 20°39N 103°19W 86 C4
Tlaxcala Mexico 19°19N 98°14W 87 D5
Tlaxcala □ Mexico 19°30N 98°10W 87 D5
Tlaxiaco Mexico 17°25N 97°35W 87 D5
Tlemcen Algeria 34°52N 1°21W 50 B5
To Bong Vietnam 12°45N 109°16E 38 F7
Toa Payoh Singapore 1°20N 103°51E 39 d
Toad → Canada 59°25N 124°57W 70 B4
Toad River Canada 58°51N 125°14W 70 B3
Toamasina Madag. 18°10S 49°25E 57 B8
Toamasina □ Madag. 18°0S 49°0E 57 B8
Toay Argentina 36°43S 64°38W 94 D3
Toba Japan 34°30N 136°51E 31 G8
Toba, Danau Indonesia 2°30N 97°30E 36 D1
Toba Kakar Pakistan 31°30N 69°0E 42 D3
Toba Tek Singh Pakistan 30°55N 72°25E 42 D5
Tobago Trin. & Tob. 11°10N 60°30W 93 K16
Tobelo Indonesia 1°45N 127°56E 37 D7
Tobermory Canada 45°12N 81°40W 82 A3
Tobermory U.K. 56°38N 6°5W 11 E2
Tobi Pac. Oc. 2°40N 131°10E 37 D8
Tobi-Shima Japan 41°12N 139°34E 30 D9
Tobin, L. Australia 21°45S 125°49E 60 D4
Tobin L. Canada 53°35N 103°30W 71 C8
Toboali Indonesia 3°0S 106°25E 36 E3
Tobol → Russia 58°10N 68°12E 28 D7
Toboli Indonesia 0°38S 120°5E 37 E6
Tobolsk Russia 58°15N 68°10E 28 D7
Tobruk = Tubruq Libya 32°7N 23°55E 51 B10
Tobyhanna U.S.A. 41°11N 75°25W 83 E9
Tobyl = Tobol → Russia 58°10N 68°12E 28 D7
Tocantinópolis Brazil 6°20S 47°25W 93 E9
Tocantins □ Brazil 10°0S 48°0W 93 F9
Tocantins → Brazil 1°45S 49°10W 93 D9
Toccoa U.S.A. 34°35N 83°19W 85 D13
Tochi → Pakistan 32°49N 70°41E 42 C4
Tochigi Japan 36°25N 139°45E 31 F9
Tochigi □ Japan 36°45N 139°45E 31 F9
Toco Trin. & Tob. 10°49N 60°57W 93 K16
Toconao Chile 23°11S 68°1W 94 A2
Tocopilla Chile 22°5S 70°10W 94 A1
Tocumwal Australia 35°51S 145°31E 63 F4
Tocuyo → Venezuela 11°3N 68°23W 92 A5
Todd → Australia 24°52S 135°48E 62 C2
Todeli Indonesia 1°40S 124°29E 37 E6
Todenyang Kenya 4°35N 35°56E 54 B4
Todgarh India 25°42N 73°58E 42 G5
Todos os Santos, B. de Brazil 12°48S 38°38W 93 F11
Todos Santos Mexico 23°26N 110°13W 86 C2
Toe Hd. U.K. 57°50N 7°8W 11 D1
Tofield Canada 53°25N 112°40W 70 C6
Tofino Canada 49°11N 125°55W 70 D3
Tofua Tonga 19°45S 175°5W 59 c
Tōgane Japan 35°33N 140°22E 31 G10
Togian, Kepulauan Indonesia 0°20S 121°50E 37 E6
Togliatti Russia 53°32N 49°24E 18 D8
Togo ■ W. Afr. 8°30N 1°35E 50 G6
Togtoh China 40°15N 111°10E 34 D6
Tohiea, Mt. Moorea 17°33S 149°49W 59 d
Tōhoku □ Japan 39°50N 141°45E 30 E10
Tōhōm Mongolia 44°27N 108°2E 34 B5
Toinya Sudan 6°17N 29°46E 51 G11
Toiyabe Range U.S.A. 39°30N 117°0W 76 G5
Tojikiston = Tajikistan ■ Asia 38°30N 70°0E 28 F8
Tojo Indonesia 1°20S 121°15E 37 E6
Tōjō Japan 34°53N 133°16E 31 G6
Tok U.S.A. 63°20N 142°59W 68 E3
Tokachi-Dake Japan 43°17N 142°5E 30 C11
Tokachi-Gawa → Japan 42°44N 143°42E 30 C11
Tokala Indonesia 1°30S 121°40E 37 E6
Tōkamachi Japan 37°8N 138°43E 31 F9
Tokanui N.Z. 46°34S 168°56E 59 G2
Tokara-Rettō Japan 29°37N 129°43E 31 K4
Tokarahi N.Z. 44°56S 170°39E 59 F3
Tokashiki-Shima Japan 26°11N 127°21E 31 L3
Tokat Turkey 40°22N 36°35E 19 F6
Tōkch'ŏn N. Korea 39°45N 126°18E 35 E14
Tokdo Asia 37°15N 131°52E 31 F5
Tokeland U.S.A. 46°42N 123°59W 78 D3
Tokelau Is. Pac. Oc. 9°0S 171°45W 64 H10
Tokmak Russia 47°16N 35°42E 19 E6
Toko Ra. Australia 23°5S 138°20E 62 C2
Tokoro-Gawa → Japan 44°7N 144°5E 30 B12
Toku Tonga 18°10S 174°11W 59 c
Tokuno-Shima Japan 27°56N 128°55E 31 L4
Tokushima Japan 34°4N 134°34E 31 G7
Tokushima □ Japan 33°55N 134°0E 31 H7
Tokuyama Japan 34°3N 131°50E 31 G5
Tōkyō Japan 35°43N 139°45E 31 G9
Tolaga Bay N.Z. 38°21S 178°20E 59 C7
Tolbukhin = Dobrich Bulgaria 43°37N 27°49E 23 C12
Toledo Brazil 24°44S 53°45W 95 A5
Toledo Spain 39°50N 4°2W 21 C3
Toledo Ohio, U.S.A. 41°39N 83°33W 81 E12
Toledo Oreg., U.S.A. 44°37N 123°56W 76 D2
Toledo Wash., U.S.A. 46°26N 122°51W 76 C2
Toledo, Montes de Spain 39°33N 4°20W 21 C3
Toledo Bend Res. U.S.A. 31°11N 93°34W 84 F8
Tolga Australia 17°15S 145°29E 62 B4
Toliara Madag. 23°21S 43°40E 57 C7

Toliara ☐ *Madag.*   21°0S 45°0E **57** C8
Tolima *Colombia*   4°40N 75°19W **92** C3
Tolitoli *Indonesia*   1°5N 120°50E **37** D6
Tollhouse *U.S.A.*   37°1N 119°24W **78** H7
Tolmachevo *Russia*   58°56N 29°51E **9** G23
Tolo, Teluk *Indonesia*   2°20S 122°10E **37** E6
Tolo Harbour *China*   22°27N 114°12E **33** G11
Toluca *Mexico*   19°17N 99°40W **87** D5
Tolyatti = Togliatti
  Russia   53°32N 49°24E **18** D8
Tom Burke *S. Africa*   23°5S 28°0E **57** C4
Tom Price *Australia*   22°40S 117°48E **60** D2
Tomah *U.S.A.*   43°59N 90°30W **80** D8
Tomahawk *U.S.A.*   45°28N 89°44W **80** C9
Tomakomai *Japan*   42°38N 141°36E **30** C10
Tomales *U.S.A.*   38°15N 122°53W **78** G4
Tomales B. *U.S.A.*   38°15N 123°58W **78** G3
Tomanivi *Fiji*   17°37S 178°1E **59** a
Tomar *Portugal*   39°36N 8°25W **21** C1
Tomaszów Mazowiecki
  Poland   51°30N 20°2E **17** C10
Tomatlán *Mexico*   19°56N 105°15W **86** D3
Tombador, Serra do *Brazil*   12°0S 58°0W **92** F7
Tombigbee → *U.S.A.*   31°8N 87°57W **85** F11
Tombouctou *Mali*   16°50N 3°0W **50** E5
Tombstone *U.S.A.*   31°43N 110°4W **77** L8
Tombua *Angola*   15°55S 11°55E **56** B1
Tomé *Chile*   36°36S 72°57W **94** D1
Tomelloso *Spain*   39°10N 3°2W **21** C4
Tomini *Indonesia*   0°30N 120°30E **37** D6
Tomini, Teluk *Indonesia*   0°10S 121°0E **37** E6
Tomintoul *U.K.*   57°15N 3°23W **11** D5
Tomkinson Ranges
  Australia   26°11S 129°5E **61** E4
Tommot *Russia*   59°4N 126°20E **29** D13
Tomnop Ta Suos
  Cambodia   11°20N 104°15E **39** G5
Tomo → *Colombia*   5°20N 67°48W **92** B5
Toms Place *U.S.A.*   37°34N 118°41W **78** H8
Toms River *U.S.A.*   39°58N 74°12W **83** G10
Tomsk *Russia*   56°30N 85°5E **28** D9
Tonalá *Chiapas, Mexico*   16°4N 93°45W **87** D6
Tonalá *Jalisco, Mexico*   20°37N 103°14W **86** C4
Tonantins *Brazil*   2°45S 67°45W **92** D5
Tonasket *U.S.A.*   48°42N 119°26W **76** B4
Tonawanda *U.S.A.*   43°1N 78°53W **82** D6
Tonb *Iran*   26°15N 55°15E **45** E7
Tonbridge *U.K.*   51°11N 0°17E **13** F8
Tondano *Indonesia*   1°35N 124°54E **37** D6
Tondoro *Namibia*   17°45S 18°50E **56** B2
Tone → *Australia*   34°25S 116°25E **61** F2
Tone-Gawa → *Japan*   35°44N 140°51E **31** F9
Tonekábon *Iran*   36°45N 51°12E **45** B6
Tong Xian *China*   39°55N 116°35E **34** E9
Tong-Yeong *S. Korea*   34°50N 128°20E **35** G15
Tonga ■ *Pac. Oc.*   19°50S 174°30W **59** c
Tonga Trench *Pac. Oc.*   18°0S 173°0W **64** J10
Tongaat *S. Africa*   29°33S 31°9E **57** D5
Tongareva = Penrhyn
  Cook Is.   9°0S 158°0W **65** H12
Tongariro △ *N.Z.*   39°8S 175°33E **59** C5
Tongatapu *Tonga*   21°10S 175°10W **59** c
Tongatapu Group *Tonga*   21°0S 175°0W **59** c
Tongchuan *China*   35°6N 109°3E **34** G5
Tongeren *Belgium*   50°47N 5°28E **15** D5
Tonggu Jiao *China*   22°22N 113°37E **33** G10
Tonghua *China*   41°42N 125°58E **35** D13
Tongjosŏn Man
  N. Korea   39°30N 128°0E **35** E15
Tongking, G. of = Tonkin, G. of
  Asia   20°0N 108°0E **38** C7
Tongliao *China*   43°38N 122°18E **35** C12
Tongling *China*   30°55N 117°48E **33** C6
Tongobory *Madag.*   23°32S 44°20E **57** C7
Tongoy *Chile*   30°16S 71°31W **94** C1
Tongres = Tongeren
  Belgium   50°47N 5°28E **15** D5
Tongsa Dzong *Bhutan*   27°31N 90°31E **41** F17
Tongshi *China*   18°30N 109°20E **38** C7
Tongue *U.K.*   58°29N 4°25W **11** C4
Tongue → *U.S.A.*   46°25N 105°52W **76** C11
Tongwei *China*   35°0N 105°5E **34** G3
Tongxin *China*   36°59N 105°58E **34** F3
Tongyang *N. Korea*   39°9N 126°53E **35** E14
Tongyu *China*   44°45N 123°4E **35** B12
Tonj *Sudan*   7°20N 28°44E **51** G11
Tonk *India*   26°6N 75°54E **42** F6
Tonkawa *U.S.A.*   36°41N 97°18W **84** C6
Tonkin = Bac Phan
  Vietnam   22°0N 105°0E **38** B5
Tonkin, G. of *Asia*   20°0N 108°0E **38** C7
Tonle Sap *Cambodia*   13°0N 104°0E **38** F5
Tono *Japan*   39°19N 141°32E **30** E10
Tonopah *U.S.A.*   38°4N 117°14W **77** G5
Tonosi *Panama*   7°20N 80°20W **88** E3
Tons → *Haryana, India*   30°30N 77°39E **42** D7
Tons → *Ut. P., India*   26°1N 83°33E **43** F10
Tønsberg *Norway*   59°19N 10°25E **9** G14
Tonto △ *U.S.A.*   33°39N 111°7W **77** K8
Tonumea *Tonga*   20°30S 174°30W **59** c
Toobanna *Australia*   18°42S 146°9E **62** B4
Toodyay *Australia*   31°34S 116°28E **61** F2
Tooele *U.S.A.*   40°32N 112°18W **76** F7
Toompine *Australia*   27°15S 144°19E **63** D3
Toora *Australia*   38°39S 146°23E **63** F4
Toora-Khem *Russia*   52°28N 96°17E **29** D10
Toowoomba *Australia*   27°32S 151°56E **63** D5
Top Springs *Australia*   16°37S 131°51E **60** C5
Topaz *U.S.A.*   38°41N 119°30W **78** G7
Topley *Canada*   54°49N 126°18W **70** C3
Topocalma, Pta. *Chile*   34°10S 72°2W **94** C1
Topock *U.S.A.*   34°46N 114°29W **79** L12
Topol'čany *Slovak Rep.*   48°35N 18°12E **17** D10
Topolobampo *Mexico*   25°36N 109°3W **86** B3
Topozero, Ozero *Russia*   65°35N 32°0E **8** D25
Toppenish *U.S.A.*   46°23N 120°19W **76** C3
Toraka Vestale *Madag.*   16°20S 43°58E **57** B7

Torata *Peru*   17°23S 70°1W **92** G4
Torbalı *Turkey*   38°10N 27°21E **23** E12
Torbat-e Heydārīyeh
  Iran   35°15N 59°12E **45** C8
Torbat-e Jām *Iran*   35°16N 60°35E **45** C9
Torbay *Canada*   47°40N 52°42W **73** C9
Torbay ☐ *U.K.*   50°26N 3°31W **13** G4
Torfaen ☐ *U.K.*   51°43N 3°3W **13** F4
Torgau *Germany*   51°34N 13°0E **16** C7
Torhout *Belgium*   51°5N 3°7E **15** C3
Tori-Shima *Japan*   30°29N 140°19E **31** J10
Torino *Italy*   45°3N 7°40E **20** D7
Torit *Sudan*   4°27N 32°31E **51** H12
Torkamān *Iran*   37°35N 47°23E **44** B5
Tormes → *Spain*   41°18N 6°29W **21** B2
Tornado Mt. *Canada*   49°55N 114°40W **70** D6
Torneå = Tornio *Finland*   65°50N 24°12E **8** D21
Torneälven → *Europe*   65°50N 24°12E **8** D21
Torneträsk *Sweden*   68°24N 19°15E **8** B18
Torngat Mts. *Canada*   59°0N 63°40W **69** F19
Tornio *Finland*   65°50N 24°12E **8** D21
Tornionjoki = Torneälven →
  Europe   65°50N 24°12E **8** D21
Tornquist *Argentina*   38°8S 62°15W **94** D3
Toro *Spain*   39°59N 4°8E **24** B11
Toro, Cerro del *Chile*   29°10S 69°50W **94** B2
Toro □ *Uganda*   1°5N 30°22E **54** C3
Toro Pk. *U.S.A.*   33°34N 116°24W **79** M10
Torodi *Niger*   13°3N 1°40E **50** F6
Toronto *Canada*   43°39N 79°20W **82** C5
Toronto *U.S.A.*   40°28N 80°36W **82** F4
Toronto Lester B. Pearson Int. ✈
  (YYZ) *Canada*   43°46N 79°35W **82** C5
Toropets *Russia*   56°30N 31°40E **18** C5
Tororo *Uganda*   0°45N 34°12E **54** B3
Toros Dağları *Turkey*   37°0N 32°30E **44** B2
Torpa *India*   22°57N 85°6E **43** H11
Torquay *U.K.*   50°27N 3°32W **13** G4
Torrance *U.S.A.*   33°50N 118°20W **79** M8
Torre de Moncorvo
  Portugal   41°12N 7°8W **21** B2
Torre del Greco *Italy*   40°47N 14°22E **22** D6
Torrejón de Ardoz *Spain*   40°27N 3°29W **21** B4
Torrelavega *Spain*   43°20N 4°5W **21** A3
Torremolinos *Spain*   36°38N 4°30W **21** D3
Torrens, L. *Australia*   31°0S 137°50E **63** E2
Torrens Cr. → *Australia*   22°23S 145°9E **62** C4
Torrens Creek *Australia*   20°48S 145°3E **62** C4
Torrent *Spain*   39°27N 0°28W **21** C5
Torreón *Mexico*   25°33N 103°26W **86** B4
Torres *Brazil*   29°21S 49°44W **95** B5
Torres *Mexico*   28°46N 110°47W **86** B2
Torres Strait *Australia*   9°50S 142°20E **62** a
Torres Vedras *Portugal*   39°5N 9°15W **21** C1
Torrevieja *Spain*   37°59N 0°42W **21** D5
Torrey *U.S.A.*   38°18N 111°25W **76** G8
Torridge → *U.K.*   51°0N 4°13W **13** G3
Torridon, L. *U.K.*   57°35N 5°50W **11** D3
Torrington, Conn., U.S.A.   41°48N 73°7W **83** E11
Torrington *Wyo.,
  U.S.A.*   42°4N 104°11W **76** E11
Tórshavn *Færoe Is.*   62°5N 6°56W **8** E9
Tortola *Br. Virgin Is.*   18°19N 64°45W **89** e
Tortosa *Spain*   40°49N 0°31E **21** B6
Tortosa, C. *Spain*   40°41N 0°52E **21** B6
Tortue, Î. de la *Haiti*   20°5N 72°57W **89** B5
Tortuguero △ *Costa Rica*   10°31N 83°29W **88** D3
Torūd *Iran*   35°25N 55°5E **45** C7
Toruń *Poland*   53°2N 18°39E **17** B10
Tory Hill *Canada*   44°58N 78°16W **82** B6
Tory I. *Ireland*   55°16N 8°14W **10** A3
Tosa *Japan*   33°24N 133°23E **31** H6
Tosa-Shimizu *Japan*   32°52N 132°58E **31** H6
Tosa-Wan *Japan*   33°15N 133°30E **31** H6
Toscana ☐ *Italy*   43°25N 11°0E **22** C4
Toshka, Buheirat en
  Egypt   22°50N 31°0E **51** D12
Toshka Lakes = Toshka, Buheirat
  en *Egypt*   22°50N 31°0E **51** D12
Toshkent *Uzbekistan*   41°20N 69°10E **28** E7
Tostado *Argentina*   29°15S 61°50W **94** B3
Tostón, Pta. de *Canary Is.*   28°42N 14°2W **24** F5
Tosu *Japan*   33°22N 130°31E **31** H5
Totana *Russia*   60°0N 42°40E **18** C7
Totnes *U.K.*   50°26N 3°42W **13** G4
Totness *Suriname*   5°53N 56°19W **93** B7
Totonicapán *Guatemala*   14°58N 91°12W **88** D1
Totoya, I. *Fiji*   18°57S 179°50W **59** a
Totten Glacier *Antarctica*   66°45S 116°10E **5** C8
Tottenham *Australia*   32°14S 147°21E **63** E4
Tottenham *Canada*   44°1N 79°49W **82** B5
Tottori *Japan*   35°30N 134°15E **31** G7
Tottori ☐ *Japan*   35°30N 134°12E **31** G7
Toubkal, Djebel *Morocco*   31°0N 8°0W **50** B4
Tougan *Burkina Faso*   13°11N 2°58W **50** F5
Touggourt *Algeria*   33°6N 6°4E **50** B7
Toul *France*   48°40N 5°53E **20** B6
Toulon *France*   43°10N 5°55E **20** E6
Toulouse *France*   43°37N 1°27E **20** E4
Toummo *Niger*   22°45N 14°8E **51** D8
Toungoo *Burma*   19°0N 96°30E **41** K20
Tournon-sur-Rhône
  France   45°4N 4°50E **20** D6
Tours *France*   47°22N 0°40E **20** C4
Toussoro, Mt. *C.A.R.*   9°7N 23°14E **52** C4
Touwsrivier *S. Africa*   33°20S 20°2E **56** E3
Towada *Japan*   40°37N 141°13E **30** D10
Towada-Ko *Japan*   40°28N 140°55E **30** D10
Towada-Hachimantai △
  Japan   40°20N 140°55E **30** D10
Towanda *U.S.A.*   41°46N 76°27W **83** E8
Tower *U.S.A.*   47°48N 92°17W **80** B7

Towerhill Cr. →
  Australia   22°28S 144°35E **62** C3
Towner *U.S.A.*   48°21N 100°25W **80** A3
Townsend *U.S.A.*   46°19N 111°31W **76** C8
Townshend I. *Australia*   22°10S 150°31E **62** C5
Townsville *Australia*   19°15S 146°45E **62** B4
Towot *Sudan*   6°12N 34°32E **54** A3
Towraghondī *Afghan.*   35°13N 62°16E **40** B3
Towson *U.S.A.*   39°24N 76°36W **81** F15
Towuti, Danau *Indonesia*   2°45S 121°32E **37** E6
Toya-Ko *Japan*   42°35N 140°51E **30** C10
Toyama *Japan*   36°40N 137°15E **31** F8
Toyama ☐ *Japan*   36°45N 137°30E **31** F8
Toyama-Wan *Japan*   37°0N 137°30E **31** F8
Toyapakeh *Indonesia*   8°41S 115°29E **37** K18
Toyohashi *Japan*   34°45N 137°25E **31** G8
Toyokawa *Japan*   34°48N 137°27E **31** G8
Toyonaka *Japan*   34°46N 135°28E **31** G7
Toyooka *Japan*   35°35N 134°48E **31** G7
Toyota *Japan*   35°3N 137°7E **31** G8
Tozeur *Tunisia*   33°56N 8°8E **50** B7
Trá Lí = Tralee *Ireland*   52°16N 9°42W **10** D2
Trá Mhór = Tramore
  Ireland   52°10N 7°10W **10** D4
Tra On *Vietnam*   9°58N 105°55E **39** H5
Trabzon *Turkey*   41°0N 39°45E **19** F6
Tracadie *Canada*   47°30N 64°55W **73** C7
Tracy *Canada*   46°1N 73°9W **72** C5
Tracy *Calif., U.S.A.*   37°44N 121°26W **78** H5
Tracy *Minn., U.S.A.*   44°14N 95°37W **80** C6
Trafalgar, C. *Spain*   36°10N 6°2W **21** D2
Trail *Canada*   49°5N 117°40W **70** D5
Trainor L. *Canada*   60°24N 120°17W **70** A4
Trakai *Lithuania*   54°30N 25°10E **9** J21
Trákhonas *Cyprus*   35°12N 33°21E **25** D12
Tralee *Ireland*   52°16N 9°42W **10** D2
Tralee B. *Ireland*   52°17N 9°55W **10** D2
Tramore *Ireland*   52°10N 7°10W **10** D4
Tramore B. *Ireland*   52°9N 7°10W **10** D4
Tramuntana, Serra de
  Spain   39°48N 2°54E **24** B9
Tran Ninh, Cao Nguyen
  Laos   19°30N 103°10E **38** C4
Tranås *Sweden*   58°3N 14°59E **9** G16
Trancas *Argentina*   26°11S 65°20W **94** B2
Trang *Thailand*   7°33N 99°38E **39** J2
Trangahy *Madag.*   19°7S 44°31E **57** B7
Trangan *Indonesia*   6°40S 134°20E **37** F8
Trangie *Australia*   32°4S 148°0E **63** E4
Trani *Italy*   41°17N 16°25E **22** D7
Tranoroa *Madag.*   24°42S 45°4E **57** C8
Tranqueras *Uruguay*   31°13S 55°45W **95** C4
Transantarctic Mts.
  Antarctica   85°0S 170°0W **5** E12
Transilvania *Romania*   46°30N 24°0E **17** E12
Transilvanian Alps = Carpaţii
  Meridionali *Romania*   45°30N 25°0E **17** F13
Transnistria = Stînga Nistrului ☐
  Moldova   47°20N 29°15E **17** E15
Transylvania = Transilvania
  Romania   46°30N 24°0E **17** E12
Trápani *Italy*   38°1N 12°29E **22** E5
Trapper Pk. *U.S.A.*   45°54N 114°18W **76** D6
Traralgon *Australia*   38°12S 146°34E **63** F4
Trasimeno, L. *Italy*   43°8N 12°6E **22** C5
Trat *Thailand*   12°14N 102°33E **39** F4
Tratani → *Pakistan*   29°19N 68°20E **42** E3
Traun *Austria*   48°14N 14°15E **16** D8
Travellers L. *Australia*   33°20S 142°0E **63** E3
Travemünde *Germany*   53°57N 10°52E **16** B6
Travers, Mt. *N.Z.*   42°1S 172°45E **59** E4
Traverse City *U.S.A.*   44°46N 85°38W **81** C11
Travis, L. *U.S.A.*   30°24N 97°55W **84** F6
Travnik *Bos.-H.*   44°17N 17°39E **23** B7
Trawbreaga B. *Ireland*   55°20N 7°25W **10** A4
Trébbia → *Italy*   45°4N 9°41E **20** D8
Třebíč *Czech Rep.*   49°14N 15°55E **16** D8
Trebinje *Bos.-H.*   42°44N 18°22E **23** C8
Trebonne *Australia*   18°37S 146°5E **62** B4
Tregaron *U.K.*   52°14N 3°56W **13** E4
Tregrosse Is. *Australia*   17°41S 150°43E **62** B5
Treherne *Canada*   49°38N 98°42W **71** D9
Treinta y Tres *Uruguay*   33°16S 54°17W **95** C5
Trelawney *Zimbabwe*   17°30S 30°30E **57** B5
Trelew *Argentina*   43°10S 65°20W **96** E3
Trelleborg *Sweden*   55°20N 13°10E **9** J15
Tremadog Bay *U.K.*   52°51N 4°18W **12** E3
Tremonton *U.S.A.*   41°43N 112°10W **76** F7
Tremp *Spain*   42°10N 0°52E **21** A6
Trenche → *Canada*   47°46N 72°53W **72** C5
Trenčín *Slovak Rep.*   48°52N 18°4E **17** D10
Trenggalek *Indonesia*   8°3S 111°43E **37** H14
Trenque Lauquen
  Argentina   36°5S 62°45W **94** D3
Trent → *Canada*   44°6N 77°34W **82** B7
Trent → *U.K.*   53°41N 0°42W **12** D7
Trento *Italy*   46°4N 11°8E **22** A4
Trenton *Canada*   44°10N 77°34W **82** B7
Trenton *Mo., U.S.A.*   40°5N 93°37W **80** E7
Trenton *N.J., U.S.A.*   40°14N 74°46W **83** F10
Trenton *Nebr., U.S.A.*   40°11N 101°1W **80** E3
Trepassey *Canada*   46°43N 53°25W **73** C9
Tres Arroyos *Argentina*   38°26S 60°20W **94** D3
Três Corações *Brazil*   21°30S 45°30W **95** A6
Três Lagoas *Brazil*   20°50S 51°43W **93** H8
Tres Lomas *Argentina*   36°27S 62°51W **94** D3
Tres Montes, C. *Chile*   46°50S 75°30W **96** F1
Tres Pinos *U.S.A.*   36°48N 121°19W **78** J5
Três Pontas *Brazil*   21°23S 45°29W **95** A6
Tres Puentes *Chile*   27°50S 70°15W **94** B1
Tres Puntas, C. *Argentina*   47°0S 66°0W **96** F3
Três Rios *Brazil*   22°6S 43°15W **95** A7
Tres Valles *Mexico*   18°15N 96°8W **87** D5
Tresco *U.K.*   49°57N 6°20W **13** H1
Treviso *Italy*   45°40N 12°15E **22** B5
Triabunna *Australia*   42°30S 147°55E **63** G4
Trianda *Greece*   36°25N 28°10E **25** C10
Triangle *Zimbabwe*   21°2S 31°28E **57** C5
Tribal Areas ☐ *Pakistan*   33°0N 70°0E **42** C4

Tribulation, C. *Australia*   16°5S 145°29E **62** B4
Tribune *U.S.A.*   38°28N 101°45W **80** F3
Trichinopoly = Tiruchirappalli
  India   10°45N 78°45E **40** P11
Trichur *India*   10°30N 76°18E **40** P10
Trichy = Tiruchirappalli
  India   10°45N 78°45E **40** P11
Trida *Australia*   33°1S 145°1E **63** E4
Trier *Germany*   49°45N 6°38E **16** D4
Trieste *Italy*   45°40N 13°46E **22** B5
Triglav *Slovenia*   46°21N 13°50E **16** E7
Trikala *Greece*   39°34N 21°47E **23** E9
Trikomo *Cyprus*   35°17N 33°52E **25** D12
Trikora, Puncak
  Indonesia   4°15S 138°45E **37** E9
Trim *Ireland*   53°33N 6°48W **10** C5
Trimmu Dam *Pakistan*   31°10N 72°8E **42** D5
Trincomalee *Sri Lanka*   8°38N 81°15E **40** Q12
Trindade *Brazil*   16°40S 49°30W **93** G9
Trindade, I. *Atl. Oc.*   20°20S 29°50W **2** F8
Trinidad *Bolivia*   14°46S 64°50W **92** F6
Trinidad *Cuba*   21°48N 80°0W **88** B4
Trinidad *Trin. & Tob.*   10°30N 61°15W **93** K15
Trinidad *Uruguay*   33°30S 56°50W **94** C4
Trinidad → *Mexico*   17°49N 95°9W **87** D5
Trinidad & Tobago ■
  W. Indies   10°30N 61°20W **89** D7
Trinity *Canada*   48°59N 53°55W **73** C9
Trinity *U.S.A.*   30°57N 95°22W **84** F7
Trinity → *Calif., U.S.A.*   41°11N 123°42W **76** F2
Trinity → *Tex., U.S.A.*   29°45N 94°43W **84** G7
Trinity B. *Canada*   48°20N 53°10W **73** C9
Trinity Hills *Trin. & Tob.*   10°7N 61°7W **93** K15
Trinity Is. *U.S.A.*   56°33N 154°25W **74** D9
Trinity Range *U.S.A.*   40°10N 118°40W **76** F4
Trinkitat *Sudan*   18°45N 37°51E **51** E13
Trinway *U.S.A.*   40°9N 82°1W **82** F2
Triolet *Mauritius*   20°4S 57°32E **53** d
Tripoli = Tarābulus
  Lebanon   34°31N 35°50E **46** A4
Tripoli = Tarābulus *Libya*   32°49N 13°7E **51** B8
Tripoli *Greece*   37°31N 22°25E **23** F10
Tripolitania = Tarābulus
  N. Afr.   31°0N 13°0E **51** B8
Tripura ☐ *India*   24°0N 92°0E **41** H18
Tripylos *Cyprus*   34°59N 32°41E **25** E11
Tristan da Cunha *Atl. Oc.*   37°6S 12°20W **49** K2
Trisul *India*   30°19N 79°47E **43** D8
Trivandrum *India*   8°41N 77°0E **40** Q10
Trnava *Slovak Rep.*   48°23N 17°35E **17** D9
Trochu *Canada*   51°50N 113°13W **70** C6
Trodely I. *Canada*   52°15N 79°26W **72** B4
Troglav *Croatia*   43°56N 16°36E **22** C7
Troilus, L. *Canada*   50°50N 74°35W **72** B5
Trois-Pistoles *Canada*   48°5N 69°10W **73** C6
Trois-Rivières *Canada*   46°25N 72°34W **72** C5
Trois-Rivières *Guadeloupe*   15°57N 61°40W **88** b
Troitsk *Russia*   54°10N 61°35E **28** D7
Troitsko Pechorsk
  Russia   62°40N 56°10E **18** B10
Trölladyngja *Iceland*   64°54N 17°16W **8** D5
Trollhättan *Sweden*   58°17N 12°20E **9** G15
Trollheimen *Norway*   62°46N 9°1E **8** E13
Trombetas → *Brazil*   1°55S 55°35W **93** D7
Tromsø *Norway*   69°40N 18°56E **8** B18
Tron *Thailand*   17°28N 100°7E **38** D3
Trona *U.S.A.*   35°46N 117°23W **79** K9
Tronador, Mte.
  Argentina   41°10S 71°50W **96** E2
Trøndelag *Norway*   64°17N 11°50E **8** D14
Trondheim *Norway*   63°36N 10°25E **8** E14
Trondheimsfjorden
  Norway   63°35N 10°30E **8** E14
Troodos *Cyprus*   34°55N 32°52E **25** E11
Troon *U.K.*   55°33N 4°39W **11** F4
Tropic *U.S.A.*   37°37N 112°5W **77** H7
Trostan *U.K.*   55°3N 6°10W **10** A5
Trou Gras Pt. *St. Lucia*   14°6N 60°53W **89** f
Trout → *Canada*   61°19N 119°51W **70** A5
Trout L. N.W.T., Canada   60°40N 121°14W **70** A4
Trout L., Ont., *Canada*   51°20N 93°15W **71** C10
Trout Lake *Canada*   56°30N 114°32W **70** B6
Trout Lake *U.S.A.*   46°0N 121°32W **78** E5
Trout River *Canada*   49°29N 58°8W **73** C8
Trout Run *U.S.A.*   41°23N 77°3W **82** E7
Trouville-sur-Mer *France*   49°21N 0°5E **20** B4
Trowbridge *U.K.*   51°18N 2°12W **13** F5
Troy *Turkey*   39°57N 26°12E **23** E12
Troy *Ala., U.S.A.*   31°48N 85°58W **85** F12
Troy *Kans., U.S.A.*   39°47N 95°5W **80** F6
Troy *Mo., U.S.A.*   38°59N 90°59W **80** F8
Troy *Mont., U.S.A.*   48°28N 115°53W **76** B6
Troy *N.Y., U.S.A.*   42°44N 73°41W **83** D11
Troy *Ohio, U.S.A.*   40°2N 84°12W **81** E11
Troy *Pa., U.S.A.*   41°47N 76°47W **83** E8
Troyes *France*   48°19N 4°3E **20** B6
Truchas Pk. *U.S.A.*   35°58N 105°39W **77** J11
Trucial States = United Arab
  Emirates ■ *Asia*   23°50N 54°0E **45** F7
Truckee *U.S.A.*   39°20N 120°11W **78** F6
Trudovoye *Russia*   43°17N 132°5E **30** C6
Trujillo *Honduras*   16°0N 86°0W **88** C2
Trujillo *Peru*   8°6S 79°0W **92** E3
Trujillo *Spain*   39°28N 5°55W **21** C3
Trujillo *U.S.A.*   35°32N 104°42W **77** J11
Trujillo *Venezuela*   9°22N 70°38W **92** B4
Truk *Micronesia*   7°25N 151°46E **64** G7
Trumann *U.S.A.*   35°41N 90°31W **85** D9
Trumansburg *U.S.A.*   42°33N 76°40W **83** D8
Trumbull, Mt. *U.S.A.*   36°25N 113°19W **77** H7
Trundle *Australia*   32°53S 147°35E **63** E4
Trung-Phan = Annam
  Vietnam   16°0N 108°0E **38** E7
Truro *Canada*   45°21N 63°14W **73** C7
Truro *U.K.*   50°16N 5°4W **13** G2
Truskavets *Ukraine*   49°17N 23°30E **17** D12
Trutch *Canada*   57°44N 122°57W **70** B4

Truth or Consequences
  U.S.A.   33°8N 107°15W **77** K10
Trutnov *Czech Rep.*   50°37N 15°54E **16** C8
Tryonville *U.S.A.*   41°42N 79°48W **82** E5
Tsandi *Namibia*   17°42S 14°50E **56** B1
Tsaratanana *Madag.*   16°47S 47°39E **57** B8
Tsaratanana, Mt. de =
  Maromokotro *Madag.*   14°0S 49°0E **57** A8
Tsaratanana △ *Madag.*   13°57S 48°52E **57** A8
Tsau *Botswana*   20°8S 22°22E **56** C3
Tsavo *Kenya*   2°59S 38°28E **54** C4
Tsavo East △ *Kenya*   2°44S 38°47E **54** C4
Tsavo West △ *Kenya*   3°19S 37°57E **54** C4
Tsentralnyy ☐ *Russia*   52°0N 40°0E **28** D4
Tses *Namibia*   25°58S 18°8E **56** D2
Tsetserleg *Mongolia*   47°36N 101°32E **32** B5
Tsévié *Togo*   6°25N 1°20E **50** G6
Tshabong *Botswana*   26°2S 22°29E **56** D3
Tshane *Botswana*   24°5S 21°54E **56** C3
Tshela
  Dem. Rep. of the Congo   4°57S 13°4E **52** E2
Tshesebe *Botswana*   21°51S 27°32E **57** C4
Tshibeke
  Dem. Rep. of the Congo   2°40S 28°35E **54** C2
Tshibinda
  Dem. Rep. of the Congo   2°23S 28°43E **54** C2
Tshikapa
  Dem. Rep. of the Congo   6°28S 20°48E **52** F4
Tshilenge
  Dem. Rep. of the Congo   6°17S 23°48E **54** D1
Tshinsenda
  Dem. Rep. of the Congo   12°20S 28°0E **55** E2
Tshofa
  Dem. Rep. of the Congo   5°13S 25°16E **54** D2
Tshwane = Pretoria
  S. Africa   25°44S 28°12E **57** D4
Tshwane *Botswana*   22°24S 22°1E **56** C3
Tsigara *Botswana*   20°22S 25°54E **56** C4
Tsihombe *Madag.*   25°10S 45°41E **57** D8
Tsiigehtchic *Canada*   67°15N 134°0W **68** D5
Tsimlyansk Res. = Tsimlyanskoye
  Vdkhr. *Russia*   48°0N 43°0E **19** E7
Tsimlyanskoye Vdkhr.
  Russia   48°0N 43°0E **19** E7
Tsinan = Jinan *China*   36°38N 117°1E **34** F9
Tsineng *S. Africa*   27°5S 23°5E **56** D3
Tsing Yi *China*   22°21N 114°6E **33** G11
Tsinghai = Qinghai ☐
  China   36°0N 98°0E **32** C4
Tsingtao = Qingdao
  China   36°5N 120°20E **35** F11
Tsingy de Bemaraha △
  Madag.   18°35S 45°25E **57** B8
Tsingy de Namaraka △
  Madag.   16°29S 45°25E **57** B8
Tsinjoarivo *Madag.*   19°37S 47°40E **57** B8
Tsinjomitondraka *Madag.*   15°40S 47°8E **57** B8
Tsirigo = Kythira *Greece*   36°8N 23°0E **23** F10
Tsiroanomandidy *Madag.*   18°46S 46°2E **57** B8
Tsitondroina *Madag.*   21°19S 46°0E **57** C8
Tsitsikamma △ *S. Africa*   34°3S 23°40E **56** E3
Tsivory *Madag.*   24°4S 46°5E **57** C8
Tskhinvali *Georgia*   42°14N 44°1E **19** F7
Tsna → *Russia*   54°55N 41°58E **18** D7
Tso Moriri, L. *India*   32°50N 78°20E **43** C8
Tsobis *Namibia*   19°27S 17°30E **56** B2
Tsodilo Hill *Botswana*   18°49S 21°43E **56** B3
Tsogttsetsiy = Baruunsuu
  Mongolia   43°43N 105°35E **34** C3
Tsolo *S. Africa*   31°18S 28°37E **57** E4
Tsomo *S. Africa*   32°0S 27°42E **57** E4
Tsu *Japan*   34°45N 136°25E **31** G8
Tsu L. *Canada*   60°40N 111°52W **70** A6
Tsuchiura *Japan*   36°5N 140°15E **31** F10
Tsuen Wan *China*   22°22N 114°6E **33** G11
Tsumeb *Namibia*   19°9S 17°44E **56** B2
Tsumis *Namibia*   23°39S 17°29E **56** C2
Tsuruga *Japan*   35°45N 136°2E **31** G8
Tsurugi-San *Japan*   33°51N 134°6E **31** H7
Tsuruoka *Japan*   38°44N 139°50E **30** E9
Tsushima *Gifu, Japan*   35°10N 136°43E **31** G8
Tsushima Nagasaki,
  Japan   34°20N 129°20E **31** G4
Tsuyama *Japan*   35°3N 134°0E **31** G7
Tsyelyakhany *Belarus*   52°30N 25°46E **17** B13
Tuaim = Tuam *Ireland*   53°31N 8°51W **10** C3
Tual *Indonesia*   5°38S 132°44E **37** F8
Tualatin *U.S.A.*   45°23N 122°45W **78** E4
Tuam *Ireland*   53°31N 8°51W **10** C3
Tuamotu, Îs.
  French Polynesia   17°0S 144°0W **65** J13
Tuamotu Arch. = Tuamotu, Îs.
  French Polynesia   17°0S 144°0W **65** J13
Tuamotu Ridge *Pac. Oc.*   20°0S 138°0W **65** K14
Tuan Giao *Vietnam*   21°35N 103°25E **38** B4
Tuao *Phil.*   17°55N 121°22E **37** A6
Tuapse *Russia*   44°5N 39°10E **19** F6
Tuas *Singapore*   1°19N 103°39E **39** d
Tuatapere *N.Z.*   46°8S 167°41E **59** G1
Tuba City *U.S.A.*   36°8N 111°14W **77** H8
Tuban *Indonesia*   6°54S 112°3E **37** G15
Tubani *Botswana*   24°46S 24°18E **56** C3
Tubarão *Brazil*   28°30S 49°0W **95** B6
Tübas *West Bank*   32°20N 35°22E **46** C4
Tubas → *Namibia*   22°54S 14°35E **56** C1
Tübingen *Germany*   48°31N 9°4E **16** D5
Tubou *Fiji*   18°13S 178°48E **59** a
Tabruq *Libya*   32°7N 23°55E **51** B10
Tubuaï, Îs.
  French Polynesia   25°0S 150°0W **65** K13
Tuc Trung *Vietnam*   11°1N 107°12E **39** G6
Tucacas *Venezuela*   10°48N 68°19W **92** A5
Tuchitua *Canada*   60°55N 129°13W **70** A3
Tuchodi → *Canada*   58°17N 123°42W **70** B4
Tuckanarra *Australia*   27°7S 118°5E **61** E2
Tucson *U.S.A.*   32°13N 110°58W **77** K8
Tucumán ☐ *Argentina*   26°48S 66°2W **94** B2

Tucumcari *U.S.A.* 35°10N 103°44W **77 J12**
Tucupita *Venezuela* 9°2N 62°3W **92 B6**
Tucuruí *Brazil* 3°42S 49°44W **93 D9**
Tucuruí, Represa de
  Brazil 4°0S 49°30W **93 D9**
Tudela *Spain* 42°4N 1°39W **21 A5**
Tudmur *Syria* 34°36N 38°15E **44 C3**
Tudor, L. *Canada* 55°50N 65°25W **73 A6**
Tuen Mun *China* 22°24N 113°59E **33 G10**
Tugela → *S. Africa* 29°14S 31°30E **57 D5**
Tuguegarao *Phil.* 17°35N 121°42E **37 A6**
Tugur *Russia* 53°44N 136°45E **29 D14**
Tui *Spain* 42°3N 8°39W **21 A1**
Tuineje *Canary Is.* 28°19N 14°3W **24 F5**
Tukangbesi, Kepulauan
  Indonesia 6°0S 124°0E **37 F6**
Tukarak I. *Canada* 56°15N 78°45W **72 A4**
Tukayyid *Iraq* 29°47N 45°36E **44 D5**
Tuktoyaktuk *Canada* 69°27N 133°2W **68 D5**
Tuktut Nogait △
  Canada 69°15N 122°0W **68 D7**
Tukums *Latvia* 56°58N 23°10E **9 H20**
Tukuyu *Tanzania* 9°17S 33°35E **55 D3**
Tula *Hidalgo, Mexico* 20°3N 99°21W **87 C5**
Tula *Tamaulipas, Mexico* 23°0N 99°43W **87 C5**
Tula *Russia* 54°13N 37°38E **18 D6**
Tulach Mhór = Tullamore
  Ireland 53°16N 7°31W **10 C4**
Tulancingo *Mexico* 20°5N 98°22W **87 C5**
Tulare *U.S.A.* 36°13N 119°21W **78 J7**
Tulare Lake Bed *U.S.A.* 36°0N 119°48W **78 K7**
Tularosa *U.S.A.* 33°5N 106°1W **77 K10**
Tulbagh *S. Africa* 33°16S 19°6E **56 E2**
Tulcán *Ecuador* 0°48N 77°43W **92 C3**
Tulcea *Romania* 45°13N 28°46E **17 F15**
Tulchyn *Ukraine* 48°41N 28°49E **17 D15**
Tūleh *Iran* 34°35N 52°33E **45 C7**
Tulemalu L. *Canada* 62°58N 99°25W **71 A9**
Tuli *Zimbabwe* 21°58S 29°13E **55 G2**
Tulia *U.S.A.* 34°32N 101°46W **84 D4**
Tulita *Canada* 64°57N 125°30W **68 E6**
Tülkarm *West Bank* 32°19N 35°2E **46 C4**
Tulla *Ireland* 52°53N 8°46W **10 D3**
Tullahoma *U.S.A.* 35°22N 86°13W **85 D11**
Tullamore *Australia* 32°39S 147°36E **63 E4**
Tullamore *Ireland* 53°16N 7°31W **10 C4**
Tulle *France* 45°16N 1°46E **20 D4**
Tullow *Ireland* 52°49N 6°45W **10 D5**
Tully *Australia* 17°56S 145°55E **62 B4**
Tully *U.S.A.* 42°48N 76°7W **83 D8**
Tulsa *U.S.A.* 36°10N 95°55W **84 C7**
Tulsequah *Canada* 58°39N 133°35W **70 B2**
Tuluá *Colombia* 4°6N 76°11W **92 C3**
Tulun *Russia* 54°32N 100°35E **29 D11**
Tulungagung *Indonesia* 8°5S 111°54E **37 H14**
Tuma → *Nic.* 13°6N 84°35W **88 D3**
Tumacacori △ *U.S.A.* 31°35N 111°6W **77 L8**
Tumaco *Colombia* 1°50N 78°45W **92 C3**
Tumakuru = Tumkur
  India 13°18N 77°6E **40 N10**
Tumatumari *Guyana* 5°20N 58°55W **92 B7**
Tumba *Sweden* 59°12N 17°48E **9 G17**
Tumba, L.
  Dem. Rep. of the Congo 0°50S 18°0E **52 E3**
Tumbarumba *Australia* 35°44S 148°0E **63 F4**
Tumbaya *Argentina* 23°50S 65°26W **94 A2**
Tumbes *Peru* 3°37S 80°27W **92 D2**
Tumbler Ridge *Canada* 55°8N 121°0W **70 B4**
Tumbwe
  Dem. Rep. of the Congo 11°25S 27°15E **55 E2**
Tumby Bay *Australia* 34°21S 136°8E **63 E2**
Tumd Youqi *China* 40°30N 110°30E **34 D6**
Tumen *China* 43°0N 129°50E **30 C4**
Tumen Jiang → *China* 42°20N 130°35E **35 C16**
Tumeremo *Venezuela* 7°18N 61°30W **92 B6**
Tumkur *India* 13°18N 77°6E **40 N10**
Tump *Pakistan* 26°7N 62°16E **40 F3**
Tumpat *Malaysia* 6°11N 102°10E **39 J4**
Tumu *Ghana* 10°56N 1°56W **50 F5**
Tumucumaque, Serra
  Brazil 2°0N 55°0W **93 C8**
Tumut *Australia* 35°16S 148°13E **63 F4**
Tumwater *U.S.A.* 47°1N 122°54W **78 C4**
Tuna *India* 22°59N 70°5E **42 H4**
Tunapuna *Trin. & Tob.* 10°38N 61°24W **93 K15**
Tunas de Zaza *Cuba* 21°39N 79°34W **88 B4**
Tunbridge Wells = Royal
  Tunbridge Wells *U.K.* 51°7N 0°16E **13 F8**
Tuncurry *Australia* 32°17S 152°29E **63 E5**
Tundla *India* 27°12N 78°17E **42 F8**
Tunduru *Tanzania* 11°8S 37°25E **55 E4**
Tundzha → *Bulgaria* 41°40N 26°35E **23 C11**
Tung Chung *China* 22°17N 113°57E **33 G10**
Tung Lung Chau
  China 22°15N 114°17E **33 G11**
Tungabhadra → *India* 15°57N 78°15E **40 M11**
Tungla *Nic.* 13°24N 84°21W **88 D3**
Tungsten *Canada* 61°57N 128°16W **70 A3**
Tunguska, Nizhnyaya →
  Russia 65°48N 88°4E **29 C9**
Tunguska, Podkamennaya →
  Russia 61°50N 90°13E **29 C10**
Tunica *U.S.A.* 34°41N 90°23W **85 D9**
Tunis *Tunisia* 36°50N 10°11E **50 A7**
Tunisia ■ *Africa* 33°30N 9°10E **51 A7**
Tunja *Colombia* 5°33N 73°25W **92 B4**
Tunkhannock *U.S.A.* 41°32N 75°57W **83 E9**
Tunliu *China* 36°13N 112°52E **34 F7**
Tunnel Creek △
  Australia 17°41S 125°18E **60 C4**
Tunnsjøen *Norway* 64°45N 13°25E **8 D15**
Tunungayualok I. *Canada* 56°0N 61°0W **73 A7**
Tunuyán *Argentina* 33°35S 69°0W **94 C2**
Tunuyán → *Argentina* 33°33S 67°30W **94 C2**
Tuolumne *U.S.A.* 37°58N 120°15W **78 H6**
Tuolumne → *U.S.A.* 37°36N 121°13W **78 H5**
Tūp Āghāj *Iran* 36°3N 47°50E **44 B5**
Tupã *Brazil* 21°57S 50°28W **95 A5**
Tupelo *U.S.A.* 34°16N 88°43W **85 D11**

Tupinambarana, I. *Brazil* 3°0S 58°0W **92 D7**
Tupiza *Bolivia* 21°30S 65°40W **94 A2**
Tupman *U.S.A.* 35°18N 119°21W **79 K7**
Tupper *Canada* 55°32N 120°1W **70 B4**
Tupper L. *U.S.A.* 44°10N 74°32W **83 B10**
Tupper Lake *U.S.A.* 44°14N 74°28W **83 B10**
Tupungato, Cerro
  S. Amer. 33°15S 69°50W **94 C2**
Túquerres *Colombia* 1°5N 77°37W **92 C3**
Tura *Russia* 64°20N 100°17E **29 C11**
Turabah *Si. Arabia* 28°20N 43°15E **44 D4**
Tūrān *Iran* 35°39N 56°42E **45 C8**
Tura *Russia* 51°55N 94°0E **29 D10**
Turayf *Si. Arabia* 31°41N 38°39E **44 D3**
Turda *Romania* 46°34N 23°47E **17 E12**
Turek *Poland* 52°3N 18°30E **17 B10**
Turén *Venezuela* 9°17N 69°6W **92 B5**
Turfan = Turpan *China* 43°58N 89°10E **32 B3**
Turfan Basin = Turpan Pendi
  China 42°40N 89°25E **32 B3**
Turfan Depression = Turpan
  Pendi *China* 42°40N 89°25E **32 B3**
Turgeon → *Canada* 50°0N 78°56W **72 C4**
Tŭrgovishte *Bulgaria* 43°17N 26°38E **23 C12**
Turgutlu *Turkey* 38°30N 27°43E **23 E12**
Turgwe → *Zimbabwe* 21°31S 32°15E **57 C5**
Turia → *Spain* 39°27N 0°19W **21 C5**
Turiaçu *Brazil* 1°40S 45°19W **93 D9**
Turiaçu → *Brazil* 1°36S 45°19W **93 D9**
Turin = Torino *Italy* 45°3N 7°40E **20 D7**
Turkana, L. *Africa* 3°30N 36°5E **54 B4**
Turkestan = Türkistan
  Kazakhstan 43°17N 68°16E **28 E7**
Turkey ■ *Eurasia* 39°0N 36°0E **19 G6**
Turkey Creek = Warmun
  Australia 17°2S 128°12E **60 C4**
Türkistan *Kazakhstan* 43°17N 68°16E **28 E7**
Türkmenabat
  Turkmenistan 39°6N 63°34E **45 B9**
Türkmenbashi
  Turkmenistan 40°5N 53°5E **45 A7**
Turkmenistan ■ *Asia* 39°0N 59°0E **28 F6**
Turks & Caicos Is. ☑
  W. Indies 21°20N 71°20W **89 B5**
Turks Island Passage
  W. Indies 21°30N 71°30W **89 B5**
Turku *Finland* 60°30N 22°19E **9 F20**
Turkwel → *Kenya* 3°6N 36°6E **54 B4**
Turlock *U.S.A.* 37°30N 120°51W **78 H6**
Turnagain *Australia* 9°34S 142°17E **62 a**
Turnagain → *Canada* 59°12N 127°35W **70 B3**
Turnagain, C. *N.Z.* 40°28S 176°38E **59 D6**
Turneffe Is. *Belize* 17°20N 87°50W **87 D7**
Turner *U.S.A.* 48°51N 108°24W **76 B9**
Turner Pt. *Australia* 11°47S 133°32E **62 A1**
Turner Valley *Canada* 50°40N 114°17W **70 C6**
Turners Falls *U.S.A.* 42°36N 72°33W **83 D12**
Turnhout *Belgium* 51°19N 4°57E **15 C4**
Turnor L. *Canada* 56°35N 108°35W **71 B7**
Tŭrnovo = Veliko Tŭrnovo
  Bulgaria 43°5N 25°41E **23 C11**
Turnu Măgurele
  Romania 43°46N 24°56E **17 G13**
Turnu Roşu, P.
  Romania 45°33N 24°17E **17 F13**
Turpan *China* 43°58N 89°10E **32 B3**
Turpan Pendi *China* 42°40N 89°25E **32 B3**
Turriff *U.K.* 57°32N 2°27W **11 D6**
Tursāq *Iraq* 33°27N 45°47E **44 C5**
Turtle Head I. *Australia* 10°56S 142°37E **62 A3**
Turtle L. *Canada* 53°36N 108°38W **71 C7**
Turtle Lake *U.S.A.* 47°31N 100°53W **80 B3**
Turtleford *Canada* 53°23N 108°57W **71 C7**
Turuépano ☑ *Venezuela* 10°34N 62°43W **89 D7**
Turukhansk *Russia* 65°21N 88°5E **29 C9**
Tuscaloosa *U.S.A.* 33°12N 87°34W **85 E11**
Tuscarawas → *U.S.A.* 40°24N 81°25W **82 F3**
Tuscarora Mt. *U.S.A.* 40°55N 77°55W **82 F7**
Tuscola *Ill., U.S.A.* 39°48N 88°17W **80 F9**
Tuscola *Tex., U.S.A.* 32°12N 99°48W **84 E5**
Tuscumbia *U.S.A.* 34°44N 87°42W **85 D11**
Tuskegee *U.S.A.* 32°25N 85°42W **85 E12**
Tuticorin *India* 8°50N 78°12E **40 Q11**
Tutóia *Brazil* 2°45S 42°20W **93 D10**
Tutong *Brunei* 4°47N 114°40E **36 D4**
Tutrakan *Bulgaria* 44°2N 26°40E **23 B12**
Tuttle Creek L. *U.S.A.* 39°15N 96°36W **80 F5**
Tuttlingen *Germany* 47°58N 8°48E **16 E5**
Tutuala *E. Timor* 8°25S 127°15E **37 F7**
Tutuila *Amer. Samoa* 14°19S 170°50W **59 b**
Tutume *Botswana* 20°30S 27°5E **53 J5**
Tuul Gol → *Mongolia* 48°30N 104°25E **32 B5**
Tuva ☐ *Russia* 51°30N 95°0E **29 D10**
Tuvalu ■ *Pac. Oc.* 8°0S 178°0E **58 B10**
Tuvuca *Fiji* 17°40S 178°48W **59 a**
Tuxpan *Mexico* 20°57N 97°24W **87 C5**
Tuxtla Gutiérrez *Mexico* 16°45N 93°7W **87 D6**
Tuy = Tui *Spain* 42°3N 8°39W **21 A1**
Tuy An *Vietnam* 13°17N 109°16E **38 F7**
Tuy Duc *Vietnam* 12°15N 107°27E **39 F6**
Tuy Hoa *Vietnam* 13°5N 109°10E **38 F7**
Tuy Phong *Vietnam* 11°14N 108°43E **39 G7**
Tuya L. *Canada* 59°7N 130°35W **70 B2**
Tuyen Hoa *Vietnam* 17°50N 106°10E **38 D6**
Tuyen Quang *Vietnam* 21°50N 105°10E **38 B5**
Tüysarkān *Iran* 34°33N 48°27E **45 C6**
Tuz Gölü *Turkey* 38°42N 33°18E **19 G5**
Tūz Khurmātū *Iraq* 34°56N 44°38E **44 C5**
Tuzigoot △ *U.S.A.* 34°46N 112°2W **77 J7**
Tuzla *Bos.-H.* 44°34N 18°41E **23 B8**
Tver *Russia* 56°55N 35°55E **18 C6**
Twain *U.S.A.* 40°1N 121°3W **78 E5**
Twain Harte *U.S.A.* 38°2N 120°14W **78 G6**
Tweed *Canada* 44°29N 77°19W **82 B7**
Tweed → *U.K.* 55°45N 2°0W **11 F6**
Tweed Heads *Australia* 28°10S 153°31E **63 D5**

Tweedsmuir ☐ *Canada* 53°0N 126°20W **70 C3**
Twentynine Palms
  U.S.A. 34°8N 116°3W **79 L10**
Twillingate *Canada* 49°42N 54°45W **73 C9**
Twin Bridges *U.S.A.* 45°33N 112°20W **76 D7**
Twin Falls *Canada* 53°30N 64°32W **73 B7**
Twin Falls *U.S.A.* 42°34N 114°28W **76 E6**
Twin Valley *U.S.A.* 47°16N 96°16W **80 B5**
Twinsburg *U.S.A.* 41°19N 81°26W **82 E3**
Twitchell Res. *U.S.A.* 34°59N 120°19W **79 L6**
Two Harbors *U.S.A.* 47°2N 91°40W **80 B8**
Two Hills *Canada* 53°43N 111°52W **70 C6**
Two Rivers *U.S.A.* 44°9N 87°34W **80 C10**
Two Rocks *Australia* 31°30S 115°35E **61 F2**
Twofold B. *Australia* 37°8S 149°59E **63 F4**
Tyachiv *Ukraine* 48°1N 23°35E **17 D12**
Tychy *Poland* 50°9N 18°59E **17 C10**
Tyler *Minn., U.S.A.* 44°17N 96°8W **80 C5**
Tyler *Tex., U.S.A.* 32°21N 95°18W **84 E7**
Tynda *Russia* 55°10N 124°43E **29 D13**
Tyndall *U.S.A.* 43°0N 97°50W **80 D5**
Tyne → *U.K.* 54°59N 1°32W **12 C6**
Tyne & Wear ☐ *U.K.* 55°6N 1°17W **12 B6**
Tynemouth *U.K.* 55°1N 1°26W **12 B6**
Tyre = Sūr *Lebanon* 33°19N 35°16E **46 B4**
Tyrifjorden *Norway* 60°2N 10°8E **9 F14**
Tyrol = Tirol ☐ *Austria* 47°3N 10°43E **16 E6**
Tyrone *U.S.A.* 40°40N 78°14W **82 F6**
Tyrone ☐ *U.K.* 54°38N 7°11W **10 B4**
Tyrrell → *Australia* 35°26S 142°51E **63 F3**
Tyrrell, L. *Australia* 35°20S 142°50E **63 F3**
Tyrrell, L. *Canada* 63°7N 105°27W **71 A7**
Tyrrhenian Sea *Medit. S.* 40°0N 12°30E **22 E5**
Tysfjorden *Norway* 68°7N 16°25E **8 B17**
Tyulgan *Russia* 52°22N 56°12E **18 D10**
Tyumen *Russia* 57°11N 65°29E **28 D7**
Tywi → *U.K.* 51°48N 4°21W **13 F3**
Tywyn *U.K.* 52°35N 4°5W **13 E3**
Tzaneen *S. Africa* 23°47S 30°9E **57 C5**
Tzermiado *Greece* 35°12N 25°29E **25 D7**
Tzukong = Zigong
  China 29°15N 104°48E **32 D5**

U

U.S.A. = United States of
  America ■ *N. Amer.* 37°0N 96°0W **75 H20**
U.S. Virgin Is. ☑ *W. Indies* 18°20N 65°0W **89 e**
Uanle Uen = Wanleweyne
  Somali Rep. 2°37N 44°54E **47 G3**
Uatumã → *Brazil* 2°26S 57°37W **92 D7**
Uaupés *Brazil* 0°8S 67°5W **92 D5**
Uaupés → *Brazil* 0°2N 67°16W **92 C5**
Uaxactún *Guatemala* 17°25N 89°29W **88 C2**
Ubá *Brazil* 21°8S 43°0W **95 A7**
Ubaitaba *Brazil* 14°18S 39°20W **93 F11**
Ubangi = Oubangi →
  Dem. Rep. of the Congo 0°30S 17°50E **52 E3**
Ubauro *Pakistan* 28°15N 69°45E **42 E3**
Ubayyiḍ, W. al → *Iraq* 32°34N 43°48E **44 C4**
Ube *Japan* 33°56N 131°15E **31 H5**
Úbeda *Spain* 38°3N 3°23W **21 C4**
Uberaba *Brazil* 19°50S 47°55W **93 G9**
Uberlândia *Brazil* 19°0S 48°20W **93 G9**
Ubin, Pulau *Singapore* 1°24N 103°57E **39 d**
Ubly *U.S.A.* 43°42N 82°55W **82 C2**
Ubolratna Res. *Thailand* 16°45N 102°30E **38 D4**
Ubombo *S. Africa* 27°31S 32°4E **57 D5**
Ubon Ratchathani
  Thailand 15°15N 104°50E **38 E5**
Ubondo
  Dem. Rep. of the Congo 0°55S 25°42E **54 C2**
Ubort → *Belarus* 52°6N 28°30E **17 B15**
Ubud *Indonesia* 8°30S 115°16E **37 J18**
Ubundu
  Dem. Rep. of the Congo 0°22S 25°30E **54 C2**
Ucayali → *Peru* 4°30S 73°30W **92 D4**
Uchab *Namibia* 19°47S 17°42E **56 B2**
Uchiura-Wan *Japan* 42°25N 140°40E **30 C10**
Uchquduq *Uzbekistan* 41°50N 62°50E **28 E7**
Uchur → *Russia* 58°48N 130°35E **29 D14**
Ucluelet *Canada* 48°57N 125°32W **70 D3**
Uda → *Russia* 54°42N 135°14E **29 D14**
Udachnyy *Russia* 66°25N 112°24E **29 C12**
Udagamandalam *India* 11°30N 76°44E **40 P10**
Udainagar *India* 22°33N 76°13E **42 H7**
Udaipur *India* 24°36N 73°44E **42 G5**
Udaipur Garhi *Nepal* 27°0N 86°35E **43 F12**
Udala *India* 21°35N 86°34E **43 J12**
Uddevalla *Sweden* 58°21N 11°55E **9 G14**
Uddjaure *Sweden* 65°56N 17°49E **8 D17**
Uden *Neths.* 51°40N 5°37E **15 C5**
Udgir *India* 18°25N 77°5E **40 K10**
Udhampur *India* 33°0N 75°5E **43 C6**
Údine *Italy* 46°3N 13°14E **22 A5**
Udintsev Fracture Zone
  S. Ocean 57°0S 145°0W **5 B13**
Udmurtia ☐ *Russia* 57°30N 52°30E **18 C9**
Udon Thani *Thailand* 17°29N 102°46E **38 D4**
Udong *Cambodia* 11°48N 104°45E **39 G5**
Udskaya Guba *Russia* 54°50N 135°45E **29 D14**
Udu Pt. *Fiji* 16°9S 179°57W **59 a**
Udupi *India* 13°25N 74°42E **40 N9**
Udzungwa △ *Tanzania* 7°52S 36°35E **54 D4**
Udzungwa Range
  Tanzania 9°30S 35°10E **55 D4**
Ueda *Japan* 36°24N 138°16E **31 F9**
Uedineniya, Os. *Russia* 78°0N 85°0E **4 B12**
Uele →
  Dem. Rep. of the Congo 3°45N 24°45E **52 D4**
Uelen *Russia* 66°10N 170°0W **29 C19**
Uelzen *Germany* 52°57N 10°32E **16 B6**
Ufa *Germany* 54°45N 55°55E **18 D10**
Ufa → *Russia* 54°40N 56°0E **18 D10**
Ugab → *Namibia* 20°55S 13°30E **56 C1**
Ugalla → *Tanzania* 5°8S 30°42E **54 D3**
Ugalla River ☐ *Tanzania* 5°45S 31°54E **54 D3**
Uganda ■ *Africa* 2°0N 32°0E **54 B3**

Ugie *S. Africa* 31°10S 28°13E **57 E4**
Uglegorsk *Russia* 49°5N 142°2E **29 E15**
Ugljan *Croatia* 44°12N 15°10E **16 G8**
Ugolnye Kopi *Russia* 64°44N 177°42E **29 C18**
Uhlenhorst *Namibia* 23°45S 17°55E **56 C2**
Uhrichsville *U.S.A.* 40°24N 81°21W **82 F3**
Uibhist a Deas = South Uist
  U.K. 57°20N 7°15W **11 D1**
Uibhist a Tuath = North Uist
  U.K. 57°40N 7°15W **11 D1**
Uig *U.K.* 57°35N 6°21W **11 D2**
Uíge *Angola* 7°30S 14°40E **52 F2**
Uiha *Tonga* 19°54S 174°25W **59 c**
Uijeongbu *S. Korea* 37°44N 127°2E **35 F14**
Ŭiju *N. Korea* 40°15N 124°35E **35 D13**
Uinta Mts. *U.S.A.* 40°45N 110°30W **76 F8**
Uis *Namibia* 21°8S 14°49E **56 C1**
Uiseong *S. Korea* 36°21N 128°45E **35 F15**
Uitenhage *S. Africa* 33°40S 25°28E **56 E4**
Uithuizen *Neths.* 53°24N 6°41E **15 A6**
Ujh → *India* 32°10N 75°18E **42 C6**
Ujhani *India* 28°0N 79°6E **43 F8**
Uji-guntō *Japan* 31°15N 129°25E **31 J4**
Ujjain *India* 23°9N 75°43E **42 H6**
Ujung Pandang *Indonesia* 5°10S 119°20E **37 F5**
Uka *Russia* 57°50N 162°0E **29 D17**
Ukara I. *Tanzania* 1°50S 33°0E **54 C3**
Uke-Shima *Japan* 28°2N 129°14E **31 K4**
Ukerewe I. *Tanzania* 2°0S 33°0E **54 C3**
Ukhrul *India* 25°10N 94°25E **41 G19**
Ukhta *Russia* 63°34N 53°41E **18 B9**
Ukiah *U.S.A.* 39°9N 123°13W **78 F3**
Ukmergė *Lithuania* 55°15N 24°45E **9 J21**
Ukraine ■ *Europe* 49°0N 32°0E **19 E5**
Ukwi *Botswana* 23°29S 20°30E **56 C3**
Ulaan-Uul *Mongolia* 44°13N 111°10E **34 B6**
Ulaanbaatar *Mongolia* 47°55N 106°53E **32 B5**
Ulaangom *Mongolia* 50°5N 92°10E **32 A4**
Ulaanjirem *Mongolia* 45°5N 105°30E **34 B3**
Ulak I. *U.S.A.* 51°22N 178°57W **74 E4**
Ulamba
  Dem. Rep. of the Congo 9°3S 23°38E **55 D1**
Ulan Bator = Ulaanbaatar
  Mongolia 47°55N 106°53E **32 B5**
Ulan Ude *Russia* 51°45N 107°40E **29 D11**
Ulanhad = Chifeng
  China 42°18N 118°58E **35 C10**
Ulaya *Morogoro, Tanzania* 7°3S 36°55E **54 D4**
Ulaya *Tabora, Tanzania* 4°25S 33°30E **54 C3**
Ulcinj *Montenegro* 41°58N 19°10E **23 D8**
Ulco *S. Africa* 28°21S 24°15E **56 D3**
Ule älv = Oulujoki →
  Finland 65°1N 25°30E **8 D21**
Ule träsk = Oulujärvi
  Finland 64°25N 27°15E **8 D22**
Uleåborg = Oulu *Finland* 65°1N 25°29E **8 D21**
Ulefoss *Norway* 59°17N 9°16E **9 G13**
Ulhasnagar *India* 19°15N 73°10E **40 K8**
Uliastay *Mongolia* 47°56N 97°28E **32 B4**
Uljin *S. Korea* 36°59N 129°24E **35 F15**
Ulladulla *Australia* 35°21S 150°29E **63 F5**
Ullapool *U.K.* 57°54N 5°9W **11 D3**
Ulleungdo *S. Korea* 37°30N 130°30E **35 F16**
Ullswater *Canada* 45°12N 79°29W **82 A5**
Ullswater *U.K.* 54°34N 2°52W **12 C5**
Ulm *Germany* 48°23N 9°58E **16 D5**
Ulmarra *Australia* 29°37S 153°4E **63 D5**
Ulonguè *Mozam.* 14°37S 34°19E **55 E3**
Ulricehamn *Sweden* 57°46N 13°26E **9 H15**
Ulsan *S. Korea* 35°20N 129°15E **35 G15**
Ulsta *U.K.* 60°30N 1°9W **11 A7**
Ulster ☐ *U.K.* 54°35N 6°30W **10 B5**
Ulubat Gölü *Turkey* 40°9N 28°35E **23 D13**
Uludağ *Turkey* 40°4N 29°13E **23 D13**
Uluguru Mts. *Tanzania* 7°15S 37°40E **54 D4**
Ulungur He → *China* 47°1N 87°24E **32 B3**
Ulungur Hu *China* 47°20N 87°16E **32 B3**
Uluru *Australia* 25°23S 131°5E **61 E5**
Uluru-Kata Tjuta △
  Australia 25°19S 131°1E **61 E5**
Ulutau *Kazakhstan* 48°39N 67°1E **28 E7**
Uluwatu *Indonesia* 8°50S 115°5E **37 K18**
Ulva *U.K.* 56°29N 6°13W **11 E2**
Ulverston *U.K.* 54°13N 3°5W **12 C4**
Ulverstone *Australia* 41°11S 146°11E **63 G4**
Ulya *Russia* 59°10N 142°0E **29 D15**
Ulyanovsk *Russia* 54°20N 48°25E **18 D8**
Ulyasutay = Uliastay
  Mongolia 47°56N 97°28E **32 B4**
Ulysses *Kans., U.S.A.* 37°35N 101°22W **80 G3**
Ulysses *Pa., U.S.A.* 41°54N 77°46W **82 E7**
Ulysses, Mt. *Canada* 57°20N 124°5W **70 B4**
Umala *Bolivia* 17°25S 68°5W **92 G5**
'Umān = Oman ■ *Asia* 23°0N 58°0E **47 C6**
Uman *Ukraine* 48°40N 30°12E **17 D16**
Umaria *India* 23°35N 80°50E **43 H9**
Umarkot *Pakistan* 25°15N 69°40E **42 G3**
Umarpada *India* 21°27N 73°28E **42 J5**
Umatilla *U.S.A.* 45°55N 119°21W **76 D4**
Umba *Russia* 66°42N 34°11E **18 A5**
Umbagog L. *U.S.A.* 44°46N 71°3W **83 B13**
Umbakumba *Australia* 13°47S 136°50E **62 A2**
Umbrella Mts. *N.Z.* 45°35S 169°5E **59 F2**
Umeå *Sweden* 63°45N 20°20E **8 E19**
Umeälven → *Sweden* 63°45N 20°20E **8 E19**
Umera *Indonesia* 0°12S 129°37E **37 E7**
Umfuli → *Zimbabwe* 17°30S 29°23E **55 F2**
Umfurudzi ☐ *Zimbabwe* 17°6S 31°40E **55 F3**
Umgusa *Zimbabwe* 19°29S 27°52E **55 F2**
Umgwenya → *Mozam.* 25°14S 32°18E **57 D5**
Umiujaq *Canada* 56°33N 76°33W **72 A4**
Umkomaas *S. Africa* 30°13S 30°48E **57 E5**
Umlazi *S. Africa* 29°59S 30°54E **53 L6**
Umm ad Daraj, J. *Jordan* 32°18N 35°48E **46 C4**
Umm al Qaywayn
  U.A.E. 25°30N 55°35E **45 E7**
Umm al Qittayn *Jordan* 32°18N 36°40E **46 C5**
Umm Bāb *Qatar* 25°12N 50°48E **45 E6**

Umm Durman = Omdurmân
  Sudan 15°40N 32°28E **51 E12**
Umm el Fahm *Israel* 32°31N 35°9E **46 C4**
Umm Keddada *Sudan* 13°33N 26°35E **51 F11**
Umm Lajj *Si. Arabia* 25°0N 37°23E **44 E3**
Umm Qasr *Iraq* 30°1N 47°58E **44 D5**
Umm Ruwaba *Sudan* 12°50N 31°20E **51 F12**
Umnak I. *U.S.A.* 53°15N 168°20W **74 E6**
Umniati → *Zimbabwe* 16°49S 28°45E **55 F2**
Umpqua → *U.S.A.* 43°40N 124°12W **76 E1**
Umreth *India* 22°41N 73°4E **42 H5**
Umtata = Mthatha
  S. Africa 31°36S 28°49E **57 E4**
Umuarama *Brazil* 23°45S 53°20W **95 A5**
Umvukwe Ra. *Zimbabwe* 16°45S 30°45E **55 F3**
Umvutyu *S. Africa* 31°38S 29°33E **57 E4**
Umzingwane →
  Zimbabwe 22°12S 29°56E **55 G2**
Umzinto = eMuziwezinto
  S. Africa 30°15S 30°45E **57 E5**
Una *India* 20°46N 71°8E **42 J4**
Una *Bos.-H.* 45°0N 16°20E **16 F9**
Unadilla *U.S.A.* 42°20N 75°19W **83 D9**
Unalakleet *U.S.A.* 63°52N 160°47W **74 C7**
Unalaska *U.S.A.* 53°53N 166°32W **74 E6**
Unalaska I. *U.S.A.* 53°35N 166°50W **74 E6**
'Unayzah *Si. Arabia* 26°6N 43°58E **44 E4**
'Unayzah, J. *Asia* 32°12N 39°18E **44 C3**
Uncia *Bolivia* 18°25S 66°40W **92 G5**
Uncompahgre Peak
  U.S.A. 38°4N 107°28W **76 G10**
Uncompahgre Plateau
  U.S.A. 38°20N 108°15W **76 G9**
Undara Volcanic △
  Australia 18°14S 144°41E **62 B3**
Underbool *Australia* 35°10S 141°51E **63 F3**
Underwood *Canada* 44°18N 81°29W **82 B3**
Ungarie *Australia* 33°38S 146°56E **63 E4**
Ungarra *Australia* 34°12S 136°2E **63 E2**
Ungava, Pén. d' *Canada* 60°0N 74°0W **69 F17**
Ungava B. *Canada* 59°30N 67°30W **69 F18**
Ungeny = Ungheni
  Moldova 47°11N 27°51E **17 E14**
Unggi *N. Korea* 42°16N 130°28E **35 C16**
Ungheni *Moldova* 47°11N 27°51E **17 E14**
Ungwana B. *Kenya* 2°45S 40°20E **54 C5**
União da Vitória *Brazil* 26°13S 51°5W **95 B5**
Unimak I. *U.S.A.* 54°45N 164°0W **74 E7**
Unimak Pass. *U.S.A.* 54°15N 164°30W **74 E7**
Union *Miss., U.S.A.* 32°34N 89°7W **85 E10**
Union *Mo., U.S.A.* 38°27N 91°0W **80 F8**
Union *S.C., U.S.A.* 34°43N 81°37W **85 D14**
Union City *Calif., U.S.A.* 37°36N 122°1W **78 H4**
Union City *N.J., U.S.A.* 40°45N 74°2W **83 F10**
Union City *Pa., U.S.A.* 41°54N 79°51W **82 E5**
Union City *Tenn., U.S.A.* 36°26N 89°3W **85 C10**
Union Dale *U.S.A.* 41°43N 75°29W **83 E9**
Union Gap *U.S.A.* 46°33N 120°28W **76 C3**
Union Springs *Ala.,*
  U.S.A. 32°9N 85°43W **85 E12**
Union Springs *N.Y.,*
  U.S.A. 42°50N 76°41W **83 D8**
Uniondale *S. Africa* 33°39S 23°7E **56 E3**
Uniontown *U.S.A.* 39°54N 79°44W **81 F14**
Unionville *U.S.A.* 40°29N 93°1W **80 E7**
United Arab Emirates ■
  Asia 23°50N 54°0E **45 F7**
United Kingdom ■ *Europe* 53°0N 2°0W **14 E6**
United States of America ■
  N. Amer. 37°0N 96°0W **75 H20**
Unity *Canada* 52°30N 109°5W **71 C7**
University Park
  U.S.A. 32°17N 106°45W **77 K10**
University Place *U.S.A.* 47°14N 122°33W **78 C4**
Unjha *India* 23°46N 72°24E **42 H5**
Unnao *India* 26°35N 80°30E **43 F9**
Unsengedsi → *Zimbabwe* 15°43S 31°14E **55 F3**
Unst *U.K.* 60°44N 0°53W **11 A8**
Unuk → *Canada* 56°5N 131°3W **70 B2**
Unzen-Amakusa △
  Japan 32°15N 130°10E **31 H5**
Uozu *Japan* 36°48N 137°24E **31 F8**
Upata *Venezuela* 8°1N 62°24W **92 B6**
Upemba, L.
  Dem. Rep. of the Congo 8°30S 26°20E **55 D2**
Upemba △
  Dem. Rep. of the Congo 9°0S 26°35E **55 D2**
Upernavik *Greenland* 72°49N 56°20W **4 B5**
Upington *S. Africa* 28°25S 21°15E **56 D3**
Upleta *India* 21°46N 70°16E **42 J4**
'Upolu *Samoa* 13°58S 172°0W **59 b**
Upper Alkali L. *U.S.A.* 41°47N 120°8W **76 F3**
Upper Arrow L. *Canada* 50°30N 117°50W **70 C5**
Upper Daly ✪ *Australia* 14°26S 131°3E **60 B5**
Upper Darby *U.S.A.* 39°55N 75°16W **81 F16**
Upper Foster L. *Canada* 56°47N 105°20W **71 B7**
Upper Hutt *N.Z.* 41°8S 175°5E **59 D5**
Upper Klamath L.
  U.S.A. 42°25N 121°55W **76 E3**
Upper Lake *U.S.A.* 39°10N 122°54W **78 F4**
Upper Liard *Canada* 60°3N 128°54W **70 A3**
Upper Manzanilla
  Trin. & Tob. 10°31N 61°4W **93 K15**
Upper Missouri Breaks
  U.S.A. 47°50N 109°55W **76 C9**
Upper Musquodoboit
  Canada 45°10N 62°58W **73 C7**
Upper Red L. *U.S.A.* 48°8N 94°45W **80 A6**
Upper Sandusky
  U.S.A. 40°50N 83°17W **81 E12**
Upper Volta = Burkina Faso ■
  Africa 12°0N 1°0W **50 F5**
Uppland *Sweden* 59°59N 17°48E **9 G17**
Uppsala *Sweden* 59°53N 17°38E **9 G17**
Upshi *India* 33°48N 77°52E **43 C7**
Upton *U.S.A.* 44°6N 104°38W **76 D11**
Uqsuqtuuq = Gjoa Haven
  Canada 68°38N 95°53W **68 D12**
Ur *Iraq* 30°55N 46°25E **44 D5**

Urad Qianqi China 40°40N 108°30E 34 D5
Urakawa Japan 42°9N 142°47E 30 C11
Ural = Uralskiy □ Russia 64°0N 70°0E 28 C7
Ural = Zhayyq ➤
  Kazakhstan 47°0N 51°48E 19 E9
Ural Australia 33°21S 146°12E 63 E4
Ural Mts. = Uralskie Gory
  Eurasia 60°0N 59°0E 18 C10
Uralla Australia 30°37S 151°29E 63 E5
Uralsk = Oral Kazakhstan 51°20N 51°20E 19 D9
Uralskie Gory Eurasia 60°0N 59°0E 18 C10
Uralskiy □ Russia 64°0N 70°0E 28 C7
Urambo Tanzania 5°4S 32°0E 54 D3
Urandangi Australia 21°32S 138°14E 62 C2
Uranium City Canada 59°34N 108°37W 71 B7
Urapuntja = Utopia
  Australia 22°14S 134°33E 62 C1
Uraricoera ➤ Brazil 3°2N 60°30W 92 C6
Urasoe Japan 26°15N 127°43E 31 L3
Urawa = Saitama Japan 35°54N 139°38E 31 G9
Uray Russia 60°5N 65°15E 28 C7
'Uray'irah Si. Arabia 25°57N 48°53E 45 E6
Urbana Ill., U.S.A. 40°7N 88°12W 80 E9
Urbana Ohio, U.S.A. 40°7N 83°45W 81 E12
Urbandale U.S.A. 41°38N 93°43W 80 E7
Urbino Italy 43°43N 12°38E 22 C5
Urbión, Picos de Spain 42°1N 2°52W 21 A4
Urcos Peru 13°40S 71°38W 92 F4
Urdinarrain Argentina 32°37S 58°52W 94 C4
Ure ➤ U.K. 54°5N 1°20W 12 C6
Urengoy Russia 65°58N 78°22E 28 C8
Ures Mexico 29°26N 110°24W 86 B2
Urewera △ N.Z. 38°29S 177°7E 59 C6
Urfa = Sanliurfa Turkey 37°12N 38°50E 44 B3
Urganch Uzbekistan 41°40N 60°41E 28 E7
Urgench = Urganch
  Uzbekistan 41°40N 60°41E 28 E7
Ürgüp Turkey 38°38N 34°56E 44 B2
Uri India 34°8N 74°2E 43 B6
Uribia Colombia 11°43N 72°16W 92 A4
Uriondo Bolivia 21°41S 64°41W 94 A3
Urique Mexico 27°13N 107°55W 86 B3
Urique ➤ Mexico 26°29N 107°58W 86 B3
Urk Neths. 52°39N 5°36E 15 B5
Urla Turkey 38°20N 26°47E 23 E12
Urmia = Orūmīyeh Iran 37°40N 45°0E 44 B5
Uroševac Kosovo 42°23N 21°10E 23 C9
Uroyan, Montanas de
  Puerto Rico 18°12N 67°0W 89 d
Urrampinyi Iltjiltarri ☼
  Australia 24°20S 132°10E 60 D5
Uruaçu Brazil 14°30S 49°10W 93 F9
Uruapan Mexico 19°24N 102°3W 86 D4
Urubamba ➤ Peru 10°43S 73°48W 92 F4
Urucará Brazil 2°32S 57°45W 92 D7
Uruçuí Brazil 7°20S 44°28W 93 E10
Uruguai ➤ Brazil 26°0S 53°30W 95 B5
Uruguaiana Brazil 29°50S 57°0W 94 B4
Uruguay ■ S. Amer. 32°30S 56°30W 94 C4
Uruguay ➤ S. Amer. 34°12S 58°18W 94 C4
Urumchi = Ürümqi
  China 43°45N 87°45E 32 B3
Ürümqi China 43°45N 87°45E 32 B3
Uruna ☼ Australia 24°3S 133°1E 60 D5
Urup, Ostrov Russia 46°0N 151°0E 29 E16
Ürzhar Kazakhstan 47°5N 81°38E 28 E9
Usa ➤ Russia 66°16N 59°49E 18 A10
Uşak Turkey 38°43N 29°28E 19 G4
Usakos Namibia 21°54S 15°31E 56 C2
Usedom Germany 53°55N 14°2E 16 B8
Useless Loop Australia 26°8S 113°23E 61 E1
Ushakova, Ostrov Russia 82°0N 80°0E 29 A8
Ushant = Ouessant, Î. d'
  France 48°28N 5°6W 20 B1
Ushashi Tanzania 1°59S 33°57E 54 C3
'Ushayrah Si. Arabia 25°35N 45°47E 44 E5
Ushibuka Japan 32°11N 130°1E 31 H5
Üshtöbe Kazakhstan 45°16N 78°0E 28 E8
Ushuaia Argentina 54°50S 68°23W 96 G3
Ushumun Russia 52°47N 126°32E 29 D13
Usinsk Russia 65°57N 57°27E 18 A10
Usk Canada 54°38N 128°26W 70 C3
Usk ➤ U.K. 51°33N 2°58W 13 F5
Uska India 27°12N 83°7E 43 F10
Usman Russia 52°5N 39°48E 18 D6
Usoke Tanzania 5°8S 32°24E 54 D3
Usolye-Sibirskoye
  Russia 52°48N 103°40E 29 D11
Uspallata, P. de
  Argentina 32°37S 69°22W 94 C2
Ussuriysk Russia 43°48N 131°59E 30 C5
Ussurka Russia 45°12N 133°31E 30 B6
Ust-Chaun Russia 68°47N 170°30E 29 C18
Ust-Ilimsk Russia 58°3N 102°39E 29 D11
Ust-Ishim Russia 57°45N 71°10E 28 D8
Ust-Kamchatsk Russia 56°10N 162°28E 29 D17
Ust-Kamenogorsk = Öskemen
  Kazakhstan 50°0N 82°36E 28 E9
Ust-Khayryuzovo
  Russia 57°15N 156°45E 29 D16
Ust-Kut Russia 56°50N 105°42E 29 D11
Ust-Kuyga Russia 70°1N 135°43E 29 B14
Ust-Maya Russia 60°30N 134°28E 29 C14
Ust-Mil Russia 59°40N 133°11E 29 C14
Ust-Nera Russia 64°35N 143°15E 29 C15
Ust-Nyukzha Russia 56°34N 121°37E 29 D13
Ust-Olenek Russia 73°0N 120°5E 29 B12
Ust-Omchug Russia 61°9N 149°38E 29 C15
Ust-Port Russia 69°40N 84°26E 28 C9
Ust-Tsilma Russia 65°28N 52°11E 18 A9
Ust-Urt = Ustyurt Plateau
  Asia 44°0N 55°0E 28 E6
Ust-Usa Russia 66°2N 56°57E 18 A10
Ust-Vorkuta Russia 67°24N 64°0E 28 C7
Ústí nad Labem Czech Rep. 50°41N 14°3E 16 C8
Ústica Italy 38°42N 13°11E 22 E5
Ustinov = Izhevsk
  Russia 56°51N 53°14E 18 C9
Ustyurt Plateau Asia 44°0N 55°0E 28 E6

Usu China 44°27N 84°40E 32 B3
Usuki Japan 33°8N 131°49E 31 H5
Usulután El Salv. 13°25N 88°28W 88 D2
Usumacinta ➤ Mexico 18°24N 92°38W 87 D6
Usumbura = Bujumbura
  Burundi 3°16S 29°18E 54 C2
Usure Tanzania 4°40S 34°22E 54 C3
Usutuo ➤ Mozam. 26°48S 32°7E 57 D5
Uta Indonesia 4°33S 136°0E 37 E9
Utah □ U.S.A. 39°20N 111°30W 76 G8
Utah L. U.S.A. 40°12N 111°48W 76 F8
Utara, Selat Malaysia 5°28N 100°20E 39 c
Utarni India 26°5N 71°58E 42 F4
Uatlan Guatemala 15°2N 91°11W 88 C1
Ute Creek ➤ U.S.A. 35°21N 103°50W 77 J12
Utena Lithuania 55°27N 25°40E 9 J21
Utete Tanzania 8°0S 38°45E 54 D4
Uthai Thani Thailand 15°22N 100°3E 38 E3
Uthal Pakistan 25°44N 66°40E 42 G2
Utiariti Brazil 13°0S 58°10W 92 F7
Utica N.Y., U.S.A. 43°6N 75°14W 83 C9
Utica Ohio, U.S.A. 40°14N 82°27W 82 F2
Utikuma L. Canada 55°50N 115°30W 70 B5
Utila Honduras 16°6N 86°56W 88 C2
Utopia Australia 22°14S 134°33E 62 C1
Utraula India 27°19N 82°25E 43 F10
Utrecht Neths. 52°5N 5°8E 15 B5
Utrecht S. Africa 27°38S 30°20E 57 D5
Utrecht □ Neths. 52°6N 5°7E 15 B5
Utrera Spain 37°12N 5°48W 21 D3
Utsjoki ➤ Finland 69°51N 26°59E 8 B22
Utsunomiya Japan 36°30N 139°50E 31 F9
Uttar Pradesh □ India 27°0N 80°0E 43 F9
Uttaradit Thailand 17°36N 100°5E 38 D3
Uttarakhand □ India 30°0N 79°30E 43 D8
Utterson Canada 45°12N 79°19W 82 A5
Uttoxeter U.K. 52°54N 1°52W 12 E6
Utuado Puerto Rico 18°16N 66°42W 89 d
Uummannaq Avannaarsua,
  Greenland 77°33N 68°52W 69 B18
Uummannaq Kitaa,
  Greenland 70°58N 52°17W 4 B5
Uummannarsuaq = Nunap Isua
  Greenland 59°48N 43°55W 66 D15
Uusikaarlepyy Finland 63°32N 22°31E 8 E20
Uusikaupunki Finland 60°47N 21°25E 8 F19
Uva Russia 56°59N 52°13E 18 C9
Uvalde U.S.A. 29°13N 99°47W 84 G5
Uvat Russia 59°5N 68°50E 28 D7
Uvinza Tanzania 5°5S 30°24E 54 D3
Uvira Dem. Rep. of the Congo 3°22S 29°3E 54 C2
Uvs Nuur Mongolia 50°20N 92°30E 32 A4
'Uwairidh, Ḥarrat al
  Si. Arabia 26°50N 38°0E 44 E3
Uwajima Japan 33°10N 132°35E 31 H6
Uwanda △ Tanzania 7°46S 32°0E 54 D3
Uweinat, Jebel Sudan 21°54N 24°58E 51 D10
Uxbridge Canada 44°6N 79°7W 82 B5
Uxin Qi China 38°50N 109°5E 34 E5
Uxmal Mexico 20°22N 89°46W 87 C7
Üydzin Mongolia 44°9N 107°0E 34 B4
Uyo Nigeria 5°1N 7°53E 50 G7
Uyûn Mûsa Egypt 29°53N 32°40E 46 F1
Uyuni Bolivia 20°28S 66°47W 92 H5
Uzbekistan ■ Asia 41°30N 65°0E 28 E7
Uzboy ➤ Turkmenistan 39°30N 55°0E 45 B7
Uzen, Bolshoi = Uzen, Mal ➤
  Kazakhstan 49°4N 49°44E 19 E8
Uzen, Mal ➤ Kazakhstan 49°4N 49°44E 19 E8
Uzerche France 45°25N 1°34E 20 D4
Uzh ➤ Ukraine 51°15N 30°12E 17 C16
Uzhgorod = Uzhhorod
  Ukraine 48°36N 22°18E 17 D12
Uzhhorod Ukraine 48°36N 22°18E 17 D12
Užice Serbia 43°55N 19°50E 23 C8
Uzunköprü Turkey 41°16N 26°43E 23 D12

V

Vaal ➤ S. Africa 29°4S 23°38E 56 D3
Vaal Dam S. Africa 27°0S 28°14E 57 D4
Vaalbos △ S. Africa 28°22S 24°20E 56 D3
Vaalwater S. Africa 24°15S 28°8E 57 C4
Vaasa Finland 63°6N 21°38E 8 E19
Vác Hungary 47°49N 19°10E 17 E10
Vacaria Brazil 28°31S 50°52W 95 B5
Vacata Fiji 17°15S 179°31W 59 a
Vacaville U.S.A. 38°21N 121°59W 78 G5
Vach = Vakh ➤ Russia 60°45N 76°45E 28 C8
Vache, Î. à Haiti 18°2N 73°35W 89 C5
Vacoas Mauritius 20°18S 57°29E 53 d
Vadakara = Badagara
  India 11°35N 75°40E 40 P9
Vadnagar India 23°47N 72°40E 42 H5
Vadodara India 22°20N 73°10E 42 H5
Vadsø Norway 70°3N 29°50E 8 A23
Vaduz Liech. 47°8N 9°31E 20 C8
Værøy Norway 67°40N 12°40E 8 C15
Vágar Færoe Is. 62°5N 7°15W 8 E9
Vagia, Akra Greece 36°15N 28°11E 25 C10
Vågsfjorden Norway 68°50N 16°50E 8 B17
Váh ➤ Slovak Rep. 47°43N 18°7E 17 D9
Vahsel B. Antarctica 75°0S 35°0W 5 D1
Váhtjer = Gällivare
  Sweden 67°9N 20°40E 8 C19
Vaï Greece 35°15N 26°18E 25 D8
Vaihiria, L. Tahiti 17°40S 149°25W 59 d
Vail U.S.A. 39°40N 106°20W 75 H18
Vairao Tahiti 17°47S 149°17W 59 d
Vaisali ➤ India 26°28N 78°53E 43 F8
Vaitogi Amer. Samoa 14°24S 170°44W 59 b
Vakh ➤ Russia 60°45N 76°45E 28 C8
Val-d'Or Canada 48°7N 77°47W 72 C4
Val Marie Canada 49°15N 107°45W 71 D7
Valaam Russia 61°22N 30°57E 8 F24
Valahia Romania 44°35N 25°0E 17 F13
Valandovo Macedonia 41°19N 22°34E 23 D10
Valatie U.S.A. 42°24N 73°40W 83 D11

Valcheta Argentina 40°40S 66°8W 96 E3
Valdai Hills = Valdayskaya
  Vozvyshennost 57°0N 33°30E 18 C5
Valdayskaya Vozvyshennost
  Russia 57°0N 33°30E 18 C5
Valdepeñas Spain 38°43N 3°25W 21 C4
Valdés, Pen. Argentina 42°30S 63°45W 96 E4
Valdez U.S.A. 61°7N 146°16W 68 F2
Valdivia Chile 39°50S 73°14W 96 D2
Valdivia Abyssal Plain
  S. Ocean 62°30S 70°0E 5 C6
Valdosta U.S.A. 30°50N 83°17W 85 F13
Valdres Norway 61°5N 9°5E 8 F13
Vale U.S.A. 43°59N 117°15W 76 E5
Vale of Glamorgan □
  U.K. 51°28N 3°25W 13 F4
Valemount Canada 52°50N 119°15W 70 C5
Valença Brazil 13°20S 39°5W 93 F11
Valença do Piauí Brazil 6°20S 41°45W 93 E10
Valence France 44°57N 4°54E 20 D6
Valencia Spain 39°27N 0°23W 21 C5
Valencia Trin. & Tob. 10°39N 61°11W 93 K15
Valencia U.S.A. 34°48N 106°43W 77 J10
Valencia Venezuela 10°11N 68°0W 92 A5
Valencia □ Spain 39°20N 0°40W 21 C5
Valencia, G. de Spain 39°30N 0°20E 21 C6
Valencia de Alcántara
  Spain 39°25N 7°14W 21 C2
Valencia I. Ireland 51°54N 10°22W 10 E1
Valenciennes France 50°20N 3°34E 20 A5
Valentim, Sa. do Brazil 6°0S 43°30W 93 E10
Valentin Russia 43°8N 134°17E 30 C7
Valentine Nebr., U.S.A. 42°52N 100°33W 80 D3
Valentine Tex., U.S.A. 30°35N 104°30W 84 F2
Valera Venezuela 9°19N 70°37W 92 B4
Valga Estonia 57°47N 26°2E 9 H22
Valier U.S.A. 48°18N 112°16W 76 B7
Valjevo Serbia 44°18N 19°53E 23 B8
Valka Latvia 57°46N 26°3E 9 H22
Valkeakoski Finland 61°16N 24°2E 8 F21
Valkenswaard Neths. 51°21N 5°29E 15 C5
Vall de Uxó = La Vall d'Uixó
  Spain 39°49N 0°15W 21 C5
Valladolid Mexico 20°41N 88°12W 87 C7
Valladolid Spain 41°38N 4°43W 21 B3
Valldemossa Spain 39°43N 2°37E 24 B9
Valle de la Pascua
  Venezuela 9°13N 66°0W 92 B5
Valle de las Palmas
  Mexico 32°20N 116°43W 79 N10
Valle de Santiago
  Mexico 20°23N 101°12W 86 C4
Valle de Zaragoza
  Mexico 27°25N 105°50W 86 B3
Valle Fértil, Sierra del
  Argentina 30°20S 68°0W 94 C2
Valle Gran Rey Canary Is. 28°5N 17°20W 24 F2
Valle Hermoso Mexico 25°35N 97°40W 87 B5
Valle Nacional Mexico 17°47N 96°18W 87 D5
Valledupar Colombia 10°29N 73°15W 92 A4
Vallehermoso Canary Is. 28°10N 17°15W 24 F2
Vallejo U.S.A. 38°7N 122°14W 78 G4
Vallenar Chile 28°30S 70°50W 94 B1
Valletta Malta 35°54N 14°31E 25 D2
Valley Center U.S.A. 33°13N 117°2W 79 M9
Valley City U.S.A. 46°55N 98°0W 80 B5
Valley Falls Oreg.,
  U.S.A. 42°29N 120°17W 76 E3
Valley Falls R.I., U.S.A. 41°54N 71°24W 83 E13
Valley of Flowers △
  India 30°50N 79°40E 43 D8
Valley Springs U.S.A. 38°12N 120°50W 78 G6
Valley View U.S.A. 40°39N 76°33W 83 F8
Valley Wells U.S.A. 35°27N 115°46W 79 K11
Valleyview Canada 55°5N 117°17W 70 B5
Vallimanca, Arroyo
  Argentina 35°40S 59°10W 94 D4
Valls Spain 41°18N 1°15E 21 B6
Valmiera Latvia 57°37N 25°29E 9 H21
Valognes France 49°30N 1°28W 20 B3
Valona = Vlorë Albania 40°32N 19°28E 23 D8
Valozhyn Belarus 54°3N 26°30E 17 A14
Valparaíso Chile 33°2S 71°40W 94 C1
Valparaíso Mexico 22°46N 103°34W 86 C4
Valparaiso U.S.A. 41°28N 87°4W 80 E10
Valparaíso □ Chile 33°2S 71°40W 94 C1
Vals ➤ S. Africa 27°23S 26°30E 56 D4
Vals, Tanjung Indonesia 8°26S 137°25E 37 F9
Valsad India 20°40N 72°58E 40 J8
Valverde Canary Is. 27°48N 17°55W 24 G2
Valverde del Camino
  Spain 37°35N 6°47W 21 D2
Vamizi I. Mozam. 11°2S 40°40E 55 E5
Vammala Finland 61°20N 22°54E 8 F20
Vamos Greece 35°24N 24°13E 25 D6
Van Turkey 38°30N 43°20E 44 B4
Van, L. = Van Gölü
  Turkey 38°30N 43°0E 44 B4
Van Alstyne U.S.A. 33°25N 96°35W 84 E6
Van Blommestein Meer
  Suriname 4°45N 55°0W 93 C7
Van Buren Canada 47°10N 67°55W 73 C6
Van Buren Ark., U.S.A. 35°26N 94°21W 84 D7
Van Buren Maine,
  U.S.A. 47°10N 67°58W 81 B20
Van Buren Mo., U.S.A. 37°0N 90°52W 80 G9
Van Canh Vietnam 13°37N 109°0E 38 F7
Van Diemen, C. N. Terr.,
  Australia 11°9S 130°24E 60 B5
Van Diemen, C. Queens.,
  Australia 16°30S 139°46E 62 B2
Van Diemen G. Australia 11°45S 132°0E 60 B5
Van Gölü Turkey 38°30N 43°0E 44 B4
Van Horn U.S.A. 31°3N 104°50W 84 F3
Van Ninh Vietnam 12°42N 109°14E 38 F7
Van Rees, Pegunungan
  Indonesia 2°35S 138°15E 37 E9
Van Wert U.S.A. 40°52N 84°35W 81 E11
Van Yen Vietnam 21°4N 104°42E 38 B5

Van Zylsrus S. Africa 26°52S 22°4E 56 D3
Vanadzor Armenia 40°48N 44°30E 19 F7
Vanavara Russia 60°22N 102°16E 29 C11
Vancouver Canada 49°15N 123°7W 78 A3
Vancouver U.S.A. 45°38N 122°40W 78 E4
Vancouver, C. Australia 35°2S 118°11E 61 G2
Vancouver I. Canada 49°50N 126°0W 78 B2
Vancouver Int. ✈ (YVR)
  Canada 49°10N 123°10W 78 A3
Vanda = Vantaa Finland 60°18N 24°56E 9 F21
Vandalia Ill., U.S.A. 38°58N 89°6W 80 F9
Vandalia Mo., U.S.A. 39°19N 91°29W 80 F8
Vandenberg Village
  U.S.A. 34°43N 120°28W 79 L6
Vandergrift U.S.A. 40°36N 79°34W 82 F5
Vanderhoof Canada 54°0N 124°0W 70 C4
Vanderkloof Dam
  S. Africa 30°4S 24°40E 56 E3
Vanderlin I. Australia 15°44S 137°2E 62 B2
Vänern Sweden 58°47N 13°30E 9 G15
Vänersborg Sweden 58°26N 12°19E 9 G15
Vang Vieng Laos 18°58N 102°32E 38 C4
Vanga Kenya 4°35S 39°12E 54 C4
Vangaindrano Madag. 23°21S 47°36E 57 C8
Vanguard Canada 49°55N 107°20W 71 D7
Vanino Russia 48°50N 140°5E 29 E15
Vankleek Hill Canada 45°32N 74°40W 83 A10
Vännäs Sweden 63°58N 19°48E 8 E18
Vannes France 47°40N 2°47W 20 C2
Vannøya Norway 70°6N 19°50E 8 A18
Vanrhynsdorp S. Africa 31°36S 18°44E 56 E2
Vansbro Sweden 60°32N 14°15E 9 F16
Vansittart B. Australia 14°3S 126°17E 60 B4
Vansittart I. Canada 65°50N 84°0W 69 D15
Vantaa Finland 60°18N 24°56E 9 F21
Vanua Balavu Fiji 17°12S 178°55W 59 a
Vanua Levu Fiji 16°33S 179°15E 59 a
Vanua Vatu Fiji 18°22S 179°15W 59 a
Vanuatu ■ Pac. Oc. 15°0S 168°0E 58 C9
Vanwyksvlei S. Africa 30°18S 21°49E 56 E3
Vapnyarka Ukraine 48°32N 28°45E 17 D15
Var □ France 43°39N 7°12E 20 E7
Var ➤ France 43°39N 7°12E 20 E7
Varāmīn Iran 35°20N 51°39E 45 C6
Varāmīn □ Iran 35°18N 51°35E 45 B6
Varanasi India 25°22N 83°0E 43 G10
Varangerfjorden Norway 70°3N 29°25E 8 A23
Varangerhalvøya
  Norway 70°25N 29°30E 8 A23
Varaždin Croatia 46°20N 16°20E 16 E9
Varberg Sweden 57°6N 12°20E 9 H15
Vardak □ Afghan. 34°0N 68°0E 40 B6
Vardar = Axios ➤
  Greece 40°57N 22°35E 23 D10
Varde Denmark 55°38N 8°29E 9 J13
Vardø Norway 70°23N 31°5E 8 A24
Varella, Mui Vietnam 12°54N 109°26E 38 F7
Varena Lithuania 54°12N 24°30E 9 J21
Varese Italy 45°48N 8°50E 20 D8
Varginha Brazil 21°33S 45°25W 95 A6
Varillas Chile 24°0S 70°10W 94 A1
Varkaus Finland 62°19N 27°50E 8 E22
Varna Bulgaria 43°13N 27°56E 23 C12
Värnamo Sweden 57°10N 14°3E 9 H16
Vars Canada 45°21N 75°21W 83 A9
Varysburg U.S.A. 42°46N 78°19W 82 D6
Varzaneh Iran 32°25N 52°40E 45 C7
Vasa = Vaasa Finland 63°6N 21°38E 8 E19
Vasa Barris ➤ Brazil 11°10S 37°10W 93 F11
Vascongadas = País Vasco □
  Spain 42°50N 2°45W 21 A4
Vasht = Khāsh Iran 28°15N 61°15E 45 D9
Vasilevichi Belarus 52°15N 29°50E 17 B15
Vasilkov = Vasylkiv
  Ukraine 50°7N 30°15E 17 C16
Vaslui Romania 46°38N 27°42E 17 E14
Vassar Canada 49°10N 95°55W 71 D9
Vassar U.S.A. 43°22N 83°35W 81 D12
Västerås Sweden 59°37N 16°38E 9 G17
Västerbotten Sweden 64°36N 20°4E 8 D19
Västerdalälven ➤ Sweden 60°30N 14°7E 8 F16
Västervik Sweden 57°43N 16°33E 9 H17
Västmanland Sweden 59°45N 16°20E 9 G17
Vasto Italy 42°8N 14°40E 22 C6
Vasylkiv Ukraine 50°7N 30°15E 17 C16
Vatersay U.K. 56°55N 7°32W 11 E1
Vati Greece 36°3N 27°53E 25 C9
Vatican City ■ Europe 41°54N 12°27E 22 D5
Vatili Cyprus 35°6N 33°40E 25 D12
Vatiu = Atiu Cook Is. 20°0S 158°10W 65 J12
Vatnajökull Iceland 64°30N 16°48W 8 D5
Vatolakkos Greece 35°27N 23°53E 25 D5
Vatoloha Madag. 17°52S 47°48E 57 B8
Vatomandry Madag. 19°20S 48°59E 57 B8
Vatra-Dornei Romania 47°22N 25°22E 17 E13
Vatrak ➤ India 23°9N 73°2E 42 H5
Vättern Sweden 58°25N 14°30E 9 G16
Vatu Vara Fiji 17°26S 179°31W 59 a
Vatulele Fiji 18°33S 177°37E 59 a
Vaudreuil-Dorion
  Canada 45°23N 74°3W 83 A10
Vaughn Mont., U.S.A. 47°33N 111°33W 76 C8
Vaughn N. Mex.,
  U.S.A. 34°36N 105°13W 77 J11
Vaujours L. Canada 55°27N 74°15W 72 A5
Vaupés = Uaupés ➤
  Brazil 0°2N 67°16W 92 C5
Vaupés □ Colombia 1°0N 71°0W 92 C4
Vauxhall Canada 50°5N 112°9W 70 C6
Vav India 24°22N 71°31E 42 G4
Vavatenina Madag. 17°28S 49°12E 57 B8
Vava'u Tonga 18°36S 174°0W 59 c
Vava'u Group Tonga 18°40S 174°0W 59 c
Vawkavysk Belarus 53°9N 24°30E 17 B13
Växjö Sweden 56°52N 14°50E 9 H16
Vaygach, Ostrov Russia 70°0N 60°0E 28 C7

Vedia Argentina 34°30S 61°31W 94 C3
Veendam Neths. 53°5N 6°52E 15 A6
Veenendaal Neths. 52°2N 5°34E 15 B5
Vefsna ➤ Norway 65°48N 13°10E 8 D15
Vega Norway 65°40N 11°55E 8 D14
Vega U.S.A. 35°15N 102°26W 84 D3
Vega Baja Puerto Rico 18°27N 66°23W 89 d
Vegreville Canada 53°30N 112°5W 70 C6
Vejer de la Frontera
  Spain 36°15N 5°59W 21 D3
Vejle Denmark 55°43N 9°30E 9 J13
Velas, C. Costa Rica 10°21N 85°52W 88 D2
Velasco, Sierra de
  Argentina 29°20S 67°10W 94 B2
Velddrif S. Africa 32°42S 18°11E 56 E2
Velebit Planina Croatia 44°50N 15°20E 16 F8
Veles Macedonia 41°46N 21°47E 23 D9
Vélez-Málaga Spain 36°48N 4°5W 21 D3
Vélez Rubio Spain 37°41N 2°5W 21 D4
Velhas ➤ Brazil 17°13S 44°49W 93 G10
Velika Kapela Croatia 45°10N 15°5E 16 F8
Velikaya ➤ Russia 57°48N 28°10E 18 C4
Velikaya Kema Russia 45°30N 137°12E 30 B8
Veliki Ustyug Russia 60°47N 46°20E 18 B8
Velikiye Luki Russia 56°25N 30°32E 18 C5
Veliko Tŭrnovo Bulgaria 43°5N 25°41E 23 C11
Velikonda Range India 14°45N 79°10E 40 M11
Velletri Italy 41°41N 12°47E 22 D5
Vellore India 12°57N 79°10E 40 N11
Velsk Russia 61°10N 42°5E 18 B7
Veluwezoom △ Neths. 52°5N 6°0E 15 B6
Velva U.S.A. 48°4N 100°56W 80 A3
Venado Mexico 22°56N 101°6W 86 C4
Venado Tuerto Argentina 33°50S 62°0W 94 C3
Vendée □ France 46°50N 1°35W 20 C3
Vendôme France 47°47N 1°3E 20 C4
Venézia Italy 45°27N 12°21E 22 B5
Venézia, G. di Italy 45°15N 13°0E 22 B5
Venezuela ■ S. Amer. 8°0N 66°0W 92 B5
Venezuela, G. de
  Venezuela 11°30N 71°0W 92 A4
Vengurla India 15°53N 73°45E 40 M8
Venice = Venézia Italy 45°27N 12°21E 22 B5
Venice U.S.A. 27°6N 82°27W 85 H13
Venkatapuram India 18°20N 80°30E 41 K12
Venlo Neths. 51°22N 6°11E 15 C6
Vennachar Junction
  Canada 45°5N 77°14W 82 A7
Vennesla Norway 58°15N 7°59E 9 G12
Venray Neths. 51°31N 6°0E 15 C6
Ventana, Punta de la
  Mexico 24°4N 109°48W 86 C3
Ventana, Sa. de la
  Argentina 38°0S 62°30W 94 D3
Ventersburg S. Africa 28°7S 27°9E 56 D4
Ventersdorp S. Africa 26°19S 26°48E 56 D4
Venterstad S. Africa 30°47S 25°48E 56 E4
Ventnor U.K. 50°36N 1°12W 13 G6
Ventotène Italy 40°47N 13°25E 22 D5
Ventoux, Mt. France 44°10N 5°17E 20 D6
Ventspils Latvia 57°25N 21°32E 9 H19
Ventuarí ➤ Venezuela 3°58N 67°2W 92 C5
Ventucopa U.S.A. 34°50N 119°29W 79 L7
Ventura U.S.A. 34°17N 119°18W 79 L7
Vénus, Pte. Tahiti 17°29S 149°29W 59 d
Venus B. Australia 38°40S 145°42E 63 F4
Venustiano Carranza
  Mexico 30°25N 115°53W 86 A1
Vera Argentina 29°30S 60°20W 94 B3
Vera Spain 37°15N 1°51W 21 D5
Veracruz Mexico 19°11N 96°8W 87 D5
Veracruz □ Mexico 19°0N 96°15W 87 D5
Veraval India 20°53N 70°27E 42 J4
Verbánia Italy 45°56N 8°33E 20 D8
Vercelli Italy 45°19N 8°25E 20 D8
Verdalsøra Norway 63°48N 11°30E 8 E14
Verde ➤ Argentina 41°56S 65°5W 96 E3
Verde ➤ Goiás, Brazil 18°1S 50°14W 93 G8
Verde ➤ Mato Grosso do Sul,
  Brazil 21°25S 52°20W 93 H8
Verde ➤ Chihuahua,
  Mexico 26°29N 107°58W 86 B3
Verde ➤ Oaxaca, Mexico 15°59N 97°50W 87 D5
Verde ➤ Veracruz,
  Mexico 21°10N 102°50W 86 C4
Verde ➤ Paraguay 23°9S 57°37W 94 A4
Verde, Cay Bahamas 23°0N 75°5W 88 B4
Verden Germany 52°55N 9°14E 16 B5
Verdi U.S.A. 39°31N 119°59W 78 F7
Verdun France 49°9N 5°24E 20 B6
Vereeniging S. Africa 26°38S 27°57E 57 D4
Verga, C. Guinea 10°30N 14°10W 50 F3
Vergara Uruguay 32°56S 53°57W 95 C5
Vergemont Cr. ➤
  Australia 24°16S 143°16E 62 C3
Vergennes U.S.A. 44°10N 73°15W 83 B11
Veria Greece 40°34N 22°12E 23 D10
Verín Spain 41°57N 7°27W 21 B2
Verkhnetulomskoye Vdkhr.
  Russia 68°36N 31°12E 8 B24
Verkhnevilyuysk
  Russia 63°27N 120°18E 29 C13
Verkhniy Baskunchak
  Russia 48°14N 46°44E 19 E8
Verkhoyansk Russia 67°35N 133°25E 29 C14
Verkhoyansk Ra. =
  Verkhoyanskiy Khrebet
  Russia 66°0N 129°0E 29 C13
Verkhoyanskiy Khrebet
  Russia 66°0N 129°0E 29 C13
Vermilion Canada 53°20N 110°50W 71 C6
Vermilion U.S.A. 41°25N 82°22W 82 E2
Vermilion ➤ Canada 53°22N 110°51W 71 C6
Vermilion B. U.S.A. 29°42N 92°0W 84 L9
Vermilion L. U.S.A. 47°53N 92°26W 80 B7
Vermillion U.S.A. 42°47N 96°56W 80 D5
Vermillion ➤ Canada 47°38N 72°56W 72 C5
Vermont □ U.S.A. 44°0N 73°0W 83 C12

Vernadsky *Antarctica* 65°0S 64°0W **5** C17
Vernal *U.S.A.* 40°27N 109°32W **76** F9
Vernalis *U.S.A.* 37°36N 121°17W **78** H5
Verner *Canada* 46°25N 80°8W **72** C3
Verneukpan *S. Africa* 30°0S 21°0E **56** E3
Vernon *Canada* 50°20N 119°15W **70** C5
Vernon *U.S.A.* 34°9N 99°17W **84** D5
Vernonia *U.S.A.* 45°52N 123°11W **78** D2
Vero Beach *U.S.A.* 27°38N 80°24W **85** H14
Véroia = Veria *Greece* 40°34N 22°12E **23** D10
Verona *Canada* 44°29N 76°42W **83** B8
Verona *Italy* 45°27N 10°59E **22** B4
Versailles *France* 48°48N 2°7E **20** B5
Vert, C. *Senegal* 14°45N 17°30W **50** F2
Verulam *S. Africa* 29°38S 31°2E **57** D5
Verviers *Belgium* 50°37N 5°52E **15** D5
Veselovskoye Vdkhr.
  Russia 46°58N 41°25E **19** E7
Vesoul *France* 47°40N 6°11E **20** C7
Vesterålen *Norway* 68°45N 15°0E **8** B16
Vestfjorden *Norway* 67°55N 14°0E **8** C16
Vestmannaeyjar *Iceland* 63°27N 20°15W **8** E3
Vestspitsbergen *Svalbard* 78°40N 17°0E **4** B8
Vestvågøya *Norway* 68°18N 13°50E **8** B15
Vesuvio *Italy* 40°49N 14°26E **22** D6
Vesuvius, Mt. = Vesuvio
  Italy 40°49N 14°26E **22** D6
Veszprém *Hungary* 47°8N 17°57E **17** E9
Vetlanda *Sweden* 57°24N 15°3E **9** H16
Vetlugu → *Russia* 56°36N 46°4E **18** C8
Vettore, Mte. *Italy* 42°49N 13°16E **22** C5
Veurne *Belgium* 51°5N 2°40E **15** C2
Veys *Iran* 31°30N 49°0E **45** D6
Vezhen *Bulgaria* 42°50N 24°20E **23** C11
Vi Thanh *Vietnam* 9°42N 105°26E **39** H5
Viacha *Bolivia* 16°39S 68°18W **92** G5
Viamão *Brazil* 30°5S 51°0W **95** C5
Viana *Brazil* 3°13S 44°55W **93** D10
Viana do Alentejo
  Portugal 38°17N 7°59W **21** C2
Viana do Castelo *Portugal* 41°42N 8°50W **21** B1
Vianden *Lux.* 49°56N 6°12E **15** E6
Viangchan = Vientiane
  Laos 17°58N 102°36E **38** D4
Vianópolis *Brazil* 16°40S 48°35W **93** G9
Vianos *Greece* 35°2N 25°21E **25** D7
Viaréggio *Italy* 43°52N 10°14E **22** C4
Vibo Valéntia *Italy* 38°40N 16°6E **22** E7
Viborg *Denmark* 56°27N 9°23E **9** H13
Vic *Spain* 41°58N 2°19E **21** B7
Vicenza *Italy* 45°33N 11°33E **22** B4
Vich = Vic *Spain* 41°58N 2°19E **21** B7
Vichada → *Colombia* 4°55N 67°50W **92** C5
Vichy *France* 46°9N 3°26E **20** C5
Vicksburg *Ariz.,*
  U.S.A. 33°45N 113°45W **79** M13
Vicksburg *Miss., U.S.A.* 32°21N 90°53W **85** E9
Victor *India* 21°0N 71°30E **42** J4
Victor Harbor *Australia* 35°30S 138°37E **63** F2
Victoria *Argentina* 32°40S 60°10W **94** C3
Victoria *Canada* 48°30N 123°25W **78** B3
Victoria *Chile* 38°13S 72°20W **96** D2
Victoria *China* 22°17N 114°9E **33** G1
Victoria *Malta* 36°3N 14°14E **25** C1
Victoria *Seychelles* 4°38S 55°28E **53** b
Victoria *Kans., U.S.A.* 38°52N 99°9W **80** F4
Victoria □ *U.S.A.* 37°0S 144°0E **63** F3
Victoria → *Australia* 15°10S 129°40E **60** C4
Victoria, Grand L.
  Canada 47°31N 77°30W **72** C4
Victoria, L. *Africa* 1°0S 33°0E **54** C3
Victoria, L. *Australia* 33°57S 141°15E **63** E3
Victoria, Mt. *Burma* 21°14N 93°55E **41** J18
Victoria Beach *Canada* 50°40N 96°35W **71** C9
Victoria de Durango = Durango
  Mexico 24°3N 104°39W **86** C4
Victoria de las Tunas = Las Tunas
  Cuba 20°58N 76°59W **88** B4
Victoria Falls *Zimbabwe* 17°58S 25°52E **55** F2
Victoria Harbour
  Canada 44°45N 79°45W **82** B5
Victoria I. *Canada* 71°0N 111°0W **68** C9
Victoria L. *Canada* 48°20N 57°27W **73** C8
Victoria Ld. *Antarctica* 75°0S 160°0E **5** D11
Victoria Nile → *Uganda* 2°14N 31°26E **54** B3
Victoria River *Australia* 16°25S 131°0E **60** C5
Victoria Str. *Canada* 69°31N 100°30W **68** D11
Victoria West *S. Africa* 31°25S 23°4E **56** E3
Victoriaville *Canada* 46°4N 71°56W **73** C5
Victorica *Argentina* 36°20S 65°30W **94** D2
Victorville *U.S.A.* 34°32N 117°18W **79** L9
Vicuña *Chile* 30°0S 70°50W **94** C1
Vicuña Mackenna
  Argentina 33°53S 64°25W **94** C3
Vidal *U.S.A.* 34°7N 114°31W **79** L12
Vidalia *U.S.A.* 32°13N 82°25W **85** E13
Vidin *Bulgaria* 43°59N 22°50E **23** C10
Vidisha *India* 23°28N 77°53E **42** H7
Vidos *Greece* 39°38N 19°55E **25** A3
Vidzy *Belarus* 55°23N 26°37E **9** J22
Viedma *Argentina* 40°50S 63°0W **96** E4
Viedma, L. *Argentina* 49°30S 72°30W **96** F2
Vielsalm *Belgium* 50°17N 5°54E **15** D5
Vieng Pou Kha *Laos* 20°41N 101°4E **38** B3
Vienna = Wien *Austria* 48°12N 16°22E **16** D9
Vienna *Canada* 42°41N 80°48W **82** D4
Vienna *Ill., U.S.A.* 37°25N 88°54W **80** G9
Vienna *Mo., U.S.A.* 38°11N 91°57W **80** F8
Vienne *France* 45°31N 4°53E **20** D6
Vienne → *France* 47°13N 0°5E **20** C4
Vientiane *Laos* 17°58N 102°36E **38** D4
Vientos, Paso de los
  Caribbean 20°0N 74°0W **89** C5
Vieques *Puerto Rico* 18°8N 65°25W **89** d
Vierge Pt. *St. Lucia* 13°49N 60°53W **89** f
Vierzon *France* 47°13N 2°5E **20** C5
Viet Tri *Vietnam* 21°18N 105°25E **38** B5

Vietnam ■ *Asia* 19°0N 106°0E **38** C6
Vieux Fort *St. Lucia* 13°46N 60°58W **89** f
Vigan *Phil.* 17°35N 120°28E **37** A6
Vigévano *Italy* 45°19N 8°51E **20** D8
Vigia *Brazil* 0°50S 48°5W **93** D9
Viglas, Ákra *Greece* 35°54N 27°51E **25** D9
Vigo *Spain* 42°12N 8°41W **21** A1
Vihowa *Pakistan* 31°8N 70°30E **42** D4
Vihowa → *Pakistan* 31°8N 70°41E **42** D4
Vijayawada *India* 16°31N 80°39E **41** L12
Vijosë → *Albania* 40°37N 19°24E **23** D8
Vik *Iceland* 63°25N 19°1W **8** E4
Vikeke = Viqueque
Viking *Canada* 53°7N 111°50W **70** C6
Vikna *Norway* 64°55N 10°58E **8** D14
Vila da Maganja *Mozam.* 17°18S 37°30E **55** F4
Vila da Ribeira Brava
  C. Verde Is. 16°32N 24°25W **50** b
Vila Franca de Xira
  Portugal 38°57N 8°59W **21** C1
Vila Gamito *Mozam.* 14°12S 33°0E **55** E3
Vila Gomes da Costa
  Mozam. 24°20S 33°37E **57** C5
Vila Machado *Mozam.* 19°15S 34°14E **55** F3
Vila Mouzinho *Mozam.* 14°48S 34°25E **55** E3
Vila Nova de Gaia *Portugal* 41°8N 8°37W **21** B1
Vila Real *Portugal* 41°17N 7°48W **21** B2
Vila-Real *Spain* 39°55N 0°3W **21** C5
Vila Real de Santo António
  Portugal 37°10N 7°28W **21** D2
Vila Vasco da Gama
  Mozam. 14°54S 32°14E **55** E3
Vila Velha *Brazil* 20°20S 40°17W **95** A7
Vilagarcía de Arousa
  Spain 42°34N 8°46W **21** A1
Vilaine → *France* 47°30N 2°27W **20** C2
Vilanandro, Tanjona
  Madag. 16°11S 44°27E **57** B7
Vilanculos *Mozam.* 22°1S 35°17E **57** C6
Vilanova i la Geltrú *Spain* 41°13N 1°40E **21** B6
Vilcheka, Ostrov *Russia* 80°0N 58°31E **28** B6
Vilcheka, Zemlya *Russia* 80°30N 60°30E **4** A11
Vileyka *Belarus* 54°30N 26°53E **17** A14
Vilhelmina *Sweden* 64°35N 16°39E **8** D17
Vilhena *Brazil* 12°40S 60°5W **92** F6
Viliya = Neris →
  Lithuania 55°8N 24°16E **9** J21
Viljandi *Estonia* 58°28N 25°30E **9** G21
Vilkitskogo, Proliv
  Russia 78°0N 103°0E **29** B11
Vilkovo = Vylkove
  Ukraine 45°28N 29°32E **17** F15
Villa Abecia *Bolivia* 21°0S 68°18W **94** A2
Villa Ana *Argentina* 28°28S 59°40W **94** B4
Villa Ángela *Argentina* 27°34S 60°45W **94** B3
Villa Bella *Bolivia* 10°25S 65°22W **92** F5
Villa Cañás *Argentina* 34°0S 61°35W **94** C3
Villa Constitución
  Argentina 33°15S 60°20W **94** C3
Villa de Arriaga *Mexico* 21°56N 101°20W **86** C4
Villa de María *Argentina* 29°55S 63°43W **94** B3
Villa de Méndez *Mexico* 25°7N 98°34W **87** B5
Villa Dolores *Argentina* 31°58S 65°15W **94** C2
Villa Frontera *Mexico* 26°56N 101°27W **86** B4
Villa Gesell *Argentina* 37°15S 56°55W **94** D4
Villa Guillermina
  Argentina 28°15S 59°29W **94** B4
Villa Hayes *Paraguay* 25°5S 57°20W **94** B4
Villa Hidalgo *Mexico* 24°15N 99°26W **87** C5
Villa Iris *Argentina* 38°12S 63°12W **94** D3
Villa María *Argentina* 32°20S 63°10W **94** C3
Villa Mazán *Argentina* 28°40S 66°30W **94** B2
Villa Montes *Bolivia* 21°10S 63°30W **94** A3
Villa Ocampo *Argentina* 28°30S 59°20W **94** B4
Villa Ocampo *Mexico* 26°27N 105°31W **86** B3
Villa Ojo de Agua
  Argentina 29°30S 63°44W **94** B3
Villa San Martín
  Argentina 28°15S 64°9W **94** B3
Villa Unión *Mexico* 23°12N 106°14W **86** C3
Villacarlos *Spain* 39°53N 4°17E **24** B11
Villacarrillo *Spain* 38°7N 3°3W **21** C4
Villach *Austria* 46°37N 13°51E **16** E7
Villafranca de Bonany
  Spain 39°34N 3°5E **24** B10
Villagrán *Mexico* 24°29N 99°29W **87** C5
Villaguay *Argentina* 32°0S 59°0W **94** C4
Villahermosa *Mexico* 17°59N 92°55W **87** D6
Villajoyosa *Spain* 38°30N 0°12W **21** C5
Villalba *Spain* 43°26N 7°40W **21** A2
Villanueva *U.S.A.* 35°16N 105°22W **77** J11
Villanueva de la Serena
  Spain 38°59N 5°50W **21** C3
Villanueva y Geltrú = Vilanova i
  la Geltrú *Spain* 41°13N 1°40E **21** B6
Villarreal = Vila-Real
  Spain 39°55N 0°3W **21** C5
Villarrica *Chile* 39°15S 72°15W **96** D2
Villarrica *Paraguay* 25°40S 56°30W **94** B4
Villarrobledo *Spain* 39°18N 2°36W **21** C4
Villavicencio *Argentina* 32°28S 69°0W **94** C2
Villavicencio *Colombia* 4°9N 73°37W **92** C4
Villaviciosa *Spain* 43°32N 5°27W **21** A3
Villazón *Bolivia* 22°0S 65°35W **94** A2
Ville-Marie *Canada* 47°20N 79°30W **72** C4
Ville Platte *U.S.A.* 30°41N 92°17W **84** F8
Villena *Spain* 38°39N 0°52E **21** C5
Villeneuve-d'Ascq *France* 50°38N 3°9E **20** A5
Villeneuve-sur-Lot *France* 44°24N 0°42E **20** D4
Villiers *S. Africa* 27°2S 28°36E **57** D4
Villingen-Schwenningen
  Germany 48°3N 8°26E **16** D5
Villmanstrand = Lappeenranta
  Finland 61°3N 28°12E **8** F23
Vilnius *Lithuania* 54°38N 25°19E **9** J21
Vilvoorde *Belgium* 50°56N 4°26E **15** D4

Vilyuchinsk *Russia* 52°55N 158°24E **29** D16
Vilyuy → *Russia* 64°24N 126°26E **29** C13
Vilyuysk *Russia* 63°40N 121°35E **29** C13
Viña del Mar *Chile* 33°0S 71°30W **94** C1
Vinarós *Spain* 40°30N 0°27E **21** B6
Vincennes *U.S.A.* 38°41N 87°32W **80** F10
Vincennes Bay *S. Ocean* 66°0S 109°0E **5** C8
Vincent *U.S.A.* 34°33N 118°11W **79** L8
Vinchina *Argentina* 28°45S 68°15W **94** B2
Vindelälven → *Sweden* 63°55N 19°50E **8** E18
Vindeln *Sweden* 64°12N 19°43E **8** D18
Vindhya Ra. *India* 22°50N 77°0E **42** H7
Vineland *U.S.A.* 39°29N 75°2W **81** F16
Vinh *Vietnam* 18°45N 105°38E **38** C5
Vinh Linh *Vietnam* 17°4N 107°2E **38** D6
Vinh Long *Vietnam* 10°16N 105°57E **39** G5
Vinh Yen *Vietnam* 21°21N 105°35E **38** B5
Vinita *U.S.A.* 36°39N 95°9W **84** C7
Vinkovci *Croatia* 45°19N 18°48E **23** B8
Vinnitsa = Vinnytsya
  Ukraine 49°15N 28°30E **17** D15
Vinnytsya *Ukraine* 49°15N 28°30E **17** D15
Vinson Massif *Antarctica* 78°35S 85°25W **5** D16
Vinton *Calif., U.S.A.* 39°48N 120°10W **78** F6
Vinton *Iowa, U.S.A.* 42°10N 92°1W **80** D7
Vinton *La., U.S.A.* 30°11N 93°35W **84** F8
Violet Valley ◎
  Australia 17°10S 127°55E **60** C4
Viqueque *E. Timor* 8°52S 126°23E **37** F7
Virac *Phil.* 13°30N 124°20E **37** B6
Virachey *Cambodia* 13°59N 106°49E **38** F6
Virachey △ *Cambodia* 14°1N 106°55E **38** E6
Virago Sd. *Canada* 54°0N 132°30W **70** C2
Viramgam *India* 23°5N 72°0E **42** H5
Virananşehir *Turkey* 37°13N 39°45E **44** B3
Virawah *Pakistan* 24°31N 70°46E **42** G4
Virden *Canada* 49°50N 100°56W **71** D8
Vire *France* 48°50N 0°53W **20** B3
Vírgenes, C. *Argentina* 52°19S 68°21W **96** G3
Virgin → *U.S.A.* 36°28N 114°21W **79** H6
Virgin Gorda *Br. Virgin Is.* 18°30N 64°26W **89** e
Virgin Is. (British) ☑
  W. Indies 18°30N 64°30W **89** e
Virgin Is. (U.S.) ☑
  W. Indies 18°20N 65°0W **89** e
Virgin Islands △
  U.S. Virgin Is. 18°21N 64°43W **89** C7
Virginia *S. Africa* 28°8S 26°55E **56** D4
Virginia *U.S.A.* 47°31N 92°32W **80** B7
Virginia □ *U.S.A.* 37°30N 78°45W **81** G14
Virginia Beach *U.S.A.* 36°49N 76°9W **81** F16
Virginia City *Mont.,*
  U.S.A. 45°18N 111°56W **76** D8
Virginia City *Nev.,*
  U.S.A. 39°19N 119°39W **78** F7
Virginia Falls *Canada* 61°38N 125°42W **70** A3
Virginiatown *Canada* 48°9N 79°36W **72** C4
Viroqua *U.S.A.* 43°34N 90°53W **80** D8
Virovitica *Croatia* 45°51N 17°21E **22** B7
Virpur *India* 21°51N 70°42E **42** J4
Virton *Belgium* 49°35N 5°32E **15** E5
Virudunagar *India* 9°30N 77°58E **40** Q10
Virunga △
  Dem. Rep. of the Congo 0°5N 29°38E **54** B2
Vis *Croatia* 43°4N 16°10E **22** C7
Visalia *U.S.A.* 36°20N 119°18W **78** J7
Visayan Sea *Phil.* 11°30N 123°30E **37** B6
Visby *Sweden* 57°37N 18°18E **9** H18
Viscount Melville Sd.
  Canada 74°10N 108°0W **69** C10
Visé *Belgium* 50°44N 5°41E **15** D5
Vise, Ostrov *Russia* 79°33N 76°50E **28** B8
Višegrad *Bos.-H.* 43°47N 19°17E **23** C8
Viseu *Brazil* 1°10S 46°5W **93** D9
Viseu *Portugal* 40°40N 7°55W **21** B2
Vishakhapatnam *India* 17°45N 83°20E **41** L13
Visnagar *India* 23°45N 72°32E **42** H5
Viso, Mte. *Italy* 44°38N 7°5E **20** D7
Visokoi I. *Antarctica* 56°43S 27°15W **5** B1
Vista *U.S.A.* 33°12N 117°14W **79** M9
Vistula = Wisła →
  Poland 54°22N 18°55E **17** A10
Vitebsk = Vitsyebsk
  Belarus 55°10N 30°15E **18** C5
Viterbo *Italy* 42°25N 12°6E **22** C5
Viti Levu *Fiji* 17°30S 177°30E **59** a
Vitigudino *Spain* 41°1N 6°26W **21** B2
Vitim *Russia* 59°28N 112°35E **29** D12
Vitim → *Russia* 59°26N 112°34E **29** D12
Vitória *Brazil* 20°20S 40°22W **93** H10
Vitória da Conquista
  Brazil 14°51S 40°51W **93** F10
Vitória de Santo Antão
  Brazil 8°10S 35°20W **93** E11
Vitoria-Gasteiz *Spain* 42°50N 2°41W **21** A4
Vitsyebsk *Belarus* 55°10N 30°15E **18** C5
Vittória *Italy* 36°57N 14°32E **22** F6
Vittório Véneto *Italy* 45°59N 12°18E **22** B5
Viveiro *Spain* 43°39N 7°38W **21** A2
Vivian *U.S.A.* 32°53N 93°59W **84** E8
Viwa *Fiji* 17°10S 177°58E **59** a
Vizcaíno, Desierto de
  Mexico 27°30N 113°45W **86** B2
Vizcaíno, Sierra *Mexico* 27°30N 114°0W **86** B2
Vize *Turkey* 41°34N 27°45E **23** D12
Vizianagaram *India* 18°6N 83°30E **41** K13
Vlaardingen *Neths.* 51°55N 4°21E **15** C4
Vladikavkaz *Russia* 43°0N 44°35E **19** F7
Vladimir *Russia* 56°15N 40°30E **18** C7
Vladimir Volynskiy = Volodymyr-
  Volynskyy *Ukraine* 50°50N 24°18E **17** C13
Vladivostok *Russia* 43°10N 131°53E **30** C5
Vlieland *Neths.* 53°16N 4°55E **15** A4
Vlissingen *Neths.* 51°26N 3°34E **15** C3
Vlorë *Albania* 40°32N 19°28E **23** D8
Vltava → *Czech Rep.* 50°21N 14°30E **16** C8
Vo Dat *Vietnam* 11°9N 107°31E **39** G6
Voe *U.K.* 60°21N 1°16W **11** A7

Vogelkop = Doberai, Jazirah
  Indonesia 1°25S 133°0E **37** E8
Vogelsberg *Germany* 50°31N 9°12E **16** C5
Voghera *Italy* 44°59N 9°1E **20** D8
Vohibinany *Madag.* 18°49S 49°4E **57** B8
Vohilava *Madag.* 21°4S 48°0E **57** C8
Vohimarina = Iharana
  Madag. 13°25S 50°0E **57** A9
Vohimena, Tanjon' i
  Madag. 25°36S 45°8E **57** D8
Vohipeno *Madag.* 22°22S 47°51E **57** C8
Voi *Kenya* 3°25S 38°32E **54** C4
Voiron *France* 45°22N 5°35E **20** D6
Voisey B. *Canada* 56°15N 61°50W **73** A7
Vojmsjön *Sweden* 65°0N 16°24E **8** D17
Vojvodina □ *Serbia* 45°20N 20°0E **23** B9
Volborg *U.S.A.* 45°51N 105°41W **76** D11
Volcán de Colima △
  Mexico 19°30N 103°40W **86** D4
Volcano Is. = Kazan-Rettō
  Pac. Oc. 25°0N 141°0E **64** E6
Volcans △ *Rwanda* 1°30S 29°26E **54** C2
Volda *Norway* 62°9N 6°5E **8** E12
Volga = Privolzhskiy □
  Russia 56°0N 50°0E **28** D6
Volga → *Russia* 46°0N 48°30E **19** E8
Volga Hts. = Privolzhskaya
  Vozvyshennost *Russia* 51°0N 46°0E **19** D8
Volgodonsk *Russia* 47°33N 42°5E **19** E7
Volgograd *Russia* 48°40N 44°25E **19** E7
Volgogradskoye Vdkhr.
  Russia 50°0N 45°20E **19** D8
Volkhov → *Russia* 60°8N 32°20E **18** B5
Volkovysk = Vawkavysk
  Belarus 53°9N 24°30E **17** B13
Volksrust *S. Africa* 27°24S 29°53E **57** D4
Volochanka *Russia* 71°0N 94°28E **29** B10
Volodymyr-Volynskyy
  Ukraine 50°50N 24°18E **17** C13
Vologda *Russia* 59°10N 39°45E **18** C6
Volos *Greece* 39°24N 22°59E **23** E10
Volosovo *Russia* 59°27N 29°32E **9** G23
Volovets *Ukraine* 48°43N 23°11E **17** D12
Volozhin = Valozhyn
  Belarus 54°3N 26°30E **17** A14
Volsk *Russia* 52°5N 47°22E **18** D8
Volta □ *Ghana* 5°46N 0°41E **48** F4
Volta, L. *Ghana* 7°30N 0°0 **50** G6
Volta Redonda *Brazil* 22°31S 44°5W **95** A7
Voltaire, C. *Australia* 14°16S 125°35E **60** B4
Volterra *Italy* 43°24N 10°51E **22** C4
Volturno → *Italy* 41°1N 13°55E **22** D6
Volzhskiy *Russia* 48°56N 44°46E **19** E7
Vomo *Fiji* 17°30S 177°15E **59** a
Vondrozo *Madag.* 22°49S 47°20E **57** C8
Vopnafjörður *Iceland* 65°45N 14°50W **8** D6
Vorkuta *Russia* 67°48N 64°20E **18** A11
Vormsi *Estonia* 59°1N 23°13E **9** G20
Voronezh *Russia* 51°40N 39°10E **19** D6
Vóroi *Estonia* 58°16N 26°3E **9** G22
Vosges *France* 48°20N 7°10E **20** B7
Voss *Norway* 60°38N 6°8E **8** F12
Vostok *Antarctica* 78°30S 106°50E **5** D8
Vostok I. *Kiribati* 10°5S 152°23W **65** J12
Votkinsk *Russia* 57°0N 53°55E **18** C9
Votkinskoye Vdkhr.
  Russia 57°22N 55°12E **18** C10
Votsuri-Shima *Japan* 25°45N 123°29E **31** M1
Vouga → *Portugal* 40°41N 8°40W **21** B1
Vouxa, Ákra *Greece* 35°37N 23°32E **25** D5
Voyageurs △ *U.S.A.* 48°32N 93°0W **80** A7
Voynitsa *Russia* 65°10N 30°20E **8** D24
Voyvozh *Russia* 62°56N 54°56E **28** C6
Vozhe, Ozero *Russia* 60°45N 39°0E **18** B6
Voznesensk *Ukraine* 47°35N 31°21E **19** E5
Voznesenye *Russia* 61°0N 35°28E **18** B6
Vrangel *Russia* 42°43N 133°5E **30** C6
Vrangelya, Ostrov
  Russia 71°0N 180°0E **29** B18
Vranje *Serbia* 42°34N 21°54E **23** C9
Vratsa *Bulgaria* 43°15N 23°30E **23** C10
Vrbas → *Bos.-H.* 45°8N 17°29E **22** B7
Vrede *S. Africa* 27°24S 29°6E **57** D4
Vredefort *S. Africa* 27°0S 27°22E **56** D4
Vredenburg *S. Africa* 32°56S 18°0E **56** E2
Vredendal *S. Africa* 31°41S 18°35E **56** E2
Vrindavan *India* 27°37N 77°40E **42** F7
Vrises *Greece* 35°23N 24°13E **25** D6
Vršac *Serbia* 45°8N 21°20E **23** B9
Vryburg *S. Africa* 26°55S 24°45E **56** D3
Vryheid *S. Africa* 27°45S 30°47E **57** D5
Vu Liet *Vietnam* 18°43N 105°23E **38** C5
Vukovar *Croatia* 45°21N 18°59E **23** B8
Vuktyl *Russia* 63°52N 57°20E **28** C6
Vulcan *Canada* 50°25N 113°15W **70** C6
Vulcan *Romania* 45°23N 23°17E **17** F12
Vulcaneşti *Moldova* 45°41N 28°18E **17** F15
Vulcano *Italy* 38°24N 14°58E **22** E6
Vulkaneshty = Vulcaneşti
  Moldova 45°41N 28°18E **17** F15
Vunduzi → *Mozam.* 18°56S 34°1E **55** F3
Vung Tau *Vietnam* 10°21N 107°4E **39** G6
Vunidawa *Fiji* 17°50S 178°21E **59** a
Vunisea *Fiji* 19°3S 178°10E **59** a
Vwaza △ *Malawi* 10°58S 33°25E **55** E3
Vyartsilya *Russia* 62°8N 30°45E **8** E24
Vyatka = Kirov *Russia* 58°35N 49°40E **18** C8
Vyatka → *Russia* 55°37N 51°28E **18** C9
Vyatskiye Polyany *Russia* 56°14N 51°5E **18** C9
Vyazemskiy *Russia* 47°32N 134°45E **29** E14
Vyazma *Russia* 55°10N 34°15E **18** C5
Vyborg *Russia* 60°43N 28°47E **8** F23
Vychegda → *Russia* 61°18N 46°36E **18** B8
Vychodné Beskydy
  Europe 49°20N 22°0E **17** D11
Vyg-ozero *Russia* 63°47N 34°29E **18** B5
Vylkove *Ukraine* 45°28N 29°32E **17** F15
Vynohradiv *Ukraine* 48°9N 23°2E **17** D12

Vyrnwy, L. *U.K.* 52°48N 3°31W **12** E4
Vyshniy Volochek
  Russia 57°30N 34°30E **18** C5
Vyshza = imeni 26 Bakinskikh
  Komissarov
  Turkmenistan 39°22N 54°10E **45** B7
Vyškov *Czech Rep.* 49°17N 17°0E **17** D9
Vytegra *Russia* 61°0N 36°27E **18** B6

W

W.A.C. Bennett Dam
  Canada 56°2N 122°6W **70** B4
Wa *Ghana* 10°7N 2°25W **50** F5
Waal → *Neths.* 51°37N 5°0E **15** C5
Waalwijk *Neths.* 51°42N 5°4E **15** C5
Waanyi-Garawa ◎
  Australia 18°2S 137°33E **62** B2
Wabakimi △ *Canada* 50°43N 89°29W **72** B2
Wabana *Canada* 47°40N 53°0W **73** C9
Wabasca → *Canada* 58°22N 115°20W **70** B5
Wabasca-Desmarais
  Canada 55°57N 113°56W **70** B6
Wabash *U.S.A.* 40°48N 85°49W **81** E11
Wabash → *U.S.A.* 37°48N 88°2W **80** G9
Wabigoon L. *Canada* 49°44N 92°44W **71** D10
Wabowden *Canada* 54°55N 98°38W **71** C9
Wabuk Pt. *Canada* 55°20N 85°5W **72** A2
Wabush *Canada* 52°55N 66°52W **73** B6
Waco *U.S.A.* 31°33N 97°9W **84** F6
Waconichi, L. *Canada* 50°8N 74°0W **72** B5
Wad Hamid *Sudan* 16°30N 32°45E **51** E12
Wad Medanî *Sudan* 14°28N 33°30E **51** F12
Wad Thana *Pakistan* 27°22N 66°23E **42** F2
Wadai *Africa* 12°0N 19°0E **48** E5
Wadayama *Japan* 35°19N 134°52E **31** G7
Waddeneilanden *Neths.* 53°25N 5°10E **15** A5
Waddenzee *Neths.* 53°6N 5°10E **15** A5
Waddington *U.S.A.* 44°52N 75°12W **83** B9
Waddington, Mt.
  Canada 51°23N 125°15W **70** C3
Waddy Pt. *Australia* 24°58S 153°21E **63** C5
Wadebridge *U.K.* 50°31N 4°51E **13** G3
Wadena *Canada* 51°57N 103°47W **71** C8
Wadena *U.S.A.* 46°26N 95°8W **80** B6
Wadeye *Australia* 14°28S 129°52E **60** B4
Wadhams *Canada* 51°30N 127°30W **70** C3
Wadhwan *India* 22°42N 71°41E **42** H4
Wādī as Sīr *Jordan* 31°56N 35°49E **46** D4
Wadi Halfa *Sudan* 21°53N 31°19E **51** D12
Wadi Rum △ *Jordan* 29°30N 35°30E **46** F4
Wadsworth *Nev.,*
  U.S.A. 39°38N 119°17W **76** G4
Wadsworth *Ohio, U.S.A.* 41°2N 81°44W **82** E3
Waegwan *S. Korea* 35°59N 128°23E **35** G15
Wafangdian *China* 39°38N 121°58E **35** E11
Wafrah *Kuwait* 28°33N 47°56E **44** D5
Wagait ◎ *Australia* 13°1S 130°5E **60** B5
Wageningen *Neths.* 51°58N 5°40E **15** C5
Wager B. *Canada* 65°26N 88°40W **69** D14
Wagga Wagga *Australia* 35°7S 147°24E **63** F4
Waghete *Indonesia* 4°10S 135°50E **37** E9
Wagin *Australia* 33°17S 117°25E **61** F2
Wagner *U.S.A.* 43°5N 98°18W **80** D4
Wagon Mound *U.S.A.* 36°1N 104°42W **77** H11
Wagoner *U.S.A.* 35°58N 95°22W **84** D7
Wah *Pakistan* 33°45N 72°40E **42** C5
Wahai *Indonesia* 2°48S 129°35E **37** E7
Wâhid *Egypt* 30°48N 32°21E **46** E1
Wahnai *Afghan.* 32°40N 65°50E **42** C1
Wahoo *U.S.A.* 41°13N 96°37W **80** E5
Wahpeton *U.S.A.* 46°16N 96°36W **80** B5
Waialua *U.S.A.* 21°34N 158°8W **75** L8
Waiau → *N.Z.* 42°47S 173°22E **59** E4
Waibeem *Indonesia* 0°30S 132°59E **37** E8
Waigeo *Indonesia* 0°20S 130°40E **37** E8
Waihi *N.Z.* 37°23S 175°52E **59** B5
Waihou → *N.Z.* 37°15S 175°40E **59** B5
Waika
  Dem. Rep. of the Congo 2°22S 25°42E **54** C2
Waikabubak *Indonesia* 9°45S 119°25E **37** F5
Waikaremoana, L. *N.Z.* 38°49S 177°9E **59** C6
Waikari *N.Z.* 42°58S 172°41E **59** E4
Waikato → *N.Z.* 37°23S 174°43E **59** B5
Waikelo *Indonesia* 9°24S 119°19E **60** A2
Waikerie *Australia* 34°9S 140°0E **63** E3
Waikokopu *N.Z.* 39°3S 177°52E **59** C6
Waikouaiti *N.Z.* 45°36S 170°41E **59** F3
Wailingding Dao *China* 22°6N 114°2E **33** G11
Waimakariri → *N.Z.* 43°24S 172°42E **59** E4
Waimate *N.Z.* 44°45S 171°3E **59** F3
Wainganga → *India* 18°50N 79°55E **40** K11
Waingapu *Indonesia* 9°35S 120°11E **37** F6
Waini → *Guyana* 8°20N 59°50W **92** B7
Wainwright *Canada* 52°50N 110°50W **71** C6
Wainwright *U.S.A.* 70°38N 160°2W **74** A7
Waiouru *N.Z.* 39°28S 175°41E **59** C5
Waipara *N.Z.* 43°3S 172°46E **59** E4
Waipawa *N.Z.* 39°56S 176°38E **59** C6
Waipiro *N.Z.* 38°2S 178°22E **59** C7
Waipoua Forest *N.Z.* 35°39S 173°33E **59** A4
Waipu *N.Z.* 35°59S 174°29E **59** A5
Waipukurau *N.Z.* 40°1S 176°33E **59** D6
Wairakei *N.Z.* 38°37S 176°6E **59** C6
Wairarapa, L. *N.Z.* 41°14S 175°15E **59** D5
Wairoa *N.Z.* 39°3S 177°25E **59** C6
Waitaki → *N.Z.* 44°56S 171°7E **59** F3
Waitangi *N.Z.* 35°16S 174°5E **59** A5
Waitara *N.Z.* 38°59S 174°15E **59** C5
Waitomo Caves *N.Z.* 38°16S 175°7E **59** C5
Waitsburg *U.S.A.* 46°16N 118°9W **76** C4
Waiuku *N.Z.* 37°15S 174°45E **59** B5
Wajima *Japan* 37°30N 137°0E **31** F8
Wajir *Kenya* 1°42N 40°5E **54** B5
Wakasa *Japan* 35°20N 134°24E **31** G7
Wakasa-Wan *Japan* 35°40N 135°30E **31** G7
Wakatipu, L. *N.Z.* 45°5S 168°33E **59** F2
Wakaw *Canada* 52°39N 105°44W **71** C7

Wakaya *Fiji* 17°37S 179°0E 59 a
Wakayama *Japan* 34°15N 135°15E 31 G7
Wakayama □ *Japan* 33°50N 135°30E 31 H7
Wake Forest *U.S.A.* 35°59N 78°30W 85 D15
WaKeeney *U.S.A.* 39°1N 99°53W 80 F4
Wakefield *Jamaica* 18°26N 77°42W 88 a
Wakefield *N.Z.* 41°24S 173°5E 59 D4
Wakefield *U.K.* 53°41N 1°29W 12 D6
Wakefield *Mass., U.S.A.* 42°30N 71°5W 83 D13
Wakefield *Mich., U.S.A.* 46°29N 89°56W 80 B9
Wakkanai *Japan* 45°28N 141°35E 30 B10
Wakkerstroom *S. Africa* 27°24S 30°10E 57 D5
Wakool *Australia* 35°28S 144°23E 63 F3
Wakool → *Australia* 35°5S 143°33E 63 F3
Wakre *Indonesia* 0°19S 131°5E 37 E8
Wakuach, L. *Canada* 55°34N 67°32W 73 A6
Walagunya ♡ *Australia* 23°10S 120°50E 60 D3
Walamba *Zambia* 13°30S 28°42E 55 E2
Wałbrzych *Poland* 50°45N 16°18E 16 C9
Walbury Hill *U.K.* 51°21N 1°28W 13 F6
Walcha *Australia* 30°55S 151°31E 63 E5
Walcheren *Neths.* 51°30N 3°35E 15 C3
Walcott *U.S.A.* 41°46N 106°51W 76 F10
Walcz *Poland* 53°17N 16°27E 16 B9
Waldburg Ra. *Australia* 24°40S 117°35E 61 D2
Walden *Colo., U.S.A.* 40°44N 106°17W 76 F10
Walden *N.Y., U.S.A.* 41°34N 74°11W 83 E10
Waldport *U.S.A.* 44°26N 124°4W 76 D1
Waldron *U.S.A.* 34°54N 94°5W 84 D7
Walebing *Australia* 30°41S 116°13E 61 F2
Wales □ *U.K.* 52°19N 4°43W 13 E3
Wales I. *Canada* 68°1N 86°40W 69 D14
Walgett *Australia* 30°0S 148°5E 63 E4
Walgreen Coast
  Antarctica 75°15S 105°0W 5 D15
Walker *U.S.A.* 47°6N 94°35W 80 B6
Walker, L. *Canada* 50°20N 67°11W 73 B6
Walker L. *Canada* 54°42N 95°57W 71 C9
Walker L. *U.S.A.* 38°42N 118°43W 76 G4
Walkerston *Australia* 21°11S 149°8E 62 b
Walkerton *Canada* 44°10N 81°10W 82 B3
Wall *U.S.A.* 44°0N 102°8W 80 C2
Walla Walla *U.S.A.* 46°4N 118°20W 76 C4
Wallace *Idaho, U.S.A.* 47°28N 115°56W 76 C6
Wallace *N.C., U.S.A.* 34°44N 77°59W 85 D16
Wallaceburg *Canada* 42°34N 82°23W 82 D2
Wallachia = Valahia
  Romania 44°35N 25°0E 17 F13
Wallal *Australia* 26°32S 146°7E 63 D4
Wallam Cr. →
  Australia 28°40S 147°20E 63 D4
Wallambin, L. *Australia* 30°57S 117°35E 61 F2
Wallangarra *Australia* 28°56S 151°58E 63 D5
Wallaroo *Australia* 33°56S 137°39E 63 E2
Wallenpaupack, L.
  U.S.A. 41°25N 75°15W 83 E9
Wallingford *Conn.,
  U.S.A.* 41°27N 72°50W 83 E12
Wallingford *Vt., U.S.A.* 43°28N 72°58W 83 C12
Wallis & Futuna, Is.
  Pac. Oc. 13°18S 176°10W 58 C11
Wallowa *U.S.A.* 45°34N 117°32W 76 D5
Wallowa Mts. *U.S.A.* 45°20N 117°30W 76 D5
Walls *U.K.* 60°14N 1°33W 11 A7
Walls of Jerusalem △
  Australia 41°56S 146°15E 63 G4
Wallula *U.S.A.* 46°5N 118°54W 76 D4
Wallumbilla *Australia* 26°33S 149°9E 63 D4
Walmsley, L. *Canada* 63°25S 108°36W 71 A7
Walney, I. of *U.K.* 54°6N 3°15W 12 C4
Walnut Canyon △
  U.S.A. 35°15N 111°20W 77 J8
Walnut Creek *U.S.A.* 37°54N 122°4W 78 H4
Walnut Ridge *U.S.A.* 36°4N 90°57W 85 C9
Walpole *Australia* 34°58S 116°44E 61 F2
Walpole *U.S.A.* 42°9N 71°15W 83 D13
Walpole-Nornalup △
  Australia 35°0S 116°45E 61 G2
Walsall *U.K.* 52°35N 1°58W 13 E6
Walsenburg *U.S.A.* 37°38N 104°47W 77 H11
Walsh *U.S.A.* 37°23N 102°17W 77 H12
Walsh → *Australia* 16°31S 143°42E 62 B3
Walsingham *Canada* 42°40N 80°31W 82 D4
Walter F. George Res.
  U.S.A. 31°38N 85°4W 85 F12
Walterboro *U.S.A.* 32°55N 80°40W 85 E14
Walters *U.S.A.* 34°22N 98°19W 84 D5
Waltham *U.S.A.* 42°23N 71°14W 83 D13
Waltman *U.S.A.* 43°4N 107°12W 76 E10
Walton *U.S.A.* 42°10N 75°8W 83 D9
Walton-on-the-Naze *U.K.* 51°51N 1°17E 13 F9
Walvis Bay *Namibia* 23°0S 14°28E 56 C1
Walvisbaai = Walvis Bay
  Namibia 23°0S 14°28E 56 C1
Wamba
  Dem. Rep. of the Congo 2°10N 27°57E 54 B2
Wamba *Kenya* 0°58N 37°19E 54 B4
Wambardi ♡ *Australia* 16°2S 130°55E 60 C5
Wamego *U.S.A.* 39°12N 96°18W 80 F5
Wamena *Indonesia* 4°4S 138°57E 37 E9
Wampana Karlantijpa ♡
  Australia 17°45S 132°10E 60 C5
Wampaya ♡ *Australia* 17°20S 135°0E 62 B2
Wampsville *U.S.A.* 43°4N 75°42W 83 C9
Wamsutter *U.S.A.* 41°40N 107°58W 76 F10
Wamulan *Indonesia* 3°27S 126°7E 37 E7
Wan Xian *China* 38°47N 115°7E 34 E8
Wana *Pakistan* 32°20N 69°32E 42 C3
Wanaaring *Australia* 29°38S 144°9E 63 D3
Wanaka *N.Z.* 44°42S 169°9E 59 F2
Wanaka, L. *N.Z.* 44°33S 169°7E 59 F2
Wanapitei L. *Canada* 46°45N 80°40W 72 C3
Wandel Sea = McKinley Sea
  Arctic 82°0N 0°0 4 A7
Wanderer *Zimbabwe* 19°36S 30°1E 55 F3
Wandhari *Pakistan* 27°42N 66°48E 42 F2
Wandoan *Australia* 26°5S 149°55E 63 D4
Wanfu *China* 40°8N 122°38E 35 D12

Wang → *Thailand* 17°8N 99°2E 38 D2
Wang Noi *Thailand* 14°13N 100°44E 38 E3
Wang Saphung
  Thailand 17°18N 101°46E 38 D3
Wang Thong *Thailand* 16°50N 100°26E 38 D3
Wanga
  Dem. Rep. of the Congo 2°58N 29°12E 54 B2
Wangal *Indonesia* 6°8S 134°9E 37 F8
Wanganella *Australia* 35°6S 144°49E 63 F3
Wanganui *N.Z.* 39°56S 175°3E 59 C5
Wangaratta *Australia* 36°21S 146°19E 63 F4
Wangary *Australia* 34°35S 135°29E 63 E2
Wangdu *China* 38°40N 115°7E 34 E8
Wangerooge *Germany* 53°47N 7°54E 16 B4
Wangiwangi *Indonesia* 5°22S 123°37E 37 F6
Wangqing *China* 43°12N 129°42E 35 C15
Wanimiyn ♡ *Australia* 15°55S 130°49E 60 C5
Wanjina Wunggurr Wilinggin ♡
  Australia 16°0S 127°0E 60 C4
Wankaner *India* 22°35N 71°0E 42 H4
Wanless *Canada* 54°11N 101°21W 71 C8
Wanleweyne *Somali Rep.* 2°37N 44°54E 47 G3
Wanneroo *Australia* 31°42S 115°46E 61 F2
Wanning *China* 18°48N 110°22E 38 C8
Wannoo Billabong Roadhouse
  Australia 27°25S 115°49E 61 E2
Wanon Niwat *Thailand* 17°38N 103°46E 38 D4
Wanqinsha *China* 22°43N 113°33E 33 F10
Wanquan *China* 40°50N 114°40E 34 D8
Wanrong *China* 35°25N 110°50E 34 G6
Wanshan Qundao
  China 21°57N 113°45E 33 G10
Wantage *U.K.* 51°35N 1°25W 13 F6
Wanxian *China* 30°42N 108°20E 32 C5
Wanzai *China* 22°12N 113°31E 33 G10
Wapakoneta *U.S.A.* 40°34N 84°12W 81 E11
Wapato *U.S.A.* 46°27N 120°25W 76 C3
Wapawekka L. *Canada* 54°55N 104°40W 71 C8
Wapikopa L. *Canada* 52°56N 87°53W 72 B2
Wapiti → *Canada* 55°5N 118°18W 70 B5
Wappingers Falls
  U.S.A. 41°36N 73°55W 83 E11
Wapsipinicon → *U.S.A.* 41°44N 90°19W 80 E8
Wapusk △ *Canada* 57°46N 93°22W 71 B10
Warakurna *Australia* 24°59S 128°17E 61 D4
Warangal *India* 17°58N 79°35E 40 L11
Waraseoni *India* 21°45N 80°2E 43 J9
Waratah *Australia* 41°30S 145°30E 63 G4
Waratah B. *Australia* 38°54S 146°5E 63 F4
Warburton *Vic.,
  Australia* 37°47S 145°42E 63 F4
Warburton *W. Austral.,
  Australia* 26°8S 126°35E 61 E4
Warburton ♡ *Australia* 26°7S 126°34E 61 E4
Warburton → *Australia* 28°4S 137°28E 63 D2
Warburton Groove
  Australia 28°18S 137°8E 63 A2
Warburton Ra.
  Australia 25°55S 126°28E 61 E4
Ward *N.Z.* 41°49S 174°11E 59 D5
Ward → *Australia* 26°28S 146°6E 63 D4
Ward Mt. *U.S.A.* 37°12N 118°54W 78 H8
Warden *S. Africa* 27°50S 29°0E 57 D4
Wardha *India* 20°45N 78°39E 40 J11
Wardha → *India* 19°57N 79°11E 40 K11
Wardsville *Canada* 42°39N 81°45W 82 D3
Ware *U.K.* 51°49N 0°0 13 F8
Ware *U.S.A.* 42°16N 72°14W 83 D12
Waregem *Belgium* 50°53N 3°27E 15 D3
Wareham *U.S.A.* 41°46N 70°43W 83 E14
Waremme *Belgium* 50°43N 5°15E 15 D5
Warialda *Australia* 29°29S 150°33E 63 D5
Wariap *Indonesia* 1°30S 134°5E 37 E8
Warin Chamrap
  Thailand 15°12N 104°53E 38 E5
Warkopi *Indonesia* 1°12S 134°9E 37 E8
Warm Springs *U.S.A.* 38°10N 116°20W 77 G5
Warman *Canada* 52°19N 106°30W 71 C7
Warmbad = Bela Bela
  S. Africa 24°51S 28°19E 57 C4
Warmbad *Namibia* 28°25S 18°42E 56 D2
Warminster *U.K.* 51°12N 2°10W 13 F5
Warminster *U.S.A.* 40°12N 75°6W 83 F9
Warmun *Australia* 17°2S 128°12E 60 C4
Warner Mts. *U.S.A.* 41°40N 120°15W 76 F3
Warner Robins *U.S.A.* 32°37N 83°36W 85 E13
Waroona *Australia* 32°50S 115°58E 61 F2
Warrabri *Australia* 21°1S 134°1E 62 C1
Warracknabeal *Australia* 36°9S 142°26E 63 F3
Warragul *Australia* 38°10S 145°58E 63 F4
Warrego → *Australia* 30°24S 145°21E 63 E4
Warrego Ra. *Australia* 24°58S 146°0E 62 C4
Warren *Australia* 31°42S 147°51E 63 E4
Warren *Ark., U.S.A.* 33°37N 92°4W 84 E8
Warren *Mich., U.S.A.* 42°28N 83°1W 81 D12
Warren *Minn., U.S.A.* 48°12N 96°46W 80 A5
Warren *Ohio, U.S.A.* 41°14N 80°49W 82 E4
Warren *Pa., U.S.A.* 41°51N 79°9W 82 E5
Warrenpoint *U.K.* 54°6N 6°15W 10 B5
Warrensburg *Mo.,
  U.S.A.* 38°46N 93°44W 80 F7
Warrensburg *N.Y.,
  U.S.A.* 43°29N 73°46W 83 C11
Warrenton *S. Africa* 28°9S 24°47E 56 D3
Warrenton *U.S.A.* 46°10N 123°56W 78 D3
Warri *Nigeria* 5°30N 5°41E 50 G7
Warrington *U.K.* 53°24N 2°35W 12 D5
Warrnambool *Australia* 38°25S 142°30E 63 F3
Warroad *U.S.A.* 48°54N 95°19W 80 A6
Warruwi *Australia* 11°36S 133°20E 62 A1
Warsa *Indonesia* 0°47S 135°55E 37 E9
Warsak Dam *Pakistan* 34°11N 71°19E 42 B4
Warsaw = Warszawa
  Poland 52°14N 21°0E 17 B11
Warsaw *Ind., U.S.A.* 41°14N 85°51W 81 E11
Warsaw *N.Y., U.S.A.* 42°45N 78°8W 82 D6
Warsaw *Ohio, U.S.A.* 40°20N 82°0W 82 F3

Warszawa *Poland* 52°14N 21°0E 17 B11
Warta → *Poland* 52°35N 14°39E 16 B8
Warthe = Warta →
  Poland 52°35N 14°39E 16 B8
Waru *Indonesia* 3°30S 130°36E 37 E8
Warumungu ♡
  Australia 19°15S 134°44E 62 B1
Warwick *Australia* 28°10S 152°1E 63 D5
Warwick *U.K.* 52°18N 1°35W 13 E6
Warwick *N.Y., U.S.A.* 41°16N 74°22W 83 E10
Warwick *R.I., U.S.A.* 41°42N 71°28W 83 E13
Warwickshire □ *U.K.* 52°14N 1°38W 13 E6
Wasaga Beach *Canada* 44°31N 80°1W 82 B4
Wasagaming *Canada* 50°39N 99°58W 71 C9
Wasatch Ra. *U.S.A.* 40°0N 111°30W 76 F8
Wasbank *S. Africa* 28°15S 30°9E 57 D5
Wasco *Calif., U.S.A.* 35°36N 119°20W 79 K7
Wasco *Oreg., U.S.A.* 45°36N 120°42W 76 D3
Waseca *U.S.A.* 44°5N 93°30W 80 C7
Wasekamio L. *Canada* 56°45N 108°45W 71 B7
Washago *Canada* 44°45N 79°20W 82 B5
Washburn *N. Dak.,
  U.S.A.* 47°17N 101°2W 80 B3
Washburn *Wis., U.S.A.* 46°40N 90°54W 80 B8
Washim *India* 20°3N 77°0E 40 J10
Washington *U.K.* 54°55N 1°30W 12 C6
Washington *D.C., U.S.A.* 38°53N 77°2W 81 F15
Washington *Ga.,
  U.S.A.* 33°44N 82°44W 85 E13
Washington *Ind.,
  U.S.A.* 38°40N 87°10W 80 F10
Washington *Iowa,
  U.S.A.* 41°18N 91°42W 80 E8
Washington *Mo., U.S.A.* 38°33N 91°1W 80 F8
Washington *N.C.,
  U.S.A.* 35°33N 77°3W 85 D16
Washington *N.J.,
  U.S.A.* 40°46N 74°59W 83 F10
Washington *Pa., U.S.A.* 40°10N 80°15W 82 F4
Washington *Utah,
  U.S.A.* 37°8N 113°31W 77 H7
Washington □ *U.S.A.* 47°30N 120°30W 76 C3
Washington, Mt.
  U.S.A. 44°16N 71°18W 83 B13
Washington Court House
  U.S.A. 39°32N 83°26W 81 F12
Washington I. *U.S.A.* 45°23N 86°54W 80 C10
Washougal *U.S.A.* 45°35N 122°21W 78 E4
Washpool △ *Australia* 29°22S 152°0E 63 D5
Wasian *Indonesia* 1°47S 133°19E 37 E8
Wasilla *U.S.A.* 61°35N 149°26W 68 E2
Wasior *Indonesia* 2°43S 134°30E 37 E8
Wāsiṭ □ *Iraq* 32°50N 46°0E 46 C5
Waskaganish *Canada* 51°30N 78°40W 72 B4
Waskaiowaka L.
  Canada 56°33N 96°23W 71 B9
Waskesiu Lake *Canada* 53°55N 106°5W 71 C7
Wasserkuppe *Germany* 50°29N 9°55E 16 C5
Waswanipi *Canada* 49°40N 76°29W 72 C4
Waswanipi, L. *Canada* 49°35N 76°40W 72 C4
Watampone *Indonesia* 4°29S 120°25E 37 E6
Watamu *Kenya* 3°23S 40°0E 54 C5
Watarrka △ *Australia* 24°20S 131°30E 60 D5
Water Park Pt.
  Australia 22°56S 150°47E 62 C5
Water Valley *U.S.A.* 34°10N 89°38W 85 D10
Waterberg Plateau △
  Namibia 20°25S 17°18E 56 C2
Waterberge *S. Africa* 24°10S 28°0E 57 C4
Waterbury *Conn., U.S.A.* 41°33N 73°3W 83 E11
Waterbury *Vt., U.S.A.* 44°20N 72°46W 83 B12
Waterbury L. *Canada* 58°10N 104°22W 71 B8
Waterdown *Canada* 43°20N 79°53W 82 C5
Waterford *Canada* 42°56N 80°17W 82 D4
Waterford *Ireland* 52°15N 7°8W 10 D4
Waterford *Calif., U.S.A.* 37°38N 120°46W 78 H6
Waterford *Pa., U.S.A.* 41°57N 79°59W 82 E5
Waterford □ *Ireland* 52°10N 7°40W 10 D4
Waterford Harbour
  Ireland 52°8N 6°58W 10 D5
Waterhen L. *Canada* 52°10N 99°40W 71 C9
Waterloo *Belgium* 50°43N 4°25E 15 D4
Waterloo *Ont., Canada* 43°30N 80°32W 82 C4
Waterloo *Qué., Canada* 45°22N 72°32W 83 A12
Waterloo *Ill., U.S.A.* 38°20N 90°9W 80 F8
Waterloo *Iowa, U.S.A.* 42°30N 92°21W 80 D7
Waterloo *N.Y., U.S.A.* 42°54N 76°52W 82 D8
Watersmeet *U.S.A.* 46°16N 89°11W 80 B9
Waterton Lakes △
  Canada 48°45N 115°0W 70 D6
Watertown *Conn.,
  U.S.A.* 41°36N 73°7W 83 E11
Watertown *N.Y., U.S.A.* 43°59N 75°55W 83 C9
Watertown *S. Dak.,
  U.S.A.* 44°54N 97°7W 80 C5
Watertown *Wis., U.S.A.* 43°12N 88°43W 80 D9
Waterval-Boven *S. Africa* 25°40S 30°18E 57 D5
Waterville *Canada* 45°16N 71°54W 83 A13
Waterville *Maine,
  U.S.A.* 44°33N 69°38W 81 C19
Waterville *N.Y., U.S.A.* 42°56N 75°23W 83 D9
Waterville *Pa., U.S.A.* 41°19N 77°21W 82 E7
Waterville *Wash., U.S.A.* 47°39N 120°4W 76 C3
Watervliet *U.S.A.* 42°44N 73°42W 83 D11
Wates *Indonesia* 7°51S 110°10E 37 G14
Watford *Canada* 42°57N 81°53W 82 D3
Watford *U.K.* 51°40N 0°24W 13 F7
Watford City *U.S.A.* 47°48N 103°17W 80 B2
Wathaman → *Canada* 57°16N 102°59W 71 B8
Wathaman L. *Canada* 56°58N 103°44W 71 B8
Watheroo *Australia* 30°15S 116°5E 61 F2
Watheroo △ *Australia* 30°15S 116°48E 61 F2
Wating *China* 35°40N 106°38E 34 G4
Watkins Glen *U.S.A.* 42°23N 76°52W 82 D8
Watling I. = San Salvador I.
  Bahamas 24°0N 74°40W 89 B5
Watonga *U.S.A.* 35°51N 98°25W 84 D5

Watrous *Canada* 51°40N 105°25W 71 C7
Watrous *U.S.A.* 35°48N 104°59W 77 J11
Watsa
  Dem. Rep. of the Congo 3°4N 29°30E 54 B2
Watseka *U.S.A.* 40°47N 87°44W 80 E10
Watson *Canada* 52°10N 104°30W 71 C8
Watson Lake *Canada* 60°6N 128°49W 70 A3
Watsontown *U.S.A.* 41°5N 76°52W 82 E8
Watsonville *U.S.A.* 36°55N 121°45W 78 J5
Wattiwarriganna Cr. →
  Australia 28°57S 136°10E 63 D2
Watuata = Batuata
  Indonesia 6°12S 122°42E 37 F6
Watubela, Kepulauan
  Indonesia 4°28S 131°35E 37 E8
Watubela Is. = Watubela,
  Kepulauan *Indonesia* 4°28S 131°35E 37 E8
Wau = Wāw *Sudan* 7°45N 28°1E 51 G11
Waubamik *Canada* 45°27N 80°1W 82 A4
Waubay *U.S.A.* 45°20N 97°18W 80 C5
Wauchope *N.S.W.,
  Australia* 31°28S 152°45E 63 E5
Wauchope *N. Terr.,
  Australia* 20°36S 134°15E 62 C1
Wauchula *U.S.A.* 27°33N 81°49W 85 H14
Waukarlycarly, L.
  Australia 21°18S 121°56E 60 D3
Waukegan *U.S.A.* 42°22N 87°50W 80 D10
Waukesha *U.S.A.* 43°1N 88°14W 80 D9
Waukon *U.S.A.* 43°16N 91°29W 80 D8
Waupaca *U.S.A.* 44°21N 89°5W 80 C9
Waupun *U.S.A.* 43°38N 88°44W 80 D9
Waurika *U.S.A.* 34°10N 98°0W 84 D6
Wausau *U.S.A.* 44°58N 89°38W 80 C9
Wautoma *U.S.A.* 44°4N 89°18W 80 C9
Wauwatosa *U.S.A.* 43°2N 88°0W 80 D9
Wave Hill = Kalkarindji
  Australia 17°30S 130°47E 60 C5
Wave Rock △ *Australia* 32°26S 118°53E 61 F2
Waveney → *U.K.* 52°35N 1°39E 13 E9
Waverley *N.Z.* 39°46S 174°37E 59 C5
Waverly *Iowa, U.S.A.* 42°44N 92°29W 80 D7
Waverly *N.Y., U.S.A.* 42°1N 76°32W 83 E8
Wavre *Belgium* 50°43N 4°38E 15 D4
Wāw *Sudan* 7°45N 28°1E 51 G11
Wāw al Kabīr *Libya* 25°20N 16°43E 51 C9
Wawa *Canada* 47°59N 84°47W 72 C3
Wawanesa *Canada* 49°36N 99°40W 71 D9
Wawona *U.S.A.* 37°32N 119°39W 78 H7
Waxahachie *U.S.A.* 32°24N 96°51W 84 E6
Way, L. *Australia* 26°45S 120°16E 61 E3
Waya *Fiji* 17°19S 177°10E 59 a
Waycross *U.S.A.* 31°13N 82°21W 85 F13
Wayland *U.S.A.* 42°34N 77°35W 82 D7
Wayne *Nebr., U.S.A.* 42°14N 97°1W 80 D5
Wayne *W. Va., U.S.A.* 38°13N 82°27W 81 F12
Waynesboro *Ga., U.S.A.* 33°6N 82°1W 85 E13
Waynesboro *Miss.,
  U.S.A.* 31°40N 88°39W 85 F10
Waynesboro *Pa.,
  U.S.A.* 39°45N 77°35W 81 F15
Waynesboro *Va., U.S.A.* 38°4N 78°53W 81 F14
Waynesburg *U.S.A.* 39°54N 80°11W 81 F13
Waynesville *U.S.A.* 35°28N 82°58W 85 D13
Waynoka *U.S.A.* 36°35N 98°53W 84 C5
Wazirabad *Pakistan* 32°30N 74°8E 42 C6
Waziristan *Pakistan* 33°0N 70°0E 42 C4
We *Indonesia* 5°51N 95°18E 36 C1
Weald, The *U.K.* 51°4N 0°20E 13 F8
Wear → *U.K.* 54°55N 1°23W 12 C6
Weatherford *Okla.,
  U.S.A.* 35°32N 98°43W 84 D5
Weatherford *Tex., U.S.A.* 32°46N 97°48W 84 E6
Weaverville *U.S.A.* 40°44N 122°56W 76 F2
Webb City *U.S.A.* 37°9N 94°28W 80 G6
Webequie *Canada* 52°59N 87°21W 72 B2
Webster *Mass., U.S.A.* 42°3N 71°53W 83 D13
Webster *N.Y., U.S.A.* 43°13N 77°26W 82 C7
Webster *S. Dak., U.S.A.* 45°20N 97°31W 80 C5
Webster City *U.S.A.* 42°28N 93°49W 80 D7
Webster Springs *U.S.A.* 38°29N 80°25W 81 F13
Webuye *Kenya* 0°37N 34°46E 54 B3
Weda *Indonesia* 0°21N 127°50E 37 D7
Weda, Teluk *Indonesia* 0°20N 128°0E 37 D7
Weddell Abyssal Plain
  S. Ocean 65°0S 20°0W 5 C2
Weddell I. *Falk. Is.* 51°50S 61°0W 96 G4
Weddell Sea *Antarctica* 72°30S 40°0W 5 D1
Wedderburn *Australia* 36°26S 143°33E 63 F3
Wedgeport *Canada* 43°44N 65°59W 73 D6
Wedza *Zimbabwe* 18°40S 31°33E 55 F3
Wee Waa *Australia* 30°11S 149°26E 63 E4
Weed *U.S.A.* 41°25N 122°23W 76 F2
Weed Heights *U.S.A.* 38°59N 119°13W 78 G7
Weedsport *U.S.A.* 43°2N 76°33W 82 C8
Weedville *U.S.A.* 41°17N 78°30W 82 E6
Weenen *S. Africa* 28°48S 30°7E 57 D5
Weert *Neths.* 51°15N 5°43E 15 C5
Wei He → *Hebei, China* 36°10N 115°45E 34 F8
Wei He → *Shaanxi,
  China* 34°38N 110°15E 34 G6
Weichang *China* 41°58N 117°49E 35 D9
Weichuan *China* 34°20N 113°59E 34 G7
Weiden *Germany* 49°41N 12°10E 16 D7
Weifang *China* 36°44N 119°7E 35 F10
Weihai *China* 37°30N 122°6E 35 F12
Weimar *Germany* 50°58N 11°19E 16 C6
Weinan *China* 34°31N 109°29E 34 G5
Weipa *Australia* 12°40S 141°50E 62 A3
Weir → *Australia* 28°20S 149°50E 63 D4
Weir → *Canada* 56°54N 93°21W 71 B10
Weir River *Canada* 56°49N 94°6W 71 B10
Weirton *U.S.A.* 40°24N 80°35W 82 F4
Weiser *U.S.A.* 44°10N 116°58W 76 D5
Weishan *China* 34°47N 117°5E 35 G9
Weiyuan *China* 35°7N 104°10E 34 G3
Wejherowo *Poland* 54°35N 18°12E 17 A10
Wekusko L. *Canada* 54°40N 99°50W 71 C9
Welch *U.S.A.* 37°26N 81°35W 81 G13

Welford △ *Australia* 25°5S 143°16E 62 D3
Welkom *S. Africa* 28°0S 26°46E 56 D4
Welland *Canada* 43°0N 79°15W 82 D5
Welland → *U.K.* 52°51N 0°5W 13 E7
Wellesley Is. *Australia* 16°42S 139°30E 62 B2
Wellesley Islands ♡
  Australia 16°32S 139°23E 62 B2
Wellingborough *U.K.* 52°19N 0°41W 13 E7
Wellington *Australia* 32°35S 148°59E 63 E4
Wellington *Canada* 43°57N 77°20W 82 C7
Wellington *N.Z.* 41°19S 174°46E 59 D5
Wellington *S. Africa* 33°38S 19°1E 56 E2
Wellington *Somst., U.K.* 50°58N 3°13W 13 G4
Wellington *Telford & Wrekin,
  U.K.* 52°42N 2°30W 13 E5
Wellington *Colo.,
  U.S.A.* 40°42N 105°0W 76 F11
Wellington *Kans., U.S.A.* 37°16N 97°24W 80 G5
Wellington *Nev., U.S.A.* 38°45N 119°23W 78 G7
Wellington *Ohio, U.S.A.* 41°10N 82°13W 82 E2
Wellington *Tex., U.S.A.* 34°51N 100°13W 84 D4
Wellington, I. *Chile* 49°30S 75°0W 96 F2
Wellington, L. *Australia* 38°6S 147°20E 63 F4
Wellington Chan. *Canada* 75°0N 93°0W 69 C13
Wells *U.K.* 51°13N 2°39W 13 F5
Wells *Maine, U.S.A.* 43°20N 70°35W 83 C14
Wells *N.Y., U.S.A.* 43°24N 74°17W 83 C10
Wells *Nev., U.S.A.* 41°7N 114°58W 76 F6
Wells, L. *Australia* 26°44S 123°15E 61 E3
Wells, Mt. *Australia* 17°25S 127°8E 60 C4
Wells Gray △ *Canada* 52°30N 120°15W 70 C4
Wells-next-the-Sea *U.K.* 52°57N 0°51E 12 E8
Wells River *U.S.A.* 44°9N 72°4W 83 B12
Wellsboro *U.S.A.* 41°45N 77°18W 82 E7
Wellsburg *U.S.A.* 40°16N 80°37W 82 F4
Wellsville *N.Y., U.S.A.* 42°7N 77°57W 82 D7
Wellsville *Ohio, U.S.A.* 40°36N 80°39W 82 F4
Wellsville *Utah, U.S.A.* 41°38N 111°56W 76 F8
Wellton *U.S.A.* 32°40N 114°8W 77 K6
Wels *Austria* 48°9N 14°1E 16 D8
Welshpool *U.K.* 52°39N 3°8W 13 E4
Welwyn Garden City
  U.K. 51°48N 0°12W 13 F7
Wem *U.K.* 52°52N 2°44W 12 E5
Wembere → *Tanzania* 4°10S 34°15E 54 C3
Wemindji *Canada* 53°0N 78°49W 72 B4
Wemyss *Canada* 44°52N 76°23W 83 B8
Wen Xian *China* 34°55N 113°5E 34 G7
Wenatchee *U.S.A.* 47°25N 120°19W 76 C3
Wenchang *China* 19°38N 110°42E 38 C8
Wenchi *Ghana* 7°46N 2°8W 50 G5
Wenchow = Wenzhou
  China 28°0N 120°38E 33 D7
Wenden *U.S.A.* 33°49N 113°33W 79 M13
Wendeng *China* 37°15N 122°5E 35 F12
Wendesi *Indonesia* 2°30S 134°17E 37 E8
Wendover *U.S.A.* 40°44N 114°2W 76 F6
Wenlock → *Australia* 12°2S 141°55E 62 A3
Wenshan *China* 23°20N 104°18E 32 D5
Wenshang *China* 35°45N 116°30E 34 G9
Wenshui *China* 37°26N 112°1E 34 F7
Wensleydale *U.K.* 54°17N 2°0W 12 C6
Wensu *China* 41°15N 80°10E 32 B3
Wensum → *U.K.* 52°40N 1°15E 12 E8
Wentworth *Australia* 34°2S 141°54E 63 E3
Wentzel L. *Canada* 59°2N 114°28W 70 B6
Wenut *Indonesia* 3°11S 133°19E 37 E8
Wenxi *China* 35°20N 111°10E 34 G6
Wenxian *China* 32°43N 104°36E 34 H3
Wenzhou *China* 28°0N 120°38E 33 D7
Weott *U.S.A.* 40°20N 123°55W 76 F2
Wepener *S. Africa* 29°42S 27°3E 56 D4
Werda *Botswana* 25°24S 23°15E 56 D3
Weri *Indonesia* 3°10S 132°38E 37 E8
Werra → *Germany* 51°24N 9°39E 16 C5
Werrimull *Australia* 34°25S 141°38E 63 E3
Werris Creek *Australia* 31°18S 150°38E 63 E5
Weser → *Germany* 53°36N 8°28E 16 B5
Wesiri *Indonesia* 7°30S 126°30E 37 F7
Weslaco *U.S.A.* 26°10N 97°58W 84 H6
Weslemkoon L. *Canada* 45°2N 77°25W 82 A7
Wesleyville *Canada* 49°9N 53°33W 73 C9
Wesleyville *U.S.A.* 42°9N 80°1W 82 D4
Wessel, C. *Australia* 10°59S 136°46E 62 A2
Wessel Is. *Australia* 11°10S 136°45E 62 A2
Wessington Springs
  U.S.A. 44°5N 98°34W 80 C4
West *U.S.A.* 31°48N 97°6W 84 F6
West → *U.S.A.* 42°52N 72°33W 83 D12
West Allis *U.S.A.* 43°1N 88°0W 80 D9
West Antarctica
  Antarctica 80°0S 90°0W 5 D15
West Baines →
  Australia 15°38S 129°59E 60 C4
West Bank ■ *Asia* 32°6N 35°13E 46 C4
West Bend *U.S.A.* 43°25N 88°11W 80 D9
West Bengal □ *India* 23°0N 88°0E 43 H13
West Beskids = Západné Beskydy
  Europe 49°30N 19°0E 17 D10
West Branch *U.S.A.* 44°17N 84°14W 81 C11
West Branch Susquehanna →
  U.S.A. 40°53N 76°48W 83 F8
West Bromwich *U.K.* 52°32N 1°59W 13 E6
West Burra *U.K.* 60°5N 1°21W 11 A7
West Canada Cr. →
  U.S.A. 43°1N 74°58W 83 C10
West Caroline Basin
  Pac. Oc. 4°0N 138°0E 64 G5
West Chazy *U.S.A.* 44°49N 73°28W 83 B11
West Chester *U.S.A.* 39°58N 75°36W 83 G9
West Coast △ *S. Africa* 33°13S 18°0E 56 E2
West Columbia *U.S.A.* 29°9N 95°39W 84 G7
West Covina *U.S.A.* 34°4N 117°54W 79 L9
West Des Moines *U.S.A.* 41°35N 93°43W 80 E7
West Dunbartonshire □
  U.K. 55°59N 4°30W 11 F4
West End *Bahamas* 26°41N 78°58W 88 A4

West Falkland *Falk. Is.* 51°40S 60°0W **96** G4
West Fargo *U.S.A.* 46°52N 96°54W **80** B5
West Fiji Basin *Pac. Oc.* 17°0S 173°0E **64** J9
West Fjord = Vestfjorden
  Norway 67°55N 14°0E **8** C16
West Fork Trinity →
  U.S.A. 32°48N 96°54W **84** E6
West Frankfort *U.S.A.* 37°54N 88°55W **80** G9
West Grand L. *U.S.A.* 45°14N 67°51W **81** C20
West Hartford *U.S.A.* 41°45N 72°44W **83** E12
West Haven *U.S.A.* 41°17N 72°57W **83** E12
West Hazleton *U.S.A.* 40°58N 76°0W **83** F9
West Helena *U.S.A.* 34°33N 90°38W **85** D9
West Hurley *U.S.A.* 41°59N 74°7W **83** E10
West Ice Shelf *Antarctica* 67°0S 85°0E **5** C7
West Indies *Cent. Amer.* 15°0N 65°0W **89** D7
West Jordan *U.S.A.* 40°36N 111°56W **76** F8
West Lamma Channel
  China 22°14N 114°4E **33** G11
West Linn *U.S.A.* 45°21N 122°36W **78** E4
West Lorne *Canada* 42°36N 81°36W **82** D3
West Lothian □ *U.K.* 55°54N 3°36W **11** F5
West Lunga → *Zambia* 13°6S 24°39E **55** E1
West MacDonnell △
  Australia 23°38S 132°59E **60** D5
West Mariana Basin
  Pac. Oc. 15°0N 137°0E **64** F5
West Memphis *U.S.A.* 35°8N 90°10W **85** D9
West Midlands □ *U.K.* 52°26N 2°0W **13** E6
West Mifflin *U.S.A.* 40°21N 79°52W **82** F5
West Milford *U.S.A.* 41°8N 74°22W **83** E10
West Milton *U.S.A.* 41°1N 76°50W **82** E8
West Monroe *U.S.A.* 32°31N 92°9W **84** E8
West Newton *U.S.A.* 40°14N 79°46W **82** F5
West Nicholson *Zimbabwe* 21°2S 29°20E **55** G2
West Odessa *U.S.A.* 31°50N 102°30W **84** F3
West Palm Beach
  U.S.A. 26°43N 80°3W **85** H14
West Plains *U.S.A.* 36°44N 91°51W **80** G8
West Point *Miss.*,
  U.S.A. 33°36N 88°39W **85** E10
West Point *N.Y., U.S.A.* 41°24N 73°58W **83** E11
West Point *Nebr., U.S.A.* 41°51N 96°43W **80** E6
West Point *Va., U.S.A.* 37°32N 76°48W **81** G15
West Point L. *U.S.A.* 33°8N 85°0W **85** E12
West Pt. = Ouest, Pte. de l'
  Canada 49°52N 64°40W **73** C7
West Pt. *Australia* 35°1S 135°56E **63** F2
West Road → *Canada* 53°18N 122°53W **70** C4
West Rutland *U.S.A.* 43°36N 73°3W **83** C11
West Schelde = Westerschelde →
  Neths. 51°25N 3°25E **15** C3
West Seneca *U.S.A.* 42°51N 78°48W **82** D6
West Siberian Plain *Russia* 62°0N 75°0E **26** B9
West Sussex □ *U.K.* 50°55N 0°30W **13** G7
West-Terschelling *Neths.* 53°22N 5°13E **15** A5
West Valley City *U.S.A.* 40°42N 111°58W **76** F8
West Virginia □ *U.S.A.* 38°45N 80°30W **81** F13
West-Vlaanderen □
  Belgium 51°0N 3°0E **15** D2
West Walker → *U.S.A.* 38°54N 119°9W **78** G7
West Wyalong *Australia* 33°56S 147°10E **63** E4
West Yellowstone
  U.S.A. 44°40N 111°6W **76** D8
West Yorkshire □ *U.K.* 53°45N 1°40W **12** D6
Westall, Pt. *Australia* 32°55S 134°4E **63** E1
Westbrook *U.S.A.* 43°41N 70°22W **81** D18
Westbury *Australia* 41°30S 146°51E **63** G4
Westby *U.S.A.* 48°52N 104°3W **76** B11
Westend *U.S.A.* 35°42N 117°24W **79** K9
Westerland *Germany* 54°54N 8°17E **16** A5
Westerly *U.S.A.* 41°22N 71°50W **83** E13
Western □ *Kenya* 0°30N 34°30E **54** B3
Western □ *Zambia* 15°0S 24°4E **55** F1
Western Australia □
  Australia 25°0S 118°0E **61** E2
Western Cape □ *S. Africa* 34°0S 20°0E **56** E3
Western Dvina = Daugava →
  Latvia 57°4N 24°3E **9** H21
Western Ghats *India* 14°0N 75°0E **40** N9
Western Isles □ *U.K.* 57°30N 7°10W **11** D1
Western Sahara ■ *Africa* 25°0N 13°0W **50** D3
Western Samoa = Samoa ■
  Pac. Oc. 14°0S 172°0W **59** b
Western Sierra Madre = Madre
  Occidental, Sierra
  Mexico 27°0N 107°0W **86** B3
Westernport *U.S.A.* 39°29N 79°3W **81** F14
Westerschelde → *Neths.* 51°25N 3°25E **15** C3
Westerwald *Germany* 50°38N 7°56E **16** C4
Westfield *Mass., U.S.A.* 42°7N 72°45W **83** D12
Westfield *N.Y., U.S.A.* 42°20N 79°35W **82** D5
Westfield *Pa., U.S.A.* 41°55N 77°32W **82** E7
Westhill *U.K.* 57°9N 2°19W **11** D6
Westhope *U.S.A.* 48°55N 101°1W **80** A3
Westland △ *N.Z.* 43°16S 170°16E **59** E2
Westland Bight *N.Z.* 42°55S 170°5E **59** E3
Westlock *Canada* 54°9N 113°55W **70** C6
Westmar *Australia* 27°55S 149°44E **63** D4
Westmeath □ *Ireland* 53°33N 7°34W **10** C4
Westminster *Calif.*,
  U.S.A. 33°45N 118°0W **79** M8
Westminster *Colo.*,
  U.S.A. 39°50N 105°2W **76** G11
Westminster *Md.*,
  U.S.A. 39°34N 76°59W **81** F15
Westmont *U.S.A.* 40°19N 78°58W **82** F6
Westmoreland *Barbados* 13°13N 59°37W **89** g
Westmorland *U.S.A.* 33°2N 115°37W **79** M11
Weston *Oreg., U.S.A.* 45°49N 118°26W **76** D4
Weston *W. Va., U.S.A.* 39°2N 80°28W **81** F13
Weston I. *Canada* 52°33N 79°36W **72** B4
Weston-super-Mare *U.K.* 51°21N 2°58W **13** F5
Westover *U.S.A.* 40°45N 78°40W **82** F6
Westport *Canada* 44°40N 76°25W **83** B8
Westport *Ireland* 53°48N 9°31W **10** C2
Westport *N.Z.* 41°46S 171°37E **59** D3
Westport *N.Y., U.S.A.* 44°11N 73°26W **83** B11
Westport *Oreg., U.S.A.* 46°8N 123°23W **78** D3

Westport *Wash., U.S.A.* 46°53N 124°6W **78** D2
Westray *Canada* 53°36N 101°24W **71** C8
Westray *U.K.* 59°18N 3°0W **11** B5
Westree *Canada* 47°26N 81°34W **72** C3
Westville *U.S.A.* 39°8N 120°42W **78** F6
Westwood *U.S.A.* 40°18N 121°0W **76** F3
Wetar *Indonesia* 7°48S 126°30E **37** F7
Wetaskiwin *Canada* 52°55N 113°24W **70** C6
Wete *Tanzania* 5°4S 39°43E **52** F7
Wetherby *U.K.* 53°56N 1°23W **12** D6
Wethersfield *U.S.A.* 41°42N 72°40W **83** E12
Wetteren *Belgium* 51°0N 3°53E **15** D3
Wetzlar *Germany* 50°32N 8°31E **16** C5
Wewoka *U.S.A.* 35°9N 96°30W **84** D6
Wexford *Ireland* 52°20N 6°28W **10** D5
Wexford □ *Ireland* 52°20N 6°25W **10** D5
Wexford Harbour *Ireland* 52°20N 6°25W **10** D5
Weyburn *Canada* 49°40N 103°50W **71** D8
Weymouth *Canada* 44°30N 66°1W **73** D6
Weymouth *U.K.* 50°37N 2°28W **13** G5
Weymouth *U.S.A.* 42°13N 70°58W **83** D14
Weymouth, C. *Australia* 12°37S 143°27E **62** A3
Wha Ti *Canada* 63°8N 117°16W **68** E8
Whakaari *N.Z.* 37°30S 177°13E **59** B6
Whakatane *N.Z.* 37°57S 177°1E **59** B6
Whale = Baleine →
  Canada 58°15N 67°40W **73** A6
Whale Cove *Canada* 62°10N 92°34W **71** A10
Whales, B. of *Antarctica* 78°0S 160°0W **5** D12
Whalsay *U.K.* 60°22N 0°59W **11** A8
Whangamata *N.Z.* 37°12S 175°53E **59** B5
Whangamomona *N.Z.* 39°8S 174°44E **59** C5
Whanganui △ *N.Z.* 39°17S 174°53E **59** C5
Whangarei *N.Z.* 35°43S 174°21E **59** A5
Whangarei Harb. *N.Z.* 35°45S 174°28E **59** A5
Wharekauri = Chatham Is.
  Pac. Oc. 44°0S 176°40W **64** M10
Wharfe → *U.K.* 53°51N 1°9W **12** D6
Wharfedale *U.K.* 54°6N 2°1W **12** C5
Wharton *N.J., U.S.A.* 40°54N 74°35W **83** F10
Wharton *Pa., U.S.A.* 41°31N 78°1W **82** E6
Wharton *Tex., U.S.A.* 29°19N 96°6W **84** G6
Wharton Basin *Ind. Oc.* 22°0S 92°0E **64** K1
Wheatland *Calif., U.S.A.* 39°1N 121°25W **78** F5
Wheatland *Wyo.*,
  U.S.A. 42°3N 104°58W **76** E11
Wheatley *Canada* 42°6N 82°27W **82** D2
Wheaton *Md., U.S.A.* 39°3N 77°3W **81** F15
Wheaton *Minn., U.S.A.* 45°48N 96°30W **80** C5
Wheelbarrow Pk.
  U.S.A. 37°26N 116°5W **78** H10
Wheeler *Oreg., U.S.A.* 45°41N 123°53W **76** D2
Wheeler *Tex., U.S.A.* 35°27N 100°16W **84** D4
Wheeler → *Canada* 57°2N 67°13W **73** A6
Wheeler L. *U.S.A.* 34°48N 87°23W **85** D11
Wheeler Pk. *N. Mex.*,
  U.S.A. 36°34N 105°25W **77** H11
Wheeler Pk. *Nev.*,
  U.S.A. 38°57N 114°15W **76** G6
Wheeler Ridge *U.S.A.* 35°0N 118°57W **79** L8
Wheelersburg *U.S.A.* 38°44N 82°51W **81** F12
Wheeling *U.S.A.* 40°4N 80°43W **82** F4
Whernside *U.K.* 54°14N 2°24W **12** C5
Whiddy I. *Ireland* 51°41N 9°31W **10** E2
Whim Creek *Australia* 20°50S 117°49E **60** D2
Whiskey Jack L.
  Canada 58°23N 101°55W **71** B8
Whiskeytown-Shasta-Trinity △
  U.S.A. 40°45N 122°15W **76** F2
Whistleduck Cr. →
  Australia 20°15S 135°18E **62** C2
Whistler *Canada* 50°7N 122°58W **70** C4
Whitby *Canada* 43°52N 78°56W **82** C6
Whitby *U.K.* 54°29N 0°37W **12** C7
White → *Ark., U.S.A.* 33°57N 91°5W **84** E9
White → *Ind., U.S.A.* 38°25N 87°45W **80** F10
White → *S. Dak., U.S.A.* 43°42N 99°27W **80** D4
White → *Tex., U.S.A.* 33°14N 100°56W **84** E4
White → *Utah, U.S.A.* 40°4N 109°41W **76** F9
White → *Vt., U.S.A.* 43°37N 72°20W **83** C12
White → *Wash., U.S.A.* 47°12N 122°15W **78** C4
White, L. *Australia* 21°9S 128°56E **60** D4
White B. *Canada* 50°0N 56°35W **73** C8
White Bird *U.S.A.* 45°46N 116°18W **76** D5
White Butte *U.S.A.* 46°23N 103°18W **80** B2
White City *U.S.A.* 42°26N 122°51W **76** E2
White Cliffs *Australia* 30°50S 143°10E **63** E3
White Hall *U.S.A.* 39°26N 90°24W **80** F8
White Haven *U.S.A.* 41°4N 75°47W **83** E9
White Horse, Vale of
  U.K. 51°37N 1°30W **13** F6
White I. = Whakaari
  N.Z. 37°30S 177°13E **59** B6
White L. *Canada* 45°18N 76°31W **83** A8
White L. *U.S.A.* 29°44N 92°30W **84** G8
White Lake *Canada* 45°21N 76°29W **83** A8
White Mountain Peak
  U.S.A. 37°38N 118°15W **77** H4
White Mts. *Calif.*,
  U.S.A. 37°30N 118°15W **78** H8
White Mts. *N.H.*,
  U.S.A. 44°15N 71°15W **83** B13
White Mts. △ *Australia* 20°43S 145°12E **62** C4
White Nile = Nîl el Abyad →
  Sudan 15°38N 32°31E **51** E12
White Otter L. *Canada* 49°5N 91°55W **72** C1
White Pass *U.S.A.* 46°38N 121°24W **78** D5
White Plains *U.S.A.* 41°2N 73°46W **83** E11
White River *Canada* 48°35N 85°20W **72** C2
White River *U.S.A.* 43°34N 100°45W **80** D3
White Rock *Canada* 49°2N 122°48W **78** A4
White Rock *U.S.A.* 35°50N 106°12W **77** J10
White Russia = Belarus ■
  Europe 53°30N 27°0E **17** B14
White Sands △ *U.S.A.* 32°46N 106°20W **77** K10
White Sea = Beloye More
  Russia 66°30N 38°0E **8** C25
White Sulphur Springs *Mont.*,
  U.S.A. 46°33N 110°54W **76** C8

White Sulphur Springs *W. Va.*,
  U.S.A. 37°48N 80°18W **81** G13
White Swan *U.S.A.* 46°23N 120°44W **78** D6
Whitecliffs *N.Z.* 43°26S 171°55E **59** E3
Whitecourt *Canada* 54°10N 115°45W **70** C5
Whiteface Mt. *U.S.A.* 44°22N 73°54W **83** B11
Whitefield *U.S.A.* 44°23N 71°37W **83** B13
Whitefish *U.S.A.* 48°25N 114°20W **76** B6
Whitefish B. *U.S.A.* 46°40N 84°55W **72** C3
Whitefish L. *Canada* 62°41N 106°48W **71** A7
Whitefish Pt. *U.S.A.* 46°45N 84°59W **81** B11
Whitegull, L. = Goëlands, L. aux
  Canada 55°27N 64°17W **73** A7
Whitehall *Mich., U.S.A.* 43°24N 86°21W **80** D10
Whitehall *Mont., U.S.A.* 45°52N 112°6W **76** D7
Whitehall *N.Y., U.S.A.* 43°33N 73°24W **83** C11
Whitehall *Wis., U.S.A.* 44°22N 91°19W **80** C8
Whitehaven *U.K.* 54°33N 3°35W **12** C4
Whitehorse *Canada* 60°43N 135°3W **70** A1
Whitemark *Australia* 40°7S 148°3E **63** G4
Whiteriver *U.S.A.* 33°50N 109°58W **77** K9
Whitesand → *Canada* 60°9N 112°28W **70** A6
Whitesands *S. Africa* 34°23S 20°50E **56** E3
Whitesboro *N.Y., U.S.A.* 43°7N 75°18W **83** C9
Whitesboro *Tex., U.S.A.* 33°39N 96°54W **84** E6
Whiteshell △ *Canada* 50°0N 95°40W **71** D9
Whiteville *U.S.A.* 34°20N 78°42W **85** D15
Whitewater *U.S.A.* 42°50N 88°44W **80** D9
Whitewater Baldy
  U.S.A. 33°20N 108°39W **77** K9
Whitewater L. *U.S.A.* 50°50N 89°10W **72** B2
Whitewood *Australia* 21°28S 143°30E **62** C3
Whitewood *Canada* 50°20N 102°20W **71** C8
Whithorn *U.K.* 54°44N 4°26W **11** G4
Whitianga *N.Z.* 36°47S 175°41E **59** B5
Whitman *U.S.A.* 42°5N 70°56W **83** D14
Whitney *Canada* 45°31N 78°14W **82** A6
Whitney, Mt. *U.S.A.* 36°35N 118°18W **78** J8
Whitney Point *U.S.A.* 42°20N 75°58W **83** D9
Whitstable *U.K.* 51°21N 1°3E **13** F9
Whitsunday I. *Australia* 20°15S 149°4E **62** b
Whitsunday Islands △
  Australia 20°15S 149°0E **62** b
Whittier *Alaska, U.S.A.* 60°47N 148°41W **74** C10
Whittier *Calif., U.S.A.* 33°58N 118°2W **79** M8
Whittlesea *Australia* 37°27S 145°9E **63** F4
Wholdaia L. *Canada* 60°43N 104°20W **71** A8
Whyalla *Australia* 33°2S 137°30E **63** E2
Wiang Kosai △ *Thailand* 17°54N 99°29E **38** D2
Wiang Sa *Thailand* 18°34N 100°45E **38** C3
Wiarton *Canada* 44°40N 81°10W **82** B3
Wiay *U.K.* 57°24N 7°13W **11** D1
Wibaux *U.S.A.* 46°59N 104°11W **76** C11
Wichian Buri *Thailand* 15°39N 101°7E **38** E3
Wichita *U.S.A.* 37°42N 97°20W **80** G5
Wichita Falls *U.S.A.* 33°54N 98°30W **84** E5
Wick *U.K.* 58°26N 3°5W **11** C5
Wickenburg *U.S.A.* 33°58N 112°44W **77** K7
Wickepin *Australia* 32°50S 117°30E **61** F2
Wickham *Australia* 20°42S 117°11E **60** D2
Wickham, C. *Australia* 39°35S 143°57E **63** F3
Wickliffe *U.S.A.* 41°36N 81°28W **82** E3
Wicklow *Ireland* 52°59N 6°3W **10** D5
Wicklow □ *Ireland* 52°57N 6°25W **10** D5
Wicklow Hd. *Ireland* 52°58N 6°0W **10** D6
Wicklow Mts. *Ireland* 52°58N 6°26W **10** D5
Wicklow Mts. △ *Ireland* 53°6N 6°21W **10** C5
Widgeegoara Cr. →
  Australia 28°51S 146°34E **63** D4
Widgiemooltha
  Australia 31°30S 121°34E **61** F3
Widnes *U.K.* 53°23N 2°45W **12** D5
Wieluń *Poland* 51°15N 18°34E **17** C10
Wien *Austria* 48°12N 16°22E **16** D9
Wiener Neustadt *Austria* 47°49N 16°16E **16** E9
Wiesbaden *Germany* 50°4N 8°14E **16** C5
Wigan *U.K.* 53°33N 2°38W **12** D5
Wiggins *Colo., U.S.A.* 40°14N 104°4W **76** F11
Wiggins *Miss., U.S.A.* 30°51N 89°8W **85** F10
Wight, I. of *U.K.* 50°41N 1°17W **13** G6
Wigston *U.K.* 52°35N 1°6W **13** E6
Wigton *U.K.* 54°50N 3°10W **12** C4
Wigtown *U.K.* 54°53N 4°27W **11** G4
Wigtown B. *U.K.* 54°46N 4°15W **11** G4
Wik and Wikway People ◇
  Australia 13°55S 142°28E **62** A3
Wilber *U.S.A.* 40°29N 96°58W **80** E5
Wilberforce *Canada* 45°2N 78°13W **82** A6
Wilberforce, C. *Australia* 11°54S 136°35E **62** A2
Wilburton *U.S.A.* 34°55N 95°19W **84** D7
Wilcannia *Australia* 31°30S 143°26E **63** E3
Wilcox *U.S.A.* 41°35N 78°41W **82** E6
Wildrose *U.S.A.* 36°14N 117°11W **79** J9
Wildspitze *Austria* 46°53N 10°53E **16** E6
Wilge → *S. Africa* 27°3S 28°20E **57** D4
Wilhelm II Coast *Antarctica* 68°0S 90°0E **5** C7
Wilhelmshaven *Germany* 53°31N 8°7E **16** B5
Wilhelmstal *Namibia* 21°58S 16°21E **56** C2
Wilkes-Barre *U.S.A.* 41°15N 75°53W **83** E9
Wilkes Land *Antarctica* 69°0S 120°0E **5** D9
Wilkie *Canada* 52°27N 108°42W **71** C7
Wilkinsburg *U.S.A.* 40°26N 79°52W **82** F5
Wilkinson Lakes
  Australia 29°40S 132°39E **61** E5
Willandra Creek →
  Australia 33°22S 145°52E **63** E4
Willapa B. *U.S.A.* 46°40N 124°0W **76** C1
Willapa Hills *U.S.A.* 46°35N 123°25W **78** D3
Willard *U.S.A.* 41°3N 82°44W **82** E2
Willare Bridge Roadhouse
  Australia 17°43S 123°38E **60** C3
Willcox *U.S.A.* 32°15N 109°50W **77** K9
Willemstad *Neth. Ant.* 12°5N 68°55W **89** D6
William → *Canada* 59°8N 109°19W **71** B7
William 'Bill' Dannelly Res.
  U.S.A. 32°8N 87°24W **85** E11
William Creek *Australia* 28°58S 136°52E **62** D2
Williams *Australia* 33°2S 116°52E **61** F2
Williams *Ariz., U.S.A.* 35°15N 112°11W **77** J7

Williams *Calif., U.S.A.* 39°9N 122°9W **78** F4
Williams Harbour
  Canada 52°33N 55°47W **73** B8
Williams Lake *Canada* 52°10N 122°10W **70** C4
Williamsburg *Ky.*,
  U.S.A. 36°44N 84°10W **81** G11
Williamsburg *Pa.*,
  U.S.A. 40°28N 78°12W **82** F6
Williamsburg *Va.*,
  U.S.A. 37°16N 76°43W **81** G15
Williamson *N.Y., U.S.A.* 43°14N 77°11W **82** C7
Williamson *W. Va.*,
  U.S.A. 37°41N 82°17W **81** G12
Williamsport *U.S.A.* 41°15N 77°1W **82** E7
Williamston *U.S.A.* 35°51N 77°4W **85** D16
Williamstown *Australia* 37°51S 144°52E **63** F3
Williamstown *Ky.*,
  U.S.A. 38°38N 84°34W **81** F11
Williamstown *Mass.*,
  U.S.A. 42°43N 73°12W **83** D11
Williamstown *N.Y.*,
  U.S.A. 43°26N 75°53W **83** C9
Willimantic *U.S.A.* 41°43N 72°13W **83** E12
Willingboro *U.S.A.* 40°3N 74°54W **81** E16
Williston *Fla., U.S.A.* 29°23N 82°27W **85** G13
Williston *N. Dak., U.S.A.* 48°9N 103°37W **80** A2
Williston L. *Canada* 56°0N 124°0W **70** B4
Willits *U.S.A.* 39°25N 123°21W **76** G2
Willmar *U.S.A.* 45°7N 95°3W **80** C6
Willmore Wilderness △
  Canada 53°45N 119°30W **70** C5
Willoughby *U.S.A.* 41°39N 81°24W **82** E3
Willow Bunch *Canada* 49°20N 105°35W **71** D7
Willow L. *Canada* 62°10N 119°8W **70** A5
Willow Wall, The *China* 42°10N 122°0E **35** C12
Willowick *U.S.A.* 41°38N 81°28W **82** E3
Willowlake → *Canada* 62°42N 123°8W **70** A4
Willowmore *S. Africa* 33°15S 23°30E **56** E3
Willows *U.S.A.* 39°31N 122°12W **78** F4
Willowvale = Gatyana
  S. Africa 32°16S 28°31E **57** E4
Wills, L. *Australia* 21°25S 128°51E **60** D4
Wills Cr. → *Australia* 22°43S 140°2E **62** C3
Willsboro *U.S.A.* 44°21N 73°24W **83** B11
Willunga *Australia* 35°15S 138°30E **63** F2
Wilmette *U.S.A.* 42°4N 87°42W **80** D10
Wilmington *Australia* 32°39S 138°7E **63** E2
Wilmington *Del.*,
  U.S.A. 39°45N 75°33W **81** F16
Wilmington *N.C.*,
  U.S.A. 34°14N 77°55W **85** D16
Wilmington *Ohio*,
  U.S.A. 39°27N 83°50W **81** F12
Wilmington *Vt., U.S.A.* 42°52N 72°52W **83** D12
Wilmslow *U.K.* 53°19N 2°13W **12** D5
Wilpena Cr. →
  Australia 31°25S 139°29E **63** E2
Wilsall *U.S.A.* 45°59N 110°38W **76** D8
Wilson *N.C., U.S.A.* 35°44N 77°55W **85** D16
Wilson *N.Y., U.S.A.* 43°19N 78°50W **82** C6
Wilson *Pa., U.S.A.* 40°41N 75°15W **83** F9
Wilson → *Australia* 16°48S 128°16E **60** C4
Wilson Bluff *Australia* 31°41S 129°0E **61** F4
Wilson Inlet *Australia* 35°0S 117°22E **61** G2
Wilsons Promontory
  Australia 38°59S 146°23E **63** F4
Wilton *U.S.A.* 47°10N 100°47W **80** B3
Wilton → *Australia* 14°45S 134°33E **62** A1
Wiltshire □ *U.K.* 51°18N 1°53W **13** F6
Wiltz *Lux.* 49°57N 5°55E **15** E5
Wiluna *Australia* 26°36S 120°14E **61** E3
Wimborne Minster *U.K.* 50°48N 1°59W **13** G6
Wimmera → *Australia* 36°8S 141°56E **63** F3
Winam G. *Kenya* 0°20S 34°15E **54** C3
Winburg *S. Africa* 28°30S 27°2E **56** D4
Winchendon *U.S.A.* 42°41N 72°3W **83** D12
Winchester *U.K.* 51°4N 1°18W **13** F6
Winchester *Conn.*,
  U.S.A. 41°53N 73°9W **83** E11
Winchester *Idaho*,
  U.S.A. 46°14N 116°38W **76** C5
Winchester *Ind., U.S.A.* 40°10N 84°59W **81** E11
Winchester *Ky., U.S.A.* 37°59N 84°11W **81** G11
Winchester *N.H.*,
  U.S.A. 42°46N 72°23W **83** D12
Winchester *Nev., U.S.A.* 36°7N 115°7W **79** J11
Winchester *Tenn.*,
  U.S.A. 35°11N 86°7W **85** D11
Winchester *Va., U.S.A.* 39°11N 78°10W **81** F14
Wind → *U.S.A.* 43°12N 108°12W **76** E9
Wind Cave △ *U.S.A.* 43°32N 103°17W **80** D2
Wind River Range
  U.S.A. 43°0N 109°30W **76** E9
Windamere, L. *Australia* 32°48S 149°51E **63** B4
Windau = Ventspils
  Latvia 57°25N 21°32E **9** H19
Windber *U.S.A.* 40°14N 78°50W **82** F6
Winder *U.S.A.* 34°0N 83°45W **85** D13
Windermere *U.K.* 54°23N 2°55W **12** C5
Windhoek *Namibia* 22°35S 17°4E **56** C2
Windidda ◇ *Australia* 26°23S 122°12E **61** E3
Windjana Gorge △
  Australia 17°51S 125°0E **60** C3
Windom *U.S.A.* 43°52N 95°7W **80** D6
Windorah *Australia* 25°24S 142°36E **62** D3
Window Rock *U.S.A.* 35°41N 109°3W **77** J9
Windrush → *U.K.* 51°43N 1°24W **13** F6
Windsor *Australia* 33°37S 150°50E **63** E5
Windsor *N.S., Canada* 44°59N 64°5W **73** D7
Windsor *Ont., Canada* 42°18N 83°0W **82** D2
Windsor *U.K.* 51°29N 0°36W **13** F7
Windsor *Calif., U.S.A.* 38°33N 122°49W **78** G4
Windsor *Colo., U.S.A.* 40°29N 104°54W **76** E11
Windsor *Conn., U.S.A.* 41°50N 72°39W **83** E12
Windsor *Mo., U.S.A.* 38°32N 93°31W **80** F7
Windsor *N.Y., U.S.A.* 42°5N 75°37W **83** D9
Windsor *Vt., U.S.A.* 43°29N 72°24W **83** C12

Windsor & Maidenhead □
  U.K. 51°29N 0°40W **13** F7
Windsorton *S. Africa* 28°16S 24°44E **56** D3
Windward Is. *W. Indies* 13°0N 61°0W **89** D7
Windward Passage = Vientos,
  Paso de los *Caribbean* 20°0N 74°0W **89** C5
Winefred L. *Canada* 55°30N 110°30W **71** B6
Winfield *U.S.A.* 37°15N 96°59W **80** G5
Wingate Mts. *Australia* 14°25S 130°40E **60** B5
Wingellina = Irrunytju
  Australia 26°3S 128°56E **61** E4
Wingham *Australia* 31°48S 152°22E **63** E5
Wingham *Canada* 43°55N 81°20W **82** C3
Winisk *Canada* 55°17N 85°5W **72** A2
Winisk → *Canada* 55°17N 85°5W **72** A2
Winisk L. *Canada* 52°55N 87°22W **72** B2
Wink *U.S.A.* 31°45N 103°9W **84** F3
Winkler *Canada* 49°10N 97°56W **71** D9
Winlock *U.S.A.* 46°30N 122°56W **78** D4
Winneba *Ghana* 5°25N 0°36W **50** G5
Winnebago, L. *U.S.A.* 44°0N 88°26W **80** D9
Winnecke Cr. →
  Australia 18°35S 131°34E **60** C5
Winnemucca *U.S.A.* 40°58N 117°44W **76** F5
Winnemucca L. *U.S.A.* 40°7N 119°21W **76** F4
Winner *U.S.A.* 43°22N 99°52W **80** D4
Winnett *U.S.A.* 47°0N 108°21W **76** C9
Winnfield *U.S.A.* 31°56N 92°38W **84** F8
Winnibigoshish, L.
  U.S.A. 47°27N 94°13W **80** B6
Winnipeg *Canada* 49°54N 97°9W **71** D9
Winnipeg → *Canada* 50°38N 96°19W **71** C9
Winnipeg, L. *Canada* 52°0N 97°0W **71** C9
Winnipeg Beach *Canada* 50°30N 96°58W **71** C9
Winnipegosis *Canada* 51°39N 99°55W **71** C9
Winnipegosis L. *Canada* 52°30N 100°0W **71** C9
Winnipesaukee, L.
  U.S.A. 43°38N 71°21W **83** C13
Winnisquam L. *U.S.A.* 43°33N 71°31W **83** C13
Winnsboro *La., U.S.A.* 32°10N 91°43W **84** E9
Winnsboro *S.C., U.S.A.* 34°23N 81°5W **85** D14
Winnsboro *Tex., U.S.A.* 32°58N 95°17W **84** E7
Winokapau, L. *Canada* 53°15N 62°50W **73** B7
Winona *Minn., U.S.A.* 44°3N 91°39W **80** C8
Winona *Miss., U.S.A.* 33°29N 89°44W **85** E10
Winooski *U.S.A.* 44°29N 73°11W **83** B11
Winooski → *U.S.A.* 44°32N 73°17W **83** B11
Winschoten *Neths.* 53°9N 7°3E **15** A7
Winsford *U.K.* 53°12N 2°31W **12** D5
Winslow = Bainbridge Island
  U.S.A. 47°38N 122°32W **78** C4
Winslow *U.S.A.* 35°2N 110°42W **77** J8
Winsted *U.S.A.* 41°55N 73°4W **83** E11
Winston-Salem *U.S.A.* 36°6N 80°15W **85** C14
Winter Garden *U.S.A.* 28°34N 81°35W **85** G14
Winter Haven *U.S.A.* 28°1N 81°44W **85** G14
Winter Park *U.S.A.* 28°36N 81°20W **85** G14
Winterhaven *U.S.A.* 32°44N 114°38W **79** N12
Winters *U.S.A.* 38°32N 121°58W **78** G5
Winterset *U.S.A.* 41°20N 94°1W **80** E6
Wintersville *U.S.A.* 40°23N 80°42W **82** F4
Winterswijk *Neths.* 51°58N 6°43E **15** C6
Winterthur *Switz.* 47°30N 8°44E **20** C8
Winthrop *U.S.A.* 48°28N 120°10W **76** B3
Winton *Australia* 22°24S 143°3E **62** C3
Winton *N.Z.* 46°8S 168°20E **59** G2
Wirlyajarrayi ◇
  Australia 21°45S 132°35E **60** D5
Wirralla *Australia* 32°24S 134°31E **63** E1
Wisbech *U.K.* 52°41N 0°9E **13** E8
Wisconsin □ *U.S.A.* 44°45N 89°30W **80** C10
Wisconsin → *U.S.A.* 43°0N 91°15W **80** D8
Wisconsin Rapids
  U.S.A. 44°23N 89°49W **80** C9
Wisdom *U.S.A.* 45°37N 113°27W **76** D7
Wiseman *U.S.A.* 67°25N 150°6W **74** B9
Wishaw *U.K.* 55°46N 3°54W **11** F5
Wishek *U.S.A.* 46°16N 99°33W **80** B4
Wisła → *Poland* 54°22N 18°55E **17** A10
Wismar *Germany* 53°54N 11°29E **16** B6
Wisner *U.S.A.* 41°59N 96°55W **80** E5
Witbank = eMalahleni
  S. Africa 25°51S 29°14E **57** D4
Witdraai *S. Africa* 26°58S 20°48E **56** D3
Witham *U.K.* 51°48N 0°40E **13** F8
Witham → *U.K.* 52°59N 0°2W **12** E7
Withernsea *U.K.* 53°44N 0°1E **12** D8
Witjira △ *Australia* 26°22S 135°37E **63** D2
Witless Bay *Canada* 47°17N 52°50W **73** C9
Witney *U.K.* 51°48N 1°28W **13** F6
Witnossob → *Namibia* 23°55S 18°45E **56** D3
Witriver *S. Africa* 25°20S 31°7E **57** D5
Wittenberge *Germany* 53°0N 11°45E **16** B6
Wittenoom *Australia* 22°15S 118°20E **60** D2
Witu *Kenya* 2°23S 40°26E **54** C5
Witvlei *Namibia* 22°23S 18°32E **56** C2
Wiwon *N. Korea* 40°54N 126°3E **35** D14
Wkra → *Poland* 52°27N 20°44E **17** B11
Wlingi *Indonesia* 8°5S 112°25E **37** H15
Włocławek *Poland* 52°40N 19°3E **17** B10
Włodawa *Poland* 51°33N 23°31E **17** C12
Woburn *U.S.A.* 42°29N 71°9W **83** D13
Wodian *China* 32°50N 112°35E **34** H7
Wodonga *Australia* 36°5S 146°50E **63** F4
Wokam *Indonesia* 5°45S 134°28E **37** F8
Woking *U.K.* 51°19N 0°34W **13** F7
Wokingham □ *U.K.* 51°25N 0°51W **13** F7
Wolf → *Canada* 60°17N 132°33W **70** A2
Wolf Creek *U.S.A.* 47°0N 112°4W **76** C7
Wolf L. *Canada* 60°24N 131°40W **70** A2
Wolf Point *U.S.A.* 48°5N 105°39W **76** B11
Wolfe Creek Crater △
  Australia 19°10S 127°47E **60** C4
Wolfe I. *Canada* 44°7N 76°20W **83** B8
Wolfeboro *U.S.A.* 43°35N 71°13W **83** C13
Wolfsberg *Austria* 46°50N 14°52E **16** E8
Wolfsburg *Germany* 52°25N 10°48E **16** B6
Wolin *Poland* 53°50N 14°37E **16** B8
Wollaston, Is. *Chile* 55°40S 67°30W **96** H3

Wollaston L. *Canada* 58°7N 103°10W **71** B8
Wollaston Lake *Canada* 58°3N 103°33W **71** B8
Wollaston Pen. *Canada* 69°30N 115°0W **68** D9
Wollongong *Australia* 34°25S 150°54E **63** E5
Wolmaransstad *S. Africa* 27°12S 25°59E **56** D4
Wolseley *S. Africa* 33°26S 19°7E **56** E2
Wolsey *U.S.A.* 44°25N 98°28W **80** C4
Wolstenholme, C.
  Canada 62°35N 77°30W **66** C12
Wolvega *Neths.* 52°52N 6°0E **15** B6
Wolverhampton *U.K.* 52°35N 2°7W **13** E5
Wondai *Australia* 26°20S 151°49E **63** D5
Wongalarroo L. *Australia* 31°32S 144°0E **63** E3
Wongan Hills *Australia* 30°51S 116°37E **61** F2
Wŏnju *S. Korea* 37°22N 127°58E **35** F14
Wonosari *Indonesia* 7°58S 110°36E **37** G14
Wonosobo *Indonesia* 7°22S 109°54E **37** G13
Wonowon *Canada* 56°44N 121°48W **70** B4
Wŏnsan *N. Korea* 39°11N 127°27E **35** E14
Wonthaggi *Australia* 38°37S 145°37E **63** F4
Wood Buffalo △ *Canada* 59°0N 113°41W **70** B6
Wood Is. *Australia* 16°24S 123°19E **60** C3
Wood L. *Canada* 55°17N 103°17W **71** B8
Woodah, I. *Australia* 13°27S 136°10E **62** A2
Woodbourne *U.S.A.* 41°46N 74°36W **83** E10
Woodbridge *Canada* 43°47N 79°36W **82** C5
Woodbridge *U.K.* 52°6N 1°20E **13** E9
Woodburn *Australia* 29°6S 153°23E **63** A5
Woodburn *U.S.A.* 45°9N 122°51W **76** D2
Woodenbong *Australia* 28°24S 152°39E **63** D5
Woodend *Australia* 37°20S 144°33E **63** F3
Woodford *Australia* 15°20S 152°47E **63** D5
Woodfords *U.S.A.* 38°47N 119°50W **78** G7
Woodlake *U.S.A.* 36°25N 119°6W **78** J7
Woodland *Calif., U.S.A.* 38°41N 121°46E **78** G5
Woodland *Maine, U.S.A.* 45°9N 67°25W **81** C20
Woodland *Pa., U.S.A.* 41°0N 78°21W **82** F6
Woodland *Wash.,*
  U.S.A. 45°54N 122°45W **78** E4
Woodland Caribou △
  Canada 51°0N 94°45W **71** C10
Woodlands *Singapore* 1°26N 103°46E **39** d
Woodlands, The *U.S.A.* 30°9N 95°29W **84** F7
Woodonga *Australia* 36°10S 146°50E **63** F4
Woodridge *Canada* 49°20N 96°9W **71** D9
Woodroffe, Mt.
  Australia 26°20S 131°45E **61** E5
Woods, L. *Australia* 17°50S 133°30E **62** B1
Woods, L. of the
  N. Amer. 49°15N 94°45W **71** D10
Woods Bay *Canada* 45°8N 79°59W **82** A5
Woodstock *Australia* 19°35S 146°50E **62** B4
Woodstock *N.B., Canada* 46°11N 67°37W **73** C6
Woodstock *Ont., Canada* 43°10N 80°45W **82** C4
Woodstock *U.K.* 51°51N 1°20W **13** F6
Woodstock *Ill., U.S.A.* 42°19N 88°27W **80** D9
Woodstock *N.Y., U.S.A.* 42°2N 74°7W **83** D10
Woodstock *Vt., U.S.A.* 43°37N 72°31W **83** C12
Woodsville *Canada* 44°9N 72°2W **83** B13
Woodview *Canada* 44°35N 78°8W **82** B6
Woodville *N.Z.* 40°20S 175°53E **59** D5
Woodville *Miss., U.S.A.* 31°6N 91°18W **84** F9
Woodville *Tex., U.S.A.* 30°47N 94°25W **84** F7
Woodward *U.S.A.* 36°26N 99°24W **84** C5
Woody *U.S.A.* 35°42N 118°50W **79** K8
Woody → *Canada* 52°31N 100°51W **71** C8
Woolacombe *U.K.* 51°10N 4°13W **13** F3
Woolamai, C. *Australia* 38°30S 145°23E **63** F4
Wooler *U.K.* 55°33N 2°1W **12** B5
Woolgoolga *Australia* 30°6S 153°11E **63** E5
Woomera *Australia* 31°5S 136°50E **63** E2
Woonsocket *R.I., U.S.A.* 42°0N 71°31W **83** E13
Woonsocket *S. Dak.,*
  U.S.A. 44°3N 98°17W **80** C4
Wooramel → *Australia* 25°47S 114°10E **61** E1
Wooramel Roadhouse
  Australia 25°45S 114°17E **61** E1
Wooroonooran △
  Australia 16°25S 146°1E **62** B4
Wooster *U.S.A.* 40°48N 81°56W **82** F3
Worcester *S. Africa* 33°39S 19°27E **56** E2
Worcester *U.K.* 52°11N 2°12W **13** E5
Worcester *Mass.,*
  U.S.A. 42°16N 71°48W **83** D13
Worcester *N.Y., U.S.A.* 42°36N 74°45W **83** D10
Worcestershire □ *U.K.* 52°13N 2°10W **13** E5
Workington *U.K.* 54°39N 3°33W **12** C4
Worksop *U.K.* 53°18N 1°7W **12** D6
Workum *Neths.* 52°59N 5°26E **15** B5
Worland *U.S.A.* 44°1N 107°57W **76** D10
Worms *Germany* 49°37N 8°21E **16** D5
Worsley *Australia* 56°31N 119°8W **70** B5
Wortham *U.S.A.* 31°47N 96°28W **84** F6
Worthing *Barbados* 13°5S 59°35W **89** g
Worthing *U.K.* 50°49N 0°21W **13** G7
Worthington *Minn.,*
  U.S.A. 43°37N 95°36W **80** D6
Worthington *Pa., U.S.A.* 40°50N 79°38W **82** F5
Wosi *Indonesia* 0°15S 128°0E **37** E7
Wote *Kenya* 1°47S 37°38E **54** C4
Wotjalum ✪ *Australia* 16°30S 123°45E **60** C3
Wotjobaluk ✪ *Australia* 37°0S 142°0E **63** C3
Wou-han = Wuhan
  China 30°31N 114°18E **33** C6
Wousi = Wuxi *China* 31°33N 120°18E **33** C7
Wowoni *Indonesia* 4°5S 123°5E **37** E6
Wrangel I. = Vrangelya, Ostrov
  Russia 71°0N 180°0E **29** B18
Wrangell *U.S.A.* 56°28N 132°23W **70** B2
Wrangell Mts. *U.S.A.* 61°30N 142°0W **68** E3
Wray *U.S.A.* 40°5N 102°13W **76** F12
Wrekin, The *U.K.* 52°41N 2°32W **13** E5
Wrens *U.S.A.* 33°12N 82°23W **85** E13
Wrexham *U.K.* 53°3N 3°0W **12** D4
Wrexham □ *U.K.* 53°1N 2°58W **12** D5
Wright *Phil.* 11°42N 125°2E **37** B7
Wright *Wyo., U.S.A.* 43°45N 105°28W **76** E11
Wright Pt. *Canada* 43°48N 81°44W **82** C3

Wrightson, Mt. *U.S.A.* 31°42N 110°51W **77** L8
Wrightwood *U.S.A.* 34°22N 117°38W **79** L9
Wrigley *Canada* 63°16N 123°37W **68** E7
Wrocław *Poland* 51°5N 17°5E **17** C9
Września *Poland* 52°21N 17°36E **17** B9
Wu Jiang → *China* 29°40N 107°20E **32** D6
Wu Kau Tang *China* 22°30N 114°14E **33** F11
Wu'an *China* 36°40N 114°15E **34** F8
Wubalawun ✪ *Australia* 15°28S 133°1E **60** C5
Wubin *Australia* 30°6S 116°37E **61** F2
Wubu *China* 37°28N 110°42E **34** F6
Wuchang *China* 44°55N 127°5E **35** B14
Wucheng *China* 37°12N 116°20E **34** F9
Wuchuan *China* 41°5N 111°28E **34** D6
Wudi *China* 37°40N 117°35E **35** F9
Wuding He → *China* 37°2N 110°23E **34** F6
Wudinna *Australia* 33°0S 135°22E **63** E2
Wudu *China* 33°22N 104°54E **34** H3
Wuguishan *China* 22°25N 113°25E **33** G9
Wugullar = Beswick
  Australia 14°34S 132°53E **60** B5
Wuhai *China* 39°47N 106°52E **32** C5
Wuhan *China* 30°31N 114°18E **33** C6
Wuhe *China* 33°10N 117°50E **35** H9
Wuhsi = Wuxi *China* 31°33N 120°18E **33** C7
Wuhu *China* 31°22N 118°21E **33** C6
Wukari *Nigeria* 7°51N 9°42E **50** G7
Wulajie *China* 44°6N 126°33E **35** B14
Wulanbulang *China* 41°5N 110°55E **34** D6
Wular L. *India* 34°20N 74°30E **43** B6
Wulian *China* 35°40N 119°12E **35** G10
Wuliaru *Indonesia* 7°27S 131°0E **37** F8
Wulumuchi = Ürümqi
  China 43°45N 87°45E **32** B3
Wundanyi *Kenya* 3°24S 38°22E **54** C4
Wunnummin L. *Canada* 52°55N 89°10W **72** B2
Wuntho *Burma* 23°55N 95°45E **41** H19
Wupatki △ *U.S.A.* 35°35N 111°20W **77** J8
Wuppertal *Germany* 51°16N 7°12E **16** C4
Wuppertal *S. Africa* 32°13S 19°12E **56** E2
Wuqing *China* 39°23N 117°4E **35** E9
Wurtsboro *U.S.A.* 41°35N 74°29W **83** E10
Würzburg *Germany* 49°46N 9°55E **16** D5
Wushan *China* 34°43N 104°53E **34** G3
Wushi *China* 41°9N 79°13E **32** B2
Wuting = Huimin
  China 37°27N 117°28E **35** F9
Wutonghaolai *China* 42°50N 120°5E **35** C11
Wutongqiao *China* 29°22N 103°50E **32** D5
Wuwei *China* 37°57N 102°34E **32** C5
Wuxi *China* 31°33N 120°18E **33** C7
Wuxiang *China* 36°49N 112°50E **34** F7
Wuyang *China* 33°25N 113°35E **34** H7
Wuyi *China* 37°46N 115°56E **34** F8
Wuyi Shan *China* 27°0N 117°0E **33** D6
Wuyuan *China* 41°2N 108°20E **34** D5
Wuzhai *China* 38°54N 111°48E **34** E6
Wuzhi Shan *China* 18°45N 109°45E **38** C7
Wuzhong *China* 38°2N 106°12E **34** E4
Wuzhou *China* 23°30N 111°18E **33** D6
Wyaaba Cr. →
  Australia 16°27S 141°35E **62** B3
Wyalkatchem *Australia* 31°8S 117°22E **61** F2
Wyalusing *U.S.A.* 41°40N 76°16W **83** E8
Wyandra *Australia* 27°12S 145°56E **63** D4
Wyangala, L. *Australia* 33°54S 149°0E **63** E4
Wyara, L. *Australia* 28°42S 144°14E **63** D3
Wycheproof *Australia* 36°5S 143°17E **63** F3
Wycliffe Well *Australia* 20°48S 134°14E **62** C1
Wye → *U.K.* 51°38N 2°40W **13** F5
Wyemandoo *Australia* 28°28S 118°29E **61** E2
Wymore *U.S.A.* 40°7N 96°40W **80** E5
Wyndham *Australia* 15°33S 128°3E **60** C4
Wyndham *N.Z.* 46°20S 168°51E **59** G2
Wynne *U.S.A.* 35°14N 90°47W **85** D9
Wynyard *Australia* 41°5S 145°44E **63** G4
Wynyard *Canada* 51°45N 104°10W **71** C8
Wyola L. *Australia* 29°8S 130°17E **61** E5
Wyoming *Canada* 42°57N 82°7W **82** D2
Wyoming □ *U.S.A.* 43°0N 107°30W **76** E10
Wyomissing *U.S.A.* 40°20N 75°59W **83** F9
Wyong *Australia* 33°14S 151°24E **63** E5
Wytheville *U.S.A.* 36°57N 81°5W **81** G13

X

Xaafuun *Somali Rep.* 10°25N 51°16E **47** E5
Xaafuun, Ras *Somali Rep.* 10°27N 51°24E **47** E5
Xaçmaz *Azerbaijan* 41°31N 48°42E **19** F8
Xai-Xai *Mozam.* 25°6S 33°31E **57** D5
Xainza *China* 30°58N 88°35E **32** C3
Xalapa *Mexico* 19°32N 96°55W **87** D5
Xangongo *Angola* 16°45S 15°5E **56** B2
Xankändi *Azerbaijan* 39°52N 46°49E **44** B5
Xanthi *Greece* 41°10N 24°58E **23** D11
Xanxerê *Brazil* 26°53S 52°23W **95** B5
Xapuri *Brazil* 10°35S 68°35W **92** F5
Xar Moron He →
  China 43°25N 120°35E **35** C11
Xátiva *Spain* 38°59N 0°32W **21** C5
Xau, L. *Botswana* 21°15S 24°44E **56** C3
Xavantina *Brazil* 21°15S 52°48W **95** A5
Xenia *U.S.A.* 39°41N 83°56W **81** F12
Xeropotamos
  Cyprus 34°42N 32°33E **25** E11
Xhora *S. Africa* 31°55S 28°38E **57** E4
Xhumo *Botswana* 21°7S 24°35E **56** C3
Xi Jiang → *China* 22°5N 113°20E **33** D6
Xi Xian *China* 36°41N 110°58E **34** F6
Xia Xian *China* 35°8N 111°12E **34** G6
Xiachengzi *China* 44°40N 130°18E **35** B16
Xiaguan *China* 25°32N 100°16E **32** D5
Xiajin *China* 36°56N 116°0E **34** F9
Xiamen *China* 24°25N 118°4E **33** D6

Xi'an *China* 34°15N 109°0E **34** G5
Xian Xian *China* 38°12N 116°6E **34** E9
Xiang Jiang → *China* 28°55N 112°50E **33** D6
Xiangcheng *Henan,*
  China 33°29N 114°52E **34** H8
Xiangcheng *Henan,*
  China 33°50N 113°27E **34** H7
Xiangfan *China* 32°2N 112°8E **33** C6
Xianggang = Hong Kong □
  China 22°11N 114°14E **33** G11
Xianghuang Qi *China* 42°2N 113°50E **34** C7
Xiangning *China* 35°58N 110°50E **34** G6
Xiangquan *China* 36°30N 113°1E **34** F7
Xiangquan He = Sutlej →
  Pakistan 29°23N 71°3E **42** E4
Xiangshui *China* 34°12N 119°33E **35** G10
Xiangtan *China* 27°51N 112°54E **33** D6
Xianyang *China* 34°20N 108°40E **34** G5
Xiao Hinggan Ling *China* 49°0N 127°0E **33** B7
Xiao Xian *China* 34°15N 116°55E **34** G9
Xiaoyi *China* 37°8N 111°48E **34** F6
Xiawa *China* 42°35N 120°38E **35** C11
Xiayi *China* 34°15N 116°10E **34** G9
Xichang *China* 27°51N 102°19E **32** D5
Xichuan *China* 33°0N 111°30E **34** H6
Xieng Khouang *Laos* 19°17N 103°25E **38** C4
Xifei He → *China* 32°45N 116°40E **34** H9
Xifeng *Gansu, China* 35°40N 107°40E **34** G4
Xifeng *Liaoning, China* 42°42N 124°45E **35** C13
Xifengzhen = Xifeng
  China 35°40N 107°40E **34** G4
Xigazê *China* 29°5N 88°45E **32** D3
Xihe *China* 34°2N 105°20E **34** G3
Xihua *China* 33°45N 114°30E **34** H8
Xili Shuiku *China* 22°36N 113°57E **33** F10
Xiliao He → *China* 43°32N 123°35E **35** C12
Xilinhot *China* 43°52N 116°2E **34** C9
Ximana *Mozam.* 19°24S 33°58E **55** F3
Xin Xian = Xinzhou
  China 38°22N 112°46E **34** E7
Xinavane *Mozam.* 25°2S 32°47E **57** D5
Xinbin *China* 41°40N 125°2E **35** D13
Xincun *China* 38°15N 117°45E **34** E9
Xing Xian *China* 38°27N 111°7E **34** E6
Xing'an *China* 25°38N 110°40E **33** D6
Xingcheng *China* 40°40N 120°45E **35** D11
Xinghe *China* 40°55N 113°55E **34** D7
Xinghua *China* 32°58N 119°48E **35** H10
Xinglong *China* 40°25N 117°30E **35** D9
Xingping *China* 34°20N 108°28E **34** G5
Xingtai *China* 37°3N 114°32E **34** F8
Xingu → *Brazil* 1°30S 51°53W **93** D8
Xingyang *China* 34°45N 112°52E **34** G7
Xinyi *China* 25°3N 104°59E **33** D5
Xinhe *China* 37°30N 115°15E **34** F8
Xining *China* 36°34N 101°40E **32** C5
Xinjiang *China* 35°34N 111°11E **34** G6
Xinjiang Uygur Zizhiqu □
  China 42°0N 86°0E **32** C3
Xinjin = Pulandian
  China 39°25N 121°58E **35** E11
Xinkai He → *China* 43°32N 123°35E **35** C12
Xinken *China* 22°39N 113°36E **33** F10
Xinle *China* 38°25N 114°40E **34** E8
Xinlitun *China* 42°0N 122°8E **35** D12
Xinmin *China* 41°59N 122°50E **35** D12
Xintai *China* 35°55N 117°45E **35** G9
Xinwan *China* 22°47N 113°40E **33** F10
Xinxiang *China* 35°18N 113°50E **34** G7
Xinzhan *China* 43°50N 127°18E **35** C14
Xinzheng *China* 34°20N 113°45E **34** G7
Xinzhou *Hainan, China* 19°43N 109°17E **38** C7
Xinzhou *Shanxi, China* 38°22N 112°46E **34** E7
Xiongyuecheng *China* 40°12N 122°5E **35** D12
Xiping *Henan, China* 33°22N 114°5E **34** H8
Xiping *Henan, China* 33°25N 111°8E **34** H6
Xique-Xique *Brazil* 10°50S 42°40W **93** F10
Xisha Qundao = Paracel Is.
  S. China Sea 15°50N 112°0E **36** A4
Xiuyan *China* 40°18N 123°11E **35** D12
Xixabangma Feng
  China 28°20N 85°40E **43** E11
Xixia *China* 33°25N 111°29E **34** H6
Xixiang *China* 33°0N 107°44E **34** H4
Xixón = Gijón *Spain* 43°32N 5°42W **21** A3
Xiyang *China* 37°38N 113°38E **34** F7
Xizang Zizhiqu □ *China* 32°0N 88°0E **32** C3
Xlendi *Malta* 36°1N 14°12E **25** C1
Xochob *Mexico* 19°21N 89°48W **87** D7
Xuan Loc *Vietnam* 10°56N 107°14E **39** G6
Xuanhua *China* 40°40N 115°2E **34** D8
Xuchang *China* 34°2N 113°48E **34** G7
Xun Xian *China* 35°42N 114°33E **34** G8
Xunyang *China* 32°48N 109°22E **34** H5
Xunyi *China* 35°8N 108°20E **34** G5
Xushui *China* 39°2N 115°40E **34** E8
Xuyen Moc *Vietnam* 10°34N 107°25E **39** G6
Xuzhou *China* 34°18N 117°10E **35** G9
Xylophagou *Cyprus* 34°54N 33°51E **25** E12

Y

Ya Xian = Sanya *China* 18°14N 109°29E **38** C7
Yaamba *Australia* 23°8S 150°22E **62** C5
Yaapeet *Australia* 35°45S 142°3E **63** F3
Yadgir *India* 16°45N 77°5E **40** L10

Yadkin → *U.S.A.* 35°23N 80°4W **85** D14
Yadua *Fiji* 16°49S 178°18E **59** a
Yaeyama-Rettō *Japan* 24°30N 123°40E **31** M1
Yagasa Cluster *Fiji* 18°57S 178°28W **59** a
Yagodnoye *Russia* 62°33N 149°40E **29** C15
Yahila
  Dem. Rep. of the Congo 0°13N 24°28E **54** B1
Yahk *Canada* 49°6N 116°10W **70** D5
Yahuma
  Dem. Rep. of the Congo 1°0N 23°10E **52** D4
Yaita *Japan* 36°48N 139°56E **31** F9
Yaiza *Canary Is.* 28°57N 13°46W **24** F6
Yakima *U.S.A.* 46°36N 120°31W **76** C3
Yakima → *U.S.A.* 46°15N 119°14W **76** C3
Yakishiri-Jima *Japan* 44°26N 141°25E **30** B10
Yakobi I. *U.S.A.* 58°0N 136°30W **70** B1
Yakovlevka *Russia* 44°26N 133°28E **30** B6
Yaku-Shima *Japan* 30°20N 130°30E **31** J5
Yakumo *Japan* 42°15N 140°16E **30** C10
Yakutat *U.S.A.* 59°33N 139°44W **68** F4
Yakutat B. *U.S.A.* 59°45N 140°45W **74** D11
Yakutia = Sakha □
  Russia 66°0N 130°0E **29** C14
Yakutsk *Russia* 62°5N 129°50E **29** C13
Yala *Thailand* 6°33N 101°18E **39** J3
Yalata *Australia* 31°59S 132°6E **61** F5
Yalata ✪ *Australia* 31°35S 132°7E **61** F5
Yalboroo *Australia* 20°50S 148°40E **62** b
Yale *U.S.A.* 43°8N 82°48W **82** C2
Yalgorup △ *Australia* 32°39S 115°38E **61** F2
Yalinga *C.A.R.* 6°33N 23°10E **52** C4
Yalkabul, Pta. *Mexico* 21°32N 88°37W **87** C7
Yalleroi *Australia* 24°3S 145°42E **62** C4
Yalobusha → *U.S.A.* 33°33N 90°10W **85** E9
Yalong Jiang → *China* 26°40N 101°55E **32** D5
Yalova *Turkey* 40°41N 29°15E **23** D13
Yalpirakinu ✪ *Australia* 22°24S 132°15E **60** D5
Yalta *Ukraine* 44°30N 34°10E **19** F5
Yalu Jiang → *China* 39°55N 124°19E **35** E13
Yam *Australia* 9°54S 142°46E **62** a
Yam Ha Melah = Dead Sea
  Asia 31°30N 35°30E **46** D4
Yam Kinneret *Israel* 32°45N 35°35E **46** C4
Yamada *Japan* 33°33N 130°49E **31** H5
Yamagata *Japan* 38°15N 140°15E **30** E10
Yamagata □ *Japan* 38°30N 140°0E **30** E10
Yamaguchi *Japan* 34°10N 131°32E **31** G5
Yamaguchi □ *Japan* 34°20N 131°40E **31** G5
Yamal, Poluostrov *Russia* 71°0N 70°0E **28** B8
Yamal Pen. = Yamal, Poluostrov
  Russia 71°0N 70°0E **28** B8
Yamanashi □ *Japan* 35°40N 138°40E **31** G9
Yamantau, Gora *Russia* 54°15N 58°6E **18** D10
Yamato Ridge
  Sea of Japan 39°20N 135°0E **30** E7
Yamba *Australia* 29°26S 153°23E **63** D5
Yambarran Ra.
  Australia 15°10S 130°25E **60** C5
Yambol *Bulgaria* 42°30N 26°30E **23** C12
Yamburg *Russia* 68°21N 77°8E **28** C8
Yamdena *Indonesia* 7°45S 131°20E **37** F8
Yame *Japan* 33°13N 130°35E **31** H5
Yamethin *Burma* 20°29N 96°18E **41** J20
Yamma Yamma, L.
  Australia 26°16S 141°20E **63** D3
Yamoussoukro *Ivory C.* 6°49N 5°17W **50** G4
Yampa → *U.S.A.* 40°32N 108°59W **76** F9
Yampi Sd. *Australia* 16°8S 123°38E **60** C3
Yampil *Moldova* 48°15N 28°15E **17** D15
Yampol = Yampil
  Moldova 48°15N 28°15E **17** D15
Yamuna → *India* 25°30N 81°53E **43** G9
Yamunanagar *India* 30°7N 77°17E **42** D7
Yamzho Yumco *China* 28°48N 90°35E **32** D4
Yana → *Russia* 71°30N 136°0E **29** B14
Yanagawa *Japan* 33°10N 130°24E **31** H5
Yanai *Japan* 33°58N 132°7E **31** H6
Yan'an *China* 36°35N 109°26E **34** F5
Yanaul *Russia* 56°25N 55°0E **18** C10
Yanbu 'al Bahr *Si. Arabia* 24°0N 38°5E **44** E3
Yanchang *China* 36°43N 110°1E **34** F6
Yancheng *Henan, China* 33°35N 114°0E **34** H8
Yancheng *Jiangsu, China* 33°23N 120°8E **35** H11
Yanchep *Australia* 31°33S 115°37E **61** F2
Yanchi *China* 37°48N 107°20E **34** F4
Yanchuan *China* 36°51N 110°10E **34** F6
Yanco Cr. → *Australia* 35°14S 145°35E **63** F4
Yandeyarra ✪ *Australia* 21°17S 118°24E **60** D2
Yandicoogina *Australia* 22°49S 119°12E **60** D2
Yandoon *Burma* 17°0N 95°40E **41** L19
Yang Xian *China* 33°15N 107°30E **34** H4
Yang-yang *S. Korea* 38°4N 128°38E **35** E15
Yangambi
  Dem. Rep. of the Congo 0°47N 24°24E **54** B1
Yangcheng *China* 35°28N 112°22E **34** G7
Yangch'ü = Taiyuan
  China 37°52N 112°33E **34** F7
Yanggao *China* 40°21N 113°55E **34** D7
Yanggu *China* 36°8N 115°43E **34** F8
Yangliuqing *China* 39°2N 117°5E **35** E9
Yangon = Rangoon
  Burma 16°45N 96°20E **41** L20
Yangpingguan *China* 32°58N 106°5E **34** H4
Yangquan *China* 37°58N 113°31E **34** F7
Yangtse = Chang Jiang →
  China 31°48N 121°10E **33** C7
Yangtze Kiang = Chang Jiang →
  China 31°48N 121°10E **33** C7
Yangyuan *China* 40°1N 114°10E **34** D8
Yangzhou *China* 32°21N 119°26E **33** C6
Yanji *China* 42°59N 129°30E **35** C15
Yankton *U.S.A.* 42°53N 97°23W **80** D5
Yankunytjatjara-Antakirinja
  Australia 27°5N 134°30E **63** A1
Yanonge
  Dem. Rep. of the Congo 0°35N 24°38E **54** B1
Yanqi *China* 42°5N 86°35E **32** B3
Yanqing *China* 40°30N 115°58E **34** D8

Yanshan *China* 38°4N 117°22E **35** E9
Yanshou *China* 45°28N 128°22E **35** B15
Yantabulla *Australia* 29°21S 145°0E **63** D4
Yantai *China* 37°34N 121°22E **35** F11
Yantian *China* 22°35N 114°16E **33** F11
Yanuca *Fiji* 18°24S 178°0E **59** a
Yanzhou *China* 35°35N 116°49E **34** G9
Yao Noi, Ko *Thailand* 8°7N 98°37E **39** a
Yao Xian *China* 34°55N 108°59E **34** G5
Yao Yai, Ko *Thailand* 8°0N 98°35E **39** a
Yaoundé *Cameroon* 3°50N 11°35E **52** D2
Yaowan *China* 34°15N 118°3E **35** G10
Yap *Pac. Oc.* 9°30N 138°10E **64** G5
Yapen *Indonesia* 1°50S 136°0E **37** E9
Yapen, Selat *Indonesia* 1°20S 136°10E **37** E9
Yapero *Indonesia* 4°59S 137°11E **37** E9
Yapuparra ✪ *Australia* 27°15S 126°20E **61** E4
Yaqaga *Fiji* 16°35S 178°36E **59** a
Yaqui → *Mexico* 27°37N 110°39W **86** B2
Yar-Sale *Russia* 66°50N 70°50E **28** C8
Yaraka *Australia* 24°53S 144°3E **62** C3
Yaransk *Russia* 57°22N 47°49E **18** C8
Yare → *U.K.* 52°35N 1°38E **13** E9
Yaremcha *Ukraine* 48°27N 24°33E **17** D13
Yarensk *Russia* 62°11N 49°15E **18** B8
Yari → *Colombia* 0°20S 72°20W **92** D4
Yarkand = Shache
  China 38°20N 77°10E **32** C2
Yarkant He → *China* 40°26N 80°59E **32** B3
Yarker *Canada* 44°23N 76°46W **83** B8
Yarkhun → *Pakistan* 36°17N 72°30E **43** A5
Yarlung Ziangbo Jiang =
  Brahmaputra →
  Asia 23°40N 90°35E **43** H13
Yarmouth *Canada* 43°50N 66°7W **73** D6
Yarmūk → *Syria* 32°42N 35°40E **46** C4
Yaroslavl *Russia* 57°35N 39°55E **18** C6
Yarqa, W. → *Egypt* 30°0N 33°49E **46** F2
Yarra Yarra Lakes
  Australia 29°40S 115°45E **61** E2
Yarram *Australia* 38°29S 146°39E **63** F4
Yarraman *Australia* 26°50S 152°0E **63** D5
Yarras *Australia* 31°25S 152°20E **63** E5
Yarrie *Australia* 20°40S 120°12E **60** D3
Yartsevo *Russia* 60°20N 90°0E **29** C10
Yarumal *Colombia* 6°58N 75°24W **92** B3
Yasawa *Fiji* 16°47S 177°31E **59** a
Yasawa Group *Fiji* 17°0S 177°23E **59** a
Yaselda *Belarus* 52°7N 26°28E **17** B14
Yasin *Pakistan* 36°24N 73°23E **43** A5
Yasinski, L. *Canada* 53°16N 77°35W **72** B4
Yasinya *Ukraine* 48°16N 24°21E **17** D13
Yasothon *Thailand* 15°50N 104°10E **38** E5
Yass *Australia* 34°49S 148°54E **63** E4
Yāsūj *Iran* 30°31N 51°31E **45** D6
Yates Center *U.S.A.* 37°53N 95°44W **80** G6
Yathkyed L. *Canada* 62°40N 90°0W **71** A9
Yatsushiro *Japan* 32°30N 130°40E **31** H5
Yatta Plateau *Kenya* 2°0S 38°0E **54** C4
Yauco *Puerto Rico* 18°2N 66°51W **89** d
Yavarí → *Peru* 4°21S 70°2W **92** D4
Yávaros *Mexico* 26°42N 109°31W **86** B3
Yavatmal *India* 20°20N 78°15E **40** J11
Yavne *Israel* 31°52N 34°45E **46** D3
Yavoriv *Ukraine* 49°55N 23°20E **17** D12
Yavorov = Yavoriv
  Ukraine 49°55N 23°20E **17** D12
Yawatahama *Japan* 33°27N 132°24E **31** H6
Yawri B. *S. Leone* 8°22N 13°0W **50** G3
Yaxian = Sanya *China* 18°14N 109°29E **38** C7
Yazd *Iran* 31°55N 54°27E **45** D7
Yazd □ *Iran* 32°0N 55°0E **45** D7
Yazd-e Khvāst *Iran* 31°31N 52°7E **45** D7
Yazman *Pakistan* 29°8N 71°45E **42** E4
Yazoo → *U.S.A.* 32°22N 90°54W **85** E9
Yazoo City *U.S.A.* 32°51N 90°25W **85** E9
Ybycuí △ *Paraguay* 26°5S 56°46W **94** B4
Ybytyruzú △ *Paraguay* 25°51S 56°11W **95** B4
Ye *Burma* 15°15N 97°15E **38** E1
Ye Xian *China* 33°35N 113°25E **34** H7
Yebyu *Burma* 14°15N 98°13E **38** E2
Yecheng *China* 37°54N 77°26E **32** C2
Yecheon *S. Korea* 36°39N 128°27E **35** F15
Yecla *Spain* 38°35N 1°5W **21** C5
Yécora *Mexico* 28°20N 108°58W **86** B3
Yedintsy = Edineţ
  Moldova 48°9N 27°18E **17** D14
Yegros *Paraguay* 26°20S 56°25W **94** B4
Yehbuah *Indonesia* 8°23S 114°45E **37** J17
Yehuda, Midbar *Israel* 31°35N 35°15E **46** D4
Yei *Sudan* 4°9N 30°40E **51** H12
Yekaterinburg *Russia* 56°50N 60°30E **18** C11
Yelarbon *Australia* 28°33S 150°38E **63** D5
Yelets *Russia* 52°40N 38°30E **18** D6
Yelizavetgrad = Kirovohrad
  Ukraine 48°35N 32°20E **19** E5
Yelizovo *Russia* 53°11N 158°23E **29** D16
Yell *U.K.* 60°35N 1°5W **11** A7
Yell Sd. *U.K.* 60°33N 1°15W **11** A7
Yellow = Huang He →
  China 37°55N 118°50E **35** F10
Yellow Sea *China* 35°0N 123°0E **35** G12
Yellowhead Pass
  Canada 52°53N 118°25W **70** C5
Yellowknife *Canada* 62°27N 114°29W **70** A6
Yellowknife → *Canada* 62°31N 114°19W **70** A6
Yellowstone
  U.S.A. 47°59N 103°59W **76** C12
Yellowstone △ *U.S.A.* 44°40N 110°30W **76** D8
Yellowstone L. *U.S.A.* 44°27N 110°22W **76** D8
Yelsk *Belarus* 51°50N 29°10E **17** C15
Yemen ■ *Asia* 15°0N 44°0E **47** E3
Yen Bai *Vietnam* 21°42N 104°52E **38** B5
Yenangyaung *Burma* 20°30N 95°0E **41** J19
Yenbo = Yanbu 'al Bahr
  Si. Arabia 24°0N 38°5E **44** E3
Yenda *Australia* 34°13S 146°14E **63** E4

Yeni Erenköy = Yialousa
  Cyprus   35°32N 34°10E **25** D13
Yenice Turkey   39°55N 27°17E **23** E12
Yenisey → Russia   71°50N 82°40E **28** B9
Yeniseysk Russia   58°27N 92°13E **29** D10
Yenyuka Russia   57°57N 121°15E **29** D13
Yeo → U.K.   51°2N 2°49W **13** G5
Yeo, L. Australia   28°0S 124°30E **61** E3
Yeo I. Canada   45°24N 81°48W **82** A3
Yeoju S. Korea   37°20N 127°35E **35** F14
Yeola India   20°2N 74°30E **40** J9
Yeong-wol S. Korea   37°11N 128°28E **35** F15
Yeongcheon S. Korea   35°58N 128°56E **35** G15
Yeongdeok S. Korea   36°24N 129°22E **35** F15
Yeongdeungpo
  S. Korea   37°31N 126°54E **35** F14
Yeongdong S. Korea   36°10N 127°46E **35** F14
Yeongju S. Korea   36°50N 128°40E **35** F15
Yeosu S. Korea   34°47N 127°45E **35** G14
Yeotmal = Yavatmal
  India   20°20N 78°15E **40** J11
Yeovil U.K.   50°57N 2°38W **13** G5
Yeppoon Australia   23°5S 150°47E **62** C5
Yerbent Turkmenistan   39°30N 58°50E **28** F6
Yerbogachen Russia   61°16N 108°0E **29** C11
Yerevan Armenia   40°10N 44°31E **44** A5
Yerington U.S.A.   38°59N 119°10W **76** G4
Yermak Kazakhstan   52°2N 76°55E **28** D8
Yermo U.S.A.   34°54N 116°50W **79** L10
Yerólakkos Cyprus   35°11N 33°15E **25** D12
Yeropol Russia   65°15N 168°40E **29** C17
Yeroskipos Cyprus   34°46N 32°28E **25** E11
Yershov Russia   51°23N 48°27E **19** D8
Yerushalayim = Jerusalem
  Israel/West Bank   31°47N 35°10E **46** D4
Yes Tor U.K.   50°41N 4°0W **13** G4
Yesan S. Korea   36°41N 126°51E **35** F14
Yeso U.S.A.   34°26N 104°37W **77** J11
Yessey Russia   68°29N 102°10E **29** C11
Yetman Australia   28°56S 150°48E **63** D5
Yeu, Î. d' France   46°42N 2°20W **20** C2
Yevpatoriya Ukraine   45°15N 33°20E **19** E5
Yeysk Russia   46°40N 38°12E **19** E6
Yezd = Yazd Iran   31°55N 54°27E **45** D7
Ygatimi Paraguay   24°5S 55°40W **95** A4
Yhati Paraguay   25°45S 56°35W **94** B4
Yhú Paraguay   25°0S 56°0W **95** B4
Yí → Uruguay   33°7S 57°8W **94** C4
Yi 'Allaq, G. Egypt   30°21N 33°31E **46** E2
Yi He → China   34°10N 118°8E **35** G10
Yi Xian Hebei, China   39°20N 115°30E **34** E8
Yi Xian Liaoning, China   41°30N 121°22E **35** D11
Yialiás → Cyprus   35°9N 33°44E **25** D12
Yialousa Cyprus   35°32N 34°10E **25** D13
Yibin China   28°45N 104°32E **32** D5
Yichang China   30°40N 111°20E **33** C6
Yicheng China   35°42N 111°40E **34** G6
Yichuan China   36°2N 110°10E **34** F6
Yichun China   47°44N 128°52E **33** B7
Yidu China   36°43N 118°28E **35** F10
Yijun China   35°28N 109°8E **34** G5
Yıldız Dağları Turkey   41°48N 27°36E **23** D12
Yilehuli Shan China   51°20N 124°20E **33** A7
Yimianpo China   45°7N 128°2E **35** B15
Yinchuan China   38°30N 106°15E **34** E4
Yindarlgooda, L.
  Australia   30°40S 121°52E **61** F3
Yindjibarndi ○ Australia   22°0S 118°35E **60** D2
Ying He → China   32°30N 116°30E **34** H9
Ying Xian China   39°32N 113°10E **34** E7
Yingkou China   40°37N 122°18E **35** D12
Yingualyalya ○
  Australia   18°49S 129°12E **60** C4
Yining China   43°58N 81°10E **32** B3
Yiningarra ○ Australia   20°53S 129°27E **60** D4
Yinmabin Burma   22°10N 94°55E **41** H19
Yirga Alem Ethiopia   6°48N 38°22E **47** F2
Yirrkala Australia   12°14S 136°56E **62** A2
Yishan China   24°28N 108°38E **32** D5
Yishui China   35°47N 118°30E **35** G10
Yishun Singapore   1°26N 103°51E **39** d
Yitong China   43°13N 125°20E **35** C13
Yixing China   31°21N 119°48E **33** C6
Yiyang Henan, China   34°27N 112°10E **34** G7
Yiyang Hunan, China   28°35N 112°18E **33** D6
Yli-Kitka Finland   66°8N 28°30E **8** C23
Ylitornio Finland   66°19N 23°39E **8** C20
Ylivieska Finland   64°4N 24°28E **8** D21
Yoakum U.S.A.   29°17N 97°9W **84** G6
Yog Pt. Phil.   14°6N 124°12E **37** B6
Yogyakarta Indonesia   7°49S 110°22E **37** G14
Yogyakarta □ Indonesia   7°48S 110°22E **37** G14
Yoho △ Canada   51°25N 116°30W **70** C5
Yojoa, L. de Honduras   14°53N 88°0W **88** D2
Yok Don △ Vietnam   12°50N 107°40E **38** F6
Yokadouma Cameroon   3°26N 14°55E **52** D2
Yokkaichi Japan   34°55N 136°38E **31** G8
Yoko Cameroon   5°32N 12°20E **52** C2
Yokohama Japan   35°27N 139°28E **31** G9
Yokosuka Japan   35°20N 139°40E **31** G9
Yokote Japan   39°20N 140°30E **30** E10
Yola Nigeria   9°10N 12°29E **51** G8
Yolaina, Cordillera de
  Nic.   11°30N 84°0W **88** D3
Yölöten Turkmenistan   37°18N 62°21E **45** B9
Yom → Thailand   15°35N 100°1E **38** E3
Yonago Japan   35°25N 133°19E **31** G6
Yonaguni-Jima Japan   24°27N 123°0E **31** M1
Yŏnan N. Korea   37°55N 126°11E **35** F14
Yonezawa Japan   37°57N 140°4E **30** F10
Yong Peng Malaysia   2°0N 103°3E **39** M4
Yong Sata Thailand   7°8N 99°41E **39** J2
Yongamp'o N. Korea   39°56N 124°23E **35** E13
Yongcheng China   33°55N 116°24E **34** H9
Yongdeng China   36°38N 103°25E **34** F2
Yonghe China   36°46N 110°38E **34** F6
Yŏnghŭng N. Korea   39°31N 127°18E **35** E14
Yongji China   34°52N 110°28E **34** G6

Yongnian China   36°47N 114°29E **34** F8
Yongning China   38°15N 106°14E **34** E4
Yongqing China   39°25N 116°28E **34** E9
Yonibana S. Leone   8°30N 12°19W **50** G3
Yonkers U.S.A.   40°56N 73°52W **83** F11
Yonne □ France   48°23N 2°58E **20** B5
York Australia   31°52S 116°47E **61** F2
York U.K.   53°58N 1°6W **12** D6
York Ala., U.S.A.   32°29N 88°18W **85** E10
York Nebr., U.S.A.   40°52N 97°36W **80** E5
York Pa., U.S.A.   39°58N 76°44W **81** F15
York, C., Australia   10°42S 142°31E **62** A3
York, City of □ U.K.   53°58N 1°6W **12** D6
York, Kap Greenland   75°55N 66°25W **69** B18
York, Vale of U.K.   54°15N 1°25W **12** C6
York Sd. Australia   15°0S 125°5E **60** C4
Yorke Pen. Australia   34°50S 137°40E **63** E2
Yorkshire Dales △ U.K.   54°12N 2°10W **12** C5
Yorkshire Wolds U.K.   54°8N 0°31W **12** C7
Yorkton Canada   51°11N 102°28W **71** C8
Yorkville U.S.A.   38°52N 123°13W **78** G3
Yoro Honduras   15°9N 87°7W **88** C2
Yoron-Jima Japan   27°2N 128°26E **31** L4
Yos Sudarso, Pulau = Dolak,
  Pulau Indonesia   8°0S 138°30E **37** F9
Yosemite △ U.S.A.   37°45N 119°40W **78** H7
Yosemite Village
  U.S.A.   37°45N 119°35W **78** H7
Yoshino-Kumano △
  Japan   34°12N 135°55E **31** H8
Yoshkar Ola Russia   56°38N 47°55E **18** C8
Yotvata Israel   29°55N 35°2E **46** F4
Youbou Canada   48°53N 124°13W **78** B2
Youghal Ireland   51°56N 7°52W **10** E4
Youghal B. Ireland   51°55N 7°49W **10** E4
Young Australia   34°19S 148°18E **63** E4
Young Canada   51°47N 105°45W **71** C7
Young Uruguay   32°44S 57°36W **94** C4
Young I. Antarctica   66°25S 162°24E **5** C11
Younghusband, L.
  Australia   30°50S 136°5E **63** E2
Younghusband Pen.
  Australia   36°0S 139°25E **63** F2
Youngstown Canada   51°35N 111°10W **71** C6
Youngstown N.Y., U.S.A.   43°15N 79°3W **82** C5
Youngstown Ohio, U.S.A.   41°6N 80°39W **82** E4
Youngsville U.S.A.   41°51N 79°19W **82** E5
Youngwood U.S.A.   40°14N 79°34W **82** F5
Youyu China   40°10N 112°20E **34** D7
Yozgat Turkey   39°51N 34°47E **19** G5
Ypacaraí △ Paraguay   25°18S 57°19W **94** B4
Ypané → Paraguay   23°29S 57°19W **94** A4
Ypres = Ieper Belgium   50°51N 2°53E **15** D2
Yreka U.S.A.   41°44N 122°38W **76** F2
Ystad Sweden   55°26N 13°50E **9** J15
Ysyk-Köl = Balykchy
  Kyrgyzstan   42°26N 76°12E **32** B2
Ysyk-Köl Kyrgyzstan   42°25N 77°15E **28** E8
Ythan → U.K.   57°19N 1°59W **11** D7
Ytyk-Kyuyel Russia   62°30N 133°45E **29** C14
Yu Jiang → China   23°22N 110°3E **33** D6
Yu Xian = Yuzhou
  China   34°10N 113°28E **34** G7
Yu Xian Hebei, China   39°50N 114°35E **34** E8
Yu Xian Shanxi, China   38°5N 113°20E **34** E7
Yuan Jiang → China   28°55N 111°50E **33** D6
Yuanqu China   35°18N 111°40E **34** G6
Yuanyang China   35°3N 113°58E **34** G7
Yuba → U.S.A.   39°8N 121°36W **78** F5
Yuba City U.S.A.   39°8N 121°37W **78** F5
Yūbari Japan   43°4N 141°59E **30** C10
Yūbetsu Japan   44°13N 143°50E **30** B11
Yucatán □ Mexico   20°50N 89°0W **87** C7
Yucatán, Canal de
  Caribbean   22°0N 86°30W **88** B2
Yucatán, Península de
  Mexico   19°30N 89°0W **66** H11
Yucatan Basin Cent. Amer.   19°0N 86°0W **87** D7
Yucatan Channel = Yucatán,
  Canal de Caribbean   22°0N 86°30W **88** B2
Yucca U.S.A.   34°52N 114°9W **79** L12
Yucca Valley U.S.A.   34°8N 116°27W **79** L10
Yucheng China   36°55N 116°32E **34** F9
Yuci = Jinzhong China   37°42N 112°46E **34** F7
Yuen Long China   22°26N 114°2E **33** G11
Yuendumu Australia   22°16S 131°49E **60** D5
Yuendumu ○ Australia   22°21S 131°40E **60** D5
Yugorenok Russia   59°47N 137°40E **29** D14
Yukon □ U.S.A.   35°31N 97°45W **84** D6
Yukon → U.S.A.   62°32N 163°54W **74** C7
Yukon Flats U.S.A.   66°40N 145°45W **74** B10
Yukon Territory □
  Canada   63°0N 135°0W **68** E5
Yukta Russia   63°26N 105°42E **29** C11
Yukuhashi Japan   33°44N 130°59E **31** H5
Yulara Australia   25°10S 130°55E **61** E5
Yule → Australia   20°41S 118°17E **60** D2
Yuleba Australia   26°37S 149°24E **63** D4
Yulin Hainan, China   18°10N 109°31E **38** C7
Yulin Shaanxi, China   38°20N 109°30E **34** E5
Yuma, Ariz., U.S.A.   32°43N 114°37W **79** N12
Yuma, Colo., U.S.A.   40°8N 102°43W **76** F12
Yuma, B. de Dom. Rep.   18°20N 68°35W **89** C6
Yumbe Uganda   3°28N 31°15E **54** B3
Yumbi
  Dem. Rep. of the Congo   1°12S 26°15E **54** C2
Yumen China   39°50N 97°30E **32** C4
Yun Xian Henan, China   35°36N 111°57E **34** G8
Yuna → Australia   28°20S 115°0E **61** E2
Yunbay Chile   17°0S 66°0W **92** G5
Yunkanjini ○ Australia   22°33S 131°6E **60** D5
Yunnan □ China   25°0N 102°0E **32** D5
Yunta Australia   32°34S 139°36E **63** E2
Yunxi China   33°0N 110°22E **34** H6

Yurimaguas Peru   5°55S 76°7W **92** E3
Yurubí △ Venezuela   10°26N 68°42W **89** D6
Yuscarán Honduras   13°58N 86°45W **88** D2
Yushe China   37°4N 112°58E **34** F7
Yushu Jilin, China   44°43N 126°38E **35** B14
Yushu Qinghai, China   33°5N 96°55E **32** C4
Yutai China   35°0N 116°45E **34** G9
Yutian Hebei, China   39°53N 117°45E **35** E9
Yutian Sinkiang-Uigur,
  China   36°52N 81°42E **32** C3
Yuxar Qarabağ =
  Nagorno-Karabakh □
  Azerbaijan   39°55N 46°45E **44** B5
Yuxi China   24°30N 102°35E **32** D5
Yuzawa Japan   39°10N 140°30E **30** E10
Yuzhno-Kurilsk Russia   44°1N 145°51E **29** E15
Yuzhno-Sakhalinsk
  Russia   46°58N 142°45E **29** E15
Yuzhnyy □ Russia   44°0N 40°0E **19** F7
Yuzhou China   34°10N 113°28E **34** G7
Yvetot France   49°37N 0°44E **20** B4

Z

Zaanstad Neths.   52°27N 4°50E **15** B4
Zāb al Kabīr → Iraq   36°1N 43°24E **44** B4
Zāb as Şaghīr → Iraq   35°17N 43°29E **44** C4
Zabaykalsk Russia   49°40N 117°25E **29** E12
Zabol Iran   31°0N 61°32E **45** D9
Zābol □ Afghan.   32°0N 67°0E **40** D5
Zābolī Iran   27°10N 61°35E **45** E9
Zabrze Poland   50°18N 18°50E **17** C10
Zacapa Guatemala   14°59N 89°31W **88** D2
Zacapu Mexico   19°50N 101°43W **86** D4
Zacatecas Mexico   22°47N 102°35W **86** C4
Zacatecas □ Mexico   23°0N 103°0W **86** C4
Zacatecoluca El Salv.   13°29N 88°51W **88** D2
Zachary U.S.A.   30°39N 91°9W **84** F9
Zacoalco de Torres
  Mexico   20°14N 103°35W **86** C4
Zacualtipán Mexico   20°39N 98°36W **87** C5
Zadar Croatia   44°8N 15°14E **16** F8
Zadetkyi Kyun Burma   10°0N 98°25E **39** G2
Zafarqand Iran   33°11N 52°29E **45** C7
Zafra Spain   38°26N 6°30W **21** C2
Żagań Poland   51°39N 15°22E **16** C8
Zagaoua Chad   15°30N 22°24E **51** E10
Zagazig Egypt   30°40N 31°30E **51** B12
Zāgheh Iran   33°30N 48°42E **45** C6
Zagreb Croatia   45°50N 15°58E **16** F9
Zāgros, Kūhhā-ye Iran   33°45N 48°5E **45** C6
Zagros Mts. = Zāgros, Kūhhā-ye
  Iran   33°45N 48°5E **45** C6
Zahamena △ Madag.   17°37S 48°49E **57** B8
Zāhedān Fārs, Iran   28°46N 53°52E **45** D7
Zāhedān Sīstān va Balūchestān,
  Iran   29°30N 60°50E **45** D9
Zahlah Lebanon   33°52N 35°50E **46** B4
Zaïre = Congo → Africa   6°4S 12°24E **52** F2
Zaka Zimbabwe   20°20S 31°29E **57** C5
Zakamensk Russia   50°23N 103°17E **29** D11
Zakhodnaya Dzvina =
  Daugava → Latvia   57°4N 24°3E **9** H21
Zākhū Iraq   37°10N 42°50E **44** B4
Zakinthos = Zakynthos
  Greece   37°47N 20°54E **23** F9
Zakopane Poland   49°18N 19°57E **17** D10
Zakros Greece   35°6N 26°10E **25** D8
Zakynthos Greece   37°47N 20°54E **23** F9
Zalaegerszeg Hungary   46°53N 16°47E **17** E9
Zalari Russia   53°33N 102°30E **29** D11
Zalău Romania   47°12N 23°3E **17** E12
Zaleshchiki = Zalishchyky
  Ukraine   48°45N 25°45E **17** D13
Zalew Wiślany Poland   54°20N 19°50E **17** A10
Zalingei Sudan   12°51N 23°29E **51** F10
Zalishchyky Ukraine   48°45N 25°45E **17** D13
Zama L. Canada   58°45N 119°5W **70** B5
Zambeke
  Dem. Rep. of the Congo   2°8N 25°17E **54** B2
Zambeze → Africa   18°35S 36°20E **55** F4
Zambezi = Zambeze →
  Africa   18°35S 36°20E **55** F4
Zambezi Zambia   13°30S 23°15E **53** G4
Zambezi △ Zimbabwe   17°54S 25°41E **55** F2
Zambézia □ Mozam.   16°15S 37°30E **55** F4
Zambia ■ Africa   15°0S 28°0E **55** F2
Zamboanga Phil.   6°59N 122°3E **37** C6
Zamora Mexico   19°59N 102°16W **86** D4
Zamora Spain   41°30N 5°45W **21** B3
Zamość Poland   50°43N 23°15E **17** C12
Zanda China   31°32N 79°50E **32** C2
Zandvoort Neths.   52°22N 4°32E **15** B4
Zanesville U.S.A.   39°56N 82°1W **82** G2
Zangābād Iran   38°26N 46°44E **44** B5
Zangue → Mozam.   17°50S 35°21E **55** F4
Zanjān Iran   36°40N 48°35E **45** B6
Zanjān □ Iran   37°20N 49°30E **45** B6
Zanjān → Iran   37°8N 47°47E **45** B6
Zante = Zakynthos
  Greece   37°47N 20°54E **23** F9
Zanthus Australia   31°2S 123°34E **61** F3
Zanzibar Tanzania   6°12S 39°12E **54** D4
Zaouiet El-Kala = Bordj Omar
  Driss Algeria   28°10N 6°40E **50** C7
Zaouiet Reggâne Algeria   26°32N 0°3E **50** C6
Zaozhuang China   34°50N 117°35E **35** G9
Zap Suyu = Zāb al Kabīr →
  Iraq   36°1N 43°24E **44** B4
Zapadnaya Dvina = Daugava →
  Latvia   57°4N 24°3E **9** H21
Zapadní Beskydy Europe   49°30N 19°0E **17** D10
Zapala Argentina   39°0S 70°5W **96** D2
Zapaleri, Cerro Bolivia   22°49S 67°11W **94** A2
Zapata U.S.A.   26°55N 99°16W **84** H5
Zapolyarnyy Russia   69°26N 30°51E **8** B24
Zapopán Mexico   20°43N 103°24W **86** C4

Zaporizhzhya Ukraine   47°50N 35°10E **19** E6
Zaporozhye = Zaporizhzhya
  Ukraine   47°50N 35°10E **19** E6
Zara Turkey   39°58N 37°43E **44** B3
Zaragoza Coahuila,
  Mexico   28°29N 100°55W **86** B4
Zaragoza Nuevo León,
  Mexico   23°58N 99°46W **87** C5
Zaragoza Spain   41°39N 0°53W **21** B5
Zarand Kermān, Iran   30°46N 56°34E **45** D8
Zarand Markazī, Iran   35°18N 50°25E **45** C6
Zaranj Afghan.   30°55N 61°55E **40** D2
Zarasai Lithuania   55°40N 26°20E **9** J22
Zárate Argentina   34°7S 59°0W **94** C4
Zard, Kūh-e Iran   32°22N 50°4E **45** C6
Zāreh Iran   35°7N 49°9E **45** C6
Zaria Nigeria   11°0N 7°40E **50** F7
Zarneh Iran   33°55N 46°10E **44** C5
Zaros Greece   35°8N 24°54E **25** D6
Zarqā', Nahr az →
  Jordan   32°10N 35°37E **46** C4
Zarrīn Iran   32°46N 54°37E **45** C7
Zaruma Ecuador   3°40S 79°38W **92** D3
Żary Poland   51°37N 15°10E **16** C8
Zarzis Tunisia   33°31N 11°2E **51** B8
Zaskar → India   34°13N 77°20E **43** B7
Zaskar Mts. India   33°15N 77°30E **43** C7
Zastron S. Africa   30°18S 27°7E **56** E4
Zavāreh Iran   33°29N 52°28E **45** C7
Zave Zimbabwe   17°6S 30°1E **57** B5
Zavitinsk Russia   50°10N 129°20E **29** D13
Zavodovski, I. Antarctica   56°0S 27°45W **5** B1
Zawiercie Poland   50°30N 19°24E **17** C10
Zāwiyat al Bayḍā = Al Bayḍā
  Libya   32°50N 21°44E **51** B10
Zāyā Iraq   33°33N 44°13E **44** C5
Zāyandeh → Iran   32°35N 52°0E **45** C7
Zaysan Kazakhstan   47°28N 84°52E **32** B3
Zaysan Köli Kazakhstan   48°0N 83°0E **28** E9
Zayū China   28°48N 97°27E **41** E20
Zazafotsy Madag.   21°11S 46°21E **57** C8
Zbarazh Ukraine   49°43N 25°44E **17** D13
Zdolbuniv Ukraine   50°30N 26°15E **17** C14
Zduńska Wola Poland   51°37N 18°59E **17** C10
Zeballos Canada   49°59N 126°50W **70** D3
Zebediela S. Africa   24°20S 29°17E **57** C4
Zeebrugge Belgium   51°19N 3°12E **15** C3
Zeehan Australia   41°52S 145°25E **63** G4
Zeeland □ Neths.   51°30N 3°50E **15** C3
Zeerust S. Africa   25°31S 26°4E **56** D4
Zefat Israel   32°58N 35°29E **46** C4
Zehak Iran   30°53N 61°42E **45** D9
Zeil, Mt. Australia   23°30S 132°23E **60** D5
Zeila = Saylac
  Somali Rep.   11°21N 43°30E **47** E3
Zeist Neths.   52°5N 5°15E **15** B5
Zeitz Germany   51°2N 12°7E **16** C7
Zelenogorsk Russia   60°12N 29°43E **8** F23
Zelenograd Russia   56°1N 37°12E **18** C6
Zelenokumsk U.S.A.   40°48N 80°8W **82** F4
Zémio C.A.R.   5°2N 25°5E **54** A2
Zempoala Mexico   19°27N 96°23W **87** D5
Zemun Serbia   44°51N 20°25E **23** B9
Zenica Bos.-H.   44°10N 17°57E **23** B7
Žepče Bos.-H.   44°28N 18°2E **23** B8
Zevenaar Neths.   51°56N 6°5E **15** C6
Zeya Russia   53°48N 127°14E **29** D13
Zeya → Russia   51°42N 128°53E **29** D13
Zêzere → Portugal   39°28N 8°20W **21** C1
Zghartā Lebanon   34°21N 35°53E **46** A4
Zgorzelec Poland   51°10N 15°0E **16** C8
Zhabinka Belarus   52°13N 24°2E **17** B13
Zhangaözen Kazakhstan   43°18N 52°48E **19** F9
Zhangagazaly Kazakhstan   45°48N 62°6E **28** E7
Zhangbei China   41°10N 114°45E **34** D8
Zhangguangcai Ling
  China   45°0N 129°0E **35** B15
Zhangjiabian China   22°33N 113°28E **33** F9
Zhangjiakou China   40°48N 114°55E **34** D8
Zhangwu China   42°43N 123°52E **35** C12
Zhangye China   38°50N 100°23E **32** C5
Zhangzhou China   24°30N 117°35E **33** D6
Zhanhua China   37°40N 118°8E **35** F10
Zhanjiang China   21°15N 110°20E **33** D6
Zhannetty, Ostrov
  Russia   76°43N 158°0E **29** B16
Zhanyi China   25°38N 103°48E **32** D5
Zhanyu China   44°30N 122°30E **35** B12
Zhao Xian China   37°43N 114°45E **34** F8
Zhaocheng China   36°22N 111°38E **34** F6
Zhaotong China   27°20N 103°44E **32** D5
Zhaoyuan Heilongjiang,
  China   45°27N 125°0E **35** B13
Zhaoyuan Shandong,
  China   37°20N 120°23E **35** F11
Zhari Namco China   31°6N 85°36E **32** C3
Zharkent Kazakhstan   44°10N 80°0E **28** E8
Zhashkiv Ukraine   49°15N 30°5E **17** D16
Zhashui China   33°40N 109°8E **34** H5
Zhayylma Kazakhstan   51°37N 61°33E **28** D7
Zhayyq → Kazakhstan   47°0N 51°48E **19** E9
Zhdanov = Mariupol
  Ukraine   47°5N 37°31E **19** E6
Zhecheng China   34°7N 115°20E **34** G8
Zhejiang □ China   29°0N 120°0E **33** D7
Zheleznodorozhnyy
  Russia   62°35N 50°55E **18** B9
Zheleznogorsk-Ilimskiy
  Russia   56°34N 104°8E **29** D11
Zhen'an China   33°27N 109°9E **34** H5
Zhengding China   38°8N 114°32E **34** E8
Zhengzhou China   34°45N 113°34E **34** G7
Zhenlai China   45°50N 123°5E **35** B12
Zhenping China   33°10N 112°16E **34** H7
Zhenyuan China   35°35N 107°30E **34** G4
Zhetiqara Kazakhstan   52°11N 61°12E **28** D7
Zhezqazghan Kazakhstan   47°44N 67°40E **28** E7

Zhidan China   36°48N 108°48E **34** F5
Zhigansk Russia   66°48N 123°27E **29** C13
Zhilinda Russia   70°0N 114°20E **29** C12
Zhitomir = Zhytomyr
  Ukraine   50°20N 28°40E **17** C15
Zhlobin Belarus   52°55N 30°0E **17** B16
Zhmerynka Ukraine   49°2N 28°2E **17** D15
Zhob Pakistan   31°20N 69°31E **42** D3
Zhob → Pakistan   32°4N 69°50E **42** C3
Zhodzina Belarus   54°5N 28°17E **17** A15
Zhokhova, Ostrov
  Russia   76°4N 152°40E **29** B16
Zhongdian China   27°48N 99°42E **32** D4
Zhongning China   37°29N 105°40E **34** F3
Zhongshan Antarctica   69°0S 39°50E **5** C6
Zhongshankong China   22°26N 113°20E **33** G9
Zhongtiao Shan China   35°0N 111°10E **34** G6
Zhongwei China   37°30N 105°12E **34** F3
Zhongyang China   37°20N 111°11E **34** F6
Zhosaly Kazakhstan   45°29N 64°4E **28** E7
Zhoucun China   36°47N 117°48E **35** F9
Zhouzhi China   34°10N 108°12E **34** G5
Zhuanghe China   39°40N 123°0E **35** E12
Zhucheng China   36°0N 119°27E **35** G10
Zhugqu China   33°40N 104°30E **34** H3
Zhuhai China   22°17N 113°34E **33** G10
Zhujiang Kou China   22°20N 113°45E **33** G10
Zhumadian China   32°59N 114°2E **34** H8
Zhuo Xian = Zhuozhou
  China   39°28N 115°58E **34** E8
Zhuolu China   40°20N 115°12E **34** D8
Zhuozhou China   39°28N 115°58E **34** E8
Zhuozi China   41°0N 112°25E **34** D7
Zhuzhou China   27°49N 113°12E **33** D6
Zhytomyr Ukraine   50°20N 28°40E **17** C15
Ziarat Pakistan   30°25N 67°49E **42** D2
Zibo China   36°47N 118°3E **35** F10
Zichang China   37°18N 109°40E **34** F5
Zidi = Wandhari
  Pakistan   27°42N 66°48E **42** F2
Zielona Góra Poland   51°57N 15°31E **16** C8
Zierikzee Neths.   51°40N 3°55E **15** C3
Zigong China   29°15N 104°48E **32** D5
Ziguéy Chad   14°43N 15°50E **51** F9
Ziguinchor Senegal   12°35N 16°20W **50** F2
Zihuatanejo Mexico   17°39N 101°33W **86** D4
Žilina Slovak Rep.   49°12N 18°42E **17** D10
Zillah Libya   28°30N 17°33E **51** C9
Zima Russia   54°0N 102°5E **29** D11
Zimapán Mexico   20°45N 99°21W **87** C5
Zimba Zambia   17°20S 26°11E **55** F2
Zimbabwe Zimbabwe   20°16S 30°54E **55** G3
Zimbabwe ■ Africa   19°0S 30°0E **55** F3
Zimnicea Romania   43°40N 25°22E **17** G13
Zinave △ Mozam.   21°35S 33°40E **57** C5
Zinder Niger   13°48N 9°0E **50** F7
Zinga Tanzania   9°16S 38°49E **55** D4
Zion □ U.S.A.   37°15N 113°5W **77** H7
Ziros Greece   35°5N 26°8E **25** D8
Zirreh, Gowd-e Afghan.   29°45N 62°0E **40** E3
Zitácuaro Mexico   19°24N 100°22W **86** D4
Zitundo Mozam.   26°48S 32°47E **57** D5
Ziwa Magharibi = Kagera □
  Tanzania   2°0S 31°30E **54** C3
Ziway, L. Ethiopia   8°0N 38°50E **47** F2
Ziyang China   32°32N 108°31E **34** H5
Zlatograd Bulgaria   41°22N 25°7E **23** D11
Zlatoust Russia   55°10N 59°40E **18** C10
Zlín Czech Rep.   49°14N 17°40E **17** D9
Zmeinogorsk Kazakhstan   51°10N 82°13E **28** D9
Znojmo Czech Rep.   48°50N 16°2E **16** D9
Zobeyrī Iran   34°10N 46°40E **44** C5
Zoba Dem. Rep. of the Congo   3°0N 25°59E **54** B2
Zoetermeer Neths.   52°3N 4°30E **15** B4
Zohreh → Iran   30°16N 51°15E **45** D6
Zolochiv Ukraine   49°45N 24°51E **17** D13
Zomba Malawi   15°22S 35°19E **55** F4
Zongo
  Dem. Rep. of the Congo   4°20N 18°35E **52** D3
Zonguldak Turkey   41°28N 31°50E **19** F5
Zonqor Pt. Malta   35°52N 14°34E **25** D2
Zorritos Peru   3°43S 80°40W **92** D2
Zou Xiang China   35°30N 116°58E **34** G9
Zouar Chad   20°30N 16°32E **51** D9
Zouérate = Zouîrât
  Mauritania   22°44N 12°21W **50** D3
Zouîrât Mauritania   22°44N 12°21W **50** D3
Zoutkamp Neths.   53°20N 6°18E **15** A6
Zrenjanin Serbia   45°22N 20°23E **23** B9
Zufār Oman   17°40N 54°0E **47** D5
Zug Switz.   47°10N 8°31E **20** C8
Zugspitze Germany   47°25N 10°59E **16** E6
Zuid-Holland □ Neths.   52°0N 4°35E **15** C4
Zuidbeveland Neths.   51°30N 3°50E **15** C3
Zuidhorn Neths.   53°15N 6°23E **15** A6
Zula Eritrea   15°17N 39°40E **47** D2
Zumbo Mozam.   15°35S 30°26E **55** F3
Zumpango Mexico   19°48N 99°6W **87** D5
Zunhua China   40°18N 117°58E **35** D9
Zuni Pueblo U.S.A.   35°4N 108°51W **77** J9
Zunyi China   27°42N 106°53E **32** D6
Zurbāṭīyah Iraq   33°9N 46°3E **44** C5
Zürich Switz.   47°22N 8°32E **20** C8
Zutphen Neths.   52°9N 6°12E **15** B6
Zuurberg △ S. Africa   33°12S 25°32E **56** E4
Zuwārah Libya   32°58N 12°1E **51** B8
Züzan Iran   34°22N 59°53E **45** C8
Zvishavane Zimbabwe   20°17S 30°2E **55** G3
Zvolen Slovak Rep.   48°33N 19°10E **17** D10
Zwettl Austria   48°35N 15°9E **16** D8
Zwickau Germany   50°44N 12°30E **16** C7
Zwolle Neths.   52°31N 6°6E **15** B6
Zwolle U.S.A.   31°38N 93°39W **84** F8
Żyrardów Poland   52°3N 20°28E **17** B11
Zyryan = Zyryanovsk
  Kazakhstan   49°43N 84°20E **28** E9
Zyryanka Russia   65°45N 150°51E **29** C16
Zyryanovsk = Zyryan
  Kazakhstan   49°43N 84°20E **28** E9
Żywiec Poland   49°42N 19°10E **17** D10

KEY TO EUROPEAN MAP PAGES

 **Large scale maps**
(>1:2 500 000)

 **Medium scale maps**
(1: 2 800 000 – 1:9 900 000)

 **Small scale maps**
(<1:10 000 000)

8 ICELAND

Arctic Circle

WORLD COUNTRY INDEX

Afghanistan	40	**G**hana	50	**O**man	47
Albania	23	Greece	23		
Algeria	50	Greenland	4	**P**akistan	40, 42
Angola	52, 53	Guadeloupe	88	Panama	88
Argentina	94, 96	Guatemala	88	Papua New Guinea	64
Armenia	19	Guinea	50	Paraguay	94–95
Australia	60–63	Guinea-Bissau	50	Peru	92
Austria	16–17	Guyana	92	Philippines	37
Azerbaijan	19			Poland	16–17
		Haiti	89	Portugal	21
Bahamas	88–89	Honduras	88	Puerto Rico	89
Bahrain	45	Hungary	17		
Bangladesh	41			**Q**atar	45
Barbados	89	**I**celand	8		
Belarus	17, 18–19	India	40–43	**R**omania	17
Belgium	15	Indonesia	36–37	Russia	18–19, 28–29
Belize	88	Iran	44–45	Rwanda	54
Benin	50	Iraq	44–45		
Bhutan	41	Irish Republic	10	**S**t. Lucia	89
Bolivia	92	Israel	46	Samoa	59
Bosnia-Herzegovina	22–23	Italy	22–23	Saudi Arabia	44–45, 47
Botswana	56	Ivory Coast	50	Scotland	11
Brazil	92–93, 95			Senegal	50
Brunei	36	**J**amaica	88	Serbia	23
Bulgaria	23	Japan	30–31	Sierra Leone	50
Burkina Faso	50	Jordan	46	Singapore	39
Burma (Myanmar)	41			Slovak Republic	17
Burundi	54	**K**azakhstan	28	Slovenia	22
		Kenya	54	Solomon Is.	64
Cambodia	38–39	Korea, North	35	Somali Republic	47
Canary Is.	24	Korea, South	35	South Africa	56–57
Cameroon	52	Kosovo	23	Spain	21
Canada	68–73	Kuwait	44–45	Sri Lanka	40
Central African Republic	52	Kyrgyzstan	28	Sudan	51
Chad	51			Suriname	92–93
Chile	94, 96–97	**L**aos	38	Swaziland	57
China	32–35	Latvia	9	Sweden	8–9
Colombia	92	Lebanon	46	Switzerland	16
Congo	52	Lesotho	57	Syria	44, 46
Congo, Dem. Rep.		Liberia	50		
of the	52–53, 54–55	Libya	51	**T**aiwan	33
Costa Rica	88	Lithuania	9	Tajikistan	28
Croatia	22–23	Luxembourg	15	Tanzania	54–55
Cuba	88–89			Thailand	38–39
Cyprus	25	**M**acedonia	23	Togo	50
Czech Republic	16–17	Madagascar	57	Tonga	59
		Malawi	55	Trinidad and Tobago	93
Denmark	9	Malaysia	36–37, 39	Tunisia	50–51
Djibouti	47	Mali	50	Turkey	19
Dominican Republic	89	Malta	25	Turkmenistan	28
		Martinique	88		
Ecuador	92	Mauritania	50	**U**ganda	54
Egypt	51	Mexico	86–87	Ukraine	18–19
El Salvador	88	Moldova	17	United Arab Emirates	47
England	12–13	Mongolia	32	United Kingdom	10–13
Equatorial Guinea	52	Montenegro	23	USA	74–85
Eritrea	47	Morocco	50	Uruguay	94–95
Estonia	9	Mozambique	55, 57	Uzbekistan	28
Ethiopia	47, 52				
		Namibia	56	**V**anuatu	64
Fiji	59	Nepal	43	Venezuela	92–93
Finland	8–9	Netherlands	15	Vietnam	38–39
France	20–21	New Zealand	59		
French Guiana	93	Nicaragua	88	**W**ales	12–13
		Niger	50–51		
Gabon	52	Nigeria	50–51	**Y**emen	47
Gambia	50	Northern Ireland	10		
Georgia	19	Norway	8–9	**Z**ambia	55, 56–57
Germany	16			Zimbabwe	55

8

14

11

11

12

10

16

15

IRELAND

UNITED KINGDOM

N

FRAN

20

21

ANDORRA

PORTUGAL

SPAIN

24

MOROCCO

AL